ENCYCLOPEDIA OF RELIGION

SECOND EDITION

3

CABASILAS, NICHOLAS
•
CYRUS II

ENCYCLOPEDIA OF RELIGION

SECOND EDITION

LINDSAY JONES
EDITOR IN CHIEF

MACMILLAN REFERENCE USA
An imprint of Thomson Gale, a part of The Thomson Corporation

THOMSON
GALE

Detroit • New York • San Francisco • San Diego • New Haven, Conn. • Waterville, Maine • London • Munich

THOMSON
GALE

Encyclopedia of Religion, Second Edition

Lindsay Jones, Editor in Chief

For more information, contact
Macmillan Reference USA
An imprint of Thomson Gale
27500 Drake Rd.
Farmington, Hills, MI 48331-3535
Or you can visit our Internet site at
http://www.gale.com

LIBRARY OF CONGRESS CATALOGING-IN-PUBLICATION DATA

Encyclopedia of religion / Lindsay Jones, editor in chief.— 2nd ed.
p. cm.
Includes bibliographical references and index.
ISBN 0-02-865733-0 (SET HARDCOVER : ALK. PAPER) —
ISBN 0-02-865734-9 (V. 1) — ISBN 0-02-865735-7 (v. 2) —
ISBN 0-02-865736-5 (v. 3) — ISBN 0-02-865737-3 (v. 4) —
ISBN 0-02-865738-1 (v. 5) — ISBN 0-02-865739-X (v. 6) —
ISBN 0-02-865740-3 (v. 7) — ISBN 0-02-865741-1 (v. 8) —
ISBN 0-02-865742-X (v. 9) — ISBN 0-02-865743-8 (v. 10)
— ISBN 0-02-865980-5 (v. 11) — ISBN 0-02-865981-3 (v. 12) — ISBN 0-02-865982-1 (v. 13) — ISBN 0-02-865983-X (v. 14) — ISBN 0-02-865984-8 (v. 15)
1. RELIGION—ENCYCLOPEDIAS. I. JONES, LINDSAY, 1954-

BL31.E46 2005
200'.3—dc22
2004017052

This title is also available as an e-book.
ISBN 0-02-865997-X
Contact your Thomson Gale representative for ordering information.

Printed in the United States of America
10 9 8 7 6 5 4 3 2 1

EDITORS AND CONSULTANTS

EDITOR IN CHIEF

LINDSAY JONES
Associate Professor, Department of Comparative Studies, Ohio State University

BOARD MEMBERS

DAVÍD CARRASCO
Neil Rudenstine Professor of Study of Latin America, Divinity School and Department of Anthropology, Harvard University

GIOVANNI CASADIO
Professor of History of Religions, Dipartimento di Scienze dell'Antichità, Università degli Studi di Salerno

WENDY DONIGER
Mircea Eliade Distinguished Service Professor of the History of Religions, University of Chicago

GARY L. EBERSOLE
Professor of History and Religious Studies, and Director, UMKC Center for Religious Studies, University of Missouri—Kansas City

JANET GYATSO
Hershey Professor of Buddhist Studies, The Divinity School, Harvard University

CHARLES HALLISEY
Associate Professor, Department of Languages and Cultures of Asia and Program in Religious Studies, University of Wisconsin—Madison

CHARLES H. LONG
Professor of History of Religions, Emeritus, and Former Director of Research Center for Black Studies, University of California, Santa Barbara

MARY N. MACDONALD
Professor, History of Religions, Le Moyne College (Syracuse, New York)

DALE B. MARTIN
Professor of Religious Studies, and Chair, Department of Religious Studies, Yale University

AZIM NANJI
Professor and Director, The Institute of Ismaili Studies, London

JACOB OLUPONA
Professor, African American and African Studies Program, University of California, Davis

MICHAEL SWARTZ
Professor of Hebrew and Religious Studies, Ohio State University

INÉS TALAMANTEZ
Associate Professor, Religious Studies Department, University of California, Santa Barbara

CONSULTANTS

GREGORY D. ALLES
Associate Professor of Religious Studies, McDaniel College
Study of Religion

SIGMA ANKRAVA
Professor, Department of Literary and Cultural Studies, Faculty of Modern Languages, University of Latvia
Baltic Religion and Slavic Religion

DIANE APOSTOLOS-CAPPADONA
Center for Muslim–Christian Understanding and Liberal Studies Program, Georgetown University
Art and Religion

DIANE BELL
Professor of Anthropology and Women's Studies, George Washington University
Australian Indigenous Religions

KEES W. BOLLE
Professor Emeritus of History, University of California, Los Angeles, and Fellow, Netherlands Institute for Advanced Studies in the Humanities and Social Sciences
History of Religions

MARK CSIKSZENTMIHALYI
Associate Professor in the Department of East Asian Languages and Literature and the Program in Religious Studies, University of Wisconsin—Madison
Chinese Religions

RICHARD A. GARDNER
Faculty of Comparative Culture, Sophia University
Humor and Religion

JOHN A. GRIM
Professor of Religion, Bucknell University and Co-Coordinator,

Harvard Forum on Religion and Ecology
Ecology and Religion

JOSEPH HARRIS
Francis Lee Higginson Professor of English Literature and Professor of Folklore, Harvard University
Germanic Religions

URSULA KING
Professor Emerita, Senior Research Fellow and Associate Member of the Institute for Advanced Studies, University of Bristol, England, and Professorial Research Associate, Centre for Gender and Religions Research, School of Oriental and African Studies, University of London
Gender and Religion

DAVID MORGAN
Duesenberg Professor of Christianity and the Arts, and Professor of Humanities and Art History, Valparaiso University
Color Inserts and Essays

JOSEPH F. NAGY
Professor, Department of English, University of California, Los Angeles
Celtic Religion

MATTHEW OJO
Obafemi Awolowo University
African Religions

JUHA PENTIKÄINEN
Professor of Comparative Religion, The University of Helsinki, Member of Academia Scientiarum Fennica, Finland
Arctic Religions and Uralic Religions

TED PETERS
Professor of Systematic Theology, Pacific Lutheran Theological Seminary and the Center for Theology and the Natural Sciences at the Graduate Theological Union, Berkeley, California
Science and Religion

FRANK E. REYNOLDS
Professor of the History of Religions and Buddhist Studies in the Divinity School and the Department of South Asian Languages and Civilizations, Emeritus, University of Chicago
History of Religions

GONZALO RUBIO
Assistant Professor, Department of Classics and Ancient Mediterranean Studies and Department of History and Religious Studies, Pennsylvania State University
Ancient Near Eastern Religions

SUSAN SERED
Director of Research, Religion, Health and Healing Initiative, Center for the Study of World Religions, Harvard University, and Senior Research Associate, Center for Women's Health and Human Rights, Suffolk University
Healing, Medicine, and Religion

LAWRENCE E. SULLIVAN
Professor, Department of Theology, University of Notre Dame
History of Religions

WINNIFRED FALLERS SULLIVAN
Dean of Students and Senior Lecturer in the Anthropology and Sociology of Religion, University of Chicago
Law and Religion

TOD SWANSON
Associate Professor of Religious Studies, and Director, Center for Latin American Studies, Arizona State University
South American Religions

MARY EVELYN TUCKER
Professor of Religion, Bucknell University, Founder and Coordinator, Harvard Forum on Religion and Ecology, Research Fellow, Harvard Yenching Institute, Research Associate, Harvard Reischauer Institute of Japanese Studies
Ecology and Religion

HUGH URBAN
Associate Professor, Department of Comparative Studies, Ohio State University
Politics and Religion

CATHERINE WESSINGER
Professor of the History of Religions and Women's Studies, Loyola University New Orleans
New Religious Movements

ROBERT A. YELLE
Mellon Postdoctoral Fellow, University of Toronto
Law and Religion

ERIC ZIOLKOWSKI
Charles A. Dana Professor of Religious Studies, Lafayette College
Literature and Religion

ABBREVIATIONS AND SYMBOLS USED IN THIS WORK

abbr. abbreviated; abbreviation
abr. abridged; abridgment
AD *anno Domini,* in the year of the (our) Lord
Afrik. Afrikaans
AH *anno Hegirae,* in the year of the Hijrah
Akk. Akkadian
Ala. Alabama
Alb. Albanian
Am. *Amos*
AM *ante meridiem,* before noon
amend. amended; amendment
annot. annotated; annotation
Ap. *Apocalypse*
Apn. *Apocryphon*
app. appendix
Arab. Arabic
ʿArakh. *ʿArakhin*
Aram. Aramaic
Ariz. Arizona
Ark. Arkansas
Arm. Armenian
art. article (pl., arts.)
AS Anglo-Saxon
Asm. Mos. *Assumption of Moses*
Assyr. Assyrian
A.S.S.R. Autonomous Soviet Socialist Republic
Av. Avestan
ʿA.Z. *ʿAvodah zarah*
b. born
Bab. Babylonian
Ban. Bantu
1 Bar. *1 Baruch*
2 Bar. *2 Baruch*
3 Bar. *3 Baruch*
4 Bar. *4 Baruch*
B.B. *Bavaʾ batraʾ*
BBC British Broadcasting Corporation
BC before Christ
BCE before the common era
B.D. Bachelor of Divinity
Beits. *Beitsah*
Bekh. *Bekhorot*
Beng. Bengali
Ber. *Berakhot*
Berb. Berber
Bik. *Bikkurim*
bk. book (pl., bks.)
B.M. *Bavaʾ metsiʿaʾ*
BP before the present
B.Q. *Bavaʾ qammaʾ*
Brāh. *Brāhmaṇa*
Bret. Breton
B.T. Babylonian Talmud
Bulg. Bulgarian
Burm. Burmese
c. *circa,* about, approximately
Calif. California
Can. Canaanite
Catal. Catalan
CE of the common era
Celt. Celtic
cf. *confer,* compare
Chald. Chaldean
chap. chapter (pl., chaps.)
Chin. Chinese
C.H.M. Community of the Holy Myrrhbearers
1 Chr. *1 Chronicles*
2 Chr. *2 Chronicles*
Ch. Slav. Church Slavic
cm centimeters
col. column (pl., cols.)
Col. *Colossians*
Colo. Colorado
comp. compiler (pl., comps.)
Conn. Connecticut
cont. continued
Copt. Coptic
1 Cor. *1 Corinthians*
2 Cor. *2 Corinthians*
corr. corrected
C.S.P. Congregatio Sancti Pauli, Congregation of Saint Paul (Paulists)
d. died
D Deuteronomic (source of the Pentateuch)
Dan. Danish
D.B. Divinitatis Baccalaureus, Bachelor of Divinity
D.C. District of Columbia
D.D. Divinitatis Doctor, Doctor of Divinity
Del. Delaware
Dem. *Demaʾi*
dim. diminutive
diss. dissertation
Dn. *Daniel*
D.Phil. Doctor of Philosophy
Dt. *Deuteronomy*
Du. Dutch
E Elohist (source of the Pentateuch)
Eccl. *Ecclesiastes*
ed. editor (pl., eds.); edition; edited by

'Eduy. *'Eduyyot*
e.g. *exempli gratia,* for example
Egyp. Egyptian
1 En. *1 Enoch*
2 En. *2 Enoch*
3 En. *3 Enoch*
Eng. English
enl. enlarged
Eph. *Ephesians*
'Eruv. *'Eruvin*
1 Esd. *1 Esdras*
2 Esd. *2 Esdras*
3 Esd. *3 Esdras*
4 Esd. *4 Esdras*
esp. especially
Est. Estonian
Est. *Esther*
et al. *et alii,* and others
etc. *et cetera,* and so forth
Eth. Ethiopic
EV English version
Ex. *Exodus*
exp. expanded
Ez. *Ezekiel*
Ezr. *Ezra*
2 Ezr. *2 Ezra*
4 Ezr. *4 Ezra*
f. feminine; and following (pl., ff.)
fasc. fascicle (pl., fascs.)
fig. figure (pl., figs.)
Finn. Finnish
fl. *floruit,* flourished
Fla. Florida
Fr. French
frag. fragment
ft. feet
Ga. Georgia
Gal. *Galatians*
Gaul. Gaulish
Ger. German
Giṭ. *Giṭṭin*
Gn. *Genesis*
Gr. Greek
Ḥag. *Ḥagigah*
Ḥal. *Ḥallah*
Hau. Hausa
Hb. *Habakkuk*
Heb. Hebrew
Heb. *Hebrews*
Hg. *Haggai*
Hitt. Hittite
Hor. *Horayot*
Hos. *Hosea*
Ḥul. *Ḥullin*
Hung. Hungarian
ibid. *ibidem,* in the same place (as the one immediately preceding)
Icel. Icelandic
i.e. *id est,* that is
IE Indo-European
Ill. Illinois
Ind. Indiana
intro. introduction
Ir. Gael. Irish Gaelic
Iran. Iranian
Is. *Isaiah*
Ital. Italian
J Yahvist (source of the Pentateuch)
Jas. *James*
Jav. Javanese
Jb. *Job*
Jdt. *Judith*
Jer. *Jeremiah*
Jgs. *Judges*
Jl. *Joel*
Jn. *John*
1 Jn. *1 John*
2 Jn. *2 John*
3 Jn. *3 John*
Jon. *Jonah*
Jos. *Joshua*
Jpn. Japanese
JPS Jewish Publication Society translation (1985) of the Hebrew Bible
J.T. Jerusalem Talmud
Jub. *Jubilees*
Kans. Kansas
Kel. *Kelim*
Ker. *Keritot*
Ket. *Ketubbot*
1 Kgs. *1 Kings*
2 Kgs. *2 Kings*
Khois. Khoisan
Kil. *Kil'ayim*
km kilometers
Kor. Korean
Ky. Kentucky
l. line (pl., ll.)
La. Louisiana
Lam. *Lamentations*
Lat. Latin
Latv. Latvian
L. en Th. Licencié en Théologie, Licentiate in Theology
L. ès L. Licencié ès Lettres, Licentiate in Literature
Let. Jer. *Letter of Jeremiah*
lit. literally
Lith. Lithuanian
Lk. *Luke*
LL Late Latin
LL.D. Legum Doctor, Doctor of Laws
Lv. *Leviticus*
m meters
m. masculine
M.A. Master of Arts
Ma 'as. *Ma'aserot*
Ma 'as. Sh. *Ma' aser sheni*
Mak. *Makkot*
Makh. *Makhshirin*
Mal. *Malachi*
Mar. Marathi
Mass. Massachusetts
1 Mc. *1 Maccabees*
2 Mc. *2 Maccabees*
3 Mc. *3 Maccabees*
4 Mc. *4 Maccabees*
Md. Maryland
M.D. Medicinae Doctor, Doctor of Medicine
ME Middle English
Meg. *Megillah*
Me 'il. *Me'ilah*
Men. *Menaḥot*
MHG Middle High German
mi. miles
Mi. *Micah*
Mich. Michigan
Mid. *Middot*
Minn. Minnesota
Miq. *Miqva'ot*
MIran. Middle Iranian
Miss. Mississippi
Mk. *Mark*
Mo. Missouri
Mo'ed Q. *Mo'ed qaṭan*
Mont. Montana
MPers. Middle Persian
MS. *manuscriptum,* manuscript (pl., MSS)
Mt. *Matthew*
MT Masoretic text
n. note
Na. *Nahum*
Nah. Nahuatl
Naz. *Nazir*
N.B. *nota bene,* take careful note
N.C. North Carolina
n.d. no date
N.Dak. North Dakota
NEB New English Bible
Nebr. Nebraska

Ned. *Nedarim*
Neg. *Nega'im*
Neh. *Nehemiah*
Nev. Nevada
N.H. New Hampshire
Nid. *Niddah*
N.J. New Jersey
Nm. *Numbers*
N.Mex. New Mexico
no. number (pl., nos.)
Nor. Norwegian
n.p. no place
n.s. new series
N.Y. New York
Ob. *Obadiah*
O.Cist. Ordo Cisterciencium, Order of Cîteaux (Cistercians)
OCS Old Church Slavonic
OE Old English
O.F.M. Ordo Fratrum Minorum, Order of Friars Minor (Franciscans)
OFr. Old French
Ohal. *Ohalot*
OHG Old High German
OIr. Old Irish
OIran. Old Iranian
Okla. Oklahoma
ON Old Norse
O.P. Ordo Praedicatorum, Order of Preachers (Dominicans)
OPers. Old Persian
op. cit. *opere citato,* in the work cited
OPrus. Old Prussian
Oreg. Oregon
'Orl. *'Orlah*
O.S.B. Ordo Sancti Benedicti, Order of Saint Benedict (Benedictines)
p. page (pl., pp.)
P Priestly (source of the Pentateuch)
Pa. Pennsylvania
Pahl. Pahlavi
Par. *Parah*
para. paragraph (pl., paras.)
Pers. Persian
Pes. *Pesahim*
Ph.D. Philosophiae Doctor, Doctor of Philosophy
Phil. *Philippians*
Phlm. *Philemon*
Phoen. Phoenician
pl. plural; plate (pl., pls.)
PM *post meridiem,* after noon
Pol. Polish
pop. population
Port. Portuguese
Prv. *Proverbs*
Ps. *Psalms*
Ps. 151 *Psalm 151*
Ps. Sol. *Psalms of Solomon*
pt. part (pl., pts.)
1Pt. *1 Peter*
2 Pt. *2 Peter*
Pth. Parthian
Q hypothetical source of the synoptic Gospels
Qid. *Qiddushin*
Qin. *Qinnim*
r. reigned; ruled
Rab. *Rabbah*
rev. revised
R. ha-Sh. *Ro'sh ha-shanah*
R.I. Rhode Island
Rom. Romanian
Rom. *Romans*
R.S.C.J. Societas Sacratissimi Cordis Jesu, Religious of the Sacred Heart
RSV Revised Standard Version of the Bible
Ru. *Ruth*
Rus. Russian
Rv. *Revelation*
Rv. Ezr. *Revelation of Ezra*
San. *Sanhedrin*
S.C. South Carolina
Scot. Gael. Scottish Gaelic
S.Dak. South Dakota
sec. section (pl., secs.)
Sem. Semitic
ser. series
sg. singular
Sg. *Song of Songs*
Sg. of 3 *Prayer of Azariah and the Song of the Three Young Men*
Shab. *Shabbat*
Shav. *Shavu'ot*
Sheq. *Sheqalim*
Sib. Or. *Sibylline Oracles*
Sind. Sindhi
Sinh. Sinhala
Sir. *Ben Sira*
S.J. Societas Jesu, Society of Jesus (Jesuits)
Skt. Sanskrit
1 Sm. *1 Samuel*
2 Sm. *2 Samuel*
Sogd. Sogdian
Soṭ. *Soṭah*
sp. species (pl., spp.)
Span. Spanish
sq. square
S.S.R. Soviet Socialist Republic
st. stanza (pl., ss.)
S.T.M. Sacrae Theologiae Magister, Master of Sacred Theology
Suk. *Sukkah*
Sum. Sumerian
supp. supplement; supplementary
Sus. *Susanna*
s.v. *sub verbo,* under the word (pl., s.v.v.)
Swed. Swedish
Syr. Syriac
Syr. Men. *Syriac Menander*
Ta' an. *Ta'anit*
Tam. Tamil
Tam. *Tamid*
Tb. *Tobit*
T.D. *Taishō shinshū daizōkyō,* edited by Takakusu Junjirō et al. (Tokyo,1922–1934)
Tem. *Temurah*
Tenn. Tennessee
Ter. Terumot
Ṭev. Y. *Ṭevul yom*
Tex. Texas
Th.D. Theologicae Doctor, Doctor of Theology
1 Thes. *1 Thessalonians*
2 Thes. *2 Thessalonians*
Thrac. Thracian
Ti. *Titus*
Tib. Tibetan
1 Tm. *1 Timothy*
2 Tm. *2 Timothy*
T. of 12 *Testaments of the Twelve Patriarchs*
Ṭoh. *ṭohorot*
Tong. Tongan
trans. translator, translators; translated by; translation
Turk. Turkish
Ukr. Ukrainian
Upan. *Upaniṣad*
U.S. United States
U.S.S.R. Union of Soviet Socialist Republics
Uqts. *Uqtsin*
v. verse (pl., vv.)
Va. Virginia
var. variant; variation
Viet. Vietnamese

viz. *videlicet,* namely
vol. volume (pl., vols.)
Vt. Vermont
Wash. Washington
Wel. Welsh
Wis. Wisconsin
Wis. *Wisdom of Solomon*
W.Va. West Virginia
Wyo. Wyoming
Yad. *Yadayim*
Yev. *Yevamot*
Yi. Yiddish
Yor. Yoruba
Zav. *Zavim*
Zec. *Zechariah*
Zep. *Zephaniah*
Zev. *Zevaḥim*

* hypothetical
? uncertain; possibly; perhaps
° degrees
+ plus
– minus
= equals; is equivalent to
× by; multiplied by
→ yields

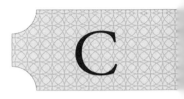

C

CABALA See QABBALAH

CABASILAS, NICHOLAS (c. 1322–1395), born Nicolaos Chamaetos Cabasilas; Greek Orthodox theologian and saint. A native of Thessalonica, Cabasilas studied there and in Constantinople. One of his teachers was his uncle Nilos Cabasilas, an adherent and successor of Gregory Palamas in the see of Thessalonica. Cabasilas served for ten years as counselor to the emperor John VI Cantacuzenos (1341–1354). In 1353 his name was put forward as a candidate for the patriarchal chair, although he was a layman. During the second half of his life, he resided in Constantinople, mostly in the monastery of Mangana, as a layman or as a monk, devoting himself to theological studies.

Gennadios Scholarios, the first patriarch after the fall of Constantinople, characterized Cabasilas's writings as "an ornament to the church of Christ." With an imposing style, apophthegmatic, prophetic, and poetical, he expresses genuine religious feeling and deep faith.

One of Cabasilas's most important works is *Interpretation of the Holy Liturgy*, a spiritual explanation of what is said and done during the Divine Liturgy, which he considers a real image of divine worship in heaven as well as of the earthly life of the incarnated God. In his thought the participation of the church in the sacraments (*mustēria*) is not symbolic, but real, as is the participation of the members of the body in the heart. By participating in the mysteries (i.e., the Body and Blood of Christ), the faithful do not incorporate these elements into the human body as they do other food; rather, the faithful themselves are incorporated into these elements. Human's union with Christ, soul with soul and body with body, brings complete peace, which makes the many one; disturbance makes the one many.

Cabasilas's second great work, *On the Life in Christ*, presents an anatomy of the spiritual life in the framework of the incarnation, repeated and continued in the sacraments of the church. Cabasilas's thought revolves around the fact of salvation through union

Clockwise from top left corner. Bronze of the Egyptian goddess Bastet, patron of Bubastis, as a cat, 713–332 BCE. Louvre, Paris. *[©Art Resource, N.Y.]*; Ninth-century Qur'ān written in Kufic script. Abbasid dynasty, Iraq. *[©Werner Forman/Art Resource, N.Y.]*; *Le Christ de l'Abbé Menasprov*. Louvre, Paris. *[©Giraudon/Art Resource, N.Y.]*; Aztec calendar stone. *[©Bettmann/Corbis]*; Fifth-century CE silver Roman shield depicting Cybele in a chariot with Attis. Archaeological Museum, Milan. *[The Art Archive/Archaeological Museum Milan/Dagli Orti]* .

with God. The destination of humankind from the moment of its creation to the end of its history is this: union with God.

For Cabasilas, the distinguishing property of God is goodness. God is good in an excelling way, and the nature of good is to pour itself out and be distributed. Thus humankind is created good from the beginning, both Godlike and Christ-like, with the purpose of being united with God in the future. The incarnate Word of God encounters a Godlike kernel in each human being and from this encounter a new life springs, which leads to perfection in life in Christ. Perfection is the supreme and complete gift of God. All things have been made for perfection.

The present world is in the process of giving birth to the inner person, who is molded and formed in the present life, but who is born only in the future world. The moment of transition is the most delightful of visions. "Christ descends from heaven to earth brilliantly, the earth raises up other suns toward the sun of justice. All is full of light" (*Life in Christ* 6.16).

In 1983 Cabasilas was canonized a saint of the Greek Orthodox church and his feast fixed on June 20. His writings are widely read in many languages.

Bibliography

Works by Cabasilas

An unsatisfactory edition of the main texts, by Fronto Ducaeus, is reprinted in *Patrologia Graeca*, edited by J.-P. Migne, vol. 150 (Paris, 1865). All modern translations of Cabasilas's two great treatises, based on this text, are necessarily unsatisfactory too. *Explication de la divine liturgie*, edited and translated by Sévérien Salaville, in *Sources Chrétiennes*, vol. 4 (Paris, 1967), follows the same text collated with one Parisian manuscript. An English translation by Joan M. Hussey and P. A. McNulty is also available as *Interpretation of the Divine Liturgy* (London, 1960). While working on my own translation into modern Greek, I prepared another, more correct original text, based on four manuscripts; see *Nikolaos Cabasilas*, no. 22 in the series "Philokalia" (Thessaloniki, 1979–).

Works about Cabasilas

Die Mystik des Nikolaus Cabasilas vom Leben in Christo, edited by Wilhelm Gass (1849; 2nd ed., Leiden, 1899), was excellent in its time. The work of Myrna Lot-Borodine, *Un maître de la spiritualité byzantine au quatorzième siècle, Nicolas Cabasilas* (Paris, 1958), in spite of its oratorical style, is very interesting. Special aspects of Cabasilas's thought are treated in Ermanno M. Toniolo's *La mariologia di Nicola Cabasila* (Vicenze, 1955); Ihor Ševčenko's "Nicolas Cabasilas' 'Anti-zealot' Discourse: A Reinterpretation," *Dumbarton Oaks Papers* 11 (1957): 79–171; and Jean Vafiadis's *L'humanisme chrétien de Nicolas Cabasilas: L'épanouissement de la personne humaine dans le Christ* (Strasbourg, 1963). For readers of modern Greek, two important works are Athanasios Angelopoulos's *Nikolaos Kabasilas Chamaetos, Hē zōe kai to ergon autou* (Thessaloniki, 1970) and Panagiotes Nellas's *Hē peri dikaiōseōs didaskalia Nikolaou tou Kabasila* (Piraeus, 1975).

Panagiotis C. Christou (1987)
Translated from Greek by Philip M. McGhee

CABTILLATION See CHANTING

CAIN AND ABEL, the first two sons of Adam and Eve, the progenitors of the race according to the Bible, after their banishment from the garden of Eden (*Gn.* 4). Cain (Heb., Qayin), the elder, was a farmer; Abel (Heb., Hevel) was a shepherd. The biblical text jumps from their birth to a later episode when both made (apparently votary) offerings to the Lord: Cain presented a meal offering of his fruits and grains, while Abel offered up the firstlings of his sheep. The offering of Cain was rejected by the Lord, and that of Abel was accepted. No reason for this is given, and generations of pious attempts to justify this event have been made by contrasting the intentions of the donors and the nature and quality of their donations. Cain's despondency led to a divine caution to resist the temptation to sin (*Gn.* 4: 6–7); presumably this refers to the jealous urges and hostile resentments Cain felt. But the elder brother was overwrought and killed his brother in the field. This led to the punishment of Cain: like his father, he would not farm a fertile earth; and, like him, he would be banished "eastward of Eden." Fearing further retribution, Cain was given a protective "sign," whose aspect delighted the fancy in later legends and art. There is a deliberate reuse of the language of the temptation and punishment of Adam and Eve (*Gn.* 3) in the ensuing account of the temptation and punishment of Cain (*Gn.* 4: 1–17).

The murder of Abel by Cain in *Genesis* 4: 1–17 is the first social crime recorded in the Bible, and it complements on the external level the inner temptation and misuse of will depicted in similar language in *Genesis* 3. The tradition of Cain's act of murder and his subsequent punishment is followed by a genealogical list that presents him as the progenitor of several culture heroes. His son, Enoch, founded the first city (*Gn.* 4: 18); and two other descendants, Jubal and Tubalcain, were respectively named the cultural ancestors of "all who play the lyre and the pipe" (*Gn.* 4: 21) and those "who forged all implements of copper and iron" (*Gn.* 4: 22). There is thus an anachronistic blending of Cain, whose name means "smith," with an ancient agricultural forebear. In so presenting Cain as the ancestor of technology and culture, the tradition displays a pessimistic attitude toward such achievements (complementing the attitude taken in the tower of Babel episode, in *Genesis* 10: 1–9) and shows a profound psychological insight into the energies and drives that underlie civilization. The episode of *Genesis* 4: 1–17 may reflect an old literary motif of debates between farmers and herdsmen as well as the fairly universal theme of fraternal pairs who represent contrasting psychological and cultural types.

Early rabbinic interpretation drew forth various elements of the story for moral and theological emphasis. The Midrash elaborates the psychology of fraternal strife (*Genesis Rabbah* 22.7), depicts Cain's impious rejection of divine justice when his offering is rejected but also notes his act of repentance in the end (*Gn. Rab.* 11.13), and shows the cycle of violence that was unleashed by Cain's act, since this deed led to his accidental death at the hands of his descendant Lamech who, in grief, accidentally killed his own son as well (*Gn.* 4: 23–24). Early Christian tradition focused on Abel as the head of a line of prophets who were killed (*Mt.* 23: 25) and emphasized his innocent blood (cf. *Heb.* 12: 24); thus they set the framework for the typology that related Abel's innocent death to that of Jesus and saw Cain as representing the children of the devil (*1 Jn.* 3: 12). For Augustine, Cain was furthermore identified with the Jews. The topos of Cain and Abel recurs in the medieval mystery plays, and the murder of Abel was a common iconographic motif in Christian and Jewish art.

BIBLIOGRAPHY

Aptowitzer, Vigdor. *Kain und Abel in der Agada den Apokryphen, der hellenistischen, christlichen und muhammedanischen Literatur.* Vienna, 1922.

Fishbane, Michael. *Text and Texture.* New York, 1979. See pages 23–27.

Ginzberg, Louis. *The Legends of the Jews* (1909–1938). 7 vols. Translated by Henrietta Szold, et al. Reprint, Philadelphia, 1937–1966. See volume 1, pages 55–59.

Réau, Louis. *Iconographie de l'art chrétien.* Vol. 2. Paris, 1956. See pages 93–100.

Speiser, E. A. *Genesis.* Anchor Bible. Vol. 1. Garden City, N.Y., 1964. See pages 29–38.

New Sources

Levin, Schneir. "The Abel Syndrome." *Jewish Bible Quarterly* 20 (1991): 111–114.

Paine, Robert. "'Am I My Brother's Keeper?' (Genesis IV:9): Violence and the Making of Society." *Qualitative Sociology* 24 (2001): 169–189.

Ratner, Robert J. "Cain and Abel, and the Problem of Paradox." *Journal of Reform Judaism* 37 (1990): 9–20.

MICHAEL FISHBANE (1987)
Revised Bibliography

CAITANYA. For half a millennium, Caitanya has been revered by millions of Hindus, especially in eastern India, as a unique human manifestation of the divine Kṛṣṇa. He is understood to be Kṛṣṇa come to bestow devotion *(bhakti)* and salvation *(uddhāra/nistāra)* upon even the lowliest of persons, while combining in himself the fair complexion and devotional sentiments of Rādhā, his divine mistress. *Caitanya* is a popular shortened form of *Kṛṣṇa-Caitanya* (whose consciousness is of Kṛṣṇa), the religious name taken at his ascetic initiation *(saṃnyāsa)* by Viśvambhara Miśra (1486–1533), an ecstatic devotee and Vaiṣṇava revivalist. To his devotees, Caitanya is the paradigm of an emotionally intense, loving devotion *(prema-bhakti)* to Kṛṣṇa—which humans may aspire to emulate while never reaching the perfection of their divine/human exemplar. He is also the object of their devout adoration, affirmed to be God, Kṛṣṇa, appearing within recent human history to establish loving devotion as the religious norm *(yuga-dharma)* of the current degenerate era, the *kaliyuga* (Kali age).

LIFE. Viśvambhara (i.e., Caitanya) was born/appeared at the onset of a lunar eclipse on the full moon day of Phālgun month, February 27, 1486, at Navadvip town, the center of Sanskrit learning in then Muslim-ruled Bengal. The second son of a Vaiṣṇava Brāhmaṇ, Jagannātha Miśra, and his wife Śacī, he became a Sanskrit *paṇḍit,* married Lakṣmī, and, after her untimely death, wed Viṣṇupriyā. At the age of twenty-two, he journeyed to Gaya to perform post-funeral rites *(śrāddha)* for his late father and first wife. While there, he was overwhelmed by devotion to Kṛṣṇa and promptly took initiation *(dīkṣā)* from a Vaiṣṇava gurū, Īśvara Purī. He returned to Navadvip overflowing with eagerness to spread devotion to Kṛṣṇa.

Viśvambhara's charismatic proselytizing led him to be readily hailed by the Vaiṣṇavas of Navadvip as their leader. For about a year, he led devotional singing, acted in devotional dramas, and even challenged the Muslim authorities by leading *saṃkīrtana* (collective religious chanting) processions through Navadvip. His behavior, both when in normal consciousness and when in ecstatic states, suggested to his followers that he was in some way God, Hari (i.e., Kṛṣṇa), manifesting himself in human guise. His engrossing passion for *bhakti* to Kṛṣṇa brought an end to his career as *paṇḍit* and soon culminated in renunciation of domestic life while still childless. He received ascetic initiation from Keśava Bhāratī in February 1510, when he took the name Kṛṣṇa-Caitanya.

Soon after taking *saṃnyāsa,* Caitanya went to the Jagannāth (Kṛṣṇa) deity (i.e., sacred image) in his great temple at Puri in Orissa. For several years, he traveled intermittently throughout India meeting adherents of diverse religious orientations—appealing all the while for devotion to Kṛṣṇa. His longest journey was through South India, toward the beginning of which he met Rāmānanda Rāya, whose spiritual sensibilities were remarkably akin to his own. It was Rāmānanda who first declared Caitanya to be not simply Kṛṣṇa, but Kṛṣṇa combined with Rādhā. A subsequent journey toward the Vraja region—locale of Mathura and Vrindavan—via Bengal was cut short after Caitanya began attracting large crowds. Caitanya subsequently did make the much-desired journey to Vraja via wooded tracts of Orissa, where he spread devotion to Kṛṣṇa among tribal peoples. While in Vraja, he visited traditional sites of Kṛṣṇa's birth, childhood, and youthful pastimes *(līlās),* and is said to have discovered still other sites.

From 1516 Caitanya remained at Puri, where he worshiped Jagannātha, engaged in his private devotions, and counseled disciples. The latter included prominent devotees from Bengal who would make an annual pilgrimage for the Jagannātha Chariot Festival *(ratha yātrā)* in June and remain with Caitanya for the duration of the rainy season. In his later years, Caitanya underwent intense and prolonged devotional states, often turbulent and ecstatic, pained by the sense of separation *(viraha)* from Kṛṣṇa. Among those who cared for him during these tormented years was Svarūpa Dāmodara, whose "notes" *(kaḍacā),* based on his intimate observations of and communication with Caitanya, had a crucial role in shaping the Vaiṣṇava theology being developed by the Gosvāmins (pastors) whom Caitanya had earlier directed to settle in and around Vrindavan. There is no confirmed report of the circumstances of his death/disappearance at Puri in the month of Āṣāṛh (possibly July 9) in 1533. But one early biographer, Jayānanda, mentions an injury that became septic. Vaiṣṇava tradition affirms his merging with the Jagannātha deity.

There are several extant accounts in Sanskrit and in Bengali of Caitanya's life and mission composed within eighty years of his passing. The earliest is the Sanskrit *Kṛṣṇa-caitanya-caritāmṛta* by a childhood friend and adult disciple, Murāri Gupta. The most informative are Vṛndāvanadāsa's *Caitanya-bhāgavata* (c. 1548; in Bengali) and Kṛṣṇadāsa Kavirāja's *Caitanya-caritāmṛta* (c. 1612; also in Bengali but containing many Sanskrit verses). As remarked by Edward C. Dimock Jr. and Tony K. Stewart in their introduction to the former's definitive translation of this masterpiece of Caitanya Vaiṣṇava literature, "it is far more than a simple biography; it is a compendium of historical fact, religious legend, and abstruse theology so complete and blended in such proportions that it is the definitive work of the religious group called Vaiṣṇava, since the time of Caitanya the most significant single religious group in all of eastern India" (1999, p. 3).

Caitanya himself, though he inspired men of great learning and piety to compose a massive corpus of Sanskrit texts, may have left at most eight Sanskrit stanzas, including the following (in Dimock's translation):

> He who knows himself as humbler than the grass, who is more forbearing than a tree, who feels no pride but gives honor to other men, he should practice always the Hari-*kīrtana.* (3:20:Sl. 5) He may crush my breasts in embracing me, a slave to his feet, he may destroy my heart by not appearing to me, he may be a libertine wherever he wants, but still he is the lord of my heart, and there is no other. (3:20:Sl. 10)

THEOLOGY. Caitanya's conception of God and humankind—as elaborated by the theologians he inspired and guided—is grounded in the *Bhāgavata Purāṇa.* The divine is understood to have three modes, in order of ascending ultimacy: *brahman* (conscious, but undifferentiated ground of being), *paramātman* (conscious divine soul indwelling all individual souls), and *bhagavān* (ultimate conscious reality, personal and possessed of all auspicious forms and qualities, encompassing and surpassing *brahman* and *paramātman*). Kṛṣṇa is understood to be the quintessential *bhagavān* (*"Kṛṣṇas tu svayam Bhagavān"; Bhāgavata Purāṇa* 1:3:28).

Human souls *(jīvas)* are minute emanations, paradoxically different and yet not different *(acintyabhedābheda)* from their divine source. A soul undergoes rebirth unless and until by divine mercy *(kṛpā)* it realizes its true nature as devoted servant of Kṛṣṇa. In the present degenerate age, Kṛṣṇa appears in the merciful guise of Caitanya to promulgate a simpler, universally accessible religious norm for the age, namely loving devotion to himself, evoked and expressed best through chanting his names *(nāmakīrtana).* In principle, all persons, and especially such disfavored classes as women, *śūdras,* and sinners, are eligible for *bhakti,* by which they may be delivered from bondage to spiritual ignorance *(avidyā),* sin *(pāpa),* and rebirth *(saṃsāra).* Devout souls may imitate the roles and sentiments displayed by Kṛṣṇa's eternal companions: his servants, parents, friends, and lovers, who are depicted in the *Bhāgavata Purāṇa* and other Vaiṣṇava texts. The goal of human life is to enter into eternal communion with Kṛṣṇa and his divine and human companions, to participate with them in his transcendent pastimes, expressive of loving devotion.

The myriad theological works in Sanskrit by the Gosvāmins whom Caitanya dispatched to Vrindavan include commentaries on the *Bhāgavata Purāṇa* by Sanātana (tenth canto) and Jīva (entire text); the *Bhaktirasāmṛtasindhu* and *Ujjvala-nīlamaṇi,* two reference anthologies by Rūpa Gosvāmin illustrating devotional dramatic theory *(bhakti-rasa-śāstra);* inspirational dramas and poems by Rūpa Gosvāmin, Raghunāthadāsa, and others; a liturgical-cum-disciplinary manual, *Hari-bhakti-vilāsa,* by Gopāla Bhaṭṭa and Sanātana; Sanātana's *Bṛhad-bhāgavatāmṛta,* a "pilgrim's progress" of a devout soul in search of ever more favored modes of devotion and ever more intimate self-disclosures of the divine; and the *Ṣaṭ-sandarbha* (or *Bhāgavata-sandarbha*), a *summa* of Vaiṣṇava theology and philosophy by Jīva (based on a prior outline by Gopāla Bhaṭṭa).

INFLUENCE. Caitanya and the movement (often called Gauḍīya or Bengali Vaiṣṇava) of which he was the fervent catalyst spread devotion to Kṛṣṇa throughout Bengal, Orissa, and Vraja and to a lesser extent Assam, with scattered circles of devotees elsewhere in India. Restoration and popularization of sites sacred to Kṛṣṇa in the Vraja region owed much to the zeal of Caitanya and his disciples. Vernaculars of eastern India, especially Bengali, are far the richer for a host of original sacred biographies and hagiographies plus songs, poems, and other Vaiṣṇava compositions; and for numerous vernacular translations and adaptations based on Sanskrit texts treating Kṛṣṇa, Caitanya, or Vaiṣṇava *bhakti.* Bengali culture as a whole, including its non-Vaiṣṇava Hindu and even Muslim sectors and as refracted through modern creative figures such a Rabindranath Tagore, has been influenced profoundly by the symbolism, ethos, values, and sensibilities of Caitanya's humane and emotionally and aesthetically refined devotion to God as Kṛṣṇa. Even practitioners of transgressive Tantric yoga—the hybrid Vaiṣṇava-Sahajiyās, many of whom sang Vaiṣṇava lyrics—have claimed to share in the heritage of Caitanya.

Through the ministering of certain of Caitanya's married associates (also called Gosvāmins), notably the egalitarian Nityānanda and the more elitist Advaita Ācārya and their descendants, as well as Vaiṣṇava ascetics, the majority of Bengali Hindus in the middle castes and considerable numbers in the upper and lower castes had come to identify themselves religiously as Vaiṣṇava in the tradition of Caitanya by the time of British Indian ethnographic and census reports. Even so, Caitanya Vaiṣṇava prestige was on the wane in urban Bengal by the late nineteenth century, despite the efforts of many to revitalize, reform, and modernize the tradition. Notable among these modernizers was Kedarnath Datta (Bhaktivinode Thakur, 1838–1914), a deputy magistrate of *kāyastha* caste. He wrote numerous Vaiṣṇava texts, launched a vigorous revitalization campaign, and sought to make traditional Kṛṣṇa-Caitanya *bhakti* comprehensible to his rationalist contemporaries in Calcutta and elsewhere. His son, Bimalprasad Datta (Bhaktisiddhanta Sarasvati, 1874–1937), founded the Gauḍīya Maṭh, a pan-Indian network of monastic communities and temples centered in Calcutta and Sri Mayapur (adjacent to modern Navadvip) and dedicated to preaching and publishing about Caitanya Vaiṣṇava *bhakti*. One of Bhaktisiddhanta's disciples, Abhaycaran De (A. C. Bhaktivedanta, 1896–1977), inaugurated the International Society for Krishna Consciousness (ISKCON) in New York in 1966. Its several thousand devotees, mostly non-Indians, currently propagate devotion to Kṛṣṇa-Caitanya worldwide using modern means of communication combined with traditional chanting of the "great prayer" *(mahā-mantra)*: "Hare Krishna, Hare Krishna, Krishna, Krishna, Hare, Hare; Hare Rāma, Hare Rāma, Rāma, Rāma, Hare, Hare."

SEE ALSO Bengali Religions; International Society for Krishna Consciousness; Kṛṣṇa, Kṛṣṇaism; Rādhā.

BIBLIOGRAPHY

An excellent source in English for studying the life, devotional image, and impact of Caitanya is the *Caitanya Caritāmṛta of Kṛṣṇadāsa Kavirāja: A Translation and Commentary* by Edward C. Dimock Jr., with an "Introduction" by Dimock and Tony K. Stewart (Cambridge, Mass., 1999). Valuable analyses of the textual sources for Caitanya's life are Sushil Kumar De's *Early History of the Vaiṣṇava Faith and Movement in Bengal,* 2d ed. (Calcutta, 1961); Bimanbehari Majumdar's *Śrīcaitanya-cariter Upādān,* 2d ed. (Calcutta, 1959); and assessments by Radhagovinda Nath in his editions of the *Caitanya-caritāmṛta,* 6 vols. (Calcutta, 1962–1963) and Vṛndāvanadāsa's *Caitanya-bhāgavata,* 6 vols. (Calcutta, 1966). Other academic studies of Caitanya and his devotees' perceptions of him include: A. K. Majumdar's *Caitanya: His Life and Doctrine* (Calcutta, 1978), Walther Eidlitz's *Kṛṣṇa-Caitanya: Sein Leben und seine Lehre* (Stockholm, 1968), Deb Narayan Acharyya's *The Life and Times of Śrīkṛṣṇa-Caitanya* (Calcutta, 1984), and the less-than-sympathetic book by Amulyachandra Sen, *Itihāsera Śrīcaitanya* (Calcutta, 1965). Sixteenth-century accounts (besides the *Caitanya-caritāmṛta*) of Caitanya and his disciples available in English translation include the *Caitanya-candrāmṛta* of Prabodhānanda, translated by Bhakti Prajnan Yati Maharaj (3d ed.; Madras, 1978), and several by Kusakratha Dasa of the Krishna Institute (Los Angeles) and by other devotees. For analysis of the tension between historicity and theology-cum-mythology as reflected in each of the sacred biographies, see Tony K. Stewart's "The Biographical Images of Kṛṣṇa Caitanya: A Study in the Perception of Divinity" (Ph.D. diss., University of Chicago, 1985).

For academic studies of the theological-philosophical tradition stemming from Caitanya, see O. B. L. Kapoor's *The Philosophy and Religion of Śrī Caitanya* (Delhi, 1978), Sushil Kumar De's *Early History of the Vaiṣṇava Faith and Movement in Bengal,* 2d ed. (Calcutta, 1961), Radhagovinda Nath's *Gauḍīya Vaiṣṇava Darśan,* 6 vols. (Calcutta, 1956–1959), Sudhindra Chandra Chakravarti's *Philosophical Foundation of Bengal Vaiṣṇavism* (Calcutta, 1969), and Mahanamabrata Brahmachari's *Vaiṣṇava Vedānta: The Philosophy of Śrī Jīva Gosvāmī* (Calcutta, 1974). Modern devotees' presentations of Caitanya and the teachings associated with him include Sisir Kumar Ghosh [Ghoshe]'s *Śrī Amiya Nimāi Carita,* 14th ed., 6 vols. (1907; Calcutta, 1975); Bhakti Vilas Tirtha's *Śrī Chaitanya's Concept of Theistic Vedānta* (Madras, 1964); and A. C. Bhaktivedanta's *The Teachings of Lord Chaitanya* (New York, 1968).

Among well-translated compositions of devotional literature in the Caitanya Vaiṣṇava tradition are *Śrī Bṛhad Bhāgavatāmṛta of Sanātana Gosvāmī,* 2 vols. (Los Angeles, 2002–2003), translated by Gopīparānadhana Dāsa; *Mystic Poetry: Rūpa Gosvāmin's Uddhava-Sandeśa and Haṁsadūta* (San Francisco, 1999), translated by Jan Brzezinski; *In Praise of Krishna: Songs from the Bengali* (Garden City, N.Y., 1967; reprint, Chicago, 1981), translated by Edward C. Dimock Jr. and Denise Levertov; and Sukumar Sen's *History of Brajabuli Literature* (Calcutta, 1935). Donna Marie Wulff's *Drama as a Mode of Religious Realization: The Vidagdhamādhava of Rūpa Gosvāmī* (Chico, Calif., 1984) and David Haberman's *Acting as a Way of Salvation: A Study of Rāgānugā Bhakti Sādhana* (New Delhi, 1988) provide detailed expositions of how Vaiṣṇava religious training *(sādhana)* draws upon devotional literature and dramatic theory.

A remarkably thorough survey of all aspects of the Vaiṣṇava tradition in Bengal from Caitanya's time through the nineteenth century is Ramakanta Chakrabarty's *Vaiṣṇavism in Bengal: 1486–1900* (Calcutta, 1985). For Orissa, see Prabhat Mukherjee's *History of the Chaitanya Faith in Orissa* (New Delhi, 1979) and for Vraja, Alan W. Entwistle's *Braj: Centre of Krishna Pilgrimage* (Groningen, Germany, 1987). Sociocultural implications of the Caitanya movement are examined by Melville T. Kennedy's *The Chaitanya Movement: A Study of Vaishnavism of Bengal* (Calcutta, 1925), Hitesranjan Sanyal's *Bāṅlā Kīrtaner Itihās* (Calcutta, 1989), and Joseph

T. O'Connell's *Religious Movements and Social Structure: The Case of Chaitanya's Vaiṣṇavas of Bengal* (Shimla, India, 1993). For the Vaiṣṇava-Sahajiyā phenomenon, see Edward C. Dimock Jr.'s *The Place of the Hidden Moon: Erotic Mysticism in the Vaiṣṇava-Sahajiyā Cult of Bengal* (Chicago, 1966). Modern developments in the Caitanya tradition in India are treated in Shukavak N. Dasa's *Hindu Encounter with Modernity: Kedarnath Datta Bhaktivinoda, Vaisnava Theologian* (Los Angeles, 1999) and in North America by J. Stillson Judah's *Hare Krishna and the Counterculture* (New York, 1974).

JOSEPH T. O'CONNELL (2005)

CAKRAS. Literally meaning a circle, wheel, or discus, the Sanskrit term *cakra* plays a key role in both Hindu and Buddhist traditions, particularly in their more esoteric Tantric forms. The term has several uses in various forms of yogic and Tantric practice. Thus cakra may refer to the circle of worship in which a particular ritual is conducted—for example, the highly esoteric *cakra pūjā* of Hindu Tantric rituals, usually performed in the dead of night in a cremation ground, involving practices that deliberately violate traditional laws of class distinctions and purity. Cakras may also refer to circular diagrams used in meditation and the worship of such specific deities as the famous Śri Cakras or Śri Yantra images associated with the goddess Tripurāsundarī.

In Hindu and Buddhist yogic practice, however, cakra has a more specific meaning. In these traditions it refers to the spiritual energy centers believed to lie within the human subtle body (*sukṣma śarīra*). The subtle body in the yogic tradition is the immaterial aspect of the living being that lies between its gross physical form and its divine spiritual essence. This subtle organism is comprised of a complex network of arteries (*nāḍīs*, usually numbered at seventy-two thousand), knots (*granthis*), and energy centers (cakras), which correspond only roughly to the arteries and organs of the physical body. The cakras are often imagined not just as wheels but also as lotus blossoms with varying numbers of petals and even in some traditions as ponds connected by an internal network of rivers.

The most widely known list of cakras in the early twenty-first century is the sixfold system, which identifies six energy centers located along the spinal column from the base of the spine to the eyebrows, with a seventh supreme cakra at the crown of the head. This sixfold list, however, is by no means the only or oldest one; it became standardized only after the publication of a translation of one relatively late text, the *Ṣaṭ-cakra-nirūpaṇa*, by Sir John George Woodroffe in 1919. The historical origin of the cakras as inner centers of subtle energy is not entirely clear. Some scholars believe that the cakras are derived from circular arrays of powerful goddesses who were originally represented externally in temples and ritual diagrams but were then gradually internalized and identified with energy centers within the body (White, 2003, p. 222). The earliest-known accounts of cakras as inner circles of energy actually come from an eighth-century Buddhist text, the *Hevajra Tantra*, which identifies four cakras in the body at the navel, heart, throat, and head respectively. These cakras are in turn identified with four geographical sites (*pīṭhas*) in India regarded as sacred to the Great Goddess, Devi or Śakti. The classic group of six cakras emerged slowly; not until the ninth or tenth century, in works like the *Kaulajñānanirṇaya*, does one find an identifiable system of six energy centers called cakras. Other yogic traditions, however, added a variety of other cakras, some listing as many as twelve.

According to the well-known sixfold system, the name and location of the cakras is as follows:

1. the *mūlādhāra*, located between the anus and the genitals, imagined as a lotus with four petals;
2. the *svādhiṣṭhānā* at the root of the genitals, with six petals;
3. the *maṇipūra* at the navel, with ten petals;
4. the *anāhata* at the heart, with twelve petals;
5. the *viśuddha* at the throat, with sixteen petals;
6. the *ājñā* between the eyebrows, with two petals.

Above these six lies a seventh and ultimate cakra, the *sahasrāra*, imagined as a thousand-petaled lotus that serves as the divine seat of Lord Śiva. Each of the cakras is also in turn enmeshed in a complex network of correspondences and is identified with a particular color, shape, element, cosmic principle, sacred syllable, and deity.

The aim of yogic practice is to awaken the divine creative energy believed to lie within every human body. This energy is imagined in the form of a coiled serpent or *kuṇḍalinī*, which represents the microcosmic presence of the divine power (*śakti*) of the goddess within each of us. When this energy is awakened through meditation, it can be made to rise upward through the body, where it successively penetrates the six cakras and awakens the various powers associated with each one. Finally, when it reaches the *sahasrāra* cakra at the crown of the head, the yogi experiences the supreme union of the divine male and female principles—Lord Śiva and the Goddess Śakti —within his or her own body.

Although the cakras do not exist as physically measurable entities in the material body, they do correspond to particular psychological states and levels of consciousness. Their opening in turn leads to "mental transformation and the opening of the psyche to hitherto inaccessible levels of consciousness" (Kakar, 1988, p. 187). On the other hand, the malfunctioning of the cakras may also lead to a variety of mental and physical problems. For example, a disorder in the *svādhiṣṭhāna* cakra at the base of the genitals can produce delusion, infatuations, and sexual disturbances among other ills (Kakar, 1998, p. 188).

One of the more remarkable figures in modern history to describe his experience of the cakras was the great Bengali holy man Sri Ramakrishna Paramahamsa (1836–1886). According to Ramakrishna, the lower three cakras associated with the anus, the sexual organs, and the navel correspond primarily to the instinctual levels of consciousness, namely greed and desire. The higher cakras, however, relate to the transcendent states of consciousness found in the heart, in mystical experience, and finally in "complete absorption in the mystic-erotic union of Śiva and Śakti" (Kripal, 1988, p. 44). As Ramakrishna described the awakening of the highest cakra, it is a state of pure ecstatic annihilation in union with the divine: "When the *kuṇḍalinī* comes here there is *Samādhi* [meditative absorption]. In this *sahasrāra*, Śiva, full of *sat* [Being] *cit* [Consciousness] and *ānanda* [Bliss], resides in union with Śakti . . . . In *Samādhi* nothing external remains. One cannot even take care of his body any more; if milk is put into his mouth, he does not swallow. If he remains for twenty-one days in this condition, he is dead" (Dimock, 1966, p. 178). For Ramakrishna then, the awakening of the seven cakras suggests that there is no rigid separation of the physical and spiritual or the sexual and transcendent dimensions of consciousness. Rather, the higher and lower cakras lie on a continuum in which "mystical union and sexual experience are different wavelengths of the same energetic spectrum" (Kripal, 1998, pp. 45–46). Through the techniques of yoga and meditation, sexual energy itself can be transformed into mystical experience, greed and desire into spiritual ecstasy.

In the early twenty-first century the cakras and techniques of awakening them are found not only in esoteric Tantric traditions but are also more widely dispersed throughout other Indian yogic practices. They have also made their way to the West and are now a regular feature in much of New Age and other alternative forms of spirituality across Europe and the United States.

SEE ALSO Kuṇḍalinī; Maṇḍalas, article on Hindu Maṇḍalas; New Age Movement; Ramakrishna; Tantrism, overview article; Yantra; Yoga.

BIBLIOGRAPHY

For good discussions of the cakras and their historical development, see David Gordon White, *The Alchemical Body: Siddha Traditions in Medieval India* (Chicago, 1996), and *Kiss of the Yoginī: "Tantric Sex" in Its South Asian Contexts* (Chicago, 2003). The classic description of the sixfold system is Sir John George Woodroffe, trans., *The Serpent Power, Being the Ṣaṭ-cakra-nirūpaṇa and Pādukā-pañcaka* (London, 1919). On Ramakrishna's description of the cakras, see Jeffrey J. Kripal, *Kālī's Child: The Mystical and the Erotic in the Life and Teachings of Ramakrishna* (Chicago, 1998); and Edward C. Dimock, *The Place of the Hidden Moon: Erotic Mysticism in the Vaiṣṇava-Sahajiyā Cult of Bengal* (Chicago, 1966). For an interesting psychological interpretation of the cakras, see Sudhir Kakar, *Shamans, Mystics, and Doctors: A Psychological Inquiry into India and Its Healing Traditions* (New York, 1982).

ANDRÉ PADOUX (1987)
HUGH URBAN (2005)

CAKRASAMVARA.

The term *Cakrasamvara,* "the binding of the wheels," designates both a Buddhist scripture and also the *maṇḍala* that it describes, which is the abode of a host of deities centering around the divine couple Śrīheruka and Vajravārāhi. The text, the *Cakrasamvara Tantra,* is also known as the *Śriheruka-abhidhāna* (The discourse of Śrīheruka) and the *Laghusamvara (Samvara* light), a name it earned because it is a short text of approximately seven hundred Sanskrit stanzas. It was composed in India during the mid-to-late eighth century, and it quickly became one of the most important Indian Buddhist Tantras, as evidenced by the large number of commentaries and associated ritual literature that it inspired. Like most Tantras, it is primarily a ritual text, dedicating most of its fifty-one chapters to the description of rites such as the production of the *maṇḍala* and the consecration ceremonies performed within it, as well as various other ritual actions such as *homa* fire sacrifices, enchantment with *mantras,* and so forth. It is a rather cryptic text, one which never gives sufficient information for the performance of these rituals and that often obscures crucial elements, particularly the *mantras,* which the text typically present in reverse order or in codes via an elaborate scheme in which both the vowels and consonants are coded by number.

The *Cakrasamvara Tantra* is classified by Buddhists as a Yoginī or Mother Tantra, a designation that reflects the focus of the text upon female deities, who constitute a significant majority of the deities in the tradition's main *maṇḍala.* It also reflects a focus on practices that, in a Buddhist monastic context at least, were deemed transgressive, such as sexual yogic practices as well as animal sacrifice and apparently even anthropophagy. Another characteristic of texts of this genre is an influence from non-Buddhist, particularly Śaiva, sources, as is most notable in the appearances of the deities themselves, who are quite similar to fierce Hindu deities such as Bhairava and Kālī. This reflects the complex origins of the text, which probably was inspired by teachings and practices of the loosely organized groups of "accomplished ones" (*siddha*), male and female practitioners of yoga who, generally speaking, do not seem to have had strongly defined religious identities. Their teachings, and the texts derived from them, seem to have been an important influence on the development of both Buddhist and Hindu Tantric traditions. The *Cakrasamvara Tantra* was particularly influenced by quasi-heretical Śaiva groups such as the Kāpālikas, who were infamous for their transgressive practices, that is, their employment of violence, meat eating, intoxicants, and sexuality as key elements of their spiritual practice.

According to the myths constructed to account for the origin of the Cakrasamvara tradition, the undeniable similarity between the Cakrasamvara deities and practices and those of their Śaiva competitors is not accidental, but a direct result of the "historical" revelation of the tradition. While there are several versions of the myth, all agree that this revelation was triggered by the takeover by Śaiva deities of twenty-four sacred sites scattered across the Indian subcontinent. There, they engaged in transgressive practices such as wanton sexuality and sacrifice of living beings. In order to put an end to their "misbehavior," the cosmic Buddha Mahāvajradhara, along with his retinue, assumed the appearance of these Śaiva deities and then subdued them, in the process transforming the Indian subcontinent into the Cakrasamvara *maṇḍala.* This myth reflects the mixed origins of the tradition and expresses a Buddhist awareness that one of their more important textual and ritual traditions shared more than superficial similarity with those upheld by rival Hindu groups.

By far the most important ritual element of the Cakrasamvara tradition is its *maṇḍala.* It is called the Three Wheeled, or *tricakra,* because its primary structural element is three wheels or concentric circles that are correlated both to the Triple World, or *trailokya,* of ancient Indian cosmology (that is, the heavens, earth, and underworlds) and to the three Buddhist psychophysical realms of body, speech, and mind. At the center of *maṇḍala,* in a palace atop the cosmic mountain, is Śrīheruka and Vajravārāhī in sexual embrace, surrounded by the Four Essence Yoginīs, Dākinī, Lāmā, Khaṇḍarohā and Rūpiṇī. They are in turn surrounded by the Three Wheels, three concentric Mind, Speech, and Body wheels, each of which has eight pairs of deities in sexual embrace, for a total of twenty-four couples, corresponding to the sacred sites. At the periphery of the wheels are eight fierce goddesses, who guard the *maṇḍala*'s gates and corners. This brings the total number of deities to sixty-two, thirty-seven of which are female. Lastly, artistic depictions of the maṇḍala usually show it as surrounded by the "eight great charnel grounds," inhabited by fearsome beasts and evil spirits.

This *maṇḍala* has been deployed in several important ways. It has been remapped across the Kathmandu Valley and Tibet, where many of the sites associated with the *maṇḍala* continue to be important pilgrimage places. Additionally, it is also mapped onto the human body, with the pilgrimage sites and associated deities linked to various parts of of the body. In the contemplative "body *maṇḍala*" practice, the adept visualizes the *maṇḍala* within her or his body, which is seen as a microcosmic version of the universe in its ideal form, as the pure abode of the *maṇḍala* deities. These practices helped ensure the successful transmission of the Cakrasamvara tradition to Nepal, Tibet, and Mongolia, where it is still practiced today.

BIBLIOGRAPHY

Davidson, Ronald. "Reflections on the Maheśvara Subjugation Myth: Indic Materials, Sa-skya-pa Apologetics, and the Birth of Heruka." *Journal of the International Association of Buddhist Studies* 14, no. 2 (1991): 197–235. An analysis of Buddhist myths of the conversion of Hindu deities.

Davidson, Ronald. *Indian Esoteric Buddhism.* New York, 2002. An overview of the history of esoteric Buddhism in India, with a useful discussion of the Cakrasamvara sacred sites and their relation to rival Hindu groups.

Dawa-Samdup, Kazi, ed. *Śri-Cakraśamvara-Tantra: A Buddhist Tantra.* Calcutta, 1919; reprint, New Delhi, 1987. Not a translation of the *Cakrasamvara Tantra* itself, but of several related ritual texts.

Huber, Toni. *The Cult of Pure Crystal Mountain: Popular Pilgrimage and Visionary Landscape in Southeast Tibet.* Oxford, 1999. A detailed study of an important Tibetan Cakrasamvara pilgrimage place.

Huntington, John, and Dina Bangdel. *The Circle of Bliss: Buddhist Meditational Art.* Chicago, 2003. A detailed study of Cakrasamvara art and iconography.

Mullin, Glenn. *Tsongkhapa's Six Yogas of Naropa.* Ithaca, N.Y., 1996. A translation of Tsongkhapa's commentary on a tradition of yoga closely associated with the Cakrasamvara.

Shaw, Miranda. *Passionate Enlightenment: Women in Tantric Buddhism.* Princeton, N.J., 1994. A study of the role of women in Buddhist Yoginī Tantra traditions.

DAVID B. GRAY (2005)

CAKRAVARTIN is a Sanskrit noun referring to an ideal universal king who rules ethically and benevolently over the entire world. Derived from the Sanskrit *cakra,* "wheel," and *vartin,* "one who turns," the term *cakravartin* (Pali, *cakkavatti*) in classical Hindu texts signifies that all-powerful monarch "whose chariot wheels turn freely" or "whose travels are unobstructed." Such a ruler's unsurpassed and virtuous rule is described as *sarvabhauma*; it pertains to all creatures everywhere. Buddhist and Jain literatures describe their enlightened founders (the Buddha or Buddhas and the *tīrthaṅkaras*, respectively) in similar terms, the notion being that religious truth transcends local or national limitations and applies to all people everywhere. This idea is particularly evident in Buddhist oral and scriptural traditions, which frequently refer to Gautama as a *cakravāla cakravartin,* an illuminator of *dharma* (life in adherence to compassionate truth) in all regions of the world. From the symbol of the turning wheel, a sign of universal sovereignty, comes the description of the Buddha as *dharmacakrapravartayati,* "he who sets the wheel of law in motion," and thus the name of his first sermon, *Dharmacakrapravartana Sūtra* (Pali, *Dhammacakkappavattana Sutta*; The sūtra on the turning forth of the wheel of dharma), in which the Buddha presents his insights into the Four Noble Truths. After his death in 480 BCE, Gautama's followers cremated his body and enshrined his relics in a stupa, just as they would have done with a universal monarch.

HISTORY OF THE CAKRAVARTIN AS AN IMPERIAL IDEAL. The general South Asian notion that the king was to have extensive rule dates at least as far back as the high Vedic era (1200–800 BCE) and possibly to the centuries preceding. The Vedic ritual coronation of the king (Rājasūya), for example, was preceded by a ceremony in which a wild stallion was left to wander at will throughout the land for an entire year, at which time it was sacrificed in the important rite known as the Aśvamedha, and all of the territory it had covered in that year was held to be the king's domain. The actual term *cakra-*

vartin was known in the late fifth and early fourth centuries BCE by the compilers of the *Maitri Upaniṣad*, who used the noun when listing the names of several kings who had renounced their royal prerogatives in favor of the life of ascetic contemplation (*Maitri Upaniṣad* 1.4).

Direct discussions of the *cakravartin* as an imperial ideal appear as early as Kauṭilya's *Artha Śāstra* (c. 300 BCE), a court manual of polity, diplomacy, economy, and social behavior. In his descriptions of the range of an emperor's influence (*cakravarti-kśetra*), Kauṭilya notes that the king should undertake any task he feels will bring him and his people prosperity and that he should have power "from the Himalayas to the ocean." Kauṭilya may have had in mind the prestige and hopes of the first Mauryan king, Candragupta, who reigned from about 321 to 297 BCE and whom Kauṭilya reportedly served as chief minister. Candragupta was perhaps the first ruler to unify all of the lands from the shores of the southern tip of India to the Himalayas in the north and the Kabul Valley in the northwest. Edicts and other lessons inscribed on pillars and cliffs describe the last Mauryan king, Aśoka (d. 238 BCE?) as a *cakravartin* under whose patronage the Buddhist Dharma spread throughout South and Southeast Asia. Chroniclers in the courts of the Śātavāhana emperors (first to second centuries CE) similarly defined their kingdoms as that world extending from the eastern, southern, and western oceans to the mountains. The Guptas, too, viewed themselves as the rulers of empires. Skandha Gupta I, who reigned from 455 to 467 CE, for example, is depicted in the Janagadh inscriptions (dated mid-fifth century CE) as a leader whose rule was the entire earth bounded by the four oceans and within which thrive several smaller countries. The Western Cāḷlukyas (sixth to eighth and tenth to twelfth centuries) described themselves as the emperors of the lands between the three seas, while the Vijayanagara rulers (fourteenth to seventeenth centuries) labeled themselves the masters of the eastern, western, southern, and northern seas.

Thus the South Asian political imagination up to the seventeenth century generally included the ideal of a unified rule, and various kings have identified themselves as universal monarchs: hence the common royal titles *samrāj* ("supreme monarch," i.e., the one who rules over all princes and principalities), *rājādhirāja* ("king above kings"), *ekarāja* ("the only king"), *parama-bhaṭṭārka* ("most venerable lord"), *disampati* ("lord of the lands"), and *digvijayin* ("conqueror of the regions").

Buddhist and Jain literatures have distinguished three types of *cakravartin*. A *pradeśa cakravartin* is a monarch who leads the people of a specific region and may be thought of as a local king. A *dvīipa cakravartin* governs all of the people of any one of the four continents (*dvīipas*, literally "islands") posited by ancient Indian cosmologies and is, accordingly, more powerful in the secular realm than the *pradeśa cakravartin*. Superior even to a *dvīipa cakravartin*, however, is the *cakravāla cakravartin*, the monarch who rules over all of the continents of the world. It is the political paramountcy of the *cakravāla cakravartin* with which the Buddha's religious supremacy is compared.

RELIGIOUS DIMENSIONS OF THE CAKRAVARTIN IDEAL. The source of the image of the king as a *cakravartin* is not to be found, however, in its political history. Rather, it is the powerful and evocative South Asian mythic and religious themes regarding the *cakravartin* with which various kings identified. According to South Asian sovereign myths (many of which suggest a solar origin), the *cakravartin*—here, a paradigmatic figure—while deep in meditation sees a peaceful and pleasantly glowing wheel (*cakra*) turning slowly in the sky above him. Knowing this wheel to be a call to unify all peoples, the king leads his armies out in all directions to the farthest horizons, all the way to the universal ring of mountains (*cakravāla*) that lie beyond the oceans and that mark the final edge of the concentric world. Guided by the celestial wheel, and borne upon the atmosphere by flying white elephants and horses, he ends all strife and suffering as he brings all people everywhere under his virtuous rule. Thus, *cakravālacakravartī cakram vartayati:* the universal monarch turns the wheel of righteousness throughout the whole world.

The mythic *cakravartin*, therefore, was a ruler in whose virtue and strength all people, regardless of their homeland, could find guidance. He was a pacifying leader whose power was embodied in his unifying skills. Hence it may be no coincidence that the religious traditions in which the *cakravartin* is given the most prestige revolve around the ideologies and aspirations of the *kṣatriya* class of Indian society, that group who were to protect society, serve as its soldiers, rule its courts, and sit on its thrones. For some *kṣatriya* communities, as, for example, those represented by the epics *Mahābhārata* and *Rāmāyāṇa* (c. 300 CE), the most appropriate person to become a universal monarch was somebody who already was a king, someone who could extend his rule through martial and diplomatic skill.

Even for some *kṣatriya* traditions, however, the true *cakravartin* renounces the political life of the secular king and guides the people through the power of his spiritual virtue. Such is the case for the early Jain and, particularly, Buddhist communities, whose histories of their founders suggest the notion that to them religious truth is more powerful and universal than political prestige. According to both Jain and Buddhist literatures, both Vardhamāna Mahāvīra (the most recent of the twenty-four Jain *tīrthaṃkaras*) and Siddhārtha Gautama (the Buddha) were born into powerful royal families, both displayed the characteristic physical signs of a *mahāpuruṣa* ("great man"), and thus were certain to become secular *cakravartins*. Both traditions further maintain that their founders, however, chose not to enjoy the political power and privileges incumbent on the universal monarch but, rather, to seek understanding of the deepest dimensions of existence itself and—especially in the case of the Buddha—to teach that understanding to all.

SEE ALSO Kingship, article on Kingship in East Asia.

BIBLIOGRAPHY

Readers interested in the history of imperial rule in India may consult any of a number of good works on the history of India. A good, if relatively short, reference is *An Advanced History of India* (London, 1948), by Ramesh Chandra Majumdar and others. For more thorough studies by various respected historians, see *The History and Culture of the Indian People,* 11 vols., under the general editorship of Ramesh Chandra Majumdar (Bombay, 1951–1969): see especially volume 2, *The Age of Imperial Unity;* volume 3, *The Classical Age,* pp. 1–360; volume 4, *The Age of the Imperial Kanauj;* and volume 5, *The Struggle for Empire.* A more impressionistic depiction of the *cakravartin* ideal is found in Heinrich Zimmer's *Philosophies of India,* edited by Joseph Campbell, "Bollingen Foundation Series," no. 26 (1951; reprint, Princeton, 1969), pp. 127–139. Finally, for an example of the *cakravartin* ideal as expressed in religious myth, see Frank E. Reynolds and Mani Reynolds's translation of a Thai Buddhist text, *Three Worlds according to King Ruang* (Berkeley, 1982), pp. 135–172.

New Sources

Bartholomeusz, Tessa J. "In Defense of Dharma: Just-war Ideology in Buddhist Sri Lanka." *Journal of Buddhist Ethics* 6 (1999).

Collins, Steven. "The Lion's Roar on the Wheel-Turning King: A Response to Andrew Huxley's 'The Buddha and the Social Contract.'" *Journal of Indian Philosophy* 24 (1996): 421–446.

Daalen, Leendert A van. "Zum Thema und zur Struktur von Vakpatis Gaudavaha: der Held als cakravartin." *Deutscher Orientalistierung* 8 (1994): 282–294.

Harvey, Peter. *An Introduction to Buddhist Ethics: Foundations, Values, and Issues.* New York, 2000.

Huxley, Andrew. "The Buddha and the Social Contract." *Journal of Indian Philosophy* 24 (1996): 407–420.

WILLIAM K. MAHONY (1987)
Revised Bibliography

CALENDARS

This entry consists of the following articles:

AN OVERVIEW
MESOAMERICAN CALENDARS
SOUTH AMERICAN CALENDARS

CALENDARS: AN OVERVIEW

The absence of a historical dimension and the scant attention paid to the religious aspect of the question are the most notable limitations of the specialized literature on calendars during the nineteenth century and into the first decade of the twentieth century. Thus, such monumental works as L. Ideler's *Handbuch der mathematischen und technischen Chronologie* (Berlin, 1825–1826), F. Ginzel's work of the same title (Leipzig, 1906–1911), and even the entry "Calendars" in James Hastings's *Encyclopaedia of Religion and Ethics,* vol. 3 (Edinburgh, 1910), although they provide indispensable information, amount to little more than unconnected descriptions of various calendars. These descriptions are not satisfactorily situated against the background of the cultures in question, but are treated as if they are solely concerned with chronology and astronomy.

The sacral aspect of the question has, however, been discussed in the subsequent scientific literature, in which the specialists are divided into two opposing camps: those who believe the calendar originated as a secular phenomenon purely utilitarian in its purposes (a view accepted by the majority of scholars), and those who believe it was originally a religious institution (Ernst Cassirer, Martin P. Nilsson, Henri Hubert and Marcel Mauss, Gerardus van der Leeuw, Mircea Eliade, and others). Less common are harmonizing positions such as that of Bronislaw Malinowski, who in an article on the calendar of the Trobriand Islanders (*Journal of the Anthropological Institute* 57, 1927, pp. 203ff.), viewed systems for computing time as meeting both practical and sacral demands.

Disagreement on the subject has been largely overcome since the publication of such works as Eliade's *Cosmos and History: The Myth of the Eternal Return* (New York, 1954) and Angelo Brelich's *Introduzione allo studio dei calendari festivi* (Rome, 1955). The reality of periodicity in the world; the religious importance of this periodicity in helping to overcome the crisis that is coextensive with human existence (the duration of which is irreversible) by establishing frequent contact with the sacred time proper to the feast or festival (which is outside of ongoing duration); the parallelism between natural and sacral periodicity, both of which have as a constant a continual renewal in the same forms, so that in even the most diverse civilizations the sacral periodicity provides an effective means of keeping a timely eye on the natural periodicity—all these ideas are now well established in our discipline. As a result, any modern work on any aspect of the vast complex of problems raised by calendars must nowadays start with the acceptance of a concept that proves to be constant across the most varied cultural contexts and the most diverse calendrical forms and manifestations, namely, that time is of interest not in and of itself and as a simple fact of nature, but only as a dimension of life that can be submitted to cultural control.

Such control is very difficult to exercise over something abstract, especially in social contexts still far from possessing even rudimentary astronomical knowledge. Nevertheless, by making use of a procedure now familiar to historians of religion, the various civilizations managed to gain this kind of control. They did so especially by *concretizing* time, whether this be understood in absolute terms or in relation to the various measurements (hours, days, months, years, etc.) that were gradually imposed on time, depending on the culture in question.

Mythology makes clear how the chronological dimension (especially if limited to the distinction and alternation of the light and dark times of the day, or to the lunar phases, which are harmoniously ordered within the arc of the month) can acquire such a material form in the minds of the peoples under study that it becomes the subject of stories without causing the least disturbance in the civilizations involved. It is told, for instance, that time was wrapped in leaves (the Sulka of New Britain); enclosed in a bag (the Micmac of Nova Scotia); kept in a box (the Tlingit of the U.S. Northwest Coast) or a trunk (the Hausa of the Sudan) and later taken out; extracted from the wattles of a fowl (the Nandi of northeastern Africa); hidden and found (the Pomo of California); hung up (the northern Paiute of Nevada); hoisted up to heaven (the Pomo; the Aleut of Alaska); pierced by arrows (the Caddo of eastern Texas); or cut up with an obsidian knife (natives of Mota in Melanesia). In each case, time is looked upon not only as something very concrete but also and especially as something capable of being handled at will.

Meanwhile the concrete treatment of time was strengthening this tendency toward materialization of the chronological sphere, for the latter was being treated in such a way as to acquire an ideal spatial coherence. As a macroscopic example, one can cite the persistent attempts to identify time with space, both in language and in the calendar, by the primitive cultures of North America—a tendency also found at a higher cultural level in the Aztec calendar, and in the Indo-European area as well (Müller, 1967). In addition, a real spatiotemporal dimension is found in Roman religion, where close, complex, and functional relations are discernible in the mythological tradition and in cult, as well as in the calendrical linking of the two, between time and Terminus (the symbol of boundaries and, at the same time, a divinity in charge of the juridical, political, and sacral aspect of territory). Moreover, the projection of a cosmic framework on the layout of the circus, and this in such a detailed form (with the aid of a rich set of symbols) as to make the circus a universe in miniature, automatically transformed the chariot races in the arena into the course of the sun through the arc of the year.

Thus, it can be a rather short step from the concretization of time to its material embodiment. The example just given shows how, while the spectator at the circus (which is assimilated to the vault of heaven) feels himself to be witnessing the calendrical rotation of the sun, the charioteer is a direct protagonist in this drama as he drives his chariot.

Yet the title "protagonist of time" belongs with greater justice to those who, through actions in which it is not easy to distinguish the sacred and profane dimensions, do not limit themselves to concretizing and materializing time but also embody it in a true calendrical system. Thus the native who in certain cultures uses knotted cords for computing time does not simply concretize this dimension by pinning it down to so many firmly fixed points of its otherwise limitless and therefore uncontrollable extension but also defines it in a calendrical manner that, though rudimentary, proves functional in relation to the needs of his society. The astronomer in ancient Peru, who used stone columns called "tools for knotting the sun" *(inti-huatana)* as a position for observing the stars, did not merely give material form to that which in and of itself would be simply the calculation of solstices and equinoxes; he also carried this materialization to a higher level by developing a calendar that was primarily a means of binding the heavenly corps in its otherwise incoherent and unusable movements. (But note, too, among the Aztecs, the "knot of years," or *xiuhmolpilli,* a great cycle of fifty-two solar revolutions subdivided into four periods of thirteen years that were described as "knotted together," *thalpilli.*) The magistrate in ancient Rome who was in charge of the ritual hammering in of the *clavus annalis* ("nail of the year") on the Ides of September (which was New Year's Day in one of the many Roman calendrical systems) thereby not only turned time from an abstraction into something that could be pinned down but also compelled it to remain, from one September to the next, within the limits of the solar year.

It is possible to view in a similar perspective those who, in civilizations already familiar with writing, either ideally or in actual fact superintended the compilation of calendars, and this specifically in the form of inscriptions. In this case the concretization of time was accomplished either by binding the dimension of time to stones and/or metals, which were moved about or incised to this end, or by imprisoning it in the no less constraining nets of the various graphic forms. Evidence here is the widespread use in the ancient Near East of the alphabet as a calendrical memorandum as early as the second millennium BCE (Bausani, 1978), as well as the example, cited above, of the *clavus annalis,* which in early Rome was regarded both as a palpable sign of the year and as a functional "writing" of a chronologico-juridical kind at a time when few people could read the symbols of the alphabet.

The key role played by human beings in these operations whereby time is concretized and straitjacketed (especially within the compass of, and for the purposes of drafting, calendrical systems that are more or less developed according to cultural level and social demands) is such that, in case of need, the materialization of time can be further specified by giving it human traits in the true and proper sense. This specification may be limited to introducing into the calendar the physiological rhythms of those who are the protagonists of time. This is seen in the assimilation, widespread and found in the most diverse cultures, of the lunar month of twenty-eight days to the menstrual cycle of the same duration; or in the projection of the period of human gestation (260 days) onto the identical time period of nine lunar revolutions, as in the Aztec *tonalamatl* or the Numan calendar at Rome.

But this process of specification can also lead to a more or less concealed identification of a segment of time (located within the calendar and thus describable in precise terms) with a part or belonging of a person who usually enjoyed an important sociocultural and, in particular, religious status. Thus, as a result of Islamic influence on the Cham of Cambodia, to give but one example, the first three days of every lunar cycle are assimilated to the three favorite wives of

Muḥammad, and every year of the twelve-year cycle is equated with one of the Prophet's members.

Finally, this process can even find expression in a personification of time in its various parts. Thus in Achaemenid Iran the retinue of the magi seems to have usually comprised 365 young men dressed in red, one for each day of the year, with the color symbolizing the lighted period of the day. At Rome, on the Ides of March (New Year's Day, according to one of the many Roman calendrical systems), all the negative aspects of the old year were eliminated through the ritual expulsion from the city of the mythical carpenter Mamurius Veturius.

This kind of progressive, and in some cases even paroxysmic, personification of time seems on closer examination to be simply an expression of the persistent tendency to *recreate,* on several distinct but complementary levels, the temporal dimension that is so important at the human level, thus asserting the priority of the unqualifiedly cultural essence of time over the mere natural fact of time.

If, on the one hand, this cultural point of reference is indispensable because it is linked to any latent or open calendrical system, on the other hand such a system, whatever its character (heliacal rising of a constellation; blooming of a species of plant; period of sowing and/or harvesting; migration of animals; etc.), becomes by this very fact a field of action for the cultural process, which immediately begins to act therein in the form of well-defined and often massive interventions. In the case, widespread in both higher and primitive civilizations, of a discrepancy between the lunar and solar years, for example, the intervention takes the form of an intercalation that makes up for the difference; in other words, a portion of human, cultural time is inserted into the living body of natural time, which is computed on the basis of the revolution of the heavenly bodies.

The awareness that the intercalated period is the work of man, and the conviction that, as such, it merits a privileged position are made manifest at various levels. This is seen in the view that the year, having been thus manipulated, is now complete as compared with nature's presumably defective version of it, whence the designation—prevalent among various primitive peoples, but also found in Mesopotamia, Rome, and China—of the year or month as "full" or "empty." It is seen too in the systematic insertion of such intercalated periods immediately after moments in the calendar that sanctioned human control over the world of nature: at Rome, for example, the intercalation came immediately after the celebration of Terminalia, a festival that appealed to mythical time in order to give sacral confirmation to the cultural definition of space. Further evidence is found in the tendency to locate during the intercalated period those events that were of capital importance for the particular civilization and that evidently could not be left to the blind and irrational course of nature's time, precisely because these events were due in the maximum degree to the human will and creativity. A prime example: the definitive liquidation of monarchic rule, which was constantly assimilated to the negativity of the period of origins, in order to make way for a republic was traditionally dated by the Romans on the very day, February 24, on which the intercalation usually began.

A negative proof pointing in the same direction is the resistance to and even rejection of intercalation in those civilizations that most clearly show the assimilation of natural time to sacred time. Such rejection was preferred despite the inevitable practical nuisances it entailed—above all, discrepancy with the rhythm of the seasons. Two examples among many can be cited. First, in ancient Egypt (which adopted the practice of intercalation only in the Alexandrian period, and then not without hindrances) an oath not to intercalate was taken by the pharaoh, who, in his capacity as the future Osiris and, therefore, an important participant in the field of action proper to the sun god Re, was probably reluctant to intervene in a dimension of reality that was projected in its ideal form onto the sacral level. Second, Muḥammad categorically prohibited changing the number of the months, which "Allāh ordained . . . when he created the heavens and the earth" (*sūrah* 9:36 of the Qurʾān), and which "Allāh has sanctified" (*sūrah* 9:37). Thus the Islamic lunar year, though without any correspondence to the seasons, has proved surprisingly functional for a religion now practiced in varying latitudes. Such interventions in the course of time became even more drastic in the great calendrical reforms of Julius Caesar (46 BCE) and Pope Gregory XIII (1582 CE).

This kind of attempt to reduce time to a cultural creation is even more pronounced in those widespread cases in which the most varied means are used to emancipate time from natural phenomena on which calendrical computation is usually based and to replace these phenomena with others. Thus, the Aztecs chose the duration of human gestation, and not the Venusian year to which astronomy bears witness, as the basis of the *tonalamatl;* the Egyptians based their calendar on the rising of Sirius (Sothis), "the second sun in the heavens," and not on the true sun; while, in the most diverse primitive cultures, it is the periodic return of the ancestors, regarded as dispensers of foodstuffs, and not the particular seasonal moment that gives a specific economic meaning to the great New Year festival. Comparable motivations probably explain the otherwise incomprehensible perseverance, on the part of the most varied types of civilization, in adopting lunisolar calendars and continuing to use them right down to the present day, despite such problems as the discrepancy between festive complex and seasonal moment, the consequent necessity of intercalating, and so on. It is as though this very difference of a few days or parts of a day represents a kind of margin of security for man, who thus has leeway to act on natural time instead of passively enduring it.

This desire to be actors rather than spectators in the development of calendrical time is even more evident in those systems in which, by highly artificial means, months are established whose duration is identical with or superior to the lunar month, and in which a short period is set apart and defined in a special way, independent of the features this period may assume from time to time in any other culture. By way of example, we may think of the five "supernumerary" *(nemontemi)* days that the Aztecs set apart at the end of the 360-day year, considering them to be *nefasti* (taboo) and unsuited for work of any kind; or, in the Egyptian calendar, of the *epagomenai* ("superadded") days that did not conclude the old year, as might have been expected, but were a prelude to the new year, a kind of "little month" directly linked to the mythical time in which the gods were born. Similarly, in the Zoroastrian religion the "days of the *Gāthās*" were added to the end of the year; on these days, the celebrants, assuming the title of Saoshyant ("rescuers"), participated ritually as protagonists in the renewal of the world. Along the same line, but at a more advanced level, is the creation of units of time comprising several or more days, months, years, centuries, or even millennia, which apparently, at least, are independent of the rhythms of nature. Examples include the very widespread seven-day week (already used in Mesopotamia); the cycles of three days and three, seven, and thirty years among the Celts; the seven-year period, the jubilee, and the groups of seven-year periods among the Hebrews; the *octaetēris* or eight-year period of the Greeks; the Aztec *xiuhmolpilli;* and the Indian *kalpa.*

But perhaps the most radical humanization of the chronological dimension (the one in which the cultural intervention into nature is the most extensive, and the dependence on nature for the computation of time is reduced to a minimum that is obscured and even deliberately ignored) is found in cases in which the historical situation determines and defines the calendar. We may pass over those restructurings that are promoted or imposed on time by important politicians (i.e., the aforementioned Julian reform). In some civilizations, the personal name of the ruler was given to the current year (eponymy among the Assyrians and in the classical world, the "regnal name" in prerevolutionary China), or events of capital importance led to a complete resystematization of the calendrical pattern, the beginning, rhythm, and shape of which, though in substance inevitably following traditional lines, had to be at least formally determined by the new order of things. The prime example here is the French revolutionary calendar, which, though it started at a particular equinox, numbered 365 days, needed periodic intercalation, and linked the new names of the months with seasonal motifs, nonetheless presented new features: a beginning (September 22) that officially coincided not with the autumn equinox but with the inauguration of the republic (September 22, 1792); the abolition of the seven-day week in favor of the decade or ten-day week; the elimination of feasts; and the nonetheless festive solemnization of five or six days (significantly called *sans-culottides*) added at the end of the year as a definitive break with Christian worship.

In connection with the historicization of time, one may also consider such phenomena as the adoption of calendrical systems belonging to other civilizations, as, for instance, the entrusting of calendar reform in China in 1629 to the Jesuits, and the adoption of the Gregorian calendar as the only valid one for civil purposes by the republican government of China in 1930; the acceptance by Japan in 1684 of the Chinese calendar as reformed by the Jesuits and then in 1873 of the Gregorian calendar; and the adoption of the Gregorian calendar by Russia after the October Revolution in 1917 and by various primitive peoples as they gradually accepted the lifestyles of the Western civilizations. Finally, there is the tendency, which practical considerations and economic reasons have made stronger than ever in our day, to create a universal and perpetual calendar that is binding on all. Such a calendar would be supremely artificial, since it seeks to be as independent as possible of natural rhythms, but for that very reason would transcend the various cultures.

SEE ALSO Chronology; Sacred Time.

BIBLIOGRAPHY

The extensive bibliography of scientific writing on the subject has been brought together and discussed splendidly by Angelo Brelich in his *Introduzione allo studio dei calendari festivi,* 2 vols. in 1 (Rome, 1955). The reader is also referred to this work for the historico-religious approach to calendrical problems. Festive time in relation to the New Year is extensively discussed and documented in Vittorio Lanternari's *La grande festa,* 2d ed. (Bari, 1976). On the concretization of time at various levels, compare the following works: Werner Müller's "Raum und Zeit in Sprachen und Kalendern Nordamerikas und Alteuropas," *Anthropos* 57 (1962): 568–590, 68 (1973): 156–180, 74 (1979): 443–464, 77 (1982): 533–558; Hugh A. Moran and David H. Kelly's *The Alphabet and the Ancient Calendar Signs,* 2d ed. (Palo Alto, Calif., 1969); Alessandro Bausani's "L'alfabeto come calendario arcaico," *Oriens Antiquus* (Rome) 17 (1978): 131–146; J. H. Scharf's "Time and Language," *Gegenbaurs morphologisches Jahrbuch* 128 (1982): 257–289; and Ulrich Köhler's "Räumliche und zeitliche Bezugspunkte in mesoamerikanischen Konzepten vom Mondzyklus," *Indiana* 7 (1982): 23–42. Also compare my *Elementi spettacolari nei rituali festivi romani* (Rome, 1965); *Terminus: I segni di confine nella religione romana* (Rome, 1974); and "La scrittura coercitiva," *Cultura e scuola* 85 (1983): 117–124. Raffaele Pettazzoni treats the primitive myths on the origin of time and provides a bibliography in his *Miti e leggende,* 4 vols. (Turin, 1948–1963). Alexander Marshak discusses Paleolithic systems of noting time in *The Roots of Civilization: The Cognitive Beginnings of Man's First Art, Symbol, and Notation* (New York, 1972). While Marshak's views are somewhat controversial, they have been widely discussed.

GIULIA PICCALUGA (1987)
Translated from Italian by Matthew J. O'Connell

CALENDARS: MESOAMERICAN CALENDARS

In 1555 Bishop Diego de Landa wrote:

> The natives of Yucatan were as attentive to the matters of religion as to those of government and they had a

> high priest whom they called Ah Kin (Daykeeper) Mai . . . . He was very much respected by the lords . . . and his sons or nearest relatives succeeded him in office. In him was the key of their learning . . . . They provided priests for the towns when they were needed, examining them in the sciences . . . and they employed themselves in the duties of the temples and in teaching them their sciences as well as in writing books about them . . . . The sciences which they taught were the computation of the years, months and days, the festivals and ceremonies, the administration of the sacraments, the fateful days and seasons, their methods of devotion and their prophecies. (Tozzer, 1941, p. 27)

When he wrote those words, Bishop Diego de Landa correctly perceived the extraordinary attention paid time and calendar by the Maya of Yucatán even several centuries after their classical heyday. It is likely that these Ah Kin were among the elite of Maya culture. One eighth-century scribe from the city of Copán received a royal burial. His remains were found elaborately laid out, ink pots, brushes, and all, next to the ruler he served. Though his trappings seem far more modest in comparison to those of his precontact predecessor, the modern Maya day keeper is still one of the most important and highly regarded members of society. Seated at a cardinally oriented table adorned with bowls of incense and lighted candles, he arranges piles of seeds and crystals drawn from his divining bag in an attempt to "borrow from the days" the answers to questions posed by his clients: Will I be cured of the disease that plagues me? Will my daughter's marriage be successfully consummated? Will my crop tide the family over this year?

Basic Calendrical Units. For the Maya a single word, *kin*, signified time, day, and sun. In both meaning and glyphic form it suggests that the art of timekeeping was intimately connected with the practice of astronomy. The directions of the petals of the floral design that makes up the *kin* glyph likely correspond to the extreme positions of the sun along the horizon. Cosmograms also exemplify the space-related time system employed by most ancient Mesoamerican cultures. Found on both pre-Columbian and colonial documents, these diagrams can be thought of as exercises in temporal completion. For example, page one of the Féjérvary-Mayer Codex from highland Mexico consists of a quadripartite glyph in the shape of a Maltese cross. Carefully positioned within the symmetric floral design are all the things that belong to each of the four sides of space: gods, plants, trees, birds, even parts of the body; moreover the four directions are color coded. But time is also spatially divided, each region of the world being assigned its share of the twenty days of the Aztec week. The so-called year bearers, the names of successive New Year's Days, are placed one at each of the tips of the cross. Circumscribing the world is the ultimate Mesoamerican number for time: 260 dots, one to each day, arrayed in 20 units of 13. These 260 days make up the Maya *tzolkin* (called by the Aztecs *tonalpohualli*), a ritual calendar known as the "count of the days."

Unique in the world, the number 260 served as the base of practically every Mesoamerican calendar that has survived. Its origin is debatable, but there can be no question that one of its factors, the number twenty, was derived from the number of fingers and toes on the body. The other factor, the number thirteen, represents the number of layers in the Maya heaven. Beyond this, however, it seems that the human body can be further implicated in the origin of the *tzolkin.* The average duration between human conception and birth is close to 260 days (on average 266). Modern Maya women in highland Guatemala still associate this sacred count with the term of pregnancy. The *tzolkin* also turns out to be a convenient approximation to the length of the basic agricultural season in many areas of southern Mexico, where it probably originated.

Celestial phenomena are also implicated in establishing Mesoamerica's fundamental time pillar. Nine moons (about 265 days) represent the 9 "bloods" taken away by the moon from pregnant women to give lives to their newborn. Lunar and solar eclipses occur at seasonal intervals commensurate with the *tzolkin* in the ratio of 2 to 3 (3 times the "eclipse year" of 173.5 days nearly equals 2 times 260 days). Thus the ancient astrologer could easily warn of certain days vulnerable to the occurrence of an eclipse. The planet Venus, the patron star of war in Teotihuacán (the ancient city of highland Mexico built around 100 BCE), was also revered by the Maya at a time when the New World's most precise calendar was being developed. The duration of its appearance as morning star averages 263 days—again close to a *tzolkin.* And if all these harmonies were not enough, in southernmost Mesoamerican latitudes the year is divisible into periods of 260 and 105 days by the (2) days in the annual calendar when the sun passes overhead.

Mesoamerican people were further cognizant of the seasonal year. Abhorring fractions, the Maya measured their year, or *haab* (Aztec, *xiuhmolpilli*), at 365 days. They divided the year into eighteen months, each of which was twenty days in length, with a concluding five-day month (an unlucky period thought to reside outside the year). Eschewing leap years, ancient Mesoamericans easily kept track of the anniversary of the tropical year within the *haab.*

Cycle building emerges as a central theme of Mesoamerican calendrics. The strategy seems to have accumulated small cycles to make bigger and bigger ones. One of the larger cycles was the calendar round, a period of 52 years consisting of 18,980 days, the lowest common multiple of the *tzolkin* and the *haab* (52 x 365 = 73 x 260). This time loop thus records the interval over which name and number combinations in both cycles repeat themselves. Perhaps not coincidentally, it is also about equal to the length of a full human life. The completion of a calendar round was quite a momentous occasion. Spanish chronicles record that Aztec priests timed this "year binding" event by proceeding to a special place outside ancient Mexico City called the Hill of the Star. There they carefully watched the Pleiades to see whether they would pass the zenith. If they did, it would be a sign from the gods that time would not come to an end. Instead, a new era would be granted to humanity.

To judge by the archaeological and epigraphic evidence, Maya mathematics was almost exclusively devoted to day keeping. About half a millennium before the beginning of the common era a system of numeration developed in southern Mesoamerica. It probably emanated about 600 BCE from the region of Monte Albán, Oaxaca, but was not without Olmec antecedents from the Gulf Coast. The Maya employed only three symbols to produce numbers written in the hundreds of millions: a dot was equivalent to one, and a horizontal bar (uniquely Maya) was equivalent to five, whereas a variety of symbols represented zero. Each of these symbols likely derived from hand gestures.

Unlike its Western counterpart, the Maya zero represented completeness rather than emptiness. Temporally it was regarded as the moment of completion of a cycle, as in the turning of a chain of nines to zeroes on the odometer of an automobile at the conclusion of a large-distance unit traveled. A seashell often represented the Maya zero, perhaps because its roundness was intended to depict the closed, cyclic nature of time. The grasping hand, which like a knot ties up or bundles the days and years together into completed packages, also serves as a zero in many of the inscriptions. The dot and bar numerals probably derived from the tips of the fingers and the extended hand respectively. The Maya expressed large time intervals in a notational system utilizing place values, quite like the Arabic system, which was developed independently in the Middle East after the fall of the Roman Empire.

STRUCTURING DEEP TIME. Just as it is part of human nature to cling to life, many societies attempt to extend their power, lineage, and legacy. Hierarchically organized societies are in the best position to do this. Often they bureaucratize time, giving it a deep structure that goes beyond the immediate confines of remembered generational experience. The Maya utilized their mathematical system to create history. They accumulated years to make scores of years. Heaping score upon score was a logical extension of their vigesimal (base twenty) system. The "long count" is a five-digit tally that marks an event in lapsed time from the most recent creation. One finds most long counts carved on stelae dating from 100 BCE to 900 CE. These display the effigy of a ruler, usually in full regalia, accompanied by a hieroglyphic text that details his or her ancestral history, described in terms of the intervals between seminal events (birth, accession, conquests, marriage, death). To add depth and historical permanence, the dating of these events often seems to have been contrived to fit with repeatable cosmic time markers, such as the reappearance of Venus as morning star, eclipses, and solstices.

To obtain the equivalent in the Gregorian calendar of any long count date appearing in the Maya inscriptions, one must be able to match with certainty at least one long count date with a date in the Gregorian calendar. Until the late twentieth century there had been considerable disagreement about just how to do this. According to the most widely accepted scheme, the so-called Goodman-Martinez-Thompson correlation, the zero point of the most recent starting position of the long count was August 12, 3114 BCE, a date on which astronomers have found no momentous celestial event to have occurred. The next cyclic overturn will take place on December 8, 2012.

CALENDARS AND CREATION. The concept of successive creation-destruction cycles is central to understanding Mesoamerican timekeeping. For example, despite the terrifying effigy at its center, the famous Aztec Sun Stone provides a pictorial narrative of a cyclic cosmogony in which people play an active role. Tonatiuh, the sun god, a flint knife depicting his lolling tongue, grips the firmament with his claws. He cries out for the blood of human sacrificial hearts that he may keep the world in motion. The four panels that surround Tonatiuh represent previous ages, or "suns," as the Aztecs called them. The first cosmogonic epoch (upper right) was the "Sun of Jaguar," named after the day "4 Jaguar" in the 260-day cycle on which it terminated (the head of the jaguar is surrounded by 4 dots within the panel). During this epoch the inhabitants of the earth, the result of the gods' first try at a creation, were giants who dwelled in caves. But they did not till the soil as expected, and so the gods sent jaguars to eat them. In the second sun, the "Sun of Wind," symbolized by the day "4 Wind" (upper left), another less than perfect human race was blown away by the wind. The gods transformed these creatures into apes that they might better cling to the world, an act said to account for the similarity between apes and people. In the third creation, the "Sun of Fire-rain" (the symbol of "4 Rain" is at the lower left), some people were permitted to survive by being transformed into birds to escape from the destruction of the world by volcanic eruptions. The fourth creation, the "Sun of Water," depicted at the lower right, ended with a flood that followed torrential downpours. But this time a transformation from people into fish kept the people from perishing entirely. The symbol "4 Water" marks this epoch. The Aztecs believed they existed in the "fifth sun," of which the symbolic date "4 Movement" houses the effigy of Tonatiuh and the other four ages. (The four large dots of this day sign's coefficient are easily recognizable on the periphery of the four panels that denote the previous suns.) According to most Mesoamerican cosmogonies, the universe was destroyed and re-created anew, each age providing an explanatory temporal framework in which to categorize different forms of life and to relate them to the present human condition.

Two distinct points about Mesoamerican concepts of time emerge in such creation stories. First is the oscillating, repetitive nature of the events taking place. Previous suns were thought to have been creative ventures that failed to achieve the necessary delicate balance between gods and people. Creation time repeats itself, but it is punctuated by periods of destruction. Second, each present contains a piece of the past. Each attempt at creation tries to account for the present state of humankind by referring to what remains in the world. Fish and birds are really human kin, the failed children from archaic creations. People were not destined to dominate them, as Old Testament *Genesis* requires. Rather, people must revere them, for nature is part of people.

According to the Aztec chronicles, the gods made sacrifices in order to bring about the world in its present condition. They performed these sacrifices at the ancient pyramids of Teotihuacán when, in the aftermath of a struggle among themselves, one of their number sacrificed himself to the ceremonial fire, thus promising to become the first rising sun. Such stories have a Darwinian ring to them: life is a struggle filled with key transitory moments. But unlike the Western view, theirs was a cosmology with a purpose. Human action, in this case blood sacrifice to the gods, was necessary to extend the fifth or present epoch. It mediated the balance of violent forces that might erupt as they still do in the fragile highland environment. After all since the gods sacrificed themselves for people, it is only reasonable that people should offer sacrifice as payment of the debt to them.

CARRYING THE BURDEN OF TIME. Perhaps no monumental imagery better expresses the essence of Maya time than Stela D of Copán. This larger than human-size monolith is dedicated to rituals conducted at the juncture of a series of important time cycles. Eight squared-off images carved in high relief confront the eye at the top of the monument. Each depicts a humanoid figure carrying an animal that represents a bundle of time. They employ tump lines, common devices used by modern Maya peasants to carry a load of wood or a sack of citrus by tying one's pack to a band that presses tightly about the forehead, thus leaving the arms to swing free and perform other tasks. Each porter is a full-figure glyph that represents a number. Thus the uppermost figure in the left block, number nine, is distinguishable by the markings on his youthful chin. He carries a heavy load of *baktuns* of time, 144,000-day periods consisting of 20 x 20 x 360 days. The old god of number 15, shown in the uppermost right block, hauls *katuns* (scores of 360-day periods). Fully transliterated, the numbered portion of Stela D reads: It was after the completion of nine *baktuns*, fifteen *katuns*, five *tuns* (360 days), zero *uinals* (20 days), and zero *kin*, reckoned since creation day, that such-and-such an event took place. Thus Stela D becomes the resting place of the numbers at the end of their long journey (*lubay* in Kekchi Maya), who finally let their burden fall 1,405,800 days (3,849 of our Gregorian years) after the last creation. Likewise *katun* prophecies from postconquest texts repeatedly refer to time as a burden: "This is the removal of his burden . . . fire is his burden . . . (In reference to the fifth katun)"; "On the day of the binding of the burden of Lord 5 Ahau." Writes one chronicler, "According to what [the Indians] say [these four first days] are those which take the road and bear the load of the month, changing in time" (Thompson, 1950, pp. 59–61). Time then appears as some sort of essence to be carried or borne along the roadway of eternity, finally seated or brought to rest at various stopping points.

Monuments such as Stela D attribute the completed cycle of time to the ruler and his dynasty. Stela D gives time a name and proclaims it to belong to the ruler, who is assigned various other titles that connect him to his otherworld ancestors. The side opposite the numbers leaves no doubt that it is the ruler who is being exalted. Dates of his accession, marriage, and victories in battle adorn the glyphic text. So high is the relief on the monument that the ruler seems almost to emerge from the cut stone, appearing larger than life, fully garbed with ritual paraphernalia in hand. He wears an enormous headdress and facial mask, his bloodletting instruments draped from his loincloth. Perhaps the ruler himself once stood before the citizenry in front of his monument performing the rite of genital bloodletting with the spine of a stingray to seal his bond with his ancestors. Here was a demonstration of the continuity of dynastic rulership that also guaranteed the continuity of time.

Two seminal qualities of the Maya concept of time from the dynastic histories comprise these time capsules wrought in stone. First, one has the sense that, whereas the arrow of time points toward the future, it is pushed from behind rather than tugged forward, a stark contrast to the teleological or purposive forward pull of time embedded in the Judeo-Christian tradition. Circumstances in the past, even before the creation of the world, had set the number gods on their journey. It was those four events, enacted in the realm of the ancestor gods, that determined the future course of human history, the creation of the lineage, the journey of the four founders of modern Maya culture to the right place to build the city. Their journey parallels in space the long arduous track along the road of time undertaken by the number gods who bear their ponderous freight. The *Popol Vuh,* the sacred book of creation of the Quiché Maya, states that the ancient word is the potential and the source for all that is done in the present world. "How should it be sown, how should it dawn?" the gods ask themselves as they contemplate the creative act (D. Tedlock, 1985, p. 73). Events that took place then, by the creators, the founders, the so-called mother-fathers, are responsible for setting time on its course toward the present.

A second seminal quality of Maya time inherent in the monumental inscriptions is more difficult to grasp, especially when contrasting it with the Western historical view of time, which clearly separates human history (arrived at via the testimony of people) from natural history determined from the testimony of things, such as events in the sky, in the landscape, signs in plants and animals. Thus events in the history of the dynasty are directly linked with cosmic events. For example, many of the paramount happenings in the life of 18 Rabbit (called Waxaklahun-Ubah-K'awil in modern orthographies), the name of the ruler depicted on Stela D, are tied directly to the appearance of the planet Venus at key positions in the sky. This habit of creating a single frame for natural and human history is quite common across Mesoamerica. It is reflected especially vividly in the Aztec year annals in which depictions of volcanic eruptions, eclipses, comets, and shooting stars appear linked to victories in battle and the deaths of emperors. Aztec history consists of like-in-kind events, both natural and civic-social, matched up repeatedly over multiple fifty-two-year cycles of time.

In many instances these astronomical events were registered in preferentially aligned calendrical, ceremonial architecture. For example, Temple 22 at Copán possesses a slot-like viewing chamber on its western facade that marks the appearance of Venus at the beginning of the rainy season. Buildings that deviate from the prevailing grid structure and buildings of unusual shape at Uxmal, Chichén Itzá, and other sites also contain Venus alignments. Classic Maya sites in the Petén rain forest include a number of solar "observatories." These specialized architectural assemblages consist of a pyramid on the west side of an open plaza that overlooks three smaller structures on the east. Viewed from the top of the former, the sun rises over each of the latter on seminal dates of the year, for example, the solstices, the equinoxes, and especially dates measured at multiples of twenty days from the passage of the sun across the zenith. In the highlands of Mexico the largest building in the Aztec capital, the Templo Mayor, was deliberately aligned with the sun at the equinox. Such structures might better be conceived as "theaters" than "observatories." They are sacred places that offer the appropriate setting for cosmically timed ritual.

Calendars and Codices. In addition to the monuments, the books (misnamed "codices") constitute a second major medium of information concerning Mesoamerican time and calendars. But here the message is quite different. If the monumental inscriptions, related to a program of public display, were intended to exalt the rulers and legitimize their descent from the gods, the content of the codices seems relatively esoteric and private, consisting of omen-bearing texts to be read only by high-status priests. Only four pre-Columbian codices have survived. Their content, expressed in what have come to be called almanacs, is almost exclusively concerned with divinatory rituals cyclically timed in remarkable detail. In a minority of cases the timings are based on astronomical phenomena encoded in tables that might properly be called ephemerides, even though their content is largely astrological.

The manifold ways the almanacs are laid out, challenging the eye of the reader to dance about the page in order to pursue a temporal journey, bespeak a playful intercourse between time and the Ah Kin. Time's arithmetic flows vertically or zigzaggedly; in some cases the black and red numbers that comprise, respectively, the intervals and resting points in a text are scattered about a single prognostic or divinatory picture like so many loose tokens dropped randomly upon it from above. In many instances the numbers seem to take on an irrational, almost mystical quality akin to the Pythagorean way of dealing with numbers.

One thinks of an almanac in the West as a compilation of useful information, most of it adapted to local space-time. One usually finds in an almanac a calendar for each month that gives all the holidays. There is also astronomical information, such as sunrise, sunset, moon phase tables, and eclipses for the year, coupled with meteorological information and tide tables for major local harbors. Information concerning weather predictions and the positions of the planetary bodies in the signs of the zodiac is also provided. Add to these data nonquantitative information on food recipes and proverbs and the modern almanac, updated and altered slightly from year to year, becomes a handy compendium that both amuses and instructs in practical matters and perhaps offers advice regarding personal behavior.

Maya almanacs feature many of these same aspects. They contain both invocations and divinations that deal with the weather, agriculture, drilling fire with sticks, and disease and medicine in addition to the fates and ceremonies. Their purpose seems to have been to bring all celestial and human activities into the realm of the sacred almanac of 260 days. As is the case in the monumental inscriptions, duration emerges as the support beam in the framework of Maya calendrics in the codices. Each phase seems to be based on a perceived forward movement of time from an event located at the start of the text, to which "distance number" intervals are added. Every round of time in a Maya almanac begins with a starting day name and number in the *tzolkin*. One then proceeds via black distance numbers to red dates, each accompanied by a picture and glyphic block that convey the appropriate debt payment and (usually) an accompanying omen. The participatory role of the Maya worshiper is also reflected in the content of the codices. The business of laying out the calendar that prescribes Maya ritual behavior must have been complex. A multitude of offerings needed to be made to the gods at the proper places and times when the gods of number dropped their loads, and the periods between ritual events surely were not arbitrary. Long thought to be endlessly cyclical in nature, many almanacs, studies suggest, may have been fixed in real time. And like modern almanacs, they may have undergone repeated revision and recopying.

The most exquisitely complex and esoteric almanacs, termed ephemerides, deal with precise astronomical prediction. Known since its rudimentary elements were deciphered early in the twentieth century, the Venus table in the Dresden Codex chronicles the appearance and disappearance dates of that planet over several centuries. Accompanying pictorials at the middle of each frame show the Venus deity Kukulcan flinging daggers of omen-bearing light on victims who lie impaled below them. A correction table enables the Venus calendar to stay on track for five hundred years with scarcely a day error. Maya astronomers seem to have been attracted by the perfect 8 to 5 commensuration between the Venus cycle of 584 days and the seasonal year of 365 days as well as by the larger commensuration between 65 Venus cycles and two 52-year calendar rounds. Adjacent ephemerides in the Dresden Codex were used to predict eclipses and to chart the movement of Mars, whose 780-day cycle commensurates with the *tzolkin* in the exact ratio of 3 to 1.

Studies suggest that other pages of the Dresden Codex as well as certain pages of the Madrid Codex also mark astronomical events. Venus deities, looking much like those in the Dresden, also appear in the Borgia group of codices from highland Mexico. In the *Anales de Quauhtitlan,* a colonial document from the Mexican highlands, are specific statements about which class of people shall suffer wounds from the piercing rays of Venus, called Quetzalcoatl in the central Mexican pantheon:

> And as they (the ancients, the forefathers) learned. When it appears (rises). According to the sign, in which it (rises). It strikes different classes of people with its rays. Shoots them, casts its light upon them. When it appears in the (first) sign, "1 alligator." It shoots the old men and women. Also in the (second) sign, "1 jaguar." In the (third) sign, "1 stag." In the (fourth) sign, "1 flower." It shoots the little children. And in the (fifth) sign, "1 reed." It shoots the kings. Also in the (sixth) sign, "1 death." And in the (seventh) sign, "1 rain." It shoots the rain. It will not rain. And in the (thirteenth) sign, "1 movement." It shoots the youths and maidens. And in the (seventeenth) sign, "1 water." There is universal drought. (Seler, 1904, pp. 384–385)

In stark contrast with the Maya texts, the so-called picture books of highland Mexico, which also include ritual ceremonial prescriptions, have generally been regarded as devoid of real-time astronomical events; that is, the Mexican codices have been characterized as celebrating time cycles, whereas the Maya books were thought to be more event specific. However, this traditional picture has been challenged by studies that offer evidence, specifically in the Codex Borgia, that real-time astronomical events were recorded in the middle of the fifteenth century. Scholars now regard Mesoamerican (especially Maya) mathematical, astronomical, and calendrical achievements to have been rather more like those of the ancient Middle East; that is, closer to the sort of quantitative science that led to modern astronomy.

SEE ALSO Aztec Religion; Maya Religion.

BIBLIOGRAPHY

As the field of Mesoamerican calendrics has remained extraordinarily specialized, most work is in journals such as the *Journal for the History of Astronomy, Archaeoastronomy, Supplement to the Journal for the History of Astronomy, Latin American Antiquity.* David H. Kelley's *Deciphering the Maya Script* (Austin, Tex., 1976) and Anthony F. Aveni's *Skywatchers: A Revised and Updated Version of Skywatchers of Ancient Mexico* (Austin, Tex., 2001) are standard texts that offer broad overviews of Mesoamerican calendrics. Somewhat more specialized are John Justeson's "Ancient Maya Ethnoastronomy: An Overview of the Hieroglyphic Sources," in *World Archaeoastronomy,* edited by Anthony F. Aveni (Cambridge, U.K., 1989); and Floyd Lounsbury's "Maya Numeration, Computation, and Calendrical Astronomy," in *Dictionary of Scientific Biography,* edited by Charles Coulston Gillespie, vol. 15, supp. 1, pp. 759–818 (New York, 1978). Alfonso Caso's "Mixtec Writing and Calendar," in *Handbook of Middle American Indians,* edited by Robert Wauchope, vol. 3 (Austin, Tex., 1965), remains the classic exposition of central Mexican calendrics. See also Rafael Tena's *El Calendario Mexica y la cronografía* (Mexico City, 1987). On other central Mexican calendars see Javier Urcid's *Zapotec Hieroglyphic Writing* (Washington, D.C., 2001). Munro S. Edmonson's *The Book of the Year: Middle American Calendrical Systems* (Salt Lake City, Utah, 1988) offers a pan-Mesoamerican comparative analysis of calendars and calendar glyphs. Contemporary Mesoamerican calendar systems are dealt with in Frank J. Lipp's *The Mixe of Oaxaca: Religion, Ritual, and Healing* (Austin, Tex., 1991); Barbara Tedlock's *Time and the Highland Maya* (Albuquerque, N.Mex., 1982; rev. ed. 1992); and Michael P. Closs, ed., *Native American Mathematics* (Austin, Tex., 1986), which also deals with North American calendars. See also Alfred M. Tozzer, ed. and trans., *Landa's Relación de las cosas de Yucatan,* vol. 18 (Cambridge, Mass., 1941), Eduard Seler, "The Venus Period in Picture Writings of the Borgian Codex Group," *Bulletin of the Bureau of American Ethnology* 28: 373–390, Dennis Tedlock's translation of *Popol Vuh: The Definitive Edition of the Mayan Book of the Dawn of Life and the Glories of Gods and Kings* (New York, 1985), and J. Eric S. Thompson, *Maya Hieroglyphic Writing* (Washington, D.C., 1950).

ANTHONY F. AVENI (2005)

CALENDARS: SOUTH AMERICAN CALENDARS

At the time of the Spanish conquest of the New World in the early sixteenth century, the peoples of Mesoamerica and the Andes were living in highly developed civilizations supported by well-integrated political and religious organizations. The Aztec, Mixtec, and Maya of Mesoamerica produced codices in which are described their gods, priests, religious paraphernalia, and so on. Their knowledge was organized by way of an elaborate calendar that bore no relationship to any kind of calendrical system known to the Spanish. The chroniclers soon realized, however, that an important aspect of these Mesoamerican calendars was the repeating succession of 260 days. The 260-day "year" was divided into thirteen "months," each comprising twenty days irrespective of observations of the sun, moon, and other celestial bodies.

Unlike the Mesoamericans, the Andean peoples did not leave codices or a hieroglyphic script (as was used, for instance, by the Maya from their early history onward). They apparently had no tradition of a historical chronology and left no dated monuments. However, a recent analysis of Peruvian *quipus*—knotted strings that were used for various administrative purposes—demonstrates that Andean peoples were capable of highly abstract, mathematical thought. Accordingly, we may assume that the conclusion reached by certain Spanish chroniclers that the *quipus* were used for calendrical purposes is valid. Indeed, José de Acosta, an early chronicler who thoroughly studied the cultures in both parts of what we now call nuclear America and who compared the Andean and Mesoamerican calendars, favored the Andean system because of its technical accomplishments. Thus it may be reasonable to assume that the political and religious needs of the Andean states crystallized into a common calendrical tradition of a complexity comparable with that of Mesoamerica; but its organizing principles may have been as different from those of the Mesoamerican tradition as these differed from the European.

Accounts by Early Chroniclers. When the Spanish conquistadors entered Cuzco, the capital of the Inca Empire, the Inca territory stretched from what is now northern Ecuador south to Chile and Argentina. Spanish chroniclers have left us some data on the astronomical and calendrical ideas of the people living on the north coast of Peru, a rich description of myths and rituals of Quechua-speaking peoples in central and southern Peru, and some bits and pieces of astronomical and calendrical lore from the Aymara-speaking peoples living around Lake Titicaca. But it was only in Cuzco that the chroniclers became aware of the rich tradition of the Inca's history, myths, and rituals, as well as of their seasonal activities (e.g., agriculture and llama husbandry) and astronomical observations and beliefs about the sun, moon, and stars. Many scattered data of critical importance in the reconstruction of the Inca calendar have survived. Nonetheless, although some chroniclers may have been aware of the importance of some of these data for the reconstruction of the calendar, they themselves recorded little more than the names of the months. They assumed that the Inca calendar comprised twelve months but barely analyzed what kinds of "months" they were in fact dealing with. The actual reconstruction of the Inca calendar—going well beyond the chroniclers' list of twelve names—enables us to realize the magnitude of the debt owed by the Inca to the states and cultures that preceded them: those of Huari, Tiahuanaco, and Chavín in the Andean highlands and those of Nazca, Mochica, and Paracas on the coast. The Spaniards' interpretations of the Inca data provide only a faint idea of what a pre-Conquest calendar might have looked like.

Some seventeen years after the Conquest, Juan de Betanzos became the first chronicler in Cuzco to attempt an account of the months. His description, however, is inextricably interwoven with a recording of Inca history, especially with those events that concern the legendary reorganization of Cuzco after the city had successfully rejected a foreign attack. He intimates the close relationship between Cuzco's calendar and its political organization, an aspect with which he was probably more familiar than any later chronicler. But he leaves the technical problem of the calendrical count unresolved. In 1574, the priest Cristóbal de Molina wrote the first detailed account of calendrical rituals in Cuzco. Juan de Polo de Ondegardo, a lawyer, had probably written a similar report some years earlier, but it was lost. In 1584, the third Council of the Peruvian Church published a shorter version of Polo's calendar; it is this version, or the knowledge of the existence of a longer report, that heavily influenced all later accounts given by the major chroniclers (e.g., Cavello de Balboa, Murua). Only the later indigenous chronicler Felipe Poma de Ayala provides substantial new information on the economic use of the calendar; and yet another indigenous chronicler, Juan de Santa Cruz, refers to the mythological data pertaining to it. The description given in 1653 by Bernabé Cobo, the last chronicler, is probably the most faithful to those of Polo and Molina.

Polo and Molina's Interpretations. Although they themselves do not seem to have grasped the calendrical problem completely, Polo and Molina give us the best evidence with which to evaluate the character of the months. Polo, for example, tells us, "[The Inca] divided the year into twelve months by the moons, and the other days that remained were added to the [different] moons themselves." Polo claims to be speaking of synodical months, that is, those that mark the period between new moons in a sequence independent from the solar year; nonetheless, he says that the eleven days that these twelve months are short of a year were added to the individual months. If he is right on this last point, we can assume that the Inca calendar had solar months, each thirty or thirty-one days long, bearing no connection to the phases of the moon. Polo refers to certain monthly observations of sunrises and sunsets that reinforce this claim. When considered together with important information from Molina, Polo's critical data underscores the fact that the Inca calendar included synodical, as well as solar, months.

According to Molina (1574), the Inca year began with the lunar month marked by the June solstice; this month started with the first new moon after the middle of May. Molina, however, was still using the Julian calendar; his "middle of May" is thus equivalent to May 25 in the Gregorian calendar, which was not introduced to Cuzco until ten years after Molina wrote his account. Accordingly, any month beginning with a new moon after May 25 would include the date of the June solstice, June 21 (Zuidema, 1982a).

Molina then describes the subsequent lunar months, stressing in particular the observations of a new moon and full moon in the fourth month. This was the month in which crops were planted and all women, including the queen, celebrated the moon. Molina then comes to the seventh month, Capac Raymi ("royal feast"), during which noble boys were initiated into manhood. During the eighth month, Capac Raymi Camay Quilla ("royal feast, moon of Camay"), rituals were dedicated to the rains, which would subside in the months to come. Molina's section on the seventh month has a day-to-day account of its ritual events but makes no reference to the moon; the eighth month, however, is described solely in terms of the lunar cycle.

Polo says that Capac Raymi originally began in January but was later moved back to December, the month "when the Sun reaches the last point on its road towards the South pole." Whatever historical information he thought could be derived from this statement, the most satisfactory reading in calendrical terms would be that Capac Raymi ended on the December solstice itself and that Camay Quilla began thereafter. Molina's description of ritual held at the end of Capac Raymi also seems to imply the same conclusion. But if both Polo and Molina were right about the lunar character of the months, then it is possible that a given Capac Raymi may not have included the December solstice at all, for the month of Inti Raymi could have begun just after May 25 (there are 211 days from May 25 to December 22; seven synodical months have only 206). From these data alone we cannot determine exactly how the Inca solved this calendrical discrepancy but we can conclude that they were aware of it and had probably devised a solution.

Later chroniclers, including modern writers, did not take into account Molina and Polo's critical data, although they sometimes opted for either lunar or solar months. Thus Clements R. Markharm (1910) interprets the calendar as consisting of solar months; the first month, he says, starts on the June solstice. John Howland Rowe, on the other hand, in his influential article "Inca Culture at the Time of the Spanish Conquest" (1946) chooses—on the authority of Polo, he claims—lunar months. Later studies on Inca culture generally follow Rowe's example. These accounts differ by as much as two months in their assessment of the location in the calendar of a particular month, making the relationship between specific ritual and seasonal activities difficult to understand.

ARCHAEOASTRONOMY AT CORICANCHA. The calendrical problem cannot be resolved on the basis of Molina and Polo's data alone. Fortunately, research on the alignment of certain Inca buildings (Zuidema, 1982a; Aveni, 1981; Urton and Aveni, 1983; Urton, 1981; Ziolkowski and Sadowski, 1984) enables us to evaluate additional types of calendrical and astronomical data. I will mention here the data based on the architecture of the Coricancha ("golden enclosure")—properly known as the Temple of the Sun—and on the rituals and myths associated with it. Located in the center of Cuzco, the Coricancha included four one-room buildings that served as temples, each facing the other two by two. The more important buildings were said to face the rising sun during the June solstice. But exact measurements by Anthony F. Aveni and myself revealed that the temples face the point on the horizon at which the sun rises on May 25. This alignment not only supports the validity of Molina's data regarding when the Inca year began but also helps us interpret other significant information. For example, in exactly the same direction of the sunrise, but just beyond the horizon, is a legendary place called Susurpuquio, well known for its important role in Inca mythology. It was here that Pachacuti Inca, the king who set the Inca on the road to conquest, had met his father, the sun god, who predicted that he and his people would share a future filled with military success. The direction toward Susurpuquio coincides closely with that of the rise of the Pleiades, the "mother" of all stars. The reappearance of the Pleiades in early June, after they had disappeared from the southern sky for some fifty days, generally marked the beginning of the year for people in central and northern Peru. In Cuzco, the full moon of the month that included the June solstice would have occurred after the Pleiades first rose in the morning sky. The Inca data on the Pleiades, the sun, and the moon replicate in detail the more general Andean concepts of celestial, calendrical, and social order established in relation to the Pleiades; we see here the Inca debt to the Andean cultures that preceded them.

CALENDRICAL SOCIAL DIVISION. Another way to further our understanding of the Inca calendar is to analyze the integration that obtained between the calendar and the empire's political hierarchy and its territorial organization. Betanzos cites this integration but gives no technical details on it. An anonymous, but rather early and well-informed, chronicler mentions how Pachacuti Inca, the king who reorganized Cuzco, divided the population of the Cuzco Valley into twelve groups. His purpose was to make each group take "account of its own month, adopting the name and surname of that lunar month, and of what it had to carry out in its month; and it was obliged to come out to the plaza on the first day of its month by playing trumpets and by shouting, so that it was known to everybody" (my translation, from Maúrtua, vol. 8, 1908). Whereas his father had brought order to the observance of lunar months, Pachacuti Inca erected pillars on the horizon from which the sun could be observed. This was an attempt to integrate the months into an account of the solar year.

THE CEQUE CALENDAR. Based on original information from Polo, Cobo describes a similar problem with the calendar and establishes the close link between customs of each Cuzco group and astronomical observations. His description is based on an important Andean political concept, which expresses the visual and directional relationship between the political divisions and their political and ritual center. For this purpose the Inca employed a system of forty-two "directions" called *ceques* ("lines").

The *ceques* were imaginary lines that radiated from Coricancha to points on the horizon. They were distributed in groups of three over four quarters of the territory; in one quarter, however, fifteen directions, that is, fourteen *ceques* (in this case, two *ceques* were taken together as one), were used. The twelve political divisions of Cuzco were individually associated not only with a different group of three *ceques* but also with one particular *ceque* in each group. Each *ceque* linked the division with the location of the land in the valley that it had been given by Pachacuti Inca. Lands in the fourth quarter were also divided between only three divisions; we notice that in this quarter the fourteen *ceques* were also rebundled into three groups of *ceques* (which had four, four, and six *ceques*, respectively).

Each of the twelve political divisions had an important ritual obligation to bring offerings to a cultic place on the horizon. The sun would then arrive at this place, either at sunset or sunrise, sometime during its annual journey. These twelve places on the horizon were called *sayhuas*; two extra ones, called *sucancas*, were necessary to comply with astronomical observations. The *ceque* system used the whole horizon, although the sun rises and sets in only part of it. Therefore a *sayhua* or *sucanca* was not necessarily located along a *ceque* that stretched between the horizon and the land of the political division that was in charge of its cult. People first worshiped a series of cultic places, called *huacas*, that were located along the three *ceques* associated with their division. They would then turn to the corresponding *sayhuas*, located in another direction, and offer the remains of whatever had been served to the *huacas*.

Cobo lists the *huacas* that were served before the *sayhuas* and *sucancas*. If this list is complete (328 *huacas*), as it indeed appears to be, then it allows us to suggest various calendrical consequences. Although it would not be appropriate here to carry out a technical analysis of Cobo's list, certain general characteristics of such a *ceque* calendar can be proposed.

One observation of the sun was made along a *ceque* radiating from the Temple of the Sun: the one toward sunrise on May 25. Perhaps one other solar observation was made along a *ceque* in the opposite direction. But all other solar observations were done from higher places just outside town. Based on our data on stars and certain *huacas* in the *ceque* system, we believe that all risings and settings of stars were observed from the Temple of the Sun. In contrast to the *sayhuas*—upright, manmade stone pillars that were used for observing the sun—the *huacas* were mostly natural topographical features whose worship was part of a cult to the earth. The rather irregular numerical distribution of the *huacas* over the *ceques* and groups of three *ceques* seems to be conditioned by their calendrical use. The number of *huacas*—on *ceques*, on groups of *ceques*, and in each of the quarters—reveals that the Inca were concerned with bringing in line the worship of the moon during its full and new phases (these phases occur every twenty-nine and one-half days) with a cult of the sun (the sun is the cause of the moon's phases), as well as with a cult of the stars (against which the moon shifts its position every night). The year can thus be divided into twelve solar months of thirty or thirty-one days each, while the moon will reach the same position among the stars every twenty-seven and one-third nights. Rituals during full and new moons carried out a balancing act between these two cycles related to the sun and the stars; one cycle occurred during the day and the other at night, while the moon can be observed both day and night.

Myths and Legends. Irrespective, however, of where a technical analysis of the *ceque* calendar leads us, the data given by the anonymous chronicler and by Polo and Cobo allow us to integrate Inca ideas of time and space with their calendrical rituals, legendary history, and myths. Each political division carried out rituals during the particular month after which it was named; we can assume, therefore, that each group's ideas about its function in society, its past, and its origin myths are relevant for an understanding of its rituals. Each group worshiped its own mythical ancestor (in the form of a mummy). Influenced by certain ideas of hierarchical order, the Inca integrated these ancestors into the legendary history of their royal dynasty. This line of thought explains why ten of the twelve political divisions were linked genealogically to the dynasty and were called *panacas* (collateral lines of descent from the royal family). The remaining two divisions represented the autochthonous population of the valley of Cuzco, which had been conquered by the Inca.

Specific myths about *panacas* and former kings should help us interpret calendrical rituals. The anonymous chronicler gives us one clue on how to proceed. He claims that each division—that is, each *panaca*—took its name from its particular month. Thus we can argue that the highest-ranked *panaca*, called *capac ayllu*, was in charge of the initiation rituals of noble youths, who were also called *capac churi* ("royal sons"). These rituals occurred during the month of Capac Raymi, which ended on the December solstice. Another *panaca*, called *aucailli* (the "victory song" that was chanted at harvest time), implying that its rituals were conducted in April. But these examples seem to be more exceptions to than confirmations of the rule, and only one chronicler (Murua) relates a myth explicitly linking two political divisions to certain months of the year and their rituals (Zuidema, 1982b).

What makes the following myth interesting is the relationship it establishes between dynastic legends and myths in Inca culture. Pachacuti Inca—who appears in the myth as the son of the first mythical founder of the royal dynasty—establishes a pact with a giant. During a month of heavy rains, the giant comes down on the rushing waters of a river some thirty kilometers from Cuzco. As the rains threaten to destroy the city, Pachacuti, who is characterized in this myth as a brash young warrior, persuades the giant to retreat, and he himself turns to stone. According to the myth, it is because of this pact with the giant that the Inca celebrated Capac Raymi in December. A sequel to the myth deals with the heroic feats of a son of Pachacuti Inca, whose conquests and marriage explain why the Inca celebrated their feast of planting (normally assigned to the month of September, but here to October 1).

Other, more legendary versions of the first myth convert Pachacuti Inca into the ninth king of the dynasty and the giant into his father, Viracocha Inca; it is these conversions that allow us to relate their *panacas* to specific months. These versions present Pachacuti Inca as the reorganizer of the city, its political system, and its calendar. Both kings are seen as historical persons, but their mythical aspects crystallize them into deities in their own right: they become the thunder god, worshiped by Pachacuti Inca as his personal god, and Viracocha, the god whom the Spanish misinterpreted as the Inca creator god. Viracocha Inca, the king, was thought to be the ancestor of the high priests of Cuzco. It may be suggested here that the giant in the myth should be associated with the society's concerns during the month of March. This was the month in which the priests of the Sun carried out rituals intended to curtail the rains and to prepare for the forthcoming dry season and harvest; they also directed the building of dams in mountain lakes to store irrigation water for use during the dry season.

No dynastic legends like those found at Cuzco were recorded for central Peru by the Spanish chroniclers, who do, however, relate stories of battles, similar to that between Pachacuti and the giant, that were fought between the thunder god and a primordial deity in the times before a great flood.

The story of Pachacuti Inca functioned on two different temporal levels in Cuzco: as a myth that was related to the yearly calendar and as a dynastic legend. It should be observed, therefore, that the temporal sequence was not the same in both cases. In the myth, the giant is associated with a calendrical concern (in March) that followed the one associated with Pachacuti Inca (in December). In the dynasty, Viracocha Inca is the father of Pachacuti Inca. Dynastic interest established a kind of causal link between the legendary versions of the stories told about succeeding kings. But the myths, as seasonal versions of the same stories, did not follow the same temporal sequence.

Here it is probably more the calendrical rituals that, in terms of a closed annual cycle, can bring unity into Inca thought, integrating the cosmological and political aspects of their society. On the basis of the data on Inca months in the chronicles, Henrique Urbano has evaluated the dialectical relationships between the gods Viracocha and Inti (Sun), who symbolize the opposing values of water and fire, respectively. Both are associated with animal symbols: Viracocha with the *amaru* ("serpent"), which is related to farming and the fertility of the earth, and Inti with the *guaman* ("falcon") and *puma* ("mountain lion"), which both represent warfare. In this occurrence, Inti is emblematic of society and of the inside, while Viracocha symbolizes nature and the outside.

RITUAL AND THE INCA CALENDAR. The analytical value of the data available allows us to study various other aspects of the Andean calendar. One aspect, that of human sacrifice, was of capital importance in the Inca state, establishing political alliances and hierarchical relationships between peoples brought under imperial rule. Victims from all parts of the empire were brought to Cuzco, either to be sacrificed there or to be sent elsewhere to be sacrificed. In journeying to and from Cuzco, they traveled along routes that were as straight as possible and that, like the lines radiating from Cuzco, were called *ceques*. The data suggest that the system of human sacrifices was integrated into the calendar. Various kinds of animals were sacrificed according to the particular occasion; they were eaten or burned, and their blood was also used. Furthermore, ashes, including those of textiles and other products, were saved so that they could be thrown into rivers at appropriate times of the year.

The most important sacrifices of all, however, were those of llamas. These animals were used for various ritual purposes according to their variety (alpaca, llama, guanaco, vicuña), color, age, and sex. The system of llama sacrifice can be reconstructed (Zuidema and Urton, 1976). Iconographic evidence from the Huari and Tiahuanaco (1–1000 CE) cultures demonstrates how deeply rooted llama sacrifices were in Andean society.

Another important aspect of Andean culture is that of divination, studied by E.-J. de Durand (1968). However, the numerous data relating to its importance for the calendar have yet to be coordinated.

CONCLUSION. The Andean calendar as an exact numerical system for computing days in the year did not survive the onslaught of Western civilization. Many rituals and calendrical customs were integrated, however, into the Catholic calendar; many scholars have reported on this syncretism (Urbano, 1974; Poole, 1984). Their studies, as well as the data from numerous monographs on present-day Andean societies, are extremely valuable in helping us to understand the symbolic values of pre-Conquest rituals. Also, the knowledge of astronomy found among present-day Andean peoples has its principal roots in pre-Conquest culture, notwithstanding the fact that their ancestors were able to integrate Spanish learned and popular notions about the sky and weather into their own systems (Urton, 1981).

The amount of ethnohistorical data that is available for reconstruction of the Inca and other Andean calendars is broader and deeper than had previously been assumed. In Peru, indigenous calendrical notions did not have the overwhelming impact on the Spaniards as they had in Mexico. Interestingly, it is those data that did not seem important to the Spaniards—that did not threaten their missionary and political interests and that lost their significance in colonial society, although they nevertheless happened to be reported—that are the most helpful in understanding pre-Conquest Andean culture and its calendar.

SEE ALSO Ethnoastronomy.

BIBLIOGRAPHY

Aveni, Anthony F. "Horizon Astronomy in Incaic Cuzco." In *Archaeoastronomy in the Americas*, edited by Ray A. Williamson, pp. 305–318. Los Altos, Calif., 1981.

Durand, E.-J. de. "Aperçu sur les présages et la divination de l'ancien Pérou." In *La divination*, edited by André Caquot and Marcel Leibovici, pp. 1–67. Paris, 1968.

Maúrtua, Victor M. *Juicio de límites entre el Perú y Bolivia.* Lima, 1908. Volume 8 contains the anonymous "Discurso de la sucesión y gobierno de los Yngas."

Molina, Cristóbal de. *Ritos y fábulas de los Incas* (1574). Buenos Aires, 1947.

Poole, Deborah A. "Ritual-Economic Calendars in Paruro: The Structure of Representation in Andean Ethnography." Ph.D. diss., University of Illinois, Urbana, 1984.

Rowe, John Howland. "Inca Culture at the Time of the Spanish Conquest." In *Handbook of South American Indians*, edited by Julian H. Steward, vol. 2, pp. 183–330. Washington, D.C., 1946.

Urbano, Henrique. "La representación andina del tiempo y del espacio en la fiesta." *Allpanchis Phuturinqua* (Cuzco) 7 (1974): 9–10.

Urton, Gary. *At the Crossroads of the Earth and Sky: An Andean Cosmology.* Austin, Tex., 1981.

Urton, Gary, and Anthony F. Aveni. "Archaeoastronomical Fieldwork on the Coast of Peru." In *Calendars in Mesoamerica and Peru,* edited by Anthony F. Aveni and Gordon Brotherston. Oxford, 1983.

Ziolkowski, M. S., and R. M. Sadowski. "Informe acerca de las investigaciones arqueo-astronómicas en el area central de Ingapirca (Ecuador)." *Revista española de antropología americana* 15 (1984): 103–125.

Zuidema, R. Tom. "Inca Observations of the Solar and Lunar Passages through Zenith and Anti-Zenith at Cuzco." In *Archaeoastronomy in the Americas,* edited by Ray A. Williamson, pp. 319–342. Los Altos, Calif., 1981.

Zuidema, R. Tom. "Catachillay: The Role of the Pleiades and of the Southern Cross and a and b Centauri in the Calendar of the Incas." In *Ethnoastronomy and Archaeoastronomy in the American Tropics,* edited by Anthony F. Aveni and Gary Urton, pp. 203–220. New York, 1982 (cited as 1982a in the text).

Zuidema, R. Tom. "The Sidereal Lunar Calendar of the Incas." In *Archaeoastronomy in the New World,* edited by Anthony F. Aveni, pp. 59–107. Cambridge, 1982 (cited as 1982b in the text).

Zuidema, R. Tom, and Gary Urton. "La Constelación de la Llama en los Andes Peruanos." *Allpanchis Phuturinqua* (Cuzco) 9 (1976): 59–119.

R. Tom Zuidema (1987)

CALIPHATE. The office of "successor" to the prophet Muḥammad as the leader of the Muslim community is a uniquely Islamic institution. Hence the anglicization *caliphate* is preferable to inadequate translations of the term *khilāfah.* (This article will not address the concept of *khilāfah* in Islamic mysticism.)

Upon Muḥammad's death in AH 11/632 CE there was in existence a self-governing, powerful Islamic community, or *ummah.* It had been shaped by the Prophet in conformity with the revelations he had received, and by the end of his life, his temporal as well as his spiritual authority was unassailable: he was the governor of the *ummah,* an arbitrator of disputes within it, the commander of its military forces, and its principal strategist. He had deputized others as his representatives to distant tribes and regions. The term *khilāfah* in the pre-Islamic sense of "deputy" was apparently used in reference to these assignees.

To the *ummah* the Prophet's death was a shocking, even inconceivable event. The Muslims were suddenly bereft of divine guidance, the source of Muḥammad's charismatic authority. Yet they were sufficiently imbued with the Islamic vision to persevere in efforts to shape the ideal society embodied in that moral imperative.

But who was to lead this society? What was to be his authority? The caliphate, the expression of the temporal leadership of all Muslims conceived as a single community, was the institutional answer. It had emerged *ad hoc,* however, in response to a crisis. Evolving practice framed theoretical constructions, especially in the absence of any agreed Qurʾānic foundation. Hence the conduct of those holding the office, the caliphs, elicited sharp and continuing controversy over not only individual moral qualitites but also the character of the institution itself.

The forces at work in this controversy may be divided for the purposes of analysis into Islamic theories of the caliphate and historical influences on the institution.

Classical Theories of the Caliphate. The majoritarian, Sunnī view of the origins of the caliphate is that Muḥammad left no instructions for the future leadership of the *ummah.* Yet on his death the community desperately required an acknowledged leader, since all the latent rivalries that the prophetic message had overwhelmed reemerged in tribal factionalism. The innermost core of the Muslims responded by acclaiming as their leader one of the earliest of their number and certainly among the most prestigious, Abū Bakr (r. 632 634). Whether he was actually proclaimed *khalīfāt rasūl Allāh* ("caliph of the messenger of God") is unclear, but all Sunnīs regard him as the first caliph. His role was to lead the *ummah* in peace and in war as the Prophet had done, and to lead the ritual prayers and conduct the pilgrimage, both of which duties he had previously performed on Muḥammad's behalf. Absent from this formulation was the prophetic role that had clothed Muḥammad's acts with nigh impeccable authority. Theoretically, a divinely guided community of Muslims selected the early Sunnī caliphs, while its act of acclamation, the *bayʿah,* constituted an elective ideal that deprecated all subsequent dynasticism.

Evolved Sunnī theory required that a caliph be an adult male from the Quraysh, the leading tribe of Mecca. Soundness of mind and body, knowledge of the religion, piety, and probity are frequently listed among Sunnī criteria. Caliphal preogatives were to lead the prayer, to be recognized in the Friday sermon as the leader of all Muslims, to coin money, to command the army, and to receive on behalf of the *ummah* a fifth of all booty. Later, the Abbasid caliphs (750–1258) arrogated to themselves the right to wear the presumed mantle of the Prophet, a sacred relic in their possession.

Sunnis generally describe the caliph's duties as follows: to defend the domain of Islam and to extend it if possible, to uphold the *sharīʿah,* the prescribed conduct for a Muslim, to ensure law and order so that Muslims might observe the *sharīʿah* in peace and security, to collect canonical taxes, and generally to administer the *ummah* in consultation with selected counselors.

The Shīʿī conception of the caliphate differs from the Sunni in the manner of origination and the consequences flowing therefrom. Out of certain verses of the Qurʾān and from selected *ḥadīth* (reports of the Prophet's words or deeds), the Shīʿah adduce that Muḥammad had indeed chosen a successor: his first cousin, son-in-law, and early convert, ʿAlī ibn Abī Ṭalib. According to the Shīʿah, a conspiracy among the companions of the Prophet denied ʿAlī his rightful position, plunging the community into error the instant Muḥammad died. That the prophet had himself selected ʿAlī establishes to Shīʾī satisfaction a leadership of far greater charismatic authority than the Sunnī version, a leadership that for most of the Shīʾī grew to incorporate impeccability and infallible interpretation of scripture.

ʿAlī did become the fourth caliph, the last of the so-called Rāshidūn or "rightly guided" caliphs, but his designation by the assassins of his predecessor, ʿUthmān ibn ʿAffān (644–656) of the clan of Umayyah, precipitated a civil war that rent forever the fabric of the community. When ʿAlī was killed in 661, the caliphate passed to the Umayyads (661–750). The Shīʿah would thereafter cleave to the view that only the ʿAlids, ʿAlī's progeny, could claim the caliphate; their claim alone was divinely sanctioned. Yet the inability of the Shīʿah never to agree on a particular candidate among ʿAlī's descendants condemned their movement to martyrdom, factionalism, and futility.

The conflict between ʿAlī and the Umayyads spawned a third interpretation of the caliphate, that of the Khārijīs. In the view of these numerically few but very active dissidents, hostile to both parties following the civil war, the caliph was liable for deposition should he deviate an iota from Muḥammad's practice. The Kharijis thus depreciated the office to no better than a tribal chieftainship. Arab nomadic groups were, in fact, the milieu from which they drew their support.

Historical Influences on the Caliphate. The evolution of the caliphate reflects in microcosm the forces molding Islamic civilization. Foremost of these was the Islamic moral imperative, expressed in the Qurʾān and the *sunnah*, or custom, of the Prophet. However visionary and inspirational these Islamic teachings were, they offered little specific guidance on the shape of Islamic leadership, principally the prophetic model and a framework of moral principles. But various non-Islamic influences heavily warped these Islamic precepts.

In the first Islamic century Arab tribalism was a continuing challenge to the developing caliphate. Inherited and/or acquired prestige, directly linked to lineage, constituted the basis of Arab leadership concepts. Traditionally power was closely associated with the numerical strength and past reputation of the lineage. Early Muslim caliphs lacked such esteem; only ʿUthmān had both tribal and Islamic prestige. His well-intentioned effort to use tribalism as well as Islamic prestige to enhance the caliph's authority was a major cause of his downfall. Mutual hostilities among the tribes plagued the early Muslim community: the Umayyads were constrained to form tribal marriage alliances to solidify their authority, but rising criticism of their reliance on Arab social custom was a crucial element in the dynasty's overthrow.

The later Umayyads and the early Abbasid dynasty were deeply affected by the tradition of imperial authority in the lands they had conquered. Its advocates, usually newly converted scribes, envisaged a rigidly hierarchical society of privileged rulers and taxpaying ruled, with the caliph as supreme arbiter in all matters. The Abbasid caliphs, therefore, withdrew within a royal city, appeared in public only on ceremonial occasions, ruled despotically and pursued a lifestyle greatly at variance with the Islamic values expressed in the Qurʾān and *sunnah*.

The Abbasids never exclusively adopted their imperial tradition inherited largely from the Sasanid Persians. They were acutely conscious of having acquired power by criticizing the alleged impiety of the Umayyads, so they patronized the *ʿulamāʾ* (religious scholars) as well as poets, musicians, and wine merchants. Even the Islamic aspects of the caliphate, however, succumbed to imperial majesty. Assuming charismatic throne-names, the Abbasids, following the later Umayyads, asserted that their authority derived directly from God, not from Muḥammad and certainly not from the *ummah*. If most of the pious shunned their patronage, still it was during the early Abbasid caliphate that Islamic civilization attained its full grandeur.

By the middle of the tenth century, however, the caliph was a virtual prisoner in his palace, his authority and his majesty evaporated. Between 945 and 1055 the Buyids, tribesmen from Iran professing Shiism, ruled the caliphal capital of Baghdad yet retained the Sunnī caliphate, perhaps recognizing that a pliant puppet symbolizing the unity of Islam was politically more useful to them than a Shīʿī caliph demanding at least their respect. Furthermore, the Buyids refused to recognize the Shīʿī Fatimid caliphate that had emerged in North Africa in 909 and was preparing to advance eastward to establish itself in Cairo (969) with the hegemony of the Muslim world as its manifest goal. As an extremist Shīʿī dynasty, the Fatimids were a menace to both Sunnī and moderate Shīʿī Muslims.

Such a threatening Shīʿī presence in North Africa evoked a response from the remnant of the Umayyad dynasty in Spain (755–1031). Heretofore content with lesser titles despite nonrecognition of their Abbasid successors, the Spanish Umayyads now claimed the caliphate in 929 as a rallying point for nearby Sunnīs. The simultaneous existence of two Sunnī caliphs presented a challenge to those religious scholars bent on accommodating their political theory to the actual historical process. Abū Manṣūr ʿAbd al-Qāhir al-Baghdādī (d. 1027), for example, argued that if an ocean should separate the *ummah* into two distant parts, a second caliph was unfortunately justifiable. This view was firmly rejected, however, by the jurist Abū al-Ḥasan al-Māwardī (d. 1058), who would condone no attenuation of the caliphal prerogatives.

Rescue, if it can be so characterized, came in the form of the Seljuk Turks, tribesmen from Central Asia who styled themselves champions of Sunnism while continuing to dominate the caliph. In the eleventh century they reversed the tide of political Shiism, yet in their train came a new influence damaging to the concept of the caliphate: visions of world domination nurtured among pastoralists of the broad Asian steppes. Incipient with the Seljuks, the view reached full force among the pagan Mongols, who would suffer no rival, however moribund, to a Mongol khanate destined to rule the earth. Their assault on Baghdad in 1258 extinguished the classical caliphate.

Although they soon became Muslim, those Mongols who ruled in Islamic lands and the Turco-Mongol dynasties that succeeded them gave little heed to the caliphate. They claimed to rule by divine right and garnished their own tradition with the Persian concepts of a functionally hierarchical society. Islamic scholarship adjusted, however reluctantly, to this new reality: henceforth the *ʿulamāʾ*, claiming to be the guardians of the *sharīʿah*, conferred the title of *khalīfat Allāh* ("deputy of God") upon any ruler who upheld that body of sacred law and ruled righteously. The once-exalted title became one of many with which Muslim rulers of succeeding centuries adorned their chancery documents.

The Mamluk sultans of Egypt, however, adopted an alleged scion of the Abbasid house as legitimator of their oligarchic rule, seemingly a residual authority during the tension-laden interlude between the death of one ruler and the consolidation of his successor. Until 1500, Indian kings used to seek investiture documents from this "shadow caliph" to bolster their tenuous legitimacy. The Ottoman conqueror of Egypt, Yavuz Sultan Selim, then took this putative Abbasid caliph to Istanbul in 1517, an event subsequently exploited by Ottoman sultans of the nineteenth century to substantiate their own caliphal claims.

By the late nineteenth century the force of European imperialism had sparked a revival of the caliphate in a new form that engendered as much controversy among Muslims as had the classical version. The Ottoman sultan, ruling a sprawling empire threatened by European powers, sought to elevate his prestige and retain a link to his lost Muslim subjects by recasting the caliphate into a spiritual office. This device appealed to Muslims under colonial rule, such as in India, tsarist Russia, the Malay Peninsula, and the Indonesian archipelago. Even in British-occupied Egypt it elicited a favorable response. But within the Ottoman empire, non-Muslim nationalists struggling for independence regarded the revived concept of the caliphate as an instrument to marshal Muslim support for their suppression. By the eve of the First World War this view was shared even by some Muslim Arabs who decried the Ottoman caliphate was a sham lacking the slightest trace of a Quraysh pedigree. Both Islamic reformers and Muslim nationalists reviled the Ottoman sultan/caliph and, citing classical scholars to support their contention, characterized the Rāshidūn as the only true caliphs.

In retrospect, it is not surprising that the most secular of the nationalist movements in Muslim countries, the Turkish, should have abolished the Ottoman caliphate in 1924; at the time it came as a shock to the entire Muslim world. The Indian Khilafat Conference (1919–1933), advocating self-rule for Indian Muslims because they owed spiritual allegiance to the caliph, found its cause hopelessly undercut. Muslims elsewhere demanding independence from colonialism had to revise their strategy once they overcame their disappointment.

In the newly independent Arab world a contest for the caliphate emerged, but the effort to revive the "true" caliphate was short-lived. Three conferences over a brief span (1926–1931) broke up in disarray. It was soon apparent that new nation-states opposed the restoration of such a vaguely defined but potentially influential institution unless their own governments could control it.

The quickened religious pulse in the Islamic world today has evoked no noticeable inclination to revive the concept of the caliphate. It would seem that however much Muslims may desire a greater sense of unity, any expression of such sentiment is unlikely to assume the caliphal form.

SEE ALSO Imamate; Modernism, article on Islamic Modernism; Ummah.

BIBLIOGRAPHY

Historical Surveys

In addition to Dominique Sourdel's comprehensive article "Khalīfa" (and its references) in *The Encyclopaedia of Islam*, new ed. (Leiden, 1960–), the only full treatment of the concept of the caliphate and its role in Islamic history is the book by Thomas W. Arnold, *The Caliphate*, the second edition of which, with an additional chapter by Sylvia G. Haim, is to be preferred (Oxford, 1965). Its heavy emphasis on classical Sunnī texts may be leavened by the insights and balance of Marshall G. S. Hodgson throughout the three volumes of his *The Venture of Islam* (Chicago, 1974). Al-Mawardi's exposition of the Sunnī caliphate is ably assessed by H. A. R. Gibb in an article, "Al-Māwardī's Theory of the Caliphate," in his *Studies on the Civilization of Islam*, edited by Stanford J. Shaw and William R. Polk (Boston, 1962). The chapter "Caliphate and Sultanate," in the pioneering *Islamic Society and the West*, vol. 1, part 1, by Gibb with Harold Bowen (Oxford, 1950), unduly reflects the views of Sunnī theoreticians of the caliphate.

Interpretive Works

Most valuable for its able exposition of the early caliphate against the background of Arab culture is H. M. T. Nagel's article, "Some Considerations concerning the Pre-Islamic and the Islamic Foundations of the Authority of the Caliphate," in *Studies on the First Century of Islamic Society*, edited by G. H. A. Juynboll (Carbondale, Ill., 1982), pp. 177–197.

The growth of Persian influences on Islamic ruling institutions is best found in the two-part article by Ann K. S. Lambton, "Quis custodiet custodes? Some Reflections on the Persian Theory of Government," *Studia Islamica* 5 (1956): 125–148;

6 (1956): 125–146. She continues her analysis into the Turko-Iranian period, but her work should be supplemented by Osman Turan's article "The Ideal of World Domination among the Medieval Turks," *Studia Islamica* 4 (1955): 77–90. The chapter "The Mongols, the Turks and the Muslim Polity" in Bernard Lewis's *Islam in History: Ideas, Men and Events in the Middle East* (London, 1973) puts Turan's thesis in a broader perspective.

Intellectual aspects of the recent phase of the history of the caliphate are perhaps best dealt with in Albert Hourani's *Arabic Thought in the Liberal Age, 1789–1939*, 2d ed. (Cambridge, 1983). The Turkish perspective is outlined in the analytical chapters of Bernard Lewis's *The Emergence of Modern Turkey*, 2d ed. (Oxford, 1968), while the abolition of the caliphate and the reaction to it in the Arab world is covered in detail in Arnold Toynbee's "The Islamic World since the Peace Settlement," in the *Royal Institute of International Affairs, Survey of International Affairs, 1925*, vol. 1 (Oxford, 1927).

Herbert L. Bodman, Jr. (1987)

CALLIGRAPHY

This entry consists of the following articles:

AN OVERVIEW
CHINESE AND JAPANESE CALLIGRAPHY
HEBREW MICROGRAPHY
ISLAMIC CALLIGRAPHY

CALLIGRAPHY: AN OVERVIEW

The term calligraphy derives from the Greek word *graphein* (to write) and *kallos* (beautiful); it has therefore often been identified with "beautiful writing." But calligraphy is more than that. It arises out of a combination of several important elements: the attitude of society to writing; the religious concepts involved; the importance and function of the text; definite, often mathematically based rules about the correct interaction between lines and space and their relationship to each other; and a mastery and understanding of the script, the writing material, and the tools used for writing. Writing and script store information essential to the political, social, and economic survival of a particular group; they are as such part of the infrastructure of society. Calligraphy makes a statement about the sum total of its cultural and historical heritage. As such it can become subject to political and nationalistic/religious expressions and pressures. In addition, calligraphy united the pictorial with the scriptorial. A calligraphic passage, or even a single Chinese character, not only provides information through its scriptorial meaning but also communicates on a more direct and archetypal level through its inherent pictorial powers. Unlike writing, calligraphy cannot be acquired simply by learning; it demands insight and individuality, but individuality expressed within strictly prescribed boundaries.

Calligraphy needs enabling tools: a smooth writing surface such as paper, parchment, or silk and instruments like a quill pen and brush to produce the variation of lines so essential for true calligraphy. The sharply yielding point of a metal stylus on wax (as used in Rome and Greece), wet clay in Mesopotamia and the Mediterranean, or palm leaves on which the script is incised in South and Southeast Asia can produce pleasing results but not calligraphy. The material and the instruments used for writing simply do not allow the production of free-flowing lines. Though stone is not the best medium, it served well to receive and preserve calligraphic copies; indeed, Western calligraphy can trace its roots to the stone inscription found on Trajan's (r. 98–117 CE) column.

The other important factor is motivation. According to the above definition, only three civilizations have produced true calligraphy: the Chinese (and those who use the Chinese script, namely Japanese and Koreans), the Arabs (and those who use the Arabic script), and Western civilization based on Roman letters, Roman laws, and the Christian church. In the case of Arabic calligraphy, it was the revelation of the Qur'ān and Islamic conquest; in the Far East artistic sensibility and political hegemony; and in the West the discipline of Roman letters and Christianity.

Calligraphy flourishes within a definite discipline. Scribal authorities such as the ones established in medieval monasteries of Europe; Ibn Muqlah's (866–940 CE) reforms of the Arabic script based on the interaction between the rhombic dot, the standard alif, and the standard cycle; and the original definition of a Chinese character based within a square. There is also a connection with dynastic elements. For example, after the fall of Rome in the fifth century, a number of "national hands" developed in the various states carved from the disintegrating empire: the Merovingian style, the Visigothic script, Carolingian minuscule, Gothic, and so on.

The Position of the Calligrapher in Society and Religion. The position of calligrapher in society and religion reflects the attitude to his craft and the level on which it is practiced. In Europe and the Arab world calligraphy has always been first and foremost in the service of God and the divine Revelation. In the West the calligrapher was "in service" too, first to a human master (Rome), then to the monastic order to which he had given his life, and eventually simply to the customer who paid him. Only in the Far East did the calligrapher exist in its own right. He did not propagate any secular or religious order; his calligraphy was, with definite restrictions, an expression of his inner self.

Though mainly practiced by men, none of the three great civilizations actively forbade women to become calligraphers. The first Chinese treatise on calligraphy, published in 320 CE, that established definite criteria, still valid today, was written by the Lady Wei Shao. It is thought that even the great Wang Xizhi (321–379 CE) was one of her students. In China and Japan calligraphy was an accomplishment practiced by the elite for the elite; a good calligraphic hand ensured success in the civil service examinations (enforced during the Tang period, 618 to 907 CE). During the Japanese Heian period (794–1185 CE) it almost took the place of an aphrodisiac in courtly circles. If the first note from a prospective lover proved indifferently written, the affair could not proceed. A special form of women's calligraphy, written in the hiragana style, developed. The Islamic world, too, knew famous women calligraphers. Some Muslim ladies achieved a high competence in calligraphy; the emperor Aurangzeb's daughter Zebunnisa (1639–1702), for example, a great patroness of art and learning, was proficient in at least three calligraphic styles. In the Maghrib (the western part of the Islamic world) women were told that they had to write at least one Qurʾān to make a good marriage. Calligraphy written by eighteenth-century Turkish women is still kept in the mosques at Istanbul. Christianity had always favored literacy in women, hoping that a good education would make them more suitable for the monastic life, should their parents decide to dedicate them. Nuns often collaborated with monks in the production of calligraphic manuscripts, but unlike in China and in the Islamic world they worked, as did the monks, anonymously. Western calligraphy, which arose simply from copying texts that were often brought back after difficult journeys from Rome or neighboring monasteries, was part of the life to which they had dedicated themselves, and, like their male colleagues, they were strictly forbidden from boasting. This was different in the Islamic countries and in China/Japan, where a long list of famous calligraphers and their biographical data were freely provided.

"Beautiful Writing." Although outside the strict discipline of calligraphy, beautiful writing is mostly based on pictorial expressions. Writing itself began mostly with pictures: in Egypt, among the Sumerians, in the Indus Valley, and in the pre-Columbian world of Central America. In the case of the Chinese this pictorial element is often still clearly visible. Though not rooted in the knowledge of traditional science and religious conviction, beautiful writing could sometimes—as, for example, in the case of the originally Indian *siddham* script—become calligraphy in the hands of Japanese masters.

But the absence of chancelleries and scribal authority had its restrictions. Judaism, for example, has produced many fine manuscripts and beautiful micrography but no calligraphy in the strict sense. During the many years of the Diaspora there were no courts or chancelleries that could establish and control definite styles. Except for the Sefer Torah, used in the synagogue, the meaning of the text has always been more important than its visual execution.

Another concept consists of writing a picture that relates to the meaning of the text. The calligrams (text pictures) of the French poet Guillaume Apollinaire (1880–1918) go however back through history to the Greek poet Simias, who, in the fourth century BCE, wrote poems in the shape of an egg or the wings of a bird. The tradition continued and was eventually introduced into Christian Europe in the sixth century by the bishop of Poitiers, who wrote a poem in the form of a cross. Text pictures remained popular right through the Middle Ages and the baroque period and surfaced again among groups like the Dadaists and some individual modern poets. Though Islam is strictly averse to visual representation, calligraphers have been skillful in writing at least the *basmalah* ("In the name of God, the Compassionate, the Merciful") in a variety of shapes. Such text pictures were also known in India and China and other parts of the world. Indeed the whole text of the Qurʾān, numbering some 77,934 words, has been written on the shell of a single egg.

Contemporary Calligraphy. In the West printing has generally been considered a move toward the end of calligraphy. But the twentieth century has seen a remarkable renewal of interest, both in Europe and, perhaps even more so, in America: exhibitions, the foundation of professional societies, teaching at art schools and colleges, and a growing circle of gifted amateurs and fine professional scribes. The roots go back to the Arts and Crafts movement of the 1880s and the work of William Morris (1834–1896) and, most of all, Edward Johnson (1872–1944). In Islamic countries and in the Far East the situation has always been different. Calligraphy has never been a disinherited art form, and printing (with wood block on which the hand of the writer could be incised) has never meant an end of calligraphic traditions. Letters, always the main basis of Western calligraphic traditions, began to appear in paintings (such as those of the cubists, surrealists, Picasso, and Joan Miró) and on newspapers (characters written by Mao Zedong on the masthead of the *Peoples Daily*) and posters. Most important, however, was a certain kind of symbiosis between the three main styles that began to appear from the middle of the last century. Western calligraphers began to take an interest in Eastern conceptions of art and calligraphy; a definite example is Mark Tobey (1890–1976). Islamic calligraphers, many educated at Western universities, have begun to look for new interpretations, which could be incorporated within the core of their own traditions. But it is mainly in Japan that calligraphy is still deeply respected. Prices for a good piece of calligraphy may start at four thousand pounds and can go up as far as one million. There, "well written" still implies calligraphic aspirations, not just textual excellence.

See Also Alphabets.

Bibliography

Brown, Michelle P. *A Guide to Historical Scripts from Antiquity to 1660.* London, 1990. An illustrated survey of the evolution of Western scripts.

Butterworth, Emma M. *The Complete Book of Calligraphy.* Wellingborough, 1981. Overview of the subject.

Catich, Edward M. *Letters Redrawn from the Trajan Inscriptions in Rome.* Davenport, Iowa, 1961. Influence of Trajan (Roman) inscription on letterforms.

Folsom, Rose. *The Calligraphers Dictionary.* London, 1990. Offers an explanation and definition of words and concepts connected with calligraphy.

Gaur, Albertine. *A History of Calligraphy.* London and New York, 1994. A comprehensive study of calligraphy in all its aspects.

Gray, Nicolette. *A History of Lettering, Creative Experiment and Lettering Identity.* Oxford, 1986. On the importance of letterforms in Western calligraphy.

Hamel, Christopher de. *Medieval Craftsmen: Scribes and Illuminators.* London, 1992. Deals with the makers of paper, parchment and inks, and with scribes, illustrators, booksellers and bookbinders.

Harris, David. *Calligraphy, Inspiration, Innovation, Communication.* London, 1991. Examines the breath of calligraphy in modern life.

Mote, Frederick W., and Hun-Lam Chu. *Calligraphy and the East Asian Book.* Edited by Howard L. Goodman. Princeton, 1988. Calligraphy before and after the start of printing in China and Japan.

Safadi, Yasin Hamid. *Islamic Calligraphy.* London, 1978. Examines the work of Islamic calligraphers from the beginning of Islam; deals also with calligraphy in Islamic architecture.

Whalley, Joyce Irene. *Writing Implements and Accessories: From Roman Stylus to the Typewriter.* Vancouver, 1975. Exhaustive study of the history of writing implements.

Yao, Min-Chi. *The Influence of Chinese and Japanese Calligraphy on Mark Tobey (1890–1976).* San Francisco, 1983. The spiritual influence of far eastern calligraphy on the American painter Mark Tobey.

Zapf, Hermann. *About Alphabets, Some Marginal Notes on Type Design.* New York, 1960. The place of calligraphy in modern type design.

ALBERTINE GAUR (2005)

CALLIGRAPHY: CHINESE AND JAPANESE CALLIGRAPHY

Four thousand years ago, it is alleged, the Chinese sage Cang Jian, whose pastime was to observe birds' footprints in the sand and trace their patterns, conceived China's first writing. These were pictographs or stenographic sketches of familiar objects, animals, or birds, still more or less easily recognized. They formed no sentences or concepts, merely incomplete ideas and phrases. In the pre-Confucian, pre-Buddhist China of the Shang dynasty (1500–1050 BCE) such scripts were used to inscribe the shells and bones used for divination. Early writing is next encountered in China during the Zhou dynasty (1122–221 BCE) in the stiff, cold, classic, formal ideograms of the "great seal" style (*da zhuan*) that covered ceremonial bronzes with messages of felicity in the afterlife. These vessels, suitable for cooking or wine, were entombed with their masters, who might need such comforts as they journeyed to join their ancestors. "Great seal" was the writing Confucius read and wrote, and it is still used in China and Japan for signature seals (chops) or ornamental inscriptions of a particularly exalted sort.

Following the unification of China in 221 BCE, the first emperor of the Qin dynasty simplified and regularized the written language into the "small seal" style (*xiao zhuan*). Writing continued in use as ceremony and religious observances, but its importance increased enormously in response to the central authority's demand for records, accounts, and the issuance of edicts and orders throughout the provinces. Within a century the "regular" style (*zhen shu*) developed and became the standard form still employed today.

Wang Xizhi (321–379 CE), China's greatest calligrapher, created a cursive or "running" script (*xing shu*). He arrived at this elegant form of speed writing, which reduces the rigid formality and clarity of "regular" style to impressionistic essentials instantly comprehensible to the expert, after studying geese. He saw in their graceful, turning, supple necks precisely the strength and flexibility required of the calligrapher's brush strokes. The result was that another convenience, and yet another level of artful beauty entered writing.

Many Chinese characters are in a sense pictures (pictographs) representing "things" such as sun, moon, tree, or house; others (ideographs) represent "ideas." But by far the majority of all Chinese characters are now recognized as "logographs," that is, as graphs that represent, strictly, neither pictorial image nor brute idea but words, through a complex system of semantic and phonemic constituents that long ago escaped from a purely visual medium of representation. By combining these graphs in an endless variety of ways to make new words and then compounding them with still others, any word or idea can be expressed. For *thunder and lightning,* for example, combine *rain* and *paddy field.* For *cash money,* put the word for *gold* next to that for a guardian *spear.* Modern notions can be incorporated into the language by the same process. For *electricity,* write *thunder and lightning,* add a tail, and make a compound with the word for *feeling.* The system suits China's monosyllabic language perfectly and adapts into Japanese most conveniently. When the Chinese or Japanese regard a character, they at once see a picture, hear a sound, and perceive a meaning.

Unabridged Chinese and Japanese dictionaries list upward of forty thousand characters today. A knowledge of five thousand is sufficient for reading a newspaper. The number of strokes within a single character ranges from one (meaning "one") to thirty-three (composed of three deer, meaning "rough," "rude," or "wild"). Each stroke is either thick or thin, strong or soft, curved or straight, heavy with ink or dry and faint, pushed against the paper or lightly withdrawn from it. A character, regardless of its number of strokes, must occupy the same amount of space within an invisible square, and must be equidistant from all others on the page. Each stroke composing the ideogram must be written in correct order—from top to bottom, left to right, vertical strokes before horizontal ones.

In 405 CE, Wani, a Korean scribe well versed in Chinese classics, was hired by the imperial court of Japan as tutor to the crown prince. Japan had no written language of its own, and it had become increasingly necessary to communicate with its powerful neighbor, the "center of the universe." Within a century China began sending presents to Japan's emperor—images of Lord Buddha, sūtras translated into Chinese from the Sanskrit and Pali, and the teachings of Confucius. Scholars arrived from China bringing with them books, music, medicines (tea among them), the craft of calendar making, and the art of divination. And with them also came the "four perfections of calligraphy"—the brush, paper, ink stick, and ink stone.

Calligraphy in Japan is called *shodō*, "way of writing," and is a way of life, a path or pursuit, like *bushidō*, the path of the warrior, *sadō*, the cult of tea, or Shintō, the way of the gods. In the Nara period (710–784 CE) priests began the practice of *shakyō*, the copying over and over of sūtras, the Buddha's teachings and commentaries thereon, a custom that continues to this day. A Chinese priest had said, "If you do not understand, write the sūtra. Then you will see its inner meaning." Obediently, priests spent lifetimes at this labor in search of enlightenment (which sometimes came in the middle of an ideographic stroke), as penance, and as a means of raising temple funds. Spiritual merit accrued not only to the writer but to the beholder and to anyone who purchased the manuscript.

Japan's earliest poems were in Chinese, but gradually the Japanese broke free and began adapting monosyllabic, short, concise, and tonal Chinese to their own spoken language, which is polysyllabic, highly inflected, and periphrastic with affixes for adjectives and prefixes for nouns. In the ninth century the women of the Heian court devised brief cursive signs called *hiragana*, a syllabary that derived from Chinese and, remotely, was probably inspired by the Sanskrit alphabet known in Chinese translation.

At present, calligraphy is held in highest esteem in Japan. Scholars practice *hitsudan*, or communicating with each other by exchanging notes across a table. (They can also communicate with modern Chinese this way without knowing the pronunciation of a single spoken word.) Great calligraphers are paid as much as fifty thousand dollars a word, and specimens of fine writing adorn shopping bags, cigarette boxes, or signs outside a shop window. *Kabuki* actors are applauded for their calligraphy, and an *onnagata* (a player of female roles) will mix a touch of lipstick in his ink to add eroticism to an autograph. *Kakizome*, the first brush writing of the new year, occurs annually on January 2, and at "calligraphy meets" more than a thousand participants ranging in age from five to sixty gather in the Great Martial Arts Hall of Tokyo to compete for prizes.

Although the typewriter and the fountain pen have removed calligraphy from the daily life of the average Japanese, many men and women practice it as a form of spiritual discipline. As Aoyama San'u, one of the greatest living calligraphers, expresses it, "In calligraphy you see the reality of the person. When you write you cannot lie, retouch, ornament. You are naked before God."

Bibliography

Chen Zhimai. *Chinese Calligraphers and Their Art.* New York, 1966.

Ecke Zong Youhe. *Chinese Calligraphy.* Philadelphia, 1971.

Hisamatsu, Shin'ichi. *Zen and the Fine Arts.* Tokyo, 1971.

Sansom, George B. *Japan: A Short Cultural History* (1931). Rev. ed. New York, 1962.

Sullivan, Michael. *The Three Perfections.* New York, 1980.

Tazawa Yutaka, ed. *Biographical Dictionary of Japanese Art.* Tokyo, 1984.

New Sources

Barrass, Gordon. *The Art of Calligraphy in Modern China.* Berkeley, 2002.

Ellsworth, Robert Hatfield. *Later Chinese Painting and Calligraphy 1800–1950.* New York, 1987.

Gaur, Albertine. *A History of Calligraphy.* London, 1994.

Sturman, Peter Charles. *Mi Fu: Style and the Art of Calligraphy in Northern Song China.* New Haven, 1997.

Zeng, Youhe. *A History of Chinese Calligraphy.* Hong Kong, 1993.

Faubion Bowers (1987)
Revised Bibliography

CALLIGRAPHY: HEBREW MICROGRAPHY

The patterning of Hebrew texts into ornamental motifs is a medieval art form that bears the modern name of micrography, "minute writing." Within an artistic tradition almost universally consigned to dependency on one dominant culture or another because of its minority status, this distinctive calligraphic device represents one of the most original aspects of Jewish art.

Emergence of the Art. Micrographic decoration can be found on manuscripts from Yemen to Germany, but its historical origins lie in the eastern Mediterranean, during the first few centuries of Muslim rule. The earliest dated example is the Cairo Codex of the Prophets written in Tiberius in 894/5 CE by the renowned scholar Moshe ben Asher. In the manner of near-contemporary Qur'āns, the manuscript contains five "carpet pages" of geometric and floral motifs, but six other full-page compositions are made up of elaborate micrographic patterns; simpler lettered designs are scattered throughout the margins of the text itself, and at the end, the patron's colophon is similarly framed with writing.

In addition to the Cairo Codex of the Prophets, patterned texts appear on at least fifteen other manuscripts and fragments dating from the tenth or eleventh century, all of which are associated with Egypt, although the scribes frequently come from elsewhere in the Muslim empire. Taken together, these early examples reflect quite clearly the dual Judeo-Muslim context that literally shaped the micrographic art. The meeting ground of the two, of course, was the veneration of the word of God, but while the Muslim scribes gave visual expression to this religious stance through the refinement of the letters that made up the divine words, their Jewish counterparts opted instead to fashion words into patterns. And here, the basic conservatism of the micrographic script, which is never regularized or embellished like the Arabic letters of the Qurʾān, may well reflect a reluctance to alter the alphabet that had been used for centuries in the writing of the Torah scroll (a practice carefully regulated in the Talmud).

The words chosen for patterning were drawn from the Bible itself and the *masorah*, the critical apparatus aimed at keeping the biblical text intact through an elaborate system of word counts. Significantly, the Cairo Codex of the Prophets is also the earliest dated Bible with *masorah*—the activities of Masoretes and scribes alike (and Moshe ben Asher was both) were devoted in their respective ways to the preservation of the sacred scripture. On the popular level, these efforts were endowed with mystical and magical significance as well, through deeply rooted notions of letter symbolism and the power of the word.

In fact, it is this last dimension that suggests a concrete source for the convention of micrographic decoration, namely the amulets and charms that were commonly inscribed, in minuscule letters, with the names of God and biblical verses often patterned around magical figures. In the early micrographic Bibles, this amuletic inspiration—and intent—is apparent throughout, from arcane marginal decorations made up of in-text *masorah* to elaborate geometric carpet pages incorporating propitious biblical verses.

Later Developments. Within the Muslim world, micrography spread from the eastern Mediterranean to Yemen, where it became a highly developed art in the fifteenth century and continued into the seventeenth. The most striking example is a 1469 Pentateuch (British Museum, MS Or. 2348), with a double-page design that fashions Psalm 119 into a Mamluk metalwork pattern of mountains and fish.

Through the Iberian Peninsula the technique reached Europe by the the thirteenth century. Spanish variants on the Near Eastern repertoire include the addition of a framing text in large letters around carpet pages and the outlining of solid decorations with micrographic borders, as well as a few representational images in micrography illustrating the adjacent Bible text. The most elaborate Spanish Bible (Bibliothèque Nationale, Paris, MS Hébreu 1314–1315) opens with eight carpet pages containing the entire biblical text in micrographic interlace.

In Germany and France, Gothic marginalia—grotesques and heraldic motifs—make their way into the micrographic tradition alongside the Near Eastern interlace, while the carpet pages at the beginning and end of the manuscript give way to full-page designs inserted between individual books of the Bible, including floral and animal motifs around the initial word of the biblical text. Full-page illustrations are also formed from micrographic text, as in the representations of Aaron found at the end of the *Book of Exodus* in a 1294/5 Pentateuch (Bibliothèque Nationale, Paris, MS Hébreu 5).

Apart from a revival of decorated marriage contracts (*ketubot*) in seventeenth-century Italy, micrography, like other manuscript arts, declined in the wake of the printed book. But the technique soon reemerged throughout eastern and western Europe in popular engravings and then lithographs, with subjects ranging from *mizraḥ* and *shiviti* designs to indicate the direction of prayer toward Jerusalem to Bible illustrations, rabbi portraits, and postcard views from Palestine, all of which were often executed in an incongruously realistic style. Renewed interest in Jewish art has drawn some modern artists back to traditional micrography techniques.

Bibliography

The most extensive work on Hebrew micrography has been done by Leila Avrin, whose essay "Micrography as Art," published along with Colette Sirat's "La lettre hébraïque et sa signification" as *Études de paléographie hébraïque* (Paris, 1981), contains many illustrations and relevant bibliography. See also Avrin's "The Illustrations of the Moshe ben Asher Codex of 985 CE." (Ph.D. diss., University of Michigan, Ann Arbor, 1974).

New Sources

Avrin, Leila. "Hebrew Micrography." *Ariel* 53 (1983): 90–100.

Metzger, Thérèse. "Ornamental Micrography in Medieval Hebrew Manuscripts." *Bibliotheca Orientalis* 43 (1986): 377–388.

Miriam Rosen (1987)
Revised Bibliography

CALLIGRAPHY: ISLAMIC CALLIGRAPHY

Calligraphy occupies the highest rank among the arts of Islam: according to the tradition of the Prophet, the calligrapher, who knows how to pen in beautiful letters the word of God or even a fragment of the Qurʾān, will certainly go to Paradise. The art of calligraphy developed at an early stage of Islamic history, and soon the ungainly characters of the Semitic alphabet were transformed into decorative letters. An angular, hieratic script developed for the preservation of the Qurʾān; although several early styles existed, it is generally called Kūfī or Kufic (from the city of Kufa in Iraq), and in pious tradition certain features of it are ascribed to ʿAlī ibn Abī Ṭālib, considered the patron of calligraphers. Early Kufic lacks the diacritical marks that were added after 685, as were the signs for vocalization (both in color). A cursive hand was also used, as numerous papyri show. This was developed into several styles for chancelery and copying purposes when the use of paper (introduced from China) became common in the Islamic world after 751. Early Kufic Qurʾāns are written on vellum with a reed pen; the format of the books is oblong, and only from about the tenth century was the normal book format adapted for Qurʾāns, apparently first in the eastern Islamic world. With this change of format, the lettering too changed: the broad, very impressive early Kufic assumed a taller, more graceful stature, and its developed forms are still used for decorative purposes.

The cursive hand was transformed into true calligraphy by the Abbasid vizier Ibn Muqlah (d. 940), who invented the system of measuring the letters by circles and semicircles, with the first letter, alif, becoming the measure for the other twenty-seven letters. As alif is basically a straight vertical line with the numerical value 1 and is used in mystical speculation as a symbol for Allāh (God), the formation of the letters "in the shape of alif" corresponds in a mystical way to the shaping of Adam "in his, God's, form." The rules of Ibn Muqlah were refined by Ibn al-Bawwab (d. 1032). Along with the circles, the square dots produced by the tip of the reed pen served as measuring units: an alif could be five, seven, or nine points high, and all the other letters had to be formed accordingly. Ṣūfī interpretation saw here the primordial dot from which everything created developed. Cursive writing replaced Kufic first in books and documents (in early days usually written as scroll), then, in the thirteenth century, also in epigraphy, where the angular letters had grown, between 800 and 1250, into multiple forms of floriated, foliated, and plaited Kufic, which became barely legible but formed exquisite geometrical ornaments. In Iran, a "hanging," slanted cursive developed from grammatical exigencies; it was refined according to Ibn Muqlah's rules to become the "bride of Islamic writings," *nastaʿlīq*, the ideal vehicle for copying Persian, Turkish, and Urdu poetry.

Calligraphy can be exercised on every material: vellum, papyrus, and paper (paper mills are found from Spain to India); it is woven into silk and linen, embroidered on velvet, used in metalwork and wood, on glass and ceramics, on stones and tiles. Brick and tile compositions result in "square" Kufic, where the names of God and the Prophet (and in Iran, ʿAlī) or religious formulas can cover whole walls in geometrical design. Calligraphy on paper (which includes the patterns for the other types of writing) is written with a reed pen; only very rarely—in early days in Central Asia and India—a brush may have been used. The trimming of the pen in distinct angles and the preparation of the various types of ink belong to the arts the calligrapher has to learn, as he has to study the shape of each and every letter for years before becoming a master who is allowed to sign works with his *katabahu*, "has written." Only in North Africa did pupils write whole words immediately, which accounts for the less "calligraphic" quality of the so-called Maghribi style.

Later calligraphers liked to form *tughrās*—originally the elaborate signature or handsign of a ruler at the beginning of a document. Subsequently the word is applied to all kinds of artistic shapes: mirrored sentences, pious formulas in the shape of birds, lions, or other creatures, faces made of sacred names, or harmonically elaborated calligrams of invocations, prayers, or divine names. The imagery of calligraphy permeates Islamic poetry, and the interpretation of letters according to their numerical value and their "mystical" qualities was, and still is, widespread.

BIBLIOGRAPHY

Numerous publications on calligraphy have been issued recently, most of which are devoted to aesthetic rather than historical purposes. A good brief introduction is Yasin H. Safadi's *Islamic Calligraphy* (Boulder, 1979). Martin Lings's *The Qur'anic Art of Calligraphy and Illumination* (London, 1976) is excellent because it dwells upon the religious character of writing. Ernst Kühnel's small but weighty book *Islamische Schriftkunst* (1942; reprint, Graz, 1972) is still very valuable for its all-around approach and interesting examples. I have provided a brief introduction to the subject in *Islamic Calligraphy* (Leiden, 1970) and delved at greater length into the history, the social situation of the calligraphers, and the uses of calligraphy in Sufism and in poetical parlance in *Calligraphy and Islamic Culture* (New York, 1984).

ANNEMARIE SCHIMMEL (1987)

CALVERT, GEORGE (1580?–1632), secretary of state and privy councillor under King James I of England; the first Lord Baltimore, principally known for his efforts in advancing religious toleration in an age that regarded pluralism as dangerous.

Calvert's commitment to religious toleration was a reflection of his unsettled religious life. Born into a Roman Catholic family that was troubled periodically for its allegiance to a proscribed church, he lived as a Catholic during the first twelve years of his life. In 1592 his father succumbed to the harassment of the Yorkshire High Commission and certified his conformity to the rites of the Church of England. George Calvert soon conformed and for the next thirty-two years lived as a Protestant.

At about the age of fourteen Calvert matriculated at Trinity College, Oxford, where he studied foreign languages. After earning his bachelor's degree, he spent three years studying municipal law at the Inns of Court. In 1603, while on a continental tour, he came to the attention of secretary of state Robert Cecil, who was in Paris. Employed as one of his many secretaries, Calvert used Cecil's influence to begin a slow but steady climb in the government of James I. He traveled overseas on a number of diplomatic missions. In Ireland he served as a member of a commission investigating the complaints of Irish Roman Catholics. In 1610 Calvert was named one of the clerks of the Privy Council. Later he assisted James in writing a tract refuting the Dutch theologian Conrad Vorstius. Two years after knighting him in 1617, James appointed Calvert as one of the secretaries of state and made him a member of the Privy Council.

During the negotiations to marry heir apparent Prince Charles to the Spanish Infanta, and to cement an alliance between Spain and England, Calvert, as secretary of state, became closely identified with both the Spanish and Roman Catholic causes. Laboring diligently to achieve the king's goal, Calvert reached the pinnacle of his power in 1621 and 1622. However, when the government scuttled the marriage treaties in 1624, Calvert lost favor at court and came under intense pressure to resign his office. During this crisis, he resolved his religious commitments, declaring his intention to live and die a Catholic. He resigned his office, selling it for three thousand pounds. James elevated him to the Irish peerage by creating him baron of Baltimore.

Out of office, Lord Baltimore turned his attention to his Irish estates and to the supervision of his Newfoundland colony, for which he had received a charter in 1621. In 1628 he returned to Newfoundland intending to colonize the region with a religiously diverse population. However, the forbidding climate and the hostility of the French convinced him to abandon his plans of permanent residency in Newfoundland. Baltimore subsequently journeyed to Virginia and, impressed by what he saw there, returned to England in 1630 to secure a charter for a colony along Chesapeake Bay.

Despite the opposition encountered from some of the Protestant settlers in Newfoundland to his policy of religious toleration, the Catholic Baltimore drew upon his own experiences in government and rejected the dominant concept of *cuius regio eius religio,* namely that the local ruler's religion must be the religion of the region. Rather, he sought to found a colony where Catholics and Protestants could work together to achieve an economically viable enterprise. He died in April 1632, shortly before the Maryland Charter passed its final seals. The founding of the colony in 1634 was left to his son Cecil, the second Lord Baltimore.

BIBLIOGRAPHY

There is to date no modern biography of George Calvert. The most thorough biography is Lewis W. Wilhelm's *Sir George Calvert, Baron of Baltimore* (Baltimore, 1884). It must be used cautiously, however, as it contains many errors. The Maryland Historical Society published the first four chapters of James W. Foster's uncompleted biography under the title *George Calvert: The Early Years* (Baltimore, 1983). Calvert's letters, mostly official, are scattered throughout the State Papers in the Public Record Office (London) and in *The Calvert Papers* in the Maryland Historical Society (Baltimore).

For Calvert's conversion to Roman Catholicism, see my short study "'The Face of a Protestant, and the Heart of a Papist': A Reexamination of Sir George Calvert's Conversion to Roman Catholicism," *Journal of Church and State* 20 (Autumn 1978): 507–531. For his religious problems in his Newfoundland colony, see R. J. Lahey's "The Role of Religion in Lord Baltimore's Colonial Enterprise," *Maryland Historical Magazine* 72 (Winter 1977): 492–511. For the role of religion in the colony founded by his heir, Cecil Calvert, see my articles "Lord Baltimore, Roman Catholics, and Toleration: Religious Policy in Maryland during the Early Catholic Years, 1634–1649," *Catholic Historical Review* 45 (January 1979): 49–75, and "'With Promise of Liberty in Religion': The Catholic Lords Baltimore and Toleration in Seventeenth-Century Maryland, 1634–1692," *Maryland Historical Magazine* 79 (Spring 1984): 21–43.

JOHN D. KRUGLER (1987)

CALVIN, JOHN

CALVIN, JOHN (1509–1564), primary Protestant reformer, biblical scholar, church organizer, and theologian. Also a humanist and linguist, Calvin helped to shape and standardize French language and literary style.

Calvin was reclusive and reticent; hence the only Calvin we know is the public figure. Of his first twenty-five years we know comparatively little. He was born at Noyon (province of Picardy), France, on July 10, 1509, the fourth of six children born to Gérard Cauvin and Jeanne Lefranc. Christened Jean Cauvin, from his university days he used the name Calvin, the latinized form of Cauvin. He spent his first thirteen years in Noyon, benefiting from the rich traditions of this historic episcopal city where his father served as attorney for the cathedral and secretary to the bishop, Charles de Hangest.

Intimately associated as a youth with the de Hangest household, Calvin developed aristocratic tastes and demeanor. Church benefices permitted him to further his education at the University of Paris; he spent nearly eleven years in Paris, participating in the intellectual life both of the university and the large circle of humanist scholars at the court of the king, Francis I.

At the university, preparing for a career in theology, Calvin had completed the master of arts degree when his father had a falling-out with the bishop. The father ordered his son to change to a career in law. Obediently Calvin moved to Orléans, where the best law faculty in France, under the leadership of Pierre de l'Étoile, was located. Though more interested in humanist studies, he completely immersed himself in the law (at Orléans, Bourges, and Paris) and took his doctorate and his licentiate in three years.

In 1531 Calvin's father died excommunicate. The struggle to secure a Christian burial for his father doubtless soured Calvin's relations with the Roman church. But for the moment the effect of his father's death was to permit him to commit himself to the uninterrupted pursuit of humanist studies.

In 1532 Calvin published his first book, a commentary on Seneca's *On Clemency.* Though distinguished for its learning, the book did not win him any acclaim. His days of humanist study in Paris were cut short when, in 1533, his close friend Nicholas Cop, rector of the University of Paris, delivered an address that incorporated ideas of the Lutheran Reformation. Reaction by the theologians at the Sorbonne was strong, and because Calvin had a hand in the composition of the address, he, along with Cop, was forced to flee for his life. Although scholarly opinion differs, it appears that shortly thereafter he underwent the "sudden conversion" he speaks about later. A marked man in France, Calvin spent the rest of his life in exile.

Having turned his considerable talents to the support of the Reformation, in early 1536 Calvin published at Basel the first edition of his epochal *Institutes of the Christian Religion.* Intended as a defense of the French Protestants to the king of France, it marked Calvin as the foremost mind of Protestantism. The desired life of solitude and study that permitted its composition could never again be Calvin's. In late July of 1536, he happened to stop in the small city of Geneva; there God "thrust him into the fray," as he was to say. Geneva had recently declared for the Protestant faith under the urging of the fiery evangelist Guillaume Farel, one of Calvin's colleagues from his Paris days. Farel, learning of Calvin's presence in the city, sought him out and urged him to join in the work of reform at Geneva. When Calvin refused, Farel thundered that God would punish him for turning his back on that work. The shaken Calvin heard it as the summons of God and agreed to stay. Except for a three-year period of peaceful study and ministry in Strasbourg (1538–1541), Calvin was henceforth associated with the city and republic of Geneva in a stormy ministry designed to bring the city into conformity with the biblical model as he understood it.

Calvin's ideal for Geneva was that church and state work hand in hand to create and govern a utopian society in which the biblical worldview was enforced. But the Genevan state was determined to keep the church under its control. A man of courage and indomitable will, Calvin took up the battle. Armed only with the power of the pulpit and of the church institutions, through persistence, adherence to biblical principles, organizational talents, and moral conviction, he managed to overcome massive resistance and to see most of his ideals realized. Geneva was transformed from a city of ill repute to one in which a strict moral code regulated the lives of all, regardless of rank or class. In spite of the radical harshness of his policies, by the end of his life Calvin was widely respected, even admired, by the Genevans. From an international perspective, Geneva became the model for the emerging Protestant states, a city of refuge for persecuted Protestants, and the so-called "Rome" of Protestantism. Of perhaps capital importance, Calvin's program—alone among the Protestant groups—included both a training center (in the University of Geneva, which he established) and an acceptance of a missionary mandate to export Calvinism throughout the world. Hence Calvinism, or Reformed Protestantism, was the only Protestant group with universalistic designs.

Unquestionably, Calvin was first and foremost a man of ideas, although he effectively blended thought and action. True to his Renaissance humanist orientation, he was interested only in what was useful. All of his ideas are designed for practical application, whether to an individual religious experience or to a specific activity of the church. Further, the rhetorical and pedagogical program of the humanists formed the basis of his thought, and their devotion to original sources determined his methodology. As a theologian he intended only to set forth scriptural teaching. He accommodated ambiguity and contradiction in his theology, for people are both limited in mental capacity and debilitated by sin, hence totally reliant upon the revelation of God in scripture.

For Calvin, the word of God in scripture is generated by the Holy Spirit and, therefore, properly interpreted only by the Holy Spirit. It is, thus, a spiritual message. Hence Calvin should not be viewed as an academic theologian, or as a theologian writing for intellectual purposes. He wrote for the church, for believers; his purpose was to edify, to form the pious mind that would emerge in reverential, grateful worship and adoration of God. He constantly warned his readers not to indulge in idle speculation, not to seek to know anything except what is revealed in the scripture, not to forget that theology is more of the heart than of the head. Consequently, being biblical, practical, and spiritual, his theology was of a different type from that of most of the later Calvinists who wrote for the university audience, for those who regarded theology as the "queen of the sciences" in the world of ideas.

The principal source for Calvin's thought is, of course, the *Institutes*. This book is best understood as a manual on spirituality. And, although the corpus of his writings is great, Calvin's ideas, whether found in sermons, biblical commentaries, or polemical literature, are consistent with what is presented in the *Institutes*.

In general Calvin had fully accepted Luther's idea that salvation is by grace alone through faith. Beyond this, scholars have been unable to establish that any one specific doctrine is central to his thought. The basic and fundamental development of his thought was not according to the traditional topics of theology, sequentially and logically developed. Formally he organized his material according to the topical format, suggesting that the key to its analysis be sought from the perspective of one or several discrete topics. Yet this approach has only led to an impasse—even to the conclusion that he was in logic and purpose inexact and ambiguous. The often-discussed doctrines of providence and predestination, for example, are presented by Calvin as the response or affirmation of a man of faith, affirming the control of God in his life, not as an epistemological program. To approach his theology from specific topics such as these has not been fruitful. There are, however, larger, general ideas or themes that run through the *Institutes* from the first page to the last like so many threads in an intricate tapestry and that point to what is essential in his thought. He understood the redemptive message to be the same in both the Old and the New Testament; hence his theology can be seen as all of a piece, permitting the dominance of the thematic approach rather than the topical.

Calvin's theological program is based on the dictum of Augustine that man is created for communion with God and that he will be unfulfilled until he rests in God. Calvin usually expresses this idea in terms of a union with the Maker and Redeemer, which is presented as essential to man's spiritual life. Thus the relationship between God and man is made the basis of all theological discourse, and this union or communion is established and maintained through what Calvin calls knowledge, a theme or idea that becomes an ordering principle of his theology. Knowledge of God the creator and knowledge of God the redeemer are the two divisions of his thought. He uses the term *knowledge* practically synonymously with the term *faith*. It comprises both the elements of objective information and its subjective appropriation, but essentially it consists of a reverential and worshipful trust in the goodness and bounty of God. As with all of his theological ideas, two poles or foci must be kept in balance: the knowledge of God and the knowledge of self. God is always—in the context of every theological discussion—at once the great, infinite, and incomprehensible being who calls all things out of nothing, as well as the loving, condescending, and revealing being who calls men and women to commune with him. God is always hidden and revealed, both beyond our comprehension and revealed to us at our level. Humans, albeit the greatest of God's creations, are always dependent creatures, both because we are created to be so and because our sin renders us totally helpless in spiritual things. Consequently God must always be the initiator of any communication with us. And hence humility, sobriety, and teachableness are our principal virtues.

Although he always keeps in mind the perfect condition in which all things were created, because of the cataclysmic event of the Fall, all of Calvin's theology is concerned with redemption, with the restoration of the state that God originally created. Christ alone is the mediator who both reveals and effects this redemption, or restoration. Human beings are in bondage to sinful nature, so anything relating to this restoration must be initiated by God through Christ. Restoration occurs when the person is united to Christ by responding in faith to the provision made through Christ's death and resurrection, but this mystical union occurs only if and when the hidden or secret work of the Holy Spirit engenders that faith. The faithful person is called to obedience, to be a servant of righteousness, to model his or her life after the incarnate Christ. In this sense Calvin's theology is Christocentric. But he did not focus attention only in the area of Christology, for all that Christ does and is, is made real to man only through the work of the Holy Spirit. Indeed, all of his soteriology is presented in the context of the work of the Holy Spirit, "the bond by which Christ effectually unites us to himself." The work of restoration, by the power of the Holy Spirit, is done in the context of the church, God's gracious provision for the activity of preaching and teaching, for the administration of the sacraments, and for the communion (and reproof) of the saints.

Calvinists were the most vital of the Protestant groups, spreading throughout Europe and the New World, triumphing in Switzerland, the Netherlands, and Scotland, and for a time in England and America. Scholarly opinion is divided over whether this success is due mainly to Calvin's theological teaching, to his training and educational program (the complete revamping of the elementary schools and the creation of the University of Geneva), or to his organizational talent. Probably all of these are contributory factors, and perhaps others, but it does seem that the vitality of the Reformed or Calvinist movement, and therefore Calvin's most enduring legacy, is due principally to the nature of his church, to its unique, adaptable, and efficient organization. Although its unique blend of theory and practicality meant that Calvin's theology could be drawn upon by a variety of different interests, it can also be shown that his theology was revised almost beyond recognition very shortly after his death and that the *Institutes* were not widely read in the late sixteenth and early seventeenth centuries. Moreover, while the educational system produced an informed and well-trained church membership that was designed to be educationally self-perpetuating, it seems undeniable that the unique organizational structure of the Calvinist church was required for the growth and development of the educational program. Calvin appears to have recognized as much, for on his return to Geneva in 1541, his first major undertaking was to secure approval of his *Ecclesiastical Ordinances,* which set forth the organization of the church.

Calvin developed a representative form of church government with the fundamental activity based in the local church. The leadership was elected from the local membership, and the power, which ultimately resided in the local membership as a whole, was vested in these elected officials, not in the clergy. While there are three higher levels of authority above the local church, established in ascending representative bodies and culminating in the national or general assembly, part of the genius of this organization lies in the ability of the local church, in times of emergency, to function without the meeting of the upper-level bodies. As a result these Calvinist churches were nearly impossible to eradicate. Silencing the minister and arresting the leadership only temporarily disrupted the church, for the minister was not an essential element in the church's continuance, and in a short time new leaders would be elected. So the church could survive, even flourish, under conditions of severe persecution. Beyond the necessary capacity to continue to exist in times when religious persecution and wars were the order of the day, the representative nature of the church responded to the psychological and political reality that humankind is more likely to be committed to a cause when participation in the decision-making process is involved. The impact of the representative nature of the Calvinist church has been significant in the development of the democratic political structures of the Western world.

Bibliography

Primary Sources

The numerous works of Calvin are available, in the original texts, in the fifty-nine volumes of the magisterial *Ioannis Calvini opera quae supersunt omnia,* edited by J. W. Baum and others (Braunschweig, 1863–1900), and in its continuation, the *Supplementa Calviniana,* a collection of subsequently discovered sermons edited by Erwin Mülhaupt and others (Neukirchen, 1961–), seven volumes to date with more to come. In English, the best edition of the *Institutes of the Christian Religion* is that of J. T. McNeill, translated by Ford Lewis Battles (Philadelphia, 1960) in two volumes. Many other works are available in English translation, including the important edition of *The New Testament Commentaries* edited by Thomas F. Torrance and David W. Torrance (Edinburgh, 1959–).

Secondary Sources

An excellent guide to the secondary literature is J. T. McNeill's "Fifty Years of Calvin Study: 1918–1968," which is prefaced to Williston Walker's *John Calvin, the Organiser of Reformed Protestantism, 1509–1564* (reprint, New York, 1969). T. H. L. Parker's *John Calvin* (Philadelphia, 1975), is fully informed and reliable, but the fullest and best biography, in spite of its hagiographic character, is Émile Doumergue's seven-volume *Jean Calvin, les hommes et les choses de son temps* (Lausanne, 1899–1927).

On Calvin's thought and influence, current scholarly opinion can be found in the proceedings of the International Congress on Calvin Research edited by W. H. Neuser in three volumes (vols. 1–2, Kampen, Netherlands, 1975, 1979; vol. 3, Bern, 1983). Benoît Giradin's *Rhétorique et théologique . . .* (Paris, 1979) is indispensable for the explication of the nature and structure of his thought, and E. A. Dowey's *The Knowledge of God in Calvin's Theology* (New York, 1952) is one of the better introductions. Richard Stauffer's *Dieu, la création et al providence dans la prédication de Calvin* (Bern, 1978) is an excellent corrective to the exclusively Christocentric interpretation of many recent scholars. On Calvin's influence, Robert M. Kingdom's *Geneva and the Coming of the Wars of Religion in France, 1555–1563* (Geneva, 1956) and *Geneva and the Consolidation of the French Protestant Movement, 1564–1572* (Geneva and Madison, Wis., 1967) are representative and excellent studies.

BRIAN G. ARMSTRONG (1987)

CAMPBELL, ALEXANDER (1788–1866), one of the founders and the foremost early leader of the Disciples of Christ. Campbell was born in County Antrim, Northern Ireland, the son of a Presbyterian minister, Thomas Campbell. He immigrated to America in 1809, joining his father, who had come two years earlier. When he arrived, Campbell discovered that his father had broken with the Presbyterian church and had begun a small, nonsectarian "Christian association." Having been exposed to similar New Testament primitivist ideas in Scotland, young Campbell embraced his father's reform and quickly became the most prominent leader of the new movement. For a time the Campbells were Baptists, and from 1823 to 1830 Alexander edited the *Christian Baptist*, a periodical that attracted many supporters in the West and South. Beginning in the 1830s Campbell and his "Reforming Baptist" supporters separated into independent churches. Campbell preferred the name Disciples of Christ, but local churches frequently were called Christian Church or Church of Christ. In 1832 the church nearly doubled in size through a union with the Christian movement led by Barton Stone of Kentucky; Campbell quickly became the dominant figure in the united denomination.

From 1830 until 1864 Campbell edited a journal called the *Millennial Harbinger*, which became a mirror of his maturing thought. The heart of Campbell's plea was an appeal for Christian union through the "restoration of the ancient order of things," that is, by restoring New Testament Christianity. Prior to 1830 Campbell was extremely iconoclastic in his attacks on the popular churches, ridiculing the clergy and seeming to attack all cooperative societies. After 1830 he became a more constructive builder and seemed confident that the millennium was about to begin, initiated by the restoration movement. In 1849 a group of Disciples leaders established the young church's first national organization, the American Christian Missionary Society, and, although he was not present at the meeting, Campbell accepted the presidency of the society.

Campbell's formal college training consisted of less than one year at Glasgow University, but he was a man of considerable erudition. He established a national reputation as a debater, especially as a result of widely publicized debates with the renowned Scottish socialist and atheist Robert Owen, in 1829, and with the Roman Catholic archbishop of Cincinnati, John B. Purcell, in 1837. Campbell became financially independent as a result of his marriage to Margaret Brown in 1811, and he spent the remainder of his life living near his wife's home in Brooke County in western Virginia. He became a moderately wealthy man, and in 1829, in his only venture into politics, he was elected a delegate to the Virginia Constitutional Convention. In 1841, Campbell established Bethany College near his home. Until his death he served as president and professor of moral sciences at the college and trained a generation of leaders for Disciples churches. Campbell traveled and preached widely throughout the United States, as well as in England and Scotland. The aging reformer was discouraged by the sectional tension caused by the slavery debate and the Civil War. He counseled moderation and believed that the restoration movement could survive the tragedy, but by the time of his death his millennial hopes had given way to pessimism.

SEE ALSO Disciples of Christ.

BIBLIOGRAPHY

No satisfactory biography of Alexander Campbell has yet been written. Probably the best source of information about the reformer is still the classic study written by his friend Robert Richardson, *Memoirs of Alexander Campbell*, 2 vols. (Philadelphia, 1868–1870). A novel based on Campbell's life is Louis Cochran's *The Fool of God* (New York, 1958). Useful specialized studies include Harold L. Lunger's *The Political Ethics of Alexander Campbell* (Saint Louis, 1954); R. Frederick West's *Alexander Campbell and Natural Religion* (New Haven, 1948); and D. Ray Lindley's *Apostle of Freedom* (Saint Louis, 1957). The most comprehensive statement of Campbell's ideas can be found in his own *The Christian System*, 4th ed. (1866; reprint, New York, 1969).

DAVID EDWIN HARRELL, JR. (1987)

CAMPBELL, JOSEPH (1904–1987). Joseph Campbell was perhaps the best-known mythologist of the twentieth century. His fame was largely due to his highly acclaimed public television interviews with Bill Moyers in 1985–1986 and his posthumously published best-selling book, *The Power of Myth* (1988), based on that series, and in no small part to movie director George Lucas, who gave Campbell credit for inspiring his movie *Star Wars* (1977). Campbell's books on myth had many admirers, from literary critics who found his analysis of hero myths interpretatively rich, to the general public, who loved Campbell's retellings of his "myths to live by." Campbell believed that the world's great myths symbolized the ultimate human spiritual goal of living joyfully and mystically, at one with one's true self and the cosmos, and generations of fans took his advice to "follow your own bliss."

EARLY YEARS. Campbell was born in New York City in 1904 to a prosperous Irish-American family who gave their gifted child every advantage. He was trained in Roman Catholicism at parochial school, but became fascinated by non-Western traditions after seeing American Indians at Buffalo Bill's Wild West Show. Campbell read widely, including many Indian myths that, he noticed, shared common motifs with stories from the Bible. After entering Columbia University in 1921, Campbell continued his studies in languages and literature, and studied anthropology with Franz Boas and philosophy with John Dewey. Campbell was introduced to Eastern religions on a trip to Europe before his college graduation. There he met Jiddu Krishnamurti and read Edwin Arnold's *The Light of Asia,* with its translations of Asian religious classics like the Upaniṣads and the life of the Buddha. Both Hinduism and Buddhism were to have a major impact on Campbell's interpretation of myths.

After graduating in 1926 with a master's degree in medieval literature, Campbell lived abroad in Paris and Munich on a two-year traveling fellowship, studying Romance philology and Sanskrit. He was deeply influenced by the contemporary European intellectual scene, and particularly intrigued by the fictional heroes of novelists James Joyce and Thomas Mann, cultural morphologist Adolf Bastian's notion of elementary ideas, ethnologist Leo Frobenius's idea of culture circles, and Sigmund Freud and Carl Jung's theories of dreaming and the unconscious. Jung's theory of collective archetypes and their role in the psychic process of self-integration had a lasting impact on Campbell's thinking.

SCHOLARLY WORK. In 1934, Campbell began his teaching career at Sarah Lawrence College, where he was a popular instructor until his retirement in 1972. His first major publication, *A Skeleton Key to Finnegans Wake* (1944, with Henry Morton Robinson), was in the field of literature, but Campbell's broad scholarly interests soon shifted to mythology. He was influenced by his friendship with the German Indologist Heinrich Zimmer, whose positive views of Indian myths as repositories of timeless spiritual truths greatly impressed him. After Zimmer's untimely death in 1943, Campbell edited his manuscripts, publishing Zimmer's *Myths and Symbols in Indian Art and Civilization* (1946) and other important books on Indian philosophy and art, along with several volumes from the Eranos conferences in Ascona, Switzerland, for the Bollingen series.

Campbell's fascination with myth, Eastern religion, and Jungian psychology finally led to his own famous study of hero myths, *The Hero with a Thousand Faces* (1949). Several other notable studies on comparative mythology followed. *The Masks of God* (1959–1968), written after an eye-opening trip to India in 1954, was a monumental four-volume survey of "primitive," "oriental," "occidental," and modern literary "creative" mythology. His goal was to write a "natural history" of myths that traced "the fundamental unity of the spiritual history of mankind" by revealing themes with a worldwide distribution, such as "fire-theft, deluge, land of the dead, virgin birth, and resurrected hero" (vol. 1, p. 3). This was followed by *The Flight of the Wild Gander* (1969), a collection of Campbell's important essays on the biological, metaphysical, and historical-cultural origins of myth as well as his own positive essay on the "secularization of the sacred" in the modern world.

After retiring from Sarah Lawrence in 1972, Campbell moved to Honolulu, where he continued writing. Books from this period include *Myths to Live By* (1972), his argument that the modern world has a desperate need for new myths; *The Mythic Image* (1974), his exploration of the intimate connection between dreams, myths, and art; *The Inner Reaches of Outer Space: Metaphor as Myth and as Religion* (1986), a collection of lectures arguing that the true meaning of myth is symbolic, universal, and mystical; *The Historical Atlas of World Mythology* (1983, 1989), a two-volume attempt to trace the historical origin and diffusion of myths; and *The Power of Myth.* Campbell died of cancer in Honolulu in 1987.

CONCEPTS OF MYTH. Campbell was hostile to organized religion. Intellectually, his antipathy owes much to John Dewey's critique of organized religion in his *A Common Faith* (1934). Dewey dismissed religion as a set of fossilized doctrines and institutions based upon a now scientifically discredited belief in the supernatural and physical immortality, weighted with historical doctrines and rituals that obscured the powerful personal experiences underlying it, and mistakenly believed to be literally rather than symbolically true. While institutional religion had little value for Dewey, however, its symbols did. They expressed the "religious moral faith" of the individual who conscientiously harmonized the self to the world through a pragmatic "adjustment" of human ethical ideals in response to an experience of the "imaginative totality" of the Universe (Dewey, 1934, pp. 18–19).

Campbell agreed with Dewey that taking such stories as the virgin birth, heaven, and resurrection as literal truths was absurd, and argued that they must be understood symbolically rather than doctrinally. In other respects, however, Campbell abandoned Dewey's self-conscious pragmatism for a Jungian perspective. Campbell saw parallels between religious and dream symbolism and followed Jung's view that dreams symbolized the collective patterns, or archetypes, of the unconscious psyche. Campbell considered dreams to be personalized myths, and myths to be depersonalized dreams. He believed that myth's symbols expressed a psychic-spiritual wisdom that could free ordinary people from the debilitating anxieties and social chaos of modern secular society.

Campbell believed that religious doctrines were nothing more than misunderstood mythology. In *The Hero with a Thousand Faces,* which he considered his most important work, Campbell drew on Freudian and Jungian psychology to argue that hero myths worldwide use a universal narrative formula to describe rites of passage, each one a local example of what James Joyce called the mono-myth, a narrative magnification of a basic three-part structure: separation, initiation, and return. Despite their various historical and cultural particularities, the stories of Jesus, Buddha, Gilgamesh, and other mythological heroes ultimately shared an underlying archetypal unity of common motifs, symbols, and themes. They also had a shared meaning—a common psychological and metaphysical reality was at work in these tales. This universality explains why ancient myths, even those of other people, are still powerful today.

Campbell believed that myth functioned as a kind of comforting second womb. He focused his work on the latter half of human life, where dealing with despair and anxiety, and especially old age, sickness, and death, is unavoidable. Myths responded to the reality of suffering and mortality by revealing a spiritual way to transcend the universal tragedies of humanity. Campbell supplemented Jung's theory of psycho-developmental integration of the unconscious and conscious with the mysticism of Hinduism and Buddhism. He believed world myths pointed to the possibility of apotheosis, of discarding personal ego and realizing an enduring oneness with the cosmos. The power of myth was its ability to shatter "forms and our attachment to the forms" and through "comedy, the wild and careless, inexhaustible joy," to evoke an ecstatic feeling of being alive (Campbell, 1949, pp. 28–29).

Campbell modified his views after his trip to India in 1954. In the latter volumes of *The Masks of God, Occidental Mythology,* and *Creative Mythology,* he rejected what he came to consider a dehumanizing monism in Eastern theology and instead embraced a Western spiritual individualism that did not dissolve the ego into a larger social and cosmic mystical whole. In *Creative Mythology,* Campbell claimed that this ideal, with origins in pre-Christian European paganism, was classically formulated in the twelfth-century Romantic literature of courtly love. Stories like those of Tristan and Isolde, in which the heroic lovers achieve an ecstatic spiritual and physical union while preserving their separate identities, exemplified the ideal of individualism. He found parallels in contemporary Western literature in the novels of James Joyce and Thomas Mann. The male heroes of Mann's *Magic Mountain* (1924) and Joyce's *Finnegans Wake* (1939) personify a kind of spiritually radical monism that is not self-sacrificing but rather a self-fulfilling realization of the "soul in the body, heaven on earth, and god in humanity" (Segal, 1990, p. 138).

CRITICAL VIEWS. Several criticisms have been lodged against Campbell's comparative mythology. Folklorist Alan Dundes argues that, like many other universalists, Campbell is prone to sweeping generalizations. To show the universality of his Belly of the Whale motif, for example, Campbell often cited stories in which a hero is swallowed. Dundes, however, points out that Campbell's motif of a fish swallowing a person is not actually found worldwide; it is not found in sub-Saharan Africa, for one, so how can it be a universal structure? He further argues that Campbell's examples include both Jonah being swallowed by a whale and Little Red Riding Hood being swallowed by a wolf. But Little Red Riding Hood is a heroine, not a hero; her story is a fairy tale, not a myth; and a wolf, not a whale, swallows her. Campbell does not explain to what level of generality an analysis can go to find the mythic pattern in myths.

Other critics, including Wallace Martin, fault Campbell for emphasizing what stories have in common, an approach that inevitably blurs distinctions "and thus makes it impossible, within the theory, to show how and why stories are different" (Martin, 1986, p. 103). Wendy Doniger O'Flaherty dismisses this as Campbell's "TV dinner approach" to myth, boiling it down to its bloodless archetypes. She sees this reductionism in *The Historical Atlas of World Mythology,* where Campbell abandoned Jungian theory for a supposedly historical analysis tracing the origin of his mythic motifs through diffusion. What Campbell forgot, O'Flaherty notes, is that a phallus, for example, may be archetypal, but it is "always someone's phallus." It is in the "banal details" of myths, their variants, and their culturally specific forms that meaning resides (O'Flaherty, 1988, pp. 34–35). Because of his decontextualizing approach, she argues, Campbell ignored indigenous interpretations and trivialized the many and often contested meanings of myths within their cultures of origin.

Although he recognized different functions of myth, his critics claim that Campbell ignored the social, political, and ethical to focus exclusively on the mystical. In *The Hero with a Thousand Faces,* Campbell left Jung behind with a metaphysical, spiritual perspective that envisaged the role of myth "not to cure the individual back again to the general delusion, but to detach him from delusion altogether and this not by readjusting the desire (*eors*) and hostility (*thanatos*)—for that would only originate a new context of delusion—but by *extinguishing* the impulses to the very root, according to the method of the celebrated Buddhist Eightfold path." (Campbell, 1949, pp. 164–165). Thus Campbell argued that the Babylonian epic of Gilgamesh told the same story as the *Dao de jing* and Indian Tantrism: that physical immortality was impossible and that the only eternity was in the realization that all was one here and now (p. 189). Hindu mysticism and the eightfold path of Buddhism provided the key for Campbell's understanding of hero myths, and he later relied upon Kuṇḍalinī Yoga and European paganism as well. This one-meaning-fits-all approach, critics claim, reveals more about Campbell's own brand of philosophy than anything else.

Several critics, including Brendan Gill and Robert Segal, have also accused Campbell of being anti-Semitic. Campbell was hostile to organized religion generally, but his critics argue that he singled out Judaism especially, using what Segal calls "the crudest of stock epithets" for his vitriolic attacks on it as chauvinistic, fossilized, tribal, patriarchal, and literalistic (Segal, 1999, p. 462). Campbell's biographers Stephen and Robin Larsen sympathetically portray him as, at most, anti-Zionist, but other critics believe Campbell's prejudices left him indifferent to the Holocaust and blind to the dangers of what the philosopher Paul Tillich describes as the "mythical powers of origin of the soil and blood" that culminated in the Nazi worship of a German paganism that lay at the heart of its terror (Tillich, 1977, pp. 13–18). Campbell's limited focus only allowed him to see this paganism nostalgically, as the source of a Western romantic individualism buried under the historical encumbrances of Christianity and Judaism.

BIBLIOGRAPHY

Campbell, Joseph. *A Skeleton Key to Finnegans Wake,* with Henry Morton Robinson. New York, 1944.

Campbell, Joseph. *The Hero with a Thousand Faces.* New York, 1949.

Campbell, Joseph. *The Masks of God.* 4 vols. New York, 1959–1968.

Campbell, Joseph. *The Flight of the Wild Gander: Explorations in the Mythological Dimension.* New York, 1969.

Campbell, Joseph. *Myths to Live By.* New York, 1972.

Campbell, Joseph. *The Mythic Image,* assisted by M. J. Abadie. Princeton, N.J., 1974.

Campbell, Joseph. *The Historical Atlas of World Mythology.* 2 vols. New York, 1983, 1989.

Campbell, Joseph. *The Inner Reaches of Outer Space: Metaphor as Myth and as Religion.* New York, 1986.

Campbell, Joseph. *The Power of Myth,* with Bill Moyers, edited by Betty Sue Flowers. New York, 1988.

Dewey, John. *A Common Faith.* New Haven, Conn., 1934.

Doniger, Wendy. "A Very Strange Enchanted Boy." *New York Times Book Review,* February 3, 1992.

Dundes, Alan, ed. *Sacred Narrative: Readings in the Theory of Myth.* Berkeley, 1984.

Ellwood, Robert. *The Politics of Myth: A Study of C. G. Jung, Mircea Eliade, and Joseph Campbell.* New York, 1999.

Friedman, Maurice. "Why Joseph Campbell's Psychologizing of Myth Precludes the Holocaust as Touchstone of Reality." *Journal of the American Academy of Religion* 66 (1998): 385–401.

Gill, Brendan. "The Faces of Joseph Campbell." *New York Review of Books* 36 (September 28, 1989): 16–19.

Larsen, Stephen, and Robin Larsen. *Joseph Campbell: A Fire in the Mind.* Rochester, Vt., 1991.

Martin, Wallace. *Recent Theories of Narrative.* New York, 1986.

Noel, Daniel, ed. *Paths to the Power of Myth: Joseph Campbell and the Study of Religion.* New York, 1994.

O'Flaherty, Wendy Doniger. *Other People's Myths.* New York, 1988.

Segal, Robert. *Joseph Campbell: An Introduction.* Rev. ed. New York, 1990.

Segal, Robert. "Joseph Campbell on Jews and Judaism." *Religion* 22 (1992): 151–170.

Segal, Robert. "Joseph Campbell as Anti-Semite and as a Theorist of Myth: A Response to Maurice Friedman." *Journal of the American Academy of Religion* 67 (1999): 461–467.

Tillich, Paul. *The Socialist Decision.* Translated by Franklin Sherman. New York, 1977.

MARK W. MACWILLIAMS (2005)

CANAANITE RELIGION

This entry consists of the following articles:

AN OVERVIEW
THE LITERATURE

CANAANITE RELIGION: AN OVERVIEW

The term *Canaanite* is variously used in both ancient and modern sources. Most popularly, it refers to the indigenous population of the southwestern Levant, which, according to biblical traditions, was displaced by Israelite conquerors late in the second millennium before the common era. This popular usage is, however, both too narrow geographically and fraught with sociohistorical difficulties. In this article, the term *Canaanite religion* will refer mainly to the one Northwest Semitic religion of the second millennium that is presently well attested, the Ugaritic. It should be borne in mind, however, that ancient sources do not necessarily support the often-asserted equation of "Ugaritic" with "Canaanite," if the terms of the equation are linguistic, ethnic, or political. And in any case, the undoubtedly idiosyncratic Ugaritic data do not facilitate a generally applicable description of "Canaanite" (or, more accurately, "Northwest Semitic") religion.

Before the late nineteenth century, there were only two sources for the study of the Canaanite religion. The first, the Hebrew scriptures, contains numerous references to the Canaanites and their practices, which are generally condemned as abominable (e.g., *Lv.* 18:3, 27–28). As early as the first century BCE, the biblical commentator Philo of Alexandria recognized that Canaan was the biblical symbol of "vice," which the Israelites were naturally bidden to despise (*De cong.* 83–85). It is generally agreed that the biblical witness to Canaanite religion is highly polemical and, therefore, unreliable; biblical evidence must at the least be used with extreme caution, and in conjunction with extrabiblical sources.

The second source for knowledge of Canaanite religion was those classical texts that preserve descriptions of aspects of it. The best known of these are the *Phoenician History* of

Philo Byblius, of which portions are preserved in Eusebius's *Praeparatio evangelica*, and *The Syrian Goddess*, attributed (perhaps falsely) to Lucian of Samothrace. The reliability of Philo Byblius, however, has been the subject of scholarly debate, and the present consensus is that the comparability of the *Phoenician History* with authentic Canaanite data should not be overstressed. At best, Philo's information probably sheds light on the religion of late Hellenized Phoenicians, and offers no direct evidence for second-millennium Canaanite religion. The same generalization applies to (Pseudo-) Lucian, despite a few scholarly claims to the contrary.

Firsthand evidence for Canaanite culture in the second millennium BCE (or, in archaeological terms, the Middle Bronze and Late Bronze periods) comes from artifactual evidence found at many archaeological sites (more than sixty for the first part of the Middle Bronze period alone—mostly tombs) and from textual evidence stemming mainly from three great discoveries: (1) the eighteenth-century royal archives of "Amorite" Mari (Tell Hariri, on the Euphrates River near the present border between Syria and Iraq); (2) the diplomatic correspondence between several Levantine vassal princes and the pharoahs Amenophis III and IV (first half of the fourteenth century), found at Tell al-ʿAmarna (about 330 km south of Cairo on the east bank of the Nile); and (3) the mainly fourteenth- and thirteenth-century texts found at Ras Shamra (ancient Ugarit) and nearby Ras Ibn Hani, both within the present-day administrative district of Latakia, on the Mediterranean coast of Syria. The artifactual evidence is crucial for understanding material culture, socioeconomic developments, population movements, and the like, and provides considerable data about funerary practices. Most significant for the study of religion are the figurines, thought to represent gods and goddesses, that have been recovered in virtually every archaeological context. These will be discussed below with other manifestations of popular religion.

The ancient city of Mari was peripheral to both the Mesopotamian and the Levantine spheres of influence. Culturally and linguistically, it was clearly West Semitic, but to label it "Canaanite" goes beyond the evidence (the designation Amorite represents, to some extent, a scholarly compromise). The Mari texts are virtually all concerned with economic, juridical, and administrative matters. One text in particular testifies to the eclecticism and heterogeneity of Mari's religious cult in the eighteenth century. It lists the sacrificial sheep distributed among the various gods and temples of Mari, and the list of gods is a mixture of Semitic and non-Semitic deities from east and west, along with some gods perhaps unique to Mari. This list of diverse gods may be supplemented by the more than one hundred forty divine names (at least two dozen of which are West Semitic) attested as components of personal names in the Mari archives.

The most striking group of Mari texts is the small collection of so-called prophetic texts. These twenty-odd letters attest to a type of oracular speaking that shows significant affinities with biblical prophecies of a millennium later. Some of this oracular speaking seems to have been done by cultic personnel, and some apparently consisted of messages transmitted by the gods through ordinary people. In either case, it clearly deviated from the normal (and presumably normative) mode of divine intermediation, which was, as generally in the ancient Near East, divination in its various forms. Local temple officials probably felt that the extraordinary behavior, and the messages transmitted by it, had to be reported to higher authorities. It may be suggested, on the basis of these Mari texts and related evidence, that the phenomenon broadly termed *prophecy* represented a peculiar and peripheral kind of divine intermediation among the West Semites generally.

Most of the Amarna letters report on Levantine military, economic, and political matters to the Egyptian court. The letters were written in Babylonian, the diplomatic language of the period, but they regularly reveal the Canaanite character of their authors—in personal names, peculiar scribal practices, and, especially, the use of characteristic Canaanite vocabulary and turns of phrase. While none of the Amarna letters is directly concerned with religion, important information can be derived from the divine names and epithets mentioned in passing (and as components of personal names), and from Canaanite religious and liturgical clichés that have been incorporated into the epistolary style. For example, the son of Aziru, prince of Amurru, writes as follows to the Egyptian court: "You give me life, and you give me death. I look upon your face; you are indeed my lord. So let my lord hearken to his servant." Such expressions, which are frequent in the correspondence, are probably borrowed liturgical formulas, perhaps from lost Canaanite prayers that were probably comparable to the biblical psalms. A systematic study of all such formulas might shed considerable light on Canaanite religious conceptions of the mid-second millennium.

Without slighting the importance of the Mari and Amarna material, by far the most significant evidence for Canaanite religion in the second millennium is found at Ugarit. From the beginning of the millennium until the city's destruction at the hands of the Sea Peoples (c. 1180–1175 BCE), Ugarit was a thriving cosmopolitan trading center. In the Middle Bronze period (2000–1600; Level II of the Ras Shamra excavations), Ugarit underwent considerable expansion. During this period, two large temples (dedicated to the gods Baal and Dagan respectively; see below) were erected on top of older ruins, forming, in effect, an acropolis in the city. The pottery of the period is predominantly Canaanite, and other material evidence demonstrates that Ugarit was in contact with Egypt, the Aegean, and Mesopotamia. At the same time, Ugarit's population was augmented by an influx of Indo-European-speaking Hurrians from the northeast.

The best-attested period at Ugarit is the last two centuries of its existence (Late Bronze III, c. 1365–1180 BCE; Level I.3 of the Ras Shamra excavations). The Ugaritic texts date from this period, although some of the religious texts are undoubtedly older, and were merely written down at this time. One of the most important developments in human history was the invention, during the reign of Niqmad II (c. 1360–1330 BCE), of a cuneiform alphabetic script (the world's oldest alphabet) adapted to the Ugaritic language. It seems likely that this invention was specifically for the purpose of setting ancient religious documents in writing, since diplomatic and administrative texts could be, and often were, written in Akkadian. At the instigation of Niqmad II, the great mythological texts that are at the heart of the Ugaritic religion were incised on clay tablets. They were preserved in the library of the high priest, which was located on the acropolis near the two temples.

In addition to the mythological texts from the high priest's library, the excavations of this and several other archives of Ugarit and Ras Ibn Hani have turned up related mythological material, descriptive ritual texts, lists of sacrificial offerings, god-lists, prayers and liturgies, incantations, divinatory texts, and dedicatory inscriptions. These may be used, with due caution, as the basis of a description of Ugaritic religion.

DEITIES. The essential information about Ugarit's deities comes from what appears to be a canonical god-list. Two nearly identical copies of the basic list have been published, along with an Akkadian "translation." In addition, the list is incorporated, with minor variations, into a list of sacrificial offerings. This list shows that the basic cultic pantheon of Ugarit numbered thirty-three or thirty-four gods. One of the most controversial problems confronting Ugaritic scholarship is the imperfect correspondence between the god-list and the gods who are prominent in the mythological texts. The myths probably represent an older stratum of Ugaritic religion, and were undoubtedly "reinterpreted" in the light of subsequent developments in the cult.

Two reasons are generally given for the order of the gods in the list: either it reflects their relative importance, or else it gives the order in which their symbols were paraded in a cultic procession. The list begins with two or three Ils (El)—the sources are evenly split on the number. *Il* is the common Semitic word for "god"; it is the proper name of the head of the Ugaritic pantheon in the mythological texts. The first Il in the god-list is associated with Mount Sapan (Tsafon), the Canaanite Olympus, which was traditionally identified with Jebel al-Aqra, about fifty kilometers north of Ugarit at the mouth of the Orontes River. (The mountain was itself deified, and appears in the god-list in place 14/15.) In all likelihood, the term *sapan,* which means "north," was taken to be a metaphor for the god's temple (as in the Bible, Psalm 48:3), and not as a simple geographical designation. Thus the *Il* of *sapan* is the numen manifest in the sanctuary, which is the earthly representation of the divine abode. Sapan, it should be noted, is not the abode of Il in the mythological texts, but of Baal.

The second Il is called *Ilib.* The Akkadian and Hurrian parallels show that this name is a portmanteau composed of the elements *il* ("god") and *ab* ("father"), but the precise significance of the combination is uncertain. Most likely the name denotes an ancestral spirit, the numen manifest in the Ugaritic cult of the dead. In the Ugaritic epic of Aqhat, the ancient worthy Danil, whose epithets mark him as one of the deified dead, seeks a son who will "erect a stela for his *ilib*"—that is, for the divine spirit of his dead father. The affinity of Il with the Ugaritic cult of the dead is shown in a mythological fragment in which the god participates in a *marzih* feast (an orgiastic revel comparable to the Greek *thiasos*), the ritual banquet of the funerary cult. Il drinks himself into a stupor (as is customary at such affairs), and has to be carried off by his faithful son. (This, too, is one of the duties of the son enumerated in the epic of Aqhat.)

The third Il is presumably to be identified with the head of the pantheon in the mythological texts. His epithets and activities in those, and in the cultic texts, provide a fair picture of his character. He is the father of the gods, who are called his "family" or "sons," and he is styled "father of humankind" and "builder of built ones." He may have been regarded as the creator of the world, but the Ugaritic evidence is inconclusive on this point. He bears the epithet "bull," a symbol of virility and power (although one mythological text casts some doubt on his sexual prowess). He is serene in his supremacy, a source of "eternal wisdom," "beneficent and benign"; a unique and problematic text that may be a prayer to Il seems even to hypostatize his "graciousness."

The three Ils comprise the three principal aspects of Ugaritic "godship," or numinous power, that are denoted by the term *il:* (1) it is the wise and sovereign power that brought gods and humans into being; (2) it abides in any sacred place; and (3) it is the tangible presence of the spirits of the dead.

The next deity on the list is Dagan. The Mari texts attest to his great importance in the Middle Euphrates region (especially Terqa). The most common explanation of his name relates it to the West Semitic word for "grain," but this is by no means certain; other (even non-Semitic) etymologies are possible. One of the two temples on the acropolis of Ugarit was evidently consecrated to Dagan. During excavations carried out in 1934, two inscribed stone slabs were found just outside the temple. The inscriptions, the only known examples of Ugaritic carved in stone, commemorate *pgr* sacrifices of a sheep and an ox offered to Dagan. Since so little is known of Dagan's character at Ugarit, and since the term *pgr* is controversial (perhaps "mortuary offering" is the best interpretation), it is not possible to say anything definitive about these stelae.

Despite his obvious prominence in the cult, Dagan plays no role in Ugaritic mythology. The god Baal bears the epithet "son of Dagan," but that is itself problematic, since Il was supposedly the father of the gods. Three explanations are possible: (1) Dagan was in some sense identified with or assimilated to Il; (2) the epithet represents a variant tradition of Baal's paternity; or (3) the epithet "son" is not to be taken literally but as an indication that Baal belongs to some class of gods exemplified by Dagan.

Following Dagan come seven Baals. The first is the Baal of Mount Sapan, who dwells in the same place as the Baal in the mythological texts (the "heights" or "recesses" of Sapan); the term *sapan* surely refers to the Baal temple of Ugarit as well. The Akkadian rendition of *Baal* is *Adad*, which is the name of the most prominent West Semitic mountain and weather god. The same Ugaritic "prayer" that mentions the graciousness of El also establishes the threefold identification of Adad (the variant Hadd occurs in the mythological texts) with Baal of Mount Sapan and Baal of Ugarit.

The significance of the other six Baals (none qualified by epithets and all identified with Adad) is uncertain, although sevenfold lists of all sorts, including divine heptads, are common throughout the ancient Near East: the number seven evidently denotes completeness or perfection. If the extra six Baals have some specific function, they might represent local manifestations or sanctuaries of Baal, separate cult symbols, or hypostatized attributes.

The name *Baal* is derived from the common Semitic noun meaning "lord, master, husband." The god's full title in the mythological texts is "prince, lord (*baal*) of the earth," and his principal epithet is "most powerful one" (*aliyan*). He is also called "high one" (*aliy*) and "rider of the clouds," both names clearly illustrating his character as a weather god.

In contrast to the numinous Il, Baal represents the divine power that is immanent in the world, activating and effectuating things or phenomena. Given the paucity of rainfall in most of the Levant, it is not surprising that the lord of the storm is the most prominent god of this type (cf. the ubiquitous Phoenician Baal Shamem, "lord of the heavens," and his famous encounter with the Israelite god in *1 Kings* 18). On his shoulders rests the burden of bringing fertility and fecundity to the land, and as such he is venerated by the rest of the gods and declared their "king."

But the kind of god who is immanent in the natural world is also subject to its flux. Thus, in the mythological texts, Baal has three enemies. The first two, Yamm ("sea") and the desert gods who are called "devourers," represent the destructive potential inherent in nature. Baal succeeds in subduing Yamm (and undoubtedly also the "devourers"), but he is in turn defeated by his third and greatest adversary, Mot ("death"; never mentioned by this name in the cultic texts). Nothing that is in the world, gods included, can escape death.

Following the seven Baals, the god-list continues with Ars wa-Shamem ("earth and heaven"). Binomial deities are common in Ugaritic; they represent either a hendiadys (as in this case) or a composite of two related gods who have been assimilated to one another. This god's function is unknown; perhaps the domain over which Baal holds sway is deified. There are also two other geographical deities: Sapan (discussed above) and "Mountain and Valley" (significance unknown, unless it defines the domain of Athtar, the god occupying the preceding place on the god-list).

The remaining divine names on the list may be grouped in four categories: individual goddesses and gods who are known or at least mentioned in the mythological texts; collective terms that designate groups of lesser deities; Hurrian deities; and otherwise unknown or poorly attested gods.

The two most prominent goddesses in the mythological texts are Athirat (Asherah) and Anat. Athirat is the consort of Il, and as such she is the highest-ranking goddess in the pantheon. Her full title is "Lady Athirat of the sea" (or perhaps "the lady who treads the sea"). She is the mother of the gods, bearing the epithet "progenitress of the gods." She is also called Ilat ("goddess"), the feminine form of Il. Athirat's activities in the mythological texts are not always clear, but she seems to specialize in zealous intervention on behalf of her divine offspring.

In contrast to the maternal goddess Athirat, Anat is a violent goddess of sexual love and war, "sister" (perhaps consort) of Baal and vanquisher of Baal's enemy Mot. Her principal epithet is "maiden," a tribute to her youth, beauty, and desirability, but pugnacity is her primary trait in the mythological texts, as well as in the epic of Aqhat; there, she secures the magic bow of the title character by arranging his death.

Iconographic evidence from Ugarit and elsewhere may be associated with both of the principal divine pairs, Il/Athirat and Baal/Anat. The first two are represented as a royal pair, either standing or enthroned. Baal is typically depicted with his arm upraised in smiting position, and Anat is naked and voluptuous, sometimes standing on a lion's back, an Egyptian Hathor wig on her head, with arms upraised and plants or animals grasped in her hands. Only the Anat figures can be identified with any certainty, because of an Egyptian exemplar that bears the inscription "Qudshu-Ashtart-Anat."

Although the precise significance of Qudshu is uncertain (perhaps she is the same as Athirat?), the Egyptian inscription seems to demonstrate the fusion of the West Semitic Anat with the great Mesopotamian goddess Ishtar (Ugaritic Athtart; the biblical Ashtoret). This fusion is apparent in the binomial Athtart wa-Anat, which occurs in two Ugaritic incantation texts and is the ultimate source of the name of the first-millennium "Syrian goddess" Atargatis. In some mythological and cultic texts, as in the god-list, Athtart still has some independent status. (Paradoxically, in Israel it is Anat who has disappeared, evidently assimilated to Ashtoret.) Her beauty is proverbial, but her principal trait is pugnacity; like Anat, she is a divine huntress.

The textual and iconographic evidence suggests that a central feature of Ugaritic religion was the veneration of two divine pairs. One pair apparently symbolized kingly and queenly sovereignty over the world—Il and Athirat; the other represented brother and sister, caught in the flux and turmoil of the world, engaged in constant struggle for survival and supremacy—Baal and Anat.

There are three other Canaanite goddesses on the god-list. Shapash is the all-seeing sun (male in Mesopotamia, but female at Ugarit), "luminary of the gods." Pid-ray ("fat"?) and Arsay ("earth," perhaps, on the basis of the Akkadian parallel, having some connection with the netherworld) are two of the daughters of Baal; the third, Talay ("dew"), does not appear on the god-list. Two other non-Canaanite goddesses are on the list, undoubtedly via the Hurrians, although the deities themselves are not necessarily Hurrian in origin: Ushharay (Ishhara), the scorpion goddess, who appears in several cultic texts but never in the myths, and Dadmish, probably a warrior goddess but very poorly attested. The one remaining goddess on the list is Uthht (pronunciation uncertain; the sex of the deity is, in fact, only surmised from the feminine ending); possibly Mesopotamian in origin, and most likely signifying a deified incense burner.

Seven male deities remain on the god-list, all but one of whom are at least mentioned in the mythological texts. Yarikh is the moon god, and he figures prominently in a poem that describes his marriage to the moon goddess, Nikkal. This text is undoubtedly a Hurrian myth in Ugaritic guise. The other clearly astral god is Shalim (the divine element in the name of the city Jeru*salem* and of King *Solo*mon), who represents the evening twilight or Venus as evening star. Since the root *sh-l-m* can signify "conclusion, completion," it is appropriate that Shalim is the last name on the list. Elsewhere, he is often paired with his sibling Shahr, who is the dawn or the planet Venus as morning star. The birth of the pair is described and celebrated in a Ugaritic poem.

Three of the gods play important roles in the mythological texts about Baal. Yamm is one of Baal's principal adversaries; he is identified with or accompanied by two fearsome sea monsters, Litan (the biblical Leviathan) and Tunnan (the biblical Tannin). The god Athtar (the masculine form of Athtart) is often associated with a prominent South Arabian astral deity, but the Akkadian translation of his name identifies him with the Hurrian warrior god Ashtabi. When Baal is killed by Mot, Athtar, styled "tyrant," is appointed king in his stead.

The god Kothar ("skilled one"; also known as Kothar wa-Hasis, "skilled and wise one") is the divine craftsman. In various sources he is a master builder, weapon maker, seaman, and magician. It has been suggested that he is the genius of technology.

The god Rashap (the biblical *Reshef,* which means both "pestilence" and "flame") is blamed in the epic of Kirta for the demise of part of the title character's family. But Rashap's real importance at Ugarit and Ras Ibn Hani emerges from the cultic texts, where he is the recipient of numerous offerings. In the late third millennium, he was one of the patron gods of the kings of Ebla. He also found his way to Egypt, where he was patron god of Amenophis II and one of the most popular gods in the cults of the nineteenth dynasty.

The Akkadian version of the Ugaritic god-list identifies Rashap with Nergal, the Mesopotamian king of the netherworld. That identification, along with other Canaanite and Egyptian evidence, leads me to suggest that Rashap is the god who, in one mythological text, is called Rapiu, the "healer," the eponymous patron of the deified dead, the *rapium* (the biblical *refa'im*). Most scholars, however, consider "Rapiu" to be an epithet of Il.

The remaining god on the list is Kinar, who is perhaps the deified lyre. Nothing is known about him, but he has been identified with the Cypriot hero Kinyras, father of Adonis.

Finally, the god-list includes four collective terms. The first, *kotharat,* designates a band of female divine singers and wet-nurses who appear on sad and joyful occasions in the Aqhat epic and the Nikkal poem, respectively (also, perhaps, in Psalm 68:7). Although their name suggests an affinity with the god Kothar, nothing further can be said about this. They bear an epithet that is problematic: the two most plausible translations are "daughters of joyous song, the swallows" and "shining daughters of the morning star [or the new moon]."

The next collective term apparently designates the "two allies of Baal," perhaps his messengers, Gapn ("vine") and Ugar ("field"). The third collective term is *puhr ilim,* the "assembly of the gods," which designates the host of lesser deities—unmentioned by name in the god-list—who constitute the progeny of Il and Athirat. In other texts, this assemblage bears other epithets, including "sons of Il" and "the family of the sons of Il"; the precise significance of these terms is much debated, but they all seem to pertain to the general Near Eastern notion of a "divine assembly" over which one god reigned supreme.

The last collective term is *malikum,* which literally means "kings." It designates the deified dead kings of Ugarit, the most important members of the larger assemblage of deified dead ancestors (*rapium,* mentioned above). The *malikum* are invoked by name in an extraordinary Ugaritic liturgy entitled the *Document of the Feast of the Protective Ancestral Spirits.* It may be inferred that the patron of the *malikum* was the ubiquitous Malik (biblical Molech), who is almost certainly to be equated with Death himself.

Many other deities who do not figure in the standard god-list are mentioned in various texts and as components of personal names. Huge, malleable pantheons characterized every major urban center of the ancient Near East, and Ugarit was no exception (see Johannes C. de Moor, "The Semitic Pantheon of Ugarit," *Ugarit-Forschungen* 2, 1970, pp. 185–228).

RITUALS AND CULTIC PERSONNEL. Most older descriptions of Canaanite religion explain it in terms of the seasonal cycle and concomitant fertility rites. The evidence for this characterization comes from first-millennium sources, especially the anti-"Canaanite" polemics of the Hebrew scriptures, and from the *a priori* claims of the "myth-and-ritual" approach to religion. When the mythic texts about the Ugaritic Baal were deciphered and pieced together, the tendency was naturally to make them conform to the older theories about Canaanite religion. Those texts were thus described as a mythic representation of the seasonal cycle, which was either recited as the accompaniment to fertility rites or served as the libretto of a fertility-cult drama.

Assuming that the biblical and related data are reliable, they evidently refer to local manifestations of first-millennium Phoenician cults (such as that of northern Israel). The simple assumption of continuity between second-millennium Canaan and first-millennium Phoenicia is unjustified—as is, more generally, the facile identification of "Canaanites" with "Phoenicians."

As for the myth-and-ritual claim, the seasonal interpretation of the Baal texts is by no means certain. There is no evidence that the Baal texts were ever used in conjunction with cultic activity. In fact, there is only one Ugaritic mythological text containing rubrics for ritual performance (discussed below); it apparently entails some sort of fertility rite, but one not necessarily connected with the seasonal cycle. Knowledge of the Ugaritic calendar and its fixed festivals is too scanty to permit the claim that Ugaritic religion was organized with respect to the agricultural year.

The Ugaritic ritual texts describe a highly organized sacrificial cult under the patronage of the king. The sacrifices seem to be of the gift or tribute type; that is, they were performed to curry favor with the gods, to secure their aid and protection. It is undeniable that offerings might have been made to deities (particularly chthonic ones) to promote the fertility of the land and the fecundity of the flocks. But the one mass public ritual that has survived, and the one attested prayer to Baal as well, both seem more concerned with protection from Ugarit's potential military opponents. In view of the shifting alliances and political instability that marked Ugarit's last two centuries, this concern seems only natural.

Most of the known Ugaritic rituals were performed by or on behalf of the king. The best-attested type of ritual is found in seven different texts. In it the king of Ugarit performs, at specified times, a ritual lustration to purify himself, and then offers a series of sacrifices to various deities. At sundown, the king "desacralizes" himself in a way that is not clear. The most interesting of these texts is evidently a prescriptive ritual to which is appended a prayer to Baal, perhaps recited by the queen, that seems to specify the occasion on which the rites were to be performed.

This text begins with a date formula and a list of offerings: "On the seventh day of the month of Ibalat [otherwise unknown]" sheep are offered to several gods, notable Baal and "the house of Baal of Ugarit." Then "the sun sets and the king performs the rite of desacralization." On the seventeenth day of the month, the king (re)purifies himself and makes another series of sacrifices, perhaps accompanied by a festal banquet (if this is the correct sense of the technical term *dbh*). (Another of the main sacrificial terms, *th*, which seems to denote "gift offering," also occurs here.) The king remains in his purified state and continues the series of offerings on the eighteenth day. Then the text breaks off. The reverse of the tablet begins with broken references to rites performed on the second day (of what, is unspecified). On the fourth, birds are offered; on the fifth the king offers a *shlmm* sacrifice to Baal of Ugarit in the temple, along with the liver of an unspecified animal (which has presumably been used for divination) and an offering of precious metal. The *shlmm* offering, well attested in biblical Hebrew and Punic cultic texts, was probably the most common type of sacrifice at Ugarit. The term is traditionally translated "peace offering," but it seems actually to have been a "gift" or "tribute" to the god. In some texts (but not this one), the *shlmm* is described as a *shrp*, which probably signifies that it was wholly consumed by fire.

On the seventh day, at sundown, the king performs the ritual desacralization, evidently aided in this case by cultic functionaries called "desacralizers." Then the queen is anointed with a libation of "a *hin* [liquid measure] of oil of pacification for Baal"; the text concludes with the following prayer, perhaps recited by the queen:

> When a strong enemy assails your gates,
> A mighty foe attacks your walls,
> Raise your eyes unto Baal:
> "O Baal, chase the strong enemy from our gates,
> The mighty foe from our walls.
> A bull, O Baal, we consecrate;
> A vow, O Baal, we dedicate;
> A firstborn [?], O Baal, we consecrate;
> A *htp* sacrifice, O Baal, we dedicate;
> A tithe, O Baal, we tithe.
> To the sanctuary of Baal let us ascend,
> On the paths to the House of Baal let us walk."
> Then Baal will hear your prayer,
> He will chase the strong enemy from your gates,
> The mighty foe from your walls.

A second type of ritual is preserved in three texts that describe the transfer of cult statues from one place to another. The clearest of these begins "When Athtart of *hr* [meaning uncertain] enters into the sanctuary [?] of the king's house. . . ." It is not clear whether the term *king* refers to Ugarit's king or to a god (perhaps both?); the "house" could be a royal palace or temple. A group of offerings is then made in the "house of the stellar gods" (meaning uncertain), including oblations, vestments, gold, and sacrificial animals. The rites are repeated seven times. The remainder of the text describes essentially the same rituals as those performed for a different collection of gods (on a different occasion?), the poorly attested *gthrm*.

One substantial ritual text is unique in the corpus, and has been the subject of many studies. It is unique in its poetic/hymnic quality and in the acts it describes. It seems to depict a great public assembly in which the entire population of Ugarit, male and female, king and commoner alike, participated. The ritual appears to have been a mass expiation or purgation of sins, or some sort of mass purification rite, designed to protect Ugarit against its threatening neighbors. A parallel has been drawn between it and the Jewish Yom Kippur, the "day of purgation [of sin]." In the Ugaritic text, the men and women of the community are alternately summoned to offer sacrifices, which they do. While the sacrifices are performed the people sing, praying that their offerings will ascend to "the father of the sons of Il" (that is, to Il himself), to the "family of the sons of Il," to the "assembly of the sons of Il," and to *Thkmn wa-Shnm*, Il's son and attendant (the one who cares for him when he is drunk; in one of his epithets, Il is called "father of *Shnm*").

Only one mythological text, the poem about the birth of Shahr and Shalim (the *ilima naimima*, "gracious gods"), includes rubrics for ritual performance. These rubrics, interspersed throughout the poem, describe the activities of the king and queen, and of cultic functionaries called *aribuma* (some kind of priests?) and *tha-nanuma* (members of the king's guard?). They offer sacrifices, participate in a banquet, and sing responsively to musical accompaniment. It seems almost certain that the poem itself was acted out as a type of ritual drama. It describes the subjugation of Death by some sort of pruning rite, followed by Il's sexual relations with Athirat and Rahmay ("womb" = Anat?). The poem concludes with the birth of Shahr and Shalim, and their youthful activities. The text and its accompanying ritual may commemorate (or attempt to foster) the birth of a royal heir to the reigning king and queen of Ugarit; they bear some relation to Mesopotamian sacred marriage rites and to Hittite rituals designed to protect the life and vigor of the king and queen.

Most difficult to reconstruct, but obviously of great importance, was the Ugaritic cult of the dead. The dead were summoned, by a liturgy accompanied by offerings, to participate in a banquet. The banquet, which was apparently a drunken orgy, was intended to propitiate the dead and to solicit the aid and protection provided by their numinous power. The most important group of the deified dead was comprised of Ugarit's kings (*malikum*). The larger assemblage, variously called "healers" (*rpim*), "healers of the netherworld" (*rpi ars*), "ancient healers" (*rpim qdmyn*), "divine spirits" (*ilnym*), and "assembly of Ditan/Didan" (*qbs dtn/ddn*), included two men who are prominent in the epic texts, Danil and Kirta, as well as several other spirits who are identified by name in a liturgical invocation of the dead.

The funerary feast itself was called a *marzih* (or *marzi*), a feast. It was held at a special location: one text describes problems concerning the rental of a *marzih* hall; a poorly preserved fragment of the Aqhat epic suggests that the *marzih* was held at a sacred "threshing floor" or "plantation," perhaps within the royal palace.

Another important text invokes the god Rapiu, "king of eternity" (that is, of the netherworld). Rapiu is clearly the patron of the deified dead; at first he is invited to drink, and at the end of the text he is asked to exert his "strength, power, might, rule, and goodness" for the benefit of Ugarit. If Rapiu is indeed to be identified with Il, this text comports well with the mythological fragment that depicts Il getting drunk at a *marzih*.

Alongside the cult of the dead must be placed the texts that apparently describe the ritual offerings to the gods of the netherworld (*ilm ars*). The clearest of these begins with an offering to Rashap and mentions several other chthonic deities. There is also a strange god-list that appears to include a collection of netherworld demons. Finally, an inscribed clay model of a liver may record a sacrifice offered to a person (or deity?) who is "in the tomb."

The considerable activity that took place in the Ugaritic cult demanded an extensive array of cultic personnel. Unfortunately, while the names of many cultic officials are known, their precise function is not. It can be assumed, of course, that "priests" participated in the royal rituals described above, but the ritual texts do not specify how. Apart from the "desacralizers," the *tha-nanuma* and *aribuma* already mentioned, several other kinds of personnel figure prominently. Except for the queen, who participated in some rituals (one broken text from Ras Ibn Hani describes a "*dbh* [sacrifical rite] of the queen"), all the important cultic functionaries attested by name or title are male.

After the king, the highest-ranking religious official was probably the *rb khnm*, the "chief of the priests." Under him were orders or guilds of *khnm* ("priests"); the term corresponds to the Hebrew *kohanim*, but there is no necessary similarity of function. The priests either were connected with the palace or they earned their living at the many shrines in Ugarite and its environs. They appear on administrative lists of personnel and on a military payroll. Other administrative texts detail allotments of oil and wine to various shrines. One of the high priests is also designated *rb nqdm*, "chief of herdsmen." In all likelihood, there was a consecrated group of herdsmen whose task was to maintain the royal flocks to be used in the cult.

The second major category of priests is called *qdshm*, "devotees" (comparison with Hebrew *qedeshim*, "cult prostitutes," is almost certainly misleading). They appear only on administrative lists, in all but one case in conjunction with *khnm*. Nothing can be said about their function at Ugarit.

Two categories of cult functionaries are attested in Akkadian texts from Ugarit, but they have no certain Ugaritic equivalents. One is the *awilu baru*, which is either an omen priest or some sort of oracular seer; one of these men is also called "priest of Adad [i.e., of Baal]." The other, aptly characterized by Anson F. Rainey (1967) as "a sort of religious brotherhood" (p. 71), is "men of the *marzi/marzih.*" Their activity was almost certainly related to the ritual feasts of the Ugaritic cult of the dead. Several other terms probably designated groups associated with the cult. There were singers, instrumentalists, and libation pourers who served as temple attendants, along with a group of uncertain function called *ytnm,* who may be compared with the problematic biblical *netinim.*

Finally, there is the well-attested and much-debated term *insh ilm.* Some scholars think that it is a divine name; others argue that it denotes cultic personnel. If the latter, then these people performed some function in the sacrificial rites, and seem to have been rewarded for their labor with "birds."

Popular Religion. As is generally the case in the ancient Near East, little can be said with any certainty about popular religion at Ugarit, since only kings, priests, and members of the elite are represented in the texts. The Ugaritic texts were apparently only a part of the larger cosmopolitan scribal tradition of Ugarit, which was modeled on the Babylonian scribal schools. The same scribes who produced the Baal texts were also trained to write in Babylonian cuneiform, and they copied Sumerian and Akkadian texts in almost every genre. Surviving evidence demonstrates that Ugarit's educated elite was conversant with the Mesopotamian Gilgamesh traditions, wisdom and proverbial literature, and legal formulas, although little of this material is reflected in texts in the Ugaritic language.

It is not at all certain, then, how much of the literary tradition might have filtered down to the commoners of Ugarit. Still, speculation about popular religion may be made in four areas: conceptions of gods reflected in personal names; the evidence of votive figurines; evidence for magic and divination; and possible religious, ethical, or "wisdom" teachings derived from the texts.

Popular conceptions of the gods may emerge from a consideration of personal names, since a great number of names are composites of divine names (or surrogates) and nominal or verbal elements. The standard collection of Ugaritic personal names, Frauke Gröndahl's *Die Personennamen der Texte aus Ugarit* (Rome, 1967), lists over fifty divine elements that appear in them. The most popular are Il, Baal, Ammu ("uncle," a surrogate for a divine name), Anat and her "masculine" equivalent Anu, Athtar, Yamm, Kothar, Malik, Pidr (masculine equivalent of Pidray?), Rapiu, Rashap, and Shapash. In some names, a god is described as father, mother, brother, sister, or uncle (e.g., *Rashapabi,* "Rashap is my father"). In others, the bearer of the name is the god's son, daughter, servant, or devotee (e.g., *Abdi-Rashap,* "servant of Rashap"). A large class of names describes characteristics of the gods; those composed with Il, for example, emphasize his kingship (*Ilimilku,* "Il is king") and justice (*Danil,* "Il judges"; *Ilsdq,* "Il is just"), his creativity (*Yakunilu,* "Il establishes"; *Yabniilu,* "Il builds") and his love (*Hnnil,* "Il is gracious").

The second class of evidence for popular religion comes from metal figurines that are generally thought to represent gods and goddesses. A comprehensive catalog of these figurines, compiled by Ora Negbi (1976), describes over seventeen hundred of them. They are considered to have been miniature copies of now-lost wooden cult statues, and were probably used as votive idols. The fact that so many have been found at cultic sites suggests that they had some ceremonial function. Negbi notes that these idols "may have been used as amulets for magic purposes in domestic and funerary cults as well" (p. 2).

As mentioned above, the figurines at Ugarit attest to the popularity of two distinct types of divine pairs, a kingly and queenly figure (Il and Athirat) and a smiting god and voluptuous goddess (Baal and Anat, with Anat occasionally portrayed as a war goddess). The latter pair is the better attested in Late Bronze Ugarit; figurines have been found in deposits from this period in and around both of the temples on the acropolis.

Some textual evidence has been recovered for magic and divination at Ugarit. There are two versions of a long and impressive incantation against the bite of a venomous serpent; several important deities are summoned from their mythical abodes during the course of the incantations.

Inscribed clay models of lungs and livers show that extispicy (divination by the examination of animal viscera) was practiced at Ugarit. The practice was undoubtedly borrowed from Babylonia, but it was given a distinctive Canaanite cast by the incorporation of West Semitic sacrificial rites. Another borrowing from the Babylonians is attested in three omen texts that describe the predictive value of unusual human and animal births. These texts clearly parallel the famous Babylonian *shumma izbu* omen series; unfortunately, they are all quite fragmentary.

Finally, one very difficult text reports a divine oracle. It begins: "When the lord of the great/many gods [Il?] approached Ditan, the latter sought an oracle concerning the child." Some individual presumably wishes to inquire of Il about his (sick?) child. (A comparable episode occurs in the Kirta epic.) Il can be reached through an intermediary, Ditan, the eponymous patron of those deified dead known as the "assembly of Ditan." The text continues with a series of instructions (broken and unclear) that will enable the inquirer to obtain the desired oracular response. The text seems to conclude with several instructions, "and afterward there will be no suffering [?]."

Taken together, these texts indicate a lively interest in the mantic arts at Ugarit. There is practically no evidence, however, about the specialists who practiced those arts; perhaps that is because they operated on the periphery of the official cultic institutions.

The most problematic aspect of popular religion is the interpretation of the Ugaritic religious texts. Assuming that they were in some way normative and that they were diffused orally, they would embody the religious "teachings" of Ugarit. There are, however, no surviving interpretations of the texts or expositions of religious doctrine that explain what those teachings might have been or what impact they had on the life of a community of believers. The Ugaritic mythic and epic texts (as opposed to the descriptive ritual texts) can be read as homilies on the nature of the world in which people live. Ancient readers or hearers of these texts would have sought their own place in the "cosmos" they describe. Ugaritic believers, like modern believers, would presumably have formulated a special application of sacred texts to their own lives.

The Baal texts punctualize eternal truths in a symbolic realm that is only superficially remote from human experience. The gods experience joy and mourning, battle and tranquillity, life and death, power and impotence. The mightiest of the gods confronts the world's challenges and surmounts them all, until he encounters Death, the one enemy to whom gods and humans alike succumb. Baal's triumphs and trials, furthermore, illustrate the contiguity and interrelationship of everything in the world: the gods, nature, the political order, and human life are all part of the same order. When Baal is vanquished, political order collapses and the earth turns infertile—not because Baal "symbolizes" order and fertility in some simplistic way, but because the intricate balance of the world has been subverted. The same upset of the natural order occurs when Kirta, a human king, becomes mortally ill.

Overarching the flux of the world, and apparently not subject to it, is the wise and beneficent Il. At critical moments in the Baal texts, the gods journey (or send emissaries) to him in order to obtain his favor and advice. After Kirta's family is annihilated by malevolent forces, Il comforts the king in a dream; later on, Il provides the cure for Kirta's terrible illness. And in the Aqhat epic, Baal implores Il to grant a son to the childless Danil. Il consents, and appears to Danil in a dream with the good news. In every case, Il manifests transcendent power that is wielded justly, in response to urgent pleas.

The epic texts (perhaps "historico-mythic" would be a better designation for them) Aqhat and Kirta parallel and supplement the mythic texts. They narrate the existential encounter of humans with the gods. Historical (or pseudohistorical) figures become exemplary or admonitory paradigms of human behavior.

The crises that move the plot of the Aqhat text demonstrate the conjunction and contiguity of the human and divine realms. Danil, who is, like Kirta, a man become god (one of the deified *rapium*—from the point of view of the reader, that is), is an embodiment of that contiguity. Danil is clearly an ideal type, pious and just; he brings his plea for a son before the gods in humble obeisance, and he is rewarded. The incubation rite performed by Danil at the beginning of the story seems to be a model of personal piety.

Other aspects of the Aqhat text suggest ethical teachings as well. The long-sought son, Aqhat, is presented as the archetypical huntsman, recipient of a magic bow fashioned by the craftsman god Kothar. But the bow is not an unequivocal blessing: it arouses the envy of Anat, and makes Aqhat so secure in his own power that he rudely dismisses the goddess. Aqhat's folly parallels Baal's when, secure in his new palace (also the work of Kothar), he presumptuously challenges Death. Even the cleverest invention affords no protection for one who oversteps his bounds and incurs divine wrath. Aqhat's death is avenged by his sister Pughat, a model of love and devotion, just as Baal's sister Anat acts on the god's behalf in the mythic texts.

The Kirta epic, like that of Aqhat, begins with its hero childless, this time because of catastrophe instead of impotence. Dramatic tension arises from the situation of a king without an heir, which could result in disruption of both the political and the natural order. The story conveys the fragility of power and the delicate relationship between humans and deities.

Kirta enjoys the favor of Il, "father of humankind," who calls the king "gracious one, lad of Il." Kirta is instructed to perform a series of rituals in order to secure victory in battle and a new wife. He does so faithfully, but he also stops to make a vow in the sanctuary of "Athirat of Tyre, goddess of the Sidonians." This act of personal piety leads to disaster: Kirta achieves his victory and builds a new family, but he is stricken with a mortal illness for his failure to fulfill the vow. His beneficent "father" Il intervenes once again in his behalf, but the story concludes with Kirta's son attempting to usurp the throne, accusing Kirta of unrighteousness (reason enough, evidently, to depose a king). The vicissitudes of kingship continue.

The texts are all firmly on the side of reward for virtue and piety, and punishment for wickedness, blasphemy, and folly. Yet even someone who is justly suffering the wrath of the gods may appeal to the gracious Il and be heard.

SURVIVALS. Survivals of Canaanite religion are observable in two first-millennium cultural spheres, the Levant and the Aegean. Phoenician religion, both in the Levant and in its wider Mediterranean sphere of influence, represents, to some extent, a continuation of Canaanite traditions. Northern Israel's official cult was among the Levantine successors of Canaanite religion. It has often been noted that biblical polemics against that cult (for example, in the *Book of Hosea*) are directed against a characteristically Canaanite feature—the idea that the god (in this case Yahveh = Baal) was immanent in nature and subject to its flux. The Israelite god was, on the other hand, comfortably assimilated to the transcendent Il.

In the Aegean area, the nature of Canaanite influence is more controversial. But there is compelling evidence for the existence of direct West Semitic contact with Mycenaean Greece, creating a legacy of Semitic names, literary motifs, and religious practices that became part of the Hellenic cultural heritage.

Bibliography

There are excellent, comprehensive articles on Amarna, Mari, and Ras Shamra in the *Dictionnaire de la Bible, Supplément,* vol. 1, cols. 207–225 (by Édouard Dhorme); vol. 5, cols. 883–905 (by Charles F. Jean); and vol. 9, cols. 1124–1466, respectively (Paris, 1928–). The Ras Shamra article, by several distinguished experts, is magisterial—the best survey to be found anywhere. In English, the journal *Biblical Archaeologist* has published a number of good survey articles: on Mari by George E. Mendenhall, vol. 11 (February 1948), pp. 1–19, and by Herbert B. Huffmon, vol. 31 (December 1968), pp. 101–124 (on the "prophetic texts"); on Amarna by Edward F. Campbell, vol. 23 (February 1960), pp. 2–22; on Ugarit by H. L. Ginsberg, vol. 8 (May 1945), pp. 41–58, and by Anson F. Rainey, vol. 28 (December 1965), pp. 102–125. All of these articles have been reprinted in *The Biblical Archaeologist Reader,* edited by David Noel Freedman and G. Ernest Wright, vols. 2 and 3 (Garden City, N.Y., 1961–1970). More recently, *Biblical Archaeologist* 47 (June 1984) is a special issue devoted to Mari.

Turning specifically to Ugarit, an excellent popular introduction is Gabriel Saadé's *Ougarit: Métropole cananéenne* (Beirut, 1979). Saadé gives a thorough account of the excavations, with complete bibliographical information and many illustrations. Most of the technical information is derived from articles in the journal *Syria,* beginning with volume 10 (1929), and from the volumes in the series "Mission de Ras-Shamra," 9 vols., edited by Claude F.-A. Schaeffer (Paris, 1936–1968). Two other useful works on the archaeological data are Patty Gerstenblith's *The Levant at the Beginning of the Middle Bronze Age* (Winona Lake, Ind., 1983) and Ora Negbi's *Canaanite Gods in Metal* (Tel Aviv, 1976).

A good detailed account of Ugarit's history is Mario Liverani's *Storia di Ugarit* (Rome, 1962), and an unsurpassed description of Ugaritic society is Anson F. Rainey's *The Social Structure of Ugarit* (in Hebrew; Jerusalem, 1967). Readers of English can consult Rainey's Ph.D. dissertation, "The Social Stratification of Ugarit" (Brandeis University, 1962).

On the study of Canaanite religion before the discovery of Ugarit, there is a fine survey by M. J. Mulder, "Von Seldon bis Schaeffer: Die Erforschung der kanaanäischen Götterwelt," in the leading scholarly journal devoted to Ugaritic studies, *Ugarit-Forschungen* 11 (1979): 655–671. The best general introduction to Canaanite religion is Hartmut Gese's "Die Religionen Altsyriens," in *Die Religionen Altsyriens, Altarabiens und der Mandäer* (Stuttgart, 1970), pp. 3–181. On the Canaanite gods, the standard work is still Marvin H. Pope and Wolfgang Röllig's "Syrien," in *Wörterbuch der Mythologie,* edited by H. W. Haussig, vol. 1 (Stuttgart, 1965), pp. 219–312. On the rituals and cultic personnel, an excellent presentation of the data is Jean-Michel de Tarragon's *Le culte à Ugarit* (Paris, 1980), which should be consulted alongside Paolo Xella's *I testi rituali di Ugarit* (Rome, 1981). There is an exceptionally interesting theoretical discussion of Canaanite religion by David L. Petersen and Mark Woodward in "Northwest Semitic Religion: A Study of Relational Structures," *Ugarit-Forschungen* 9 (1977): 232–248. The outstanding representative of the myth-and-ritual approach is Theodor H. Gaster's *Thespis,* 2d ed. (1961; New York, 1977).

There is not yet an adequately introduced and annotated English translation of the Ugaritic texts. The best English translations are those of H. L. Ginsberg, in J. B. Pritchard's *Ancient Near Eastern Texts relating to the Old Testament,* 3d ed. (Princeton, 1969), pp. 129–155, and those in J. C. L. Gibson's revision of G. R. Driver's *Canaanite Myths and Legends,* 2d ed. (Edinburgh, 1978). The serious student should consult *Textes ougaritiques,* translated and edited by André Caquot and others (Paris, 1974), and the even more comprehensive Spanish work by Gregorio del Olmo Lete, *Mitos y leyendas de Canaán según la tradición de Ugarit* (Madrid, 1981), complemented by the same author's *Interpretación de la mitología cananea* (Valencia, 1984). A more popular introduction and translation that is both readable and of high quality is Paolo Xella's *Gli antenati di Dio* (Verona, 1982). A comparable but inferior volume in English is *Stories from Ancient Canaan,* edited and translated by Michael D. Coogan (Philadelphia, 1978).

Works on Ugarit and the Bible are legion. The serious student is directed to *Ras Shamra Parallels,* edited by Loren R. Fischer, 2 vols. (Rome, 1972–1975). The contributions are uneven in quality, but the many proposed parallels are presented with full bibliographic information. A convenient survey of comparative studies is Peter C. Craigie's "Ugarit and the Bible," in *Ugarit in Retrospect,* edited by Gordon Douglas Young (Winona Lake, Ind., 1981), pp. 99–111. John Gray's *The Legacy of Canaan,* 2d ed. (Leiden, 1965), has become a standard work in this area; its great learning and originality are marred by eccentricity, especially in the translation of the Ugaritic texts. On the most important classical account of "Canaanite" religion, see the definitive work by Albert I. Baumgarten, *The Phoenician History of Philo of Byblos* (Leiden, 1981). Semitic influence on the Aegean world is one of the main topics of Cyrus H. Gordon's stimulating book *Before the Bible: The Common Background of Greek and Hebrew Civilizations* (London, 1962); a more technical work on the subject is Michael C. Astour's brilliant *Hellenosemitica* (Leiden, 1967).

New Sources

The period 1985–2004 has produced a wealth of new information and scholarly analysis concerning Ugaritic religion. Important new reference works include the *Handbook of Ugaritic Studies,* edited by Wilfred G. E. Watson and Nicolas Wyatt (Leiden, 1999), and the revised edition of the *Dictionary of Deities and Demons in the Bible,* edited by Karel van der Toorn, Bob Becking, and Pieter W. van der Horst (Leiden, 1999). These books provide extensive bibliographic references to previous studies of Ugaritic religion and deities.

Excellent English translations of the mythological texts are conveniently gathered in Simon Parker's edited volume, *Ugaritic Narrative Poetry* (Atlanta, 1997), and in Nick Wyatt's *Religious Texts from Ugarit* (2d ed., Sheffield, 2002). Scholarly advances in the study of religious iconography are represented by the landmark book by Othmar Keel and Christoph Uehlinger, *Gods, Goddesses, and Images of God in Ancient Israel* (Minneapolis, 1998). The cultic and ritual texts from Ugarit have also received renewed attention, culminating in

Dennis Pardee's massive study, *Les textes rituels* (Paris, 2000). Non-specialists may find Pardee's shorter presentation, *Ritual and Cult at Ugarit* (Atlanta, 2002), more accessible yet equally authoritative. Gregorio del Olmo Lete's useful book, *Canaanite Religion: According to the Liturgical Texts of Ugarit* (Bethesda, Md., 1999), offers a comprehensive analysis of Ugaritic religion, while Mark S. Smith's survey, *The Early History of God: Yahweh and the Other Deities in Ancient Israel* (2d ed., Grand Rapids, 2002), explores the relationship between Ugaritic religion and the biblical record. Important studies of aspects of Ugaritic religion can also be found in the following books:

Day, John. *Yahweh and the Gods and Goddesses of Canaan.* Sheffield, 2000.

Dietrich, Manfried, and Oswald Loretz. *Studien zu den ugaritischen Texten.* Münster, 2000.

Hadley, Judith M. *The Cult of Asherah in Ancient Israel and Judah.* Cambridge, 2001.

Lipiński, Edward. *Dieux et déesses de l'univers phénicien et punique.* Leuven, 1995.

Mettinger, Tryggve N. D. *The Riddle of Resurrection: "Dying and Rising Gods" in the Ancient Near East.* Stockholm, 2001.

Niehr, Herbert. *Religionen in Israels Umwelt: Einführung in die nordwestsemitischen Religionen Syrien-Palästinas.* Würzburg, 1998.

del Olmo Lete, Gregorio. *El continuum cultural cananeo. Pervivencias cananeas en el mundo fenicio-púnico.* Sabadell, 1996.

del Olmo Lete, Gregorio. *Mitos, leyendas y rituales de los semitas occidentales.* Madrid, 1998.

Pardee, Dennis. *Les textes para-mythologiques de la 24e compagne (1961).* Paris, 1988.

Schmidt, Brian B. *Israel's Beneficent Dead.* Tübingen, 1994.

Smith, Mark S. *The Ugaritic Baal Cycle, I.* Leiden, 1994.

Smith, Mark S. *The Origins of Biblical Monotheism: Israel's Polytheistic Background and the Ugaritic Texts.* Oxford, 2001.

Wyatt, N., W. G. E. Watson, and J. Lloyd, eds. *Ugarit, Religion, and Culture.* Münster, 1996.

Yon, Marguerite. *La cite d'Ougarit sur le tell de Ras Shamra.* Paris, 1997.

Alan M. Cooper (1987)
Revised Bibliography

CANAANITE RELIGION: THE LITERATURE

The scope of this article needs definition. The term *Canaanite* designates the culture of the region often known as the Levant, roughly comprising the modern entities of Syria, Lebanon, Jordan, Israel, and Palestine, beginning with the earliest extensive written records in the third millennium BCE and ending with the start of the Hellenistic period in the fourth century BCE. "Canaanite" did not have such a broad definition in antiquity; generally, and especially in the Bible, Canaan is the southwestern part of this region. The sources are not consistent in this usage, however, and many modern scholars apply it to the regions that in the first half of the first millennium BCE were divided into the political units of Phoenicia, Israel (later Israel and Judah), Ammon, Moab, Edom, and not infrequently, Aram, especially Aram-Damascus.

The term *literature* is used here to mean extended works composed in poetic style, specifically several dozen clay tablets, inscribed with an alphabetic cuneiform script, that have been found at ancient Ugarit (modern Ras Shamra) on the Syrian coast in excavations since 1929. The much larger body of material found there, and at nearby Ras Ibn Hani, apparently a royal palace, includes a variety of documents not germane to the topic of this article, such as diplomatic correspondence, lists of ritual offerings, economic texts, and notes for the care and treatment of horses. But even these contain valuable evidence for religious practice, especially in the names of the gods listed as recipients of offerings, names that were also used as components of personal names.

Most of the literary texts were found in the temple precinct of ancient Ugarit, on the city's acropolis. This is not merely a result of scribal activity in the sacred quarter, because the secular archives were found in the royal palace area and other libraries existed elsewhere in the city; rather, the presence of these texts in a religious context indicates that they had a religious function. Unhappily, few of them have any rubrics, and other, specifically ritual texts, such as the lists of offerings and the inscriptions on clay models of livers and lungs used for divination, provide no clue to the cultic setting in which the literary texts were used. Presumably, at least some of them were read or recited periodically at festivals, as were the Homeric poems in ancient Greece; others may have been actual librettos for ritual activities.

Characteristics of the Texts. The major mythological and epic texts were written on clay tablets that were fired after having been inscribed on both sides in from one to four columns. The lines are written continuously, with divisions between the words but without other spacing except for occasional dividing lines between sense units and episodes; these, however, are not used systematically. Not infrequently, the tablets have a title at the beginning; thus, two of the three parts of the Kirta cycle are marked "Concerning Kirta," and one tablet of each of the Baal and Aqhat cycles has a similar heading. Such a cataloging device may have been used more regularly, but because a significant number of the tablets are broken at the edges, one cannot be sure. The incomplete preservation of many of the tablets also makes it more difficult to follow the sequence of the narratives and hence to interpret them; this explains the conjectural analyses below.

Five tablets have concluding notations; the most complete reads: "The scribe was Ilimilku from Shubanu, the apprentice of Attanu-Purlianni, the chief priest, the chief herdsman; the sponsor was Niqmaddu, king of Ugarit, master of Yargub, lord of Tharumani." As this colophon indicates, the texts were written under royal patronage, illustrating the close connection between palace and temple. The king in question was Niqmaddu III, the second-last ruler of Ugarit, who lived in the late thirteenth century BCE. Ilimilku may have been more than just a scribe to whom the contents of the tablets were dictated. Although the texts show signs of having originally been oral compositions, Ilimilku may have been a writer in the modern sense, one who, like Homer in Greece a few centuries later, took an oral tradition and creatively revised it for a written medium.

Among the characteristics that Canaanite literature shares with other oral literatures is the use of stock epithets for human and divine characters, a technique most familiar from the *Iliad* and the *Odyssey.* Thus, El, the head of the pantheon, is variously called "the bull," "the creator of creatures," "the father of years," "the kind, the compassionate," and "the king"; the storm god Baal is "the prince," "the conqueror (of warriors)," and "the lord of the earth"; Kirta, the hero of the epic called by his name, is "the gracious one," "the noble," and "the servant of El"; and Danel, the father of the title character of *Aqhat,* is "the hero" and "the Healer's man." The poets apparently chose the epithet that was most appropriate for the context and that best fit the meter.

Another device familiar from the Homeric poems is the use of formulaic units to narrate standard scenes: the offering of a sacrifice; the harnessing of a donkey; the preparation of a banquet; the journey of a god or goddess to El's abode. Thus, with appropriate changes of number and gender, the following lines occur some half dozen times in the extant corpus:

> Then she headed toward El, at the source of the two rivers, in the midst of the two seas' pools; she opened El's tent and entered the shrine of the King, the Father of Years. At El's feet she bowed down and adored; she prostrated herself and worshiped him.

Also characteristic of Ugaritic literature is the almost verbatim repetition of large blocks of lines; this is found in the giving of a command and its execution, the occurrence of a dream and its telling, and in various specific narratives.

Finally, like other ancient eastern Mediterranean literatures, this originally oral Canaanite literature was poetic. Because the texts were written almost entirely without vowels, it has so far not been possible to establish the metrical principles underlying the poetry, and rhyme was not used. But one formal characteristic can be identified, traditionally called parallelism and fortunately not obscured by translation. In Canaanite poetry the basic element is a unit of two or three lines in which one thought is extended by repetition, paraphrase, or contrast. Thus, in a speech by the craftsman god Kothar-wa-Hasis, the lines

> "Let me tell you, Prince Baal, let me repeat, Rider on the Clouds: behold, your enemy, Baal, behold, you will kill your enemy, behold, you will annihilate your foes; you will take your eternal kingdom, your dominion forever and ever"

consist of three units, each of which expresses a complete thought. This stylistic feature is familiar from the other major source of Canaanite literature, the Hebrew scriptures, for the same building blocks of Canaanite verse—parallel pairs—are used there as well:

> Behold, your enemies, Yahweh, behold, your enemies have perished, all evildoers have been scattered. (*Ps.* 92:9)

> Your kingdom is an eternal kingdom, your rule is forever and ever. (*Ps.* 145:13)

The reason for this similarity of form and content is cultural: notwithstanding the significant geographical and temporal differences between Ugarit and Israel, they were part of a larger cultural entity that shared a common poetic and religious vocabulary.

This commonality is significant, for the literature of ancient Israel preserved in the Bible is able to shed much light on obscurities and gaps in the Canaanite literature from Ugarit. Conversely, the Ugaritic texts enable us to understand the Canaanites better on their own terms instead of through the often virulent polemics of the biblical writers. Each body of literature thus illumines the other, as will be seen below.

Mythological Texts. The texts in this category make no reference to human persons or actual societies. The protagonists are divine and there is no historical time frame.

The Baal cycle. The major cycle of preserved Canaanite literature from Ugarit has to do with the deity Baal, the most important god in the Ugaritic pantheon. Although the high god El was worshiped at Ugarit, as throughout the Semitic world, and figures in a number of texts, Baal seems to have supplanted him as the major deity by the late second millennium BCE; this is confirmed both by nonliterary sources, such as ritual lists and personal names, and by the Baal cycle, whose theme in brief is the affirmation "Baal the Conqueror is our king!"

More than a dozen tablets contain various episodes or variants of the Baal cycle, indicating the god's importance at Ugarit, but many of them are fragmentary, and so any sustained development of the plot of the cycle is difficult to determine. What is clear is the main plot of three episodes: Baal's battle with Sea; the construction and dedication of Baal's house; and Baal's encounter with Death.

Baal and Sea. El, the head of the pantheon, had apparently shown preference to his son Sea (Yamm)—called "El's beloved" and also by the parallel titles Prince Sea and Judge River—over Baal, the son of Dagan (whose name means "grain"). Initially, Sea seems to have gained the upper hand, with El's support. He sends the council of the gods, over which El presides, an ultimatum:

> "Message of Sea, your master, your Lord, Judge River: 'Give up, O gods, the one you are hiding, the one you are hiding, O multitude; give up Baal and his powers, the son of Dagan: I will acquire his gold.'"

Although El and the divine assembly are willing to capitulate to Sea's demand, Baal is not, and he proceeds to engage Sea in battle. With the help of magical clubs fashioned for him by Kothar wa-Hasis ("skillful and wise"; the divine craftsman, the Canaanite equivalent of the Greek Hephaistos), Baal defeats his adversary:

> The club danced in Baal's hands, like a vulture from his fingers; it struck Prince Sea on the skull, Judge River between the eyes; Sea stumbled; he fell to the ground; his joints shook; his frame collapsed. Baal captured and drank Sea; he finished off Judge River.

This brief episode cannot be fully understood without reference to similar and more detailed Near Eastern myths, especially that preserved in the Babylonian *Enuma elish.* There the council of the gods is threatened by Tiamat (Deep), the primeval goddess of saltwater. The only deity able to rescue the gods is the young storm god, Marduk, who agrees to do so only if he is given complete authority over gods and human beings. Following their battle, described in lavish detail, Marduk forms the elements of the cosmos from the corpses of his defeated adversaries and is proclaimed supreme ruler. Despite differences between the Babylonian and Ugaritic texts, there seem here to be two versions of a single story that tells how a younger god comes to assume leadership over his fellows; similar myths are found in ancient Anatolia, Greece, and India. Like Marduk, Baal is a storm god: he is called the "rider on the clouds" (compare the Homeric epithet of Zeus, "the cloud-gatherer"); his weapon is the lightning bolt; and he is responsible for the rains in their season.

Many of these aspects of Baal are also attributed to the Israelite Yahweh. Thus, he too is the "rider on the clouds" (*Ps.* 68:4); he

> makes the clouds his chariot, walks on the wings of the wind, makes the winds his messengers, fire [and] flame his ministers. (*Pss.* 104:3–4)

There are also allusions in various biblical passages to a primeval conflict between Yahweh and the sea; especially noteworthy is *Job* 26:12–13:

> With his power he stilled the sea, with his skill he smote Rahab, with his wind he put Sea in a net, his hand pierced the fleeing serpent.

(Compare *Psalms* 89:9–10 and *Isaiah* 27:1.)

The Bible does not, however, present a completely developed version of this primeval struggle, for in ancient Israelite tradition the normative event was not mythical but historical: the defeat of the Egyptian army at the Red Sea. But frequently the language used to celebrate this event was derived from Canaanite myth. Thus, *Psalms* 77:15–20 incorporates into a remembrance of God's ancient deeds the following:

> With your arm you redeemed your people, the sons of Jacob and Joseph. The waters saw you, God, the waters saw you and writhed, indeed, the deeps trembled; the clouds poured out water, the thunderheads sounded their voice, your arrows were in constant motion. . . . Through the sea was your way, and your path through the mighty waters. . . . You led your people like a flock, by the hand of Moses and Aaron.

(Compare *Isaiah* 51:9–10.)

Furthermore, the same parallel terms used of Baal's adversary are put into service by biblical poets, as in *Habakkuk* 3:8:

> Were you not angry at the river, Yahweh, was your rage not against the river, was your wrath not against the sea?

And in *Psalms* 114:1–3 the formulaic pair "sea/river" is partially historicized:

> When Israel came out of Egypt, the house of Jacob from people of a different language . . . the sea saw and fled, the Jordan turned back.

In the more fully elaborated prose accounts of the story of Israel's deliverance, the splitting of the Red Sea is repeated at the crossing of the Jordan, again reflecting the ancient parallelism.

The ancient Israelites thus made frequent use of the broader ancient Near Eastern myth of the defeat of the primeval sea by the storm god. In the Bible, as in Ugaritic, the watery adversary of the deity is also called Leviathan, the multiheaded monster (*Pss.* 78:13–14; cf. *Jb.* 41). Behemoth and Rahab, other biblical names for the sea, have not yet turned up elsewhere. This myth is transformed in the apocalyptic visions of Jewish and Christian writers: in the end of time, the sea will finally be defeated (see *Is.* 27:1; *Rv.* 21:1).

Baal's house. After a considerable gap, the Baal cycle continues with a description of Baal's victory banquet. One of Baal's servants prepares an appropriate spread for "Baal the Conqueror, the Prince, the Lord of the Earth":

> He put a cup in his hand, a goblet in both his hands, a large beaker, manifestly great, a jar to astound a mortal, a holy cup that women should not see, a goblet that Asherah must not set her eye on; he took a thousand jugs of wine, he mixed ten thousand in his mixing bowl.

Another break in the text occurs here, and there follows a lengthy account of a battle waged by Anat, the most vividly described of the three major goddesses in the Ugaritic texts. The other two, Asherah (Athiratu in Ugaritic) and Astarte (Athtartu), appear only infrequently and generally in formulaic passages that shed little light on their characters. Anat, on the other hand, is a major figure in the Baal cycle, a position that is appropriate in view of her relationship to Baal: she is his sister and his wife. As this description of her martial style indicates, Anat is a violent deity:

> Heads rolled under her like balls, hands flew over her like locusts, the warriors' hands like swarms of grasshoppers. She fastened the heads to her back, she tied the hands to her belt. She plunged knee-deep in the soldiers' blood, up to her hands in the warriors' gore; with a staff she drove off her enemies, with the string of her bow, her opponents.

After this gory battle Anat purifies herself:

> She drew water and washed, the heavens' dew, the earth's oil, the rain of the Rider on the Clouds, dew that the heavens pour on her, rain that the stars pour on her.

In the next scene, Baal sends messengers to summon Anat; this invitation, which includes one of those extended formulae that recur in the texts, is lyrical in tone:

> "Message of Baal the Conqueror, the word of the Conqueror of Warriors: 'Remove war from the earth, set love in the ground, pour peace into the heart of the earth, rain down love on the heart of the fields. Hasten! hurry! rush! Run to me with your feet, race to me with your legs; for I have a word to tell you, a story to recount to you: the word of the tree and the charm of the stone, the whisper of the heavens to the earth, of the deeps to the stars. I understand the lightning that the heavens do not know, the word that human beings do not know, and earth's masses cannot understand. Come, and I will reveal it: in the midst of my mountain, the divine Zaphon, in the sanctuary, in the mountain of my inheritance, in the pleasant place, in the hill I have conquered.'"

When Anat sees Baal's messengers approaching, she is overcome with fear that another enemy threatens Baal. She lists the various enemies of Baal who have been defeated; first among them is Sea, who is given a full range of epithets, including "the dragon," "the twisting serpent," and "the seven-headed monster." Curiously, Anat herself claims credit for Sea's defeat, as for that of the other enemies named. Clearly, there was more than one version of Baal's defeat of Sea, for the one discussed above does not depict Anat as a participant in the battle; similarly, there is no account of combat between Baal and such adversaries as "the divine calf, the Rebel" or "El's bitch, Fire." These gaps in knowledge are salutary reminders of the limited nature of the sample of Ugaritic literature as yet discovered, and of the difficulty of combining the several tablets of the Baal cycle into a continuous narrative.

When Baal's messengers assure Anat that there is no danger and issue Baal's invitation, Anat proceeds to visit Baal. Again a section is missing, and as the text resumes, the main plot line of this tablet is developed: the construction of a permanent abode for Baal. In the gap he apparently complains to Anat that despite his victory over Sea, he has no house like the other gods. The word *house* in Ugaritic, as in Hebrew, has several senses; here it means not just a dwelling but a permanent abode for the god, hence a temple. The construction of a temple for the god who has been victorious over the forces of chaos is a typical motif; in *Enuma elish* in particular, after Marduk establishes cosmic order and creates human beings from the blood of Tiamat's spouse, the gods themselves build a temple for Marduk, and after its completion they are his guests at an inaugural banquet. Baal's elevation to kingship over the gods and human beings is therefore incomplete as long as he has no house like the other gods.

Anat goes to El to obtain his approval for the erection of a temple for Baal; her request includes a characteristic threat of violence if she is refused:

> "I'll smash your head; I'll make your gray hair run with blood, your gray beard with gore."

Before El can give his assent, however, his consort Asherah has to agree; mollified by a bribe of marvelous gifts specially fashioned by Kothar, the divine craftsman, she intercedes for Baal:

> "You are great, El, you are truly wise; your gray beard truly instructs you. . . . Now Baal will begin the rainy season, the season of wadis in flood; and he will sound his voice in the clouds, flash his lightning to the earth. Let him complete his house of cedar! let him construct his house of bricks!"

Anat brings the news of El's approval to her brother; Baal then gathers appropriate building materials—silver, gold, lapis lazuli—and commissions Kothar to begin work. As they discuss the plans, Kothar recommends that a window be included; despite his repeated urgings, however, Baal refuses. The house is built, and with the other gods Baal celebrates its completion at a banquet, after which he goes on a triumphal tour of his domain. When he returns, he has apparently changed his mind about the window, and at his request Kothar makes one; from this window, appropriately described as a slit in the clouds, Baal thunders, the earth quakes, and his enemies flee. Baal's enthronement as king is complete.

Baal and Death. Near the end of the tablet on which the above episode occurs, Baal proclaims:

> "No other king or non-king shall set his power over the earth. I will send no tribute to El's son Death, no homage to El's Beloved, the Hero. Let Death cry to himself, let the Beloved grumble in his heart; for I alone will rule over the gods; I alone will fatten gods and human beings; I alone will satisfy earth's masses."

This challenge to Death is best explained by the incomplete nature of Baal's triumph: while he has defeated Sea and has been proclaimed king by the divine assembly, the major force of Death is still not subdued.

Like Sea, Death is El's son; apparently, Baal's accession to kingship over the gods requires the elimination of this rival as well. The enigmatic dispute between Baal and Kothar about whether Baal's house is to have a window may be an indication of Baal's awareness of this requirement. Baal's initial reluctance can be better understood by reference to *Jeremiah* 9:21:

> Death has come up through our windows, he has entered our fortresses, cutting down the children in the street and the young men in the squares.

Since the decipherment of Ugaritic it has become clear that in many biblical passages that mention death, there is at least indirect reference to the Canaanite deity representing death (Hebrew and Ugaritic, *mot*) and not merely a designation of the cessation of life. The verse in *Jeremiah* is one such passage, and may reflect a popular belief that the god Death entered a house through the window. Seen in this light, Baal is at first unwilling to include a window in his house because he fears giving Death access; later, after his inaugural banquet and triumphal march, his grasp of power is, he thinks, more secure.

In any event, having proclaimed his supremacy, Baal sends messengers to Death; their names are Gapn and Ugar ("vine" and "field," appropriately reflecting Baal's aspect as god of the storm that brings fertility and thus anticipating the coming contest with its antithesis). Baal directs them:

> "Head toward the midst of his city, the Swamp, Muck, the throne where he sits, Phlegm, the land of his inheritance."

Death's underworld domain is, like the grave, a damp, dark, unpleasant place; it is reached from his earthly territory, the barren, hot desert, where (Baal continues)

> "Sun, the gods' lamp, burns, the heavens shimmer under the sway of El's Beloved, Death."

Suitably warned and instructed, Baal's two messengers leave. Because the text is broken here and even an entire tablet may be missing, it is not wholly clear what the gist of Baal's message is; a plausible guess is that Baal wishes to invite Death to his new palace. But Death will have none of such niceties; Baal is condemned for his destruction of Sea and its cosmic consequences, and the sentence is death at Death's hands. Gapn and Ugar return with Death's reply:

> "One lip to the earth, one lip to the heavens; he stretches his tongue to the stars. Baal must enter inside him; he must go down into his mouth, like an olive cake, the earth's produce, the fruit of the trees."

Without any sign of resistance, Baal agrees:

> "Hail, El's son Death!"
>
> "I am your servant; I am yours forever."

The tablet is very fragmentary here, leaving only the skeleton of a plot. Baal is to take with him all his companions and accoutrements—cloud, winds, lightning bolts, rain—and to proceed to the underworld; then "the gods will know that you have died." Apparently he does so, for when a readable text resumes, two messengers are reporting to El:

> "We arrived at the pleasant place, the desert pasture, at the lovely fields on Death's shore. We came upon Baal: he had fallen to the ground. Baal the Conqueror has died; the Prince, the Lord of the Earth, has perished."

El's reaction is, initially, one of grief:

> He poured earth on his head as a sign of mourning, on his skull the dust in which he rolled; he covered his loins with sackcloth. He gashed his skin with a knife, he made incisions with a razor; he cut his cheeks and chin, he raked his arms with a reed, he plowed his chest like a garden, he raked his back like a valley. He raised his voice and shouted: "Baal is dead: what will happen to the peoples? Dagan's son: what will happen to the masses?"

Meanwhile, Anat independently discovers Baal's corpse, and she too mourns in the same formulaic fashion. Afterward, with the help of Sun, she brings Baal's body back to Mount Zaphon, where she buries him and offers the appropriate funerary sacrifice. Then she heads toward El's abode, where her announcement of Baal's death occasions El's suggestion to Asherah that one of her sons replace Baal as king; at least two try and are found wanting.

After a considerable gap in the text, Anat is described as she is about to encounter Death:

> Like the heart of a cow for her calf, like the heart of a ewe for her lamb, so was Anat's heart for Baal.

Anat grabs Death's clothes and insists that he give up her brother; Death refuses, or at least is unable to grant her request. Time passes; in Baal's absence the forces of drought and sterility are dominant; "the heavens shimmered under the sway of El's son, Death." Again Anat approaches Death; no words are exchanged, but this time Baal's sister is as violent in grief as she is in battle:

> She seized El's son, Death: with a sword she split him; with a sieve she winnowed him; with a fire she burned him; with a hand-mill she ground him; in the field she sowed him.

This agricultural imagery is striking: for Baal, the dead god of fertility, to be restored to life and for Death, the living god of sterility, to be destroyed, the mysterious processes of the natural cycle have to be ritually repeated. It is important to note that this is not the ordinary annual cycle but rather the periodic disaster that a prolonged drought can cause; if the life-giving winter rains are to fail, there will be no crops, no food for animals or humans. In myth this is represented by the struggle between Baal and Death; with Baal dead, the forces of sterility prevail, and Baal can be revivified only by Death's death. Only if Death, whose appetite is insatiable, whose gaping jaws have swallowed up Baal like a lamb or a kid, is himself swallowed up, can Baal's power return.

In the next scene, El has a prophetic dream in which he foresees Baal's restoration and its effects:

> In a dream of El, the Kind, the Compassionate, in a vision of the Creator of Creatures, the heavens rained down oil, the wadis ran with honey.

Baal is restored to power, and as a later heir of Canaanite tradition would put it (*1 Cor.* 15:54–55):

> Death is swallowed up in victory. Where, O Death, is your victory? Where, O Death, is your sting?

(Compare *Isaiah* 25:8 and *Hosea* 13:14.)

The Baal cycle does not quite end here; there remain his revenge on his rivals and yet another successful struggle with Death after a seven-year interval. The latter confirms the analysis of this last episode as the mythical representation of an occasional rather than an annual event.

The relationship between El and Baal is complex. On a narrative level, it is difficult not to sense El's less than enthusiastic acceptance of Baal's dominion. In the first episode he is willing to hand Baal over to Sea, "El's Beloved"; in the second, both he and Asherah are scornful of Baal's position, for "he has no house like the other gods"; and in the third, despite his real (although stylized) grief at Baal's death, he is quick to suggest replacements from his own family. Furthermore, throughout the cycle El remains the head of the pantheon and presides over the council of the gods. Yet this very cycle, the most extensive among the surviving texts from Ugarit, tells of Baal's rise to some kind of preeminence. At the very least it can be suggested that Canaanite ideology was not static, and the mythological literature reflects this fluidity. While Baal had become the patron god of Ugarit, this did not mean that its citizens rejected either the worship of El or the traditional understanding of his role in the world of the gods.

Other mythological texts. In other texts from the same archaeological context as the Baal cycle, El has a dominant, sometimes even an exclusive, role. There follows a discussion of some of the better-preserved texts that also have to do with the Canaanite gods.

Birth of the beautiful and gracious gods. Unlike the other texts treated here, this tablet (of which some seventy-six lines survive) combines mythological material with ritual rubrics; the former is apparently the accompanying libretto for the action prescribed by the latter.

The central portion of the tablet describes the conception and birth of the deities Dawn (Shahar, probably the morning star) and Dusk (Shalim, the evening star). As it opens, El is at the seashore, where two women became aroused as they observe his virility:

> El's hand [a euphemism] grew as long as the Sea, El's hand as long as the Ocean.

In language full of double entendre, the text relates how El shoots and cooks a bird, and then seduces the women:

> The two women became El's wives, El's wives forever and ever. He bowed low, he kissed their lips; behold, their lips were sweet, as sweet as pomegranates. When they kissed, they conceived, when they embraced, they became pregnant; they began labor and gave birth to Dawn and Dusk.

Two divine sons are thus sired by El, who is in full possession of his vigor and virility. As his offspring, they "suck nipples of the Lady's breasts"; "the Lady" is El's principal consort, the goddess Asherah. But the two young gods have insatiable appetites, comparable (because the same formula is used) to that of Death himself:

> One lip to the earth, one lip to the heavens: into their mouths entered the birds of the heavens and the fish in the sea.

So, at El's command, they are banished to the desert; after seven years they are finally allowed to reenter the land by "the guard of the sown." Here the text breaks off.

This summary does not begin to deal with the many problems of interpretation posed by the laconic text, nor is it clear how the first portion of the tablet is related to the material just recounted. The tablet begins with a first-person invocation to "the beautiful and gracious gods," almost certainly Dawn and Dusk, who are minor but established figures in the Ugaritic pantheon; Dawn also occurs in biblical tradition (*Is.* 14:12). Their exile in the desert may be a mythical explanation of their perceived origin: in the ancient view both day and night rose in the east, and from the Canaanites' perspective the eastern limit of their territory was the great Syrian desert.

The details of the ritual, in which particular words and actions are to be repeated seven times and performed in the presence of the king, queen, and royal court, are highly obscure. Various deities are mentioned, various sacrifices are to be offered, and while there are some verbal connections with the mythic section, it is difficult to interpret the whole with coherence; yet it is improbable that the two parts are not somehow related. What is clear is that the myth depicts El with full enjoyment of his generative powers, and it is likely that the concern underlying both the ritual and the narrative parts is the maintenance of fertility.

Marriage of Nikkal and the moon god. This relatively brief text is a kind of epithalamium, or wedding hymn, celebrating the marriage of the moon god (Yarih), "the heavens' lamp," to Nikkal wa-Ib. The first part of the latter's composite name is ultimately derived from the Sumerian title of the moon goddess Ningal, "great lady," and its second half is connected with the word for "fruit." The tablet opens with an invocation of Nikkal and Hirhib, an otherwise unknown deity called "the king of summer," and then tells of the Moon's passion for Nikkal. To obtain his intended bride he uses the services of Hirhib, the divine marriage broker, offering to pay her father as bride-price a thousand silver pieces, ten thousand gold pieces, and gems of lapis lazuli.

Hirhib suggests that Moon marry instead Baal's daughter Pidray ("misty") or someone else, but Moon is adamant; the marriage with Nikkal is arranged, and the bride-price is paid:

> Her father set the beam of the scales; her mother the trays of the scales; her brothers arranged the standards; her sisters took care of the weights.

This portion of the tablet ends with another invocation: "Let me sing of Nikkal wa-Ib, the light of Moon; may Moon give you light."

The brief second part of the tablet consists of another hymnic invocation of the goddesses of childbirth, the Wise Women (Kotharatu). Their presence, as in the account of the birth of Aqhat (see below), guarantees the conception and safe delivery of babies.

El's banquet. This short tablet provides a candid glimpse of the gods, and especially El, as they participate in a ritual symposium. El invites the gods to his house, where he has prepared a feast; among those present are Moon, Astarte, and Anat.

> The gods ate and drank; they drank wine until they were full, new wine until they were drunk.

At this point the party becomes rowdy, and El's gatekeeper rebukes the guests; El too is chided, apparently for allowing the unruly behavior. Then, however, El himself becomes intoxicated and decides to retire; en route he has an alcoholic hallucination of a figure with two horns and a tail (a possible satanic prototype). Despite the support of two attendants,

> He fell in his excrement and urine, El fell like a dead man, El, like those who go down into the earth.

In other words, he is dead drunk. The reverse side of the tablet is extremely fragmentary, but, appropriately, it seems to contain a remedy for hangovers.

In the middle of the text, El is described as seated, or enthroned, in his *mrzḥ* ("symposium"). The *mrzḥ* (Hebrew *marzeaḥ*) was a chronologically and geographically widespread ritual institution, mentioned several times in texts from Ugarit (including once in the fragmentary Rephaim texts, discussed below), twice in the Bible (*Jer.* 16:5, *Am.* 6:7), and in Phoenician/Punic texts from Sidon and Marseilles. It is also mentioned in Aramaic texts from Elephantine in Egypt, from Petra in Jordan, and from Palmyra in Syria. Scholars disagree as to the precise character of this institution, especially its possible connection with funereal practices and memorials; there is no doubt that this text contains at least part of its mythological background.

EPIC TEXTS. The two major Canaanite literary cycles with human protagonists are *Aqhat* and *Kirta.* As in more familiar classical heroic epics, however, and as in other ancient Near Eastern sources, such as the Mesopotamian Gilgamesh epic, the gods play a significant role in the narrative; from a temporal point of view, actions in both the divine and human realms occur on a single continuum. Thus, while a specific time is not indicated in either of these two texts, the time frame in which the narrative takes place is historical at least in the sense that the cosmic order has been established.

Aqhat. This title is an ancient one, appearing as a cataloging device at the beginning of the third major tablet of the cycle that is preserved. Nevertheless, the story is part of a larger one about Aqhat's father, Danel, a royal figure whose righteousness and wisdom were legendary (see *Ez.* 14:14, 20; 28:2). The surviving remnants of the cycle deal with the relationship of Danel and his son, and as the extant story begins, Danel is described performing a seven-day incubation ritual, occasioned by his lack of progeny.

A period of seven days or seven years occurs some five times in *Aqhat,* and elsewhere in the Ugaritic corpus as well: Baal's initial defeat of Death lasted seven years, and in the Aqhat text (see below), Danel cursed the land by calling for an absence of Baal's generative powers:

> "For seven years let Baal fail, eight, the Rider on the Clouds: no dew, no showers, no surging of the double deep, no benefit of Baal's voice."

This is reminiscent of the alternation of seven years of plenty and seven of famine in the biblical story of Joseph. The frequent use of the number seven applies to days as well; in both the Ugaritic texts and the Bible, seven days is the conventional length of a journey, and the revelation about to be made to Danel recalls God's call to Moses on the seventh day *(Ex.* 24:16). Other biblical examples include the seven days of creation at the beginning of *Genesis* and the literal tour de force of the collapse of Jericho, which occurred on the seventh day after seven priests blowing on seven trumpets had marched seven times around the city. It is unlikely that this repeated use of seven is much more than literary convention, but its frequent occurrence in Ugaritic and biblical literatures underscores the close relationship between them.

On the seventh and final day of Danel's ritual, Baal, Danel's patron, addresses the assembly of the gods on Danel's behalf:

> "Unlike his brothers, he has no son; no heir, like his cousins; yet he has made an offering for the gods to eat, an offering for the holy ones to drink."

In response, El blesses Danel and then catalogs the benefits that a son will provide:

> "When he kisses his wife she will become pregnant; when he embraces her she will conceive: she will become pregnant, she will give birth, she will conceive; and there will be a son in his house, an heir inside his palace, to set up a stela for his divine ancestor, a family shrine in the sanctuary; to free his spirit from the earth, guard his footsteps from the Slime; to crush those who rebel against him, drive off his oppressors; to eat his offering in the temple of Baal, his portion in the temple of El; to hold his hand when he is drunk, support him when he is full of wine; to patch his roof when it leaks, wash his clothes when they are dirty."

Heartened by the divine promise, Danel returns to his palace, where with the assistance of the Wise Women, the goddesses of marriage and childbirth, conception occurs after seven days.

This list of ritual and personal filial duties suggests that one of the epic's purposes was didactic: to school its audience in proper social behavior, which included not only the responsibilities of a son to his father but the model conduct of kings, of daughters and sisters, and in fact, of all humans in their complex relationships with one another and with the gods.

The picture of the childless patriarch is a commonplace in Canaanite literature. In the Ugaritic texts, the opening of *Kirta* (see below) is remarkably similar to that of the Danel cycle, and in *Genesis,* Abraham, Isaac, and Jacob each are initially either childless or lacking descendants from their favorite or principal wives. In each case, offspring are promised by their patron deity: in Abraham's case, in the context of a nocturnal revelation, like Danel's (*Gn.* 15), and in Isaac's, in response to a prayer by the patriarch (*Gn.* 25:21). In the more extensive Jacob cycle, the promise of numerous descendants is made at night (*Gn.* 28:11–17) and is granted in response to Jacob's favorite wife Rachel's specific prayer (*Gn.* 30:22). The stories of Hannah (Samuel's mother), of Samson's parents, and to some extent of Job are further variations of this motif. In the biblical narratives of Israel's ancestors as preserved in *Genesis* it is further significant that the patron deity who pronounces the blessing on each patriarch, although called Yahweh in the present sources, is elsewhere unequivocally identified as El (see *Ex.* 6:3; cf. *Gn.* 14:19–20; 49:25). As his epithets in biblical literature and especially in Genesis make clear, this is none other than the head of the Canaanite pantheon. It is noteworthy that in *Aqhat,* even though Baal is Danel's patron (as his epithet, "the Healer's man," indicates), the blessing is given by El; Baal acts only as mediator between the childless king and "El, the Bull, the Creator of Creatures."

The middle third of this first of the cycle's three tablets is missing; in this section the birth of Danel's son Aqhat must have been related. The story then resumes. As Danel is engaged in typical royal judicial activity at the city gate, judging the cases of widows and orphans, he sees Kothar approaching with a bow and arrows. The divine craftsman gives this weapon to Danel as a gift for his son; after a suitable feast, prepared by Danel's wife for their divine guest, the god departs.

In the next episode Anat, having seen the wonderfully crafted weapon, offers to buy it from Aqhat; the latter refuses, proposing instead that he will supply the raw materials necessary for the construction of another one by Kothar. Anat goes further:

> "If you want life, Aqhat the Hero, if you want life, I'll give it to you, immortality—I'll make it yours. You'll be able to match years with Baal, months with the sons of El."

Again Aqhat refuses, and this time his response goes beyond the proper limits:

> "Don't lie to me, Virgin, for to a hero your lies are trash. A mortal—what does he get in the end? what does a mortal finally get? Plaster poured on his head, lime on top of his skull. As every man dies, I will die; yes, I too will surely die. And I have something else to tell you: bows are for men! Do women ever hunt?"

The first part of Aqhat's response, while realistic, is bad enough: he implicitly denies Anat's ability to provide what she had promised, because from his perspective, old age and death are inescapable. But in insulting her prowess with such weapons, Aqhat is challenging the goddess's very essence. Anat replies with a characteristically furious threat, and goes to report the matter to El.

The second and shortest tablet of the cycle retains only two of its original four columns. In the first column El accedes, apparently with reluctance, to Anat's insistence on revenge, and in the last Anat carries out her threat:

> When Aqhat sat down to eat, the son of Danel to his meal, vultures swooped over him, a flock of birds soared above. Among the vultures swooped Anat; she set him [Yatpan, Anat's henchman] over Aqhat. He struck him twice on the skull, three times over the ear; like a slaughterer he made his blood run, like a butcher, run to his knees. His breath left him like wind, his spirit like a breeze, like smoke from his nostrils.

The end of this tablet and the beginning of the next are badly broken; apparently Anat regrets her action, at least in part because while Aqhat was being killed his bow dropped into the sea.

When the text becomes legible, Danel is again sitting at the gate presiding over legal matters. His daughter Pughat notices that the vegetation has withered and that vultures are swooping over her father's house; both are clear signs of violent, unnatural death. With his clothes torn in mourning, Danel

> cursed the clouds in the still heat, the rain of the clouds that falls in summer, the dew that drops on the grapes.

Thus, Danel invokes a seven-year drought (see above), the absence of Baal's pluvial benefits. Then, at her father's instructions, Pughat,

> who got up early to draw water, who brushed the dew from the barley, who knew the course of the stars, in tears she harnessed the ass, in tears she roped up the donkey, in tears she lifted her father, she put him on the ass's back, on the splendid back of the donkey.

At this point neither Danel nor Pughat is aware of Aqhat's death; together they set out on a tour of the blasted fields. There, Danel poignantly wishes that they could be restored, so that

> "the hand of Aqhat the Hero would harvest you, place you in the granary."

While they are still in the fields, messengers appear and relate the facts of Aqhat's death. Danel is stricken:

> His feet shook, his face broke out in sweat, his back was as though shattered, his joints trembled, his vertebrae weakened.

Finally, Danel lifts up his eyes, sees the vultures overhead, and curses them:

> "May Baal shatter the vultures' wings, may Baal shatter their pinions; let them fall at my feet. I will split their gizzards and look: if there is fat, if there is bone, I will weep and I will bury him, I will put him into the hole of the gods of the earth."

Three times Danel examines the innards of various vultures for remains of Aqhat; they are found at last inside Samal, the mother of vultures, and presumably are given proper burial. Danel then curses the three cities near the scene of the crime and returns to his palace to begin the mourning period. For seven years the mourning goes on, and at its conclusion Danel dismisses the mourners and offers the appropriate sacrifice.

In the last surviving brief episode, Pughat asks her father's benediction:

> "Bless me, that I may go with your blessing; favor me, that I may go with your favor: I will kill my brother's

killer, put an end to whoever put an end to my mother's son."

The blessing having been given, Pughat, like the Jewish heroine Judith, applies cosmetics and puts on her finery, under which she hides a sword. She reaches Yatpan's tent at sundown, and he welcomes her, boasting:

"The hand that killed Aqhat the Hero can kill a thousand enemies."

Our text ends tantalizingly:

Twice she gave him wine to drink, she gave him wine to drink.

Interpretation of this epic is difficult because of the gaps in the narrative and the abrupt break at the end of the preserved portion, but some light is shed on the main lines of the story by other ancient sources. The encounter between Anat and Aqhat is reminiscent of similar episodes in classical literatures, and especially of a portion of the Gilgamesh epic. There, the goddess Ishtar (Inanna) tries to seduce Gilgamesh; he repudiates her advances and reminds her in arrogant, insulting detail how she had behaved toward other mortals she had loved after she had finished with them. Ishtar is naturally furious and complains bitterly to her father, Anu, the head of the pantheon. At first he resists her desire to take revenge on Gilgamesh by setting against him a powerful animal adversary, the Bull of Heaven, telling her that if her request is granted there will be seven years of drought. Finally, however, Anu relents, when Ishtar tells him that she has stored up sufficient grain and fodder.

The parallels between this episode and *Aqhat* are numerous and striking, but there are also significant differences. While Ishtar is the Mesopotamian counterpart of Anat, a goddess of love and of war, Gilgamesh and Aqhat are not simply literary cultural variants. In particular, it seems unlikely that the bow in the Ugaritic epic is a symbolic substitute for Aqhat's sexual organ: because it had been manufactured by Kothar, a substitute could be made for it, and after Aqhat's death it dropped into the sea.

The Egyptian myth of Osiris offers another avenue of comparison. In that tale Isis, the sister (and wife) of the dead Osiris, retrieves the murdered corpse of her brother, gives it a proper burial, and then encourages their son Horus to avenge his father's death; Osiris is, significantly, the god of the regenerating vegetation.

It seems, then, that the Gilgamesh, Osiris, and Aqhat cycles have a common thread, the threat to continued fertility. Extrapolating from these links, it is likely first that Pughat does avenge her brother's death, probably by destroying Anat's henchman Yatpan—it turns out that women hunt after all! Second, given the importance assigned to Danel's lack of an heir and the positive recollection of him in *Ezekiel*, it is difficult not to assume that he, like Job, is granted rehabilitation, that the land is restored to production, and that a substitute son is born, all in other episodes of the Danel cycle not yet discovered.

The Rephaim texts. Three other tablets, extremely fragmentary ones, give some hint of the outcome of the story. Like most of the texts treated in this article, they were written down by Ilimilku, and because one of them mentions Danel by name, they are part of the larger Danel tradition. Most scholars refer to them as the Rephaim texts, after the Hebrew pronunciation of the name of their principal figures, the Rephaim; this title is probably to be translated (despite the Hebrew vocalization) as "the Healers," although some scholars prefer "the Healthy (or Healed) Ones." These "Healers" seem to have been minor deities of the underworld. (See *Job* 26:5; in other biblical passages the term *Rephaim* is used for the legendary pre-Israelite inhabitants of the land of Canaan, probably by extension from the sense of the deified dead.) They also seem to have been connected with Baal; recall Danel's epithet, "the Healer's man."

In these texts the Healers visit Danel's threshing floor and plantation, presumably to restore them. Four broken lines read as follows:

"Behold your son, behold . . . your grandson . . . the small one will kiss your lips."

It is tempting to see here the promise, if not the fact, of a new heir for Danel. It has even been conjectured that Aqhat himself was restored to life, somewhat analogously to Baal's resurrection, but this is unlikely because Aqhat was human, not divine, and he himself had stated the Canaanite view of mortality: "As every man dies, I will die."

Kirta. This epic, consisting of three tablets, is incomplete: at least one additional tablet is missing, for the third ends abruptly in mid-sentence. Its eponymous hero, Kirta (a name also vocalized as Keret), was, like Danel, a king, and as the story begins he too has no heir. As he laments his lot, he has a revelatory dream in which El appears to him; parallels in *Aqhat* and in the ancestral stories of *Genesis* indicate that his sleep may have been part of a formal incubation ritual. El's instructions to Kirta amount to more than ninety lines of text, and they are immediately repeated, with only minor variations, as the childless ruler carries out the divine commands.

First, Kirta offers a sacrifice to the gods, and then he prepares an army for his campaign against King Pabil of Udm, whose daughter, the Lady Hurraya, is to be given to Kirta as his wife. There is almost universal conscription:

The bachelor closed his house; the widow hired a substitute; the sick man carried his bed; the blind man was assigned a station; even the new husband came out: he led his wife to another, his love to a stranger.

This army proceeds like a swarm of locusts for three days, after which it arrives at the sanctuary of Asherah of Tyre. There Kirta vows that if his suit is successful, he will donate double the bride-price to the goddess. On the evening of the seventh day he reaches Udm and lays siege to the city:

They attacked the cities, they raided the towns; they drove the woodcutters from the fields, and the gatherers

> of straw from the threshing floors; they drove the water carriers from the well, and the women filling their jars from the spring.

After seven days of siege Pabil begins to negotiate, offering Kirta silver, gold, slaves, and chariots. But Kirta rejects these, insisting that there is only one thing he wants:

> "Give me rather what is not in my house: give me the Lady Hurraya, the fairest of your firstborn: her fairness is like Anat's, her beauty is like Astarte's, her eyebrows are lapis lazuli, her eyes are jeweled bowls."

This is the end of the narrative of Kirta's fulfillment of El's command, and also the conclusion of the first tablet. The beginning of the second tablet is damaged; as the text resumes, Pabil accedes to Kirta's suit, with regret:

> "As a cow lows for her calf, as recruits long for their mothers, so will the Udmites sigh."

After some missing lines, the council of the gods assembles in procession. Some of them are listed: the Bull (El), Baal the Conqueror, Prince Moon, Kothar-wa-Hasis, the Maiden (Anat), and Prince Resheph. This assembly gathers to witness El's blessing, at Baal's behest, of Kirta's marriage:

> "Kirta, you have taken a wife, you have taken a wife into your house, you have brought a maiden into your court. She will bear seven sons for you, she will produce eight for you; she will bear Yassib the Lad, who will drink the milk of Asherah, suck the breasts of the Virgin Anat, the two wet nurses of the gods."

The close association with the gods of the offspring of royal but human parents is a feature of the Canaanite ideology of kingship.

Seven years passed, and El's blessing proves effective, but Asherah is angry because Kirta has forgotten his vow. Meanwhile, Kirta plans a feast for his nobles, but during its preparation he is stricken with a mortal disease, apparently as a punishment from Asherah.

As the third tablet opens, Kirta's son Ilha'u is expressing consternation at his father's illness:

> "How can it be said that Kirta is El's son, an offspring of the Kind and Holy One? Or do the gods die? Do the Kind One's offspring not live on?"

Ilha'u shares his dismay with his sister Thitmanit ("the eighth," or Octavia), who repeats her brother's words of confusion. After another gap the text tells of the disastrous consequences of Kirta's illness:

> The plowmen lifted their heads, the sowers of grain their backs: gone was the food from their bins, gone was the wine from their skins, gone was the oil from their vats.

Again there is a break in the text, and then El intervenes personally; he asks the divine council seven times if any of their number can cure Kirta, "but none of the gods answered him." Finally he takes the task upon himself:

> "I will work magic, I will bring relief; I will expel the sickness, I will drive out the disease."

To do so he takes clay and creates the goddess Shataqat (whose name means "she causes [disease] to pass away"), then sends her to Kirta. She succeeds; "Death was broken," and Kirta's appetite returns.

In the final scene, after Kirta has been restored to his throne, his rule is challenged by one of his sons on the ground that because of his weakness, he has ceased to perform the expected functions of a king:

> "You do not judge the cases of widows; you do not preside over the hearings of the oppressed; you do not drive out those who plunder the poor; you do not feed the orphan before you, the widow behind your back."

Kirta's response is to curse his son, praying that Horon, an underworld deity, and Astarte, "the name of Baal," will smash his son's skull.

The plot of the *Kirta* cycle is relatively straightforward (at least where the text is continuous). *Kirta* also provides a perspective on the Canaanite ideology of kingship. Among the duties of the king was to maintain the social order; he did so by his effective support of the powerless in society—the poor, widows, orphans—all groups who are mentioned in innumerable ancient Near Eastern sources as the special responsibility of kings, both divine and human. Thus, his son's attempted coup to seize Kirta's throne was motivated by the alleged lack of justice for the powerless; Absalom's revolt against his father, King David, in *2 Samuel* 15 was initially successful because Absalom was able to appeal to a similar failure in the royal administration of justice. Another aspect of the maintenance of the social order was the provision for an orderly succession; Kirta's (and Danel's) desire for male descendants was prompted by the recognition of this royal responsibility.

The most complex feature of Canaanite royal ideology, however, was the quasi-divine status of the king; as the repeated question of Kirta's children—"Do the Kind One's offspring not live on?"—shows, it was puzzling to the Canaanites as well. The *Kirta* cycle probably recounts the legendary tale of the founder of a Canaanite dynasty. While there is evidence that the kings of Ugarit, like those of the Hittites, were deified after their death, there is no suggestion of actual divine parentage for them. Kirta's epithet "El's son" must therefore have a nonbiological sense, expressing in mythological language the close connection between human and divine rule. Thus, just as Baal was responsible for the continuing fertility of the earth, which failed during the period of his subjugation to Death, so the king shared in this responsibility; when Kirta was ill, the natural order was upset. (Psalm 72, one of the Israelite royal hymns, is an extended elaboration of the positive connection of natural prosperity with the king.)

The evidence of a number of biblical passages that speak of the king as the son of Yahweh is instructive here. The language of divine sonship is not just a literary device but seems to have been part of the actual coronation ceremony, in which the newly anointed king would proclaim:

> "I will tell of Yahweh's decree. He said to me, 'You are my son; this day I have given birth to you.'" (*Ps.* 2:7)

Similar language is found in *2 Samuel* 7:14 and in *Isaiah* 9:2–7, a prophetic coronation oracle, the divine council itself proclaims:

> "To us a child has been born, to us a son has been given."

The language of sonship also occurs in *Psalms* 89:26, immediately after a passage that expresses in the clearest way the close relationship between deity and king. Earlier in the psalm Yahweh is praised as the one who (like Baal) rules the raging of the sea, scattering his enemies with his mighty arms (vv. 9–10); in verse 23, using the traditional parallel formula for the storm god's enemy, the deity states that he will share his cosmic powers with the Davidic king:

> "I will set his hand on the sea, and on the rivers his right hand."

CONCLUSION. This article has dealt primarily with the corpus of Canaanite literature from Ugarit and has not discussed in detail the many other Canaanite sources extant. Most prominent among these are hundreds of inscriptions from the first millennium BCE in the Phoenician, Aramaic, Hebrew, Moabite, Ammonite, and Edomite languages; references to Canaanite religion in various Greek and Roman writers; and, more remotely, scattered material in Mesopotamian sources. It should be realized, however, that with rare exceptions, this material is not literature in the sense in which the term has been interpreted above.

Throughout this article there has also been an effort to adumbrate the significance of the Ugaritic texts for the interpretation of the other great corpus of literature that may be subsumed in the designation *Canaanite*—the Bible. Much more could be added on this topic, including discussion of the council of the gods; the enthronement festival of the deity as represented in *Psalms*; and, in general, the pervasive use of Canaanite imagery, formulas, and ideology by biblical writers, especially when describing the character and activity of Yahweh. The writers were themselves aware of this relationship and the problems it raised; this partially explains the consistent portrayal of ancient Israel as—at least in the ideal—a people set apart from their historical context, their hostility toward their non-Yahwistic neighbors, and the insistence on the uniqueness of Yahweh. Yet biblical tradition can, on occasion, be remarkably candid about the origins of Israel and its culture. In the light of Canaanite religious and mythological literature, the declaration of the prophet Ezekiel to Jerusalem is strikingly apposite: "Your origin and your birth are of the land of the Canaanites" (*Ez.* 16:3).

BIBLIOGRAPHY

The official publication of the major Ugaritic texts is Andrée Herdner, *Corpus des tablettes en cunéiformes alphabétiques découvertes à Ras Shamra-Ugarit de 1929 à 1939* (Paris, 1963); the first volume contains the texts, preceded by extensive bibliographies and copiously annotated, and the second contains photographs and hand copies. The standard edition used by most scholars is Manfred Dietrich, Oswald Loretz, and Joaquín Sanmartín, *The Cuneiform Alphabetic Texts from Ugarit, Ras Ibn Hani, and Other Places,* 2d ed. (Munster, Germany, 1995); it is generally abbreviated as *CAT* (or sometimes *KTU,* from the title of the original German edition).

Several accessible translations for the general reader exist. The translations in this article are the author's own, revised from those first published in Michael David Coogan, *Stories from Ancient Canaan* (Philadelphia, 1978) and used by permission of Westminster John Knox Press. That work also includes helpful introductions to each of the four cycles that are translated, as well as to the Canaanite material from Ugarit in general. The best recent translation of the Ugaritic texts into English is Simon B. Parker, ed., *Ugaritic Narrative Poetry* (Atlanta, 1997), in which translations by a number of scholars are juxtaposed to transcriptions of the original Ugaritic; unfortunately there is no consistency in this volume, so that the same Ugaritic words and phrases are translated differently by different scholars. Also important are Gregorio del Olmo Lete, *Mitos, leyendas y rituales de los semitas occidentales,* 2d ed. (Madrid, 1998), and the translations, mostly by Dennis Pardee, found in William W. Hallo, ed., *The Context of Scripture,* vol. 1, *Canonical Compositions from the Biblical World* (Leiden, 1997), pp. 237–375. Nicolas Wyatt, *Religious Texts from Ugarit: The Words of Ilimilku and His Colleagues,* 2d ed. (London and New York, 2002), which includes a number of ritual texts as well as the myths and epics considered here, is often idiosyncratic. Among older versions, especially valuable are *Textes ougaritiques,* vol. 1 of *Mythes et légendes,* by André Caquot, Maurice Sznycer, and Andrée Herdner (Paris, 1974), and *Canaanite Myths and Legends,* by John C. L. Gibson, 2d ed (Edinburgh, 1978).

A number of studies have been devoted to individual myths and epics. Among the best are Mark S. Smith, *The Ugaritic Baal Cycle* (Leiden, 1994), and Simon B. Parker, *The Pre-biblical Narrative Tradition: Essays on the Ugaritic Poems Keret and Aqhat* (Atlanta, 1989). It is also important to understand the myths and epics in the larger context of the ritual texts from Ugarit; a good starting point is Gregorio del Olmo Lete, *Canaanite Religion according to the Liturgical Texts of Ugarit* (Bethesda, Md., 1999), translated by W. G. E. Watson.

Grammars and dictionaries are also important resources. Among the most comprehensive are Gregorio del Olmo Lete and Joaquín Sanmartín, *A Dictionary of the Ugaritic Language in the Alphabetic Tradition* (Leiden, 2003), translated by Wilfred G. E. Watson, and Josef Tropper, *Ugaritische Grammatik* (Munster, Germany, 2000).

Since their discovery and decipherment, the Ugaritic texts have been the focus of a steady stream of investigation. A useful summary of the history of scholarship is Mark S. Smith, *Untold Stories: The Bible and Ugaritic Studies in the Twentieth Century* (Peabody, Mass., 2001). A fuller view of Ugaritic studies at the turn of the millennium is provided by the essays in *Handbook of Ugaritic Studies,* edited by Wilfred G. E. Watson and Nicolas Wyatt (Leiden, 1999). See also the lengthy review of that volume, providing many corrections especially on matters of detail, by Dennis Pardee, "Ugaritic Studies at the End of the 20th Century," *Bulletin of the*

American Schools of Oriental Research 320 (November 2000): 49–86.

MICHAEL D. COOGAN (1987 AND 2005)

CANDOMBLÉ SEE AFRO-BRAZILIAN RELIGIONS

CANDRAKĪRTI

CANDRAKĪRTI (Tib., Zla ba grags pa; Chin., Yuecheng; Jpn., Gesshō), Indian Buddhist dialectician. Scholars have identified at least three Candrakīrtis. The first, who will be referred to as "Candrakīrti I," was a renowned Madhyamaka (Mādhyamika) philosopher who lived around 600–650 CE; the second, "Candrakīrti II," was a Tantric master assumed to have lived slightly later than the former; and the third, "Candrakīrti III," was a Buddhist thinker of the eleventh century. Biographies are available only in Tibetan sources such as the histories of Bu ston, Tāranātha, and Sumpa mkhan po. These sources are not particularly helpful to the historian, for they tend to confuse history and legend and freely interchange the lives of the three Candrakīrtis. This did not pose a great problem in Tibet, however, for the Tibetan tradition acknowledges only one Candrakīrti, who lived for three or four hundred years.

Candrakīrti I wrote several important commentaries on the works of Nāgārjuna and Āryadeva: (1) the *Prasannapadā* (available in Sanskrit in Bibliotheca Buddhica 4, hereafter cited as Bibl. Bud.), a commentary on Nāgārjuna's *Mūlamadhyamakakārikā*; (2) the *Yuktiṣaṣṭikāvṛtti* (Derge edition of the Tibetan Tripiṭaka 3864, hereafter cited as D.; Beijing edition of the Tibetan Tripiṭaka 5265, hereafter cited as B.); (3) the *Śūnyatā-saptativṛtti* (D. 3867, B. 5268); and (4) the *Catuḥśatakaṭīkā* (D. 3865, B. 5266, partially available in Sanskrit), a commentary on Āryadeva's *Catuḥśataka.* He also composed works of his own inspiration: (1) the *Madhyamakāvatāra,* with its autocommentary, the *Madhyamakāvatārabhāṣya* (Tib. edition in Bibl. Bud. 9), an introduction to the basic Madhyamaka treatise of Nāgārjuna; and (2) the *Pañcaskandhaprakaraṇa* (Tib. edition, Lindtner, 1979), a treatise on Abhidharma topics (five aggregates, twelve bases, and eighteen elements) from the Madhyamaka point of view. Opinions differ concerning the authorship of the work titled *Triśaraṇa[gamana]saptati* (D. 3971, 4564; B. 5366, 5478). According to Lindtner it was composed by Candrakīrti I, but according to Ruegg (1981), by Candrakīrti II. As to the chronological order of these treatises, one can only state with certainty that the *Madhyamakāvatāra* (probably with the autocommentary) was composed before the two large commentaries, the *Prasannapadā* and the *Catuḥśatakaṭīkā,* since both of the latter refer to the former.

Candrakīrti I expounded the Madhyamaka philosophy of Nāgārjuna and defended the position of Buddhapālita (c. 470–540) against the criticism of Bhāvaviveka (c. 500–570), who had wanted to adopt independent inferences. Candrakīrti I thus tried to reestablish the *prasaṅga* method of reasoning. Tibetan doxographers accordingly classified him with Buddhapālita as representative of the Prāsaṅgika school. He also lodged criticism against the doctrines of the Buddhist logico-epistemological school and the metaphysical and gnoseological theories of the Yogācāra-Vijñānavāddins.

Candrakīrti II composed a few Tantric works, the most important of which is the *Pradīpoddyotana* (D. 1785, B. 2650), a commentary on the *Guhyasamāja Tantra.* Candrakīrti III composed the *Madhyamakāvatāraprajñā* or *Madhyamakaprajñāvatāra* (D. 3865, B. 5264) and together with the translator 'Gos khug pa lhas btsas translated it into Tibetan. If the identification of Dpal ldan zla ba with Candrakīrti III is correct, this same pair of translators also translated Kṛṣṇapāda's commentary on the *Hevajra Tantra* (D. 1187, B. 2317). 'Gos khug pa lhas btsas also translated the *Pradīpoddyotana* with Rin chen bzang po (958–1055) and others. We can thus fix the date of Candrakīrti III within the eleventh century.

Although Candrakīrti I and III are certainly two different people, it may be possible that Candrakīrti II is identical with either Candrakīrti I or III. Research on this point remains open.

SEE ALSO Mādhyamika.

BIBLIOGRAPHY

Lindtner, Christian. "*Candrakīrti's Pañcaskandhaprakaraṇa.*" *Acta Orientalia* 40 (1979): 87–145.

May, Jacques, trans. *Candrakīrti, Prasannapadā Madhyamakavtti: Commentaire limpide au traité du milieu.* Paris, 1959.

Ruegg, David S. *The Literature of the Madhyamaka School of Philosophy in India.* Wiesbaden, 1981.

New Sources

Āryadeva, Candrakīrti, and Karen Lang, "Aryadeva and Candrakīrti on Self and Selfishness" In *Buddhism in Practice,* edited by Donald S. Lopez, Jr., pp. 380–398. Princeton, 1995.

Jong, J. W. de. "Materials for the Study of Aryadeva, Dharmapala and Candrakirti: The Catuhsataka of Aryadeva, Chapters 12–13, 2 V." *Indo Iranian Journal* 36 (1993): 150–153.

Scherrer Schaub, Cristina. "Tendance de la pensee de Candrakirti, Buddhajnana et Jinakriya." *Buddhist Forum* 3 (1994): 249–272.

MIMAKI KATSUMI (1987)
Revised Bibliography

CANISIUS, PETER

CANISIUS, PETER (1521–1597), doctor of the church, Jesuit priest, educator, theologian, and saint. Born at Nijmegen, Peter Canisius was educated at the University of Cologne. Sent by his father, Jakob Kanijs, to study law at Louvain in 1539, Peter, determined to be a priest, returned to Cologne and in 1541 became the first German Jesuit. He helped to found the first German Jesuit house at Cologne and in 1546 was ordained a priest. In 1547, Cardinal Truchsess of Augsburg appointed Canisius as his theologian at the Council of Trent. Between the first and second sessions of the council, Canisius went to Rome for further spiritual training with Ignatius Loyola, founder of the Society of Jesus. From 1548 to 1580 Canisius worked out of Germany, traveling to Austria and Poland as Jesuit provincial, counselor to princes, and founder of Jesuit schools. Three times Emperor Ferdinand I (1556–1564) asked Canisius to become bishop of Vienna, but each time he refused. From 1556 to 1569 Canisius served as the first Jesuit provincial of upper Germany. In 1580 he was sent to Fribourg in Switzerland to help found a Jesuit college; it was his last assignment.

Canisius's primary work was reestablishing Roman Catholicism or strengthening it where it was threatened by Protestantism, especially in Germany, Austria, and Poland. His means were manifold, but chief among them was education through the establishment of twenty Jesuit colleges between 1549 and 1580. From these colleges came staunchly Roman Catholic political and spiritual leaders.

Frequently, Canisius had to deal directly with Protestants, as at Worms in 1557 and at Augsburg in 1566, or indirectly through his advice to Catholic princes to whom he was appointed secret nuncio by the pope. While he dealt severely with heretical books and what he deemed overly lenient policies on the part of princes, he distinguished between obdurate heresy and that of people who had been led astray. These latter should not be coerced, he argued, but persuaded. To prepare Catholics to meet Protestant arguments, Canisius drew up catechisms that, while not attacking Protestants frontally, gave Catholics a thorough grounding in the Catholic side of controversial issues such as justification and the Lord's Supper. Canisius also answered Protestant controversialists, especially the Centuriators, Flacius Illyricus and Johann Wigand, who had prepared the *Magdeburg Centuries*, a century-by-century history interpreted from a Lutheran perspective.

Toward his flock, Canisius was a kindly and practical superior and pastor. He served as cathedral preacher at Augsburg, Innsbruck, and Fribourg, and through his direct and pious sermons won back thousands to the Roman Catholic sacraments. Pope Leo XIII (1898–1903) dubbed Canisius "the second apostle of Germany after Boniface." He was canonized on May 21, 1925 and declared a doctor of the Catholic church by Pope Pius XI.

Bibliography

The best source for Canisius's life is a multivolume edition edited by Otto Braunsberger, *Beati Petri Canisii Societatas Iesu epistulae et acta*, 8 vols. (Freiburg, 1896–1923). Friedrich Streicher has edited a critical edition of Canisius's catechisms: *S. Petri Canisii doctoris ecclesiae catechismi Latini et Germanici*, 2 vols. (Munich, 1933–1936). The *Bibliothèque de la Compagnie de Jésus*, compiled by Carlos Sommervogel (1891; reprint, Paris, 1960), contains a bibliography of Canisius's publications in volume 2, pages 617–688. The standard life of Canisius is by James Brodrick, *St. Peter Canisius, S.J., 1521–1597* (1935; reprint, Baltimore, 1950).

Jill Raitt (1987)

CANNIBALISM is both a concept and a practice that may involve diverse themes of death, food, sacrifice, revenge, aggression, love, and destruction or transformation of human others. The many and varied examples of cannibalism are difficult to summarize, except in terms of the widespread idea of the human body as a powerful symbolic site for defining relations between oneself and others and marking the boundaries of a moral community. In violating the bodily integrity that prevails in ordinary social life, cannibalism signifies an extraordinary transformation or dramatization of relations between those who eat and those who are eaten. When it occurs in religious contexts, the act of consuming human substance commonly represents an exchange between people and cosmic powers, promoting union with the divine or renewing life-sustaining spiritual relations. Such religious meanings may overlap with the social and political significance of consuming enemies to mark one's dominance and superiority—or consuming kin to express love, to distance the spirit of the deceased from the world of the living, or to acquire physical or spiritual qualities contained in the corpse. Thus sacrifice, the aggressive destruction of enemies, and the devoted incorporation or anxious destruction of a loved one's body are all facets of cannibalism that may be present in different cultural contexts.

Cannibalism and Its Complexity of Form. Anthropologists distinguish between endocannibalism, eating a member of one's own social group, and exocannibalism, eating a member of some other group, frequently an enemy. Endocannibalism is most often associated with funerals or other mortuary rites and with themes of sacrifice, familial devotion, reincarnation, and regeneration, as well as group welfare, reproduction, and continuity. Exocannibalism commonly signifies domination, revenge, or destruction of enemies. The distinction between exo- and endocannibalism has limited value in describing the complex forms in which people have ingested human body substances.

The symbolism of the sacrifice and consumption of human offerings pervades religious thought in European and Middle Eastern traditions; this symbolism is explored by Walter Burkert in *Homo Necans* (1983). Cannibalism is a common theme in mythology and folk tales (see Lévi-Strauss, 1969) and, as a practice, it has been reported in Europe, Polynesia, Melanesia, North and South America, and Africa (see Tannahill, 1975; Sanday, 1986; Gordon-Grube, 1988). The occurrences have no simple correlation with patterns of subsistence, ecology, food supply, or other cultural conditions.

In popular imagination and in psychoanalytic analyses such as that of Eli Sagan (1974), cannibalism has commonly been seen as characteristic of primitive communities and magical thought rather than civilization and religion. Such assumptions ignore the variety of cannibalistic practices in complex societies, such as the western European tradition of using human body parts as medicines and the Aztec practice of human sacrifice. As William Arens (1979) has emphasized, exaggerated or unfounded reports of cannibalism are widespread and often have been used as racist propaganda and justification for colonial domination of native peoples. Arguments persist about when and where cannibalism really has existed as an institutionalized, socially accepted practice. Some of the most heated of these debates have focused on Fiji and the circumstances surrounding the death of Captain James Cook in Hawai'i, and on the interpretation of archaeological remains of the ancient Anasazi culture of the southwestern United States. Anthropological scholarship on some of the better-described ethnographic and historical cases has focused on elucidating the cultural beliefs reflected in the diverse historical practices of consuming human body substances.

CANNIBALISM AND THE AZTEC RELIGION. Perhaps the most widely known large-scale practice of human sacrifice and cannibalism is that of the ancient Aztec, as recorded by many early reports. The Aztec religion involved many kinds of offerings, but the Sun, patron of warriors, required human hearts and human blood for nourishment; human sacrifice was therefore essential. The victims were usually prisoners or purchased slaves; during the rituals, their hearts were removed and placed in vessels, and their heads were placed in skull racks. The limbs, and sometimes other portions of the victims' bodies, might be cooked and eaten by the nobles, priests, and wealthy elite, as well as by successful warriors and guests invited to celebratory feasts. Aztec priests also practiced autosacrifice, drawing their own blood as an offering.

Michael Harner (1977) and Marvin Harris (1977) argue that Aztec cannibalism had a nutritional purpose, because the Aztecs of the late prehistoric and early historic period had depleted their game supply and lacked domestic herbivores. Harner and Harris suggest that cannibalism was a response to the pressure of overpopulation and meat shortage, disguised as propitiation of the gods. Their reasoning and claims about the scale of both human sacrifice and food shortages have been disputed by other scholars who emphasize that the public ritual of blood sacrifice was vital in the Aztec religion.

CANNIBALISM IN SYMBOLISM AND MYTH. Among the Kwakiutl of the northwest coast of North America, a major feature of the winter ceremonies was the Hamatsa dancer, who symbolized hunger, craving for human flesh, the fire that transforms, and regurgitation (rebirth), and who was later tamed so as to become a member of society. Here the cannibalistic image is the key to the relation between man and supernatural forces. In the Great Lakes region of Canada and the United States, northern Algonkian legends describe a cannibalistic Windigo monster. Under conditions of winter isolation and the threat of starvation, individuals sometimes developed delusions of being transformed into such a monster (Marano, 1985). The idiom of cannibalism in myth is worldwide and has an extensive range of context and meaning. Claude Lévi-Strauss (1969) points to the universe of oppositions, associations, and transformations of humans and animals: death and rebirth, cooked and raw food, death and rotting, cannibal and ogre. South America is one of the areas where these themes have been elaborated in myths and, in the past, were expressed by a number of native societies through practices of endocannibalism and exocannibalism.

ENDOCANNIBALISM AND EXOCANNIBALISM IN SOUTH AMERICA. For some native peoples in lowland South America, endocannibalism was a ritual act that honored the deceased by sparing the corpse from the horror of burial and decay. Eradicating the body by consuming it was thought to protect against the negative effects of death and the twin dangers associated with the corpse: the danger that the body's presence would attract the dead person's soul to attack living people, and the danger of excessive grief among mourners for whom the body is a constant reminder of their loss (Conklin, 2001). South American endocannibalism took several forms, from eating the flesh (among the Guayaquí of Paraguay and the Wari' of Brazil) to cremating the flesh and grinding the roasted bones into a powder to be mixed with food or beverage and consumed (Clastres, 1974; Conklin, 2001; Dole, 1962; McCallum, 1999; Vilaça, 2000). Among the Wari' of Brazil, who believed that ancestors' spirits become game animals that offer their flesh to feed their living relatives, the act of consuming the corpse at the funeral evoked religious beliefs about life-supporting reciprocity between the living and the dead, and between people and animal spirits.

For the Tupinamba and other native peoples of lowland South America, exocannibalism was traditionally associated with intertribal and intercommunity warfare. War was highly ritualized, being preceded by dreams and magical rites, and victory was celebrated with further rites, cannibal feasts, and a display of head trophies by the victors. Prisoners might be kept for a long time, adopted or married into a local family, and then tortured before being killed and eaten. Eduardo Viveiros de Castro (1992) has shown how the Tupinamba treatment of war captives embodied cultural ideas about self and other, nature and culture, marriage and alliance. Carlos Fausto (1999) sees cannibalism as a key mechanism and metaphor through which Amazonian peoples transformed enemies into kin, or mortals into immortals, by taming, socializing, or perfecting that which is wild or culturally inferior.

CANNIBALISM IN THE PACIFIC ISLANDS. The raiding of enemy villages and consumption of enemy dead—or the taking of captives who were later killed and eaten—also has been documented in Melanesia and Polynesia. The discovery and control of Pacific islanders from the eighteenth century onward brought exploratory expeditions, missionaries, administrators, magistrates, and, later, anthropologists into contact with local informants who described and explained their beliefs and practices related to consuming human substances. Ross Bowden (1984) reports that in New Zealand, Maori cannibalism in warfare not only provided contributions to the warriors' diet but also had a profound symbolic significance: to degrade the slain enemy, whose flesh was converted into food and whose bones were turned into objects of common use. The victors especially relished desecrating the corpse of a chief.

In Fiji, myth and historical practices together provide an understanding of the interconnections between the Fijians' surrender of their sisters to foreign husbands in exchange for marriage payment of valuable whale teeth and their capture of foreign war prisoners for cannibalism. Human sacrifice accompanied the building of sacred houses and canoes and the ceremonial visits of allied chiefs. A Fijian chief oversaw an exchange cycle that included the symbolic transfer of valued objects—women (as wives) and men (as cannibal victims); by this process, political alliances were confirmed. The cannibal victims were consecrated to the major war god, who was represented by the chief.

In parts of Melanesia, anthropologists have documented native informants' accounts of cannibalistic practices that continued into the mid-twentieth century. In the northern Fore region of the New Guinea highlands, dead enemies were eaten by men and women, and in the southern region women and children ate kin and members of the residential group who had died. Similarly, Gimi women cooked and ate the dead of the local group. The Fore people reportedly valued enemy flesh as food, but cannibalism carried ritual meanings as well. When Gimi women ate human flesh they prevented the ravages of decomposition and alleviated the hunger they believed to be caused by intense sorrow. Gimi practices were structured by kinship relations, ideas about exchange transactions between men and women, and myths that associate cannibalism with wildness and uncontrolled or rapacious female sexuality.

Elsewhere in the New Guinea highlands, warfare cannibalism reflected concerns with fertility and gender. The Bimin-Kuskusmin (see Poole, 1983) and the neighboring Miyanmin reportedly ate enemies killed in war. The latter ate the whole body, whereas the former group dismembered bodies, buried heads, and ate to defile the enemy. The Bimin-Kuskusmin distinguished between hard body parts that were considered male and were eaten by men, and those parts, flesh and fat, that were considered female and were eaten by women. The Great Pandanus Tree Rite was an occasion for feasting upon game and human victims obtained by raiding a nearby group. Fitz John Porter Poole's interpretation of this ritual emphasizes the cultural meaning of male and female substances, ritual expression of myth, relations between the sexes, fertility, and death.

Cannibalism and the Occult. Among the Asmat, the consumption of enemies was associated with the construction of masculinity through head-hunting and initiation rituals. In West Africa, among the Sherbro, for example, certain secret societies, such as the Human Leopard and Alligator, reportedly required head-hunting and cannibalism as a qualification for membership (see MacCormack, in Brown and Tuzin, 1983). Witches and sorcerers acquired and renewed their powers by consuming human flesh and thereby absorbing the powers of the deceased. Accusations of cannibalism are a political weapon still powerful among the contemporary Sherbro of Sierra Leone.

Witchcraft is in various ways commonly associated with cannibalism. In the Strickland/Bosavi region of the New Guinea highlands, among a number of groups, including the Onabasulu (see Ernst, in Goldman, 1999), witches who were executed were cooked and consumed in a symbolic denial of the individual's humanity and status as a moral person. Elsewhere, witches themselves are often thought to be cannibals who obtain personal mana (power) by consuming a victim. The notion that witches feed upon the blood and body of their victims and that death results from this loss of body substance is noted in many areas among unrelated peoples. In some places a cult group of witches is believed to teach and share techniques and cannibalistic acts, real or symbolic, but a belief in a solitary cannibal-witch also exists. Neil Whitehead (2002) describes how sorcerers in the highlands of Guyana extract and sip fluids from decomposing corpses. The act is the sorcerer's gift to divine beings of the cosmos, given to ensure the fertility of plants, fish, and animals.

Conclusion. The theme of cannibalism as an exchange that feeds and renews sources of life and fertility appears in a wide range of contexts, from the hostile relations of Guyanese sorcery and Aztec warfare and human sacrifice to the loving and honorable funerary rites of native peoples in Melanesia and lowland South America. Although Eli Sagan (1974), I. M. Lewis (1986), and other psychological theorists see in aggression and interpersonal conflict the source and meaning of cannibalism, the trend among most anthropologists and historians has been to demonstrate the diversity of cultural meanings. In both practice and imagination, cannibalism is clearly an emotionally charged and culturally significant act, but it has no single meaning. Cannibalism's multifaceted symbolism and its connections with mythic themes of sacrifice, destruction, regeneration, and social reproduction are understood best within a specific cultural context.

See Also Aztec Religion; Human Sacrifice, overview article.

Bibliography

Books and articles on cannibalism may be theoretical or interpretive general works or they may present descriptive case studies that analyze cannibalism in particular cultural settings. Many works combine both features, applying a theoretical or interpretive approach to particular case studies.

General Works

Arens, William. *The Man-Eating Myth: Anthropology and Anthropophagy.* New York, 1979. Finds the evidence for cannibalism unconvincing.

Goldman, Laurence R., ed. *The Anthropology of Cannibalism.* Westport, Conn., 1999. Presents a series of articles with critiques of Arens's position, analyses of the politics of ethnographic representations of cannibalism, and case studies cited in the text of this article: Kantner on the Anasazi, Zubrinich on the Asmat, and Ernst on the Onabasulu.

Harris, Marvin. *Cannibals and Kings: The Origins of Culture.* New York, 1977. Presents a materialist-ecological explanation of cannibalism.

Lewis, I. M. "The Cannibal's Cauldron." In Lewis's *Religion in Context: Cults and Charisma,* pp. 63–77. New York, 1986. Highlights symbolic themes of sexuality and oral aggression.

Sagan, Eli. *Cannibalism: Human Aggression and Cultural Form.* New York, 1974. A popular psychoanalytic study of cannibalism in general, relating it to aggression and sublimation of aggression.

Sanday, Peggy Reeves. *Divine Hunger: Cannibalism as a Cultural System.* New York, 1986. Surveys cross-cultural cannibalism and analyzes its relation to cultural concepts of self-other relations and the reproduction of society.

Tannahill, Reay. *Flesh and Blood: A History of the Cannibal Complex.* New York, 1975.

Studies of Areas and Cases

Bowden, Ross. "Maori Cannibalism: An Interpretation." *Oceania* 55 (1984): 81–99.

Brown, Paula, and Donald Tuzin, eds. *The Ethnography of Cannibalism.* Washington, D.C., 1983. Presents a group of case studies, some cited in the text of the article: Poole on the Bimin-Kuskusmin, MacCormack on the Sherbro, and Sahlins on the Fijians, with a commentary by Shirley Lindenbaum.

Burkert, Walter. *Homo Necans: The Anthropology of Ancient Greek Sacrificial Ritual and Myth.* Berkeley, Calif., 1983. Essentially a study of the ritualization of sacrifice. Cannibalism as imagery rather than practice.

Clastres, Pierre. "Guayakí Cannibalism." In *Native South Americans: Ethnology of the Least Known Continent,* edited by Patricia J. Lyon, pp. 309–321. Boston, 1974.

Conklin, Beth A. *Consuming Grief: Compassionate Cannibalism in an Amazonian Society.* Austin, Tex., 2001.

Dole, Gertrude. "Endocannibalism among the Amahuaca Indians." *Transactions of the New York Academy of Sciences* 24 (1962): 567–573.

Fausto, Carlos. "Of Enemies and Pets: Warfare and Shamanism in Amazonia." *American Ethnologist* 26, no. 4 (1999): 933–956.

Forsyth, Donald W. "The Beginnings of Brazilian Anthropology: Jesuits and Tupinamba Cannibalism." *Journal of Anthropological Research* 39 (1983): 147–178.

Gillison, Gillian. *Between Culture and Fantasy: A New Guinea Highlands Mythology.* Chicago, 1993.

Gordon-Grube, Karen. "Anthropophagy in Post-Renaissance Europe: The Tradition of Medicinal Cannibalism." *American Anthropologist* 90, no. 2 (1988): 405–409.

Harner, Michael J. "The Ecological Basis for Aztec Sacrifice." *American Ethnologist* 4 (1977): 117–135.

Lévi-Strauss, Claude. *The Raw and the Cooked.* New York, 1969. Discusses myths of cannibalism and the symbolism of raw, cooked, and rotten food, especially among South American tribes.

Lindenbaum, Shirley. *Kuru Sorcery: Disease and Danger in the New Guinea Highlands.* Palo Alto, Calif., 1979. A discussion of the importance of sorcery belief in the reactions of the Fore to the kuru disease, which was spread by contact with victims of the disease, mainly through cannibalism.

McCallum, Cecelia. "Consuming Pity: The Production of Death among the Cashinahua." *Cultural Anthropology* 14, no. 4 (1999): 443–471.

Marano, Lou. "Windigo Psychosis: The Anatomy of an Emic-Etic Confusion." In *Culture-Bound Syndromes,* edited by Ronald C. Simons and Charles C. Hughes, pp. 411–448. Dordrecht, 1985.

Métraux, Alfred. "The Tupinamba." In *Handbook of South American Indians,* edited by Julian H. Steward, vol. 3. Washington, D.C., 1949.

Métraux, Alfred. "Warfare, Cannibalism, and Human Trophies." In *Handbook of South American Indians,* edited by Julian H. Steward, vol. 5. Washington, D.C., 1949.

Obeyesekere, Gananath. "Cannibal Feasts in Nineteenth-Century Fiji: Seaman's Yarns and the Ethnographic Imagination." In *Cannibalism and the Colonial World,* edited by Francis Barker, Peter Hulme, and Margaret Iversen, pp. 63–86. New York, 1998.

Poole, Fitz John Porter. "Cannibals, Tricksters, and Witches: Anthropophagic Images among Binim-Kuskusmin." In *The Ethnography of Cannibalism,* edited by Paula Brown and Donald Tuzin, p.13. Washington, D.C., 1983.

Sahlins, Marshall. "Raw Women, Cooked Men, and Other 'Great Things' of the Fiji Islands." In *The Ethnography of Cannibalism,* edited by Paula Brown and Donald Tuzin. Washington, D.C., 1983.

Strathern, Andrew. "Witchcraft, Greed, Cannibalism and Death: Some Related Themes from the New Guinea Highlands." In *Death and the Regeneration of Life,* edited by Maurice Bloch and Jonathan Parry, pp. 111–133. New York, 1982. Compares and discusses the themes of cannibalism, witchcraft, sacrifice, exchange, recreation, and the enemy.

Vilaça, Aparecida. "Relations between Funerary Cannibalism and Warfare Cannibalism: The Question of Predation." *Ethnos* 65, no. 1 (2000): 83–106.

Viveiros de Castro, Eduardo Batalha. *From the Enemy's Point of View: Humanity and Divinity in an Amazonian Society.* Chicago, 1992. An interpretation of Tupi-Guarani ritual cannibalism, emphasizing how society is constructed through the incorporation of enemy others.

Walens, Stanley. *Feasting with Cannibals: An Essay on Kwakiutl Cosmology.* Princeton, N.J., 1981. A symbolic analysis of Kwakiutl cannibalistic spirits and dances.

Whitehead, Neil L. *Dark Shamans: Kanaimà and the Poetics of Violent Death.* Durham, N.C., 2002.

Zerries, Otto. "El endocanibalismo en la América del Sur." *Revista do Museu Paulista* (Sao Paulo) 12 (1960): 125–175.

PAULA BROWN (1987)
BETH A. CONKLIN (2005)

CANON. Because employment of the term *canon* (usually as a synonym for *scripture*) in comparative religious studies is both commonplace and subject to a growing scholarly debate, the classic usage will be considered at the outset. Subsequently, a consideration of contemporary applications of the term within the study of world religions will follow in order to illustrate its usefulness and to show some of the hermeneutical issues implicit in such usage. Since the use of *canon* to mean both a norm and an attribute of scripture arose first within Christianity, some special attention must necessarily be given to present debates in the study of that religion. However, the focus of this treatment is on the wider implications concerning the value of this term in a comparativist description of world religions.

ETYMOLOGY AND EARLIEST HISTORICAL USAGES. The Greek word *kanōn*, which gave rise to its later European and English equivalents, is a Semitic loanword basically signifying a reed, as seen in biblical passages such as *1 Kings* 14:15 and *Job* 40:21. The semantic usage that occurs in Hebrew (*qaneh*), Assyrian (*qanu*), Ugaritic (*qn*), and similarly in Aramaic, Syriac, Arabic, and modern Hebrew, derives in turn from the even more ancient non-Semitic Sumerian (*gi, gi-na*), with the same import. In the above Semitic languages, the basic conception of a reed generated a semantic field that included in Hebrew, for example, the description of either a standard of length or a straight or upright object. Images of a standard of length that occur in biblical passages are the measuring rod (*qeneh ha-middah*) in *Ezekiel* 40:3 and 40:5 and a full reed of similar length in *Ezekiel* 41:8. The straight or upright object is exemplified as the shaft of a lampstand in *Exodus* 25:31, the branches of a lampstand in *Exodus* 25:32, and a shoulder blade in *Job* 31:22.

The Greek usage of this common Semitic term extended these derivations to include a great variety of figurative applications. Besides associating this term with various instruments of measure and design, Greeks came to regard lists, catalogs, or tables in the sciences as "canons." Likewise, the humanities and anthropology sought to describe "the norm" (*ho kanōn*), for example, in grammar, aesthetics, music, physical beauty, ethics, the perfection of form in sculpture, and so forth. Epicurus wrote a book, now lost, entitled *Peri kritēriou hē kanōn*, focused on the "canonics" of logic and method. Epictetus, and the Epicurians similarly, sought to find a formal basis (*kanōn*) for distinguishing truth from falsehood, the desirable from the undesirable.

In the area of religion, Christianity drew heavily from this Hellenistic milieu and came to assign a new and unique role to the term *canon.* In the New Testament itself, the Greek term is used only by the apostle Paul as a standard of true Christianity in *Philippians* 3:16 and in a late text, *Galatians* 6:16, and as a divinely delimited mandate or authorization in *2 Corinthians* 10:13–16. Nonetheless, in the Roman church during the first three centuries, the term occurs frequently and can signify almost any binding norm of true Christianity, expressed with a variety of technical nuances. For instance, Irenaeus, in the second century, could already speak of various familiar canons: "the canon of truth" (in preaching), "the canon (rule) of faith" (Lat., *regula fidei,* or the essential truth of the gospel), and "the ecclesiastical canon" (Lat., *regula veritatis,* expressing both true confession and correct ritual participation in the church). Likewise, the term could characterize any authorized list or collection of decisions or persons. Thus one could speak of a "canonical" set of laws, a list or collection of "canonized" saints, papal decretals (ninth century), church leaders, monks, nuns, and so on. Hence, early in the history of Christianity, the Greek *kanōn* was carried over as *canon* or *regula* in the Latin used in churches of the East and the West. By the Middle Ages, the whole collection of binding decisions by the Roman church came to be regarded as the *ius canonicum* (canonical laws), either touching on secular matters (Lat., *lex;* or Gr., *nomos*) or belonging to the juridical, religious, and ethical canons of the church. Gratian's *Decretum* (1139–1142 CE) provided the foundation for canon law in Roman Catholicism.

The relationship between "canon" and "scripture" in Christianity is more complicated. The earliest Christian scripture was either the Hebrew Bible of Judaism or the old Greek version of it (the so-called Septuagint). Within Judaism, neither prerabbinic nor rabbinic literature ever chose to refer to this scripture as a "canon." At about the same time as the flowering of rabbinic Judaism in the second century, Irenaeus—probably borrowing the use of the term from Marcion, his gnostic competitor—began to speak of a "New Testament" as a group of "inspired" Christian traditions distinct from the "Old Testament" inherited as scripture from Judaism. The Christian terminology of "inspiration," although grounded in Jewish understanding, occurs first in the later Pauline traditions and undoubtedly reflects influence from related Hellenistic conceptions that had previously been applied to the *Iliad* and the *Odyssey.* However, not until shortly after 450 CE did the term *canon* begin to be used by Christians, apparently first by Athanasius, to designate the biblical books of scripture.

Within rabbinic Judaism, the Hebrew scripture began to be called Miqra' ("that which is read"), and the entire collection came to be referred to as Tanakh, an acronym of the names of the three major divisions of the Hebrew scriptures: Torah (Pentateuch), Nevi'im (Prophets), and Ketuvim (Writings). Instead of speaking about "canonization," as was typical later in Christianity, Jewish sources describe an endeavor to determine which books "defile the hands" and, therefore, constitute sacred scripture, as distinguished from other normative traditions. The extrabiblical traditions in the Mishnah and Talmud were, consequently, authoritative (arguably "canonical" in that sense) but considered to be "oral law," which did not defile the hands, in contrast to the scripture or "written law." Prior to these designations within Judaism and Christianity, the Hebrew Bible (Old Testament) was denoted by a variety of diverse expressions, such as "the law and the prophets and the other books of our fathers" (Prologue to *Ben Sira*); "the law and the prophets" (e.g., *Mt.* 5:17); "the law of Moses, the prophets, and the psalms" (*Lk.* 24:44); the "oracles of God" (*Rom.* 3:2); "the scripture" (e.g., *Mk.* 12:24); "the holy scriptures" (Philo Judaeus, *On Flight and Finding* 1.4); "the book"; "the sacred book"; and others. In view of this evidence scholars continue to disagree whether the weight of the later Christian references to the term *canon* for scripture turns primarily on the term's denotation of either a binding "norm" or an ecclesiastically approved "list" of inspired books.

In Islam, another "religion of the Book" associated with the children of Abraham, the Qurʾān replaces the imperfect rendering of revelation in Judaism and Christianity. While Muslim interpreters never traditionally identified the Qurʾān as a "canon," they did employ the term to designate the law, in a manner reminiscent of some early Christian understandings of the biblical law of God.

Contemporary Usage. Certainly, the use of the term *canon,* despite its association with Christianity, can prove to be an illuminating heuristic device in describing other world religions and their principal texts. The analogies with the formation of Western religious canons provides an attractive, yet to be fully explored, way of thinking about religion in general. For example, such terminology can be helpful in understanding aspects of Eastern religions. Although Confucius (Kongzi), who died in the fifth century BCE, claimed of his teaching, "I have transmitted what was taught to me without making up anything of my own" (*Lun-Yü* 7.1), the "Five Classics" as we now know them only became a scripturelike guide to Confucianism from the first century CE onward. Obviously innovations entered into this work long after the death of Confucius. Moreover, competing views within Confucianism led to some groups' diminishing the importance of this work or adding to it new canons that were viewed as complementary (e.g., Ssu Shu, or "Four Books," and still later in the Chʿing era, the "Thirteen Classics"), almost in the same manner as Christianity added the New Testament to the "Old."

Just as Christians debated whether the Old Testament "canon" should be the Hebrew version, with Judaism, or the expanded old Greek version, language and culture influenced the formation of "canonical" distinctions in many religions. Centuries after the death of the Buddha, ancient traditions were combined in South Asia to form what is presently called the "Pali canon" (c. 29–17 BCE). A century or so later, a different "canonical" literature developed in India, written in Sanskrit and eventually translated into Chinese and Tibetan, which became foundational for Mahāyāna Buddhism. In contrast to adherents of the Pali canon, these Buddhists regarded the sūtras of the Mahāyāna ("great vehicle") as an alternative canon, the only true authority regarding what the Buddha himself taught. Even within later Zen Buddhism, where the idea of a canon seems antithetical, one may consider the lists of *kōans,* questions and answers developed in regional monasteries for training and testing students, as attaining "canonical" status as a constant feature of the instructions given by particular Zen masters.

Just as some "Christian" gnostics dismissed the Hebrew Bible in favor of a "New Testament," one may find an analogy with the development of Hinduism as a reaction against certain aspects of Vedic religion. Similar to the Jewish distinction between written and oral law was the distinction made by brahmans between two kinds of "canonical" literature. *Śruti* ("heard") generally refers to the ritualistic literature found in the Upaniṣads and is believed to be revealed directly from divinity, while *smṛti* ("remembered") designates the epics, the later Purāṇas and other legal and philosophical writings touching on practical matters of personal, social, and domestic conduct. Even if *śruti* has a higher status, it can be viewed as a lower kind of ritualistic knowledge in comparison with the immediate moral implications of *smṛti.* So, too, even if the oral law does not defile the hands, it may provide a more explicit and pragmatically significant register of the demands of a holy life in Judaism than one can find by simply reading the written law.

Hermeneutical Implications. The above descriptions adumbrate some of the possibilities and problems in the use of *canon* as a technical term in the study of religion. The term inherently vacillates between two distinct poles, in both secular and religious usage. On the one hand, it can be used to refer to a rule, standard, ideal, norm, or authoritative office or literature, whether oral or written. On the other hand, it can signify a temporary or perpetual fixation, standardization, enumeration, listing, chronology, register, or catalog of exemplary or normative persons, places, or things. The former dimension emphasizes internal signs of an elevated status. The latter puts stress on the precise boundary, limits, or measure of what, from some preunderstood standard, belongs within or falls outside of a specific "canon." For the purpose of illustrating these significant differences, I shall call the former "canon 1" and the latter "canon 2." This "ideal" distinction only demarcates poles in a continuum of options, since the essential nature and status of a normative tradition or a "scripture" within a religion inevitably emerges through its own unique, dialectical interplay between these polarities. The interplay itself engenders a systemic ambiguity in any discussion of religious canons and helps account for the variety of ways, sometimes conflicting, in which the term *canon* has been employed in recent scholarship.

Canon 1. In its first usage as rule, standard, ideal, or norm, the term *canon* in the secular domain may apply to a wide range of fields in which a standard of excellence or authority governs the proper exercise of a discipline. For example, it can reflect criteria by which one makes decisions within a field of inquiry, whether these choices conform to grammatical and mathematical principles or indices of aesthetic excellence in rhetoric, art, or music. Implicit in such canons is some political and social theory of intellectual consensus about the quality, worth or preservation, and validity of that which is being judged and remembered. Likewise, religious iconography, Buddhist organization of a city, and church architecture reflect implicit canonical assumptions. The success of "pop art" in the 1960s may have resided partly in its ability to make our implicit canons explicit. The Campbell's Soup can we had accepted in some unconsciously canonical sense suddenly appears before us in an explicitly canonical form through the medium of art. The dynamism possible within such canons becomes evident when, for instance, one surveys the changing collections of art museums and contrasts their content with the work being done in artists' studios.

In examining religious scriptures as "canons," one may generalize that the founding leaders of religions almost never compose for their disciples a complete scripture. The one obvious exception is that of the third-century Mani, founder of Manichaeism. There are usually substantial periods after the death of a leader or founder when oral and/or written traditions function authoritatively as canonical, in the sense of representing a scripture without specific dimension. This dynamic process may be influenced greatly by later disciples, and the scriptures may for long periods of time, if not indefinitely, lack the public form of a fixed list of books or a standardized "text." At the same time, canonical criteria, such as "inspiration," incarnation of the Dharma, and so on, are sufficient for them to sustain their scriptural status. The initial recognition of some traditions as being crucially foundational or scriptural sets in motion political and economic pressures within the religion that usually lead to the formation of a scripture in the latter sense of *canon* (canon 2).

From the standpoint of Christian history, one may argue that the term *canon* has been and may continue to be useful in the designation of extrabiblical oral or written decisions that are binding in matters of faith and practice, as part of a church's teaching magisteria. Certainly, prior to the fourth century, some Christian traditions were explicitly canonical (canon 1) in the sense that they provided normative religious guidance outside of the Hebrew Bible. Justin Martyr cites from the "Sayings of the Lord" source as authoritative alongside the Hebrew Bible and arguably refuses to do the same with the Gospel narratives or Paul's letters. It is unlikely that these "sayings" belong to a fixed list. Therefore, one can say that Christian scripture had a canonical status (canon 1) long before the church decisions of the fourth century delimited a fixed list of books (canon 2). More precisely, the canonization (canon 2) is by degree, since even in the fourth and fifth centuries the standardization of the actual text had not taken place.

Despite the silence of the rabbinic tradition on the subject, recent studies of Judaism commonly refer to "canon(s)" and "canonization." In a provocative study, Sid Leiman regards a religious book as "canonical" if it is "accepted by Jews as authoritative for religious practice and/or doctrine . . . binding for all generations . . . and studied and expounded in private and in public" (Leiman, 1976, p. 14). Because this definition conforms to criteria of canon 1, Leiman can claim that the oral law is "canonical," although it both is "uninspired" and does not defile the hands as scripture. Relying on this principle of normativeness, Leiman can distinguish between different kinds of books: "outside" or banned books; secular or "Homeric" books that deserve reading; inspired canonical books (scripture); and uninspired canonical books (oral law, i.e., Mishnah/Talmud). Consequently, the Jewish discussion at the end of the first century CE at Yavneh over the status of the *Book of Ecclesiastes* concerned only its "inspiration," not its canonicity, for it could continue to be cited as normative even if not as "scripture."

Conversely, other scholars, (see, for example, Jacob Neusner, 1983, pp. 11–37) argue that the ritual difference, "defiling the hands," did not produce any clear levels of canonical authority between the Hebrew Bible, the Mishnah/Talmud, other religious books, and the "inspired" commentary of a rabbi. If canonicity (canon 1) is determined by the norm of revelation itself, then distinctions either among levels of canonicity or between canonical and noncanonical literature begin to blur. If, as Neusner suggests, the rabbis themselves embodied the *torah* (law), then for students of religion there is only limited value in a descriptive appeal to certain texts as "canonical." If the meaning of these texts resides in a spiritual or "Midrashic" sense held by consensus among "inspired" rabbis rather than in a "plain" literary, or *peshaṭ*, sense, then the semantic import is not publicly available through a reading of the scripture per se. Similarly, some Catholic scholars currently locate the canonical sense of Christian scripture in the teaching magisterium (canon 1) of the church hierarchy rather than in either a literary or historical-critical assessment of biblical texts themselves. In such an approach, a scripture may be viewed as the deposit of a variety of historical traditions, any of which may or may not be "canonical" (canon 1) according to an "inspired" norm or standard inherent within the leadership of the religion itself. In this case, identifying a scripture may shed only modest light on the beliefs of a religion.

From a historical perspective, the final formation of a scripture (canon 2) usually results from an earlier, often obscured process of redaction, expansion, and selection of texts (canon 1), whether one thinks of the *Dao de jing* of Daoism, the various Buddhist canons, the extensive collection of Jain "canonical" literature, or the Hindu *Mahābhārata* and the *Bhagavadgītā* along with the older Vedas.

Often some underlying traditions of a scripture were considered normative or "canonical" for the earliest disciples, while other traditions gain an elevated status as scripture not anticipated by their celebrated founders, as, for example, through the posthumous deification of Lao-tzu. Repeatedly one finds evidence of how earlier oral or written traditions or writings, whose normativeness depended originally on more modest criteria, gradually gain greater authority, in terms of a later perception of religious genius, inspiration, revelation of the law (e.g., *dharma*), or the presence of ultimate reality, perfection, or some other transcendent value. This adjustment in the believers' vision of canonical traditions within a religion often entails a radical shift in the perception, understanding, and significance of older traditions when they are caught up into the new context of a scripture.

Most often, canon and community are related dialectically in a process of semantic transformation. The steps taken by editors in this process may go unrecognized by the believers or may be seen as essential elements in the orchestration of the traditions in order to protect them from heretical misinterpretation. In sum, the recognition of canon 1 materials, defined as traditions offering a normative vehicle or an ideal standard, occurs in most world religions and usually contributes momentum to an impulse within the history of a religion to totalize, to circumscribe, and to standardize these same normative traditions into fixed, literary forms typical of canon 2.

Canon 2. The second usage of the term *canon* will be in the sense of a list, chronology, catalog, fixed collection, and/or standardized text. Scholars of comparative religion such as Mircea Eliade and Wilfred Cantwell Smith have placed emphasis on the full appearance of a religion complete with its "scripture," reflecting whatever norms of excellence, truth, goodness, beauty, or revelation may be affirmed by the respective religious adherents. In religious studies, the foundational religious documents are most easily approached at this more developed stage, when they constitute a publicly available, delimited canon (canon 2) in the maturity of particular religious movements. Of course, only the most presumptuous type of "protestant" interpretation of other religions would presume that the ideas and beliefs of a religion can be grasped solely by a literary study of such religious canons. Smith has amply illustrated the problems that arise in the study of Islam because of this naïveté.

As already noted, the normativeness of religious traditions is usually acknowledged long before these same traditions attain a fixed dimension and textual standardization, the elements of canon 2. So, for example, after the death of the Buddha the disciples sought, although not without controversy, to envision the diverse sermons (canon 1) of the Blessed One as part of a larger collection (canon 2), a larger normative and publicly recognized canon.

Conversely, Mani claimed to write by inspiration "my scriptures," which combined the essence of older books or scriptures into one "great wisdom" (*Kephalaia* 154). His work remains exceptional in part because he is perhaps the only founder of a major religion who was self-consciously "inspired" to compose a complete "scripture." His work represents the best-known example of a canon that attained both normative authority and distinct literary boundaries at the same time. Even so, other generations of believers expanded and modified the canon. Mani's use of the Judeo-Christian concept of scripture corresponds to his hope of absorbing these two religions into his own, much as Islam aspired in its early development to bring Jews and Christians into its more universal fold.

Unlike most other religious canons, completed centuries after their founders had died, Islam settled most dimensions of the Qurʾān within only twenty-three years after the death of Muḥammad. One of the significant differences in the comparison of Islam with Judaism, Christianity, and Manichaeism is that the Qurʾān is not a "scripture" in the sense of an inspired, historically accommodated writing. The Qurʾān is the actual word of God, representing an eternal archetype of revelation cast in heavenly language. Unlike Christianity's scripture of "books" (*ta biblia*), the Qurʾān is more simply "the Book." Nevertheless, during the lifetime of the Prophet, his disciples did not have the book of the Qurʾān as we now know it. The order of the chapters and other significant editorial influence belongs to the hands of the disciples who succeeded the Prophet. Moreover, the later collections of the *sunnah* (customary practice of the Prophet), now found in the *ḥadīth*, provided a normative and, therefore, "canonical" (canon 1) guide to Muslim exegesis. As with the Jewish Karaites and the Antiochene Christian exegetes, many "spiritualists" within Islam could lay claim to their own direct insight upon scripture in a manner that diminished the significance of the *ḥadīth* and could appear to assign normative, and in that sense, "canonical" status to the Qurʾān alone.

Regarding the final delimitation of the Hebrew scriptures, most scholars agree that the promulgation by Ezra of a five-book Torah in the early postexilic period constituted a decisive moment in the formation of Judaism. Unlike the later case of the Christian Gospels, the Pentateuch comprised a single, allegedly Mosaic "book of the Torah" (*Jos.* 1:7–8). From a traditional-historical standpoint, this Mosaic Torah appears to combine multiple older, normative *torot*, or laws, in the sense of canon 1 and/or canon 2 (e.g., *Proto-Deuteronomy*) into a fixed and integrated collection of books (canon 2). This combination of traditions most likely reflects the legislation preserved and venerated by two different groups from the Babylonian exile—bearers of Jerusalemite priestly tradition (e.g., the laws in *Exodus* 22ff.) and deuteronomistic interpreters (e.g., the Decalogue in *Deuteronomy* 5 and the subsequent laws). The effect would be to make much private tradition public and to set all of the laws forward to be interpreted together as parts of the same revelation of law delivered by God to Moses prior to the conquest of Palestine.

Similar to the codification by the Egyptians of the Fifth Pharaonic Law early in the same period, the promulgation of the Mosaic Torah probably occurred in response to a benevolent policy under Persian sovereignty. As a reward for this codification and public promulgation of the private or secret religious law, the Persians sanctioned the right of Jewish leaders to make juridical decisions according to it in exchange for obedience to Persian civil and international law. In any case, these events undoubtedly helped to accelerate the forces behind the formation of a part of a religious canon.

The compilation of the exact list of books that make up the completed Hebrew Bible could not be completed until late in the first century, perhaps not until the second. Furthermore, the textual standardization of the Bible continued up to the end of the first millennium, culminating in a relatively uniform consensus regarding the orthography, punctuation, and vocalization of the so-called Masoretic text of the Tanakh, the Hebrew scriptures. Here, as in the case of Christianity and many other religions, the process of canonization in the sense of canon 2 entails a resolution of the limits of the collection before a full standardization of the text can take place. Centuries might elapse during this process of full canonization (canon 2), and it may be much easier for believers to debate the authority of the latest stages in the process of the text's stabilization than it is for them to reopen the question of whether a book really belongs in the scripture at all. The length of the process of full canonization may often affect the believer's assessment of what represents the final text.

The semantic import of the formation of a canon 2 should not be underestimated. Christianity and Judaism amply illustrate this feature. Unlike the above-mentioned instance of the Pentateuch, the individual Christian Gospels retained their independence from one another despite the assumption that they collectively convey the same "one" gospel of Jesus Christ. Perhaps the late ending of Mark attests to an effort at bringing that work into greater harmony within the canonical collections of gospels. Paul's letters illustrate a different feature, for they include in a single collection some original letters in edited and unedited form, for example, *Galatians, Romans, 1* and *2 Corinthians,* together with deutero-Pauline traditions reflective of a later generation, for example, *2 Thessalonians.* The original Pauline letters, which were written before the composition of the Gospels, were, through canonization, subordinated to the Gospels as commentary upon them. Similarly, the *Gospel of John* is read contextually within scripture in connection with the so-called Johannine letters (*1, 2,* and *3 Jn.*), even though the historic evidence of common authorship is extremely weak. Again, this type of canonization alters the religious vision of the preceding authoritative traditions (canon 1) as being part of a larger "inspired" New Testament. The terms *New Testament* and *Old Testament* likewise signal a change in the perceived significance of the Hebrew Bible when read as part of a Christian text in the context of a purportedly new revelation. The difference in religious visions of the "shared" scripture implies profound distinctions between the import of the Tanakh within Judaism and that of an "Old Testament" within Christian interpretation.

SCRIPTURE AND CANON. These ideal distinctions between canon as a norm and canon as a list or standardization of text usually overlap in the actual assessment of a particular religion. For example, in the Tanakh and the New Testament one can detect evidence of "canon-conscious redactions," whereby assumptions about the normativeness (canon 1) of the traditions and of their being read together in a specific collection (canon 2) coincide.

Historicized titles added to the psalms assigned to David link these prayers contextually to the narrative about David in *1* and *2 Samuel.* The epilogue to *Ecclesiastes* summarizes the essence of the book in a manner that puts the "wisdom," or Solomonic, books in full continuity with the Torah. The addition of titles to some of the Christian Gospels makes their character and common witness together as Gospels more explicit than their original authors could have envisioned. The *Gospel of Luke* in the Western tradition has now been separated from its original sequel, *Acts of the Apostles,* by the *Gospel of John.* In this way, the Gospels were read collectively and *Acts* came to mark a transition from the teachings of Jesus to that of the apostle Paul. This type of organization of highly diverse traditions into partially harmonized canons of literature is also common to the canons of other world religions.

As has already been shown, considerable differences of opinion exist among scholars over the appropriate relationship between the terms *scripture* and *canon.* At a minimum, these terms both gain and lose some of their historical significance when they are taken away from the specific religious vocabulary of Judaism and Christianity for the purpose of an etic assessment of world religions. Frequently scholars have used *scripture* and *canon* synonymously, although ambiguity in both terms, particularly in the latter, suggests the need for more careful definitions and historical finesse. In the application of both terms to a religion, the interpreter stands within a hermeneutical circle. Only by some prior judgment regarding the identity of the believers of a given religion can any description be proffered regarding their "canons" and their modes of interpreting the same. Moreover, this judgment is hindered by the ethnocentrism of the outside observer, as well as by the difficulty in taking a term indigenous to one religion and assigning to it a technical usage appropriate for describing features of other religions.

Nevertheless, contemporary efforts to understand how canons achieve formation and exercise significance within a religion has already proved unusually illuminating as a way to describe and to compare religions generally. The interpretation of religion must inevitably assume some operational certitude regarding the identity, the economic character, and the literary sources of revelation or truth to which religions lay claim in the world. It must be carried out with an acute awareness that the heretics and noncanonical sayings of some will likely be viewed as the saints and scripture of others.

SEE ALSO Authority; Scripture.

BIBLIOGRAPHY

Beyer, Hermann W. "Kanon." In *Theological Dictionary of the New Testament,* edited by Gerhard Kittel. Grand Rapids, Mich., 1965. An excellent word study of the Greek term in secular and Christian sources.

Bleeker, C. Jouco, ed. *Historia Religionum: Handbook for the History of Religion,* vol. 2, *Religions of the Present.* Leiden, 1971. An excellent overview of religions with careful attention to the historical appearance of normative traditions in each.

Brown, Raymond E. *The Critical Meaning of the Bible.* New York, 1981. A significant Catholic example of the modern attempt to distinguish between the "literal" and the "canonical sense" of the biblical text.

Campenhausen, Hans von. *The Formation of the Christian Bible.* Philadelphia, 1972. A classic study of the canonization of the New Testament.

Childs, Brevard S. *Introduction to the Old Testament as Scripture.* Philadelphia, 1979. An examination of how the canonization of the Hebrew Bible (Old Testament) influenced the "shape" and semantic import of biblical books.

Childs, Brevard S. *The New Testament as Canon: An Introduction.* Philadelphia, 1985. A study of the New Testament from the perspective of the role played by canonization in its formation as scripture.

Eliade, Mircea. *A History of Religious Ideas,* vol. 2, *From Gautama Buddha to the Triumph of Christianity.* Chicago, 1982. A monumental overview in which "canon" and "scripture" are employed as categories to interpret major world religions.

Leiman, Sid Z. *The Canonization of Hebrew Scripture.* Hamden, Conn., 1976. A controversial reexamination of the primary evidence for the canonization of the Hebrew Bible. Leiman helpfully collects and translates relevant texts from the Mishnah, the Talmud(s), and other sources.

Neusner, Jacob. *Midrash in Context.* Philadelphia, 1983. A provocative study of how the oral law came to accompany Jewish scripture in the history of that religion, as well as the implications of "canon" for the same.

Peters, F. E. *Children of Abraham: Judaism, Christianity, Islam.* Princeton, 1982. A comparative investigation into the three "religions of the book," including concern with issues of scripture and tradition.

Sanders, James A. *Canon and Community: A Guide to Canonical Criticism.* Philadelphia, 1984. An attempt to understand the dynamic of religious interpetation in Judaism and Christianity through a hermeneutical theory of canonization.

Sheppard, Gerald T. *Wisdom as a Hermeneutical Construct: A Study in the Sapientializing of the Old Testament.* Berlin and New York, 1980. A monograph that examines the canonical understanding of "wisdom" and "wisdom books" in prerabbinic Judaism and explores similar examples of late "canon conscious redactions" within the Hebrew Bible itself.

Sheppard, Gerald T. "Canonization: Hearing the Voice of the Same God through Historically Dissimilar Traditions." *Interpretation* 36 (January 1982): 21–33. An examination of the semantic import of the selection and editing of traditions in the formation of both the Hebrew Bible and the New Testament.

Smith, Wilfred Cantwell. "The Study of Religion and the Study of the Bible," *Journal of the American Academy of Religion* 39 (June 1971): 131–140. A general theory regarding the proper understanding of "Bible" in the study of comparative religions.

Smith, Wilfred Cantwell. "The True Meaning of Scripture: An Empirical Historian's Nonreductionist Interpretation of the Qur'ān." *International Journal of Middle East Studies* 11 (July 1980): 487–505. A consideration of the problem of understanding what constitutes viable religious interpretation from a history of religions perspective.

Sundberg, Albert C., Jr. *The Old Testament of the Early Church.* Cambridge, 1964. An argument, based on an examination of early Christian appeals to "scripture," that the conception of a "scripture" without specific dimensions preceded the later ecclesiastical decisions regarding a "canonical" Bible conforming to a specific list of books.

New Sources

Assmann, Aleida, and Jan Assmann, eds. *Kanon und Zensur.* Munich, 1987. Proceedings of two conferences on canonization and censorship, including contributions in both sociological and historical perspectives.

Farneti, Roberto. *Il canone moderno. Filosofia politica e genealogia.* Turin, Italy, 2002.

Kooij, Arie van der, and Karel van der Toorn. *Canonization and Decanonization. Papers presented to the International Conference of the Leiden Institute for the Study of Religions.* Leiden, 1998. This important volume includes a first section on "(De)canonization and the History of Religions" and a second section on "(De)canonization and Modern society." An annotated bibliography compiled by J. A. M. Snoek (pp. 436–506) makes this book an indispensable tool for any future study on the topic.

GERALD T. SHEPPARD (1987)
Revised Bibliography

CAO DAI is a syncretistic modern Vietnamese religious movement founded in 1926 by Ngo Van Chieu (1878–1932; also known as Ngo Minh Chieu). An official of the French colonial administration, Chieu was widely read in both Eastern and Western religion, and had a particular interest in spiritism. The movement began during séances conducted by Chieu and a group of friends of similar background as Vietnamese intellectuals. An entity called Cao Dai (literally, "high tower," a Daoist epithet for the supreme god) appeared and delivered to the group the fundamental features of the religion: universalism, vegetarianism, the image of an eye in a circle (which became its central symbol), and various details of worship. On November 18, 1926 the movement was inaugurated in a dramatic ceremony that drew some fifty thousand people. Though resisted by Buddhists and French officials, who perceived its nationalistic potential, Cao Dai grew phenomenally. By 1930 it numbered a half million by conservative estimate, and soon had garnered over one million followers, embracing at least one-eighth of the population in what was to become South Vietnam. The remarkable appeal of the eclectic, spiritist faith undoubtedly reflected the yearning of an oppressed Vietnamese population for something new, immediate, indigenous, and idealistic in a situation in which Catholicism was the religion of the alien colonizers, Buddhism was moribund, and Confucianism was linked to a social order clearly passing away.

Cao Dai met those criteria. The substantial Chinese cultural influence in Vietnam is evidenced in the fundamental similarity of Cao Dai to religious Daoist sectarianism in its spiritism, political overtones, and colorful liturgy. Furthermore, like most Chinese religious movements of recent centuries, it also sought to unify the "three faiths," and so it incorporated Confucian morality, Buddhist doctrines such as *karman* and reincarnation, and Daoist occultism. Also like some of its Chinese counterparts, it further sought to unify the religions of the world, seeing them all as coming from the same source, and heralding a new age of world harmony. Its elaborate organizational structure, headed by a pope, cardinals, and archbishops, was patently inspired by Roman Catholicism. Besides the supreme god, Cao Dai, the faith also honored a great company of spirits, not only Eastern figures like the Buddha, Lao-tzu, Confucius, and Sun Yat-sen, but also such Westerners as Jesus, Muḥammad, Joan of Arc, and Victor Hugo.

Cao Dai worship centers on rituals performed in temples four times daily and celebrated with even greater elaborateness on festivals. The rituals consist of prayer, chants, and such simple offerings as incense, tea, and wine presented with highly stylized ceremony. Séances are held separately and are restricted to set occasions and to mediums appointed by the hierarchy. Despite these rules, Cao Dai has generated a number of sizable subsects, frequently inspired by fresh mediumistic communications.

Cao Dai is headquartered in a sacred city, Tay Ninh, northwest of Saigon. Here it boasts a large main temple and many administrative and ritual offices. Before the unification of Vietnam under the communist Hanoi regime in 1975, the "Holy See" was responsible not only for spiritual and ecclesiastical matters, but also for managing the sect's considerable agricultural and business holdings. During the several decades of strife before 1975, Cao Dai exercised effective control of its headquarters province and, until its forces were disbanded by President Ngo Dinh Diem in 1955, fielded its own army. Although its alliances shifted among the contending groups, Cao Dai basically labored for an unaligned nationalism.

Accused by the new communist state of being both politically oriented and "superstitious," after 1975 Cao Dai was severely repressed A high proportion of its churches were confiscated, and clergy arrested or laicized. The Holy See became virtually inactive. However, a gradual liberalization of policy toward religion commenced in the late 1980s. In 1997, in a grand ceremony at Tay Ninh, the regime officially made Cao Dai a recognized religion, though its governance was placed firmly under state control; many believers resisted recognition at that price. Outside Vietnam, Cao Dai temples and worship centers flourish in Vietnamese immigrant communities. Estimates put the faith's worldwide numbers at between two and four million.

See Also Vietnamese Religion.

Bibliography

Blagov, Sergei. *The Cao Dai: A New Religious Movement.* Moscow, 1999.

Bui, Hum Dac, and Ngasha Beck. *Cao Dai: Faith of Unity.* Fayetteville, Ark., 2000.

Oliver, Victor L. *Caodai Spiritism: A Study of Religion in Vietnamese Society.* Leiden, 1976.

Werner, Jayne Susan. *Peasant Politics and Religious Sectarianism: Peasant and Priest in the Cao Dai in Viet Nam.* New Haven, 1981.

Robert S. Ellwood (1987 and 2005)

CAPPS, WALTER. Born in Omaha, Nebraska, of Swedish-American background, Walter Holden Capps (1934–1997) was a professor in the Department of Religious Studies, University of California, Santa Barbara, from 1963 to 1996. Beginning with his academic training and intellectual interests in European Christian theology and philosophy of religion, Capps proceeded to develop innovative research and teaching on the intersections of religion with American culture, society, and political life. He emerged as a public intellectual through his academic and administrative leadership of the Council on the Study of Religion (1977–1984), the California Council for the Humanities (1983–1985), and the National Federation of State Humanities Councils (1985–1987). Elected in California to the U.S. House of Representatives in 1996, Walter Capps served in the Congress for ten months before his untimely death of a heart attack in October 1997. The Walter H. Capps Center at the University of California, Santa Barbara, was established in 2002 to continue his legacy by advancing the study of religion and public life.

From the philosophy of religion developed in Uppsala, Sweden, by Anders Nygren (1890–1978), Capps distilled an intellectual program for the study of religion, based on a Kantian framework, that remained remarkably consistent throughout his life. Immanuel Kant's three critiques represented for Capps three different but complementary entry points into the study of religion: with echoes of the ancient Greek trinity of the true, the good, and the beautiful, as Capps often observed, Kant's *Critique of Pure Reason* (1781) raised the problem of theoretical knowledge; his *Critique of Practical Reason* (1788) focused on ethics; and his *Critique of Judgment* (1790) engaged the world of aesthetics. Adopting this multidimensional Kantian mandate, Capps pursued these three threads—theoretical, practical, and aesthetic—through his publications and teaching in the study of religion.

Although his earliest books were on contemporary developments in Christian theology, Capps had a consistent interest in theory and method in the study of religion and religions. In part, this interest was informed by Nygren's philosophy of religion, which sought general, formal, and even scientific terms in which "to identify and examine the content of religion" (Capps, 2000, p. 21). But Capps was also convinced that the academic study of religion was a collective, cumulative, intellectual enterprise in asking certain basic questions about the essence, origin, structure, function, and language of religion. From *Ways of Understanding Reli-*

gion (1972), his edited collection of theoretical approaches to these questions, to his landmark history of the study of religion, *Religious Studies: The Making of a Disciple* (1995), Capps rigorously and perceptively examined the diversity of theoretical approaches to the study of religion.

Moving from the theoretical to the practical, Capps developed work on religion and politics, first through his interest in the impact of the Vietnam War on American society, which produced a groundbreaking book, *The Unfinished War: Vietnam and the American Conscience* (1982), and an extraordinary university course, "Religion and the Impact of the Vietnam War," which received national attention in the United States by being featured on the popular television show *60 Minutes.* Subsequently, in his research on right-wing, conservative Christian politics, which resulted in the book *The New Religious Right: Piety, Patriotism, and Politics* (1990), Capps emerged as an acute analyst of religious and political tensions in American society. Although his work on the practical implications of religion primarily focused on the United States, Capps's interest in the political, social, and ethical implications of religion was never parochial, as witnessed by his skill in surveying global, cross-cultural, and multireligious relations between religion and society.

Alongside theory and practice, Capps was consistently interested in aesthetics, structures of feeling, and varieties of experience. From 1968 to 1969, as a visiting scholar at one of the world's preeminent centers for art history, the University of London's Warburg Institute, Capps was able to develop his enduring interest in aesthetics. In his studies of religion, this aesthetic sensibility was clearly evident in his abiding theoretical concern that most accounts of religion failed because they were frozen in time—like still photographs—instead of providing moving pictures that might track the dynamic, experiential character of religion. In thinking about religious experience, Capps was more interested in processes of change, as explored by the psychoanalyst Erik Erikson (1902–1994), who tracked the psychological transitions in the human life cycle, than in establishing deep psychological structures. At the same time, however, Capps's interest in aesthetics, feeling, and religious experience informed his research on the stillness of religious contemplation and religious solitude, as evident in his edited volume on Christian mysticism and his explorations of Christian monasticism.

For the study of religion, these three strands—theoretical, practical, and aesthetic—represent a research program, as Capps argued, that fits the multidimensional character of religion. In a 1997 article on the Czech philosopher, political activist, and creative artist Václav Havel, Capps demonstrated that these three strands could be woven together in a single life. His own life, as academic, politician, and person, was similarly woven.

Bibliography

Capps, Walter. *Time Invades the Cathedral: Tensions in the School of Hope.* Philadelphia, 1972.

Capps, Walter, ed. *Ways of Understanding Religion.* New York, 1972.

Capps, Walter. *Hope Against Hope: Moltmann to Merton in One Decade.* Philadelphia, 1976.

Capps, Walter, and Wendy Wright, eds. *Silent Fire: An Invitation to Western Mysticism.* San Francisco, 1978.

Capps, Walter. *The Unfinished War: Vietnam and the American Conscience.* Boston, 1982; 2d ed., 1990.

Capps, Walter. *The Monastic Impulse.* New York, 1983.

Capps, Walter. *The New Religious Right: Piety, Patriotism, and Politics.* Columbia, S.C., 1990.

Capps, Walter. *Religious Studies: The Making of a Discipline.* Minneapolis, Minn., 1995.

Capps, Walter. "Interpreting Václav Havel." *Cross Currents* 47 (1997): 301–316.

Capps, Walter. "Introduction to *Religious Apriori.*" In *Anders Nygren's Religious Apriori*, edited by Walter H. Capps and Kjell O. Lejon, pp. 17–35. Linköping, Sweden, 2000. Available from http://www.ep.liu.se/ea/rel/2000/002/rel002-contents.pdf.

David Chidester (2005)

CARDS function in the religious context both as instruments for performing divination rituals and as repositories of esoteric sacred teaching. Current historical evidence suggests that cards originated in China and that their sacred usage developed from shamanistic or Taoist divinatory rituals that predated cards themselves. The oldest extant card, found in Chinese Turkistan, dates from no later than the eleventh century. The design of Chinese cards was copied from paper money first used in the Tang dynasty (618–908 CE). The design of an arrow on the back of the oldest Korean cards suggests that those cards developed from a divination technique for interpreting the pattern of arrows randomly cast onto a circle divided into quadrants.

Number and pattern, and their orderly transformations, are in sacred mathematics symbolic expressions, or hierophanies, of the eternal divine essences and processes that manifest themselves to us in time as the visible cosmos. The pack of divination cards is a homologue of the set of divine mathematical potentialities that can manifest itself in the time and space of the cosmos. The spontaneous play of the cards, like in any other particular act of divination, reveals a meaningful structure homologous to the divine creative process, which manifests itself within worldly events. The interpretation, or reading, of any particular play of cards is essentially a matter of intuiting from the sacred mathematical symbolism of the cards the worldly events whose structure corresponds to that symbolism.

It is not certain when and where cards first appeared in Europe. One hypothesis is that they were brought into southern Europe by the Moors as early as the eighth century. The earliest mention of numbered cards is in Covelluzzo's

Istoria della città di Viterbo (1480). Covelluzzo says that they were brought to the city of Viterbo by the Saracens in 1379. In her extensive study *A History of Playing Cards* (New York, 1966), Catherine P. Hargrave says that these early numbered cards were probably European copies of Chinese cards that arrived through Venice. The oldest extant European cards are several tarot cards from a pack designed for Charles VI of France in 1392.

The two most prominent packs of cards used in Europe for divination are the ordinary pack, consisting of fifty-two cards, and the tarot pack, consisting of seventy-eight cards. The ordinary pack is divided into four suits—diamonds, clubs, hearts, and spades. Joseph Campbell (in Campbell and Roberts, 1979) has suggested that the four suits represent the four estates, or classes, of the medieval social order: clergy (hearts), knights (spades), merchants (diamonds), and peasants (clubs). The four suits of the ordinary pack possibly developed under Protestant influence from the earlier tarot suits of chalices, swords, coins, and staves. The fact that the four suits of the ordinary pack culminate in the figures of knave, queen, and king leads Campbell to suppose that the pictorial symbolism of the cards expresses a medieval esoteric initiatory tradition wherein ascent along any of the four lines represented by the suits leads to spiritual realizations of equivalent value and importance.

The tarot pack falls into two sections: the "minor arcana" of fifty-six cards, divided equally into four suits, and the "major arcana" of twenty-one numbered picture cards and one unnumbered card, the Fool. The origin of the tarot deck is not known. The first history of the tarot, *Le jeu des tarots* (Paris, 1781), was written by Court de Gebelin. Gebelin claims that the deck originated in ancient Egypt and represents the esoteric teaching of the god Thoth, recorded and expressed in a hieroglyphic alphabet, in which all the gods are symbolized by pictorial signs and numbers. While Gebelin's theory of Egyptian origins is clearly itself of a mythic nature (the Rosetta Stone, which made translation of hieroglyphics possible, was not discovered until 1790), the evidence of recent research on the history of symbols indicates that the deck is indeed, as Gebelin supposed, a repository of sacred teaching and esoteric knowledge. The pictorial symbolism of the deck is known to have much in common with the symbolism of spiritual initiation rites and instruction in Hellenistic mystery cults, ancient astrology, and medieval alchemy, wherein the processes of manifesting divine energies are represented in the progression of visual and numerical symbols.

BIBLIOGRAPHY

Tarot Revelations by Joseph Campbell and Richard Roberts (San Anselmo, Calif., 1979) is a detailed work summarizing the phenomenological evidence linking the tarot to Hellenistic religion and alchemy as well as the tarot's place in nineteenth-century esoteric societies.

New Sources

Baird, Merrily. "Card Games." In her *Symbols of Japan: Thematic Motifs in Art and Design.* New York, 2001.

Giles, Cynthia. *The Tarot: History, Mystery, and Lore.* 1992; reprint. New York, 1994.

Preston, Cathy Lynn and Michael Preston. "Catholic Holy Cards: Visual, Verbal, and Tactile Codes for the (In)visible." In their *The Other Print Tradition: Essays on Chapbooks, Broadsides, and Related Ephemera,* pp. 266–283. New York, 1994.

RICHARD W. THURN (1987)
Revised Bibliography

CARGO CULTS [FIRST EDITION]. In 1980, a motorcade drove into Madang, a provincial capital in Papua New Guinea (independent since 1975), and stopped outside the local branch of the national bank. The drivers and passengers came from a Catholic village sixty kilometers to the west. Their spokeswoman, Josephine Bahu (about twenty-eight at the time), asked the bank manager, a European, to give her the keys to his vaults, for God had revealed to her the truth about money—its true source and its proper use as a road to economic development.

This incident was a recent example of cargoism, the most common form of millenarianism in Melanesia since the nineteenth century, when colonial rule reduced its inhabitants to the status of cheap labor for European employers. The millennium, as it has inevitably come to be manifested in this context, is the anticipated arrival of bulk supplies of European goods (cargo)—civilian stock, such as tinned meat, cotton cloth, steel tools, and motor vehicles; and military equipment, especially rifles and ammunition—which many of the people believe to be made not by human beings but by a deity or deities aided by the spirits of the dead. This conception of the millennium may give rise to a cargo cult or movement whose devotees perform ritual to induce the cargo god(s) to send the ancestors with supplies of the new wealth (and nowadays, as the initial example suggests, money) for immediate distribution. I begin by describing overt cargo phenomena and then discuss some of the best-known approaches to their study by Western scholars.

OVERT CARGO PHENOMENA. Western scholars first learned about cargo phenomena in 1857 through the publication of the Mansren myth of the Koreri in the Biak-Numfoor area of Irian Jaya, probably the oldest cargo movement in the whole region, although there were manifestations in Samoa in the 1830s and in Fiji in the 1880s. In Papua New Guinea the first known cults were the Baigona, reported in 1912, and the Vailala Madness, reported in 1919, although one movement, centered on Madang, can be dated from 1871 and continues to the present day. Cargoism began to proliferate just before World War II. In Papua New Guinea there has been a plethora of cults; in the Solomon Islands, Marching Rule; and in Vanuatu, the John Frum movement. In recent times the region has seen the rise of various alternatives to cargoism, specifically Pentecostalism and other Christian cults that are independent of the established European missions and that lay stress on healing and salvation. Although it is hard to draw a firm line between cargoism and other modern religious developments in Melanesia, I concentrate on cargo cults as such.

The many forms that cargo cults take depend on a number of variables: (1) a people's socioeconomic structure, basic personality, and traditional religion, which factors together determine the strength of their desire for the new wealth and the extent to which they are prepared to test or reject theological experiments; (2) the nature of the introduced religion, which they may or may not readily interpret as cargo doctrine; and (3) the pattern of initial contact and subsequent relations with Europeans (the actual purveyors of cargo), which underlie the political aspects of the people's responses. Thus, as we learn from the early ethnographic accounts of the Papua New Guinea Highlands—which were brought under administration only after 1933, when Europeans had gained some experience in Melanesian affairs—for some years it seemed likely that strong social structures, hard-headedness, and the predilection for secularism rather than religion, together with good race relations, accounted for the general paucity of cargo cults in the area. On the seaboard, incorporated within colonial administrations soon after 1884, a contrary situation obtained. Relatively weak social structures, an induced inferiority complex, an intellectual system dominated by theology, and often traumatic race relations had created the conditions in which cargoism was bound to flourish. Yet, although differences of this kind do exist, the neat geographical distinction suggested is probably overdrawn. In recent years cargoism, like Pentecostalism, has made inroads into the Highlands, forcing a reappraisal of previous interpretations.

The most obvious signs of a cargo cult's emergence are generally its devotees' preparations for the arrival of the goods they expect. Especially early on, when all cargo came by ship, they built wharves and storehouses in coastal villages. During and after the Pacific war, when the importance of aircraft became apparent, they cleared airstrips. Cargo may also be expected to appear in local cemeteries, which devotees assiduously keep clean and tidy, on altars in churches, which they regard as particularly holy, or at other places the leaders designate. In addition, there have been "flagstaffs," "radio masts," and even "telephones," by means of which the leaders could make contact with the deity and ancestors for news of the goods' arrival. Sometimes both leaders and followers have "demonstrated" the reality of this contact by simulating spirit possession, including shaking fits and other forms of violent seizure.

Yet cargo cannot come by itself: its arrival has to be ensured by means of religious ritual. A cult normally begins when, after a dream, waking vision, or some other extraordinary experience, its leader announces that he has been in touch with the deity, who has revealed to him the source of the desired wealth, the methods by which those who have so far monopolized it (generally Europeans) have defrauded the people of their rights, and the new ritual procedures necessary to redress the balance. Most leaders have been men, but there have been some outstanding women: Josephine Bahu in the 1980s, Philo of Inawai'a village (of the Mekeo language group, Papua) in 1941, and Polelesi of Igurue village (of the Garia language group, New Guinea) in 1947.

In this context, it is essential to distinguish between cults based on paganism, Christianity, and syncretic Christian-pagan doctrine. In a purely pagan cult, the leader has the difficult task of persuading the followers that traditional myths have a meaning which was not mentioned in the past but which has now been revealed to him alone. In quasi-Christian cults the problem is not so great. Christianity is not enshrined in tradition and can be interpreted with greater flexibility. The leader may claim to have visited God in heaven and returned as the Black Jesus. Again, in the course of some such experience, he may have learned that the secret of the cargo is the identification of an indigenous deity with God or Jesus Christ.

These basic differences, which are generally the result of the degree of administrative and more particularly mission influence, determine the nature of the ritual instructions the leader invariably claims to have received from the deity. In a pagan cult, where cultural change is minimal, the leader is likely to do no more than order the performance of mainly traditional rituals in honor of deities and the dead (possibly with a few foreign embellishments), albeit in an intensified form, as happened in the eastern Highlands of Papua New Guinea. But where there has been acculturation, ritual incorporates new forms and becomes more elaborate. Cults based on Christianity may have mass village assemblies with marathon church services and prayers to God, "the Cargo Giver." Disbelievers are threatened with hellfire, and the Second Coming of Our Lord is prophesied as imminent, with all the wealth of Europe going to the faithful. There are mass conversions and baptisms. Polygyny and sexual promiscuity are forbidden, although in some villages in the southern Madang Province in the 1940s cult leaders experimented with wife exchange on the ground that this eliminated the quarrels over adultery that so displeased God. The sanctuaries of traditional deities are often desecrated or destroyed, and all forms of indigenous dancing and exchange outlawed. Christian fervor may go to extremes: in the early 1960s, in a village north of Madang, a man acquiesced in having his throat slit in front of a completely unsuspecting Catholic archbishop. It eventuated that this was a ritual reenactment of the Crucifixion: the victim was the Black Jesus, who was to intercede with God for the economic advantage of his people just as the White Jesus had done for Europeans.

In Christian-pagan syncretic cults, ritual, like doctrine, tends to borrow from both religions. Cults of this degree of sophistication often have two interesting features. First, devotees may root out their crops, cut down their palms and fruit trees, and slaughter their livestock. No ubiquitously satisfactory explanation for this behavior has been found, but in one area, the southern Madang Province, the reason given is that the people want to stress their poverty to the cargo deity and ancestors, thereby hastening the arrival of the new goods. Second, especially in communities which value money as a means of access to cargo, leaders may persuade their followers to place spare cash in a case or chest on the promise that their ritual will increase the sum deposited many times over. Finally, in some areas the people have totally rejected Christianity and its syncretic modifications in favor of paganism for cargoist ends. This heralds the reintroduction of traditional ritual with modern borrowings.

WESTERN ANALYSES OF CARGO PHENOMENA. The extensive literature on cargoism primarily consists of accounts of single cults, although there are several important comparative analyses. Space precludes detailed consideration of these general works, so I have selected for discussion the approaches of several Western scholars since World War I to indicate the trends in our thinking about the problem.

It took many years to complete detailed studies of cargo cults in which the participants could speak for themselves. Inevitably, therefore, the first European interpretations were ethnocentric. Francis E. Williams, who was from 1922 until 1943 the government anthropologist in Papua, wrote essays in 1922 and 1934 that examined the facts of cargo phenomena in light of the assumptions of his own society. He wrote only about the disturbances in the Gulf Province, the so-called Vailala Madness, a title which, significantly, he never challenged. Although a meticulous field-worker, he never comprehended Melanesian values and epistemology. He made careful notes about the external features of the cult: the people's imitation of European dress, eating habits, and house decoration; their use of Christian beliefs as part of their doctrine; their make-believe Western technology; and their periodic hysteria. But the meaning of it all eluded him: nothing in his personal or academic experience had prepared him for this kind of behavior. He concluded that the people were temporarily insane as a result of misunderstood Christianity and boredom caused by the loss of traditional activities, such as warfare and religious ceremonies. The cure he advocated was the Anglo-Australian boarding-school nostrum: some form of intervillage sport like football.

Peter Worsley, writing in the 1950s, had at his disposal a far larger body of cargoist literature, which he presented with great thoroughness. Yet much of the material was of doubtful value, based as it was on superficial accounts by untrained onlookers during and after World War II. Many of the observations were made when, after a period of optimistic but unproductive cooperation with Europeans (which the authors never appreciated), the people were finally hostile to whites. Hence it was easy for Worsley to offer a Marxist explanation: the cults were an embryonic form of class struggle against economic and political oppression, that is, the people's protest against their colonial overlords.

There are two objections to this kind of analysis. First, although one aspect of cargoism is undeniably its political statement, we have no evidence that cargoism is invariably anti-European. After a bad period, mainly in the nineteenth and early twentieth centuries, colonial rule—certainly as it was known in Papua New Guinea—was relatively benign. Many villagers have adopted cargoism as a means of explaining and manipulating the new order long before unfulfilled hopes have made them antagonistic. As indicated, cargoism can express the desire to fraternize with white men. Second, the Marxist approach to issues raised by cargoism is basically secular and so barely touches on the question of why the people have used religion, virtually on its own, to explain and try to cope with the colonial and postcolonial situations. Many cults are based on intricate philosophies, which cannot legitimately be ignored.

Between 1960 and 1972 three other scholars—Ian Jarvie, Freerk Kamma, and Kenelm Burridge—did much to offset this imbalance. Jarvie, a philosopher with a deep interest in social anthropology and an appreciation of Melanesian religion, approaches cargoism from an uncompromisingly intellectualist point of view. Although he does not deny the importance of the political issues raised by Worsley, he makes it quite plain that his interest lies in the structure of cargo doctrines as means of "teaching" the people the source of European wealth and giving them the prescription for getting it. In the sense that they are based on traditional assumptions and modes of thought, cargo cults are completely logical.

Kamma, a missionary who studied the Koreri movement in the northwestern sector of Irian Jaya, argues that it is a direct continuation of religious traditions aimed at maintaining and improving the people's way of life. With the arrival of European missionaries in the nineteenth century, the people wove Christianity into these traditions and treated cargo as the symbol of the improved way of life. His argument is echoed by John Strelan, another missionary, who reasons that for Melanesians cargo is salvation, an idea akin to Calvin's dictum that worldly success is the basis of *certitudo salutis.*

Burridge, who studied the Tangu in the northern Madang Province, sees cargo cults as the Melanesians' attempt to achieve full human dignity through attainment of economic and sociopolitical equality with Europeans. Their purpose is to create the "new society" and the "new man" able to maintain this principle of equivalence with whites. He stresses the importance of the "myth-dream," in both traditional religions and quasi-Christian cults, as the revelation of the origin of cargo and the secret of the ritual that will make it available.

A COMPOSITE APPROACH TO CARGO PHENOMENA. I have developed a composite approach based on my own research in the southern Madang Province after 1949. I regard it as essential to take all the issues raised by the foregoing scholars and combine them in a way that keeps each one in proper perspective. Broadly, cargoists try to recreate in the modern situation the same kind of predictable cosmic order they knew in the past: an order the gods ordained and human beings maintain by fulfilling social obligations among themselves and ritual obligations toward deities and ancestors. This recreation will give them the key to the new wealth and ensure its fair distribution. In a word, they retain their old cosmic values of anthropocentrism and materialism: man is the center of the cosmos, which exists for his benefit. Cargoism, thus conceived, is a dialogue between the old sociocultural system and the economic, political, and religious policies introduced by colonial administrations. A most important factor is that, although they enabled the people to acquire limited supplies of the new goods, these policies actually achieved few changes in village life. Despite a century of European control, the pattern of economic and sociopolitical life has remained very much intact. The people still have minimal knowledge of the European world, so that their reactions to, and interpretations of, cargo are based primarily on tradition. To this extent, cargoism is conservative.

My "composite approach" to cargoism raises three questions relating to *motivation, conceived means,* and *effects* in cargo cult. Why do the people desire European goods so much that they waste decades in trying to acquire them by obviously futile procedures? Why do they rely on religious ritual rather than secular activity? What have cargo cults done to indigenous society?

MOTIVATION. In absolute terms, Melanesians have never been poor. They have rarely known hunger. Hence cargoism is an expression of relative deprivation. The people want Western goods for two reasons: their obvious utility and technical superiority over indigenous products; and their sociopolitical significance. They quickly saw the practical value of European artifacts, especially steel axes and knives, nails, and cloth. In the nineteenth century European traders took great pains to provide the kinds of goods the people wanted. These traders were always on guard against theft, for the demand for their goods was great, and Melanesians were skillful fighters. By 1900, most Melanesians under colonial administration had adopted steel tools, some Western clothing, and such luxuries as glass beads and mirrors.

This pragmatic incentive has its sociopolitical counterpart, which can be understood only by considering the role of wealth in traditional society. Beyond its usefulness, wealth is a vital content of all social relationships. Bonds between local descent groups, kinsmen, and affines—the prime constituents of social structure—are strengthened by the periodic exchange of goods and services, particularly pigs and valuables. For one party to fail in its commitments is cause for tremendous shame, which nothing can alleviate. The people desire exactly this kind of egalitarian relationship with Europeans, and cargo is the most important part of the goods and services to be exchanged. One cargo leader put it to an Australian officer thus: "We are doing no harm. All we want is to live well—like white men!" Yet the structure of the modern economy necessitates marked inequalities between foreign employers and indigenous employees. European monopoly of the new wealth has become the symbol of this imbalance and hence a primary cause of political unrest.

Although the pragmatic incentive to acquire cargo is a constant, sociopolitical motivation correlates with the climate of race relations, which in its turn determines the kinds of goods the people desire and the political significance of cult activity. This has been documented for one area of Papua New Guinea. In the southern Madang Province, which comprises a large number of separate language groups or virtually autonomous societies, the cargo movement has since 1871 passed through five broad stages that have expressed varying attitudes toward Europeans (ranging from friendship to hostility) and shifting preferences for specific types of goods, civilian or military.

The first stage (1871–c. 1900) began with the arrival of the first European settler, the Russian scientist Baron Miklouho-Maclay, who won the people's friendship by establishing a fair trading partnership with them. He introduced Western civilian goods and new food plants, all of which were enthusiastically received. In 1884 he was followed by German settlers, whose behavior was a complete antithesis: they were arrogant; they alienated a disproportionate amount of coastal land for plantations; and they paid badly for labor. Friendship gave way to hostility, which was the leitmotif also of the second stage (c. 1900–c. 1914). The people now wanted to acquire rifles and ammunition with which to expel the foreigners. In 1904 the administration put down a serious uprising in Madang and in 1912, fearing another emergency, exiled a large part of the local population.

The third stage (c. 1914–c. 1933) saw a *volte-face.* The new Australian administration permitted the exiles to return home, and the people sought an accommodation with the whites, hoping to live in peace with them and acquire civilian goods. Certainly the last expectation was unreal, so that the fourth stage (c. 1933–c. 1945) witnessed a return to enmity toward Europeans and a desire for military equipment. Some cultists collaborated with the Japanese (who occupied the area between 1942 and 1944), armed themselves with discarded Japanese weapons, and set up a quasi-military camp. For a brief time after 1945 the people, under the leadership of Yali Singina, who had served in the Australian army, once again expressed goodwill toward Europeans. Because of a misunderstanding, Yali believed, and so had persuaded his people, that in return for the loyalty of native troops the Europeans would reward the people with bulk cargo. These hopes were dashed in 1947, when it transpired that the "bulk reward" was to be development in the form of hospitals and schools—benefits that ordinary villagers could not then appreciate. This inaugurated the fifth stage (1948–1950), which expressed renewed hostility and, for some of the regional population at least, the hope of getting modern weapons with which to fight the Europeans.

Regrettably, there is no comparable account of this alternating pattern of friendly and hostile race relations elsewhere in Melanesia. Yet the Madang evidence stresses the falsity of the view that cargoism always expresses hostility toward Europeans. Another recent incident supports this argument. In a major cargo cult in the East Sepik Province of Papua New Guinea in 1971, some six thousand people formed a chain gang to remove from the summit of Mount Hurun some military concrete markers, which were believed to be demons impeding the cargo millennium. Before the event local Europeans widely predicted that they would be the target of popular animosity. Yet there was no evidence of this. Cult devotees brought the markers to the station of the local European patrol officer and then peacefully dispersed. Significantly, a year later a similar operation was planned near Madang: the destruction of the monument erected in honor of the German governor von Hagen after his death in 1897 and said to be preventing the arrival of the cargo deity. The sponsors stressed their desire for racial harmony by inviting Europeans and Chinese to take part. They tried to get a message to this effect broadcast over Radio Mandang.

Conceived means. As attacks on trading vessels and uprisings around Madang suggest, Melanesians are prepared to use physical force to gain their economic and political ends. Hence it is perhaps puzzling that at the same time they consistently rely on religious ritual as a means of getting cargo in the face of recurrent failure. It can be said, of course, that once they appreciate the power of colonial administrations they are afraid to take direct action. But this does not explain why they are convinced that religion will provide a solution or why, in some cases, they combine it with secular economic activity. For instance, the people of Karkar Island and Mount Hagen, now rich from cash crops, either believe in or actually practice cargo ritual.

The only possible answer is that Western contact has not destroyed the people's traditional intellectual assumptions: that religion is the source of "true knowledge" and that ritual is a pragmatic technology with no mystical attributes. The forces that governed the old cosmic order should govern the new one. This idea was expressed to me early in my research by a highly intelligent informant: "Everything that we have was invented by a deity: taro, yams, livestock, artifacts. If we want taro to grow, we invoke the taro goddess, and so forth. Well, then, you people come to us with all your goods, and we ask, 'Where is the god of the cargo and how do we contact him?'" The continuing search for the divine source of Western goods after each negative result is consistent with this statement.

Here again the southern Madang Province is illustrative, as the area saw a succession of five cargo beliefs or doctrines that correlated more or less with the sociopolitical stages already summarized. The first of these beliefs (1871–c. 1900) expressed the people's conclusion that the early European visitors were indigenous gods suddenly appearing in their midst. Miklouho-Maclay was either Kilibob or Manup, the two deity brothers who between them were said to have created all the sociocultural systems of the region's seaboard. He had invented the new goods he brought especially for them, and as a measure of their friendship they had to reciprocate with gifts of food. They do not appear to have honored him with ritual while he was living in their midst. Ordinary social behavior sufficed. Although they at first expected to establish comparable exchange ties with the Germans, ultimately they came to regard them, because of their haughtiness, as hostile gods whose purpose was to enslave them with their rifles. But, as the second cargo belief (c. 1900–c. 1914) indicated, they decided that the Germans were human beings who, because of a cosmic accident, had acquired sole access to the cargo deity, Kilibob or Manup, and so misappropriated the wealth properly destined for Madang.

The third cargo belief (c. 1914–c. 1933) expressed the people's renewed goodwill toward Europeans because the missionaries had consistently shown concern during their exile and the new administration had brought them home, which they interpreted as signs that the cargo secret would be revealed to them. To this end, they adopted Christianity and revised it as a cargo religion. God, Jesus Christ, and the ancestors lived in Heaven (a suburb of Sydney, Australia), where they made cargo. Baptism and assiduous worship of the kind already described would induce God to send the ancestors with cargo to the ships (and later aircraft) that would deliver it to the Madangs. But after twenty years the people were no better off. Thus the fourth cargo belief (c. 1933–c. 1945) spelled out their distrust of, and enmity to, Europeans, especially the missionaries, who had hidden the truth from them. The new doctrine and ritual were syncretic. Kilibob and Manup were equated with God and Jesus Christ, the cargo deities kept prisoner by the whites in Australia. The aim was to honor them in such a way as to ensure their return: through church services, dancing, feasting, and food offerings. The Japanese soldiers, of course, were either spirits of the dead or emissaries of the cargo god sent to punish the Europeans for their duplicity. The fifth cargo belief (1948–1950) marked the end of dependence on a foreign religion. All the traditional gods of the southern Madang Province were now proclaimed cargo deities. The missionaries had hidden them in Australia, but Manup (alias Jesus Christ) had found them and taught them to make cargo. It was now the people's duty and interest to get them back to Madang to establish the millennium. To do this, they had to reject all Christian teaching and worship, and return to traditional ritual, especially dancing, feasting, initiatory ceremonies, and food offerings to gods and ancestors set out on specially prepared tables.

Effects. Until recently a main interest of Anglo-Australian social anthropology has been the study of political structure and function, and it is not surprising that the effect of cargoism on traditional society has been evaluated predominantly in that field. Early suggestions were that cargoism might help lay the foundations of future nationalism in two ways: by uniting the populations of whole regions and thereby breaking down sectionalism based on clan, village, and language group; and by preparing the people to accept genuine development when it was presented to them in realistic administrative projects. We should be careful on both these counts.

In the first context, although cargo cults have at times brought together social aggregations far larger than was possible before contact, it is doubtful whether this process has been universal and automatic or whether the leaders have deliberately fostered it. The evidence suggests rather that these aggregations occur only when their members have a single doctrine to unite them. When this is lost, the aggregations disperse. I consider again the southern Madang Province. In the second stage of the cargo movement, although the people of the whole coast under administration may have been hostile to the Germans and may have hoped for a return of Kilibob or Manup, they did not form a grand alliance. The politico-military groups in the revolts of 1904 and 1912 appear to have been based on old rather than new alignments: traditional clan alliances and marriage or kinship ties. In the third stage, widespread conversion to Christianity gave the people of the whole region a sense of common consciousness: together with Europeans, they were all descended from Adam, Eve, and Noah. Yet there was no attempt to create a wide political organization to exploit the new attitude. In the fourth stage, this widespread common consciousness was considerably attenuated because the new syncretic doctrines based on the amalgam of the Kilibob-Manup myth and Christianity were restricted entirely to the littoral. The quasi-Christian cargoists of the inland, who had no rights to the traditional myth, were at once excluded. Nevertheless, the coastal villagers following the new doctrine did evince a degree of solidarity never known in the past. Finally, in the fifth stage, Yali Singina agreed to become the movement's leader only when he was satisfied that Jesus-Manup had transferred the power to make cargo to all the indigenous deities so that he, as an inland dweller, could not be accused of theft for meddling with a coastal myth. The new doctrine had the potential to unite the people of the whole region in a mass anti-European cult. Yet, although antagonism was rife, Yali's organization was too inefficient and parochial to turn it into an effective political force. In short, the process of expanding political cohesion is probably unconscious and haphazard rather than deliberately planned.

In the second context, there appears to be even less evidence to support the view that cargoism arouses among the people such energy and enthusiasm for modernization that it helps facilitate the change to indigenous government and administration. Indeed, the facts suggest that cargoism is—and that its devotees see it as—ontologically quite different from the national structure established and bequeathed by the former colonial power, and that cargoism cannot easily be assimilated to that structure, which, moreover, it may deliberately impede. By presenting itself as a seemingly logical alternative system, the movement offers those unwilling to experiment with new ideas the opportunity to engage in activities which may be consistent with tradition but are bound to be sterile—an argument relevant not only to the political field but to the economic and educational fields as well.

In the field of politics, it is necessary to consider the behavior of cargoists in two situations; in the electorate at large; and within parliament and local government councils. During election campaigns cargoists have indeed made extravagent claims. In 1967–1968 Yali Singina, who now prefixed his name with the title god-king, campaigned for a seat in the national parliament in Port Moresby on the following platform. He would go to the House, where he would discover the indigenous deities, whom the administration had now placed there in a secret room. He would occupy the Speaker's Chair, take control of the Mace, and liberate the gods, with whom he would return to Madang, where he would usher in the cargo millennium and proclaim self-government, administering the country with the aid of those European officers of whom he approved. He was not elected. Again, in 1971, he rejected an offer of an electoral alliance from the Madang representatives of Pangu Pati (the senior government party) on the grounds that as "king" of Papua New Guinea he could not share power. Yet, in 1972, he belatedly but unsuccessfully tried to take up the offer because he believed that Pangu was a cult organization like his own. Matias Yaliwan, the chief cargo prophet in the East Sepik Province, claimed to have been told in a dream that he had been appointed leader of the country. He was elected to parliament in 1972 and subsequently told his followers that it was through his special aura that self-government was achieved. By the same token, in the 1980s Josephine Bahu's senior followers wrote to the prime minister that she should be made head of state.

Apart from Matias Yaliwan, a number of known cargoists have been elected to parliament and local government councils, where their behavior has generally been far more circumspect. Real politics does not provide an arena in which they can operate with success. Matias resigned his seat when he realized that his claim to personal leadership was being quietly ignored. Other cargoists have remained largely quiescent, making few speeches and little contribution to proceedings beyond voting. In the same way, Yali Singina and his "deputy" Dui Yangsai sat for many years on the Rai Coast Council but, despite their flamboyant pronouncements elsewhere, never advocated cargoist policy in the chamber.

A comparable conflict of interest and interpretation obtains in the fields of economic development and education. Although on Karkar and at Mount Hagen the people have succeeded in cash cropping while at the same time engaging in cargoism, there are many other cases in which cargoists and developers are continually at loggerheads. The cargoists assert that the developers prevent the millennium by paying all their attention to their plantations and denying the cargo god the ritual honor due to him. Also, it is questionable how genuine economic success on Karkar and at Mount Hagen can be when many people still appear to regard purely secular activity as a poor second best. Cargoism could well hold them back from innovations that might lead to expansion, so that they may remain always the satellites of European businessmen, who still provide all the initiatives. Finally, many people misunderstand and are disenchanted with modern education. In the past, parents have taken their children away from mission schools when they discovered that the cargo secret was not in the curriculum. Some have even denied the value of mission schools, which are attended by children of both sexes: genuine education—that is, powerful religious secrets—is given only to males during and after initiation. In cargoist areas secular education has been equally badly received. Many children see no point in it, and the dropout rate for secondary schools is very high. Unsuccessful pupils have been drawn into cargo organizations as "secretaries" and "clerks." With their smattering of Western knowledge, these young members give the cults an appearance of increased sophistication and provide explanatory systems so persuasive that the ordinary villager finds it hard to fault them. It is no wonder that both national and provincial politicians and public servants, concerned for the future of their country, view these counterintellectuals with disquiet, as a fifth column that can vitiate genuine achievement.

SEE ALSO New Guinea Religions.

BIBLIOGRAPHY

Berndt, Ronald M. "A Cargo Movement in the Eastern Central Highlands of New Guinea." *Oceania* 23 (September 1952): 40–65; (December 1952): 137–158; (March 1953): 202–234. An early paper describing what was until recently one of the few cargo cults in the Highlands of Papua New Guinea.

Burridge, Kenelm. *Mambu: A Melanesian Millennium.* London, 1960. A humane and sophisticated analysis of cargo activity in the northern Madang Province of Papua New Guinea. Emphasizes the people's efforts to reestablish their self-respect by achieving socioeconomic and political equality with Europeans. Burridge expands and projects his argument into the field of international millenarianism in his *New Heaven, New Earth* (New York, 1969).

Cochrane, Glynn. *Big Men and Cargo Cults.* Oxford, 1970. An analysis of the role of leaders in cargo cults, with emphasis on Papua and the Solomon Islands.

Guiart, Jean. *Un siècle et demi de contacts culturels à Tanna, Nouvelles-Hebrides.* Paris, 1956. An important historical analysis of administrative and mission influence and popular response (including cargoism) in Vanuatu.

Hanneman, E. F. "Le Culte du Cargo en Nouvelle-Guinée." *Le monde non Chretién,* n. s. 8 (October–December 1948): 937–962. An early demonstration of the possibilities of an intellectualist approach to cargoism. A classic work.

Harding, Thomas G. "A History of Cargoism in Sio, North-east New Guinea." *Oceania* 38 (September 1967): 1–23. A paper important not only for its ethnographic content: here Harding coins the term cargoism and establishes the movement as a philosophy in its own right.

Jarvie, Ian C. *The Revolution in Anthropology* (1964). New York, 1967. A prominent work: the first internationally recognized study of cargoism in intellectualist terms and, at the same time, an astute critique of positivist social anthropology.

Kamma, Freerk C. *Koreri.* The Hague, 1972. A detailed history and analysis of cargoism in western Irian Jaya, with a most valuable summary and assessment of other works on the general subject.

Lawrence, Peter. *Road Belong Cargo.* Manchester and Melbourne, 1964. A full history of the cargo movement in the southern Madang Province of Papua New Guinea, with a rounded analysis of the movement in its economic, sociopolitical, and intellectual contexts. The analysis of the people's intellectual interpretation of cargo and the right way to get it, independently parallels and endorses Jarvie's argument in *The Revolution in Anthropology,* mentioned above.

May, Ronald J. "Micronationalism in Perspective" and "Micronationalism: What, When, and Why?" in *Micronationalist Movements in Papua New Guinea,* edited by Ronald J. May. Canberra, 1982. The most recent and precise analysis of the relationship between cargoism and nationalism in Papua New Guinea.

McSwain, Romola. *The Past and Future People.* Oxford, 1977. A thorough examination of a Papua New Guinea society (Karkar Island) undergoing development preparatory to becoming part of a new independent nation-state; discusses the way in which the people have interwoven new economic, political, and educational projects with cargoism.

Ogan, Eugene. *Business and Cargo.* Canberra, 1972. A most valuable account of the relationship between commercial development and cargoism among the Nasioi of Bougainville, Papua New Guinea, a people living in the shadow of a major mining venture to which much of the local economy was tied.

Plutta, Paul, and Wendy Flannery. "'Mama Dokta': A Movement in the Utu Area, Madang Province." In *Religious Movements in Melanesia,* edited by Glen W. Bays. Goroka, Papua New Guinea, 1983. A vivid description of cargoist activity in modern postindependence setting; illustrates the uneasy relationship between cult devotees and the indigenous government.

Schwartz, Theodore. "The Paliau Movement in the Admiralty Islands, 1946–1954," *Anthropological Papers of the American Museum of Natural History* 49 (1962): 211–421. An important work. Describes and analyzes an indigenous, as against a government-sponsored, development movement and its ambivalent relationship with a cargo cult.

Steinbauer, Friedrich. *Melanesian Cargo Cults.* Saint Lucia, Australia, 1979. A most comprehensive survey and discussion of the literature on cargo cults and of European scholars' approaches to them.

Strathern, Andrew. "The Red Box Money-Cult in Mount Hagen 1968–71." *Oceania* 50 (December 1979): 88–102; (March 1980): 161–175. A paper important for dispelling the mistaken notion that Highlands societies in Papua New Guinea are not prone to cargoism; valuable too for showing how the people experiment with cargo activity while engaging in vigorous cash cropping.

Strelan, John G. *Search for Salvation.* Adelaide, Australia, 1977. An enterprising general analysis of cargoism from a Christian missionary's point of view. Strelan suggests that Melanesians are now working out their own distinct theology.

Williams, Francis E. "The Vailala Madness" and "The Vailala Madness in Retrospect." In *Francis Edgar Williams: The Vai-*

lala Madness and Other Essays, edited by Erik Schwimmer, pp. 351–384 and pp. 385–395. London, 1976. Two early accounts of cargo cult, most valuable for their careful description of its external features but lacking insight into its socioeconomic, political, and epistemological bases.

Worsley, Peter. *The Trumpet Shall Sound: A Study of "Cargo" Cults in Melanesia* (1957). New York, 1968. An early general work important because it did much to bring the phenomenon of cargoism to the attention of Western scholars. Describes many of the outbreaks of cargo cult up to the 1950s. The first edition is written from a strictly Marxist perspective, at least part of which the author renounces in the second.

PETER LAWRENCE (1987)

CARGO CULTS [FURTHER CONSIDERATIONS].

Since Peter Lawrence wrote his confident, empirically rich discussion of the cargo cult for the first edition of this encyclopedia in 1987, the terrain of Pacific religion and politics has changed, as has the terrain of scholarly analysis. It is no longer so clear that "cargo cults" ever existed, or at least whether the analytic category is valuable.

Over the past fifty years in the Pacific, the post–World War II decolonization imperative has proceeded apace. New nation-states, multinational corporations, nongovernmental organizations, proliferating evangelical groups, and other postcolonial institutions and agents populate the islands. The imperial world system entanglements of the era of European capitalist and colonial expansion are replaced by global interconnections of the post–World War II United Nations world, including regional nation-state alliances, aid and development programs, migration, tourism, multinational corporate penetration, consumption, and media flows. Yet, Pacific people have not ceased to innovate politically and religiously. How are we to understand these innovations? What particular issues of religion, power, and sovereignty are raised by the nation-state and how might this implicate the concept of the cargo cult?

In scholarship, the "cargo cult" is now treated far more skeptically by many scholars than in Lawrence's account. In the mid-twentieth century, scholars unproblematically wrote books and articles defining cargo cults, giving examples of cargo cults, arguing over their nature and causes, and proposing explanations of their causes. While many important studies still use the category (and while Pacific peoples themselves may use the term—positively, neutrally, or pejoratively), many of the analytic issues have turned from ontology to epistemology, from questions about what cargo cults are, to questions about the knower, and to the effects of claiming that cargo cults do exist or the effects of seeking to specify their characteristics. For example, some anthropologists now argue that "cargo cults do not exist," finding the so-named phenomena better understood instead in terms of ongoing trajectories of Pacific history-making (including that long predating the colonial encounter), while others find their origin not in Pacific sociology or cosmology but in the Western imagination. Finally, serious scholarly thinking about the nature of states and cults that finds the state as enchanted as any millenarian movement has made the melding of politics and religion in these Pacific movements less surprising and all the more useful to study of general issues of present and future religious life.

This entry reviews three analyses that exemplify some of these trends in interesting ways, beginning with a summary of Martha Kaplan's chronicle of the Fijian Tuka movement, *Neither Cargo nor Cult: Ritual Politics and the Colonial Imagination in Fiji* (1995). The work is fully committed to understanding an ongoing, dynamic ritual-political history making of Fijians, and it is also highly skeptical of the analytic utility of the concept of the cargo cult, finding its origins in British colonial discourse of order and disorder. It thus takes a Bakhtinean, dialogical approach to this colonial and postcolonial history. Dialogical does not mean a friendly or consensus-seeking interchange, but rather explores the semiotic and cultural consequences of interactions of sharply opposed agents, parties, and classes. Thus, a dialogical history is a history in which none of the agents is unaffected by the interaction (see Kelly and Kaplan, 1990).

Next is a summary of Lamont Lindstrom's important *Cargo Cult: Strange Stories of Desire from Melanesia and Beyond* (1993), which argues that cargo cults do exist (or at least that there is a cross-cultural unity among certain events of collective action in which people seek to fulfill rational desires through irrational means). But Lindstrom does not seek to elaborate the characteristics of this category. Rather, Lindstrom's poststructuralist psychoanalytic approach draws our attention to what he calls the Western discourse of cargoism, in which, he argues, non-Melanesians map onto Melanesians their own fantasies concerning love, longing, and unrequited desire.

Finally, a brief summary is presented of an article in which discourse about cargo cults figures in decolonization history. Robert J. Foster's "Your Money, Our Money, the Government's Money" (2002) is an evocative historical ethnography of money and the state in decolonizing and independent Papua New Guinea (PNG), in which the enchantments of a national monetary system emerge in a complex and dialogical postcolonial history.

This description of the current field is, by design, selective. The examples have been chosen to contrast with Lawrence's approach. Readers interested in a wider spectrum of important turn-of-the-millennium writing on cargo cults in the Pacific, and on cargo cults and revitalization movements more generally, will find the collections by Holger Jebens, *Cargo, Cult, and Culture Critique* (2004), and Michael E. Harkin, *Reassessing Revitalization Movements: Perspectives from North America and the Pacific Islands* (2004), most useful.

PROBLEMATIZING THE ANALYTIC CONCEPT. Important scholars have seen the Fijian Tuka of the 1880s as the flagship example of a cargo cult (Worsley, 1957, 1968) or millenarian movement (Burridge, 1969). Tuka would seem to have features similar to those Lawrence describes. Led by a hereditary oracle priest called Navosavakadua or Mosese Dukumoi (d. 1897) oriented in opposition to eastern coastal Fijian kingdoms and colonial rulers, 1880s colonial accounts of the movement described anticipation of the return of Fijian gods (notably the twin gods Nacirikaumoli and Nakausabaria, newly understood as Jesus and Jehovah) and a transformed political and material order. One could then, following Lawrence, see Tuka as one of his syncretic rather than pagan or Christian movements. One could also, with Peter Worsley and later Fiji scholars Simione Durutalo (1985) or ʻAtu Emberson-Bain (1994), see Tuka as protonationalist, prefiguring twentieth-century incipient union movements or Labour Party politics. Or, with Kenelm Burridge (1969), one could see the movement as a strategy to obtain moral recognition in an oppressive colonial context. However, chronicling Tuka via field research in Fiji (with descendants of the leader and his followers) and via examination of the colonial records at the National Archives of Fiji and beyond, Kaplan has argued instead that there was neither a cargo nor a cult at issue. The very attempt to define and explicate a general category of "cargo cult" seems to reify and occlude the complexities of this dialogical history.

On the one hand, theorists of "cargo cults" or "millenarian movements" were among the first scholars to have acknowledged and politically engaged the issue of the agency of "Others" in cultural change in colonial contexts. Such studies initiated basic discussions about agency and history in colonial societies that have inflected most later anthropological considerations, including this one. (Indeed, over the years since Lawrence's entry for this encyclopedia was written, Worsley's approach, downplayed by Lawrence, seems to have been prescient of the strong political voice that emerged in the anthropology of the 1980s, an anthropology much focused on Gramscian questions [via Raymond Williams] of hegemony and resistance or Foucaultian questions of knowledge/power.) Problematic, however, is the way that these studies drew boundaries around the phenomenon to be studied and the way they reified the category of cult, lumping together ostensibly similar events throughout Fiji and the Pacific, identifying and abstracting "cults" as a general phenomenon, or treating cults as a transitional stage between tradition and inevitable modernity (see Kelly, 2002; Pletsch, 1981).

Dissolving the Cargo Cult into the Fabric of Pacific History-Making. The analytic concept of cult itself has been called into question in a range of ways. For example, quite pointedly, Nancy McDowell argues with reference to Claude Lévi-Strauss's famous argument on totemism that "cargo cults do not exist or at least their symptoms vanish when we start to doubt that we can arbitrarily extract a few features from context and label them an institution" for "just as totemism did not exist, being merely an example of how people classify the world around them, cargo cults too do not exist, being merely an example of how people conceptualise and experience change in the world" (1988, pp. 121–122). For example, concerning Navosavakadua and Tuka in Fiji, why in seeking to study millenarianism did scholars such as Burridge problematize "Tuka" for study, rather than the massive Fijian Christian conversion of the 1830s and 1850s? Indeed, Marshall Sahlins (1985) chronicles this conversion as part of a ritual-political kingship politics in Fiji without finding any need to refer to "cults." Reconsidered in these ways, "cults" dissolve into far more complex histories of indigenous history making of colonial encounter and of the making of new cultural-political systems. For some scholars, this becomes an opportunity to reconsider cargo cults as examples of a culturally Melanesian form of history making, whereby external intrusions are encompassed and remade culturally. Such an approach can run the risk of presenting Pacific people as unchangingly culturally separate, but the argument that there are plural ways of making history can also serve as a strong, politically inflected argument for the autonomy and power of non-Western peoples, even in the face of hegemonizing discourses. Indeed, as Sahlins (1988) and others point out, globalization itself can impel or support diversification and difference.

And indeed, in the events called "Tuka," Fijians mobilized a Fijian grammar for history making, invoking a long-standing ritual political opposition of "People of the Land" against eastern coastal chiefs and other culturally constructed foreigners, as well as against labor recruiters, missionaries, and colonial administration Yet, it is not enough simply to see Navosavakadua and Tuka as encompassed in an essentially Fijian form of local history making. For, reconsidering cargo cults in the context of local histories entails attention to a dialogical history, in which the local and the colonial, the local and the global are never unaffected by each other.

Cults and Movements in the Colonial Imagination. While *Neither Cargo nor Cult* (1995) argues that the analytic categories of "cargo cults" or "millenarian movements" are scholarly reifications, it also argues that (despite McDowell's elegant borrowing of Lévi-Strauss) cults and movements *do* exist. They exist, not necessarily as Pacific or non-Western phenomena, but rather as a category in Western culture and colonial practice. "Tuka" was a thing to colonial officers and has come down to us as such. In the colonial imagination it incited the drafting of ordinances for its criminal prosecution and the deportation of its practitioners, gaining its own sites in colonial archival files and indexes and in local responses to colonial criminalization.

When Tuka as cult—separate, irrational, and nonorthodox—came into being via British colonial discourse and practice, a coalition of eastern coastal Fijian chiefs and colonial officials simultaneously brought into being another entity: a colonial state founded on a system that would (with self-proclaimed humanity and cost-effectiveness) rule Fijians through their traditional chiefs, institutions, and customs. An understanding of the dependence of states (from kingdoms to colonies to nation-states) on ritual or magical constitution of cosmology and authority shifts our attention from the enchantments of the marginalized to the enchantments required to routinize the major and central power (e.g., see Abrams, 1988; Kelly and Kaplan, 1990; Sahlins, 1985; Tambiah, 1985; Taussig, 1992). Certainly, neither colonial state nor cult was real before the dialogical history of Fiji of the late 1800s. Both were founded and routinized in ritual politics.

Thus, in *Neither Cargo nor Cult* (1995) Kaplan presents a composite analytic approach, but the analytic components are quite different from Lawrence's empirical, causal conditions. This view is one that is confident of the reality of Fijian and colonial historical agencies, in dialogical relation, though it is skeptical that separating out inquiry about cults in particular will tell us enough about this complex history and the enchantments of both the colonially routinized state and the criminalized resistant counterpolity that Navosavakadua envisioned and tried to make real. It does, however, attend to the pull, the feeling of obviousness, to find cults real, since, ethnographically, they were very real to colonial agents. Still, it is important to recognize that that reality was generated initially not in Fijian practice or intent, but rather in the colonial imagination.

Cargoism: Western Discourse about "Cargo Cults." It is this Western certainty that cargo cults do exist that Lindstrom explores, taking us from the twentieth-century arenas of colonial discourse and practice in which they coalesced for scholars of Melanesia to an American and global popular imagination. In *Cargo Cult: Strange Stories of Desire from Melanesia and Beyond*, Lindstrom, invoking post-structuralist theory and literary deconstructionism (1993, p. 10), focuses attention on the literal term *cargo cult*. Tracing the term, Lindstrom cagily proclaims that he will not say anything about Melanesian ethnographic realities. "Cargo cult—or something like this under another name—may actually exist on Melanesian islands—or it may not" (p. 12). On the other hand, Lindstrom later asks, looking at discourse about "cargo cults," what common denominator is to be found in the phenomena to which the term is applied? If there is a general phenomenon, it is a "variety of desires for collective benefit coupled with apparently irrational strategies to attain those desires," he concludes (p. 189). Yet, it is not so much the quest for an essence of cargo cult, a common denominator in the events and actions of different peoples in Melanesia and beyond, but rather a common denominator in what Westerners perceive in these events and the implications of naming something a cargo cult that fascinates Lindstrom. He borrows the term *cargoism,* coined initially to denote "real" Melanesian activities, to instead denote discourse about cargo cults, especially Western discourse. Lindstrom's interest is, adamantly, in the uses of the term, which he considers to be a Western projection of unfulfilled desire. The term had, and still has, a complex life: it was at first a Western term projected onto Melanesians, but more recently it has been used by Melanesians about themselves and by Westerners about Melanesians, about the Third World, and about themselves.

The term *cargo cult,* Lindstrom tells us, first appeared in 1945 in the pages of the colonial news magazine *Pacific Islands Monthly* (1993, pp. 15–16) and was used as an epithet, interchangeably with "madness." Soon, Lindstrom notes, missionaries, planters, and administrators traded accusations as to who was responsible for cargo cults. Soon, too, the term entered anthropological usage, from missionary-anthropologists in New Guinea to Australia-based anthropologists, and by the 1950s the literature was copious enough that a bibliography was compiled by a South Pacific Commission librarian (p. 38). He argues that the term is then projected back, anachronistically, as when Lawrence wrote of early nineteenth-century movements as cargo cults (p. 38), though, one might argue that more could be said of the reifications already extant in British colonial discourse.

Lindstrom goes on to chronicle the history of uses of the term in anthropological analysis (up to and including the argument that "cargo cults do not exist"). He suggests that anthropologists extended the features of the ostensible cults to all of Melanesian society, seeking to show that care for cargo and use of cultic, religious means was itself a general Melanesian characteristic. To sympathetically explain cults, Lindstrom says, anthropology claims that the colonial's exceptional and fearful cult is in fact normal Melanesian culture. Thus, he says, for anthropologists, "Cults are not—or not just—aberrant ritualized reaction to a powerful European presence. Anthropology instructs us, rather, that cults are normal, creative Melanesian institutions of cultural dynamism and change" (1993, p. 61). Other anthropologists would argue that in fact the anthropological problematic of valuables, exchange, and cosmology in the Pacific, made famous by Bronislaw Malinowski in 1922 and Marcel Mauss in 1925, predates "cargo cult" discussions and that Lindstrom homogenizes and simplifies anthropological scholarship of the Pacific, in his quest to delineate a single, general Western obsession with cargo cults.

Lindstrom also discusses political uses of the term in independent Papua New Guinea, where it is used in political discourse, sometimes to signify positive kastam, or tradition, other times as a negative epithet to disparage political opponents. But he reserves special interest for the term's wider spread in popular discourse (film, tabloids, and news media) in the United States and globally. Most interesting to Lindstrom are the consequences of calling phenomena "at home" in the West cargo cults. He concludes, "The cargo cult is an allegory of desire" (1993, p. 184). He finds this desire, projected onto "others," but really about the self, in the Western psyche and in love of commodities, an unfulfillable desire, an unrequitable love.

"Cargo Cult is fascinatingly trivial," Lindstrom wrote provocatively on page three of his 246-page book. His fascination draws us to chronicle a world of talking about cargo cults. The work's focus on cargo cults, even when the focus is on discourse about cargo cults, may once again reify its object, now risking solipsism. What more, beyond unrequited love, might animate the projects and events that are folded into this way of narrating unrequited love? What of desires and successes for freedom, for self-determination, for Burridge's "moral redemption," for . . .? It is Lindstrom's intention to produce a Foucaultian genealogy of a term's contextual origins and the consequences of its use. However, diagnosing Western unrequited longing may not lead us into greater insights into anything else.

DIALOGICAL HISTORIES FOR A DECOLONIZING AND GLOBALLY INTERCONNECTED WORLD. The big story of the twentieth century for places like the Pacific is the end of the era of empires and the coming into being of the nation-state as the normal polity form. Not just the former colonies, but also the former colonizers were reconstituted as nation-states. Massive new secular rituals, state myths, and authorizing accounts have been mobilized to routinize and to make real these new polity forms. Familiars for the state and nation are born: flags that seem the living body of the state and anthems and pledges of and for the nation that serve as charms binding members to national citizenship (on state familiars, see Kaplan, 2003). What is the place of matters once called cargo cult in this history?

The most intriguing of more recent studies of cargo cults are those that are not about cargo cults at all, but rather about complex local and global histories in which the term figures historically. In this category would fall, for example, studies like Foster's "Your Money, Our Money, the Government's Money: Finance and Fetishism in Melanesia" (2002). This is an analysis, not of a cargo cult, but of the enchantments found in the putatively modern, Western, disenchanted, and practical world of nation-states, nation-building, development agencies, financial institutions, and national economy. Foster's overall point is that by assuming that Melanesians were confused about the real and true origins and value of material things, colonizers were also able to assume that they themselves lived in a Western world in which the real and true value of material things was self-evident and irrefutable, a world without fetishes (pp. 36–37). Foster's analysis shows that the New Guinea state, and indeed all states, depends on the workings of state familiars like money; that is, on the public belief that only the state-issued tokens are appropriate tender for all debts, public and private.

In the mid-twentieth century, colonizers in New Guinea began distributing educational material about money, seeking to counter cargo-cult thinking, the perceived "native" misunderstanding of the origin of goods. In the 1960s the Administration and the Reserve Bank of Australia produced booklets and films to provide people with "an understanding of the management of money." Addressing individuals with advice about "your money," they presupposed and naturalized "modern" individuals who would relate to money and define themselves via work and monetary wealth, rather than in relation to other people. Ironically, urging people to abandon the materiality of traditional wealth items, colonial advice nonetheless proffered a material form for the wealth of the people of Papua New Guinea: the bank book. At the lead up to independence in 1975, colonial education about money turned to "our money" and the national wealth, with money serving as a token of the nation-state that was just coming into being.

Where Lindstrom was critical of approaches that lent reality to cargo cult beliefs and practices, believing that they implied a diagnosis that the "natives" were mad, not rational, Foster follows William Pietz (1985, 1987, 1988), not Lindstrom, in seeing the cardinal fantasy endorsed by cargo-cult theory (and all imputations of fetishism to "others") as the idea that "We" have or can have a society without fetishes, a purely rational society of enlightenment. Foster's argument can be carried further, thinking about alleged "cargo cults'" in particular. Something becomes known as a "cargo cult" precisely when it is objectified, criminalized, and subject to scrutiny, criticism, and counterargument; when its premises do not seem natural and inevitable; and when its modes do not readily persuade official observers. But, as Foster argues, we all live with tokens of the state (we might call them state familiars), including our money, that for others have not successfully routinized into obvious utility. Foster cites U.S. survivalists who question U.S. government legitimacy and question the legitimacy of U.S. paper money. And, in Papua New Guinea, Foster shows, questions about money question the state as well, whether debating the figures portrayed on notes, maintaining shell money and using it to pay taxes, or using bills and notes as ceremonial exchange valuables. These kinds of usages bring together what colonial and postcolonial administrators "hell bent on modernization" (Foster 2002, p. 60) tried so hard to keep apart. One could propose that this is an example of Melanesian confusion, or, preferably, that it is an example of the very potential that all powerful systems (states, finance systems, and cosmologies) must trade in reliance on modes of routinzation, on tokens of existence, and on familiars that render them subject to being recognized as constructs, challenged and sometimes remade. That is, one could take the point to be that nations, states, and religions rely on the same kinds of enchantment of symbols and institutions that get undermined in criticism of cults.

GODS AND NATION-STATES. Whether or not cargo cults and the cargo cult literature is adduced, much of the scholarship since the 1980s in the Pacific has focused on postcolonial histories of nation and state as locally understood and lived in the Pacific Islands, describing predicaments and novel local solutions in ritual, economics, kinship, and religious life that connect to matters of sovereignty and its infringements, and the reconfiguration of old and new institutional forms. The literature that explicitly continues the study of cargo cults also connects new cosmologies to postcolonial as well as colonial history and sees millenarian movements growing in entwined response to increasingly diverse Christian evangelizing and/or to development discourse, electoral politics, and political crises.

Commonly, conflicts over power begun in precolonial and colonial eras are of continuing import. This is especially clear in the example of Tuka in Fiji's history. Tuka was about questions of local sovereignty (though not nation-state sovereignty) and it was also, for Navosavakadua, about identifying one's own gods. For Navosavakadua, the twin gods Nacirikaumoli and Nakausabaria had been misunderstood as Jesus and Jehovah. For some of his descendants, Navosavakadua was himself Jesus, returned. For some Fijians, more generally, Fiji and Fiji Christianity are special and traditional and entitle Fiji's indigenes to special political privilege in the island's nation-state (Kelly and Kaplan, 2001). What we learn from Tuka, we can bring to the study of the United Nations and the nation-state. These putatively disenchanted institutions have, in fact, their own rituals and even their own familiars.

For Lawrence, the variables for considering cargo cults were the characteristics of local society, the nature of introduced religion, and the character of contact with Europeans. But the world-system entanglements of the era of European capitalist and colonial expansion are replaced by global interconnections of the post–World War II, United Nations, nation-state world. People everywhere in this world face dilemmas of belief over the question of how nation-states or other political entities are to be authorized. On what basis is legitimate sovereignty made? Does it come from "we the people"? From a god or gods? From previous or external powerful political forms, like empires or the United Nations? People in nation-states are confronting these questions. Monotheism and the idea of a universal god is not always congruent with bounding the local nation-state. The relations of church and state, and of God and the nation are often in tension.

CONCLUSION. Earlier scholarship that defined *cargo cults* (including the work of Peter Lawrence), addressed matters of subjectivity and the imagination, and of emotional life entwined with reason and social institutions, mostly as matters located in local, non-Western institutions in transition toward a generalized modern life. Those studies neglected the degree to which colonials, and then scholars, imposed their own subjectivity, images, categories, and desires into their frameworks of description and analysis. Later, so-called postmodern scholars demonstrated the powers and limits of intrinsically political discourse everywhere. They tended to refocus attention from the people studied to the people studying. But scholars of the cargo cult and beyond now ponder both scholarly (and other) imaginings and the actual fabric of the world's interconnected histories—that is, they can ponder both the elements of actually complex and variegated Western imaginaries (religious, political and scholarly, local and global, colonial and postcolonial, Western and not) and the careers of those ideas everywhere.

BIBLIOGRAPHY

Abrams, Philip. "Notes on the Difficulty of Studying the State." *Journal of Historical Sociology* 1, no. 1 (1988): 58–89.

Burridge, Kenelm. *New Heaven, New Earth: A Study of Millenarian Activities.* Oxford, 1969.

Durutalo, Simione. "Internal Colonialism and Unequal Regional Development: The Case of Western Viti Levu, Fiji." Master's thesis, University of the South Pacific, 1985.

Emberson-Bain, ʻAtu. *Labour and Gold in Fiji.* Cambridge, U.K., 1994.

Foster, Robert J. "Your Money, Our Money, the Government's Money: Finance and Fetishism in Melanesia." In *Materializing the Nation: Commodities, Consumption, and Media in Papua New Guinea.* Bloomington, Ind., 2002.

Harkin, Michael E., ed. *Reassessing Revitalization Movements: Perspectives from North America and the Pacific Islands.* Lincoln, Neb., 2004.

Jebens, Holger, ed. *Cargo, Cult, and Culture Critique.* Honolulu, 2004.

Kaplan, Martha. Neither Cargo nor Cult: Ritual Politics and the Colonial Imagination in Fiji. Durham, N.C., 1995.

Kaplan, Martha. "The Magical Power of the Printed Word (in Fiji)." In *Magic and Modernity: Interfaces of Revelation and Concealment,* edited by Birgit Meyer and Peter Pels. Stanford, Calif., 2003.

Kelly, John D. "Alternative Modernities, or Alternatives to Modernity? Getting out of the Modernist Sublime." In *Critically Modern: Alternatives, Alterities, Anthropologies,* edited by Bruce M. Knauft. Bloomington, Ind., 2002.

Kelly, John D., and Martha Kaplan. "History, Structure, and Ritual." *Annual Review of Anthropology* 19 (1990): 119–150.

Kelly, John D., and Martha Kaplan. *Represented Communities: Fiji and World Decolonization.* Chicago, 2001.

Lindstrom, Lamont. *Knowledge and Power in a South Pacific Society.* Washington, D.C., 1990.

Lindstrom, Lamont. *Cargo Cult: Strange Stories of Desire from Melanesia and Beyond.* Honolulu, 1993.

Malinowski, Bronislaw. *Argonauts of the Western Pacific.* London, 1922.

Mauss, Marcel. *The Gift: The Form and Reason for Exchange in Archaic Societies* (1925). Translated by W. D. Halls. New York, 1990.

McDowell, Nancy. "A Note on Cargo Cults and Cultural Constructions of Change." *Pacific Studies* 11, no. 2 (1988): 121–134

Pietz, William. "The Problem of the Fetish." Part 1, *Res* 9 (1985); Part 2, *Res* 13 (1987) 23-45; Part 3, *Res* 16 (1988) 105–123.

Pletsch, Carl. "The Three Worlds, or, The Division of Social Scientific Labor, circa 1950–1975." *Comparative Studies in Society and History* 23, no. 4 (1981): 565–590

Sahlins, Marshall. *Islands of History.* Chicago, 1985.

Sahlins, Marshall. "Cosmologies of Capitalism: The Trans-Pacific Sector of 'The World System.'" *Proceedings of the British Academy* 74 (1988): 1–51.

Tambiah, Stanley Jeyaraja. *Culture, Thought, and Social Action: An Anthropological Perspective.* Cambridge, Mass., 1985.

Taussig, Michael. "Maleficium: State Fetishism." In *The Nervous System,* pp. 111–140. New York, 1992.

Worsley, Peter. *The Trumpet Shall Sound: A Study of "Cargo" Cults in Melanesia.* London, 1957; 2d ed. New York, 1968.

MARTHA KAPLAN (2005)

CARIBBEAN RELIGIONS

This entry consists of the following articles:

PRE-COLUMBIAN RELIGIONS
AFRO-CARIBBEAN RELIGIONS

CARIBBEAN RELIGIONS: PRE-COLUMBIAN RELIGIONS

European explorers noted three major aboriginal groups in the Caribbean at the time of contact (1492 and the years immediately following): Island Arawak, Island Carib, and Ciboney. There is an abundance of information concerning the religious practices of the Island Arawak and Island Carib, but very little is known of Ciboney religion. Our knowledge of the Ciboney has increased somewhat, especially through the work of Cuban archaeologists such as Osvaldo Morales Patiño, but there remain many gaps in the archaeological and ethnohistorical records.

This essay will focus on the Island Arawak and the Island Carib. The Island Arawak were concentrated in the Greater Antilles, a group of large, mainly sedimentary islands. The principal islands of the Greater Antilles are, moving from east to west, Puerto Rico, Hispaniola (now divided between Haiti and the Dominican Republic), Jamaica, and Cuba. The Island Carib inhabited the small, mainly volcanic islands of the Lesser Antilles (Saint Christopher-Nevis, Antigua, Guadeloupe, Dominica, Martinique, Saint Lucia, Barbados, Grenada, Saint Vincent, and Tobago). Trinidad, Margarita, Cubagua, and Coche are usually considered a part of the Caribbean region, but culturally these islands have much in common with the South American mainland (Glazier, 1980b; Figueredo and Glazier, 1982).

Earlier scholars, such as Hartley B. Alexander (1920), emphasized differences between Island Arawak and Island Carib religions. This tradition continued in the work of scholars such as Fred Olsen (1974) and Charles A. Hoffman (1980), for example, who postulated strong Maya influence on the religious systems of the Greater Antilles. Later, scholars paid greater attention to the similarities in Arawak and Carib belief systems—for example, the many parallels in Arawak and Carib shamanism—than to their differences.

Both the Island Arawak and the Island Carib originally migrated from the South American mainland (Rouse, 1964). The Island Arawak settled in the Greater Antilles at about the beginning of the common era and were followed several hundred years later by the Carib, who claimed to have begun their migrations into the Lesser Antilles only a few generations before the arrival of Columbus. The Island Carib asserted that they conquered the Arawak of the Lesser Antilles, killing the men and marrying the women. Douglas M. Taylor (1951) suggests that the women's language prevailed, because the language spoken by the descendants of the Island Carib belongs to the Arawakan family of languages. Of course, another possible explanation is that all the peoples of the Lesser Antilles were of Arawak origin.

It should not be assumed that the Island Arawak of the Greater Antilles and the Arawak of the South American mainland are members of the same ethnic group. The Island Arawak and Arawak proper did not speak the same language. Irving Rouse points out that their two languages were "no more alike than, say, French and English" (Rouse, 1974). Moreover, inhabitants of the Greater Antilles thought of themselves not as "Arawak" but as members of local chiefdoms, each of which had its own name. Since each chiefdom was totally independent of all others, the group we know as the Island Arawak had no need for an overall tribal name.

In 1920, Hartley Alexander suggested that the sea must have been a tremendous barrier to cultural transmission in the Caribbean. Contemporary archaeologists, however, recognize that water did not constitute a barrier for these peoples. Therefore, archaeologists no longer study individual islands in isolation. This has many implications for the study of aboriginal Caribbean religions as it becomes increasingly apparent that religious developments on one island were likely to have affected religious developments elsewhere in the region. Various island groups seem to have been in constant contact with one another.

Archaeologists have since established a firmer and more comprehensive chronology for the Caribbean region (Rouse and Allaire, 1978). They also have discovered much greater variation in religious artifacts than was previously thought to exist, which in turn hints at a greater variation within the religious traditions of the Island Arawak and the Island Carib than was previously supposed. Arawak and Carib traditions, for example, may have differed from settlement to settlement on the same island.

DEITIES. Both the Island Arawak and the Island Carib possessed a notion of a high god, though, as the chroniclers' reports make clear, their high god differed conceptually from the God of Christianity. We know, too, that aboriginal high gods were thought to exert very little direct influence on the workings of the universe. Many of the early chroniclers, including Fray Ramón Pané, Gonzalo F. de Oviedo, and Raymond Breton, refer to Arawak and Carib high gods as kinds of *deus otiosus;* that is, they are inactive gods far removed from human affairs and concerns. Neither the Island Arawak nor the Island Carib conceived of their high god as creator of the universe, and it is unclear how powerful the high god was thought to be. Was it that their high god was able to interfere directly in world affairs but chose not to do so, or was he thought to be totally ineffectual? Chroniclers differ somewhat on this. Pané suggests that the high god was a powerful deity who chooses to be inactive. Other chroniclers stress the inactivity of the high god and the lack of attention accorded him. The bulk of the evidence, including what we know of other American Indian religions (Hultkrantz, 1979), supports the latter interpretation.

Island Arawak. The identification of Island Arawak deities is often a problem. Their high god was known by two names: Iocauna and Guamaonocon (spellings differ from chronicler to chronicler). Peter Martyr reports that the Arawak supreme being was not self-created but was himself brought forth by a mother who has five names or identities: Attabeira, Mamona, Guacarapita, Iella, and Guimazoa. He also reports other appellations for the high god, including Jocakuvaque, Yocahu, Vaque, Maorocon, and Macrocoti. Pané provides an equally complex list of male and female deities, and it is apparent that most deities in the Arawak pantheon were recognized by a number of appellations. Henri Pettitjean-Roget (1983) has suggested that the various names be interpreted as different incarnations of the same deity, as in the Hindu tradition. Another possible explanation is that different names simply represent local variants.

A number of interpreters (Joyce, 1916; Alexander, 1920) have posited that the Island Arawak possessed a conception of an earth mother and a sky father similar to that of other American Indian groups. This has been called into question. While there are many similarities between the goddess Attabeira and the earth mother of American Indian mythology, there are also many differences. Attabeira does seem to have been associated with fertility, and as Fred Olsen (1974) suggests, her many Arawakan names describe her various functions: mother of moving waters (the sea, the tides, and the springs), goddess of the moon, and goddess of childbirth. Representations of Attabeira frequently show her squatting in the act of parturition, and archaeologists have been greatly impressed with the vividness of these portrayals. Her hands are holding her chin while her legs press into her sides as she struggles in childbirth. In several representations her open mouth and heavy eyebrows ridging over wide-open eyes convey successfully the intensity of her efforts. But there are other characteristics of Attabeira that are not at all like those of an earth mother. Sven Lovén (1935) concludes that Attabeira cannot be identified as a goddess of the earth because she seems to have dwelt permanently in the heavens. He concedes that Attabeira may have been an all-mother, but this does not necessarily imply that she was an earth goddess.

Lovén (1935) also points out that Iocauna was not an all-father. As noted previously, native conceptions of Iocauna would have precluded procreative activities. It is possible that one of Iocauna's names, Yocahu, is related to the yuca (cassava) plant (Fewkes, 1907). Yocahu may have been the giver of yuca or the discoverer of yuca, but he was not believed to be the creator of yuca (Olsen, 1974). It is clear from all accounts that after yuca was given to the Island Arawak, it was cultivated through the cooperation of *zemi* spirits and was not at all dependent on the cooperation of Yocahu.

Other prominent Island Arawak deities include: Guabancex, goddess of wind and water, who had two subordinates: Guatauva, her messenger, and Coatrischio, the tempest-raiser; Yobanua-Borna, a rain deity; Baidrama (or Vaybruma), a twinned deity associated with strength and healing; Opigielguoviran, a doglike being said to have plunged into the morass with the coming of the Spanish; and Faraguvaol, a tree trunk able to wander at will. One difficulty with the various listings provided by the chroniclers is that they do not distinguish mythical beings and deities. This is unfortunate because the Island Arawak themselves seem to have made such a distinction.

As Alexander (1920) has pointed out, there is some evidence that nature worship and/or a vegetation cult existed among the Island Arawak. This remains, however, a much neglected aspect of Island Arawak religion. Pané's elaborate description of the manufacture of wooden religious objects suggests some similarities between the production of these objects and the construction of wooden fetishes in West Africa. While the analogy is not complete, it has been noted that many aspects of Caribbean religions seem to derive from similar attitudes toward material objects (Alexander, 1920).

One of the most important differences between Arawak and Carib religions is that among the Island Arawak nature worship seems to have been closely associated with ancestor worship. The bones of the Island Arawak dead, especially the bones of their leaders and great men, were thought to have power in and of themselves. This notion also existed among the Island Carib, but their ceremonies and representations were not so elaborate. In addition, most chroniclers mention that the Island Arawak painted their bodies and faces, especially in preparation for war. The chroniclers are in agreement that the painted figures were horrible and hideous, but there is little agreement as to what the figures were supposed to represent. Jesse W. Fewkes (1907) has suggested that body paintings had religious importance; most other sources suggest that markings served to distinguish members of the same clan. The practice may have been a form of ancestor worship.

Island Carib. Like the Island Arawak, the island Carib recognized a multitude of spirit beings as well as a high god whose name varies according to text. Sieur de La Borde (1704) refers to their high god as Akamboüe. According to Raymond Breton (1665), however, Akamboüe means "carrier of the king," and the highest deity in the Island Carib pantheon was the moon, Nonu-ma. Breton argues that the moon was central in Island Carib religion because the Carib reckoned time according to lunar cycles. The sun, Huoiou, also occupied an important place in the Island Carib pantheon. Although the sun was said to be more powerful than the moon, Huoiou was also said to be more remote from human affairs and therefore less significant.

Of the spirits directly involved in human affairs, Icheiri and Mabouia are the most frequently mentioned. Icheiri, whose name comes from the verb *ichéem*, meaning "what I like" (Breton, 1665, p. 287), has been interpreted as a spirit of good, while Mabouia, from the same root as the word *boyé*, or "sorcerer," has been interpreted as a spirit of evil. The Carib informed Breton that it was Mabouia who brought about eclipses of the sun and caused the stars to disappear suddenly.

The terms *icheiri* and *mabouia* have been widely discussed in the secondary literature. I believe that these were not names of spirits, but were general categories within the spirit world, and that spirits were classified primarily according to their relation to the individual. One man's *icheira* (helper) could be another man's *mabouia* (evil spirit) and vice versa (Glazier, 1980a). The most important consideration, as far as the Carib were concerned, was to get a particular spirit on one's side.

Another major category in the Island Carib spirit world was that of the *zemiis. Zemi*, too, appears to have been a very general term; the word is of Arawak origin and indicates the strong influence of Island Arawak language and culture on the Island Carib. Among the Carib, to get drunk, *chemerocae*, literally meant "to see *zemiis*." *Zemiis* were thought to live in a paradise far removed from the world of the living, but every so often, according to La Borde (1704), Coualina, chief of the *zemiis*, would become angry about the wickedness of some *zemiis* and drive them from paradise to earth, where they became animals. This is but one example of the constant transformations from deity to animal in Island Carib mythology.

Zemiis were frequently represented by, and in many cases were identical with, conical objects that have been found at both Island Arawak and Island Carib sites. The most common types are triangular (the so-called three-pointers) and/or humpback in shape. Some are elaborately carved, but a majority of *zemiis* are plain. Archaeologists have discovered *zemiis* made of wood, conch shell, and stone, but stone *zemiis* are the most prevalent.

Fewkes (1907) was among the first to suggest the religious import of these objects. He posited that they may have had a magical function, especially in reducing pains associated with childbirth. Olsen (1974) offers a more materialistic explanation. He suggests that the conical shapes of these stones represented the Caribbean islands themselves dramatically rising out of the sea with their pronounced volcanic peaks. Pettitjean-Roget (1983) provides a broader interpretation than Fewkes or Olsen. He postulates that these conical objects were nothing less than an encapsulation of the entire cosmos.

AFTERLIFE. Both the Island Arawak and the Island Carib had a notion of the afterlife. The Island Arawak conceived of spirits of the dead, called *opias* or *hubias*, who were said to wander about the bush after dark. Occasionally *opias* joined the company of the living and were said to be indistinguishable from the living, except for the spirits' lack of navels. In both Arawak and Carib religions, the activities of the dead were thought to resemble the activities of the living. *Opias*, for example, passed their time feasting and dancing in the forest. Their behaviors were similar to native ceremonies.

Pané reports that the Arawak of Haiti believed in a kingdom of death, Coaibai, which was situated on their own island. Every leader of importance had his own kingdom of death, usually located within his own dominion. In addition, there were uninhabited places where the spirits of evil people were said to roam.

The Island Carib, on the other hand, had a much more diffuse notion of the afterlife. All spirits of the body, *omicou*, went to the seashore or became *mabouias* in the forest. There was no concept of an underworld, nor were spirits associated with specific locations, as among the Island Arawak. Each individual was said to possess three souls: one in the heart, one in the head, and one in the shoulders. It is only the heart-soul that ascends to the sky, while the other two souls wander the earth for eternity. The Island Carib asserted that only valiant heart-souls ascended; the implication here is that even the heart-souls of the less valiant sometimes became *mabouias* and roamed the earth.

Elaborate burial ceremonies were noted among both the Island Arawak and the Island Carib. Archaeological evidence indicates that the Island Arawak performed several types of burials: (1) direct interment, with the skeleton in a sitting or flexed position; (2) interment within a raised mound, with the body in a crouched position; (3) interment within a grave covered with an arch of branches topped with earth; and (4) burial in caves, with skeletons in a flexed position. Secondary burials were also prevalent (Lovén, 1935).

Christopher Columbus summarized the different burial customs on Hispaniola as follows: "They open the body and dry it by the fire in order that it may be preserved whole. Often, depending on rank, they take only the head. Others are buried in caves. Others they burn in their houses. Others they drive out of the house; and others they put in a hammock and leave them to rot" (Lovén, 1935). It is apparent that Arawak burial customs differed markedly and that burials for leaders were much more elaborate than burials for the masses. From the archaeological record, it is also apparent that the Island Arawak buried a majority of their dead in crouching or flexed positions. In this they differed from the Ciboney, who buried their dead lying straight (Lovén, 1935).

Burial customs among the Island Carib were not so varied. Breton (1665) noted that the Island Carib dreaded death, and that it was forbidden to utter the name of the deceased. The Island Carib referred to the dead indirectly (e.g., "the husband of so-and-so") because to do otherwise would cause the deceased to come back to earth.

When an Island Carib male died, the women painted his cheeks and lips red and placed him in a hammock. After some time the decomposed body was brought inside a hut, where it was then lowered into a shallow grave. Burial was in the flexed position, with the body sitting on its heels, and with the elbows resting on the knees and hands folded to the breast. Important men were buried with cooking pots and utensils, their dogs, and slaves who were killed so they might continue to serve their masters in the next life. La Borde (1704) notes that the Island Carib frequently burned the bodies of their leaders and mixed the ashes with their drinks. This may not be accurate, for there is little archaeological evidence for cremation among the Island Carib.

ORIGIN MYTHS. We possess no creation myths for Caribbean peoples. Both Island Arawak and Island Carib seem to have assumed that the universe had always been in existence. They did, however, have many stories concerning the earliest peoples of their respective groups.

Island Arawak. According to the aborigines of Haiti, the earliest people appeared out of two caves. A majority of the people emerged from a cave known as Cicibagiagua, while another, smaller group emerged from the cave Amaiacuva. Alexander (1920) suggests that these two caves represent two different races or tribes. Lovén (1935) argues to the contrary: there is, he says, but one tribal group. Since most of the people emerged from Cicibagiagua, those who emerged from Amaiacuva constituted an elite, the Taino. I find Lovén's interpretation the more plausible. These caves, situated on the mountain of Cauta in the region of Caunana, were believed to actually exist and may have been located in the area of present-day Sierra de Coonao. Where caves did not exist, Island Arawak stress appearance out of the ground.

Island Arawak legends also account for the first appearance of the sun and the moon from a grotto known as Giovaua, and for the origin of fish and the ocean. According to the legend:

> There was a certain man, Giaia, whose son, Giaiael, undertook to kill his father, but was himself slain by the parent, who put the bones into a calabash, which he hung on top of his hut. One day he took the calabash down, looked into it, and an abundance of fishes came forth. The bones had changed into fish. Later, when Giaia the parent was absent, his four sons took the calabash and ate some of the fish. Giaia returned suddenly and in their haste the sons replaced the calabash badly. As a result, so much water ran from it that it overflowed all of the country, and with the water came an abundance of fish. (Fernández Méndez, 1979; my trans.)

Other stories tell how the four brothers obtained manioc and tobacco from people whom they visited (see Fernández Méndez, 1979). Rouse (1948) suggests that these stories may have been put to song.

The stories of the emergence from caves and the origin of fish are, in Pané's account, followed by stories concerning the adventures of Guaguigiana, a culture hero, and his comrade. Giadruvava. Guaguigiana appears to have been something of a trickster figure, and his adventures resemble those of trickster-fixers associated with other American Indian groups. It is to Pané's credit that he attempted to present stories in the order in which the Island Arawak themselves presented them, even when that order made little intuitive sense to him (Deive, 1976).

Island Carib. Among the Island Carib the first man, Louguo, was said to have descended from the sky. Other men came out of his navel and his thighs. Louguo created fish by throwing cassava scrapings into the sea, and according to La Borde (1704), many of the first men were later transformed into stars.

The constellations were accorded great importance in Island Carib thought: Chiric (the Pleiades) was used to number their years; Sauacou, who changed into a great blue heron, was sent to heaven where he forms a constellation announcing hurricanes; the Great Bear is the heron's canoe; the constellation Achinaou announces gentle rains and high winds; the constellation Cauroumon is associated with heavy waves; the constellation Racumon was changed into a snake; and Baccamon (Scorpio) foretells high winds (Breton, 1665). It is clear that the various constellations were used to divine the future, but it is unclear whether or not the constellations were actually believed to cause earthly events.

RITES AND CEREMONIES. The most important ceremonies among the Island Arawak pertained to rain and the growth of crops, but there were also important ceremonies for success in war, burial of the dead, curing of the sick, canoe building, cutting hair, the births of children, marriage, and initiation. In most instances these rites took the form of elaborate dances known as *areitos.* Fewkes (1907) notes that dramatization played a part in all ceremonies. For example, in their war dances the entire war sequence was portrayed: the departure of the warriors, surprise of the enemy, combat, celebration of victory, and return of the war party. Singing also played a part in all ceremonies, and some of the early chroniclers incorrectly restricted their use of the term *areitos* to funeral chants or elegies in praise of heroes.

The island Carib conducted ceremonies on many of the same occasions as did the Island Arawak. According to La Borde, the Island Carib held rites whenever a council was held concerning their wars, when they returned from their expeditions, when a first male child was born, when they cut their children's hair, when their boys became old enough to go to war, when they cut down trees, and when they launched a vessel. Some authorities mention other ritual occasions: when a child reached puberty, when a parent or spouse died, when the Island Carib were made captives, and when they killed one of their enemies.

Island Carib rites met individual as well as societal needs. Each individual had his own personal deity or *zemi.* These personal deities were thought to reveal things to the individual, and it is reported that individuals customarily withdrew from society for six or seven days, without taking any sustenance save tobacco and the juice of herbs. During this period, the individual experienced visions of whatever he or she desired (victory over enemies, wealth, and so on).

Much has been written on alleged cannibalism among the Island Carib (the word *cannibal* is a corruption of *Caribal,* the Spanish word for "Carib"). The Island Arawak told Columbus that they were subject to raids by man-eating Indians known as Carib, and Columbus directed his second voyage to the Lesser Antilles, where he had been told the Carib lived, in order to confirm Arawak reports. Rouse (1964) credits Columbus with confirming that the Carib practiced ritual cannibalism, that is, they ate captives in order to absorb their fighting ability. Recently the anthropologist William Arens (1979) has suggested that Columbus had no direct evidence for this assertion, and in fact did not really believe that the Carib were cannibals, but he perpetuated the myth of Carib cannibalism for political reasons. The early chroniclers provide some support for this position. In his *Historia general de las Indias, 1527–61,* Bartolomé de Las Casas flatly denies that the Carib were cannibals. Whatever the status of Carib cannibalism, there is agreement that it was not an everyday practice and was largely confined to ritual occasions.

One other Island Carib rite attracted considerable attention in the early literature, and that was the practice of the *couvade.* At the birth of a child, Jean-Baptiste Dutertre reports, Carib fathers would rest as if it were they who were suffering labor pains. For forty days and nights fathers remained isolated from society, fasting or consuming a meager diet. At the end of this period there was a great feast at which the invited guests lacerated the father's skin with their fingernails and washed his wounds with a solution of red pepper. For an additional six months the father was expected to observe special dietary taboos (e.g., it was believed that if the father ate turtle, the child would become deaf). Dutertre records a number of other taboos involving birds and fish.

DRUGS. Tobacco, narcotics, and stimulants played an important part in both Island Arawak and Island Carib rites. Tobacco, called *cohiba,* was used in a number of different forms in all ceremonies. Among the Island Arawak, tobacco smoke was used as an incense to summon the gods. Tobacco was sprinkled on the heads of idols as an offering. Religious leaders among the Island Arawak and Island Carib "stupefied" themselves with tobacco when they consulted their oracles; they also used tobacco in curing rituals.

As Breton (1665) reports, the Island Carib "know tobacco but do not smoke it." They would dry it by a fire, pound it into a powder, add a little seawater to it, and then place a pinch of the snuff between their lips and gums. The Island Arawak, on the other hand, sometimes did inhale tobacco smoke through their nostrils. But its use was limited. Generally there is no evidence that tobacco was burned during ceremonies.

Throwing *aji* (pepper) onto live coals was part of Island Arawak and Island Carib preparations for warfare. Ricardo E. Alegría (1979) contends that the pepper caused irritation of the mucous membrane, a racking cough, and other discomforts that were thought to induce the proper psychological state for war.

SHAMANISM. The distinction between shamans, who are said to obtain their power directly from the supernatural, and priests, who must learn a body of ritual knowledge from established practitioners, is not useful in distinguishing Island Arawak religious leaders (variously known as *piaies, behutios, buhitihus, behiques*) from Island Carib leaders known as *boyés.* Although the role of the *piaie* appears to have been more priestlike than that of the *boyé,* similarities among *piaies* and *boyés* far exceed their differences.

Island Arawak. Major duties of the Arawak *piaie* were to divine the future by consulting their personal *zemiis* and to direct offering to *zemiis* during public ceremonies. In both of these duties, they served as intermediaries between the Island Arawak and their gods (Deive, 1978).

Accounts of Arawak shamanism provide very little detail concerning the *piaie's* role in public ceremonies, and it is unclear whether or not all *piaies* were able to conduct public ritual. It is possible that some *piaies* functioned solely as curers or diviners and could not perform other rites.

Pané provides a lengthy account of Arawak healing practices. The curer, he notes, began his treatment of the patient by prescribing a special diet and was himself expected to observe the same diet as his patient. Herrera gives a condensed description of curing procedures:

> When any leading man is sick, he calls a medicine man, who is obliged to observe the same dietary rules as the patient. It is customary for the medicine man to purge himself with an herb that he takes by inhaling until he believes himself inspired. In this condition he says many things, giving the sick to understand that he is talking with an idol. Then the Indians anoint their faces with oil and purge the sick who stand by in silence. The medicine man first makes two circuits about the patient and, pulling him by the legs, goes to the door of the house, which he shuts, saying: "Return to the mountain or whither you wish; blow and join hands and tremble, and close the mouth." Breathing on his hands, he then sucks the neck, the shoulders, the stomach, and other parts of the body of the sick man, coughing and grimacing; he spits into his hands what he had previously placed in his mouth and tells the sick man that he has taken from the body that which is bad. He also says that the patient's *zemi* had given it to him because he had not obeyed him. The objects that the doctors take from their mouths are for the most part stones, which they often use for childbirth or other special purposes, and which they also preserve as relics. (Herrera, 1937, p. 69; my trans.)

If a patient died, it was thought to be because the *piaie* had not observed the proper diet. The Island Arawak were not very tolerant of unsuccessful healers, and it was not uncommon for a healer to be seized by a deceased person's relatives who would strike him with a stick until his arms and legs were broken, gouge out his eyes, and lacerate his private parts.

Alfred Métraux (1949), in his overview of shamanism in South America, states that in most instances the role of the religious leader was distinct from that of the political leader, but this distinction between political and religious authority does not seem to have been as pronounced among the Island Arawak. For example, Rouse (1948) points out that it is unclear whether the chief and his attendants (the principal men of the village) were also shamans. The attendants, he notes, had a special name, *bohuti,* and were of such high status that they customarily refused to accept commoners as patients.

Island Carib. The Island Carib maintained a rigid distinction between political and religious authority. There are no reports of healers becoming chiefs or chiefs becoming healers. But even in the Lesser Antilles, a certain complicity between religious and political leaders is apparent. For example, a political leader needed a *boyé's* support in order to wage war, and *boyés* derived direct economic benefits through their association with chiefs.

The Carib never went to war without first consulting the spirit world to find out if conditions were favorable for victory. Since chiefs were unable to make direct contact with spirits, they required the services of a *boyé* whose predictions had tremendous impact on public opinion. It would be difficult for a war chief to override a *boyé's* predictions and carry out expeditions believed to be inauspicious. Shamans never gained an upper hand, however, for if a chief was dissatisfied with one *boyé's* prediction, he was free to consult others. Often, several *boyés* were consulted at once, and the old war chief chose the most "correct" prediction. Given the circumstances, it was advantageous for both parties when a chief developed a working relationship with a particular shaman who could be counted on to support his war policies. These relationships often followed kinship lines.

Boyés also needed to develop working relationships with chiefs to defray the high costs of apprenticeship. We have no clear notion of the actual length of apprenticeship for shamans among the Island Carib, though in some tribes of the Guianas apprenticeship is said to have lasted from ten to twenty years (Métraux, 1949). This period of training was probably considerably shorter among the Carib, but we lack details for all but the final months of preparation:

> After a fast of five months, the candidate is brought into the *carbet* (a place in which things have been set aside) before a table on which manioc bread, *ouicou* (sweet potato and manioc beer), and the first fruits of the season are placed. An older shaman chants and blows tobacco smoke to summon his familiar spirit who descends and sits on a hammock to receive offerings (*anaeri*). The elder shaman asks for another spirit to descend and become his apprentice's familiar. (Dutertre, 1667–1671, vol. 2, pp. 365–366; my trans.)

From this passage, it is clear that five months of training (and possibly more) was required of the would-be shaman. This would constitute a hardship for the apprentices family, for others had to assume his workload and provide for him while he was in training. Also, they had to provide offerings for sacrifice and make payments to senior *boyés*.

Boyés were a professional class in Island Carib society. They charged for all services, and I contend that they did not train new shamans without demanding something in return. War chiefs and their families, as wealthier members of their society, were in the best position to take on obligations to senior *boyés* (Glazier, 1980).

Island Carib shamanism was not flexible. It was not possible to go off on one's own and become a *boyé*. A would-be shaman had to do an apprenticeship under an established *boyé* and had to undergo formal rites of initiation in order to receive a spirit familiar. Shamans who claimed that their knowledge derived solely from their relationship with spirits probably glossed over their arduous training, wanting instead to stress mystical aspects of their careers. The picture they present of shamanism in the Lesser Antilles is inaccurate.

There is, however, no ambiguity concerning the *boyé's* authority. While the authority of the war chief may have been that of a charismatic leader, the authority of the *boyé* was clearly that of formal investiture. Breton (1665) put it succinctly: "The *boyés* make other people *boyés*."

Boyés were perhaps the wealthiest members of their society. While war chiefs and families had considerable control over the distribution of some resources and war booty, *boyés* had control over the distribution of goods outside kinship obligations. A *boyé's* clientele was not restricted to his kin group, and his reputation could well transcend his own island. The *boyé* Iris's reputation, for example, extended beyond his native Dominica (Du Puis, 1972).

The *boyés* had great potential for wealth, for there was always demand for their services. In times of trouble, they were called upon to dispel evil spirits; in times of prosperity, they were called upon to insure its continuance; and when there was doubt, they gave assurances for the future. Major religious activities were sacrifice and offerings, both of which were ultimately appropriated by the *boyés* (Rochefort, 1665). Offerings consisted of foodstuffs and some durable goods, a portion of which went directly to the shaman in return for his services; the remainder, ostensibly for the gods, was appropriated later for the shaman's use. Thus shamans had numerous occasions to accumulate wealth, and in some cases a shaman may have gotten too wealthy and would be forced by public opinion to redistribute part of his property.

Under certain conditions, senior war chiefs were allowed to join with the *boyés* in appropriating offerings intended for the gods. This further differentiates the roles of *boyé* and chief. Only the most senior war chief had the right to do what any *boyé* could do from the moment of his initiation.

BIBLIOGRAPHY

Alegría, Ricardo E. "The Use of Noxious Gas in Warfare by the Taino and Carib Indians of the Antilles." *Revista/Review Interamericana* 8 (1979): 409–415.

Alegría, Ricardo E. *Ball Courts and Ceremonial Plazas in the West Indies.* New Haven, 1983.

Alexander, Hartley Burr. "The Antilles." In *The Mythology of All Races*, edited by Louis Herbert Gray, vol. 11, *Latin-American Mythology*, pp. 15–40. Boston, 1920.

Arens, William. *The Man-Eating Myth: Anthropology and Anthropophagy.* Oxford, 1979.

Benzoni, Girolamo. *History of the New World* (1595). Translated by W. H. Smyth. London, 1857.

Breton, Raymond. *Dictionnaire caraïbe-françois.* Auxerre, 1665.

Charlevoix, Pierre-François de. *Histoire de l'Ile Espagnole ou de Saint-Dominique.* 2 vols. Paris, 1930–1931.

Deive, Carlos Esteban. "Fray Ramón Pané y el nacimiento de la etnografía americana." *Boletín del Museo del Hombre Dominicano* 6 (1976): 136–156.

Deive, Carlos Esteban. "El chamanismo taíno." *Boletín del Museo del Hombre Dominicano* 9 (1978): 189–203.

Du Puis, Mathias. *Relation de l'establissement d'une colonie françoise dans la Gardloupe isle de l'Amérique, et des mœurs des sauvages* (1652). Reprint, Basse-Terre, 1972.

Dutertre, Jean-Baptiste. *Histoire générale des Antilles habitées par les François* (1667–1671). 4 vols. Fort-de-France, Martinique, 1958.

Fernández Méndez, Eugenio. *Art y mitologia de los indios Tainos de las Antillas Mayores.* San Juan, Puerto Rico, 1979.

Fewkes, Jesse Walter. *The Aborigines of Porto Rico and Neighboring Islands.* Annual Report of the Bureau of American Ethnology, no. 25. Washington, D.C., 1907. See especially pages 53–72.

Figueredo, Alfredo E., and Stephen D. Glazier. "Spatial Behavior, Social Organization, and Ethnicity in the Prehistory of Trinidad." *Journal de la Société des Américanistes* 68 (1982): 33–40.

García Valdés, Pedro. "The Ethnography of the Ciboney." In *Handbook of South American Indians,* edited by Julian H. Steward, vol. 4, pp. 503–505. Washington, D.C., 1948.

Glazier, Stephen D. "The Boyé in Island-Carib Culture." In *La antropología americanista en la actualidad: Homenaje a Raphael Girard,* vol. 2, pp. 37–46. Mexico City, 1980. Cited in the text as 1980a.

Glazier, Stephen D. "Aboriginal Trinidad and the Guianas: An Historical Reconstruction." *Archaeology and Anthropology: Journal of the Walter Roth Museum* (Georgetown, Guyana) 3 (1980): 119–124. Cited in the text as 1980b.

Gullick, C. J. M. R. *Exiled from St. Vincent.* Valletta, Malta, 1976.

Herrera y Tordesillas, Antonio de. *Historia general de los hechos de los Castellanos en las islas y Terrafirme del Mar Océano.* 17 vols. Madrid, 1934–1957.

Hoffman, Charles A. "The Outpost Concept and the Mesoamerican Connection." In *Proceedings of the Eighth International Congress for the Study of the Pre-Columbian Cultures of the Lesser Antilles,* pp. 307–316. Tempe, Ariz., 1980.

Hultkrantz, Åke. *Religions of the American Indians.* Los Angeles, 1979.

Joyce, Thomas A. *Central American and West Indian Archaeology.* London, 1916.

La Borde, Sieur de. *Voyage qui contient un relation exacte de l'origine, mœurs, coûtumes, réligion, guerres, et voyages des Caraïbes, sauvages des isles Antilles de l'Amérique.* Amsterdam, 1704.

Las Casas, Bartolomé de. *Historia general de las Indias, 1527–61.* 2 vols. Edited by Juan Perez de Tudela and Emilio Lopez Oto. Madrid, 1957.

Layng, Anthony. *The Carib Reserve: Identity and Security in the West Indies.* Lanham, Md., 1983.

Lovén, Sven. *Origins of the Tainan Culture, West Indies.* Göteborg, 1935.

Métraux, Alfred. "Religion and Shamanism." In *Handbook of South American Indians,* edited by Julian H. Steward, vol. 5, pp. 559–599. Washington, D.C., 1949.

Morales Patiño, Osvaldo. "Arqueología Cubana, resumen de actividades, 1946." *Revista de arqueologia y etnografia* (Havana) 1 (1947): 5–32.

Olsen, Fred. *On the Trail of the Arawaks.* Norman, Okla. 1974.

Oviedo y Valdés, Gonzalo Fernández de. *Historia general y natural de las Indias* (1535). 5 vols. Edited by Juan Perez and Tudela Bueso. Madrid, 1959.

Pané, (Fray) Ramón (Father Ramón). *Relación acerca de las antigüedades de los Indios, 1571.* Edited by José Juan Arrom. Mexico City, 1978.

Pérez de Oliva, Fernán. *Historia de la inuención de las Yndias.* Edited by José Juan Arrom. Publicaciones del Instituto Caro y Cuerva, no. 20. Bogotá, 1965.

Pettitjean-Roget, Henri. "De l'origine de la famille humaine ou contribution à l'étude des Pierres à Trois-Pointes des Antilles." In *Proceedings of the Ninth International Congress for the Study of Pre-Columbian Cultures of the Lesser Antilles,* pp. 511–530. Montreal, 1983.

Rochefort, Charles César de. *Histoire naturelle et morale des iles Antilles de l'Amérique.* 2d ed. Rotterdam, 1665.

Rouse, Irving. "The West Indies." In *Handbook of South American Indians,* edited by Julian H. Steward, vol. 4, pp. 49–565. Washington, D.C., 1948.

Rouse, Irving. "Prehistory of the West Indies." *Science* 144 (1964): 499–513.

Rouse, Irving. "On the Meaning of the Term 'Arawak.'" In *On the Trail of the Arawaks,* by Fred Olsen, pp. xiii–xvi. Norman, Okla., 1974.

Rouse, Irving, and Louis Allaire. "Caribbean." In *Chronologies in New World Archaeology,* edited by R. E. Taylor and C. W. Meighan, pp. 431–481. New York, 1978.

Taylor, Douglas M. *The Black Carib of British Honduras.* New York, 1951.

Wilbert, Johannes. "Magico-Religious Use of Tobacco among South American Indians." In *Spirits, Shamans and Stars: Perspectives from South America,* edited by David L. Browman and Ronald A. Schwarz, pp. 13–38. The Hague, 1979. This article also appears in *Cannabis and Culture,* edited by Vera D. Rubin (The Hague, 1975), pp. 439–461.

STEPHEN D. GLAZIER (1987)

CARIBBEAN RELIGIONS: AFRO-CARIBBEAN RELIGIONS

Most West Indians of African descent are affiliated, at least nominally, with a historic Christian denomination or with one of the newer sects. In many areas of the West Indies, however, a number of hybrid religions have attracted large numbers of followers. In Haiti, virtually the entire population is in some way involved in vodou. In Jamaica, the Revivalist, Kumina, and Convince cults continuously attract a small number of adherents. Wherever such cults are found, some persons participate more or less regularly in both a Christian church and a cult, and in times of crisis many who ordinarily ignore the cults become involved in their healing or magical rituals.

This essay will concentrate on four types of syncretic religious cults found in the Caribbean region, which will be called the *neo-African cults*, the *ancestral cults*, the *revivalist cults*, and the *religio-political cults*. The experience of Caribbean blacks under the political, economic, and domestic conditions of slavery modified character in a stressful direction, and those who were most sensitive to the stress advanced innovative religious and secular systems to deal with their anxiety. The new religious institutions consisted of elements of African and European beliefs and practices, and, in some cases, parts of American Indian and South Asian religious traditions. A number of new religions arose from the interaction of three major variables: socioeconomic, psychological, and cultural. Contingent factors in the development of these hybrid religions include such ecological and demographic variables as the degree to which a group of people had been isolated physically and socially from other segments of the population and the proportion of the total population constituted by various ethnic and racial groups (Simpson, 1978). Successful religions spread, adapt, and persist after the conditions that gave rise to them have changed (or changed to some extent), and individuals are socialized into accepting the revised beliefs and procedures. When this happens, a religion acquires new meanings for its members, and it takes on new functions, the most universal of which is the satisfaction that comes from group activities.

Neo-African Cults. These cults developed during the early stages of cultural contact between persons of European and African origin, because members of the subordinate group could neither acquire the religion of the dominant group nor participate as comembers in the historic Christian denominations. The major cults of this type are Haitian vodou, Cuban Santería, and Trinidadian Shango. From the viewpoint of cultural content, these religions represent the most extensive blend of African and European traditions and rituals in the Caribbean region.

Haitian vodou. The African dances that were performed in the seventeenth century by slaves in the western part of the island of Hispaniola and the religious beliefs of the Fon, Siniga, Lemba, Yoruba, and other African peoples who had been brought to Hispaniola were combined with certain beliefs of European folk origin about Roman Catholic saints, and, as a result, the neo-African religion of vodou developed. As James G. Leyburn (1966) has noted, the period from 1780 to 1790, when the importation of slaves to Hispaniola was increasing, saw the emergence of vodou, with a gradual ascendancy of Fon ideas. Finding the rites useful for their cause, revolutionary leaders in the last decades of the eighteenth century and the early years of the nineteenth century brought about further syntheses.

The supernatural phenomena of greatest importance in vodou are the *lwa*, also known as *zanj*, *mistè*, and other names. Many of these have names derived from old African gods, but other deities have names derived from African tribal or place names, names of Haitian origin, or names of Catholic saints; others have names of uncertain origin. The confusions and contradictions in the beliefs about these beings are due in part to contradictions in the Fon religious system that the Haitians adopted, and in part to the merging of the Fon system with that of the Yoruba (Courlander, 1960). But the endless variations in these and other beliefs concerning the ultimate reality are also the result of the absence of a hierarchy in the cult and of written documents. Erika Bourguignon (1980) suggests that variety and inconsistency in Haitian vodou have developed, and continue to develop, in part through the mechanism of altered states of consciousness, particularly in the forms of possession-trance and dreams. In Haiti, possession-trance is not highly stereotyped and prescribed. During possession-trance, cult leaders and members speak and act in the names of the spirits, behaving in ways that may modify the future performance of the ritual or the adherents' perception of the spirits.

The grand *lwa* comprise both nature spirits and functional spirits that are of African origin. Prominent among the nature spirits are Dambala, the serpent spirit identified with the rainbow and associated with floods; Bade, spirit of the winds; Sogbo, a Fon spirit of thunder; Shango (Yor., Ṣango), the Yoruba spirit of thunder and lightning; and Agwé, spirit of the sea. The functional *lwa* include Legba, the Fon guardian of crossroads and all barriers; the Ogou (Yor., Ogun) family, spirits associated with war; Zaka, associated with crops and agriculture; Ezili, a sea goddess among the Fon, but transformed in Haiti into the personification of feminine grace and beauty; the members of the Gèdè family, the spirits of death; Adja, skilled in the fields of herbs and pharmacy; and Obatala (Yor., Ọbatala), the Yoruba divinity responsible for forming children in the womb (Herskovits, 1937b; Courlander, 1939; Simpson, 1945, 1978; M. Rigaud, 1953; Métraux, 1959).

The *lwa* are also identified with Catholic saints. Thus, Legba is often believed to be the same as Anthony the Hermit, but some say that he is Saint Peter, the keeper of the keys. Dambala is identified with Saint Patrick, on whose image serpents are depicted. Ogou Ferraille is equated with Saint James; while Ogou Balanjo, the healer, is associated with Saint Joseph, who is pictured holding a child whom he blesses with an upraised hand. Obatala becomes Saint Anne; and Ezili, who is believed to be the richest of all the spirits, is identified with Mater Dolorosa and is represented as richly clothed and bejeweled. The *marassa*, spirits of dead twins, are believed to be the twin saints Cosmas and Damian (Price-Mars, 1928; Herskovits, 1937a).

The relationship between vodou adherents and the *lwa* is thought to be a contractual one; if one is punctilious about offerings and ceremonies, the *lwa* will be generous with their aid. The *lwa* must be paid once or twice a year with an impressive ceremony, and small gifts must be presented frequently. It is thought that the *lwa* like blood and that animal sacrifices are the means by which favors may be obtained. It is believed also that neglect of one's *lwa* will result in sickness, the death of relatives, crop failure, and other misfortunes (Simpson, 1980).

In West Africa, concepts of the "soul" are highly elaborated. In traditional Fon belief, all persons have at least three souls, and adult males have four (Herskovits, 1938). In Haitian vodou, every man has two souls: the *gro bonanj*, which animates the body and is similar to the soul in the Christian sense, and the *ti bonanj*, which protects a person against dangers by day and by night (Métraux, 1946). "Bad" souls are said to become "bad" *lwa* who divide their time between suffering in hell and doing evil deeds on earth (Simpson, 1945).

Adherents fear the power of the dead and observe funerary and postfunerary rites meticulously. A wake is held on the night of death; the funeral itself follows and, if possible, is held in accordance with the rites of the Catholic Church. On the ninth night after death is the "last prayer," and on the tenth night a ritual is held in which sacrifices are offered to all the family dead (Métraux, 1959; Herskovits, 1937b). Also, a family must honor its dead by mentioning their names at subsequent ceremonies and, if family finances permit, by holding memorial services for them annually. In vodou belief, the dead rank second only to the *lwa*, and to neglect or anger them is to invite disaster. (For accounts of vodou cermonies, see Herskovits, 1937b, pp. 155–176; Simpson, 1940; Simpson, 1946; Rigaud, 1946; Métraux, 1959, pp. 157–212; Courlander, 1960, pp. 41–74.)

François Duvalier, the dictatorial president of Haiti from 1957 to 1971, successfully exploited vodou for political purposes (Rotberg, 1976). Nevertheless, most observers agree that the cult has been weakened in recent years. An important factor in its decline has been the decay of the large extended family in the rural areas. Many of the large cult centers have split up into minor sects under priests whose training has been inadequate. A deepening economic poverty in the countryside has brought about the impoverishment of ritual there, and with the expansion of urbanization there have emerged innovative cult leaders who deal with the problems of a heterogeneous clientele rather than with the traditional concerns of farming or the demands of ancestral spirits (Bastide, 1971; Métraux, 1959; Bourguignon, 1980).

Cuban Santería. Most of the non-European elements in the Afro-Cuban syncretic religion known as Santería are derived from Yoruba beliefs and rituals. Animals are sacrificed to Yoruba deities, Yoruba music is played on African-type drums, songs with Yoruba words and music are sung, and dancers are possessed by the *orisha* (Yor., *orișa*, "spirit"). Yoruba foods are cooked for the gods and for devotees, beads of the proper color are worn, and leaves with Yoruba names are used in preparing medicines and in washing the stones of the *ori-sha* and the heads of cult members. In Santería, Elegba (Yor., Eșu or Ẹlẹgba) is identified with Saint Peter, and Shango (Yor., Șango), god of thunder, is identified with Saint Barbara. Shakpana (also Babaluaiye; Yor., Șọ-pọna) is equated with Saint Lazarus. Oya (Yor., Ọya), one of Shango's wives, is the equivalent of Saint Teresita. Obatala (Yor., Ọbatala) is Our Lady of Mercy, and Yemaja (Yor., Yemọja) is identified with the Virgin of Regla (a suburb of Havana). Osun (Yor., Ọșun) is associated with the Virgin of Cobre (a town in eastern Cuba), and Osanyin (Yor., Ọsanyin) known for his skill in healing, is identified with Saint Raphael. Ifa, or Orunmila (Yor., Ọrunmila), the god of divination, is linked with Saint Francis of Assisi. The Ibeji (Yor., "twins"), who behave like young children, are the counterparts of the twin saints Cosmas and Damian. Ogun, the Yoruba god of war and iron, is equated with John the Baptist (Bascom, 1951, 1972).

During a Santería ceremony, the blood of animals sacrificed to the gods is allowed to flow onto the sacred stones of the *santero* (Santería priest). Many instances of spirit possession during a given cermony indicate that the *orishas* have been well fed and are satisfied with the ritual offerings. The herbs serve to cleanse, refresh, and prepare the devotees and ritual objects for contact with the *orisha.* The blood is the food of the deities, and the stones are the objects through which they are fed and in which their power resides (Bascom, 1950). The *lucumis* (Afro-Cubans of Yoruba extraction) honor each of the gods with choral dances and pantomime in accordance with authentic Yoruba tradition (see Ortiz, 1951, for a detailed and vivid account of *lucumi* dances; and Simpson, 1978).

The regime of Fidel Castro has not assisted the Afro-Cuban cults and has taken some measures to control their expansion (Barrett, 1982). Although in recent years Santería has declined in Cuba, the presence of Cuban refugees has stimulated the worship of Shango and the other Yoruba *orisha* in the United States. Today many priests and priestesses officiate in Miami, New York City, Newark, Detroit, Chicago, Savannah, Gary, and other cities (Bascom, 1972).

The Shango cult in Trinidad. In southwestern Nigeria, each Yoruba deity, including Șango, god of thunder and lightning, has his or her own priests, followers, and cult centers. In the Shango cult in Trinidad, Shango is only one of several dozen "powers," which include twenty or more Yoruba deities (Lewis, 1978). Several non-Yoruba powers—especially Gabriel and Mama Latay—are popular in Trinidad. Ancient African gods are identified with certain Catholic saints, as occurs in Haiti, Grenada, parts of Brazil, Cuba, and other countries in the New World. Among these pairings in Trinidad are Obatala and Saint Benedict; Shango and Saint John; Shakpana and, variously, Moses or Saint Francis or Saint Jerome; Oshun and Saint Philomena or Saint Anne; Béji (Ibeji) and Saint Peter; Emanja and Saint Catherine or Saint Anne; Oya and Saint Philomena or Saint Catherine. Each god has his or her favorite colors, foods, and drinks; each is thought to have certain physical traits and to possess certain powers. In Shango, as in vodou and Santería, participants can recognize the major spirits who are well known throughout the country, or the principal spirits known in a given locality, by the stylized behavior of devotees possessed by them (Bourguignon, 1980). For example, Ogun, the god of iron and war, is believed to prefer the colors red and white (also the favorite colors of Shango), and rams and roosters are his preferred offerings. When possessed by Ogun, a Shangoist brandishes a sword and behaves in a violent way (Simpson, 1978).

Each Shango cult center holds an annual ceremony in honor of the *orisha* known to its worshipers. The four-day ritual begins with the recitation of original prayers, followed by several repetitions of the Lord's Prayer, Hail Mary, and the Apostle's Creed. The leader then recites in succession prayers such as Saint Francis's prayer, Saint George's prayer, and Blessed Martin's prayer; he recites each prayer line-by-line, and the worshipers repeat each line after him. Next, in an act of dismissal, food for the deity Eshu is placed outside the ceremonial area. (The Yoruba deity Ẹṣu is thought both to serve as a messenger among the gods and to be a trickster.) After Eshu's ejection, the worshipers invite other powers to the ceremony by drumming the powers' favorite rhythms. Ogun's rhythm is the first to be played. Drumming, dancing, singing, and spirit possession continue through the night; the climax comes at dawn with the sacrificing of pigeons, doves, chickens, agoutis, land turtles, goats, and sheep. Similar rites are performed on the following three nights, and often a bull is sacrificed. Aspects of Trinidadian cult life that are closely related to African religious behavior include divination, conjuring, and folk medicine, which are often strikingly similar to West African procedures (Simpson, 1978).

In recent decades, traditional religious, magical, and medical beliefs have been undermined to some extent by the expansion of education, the growth of medical and social services, and the influence of mass communication. Trinidadian Shango has also been modified by the intermixture of some of its aspects with the Spiritual Baptist (Shouters) complex (Simpson, 1978). There are many similarities between the Shango cult of Trinidad and that of Grenada (Pollak-Eltz, 1968; Simpson, 1978).

Ancestral Cults. The second type of hybrid religious cult in the Caribbean, called the *ancestral cult*, has fewer African and more European components than does the neo-African-type religion. The Kumina and Convince cults and the Kromanti Dance in Jamaica, the Big Drum Dance of Grenada and Carriacou, Kele in Saint Lucia, and the religion of the Black Carib of Belize exemplify this kind of syncretic religion.

Kumina. According to Monica Schuler (1980), Kumina did not originate among plantation slaves of the eighteenth century but was brought to Jamaica by post-emancipation immigrants from central Africa who chiefly settled in the eastern parish of Saint Thomas. Kumina is primarily a family religion, and each group honors a number of family spirits in addition to other divinities. The three ranks of Kumina spirits (known as zombies) are the sky gods, the earthbound gods, and ancestral zombies. Among the thirty-nine sky gods listed by Joseph G. Moore (1953), only one (Shango) clearly has the name of a West African deity, but some Kumina gods appear to serve tribes or "nations" that are African. Of the sixty-two earthbound gods given by Moore, at least seven have biblical names (e.g., Moses, Ezekiel). The twenty-one ancestral zombies are the spirits of men and women who, in their lifetimes, were dancing zombies (persons who experienced possession by a god and who danced while possessed), *obeah* men (sorcerers), and drummers (Moore and Simpson, 1957). Most Kumina dances are memorial services held to pay respects to the dead ancestors of the participants, but ceremonies are performed on other occasions, such as betrothal, marriage, burial, the naming of a baby, the anniversary of emancipation, and Independence Day (Moore, 1953; Schuler, 1980).

All zombies are invoked through drumming and singing. Songs are of two types: *bilah* songs, which are sung in a dialect of English; and country songs, which are sung in a language referred to as *African* (accent on the last syllable). Kumina ritual ends with the sacrifice of a goat and the dance of the Queen of the Kumina and her attendants. In performing ritual, the living members of a family convey their wishes to the ancestors (Moore and Simpson, 1957, 1958).

Convince. The Convince ritual practiced in the Jamaican parishes of Saint Thomas and Portland has a number of Christian elements, but its principal powers are the spirits of persons who belonged to the cult during their lifetime. The most powerful *bongo* ghosts come from Africa, but the spirits of ancient Jamaican slaves and the Maroons (descendants of runaway slaves), who perpetuated the cult until recent times, are also of importance. The spirits of Jamaicans more recently departed are less powerful than the other ghosts, but those who practiced *obeah* ("conjuration") in their lifetime are used by *bongo* men (i.e., Convince devotees) as partners in divination and conjuring. Each *bongo* man operates independently, and each has one or more assistants called apprentices or grooms. In addition, a number of lesser followers are attached to each cult group, including some persons who are devout Christians (Hogg, 1960).

Each *bongo* man holds a sacrificial ceremony annually and conducts Convince rites as the need for them arises. Christian prayers, the reading of Bible passages, and hymn singing precede the main ceremony. Special *bongo* songs, hand clapping, and dances performed by *bongo* men call the spirits to the ceremony. Later, the spirits of the ancestors (that is, devotees possessed by the ghosts) dance.

According to Donald Hogg (1960), such traits as blood sacrifice, vigorous possession-trance behavior, the materialistic purposes of ceremonies, the involvement with divination and conjuring, religious dancing, the worship of ancestral spirits, and the propitiation of potentially malevolent beings almost certainly have African antecedents. In these respects Convince, like Kumina, shows greater African influence than do the Revival Zion, Pocomania, and Rastafarian cults in Jamaica. Once a nativistic movement, Convince has so declined since the 1950s that it now provides mainly jollification and catharsis.

The Kromanti Dance. The traditional religion of the descendants of "Maroons," escaped slaves of the seventeenth and eighteenth centuries in Jamaica, is known as the Kromanti Dance. One supreme deity, Yankipong, is believed to be remote from human affairs. The spirits of the dead, called *duppies, jumbies,* or *bigi-man,* have the power to work good or evil in the daily lives of their descendants, and this power is referred to by the term *obeah* or by the more modern term *science.* No Kromanti Dance can be successful without one or more of the participants becoming possessed by the spirit of an ancestor. Most Kromanti Dance ceremonies require the sacrifice of an animal to the *pakit* (ancestral spirit) of the *feteman* (ritual specialist). Although the Kromanti Dance is a separate tradition, it bears some similarity to both Kumina and Convince (Bilby, 1981, pp. 52–101).

The Big Drum Dance in Grenada and Carriacou. For numerous residents of Grenada and Carriacou, performing the Big Drum Dance (also known as the Nation Dance, or Saraca—"sacrifice") is a show of respect to their ancestors. In Carriacou, many persons can still recount the African "nations," traced patrilineally, to which they belong. Usually this ceremony is a family occasion, but it may be put on by members of an occupational group—for example, fishermen. Various reasons are given for organizing a festival: to counter the ill health or misfortune of a friend or relative, to dedicate a tombstone for a deceased family member, to start a critically important undertaking, or to launch the marriage preparations of a son or daughter. Offerings of food are prepared for the ancestors and the guests, a space is provided where the spirits of the ancestors can dance, the ancestors are summoned, and the "beg pardon" dance is performed, during which family members kneel and sing, asking the ancestors to pardon them for any wrongdoing (Pearse, 1956). In Carriacou, as M. G. Smith (1971) has noted, Christianity and the ancestral cult are complementary, each supplying what the other lacks.

The Kele cult in Saint Lucia. The Kele ceremony in Saint Lucia resembles, in attenuated form, the Shango ritual in Trinidad. The ritual is performed to ask the ancestors of devotees for health, protection against misfortune in agriculture, and success in important undertakings, as well as to thank the forebears for past favors. The paraphernalia essential for the Kele rite consists mainly of Amerindian polished stone axes (which are called *pièrres tonnerres,* "thunderstones," by devotees, who believe them to have fallen from the sky), drums, and agricultural implements such as machetes, axes, hoes, and forks. Several of the stone axes are placed on the ground to form a cross, with additional axes arranged around the central grouping (Simpson, 1973; Simmons, 1963).

The stone axes, addressed as "Shango," symbolize the African ancestors of the Saint Lucians who participate in Kele. Thunderstones constitute one of the principal symbols of Shango in West Africa, Haiti, Cuba, Trinidad, Grenada, and urban areas of the United States that are heavily populated by immigrants from the Caribbean. Present-day devotees in Saint Lucia seem to be unaware that Shango (Ṣango) is the deity of thunder and lightning in traditional West African belief. To these believers, Shango is simply the name of the thunderstones that enable the living to get in touch with their African ancestors.

Following some preliminary drumming, singing, and dancing, the leader of a Kele ceremony asks the ancestors to intercede with God on behalf of the sponsor of the occasion. A ram is then sacrificed to the ancestors. Communication with God is achieved through possession; the ancestors enter the bodies of some of the men participating in the ceremony. After the ram has been cooked, morsels of the meat, as well as portions of yams, rice, and other foods, are thrown on the ground as offerings to Shango—that is, to the African ancestors. Saint Lucia is a predominantly Catholic country, and some devotees of the cult are active Catholics.

Ancestral cult of the Black Carib of Belize. The Black Carib of Belize are descendants of African slaves who escaped from other parts of the West Indies and settled first among the Island Carib in Saint Vincent. At the end of the eighteenth century, they were deported by the English to Roatan, an island in the Gulf of Honduras, and later they spread out along the coast of the mainland. The Black Carib of Belize speak a South American Indian language, and, as Douglas MacRae Taylor has noted, their "outward cultural manifestations differ but little, in the main, from their neighbors" (Taylor, 1951, p. 37; Stone, 1953, pp. 1–3).

The supernatural beliefs, rites, and practices of the Black Carib are a mixture of African and non-African elements. Singing, drumming, and dancing are intended to placate the ancestors of the family giving the ceremony, and some participants become possessed by the spirits of their deceased ancestors, as occurs in Kumina and Convince in Jamaica, the Big Drum in Grenada and Carriacou, and Kele in Saint Lucia. Sacrifices of food and drink are offered periodically to the spirits of the ancestors; some offerings are taken out to sea and thrown into the water.

Most of the Black Carib are professed Christians and, in the main, Catholics. They see no inconsistency between their Christian faith and non-Christian beliefs. The ancestral spirits are regarded as subordinate to the Christian God, and the evil forces of the universe are manifestations of Satan (Taylor, 1951).

REVIVALIST CULTS. The third type of Afro-Caribbean religious syncretism, the *revivalist cult,* descends from the Afro-Protestant cults of the late eighteenth century and, in the case of Jamaica, from the Great Revival of 1861–1862. Revival Zion in Jamaica, the Spiritual Baptists (Shouters) of Trinidad, and the Shakers of Saint Vincent typify this kind of cult.

Revival Zion. For nearly a hundred years after England acquired Jamaica in 1655, no missionary work was carried on on the island. The official missionary movement did not begin until the 1820s. A religious movement known as

Myalism emerged in the 1760s to protect slaves against European sorcery. This "native" Baptist movement was without serious competition during the forty-year period (1780–1820) when a reinterpretation of Christianity spread across Jamaica. Rent and wage disputes between planters and workers were common after the abolition of apprenticeship in 1838. In 1841–1842, Myalists preached the millenarian message that they were God's angels, appointed to do the work of the Lord, and their wrath was directed against both planters and missionaries. The authorities took severe measures against the movement. Popular interest in separatist churches, as well as in regular missions, was stimulated by the Great Revival which swept over the island in 1861–1862, but the enthusiasm dwindled within a short time. The hybrid religion of the Myalists, or Black Baptists, which included dancing, drumming, and spirit possession, resurfaced in 1866. Subsequently, the vitality of this movement was seen in the multiplication and flourishing of black revivalist cults (Curtin, 1955; Schuler, 1979).

Adherents of Revival Zion and the related sects of Revival and Pocomania do not identify old African gods with Christian saints as do participants in vodou (Haiti), Santería (Cuba), and Shango (Brazil, Trinidad, Grenada). The Holy Spirit possesses followers during revivalist ceremonies, as do the spirits of Old Testament figures such as Jeremiah, Isaiah, Joshua, Moses, Shadrach, Meshach, and Abednego; New Testament apostles and evangelists such as Matthew, Mark, Luke, John, Peter, and James; the archangels Michael, Gabriel and Raphael; Satan and his chief assistant, Rutibel; beings from Hebrew magical tradition, such as Uriel, Ariel, Seraph, Nathaniel, and Tharsis; Constantine, Melshezdek, and the Royal Angel; and the dead, especially prominent revivalist leaders of the past (Moore and Simpson, 1957; Simpson, 1978).

Drumming, hymn singing, hand clapping, praying, Bible reading, spirit possession, and intermittent commentary by the leader are main features of the weekly services, as is "spiritual" dancing, in which leading participants circle the altar counterclockwise, stamping first with their right feet and then with their left, bending their bodies forward and then straightening up, hyperventilating, and groaning rhythmically. Special revivalist rituals include baptismal ceremonies, death rites (wake, funeral, "ninth night," "forty days," and memorial services held after one or more years have passed since the death), and the dedication of a meeting place. "Tables" (feasts) are given to thank the spirits for assistance or to seek deliverance from trouble (Simpson, 1956).

Spiritual Baptists (Shouters) of Trinidad. In many ways, the Spiritual Baptist cult (Shouters) in Trinidad is similar to Revival Zion in Jamaica, but there are several noteworthy differences. Among the Shouters, no drums or rattles accompany hymn singing. Spiritual Baptists do not become possessed by the wide variety of spirits that possess Revivalists in Jamaica; as a rule, devotees are possessed only by the Holy Spirit. Certain groups among the Shouters do, however, make ritual offerings to the spirits "of the sea, the land, and the river," and occasionally a Shango "power" may enter a person who is taking part in a ritual. In Trinidad, important relationships exist between Spiritual Baptists and Shango groups. (The Shango cult is not found in Jamaica). Shangoists as well as Shouters need to be baptized, and only a Shouters pastor of some standing can perform this service. In addition, "mourning" and "building"—optional rites taken by some members of both cults—are conducted by Spiritual Baptist leaders. Many Shouters attend the annual ceremonies staged by different Shango cult groups, and like their counterparts in syncretic cults elsewhere in the Caribbean, some adherents participate at times in the services of more orthodox religions (Simpson, 1978; Glazier, 1983).

Spiritual Baptists are often men and women of the lower classes. Most are of African descent, but a few East Indians do participate in the cult. Throughout the Caribbean in recent decades, most of the neo-African cults, the ancestral cults, and the revivalist cults, as well as many of the historical churches, have lost membership, while the Pentecostal, Holiness, and Adventist sects and the Rastafarian movement have made impressive gains (Simpson, 1978).

The Shakers of Saint Vincent. English rule of the island of Saint Vincent began in 1783, and the first direct religious influence intended for the slave population was brought to the island by a Methodist missionary in 1787. The Shaker cult, which goes back to at least the early part of the twentieth century, has a Methodist base, with an admixture of elements of other Christian denominational traditions (Anglicanism, Roman Catholicism, Pentecostalism), modified African religious traits, and elements developed locally. An important feature of this religion is the mild state of dissociation, attributed to possession by the Holy Ghost, that some of its adherents experience. The range of Shaker services and the rituals themselves are similar to those of the Spiritual Baptists of Trinidad (Henney, 1974).

RELIGIO-POLITICAL CULTS. The fourth cult type appears when a society is undergoing severe reorganization, as was the case in Jamaica with the unrest that accompanied the Great Depression of the 1930s. The Rastafarian movement, which appeared in the island during this period, is a mixture of social protest and religious doctrine and so may be called a *religio-political cult.*

Rastafarianism. An important factor underlying the rise of Rastafarianism is that, since at least the beginning of the twentieth century, Jamaican blacks have identified with Ethiopia on account of its biblical symbolism. The verse most often cited is *Psalms* 68:31: "Princes come out of Egypt; Ethiopia shall soon stretch out her hands unto God." Between 1904 and 1927, Ethiopianism came to the attention of Jamaicans through several essays, articles, and books published in Jamaica and in the United States. The early 1930s saw the founding of a number of associations for black people and the emegence of the Rastafarian movement, named after Ras ("prince") Tafari, who was crowned emperor Haile

Selassie of Ethiopia (Abyssinia) in November 1930. Marcus Garvey had formed the Universal Negro Improvement Association in Jamaica in 1914, and his doctrine of racial redemption, together with the coronation of Haile Selassie, furthered interest in the Ethiopian tradition (Hill, 1980).

Since emancipation, persons on the lower rungs of Jamaican society have struggled continuously against exploitation. Higher wages, the granting of civil and political rights, and other gains have come slowly, and often against bitter opposition. In the early 1930s, the basic issues for rural Jamaicans were land, rent, and taxation, and their struggles over these questions gave rise to the millenarian visions of the Rastafarian movement. In that period, Rastafarians were subjected to intense police pressure in Saint Thomas and neighboring parishes. It is likely that the Rastafarian millenarianism, with its vision of black domination, served as a catalyst in bringing about the labor uprisings of 1938 (Hill, 1981).

In 1953, Rastafarianism bore strong resemblance to revivalism in organizational and ritual patterns. The small, independent groups of both movements had similar sets of officers, festivals, and ritual procedures, including the reading of passages from the Bible and the singing of hymns (modified in the case of the Rastafarians to fit the doctrines of the cult), but important differences existed. Drumming, dancing, and spirit possession were prominent features of revivalism, but they never occurred in a Rastafarian gathering (Simpson, 1955). Beards and dreadlocks were present among Rastafarians but were not important aspects of the movement in the early fifties, nor was the place given to *ganja* (marijuana). Rastafarianism was, however, antiestablishment and bitter on the racial question (Chevannes, 1977). Revivalism had no political significance in 1953; its adherents were mainly concerned about personal salvation (Simpson, 1956).

According to Rastafarian doctrines in 1953, (1) black people were exiled to the West Indies because of their transgressions; (2) the white man is inferior to the black man; (3) the Jamaican situation is hopeless; (4) Ethiopia is heaven; (5) Haile Selassie is the living God; (6) the emperor of Abyssinia will arrange for expatriated persons of African descent to return to the homeland; and (7) black men will soon get their revenge by compelling white men to serve them (Simpson, 1955). These remain the basic beliefs of the movement, but not all adherents subscribe to all of them, nor do they give them equal emphasis. Rastafarians reinterpret the Old Testament in claiming that they are true present-day prophets, the "reincarnated Moseses, Joshuas, Isaiahs, and Jeremiahs." They also believe that they are "destined to free the scattered Ethiopians who are black men" (Nettleford, 1970, pp. 108–109).

As revivalism began to decline in the mid-1950s, many of its followers were attracted to Rastafarianism and became active participants in the movement, or sympathizers (Smith, Augier, and Nettleford, 1960). Between 1953 and 1960, the Rastafarian movement grew rapidly and became more complex doctrinally. This growth continued through the 1970s and the early 1980s. Membership—both the fully committed and partially committed—came to be drawn from all levels of the society. The more militant Rastafarians insisted that deliverance from poverty, unemployment, and humiliation must come from forces within Jamaica and not from Haile Selassie or Haile Selassie's spirit. Repatriation to Africa received less emphasis as some bands began to stress black power and "the africanization of Jamaica" (employment, education, and use of the country's resources are to benefit persons of African descent; see Nettleford, 1970; Barrett, 1974; Simpson, 1978).

The militancy of present-day Rastafarianism is seen clearly in its concept of a modern Babylon that includes Britain, the former colonial power; the United States, the present major industrial power; the bourgeois state of Jamaica; and the church. Babylon is said to be the source of Jamaica's misfortunes (Chevannes, 1977). A recent theme of the movement has to do with its concept of nature. In Rastafarian thought nature is nonindustrial society; and this underlies certain aspects of Rastafarian lifestyle—for example, dietary rules, uncombed locks and beards, and the importance of *ganja* (Chevannes, 1977).

Since the early 1960s, Rastafarianism has played an important role in the evolution of Jamaican popular music. The rhythm of the Rastafarians' *akete* drums influenced the development of the fast rhythm called *ska,* and the ska form has developed into reggae. Most reggae songs contain caustic social comments, but they also praise Ras Tafari, Jamaican heroes, freedom, and *ganja* (Barrett, 1977; Chevannes, 1977). In the poetry and prose written by contemporary Rastafarians awareness of an African identity and of Africa itself is a main theme (Johnson, 1980).

Rastafarianism is not a unified movement (Campbell, 1980). Many of the brethren gather in small, informal bodies and are not affiliated with organized groups. Many Rastafarians refuse to take part in elections on the grounds that neither of Jamaica's two political parties represents them. In recent times, however, some Rastafarians have played an increasingly active role in politics (Smith, Augier, and Nettleford, 1960; Chevannes, 1977).

Rastafarian culture has spread to other parts of the Caribbean, and Rastafarian art, poetry, music, and philosophy are well known in London, Paris, and other cities in Western Europe and the United States. Rastafarian music has been diffused to a number of African countries (Campbell, 1980).

The dethronement of Haile Selassie in 1974 and his death the following year have not resulted in a decline of the movement. Rastafarianism arose out of certain conditions in Jamaica and in other countries of the Caribbean and has continued because those conditions, as well as the international situation, have not changed appreciably (Barrett, 1977).

SEE ALSO Christianity, article on Christianity in the Caribbean Region; Fon and Ewe Religion; Santería; Vodou; West African Religions; Yoruba Religion.

Bibliography

Barrett, David B., ed. *World Christian Encyclopedia: A Comparative Study of Churches and Religions in the Modern World, AD 1900–2000.* Oxford, 1982.

Barrett, Leonard E. *Soul-Force: African Heritage in Afro-American Religion.* New York, 1974.

Barrett, Leonard E. *The Rastafarians: Sounds of Cultural Dissonance.* Boston, 1977.

Bascom, William R. "The Focus of Cuban Santeria." *Southwestern Journal of Anthropology* 6 (Spring 1950): 64–68.

Bascom, William R. "The Yoruba in Cuba." *Nigeria* 37 (1951): 14–20.

Bascom, William R. *Shango in the New World.* Austin, Tex., 1972.

Bastide, Roger. *African Civilisations in the New World.* New York, 1971.

Bilby, Kenneth M. "The Kromanti Dance of the Windward Maroons of Jamaica." *Nieuwe West-Indische Gids* (Utrecht) 55 (August 1981): 52–101.

Bourguignon, Erika. "George E. Simpson's Ideas about Ultimate Reality and Meaning in Haitian Vodun." *Ultimate Reality and Meaning* (Toronto) 3 (1980): 233–238.

Chevannes, Barry. "The Literature of Rastafari." *Social and Economic Studies* 26 (June 1977): 239–262.

Courlander, Harold. *Haiti Singing.* Chapel Hill, N.C., 1939.

Courlander, Harold. *The Drum and the Hoe: Life and Lore of the Haitian People.* Berkeley, 1960.

Curtin, Philip D. *Two Jamaicas: The Role of Ideas in a Tropical Colony, 1830–1865.* Cambridge, Mass., 1955.

Davis, E. Wade. "The Ethnobiology of the Haitian Zombie." *Journal of Ethnopharmacology* 9 (1983): 85–104.

Glazier, Stephen D. *Marchin' the Pilgrims Home: Leadership and Decision-Making in an Afro-Caribbean Faith.* Westport, Conn., 1983.

Henney, Jeannette H. "Spirit-Possession Belief and Trance Behavior in Two Fundamentalist Groups in St. Vincent." In *Trance, Healing, and Hallucination: Three Field Studies in Religious Experience*, by Felicitas D. Goodman, Jeannette H. Henney, and Esther Pressel, pp. 6–111. New York, 1974.

Herskovits, Melville J. "African Gods and Catholic Saints in New World Negro Belief." *American Anthropologist* 39 (1937): 635–643. Cited in text as 1937a.

Herskovits, Melville J. *Life in a Haitian Valley.* New York, 1937. Cited in text as 1937b.

Herskovits, Melville J. *Dahomey: An Ancient West African Kingdom.* 2 vols. New York, 1938.

Hill, Robert A. "Dread History: Leonard Howell and Millenarian Visions in Early Rastafari Religions in Jamaica." *Epoche* 9 (1981): 30–71.

Hogg, Donald. "The Convince Cult in Jamaica." *Yale University Publications in Anthropology* 58 (1960): 3–24.

Johnson, Howard. "Introduction." In *Boy in a Landscape: A Jamaican Picture*, by Trevor Fitz-Henley. Gordon Town, Jamaica, 1980.

Laguerre, Michel S. *Vodou Heritage.* Beverly Hills, Calif., 1980.

Lewis, Maureen Warner. "Yoruba Religion in Trinidad: Transfer and Reinterpretation." *Caribbean Quarterly* 24 (September–December 1978): 18–32.

Leyburn, James G. *The Haitian People.* Rev. ed. New Haven, 1966.

Métraux, Alfred. "The Concept of Soul in Haitian Vodu." *Southwestern Journal of Anthropology* 2 (Spring 1946): 84–92.

Métraux, Alfred. *Vodou in Haiti.* New York, 1959.

Moore, Joseph G. "Religion of Jamaican Negroes: A Study of Afro-American Acculturation." Ph.D. diss., Northwestern University, 1953.

Moore, Joseph G., and George E. Simpson. "A Comparative Study of Acculturation in Morant Bay and West Kingston, Jamaica." *Zaire* 11 (November–December 1957): 979–1019, and 12 (January 1958): 65–87.

Nettleford, Rex M. *Mirror, Mirror: Identity, Race and Protest in Jamaica.* Kingston, Jamaica, 1970.

Ortiz Fernández, Fernando. *Los bailes y el teatro de los negros en el folklore de Cuba.* Havana, 1951.

Pearse, Andrew C. *The Big Drum Dance of the Carriacou.* Ethnic Folkways Library P 1011.

Pollak-Eltz, Angelina. "The Shango Cult in Grenada, British Westindies." In *Proceedings of the Eighth International Congress of Anthropological and Ethnological Sciences*, vol. 3, pp. 59–60. N.p., 1968.

Price-Mars, Jean. *So Spoke the Uncle.* Washington, D.C., 1983. A translation, with introduction and notes, by Magdeline W. Shannon of *Ainsi parla l'oncle* (Paris, 1928).

Rigaud, Milo. *La tradicion vaudoo et le vaudoo haitian: Son temple, ses mystères, sa magie.* Paris, 1953.

Rigaud, Odette M. "The Feasting of the Gods in Haitian Vodu." *Primitive Man* 19 (January–April 1946): 1–58.

Rotberg, Robert I. "Vodun and the Politics of Haiti." In *The African Diaspora: Interpretive Essays*, edited by Martin L. Kilson and Robert I. Rotberg, pp. 342–365. Cambridge, Mass., 1976.

Schuler, Monica. "Myalism and the African Religious Tradition in Jamaica." In *Africa and the Caribbean: The Legacies of a Link*, edited by Margaret E. Crahan and Franklin W. Knight, pp. 65–79. Baltimore, 1979.

Schuler, Monica. *"Alas, Alas, Kongo": A Social History of Indentured African Immigration into Jamaica, 1841–1865.* Baltimore, 1980.

Simmons, Harold F. C. "Notes on Folklore in St. Lucia." In *Iouanaloa: Recent Writing from St. Lucia*, edited by Edward Braithwaite, pp. 41–49. Saint Lucia, 1963.

Simpson, George E. "The Vodun Service in Northern Haiti." *American Anthropologist* 42 (April–June 1940): 236–254

Simpson, George E. "The Belief System of Haitian Vodun." *American Anthropologist* 47 (January 1945): 35–59.

Simpson, George E. "Four Vodun Ceremonies." *Journal of American Folklore* 59 (April–June 1946): 154–167.

Simpson, George E. "Political Cultism in West Kingston." *Social and Economic Studies* 4 (June 1955): 133–149.

Simpson, George E. "Jamaican Revivalist Cults." *Social and Economic Studies* 5 (December 1956): 321–442.

Simpson, George E. "The Kele Cult in St. Lucia." *Caribbean Studies* 13 (October 1973): 110–116.

Simpson, George E. *Black Religions in the New World.* New York, 1978.

Simpson, George E. "Ideas about Ultimate Reality and Meaning in Haitian Vodun." *Ultimate Reality and Meaning* (Toronto) 3 (1980): 187–199.

Smith, M. G. "A Note on Truth, Fact, and Tradition in Carriacou." *Caribbean Quarterly* 17 (September–December 1971): 128–138.

Smith, M. G., Roy Augier, and Rex M. Nettleford. *The Ras Tafari Movement in Kingston, Jamaica.* Mona, Jamaica, 1960.

Stone, Doris. *The Black Caribs of Honduras.* Ethnic Folkways Library P 435.

Taylor, Douglas MacRae. *The Black Carib of British Honduras.* New York, 1951.

GEORGE EATON SIMPSON (1987)

CARMATHIANS SEE QARĀMIṬAH

CARNIVAL.

The Christian festival called Carnival takes place on Shrove Tuesday, the eve of Ash Wednesday. In its widest sense, however, the Carnival period is of much longer duration, beginning right after Christmas, the New Year, or the Feast of Epiphany, depending on the region.

The etymological roots of the name *Carnival* may be the Latin *caro* ("meat") and *levara* ("to remove, to take away"), which in vulgar Latin became *carne levamen,* and afterward *carne vale.* Some etymologists also link it to *carnis levamen,* "the pleasure of meat," the farewell to which is celebrated in the festivities that come immediately before the prohibitions of Lent. Another hypothesis links it etymologically to the *carrus navalis,* the horse-drawn, boat-shaped carriage that was paraded in Roman festivals in honor of Saturn, carrying men and women who, in fancy dress and wearing masks, sang obscene songs.

If it is problematic to identify the etymological roots of *Carnival,* it becomes even more difficult to determine the historical origins of the celebration itself. However, the Roman feasts of Saturn, the Saturnalias, are generally recognized as the ancient forerunner of Carnival festivities. They embodied the essential carnival spirit, strongly characterized by the transgression of daily conventions and excesses of behavior. In these feasts, which took place in the midst of great licentiousness, slaves banqueted together with their masters, whom they insulted and admonished. From among them was elected a King of Chaos who, for the period of Saturnalia only, enjoyed full rights to his master's concubines, and gave ridiculous orders that had to be obeyed by everyone. At the end of the festivities, however, he was unthroned and, in the earliest form of the rite, sacrificed to signal a return to order.

Although far in meaning from the Christian Carnival, these Roman rituals contained some elements that would come to define the later and more universal concept of the feast. The inversion of prevailing norms—as when servants rule masters—is of particular importance; the burlesque parodies of power and order, as seen in the dramatization of the Jester King, and the element of exaggeration, both in terms of libidinous excesses and in the inordinate consumption of food and drink, have also become prominent characteristics of Carnival. This unruliness that temporarily suspends the recognized world order has the corollary of introducing a contrast to the parameters of daily life. In other words, these cyclical rituals of disorder and rebellion show themselves incapable of administering real life because they foster the confusion of roles, licentiousness, and the mockery of power; they thus serve as a reminder of the necessity for order, which is reestablished at their conclusion.

In *Rabelais and His World* (Cambridge, Mass., 1968) the Russian essayist Mikhail Bakhtin presents an interesting interpretation of the meaning of Carnival in the context of the Middle Ages and the Renaissance. He treats Carnival as the most evident expression of a joking popular culture with its roots in the Roman Saturnalias, which reflected the playful, irreverent side of human nature and the indestructible festive element in all human civilizations. During the whole of the Middle Ages and the Renaissance, this culture of laughter resisted the official, serious culture. In opposition to the mysticism and dogmatism of the ecclesiastical culture and rigidity of the prevailing political structures, the joking popular culture revealed a world in which a playful mutability was possible and provided an experience, at once symbolic and concrete, of the suspension of social barriers. By dramatizing the comic and relative side of absolute truths and supreme authorities, it highlighted the ambivalence of reality, coming to represent the power of both absolute liberty and farce.

Using these distinctions, Bakhtin contrasts the official and ecclesiastical ceremonies of ordered society with the festivities of carnivalesque culture. He characterizes the former as rituals of inequality because they reinforce the dominant order and seek justification of the present in the past. The latter he regards as rituals of equality because they parody the stratification of power and the cult of religion, as well as provide a symbolic suspension of norms and privileges, harboring a seed of social reaction in satire.

Thus, inversion is universally at the root of Carnival symbolism, and explains the presence of such customs as transvestite costume, or clothes worn inside out, the poor playing the role of the rich, and the weak that of the powerful. This interpretive perspective also makes sense of the symbolism of death, common in Carnival celebrations; here it implies revitalization. Similarly, the dethroning and burning in effigy of the Jester King marks the end of a cycle and suggests the commencement of another, and the scatological aggressions with bodily materials like urine are a symbolic component implying fertilization. From this point of view, one can also amplify the concept of "carnivalization" to include all the symbolic processes that bring about transformations in the representation of social reality.

The most notable carnivalization of late medieval European society was to be found in the Feast of Fools, also called the Feast of Innocents. Although it took place in churches between Christmas and Epiphany, this festival was both an extreme satire of the mannerisms and mores of the court and the high church and a radical mockery of ecclesiastical structure and religious doctrine. The low church and the lower orders played an important part in it, while the high church and the nobility were its principal targets.

For the festival, a King of the Fools or a Boy Bishop, chosen from among the local choir boys, was elected to act out a parody of episcopal functions, including the distribution of blessings to the crowd from a balcony. A comic version of the holy mass was enacted, in which obscene parodies such as "The Liturgy of the Drunkards," "The Liturgy of the Gamblers," and "The Will of the Ass" were substituted for the canticles and prayers. Masked and painted, wearing the garb of the high church or dressed up as women, the revelers danced freely in the cathedrals and banqueted on the altars. The burning of old shoes and excrement replaced incense. Meanwhile, riotous processions of other revelers, wearing goat and horse masks, paraded dancing and singing through the streets.

Dances in churches are not totally unheard of in the history of Christianity; so-called shrine dances, for example, were frequent in the first centuries of its development. However, with the consolidation and institutionalization of the church, these dances were gradually abolished. In any case, the Feast of Fools had an entirely different sense. Its most striking characteristic was that of grotesque buffoonery, and in it the carnivalesque inversion was carried to its ultimate extreme. Focusing on the ecclesiastical hierarchy and religious ethics, the Feast of Fools pointed out the critical relations of medieval society and demonstrated that such a society was capable of self-criticism.

The Feast of the Ass, which took place principally in France, was a variation within the same category of rituals of carnivalesque inversion. Also part of the Christmas cycle, it theoretically commemorated Mary's flight to Egypt. The central character was, however, the ass, or rather the Ass Prince, who was richly adorned and brought in procession under a luxurious canopy to the church, where a mass was celebrated in its honor, punctuated with braying noises to which the celebrants responded by also braying.

For almost a millennium, the Roman Catholic church attempted, with perceptible difficulty, to control or ban the Feast of Fools. One of the first recorded proscriptions dates from the seventh century in Toledo, Spain. That this had little success can be measured by the numerous subsequent proscriptive edicts up to the sixteenth century, like that of Dijon, France, in 1552. The Feast of Fools died out only with the advent of the Reformation and Counter-Reformation. Until then, just as it had come under severe attack, it had also produced its enthusiastic apologists, such as those who wrote the circular of the Theology School of Paris in 1444. This circular maintained that just as fermenting barrels of wine sometimes need ventilation to prevent them from exploding, the wine of human madness must have an outlet at least once a year in order to transform itself into the good wine of pious devotion.

The Feast of Fools continued for a long time in France. It was still a solidly institutionalized event in Nice in the seventeenth century, when various secular laws were passed to regulate the structuring of the profane "Abbeys of the Fools" and to formalize the powers of the "Abbots of the Fools." At the same time, ecclesiastical decrees attempted to prevent the previously uncontrolled participation of the low church in the carnivalesque festivities and dances and bind them to their liturgical duties on the relevant days.

As a result of the Nice ordinance in 1539, the carnivalesque balls were subdivided into four categories, namely, those of the nobles, the merchants, the artisans, and the laborers. Each was the responsibility of one Abbot of the Fools, aided by a certain number of "monks," who policed the ball. The "abbots" were responsible for maintaining order, for making sure that only those suitably dressed, unarmed, and wearing masks, entered, and for preventing members of a different category from attending the wrong ball. The ruling of 1612 increased the number of Abbeys of the Fools to ten and gave the Abbots of the Fools the artistic function of directing the musicians as well as the right to dance at the balls.

The Abbots of the Fools also had the right to collect *charavilh,* a tax paid by betrothed widows upon remarriage. *Charavilh* itself sometimes brought about a sort of carnival, whenever the bridegroom was reluctant to pay it. In such an instance, the "abbot" would barricade the entrance to his house and orchestrate a deafening racket with trumpets and various improvised percussion instruments, such as saucepans and frying pans, until the recalcitrant newlyweds agreed to pay. Although *charavilh* was prohibited in Nice in 1721, it was so deeply rooted in the popular customs of the region that there are records of its occurrence until the end of the nineteenth century.

Nevertheless, by the end of the Middle Ages, the trend everywhere was to discipline Carnival, restricting the extremes of its licentiousness and violence, while encouraging its artistic aspects. To control carnivalesque rebelliousness was, however, the work of centuries. The introduction of masked balls in the sixteenth century in Italy was the first step on the festival's path to a predominantly poetic character. Parades of floats began to compete for a place in the disorderly street processions. From the combination of these two new currents flowered the fusion of carnival with art.

The rise of the Italian *commedia dell'arte* played an important role in the consolidation of the use of masks, lending them an artistic character and codifying human types. Previously, a wide variety of masks had already been featured in Carnival, so that they were easily assimilated into the *commedia dell'arte,* a theatrical genre with a close popular affinity to the festival, imbued with a similar spirit of social satire. The *commedia dell'arte* selected several types of masks from the carnivalesque repertory and reduced these to a certain number of character types, translating regional and psychological characteristics which, as they evolved, became more abstract and universal. It drew strongly on regional inspiration and referred to events in the day-to-day Italian life of the time, as is the nature of improvised theater. From these traditions emerged its famous characters, who, in a stylized form, dominated the three subsequent centuries of the carnivalesque scenario in Europe. The characters of the *commedia dell'arte* embodied various satirical social types of the Italy of that period: Pantaloon, for example, was the rich, greedy, and libidinous merchant; the Doctor represented the pedantic drunkard and charlatan; and the Captain was boastful and full of bravado, but a complete coward. Harlequin, Colombine, and Pulcinella are the most famous of these figures. With time, all modified their characteristics. Initially, Harlequin represented the ignorant rustic who thought himself intelligent and whose poverty was evident in the patches, later sophisticated into lozenges, on his clothes. Pulcinella belonged to the same category of clowns and buffoons, though he was also crafty, as did Colombine, who evolved from a simple peasant girl to a calculating and extremely cunning maidservant. From the fusion of the *commedia dell'arte* with the masquerades of other cultures came a number of other characters, such as Pierrot, from France, who became an eternally present and central character in Carnival.

The *commedia dell'arte* and the Italian Carnival had much in common, as a result of their shared spirit of buffoonery and improvisation, each making the other more colorful and fertile. In Renaissance Florence, Carnival songs made fun of the private lives of certain social groups, with themes like "the goldsmith's song," "the song of the poor who accept charity," and "the song of the young wives and the old husbands"; by means of their festive ambivalence, they revealed the ridiculous—and usually censored—side of social conventions. Under the patronage of the Medici family, the Florentine Carnival was typified by the singing of these songs on flower-covered, ornamented triumphal carts, which were the models for the later Carnival floats of the Baroque and Romantic periods. In Turin, too, there were parades of flower-covered carts and floats as well as tournaments and cavalcades. In Venice, as throughout the Italian Peninsula, masks were the distinguishing feature of Carnival. Celebrated with the great solemnity afforded by the presence of the doge and Signoria and accompanied by a fireworks display, it contrasted with what happened in the streets, where there were battles between rival groups and a bull was sacrificed. Another element of Venetian Carnival was the flight of a man on ropes to the top of the campanile of Saint Mark's, since Carnival was also a time to challenge and exorcise the forces of nature.

Carnival in Rome was typified by a complex symbolism of violence, death, and resurrection. In Pope Paul II's time, in the fifteenth century, it was transferred to the Via Latta, which became the traditional setting for the carnivalesque parades called Corso. The Roman Carnival was essentially a series of masquerades and horse parades—these abolished only in 1833—culminating on Shrove Tuesday with an impressive candlelight procession, in which the participants, shouting "Death to him who has no candle," tried in whatever ways they could to put out one another's candles. In the carnivalesque revelry, the literal meaning of the threat of death was tempered, blending into the essential ambivalence of Carnival imagery. The procession ended with a Pantagruelian feast in the early morning of Ash Wednesday, during which immense quantities of meat were consumed in anticipation of the Lenten fast to follow.

As a result of the Romantic movement, the following centuries saw a growing beautification of Carnival. Flowered carriages, parades, allegorical floats that grew ever more majestic and complex, and fancy-dress balls became permanent features of the celebration, wherever it still existed. The elements of violence lessened: fighting, verbal abuse, and the various forms of mock aggression—water jets, the hurling of oranges, plaster confetti—gradually gave way to battles of flowers and colored paper confetti that were the new and prominent aspect of nineteenth-century street Carnival. In this way, the masses of revelers were gradually transformed from participants to spectators, to the detriment of the heterogeneous character of the festival, which had been for everyone and everywhere, unfocused and without privileged actors. In proportion as the crowds grew more controlled, the festival became spatially more limited, subordinated to rational organization, diminishing the spirit of carnivalesque improvisation and burlesque satire. In Nice, for example, where Carnival still preserved its rich tradition, a festival committee was set up in 1873. The functions of this committee were to organize the festivities, parades, and flower battles and to award prizes for the allegorical floats, functions that still exist today.

These artistic and commercial innovations passed by the Carnival in Portugal. The typical form of Portuguese Carnival, like that of the whole Iberian Peninsula, was the Entrudo, a rowdy celebration in which flour, eggs, lupines, mud, oranges, and lemons were thrown on passersby. Dirty water, glue, and various other liquids were also poured onto the crowd, and gloves heavy with sand were dropped from windows. Repeating a common New Year custom, pots and pans and all sorts of useless kitchen utensils were also thrown out of the windows, perhaps symbolizing the discarding of the old, or perhaps heralding the Lenten fast. Fierce battles were waged with plaster eggs, wax lemons, corncobs, and beans blown fiercely through glass or cardboard straws. Blows with brooms and wooden spoons were dealt out liberally. Apart from the violence and filth, the Entrudo was also a Carnival of gluttony: in the better stocked houses—from whose windows cakes and pastries were pitched—guests feasted sumptuously. Even in the convents cakes were widely distributed.

The apogee of the Portuguese Entrudo was in the eighteenth century. This coincided with the period of the greatest popularity and prestige of masked balls in the European courts; in 1715, the Royal Music Academy of Paris transformed its opera hall into a ballroom, in use three times a week throughout the year. Masks had been prohibited in Portugal since 1689, exactly when they were at the height of fashion in the rest of Europe. The first masked ball in Lisbon took place only in 1785, offered by the Spanish ambassador in commemoration of the marriage of Princess Carlota Joaquiná with Prince João, but further masques were prohibited again immediately afterward. So the Entrudo continued to reign largely without rivals.

In Galicia, Spain, the Carnival of flour, eggs, and water was similar. It began with a chariot attack by one neighboring village on another and ended with the burial of Señhor Antroido, for whom a eulogy was written, satirizing the most notable local people and the most notorious events of the previous year.

In nineteenth-century Portugal, there were flower battles in Oporto and Lisbon. Nevertheless, the form of Carnival introduced into the American colonies by Portugal and Spain was, in substance, the Entrudo.

In Europe, it was a weakened Carnival that greeted the contemporary age. In the scientific dogmatists of the end of the nineteenth century, Carnival inspired suspicion and contempt and was viewed as an irrational, primitive, and inexplicable rite. Lacking spontaneous popular support in Europe, Carnival has, with rare exceptions, gradually lost its force in the twentieth century, until it has become a subject of interest chiefly for academics and those who have a strong affection for the past.

In Brazil, meanwhile, Carnival assumed the proportions of a national festival. Because of Brazil's multiethnic population and nearly continental proportions, its Carnival drew on many different cultural and folkloric sources, becoming the melting pot of indigenous, African, and European influences. Instead of surviving merely as a curious anachronism, it is today a living, dynamic phenomenon, modifying itself even in conjunction with the modern resources of mass communications. The Brazilian Carnival, like those of all Hispanic America, stems from the Iberian Entrudo. Begun with the Portuguese colonization in the sixteenth century, the Entrudo lasted more than three centuries before collapsing in the first years of the Brazilian republic. Prohibitions against it, however, date from its very introduction. The first recorded one is a decree of 1604, the first of many that produced no result, despite the stipulated punishments. A decree of 1853 imposed fines and detention for free men and caning and prison sentences for slaves participating in the Entrudo; nevertheless, another with identical content had to be issued in 1857.

The Brazilian Entrudo was very close to its Portuguese source: it involved the throwing of a lot of water and various small projectiles, later substituted by wax lemons. During the Entrudo, so much water was used in Rio de Janeiro that the newspapers invariably warned about risks to the city's water supply. The Entrudo was played even in the imperial palace, and whole families with their slaves dedicated weeks on end to the fabrication of wax lemons. Daniel Kidder, an American missionary who visited Brazil in the nineteenth century, advised in his *Sketches of Residence and Travel in Brazil* (Philadelphia, 1845) that people leaving their houses on these days should take their umbrellas with them to protect themselves against missiles and water.

In the mid-nineteenth century, the Brazilian Carnival showed clear signs of transformation. Masked balls were held, though the use of masks had been prohibited during the whole of the colonial period, just as in Portugal. Processions of allegorical carriages made their first appearance in 1855, in a pompous parade sponsored by competing groups known collectively as the Great Carnivalesque Societies, and this contrasted so strongly with the disorder of the Entrudo that from then on the characteristics of the street Carnival began to change. Originally, among these societies there were a considerable number of intellectuals; one of the relevant features of the parade each year was the presence of a "Float of Criticism," satirizing some important recent political event, about which satirical poems were also distributed.

With the abolition of slavery at the end of the nineteenth century, massive rural contingents migrated to the larger urban centers, bringing with them a great variety of regional folkloric contributions. In the first decades of the twentieth century, the activities involved in Carnival expanded, and a multiplicity of organizations, structured to a greater or lesser extent, began to make their presence felt in the street Carnival.

The Congo, a popular festivity with African roots alluding to the coronation of the "Congolese kings," began to make its contribution at this time. It was made up of several elements, among which were processions and warlike dances. From these came the majestic Maracatus, making their appearance in the Carnival of northeastern Brazil; these are choreographed processions derived from the Congo, with king, queen, and a court of princes, ladies, ambassadors, and standard- and sunshade-bearers, along with a percussion section of rhythmic drums and triangles. There was also an increase in the number of *cordões*—loose groupings of people with masks depicting old people, the Devil, kings, queens, clowns, Bahian women, Indians, bats, Death, and so forth, who sang and danced frenetically to the accompaniment of percussion instruments.

An innovation in the Carnival of the south of Brazil were the *ranchos de reis,* which were taken from devotional Christmas dramatizations performed in procession, reproducing the journey of the Three Kings to Bethlehem to visit the infant Jesus. They were, however, stripped of their religious allusions, carnivalized, and took the form of *rancho carnavalesco*—a slow-march procession accompanied by brass and string instruments, during which costumed male and female choruses, carrying small allegorical images, narrate lyrical stories while singing and dancing.

The most complete expression of the contemporary Brazilian Carnival is the samba school. These schools, which are actually associations, present a kind of mobile popular opera, each year worked around a different theme. This theme is narrated through the music and words of the Carnival samba song *(samba-enredo),* and the characters are represented collectively by groups of dancers and singers in costume, with the scenery mounted on allegorical floats. A samba school is divided into three basic sections: first comes the drum section *(bateria),* which has between two hundred and four hundred instrumentalists, who play big bass drums *(surdos),* side drums, tambourines, triangles, *cuícas,* and bells, among other percussive instruments; second is the group *(ala)* of composers; and last is the main body of dancer-singers and other performers of the school. Schools compete with one another during the festival. The increasing complexity of the parade, and its internal regulation, have brought about the creation of a great number of both financial-administrative and technical-artistic posts, organzing the samba schools to meet certain commercial norms. There are more than a hundred samba schools, concentrated principally in Rio de Janeiro, where they originated, each one with between two thousand and four thousand members.

The rapid rise of the samba schools is an interesting sociological phenomenon. They sprang up in Rio de Janeiro in the 1930s, from the lowest social strata. At that time, the Carnival in Rio de Janeiro was visibly stratified: the upper classes amused themselves with costumed saloon-car processions, tossing confetti and paper ribbons; working-class districts celebrated with *ranchos;* while the samba schools, which were still embryonic associations, attracted the remaining peripheral elements.

At first these associations suffered great persecution. Their participants, the *sambistas,* sometimes had to hide themselves in the centers of Afro-Brazilian cults recognized by the police, where they held clandestine samba parties. There was still a lot of violence and disorder in the Brazilian Carnival; on the one hand, fights and shoot-outs and, on the other, strong police repression, particularly against the lowest social elements.

The samba schools came from the carnival blocks *(blocos carnavalescos),* which were conglomerations of barely organized masked dancers, modelled on the *ranchos* but with rather more limited financial resources. From the *ranchos* they adopted the processional form, the thematic structure, the master of ceremonies and flag-bearer, and the allegories, but the brass instruments were eliminated and the rhythm section increased to correspond to the beat of the samba.

The samba schools soon caught the attention of the governing authorities because of their populist potential, and when Carnival was made official in 1935, it became obligatory to enact national and historic themes. In the 1960s, the intellectuals and the urban middle class became involved in the samba schools, recognizing them as a genuine focus of popular national character. Their complete acceptance by the higher social classes coincided with the aspiration of the poorer element to be accepted and, as a result, the samba schools received a fresh and definitive impulse on the road of growth and social valuation.

The samba schools have now developed into extraordinarily complex institutions, in both their actual parades and their daily organization. They continue to function throughout the year as modest community clubs, always, however, with an eye to raising money for their Carnival expenses. As Carnival draws closer, they open up to allow the participation of the upper classes, until the parade at the climax festival, which is itself a rite of total social integration. Afterward, they retract again to their more modest dimensions. The themes of the parade refer to folkloric tales and events from Brazil's history, which, in the language of Carnival, are translated into an idealized vision of Brazil, depicted as a rich and generous mother country in which the contributions of the three races—white, black, and indigenous—join them in harmony, and where there is always room for hope and optimism. In reality, Brazil is a country marked by deep inequalities, still struggling in its uphill battle for development.

In its historical and contemporary manifestations, the common denominator of Carnival is still the process of the inversion of reality. This inversion is of a symbolic and temporary nature, which classifies as a process of ritual transformation. As a ritual, Carnival allows a glimpse of the axiomatic values of a given culture, as well as its underlying contradictions. The language that relates these contradictions to one another is principally that of satire. But the carnivalesque inversion can equally be expressed through violence and exaggeration. In the Carnival context, violence symbolizes an attack on order, classifying the festival, in this case, as a ritual of rebellion, of which the Entrudo is the clearest example. Carnival retains a close correlation with daily life, though during its celebration the normal and quotidian are inverted and lived as a festival. In this way, carnivalesque rebellion and provocation become a parody of true rebellion and provocation. In any case, ambivalence is inherent in Carnival symbolism, since Carnival itself is on the threshold between order and disorder, hierarchy and equality, real and ideal, sacred and profane. Essentially, Carnival represents confrontation of the antistructure with the structure of society, constituting a channel through which utopian ideals of social organization find expression and suppressed forms of human behavior are released from the restrictions of daily life.

The inversion of the social order inherent in Carnival, when amplified to a larger scale, represents the inverted, profane extreme of the sacred religious festival that Carnival immediately precedes. The two are inextricably interwoven and find their opposites in each other.

See Also Masks.

Bibliography

One of the most complete interpretations of the meaning of contemporary Carnival in Brazil is Roberto DaMatta's *Carnavais, malandros e heróis* (Rio de Janeiro, 1979). The same author analyzes the costumes and gestures of Brazilian Carnival in *Universo do Carnaval* (Rio de Janeiro, 1981). For a knowledge of samba schools, their internal organization and ideology, see my *O palácio do samba* (Rio de Janeiro, 1975) and José Sávio Leopoldi's *Escola de samba, ritual e sociedade* (Petrópolis, 1978). For the carnivalization of a sacred rite, refer to Isidoro Maria da Silva Alves's *O Carnaval devoto* (Petrópolis, 1980), which deals with the profane aspects of a religious procession.

For a view of contemporary Carnival in Europe, see Annie Sidro's *Le Carnaval de Nice et ses fous* (Nice, 1979). The catalog edited by Samuël Glotz, *Le masque dans la tradition européenne* (Mons, Belgium, 1975), provides important information about the use of masks at Carnival.

A broad definition that allows a vision of Carnival as a ritual phenomenon can be found in the article by Edmund R. Leach, "Ritualization in Man in Relation to Conceptual and Social Development," in *Philosophical Transactions of the Royal Society of London* 251 (December 1966): 403–408. For notions of structure and antistructure and for a discussion of the symbolic properties and transformation processes of ritual phenomena, essential reading is Victor Turner's *The Ritual Process* (Chicago, 1969).

New Sources

Béhague, Gerard. "*Popular Music.*" In *Handbook of Latin American Popular Culture*, edited by Harold E. Hinds Jr. and Charles Tatum, pp. 3–38. Westport, Conn., 1985.

Cunha, Maria Clementina Pereira. *Ecos da folia: uma história social do carnaval carioca entre 1880–1920* (Echos of folly: a social history of carnival between 1880 and 1920). São Paulo, 2001.

Dudley, Shannon. *Carnival Music in Trinidad: Experiencing Music, Expressing Culture.* Oxford, 2003.

Eisenbichler, Konrad, and Wim Hüsken, editors. *Carnival and the Carnivalesque: The Fool, The Reformer, The Wildman, and Others in Early Modern Theatre.* Amsterdam and Atlanta, 1999.

Eneida, Haroldo Costa. *História do Carnaval Carioca (History of Carnival).* Rio de Janeiro, 1987.

Harris, Max. *Carnival and Other Christian Festivals: Folk Theology and Folk Performance.* Austin, 2003.

Orloff, Alexander. *Carnival: Myth and Cult.* Wörgl, Austria, 1981.

Scher, Philip W. *Carnival and the Formation of a Caribbean Transnation.* Gainesville, Fla., 2003.

Maria Julia Goldwasser (1987)
Revised Bibliography

CARO, JOSEPH See KARO, YOSEF

CARROLL, JOHN

CARROLL, JOHN (1735–1815), first Roman Catholic bishop of the United States (1789). Carroll attended Saint Omer College in French Flanders in 1748 and a few years later joined the Jesuits. By 1771 he had been ordained a priest and made his final vows in the order. When Pope Clement XIV suppressed the Jesuits in 1773, Carroll was briefly under arrest. The next year he returned to his family estate in Maryland, ministering as best he could under the uncertain jurisdiction ex-Jesuits then faced. He joined his cousin, Charles Carroll, and Benjamin Franklin in an attempt at winning Canadian support for political independence, which would open the way for an American Catholic church.

Carroll's church leadership emerged in 1782–1783, inspired by concepts of church-state separation drawn from the writings of Roberto Bellarmino, Francisco Suárez, and English Catholic commentators on the subject. Carroll viewed the relationship between the pope and Roman Catholic congregations as principally spiritual rather than administrative; thus his plan for the American Catholic church placed church property in the United States in its own corporations, both clerical and lay, in this way guarding against foreign intrusion. Carroll also emphasized the spiritual nature of the office of bishop, a view he would explain in a disciplinary decree published in 1797.

In order to ensure against a nonresident appointee by Rome, Carroll advocated electing the first American bishop by vote of the clergy. Thereafter, he expected, the American hierarchy could follow more common ecclesial practices. However, the first American see, Baltimore, remained under the administrative control of the Congregation of the Propagation of the Faith, a body administered by Rome, thus weakening American control over episcopal appointees. Later, as first archbishop of Baltimore (1808–1815), Carroll was to acknowledge the lack of suitable American candidates to fill offices created by four new dioceses.

Consistent with Maryland Catholic tradition, Carroll held that no one should be molested in the free exercise of his religion. He believed that the Maryland constitution honored this principle. He wrote against states with laws that favored Protestantism (1789), arguing that such laws went beyond what was just in interpreting the role of religion in the state's promotion of public morality. In *An Address to the Roman Catholics* (1784), Carroll responded to what he considered distortions of Catholic teachings in these and other areas. His arguments were effective in the era before the rise of Nativism—a movement characterized by hostility toward immigrants, particularly Irish Catholics.

John Carroll was also eminent as a builder of the church in visible form. Emerging into the world of public worship after 1776, the Catholic community under his leadership determinedly built parishes and institutions. Among the lasting legacies of his episcopacy were the establishment of Saint Mary's Seminary, the recruitment of priests from Europe, and the founding of Georgetown College for the laity of all faiths. He placed high value on the ministry and education of women, as seen in his sponsorship of Elizabeth Ann Seton's founding of the Daughters of Charity and of parochial schools. He also sponsored establishments of the Carmelite and Visitation orders. Carroll also contributed his services to Saint John's and Washington colleges and to what became the University of Maryland.

BIBLIOGRAPHY

The primary source for Carroll's writings is *The John Carroll Papers*, 3 vols., edited by Thomas O'Brien Hanley (Notre Dame, Ind., 1976). Arranged in chronological order, it has title and date listings for each volume, useful for the references made above. Annabelle M. Melville's *John Carroll of Baltimore* (New York, 1955) to some extent abridges Peter K. Guilday's biography, *The Life and Times of John Carroll*, 2 vols. (1922; reprint, Westminster, Md., 1954). Joseph Agonito has made the most extensive use to date of the Carroll papers in "Ecumenical Stirrings: Catholic-Protestant Relations during the Episcopacy of John Carroll," *Church History* 45 (1976): 358–373.

THOMAS O'BRIEN HANLEY (1987)

CĀRVĀKA. A school of "materialists" thought to have been contemporary with early Buddhism, the Cārvāka school, or Cārvākas, has only scant evidence to attest to its existence. Writing in Hastings's *Encyclopaedia of Religion and Ethics*, Louis de La Vallée Poussin noted that "a materialistic school, a system in the exact sense of the term" did not exist in India. Such an opinion was based not upon the failure of scholars to recognize such terms as *lokāyata* ("world-extended"?) or *cārvāka*, or the schools known by these names, but upon the ambiguity and obscurity that certainly surround their origin and exact connotation. In earlier literature the term *lokāyata* did not stand for a doctrine that is necessarily materialistic. In the Buddhist collection *Saṃyutta Nikāya*, two *brahmans* are described as followers of the Lokāyata view, proponents of which are credited with holding one or more of the following four propositions: everything exists; nothing exists; everything is a unity; and everything is a plurality. Buddhaghosa's commentary identifies the first and third propositions as "eternalist views" (*sassata-ditthiyo*) and the second and fourth as "annihilationist views" (*uccheda-ditthiyo*). Later, the Annihilationist views were regarded as consonant with materialism.

The use of the word *cārvāka* was also initially obscure. Some say that *cārvāka* was a name. Others propose a fanciful etymology, joining *caru* ("beautiful") with *vāk* ("speech") to render a compound connoting "attractive discourse"; thus understood, the doctrines of this school, which denounce religion and religiously founded morality as useless, would have been found attractive by the common man, himself a materialist at heart. In later writings, the name *Lokāyata* came to refer to the Cārvāka school, which was traced to a mythical founder Bṛhaspati. In the latter part of the twentieth century, a number of Lokāyata *Bārhaspatya sūtras* were collated from various sources, but their authenticity is open to question.

According to the available sources, the Cārvāka taught that the world is as we see it, that is, as perceived by our sensory organs, and is devoid of all but a purely mechanical order or principle that can be confirmed by recourse to sense evidence alone. A moral or ethical order, admitted in one form or another by all other Indian schools (as in, for instance, their use of the paired terms *dharma* and *adharma*), is thus denied as incompatible with empirical evidence. So too, an omniscient being, God, life after death, and ultimate reward or punishment for one's actions are all denied. It is for this reason, and for the fact that it denies the authority of the Vedas, that the school is termed *nāstika*, or negativist.

Cārvāka ethics, as might be expected, do recognize the claims of superior force and authority. Obedience to the king and to the state are recommended as a practical means of self-preservation; otherwise, a life given to the pursuit of pleasure and wealth is considered the ideal. Political power was deemed by the materialists to derive from the approval of the governed (*lokasiddha bhavet rājā*); as a consequence, the ruler's mandate to govern was regarded as without divine or transcendental sanction. Cārvāka cosmology recognized four elements—earth, water, fire, and air—as fundamental constituents of all things; when called on to explain the appearance of life or consciousness in material things when the elements themselves are devoid of any such powers or properties, the Cārvāka had recourse to a theory whereby the conjunction of certain elements is accidentally invested with properties missing in the original constituents. As evidence of this, they pointed to the power in the fermented drink to intoxicate, which is missing in the unfermented constituents. This empirical methodology might have been the precursor of scientific thought in India.

Cārvāka epistemology regards perception as the only valid source of knowledge and explicitly rejects inference. Eventually, the school produced a very sophisticated philosophical critique of the inductive premise in each act of inference. Sometimes the Cārvāka view is represented as a skeptical critique of knowledge, for, according to Jayarāśi, probably a proponent of Cārvāka doctrines, even sense evidence can mislead.

It is doubtful whether there was ever a well-entrenched traditional "school" called Cārvāka or Lokāyata, for we do not have available to us any independent texts of the classical period that are expressly affiliated with this school. The notable exception is the text of Jayarāśi called *Tattvopaplavasiṃha*, discovered and edited in 1940. In it, the author is revealed as a gifted dialectician. The work itself is a highly sophisticated critique of all the *pramāṇas*, or valid sources of knowledge, criticizing both Vedic and non-Vedic schools. Theories of perception and inference of the Nyāyā, Buddhist, Sāṃkhya, Mīmāṃsā, and Jain traditions are all faulted. If this text belongs to the Cārvāka-Lokāyata school, then we have to admit that this tradition consists not only of materialism, but combines elements of skepticism and agnosticism as well. In this light, it would be incorrect to credit the Cārvākas with advocacy of pure license and hedonism, charges that, after all, are found only in the writings of their opponents (as, for instance, Haribhadra and Mādhava). All told, the Cārvākas probably represent an anti-religious tradition that rejected religious and spiritual pursuits and sought the basis of moral and social order in human rationality.

SEE ALSO Materialism.

BIBLIOGRAPHY

Summary accounts of this school can be found in such compendia of Indian philosophy as Haribhadra's *Ṣaḍdarśanasamuccaya* (seventh century) and Madhava's *Sarvadarśanasaṃ-graha* (fourteenth century). Haribhadra was a Jain and hence belonged to a non-Vedic school; Mādhava was a Vaidika, probably a Vedāntin.

Modern studies include Hara Prasad Shastri's *Lokayata* (Oxford, 1925), a pioneering work that is both suggestive and illuminating; Dakshinaranjan Shastri's *A Short History of Indian Materialism, Sensationalism and Hedonism*, 2d ed. (Calcutta, 1957), a tenuous historical reconstruction of the school; and Debiprasad Chattopadhyaya's *Lokāyata: A Study in Ancient Indian Materialism* (New Delhi, 1959), a Marxist analysis of the history of Indian materialism, including useful materials from nonphilosophical literature.

BIMAL KRISHNA MATILAL (1987)

CASSIAN, JOHN (c. 365–c. 435), monastic leader, founder of ascetic theology in the Latin church. According to Gennadius of Marseilles, John Cassian came from Scythia Minor (modern-day Dobruja), a province of the early Byzantine empire. Born of a rich Scythian family, Cassian received a good education. After he moved to Palestine, he entered a monastery in Bethlehem, together with his friend Germanos. Receiving permission for a temporary absence, the two men left the monastery for a short visit to the monastic colonies of Egypt. After they met the first prominent elders there, they were so fascinated that they forgot their promise to return to their monastery in Bethlehem. They continued on their travels as far as the region of Scetis, where they settled. From time to time they made visits to other monastic areas, but they do not seem to have realized their original intention of visiting the Pachomian monasteries at Thebais. Cassian and Germanos stayed in Egypt for over thirteen years, with only a short break to settle the matter of their permission to leave Bethlehem.

During the anti-Origenist persecution of 399 the two men were forced to abandon Egypt because of their association with Origenist monks, whose theological exponent was Evagrios of Pontus. They fled to Constantinople, where they were well received by the archbishop John Chrysostom. There Germanos was ordained a priest and Cassian a deacon. At the beginning of 405, they went to Rome on behalf of Chrysostom to deliver a letter to Pope Innocent I.

After 415 Cassian, now a priest, moved to Marseilles, where he established two monasteries, one for men and one for women. The last record of him is Prosper of Acquitaine's theological attack on him, in about 433. A short time after the attack Cassian died; his last words, reported in *Sayings of the Fathers*, were "I have never done my own will, nor taught anyone something which I had not previously carried out."

Cassian came very late to writing, and he wrote only when requested to do so by important persons. Generally he used the same material as did Evagrios, but he gave it his own personal imprint. More synthetical than Evagrios, he arranged his sources in extensive collections. He was a brilliant Latin stylist, distinguished for his clarity and elegance. Three of his works are still read today with great interest.

1. *Institutes of the Cenoby and the Remedies for the Eight Principal Vices*, written around 420 at the request of Castor, bishop of Apt in Provence, consists of two distinct sections. Books 1–4 discuss clothing, prayer, psalmody, and rules of monastic life; books 5–12 are a moral exposition of the eight evil thoughts, or vices—gluttony, luxury, avarice, wrath, sloth, *acedia* (negligence), vainglory, and pride—and their remedies.
2. *Conferences of the Fathers* has three sections. Conferences 1–10, written around 422 and dedicated to Leo, bishop of Fréjus, and the monk Helladius, recount Cassian's conversations with famous elders from Scetis on the fundamental principles of the ascetic and spiritual life. Conferences 11–17, written around 424 at the request of Honoratus, founder of Lérins monastery, and the monk Eucherius, recount Cassian's conversations with elders of the Nile delta on problems of spiritual theology. Conferences 18–24, written around 426 and dedicated to a group of Gallican monks, present conversations with elders of the Nile delta and Scetis on particular problems of the ascetic life.
3. *On the Incarnation against Nestorius*, written in 430 at the request of the future pope Leo, constitutes the single Western refutation of Nestorian teachings, which Cassian considered a result of Pelagian influence.

Cassian is the first monastic leader in the West to have set forth the theological principles of monastic life. Although his works encompass not only the anchoritic but also the cenobitic form of monasticism, his real interest lay in anchoritism. On questions of monastic organization, his sources are the institutions of the monastic centers in the East, chiefly Egypt and Palestine. In the theoretical area, he has as his guide the great teacher of ascetical theology, Evagrios, although, because Evagrios had been condemned as a heretic, Cassian avoided citing his name.

Cassian's thought revolves around the spiritual perfection of ascetics, following the classical twofold distinction of the stages of the spiritual life, the active and the contemplative way, for which he used the Greek terms *praktikē* and *theoretikē*. Complete renunciation leads to the active way: "We have two fathers, one to abandon, the other to follow" (*Conf.* 3.6). In the preliminary stage a fierce struggle develops against the passions caused in us by demons and evil thoughts. *Praktikē* becomes the way through which the cleansing of the passions and the establishment of the virtues are effected. *Theoretikē* is the higher stage, in which the contemplation of the divine realities and the acknowledgment of the most secret signs are acquired (*Conf.* 14.1).

Like all ascetic writers, Cassian demands from Christians a hard struggle for the attainment of perfection. This struggle, in turn, requires a strong and free will. Cassian rejected two important theories of his day. He regarded the volitionism of Pelagius as heretical, and the absolute predestination of Augustine of Hippo as sacrilegious. According to Cassian, humankind preserved even after the Fall the ability to turn toward the good and to accept or reject the salvation offered by God.

In the West, Cassian's teaching was criticized by Prosper of Aquitaine, a disciple of Augustine, and later it was condemned by the Council of Orange (529). It is still regarded today as semi-Pelagian. Cassian, however, was an Eastern theologian in the Latin West, and his teaching must be judged by Greek theological criteria. From this point of view, he was in agreement with the entire Eastern tradition and especially with the views of John Chrysostom.

In his last years, Cassian was regarded as one of the leading theologians of the West. Even though his opposition to Augustine kept him out of the mainstream of the Western church, his authority was unofficially accepted. Abridged redactions of his writings were made in both Latin and Greek, while eight of his sayings were preserved in *Sayings of the Fathers.* Through Benedict of Nursia his influence was spread throughout the West.

Gennadius of Marseilles calls Cassian a saint, but in the West he is not venerated, except in Marseilles, where his feast is celebrated on July 23. In the East the feast is generally celebrated on February 29.

BIBLIOGRAPHY

Works by Cassian

Guy, Jean-Claude, ed. and trans. *De institutis / Institutions cenobitiques.* Vol. 109 of *Sources chrétiennes.* Paris, 1965.

Migne, J.-P., ed. *Opera omnia.* Vols. 49 and 50 of *Patrologia Latina.* Paris, 1874 and 1863.

Petschenig, Michael, ed. *Opera omnia.* Vols. 13 and 17 of *Corpus Scriptorum Ecclesiasticorum Latinorum.* Vienna, 1886 and 1888.

Pichery, Eugène, ed. and trans. *Conlationes Patrum (Conférences).* Vols. 42, 54, and 64 of *Sources chrétiennes.* Paris, 1955–1959.

Works about Cassian

Cassian's doctrines on nature and grace in opposition to Augustine's view of predestination is the central concern of Alexander Hoch's *Lehre des Johannes Cassianus von Natur und Gnade: Ein Beitrag zur Geschichte des Gnadenstreites im fünften Jahrhundert* (Freiburg im Breisgau, 1895), and Joseph Laugier's *S. Jean Cassien et sa doctrine sur la grâce* (Lyons, 1908). A general picture of the personality and the work of Cassian is given under "Cassien" in *Dictionnaire de spiritualité* (Paris, 1937). Owen Chadwick's *John Cassian: A Study in Primitive Monasticism* (1950; 2d ed., London, 1968) is very important. A number of other studies on special aspects of his monastic activities may be mentioned, such as Hans Oskar Weber's *Die Stellung des Johannes Cassianus zur ausserpachomianischen Mönchstradition* (Munich, 1961), Salvatore Pricoco's *L'isola dei santi: Il cenobio di Lerino e il origini del monachesimo gallico* (Rome, 1978), and Philip Rousseau's *Ascetics, Authority and the Church in the Age of Jerome and Cassian* (Oxford, 1978). Some new studies on the theological teachings are Victor Codina's *El aspecto cristológico en la espiritualidad de Juan Casiano,* "Orientalia Christiana Analecta," vol. 175 (Rome, 1966), and Paul Christophe's *Cassien et Césaire: Prédicateurs de la morale monastique* (Gembloux, 1969).

PANAGIOTIS C. CHRISTOU (1987)
Translated from Greek by Philip M. McGhee

CASSIRER, ERNST (1874–1945), German philosopher of culture. Cassirer was born in Breslau, Silesia. He studied at the universities of Berlin, Leipzig, Heidelberg, and Marburg and completed his inaugural dissertation under the direction of the Neo-Kantian Hermann Cohen at Marburg in 1899. Between 1903 and 1919 Cassirer taught as privatdocent at the University of Berlin, and in 1919 he assumed the chair of philosophy at the newly founded University of Hamburg. Cassirer left Germany in 1933 with the rise of Nazism; he taught for two years at Oxford before accepting a professorship at the University of Göteborg in Sweden in 1935. Cassirer left Sweden for the United States in the summer of 1941, teaching first at Yale and then at Columbia.

Cassirer's published writings comprise nearly 125 items, ranging from short articles to books of eight hundred pages. They treat a wide range of subjects in history, linguistics, mythology, aesthetics, literary studies, and science. Because he wrote continuously on so many subjects it is difficult to form a sense of Cassirer's thought as a whole. The largest division within his writings is between his works on the history of philosophy and those that state his own philosophical position. In addition to these are subcategories of works on literary figures, especially Goethe, and on the philosophy of science.

The center of Cassirer's work in the history of philosophy is his four-volume study *Das Erkenntnisproblem in der Philosophie und Wissenschaft der neuern Zeit* (The Problem of Knowledge in Philosophy and Science in the Modern Age). The first two volumes (1906–1907) trace the problem of knowledge from Nicholas of Cusa to Kant. The third (1920) and fourth (first published in English translation in 1950) continue the theme through Hegel and into the first decades of the twentieth century. In addition to this large study, Cassirer's works on the Enlightenment, the Renaissance, Descartes, and Leibniz have become classics in their areas. The central work of Cassirer's original philosophy is his three-volume *Philosophie der symbolischen Formen* (The Philosophy of Symbolic Forms; 1923–1929), the groundwork of which was laid in his theory of scientific concept formation in *Substanzbegriff und Funktionsbegriff* (Substance and Function) in 1910. He extended his theory of concept formation to humanistic thought in *Zur Logik der Kulturwissenschaften* (The Logic of the Humanities; 1942). Cassirer recast his conception of symbolic forms in *An Essay on Man* (1944). This was followed by *The Myth of the State* (1946); both works were written in English.

Cassirer regards religion as part of the symbolic form of myth. In *An Essay on Man* he labels this as the symbolic form of "myth and religion" within a series of symbolic forms that includes also language, art, history, and science. Each of these areas of human culture represents a way in which people form their experience through symbols. Cassirer defines the human as an "animal symbolicum." Consciousness forms its object in many different ways. No one mode of formation offers a "literal" presentation of the real; all human activities are equally "symbolic." The symbol is the medium of all people's cultural activity, whether mythic-religious, linguistic, artistic, historical, or scientific. The interrelationships of all these manners of symbolizing form the system of human culture.

Religion arises as a stage within the mythical mode of symbolizing. In the second volume of *Philosophie der symbolischen Formen* (see part 4) Cassirer says that the break between religious consciousness and the mythical symbol occurs when consciousness begins to regard the images and signs of myth as pointing to meanings beyond immediate existence. Like true linguistic signs, Cassirer says, religious signs are understood as referring to an order of reality beyond the plane of immediate sensuous existence. In mythical consciousness the dancer who wears the mask of the god *is* the god; he does not signify the god who exists in another realm of being. Religion introduces a distinction between a finite and an infinite realm, a distinction that is beyond the power of the mythic symbol. For mythical consciousness, symbol and symbolized occupy a single plane of reality. In religious consciousness the sensuous and the spiritual divide, but they remain in this division as continuously pointing to each other in a relationship of analogy.

In *An Essay on Man* Cassirer approaches the relationship between myth and religion less in terms of the epistemology of the symbol and more in sociocultural and moral terms: "In the development of human culture we cannot fix a point where myth ends or religion begins. In the whole course of its history religion remains indissolubly connected and penetrated with mythical elements" (p. 87). Cassirer says that myth and religion originate in the "feeling of the indestructible unity of life" and in the fear of death as a break in this unity. In his phenomenology of the third volume of *Philosophie der symbolischen Formen,* Cassirer connects myth with the *Ausdrucksfunktion* of consciousness, with the primordial phenomenon of "expression." Religion never loses its roots as an expression of the unity of life and the fear of death.

Religion also has roots in the "sympathy of the Whole" that underlies magical practices in primitive societies. But religion arises, Cassirer says in *An Essay on Man,* when the totem and taboo system of society based on magical practices begins to break down. In the taboo system the individual has no responsibility for his own actions. Religion gives scope to a new feeling, that of individuality. Cassirer regards the prophetic books of the Old Testament as an example of the rise of the new ideal of individual moral responsibility that marks the appearance of religious consciousness out of the taboo system. In religion there develops this first sense of the moral self.

Bibliography

Works by Cassirer

There are two comprehensive bibliographies of Cassirer's writings: a topical arrangement can be found in *Philosophy and History: Essays Presented to Ernst Cassirer,* edited by Raymond Klibansky and H. J. Paton (Oxford, 1936), pp. 338–353, and a chronological listing appears in *The Philosophy of Ernst Cassirer,* edited by Paul A. Schilpp (Evanston, Ill., 1949), pp. 881–910. Of particular interest to the study of Cassirer's conception of myth and religion are the following: *Philosophie der symbolischen Formen,* 3 vols. (Berlin, 1923–1929), translated by Ralph Manheim as *The Philosophy of Symbolic Forms,* 3 vols. (New Haven, 1953–1957), especially volume 2, *Mythical Thought; Sprache und Mythos* (Leipzig, 1925), translated by Suzanne K. Langer as *Language and Myth* (New York, 1946); *Zur Logik der Kulturwissenschaften: Fünf Studien* (Göteborg, 1942), translated by C. S. Howe as *The Logic of the Humanities* (New Haven, 1961); *An Essay on Man: An Introduction to a Philosophy of Human Culture* (New Haven, 1944); and *The Myth of the State* (New Haven, 1946). *Symbol, Myth, and Culture: Essays and Lectures of Ernst Cassirer 1935–45* (New Haven, 1949), edited by Donald Phillip Verene, is a volume of Cassirer's previously unpublished papers. It includes a description of the corpus of Cassirer's manuscripts housed at Yale University.

Works about Cassirer

For bibliographies of critical work on Cassirer, see "Ernst Cassirer: A Bibliography," *Bulletin of Bibliography* 24 (1964): 103–106, and "Ernst Cassirer: Critical Work 1964–1970," *Bulletin of Bibliography* 29 (1972): 21–22, 24, both compiled by Donald Phillip Verene, and "Bibliographie des textes sur Ernst Cassirer," *Revue internationale de philosophie* 28 (1974): 492–510, compiled by Robert Nadeau. These bibliographies list critical works on Cassirer in all languages. The main source for critical views on Cassirer's thought remains *The Philosophy of Ernst Cassirer,* edited by Paul A. Schilpp (Evanston, Ill., 1949). The essays in this volume cover all aspects of Cassirer's thought, but most are expository. Other book-length works are Carl H. Hamburg's *Symbol and Reality: Studies in the Philosophy of Ernst Cassirer* (The Hague, 1956); Seymour W. Itzkoff's *Ernst Cassirer: Scientific Knowl-*

edge and the Concept of Man (Notre Dame, Ind., 1971) and *Ernst Cassirer: Philosopher of Culture* (Boston, 1977); and David R. Lipton's *Ernst Cassirer: The Dilemma of a Liberal Intellectual in Germany, 1914–1933* (Toronto, 1978). There are two biographies of Cassirer in essay form, one by Dimitry Gawronsky in *The Philosophy of Ernst Cassirer,* the other by Cassirer's wife, Toni Cassirer, *Mein Leben mit Ernst Cassirer* (1950; reprint, Hildesheim, 1981).

New Sources

Bayer, Thora Ilin. *Cassirer's Metaphysics of Symbolic Forms: A Philosophical Commentary.* New Haven, Conn., 2001.

Friedman, Michael. *A Parting of the Ways: Carnap, Cassirer, and Heidegger.* Chicago, 2000.

Graeser, Andreas. *Ernst Cassirer.* Munich, 1994.

Itzkoff, Seymour W. *Ernst Cassirer: Scientific Knowledge and the Concept of Man.* 2nd ed. Notre Dame, Ind., 1997.

Krois, John Michael. *Cassirer, Symbolic Forms and History.* New Haven, Conn., 1987.

Lofts, Steve G. *Ernst Cassirer: A "Repetition" of Modernity.* Albany, N.Y., 2000.

Strenski, Ivan. *Four Theories of Myth in 20th Century History: Cassirer, Eliade, Lévi-Strauss and Malinowski.* Iowa City, Iowa, 1987.

Sundaram, K. *Cassirer's Conception of Causality.* New York, 1987.

Wisner, David A. "Ernst Cassirer, Historian of the Will." *Journal of the History of Ideas* 58 (1997): 145–161.

DONALD PHILLIP VERENE (1987)
Revised Bibliography

CASTE SYSTEM SEE VARṆA AND JĀTI

CASTRATION.

CASTRATION. Castration is a custom found both in mythological tales and in ritual practices of peoples of various origins, cultural levels, and geographical locations. Because there is a preponderance of documentation of the custom in the ancient Near East and Mediterranean cultures, the origin and propagating center of this custom has often been ascribed to ancient Semitic culture. But evidence of castration has also been found in other, different cultures that were never influenced by Semitic culture, which seems to rule out a hypothesis of diffusion. Besides, the act of castration, both mythological and ritual, is naturally connected with other practices, beliefs, and doctrines that are all related in some way to sex and sexuality. Their connections (with circumcision, bisexuality, virginity, and celibacy) constitute a kind of compact but multivariegated "symbolic universe."

MYTHS. Many of the cosmogonic myths are based on two cosmic entities, Sky and Earth, who are originally united in a sexual embrace from which violent action alone can separate them. A tale of the Maori in New Zealand says that offspring born of the endless mating of Rangi ("sky") and Papa ("earth") are held in darkness and spacelessness. Finally the offspring decide to separate their parents, cutting the father's "tendons" (probably a euphemism) and pushing him up to achieve the present separation of sky and earth. The cosmogonic motif of the primordial couple is found in almost all Oceanic civilizations and widely in Africa and the Americas. But the act of violent separation of the two cosmic entities is seldom clearly described as a real act of castration, even if its symbolic verisimilitude leads one to think of it in this way. An example of castration presented in a straightforward manner is in the Greek cosmogonic myth, Hesiod's *Theogony.* The god Ouranos ("sky") and the goddess Gaia ("earth") conceive a breed of divine beings, but the god exhausts his paternal role in procreation and keeps his children from any kind of activity, thrusting them again into their mother's womb. At last one of them, Kronos, makes an ambush and cuts off his father's sexual organ, throwing it behind his own back. The goddess Gaia is fertilized by the blood of Ouranos, while from his sexual organ, which falls into the sea, is born the goddess of love, Aphrodite. Thus the only way to eliminate Ouranos, whose existence consisted of mere sexual and procreative activity, was to castrate him: this is the only opportunity to "murder," in some sense, an immortal god. This castration is a positive event because it breaks the cycle of endless and useless reproduction and gives Ouranos's offspring a living space between sky and earth. It represents moreover a fundamental moment in the establishment of the real and ordered world. From the morphological point of view, the myth of Ouranos's castration is typical of the image of the heavenly divine being who, after his initial performance, leaves the stage, becoming a *deus otiosus.*

Comparative analysis has pointed out important resemblances to the myth of the impotence of Varuṇa, an Indo-Iranian god, and also to the investiture ritual of the king in India (Dumézil, 1948). Analogies exist also with the Navajo creation myth (*Dine Bahane*), in which the First Woman gives birth to twins with her husband. These twins, who are *nadleeh* (intersexed, neither male nor female), ordered the world, slayed the dragons, and invented pottery and all sort of tools. Historical analysis, on the other hand, has indicated some parallel cases in cosmogonic myths of the ancient Near East. The Mesopotamian creation epic, *Enuma elish,* tells of the god Enki, who defeats and annihilates his enemy Mummu, taking off his crown, smashing his head, and finally cutting off his penis. The Hittite myth of Kumarbi contains even more similarities to Ouranos's story. This cosmogony, combining one of the earliest Hurrian stories with some elements of Assyro-Babylonian mythology, deals with a succession of children's rebellions against their fathers. In this myth Kumarbi pursues his father, Anu, who seeks safety by flying toward the sky, but the son grabs his father's feet, dragging him to the ground. Then, seized by excitement, Kumarbi bites his father's penis, tears it off, and swallows it, laughing and boasting of his bravado. But the swallowed sexual organ makes him pregnant with terrifying gods who will soon defeat him in turn.

Scholars are in agreement that the similarity between Greek and Hittite myths can be explained as an indication of direct historical derivation on the grounds of similar general structure and the common presence of castration. Nevertheless there are significant differences between these myths, and there remains a notable uncertainty about how the motif spread. A recurrence of Ouranos's castration can be found in the cosmogony of Philo of Byblos, a late Phoenician author who claims a reference to Sanchuniathon, an ancient Phoenician author. Mixing local information with Greek conceptions in a syncretic and euhemeristic way, Philo ascribes to the god El-Kronos an act of castration against his father. The Hellenic pattern is clearly apparent, but archaeological discoveries at Ugarit (Ras Shamra) in Phoenicia, dating from the second millennium BCE, seem to confirm to some extent the authenticity and antiquity of the myth. In a different case in the Prose Edda, an ancient Germanic cosmogony, the "father of everything," a personal entity with creative power, is also called "the castrated" with no further explanation. Scholars agree that many features of this divine being are not original but derived from Christian influences, and they think also that the castration element can be dated back to the earliest Greek tradition of Ouranos.

Besides these cosmogonic myths other kinds of myths in which castration constitutes a pattern of ritual action deserve mention. The close connection between myth and rite in these cases arouses the rightful suspicion that the myth may have been constructed in order to provide a motivation for the ritual practice. The most famous myth is the Greco-Roman story of the goddess Cybele and the god Attis. Cybele, venerated in Rome and in the Roman Empire under the name of Great Mother (Magna Mater), was an ancient goddess of fertility known in Anatolia since the second millennium BCE under the name of Kubaba. Some iconographic and onomastic evidence suggests an even more remote origin going back to the Anatolian Neolithic and perhaps Mesopotamian civilization. The young servant-lover Attis, on the other hand, seems to have been introduced along with his mate only after the arrival in Anatolia of the Phrygians (c. eighth century BCE). There are several mythical versions of Attis's castration (Hepding, 1903/1967). It is easy to follow a constant line of development from more ancient tales—much more intricate and grotesque—to the embellished and romantic later versions. The original stories take place in an environment of unnatural primitiveness, monstrous procreations, violent loves, and bloody punishments. All these versions culminate in the story of Attis, who castrates himself in a fit of madness or out of a desire for absolute chastity. Sometimes Attis's castration is attributed to a wild boar or to a jealous entity who wants to punish him for his amorous exploits.

Similar is the Egyptian myth of the mystical couple Isis and Osiris, but here the mythical castration apparently does not constitute a pattern of ritual action. The god Osiris was dismembered, and fourteen pieces of his body were strewn all over Egypt. His wife, the goddess Isis, found the body. But Osiris's penis was thrown into the Nile and eaten by a fish, so Isis is forced to construct with sycamore wood a facsimile of his phallus. The Phoenician and Cypriot and in any case Semitic Adonis that lives out his short season seducing and being seduced by Aphrodite, whose vitality is overpowering, bled to death in a boar hunt. But his castration is only hypothetical, and above all there is no evidence that his priests practiced ritual castration. Two basic events, emasculation and death, therefore mark the mythical personalities of these young gods (but only problematically the concrete ritual castration of their followers) and signify the depotentiation of divine life and its inevitable repercussions on the life of the cosmos, which seems to imitate the vicissitude of the divine body (Casadio, 2003).

RITUALS. The documentation related to ritual practices records, first of all, that the act of castration can sometimes be the result of temporary exaltation or religious fanaticism. The religio-historical as well as ethnographic literature cites some examples, but their rarity and especially their complete isolation from myths, doctrines, and institutionalized interpretations make them subjects for studies in psychology (or psychopathology). The history of religions, on the other hand, is concerned with institutionalized acts of castration, for instance, within the so-called pubertal cults. All these practices belong to a broader category of ritual mutilations, like the custom of removal of one testicle, which is practiced almost exclusively among Camitic populations in Africa, where it seems to serve as a substitute for circumcision, a practice completely unknown to them. In the initiation rites of primitive peoples different practices involving male genitalia are frequent (circumcision, subincision), as are those involving female genitalia (clitoridectomy, infibulation), and their origin and significance seem rather difficult to establish. According to some scholars, these practices constitute symbolic equivalents of castration.

Another category of castration is the custom, widespread in the ancient Near East and in Semitic cultures, of castrated priests. The *kurgarru,* for instance, is a eunuch priest of Ishtar who officiates at the orgiastical rites in honor of the god Marduk. Many of the clergy of Hekate in Stratonicea, Caria, and in Laginas and the clergy of Artemis in Ephesus and of Atargatis in Hierapolis, Syria, were castrated. Some sporadic cases of analogous priestly castration have been reported in Brahmanic India, particularly in the northern mountains, and also in Nepal and Tibet. Usually the castrated priests are connected with a powerful and fertile goddess, sometimes with astral characteristics, and at other times with the features of a goddess of animals, who is conventionally called Mother Goddess.

Finally, there is a series of examples in which the ritual of castration appears entirely institutionalized, justified according to the myths of foundation or in accordance with precise beliefs and doctrines. Within the Cybele and Attis cult, the mythical castration of Attis is the foundation of the practice of castration of his priests (and perhaps of believers too), which is a kind of sacrament of consecration, a sacrifice recalling the god's passion, and sometimes a votive offering. The Galli—as these priests are most commonly called—dedicated themselves to the goddess Cybele after willingly castrating themselves during ritual performances in which, in a frenzy of dances, obsessive beating of drums, and self-flagellation, they reached paroxysms of exaltation. The Galli wore female clothing and heavy makeup, their hair was long and loose, and they lived in a wandering missionary community, supporting themselves with alms they received for offering predictions and prognostications. At Pessinus in Asia Minor they ruled sacerdotal city-states in which temples and royal palaces were unified. In Greece they were generally despised and driven away because of their mutilation and their appearance; they were never fully assimilated into official religion. In Rome, where the cult of Cybele was introduced in 204 BCE, and in the Roman Empire they were at first strictly regulated and controlled by the state; then they acquired, little by little, more importance and autonomy. The Roman distaste for eunuchism slowly faded away because of the approval of some emperors of the practice and because of a certain lessening of bloodier and crueler aspects of the cult.

Thus the cult of Cybele and Attis had its temples and its brotherhood in Rome, and its feasts included in the sacral calendar. Little by little, under the influence of a certain spiritualism and new symbolic interpretations, the cult assumed a mystic character and became a kind of mystery cult like other cults of Oriental origin. The castration of believers was easily explained as a sign of the search for perfection, a voluntary renunciation of the pleasures of the flesh, and the Attis figure became more and more spiritualized. During the later Roman Empire the self-castration of believers was probably replaced or integrated into the bloody and spectacular rite called the Taurobolium. A bull was slain and (probably) castrated, and its blood was shed over the believer as a lavation of intensified achievement, regenerative and purifying. Important mystical interpretations of relevant myths also were given in late antiquity by Naassene Gnostics, for example, by which "the mutilation of Attis means that he was separated from the low earthly regions of creation" (Cosi, 1986, pp. 111–113). For Julian the Apostate the castration of Attis means "a pause in the rush towards the infinite" (Cosi, 1986, pp. 111–113).

Castration appears sporadically in practices of groups, sects, and isolated thinkers that link it to doctrines preaching asceticism and sexual abstinence and regard it as an escape from the temptations of the flesh. Such doctrines—which have remarkable precedents and parallels within the pagan as well as the Judaic world—developed during the first centuries of the Christian era and were inclined to radicalize the pronouncement by Matthew on eunuchs (*Mt.* 19:12) as well as the orthodox position (of Paul, for instance) on the prestige of virginity. Strongly connected with sexual and marital morality, bound to the theme of ecclesiastical celibacy, and intertwined with the rise of monasticism, this topic is evinced in some authors as a preaching of the *enkrateia* (continence), understood as the complete rejection of any kind of sexual intercourse. If within the ecclesiastical and orthodox line virginity and chastity are recommended solely on the basis of motivations, such as the imitation of Christ or in anticipation of the kingdom of heaven, according to these doctrines sexual abstinence becomes a necessary condition of salvation and is based on ontological and protological motivations of the dualistic and Platonic mold. According to some writers, the Greek father Origen (third century CE) and other ecclesiastic authorities castrated themselves in order to extinguish definitively any desire for sexual intercourse. At the same time, in the mysterious sect of the Valesians (from Valesius, the founder), castration was a normal practice. Epiphanius, bishop of Salamis, refuted the sect and accused it of heresy. It also seems that among the Manichaeans the current obligation of chastity was transformed in some cases into the practice of self-castration. The phenomenon must have been rather widespread, because it was addressed by the Council of Nicaea (325 CE) and a bull of Pope Leo I (c. 395 CE).

A renewal of the practice of castration for the sake of proselytism and asceticism (a call to remove the "organs of sin") is found among the Skoptsy (the castrated), a Russian sectarian community that developed from the complex movement of the Raskol schism during the mid-eighteenth century. The Skoptsy were long persecuted, but they spread throughout Russia during the next century and survived in some Romanian peasant communities until 1950.

ORIGINS. From this brief review of facts relative to castration in some myths and ritual practices, it becomes clear that even if the ancient Semitic (and Mediterranean) world offers the majority of the documentation and shows some cases of dependence and evolution, it cannot be considered the unique source of the diffusion of this practice. In the same way it is impossible to decide on a univocal interpretation of the practice of castration that can explain in all cases its causes and motivations. Sometimes the connection with themes of fertility and procreation is primary, so that castration of a "vegetation spirit" ("Dying and rising god," in the words of James George Frazer [1890, I, pp. 278–279]) constitutes a dramatic event stopping the flow of life or containing it within more orderly boundaries. "Functional" is otherwise the explanation provided by Walter Burkert (1979): the act of castration, producing neither man nor woman but "nothing," puts a man outside archaic society and makes apostasy impossible. At other times, on the basis of doctrinary principles, castration is instead related to a search for asexuality understood as a privileged condition. In some cases this asexuality resolves into a kind of symbolic bisexuality that aims to reproduce in the believer the powerful joint presence of both sexes that is found in certain androgynous primordial figures. Interpretations influenced by psychoanalysis have often been offered to explain these themes. Finally, in many cases castration is clearly demanded as an extreme form of mystical practice in currents of thought that celebrate abstention as a choice in life and as a condition of salvation.

See Also Androgynes; Clitoridectomy; Cybele; Dying and Rising Gods; Hierodouleia; Virginity.

Bibliography

For "Dying and rising gods," see James George Frazer, *The Golden Bough*, I-II (London, 1890). For a discussion of castration as a form of substitution sacrifice, see Henri Graillot's treatment of the myth and the ritual of Cybele and Attis in his now classic *Le culte de Cybèle, mère des dieux, à Rome et dans l'Empire romain* (Paris, 1912). For a more modern treatment, see Maarten J. Vermaseren's *Cybele and Attis: The Myth and the Cult* (London, 1977). Vermaseren compiled archaeological and literary documents concerning the cult in *Corpus cultus Cybelae Attidisque*, 7 vols. (Leiden, 1977–1989). See also Walter Burkert, *Structure and History in Greek Mythology and Ritual* (Berkeley, Calif., 1979); Dario M. Cosi, *Casta Mater Idaea: Giuliano l'Apostata e l'etica della sessualità* (Venice, 1986); Shaun Tougher, ed., *Eunuchs in Antiquity and Beyond* (London, 2002); and Maria Grazia Lancellotti, *Attis: Between Myth and History; King, Priest, and God* (Leiden, 2002), a radically historicizing treatment of myth and ritual. For a discussion of Ouranos and Kumarbi, see Hans Gustav Güterbock, ed., *Kumarbi: Mythen vom churritischen Kronos aus den hethitischen Fragmenten zusammengestellt* (Zurich, 1946). For a reappraisal of the evidence of Dionysos, see Eric Csapo, "Riding the Phallus for Dionysus," *Phoenix* 51 (1997): 253–295. The literary sources for Attis are in Hugo Hepding's *Attis, seine Mythen und sein Kult* (Giessen, 1903; reprint, Giessen and Berlin, 1967). A comparative study of Indian and Iranian ritual is Georges Dumézil, *Mitra-Varuna*, 4th ed. (Paris, 1948). The theme of sexual abstinence is addressed in Ugo Bianchi, ed., *La tradizione dell'enkrateia: Motivazioni ontologiche e protologiche* (Rome, 1985). See in general Walter Burkert, *Creation of the Sacred: Tracks of Biology in Early Religions* (Cambridge, Mass., 1996); Gary Taylor, *Castration: An Abbreviated History of Western Manhood* (New York, 2002); and Giovanni Casadio, "The Failing Male God: Emasculation, Death, and Other Accidents in the Ancient Mediterranean World," *Numen* 50 (2003): 231–268.

Dario M. Cosi (1987 and 2005)

CASTRÉN, MATTHIAS ALEXANDER (1813–1852)

CASTRÉN, MATTHIAS ALEXANDER (1813–1852) was a scholar of Finno-Ugric languages and the founder of the Finnish School of Ethnography of Religion. His studies of remote north Eurasian peoples helped establish a discipline that he named Altaic in accordance with his theory of their *urheimat* (point of common origin) in the Altai Mountains. Now called Finno-Ugrics or Uralics, the discipline, in Castrén's broad definition, embraces comparative studies of Finnish and Finno-Ugric languages, literature, ethnology, folklore, and religion.

Castrén began his studies at the University of Helsingfors (now Helsinki) as a student of Greek and Hebrew. Before long, however, this was subsumed by an interest in Finnish and other regional languages. He traveled twice throughout Eurasia, including a journey through Siberia proposed by his Finnish colleague A. J. Sjögren (1794–1855), an academician in Saint Petersburg. During his visits among the small populations in the huge, sparsely populated territory between the Ural Mountains and the southwestern Chinese border, Castrén recorded local folk songs, proverbs, legends, and other traditions. These were published by Anton Schiefner (1817–1879), another linguist from Saint Petersburg, in the twelve-volume series *Nordische Reisen und Forschungen*, between 1853 and 1862.

Castrén collected folklore mainly among the Samoyed peoples of Siberia; most of this work was published in 1960 by Toivo Lehtisalo (1887–1962) as *Samojedische Sprachmaterialien: Gesammelt von M. A. Castrén und T. Lehtisalo.* Publications on Castrén's voyages by Aulis J. Joki (1913–1989) show how Castrén carried out his fieldwork, collecting such linguistic artifacts as Turkish epics among the Tatars of Minusinsk steppe at Akaban (Schiefner, 1853–1862, vol. 2, pp. 305–306).

Castrén had a rare ability to learn to communicate in foreign languages in a short time, and he spent three to six months at each key station. Although he was criticized by later philologists for both his Altaic *urheimat* theory and his overeagerness to find new languages, both of these can be understood in the context of the nationalistic Pan-Finno-Ugric trend of his time, which sought new relatives on the family tree of the recently established Finnish nation.

The study of Finno-Ugric religion, particularly shamanism, was central to Castrén's fieldwork between 1841 and 1849. He wrote:

> All the religion proper of the Altaic peoples has been called shamanism. Unfortunately this far attention has more been paid on the naming and outer features of the phenomenon, not on the inner disposition, the essential nature of it. . . . I would not consider shamanism as a form of religion of its own, but rather as a moment of the folk religious divine doctrine. (Castrén, 1853, p. 1)

A professor at the University of Helsingfors in the last years of his life, Castrén was appointed chair of Finnish language and literature studies. As a professor Castrén devoted most of his lectures to the folklore and mythology of northern peoples. In one of his last lectures he defined ethnography as:

> a new name for an old thing. It means the scientific study of the religion, society, customs, way of life, habitations of different peoples, in a word: everything that belongs to their inner and outer life. Ethnography could be regarded as a part of cultural history, but not all nations possess a history in the higher sense; instead their history consists of ethnography. (Castrén, 1857, p. 8)

Castrén's untimely death at the age of thirty-nine left much of his work unfinished. He is remembered most for his linguistic studies that identified the Finno-Ugric and Samoyedic languages as members of the larger Uralic family.

SEE ALSO Finnish Religions; Finno-Ugric Religions.

BIBLIOGRAPHY

Castrén, Matthias Alexander. *Nordiska resor och forskningar,* vol 2: *Föreläsningar i finsk mytologi.* Helsinki, 1853.

Castrén, Matthias Alexander. *Tutkimusmatkoilla Pohjolassa; Matias Aleksanteri Castrénin matkakertomuksista suomentanut ja johdan non kirjoittanut Aulis J. Joki.* Helsinki, 1853.

Castrén, Matthias Alexander. *Nordiska resor och forskningar,* vol. 3: *Ethnologiska föreläsningar.* Helsinki, 1857.

Castrén, Matthias Alexander, and Toivo Lehtisalo. *Samojedische Sprachmaterialien: Gesammelt von M. A. Castrén und T. Lehtisalo.* Helsinki, 1940.

Estlander, Bernhard. *Mathias Aleksanteri Castrén: Hänen matkansa ja tutkimuksensa.* Helsinki, 1929.

Joki, Aulis J. "M. A. Castrénin elämäntyö." *Virittäjä* 67 (1963).

Pentikäinen, Juha. "Northern Ethnography: On the Foundations of a New Paradigm." In *Styles and Positions: Ethnographical Perspectives in Comparative Religion.* Comparative Religion 8. Helsinki, Finland, 2002.

Schiefner, Anton. *Nordische Reisen und forschungen.* Saint Petersburg, 1853–1862.

JUHA PENTIKÄINEN (2005)

CASUISTRY.

CASUISTRY. Moral knowledge comprises general principles and propositions: for example, "Do unto others as you would have them do unto you," "Honest persons do not lie or steal," and so forth. However, moral knowledge also bears on choices to act in specific ways in unique situations. Thus, general principles must be transformed into particular choices: "I should not make this offensive remark about him because I would not want him to say such a thing about me in the hearing of those people," "I could not consider myself honest if I told her she was capable enough to deserve promotion," and so forth. Casuistry is concerned with the transition from general moral knowledge to particular moral choices. It can be defined as "the technique of reasoning whereby expert opinion is formulated concerning the existence and stringency of particular obligations in light of general moral maxims and under typical conditions of the agent and circumstances of the action."

Religious moralities that rest upon strong divine commands and prohibitions are fertile ground for a casuistry. Unless a divine imperative is couched in terms that direct a particular person to perform or refrain from a particular act at a particular time (e.g., "Moses, you must proclaim the Commandments to the people when you descend the mountain"), interpretation of the general statement of a divine command is necessary. Does, for example, the command "Thou shalt not kill" apply to David facing Goliath? However, it is not only divine commands and prohibitions that generate the need for casuistry. All statements of moral principle are expressed in universal terms; thus, any ethical system, if it is to take effect in the lives and actions of its adherents, must have its universal principles fitted to the various situations in which decisions are to be taken.

CASUISTRY IN NON-CHRISTIAN CONTEXTS. In the three major ethical monotheisms, Judaism, Christianity, and Islam, certain persons have assumed the role of interpreting to the faithful the overarching moral injunctions of the Lord God. In Judaism, the written law, collected in the five books of the Torah, and the oral law, taught by Moses to the Israelites, were expounded by the scribes. These detailed interpretations of the law, collected in the two Talmuds, were themselves commented upon by the learned teachers of the people. This immense body of literature, as well as the intellectual tradition enshrined in it and continued by the rabbis in the life of the people of Israel, is called *halakhah* ("the way"). Concerned with fidelity to the law in every aspect of daily life, it is the casuistry of Judaism. However, within this tradition, a special form of reasoning, employing very sharp distinctions and clever logic, came to be called *pilpul* ("pepper"). Flourishing in the late Middle Ages, it was criticized by the great rabbi Eliyyahu ben Shelomoh Zalman (1720–1797) and others for twisting the plain truth "like shaping a wax nose." In this respect, *pilpul* resembles the Roman Catholic casuistry of the seventeenth century that gave rise to the pejorative connotation of the word.

Sharīʿah (lit., "the path toward water") designates the holy law of Islam revealed in the Qurʾān. More particularly, the word refers to forms of ritual and social behavior to be observed by the faithful. In the eighth and ninth centuries, schools of interpretation coalesced: they attempted to define precisely the exact content and stringency of the law. The teachers of Islam, *muftīs*, issued *fatwās*, considered opinions for the guidance of the faithful, distinguishing moral acts as obligatory, recommended, permitted, reprehensible, or forbidden. Since God's will is inscrutable, it is permitted to find *hiyal* ("stratagems") to avoid the letter of the law in favor of the spirit. Again, it is this aspect of Muslim casuistry that recalls the reprehensible approach that gave casuistry its bad name.

In the Western philosophical and theological tradition, two sources of casuistry are manifest. Socrates suggested cases to test whether the general definitions of virtue proposed by his interlocutors were adequate (e.g., in *Euthyphro, Laches*). Aristotle noted, as the premier methodological point of his *Nicomachean Ethics* that, while the nature of the human good and of virtue can be stated in general, "fine and just *actions* exhibit much variety and fluctuation" (*Nicomachean Ethics* 1.3). The Stoics proposed the most general precepts (e.g., "Follow nature"), and their opponents, particularly the Cynics, retorted with cases to show that rules of such generality could lead to no definite conclusions for action, or even to contradictory ones. Certain questions that become perennial first appear in this debate: for example, "Which of two shipwrecked men clinging to a spar has a right to it?" and "Should a merchant reveal defects of his merchandise?" Cicero recalls these questions and employs them to illustrate his theses regarding the priority of virtue over expedience. The third book of his *On Duties* is, in effect, the first book of casuistry in Western moral philosophy, even though it contains much material from authors of the Late Stoa.

Casuistry in the Christian Era. The teachings of Christ contain many "hard and impossible" commands: "If you will follow me, leave father and mother," "Turn the other cheek," "It is as hard for a rich man to enter heaven as for a camel to pass through the eye of a needle." Those dedicated to following his ideals of love and mercy had to discern how these difficult and paradoxical commands were to be carried out in daily life. They also faced the problem of whether they and all converts from Judaism and paganism were bound by the law of the Jews. There is therefore some casuistry in the Gospels, in the *Acts of the Apostles,* and in the epistles of Paul, all of it employing reasoning of the type familiar to the rabbinical schools. In the early centuries of the church, many Christian writers faced the problem of how the Christian should live. In *Can a Rich Man Be Saved?* Clement of Alexandria advises that the severe words of Jesus do not condemn those who, while rich in goods, are poor in spirit. Augustine's *On Lying* is a premier work of casuistry in which appears the question analyzed centuries later by Kant: "Should a person lie to conceal an innocent person from persecutors?"

In the history of Christianity, casuistry was given its greatest impetus by the practice of confession of sins and absolution by a priest. When private confession first appeared, in the sixth to the eighth centuries, books of direction were written for priests advising them what penances to impose. These "penitential books," while lacking precise analysis of moral acts, show an incipient sense of discrimination regarding the moral seriousness of certain acts and the circumstances that modify or excuse. In the twelfth century the canon law of the church, working with the large corpus of ecclesiastical case law, as well as with rediscovered Roman law, provided distinctions and categories for a more refined casuistry, as did the speculative theology of the thirteenth century. The books for confessors published from the late thirteenth through the fifteenth centuries manifest this influence in careful but succinct delineations of the nature of conscience, of law, and of imputability. These later volumes were stimulated by a universal law of the church requiring that all confess at least yearly and that the confessor deal with penitents "as a prudent physician of the spirit" (Fourth Lateran Council, 1215). These books present innumerable cases involving marriage, commerce, feudal obligations, and justice. In each example the purpose is to assist the confessor in judging whether a particular act that appeared to violate a moral commandment of church law did in fact do so in the particular circumstances of its commission. Raymond Pennafort, Peter the Cantor, Alain of Lille, William of Chobham, and Peter of Poitiers were the principal authors of this genre. In the fourteenth and fifteenth centuries, certain *summae* that presented material in alphabetical order (e.g., from *Absolution* to *Uxoricide*) became immensely popular: the *Summa Astesana,* the *Summa Sylvestrina,* and the *Summa Angelica.*

During the Reformation, casuistry was stimulated by several circumstances. The Council of Trent (1551) required Roman Catholics to confess sins by kind and number, a reaction to Protestant rejection of confession to a priest. The Society of Jesus, founded in 1540, dedicated itself to propagating the proper use of the sacrament of penance and to the education of the Catholic laity and clergy. In the religious turmoil of the last half of the sixteenth century, many settled moral positions were upset. Catholics faced novel problems of personal relationship (e.g., how to deal with non-Catholics) and of public moment (e.g., how to continue to observe traditional prohibitions regarding money lending in the new mercantile economy, how to govern newly discovered lands, whether to give allegiance to rulers of newly formed national states). The Jesuits and other theologians undertook to analyze these problems, both in speculative treatises and in more practical case presentation. They produced a vast literature, known collectively as "cases of conscience." In the century between 1565 and 1665, over six hundred titles appeared, many of them in multiple editions.

In 1663 Blaise Pascal, the great mathematician and physicist who had taken the side of the Jansenists (a Catholic sect of extreme piety and rigor) against the Jesuits, published the *Provincial Letters.* In this brilliant satire, he attacked the Jesuit casuists, citing case after case in which ingenious analysis led to outrageous moral conclusions. The casuists, with their clever distinctions, seemed able and willing to dispense with all moral probity, allowing killing, adultery, and lying, if only the circumstances were right. The criticism, justified to some extent, was too far-reaching: it condemned the entire enterprise of casuistry for the faults of some of its authors and the weakness of some aspects of its methodology. From that time onward, casuistry has carried the opprobrious sense of moral sophistry.

Casuistry continued to be an integral part of Catholic moral theology. Alfonso Liguori (1696–1787), a most revered Catholic moralist, was a master casuist. By the mid-nineteenth century, however, casuistry had become sterile and was much criticized, within and without the church, for its failure to promote moral ideals and its dwelling on minimal obligation. Nevertheless, some fine casuistic analyses continued to appear: about the just war, the just wage, abortion, and so forth.

Protestant theology showed little interest in casuistry—indeed showed early antipathy. (Luther cast the *Summa Angelica* into the flames, calling it the "Summa Diabolica.") Anglican theologians engaged in a vigorous casuistry in the seventeenth century, with Jeremy Taylor and William Perkins being the leading authors. In the twentieth century, *Conscience and Its Problems* (1927), one of the very few modern English works on casuistry, was written by an Anglican theologian, Kenneth E. Kirk.

In the 1970s, interest in medical ethics led to the revival of a sort of casuistry both within and without the theological context. The occurrence of many cases of note, such as that of Karen Ann Quinlan, brought theological and philosophical moralists to analyze the ethical issues. The National

Commission for Protection of Human Subjects of Biomedical and Behavioral Research (1974–1978) employed a method of case analysis to develop the ethics of research. In the 1980s, concern about nuclear armaments further stimulated casuistry, and a case analysis of various "scenarios" of defense was developed. *The Church and the Bomb* (1983), a publication of the Church of England, and the pastoral letter on nuclear warfare (1984) of the American Catholic bishops are both examples of sound casuistry.

METHODOLOGY OF CASUISTRY. Casuistry differs from moral philosophy in a number of ways. The work of the casuist is discrimination; that of the moral philosopher, generalization. Casuists discuss moral problems; moral philosophers discuss moral reasoning. Casuists analyze the morality of choice in circumstances; moral philosophers analyze the meaning of moral principle in general. While the work of moral philosophers has been richly described and many methodologies have been proposed, the work of casuists—although we are all, in a sense, casuists in our personal moral deliberations—is hardly understood, and it has no accepted methodology. Even the casuists of the seventeenth century developed no overall method of resolution of moral problems. Inspection of their work, however, reveals the outline of their method.

Casuists developed positions by first stating a case in which the moral obligations entailed by a rule were most clear and then moving, step by step, to more complex cases. These steps were taken by adding various circumstances and weighing their relevance to the stringency of the rule. They assessed the degree of credence that various options deserved and the consequent weight of moral obligation. They aimed at resolving the case not by settling theoretical problems but by practical advice concerning how seriously a person involved in certain sorts of circumstances should consider himself bound by or excused from the moral principles generally incumbent. The strength of the casuists' method lay in an appreciation of exceptions and excuses generated by different circumstances; the weakness lay in the absence of any theoretically established boundaries of this appreciation. Casuistry at its best is vigorous moral common sense; at its worst, it is moral sleight of hand.

SEE ALSO Christian Ethics.

BIBLIOGRAPHY

Häring, Bernhard. *The Law of Christ,* vol. 1, *General Moral Theology.* Translated by Edwin G. Kaiser. Westminster, Md., 1961. See especially chapter 1.

Jonsen, Albert R., and Stephen Toulmin. *The Abuse of Casuistry.* Berkeley, 1988.

Kirk, Kenneth E. *Conscience and Its Problems: An Introduction to Casuistry.* London, 1927.

Long, Edward L. *Conscience and Compromise: An Approach to Protestant Casuistry.* Philadelphia, 1954.

New Sources

Gallagher, Lowell. *Medusa's Gaze: Casuistry and Conscience in the Renaissance.* Stanford, Calif., 1991.

Keenan, James F., and Thomas Shannon, eds. *The Context of Casuistry.* Washington, D.C., 1995.

Leites, Edmund, ed. *Conscience and Casuistry in Early Modern Europe.* New York, 1988.

Miller, Richard P. *Casuistry and Modern Ethics: A Poetics of Practical Reasoning.* Chicago, 1996.

Vallance, Edmund, and Harald Braun, eds. *Conscience in the Early Modern World, 1500–1700.* New York, 2003.

ALBERT R. JONSEN (1987)
Revised Bibliography

CATHARI. Catharism (from *cathari,* "the pure") was distinguished from the other heresies of the Middle Ages by its rejection of basic Christian beliefs, although its adherents claimed that in their pursuit of a pure life they were the only true Christians. In contrast to the Waldensians and other gospel-inspired movements of the twelfth century, the basis of Catharism was a non-Christian dualism deriving ultimately from Gnosticism. In place of the Christian conception of an inherently good universe that was wholly God's creation and embraced all existence, spiritual and material alike, this dualism posited two principles: one good, governing all that was spiritual, the other evil, responsible for the material world, including man's body. The consequence was the denial of the central Christian doctrines of the incarnation, Christ's two natures and the virgin birth, bodily resurrection, and the sacraments, all of which involve the acceptance of matter as part of God's design, as well as nullifying the doctrine of the Trinity and the very idea of God's omnipotence.

By the time it reached the West from Byzantium, Catharism had taken two forms, a mitigated and a radical dualism. Mitigated dualism originated with the Bogomils in Bulgaria in the tenth century, spreading to the Byzantine empire, whence it was carried to western Europe. It was closer to Christianity in recognizing only one God, the good God who had created everything good, including Satan, who had been his eldest son Lucifer before he had rebelled against his father. Satan had therefore corrupted himself by his own free will, and that freedom was held, somewhat inconsistently, to belong also to the souls that Satan subsequently imprisoned in bodies. Adapting the Old Testament account of creation in *Genesis,* the Bogomils, and later the Cathari, substituted Satan for God as creator of the firmament and the visible world, although Satan made it from preexisting matter created by God from nothing.

The world was therefore Satan's domain, and the Old Testament was the witness to his tyrannical rule. Hence the Cathari rejected the Old Testament as God's word—one of their distinguishing traits. Although they accepted the New Testament, its meaning was transformed as part of a syncretism of Christian and non-Christian beliefs, expressed as allegories and fables that were the preserve of the initiated—the perfect. Catharism thus not only had its own tenets and practices but also its own canonical literature.

The only thing that Satan had been unable to make was the human soul; it came from the angels and was variously described in the different Cathar fables as having been captured or stolen from heaven and then put in a body. The first two imprisoned souls were Adam and Eve, who by succumbing to Satan's temptations, depicted in strongly sexual imagery, became the progenitors of the human race. The penalty for their fall, which for the Cathari was identified particularly with sexuality, was the procreation of individual souls with their bodies, so that all men were born as souls imprisoned in a body. The whole of Cathar religious practice was directed toward releasing the soul from the body, thereby liberating it from Satan's rule and enabling it to return to its place in heaven. That was also the reason why God, taking pity on the fallen angels, represented by mankind suffering for Adam and Eve's sin, had sent not only Christ, his second son, but also the Holy Spirit into the world to help redeem them. Although they, too, according to some mitigated dualists, were part of God's nature, they were inferior to God. Moreover, as a spirit, Christ in his human form did not have a real body: it was either, according to some, a phantom, or, according to others, some kind of angelic covering. Whatever the case, though, the human Christ of the Cathari was not the word made flesh. He had not been born of Mary but had entered through her ear. Nor did he suffer on the cross, another of the material objects, together with images and the material properties of the Christian sacraments, rejected by the Cathari. The true Christ suffered for mankind in heaven. In this world his role was to show the way and reestablish the truth of God's word. In that sense there was, in keeping with their docetic belief, only one Christ, in heaven; he was not to be found in churches, which were not his house: one more Cathar trait, shared with the Waldensians, although by the late twelfth century in Languedoc, the Cathari did use churches as meeting places for their ceremonies. The struggle of the soul with Satan would finally end not as in the orthodox Christian belief, in the body's resurrection with the soul, but in the body's destruction with all of Satan's handiwork and the soul's ascent into heaven.

The main divergence of radical dualism from the mitigated form lay in its making the opposition between the principles of good and evil absolute and eternal. Good and evil and their creations had always coexisted. And as the good God's creation was heaven, so the visible world created by Satan was hell. Hence to live in this world was to be in hell, in man's case through having a body in which, as with the mitigated dualists, Satan had initially imprisoned the souls of angels taken from heaven. Free will thus played no part in Satan's original fall; and the power of God was correspondingly restricted in never having had control over evil, which was completely autonomous. Nor did individuals have the means of directly returning to God. Although Christ taught the way of salvation, individuals had first to undergo a series of reincarnations until they came to recognize evil by becoming perfect, thereby freeing their souls from the devil. Christ himself, and generally Mary, were regarded as angels, neither having a real body. For both absolute and mitigated dualists, as indeed for orthodox Christians, all souls would at the end be saved or damned. But for the absolute dualists free will seems to have played no part in salvation. At the end the visible world would fall into material chaos from which all souls would have departed, whereas for the mitigated dualists Satan would be captured and all things would return to order.

Accordingly the Cathari shunned all contact with the material, beyond that which was unavoidable to their existence as human beings. That meant the rejection of marriage, of all foods that were the product of sexual generation, of all material elements in worship, and of all involvement in things of this world, whether love of material goods or worldly behavior, including any kind of violence or taking of life, the exercise of jurisdiction, or the swearing of oaths. The result was an extreme asceticism and austerity, which in their moral and practical expression had close affinities with the Christian ideal of evangelical perfection. The Cathari exhibited the same sense of material renunciation and spiritual devotion, and that probably more than anything else accounted for the hold that the Cathari were able to gain in southern France and northern Italy in the twelfth and thirteenth centuries.

Because the demands of Catharism were exceptional, strict practice was confined to a small minority of adepts, the perfect. They represented the Cathar hierarchy; unlike the Christian hierarchy, however, they were a very small elite who had to prove themselves all the time. The mass of ordinary Cathar believers were able to live ordinary lives while accepting the spiritual ministrations and authority of the perfect.

The great dividing line between the perfect and the believers was the reception of the *consolamentum:* the initiation rite of spiritual baptism by the laying on of hands that admitted the recipient into the ranks of the perfect. It was usually performed after a year's probation and the full revelation of Cathar teaching, which was not accessible to the ordinary adherents. Once received, the *consolamentum* remitted the consoled's sins and the consequences of the soul's imprisonment in a body, reuniting his soul with his spirit in heaven and releasing him from Satan's rule. It was then that his testing really began. Any lapse into forbidden sins—and for the Cathari they were all equal—meant the loss of the *consolamentum* both for the sinner and for those who had been consoled by him. He could be reconsoled only after severe penance. But so long as he remained firm to his obedience, he was effectively among the saved, one of the perfect, and revered as such by ordinary believers. For the latter a special *consolamentum* was administered before death to remit their sins and bring salvation; should they recover, a further *consolamentum* was needed. The *consolamentum* thus conferred a Gnostic-like certainty of salvation which challenged orthodox Christian revelation.

The precise date of the appearance of Catharism in western Europe has been keenly debated; there is no universal agreement even now. The generally accepted view is that the first firm evidence of Cathari appears at Cologne in 1143 or 1144. That opinion could well be modified in the future. What can be said is that by the 1150s they were in southern France and northern Italy; by the 1160s they were firmly established in both regions. These became their two chief areas, especially Languedoc in the lands of the count of Toulouse. In 1176 a great council of Cathari is reported to have been held at Saint-Félix-de-Caraman where, in addition to an already existing Cathar bishopric at Albi, three more bishoprics were established for Cathar territories. It was from Albi that the southern French Cathari received their name of Albigensians (Albigenses). By 1170 they had become the main heresy to be combated. The papacy sent a succession of preaching missions, including Waldensians, Cistercians, and the founder of the Dominican order, Dominic. As early as 1181 Alexander III's cardinal legate, Henry, abbot of Clairvaux (before whom Valdès also appeared), besieged a castle at Lavaux sheltering two heretics. Alexander's successor, Innocent III, intensified the pressure, using both sanctions and persuasion. Matters came to a head in January 1208, when one of Innocent's legates, Peter Castelnau, was assassinated. Innocent, who had already called upon the king of France to make war against the Cathari, then launched his own crusade under the abbot of Cîteaux. That marked the beginning of the Albigensian crusade, in which the lands of the count of Toulouse were overrun. Although the crusade severely weakened the Cathari, they survived and regrouped. It was not until 1243 that they were effectively destroyed as an organized church with the capture of over 200 perfect at Montségur. Their strength had lain in the widespread support they had received in both town and countryside from the nobles as well as from artisans and members of the professions. For a time before the Albigensian crusade they had overshadowed the Roman Catholic church in southern France.

In Italy, the Cathari never enjoyed the same cohesion as those in Languedoc. They were driven by the conflicts that began early in the 1160s between adherents of the two forms of dualism. They were also mainly located in the cities, where they owed their survival to the opposition of the cities to both imperial and papal authority. It was only in the second half of the thirteenth century, after the ending of the wars between the popes and Frederick II, the German emperor, that the way was cleared for papal action against the Cathari. A series of trials in the larger Italian cities had largely extirpated them by the beginning of the fourteenth century, at which time they also disappeared from Languedoc.

See Also Dominic; Waldensians.

Bibliography

Borst, Arno. *Die Katharer.* Stuttgart, 1953. The standard work on the subject.

Lambert, Malcolm. *Medieval Heresy: Popular Movements from Bogomil to Hus.* London and New York, 1977. The fullest and most up-to-date account of medieval popular heresies. Particularly strong on the Cathari.

Moore, R. I., ed. *The Birth of Popular Heresy.* London, 1975. A representative selection of translated sources, mainly from the twelfth century, with a useful introduction.

Obolensky, Dimitri. *The Bogomils: A Study in Balkan Neo-Manichaeism.* Cambridge, 1948. The standard account in English.

Russell, Jeffrey B. *Dissent and Reform in the Early Middle Ages.* Berkeley, 1965. A useful, wide-ranging survey of early medieval heresies to the end of the twelfth century.

Thouzellier, Christine. *Catharisme et Valdéisme en Languedoc.* Louvain and Paris, 1969. A very full analysis of the sources.

Wakefield, Walter L. *Heresy, Crusade and Inquisition in Southern France, 1100–1250.* Berkeley, 1974. A clear, brief account with a good bibliography.

Wakefield, Walter L., and Austin P. Evans, eds. *Heresies of the High Middle Ages.* New York and London, 1969. The largest collection of translated sources, particularly valuable for their fullness.

Gordon Leff (1987)

CATHARSIS.

The Greek *katharsis* is an action noun corresponding to a verb that literally means "to prune, to clean, to remove dirt or a blemish [*katharma*] for the purpose of rendering some thing, place, or animate being pure [*katharos*]." As denoting the general process of purification, *catharsis* could of course be applied to a very broad range of phenomena in the history of religions. In this article, however, the focus will be specifically on the Greek conception. Although the meaning of *catharsis* and the exact techniques or modalities of purification (*katharmoi*) differ according to context, the sense of *catharsis* always remains negative: it refers to separating, evacuating, or releasing. Whether performed in a strictly ritual setting or understood as a spiritual concept, catharsis maintains this negative meaning of ridding either oneself or an object of something impure or unclean.

Catharsis originally appears as a ritualized process of quasi-material purification that makes use of a variety of substances as purifying agents. Chief among these are the elements water, fire, and sulfur, followed by oil, clay, and bran. Certain other vegetable substances, such as laurel, myrtle, and olive are also used, especially as prophylactics (coronets of leaves) or as supports of cleansing waters (aspersions). Since ceremonial purifications are usually conducted out in the open, the element of air also plays a role.

In the selection and use of such purifying agents, the symbolism of numbers sometimes comes into play, especially of the numbers three, seven, and nine. The gestures involved in aspersions, ablutions, fumigations, and the like, may be repeated a set number of times; a definite number of sacrificial victims may be required; and even the source of the water used in the rite may be determined on the basis of numbers (water coming from a river that arises from three springs was preferred).

When a sacrificial victim was required for purification, the pig was the most frequently sacrificed animal. However, once a year, the Athenians purified their city with the sacrifice of two human victims, *pharmakoi,* one bearing the guilt of all the Athenian men, the other bearing the guilt of all the Athenian women. As a general rule whatever served for the purification had to be completely destroyed. Human victims were burned.

The idea of defilement is closely linked to the perception of a disturbance of the natural order or a breach of the day-to-day routine. Contacts or experiences that call into question the physical integrity of the individual or of the general environment require a catharsis. Since health is understood to be normal, illness is seen as something abnormal, as a physical or mental stain requiring purification. Madness, too, and breaches of morality are seen as illnesses and therefore as defilements; thus an army in violation of the law or in revolt can be called back to order, cured of its illness, through purifications. Examples of this "psychosomatic" use of purification are numerous. The Proetides were purified of their madness by the magus Melampus. To cure the Lacedaemonian women struck with nymphomania required the intervention of a *kathartēs* Bakis, delegated by Apollo, the god of healing and purification. The women of Samos were liberated from their sexual exaltation thanks to the *katharmos* of Dexikreon.

The Bacchants were liberated from their maladies quite differently, however—in the orgy, which temporarily identified them with Dionysos, the god of *mania.* The Dionysian orgy is cathartic to the extent that it releases the urges repressed by social and moral constraints. The ritual release of the Dionysian rite is a purification: "Blessed are the dancers and those who are purified, who dance on the hill in the holy dance of god" (Euripides, *The Bacchae* 75ff.). Intoxication from wine or from dance purges the individual of irrational impulses which, if repressed, would be noxious. Ritual madness can also cure internal madness. Music, too, can have a cathartic function (Quintilianus Aristides, *Peri mousikēs* 3.23). The Aristotelian theory of tragedy—initially Dionysiac—defined catharsis from this same perspective: The satiation of the passions by the spectacle of the theater is a therapeutic based, like the Bacchic *ekstasis,* on purgative and liberating homeopathy.

Contact with death requires purification, whether it is a death one has caused, the death of a family member, or any other contact with the dead. The murderer, whether the act was voluntary or involuntary, is defiled. Herakles had to be purified of the deaths of Iphitos, the Meropes, the sons of Proteus, and the centaurs; Achilles of the murder of Thersites (according to Arctinos of Miletus); Jason and Medea of the murder of Apsyrtos; and Theseus of the murder of the Pallantides. In certain cases, only the gods can cleanse the criminal of his wrongdoing. Ixion was apparently the first murderer purified by Zeus. Patricide constituted a particularly grave case, whether of Oedipus or Orestes; the latter was purified by Apollo himself. The stain of death may also be collective, as in the case of the Athenians after the deaths of Androgeus or the Cylonians. In this case a collective purification may be necessary. Even the quelling of malefic creatures such as the brigands killed by Theseus, the dragon killed by Cadmus, or the serpent Python killed by Apollo demands purification.

However, Homer presents us with a somewhat different picture. Odysseus, after having executed the suitors of Penelope, asks that sulfur and fire be brought "to disperse the bad air" (*Odyssey,* 22.481). This is meant to purify the house but not particularly those who have been killed or have done the killing. It is as if the cadaver that defiles a house takes precedence over the idea of moral responsibility for homicide.

Throughout antiquity the sentiment prevails that the contact with death, the presence of the dead under the family roof, demands purification. Iamblichus writes around 300 CE: "It is impious to touch human bodies from which the soul has departed," since "the nonliving mark the living with a stain." Thus the domicile of the deceased should be ritually disinfected. In the morning, vases of lustral water that had to be borrowed from another house were placed at the door of the deceased's home. These were then interred with the dead. The funeral and the subsequent rites had the ultimate purpose of purifying the family and consecrating the boundary that would henceforth separate the dead from the living; any dead person deprived of a tomb thus remained a *katharma.*

Certain sacred places prohibit the presence of tombs. Pisistratus, instructed by the oracles, purified the island of Delos by having the dead disinterred "anywhere in the region within visual range of the sanctuary" (Herodotus, 1.64). Later, in 426, all of the dead found on the island were disposed of (Thucydides, 1.8, 3.104, 5.1). The authorities of Eleusis had the body of a dead man found on the plain of Rharos removed and had the entire plain purified by a *kathartēs.* Contact with the world of the dead was not permissible without prior lustrations (Homer, *Odyssey* 11.25ff.; Lucian, *Nekuomanteia* 7). Conversely, one who was resuscitated had to be washed and nursed like a newborn (Plutarch, *Quaestiones Romanae* 5). Even encountering the dead in a dream requires purification (Aristophanes, *Ranae* 1340). Finally, contact with and, particularly, the eating of dead animals were impure in the eyes of the Orphics, the Pythagoreans, the initiates of the cult of Zagreus (Euripides, *The Cretans* 472), as well as for candidates for certain initiations (Porphyry, *De abstinentia* 4.16; Apuleius, *Metamorphoses* 11.23.2). There was also a blood taboo, which legitimated excluding criminals from the Eleusinian mysteries, but the Lesser Mysteries of Agra prepared them for initiation into the Greater.

The blood taboo explains the relationship of menstruation, generation, and parturition to catharsis. Hippocrates gives the menstrual periods the name *katharsis* because they relieve women of their menstrual blood. The houses of women giving birth also require purification. Miscarriages require forty days of lustrations. When Delos was purified in 426 all lying-in on the island was forbidden. To approach a woman in labor was, for the superstitious character in Theophrastus (*Characteres* 16.9), as serious as walking on a grave or touching the dead (the two injunctions are often in tandem). The initiates of Ida whom Euripides places on stage in *The Cretans* avoid "assisting at birth or approaching a coffin." The newborn, too, must be purified. By means of several lustrations the Amphidromies of the Greeks and the rites of the *dies lustricus* of the Romans integrate the newborn into the community and preserve him from evil spirits attracted by the blood present at birth.

Sexual contacts demand catharsis just as those with death or the dead. Anyone wishing to approach the chapel of Men-Lunus had to be purified if he had eaten pork or garlic or touched a woman or corpses. Matrimonial rites derive from concerns connected with the taboos of blood, sex, or life. They consist of preliminary lustrations (baths, aspersions, circulating fumigations, the wearing of white vestments and of crowns), which were to safeguard the couple (Euripides, *Iphigenia in Aulis* 1111; Valerius Flaccus, *Argonautica* 8.245f.).

More radically, life itself can appear impure, inasmuch as life comes from a mixture of body and soul, Dionysiac and Titanic elements which, according to Orphism, are implicit in the human makeup. Life is also impure when compared to that of the gods. Contact with the gods thus requires certain lustrations. Access to sacred enclosures (and especially to the *aduton*, the inner sanctum) is forbidden to those who have not undergone the ritual catharsis. Pools of water for this purpose are located at the entrances to sanctuaries, reminiscent of the holy water fonts of Christian churches. The sacrificial ceremony itself includes purifications of the officiates, of the participants, the victim, the liturgical vessel, the instruments of immolations, and the altar near which the animal is to be slaughtered.

The initiations, which permit man to establish a closer bond with the world of the gods, indeed, to be assimilated to the gods in certain cases, impose on the candidate a rigorous catharsis. Examples include the rituals of Andania and Agra, various types of abstinences, baths in the sea with a sacrificial pig for the candidates for the mysteries of Eleusis, and the continences, abstinences, and ablutions for the initiates of Isis, Mithra, and Dionysos. The Bacchic mysteries could even be regarded as being essentially cathartic. These rites suppose that man himself is too unclean to enter into relationship with the gods. Moreover, he cannot himself proceed with his own purification; he needs to have recourse to the techniques of a priest or of a *kathartēs*.

The philosophers, however, shifted emphasis in the understanding of catharsis, viewing it more in terms of spiritual purification. An inscription at Epidaurus recommends that one approach the gods with a pure spirit (Porphyry, *De abstinentia* 2.19; cf. Cicero, *De legibus* 2.24: "The law bids one approach the gods purely, with a spirit that is in which all things are"). The speculations of the Orphics were particularly important to this change of emphasis. Orphic mythology places a hereditary taint on humanity that has been compared to a sort of original sin. It is said that Zeus, hurling a bolt of lightning, reduced the race of Titans to cinders for having eaten Dionysos Zagreus. The human race is then born from these cinders. Consequently, human beings must be delivered from this Titanic contamination in order to recover their true Bacchic essence. Toward this end, Orphic catharsis serves to actually reinstate the divine life through the practice of continual asceticism. Similarly, Plato (*Phaedo*, 67c) refers to an "ancient tradition" for the purification *par excellence:* the separation of the soul from the body. The *kathartēs* whom Plato ridicules in *The Republic* (364e) and the Orpheotelestes of Theophrastus (*Characteres* 16.11) offer ritual recipes. The "Orphic life" implies a *spiritual* discipline, a kind of personal sacrifice. Similarly, the Platonists and, later, the Neoplatonists, were to preach the liberation of the spirit. This catharsis is reserved, however, for the elite sages, and with the last of the Neoplatonists the techniques of theurgy tended to overshadow intellectual purification.

After physical death (which the philosopher can anticipate while still in the body), the soul must be stripped of the garments that it has donned in its descent through the planetary spheres (Cumont, 1949, pp. 358, 364; Festugière, 1953, pp. 128ff.). Posthumous catharsis, as understood by the Orphics and Neoplatonists, consists in separating the soul from all heterogeneous elements. Vergil's hell (*Aeneid*, 6.740ff.), which tries the souls by wind, water, and fire, reminds us of the *katharmoi* of Empedocles (frag. 115). Seneca (*Ad Marciam de consolatione* 25.1), by contrast, gives a moral explanation for posthumous purification. The funeral pyre is thought by some to purify the soul from the body. Lightning is also thought to confer apotheosis (Cumont, 1949, p. 330). For others, the universe as a whole is subject to periodic purifications, which in Stoic cosmology consist of deluges and conflagrations (Origen, *Against Celsus* 4.12, 4.21, 4.64, 4.69).

From birth to death, through marriage and initiations, catharsis thus sanctioned the major steps of life. From its therapeutic, magic, or prophylactic functions, catharsis tended to shift in time to a moral and mystical exercise, especially in stipulating the conditions for salvation or apotheosis through radical ablation or liberation.

SEE ALSO Blood; Fire; Purification; Water.

BIBLIOGRAPHY

Bouché-Leclercq, Auguste. "Lustratio." In *Dictionnaire des antiquités grecques et romains* (1904), edited by Charles Daremberg et al., vol. 3. Graz, 1963.

Boyancé, Pierre. *Le culte des muses chez les philosophes grecs.* Paris, 1937.

Boyancé, Pierre. "Platon et les cathartes orphiques." *Revue des études grecques* 55 (1942): 217–235.

Cumont, Franz. *Lux perpetua.* Paris, 1949.

Dodds, E. R. *The Greeks and the Irrational.* Berkeley, 1951.

Fehrle, Eugen. *Die kultische Keuschheit im Altertum.* Giessen, 1910.

Festugière, A.-J. *La révélation d'Hermès Trismégiste,* vol. 3. Paris, 1953.

Festugière, A.-J. *Études de religion grecque et hellénistique.* Paris, 1972.

Jeanmaire, Henri. *Dionysos: Histoire du culte de Bacchus.* Paris, 1951.

Moulinier, Louis. *Le pur et l'impur dans la pensée des Grecs, d'Homère à Aristote.* Paris, 1952.

Nilsson, Martin P. *Geschichte der griechischen Religion,* vol. 2, *Die hellenistische und römische Zeit.* 3d rev. ed. Munich, 1974.

Parker, R. *Miasma: Pollution and Purification in Early Greek Religion.* Oxford, 1983.

Places, Édouard des. *La religion grecque.* Paris, 1969.

Rohde, Edwin. *Psyche: The Cult of Souls and Belief in Immortality among the Greeks* (1925). Translated by W. B. Hillis. London, 1950.

Spiegel, N. "The Nature of Katharsis according to Aristotle: A Reconsideration." *Revue belge de philologie et d'histoire* 43 (1965): 22–39.

Trouillard, Jean. *La purification plotinienne.* Paris, 1955.

Turcan, Robert. "Un rite controuvé de l'initiation dionysiaque." *Revue de l'histoire des religions* 158 (1960): 129–144.

Turcan, Robert. "*Bacchoi* ou bacchants? De la dissidence des vivants à la ségrégation des morts." *L'association dionysiaque dans les sociétés anciennes* (Coll. De l'Ecole française de Rome, 89), Rome, 1986, pp. 227–244.

Wächter, Theodor. *Reinheitsvorschriften im griechischen Kult.* Giessen, 1910.

ROBERT TURCAN (1987 AND 2005)
Translated from French by Marilyn Gaddis Rose and William H. Snyder

CATHEDRAL

SEE BASILICA, CATHEDRAL, AND CHURCH

CATHERINE OF SIENA

CATHERINE OF SIENA (1347–1380), Caterina da Siena; Italian mystic and Christian saint. The particular genius of the spirituality of Catherine of Siena had its earliest beginnings in a visionary experience of Christ when she was six years old, and her subsequent childish yet serious vow of virginity. She persisted in her purpose in spite of family opposition until she was accepted as one of the Mantellate, a Dominican third-order group comprising, up to then, only widows. For about three years thereafter she gave herself to prayer and asceticism in almost complete seclusion, until her very prayer (which had become deeply mystical) led her out, first to serve the poor and the sick in her own city, and gradually into wider and wider spheres.

She had learned in her solitude to read, and now she became an enthusiastic conversationalist, feeding insatiably on the theological knowledge of friends she attracted among Dominicans, Augustinians, Franciscans, and Jesuits. She began, too, to draw as disciples people from every walk of life, a circle she would call her *famiglia.* She found an ideal mentor in the Dominican friar Raymond of Capua. Raymond was an astute theologian and diplomat, under whose guidance and in whose company Catherine's scope broadened to include the ecclesiastical and the political—in her mind always of one piece with the spiritual, and all ultimately oriented to the same spiritual ends.

Unlike her contemporary Birgitta of Sweden, Catherine was an ardent promoter and recruiter for the crusade projected by Pope Gregory XI and his successor, Urban VI. A holy war seemed to her a perfect means of uniting in a common cause Christians now at odds among themselves and with the papacy. She saw Palestine as a Christian trust, and she believed with many that the advance of the Turks toward Europe must be halted. A main object of the crusade would be the conversion of the Muslims, who would in their new faith be a leaven to reinvigorate a sick church. And it would provide her and others (she apparently intended to go along) the opportunity to pay Christ "blood for blood."

It was the dissension between Florence and Gregory XI that brought Catherine to that city in 1376 to attempt to mediate a reconciliation. On the mandate, probably, of only certain Guelphs she traveled to Avignon (where the popes had resided since 1309) with no official credentials, only to be ignored by Florentine ambassadors who came later. In subsequent efforts, also, she failed to influence the Florentines significantly in this dispute, which was to her essentially religious but was to them a matter of political survival.

Once rebuffed by Florence, Catherine turned her energy toward the two issues she considered the root of the dissension: the continuing absence of the popes from Rome and clerical corruption. If the pope would return to Rome, she reasoned, Christians would have no more cause for rebellion, and reform could begin. Gregory XI had in fact so resolved but had repeatedly, in fear, put off taking action. Catherine can surely be credited with finally moving him. In fact, when dissent deepened after his return to Rome, many including the pope blamed Catherine's advice.

Gregory XI died on March 27, 1378, and within months his successor, Urban VI, was being denounced by a growing number of the cardinals, who in September of that year elected Clement VII as antipope, thus effectively splitting the church. At Urban's invitation Catherine came to Rome to support his cause. Though her health was by this time failing under her fierce asceticism and exertion, she continued to pray and work tirelessly for unity and reform, both of which seemed to her ever more elusive. The weight of this sense of failure surely contributed to her early death on April 29, 1380. She was canonized in 1461 and proclaimed a doctor of the church in 1970; she and Teresa of Ávila were the first women to receive that title.

Catherine used letters prodigiously as a favored vehicle of influence. The nearly four hundred letters that have been collected and edited date mostly from 1375 to 1380. They are addressed to persons as diverse as popes, high-ranking clergy, nobles, relatives, disciples, prisoners, and prostitutes. Unfortunately, the early compilers' purposes of simple edification led them to delete much that was personal from the letters, but still they open a revealing window on Catherine's evolving thought and on her warm and spontaneous personality.

In 1377 and 1378, in addition to all her other activities, Catherine composed the work since known as *The Dialogue* (because she cast it as an exchange between God and herself). Her intent in writing it was to share with her disciples and others the insights she had gained in prayer and in her own experience. In it she approaches the way of holiness from several vantage points, and develops at length the themes of God's providence, the role of Christ as redeemer and mediator, and the church. Finally, during the last three and a half years of Catherine's life, her secretaries sometimes recorded her prayers when she spoke in ecstasy. Twenty-six such prayers have been preserved.

Through her reading and her associations, Catherine gained a knowledge of the Christian tradition remarkable in an otherwise unschooled person. In her works she draws freely not only from scripture but from Augustine, Gregory the Great, Bernard, and Thomas Aquinas (to name only those most frequently reflected), as well as from contemporaries such as Ubertino of Casale, Domenico Cavalca, Iacopo Passavanti, and Giovanni Colombini. Her own writing, however, is not speculative or systematic or analytical. Rather, she synthesizes into an integrated whole all of the various aspects of Christian faith on which she dwells. Her purposes are eminently practical, her tone warm and personal. She resorts for clarification not to conceptual argumentation but to literary images, developing the meaning of each as she goes and interweaving them one with another.

The central principles around which Catherine's teaching revolves are everywhere evident in her writings: God alone is absolute being, and God's being is at once love and truth—love that is truth and truth that is love. When humankind cut itself off from God by sin, God's endlessly creative and re-creative being took flesh in Jesus Christ, who in himself repaired the breach. The foundation of all spiritual life is knowledge of oneself in God and of God in oneself. Human nature is God's creation and as such is essentially good, and Catherine is therefore understanding and compassionate of human weakness even as she denounces sin. Desire for the truth and love that is God puts all in order, and what God asks of the human heart is infinite desire.

Bibliography

Works by Catherine of Siena

The most complete recent edition of Catherine's letters is *Le lettere di S. Caterina da Siena*, 4 vols., translated and edited by Nicoló Tommaseo, revised by Piero Misciattelli (1860; reprint, Florence, 1940). The first volume of the only truly critical edition was prepared by Eugenio Dupré Theseider, *Epistolario di Santa Caterina da Siena*, vol. 1 (Rome, 1940); the work on this critical edition is being pursued by Antonio Volpato. A complete English translation from the critical edition is in progress under my editorship. I have translated Giuliana Cavallini's critical editions of *Il dialogo* (Rome, 1968) and *Le orazioni* (Rome, 1978) as *The Dialogue* (New York, 1980) and *The Prayers of Catherine of Siena* (New York, 1983), respectively.

Works about Catherine of Siena

A useful primary source for the life of Catherine of Siena is Raymond of Capua's *The Life of Catherine of Siena (1385–1389)*, translated by Conleth Kearns (Wilmington, Del., 1980); other biographies in English are *History of St. Catherine of Siena and Her Companions*, by Augusta Theodosia Drane (London, 1899), good for its inclusion of primary source material not otherwise available in English; *Saint Catherine of Siena: A Study in the Religion, Literature and History of the Fourteenth Century in Italy*, by Edmund G. Gardner (New York, 1907), complete on historical contexts and well indexed; and Arrigo Levasti's *My Servant, Catherine*, translated by Dorothy M. White (Westminster, Md., 1954), which concentrates on Catherine's psychology and spirituality and also gives an excellent bibliography. Eugenio Dupré Theseider's entry "Catherine da Siena, Santa," in *Dizionario biographico degli Italiani* (Rome, 1979), covers very well Catherine's life and theology, including debated points, and offers a very comprehensive bibliography.

Suzanne Noffke (1987)

CATHOLIC CHURCH See ROMAN CATHOLICISM

CATS

CATS seem to be surrounded by a special power. Their graceful movements, their liveliness at night, and their inaudible steps as well as their independent spirit have enchanted poets and painters and storytellers in many cultures, but these very traits account also for the aversion many people have had to them. Throughout history, cats have rarely been regarded with indifference; they have generally been considered either sacred or demonic. The earliest known center of their veneration, and probably also of their domestication, was ancient Egypt, where they are documented from 1600 BCE onward. Bast, a popular goddess of pleasure, was represented with a cat's head. Numerous sacred cats lived around her sanctuary in Bubastis, and thousands of mummified cats have been found in that area.

Other goddesses with feline attributes have also been connected with cats. In a Roman myth, Diana assumes the form of a cat, and in Germanic mythology, Freyja's carriage is drawn by cats. In Bengali Hinduism, Ṣaṣṭi rides or stands on a (usually black) cat. Should a mother be disrespectful to the goddess, a cat will kill her children; such revenge can be averted by pouring sour milk over a black cat and licking it off.

Cats are frequently perceived as malevolent creatures. The idea that a cat can "suck the breath" of sleeping children (i.e., suffocate them) is widely prevalent, and in some myths the cat is represented even as a bloodsucking ogre. Some people think that to swallow a cat's hair will result in tuberculosis. But a cat's tooth can serve as a talisman, for cats have not only "nine lives" but supernatural powers. In Ireland, for example, it is thought that the devil can assume the form of a cat; in China, it is believed that cats can see spirits at night and that a dead cat can turn into a demon. In many places it is thought that cats can sense the presence of death, that they can smell the guiding spirit come to conduct away the departing soul. Because of their supernatural abilities, cats are connected with witches and sorcerers; in fact, they are—especially black ones—typical familiars of witches. In medieval Europe, every owner of such an animal was therefore suspect.

As an agent of the supernatural, the cat became a sacrificial animal in some cultures. In medieval Europe, cats were killed as an expiation in times of plague or were thrown into the Saint John's fire at the summer solstice. As late as the mid-seventeenth century, in the ceremony of the Taigheirm in the West Highlands of Scotland, black cats were roasted on spits to raise the infernal spirits. In Japan, however, as in ancient Egypt and other cultures, it has been thought inadvisable to kill a cat, owing to its special power. Such an act would bring misfortune, or would have to be atoned for (in Muslim Bengal, with five pounds of salt).

In European lore, cats can function as house goblins and are also counted among the shapeshifters; they can assume enormous proportions in case of danger or in order to rescue their benefactor from equally enormous rats. Thus their role can be beneficial as well: friendly cat demons can produce gold and treasures for those who have been kind to them, and cats—especially tricolored cats (which are believed to be always female)—can protect a house from fire and guarantee marital happiness.

In many cultures it is considered a bad omen to see a cat, especially a black one, when leaving a house; likewise, to dream of a black cat, or to cross its path, means misfortune. But the black cat's body serves both medical and magical purposes; a meal of cat's brains may arouse love in someone, or strengthen a man's sexual power, or restore sight. Pulverized cat's gall rubbed into the eyes enables one to see at night, or to see *jinn.* Certain parts of a black cat, prepared with other ingredients, can make a person invisible.

The behavior of cats is also often regarded as an omen. In Germany, if a cat washes itself, a guest will come. In China, the arrival of a strange cat in a house portends poverty, because that cat is believed to have a premonition that many mice will come to live in that house. The cat's sensitivity to atmospheric changes has led, in many places, to belief that it can predict—or, indeed, is responsible for—the weather. In Turkey, if a cat purrs loudly, a severe winter is impending; in England, if a cat sits with its back to the fire, there will be frost. In Java and Sumatra, bathing two cats or throwing one into a river can bring rain.

Folklore often talks about the hypocritical cat. "The cat weeps at the mouse's death," according to a Chinese proverb. The story of the "repentant" cat that appears as a pious ascetic in order to cheat the mice has been told from ancient Egypt to modern Mongolia, and it occurs frequently in Persian literature (see ʿUbayd-i Za-kānī's little epic *Mouse and Cat* from the fourteenth century). Hence, in Persian and Ottoman Turkish urban poetry, the term *cat* is sometimes used to characterize a sly person of high rank. The friendship of a cat with a mouse or other weaker animal, or with its archenemy the dog, lasts only so long as both are in danger, as *Ka-līlah wa-Dimnah* (The fables of Bidpai) tells us; once safe, the cat usually eats the mouse. This "hypocrisy" has been expressed in many proverbs that warn against trusting the cat, which may first lick one's hand and then scratch it. The motto of the Mackintosh clan of Scotland is "Touch not a cat but [i.e., without] a glove."

Nevertheless, the cat has many positive aspects. In ancient Rome, the cat was a symbol of liberty, for no animal has so independent a spirit or is so resistant to restraint as a cat. In China, the association of the sign for cat, *mao,* with that for the number eighty has made the cat a symbol of long life.

In Islamic tradition, the cat is born in Noah's ark from the lioness's sneeze, or else she is the lion's, or tiger's, aunt who teaches him various tricks but withholds the last one, that is, how to climb a tree. The positive evaluation of cats in the Islamic world is due to the prophet Muḥammad's fondness for cats. Because he stroked the back of a cat that saved him from a snake's wiliness, cats never fall on their backs, and the trace of his fingers is visible in the dark stripes that appear on the foreheads of most cats. The cat is clean and does not spoil man's purity for prayer (as does the dog), and its drinking water can be used for ritual ablutions. Many Ṣūfīs have had cats as companions, animals that have sometimes performed wonderful feats of clairvoyance or self-sacrifice to save others from danger or death. The most remarkable cult of cats is connected with the North African beggars' order of the Heddawa, in which cats are treated like humans; however, once in a while a cat is ritually killed by the brethren. Cats can assume the shape of saints or helpers, as in pre-Islamic Arabia, where desert demons, *ghūl,* were visualized with cats' heads. Even the Sakīnah, God's presence, appeared to the Prophet in the shape of a white cat.

Caterwauling, not always appreciated by most people, has sometimes been interpreted as mysterious music. An early Arabian musician learned some superb songs from a black cat in his dreams. Nursery rhymes sing of the cat's fiddling, and the cat's purr has sometimes been interpreted as its prayer.

Benevolent cats occur frequently in folk tales. The Dick Whittington motif of the cat that proves useful in a country without cats is known in the East and the West. The friendly, clever tomcat, manifested in *Puss in Boots*, is a common topic of folk tradition. It is always the youngest of three sons who inherits the resourceful cat. Thus, the cat often uses its magic properties for positive ends and appears as a mediator between the hero and the supernatural world. This expresses best the good side of the cat's ambivalent character and of its role as an animal that is powerful in the three realms of activity: demonic, human, and divine.

BIBLIOGRAPHY

Carl Van Vechten's *The Tiger in the House*, 3d ed. (New York, 1936), includes interesting chapters on cats in the occult and in folklore as well as an extensive, classified bibliography. Since publication of this work, the literature about cats has increased enormously and at present is growing almost daily. Excellent surveys can be found in *Nine Lives: The Folklore of Cats*, by Katharine M. Briggs (New York, 1980), and in *Le chat dans la tradition spirituelle*, by Robert de Laroche (Paris, 1984). For Islamic cat lore, see my discussion in *Die orientalische Katze* (Cologne, 1983).

New Sources

Loibl, Elisabeth. *Deuses Aimais.* São Paulo, 1984.

ANNEMARIE SCHIMMEL (1987)
Revised Bibliography

CATTLE. By *cattle* is here meant those bovines that have been brought under domestication (*Bos taurus*, *Bos longifrons*, *Bos brachyceros*, *Bos indicus*) and not merely bovines or domesticated livestock in general. The first datum that must thus concern anyone interested in the religio-historic importance of cattle is the very fact of the domestication of wild bovines, which was one of the central cultural accomplishments of the "Neolithic revolution," now dated in the period roughly between the tenth and sixth millennium BCE. Since the nineteenth century, a debate has continued between those who have argued in favor of a religious motivation for the domestication of this species and those who have stressed material and economic factors. The former position, initially formulated by Eduard Hahn, emphasized the common use of cattle as sacrificial victims throughout ancient Mesopotamia, arguing from this datum that cattle were tamed in order to ensure a regular and adequate supply of victims for the sacrificial cult. While some still maintain this theory, more generally accepted is the opposing point of view, which holds that obtaining reliable sources of milk, meat, and traction power for nonreligious purposes was the primary motive for the initial domestication.

Once tamed, cattle quickly came to occupy a highly important place within both the agricultural and the pastoral economies of Neolithic societies. In those areas where sufficient rainfall and a long growing season made the production of crops feasible, cattle were harnessed to the yoke and used for plowing, a process that greatly increased the agricultural yield. This combination of cereal agriculture and cattle-drawn plows was an extremely dynamic one: increased agricultural production made it possible to feed ever larger herds of cattle (as well as ever more people), which in turn made it possible to bring ever larger areas of land under the plow. As irrigation techniques were mastered, still greater production resulted, ultimately making possible the emergence of urban civilization.

Elsewhere, in terrains less conducive to agricultural production, with perhaps an inadequate water supply and/or a short growing season, pastoral economies proper developed. Here, herds of cattle were exploited more as a source of food and raw materials than for their labor. Milk, butter, cheese, and sometimes the blood of cattle served as chief items of diet, although agricultural products might also be obtained by way of trade. Meat, for pastoralists as for those who practiced mixed herding and agriculture, remained always a highly specialized and prestigious item of diet, the consumption of which was surrounded by religious attitudes and ritual procedures.

Beyond food, cattle provided numerous other necessities of life for such pastoral peoples as the Nilotic tribes of East Africa, the Israelites of the patriarchal period, and the early Indo-Europeans. Among the products derived from cattle were leather hides, used for clothing, shelter, defensive armament, thongs, and the like; bone tools; dung, which served as fuel for slow-burning fires in areas where wood was scarce; and urine, often used as an all-purpose disinfectant. It is thus no overstatement to say that for cattle-herding pastoralists, cattle formed the very means of production, being in effect machines for the conversion of grass into multiple usable forms.

Equally important, however, is the fact that cattle served as the standard measure of wealth and means of exchange. Nor is exchange to be understood as simply trade: rather, the transfer of cattle from one person or group to another establishes a continuing relation between them, the exchange having social, ritual, and sentimental dimensions as well as economic. Convenient examples of this are found in the institutions of bridewealth and wergild, whereby one social group that has caused another group to lose a valued member compensates the latter by bestowing a prescribed number of cattle upon them. These cattle not only restore the economically productive value of the lost individual, but also replace him or her in the affections of the group that receives them. As a result of this exchange, the two groups—one of which would otherwise benefit at the expense of the other—remain in balance and harmony.

Cattle are thus a crucially important part of any pastoral society, for in truth they make social life possible. All moments of passage—births, deaths, marriages, initiations—are marked by an exchange of cattle. And, in addition to horizontal exchanges of cattle (i.e., those between humans, all of whom occupy the same level of the cosmos), vertical exchanges are also frequent, sacrifice being in part an exchange between humans and gods—as for instance in sacrifices performed on behalf of those suffering from disease, in which cattle are given to deities, who in return restore the afflicted person to his or her social group.

One can thus readily see that there exists a constant demand for cattle within pastoral societies, given their enormous importance as means of production, means of exchange, measures of wealth, and signs of prestige. New supplies are obtained through normal reproduction and breeding, of course, but also through violence, for the raiding of neighboring people's herds is an extremely common practice among pastoralists. Such raids stand in marked opposition to the types of exchange discussed above. Involving no reciprocity, they create or perpetuate imbalance and disharmony between the raiding and raided groups, reciprocity and balance (but never harmony) appearing only when the tables are turned and the previously raided group turns raider itself. To ensure success in raids, warrior values and patterns of organization—militarized age-sets, *Männerbünde,* and the like—are particularly cultivated. Specialized training, initiatory rituals, and magical apparatuses prepare young men to go forth on raids, these being not simply expeditions born of socioeconomic utility, but also—from the point of veiw of those who participate, at any rate—sacred, ritual ventures.

The chief means whereby raids are elevated to ritual status is through the propagation of myths that offer a divine precedent for the deeds of warriors. Such myths, in which the exploits of a deity, hero, or primordial ancestor are celebrated, serve to charter and legitimate similar raiding activity, as warriors come to identify with, and pattern themselves after, the mythic models. A case in point is a celebrated Nuer myth, which tells of the first cattle raid launched by the first Nuer against the first Dinka, at the command of God himself:

> There were still no cattle on the earth. Then God collared Nuer and gave him a cow and a calf with the instructions to share them with Dinka—to give the cow to Dinka and to keep the calf himself. Then, he secretly gave Nuer the direction to come to him early in the morning in order to receive his calf. But, unobserved, Dinka had overheard this speech. Very early—still by night—Nuer came to God's dwelling and said, "Gwah, my Father, I have come; give me my calf." "Who are you?" asked God. Whereupon the Nuer said, "I am Nuer." "But now, who was it who came to me a little while ago and said he was Nuer, and to whom I consequently gave the calf?" God now asked. The astonished Nuer replied, "I did not come. That must have been Dinka. This was Dinka cunning; he has out-witted me." Then God said to Nuer, "Good, now you take the cow for the present; then follow Dinka. When you have overtaken him, you may kill him and take the calf from him." Since that time date the struggles of the Nuer against the Dinka to gain possession of their cattle. (Crazzolara, 1953, pp. 68–69; my trans.)

As the last sentence of this highly significant text indicates, the Nuer—who are militarily superior to their Dinka neighbors—make use of this myth to justify their raiding activity, for the myth permits them to claim that such aggression (1) sets right an ancient wrong, in which Dinka initially cheated Nuer of his calf, and (2) fulfills a commandment spoken by God. Such an ideology permits the Nuer to make use of their superior force with a sense of perfect self-righteousness; it seems probable that the Dinka herds would be thoroughly depleted by Nuer attacks, were it not for the fact that the Dinka tell more or less the same myth, interpreting it, however, as establishing a sacred charter and precedent for their own continuing theft of Nuer cattle through stealth and guile, qualities in which they exceed their Nuer enemy.

Similar stories are found among many other peoples for whom cattle are a mainstay of the society and economy. Sometimes these circulate in secular versions, as in Ireland, where numerous tales, including the great national epic *Táin Bó Cuailnge* (The Cattle Raid of Cuailnge) celebrate the raiding exploits of human, if prodigious, warriors. Elsewhere, demigods appear as the prototypical heroes of cattle raids, as with the Greek tale of Herakles and Geryon, or its Roman counterpart, in which Hercules vanquishes Cacus. Both of these are quite similar to the pattern of the Nuer myth, telling how a foreigner stole cattle, which the national or ethnic hero then recovered in a fully justified raid. Yet again, the central figure of raiding myths may himself be a deity, as in numerous myths of Vedic India, in which the warrior god Indra recovers stolen cattle from such enemies as the *paṇis,* Vṛtra, and Vala. In these myths, the cattle raid is lifted to cosmogonic significance, for it is regularly told that in recovering lost cattle, Indra also set free imprisoned waters and light, rescuing the cosmos from possible disaster. Here the rains and the sun's rays are homologized to cattle; they are the cows of the atmosphere and of the heavens respectively, these having been penned up by drought and night but set free by the god's successful cattle raid—a raid that makes all life and prosperity possible and on which human raiding is patterned.

A certain moral ambiguity frequently surrounded raiding, however, in myth as in actual practice. Thus, for instance, the Homeric *Hymn to Hermes* tells how the god Hermes, while still an infant, stole cattle from his brother Apollo. Yet for all that the exploit is celebrated and helped Hermes win elevation to full divine stature (the common initiatory value of raiding is here evident), Hermes' action is also called into question. According to the hymn, he was hunted down by Apollo, forced to stand trial, and ultimately had to make restitution to his brother before peace could be established between them.

Part of the problem was that Hermes had killed some of the cattle that he stole, and the unrightful slaughter of cattle is always a most serious crime among cattle-herding peoples. Thus, for instance, Enkidu was condemned to death for his part in slaying the Bull of Heaven, according to the *Epic of Gilgamesh*, and the men of Odysseus's last ship were all destroyed by a thunderbolt for having killed and eaten the cattle of the sun god Helios, which were pastured on the island of Thrinacia. Again, among Nuer and Dinka alike, any cattle killed for food outside of sacrifice are said to be slain "just for nothing" (*bang lora*), and it is expected that they will return to haunt their slayer.

The same point is made in this Nuer-Dinka belief as in the story of Odysseus's men: however much hunger may drive one to desire meat, lethal violence directed against cattle constitutes a sacrilege unless it is set within a ritual context—that is to say, carried out with a certain etiquette, solemnity, and decorum (often by specialists), and legitimated by reference to some set of sacred precedents, symbolic constructs, or transcendent principles. These conditions being met, the slaughter of cattle and subsequent distribution of meat is considered sacrifice; these lacking, it is wanton butchery.

Cattle sacrifice is ideologically the most prestigious and significant ritual performed among pastoral peoples, although in practice offerings of lesser economic value (sheep, goats, milk products, cakes, etc.) are often substituted. In part, as has been discussed above, sacrifice always includes among its significances and functions the consecration of meat and the legitimation of the violence requisite for the procurement of meat. Sacrifice is no more a straightforwardly utilitarian procedure, however, than it is a simple or univocal one. Rather, complex symbolisms and multiple dimensions are always present, however much these may differ from one culture area, historical period, or sacrificial performance to another.

Cattle sacrifice in ancient Babylon, for example, while clearly part of the general "care and feeding of the gods" enjoined upon mankind, was also in part a remembrance or repetition of the cosmogony. For as tablet 5 of the creation account *Enuma elish* makes clear, the deity Tiamat—whose death marks the beginning of the cosmos as we know it—was understood to take the form of a cow, although other passages of the text present her as a monstrous, chaotic being. (A similar account of a being simultaneously monstrous and bovine, which must be put to death in order for a proper cosmos and society to emerge, is the golden calf of *Exodus* 32.) Moreover, the sacrifice of cattle was cast as a divine act, as is clear in the declaration of the Babylonian priest who offers an ox, the skin of which will be made into the covering for a temple drum: "These acts—it is the totality of the gods who have performed them, it is not really I who performed them."

Again, the cattle sacrifice of the Greek *polis* (city-state) was informed by myths of the first sacrifice, particularly that performed by Prometheus, as described by Hesiod, which—as Marcel Detienne and Jean-Pierre Vernant (1980) have demonstrated—served to define the essential human position in the universe as that intermediate to those of beasts and gods. Of particular interest in myth and practice alike is the precise definition of portions allocated to the gods—the victim's bones, wrapped in a single layer of fat—and those reserved for humans—the rest of the meat, wrapped within the animal's stomach. In this, some scholars have seen a reminiscence of archaic hunters' rites, the bones being preserved so that the dead animal might be resurrected. Detienne and Vernant have argued, however, for a different line of interpretation, in which bones are contrasted to meat as the undecaying (or immortal) portion of the victim to the decaying (or mortal) portion. The contrast of meat and bones thus replicates and comments upon the contrast of gods and men; the inclusion of the stomach in the human portion further stresses man's need to eat, which spurs him on to kill.

Social processes also figure prominently in the logic and structure of cattle sacrifice, for the distribution of meat tends to be differential and hierarchic, either in the nature of the portions assigned to individuals or in the order in which portions are presented, or both. A clear case in point is the Roman Feriae Latinae, an annual ceremonial to which all members of the Latin League sent representatives and contributions. The central act was the sacrifice and dismemberment of a white bull, pieces of meat from which were assigned to the representatives according to the relative importance of their cities. Change over time was also reflected in the proceedings of the Feriae Latinae, for as a city grew or shrank in size and stature, its portion of meat seems to have been adjusted accordingly. Other societies also possessed mechanisms whereby social hierarchy could not only be signified within a sacrificial context, but could also be contested, as seen in the accounts of brawls and duels fought over the "champion's portion" among the Greeks and Celts.

Cattle sacrifice was also a highly important part of Indo-Iranian religion, reflecting the prominent position of cattle within the society and economy of India and Iran alike. Certainly, cattle figure almost obsessively in the earliest religious texts from India and Iran (the *Ṛgveda* and the *Gāthās* of the Avesta respectively), although some scholars have maintained that most references to cattle should be taken metaphorically or allegorically, while granting that the stimulus for bovine imagery would still come from the real possession of cattle. Controversy also exists as to whether Zarathushtra (Zoroaster) condemned cattle sacrifice in Iran—as some of the Gathic texts seem to indicate—or if it remained always a part of the Zoroastrian cultus.

The rejection of cattle sacrifice is attested elsewhere in history, particularly in cases where a previously pastoral population has abandoned its earlier mode of production and consequent way of life. Thus, for instance, within the Athenian *polis*, details of the foremost cattle sacrifice—the Bouphonia ("ox-slaying")—reveal a profound uneasiness over the violence and bloodshed inherent in the rite. Toward the end of each Bouphonia, a trial was thus held to assess the guilt of those responsible for the victim's death, such guilt ultimately being assigned to the sacrificial knife with which it was killed, the knife then being punished (and purified) by being thrown into the sea.

However much the ritual slaughter of cattle prompted a certain moral disquietude, the practice continued unabated throughout the history of ancient Greece, insofar as sacrifice was a central mechanism for the periodic renewal of social hierarchy and integration within the *polis.* The criticism of sacrifice implicit in the Bouphonia, however, was given a more articulate and aggressive formulation by certain philosophers and mystics possessed of a radically different vision of what the *polis* ought to be and of the guilt incurred through sacrificial violence. Chief among these were Pythagoras and Empedocles, the latter of whom condemned sacrifice in the following terms, contrasting it with an imagined paradisal sort of offering that took place in the distant past and—given his theories of cyclical time—would once again replace the bloody rituals:

> Ares was not a god for them, nor was Battle-din,
> Nor was Zeus the king, nor Kronos, nor Poseidon,
> But Aphrodite was queen.
> They appeased her with pious gifts:
> With painted animal figurines, with perfumes,
> With sacrifices of unmixed myrrh and fragrant frankincense,
> Pouring libations of golden honey to the ground.
> The altar was not smeared with the unmixed gore of bulls.
> Rather, that was the greatest defilement for men:
> Taking away the life-force in order to eat the noble limbs.

Although these Greek opponents of sacrificial ritual remained always in a minority—often, what is more, a suspect minority—others were more successful in India, where the doctrine of *ahiṃsā,* "noninjury" to all living creatures, gradually displaced older sacrificial ideology, particularly in the wake of Buddhist and Jain challenges to Brahmanic doctrines and practice. Thus, the Sanskrit legal texts—as Ludwig Alsdorf (1962) first demonstrated—show a clear process of development, in which the eating of meat obtained from sacrifices was first freely permitted, but later came to be condemned.

Although the privileged status of the "sacred cow" in India is in some measure related to the emergence of the *ahiṃsā* ethic, its sources are considerably older. For already in the *Ṛgveda* and also in the Avesta, cows are referred to as "beings not to be killed" (Skt., *aghnya;* Av., *agenya*), a correspondence that indicates that this was already an item of Indo-Iranian belief at the beginning of the second millennium BCE. One must stress, however, that it is only cows—that is, female bovines—that are so designated, and not cattle in general, and it appears likely that the symbolic, sentimental, and socioeconomic importance of the cow as the source of both milk and new bovine life led to the formulation of religious principles protecting it against slaughter, even slaughter within the context of sacrifice.

Within modern Hinduism, however, the "sacred cow" has been treated as the foremost example of the more general principle of *ahiṃsā,* as for instance in a celebrated treatise by Mohandas K. Gandhi entitled "How to Serve the Cow." Vast numbers of cattle roam the Indian subcontinent free from any threat to their well-being (urban riots have been provoked by attempts to drive cattle from busy streets or markets), and numerous homes have been founded for the care of old and sick cattle.

Western technocrats, colonial authorities, and others have generally viewed the "sacred cow" of India as a classic example of the ways in which religious principles can lead large populations into modes of habitual behavior and social organization that are irrational and counterproductive in strictly economic terms. Yet this view has been challenged, largely by the research of Marvin Harris, and a lively debate has resulted, which is still to be resolved. For it is Harris's contention that when one considers the full range of ways in which cattle resources are exploited within India (traction, dung for fuel, milk and milk products, etc.) and the ways in which cattle are fed (scavenging, use of stubble from the fields, etc.), as well as other important seasonal and ecological factors, one is forced to conclude that the prohibition on killing cattle is both rational and productive, even in the most narrow economic sense. Debate still rages over many details of Harris's argument, as well as on his general conclusion, but his writings have been a valuable corrective to studies that emphasize the divergence between religious and socioeconomic considerations. Rather than being contradictory, even in the case of the "sacred cow," these matters are intimately correlated, in ways far richer and more complex than is generally understood.

SEE ALSO Bones; Neolithic Religion; Sacrifice.

BIBLIOGRAPHY

On the religious significance of cattle within pastoral cultures, see my *Priests, Warriors, and Cattle: A Study in the Ecology of Religions* (Berkeley, 1981). A good discussion of the domestication of the species is found in Frederick E. Zeuner's *A History of Domesticated Animals* (New York, 1963). Eduard Hahn's theories on the religious origin of domestication were set forth in a number of publications, most important of which was *Die Haustiere und ihre Beziehungen zur Wirtschaft des Menschen* (Leipzig, 1896).

The importance of cattle in the life and religion of the peoples of East Africa has been treated in a number of excellent publications, among which should be noted Melville J. Herskovits's "The Cattle Complex in East Africa," *American Anthropologist* 28 (1926): 230–272, 361–388; E. E. Evans-Pritchard's *Neur Religion* (Oxford, 1956); Godfrey Lienhardt's *Divinity and Experience: The Religion of the Dinka* (Oxford, 1961); Peter Rigby's *Cattle and Kinship among the Gogo* (Ithaca, N.Y., 1969); Pierre Bonte's "Il bestiame produce gli uomini: Sacrificio, valore e feticismo del bestiame nell' Africa orientale," *Studi storici* 25 (1984): 875–896; and J. P. Crazzolara's *Zur Gesellschaft und Religion der Nueer* (Vienna, 1953).

On sacrifice in general, see Walter Burkert's *Homo Necans* (Berkeley, 1983); *La cuisine du sacrifice en pays grec,* edited by Marcel Detienne and Jean-Pierre Vernant (Paris, 1980); and the papers on the theme "Sacrificio, organizzazione del cosmo, dinamica sociale," *Studi storici* 25 (1984): 829–956.

On the use of cattle as metaphor, see Wolfgang E. Schmid's "Die Kuh auf der Weide," *Indogermanische Forschungen* 64 (1958–1959): 1–12; George G. Cameron's "Zoroaster the Herdsman," *Indo-Iranian Journal* 10 (1968): 261–281; and Boris Oguibenine's "Le symbolisme de la razzia d'après les hymnes vediques," *Études indo-européennes* (1984): 1–17.

On cattle raiding, see Peter Walcot's "Cattle Raiding, Heroic Tradition, and Ritual: The Greek Evidence," *History of Religions* 18 (May 1979): 326–351; Françoise Bader's "Rhapsodies homériques et irlandaises," in *Recherches sur les religions de l'antiquité classique*, edited by Raymond Bloch (Paris, 1980); and Doris Srinivasan's *The Concept of Cow in the Rigveda* (Delhi, 1979).

On *ahiṃsā* in India, see Ludwig Alsdorf's *Beiträge zur Geschichte von Vegetarismus und Rinderverehrung in Indien* (Wiesbaden, 1962). The debate on the sacred cow has taken place largely in the pages of *Current Anthropology* (Chicago) from 1966 on. Marvin Harris's arguments are conveniently summarized in *Cows, Pigs, Wars and Witches* (New York, 1974). On the Indian homes for indigent cattle, see Deryck O. Lodrick's *Sacred Cows, Sacred Places* (Berkeley, 1981).

New Sources

Peires, J. B. *The Dead Will Arise: Nongqawuse and the Great Xhosa Cattle-Killing Movement of 1856–7.* Bloomington, 1989.

Bruce Lincoln (1987)
Revised Bibliography

CAUSATION

See FREE WILL AND DETERMINISM; OCCASIONALISM

CAVES.

In all cultures and in almost all epochs the cave has been the symbol of creation, the place of emergence of celestial bodies, of ethnic groups and individuals. It is the great womb of earth and sky, a symbol of life, but also of death. It is a sacred place that constitutes a break in the homogeneity of space, an opening that is a passage from one cosmic region to another, from heaven to earth or, vice versa, from earth to the underworld (Eliade, 1959, p. 37).

All caves are sacred. Some, like cosmic mountains or important sanctuaries, are considered the center of the universe. Where the sacred manifests itself, the world comes into existence (Eliade, 1959, p. 63). Every religious person places himself at the center of the world, "as close as possible to the opening that ensures him communication with the gods" (ibid., p. 65). Earth gods live in caves, which are often called "the earth's navel." As the world center, the *axis mundi*, the cave at times blends in religious symbolism with the mountain. Of the elements in Asian geomancy that determine the quality of a place for a settlement, a home, or a tomb, mountains are considered the most important. Their vital energy gives them the name of "dragon." This magical energy flows into a cave, which is not always a real opening but represents an auspicious site. Geomantic caves are those surrounded by mountains, where wind is stored and where water, which maintains the spiritual energy, is close by. The mountains are believed to have been created in order to form geomantic caves (Yoon, 1976, pp. 28–34). This mountain-cave-water-energy tradition is similar to the ancient Mexican belief that water was contained within mountains, the womb of the water goddess Chalchiuhtlicue, whence it flowed in the form of the rivers and lakes necessary to human settlement.

The Cave as *Axis Mundi*. The cave as a sacred spot that marks the place for a major religious structure and even for a great city, the *axis mundi* of its time, is well illustrated at Teotihuacán, Mexico. The most impressive monument here (built c. 100 BCE, destroyed c. 750 CE) is the Pyramid of the Sun, built shortly before the beginning of the common era over a primitive shrine, which was itself built over a subterranean cave. The cave has the form of a four-petaled flower, one of Teotihuacán's most popular art motifs, possibly symbolizing the four world quarters. The great Sun Pyramid was constructed in such a way that the four-petaled cave lies almost directly beneath its center. Although the cave was ransacked in ancient times, the few remains within suggest that it may have been a cult center for water gods. Or, inasmuch as a sixteenth-century document labels the place in front of the pyramid "Moctezuma's oracle," an oracle may well have dwelt here. Whatever the answer, the sacredness of this cave was such that it had to be preserved by building a shrine over it, then by constructing the immense pyramid over this. Sacred space was thus preserved for all time.

Birth and Creation. Because of its volcanic formation, Mesoamerica is honeycombed with caves. Each is revered, and many are associated with the emergence myth. Chicomoztoc ("seven caves") was the place of creation of many ethnic groups, particularly the Aztec. Its seven caves are represented in ancient pictorial manuscripts and in oral tradition. But before the creation of people, the sun and the moon were made in a grotto. In the myth of the creation of the Fifth Sun (the name given the present era by the Aztec), some chronicles state that after one god threw himself into a fire and became transformed into the sun, another god went into a cave and came out of it as the moon. In a legend of Española (Hispaniola), all men were created in one cave, all women in another (Fray Ramon Pané, in Heyden, 1975). Sustenance, also, originated in caves, according to popular belief. Some caves were called *cincalco*, "house of maize"; in them corn was kept by the gods. A sixteenth-century Mexican chronicle, *Historia de México*, relates that Centeotl, a maize god, was born in a cavern; from different parts of his body cotton and many edible plants grew. According to another early chronicler, Fray Geronimo de Mendieta, a flint knife fell from heaven and landed in Chicomoztoc, where it broke into sixteen hundred pieces, from which that number of gods was created. The cave, then, is a symbol of the womb. According to Fray Bernardino de Sahagún's *Historia general de las cosas de la Nueva España* (the so-called Florentine Codex), a saying is ascribed to Aztec women of the sixteenth century: "Within us is a cave, a gorge . . . whose only function is to receive."

The Emergence Place. The cave as the center of the world and place of emergence is found in many traditions. Hopi mythology tells of three worlds under the earth where the Hopi lived with the Ant People before they found their way up to the fourth, or present, world. The Zuni, with the same traditions, call the place of emergence *hepatina* ("the middle place") and the last world (which they classify as still underground) the "fourth womb." The modern kiva of these and other Pueblo Indian groups is an artificial cave, the ceremonial center of the village, in which there is also a small hole in the ground, symbolic of the place of emergence. Kiva ritual follows a man from life to death. As soon as he is born a boy is symbolically initiated into the ritual life and pledged to his father's kiva. Zuni society has six divisions, associated with the four world directions, the zenith, and the nadir. Each division has its own kiva, around which religion revolves (Leighton and Adair, 1966). The kiva evidently has been basic to ritual for many centuries. During the Pueblo Classic period (1050–1300) the underground kivas were of tremendous size, as can be seen in the ruins of Mesa Verde and Chaco Canyon. They were caves within caves, partially natural grottoes and partially hacked out of the rocks. A maze design carved on rocks in Arizona—much like the Minoan maze—represents the myth of emergence. It is the Mother Earth symbol, according to the modern Hopi; the maze represents the paths a person will follow on the road of life (Campbell Grant, 1967, p. 65).

Cave Gods and Rites. Since the rites and deities of different parts of the world, many of them associated with caves, are dealt with in numerous articles of this encyclopedia, this brief section is focused on Mesoamerica, which, in general, is less well known than Europe or the Orient.

Tlaloc, the Aztec rain and earth deity, was also called Path under the Earth, or Long Cave, according to the sixteenth-century chronicler Fray Diego Durán. This name refers to the god's character as fertilizer of the earth with gentle rain, and also to rites in caves where water deities were propitiated. Rain, lightning, and thunder were thought to be controlled in caves and on mountain tops. Toribio Motolinía, another colonial chronicler, describes ceremonies to Tlaloc each year during which four children were sacrificed and their bodies placed in a cave; this was then sealed until the following year, when the rite was repeated. Children were considered special messengers to the water gods.

Oztoteotl literally means "god of caves"; this was the name of a god venerated in a sacred cave at Chalma, a site about two days' march from Mexico City that was the scene of important pilgrimages. Oztoteotl has been supplanted by the Christian Lord of Chalma (a representation of Christ), who is no less venerated, both in the cave and in a church erected here. One rite in Chalma is the leaving of umbilical cords in two caves, one at the top of the hill, one at the bottom, in order to ensure the infants of good fortune in life.

Vegetation gods frequently had rites performed in their honor in caves. For example, the skins of flayed victims (symbolizing corn husks or those of other plants) were stored in an artificial cave at the foot of the Yopico pyramid in Tenochtitlán, the Aztec capital, and bodies of young women sacrificed to Xochiquetzal, the vegetation goddess, were placed in a cave called a "mist house." These instances may constitute a ritual metaphor for seed germination, which takes place in a dark area, comparable to the cave-womb.

Regarding ceremonies, the fabulous grotto of Balankanché, immediately southeast of the ancient Maya city of Chichén Itzá in Yucatán, has revealed a wealth of offerings to the rain god Tlaloc (Chac, among the Maya) and chamber after chamber of ceremonial settings for rites. These date mainly from the ninth century CE, when highland Mexican influence was strong (hence the presence of the god Tlaloc rather than Chac), although the grotto was used for ritual purposes mainly by the Maya, through 3,000 years. Six offertory foci are directly associated with either underground pools or stalagmitic formations, caused by the action of the water (Andrews, 1970, p. 9). These natural formations have the appearance of altars and were used as such. In the major chamber, floor and ceiling are united by a stalactite-stalagmite "tree" that suggests the ceiba (silk-cotton), the sacred Maya tree that unites earth, sky, and underworld. This structure is called by the modern—and undoubtedly by the ancient—Maya the "throne of the *balam,*" that is, of the Jaguar Priest. When the inner chambers were discovered in 1959, this altar-throne was found to be covered with effigy censers, most of them in the form of Tlaloc, some wearing flayed skins and some suggestive of the Aztec vegetation deity Xipe Totec. Other offerings here and in various chambers include miniature vessels, grinding stones, and spindle whorls, perhaps symbolic offerings for use in the otherworld. Enigmatic handprints in red ocher (as suggested below, perhaps evidence of a rite of passage) are on the central, treelike column and on the ceiling of low tunnels. Other chambers with stalagmitic altars yielded many more Tlaloc effigy censers, quantities of shells, jade beads, fragments of a wooden drum, and charcoal from burnt offerings. Numerous fire pits and the charcoal in the censers seem to be evidence of both illumination and ritual hearth use. Inasmuch as smoke was one of the messengers to the gods, the fires may have been intended solely for communication. That this was a major ritual center is indicated by the insistence of the *H-men* (the practitioner of native folk religion) from a village near Balankanché that, because of the cave's sacred nature, when the sealed chambers were discovered, it was necessary to propitiate the deities within in order to ward off supernatural retribution for the profanation. Rites were held involving the ritual drinking of honey-based *balché,* the sacrifice of chickens, and, among other things, the imitation of frogs by two small boys: the entrance to the cave home of the rain god was traditionally guarded by a frog (Andrews, 1970, pp. 70–164).

This type of ceremony is not unique to the cenotes of Yucatán. Marion Oettinger (in a personal communication) records a cave rite in the state of Guerrero dedicated to the water god; in it, stalactites and stalagmites are revered as deities. Corn is believed to come from hollows on the cave floor made by dripping water. Rites dedicated to supernatural beings who control water and vegetation are still held within the cave.

RITES OF PASSAGE. Since Paleolithic times caves have been preferred places for many rites of passage. Symbols of passage into another world, of a descent to the underworld, they are the scene of initiation rites for shamans—among the Australian medicine men, among the Araucanian of Chile, among the Inuit (Eskimo), and among peoples of North America, to mention but a few (Eliade, 1964, p. 51). The *iruntarinia* ("spirits") of central Australia create a medicine man when an Aranda (Arunta) candidate goes to sleep at the mouth of a cave; he is dragged into it by one of the spirits and dismembered, and his internal organs are exchanged for others. For example, a fragment of rock crystal, important to shamanic power (a detail reported in Oceania and the Americas also), is placed in his body, which is then returned to his village (Eliade, 1964, pp. 46, 139). Eliade tells also of the initiatory dream-journey of a Nenets (Yurak Samoyed) in his transition from candidate to shaman. In one important episode, the initiate was led into a cave covered with mirrors; there he received a hair from each of two women, mothers of reindeer, with which to shamanize for the animal (p. 41).

In British Columbia, as each Salish adolescent concluded a puberty rite, he or she imprinted a red hand on a cave wall. Furthermore, these and other images painted in red on rock walls recorded remarkable dreams. A spirit quest by a Salish boy led him into the hills, usually to a cave, where, through praying and fasting, he would dream of a supernatural being who would be his guardian in later life (Grant, 1967, p. 29). Among the Dogon in Africa, circumcision rites are recorded by ritual signs and paintings on the rocks; these are also related to ceremonies for the renewal of the cosmos every sixty years. In Mexico's Malinalco rock temple, carved altarlike felines and eagles stand against the walls; the military orders of the Jaguar and the Eagle must have held ceremonies here, such as the initiation of new members into their select ranks.

A rite of passage from illness to health is performed at the grotto at Lourdes, France. The healing waters of Lourdes's spring and the story of the apparition of the Virgin Mary to Bernadette have made this an important pilgrimage center since 1858.

In Mexico, until early this century, a boy child born in the vicinity of the Teotihuacán pyramids was placed in a cave. An animal, it was said, came out from the dark interior and licked his face; if the baby did not cry, he automatically acquired the right to be a *granicero. Graniceros* perform curing ceremonies and control rain from within caves. Thus the child experienced two rites of passage, a kind of baptism and initiation into this special group. In a part of Chiapas, as soon as a child moves within his mother's womb, he is said to possess a spirit, and this dwells in caves (Esther Hermitte, cited by Heyden, 1976). At times a cave steals this spirit or that of an adult, whereupon a *curandero,* a healer, must perform a rite in the cave. In one case he captures the lost spirit in a piece of the spirit-owner's clothing and manages to pull it out of the cave (Guido Münch, personal communication, referring to Oaxaca). In these cases of soul loss and recuperation, the rite of passage is a hazardous one between life and death. People also become ill from cave "winds," and *graniceros* can cure them by making offerings to the owners of the caves. A rite associated with these ceremonies is that of dying and resuscitating; the usual way to become a *granicero* is to be struck by lightning, be pronounced dead, and then come to life again. In some regions the healer must "die" twice a year; then his spirit goes to a special cave, where he receives instructions (William Madsen, cited by Heyden, 1976). Exorcism is yet another rite practiced in caves, frequently by saying a mass in the interior, in the presence of the affected person.

RELIGIOUS CAVE ART. Paintings on the walls of ancient caves, or sculptures hewn out of rock within caverns, have been called "invisible art" and likened to "silent music" (Carpenter, 1978, pp. 90–99). That is, such art was created for the initiated few and did not need to be public. Esoteric it is, and it has generally been conceived to possess sympathetic magic. For example, depicting a speared deer would ensure success in the hunt. Undoubtedly this is one meaning, but it is not the only one. Some cave images may be a way of keeping a record of rites. They may also relate to the animal double that each person possesses. Among the North American Indians, a young man, as part of a spirit quest, often gave thanks to his spirit guardian by painting or carving figures on cliff walls or in dark caves. These were addressed to his spirit guardian and were not meant to be seen by living humans; exposure would diminish their powers. Carpenter suggests that many anthropomorphic figures, depicted at times in coitus, in caves or in earth sculpture on mountaintops or desert floors, probably represent the original tribal ancestors and, by extension, the beginning of the world.

European cave paintings dating from the Upper Paleolithic period (c. 35,000–19,000 years ago), among them those at Altamira in Spain and at Lascaux, Cap Blanc, Les Trois Frères, Cougnac, and Rouffignac in France, portray mainly animals. Although Henri Breuil had interpreted these as belonging to hunting-gathering magic, recent studies propose that such art is part of Paleolithic cosmology. Leroi-Gourhan (1965) sees this worldview as based on a male-female division, with sections of the caves, as well as the animals and symbols, divided according to gender. Alexander Marshack interprets certain forms in cave art as calendrical and incisions on bones and antlers as notational; he also claims that some representations have seasonal and ecological significance, symbolized, for example, by flora and fauna typical of certain seasons and regions (cited by Conkey, 1981, p. 23). Ritual art, then, is often a key to the daily life and economy of a people, as well as to their religion.

At El Castillo in Cantabrian Spain, about fifty negative handprints were painted on a wall by blowing red ocher around a hand held there. Although this symbol has not been clearly interpreted by students of the period, it is reminiscent of red handprints on walls in the Maya region of Mexico, prints that according to popular tradition were placed there by slaves who were to be sacrificed. This interpretation may be fantasy, however, for in Pueblo belief (where Mexican influence is often found) the handprint is a "signature" that attracts supernatural blessings or marks the completion of a rite. Some animal representations, evidently men dressed in skins and antlers, have been thought to depict sorcerers. Clusters of bison on the ceiling at Altamira could symbolize different human groups that went to the cave for various reasons and rites. Thus the cave could have been a seasonal aggregation site for people who were dispersed throughout the region (Conkey, 1981, p. 24). Could Altamira have been an early Magdalenian pilgrimage center?

René Huyghe, in discussing Paleolithic cave art, points out that the facsimile is effective in the beliefs of the people who create these magic images. He further explores the function of the facsimile, citing paintings on the walls of Egyptian tombs, where representations of foodstuffs and furniture sometimes substituted for the actual articles needed for life after death. Huyghe has stated that the accomplished technique with which the cave paintings were executed indicates probable teaching by sorcerer-priests (1962, pp. 16, 18). With the transition to the Mesolithic and Neolithic periods, cave art became more realistic and depicted human beings in communal activities. Paintings of this sort are found at the entrance to caves, accessible to the larger group, instead of in dark interiors, where formerly esoteric rites must have been held. This different religio-social art is characteristic of the Iberian coast facing Africa, and its tradition has continued to the present time among the African San. The paintings convey great action, expressed by few, almost abstract lines (running warriors at Teruel, for example), side by side with incipient architecture (the menhir, probably intended as a receptacle for the soul of the deceased). Both reflect more settled activities of Neolithic peoples: flock keeping and agriculture, which spurred new ideas and customs (Huyghe, 1962, pp. 21–24).

America holds a wealth of cave and rock art, from Alaska to South America. Most of it dates from about 1000 CE to the late 1800s. Its subjects are animals, humans, supernatural beings, and abstract designs. Although some scenes are historical or narrative (depicting Spanish horsemen, for example), much of this art is religious. Hunting magic is represented by a heart line drawn within an animal and sometimes pierced by an arrow. The mythical Thunderbird, thought to control thunderstorms but also a clan symbol and sacred ancestor guardian among the Hopi, is often represented. The plumed serpent, known as the god Quetzalcoatl in Mexico, was the guardian of springs and streams in the Southwest, and is seen on kiva wall paintings or in rock carvings. In the San Francisco Mountains of Baja California a sixteen-foot-long plumed serpent is the object of a ceremony involving red and black men and deer. However, Uriarte sees this great figure as a serpent-deer, joining the natural forces of both creatures (1981, p. 151). The men surrounding it wear serpent-deer headdresses and therefore must be members of a cult group. Uriarte suggests also that the two-in-one animal may represent a male-female creation myth. Hundreds of handprints found in Arizona, Utah, and northern California must have had ceremonial significance. The Chumash of California painted supernatural figures, believed to be related to dreams and visions, in remote mountainous areas. A ceremonial liquor used by the Chumash and other groups was made of the hallucinogenic jimsonweed, which could have spurred such ritual art. Rock paintings by the Navajo marked sacred places where mythological events occurred; these paintings often depicted the *yei,* equivalent to the Pueblo kachina, a divine creature usually associated with maize agriculture. Campbell Grant (1967) suggests an important reason for some of the rock art symbols: they were mnemonic devices for rites, and records of certain events. Among present-day Ojibwa, tobacco, prayer sticks, and cloth are placed on rocks below paintings as offerings to the supernatural beings depicted there. The Ojibwa believe that a shaman can enter the rock and trade tobacco with the spirit there for special medicine (Grant, 1967, pp. 32, 147).

In central Baja California, Uriarte (1981) records 72 caves painted with 488 figures or sets of figures, many with the bodies adorned in body paint of various colors. Similar colors are also typical of cave paintings in northwestern Australia. Among the Kulin there, Bunjil was the supreme mythological being, who with all his people turned into stars and whose son was the rainbow. Bunjil's favorite place was Angel Cave; he created it when he spoke to rocks, which then opened up (Aldo Massola, 1968, pp. 59, 106).

Artificial Caves. Some of the world's most renowned painted caves are in India. At Ajantā the Gupta style of the fifth and sixth centuries was the peak of a golden age, although the caves themselves existed by the second century BCE, and painting continued through the eighth century CE. Portrayed on the walls are scenes from the lives of Gautama Buddha, the *bodhisattvas,* and other divine beings conceived in the manner of the palace life of the time. The jātaka tales painted here illustrate the Buddha's previous earthly experiences. That some of the people are engaged in religious conversation is apparent from the occasional *mudrās* (hand positions). But perhaps the most extraordinary thing about these caves, as well as at Ellora and elsewhere, is that they were carved out of sandstone rock. Entire mountains were turned into sanctuaries by devoted and anonymous sculptor-architects to be used as monastic retreats. The thirty Ajantā caves, excavated in the semicircular face of a mountain in the Deccan region near Aurangabad, are either *caityas* (chapels) or *vihāras* (monasteries). The *caityas* consist of an apse, side aisles, and a central nave in the center of which is a stupa, all hewn out of living rock. In the *vihāras* there are a congregation hall and monks' cells. In the early caves, the Buddha was represented not in his bodily form but with symbols, such as the bodhi tree or a set of footprints. Sculpture in relief and in the round later filled the caves and covered the doorways with large figures of the Buddha and the *bodhisattvas* as well as an exuberance of elephants, buffalo, men and women in different positions, lotus medallions, and other floral motifs. The happy marriage at Ajantā of architecture, painting, and sculpture produced an insuperable monument to the Buddhist faith.

Also hewn out of a mountain (sometime between the fourth and ninth centuries CE), the caves at Ellora are a miracle of carving. Unlike the Buddhist caves at Ajantā, these are dedicated to three faiths: the early caves, before 800, are Buddhist; the Hindu caves overlap (600–900), and the Jain caves cover the period from 800 to 1000. At Ellora the great Hindu Kailash temple dedicated to Śiva represents Mount Kailash, where the gods dwell. In the early Buddhist caves, the vast number of Buddhas, *bodhisattvas*, and *śaktis* express the Vajrayāna philosophy, wherein Buddhahood was obtained through self-discipline and meditation. The Hindu caves are dedicated to Śiva, who is worshiped symbolically in the phallic symbol called the lingam, found always in the shrine. Sculptures of Śiva also represent him in many of his manifestations, as the personification of death and time, as Creator, Destroyer, Divine Lover, and Lord of the Dance. Śiva's wife Pārvatī, goddess of love and beauty, accompanies him, as does his son Gaṇeśa, the elephant-headed god of wisdom. Śiva is sometimes represented in his half-male, half-female form. Brahmā and Viṣṇu are also portrayed in various forms. The composition of Ajantā paintings is at times reminiscent of the *maṇḍala* (or cosmic diagram), while Jain sculpture at Ellora borrowed freely from Hinduism and depicts Hindu deities.

Undoubtedly the most spectacular of the many caves carved out of solid rock in China is the complex known as Longmen Grottoes at Luoyang, in Honan Province. Begun in the fifth century CE, the grottoes continued to be carved over a period of four hundred years. Twenty-one hundred caves and niches and more than forty pagodas house more than one hundred thousand sculptures, the largest 17.4 meters, the smallest only 12 centimeters high. Statues in these grottoes mainly portray the Buddha. Also represented are attendant figures, warriors, the Buddha's disciples, *bodhisattvas*, and a giant lotus—symbol of divine birth, purity, creative force, and Buddha's footsteps—on a ceiling. The walls of one cave, that of the Ten Thousand Buddhas, are covered with a myriad of tiny relief-carved figures of the divinity, which envelop the viewer with an awesome sense of the sacred.

ROCK TEMPLES AND TOMBS. The hypogea, rock-cut tombs of Egypt, attest to the use of natural materials available for building. Stone, abundant in Egypt, was used for the great monuments. From the Middle Kingdom on, tombs were hollowed out of cliffs alongside the Nile for high officials of Upper Egypt. By the time of New Kingdom, the Valley of the Kings, on the Nile's west side facing Luxor, had become the necropolis of pharaohs, who lay in rock-cut tombs on both sides of the valley. The funerary temple of Queen Hatshepsut at Deir al-Bahri was carved out of the mountain on different levels. Under Ramses II, in the nineteenth dynasty, the spectacular rock temple at Abu Simbel was hewn out of a mountain in Upper Egypt.

In Persia, royal rock tombs at Naksh-i-Rustam, near Persepolis, date from the sixth to the fourth centuries BCE. Here the king is represented before a fire altar, above which is the god Ahura Mazdā, whose face is surrounded by a circle, symbol of eternity. At Petra, in modern Jordan, the Nabateans more than two thousand years ago carved their capital city out of rock. Along with temples and civil buildings, some of these artificial caves are tombs for the kings.

In Mexico, shaft tombs—the shaft hollowed out of the earth, ending in a side chamber for the cadaver—were definitely cave representations, the deceased returning to the earth that gave him life. The *temazcal,* the purifying sweat bath, used for millennia in this region, was "the house of flowers" in pre-Columbian times, the flower symbolizing both the womb and the cave.

An outstanding example of funerary caves, albeit in this case artificial, is that of Rome's catacombs. These were Christian cemeteries begun in the first century CE. They were twice confiscated, during the third century and at the beginning of the fourth; after a bloody persecution by Diocletian, peace was finally granted by Constantine in 313. From then on, catacomb excavations were enlarged and embellished with paintings and inscriptions referring to Christian martyrs; they became the goal of pilgrims.

In the sub-Saharan region of Mali, the Tellem people, who flourished from the eleventh to the sixteenth centuries, buried their dead, accompanied by grave furniture and clothing for the otherworld, in special caves. Objects were ritually destroyed, as they are in other parts of the world, in order to release the spirit. One cave contained three thousand skeletons. Among the offerings left in these high cliff caves were skeletal remains of a crowned crane and of a turtle, both figures in the mythology of the Dogon, who came to the region after the Tellem (Bedaux, 1982, pp. 28–34).

In the lowland Maya region of Mexico and Central America, the limestone floor is honeycombed with cenotes. Perhaps because these are the main sources of water in the largely riverless Yucatán Peninsula, they were highly venerated as sacred sites; one of their functions was that of funeral chamber. The great cenote at Chichén Itzá is well known, as are tales of fair maidens thrown into the water at this cave-well. It actually was a place of sacrifice to aquatic deities, but adolescents of both sexes were the victims. A sixteenth-century account by Fray Diego de Landa tells of young boys whose hearts were extracted before their bodies were deposited in the cenote; propitiation of water gods by child sacrifice was a common rite. The victims were accompanied by incense balls, gold jewels, and the even more highly prized jade, symbol of water and of all that is precious. These sacrificial rites were related to maize agriculture, but also had divinatory and prophetic purposes. Before the rainy season, or during times of drought, child sacrifices increased. Some accounts relate that the victims were lowered alive into the cave-well so that they could communicate with the god, then left to drown. A procession went from the main temple to a shrine next to the cenote; there the priests instructed the victim as to the message to be given to the gods; then they consummated the sacrifice. The walls of Guatemala's spectacular Naj Tunich cavern are covered with eighth-century paintings of the ritual ball-game (with celestial and life-death significance), ritual bloodletting, dwarfs (associated with both heavens and the underworld), shells (symbols of birth and of death), and long columns of hieroglyphs, mainly calendrical. George Stuart (1981, pp. 220–235) points out that the Classic Maya considered the numbers and days in their calendar as a procession of gods who marched along an eternal and endless trail. The Maya believed that caves, like the roots of the sacred ceiba tree that held earth and sky together, reached far down into the underworld. Caves were the entrance to this place, called Xibalba, where underworld gods dwelt. Stuart suggests that the great cavern of Naj Tunich was the embodiment of Xibalba, place of death.

SEE ALSO Labyrinth; Mountains; Neolithic Religion; Paleolithic Religion.

BIBLIOGRAPHY

Andrews, Edward Wyllys. *Balankanché, Throne of the Tiger Priest.* New Orleans, 1970.

Bedaux, Rogier M. A. "Rediscovering the Tellem of Mali." *Archaeology* 35 (1982): 28–34.

Carpenter, Edmund. "Silent Music and Invisible Art." *Natural History* 87 (1978): 90–99.

Conkey, Margaret W. "A Century of Palaeolithic Cave Art." *Archaeology* 34 (1981): 20–28.

Eliade, Mircea. *The Sacred and the Profane.* New York, 1959.

Eliade, Mircea. *Shamanism: Archaic Techniques of Ecstasy.* Rev. & enl. ed. New York, 1964.

Grant, Campbell. *Rock Art of the American Indian.* New York, 1967.

Heyden, Doris. "An Interpretation of the Cave underneath the Pyramid of the Sun in Teotihuacán, Mexico." *American Antiquity* 40 (1975): 131–147.

Heyden, Doris. "Los ritos de paso en las cuevas." *Boletín Instituto Nacional de Antropologia e Historia* (Mexico City) 2 (1976): 17–26.

Huyghe, René. "Prehistoric Art: Art Forms and Society" and "Primitive Art: Art Forms and Society." In *Larousse Encyclopedia of Prehistoric and Ancient Art,* edited by René Huyghe, pp. 16–25, 72–77. London, 1962.

Leighton, Dorothea C., and John Adair. *People of the Middle Place: A Study of the Zuni Indians.* New Haven, 1966.

Leroi-Gourhan, André. *Treasures of Prehistoric Art.* New York, 1965.

Massola, Aldo. *Bunjil's Cave: Myths, Legends and Superstitions of the Aborigines of South-East Australia.* Melbourne, 1968.

Stuart, George E. "Maya Art Treasures Discovered in Cave." *National Geographic* 160 (1981): 220–235.

Uriarte, Maria Teresa. *Pintura Rupestre en Baja California.* "Colección Científica," no. 106. Mexico City, 1981.

Yoon, Hong-key. *Geomantic Relationships between Culture and Nature in Korea.* Taipei, 1976.

New Sources

Berkson, Carmel. *Elephante, the Cave of Shiva.* Princeton, N.J., 1983.

Bonor, Juan Luis. *Las cuevas mayas: simbolismo y ritual.* Madrid, 1989.

Loubser, J. H. N. *A Guide to the Rock Paintings of Tandjesberg.* Bloemfontein, Republic of South Africa, 1993.

Rutkowski, Bogdan, and Krzysztof Nowicki. *The Psychro Cave, and Other Sacred Grottoes in Crete.* Warsaw, 1996.

Whitehouse, Ruth. *Underground Religion: Cult and Culture in Prehistoric Italy.* London, 1992.

DORIS HEYDEN (1987)
Revised Bibliography

CAYCE, EDGAR. Edgar Cayce (1877–1945) was an American spiritual healer and teacher. Celebrated for trance readings, diagnosing illnesses, and for prescribing unorthodox but reputedly effective treatments, Cayce (pronounced "Casey") was a seminal figure for the mid- to late twentieth-century revival of interest in psychic phenomena and the New Age movement. In addition to Cayce's healing work, the New Age movement was inspired particularly by trance teachings offered by the "sleeping prophet," as Cayce was called. These included "life readings," interpreting the lives of individuals in light of previous incarnations, and discourses involving future history and "earth changes." Cayce was relatively little known until the appearance late in his life of a best-selling biography by Thomas Sugrue, *There Is a River* (1942); Cayce's life and work thereafter became the subject of many publications.

Cayce was born in Hopkinsville, Kentucky, in modest circumstances, the son of a farmer and sometime small shopkeeper. Edgar Cayce's formal education did not extend beyond grammar school. He and his family were faithful members of the (Campbellite) Christian Church. Deeply religious, Edgar read the Bible regularly and taught Sunday school for many years. He married Gertrude Evans in 1903 and was the father of three sons: Hugh Lynn, Milton Porter (who died in infancy), and Edgar Evans. As a young adult, Cayce was employed as a salesman in a bookstore and in other enterprises. After moving to Bowling Green, Kentucky, in 1903, he worked as a photographer. He lived in Alabama, chiefly in Selma, from 1909 to 1923, then moved to Dayton, Ohio, and finally in 1925 to Virginia Beach, Virginia, where he spent the remainder of his life engaged in his psychic work.

The trances began around 1901, when Cayce was hypnotized in Hopkinsville by Al C. Layne, an osteopath and amateur hypnotist, in connection with treatment for a throat disorder. Reportedly, the entranced patient diagnosed his own condition and prescribed an effective cure by suggestion. As news of this occurrence spread, Cayce was persuaded by Layne to work with him in treating other patients in a similar way. Layne would put Cayce into a hypnotic state, during which the latter would characteristically say, "We have the body," and proceed to describe the ailment in specific anatomical terms. The healing methods he recommended varied greatly from individual to individual and included unique combinations of osteopathy, chiropractic, electrotherapy, vibrations, massage, foods and diets, and herbal treatments. Experience showed that the work was equally effective whether the patient was in the same room with Cayce, in an adjoining room, or miles away. For some years, however, Cayce's trance readings were only occasional. During his years in Alabama, he also attempted to use his psychic powers to find oil in Texas, but without success.

In 1923 Cayce met Arthur Lammers of Dayton, Ohio, a prosperous printer and student of theosophy. Deeply impressed by his conversations with Lammers, Cayce moved to Dayton, and soon afterwards his readings began to include references to reincarnation, Atlantis, Gnostic Christianity, and other features of the theosophical and occult worldview. He began to give "life readings," relating physical and other problems of clients to their past lives.

In 1925, following what he believed were psychic leadings, Cayce moved to Virginia Beach where, with the support of wealthy backers, he was able to devote himself exclusively to his spiritual calling and to establish complementary works. Chief among his supporters was Morton Harry Blumenthal, a young Jewish stockbroker from New York. They founded a Cayce Hospital in 1928 and Atlantic University in 1930, but both failed during the Great Depression. On the other hand, the Association for Research and Enlightenment (ARE), a membership organization incorporated in 1932, has remained a major pillar of Cayce's work and legacy. It provided for continuing stenographic recordings of Cayce's readings (begun in 1923), for the dissemination of a newsletter and other literature, and, in time, for the establishment of Cayce study groups around the nation and the world. Some fifteen thousand transcripts of readings are kept in the ARE library in Virginia Beach, a collection available to researchers and unique in the annals of mediumship. A study by Edgar Cayce's sons based on this material, *The Outer Limits of Edgar Cayce's Power* (1971), presents a remarkably candid assessment of their father's successes and failures.

Edgar Cayce's older son, Hugh Lynn Cayce (1907–1982), a gifted organizer, did much to develop the ARE, heading it in the postwar years following his father's death. It was largely through Hugh Lynn's books, lectures, and energetic promotional activities that Cayce and the ARE acquired a central position in the new spiritual consciousness of the 1960s and the New Age movement. The association regained control of the hospital building in 1956 and converted it into office spaces for the ARE. Atlantic University was reopened in 1985 as a distance learning institution, offering courses and degree programs in New Age topics. By 2004 the extensive headquarters campus of the movement in Virginia Beach included a library, a bookstore, a conference center, alternative healing facilities, and a day spa. Hugh Lynn Cayce was succeeded in the leadership of the movement by his son, Charles Cayce (b. 1942).

Edgar Cayce is a figure unique in American spirituality. He represents a link between the biblical and folk Christianity of the middle South out of which he came and which was always a part of his world, and the theosophical ideas he also espoused. Reincarnation and other such concepts seemed much less alien to many Americans when expressed by a seer of Cayce's background and earthy character. Cayce also was a living link between the Spiritualism of the nineteenth century, with its trance mediumship, and the New Age era of the late twentieth century. Because of him, ideas from all these quarters came together to form the groundwork of a distinctive American esotericism.

See Also Association for Research and Enlightenment.

BIBLIOGRAPHY

Bro, Harmon Hartzell. *A Seer out of Season: The Life of Edgar Cayce.* New York, 1989.

Cayce, Charles Thomas, and Jeanette M. Thomas, eds. *The Works of Edgar Cayce as Seen through His Letters.* Virginia Beach, Va., 2000.

Cayce, Edgar. *My Life As a Seer: The Lost Memoirs.* Compiled and edited by A. Robert Smith. New York, 1971.

Cayce, Edgar Evans, and Hugh Lynn Cayce. *The Outer Limits of Edgar Cayce's Power.* New York, 1971.

Cayce, Hugh Lynn. *Venture Inward.* New York, 1964.

Cayce, Hugh Lynn, ed. *The Edgar Cayce Reader.* New York, 1969.

Johnson, K. Paul. *Edgar Cayce in Context: The Readings, Truth and Fiction.* Albany, N.Y., 1998.

Kirkpatrick, Sidney D. *Edgar Cayce: An American Prophet.* New York, 2000.

Sugrue, Thomas. *There Is a River: The Story of Edgar Cayce.* New York, 1942; rev. ed., 1945.

Robert S. Ellwood (2005)

CELIBACY, the deliberate abstinence from sexual activity, derives its religious value from the vital human significance of sex itself. The different roles played by celibacy in the world's religions then reflect different attitudes toward procreation and earthly existence. Thus, traditions oriented toward fecundity and wordly success, like those of most nonliterate peoples, rarely if ever enjoin permanent celibacy for anyone; only periods of temporary celibacy preceding and following childbirth and at crucial communal rituals are prescribed. The great traditions of Hinduism, Buddhism, and Christianity, on the other hand, all oriented toward otherwordly goals, have firmly established roles for celibate monks working out their salvation. And smaller, extreme groups with radically negative views of life in the world may prescribe celibacy as an ideal for all. The reasons offered for celibacy consequently range from concerns for personal physical health to a total rejection of the physical body. Religious institutions, moreover, differ both in the ways of life that they prescribe for the celibate and in the image of the celibate that they present to laypersons.

Traditional Perceptions. The placement of deliberate religious restraints on physical behavior, celibacy is often explained within tradition through physiological as well as metaphysical concepts. Asian esoteric texts, moreover, can be most explicit about the spiritual potentials of reproductive energies. Traditional understandings of celibacy, then, present a continuity that spans ideas about marriage and procreation, spiritual powers, spiritual purity, and chaste marriage to the divine.

Temporary concentration of reproductive energies. The perception that sexual intercourse during pregnancy and lactation will harm an infant is found in many cultures, including some contemporary Western folk traditions. The larger worldviews in which this perception is embedded may thus vary immensely. For the Arapesh of New Guinea, the practice of temporary celibacy has a positive religious significance for procreation. According to Arapesh ideas, the fetus is shaped and nurtured by both parents through several weeks of frequent and purposeful intercourse after the mother's menstruation stops. Yet once the mother's breasts enlarge in the first obvious sign of pregnancy, the child is considered fully formed and all intercourse must cease. After the child is born, the parents are supposed to sleep together with it, devote their energies to it, and give it special attention. If either parent indulges in sexual activity—even with other partners—before the child can walk, they say that it will become weak and perhaps die. With infanticide common among the Arapesh, choosing to keep a child is a deliberate decision, and this extended celibacy surrounding childbirth, once chosen, is normally kept. Celibacy then appears to represent here a conscious channeling and concentration of the reproductive power of both parents for the good of the child, lineage, and community.

The power of holy persons. Adepts in the esoteric traditions of Asia are often aware of transmuting their reproductive power into spiritual power and channeling it within. This perception lies behind certain occult meditation techniques found in both India and Daoist China that draw on a tension between continence, in a strict sense, and sexual intercourse. Through entering a woman and still remaining continent, the male adept arouses sexual energy in both partners, which can then be absorbed inwardly for spiritual transformation. More often, however, adepts practice techniques that entail only physiological imagery: Daoist spiritual alchemy may lead to the generation of an immortal fetus; Hindu yogins speak of channeling the seed upward through higher centers of the body. For most adepts, then, total celibacy is crucial in order to preserve the spiritual potencies of their own seed, a point also affirmed in popular tradition: Hindu mythological texts are full of stories of ascetics who succumbed to lust and lost their powers.

Thus, the power of holy persons also depends in good part on their self-control. The word *yoga,* in fact, deriving from a root meaning "to yoke," can often be best understood in a very concrete sense: a willful harnessing of the vital energies, which are considered prone to rage like beasts. So even in traditions like Christianity that do not explicitly posit a direct continuity between sexual and spiritual energies, celibacy still appears as a measure of powerful mastery over the senses. Latin Catholicism gives us stories of triumphant (and faltering) ascetics struggling with incubi or succubi, attractive male or female spirits bent on seducing them. Among the American Shakers, a struggle with sexual desire became the distinctive focal point through which an active Protestant sect sought to reform human existence. For the Shakers, the world of sensual experience itself was so overwhelming that a break with it required radical means: absolute abstention. In this instance, perfect celibacy expresses an attempt at total self-mastery.

Separation from the impure. Ascetics who aim to subjugate the flesh usually have no high opinion of the gross physical matter that constitutes it. The eventual aim of controlling the sexual nature for many can then become the achievement of distance from a fundamentally impure, degenerate, and transient world. The perception of the physical body itself as disgusting and ultimately worthless may be actively cultivated in monastic traditions, sometimes through deliberate meditation practice. In the near-canonical *Visuddhimagga,* Theravāda Buddhist monks are enjoined to detach themselves from sensual desire by contemplating the dead body in various stages of decomposition (swollen, bluish, gnawed, worm-eaten) and the live body as filled, among other things, with intestines, excrement, bile, pus, fat, mucus, and urine (chaps. 6, 8). Sexual activity in this context can easily be seen as another disgusting physical function from which all wise people should abstain.

In nonliterate cultures, which usually have fewer qualms about the physical body, the impurity attributed to sex may stem in part from its potential danger to the social fabric. Built up out of kinship bonds, tribal societies may splinter over family tensions and conflicts about women. Temporary celibacy is thus often enjoined at crucial public rituals that highlight communal solidarity—initiations, hunting expeditions, the start of a group journey.

The image of chaste asexuality encompassing the common good is also found in Western religious institutions. Roman state religion, which is often, in fact, understood to derive from the religion of family and clan, exalted the Vestal Virgins. The keepers of Rome's communal hearth, the Vestal Virgins were legally neither men nor women. Buried alive if they violated their chastity, their most crucial obligation was celibacy itself. People in literate as well as nonliterate cultures, then, may believe that sacred institutions maintaining the welfare of humanity as a whole should depend on individuals in an extraordinary state, beyond human sexuality.

Ideas about the impurity of sex known both to the Roman world's ascetics and in its politico-religious institutions were assimilated and transformed by early Christians, who by the fourth century had recognized the source of their own religious institution in the virgin son of a virgin mother. For Christians, then, maintaining virginity can be an imitation of divine models and the purity of permanent celibacy can offer a constant tie to what is realized as primal in religious experience. Appearing as the original state of man born of the spirit, celibacy in Christianity, as in other traditions, promises innocence—eternal childhood in the Lord.

Exclusive attachment to the divine. Being an eternal child in God can free the celibate from many worldly responsibilities. Luke's reference to chaste persons as "equal to angels" (20:35–36) suggests not only the innocence of celibates, but also their roles as agents of God, in no way beholden to man. Certainly, the ability to devote all of one's efforts to spiritual matters without the burden of family obligations is a very frequently voiced justification for celibacy in the East as well as in the West. In India, the practical implications of celibacy for a life devoted to religious pursuits has explicit expression in the semantic range of the Sanskrit word *brahmacarya,* which occurs very frequently in religious writings. Used most often to refer to sexual abstention, *brahmacarya* literally means "walking with *brahman,*" the primal divine essence; at the same time, *brahmacarya* may be used to refer specifically to the first stage in the traditional Hindu life cycle, which is supposed to be devoted to religious study. Thus, a word suggesting adherence to first divine principles explicitly links the concept of celibacy to distinctly religious pursuits and the absence of worldly, adult responsibilities.

In a highly dualistic theology, strict adherence to first principles can demand an absolute withdrawal from involvement in earthly endeavors. Abstinence from sex is required less to follow active religious pursuits freely than to desist from physical procreation. For a gnostic like Marcion (d. 160?), the physical world is the creation of a false god, not the true one; trapped in physical bodies, souls cannot return to their real, original home. From this perspective, making more physical bodies only means making more prisons for human souls, and keeping celibate represents a refusal to further the false, earthly creation.

By inhibiting fruitful physical unions, celibacy may also strengthen the devotee's spiritual union with the Lord. Indeed, in devotional traditions, physical sexual abstinence is often a sign of faithful attachment to the divine beloved. Hindu devotional poetry idealizes the stalwart devotee as the Lord's faithful wife, a concept institutionalized in Catholic orders that identify nuns as brides of Christ. Moreover, Christian as well as Hindu mystics sometimes express themselves in terms of nuptial ecstasy. Though the patriarchal heritages of East and West usually present the aspiring soul in feminine guise, dependent on the will of her Lord, men too can adopt a passionate devotional attitude. In India, both male and female devotees of Kṛṣṇa understand the highest spiritual state in terms of romantic love, and make much of Kṛṣṇa's amorous dalliance with the adoring milkmaids of his pastoral childhood home. Some theologians of Kṛṣṇa worship have further pointed out that the milkmaids were in fact married women, and that the most intense desire between men and women actually takes place outside routinized marriage, between clandestine lovers. So, paradoxically, the milkmaids' passionate attachment to Kṛṣṇa —an important ideal for a large tradition of Indian celibates—is frequently represented as wives' unchaste betrayal of their husbands. Thus, as radical departures from ordinary convention, both celibacy and sexual abandon become religious parallels to one another.

The Place of Celibacy in Society. Like total sexual abandon, moreover, total abstinence is not a generally recommended practice in most traditions, and the social regulation of sexual behavior may entail curbs on celibacy as well as on indulgence. Indeed, traditional cultures often present celibacy and procreation in a complementary relationship, which can be ordered according to the calendrical cycle, the life cycle, or divisions in the society as a whole. At the same time, separate communities of celibates have their own norms of sexual propriety, and the maintenance of these norms is often crucial for the image of the celibate in the eyes of laypersons.

Procreation and abstinence in traditional societies. Clearly, no civilization can survive for long without some provision for procreation, and religious traditions with strong ethnic roots, like Confucianism and Judaism, may have no place at all for the permanent celibate. Although traditional Judaism proscribes sexual relations outside marriage, all Jews are expected to marry and engage regularly in conjugal relations. Indeed, the Sabbath itself is thought of as a bride, and to celebrate its arrival Jewish husbands are enjoined to have intercourse with their wives joyously on Sabbath eve. In Judaism, then, controlled religious pursuits should also embrace sanctified procreation throughout a mature person's life.

The most highly structured relationships between abstinence and procreation are found in traditional India, where classical Hindu tradition sees these relationships ordered not, as in Judaism, in a lifelong weekly cycle, but in the cycle of each individual life. The life stages of classical Hinduism are fourfold: (1) *brahmacarya,* a period of celibate study; (2) *gṛhastha,* the householder stage, in which traditional Hindus were expected to marry and have many children, particularly sons who would perform their death rites; (3) *vanaprastha* ("forest dwelling"), the later stage of marriage, after the children were fully raised and had received most of their inheritance, and when abstinence was prescribed; and finally (4) *saṃnyāsa,* the stage of total renunciation of settled life as well as sex. The classical Hindu life cycle, then, begins and ends in celibacy, but prescribes a sexually fruitful period of life as a householder in between.

Giving celibacy an explicit place in the individual life cycle, Hindu tradition also gives celibate individuals an explicit place in society. Hindus recognize that exceptional individuals will want to live all their lives as celibate ascetics, either prolonging their studies indefinitely as *brahmacārins* or bypassing the householder stage by making early formal renunciation. Today, Hindus tend to collapse the first and last stages of the cycle and ignore the third, thus resolving the four stages of the life cycle into two social states: householders fruitfully participating in society, nurturing new souls, and supporting ascetics; and solitary celibates outside society, working out their own salvation. In most Indian cosmologies, the participation of householders as well as celibates is required in the proper economy of salvation in the cosmos.

Sexual norms in celibate groups. In Theravāda Buddhism, the complementary roles of the householder and celibate were institutionalized and given a distinctive religious valuation. The community of monks—the *saṃgha*—should be supported by the laity, but the proper ordering of the cosmos (and so the welfare of the laity) depends on the *saṃgha's* purity, conceived in good part as its sexual purity. Thus, in the Vinaya Piṭaka, the monastic disciplinary code, specific rules governed everyday practices that had even the most subtle sexual implications, from propriety in dress to contact with women. Atonement for even minor sexual infractions required not only confessions but also a formal legal decision handed down in a meeting of the community. Sexual intercourse with a woman was one of the few grounds for immediate expulsion from the *saṃgha.*

Perhaps more crucial than the rules regulating the contact between members of a celibate community and potential sexual partners outside it are those controlling the relationships among the community members themselves. These rules can be especially complex in celibate communities of mixed sex. The Shakers, a mixed celibate community founded by a woman, maintained strict segregation between the sexes; men and women were even to avoid passing each other on stairways. Taking in children and youths to raise, they kept them under tight control. Children were not allowed out at night except for some specific reason (and not for any reason on Saturday evenings); lest they be tempted, children even of the same sex were not to be left unattended at their weekly bath. In whole communities of the same sex, too, provisions are often made to inhibit physical contact among members. Though the *Rule of Saint Benedict,* which stands behind much of Western monastic life, has little explicit to say about celibacy itself, it does include provisions apparently aimed at the prevention of homosexuality. Monks should sleep in separate beds, clothed and with a light burning; though inmates of monasteries should sleep in groups, young monks should not sleep alone as a group but should be together with older ones (chap. 22). The abbots seemed to recognize that ideals of spiritual love among members of their communities could stand in practical tension with vows of celibacy.

Yet more often than not, the physical chastity of cloistered monks is rarely tested; the crucial spiritual role of sexual restrictions on celibates is less the prevention of sexual activity than of sexual thoughts. For celibates living outside the cloister, continually interacting with laypersons, temptation and desire can become particularly problematic. Necessary celibacy for diocesan priests has been frequently questioned, both inside and outside the Roman Catholic church. In pre-Reformation Europe, many priests openly took concubines, and the last half of the twentieth century has heard continuing discussion of the value of requiring celibacy for all priests. The tensions facing the modern priest are understandable: living in a sexually open society and as a confessor hearing detailed accounts of the intimate lives of individuals, he is nevertheless expected to exercise the same sexual discipline—both mentally and physically—of the cloistered monk.

The image for the layperson. The persistence of sacerdotal celibacy in Roman Catholic tradition may lie, in part, in the image that the priest holds for the laity. As an administrator of divine office, the priest is seen to function within the holy mother church and should reflect her virginal purity. The ideal of virginal purity for its officiants is maintained even in the Eastern Orthodox church: though married men are allowed to become priests, they are not allowed to rise to the highest episcopal office, and once a man has become a priest he may not take a wife. As representatives of a sacred institution regarded as pure, Buddhist monks project a similar image of chaste holiness in Theravāda society. Like priests, monks are formal participants in Theravāda ritual, much of which involves the feeding of monks by laypersons. The religious power of the rite for laypersons depends in part on the monks' perceived purity.

A vow of celibacy, moreover, can make individuals appear remarkable beyond the confines of sanctified ritual. No longer appearing as ordinary mortals, celibates can be relaxed in their socioreligious roles. The Roman Catholic priest can joke and gossip with parishioners and not have to worry too much about a decorous image. A Theravāda monk, even if he is not particularly charismatic, at least withstands the rigors of chastity—an experience familiar to many male Theravadins who have temporarily taken the robe. Among Hindu gurus, the married ones may feel constrained to appear particularly scrupulous in financial matters; celibate gurus, on the other hand, not burdened by family responsibilities, are said to be more easily trusted. And in all traditions, celibate hermits who do not interact readily with laypersons may, through their renunciation of society, seem awesome and powerful.

CONCLUSION. In setting individuals apart from normal life, deliberate celibacy can render them extraordinary both to themselves and to others. In crucial situations, temporary abstinence is undertaken by members of many cultures, either to achieve distance from impurity during rituals or to channel reproductive energy at the birth of a child. In religions oriented toward salvation, more permanent vows of celibacy affirm the links of individuals to powers higher than this world, often as members of sanctified institutions. In these ways, celibacy makes people seem less grossly, physically human, and thus, sometimes, more divine.

SEE ALSO Asceticism; Desire; Kuṇḍalinī; Saṃnyāsa; Tantrism; Virginity.

BIBLIOGRAPHY

For an extensive survey of celibacy in Christianity with a brief treatment of Asian traditions see Elizabeth Abbott, *A History of Celibacy* (New York, 2000). For small-scale societies, see the essays in *Celibacy, Culture, and Society: The Anthropology of Sexual Abstinence* (Madison, 2001) edited by Elisa Janine Sobo and Sandra Bell. In *Taoist Yoga: Alchemy and Immortality* (New York, 1970), Charles Luk presents a translation of a turn-of-the-century Chinese text that treats the spiritual transformation of sexual energies. Mircea Eliade, *Yoga: Immortality and Freedom* (Princeton, 1969), treats this dimension of celibacy along with many others in Hindu religious traditions. Social-scientific insight on the role of celibate monks in Theravāda Buddhist culture is presented in S. J. Tambiah, *Buddhism and the Spirit Cults in North-east Thailand* (Cambridge, 1970). A socio-religious perspective on the Shakers is given by Louis J. Kern, who presents them as a radical Protestant community: *An Ordered Love* (Chapel Hill, 1981).

Incisive accounts of issues surrounding celibacy in the first Christian centuries are offered by Peter Brown, *The Body and Society: Men, Women, and Sexual Renunciation in Early Christianity* (New York, 1988). Later Christian traditions are treated in the essays in *Medieval Purity and Piety: Essays on Medieval Clerical Celibacy and Religious Reform* (New York, 1998), edited by Michael Frassetto. Contemporary concerns about celibacy in Catholicism, together with a concise historical survey, are presented by Thomas McGovern, *Priestly Celibacy Today* (Princeton and Chicago, 1998).

DANIEL GOLD (1987 AND 2005)

CELTIC RELIGION

This entry consists of the following articles:

AN OVERVIEW
HISTORY OF STUDY

CELTIC RELIGION: AN OVERVIEW

Historical references to the Celts begin in the fifth century BCE. Herodotus and Hecataeus of Miletus are the forerunners of a long series of Greek and Latin writers whose reports and comments, both well- and ill-informed, reflect the changing fortunes of the Celtic peoples during the pre-Christian era and their impact on the Greco-Roman world. Herodotus and Hecataeus confirm that by about 500 BCE the Celts were already widely dispersed over central and western Europe, including perhaps Gaul and the Iberian Peninsula, and evidence from the fifth century testifies to further territorial expansion. About 400 BCE this process quickened as tribal bands invaded northern Italy and established settlements that, in due course, became the Roman province of Gallia Cisalpina. Some Celtic bands raided farther south, as far as Rome and Apulia and even Sicily, and around 387 they captured and sacked the city of Rome, an event of traumatic importance in Roman history.

To the east, other Celtic tribes penetrated into the Carpathians and the Balkans during the fourth century BCE. In 279 some of them entered Greece and plundered the shrine at Delphi, and in the following year three Celtic tribes, known collectively to the Greeks as Galatae, crossed into Asia Minor and eventually settled in the region that still bears the name Galatia. In Britain, the final phase of Celtic settlement came with the arrival of the Belgae in the first century BCE, although there is archaeological evidence of earlier immigrations dating back as far as the fifth century BCE. For Ireland, the evidence is complicated, and one cannot confidently infer a Celtic presence before the third century BCE.

By the early third century BCE the Celts extended across the length of Europe from Britain to Asia Minor, and they were considered one of the three or four most important barbarian peoples in the known world. Thereafter, however, their history is one of decline. Harried by Germans in the north, Dacians in the east, and Romans in the south, the continental Celts saw their widespread dominion disintegrate and contract until their realm came to be associated solely with Gaul, where they maintained their independence until their conquest by Caesar (100–44 BCE) in the mid–first century BCE (58–51 BCE).

In Britain and Ireland the process was longer drawn out, but there too Celtic society was gradually eroded and submerged by foreign domination. By the beginning of the twenty-first century, Celtic languages were being spoken only on the western periphery, in restricted areas of Ireland, Scotland, Wales, and Brittany. The insular languages belong to two distinct branches of Celtic and perhaps reflect an older dialectal division among the Celtic-speaking peoples of Europe: Goidelic, which comprises Irish and Scottish Gaelic (and formerly Manx), and British or Brythonic, comprising Welsh and Breton (and formerly Cornish). However, Breton, which is largely the product of immigration to Brittany from southwest Britain from around the fourth to the seventh century CE, may also have absorbed surviving elements of Gaulish speech.

The entry of the Celts into the written record coincides with the first evidences of the Second Iron Age, also known as La Tène culture, which refers broadly to those areas of Europe historically associated with the Celts. However, the further back beyond the fifth century BCE one goes, the more difficult it becomes to use the term Celts with reasonable confidence, because the correlatives of language and written reference are lacking. The cultural phase which preceded La Tène, known as Hallstatt, dates from the ninth century BCE and covers an expanse of territory extending at least from Burgundy to Bohemia. Hallstatt culture is characterized by elaborate chariot burials and by the use of iron rather than bronze for arms and utensils. It is the product of a warrior aristocracy that is generally recognized as Celtic, or at least as the direct ancestor of the Celts of the following period. Obviously, the definition of a Celtic identity was the product of a long period of linguistic and cultural evolution, and some archaeologists have ventured to identify as proto-Celtic the peoples of the Urnfield culture and of the Tumulus culture that preceded it in the second millennium BCE, or even the peoples of the Beaker and Battle-Axe cultures of the third millennium BCE. However, this is mere speculation; the point in the archaeological record at which the Indo-Europeans made their appearance in central and western Europe cannot be known with certainty. And yet most scholars discern in the culture of the Tumulus peoples features that are echoed in that of La Tène.

SOURCES. The sources for Celtic religion fall broadly into two categories. The first category comprises the various monuments relating to the Celts on the continent, particularly in Gaul and in Roman Britain, and the second category comprises the insular Celtic literatures that have been preserved in writing. The two types pose problems that are very different in character. Most dedicatory inscriptions, images of Celtic deities, and commentaries by classical authors belong to the Roman period and probably reflect in varying degrees the effect of Roman influence on Gaulish institutions. For example, because Gaulish sculpture is based for the most part on Greco-Roman models, it is often difficult to assess and interpret its relevance to native belief. Even cases in which motifs and figures seem clearly to derive from pre-Roman religious tradition, as in some of the Celtic coins of the third and second centuries BCE, they are not easily related to what is known of insular Celtic myth and ritual.

The difficulty lies in the lack of the literature that would provide a context for the iconography as well as a key to its understanding. The druids, as Caesar records, accorded primacy to the spoken word and refused to commit their teaching to writing. Consequently, the whole of the traditional literature, including the mythology that gave the iconography its meaning, was confined to oral transmission and perished with the extinction of the Gaulish language. The total loss of this vernacular literature, which was doubtless comparable in volume and variety with that of early Ireland, renders all the more significant the testimony of those classical authors who recorded their own or others' observations on the Celts. Probably the most important was Posidonius (c. 135–c. 50 BCE), who had firsthand knowledge of diverse cultures, including the Celtic in southern Gaul, and who devoted the twenty-third chapter of his lost *Histories* to Celtic ethnography. Much of his account of the Celts survives in the work of later writers who borrowed from him, such as the historian Diodorus Siculus (died after 21 BCE,), the geographer Strabo (c. 63 BCE–24 CE), and, most notably of all, Julius Caesar, whose account is crucial for the study of Gaulish religion.

The limitations of the classical sources are obvious. Most of the reports come at second- or third-hand and are subject to the prejudices and preconceptions born of classical civilization—or even, as in the case of Caesar, of internal Roman politics—but they are not without substance, as on many points they harmonize remarkably with the later insular sources. For example, classical sources note that in Gaul there were three classes associated with literature and learning: the druids, the bards, and, between them, an order that seems to have been best known by the Gaulish term **vātis* (cognate with Latin *vatis*; * denotes a form not appearing in epigraphs and reconstructed from the quotations of Greek and Latin authors), which is not clearly distinguishable from the druids. Far removed in time and space, the same threefold arrangement occurs in medieval Ireland, comprising here druids (*druïdh*), *filidh*, and bards (*baird*). The term *fáith* (prophet) is the Irish cognate of Gaulish **vātis* and appears frequently as a near synonym of *fili* (plural, *filidh*).

Manuscripts. The second main body of evidence, the insular Celtic literatures, is at first glance far removed from the pre-Roman world of the continental Celts. The great historian of Gaul, Camille Jullian (1859–1933), questioned whether it was valid to use Irish and Welsh literary sources to interpret Latin and Greek references to Gaulish institutions and concluded that one could not rely on documents written so long after the Celtic migration to Ireland. In fact, the gap is much narrower than the twelve centuries that he supposed, because much of the relevant material is linguistically older than the period of the manuscript collections in which it is now preserved. Further, there is no evidence that Christianity was introduced to any part of Ireland before the second half of the fourth century CE, or that it impinged much on the traditional culture of the country before the sixth century. Moreover, one must reckon with the highly conservative character of Irish learned tradition, which, thanks to the assiduousness of the hereditary *filidh*, survived far into the Christian period and transmitted innumerable elements of form and content, particularly in the area of social institutions, which find their closest detailed analogues in the sacred texts of Vedic and classical Sanskrit.

Written literature in Irish dates from the second half of the sixth century CE, when monastic scholars adapted the Latin alphabet for that purpose, and it gradually increases in volume during the following centuries. In addition to a good deal of typically monastic learning, both religious and secular, the literature comprises a vast amount of varied material recorded or adapted from oral tradition. However, only fragments of this literature survive in contemporary manuscripts, mostly in the form of annals or notes and glosses accompanying Latin texts; all the vernacular manuscripts written before the end of the eleventh century, some of them known by name, have perished through usage or spoilage caused by warfare. Then around 1100 came *Lebhor na hUidhre* (The book of the dun cow), probably written in the monastery of Clonmacnois and the first of a series of great vellum manuscript compilations that were part of a conscious endeavor in the face of ominous political and social change to conserve the monuments of native tradition. It was followed around 1130 by an untitled collection now at the Bodleian Library at Oxford University and around 1150–1200 by *Lebhor na Nuachongbála* (known commonly as the Book of Leinster), probably compiled in the monasteries of Glendalough and Terryglass, respectively. Over the next couple of centuries a number of major manuscripts appeared, of which the most important are the Great Book of Lecan, Yellow Book of Lecan, Book of Ballymote, Book of Lismore, and Book of Fermoy. These capacious *bibliothecae* embrace all the various genres of traditional literature: hero and king tales, mythological tales, origin legends, genealogies, onomastic (the study of proper names) and etymological lore, gnomic texts, legal tracts, eulogy and elegy, battle tales, birth tales, death tales, tales of the otherworld, and so on. It is important to remember that, although the surviving manuscripts date from a relatively late period, the matter they contain has generally been copied more or less faithfully from earlier manuscripts. The result is that the initial redaction of the individual texts can be dated with a fair degree of accuracy on the basis of linguistic criteria. Thus the texts are often demonstrably centuries older than the extant manuscripts.

Along with these manuscript collections, several specialized compilations, including *Leabhar Gabhála Éireann* (The book of the taking of Ireland), commonly known as the Book of Invasions, an amalgam of myth and pseudohistory, which purports to recount the coming of the Gaels to Ireland as well as the several immigrations that preceded it; the *Cóir Anmann* (Fitness of names), a catalog of names of "historical" personages with many imaginative etymologies and references to traditional legends; and the *Dinnshenchas* (Lore of famous places), which provides a much fuller and more elaborate examination of place names than the *Cóir Anmann* provides for personal names. The features of the Irish landscape and their names, if properly construed, were thought to reveal the history of the country and its peoples from their beginnings. From the first shaping and definition of the land—the clearing of plains, the creation of rivers and lakes, and the assigning of names (as related in *Leabhar Gabhála*)—each place was linked indissolubly to momentous events by an association that conferred on it an enduring psychic resonance. The onomastic element is pervasive in Irish (and Welsh) literature, and in poetic tracts dating from around the tenth century, the history of *dinnshenchas* is included in the course of study prescribed for apprentice *filidh*. During the eleventh and twelfth centuries, a period of intensive compilation, a comprehensive volume of these onomastic legends was assembled. This mythological gazetteer of Irish place names exists in several recensions (critically revised texts that use varying sources), both prose and verse. Among the many other miscellaneous sources are the lives of the saints, particularly those later ones compiled or redacted from the eleventh century onward (of which it is sometimes said that they contain more pagan mythology than Christianity).

Evidence indicates that the early oral literature of Wales was comparable in volume and variety with that of Ireland. Unfortunately, because of a weaker scribal tradition, Welsh literature is less well documented for the pre-Norman period, prior to the eleventh century. This applies particularly to prose, which in the Celtic languages is the standard medium for narrative and hence for most heroic and mythological literature. Of the compositions ascribed to the fathers of Welsh poetry, Taliesin and Aneirin, who belonged to the second half of the sixth century, only a modest proportion is likely to be authentic, and all of that consists of eulogy and heroic elegy. However, from the ninth or tenth century onward Taliesin became the focus of poems and stories (extant only in much later versions) that represent him as a wonder child, seer, and prophet; some of these motifs clearly derive from native mythological tradition. There is no evidence of written Welsh narrative prose before the eleventh century, the period to which most scholars assign the first redaction of the earliest of the group of tales known as the *Mabinogi* or *Mabinogion.* However, the earliest manuscripts containing this prose material date from considerably later. Apart from two manuscript fragments from the late thirteenth and early fourteenth centuries, the main texts are the "White Book of Rhydderch" from the mid–fourteenth century and the "Red Book of Hergest" from the late fourteenth or early fifteenth century. Another important source is the *Trioedd Ynys Prydein* (The triads of the island of Britain), which contains numerous references to mythological as well as historical characters and events; it may have been compiled in the twelfth century, but much of the contents must have existed in oral tradition before then. Also of mythological interest are the poems compiled as part of the "Black Book of Carmarthen" in the mid-thirteenth century, some of the contents of which may be dated on linguistic grounds to the ninth or tenth century.

Given the diversity of these sources, it is unrealistic to expect from them a clear image of religious and mythological unity. On one hand, Gaulish epigraphy and iconography belong preponderantly to the period of Roman domination when native religion was being progressively modified by Roman influence. On the other hand, the insular literatures, although exceedingly conservative in many respects, were recorded and redacted by monastic scribes and scholars who, however well disposed toward their own vernacular tradition, were nonetheless educated Christians, who on matters of crucial importance doubtless gave priority to Christian teaching over pagan tradition. In short, the integral tradition as it would have been transmitted and commented on by the druids in an independent Celtic society does not exist. Even among the insular Celts, history created important disparities. For instance, Ireland escaped the immediate physical presence of Rome, which left its imprint so clearly on medieval language and thought in Britain and Wales. One must also acknowledge the imponderable but obviously considerable survival of pre-Celtic religion in Celtic belief and practice in the several areas of Celtic settlement. Yet, despite these sources of dissimilation, the underlying structural and thematic unity of British and Irish ideology is more striking than the superficial differences.

Artifacts. The plastic art of the Celto-Roman period is so evidently based on that of Rome that it might appear at first glance to have been borrowed whole and unchanged, but on closer scrutiny it reveals many elements that derive from the Celtic rather than from the Roman tradition. On one hand, there are forms quite foreign to classical art, such as the tricephalic (three-headed) god, the god with stag's antlers, and the god depicted in the Buddha-like cross-legged position. On the other hand, there are images more or less in the classical mode but with features not associated with the corresponding deities of Greco-Latin religion: the wheel, for instance, or the mallet. The wheel is seen by some as representing the thunderbolt, by others as representing the sun, and in some cases it may also be the emblem of the god of the underworld. Similarly, the mallet or hammer is thought to have several connotations: it symbolizes thunder and the sky from which it emanates, but it also functions as an apotropaic (able to prevent evil or bad luck) symbol and as the emblem of an underworld god of fecundity. The cornucopia, or horn of abundance, is not particularly Celtic, but it appears as a common attribute of the Celtic mother goddess, perhaps the most important divinity of the primitive Celtic pantheon. Animal horns are commonly regarded as signs of fertility, and the antlers that the Celtic deity wears on the Gundestrup Caldron, a first-century BCE vessel found in Denmark, and elsewhere are taken to symbolize his power and fecundity. Another frequent emblem of divinity is the ornamented torque, which is interpreted to denote a powerful god who is able to provide protection from evil spirits. Although it is usually worn around the neck as a metal collar, the torque is sometimes held in the hand, and, on the relief of the Celtic god Cernunnos in the Musée de Cluny in Paris, the deity carries two torques suspended on his horns.

Probably the most notable element in the religious symbolism of the Celts is the number three; the mystic significance of the concept of threeness is attested in most parts of the world, but it seems to have had a particularly strong significance for the Celts. This is confirmed both by Celto-Roman iconography, which has its three-headed and three-faced deities (and even a triphallic Mercury) and its triads of mother goddesses, and by the insular literary tradition, which has an endless variety of ternary groups in which the triad is an expressive restatement of an underlying unity. Examples include goddesses such as the three Brighids and inseparable brothers such as the three companions of the tragic heroine Deirdre. It is commonly accepted that ternary repetition has an intensifying force, expressing totality or omnipotence, although its symbolism may be even more complex and subtle.

Continental Deities and Insular Equivalents. Given that the bulk of the relevant evidence belongs to the Roman period, the Gaulish religion is for the most part as seen through Roman eyes, which means that it is perceived and presented in terms of Roman religion. A classical example is the passage in Caesar's *Gallic Wars* in which he lists and defines the principal gods of the Gauls:

> Of the gods they worship Mercury most of all. He has the greatest number of images; they hold that he is the inventor of all the arts and a guide on the roads and on journeys, and they believe him the most influential for money-making and commerce. After him they honor Apollo, Mars, Jupiter, and Minerva. Of these deities they have almost the same idea as other peoples: Apollo drives away diseases, Minerva teaches the first principles of the arts and crafts, Jupiter rules the heavens, and Mars controls the issue of war. (*Gallic Wars,* 6.17)

What Caesar offers us here is a thumbnail sketch of the Gaulish pantheon modeled on that of Rome. As part of this glaringly Roman interpretation, he refers to each deity not by his proper Celtic name but by that of a Roman deity to which it is most easily equated. At the same time he introduces a neat schematism, which is quite foreign to all that is otherwise known of Celtic religion. In thus equating gods and divine functions that are not really equal, he has posed many problems for modern scholars who seek to identify Caesar's Roman gods in continental Celtic iconography and insular Celtic mythology.

To confound matters further, modern scholars have tended to depreciate Caesar's testimony on the Gauls; first, on the grounds that he distorted the facts to enhance his own achievements, and second, on the grounds that he took his information from Posidonius, but used it inaccurately. It has been argued, for example, that Caesar—and even Posidonius—exaggerated the social and political importance of the druids, assigning them a dominant role that they never in fact possessed. Yet in this regard, as in others, Caesar's version of things is largely confirmed by the independent evidence of the insular literatures. Once allowance is made for the synoptic nature of his comment, his inevitable professional bias, and the limitations of his interest in Gaul, there is no reason to assume that his account is not largely authentic. By the time he wrote his account, he had had eight years' experience of the country, and most likely he derived much of his information from personal observation and from the reports of colleagues and acquaintances; certainly there is little basis for the common assumption that he was totally indebted to Posidonius for his knowledge of the land and its people.

The concise precision of Caesar's testimony makes it difficult to correlate with other evidence. Georges Dumézil (1898–1986) remarked that one of the many traits the early Irish shared with the Indians is that they were both fond of classification and careless of order. The result is that Irish literature is often a curious mixture of meticulous detail and incoherence that finds its closest parallel in some of the Indian epics. One must therefore adjust one's mental perspective considerably as one moves from Caesar to the vernacular literatures. It may be that something of this prodigal disorder is reflected in the continental Celtic iconography, which may help to explain why identifications with Caesar's deities are often more a matter of speculation than of demonstration. But perhaps a more important consideration is that Caesar's account and the iconography refer to quite different stages in the history of Gaulish religion. Periods of profound cultural and political change often bring into prominence popular forms of belief and practice that have hitherto been concealed by the dominant orthodoxy. It seems probable that the religion represented in Gallo-Roman plastic art was less clearly structured and delimited than that maintained by the druids in the days of independence before Caesar's conquest.

Modern scholars have often noted, and sometimes exaggerated, a discrepancy between Caesar's account and the Gallo-Roman evidence, claiming that the evidence does not substantiate Caesar's account of a pantheon of major deities who were worshiped throughout Gaul. In Gallo-Roman dedications, deities may be assigned a Roman name, a native Gaulish name, or a Roman name accompanied by a native epithet. The last two cases clearly have to do with indigenous gods, and even the first group may also. For example, the numerous statues and reliefs of Mercury in the guise of the Greco-Roman god might have been intended to honor that god, but equally they might have been intended to honor a native god by borrowing the classical form together with the classical name. Indeed, many of these images have certain features that betray their essential non-Roman character. It has been observed that the great majority of the several hundred names containing a Gaulish element occur only once. Those that occur more frequently tend to do so in regional or tribal groupings, and many of them have a clear local reference (e.g., Mars Vesontius pointing to Vesontio and Dea Tricoria referring to a goddess of the Tricorii). The inference drawn by some scholars, including Joseph Vendryes and Marie-Louise Sjoestedt, is that, although the Celts had a multiplicity of gods, their cults were local and tribal rather than national. Scholars also cite Lucan's (39–65 CE) mention of the deity name Teutates, which they interpret as "God of the Tribe" based on the etymologies of Celtic word **teutā* (tribe) and an oath formula from Irish hero tales, *Tongu do dia toinges mo thuath* (I swear to the god to whom my tribe swears).

But this evidence is susceptible of a different interpretation. A large proportion of the Gaulish forms attested in dedications are mere epithets or bynames; even of those that may be taken to be proper names, it would be quite erroneous to suppose that each indicates a separate deity. As Dumézil remarked in *Dieux des Indo-Européens* (1952), the names of deities are easily reinvented, and the insular literatures offer examples of major gods known by several different names. As for the form *Teutates*, it may be a title linking the god to the tribe but does not necessarily confine him to it. By the same token, in early Irish law the small tribal kingdom, the *tuath* (from **teutā*), was the unit of jurisdiction, and rules of law were explicitly stated to apply *i tuaith* (within a *tuath*). Presumably, then, laws originally applied with equal validity only between members of the same tribe; however, substantially the same law—formulated by the same learned class of jurists related to the druids and *filidh*—was common to all the tribal kingdoms. Similarly, in primitive Ireland the vital ritual of inauguration was founded in the first place on the small tribal kingdom (*tuath*), as is enunciated in the law tracts, but it is also replicated at different levels throughout the wider cultural community. And as for the alleged lack of great divinities common to all the Celtic peoples, this is gainsaid even in terms of nomenclature by such insular gods as Lugh and Brighid and their continental equivalents. In short, there is a growing awareness that, despite its all too obvious complexities, the seeming throng of Celtic gods is both less amorphous and more universal than was formerly believed.

Another criticism levelled at Caesar is that he assigned separate functions to the several Gaulish deities in contradiction of the evidence. Some scholars hold that the deities were polyvalent (they can be understood in more than one way) tribal gods, and that to seek to restrict them to distinct spheres of activity is pointless. Others hold that all the various attested gods may be reduced ultimately to a single deity who is both polyvalent and polymorphic (i.e., taking more than one form). Thomas F. O'Rahilly, one of the two principal exponents of this view, believed that the core of Irish and Celtic mythology was the conflict in which this universal deity was slain by a youthful hero using the god's own sacred weapon, the thunderbolt. Pierre Lambrechts, the other principal exponent of this view, believed that originally Celtic religion was bound up with one great deity, possibly a ternary (three-formed) deity endowed with multiple and comprehensive attributes and that during the Roman period this largely undefined and impersonal deity was fragmented into a number of smaller, specialized deities through contact with the Greco-Roman world.

This notion of a single all-encompassing god, endlessly varied in form and function, has perhaps a certain plausibility. Because the Celtic gods were not clearly departmentalized, it is difficult to pair them off neatly with their Roman counterparts, and so one finds such evident anomalies as the occasional use of the same Gaulish byname (e.g., Iovantucarus and Vellaunus) with different Roman deity names (e.g., Mars and Mercurius). However, although the functional roles of the several deities are not clearly defined and delimited and frequently overlap with one another, it does not follow that they may be reduced to a single, all-purpose divine overlord. It has often been remarked that in polytheistic systems each god tends to move beyond his or her normal functional field toward a kind of universalism. Yet, despite this tendency toward the assimilation of roles, the insular Celtic gods are far removed from functional indifferentism, and there are some, like Goibhniu (The Smith) and Dian Cecht (The Leech) whose central responsibilities are defined very precisely. The assumption of undifferentiated polyvalence that underlies the conflicting interpretations of Vendryes and O'Rahilly (i.e., tribal and polytheistic) or Lambrechts (i.e., vaguely monotheistic) has not been substantiated. In fact, more recent scholars, notably Françoise Le Roux and Anne Ross, have moved in the direction of a typological classification of the gods based on criteria of function. The scheme put forward by Le Roux is in close conformity with the principles established in Dumézil's functional theory of Indo-European mythology. Indeed, it could be argued that this typological approach had already been anticipated by Caesar in his brief account of the characteristic activities of the major Gaulish deities.

Mercury or Lugh. Caesar's observation that Mercury was the deity with the greatest number of images in Gaul is confirmed by the surviving evidence of inscriptions, stone statues and reliefs, bronze statuettes, and terra-cotta figures. His image often appears in the mode of the classical Mercury: youthful, naked, and beardless; equipped with caduceus (rod entwined with a pair of snakes), petasos (wide-brimmed hat), and purse; and accompanied by cock, ram, or tortoise. But his image is also found in Gallo-Roman guise: mature, bearded, and dressed in a heavy cloak. Sometimes, as in the east and the north of Gaul, he has three heads. Unlike his Roman counterpart, he has a frequent consort named Maia or Rosmerta (The Provider) and includes the art of war in his range of competence.

One cannot assume that Caesar's Mercury coincides with a single native deity throughout the Celtic areas, but there is quite strong evidence for identifying him substantially with the Irish god Lugh (although some doubts have been expressed in this regard by Bernhard Maier). First, Lugh's name and cult were pan-Celtic. Further, Caesar speaks of Mercury as *omnium inventorem artium* (inventor of all the arts), a close paraphrase of Lugh's sobriquet in Irish, *(sam)ildánach* (skilled in many arts together). In fact, an episode in the tale of the mythological Battle of Magh Tuiredh dramatically sets forth Lugh's claim as the only god who was master of all the arts and crafts. At Osma in Spain an inscription was found with a dedication on behalf of a guild of shoemakers to the Lugoves, whose name is the plural of Lugus, an older form of Lugh. Most likely these divinities, who recur in an inscription from Avenches in Switzerland, are simply the pan-Celtic Lugus in plural, perhaps triple, form. The Middle Welsh tale *Math vab Mathonwy* may well echo this connection with shoemaking, for Lleu, the Welsh cognate of Lugh, operates briefly as a high-class practitioner of the craft.

In Ireland, Lugh was the youthful victor over malevolent demonic figures, and his great achievement was to kill the cyclopean Balar with a slingshot. Lughnasadh, his feast, was a harvest festival, and at least two of its principal sites, Carmun and Tailtiu, were the burial places of goddesses by the same names, who were associated with the fertility of the earth (as was, apparently, the Gaulish Mercury's consort Rosmerta). Lugh was the divine exemplar of sacred kingship, and in the tale *Baile in Scáil* (The Phantom's Vision) he appears seated in state as king of the otherworld and attended by a woman identified as the sovereignty of Ireland, reminiscent of Rosmerta. His usual epithet, *lámhfhada* (of the long arm), relates to his divine kingship. In the Christian period Lugh survived in the guise of several saints known by variants of his name—Lughaidh, Molua, and others—and the motif of the arm is reflected in these Christian traditions as well.

Gaulish Mars. A famous passage in Lucan's (39–65 CE) *Civil War* refers to the bloody sacrifices offered the three Celtic gods: Teutates, Esus, and Taranis. A later commentator on Lucan clearly illustrates the difficulty of identifying individual Gaulish and Roman gods, for one of his two main sources equated Teutates with Mercury, the other with Mars. But if, as seems likely, *teutates* is primarily a title ("god of the tribe") rather than a name, then such confusion is explainable: the god of sovereignty and the arts, Mercurius, will also function as a warrior, whereas the god of war, Mars, will often function as the protector of the tribe. Consequently, their functions will sometimes overlap, and it may be a matter of chance or circumstance which is given preeminence in a given time or place. A further complication is that many of the Gallo-Roman dedications to Mars present him not only as a god of war but also as god of healing and guardian of the fields, but this may reflect an extension of his role in the Roman period and does not necessarily discredit Caesar's description of him as god of war. So far as the insular tradition is concerned, a god of war does not come into clear focus, perhaps because fighting is a more or less universal rather than a differentiating feature in the heroic context. Thus one cannot easily define the role of Mars, and one cannot so easily assign him a pan-Celtic identity as one can Lugh.

Gaulish Apollo. The classical form of Apollo in Romano-Celtic monuments only partly conceals the several native deities who have been assimilated to him. The use of the plural is probably justifiable, because several of the fifteen or more epithets attached to Apollo's name have a wide distribution, which might suggest that they were independent gods. Yet some of these epithets may have referred to a single deity. Belenus was especially honored in the old Celtic kingdom of Noricum in the eastern Alps, as well as in northern Italy, southern Gaul, and Britain. The solar connotations of the stem *bel-* (shining, brilliant) would have confirmed the identification with the Greco-Roman Apollo. Grannus, whose name is of uncertain etymology, has a widespread cult with one of its principal centers at Aachen. He is sometimes accompanied by a goddess named Sirona. Borvo, or Bormo, whose name denotes boiling or seething water, is associated with thermal springs, as at Bourbonne-les-Bains and other sites named after him. His consort is Damona (Divine Cow) or Bormana.

This association of healing with springs and wells, which was subsequently taken over into Christian or sub-Christian usage throughout the Celtic countries, tended to encourage localized cults, and it is all the more remarkable that these early names had such an extensive currency. Unlike those already mentioned, Maponos (Divine Son/Youth) occurs mainly in northern Britain, although it is also attested in Gaul near healing springs. Maponos appears in medieval Welsh literature as Mabon, son of Modron, that is, of Matrona (Divine Mother), eponymous goddess of the river Marne in France. A brief but significant episode in the tale of *Culhwch and Olwen* casts him in the role of hunter and alludes to a myth attested elsewhere in insular literature of the youthful god carried off from his mother when three nights old. That his legend was once more extensive in oral tradition than appears from the extant literature is borne out by the survival of his name into Arthurian romance under the forms Mabon, Mabuz, and Mabonagrain.

His Irish equivalent was Mac ind Óg (Young Lad/Son), otherwise known as Oenghus, who was believed to dwell in Bruigh na Bóinne, the great Neolithic and therefore pre-Celtic, passage grave of Newgrange. He was the son of Daghdha, chief god of the Irish, and of Boann, eponym of the sacred river of Irish tradition (Boyne, in English). As his name and relationship suggest, he is a youthful god, and, perhaps in keeping with this, he is often treated with a certain affection in the literature, particularly in his familiar roles of trickster and lover. But he is nowhere presented as a god of healing, which merely underlines the impossibility of exactly equating Celtic and Roman gods in terms of their functional range.

Gaulish Minerva: Irish Brighid. The goddesses of insular Celtic tradition are involved in a wide range of activities that are only partly reflected in Caesar's succinct comment that Minerva concerned herself with teaching "the first principles of the arts and crafts" (*Minervam operum atque artificiorum initia tradere*), even though expertise in arts and crafts enjoyed high status in Celtic society and covered a broad swathe of competences. It is very probable that Caesar chose a single widely revered deity to represent the whole category of goddesses, national and regional. Dedications to Minerva are found throughout the Celtic areas of the continent and in Britain. At Bath she was identified with the goddess Sulis who was worshiped there in connection with the thermal springs and has been identified as a solar deity. The name Minerva is frequently accompanied by the epithet *belisama* (very brilliant), which suggests a rapport with the Gallo-Roman Apollo, who is sometimes named Belenus (The Shining One). The related plural *suleviae* is applied to triads of mother-goddesses at sites on the Continent and in Britain. Sulis Minerva is also related to the widespread and important category of mother-goddesses: Matres Suleviae and Suleviae Iunones.

In the Irish context the single goddess who answers best to Caesar's Minerva by virtue of her functional repertoire and wide-ranging cult is the goddess Brighid (from earlier **Brigentī*). According to the *Glossary of Cormac mac Cuilennáin* (c. 900) she was the daughter of the father-god, the Daghdha (literally, Good God), and was worshiped by the *filid*, the exclusive fraternity of learned seer-poets. In keeping with the Celtic penchant for triadic repetition, she had two sisters, also called Brighid—the one associated with healing, the other with the smith's craft—and their combined fame was such that among all the Irish a goddess used to be called Brighid (a statement that invites comparison with Caesar's use of Minerva as an inclusive term for the goddesses of Gaul). Thus, Brighid was patroness of the artistic inspiration of the poets as well as of healing and craftsmanship. Minerva, for her part, is associated with healing, as at the shrine of Bath, and she is also combined on reliefs with Mercury, the master of all the arts, and Vulcan, more specifically connected with the craftsmanship of the smith. It seems clear that Brighid is merely the Irish reflex of a pan-Celtic deity. Her name, which meant originally "The Exalted One," has its close linguistic correspondent in **Brigantî*, latinized as *Brigantia*, the name of the tutelary goddess of the Brigantes, who formed an important federation in northern Britain. She has also a remarkable Christian (or Christianized) double in the person of her namesake Brighid, the great sixth-century abbess of the monastery of Kildare. The legend of the saint is inextricably fused with that of her pagan alter ego, and as she is inevitably accorded a much fuller documentation by monastic redactors, there is the curious irony that the richest source for the mythology of the goddess is the hagiography of the saint together with the prolific folklore that commemorates her in popular tradition. Both the saint's *Lives* and her folklore suggest a close connection with livestock and the produce of the soil, and, appropriately, her feastday, February 1, coincides with Imbolg, the pagan festival of spring. In a passage of the *Topographia Hiberniae* that evidently draws on this conflate tradition, the twelfth-century Norman cleric Gerald of Wales (c.1146–c.1223; also known Giraldus Cambrensis) reports that Brighid and nineteen of her nuns at Kildare took turns in maintaining a perpetual fire surrounded by a hedge within which no male might enter. Also, it is a significant coincidence that already in the third century Iulius Solinus, associating Minerva with the healing springs of Sulis, mentions in *Collectanea Rerum Memorabilium* that perpetual fires burned in her sancuary also. In secular texts Brighid is sometimes made to aid and encourage the men of Leinster when they were engaged in crucial conflicts, a reflection perhaps of her pristine role as territorial goddess like those other Celtic deities indicated by such nicknames as Dea Tricoria of the Tricorii in the Narbonnaise, Dea Nemetona of the Nemetes in the Rhine region, or even Dea Brigantia of the British federation.

Celtic Vulcan. Although Caesar does not mention a Gaulish Vulcan, his cult was evidently known to all the Celtic peoples; indeed, the evidence suggests that he enjoyed a higher status than his Roman counterpart. Because he functioned as a very specialized deity, there is a strong probability that his native name among the continental Celts made reference to his craft, as it did in Ireland and Wales, where he was known as Goibhniu and Gofannon, both names derived from the word for *smith.* The weapons Goibhniu forged with his fellow craft gods, Luchta the Wright and Creidhne the Metalworker, were unerring in aim and fatal in their effect. Further, those who attended the Feast of Goibhniu and partook of the god's sacred drink were thereby rendered immune to age and decay. He was known for his healing powers, and he is invoked in an Old Irish charm for the removal of a thorn. Until the nineteenth century, and in some areas even into the twentieth century, the country smith was still believed to retain something of his ancient preternatural faculty, and he was constantly called on for the healing effects of his charms and spells. In the early tradition, Gobbán Saer (Gobbán the Wright; Gobbán is a hypocoristic form of Goibhniu) was renowned as a wondrous builder, and under the modern form, Gobán Saor, he is the skillful and resourceful mason who outwits his rivals and enemies by his clever stratagems.

Gaulish Hercules or Irish Oghma. Hercules is well represented in Celto-Roman iconography and has a number of regional epithets assigned to him. Doubtless his popularity derives largely from his identification with native Celtic gods who correspond approximately to his classical character. One of these is mentioned in a curious passage by the Greek writer Lucian in the second century CE, who, when describing a Gaulish picture of Hercules, notes that the Celts call him Ogmios. It showed him armed with his familiar club and bow but pictured him uncharacteristically as an old man, bald and gray with his skin darkened and wrinkled by the sun. He pulled behind him a willing band of men attached by slender chains that linked their ears to the tip of his tongue. The explanation, according to Lucian's Gaulish informant, was that eloquence reaches its apogee in old age: the Celts did not identify eloquence with Hermes, as did the Greeks, but with Hercules, because he was by far the stronger.

A question much debated is whether this hoary champion can be identified with the Irish god Oghma, despite the fact that the phonological correspondence is not exact. The functional parallel is adequate: Not merely is Oghma known as a *trénfher* (strong man, champion), but he is also credited with the invention of the Ogham letters. This system of writing was based on the Latin alphabet and can hardly be older than the fourth century CE, but it probably replaced an older system of magical symbols of the same name.

Gaulish Dis Pater or Irish Donn. Caesar mentions Dis Pater separately from the other gods and states that all the Gauls believed with their druids that they were descended from him. The reference is brief but is sufficient to indicate at least an analogy between the Gaulish god of the dead and his Irish counterpart Donn (Brown/Dark One), whose dwelling place was a small rocky island off the southwest coast of Ireland known as Tech nDuinn (House of Donn). Its English name, the Bull, echoes its other name in early Irish, Inis Tarbhnai (Island of Tarbnae). *Tarbhnae* derives from *tarbh* (bull), which perhaps suggests a connection between the god Donn and the great brown bull (the Donn) of Cuailnge, which provides the central motivation for the saga *Táin Bó Cuailnge* (The cattle raid of Cuailnge).

In his role as god of death, Donn is a rather retiring figure in the early literature. Like Dis Pater, he seems to stand apart from the other deities, but his importance is confirmed by his status in modern folk tradition, in which he is represented as the underworld god who creates storms and shipwrecks but also protects cattle and crops. Both early and late sources record the belief that the dead made their way or were ferried to his island after death. As one early text makes clear, these travelers were regarded as Donn's descendants returning to their divine ancestor. The parallel with Dis Pater is evident and is a further argument for the general authenticity of Caesar's account of the Gaulish deities. Donn's importance in indigenous religious tradition is implicitly recognized in the fact that he is included in the pseudo-history of *Leabhar Gabhála Éireann* as chief of the Gaels, the Sons of Míl, last of the several peoples to settle in Ireland, but his religious significance presented a problem of how to accommodate him within what was essentially a project of Christianizing native mythic history. The solution the redactors opted for was to dispose of him by having him drown in the sea off the southwest coast and be subsequently brought for burial to a rocky islet nearby that has been known ever since as the Island of Donn.

Sucellus and Nantosvelta. Some two hundred monuments, mostly in Gaul, show a deity holding a hammer, and a number name him as Sucellus (The Good Striker). Besides the characteristic hammer or mallet, he is often depicted with a cask or drinking jar and accompanied by a dog. He is sometimes paired with the goddess, Nantosvelta, whose name suggests an association with water (cf. Welsh *nant,* meaning *brook*). Particularly in the Narbonnaise, Sucellus is frequently assimilated to the Roman Silvanus, guardian of forests and patron of agriculture. Because of these associations and attributes, he has been seen as controlling fecundity, not an unusual function for an underworld deity. He has also been equated with the Celtic Cernunnos and the Irish Daghdha, but although there are certain broad similarities between them, the evidence does not suffice to prove a closer connection.

Goddesses and divine consorts. In continental iconography, the frequent pairing of god and consort represents the goddesses as complementary to the male deities, and this image may overlap with the ideal coupling of king and territorial goddess so widely portrayed in medieval Irish literature.

It seems impossible to draw any clear distinction between specific named goddesses and the *matres* or *matronae* who appear so frequently in Celtic iconography, often in triadic form like the goddesses of Irish tradition. Both goddesses and *matres* are concerned with fertility and with the seasonal cycle of the earth, and the insular goddesses are sometimes identified with the land and cast in the role of its protective deities. This intimate connection with the land and its physical features is reflected in the exceptional importance of the feminine element in the *dinnshenchas,* the vast accumulation of prose and verse, which constitutes a virtual mythological topography of Ireland. A goddess's concern for the land in general also becomes a responsibility for the particular region or kingdom with which she is especially associated. Each goddess ensures the material well-being, sovereignty, and physical security of her particular domain, just as Brighid, in the guise of her saintly namesake, protects Leinster both as goddess of war and as goddess of peace. The mother-god specifically titled as such, Mâtrona, gave her name to the river that is now the Marne in France. She was the mother of Maponos (The Youthful/Son God) known in Welsh as Mabon, son of Modron. In Irish tradition the corresponding role belonged to Boann, eponym of the river Boann (anglicized Boyne); she was the mother of the Irish divine youth par excellence, Mac ind Óc, whose name is the semantic equivalent of the Welsh and Celtic Mabon/Maponos. As mother, the goddess is sometimes represented in Irish texts as ancestress of a distinguished line of descent, and this is presumably what is intended by the author of the medieval Welsh tale "Branwen Daughter of Llŷr" in which he describes Branwen as one of the three great ancestresses of the island of Britain.

In keeping with their title—Matres, Matrae, Matronae—the mother-goddesses attested throughout the Romano-Celtic world are characteristically represented with the various symbols of their maternal and creative function: carrying or caring for infants or bearing such familiar symbols of prosperity as the cornucopia or the basket of fruits. They were also thought of as nourishing and watching over specific peoples and regions and were named accordingly the Matres Glanicae at Glanum (Saint-Rémy-de-Provence), for example, or the Matres Treverae among the Treveri. They would seem to have survived cultural and religious change in the guise of the *mamau* (mothers) and the formidable *cailleacha* (old women) of Welsh and Irish-Scottish popular tradition respectively.

Nature associations. Underlying the tradition of *dinnshenchas* is the belief that prominent places and geological features throughout Ireland were the scene of mythic events or the abode, even the embodiment, of mythic personages. Many of the numerous women who populate this world of onomastic legend are clear reflexes of the multifaceted goddess whose origins are bound up with the physical landscape—figures like Tailtiu and Carmun whose burial places were named after them—were the sites of great royal assemblies. In most of the Celto-Roman world the early onomastic lore disappeared with the indigenous languages, but something of it remained in the divine nomenclature of these areas.

Apart from the general cult of the earth goddess, an extensive repertory of deity names attached to individual places or topographical features also exists. Hilltops and mountain tops are considered particularly appropriate settings for the sacred, as evidenced by dedications to Garra and Baeserta in the Pyrenees and to Vosegus in the Vosges. There was a god of the clearing or cultivated field (Ialonus), of the rock (Alisanos), of the confluence (Condatis), of the ford (Ritena), and of the fortified place (Dunatis). Water, particularly the moving water of rivers and springs, had its special deities, which were generally female in the case of the rivers. One can perhaps glimpse the lost mythology of such rivers as the Seine (Sequana), the Marne (Matrona), and the Saone (Souconna) through the legends of insular equivalents like the Boyne (Boann). The names of many rivers throughout the Celtic lands, such as the French Dives or the Welsh Dyfrdwy, are derived from the stem *dev-* and mean simply "the divine one." Sacred springs are deified as, for example, Aventia (Avenches), Vesunna (Périgeux), and Divona (Cahors). Further, there were many divine patrons of thermal waters, such as the god Borvo, and this particularly widespread cult is reflected in the countless holy and healing wells (some twelve hundred in Wales alone, and no one has yet added up the Irish instances) that made the transition from paganism to Christianity with little essential change. However, the abundant material evidence for this pan-Celtic phenomenon is not matched by the early insular literary evidence: many Irish tales mention wells with preternatural powers and associations, but there is hardly anything about healing wells as such. Unless this is due to suppression by the monastic redactors of the literature, the only explanation would seem to be that the frequenting of healing wells had always been regarded, even in pagan times, as a popular practice to be distinguished from the more official tribal cults, or simply that it was so familiar as to be unremarkable.

In many instances the holy wells of the Christian period stand close to a specific tree that shares their supernatural aura. Obviously, this is one aspect of the widespread cult of sacred trees. In the Pyrenees there are dedications to the beech (Deo Fago) and to the Six Trees (Sexarbori deo, Sexarboribus) and at Angoulême to the oak (Deo Robori). The Romano-Celtic name of the town of Embron, *Eburodunum,* contains the name of the deified yew tree. Such continental forms are supplemented by a vast dossier of insular evidence. There were, for example, scores of Christian foundations in Ireland evidently located on the sites of pagan cult centers, each with its sacred tree nearby. The literature frequently mentions several great trees that were particularly honored in tradition: the Tree of Tortu (an ash), the Oak of Mughna, the Yew of Ross, the Bough of Dathí (an ash), the Ash of Uisnech, among others. There was even a special term for such trees, *bile,* and this term was sometimes used for the great tree that marked each of the inauguration sites of tribal and provincial kings. Standing theoretically at the center of its kingdom like the *axis mundi* in its greater cosmos, the *bile* symbolized the integrity and independence of the kingdom. When it happened, as it did occasionally, that it was attacked and felled by a hostile neighbor, this doubtless dealt a severe blow to communal pride and self-respect.

Zoomorphic gods. Celto-Roman iconography contains a rich abundance of animal imagery, frequently presenting the deities in combinations of zoomorphic and anthropomorphic forms. Already noted is the probable connection between Donn, the Irish Dis Pater, and the bull of the same name in the epic *Táin Bó Cuailnge*. Neither of the two bulls whose conflict forms the climax of the tale is of natural origin. According to other texts, they had previously undergone many metamorphoses—as ravens, stags, champions, water beasts, demons, and water worms—and in the beginning they had been the swineherds of the lords of the otherworld. This kind of shape shifting, a continuing expression of the unity of the living world of creation, is commonplace in insular Celtic tradition and serves to invest a given deity or heroic demigod with the attributes traditionally ascribed to certain birds and animals. For instance, the bond between animal and human is implicit in the archetype of the divine swineherds, who are doubtless avatars of the great herdsman god. Further, the Brown Bull of Cuailnge cannot be wholly dissociated from the Tarvos Trigaranus (The Bull of the Three Cranes), pictured on reliefs from Trèves and Notre-Dame-de-Paris and presumably the subject of a lost Gaulish narrative. Among the Celts, as among many other cattle-rearing peoples, the bull was a vivid symbol of power and fertility and appears frequently as a trope in the eulogy of the medieval Irish court poet. It is hardly surprising, therefore, that a god representative of royal and heroic functions should have been represented by this image. Donnotarvos (Brown Bull), the king of the Helvetii mentioned by Caesar, bore a name of great mythic resonance among the Celts, most probably derived from the same deity who appears in the Irish saga as the Brown Bull of Cuailnge.

The animal connections of the Celtic gods are extensive and varied. The iconography shows Cernunnos (The Horned One) associated with the stag, the ram-headed serpent, the bull, and, by implication, with the whole animal world. The iconography also includes boars, horses, dogs, and bears, as well as fish and various kinds of birds—all connected more or less closely with certain deities. This rich diversity is reproduced in even greater abundance in the insular tradition, creating a complex web of connotations and relationships that defy any neat classification. For example, the boar is quite well represented in Celto-Roman sculpture, as in the figure from Euffigneix, Haute-Marne, of a god carrying a boar before him. In insular literature it appears almost ubiquitous. It sometimes leads its pursuers into the otherworld, and often it is in fact a human who was transformed through some mischance or misdeed. Pork was the choice food of the Celts, and, appropriately, in Irish tales the unfailing food of the otherworld is a pig, which, although cooked each night, remains alive and whole each morning.

The horse, index and instrument of the great Indo-European expansion, has always had a special place in the affections of the Celtic peoples. Sometimes in insular tradition, particularly in folk tales, he is the bearer of the dead to the otherworld, a role probably reflected in some monuments in southern Gaul, such as the frieze of horses' heads on a lintel from the Celto-Ligurian sanctuary of Roquepertuse, Bouches-du-Rhone. Epona (from **epos*, meaning *horse*) was an important Celtic deity and was particularly favored as patron of the cavalry of the Roman army. She has insular analogues in the Welsh Rhiannon and in the Irish Edaín Echraidhe (*echraidhe*, meaning *horse riding*) and Macha, who outran the fastest steeds. There was also a Dea Artio (as well as a Mercurius Artaios), whose name connects her with the bear (Irish, *art*, meaning *bear*); a little bronze group from Bern shows her seated before a large bear with a basket of fruit by her side. Dea Arduinna, who appears seated on a wild boar, may be compared with the Irish goddess Flidhais, who ruled over the beasts of the forest and whose cattle were the wild deer.

Gaulish monuments that show a god or goddess with two or more birds seated on their shoulders call to mind the supernatural birds that are a familiar feature of insular tradition, in which some deities assume bird form occasionally; others, like the war goddesses, do so constantly. The insular catalog of bird imagery is endless. King Conaire's supernatural father came to his mother in bird form, Fann and Lí Ban came to Cú Chulainn as two birds joined by a golden chain, emissaries from the otherworld. Indeed, such wondrous birds are a recognized symbol of the supernatural world. Examples include the three birds of the Irish goddess Cliodhna with their magic song and the three birds of the Welsh Rhiannon who "wake the dead and lull the living to sleep." They all form part of that rich imaginative intuition that envisaged animals, birds, and the whole domain of nature as a mediating element between gods and men and that underlies Celtic literary tradition as well as the fluid discipline of early Irish art.

INVASIONS OF GODS AND MEN. When Irish monastic scholars began recording native mytho-historical tradition, probably in the second half of the sixth century, they experienced the same difficulty that Christian historiographers have encountered elsewhere in dealing with traditional sources: how to resolve the conflict between Christian and native versions of cosmic origins. Their solution was the familiar one of substituting the biblical doctrine for the earlier part of the native legend, so that it would seem that the legend derived from the doctrine. The fact that the scholars controlled the art of writing invested their new composite history—incrementally elaborated under the influence of the chronicles of Orosius (c. 385–420) and Eusebius of Caesarea (c. 260–c. 330 CE) and Isidore of Seville's (c. 560–636) *Etymologiae*—with an authority it might not otherwise have acquired so quickly.

As Christian scholars developed an increasingly close accommodation over the next few centuries with the custodians of native learning, the *filidh*, their revised version gradually won universal acceptance. Although it did not erase all trace of the earlier tradition, it cancelled out the substance of the original cosmogonic myth. For instance, although the primary ancestral role of Donn, Nuadhu, and others was not forgotten, Adam was accepted as the progenitor of mankind.

The Book of Invasions. The formulation of this revised teaching is attested in poems of the seventh century or earlier, but it was in the twelfth century that it reached its culmination in the pseudohistory entitled *Leabhar Gabhála Éireann* (The Book of the Taking of Ireland), commonly known as the "Book of Invasions," a cumulative enterprise that carried the tale of Ireland's history from Noah to the Norman conquest. The "taking" in question evidently refers to the coming of the Gaels (or Goidels), but in the extant compilation this is preceded by five other immigrations. The first came before the Flood and was led by either Cesair, a daughter of Bith, who was a son of Noah, or by Banbha, one of the eponyms of Ireland. But the only one to survive the Flood was Fintan (The White Ancient One), who outlived innumerable generations until finally in the Christian period he bore witness to the events of the distant past. The next two settlements were led by Partholón and Nemhedh, respectively. During both, various crafts and social practices were introduced, many lakes were formed, and plains were cleared. These advances indicate in the familiar manner of myths of beginnings how Ireland attained the reality of permanent morphological definition in those times. Both peoples had to withstand the attacks of the Fomhoire, a race of demonic beings who from their haunts beyond the sea posed a perpetual threat to the existence of ordered society.

The main innovations credited to the fourth settlement, comprising the Fir Bholg, the Gailióin, and the Fir Dhomhnann, were sociopolitical in character. By dividing the country into five they instituted the provinces (literally, *fifths* in Irish), and they introduced the concept of sacred kingship and the relationship between the justice of the king and the fertility of the land. They were followed by the Tuatha Dé Danann (The Tribes/Peoples of the Goddess Danu), who came skilled in the arts of druidry and magic. They brought with them four talismans: the Stone of Fál, which shrieked under the true pretender to kingship; the spear of Lugh, which ensured victory; the sword of Nuadhu, which none escaped; and the caldron of the Daghdha, from which none went unsatisfied. They defeated the Fir Bholg in the First Battle of Magh Tuiredh, but soon they had to take up arms against the Fomhoire.

The Second Battle of Magh Tuiredh. There is also an independent account of the Second Battle of Magh Tuiredh in a text that is perhaps the single most important source for Irish mythology. In it the genesis of the conflict is traced to the First Battle of Magh Tuiredh, in which Nuadhu, king of the Tuatha Dé Danann, lost his arm. Because a personal defect, physical or moral was incompatible with the notion of true kingship, he was obliged to abdicate and was succeeded by Bres (The Beautiful), who had been fathered by Elatha, a king of the Fomhoire, with a woman of the Tuatha Dé, among whom he was reared. But his rule brought only hardship and oppression for the Tuatha Dé, and there was an end to the generosity and hospitality that characterized a true king. Finally he was lampooned by the poet Coirbre in the first satire composed in Irish, and he was asked to give up the kingship. His response was to go to the Fomhoire to seek their support.

Meanwhile, Nuadhu was fitted with a silver arm by Dian Cécht (The Leech) and restored to sovereignty, and from that time forth he was known as Nuadhu Airgedlámh (Nuadhu of the Silver Arm). But when Lugh came to the royal court of Tara and gave proof of his mastery of all the arts, Nuadhu immediately gave way so that Lugh might lead the Tuatha Dé to victory. In the battle itself Lugh called on all the preternatural powers of the craftsmen and magicians of the Tuatha Dé, while Dian Cécht used his own healing magic to revive the slain. The dreaded Balar of the Fomhoire had a "baleful eye" which could destroy armies, but Lugh struck it with his slingstone and killed him. The Fomhoire were then expelled from Ireland forever, and Bres himself was captured, but his life was spared on condition that he divulge to the Tuatha Dé the proper times for plowing, sowing, and reaping.

The Gaels and the Tuatha Dé. The primary subject of the "Book of Invasions" was perhaps the final settlement of prehistoric Ireland, that of the Gaels, or Irish Celts. Because its underlying purpose was to biblicize the origins of the Gaels, it began, as it were, at the beginning, following them in their long journey from Scythia to Egypt and to Spain, whence they finally came to Ireland under the leadership of Míl Espáine (Míl of Spain). The account of this early odyssey is a learned fiction modeled on the story of the wandering of the Israelites in the book of Exodus. But as the narrative approaches Ireland, it undergoes a sea change and begins to draw more overtly on native tradition. The crucial role in the landing is assigned to the poet-seer and judge Amhairghin. By virtue of his wisdom and his mantic power he overcomes the opposition of the Tuatha Dé and becomes the first Gael to set foot on Irish soil. As he does so—on the Feast of Beltene (May Day)—he sings a song of cosmic affirmation in which he subsumes within himself the various elements of the created universe: "I am an estuary into the sea / I am a wave of the ocean / I am the sound of the sea / . . . I am a salmon in a pool / I am a lake in a plain / I am the strength of art." Like Kṛṣṇa in the Indian tradition and Taliesin in the Welsh, he embodies the potential of all creation, and the timing of his song is particularly appropriate and decisive. Sung as he arrives at the land's edge from the ocean of nonexistence, his words are the prelude to the creation of a new order of which he is the shaper and the source. Through them and through the judgments he pronounces in the succeeding narrative, the Ireland of history is summoned into being.

Having defeated the Tuatha Dé, the Sons of Míl go to the royal center of Tara and on the way meet the three divine eponyms of Ireland—Banbha, Fódla, and Ériu. At Tara the three kings of the Tuatha Dé—Mac Cuill, Mac Cécht, and Mac Gréine—ask for a respite before surrendering sovereignty. Significantly, they refer the conditions to the judgment of Amhairghin. He decides that the Sons of Míl should reembark and retire beyond the ninth wave, which for the Celts constituted a magic boundary. But when they try to land again, the Tuatha Dé create a magical wind that carries them out to sea. Then Amhairghin invokes directly the land of Ireland, and immediately the wind abates. The Sons of Míl come ashore and defeat the Tuatha Dé at Tailtiu, site of the annual festival instituted by Lugh.

Although defeated, the Tuatha Dé still use their magic powers to extract a reasonable settlement from the Gaels. They agree to divide the country into two parts, the lower half going to the Tuatha Dé and the upper half to the Gaels. Thus is explained the traditional belief that the ancient gods—the *sídheóga* (fairies)—lived underground in *sídhe*, or fairy mounds. That this belief was traditional already in the seventh century is evidenced by Bishop Tírechán, biographer of Saint Patrick, who noted that the *sídh*, or gods, dwell in the earth.

GODS OF BRITAIN. Early Welsh literary tradition, like the medieval Welsh language, seems further evolved from its archaic roots than its Irish counterpart. This is probably due partly to the cultural effects of the Roman colonization of Britain from the first to the fifth century and partly to the late redaction of the extant material, particularly the prose. But whatever the causes, the result is that Welsh mythological narrative, although preserving some remarkably archaic elements, nonetheless lacks the extensive context found in Irish narrative and betrays the hand of a later redactor or redactors not wholly familiar with the mythological framework from which their materials derived.

Family of Dôn. The main source for Welsh mythological tradition is the collection of tales known as the *Mabinogi* or *Mabinogion*, especially the group known as the "Four Branches." These four tales, which were probably redacted toward the end of the eleventh century, take the gods of Britain as their dramatis personae. The last of the four, "Math Son of Mathonwy," deals in particular with the group of gods sometimes referred to as the family of Dôn. The Math of the title is lord of Gwynedd in north Wales. His peculiarity is that he must keep his feet in a virgin's lap except in time of war. When his virginal foot-holder is violated by his sister's son—Gilfaethwy, son of Dôn—with the connivance of his brother Gwydion, son of Dôn, Math turns the two brothers into male and female animals—stags, boars, and wolves—for three years, during which time they give birth to three sons.

Subsequently, Math seeks a new foot-holder, and Gwydion suggests his sister, Aranrhod, daughter of Dôn. Math asks her to step over his magic wand as a test of her virginity, and as she does so, she drops a yellow-haired boy and something else, which Gwydion promptly conceals in a chest. The boy is baptized Dylan and immediately makes for the sea and takes on its nature, for which reason he is henceforth called Dylan Eil Don (Dylan son of Wave). The object concealed by Gwydion turns out to be another male child, who in due course is given the name Lleu Llaw Gyffes (Lleu of the Skillful Hand). The rest of the tale is taken up with Lleu's relations with his mother, Aranrhod, and with his beautiful but treacherous wife, Blodeuwedd (Flower-aspect), who had been created for him by Gwydion from the flowers of the oak, the broom, and the meadow sweet. The name Lleu is, of course, the cognate of the Irish Lugh and the Gaulish *Lugus.

The same tale refers incidentally to Gofannon, son of Dôn (Divine Smith), whose name is cognate with the Irish Goibhniu. There is mention elsewhere of Amaethon, son of Dôn, the divine plowman, and there are various references in medieval poetry that indicate the existence of extensive oral tradition about the family of Dôn. Their communal association with magic is reminiscent of the Irish Tuatha Dé Danann, and it has been suggested that Dôn is the equivalent of Irish Donu (Mother of the Gods), the original form of the name Danann.

Family of Llŷr. The three members of the family of Llŷr—Branwen, Bendigeidvran (Bran the Blessed), and Manawydan—appear in the "Second Branch" of the *Mabinogi,* although it is only in the "Third Branch" that Manawydan assumes an independent role. The tale is dominated by the enormous figure of Bendigeidvran. When his sister Branwen is ill treated in Ireland, where she has gone as the wife of Matholwch, king of Ireland, he goes with an army to exact vengeance. The British gain victory in a fierce battle with the Irish, but only seven of them survive beside Bendigeidvran, who is wounded in the foot by a poisonous spear. He commands his companions to cut off his head and to bury it at the White Mount in London as a safeguard against invasions. They set out for London and on the way enjoy two periods of otherworldly peace and joy in the presence of his uncorrupted head, at Harlech and on the isle of Gwales.

Clearly, the children of Llŷr are not comparable with those of Dôn: in no sense do they form a pantheon of deities; indeed, Branwen's antiquity is not beyond question. But the association of Bran (as Bendigeidvran was known earlier) and Manawydan is old, and there is an early verse reference to them presiding together over the otherworld and its feast. Manawydan's Irish counterpart is Manannán mac Lir (Son of the Sea), and it is a curious and perhaps significant coincidence that Manannán figures with an Irish Bran in an early lyric tale, which tells of a journey made by Bran to the otherworld. But Manannán is represented as god of the sea, probably replacing the god Nechtan in this role, whereas Manawydan has no such function in Welsh in the extant Welsh texts.

Pwyll, Rhiannon, and Pryderi. In the "First Branch" of the *Mabinogi*, Pwyll, Lord of Dyfed in southwest Wales, comes to the aid of Arawn, king of Annwn, by slaying his otherworld enemy Hafgan in a single combat that is, in fact, an ordeal by battle of the kind known in early Irish as *fír fer* (truth of men or heroes). As a result he is henceforth known as Pwyll the Head of Annwn. The *Mabinogi* represents him here as a mortal, but because his name literally means *wisdom* and because he is designated Lord of Annwn (the Otherworld), it is probable that he was originally a deity. The latter part of the tale is concerned with the death of the hero Pryderi. Pwyll marries the lady Rhiannon, who first appears to him riding a white horse, and from their union Pryderi is born. But the newborn child is mysteriously abducted, to be discovered later by Teyrnon, Lord of Gwent Is-coed, and reared by him and his wife for several years until they realize the child's true origins and restore him to Pwyll and Rhiannon. After Pwyll's death Pryderi succeeds to the lordship of Dyfed. Later, in the "Third Branch," Rhiannon becomes the wife of Manawydan.

The above merely sketches a complicated narrative whose reference to the underlying mythology is extremely difficult to decipher with any confidence. Teyrnon's name (from **Tigernonos*; Great/Divine Lord) implies a more important role than the one he plays in the tale and, in fact, is a more appropriate title for the lord of the otherworld. Rhiannon (whose name derives from **Rīgantona*; Great/Divine Queen) may be an equivalent of Epona, the Celtic horse goddess, whereas Rhiannon and Pryderi seem to offer a parallel to the pairing of Modron (Great/Divine Mother) and Mabon (Great/Divine Son). The problem is similar to that posed by much of the Welsh mythological evidence in the medieval poetry and the collections of triads: There are numerous references to mythological persons, objects, and events, but these appear without sufficient accompanying matter to set them in context.

GODDESSES OF THE INSULAR CELTS. In *The Aran Islands* (1907) John M. Synge said of the Aran islanders of the beginning of the twentieth century that they were interested in fertility rather than eroticism, and on the evidence of the extant monuments and literature, his observation could apply to those people who created the mythology of the Celtic goddesses. The Celts had no goddess of love, and so far as one can judge from insular tradition, the numerous sexual liaisons of the goddesses were generally motivated by ritual or social causes, not by erotic ones. Their sexuality was merely the instrument of their fertility, whether in terms of progeny or of the fruitfulness of the land with which they were so often identified.

The cult of the mother goddess, attested in Gaul from prehistoric times, underlies a great deal of Irish and Welsh tradition. The "Second Branch" of the *Mabinogi* describes Branwen daughter of Llŷr as "one of the three great ancestresses of Britain." The other two presumably are Rhiannon and Aranrhod, and it is clear from Irish literature that the typical goddess figure was often esteemed as the genetrix of peoples. Her personification of the earth tended to be defined and delimited by cultural and political boundaries: The eponymous triad of Ériu, Fódla, and Banbha represent both the reality and the concept of Ireland in its totality, but a multitude of analogous characters also exist that are connected with lesser areas—a province, a district, or a particular locale. Some of the latter, such as Áine, Aoibheall, and Cliodhna, have retained their niche in popular tradition and in place names to the present day. In this domain the supernatural female often becomes a dominant figure overshadowing her male counterpart.

One of the most enduring myths of the Celts was that of the solemn union between a ruler and his kingdom, in which the kingdom is conceived in the form of a divine woman. It appears, slightly veiled, in the Arthurian romances and may be reflected at times in the frequent pairing of god and goddess in Celto-Roman sculpture, but its influence is most profound and most widely documented in Irish tradition. The normal way of reporting the inauguration of a king was to say that he was married to (literally, "slept with") his kingdom. From the hundreds if not thousands of references and allusions to this theme, one gains some idea of the ritual union of king and consort as it must have been performed before the effective Christianization of the political establishment in the sixth century. The ritual union had two main elements: first, a libation offered by the bride to her partner, and second, the sex act. The divine nature of Queen Medhbh of Connacht is evidenced by her name as well as by her actions: She who was famed for the number of her successive husbands was called Medhbh (The Intoxicating One), and, under the slightly variant name Medhbh Lethdherg, it was said of her that "she would not permit a king in Tara unless he had her for his wife." The central element was the sexual meeting, and its profound significance is brought out in countless poems and narratives in which the woman is transformed from repulsive age and ugliness to radiant youth and beauty by the act of intercourse with her ordained mate.

As leader of the Connacht armies, Medhbh is associated with war as well as with sovereignty, but, in general, the warlike aspect of the goddess is manifested indirectly: she influences the fortunes of war rather than actually participating. Other goddesses teach the art of fighting, including Buanann (The Lasting One); Scáthach (The Shadowy One), from whom Cú Chulainn acquired his heroic skills; and the formidable trio of Morríghan (Phantom Queen), Bodhbh (Scald-Crow), and Nemhain (Frenzy) or Macha, who haunt the battlefield to incite the fighters or to hinder them by their magic. These had their equivalents throughout the Celtic world: The name Bodhbh Chatha (Crow/Raven of Battle) is the exact cognate of Cathubodua, attested in Haute-Savoie, and the trio of war goddesses recurs in Britain at Benwell in the inscription "*Lamiis tribus*" (to the three Lamiae).

In direct contrast to these ruthless furies are those charming women who inhabit the happy otherworld in such numbers that it came to be called Tír inna mBan (The Land of Women) in some contexts. Sometimes they come as emissaries from the land of primeval innocence where the pleasures of love are untainted by guilt and where sickness and disease are unknown. Conla son of Conn is induced to go there by "a young and beautiful woman of noble race whom neither death awaits nor old age," and Bran son of Febhal is similarly persuaded by a woman bearing a silvery branch from the wondrous apple tree, which is a characteristic feature of the Celtic otherworld. The multiforms of the insular Celtic goddesses are endless, and sometimes the named figure changes her role from one context to another. For example, in *Mythe et épopée* (1968), Georges Dumézil has sought to demonstrate from three separate tales that the goddess Macha, eponym of the old pagan center of Emhain Mhacha and of the Christian metropolis of Ard Macha (modern Armagh), reflects in her several roles the Indo-European trifunctional system of religion, warrior prowess, and fertility. Although his argument is open to question, it is nonetheless true that several of the prominent goddesses have widely varying epiphanies.

MYTHIC SPACE AND TIME. In a tradition in which the natural and the supernatural realms frequently converge, it is not surprising that there is a constant awareness of the relativities of time and space. This is particularly true of texts relating explicitly to the otherworld, but it is common throughout Irish and much of Welsh literature. The land of Ireland itself, with its place names and physical features, seems to shift with enigmatic ease between the two levels of perception. The early redactors of the written texts were fascinated by the contrasting effects of changing perspective, as when the god Manannán describes the sea as a flowery plain or the monks of Clonmacnois observe a boat sail in the sky over their head and drop its anchor by their church door.

But certain places are permanently set apart from their secular environment: cult sites, the precincts of sacred festivals, and, above all, the notional center of the ethnic world of native tradition. This concept of the center is one of the constants of Celtic ideology, and it retained a good deal of its ancient symbolism in Irish learned literature as late as the seventeenth century. Caesar reports that the Gaulish druids assembled each year at a holy place in the lands of the Carnutes, which was regarded as the center of Gaul. His term *locus consecratus* may well translate the word *nemeton* (sacred place),which is found in place-names throughout the Celtic world. According to Strabo (c. 63 BCE–24 CE), the Council of the Galatians met at a place known as Drunemeton (Oak Sanctuary). In Ireland the druids were closely associated with Uisnech, the "navel" of Ireland, the location of the primal fire, and reputedly the site of a great festival. The focus of sacral kingship was at Tara in the central province of Midhe (Middle) and it was entirely fitting that St Patrick's late seventh-century biographer, Muirchú maccu Machtheni, who describes Tara as *caput Scotorum* (the capital of Ireland), should have him travel there to demonstrate his superiority over the druids of Loegaire mac Néill, *imperator barbarorum* and "ancestor of the royal stock of almost the whole of this island."

The great social assemblies of ancient Ireland were generally held at one of the seasonal festivals. The Irish year, like the Indo-European year, was divided into two halves, *samh* (summer) and *gamh* (winter). The summer half began at Beltene or Cédshamhain, the first of May, and the winter half at Samhain, the first of November. These halves were further subdivided by the quarter days of Imbolg, the first of February and the beginning of spring, and Lughnasadh, the first of August and the start of the harvest festival associated with the god Lugh. The old binary division is found also in the famous bronze calendar discovered at Coligny, near Bourg, which probably dates from the early first century CE or late first century BCE. Judging from the calendar, the Gaulish druids divided the year into two halves beginning with the months Samon(i-) and Giamon(i-). Of the two names for the beginning of summer, Beltene may have referred originally to the fire ritual traditionally held at that time: *bel-* probably means *shining* or *bright*, and *tene* may be related to the Irish word for *fire*. In the course of time, however, Beltene displaced the older term Cédshamhain or Cédamhuin (cf. the Welsh cognate Cyntefin) as the name for the festival season itself.

KINGSHIP. In Caesar's time the institution of kingship was already on the way to dissolution in Gaul, having been widely displaced by the secular office of *vergobret* (chief magistrate), although it is clear from the extant evidence that all the tribal territories, the *civitates* of Caesar's time, had earlier been ruled by kings in the mold of those of early Britain and Ireland. The medieval Irish king tales inevitably share in some degree the values of the general heroic literature, but these are not their main preoccupation. They are concerned rather with the affirmation of political and social realities and with the safeguarding of traditional institutions: the status and functions of the king and the sacred ritual of inauguration that set the seal on his accession to power, the origins of tribes and dynasties and exemplary tales of their internecine conflicts, the deeds and judgements of famous rulers of the past, and so on. The sacral kingship was both the pivot and the foundation of the social order, and the king was its personification. If his conduct or even his person were blemished in any way, the effect of his blemish would be visited on his kingdom, diminishing its integrity and prosperity; conversely, fortune favored the righteous ruler and his people flourished and his territory became rich and fertile. As the instrument of justice, the king must be seen to be fair and flawless in his decisions and several of the famous kings of legend are frequently presented as models of regal wisdom and justice. Thus, Cormac mac Airt is pictured as a paragon of kingship and as an Irish Solomon. His accession came about when he proposed a just judgement after his predecessor Lughaidh mac Con had been deposed for delivering an unjust one. Conaire Mór is likewise an exemplary king whose reign brings peace and well-being to the land until he tempers justice with excessive mercy in the case of his three marauding foster brothers. Immediately a train of events is set in motion that leads inexorably to his death in a welter of violence.

As the central pillar of his kingdom the sacral king was its primary point of contact with the world of the supernatural in pre-Christian time, and as such it was necessary to insulate him from harmful intervention from whatever source. Thus each of the five provincial kings was subject to a set of *gessa* (taboos), which made manifest the transcendent nature of his role and were presumably intended to hedge him from unnecessary danger. When, however, as in the case of Conaire Mór, he unavoidably or unwittingly violates his *gessa*, he is already doomed to disaster and death. The crucial touchstone of a king's reign was the *fír flathemon* (the ruler's truth/righteousness) with which he discharged the responsibilities of his office. The analogy between the *fír flathemon* and the Indic "act of truth" has long been recognized and there is acceptance that together they represent an Indo-European institution. The concept of the Ruler's Truth is referred to frequently in Irish literature, most notably in *Audacht Morainn* (The Testament of Morann, a legendary law-giver), an early example of the literary genre of the *speculum principum* (literary, "mirror of princes"), which was designed to give counsel and guidance to a king. The *Audacht* was probably written toward the end of the seventh century CE, but the genre was already long established in oral tradition, and it is widely accepted that the European *speculum principum* derives partly from the Irish model and that the *Audacht* itself contains much that is referable to Irish kingship in the pre-Christian period.

As a genre the *speculum* was evidently associated with the rite of royal inauguration and was probably recited publicly by a druid or *fili* in the course of the ritual ceremony. In the pre-Christian and early Christian period, as reflected in the classical law tracts, there were three grades of kingship: the *rí tuaithe* (king of a *tuath;* literally, "*people*" or "*tribe*"), the smallest political entity; the *ruiri* (great king or overking), who, as well as ruling over his own petty kingdom, received tribute from several other *tuatha;* and finally the *rí ruirech* (king of overkings), who is equated to the *rí cóicid* (king of a province). Despite the wide disparity of these kingships in range and importance, each of them had its own sacred king and its own inauguration site. However, it is clear that Tara—as the ideological focus of sacral kingship and at the heart of the Irish cosmographic system—enjoyed a special prestige as a kind of *primus inter pares* (first among equals) among royal sites and thus became the goal, real or notional, of ambitious kings throughout the early Middle Ages. Feis Temhra (The Feast/Wedding Feast of Tara) was the great festival held in pagan times to confirm a new king and to celebrate his ritual marriage to his kingdom. At Tara stood the Lia Fáil (Stone of Fál), the "stone penis" that cried out when it came in contact with the man destined to be king. *Feis,* verbal noun of the verb *foaid,* means literally "to sleep, spend the night," and, in the context of the royal confirmation, it refers to the ritual marriage of the king and his kingdom, as underlined in the alternative expression *banais rígi* (wedding feast of kingship), in which *banais* is compounded of *ben* (woman) and *feis.* This terminology continues to be used of various royal inaugurations in annalistic and other texts, even in the Anglo-Norman period. One can only speculate as to the precise form the marriage ritual may have assumed in pre-Christian times—actual union with a surrogate bride or a simulated union that included the proffering of the drink of sovereignty. The earliest list of reigning kings for the kingship of Tara is furnished by the seventh-century text *Baile Chuind* (The vision of [King] Conn [Cétchathach]), which purports to prophesy the individual kings who were to reign in Tara from the time of his son Art onward. Its literal formula for "*X* shall reign" is "*X* shall drink it," in which the formal potion presented to the ordinand is employed as a synonym for the combined ceremony of sacral investiture and the exercise of kingship. The text is devoid of explanatory introduction and is presumably to be understood as spoken by Conn himself, but when it was reworked and expanded in a more narrative and iconically stylized context in the ninth century in the tale *Baile in Scáil* (The phantom's vision), the prophecy is spoken by the god Lugh, the Irish (and Celtic) divinity traditionally regarded as personifying the ideal of kingship. It tells how Conn went on a circuit of the rampart of Tara accompanied by his three druids to guard against hostile incursions by forces from the otherworld, perhaps a reference to the familiar taboo that forbade the king to let the sun rise on him in Tara. One recalls, for example, the story of Aillén mac Midgna from the otherworld mound of Síd Finnachaid who came regularly to Tara at Samain (Hallowe'en), lulled its people to sleep with his supernatural music (*ceol sídhi*) and burned it down with a pillar of fire, until finally he was slain by the leader of the Fiana, Fionn mac Cumaill. So, when Conn mounts the rampart of Tara in *Baile in Scáil,* he comes into direct contact with the otherworld, although, in this instance, under one of its more benign aspects. A magic mist enveloped the king and his companions and a horseman (the *scál* or phantom) approached and asked them to accompany him to his dwelling. Within they found a girl seated on a chair of crystal and wearing a golden crown. Beside her stood a vessel of gold with a golden cup nearby. The phantom, seated on his throne, identified himself as the god Lugh and declared that he had come to announce to them the names of Conn's successors and the duration of their reigns. The young woman was the sovereignty of Ireland and when she asked to whom she should offer the cup of red ale (*dergfhlaith*), the phantom enumerated his catalog of the kings who would follow Conn.

The terminology used in reference to the *hieros gamos* (sacred marriage) of king and goddess points to some sort of sexual union taking place in pre-Christian times, as do the several tales of the loathsome hag who is transformed to youth and beauty by intercourse with the rightful candidate for kingship, a theme that is exploited for political dynastic ends in extant medieval versions. But accounts of the actual inauguration ceremony are of later date and betray some degree of ecclesiastical influence. Inevitably the Christian Church, conscious of the pivotal significance of the sacral kingship to native society, sought to arrogate to itself a central role in "ordaining" the ruler, and thus to sanitize the most incompatible elements of the traditional ritual. But tradition was tenacious. According to a quite late prose account (fourteen to sixteenth century) of the ceremonial inauguration of the Ó Conchubhar kings of Connacht, many clerics and all the subkings of the province were present, yet it was Ó Maoil Chonaire, the *fili*, modern proxy of the ancient druid, who installed him as king (*aga ríghadh*) by presenting him with the rod of sovereignty, and, the text adds, none but Ó Maoil Chonaire had the right to be with the king on the inauguration mound apart from the keeper of the mound.

Moreover, the gradual revision of the inauguration ceremony during the pre-Norman centuries may not have proceeded as regularly and universally as most later accounts might suggest. In a well-known passage of his *Topographia Hiberniae*, which is based on information garnered during his stay in Ireland in the late twelfth century, Gerald of Wales describes a "barbarous and abominable" rite of inauguration practiced in what is now County Donegal. A white mare is brought to the midst of the assembled people, the future chief has sexual union with the mare, which is then killed, cut in pieces, and boiled. The chief then sits in this bath, eats of the mare's meat and drinks of the broth, and thus kingship and power is conferred on him. Despite the lack of supporting native testimonies, it is difficult to discount the striking analogy this bizarre ritual presents to the Indic *asvamedha* (horse sacrifice), one that is accepted by most comparatists. The main disparity is that in the Irish version the sex act involves the king and a mare instead of the queen and a stallion, as in India, but some scholars would, in fact, argue that the Indo-European inauguration was primarily between king and mare. However, even if the essential authenticity of Gerald's account is accepted, it does not follow, as some have assumed, that such a rite was practiced in or close to his time. Elsewhere he draws on reports—some fabulous, others more factual—gathered from a variety of sources, oral as well as written. In this particular instance, it is a piece of *seanchas* (oral history), referring to an already more or less obsolete era. Nonetheless, it is a useful reminder that the version of native belief and ideology mediated to modern readers by the redactors of the medieval monasteries is less than comprehensive.

Another archaic institution associated with royal inauguration was the *crech ríg* (royal foray), which is still attested in the post-twelfth century Anglo-Norman period. As in ancient India, such a cross-border raid was a recognized occasion for the new king to demonstrate his fitness for office and at the same time to acquire the means to make appropriate show of his largesse.

The heroic ideal: The Ulster Cycle. Like the sacral king of prehistoric tradition, the hero occupied an ambiguous status between god and men. Typically, he has a divine as well as a human father, and his trials and achievements bring him into contact with supernatural powers more frequently than other mortals. He has many incarnations in insular Celtic literature, but it is above all the Ulster Cycle that represents him in the quintessential heroic setting.

The cycle is set in the province of Ulster when it was dominated by the Ulaidh, the people from whom the province derived its name, at a time somewhere between the coming of the Celts, perhaps as late as the third century BCE, and the conquest of the Ulaidh, which may have taken place in the early fifth century CE. The cycle portrays an aristocratic warrior society with a La Tène (Second Iron Age) type material culture, and in many respects the society shows striking correspondences with what is reported of independent Gaul. The king of the Ulaidh at this time was Conchobhar mac Nessa, who had his royal court at Emhain Mhacha near the present city of Armagh. He presided over a numerous company, which included the youthful Cú Chulainn, the senior heroes Conall Cernach and Ferghus mac Roich, and such others as the druid Cathbhadh, the wise peacemaker Sencha mac Ailella, and the inveterate mischief-maker Bricriu, known as Nemhthenga (Poison-tongue). These characters constitute the cast of an extensive literature of which the centrepiece is the great saga *Táin Bó Cuailnge* (The cattle raid of Cuailnge). It tells of Queen Medhbh of Connacht's incursion into Ulster with the object of seizing the great Brown Bull of Cuailnge, which was of divine origin. As a result of a curse by the goddess Macha, the Ulstermen are unable to resist the attack, and it falls to the young Cú Chulainn to defend the province single-handedly. By engaging in a series of single combats with heroes of the Connacht army, he hinders their advance until the Ulstermen recover their strength and rout their enemies. The climax and finale of the tale is the tremendous encounter in which the bull of Cuailnge slays the Finnbhennach, the white-horned bull of Connacht.

As the heroic milieu par excellence, the court of Conchobhar at Emhain became the focus for a wide variety of tales reflecting the different facets of the heroic ethos, and as the quintessential hero Cú Chulainn became the subject of many narratives exploring the nature of the hero's mediating role between gods and men and his singular relationship with his own community. Cú Chulainn experiences the perennial dilemma of the supreme hero caught in the insoluble contradictions of his ambiguous status. Neither divine nor merely human, Cú Chulainn lives within the tribe and yet does not wholly belong; a member of a heroic confraternity, he characteristically stands alone. His initiation to the heroic circle is recounted in a section of *Táin Bó Cuailnge* that narrates his boyhood deeds (*macghnímhartha*), which, linguistically, is not part of the oldest stratum of the text (it may belong to the ninth century), although its content is part of an archaic tradition. For his first exploit, Cú Chulainn slays the three fearsome sons of Nechta Scéne who have been a scourge on the Ulstermen. Here the narrative appears to reproduce an old Indo-European motif of the hero's victory over a trio of adversaries or a three-headed monster. He also, for the first time, experiences the *riastradh* (grotesque distortion) and the phenomenal body heat that are the external manifestations of his battle fury and that mark him in Irish tradition as a hero above heroes. These traits also have old and widespread analogues.

Cú Chulainn's career is a short one, but because it constitutes a paradigm of the hero, the mythmakers and storytellers have taken the critical stages of his life and woven a web of narrative around each: his threefold birth distinguished by incest and divine paternity, familiar marks of the sacred conception of the hero; his martial training with the otherworldly Scáthach; his wooing of Emher and his marriage; and finally his death, which, because he was invincible by merely human means, could only be effected through trickery and sorcery. This framework has also accommodated a number of other more occasional tales, such as those of his adventures in the otherworld or the tragic *Aided Aenfhir Aífe* (The death of Aífe's only son), which brings Cú Chulainn to slay his own son through a combination of moral compulsion and mistaken identity.

But Cú Chulainn and his life cycle are only a part of the larger cycle of the Ulster tales and in many he plays a relatively small role or none at all. His singular importance is that he epitomizes the heroic virtues and values. By the seventh century CE he had become a focus in the written literature for archaic traditions pertaining to what Dumézil defined as the second of the Indo-European social functions—that of the warrior.

The Fionn Cycle. In early Irish, the Fionn Cycle was also known as the *Fianaighecht.* It comprises a complex of stories and traditions about the Fian, the band of hunter-warriors led by Fionn mac Cumhaill. The cycle is commonly called the Fenian Cycle, a modern Anglicization, or the Ossianic Cycle, after Fionn's son Oisin (or Ossian). Etymologically, the term *fian* (plural, *fiana*) embodies the notion of living by the hunt or by force of arms, and this notion corresponds exactly with the role of the Fiana in Irish tradition. Originally there were several groups of Fiana, but the fame of Fionn's company relegated the others to obscurity. Each *féinnidh* (individual member of the Fian) was required to undergo initiatory trials of his skill and endurance before admittance, and once accepted he had to sever his legal and social connections with his kin and his tribe and abandon the associated rights and responsibilities. Yet although he placed himself outside the tribal community, he did not place himself outside the law, for the Fiana were recognized by law and tradition as fulfilling a legitimate function. Many legends picture the Fiana as the defenders of Ireland against the incursions of foreign—that is, in effect, supernatural—enemies. From the eleventh or twelfth century onward, and perhaps even earlier, these enemies are often identified in an ambiguous, mythopoeic (relating to mythmaking) fashion with the Viking raiders of the ninth century.

Some have recognized the Celtic form **vindos* (white, fair)—the source of Irish Fionn and Welsh Gwynn—in the Celtic deity name/epithet Vindonnus, and thus concluded that Fionn himself was originally divine, although this is questionable. **Vindos* is related to the Indo-European stem **ui-n-d* (finds out, knows). It also has been suggested that Fionn's name means "he who finds out, he who knows." This accords with his role in tradition, which represents him as poet and seer as well as warrior-hunter, perhaps like his Welsh counterpart Gwynn ap Nudd, who appears fleetingly in Welsh tradition as a "magic warrior-huntsman." Fionn is sometimes said to have acquired his supernatural knowledge by tasting the otherworldly liquor. His normal means of divination was simply to chew his thumb, with which he had once touched the Salmon of Knowledge, which he was cooking for his master in poetry and magic. Moreover, poetry and preternatural vision have always been characteristic attributes of the Fionn cycle as a whole.

Like Cú Chulainn, Fionn is also the subject of a narrative recounting his boyhood deeds. His birth followed soon after his father's death at the hands of the rival band of the Sons of Morna. He was reared secretly in the forest by two female warriors until he was ready to assert his precocious claim to the leadership of the Fian. He killed a malevolent being called Aillén mac Midgna, who came each year to burn down the royal court of Tara (one of several variants of a myth in which Fionn figured as conqueror of a supernatural one-eyed arsonist). Even within the Fian his archrival was Goll (one-eyed) mac Morna, also known as Aodh (Fire). There is an obvious analogy here with the myth of Lugh's defeat of Balar, and it has, in fact, been argued that Fionn was simply another name and persona for that deity. However, although Lugh is represented as being closely associated with the sacred function of kingship, Fionn's relationship to kingship is, at the very least, ambiguous. It is true that he and his followers became closely associated with the king of Tara as a kind of standing army, but it has been suggested that this is a fairly late development. Earlier their role as mercenaries appears to have been more marginal and ambivalent.

This marginal status may partly explain why the *Fianaighecht* was accorded little space in the written texts before the eleventh and twelfth centuries, although it is attested as early as the Ulster Cycle. By and large the literature of prestige such as the Ulster Cycle reinforced the structures and usages of organized aristocratic society within its clearly defined political boundaries. But the Fian's environment was outside and beyond this cultivated domain in the forest and the wilderness. Here they roamed at will, on foot or on horseback, unlike the Ulster heroes, who traveled in chariots. Intimately connected with nature, both animate and inanimate, their world blurred and often dissolved the boundaries of social and natural categories. For example, several of the *feinnidi* were born of mothers in animal form, and the Fian's great hounds, Bran and Sgeolang, had a human mother. It is hardly surprising that Fian mythology has always had a firm hold on the popular imagination and that it only gained prominence in the written tradition when the learned class began to react to the pressure of sociopolitical change in the eleventh and twelfth centuries.

The ambiguous nature of the region inhabited by the Fian emerges clearly in their relations with the otherworld. Whereas in the Ulster tales the association of the two worlds tends to happen at specific times—at the great calendar festivals, for instance, or during initiation rituals—among the Fian these associations are casual and continual. The Fian's liminal status ensures that they can participate freely in both the natural and the supernatural world as they are able to easily cross the threshold between worlds. In this as in much else they correspond to the heroes of Arthur's court and there can be little doubt that the cycles of Fionn and Arthur, whatever their later vicissitudes, derive from the same sector of insular mythology.

The "Elopement of Diarmaid and Gráinne," one of the most popular tales in the *Fianaighecht*, tells how the mature Fionn loses the beautiful Gráinne to Diarmaid ua Duibhne (The Master and Charmer of Women), just as Arthur loses Gwenhwyfar (Guinevere) to Medrawd (Melwas). The tale is one of several Irish analogues of the romance of Tristan and Iseult, and it also ends in tragedy, when Diarmaid is killed by the magic boar of Beann Ghulban with Fionn's connivance. It has been suggested that Gráinne's name, which can mean literally *ugliness*, obliquely identifies her with the version of the sovereignty goddess who appears as a repulsive hag until she is transformed to youthful beauty by union with her rightful and royal mate. Diarmaid Donn (Brown, Dark) may originally have been the god Donn who ruled the otherworld of the dead.

The most comprehensive source for the *Fianaighecht* is a long frame story entitled *Agallamh na Senórach* (The converse of the old men), which was probably compiled near the end of the twelfth century. The title indicates the convenient device on which the massive narrative rests: Caoilte mac Rónáin, one of the principal members of the Fian, long outlives his contemporaries and eventually meets with St. Patrick, who is on his mission of Christianization. Caoilte accompanies Patrick on his journey throughout the Irish countryside and, at the saint's request, tells him the stories associated with its hills, rivers, plains, and other natural features. The result is a vast thesaurus of place-name lore (*dinnshenchas*), which brings together the several streams of learned and popular tradition that went into the making of the Fionn Cycle.

SYSTEM OR CHAOS. Matthew Arnold admired the Celts for their lyric gifts, but he claimed, perhaps not without some reason, that they lacked the sense of architecture in their literary compositions. It is a sentiment that has been echoed by many students of Celtic religion and mythology when confronted with the frustratingly formless and unfinished character of the rich corpus of evidence. This feeling has been aptly expressed by Marie-Louise Sjoestedt in her *Gods and Heroes of the Celts* (1949):

> In travelling through the dense forest of the insular legends, and stirring the ashes of the continental Celtic world, we did not hope to uncover the plan of a vast edifice, a temple of the Celtic gods, partly overrun by the luxuriant wilderness and partly ruined by invaders. The indications are that this edifice never existed. Other people raised temples to their gods, and their very mythologies are temples whose architecture reproduces the symmetry of a cosmic or social order—an order both cosmic and social. It is in the wild solitude of the nemeton and sacred woodland, that the Celtic tribe meets its gods, and its mythical world is a sacred forest, pathless and unbounded, which is inhabited by mysterious powers. . . . We seek for a cosmos and find chaos. . . . The investigation of the insular tradition leaves one with a sense of something missing. One searches in vain for traces of those vast conceptions of the origin and final destiny of the world which dominate other Indo-European mythologies. Was there a Celtic cosmogony or eschatology? Must we suppose from the few allusions, vague and banal as they are, which Caesar or Pomponius Mela have made to the teaching of the druids, that a whole aspect, and an essential aspect, of this mythical world is hidden from us and will remain hidden? Should we explain the silence of our texts by the censorship of Christian monks, who were nevertheless liberal enough to allow the preservation of episodes much stained with paganism, and features most shocking to the Christian mentality? (p. 92)

Sjoestedt's own reply to this last rhetorical question would have been a clear negative, but some more recent studies suggest a qualified affirmative. In fact, there are grounds for believing that the early monastic redactors, for all their undoubted empathy and tolerance, did censor pagan learned tradition by omission as well as by critical editing, and that their omission most seriously affected those areas in which conflict of doctrines was least acceptable to Christian orthodoxy: ritual, cosmogony, and eschatology.

In 1918 Joseph Vendryes demonstrated in an important article that the Celtic languages, and particularly early Irish, preserve the remnants of an old Indo-European religious vocabulary originating with the hieratic ancestors of *brahmans*, pontifs, and druids. Since then it has become increasingly clear that these particularities of terminology are not to be seen as isolated fossils but rather as reflecting interrelated elements of a system of socioreligious thought and practice, which must have persisted substantially unchanged until a relatively late date, perhaps—in Ireland at least—until the establishment of Christianity. The numerous survivals of archaisms from Indo-European ideology, ritual, and liturgy in early Irish recorded tradition strongly support this conclusion. So also does the "deep structure" of early Irish narrative that is gradually being uncovered by the close analysis of individual texts. In the context of such fundamental and constantly recurring themes as the sacral kingship, the king as mediator between the secular and the supernatural world, the antinomy of ideological unity and political fragmentation, and the concept of social or cosmic order, these early texts often reveal a complex weave of structured allusion that presupposes in the not too distant past a coherent and authoritative system of politico-religious and juridico-religious belief and speculation.

However, it would be wrong to assume that the texts offer a complete and consistent record of that system, not merely because monastic redactors practiced conscious censorship and selectivity but also because the texts were recorded long after druidic paganism had ceased to be the official and uncontested religion of the country. By reason of this remove in time and motivation, the early Irish documentation belongs largely to the category to which Georges Dumézil has applied the term *mythologie littérarisée* It is the concern of contemporary scholars to analyze and interpret this rich documentation and to restate it in mythico-religious rather than literary terms.

SEE ALSO Druids; Fomhoire; Mabinogion; Matres; Sídh; Táin Bó Cuailnge; Tuatha Dé Danann.

BIBLIOGRAPHY

Arnold, Matthew. *On the Study of Celtic Literature.* London, 1867.

Bieler, Ludwig, ed. *The Patrician Texts in the Book of Armagh.* Dublin, 1979.

Binchy, Daniel A. *Celtic and Anglo-Saxon Kingship.* Oxford, 1970.

Birkhan, Helmut. *Kelten: Versuch einer Gesamtdarstellung ihrer Kultur.* Vienna, 1997. A comprehensive and detailed account of ancient and medieval Celtic culture with generous treatment of religion, mythology, and institutions.

Bromwich, Rachel. *Trioedd Ynys Prydein: The Welsh Triads.* 2d ed. Cardiff, 1978. This edition of the medieval triads and the rich commentary and notes that accompany it are an invaluable source of information on early Welsh and British history, myth, and legend.

Duval, Paul-Marie. *Les dieux de la Gaule.* Rev. ed. Paris, 1976. A convenient compendium of what is known and surmised about the Gaulish gods.

Dumézil, Georges. *Horace et les Curiaces.* Paris, 1942.

Dumézil, Georges. *Naissance de Rome.* Paris, 1944.

Dumézil, Georges. *Dieux des Indo-Européens,* Paris, 1952.

Dumézil, Georges. *Mythe et épopée.* Vol. 1. Paris, 1968.

Gray, Elizabeth A. *Cath Maige Tuired: The Second Battle of Mag Tuired.* London, 1982. An edition of this important mythological text. Gray's "Cath Maige Tuired: Myth and Structure," *Éigse* 18 (1981): 183–209 and 19 (1982–1983): 1–35, 230–262, presents a detailed interpretative analysis of the content of the tale.

Lambrechts, Pierre. *Contributions a l'étude des divinités celtiques.* Bruges, 1942.

Le Roux, Françoise, and Christian J. Guyonvarc'h. *La Civilisation celtique Rennes: La société celtique: dans l'idéologie trifonctionnelle et la tradition religieuse indo-européennes.* Rennes, France, 1991.

Le Roux, Françoise, and Christian J. Guyonvarc'h. *Les fêtes celtiques.* Rennes, France, 1995.

Lucas, A. T. *Cattle in Ancient Ireland.* Kilkenny, Ireland, 1989.

Mac Cana, Proinsias. *Celtic Mythology.* Rev. ed. Feltham, U.K., 1983. A short survey of the subject with illustrations of sculpture, metalwork, and so on.

MacCulloch, J. A. *The Religion of the Ancient Celts.* Edinburgh, 1911. Reprinted as *Celtic Mythology* (Boston, 1918). Still useful if read in conjunction with more recent accounts.

MacNeill, Máire. *The Festival of Lughnasa.* Oxford, 1962. A comprehensive inventory of all the local festivals in Ireland that can be shown to continue the Celtic feast of Lugh, together with a very helpful commentary and a rich collection of texts, largely from the oral tradition.

Maier, Bernhard. "Is Lug to be identified with Mercury? (*Bell. Gall.* VI, 17,1): New Suggestions to an Old Problem." *Ériu* 47 (1996): 127–35.

Maier, Bernhard. *Dictionary of Celtic Religion and Culture.* Woodbridge, U.K., 1997. Translation of *Lexikon der keltischen Religion und Kultur* (Stuttgart, Germany, 1994; reprint, 1997). A useful and accurate work of reference covering the continental and insular evidence—literature, iconography, archaeology.

Meyer, Kuno, ed. and trans., and Alfred Nutt. *The Voyage of Bran, Son of Febal, to the Land of the Living.* 2 vols. London, 1895–1897. Includes a long commentary on the Celtic concept of the otherworld and the doctrine of rebirth. Largely superseded by more recent studies, it still contains many useful insights.

Murphy, Gerard, ed. and trans. *Duanaire Finn: The Book of the Lays of Fionn.* Vol. 3. Dublin, 1953. Includes a long and valuable commentary on the history of the Fionn Cycle and on the relationship between medieval manuscript and modern oral versions.

Nagy, Joseph Falaky. *The Wisdom of the Outlaw: The Boyhood Deeds of Finn in Gaelic Narrative Tradition.* Berkeley, Calif., 1983. An excellent interpretative commentary on the Irish Fionn Cycle, the first extended study of the cycle in terms of modern mythological theory. It explores the internal consistency of the cycle as reflected in some of its constituent narratives and brings out the markedly liminal character of Fionn and his followers.

Ó Cathasaigh, Tomas. *The Heroic Biography of Cormac mac Airt.* Dublin, 1977. A perceptive exposition of the status and function of the Irish hero-king as reflected in the legends of Cormac mac Airt.

O'Flaherty, Wendy Doniger. *Women, Androgynes, and Other Mythical Beasts.* Chicago, 1980. In particular, see chapter 6, "The Indo-European Mare."

O'Rahilly, Thomas F. *Early Irish History and Mythology.* Dublin, 1946. Valuable for its coverage of Irish literary resources in all periods and for its brilliant analyses of medieval texts, but sometimes rather outmoded and idiosyncratic in its treatment of essentially mythological narratives as reflections of historical events.

Ó Riain, P. "Traces of Lug in Early Irish Hagiographical Tradition." *Zeitschrift für celtische Philologie* 36 (1978): 138–55.

Ó Riain, Pádraig. "The 'Crech Ríg' or 'Regal Prey.'" *Éigse* 15 (1973): 24–30.

Puhvel, Jaan. "Aspects of equine functionality." In *Myth and Law among the Indo-Europeans,* edited by Jaan Puhvel, pp. 169–69. Berkeley, Calif., 1970.

Rees, Alwyn, and Brinley Rees. *Celtic Heritage.* London, 1961. An important and stimulating work that seeks to structure insular Celtic tradition in terms of a number of ideological concepts and motivations. It is inspired by the Dumézilian system of analysis, applied in a flexible and imaginative fashion.

Ross, Anne. *Pagan Celtic Britain.* London, 1967. Surveys the British repertory of images for the Celtic gods and their attributes. Contains an extensive discussion of the several main categories of deity: horned god, warrior god, divine animals, among others. Useful also for its rich comparative documentation from insular literary and folklore sources.

Scowcroft, R. Mark. "*Leabhar Gabhála.* Part II: The Growth of the Tradition." *Ériu* 39 (1988) 1–66. Offers an excellent analytic commentary on the new synthetic mythology that emerged from the fusion of pagan myth and legend with the Latin-mediated learning of clerics and schoolmen.

Sjoestedt, Marie-Louise. *Dieux et héros des Celtes.* Paris, 1940. Translated by Myles Dillon as *Gods and Heroes of the Celts* (London, 1949). A short but perceptive survey of Celtic, mainly Irish, mythology and hero tales. At the time of its publication it offered fresh insights into the nature of Celtic myth and is still necessary reading.

Synge, John M. *The Aran Islands.* Drawings by Jack B. Yeats. Dublin, 1907.

Vendryes, Joseph. "Les correspondances de vocabulaire entre l'indo-iranien et l'italo-celtique." *Mémoires de la Société de Linguistique de Paris* 20 (1918): 265–285.

Vendryes, Joseph. *Les religions des Celtes* (1948). Revised by Pierre-Yves Lambert. Vol. 1. Spézet, France, 1997. It is primarily an exhaustive catalogue of the varied data, both continental and insular, relating to Celtic religion. More descriptive than theoretical, it is still a useful source of information.

Vries, Jan de. *Keltische Religion.* Stuttgart, Germany, 1961. A comprehensive treatment of the whole of Celtic religion. It is well documented and strong on Indo-European and other comparative aspects, less so on the insular tradition, although the latter is given fairly generous coverage.

PROINSIAS MAC CANA (1987 AND 2005)

CELTIC RELIGION: HISTORY OF STUDY

The terms *Celt* and *Celtic* were originally used by ancient Greek and Roman writers to refer to an extensive network of tribes located primarily in Gaul (roughly modern-day France, Belgium, and northern Italy) who claimed, or were thought by their neighbors, to share a common descent. These terms, however, were never used in reference to the peoples of Britain and Ireland, even though it is now known that they did (and some still do) speak Celtic languages. Some classical writers did note traits common to both the Celts and the Britons, such as the institution of druids and druidism, which, according to Caesar, originated in Britain. The use of the ethnonym Celtic to refer to related languages both modern and ancient (that in turn constitute a subset of the Indo-European family of languages) dates back to the eighteenth century, arising in the wake of the scholarly discovery of the family resemblance among the still-living Irish, Scottish Gaelic, Manx, Welsh, Cornish, and Breton languages and the long-dead languages of the continental Celts.

EARLY DEVELOPMENT OF CELTIC RELIGION STUDIES. Soon after the discovery of the common descent of ancient and living Celtic languages circa 1700, ambitious attempts were launched to expand the "Celtic connection" beyond the realm of linguistics and specifically to establish Celtic common denominators in the areas of religion, worldview, and myth. Central to these attempts to understand what the pagan Celts believed, who their gods were, and how they worshiped them was the figure of the druid, famously described in classical sources as a barbarian philosopher and also as a presider over sometimes grisly sacrifices, pointedly conducted in the realm of nature as opposed to the cultural confines of temples. John Toland (1670–1722), the English pantheist and biographer of John Milton, wrote admiringly of the druids of ancient Britain and of the enlightened religion they promulgated. Later on in the mysticism of the poet William Blake (1757–1827) the not-really-pagan British priests played an important role in Blake's vision of the salvific link between "Albion" and Jerusalem.

In time druids (including those who occasionally appeared in medieval Irish literature) merged in the scholarly and popular imagination with the figure of the Celtic bard, the practitioner of the verbal and musical arts toward which, according to popular notions that linger into the early twenty-first century, the Celts are naturally inclined. The impression of an artistic as well as a "druidic" (philosophical, mystical, and perhaps even savage) bent to pre-Christian Celtic religion, and even to Christianity as it developed among the Celts, gained strength from the popularity of the works of the Scottish writer James Macpherson (1736–1796), who fabricated an ancient Celtic poet "Ossian" to evoke a dramatic world of ancient Highland heroes and heroines prone to romantic melancholy and pronouncements worthy of the Enlightenment's noble savage.

Even in the early twenty-first century most of the popular, Neopagan, and some academic treatments of the topic of Celtic religion are fueled by a druidocentric desire to recapture a mystical wisdom that supposedly informs Celtic culture and art. This popular tendency to view the religion along with the art of the Celts as sources of atavistic truth for modern seekers to rediscover can also be traced to the widely influential literary characterizations of Celts and their worldview developed by the Breton scholar of religion Ernest Renan (1823–1892), the English critic Matthew Arnold (1822–1888), and the Irish poet William Butler Yeats (1865–1939). The romantic image of the Celts and their religious traditions has now been compounded by the widespread impression (based on ambiguous evidence) that the Celts privileged women and honored their goddesses to an extent that set them apart from other ancient peoples.

It is important to note that most of the serious Celtic scholarship from the mid–nineteenth century on has been devoted to locating and organizing the available data on the Celts—their languages, histories, cultures, literatures, and the physical record they left behind—and not to tackling broad, harder-to-define, and controversial concepts such as "Celtic religion" and "mythology." Larger questions such as these have in fact been ignored or even treated with scorn by many if not most scholars in the field. Undeniably this neglect in part reflects the difficulty of accurately describing Celtic religious beliefs, practices, and myths, given that the pre-Christian Celts left relatively little in the way of a written record and the agenda of medieval Christian Celts often overruled the ethnographic impulse in what they wrote about their pre-Christian past. And yet the relative dearth of serious study of Celtic religion, by definition an interdisciplinary venture, also points to the rather sparse communication among Celticists working in different languages and literary traditions (such as Irish and Welsh) and between those who work on Celtic languages, literatures, and history and those who work on Celtic archaeology and prehistory.

The earliest attempts to discover what the pagan Celts believed, who their gods were, and how they worshiped them that are still worth consulting in the early twenty-first century, though cautiously, were authored by the first Oxford professor of Celtic, Sir John Rhŷs (1840–1915), and the enterprising Englishman Alfred Nutt (1856–1910). The attention of these scholars was directed primarily toward the texts produced by the medieval Welsh and Irish, and their primary working assumption was that the "waifs and strays" of pre-Christian beliefs, myths, and rituals were embedded in this literature and to some extent were reconstructible. There was also considerable interest (especially on the part of Rhŷs) in the folklore of contemporary Celts—their superstitions, stories, and customs—as reflecting many of these same vestiges. Rhŷs and Nutt, like their scholarly coevals, were profoundly affected by a nineteenth-century view of premodern religion (particularly of the polytheistic Indo-European kind) as a prescientific system for explaining natural phenomena—a system that, the theory went, was prone to misinterpretation and breakdown as it was passed down through the generations. These early pioneers of the study of Celtic religion freely compared their data with the pre-Christian religious traditions of other Indo-European peoples and employed many of the terms and concepts developed in the nineteenth century by Jacob Grimm (1785–1863) and Wilhelm Grimm (1786–1859), Johann Georg von Hahn (1811–1869), and Friedrich Max Müller (1823–1900).

These nineteenth-century tendencies, both stimulating and confining, were still in evidence in early twentieth-century scholarship on Celtic religion. Also influencing these works—including Georges Dottin's *La religion des Celtes* (1904), John Arnott MacCulloch's *The Religion of the Ancient Celts* (1911), and Joseph Vendryes's *La religion des Celtes* (1948)—was the inclination, derived from classical authors writing on their Celtic neighbors, to interpret Celtic religious traditions in terms borrowed from Greek and Roman religion (e.g., the search for a Celtic "pantheon"). Some Irish and British scholars of the first half of the twentieth century attempted, sometimes to the point of obsession, to reconstruct insular Celtic divinities consonant with their continental cousins from what they considered to be the garbled medieval record produced by Christians no longer in touch with pre-Christian religious sensibilities. The philologist Thomas O'Rahilly's never completed *Early Irish History and Mythology* (1946) cast a spell on a whole generation of scholars as it looked relentlessly for solar deities and heroes, although, as the title suggests, historical peoples and forces were also discernible behind some members of O'Rahilly's mythological cast of characters. William John Gruffydd (1881–1954), in his still influential reconstructions of narratives about gods and goddesses underlying the Four Branches of the Welsh Mabinogi, applied some of Frazer's formulations of "primitive" magical and religious thought (Nagy, 2001) and recycled the "heroic biography" paradigm of mythic narrative previously used by Nutt. Later studies that still employ but fine-tune the biographic-mythic paradigm include Tomás Ó Cathasaigh's *Heroic Biography of Cormac mac Airt* (1977) and Joseph Falaky Nagy's *The Wisdom of the Outlaw: The Boyhood Deeds of Finn in Gaelic Narrative Tradition* (1985), both studies of Irish narrative characters whose story cycles have religious implications.

TWENTIETH-CENTURY DEVELOPMENTS. As the twentieth century unfolded, Celtic scholars, pursuing questions raised by earlier scholars and their particular approaches to religion, had access to new resources and tools. Major strides in the uncovering and cataloging of the remains of ancient Celtic peoples made it much more feasible and productive to compare and contrast ancient images with medieval tales and narrative characters, for example, in the work of Marie-Louise Sjoestedt (1900–1940) and Anne Ross's *Pagan Celtic Britain: Studies in Iconography and Tradition* (1967). Meanwhile the tireless collecting activities of the Irish Folklore Commission made it possible to study the diachronic development of Irish narratives, beliefs, and customs that arguably derive from the pre-Christian religious tradition and that, by adapting to changing cultural circumstances, have survived or even flourished down to modern times. Máire MacNeill's 1962 study of the Irish harvest festival of Lughnasa and the stories and rituals associated with it through the centuries and Patricia Lysaght's 1986 monograph on the enduring figure of the banshee demonstrate the chronological span over which studies of the pre-Christian religious tradition and its protean afterlife can now range.

The profound twentieth-century shift in the scholarly paradigm of religion, sparked by the contributions of Max Weber (1864–1920) and Émile Durkheim (1858–1917) to religious studies, and the structuralist approach to the study of symbolic aspects of human culture (deriving from linguistics and semiotics) slowly but surely penetrated Celtic studies in the twentieth century. When Celtic scholars began to view society rather than nature as the primary focus of religion and negotiation among cultural values rather than explanation of natural phenomena as the basic task of religion, solar deities gave way to ideological concepts, especially under the influence of the linguist Émile Benveniste (1902–1976), who pioneered the techniques of a lexically based search for shared Indo-European institutions and elements of worldview, and of the scholar of religion Georges Dumézil (1898–1986), who compellingly excavated a model of society consisting of three "functions" out of the religious data available from various ancient and medieval Indo-European cultures (including Celtic).

Heralding these new approaches, *Celtic Heritage* by Alwyn Rees and Brinley Rees (1961) presented an ambitiously comprehensive and fundamentally religious interpretation of medieval Celtic literature. As argued by Rees and Rees, who were inspired by the work of Mircea Eliade (1907–1986) as well as by Dumézil, the Christian milieu of medieval Celtic literary composition hardly deterred the rich body of story preserved thereby from refining and applying the inherited sacred model of the Indo-European "tripartite" society, mapped onto the landscape by way of place names and local associations and traced in the contours of a historicized but still fundamentally mythic past. The reflections and refractions of social structure and thought on display in religious symbolism as expressed through story and image also loom large in Jan de Vries's *Keltische Religion*, also published in 1961, which focuses primarily on the available evidence concerning the continental Celts and their modes and objects of worship. Druids staged a dramatic comeback on the scholarly scene, this time viewed from a more archaeologically and sociologically informed perspective, in Stuart Piggott's *The Druids* (1968) and Françoise Le Roux's *Les druides* (1961).

Proinsias Mac Cana's perennial *Celtic Mythology* (1970) inaugurated a golden age of scholarship informed by a confidence that key themes and motifs in Celtic religion and mythology could be securely identified and interpreted (Gray, 1981–1983; Sayers, 1985; Sterckx, 1981). Such studies judiciously combined an openness to the nuances of the linguistic, literary, and archaeological evidence with those elements of Dumézil's and Sjoestedt's approaches that served the Celtic materials best—such as viewing sovereignty myths and rituals as fundamentally religious, making a distinction between culture heroes who operate within the social realm and those who ambivalently dwell on its borders, and appreciating the "multitasking" that characterizes the careers of goddesses and other mythological females. Busying themselves more with the details than with the big picture, scholars of the latter half of the twentieth century prudently shied away from perpetuating a monolithic concept of Celtic "religion" or "mythology" and grew more sensitive to the diversity of religions and mythologies that historically developed among the Celts, who themselves were never a single people.

A major contribution of the second half of the twentieth century to the evolving understanding of Celtic religious traditions has been a heightened awareness of the delicate artifice underlying both the modern scholarly concept of Celtic and the reports of pre-Christian belief, practice, and myth conveyed in early medieval texts. Careful probings of "Celticity" punctuate Patrick Sims-Williams's (1990) salutary sorting-out of concepts of the otherworld as they were supposedly shared among the insular Celts. Bernhard Maier's *Die Religion der Kelten* (2001) similarly displays a healthy skepticism concerning the literary evidence that, on religious matters especially, can be as intentionally misleading as it is enlightening about the preliterary past.

The boldness behind the medieval Irish project to construct a picture of pre-Christian Ireland and its religion that would appear consistent with biblical history and early medieval, not exclusively Celtic, notions of how pagans worshiped and what they believed in was the focus of Kim McCone's revisionist *Pagan Past and Christian Present in Early Irish Literature* (1990). In light of what is now known both about continental Celtic religious belief and practice (particularly as these engaged in cultural dialogue with those of the Greeks, Etruscans, and Romans) and about medieval Irish and Welsh cultures engaged in lively cross-cultural communication on the northwestern edge of Christendom, it is no longer scholarly wisdom, as it once was, to view the Celtic peoples as having been compulsively conservative in regard to their religious traditions. Indeed the tendency is now to highlight the syncretistic trends that have produced what were once thought to be characteristically Celtic religious concepts of either the pre-Christian or Christian era or concepts that seem to straddle both (Borsje, 1996; Mackey, 1989; Sjöblom, 2000). Stemming in part from hyperrevisionist critiques of Celtic and Indo-European as cultural categories, an even more radical scholarly approach to the study of Celtic religious traditions emerged in 1999, spearheaded by Simon James. Receiving considerable attention but not immediately widely embraced, James's approach highlights the impact of the geographic contiguity or proximity of peoples over linguistic and cultural inheritance as a factor in determining the outcome of cultural development, including religion.

A controversy over a familiar and formulaic phrase from medieval Irish literature serves as a demonstration of some of the key shifts in perspective and agenda that have shaped scholarship on Celtic religions. A recurring preface to heroic boast or assertion in a body of late Old Irish and early Middle Irish tales constituting what is called the Ulster Cycle, having to do with heroes and situations pertaining to a period well before the coming of Christianity, is, to the effect, "I swear by the god(s) my people swear by." This expression was considered an example of what much in the Ulster Cycle seems to offer, namely, "a window on the Iron Age" (Jackson, 1964), replete with a pre-Christian worldview, tribal gods for one's people to swear by (parallel perhaps to the continental Celtic deity Teutates "God of the People"), and other elements of belief and practice that seemed more reflective of pre-Romanized Gaul than of early Christian Ireland. In the late twentieth century this attractive reading of the Ulster Cycle as a portal into the Celtic past was challenged, and the argument made that the "I swear" expression is a Christian-era invention meant to evoke the flavor of an imagined pre-Christian past (Ó hUiginn, 1989). A scholarly battle ensued, with the original interpretation of the phrase stoutly defended by Calvert Watkins (1990).

Whatever the outcome of this controversy and whether or not the expression is authentically pre-Christian, there is still much to be learned about the religious traditions of the continental and insular Celtic peoples. Surprisingly, or perhaps not so, the increasing availability of different types of data (textual, archaeological, and folkloric) and the increasing confidence in understanding and using them has made Celtic scholars more hesitant to treat sources as unambiguous time capsules and more leery of blanket statements of the sort that used to characterize the study of Celtic religion and that still, alas, bedevil the seemingly endless stream of popular published treatments of the subject. At this stage of knowledge of Celtic religion, those who truly know their Celtic archaeology or their Celtic literatures are hardly ready to swear to anything, by any god.

BIBLIOGRAPHY

Borsje, Jacqueline. *From Chaos to Enemy: Encounters with Monsters in Early Irish Texts; An Investigation Related to the Process of Christianization and the Concept of Evil.* Turnhout, Belgium, 1996.

Gray, Elizabeth A. "Cath Maige Tuired: Myth and Structure." *Éigse* 18 (1981): 183–209; 19 (1982–1983): 1–35, 230–262.

Gruffydd, William John. *Math vab Mathonwy: An Inquiry into the Origins and Development of the Fourth Branch of the Mabinogi with Text and a Translation.* Cardiff, 1928.

Jackson, Kenneth Hurlstone. *The Oldest Irish Tradition: A Window on the Iron Age.* Cambridge, U.K., 1964.

James, Simon. *The Atlantic Celts: Ancient People or Modern Invention?* London, 1999.

Le Roux, Françoise. *Les druides.* Paris, 1961. Later editions, coauthored with Christian Guyonvarc'h, are considerably expanded but not necessarily improvements on the original.

Lysaght, Patricia. *The Banshee: The Irish Death-Messenger* (1986). Boulder, Colo., 1997.

Mac Cana, Proinsias. *Celtic Mythology* (1970). Rev. ed. New York, 1983.

MacCulloch, John Arnott. *The Religion of the Ancient Celts.* Edinburgh, 1911.

Mackey, James P., ed. *An Introduction to Celtic Christianity.* Edinburgh, 1989.

MacNeill, Máire. *The Festival of Lughnasa: A Study of the Survival of the Celtic Festival of the Beginning of Harvest.* London, 1962.

Maier, Bernhard. *Lexikon der keltischen Religion und Kultur.* Stuttgart, 1994. Available in English as *Dictionary of Celtic Religion and Culture.* Translated by Cyril Edwards. Rochester, N.Y., 1997. Contains entries on and brief bibliographies for most of the concepts and authors mentioned in this article.

Maier, Bernhard. *Die Religion der Kelten: Götter-Mythen-Weltbild.* Munich, 2001. An up-to-date and reliable survey of the subject; the opening chapter deftly covers some of the major intellectual trends that have influenced the study of Celtic religion.

McCone, Kim. *Pagan Past and Christian Present in Early Irish Literature.* Maynooth, Ireland, 1990.

Meyer, Kuno, and Alfred Nutt. *The Voyage of Bran, Son of Febal to the Land of the Living: An Old Irish Saga.* 2 vols. London, 1895–1897. As well as an edition and translation of this and other texts that are important for an understanding of the concept of the otherworld that inhabits early Irish literature, this work contains Nutt's characteristic "Essay on the Irish Vision of the Happy Otherworld and the Celtic Doctrine of Rebirth."

Nagy, Joseph Falaky. *The Wisdom of the Outlaw: The Boyhood Deeds of Finn in Gaelic Narrative Tradition.* Berkeley, Calif., 1985.

Nagy, Joseph Falaky. "Folklore Studies and the *Mabinogion.*" In *150 Jahre "Mabinogion"—Deutsche-Walische Kulturbeziehungen,* edited by Bernhard Maier and Stefan Zimmer, with Christiane Batke, pp. 91–100. Tübingen, Germany, 2001.

Ó Cathasaigh, Tomás. *The Heroic Biography of Cormac mac Airt.* Dublin, 1977.

Ó hUiginn, Ruairí. "Tongu do dia toinges mo thuath and Related Expressions." In *Sages, Saints, and Storytellers: Celtic Studies in Honour of Professor James Carney,* edited by Donnchadh Ó Corráin, Liam Breatnach, and Kim McCone, pp. 332–341. Maynooth, Ireland, 1989.

O'Rahilly, Thomas F. *Early Irish History and Mythology.* Dublin, 1946.

Piggott, Stuart. *The Druids.* London, 1968. The latter half of the book includes a helpful survey of early modern popular and scholarly attitudes toward druids and Celtic religion in general.

Rees, Alwyn, and Brinley Rees. *Celtic Heritage: Ancient Tradition in Ireland and Wales.* London, 1961.

Rhŷs, Sir John. *Lectures on the Origin and Growth of Religion as Illustrated by Celtic Heathendom.* London, 1888.

Ross, Anne. *Pagan Celtic Britain: Studies in Iconography and Tradition.* London, 1967.

Sayers, William. "Fergus and the Cosmogonic Sword." *History of Religions* 25 (1985): 30–56.

Sims-Williams, Patrick. "Some Celtic Otherworld Terms." In *Celtic Language, Celtic Culture: A Festschrift for Eric P. Hamp,* edited by A. T. E. Matonis and Daniel F. Melia, pp. 57–81. Van Nuys, Calif., 1990.

Sjöblom, Tom. *Early Irish Taboos: A Study in Cognitive History.* Helsinki, Finland, 2000.

Sjoestedt, Marie-Louise. *Gods and Heroes of the Celts.* Translated by Myles Dillon. London, 1948. Dillon's English translation of *Les dieux et héros des Celtes* (1940).

Sterckx, Claude. *La tête et les seins: La mutilation rituelle des enemis et le concept de 1'âme.* Saarbrücken, Germany, 1981.

Vendryes, Joseph. *La religion des Celtes* (1948). Spézet, France, 1997. An additional critical apparatus (including bibliography) supplied by Pierre-Yves Lambert adds to the value of this reissue of Vendryes's work.

Vries, Jan de. *Keltische Religion.* Stuttgart, 1961.

Watkins, Calvert. "Some Celtic Phrasal Echoes." In *Celtic Language, Celtic Culture: A Festschrift for Eric P. Hamp*, edited by A. T. E. Matonis and Daniel F. Melia, pp. 47–56. Van Nuys, Calif., 1990.

JOSEPH F. NAGY (2005)

CENTER OF THE WORLD. The importance of the symbolism of the center of the world can hardly be overstated, for it establishes the order of the universe, drawing together the spiritual destiny of collective humankind and that of the individual human being. The term *center of the world* refers to that place where all essential modes of being come together; where communication and even passage among them is possible. The center of the world is the heart of reality, where the real is fully manifest. The nature of this manifestation may vary greatly from one culture to another, taking the form of a vague, undefined power or of the direct appearance of a divinity. Since this center stands apart as the extraordinary place where the real is integral, it is always a sacred place, qualitatively different from mundane space. In the religious world view, every ordered and habitable area possesses such a center, a space that is sacred above all others. For this reason, the center of the world should not be portrayed in purely geometric terms or forms. It is because the center of the world is defined by its special relationship to the sacred that there can be multiple centers in any cosmos or microcosm. Cultures in Mesopotamia, India, and China, for example, saw no inconsistency in recognizing a large number of sacred places, each one called "the center of the world." The center of the world is a locus in mythic geography, a symbolic portrayal of the real, known, and essential aspects of the world, rather than a detached and objective reckoning of abstract space.

In cultures that conceive of the universe as multiple realms of heavens, hells, and strata for various kinds of beings, the center of the world is that point where all realms intersect and where the most direct contact with the sacred is obtained. Existence of a sacred center allows for the establishment of a world system, a body of imaged realities that are related to one another: a sacred point that stands apart from the homogeneity of general space; symbolic openings from one level of reality to another; an *axis mundi* (tree, mountain, ladder, vine, or pillar) that symbolizes the communication between cosmic regions; and the extension of an organized and habitable world that exists around the center. This cosmos constructed around a sacred center lies in opposition to the chaotic space beyond it, which has neither been ordered by the gods nor consecrated in rituals imitating the divine creative acts. That indeterminate space beyond the cosmos remains uninhabitable by human beings because it is a place where communication with the supernatural world is impossible. In the "other world" dwell demonic beings, ghosts, monsters, souls of the dead, or foreigners.

SYMBOLIC FORMS. In order to illustrate how widespread is the concept of the center of the world and how constant is its basic meaning, some of its most common symbolic forms may be noted. Amond these are the sacred mountain; the cosmic tree; the bridge or ladder connecting cosmic realms; sanctuaries, temples, tombs; sacred cities; domestic space; personal space; and sacred sound.

In Asia one finds the elaborate religious symbolism of Mount Meru, the cosmic mountain whose complex symbolic meanings are put forth especially in the post-Vedic literature of India, particularly in the Purāṇas of Hinduism, and in certain Buddhist texts. On its peak lie the cities of the gods. It has existed since the beginning of time. Upon its slopes the waters of immortality are stored in Lake Anavatapta. The sacred river Ganges flows from Mount Meru. It is the fixed point about which revolve the sun and the stars. Around it are gathered other sacred mountains. In ascending the slopes of Mount Meru, one passes through all possible spiritual states of being until, arriving at the summit, one transcends the particularities of any of them. Similarly, in early Daoism, Kunlun is a cosmic mountain paradise connecting heaven and earth. In some accounts concerning the primordial human being named Pangu, Kunlun makes its appearance from out of the chaotic flood waters that deluged the earth. It was here at the center of the universe that human life was created and the world regenerated.

In the *Zhuangzi* and *Liezi*, Kunlun is the place where the Yellow Emperor "dies" to the mundane world and flies to heaven in the immortal form of a bird-man. Also in the *Liezi* is a description of the mountain Hu-ling, which forms the center of a paradise whose inhabitants are rejuvenated by the water bubbling forth from the sacred spring on its summit. The spirit is the only vehicle that can transport one on a journey across the slopes of this cosmic mountain. To find one's way to this mountain is to return to the beginning of time, where one's adult body becomes once again virginal, and one's mind attains undifferentiated knowledge, limitless as a bottomless spring. The ascent transcends all particular states and attains the mode of preexistence, the condition of the "spirit man" *(shen-jen),* spoken of as the Daoist ideal of the holy man in the *Liezi, Huainanzi,* and the *Zhuangzi.*

Examples of cosmic mountains that stand at the center of the world make up a very long list. The central mountain of Uralo-Altaic cosmology, Sumbur, Sumur, or Semeru, lay directly under the North Star, which fixed the central point of the heavens. In Norse mythology, Hininbjörg, the "heavenly mountain," lies at the center of the earth, where the rainbow touches the celestial vault. In the Hebrew Bible (*Jgs.* 9:37) Mount Gerizim is referred to as *ṭabur ha-arets,* "the navel of the earth." Indeed, there are traditions that report that the land of Palestine is so high, located as it is near the heights of the cosmic mountain, that it alone remained unflooded during the Deluge. Mount Tabor, in its very name, may share associations with the navel, *ṭabur,* of the earth. A ninth-century Islamic tradition argued by al-Kisāʾī of Kufa holds the sacred Kaʿbah to be the highest place on earth, located directly beneath the North Star (i.e., at the center of the world). In a Christian tradition from the Syrian *Book of the Cave of Treasures,* Golgotha was the center of the world, the summit of the cosmic mountain, and the culmination of salvation history. It was there that Adam was created and buried, in the same place in which the blood of Christ was shed to redeem the world. The image of the cosmic mountain immediately introduces us to the concept of *axis mundi,* the "hub of the world," which symbolizes the communication between cosmic realms. It likewise brings up the symbolism of ascension, since one may transcend the planes of existence along a vertical axis.

Another widely known symbol of the center of the world is the cosmic tree, which transfixes the levels of the world, making communication and passage among them possible. At the center of the world in the Baltic religious traditions stood the Saules Koks, the "tree of the sun." It grew out of the top of the mountain of heaven, the farmland of the heavenly supreme being Dievs. It is the source of life. Although earthly species of tree may represent the tree of the sun, it is unique and inaccessible, it may be described as made of precious metal, gold, or silver. A supernatural orb descends through its branches, perhaps associated with Saule, the sun herself, who is the mother of all life. Likewise, among the Maya of Mesoamerica during the Classic period (300–900 CE) the universe was centered on Yaxche, the "first, or green, tree," extending upward to the zenith (the white interval between east and west) and downward to the nadir (the yellow interval between west and east).

Certain Babylonian inscriptions refer to the black tree named Kiskanu that grows at Eridu, a place at the center of the world. This sacred tree is described in cosmic terms: it shines with the lapis-lazuli radiance of the starry night and spreads its boughs out toward the cosmic ocean that encompasses the world. It is the place where Ea (Enki), the god of fertility and of cultural skills, is present, and the resting place of Bau, Ea's mother, the goddess of abundant flocks and agriculture. The *Vǫluspá,* the Scandinavian creation story, tells of Yggdrasill, the cosmic tree whose roots penetrate the center of the earth. Óðinn (Odin) leaves his eye in the Spring of Mmir ("memory" or "meditation"), located near Yggdrasill, in exchange for the privilege of refreshing his wisdom there whenever he returns. Near the foot of Yggdrasill, at the spring of Urðr (Urd) located there, the divinities pronounce judgments. Water is drawn from the spring of Urðr by three Norns, maidens who govern the fate of humans. In the branches of Yggdrasill, which spread out across heaven and earth, live supernatural animals. At the foot of the tree lies the enormous cosmic serpent, Niðhǫggr (Nidhogg), who threatens the very existence of the tree by gnawing continually upon it. At the very top of the tree perches an eagle who does daily battle with the destructive serpent. The *Vǫluspá* describes not only the creation of the world but its demise when it gives way to a paradisal epoch. Even at that time, Yggdrasill will endure.

The symbolism of the center of the world may be expressed through a range of other symbols—a ladder, a vine, a rope, a bridge—all of which serve as an *axis mundi* connecting heaven and earth or various cosmic realms of being. For example, for the Desana, a Tucano-speaking group of the Vaupés River area of southern Colombia, the center of the world is occupied by the Go'a-mëe, which transfixes all zones of the universe through their center. Go'a-mëe is likened to the penis of the creator Sun Father. In the image of a tubular bone *(ve'e go'á),* it joins all the cosmic levels together in an act of continuous intercourse. This immense phallus at the center of the world is a fundamental part of the creation, since it carries the "yellow intention," the solar semen of the creator, into the cosmic uterus, Ahpikondía ("river of milk"), from which all life comes.

The image of the center as the locus of all powers and passage makes clear the religious significance of a range of holy sites, from informal sanctuaries to temples, cathedrals, or even whole cities. The Mandan, a Plains Indian group now living in North Dakota, placed a circular shrine in the center of each of their villages. It was constructed of wood panels nearly two meters in height. In the center of the shrine stood a cedar post, the image of the supernatural being named One Man, who lived in the times spoken of in myth. One Man was the brother of the first human being. The Achilpa, an Aranda (Arunta) tribe in Australia, install Kauwa-auwa, a sacred pole fashioned from the trunk of a gum tree, in their settlements. It is the pillar that their legendary ancestor Numbakula constructed, anointed with blood, and used to ascend into the sky during the mythic period. It is the means of communication between this world and the world above; between this period of time and the mythical time of the ancestor. Whenever the Achilpa wander as a group, they carry Kauwa-auwa with them and head in the direction toward which the sacred pole inclines. In this way communication with the supernatural will always be possible.

Standing at the center of the world, the temple too spans all levels of reality. The Rock of Jerusalem reaches down into the waters below the earth (Heb., *tehom*). Directly over this watery chaos, the Mishnah locates the Temple. The Rock of the Temple of Jerusalem thus closes "the mouth of the *tehom.*" The Babylonian sanctuaries of Nippur and Larsa were given the title *duranki,* "link between heaven and earth." In ancient Babylon the temple also served to connect heaven and earth: it was built upon *babapsu,* "gate of *apsu,*" the watery chaos that existed before creation. The stupa of Borobudur in Java was built in the form of a mountain occupying the center of the cosmos. It is here at the center of the universe that one may have the most direct contact with Buddhahood. By ascending the stages of the stupa, the pilgrim passes through all realms of reality.

In some cases, a city becomes the sacred place where heaven and earth come together. Architects designing sacred capitals oriented the sites to the cosmic powers that filled them with their sacred force and rendered them habitable.

Ritual actions focused the supernatural power of a kingdom within the city confines. In Thailand a new monarch performed a ceremonial tour *(liap mo'aṅ)* around his capital. In Egypt, a ceremony called the Circuit of the White Wall was celebrated when a new pharaoh came to Memphis. The practice was modeled on the actions of Menes, who had designed the sacred city. When Romulus determined the circumference of Rome, he plowed a furrow in such a way as to form the city on the model of the cosmos as a whole. This line, the *pomerium,* was marked then by stones and considered holy. Not only was the capital city made habitable by its consecration as a sacred place, the capital itself became the center for diffusion of sacred forces throughout the wider kingdom. Through the city gates, sacred power, generated at the center of the capital during its ceremonies, passed out to the extended world. In this way, the city, often built on a heavenly model, becomes a source of resanctification and sacred renewal for a world corrupted over time. Such was the function of the sacred cities of Cuzco, the Inca capital in the Andes of South America, and Tenochtitlán, the Aztec capital and center of life forces throughout Mesoamerica in the early sixteenth century CE. Tenochtitlán was called "the root," "the navel," and "the heart" of the earthly layer in the cosmos. It was the "supreme" place in which the world of humans was joined with the Giver of Life, for it supported the multiple layers of the celestial realm and communicated with the underworld. As the Aztec adage says: "Who would conquer Tenochtitlán? Who could shake the foundation of heaven?" (cited in Miguel León-Portilla, *Pre-Colombian Literatures of Mexico,* Norman, Okla., 1968, p. 87).

The symbolism of the center of the world is by no means limited to extravagant cases. The house often contains the center of the world. The Barasana of the northwest Amazon conceive of their *maloca,* the longhouse in which an extended family lives, in the image of the universe, especially at the time of the Yurupary festival. During the rites known as He, the longhouse becomes the center of the universe, where life began when a mythic ancestor anaconda swam there and disintegrated into the many separate parts which formed the separate lineages of the tribe. From his long bones came the sacred flutes and long trumpets played during the festival. These instruments are laid end to end to reconstruct—literally to remember—the ancestor as he was, whole and entire, at the beginning of time at the center of the house-universe. In the Barasana tradition the whole house is "cosmicized" for the cermonial occasion. In other cultures, some structure in the house serves as an image of the center of the world; a central beam, center post, or chimney, the smoke hole or hearth, and so on.

The tendency to find the center of the universe in multiple locations may be carried as far as the discovery of it within one's own body. Such is the case in certain Tantric schools that rejected the validity of an external *maṇḍala* but insisted rather on locating the center of the *maṇḍala* within the yogin. The interior *maṇḍala,* an image of the universe, enabled the yogin to identify his "mystical body" as a whole microcosm. As each internal *cakra,* the "wheel" where cosmic life and psychic life intersect, is activated, the practitioner progressively penetrates into the center of an interior *maṇḍala,* an image of the universe.

There is an impulse to replicate the image of the center of the universe in multiple forms. At one stage in the creation of the universe, according to the Dogon of Mali, a supernatural being connected the heavenly and earthly realms with thread fibers into which he wove symbols of the creative word spoken by Amma, the supreme being. The symbolism of fibers passing back and forth from heaven to earth is repeated in the image of a special drum, whose two heads are bound together in an intricate pattern of thread fibers. The same meaning is continued in children's games in which the child's hands are identified with the hands of the supernatural being, and the "cat's cradle" of thread drawn between the child's fingers imitates the creative word-threads communicated between heaven and earth. Weaving itself, and the loom, are invested with the same symbolic value. Rains are imagined to be moist breath-threads rewound into the heavens along the sun's rays by the copper spirals of moisture that entwine the sun. This sort of replication of the image of the *axis mundi* in village sites, house plans, ritual furnishings, personal ornaments, games, and cooking utensils tends to identify the fullness of being characteristic of the center of the world with the universe as a whole.

Although emphasis falls on the center of the world as a point of contact with the heavenly world and, therefore, associated with the symbolism of ascent, it should be made clear that, at the center of the world, one also communicates with underground realms of being. Insofar as these underground realms may be connected with death and the descent of the soul at death, rituals that employ symbolic death (such as initiations) often take place at the center of the world. Death requires passage from one state of being to another. On the Northwest Coast of North America the Kwakiutl candidate, undergoing a symbolic death during his initiation into a dancing society, declares "I am at the center of the world!" He stands at the foot of a cedar "cannibal pole" wrapped in red bark, which imbues it with supernatural power, *nawalak.* On the other hand, the kind of death associated with the center of the world may be more literally conceived. In these cases, the tomb comes to be the center of the world.

Intriguing also is the suggestion that at the center of the world is found a sound or set of sounds, usually sacred music of some sort, which effects the transition between world levels. Already mentioned is the image of the Dogon drum, the percussive instrument that effects transition and embodies the image of the *axis mundi* in its own construction. In the universe of the Warao Indians of the Orinoco Delta of Venezuela, transition from one realm of the cosmos to another is made by crossing a snake-bridge. The snake has musical bells on its horns. The shaman learns how to pass from one cosmic zone to another by singing the sounds he hears (sung by flowers, insects, supernatural beings) when he first makes the journey. The Chiripá shamans of eastern Paraguay sing a sacred song that is said to be "like a bridge" that permits communication between the heavenly and earthly worlds. Especially in religious worldviews wherein every kind of being possesses sounds unique to it, ritually controlled combinations of sound in sacred music "convocalize," or convoke, different realms of being by bringing them together at one time. The spatial images discussed earlier bring multiple realms of being together in the same place; sacred music and sound may bring together multiple realms of being in the same time.

Associated Actions and Attitudes. Even these few illustrations demonstrate a number of actions consistently appropriate to the range of ideas and symbols associated with the center of the world. To begin with, the sacred place, the locus of the center of the world, is set apart, deliberately made sacred; that is, in spite of its ordinary and profane aspects it is a place where communication with extraordinary beings is possible. The place may be made sacred by the arbitrary and unprovoked appearance of a supernatural power (kratophany), or the sacralizing event may be the appearance of a god (theophany). Generally speaking, we may say that a place may be set apart by an appearance of the sacred (hierophany). A second means of setting a place apart from profane space is through acts of deliberate consecration carried on by human beings in ritual. The examples cited show how closely the center of the world is associated with creation. This makes it easier to understand why the ritual construction of sacred spaces repeats, in stylized and symbolic form, the actions of the cosmogony. Just as the primordial moment of creation underlies all creative instances, so too does the place of origin become the point toward which all other life-filled space is oriented.

In the rites of Vedic sacrifice, for example, "the sacrificer makes himself a ladder and a bridge to reach the celestial world" (*Taittirīya Saṃhitā* 6.6.4.2). Before he (sometimes in company with his wife) can ascend to the upper world, the sacrificer must first prepare and consecrate the sacrificial stake, the *yūpa*. This is fashioned from a tree likened to the cosmic tree. After the *yūpa* is made, it is installed as a cosmic pillar, upholding and connecting all realms of being: "Lift thyself up, O Lord of the Forest, unto the summit of the earth!" (*Ṛgveda* 3.8.3.) The idea is made explicit in the *Śatapatha Brāhmaṇa* (3.7.1.4): "With thy summit thou dost hold up the heavens, with thy branches thou fillest the air, with thy foot thou steadiest the earth." While ascending the stake, he may extend his arms, just as a bird stretches out its wings, and exclaim, "I have attained to heaven, to the gods: I have become immortal!" (*Taittirīya Saṃhitā,* 1.7.9.)

The consecration of sacred space undertakes to create the world, in symbolic terms, and thus make it habitable; that is, make communication possible with powerful beings who are the source of creativity. Consecration, then, involves installation of the structures of the cosmos. The sacred lodge of the Algonquin people of North America embodies the essential structures of the universe. The construction itself is the cosmogony: the doors and windows are the four cardinal directions, each with its own color. The roof is the vault of heaven, the floor the earth. Human beings situate their cultic life at the center of this microcosm. The rites of the center include not only constructions reenacting the cosmogony but also rites of ascent, descent, and transition between states of being. Rites of sacrifice are properly celebrated at this point, where the spirit of the victim may pass from one plane to another. Construction sacrifices consecrate foundations and give life to the forms of buildings and bridges by using the cosmogony as their model. Curing rituals are often performed at the center, where life can be regenerated, powerful and fresh, just as it was once generated for the first time at the moment of creation.

All of these symbolisms of the center reflect the spiritual need for orientation to what is sacred. It is this proximity to the sacred that makes human life possible, for it satisfies the mature spiritual need for what is real and has meaning.

The examples depict an ambivalence inherent in the symbolism of the center. The spatial images themselves suggest two things at the same time: communication and distant separation. The very cosmic tree and mountain that join heaven and earth together also hold them apart from one another. This ambivalence of the center describes well a primary quality of religious experience. On the one hand, the journey to the center may be arduous and dangerous. No one may have access to the center, to different states of being, without careful preparation and spiritual strength. The journey to the center may require a complete transformation of one's spiritual being. On the other hand, the image of the center of the world is replicated in multiple forms. This ensures that communication with the fullness of reality is everywhere possible. Easy access to other modes of being is reminiscent of the paradisiacal state of the universe when it first came into being. The difficulty of passage to the center appears to be founded on the experience that communication with or acquisition of new states of being means a cessation, or "death," of one's profane state of being. Nevertheless, the ease with which one may enter the center of the world draws upon a profound knowledge of the nature of religious symbolism, in this case, the symbolism of the center: its multivalent character makes it capable of extending its significance to multiple levels of meaning and planes of reference. For example, the symbolism of the center, with great consistency of meaning, applies to the center of the universe, the center of the residential unit, the center of the village, the home, the ritual space, the human physiology mystically conceived, and the act of spiritual concentration. On every plane, the significance of the symbolism of the center of the world underlines the fact that at the heart of existence lies an experience and a mode of being entirely different from the ordinary world centered on it. Paradoxically, it is from this conjunction of beings that the reality of this world derives.

SEE ALSO Axis Mundi; Bridges; Cities; Consecration; Home; Mountains; Orientation; Temple; Trees.

BIBLIOGRAPHY

Extensive bibliography and lucid discussion of the symbolism of the center of the world can be found in Mircea Eliade's *Patterns in Comparative Religion* (New York, 1958), esp. pp. 367–387. See also Eliade's *The Sacred and the Profane: The Nature of Religion* (New York, 1959), pp. 20–67, and his *Images and Symbols: Studies in Religious Symbolism* (New York, 1969), pp. 27–56.

Other studies, with helpful bibliographies, investigate specific images and instances of the center of the world. On the cosmic mountain, see Joseph W. Bastien's *Mountain of the Condor: Metaphor and Ritual in an Andean Ayllu* (Saint Paul, Minn., 1978), and I. W. Mabbett's "The Symbolism of Mount Meru," *History of Religions* 23 (August 1983): 64–83. On the cosmic tree, see Y. T. Hosoi's "The Sacred Tree in Japanese Prehistory," *History of Religions* 16 (November 1976): 95–119. For a discussion of ways in which the mountain, cosmic tree, city, cave, and temple may be drawn together and overlap in the symbolism of the center, see the essays in *Mesoamerican Sites and World-Views,* edited by Elizabeth P. Benson (Washington, D.C., 1981). Regarding the personalization of cosmic space, see Catherine L. Albanese's "The Multi-Dimensional Mandala: A Study in the Interiorization of Sacred Space," *Numen* 24 (April 1977): 1–25. On the image of a city, see Werner Müller's, *Die heilige Stadt: Roma quadrate, himlisches Jerusalem und die Mythe vom Weltnabel* (Stuttgart, 1961); Paul Wheatley's *The Pivot of the Four Quarters: A Preliminary Enquiry into the Origins and Character of the Ancient Chinese City* (Chicago, 1971); and Paul Wheatley and Thomas See's *From Court to Capital: A Tentative Interpretation of the Origins of the Japanese Urban Tradition* (Chicago, 1978). See also Davíd Carrasco's "City as Symbol in Aztec Thought: The Clues from the Codex Mendoza," *History of Religions* 20 (February 1981): 199–223. For a comparative treatment of the role of city as center in religious literature and poetry, see James Dougherty's *The Fivesquare City: The City in the Religious Imagination* (Notre Dame, Ind., 1980). For a discussion of the center of the world as that place where the creative act imposes order on chaos, see N. J. Girardot's *Myth and Meaning in Early Taoism: The Themes of Chaos* (Berkeley, 1983).

For Buddhist cosmographies and descriptions of Mount Meru as the center of all world systems, see Georges Coedès's *Les trois mondes* (Paris, 1973). For treatment of the cosmic symbolism applied to the residence space, see Werner Müller's *Die blaue Hütte* (Wiesbaden, 1954). Concerning the "paradise" found as a sacred mountain in the center of the universe, see Michel Soymié's "Le Lo-feou chan: Étude de géographie réligieuse," *Bulletin de l'École Française d'Extrême-Orient* 48 (1956): 1–139. On the conception of the house as a microcosm, with the hearth or dance plaza as the center for ritual, see Anthony Jackson's *Na-khi Religion: An Analytical Appraisal of Na-khi Ritual Texts* (The Hague, 1979) and Christine Hugh-Jones's *From the Milk River: Spatial and Temporal Processes in Northwest Amazonia* (Cambridge, 1979), pp. 40–49, 235–282. For a discussion of sacred sound as an image of the *axis mundi,* see Lawrence E. Sullivan's "Sacred Music and Sacred Time," *World of Music* (Berlin) 26, no. 3 (1984): 33–52; and Rodney Needham's "Percussion and Transition," *Man* 2 (December 1967): 606–614. For a discussion of how the cosmic winds of the four quarters become centered and "holy" in the sacred sounds of ritual speech, see James K. McNeley's *Holy Wind in Navajo Philosophy* (Tucson, 1982) and Gary Witherspoon's "The Central Concepts of Navajo World View," *Linguistics* 119 (1972): 41–59. On the temple as a locus of the union of beings, see David Dean Shulman's *Tamil Temple Myths: Sacrifice and Divine Marriage in the South Indian Saiva Tradition* (Princeton, 1980).

For a consideration of the way in which the sacredness of the center relates, in a paradoxical way, to the boundaries of space, see Victor Turner's "The Center Out There: Pilgrim's Goal," *History of Religions* 12 (February 1973): 191–230, and Gerardo Reichel-Dolmatoff's *Amazonian Cosmos: The Sexual and Religious Symbolism of the Tukano Indians* (Chicago, 1971), esp. pp. 47–55, 116–117.

New Sources

Nasr, Seyyed Hossein. "To Live in a World with No Center—and Many." *Cross Currents* 46, no. 3 (Fall 1996): 318–325.

MIRCEA ELIADE (1987)
LAWRENCE E. SULLIVAN (1987)
Revised Bibliography

CENTRAL ASIAN RELIGIONS

SEE BUDDHISM, *ARTICLE ON* BUDDHISM IN CENTRAL ASIA; INNER ASIAN RELIGIONS; ISLAM, *ARTICLE ON* ISLAM IN CENTRAL ASIA

CENTRAL BANTU RELIGIONS.

The term *central Bantu,* as used here, refers to speakers of languages belonging to the Bantu branch of Niger-Congo who live in the Congo Basin. They are spread over thousands of square miles stretching from the mouth of the Congo River on the Atlantic to Lake Malawi and the Shire Basin in the east, lying between 4° and 17° south latitude. They occupy much of the Democratic Republic of the Congo (formerly Zaire), Angola, Zambia, and Malawi, spilling over into the Congo Republic, Tanzania, and Zimbabwe. Much of the region is forested savanna interspersed with grasslands, except where the great equatorial forest thrusts southward into Kuba and Lele territory in the northern part of the Democratic Republic of the Congo.

In 1980 the central Bantu peoples were estimated to number around ten million, divided among many groups varying in size from half a million to a few hundred. The best known are the Bakongo, Basuku, Bakuba (including the Bushong), Basilele, Baluba, Basongye, Balunda, Bachokwe, Bandembu, Balubale, Balozi, Baila, Batonga, Balamba, Babemba, Babisa, Bachewa, and Bafipa. The nominal prefex *ba* is frequently dropped and the groups are referred to simply as Kongo, Suku, and so on. Lele and Ndembu religions, through the writings of Mary Douglas and Victor Turner, have done much to shape current thought on religious symbols and the nature of ritual.

The Luba and Lunda stress patrilineal descent. The Lozi have a bilateral system. The other central Bantu are matrilineal, but residence upon marriage varies: in the Democratic Republic of the Congo, Angola, and south and west Zambia, the rule was that a wife moved to her husband's residence, and her sons returned to her brothers at maturity. In northern Zambia and Malawi, on the other hand, men joined their wives, and the long-lasting links were those between women. During the twentieth century, residence became more flexible. Prior to the late nineteenth century (before the colonial period) political organization varied. The Bushong, Luba, Lunda, and Kongo (Democratic Republic of the Congo), Lozi and Bemba (Zambia), and Chewa (Zambia and Malawi) had created centralized states dominated by royal courts. Others, such as the Tonga of Zambia, lived in small communities whose leaders depended on personal influence. In the Democratic Republic of the Congo, Angola, and western Zambia, religious systems emphasized the central importance of charms in both public and private rituals and made the spiritual realm manifest with carved figurines and masked dances. Elsewhere charms were used primarily in the private search for power, while public rituals centered on prayer and offering. Despite the differences, the social and religious systems of the savanna region had a common base.

COMMON BASE. A comparison of the myths and ritual symbols of the Kuba, Luba, and Lunda of the Democratic Republic of the Congo and the Bemba of Zambia led Luc de Heusch to the conclusion that the savanna peoples share a common symbolic vocabulary. He attributes this to their common ideological heritage from proto-Bantu ancestors. This common heritage was reinforced with the expansion of centralized states, which tended to imitate each other, and the growth of trading networks, which by the seventeenth century linked much of the region into one great system. Myths, he suggests, moved along the trade routes like merchandise (de Heusch, pp. 245–247). In fact, given the importance of charms or fetishes, which could be bought or sold, much ritual material was merchandise, encouraging the spread of cultic objects and organizations.

These materials could be accepted more easily because before the period of colonial rule the religious systems of the region shared common values and beliefs about the nature of the cosmos and the role of humans, spirits, and impersonal powers in the cosmic order. All were based on the assumption that a good human life is part of the natural order laid down at creation. The supreme being, or creator, was seen as beneficent but remote. Spirits active in relation to human interests, whether ancestral spirits or spirits of nature, were beneficent in principle. Power also existed throughout the cosmos and was inherent in all phenomena—in plants, animals, rocks, streams, and pools. It lay ready to be tapped and used by those who learned the correct techniques, and when it was converted into magic or a charm it could then be used to enhance human felicity or to destroy it.

Another common feature of central Bantu religions was the belief that human disorder disturbed the cosmic order. Drought, other natural disorders, infertility, and illness occurred because of human failure or evil. Malevolent and ambitious men and women who harnessed power for their own ends brought about suffering, death, and social and natural chaos. Evil, then, was due to human intervention and was seen as a perversion of the natural order. This was witchcraft. The natural order could be preserved or restored only by controlling the human disorder. When deaths or illnesses mounted, drought persisted, or general malaise afflicted a community, people first appealed to known spirits in rituals that cast out anger and demonstrated solidarity while in turn, the spirits were asked to cool their wrath. In case of failure, people tried extraordinary measures, replacing charms and rituals that had lost power with new, vigorous ones or summoning those who claimed to be able to identify and strip witches of their magic. As the community was purified and revitalized, the natural order was restored. De Craemer, Vansina, and Fox believe that the religious history of the Congo Basin has been marked by a sequence of revitalization cults conforming to the same pattern.

Central Bantu religions were also pragmatic, emphasizing ritual and practice rather than doctrine. Heresy could not exist. Rituals, moreover, were a means to immediate practical ends and were not intended to merge the human with the divine. They were performed to obtain rain, fertility of crops and women, success in hunting, protection from misfortune, recovery from illness, and to regulate the transition of community members from one life phase to another (especially from death to protecting ancestor status). Researchers in the region have not reported the existence of highly developed mythologies, and theories about the nature, origin, or history of spiritual beings appear not to have been elaborated. What spirits did—not what they were—was important. Spirits were identified by effect, and when in doubt a diviner was consulted. In the area that has become the Democratic Republic of the Congo, Angola, and western Zambia, Bantu-speaking peoples who used images and masks were concerned with symbolic statement about action rather than with a representation of substance. The majority of peoples who lived in the area that is now Zambia and Malawi made no images. They agreed with the Tonga, who said, "We call all spirits wind. Like wind we cannot see them. We only know what they are by what they do."

A further common characteristic has been isolated by MacGaffey (1980), but he concludes that it was common to all Bantu speakers with the exception of the Nyakyusa. According to MacGaffey, all religions of the Bantu-speaking peoples distinguished between good and evil in terms of effects rather than means, and thus had a similar structure. An act was good or bad depending upon the consequences. Diviners, herbalists, rulers, and great hunters were akin to witches in that they sought and use extraordinary power. If evil resulted, then they were witches. All use of power for purely private ends were assumed to be at the expense of others and therefore evil.

These values and the view of a cosmos pervaded with power continue to hold, although today many central Bantu are Christians and a few are Muslims, and many beliefs and rituals reported in the early ethnographies disappeared during the radical political and economic changes of the twentieth century. What follows, therefore, is a reconstruction based on what we know of nineteenth-century practices.

SOCIAL SETTING. By the beginning of the twentieth century, most central Bantu were subsistence cultivators, and their religions echoed their concerns. In general the countryside was well watered, but during the long dry season people depended upon springs and pools, especially in the more arid southeast. Rainfall was problematic, again especially in the southeast where droughts are frequent. It is no accident that so much communal ritual was associated with appeals for rains, while spirits linked to territorial cults were thought to dwell in pools and springs or moist caverns.

Because they are subject to leaching, tropical soils lose fertility rapidly. Most soils of the Congo Basin, except for river alluvials, are poor in nutrients and require long-term fallow. Tsetse flies inhibited the keeping of cattle and sometimes small stock except in a few grassland areas. The Lozi, Ila, Tonga, and a few others had herds of cattle, but most central Bantu depended on hunting and fishing for animal protein. As a result population densities were low, averaging about 6.9 to the square mile in the 1960s after considerable population increase.

Cultivators lived in small villages, ranging in size from forty to five hundred inhabitants, a size that left them highly vulnerable to natural disasters and demographic failure. High value was placed on fecundity and protection against accidents or epidemics. Villages moved to new sites every few years as soils became exhausted and game depleted. Those individuals dissatisfied with village morale or leadership moved away to join kin elsewhere. Since neither permanent buildings nor ownership of land tied people to a single place, communities were fragile, easily disrupted by quarrels or by events that aroused the fear that witches were at work.

Archaeological evidence for agriculture dates back to the early years of the first millennium. Most crops were annuals, although the Kongo had stands of palm oil and kola nut while the Kuba and Lele grew raffia palm. Staple crops were the millets and sorghums first domesticated in Africa, and many agricultural rituals centered on these. By the end of the nineteenth century they were being displaced by maize and cassava, which were first introduced from America to the Atlantic coast in the sixteenth century.

The village and its associated fields were viewed as domestic space subject to human control under the protection of the spirits of the dead. The surrounding bush was untamed space, controlled by nature spirits with whom humans had to come to an understanding since they depended upon the bush even more than upon their fields. The bush provided fuel, building materials, medicines, materials for crafts, and a substantial amount of food. Until the twentieth century game was usually abundant and hunting important. The contrasts between village and bush, domestic and wild, farming and hunting, and birth and death were common ritual motifs.

CULTS AND SPIRITS. Secret cults associated with initiation schools and masked performances existed in the area that has become the Democratic Republic of the Congo and Angola and among Luvale, Chokwe, and Ndembu immigrants near the upper reaches of the Zambezi River. Their theme was access to power. The Chewa near Lake Malawi also used masks in the Nyau cult, which mimed the invasion of domestic space by the spirits of the wild and the reign of disorder. Many central Bantu religions lacked such cults, but there were other cults that existed throughout the region. These have been classified into four cult types: domestic or kinship, territorial, professional, and healing. Each was the expression of a particular community of interest—kinship, residence, occupation, and common suffering—and might have its own set of shrines and mediators. Appeals were addressed to ancestors, dead heroes and rulers, and the spirits of nature through these cults.

Absence of a cult of the creator. The creator—known as Nzambe in much of the Democratic Republic of the Congo, Lesa over much of present-day Zambia, and Mulungu among those in contact with Swahili speakers—was the ultimate source of life and the initiator of universal order. Oaths used the creator's name, and the will of the creator provided the ultimate explanation when other explanations had failed. Rain, thunder, and lightning were manifestations of the creator; the falling rain was greeted with "The creator falls." But there was no expectation that the creator was concerned with human affairs, and a cult with shrines, priests, and offerings was not provided. J. Matthew Schoffeleers believes that the Mbona cult of the southern Chewa was initially a cult of the creator. If so, this would be a unique instance; by historical times Mbona conformed to the pattern common among central Bantu-speaking peoples of offering devotion to a spirit believed to be a former ruler or spirit medium.

Because central Bantu peoples did not personify the creative force, they had no need to attribute gender to the creator. Bantu languages, which all lack grammatical gender, do not force the speaker to make such distinctions. When the creator became identified with the Christian God through the teaching of missionaries, many came to think of the creator as male and father, but for the most part, the sex of the creator is seen as a matter unknowable to humans.

Spirits that dealt directly with humans might be given sexual attributes, even if it was never believed that they were once human beings. They could be thought to have a definite form, even if it was invisible, and diviners, mediums, and witches were sometimes said to be able to see them. They were given names and sometimes linked through genealogies or arranged in hierarchical ranks of power.

Ancestral spirits and domestic cults. The Kuba and Lele were unique in having no ancestral cults. According to Vansina, this is a recent development among the Kuba, one that is tied to the disappearance of lineage organization. Their dead were thought to be reincarnated after only a brief existence as ghosts.

Other central African peoples who believed in reincarnation thought of the reincarnated spirits as free to come and go in the homesteads of their kin. These spirits were invoked in domestic rituals of households and lineages and also in the professional cults of specialists. It was believed that such spirits affected the welfare of their descendants and members of their descent groups. Whatever the system of descent, children owed service to the spirits of their dead parents, grandparents, and siblings. These spirits were installed as guardians of their households, and they protected their dependents against intruding spirits and against charms sent by human malice. Periodically they were given offerings to assure them that they were remembered and cared for.

Illness or personal misfortune, while it might be attributed to witchcraft, also signified a breach between the dead and the living caused by a living person's neglect or wrongdoing. Divination discovered which ancestor or ancestors harbored anger and why. The offender then made an offering with a prayer for renewed favor. Divination usually named those who had died recently, but the recent dead were asked to bring with them to share in the offering all those they knew who were no longer known to the living. Beyond that range the dead had lost all community with the living and existed only as malevolent wandering shades who could be enlisted by witches.

Since the spirits had the same tastes as the living, the Kongo offered them palm wine and kola nuts, a common provision for honored guests among the Kongo. Elsewhere the offering was of meal and water or beer or kaolin powder. The Tonga first offered meal and water, and if conditions improved (meaning that the right spirit had been identified), they offered beer. The beer had to be brewed from grain grown by the members of the household for which the appeal was being made. Because it was won with their sweat, it was endowed with their life force. Offering, therefore, had an element of sacrifice.

The common place of offering in domestic cults was the doorway of the dwelling, which was associated with the coming and going of the spirits. Most offerings took place in early morning before spirits and people had dispersed for the day. The dwelling itself was a shrine to domesticity, for those who lived within were continuing the domestic life laid down by the ancestors. The sexual activity of the married couple, which created new life, was therefore made sacred, as was the cooking fire that helped to sustain life.

Lineages, where they existed, were ritual communities focused on common ancestors, led by elders who themselves had known many of those whose spirits they now summoned. The elder's dwelling could serve as a lineage shrine as well as his household shrine, but special shrines also existed. They took the form of a simple post, a tree planted when the homestead was built, a miniature dwelling, or a gateway formed of two posts with a crossbar. Like all central Bantu shrines they were simple, impermanent, and could be built again when need arose. First fruits were laid at the shrine. At harvest or before sowing, lineage members gathered to make offerings. This might include the ritual killing of a chicken, which then provided a communion meal. But residential patterns led to the dispersal of lineage members and only those who lived nearby came to the shrine. As a result, most lineages had few members and a shallow time depth.

Individuals who had special skills bestowed upon them by an ancestor dedicated shrines to their spirit sponsor. Here the spirit was invoked before the person embarked on the hunt or other activity, and it was thanked for success in the enterprise. Such shrines also served as reminders that the living followed a way of life created by those now dead and that they could depend upon the knowledge the dead had acquired.

Territorial cults, heroes, and nature spirits. Because villages had populations of diverse origin owing service to different sets of ancestors, lineage cults based on devotion to common ancestors could not serve village or neighborhood interests. Their common interests were the basis of territorial cults whose rituals dealt with rain, the ensurance of a harvest, the communal hunt, and vulnerability to epidemic.

Some territorial cults had no permanent shrines but rather centered on spirit mediums who spoke under possession as the embodiment of nature spirits, of those who had first settled the land, or of ancient heroes or former rulers who had once had some interest in the territory. Other cults used natural shrines that were seen as places where spirits manifested themselves. These were usually deep pools, waterfalls, caves, and high places. Here offerings of black cloth, black beads, beer, domestic stock, meal, and water were made. Hoes and spears, the essential tools of cultivation and the hunt, were also appropriate offerings. Some communities supplemented the natural shrines with miniature dwellings or shelters, set apart from the village, where they appealed to spirits thought to have once lived as members of their social group. Often these were identified as the first couple who had settled in the area and had first come to terms with the spirits of the land, making them proper intermediaries.

Officiants in the territorial cults were priests, priestesses, and mediums. The former, if representative of first settlement, are usually called earth priests. They were of particular importance among acephalous peoples, but even in the centralized kingdoms where royal shrines catered to public concerns, earth priests led local communities.

The earth priest was chosen from the lineage associated either with settlement or with some later community leader. He had a ritual wife who represented the first wife, and together they followed the routine believed to have been established with the foundation of the community. They carried out the rites that organized the agricultural year, initiating clearing of fields, planting, weeding, bird scaring, eating of first fruits, and harvest. Often wild spinach and fruits were brought to them as they came into season, as well as the first cut of thatching grass. When the community moved, their house was the first to be built, and it was from their rekindled fire that fire was taken by others. Since they were associated with fertility, their ritual intercourse gave validity to the promise of reward for hard agricultural labor. Seeds placed beneath their bed were imbued with vitality and were distributed for planting.

The permission of the earth priest and his wife might also be sought for the felling of large trees associated with spirits or regarded as the embodiment of power or for any disturbance of the earth. They gave permission to hunters to use the bush. Adherents of the local cult would make the first appeal for rain before their house, asking them in turn to appeal to the spirits of the first couple to intervene with the natural spirits to preserve the community that they had founded. Carrying drums and singing, the petitioners subsequently went to the shrine at the gravesite of the first settler or to one of the natural shrines to renew the appeal.

Priests and priestesses gave continuity, but mediums provided for communication and innovation. At regular offerings, men and women told the spirits what they desired; the spirits, in turn, made their own demands and gave warnings through mediums. The spirits chided earth priests and priestesses for ritual neglect or abandonment of ancestral ways. They called for new shrines to be built, instigated changes in routines, and demanded offerings for themselves and their mediums. Sometimes they announced the arrival of previously unknown spirits or threatened to abandon the community. When rain was at stake, black beads and black cloth were appropriate offerings to the mediums, for black symbolized the rain clouds. White was offered when they were asked to stop overly abundant downpours. When the spirits demanded sacrifices, black animals were provided.

Although some of the most powerful mediums lived separately and could be approached only through their attendants, the majority lived as ordinary men and women except when they were possessed. During possession, people clapped before them as they did before the shrines or in the presence of a ruler.

Just as first settlers continued to watch over their communities, so dead kings and queens continued to oversee their realms. These royal spirits were often associated with regional shrines. While Bemba kings were buried in one royal cemetery, rulers elsewhere were buried at their capitals. Since each ruler built a new capital, royal shrines were widely scattered. Initially the royal shrine was cared for by retired officers of the dead king and by royal widows; the office then became hereditary to their descent lines. The dead ruler might also speak through a medium attached to the shrine, a medium whose post was not usually hereditary. Periodically the living king or queen sent offerings to all the royal shrines throughout the kingdom to invoke the protection of the new ruler. Their anger at his bodily failure or neglect could bring disaster upon the realm.

Some territorial shrines served only a neighborhood, while others served a large region as places of last appeal. Shrines might be interlinked because they were associated with the same spirit, or because mediums in many places claimed possession by the same spirit. The most famous spirits had many mediums. When nearby shrines and mediums failed to give satisfaction, communities sent delegations to distant shrines and mediums, crossing linguistic and political boundaries. This gave witness that in the last analysis all shared the same human interests. Homogenization of belief and rituals was inevitable.

Professional cults. Many types of professional guilds existed in what is now the Democratic Republic of the Congo, each with its own cult. Elsewhere we have good evidence only for hunting cults and sometimes cults of diviners and smiths. Individual cult members could count upon assistance from a sponsoring ancestor, but the guild also had a variety of guild rituals, including those for the initiation of new members. They were taught medicines and spells needed to handle the power inherent in the earth, water, large trees, and big game. Because they dealt with power, guild members were regarded as dangerously close to the temptation of witchcraft. A breaking of the normal rules was attributed to hunters, who in the reckless search for power engaged in incest and sacrificed kin to obtain spirit companions in the hunt. The very presence of the hunter, linked as he was with blood and death as well as with extraordinary power, was dangerous to small children and pregnant women.

Many central Bantu thought that witches, too, had professional guilds. It was a common belief that witches offered human flesh as a feast and delighted in the evil that they had orchestrated.

Cults of suffering. Cults of suffering, or of affliction as Victor Turner called them, may have been of minor importance prior to the twentieth century. During that century, however, these cults proliferated. They are based on the belief that various kinds of spirits seize upon or enter human victims, who then must come to terms with them. Treatment requires identification of the spirit and instruction in how to meet its demands. Thereafter the sufferer becomes an adept able to treat new victims. All adepts in the locality are expected to help their fellow sufferers, and this joins them in a ritual community. As the people of surrounding areas become suspicious that the new spirit has begun work in their community, adepts are summoned to diagnose and treat, and so the cults spread rapidly.

In the west, in the Democratic Republic of the Congo, Angola, and western Zambia, cults of suffering are associated with spirits known as *mahamba.* Elsewhere in Zambia and in Malawi they are more likely to be referred to as *masabe. Mahamba* and *masabe* spirits may be identified as former members of alien ethnic groups who ask those possessed to speak in their own tongue and don their costume. *Mahamba* cults may also invoke the spirits of the sufferer's own ancestors.

Early cults of affliction were concerned with the incursion of animal spirits and spirits of the bush and may have developed out of hunting cults. More recent ones are linked to the uncertainties of alien modern experiences; cults centered on such things as the airplane, railroad, city life, warfare, angels, and on those people taken away as slaves to Europe and America have appeared in the last few decades. Each spirit is identified with its own drum rhythms, songs, medicines, and sometimes costume. Cults are most elaborate, and seem to have greater permanence, in the area inhabited by the west-central Bantu peoples. Elsewhere they came and went with great rapidity until the 1970s and 1980s, when some of the cults of affliction began to take on the semblance of a church and to make claims about their ability to go beyond the control of invading spirits. Some cult leaders now claim that they have the power to heal, provide protection against witches, and control the rains. They often have many spirits, which are seen as helpers.

Although men and women of all ages may be initiated into cults of suffering, the majority of initiates are women. Lewis attributes this to the peripheral role women have in the public sphere. But among the central Bantu peoples, only the Lele barred women from participation in public religious actions. In general, central Bantu religions provided women with important ritual and political roles. Women were sometimes political rulers and held offices in both territorial and kinship cults. On death they became ancestral spirits, and living women could make offerings to the ancestors. Lineage offerings usually required the collaboration of a man and woman elder. Women became diviners and herbalists, and some of the most famous mediums were women. The Luba are reported as saying that no man had a body strong enough to support possession by the greatest spirits—only the women were strong enough to withstand such power.

Central Bantu peoples differed in their judgment concerning the association of women with the possibility of evil. Some are reported to have connected maleness with power and death, femaleness with fertility and life. Yet some attributed witchcraft to women. Among the Luba those accused of witchcraft were usually women. The Lamba thought men and women were equally likely to be witches. The Bemba, Tonga, and Chewa usually accused men because men were thought to compete with one another through ambition, and so it was through them that evil disrupted the world.

Religious Transformation. De Craemer, Vansina, and Fox believe the basic elements and symbols of central African religions have been stable over the centuries (perhaps for millennia), although specific religious movements have come and gone. Nevertheless the last four centuries have been marked by religious questioning and transformation, paralleling the turmoil and transformation in political and economic regimes. The Kongo on the Atlantic coast first encountered the Portuguese and Christianity at the end of the fifteenth century. Many Kongo people were baptized, and the cross was adopted as a powerful charm. In the sixteenth century the Portuguese also began pushing up the Zambezi River from the Indian Ocean. By that time central Africa had long had trade links with Islamic settlements on the East African coast. Exchange of ideas was inevitable. By the early nineteenth century trading caravans in search of slaves and ivory were disturbing even the most remote areas.

The slave trade brought about the destruction of many of the ancient kingdoms. The Kongo kingdom disintegrated in the sixteenth century in the turmoil provoked by Portuguese slavers. In the mid-nineteenth century Chokwe slave raiders from Angola overran the Lunda and Luba empires. The weakened Chewa kingdoms had already fallen easily to nineteenth-century Ngoni invaders from the south. Royal cults associated with the old kingdoms either disappeared in the chaos or persisted by transforming themselves into other forms of territorial cults.

The dispersal of fleeing populations and the caravan movements led to a spread of epidemic disease on an unprecedented scale and to a questioning of the efficacy of existing religion. At the end of the nineteenth century central Africa was carved up among European powers, and formerly independent rulers became suspect as ritual leaders when they were transformed into bureaucrats in colonial governments. Between 1950 and 1980, independence movements brought African governments into power, but these were no more willing to accept claims to authority based on religious inspiration or cultic position than were the colonial governments.

In the twentieth century people came to depend on the cash economy and world trade. Market conditions are now as important as rainfall in determining well-being. New crops and agricultural techniques dominate the scene; consequently, territorial cults associated with agriculture have become less important. Hunting had little importance by the late 1980s since game had been largely depleted except in a few refuge areas. Hunting cults, not surprisingly, have largely vanished. And as cheap imported goods have spread and undercut local products, rituals associated with other crafts have also faded.

Many adults have been trained in mission schools or otherwise influenced by Christianity. Their children attend government schools where dependence upon ancestors or territorial cults is derided, although the power of charms and witches continues to be admitted.

Religious life has had to adjust to the fact that the central Bantu-speaking peoples are no longer primarily based in rural areas supported by agriculture and the produce of the bush. Many are now wage earners. Most men and women have spent some years in the cities that grew up around mines and trading and administrative centers. A substantial portion of the population is now permanently urbanized. Cities are becoming arbiters of the good life. The twentieth century saw a loss of faith, and people no longer even know about many of the beliefs that were an important part of their forebears' lives in 1900. It also saw the rise and rapid spread of new religious movements that promise to free people from the threat of witchcraft and to provide an understanding of the human experience.

Religious systems are not direct reflections of the social order, nor are they compelled solely by economic considerations. Yet they relate to the concerns of those who live in a given time and place. A viable religion must reflect people's desires, fears, and visions of what life ought to be like; provide rituals that speak to these concerns; and somehow link the transitory human experience with some enduring guarantee of order.

It is not surprising that many new religious movements have arisen among migrants in ethnically diverse cities or that these movements center upon the individual's search for a community of the purified rather than on the community of kinship or the common interests of a rural neighborhood. Many people today find religious community through conversion linked with healing and purification, and it is among those who share this experience that they find help to face illness and death and a shield against fears of loneliness, joblessness, and the envy of others.

Many of the new religions have their roots in Christianity, but their founders adapt Christian elements to what they see as African needs and wisdom. Unlike the mission churches, they accept the efficacy of charms and the power of witches and arm their adherents against these dangers. They recognize the continuing existence of the dead and the possibility of possession. They identify the creator with the Christian God but announce that the creator now cares about humanity and is actively at work in the world. Many of these new religions base themselves upon a visionary experience in which the creator appeared to be the founder and seek to provide either a new explication of the Bible or to replace it with a new message for Africans. Such was the Antonine movement founded in 1704 by Dona Béatrice, a Kongo woman, as a response to the disintegration of the Kongo world (Balandier, pp. 257ff.). The churches of Simon Kimbangu (Kimbanguist Church), Alice Lenshina (Lumpa Church), John Maranke (Apostolic Church of John Maranke), and John Masowe (Apostolic Church of John Masowe) were comparable responses in the twentieth century. Fernandez describes their theology as "lived, sung, and pictured in images, not formulated" (p. 222).

Cults of suffering and witch-finding movements also proliferated in the twentieth century as the old religious foundations crumbled, but they are more likely to operate in rural areas. Witch-finding movements aim at purification of existing communities to restore them to working order and usually vanish, to be replaced by a successor, when pain and suffering are again found to be the human portion. The Muchapi movement, which swept Malawi and Zambia in the 1920s, was short-lived, as was the Mikom iyool current among Luba, Bushong, and Lele in the 1940s (Douglas, pp. 245ff.). Their successors have also not lasted long. But they attest to a continued belief that the world is basically good and that all will be well if humans can be induced to discard malice and control ambition.

See Also Affliction, article on African Cults of Affliction; African Religions, article on New Religious Movements; Bemba Religion; Kimbangu, Simon; Kongo Religion; Lenshina, Alice; Luba Religion; Maranke, John; Ndembu Religion; Witchcraft, article on African Witchcraft.

Bibliography

Balandier, Georges. *Daily Life in the Kingdom of the Kongo.* Translated by Helen Weaver. London, 1968.

Beattie, John, and John Middleton, eds. *Spirit Mediumship and Society in Africa.* New York, 1969.

De Craemer, Willy, Jan Vansina, and Renée C. Fox. "Religious Movements in Central Africa: A Theoretical Study." *Comparative Studies in Society and History* 18 (October 1976): 458–475.

de Heusch, Luc. *The Drunken King, or The Origin of the State.* Translated by Roy G. Willis. Bloomington, Ind., 1982.

Douglas, Mary. *The Lele of the Kasai.* London, 1963.

Fernandez, James W. "African Religious Movements." *Annual Review of Anthropology* 7 (1976): 195–234.

Lewis, I. M. *Ecstatic Religion: An Anthropological Study of Spirit Possession and Shamanism.* Harmondsworth, U.K., 1971.

MacGaffey, Wyatt. "Comparative Analysis of Central African Religions." *Africa* 42 (1972): 21–31.

MacGaffey, Wyatt. "African Religions: Types and Generalizations." In *Explorations in African Systems of Thought,* edited by Ivan Karp and Charles S. Bird, pp. 301–328. Bloomington, Ind., 1980.

Schoffeleers, J. Matthew. "The Interaction of the M'Bona Cult and Christianity, 1859–1963." In *Themes in the Christian History of Central Africa,* edited by T. O. Ranger and John Weller, pp. 14–29. Berkeley, Calif., 1975.

Schoffeleers, J. Matthew, ed. *Guardians of the Land: Essays on Central African Territorial Cults.* Gwelo, Rhodesia, 1978.

Turner, Victor. *The Forest of Symbols: Aspects of Ndembu Ritual.* Ithaca, N.Y., 1967.

Turner, Victor. *The Drums of Affliction: A Study of Religious Processes among the Ndembu of Zambia.* London, 1968.

Turner, Victor. *The Ritual Process: Structure and Anti-Structure.* Chicago, 1969.

van Binsbergen, Wim. "Explorations in the History and Sociology of Territorial Cults in Zambia." In *Guardians of the Land,* edited by J. Matthew Schoffeleers, pp. 47–88. Gwelo, Rhodesia, 1978.

Werbner, R. P., ed. *Regional Cults.* New York, 1977.

Willis, Roy G. "Instant Millennium: The Sociology of African Witch-Cleansing Cults." In *Witchcraft Confessions and Accusations,* edited by Mary Douglas, pp. 129–140. New York, 1970.

New Sources

Fardon, Richard. *Between God, the Dead and the Wild: Chamba Interpretation of Ritual and Religion.* Edinburgh, U.K., 1990.

Mudimbe, V. Y. *Parables and Fables: Exegesis, Textuality and Politics in Central Africa.* Madison, Wis., 1991.

ELIZABETH COLSON (1987)
Revised Bibliography

CERAMESE RELIGION SEE SOUTHEAST ASIAN RELIGIONS, *ARTICLE ON* INSULAR CULTURES

CEREMONY is conventionally defined as a highly formalized observance or practice prescribed by custom and undertaken by a collective, or as customary observances and practices considered as a whole. In contrast to conventional usage, in which the term *ceremony* is interchanged indiscriminately with *ritual*, in theoretical discussion, the terms are increasingly distinguished; *ceremony* is identified as a genre or type of ritual that is distinguished from other genres by its object. A prevalent trend identifies ceremony with secular interests, that is, the symbolic representation of sociocultural arrangements as opposed to religious or sacred ones. In addition, ceremony is differentiated by its essentially conservative social role: the maintenance of existing sociocultural arrangements over against their transformation. Presidential inaugurations in the United States, for example, transfer power from one political party to another in order that the democratic political system remains intact. Key to transferal of power is legitimation of the new regime. This is achieved both by election and by securing God's blessing at the swearing in of the new president.

The question has been raised whether it is not more proper and useful to approach ceremony as a ritual attitude as opposed to a distinct ritual type. Ronald L. Grimes argues that standard analytic or classificatory distinctions among types of ritual—differentiation between "sacred" and "profane" activity, and so on—are insufficient in the analysis of ritual, since they fail to take into account a variety of "embodied attitudes" that emerge during the course of a ritual, such as ceremony, decorum, and ritualization. Ceremony is not so much an analytic type as it is a layer, attitude, sensibility, or "mode" of ritual, contends Grimes. He suggests that when one or another mode becomes dominant, it is proper to speak of a ritual of ceremony, and so forth (Grimes, 1982, pp. 223, 235, 241).

This entry gives an overview of the theoretical discussion, devoting special attention to the relationship between ceremony and political power, and that between ceremony and religion, both central concerns in the theories. In contrast to theorists who identify ceremony as a strictly secular ritual, this entry suggests that inasmuch as sociopolitical (or secular) and religious (or sacred) interests overlap and even converge, the relationship between ceremony and religion is problematic; they are not always distinct.

THEORIES OF CEREMONY. Theorists call attention to features of ceremony that are characteristic of such rituals. Formalization and stylization (i.e., specification of time and place, formulaic speech and gesture, etc.) are indicative of ceremony's scripted character as "intentional" (Grimes, 1982, p. 41) or self-conscious behavior. Ceremony is fundamentally self-reflective performance. As such, ceremony is essentially "self-symbolizing" (Goffman, 1974, p. 58); it has representational intent. Like all symbolic behavior, ceremony points to a larger framework of action. The public character of ceremony is an indication that its more general context is social and cultural life. According to Erving Goffman, ceremony provides a symbolic means whereby participants represent themselves in one of their central social roles (1974, p. 58). Through dramatization and other representational means ceremony presents those ideologies, values, and the social institutions to which they are bound, as well as other sociocultural constructs that constitute social and cultural life or group life, in the case of ceremonies undertaken on a smaller scale.

The underlying motivation in the ceremonial representation of the various social and cultural constructs is said to be the confirmation and reinforcement of those organizing frameworks that order sociocultural life in a normative way. Steven Lukes explains that:

> the symbolism of political ritual *represents* . . . particular models or political paradigms of society and how it functions. In this sense, such ritual plays, as Durkheim argued, a cognitive role, rendering intelligible society and social relationships. . . . In other words, it helps to define as authoritative certain ways of seeing society: it serves to specify what in society is of special significance, it draws people's attention to certain forms of relationships and activity—and at the same time, therefore, it deflects their attention from other forms, since every way of seeing [is] also a way of not seeing. (Lukes, 1975, p. 301)

"Ceremony," writes Victor Turner, "constitutes an impressive institutionalized performance of indicative, normatively structured social reality" (1982, p. 83). In his view, ceremony's indicative role gives it a conservative character that distinguishes it from ritual. "Ceremony *indicates*, ritual *transforms*," Turner emphasizes (1982, p. 80). Ritual is "a transformative self-immolation of order as presently constituted, even sometimes a voluntary *sparagmos* or self-dismemberment of order, in the subjunctive depths of liminality" (1982, p. 83). "Without taking liminality into account ritual becomes indistinguishable from 'ceremon'" (1982, p. 80). Ritual derives its liminal quality from separating participants from their everyday social-structural identity and, consequently, from creating an ambiguous social status as the ritual prepares participants to undergo a transition to a new social identity (1982, pp. 80–85). Turner contends that ritual exists in dialectical relation to everyday social structure; ritual is fundamentally "anti-structure" (Turner,

1974). By relaxing social structural requirements, ritual liminality makes possible experimentation with social structure, and with it, structural and cultural innovation. Thus, ritual enables sociocultural systems to change and grow as new demands, particularly for egalitarian and direct (or "communitarian") social interchange, challenge existing social-structural arrangements. Turner's conceptualization of ritual liminality helps explain why spontaneity and disorder seldom emerge during the course of ceremony, and then only during prescribed times or in established places: the intent to conserve the social-structural status quo requires that ceremony's liminal aspects be narrowly circumscribed or kept in check.

Ceremony's confirmatory or conservative role makes it especially suited to exploitation in times of social conflict or potential crisis, when existing norms are challenged or under threat. Since formalization conveys legitimacy, ceremony lends itself to portraying as indisputable and fixed those ideologies and social institutions that are most in doubt during times of social crisis. Sally F. Moore and Barbara G. Myerhoff note that ceremony's authoritative presentation of its material as axiomatic is paradoxical, since it is the most obviously contrived and hence arbitrary social interaction. They note that preoccupation with order by implication points to the possibility of disorder, chaos, and most importantly, open choice of other cultural configurations. While ceremony may be intended to mask contradiction, on a more subtle, less conscious level, it may give it expression (Moore and Myerhoff, 1977, pp. 16, 18; cf. Lukes, 1975, pp. 296–302).

A more fundamental motivation in the ceremonial representation of social and cultural constructs identified by Moore and Myerhoff is the cultural declaration of order over against indeterminacy. Ceremony is intended to proclaim "cultural order as against a cultural void," which exist in dialectical tension. It "banishes from consideration the basic questions raised by the made-upness of culture, its malleability and alterability." As formalized behavior, ceremony is essentially an attempt to assert order: "Through order, formality, and repetition it seeks to state that the cosmos and social world, or some particular small part of them are orderly and explicable and for the moment fixed" (Moore and Myerhoff, 1977, pp. 16–17). Formality thus allows ceremony to authenticate its message, conferring permanence and legitimacy on what is in fact a social construction. "Its medium is part of its message" (1977, p. 8).

While ceremony symbolizes or reflects the socially and culturally normative, it is not a mere mirror image. Ceremonies, notes Moore, are not simply dramatizations of social and moral norms: they are "performative acts." Ceremonies do not simply communicate information, nor are they merely analogies; "they *do* something," putting into action what they symbolize (Moore, 1977). Clifford Geertz explains that by presenting an ontology, a demonstration of being or existence, ceremony serves "to make it happen—make it actual" (1980).

Ceremony models or shapes sociocultural life in a twofold sense, Geertz observes. It offers idealized representations of normative social arrangements that are to be emulated; it also encourages participants to conform their behavior to these arrangements by showing that the way of life that is presented is adapted to the world as it actually exists. Hence ceremony is paradigmatic in a dual sense: it is both a model of and a model for social and cultural life (Geertz, 1980 and 1973).

Inextricably linked to ceremony's corroborative and legitimating functions is the assertion and securing of power. As Grimes observes, "ceremony consists of power negotiations in ritual form. . . . Ceremonial gestures are bids for authority, prestige, recognition, and control" (1982, p. 224). The underlying interest in asserting and securing power gives ceremony a serious tone, which remains dominant even when ceremony manifests festive aspects. Grimes observes that because ceremony implies a distinction between the group that is symbolically asserting its power and the "other side, it is manifestly competitive, sometimes conflict-laden" (1982, p. 42). The successful symbolization of power requires that the social contradiction inherent in the arbitrary assertion of power be masked and only righteous or legitimate properties be exposed. The potential for power to be a source of conflict and not solely a means of conflict resolution must also be concealed. Other theorists point out that ceremony is not simply a disguise for power; it is the assertion of power, or power in action. The fact that ceremony is imbued with the authority of groups that are already in a position of power or that are emerging as a dominant power explains in part why it is one of the predominant frames, or principles of organization, by which social arrangements are ordered (Goffman, 1974, pp. 10–11, 48).

Ceremony and Political Power. Political rituals are the most obvious examples of ceremony as it relates to power. Catherine Bell defines "political rites" as "ceremonial practices that specifically construct, display and promote the power of political institutions (such as king, state, the village elders) or the political interests of distinct constituencies and subgroups" (1997, p. 128). Bell draws from Geertz in her observation that political rituals create power by establishing a ruler or political institution's "iconicity" with the order of the cosmos (Bell, 1997, pp. 128–130; Geertz, 1980). Geertz observes that ceremony demonstrates that a political regime is an image of the cosmic order itself, and thus is congruent with the cosmic order. Showing the ruling political power to be part of the cosmic order, and hence part of the natural order of things, establishes its legitimacy.

Congruence between political power and cosmic order is demonstrated by way of an elaborate argument communicated in symbolic performance or display. Geertz offers the example of the display of vast wealth by the "theater state" of ancient Java or Bali, to which kings devoted most of their time. The continual display of the ruler's wealth through a variety of state rituals demonstrated that his rule was "a microcosm of the supernatural order . . . and the material embodiment of the political order" (Bell, 1997, p. 129, citing Geertz, 1980, p. 13). In his classic essay on religion as a cultural symbol system, Geertz (1973) observes that ritual performance goes beyond giving ideational veracity, via argument, to a particular view of the world and ethos or style of life. Ritual provides further validation by evoking specific emotions that give firsthand, experiential evidence that the world is actually constituted as claimed by intellectual argument, and consequently that the lifestyle the argument shows to be ideally fitted to the world is in fact suited to it. Intellectual argument and emotional experience are mutually reinforcing.

Geertz argues that ceremony as practiced by the Balinese kingship is more than a symbolic disguise of "real" power residing in physical force or the threat of violence; it is more than artifice (Bell, 1992, pp. 192–193; Geertz, 1980, pp. 122–136 passim). Bell issues the caveat that some political rituals, as in the case of China, do disguise the source and exercise of power while also serving overt political purposes (Bell, 1992, p. 194). Geertz's insight runs counter to the once prevailing view of sacred kingship developed by James G. Frazer and A. M. Hocart, namely, that ritual legitimates real political power (Bell, 1992, p. 193). In Geertz's view, ritual legitimation is not distinct from political power, but is itself an expression of power that is used to achieve political ends. For Geertz, the ability to perceive that the ritual performances of the Balinese state are real political power depends upon not opposing the symbolic and the real or aesthetic performance to action. Power must be seen as not existing outside the mechanisms through which it works (i.e., ritual). Bell notes that Michel Foucault makes the same observation regarding the mechanisms and dynamics through which ritual works (Bell, 1997, p. 132; and 1992, chap. 9). David Cannadine's and Maurice Bloch's analyses of ritual develop Geertz's understanding of ritual as legitimation of power and, hence, as real and efficacious power (Bell, 1992, pp. 194–195; Cannadine, 1987; Bloch, 1987).

"In other words," Bell writes, "political rituals do not refer to politics, as Geertz has strained to express, they *are* politics. Ritual is the thing itself. It *is* power; it acts and it actuates" (Bell, 1992, p. 195). "In sum, it is a major reversal of traditional theory [for Geertz and others] to hypothesize that ritual activity is not the 'instrument' of more basic purposes, such as power, politics, or social control, which are usually seen as existing before or outside the activities of the rite. It puts interpretive analysis on a new footing to suggest that ritual practices are themselves the very production and negotiation of power relations" (1992, p. 196). Viewing ritual legitimation as an expression of power that is more efficacious than "brute force," as Geertz, Cannadine, Bloch, and others have done, makes ritual an important tool in the analysis of politics (Bell, 1992, p. 195).

Drawing on Foucault, Bell argues more specifically that political rituals construct power by creating a "power relationship" of domination and submission (Bell, 1997, p. 132; 1992, chap. 9). Political rituals are not simply "secondary reflections" of relationships of domination and submission that guide exchanges between ruler and subject; "They create these relations [dominance and submission]; they create power in the very tangible exercise of it" (1997, p. 136). According to Bell, ritual's effectiveness as a form of power lies in its capacity to create nuanced relationships of power in which those who dominate and those who submit negotiate power (1992, pp. 196–218). Nuanced relationships involve both acceptance of and opposition or resistance to those whom ritual empowers.

Bell notes that Foucault argues that power does not exist in a simplistic dominant-dominated relationship (Bell, 1992, chap. 9). Power, of necessity, requires choice. Distinct from force or coercion, power depends upon freedom or resistance, which provokes it and legitimates its use. Those who submit are free to act in contrary ways. Thus, those who dominate only indirectly shape the field of actions of others. Bell points out that Geertz's rejection of the distinction between ritual (or symbol) and real power dismisses the simplistic view of power as the assertion of the ruler's or political power's will upon the dominated (Bell, 1992, p. 194). Power depends upon the dominant and the dominated choosing various courses of action to maintain the relationship as one of power. Individuals submit to political domination while recognizing that they are still free to create their own personal path of freedom, especially in the form of dissenting private thoughts, as in the case of mental dissent from a totalitarian regime. Calling attention to the fact that Foucault has been criticized for eliminating coercion, Bell argues that his analysis of power discloses an important aspect of power that has been minimized—reciprocity (Bell, 1992, p. 204).

Elaborating on the process by which ritual allows society to create itself in the image of power relations, Bell adds that ritual participants project, and thereby objectify, relationships of power that are drawn from society (Bell, 1992, 204–218). Participants do not view themselves as projecting these relationships; they view themselves as responding instinctively to the natural social order instead. Participants then reembody these projected or objectified schemes. Through objectification and embodiment, ritual creates a society that actually consists of these relationships of power. The process of objectification, embodiment, and resistance empowers those who submit, even as it empowers those who dominate. Thus, negotiating and giving nuance to power relations actually empowers those who appear to be controlled by them.

Bell offers the example of the Japanese enthronement ceremony (1997, pp. 130–133). Overseen by the imperial state and supported by state Shintō, the enthronement ceremony heightens the relationship between the emperor and the cosmic order by giving him semidivine status. Through a series of elaborate associated rituals, enthronement appeals to "a sense of cosmological fit" between the emperor and divine beings (Bell, 1997, p. 132). The rituals include food offerings to Amaterasu, the sun goddess, who is ancestor of the royal clan, according to tradition. The emperor is considered to be her "grandson." The offerings symbolize sexual relations between the emperor as "bridegroom" and Amaterasu that result in his ritual rebirth prior to the swearing in. Thus, the goddess's divine grandson is reborn in the form of a human emperor. Hirohito, who was emperor of Japan from 1926 to 1989, undertook symbolic sexual relations with the sun goddess during his formal enthronement in 1928, when Japan was ruled by the imperial government, which gained support from state Shintō, the national religion. (Hirohito was forced to renounce his divine status under the post–World War II constitutional government.) According to Bell, the ritual decorum or etiquette governing the behavior of those granted a royal audience creates relationships that empower the emperor. Etiquette and ceremony are not merely symbolic or "empty"; rather they create relationships of power involving political dominance and submission. Political rituals "create political reality." Furthermore, the symbolic action that constitutes such rituals makes political forces visible, and makes it possible for participants to identify with and to understand these forces, which are otherwise too complex to comprehend (Bell, 1997, p. 133; Kertzer, 1988, pp. 1–2). Bell points out that although political leaders in modern societies are elected, ceremonial display nevertheless makes an appeal to the cosmic order. She notes that an important function of the inaugural address of a newly elected American president is establishing the president's moral leadership, whereby his election is transmuted into an event that is not an accident of history.

The link between the ceremonial confirmation and maintenance of social and cultural norms and the negotiation of power is clearly evident in national or civic ceremonies, as well as in mass political rallies. Illustrative examples are found in the parades, processions, pageants, theatrical performances, and other ceremonious events that are associated with independence day celebrations in the United States (Bellah, 1967), Mexico (Vogt and Abel, 1977), and Indonesia (Peacock, 1968). Other examples are May Day, the anniversary of the October Revolution, and Victory Day in the former Soviet Union (Lane, 1981). On a smaller scale, examples are found in "political ceremonials," such as ritualized town or public meetings among the Indians and mestizos of Mexico (Hunt, 1977) and the villagers of Kilimanjaro in Tanzania (Moore, 1977). The Native American powwow has been interpreted as a public arena of power and politics in which participants negotiate conflicts regarding the participation of women and girls in the powwow, spiritual versus secular uses of powwow (e.g., turning the powwow into political protest), and relations with non-Indian participants (Mattern, 1996).

Other political rituals challenge the political status quo (Bell, 1997, p. 134). Bell points out that "rites of rebellion," as analyzed by Max Gluckman, and other rituals engage symbolic interaction in a different way; they must mobilize people as a political movement or force in opposition to the ruling regime. Bell gives as examples the cargo cults of New Guinea and Melanesia, which fused religious and political interests, and the Mau-Mau rebellion against British colonial power in Kenya. Another example is the reconstructed May Day demonstrations in Hungary under Soviet domination (Kurti, 1990). Originally observing the Soviet revolution, May Day in Hungary acquired new nationalist meaning in the hands of opponents of Soviet rule in the late 1980s, when opposition leaders incorporated images of leaders of the October 23, 1956, uprising against Soviet occupation.

On a much smaller scale, institutional ceremonies offer constituents an opportunity to resist official state ideology, as well as forms of authoritative ideology at the local level. An example was the awards ceremony at a girls' public primary school in Mombasa, Kenya (Porter, 1998). The ceremony had unintended consequences regarding the enactment of power and cultural identity as different participants used it simultaneously to produce cultural meanings that sustain the state as well as local authorities, and to produce alternative interpretations of national and local culture that challenged power at both levels. The postcolonial state has used the secular public schools, their curricula, and their ceremonies to develop a homogeneous national identity and national unity to advance its nation-building efforts. The awards ceremony offered the school's Muslim female students, who are Swahili, an opportunity to resist state efforts as representatives of an ethnic minority who lost political and economic power to the postcolonial state. At the ceremony, the girls performed Swahili poems and expressed their devotion to their religion. Public expressions of religion, performances of poetry, and pursuit of education are typically activities of Swahili men, and not women. By reciting poetry in this public and educational setting, the schoolgirls challenged the traditional gender expectations for adolescent Swahili girls. This in itself was a challenge to the normative relationship between adolescent Swahili females and their male elders. The girls presented an additional challenge to their traditional Muslim culture and the state when the headmistress declared the new school uniform to be the old cotton dress uniform refitted to wear more loosely, with the addition of the traditional Muslim *ḥijāb*, a large headscarf, and *suruali*, long pants. While the adolescent girls proclaimed their devotion to their religion by wearing the traditional dress, about which they sang in their performance, they reinterpreted the meaning of wearing it. In their performance, the girls declared wearing the dress to be a sign of their being modern girls. For these Swahili adolescents, the wearing of traditional dress and experimentation with colors and textured or beaded fabrics were efforts to be fashionable in their youth culture.

The novel *Ceremony* by the Native American author Leslie Marmon Silko (1977) has been viewed as a kind of rite of rebellion against the dominant white social and political order that reconstructs power relations between Native Americans and whites. James Ruppert characterizes *Ceremo-*

ny as "a protest novel" that calls attention to the oppression of Laguna peoples by "an indifferent and often hostile dominant culture" (Ruppert, 2002, p. 177). Silko's novel presents the healing of an interracial Native American war veteran who despairs over his treatment by white society and the loss of meaning that has resulted from his loss of connection to his Native American community and its traditional ways. Allan Chavkin notes that the novel's protagonist is restored by a traditional curing ritual, which is based on the Navajo Antway, a purification ritual performed for returning veterans; the ritual uses chant to reenact myth and through it impart meaning or a spiritual understanding of events (Chavkin, 2002). The novel concludes with the protagonist's vision quest. He undergoes a visionary experience that restores meaning by reaffirming the Native American view that the spiritual world that is disclosed in myth is reality.

Drawing on Elaine Jahner, Ruppert views the structure of Silko's novel as a ritual chant or prayer that engages Native American and white implied readers as ritual performers who become part of the telling of the mythic story at the center of the novel through the act of reading. Readers assume the position of priests who sing and pray. Reading the novel "becomes a new ceremony in itself" as readers undergo new experiences that alter their perspectives (Ruppert, 2002, p. 184). The novel engages Native American and white readers in learning about the other's worldview as the text translates each group's discourse. In the process, the text mediates each group's experiences of the other. Mediation validates each group's perspective while calling attention to its strengths and limitations. In addition, mediation encourages each group to fuse both perspectives, thus creating a new point of view. White readers learn the mythic view of Native Americans, and Native American readers learn the sociological view of white Americans. The mythic outlook of Native Americans encourages white readers to adopt a spiritual vision of reality in order to restore meaning and avoid self-destruction through unbridled power, particularly war and atomic weapons. In this view, all living things, including the earth, are connected and shown to be part of a larger, inclusive reality. White society's sociological analysis may give Native Americans insight into how they have internalized the view that Native Americans are inferior. In Ruppert's view, Silko attempts to join Native Americans and whites in fighting against common enemies—Silko's "Destroyers," or forces of evil—who threaten to annihilate both. Silko does so by creating a new ceremony that erases all boundaries between peoples by fusing the perspectives and experiences of Native Americans and whites.

As a group, scholars of Native American religions have traditionally used the term *ceremony* to refer to Native American ritual. They do not make the distinction between ceremony and ritual found in the theoretical literature; hence they use the terms *ceremony* and *ritual* interchangeably.

CEREMONY AND RELIGION. Two distinct tendencies in identifying the object of ceremony can be found in the theoretical literature. Ceremony is either identified with secular interests exclusively, or it is associated with both secular and religious concerns, which sometimes converge. Jack Goody and Max Gluckman represent the first trend. They contend that although conventionalized nonreligious and religious activities are the same analytic type of behavior (i.e., formalization that has nonrational ends or is of a nontechnical nature) and play similar roles, they entail disparate beliefs and therefore should be differentiated. Conventional action that is addressed to spiritual beings or concerned with the ultimate is designated "religious." Objecting to the tendency to identify formalized collective activity with religious ritual, established as a precedent by Durkheim, Goody distinguishes activity of an "exclusively secular significance." He identifies conventional activity of a nonreligious nature, such as the anniversary of the October Revolution, as "ceremonial." Goody treats *ceremony*, like formalized "religious" activity, as a subcategory of *ritual*, the term by which he designates the most general category of conventional behavior (1961, p. 159). Gluckman prefers *ceremony* as the inclusive term for conventional and stylized, or "ceremonial," behavior. He uses the term *ceremonious* to distinguish nonreligious formal activity, and reserves the term *ritual* for the subcategory of ceremonial activity referring to "mystical notions" (1962, pp. 22–23).

Goody avoids the terms *sacred* and *profane* in his distinction between religious and ceremonial rituals. Because the dichotomy they represent is a foreign concept within many cultures, he believes these terms have limited application as rubrics for analytic categories. The fact that the sacred-profane polarity is not universally recognized suggests, as Goody notes, that these are external categories, imposed by an outside observer, rather than categories held by participants themselves.

As recognized by ceremony theorists who associate ceremony with both secular and religious interests, a strict distinction between secular and religious activity is problematic. Historical phenomena do not exhibit the discrete boundaries that are found in precise theoretical categories. Although they are not sponsored by institutionalized religion, many secular ceremonies make reference to and even depend upon religious belief or religious symbols. The appeal to religious belief and the use of religious symbols in such ceremonies is an indication and expression of the convergence of religious and political interests, even when religion and the state are legally separated. Their convergence is critical when the political order seeks to legitimate its authority through divine sanction, thus giving religion a central place within the public sphere, even where church and state are separate.

Ceremonies associated with civil religion are noteworthy examples. *Civil religion* is Robert Bellah's term designating a form of religion that is characteristic of highly secularized and technologically oriented modern nation states; civil religion is said to exist independently of institutionalized religion, although it is dependent on organized religion for many of its symbols (Bellah, 1967). Invoking God in presidential inaugurations in the United States, and swearing to uphold the Constitution on the Bible (Bellah, 1967; Wilson, 1979), and in Memorial Day observances (Warner, 1959), for example, is intended to secure the continuation of divine blessing on the social and political order (Bellah, 1967; Cherry, 1970; Warner, 1959; and Wilson, 1979). Appealing to God and scripture during coronations in Great Britain is intended to accomplish the same effect (Bocock, 1974).

The convergence of religious and political interests in ceremony is most evident in religio-political systems. There ceremony occupies a central public place by virtue of its legitimating role. State ceremonies that are associated with divine kingship, long established as a state cult in Asia, the Middle East, Africa, and elsewhere, are illustrative. The "state ceremonials" of nineteenth-century Bali (royal dedications of palace temples, royal ordinations, royal cremations, and other "state ritual") appropriated Hindu cosmology in order to depict the king as a manifestation of divine power and thereby secure power by the state (Geertz, 1980). Ceremonies drawing attention to "divine election" and divinization in imperial Rome provide instructive premodern examples of securing state power by ritually cosmologizing a political office (MacCormack, 1981).

The blurring of boundaries between religious and political interests is found on a smaller scale in numerous civic ceremonies. Fiesta, a citywide celebration of the establishment of Santa Fe, New Mexico, as a Spanish city, is an illustrative example (Grimes, 1976). Religious symbols play a central role in the ceremonial negotiation of power among Native American, Hispanic-American, and other Euro-American members of the community not simply because they help to establish group identity, but because they help to legitimate sociopolitical interests. Links between Roman Catholicism and the historic domination of Native Americans by the Spanish are exploited in the Fiesta Mass, the procession of *La Conquistadora* (the Virgin), and other church-sponsored events, as Hispanic Americans assert their power over Native Americans.

It has been suggested that if societies do in fact tend to look to the cosmic order as their ideal for the social order, then secular ritual would always manifest sacred aspects. "If this is the case it may not be possible to speak of purely religious ritual or of purely secular ceremonial," argues Eva Hunt. Furthermore, if the secular and religious orders are interdependent, so that the secular models and shapes the religious, which in turn models secular behavior, then "secular and sacred may not be different behaviors but different analytic aspects of the same behaviors" (Hunt, 1977, p. 143).

Moore and Myerhoff define the sacred in broader terms by which they distinguish it from religion. By *sacred* they mean unquestionability or being inviolable and traditionalizing. According to their definition, secular rituals exhibit a sacred dimension when they present ideology, doctrine, and so on as authoritative and incontrovertible, and in so doing secular rituals serve as a tradition-making force. Moore and Myerhoff distinguish ceremony from religious ritual by the absence of otherworldly or ultimate explanations, which are said to be the distinct province and function of religious ritual. The scope of ceremony is restricted to specialized aspects of social and cultural life and to its immediate concerns. In their view, ceremony, unlike religious ritual, does not act on the other world in order to influence this world; it acts solely on this world. Ceremony is distinguished by its "meaning and effect," which are sacred but not religious (Moore and Myerhoff, 1977, p. 8).

Moore and Myerhoff propose and oppose the analytic categories *religious* and *nonreligious*, *sacred* and *nonsacred* in order to take account of secular rituals that manifest a sacred dimension and those that do not, rituals that make use of religious symbols, and other possible combinations, including the presence of secular concerns within religious life (Moore and Myerhoff, 1977, pp. 3, 10–15, 20–22). Insofar as religious and sociopolitical interests intersect and even converge, distinguishing ceremony from religion will remain problematic, however.

Returning to Grimes' argument, if ceremony is treated as a mode of ritual rather than a type of ritual, then distinguishing ceremony from religion becomes even more problematic. He argues that rituals that are explicitly religious can demonstrate ceremonious aspects and do so when they are placed in the service of social and political interests (Grimes, 1982, p. 42). Timely examples are found in the rituals associated with the convergence of theology and political ideology in contemporary fundamentalist Christianity in the United States and fundamentalist Islam in the Middle East and elsewhere. Use of the pulpit by fundamentalist Christians to promote rightist interests during national and state elections in the United States has received much attention in political and scholarly circles as well as in the media. Although the role of fundamentalist Islam in the revitalization of conservative and even extremist Muslim and Arab ideology has received equal attention, less attention has been given the role of religious ritual. An example is the use of ʿĀshūrāʾ, the ritual dramatization and commemoration of the martyrdom of Muḥammad's grandson, Ḥusayn ibn ʿAlī, to legitimate Shīʿī ideology and rule in Iran (Hegland, 1983). Reinterpreting Ḥusayn's death as the final outcome in the struggle of a righteous man against the corruption of true religion by political rulers, the Shīʿah found in ʿĀshūrāʾ a powerful symbol in the service of the revolution of 1979. By giving the ritual new ideological content, identifying the monarchy and allied power structures as forces hostile to Islam and themselves as preservers of true faith, the Shīʿah in Iran made use of ʿĀshūrāʾ in their ascendancy to power.

The 1993 state funeral of Turkey's President Turgut Ozal offered an example of three competing versions of the convergence of religious and political interests in ceremony. Gunter Seufert and Petra Weyland (1994) report that three rival groups symbolically expressed three divergent views of the sacred cosmic order and of the place and power of religion within the state. President Ozal's funeral was the first high-level state ceremony in which secular and official religious representatives of the secular state and representatives of nonstate-sponsored religion appeared together since the founding of the Republic of Turkey in 1923 by President Mustafa Kemal. Representatives of the state, both secularists and those representing the official version of Islam, gave Islam an ambiguous place within the cosmos, a modified version of the Kemalist secular cosmos. They had appropriated Islamic symbolism increasingly in order to regain support of average Muslims and had tolerated the existence of the Islamic brotherhoods and their participation in state institutions. The state representatives allowed the brotherhoods, especially the Naksibendiyye, to take part in the state funeral and even to perform some of the rituals associated with it, in spite of an official ban against public appearances by members of the brotherhoods. The brotherhoods had been banned under President Kemal's regime, which reconstructed Turkey as a secular state in which the state government tightly regulated religion. President Ozal, a pious Muslim who had found Islam and the secular state compatible, restored Islam to public life. The Naksibendiyye gave Islam a central place within the cosmos but accommodated it to the state. Hostile political factions opposing the state, who were not permitted an official role in President Ozal's funeral but who demonstrated outside the mosque where his funeral was held, gave Islam a supreme place.

Seufert and Weyland interpret the inclusion of the Naksibendiyye by the state as an effort by the state to co-opt, within certain limits, this particular religious group and its traditional version of Islam in order to give the state legitimacy in the eyes of Muslims as part of the state's effort to maintain its version of the sacred cosmos and its power within it. Historically, the Naksibendiyye had alternately supported or opposed the state, and had won popular support for the ruling power. More important, Seufert and Weyland view the inclusion of the Naksibendiyye as an effort by the state to use this group's popularity among the masses to control popular Islam, especially fundamentalist male youths. Their sympathies lay with opponents of the state, especially Kurdish and fundamentalist parties, and their alternative versions of Islam. Seufert and Weyland also interpret the inclusion of the Naksibendiyye as an attempt by the state to gain greater acceptance within the wider Muslim world. The authors argue that the Naksibendiyye were willing to cooperate with the state in order to regain influence, to promote internationalism among Muslims, and to strengthen religious orthodoxy in response to alternative religious views. The authors conclude that while the political elite used President Ozal's funeral to retain their legitimacy and power by enacting the official version of the sacred cosmos, they could not control how the Naksibendiyye Muslims or Muslim opponents would promote their own versions, or how average Muslims would consume the various versions that were available to them. Thus Ozal's state funeral reflected the existence of multiple views of the cosmic order among members of the Turkish state.

CONCLUSION. Any attempt to define ceremony must take into account the interpenetration of traditional ritual categories: sacred and secular, religious and political, and the like. As demonstrated in the examples presented above, historical phenomena cannot be compartmentalized as neatly as a number of theoretical treatments of ceremony suggest. Any effort to analyze ceremony also must take note that formalization, corroborative tendencies, and other aspects of ceremoniousness are inherent to ritual. As suggested in the examples offered above, the ceremonious mode can be expected to dominate when ritual has been placed in the service of tradition or the legitimation of power. In this instance, as Turner observes, ritual's liminal features have been circumscribed in order to contain the threat to the established social order.

SEE ALSO Ritual.

BIBLIOGRAPHY

Bell, Catherine. *Ritual Theory, Ritual Practice.* New York, 1992.

Bell, Catherine. *Ritual: Perspectives and Dimensions.* New York, 1997.

Bellah, Robert N. "Civil Religion in America." *Daedalus* 96 (1967): 1–21.

Bloch, Maurice. "The Ritual of the Royal Bath in Madagascar." In *Rituals of Royalty: Power and Ceremonial in Traditional Societies,* edited by David Cannadine and Simon Price, pp. 271–297. Cambridge, U.K., 1987.

Bocock, Robert. *Ritual in Industrial Society: A Sociological Analysis of Ritualism in Modern England.* London, 1974.

Cannadine, David. "Introduction: Divine Right of Kings." In *Rituals of Royalty: Power and Ceremonial in Traditional Societies,* edited by David Cannadine and Simon Price, pp. 1–19. Cambridge, U.K., 1987.

Chavkin, Allan. "Introduction." In *Leslie Marmon Silko's* Ceremony*: A Casebook,* pp. 3–15. New York, 2002.

Cherry, Conrad. "American Sacred Ceremonies." In *American Mosaic: Social Patterns of Religion in the United States,* edited by Phillip E. Hammond and Benton Johnson, pp. 303–316. New York, 1970.

Geertz, Clifford. "Religion as a Cultural System." In *The Interpretation of Cultures: Selected Essays,* pp. 87–125. New York, 1973.

Geertz, Clifford. *Negara: The Theatre State in Nineteenth-Century Bali.* Princeton, 1980.

Gluckman, Max. "Les Rites de Passage." In *Essays on the Rituals of Social Relations,* edited by Max Gluckman, pp. 1–52. Manchester, UK, 1962.

Goffman, Erving. *Frame Analysis: An Essay on the Organization of Experience.* New York, 1974. Discusses ceremony on pages 43–44, 48, 58, and 126. Reprint, Boston, 1986.

Goody, Jack. "Religion and Ritual: The Definitional Problem." *British Journal of Sociology* 12 (1961): 142–164.

Grimes, Ronald L. *Symbol and Conquest: Public Ritual and Drama in Santa Fe, New Mexico.* Ithaca, N.Y., 1976.

Grimes, Ronald L. "Modes of Ritual Sensibility" and "Two Public Celebrations." In *Beginnings in Ritual Studies*, pp. 35–51 and pp. 221–231. Lanham, Md., 1982; rev. ed., Columbia, S.C., 1995.

Hegland, Mary. "Ritual and Revolution in Iran." In *Political Anthropology*, edited by Myron J. Aronoff; Vol. 2: *Culture and Political Change*, pp. 75–100. New Brunswick, N.J., 1983.

Hunt, Eva. "Ceremonies of Confrontation and Submission: The Symbolic Dimension of Indian-Mexican Political Interaction." In *Secular Ritual*, edited by Sally F. Moore and Barbara G. Myerhoff, pp. 124–147. Assen, Netherlands, 1977.

Kertzer, David I. *Ritual, Politics, and Power*. New Haven, 1988.

Kurti, Laszlo. "People vs. the State: Political Rituals in Contemporary Hungary." *Anthropology Today* 6, no. 2 (1990): 5–8.

Lane, Christel. *The Rites of Rulers: Ritual in Industrial Society, The Soviet Case*. Cambridge, U.K., 1981.

Lukes, Steven. "Political Ritual and Social Integration." *Sociology* 9 (1975): 289–308.

MacCormack, Sabine G. *Art and Ceremony in Late Antiquity*. Berkeley, Calif., 1981.

Mattern, Mark. "The Powwow as a Public Arena for Negotiating Unity and Diversity in American Indian Life." *American Indian Culture and Research Journal* 20, no. 4 (1996): 183–201.

Moore, Sally F. "Political Meetings and the Simulation of Unanimity: Kilimanjaro 1973." In *Secular Ritual*, edited by Sally F. Moore and Barbara G. Myerhoff, pp. 151–172. Assen, Netherlands, 1977.

Moore, Sally F., and Barbara G. Myerhoff. "Secular Ritual: Forms and Meanings." In *Secular Ritual*, edited by Sally F. Moore and Barbara G. Myerhoff, pp. 3–24. Assen, Netherlands, 1977.

Peacock, James L. *Rites of Modernization: Symbolic and Social Aspects of Indonesian Proletarian Drama*. Chicago, 1968.

Porter, Mary A. "Resisting Uniformity at Mwana Kupona Girls' School: Cultural Productions in an Educational Setting." *Signs: Journal of Women in Culture and Society* 23, no. 3 (1998): 619–643.

Ruppert, James. "No Boundaries, Only Transitions: *Ceremony*." In *Leslie Marmon Silko's* Ceremony*: A Casebook*, edited by Allan Chavkin, pp. 175–191. New York, 2002.

Silko, Leslie Marmon. *Ceremony*. New York, 1977.

Seufert, Gunter, and Petra Weyland. "National Events and the Struggle for the Fixing of Meaning: A Comparison of the Symbolic Dimensions of the Funeral Services for Ataturk and Ozal." *New Perspectives on Turkey* 11 (1994): 71–98.

Turner, Victor. *Dramas, Fields, and Metaphors: Symbolic Action in Human Society*. Ithaca, N.Y., 1974.

Turner, Victor. *From Ritual to Theatre: The Human Seriousness of Play*. New York, 1982. See pages 80–84.

Vogt, Evon Z., and Suzanne Abel. "On Political Rituals in Contemporary Mexico." In *Secular Ritual*, edited by Sally F. Moore and Barbara G. Myerhoff, pp. 173–188. Assen, Netherlands, 1977.

Warner, William Lloyd. *The Living and the Dead: A Study of the Symbolic Life of Americans*. New Haven, 1959.

Wilson, John F. *Public Religion in American Culture*. Philadelphia, 1979.

BOBBY C. ALEXANDER (1987 AND 2005)

CERULARIOS, MICHAEL

CERULARIOS, MICHAEL (c. 1000–1058), patriarch of Constantinople. Cerularios typified the Byzantine prelate in that he was characterized by experience in imperial and ecclesiastical matters, intellectual inclinations (which included an interest in occultism), and private monastic devotion. But he had one flaw: he was arrogant and relentless in increasing his see's ecclesiastical prerogatives.

Born in Constantinople of a senatorial family, Cerularios rose to power as a civil servant. His tenure was marked by his direct involvement in the conspiracy to depose Emperor Michael IV (1040) in favor of Constantine IX Monomachus. To avoid political banishment, he became a monk. Elected to the patriarchate in 1043, Cerularios held this position until 1058 through the reigns of four emperors.

The events of 1054 caused Cerularios to be viewed as one of the most controversial of patriarchs. His critics do not agree as to the extent of his responsibility for the schism between Rome and Constantinople. The patriarch's relations with Rome, however, must be seen in the greater context of the growing ideological rift that existed between Eastern and Western Christendom and that was manifest in the political, cultural, and theological misunderstandings of the eleventh century. An assessment of Cerularios solely in the light of this dispute unduly minimizes his role as a patriarch who attempted to extend his powers over the state.

The legacy of Cerularios, then, remains a mixed one. Admired by his flock as a champion of orthodoxy and celebrated as a confessor of the faith, Cerularios's aura reminded the faithful, especially during the Fourth Crusade (1204), that compromise with the West was inadmissible. Yet he is not commemorated as a saint. Moreover, he was able, unlike his predecessors, to elevate himself to a position of supra-imperial authority, as evidenced by his wearing of the purple buckskins reserved for the emperor. Ironically, Cerularios was forced to abdicate in 1058 at the height of his glory by the very Isaac I Commenus whose position as emperor he had secured.

BIBLIOGRAPHY

The published works of Cerularios can be found in *Patrologia Graeca*, edited by J.-P. Migne, vol. 120 (Paris, 1864). For Michael Psellus's denunciatory address against Cerularios, see Louis Bréhier's "Un discours inédit de Psellos," *Revue des études grecques* 16 (1903): 375–416 and 17 (1904): 35–75; for Psellus's funeral oration to Cerularios, see Konstantinos N. Sathas's *Mesaionike bibliotheke e sylloge anekdoton mnemeion tes Hellenikes historias*, vol. 4 (Paris, 1874), pp. 303–387.

An older but reliable essay on Cerularios is J. B. Bury's "Roman Emperors from Basil II to Isaac Komnenos," in *Selected Essays of J. B. Bury,* edited by Harold Temperley (1930; reprint, Chicago, 1967), pp. 210–214. The classic narrative of the patriarch's role in the schism remains Steven Runciman's *The Eastern Schism: A Study of the Papacy and the Eastern Churches during the Eleventh and Twelfth Centuries* (1955; reprint, Oxford, 1963). A well-documented account of his role in the azyme controversy with updated bibliography is Mahlon H. Smith III's *And Taking Bread: Cerularius and the Azyme Controversy of 1054,* "Théologie historique," vol. 47 (Paris, 1978).

John Travis (1987)

CEYLONESE RELIGION See SINHALA RELIGION

CHAITANYA See CAITANYA

CHALCEDON, COUNCIL OF See COUNCILS, *ARTICLE ON* CHRISTIAN COUNCILS

CHAN. The Chan school of Buddhism developed in China beginning in the sixth century CE, spread to Korea, Japan, and Vietnam beginning in the ninth century, and has moved to Europe, the United States, and other parts of the world in modern times. The name Chan (Sŏn in Korean, Thiền in Vietnamese, and Zen in Japanese) is the Chinese transliteration of the Indian word for concentration meditation, dhyāna in Sanskrit and jhāna in Pali (and similar forms in other *prakrits* or vernacular Indian languages).

Although Chan is thus named after a type of Buddhist meditation, it does not by any means have a monopoly on the practice of meditation in East Asia, nor is its own identity as a school limited to meditation alone. The best key to understanding Chinese Chan is actually the genealogical quality of its historical identity and style of spiritual cultivation. Like other Buddhist schools, Chan defines itself not as one among many schools or interpretations of Buddhism but as the authentic teaching of Śākyamuni Buddha. In the case of Chan, this teaching is understood as having been transmitted from Śākyamuni through an unbroken sequence of Indian and Chinese patriarchs and down to the masters of the present age. This transmission took place, advocates of the school assert, without words and from mind to mind, entirely apart from the translation and exposition of written scriptures. And, just as each recognized member of the Chan lineage thus identifies himself (or, much less commonly, herself) according to a specific genealogy of masters and disciples, so is the religious practice of Chan framed within a patriarchal structure resembling a father-son succession. Chan teachers and students are often depicted as engaging in "encounter dialogue," conceived of as a spontaneous oral interchange in which masters use a variety of verbal and physical strategies to provoke their followers out of limited, patterned thinking and propel them into a direct realization of the truth. From the twelfth century onward it became common to use such anecdotes as foci of meditative concentration, called *gongan* (public cases, or precedents; Jpn., kōan). Since the anecdotes chosen for such instruction were often derived from the teacher's own lineage, students were thus encouraged to examine and in some ways emulate the enlightened behavior of their own genealogical predecessors.

The historical development of Chinese Chan may be divided into six overlapping stages: (1) proto-Chan, referring to the activities of the founding patriarch Bodhidharma (d. c. 530) and the loosely connected group of wandering ascetics who venerated him; (2) early Chan, from the mid-seventh through the end of the eighth century, when a number of stable community groups and competing factions emerged and the basic terms of the school's teachings and historical self-identity were first elaborated in writing; (3) middle Chan, from the latter part of the eighth through the tenth century, when encounter dialogue emerged as the primary mode of Chan religious expression; (4) Song-dynasty Chan, the pinnacle of Chan activity in the tenth to thirteenth centuries, when the school dominated Chinese monastic institutions and created its most characteristic ideals (including the "classical" image of middle-period masters as enlightened sages); (5) later imperial Chan, from the end of the thirteenth to the beginning of the twentieth century, when there occurred a number of variations on earlier themes and new combinations with other forms of Buddhist activity, in particular Pure Land Buddhism; and (6) modern Chan in the twentieth and twenty-first centuries, when various individuals and groups worked to identify with or capitalize upon the reputation Chan achieved through its encounter with the modern, and in particular the Western, world.

Knowledge about the first two phases of Chan has been aided immeasurably by the discovery of Chan-related manuscripts at Dunhuang, China, which have provided insight into the tradition unfiltered by perspectives from the Song dynasty and later. The middle period, in contrast, which is inevitably described by anecdotes concerning some of the most famous sages of the Chan tradition, is known almost exclusively through Song-dynasty materials and thus represents the most difficult challenge to historical scholarship. And, although there are massive quantities of primary-source material for the Song dynasty and later, these have not yet been thoroughly studied, especially in Western languages. In spite of an abundance of source material, including publications by Chinese Buddhist teachers identifying themselves as Chan monks, there is as yet relatively little scholarly analysis of how Chan might function as a coherent set of themes and practices in the contemporary world, especially given the complex interrelationships between Chinese Chan, Japanese Zen, Korean Sŏn, Vietnamese Thiền, and their offspring traditions in Western countries.

Proto-Chan. Bodhidharma is universally revered as the founding patriarch of Chan, but very little is known about him. Traditionally, he is identified as the son of a *brahman* king of southern India, who arrived in southern China during the reign of the pro-Buddhist sovereign, Emperor Wu of the Liang dynasty (r. 501–549). Asked by Emperor Wu about the religious value of his support for Buddhism, Bodhidharma is supposed to have replied, "No merit whatsoever." Following this, Bodhidharma crossed the Yangzi River and took up meditation in a cave at Shaolinsi on Mount Song (Henan province). His most famous student and eventual successor, Huike (c. 485–555/574), is supposed to have cut off his own arm in his zeal to persuade Bodhidharma to convey the Buddhist teachings.

It is important to recognize that Chan stories such as the preceding are generally without historical basis, and simultaneously to appreciate the profoundly important role such creations played within the growth of the Chan tradition. Rather than undercutting their importance, the fictive quality of such anecdotes actually enhances their significance as imaginative scriptings of enlightened behavior. That is, rather than events involving one or two historical figures, they were molded by mythopoeic processes that involved thousands upon thousands of people, and which served to mold the basic conceptual patterns by which the school developed. This relationship between the triviality of journalistically accurate history and the profound importance of mythological and legendary themes is not restricted to Bodhidharma or proto-Chan, but actually applies to all of Chinese Chan Buddhism: what is not "true" is often demonstrably more important. With regard to Bodhidharma, we know that his role within the Chan movement was essentially legendary, that is, the school was built as much on the idea of him as a foreign meditation master as on the basis of any specific teachings or accomplishments.

There exists a text attributed to Bodhidharma known as the *Treatise on the Two Entrances and Four Practices* (Erru sixing lun), which establishes the basic configuration of Chan religious thought. The "entrance of principle" *(liru)* is explained using the concept of the buddha-nature, the fully enlightened mind that all sentient beings harbor within the recesses of their own identities, obscured by deluded thinking and dualistic conceptualization. The text's explanation of how to undertake this approach is vague, especially in its use of the term *wall-contemplation (biguan),* which initially seems to have referred to a state of being firmly closed off from outside sensory influence. (In later years this term was understood simplistically as "sitting facing a wall.") The "entrance of practice" *(xingru)* is described as a set of attitudes of nonattachment to one's states of suffering and happiness, so that one eventually acts fully in accord with the *dharma* in all situations. This text's use of the buddha-nature concept and the pairing of the two entrances, one meditative and focused inwardly, and the other active and focused on outward behavior, represented the building blocks from which Chan discourse developed.

Little is known about the early followers of Bodhidharma; they consisted of individuals and small groups of wandering ascetics associated with various sites in north China. They were apparently devoted to the *Treatise on the Two Entrances and Four Practices,* and the Dunhuang manuscript of this text includes a number of letters and dialogues they appended to it. In later years (after about the end of the eighth century), however, this text came to be de-emphasized, since it was no longer compatible with the hagiographic image of Bodhidharma as an inspired raconteur.

Early Chan. This phase of Chan includes a number of distinct communities and factions, to be dealt with here in succession.

East Mountain teaching. The meditation instructors Daoxin (580–651) and Hongren (601–674) spent exactly half a century (624–674) in the same monastic complex in Huangmei (Hubei province). To this may be added another quarter century of residence (675–701) by Hongren's student Shenxiu (c. 606–706) at Yuquansi in Jingzhou (also Hubei). Thus the East Mountain community developed for fully seventy-five years in provincial locations. At Huangmei, Daoxin and Hongren taught meditation to an increasing number of Buddhist monks and nuns of various backgrounds; there is no evidence that they engaged in any Buddhist activity other than this. In contrast to the handful of names associated with Bodhidharma and Huike, there are about a dozen associated with Daoxin and twice the number associated with Hongren.

Northern school. In 701 Shenxiu traveled to Luoyang (Henan province), one of the two capitals of medieval China, where he had been invited to teach in the palace by the only woman to rule China in her own name, Empress Wu (r. 684–705). Here Shenxiu proclaimed himself a successor to Hongren's "pure teaching of East Mountain," explaining that the essence of Buddhism was "contemplation of the mind" and interpreting any and all Buddhist doctrines as metaphors for this practice. For example, he wrote metaphorically, "those who seek emancipation always consider the body as the lamp's stand, the mind as the lamp's dish, and faith as the lamp's wick. . .If one constantly burns such a lamp of truly suchlike true enlightenment, its illumination will destroy all the darkness of ignorance and stupidity." Shenxiu thus emphasized that one should constantly remain in meditation while constantly working to aid sentient beings—an explanation of the *bodhisattva* ideal of Mahāyāna Buddhism. His teachings were spectacularly popular in the sophisticated society of the Chinese imperial capitals (at both Luoyang and Chang'an), and after his death the most prominent of his more than seventy students continued as instructors to court society throughout the 730s, as did their students and later successors (with somewhat lesser prominence) after that.

Shenxiu and his students carried with them a written explanation of their master Hongren's teachings known as the *Treatise on the Essentials of Cultivating the Mind* (Xiuxin yao lun), which they edited after Hongren's death in memory of his legacy. Here the buddha-nature concept introduced in the *Treatise on the Two Entrances and Four Practices* was clarified by means of a metaphor of sun and clouds: Just as the sun is constantly shining even when obstructed by clouds, so the practitioner should maintain awareness of the existence of the buddha-nature within, even if it is obscured by human ignorance. The *Treatise on the Essentials of Cultivating the Mind* includes two different specific practices of meditation, framed within a combination of seemingly contradictory exhortations to make an effort in spiritual cultivation, on the one hand, and to avoid positing enlightenment as an objectified goal, on the other.

The text attributed retrospectively to Hongren was only the first of several to be composed after his students began moving into the two capitals. The most important of these texts, the earliest of the "transmission of the lamp" genre, narrated the transmission of Buddhism by a sequence of meditation masters. Although these works discussed only teachers active in China (and not their Indian predecessors) and differed among themselves in the specifics of the transmission, they contained the first written expressions of the Chan lineage theory. The individual described as the "third patriarch" in traditional Chan sources, Sengcan, is only mentioned for the first time in a text from 689 CE; the justifiably famous *Inscription on Believing in Mind* (Xinxin ming) attributed to him was composed sometime in the middle of the eighth century.

Southern school. Beginning in 730 a monk named Shenhui (684–758) attacked Shenxiu's students as belonging to a nonmainstream lineage and advocating an inferior teaching. He asserted boldly that his own teacher, the hitherto obscure Huineng (638–713) of Caoqi in the far south (Guangdong province), was Hongren's only fully authorized successor and was the "sixth patriarch" of Chan Buddhism, and that only this single lineage was legitimate. It was Shenhui who labeled Shenxiu and his successors the "Northern school" and Huineng's teaching the "Southern school," based on the geographical locations where the two masters taught. (Shenxiu's successors did not refer to themselves in this fashion until decades later.)

Shenhui himself was not a meditation instructor, but an evangelist; he had no long-term relationships with students, and for him religious wisdom was something to be achieved immediately, in an instantaneous flash of insight, rather than requiring nurturing over lengthy periods of self-cultivation. A gifted storyteller, Shenhui inspired his students and listeners with a message of nondualistic wisdom that he described as the teaching of sudden enlightenment. Although his doctrinal innovations and entertaining public presentations were very appealing, the factionalist and even ad hominem quality of his campaign against the alleged gradualism of the Northern school created a crisis in early Chan.

Oxhead school and Platform Sūtra. The factionalist crisis fomented by Shenhui was resolved by the Oxhead school and the capstone text of early Chan, the *Platform Sūtra* of the Sixth Patriarch (Liuzu tan jing). Although the Oxhead school had its own fictive lineage, tracing itself back to a student of Daoxin's, its members adopted the legendary image of Huineng as sixth patriarch. Oxhead school figures tended to downplay any differences between the Northern and Southern schools, making statements such as "the mind is the central principle" (using the term *zong,* which is also used with the meaning "school"). The most representative Oxhead text is the *Treatise on the Transcendence of Cognition* (Jueguan lun), which presents a dialogue between a fictional student and teacher proceeding in three stages: (1) questions and answers about the *dharma,* (2) the student's perception of the nonexistence of all things, and (3) the student's final realization of the ultimate truth.

This threefold structure is also apparent in the famous *Platform Sūtra,* the earliest version of which appeared about 780. This text draws on Shenhui's acceptance of Huineng as Hongren's only successor but effectively writes Shenhui out of the story, saying nothing of his famous campaign and belittling him as a foolish young monk. The *Platform Sūtra* story is, like the anecdotes about Bodhidharma, demonstrably ahistorical: Shenxiu studied with Hongren in the 650s, not toward the end of the master's life, and the very notion of selecting a single successor was only conceivable after Shenhui's campaign. However, the text has been widely influential as a religious scripture, known especially for its inspired depiction of Huineng as an unlettered sage.

MIDDLE CHAN. In south-central China in the latter half of the eighth century there emerged two lineages of Chan practitioners that came to embody a new approach to Buddhist spiritual cultivation based on lively interaction between teachers and students and often iconoclastic behavior, a style of discourse known as encounter dialogue. The chief figures in this new development were Shitou Xiqian (710–790) in Hubei and Mazu Daoyi (709–788) in Jiangxi, who are remembered as progenitors of the Caodong (Jpn., Sōtō) and Linji (Jpn., Rinzai) lineages, respectively. Many of the most memorable anecdotes of Chinese Chan derive from Mazu's so-called Hongzhou school (a name based on his residence in what is now Jiangxi province), which includes Zhaozhou Congshen (c. 778–897), Baizhang Huaihai (749–814), and Nanquan Puyuan (748–834). Virtually all accounts of Chinese Chan include references to Zhaozhou's negative response to the question of whether dogs have the buddha-nature (he replied, "No!"); Baizhang's supposed maxim, "A day without work is a day without food"; and Nanquan's outrageous killing of a cat as a challenge to other trainees. The most famous representative of this style of Chan was Linji Yixuan (d. 867; Jpn., Rinzai Gigen), whose recorded sayings contain memorable phrases such as "the true man of no rank" and shocking lines such as "if you meet the Buddha, kill him!"

There would appear, at first glance, to be a close correspondence between the "encounter dialogue" style of such

Hongzhou-school figures and the religious doctrines of the school. Mazu's teachings are described as holding that "the arising of mental activity, the movement of thought, even snapping the fingers or moving the eyes—all actions and activities are the functioning of the entire essence of the buddha-nature." Thus Mazu and his students are supposed to have emphasized dynamic interaction using lively repartee, physical gestures, and even loud shouts and physical blows. The problem, however, is that such events—which are supposed to have taken place a few decades before or after the year 800—are not recorded in any written text until 952. This is the date of the very important *Anthology of the Patriarchal Hall* (Zutang ji), which is the first text to contain any written transcription of oral Chan dialogue. Preserved only in Korea, this anthology established the basic pattern of all later "transmission of the lamp" texts by providing entries for the entire lineage from the seven Buddhas of the Past (i.e., from its ancient predecessors in India) to the present.

Although there are substantial materials concerning the Honzhou school that date from its own time, none of these texts (nor any of the manuscripts from Dunhuang) contain transcriptions of encounter dialogue. It does appear that the lineages of Shitou and Mazu represented a new spirit of Chan that arose in the latter half of the eighth century in south-central China. However, it is also clear that the "traditional" image of Shitou, Mazu, and their immediate generations of disciples was not generated until the Song dynasty. The questions that confront scholars now are: When and how did encounter dialogue actually develop? What were the contemporaneous historical identities of Shitou, Mazu, and others?

SONG-DYNASTY CHAN. The Song dynasty witnessed the Chan school's greatest efflorescence in China, and it was during this period that there emerged the school's mature configuration, not a fixed pattern but a dynamic interplay of elements, rather like the "climax paradigm" of complex biological systems. This success should be understood against the background of larger political and social changes that allowed Chan to flourish even as they set the stage for a fundamental transformation in Chinese Buddhism as a whole.

The Northern Song (960–1127) reestablished the centralized imperial state, and its rulers did their best to emulate their illustrious Tang-dynasty predecessors. However, the world had changed, and the Song court was forced to pay deference to the competing Liao (916–1125) and Jin (1115–1234) regimes. (The Song even paid material tribute to the Jin.) After the Jin conquest of north China, the Southern Song (1127–1279) was wracked by abortive social and political reforms and a never-ending debate about military action to retake the north. Although the Jin and the Southern Song collaborated to eliminate the Liao, they were swallowed up in turn by the Mongolian Yuan dynasty (1206–1368). Where earlier generations of scholars focused on the An Lushan rebellion of 755 to 763 as an important watershed in the transition from medieval aristocratic centralism to premodern regionalism, in recent years historians have begun to pay attention to the twelfth-century emergence of elites focused not on national political service but on building power and wealth for their respective clans in local and regional settings.

At the beginning of the Northern Song the Chan school found itself in a surprisingly dominant position. As a movement that only began to achieve national prominence in the eighth century and which remained subordinate throughout the Tang, by the end of the tenth century and the beginning of the eleventh the category of "Chan master" (or "meditation master") accounted for some three-quarters of the most prominent members of the *saṃgha.* One reason for this popularity was the effective collapse of the translation enterprise, which had been the primary focus of imperial support for Buddhism ever since the end of the fourth century. Although there was a flurry of effort in the late tenth century setting up the necessary government offices and collecting all the available Indic manuscripts, after a mere two decades of work (980–1000) there simply were no more texts arriving from the "western regions" for translation. In effect, the translation enterprise had ended at the beginning of the ninth century, and the brief period of Song activity was only an exceptional final gasp. The increasing prominence of Chan texts over this period, and especially their imperial recognition and circulation in woodblock editions, should be understood against this background.

From the beginning of the Song dynasty, Chan monks played a role very different from the rustic ideal associated with Huineng, Mazu, and other Tang figures: they served as abbots of some 90 percent of the largest monastic institutions ("monasteries of the ten directions," *shifang conglin,* often referred to as "public monasteries") in China, directing practice in meditation and functioning as fund-raisers for their temples. In previous scholarship this has been interpreted as evidence of the degeneration of Chan, but it now seems more reasonable to view this period as the high point of the school's efflorescence in China. Indeed, the romantic image of the Tang-dynasty sages is now understood to be a Song-dynasty creation, and the quest for "pure Chan" a function of Japanese sectarian interests.

Song-dynasty writers used various labels in reference to different lineage-based styles of Chan from the late Tang onward, and there are observable shifts in the relative vitality of different factions over time. Thus we read of the so-called five houses (*wujia;* Jpn., *goke*), the Fayan, Guiyang, Yunmen, Caodong, and Linji lineages, which never coexisted except in written summaries of Chan teachings. The Caodong lineage was tenuous for a time and was always overshadowed by the Linji school, which itself spawned the Huanglong and Yangchi sublineages. Linji, or Rinzai, predominated among lineages transmitted to Japan from the end of the twelfth century onward, although one of the two Caodong, or Sōtō, lineages (that associated with Dōgen Kigen [1200–1253]) eventually became widespread there as well.

The most important Chan figure during the Song dynasty was Dahui Zonggao (1089–1163), who as abbot in successive appointments at some of the largest monasteries in China taught hundreds, sometimes even thousands, of students at a time. Dahui is known for an energetic and personal style, addressing much of his attention to literate laymen and accepting as his students nuns as well as monks. In fact, it was in teaching a nun, Miaodao (fl. c. 1134–1155), that he developed his most characteristic teaching style: the use of intense contemplation of the "critical phrase" *(huatou)* of what came to be called *gongan.*

Dahui had Miaodao consider a phrase attributed to Mazu: "It is not mind, it is not Buddha, it is not a thing." In his instructions Dahui said, "You must not take it as a statement of truth. You must not take it to be something you do not need to do anything about. Do not take it as a flint-struck spark or a lightning flash. Do not try to divine the meaning of it. Do not try to figure it out from the context in which I brought it up. 'It is not the mind, it is not the Buddha, it is not a thing; after all, what is it?'" Dahui thus prohibited all potentially rational approaches to solving the problem, and he rejected Miaodao's first attempts to demonstrate her understanding, sometimes with loud shouts. Eventually she understood, and from that point on Dahui began teaching all his students using the *huatou* method. Dahui was also an outspoken advocate of vigorous effort in meditation practice, and he railed publicly against contemporary Chan teachers of the Caodong lineage who taught "silent illumination" *(mozhao).* This was anathematic for Dahui whenever it was taken to mean merely sitting like dead wood, waiting for enlightenment to happen someday.

The extensive literature of the Song-dynasty Chan school may be approached in terms of several different genres. First, "recorded sayings" *(yulu,* also referred to as "discourse records"; Jpn., *goroku)* were published for individual Chan teachers, initially after their demise (as with the *Treatise on the Essentials of Cultivating the Mind)* but eventually during the masters' lifetimes and with their active collaboration. (There is a famous rant in the *Record of Linji* against students who take notes during sermons, transforming the teacher's "live words" into dead ones, but this injunction came to be ignored.)

Second, "transmission of the lamp" histories *(chuandeng shi,* or simply *dengshi;* Jpn., dentōshi or tōshi) are texts that organize information about Chan teachers and their teachings into generational hierarchies. The earliest texts of this genre appeared in the early eighth century; the best-known examples are the *Anthology of the Patriarchal Hall* of 952 and the *Record of the Transmission of the Lamp [compiled during the] Jingde [era]* (Jingde chuandeng lu; Jpn., Keitoku dentōroku) of 1004. A handful of texts published in the twelfth to the thirteenth centuries effectively supplemented and extended the *Record of the Transmission of the Lamp;* that these texts were presented to the imperial court and officially included in the Buddhist canon indicates their status as public documents describing the lineage identities used in negotiating appointments as abbots to public monasteries.

Third, given the great proliferation of Chan anecdotes transcribed in the preceding genres, there developed shorter collections of favorite examples, known as "precedent anthologies" *(gongan ji;* Jpn., kōan shū). The most important of these are the *Emerald Cliff Record (Biyan lu;* Jpn., *Hekigan roku),* which contains several layers of teachers' commentaries on a hundred different anecdotes drawn primarily from the *Record of the Transmission of the Lamp of* 1004 compiled by Yuanwu Keqin (1063–1135) and the *Gateless Barrier (Wumen guan;* Jpn. *Mumonkan)* by Wumen Huikai (1183–1260; the title is a pun on his name). The latter text contains forty-eight anecdotes (some of them identical to those of the *Emerald Cliff Record)* presented with less structural complexity but perhaps greater religious eloquence.

Fourth, there is a wide variety of other Chan texts, including poems, essays, monastic regulations, and historical documents.

LATER IMPERIAL CHAN. The founding emperor of the Ming dynasty (1368–1644) supported a revitalization of Chinese Buddhism (along with strict government control of the religion), promoting what were thought to be the most important scriptures and supporting basic forms of Buddhist education. In this context Chan masters wrote commentaries on scriptures such as the *Heart Sūtra* and *Diamond Sūtra,* explaining their doctrines using Chan rhetoric. Toward the end of the dynasty a number of prominent Chan teachers appeared who worked to "revive" the fortunes of the school, sometimes in combination with Pure Land devotional practices oriented to laypeople. In the Qing dynasty (1644–1911) members of the Huangbo lineage struggled to reinvent Chan, bypassing the Song synthesis and reaching back to Linji Yixuan. The Huangbo school figure Yinyuan Longqi (1592–1673; Jpn., Ingen Ryūki) and some of his followers emigrated to Japan in 1654, stimulating a reconfiguration of Zen there through his combined use of Pure Land practices.

MODERN CHAN. This era includes a wide range of different phenomena. In the pre-1949 period there remained a small number of strong meditation centers at Chinese monasteries, many of them perpetuating Chan styles of practice, but the specifics of their religious identities are still unclear. Xuyun (1840–1959) is famous for having initiated himself into several long-defunct lineages, while the monk Zhang Shengyan (b. 1930) established centers for Chan meditation and Buddhist study in New York in self-conscious preparation for the extension of his teaching activities to Taiwan. Although there are numerous Chinese (as well as Korean and Vietnamese) teachers active in Taiwan, Hong Kong, mainland China, and abroad who identify themselves as representing the Chan school and its teachings, many of whom adopt Chan-style rhetoric and meditation practices, they often adopt characteristics of Japanese Zen in the West.

SEE ALSO Buddhism, Schools of, article on Chinese Buddhism; Buddhist Philosophy; Jingtu; Nirvāṇa; Prajñā; Zen.

BIBLIOGRAPHY

The modern study of Chinese Chan Buddhism derives in large part from a group of research project undertaken in Kyoto, Japan, organized and supported by Ruth Fuller Sasaki (1893/1894–1967). Participants in this project included the Chan scholar Yanagida Seizan, the Chinese linguist Iriya Yoshitaka (1910–1998), Chan scholar Philip B. Yampolsky (1920–1996), translator Burton Watson, and the poet Gary Snyder. In addition to producing a translation of the recorded sayings of Linji Yixuan, translated by Ruth Fuller Sasaki as *The Recorded Sayings of Ch'an Master Lin-chi Hui-chao of Chen Prefecture* (Kyoto, 1975), this group transformed the study of Chinese Chan by reading its texts as colloquial Chinese, rather than through the formalized traditions of Japanese Zen.

Of this group it was Yanagida who made the most extensive and profound contributions to the study of Chinese Chan in the twentieth century. A summary of his major works is available in John R. McRae, "Yanagida Seizan's Landmark Works on Chinese Ch'an," *Cahiers d'Extême-Asie* 7 (1993–1994): 51–103. Otherwise, relatively little of Yanagida's research is available in English: see "The Development of the 'Recorded Sayings' Texts of the Chinese Ch'an School," in Whalen Lai and Lewis R. Lancaster, eds., *Early Ch'an in China and Tibet* (Berkeley, 1983), pp. 185–205; "The Li-tai fa-pao chi and the Ch'an Doctrine of Sudden Awakening," also in Lai and Lancaster, pp. 13–49; and "The Life of Lin-chi I-hsüan," *Eastern Buddhist* n.s. 5, no. 2 (1972): 70–94.

In English, the most influential contribution to study of Chinese Chan has been Philip B. Yampolsky, *The Platform Sutra of the Sixth Patriarch: The Text of the Tun-huang Manuscript with Translation, Introduction, and Notes* (New York and London, 1967), which includes a masterful introduction outlining the development of both the myth of Huineng and the text bearing his name. Although Yampolsky's translation is the most widely used, Wing-Tsit Chan, *The Platform Scripture* (New York, 1963), is still worthy of reference for the Dunhuang version of the text, and John R. McRae, *The Platform Sūtra of the Sixth Patriarch* (Berkeley, 2000), may be consulted for the Ming-dynasty edition.

For Bodhidharma, and for the development of Chan hagiography in general, an insightful treatment is Bernard Faure, "Bodhidharma as Textual and Religious Paradigm," *History of Religions* 25, no. 3 (1986): 187–198. For a translation of the treatise attributed to Bodhidharma, as well as the material appended to the master's words in Dunhuang manuscripts, see Jeffrey L. Broughton, *The Bodhidharma Anthology: The Earliest Records of Zen* (Berkeley, 1999).

Studies of early Chinese Chan include John R. McRae, *The Northern School and the Formation of Early Ch'an Buddhism* (Honolulu, 1986), and Bernard Faure, *The Will to Orthodoxy: A Critical Genealogy of Northern Chan Buddhism* (Stanford, Calif., 1997). While these two books focus on the Northern school, Faure's two volumes, *The Rhetoric of Immediacy: A Cultural Critique of Chan/Zen Buddhism* (Princeton, 1991) and *Chan Insights and Oversights: An Epistemological Critique of the Chan Tradition* (Princeton, 1993), include a far-ranging postmodernist inquiry into the overarching themes of Chinese Chan. Robert E. Buswell Jr., *The Formation of Ch'an Ideology in China and Korea: The Vajrasamādhi-Sūtra, a Buddhist Apocryphon* (Princeton, 1989), contains an intriguing hypothesis concerning the probable Korean authorship of a Chan-related text. Other important studies are found in R. M. Gimello and P. N. Gregory, eds., *Studies in Ch'an and Hua-yen* (Honolulu, 1983), and Peter N. Gregory, ed. *Sudden and Gradual: Approaches to Enlightenment in Chinese Thought* (Honolulu, 1987). A masterful summary of many of the issues of early and middle Chinese Chan is found in Peter N. Gregory, *Tsung-mi and the Sinification of Buddhism* (Princeton, 1991).

The most substantial source of information about Chinese Chan prior to the Song dynasty available in English is certainly Heinrich S. Dumoulin, *Zen Buddhism: A History,* vol. 1, India and China, translated by James W. Heisig and Paul Knitter (New York, 1989; rev. ed., 1994), although the romanticism that imbues Dumoulin's account is criticized severely in John R. McRae's *Seeing through Zen: Encounter, Transformation, and Genealogy in Chinese Chan Buddhism* (Berkeley, 2003), which both traces the overall evolution of Chinese Chan and works to change how readers think about the subject. Dumoulin's presentation is largely a synthesis of the semi-scholarly writings of D. T. Suzuki (1870–1966) and the historical analysis of Hu Shih (1891–1962); the best source for the strikingly different positions of these two figures are Hu's "Ch'an (Zen) Buddhism in China: Its History and Method," *Philosophy East and West* 3, no. 1 (1953): 3–24, and Suzuki's rejoinder, "Zen: A Reply to Hu Shih," pp. 25–46 of the same issue. Analytical critiques of these two scholars are available in Robert Sharf, "The Zen of Japanese Nationalism," in Donald S. Lopez Jr., ed., *Curators of the Buddha: The Study of Buddhism Under Colonialism* (Chicago, 1995), pp. 107–160; and John R. McRae, "Religion as Revolution in Chinese Historiography: Hu Shih (1891–1962) on Shen-hui (684–758)," *Cahiers d'Extême-Asie* 12 (2001): 59–102. Although there is as yet no adequate single volume on middle-period Chan, Robert E. Buswell Jr., *The Korean Approach to Zen: The Collected Works of Chinul* (Honolulu, 1983), and Cuong Tu Nguyen, *Zen in Medieval Vietnam: A Study and Translation of Thiền uyển tập anh* (Honolulu, 1997), both include important information concerning both Chinese Chan and its diffusion to Korea and Vietnam, respectively.

For later periods of Chan there is rather less available. One very influential article is T. Griffith Foulk, "Myth, Ritual, and Monastic Practice in Sung Ch'an Buddhism," in Patricia Buckley Ebrey and Peter N. Gregory, eds., *Religion and Society in T'ang and Sung China* (Honolulu, 1993), pp. 147–208. An extensive study of the earliest text of Chinese monastic regulations, from 1103, is found in Yifa, *The Origins of Buddhist Monastic Codes in China: An Annotated Translation and Study of the Chanyuan qinggui* (Honolulu, 2002). Dale S. Wright has contributed a trenchant guide to reading Chan texts in his *Philosophical Meditations on Zen Buddhism* (Cambridge, UK, 1998). Steven Heine and Dale S. Wright have edited a valuable anthology, *The Kōan: Texts and Contexts in Zen Buddhism* (New York, 2000), several of the contributions to which provide the best recent scholarship on Chinese "encounter dialogue" and *gongan* introspection. A number of specialized articles are included in Peter N. Gregory and Daniel A. Getz Jr., eds., *Buddhism in the Sung* (Honolulu, 1999), including Miriam Levering's "Miao-tao and Her Teacher Ta-hui," pp. 188–219. Also see

Miriam Levering, "Lin-chi Ch'an and Gender: The Rhetoric of Equality and the Rhetoric of Heroism," in José Ignazio Cabezón, ed., *Buddhism, Sexuality, and Gender* (Albany, N.Y., 1992), pp. 137–156. For Ming-dynasty Chan consult Yü Chün-fang's *The Renewal of Buddhism in China: Chu-hung and the Late Ming Synthesis* (New York, 1981). For Chan in contemporary China, an anecdotal evocation is available in *Empty Cloud: The Teachings of Xu Yun, a Remembrance of the Great Chinese Zen Master,* by Jy Din Sakya as related to Chuan Yuan Shakya and Upasaka Richard Cheung (Albany, N.Y., 1992).

A large number of Chan texts are available in English translation, although not always in reliable form. One of the best is Urs App, *Master Yunmen: From the Record of the Chan Teacher "Gate of the Clouds"* (New York, Tokyo, and London, 1994). The best treatment of the Song-dynasty development of Chan literature is Christian Wittern, *Das Yulu des Chan-Buddhismus: Die Entwicklung vom 8.–11. Jahrhundert am Beispiel des 28, Kapitels des Jingde Chuandenglu (1004)–* (Bern, Germany, and New York, 1998).

JOHN R. MCRAE (2005)

CHANCE, in the most general sense of the word, is the negation of necessity and the opposite of determinism. The word "chance," derived from the Latin *cadere* ("to fall"), has a wide spectrum of meanings encompassing randomness, probability, coincidence, contingence, fluke, accident, incident, fortuity, serendipity, hazard, risk, opportunity, luck, fortune, and fate. Many words related to chance, such as *coincidence, contingence,* or the German *Zufall,* indicate a binary structure, the coming together of two causally independent series of events. Something happens, or a certain situation or person is encountered by chance. (The word "incident" derives from Latin *incidere,* "to befall, to fall out.")

The awareness of chance is an integral part of worldviews, both indeterministic and deterministic. Chance may be regarded positively as "an essential aspect of any real process" (Bohm, p. 141); negatively as the lack of causality or knowledge of such; and neutrally as the law of probability.

To some, chance denotes human freedom, but to others, fate. Chance can be haphazard; it can be fortunate or unfortunate. It is a highly equivocal, bifacial term, in that one meaning can easily turn into its opposite. This ambivalence may be traced back to the essential unpredictability and unknowability of any happening. The insurance business, for instance, rests on its customers' belief in chance (in the sense of unpredictability), but itself uses the theory of chance—that is, probability—to calculate its risks and price its policies (see Knight).

Although in the early twenty-first century the theory of probability predicts the course of class events to a great extent, the ultimate unknowability and uncertainty of individual events can never vanish from the realm of human experience (see Von Mises). This persistent presence of chance elements can be argued from the contingent nature of one's existence or from free will. Again, the uncertainty and indeterminateness of reality can be the source of inspiration for art or enterprise. The spirit of gambling, for instance, deliberately creates uncertain situations for the enjoyment of the risks themselves (see Rothbard, p. 500).

CHANCE, GREEK VIEWS. Dante noted that Democritus "ascribes the world to chance" (*Inferno* 4.136; cf. Cioffari, chap. 1). Aristotle also observed that for Democritus the cosmos was ordered by chance (*automaton*), that is, out of itself (*auto*) without any reason or purpose (*maton*). (For the etymology of *automaton,* see *Physics* 197b.) In opposition to this view of chance as a spontaneous event, or as "a cause that is inscrutable to human intelligence, as being a divine thing and full of mystery" (*Physics* 196b), Aristotle considered chance (*tuchē* and *automaton*) as an accidental cause of the "efficient order" and what happens "by accident" (*kata sumbebēkos*). Chance is indeterminate, changeful, and unstable. It is whatever comes about, neither always nor usually, but rarely (*Metaphysics* 1026b–1027a, 1065a; *Physics* 196b–198a).

Aristotle moreover distinguished two types of chance events, *tuchē* and *automaton.* Illustrating this distinction, Alexander of Aphrodisias, a third-century commentator, gave the example of a lost horse recovered by chance by his former owner. For the owner, the event is fortunate (*tuchē*), but for the horse it is simply fortuitous (*automaton*). *Automaton* has a broader range of meanings than *tuchē,* as it is applicable both to the natural and human worlds, whereas *tuchē* applies only to the latter (see Kuki, pp. 63–67).

Regarding luck and chance, Aristotle observed: "We speak of 'good luck' when luck brings us something good, and 'bad luck' in the opposite event, or, in serious cases, of 'good fortune' [*eutuchia*] or 'misfortune' [*dustuchia*]" (*Physics* 197a). Good fortune or chance for Aristotle comprised such qualities as noble birth, good children, wealth, political power, friends, and beauty (cf. *Rhetoric* 1389a). Fortune or chance is the cause of these external goods (*Politics* 1322b). The ethical virtues of justice, courage, temperance, and wisdom, however, lie outside the realm of chance, that is, within human control (cf. *Politics* 1323a).

The Greek word for chance, *tuchē,* contains the long history of poets' and writers' reflections on the subjects of luck, fate, the vicissitudes of life, and the gods' share in such human events. For Pindar, Soteira Tyche (Fortune the Savior) is "heaven-sent good fortune," the "kindly power who may crown the efforts of man" (Greene, pp. 72–73). Plato talked about a *theia tuchē,* a divine chance (*Timaeus* 25e), who comes to save human beings from their folly. Many Greeks worshipped Agathe Tyche, the goddess of good fortune (*Timaeus* 26e; Greene, p. 299). Aristotle admitted that chance has a religio-ethical significance in that fortune and happiness (*eudaimonia*) are often synonymous, that "happiness is a divine gift" (*Nicomachean Ethics* 1099b; Greene, p. 325), and that "the lucky seem to succeed owing to God" (*Ethica Eudemia* 1248b; Cioffari, p. 27).

But Goddess Tyche is not always benevolent or dependable. Archilochus (c. 700–650 BCE) is said to have introduced the idea of *tuchē* into the discourse, along with the already familiar Homeric notion of *moira* (fate), to account for what controlled human destiny. According to Orphic doctrines, fate was the law that controlled the conditions of human beings' birth, death, and reincarnation, but by the fifth and fourth centuries BCE, goddess Tyche became increasingly important. An anonymous poet wrote: "Fortune [Tyche], beginning and end of human beings. Thou sittest in the seats of wisdom, and grantest honor to human deeds . . . thou most excellent of gods" (Loeb ed., *Lyra Graeca*, vol. 3, p. 477). In Greek tragedies, the role of *tuchē* was considerable. Euripides's Ion exclaims: "O Tyche, thou who hast brought change to myriads of human beings, causing them now to suffer misfortune, and now to fare well, by what a narrow margin have I escaped slaying my mother!" (Euripides, *Ion* 1512–1515). Tyche, as the goddess of chance, was associated with Lachesis, one of the Moirai (Fates) and the "dispenser of human lots" (Hesiod), and took on a fickle, unpredictable character.

CHANCE, THE ROMAN VIEW. The cult of the native Italian goddess Fortuna was revived when she was identified with Tyche. Pliny the Elder noted:

> Everywhere in the whole world, at every hour by everyone's voices Fortuna alone is invoked and named, alone accused, alone impeached, alone pondered, alone applauded, alone rebuked and visited with reproaches; deemed volatile and indeed by most people blind as well, wayward, inconstant, uncertain, fickle in her favors and favoring the unworthy. . . . We are so much at the mercy of chance that Chance herself takes the place of god. (*Natural History* 2.22)

The belief in Fortuna persisted well into Renaissance Europe; she was often depicted with wings, bearing a rudder and wheel, symbolizing swiftly changing fortune.

CHANCE IN CHRISTIANITY AND RATIONALIST PHILOSOPHY. Christian views on chance vary somewhat. Whereas Augustine denied any possibility of chance or fortune in view of all-controlling providence (*City of God* 5.1), Aquinas admitted chance (*contingens*) within the providential scheme. Things "happen necessarily or contingently according to God's will" (*Summa theologiae* 1.19.8).

Spinoza spoke of chance "with reference to a deficiency in our knowledge [of the cause]" (*Ethics* 1.33.1); likewise, Laplace took it as the expression of "our ignorance as to the causes of phenomena." Hume declared that "there is no such thing as chance," but "our ignorance of the real cause of any event begets this sort of belief or opinion" (*Concerning Human Understanding* 6). Chance thus understood has merely a subjective reality. Leibniz, on the other hand, considered the world as "the whole assemblage of *contingent* things" that has its necessary and eternal substance (i.e., God) for its existence ("Essays on the Justice of God and the Freedom of Man in the Origin of Evil," 1.7); also he distinguished two kinds of truths and held that "truths of fact are contingent," while "truths of reasoning are necessary" (*Monadology* 33).

CHANCE AS SERENDIPITY. In opposition to the mechanical necessitarianists of the late nineteenth century, C. S. Peirce developed a philosophical position that he called "tychism." It preserves the necessary presence of chance (Gr., *tuchē*), "a spontaneity which is to some degree regular," in the evolutionary process of the world, and this accounts for the individual specification (1923, pp. 200–201). Max Born, from the standpoint of quantum mechanics, likewise took chance to be mixed with "certain regularities," and nature to be "ruled by laws of cause and laws of chance." Distinguishing causality from determinism, Born incorporated chance into the consideration of causality, and thereby gave quantum mechanics indeterministic foundations (cf. Heisenberg's "principle of indeterminacy" or Niels Bohr's "principle of complementarity"). This indeterministic position was rejected by Einstein, who was convinced that God was not a "dice-playing God" (Born, pp. 3, 109, 122–123). The Nobel laureate biologist Jacques Monod declared that "chance alone is at the source of every innovation, of all creation in the biosphere" (p. 112). Objectors to this view hold that Monod's equation of "chance and man's freedom to choose his own ethical value" is erroneous (see MacKay, p. 31), or that "physico-chemical determinism" is not synonymous with the "absence of choice and freedom" (Schoffeniels, p. xix).

Not only the old question of divine providence, human freedom and chance, but the question of scientific discoveries and their philosophical implications occupy the contemporary mind. The current trend is in agreement with the worldview that is fast moving towards indeterminism, and chance, understood as serendipity, is considered instrumental in biological and other scientific discoveries and breakthroughs (see works by J. H. Austin and A. Kantorovich, for instance).

RADICAL CONTINGENCY: A BUDDHIST VIEW. The Buddhist doctrine of dependent co-origination (*pratītya-samutpāda*) may be interpreted as a theory of radical contingency. It holds that there are "no accidental occurrences" and that everything in the world is produced "causally conditioned." Buddhists deny any theory of creation by a transcendental agent or anything such as fate. Moreover, things, causally produced in this fashion, have no "self-nature" (*svabhāva*). This view diametrically opposed the determinism of the Indian materialists, the Ājīvikas, as well as the syncretic view of the theory of inner and outer causation held by Jains (see Kalupahana).

From a certain perspective, this Buddhist doctrine appears to be a deterministic view in that it asserts that everything is subject to the law of causation. But from a reverse perspective, the convergence of causal factors is thoroughly indeterminate; it rests on a radical contingence of various factors, both of the spatio-temporal and psycho-mental nature. Innumerable conditioning elements come together in the arising of a single event at each moment.

JUNG'S VIEW ON SYNCHRONICITY. C. G. Jung coined the term "synchronicity" to designate the phenomenon of the coincidence of events and subjective psychic states. It "takes the coincidence of events in space and time as meaning something more than mere chance, namely, a peculiar interdependence of objective events among themselves as well as with the subjective (psychic) states of the observer or observers" (1967, p. xxiv). Jung was inclined to value the "practical result of chance" more highly than the "theoretical considerations of cause and effect" (p. xxiii), and hence, "we must admit that there is something to be said for the immense importance of chance" (*ibid.*, p. xxiv).

DIVINATION. Belief in fortune opens the way for divination. Throughout the history of humankind, recourse to divination has been practiced in times of trouble or uncertainty. Divination was originally a means to obtain answers to questions that are insoluble by rational reasoning. A story is recorded in Plutarch of the successor to the throne of the Thessalian kingdom being chosen by casting lots at Delphi. In Shang China, divination originated in a human attempt to fathom the mind of the deity; during the Zhou period the art of divination was given philosophical foundation (see *The Book of Changes* or *Yijing*). In Japan well into the thirteenth century, shrine virgins known as *saigū*, who served at the most auspicious shrine of all, the Ise Shrine, were chosen from among eligible princesses by divination.

It appears that only later did divination come to be interpreted as dealing with chance or randomness. It is noteworthy in this connection that Apollo, the Greek god of knowledge, despised the uncertainty of the lot and handed over the divination dealing with the chances of the dice to Hermes, who thus became the gambler's god.

Belief in chance has a double role to play in the practice of divination—in the method (as the principle of randomness) and in the interpretation (as the principle of coincidence). A deterministic worldview that negates chance can nevertheless employ divination. For example, an African system of divination, Ifa, is based on the assumption that individuals basically cannot change their own destiny, but just as they can spoil it to a degree, so can the practice of Ifa improve it. Even Stoics, who were thoroughgoing determinists, eagerly sought knowledge of the future that fell outside the prediction of scientists, physicians, and other experts. The harmony between the human soul and the divine soul provided them with the basis for divination as a means of communication with God in order that human beings "might know the divine will in advance and obey it" (William A. Falconer, introduction to Cicero's *De divinatione*, Loeb ed., 1923, p. 216).

Like the widely practiced throwing of pebbles or stones for divinatory purposes, the method of the Chinese *yijing* divination consists in casting yarrow stalks (or coins) to yield randomly determined odd or even numbers. The philosophers of the later Song period maintained that this randomness was essential, for "some truths could only be sought by means of the random cast of the stalks and the evolution of the all-informing hexagram; this was achieved by means that were anything but systematic or responsive to reason" (Loewe, in Loewe and Blacker, p. 52).

Be it bibliomancy, a random opening of books such as the Bible, the Qurʾān, or Vergil's *Aeneid;* rhapsodomancy, which consists in writing out passages from books on separate slips and drawing one of them at random; or kledonomancy, appealing to a chance word overheard—all rest on randomness as the vehicle. (Incidentally, the Latin word for fate, *fatum,* comes from *for,* "to speak," "to say." *Fatum* is "what is said.") As chance is unknowable in essence, so does randomness, a form of chance, appear as an appropriate means to grasp the unknown. The mathematical doctrine of chance can be applied to calculating the outcome of random throwing of dice, for instance, but it does not replace the purpose of divination, which is to provide an answer to a question brought to it.

A skilled interpretation of such signs as those mentioned above is of central importance for divination and may be said to rely on the principle of coincidence or correspondence, according to which signs are somehow related to the human situation under consideration. It is assumed not only that there is a certain correspondence between the method of divination and the meaning obtained through it but that there is a correspondence between human affairs and the larger cosmic movement (as in, for example, *The Book of Changes*) or the divine will. "The casting of lots is familiar in the Old and New Testaments as a method of ascertaining divine will" (Halliday, p. 206; cf. *Jos.* 6:14, *Jon.* 1:17, *Acts* 1:26, *Prv.* 16:33), and a divinatory message was regarded as sacred and mysterious (*Prv.* 16:10).

MIRACLE. An extremely rare or unusual occurrence may be considered a miracle. Aquinas summarized the traditional Christian understanding of miracle as: "When anything is done outside the order of created nature by a power unknown to us, it is called a miracle as regards ourselves" (*Summa theologiae* 1.110.4.2). He argued that just as ignorance of the cause is the source of amazement, so also when the cause is completely hidden, as God is, a thing is wondrous in an unqualified way, and this is a miracle—"what is of itself filled with admirable wonder" (*Summa contra gentiles* 3.101; cf. Augustine, *City of God* 21.8). For Hume, who denied chance, a miracle is "a violation of the laws of nature" supported by human testimony and sustained by belief (*Concerning Human Understanding* 10). Over against the Humean interpretation, Peirce found Butler's position that "the order of nature is a law to the doctrine of miracles" to affirm miracles and to be "in consonance with the higher teachings of modern science" ("Hume on Miracles," *Collected Papers* 6.546–547). Contemporary theists argue that a "dynamically stable world," which embraces chance, affords the possibility of miracles.

CHANCE AND THE UNKNOWN. Chance events, beyond human ratiocination and calculations, disclose the radical uncertainty present at the heart of reality. The interpretation of chance depends on whether one's worldview is religious or nonreligious. The fundamental unknowability of events—their mystery—can inspire awe. The religious mind has perceived in chance something sacred or a manifestation of the divine will. Some have placed chance within the governance of divine providence. Others reject it in deference to the same divine providence, arguing that what happens has already been determined by the transcendent scheme. Hence a seemingly chance occurrence, either fortunate or unfortunate, takes on the meaning of fate. In contrast, chance seen as pointing out the utter indeterminateness of things would signify the presence of free will. From a strictly fatalistic point of view, of course, there is no room for chance, for everything is already predetermined prior to the occurrence of events, and everything is already fated. Chance and fate—these initially contradictory notions are but two counter-interpretations of the experience of unexpected coincidence or happenings that seem arbitrary but nevertheless have a decisive impact on one's life and in some cases totally change it.

See Also Divination; Fate; Gambling; Miracles; Pratītya-samutpāda.

Bibliography

Comprehensive works on chance in English are few. In other languages, one may profitably consult Kuki Shūzō's *Gūzensei no mondai* [The problem of contingency] (1935; Tokyo, 1976), translated as *Le problème de la contingence* (Tokyo, 1966), and Wilhelm Windelband's *Die Lehren vom Zufall* (Berlin, 1870).

On the economic theory of risk, probability, and uncertainty, see Frank H. Knight's *Risk, Uncertainty and Profit* (New York, 1921). On the distinction between "class probability" and "actual singular events," see Ludwig Von Mises's *Human Action*, 3d rev. ed. (Chicago, 1963), and M. N. Rothbard's *Man, Economy, and State*, 2 vols. (Princeton, 1962).

For a popular, readable introduction to the laws of chance and probability, see Darrell Huff's *How to Take a Chance* (New York, 1959), and Deborah J. Bennett, *Randomness* (Cambridge, Massachusetts & London, 1998). For a philosophical treatment of this subject, see D. H. Mellor's *The Matter of Chance* (Cambridge, 1971).

On the ancient Greek view of chance and fate, see William C. Greene's *Moira: Fate, Good and Evil in Greek Thought* (Cambridge, Mass., 1944). On Aristotle and the Scholastics, see Vincenzo Cioffari's *Fortune and Fate: From Democritus to St. Thomas Aquinas* (New York, 1935). On Leibniz's view of contingency, see *Theodicy* (London, 1951); also "Monadology" in Leroy E. Loemker, trans. & ed., *Philosophical Papers and Letters* (Chicago, 1956). For C. S. Peirce's philosophy of chance, see his *Chance, Love and Logic* (1923; New York, 1949).

On the Buddhist view of chance and causation, see David J. Kalupahana's *Causality: The Central Philosophy of Buddhism* (Honolulu, 1975); G. C. Pande, "Causality in Buddhist Philosophy," Eliot Deutsche & Ron Bontekoe, ed., *A Companion to World Philosophies* (Oxford, 1997), pp. 370–380.

For a contemporary view of chance from a scientific perspective, see Max Born's *Natural Philosophy of Cause and Chance* (Oxford, 1951) and David Bohm's *Causality and Chance in Modern Physics* (Princeton, 1957). Jacques Monod's position is stated in his *Chance and Necessity* (New York, 1971), and Ernest Schoffeniels's critique is in his *Anti-Chance* (Oxford, 1976). On the role of serendipity in scientific discoveries, see James H. Austin, *Chase, Chance, and Creativity: The Lucky Art of Novelty* (New York, 1978), and Aharon Kantorovich, *Scientific Discovery: Logic and Tinkering* (Albany, N.Y., 1993).

For a theistic position on chance, see Donald M. MacKay's *Science, Chance, and Providence* (Oxford, 1978), and William G. Pollard's *Chance and Providence* (New York, 1958).

On divination, see *Greek Divination* by W. R. Halliday (1913; Chicago, 1967); *Oracles and Divination*, edited by Michael Loewe and Carmen Blacker (New York, 1981), contains a wide range of material from many cultures.

On the idea of synchronicity, see C. G. Jung's foreword to *The I Ching [Yijing], or Book of Changes*, 3d ed., translated by Cary F. Baynes (Princeton, 1967), and Jung's essays "Synchronicity: An Acausal Connecting Principle" and "On Synchronicity," in *The Structure and Dynamics of the Psyche*, 2d ed. (Princeton, 1969), vol. 8 of *The Collected Works of C. G. Jung*.

On miracles, see Antony Flew's "Miracles," in *The Encyclopedia of Philosophy*, edited by Paul Edwards (New York, 1967), vol. 5, and C. S. Peirce's "Hume on Miracles," in the *Collected Papers of Charles Sanders Peirce*, edited by Charles Hartshorne and Paul Weiss (Cambridge, Mass., 1960), vol. 6. Richard Swinburne's *The Concept of Miracle* (London, 1970) deals with the problem from the standpoint of philosophy of religion.

Michiko Yusa (1987 and 2005)

CHANG CHÜEG See ZHANG JUE

CHANG HSÜEH-CH'ENG See ZHANG XUECHENG

CHANG LU See ZHANG LU

CHANG TAO-LING See ZHANG DAOLING

CHANG TSA See ZHANG ZAI

CHANNING, WILLIAM ELLERY, American Unitarian minister. Channing was born on April 7, 1780 in Newport, Rhode Island, of a distinguished family. He entered Harvard College in 1794, graduated in 1798, and was elected a regent of Harvard in 1801. He began his lifelong ministry at Boston's Federal Street Congregational Church in 1803. Channing defended the liberal Congregationalist ministers in 1815 against an attack in *The Panoplist* by Jedidiah Morse, who accused them of covertly holding the views of the English Unitarian Thomas Belsham, who held that Christ was strictly human in nature, with human imperfections. Channing replied that the liberals were Arians and hence believed that Christ's character included intellectual, ethical, and emotional perfection. Thrust into prominence by this defense, Channing was asked to prepare a manifesto for the liberals, which he did in "Unitarian Christianity," his 1819 ordination sermon for Jared Sparks in Baltimore. This sermon unified the liberals around Channing's leadership; yet when the American Unitarian Association was organized in 1825, he refused the office of president, because he did not want Unitarianism to become a sect.

Channing was the outstanding representative of early American Unitarian theology in the period prior to the Transcendentalist controversy. He emphasized the authority of reason and revelation, the unique and infallible authority of Jesus, human educability to a Christlike perfection, and human essential similarity to God. His thought includes a modified Lockean philosophy, an Arian Christology, and an optimistic view of human nature.

John Locke's influence is present in Channing's arguments for the rational character of revealed religion and his emphases on miracles and fulfilled prophecies as evidences for the truth of Christianity. In his 1819 sermon "Unitarian Christianity," he called for a careful use of reason in interpreting scripture. Channing held that reason judges even the claim of a revelation to authority. Reason approves the claim of the Christian scriptures to authority. Rationally interpreted, these scriptures yield the doctrines of the unipersonality and moral perfection of God.

Channing modified his Lockean epistemology when he became acquainted with the Scottish common-sense philosophy of Thomas Reid, Adam Ferguson, and Francis Hutcheson. In his opinion, Richard Price corrected Hutcheson's thought in a way that more effectively met the arguments of David Hume, thus making room for new ideas other than those derived from sensation and reflection. Disagreements exist, however, about the extent to which Channing's later thought became more akin to that of the Transcendentalists.

Channing's Arian Christology and his optimistic view of human nature were closely related. He viewed Christ as morally perfect. He based his Christology on scriptural evidences of Christ's perfection and his own belief in the freedom of the will. Christ exemplified the perfection to which others can attain. In order to account for Christ's flawless moral perfection, Channing inferred from it Christ's preexistence; yet he maintained that others should aspire to, and can achieve, a similar perfection.

Channing advocated prison reform and opposed alcoholism and other social evils, but he was reluctant to speak out openly against slavery. He acknowledged the fairness of rebukes for his silence. In 1835 he published *Slavery*, which had a marked effect in arousing public opinion against the slave system; thereafter his outspoken opposition to slavery cost him friends and support. His writings during this period show that his optimism and his rejection of the doctrine of depravity in no way blinded him to the reality of sin.

Channing's essays made him famous on both sides of the Atlantic Ocean. These, along with his sermons, lectures, and *Slavery*, were translated into German, French, Hungarian, and other languages. Channing became ill on a vacation trip and died at Bennington, Vermont, on October 2, 1842.

Bibliography

Works by Channing

The most accessible editions are *The Works of William Ellery Channing*, 6 vols. (Boston, 1903), and *The Works of William E. Channing, D. D., with an Introduction; New and Complete Edition, rearranged; To Which Is Added, The Perfect Life* (Boston, 1886).

Works about Channing

Conrad Wright has written a balanced introduction to Channing's thought in "The Rediscovery of Channing," chapter 2 of his *The Liberal Christians: Essays on American Unitarian History* (Boston, 1970). The most complete study of Channing's philosophy and theology is Robert L. Patterson's *The Philosophy of William Ellery Channing* (New York, 1952), with detailed, informative footnotes. Channing's concern for social issues is emphasized by Jack Mendelsohn in *Channing: The Reluctant Radical* (Boston, 1971). The most recent study is Andrew Delbanco's *William Ellery Channing: An Essay on the Liberal Spirit in America* (Cambridge, Mass., 1981).

JOHN C. GODBEY (1987)

CHANTEPIE DE LA SAUSSAYE, P. D. (1848–1920), Dutch theologian, philosopher, and historian of religions.

Pierre Daniël Chantepie de la Saussaye, who was of Huguenot descent, studied theology at the University of Utrecht, where he obtained his doctorate in 1871. After a short stay in Bonn and Tübingen, where he worked with J. T. Beck, he served as a minister in the Dutch Reformed church (1872–1878). In 1878 he was appointed to the new Chair of the History of Religions in the faculty of theology at the University of Amsterdam. There he stayed until 1899, when he was appointed to the Chair of Theological Encyclopaedia, Doctrine of God, and Ethics in the faculty of theology at the University of Leiden, a post that he held until his retirement in 1916. Chantepie de la Saussaye was one of the representatives of the movement in Dutch Protestantism called "ethical theology," which stressed the value of religion both as a reality of the heart and as an existential datum with ethical implications.

Chantepie de la Saussaye defended the autonomy of the new science of religion, but he was always sensitive to its presuppositions and limitations. He had no knowledge of Asian languages; his own historical research concentrated on Old Germanic religion. After his appointment in Leiden, he practically left the field of history of religions and paid attention thereafter primarily to questions of faith and ethics. Among his students in Leiden, Gerardus van der Leeuw seems to have been the most sensitive to what Chantepie de la Saussaye saw as the direction that science of religion in a theological faculty should take.

Chantepie de la Saussaye's major work, the two-volume *Lehrbuch der Religionsgeschichte* (1887–1889; translated as *Manual of the Science of Religion,* 1891), is a handbook of the science of religion in a broad sense. As one of the first of such works, it is one of the discipline's great historical documents, and it deserves close attention. In its first edition the *Lehrbuch* was divided into four sections: an introduction followed by phenomenological, ethnographical, and historical parts. In the introductory section Chantepie de la Saussaye, distancing himself from the philosophical systems and general reductive theories of religion current at the time, discusses the new science of religion. He ascribes its rise to the discovery of many new source materials for ancient religions; to the fact that world history can now be described as an entity; and in particular to the modern philosophical view of religion as one whole. Over against theological distinctions, he asserts, modern philosophy recognizes "the unity of religion in the variety of its forms" and considers religion as a single phenomenon subject to "philosophical knowledge." Significantly, he pays tribute here to G. W. F. Hegel, who distinguished "the various modes for studying religion (metaphysical, psychological and historical) and made us see the harmony between the idea and the realization of religion." For Chantepie de la Saussaye the empirical science of religion is distilled, so to speak, from philosophy of religion as Hegel conceived it.

Chantepie de la Saussaye distinguishes more sharply than Hegel, however, between philosophy and history of religion, and between the "essence" and "manifestations" of religion: whereas philosophy of religion is concerned with the "essence" of religion, history of religion as an empirical discipline studies its "manifestations." History of religion is subdivided into an ethnographical section treating peoples "without history," and a much larger section treating the religions of peoples with written documents.

As for philosophy of religion, it treats religion in both its subjective and its objective aspects, and consequently consists of what Chantepie de la Saussaye calls a "psychological" and a "metaphysical" part. Metaphysical philosophy of religion stresses God's objective speaking in nature and life, whereas psychological philosophy of religion stresses the human's subjective reaching out to God. For Chantepie de la Saussaye, as for C. P. Tiele and van der Leeuw, "psychological" denotes not so much an empirical, verifiable reality as a philosophical category indicating the subjective side of human experience. It is important to see how large Hegel still looms in the background of Chantepie de la Saussaye's thinking on religion and consequently his phenomenology.

The *Lehrbuch* was an important contribution to the new science of religion in another respect, too. The phenomenology of religion contained in its second section was the first of its kind and drew largely on Hegel; it was published in 1887 before the work of Franz Brentano and Edmund Husserl, who were to conceive of phenomenology in a totally different way. Appropriately, given the clear distinction that Chantepie de la Saussaye made between philosophy and history of religion—he viewed the latter as an empirical discipline—he conceived of phenomenology as a discipline mediating between history on one hand and philosophy on the other. Its task was to collect and classify the various religious phenomena, and to establish the meaning of the different classes of phenomena.

At the very beginning of the phenomenological section of the *Lehrbuch,* Chantepie de la Saussaye points out that a phenomenology of religious forms deals with facts of human consciousness; that these outward forms of religion can be understood only on the basis of "inward processes"; and that it is their particular "inward relation" that distinguishes religious from nonreligious acts, ideas, and sentiments. Consequently, phenomenology of religion was in principle closely connected with psychology. This was the line taken by his pupil Gerardus van der Leeuw, who was to develop explicitly this psychological-phenomenological research of religion.

Chantepie de la Saussaye himself does not go so far, treating only the forms and not the contents of religious consciousness. Already in his dissertation of 1871 he had considered religion as a kind of species comprising a number of different forms. To develop a classification of these forms, he distinguishes three sectors in religion—cult, doctrine, and religious feeling, of which the first is the most stable sector and the last is practically limited to the present. The *Lehrbuch*'s phenomenological section describes (1) objects of worship, religious acting, sacred persons, religious communities, and sacred writings and (2) religious thinking (myth and doctrine). Religious feeling does not receive separate treatment.

It has often been noted that this phenomenological section was entirely dropped in the second edition of the *Manual.* Chantepie de la Saussaye explained that in his view this section had to be either considerably enlarged or omitted. He chose to omit it for reasons of space, and also because phenomenology constituted a border discipline between history and philosophy requiring separate treatment in a new book. Unfortunately—and significantly—this book never appeared. It was his pupil van der Leeuw who worked in this direction and developed phenomenology of religion as a special branch of the study of religion.

In point of fact, Chantepie de la Saussaye's wish to develop a phenomenology of religion as a special field between history and philosophy—between empirical facts and systematic thought—did not achieve much more than an outward classification and systematization of religious forms. This he did on the basis of the Hegelian legacy, with its distinction between the essence and the manifestations of religion. His phenomenology—which was quite independent of the phenomenological movement started by Franz Brentano, Edmund Husserl, and others—was a very formal discipline relegating the problem of religious meaning mainly to philosophy or to the scholar's intuition, or, worse, to the scholar's personal religious views and convictions.

See Also Leeuw, Gerardus van der; Phenomenology of Religion.

Bibliography

For bibliographic data on Chantepie de la Saussaye's person and work, see my book *Classical Approaches to the Study of Religion,* vol. 2, *Bibliography* (The Hague, 1974), pp. 37–38.

Two books by Chantepie de la Saussaye exist in English translation. *Manual of the Science of Religion* (London, 1891) is the English translation of the first edition of the *Lehrbuch der Religiongeschichte,* 2 vols. (Freiburg im Breslau, 1887–1889). The second and third editions of the *Lehrbuch,* of which Chantepie de la Saussaye was no longer the author but the editor, have not been translated into English. *The Religion of the Teutons* (Boston, 1902) is a considerably expanded translation of a book published in Dutch in 1900.

New Sources

James, George Alfred. *Interpreting Religion: The Phenomenological Approaches of Pierre Daniel Chantepie de la Saussaye, W. Brede Kristensen, and Gerardus van der Leeuw.* Washington, D.C., 1995.

Plantinga, Richard J. "In the Beginning: P. D. Chantepie de la Saussaye on Religionswissenschaft and Theology." *Religious Studies and Theology* 8 (1988): 24–30.

Ryba, Thomas. "Comparative Religion, Taxonomies and 19th Century Philosophies of Science: Chantepie de la Saussaye and Tiele." *Numen 48,* no. 3 (2000): 309–338.

Jacques Waardenburg (1987)
Revised Bibliography

CHANTING

CHANTING. Many scholars trace chanting to the earliest stages of human development, a time when speech was presumably not differentiated from chant. Even today Saami (Lapp) women in Finland, Jewish women in Morocco, and Santali women in Bihar, India, unconsciously replace sobbing with chanting while lamenting their dead. Australian Aborigines, when excited, break into a torrent of words governed by rhythms and cadences resembling chant. Hungarian dirges and some Khanty (Ostiak) and Mansi (Vogul) tribal melodies of Siberia consist of sung declamations, while the Zulu, Yoruba, Igbo, and Bantu-speaking peoples possess real "melody languages." Contemporary shamans and medicine men on several continents are known to chant sacred rites in a secret language, often invented by themselves. Furthermore, not only American Indian Navajos, African Khoi, and Liberian Jabos use tone levels in their speech: contemporary Burmese, Siamese, Annamese (Vietnam), and Chinese recognize two to nine different tone levels in their languages. The ancient Chinese even distinguished whole families and clans by musical signs conferred upon them by tradition.

Close observation of ordinary conversation in any culture shows that musical intervals recur in the simplest of sentences. A middle pitch is usually maintained, and emphatic words, clauses, and conclusions are indicated by change of pitch. When a speaker addresses an audience, the pitches become more pronounced, and a "melody of speech" emerges. It is reported that the Greek orator Demosthenes (fourth to third century BCE) employed an assistant to blow a whistle (*tonorion*) during his speeches to remind him of certain pitch levels. Cicero and Gellius (author of *Noctes Atticae*) wrote that some classical authors memorized and performed their speeches with the aid of a flute player to insure the right intonation of the melodic line. Isocrates (436–338 BCE), the Athenian orator and teacher, insisted that the perfect oration was really a musical composition. It is therefore entirely possible that formalized chanting and cantillation of holy scriptures were derived from "singing to speech."

The modern definitions of chant (from Latin *cantare,* "to sing, to intone") and cantillation (from Latin *cantillare,* "to sing low, to hum") apply to the recitation of sacred writings with musical tones, usually improvised, as in synagogues, churches, mosques, and Asian temples. Chant in all these liturgies is usually monophonic, unaccompanied, and in so-called free rhythm, which results from the recitation of prose texts. The term *chant* applies in particular to the liturgical melodies of the Jewish and Samaritan synagogues, and to the Byzantine, Russian, Armenian, Syrian, Ambrosian, Gallican, Mozarabic, and Roman churches. The latter is better known as Gregorian chant and plainsong. *Chant* also refers to the traditional method of singing psalms and canticles in the daily offices of the Roman and Anglican churches. Chanted also are the Islamic Qur'ān, the Indian Vedas, and Buddhist scriptures.

Hebrew Chant. The term *cantillation* applies primarily to the recitation of the Hebrew Bible by Jews and Samaritans. Cantillation of the Bible on special occasions is already attested to in *Deuteronomy* 31:12, *2 Kings* 22:1–13, and *Nehemiah* 8:1–8. But regular biblical readings were established only in the fifth century BCE, when Ezra the Scribe chanted from the Law in the Jerusalem Temple twice a week on market days to all the people assembled there. This is the earliest evidence of regular biblical recitation in public. Since the reader had to amplify his voice in order to be heard, his unconscious chanting established the first biblical cantillation.

Cantillation gave particular expression to word meaning (accent) and phrasing (syntax). The importance of melody was prescribed in no uncertain terms by the Talmud (*Meg.* 32a), where Yoḥanan (second century) says, "He who reads [the Bible] without a melody and studies without a tune is referred to by the verse 'Wherefore I gave him statutes that are not good . . .' (*Ez.* 20:35)." The melody was logogenic, or word-bound; in other words, the interpolation of extraneous syllables or words into the text was forbidden. Cantillation was not a prominent practice in the Jerusalem Temple but in the course of time became the most important part of the synagogue service. The Jews preserved biblical cantillation in oral tradition for at least one thousand years (fifth century BCE to fifth century CE).

Melodic patterns or motifs were indicated by a system of finger and hand movements called cheironomy (from Greek *cheir,* "hand"), a practice depicted by Sumerians and Egyptians on bas-reliefs and in tombs in the fourth and third millennium BCE. These gestures were intended to refresh the memory of those who had previously learned the melodies by ear. Cheironomy remained in use until the seventeenth century in Greek monasteries, although modern musical notation was available. Hindus and Jews employ cheironomic signs even today, and various systems have been developed by different groups.

The first cheironomic signs were simple: the rise of the melody was signaled by an upward stroke of the hand (/), the fall by a downward stroke of the hand (\), and the rise and the fall on a single syllable by the junction of the two signs (/\). Various combinations of these basic symbols followed. It was musical notation written on the air.

When Hebrew ceased to be a living language, the Masoretes, transmitters of the biblical tradition, devised written symbols to safeguard the proper pronunciation, phrasing, and melodies of biblical Hebrew. The task took five centuries to complete (fifth to tenth century CE). The Masoretes transferred the cheironomic signs from the air to parchment and paper. It must be noted that other cultures employed similar symbols for similar purposes; indeed, scholars disagree as to which culture was the first to transfer hand movements form the air to parchment. Greece, India, the Middle East, and Europe have all been suggested. But the symbols are so elementary that any culture could have invented them independently without outside influence.

These first ekphonetic signs (from Greek *ekphōnēsis,* "pronunciation") were later refined, became more complicated, and gave way to neumes (from Greek *neuma,* "nod, sign"). By combining and recombining ekphonetic signs a variety of melodic motifs were created and became neumes. The major difference between ekphonetic signs and neumes is that ekphonetic signs indicate not a freely invented melody but a succession of fixed melodic formulas. Sometimes ekphonetic signs occurred only in the beginning and end of a phrase, as in Samaritan biblical changing or psalmtones of Gregorian chant.

The *ṭa'amei ha-miqra',* the Hebrew accents, were invented by grammarians, and many scholars believed in the past that their sole purpose was grammatical. Jews call the oral renditions, the vocal utterances of the biblical text, "cantillation," while the written symbols are called "accentuation." Three different systems of accentuation were developed by the Masoretes. The Palestinian system consisted almost entirely of dots and numbered only ten basic accents. The Babylonian system consisted predominantly of letters positioned above the word (supralinear). Each letter represented the initial of a musical term, such as *z* for *zarqa'* or *t* for *tibra* (*yetib*). This system became very popular in the Middle East and was employed, for example, by the Yemenite Jews until they emigrated to Israel in 1948. The Tiberian system of twenty-eight accents, universally in use today, consists of a combination of dots and other symbols.

The accents were provided for the books of the Bible that were read in public, namely: the Pentateuch, the Prophets, *Esther, Lamentations, Ruth, Ecclesiastes, Song of Songs, Psalms,* and in some communities *Job* and *Proverbs.* While the Hebrew accents are identical in all the Jewish Bibles of the world, their musical interpretation differs from place to place. The reason for this phenomenon is the indefinite nature of nondiastematic ekphonetic signs, which do not indicate musical intervals or pitches. Hebrew accents never developed an exact pitch notation, unlike the neumes of medieval European churches, which employed signs for single notes as well as for groups of notes.

Four accents in the oral traditions of Babylonian and Yemenite Jews can be compared. Neither interval structures nor directions of the melodies agree. This extreme divergence in cantillation motifs was caused by the total isolation of Yemenite Jews. Whereas written communication with Babylonia or Egypt existed, personal encounters were extremely rare. Thus an exchange or transmission of oral musical tradition was curtailed. By contrast, large areas of North Africa, northern Arabia, Persia, and Central Asia (Bukhara) as well as the Mediterranean show similarities in biblical cantillation. Furthermore, these cantillations seem closely related to the Babylonian type discussed previously.

The eastern European types of cantillation practiced by Polish, Lithuanian, Hungarian, and Russian Jews are related. These are, however, unrelated to German, Italian, French, or Sephardic (Spanish-Portuguese) cantillations: the latter four are also not related to one another. How is it, then, that Hebrew cantillation is instantly recognizable anywhere in the world? The reasons are unvarying text (Hebrew) and the ekphonetic symbols that are prescribed for every word of the sentence and have a syntactical as well as a musical function. They provide a solid structural basis for cantillation.

In addition to biblical cantillation, Jews recognize formalized chanting without ekphonetic symbols, namely that employed in blessings, certain prayers in the synagogue and at home, the study of Mishnah, the study of the *gemara',* and the study of the Zohar. In addition, Yemenite Jews recite from the Aramaic translation of the Bible on the Sabbath and on holidays in the synagogue. It is worth nothing that the Yemenite Jews are the only ones to perpetuate this Second Temple tradition and translate every Hebrew sentence into the Aramaic vernacular of the time.

Chanting in all these cases is based on a melody that consists of an opening motif (*initium*), followed by an undifferentiated two-tone motif (*tenor*) and a final cadence (*finalis*). The melody varies in length according to the number of words in the sentence, but the melodic motifs do not vary.

A. Z. Idelsohn (1921–1922) demonstrates the similarity of Yemenite Jewish cantillation and Gregorian chant, showing their common origins, perhaps from Temple times. In Eastern melodies the formulas are less rigid than those of Gregorian psalmody. In Byzantine melodies the same formulas can be used at the beginning, the middle, or the end of a chant.

The Samaritans cantillate the Hebrew Bible according to *sidra' miqrata'* (the Aramaic form of the Hebrew *seder ha-miqra'*), nondiastematic ekphonetic symbols. There are ten in number, but only three basic ones are remembered (see Spector, 1965, pp. 146–147): *arkenu-enged* (has the function of a colon), *afsaq* (full stop), and *anau* (pause, with the function of a semicolon). The Samaritan high priest Amran ben Ishaq still practiced the dynamic interpretations of *shayala'* (question), *z'iqa* (shouting), and *ba'u* (supplication) and sang them into a tape recorder for posterity (recorded 1951–1953).

Of ten extant cantillation styles, two are most prominent. The *logogenic*, or word-bound style, does not permit the inclusion of extraneous syllables or words. It was originally practiced by priests only and forbidden to the laity. It was intervallically stepwise, syllabic, and without ornamentation of the melody. The *pathogenic-melogenic* style, derived from passionate emotion and melody, permits the interpolation of extraneous nonsense syllables into the text if the text is shorter than the melody. It is particularly effective in the public reading of the Decalogue on the Festival of Shavu'ot. In this recitation the melody often overshadows the text. The nonsense syllables are "*ee-no-a.*"

BYZANTIUM. Scholars apply the term *Byzantine music* to Eastern ecclesiastical chant sung in Greek. In spite of the language it is maintained that this music was not a continuation of ancient Greek music but contained Near Eastern musical elements. (The Hellenized Near East was part of the Byzantine empire.)

Byzantine ecclesiastical music, like Near Eastern music, was entirely vocal, monophonic, unaccompanied, and devoid of meter. The use of organs and other musical instruments was forbidden inside the churches, similar to the prohibition in synagogues and (later) mosques. The liturgical books intended for chanting of lessons were performed in ekphonetic style, midway between recitation and singing. On solemn occasions actual singing replaced the cantillation. For training Christian congregations in singing, Jewish readers and precentors from synagogues were chosen who had previously converted to Christianity. Especially trained for the office, they made it possible to introduce into Christian worship not only chanting but also antiphonal singing, particularly psalms for solo voice with congregational responses. Performances varied from simple recitation to elaborate cantillation. The musical structure of the psalm melody consisted of (1) an initial clausula (*initium*), leading to the note on which the verse is chanted, (2) a repeated or slightly changed note of the recitation (*tenor*), (3) an occasional *mediant*, or half clause, and (4) the *finalis*, a cadence marking the end of the verse. In Eastern melodies the formulas are less rigid than those of Gregorian psalmody. In Byzantine melodies the same formulas can be used at the beginning, the middle, or the end of a chant.

The rise of the Kontakion is closely associated with the name of Romanus, who was a Jew by birth (d. 555 CE). Born in Syria, he became deacon of the Christian church in Phoenicia and went to Constantinople. He was culturally a Near Eastern musician-priest. It is reported that Romanus composed more than one thousand Kontakia. The first part of a monostrophic hymn in his honor has been preserved; it was sung on the first day of October, when the Byzantine church celebrates the Feast of Saint Romanus.

GREGORIAN CHANT. Gregorian chant is the traditional music of the Roman Catholic Church. Scholars maintain that it is rooted, like the music of the Byzantine church, in the pre-Christian service of the Jews. It acquired distinctive characteristics in the third and fourth centuries and was fully developed by the seventh century. It deteriorated in the sixteenth century and was revived in the nineteenth.

Many Gregorian practices were taken from the synagogue. The hours of the daily office are modeled after the prayers of the Jews, beginning with the evening prayer after sunset. The *Book of Psalms*, already used in the Jerusalem Temple, was made even more prominent by the church. The terms *Alleluya* and *Amen* are Hebrew. The Sanctus of the Mass was derived from the Qiddush of the Jews, as demonstrated by Eric Werner (1946, p. 292). The melodies show stepwise movement. Melodic rises or falls of the intervals of a second and a third are common, but those of a fifth are rare. The melodies can be classified as syllabic (one note to a syllable), neumatic (two to five notes to a syllable), and melismatic (long, highly ornamented phrases). The chant consists of one melodic line with neither harmony nor polyphony to support it.

Similarities between Yemenite Jewish psalmody and the first Gregorian psalmtone can be shown. A. Z. Idelsohn (1921–1922) shows parallels between Babylonian, Persian, Yemenite, and Oriental Sephardic melodies of the Jews and Gregorian chant. Not only are the same motifs employed but similar modes as well. The mode, the Greek Dorian, an E-mode, is the Pentateuch mode of the Jews, and is in widespread use in Middle Eastern and Mediterranean countries.

ARMENIA. The Armenian ekphonetic signs and neumes called *khaz* have never been deciphered, although rich source materials from the ninth to the twelfth centuries exist in Armenian, European, and Israeli libraries and museums. Contemporary scholars (e.g., Robert Atajan, 1978) believe in an independent origin of the *khaz* and reject an earlier theory (see, for example, Fleischer, 1895–1904) that the Armenian *khaz* were derived from Greek neumes. The Armenian *khaz* consist of two independent systems, a prosodic system for recitation and a musical system for singing according to *khaz*. The Hebrew and Samaritan ekphonetic signs discussed previously have no such division: one system governs both prosody and melody.

The Armenian *khaz* numbers ten symbols, five prosodic (*thaw, sosk, aibatatz, entamna,* and *storat*) and five musical (*erkar, ssuch, shesht, olorak,* and *buth*). According to Robert Atajan, the prosodic *khaz* relate to the peculiarities of Armenian phonetic pronunciation and have no bearing on the music. Syntactic symbols in the prosodic system, however, are of particular significance in the musical structure of the sentence: *storaket* ("deep point") is a comma, *mitshaket* ("middle point") is a semicolon or colon, and *vertchaket* ("final point") is a period. The musical signs *erkar* and *ssuch* indicate a lengthening or shortening of tone duration. The other three, *shesht, olorak,* and *buth,* represent tone pitches or rather melodic formulas based on Armenian folk tunes.

Armenian musical notation was already mentioned in the fifth century CE by Kasar Parbezi in his *History of Armenia,* but no musical symbols were preserved. From the tenth to the twelfth centuries art and music flourished, and twenty-five neumes were developed to indicate pitch, volume, duration, tone color, ornamentation, syntax, and prosody. From 1400 to 1600, *khaz* notation went into decline; it was revived only in the nineteenth century by the music theorist Baba ("father") Hamparzum (born Hamparzum Limonjian) in Constantinople. In this new and simplified *khaz* notation a great number of liturgical chants and folksongs were written down by the musicologist Komitas and are thus preserved for future generations.

The Qurʾān. The chanting of the Qurʾān is regulated not by ekphonetic signs or neumes but by oral tradition, which varies from place to place. The word is paramount, and no ornamentation is permitted. Sudden stops within the Qurʾānic sentence are a special feature. The call to prayer varies from country to country. Syllabic, elaborate melismas are often incorporated.

INDIA. The Vedas (from Sanskrit *vid,* "to know, to understand"), the sacred texts of the Hindus, were probably composed by Aryan tribes who invaded India from the northwest around 1500 BCE. The sacred texts had been handed down in oral tradition with accents at least since the fourth century BCE, as reported by the grammarian Pāṇini, who presumably knew the living practice. The interpretation of the accents is by no means uniform. Pāṇini wrote: "A vowel pronounced in a high register is called *udātta,* a vowel pronounced in a low register is called *anudātta,* and the connection of both is called *svarita.*" Some modern scholars maintain that *udātta* is a middle tone, higher than *anudātta,* and that *svarita* is higher than *udātta.* Only male members of the priestly *brahman* caste are eligible to recite the Vedas.

The Vedas were for hundreds of years handed down orally and not committed to writing, unlike the sacred books of the Jews, Christians, and Muslims. The Hindus relied on the spoken word for three thousand years, and even today the Vedas are recited from memory; every precaution is observed to avoid the smallest error, which, it is believed, may produce disaster. This belief is similar to the one held by the Jews of Yemen, who maintain that a mistake in the public reading of the Bible in the synagogue can cause the death of little children. To avoid catastrophe the precentor who commits an error has to repeat the entire verse in the synagogue.

As the Vedic language evolved into classical Sanskrit, the priests feared that the archaic language of the Vedas might become corrupt and the meaning of the texts forgotten. Consequently the Vedas were written down. The earliest surviving manuscripts date from the eleventh century.

Four compilations of the Vedas exist: (1) the *Ṛgveda,* the Veda of verses, contains more than 1,000 hymns; (2) the *Yajurveda,* the Veda of sacrificial sayings (*yajus*), contains verses and formulas dealing with sacrifices; (3) the *Sāmaveda,* the Veda of songs (*sāman*), contains verses of the *Ṛgveda* set to notated melodies for singer-priests; (4) the *Atharvaveda* is a collection of magical formulas and spells, little known today. The Vedas occur in two forms: the form in which they are recited for the purpose of preservation and transmission to students, and the form in which they are recited at sacrifice. Since large-scale sacrifices are infrequent today, little is known about the sacrificial form.

The *Ṛgveda* is recited to three tones: the "raised" (*udātta*), the not raised (*anudātta*), and the "sounded" (*svarita*). The *svarita* is marked with a perpendicular line over the syllable, the *anudātta* with a horizontal line beneath; the *udātta* and *pracaya* ("accumulated tone" following *svarita*) are unmarked. The *Yajurveda* is recited on the notes D, E, F or F.

The *Sāmaveda* is the most musical of all. It alters and expands the words of the *Ṛgveda* to make them suitable for chanting. The original text was often distorted by the insertion of meaningless words and syllables. The grammatical and prosodic specifications of the *Ṛgveda* have been given a musical meaning. The practitioners of the *Sāmaveda* believe that the *sāman* is a melody to which words were found, not the other way around. The three-tone nucleus (C–E) of the *Ṛgveda* and *Yajurveda* was extended both upward and downward by approximately semitone in each direction (B–F). The *Atharvaveda* does not seem to be recited according to set rules.

TIBET. Tibetan Buddhist chants are divided into *'don,* recitation chants; *rta,* melodic chants; and *dbyaṅs,* tone contour chants. The general designation for the monastic chant repertoire is *'don cha.* The recitation chants are stylized recitations that employ reiterating pitch and rhythmic patterns according to the words in the sentences.

Rta are melodic chants with distinctly patterned melodies. Unlike *'don,* they are relatively independent of their texts; unlike *'don* they are considered melodic and musical. However, their performance is called "speaking." They are similar to melodies in Western and non-Tibetan performance traditions.

Dbyaṅs are tone contour chants and are considered the most beautiful chants used in Tibetan music. They are very slow, low-pitched, and most complex. In contradistinction to *'don* and *rta*, which are "spoken," the *dbyaṅs* are "intoned." They include changes in intonation, pitch, loudness, and (most remarkably) overtone mixtures, which are perceived as two or more pitches produced simultaneously by one singer. Unlike the simpler *'don* and *rta*, they are notated. The melodic contour is defined by thickening lines that indicate increasing loudness; rising lines indicate rising pitch, falling lines falling pitch; sharp angles indicate interruptions, breath pauses, and so forth. (All Western notations are by Ter Ellingson.)

SECULAR CHANT. Secular chanting is prominent in the epic poetry of many countries; thus it is used for the most dignified and elaborate form of narrative poetry dealing with heroic, legendary, and historical events as well as with the drama and romance of love. Epics are usually chanted by a single performer, but in some Asian countries contests between two rival performers are customary and may last several days. In ancient times the narrator of epics chanted without instrumental accompaniment. This custom survives in certain areas, for example Tibet and Kurdistan. (The Jews of Kurdistan have epics of their own, such as *David and Goliath* and the *Crossing of the Red Sea*, whose narratives are distinct from the biblical texts.) Contemporary performers, however, accompany themselves on a stringed instrument, preferably a violin (Persian, *kemanje*; Turkmen, *ghyjjak*) or a lute (Kirghiz, *kobuz*; Turkmen, *dutar*; Tajik and Uzbek, *dumbura*). Melodies are word-bound (logogenic), and the musical structure admits of little improvisation. The melodies tend to be predictable and repetitious.

Chant is usually defined as an intermediate stage between speaking and singing. Some writers call chant "elevated speech." Chant, however, can take many forms—from speaking on one tone (*Sprechgesang*) to singing in full voice, as in some churches. The melody is always word-bound and moves usually stepwise within intervals of fourths or fifths. Notation for chant developed from hand movements (cheironomy) to ekphonetic notation and neumes. Today, chant is written in contemporary musical notation.

SEE ALSO Music, article on Music and Religion in Japan; Tilawah.

BIBLIOGRAPHY

Apel, Willi. *Gregorian Chant* (1958). Bloomington, Ind., 1970.

Atajan, Robert. "Armenische Chasen." In *Essays on Armenian Music*, edited by Vrej Nersessian, pp. 131–148. London, 1978.

Belayev, Victor M. *Ocherki po istorii muzyki narodov SSSR.* 2 vols. Moscow, 1962–1963.

Ellingson, Ter. " '*Don rta dbyangs gsum*: Tibetan Chant and Melodic Categories." *Asian Music* 10 (1979): 112–156.

Fleischer, Oskar. *Neumen-Studien.* 2 vols. Leipzig, 1895–1904.

Fox-Strangways, A. H. *The Music of Hindostan* (1914). Oxford, 1967.

Høeg, Carsten. *La notation ekphonétique.* Copenhagen, 1935.

Idelsohn, A. Z. "Parallelen zwischen gregorianischen und hebraeisch-orientalischen Gesangsweisen." *Zeitschrift für Musikwissenschaft* 4 (1921–1922): 515–524.

Idelsohn, A. Z. *Jewish Music in Its Historical Development* (1929). New York, 1967.

Jairazbhoy, N. A. "An Interpretation of the Twenty-two Srutis." *Asian Music* 6 (1975): 38–59.

Lachmann, Robert. *Die Musik des Orients.* Breslau, 1929.

Spector, Johanna. "A Comparative Study of Scriptural Cantillation and Accentuation (Pentateuch)." Ph.D. diss., Hebrew Union College, 1951.

Spector, Johanna. "The Significance of Samaritan Neumes and Contemporary Practice." In *Studia Musicologica*, edited by Zoltan Kodály, vol. 7, pp. 141–153. Budapest, 1965.

Spector, Johanna. "Musical Tradition and Innovation." In *Central Asia: A Century of Russian Rule*, edited by Edward Allworth, pp. 434–484. New York, 1967.

Szabolcsi, Bence. *A History of Melody.* Translated by Cynthia Jolly and Sara Karig. London, 1965.

Wagner, Peter. *Einführung in die gregorianischen Melodien.* 3 vols. Leipzig, 1895–1921. Volume 1 has been translated as *Origin and Development of the Forms of the Liturgical Chant* (London, 1901).

Wellesz, Egon. *A History of Byzantine Music and Hymnography.* 2d ed. Oxford, 1961.

Werner, Eric. "The Doxology in Synagogue and Church, a Liturgico-Musical Study." *Hebrew Union College Annual* 19 (1946): 275–351.

New Sources

Astrauskas, Rimantas. *Ritual and Music: Papers Presented at the International Ethnomusicologist Conference Held in Vilnius, Lithuania, December 11–12, 1997.* Vilnius, 1999. Crocker, Richard L. *An Introduction to Gregorian Chant.* New Haven, 2000.

Gass, Robert, and Kathleen A. Brehony. *Chanting: Discovering Spirit in Sound.* New York, 1999.

Jacobson, Joshua R. *Chanting the Hebrew Bible: The Art of Cantillation.* Philadelphia, 2002.

McDannell, Colleen, ed. *Religions of the United States in Practice.* Princeton, 2001.

Nelson, Angela M. S. *This Is How We Flow: Rhythm in Black Culture.* Columbia, 1999.

Perera, G. Ariyapala. *Buddhist Paritta Chanting Ritual: A Comparative Study of the Buddhist Benedictory Ritual.* Dehiwela, 2000.

Wilson, Ruth Mack. *Anglican Chant and Chanting in England, Scotland, and America, 1660 to 1820.* Oxford, 1996.

JOHANNA SPECTOR (1987)
Revised Bibliography

CHAOS, in the history of religions, refers primarily to the primordial condition, precosmic period, or personified being found in many oral and literary mythologies. It is commonly, although not always legitimately, taken to mean the horribly confused state, muddled matrix, vacuous condition, or monstrous creature preceding the foundation of an organized world system. By extension, the idea of chaos in myth and ritual may also apply to any anomalous condition, event, or entity outside conventionally sanctioned codes of order. The meaning and significance of chaos in world mythology has, moreover, a special thematic relationship with the idea of the beginnings of the world, or of any structured condition. The word *beginning* is, in fact, etymologically connected with the Old English *on-ginnan* and the Old Norse *gina*, in both of which lurks the mythological image of the cosmogonic Ginnungagap, the primordial void that spawned the giant Ymir (the Primordial Man) in ancient Norse tradition. From a cross-cultural perspective, the image of chaos is therefore especially prominent in cosmogonic and anthropogonic myths, as well as in many types of origin myths and passage rituals concerned with some transitional situation in human life or with some significantly altered state of affairs, whether for well or ill. Chaos appears, for example, within the context of the condition of death or the dream time of sleep, flood mythology, apocalyptic imagery in general, or foundational legends and rites pertaining to a new sociopolitical tradition.

The English word *chaos* derives directly from the Greek *chaos*, which in Hesiod's *Theogony* (c. eighth century BCE) denoted a cosmogonic "yawning gap, chasm, or void," from which generated the successive worlds of the gods and mankind. Hesiod, who drew upon earlier mythological sources, rather neutrally depicted the original chaos as merely the empty, dark space that allowed for the penetrating movement of erotic desire and for the appearance of Earth (Gaia) as the secure home for all subsequent created forms and beings. But the *Theogony* also displays the mythological premise for a more negative evaluation of chaos, since the earliest generations of Titanic gods, most closely identified with the untrammeled passion and anarachy of the primitive chaos condition, must be violently defeated by Zeus to insure the permanence and universality of the Olympian order. The primal chaos is itself only the blind abyss necessary for the creation of the physical world, but *chaos* here also refers to the mythic period—and, by implication, to a kind of "chaos-order" or condition—of the pre-Olympian gods who struggle against the imposition of Zeus's all-encompassing rule.

Because of their general impact on the colorations of meaning popularly conjured up by the modern use of the term *chaos*, it is worth citing two other ancient Western documents. In the priestly tale of *Genesis* (c. fourth century BCE) found in the Hebrew scriptures, chaos is reduplicatively called *tohu va-vohu*, a dark, watery, formless waste or "limbo-akimbo" that must be wrested into order by the willful fiat of a god completely separate from the stuff of creation. In a somewhat similiar vein, although more somberly stressing a hostile jumble of primal matter over blank vacuity, Ovid (43 BCE–18 CE), in his poetic compendium of mythology known as the *Metamorphosis*, describes chaos as "all ruse and lumpy matter . . . in whose confusion discordant atoms warred." As in the biblical version, Ovid's creation requires a nameless god, or "Kindlier Nature," who brings order out of the formless chaos.

The above-mentioned accounts serve to exemplify the commonplace tendency to dichotomize the meaning of existence into the negative-positive polarities of chaos and cosmos, confusion and order, death and life, evil and good, or, more theologically, into some dualistic distinction between the absolutely sacred and creative being of a transcendent "kindlier" God, on the one hand, and the utterly profane nothingness and nonbeing of a passively neutral or actively belligerent chaos. Clearly, these distinctions have both ontological and moral implications, so that it may also be said that the polarized evaluation of the mythic chaos is the backdrop for the theological and philosophical elaborations on such problems as *creatio ex nihilo* and theodicy. Indeed, the overall issue here directly affects the modern academic understanding of religion, since a whole tradition of Western scholarship defines religion as the contrast between the sacred and the profane, or, to use Peter Berger's more straightforward sociological formulation, as the "establishment through human activity of . . . a sacred cosmos that will be capable of maintaining itself in the ever-present face of chaos" (*The Sacred Canopy*, New York, 1967, p. 51).

A comparative assessment of world mythology shows, however, that such pat divisions are not always warranted, so that, for instance, the apparently fundamental contrast between chaos and cosmos may reveal more of a dialectical relationship. This ambivalence is at least suggested by the observation that the Greek root of the term *kosmos* does not so much refer to the creation of an absolute, universal, and final world order (although with Pythagoras in the sixth century BCE it will take on this sense as its basic meaning) as to the more relative and transitive idea of the "cosmetic" alteration of some more natural, plain, and primitive condition. *Cosmos* in this sense is the differentiated, deferential, and ornamental order; it is the painted and tattooed body of chaos—pretty and pleasing primarily to the eye of the beholder. One tradition's chaos, in other words, is another's cosmos, and vice versa. It depends on the vantage point, or, at least, on whether the original cosmogonic chaos is conceived advantageously. In the broadest sense, chaos stands for the root "otherness" and "strangeness" of existence and the ironic indeterminacy of all human constructs.

"Creation out of chaos," in like manner, may not just refer to the appearance of order and reality out of the void, but the creative possibility of many different orders and worlds. As the hidden sum of all potential *kosmoi*, chaos is intrinsically linked to the transformative nature of phenomenal and cultural existence. The tensed relationship of "chaos and cosmos," then, usually has sociopolitical as well as metaphysical implications, and this, it would seem, has much to do with the interpretation of chaos seen in particular myths and cultural traditions. This, of course, begs the question as to the ultimate premise of world construction, but it is exactly the fundamental existential puzzles of "something from nothing" and the interrelationship of unity and multiplicity, plenitude and limitation, that give rise to a moot diversity of possible answers and that are always addressed to some extent in chaos mythology.

Images of Chaos. Any excessive or transitional aspect of the natural world (e.g., the untamed vegetation of a jungle, the blurring of light and dark at twilight, the frenzied winds of a storm, and so on) may be taken as a cipher for the mythological chaos; but, as already suggested by the biblical allusions, the most prevalent natural metaphor for chaos is water. Given water's infinite fluidity, its protoplasmic vitality, as well as its lethal and regenerative potencies, it is hardly surprising that images of a vast ocean, a turbulent sea, or some other murky, cloudy, frothy, and misty mixture of air and water is used in many myths to depict the original broth of creation.

Common also are references to the moist darkness and foggy gloom of the precosmic condition, along with various depictions of a swirling vortex or whirlpool that links the water imagery with the more abstract ideas of the abysmal void. Other traditions speak of a primal muddle of earth and water, as in the "earth diver" myths that tell of a fragment of muddy soil (often imagined as a central hillock or mountain) rescued from the depths by some animal god or sky deity. Both in tribal cultures and in ancient civilizations there are descriptions of a watery, labyrinthine underworld of the dead, and accounts of limitless seas and rivers surrounding and penetrating the inhabited world; these imply that the dark waters of creation continue to flow around, through, and beneath the hollows of the established cosmos. Finally, there are the worldwide myths of a great flood (or of excessive heat and drought) in the distant past or apocalyptic future that are clearly charged with the cosmogonic idea of a regression to an initial state of total solvency. In these myths, the twin potency of chaos comes to the fore, since the deluge is devastating to the existing world yet simultaneously establishes the necessary precondition for a new creation.

Another important category of chaos symbolism concerns the universal imagery of an embryonic condition or womblike form. This is especially exemplified in the so-called cosmic egg myths (along with the analogous myths involving a bloody lump of flesh or a creatively fertile yet "empty" vessel, such as a pot, sack, gourd, cocoon, or drum), that stress the preexistence of some ovarian matrix within which is mysteriously harbored the structured multiplicity of all cosmic forms. While they sometimes involve an external agent of creation responsible for the production and development of the cosmic zygote, these myths often emphasize the organic conjunction of cosmogonic unity and phenomenal duality as well as the spontaneous self-sufficiency of the creation. It is in this way that the undifferentiated unity and implicate order of the cosmic egg can be said to come before any divine chicken, or, in the words of Samuel Butler, "a hen is only an egg's way of making another egg."

Theriomorphic and anthropomorphic personifications of chaos are often imagined as the gigantic and misshapen offspring of the primal waters, embryonic condition, or dark void. Recalling Hesiod's portrait, such creatures represent the individualized embodiments of chaos within the differentiated world. The actions of these creatures, moreover, show that chaos has a "history" that continuously impinges upon human history. The primary denizens of the chaos time can be categorized as: (1) dragon-serpent figures, often having composite avian-aquatic features (e.g., Vṛtra in Vedic mythology); (2) animal or hybrid man-animal trickster figures (e.g., Raven and Crow in North American Indian tradition); (3) a female demoness, a terrible mother, or chaos hag who has associations with the primal waters and "mother earth" imagery (e.g., Tiamat in Babylonian myth); (4) cosmic giant figures who, while theoretically androgynous, are often more male than female (e.g., Pangu in Chinese tradition); and (5) an incestuous brother and sister couple or a set of divine twins of ambiguous sexuality (e.g., Izanagi and Izanami in Japanese mythology). All of these chaos creatures are particularly related to cosmogonic and other origin myths, are often combined within a single mythic tradition, and are frequently portrayed in rituals concerned with significant seasonal and social transitions (e.g., worldwide celebrations of the New Year). While they may be suppressed, hidden, and transformed in various ways, all of them have popular folkloric surrogates (e.g., the revenant, demon, witch, and fool) and continue their ambivalent careers at the margins of the human world.

The underlying logic that emerges from this rapid cross-cultural survey suggests that chaos is both prior to the world as its cosmogonic source and existentially interstitial to the world as its transformative ground. Because it lies before and between any single order, or always "in relation" to any explicit world, the religious meaning of chaos remains profoundly ambiguous. By its very nature, then, chaos can be variously imagined as simply before and other than, as negatively destructive of, or as creatively challenging to, some ordered world system. Given this queasy multivalence, it is also possible to see why in cultural history any single cosmological tradition will most often seek to deny the relativity of its own vision of order by officially upholding a predominantly negative image of chaos.

Negative and Positive Evaluations. The negative evaluation of chaos commonly takes the form of a mythic and ritual scenario of combat, which was first delineated in relation to ancient Near Eastern and biblical materials. But this pattern is not restricted to the ancient Near East; it is clearly found in many diverse oral and literate traditions. While the combat pattern of myth displays many permutations depending on the particular cultural context, the basic plot is typified by the Babylonian *Enuma elish* (dating back, in part, to the second millennium BCE), which tells of the struggle between a chaos monster associated with the primal waters (i.e., the demoness Tiamat and her forces) and a triumphant sky deity responsible for some significant cultural innovation (the warrior god Marduk, who slays Tiamat, divides her carcass to form the world, and establishes the central temple and righteous rule of the city-state of Babylon).

In the *Enuma elish*, Tiamat and her monstrous cohorts represent the older, otiose generation of gods that resist the noisy, rambunctious creative activity of the younger gods championed by Marduk. From this perspective—and it is an interpretive judgment found in many other versions of the combat myth—chaos and its first generation of creatures refer to the impotency of a form that, in time, is drained of its initial creative energy. Tiamat, in other words, stands for the dangerous principle of entropy, the negative, polluting force that seeks to dissolve all new life forms back into the silent slumber and amniotic inertia of death.

The law of cosmic life in this sense is the organic rule of chaotic disintegration that is necessary for new life. Such a cyclic return to chaos may be delayed, but even the younger gods, as part of a cosmos connected by origins with the principle of chaos, are still ultimately subject to the cosmic weariness and senility first displayed by Tiamat. One way to resolve this dilemma, which is seen prominently in monotheistic traditions, is to discover the reality of a dualistic separation between chaos and an absolutely transcendent, wholly spiritual or divine order impervious to the inevitable temporal change and collapse of all cosmic forms. Monistic theories asserting the fundamental unreality or illusory nature of chaos/cosmos represent another strategy.

The combat pattern is also witnessed in many tribal traditions, although the intensity of the antagonistic relationship between chaos and the human order (and consequently the dualistic translation of this as the polarity between death and life, evil and good, demon and god) is ordinarily heightened within the context of the classical or historical religions. Thus, such traditions often suggest that ritual remembrances of the mythic skirmish primarily function to celebrate the victory over chaos and the heroic finality of some authoritarian order. There is an emphasis here on the permanent suppression of chaos, or at least a denial that the primordial enemy possesses any positive attributes. The problem, as previously indicated, is that chaos is never completely overcome in ordinary cosmic life, although for some religions a postmortem heavenly existence (as well as a climactic apocalyptic purification of the cosmos) can be interpreted as a final and total victory over chaos.

While it is true that festivals of licensed folly are found in both tribal and classical traditions, the former tend to accept more readily the instrinsic value and positive ambiguity of a periodic ritual return to a chaotic or "liminal" condition. The danger perceived by such peoples is not so much chaos in the sense of the end of order and life but rather the social entropy and tension of too much deadening order. Chaos in this "primitive" sense is the pivot of cosmic and social equilibrium, and refers to the ritual reappearance of unstructured freedom and sheer potentiality. To refresh life, chaos must be disciplined and periodically embraced, not simply defeated.

The contemporary American satirist Peter De Vries has perversely suggested that if "in de beginning was de void, and de void was vit God," then it is probably the case that one "mustn't say de naughty void" (*Blood of the Lamb*, Boston, 1962, p. 181). In like manner, even when an implacably vile and naughty chaos is portrayed—as in some versions of the combat myth—there is often the contradictory implication that the divine champions are finally congenerous with their primordial foes. The forces of chaos and the watery void are always, it seems, the enemies of righteous order yet originally and simultaneously "vit God."

Chaos, it must be said, is both naughty and nice, or to borrow appropriately enough from Rudolf Otto's classic definition of the sacred (*The Idea of the Holy*, [1917] 1958), chaos is both repulsive and attractive in its awful appeal to the religious imagination. Its repugnant aspects are clearly seen in the many worldwide adumbrations of the combat scenario, but it remains to indicate the somewhat more muted allure of chaos as a positive and beneficial religious principle. Thus, there are what might be called "pro-chaos" religious traditions that in different ways espouse chaos as a goal. Of these there are, in general, three—sometimes overlapping—possibilities: (1) chaos may symbolize the final attainment of, and fusion with, some perfectly unconditioned unity and bliss totally beyond cosmic existence—a "nothingness that glistens with plentitude" (E. M. Cioran, *The Temptation to Exist*, Chicago, 1968, p. 155); (2) chaos may be experienced as a stage, threshold, or "dark night of the soul" at the ultimate edge of cosmic reality that leads to a distinct and higher vision of the absolutely transcendent Divine; and (3) chaos may represent the experience of a more paradoxical state, or *coincidentia oppositorum*, merging transcendent unity and cosmic multiplicity and functioning not as an end, but as a healing way station for a more harmonious inner and social life.

Such options obviously relate to "mystical" forms of world religions, but it should be recalled that a positive attitude toward chaos was already forecast by tribal rituals that periodically welcomed a twilight zone back into the human fold. Because of this sympathy, mystical forms of religion (along with other types of shamanistic-ecstatic, individualistic, and revolutionary religious movements) often manifest a kind of "primitive" sentiment toward chaos that contrasts and challenges the more one-sidedly negative evaluations seen in institutionalized religion.

One instance of these contrasting interpretations within a single tradition is found in India, where some radical forms of Upanisadic, Buddhist, and *bhakti* mysticism seek a supreme integration with the sacred "emptiness" of chaos. These forms can, in turn, be distinguished from the dharmic system of rigidly differentiated castes seen in Vedic and Puranic Hinduism. Within Western tradition—and frequently in tension with mainstream Christian, Jewish, and Islamic institutions—there are also movements that stress the mystical conjugation of the divine and chaos. Conceptions arising from such movements include, in Christianity, the *Ungrund* (the "unground" or abyss that gives rise to God's self-consciousness), described by Jakob Boehme (1575–1624); the qabbalistic idea of *tsimtsum*, the creative "gap" within God, in sixteenth-century Judaism; and the alchemical *massa confusa* (the prime matter, often imagined as an egg or coiled snake) in both Christian and Islamic esoteric circles after the Renaissance. All allude in some degree to the mythological chaos as a strangely positive image.

There are other cases of this pro-chaos persuasion, but one of the more striking examples is found in Chinese tradition. In ancient China during the Eastern Zhou period (c. eighth through second centuries BCE) the mythological chaos was called *hundun*, which connoted the image of a Humpty-Dumpty-like, closed, embryonic condition or creature. Confucian thought and the ancient classics stressed the role of a succession of semidivine Sage-Kings who disciplined the chaotic forces of the natural world and carved the hierarchical order of the Middle Kingdom out of the carcass of the primitive condition of *hundun*. As a counterpoint to this point of view, the early Daoist texts suggest the existence of a veritable cult of chaos, since for these works the attainment of an authentically spontaneous and harmonious life required the rejection of conventional standards of propriety and recommended a return to an experience of primitive unity by means of the mystical "arts of *hundun*." Thus, in early Daoist texts (as distinct from the later institutionalized Daoist religion), the mythical *hundun* can be identified with the ultimate principle of the Dao as the rhythmic source and ground of life. Because of his periodic journeys in mind and heart back to the time of chaos, the Daoist mimics the seasonal regeneration of nature and the ritual regeneration of primitive cultural life and is able, therefore, to remain fresh and whole in the world.

Affirmations of the saving power of chaos have had a significant, although largely unorthodox, role to play in the history of religions; and, as broadly protesting all conventionalized truth, the cult and cultivation of chaos can be said to have inspired a whole spectrum of countercultural irruptions, "interstitial events," or "liminoid phenomena" throughout history. Because it rubs against the customary order of things, the religious, philosophical, artistic, and political "art of chaos" is always a risky enterprise, as indicated by the checkered careers of assorted Daoist mystics, Zen monks, holy fools, clownish alchemists, utopian Ranters, Romantic poets, Nietzschian nihilists, frenzied surrealists, neo-pagan anarchists, the Maoist "Gang of Four," and deconstructionist critics.

CONCLUSION. Perhaps the most responsible way to end an investigation of chaos is to refuse the temptation to parse a subject so hopelessly ironic. It is, after all, the principle of chaos that opens the abyss of indeterminacy and undecidability in all interpretive endeavors. Suffice it to say that, despite its decidedly negative public reputation, the image of chaos may be found in fact to have positive religious value. Even more important is the recognition that the idea of chaos represents one of the honored ways religions have tried to imagine the ambiguous origins and equivocal nature of existence. For this very reason the meaning of chaos in the history of religions maintains its imaginative integrity by remaining chaotic. Respecting the root topsy-turviness of chaos should not, however, prevent careful reflection on its imaginative history since, even in its most negative guise, the phantomlike shapes of chaos are directly related to the way particular religions have envisioned reality. The nature and significance of chaos, therefore, touches upon a number of issues that are central to the overall interpretive understanding and definition of religion.

SEE ALSO Cosmogony; Dragons; Egg; Water.

BIBLIOGRAPHY

Concerning the general theoretical background to the religious and philosophical understanding of chaos and order, see *The Concept of Order*, edited by Paul G. Kuntz (Seattle and London, 1968), for an eclectic selection of articles—especially pertinent are James K. Feibleman's "Disorder" (pp. 3–13) and, for the religious context, Charles Hartshorne's "Order and Chaos" (pp. 253–267) and Joseph M. Kitagawa's "Chaos, Order, and Freedom in World Religions" (pp. 268–289). See also David L. Hall's *Eros and Irony* (Albany, 1982), which provocatively analyzes cultural history in relation to varying conceptions of creation, chaos, and cosmology.

Barbara C. Sproul's *Primal Myths: Creating the World* (San Francisco, 1979) is a convenient sourcebook for the more important creation myths and includes some abbreviated, but helpful, commentary on the different religious images of chaos. More valuable for their discussions of the relation between the ideas of "creation" and "chaos" are Mircea Eliade's *Myth and Reality* (New York, 1963), which investigates the mythological and ritual meaning of chaos as correlated with the author's theory concerning the "prestige" of cosmogony, and Charles H. Long's *Alpha: The Myths of Creation* (New York, 1963), which includes some of the important mythological source materials as well as an extensive comparative examination of the structural significance of chaos imagery. For the ritual themes of "liminality" and "pollution" as suggestively analogous to the mythic idea of chaos, especially among tribal traditions, see Victor Turner's *The Ritual Process* (Ithaca, N.Y., 1977) and Mary Douglas's *Purity and Danger: An Analysis of Concepts of Pollution and Taboo* (New York, 1966).

The myth and ritual theme of combat that promotes a negative and dualistic evaluation of chaos is classically presented for ancient Near Eastern and biblical materials by Hermann Gunkel's *Schöpfung und Chaos in Urzeit und Endzeit* (Göttingen, 1895). But see also the more recent studies by Bernhard W. Anderson, *Creation versus Chaos* (New York, 1967), which emphasizes the biblical context; Mary K. Wakeman, *God's Battle with the Monster* (Leiden, 1973), which comparatively reexamines the ancient Near Eastern documentation; and Joseph Fontenrose, *Python: A Study of Delphic Myth and Its Origins* (Berkeley, 1959), which focuses on Greek tradition but draws upon a broad assortment of cross-cultural materials (i.e., Indo-European, ancient Near Eastern, East Asian, American Indian, etc.).

For studies that examine the more positive and ambiguous dimensions of chaos symbolism, along with related imagery, see, for India, Wendy Doniger O'Flaherty's *Women, Androgynes, and Other Mythical Beasts* (Chicago and London, 1980) and, for the ancient Chinese theme of *hundun*, my own *Myth and Meaning in Early Taoism: The Theme of Chaos* (Berkeley and London, 1983). In addition to their primary subject areas, both of these works comparatively cite a broad range of cross-cultural materials. Finally it is worth noting, among other possibilities, William Willeford's *The Fool and His Scepter* (London, 1969) and Mircea Eliade's *Mephistopheles and the Androgyne: Studies in Religious Myth and Symbol* (New York, 1965). The former is a fascinating literary study of the folkloric and popular embodiments of chaos in the Western tradition of the fool or jester, and the latter is a rich comparative study of different symbolic themes touching on the religious ideas of duality and the "coincidence of opposites."

NORMAN J. GIRARDOT (1987)

CHAOS THEORY.

In the *Principia* (1687), Isaac Newton gave an account of mechanics formulated in terms of precise equations of motion. Given the initial conditions of a system, it was possible to predict completely its future behavior and to retrodict its past. Newton himself did not take a purely mechanical view of the world. There was the mysterious force of gravity, concerning whose origin and nature he declined to frame a hypothesis, and he also believed that the maintenance of the stability of the solar system would require occasional angelic intervention. Newton's eighteenth-century successors, however, had different opinions, and they celebrated the triumph of mechanical thinking. Julien de La Mettrie (1709–1751) wrote his book *Man the Machine* (1748), and Pierre-Simon de Laplace (1749–1827), in his great work on celestial mechanics, believed that he had established the natural stability of the solar system, so that appeal to the hypothesis of divine assistance in its preservation was no longer necessary.

The nineteenth-century development of field theories, inspired by the insights of Michael Faraday (1791–1867) and James Clerk Maxwell (1831–1879), did not essentially change the picture. The partial differential equations of a field theory are as deterministic in consequence as are the ordinary differential equations of Newtonian mechanics. Classical physics, as this whole body of theory is called, appeared to present the image of a clockwork universe, whose Creator could be no more than the Cosmic Clockmaker.

UNPREDICTABILITIES. Twentieth-century physics, however, saw the death of a merely mechanical understanding of the world. This came about through the discovery of widespread intrinsic unpredictabilities present in physical process, of a kind resulting from the way things actually are and not simply from deficiencies in experimental or calculational techniques. These unpredictabilities first manifested themselves in quantum theory's account of atomic and subatomic phenomena. In considering, for instance, the decay of a radioactive nucleus, scientists could do no more than assign a certain probability that such decay might occur in a given period of time. Newton's predictive style of reasoning had to be replaced by a purely probabilistic approach. Quantum effects, however, were only directly observable at the level of microscopic process, remote from the macroscopic experience of everyday reality. The latter was still the realm of classical physics.

In the 1960s many scientists began to realize that even classical physics was not as tame and controllable as had been supposed. There are certainly many systems that behave as if they were reliably predictable "clocks," but there are also other systems that behave like "clouds," that is to say their behavior is so sensitive to the fine detail of their circumstances that the slightest disturbance will radically alter their future behavior. One of the pioneers in making this discovery was the theoretical meteorologist Edward Lorenz (1917–). Lorenz had been studying certain equations that corresponded to a highly simplified model of a weather system. He determined that very slight changes in the input of initial conditions into his equations would totally change the character of their output predictions. This exquisite sensitivity to detail has come to be expressed through a serious scientific joke, the *butterfly effect*: the Earth's weather systems can be in so sensitive a state that a butterfly, stirring the air with its wings in the Amazonian jungle today, could produce effects that escalate until they result in a storm over New York City in about three weeks time! Obviously, according to this model, long-term weather forecasting is never going to work; future storms are intrinsically unpredictable because no one can know about all those butterflies.

Lorenz's surprising discovery had been anticipated by the French mathematician, Jules-Henri Poincaré (1854–1912). In 1889 he published a study of the gravitational three-body problem in which he showed that it did not always possess smoothly predictable solutions of the kind that Laplace had assumed.

CHAOS THEORY. The analysis of the sensitive and unpredictable behavior of various systems has been called chaos theory. Typically its occurrence is found to arise from equations that have the properties of reflexivity (they turn back upon themselves) and nonlinearity (doubling the input does not double the output, but it changes it in a much more radical way). In principle, the equations are exactly deterministic, in the sense that an absolutely precise input will yield an absolutely precise output, but in practice, because in the real world no initial conditions can be known with arbitrary accuracy, unpredictability results from the uncontrollable effects of residual ignorance. *Deterministic chaos,* as it is often called, gives rise to apparently random behavior.

In fact, the term *chaos* was somewhat ill chosen. Systems of this kind exhibit a kind of interlacing of order and disorder, which can best be illustrated by the case of dissipative systems that feature a degree of friction acting in the process. In this case, the future behavior is not totally haphazard; rather, its possibilities are contained within an extensive though limited portfolio of options called a *strange attractor.* The word "attractor" expresses the system's rapid convergence onto this range of possibilities, and "strange" refers to the mathematically intricate shape of this form of possibility. It turns out that the latter is characterized by fractal geometry, a "jagged" range of possibilities in striking contrast to the smoothly varying expectations of conventional classical physics. A fractal presents a pattern that appears essentially the same on whatever scale it is sampled—one might think of them as saw-teeth, themselves saw-toothed; the pattern continues to infinity. The interlacing of order and disorder in chaos theory connects with an important scientific insight. It has come to be recognized that the emergence of novelty requires a state of affairs that can be characterized as being "at the edge of chaos." To be too much on the orderly side of that border would correspond to a situation possessing a degree of rigidity that permitted only rearrangements to occur but did not allow the emergence of genuine novelty. On the other hand, to be too far on the haphazard side of the border would correspond to a situation so unstable that no novelty could persist. Fruitfulness requires a subtle balance between order and openness.

METAPHYSICS. The unpredictability in chaos theory is an epistemological property, telling us that we cannot know beforehand what the future behavior of a chaotic system will prove to be. There is no inescapable connection between epistemology (what we know) and ontology (what is the case). No logical entailment links the two together. Instead, the relationship is a matter for metaphysical decision (and so, for philosophical argument).

Immanuel Kant (1724–1804) maintained that the appearances of phenomena are no guide to the nature of noumena, or the character of things in themselves. On the other hand, most scientists, either consciously or unconsciously, assume a realist position, believing that scientific knowledge gives access to the nature of the physical world.

In the case of the intrinsic unpredictabilities of quantum theory, almost all physicists have adopted a realistic interpretation of phenomena. Werner Heisenberg's uncertainty principle is not regarded simply as an epistemological principle of ignorance, but it is taken to be an ontological principle of actual indeterminacy. The fact that the work of quantum physicist David Bohm (1917–1992) has provided an alternative option, of equal empirical adequacy, which offers a deterministic interpretation of quantum phenomena, shows that the majority position is indeed a matter of metaphysical choice rather than physical necessity.

In the case of the intrinsic unpredictabilities of chaos theory, however, the majority decision has gone the other way. Most physicists disconnect epistemology and ontology, concluding that the theory shows that deterministic equations are consistent with the appearance of random behavior. "Deterministic chaos" is indeed the way they think about the theory. This absence of any willingness to question the assumption of underlying determinism seems to have been influenced by the feeling of deep respect accorded to the historic equations of classical physics.

Yet a different strategy is metaphysically possible. This would involve interpreting the unpredictabilities as signs of ontological openness. In turn, this strategy would necessitate a reinterpretation of the equations of "deterministic chaos." The sensitivity of chaotic systems to the details of their circumstances provides a way in which such a reinterpretation can be accomplished. Because of such sensitivity, chaotic systems can never properly be treated in isolation. Their vulnerability to the slightest disturbance means that they are intimately linked to their environment. Yet the experimental support that "verifies" the laws of classical physics has all been obtained through investigations of situations in which the assumption of isolatability is an acceptable idealization. Otherwise, analysis of what was going on would have been too complex to be feasible. It is perfectly possible, therefore, to make the metaphysical conjecture that the supposed laws of classical physics are actually no more than approximations of the behavior of what may be conceived actually to be a more subtle and supple physical reality. The approximation involved could be called *downward emergence,* because it would relate to behavior observable only in the idealized circumstance of an isolated system.

In this metaphysical scheme, epistemological unpredictability is the sign of an ontological openness. Such openness is not meant to imply that the future is some sort of random lottery, but rather that the causal principles involved are more than those described simply by the conventional physical picture of the exchange of energy between constituents. The unisolatibility of chaotic systems means that though such systems may be made up of components, they also must be considered holistically, in the context of their totality. The variety of the different possible patterns of their future behavior, represented by the different ways in which a chaotic system might traverse its strange attractor, are not discriminated from each other by energy differences, but by differing patterns of dynamical behavior, characterized by different expressions of "information." These considerations led to the metaphysical conjecture that chaos theory should be interpreted as affording scope for a new kind of causal agency, having the character of being top-down (influence of the whole upon the parts) and corresponding to an input of information (specification of patterned dynamical behavior). One might summarize the proposal as suggesting the concept of holistic causality through *active information.*

Two general considerations may be offered in support of such a metaphysical project. One is that the stance taken accords with the realist strategy followed by almost all physicists in the case of quantum theory. There is no apparent reason to treat quantum theory and chaos theory differently in this respect. Second, human experience of agency, of the willed execution of the intentions of the whole person, encourages the belief that an account of the causal nexus of the world is needed, an account that goes beyond simple constituent notions. The concept of top-down causality, operating through the input of information, offers the glimmer of a prospect of how one might begin the task of reconciling the scientific account of process with the human experience of agency.

The theologian may also find these ideas to be of use in thinking about divine providential interaction with creation. If the causal grain of nature is open in the way suggested, there seems to be no difficulty in believing that the Creator also interacts with the unfolding history of creation through the input of active information.

QUANTUM CHAOLOGY. At first sight it might seem that the metaphysical problems discussed above might readily be solved by combining the insights of quantum physics and chaos theory.

The behavior of chaotic systems quite rapidly comes to depend upon the details of circumstances lying at the level of Heisenberg uncertainty or below. It might seem attractive, therefore, to appeal to the generally accepted indeterministic character of quantum process to induce openness in the behavior of chaotic systems. Yet this approach faces serious difficulties, resulting from a lack of understanding of how one might consistently combine quantum theory and chaos theory. Indeed, these theories appear to be mutually incompatible.

Quantum theory possesses an intrinsic scale, set by Max Planck's fundamental constant. As a result, in quantum thinking it is possible to give a meaning to terms such as *large* or *small*. We have seen that chaos theory, on the contrary, is scale-free because of its fractal character, implying that everything looks roughly the same on whatever scale it is surveyed. Clearly some significant modification of thinking would be required to bring the two theories together. Modern physics has only a rather patchy picture of the causal nature of reality, and is far from being able to offer an integrated account, applicable at all levels.

The complexity of the considerations involved can be illustrated by the behavior of Hyperion, one of the moons of Saturn. It is an irregularly shaped piece of rock about the size of New York City, which is observed to be tumbling chaotically. Quantum effects, with their imposition of scale, would be expected to suppress this chaotic motion very effectively for so large an object. Calculations made on this basis indicate that tumbling should last for only about thirty-seven years. However another effect, called decoherence, due to the environmental influence of the radiation that bathes Hyperion, in its turn suppresses the quantum effects and explains why the moon's chaotic behavior can be expected to continue almost indefinitely. The causal nexus of the world is very complex, with a variety of effects interlacing.

SEE ALSO Physics and Religion.

BIBLIOGRAPHY

Gleick, James. *Chaos: Making a New Science.* London, 1988. An excellent introduction to chaos theory for the general reader.

Peitgen, Heinz-Otto, and Peter Richter. *The Beauty of Fractals.* Berlin, 1986. Lavishly illustrated account of fractal geometry.

Polkinghorne, John. *Belief in God in an Age of Science.* New Haven, Conn., 1998. Chapter 3 gives an account of divine action based on an ontological interpretation of chaos theory.

Prigogine, Ilya. *The End of Certainty: Time, Chaos, and the New Laws of Nature.* New York, 1997. A Nobel laureate's account of the openness of physical process.

Ruelle, David. *Chance and Chaos.* Princeton, N.J., 1991. Accessible survey by a distinguished mathematical physicist.

Russell, Robert, Nancey Murphy, and Arthur Peacocke, eds. *Chaos and Complexity: Scientific Perspectives on Divine Action.* Vatican City, 1995. Conference proceedings reporting a variety of points of view and focusing on questions of divine action.

Saunders, Nicholas. *Divine Action and Modern Science.* Cambridge, UK, 2002. A careful and comprehensive survey of current issues.

JOHN POLKINGHORNE (2005)

CHARDIN, PIERRE TEILHARD DE SEE TEILHARD DE CHARDIN, PIERRE

CHARISMA. The word *charisma* [plural *charismata*], originally used by St. Paul in the New Testament—to describe "spiritual gift[s]," has expanded its definition in the past hundred years. Academics, journalists, and the general public now use the term and its adjective, *charismatic*, to refer to any extraordinary leadership or authority. German sociologist Max Weber (1864–1920) deliberately began using the term this way in his scientific articles that were published in the early twentieth century. Weber did not foresee, however, the subsequent broad application of the word; charisma has since been attributed to religious and political leaders, dictators, cult leaders, CEOs, salespeople, popular entertainers, athletes—even race horses. Weber laments that the "attempt to explain charisma is clearly hampered by variation in the range of meaning attached to the term."

The following entry discusses the sociological applications of charisma, reviews charisma and analogous concepts that express spiritual virtuosity in world religions, and identifies the specific meanings of *charisma* and *charismata* in the New Testament and in subsequent Christian theology and ecclesiology.

CHARISMA AS A SOCIOLOGICAL CONCEPT. Max Weber, the German social thinker perhaps best known for his book *The Protestant Ethic and the Spirit of Capitalism* (1904–5), introduced the term charisma as a descriptive concept throughout his writings. He seems to assume that the reader already understands the idea; therefore, rather than defining it or explaining it, he devotes his energies to analyzing the consequences and outcomes of charismatic authority. His most frequently quoted passage comes from the posthumously published compilation *Wirtschaft und Gesellschaft*, translated by Roth and Wittich as *Economy and Society*:

> The term *charisma* will be applied to a certain quality of an individual personality by virtue of which he is considered extraordinary and treated as endowed with supernatural, superhuman, or at least specifically exceptional powers or qualities. These are such as are not accessible to the ordinary person, but are regarded as of divine origin or as exemplary, and on the basis of them the individual concerned is treated as a "leader."

Some critics have felt that Weber's definition essentially perpetuates the "great man" approach to history as developed by his predecessors, Scottish historian Thomas Carlyle (1795–1881) and German philosopher Friedrich Nietzsche (1844–1900). Yet Weber also noted, "What is alone important is how the individual is actually regarded by those subject to charismatic authority, by his 'followers' or 'disciples'." With this caveat, he emphasizes the influence, or perhaps the susceptibility, of the great person's followers.

Weber introduces charisma as one of the three basic sources of legitimate societal authority; the other two are tradition and rationalized or codified law. Weber believes charisma is the most vital, but is also inherently unstable; consequently, he places special emphasis on the question of how a charismatically-based authority can preserve continuity, especially during modern times, an era of rationalization, or an age of disenchantment (*Entzauberung*). Weber proposed *Veralltäglichung* as the mechanism to maintain charismatic authority. The term is usually translated as "routinization," although that conveys a more bureaucratic tenor than Weber intended. One type of routinization would be a direct transfer of charisma from one person to a successor, the sort of lineage charisma used to determine the succession of Dalai Lamas. The method also applies to the general idea of "sacral kingship," found in peoples of the ancient Near East, ancient China, and medieval Europe. The other, more modern form of routinization, according to Weber, took the form of depersonalization (*Versachlichung*), producing the charisma of office. In this instance, charismatic authority is more or less independent of the personal qualities of the person holding the office.

Charisma, according to Weber, tends by its very nature to be non-rationalized and upsetting to an established order. One example of this instability would be the violence inspired by the French revolutionary Maximilian-François Marie-Isidore de Robespierre (1758–1794). Yet a charismatic challenge can also be made in the name of restoring an older or more traditional order, as in the recent case of the Muslim fundamentalist and Iranian revolutionary leader Ayatollah Ruhollah Khomeini (1902–1989).

Weber's analysis, while secular, grew from his fundamentally Protestant perspective; according to this outlook, personal charisma would always hold more vitality and authenticity than a routinized charisma of office, such as that claimed by priests and bishops in the Catholic Church. In fact, Weber's immediate source for his studies of charisma was the German Protestant theologian Rudolph Sohm (1841–1917). German sociologist Werner Stark published a four-volume critique of Weber's theories; he argues that Weber, because of this Protestant orientation, was unable to appreciate the dynamics of vitally charismatic communities, whether they were composed of Catholics, Asians, or indigenous people.

A few commentators have argued that, for the sake of clarity, the concept of charisma should remain in the context of religious discourse. Most, however, have followed Weber's lead into extended usage. Most notably, Edward Shils connects the concept of charisma to a seemingly inherent responsiveness in human nature to the idea of order, whether cosmological or social. Shils argues:

> The generator or author of order arouses the charismatic responsiveness. Whether it be God's law or natural law or scientific law or positive law or the society as a whole, or even a particular corporate body or institution like an army, whatever embodies, expresses or symbolizes the essence of an ordered cosmos or any significant sector thereof awakens the disposition of awe and reverence, the charismatic disposition.

In a careful critique, his colleagues Bensman and Givant argue that Shils's analysis is so broad and all-encompassing (especially because he applies charisma both to reverence for order and to challenge to order) that the concept becomes too diffuse to be useful. On the other hand, scholars such as Tambiah have extended the concept even more broadly applying it to fetish objects such as the amulets of Theravādan Buddhist saints in Thailand and Burma.

Another approach, carefully articulated by Bryan Wilson and widely accepted, corrects the implication that charisma is something that resides in a person; rather, it emphasizes that charisma is something inherently relational or, as Downton puts it, "transactional." Someone who has no followers cannot be called charismatic. As Constantin has put it, the ecology of charisma involves the social production of sainthood. Other scholars, including Downton, Jacobs, and Post, have developed a psychoanalytic reading of the charismatic relationship, building upon the Freudian concepts of the idealized self, identity diffusion, and narcissism. These researchers see the weak ego boundaries of the charismatic leader and his or her submissive followers as perfect and dangerous complements to each other.

Considering this relationship between leader and followers caused Wilson to analyze the social construction of charisma. He hypothesized that certain types of communitarian cultures were peculiarly susceptible to charismatic relationships. In his provocatively titled monograph *The Noble Savages: The Primitive Origins of Charisma*, he refers to these cultures as tribal, or "primitive." Many other scholars, however, have investigated charisma in modern political contexts, developing case studies of leaders such Cuba's Fidel Castro, Germany's Adolf Hitler, Italy's Benito Mussolini, the United States' Franklin Roosevelt, and Iran's Ayatollah Khomeini. As these studies show, the motif of charismatic political leadership tends to be invoked as a value-neutral concept, although some writers selectively invoke such terms as pseudo-charisma or manufactured charisma.

Beyond politics, the use of the term charisma has become quite entrenched in organizational and leadership research. Some scholars in the New Leadership movement view charisma as a component of a specific leadership style. Rather than management-focused or transactional, this mode is described as transformational and visionary. Other researchers, however, question whether a vision that encompasses company and personnel management, bottom-line profits, and market strategies—no matter how creative it may be—can relate to charisma. Nevertheless, from the first appearance of the word "charismatic" in American journalism (in a 1949 *Fortune* magazine reference to John L. Lewis, head of the United Mine Workers), through references to CEOs such as Lee Iacocca of Chrysler and Steve Jobs of Apple Computer, the term has become entrenched in discourse about the corporate world.

Charisma and its Analogues in World Religions. Weber drew his use of charisma as a sociological concept from its preexisting use in biblical studies. In the Bible, the Greek term *charisma* (spiritual gift), and the root word from which it is derived, *charis* (grace or favor), are confined to the Greek translation of the Old Testament (the Septuagint) and to the New Testament. The *idea* of charismatic leadership, however, is archetypal in the Old Testament. This idea is generally signaled in the Hebrew text by the use of the noun *hen* (favor) or the verb *hanan* (to show favor). Thus, the paradigmatic image of the charismatic hero is the unlikely, apparently unqualified, figure who has received God's favor. Hebrew scripture contains many charismatic figures, such as Moses, Samson, Saul, David, Elijah, and Elisha. These chosen ones experience the visitation of *ruah*, the divine spirit; they may also become, as did Saul and David, "the anointed of the Lord." These charismatic figures overcome all odds and obstacles and achieve spectacular triumphs in the name of the Lord, as did Moses over Pharaoh (*Exod.* 14), David over Goliath (1 *Sam.* 17) or Elijah over the priests of Baal (1 *Kings* 18). David's many triumphs over Saul exemplify the dynamics of the transfer of charisma from one personage to another. The medieval and Renaissance city-state of Florence adopted David as its charismatic icon par excellence, immortalizing his image in sculptures by Donatello, Verocchio, and, of course, Michelangelo.

In terms of religious rather than political leadership, the prototypical charismatic hero in Hebrew scripture is Moses, called by God despite his own infirmities to lead the children of Israel out of Egypt (*Exod.* 1–4). After Moses returned from his theophanies on Mount Sinai (*Exod.* 19 and 32–33), so numinous was his presence and so transfigured was his face by glory that he had to wear a veil among the people (*Exod.* 34:33–35). Extraordinary as is the scriptural account of Moses, Jewish legend and folklore magnify it even further, enhancing his miraculous birth story, the signs and wonders of his commission, the events of the Exodus, and the mystery of his death.

The New Testament contains direct typological parallels to the charismatic initiations of the Hebrew scripture, in the gospel accounts of the Jesus' baptism (*Matt.* 3) and his transfiguration, in which Peter, James, and John see Jesus as radiant with light, appearing together with Moses and Elijah (*Matt.* 17:1–8). On both occasions, a voice from heaven proclaims that Jesus is "my beloved Son, in whom I am well pleased." Another parallel to the Old Testament messages indicating that someone has found great favor with the Lord is found in the angel Gabriel's well-known greeting to Mary as "full of grace" (*kecharitomene*, or exceedingly favored; *Luke* 1:28). This term marks her as a charismatic figure in her own right. It should also be noted, however, that the word *charis*, "grace," also became part of a standard early Christian salutation of "grace and peace of our Lord Jesus Christ be unto you," throughout New Testament epistolary literature (*Rom.* 1:7 and *I Thess.* 5:28). The descent of the Holy Spirit and the gift of speaking in tongues at Pentecost, as described in *Acts* 2:1–4, is the paradigm for all subsequent Christian discourse on *charismata*, or spiritual gifts.

Charisma, in the general sense of inspired religious leadership or virtuosity, is a lens through which any and all religious traditions can be viewed. In biblical tradition, the chain of charismatic leaders continues in the Hebrew scripture with the prophets, followed later by such religio-nationalistic figures as Judas Maccabaeus and Simeon bar Kokba. Bar Kokba illustrated the dark side of ultra-nationalistic and messianic charismatic leadership, since his leadership resulted in the final devastation of Jerusalem and Israel by the Roman emperor Hadrian's legions. Charismatic Judaism is a modern term given to that putative type of Second Temple Judaism, which has been led by latter-day prophets, such as Honi the Circle Maker and Hanina ben Dosa, who claim to emulate Elijah and Elisha. As Neusner describes, they "were known for miracles, primarily healing and control over the weather. . . . [This] Charismatic Judaism is judged to stand in contrast to the *halakhic* Judaism of the Pharisees and other levitical [sic] groups and to derive from Galilee." Some scholars have proposed including Jesus of Nazareth in this circle, but Neusner notes, "Though still in use, the category charismatic Judaism has lost most of its analytic force."

For the most part, rabbinic Judaism has been wary of charismatic religious leadership, especially given outbreaks of messianism such as in the unfortunate case of the Jewish mystic Shabbetai Tsevi (1626–1676), who claimed to be the savior of his people. An exception to the general rabbinic avoidance, however, is the Hasidic movement, a Jewish tradition which embraces charismatic expression. Hasidic Judaism offers a constructive response to world disenchantment, defends personal inner freedom, welcomes a collective, experiential, and experimental approach to religiosity, and accepts its *tsaddiqim* as charismatic leaders.

The nineteenth-century *tsaddiq* Menachem Mendl of Kotske, also called the Kotsker, lost his disciples when he violated Sabbath traditions, however. Although Hasidic followers are very loyal to their *tsaddiq*, they remain bound by strict orthodoxy. Hence, the *tsaddiq* is what Berger terms a "chained charismatic." Contemporary neo-Hasidim, as embodied in the *rebbe* Menachem Mendl Schneersonn, *tsaddiq* of the Lubavitch sect, combines a dedication to intense personal religious experience with "the most fervent and animated observ[ance] of Judaic rituals and *halakhic* standards."

Closer to mainstream Judaism is the elevation of scholarly study of Torah to a charisma of reason, exemplified by the *maskil*, or the religious scholar. In a Weberian analysis of the charismatic aspects of the religious kibbutz movement in modern Israel, Fishman illustrates what he calls the "charismatic power of Torah." Appropriating the idea that charisma is "anti-establishment," kibbutz leaders speak of "the holy rebellion" of following Torah, as "With a quiver of holiness, the tractor opened the new land." Fishman shows how the "primeval charisma" of the early Bund stage of the kibbutz movement was transformed under increasingly rationalized organization into an abated form of "routinized charisma" in the Commune stage.

Christian tradition, once it entered the multicultural gentile world, experienced a more common but equally conflicted tradition of charismatic religious leadership. Beginning with St. Paul's attempt to settle disputes over charismatic expression within the Christian community at Corinth, and continuing through the era of controversy between different strains of Christianity, or as some scholars would now prefer to put it between different or "alternative" Christianities, each led by competing charismatic figures, the story of Christianity can be seen as an ongoing cycle of conflicts between charismatic personages, variously labeled as heretics, prophets, mystics, reformers and cult leaders, on the one hand, and the institutional church (whether Catholic, Orthodox, or Protestant) with its proclaimed *magisterium* or teaching authority on the other. Sainthood itself, from the age of the apostles through the era of martyrdom and the Catholic Church after the Roman emperor Constantine, continuing into the age of asceticism, monasticism, and other forms of extreme religious virtuosity, became a charismatic phenomenon.

Medieval Catholics believed that the shrines and relics of saints could transfer their charisma to pilgrims and devotees. Charismatic sainthood in the early modern and modern eras has been associated with founders and reformers of religious orders (Francis of Assisi and Teresa of Ávila), apocalyptic New Age visionaries (Joachim of Flora), spellbinding preachers (Savonarola), cult leaders (Jim Jones and David Koresh), prophetic ministers and witnesses for peace (Martin Luther King Jr., Dorothy Day, Oscar Romero, and Philip Berrigan), as well as the "official" or canonized saints who were honored for their piety, good works, and attributed miracles, and church leaders, such as Pope John XXIII and Pope John Paul II, who aptly exemplify what Weber called "charisma of office."

As with Judaism, Sunnī Islamic tradition is wary of charismatic religious leadership; in fact, the religion Sunnī recognizes no formal hierarchy. As Lindholm explains, Sunnī Islam, like Judaism, is an "emissary" rather than an "exemplary" religious tradition: the religious teacher is a conveyor of the word of God, not an awe-inspiring religious virtuoso. The closest analogue to the Greek *charisma* in Islamic Arabic is the term *baraka*, for "a benign force, of divine origin, which bestows physical superabundance and prosperity, and psychological happiness." In mainstream Sunnī tradition, charisma or *baraka* was concentrated in the Qurʾān itself, and in the person of the prophet Muḥammad. As Lindholm notes, a "felt charismatic bond with the Prophet drew Muslims into the community of believers and simultaneously gave them a sense of personal spiritual expansion that is the hallmark of charismatic discipleship. At the same time. . . the actual message carried by Muḥammad modestly downplayed and even denied his own charismatic role." Nevertheless, the Prophet's life became progressively mythologized over time: Padwick comments, "increasingly, he was portrayed as pure, infallible, capable of foreseeing the future, of cursing his enemies, of splitting the moon in the sky, of ascending to heaven while still alive, and, above all, of interceding for the frightened faithful on the terrible day of judgment." This mystical life of Muḥammad became rich source material for the flowering of Islamic schools of mysticism in the Middle Ages, including the Ṣūfī traditions discussed below.

In the meantime, the great competing sect of Islam, the Shīʿah, has always been much more open to charismatic religious expression. Emphasizing the religious lineage of the Prophet's family, through the martyrs Ali and Hussein, and many subsequent saints and martyrs (*sheikhs*, or *pirs*), Shīʿahs venerate saints, travel on pilgrimages to their tombs, and participate in ecstatic "passion dramas" or commemorations. Moreover, unlike the Sunnī tradition, Shīʿahs exalt charismatic religious leaders, *mullahs* and *ayatollahs*, the most familiar of whom are the late Ayatollah Khomeini of Iran and the present Ayatollah al-Sistani of Iraq.

The other, ostensibly non-political or non-sectarian outlet for abundant expression of charismatic religious experience in Islam has been the Ṣūfī movement, originating in the late eighth century. These "friends of God," or *walī*, "did not just recite the traditions, but believed they could achieve spiritual transformation" through controlling the passions and emulating the Prophet. By the twelfth century, Ṣūfī saints (*sheikhs*, or *pirs*) began to found lodges (*tariqas*, or pathways) for students. These wayfarers, or spiritual seekers, would follow the Ṣūfī quest of seeking to know God intuitively, the potential solipsism countered by a deep-seated and self-abnegating communalism. According to Ṣūfī mysticism, Muḥammad was not only the Prophet, but the perfect man, a cosmic pivot (*qutb*) who serves to bring the world to perfection. Moreover, Lindholm notes that an invisible *qutb* "must exist for every generation, even though, as 'God's bride' he was veiled from ordinary men, and discerned only by the purified elite. . . . The only problem was that the members of the secret sanctified order could only be recognized by their charismatic aura, since they had no objective credentials."

While best known in the West through medieval poets such as Jalāl al-Dīn Rūmī (1207–1273) and New Age neo-Ṣūfī teachings, Sufism is virtually non-existent in the Middle East in the early twenty-first century. Ṣūfī lodges continue to be prominent, however, in South Asia and North Africa, in socio-cultural contexts that are more conducive to charismatic devotional practice. Werbner and Basu's 1998 anthology, *Embodying Charisma: Modernity, Locality, and the Performance of Emotion in Sufi Cults* contains essays on charismatic Ṣūfī religious practices in Pakistan, Bangladesh, Tamil Nadu, Gujarat, and elsewhere in South Asia, while the 1988 anthology edited by Donal Cruise O'Brien and Christian Coulon, *Charisma and Brotherhood in African Islam*, contains case studies of charismatic Ṣūfī lodges in East and West Africa. As O'Brien and Coulon explain in their introduction, in African Ṣūfī lodges such as the *Qadiriyya* of Nigeria, *baraka* designates "a power relation of the charismatic type" in which piety, spirituality, moral fiber, and therapeutic powers can be transmitted or inherited from person to person. Moreover, in the context of colonialism, the Ṣūfī lodges sometimes used charisma as a political instrument. Ironically, European colonial involvement had the unintended effect of enhancing the role of charismatic Islam in Africa. Coulon's essay focuses on the case study of a Senegalese woman *sheikh*, Sokhna Magat Diop, who inherited her *baraka* from her parents and who, while she has no standing in and does not even attend the local mosque, exercises religious authority over both male and female disciples through the power she gains from her mystic religious retreats (*khalw-as*).

The association of Ṣūfī saints in Africa with medicine and healing naturally suggests the survival and incorporation of pre-Islamic African cultural traditions. Kramer's *The Red Fez: Art and Spirit Possession in Africa* discusses examples of charismatic spirit possession in North and Central Africa, and their occasional connection with anti-colonial movements, although it is also true that these possession cults caused "difficulties for the politically conscious because of their anarchic character." Other religio-political movements in Africa were led by figures who claimed an Afro-Christian charisma, such as Simon Kimbangu in the Belgian Congo and, in his wake, André Matswa in the French Congo.

Indigenous African cultural traditions contain analogues to charisma in the art and ceremonies of secret societies, as well as in the role of diviners, healers, and sorcerers. Among the spirit-possessed Nuer prophets of the Sudan, Ngundeng of the Lou tribe became widely famous for his healing, cursing, trickery, and extreme feats of asceticism by which he accessed the power of the bush, and who after his death in 1906 passed on his spirit power to his son. Evans-Pritchard's classic *Nuer Religion* (1956) remains a standard source, although Beidelman has countered his view that the tradition of charismatic Nuer prophecy is a recent development. The story of African spirit possession and charismatic religious authority can also be pursued through the African diaspora, in syncretistic traditions such as Shango in Brazil, vodou in Haiti, and Santeriá in Cuba.

Analogous traditions of trance, ecstasy, divination, and other aspects of charismatic religious authority can be documented from Australia and Oceania, such as the Aborigine *karadji, wiri:nan, or bug:nja*—different tribal names for a "clever man" or spirit-man—or the concept of *mana* in Melanesia, a very overworked term that encompasses aspects of what we could call charismatic power. Malinowski argued that the cosmological vision implied by the concept of *mana* had nothing to do with the manipulations of magic, because, quoting Codrington, *mana* "acts in all ways for good and evil. . . [and] shows itself in physical force or in any kind of power and excellence which a man possesses."

Power naturally includes social leadership, authority, and mobilization. In Polynesia, people approved their rulers by appealing to their *mana*, or 'spirit-authority'. . . . *Mana* accompanied the totality of power, victory, and continued security because a mandate of an individual's rule would be confirmed by the spirit-world.

An analogous concept in Native North American vocabulary would be the Dakota term *wakan*. Malinowski quotes, "all life is *wakan*. So also is everything which exhibits power, whether in action, as the winds and drifting clouds, or in passive endurance, as the boulder by the wayside. . . . It embraces all mystery, all secret power, all divinity." Wilson illustrates Native American charismatic leadership in essays on the Ottawa chief Pontiac, the Shawnee chiefs Tecumseh and Tenskwatawa. On the other hand, Wilson argues that military leaders such as the Lakota chief Sitting Bull "were not charismatic figures: their status did not depend on some claim to supernatural legitimation."

In the context of world religion, I. M. Lewis offers perhaps the most broadly framed and all-encompassing definition of charisma, in the preface to his *Religion in Context: Cults and Charisma*:

> The beliefs and behavior conventionally distinguished as "witchcraft," "spirit-possession," "cannibalism," and "shamanism" seem at first sight to have little in common. Anthropologists and other students of comparative religion regularly treat these phenomena as totally unrelated and even mutually exclusive, objectified "things" characteristic of different cults and of distinct types and stages) of culture and society. This book takes a different view. It argues that, on the contrary, these are actually closely related expressions of mystical power, or "charisma."

This interpretation suggests a much broader use of the term than appears in most of the literature on the subject, but Carrasco has expanded it even further. He invokes charisma as a rubric for understanding and interpreting some of the most gruesome rituals of Aztec ceremonialism. Carrasco reads the bloodiest of all Aztec rituals, *Tlacaxipeualiztli*, the Feast of the Flaying of Men, as a ritual of the transfer and "redistribution of the charisma of the [ritually sacrificed] warrior throughout the ceremonial landscape of Aztec Mexico." During the ritual, the captive is slain within the ritually controlled environment of the gladiatorial stone (*temalacatl*). The priests extract from the victim's chest his still-pulsating heart (the "precious-eagle-cactus-fruit"), place it in a ceremonial bowl (*cuauhxicalli*, or "eagle-vessel"), flay and dismember the victim, and distribute his body parts to be ritually eaten. A "deity impersonator" wears the flayed skin in the name of the captor. The progress, or "career," as Carrasco calls it, of the flayed skins as they are paraded through the center and peripheries of the Aztec capital "are motivated by the Aztec need for charisma–living, pulsating gifts of gods," and the transferences and exchanges of this charisma spread the "gifts" throughout the community in a "public accumulation of charisma. "

Carrasco's interpretation draws upon López Austin's analysis of the "body as charisma" in Aztec ideology, Johanna Broda's insights into Aztec ceremonial rites, and Stanley Tambiah's analysis of the transfer of charisma in Thai Buddhism through the medium of charismatic amulets, or sacra, which radiate and impart embodied charisma to their wearers. Similarly, "in Aztec society the charisma, or the objectification of power so that it can be perceived, was expressed in a fecund variety of sacred objects, one of the most powerful being the sacrificed human body and in particular the skin and body parts of the sacrificed warrior," while the ritual cannibalism amounts to "the eating of charisma," in "a ritual of complete absorption and incorporation."

In the early twenty-first century, applying the concept of charisma to the Aztec Feast of Flaying or to Melanesian head-hunting remains controversial. Most scholars agree, however, that charisma can be ascribed to any figure who is accepted by the community to have accessed supernatural power—whether through trance, vision quest, intense prayer, heroic asceticism, or any other means—and who manifests those powers to such a degree that followers accept his or her religious authority or leadership with submissive awe or unquestioning loyalty. Such a definition encompasses the whole array of traditions of "shamanism," as the term is now globally applied. Vast literature on shamanism has accumulated in recent decades, but the indispensable starting point for research (even though it has been roundly criticized by contemporary scholars for being a-historical) is Mircea Eliade's (1907–1986) magisterial volume *Shamanism: Archaic Techniques of Ecstasy*. Grounding his survey in the cultural worlds of Central and North Asia—the presumed diffusion area for the global spread of shamanism to North and South America, Oceania, Tibet, Southeast Asia, and the Far East—Eliade discusses shamanic vocation and initiation, shamanic dream-visions, flights to the celestial worlds and underworlds, spirit combats, and healing rituals.

This virtually global context could attach charisma to a Tibetan or Navajo sand-painting ritual, or to an Inuit *tunghalik* (shaman), or to an *ajk'ij* (Quiché Maya daykeeper), or to the companion-spirits called *wayob* by the Maya and *nahualli* by the Aztec. Pre-Buddhist shamanistic traditions have survived in Korea and Japan (including *miko*, the female shamans of Japan who practice trance and spirit-possession), and have syncretically combined with popular forms of Buddhist devotion as enduring expressions of the "little tradition." Initially despised or treated as a curiosity in modern times by Japanese and Korean intellectuals, whether from the stance of modernism or Marxism, the shamanic traditions have come to be courted in Korea as vehicles of counter-hegemonic popular expression (as in *madang kut*, street protest performance), or as nationalist symbols of folk patriotism. The popular superstar Korean shaman Nami was even declared to be a national cultural treasure.

In addition to Asiatic shamanism, the so-called higher religions, or great traditions, of Asia, such as Hinduism and Buddhism, also have traditions of religious virtuosity and leadership that can be analyzed in terms of charisma. In fact, Max Weber himself devoted treatises specifically to these two great traditions, although his understanding of them has been greatly contested. The tradition of the guru in Hinduism, as a charismatic alternative to the entrenched Brahmanic priesthood, is the major case in point, beginning in the era of the Upaniṣads and continuing into the early twenty-first century. Many Hindu gurus relocated to Europe and America beginning in the nineteenth century.

The best starting point for research on charismatic religious leadership in India is the anthology *Charisma and Canon: Essays on the Religious History of the Indian Subcontinent* (2001). This work contains a theoretical essay by Heinrich von Stietencron, to whom the volume is dedicated, and case studies on medieval, premodern, and modern gurus and prophets. Among the latter are essays on such early figures as Sankara (c. 788–820), and on the transfer and institutionalization of charisma in medieval traditions derived from founding gurus, as well as case studies of more recent charismatic religious figures such as the Sikh guru Nanak, Mahatma Gandhi, and Sathya Sai Baba. Other, more theoretical essays include studies of the intersections of the charismas of texts, rituals, and performances, and the crossings between Hinduism, Ṣūfīsm, and other Islamic charismas on the Indian subcontinent.

A particularly interesting case of the failure to routinize the charisma of a guru is provided by Śrī Aurobindo. Aurobindo himself personally passed on his charisma to his associate Mirra Richard, whom he called the Spirit Mother. Not all of his followers recognized her authority, however; some of these dissidents founded an idealized anarchic community called Auroville, recognized by the Indian government. Auroville ultimately foundered in divisive legal quarrels between the Śrī Aurobindo Society and the Aurovillians over the matter of who had received the guru's charisma. In another well-known instance, that of Krishnamurti, the guru himself renounced the charisma attributed to him by his "handlers" and subsequently embarked on a "non-charismatic" career as a spiritual teacher. Other gurus who projected their charismatic leadership onto a global stage and often became embroiled in controversies and legal issues have included Maharishi Mahesh Yogi (b. 1911) and the Transcendental Meditation movement; Bhagwan Shree Rajneesh (1931–1990) and the Rajneeshpuram community; and the Rev. Sun Myung Moon (b. 1920) and the Unification Church.

Buddhism presents a very different picture of charisma compared to Hinduism. In its origins, despite the obviously charismatic personality of Siddhārtha Gautama (c. 563–c. 483 BCE), or the Buddha, the basic Theravādan teachings of the Pali canon emphasized the necessity of individual realization—as the Buddha urged in his farewell sermon, "be ye lamps unto yourselves!" The Mahāyāna and Vajrayana versions of Buddhism, however, as they spread to Tibet, China, Korea, and Japan, transformed the severe "agnostic" Theravādan teachings into the richly pietistic venerations of the buddhas and *bodhisattvas* as gods and god-like saints. In relics, statues, and *tankas* (painted Tibetan meditation cosmograms) these Mahāyāna spirit-beings freely offered access to their limitless charisma by virtue of their infinite compassion. Ironically, however, the Theravādan traditions of Southeast Asia developed the most powerful traditions of human charismatic spirituality, despite—indeed, because of—the severity of monastic dedication to the original four noble truths and noble eightfold path. Tambiah has shown that the spiritual virtuosity of the forest-dwelling monks of Thailand, Malaysia, and Myanmar (Burma), and their emblems and artifacts, became sought-after sources of charisma by the lay communities. The suggestive sociological comparisons between Theravādan monasticism and medieval Catholic monasticism, especially with regard to charismatic leadership, have been fully explored in Silber's *Virtuosity, Charisma, and Social Order: A Comparative Sociological Study of Monasticism in Theravāda Buddhism and Medieval Catholicism.*

Charisma also appears in the traditional religions of China. The early biography of Confucius (Kongzi, 551–479 BCE) by Szema Ch'ien, for example, describes the sage as having had a wondrous birth and an almost inexplicable impact on all those who met him. Confucius also attracted a dedicated band of followers in life who gathered at his grave after his death. Even more miraculous tales are told about the legendary Laozi (fl. sixth century BCE), the reputed author of the *Dao de jing*; his Daoist disciple Chuangzi composed fictional conversations in which Confucius lauded Laozi as a spiritual master. The two sages are frequently featured in Chinese landscape painting.

Scholars frequently emphasize the basically secular nature of Confucian tradition, although in practice, the Confucian shrine or temple has all the earmarks of a religious space. Interestingly, then, Feuchtwang and Mingming's recent study of four modern Chinese charismatic leaders—Wansheng, Wumu, Lin Qingbiao, and Gao Bineng—operating variously under colonial, nationalist and communist regimes, emphasizes the intersection of modern grassroots politics with traditional religious worldview. The editors point out that the word for "charisma" used on mainland China and in Taiwan is not the one in the official dictionaries; rather, it is a term that conveys "the religious aspect of being able to get things done. . . . It would be *lingyan*—said of the efficiency and responsiveness of gods who have been human, and also of the images in whom that efficacy and responsiveness has been injected by means of a ritual of initiation and insertion. If *lingyan* were transliterated back into secular English, it would be 'proven efficacy of an uncanny intelligence.'" An archaic Chinese analogue to the concept of charismatic leadership is the concept of the Mandate of Heaven: the manifest legitimation of authority, apparent to all, which passes inexorably from one leader to another.

CHARISMA AND _CHARISMATA_ IN PAULINE AND CHRISTIAN CHURCH TRADITION. Earlier sections of this article have reviewed charisma and charismatic figures in the Bible using the generalized Weberian sense of the term. But the New Testament, and specifically the Pauline corpus, introduced a much more specific use of the Greek words *charisma* and *charismata.* These terms were employed as derivatives of the root word *charis* (grace), or "spiritual gift(s)" that were bestowed by the Holy Spirit upon individuals or groups. When used in this highly specific way, the two terms are not translated but merely transliterated into English (or other modern languages) as "charism" and "charismata."

Acts 2 contains the prototypical New Testament account of the bestowal of gifts by the Holy Spirit. On Pentecost, amid a rushing sound as of a violent wind, tongues of fire come to rest upon the head of each apostle. After this event, when the apostles speak, each listener hears the words in his or her own language. Evidently, the idea that the Holy Spirit endows Christians with miraculous abilities took powerful hold among the early Christian congregations, and nowhere more so than at Corinth, where apparently there was a Christian congregation with Gnostic tendencies and also with a powerful antinomian sense of living out a new liberated Christian life. Among the hallmarks of this liberated Christian practice were women who chose to appear in church without their heads veiled and a congregation that was open to the spiritual leadership of individuals who had received that particular gift of the Holy Spirit (the gift of "speaking in tongues"). These roles would be filled spontaneously, by inspiration, rather than by the careful passing on of the charisma of office customary in the apostolic laying-on of hands or the selection of deacons.

The challenge this posed to the evolving organizational church would become evident. Paul addressed this challenge, as he had done in relation to the Judaic character of the early church. He entered decisively into the Corinthian controversy over what would be called in modern parlance a "charismatic community of worship." The key passage occurs in *1 Corinthians* 12–14, in a passage concerning spiritual gifts. Paul, trying to bring order out of creative anarchy, acknowledges the variety of spiritual gifts (speaking wisdom and knowledge, healing, working miracles, prophesying, discerning spirits, speaking in tongues, and interpreting tongues), but he emphasizes that the bestowing Spirit is one, and that such gifts are given "for the common good" (12:7) and for "edification and encouragement and consolation" of others (14:3). Paul interjects his famous hymn to love (*agape*): "If I speak in the tongues of mortals and of angels, but do not have love, I am a noisy gong or a clanging cymbal." (13:1). In this way, Paul answers those who might have exulted in their particular spiritual gift; he especially rebukes those who may have exulted in their ability to speak in tongues, now no longer meaning other languages, but rather glossolalia. He places that particular charism at the bottom of the list, as having the least benefit of edification of others, and follows it with the gift of interpretation of tongues in order to emphasize the priority of catechesis over ecstatic enthusiasm. Other passages addressing the same issue of spiritual gifts occur at *Romans* 12, *Ephesians* 4, and 1 *Peter* 4.

The contentious subject of charismatic gifts continued to trouble the Catholic Church from the Patristic through the medieval periods. It also caused concern among the Protestant reformers, who were just as concerned as the Catholic hierarchy with maintaining faith and order in their churches. German Catholic theologian Karl Rahner (1904–1984), both looking back to Patristic and Scholastic sources and at modern Church documents, outlines a more harmonious history: in the earliest period, he says, "there was no sign of hostility between ecclesiastical authority and charisms," until the second century challenge of Montanism, named for Montanus, a claimant of independent charismatic authority. Thomas Aquinas' codification of Pauline teaching was that charisms, although bestowed as a God-given grace, do not partake of the fullness of perfection of "sanctifying grace." In a sense, the Catholic church co-opted charisma by recognizing, alongside the official charisms of the priesthood and sacraments, the independent charisms of martyrdom, virginity, asceticism, monasticism, and wonder-working sainthood, although, as Rahner notes, the comprehensive history of Christian charisma has yet to be written.

For contemporary Catholic teaching, Rahner and others cite Pope Pius XII's encyclical *Mystici corporis*, which develops the Pauline metaphor of the church as the body of Christ and the people of God as a "holy people" who contribute in an "orderly" way to the teaching *magisterium* of the Church. The role of the laity and their charisms was of course further enhanced by the documents of Vatican II, subsequently scaled back in practice by the relatively conservative mood of the Catholic Church from the 1980s through the early twenty-first century. Meanwhile, however, both the Catholic and Protestant churches witnessed a worldwide phenomenon of religious renewal in the form of the charismatic movement. Based on the ecstatic practices of earlier Pentecostal and "Holiness" religious sects in the United States in the nineteenth and early twentieth century, the neo-Pentecostal movement arose within the mainstream denominations of Protestantism and Catholicism in the 1960s. The movement, based on an emotional style of worship, sometimes including glossolalia (speaking in tongues), spread rapidly during the 1980s, when it peaked in the United States and Europe. It continued to expand in Latin America, Asia, and Africa, however, where it sometimes combined syncretically with indigenous religious traditions in independent congregations, some of whom identified themselves as Christian and others who did not. A vast scholarly literature on the charismatic church movement has accumulated, including individual case histories of sects and congregations. A particularly important theoretical contribution is Csordas's *Language, Charisma, and Creativity*, a sociological analysis of the Catholic charismatic movement.

When invoked as a global concept, charisma has many different meanings. Many scholars agree with Tambiah, who asserts that there is no identifiable original charisma; rather, there are social constructions and cultural traditions of charismas, each with their distinctive worldviews, psychologies, and sociopolitical implications.

SEE ALSO Pentecostal and Charismatic Christianity; Rahner, Karl.

BIBLIOGRAPHY

The essential texts by Max Weber presenting his sociological concept of charisma can be found in reliable English translation in: *Economy and Society: An Outline of Interpretive Sociology*, 2 vols., ed. and trans. by Guenther Ross and Claus Wittich (Berkeley, Calif., 1978); and *On Charisma and Institution Building*, ed. S. N. Eisenstadt (Chicago, 1968). Important studies and revisions of Weber's ideas on charisma can be found in the following: Wolfgang Schluchter, *Rationalism, Religion, and Domination: A Weberian Perspective*, tr. Neil Solomon (Berkeley, Calif., 1989); Werner Stark, *The Sociology of Religion: A Study of Christendom*, 4 vols. (London,

1966); Charles Lindholm, *Charisma* (Oxford, 1990); Edward Shils, *Center and Periphery* (Chicago, 1975), and "Charisma, Order and Status," *American Sociological Review* 30 (1965): 199–213; Stephen Turner and Regis Factor, *Max Weber: The Lawyer as Social Thinker* (London, 1994); Bryan R. Wilson, *The Noble Savages: The Primitive Origins of Charisma and Its Contemporary Survival* (Berkeley, Calif., 1975).

Important essays are found in the following four anthologies: *Recent Research on Max Weber's Studies of Hinduism*, ed. by Detlef Kantowsky (Munich, Germany, 1986); *Charisma: Theorie/Religion/Politik*, ed. by Winfried Gebhardt, Arnold Zingerle, and Michael Ebertz (Berlin, 1993); *Secularization, Rationalism, and Sectarianism: Essays in Honour of Bryan R. Wilson*, ed. by Eileen Barker, James Beckford, and Karel Dobbelaere (Oxford, 1993), including a key essay by Roy Willis, "Charisma and Explanation," pp.167–80; and *Charisma, History and Social Structure*, ed. by Ronald Glassman and William Swatos (New York, 1986), containing the following key essays: Joseph Bensman and Michael Givant, "Charisma and Modernity: the Use and Abuse of a Concept," pp. 27–56; William Swatos, "The Disenchantment of Charisma: On Revolution in a Rationalized World," pp. 129–46.

For discussions focusing on the topic of charismatic leadership in politics, business, and religious cults, see Ann Ruth Willner, *The Spellbinders: Charismatic Political Leadership* (New Haven, Conn., 1984); David Aberbach, *Charisma in Politics, Religion and the Media: Private Trauma, Public Ideals* (London, 1996); James Downton, *Rebel Leadership: Commitment and Charisma in the Revolutionary Process* (New York, 1973); Carl Friedrich, "Political Leadership and the Problem of Charismatic Power," *Journal of Politics* 23 (1961): 3–24; Gary Wills, *Certain Trumpets: The Call of Leaders* (New York, 1994); J. A. Conger and R. N. Kanungo, eds. *Charismatic Leadership: The Elusive Factor in Organizational Effectiveness* (San Francisco, 1988); Alan Bryman, *Charisma and Leadership in Organizations* (London, 1992); Benjamin Zablocki, *Alienation and Charisma: A Study of Contemporary American Communes* (New York, 1980); Janet Liebman Jacobs, *Divine Disenchantment: Deconverting from New Religions* (Bloomington, Ind., 1989); Anthony Storr, *Feet of Clay: A Study of Gurus* (London, 1996); Hans-Georg Soeffner, *The Order of Rituals: The Interpretation of Everyday Life* (New Brunswick, Canada, 1997); Lewis Carter, *Charisma and Control in Rajneeshpuram* (Cambridge, U.K., 1990); Alan Berger, "Hasidism and Moonism: Charisma in the Counterculture," in Glassman and Swatos, pp. 83–100; Eileen Barker, "Charismatization: The Social Production of 'An Ethos Propitious to the Mobilisation [sic] of Sentiments,'" in Barker, Beckford, and Dobbelaere, pp. 181–202; and Jerrold Post, "Charisma," in *Encyclopedia of Millenialism and Millenial Movements*, ed. Richard Landes (New York, 2000): 65–69.

On the subject of sacred charismatic kingship, see James Frazer, *The Golden Bough*, abridged edition (New York, 1958); Fritz Taeger, *Charisma: Studien zur Geschichte des Antiken Herrscherkultes*, 2 vols. (Stuttgart, 1957); A. D. Nock, "Notes on Ruler Cult, I-IV," *Journal of Hellenic Studies* XLVIII (1928): 21–43; E. H. Kantorowicz, *The King's Two Bodies: A Study in Medieval Political Theory* (Princeton, N.J., 1957); and David Freidel, Linda Schele, and Joy Parker, *Maya Cosmos* (New York, 1995).

On charismatic leadership in the Old Testament and in Judaism, see (in addition to the standard commentaries): Robert Alter, *The David Story* (New York, 1999); Theodor H. Gaster, *Myth, Legend and Custom in the Old Testament*, 2 vols. (New York, 1969); Joshua Trachtenberg, *Jewish Magic and Superstition* (New York, 1970); Louis Ginzberg, *The Legends of the Jews*, 7 vols. (Philadelphia, 1909–38); Louis Finkelstein, *Akiba: Scholar, Saint and Martyr* (New York, 1970); Aryei Fishman, *Judaism and Modernization on the Religious Kibbutz* (Cambridge, UK, 1972); "Charisma," in *Dictionary of Judaism in the Biblical Period: 450 BCE to 600 CE*, ed. Jacob Neusner and William Scott Green (New York, 1996): 117–18; and Berger, "Hasidism and Moonism," cited above.

On charisma and Christian sainthood, important sources include Peter Brown, *Society and the Holy in Late Antiquity* (Berkeley, Calif., 1981); *Saints and Their Cults: Studies in Religious Sociology, Folklore and History*, ed. Stephen Wilson (Cambridge, UK, 1983); Ilana Friedrich Silber, *Virtuosity, Charisma, and Social Order: A Comparative Sociological Study Of Monasticism In Theravada Buddhism And Medieval Catholicism* (Cambridge, UK, 1995); Donald Weinstein and Rudolph Bell, *Saints and Society: The Two Worlds of Western Christendom, 1000–1700* (Chicago, 1982); Jean Séguy, "The Apocalyptic Theme in Religious Orders," in Barker, Beckford, and Dobbelaere, (203–22); and Leonardo Boff, *Liberating Grace* (Maryknoll, N.Y., 1981).

Two key anthologies address charisma in Islam. The more recent is *Embodying Charisma: Modernity, Locality And The Performance Of Emotion In Sufi Cults*, ed. by Pnina Werbner and Helene Basu (London, 1998), which includes the key essay by Charles Lindholm, "Prophets and *pirs*: Charismatic Islam in the Middle East and South Asia," 209–33. The other is *Charisma and Brotherhood in African Islam*, ed. by Donal Cruise O'Brien and Christian Coulon (Oxford, 1988), which includes the following cited essays: Louis Brenner, "Concepts of *Tariqa* in West Africa: the Case of the Qadiriyya," pp.33–52; François Constantin, "Charisma and the Crisis of Power in East Africa," pp. 67–90; and Christian Coulon, "Women, Islam and *Baraka*" pp. 113–34. An older ethnographic source is Edward Westermarck, *Ritual and Belief in Morocco*, 2 vols. (London, 1926); also see C. E. Padwick, *Muslim Devotions* (London, 1961); and the essay by Michael Kimmel and Rahmat Tavakol, "Against Satan: Charisma and Tradition in Iran," in Glassman and Swatos, pp. 101–14.

For charisma and spirit-possession in African society and religion, see Fritz Kramer, *The Red Fez: Art and Spirit Possession in Africa* (London, 1993); Dominique Zahan, *The Religion, Spirituality, and Thought of Traditional Africa* (Chicago, 1979); Benjamin Ray, *African Religions* (Englewood Cliffs, N.J., 1976); John Mbiti, *Introduction to African Religion* (Oxford, 1991); and Mary Nooter, *Secrecy: African Art that Conceals and Reveals* (Munich, Germany, 1993). A relevant classic African ethnography is E. E. Evans-Pritchard, *Nuer Religion*, 2 vols. (Oxford, 1956); also see T. O. Beidelman, "Nuer Priests and Prophets: Charisma, Authority, and Power Among the Nuer," in *The Translation of Culture*, ed. T. O. Beidelman (London, 1971). On Haitian vodou, see Alfred

Metraux, *Voodoo in Haiti* (1959), tr. Hugo Charteris (New York, 1972); Milo Rigaud, *Secrets of Voodoo* (1953), tr. Robert Cross (San Francisco, 1985); and Pierre Pluchon, *Vaudou: Sorciers Empoisonneurs* (Paris, 1987).

With reference to Oceania and the analogous concept of *mana* as charisma, see Bronislaw Malinowski, *Magic, Science and Religion* (New York, 1948); R. H. Codrington, *The Melanesians: Studies in their Anthropology and Folklore* (Oxford, 1891); Garry Trompf and Tony Swain, *The Religions of Oceania* (London, 1995); and Marshall Sahlins, *How "Natives" Think: About Captain Cook, for Example* (Chicago, 1995). For Aboriginal Australia, see James Cowan, *The Aborigine Tradition* (Rockport, Mass., 1992).

The subject of charisma in other indigenous traditions is discussed in I. M. Lewis, *Religion in Context: Cults and Charisma* (Cambridge, UK, 1986); and, for application to Aztec culture, Davíd Carrasco, *City of Sacrifice: The Aztec Empire and the Role of Violence in Civilization* (Boston, 1999). On the subject of shamanism, the indispensable starting point remains Mircea Eliade, *Shamanism: Archaic Techniques of Ecstasy* (Princeton, N.J., 1964). For shamanism among the Maya, see Barbara Tedlock, *Time and the Highland Maya* (Albuquerque, N.M., 1982); and Freidel and Schele, *Maya Cosmos*, cited above. For shamanism in Japan, see Carmen Blacker, *The Catalpa Bow* (London, 1975); and H. Byron Earhart, *Religion in the Japanese Experience: Sources and Interpretations* (Encino, Calif., 1974); and for Korea, *Shamanism: the Spirit World of Korea*, edited by Richard Guisso and Chai-shin Yu (Berkeley, Calif, 1988); Laurel Kendall's *Shamans, Housewives, and Other Restless Spirits* (Honolulu, Hawaii, 1985); and Daniel Kister's *Korean Shamanist Ritual: Symbols and Dramas of Transformation* (Budapest, Hungary, 1997).

The literature on charismatic religious leadership in India and Indian-derived traditions, Hindu and Buddhist, is vast. A key work that focuses specifically on charisma is Stanley Jeyaraja Tambiah's *The Buddhist Saints of the Forest and the Cult of Amulets: A Study in Charisma, Hagiography, Sectarianism, and Millenial Buddhism* (Cambridge, UK, 1984). Also see Robert Minor, "Routinized Charisma: the Case of Aurobindo and Auroville," in *Religion and Popular Culture: Encounters and Identities in Modern South India*, ed. by Keith Yandell and John Paul (Richmond, Surrey, UK, 2000): 130–48. Popular accounts of Indian gurus appear in Peter Brent, *Godmen of India* (London, 1972).

An important recent anthology on the topic is *Charisma and Canon: Essays on the Religious History of the Indian Subcontinent*, edited by Vasudha Dalmia, Angelika Malinar, and Martin Christof (Oxford, 2001), which includes the following cited essays: Heinrich von Stietencron, "Charisma and Canon: The Dynamics of Legitimization and Innovation in Indian Religions," pp. 14–40; Peter Schreiner, "Institutionalization of Charisma: The Case of Sahajananda," pp.155–70; Monika Horstmann, "Charisma, Transfer of Charisma and Canon in North Indian Bhakti," pp. 171–82; Dennis Matringe; "The Re-enactment of Guru Nanak's Charisma in an Early-Twentieth Century Punjabi Narrative," pp. 205–22; Dieter Conrad, "Gandhi as Mahatma: Political Semantics in an Age of Cultural Ambiguity," pp. 223–49; Smriti Srinivas, "The Advent of the Avatar: The Urban Following of Sathya Sai Baba and its Construction of Tradition," pp. 293–312; Heidrun Brückner, "Fluid Canons and Shared Charisma: On Success and Failure of a Ritual Performance in a South Indian Oral Tradition," pp. 313–27; Gian Giuseppe Filippi and Thomas Dähnhardt, "Ananda Yoga: A Contemporary Crossing between Ṣūfīsm and Hinduism," pp. 350–59; and Jamal Malik, "Canons, Charismas and Identities in Modern Islam," pp. 376–87.

Other works that focus on charisma in the context of Buddhism are: J. L. Taylor, *Forest Monks and the Nation-State* (Singapore, 1993); and Raymond Lee, *Sacred Tensions: Modernity and Religious Transformation in Malaysia* (Columbia, S.C., 1997); and Silber's *Virtuosity, Charisma and Social Order*, cited above. For China, see Laurence Thompson's *Chinese Religion* (Belmont, Calif., 1979) and *The Chinese Way in Religion* (Belmont, Calif., 1973); and on Daoism, Holmes Welch, *The Parting of the Way* (London, 1957). For modern Chinese charismatic leadership, see Stephan Feuchtwang and Wang Mingming, *Grassroots Charisma: Four Local Leaders in China* (London, 2001).

On the highly specific use of the words *charisma* and *charismata* in the New Testament, the first work that should be consulted is the entry authored by Hans Conzelmann in *Theological Dictionary of the New Testament* [TDNT], ed. by Gerhard Friedrich, tr. by Geoffrey Bromiley (Grand Rapids, Mich., 1974), vol. IX: 402–15; and the entries under "Charisma" authored by Carl Heinz Ratschow, Ludwig Schmidt, Nico Oswald, John Schütz, and Rudolf Landau in *Theologische Realenzyclopädie* (Berlin, 1981), bd. VII: 681–98; also Hans Gasper's article on "Charisma" in *Religion in Geschichte und Gegenwart: Handwörterbuch für Theologie und Religionswissenschaft*, Bd. 2, ed. by Hans Dieter Betz, et al. (Tübingen, Germany, 1957): cols. 112–120; and "Grace," in John L. McKenzie, *Dictionary of the Bible* (Milwaukee, 1965), 324–326.

For commentary on the "spiritual gifts" passage in 1 Corinthians, see: Hans Conzelmann, *1 Corinthians: A Commentary on the First Epistle to the Corinthians*, tr. James Lietch (Philadelphia, 1975); John Coolidge Hurd, *The Origin of 1 Corinthians* (London, 1965); William Orr and James Arthur Walther, *1 Corinthians: A New Translation. . . and Commentary. The Anchor Bible* (New York, 1976); David Horrell, *The Social Ethos of the Corinthian Correspondence* (Edinburgh, 1996); and Antoinette Clark Wire, *The Corinthian Women Prophets: A Reconstruction through Paul's Rhetoric* (Minneapolis, 1990).

Subsequent Catholic theological usage is covered in articles by Karl Rahner: "The Charismatic Element in the Church," in *A Rahner Reader*, ed. Gerald McCool (New York, 1985), pp. 293–6; and the entries "Charism," in *Encyclopedia of Theology: The Concise Sacramentum Mundi*, ed. Karl Rahner (New York, 1982), pp.184–6; and "Charisma," in *Lexicon für Theologie und Kirche* (Freiburg, Germany, 1958): Bd. 2, cols. 1025–30. Also see Henri Leclercq, "Charismes," in *Dictionnaire D'Archéologie Chretienne et de Liturgie*, ed. Fernand Cabrol and Henri Leclercq (Paris, 1913): vol. 3, cols. 579–98; and J.-V.-M. Pollett, "Charisme," in *Catholicisme: Hier Aujourd'hui Demain: Encyclopédie en sept volumes*, ed. G. Jacquemet (Paris, 1947), vol. 2, col. 956–9; and the following entries by R. J. Tapia: "Charism," in *Encyclopedic Dictionary of Religion*, ed. Paul Meagher, Thomas O'Brien and Sr. Consuelo Maria Aherne (Washington, D.C., 1979): 711–2; and "Charism—Given to Individual," in *New Catholic Encyclopedia* (San Francisco, 1967): vol. III, 460–2.

An important theoretical study of the charismatic movement is Thomas J. Csordas, *Language, Charisma, and Creativity: The Ritual Life of a Religious Movement* (Berkeley, Calif., 1997).

George L. Scheper (2005)

CHARISMATIC CHRISTIANITY See PENTECOSTAL AND CHARISMATIC CHRISTIANITY

CHARITY.

CHARITY. The word *charity* derives from the Latin *caritas* and can be traced to the Greek *charis.* In the Western religious tradition, *charity* has become synonymous with the Greek terms *agape, philanthopia, eleemosune* (or *eleos*), and even *philia* and *eros*; with the Hebrew words *zedakah, gemilut hesed,* and *aheb*; and with the Latin *amor, amicitia, beneficia,* and *caritas* (or *carus*). Thus, as a theoretical conception, charity has meant both possessive and selfless love, as well as favor, grace, mercy, kindness, righteousness, and liberality. In its practical application charity denotes the distribution of goods to the poor and the establishment and endowment of such social-welfare institutions as hospitals, homes for the aged, orphanages, and reformatory institutions.

Documents of ancient Mesopotamia and Egypt indicate that charity in the sense of social justice was considered a divinely decreed principle. The reforms of King Urukagina (c. 2400 BCE) were praised because "he freed the inhabitants of Lagash from usury. . .hunger. . . . The widow and the orphan were no longer at the mercy of the powerful." But ideals of charity and social justice and the principle of social consciousness developed not only because the divinity had so ordained but also because social circumstances, human oppression, and suffering demanded them. The goddess Nanshe and later the god Utu (or Shamash), the orphan's mother and father, were the guarantors of justice, cared for the widow, sought out justice for the poorest, and brought refugees shelter. King Hammurabi (d. circa 1750 BCE) sought through legislation to eliminate the social inequity that had been created by the malpractices of businessmen or other members of the enterprising Babylonian society. In ancient Egypt charity was perceived as an inner disposition toward fellow human beings and as a way to propitiate the gods for the purpose of achieving immortality, but it also meant, as *The Book of Going Forth by Day* indicates, "giving bread to the hungry, water to the thirsty, clothes to the naked and even a boat to the one who had none."

There is little doubt that early Hebrew thought was greatly influenced by the Babylonian, Egyptian, and other peoples of the ancient Near East. But the Hebrews molded what they inherited and added their own religious and social thought as set forth in their scriptures, particularly the Hebrew Bible. The Hebrew root *aheb* refers primarily to love between man and woman, but in its theological use it denotes God's love for humankind, humankind's love for God, and love among human beings. God's love for humankind is caused by its need but also by God's innate qualities (*Deut.* 10:17–18; *Ps.* 145:15–16). A person's love for God is a response to God's love, a gratitude that is also expressed through one's love for other people.

As an applied virtue, charity is expected of everyone, for whoever gives charity will be blessed by the Lord (*Deut.* 15:7–10). In medieval Judaism, almsgiving to the needy poor was considered essential. For Moses Maimonides the highest form of charity was to help the poor Israelites rehabilitate themselves by lending them money, taking them into partnership, or employing them, for in this way the desired end is achieved without any loss of self-respect for the recipient. Lending money "to the poor man so as to alleviate his poverty and afford him generous support" was considered an obligatory mode of charity. Notwithstanding occasional references to liberality toward the Gentiles, as we find in the Babylonian Talmud (Gittin 61a), in Jewish tradition "charity begins at home," and for many centuries the object of charity was the fellow Jew. Almsgiving was advocated by the Torah, but it was directed toward fellow Jews, "the descendants of the seed of Abraham. . .of pure Israelite descent." "Hard-heartedness is only found among the gentiles," as it is said that "they are cruel and have no compassion," in the words of Maimonides, who cites several passages from the Hebrew Bible in support of his views, such as Deuteronomy 15:3, Deuteronomy 15:11, Deuteronomy 14:1, and Jeremiah 6:23. The behavior of the Israelite toward the Gentile is different because Israelites are "the children of the Lord." Thus, Israelites must be generous to fellow Israelites.

In ancient Greek society charity was synonymous with love (*agape*), *philanthropia, eleos,* and *philoxenia,* and it was manifested through benevolent deeds on behalf of those in need. In a variety of forms charity is present in the earliest Greek poetry, drama, and philosophy. Compassion for the afflicted and loving hospitality were greatly emphasized in Mycenaean and archaic Greek society (1400–700 BCE). The care of strangers and suppliants was an ethical imperative because such people had been placed under the direct aegis of the divinity. Zeus became known as Xenios, "protector of strangers." This imperative is expressed in Homer's *Odyssey*: "Receive strangers regardless of who they may be; that man is sacred who welcomes a wayfaring stranger."

It was believed that when a poor person was expelled form the table of the rich or even rudely handled, the vengeance of the "gods and Furies would be visited upon the heartless miscreant," for "gods and Furies exist for beggars." To be merciful and to act out of love were common ethical admonitions. Hesiod (c. 700 BCE) was even more pronounced in his concern for the poor, though he lauded hard work and stressed moderation in the practice of charity while advocating philanthropy, righteous deeds, and reverence for the stranger and the poor. Hesiod writes that in offering hospitality one should "be neither too lavish nor too parsimonious" and that one should not "taunt anyone for his poverty which eats out the heart—even cursed poverty is sent by the immortal gods."

The most important characteristic of Greek thought as early as the Homeric age is ethical in nature. In the classical Greek city-states, whether in Athens, Thebes, or remote Acragas, charity in the sense of selfless love, almsgiving, pity, and concern for the orphan, the widow, and the elderly was widely and generously practiced. The Greek *charis* originally denoted a gift of favor inspired by the Charites (the three Graces), goddesses who personified not only physical attributes such as charm, grace, and beauty but also kindness, goodwill, and gratitude.

Under the influence of the great philosophers Socrates, Plato, and Aristotle, and of the Stoics, charity was perceived as a duty toward all "broken and destitute humanity wherever found." It was a normal and religious obligation, a social and economic need. The pre-Socratic philosophers had held that justice and equality were principles of divine origin. Pythagoras, in particular, emphasized equality and harmony in social relationships. "All human laws are nourished by one, which is divine," adds Heraclitus. There are no political or economic laws, only moral laws.

For the great thinkers of the fifth and the fourth centuries BCE, doing good for the sake of goodness was the only moral ground for charity. A cardinal principle of Greek religion and social thought was that the divinity is good and the cause of good. Plato writes that for "the cause of evil we must look in other things and not in God" (*Republic* 2.18). Neither God nor man can be really good without in some way communicating his goodness to others. Aristotle adds, "If all men vied with each other in moral nobility and strove to perform the noblest deeds, the common welfare would be fully realized, while individuals also could enjoy the greatest of goods, inasmuch as a virtue is the greatest good" (*Nicomachean Ethics* 9.8.7). Thus, "the conferring of a benefit where a return is not sought is morally acceptable, and the value of the gift is not to be judged by its intrinsic worth but by the spirit of one giver." Aristotle insisted on the idea of "the cheerful giver." Being good meant doing good.

Poverty should not be tolerated, for, according to Aristotle, it leads to the erosion of a democratic state and constitutes the basis of social revolts (*Politics* 6.3.4). Professional beggars were banned by Homeric society and Solon's and Plato's Athens as well as by Sparta. Nevertheless, poverty was accepted as a fact of life, and charity a means for its relief. The Greeks invoked curses upon men "who failed to provide water for the thirsty, fire for anyone in need of it, burial. . . , [hospitality, or] directions for a lost stranger."

Much of Greek religious and social thought was adopted by such Roman thinkers as Cicero and Seneca, who in their exposition of *caritas* and *beneficia* echo Aristotle's teachings and the Greek understanding of *philanthropia*. Whether for the sake of honor or other motives, much charity was practiced in the Roman Empire, especially in the *alimenta*, measures introduced to assist orphans and poor children. Initiated by private philanthropists, the system was adopted by the imperial government after the reign of Nerva (CE 96–98).

Charity in Christianity is synonymous with *agape*, or love. Whether it was a new commandment, as Christ had taught (*John* 13:34), is controversial. One thing is certain: Christianity proved more ecumenical and proclaimed that "there is neither Jew nor Greek, there is neither slave nor free, there is neither male nor female. . .but all [are] one in Christ Jesus" (*Gal.* 3:28). In its practical application charity went beyond Jews, Greeks, and Romans. It stressed that "love is of God, and he who loves is born of God and knows God. He who does not love does not know God; for God is love" (*1 John* 4:7–8). God's love requires that human beings love one another (*1 John* 4:11). There is no better account of the nature and the fruits of Christian charity than the thirteenth chapter of Paul's First Letter to the Corinthians. Charity is defined as the love of God expressed through the God-made-man event in Christ and as humans' love of neighbor, the solvent of hatred of the enemy.

In postapostolic and medieval Christian thought, charity was the will of God, an act of propitiation to a means of eternal reward, a social obligation, and an act of righteousness. The motives might be selfless altruism, desire for fame, inner satisfaction, or a desire to imitate the divinity. Byzantine society, its government and church, monastic communities and individuals, made charity a major concern and established numerous institutions for the sick, orphans, widows, indigent, and others in need of rehabilitation and assistance. The Greek Christian tradition of charity, as selfless love and as acts of alms deeds, was established by the great Church fathers of the fourth century. To possess and practice charity is to imitate God, who is absolute and who has manifested love. Thus, Gregory the Theologian's admonition: "Prove yourself a god. . .imitating the mercy of God. There is nothing more godly in man than to imitate God's beneficent acts" (Homily 14).

Charity was also a cardinal feature of medieval Western European society, which was guided by the Church there. Augustine of Hippo, who exerted a major influence on the ethics of Latin and Western Christianity, writes that charity must be an inward quality of a person before it can be expressed outwardly as love and alms deeds. One cannot love others if one does not love oneself. Selfless charity works no evil. Eleemosynary deeds without selfless charity are not a guarantee of divine favor. God considers not the person to whom the gift is given, but the spirit in which it is made (*The City of God*, Book 21, 27). And Caesarius of Arles, nearly a century of later, added that "if you possess charity [in the sense of selfless love], you have God; and if you have no God, what do you possess?" (Homily 22).

Charity as a synonym for love, either as God's love for man or man's reciprocal love for God expressed in acts of love for fellow men, a conception central to the Western tradition, is not explicitly stated in Buddhism, Hinduism, or Islam. Nor do we find definitions of charity similar to conceptions of *philanthropia* (Plato, Plutarch) or *agape* (New Testament). The Buddha's four noble truths *(catvāri-ārya-satyāni)* inherently include love and compassion toward fellow human beings. Buddhism sees suffering as a universal reality, but a reality with a cause. Suffering may be relieved through application of three principles: *metta* or *maitri*, loving kindness actively pursued; *karuna*, compassion or mercy, which does not repay evil with evil; and *mudita*, a feeling of approval of other people's good deeds. These principles find their expression in works of social welfare, including public works projects and the maintenance of hospitals and shelters or hospices.

The meaning of charity in Hinduism depends upon the interpretation of *dharma*, "the primary virtue of the active life of the Hindu." *Dharma* is the inner disposition and the conserving Idā, while the action by which it is realized is known as *karman*, which is expressed in physical, verbal, and mental forms. The physical forms consist of good deeds such as hospitality, duties to wife and children, and assistance to those in need. Verbal charity is identified with proper or gentle speech and courteous behavior. Mental charity is synonymous with piety.

Hinduism had given a primary position to personal ethics. And the Upaniṣads clearly indicate that each person is responsible for his economic or social condition. If individuals are moral and perfect and economically safe, society will ultimately be perfect. Thus, personal charity is enjoined to a degree that makes organized charity unnecessary.

If a human is a creature good by nature, then humans can develop ethics of benevolence, justice, or righteousness. Jainism, in particular, which stresses self-cultivation more than social involvement, sees self-perfection as the best means of alleviating social misery. The value of charity as an act of benevolence is judged by the degree of personal cultivation and sacrifice involved. It is a spontaneous and personal virtue, instinctive rather than acquired. "To love your neighbor as yourself" is inherent in the Vedic formula of unity with the absolute self, "That art thou" *(tat tvam asi)*. Because one loves oneself, one is bound to love one's neighbor, who is not different from oneself.

Charity in Islam depends on the belief in an omnipotent God, master of humankind, which not only receives God's mercy but is always in danger of incurring his wrath. Thus, mankind needs to serve God by means of good works, including almsgiving, both voluntary offerings (*sadaqat*) and legally proscribed ones (*zakāt*), kindness, and good treatment of parents, orphans, and the elderly. A summary of Islam's moral code bearing on charity is found in the Qur'ān's seventeenth *sūrah*, lines 23–30. "The Lord has decreed . . . kindness to parents. . . . Give the kinsman his due, and the needy, and the wayfarer. . . . Come not near the wealth of the orphan. . . ." These and other similar admonitions constitute the outward signs of piety, the means of expiating offenses, and the path to ultimate salvation. The specific forms of charity in Islam were also given institutional expression through endowments known as a *waqf*.

Whether or not influenced by religious traditions or humanistic motives inherent in natural law, there are in today's world hundreds of national and international organizations dedicated to some forms of charitable activity. A few of the better known charitable agencies would include CARE, Oxfam, UNICEF (United Nations Children's Fund), and Civil Society International.

CARE, an international consortium of member states, is devoted to distribution of food and clothes to the needy but also dedicated to the reduction of poverty among the world's poorest countries. Like CARE, Oxfam, in addition to practical daily charities, tries to find solutions to overcome poverty and improve health. It responds to needs of countries that have suffered from earthquakes, floods, and epidemics.

UNICEF, under the aegis of the United Nations, is committed to charity affecting poor and destitute children. Health care, improved nutrition, clean water, education are some of UNICEF's priorities.

Among its various missions, the works of Civil Society International includes aid to the poor, the orphaned, the elderly, the sick, and the disabled.

SEE ALSO Almsgiving; Grace; Hospitality; Zakāt.

BIBLIOGRAPHY

Berry, Thomas. *Religions of India: Hinduism, Yoga, Buddhism.* New York, 1971.

Berry, Thomas. *Buddhism.* New York, 1975.

Betsworth, Roger G. *Social Ethics. An Examination of American Moral Tradition.* Louisville, Ky., 1990.

Brenner, Robert. *Giving: Charity and Philanthropy in History.* Somerset, N. J., 1996.

Chaudhuri, Nirad C. *Hinduism.* London, 1979.

Constantelos, Demetrios J. *Byzantine Philanthropy and Social Welfare.* New Brunswick, N.J., 1968.

Constantelos, Demetrios J. *Poverty, Society and Philanthropy in the Late Medieval Greek World.* New Rochelle, N.Y., 1992, pp. 39–52.

Constantelos, Demetrios J. "Zakāt in Islam and Philanthropia in Greek Orthodox Christianity." In *Kairos. Epistemoniki Epeterida Panepistemiou Thessalonikis,* no. 4, pp. 693–702. Thessaloniki, 1994.

Conze, Edward. *Buddhism: Its Essence and Development.* Oxford, 1951.

Hands, A. R. *Charities and Social Aid in Greece and Rome.* Ithaca, N.Y., 1968.

Haramantides, Agathangelos, ed. *He Martyria tes Agapes (The Witness of Love).* Athens, 2001.

Ilchman, Warren, and Edward L. Queen, eds. *Philanthropy in the World's Traditions.* Bloomington, Ind., 1998.

Jeffrey, Arthur, ed. *Islam: Muhammad and His Religion.* New York, 1958.

May, Herbert G., and Bruce M. Metzger, eds. *The New Oxford Annotated Bible with the Apocrypha,* rev. ed. New York, 1977.

May, William F., and A. Lewis Soens Jr., eds. *Ethics of Giving and Receiving. Am I My Foolish Brother's Keeper?* Dallas, Tex., 2000.

Minkin, Jacobs. *The World of Moses Maimonides.* New York and London, 1968.

Nikhilananda. *Essence of Hinduism.* Boston, 1948.

Nygren, Anders. *Agape and Eros,* rev. ed. Translated by Philip D. Watson. Philadelphia, 1953.

Oates, Mary. *Catholic Philanthropic Tradition in America.* Bloomington, Ind., 1995.

Olasky, Marvin. *Tragedy of American Compassion.* Wheaton, Ill., 1995.

Organ, Troy. *The Hindu Quest for the Perfection of Mani.* Athens, Ohio, 1970.

Pétré, Héléne. *Caritas: Étude sur le vocabulaire Latin de la charité chrétienne.* Louvain, Belgium, 1948.

Pickthall, James B., ed. *The Ancient Near East.* 2 vols. Princeton, N.J., 1973–1975.

Quell, Gottfried, and Ethelbert Stauffer. "Agapao, Agape, Agapetos." In *Theological Dictionary of the New Testament,* edited by Gerhard Kittel, vol. 1, pp. 21–55. Grand Rapids, Mich., 1964.

Scott, Anthony, ed. *Good and Faithful Servant.* Crestwood, N.Y., 2003.

Singer, Amy, and Mine Ener, eds. *Poverty and Charity in Middle Eastern Contexts.* Albany, N.Y., 2001.

Smith, Bradford, and Sylvia Shue, eds. *Philanthropy in Communities of Color.* Bloomington, Ind., 1999.

DEMETRIOS J. CONSTANTELOS (1987 AND 2005)

CHARLEMAGNE (c. 742–814), also known as Charles the Great and Carolus Magnus; king of the Franks (768–800) and first emperor of a revived Empire in the West (800–814). For three years after the death in 768 of Pépin III (the Short), the *regnum Francorum* was divided between his two sons, but in 771 the elder, Charlemagne, became sole ruler, although not without opposition. His unusually long reign was of major importance in the history of western Europe and the Christian church and the Latin culture associated with it. In 773–774, responding to papal appeal, Charlemagne invaded the Lombard kingdom, annexed it to his own and then visited Rome, where he was ceremonially received and given an "authoritative" text of church law. On a second visit (781) his two sons were baptized by the pope and given subordinate kingdoms.

Involuntary conversions and the establishment of an organized church followed Charlemagne's military victories over the Saxons (beginning in 772), but Saxony was for years beset by bloody and destructive rebellions. Nevertheless, the monastery of Fulda, the bishopric of Würzburg, and new settlements such as Paderborn became centers of organized missionary activity. In 785 the leaders of Saxon resistance accepted baptism, although it may be doubted whether many Saxons followed their example until further pressures, including severe punishment for "pagan" practices, had been employed. The conversion of the Frisians was simultaneously being achieved, although with less violence.

A succession of campaigns (led first by the king himself and then by subordinate commanders) against the Asiatic Avars west of the middle Danube and against Slav tribes to their south ended Avar independence and opened up the region to missionary activity from Salzburg and Aquileia. Campaigns were also conducted intermittently against northern Slav peoples, who then received clergy from the new Saxon bishoprics, and late in the reign the Franks were also in both military and peaceful contact with the Danes. In the southwest, a campaign into Muslim Spain in 778 ended disastrously, supposedly at Roncevalles in the Pyrenees. Subsequently, however, local commanders gradually extended Frankish authority over the predominantly Christian lands as far south as the Ebro (the region of Navarre and the later Catalonia).

Charlemagne inherited a concept of kingship that emphasized the obligation and legitimacy of extending the Christian faith by force of arms while also securing it at home. To these ends came also the utilization of the church hierarchy as well as lay officials as a means of social control; both groups were expected to give effect to the legal rules and pious exhortations expressed in capitularies promulgated in Latin by the assemblies that brought together bishops, abbots, and leading laymen in 779, 789, and frequently in later years. The king's personal devotion to *religio Christiana,* with which he is credited by his biographer Einhard (writing c. 829), was essentially expressed in observance of the externals of worship as provided by the court chaplains, with little regard for spirituality or personal morality. Even before 779, however, church authorities were making the king aware that among his responsibilities should be the encouragement of learning (*eruditio*) as a basis for more effective government and the more correct understanding of the texts on which the Christian faith was grounded.

Peter of Pisa, remembered as the person who taught Charlemagne "Latin grammar," and other learned Italians joined the still-itinerant court. Around 780 Charlemagne seems to have invited churches and monasteries to supply copies of books in their possession; this was the beginning of a court library that by 790 included a range of patristic writings as well as a remarkable collection of pre-Christian classical texts. A small number of manuscripts, mostly liturgical, were decorated in a distinctive and eventually influential style by resident artists. The circle of scholars was notably enlarged by the arrival of Alcuin and other Englishmen and of the Visigothic Theodulf (later bishop of Orléans). Theodulf is generally accepted as the principal author of the remarkable first example of court scholarship, the so-called *Libri Carolini,* composed and revised (792–793) to counter the current Byzantine and papal concept of images and the adoration due them.

The heterodox views of Spanish ecclesiastics on Christ's relationship with God the Father (adoptionism) were condemned in Frankish councils and challenged in detail by Alcuin, apparently with ultimate success. An increasing concern also with unity of practice in the church was expressed in the provision of standard service texts. However, the "Gregorian" sacramentary sent from Rome was in fact ill suited to the needs of churches in Francia and had to be supplemented; in practice, mixed and divergent books were in use for private and public devotion and study for many decades.

In the 790s the court was providing adolescents (including laymen, e.g., Einhard) who had received a basic education elsewhere with more advanced instruction based on the antique tradition of the "liberal arts" and especially the trivium of grammar, rhetoric, and dialectic. The importance to church and kingdom of correct Latin was emphasized in a royal circular letter, but since this Latin was to be pronounced as spelled, a gap was opened between the language of scholarship and worship on the one hand and everyday speech in Romance (as well as Germanic) regions on the other. Serious attempts were nonetheless made to communicate the elements of the faith to the laity in their vernacular.

Charlemagne and his court increasingly remained at Aachen, where an impressive group of palace buildings including an octagonal chapel was built. This was accompanied by speculation on the nature of the Frankish king's authority over an *imperium Christianum.* In 799 Pope Leo III was the victim of a violent attack in Rome, and he appealed to Charlemagne; the latter's representatives cleared the pope of unspecified charges leveled against him, but final judgment on his attackers was reserved for the king. In the summer of 800 Charlemagne visited Saint-Martin's, Tours, and its abbot, Alcuin, and then journeyed via Ravenna to Rome. On December 23 he presided over an assembly at which the participating bishops declared that they could not pass judgment on the pope. The latter took an oath of innocence, and the Roman rebels were dealt with. On December 25 at mass in Saint Peter's the pope crowned Charlemagne, as he prayed and those present acclaimed him, "Augustus, great and powerful emperor of the Romans."

The ceremonies had obviously been carefully planned to recognize Charlemagne's unique authority and achievements, but he may well have been unprepared for the precise way in which he was made "emperor in the West." Even if he was worried about the reactions of the imperial court at Constantinople, however, his new title was very soon used in official documents and was subsequently carried on a distinctive new coin. Moreover, the almost annual promulgation of capitularies after 802 and his complaints that many were regularly ignored suggest that the emperor felt that he had assumed new responsibilities toward his Christian subjects.

The resident scholars and advisers were now predominantly younger men; the older generation had left the court for bishoprics and abbeys, and offered their views on doctrinal matters, in writing or at special assemblies. In 806 Charlemagne planned to divide his territorial empire, probably without passing on the title. The death of two of his sons left him with a single heir, Louis, and in 813 he was personally crowned by his father at Aachen. In the same year councils were held simultaneously in different parts of Francia to make more detailed regulations for church organization and practice. When Charlemagne died on January 28, 814, he was buried at Aachen in a tomb whose form and simple inscription are known only from Einhard. His death did not constitute the sharp break often supposed: some of the old courtiers remained and there was continuity of artistic activity at the new emperor's court. Louis did, however, have a deeper concern for Christian spirituality, and the fullest flowering of Carolingian learning took place when the territorial and political unity of the empire was already past history.

BIBLIOGRAPHY

The major historical, literary, and documentary sources for the reign of Charlemagne have been edited, some of them several times, in the various series of the "Monumenta Germaniae Historica" (1826–). The Council of Europe Exhibition devoted to Charlemagne and his heritage that took place at Aachen in 1965 was the occasion of the publication of the magnificent *Karl der Grosse: Lebenswerk u. Nachleben,* 4 vols. plus index, edited by Wolfgang Braunfels and others (Düsseldorf, 1965–1968), whose 2,400 pages provide authoritative accounts of almost every aspect of the man and the age. The history of the church is dealt with in volume 1 (organization), volume 2 (learning), and volume 3 (art and architecture). A concise semi-popular account is my *The Age of Charlemagne,* 2d ed. (New York, 1973), to be read in conjunction with my " 'Europae Pater': Charlemagne and His Achievement in the Light of Recent Scholarship," *English Historical Review* 85 (1970): 59–105. The most recent English-language account of the reign is Rosamond McKitterick's *The Frankish Kingdoms under the Carolingians, 751–987* (New York, 1983), chaps. 3, 4, and 6.

DONALD A. BULLOUGH (1987)

CHASTITY. A central virtue in the Greek, Roman, and Christian traditions, chastity (Gk. *sōphrosunē,* Lat. *castitas*) reflects the values of purity, blamelessness, and order. The term is sometimes misunderstood as referring to asceticism or sexual abstinence, but the relationship between chastity and renunciation is one of tension and in many cases opposition. In its original context in the ancient Mediterranean, chastity is marked by a connotation of fertility and reproduction, and this has persisted in Christianity across its history, though with important and complicating developments described below.

GREEK *SŌPHROSUNĒ* AND ROMAN *CASTITAS*. From archaic times, the Greek poets had celebrated the virtue of mental balance and self-mastery, *sōphrosunē*. *Sōphrosunē* stood for the moderation and good sense of an Odysseus, in contrast both to *megalopsychia*, the high-minded boldness and honor of a warrior hero such as Ajax or Achilles, and to *hybris*, the unwary pride that could only lead to *nemesis*, destruction. Where men are concerned, it is not until fifth-century Athens that this idea of balance begins to include emphasis on moderation (though by no means rejection) of the sexual appetites. For women, however, the sexual loyalty and self-control implicit in the male version of *sōphrosunē* is explicit in the earliest sources. The *Odyssey*'s description of Penelope—in her faithful rejection of suitors when her husband Odysseus was believed dead, and her initial caution on being told that he had been seen alive—was accepted by all later writers as the classic example of the virtue.

In their origin, the values of sound-mindedness, moderation, and balance denoted by *sōphrosunē* bear no relation to Greek ideas of ritual purity (*hagnotēs*) and pollution, but by the early fifth century BCE purity had come to have a moral connotation, and this had repercussions for *sōphrosunē*. Plato (d. 347 BCE) developed this further, according a role to *sōphrosunē* in his idea of *katharsis* (purification). In later antiquity, Neoplatonists such as Plotinus (d. 269/70 CE) and the Christian Gregory of Nazianzus (d. 389 CE) would redefine *sōphrosunē* as a means of purifying the soul and elevating it towards union with the One. But for the orators of the classical and Hellenistic periods, masculine *sōphrosunē* was essentially a civic virtue, the quality allowing the good citizen to cooperate with his peers and rivals on behalf of the common good. At the same time, *sōphrosunē* is the most common virtue attributed on memorial reliefs and tombstones for Greek women, both married and unmarried.

Different aspects of *sōphrosunē* correspond to distinct Latin equivalents. The male civic virtue of self-control corresponds to *temperantia* and *moderatio*, virtues which are commended by the Latin orators in terms similar to Greek praise for *sōphrosunē*. But chastity (*castitas*), the domestic or sexual aspect, comes from the Latin vocabulary of ritual purity. Corresponding to the Sanskrit Śiṣṭah (instructed) and originally denoting conformity to religious law or rite, the adjective *castus* (from which *castitas* is derived) acquired, in classical Latin, an ethical dimension through its similarity with the participial form of *careō* (to lack). In writers such as Cicero (d. 43 BCE) *castus* could be taken to mean "without fault," attested alongside the earlier meaning of ritual conformity or expertise. The range of meanings of *castus* is reflected in its antonym *incestus*, which denotes both ritual and moral impurity. For Roman women, *castitas*, like *sōphrosunē*, was the virtue of wisdom and fidelity in marriage, with a strong connotation of fertility (and specifically of producing children whose paternity was not in doubt). The chaste, fertile wife was a prized figure in Roman society, a cherished icon of *romanitas*.

CHRISTIANITY. It is through Latin Christianity that *castitas* exerted its greatest influence in the European tradition, and developments in late antiquity reflect an emerging tension over how to define the virtue. From earliest times, both *sōphrosunē* and *castitas* had been applicable to both the married and the unmarried. To the degree that restraint of sexuality was an important dimension, this was in service of the civic values of monogamy and fertility. A virgin's chastity foretold its own fulfilment at the next, married, stage of life in harmonious domesticity and the production of legitimate offspring. Earliest Christianity did not challenge the ancient definitions of *sōphrosunē* and *castitas*. Although many New Testament and early Christian writers perceived an eschatological value in sexual continence (*enkrateia*), the second-century author of the Pastoral Epistles of the New Testament embraces a traditional Greek idea of *sōphrosunē* as a civic virtue, and even the proponents of *enkrateia* do not define it as a synonym of *sōphrosunē*. But in the fourth and fifth centuries Christian ascetic writers sought to redefine *sōphrosunē* and *castitas* in ascetic terms. In the case of Latin Christianity this would have significant repercussions up to and beyond the Reformation.

A minority of Latin Christian writers, among them the brilliant but famously intemperate biblical scholar Jerome (d. 420 CE), argued that it was the ascetic, not the legitimately married householder, who best exemplified the virtue of *castitas*. The more traditionally-minded Ambrose of Milan (d. 397 CE) found the winning formula, reasserting the ancient compatibility between premarital and marital aspects of *castitas*, yet describing *castitas* as taking three forms. Conjugal, widowed, and virginal *castitas* were, however, ranked according to an ascending order of virtue, in terms which evoked the New Testament hierarchy of the thirty-fold, sixty-fold, and hundred-fold fruits. This definition would endure through the Latin Middle Ages, and the Benedictine monastic commitment to poverty, chastity, and obedience draws on this "inclusive" definition. Perhaps the most important medieval contribution is that of Thomas Aquinas (d. 1273 CE), who defined *castitas* as an aspect of the cardinal virtue of temperance, moderating the sense appetite of both body and soul. (While the less perfect virtue of continence strengthens the soul against the assaults of passion, *castitas* operates at a deeper level, tranquilizing the impulse itself. *Castitas* thus sanctifies both the married couple in legitimate sexual union, and the ascetic in sexual renunciation.)

Since the early Modern period, the Protestant Reformed Churches have returned to a more ancient emphasis on the chastity of the married in their refusal to endorse clerical and monastic sexual renunciation. Catholic theology up to the Second Vatican Council (1962–1965) followed Aquinas in defining virginity as the highest form of chastity, while post-Vatican II theologians have asserted the moral value of sexual union in marriage as a sign and expression of conjugal and procreative charity.

JUDAISM AND ISLAM. Biblical, Hellenistic, and Rabbinic Judaism do not have a concept precisely analogous to *sōphrosunē* and *castitas,* though sexual virtue is understood as a matter both of ritual purity and of ethics. Although ancient Israelite warriors had been required to practice sexual abstinence in preparation for battle, throughout Jewish history the procreative union of legitimate marriage has been prized as a response to the biblical dictum, "Be fruitful and multiply." In early Israel, the high priest was a married householder, and his family's behavior was scrutinized along with his own for sexual and ethical purity. Up to and including the Rabbinic period, polygyny meant that sexual fidelity to a single partner was required in women rather than in men; adultery, for example, was defined as extra-marital union involving a married woman. (A married man was not legally an adulterer unless his partner was another man's wife.) Fertility and secure paternity seem to have been the object. Though a wife's sexual virtue was highly valued, this aspect is not persistently singled out for praise in Biblical literature. The good wife of *Proverbs* 31, for example, whose price is celebrated as having been above that of jewels, was in fact praised for her shrewd business sense rather than for sexual virtue, though the latter is likely to have been taken as a given.

Islamic ideas surrounding sexual virtue are broadly compatible with those of Biblical Judaism. This is reflected in the idea that marriage, householding, and reproduction are a central ethical duty for men as well as women, and in the acceptance of polygyny, with the corresponding asymmetry in the definition of male and female sexual virtue. Legitimate conjugal sexuality includes periods of abstinence such as the fasting days of Ramaḍān or the pilgrimage to Mecca, but permanent sexual continence is not favored.

Most literature on chastity in Islam deals with its legal aspect, the regulation of sexual activity for both men and women in conformity with notions of ritual purity or *ṭahārah.* Female seclusion, *haram* (Eng., "harem"), along with specific forms of dress designed to signal married and particularly wifely chastity, are practiced in culturally diverse forms (and in varying degrees) in many Islamic communities, underlining the cultural centrality of sexual virtue. (*Haram,* the area wherein things prohibited to immortality are present, is a term also used to describe the sanctuary area around mosques and religious sites such as the Kaʿbah in Mecca.)

According to the Qurʾān *iḥtisham,* modesty in personal appearance, is required of both men and women. For women, the adoption of severe forms of self-covering such as facial veiling, particularly by groups living in proximity to Muslim or non-Muslim communities whose female dress is comparatively relaxed, can serve as a means of marking a community's boundary, and even of broadcasting its dissent from a dominant culture in politically charged terms. By contrast, in South Asia seclusion of women, commonly referred to in English as "purdah" (*pardā* in Hindi and Urdu, from the Persian *parde,* "curtain") occurs in both Muslim and non-Muslim contexts, including Christian communities.

Hinduism. The broad array of South Asian traditions, sects, and religious-philosophical schools which are referred to under the umbrella term 'Hinduism' share no single defining feature. In general it can be said that their mode of defining the relationship between sexual and ritual purity is decidedly different from that of the religious traditions springing from the ancient Mediterranean empires. However, in the case of Islam a millennium of proximity between Islam and indigenous traditions in South Asia has not been without effect (so, for example, South Asian Muslim and Hindu approaches to purdah often reflect mutual influence).

While European writers such as Max Weber have tended to emphasize the traditions of the world-renouncing ascetic in South Asia in terms which highlight its superficial commonalities with European asceticism, these tradition are neither so dominant in South Asian religious practice, nor so similar to their European counterparts, as has been implied. Important in this respect is the fact that in South Asian traditions the purity/impurity binary coexists with the binary of auspiciousness and inauspiciousness. Despite their structural similarity, these binaries often work across each other rather than in parallel. Thus sexuality is generally defined as impure rather than pure, but as auspicious rather than inauspicious. The identification of *śakti,* the generative and vital principle, with women means that maternity, like sexuality, is seen as powerfully auspicious, and as a positively valued arena of female agency, at the same time as childbirth and the sexual act are ritually impure. Though householdership is perceived as normative for women in most South Asian traditions, with devotion to the health, longevity, and prosperity of husband and sons the core duty (*dharma*), it is generally held that for both men and women *dharma* may be defined according to life-stage. Post-reproductive asceticism for women is widely valued, with the rejection altogether of the householder *dharma* for women a minority position. Since antiquity, a strand of tradition has venerated the Hindu widow as an exemplar of perfect wifely loyalty and devotion if on the death of her husband she became *satī* by throwing herself on her husband's funeral pyre. The practice, never widely attested, nonetheless is intermittently attested as having elicited considerable religious devotion. It continues sporadically to the present, and has been the subject of international concern and controversy in the aftermath of the death of Roop Kanwar, a young Rajasthani widow, in 1987.

Bibliography

Ahmed, Leila. *Women and Gender in Islam: Historical Roots of a Modern Debate.* New Haven, Conn. 1993.

Babb, Lawrence A. *The Divine Hierarchy: Popular Hinduism in Central India.* New York, 1970.

Banerjee, Pompa. *Burning Women: Widows, Witches, and Early Modern European Travelers in India.* New York, 2003.

Cooper, Kate. *The Virgin and the Bride: Idealized Womanhood in Late Antiquity* Cambridge, Mass., 1996.

Denton, Lynn Teskey. "Varieties of Hindu Female Asceticism." In *Roles and Rituals for Hindu Women,* edited by Julia Leslie. London, 1991.

Hawley, John Stratton. *Sati, The Blessing and the Curse: The Burning of Wives in India.* New York, 1994.

Jamison, Stephanie W. *Sacrificed Wife, Sacrificer's Wife: Women, Ritual, and Hospitality in Ancient India.* New York, 1996.

North, Helen. *Sophrosune.* Ithaca, N.Y., 1966.

Peristany, J.G., ed. *Honour and Shame: The Values of a Mediterranean Society.* Chicago, 1966.

Mandelbaum, David G. *Women's Seclusion and Men's Honor: Sex Roles in North India, Bangladesh and Pakistan.* Tucson, Ariz., 1988.

Marglin, Frédérique Apffel. "Power, Purity, and Pollution: Aspects of the Caste System Reconsidered." *Contributions to Indian Sociology* n.s. 11:2 (1977).

Marglin, Frédérique Apffel. "Female Sexuality in the Hindu World." In *Immaculate and Powerful: The Female in Sacred Image and Social Reality.* Edited by Clarissa W. Atkinson, Constance H. Buchanan, and Margaret R. Miles. Boston, 1985.

Matthews, Victor H., and Don C. Benjamin, eds. "Honor and Shame in the World of the Bible." *Semeia: An Experimental Journal for Biblical Criticism* 68 (1994).

Moulinier, Louis. *Le pur et l'impur dans la pensée des Grecs.* Paris, 1952.

Roper, Lyndal. *The Holy Household: Women and Morals in Reformation Augsburg.* Oxford, 1989.

KATE COOPER (2005)

CHENG HAO

CHENG HAO (1032–1085) and his younger brother Cheng Yi were two of the most important thinkers of Song dynasty (960–1279) China, and their writings in such fields as cosmology, philosophy, self-cultivation, ethics, ritual, governance, and classical studies influenced the course of East Asian thought for centuries. Much of their work was transmitted orally and compiled by their students, who did not always attribute a particular saying to either of the brothers but simply credited it to "Master Cheng." Hence one cannot always distinguish between the thought of Cheng Hao and Cheng Yi, who nonetheless shared many ideas in common.

HISTORICAL CONTEXT. The Chengs spent much of their lives near the capitals of Luoyang and Kaifeng and were personally acquainted with other important thinkers from that region of central China, such as Shao Yong (1011–1077), Zhou Dunyi (1017–1073), and Zhang Zai (1020–1077). The Chengs hailed from a family that had served as scholar-officials for the Song rulers since the beginning of the dynasty. Their first teacher was their mother, nee Hou, who was herself highly educated, and they were later influenced by her attitudes toward folk religious beliefs. One of the official residences the Cheng family occupied was initially believed by the household staff to be inhabited by monstrous apparitions. When Ms. Hou calmly dismissed such notions, the "hauntings" ceased.

In their teens, the Cheng brothers studied for a year with Zhou Dunyi. Zhou understood the universe as a living entity that is always in motion, producing and reproducing creatures endlessly, and he apprehended its energies so intimately that he refused to cut down the weeds that grew outside his window. The Chengs displayed a similar affinity for living things: Cheng Hao, like Zhou, did not clear the weeds outside his window, and Cheng Yi in his early twenties wrote an essay describing his efforts to save small fish from the predations of hungry cats and human beings. (Later in life, however, Cheng Yi deemed his youthful writings overwrought.)

As a young man, Cheng Hao attended the Imperial Academy in Kaifeng. In that city he met the scholar Zhang Zai (who was also his relative) and impressed Zhang with his understanding of the *Book of Changes*, an ancient and arcane divinatory text that had inspired many layers of philosophical commentaries. In his early twenties Cheng Hao attained the "presented scholar" *(jinshi)* degree, a mark of scholarly achievement that also facilitated his entry into government service. He served in various official capacities in Shaanxi, Jiangsu, Sichuan, and Henan and earned a reputation as an effective practitioner of good governance who educated the people and promoted their welfare.

Like his mother, he tried to disabuse the common people of folk beliefs he perceived as harmful to their well being. When he first took up his post in Huxian in Shaanxi, for example, rumors abounded of a statue of a stone Buddha whose head emitted rays of light. This at once fascinated and frightened the local populace. But after Cheng Hao ordered a monk to cut off the Buddha's head and bring it to his office so that he, too, could witness it the next time it glowed, the radiance stopped. The Chengs were also critical of some forms of contemporary Buddhism, which they decried as false teachings that intimidated the common people with fears of death. Moreover, they claimed, Buddhists were either too wanton or too rigid, tended to be selfish, were afraid of life and death, and were disconnected from reality.

Cheng Hao served at court in the capital of Kaifeng for a time in his thirties, but his promotion of idealistic models of good governance—sage rulers who embodied humaneness, righteousness, and integrity—eventually clashed with those of reformist political rivals such as Wang Anshi (1021–1086). He was again stationed in various postings outside the capital, and during a sojourn in Luoyang he spent considerable time with his neighbor Shao Yong, who was known for his prognosticatory writings on the *Book of Changes.* In the later years of their careers, the Chengs focused more on teaching and developed a following of disciples, among them the scholars Lü Dalin (1040–1092), Xie Liangzuo (c. 1050–c. 1120), You Zuo (1053–1123), and Yang Shi (1053–1135). Cheng Hao became known as Master Mingdao, or "The Master who Illuminates the Way."

COSMOLOGY. Cheng Hao's cosmology was greatly influenced by Zhang Zai's *Western Inscription (Ximing),* a short text that describes the universe as a large family wherein a human being is a child of heaven and earth, all people are one's siblings, and all creatures are one's companions. One's own body is coextensive with the powers of the universe, and one's nature is at one with its operations. Cheng Hao was inspired by this vision but particularly emphasized the role of human values in sustaining the subtle consubstantiality of the individual and the cosmos. In his discussion of humaneness (*ren*, also translated as benevolence), Cheng Hao asserted that people who could understand this integral virtue of humaneness could do nothing less than form one body with all things and participate fully in the operations of the universe. Following the classical thinker Mengzi, he believed that human beings were also responsible for adhering to the cardinal virtues of righteousness *(yi),* ritual propriety *(li),* wisdom *(zhi),* and trustworthiness *(xin)* and implementing them with integrity (*cheng*, or sincerity) and reverence (*jing*, or seriousness). A profound pattern of an underlying commonality that Cheng understood as "principle" (*li*, or pattern) permeated human nature (*xing*), heaven and earth, the Way (*dao*), and, in fact, all things. Principle was one, but it manifested itself in the world in multiple ways.

Human nature was bestowed by heaven, and being in accord with that nature was the Way, an ineffable path beyond the realm of physical form. Human nature was essentially good, but Cheng Hao (unlike his brother) did not disallow that evil (*e*) was not part of principle or the nature. Humans were also susceptible to negative deficiencies in their *qi* (the vital energy, vital force, or material force that suffuses all living things), flaws that were metaphorically described as muddied, turbid, or clouded conditions within what otherwise would be clear water. Desires led one astray, but they could be readily overcome with reverence and humaneness. The Chengs spoke often of Confucius's idea of "controlling the self and returning to ritual" (*Analects* 12:1), a program that itself constituted humaneness. All solutions to the problem of excessive desires were already complete within one, provided one only made the effort to eliminate selfishness.

The Chengs understood ritual at one level as an innate sense of propriety and decorum that guided daily human interactions; it was also the body of institutionalized, regularized rituals and ceremonies performed at occasions that required communication between human beings and the numinous powers that suffused their world. Cheng Hao warned that one should not become too involved in the external particulars of rites; it was more important that one turn inward and understand their principle. Rites would then channel human emotions in appropriate directions and provide direction for the nature. But Cheng Hao was nonetheless noted for his superb grasp of ritual institutions, and the Chengs were sought out for their expert advice on such matters. They were versed both in historical minutiae and contemporary ritual usages and were consulted on such matters as sacrificial offerings, rites of passage, burial practices, geomancy, monstrosities and prodigies, and the construction of altars and temples to various kinds of spirits.

The Chengs' views on ghosts *(gui)* and spirits *(shen)* derived especially from classical texts such as the *Book of Changes*, the *Book of Odes* (*Shijing*), and the *Book of Rites (Liji),* particularly the chapter of the *Rites* that became known independently as the *Centrality and Equilibrium* (*Zhongyong*, or *Doctrine of the Mean*). They understood spirits as manifestations of the operations of heaven and the transformative powers of creation, which is not to say that spirits were merely depersonalized forces. The Chengs implicitly understood ancestral spirits as individual entities that should be fed and given places to rest during sacrificial offerings. When presenting sacrificial offerings, for example, food must be divided into individual portions, for the spirits cannot merge into one to enjoy them. These two perspectives—that spirits are cosmic powers and particularized entities—are not necessarily contradictory, given Cheng's larger vision that principle is one but its manifestations are many.

Although Cheng Hao's teachings were proscribed for a number of years after his death, his spirit was posthumously elevated in rank in the thirteenth century and was given offerings thereafter in Confucian temples throughout East Asia.

See Also Cheng Yi; Li.

Bibliography

English translations of selected works by the Chengs are included in Wing-tsit Chan's *A Source Book in Chinese Philosophy* (Princeton, 1963), his *Reflections on Things at Hand* (New York, 1967), and William Theodore De Bary and Irene Bloom, eds., *Sources of Chinese Tradition from Earliest Times to 1600*, 2d ed. (New York, 1999). Excerpts from their writings on spirits were included in the thirteenth-century text translated by Wing-tsit Chan as *Neo-Confucian Terms Explained* (New York, 1986), but their views on matters religious have otherwise been little studied in the West. One of the best secondary studies of their work is still A. C. Graham's *Two Chinese Philosophers: Ch'eng Ming-tao and Ch'eng Yi-ch'uan* (London, 1958), which was republished in 1992 as *Two Chinese Philosophers: The Metaphysics of the Brothers Cheng* (La Salle, Ill.) and translated into Chinese by Cheng Dexiang as *Er Cheng xiongdi de xin Ruxue* (The Neo-Confucianism of the Cheng Brothers; Zhengzhou, China 2000). Graham is a philosopher rather than a scholar of religion, and his treatment of spiritual beings reflects that perspective. For biographical information, see *Sung Biographies* edited by Herbert Franke (Wiesbaden, 1976) and the *RoutledgeCurzon Encyclopedia of Confucianism* edited by Yao Xinzhong (London, 2003), which includes entries on specific concepts and thinkers noted above. Recent articles include Yong Huang's "Cheng Brothers' Neo-Confucian Virtue Ethics: The Identity of Virtue and Nature," *Journal of Chinese Philosophy* 30 (2003): 451–467; Wai-ying Wong's "The Status of Li in the Cheng Brothers' Philosophy," *Tao: A Journal of Comparative Philosophy* 3 (Winter 2003): 109–119, which explores the notion of ritual; and Thomas Selover's "Forming One Body: The Cheng Brothers and Their Circle," in Tu Weiming and Mary Evelyn Tucker, eds., *Confucian Spirituality*, vol. 2 (New York, 2004 pp. 56–71). For Chinese sources, see the entry on Cheng Yi.

Deborah Sommer (1987 and 2005)

CHENG YI (1033–1107), like his older brother Cheng Hao, was one of the most important figures in the history of Chinese thought. He spent most of his life accompanying his father or brother in their official postings, establishing academies and teaching disciples.

Historical Context. His early years followed the same direction as those of his brother. An essay he composed while still a student at the Imperial Academy in Kaifeng received accolades from examiner Hu Yuan (993–1059), who offered him a position there. Cheng soon became noted for his scholarship, and he attained the "presented scholar" (*jinshi*) degree in his twenties. This achievement provided him entry into government service, but for most of his life he showed little interest in official rank or the remuneration it offered.

But in his fifties his fame as a learned scholar and person of character earned him for two years the position of lecturer on the classics to the twelve-year-old Emperor Zhezong (r. 1086–1100)—or more accurately, to the boy's regent, Empress Dowager Xuanren (d. 1093). Cheng admonished them to model themselves after the sage rulers of antiquity and adhere to moral values. His uncompromising nature gained him enemies, whereas his writings and lectures attracted many followers from high office and distant places. He spent much of his life in the Luoyang region, but in 1097 he was banished to Sichuan for several years, and his teachings were prohibited. There he completed a commentary on the *Book of Changes* around 1099 (the only major work he compiled himself), and according to local folk tradition he wrote it while living in a cave in Fuling (near modern Chongqing). He was pardoned a year before his death, but the political situation was still such that only a handful of his followers ventured to attend his funeral.

Influences and Cosmology. Like his brother Cheng Hao, Cheng Yi was much influenced by the classical thought of such texts as the *Analects* of Confucius, the *Mengzi,* the *Book of Rites* (of which the *Great Learning* and *Centrality and Equilibrium,* or *Doctrine of the Mean,* are two chapters), and the *Book of Changes.* The brothers shared many ideas about cosmology and human nature, but Cheng Yi did not allow that negative tendencies, or evil (*o,* a term that means "not good" but that does not necessarily carry the sense of moral turpitude or depravity present in some Christian notions of evil), were originally present in human nature. They might nonetheless be present in the *qi,* or vital energy, that suffused all things. The human mind or heart (*xin*) was originally good, and human beings were endowed with moral virtues that allowed them, with effort, to overcome the potential selfishness of human desires that might arise as they interacted with the external world. Through reverent attentiveness (*jing*), integrity (*cheng*), and adherence to ritual, they could realize their true natures, abide in the Way (*dao*), and become sages. Underlying all the multiple phenomena of the universe in its myriad fluctuations was a oneness or common pattern called principle *(li)* or heavenly principle (*tian li*). Principle was a notion present even in early classical texts, but the Chengs made it integral to a system of thought that emphasized an essential commonality between the human realm and the operations of the cosmos.

Sagehood was accessible to all and need not be reached through book learning. In his early essay "On What Master Yan Loved to Learn," Cheng Yi emphasized that thousands of Confucius's disciples had mastered texts, but only Master Yan, or Yan Hui, was lauded for his love of learning—learning to become a sage. For Cheng Yi, learning to be a sage meant looking inward and developing one's own inherent moral potential (which was informed by the same principle that directed the natural growth and fruitfulness of the cosmos) to the point where the process became spontaneous and joyful. One learned by following the *Great Learning*'s program of attentively "investigating things" (*ge wu;* "things" meaning material things, living things, and events) to elucidate their principles.

The greatest numinous power in the Chengs' cosmological system was heaven (*tian*), which they understood as a life-giving, impartial, and generous source that bestowed on human beings their nature. The human mind was moreover one with the mind of heaven; human principle, one with the principle of all things. *Heaven* was one term given to a range of ineffable powers that existed in various valences. When once asked about the meaning of the ancient expression "August Heaven, the Lord on High *(haotian shangdi),*" Cheng Yi replied that when one spoke of such things in terms of form and substance, one called it "heaven"; in terms of a master, "Lord"; in terms of function, "ghosts and spirits"; in terms of subtlety, "spirit"; and in terms of nature and emotion, *"qian,"* the first hexagram of the *Book of Changes,* which denoted primal forces of the cosmos.

Cheng Yi was consulted on many matters that in the West would be called religious: people looked to him for answers to their questions about divining with tortoiseshells, selecting burial sites, performing mortuary rites, constructing ancestral temples and sacrificial halls, conducting sacrificial offerings and other rites, avoiding wanton sacrifices and spectral monstrosities, understanding the nature of spiritual beings and souls, and interpreting ancient ritual texts. He was consulted not only for his understanding of archaic rituals but also for his views on how one might interpret ancient models for contemporary needs. Cheng Yi determined a particular usage's appropriateness by the criteria of rightness or righteousness *(yi),* principle *(li),* and ritual propriety (*li,* a character different from the *li* of principle). He allowed that most, but not all, ancient usages were informed by principle.

Cheng Yi believed that commemorative votive offerings *(ji si)* presented to spiritual beings were not merely a product of human endeavor but were ultimately rooted in heavenly principle, the heavenly nature, and the human mind. Even otters, wolves, and eagles made sacrificial offerings, he asserted, following long-held beliefs about animal behavior described in the *Book of Rites,* so how much more should one expect humans to show respect to their ancestors and recompense their kindness with food offerings. Votive rites were patterned on the processes of the cosmos itself as manifested in the hexagrams "Dispersion" (*huan*) and "Congregation" *(cui)* in the *Book of Changes.* Offerings presented at ancestral temples countered the centrifugal forces of dispersion and congregated the minds of human beings into a unified direction. Whereas Cheng Yi acknowledged that the principles of votive offerings were difficult to fathom, he criticized his wealthy contemporaries for enjoying this-worldly pleasures at the expense of properly maintaining ancestral temples. Such people were no better than birds and beasts.

Cheng Yi was often queried about ghosts (*gui,* a term that in antiquity usually referred to ghosts of deceased human beings) and spirits (*shen,* which in ancient times might refer to human spirits but could also refer to numinous powers of all kinds). He was well known for stating that they are "creative transformations" (*zao hua*), a notion taken from the *Book of Changes.* This is not to say that for Cheng Yi spiritual beings did not exist, but that they were very subtle. When asked whether one could resonate with and invoke the spiritual and luminous realm (*shen ming*), Cheng Yi replied that it was possible; filial piety (*xiao*) and sibling amity *(di)* allowed one to communicate with ancestral spirits. Filiality and amity were precisely the "principle" of the spiritual realm.

Reverence was the proper attitude toward spirits with which one had no kin relationship, such as the spirits of mountains and rivers, which were thought to produce rain. Cheng Yi found irreverent the folk practice of worshipping sculpted anthropomorphic images believed to represent those powers; it was not the wood or clay images that produced rain, he said, but the mountains themselves, and it was they, not the images, that deserved reverence. Cheng Yi criticized other folk, Buddhist, and Daoist practices and beliefs that he believed were far removed from classical antecedents. He derided the Buddhists for "hating things" and attempting to remove themselves from the matrix of continuous creation and found laughable, for example, the Daoist (*Daojia*) notion that each sense faculty of the human body has its own spirit.

Cheng Yi's views on matters religious were influential throughout Asia for centuries. By the thirteenth century, both he and his brother were themselves venerated as sages, and they received commemorative offerings in Confucian temples throughout China and East Asia until modern times. Cheng Yi outlived Cheng Hao by over twenty years and left behind a much larger body of work, mostly in the form of oral teachings recorded by his followers.

See Also Cheng Hao; Li.

Bibliography

One of the most complete studies of Cheng Yi's thought in English is still Ts'ai Yung-ch'un's "The Philosophy of Ch'eng I: A Selection of Texts from the Complete Works" (Ph.D. diss., Columbia University, 1950), which contains a chapter on his notions of spirits. For Cheng Yi's commentaries on the *Book of Changes,* see Tze-ki Hon's "Northern Song 'Yijing' Exegesis and the Formation of Neo-Confucianism" (Ph.D. diss., University of Chicago, 1992). Cheng Yi's notion of principle is discussed by Kidder Smith, Jr., in his "Ch'eng I and the Pattern of Heaven-and-Earth," in *Sung Dynasty Uses of the I Ching,* edited by Kidder Smith, Jr. et al. (Princeton, 1990). Cheng's Yi's views on sage rulers are examined in Marie Guarino's "Learning and Imperial Authority in Northern Song China (960–1126): The Classics Mat Lectures" (Ph.D. diss., Columbia University, 1994). For other English sources on the Chengs, see the entry on Cheng Hao.

Selected primary sources by the Chengs are introduced in *A Sung Bibliography* edited by Yves Hervouet (Hong Kong, 1978). Recent editions of their major writings include the four-volume *Er Cheng ji* (Collected works of the two Chengs; Beijing, 1981) and the *Er Cheng yi shu, Er Cheng wai shu* (Transmitted writings of the two Chengs, Miscellaneous writings of the two Chengs; Shanghai, 1992). Although research in English on the Chengs little addresses their thought on religious subjects, some Chinese studies do. See Jiang Guanghui's "Lixue de guishen guan" (Concepts of ghosts and spirits in the School of Principle) in his *Lixue yu Zhongguo wenhua* (The School of Principle and Chinese culture; Shanghai, 1994): 367–384; Li Rizhang's *Cheng Yi Cheng Hao* (Taipei, 1986); Pang Wanli's *Er Cheng zhexue tixi* (The Cheng's philosophical system; Beijing, 1992); and Wang Binglun's "Guanyu er Cheng pochu shisu mixin sixiang shiji shuping" (On the Chengs' eradication of folk superstitious thought) in *Luoxue yu chuantong wenhua* (The Luo School and traditional thought), edited by the Henan Province Philosopher's Association (Henansheng zhexue xuehui; Zhengzhou, 1989): 228–239 and Deborah Sommer's "Er Cheng xiongdi lun jisi yu guishen" (The Cheng brothers on sacrifice and spirits) in Cheng Dexiang, ed., *Er Cheng xinrujia xinlun* (New studies of the Neo-confucianism of the Cheng brothers; Zhengzhou, c. 2005).

Deborah Sommer (1987 and 2005)

CHEN-JEN *See* ZHENREN

CHEN-YEN *See* ZHENYAN

CHEROKEE RELIGIOUS TRADITIONS.

The Cherokee, an Iroquoian-speaking people, refer to themselves as *Aniyvwiya,* "the Real People," or as *Anitsalagi,* their traditional name. Today, they comprise the largest Native American group in the United States. According to the 2000 U.S. Census, approximately 281,060 people identify as being of Cherokee descent, and 260,000 of those are federally recognized tribal members. Over 230,000 Cherokee are citizens of the Cherokee Nation, located in Oklahoma. The Eastern Band of Cherokee Indians, in North Carolina, has approximately 12,000 members and the United Keetoowah Band has about 16,000. Cherokee citizens can be found living throughout the United States as well as within the jurisdictional boundaries of the Cherokee Nation and the Eastern Band of Cherokee Indians.

The Cherokee originally occupied territory now comprising Tennessee and parts of Alabama, Georgia, Kentucky, North Carolina, South Carolina, and Virginia. In response to American expansionism, groups of Cherokee began emigrating to Arkansas Territory as early as 1810. In 1817 the U.S. government finalized the first treaty that called for cessions of Cherokee land in exchange for a tract of land in Arkansas for those who voluntarily emigrated west. Nineteen years later, in 1836, the U.S. Senate ratified the Treaty of New Echota, which authorized the removal of the Cherokee. Beginning in 1838, the United States sent troops, militia, and volunteers to forcibly remove the Cherokee to Indian Territory, which later became the state of Oklahoma. Those Cherokee who marched west endured hunger, extreme cold, inadequate clothing and shelter, and sickness. One-quarter of those removed, or approximately 4,000 Cherokee, died on what became known as the Trail of Tears. Only a few remnant groups, totaling approximately 1,400, avoided the removal west.

Prior to removal, the Cherokee had an agriculturally based society. They followed a ceremonial cycle linked to agricultural seasons, such as the first green grass and the first harvest of green corn. The Cherokee grew two types of corn as well as beans and squash, peas, potatoes, and pumpkins. They also gathered wild foods such as fruits and nuts, and they collected honey. The women, in the matrilineal and matrilocal world of the Cherokee, had primary responsibility for the fields and wild plant foods. Men hunted deer and other game during the fall months and assisted the women at planting and harvesting time. Husbands moved into the homes of their wives, who held proprietary responsibility for the houses, fields, and children. Such control afforded women an important place in the economic, political, and religious life of the Cherokee, which depended, in great part, upon the production of corn.

The Green Corn ceremony, the most important ceremony among the Cherokee, celebrated the harvesting of corn in late July or August. Everyone abstained from eating the new corn until they had performed the ceremony. The Green Corn ceremony marked a time of purification and renewal of individuals and society. Women swept out their homes, cleaned their fireplaces, and discarded old food and clothing. The men swept out the council house and removed the old ashes from the central hearth, whitewashed the buildings, and brought in new dirt for the ceremonial square ground. Purification rituals included fasting, scratching the body, vomiting induced through the use of emetics, and a type of bathing referred to as "going to water." Renewal involved restoration of harmony through forgiveness of wrongs and reconciliation of differences. The council also met during the Green Corn ceremony to consider national interests for the coming year.

Rituals and observances during the Green Corn ceremony reinforced the beliefs and values of the Cherokee and insured the continued well-being of the community. The ceremony recognized Selu or Corn Woman who, through the sacrifice of her body, gave the gift of corn to the Cherokee. Selu and Kanati ("The Lucky Hunter") symbolized the interdependent and complementary aspects of Cherokee society, including female and male roles, agriculture and hunting, and birth and death. They provided models for human behavior.

Cherokee regularly engaged in purification rituals before and during major events including the Green Corn ceremony, in order to restore balance and harmony to society. Scratching involved drawing a comb-like instrument across the arms, legs, and torso of the body until the blood flowed, thus purifying the body of impure or bad blood. Scratching was followed by "going to water," or submerging oneself four times in a moving stream to reinforce health and strength and to ensure long life. The men also purified themselves with White Drink, commonly referred to as Black Drink by Euro-Americans because of its dark color. Beloved women typically prepared this emetic, which the men consumed in great quantities and then vomited up, thus cleansing themselves.

During the Green Corn ceremony and other ceremonials the Cherokee drew upon elements from the Above and Below World to purify and renew themselves and This World. Fire, the symbol of purity, is understood by the Cherokee to be the messenger between human beings and the Provider. The smoke of the fire carries prayers upward. The Cherokee also use tobacco in their rituals to disseminate the power of their thoughts. According to Cherokee belief, the power to create resides in thought, and tobacco that has been made efficacious through thoughts that have been spoken or sung is, in turn, burned during rituals for protection or curing.

Approaches to Ethics and Daily Conduct. The Cherokee emphasis on maintaining harmonious or peaceful relations between human beings and between humans beings and animals or supernatural beings is reflected in Cherokee social conventions. The Cherokee reinforce amiable relations by sharing their time and material goods with each other. They reinforce harmony among themselves through acts of reciprocity and redistribution, of giving to others. The idea is that if everyone gives, everyone will receive according to their needs. Thus, one who has been fortunate in obtaining goods would share those goods with others less fortunate.

The structures of Cherokee society also serve to maintain balance between individuals, towns, and outsiders. Historically, their clan system, which consists of the Wolf, Deer, Bird, Paint, Blue, Wild Potato, and Long Hair clans, determined social, political, and religious responsibilities. Cherokee society was also organized on the basis of either the White or the Red Path. The White Path is the path of peace and the Red Path is the path of victory or war. In historical times the state of affairs (peace or the disruption of it) determined the leadership of Cherokee towns. During times of peace, White leaders oversaw the daily concerns of Cherokee society. However, during times of conflict, Red leaders became prominent in the decision making. Certain highly respected men and women, referred to as Beloveds, were charged with mediating for peace and mitigating bloodshed. They were expected to extend hospitality to all who came to their homes or their Mother Towns, beloved sacred places. The most well-known beloved Cherokee woman is Nancy Ward, a Supreme Beloved Woman, who protected American captives and military personnel as well as Cherokee during the American Revolution. Balance was maintained during wartime through a division of responsibility based on council status, gender, and age. War councils declared war and the women's council decided how war was to be conducted. Red leaders (young warriors) and White leaders (elders) sat opposite each other during council meetings, and Beloved women had special seats within the council chamber.

Religious Resistance Movements. In response to changes brought about by contact with Europeans and, later, Americans, Cherokee people struggled with issues surrounding acculturation to Euro-American ways and retention of indigenous cultural characteristics. Various ceremonial practices reflected the changes that the Cherokee underwent. A number of winter dances, for example, featured masked dancers symbolizing visitors from distance places. They danced to protect themselves from malevolent people and to prevent disease. By the late nineteenth century the repertoire of masked winter dances had expanded to include masked caricatures of Europeans called "Boogers." The Booger Dance developed in response to devastating diseases introduced by Europeans and the disrespectful treatment of Cherokee women by white males.

The eighteenth century, an era of tumultuous change for the Cherokee, witnessed the rise of several religious movements. In February 1811, three Cherokee—a man and two women—had a vision in which the Provider, the Supreme Being, warned the Cherokee to return to their former way of life and to rid themselves of the trappings of white society. Ten months later another Cherokee man told of receiving a vision in which the Provider expressed displeasure that whites had built a house on a sacred hill and that the Cherokee people were no longer expressing thanks for the fruits of the land. By February 1812, stories of apocalyptic visions were spreading among the Cherokee. These prophecies arose at a time when Tenskwatawa, the Shawnee Prophet, and his brother, Tecumseh, were urging native people throughout the Ohio and Mississippi Valleys to join a confederacy of tribal nations to resist American encroachments. Some Cherokee responded to both Cherokee and Shawnee prophecies; however, the outbreak of the War of 1812 diverted attention away from the prophecies.

The concern of the Cherokee continued to increase as land cessions and emigrations to the west signaled major disruptions in their way of life. A movement that became known as White Path's Rebellion arose in 1827 when a group of traditionalists again tried to halt rapid acculturation by advocating the abolishment of the newly formed Cherokee constitutional government and a return to the practice of traditional dances and rituals. The traditionalists agreed to discontinue holding meetings in opposition to the Cherokee council's actions in order to present a united front against the United States' efforts to remove them from their homelands.

Those Cherokee who survived the forced removal to Indian Territory faced the uncertainties of living in an unfamiliar region. They no longer had access to their sacred places, and many of their elders, the carriers and purveyors of ritual knowledge, had died on the march. Many turned to missionaries for spiritual comfort, and Cherokee leaders advocated Western education as a means to survival. Over time the clan system declined, and ceremonies like the Green Corn ceased to be practiced among the Western Cherokee, although remnants of the ceremony remained among the Eastern Cherokee. For many rural fullbloods, Baptist churches replaced ceremonial grounds as social and religious centers. In 1859 Evan Jones, a Baptist missionary among the Western Cherokee, organized the Keetoowah Society among the fullbloods, many of whom became resistance fighters in the period before and after the Civil War. Many fullbloods did not like the political focus of the society, however, and in 1879 an amendment was drawn up to make it a religious group as well.

Shortly after the Civil War ended a number of medicine people told of a prophecy they had received through which they had learned that the son of Pig Smith would lead the Cherokee through difficult times. As a result, Pig Smith arranged for his son, Redbird, to be taught in the ways of the Keetoowah. Redbird Smith and his followers formed their own organization, known as the Nighthawk Keetoowahs. Redbird Smith turned to medicine people and their sacred formulas (ritual prayers) to access traditional Cherokee knowledge. The invention of the Cherokee syllabary in 1821 by Sequoyah (George Guess) enabled the medicine people to record their formulas, which they carried with them to Indian Territory. Through use of medical knowledge, seven sacred wampum belts, and the clan system, Redbird Smith taught the Cherokee the way of the White Path. In 1902 he built the first stomp ground of the Nighthawk Keetoowah. Soon the Cherokee had twenty-two ceremonial stomp grounds.

Contemporary Contexts. Today, the stomp dance remains the major Cherokee traditional ceremonial. Stomp dances are held primarily during the summer season. Each year Cherokee from all over the country gather in the southern part of the Cherokee Nation of Oklahoma for a major stomp dance held on the anniversary of Redbird Smith's birthday. Another major stomp dance is held each year during the Cherokee National Holiday on Labor Day weekend.

Stickball games, once a means for resolving disputes between towns, are now a way of reinforcing harmony and community among the Cherokee. Communal feasts reflective of the Green Corn Dances of earlier times promote ideals of sharing and reciprocity. Wampum belts, White Drink, tobacco, fire, and doctoring remain strong elements of Cherokee ceremonial life.

Protestant churches, especially Baptist churches, also continue to be an important part of Cherokee religious life. Missionization among the Cherokee began as early as 1736, when Christian Priber, a Jesuit, went to Cherokee country. In 1801 the Moravians, or United Brethren, established a mission at Springplace, Georgia. Two years later Gideon Blackburn, a Presbyterian, arrived among the Cherokee, followed by the Baptists of Georgia in 1815. By 1817 the American Board of Commissioners for Foreign Missions had established its first mission among the Cherokee at Brainerd, in Tennessee. The Cherokee syllabary also enabled translations of the New Testament, hymnbooks, and other religious works in the Cherokee language, thus facilitating missionary work. By 1832, 5 to 6 percent of the 5,000 or 6,000 Cherokee in Evan Jones's mission region were Baptists and a slightly greater number were Methodists.

Today, Baptist and Methodist churches flourish among the Cherokee people. Cherokee gospel-singing is popular, and large tents filled to overflowing with audiences gathered to hear Cherokee gospel songs can be seen at the annual Oklahoma Cherokee festival held on Labor Day weekend. In 1985, Eastern and Western Cherokee reunited at Red Clay in Tennessee. The reunion emphasized traditional ritual symbolism, including the use of sacred fire in a Ceremony of Flame held in Cherokee, North Carolina. The following year the two groups met in Tahlequah, Oklahoma, again reuniting relatives who had been separated since the removal of 1838.

Revivals and gospel-singing are popular events in Cherokee country, East and West. For some Cherokee, Christian churches provide the structure for maintenance of Cherokee identity and culture that the Green Corn ceremony and stomp grounds once did. The church is the place where Cherokee can gather for communal feasts, share stories, and hear the language spoken and sung. However, it is not unusual to find Cherokee who are participants in both Christian churches and traditional stomp grounds. Cherokee healers are valued as much as Western doctors by many Christian and traditional Cherokee. For both groups, relationships to the land in Northeastern Oklahoma or in North Carolina remain integral to their identity as Cherokee.

BIBLIOGRAPHY

Journal of Cherokee Studies. Published by the Museum of the Cherokee Indian in cooperation with the Cherokee Historical Association.

Kilpatrick, Jack Frederick, and Anna Gritts Kilpatrick. *Run toward the Nightland: Magic of the Oklahoma Cherokee.* Dallas, Tex., 1967.

McLoughlin, William G. *The Cherokees and Christianity, 1794–1870: Essays on Acculturation and Cultural Persistence.* Athens, Ga., 1994.

Mooney, James. *Myths of the Cherokee and Sacred Formulas of the Cherokees.* Nashville, 1982. "Myths of the Cherokee" was originally published as the *Nineteenth Annual Report of the Bureau of American Ethnology, 1897–1898,* pp. 3–576, (Washington, D.C., 1900); and the "Sacred Formulas of the Cherokees" was originally published in the *Seventh Annual Report of the Bureau of American Ethnology, 1885–1886,* pp. 301–397, (Washington, D.C., 1891).

Perdue, Theda. *Cherokee Women: Gender and Culture Change, 1700–1835.* Lincoln, Neb., 1998.

Thomas, Robert. *The Origin and Development of the Redbird Smith Movement.* M.A. thesis, University of Arizona, Tucson, 1953.

Wahnenauhi [Lucy L. Keys]. "The Wahnenauhi Manuscript: Historical Sketches of the Cherokees, Together with Some of Their Customs, Traditions, and Superstitions." Edited by Jack Frederick Kilpatrick. In *Smithsonian Institution Bureau of American Ethnology Bulletin* 196, *Anthropological Papers,* no. 77, pp.179–213. Washington, D.C., 1966.

MICHELENE E. PESANTUBBEE (2005)

CH'I SEE QI

CHIAO SEE JIAO

CHIBCHA RELIGION SEE MUISCA RELIGION

CHIH-I SEE ZHIYI

CHIH-YEN SEE ZHIYAN

CHILD. The child is a universal symbol of future potentiality as well as the carrier of the heritage of the past. The child is symbolic of the past, coming into being from generative forces that preceded it, yet for it the future is an open possibility. In *Essays on a Science of Mythology* (1949), Károly Kerényi states that the image of the primordial child represents the childhood of the world itself, even the origin of life. There is a mystery about the child, for what it will be as an adult is not yet and cannot be known. The child represents innocence, purity, wonder, receptivity, freshness, noncalculation, the absence of narrow ambition and purpose. As yet innocent of life, the child portrays the beginning, the origin of all. It symbolizes a primordial unity, before differentiation has taken place. Gender differences are mainly in potentiality; consciousness has not been separated out from the unconscious; choice has yet to become a burden and a responsibility.

In the alchemical tradition of medieval Europe, a child wearing a crown or regal garments was a symbol of the philosopher's stone, that is, of a wholeness realizing the mystical union of the inner spirit with the eternal spirit. Something of this feeling may sustain the devotion to the Infant Jesus of Prague, whose statue, preserved since 1628 in the Church of Our Lady of Victory in Prague, portrays the infant Jesus as Christ the King, with his left hand encircling a miniature globe surmounted by a cross and his right hand bestowing a blessing.

Because the child requires care and nurture, it represents the needs and demands of utter dependency. The child's closeness to nature is indicated in numerous stories telling of a special child being cared for by animals. Children are further associated with the Great Mother, and thus with maternal elements such as water; in legend, then, one finds children brought by fishers such as the stork, or by water dwellers such as the frog, or born from Mother Earth under a bush or in a cave. Children are often used to personify the seasons: Spring, amid leaves and flowers; Summer, holding ears of corn; Autumn, with fruit; Winter, wrapped in a cloak. Growth and development are implicit, for childhood is a temporary state. The child represents incredible power, vitality, and persistence toward growth; one grows up physically, whether one wishes to or not. Furthermore, there is rejoicing at growth, no matter how charming a child may be. There is grief at the death of a child but not at the loss of a child to adulthood.

Children and old people have something in common and usually get along well with one another; both must accept dependency. The child also symbolizes that stage of life in which the old person, transformed, acquires a new simplicity. Together, they represent the continuity and flow of life. The child symbolizes a higher transformation of individuality, the self transmuted and reborn into perfection. Thus, not surprisingly, the motif of the child is found in religions and mythologies from earliest times and all around the world. In Christianity, for example, the baby in the crèche and the adult on the cross are the two poles between which the liturgical year moves, each in different ways pointing to the tasks of human life for spiritual development.

The Child in Mythology. The symbolism of the child implies a connection with the mythology of the hero. The potential of the child is indicated in many myths depicting heroic nature as predestined rather than simply achieved. Almost invariably, the hero is described as endowed with extraordinary powers from the moment of birth, if not of conception.

In *The Myth of the Birth of the Hero* (1959), Otto Rank identifies many of the principal motifs associated with the divine child. Typically, the child has parents of royal or noble lineage. In many stories the father is a god and the mother a human, or some other miraculous quality characterizes the birth. Since extraordinary difficulties attend the birth of a hero, the child is endangered. Often the father is the source of danger, or a ruler who has been warned that the child will kill or supplant him. The infant is abandoned, exposed, or sent away. In every myth of sanctified childhood, the world assumes the care of the child. However rejected, the child is rescued by a providential act of nature or by rural people close to nature. Upon maturity the child discovers his or her true identity and sets up a new order, rectifying previous wrongs.

Not all hero myths have birth stories, but most of them do, and the same motifs are found throughout the world, as Joseph Campbell demonstrates in *The Hero with a Thousand Faces* (1968). In a story from the Hindu epic *Mahābhārata*, the hero, Karṇa, is born of a virgin and the sun god, Sūrya. According to one account, the bodhisattva who later became Gautama Buddha entered his mother's womb from the right side, and at the end of ten months left the right side of his mother again in full consciousness. The North American Algonquin tell a story of the miraculous birth of Michabo, who, in one form of the myth, is said to be the grandson of the Moon and the son of the West Wind and a maiden who had been miraculously fecundated by the passing breeze. His mother died in giving birth, but he did not need the fostering care of a parent, for he was born "mighty of limb and with all the knowledge that it is possible to attain." The mother of the Aztec hero Quetzalcoatl also died at his birth, but the newborn at once possessed speech, reason, and wisdom.

A rather common incident in the stories of American Indian heroes is their immediate growth from early childhood to manhood, as in the case of Young Rabbit of the Sioux, Bloodclot Boy of the Blackfeet, and the Divine Twins of the Pueblo Indians. In Roman mythology, Romulus and Remus were born of a king's daughter and the war god, Mars. In Greek mythology, King Acrisius of Argos, having been warned by an oracle against male descendents, locked his daughter in an iron chamber; but Zeus penetrated the roof in the guise of a golden rain, and Danaë became the mother of Perseus. In Christian tradition, Jesus was born of the Virgin Mary by the power of the Holy Spirit.

The extraordinary difficulties at the hero's birth take a variety of forms. Sometimes the father is the child's enemy, as was Kronos, who devoured his children to prevent his predicted demise by a child of his; or the father may be merely absent, as Zeus was when Dionysos was being torn to pieces by the Titans. Jesus was threatened by the edict of Herod, who, having heard of the birth of a king, ordered all male children under two years of age put to death. The infant Moses, being in similar danger from the Egyptian pharaoh, was placed in a basket to float down the Nile. In the Hindu story, Karṇa was likewise placed in a basket on a river, while in an Old Norse saga, Siegfried was put in a glass vessel to float down a stream to the sea. Romulus and Remus, when condemned by the king, were set afloat in a tub on the river Tiber. The delivery of the hero from danger is frequently effected by the waters of a river or sea. In Oceanic mythology, the hero Māui was cast into the sea by his mother, because he was so small and scrawny that she thought he was dead. The father of Oedipus ordered him exposed to die, because an oracle had advised him that he would be killed by his own son.

Typically, the rejected child is rescued either by animals or by simple, rural folk. In a Greek story about a hero of the Medes, Cyrus, the baby, upon being ordered exposed by his royal grandfather, was raised by a herder who did not carry out the order but substituted his own still-born child. In another Greek story, Paris, the son of Priam of Troy, was ordered exposed by his father and was left on a mountaintop; a she-bear nursed the child for five days, and when he was found still alive, the servant who had left him there took him home to raise him himself. Kṛṣṇa, an incarnation of the Hindu god Viṣṇu, grew up among cowherders and is famed for his sport with the *gopīs*, or cowherdesses. A child that is abandoned to nature, then saved and brought up by her, no longer shares the common experience of humankind, for as Mircea Eliade points out in *Patterns of Comparative Religion* (1958), the abandoned child has reenacted the cosmological instant of beginning and grows up not in the midst of a family but in the midst of the elements. He is dedicated to a destiny that no ordinary person could attain.

These stories commonly present the exile or the despised one as handicapped, or make the hero an abused son or daughter, orphan or stepchild. The child of destiny has to face a long period of obscurity. This is a time of extreme danger, with many obstacles. The myths agree that an extraordinary capacity is required to face and survive such experience: heroic infancies abound in anecdotes of precocious strength, cleverness, and wisdom.

In time, the hero, now a youth, returns to his proper home, often to overthrow his father and set himself in his place, as did Oedipus and Perseus. Jesus said that he did not come to abolish the Law but rather to fulfill it; however, his followers understood his teaching to be a new covenant as the basis of relationship with God. Gautama Buddha, rejecting the scriptures and the caste system of traditional Hinduism, offered a new way, the Eightfold Path, for dealing with the problems of life.

Psychological Interpretation. Many students of mythology, such as Károly Kerényi and Joseph Campbell, have made use of C. G. Jung's concept of archetypes to interpret the worldwide occurrence of motifs like that of the child. In Jung's view, an archetype is a pattern through which human nature has repeatedly expressed itself, employing different imagery in different cultures but reflecting in each case a recognizable form common to all humankind. In his essay "The Psychology of the Child Archetype" (1949), Jung suggests that one function of the child motif in the adult psyche is to compensate or correct, in a meaningful manner, the one-sidedness and extravagances of the conscious mind, by revealing the possibility for future development.

The symbolism of the child has no one meaning but on the other hand it is not unlimited. Most personality theories assume that the psyche, like the body, has a built-in mechanism for healing itself. Just as the body produces antibodies to ward off attack from foreign invaders, so the psyche produces images that are suggestive or corrective for its health. The motif of the child, when occurring in the unconscious of an individual (as in a dream, an obsession, or a fascination) or in the mythologies and fables of a culture, may suggest a future potential development for the individual or the culture.

The child symbolizes movement toward maturity. Being itself the product of the union of two opposites, male and female, it is a symbol of wholeness. In the mythologies of the divine child, there is a union of the divine and human; spirit and body have become one, which is the essence of the human experience. The miraculous element in the stories indicates that a special manifestation of the immanent divine principle has become incarnate in the world. The child is a symbol, then, of the wholeness toward which life moves. The mythologies of the child hero or divine child illustrate the problems encountered in psychological growth and development toward wholeness. As a "miraculous" conception the future potential is a given element, yet it is also precarious: the child as future possibility is abandoned daily. Many difficulties and obstacles have to be overcome in any movement of the psyche toward wholeness.

The motif of the child may also occur as a corrective to a conscious attitude that has become too rigid, too fixed, or stagnated. The child suggests something evolving toward independence, which necessitates detachment from its origins. In this sense, abandonment, though painful, is necessary for the future potential.

The child has a naive view of life, is typically interested in learning more about life, and has a lot of energy for that task. It represents one of the strongest urges in every being, namely, the urge to realize itself. There is an invincibility and uncomplicated vitality about the child that the stories describe in various ways. The obscurity in which the child is typically raised points to the psychological state of nonrecognition, the naive condition of the beginning, before consciousness has become differentiated from the unconscious. As such, the child symbolizes the goal of human development, when there has been a reintegration of consciousness with the unconscious or nature. The wisdom of old age is a state in which the opposites and tensions of life and growth have become reconciled and are more or less at peace. "You must become as little children," Jesus taught. Maturity can be seen as the unclouded joy of the child at play who takes it for granted that he or she is at one, not only with playmates, but with all of life.

The symbol of the child is a source of energy for a new development. In "Reveries toward Childhood" in his *Poetics of Reverie* (1969), Gaston Bachelard says, "The great archetype of life beginning brings to every beginning the psychic energy which Jung has recognized in every archetype, . . . for the archetypes are reserves of enthusiasm which help us believe in the world, love the world, create the world" (p. 124).

SEE ALSO Jesus; Kṛṣṇa; Heroes.

BIBLIOGRAPHY

The Hungarian classicist Károly Kerényi has published extensively on mythology; his essay "The Primordial Child in Primordial Times," in Kerényi and C. G. Jung's *Essays on a Science of Mythology* (1949; rev. ed., New York, 1963), has explored the theme of the divine child, drawing primarily on Greek, Roman, Finnish, Russian, and Indian mythologies. Daniel G. Brinton's collection of hero myths of American Indians, *American Hero Myths* (Philadelphia, 1882), demonstrates the presence of similar motifs among the indigenous peoples of the Western Hemisphere. Joseph Campbell's classic work *The Hero with a Thousand Faces* (Princeton, 1968) describes the basic pattern of myths of the hero. Otto Rank's *The Myth of the Birth of the Hero* (New York, 1959) outlines the basic motifs of its subject and offers a psychoanalytic interpretation. Joseph Campbell's *The Mythic Image* (Princeton, 1974) reexamines the motifs Rank identified and offers some illustrations and interpretation in a section on "Infant Exile." C. G. Jung's essay "The Psychology of the Child Archetype" can be found in *Essays on a Science of Mythology* (cited above) and in volume 9 of *The Collected Works of C. G. Jung* (New York, 1959); it provides a psychological interpretation of this worldwide motif. Mircea Eliade's *Patterns in Comparative Religion* (New York, 1958) has in section 87, "Man's Descent from the Earth," a brief discussion of the meaning of the motif of the abandoned child. A philosophical reverie on the meaning of childhood can be found in Gaston Bachelard's "Reveries toward Childhood," in *Poetics of Reverie* (New York, 1969). The fourth issue of the journal *Parabola: Myth and the Quest for Meaning* (August 1979) is devoted to the meaning of the child and childhood.

WALLACE B. CLIFT (1987)

CHILD, LYDIA MARIA. Lydia Maria Child (1802–1880) was a prolific author and a founder of the American abolitionist movement. Child wrote two books on religion: *The Progress of Religious Ideas* (1855), which offered a history of the world's religions and sought to put Christianity on a level footing with other religions; and *Aspirations of the World: A Chain of Opals* (1878), which collected what Child considered the most valuable religious texts, including many more excerpts from Greco-Roman, Buddhist, Persian, and Hindu sources than from the Bible. Child's radically universalist religious sensibility informed her life-long quest to eradicate racial prejudice.

Child did not fit easily into religious categories. She was born in Medford, Massachusetts, the daughter of a baker, and she rejected her parents' Calvinism as an adolescent. The older brother who educated her, Convers Francis, became a Unitarian minister, but she found Unitarianism cold and intellectual. She was attracted to Swedenborgian mysticism, but felt that it fed her imagination more than her heart or her intellect.

Child published her first novel, *Hobomok: A Tale of Early Times* (1824), a controversial story about an Indian-white romance and marriage, when she was twenty-two, and was soon feted as a promising young author. She wrote a book or two per year while editing the first successful children's magazine, and she married David Lee Child, an idealistic and debt-prone political activist.

In 1833 Child published *An Appeal in Favor of That Class of Americans Called Africans*, the first significant study of slavery, emancipation, and American racism. This ardent yet well-researched plea for the eradication of slavery established her as a leader of the abolitionist movement. She went on to edit the *National Anti-Slavery Standard*, thus becoming the first female editor of a national political newspaper. During this time, Child concluded that Swedenborgianism was not a true religion because so many of its followers accepted slavery. She attended numerous religious institutions, including a Catholic cathedral and a Jewish synagogue, but felt they were all too narrow-minded.

Child took seven years to write her three-volume *Progress of Religious Ideas,* in which she argued that all religions are revelations of the divine spirit. People throughout history have asked the same questions and expressed the same hopes, and the divine spirit has spoken to them using whatever forms they were best able to receive. Symbols that may seem odd to an outsider—the Egyptians' golden scarab, the Christians' cross—feel quite different when viewed from inside a tradition. People should therefore respect all the world's religions, acknowledging their weaknesses but cherishing the ways in which they partake of truth and goodness. True religion is a matter of faith and hope, not theological arguments or sectarian divisions.

Christianity, Child suggested, has no privileged status. Each religion builds upon the spiritual insights of earlier eras, and Christianity is rooted in Jewish, Greek, and Persian thought. It may, furthermore, eventually be superseded by new, more true, beliefs that cannot yet be imagined. Child warned against holding too tightly to old revelations. Each revelation is designed to be comprehensible in a specific time and place, and once people move too far past that state of society a written revelation may hinder, not help, further spiritual growth.

Child conceded that Christianity can have unusually good practical results. All religions have an iniquitous tendency to divide humanity into competing sects, but Christianity alone sometimes preaches universal sympathy and benevolence. Christians often fall into divisiveness, bigotry, and war, but Christianity can encourage them to see all people, even non-Christians, as one family. Christian sympathy, for example, led England to abolish slavery. Christianity is thus desirable not because it is more truthful than other religions, but because it is potentially more moral.

Many reviewers protested Child's refusal to give Christianity any preferential divine origin, but two of the abolitionist ministers whom Child most respected—Theodore Parker and Samuel May—enthusiastically praised her work. Forty years later, Elizabeth Cady Stanton echoed Child's views in her *Woman's Bible* (1895–1898). Child's readership was not large, but she gave courage to some of the nineteenth century's most rebellious religious thinkers.

When Child was in her seventies, she finally found a compatible religious community. The Free Religious Association was founded by a group of progressive Unitarians who wanted a place for people of all religions, including agnostics, to come together in an unconstrained pursuit of truth. Child found its gatherings inspiring and thought-provoking.

She had become particularly interested in Buddhism, and avidly read new translations of Asian texts. In two *Atlantic Monthly* articles, written at a time of rising anti-Asian racism, she portrayed Buddha and Jesus as almost identical figures. Both, she explained, identified with the poor and outcast and sought to open "the road to holiness" to everyone. No longer did Child claim that only Christianity teaches universal sympathy.

Child's last book was *Aspirations of the World: A Chain of Opals.* Its goal, she explained, was to illuminate the soul's universal aspirations and intuitions. Most of the book consists of selections from the world's sacred scriptures, grouped into subject headings such as "Ideas of the Supreme Being," "Moral Courage," and "Fraternity of Religions," and arranged in chronological order under each heading. Child included only the passages that she found most wise, beautiful, and intellectually and imaginatively satisfying. This "Eclectic Bible," she suggested, offered guidance and inspiration from the best aspects of all the world's religions. In this work, as in all her religious and political writings, Child sought to eradicate divisions within the human race and help readers see everyone as equal parts of one humanity.

BIBLIOGRAPHY

Child, Lydia Maria. *An Appeal in Favor of That Class of Americans Called Africans* (1833). Edited by Carolyn Karcher. Amherst, Mass., 1996.

Child, Lydia Maria. *The Progress of Religious Ideas: Through Successive Ages.* 3 vols. New York, 1855.

Child, Lydia Maria. *Aspirations of the World: A Chain of Opals.* Boston, 1878.

Child, Lydia Maria. *Hobomok and Other Writings on Indians.* Edited by Carolyn Karcher. New Brunswick, N.J., 1986.

Karcher, Carolyn. *The First Woman in the Republic: A Cultural Biography of Lydia Maria Child.* Durham, N.C., 1994.

Karcher, Carolyn, ed. *A Lydia Maria Child Reader.* Durham, N.C., 1997.

LORI KENSCHAFT (2005)

CHINESE PHILOSOPHY. The major developments in Chinese philosophy during the past three thousand years will be outlined here; ideas that are essentially religious, treated elsewhere, will be noted only as may be necessary to show the religious relevance and historical context of philosophical themes. This overview will be at once chronological and topical, as follows:

1. The pre-Classical background (to the sixth century BCE)
2. Classical philosophy (late sixth to late third century BCE)
3. The first imperial era (to the third century CE)
4. The development of Buddhism in China (to the ninth century)
5. The Confucian revival (Tang and Song periods)
6. The later empire (since the fourteenth century)

THE PRE-CLASSICAL BACKGROUND. China circa 550 BCE consisted only of what is now North China; even the states of the Yangtze River valley did not speak the language of what was recognized as the civilized heartland to the north. This known "world" had been in anarchy for more than two centuries, since the overthrow of the last Western Zhou king (in present-day Xi'an) in 771 BCE. By about the sixth century BCE there was a nominal quasi-feudal hierarchy under a powerless successor Zhou "king" in Luoyang, but in fact, the political landscape was dotted with a patchwork of small quarreling states under local lordlings who themselves often had no real power. China was still emerging from the Bronze Age (iron casting had begun circa 700 to 600), but its civilization was old, stretching back in time beyond memory or reliable record. The Zhou dynasty had begun about five hundred years earlier with a conquest by a western Chinese state. Archaeology has now validated the tradition of a Shang dynasty before that, centered in Henan, which may have lasted another five hundred years. The tradition of a still earlier Xia dynasty, again of almost five hundred years, continues to be debated; it was supposed to have started with three marvelously wise rulers, Yao, who chose his own successor, Shun, who in turn selected Yu, the first ruler of the Xia.

Speculative philosophy was soon to fill the third millennium BCE with still more (timeless) civilization-creating emperors. The Chinese venerated their past, cherished what they had, and invented what they needed. In the sixth century BCE there existed a modest ancient literature, in large part anonymous: the earliest philosophers often quote the "Odes" *(Shi)* or the "Documents" *(Shu)* to make a moral point; some of these still exist. The earliest known writing, discovered on pieces of shell and bone used by Shang royal diviners, dates from about 1200 BCE, and a few traditional texts surviving even now may date to the eleventh century BCE. There was a wealth of learning for learned men to know. Such persons were among the well born, if not so well born that all their time was taken in ruling or fighting. Most people, then as now, were farmers, and it is said that only the aristocrats kept family records and sacrificed to ancestors.

In the Shang, sacrifices to royal ancestors were often of human beings, and in the Zhou it still was common to bury a lord with attendant sacrifices and to sacrifice war captives at one's local altar to the soil. The earliest philosophers denounced these practices. A high god, called Tian (Heaven), or (earlier) Shangdi, was worshiped by the king who in theory held from Tian his "mandate" *(ming)* to rule as long as he maintained the "virtue" *(de)* of the founder of the dynastic line. Increasing population and the growth of urban centers, combined with constant war, eliminated smaller domains, producing a class of unattached petty "gentlemen" *(shi)* who in an earlier age would have been knights or minor hereditary court officers and who had or aspired to some education. The first philosophers and their disciples are from this group. Dissatisfied with present conditions, they looked back to an imagined better past in which they would have had secure roles, and were critical of the higher aristocrats whose power came from their connections rather than from real ability or character.

THE AGE OF CLASSIC PHILOSOPHY: THE FIRST PHASE. The first philosophers were moralists, motivated by perceived political and social ills. For them the basic ill was disorder, brought about by the greed of local lords or heads of powerful families and by their attempts to seek status to which they had no right. These philosophers were not revolutionary; they accepted the existing authorities, and if they looked for remedies they sought positions for themselves or their students as advisers and ministers. We can distinguish three positions. (1) Confucius (Kong Qiu; traditional dates 551?–479 BCE) would have real political power in the hands of men of cultivated moral character and sought to train his students (and himself) in traditional morals and etiquette to make them employable in court positions. (2) Mozi (c. 450–c. 380 BCE), in training his students for office, worked out a specific political program with a supporting philosophical argument that ignores the problem of moral character; for him, an official was "worthy" of his job if he discharged his duties effectively. (3) Yang Zhu (fl. c. 400–350 BCE) concluded that the times could not be remedied. For him, the only reasonable course was withdrawal and the choice of an optimally satisfactory style of personal life.

Confucius. Confucius (the Latinized form of Kong Fuzi, or Master Kong) stressed the importance of developing traditional virtues, such as filial piety *(xiao)*, courage, honesty, loyalty, kindliness *(ren)*, and familiarity with the rules of traditional polite behavior and ceremonial *(li)*. In politics he was a legitimist, supporting the Zhou king and the rightful authority of the duke of Lu (his native state), which had slipped into the hands of three collateral ducal families, and deploring any behavior in powerful persons that implied an improper claim to status. The good society of the past was to be restored by making traditional standards and values real again. This was Confucius's concept of "rectifying names" *(zheng ming)*, that is, making the referents of such terms as *father* and *ruler* really correspond to their meaning. Accordingly, traditional religious rituals had great value for him and he held *tian* (Heaven) in genuine awe; but he usually turned aside substantive religious queries. His moral philosophy is self-cultivationist: a good life, he held, is one of constant self-improvement. And it is deontological: the world would be better if we were good and always did what is right but that is not what determines what is good and right. Confucius had devoted disciples, but how to teach virtue was a problem for him. He admitted that he taught only eager students and evinced exasperation when a student grasped his teaching but remained unmoved.

Mozi. In sharp contrast to Confucius, Mozi (who may have been originally a wheelwright) is utterly "practical." The earliest strata of the *Mozi* text show him unconcerned with the cultivation of character. He wrote, for example, that officials will be loyal if they are well paid; music—prized by the Confucians for its harmonizing effect on the emotions and the self—he dismissed as a useless expense. An idea or policy is approvable, according to Mozi, if it promotes one of three basic social goods: order, wealth, and population growth. He devotes a whole chapter to ghosts and spirits and another to "the will of Heaven." These entities must be obeyed and sacrificed to lest they punish or withhold gifts such as long life—contrast Confucius, who is willing to "die in the evening" if he can "hear the Way" in the morning—but there is no tone of awe in what we read. The fundamental good is order, its antithesis is offensive war (defensive war is approved; the Moists became experts in its techniques). But each human naturally pursues his or her own interest and takes as "right" *(yi)* that which serves it, fighting with his or her neighbors. It is the function of the state, by meting out rewards and praise or punishments and censure, to impose one standard of right, which is to be the "will of Heaven." And Heaven's will is that people "love one another impartially" *(jian ai)*. If you love your neighbor's family, city, and state as you love your own, then all fighting will cease. Shown the cool advantages of adopting this attitude toward others, it is inconceivable that an intelligent human will not do so; and rulers know well how to get their subjects to comply with their wishes and favor their ends. Condemning fatalism—a doctrine that, he says, deceives men into thinking human effort is useless—Mozi implies that one can adopt an attitude at will. But his stark logic has at least one flaw: although he demanded absolute obedience and dedication from his followers, nothing in Mozi's system shows them why they should make this sacrifice. Nonetheless, there are accounts of followers giving up their lives for his cause. The Moists were tightly organized and were a force in the world of thought for two centuries, before eventually disappearing by the time of the Qin unification of 221 BCE.

Yang Zhu. Although none of Yang Zhu's writings has survived, his views can be gleaned from other books. He was among the many in this period who concluded that nothing could be done to right the world and that no interest of one's own was served by seeking to advance oneself in it. The best course, therefore, was to keep out of harm's way and "nourish one's life," avoiding office. Although some who shared these views with Yang Zhu were hedonists, Yang himself probably was not; he believed that a measured asceticism might well be the wisest way to conserve life and optimize satisfactions. In one account of this type of thought the greatest satisfaction to be enjoyed is *yi.* It is probably "honor," rather than "righteousness," that is meant here, and to the extent that others' *yi* meant social dutifulness, it would have to be deemed by the follower of Yang as incompatible with life or nature. But such persons who withdraw from society can be seen as engaging in a kind of self-cultivation; their stance is not far from that of the Confucian-minded person who judges that the Way *(dao)* does not prevail in his time and so withdraws into private life to cultivate a personal "purity" uncorrupted by the world's temptations. Yang appears in the pages of the *Zhuangzi,* and there is reason to think that Zhuangzi may have at first been a follower. It is plausibly argued that recluses of this kind were the first Daoists.

THE AGE OF CLASSICAL PHILOSOPHY: THE HUNDRED SCHOOLS. By 350 BCE no one took the feeble Zhou king seriously. Sometimes tentatively, in the wake of a military victory, and sometimes by mutual agreement, the stronger of the local "dukes" declared themselves "kings" *(wang),* each thus implying an intention to succeed the Zhou. By 320 there were at least eight such "kings." One of the most ambitious was the ruler of Qi (modern Shandong Province). Of course, such ambition could only be realized in the end by military action. In the meantime, however, a "king" had to build his prestige by a display of his royal "virtue" *(de),* and the ruler of Qi ostentatiously opened his ears to the advice of all the wise men he could entice into his court. Hundreds of wandering philosophers and their disciples were housed in a suburb of Jixia, the Qi capital. (An early philosophical encyclopedia, the *Guanzi,* may be a residue of their work.) Other new "kings" and lesser lords, especially the king of Wei in Daliang (Kaifeng), tried to keep pace. Philosophy thrived in great variety. By the third century BCE the main body of Moists had split into three sects, each with its own text of the doctrine. One specialized group developed the science of military defense and had its own texts. Others were experts in the theory of argument; their canons and explanations are, in effect, treatises on logic and epistemology.

Other philosophers, perhaps following the lead of the Moist logicians, made reputations for their ability to baffle audiences with clever arguments for impossible theses. The most famous are Hui Shi ("The sun at noon is the sun setting" and other paradoxes) and Gongsun Long ("A white horse is not a horse"). Proto-Daoists such as Shen Dao argued that a conceptual knowledge impedes real understanding. The Confucians had their schools, which stressed ritual, filial piety, or moral psychology and derived from one or another prominent disciple of Confucius. A school of social primitivists, led by one Xu Xing, held that market prices should be standardized to prevent cheating and that a good ruler must not be supported by his people but should work in the fields with them. Zou Yan amazed his lavish royal hosts with grand speculations about the patterns of history and the geography of the world, based on the theories of yin and yang and the "five powers" *(wu de* or *wu xing).* Perhaps for the first time, an old manual of divination was caught up in philosophy, with a (now lost) commentary based on yin-yang *wu xing* theory. This same manual later acquired a moral commentary attributed to Confucius and, as the *Yi jing,* became the ranking book in the Confucian classics. In this combination of divination and metaphysics we see a perennial Chinese concept of "resonant causality," one thing in the universe causing something else "like" it—a celestial object or an *Yi jing* hexagram—to be activated in response.

Mengzi. This is the setting of the career of Mengzi (Mencius), the ancient philosopher with probably the greatest influence on later Chinese philosophical thought. Mengzi belongs to the moral-psychological line of philosophical descent from Confucius. The *Mengzi* opens with him, an old man, in conversation with the kings of Wei (known also as Liang) in the year 320, and Qi in the year 319, urging them to desist from warfare and to lighten the burdens on their people. He boldly argues that a bad ruler may be justly deposed or killed, but he is in no way egalitarian, arguing (against Xu Xing's followers) that rulers and educated men deserve their privileged place in society because they "work with their minds," having the duty of caring for the mass of humanity through a government of foreseeing benevolence. Mengzi is best known for his theory of the innate goodness of people: we are all born with psychological "sprouts" implanted in us by Heaven, that if encouraged to grow naturally develop into the virtuous dispositions *(xin)* of benevolence *(ren),* dutifulness *(yi),* sense of propriety *(li),* and moral "knowledge" (*zhi,* sense of right and wrong). (Thus, Mengzi solves the problem of the teachability of virtue.) Human evil results from the stunting of our originally good "nature" *(xing)* owing to harsh conditions. Thus, a good government would restore humanity to goodness by improving the people's lot and educating them.

Mengzi attacked both the Moists—their "universal love," he argued, denies the special duties we have to parents—and the Yangists, whose "egoism" denies our duties to rulers. He nonetheless draws from both. A life of virtue he held, would be in accord with our nature and would be what we would naturally most enjoy. As for the Moists, by Mengzi's time they were coming to see that their doctrinaire program of universal love required a concession to self-cultivation ethics. One must first develop a capacity for loving, which has a natural "root" in affection for parents; at the bidding of doctrine, one can then apply it impartially. It is to this that Mengzi objects: the "root" of benevolence, he says, is indeed innate, but it has a deep structure and can be developed and "extended" in only one way, diminished in due degree at removes from the self. Against Gaozi, he argues that not only our affective nature but also our sense of duty and respect is "internal" (innate). We can encourage our virtues to grow because we enjoy them; they develop and thrive with practice without being forced.

Zhuangzi. The *Zhuangzi* is now recognized to be composite, the later syncretic parts perhaps actually dating to early Han, and other parts, such as a primitivist stratum, dating to the end of the third century BCE. It is usually held that the first seven chapters are by a man named Zhuang Zhou, about whom almost nothing is known. In any case, these chapters seem to be the earliest. It is necessary to date them after Mengzi (the opening of chapter 4 contains an obvious parody of the opening of book 2 of *Mengzi)*; they were probably written in the early third century BCE (chapter 2 satirizes Gongsun Long without naming him; he was a client of a prince of Zhao active as late as c. 250 BCE). The *Zhuangzi* uses a novel medium in philosophy. Whereas the *Lunyu* (Analects) and *Mengzi* are collections, over time, of conversations and sayings, and the *Mozi* a series of reasoned treatises (a mode shortly to be copied by Xunzi and Han Feizi), the *Zhuangzi* makes its points through the use of fiction, sometimes fantastic and often quite funny. Confucius himself is often stolen as a fictional character. It is reasonably argued (by A. C. Graham) that Zhuang Zhou began as a follower of Yang Zhu's school of egoist withdrawal but then had a traumatic "conversion experience." This seems to have shown him that literal withdrawal from the world is merely another posture of involvement; genuine withdrawal must have the form of detachment while one plays the game of life, "walking without touching the ground." In this spirit one may even accept political, social, and familial commitments.

Zhuangzi carries this attitude to the deepest philosophical level. According to him, we must use language, but we must not suppose that our words really fit, for there is nothing absolutely right about them. This is true of all of our evaluative concepts that we articulate in words; the moral concepts of the Confucians are prejudices, time determined. This applies even to such distinctions as dreams versus reality or life versus death (which may be better than life, for all we know). The favorite word of the moral philosophers, *dao,* or "way," becomes for Zhuangzi the Way of all nature, of which the wise man sees himself a part in both life and death. He accepts both joyfully, using his mind as a mirror to reflect reality just as it is, without any distorting preconceptions or preferences and "without injury to himself." The book has been perennially popular; the most important philosophical commentary (by Guo Xiang or Xiang Xiu) dates to circa 300 CE. Zhuangzi's epistemological-metaphysical outlook anticipates that of the Mādhyamika Buddhist philosophy, which was transmitted to China in the early fifth century CE. Later still, Chan Buddhism inherited his provocative blend of humor and paradox.

Xunzi. The active life of Xunzi extends from the early third century BCE to 238, when he was forced to retire from a magistracy in Chu. A native of Zhao, he twice spent time in the philosophical center of Jixia in Qi, where he was recognized as a successor to and rival of Mengzi. Explicitly Confucian, Xunzi was actually eclectic. One probably early essay ("Dispelling Obsessions") describes the mind as a mirror, but unlike Zhuangzi, Xunzi believed that the mind not only reflects but also stores and, if properly used, leads one not to an uncommitted attitude but to the truth, which is the Confucian Way. As in *Mengzi* (6A.15), one can be "obsessed" *(bi)* if one does not reflect carefully; but unlike Mengzi, Xunzi held that such obsession is likely to be an unwise intellectual commitment rather than an unevaluated sense appetite. Accordingly, Xunzi is authoritarian; he believed that one must be protected from wrong ideas. This, he maintains, is the business of the state. The moral order itself (*li yi,* "rites and right," for Xunzi) was created by the sage-kings, on whose teachings we therefore depend if we are to be moral.

Xunzi directly opposes Mengzi not only in this but also in his related view that "human nature is evil": we are composed, according to Xunzi, of an appetitive "nature" *(xing)* that if uncontrolled causes men to quarrel for satisfactions (as in Mozi), as well as a capacity for intelligent action *(wei),* which enabled the wisest (the sage-kings) to see that rules must be ordained if a tolerable social life is to be possible for humankind. Mengzi has the problem of explaining convincingly how evil is possible given the goodness of human nature; Xunzi has the converse problem of explaining how morality is possible at all. The sages' *li yi* are justified by their utility, but to be moral we, and they, have to accept them as right. Mozi solves this problem (perhaps he did not recognize it) by requiring that the state-imposed *yi* shall be what Heaven wills; Xunzi's Heaven, however, is merely the sky above and the order of Nature, and only the uneducated believe it has divine power. What Xunzi says is that humans differ from animals in having *yi* not, it seems, in the Mencian sense of an innate disposition to particular duties, but in an innate capacity to be socialized. The wise person will calculate, at a metamoral level, that only a life according to the Confucian Way can give optimum satisfaction; seeing this, the individual will necessarily choose it, and will choose to be educated so as to become the sort of person who can live it. At the same time, one sees that it really is right that there should be such standards: given the order of all nature, they are the only solution to the human predicament. Thus the "rites" can be seen as the continuation in the human realm of the natural order of the heavens, and Xunzi writes fervent passages to this effect, religious in tone if not in content. In this way the problem implicit in (and ignored by) Mozi—how we can make a calculated choice of our own attitudes—is avoided without recourse to Mengzi's solution to the paradox of virtue (that virtue cannot be taught unless one is virtuous already, as Mencian man is).

Xunzi can be called the first Chinese academic philosopher—reviewing his predecessors, criticizing, picking and choosing, solving problems. He was much appreciated in the ensuing Han era, but by the time Han Yu read him and wrote about him in the ninth century, Xunzi had almost become a curiosity. Still, the more authoritarian of the Neo-Confucians in following centuries are often closer to him than they realized.

Han Feizi. Two of Xunzi's students were Li Si, later prime minister to the First Emperor of Qin, and Han Fei, a prince of the Han state and last of the major preimperial philosophers. The last two Zhou kings had been deposed by Qin in 256 and 249 BCE, and after three more decades the last of the resisting states were absorbed. The political philosophy that guided the new order was what Chinese bibliographers call Legalism (Fa jia), the doctrine that the function of the state is to maximize its strength in agricultural production and in military power by eliminating useless classes (including philosophers) and regimenting the population with a rigidly enforced code of law, using rewards for desired behavior and severe punishments (mutilation or worse) for violations. This would benefit the people and give them order: standing in fear of the state they would behave so that its terrors need never be used. The power of the ruler was to be exalted, but at the same time the ruler was advised to avoid action, keeping his officials in doubt about his intentions lest they combine against him. Thus a curious, quasi-Daoist philosophy of inaction, what H. G. Creel, in his *What Is Taoism?* (Chicago, 1970), calls "purposive Taoism," was the basis of a philosophy of power.

Han Feizi and Li Si were both Legalists. The one recommended philosophically, and the other eventually carried out, the infamous "burning of the books" of proscribed philosophical schools, including especially Confucian texts, in 213 BCE. Legalism strongly influenced the development of Chinese law, but as a philosophy it was usually condemned by the Confucians, who became dominant a century later. Han Feizi continued to be read and was esteemed highly for his literary style.

Laozi. The Daoist bent in Han Feizi is genuine. The book that collects his writings includes a Legalist commentary to selections from a short text that stands first among the Daoist classics: the *Dao de jing.* It is ascribed to a certain Laozi, alias Li Er or Li Dan, supposed to have been an elder contemporary of Confucius and an archivist in the royal Zhou court. In fact, a myth was invented sometime in the third century BCE that Confucius had made a trip to Luoyang to consult him. Although these things are still believed by some scholars, many now take the book to be a third-century work, probably later than the earlier parts of the *Zhuangzi.* The most radical view, that of D. C. Lau (*Tao-te Ching,* Hong Kong, 1982), sees it as a collage of short fragments of Daoist "hymns" and other lore that got assembled in an editorial tradition into the present booklet of brief, sometimes rhymed sections. According to this view, Laozi is a complete fiction, yet he has become the patron saint of Daoism, even a god. The *Dao de jing* has become incredibly popular in the West—there are more translations of it than of almost any other book in the world—but no two interpretations are alike. Although Han Feizi saw Legalism in it, Arthur Waley (*The Way and Its Power,* London, 1935) sees it as the work of a late Warring States "quietist" who was opposed to Legalism. The dominant view is that it is filled with the profoundest wisdom concerning life and being. It is conventionally ordered in two parts, the first opening with a meditation on Dao, the second, with one on *de,* hence the title; however, archaeology has now yielded Han texts that reverse the order.

In the *Dao de jing* we find again Zhuangzi's conceptual relativism: the Dao itself is nameless; contrasting concepts generate each other. Many of the sections recommend inaction, nonstriving, not reaching for too much (lest from success one fall back to nothing: "reversion is the order of the Dao"), and adopting a "female," seemingly nonresisting, posture in life and in state policy. The desirable society is one in which the people are kept ignorant and simple. Often the book deals explicitly with the way a ruler should govern his state, suggesting that the way to effective power is inaction. A theme echoing Shen Dao condemns cleverness and "knowledge": "He who speaks does not know; he who knows does not speak." The first virtue is simplicity, like that of a newborn baby or of an "uncarved block" of wood. "The highest virtue *(de)* does not 'virtue' [*de*—i.e., display itself as virtue]; therefore it has virtue" (cf. *Zhuangzi,* chap. 5). The book teems with such simply stated teasing paradoxes.

THE FIRST IMPERIAL ERA. The late Zhou era of contending states was terminated by the Qin conquest, complete by 221 BCE; Qin disintegrated after the death of its first emperor. The succeeding Han dynasty, from 206 BCE to 220 CE (interrupted by Wang Mang, 9–22) but ineffective after about 190, was followed by a division into Three Kingdoms (221–279). An unstable reunification was ended in 317, when defeats by non-Chinese northern "barbarians" drove the Jin court south to the Yangtze River valley, then still a border area with only a tenth of China's people. At the beginning of the Han dynasty, Legalist political ideas were defended, sometimes vigorously, by some court officials into the first century BCE. Daoism as a personal and political philosophy continued in favor and is represented by the *Huainanzi* (c. 130 BCE), an encyclopedic book assembled under the support of Liu An, one of the Han princes. A syncretic Daoism, drawing from all of late Zhou thought, is represented by chapter 33 of the *Zhuangzi* (second century BCE). Prominent early Han Confucians include Jia Yi (200–168 BCE) and, especially, Dong Zhongshu (179–104 BCE). With the latter, Confucianism gained imperial favor under the emperor Wudi. A system of recruiting scholars for official service was decreed, and court scholars on the Confucian classics were established.

The New Text school. The Qin burning of the books left Confucians with the task of recovering their revered texts. This produced a rich scholarship of commentary (much of it now gone) on various textual traditions of this or that classic. It also, more significantly, led to a lasting division between the so-called New Text schools, which used texts existing only in the "new" reformed Qin-Han script, and the Old Text traditions, which were based on manuscripts in antique script that (allegedly) had survived the Qin suppression. The two sides had opposed philosophical orientations, as well as their own favored texts. The New Text partisans favored the *Gongyang Commentary* on the *Chun qiu*

(Spring and autumn annals of Lu, ascribed to Confucius). They held that Confucius had been a "throneless king," founder of a theoretical "dynasty" intervening between Zhou and Han. In his *Chun qiu,* New Text thinkers claimed, Confucius had actually used "subtle" language to lay down the moral and ritual rules of an ideal world order and had predicted the rise of Han. This theory was fitted into a speculative philosophy of history in Dong's *Chun qiu fanlu,* further developed by the later Han writer He Xiu (129–182), according to whom history goes through three great stages, culminating in an era of "great peace" *(tai ping).* A similar idea occurs in the classic called the *Li ji,* composed of short prose pieces probably by Han court ritualists; as a millenarian concept, it has repeatedly surfaced in philosophy, religion, and popular rebel ideology during the past two thousand years.

The New Text persuasion saw Heaven as a personal deity. Any unusual celestial phenomenon—such as a comet or unpredicted eclipse—was Heaven's sign of displeasure with the behavior of the ruler. Heaven and human affairs were intimately linked by way of yin-yang and Five Elements *(wu xing)* metaphysics, which grouped all aspects of the world in groups of fives (into which fours were forced); thus, water, black, winter, north, anger, and storing are in the same interacting category. The middle and late Han "apocrypha" *(wei shu),* representing Confucius as quasidivine, are also the result of this type of thought, which was markedly numerological; for example, the Shiqu and Bohu imperial conferences on the classics, 51 BCE and 79 CE, were convoked on the five hundredth anniversary of Confucius's supposed birthdate (and probably the one thousandth anniversary of the supposed date of the beginning of the Zhou) and on the eight hundredth anniversary of the first year of the *Chun qiu* chronicle, respectively. Divination was in great vogue; this was the age when the *Yi jing* became the foremost classic. In moral philosophy and moral psychology, Dong Zhongshu and his persuasion were more or less in accord with Mengzi, holding that we are at least potentially "good" by nature.

The Old Text school. The Old Text faction in scholarship includes Liu Xin, court librarian in the Wang Mang era, who was later charged with forging some of these texts (notably the *Zuo zhuan* commentary to the *Chun qiu*). A type of philosophy contrasting with the Dong and He Xiu sort is usually typed Old Text. Naturalistic and skeptical, its major writers were Yang Xiong, who held that human nature is a mixture of good and bad, and, especially, Wang Chong (27–c. 100), who thought that Mengzi, Xunzi, and Yang were each right about the natures of some people. Like Xunzi, these thinkers take Heaven to be a natural entity, not a being with intentions intervening in human affairs. Wang's *Lun heng* admits that portents foretell important historical changes but holds that they are the spontaneous effect of *qi* (matter-energy); Heaven's Way is "nonactivity." Wang holds a bleak fatalism: to him, nothing we do can alter what will happen in our individual lives or in history (here he is unlike Xunzi). He does not hesitate to criticize Confucian doctrines and texts, and explicitly approves the naturalism of philosophical Daoism.

Daoism. Daoism in this age and later was of two sorts. One, which became a religion, shared with New Text Confucianism the correspondence metaphysics of yin-yang and *wu xing* but was aimed at individual survival. For the person who could afford it, this Daoism meant adopting a regimen of life, breathing exercises, diet, and alchemy designed to make one's physical body immortal. For others, there was the possibility of getting one's life prolonged as a reward for good deeds—an idea found in early Zhou bronze inscriptions, in the *Shang shu,* and in Mozi but not in the work of other Zhou philosophers—or of getting reborn as an immortal after death. In time, this cult developed a system of gods, rituals, heavens, and hells.

A second, quite different type of Daoist thought continues or revives the Daoism as personal philosophy found in early Han texts and in the *Zhuangzi.* The naturalistic skepticism of Wang Chong moves in this direction, but whereas Wang's thought was a fatalism of despair, the revived interest in Zhuangzi and Laozi of the end of Han and following centuries was a naturalism of detachment. Wang Bi (226–249) is the author of the standard commentary to *Laozi* and of a commentary to the *Yi jing (Zhou yi yueli).* An important philosophical commentary to the *Zhuangzi* is attributed to both Xiang Xiu (late third century) and Guo Xiang (d. 312). These and others who applied themselves to "the study of the Mysterious" *(xuan xue)* actually continued to take Confucius as the greatest sage, but he became for them a Daoist in fact (in the *Zhuangzi* he had been a Daoist in humorous fiction). He surpassed even Laozi in his attainment of "nothing" *(wu),* that is, "nonattachment" and "desirelessness," since he had passed beyond the desire even for these things.

The interest in semantics and metaphysical paradoxes of the early third century BCE was also revived; most of the extant text attributed to Gongsun Long was fabricated at this time. These interests were expressed in a fashion of precious philosophical conversation that came to be called "pure talk" *(qing tan).* Other important additions to philosophical literature, probably from the third century CE, are the *Liezi,* another Daoist classic similar to *Zhuangzi* and pretending to be a Zhou work, and the forged Old Text chapters of the *Shang shu.* The *Liezi,* like the Xiang-Guo commentary, praises an ethic of following one's nature, which, when practiced among the aristocracy, led from aestheticism to eccentric hedonism. Ge Hong (c. 250–330) criticized this ethic—from a Confucian point of view—as well as the Daoist philosophical anarchism of his contemporary Bao Jingyan. Ge, however, was eclectic, and his own book *Baopuzi* is, among other things, an important work on alchemy as a method of attaining immortality.

THE DEVELOPMENT OF BUDDHISM IN CHINA. There is evidence of a Buddhist presence in China from as early as the late Western Han dynasty. In the Eastern Han period there were centers of Buddhism in a few cities, including Luoyang, where a Parthian, An Shigao, arrived circa 148 and began translating texts in meditation in the Hīnayāna tradition of escape from psychic causation *(karman).* More popular among philosophically minded Chinese Buddhists and their Daoist friends were "wisdom" *(prajñā)* treatises, and later texts, in the Mādhyamika tradition of Nāgārjuna (second century CE), which teach that the elements of phenomenal existence and our concepts of them are conditioned, relative, and impermanent and thus "empty" *(śūnya).* Realization of this concept leads to a saving mental detachment; thus this kind of thought converged with philosophical Daoism. Early Chinese philosophical Buddhists of this kind include Zhi Dun (314–366) in the South and Sengzhao (384?–414) in the North.

Six Dynasties period. Sengzhao was a disciple of Kumārajīva (344–413), a Central Asian who was brought to Xi'an in 401 and is famous as a translator, especially of Mādhyamika texts. Another important northerner was Dao'an (312–385), who was learned in all aspects of Buddhism and philosophical Daoism and the author of an early catalog of translations. Among Dao'an's many disciples was Huiyuan (334–416) in the South, a believer in Amitābha and his Pure Land *(jingtu)* paradise and the author of a treatise on immortality.

By the sixth century, cults of salvation by faith came to assume a "three ages" theory of history, in which the present epoch was regarded as a final, degenerate age in which men can no longer save themselves by adhering to the pristine Buddhist message as taught by Śākyamuni Buddha. This idea combined with the Mādhyamika concept of multiple truth (see, for example, Jizang, 549–623), which holds that the mind must move through stages of ordinary thought before it can grasp emptiness, greatly increasing the speculative range of Buddhist philosophy. Huiyuan's most famous disciple was Daosheng (c. 360–434), another southerner, whose theories anticipate important ideas in the Tiantai and Chan schools of the Tang era and prefigure central issues in Neo-Confucianism. Drawing on the *Mahāparinirvāṇa Sūtra,* Daosheng argued that all beings have the "Buddha nature," which he identified with "emptiness" *(śūnyatā)* and with the "true self" *(zhen wo).* Enlightenment has to be "sudden" (but after gradual training), since ultimate wisdom cannot be analyzed. Another major translator was Paramārtha (499–569, arriving at the southern court of Liang in 548), who rendered important Yogācāra (idealistic) texts of fully developed Mahāyāna Buddhism.

Since Buddhist thought in China of this period flows in large part from the introduction and translation of texts, texts themselves rather than great teachers are often the focus of schools. These schools did not endure as distinct ideological traditions but represented a major intellectual development toward the sort of "systematic theology" found in the great schools of the Tang era. Mādhyamika thought is the focus of the San-lun (Three Treatises) school, based on three treatises translated by Kumārajīva, and noteworthy for its concept of three levels of truth at successively more complete stages of negation. The Niepan, or Nirvāṇa, school, based on the *Mahāparinirvāṇa Sūtra,* developed out of the interests of Daosheng, until it was absorbed later into Tiantai. The so-called Dilun school was based on the *Shidi jinglun,* a translation, popular in the North, of a treatise by Vasubandhu on a sūtra describing the ten stages of a *bodhisattva.* The Dilun school merged in the Tang with Huayan. The Shelun school was based on Asaṅga's *Mahāyānasaṃgraha* through Paramārtha's translation in 563, and was later superseded by the Faxiang, or "mere ideation," school. Another well-known philosophical text in this tradition, widely read even by non-Buddhists, is the *Dasheng qixin lun* (Treatise on awakening of faith in the Mahāyāna), which was important both for Faxiang and Huayan adherents.

During the long period of North-South division (317–588), Buddhism became the dominant religion in China, but it developed differently in the two areas. In the North, Buddhist institutions were wholly under the control of the state and were even used as a means of control of the populace. In the South, temples were lavishly patronized by emperors (especially Wudi), but monks maintained much independence, and there was a more active climate of debate between Confucians and Daoists; of special interest is the debate over the immortality of the soul. A Confucian, one Fan Zhen, wrote *Shenmie lun* (On the mortality of the soul, c. 500), an essay attacking the Buddhist view (for example, that of Huiyuan) and arguing that the soul is to the body as function *(yong)* is to essence/structure *(ti)* or as sharpness is to a knife. (Buddhists continued to deny the permanence of the phenomenal self, regarding it as mere appearance or "function" *[yong],* as distinct from the real self which is "essence" *[ti],* or Buddha nature; popular faith, however, ignored the distinction. Here, Fan provocatively alters the categories *ti* and *yong.*) Many vigorous replies to Fan are preserved. In the South, critics of the new religion warred with words; in the North, however, there were episodes of state repression, instigated by Confucian and religious Daoist advisers to the emperor, in 446 and between 574 and 577. The most severe of these came later, in 845, under a Daoist Tang emperor.

Sui-Tang period. It was under the reunified empire of the Sui (589–618) and Tang (618–907) that Buddhism reached its greatest strength. The Sui emperors used Buddhism as an official ideology to support the throne, while the Tang emperors claimed descent from Laozi and favors to Buddhism were made more cautiously. But it is in the philosophical schools that flourished in the Tang that fully developed Chinese Buddhism is seen best. The Sanjie jiao, a sect based on the concept of the three ages, started in the Sui by Xinxing (540–594), was suppressed in 713. One of the most important schools of doctrine was Tiantai, systematized by the monk Zhiyi (538–597). Tiantai synthesizes the great variety of Buddhist *sūtras* and doctrines by holding there are different levels of truth and that the Buddha went through different stages of teaching offering different means to salvation. For followers of Tiantai, the *Lotus Sutra (Saddharmapuṇḍarīka Sūtra)* is said to represent the final and most complete teaching of the Buddha. The school is often characterized as holding that the world is universal mind, comprising both a universal, pure (Buddha) nature (compare Daosheng) and an impure nature that produces ordinary phenomena, attachment, and evil. Zhiyi himself, however, was much more a Mādhyamika than an idealist. He emphasized that mind and object are both "ungraspable" (i.e., empty), and that delusion is not ultimately different from enlightenment; perhaps the most famous metaphysical dictum of Tiantai is that "all phenomena are (ultimately) real" *(zhu fa shi xiang)*. A later master, Zhanran (711–782) held that even inanimate things have the Buddha nature.

Another master, Xuanzang (596–664), was the most famous of the Chinese who went to India, brought back texts, and recorded their travels (others were Faxian, who left in 399, and Yijing, who traveled in the seventh century). With his translations, Xuanzang and his disciple Kuiji (632–682) started the Faxiang ("dharma-appearance"), or Weishi ("mere ideation"), school, based on the views of Asaṅga and Vasubandhu that the external world is illusory. There has been a recent revival of this idealist philosophy in China led by Ouyang Jingwu (1871–1943) and the monk Taixu (1889–1947.)

The important masters of another prominent Tang school, the Huayan (Avataṃsaka), were Fashun, or Dushun (557–640), Zhiyan (602–668), Fazang (643–712), and Chengguan (738?–820?). Huayan thinkers held all reality to be a blend of a "world of principle *(li)*" and a "world of things *(shi)*," all phenomena being manifestations of one ultimate principle. Even more than the Tiantai scheme, this suggests the dominant metaphysics of the Neo-Confucianism of the following dynasties. The usually dominant Cheng-Zhu school of Neo-Confucianism, however, tended toward a metaphysical dualism; monistic varieties of Neo-Confucianism are, perhaps, closer to Huayan, which appeals to the fundamental "non-obstruction" of *li* and *shi (lishi wuai)*. The last master of Huayan was Zongmi (780–841). Another tradition of dualistic monism that leaves its mark on Buddhist art, if not on wider philosophy, is the Zhenyan (Tantric) school, whose maṇḍalas and sexual imagery represented wisdom and compassion in a female-male (yin-yang?) relation.

The most important schools, after the persecution of 845, were the Pure Land (Jingtu) and Chan. The former, preaching that one can be reborn in paradise by reciting the name of Amitābha, had as its early master (after Huiyuan) the northern monk Tanluan (476–542); important Tang masters were Daochuo (562–645) and Shandao (613–681). The Chan school represents itself as deriving from an Indian monk, Bodhidharma, said to have come to China about 520, who was a master of meditation (*dhyāna*, hence the name Chan); the school also sees itself as preserving a "mental transmission" of true insight from the Buddha himself. The school recognized a series of "patriarchs," the sixth, according to some northern texts, being Shenxiu (seventh century); his status was challenged by a southern monk, Shenhui (670–762), who claimed that the actual sixth patriarch was a certain Huineng (638–713). The *Platform Sūtra* attributed to Huineng is one of the most widely read and influential texts in and beyond Buddhism. All of the major Neo-Confucian masters from the Song dynasty onward were probably familiar with it, and many had experimented with Chan early in their careers. The Chan religious goal is enlightenment rather than rebirth in a ("Pure Land") paradise, and the Huineng episode marks a division between "northern" and "southern" Chan, the alternatives being final insight reached gradually through meditation and a direct and sudden insight into the real nature of the self and phenomena in the midst of ordinary activity. Two schools have been prominent since 845, the Caodong and the Linji. (Of three others, the Yunmen was active in the Northern Song dynasty.) Linji makes use of physical shocks and baffling, often humorous puzzles to break the mind loose from ordinary thinking; while iconoclastic, it actually owes much to Mādhyamika and to the Daoism of Zhuangzi.

The Confucian Revival. Han Yü (768–824) strongly criticized Buddhism as socially parasitic, and in eloquent essays and letters regarded as models of style he represented himself as reviving the pre-Buddhist Confucianism of Zhou times. Confucians of the Song dynasty (960–1279) regarded him and Li Ao (d. 844) as their precursors. A revival of Confucian thought, as the primary philosophy of social and political participation, was stimulated by the reconstitution of the imperial state in Sui-Tang and the development of the modern civil service examination system, which from the Song onward required a thorough knowledge of the Confucian classics. Other factors contributed: the growth of cities, the invention of printing, and especially the development of the Confucian "academies" (*shuyuan*, perhaps on the model of Buddhist temple schools), which began to appear in the Five Dynasties period (906–959) and multiplied in Song and later. Funded both by the state and by private donors, the Confucian academies were the primary forums of philosophical discussion, and in the late Ming (1368–1644) they became partly political, with famous lecturers drawing huge audiences from distant parts. In the Song the new Confucianism took two forms: One was political, social, and reformist; the other, speculative and metaphysical.

Since the new Confucian thought identified itself as a revival of very ancient ideals, in its reformist aspect it was simultaneously both antiquarian and radical. Fan Zhongyan (989–1052) is known for his adaptation of the *bodhisattva*'s vow—to be the first to suffer hardship and the last to be "saved"—to social service. Ouyang Xiu (1007–1072), best known as a historian, criticized Buddhism as a foreign intrusion and a sickness in society that must be cured by the revival, by the state, of ancient customs, communal spirit, and "rites." In this way "government and doctrine" would once again proceed from the same source: state and society would revitalize each other by recombining. This vision of a benevolent and selfless, albeit totalitarian, utopia has bewitched major Confucian philosophers—among them Zhu Xi, Wang Yangming, Zhang Xuecheng, and Kang Youwei—to the present. Wang Anshi (1021–1086), when directing the government, was the center of a storm of controversy over his reform program. Zhu Xi (1130–1200) too had his reformist side (neglected in later attention to his thought), arguing for a complete revision of the examination and education system.

The other aspect of Song thought was its speculative metaphysics and moral psychology. The fertile eleventh century has three who can be called cosmologists. Zhou Dunyi (1017–1073) offered the *Taiji tu* (Diagram of the supreme ultimate), showing all things as evolved from a first principle that differentiates itself into the yin and yang, then into the "five elements," and so on. Zhang Zai (1020–1077) saw all things as continually condensing out of and dissolving back into a primordial *qi* and drew the moral conclusion that we and all things are one family. Finally, Shao Yong (1011–1077) tried to explain the universe through *Yi jing* binary numerology. Moral psychology includes monists Cheng Hao (1032–1085) and Lu Jiuyuan (Xiangshan) and dualists Cheng Yi (Hao's brother, 1033–1108) and Zhu Xi. The latter tried to synthesize the work of his precursors, and his system became orthodox for the imperial civil service examinations in the Yuan and later dynasties.

The preeminence of Zhu's thought was confirmed by the imperial publication of the encyclopedia *Xingli daquan* in 1415. Zhu's idea resembles Huayan metaphysics: there is a realm of "principle" *(li)* and a realm of "embodiment" *(qi,* literally, "vessel," but in effect "matter," as in the homophonous graph *qi)*. In the human individual, our moral "nature" *(xing)* is our principle, identified with Dao, so that (with Mengzi) we are by "nature" good; evil and selfish tendencies in us are the consequence of "impure" *qi,* different in different individuals, which must be purified by moral cultivation. Long study, for example, of the classics, increases the sum of principle in the mind until a moment of synthetic moral illumination is attained (here is the Cheng-Zhu adaptation of the Buddhist "gradual attainment—sudden enlightenment" problem). Later philosophers debated endlessly on the relation between these entities and their relation to the mind, which Lu and later Wang Yangming identified with principle. Whatever their metaphysics, such thinkers were moral self-cultivationists who saw the primary moral-religious "task" *(gongfu)* as the "correcting of the mind," following the *Li ji* chapter *Da xue* (Great learning). This became for them the foremost of the classic texts. The usual program was to "watch oneself" and to scotch each "selfish thought" *(si yi)* as it arose, recalling the Buddhist anxiety about thoughts of "attachment" being the source of (bad) *karman.* Noteworthy after Zhu are his student Zhen Dexiu (1178–1235) and the Yuan moralist Xu Heng (1209–1281). This "mind learning" was pursued in some form by all the leading moralists of the ensuing Ming dynasty.

The Later Empire. The most important Ming philosopher was Wang Yangming (1472–1529, personal name, Shouren). His most arresting ideas, simple but puzzling enough to provoke a century and a half of controversy, are as follows. (1) We all have, or share, a mental faculty of moral intuition *(liang zhi),* and there are no "principles" *(li)* other than the renditions of this faculty, if we only learn to let it operate without "obscuration" *(bi),* which is the source of evil. Thus, "mind" *(xin)* is "principle" *(li),* and ethics is situational. (2) Complete experience and fully engaged practice involve the operation of this faculty. We do not first apprehend something and then (perhaps consulting a set of rules) decide how to judge it; thus, there is a "unity of knowledge and practice" *(zhi xing heyi).* (3) A "four-sentence teaching" (based on the *Da xue*) explains that the mind in "essence" *(ti)* is uninvolved in good and evil and that these predicates apply only to its activities of thought and judgment.

Was Wang really a Buddhist? No, but his *liang zhi* was the "sun," and "obscuration" was the "clouds" (the images are Huineng's). For Wang mind is Mind, universal, as in Tiantai. And it is in the context of ordinary activity that *liang zhi* reveals to itself a "principle" that eludes abstraction; but the context, and the revelation, are moral. Indeed, as Feng Youlan suggests, if the Chan Buddhist could have accepted family and social relationships as the ordinary activity that is the locus of his Dao, he would have become a Neo-Confucian. But the problematic of Buddhism continues to be played out within Wang's Confucianism. Moralists after Wang were split, some calling for a moral cultivation of strict discipline and others holding that intuition must be allowed to function without forcing or intervention, "here and now" *(dangxia).* Among the latter were Wang Ji (1498–1583), and also Wang Gen (1483–1540) and his followers of the Taizhou school, including He Xinyin (1517–1579) and Li Zhi (1527–1602), both of whom were so boldly individualistic that they died in prison.

China concurrently was experiencing one last intellectual revival of Buddhism, prominent teachers being Zhuhong (1535–1615) and Deqing (1546–1643). There was a marked syncretist tendency everywhere, and experiments in combining the Three Teachings (Confucianism, Daoism, and Buddhism) were thought interesting. (It was perhaps for this reason that Matteo Ricci, himself a friend of Li Zhi, was easily accepted in Chinese intellectual circles.) Some, on the far "left" among post-Wang Confucians, whose *dangxia* ethics tended to be antinomian, were known as "mad Chanists." Li himself actually donned monk's garb and played with Legalist ideas. The last decades of the Ming were scarred by factional strife, especially involving the Confucians of the Donglin Academy group, many of whom lost their lives in their conflict with court eunuchs.

After the Manchu conquest and establishment of the Qing dynasty in 1644, the freewheeling Ming style of philosophy ceased. The academies were absorbed into the government school structure, and at first the outstanding thinkers were men who avoided government service. Such were Huang Zongxi (1610–1695), noted historian of Song, Yuan, and Ming philosophy and advocate of limitations on imperial power; Gu Yanwu (1613–1682), a philologist who accepted Zhu Xi's views but favored "search for evidence" ("the study of *li* is the study of the classics"); Wang Fuzhi (1619–1692), recluse and anti-Manchu philosopher of history; and Yan Yuan (1635–1704), a "pragmatist" who rejected Song-Ming metaphysics as impractical and meaningless. Gu set the intellectual tone for the next two centuries, which prized philological scholarship (often patronized by the imperial court or by wealthy officials who financed expensive projects of compilation, drawing many scholars together) and tended to disparage mere "empty words," that is, speculative philosophy. But the Qing emperors vigorously promoted Cheng-Zhu moral philosophy for its disciplinary value, and they were assured by flatterers that at last, as in the golden age of antiquity, "government" *(zhi)* and true "doctrine" *(jiao)* were again one.

This echo of Ouyang Xiu stirred the imagination of a genuinely independent thinker of the next century, Zhang Xuecheng (1738–1801), a local historian whose philosophy of history pictured antiquity as a concrete "unity of knowledge and practice" ("the Six Classics are all history") or of Dao and *qi.* Zhang much admired the experiments in Mencian ethics of his contemporary Dai Zhen (1724–1777), but he censured Dai for his impatience with Zhu Xi. Intellectualist and not at all self-cultivationist, the famous philological scholar Dai held that principles and human desires are not antithetical and that to become a sage one must feed the mind with knowledge, testing candidate principles by applying the Confucian golden rule *(shu)* until what is only "natural" *(ziran)* is seen to be "necessary" *(biran).* For Dai, the prime form of evil is to mistake one's own mere "opinions" *(yijian)* for true principles and to force them on others.

What had happened in the Qing dynasty turn in thought was both a reaction against the speculative and introspective temper of earlier Neo-Confucianism and, at the same time, a further development of its implications. Wang Yangming had insisted that principles cannot be grasped abstractly apart from concrete moral experience; the Qing intellectualist translation of this idea was that philosophical insight cannot be separated from historical and philological "solid learning."

Neither Zhang nor Dai received philosophical recognition until the twentieth century. Meanwhile, another intellectual movement was gathering force: Qing philology. Leading many to reject "Song studies" *(Song xue)* for "Han studies" *(Han xue),* Qing philology in time led to a reassessment of the Han era New Text philosophy of history of Dong Zhongshu and He Xiu. Their ideas were taken up by Kang Youwei (1858–1927) and others among the group of Confucian intellectuals pushing radical political reforms at the end of the nineteenth century. Kang urged a revisionist view of the classics (in which the Han court librarian Liu Xin figured as villain, forging half of them) that portrayed Confucius as a reformer, holding a historical, Western-style theory of progress. Confucianism was to be a religion, since the model of the West showed that a lively religious faith was necessary for progress and national strength. This idea lingered into the twentieth century, naturally enough among the Chinese, for whom the West for generations had been represented by missionaries, and who failed to see that the Western faith that sent the missionaries to China was already waning.

The Twentieth Century. The 1920s saw the first real impact of American and European contemporary academic philosophy, notably in the lively controversy on "science and philosophy of life" in 1923. A primary problem for twentieth-century thinkers was how to reconcile their commitments to historical Chinese values with Western intellectual temptations. Thus, Hu Shi (1891–1962), a student of John Dewey, hunted through Chinese philosophy for examples of pragmatism and logical method. Thus also, Marxists of the Liberation period (c. 1949) wrote one another little essays on "how to study" *(xuexi),* and on how to reform "individual nature" *(ge xing)* into "party nature" *(dang xing),* picking into ancient Confucian (and even Buddhist) self-cultivationist literature. Those who saw Communism as a new religion, and the hallmark of religion as the desire for self-change, should not have been surprised. Twentieth-century thought sometimes continued the past and sometimes merely used it, but it seldom ignored it. There have been the non-Marxists (Xiong Shili, Confucian-Buddhist; Feng Youlan and He Lin, Neo-Confucian; Hu Shi, pragmatist; Zhang Dongsun, Neo-Kantian), the Marxists (Li Dazhao, Chen Boda, Liu Shaoqi, Mao Zedong himself), both at once (perhaps, Liang Shuming), and both by turns (Feng again). Such deeply thoughtful men as Xu Fuguan and Mou Zongsan (students of Xiong) and the late Tang Junyi can genuinely be called contemporary religious philosophers within the Confucian mold.

See Also Afterlife, article on Chinese Concepts; Alchemy, article on Chinese Alchemy; Buddhism, article on Buddhism in China; Buddhism, Schools of, article on Chinese Buddhism; Buddhist Books and Texts, article on Exegesis and Hermeneutics; Cheng Hao; Cheng Yi Chinese Religion, overview article; Confucianism, overview article; Confucius; Dai Zhen; Dao and De; Daoism; Dong Zhongshu; Ge Hong; Guo Xiang; Gu Yanwu; Han Fei Zi; Kang Youwei; Laozi; Legalism; Li; Liu An; Mappō; Mengzi; Mozi; Nāgārjuna; Qi; Shangdi; Taiji; Taiping; Tian; Wang Bi; Wang Chong; Wang Fuzhi; Wang Yangming; Xian; Xiao; Xunzi; Yao and Shun; Yinyang Wuxing; Yu; Zhang Xuecheng; Zhang Zai; Zhou Dunyi; Zhu Xi; Zhuangzi; Zhuhong.

Bibliography

Briere, O. *Fifty Years of Chinese Philosophy, 1898–1950.* Translated by Laurence G. Thompson and edited by Dennis J. Doolin. London, 1956.

Chan, Wing-tsit. *An Outline and an Annotated Bibliography of Chinese Philosophy.* New Haven, 1961.

Chan, Wing-tsit, trans. and comp. *A Source Book in Chinese Philosophy.* Princeton, 1963. Includes an especially useful bibliography.

Ch'en, Kenneth. *Buddhism in China: A Historical Survey.* Princeton, 1964. Includes an especially useful bibliography.

Cua, Antonio S., ed. *Encyclopedia of Chinese Philosophy.* New York and London, 2003. Valuable for the study of contemporary thinkers.

de Bary, Wm. Theodore, ed. *Self and Society in Ming Thought.* New York, 1970.

de Bary, Wm. Theodore, ed. *The Unfolding of Neo-Confucianism.* New York, 1975.

de Bary, Wm. Theodore. *Neo-Confucian Orthodoxy and the Learning of the Mind-and-Heart.* New York, 1981.

de Bary, Wm. Theodore, Wing-tsit Chan, and Burton Watson, comps. *Sources of Chinese Tradition.* New York, 1960.

de Bary, Wm. Theodore, and Irene Bloom, comp. *Sources of Chinese Tradition,* vol. 1, 2d ed. New York, 1999.

Forke, Alfred. *Geschichte der alten Chinesischen Philosophie; Geschichte der Mittelalterlichen Chinesischen Philosophie; Geschichte der Neueren Chinesischen Philosophie.* Hamburg, 1927, 1934, 1938.

Fung Yu-lan. *A History of Chinese Philosophy.* 2 vols. 2d ed. Translated by Derk Bodde. Princeton, 1952–1953. Includes an especially useful bibliography.

Furth, Charlotte, ed. *The Limits of Change: Essays on Conservative Alternatives in Republican China.* Cambridge, Mass., 1976.

Graham, A. C. *Two Chinese Philosophers: Ch'êng Ming-tao and Ch'êng Yi-ch'uan.* London, 1958.

Graham, Angus C. *Disputers of the Tao: Philosophical Argument in Ancient China,* La Salle, Ill., 1989.

Hsiao Kung-chuan. *A History of Chinese Political Thought,* vol. 1, *From the Beginnings to the Sixth Century A.D.* Translated by F. W. Mote. Princeton, 1979.

Loewe, Michael, and Edward L. Shaughnessy, editors. *The Cambridge History of Ancient China: From the Origins of Civilization to 221 B.C.* Cambridge, U.K., 1999.

Metzger, Thomas A. *Escape from Predicament: Neo-Confucianism and China's Evolving Political Culture.* New York, 1977.

Needham, Joseph. *Science and Civilisation in China,* vol. 2, *History of Scientific Thought.* Cambridge, U.K., 1956. Includes an especially useful bibliography.

Nivison, David S., and Arthur F. Wright, eds. *Confucianism in Action.* Stanford, Calif., 1959.

Nivison, David S., Bryan W. Van Norden, eds. *The Ways of Confucianism: Investigations in Chinese Philosophy.* Chicago, 1996.

Schwartz, Benjamin I. *The World of Thought in Ancient China.* Cambridge, Mass., 1985.

Wright, Arthur F., ed. *Studies in Chinese Thought.* Chicago, 1953.

Wright, Arthur F. *Buddhism in Chinese History.* Stanford, Calif., 1959. Includes an especially useful bibliography.

David S. Nivison (1987 and 2005)

CHINESE RELIGION

This entry consists of the following articles:

AN OVERVIEW
POPULAR RELIGION
MYTHIC THEMES
HISTORY OF STUDY

CHINESE RELIGION: AN OVERVIEW

This article provides an introduction to the rise and development of various religious movements, themes, and motifs over time. Its emphasis is on historical continuities and on the interaction of diverse currents of Chinese religious thought and practice from the prehistoric era to the present.

The study of Chinese religion presents both problems and opportunities for the general theory of religion. It is therefore instructive, before embarking on a historical survey, to outline a theoretical approach that will accommodate the wide variety of beliefs and practices that have traditionally been studied under the rubric of religion in China.

One indicator of the problematic nature of the category "religion" in Chinese history is the absence of any premodern word that unambiguously denotes the category. The modern Chinese word *zongjiao* was first employed to mean "religion" by late-nineteenth-century Japanese translators of European texts. *Zongjiao* (or *shūkyō* in Japanese) is a compound consisting of *zong (shū),* which is derived from a pictogram of an ancestral altar and most commonly denotes a "sect," and *jiao (kyō),* meaning "teaching." (The compound had originally been a Chinese Buddhist term meaning simply the teachings of a particular sect.) *Zongjiao/shūkyō* thus carries the connotation of "ancestral" or sectarian teachings. The primary reference of this newly coined usage for *shūkyō* in the European texts being translated was, of course, Christianity. And since Christianity does in fact demand exclusive allegiance and does emphasize doctrinal orthodoxy (as in the various creeds), *zongjiao/shūkyō* is an apt translation for the concept of religion that takes Christianity as its standard or model.

Part of the problem arising from this situation is that Chinese (and Japanese) religions in general do not place as much emphasis as Christianity does on exclusivity and doctrine. And so Chinese, when asked to identify what counts as *zongjiao* in their culture, are often reluctant to include phenomena that westerners would be willing to count as religion, because the word *religion*—while notoriously difficult to define—does not carry the same connotations as *zongjiao.*

Before the adoption of *zongjiao, jiao* itself ("teaching") came closest in usage to the meaning of "religion." Since at least the Ming dynasty (1368–1644), the standard rubric for discussing the religions of China was *san jiao,* or the "three teachings," referring to Confucianism, Daoism, and Buddhism. Yet this is problematic too, as it excludes what today is usually called "popular religion" (or "folk religion"), which throughout Chinese history has probably accounted for more religious behavior than the "three teachings" combined. This exclusion is more than a matter of usage: *jiao* does not apply well to popular religion because popular religion is strongly oriented toward religious action or practice; it has very little doctrine and, apart from independent sects, no institutionally recognized canonical texts in which doctrines would be presented.

Confucianism also presents problems. Although constituting a standard chapter in modern Western surveys of Chinese religion, Confucianism is very often described as something other than a religion in the strict (yet poorly defined) sense. There was a time in Western scholarship when Buddhism was occasionally described in similar fashion, although outside the most conservative theological frameworks that is no longer the case. But the status of Confucianism, even in academic circles focused on Chinese religion, is still disputed.

The problematic nature of Confucianism vis-à-vis religion is the most compelling reason to suggest at the outset a conceptual framework in which all the varieties of Chinese religion can be understood. In effect this is a "definition" of religion, although it should not be considered an exclusive definition. It is, instead, one way of conceptualizing religion that is well suited to its subject—that is, that makes particularly good sense of *Chinese* religion—and that sheds light not only on the noncontroversial forms of Chinese religion but also on those forms that might be excluded by some definitions. But it should be acknowledged that, since religion is a multidimensional set of complex human phenomena, no single definition (short of a laundry list of common characteristics) should be expected to capture its essence. Indeed, perhaps religion has no essence.

The concept of religion that will be presumed here is that *religion is a means of ultimate transformation and/or ultimate orientation.* This is an elaboration of a definition proposed by the Buddhologist Frederick Streng, who suggested that religion is "a means to ultimate transformation" (Streng, 1985, p. 2). "Ultimate transformation" implies (1) a given human condition that is in some way flawed, unsatisfactory, or caught in a dilemma; (2) a goal that posits a resolution of that problem or dilemma; and (3) a process leading toward the achievement of the goal. This formula is well suited to Chinese religions because the concept of transformation (*hua*) is in fact a highly significant element in Confucian, Daoist, and Chinese Buddhist thought and practice. The qualifier "ultimate" means that the starting point, process, and goal are defined in relation to whatever the tradition in question believes to be absolute or unconditioned. "Ultimate orientation" introduces an aspect of Mircea Eliade's theory of sacred space and sacred time: spatial orientation to an *axis mundi,* a symbolic connection between heaven and earth; or temporal orientation marked in reference to periods of sacred ritual time, such as annual festivals. This addition to Streng's definition accounts for certain popular practices that are not conceived in terms of ultimate transformation. Much of the contemporary practice of Chinese popular religion—such as worship and sacrifice for such mundane ends as success in school or business—can be explained in terms of ultimate orientation. And Confucianism, the most problematic strand of Chinese religion, can clearly be seen as a "means of ultimate transformation" toward the religious goal of "sagehood" (*sheng*), a term whose religious connotations are suggested, for example, by the use of the same word to translate the Jewish and Christian "Holy Scriptures" (*shengjing*).

The geographic scope of Chinese religions extends from mainland China to Taiwan, Singapore, Southeast Asia, and scattered Chinese communities throughout the world. Although religion in the People's Republic of China on the mainland was harshly suppressed from the 1950s through the 1970s, and indeed almost disappeared during that period, there has been considerable (although not untroubled) revitalization since the early 1980s. Our discussion of religion in Chinese history will focus on mainland China and, after the nineteenth century, Taiwan.

Contemporary Chinese religion is the product of continuous historical development from prehistoric times. In that period the area of present-day China was inhabited by a large number of tribal groups. In around 5000 BCE several of these tribes developed agriculture and began to live in small villages surrounded by their fields. Domesticated plants and animals included millet, rice, dogs, pigs, goats, sheep, cattle, and silkworms. The physical characteristics of these early agriculturalists were similar to those of modern Chinese. The archaeological record indicates gradual development toward more complex technology and social stratification. By the late Neolithic period (beginning around 3200 BCE) there were well-developed local cultures in several areas that were to become centers of Chinese civilization later, including the southeast coast, the southwest, the Yangzi River valley, the northeast, and the northern plains. The interaction of these cultures eventually led to the rise of literate, bronze-working civilizations in the north, the Xia (before 1500 BCE) and Shang (c. 1500–1050 BCE). The existence of the Xia kingdom is attested in early historical sources that have otherwise been shown to accord with archaeological discoveries. However, archaeologists are still debating whether the Xia period constituted a state-level "dynasty," as it has traditionally been described. The Shang has been archaeologically verified, beginning with the excavation of one of its capitals in 1928.

There is some evidence for prehistoric religious activities, particularly for a cult of the dead, who were often buried in segregated cemeteries, supine, with heads toward a single cardinal direction. In some sites houses and circles of white stones are associated with clusters of graves, while in others wine goblets and pig jaws are scattered on ledges near the top of the pit, perhaps indicating a farewell feast. There seems to have been a concern for the precise ordering of ritual acts, perhaps an early version of the importance of universal order or pattern in later Chinese cosmology. In the Wei River area, secondary burial was practiced, with bones from single graves collected and reburied with those of from twenty to eighty others. Grave offerings are found in almost all primary burials, with quantity and variety depending on the status of the deceased: tools, pottery vessels, objects of jade and turquoise, dogs, and, in some cases, human beings. Jade, in particular—a substance that does not break down and requires extraordinary skill and effort to carve with the simplest of tools—was associated with high-status burials and perhaps symbolized the eternity of the afterlife. The *bi* (a flat disk with a central hole) and *cong* (a tube, square on the outside and circular inside) were jade mortuary objects—apparently not used in life—whose meanings have not been determined. The bodies and faces of the dead were often painted with red ochre, a symbol of life. All of these practices constitute the prehistoric beginnings of Chinese ancestor worship. Other evidence for prehistoric religion includes deer buried in fields and divination through reading cracks in the dried shoulder bones of sheep or deer. This form of divination, attested in what is now northeast China by 3560–3240 BCE, is the direct antecedent of similar practices in historical times. Buried deer suggest offerings to the power of the soil, a common practice in later periods.

Early Historical Period. The early historical period (Shang and Zhou kingdoms) saw the development of many of the social and religious beliefs and practices that continue to this day to be associated with the Chinese. Although obvious links with the earlier period persist, it is with the emergence of these kingdoms that the religious history of the Chinese properly begins.

The Shang. The formation of the Shang kingdom was the result of technological innovation such as bronze casting and to the development of new forms of social and administrative control. Extant evidence provides information about the religion of the Shang aristocracy, characterized in the first place by elaborate graves and ceremonial objects for the dead. Grave offerings include decapitated human beings, horses, dogs, large numbers of bronze vessels, and objects of jade, stone, and shell. Some tombs were equipped with chariots hitched to horses. These tomb offerings indicate a belief that afterlife for members of the royal clan was similar to that of their present existence but in a heavenly realm presided over by the Shang high god Di ("Lord") or Shangdi ("Lord on High").

The major sources for our understanding of Shang religion are inscriptions on oracle bones and in bronze sacrificial vessels. From these we learn that the most common recipients of petition and inquiry were the ancestors of the royal clan. These deified ancestors were believed to have powers of healing and fertility in their own right, but they also could serve as intermediaries between their living descendants and more powerful gods of natural forces and Shangdi. Ancestors were ranked by title and seniority, with those longest dead having the widest authority. Since they could bring harm as well as aid to their descendants, it was necessary to propitiate the ancestors to ward off their anger as well as to bring their blessing. Nature deities named in the inscriptions personify the powers of rivers, mountains, rain, wind, and other natural phenomena. Shangdi, whose authority exceeded that of the most exalted royal ancestor, served as a source of unity and order.

To contact these sacred powers the Shang practiced divination and sacrificial rituals, usually closely related to each other. In divination, small pits were bored in the backs of turtle plastrons or the shoulder blades of oxen or sheep. Heated bronze or wooden rods were placed in these impressions, causing the bones to crack with a popping sound. Diviners then interpreted the pattern of the cracks on the face of the bone, perhaps combined with the sound of the popping, to determine yes or no answers to petitions. The subjects of divination include weather, warfare, illness, administrative decisions, harvests, royal births (with the preference for sons that was to continue throughout Chinese history already present), and other practical issues, but the most frequent type of inquiry was in reference to sacrifices to ancestors and deities. Sacrifices to ancestors and spirits residing above consisted mainly of burning meat and grain on open-air altars; gods of the earth were offered libations of fermented liquors, and those of bodies of water given precious objects such as jade. Sacrificial animals included cattle, dogs, and sheep. Human beings were sacrificed during the funeral rituals of kings, presumably to serve them in the afterlife. At least one powerful woman was also buried with human sacrifices, in addition to thousands of precious objects (bronze and jade objects, cowrie shells). This was Fu Hao (Lady Hao), the wife of King Wuding, around 1200 BCE, who apparently commanded an army during her lifetime and was given sacrifices after her death.

The Shang had a ten-day week, and the titles of the deified royal ancestors corresponded to the day on which sacrifice was made to them. Thus, their personal characteristics were less significant than their seniority and their place in the ritual cycle. In the sacrifices themselves what was most important was the proper procedure; the correct objects offered in the right way were believed to obligate the spirits to respond. Thus, in Shang sacrifice we already see the principle of reciprocity, which has remained a fundamental pattern of interaction throughout the history of Chinese religions. In Shang theology the king played the role of intermediary between the human and heavenly realms. He was responsible for maintaining harmonious relations with his ancestors, Di, and the other deities, and so ensuring their blessings on the realm. The considerable expenditures of time and resources devoted to sacrifice and divination in the Shang court suggest that the authority of the king depended in part on his role as the pivot between heaven and earth.

The Zhou. There are many references in Shang oracle bone texts to a people called Zhou who lived west of the Shang center, in the area of modern Shanxi province. The Zhou, who were considered to be an important tributary state, were at first culturally and technologically inferior to the Shang, but they learned rapidly and by the eleventh century BCE challenged the Shang for political supremacy. The final Zhou conquest took place in about 1050 BCE. Remnants of the Shang royal line were allowed to continue their ancestral practices in the small state of Song, in exchange for pledging loyalty to the Zhou.

The Zhou system of government has been loosely called "feudal," but it differed from European feudalism in that the peasants were not bound to the land, and the local lords (*gong*, or "dukes") owed allegiance to the central king (*wang*) based not on law but on bonds of kinship. The king directly ruled only a small territory around the capital city, Chang'an, which was located in the Wei River valley near present-day Xian. He controlled an army, which frequently was joined by armies of the various dukes. The Zhou kings were the first to call themselves "Son of Heaven" (*tianzi*), a term that continued to be applied to the later emperors of China up to the early twentieth century. Corollary to their identity as Son of Heaven, they alone had the right and responsibility to make annual sacrifices to heaven. This too was a practice that lasted until the twentieth century.

The Zhou dynasty lasted nominally almost eight hundred years, making it the longest-lasting dynasty in world history. But in fact their power and their territory remained intact only until 771 BCE, when the king was assassinated and the capital was moved eastward to the more easily defended Luoyang. The periods corresponding to these two capitals are called Western Zhou (1150–770 BCE) and Eastern Zhou (771–221 BCE). The Eastern Zhou was a period of increasing fragmentation and is further divided into the Spring and Autumn period (722–403 BCE) and the Warring States period (403–221 BCE). The former is named after a chronicle of the state of Lu, in contemporary Shandong province, covering these years and traditionally attributed to Confucius (Lu was Confucius's home state). The latter period, as the name implies, saw almost constant warfare, as the last seven major states (formerly Zhou fiefdoms) battled it out until only one was left standing, the Qin.

The Western Zhou period, especially the periods of the earliest kings, was regarded by later Chinese thinkers as a golden age of enlightened, benevolent rule by sage-kings. They especially revered the first two kings, Wen and Wu (whose names mean "culture" and "military," respectively), and King Wu's brother, the duke of Zhou, whose "fief" was the state of Lu. But it was the Eastern Zhou, the period of political disintegration, that witnessed the origins of classical Chinese civilization. It was during this era—sometimes called the Period of the Hundred Philosophers—that Confucianism, Daoism, and many other schools of thought began.

Unlike the sources available to us regarding Shang religion, which are limited to oracle bones and inscriptions on bronze ritual vessels, there are enough Zhou sources to allow us say something about the religion of common people as well that of the aristocracy. Both commoners and elite believed in gods, ghosts, ancestors, and omens (the significance to human beings of unusual phenomena in nature) and practiced divination, sacrifice, and exorcism. The common ground shared by the elite and the common people was much more extensive than their differences, which for the most part were differences in emphasis and interpretation. These distinctions begin to emerge in the Western Zhou and become clearer in the Eastern Zhou, or Classical, period.

The early Zhou elite, as might be expected, were chiefly concerned with their aristocratic ancestors, the powerful ruling gods, and political matters, while the common people had more interaction with lower gods, demons, and ghosts that inhabited the world and generally made trouble for people. The Zhou ancestors were believed to reside in a celestial court presided over by Tian, "Heaven," the Zhou high god, similar to Shangdi in scope and function although less personalized. The ancestors had power to influence the prosperity of their descendants, their fertility, health, and longevity. Through ritual equation of natural forces with deities, the ancestors could also influence the productivity of clan lands. In addition, royal ancestors served as intermediaries between their descendants and Tian.

Ancestral rituals took the form of great feasts in which the deceased was represented by an impersonator, usually a grandson or nephew. In these feasts the sharing of food and drink confirmed vows of mutual fidelity and aid. The most important ancestor worshiped was Houji, who was both legendary founder of the ruling house and the patron of agriculture. As was true for the Shang, Zhou rituals were also directed toward symbols of natural power such as mountains and rivers; most significant natural phenomena were deified and worshiped. The proper time and mode of such rituals were determined in part by divination, which in the Zhou involved both cracking bones and turtle plastrons and the manipulation of dried stalks of the yarrow or milfoil plant. Divination was also employed in military campaigns, the interpretation of dreams, the siting of cities, and in many other situations involving important decisions.

Milfoil divination became the method at the core of the *Zhouyi,* or *Changes of Zhou,* a divination manual that acquired philosophical commentaries and became known as the *Yijing,* or *Scripture of Change,* part of the earliest Confucian canon. The *Yijing* classifies human and natural situations by means of sixty-four sets of six horizontal lines (hexagrams), each of which is either broken or solid. The solid lines represent *qian,* or Heaven, the creative or initiating force of nature, while the broken lines represent *kun,* or earth, which receives and completes. The permutations of these fundamental principles, according to early Chinese cosmology, constitute the patterns or principles of all possible circumstances and experiences. Through ritual manipulation involving chance divisions, the milfoil stalks are arranged in sets with numerical values corresponding to lines in the hexagrams. One thereby obtains a hexagram that reflects one's present situation; additional line changes indicate the direction of change, and thus a potential outcome. Contemplation of these hexagrams clarifies decisions and provides warning or encouragement.

The *Yijing* is essentially a book of wisdom for personal and administrative guidance, used since at least the seventh century BCE. However, from the sixth century BCE on commentaries were written to amplify the earliest level of the text, and by the first century CE there were seven such levels of exposition, some quite philosophical in tone. The *Scripture of Change* was believed to reflect the structure of the cosmic order and its transformations, and hence became an object of reverent contemplation in itself. Its earliest levels antedated all the philosophical schools, so it belonged to none, though the Confucians later claimed it as sacred scripture. The polarity of *qian* and *kun* provided a model for that of yang and yin, first discussed in the fourth century BCE. The *Yijing*'s sometimes obscure formulations gave impetus to philosophical speculations throughout the later history of Chinese thought.

A third focus of Zhou worship, in addition to ancestors and nature gods, was the *she,* a sacred earth mound located in the capital of each state and in at least some villages. The state *she* represented the sacred powers of the earth available to a particular domain and so was offered libations upon such important occasions in the life of the state as the birth of a prince, ascension to rule, and military campaigns. Beside the earth mound stood a sacred tree, a symbol of its connection to the powers of the sky. The *she* was an early form of the shrine to the earth-god, or *tudi gong,* which is a prominent part of Chinese popular religion today.

The early Zhou aristocracy carried out sacrificial rituals to mark the seasons of the year and promote the success of farming. These sacrifices, performed in ancestral temples, were offered both to the high god Tian and to ancestors. These and other Zhou rituals were elaborate dramatic performances involving music, dancing, and archery, concluding with feasts in which much wine was consumed.

The most distinctive early Zhou contribution to the history of Chinese religions was the theory of *tianming,* the "Mandate of Heaven," first employed to justify the Zhou conquest of the Shang and attributed to the duke of Zhou. According to this theory, Heaven as a high god wills order and peace for human society. This divine order is to be administered by virtuous kings who care for their subjects on Heaven's behalf. These kings are granted divine authority to rule, but only so long as they rule well. If they become indolent, corrupt, and cruel, the Mandate of Heaven can be transferred to another line. This process can take a long time and involve many warnings to the ruler in the form of natural calamities and popular unrest. Those who heed such warnings can repent and rehabilitate their rule; otherwise, the mandate can be claimed by one who promises to restore righteous administration. In practice it is the victors who claim the mandate, as did the founding Zhou kings, on the grounds of the alleged indolence and impiety of the last Shang ruler. The idea of the Mandate of Heaven has gripped the Chinese political imagination ever since. It became the basis for the legitimacy of dynasties, the judgment of autocracy, and the moral right of rebellion. This status it owed in part to its support by Confucius and his school, who saw the Mandate of Heaven as the foundation of political morality. The corollary notion that Heaven has a moral will was the first formulation of what later became a foundation principle of Confucian thought: that human moral values are grounded in the natural world.

Commoners during the Zhou period had less reason to trust in the moral will of Heaven, as the lives they led were more subject to hardships imposed by capricious natural phenomena than those of the ruling elite. The *Scripture of Odes* (*Shijing*), for example, contains the following verse that probably reflects the feelings of common people:

> Great Heaven, unjust, Is sending down these exhausting disorders. Great Heaven, unkind, Is sending down these great miseries. (Translated by Poo, 1998, p. 37)

While such sentiments were undoubtedly not limited entirely to the common people, they are strikingly at odds with the concept of a moral, just Heaven. Commoners' beliefs were closely tied to the agricultural cycle and the negative or dangerous spiritual forces inhabiting the world. In contrast to the more abstract Heaven, these forces took the form of an astonishing variety of gods, demons, and spirits. These included the gods of particular mountains, rivers, and seas (usually depicted in hybrid animal or animal-human forms), earth gods (*tu shen*), a sacred serpent, a thorn demon, a water-bug god, hungry ghosts, and the high god, called Shangdi (High Lord, the same term used during the Shang dynasty), Shang Huang (High Sovereign), or Shang Shen (High God). With the possible exception of the high god, these deities were not immortal. Nor were they concerned with human morality; unlike Tian, they responded only to properly performed sacrifices. Sacrifice by commoners was generally performed for personal and familial welfare, unlike the predominant concerns among the elite for affairs of state.

When the early Zhou political and social synthesis began to deteriorate in the eighth century and competing local states moved toward political, military, and ritual independence, rulers from clans originally enfeoffed by Zhou kings also lost their power, which reverted to competing local families. This breakdown of hereditary authority led to new social mobility, with status increasingly awarded for military valor and administrative ability, regardless of aristocratic background. There is some evidence that even peasants could move about in search of more just rulers. These political and social changes were accompanied by an increase in the number and size of cities and in the circulation of goods between states. But as warfare increased throughout this period, commoners were repeatedly conscripted into various armies, playing havoc with local agricultural economies (not to mention social morale and family life) as able-bodied men were forcibly taken away from their fields. There were numerous shifting alliances among the powerful states (as the former fiefdoms could now be called), and gradually their number decreased as the most powerful gobbled up the weaker ones.

During the final century or so of the Warring States period, some of the dukes began calling themselves kings (*wang*), usurping the title reserved for the central monarch under the Zhou system.

This time of social mobility and political chaos was a fertile period in the history of Chinese religion and philosophy. There began to appear a new class of intellectual elite, who would eventually produce the texts that formed the foundations of the Classical tradition. The intellectuals, like the ruling elite, were interested in the abstract notion of a moral Heaven, although they understood it less as a doctrine of political legitimation and more as a religious basis for a system of ethical thought and practice. The ruling elite, on the other hand—finding that the need for legitimation of their military takeover of the Shang (now over two hundred years in the past) was not as pressing as it once had been—seem to have lost interest in the idea and concentrated more on the older systems of worship of royal ancestors and spirits of nature. These older rituals became more elaborate and were focused on the ancestors of the rulers of the states rather than on those of the Zhou kings.

Some intellectuals in this era were led to question the power of the gods. In theory, the loss of a state was ultimately the result of ritual negligence by the ruler, while the victors were supposed to provide for sacrifices to the ancestors of the vanquished. But in practice, many gods charged with protection were deemed to have failed while their desecrators flourished. The worldviews of the elite and the commoners were not radically distinct: the panoply of spiritual beings was known to all, and to the extent that members of the elite had family roots in the agricultural tradition, they too engaged in the ritual forms of propitiation of and communication with the various gods, ghosts, and spirits. The religious worldview was a continuous whole, in which differences in emphasis corresponded to differences in the immediate concerns and interests of its participants.

By the sixth century many intellectuals had developed a more rationalistic perspective, accompanied by a turning away from gods and spirits to the problems of human society and governance. The collapse of the Zhou system persuaded the majority of intellectuals that there was a critical need for a new political and ideological foundation for the state. There were, essentially, two aspects to the intellectual problem posed by the Zhou breakdown: theoretical and practical. The theoretical problem stemmed from the doctrine of the Mandate of Heaven: if Heaven indeed has (or is) a moral will, and if Heaven has the power to influence human events by replacing evil rulers with good ones, how can such violence and suffering continue? This question and the question of the nature and origin of evil, usually posed as the question of human nature, became central to the Confucian tradition by the end of the Zhou period. The practical problem, which on the whole received more attention than the theoretical one, was simply, how are social and political order and harmony to be restored? What is the proper role of government in human life, and how should society and government be organized and run? How can rulers discharge their moral responsibilities to their people and to Heaven? How can they maintain their legitimacy in light of the Mandate of Heaven?

Confucius. It was in this context that we find the beginnings of Chinese philosophy. Confucius (c. 551–479 BCE) was born in the small state of Lu, near the present city of Qufu, in present-day Shandong province. His given name was Kong Qiu; as an adult he was commonly known as Kong Zhongni, although many called him by the honorific name Kongzi, or Master Kong. "Confucius" is a latinized name invented by seventeenth-century Jesuit missionaries in China, based on a very rarely used honorific name, Kongfuzi. Lu was a state in which the old Zhou cultural traditions were strong but that was buffeted both by repeated invasions and by local power struggles. Confucius's goal was the restoration of the ethical standards, just rule, and legitimate government—the *dao,* or "Way"—of the early Zhou period as he understood them. The models for the restoration of the *dao* were the founding kings of the Zhou dynasty, who had ruled with reverence toward their ancestors and kindness toward their people, ever fearful of losing Heaven's approval. These models had mythic force for Confucius, who saw himself as their embodiment in his own age.

The sources from which the Way of the ancient kings could be learned were ritual, historical, literary, and oracular texts, some of which later came to be known as the Five Scriptures (*wujing*). ("Five Classics" is the usual translation, but they certainly were regarded by Confucius and his followers as sacred texts, so "scriptures" is more accurate.) In addition to the *Yijing,* the divination text discussed above, they included the *Shijing* (Scripture of Odes), a collection of folk and aristocratic songs allegedly collected by Confucius; the *Shujing* (Scripture of Documents), purporting to consist of official documents from the ancient Xia dynasty (still historically undocumented) up through the Shang and early Zhou dynasties; the *Chunqiu* (Spring and Autumn), the terse history of Confucius's home state of Lu; and the *Liji* (Record of Ritual), which describes not only the formal rituals of the early Zhou but also the modes of behavior, customs, dress, and other aspects of the lives of the early kings. A sixth one, the *Yuejing* (Scripture of Music), is no longer extant but sections of it survive in the *Liji.*

Although several parts of the Five Scriptures were later attributed to Confucius, it is not likely that he wrote anything that survives. The best source of his teachings is the *Lunyu* (*Analects*), a collection of his sayings recorded by his disciples after his death. Since the compilation of this text continued for over a century, much of it is not historically reliable. Nevertheless, throughout Chinese history until recent times it has been regarded as the definitive teachings of Confucius, so in terms of its influence on Chinese culture it can be read as a whole.

Confucius believed that society could be transformed by the moral cultivation of those in power, because virtue (*de*) has a natural transformative effect on others. This inner moral power or potential was "given birth to" in the individual by Heaven, and it was this that Heaven responded to, not merely the outward show of ritual or the exercise of force. Thus, government by virtue—that is, by setting a moral example—was actually more effective in the long run than government by force or the strict application of law and punishment. *De* had earlier referred simply to the power of a ruler to attract and influence subjects—his charisma, in the Weberian sense—so in this and several other respects Confucius's innovation was to moralize a concept that hitherto had been ethically neutral. The moral perfection of the individual and the perfection of society were coordinate goals, for the moral perfection of the self *required* a morally supportive social environment, in the form of stable and loving families, opportunities for education, and good rulers to serve as models. Society as a whole could best be perfected from the top down, and in terms of the political situation it was most important to establish a government staffed by virtuous men (women did not serve in government). For these reasons Confucius directed his teaching toward local rulers and men whose goal was to serve in government. Literacy was a prerequisite of the moral cultivation that he taught, and so he did not bring his message to the masses, the great majority of whom at that time were illiterate.

He gathered a small group of disciples whom he taught to become *junzi* (superior men), men of ethical sensitivity and historical wisdom who were devoted to moral self-cultivation in preparation to become humane and able government officials. The term *junzi* had originally referred to hereditary nobility, but Confucius used it to mean a kind of moral nobility. Likewise, he expanded the meaning of *li,* or "ritual," to mean proper behavior and a kind of reverent seriousness in one's every action. The highest virtue was *ren,* "humanity" or "humaneness," which Confucius understood to be the perfection of being human. *Ren* described the inner moral character that was necessary in order for one's outward behavior, or *li,* to be authentic and meaningful. Confucius regarded *ren* as a nearly transcendental quality that only the mythic sages of the past had actually attained, although later Confucians claimed it was attainable by anyone.

Thus, Confucius initiated a new level of ethical awareness in Chinese culture and a new form of education, education in what he believed were universal principles for mature humanity and civilization. He assumed that the criteria for holding office were intelligence and high moral principles, not hereditary status, and so further undermined the Zhou feudal system that was crumbling around him. His ethical teachings were intended to describe the Way (*dao*) of the superior or morally noble person, a way that originated in the will of Heaven for its people. Although this Way had been put into practice by the glorious founders of the Zhou dynasty, it was not presently being practiced. The absence of the Way was manifested by widespread conflict and a breakdown of ritual and propriety (*li*), indicating a breach not only in the social order but also in the cosmic order. Ritual or ritual propriety, therefore, was not merely a means of enforcing social order, nor was Confucius's innovation a turn from religion to philosophy; rather, it was a philosophical deepening of a fundamentally religious worldview. Despite the fact that he urged his followers to pay more attention to human affairs than to worshiping the variety of traditional spiritual beings, he denied neither their existence nor the importance of worshiping ancestors. He redirected the religious sense of awe and reverence that had traditionally been focused on the realm of gods and spirits to the human social and political sphere.

The followers of Confucius came to be known as *ru,* or "scholars," signifying their relationship with the literary tradition. They were in a sense custodians of and experts in the literate cultural tradition (*wen*), especially in the areas of court ritual, official protocol, and history. By the fourth and third centuries BCE other schools of thought were developing. They included a school of natural philosophy based on the concept of the *yin* (dark, quiescent) and *yang* (light, active) phases of *qi* (psycho-physical substance); an early form of Daoism (Taoism); a school of Legalism that taught the strict application of law and punishment as the solution to the era's disorder; a school based on the investigation of names and their meanings; and several others. In the culture at large religious beliefs and activities continued unabated; divination and rituals accompanied every significant activity, and a quest for personal immortality was gaining momentum. One of the new schools of thought that reflected these religious concerns was that of Mozi.

Mozi. Mozi (Master Mo, fifth century BCE), a thinker from an artisan background, was a thoroughgoing utilitarian who taught that the fundamental criterion of value was practical benefit to all. He was from Confucius's home state of Lu and was educated in the emerging Confucian tradition, but he turned against what he perceived to be its elitism and wasteful concern with elaborate rituals. In his ethical teaching Mozi reinterpreted along utilitarian lines such Confucian principles as righteousness and filial reverence, focusing on the theme of universal love without familial and social distinctions. He also attracted a group of disciples whom he sent out to serve in various states in an attempt to implement his teachings.

For the history of Chinese religions the most significant aspect of Mozi's thought is his concern to provide theological sanctions for his views. For Mozi Tian, or Heaven, is an active creator god whose will or mandate extends to everyone; what Heaven wills is love, prosperity, and peace for all. Heaven is the ultimate ruler of the whole world; Tian sees all, rewards the good, and punishes the evil. In this task it is aided by a multitude of lesser spirits who are also intelligent and vital and who serve as messengers between Tian and human beings. Mozi advocated that since this is the nature of divine reality, religious reverence should be encouraged by the state as a sanction for moral order.

To protect himself from intellectual skeptics Mozi at one point allowed that even if deities and spirits do not exist, communal worship still has social value. Although his whole attempt to argue for belief in Heaven on utilitarian grounds could be understood as a last stand for traditional religion within a changing philosophical world, there is no reason to doubt that Mozi himself believed in the gods.

The fourth century BCE was a period of incessant civil war on the one hand and great philosophical diversity on the other. A variety of thinkers arose, each propounding a cure for the ills of the age, most seeking to establish their views by training disciples and attaining office. Some advocated moral reform through education, others through authoritarian government, laissez-faire administration, rationalized bureaucracy, agricultural communes, rule in accord with the powers of nature, or individual self-fulfillment. Religious concerns were not paramount for these thinkers; indeed, for some they do not appear at all. The two traditions of this period that do warrant discussion here are the Confucian, represented by Mengzi (Mencius, c. 391–308 BCE) and that of the mystically inclined individualists, traditionally known as the school of Dao (*daojia*).

Mengzi. Master Meng, whose given name was Meng Ke, was a teacher and would-be administrator from the small state of Zou who developed Confucius's teachings and placed them on a much firmer philosophical and literary base. Mengzi was concerned to prepare his disciples for enlightened and compassionate public service, beginning with provision for the physical needs of the people. He believed that only when their material livelihood is secure can the people be guided to higher moral awareness. This hope for moral transformation is grounded in Mengzi's conviction that human nature contains the potential for goodness. What is needed are rulers who nourish this potential as "fathers and mothers of the people." These teachings Mengzi expounded courageously before despotic kings whose inclinations were quite otherwise.

Tian, or Heaven, for Mengzi is an expression of the underlying moral structure of the world, so that in the long run "those who accord with Heaven are preserved, and those who oppose Heaven are destroyed." Heaven's will is known through the assent or disapproval of the people—a proto-democratic aspect of Mengzi's thought. The human mind possesses an innate potential for moral awareness, a potential bestowed by Heaven at birth, so that "to understand human nature is to understand Heaven" and "to preserve one's mind and nourish one's nature is to serve Heaven." This potential is more than mere possibility; it comprises innate and concrete emotional dispositions that, when nourished or developed, become the core virtues of humanity *(ren)*, rightness or appropriateness *(yi)*, propriety *(li)*, and moral wisdom *(zhi)*. This natural course of human development, rather than a static essence, is what constitutes human nature for Mengzi. In cultivating our moral capacities we become fully human and actualize the moral potential of the cosmos. But this process requires a supportive, nourishing environment: a loving and supportive family, opportunities for education, and a humane government.

As had Confucius, Mengzi assumed that ancestor worship was a basic requirement of civilized life, but neither thinker emphasized such worship as much as did later texts like the *Xiaojing*, the *Scripture of Filiality* (third century BCE). And while Confucius had relied largely upon the power of the cultural tradition—in particular the words and examples of the ancient sages preserved in the Five Scriptures—to serve as agents of individual and social transformation, Mengzi's theory could be characterized as a developmental moral psychology. Mengzi represents both a further humanization and a further spiritualization of the Confucian tradition, and his emphasis on the powers of human nature did much to shape the religious sensibilities of Chinese philosophy. In a third century BCE text closely associated with the Mencian school, the *Zhongyong* (The mean in practice or Centrality and commonality), these tendencies were developed to a point not seen again until the eleventh- and twelfth-century revival of Confucianism:

> Only that one in the world who is most perfectly authentic is able to give full development to his nature. Being able to give full development to his nature, he is able to give full development to the nature of other human beings and, being able to give full development to the nature of other human beings, he is able to give full development to the natures of other living things. Being able to give full development to the natures of other living things, he can assist in the transforming and nourishing powers of Heaven and Earth; being able to assist in the transforming and nourishing powers of Heaven and Earth, he can form a triad with Heaven and Earth.

Xunzi. The third most important Confucian philosopher before the Han dynasty (206 BCE–220 CE) was Xunzi (Xun Qing, c. 310 to c. 220 BCE), a scholar from the state of Zhao who held offices for a time in the larger states of Qi and Chu. Xunzi's thought was influenced by several of the traditions that had developed before his time, including those of the Logicians, Daoists, and Legalists. Xunzi agreed with the Legalist emphasis on the need for strong centralized rule and a strict penal code. He also shared their low estimate of human nature, which in his view tended toward selfishness and competition. Nonetheless, Xunzi believed that human attitudes and behavior are perfectible by dint of much discipline and effort, so his differences with Mengzi on this point are those of degree. Both thinkers claimed that the ordinary person can become a "sage" (*shengren*), one who fully exemplifies the virtue of humanity (*ren*). But for Mengzi this was a developmental process, while for Xunzi it was a transformation (*hua*) requiring the external leverage, so to speak, of past sages.

Xunzi's chief contribution was his reinterpretation of Tian as the order of nature, an order that has no consciousness and is not directly related to human concerns. This interpretation is parallel to the views of the *Laozi (Daodejing)* and *Zhuangzi* texts concerning the cosmic "Way" (*dao*). Xunzi was concerned to separate the roles of heaven, earth, and man, with human attention directed toward ethics, administration, and culture. In this context rituals such as funeral rites are valuable channels for emotions but have no objective referent; their role is social and psychological, not theological. Ignorant "petty people" who believe in the literal efficacy of rain dances and divination are to be pitied; for the gentleman such activities are "cultural adornment."

Xunzi thus gave impetus to the skeptical tradition in Chinese thought that began before Confucius and was reinforced by later thinkers such as Wang Chong (c. 27–100 CE). Xunzi's teachings at this point provided a theoretical basis for a rough bifurcation between elite and popular attitudes toward religion and for sporadic attempts to suppress "excessive cults." Xunzi's epistemology also set up the intellectual framework for a critique of heresy, conceived as inventing words and titles beyond those employed by general consensus and sanctioned by the state. These themes had important implications for the remainder of Chinese history, including official attitudes toward religion today.

Early Daoist thought. The earliest extant writings focused on the mysterious cosmic "Way" (*dao*) that underlies all things are the first seven chapters of the extant *Zhuangzi*, a text attributed to a philosopher named Zhuang Zhou of the fourth century BCE, and a few sections of the *Guanzi*, another fourth-century text. Zhuang Zhou, or Zhuangzi (Master Zhuang), was convinced that the world in its natural state is peaceful and harmonious, a state exemplified by the growth of plants and the activities of animals. Disorder is the result of human aggression and manipulation, a tendency that finds as much expression in Confucian and Moist moralizing as in cruel punishments and warfare. Such moralizing in turn is rooted in a false confidence in words, words that debators use to express their own limited points of view and thus to dichotomize our understanding of the world. Indeed, all perspectives are limited and relative, conditioned by the interests and anxieties of species, social positions, and individuals. The answer to this problem is to understand and affirm the relativity of views, and thus harmonize them all. This the sage does by perceiving the constant rhythms of change within all life and identifying with them. In his view all dichotomies are unified; hence, there is no need for struggle and competition. The sage intuits the *dao* within and behind all things and takes its all-embracing perspective as his own. This perspective allows him to achieve a state of emotional equanimity, which even a serious illness or the death of a loved one cannot disturb. Indeed, such events illustrate the ultimate truth of the Way—change and transformation—and can therefore provide opportunities to rejoice in one's participation in what is fundamentally real.

The *Guanzi* is a long, composite text attributed to a famous statesman of the seventh century BCE, but it was probably written or compiled from the fourth to the second centuries BCE, and its actual authors are unknown. Its earliest sections focus on the cosmological and physiological bases of self-transformation according to the Way, using such concepts as *qi* (the psycho-physical substance of all things), *jing* (life-giving essence), and *shen* (spirit), all of which remained central to the Daoist religion in its later development.

The best-known book devoted to discussing the *dao* behind all things is the early third-century BCE *Daodejing* (The Way and Its Power), also known as the *Laozi*, after its reputed author, a mythical sage known simply as the "Old Master," said to have been an older contemporary of Confucius. The *Laozi* discusses the Way in more direct, metaphysical terms than does the *Zhuangzi*, all the while protesting that such discussion is ultimately futile. Here we are told that the *dao* is the source of all things, "the mother of the universe," the ineffable cosmic womb out of which all emerges. The *dao* also "works in the world," guiding all things in harmonious development and interaction. As both source and order of the world the *dao* serves as a model for enlightened rulers who gain power by staying in the background and letting their people live spontaneously in response to their own needs. The *dao* is the vital force of life perceived at its utmost depth; it works mysteriously and imperceptibly, and yet there is nothing it does not accomplish. Its symbols are water rather than rock, valleys rather than hills, the female rather than the male. Although its perspective is profound, its author intended this book to be a handbook of wise and successful living, living characterized by a natural, spontaneous action that does not prematurely wear itself out.

These texts were the sources of a persistent tradition of naturalistic mysticism in the history of Chinese religions. They were the inspiration for much poetry, romantic philosophy, and meditation, all intended as a corrective for the bustle and competition of life, a means to peace of mind, and a clarification and broadening of perspective. They describe the enlightened person as living peacefully and long because he does not waste his vital powers on needless contention and aggression. In the *Laozi*, for example, we are told that "He who knows when to stop is free from danger; therefore he can long endure" (chapter 44), and that one who is "a good preserver of his life" cannot be harmed, "because in him there is no room for death" (chapter 50). Although in some passages of the *Zhuangzi* an enlightened perspective leads to acceptance of death, a few others provide poetic visions of immortals, those who have transcended death by merging with the *dao*. One of the terms Zhuangzi uses for these individuals is *zhenren*, "perfected people," a term that later became important in the fully developed Daoist religion that took shape after the second century CE. These indications of immortality in the earliest Daoist texts provided the chief point of contact between the Classical tradition and those who sought immortality by more direct means, including later practitioners of Daoist religion.

The quest for immortality. An explicit concern for long life (*shou*) had already appeared on early Zhou bronzes and in poems in the *Scripture of Odes.* Beginning in the eighth century BCE we find terms expressing a hope for immortality, such as "no death," "transcending the world," and "becoming an immortal." By the fourth century BCE there is evidence of an active quest for immortality through a variety of means, including exercises imitating the movements of long-lived animals, diets enforcing abstinence from grains, the use of food vessels inscribed with characters indicating longevity, the ingestion of herbs and chemicals, and petitions for the aid of immortals residing in mountains or distant paradises. It was in this context that Chinese alchemy began. The alchemical quest became the most dramatic form of the quest to transcend death, growing in popularity during the Qin (221–206 BCE) and Western Han (206 BCE–9 CE) dynasties.

The goal of all these practices was to return the body to its original state of purity and power with its *yin* and *yang* forces vital and in proper balance. The fact that some of the compounds used were poisonous did not deter the experimenters; those who died were believed by devotees to have transferred themselves to another plane of existence, that of the immortals (*xian*). All this effort and expense were considered necessary because in ancient China the person was understood to be a psycho-physical whole, composed throughout of one vital substance, *qi,* in different modes and densities. Corresponding to the *yin* and *yang* phases of *qi* there were thought to be two "souls," the *po* and *hun,* respectively. The *po,* associated with the gross physical body, would ideally remain with the body after death, or would descend to a murky underworld, the Yellow Springs. The *hun,* associated with the more intelligent and spiritual aspect of the person, would rise up to heaven and would retain its integrity only as long as it was ritually acknowledged and "nourished" through ancestor worship.

These forms of continuation after death were perceived by some to be tenuous and limited, so they attempted to make the entire person/body immortal by transforming its substance. There was no doctrine of an eternal, immaterial soul to fall back on as in India or the Hellenistic world, so the only alternative was physical immortality. In China this tradition continued to develop through the Eastern (Latter) Han dynasty (25–220 CE) and produced texts of its own full of recipes, techniques, and moral exhortations. As such, it became one of the major sources of the Daoist religion that emerged in the second century CE.

Spirit mediums. The other important expression of Chinese religious consciousness before the Han dynasty was shamanism, which most commonly took the form of deities and spirits possessing receptive human beings. Spirit mediums both female and male are mentioned in discussions of early Zhou religion as participants in court rituals, responsible for invoking the descent of the gods, praying and dancing for rain, and for ceremonial sweeping to exorcise harmful forces. They were a subordinate level of officially accepted ritual performers, mostly women, who spoke on behalf of the gods to arrange for sacrifices. In conditions of extreme drought they could be exposed to the sun as an inducement to rain. Female mediums were called *wu,* a word etymologically related to that for dancing; male mediums were called *xi.* In the state of Chu, south of the center of Zhou culture, there were shamans believed able to practice "spiritual flight," that is, to send their souls on journeys to distant realms of deities and immortals.

Han historical sources indicate that by the third century BCE there were shamans all over China, many of whom were invited by emperors to set up shrines in the capital. This was done in part to consolidate imperial control but also to make available fresh sources of sacred power to support the state and heal illness. Sporadic attempts were also made by officials to suppress shamanism. These began as early as 99 BCE and continued in efforts to reform court rituals in 31–30 BCE and to change local practices involving human sacrifice in 25 CE. However, it is clear that shamanism was well established among the people and continued to have formal influence at court until the fifth century CE. Shamans were occasionally employed by rulers to call up the spirits of royal ancestors and consorts, and incidents of court support continued into the eleventh century. Owing in part to the revival of Confucianism in that period, in 1023 a sweeping edict was issued that all shamans be returned to agricultural life and their shrines be destroyed. Thus, the gradual Confucianization of the Chinese elite led to the suppression of shamanism at that level, but it continued to flourish among the people, where its activities can still be observed in China, Taiwan, and other Chinese communities.

THE BEGINNINGS OF EMPIRE. In the fifth century BCE the disintegration of the Zhou feudal and social order quickened under the pressure of incessant civil wars. The larger states formed alliances and maneuvered for power, seeking hegemony over the others, aiming to reunify the area of Zhou culture by force alone. In 256 BCE the state of Qin, under the influence of a ruthlessly applied ideology of laws and punishments suggested in the fourth century BCE by Shang Yang, one of the founders of the Legalist school, eliminated the last Zhou king and then finished off its remaining rivals. Finally, in 221 the state of Qin became the empire of Qin (221–206 BCE), and its ruler took a new title, "First Emperor of Qin" (*Qin shi huangdi*). With this step China as a semicontinental state was born. There were many periods of division and strife later, but the new level of unification achieved by the Qin was never forgotten and became the goal of all later dynasties.

The Qin emperors attempted to rule all of China by the standards long developed in their own area; laws, measurements, written characters, wheel tracks, thought, and so forth were all to be unified. Local traditions and loyalties were still strong, however, and Qin rule remained precarious. After the emperor died in 209, he was replaced by a son who proved unequal to the task. Rebellions that broke out in that year severely undermined Qin authority, and by 206 one of the rebel leaders, a village head named Liu Bang, had assumed de facto control of state administration. In 202 Liu Bang was proclaimed emperor of a new dynasty, the Han (202 BCE–220 CE), built upon Qin foundations but destined to last, with one interregnum, for over four hundred years.

The Qin. The Qin was noteworthy both for its suppression of philosophy and its encouragement of religion. The Legalist tradition dominant in the state of Qin had long been hostile to the Confucians and Moists, with their emphasis on ethical sanctions for rule. For the Legalists the only proper standard of conduct was the law, applied by officials concerned with nothing else, whose personal views were irrelevant as long as they performed their task. The only sanctions the state needed were power and effective organization. Not long after Qin became an empire, it attempted to silence all criticism based on the assumption of inner standards of righteousness that were deemed to transcend political power and circumstance. In 213 BCE the court made it a capital offence to discuss Confucian books and principles and ordered that all books in private collections be burned, save those dealing with medicine, divination, and agriculture, as well as texts of the Legalist school. In this campaign, several scores of scholars were executed, and a number of philosophical schools were eliminated as coherent traditions, including the Moists and the Dialecticians. In the early Han dynasty both Daoist philosophy and Confucianism revived, and Legalism continued to be in evidence in practice if not in theory. But a unified empire demanded unified thought, a dominant orthodoxy enforced by the state. From this perspective variety was a threat to the Qin, and furthermore, there were no independent states left to serve as sanctuaries for different schools.

Qin policy toward religion, by contrast, encouraged a variety of practices to support the state. To pay homage to the sacred powers of the realm and to consolidate his control, the First Emperor included worship at local shrines in his extensive tours. Representatives of regional cults, many of them spirit mediums, were brought to the court, there to perform rituals at altars set up for their respective deities. The Qin expanded the late Zhou tendency to exalt deities of natural forces; over one hundred temples to such nature deities were established in the capital alone, devoted to the sun, moon, planets, several constellations, and stars associated with wind, rain, and long life. The nation was divided into sacred regions presided over by twelve mountains and four major rivers, with many lesser holy places to be worshiped both by the people and the emperor. Elaborate sacrifices of horses, rams, bulls, and a variety of foodstuffs were regularly offered at the major sites, presided over by officials with titles such as Grand Sacrificer and Grand Diviner. Important deities were correlated with the Five Phases (*wuxing*), the modes of interaction of natural forces, the better to personify and control these powers.

A distinctive feature of Qin religion was sacrifices to four "Supreme Emperors" responsible for natural powers in each of the four quarters. Only the emperor could worship these deities, a limitation as well for two new rites he developed in 219, the *feng* and *shan* sacrifices. These were performed on sacred Mount Tai, in modern Shandong province, to symbolize that the ruler had been invested with power by Heaven itself. Another driving force behind Qin encouragement of religious activities was the First Emperor's personal quest for immortality. We are told that in this quest he sent groups of young people across the China Sea to look for such islands of the immortals as Penglai.

The Han. The defeat of Qin forces in the civil wars leading up to the founding of the Han dynasty deposed Legalist political thought along with the second and last Qin emperor. It took several decades for the new Han dynasty to consolidate its power. Since the Legalists had developed the most detailed policies for administering an empire, many of these policies were followed in practice in modified form.

Some early Han scholars and emperors attempted to ameliorate royal power with a revival of Confucian concern for the people and Daoist principles of noninterference (*wuwei*). For example, a palace counselor named Jia Yi (200–168 BCE) echoed Mengzi in his emphasis that the people are the basis of the state, the purpose of which should be to make them prosperous and happy so as to gain their approval. A similar point of view is presented in more Daoist form in the *Huainanzi,* a book presented to the throne in 139 BCE by a prince of the Liu clan who had convened a variety of scholars in his court. This book discusses the world as a fundamentally harmonious system of resonating roles and influences. The ruler's job is to guide it, as an experienced charioteer guides his team.

Both Jia Yi and the *Huainanzi* assume that the rhythms that order society and government emanate from the cosmic *dao.* The ruler's task is to discover and reinforce these rhythms for the benefit of all. This understanding of a Daoist "art of rulership" is rooted in the teachings of the early Daoist texts discussed above *(Zhuangzi, Guanzi,* and *Laozi),* which in the early Han were called the Huang-Lao school, the tradition of the Yellow Emperor (Huangdi) and Laozi. Four other Huang-Lao texts were rediscovered in 1973 at Mawangdui, in a tomb sealed in 168 BCE. This early form of Daoism, which was adopted by the early Han emperors, is concerned with the *dao* as the creative source of both nature and humanity, their patterns of order, and the ontological basis of law and administration. Here we see an attempt to apply Daoist philosophical principles to the ordering of society by blending them with Legalist ideas.

Some Confucian books had escaped the flames of 213 BCE, and those that did not were reconstructed or written anew, with little but the old titles intact. By this time scholars such as Xunzi had already incorporated the best thought of their day into fundamentally Confucian expositions that advocated a strong centralized state and an ethical teaching enforced by law. This expanded interpretation of Confucius's teachings served his followers well in the early Han. They occupied the middle ground between Legalism and Daoist laissez-faire. There was room in their perspective for political power, criminal law, advocacy of benevolent rule, moral suasion, religious rituals, and personal ethical development, all supported by a three-century tradition of training disciples to study sacred texts and emulate the models they provided. In addition, the philosopher Dong Zhongshu (c. 179–104 BCE) incorporated into Confucianism the theories of Zou Yan and the "Naturalists," who in the fourth century BCE had taught that the world is an interrelated organic whole that operates according to the cosmic principles of *yinyang* and *wuxing* (Five Phases). The *Huainanzi* had already given this material a Daoist interpretation, stressing the natural resonance between all aspects of the universe. In the hands of Dong Zhongshu this understanding became an elaborate statement of the relationship of society and nature, with an emphasis on natural justification for hierarchical social roles, focused on that of the ruler.

Dong Zhongshu provided a more detailed cosmological basis for Confucian ethical and social teachings and made it clear that only a unified state could serve as a channel for cosmic forces and sanctions. Dong was recognized as the leading scholar of the realm and became spokesman for the official class. At his urging, the sixth Han emperor, Wudi (r. 140–87 BCE), shifted his allegiance from Huang-Lao Daoism to Confucianism. In 136 BCE the Confucian classics were made the prescribed texts studied at the imperial academy. Texts of other schools, including the Daoist theories of administration noted above, were excluded. This meant in effect that Dong Zhongshu's version of Confucianism became the official state teaching, a status it retained throughout the Han dynasty. So it was that the humble scholar of Lu, dead for over three hundred years, was exalted as patron saint of the imperial system, a position he retained until 1911. State-supported temples were established in Confucius's name in cities all over the land, and his home at Qufu became a national shrine. In these temples, spirit tablets of the master and his disciples (replaced by images from 720 to 1530) were venerated in elaborate and formal rituals. As the generations passed, the tablets of the most influential scholars of the age came to be placed in these temples as well, by imperial decree, and so the cult of Confucius became the ritual focus of the scholar-official class.

Dong Zhongshu's incorporation of *yinyang* thought into Confucian philosophy had the unfortunate effect of legitimating and accentuating what was already a patriarchal social system. The root meanings of *yin* (dark) and *yang* (light) were not gendered, but neither did they necessarily imply a complementarity of equals. The predominant interpretation of the *yin-yang* polarity throughout Chinese history (with a few texts like the *Laozi* as prominent exceptions) understood the relationship as a *hierarchical* complementarity, with *yin* as quiescent and sinking and *yang* as active and rising. The general preference for *yang* over *yin*, combined with the patriarchal association of women with *yin* and men with *yang*, provided philosophical justification for the subservience of women to men. Educated women as well as men accepted this as a fact of nature. Ban Zhao (45–114 CE), the most famous female intellectual in Chinese history, wrote an influential book called *Lessons for Women* (*Nujie*), which emphasized the propriety of women's humility and subservience, although her support of education for girls could, in its context, be considered a "feminist" position. In general, Confucians believed that women could become sages, but only by perfecting the virtues of the "woman's Way" as wives and mothers.

Han state rituals were based upon those of Qin but were greatly expanded and more elaborate. The first Han emperor, Gaozu, instituted the worship of a star god believed to be associated with Houji, the legendary founder of the Zhou royal line. Temples for this deity were built in administrative centers around the realm, where officials were also instructed to worship gods of local mountains and rivers. Gaozu brought shamans to the palace and set up shrines for sacrifices to their regional deities. He also promoted the worship of his own ancestors; at his death temples in his honor were built in commanderies throughout the empire.

These efforts to institute an imperial religious system supported by officials at all levels were energetically continued by Emperor Wu, during whose fifty-four-year reign the foundations of imperial state religion were established for Chinese history into the twentieth century. The emperor's religious activities were in turn supported by the philosophy of Dong Zhongshu, with its emphasis on the central cosmic role of the ruler. Emperor Wu revived the *jiao* or suburban sacrifice at the winter solstice to express imperial support for the revival of life forces. He also began to worship Taiyi, the "Supreme One," a star deity most noble in the heavens, an exalted version of a Zhou god. Taiyi was coequal with Heaven and earth, a symbol of both cosmic power and the emperor's status. In the period 112–110 BCE Emperor Wu renewed the *feng* and *shan* sacrifices at Mount Tai, the sacred mountain of the east, a key place of direct communication with Heaven for the sake of the whole realm. In 109 BCE he ordered that a *ming tang* (hall of light) be built at the foot of Mount Tai as a temple where all the major deities of China could assemble and be worshiped. Emperor Wu also toured the realm, sacrificing at important shrines along the way, all to express his religious convictions and assert his authority.

Detailed instructions for these Han rituals were provided by handbooks of ritual and etiquette such as the *Liji* (Record of Ritual), the present version of which was compiled in the second century BCE but includes earlier material as well. Here we find descriptions of royal rituals to be performed at the solstices and the equinoxes, as well as instructions for such matters as the initiation ("capping") of young men and the worship of ancestors. The emphasis throughout is on the intimate correlations of nature and society, so that social custom is given cosmic justification. The *Liji* complements Dong Zhongshu's philosophy by extending similar understandings to the social life of the literate elite. In this context periodic rituals served as concentrated reminders of the cosmic basis of the whole cultural and political order. Thus did the imperial ruling class express its piety and solidify its position.

It should be noted, however, that the old Zhou concept of the "Mandate of Heaven" continued to influence Han political thought in a form elaborated and attenuated at the same time. Particularly in the writings of Dong Zhongshu, evidence for divine approval or disapproval of the ruler was discerned in natural phenomena, such as comets or earthquakes, interpreted as portents and omens. In accord with this belief, officials were appointed to record and interpret portents and to suggest appropriate responses, such as changes in ritual procedure and the proclamation of amnesties. The developing tradition of political portents recognized the importance of divine sanctions but provided a range of calibrated responses that enabled rulers to adjust their policies rather than face the prospect of rejection by Heaven. The Mandate of Heaven in its earlier and starker form was evoked chiefly as justification for rebellion in periods of dynastic decay. Nonetheless, portent theory in the hands of a conscientious official could be used in attempts to check or ameliorate royal despotism, and hence was an aspect of the state religious system that could challenge political power as well as support it.

The Han emperor Wu devoted much effort to attaining immortality, as had his Qin predecessor. As before, shamans and specialists in immortality potions were brought to court, and expeditions were sent off to look for the dwelling places of those who had defeated death. The search for immortality became quite popular among those who had the money and literacy to engage in it. In part this was the result of the transformation of the Yellow Emperor (Huangdi) into the patron deity of immortality, the earliest popular saving deity of this type in China. This transformation, fostered by magicians or "technique specialists" *(fangshi)* at Emperor Wu's court, included stories that the Yellow Emperor had ascended to Heaven with his whole retinue, including a harem of over seventy.

A more common expression of hope for some sort of continuity after death may be seen in tombs of Han aristocrats and officials, many of which were built as sturdy brick replicas of houses or offices, complete with wooden and ceramic utensils, attendants, and animals, as well as food, drugs, clothing, jade, bamboo books, and other precious objects. To a large extent this was a modification of Shang and Zhou traditions. However, in a few Han tombs were tightly sealed coffins filled with an embalming fluid in which even the skin and flesh of the bodies have been preserved. On top of one of these coffins has been found an elaborate silk banner from the southern state of Chu, painted with a design evidently intended to guide the occupant to a paradise of the immortals, perhaps that of the Queen Mother of the West, Xi Wang Mu.

Another destination for the dead was an underworld that was a Han elaboration of the old myth of the Yellow Springs, a shadowy place beneath the earth referred to as early as the eighth century BCE. From the Han period, there are tomb documents by which living officials transferred the dead in their jurisdiction to those of their counterparts in the underworld. There are also references to a realm of the dead inside Mount Tai. The god of this mountain keeps registers of the life spans of all, and death may be referred to as "to return to the Eastern Peak." By the third and fourth centuries CE it was believed that there was a subterranean kingdom within Mount Tai, where judges decided the fate of the dead. These alternative beliefs represent the state of Chinese understandings of afterlife before Buddhist impact.

What came to be called the Former Han dynasty ended in 8 CE when the throne was occupied by a prime minister named Wang Mang (r. 9–23 CE), who established a Xin ("new") dynasty that was to last for fourteen years. Wang's chief contribution to the history of Chinese religions was his active promotion of prognostication as a way of understanding the intimate relationship between Heaven and the court. In 25 CE Liu Xiu (r. 25–57), a member of the Han royal line, led a successful attack on Wang Mang and reestablished the (Latter) Han dynasty. Like Wang Mang, he actively supported prognostication at court, despite the criticism of rationalist scholars such as Huan Tan (43 BCE–28 CE), who argued that strange phenomena were a matter of coincidence and natural causes rather than messages from Heaven.

A related development was controversy between two movements within Confucian scholarly circles, the so-called New Text school of the Former Han and a later rationalistic reaction against it, the Old Text school. The New Text school developed out of Dong Zhongshu's concern with portents. Its followers wrote new commentaries on the classics that praised Confucius as a superhuman being who predicted the future hundreds of years beyond his time. By the end of the first century BCE this interpretation of the sage in mythological terms was vigorously resisted by an Old Text school that advocated a more restrained and historical approach. These two traditions coexisted throughout the remainder of the Han dynasty, with the New Text scholars receiving the most imperial support through the first century CE. After Huan Tan, the best known rationalist was Wang Chong, whose *Lunheng* (Balanced Essays) fiercely criticizes religious opinions of his day, including prognostication and belief in spirits of the dead. Although Wang Chong was not well known by his contemporaries, his thought was rediscovered in the third century and established as a key contribution to the skeptical tradition in Chinese philosophy. An important religious legacy of the New Text school was the exalted interpretation of Confucius as a semidivine being, which was echoed in later popular religion. Its concern with portents and numerology also influenced Daoism.

We have noted the appearance of the Yellow Emperor as a divine patron of immortality and as a representative of a new type of personified saving deity with power over a whole area of activity. In the latter half of the Han dynasty the number and popularity of such deities increased, beginning with the cult of the Queen Mother of the West (Xi Wang Mu). She was associated with the Kunlun Mountains in the northwest, where she presided over a palace and received a royal visitor, King Mu of the Zhou dynasty, who she predicted would be able to avoid death. In 3 BCE Xi Wang Mu's promise of immortality to all became the central belief of an ecstatic popular cult in her name that swept across North China. Although this movement abated in a few months, the Queen Mother herself is commonly portrayed in Latter Han iconography. Kunlun is described as the center pillar of the world, from where she controls cosmic powers and the gift of immortality. This goddess has continued to have an important role in Chinese religion until the present day.

Mountain-dwelling immortals constituted another source of personal deities in this period. These beings were believed to descend to aid the ruler in times of crisis, sometimes with instructions from the Celestial Emperor (Tiandi), sometimes themselves identified with the "perfect ruler" who would restore peace to the world. By the second century CE the most important of these figures was Laozi, the legendary author of the *Daodejing,* who appears as a deity called Huang Laojun (Yellow Lord Lao) or Taishang Laojun (Most High Lord Lao). By this time Laozi had been portrayed for centuries in popular legend as a mysterious wise man who disappeared without a trace. We have seen that the book in his name contains passages that could be interpreted as support for the immortality cult, and by the first century he was referred to as an immortal himself. In an inscription of 165 CE Laozi is described as a creator deity, equal in status to the sun, moon, and stars. A contemporary text assures his devotees that he has manifested himself many times in order to save humankind, that he will select those who believe in him to escape the troubles of the age, and that he will "shake the Han reign." It is this messianic theme that provided the religious impetus for two large popular religious movements in the late second century CE that were important sources of later Daoist religion and the popular sectarian tradition. These movements were the *Tianshi dao* (Way of the Celestial Masters) in the west and the *Taiping dao* (Way of Great Peace) in the north.

The Way of the Celestial Masters began with a new revelation from the Most High Lord Lao to a man named Zhang Daoling in 142 CE. In this revelation Zhang was designated as the first "Celestial Master" and was empowered to perform rituals and write talismans that distributed this new manifestation of the *dao* for the salvation of humankind. Salvation was available to those who repented of their sins, believed in the *dao,* and pledged allegiance to their Daoist master. The master in turn established an alliance between the gods and the devotee, who then wore at the waist a list or "register" of the names of the gods to be called on for protection. The register also served as a passport to heaven at death. Daoist ritual consists essentially of the periodic renewal of these alliances by meditative visualization, ritual confession and petition, and sacrificial offering of incense and sacred documents. Daoist texts are concerned throughout with moral discipline and orderly ritual and organization.

Under Zhang Daoling's grandson, Zhang Lu, the Way of the Celestial Masters established a theocratic state in the area of modern Sichuan province with an organization modeled in part on Han local administration. The administrative units or "parishes" were headed by "libationers," some of whom were women, whose duties included both religious and administrative functions. Their rituals included reciting the *Laozi,* doing penance to heal illness, and constructing huts in which free food was offered to passersby. Converts were required to contribute five pecks of rice, from which the movement gained the popular name of "the Way of Five Pecks of Rice" (*Wudoumi dao*). In 215 Zhang Lu pledged allegiance to a Han warlord (Cao Cao), whose son founded the new state of Wei in 220. The members of the sect were required to disperse their self-governing community in Sichuan, but they were allowed to continue their activities and taught that Wei had simply inherited divine authority from the Celestial Master Zhang and his line. By the fourth century the Celestial Masters developed more elaborate collective rituals of repentance, retrospective salvation of ancestors, and the strengthening of vital forces through sexual intercourse. Eventually all branches of Daoism traced their origins to the Way of the Celestial Masters.

We know less about the practices of the Way of Great Peace because it was destroyed as a coherent tradition in the aftermath of a massive uprising in 184 CE. Its leader, also named Zhang (Zhang Jue, d. 184 CE), proclaimed that the divine mandate for the Han rule, here symbolized by the wood (green) phase (of the Five Phases), had expired, to be replaced by the earth phase, whose color is yellow. Zhang Jue's forces thus wore yellow cloths on their heads as symbols of their destiny, and hence the movement came to be called the Yellow Scarves (often misleadingly translated as Yellow Turbans). The Han court commissioned local governors to put down the uprising, which was soon suppressed with much bloodshed, although remnants of the Yellow Scarves continued to exist until the end of the century.

The Yellow Scarves are better understood as a parallel to the Celestial Master sect rather than as connected to it, although the two movements shared some beliefs and practices, particularly healing through confession of sins. The Way of Great Peace employed a scripture known as the *Taipingjing* (Scripture of Great Peace), which emphasizes the cyclical renewal of life in the *jiazi* year, the beginning of the sixty-year calendrical cycle. Both sects were utopian, but the Yellow Scarves represent a more eschatalogical orientation. In retrospect, both of these groups appear as attempts to reconstruct at a local level the Han cosmic and political synthesis that was collapsing around them, with priests taking the place of imperial officials.

The most important legacy of the late Han popular religious movements was their belief in personified divine beings concerned to aid humankind, a belief supported by new texts, rituals, and forms of leadership and organization. This belief was given impetus by the expectation that a bearer of collective salvation was about to appear in order to initiate a new time of peace, prosperity, and long life. From the third century on this hope was focused on a figure called Li Hong, in whose name several local movements appeared, some involving armed uprisings. This eschatological orientation was an important dimension of early Daoism, which at first understood itself as a new revelation, intended to supplant popular cults with their bloody sacrifices and spirit mediums.

In addition to such organized movements as the Yellow Scarves, Han popular religion included the worship of local sacred objects such as trees, rocks, and streams, the worship of dragons (thought to inhabit bodies of water), the belief that spirits of the dead have consciousness and can roam about, and a lively sense of the power of omens and fate. By the third century there are references to propitiation of the spirits of persons who died violent deaths, with offerings of animal flesh presided over by spirit mediums.

Feng-shui (wind and water), or geomancy, also developed during the Han as a ritual expression of the *yin-yang* and five-phases worldview. It is the art of locating graves, buildings, and cities in auspicious places where there is a concentration of the vital energies *(qi)* of earth and atmosphere. Spirits of the dead in graves so located, by virtue of being part of the natural flow of *qi* through the earth, are less likely to roam the world as ghosts and harm their descendants. Likewise, homes and cities harmoniously oriented with the flow of *qi* benefit the living directly; to be in harmony with the natural order is "auspicious." The earliest extant *feng-shui* texts are attributed to famous diviners of the third and fourth centuries. Chinese religion was thus developed at a number of levels by the time Buddhism arrived, although Buddhism offered several fresh interpretations of morality, personal destiny, and the fate of the dead.

THE PERIOD OF DISUNION. By the time the first Buddhist monks and texts appeared in China around the first century CE, the Han dynasty was already in decline. At court rival factions competed for imperial favor, and in the provinces restless governors moved toward independence. Political and military fragmentation was hastened by the campaigns against the Yellow Scarves uprising, after which a whole series of adventurers arose to attack each other and take over territory. In the first decade of the third century three major power centers emerged in the north, southeast, and southwest, with that in the north controlling the last Han emperor and ruling in his name. By 222 these three centers each had declared themselves states (the "Three Kingdoms" of the famous fourteenth-century historical novel by Luo Guanzhong), and China entered a period of political division that was to last until late in the sixth century. This is known as the Six Dynasties period, or alternatively, the Wei-Jin and Northern-Southern Dynasties periods. In this time of relatively weak central government control, powerful local clans emerged to claim hereditary power over their areas.

The beginnings of Buddhism in China. With the gradual expansion of Buddhism under the patronage of the Kushan rulers (in present-day northwest India, Pakistan, and Afghanistan) into the oasis states of Central Asia, and with the corresponding expansion of Chinese influence into this same region, it became inevitable that Buddhism would be introduced into East Asia. Over a thousand-year period from the beginning of the common era until the close of the first millennium, the opportunities for cultural exchange with South and West Asia afforded by the so-called Silk Road—actually a whole network of trade routes throughout Asia and connecting it with Europe—nourished vibrant East Asian Buddhist traditions. These began with earnest imitation of their Indian antecedents and culminated in the great independent systems of thought that characterize the fully developed tradition: Huayan, Tiantai, Jingtu, and Chan.

From about 100 BCE on it would have been relatively easy for Buddhist ideas and practices to come to China with foreign merchants, but the first reliable notice of it in Chinese sources is dated 65 CE. In a royal edict of that year we are told that a prince administering a city in what is now northern Jiangsu province "recites the subtle words of Huang-Lao, and respectfully performs the gentle sacrifices to the Buddha." He was encouraged to "entertain *upāsakas* and *sramanas,*" Buddhist lay devotees and initiates. In 148 CE the first of several foreign monks, An Shigao, settled in Luoyang, the capital of the Latter Han. Over the next forty years he and other scholars translated about thirty Buddhist scriptures into Chinese, most of them from pre-Mahāyāna traditions, emphasizing meditation and moral principles. However, by about 185 three Mahāyāna *prajñāpāramitā* (Perfection of Wisdom) texts were translated as well.

A memorial dated 166, approving Buddhist "purity," "emptiness," nonviolence, and control of sensual desires, further informs us that in that year the emperor performed a joint sacrifice to Laozi and the Buddha. In 193–194 a local warlord in what is now Jiangsu erected a Buddhist temple that could hold more than three thousand people. It contained a bronze Buddha image before which offerings were made and scriptures were read. During ceremonies in honor of the Buddha's birthday, thousands came to participate, watch, and enjoy free food and wine. Thus, by the end of the second century there were at least two centers of Buddhist activity, Luoyang in the north and an area in the southeast. At court Buddhist symbols were used in essentially Daoist rituals, but in the scriptures the novelty and differences of Buddhism were made clear in crude vernacular translations. Injunctions to eliminate desires, to love all beings equally, without special preference for one's family, and to regard the body as transitory and doomed to decay rather than an arena for seeking immortality were not without precedent in Chinese thought, but they did challenge the Han Confucian orthodoxy.

Although early sources mention terms for various clerical ranks, rules for monastic life were transmitted in a haphazard and incomplete fashion. Monks and nuns lived in cloisters that cannot properly be called monasteries until a few centuries later. Meanwhile, leadership of the Chinese clergy was provided first by Central Asian monks, then by naturalized Chinese of foreign descent, and by the fourth century, by Chinese themselves. Nuns are first mentioned in that century as well.

The movement of Buddhism to China, one of the great cultural interactions of history, was slow and fortuitous, carried out almost entirely at a private level. The basic reason for its eventual acceptance throughout Chinese society was that it offered several religious and social advantages unavailable to the same extent in China before. These included a full-time religious vocation for both men and women in an organization largely independent of family and state, a clear promise of life after death at various levels, and developed conceptions of paradise and purgatory, connected to life through the results of intentional actions (*karma*). Many women found Buddhism an attractive alternative to the "woman's Way" supported by Confucianism, with its limited options for fulfillment as wives and mothers. Buddhism also offered the worship of heroic saviors in image form, supported by scriptures that told of their wisdom and compassion. For ordinary folk there were egalitarian moral principles, promises of healing and protection from harmful forces, and simple means of devotion; for intellectuals there were sophisticated philosophy and the challenge of attaining new states of consciousness in meditation, all of this expounded by a relatively educated clergy who recruited, organized, translated, and preached.

In the early fourth century North China was invaded by the nomadic Xiongnu, who sacked Luoyang in 311 and Chang'an in 316. Thousands of elite families fled south below the Yangzi River, where a series of short-lived Chinese dynasties held off further invasions. In the north a succession of kingdoms of Inner Asian background rose and fell, most of which supported Buddhism because of its religious appeal and its non-Chinese origins. The forms of Buddhism that developed here emphasized ritual, ideological support for the state, magic protection, and meditation.

It was in the south, however, that Buddhism first became a part of Chinese intellectual history. The Han imperial Confucian synthesis had collapsed with the dynasty, a collapse that encouraged a quest for new philosophical alternatives. Representatives of these alternatives found support in aristocratic clans, which competed with each other in part through philosophical debates. These debates, called *qingtan,* or "pure conversation," revived and refined a tradition that had been widespread in the period of the so-called Hundred Philosophers (sixth and fifth centuries BCE), a tradition with precise rules of definition and criteria for victory. By the mid-third century these debates revolved around two basic perspectives, that of rather conservative moralists called the "school of names" (*mingjiao*) and that of those advocating "spontaneous naturalism" (*ziran*). By the early fourth century Buddhist monks were involved in these debates, supported by sympathetic clans, advocating a middle ground between the conservatives and libertarians, spiritual freedom based on ethical discipline. Although Buddhism was still imperfectly understood, it had gained a vital foothold.

Chinese intellectuals first attempted to understand Buddhism through its apparent similarities to certain beliefs and practices of Daoism and immortality cults. Thus, *bodhisattvas* and buddhas were correlated with sages and immortals, meditation with circulation of the vital fluids, and *nirvāṇa* with *wuwei,* spontaneous, nonintentional action. However, Indian Buddhism and traditional Chinese thought have very different understandings of life and the world. Buddhist thought is primarily psychological and epistemological, concerned with liberation from *saṃsāra,* the world perceived as a realm of suffering, impermanence, and death. For the Chinese, on the other hand, nature and society are fundamentally good; our task is to harmonize with the positive forces of nature, and enlightenment consists in identifying with these forces rather than in being freed from them. The interaction of these worldviews led Chinese Buddhists to interpret psychological concepts in cosmological directions. For example, the key Mahāyāna term "emptiness" (*śūnyatā* in Sanskrit, *kong* in Chinese) refers primarily to the interdependence of all things—that is, their lack of any independent nature or being—and to the radically objective and neutral mode of perception that accepts the impermanence and interdependence of things without trying to control them or project onto them human concepts and values. Indeed, the first discussions of this term used it as a logical tool to destroy false confidence in philosophical and religious concepts, particularly earlier Buddhist ones. All concepts, according to this doctrine, are mutually contradictory and refer to nothing substantial; hence they are "empty." In China, however, "emptiness" immediately evoked discussion about the origin and nature of the phenomenal world. "Emptiness" was equated with "nonbeing" (*wu*), the fecund source of existence, and "vacuity" (*xu*), the absence of concrete existence or cognitive preconception, both of which are prominent concepts in the *Laozi.* As their understanding of Buddhism deepened, Chinese thinkers became more aware of the epistemological force of the term "emptiness" but continued to see it primarily as a problem in interpreting the world itself. In that respect it was somewhat consistent with certain Confucian and Daoist ideas, such as the notion that persons and things are defined by their relationships with others or their positions in the overall pattern of things—the *dao.*

Buddhist thought was already well developed and complexly differentiated before it reached China. Likewise, Chinese culture, religion, and philosophy were mature and highly developed when Buddhism entered China. So the story of Buddhism in China was a case of two mature cultural systems, with some rather fundamental linguistic and social differences, interacting and transforming each other. But at first the Chinese knew of Buddhism only through scriptures haphazardly collected in translations of varying accuracy, for very few Chinese learned Sanskrit. Since all the sūtras claimed to be preached by the Buddha himself, they were accepted as such, with discrepancies among them explained as deriving from the different situations and capacities of listeners prevailing when a particular text was preached. In practice, this meant that the Chinese had to select from a vast range of data those themes that made the most sense in their preexisting worldview. For example, as the tradition develops we find emphases on simplicity and directness, the universal potential for enlightenment, and the Buddha mind as source of the cosmos, all of them prepared for by similar ideas in indigenous thought and practice.

The most important early Chinese Buddhist philosophers, organizers, and translators were Dao'an (312–385), Huiyuan (334–417), and Kumārajīva (334–413), each of whom contributed substantially to the growth of the young "church." Dao'an was known principally for his organizational and exegetical skills and for the catalog of Buddhist scriptures he compiled. His disciple Huiyuan, one of the most learned clerics in South China, gathered a large community of monks around him and inaugurated a cult to Amitābha, a popular Buddha. Kumārajīva, the most important and prolific of the early translators, was responsible for the transmission of the Mādhyamika (*Sanlun*) tradition to China. His lectures on Buddhist scripture in Chang'an established a sound doctrinal basis for Mahāyāna thought in the Middle Kingdom. Another formative early figure was Daosheng (d. 434 CE), a student of Kumārajīva. He is known for his emphasis on the positive nature of *nirvāṇa,* his conviction that even nonbelievers have the potential for salvation, and his teaching of instantaneous enlightenment. Like the concept of emptiness, these ideas resonated well with certain Confucian and Daoist concepts, such as the goodness of human nature in Mengzi and the Daoist notion of spontaneity. Such themes helped lay the foundation for Chan (Japanese, Zen) Buddhism in the seventh and eighth centuries.

The history of monastic Buddhism was closely tied to state attitudes and policies, which ranged from outright suppression to complete support, as in the case of Emperor Wu of the Liang dynasty (r. 501–549), who abolished Daoist temples and built Buddhist ones, and three times entered a monastery himself as a lay servitor. However, by the fifth century Buddhism was becoming well established among people of all classes, who, to gain karmic merit, donated land and goods, took lay vows, served in monasteries, and established a variety of voluntary associations to copy scriptures, provide vegetarian food for monks and nuns, and carve Buddha images. The most important image-carving projects were at Yungang in Shanxi and Longmen in Henan, where huge figures, chiefly those of Śākyamuni, Amitābha, and Maitreya, were cut into cliffs and caves. Such major projects of course also involved large-scale official and clerical support.

It was in the fifth century as well that Chinese Buddhist eschatology developed, based in part on predictions attributed to the Buddha that a few hundred years after his entry into *nirvāṇa* the *dharma* (the Buddha's teachings) would lose its vigor, morals would decline, and ignorant, corrupt monks and nuns would appear. In addition, from its inception as a full-fledged religion in the second century, Daoism had proclaimed itself to be the manifestation of a new age of cosmic vitality, supported by pious devotees, "seed people." A combination of these motifs led to the composition in China of Buddhist scriptures saying that since the end of the age had come, more intense morality and piety were required of those who wished to be saved. These texts also promised aid from saving *bodhisattvas* such as Maitreya, the next buddha-to-be. In some cases the apocalyptic vision of these texts inspired militant utopian movements, led by monks but with lay membership. By the early seventh century a few of these groups were involved in armed uprisings in the name of Maitreya, which led eventually to a decline in official support for his cult, although he remained important in popular sectarian eschatology.

The first important school of Buddhist thought developed in China was the Tiantai, founded by the monk Zhiyi (538–597). This school is noted for its synthesis of earlier Buddhist traditions into one system, divided into five periods of development according to stages in the Buddha's teaching. According to Tiantai, the Buddha's teachings culminated in his exposition of the *Lotus Sūtra,* in which all approaches are unified. Zhiyi also systematized the theory and practice of Mahāyāna meditation. His most important philosophical contribution was his affirmation of the absolute buddha mind as the source and substance of all phenomena. In Zhiyi's teaching the old Mādhyamika logical destruction of dualities is replaced by a positive emphasis on their identity in a common source. So, in impeccably Buddhist language, he was able to justify the phenomenal world, and thus to provide an intellectual foundation for much of the later development of Buddhism in China.

In 581 China was reunified by the Sui dynasty (581–618) after three and a half centuries of political fragmentation. The Sui founder supported Buddhism, particularly the Tiantai school, as a unifying ideology shared by many of his subjects in both north and south. After four decades of rule the Sui was overthrown in a series of rebellions, to be replaced by the Tang (618–907). Although the new dynasty tended to give more official support to Confucianism and Daoism, Buddhism continued to grow at every level of society.

The rise of Daoist religion. By the fourth century Daoism was characterized by a literate and self-perpetuating priesthood, a pantheon of celestial deities, complex rituals, and revealed scriptures in classical (literary) Chinese. Although the first elements of this tradition appeared in the second-century popular movements discussed above, the tradition underwent further development at the hands of gentry scholars versed in philosophy, ethical teachings, and alchemy. These scholars saw themselves as formulators of a new, more refined religion superior to the popular cults around them. This new system was led by priests who, though not officials, claimed celestial prerogatives.

Daoism is fundamentally rooted in the concept of *qi,* the psycho-physical-spiritual substance out of which nature, gods, and humans evolve. The source and order of this vital substance is the *dao,* the ultimate basis of life in the universe. The gods are personified manifestations of *qi,* symbolizing astral powers of the cosmos and organs of the human body with which they are correlated. Under the conditions of ordinary existence *qi* becomes stale and dissipated, so it must be renewed through ritual and meditative processes that restore its primal vitality. Some of these practices consist of visualizing and calling down the cosmic gods to reestablish their contact with their bodily correlates. In this way the adept ingests divine power and so recharges his or her bodily forces for healing, rejuvenation, and long life. In others, the substances of the human body—*jing* (life-giving "essences," such as sexual fluids), *qi* ("vital breath," in a more specific sense than the general *qi* of which all things are composed), and *shen* (spirit)—are manipulated and purified through visualization and meditation. Physical exercises and dietary practices (such as abstinence from grains, which are thought to contain the dark *yin* power of the earth) are also parts of the Daoist regimen. The general aim of these practices is to enhance spiritual and physical health. Accomplished practice results in the purification of the psycho-physical being into the embryo of a new, immortal self. Rituals are also performed for an entire community; Daoist masters can release their cosmic power through ritual actions that revive the life forces of the community around them.

When the Celestial Master sect was officially recognized by the state of Wei (220–265) in the early third century, its leadership was established in the capital, Luoyang, north and east of the old sect base area in modern Sichuan. In the north remnants of the Yellow Scarves still survived, and before long the teachings and rituals of these two similar traditions blended together. A tension remained, however, between those who saw secular authority as a manifestation of the Way and those determined to bring in a new era of peace and prosperity by militant activity. Uprisings led by charismatic figures who claimed long life and healing powers occurred in different areas throughout the fourth century and later.

Meanwhile, in the southeast another tradition emerged that was to contribute to Daoism, a tradition concerned with alchemy, the use of herbs and minerals to attain immortality. Its chief literary expression was the *Baopuzi* (The Master Who Embraces Simplicity) written by Ge Hong in about 320. Ge Hong collected a large number of alchemical formulas and legends of the immortals, intended to show how the body can be transformed by the ingestion of gold and other chemicals and by the inner circulation of the vital *qi,* special diets, and sexual techniques, all reinforced by moral dedication. Ge Hong's concerns were supported by members of the old aristocracy of the state of Wu (222–280) whose families had moved south during the Latter Han period.

When the northern state of Jin was conquered by the Xiongnu in 316, thousands of Jin gentry and officials moved south, bringing the Celestial Master sect with them. The eventual result was a blending of Celestial Master concern for priestly administration and collective rituals with the more individualistic and esoteric alchemical traditions of the southeast. Between the years 364 and 370 a young man named Yang Xi claimed to receive revelations from "perfected ones" *(zhenren,* a term from the *Zhuangzi)* or exalted immortals from the Heaven of Supreme Purity (Shangqing). These deities directed Yang to make transcripts and deliver them to Xu Mi (303–373), an official of the Eastern Jin state (317–420) with whom he was associated. Yang Xi believed his new revelations to be from celestial regions more exalted than those evoked by the Celestial Master sect and Ge Hong. The Perfected Ones rewrote and corrected earlier texts in poetic language, reformulated sexual rites as symbols of spiritual union, and taught new methods of inner cultivation and alchemy. These teachings were all presented in an eschatological context, as the salvation of an elect people in a time of chaos. They prophesied that a "lord of the Way, [a] sage who is to come" would descend in 392. Then the wicked would be eliminated and a purified terrestrial kingdom established, ruled over by such pious devotees as Xu Mi, now perceived as a priest and future celestial official. It is perhaps not accidental that these promises were made to members of the old southern aristocracy whose status had recently been threatened by the newcomers from the north.

Xu Mi and one of his sons had retired to Maoshan, a mountain near the Eastern Jin capital (modern Nanjing); hence, the texts they received and transcribed came to be called those of a Maoshan "school." In the next century another southern scholar, Tao Hongjing (456–536), collected all the remaining manuscripts from Yang Xi and the Xu family and edited them as the *Zhengao* (Declarations of the Perfected). With this the Maoshan/Shangqing scriptures were established as a foundation stone of the emerging Daoist canon.

In the meantime another member of Ge Hong's clan had written a scripture in about 397, the *Lingbaojing* (Scripture of the Sacred Jewel), which he claimed had been revealed to him by the spirit of an early third-century ancestor. This text exalted "celestial worthies" (*tianzun*), who were worshiped in elaborate collective rituals directed by priests in outdoor arenas. The *Lingbaojing* established another strand of Daoist mythology and practice that was also codified in the south during the fifth century. Its rituals replaced those of the Celestial Master tradition while remaining indebted to them. Lingbao texts were collected and edited by Lu Xiujing (406–477), who wrote on Daoist history and ritual.

Daoism was active in the north as well, in the Northern Wei kingdom (386–534), which established Daoist offices at court in 400. In 415 and 423 a scholar named Kou Qianzhi (365–448) claimed to have received direct revelations from Lord Lao while he was living on a sacred mountain. The resulting scriptures directed Kou to reform the Celestial Master tradition; renounce popular cults, messianic uprisings, and sexual rituals; and support the court as a Daoist kingdom on earth. Kou was introduced to the Wei ruler by a sympathetic official named Cui Hao (d. 450) in 424 and was promptly appointed to the office of "Erudite of Transcendent Beings." The next year he was proclaimed Celestial Master, and his teachings "promulgated throughout the realm." For the next two decades Kou and Cui cooperated to promote Daoism at the court. As a result, in 440 the king accepted the title Perfect Ruler of Great Peace, and during the period 444 to 446 proscribed Buddhism and local "excessive cults." Although Cui Hao was eventually discredited and Buddhism established as the state religion by a new ruler in 452, the years of official support for Daoism clarified its legitimacy and political potential as an alternative to Confucianism and Buddhism.

The Consolidation of Empire: Seventh to Fourteenth Centuries. The Chinese religious traditions that were to continue throughout the rest of imperial history all reached maturity during the Tang (618–907) and Song (960–1279) periods. These traditions included Buddhism, Daoism, neo-Confucianism, Islam, and popular religion in both its village and sectarian forms. It was in these centuries as well that other foreign religions were practiced for a time in China, particularly Manichaeism, Nestorian Christianity, and Judaism (one Jewish community continued to flourish until the nineteenth century). Rituals performed by the emperor and his officials continued to be elaborated, with many debates over the proper form and location of altars and types of sacrifices to be offered. During the Tang dynasty, cults devoted to the spirits of local founders and protectors were established in many cities. These city gods (*chenghuang shen*) were eventually brought into the ranks of deities to whom official worship was due.

Manichaeism, Nestorian Christianity, Judaism, and Islam. The area of the Tang dynasty rivaled that of the Han, with western boundaries extending far into Central Asia. This expansion encouraged a revival of foreign trade and cultural contacts. Among the new foreign influences were not only Buddhist monks and scriptures but also the representatives of other religions. There is evidence for Zoroastrianism in China by the early sixth century, a result of contacts between China and Persia that originated in the second century BCE and were renewed in an exchange of envoys with the Northern Wei court in 455 and around 470.

A foreign tradition with more important influence on the history of Chinese religions was Manichaeism, a dynamic missionary religion teaching ultimate cosmic dualism founded by a Persian named Mani (216–277?). The first certain reference to Manichaeism in a Chinese source is dated 694, although it may have been present about two decades earlier. As was true with Zoroastrianism, Manichaeism in its early centuries in China was primarily practiced by foreigners, although its leaders soon composed catechisms and texts in Chinese stressing the congruence of their teachings with Buddhism and Daoism. In 755 a Chinese military commander named An Lushan led a powerful rebellion that the Tang court was able to put down only with the help of foreign support. One of these allies was the Uighur, from a kingdom based in what is now northern Mongolia. In 762 a Uighur army liberated Luoyang from rebel forces, and there a Uighur *kaghan* (king) was converted to Manichaeism. The result was new prestige and more temples for the religion in China.

However, in 840 the Uighurs were defeated by the Kirghiz, with the result that the Chinese turned on the religion of their former allies, destroyed its temples, and expelled or executed its priests. Nonetheless, at least one Manichaean leader managed to escape to Quanzhou in Fujian province on the southeast coast. In Fujian the Manichaeans flourished as a popular sect, characterized by their distinctive teachings, communal living, vegetarian diet, and nonviolence, until the fourteenth century. They were called the Mingjiao ("religion of light"). They disappeared as a coherent tradition as a result of renewed persecutions during the early Ming dynasty (1368–1644). Several Manichaean texts were incorporated into the Daoist and Buddhist canons, and it is likely that Manichaean lay sects provided models for similar organizations that evolved out of Buddhism later. Manichaean dualism and demon exorcism may have reinforced similar themes in Daoism and Buddhism as they were understood at the popular level.

According to a stone inscription erected in Chang'an (present-day Xian) in 781, the first Nestorian missionary reached China in 635 and taught about the creation of the world, the fall of humankind, and the birth and teaching of the Messiah. The ethics and rituals described are recognizably Christian. Chinese edicts of 638 and 745 refer to Nestorianism, which appears to have been confined to foreign communities in large cities on major trade routes. In 845 Nestorianism was proscribed along with Buddhism and other religions of non-Chinese origin, but it revived in China during the period of Mongol rule in the thirteenth and fourteenth centuries. In 1289 the court established an office to supervise Christians, and a 1330 source claims that there were more than thirty thousand Nestorians in China, some of them wealthy and in high positions, no doubt a result of the Mongol policy of ruling China in part with officials of foreign origin. In this period the church was most active in eastern cities such as Hangzhou and Yangzhou. The Nestorians were expelled from China with the defeat of the Mongols in the mid-fourteenth century, and no active practitioners were found by the Jesuits when they arrived about two hundred years later. So the first Christian contact with China expired, leaving no demonstrable influence on Chinese religion and culture.

There is no certainty regarding the date of Judaism's entrance into China. Two of the four surviving commemorative stelae from the synagogue in Kaifeng trace it to the Han dynasty, suggesting that the emigration might have followed the destruction of the Jerusalem Temple in 70 CE But most scholars agree that it was more likely during the Tang that Jewish merchants from Persia or Bukhara first settled in Kaifeng, on the Yellow River in Henan province. Other premodern Jewish communities existed in Ningbo, Hangzhou, Yangzhou, and Guangzhou, all probably established by merchants arriving by sea, but the Kaifeng community was the most successful. Kaifeng was the capital of the Northern Song dynasty (960–1127), and at some point during that period the emperor received representatives of the Jewish community at court and bestowed upon them Chinese surnames, one of which was his own (Zhao). In 1163, under the Jurchen Jin dynasty that had conquered northern China, the Jews built their first synagogue, with approval from the government. Over the ensuing centuries the synagogue was destroyed by floods, rebuilt, and expanded several times.

The Chinese first learned of Islam in 638 from an emissary of the last Sassanid king of Persia, who was seeking their aid against invading Arab armies. This the Chinese refused, but a number of Persian refugees were admitted a few years later after the Sassanid defeat and allowed to practice their Zoroastrian faith. In the early eighth century Arab armies moved into Central Asia, and in 713 ambassadors of Caliph Walid ibn Yazīd were received at court in Chang'an, even though they refused to prostrate themselves before the emperor. However, in 751 a Chinese army far to the west was defeated in the Battle of Talas by a combination of Central Asian states with Arab support. This defeat led to the replacement of Chinese influence in Central Asia with that of the Arabs and the decline of Buddhism in that area in favor of Islam. In 756 another caliph sent Arab mercenaries to aid the Chinese court against An Lushan; when the war ended many of these mercenaries remained, forming the beginning of Islamic presence in China, which by the late twentieth century totaled about thirty million people, one of the five main constituencies of the People's Republic. The eighth-century Arab population was augmented by Muslim merchants who settled in Chinese coastal cities, for a time dominating the sea trade with India and Southeast Asia.

The major influx of Muslim peoples occurred during the Yuan dynasty (1206–1368) when the land routes across Central Asia were secure and the Mongols brought in large numbers of their non-Chinese subjects to help administer China. It was in this period that Islam spread all over China and established major population bases in the western provinces of Yunnan and Gansu. Here their numbers increased through marriage with Chinese women and adoption of non-Muslim children, all converted to Islam. Although the result was a dilution of Arab physical characteristics, the use of the Chinese language, and the adoption of some Chinese social customs, for most the Islamic core remained. Muslims did not accept such dominant Chinese traditions as ancestor worship and pork eating, and they kept their own festival calendar. This resistance was the result in part of the tenacity of their beliefs, in part of the fact that their numbers, mosques, and essentially lay organization permitted mutual support.

Muslims in China have always been predominantly Sunnī, but in the sixteenth century Sufism reached China through Central Asia. By the late seventeenth century Ṣūfī brotherhoods began a reform movement that advocated increased use of Arabic and a rejection of certain Chinese practices that had infiltrated Islam, such as burning incense at funerals. Sufism also emphasized ecstatic personal experience of Allāh, the veneration of saints, and the imminent return of the *mahdī,* who would bring a new age, this last theme due to Shīʿī influence as well.

These reformist beliefs, coupled with increased Chinese pressure on Islam as a whole, led eventually to a powerful uprising in Yunnan between 1855 and 1873, an uprising allowed to develop momentum because of old ethnic tensions in the area and the distraction of the Chinese court with the contemporary Taiping rebellion (1851–1864). The Yunnan rebellion was eventually put down by a combination of Chinese and loyalist Muslim forces, and the Muslims resumed their role as a powerful minority in China, called the Hui people.

The chief role of Islam in China was as the religion of this minority group, although in some twentieth-century popular texts it was recognized as one of the "five religions" whose teachings were blended into a new synthetic revelation, along with Confucianism, Daoism, Buddhism, and Christianity. Another aspect of Islam's historical impact was to sharply reduce Chinese contact with India and Central Asia after the eighth century, and thus to cut off the vital flow of new texts and ideas to Chinese Buddhism. And since the 1980s, mostly in the Uighur Autonomous Region of Xinjiang, there has been increasing pressure, fueled by Islamic militancy, for independence from the People's Republic of China.

Tang Buddhism. The first Tang emperor, Gaozu (r. 618–626), approved of a plan to limit both Daoist and Buddhist temples. His son Taizong (r. 626–649) agreed with the Daoist contention that the imperial family was descended from Laozi, whose legendary surname was also Li; however, Taizong also erected Buddhist shrines on battlefields and ordered monks to recite scriptures for the stability of the empire. Buddhist philosophical schools in this period were matters of both belief and imperial adornment, so, to replace the Tiantai school, now discredited on account of its association with the Sui dynasty, the Tang court turned first to the Faxiang or Weishi ("consciousness only") school, an idealist teaching known in Sanskrit as Yogācāra or Vijñanavada. Some texts of this tradition had been translated earlier by

Paramartha (499–569), but it came to be thoroughly understood in China only after the return of the pilgrim Xuanzang in 645 from his sixteen-year-long overland journey to India. Xuanzang was welcomed at court and provided with twenty-three scholar-monks from all over China to assist in translating the books he had brought back. The emperor wrote a preface for the translation of one major Vijñanavada text, and his policy of imperial support was continued by his son Gaozong (r. 650–683).

However, the complex psychological analysis of the Vijñanavada school, coupled with its emphasis that some beings are doomed by their nature to eternal rebirth, were not in harmony with the Chinese worldview, which had been better represented by Tiantai. Hence, when imperial support declined at Gaozong's death in 683, the fortunes of the Faxiang school declined as well, despite the excellent scholarship of Xuanzang's disciple Kuiji (632–682). At the intellectual level it was replaced in popularity by the Huayan ("flower garland") school as formulated by the monk Fazang (643–712). This school, based on a sūtra of the same name (Sanskrit, *Avataṃsaka*), taught the emptiness and interpenetration of all phenomena in a way consonant with old Chinese assumptions. Furthermore, in Huayan teaching the unity and integration of all things is symbolized by a Buddha called Vairocana who presides over his Pure Land in the center of an infinite universe. However dialectically such a symbol might be understood by Buddhist scholars, at a political and popular level it was appropriated more literally as a Buddhist creator deity.

It is no accident that the Huayan school was first actively supported by Empress Wu Zhao (Wu Zetian, r. 684–704) who took over the throne from her sons to set up her own dynasty, the Zhou. Since Confucianism did not sanction for female rulers, Empress Wu, being a devout Buddhist, sought for supporting ideologies in that tradition, including not only Huayan but also predictions in obscure texts that the Buddha had prophesied that several hundred years after his death a woman would rule over a world empire. Monks in Wu Zetian's entourage equated her with this empress and further asserted that she was a manifestation of the future Buddha Maitreya.

When Empress Wu abdicated in 704, her son continued to support the Huayan school, continuing the tradition of close relationship between the court and Buddhist philosophical schools. However, during this period Buddhism continued to grow in popularity among all classes of people. Thousands of monasteries and shrines, supported by donations of land, grain, cloth, and precious metals, were built by convict workers, the poor, and serfs bound to donated lands. Tens of thousands of persons became monks or nuns, elaborate rituals were performed, feasts provided, and sermons preached in both monastery and marketplace. Buddhist observances such as the Lantern Festival, the Buddha's birthday, and the Ghost Festival became widely practiced, while pious lay societies multiplied for carving images and inscriptions and disseminating scriptures. Wealthy monasteries became centers of money lending, milling, and medical care, as well as hostels for travelers and retreats for scholars and officials. In high literature the purity of monks and monasteries was admired, while in popular stories *karma,* rebirth, and purgatory became unquestioned truths. The state made sporadic attempts to control this exuberance by licensing monasteries, instituting examinations for monks, and issuing ordination certificates, but state control was limited and "unofficial" Buddhist practices continued to flourish.

An important factor in this popularity was the rise of two more simple and direct forms of Chinese Buddhism, much less complex than the exegetical and philosophical schools that were dominant earlier. These were the Pure Land (Jingtu) school, devoted to rebirth in Amitābha's paradise, and the Chan ("meditation") school, which promised enlightenment in this life to those with sufficient dedication. These traditions were universalist and nonhierarchical in principle yet came to have coherent teachings and organizations of their own appealing to a wide range of people. Both should be understood as products of gradual evolution in the seventh and eighth centuries, as a positive selection from earlier teachings, particularly Tiantai, and as a reformist reaction against the secularization of the Tang monastic establishment.

By the third century CE texts describing various "pure realms" or "Buddha lands" had been translated into Chinese, and some monks began to meditate on the best known of these "lands," the Western Paradise of the Buddha Amitābha. In the fourth century Zhi Dun (314–366) made an image of Amitābha and vowed to be reborn in his paradise, as did Huiyuan in 402. These early efforts concentrated on visualization of buddha realms in states of meditative trance. However, in two Pure Land sūtras describing Amitābha and his realm, devotees are assured that through a combination of ethical living and concentration on this buddha they will be reborn at death in his realm, owing to a vow he had made eons ago to create out of the boundless merit he had accumulated on the long path to Buddhahood a haven for sentient beings. This promise eventually led some monks to preach devotion to Amitābha as an easier way to salvation, available to all, through a combination of sincere thinking on the Buddha and the invocation of his name in faith. To strengthen their proclamation, these monks argued that in fact Amitābha's Pure Land was at a high level, beyond *saṃsāra* (the cycle of rebirth), and thus functionally equivalent to *nirvāṇa* for those less philosophically inclined.

Philosophers of the fifth and sixth centuries such as Sengzhao and Zhiyi discussed the Pure Land concept as part of larger systems of thought, but the first monk to devote his life to proclaiming devotion to Amitābha as the chief means of salvation for the whole of society was Tanluan (476–542), a monk from North China where there had long been an emphasis on the practical implementation of Buddhism. Tanluan organized devotional associations whose members both contemplated the Buddha and orally recited his name. It was in the fifth and sixth centuries as well that many Chinese Buddhist thinkers became convinced that the final period of Buddhist teaching for this world cycle was about to begin, a period (called in Chinese *mofa,* the Latter Days of the Law) in which the capacity for understanding Buddhism had so declined that only simple and direct means of communication would suffice.

The next important preacher to base his teachings solely on Amitābha and his Pure Land was Daochuo (562–645). It was he and his disciple Shandao (613–681) who firmly established the Pure Land movement and came to be looked upon as founding patriarchs of the tradition. Although both of these men advocated oral recitation of Amitābha's name as the chief means to deliverance, such recitation was to be done in a concentrated and devout state of mind and was to be accompanied by confession of sins and the chanting of sūtras. They and their followers also organized recitation assemblies and composed manuals for congregational worship. Owing to their efforts, Pure Land devotion became the most popular form of Buddhism in China, from whence it was taken to Japan in the ninth century. Pure Land teachings supported the validity of lay piety as no Buddhist school had before, and hence both made possible the spread of Buddhism throughout the population and furthered the development of independent societies and sects outside the monasteries.

The last movement within orthodox Buddhism in China to emerge as an independent tradition was Chan (Japanese, Zen), characterized by its concentration on direct means of individual enlightenment, chiefly meditation. Such enlightenment had always been the primary goal of Buddhism, so in a sense Chan began as a reform movement seeking to recover the experiential origins of its tradition. Such a reform appeared all the more necessary in the face of the material success of Tang Buddhism, with its ornate rituals, complex philosophies, and close relationships with the state. Chan evolved out of the resonances of Mahāyāna Buddhism with the individualist, mystical, and iconoclastic strand of Chinese culture, represented chiefly by the philosophy of the *Laozi* and *Zhuangzi,* especially the latter. This philosophy had long advocated individual identification with the ineffable foundations of being, which cannot be grasped in words or limited by the perspectives of traditional practice and morality. Such identification brings a new sense of spiritual freedom, affirmation of life, and acceptance of death. The importance of meditation had long been emphasized in Chinese Buddhism, beginning with Han translations of sūtras describing the process. The Tiantai master Zhiyi discussed the stages and positions of meditation in great detail in the sixth century. Thus, it is not surprising that by the seventh century some monks appeared who advocated meditation above all, a simplification parallel to that of the Pure Land tradition.

The first references to a "Chan school" appeared in the late eighth century. By that time several branches of this emerging tradition were constructing genealogies going back to Śākyamuni himself; these were intended to establish the priority and authority of their teachings. The genealogy that came to be accepted later claimed a lineage of twenty-eight Indian and seven Chinese patriarchs, the latter beginning with Bodhidharma (c. 461–534), a Central Asian meditation master active in the Northern Wei kingdom. Legends concerning these patriarchs were increasingly elaborated as time passed, but the details of most cannot be verified. The first Chinese monk involved whose teachings have survived is Daoxin (580–651), who was later claimed to be the fourth patriarch. Daoxin specialized in meditation and monastic discipline and studied for ten years with a disciple of the Tiantai founder, Zhiyi. He is also noted for his concern with image worship and reciting the Buddha's name to calm the mind.

One of Daoxin's disciples was Hongren (601–674), who also concentrated on meditation and on maintaining "awareness of the mind." His successor was Faru (d. 689), whose spiritual heir in turn was Shenxiu (d. 706), who had also studied with Hongren. Shenxiu was active in North China, where he was invited to court by the Empress Wu and became a famous teacher. In the earliest and most reliable sources Hongren, Faru, and Shenxiu are described as the fifth, sixth, and seventh Chan patriarchs, with Faru eventually omitted and replaced in sixth position by Shenxiu. However, in the early eighth century this succession, based in the capitals of Luoyang and Chang'an in the North (and hence retrospectively referred to as the "Northern school"), was challenged by a monk named Shenhui (670–762), who had studied for several years with a teacher named Huineng (638–713) in a monastery in Guangdong province in the south. Shenhui labored for years to establish a new form of Chan, a "Southern school," centered on recognizing the buddha nature within the self, and thus less concerned with worship, scripture study, and prescribed forms of meditation.

Shenhui's most lasting achievement was the elevation of his teacher Huineng to the status of "sixth patriarch," displacing Shenxiu. This achievement was textually established through the composition of a book entitled *The Platform Sūtra of the Sixth Patriarch* (*platform* here means the high chair on which the abbot sits while giving *dharma* talks) in about 820 by members of Shenhui's school. Portions of this book are very similar to the teachings of Shenhui, who did not cite any writings by Huineng, although he was no doubt influenced by his study with him. In the *Platform Sūtra* Huineng is portrayed as a brilliant young layman of rustic background who, although he is only a kitchen helper in the monastery, confounds Shenxiu and is secretly given charge of the transmission by Hongren, the fifth patriarch. This book teaches instantaneous enlightenment through realization of inner potential while criticizing gradualist approaches that rely on outer forms such as images and scriptures. As such it is an important source of the Chan individualism and iconoclasm well known (and often exaggerated) in the West.

Although Buddhism flourished at all levels of Chinese society in the Tang period, an undercurrent of resentment and hostility toward it by Confucians, Daoists, and the state always remained. Han Yu (768–824), one of China's great writers, campaigned against Buddhist influence and argued for a revival of the teachings of Confucius and Mengzi. This hostility came to a head in the mid-ninth century, strongly reinforced by the fact that Buddhist monasteries had accumulated large amounts of precious metals and tax-exempt land. From 843 to 845 Emperor Wuzong (r. 840–846), an ardent Daoist, issued decrees that led to the destruction of 4,600 monasteries and 40,000 temples and shrines, and the return of 260,500 monks and nuns to lay life. Although this suppression was ended in 846 by Wuzong's successor, monastic Buddhism never fully regained its momentum. Nonetheless, Buddhist ideas, values, and rituals continued to permeate Chinese society through the influence of the Chan and Pure Land schools, which survived the 845 persecution because of widespread support throughout the country.

Tang Daoism. Daoism continued to develop during the Tang period, in part because it received more support from some emperors than it had under the Sui. As noted earlier, Taizong claimed Laozi as a royal ancestor, and in 667 the emperor Gaozong (r. 650–683) conferred on Laozi the title of emperor, thus confirming his status. Empress Wu, Gaozong's wife, swung the pendulum of support back to Buddhism, but Daoism was favored in later reigns as well and reached the high point of its political influence in the Tang with the suppression of Buddhism and other non-Chinese religions in the 840s.

The most important Daoist order during the Tang was that based on Maoshan in Jiangsu, where temples were built and reconstructed, disciples trained, and scriptures edited. Devotees on Maoshan studied Shangqing scriptures, meditated, practiced alchemy, and carried out complex rituals of purgation and cosmic renewal, calling down astral spirits and preparing for immortality among the stars. These activities were presided over by a hierarchical priesthood, led by *fashi,* "masters of doctrine," the most prominent of whom came to be considered patriarchs of the school.

Daoism in the Song and Yuan periods. The old Tang aristocracy had begun to lose its power after the An Lushan rebellion in the eighth century. The turmoil of the ninth and tenth centuries sealed its fate and helped prepare the way for a more centralized state in the Song, administered by bureaucrats who were selected through civil service examinations. This in turn contributed to increased social mobility, which was also enhanced by economic growth and diversification, the spread of printing, and a larger number of schools. These factors, combined with innovations in literature, art, philosophy, religion, science, and technology, have led historians to describe the Song period as the beginning of early modern China. It was in this period that the basic patterns of life and thought were established for the remainder of imperial history.

During the tenth through thirteenth centuries Daoism developed new schools and texts and became more closely allied with the state. The Song emperor Chenzong (r. 990–1023) bestowed gifts and titles on a number of prominent Daoists, including one named Zhang from the old Way of the Celestial Masters, based on Mount Longhu in Jiangxi province. This led to the consolidation of the Zhengyi (Orthodox Unity) sect led by hereditary Celestial Masters. The other official Daoist ordination centers in this period were those at Maoshan and the Lingbao center in Jiangsu.

A century later, during the reign of Emperor Huizong (r. 1101–1125), the most famous imperial patron of Daoism, three new Daoist orders appeared, one with a popular base in southeastern Jiangxi, another a revival of Maoshan teachings, and the third the Shenxiao Fa (Rites of the Divine Empyrean), initiated by Lin Lingsu, who was active at court from 1116 to 1119. Lin's teachings were presented in a new, expanded edition of a fourth-century Lingbao text, the *Durenjing* (Scripture of Salvation). The scripture proclaimed that a new divine emperor would descend to rule in 1112, thus bestowing additional sacred status on Huizong. This liturgical text in sixty-one chapters promises salvation to all in the name of a supreme celestial realm, a theme welcome at a court beset with corruption within and foreign invaders without. The Jiangxi movement, called Tianxin (Heart of Heaven) after a star in Ursa Major, was most concerned with the ritual evocation of astral power to exorcise disease-causing demons, particularly those associated with mental illness. The first edition of its texts was also presented to Huizong in 1116.

In 1126 the Song capital Kaifeng was captured by the Jurchen, a people from northeastern Manchuria who, with other northern peoples, had long threatened the Song. As a result the Chinese court moved south across the Yangzi River to establish a new capital in Hangzhou, thus initiating the Southern Song period (1127–1279). During this period China was once again divided north and south, with the Jurchen ruling the Jin kingdom (1115–1234). It was here in the north that three new Daoist sects appeared, the Taiyi (Grand Unity), the Dadao (Great Way), and the Quanzhen (Complete Perfection). The Taiyi sect gained favor for a time at the Jin court because of its promise of divine healing. Dadao disciples worked in the fields, prayed for healing rather than using charms, and did not practice techniques of immortality. Both groups were led by a succession of patriarchs for about two hundred years but failed to survive the end of the Yuan dynasty. Both included Confucian and Buddhist elements in a Daoist framework.

The Quanzhen sect was founded in similar circumstances by a scholar named Wang Zhe (1113–1170) but continues to exist. Wang claimed to have received revelations from two superhuman beings, whereupon he gathered disciples and founded five congregations in northern Shandong. After his death seven of his leading disciples continued to proclaim his teachings across North China. One of them was received at the Jin court in 1187, thus beginning a period of imperial support for the sect that continued into the time of Mongol rule, particularly after another of the founding disciples visited Chinggis Khan at his Central Asian court in 1222.

In its early development the Daoist quest for personal immortality employed a combination of positive ritual techniques: visualization of astral gods and ingestion of their essence, internal circulation and refinement of *qi,* massage, ingesting elixirs of cinnabar, mica, or gold in suspension, all accompanied by taboos and ethical injunctions. During the Song and Yuan periods, the ingestion of elixirs, called *waidan* (external alchemy), was replaced by forms of meditation and visualization in which the bodily substances and meditative exercises were expressed in alchemical terms. This new form of practice, called *neidan* (internal alchemy), is well expressed in the writings of Zhang Boduan (983–1082). Under Confucian and Chan influence the Quanzhen school further "spiritualized" the terminology of the older practices, turning their physiological referents into abstract polarities within the mind, to be unified through meditation. Perhaps in part because of this withdrawal into the mind, Quanzhen was the first Daoist school to base itself in monasteries, although celibacy to maintain and purify one's powers had been practiced by some adepts earlier, and some Daoist monasteries had been established in the sixth century under pressure from the state and the Buddhist example.

The Quanzhen sect reached the height of its influence in the first decades of the thirteenth century, and for a time it was favored over Chinese Buddhism by Mongol rulers. Buddhist leaders protested Daoist occupation of their monasteries and eventually regained official support after a series of debates between Daoists and Buddhists at court between 1255 and 1281. After Buddhists were judged the winners, Kublai Khan ordered that the Daoist canon be burned and Daoist priests returned to lay life or converted to Buddhism. In the fourteenth century the Quanzhen sect merged with a similar tradition from South China, the Jindandao (Golden Elixir Way) also devoted to attaining immortality through cultivating powers or "elixirs" within the self. The name Quanzhen was retained for the monastic side of this combined tradition, whereas the Jindandao continued as a popular movement that has produced new scriptures and sects since at least the sixteenth century. The older Daoist schools continued to produce new bodies of texts from the eleventh century on, all claiming divine origin, powers of healing, exorcism, and support for the state.

The revival of Confucianism. Confucianism had remained a powerful tradition of morality, social custom, and hierarchical status since the fall of the Han, but after the third century it no longer generated fresh philosophical perspectives. There were a few Confucian philosophers such as Wang Tong (584?–617), Han Yu, and Li Ao (fl. 798), but from the fourth through the tenth centuries Buddhism and Daoism attracted a great many intellectuals; the best philosophical minds, in particular, were devoted to Buddhism. However, in the eleventh century there appeared a series of thinkers determined to revive Confucianism. In this task they were inevitably influenced by Buddhist theories of mind, enlightenment, and ethics; indeed, most of these men went through Buddhist and Daoist phases in their early years and were "converted" to Confucianism later. Nonetheless, at a conscious level they rejected Buddhist "emptiness," asceticism, and monastic life in favor of a positive metaphysics, ordered family life, and concern for social and governmental reform. With a few exceptions the leaders of this movement, known in the West as neo-Confucianism, went through the civil service examination system and held civil or military offices.

Early neo-Confucianism had both rationalistic and idealistic tendencies; the aim of both was to actualize the inherent sagehood of every human being by realizing and acting upon the ultimate principle *(li)* of the natural/moral order. The more rationalist school believed that this order or principle was present in humans as their fundamental, metaphysical nature (*xing*), but that the physical nature of the mind (*xin*) obscured the metaphysical nature and hindered our awareness of it. This line of thinking was developed by Cheng Yi (1033–1107) and Zhu Xi (1130–1200) and became known as the Cheng-Zhu school. The idealistic approach, which later became known as the Lu-Wang school after Lu Jiuyuan (1139–1193) and Wang Yangming (1472–1529), said that the fundamental natural/moral order was fully present to awareness in the active, functioning mind and so did not require intellectual learning to be known. Thus, both schools focused on the mind; their differences concerned whether *li* was already present in the mind and needed only to be acted upon, or whether it first had to be intellectually induced through the rational investigation of human nature and the natural world. Interaction between these poles provided the impetus for new syntheses until the seventeenth century. But Zhu Xi's version—synthesizing the teachings of not only Cheng Yi but also his brother Cheng Hao (1032–1085), their former teacher Zhou Dunyi (1017–1073), their uncle Zhang Zai (1020–1077), and their friend Shao Yong (1011–1077)—was made the basis of the civil service examinations in 1313 and hence came to have a powerful influence throughout literate society that lasted until the examination system was abolished in 1905.

In the history of Chinese religions, the impact of neo-Confucianism is evident at different levels. The intellectual and institutional success of this movement among the Chinese elite led many of them away from Buddhism and Daoism toward a reaffirmation of the values of family, clan, and state. While the elite were still involved in such popular traditions as annual festivals, geomancy, and funeral rituals, the rational and nontheistic orientation of neo-Confucianism tended to inhibit their participation in ecstatic processions and shamanism. These tendencies meant that after the eleventh century, sectarian and popular forms of religion were increasingly denied high-level intellectual stimulation and articulation. Indeed, state support for a new Confucian orthodoxy gave fresh impetus to criticism or suppression of other traditions. Another long-term impact of neo-Confucianism was the Confucianization of popular values, supported by schools, examinations, distribution of tracts, and lectures in villages. This meant that from the Song dynasty on the operative ethical principles in society were a combination of Confucian virtues with Buddhist *karma* and compassion, a tendency that became more widespread as the centuries passed.

All of these developments were rooted in the religious dimensions of the neo-Confucian tradition, which from the beginning was most concerned with the moral transformation of self and society. This transformation was to be carried out through intensive study and discussion, self-examination, and meditation, often in the social context of public and private schools and academies, where prayers and sacrificial offerings to former Confucian "sages and worthies" accompanied study and discussion. Through the process of self-cultivation one could become aware of the patterns of moral order within the mind and in the cosmos, an insight that itself became a means of clarifying and establishing this cosmic order within society. So Confucianism became a more active and self-conscious movement than it ever had been before.

Song Buddhism. Song Buddhist activities were based on the twin foundations of Chan and Pure Land, with an increasing emphasis on the compatibility of the two. Although the joint practice of meditation and invocation of the Buddha's name had been taught by Zhiyi and the Chan patriarch Daoxin in the sixth and seventh centuries, the first Chan master to openly advocate it after Chan was well established was Yanshou (904–975). This emphasis was continued in the Yuan (1279–1368) and Ming (1368–1644) dynasties, so that by the late traditional period meditation and recitation were commonly employed together in monasteries as two means to the same end of emptying the mind of self-centered thought.

During the Song dynasty Buddhism physically recovered from the suppression of the ninth century, with tens of thousands of monasteries, large amounts of land, and active support throughout society. By the tenth century the Chan school was divided into two main branches, both of which had first appeared earlier, the Linji (in Japanese, Rinzai), emphasizing *gongan* practice and dramatic, spontaneous breakthroughs to enlightenment in the midst of everyday activities, and the Caodong (in Japanese, Sōtō), known for a more gradual approach through seated meditation, or *zuochan* (in Japanese, *zazen*). The most prominent Song representative of the Linji lineage was Dahui Zonggao (1089–1163), a popular preacher to laypeople as well as a meditation master. In the Caodong lineage the most prominent teacher was Hongzhi Zhengjue (1091–1157), who taught meditation as "silent illumination" (*mozhao*).

Although the Tang dynasty has traditionally been called the Golden Age of Chan Buddhism, it was actually during the Song that Chan became firmly established and developed the styles today associated with it. Notwithstanding its often colorful and iconoclastic teaching methods, Chan has always been characterized by disciplined communal living in monasteries, centered on group meditation but with a strong emphasis on traditional Buddhist ethics. The hallmarks of Chan monasticism have traditionally been ascribed to Baizhang Huaihai (749–814). These include the rejection of a central Buddha hall containing images in favor of a *dharma* hall, where the abbot would lecture and conduct services; a *saṃgha* or monks' hall, with platforms along the sides for sleeping and meditation; private consultations with the abbot; and shared responsibility for manual labor, including agricultural work to reduce dependence on outside donations with the reciprocal obligations they involved. Evaluating this traditional view, historians have noted that the earliest extant text containing Baizhang's rules dates from the late tenth century, and the earliest extant detailed code of monastic conduct is dated 1103 or 1104; thus, we have Song dynasty texts purporting to describe Tang dynasty monasteries. Research has also found that the allegedly unique features of Chan monasteries were also found in Tiantai monasteries and that the claim of a distinct style dating back to the Tang, a style actually common to the majority of monasteries, served as support for the Song policy by which all publicly supported monasteries were designated as Chan and their abbacies restricted to monks in a Chan lineage. This policy took effect during the Northern Song. After Chan thus became the "established" sect, agricultural labor was reduced as Chan monasteries received donations of land and goods from wealthy patrons.

During the Song Chan produced new genres of Buddhist literature that eventually became more central to its teaching than the older Mahāyāna sūtras. The "recorded sayings" (*yulu*) of patriarchs and abbots with their disciples were an adaptation of an older Chinese form whose most notable example was the *Analects* (*Lunyu*) of Confucius. From these were extracted shorter sayings and conversations demonstrating the struggle to attain enlightenment. These records, codified as "public cases" (Chinese, *gongan;* Japanese, *kōan*), were meditated upon by novices as they sought to experience reality directly. And "Lamp Records" (*denglu*) were compilations of the saying of various lineages, demonstrating what Chan teachers called the "mind-to-mind transmission" that connected them with Śākyamuni Buddha. This doctrine also supported the Chan claim to represent a more authentic form of Buddhism than the other major Chinese schools (Tiantai, Huayan, and Pure Land), each of which focused on a particular sūtra (the *Lotus,* the *Avataṃsaka* or Huayan, and the three Pure Land sūtras, respectively). Thus, Chan Buddhism constructed what we might call a mythic history of itself that had important "political" ramifications.

One of the most important developments in Song Buddhism was the spread of lay societies devoted to good works and recitation of the Buddha's name. These groups, usually supported by monks and monasteries, ranged in membership from a few score to several thousand, including both men and women, gentry and commoners. In the twelfth century these societies, with their egalitarian outreach and congregational rituals, provided the immediate context for the rise of independent popular sects, which in turn spread throughout China in succeeding centuries. The Song associations were an organized and doctrinally aware means of spreading Buddhist ideas of salvation, paradise and purgatory, *karma,* and moral values to the population at large, and so they contributed to the integration of Buddhism with Chinese culture.

Popular religion. The other major tradition that took its early modern shape during the Song period was popular religion, the religion of the whole population other than orthodox Daoist priests, Buddhist monks, Confucian scholars, and state officials in their public roles (although elements of popular religion overlapped with these more specialized vocations). Zhou and Han sources note a variety of religious practices current throughout the population, including ancestor worship, sacrifices to spirits of sacred objects and places, belief in ghosts, exorcism, divination, and the activities of spirit mediums. Many of these practices began in prehistoric times and formed the sea out of which more structured and focused traditions gradually emerged, traditions such as the state cult, Confucian philosophy, and Daoist religion. Each of these emerging traditions was associated with social elites who had to define themselves as different from their peasant and artisan surroundings. In the process they often came to criticize or even suppress cults active among common folk devoted to local spirits and concerned primarily with efficacious response to immediate needs. Since the Chinese state had always claimed religious prerogatives, the most important factor was official authorization by some level of government. Unauthorized cults were considered "excessive," beyond what elite custom and propriety admitted. Nonetheless, such distinctions were of importance primarily to the more self-conscious supporters of literate alternatives; to their less theologically inclined peers, "popular religion" was a varied set of customs that reflected the way the world was.

Popular religious practices were diffused throughout the social system, based in family, clan, and village, at first devoted only to spirits with limited and local powers. By the Han dynasty personified deities of higher status appeared, along with organized sects such as the Way of the Celestial Masters, with ethical teachings and new myths of creation and world renewal, all reinforced by collective rituals. These developments were produced by literate commoners and minor officials at an intermediate level of education and status, and show remarkable resemblance to the first records of such middle-class thought in the writings of Mozi, six hundred years earlier. This level of Chinese religious consciousness was strongly reinforced by Mahāyāna *bodhisattvas,* images, offering rituals, myths of purgatory, and understandings of moral causation. By the fourth century, Daoist writers were developing elaborate mythologies of personified deities and immortals and their roles in a celestial hierarchy.

During the Song period all these various strands came together to reformulate popular religion as a tradition in its own right, defined by its location in the midst of ordinary social life, its pantheon of personified deities, views of afterlife, demonology, and characteristic specialists and rituals. Its values were still founded on pragmatic reciprocity, but some assurances about life after death were added to promises for aid now.

This popular tradition is based on the worship or propitiation of gods, ghosts, and ancestors. The boundaries between these categories are somewhat fluid. Under ideal circumstances, when a person dies the *hun,* or *yang* soul, rises to heaven and becomes an ancestor (*zu* or *zuxian*) and the *po,* or *yin* soul, remains with the body in the earth—provided that the death was normal, the body was buried in a proper funeral, and subsequent memorial services or ancestral sacrifices are properly made by blood or ritually adopted descendants. If these conditions are not met, either the *hun* or the *po* (depending on local beliefs) can become a ghost *(gui).* Ghosts can be ritually adopted or—in the case of unmarried women—posthumously married, thereby becoming ancestors; they can even be enshrined and worshiped as minor gods. Although scholars differ on whether the propitiation of ancestors should be called worship or veneration (since they are not gods), the basic ritual actions performed for gods and ancestors (burning incense, praying, offering food or "spirit money") are virtually identical. The status of the particular recipient is indicated by certain variations, such as offering uncooked food for a god but cooked food for an ancestor; cooked food implies a meal being shared, and ordinary people do not presume to invite gods into their homes for meals. Phenomenologically, the difference between a god and an ancestor is that the former has more numinous power (*ling*) and can therefore exert influence on a circle of the living wider than his or her own family.

Beyond the household popular religion is practiced at shrines for local earth-gods and at village or city neighborhood temples. Temples are residences of the gods, where they are most easily available and ready to accept petitions and offerings of food and incense. Here, too, the gods convey messages through simple means of divination, dreams, spirit mediums, and spirit writing. The most common forms of divination are the use of "moon-blocks" *(shengbei)* and divinationslips (*quia*). Divination usually accompanies sacrificial offerings to ascertain whether they are pleasing. Great bronze incense burners in temple courtyards are the focal points of ritual communication, and it is common for local households to fill their own incense burners with ashes from the temple. All families residing in the area of the village or the city neighborhood are considered members of the temple community.

Most of the deities characteristic of this tradition are human beings deified over time by increasing recognition of their efficacy and status. Having once been human they owe their positions to veneration by the living and hence are constrained by reciprocal relationships with their devotees. Many of the deities of popular religion are responsible for specific functions such as providing rain or healing diseases, while others are propitiated for a wide variety of reasons—sometimes simply for general good fortune, or to maintain a harmonious relationship with the unseen world (an example of "ultimate orientation"). Under Daoist influence the pantheon came to be organized in a celestial hierarchy presided over by the Jade Emperor, a deity first officially recognized as such by the Song emperor Zhenzong in the beginning of the eleventh century. The Jade Emperor is called Yuhuang dadi (Jade Emperor Great Lord) or Yuhuang shangdi (Jade Emperor High Lord)—the latter incorporating the name of the high god of the Shang dynasty.

Gods are symbols of order, and many of the gods of Daoism and popular religion are equipped with weapons and troops. Such force is necessary because beneath the gods is a vast array of demons, hostile influences that bring disorder, disease, suffering, and death. Although ultimately subject to divine command, and in some cases sent by the gods to punish sinners, these demons are most unruly and often can be subdued only through repeated invocation and strenuous ritual action. It is in such ritual exorcism that the struggle between gods and demons is most starkly presented. Some demons are ghosts *(gui)*, or the spirits of the restless dead who died unjustly or whose bodies are not properly cared for; they cause disruption to draw attention to their plight. Other demons represent natural forces that can be perceived as hostile, such as mountains and wild animals. Much effort in popular religion is devoted to dealing with these harmful influences.

There are three different types of leadership in this popular tradition—hereditary, selected, and charismatic—although of course in any given situation these types can be mixed. Hereditary leaders include the fathers and mothers of families, who carry out ancestor worship in the clan temple and household, and sect leaders, who inherit their positions. Hereditary Daoist priests also perform rituals for the community. Village temples, on the other hand, tend to be led by a village elder selected by lot on a rotating basis. Charismatic leaders include spirit mediums, spirit writers, magicians, and healers, all of whom are defined by the recognition of their ability to bring divine power and wisdom directly to bear on human problems.

Popular religion is also associated with a cycle of annual festivals, funeral rituals, and geomancy *(feng-shui)*. Popular values are sanctioned by revelations from the gods and by belief in purgatory, where the soul goes after death, there to be punished for its sins according to the principle of karmic retribution. There are ten courts in purgatory, each presided over by a judge who fits the suffering to the crime. Passage through purgatory can be ameliorated through the transfer of spirit money by Buddhist or Daoist rituals. When its guilt has been purged, the soul advances to the tenth court, where the form of its next existence is decided. This mythology is a modification of Buddhist beliefs described in detail in texts first translated in the sixth century.

The period of Mongol rule. The Mongols under Chinggis Khan (1162–1227) captured the Jin capital of Yanjing (modern Beijing) in 1215 and established the Yuan dynasty (1279–1368).

From China they ruled their vast domain, which extended all the way to central Europe. For the next several decades the "Middle Kingdom" was the eastern end of a world empire, open as never before to foreign influences. In the realm of religion these influences included the Nestorians, a few Franciscan missionaries in the early fourteenth century, the growth of the Jewish community in Kaifeng, and a large number of Tibetan Buddhist monks.

The first Mongol contact with Chinese Buddhism was with Chan monks, a few of whom attained influence at court. In the meantime, however, the Mongols were increasingly attracted by the exorcistic and healing rituals of Tantric Buddhism in Tibet, the borders of which they also controlled. In 1260 a Tibetan monk, 'Phags-pa (1235–1280), was named imperial preceptor and soon after chief of Buddhist affairs. Tibetan monks were appointed as leaders of the *saṃgha* all over China, to some extent reviving the Tantric (Zhenyan) school that had flourished briefly in the Tang.

By the early fourteenth century another form of popular religion appeared, the voluntary association or sect that could be joined by individuals from different families and villages. These sects developed out of lay Buddhist societies in the twelfth century, but their structure owed much to late Han religious associations and their popular Daoist successors, Buddhist eschatological movements from the fifth century on, and Manichaeism. By the Yuan period the sects were characterized by predominantly lay membership and leadership, hierarachical organization, active proselytism, congregational rituals, possession of their own scriptures in the vernacular, and mutual economic support. Their best known antecedent was the White Lotus sect, an independent group founded by a monk named Mao Ziyuan (1086–1166). Mao combined simplified Tiantai teaching with Pure Land practice, invoking Amitābha's saving power with just five recitations of his name. After Mao's death the sect, led by laymen who married, spread across south and east China. In the process it incorporated charms and prognostication texts, and by the fourteenth century branches in Guangxi and Henan were strongly influenced by Daoist methods of cultivating the internal elixirs. This led to protests from more orthodox leaders of the Pure Land tradition, monks in the east who appealed to the throne that they not be proscribed along with the "heretics." This appeal succeeded, and the monastic branch went on to be considered part of the tradition of the Pure Land school, with Mao Ziyuan as a revered patriarch.

The more rustic side of the White Lotus tradition was prohibited three times in the Yuan but flourished nonetheless, with its own communal organizations and scriptures and a growing emphasis on the presence within it of the future buddha Maitreya. During the civil wars of the mid-fourteenth century this belief encouraged full-scale uprisings in the name of the new world Maitreya was expected to bring. The Ming founder Zhu Yuanzhang (1328–1398) had for a time been an officer in one of the White Lotus armies, but after his victory he tried to suppress the sect. It continued to multiply nonetheless under a variety of names.

The first extant sectarian scriptures, produced in the early sixteenth century, indicate that by that time there were two streams of mythology and belief, one more influenced by Daoism, the other by Buddhism. The Daoist stream incorporated much terminology from the Golden Elixir school (Jindandao) and was based on the myth of a saving mother goddess, the Eternal Venerable Mother, who is a modified form of the old Han-dynasty Queen Mother of the West, a figure mentioned in Quanzhen teachings as well. The Buddhist stream was initiated by a sectarian reformer named Luo Qing (1443–1527), whose teachings were based on the Chan theme of "attaining Buddhahood through seeing one's own nature." Luo criticized the White Lotus and Maitreya sects as being too concerned with outward ritual forms, but later writers in his school incorporated some themes from the Eternal Mother mythology, while other sectarian founders espousing this mythology imitated Luo Qing's example of writing vernacular scriptures to put forth their own views. These scriptures, together with their successors, the popular spirit-writing texts of the nineteenth and twentieth centuries, constitute a fourth major body of Chinese sacred texts, after those of the Confucians, Buddhists, and Daoists.

The number of popular religious sects increased rapidly during the sixteenth and seventeenth centuries, all part of the same general tradition but with different founders, lines of transmission, texts, and ritual variations. Such groups had been illegal since the Yuan, and some resisted prosecution with armed force or attempted to establish their own safe areas. In a few cases sect leaders organized major attempts to overthrow the government and put their own emperor on the throne, to rule over a utopian world in which time and society would be renewed. However, for the most part the sects simply provided a congregational alternative to village popular religion, an alternative that offered mutual support and assurance and promised means of going directly to paradise at death without passing through purgatory.

Popular religious sects were active on the China mainland until the start of the Cultural Revolution in 1966, and they continue to multiply in Taiwan, where they can be legally registered as branches of Daoism. Since the late nineteenth century most sectarian scriptures have been composed by spirit writing, direct revelation from a variety of gods and culture heroes.

MING AND QING RELIGION. Mongol rule began to deteriorate in the early fourteenth century because of struggles between tribal factions at court, the decline of military power, and the devolution of central authority to local warlords, bandit groups, and sectarian movements. After twenty years of civil war Zhu Yuanzhang, from a poor peasant family, defeated all his rivals and reestablished a Chinese imperial house, the Ming dynasty (1368–1644). Zhu (Ming Taizu, r. 1368–1398) was an energetic ruler of strong personal religious beliefs who revised imperial rituals, promulgated strict laws against a variety of popular practices and sects, and recruited Daoist priests to direct court ceremonies. For him the Mandate of Heaven was a living force that had established him in a long line of sacred emperors; his ancestors were deemed powerful intermediaries with Shangdi. He elaborated and reinforced the responsibility of government officials to offer regular sacrifices to deities of fertility, natural forces, and cities, and to the spirits of heroes and abandoned ghosts.

Ming dynasty. Under the Ming, such factors as the diversification of the agricultural base and the monetization of the economy had an impact on religious life; there were more excess funds for building temples and printing scriptures, and more rich peasants, merchants, and artisans with energy to invest in popular religion, both village and sectarian. Sectarian scriptures appeared as part of the same movement that produced new vernacular literature of all types, morality books to inculcate neo-Confucian values, and new forms and audiences for popular operas. More than ever before the late Ming was a time of economic and cultural initiatives from the population at large, as one might expect in a period of increasing competition for resources by small entrepreneurs. These tendencies continued to gain momentum in the Qing period.

Ming Buddhism showed the impact of these economic and cultural factors, particularly in eastern China, where during the sixteenth century reforming monks such as Yunqi Zhuhong (1535–1615) organized lay societies, wrote morality books that quantified the merit points for good deeds, and affirmed Confucian values within a Buddhist framework. Zhuhong combined Pure Land and Chan practice and preached spiritual progress through sparing animals from slaughter and captivity. The integration of Buddhism into Chinese society was furthered as well by government approval of a class of teaching monks, ordained with official certificates, whose role was to perform rituals for the people.

Buddhism also had a synergetic relationship with the form of neo-Confucianism dominant in the late Ming, Wang Yangming's "learning of the mind." On the one hand, Chan individualism and seeking enlightenment within influenced Wang and his disciples; on the other hand, official acceptance of Wang's school gave indirect support to the forms of Buddhism associated with it, such as the teachings of Zhuhong and Hanshan Deqing (1546–1623).

Daoism was supported by emperors throughout the Ming, with Daoist priests appointed as officials in charge of rituals and composing hymns and messages to the gods. The Quanzhen sect continued to do well, with its monastic base and emphasis on attaining immortality through "internal alchemy." Its meditation methods also influenced those of some of Wang Yangming's followers, such as Wang Ji (1497–1582). However, it was the Zhengyi sect led by hereditary Celestial Masters that had the most official support during the Ming and hence was able to consolidate its position as the standard of orthodox Daoism. Zhengyi influence is evident in scriptures composed during this period, many of which trace their lineage back to the first Celestial Master and bear imprimaturs from his successors. The forty-third-generation master was given charge of compiling a new Daoist canon in 1406, a task completed between 1444 and 1445. It is this edition that is still in use today.

By the seventeenth century, Confucian philosophy entered a more nationalistic and materialist phase, but the scholar-official class as a whole remained involved in a variety of private religious practices beyond their official ritual responsibilities. These included not only the study of Daoism and Buddhism but also the use of spirit-writing séances and prayers to Wenchang, the god of scholars and literature, for help in passing examinations. Ming Taizu had proclaimed that each of the "three teachings" of Confucianism, Buddhism, and Daoism had an important role to play, which encouraged synthetic tendencies present since the beginnings of Buddhism in China. In the sixteenth century a Confucian scholar named Lin Zhao'en (1517–1598) from Fujian took these tendencies a step further by building a middle-class religious sect in which Confucian teachings were explicitly supported by those of Buddhism and Daoism. Lin was known as "Master of the Three Teachings," the patron saint of what became a popular movement with temples still extant in Singapore and Malaysia in the mid-twentieth century. This tendency to incorporate Confucianism into a sectarian religion was echoed by Zhang Jizong (d. 1866) who established a fortified community in Shandong, and by Kang Youwei (1858–1927) at the end of imperial history. Confucian-oriented spirit-writing cults also flourished in the late nineteenth and early twentieth centuries, supported by middle-level military and civil officials and producing produced tracts and scriptures of their own. These "Phoenix Halls" (*luantan*) spread to Taiwan in the second half of the nineteenth century and continue to exist in the twenty-first.

During the sixteenth century Christian missionaries tried for the third time to establish their faith in China, this time a more successful effort by Italian Jesuits. In 1583 two Italian Jesuits, Michael Ruggerius and Matteo Ricci (1552–1610), were allowed to stay in Zhaoqing in Guangdong province. By their knowledge of science, mathematics, and geography they impressed some of the local scholars and officials; Ricci eventually became court astronomer in Beijing. He also made converts of several high officials, so that by 1605 there were two hundred Chinese Christians. For the next several decades the Jesuit mission prospered, led by priests given responsibility for the sensitive task of establishing the imperial calendar. In 1663 the number of converts had grown to about one hundred thousand. The high point of this early Roman Catholic mission effort came during the reign of the Kangxi emperor (r. 1662–1722), who, while not a convert, had a lively curiosity about European knowledge.

Nonetheless, Chinese suspicions remained, and the mission was threatened from within by rivalries between orders and European nations. In particular, there was contention over Jesuit acceptance of the worship of ancestors and Confucius by Chinese Christian converts. In 1645 a Franciscan obtained a papal prohibition of such "accommodation," and this "rites controversy" intensified in the ensuing decades. The Inquisition forbade the Jesuit approach in 1704, but the Jesuits kept on resisting until papal bulls were issued against them in 1715 and 1742. Kangxi had sided with the Jesuits, but in the end their influence was weakened and their ministry made less adaptable to Chinese traditions. There were anti-Christian persecutions in several places throughout the mid-eighteenth century; however, some Christian communities remained, as did a few European astronomers at court. There were several more attempts at suppression in the early nineteenth century, with the result that by 1810 only thirty-one European missionaries and eighty Chinese priests were left, but church membership remained at about two hundred thousand.

The first Protestant missionary to reach China was Robert Morrison, sent by the London Missionary Society to Guangzhou in 1807. He and another missionary made their first Chinese convert in 1814 and completed translating the Bible in 1819. From then on increasing numbers of Protestant missionaries arrived from other European countries and the United States.

Christian impact on the wider world of Chinese religions has traditionally been negligible, although there is some indication that scholars such as Fang Yizhi (1611–1671) were influenced by European learning and thus helped prepare the way for the practical emphases of Qing Confucianism. Zhuhong and Ricci had engaged in written debate over theories of God and rebirth, and even the Kangxi emperor was involved in such discussions later, but there was no acceptance of Christian ideas and practices by Chinese who did not convert. This is true at the popular level as well, where in some areas Chinese sectarians responded positively to both Roman Catholic and Protestant missionaries. Christians and the sectarians were often persecuted together and shared concerns for congregational ritual, vernacular scriptures, and a compassionate creator deity. Yet nineteenth-century sectarian texts betray few traces of Christian influence, and even when Jesus speaks in later spirit-writing books, it is as a supporter of Chinese values.

Chinese Judaism thrived, at least in Kaifeng, through the Ming and part of the Qing dynasties. The Ming, in fact, has been called a "Golden Age" of Judaism in Kaifeng. Many members of the community achieved success in the civil service examinations and were appointed to relatively high government positions; good relations with Chinese officials helped the community to rebuild its synagogue after floods six times during the Ming.

In 1605, a Kaifeng Jew named Ai Tian visited the capital at Beijing and, having heard that there were westerners there who worshiped one god but were not Muslims, paid Matteo Ricci a visit, thinking that these westerners might be fellow Jews. After some awkward conversation, in which Ai thought Ricci was a Jew and Ricci thought Ai was a Christian, the truth emerged and the Chinese Jews came to the attention of the Western world for the first time. During the Rites Controversy the Jesuits consulted with the Kaifeng Jews on their practice of honoring ancestors in the synagogue and used that as part of their argument for toleration of the custom.

There were unsuccessful missionary efforts to convert the Jews to Christianity, but the Jews suffered neither discrimination from Chinese society nor repression from the Chinese government, except for a few slightly restrictive decrees concerning kosher slaughter during the Yuan dynasty. Nonetheless, the high level of involvement of Kaifeng Jews in the civil service examination system, which required a heavy investment of time in the study of Chinese classics, history, and literature, resulted in fewer educated Jews studying Hebrew. This eventually contributed to their complete assimilation in Chinese society and the disappearance of Jewish practice in China. Another factor was the expulsion of the Christian missionaries after the Rites Controversy, as they had been the Chinese Jews' major link to the world outside China.

Qing dynasty. The Manchus, a tribal confederation related to the Jurchen, had established their own state in the northeast in 1616 and named it Qing in 1636. As their power grew, they sporadically attacked North China and absorbed much Chinese political and cultural influence. In 1644 a Qing army was invited into China by the Ming court to save Beijing from Chinese rebels. The Manchus not only conquered Beijing but stayed to rule for the next 268 years. In public policy the Manchus were strong supporters of Confucianism and relied heavily on the support of Chinese officials, but in their private lives the Qing rulers were devoted to Tibetan Buddhism. Most religious developments during the Qing were continuations of Ming traditions, with the exception of Protestant Christianity and the Taiping movement it helped stimulate.

Before their conquest of China the Manchus had learned of Tibetan Buddhism through the Mongols and had a special sense of relationship to a *bodhisattva* much venerated in Tibet, Mañjuśrī. Nurhachi (1559–1626), the founder of the Manchu kingdom, was considered an incarnation of Mañjuśrī. After 1644 the Manchus continued to patronize Tibetan Buddhism, which had been supported to some extent in the Ming as well, in part to stay in touch with the dominant religion of Tibet and the Mongols. In 1652 the Dalai Lama was invited to visit Beijing, and in the early eighteenth century his successors were put under a Qing protectorate. In 1780 the Panchen Lama paid a visit to the Qianlong emperor (r. 1736–1795) on his seventieth birthday at the imperial retreat of Rehe (formerly written Jehol, now called Chengde), northeast of Beijing. At Rehe the earlier Qing emperors had built a dozen Tibetan Buddhist temples (in addition to a Confucian temple and school), including a smaller replica of the Potala Palace in Lhasa.

Early Qing emperors were interested in Chan Buddhism as well. The Yongzheng emperor (r. 1723–1735) published a book on Chan in 1732 and ordered the reprinting of the Buddhist canon, a task completed in 1738. He also supported the printing of a Tibetan edition of the canon, and his successor, Qianlong, sponsored the translation of this voluminous body of texts into Manchu. The Pure Land tradition continued to be the form of Buddhism most supported by the people. The most active Daoist schools were the monastic Quanzhen and the Zhengyi, more concerned with public rituals of exorcism and renewal, conducted by a married priesthood. However, Daoism no longer received court support. Despite repeated cycles of rebellions and persecutions, popular sects continued to thrive, although after the Eight Trigrams uprising in 1813 repression was so severe that production of sectarian scripture texts declined in favor of oral transmission, a tendency operative among some earlier groups as well.

The most significant innovation in Qing religion was the teachings of the Taiping Tianguo (Celestial Kingdom of Great Peace), which combined motifs from Christianity, shamanism, and popular sectarian beliefs. The Taiping movement was begun by Hong Xiuquan (1814–1864), a would-be Confucian scholar who first was given Christian tracts in 1836. After failing civil service examinations several times, Hong claimed to have had a vision in which it was revealed that he was the younger brother of Jesus Christ, commissioned to be a new messiah. Hong proclaimed a new kingdom upon earth, to be characterized by theocratic rule, enforcement of the Ten Commandments, the brotherhood of all, equality of the sexes, and redistribution of land. Hong and other Taiping leaders were effective preachers who wrote books, edicts, and tracts proclaiming their teachings and regulations and providing prayers and hymns for congregational worship. They forbade the worship of ancestors, Buddhas, and Daoist and popular deities. Wherever the Taipings went they destroyed images and temples. They rejected geomancy and divination and established a new calendar free of the old festivals and concerns for inauspicious days.

In the late 1840s Hong Xiuquan organized a group called the God Worshipers Society with many poor and disaffected among its members. They moved to active military rebellion in 1851, with Hong taking the title "Celestial King" of the new utopian regime. Within two years they captured Nanjing. Here they established their capital and sent armies north and west, involving all of China in civil war as they went. Although the Qing government was slow to respond, in 1864 Nanjing was retaken by imperial forces and the remaining Taiping forces slaughtered or dispersed. For all of the power of this movement, Taiping teachings and practices had no positive effect on the history of Chinese religions after this time, while all the indigenous traditions resumed and rebuilt.

The Qing also witnessed the decline of Chinese Jewish religious life. By the mid-nineteenth century in Kaifeng there were no Jews left who could read Hebrew. Without a rabbi there was little reason to keep the Kaifeng synagogue in repair, so the community sold the property to the Canadian Anglican mission. Today on the site is a hospital, behind which is "South Teaching the Torah Lane" (*Nan jiaojing hutong*), formerly the heart of Kaifeng's Jewish quarter. Two or three hundred Jews still live in Kaifeng, and others are spread throughout the country, but aside from the their ethnic self-identification they have little knowledge of or contact with Judaism. Since the 1980s there has been a revival of interest in this tradition, both among Chinese Jews themselves and in the academic world. Since the 1990s several institutional centers of Judaic studies have been established at major universities in China.

The End of Empire and Postimperial China. In the late nineteenth century some Chinese intellectuals began to incorporate into their thought new ideas from Western science, philosophy, and literature, but the trend in religion was toward reaffirmation of Chinese values. Even the reforming philosopher Kang Youwei tried to build a new cult of Confucius, while at the popular level spirit-writing sects proliferated. In 1899 a vast antiforeign movement began in North China, loosely called the Boxer Rebellion because of its martial arts practices. The ideology of this movement was based on popular religion and spirit mediumship, and many Boxer groups attacked Christian missions in the name of Chinese gods. This uprising was put down in 1900 by a combination of Chinese and foreign armies after the latter had captured Beijing.

The Qing government attempted a number of belated reforms, but in 1911 it collapsed from internal decay, foreign pressure, and military uprisings. Some Chinese intellectuals, free to invest their energies in new ideas and political forms, avidly studied and translated Western writings, including those of Marxism. One result of this westernization and secularization was attacks on Confucianism and other Chinese traditions, a situation exacerbated by recurrent civil wars that led to the destruction or occupation of thousands of temples. However, these new ideas were most influential in the larger cities; the majority of Chinese continued popular religious practices as before. Many temples and monasteries survived, and there were attempts to revive Buddhist thought and monastic discipline, particularly by the monks Yinguang (1861–1940) and Taixu (1890–1947).

Since 1949 Chinese religions have increasingly prospered in Taiwan, particularly at the popular level, where the people have more surplus funds and freedom of belief than ever before. Many new temples have been built, sects established, and scriptures and periodicals published. The same can be said for Chinese popular religion in Hong Kong, Macao, and Singapore. The Daoist priesthood is active in Taiwan, supported by the presence of hereditary Celestial Masters from the mainland who provide ordinations and legitimacy. There are also several large and prosperous Chan organizations with branches all over the world. Another rapidly growing Buddhist sect in Taiwan is the Buddhist Compassion Relief (Ciji) Foundation, founded by the nun Cheng Yan in 1966 to mobilize social work and education from a Mahāyāna Buddhist perspective.

The constitution of the People's Republic establishes the freedom both to support and oppose religion, although proselytization is illegal. In practice religious activities of all types declined drastically there after 1949 and virtually disappeared during the Cultural Revolution of 1966 to 1976. In official documents and state-controlled media religion was depicted along Marxist lines as "feudal superstition" that must be rejected by those seeking to build a new China. Nonetheless, many religious activities continued until the Cultural Revolution, even those of the long-proscribed popular sects. The Cultural Revolution, encouraged by Mao Zedong and his teachings, was a massive attack on old traditions, including not only religion but also education, art, and established bureaucracies. In the process thousands of religious images were destroyed, temples and churches confiscated, leaders returned to lay life, and books burned. At the same time a new national cult arose, that of Chairman Mao and his thought, involving ecstatic processions, group recitation from Mao's writings, and a variety of quasi-religious ceremonials. These included confessions of sins against the revolution, vows of obedience before portraits of the chairman, and meals of wild vegetables to recall the bitter days before liberation. Although the frenzy abated, the impetus of the Cultural Revolution continued until Mao's death in 1976, led by a small group, later called "the Gang of Four," centered around his wife, Jiang Qing (1914–1991).

This group was soon deposed, a move followed by liberalization of policy in several areas, including religion. Since 1980 many churches, monasteries, and mosques have reopened and religious leaders reinstated, in part to establish better relationships with Buddhist, Christian, and Muslim communities in other countries. There has been an accelerating revival of popular religion as well, spurred in part by the return of market capitalism under Deng Xiaoping (1905–1997). This occurred primarily in the southeast at first; since the early 1990s Taiwanese have been allowed to travel to the mainland, and many have financially supported the reconstruction of local temples, especially in Fujian province, from which most mainland Taiwanese emigrated. But the revival of popular religion is occurring throughout China, most notably in rural areas.

The official line on religion has moderated, the government now acknowledging that some aspects of China's traditional culture are worth preserving; also that religion will eventually disappear on its own when the perfect socialist state is realized, so it is unnecessary to forcefully hasten the process. Along with the booming capitalist economy that developed in the 1990s and into the twenty-first century, "socialism with Chinese characteristics"—a popular slogan of Deng Xiaoping—allows the state to tolerate and support religion, within limits.

The religious revival includes many groups devoted to various forms of *qigong,* the "manipulation of *qi,*" which has roots in Daoist self-cultivation. In 1999 the government began a severe crackdown on one such cult, Falun Dafa (Great Law of the Dharma Wheel), commonly referred to in the West as Falun Gong (Exercise of the Dharma Wheel), which more accurately denotes their Buddho-Daoist-inspired form of mental and physical cultivation. Founded in 1992 by Li Hongzhi (b. 1951), Falun Dafa attracted practitioners in the tens of millions in part because of its claims to improve health and lengthen life in the context of the aging of the Chinese population and the collapse of state-supported cradle-to-grave health care. In April 1999 the organization, largely through the medium of e-mail, secretly organized a silent demonstration by more than ten thousand practitioners outside the residence compound of China's top leaders in Beijing to protest what they said was a slanderous magazine article and the refusal of the authorities to let them register as a voluntary association, as required by law. The group's ability to mobilize such large numbers and the fact that Li Hongzhi had emigrated to the United States in 1998 apparently motivated the repression.

Other sensitive areas of religious life in China include illegal Christian "house churches," Buddhists in Tibet (an "autonomous province" of China), and Muslims in the far-western autonomous province of Xinjiang. The latter two cases are related to the government's fear of forces that could support independence movements. The Christian churches, given the long and problematic history of missionary activity and colonialism in China, are suspect for their potential ties to the West. Although Catholicism is one of the five officially recognized religions (Buddhism, Daoism, Islam, Protestant Christianity, and Catholic Christianity), the Roman Catholic Church is outlawed because of its allegiance to the Vatican; only the Chinese Patriotic Catholic Association is recognized. The other four religions likewise have government-supported associations as the means of government control. Popular religion and Confucianism are not officially designated as religious in China: popular religion is considered "superstition" (*mixin*), and Confucianism is considered an "ideology," although not necessarily (any longer) a "feudal" ideology. There is in fact renewed interest in Confucianism among intellectuals, many of whom sense a moral vacuum in China since Marxist/Maoist thought ceased to exert any influence outside government. A modernized, less patriarchal form of Confucianism, they believe, might provide a set of moral principles better suited to Chinese culture than one imported from the West. Although China was once thought by westerners to be a "timeless" realm in which nothing changed, the story of religion in China, as far back as we can see, has been one of constant change.

SEE ALSO Afterlife, article on Chinese Concepts; Alchemy, article on Chinese Alchemy; Amitābha; Ancestors, article on Ancestor Worship; Bodhidharma; Buddhism, articles on Buddhism in Central Asia and Buddhism in China; Buddhism, Schools of, article on Chinese Buddhism; Chan; Chinese Philosophy; Chinese Religious Year; Christianity, article on Christianity in Asia; Confucianism, overview article; Confucius; Dao and De; Daochuo; Daoism, overview article; Daosheng; Domestic Observances, article on Chinese Practices; Dong Zhongshu; Fangshi; Fazang; Flight; Ge Hong; Han Fei Zi; Huangdi; Huayan; Huineng; Huiyuan; Inner Asian Religions; Islam, article on Islam in China; Jesuits; Jiao; Jingtu; Judaism, article on Judaism in Asia; Kang Youwei; Kou Qianzhi; Kuiji; Kumārajīva; Legalism; Li; Liang Wudi; Linji; Liu An; Lu Xiujing; Mahāvairocana; Maitreya; Manichaeism; Mañjuśrī; Mappo; Mengzi; Millenarianism, article on Chinese Millenarian Movements; Mongol Religions; Morrison, Robert; Mozi; Nestorianism; Nianfo; Pure and Impure Lands; Qi; Ricci, Matteo; Sacrifice; Sengzhao; Shamanism, overview articles; Shandao; Shangdi; Soul, article on Chinese Concepts; Taiping; Taixu; Tanluan; Tao Hongjing; Theodicy; Tian; Tiantai; Wang Chong; Wang Zhe; Xian; Xi Wang Mu; Xunzi; Yinyang Wuxing; Yogācāra; Yuhuang; Zhang Daoling; Zhang Lu; Zhang Zai; Zhenren; Zhenyan; Zhiyi; Zhou Dunyi; Zhuangzi; Zhu Xi; Zoroastrianism.

BIBLIOGRAPHY

Adler, Joseph A. *Chinese Religious Traditions.* Upper Saddle River, N.J., 2002.

Allan, Sarah. *The Shape of the Turtle: Myth, Art, and Cosmos in Early China.* Albany, N.Y., 1991.

Allan, Sarah, and Alvin P. Cohen, eds. *Legend, Lore, and Religion in China: Essays in Honor of Wolfram Eberhard on His Seventieth Birthday.* San Francisco, 1979.

Barrett, Timothy Hugh. *Li Ao: Buddhist, Taoist, or Neo-Confucian?* Oxford and New York, 1992.

Barrett, Timothy Hugh. *Taoism under the T'ang: Religion and Empire during the Golden Age of Chinese History.* London, 1996.

Benn, Charles D. *The Cavern-Mystery Transmission: A Taoist Ordination Rite of AD 711.* Honolulu, 1991.

Berling, Judith A. *The Syncretic Religion of Lin Chao-en.* New York, 1980.

Berthrong, John H. *Transformations of the Confucian Way.* Boulder, Colo., 1998.

Bokenkamp, Stephen R. *Early Daoist Scriptures.* Berkeley, Calif., 1997.

Chang, K. C. *Art, Myth, and Ritual: The Path to Political Authority in Ancient China.* Cambridge, Mass., 1983.

Chang, Maria Hsia. *Falun Gong: The End of Days.* New Haven, Conn., 2004

Chappell, David W., ed. *Buddhist and Taoist Practice in Medieval Chinese Society.* Honolulu, 1987.

Cheng Chien Bhikshu. *Sun Face Buddha: The Teachings of Ma-tsu and the Hung-chou School of Ch'an.* Berkeley, Calif., 1992.

Ching, Julia. *Probing China's Soul: Religion, Politics, and Protest in the People's Republic.* San Francisco, 1990.

Ching, Julia. *Chinese Religions.* Maryknoll, N.Y., 1993.

Ching, Julia. *Mysticism and Kingship in China: The Heart of Chinese Wisdom.* Cambridge, UK, 1997.

Ching, Julia. *The Religious Thought of Chu Hsi.* Oxford, 2000.

Chow, Kai-wing. *The Rise of Confucian Ritualism in Late Imperial China: Ethics, Classics, and Lineage Discourse.* Stanford, Calif., 1994.

Csikszentmihalyi, Mark, and Philip J. Ivanhoe, eds. *Religious and Philosophical Aspects of* Laozi. Albany, N.Y., 1999.

Dean, Kenneth. *Taoist Ritual and Popular Cults of Southeast China.* Princeton, N.J., 1993.

de Bary, Wm. Theodore, and Irene Bloom, eds. *Sources of Chinese Tradition,* 2d ed. Vol. 1. New York, 1999.

de Bary, Wm. Theodore, and Richard Lufrano, eds. *Sources of Chinese Tradition,* 2d ed. Vol. 2. New York, 2000.

De Meyer, Jan A. M., and Peter M. Engelfriet, eds. *Linked Faiths: Essays on Chinese Religions and Traditional Culture in Honour of Kristofer Schipper.* Leiden, 2000.

Dillon, Michael. *China's Muslim Hui Community: Migration, Settlement and Sects.* Richmond, U.K., 1999.

Dumoulin, Heinrich. *Zen Buddhism: A History.* Vol. 1: *India and China.* New York and London, 1988.

Ebrey, Patricia Buckley, and Peter N. Gregory, eds. *Religion and Society in T'ang and Sung China.* Honolulu, 1993.

Feuchtwang, Stephan. *Popular Religion in China: The Imperial Metaphor.* Richmond, U.K., 2001.

Fingarette, Herbert. *Confucius: The Secular as Sacred.* New York, 1972.

Gardner, Daniel, trans. *Learning to Be a Sage: Selections from the Conversations of Master Chu, Arranged Topically.* Berkeley, Calif., 1990.

Gernet, Jacques. *China and the Christian Impact.* Translated by Janet Lloyd. 1982; Eng. trans. Cambridge, UK, 1985.

Girardot, Norman. *Myth and Meaning in Early Taoism.* Berkeley, Calif., 1983.

Girardot, N. J., James Miller, and Liu Xiaogan, eds. *Daoism and Ecology: Ways within a Cosmic Landscape.* Cambridge, Mass., 2001.

Graham, A. C. *Yin-yang and the Nature of Correlative Thinking.* Singapore, 1986.

Graham, A. C. *Disputers of the Tao: Philosophical Argument in Ancient China.* LaSalle, Ill., 1989.

Granet, Marcel. *Festivals and Songs of Ancient China.* Translated by E. D. Edwards. New York, 1975.

Granet, Marcel. *The Religion of the Chinese People.* Translated by Maurice Freedman. Oxford, 1975.

Gregory, Peter N., ed. *Sudden and Gradual: Approaches to Enlightenment in Chinese Thought.* Honolulu, 1987.

Gregory, Peter N., and Daniel A. Getz, Jr. *Buddhism in the Sung.* Honolulu, 1999.

de Groot, J. J. M. *The Religious System of China, Its Ancient Forms, Evolution, History and Present Aspect, Manners, Custom and Social Institutions Connected Therewith.* 6 vols. 1892–1910; reprint New York, 1969.

Guisso, Richard W., and Stanley Johannesen, eds. *Women in China: Current Directions in Historical Scholarship.* Youngstown, N.Y., 1981.

Hansen, Valerie. *Changing Gods in Medieval China, 1127–1276.* Princeton, N.J., 1990.

Hunter, Alan, and Kim-Kwong Chan. *Protestantism in Contemporary China.* Cambridge and New York, 1993.

Hymes, Robert. *Way and Byway: Taoism, Local Religion, and Models of Divinity in Sung and Modern China.* Berkeley, Calif., 2002.

Ivanhoe, Philip J. *Confucian Moral Self Cultivation,* 2d ed. Indianapolis, 2000.

Ivanhoe, Philip J., and Bryan W. Van Norden, eds. *Readings in Classical Chinese Philosophy.* New York, 2001.

Jochim, Christian. *Chinese Religions: A Cultural Perspective.* Englewood Cliffs, N.J., 1986.

Jordan, David K. *Gods, Ghosts, and Ancestors: Folk Religion in a Taiwanese Village.* Berkeley, Calif., 1972.

Jordan, David K., and Daniel L. Overmyer. *The Flying Phoenix: Aspects of Chinese Sectarianism in Taiwan.* Princeton, N.J., 1986.

Keightley, David N. *Sources of Shang History: The Oracle Bone Inscriptions of Bronze Age China.* Berkeley, Calif., 1978.

Keightley, David N. *The Ancestral Landscape: Time, Space, and Community in Late Shang China, ca. 1200–1045 BC.* Berkeley, Calif., 2000.

Kindopp, Jason, and Carol Lee Hamrin, eds. *God and Caesar in China: Policy Implications of Church-State Tensions.* Washington, D.C., 2004.

Kleeman, Terry F. *A God's Own Tale: The Book of Transformations of Wenchang, the Divine Lord of Zitong.* Albany, N.Y., 1994.

Kleeman, Terry F. *Great Perfection: Religion and Ethnicity in a Chinese Millennial Kingdom.* Honolulu, 1998.

Kohn, Livia. *Daoism and Chinese Culture.* Cambridge, Mass., 2001.

Kohn, Livia, ed., *Taoist Meditation and Longevity Techniques.* Ann Arbor, Mich., 1989.

Lagerwey, John. *Taoist Ritual in Chinese Society and History.* New York, 1987.

Leighton, Taigen Daniel, with Yi Wu, trans. *Cultivating the Empty Field: The Silent Illumination of Zen Master Hongzhi.* San Francisco, 1991.

Lopez, Donald S., Jr., ed. *Religions of China in Practice.* Princeton, N.J., 1996.

Mair, Victor H., ed. *Experimental Essays on Chuang-tzu.* Honolulu, Hawaii, 1983.

Maspero, Henri. *Taoism and Chinese Religion.* Translated by Frank A. Kierman Jr. Amherst, Mass.,1981.

Miller, James. *Daoism: A Short Introduction.* Oxford, 2003.

Munro, Donald J., ed. *Individualism and Holism: Studies in Confucian and Taoist Values.* Ann Arbor, Mich., 1985.

Naquin, Susan. *Millenarian Rebellion in China: The Eight Trigrams Uprising of 1813.* New Haven, Conn., 1976.

Naquin, Susan, and Chün-fang Yü, eds. *Pilgrims and Sacred Sites in China.* Berkeley, Calif., 1992.

Overmyer, Daniel L. *Folk Buddhist Religion: Dissenting Sects in Late Traditional China.* Cambridge, Mass., 1976.

Overmyer, Daniel L. *Religions of China: The World as a Living System.* San Francisco, 1986.

Overmyer, Daniel L., ed. *Religion in China Today.* Cambridge, U.K., 2003.

Paper, Jordan. *The Spirits Are Drunk: Comparative Approaches to Chinese Religion.* Albany, N.Y., 1995.

Poo, Mu-chou. *In Search of Personal Welfare: A View of Ancient Chinese Religion.* Albany, N.Y., 1998.

Powell, William F., trans. *The Record of Tung-shan.* Honolulu, 1986.

Robinet, Isabelle. *Taoist Meditation: The Mao-shan Tradition of Great Purity.* Translated by Julian F. Pas and Norman J. Girardot. Albany, N.Y., 1993.

Robinet, Isabelle. *Taoism: Growth of a Religion.* Translated by Phyllis Brooks. Stanford, Calif., 1997.

Ropp, Paul S., ed. *Heritage of China: Contemporary Perspectives on Chinese Civilization.* Berkeley, Calif., 1990.

Saso, Michael. *Taoism and the Rite of Cosmic Renewal,* 2d ed. Pullman, Wash., 1990.

Saso, Michael, and David W. Chappell, eds. *Buddhist and Taoist Studies.* Honolulu, 1977.

Schipper, Kristofer. *The Taoist Body.* Translated by Karen C. Duval. Berkeley, Calif., 1993.

Schwartz, Benjamin I. *The World of Thought in Ancient China.* Cambridge, Mass., 1985.

Shahar, Meir, and Robert P. Weller, eds. *Unruly Gods: Divinity and Society in China.* Honolulu, 1996.

Shryock, John K. *The Origin and Development of the State Cult of Confucius.* 1932; reprint New York, 1966.

Smith, Kidder, Jr., Peter K. Bol, Joseph A. Adler, and Don J. Wyatt. *Sung Dynasty Uses of the* I Ching. Princeton, N.J., 1990.

Smith, Richard J. *Fortune-Tellers and Philosophers: Divination in Traditional Chinese Society.* Boulder, Colo., 1991.

Sommer, Deborah. *Chinese Religion: An Anthology of Sources.* New York, 1995.

Streng, Frederick J. *Understanding Religious Life,* 3d ed. Belmont, Calif., 1985.

Taylor, Rodney L. *The Cultivation of Sagehood as a Religious Goal in Neo-Confucianism: A Study of Selected Writings of Kao P'an-lung (1562–1626).* Missoula, Mont., 1978.

Taylor, Rodney L. *The Way of Heaven: An Introduction to the Confucian Religious Life.* Leiden, 1986.

Taylor, Rodney L. *The Religious Dimensions of Confucianism.* Albany, N.Y., 1990.

Teiser, Stephen F. *The Scripture on the Ten Kings and the Making of Purgatory in Medieval Chinese Buddhism.* Honolulu, 1994.

Teiser, Stephen F. *The Ghost Festival in Medieval China.* Princeton, N.J., 1998.

Thompson, Laurence G. *Chinese Religion: An Introduction,* 5th ed. Belmont, Calif., 1996.

Tu, Ching-i, ed. *Classics and Interpretations: The Hermeneutic Traditions in Chinese Culture.* New Brunswick, N.J., 2000.

Tu Wei-ming. *Humanity and Self-Cultivation: Essays in Confucian Thought.* 1978; reprint Boston, 1998.

Tu Weiming, and Mary Evelyn Tucker, eds. *Confucian Spirituality.* New York, 2003 (vol.1) and 2004 (vol. 2).

Tucker, Mary Evelyn, and John Berthrong, eds. *Confucianism and Ecology: The Interrelation of Heaven, Earth, and Humans.* Cambridge, Mass., 1998.

Wang, Robin R., ed. *Images of Women in Chinese Thought and Culture: Writings from the Pre-Qin Period through the Song Dynasty.* Indianapolis, 2003.

Welch, Holmes, and Anna Seidel, eds. *Facets of Taoism: Essays in Chinese Religion.* New Haven, Conn., 1979.

Weller, Robert P. *Unities and Diversities in Chinese Religion.* Seattle, 1987.

Wilson, Thomas A. *Genealogy of the Way: The Construction and Uses of the Confucian Tradition in Late Imperial China.* Stanford, Calif., 1995.

Wilson, Thomas A., ed. *On Sacred Grounds: Culture, Society, Politics, and the Formation of the Cult of Confucius.* Cambridge, Mass., 2002.

Wolf, Arthur P., ed. *Religion and Ritual in Chinese Society.* Stanford, Calif., 1974.

Xu Xin. *The Jews of Kaifeng, China: History, Culture, and Religion.* Jersey City, N.J., 2003.

Yao, Xinzhong. *An Introduction to Confucianism.* Cambridge, UK, 2000.

Yates, Robin D. S. *Five Lost Classics: Tao, Huang-Lao, and Yin-Yang in Han China.* New York, 1997.

Yü, Chün-fang. *Kuan-yin: The Chinese Transformation of Avalokiteśvara.* New York, 2001.

Zürcher, Erik. *The Buddhist Conquest of China.* 2 vols. Leiden, 1959.

DANIEL L. OVERMYER (1987)
JOSEPH A. ADLER (2005)

CHINESE RELIGION: POPULAR RELIGION

Chinese popular religion is a scholarly construct which does not correspond to any traditional Chinese notion or institution. Scholars in China, in Japan, and in the West give it different meanings; while several historians or anthropologists have tried to define it, most authors use the phrase loosely to refer to whatever religious idea or practice does not fall clearly within the purview of China's three institutionalized religions, Buddhism, Daoism, and Confucianism. The fundamentally ambiguous word "popular" sometimes refers to any widespread or commonly held idea or practice, and is sometimes used more narrowly in contrast to "elite" religion. This ambiguity is both creative and confusing; the confusion is further compounded by the very frequent use of phrases such as "popular Buddhism," "popular Daoism," and "popular Confucianism." Whether these are similar or different from "popular religion" is a matter of opinion.

As a consequence of such loose and varied usage, words such as "popular religion" or "folk religion," although often used in a similar way, might arguably be totally eliminated. Yet scholars and observers need hermeneutical tools to understand the religious field in Chinese history, and "popular" should be useful if defined properly. This essay considers the elements of popular religion in the context of Chinese religion, and it attempts to delineate what "popular" implies by looking at the roles of clerical institutionalized religions, local lay communities, and individual specialists and devotees.

DEFINITIONS. With the exception of religions, notably Islam and Christianity, that arrived in China from elsewhere and could not become fully integrated because of exclusive claims of truth, most religious practices, beliefs, and organizations in China can be described as belonging to a single system, best termed "Chinese religion" (sometimes called "Chinese traditional religion"). This organic, non-hierarchical system integrates traditions of individual salvation (self-cultivation through meditation and body techniques, morality, and spirit-possession techniques, including spirit-writing), communal celebration (cults to local saints and ancestors), and death rituals together with the three institutionalized religions, Buddhism, Daoism, and Confucianism.

The three institutionalized religions are precisely defined, each with a distinctive clergy, a canon (scriptures that define orthodoxy), a liturgy, and training centers (monasteries and academies where the canon is kept and the clergy is trained and ordained). The institutions defined by these four characteristics can be referred to as "Buddhism," "Daoism," and "Confucianism" *stricto sensu.* Confucianism, Buddhism, and Daoism within Chinese religion do not function as separate institutions that provide their members an exclusive way to salvation, as in the nineteenth-century Western concept of religion; rather, their purpose is to transmit their tradition of practice and make it available to all, either as individual spiritual techniques or liturgical services to whole communities. In late imperial times and well into the twentieth century, only clerics and a small number of retired laymen *(jushi)* would declare themselves as Buddhists or Daoists, but very few Chinese indeed have never engaged in Buddhist or Daoist practices. The wide acceptance and official status of the doctrine of the three religions' coexistence has made them complementary to one another.

The three institutionalized religions serve the whole of Chinese religion, which is not "syncretism" as it is too often described (the word syncretism should be reserved to certain sectarian traditions): they are expected to coexist but not mingle, and people do not confuse them. The many independent communities that form the social structure of Chinese religion choose from among the shared repertoire of beliefs and practices those services offered by the three religions that give them relevant meaning, and their choices hinge on socio-economic, ideological, and theological considerations much more complex than an elite/popular dichotomy can suggest. Therefore, the large majority of communities that are not Confucian, Buddhist, or Daoist can be labeled as Chinese popular religion, but this term does not necessarily imply any social class, lack of intellectual sophistication, or heterodoxy. On the other hand, while the three religions have nationwide institutions, cult communities are fundamentally local in nature, and they have been therefore aptly described as "local religion. "

HISTORICAL CONSTRUCTION. Most of the fundamental elements of Chinese religion began to be observed during antiquity, that is, in the period before the unification of the Chinese world under the Qin empire (221 BCE). Religious beliefs and practices of the ancient royalty and nobility have been documented through partly transmitted liturgical manuals and archaeological evidence, but local cults and commoners' practices have also been reconstructed through fragmentary evidence, notably recently excavated manuscripts. Shared practices among various social classes and regions have led scholars to speak of a "common religion" for the late antiquity and the Han dynasty (206 BCE–220 CE). The major features of this common religion include care for the dead, addressing both the corpse (hence the importance of grave maintenance, and in later times geomancy) and souls that go through a netherworld administration and can either be installed as ancestors, or, if not given proper rituals, suffer as ghosts or demons. A bureaucratic vision of the universe, and particularly of the netherworld, had already been formed by the Han, and it would be further developed by Daoism. It informs the contracts and formal demands to netherworld officials concerning the fate of the dead, the prolongation of the living person's life-span, and the cure of illnesses caused by ghosts or demons. Ancestors as well as gods can be requited through sacrifices of alcohol, grains, and most importantly, meats; the offerings differ by type of sacrificial animal or cooking methods according to the relationship between the person and the ancestor or god. Sacrifices are preceded by ritual purification (*zhaijie*), including abstinence from alcohol, meat, sex, and unclean activities. Incense, first used as a purificatory fumigant, would later gradually become the most basic and common offering (in ancient time as powder, and later as sticks). Gods or ancestors can possess the living so as to participate in the sacrificial banquet or speak to humans; spirit-mediums (*wu*), or shamans as they are sometimes called (somewhat problematically) in Western languages, were recognized intermediaries, but it also happened that non-specialists, and indeed children, could be possessed. Possession played a major role in exorcisms from ghosts or demons; the exorcising deities are themselves usually former ghosts or demons. All of these features of the common religion of late antiquity still comprise the basic elements of Chinese religion in the twenty-first century.

Confucianism formed during the Han dynasty as the self-proclaimed heir of the elite sacrificial religion of antiquity, became the state religion during the Han, and would remain so until the end of the empire in 1911. Meanwhile, during the second century BCE, Daoism gradually organized into communities and a distinctive liturgy, and Buddhism began to flow into China from Central Asia. These three religions often conflicted with one another until a doctrine of their equal orthodoxy and coexistence was formulated during the Tang era (618–907). At the same time, all three attempted to control the pre-existing local cults by integrating them into their clerical structures and reforming their practices, but with limited success; for example, Buddhism and Daoism notably attempted, but failed, to suppress animal sacrifices. From the third to the tenth centuries, Buddhist and Daoist monasteries were the largest religious institutions, and clergy-led pious associations were omnipresent in rural and urban China, but local cults continued to practice as well.

The modern religious organization of Chinese society, still existing despite twentieth-century upheavals, gradually took shape between the tenth and the thirteenth centuries. This process included the growth of the cult of local saints which superseded clerical institutions (monasteries) as the religious centers of society; the appearance of the large temple festivals and opera performances; the adoption of local saints within the liturgical pantheons of Confucianism, Buddhism and Daoism (through the process of state and Daoist canonization of local gods); the growth of lineages and corporations as powerful religious and economic institutions; the employment of Buddhist and Daoist clerics in temples of local saints, lineages, and corporations as contractual managers; the democratization of salvation techniques (meditation, inner alchemy); the phenomenal growth of spirit-writing (*fuji*, *fuluan*) and the formation of a common ethics shared by the whole of Chinese religion based on spirit-writing revelations and expressed in morality books, *shanshu*. Spirit-writing is fairly uniform as a technique, but it is used by many different kinds of groups, including immortality cults, gentry morality cults, and sectarian movements.

The early modern religious organization of Chinese society was dramatically upset by twentieth-century political revolutions. As early as the 1898 reforms, an edict called for the seizure of all local temples to be turned into schools, and although promptly revoked, this measure was again adopted after 1901. Political reformists considered temple cults as the center of local identities and autonomy, and an obstacle to nation-building: they wanted to destroy temples and associations in order to seize their material and symbolical resources and build a modern nation-state. At the same time, the introduction around 1901 of the Western notions of religion and superstition caused a complete reformulation of the imperial religious policies: now, major world religions (with a church structure, a canon, and a philosophy) were tolerated, but superstitions were targeted for destruction. This became the official stance of the Republic of China (1912–) and the People's Republic (1949–) that gave relative recognition to five religions (Buddhism, Daoism, Islam, Catholicism, Protestantism, with the first two defined in a narrow, monastic sense) but actively suppressed all local cults, temples, and festivals. Because of destructions and financial ruin, local cults gradually declined, which opened the way for many sectarian movements to flourish. Such movements offered conventional services (healing, morality teachings, and liturgical services such as death rituals) but at the same time fully embraced the modern discourse of religion against superstition. This was notably the case with movements that practiced spirit-writing and proselytized on a very large scale, such as Tongshan she, Daoyuan, or Yiguandao. The Qigong movement of self-healing, first supported by the Communist authorities, also occupied the vacant space. Progressive liberalization on the mainland since the 1980s, however, has allowed a remarkable renewal of local cults on a scale unexpected by most scholars, and the Chinese religious field is gradually recovering its erstwhile diversity.

SOCIAL STRUCTURES. Western descriptions of Chinese religious life have long tended to emphasize its motley, disorganized nature. Closer examination, however, reveals that it is based on well-defined social structures, some of which are coterminous with local society (village, clans) and others which are more purely religious: thus, even though religious groups are strongly linked to secular social organizations, the former do not merely reflect the latter, and religious communities have their own logic and agency. What best characterizes the social organization of Chinese religion is the communities' fundamental autonomy. While they can, and often do, negotiate alliances and build networks, for both religious (large-scale celebrations) and secular purposes (order-maintenance, infrastructure building, arbitrating local tensions, and conflicts), all temples, communities, and other religious groups are independent, refusing to take any order from any external authority, secular or spiritual. Some scholars have described the networks of cult communities as China's civil society.

The typology and relative importance of the social structures of Chinese religion vary among different regions of the Chinese world, between rural and urban areas, and between Chinese residents and the diaspora; it is possible, however, to distinguish basic types. The most fundamental distinction opposes ascriptive communities, where adhesion is compulsory and by household relative to social status, and congregations characterized by free, individual participation. Three main types of ascriptive communities exist: the territorial communities, the clans, and the corporations.

Of the three, the territorial communities are the most prevalent and also the most ancient direct descendants of the earth god cults, *she*, of antiquity. According to one of the oldest and most fundamental principles of Chinese religion, all persons living within a given area must take part in the cult of the territorial god of that region, or domain (*jing*). In many places, the generic impersonal *she*, or *tudi gong* in modern parlance, evolved during the Song (960–1279) into local saints, each of which was given its own individual name, birthday, and history, and *she* altars became elaborate temples with statues. The imperial state, notably under the first emperor (r. 1368–1398) of the Ming dynasty (1368–1644), tried to revert the territorial cults to canonical *she* altars, but with limited success. During the modern period, territorial communities exist at different levels: while streets, or small neighborhoods maintain modest shrines to an anonymous generic *tudi gong*, many larger villages and urban neighborhoods have one communal temple for the cult of a saint embodying local identity and history. Walled cities have a temple for the territorial cult of the whole city, the Chenghuang (god of the moat and walls, or, more commonly, city god), a cult that appeared during the Tang period and became fully institutionalized and universal during the early Ming. In all cases, the territorial temple is built and owned in common, and all households have a duty to contribute to it, often through a poll tax (*dingkou qian*).

The clans or lineages are of more recent origin. Even though the ancestral cult has been a fundamental element of Chinese religion throughout recorded history, it was organized at the family level (*jia*, or household) only. The advent of very large kin groups based on common descent (proved or supposed) from a common ancestor, and pooling resources for cults to this ancestor, seems to be a twelfth-century innovation. Although not canonical institutions, these clans shared the neo-Confucianism ideology, and rose to prominence between the Song and the Ming to become influential on the economic, social, and religious scenes. Modern worship focuses on the ancestral cults using Confucian liturgy, but many clans also sustain cults to local saints and employ a variety of religious specialists.

The emergence of corporations is also a Song phenomenon, but one that reached maturity only by the late Ming, since it was strongly linked to the commercial and urban development that characterized these two periods. Professional and commercial guilds, called *hui* or *zuo*, managed relations with the state; regulated competition, prices, and wages; supervised training and confirmation of apprentices, and were organized as cults to patron saints (*zushiye*). A related type of organization, not well attested before the Ming, is the common-origin association, usually called *huiguan* or *gongsuo*. Most of the time, *huiguan* were also trade guilds, since numerous trades were comprised of monopolies of people from certain districts. Larger cities, however, also contained larger provincial *huiguan* that welcomed people from different trades. Both guilds and common-origin associations established halls in which members could meet and unite in ritual celebration. The most affluent groups built their own place, with a temple and facilities (such as a hotel, meeting rooms, and an opera stage). The poorer guilds constructed a hall or chapel within a larger temple.

These three kinds of ascriptive communities are quite different from congregations characterized by free adhesion. In the former, one, or rather one's household, had to join a particular clan, trade guild, and territorial community whether one liked it or not; on the other hand, in the latter, joining a devotional group was an extra, an individual option. Those who chose to join one of these groups received social approval; their participation was seen as a mark of piety and moral dedication. On the other hand, the imperial state did not approve of such congregations. The religious policy of the late imperial state drew a line between ascriptive communities, which respected the natural patriarchal structures of local society and recognized them as orthodox, and devotional congregations, which were outlawed. In practice, however, most congregations were left to themselves and operated openly, since it proved impossible for the authorities to clearly separate the two kinds of groups.

The congregations were extremely varied. Many originated in medieval Buddhist and Daoist pious societies (*yi* or *she*). The societies financed, within or without monasteries, activities such as rituals, the making of scriptures or icons, or and mutual aid between members. They were often under clerical leadership. In the early twenty-first century, such societies continue to exist; after the tenth century, however, they became less numerous than other congregations—often called *xianghui*, or incense communities—that worshiped local saints and were housed in temples. These devotional groups may organize rituals to celebrate the birthday of their saint or contribute to the upkeep of a temple by making specific offerings or by maintaining and cleaning chapels; the best-endowed congregations built their own temples. Pilgrimage associations also developed on a major scale, as pilgrimages to holy mountains (such as Taishan, Wudang shan, Xishan, and Miaofeng shan near Beijing) drew hundreds of thousands of pilgrims a year during the period between the sixteenth and the nineteenth centuries. Amateur troupes also perform during temple festivals, processions, or pilgrimages. Many congregations run charitable programs (offering tea or food to pilgrims or beggars, and providing medicine, clothes, or coffins to the needy). Devotional groups focused on charitable acts developed and institutionalized themselves between the sixteenth and the nineteenth centuries; they eventually became large philanthropic foundations, *shantang*, but never lost their devotional dimension.

Finally, many congregations were oriented towards individual salvation and spiritual practice. This category includes groups that were led by clergy and geared towards lectures and meditation practice. In addition, increasingly after the sixteenth century, the category added spirit-writing cults formed of laypersons, with one or several spirit-mediums receiving direct revelations from gods and saints and publishing these revealed communications in book form. Many such texts were morality books; consequently, these cults also engaged in charity, and their roles largely overlapped with philanthropic foundations. Another sub-category was the sectarian tradition, also geared towards revelation, study of sacred texts, and meditation, but with a distinctive theology and body of scriptures, called *baojuan*.

Sectarian groups are often called *minjian zongjiao*, literally "popular religions", in scholarly Chinese publications. This label is confusing, because the Western-language term "popular religions" encompasses much more than just the sectarian tradition. Some scholars, considering the distinctiveness of the theology and scriptures of the sectarian tradition, have considered it to be China's fourth religion. On the other hand, fieldwork observation shows that most sectarian groups are not marginalized or exclusive communities. Rather, they are devotional associations whose leaders provide—to members and outsiders alike—services such as healing, teachings on morality, death rituals, and local leadership in village affairs. These social services are very similar to those offered by other groups.

Although ascriptive communities and voluntary congregations, including sectarian groups, are clearly different, they share much in common in terms of organization, such as the nomination processes for leaders, modes of financing, rules, and ritual celebrations. Through these groups, individuals receive access to a large range of religious services, to specialists, and to salvation. All sorts of them can be found throughout the Chinese world, but their relative importance varies by region (for instance, clans are much more prevalent in South China), and even from village to village. In places where some types of organizations are rare or weak, others tend to take over their role, and there have been instances of sectarian groups acting as a village's territorial community.

TEMPLES AND SPECIALISTS. Most religious communities build a temple, but this is not absolutely necessary for the purpose of the cult. Many groups, either because they cannot afford it, or because they are illegal and cannot have highly visible meeting places, have no shrine of their own. Each religious group, however, must have an incense burner (*xianglu*) and a material support for their deity (a statue, a name tablet, or a painting that has to be consecrated, *kaiguang,* a ritual normally done by a Daoist or a Buddhist cleric). Families also have a domestic altar in the house's main room, which contains statues or tablets of ancestors as well as some protective deities. Most faith communities build their own temple, or a chapel or hall within an existing temple. Many such temples were constructed (probably over one million as of 1900), most of which had many different cults beside the main deity that gave the temple its name; separate chapels and icons were erected by sub-groups or individuals within the community. All Chinese temples conformed to a single general model in terms of architecture, layout, and symbolic vocabulary. A temple belongs either to the clerical, or more often, the lay community that built it, so most temples can not be deemed Daoist, Buddhist, or Confucian—or even "syncretic"—rather, they are the meeting place for communities constituted in their alliance with their saints. Only temples built by clerical communities—that is, Buddhist and Daoist monasteries, and Confucian academies—can be said to belong to a definite religion. Temple community leaders are chosen, usually every year, by a combination of bids (leaders are usually wealthy locals who pay dearly for the symbolic capital of religious leadership), rotation, and election by the god (divination, drawing by lots); they preside over the rituals and manage temple assets and regulations.

Temples can hire religious specialists, and many of the larger temples who can afford it do so. Among specialists, Buddhists or Daoists are hired as temple managers (*zhuchi*) on a contractual basis: they are financially supported (by temple land endowments and community taxes) and can adopt and train the disciples of their choice; they have to manage the temple's day-to-day liturgical life, under the supervision of temple community leaders. They might lose their positions if they appropriate temple property or gravely misbehave. Occasionally, Buddhist managers are replaced with Daoist ones and vice versa, so the confessional affiliation of the resident cleric and that of the temple are two clearly separate questions. Male or female clerics can be temple managers; in the early twenty-first century, estimates of the proportion of women in these roles range between 25 and 30 percent. Buddhists and Daoists not living in the temple can be contracted to perform scheduled rituals; they are also available to families and individuals for death rituals and other services (such as exorcisms or consecrations). Parish systems are rare, and families are free to hire the cleric of their choice if they can afford it. Confucian clerics (*lisheng,* males only) almost never work as temple managers, but they may be invited to preside over sacrifices or family rites (notably funerals).

Other non-clerical specialists also work full-time or by invitation in temples and for families. Diviners help laypersons to interpret oracles, notably those communications obtained through divination sticks (*lingqian,* sets of oracular poems; some sets are devoted specifically to medical queries, *yaoqian*). Some Buddhists and Daoists double as diviners, but this service is often provided by professional diviners, *yinyang xiansheng,* sometimes doubling as geomancers. Spirit-mediums, trained and ordained by Daoists, are important temple specialists, acting either during festivals or on a regular schedule (for example, holding sessions once a week). Laypersons can come and ask questions (such as advice on upcoming decisions or requests for cures) to the god through the medium; the latter answers either verbally (with an interpreter at hand) or writes a talisman (sometimes with his or her own blood) that can protect or heal. In the village world, many spirit-mediums and healers work at home, independently from temples: they maintain an altar with their own favorite deities, and can heal petitioners' illnesses through a combination of divination, propitiations, and exorcism. Both men and women can become spirit-mediums or healers; they need only to be called by the gods (a vocation which is often resisted), and to develop charisma; in modern times, women healers seem to have become more numerous. Spirit-mediums and healers' own deities are extremely varied, but fox spirits are very common throughout Northern China, and groups of five exorcistic deities (Wutong, Wuchang) predominate in southern China.

Yet another category of specialist is the spiritual master who teaches self-development techniques, from *yangsheng,* cultivation of health to achieve long life (through breathing techniques, dietetics, gymnastics, and sexual techniques) to more elaborate and demanding body-and-mind practices designed to produce supra-normal powers and eventually salvation (as an immortal). Among these masters, Daoists and Buddhists compete with sectarian leaders, martial artists, and doctors of Chinese medicine.

POPULAR RELIGION, STATE AND SOCIETY. Popular religion and the state have a long history of complicated relationships. Until the twentieth century, anti-superstition campaigns, Chinese religion, and local cults in particular had never been completely banned: territorial, clan, and corporation cults were mostly recognized as orthodox, and their liturgy, notably sacrifices, was Confucian, that is, the same as that practiced by the state cults. On the other hand, the imperial state has always tried to curtail the number and the size of temple cults, for a host of theological, economic, and socio-political reasons. Most often, the state has limited the number of cults in which commoners were allowed to participate, even though such laws seem to have been consistently ignored throughout history. The state has recognized certain local cults by integrating them into its own register of sacrifices(*sidian*); all other cults were deemed *yinsi*, a complex notion meaning "profligate," "immoral," or "wanton," that is, causing financial and emotional excesses and eventually bearing no graces but only harm. Such immoral cults were forbidden but nonetheless remained extremely common; usually, state toleration and accommodation alternated with occasional repression, and stories of officials destroying "immoral" temples are common from the Han dynasty to the modern period. Officials also attempted to distinguish orthodox local territorial gods from forbidden devotional congregations, notably those involving women. Late imperial law forbade women to visit temples (Confucian orthodoxy aspired to confining them at home), which they nonetheless did in great numbers; large-scale women-only pilgrimage associations also were formed. Nighttime celebrations and participation of mediums were also targeted by officials, with equally little success.

Attempts at curtailing the celebrations of local temple cults were linked to a growing Confucian fundamentalism during the Ming and Qing periods. At the same time, sectarian movements were banned outright because of rebellions. For this reason, some scholars have looked at Chinese popular religion as a field of resistance to state power. For the most part, local cults do not develop an ideology of opposition and resistance; the vast majority of communities align themselves with law and order, but because religious groups were the only natural and tolerated form of social organization in imperial China, and as the individual temple communities incarnated local identity and autonomy, it is only natural that resistance movements came to be religiously organized. The twentieth-century anti-superstition destructions had much more effect on popular religion than did imperial policies, and also caused more resistance among the people.

THEOLOGY. As Chinese religion does not have a common canon and spiritual authorities, there is no unified formal theology. All cults and specialists, however, share a common cosmology. This cosmology, formed during late antiquity and the Han period, dictates that the material and spiritual realms are not separate. The universe is a whole organic system, constantly evolving according to known rules, described through operative symbols (including *yin* and *yang*, five phases, and trigrams). All beings are in constant interaction (*ganying*), even at long distances. Due to their different inherent qualities and histories, beings are more or less pure and endowed with spiritual power, *ling*, meaning efficacy and charisma. All beings—humans, animals and even plants—can purify themselves (through morality and self-cultivation) before and after death, and thereby ascend the ladders of the spiritual hierarchy and increase their *ling*. Miracles and the answering of prayers are manifestations of *ling*. Beside these basic principles, the formulation of cosmological and theological thinking is entrusted to clerical specialists (Buddhists, Daoists, Confucians, and sometimes sectarian leaders): that is why these specialists are invited by cult communities to write texts (such as stele inscriptions, scriptures, hagiographies, and liturgical hymns) to justify their cults and practices and place them in a larger orthodox framework. These sources, in particular the stele inscriptions which are the records of temple communities, mix the external discourse of literate clerical specialists and the internal discourse of the community.

Communities and individuals by and large share similar values, especially since the Song period, which included the advent of a common ethics (integrating elements of Confucian, Daoist and Buddhist origins) that was expressed in morality books. All practitioners agree that actions carry retribution (conceived either as automatic *karma* accounting, or, more often, as a post-mortem judicial process administered in courts of hell), and this concept determines the fate of each human (and animal) being after death. The theological exegesis provided by specialists is supplemented by an abundance of "popular theology," mostly in accord with clerical formulations, that expresses itself in genres such as the novel or the opera. Vernacular novels such as *Fengshen yanyi*, *Xiyou ji*, or *Shuihu zhuan*, have played a major role in transmitting lore on gods and ritual; moreover, their authors have even been accused by some officials of encouraging heterodoxy and inspiring rebellions.

Who are the deities? Anthropologists have found that most Chinese divide the realm of other-worldly beings into three categories—gods, ghosts and ancestors—and indeed, similar distinctions already existed before the Han period. These are not strictly separate categories, however, as the ancestors of one group are the ghosts of another, and as both ghosts and ancestors can become gods. Ancestors are those who, having gone through a good death, and being subsequently fed by their patrilineal descendants, stay with them at a carefully maintained distance. Ghosts and demons are those who have suffered a bad death (early death, suicide, dismemberment, and other unnatural circumstances—the demonology is very rich) and who could not be ritually installed as ancestors. They roam around, seeking vengeance, and they can cause illnesses and accidents. Ghosts and demons have to be kept at bay, which includes being bribed by sacrifices (notably during their seventh-month propitiation ceremony) and disempowered by exorcisms. Gods (*shen*) are also dead human beings endowed with exceptional *ling* (due to morality and fortitude). Although many gods are, like ghosts, victims of bad death, unlike ancestors, they are thought to work mostly for the good of humans, especially those orthodox gods (*zhengshen*) who have a privileged position in the spiritual bureaucracy. Nearly all gods, ghosts, and ancestors are dead humans, with a history, birthdays and death days to be celebrated, and traces left on earth (places where they committed such and such acts of prowess; however, there is little cult worship of relics outside of the Buddhist context). For this reason, local gods, notably those who were canonized by the state or by the Daoists, can also be referred to as saints. In addition, there are a few nature gods and pure Daoist stellar deities that are not dead humans.

All cults are reciprocal, contractual relations between a human community and a deity. The community nourishes (through sacrifices) and houses (in temples) the deity in exchange for the god's support. If support and miracles fail to happen, the cult dies out, and new cults arise. Since each community contracts its own relationship with its deity and freely elaborates its hagiography and iconography, there is no cohesive pantheon structuring all of the deities. There are many concurrent pantheons: the liturgical pantheons of the Daoists, Buddhists, and Confucians, which are more or less unified throughout China, as well as those of the innumerable communities; there are also regional pantheons integrating local gods in the framework of common rituals, myths, and temple cult alliances within one area. Although they only overlap partially, these various pantheons do not really contradict one another. Many gods are known nationwide, whereas most local saints are unheard of outside of their home county. Nationwide gods usually have been canonized by both the state and Daoism, and most of them rose to regional and national status during the pivotal Song-Yuan period. The most common ones include emperor Guan (Guandi, full name Guan Yu, a martial and upright hero, known as the god of war), Zhenwu (a Daoist saint, also a martial deity), Mazu (a fisherwoman patron saint of boatmen), Eastern Peak (Mount Taishan, head of the netherworld courts), Lü Dongbin (an alchemist saint, healer, and instructor through spirit-writing), Wenchang (a Daoist patron saint of scholars and spirit-writing morality books). Some gods are specialized in certain services (such as healing or granting rain) but most local saints will answer any prayer. It is, moreover, difficult to associate a god with definite values or beliefs, as a god can mean very different things in different communities.

One fundamental structure of Chinese pantheons is the bureaucratic metaphor, that is, the idea that gods fill positions in a bureaucracy, are promoted or demoted, and have to answer to higher authorities. The head of this pantheon is Yuhuang, the Jade emperor god, commonly called Heaven. Yet, whereas many authors have taken this bureaucratic metaphor as a way to project human society and the imperial political system onto the other world (a thesis followed by scholars who think that religion merely reflects sociopolitical realities without any autonomous agency), there are many differences between the human world, even in idealized form, and the way the Chinese say the other world works. First, many deities, notably territorial gods (Chenghuang and *tudi gong*), are mostly officials within a hierarchical system (the Chinese often say "our gods are our officials"), but many others work from outside the spiritual bureaucracy, either as benevolent mediators (Guanyin and the Daoist immortals) or as outsiders, helping their devotees in an exclusive relationship that is not validated by inclusion in larger symbolical schemes. The bureaucratic metaphor accommodates both integration with larger, pan-Chinese political and symbolical systems and of the need for autonomy and self-defense from the intrusions of such systems. At the same time, there is a gendered aspect of such oppositions: male deities tend to be territorial and bureaucratic, and ascriptive communities are often managed by male worthies; while female deities tend to operate from outside hierarchical pantheons, and voluntary congregations are the main venues for the activities of women. Both men and women, however, share the same goal: salvation through becoming ancestors or gods.

LITURGY. The Chinese religion's economy of salvation offers several channels for both individual and communal interaction with deities, thereby fulfilling worldly needs and providing ultimate salvation. Temples are not open at all times to individuals. People tend to visit on certain occasions: the temple festival, New Year's Day, and on the first and fifteenth day of each month in the lunar calendar—the official suppression of which during the late 1920s was meant to eradicate superstitions. People usually visit temples when they have a prayer to address to deities, as there is no compulsory attendance in Chinese religion (however, all must pay taxes to the local territorial temple and clan shrine). Beside burning incense, devotees bring offerings (foodstuffs, candles, flowers, and cash donations) and formulate their prayer, either orally or, if there is a clerical specialist present, in a formal written request (*shu*), prepared by the cleric and burnt (all messages and offerings to gods are sent to them through fire). Written petitions to deities existed as early as late antiquity and have been developed by Daoism; they are used particularly when the devotee feels he or she has been the victim of wrongdoing and seeks justice through the gods; ordeals may also be staged. The objects of prayers are naturally those of most common concern to Chinese people: health, prosperity, children and continuation of lineages, favorable weather and agriculture, and business success.

Prayers are normally accompanied by a vow (*yuan*). When praying, the devotee promises (*xuyuan*) to do something (give a donation, build a new temple, engage in charity, make a pilgrimage, or become a vegetarian); if the prayer is answered, she or he returns to the temple to make good on the promise (*huanyuan*). Temples, as well as home altars of spirit-mediums and other specialists are full of votive offerings (such as wooden boards, furniture, banners, and other decorative elements) carrying the name and words of thanks of those who did *huanyuan* and bear witness to the god's efficacy. People who have been cured by a religious specialist or a god often become the adopted son or daughter of the specialist or god through ritual adoption. Healing seems to have always been the most common cause for an individual converting to a community or a cult.

The communal liturgy of Chinese local cults is the temple festival, *miaohui* or *saihui*, usually held to commemorate the birthday of the main god. A festival combines several elements: clerical liturgy, sacrifice, performing arts and processions, as well as socio-economic functions (a temple fair or market is organized, and allied communities are invited). Daoists or Buddhists are often contracted to perform grand classical liturgy, which is fundamental for integrating the cult in the larger scheme of Chinese civilization, notably the Daoist *jiao* ritual that places the community and its gods into a cosmic alliance and its economy of universal salvation. For this reason, scholars have described Daoism as the liturgical framework of local cults. Local saints, except for some Buddhist and Daoist vegetarian saints, are also honored with animal sacrifices. Since the Song period, after the formation of the beef taboo (which reserved sacrifices of oxen or buffalo and consumption of beef to certain imperial and purely Confucian cults), sacrificial victims are pigs, sheep or goats, and smaller animals (such as poultry or fish). As in sacrificial traditions worldwide, the meat is first tasted by the deities, thereby sanctified, and eventually shared by the community during a banquet. Buddhists and Daoists usually take little part in this sacrifice, however, that often follows a Confucian liturgy. The ostentatious and competitive aspect of festivals is apparent; different families or congregations compete to see who can provide the largest and most spectacular offerings.

At the same time, local vernacular liturgy is performed outside the temple. Processions are an important part of temple festivals, particularly for territorial cults; these processions precisely follow the boundaries of the territory or jurisdiction of the god; they have also an exorcistic value (expelling ghosts and demons and all pestilence from the community) and spirit-mediums play a major role. Processions also include voluntary devotional associations that perform martial art, farces, stilt walking, lion dances, and other kinds of popular shows. In front of the temple, operas are performed for the gods and community members. One particularly important opera, found throughout China, is the Mulian cycle, which tells the story of the monk who visited the hells looking for her sinful mother and managed to save her, as well as all the other suffering souls. Mulian plays are staged during the seventh month at the same time as the large-scale celebrations (which are colloquially known as ghost festivals) that try to save all suffering (and potentially malefic) ghosts and demons of the community, thus serving as communal exorcism, remembrance, and expiation of bad conscience. Mulian plays are dramatic, entertaining, and highly didactic, as the travel through the hells allows the actors to dramatize their values and beliefs regarding morality and retribution.

SCHOLARSHIP AND HISTORIOGRAPHY. Because Chinese official historiography documents poorly and in a very biased way all local, non-clerical religious institutions and practices (in fact, most of them document repression and conflict), historians have long underestimated the extent, variety, and vitality of local religion. Only a few historians and folklorists (such as Sawada Mizuho), who study anecdotes and other narrative sources, have been able to address the complexity of past religious culture. The study of popular religion has been conducted mostly by anthropologists, first in Taiwan, Hong Kong, and overseas communities, and since the 1980s in mainland China. Among the pioneers were K. Schipper, S. Feuchtwang, D. Jordan, and S. Sangren, all of whom worked in Taiwan, following up on late nineteenth-century and early twentieth-century observers, often missionaries (J. de Groot, C. Day, J. Shryock, W. Grootaers). Since the 1970s, historians have supplemented the theories of anthropologists with written material, notably regarding sectarian movements (S. Naquin, D. Overmyer, B. ter Haar) or local cults (P. Katz). One very influential paradigm, formulated mostly from a sociological perspective by C.K. Yang, was that Chinese popular religion was "diffuse" (transmitted by families and through shared values, rather than through institutions). With the renewal of temple cults and other large-scale organizations on the mainland since the 1980s, however, and the discovery of huge amounts of written material produced by these cults and found in the field, social scientists have had to reconsider the importance, not only of the religious beliefs and values, but also of the social structures of local religion in premodern and modern Chinese society. During the 1990s, researchers led important efforts to collect and publish written material found in the context of local cults; these studies have greatly expanded knowledge of the field, notably the Taiwanese-led projects around the journal *Minsu quyi* and related collections. Materials include scripts of rituals (performed by local Daoist lineages or other specialists) and operas, hagiographies, stele inscriptions, and records of pious associations.

At the same time, theories elaborated on the basis of early fieldwork in Taiwan and Hong Kong are beginning to be challenged or refined, thanks to observations in inland provinces; some of these provinces, although inhabited by tens of millions of people, are still poorly documented. Much research on Chinese popular religion has dealt with the question of diversity: Are popular and elite religious ideas and practices different enough to justify the notion of two different religions, or are they just varying expressions of a fundamentally unique religious tradition? This debate has been brought to more subtle levels by discussing ways in which attempts, mostly by late imperial and modern elite, to bring unity (hegemony) to religious representations and practices partially succeeded, shaping the discourse of the villagers in a Confucian framework, and partially failed, as villagers are able to maintain their cults and rituals under the appearance of Confucian orthodoxy. Another topic of Chinese religion with questions of unity or diversity is the liturgical calendar. The basic structure of the calendar is the same throughout the Chinese world, with the new year event (a family celebration of renewal and settling accounts with both humans and Heaven), rites for ancestors, propitiation of ghosts and demons during the seventh month; yet at the same time, much variety exists among regional and local yearly events.

SEE ALSO Afterlife, article on Chinese Concepts; Ancestors, article on Ancestor Worship; Divination; Domestic Observances, article on Chinese Practices; Millenarianism, article on Chinese Millenarian Movements; Soul, article on Chinese Concepts.

BIBLIOGRAPHY

Clart, Philip. "Confucius and the Mediums: Is There a 'Popular Confucianism'?" *T'oung Pao* 89, nos. 1–3 (2003): 1–38. On twentieth-century spirit-writing cults as popular Confucianism.

Cohen, Myron. "Shared Beliefs: Corporations, Community and Religion among the South Taiwan Hakka during the Ch'ing." *Late Imperial China* 14, no. 1 (1993): 1–33. A sociological approach of religious organizations.

Dean, Kenneth. *Daoist Ritual and Popular Cults of South-east China.* Princeton, N.J., 1993. A superb fieldwork and comprehensive description of how Daoists provide a "liturgical framework" for local cults.

Dean, Kenneth. "Transformations of the *She* (Altars of the Soil) in Fujian." *Cahiers d'Extrême-Asie* 10 (1998): 19–75. A history of territorial cults and their evolution through the early modern period.

Durand-Dastes, Vincent. "Prodiges ambigus. Les récits non-canoniques sur le surnaturel entre histoire religieuse, histoire littéraire et anthropologie." *Revue bibliographique de sinologie* (2002): 317–343. An excellent historiographic discussion on the use of narrative literature for the study of popular religion.

Feuchtwang, Stephan. *Popular Religion in China: The Imperial Metaphor.* London, 2001. A classic, theoretically complex, but comprehensive discussion of popular religion in a Taiwanese village.

Goossaert, Vincent. *Dans les temples de la Chine: Histoire des cultes, vie des communautés.* Paris, 2000. A synthetic introduction to Chinese temples.

Goossaert, Vincent. "Le destin de la religion chinoise au 20e siècle." *Social Compass* 50, no. 4 (2003): 429–440. A first discussion of the modern history of Chinese religion, faced with anti-superstition campaigns, temple destruction, and the birth of scholarly study of local cults.

Guo, Qitao. *Exorcism and Money: The Symbolic World of the Five-Fury Spirits in Late Imperial China.* Berkeley, Calif., 2003. How ambiguous exorcist gods became integrated in orthodox local ritual in sixteenth-century Huizhou (Anhui province).

ter Haar, Barend. "Local Society and the Organization of Cults in Early Modern China: A Preliminary Study." *Studies in Central and East Asian Religions* 8 (1995): 1–43. Temple cults and their social organization as seen by an historian.

Hansen, Valerie. *Changing Gods in Medieval China, 1127–1276.* Princeton, N.J., 1990. An authoritative study on the birth of regional and national cults.

Katz, Paul. *Demon Hordes and Burning Boats: The Cult of Marshal Wen in Late Imperial Chekiang.* Albany, N.Y., 1995. A local cult, seen through history, hagiography, and ritual.

Lopez, Donald S., ed. *Religions of China in Practice.* Princeton, N.J., 1996. A very readable selection of important primary sources from antiquity to the present.

Naquin, Susan. *Peking: Temples and City Life, 1400–1900.* Berkeley, Calif., 2000. A very detailed study of urban temples, their history, and their functions.

Overmyer, Daniel. "From 'Feudal Superstitions' to 'Popular Beliefs': New Directions in Mainland Chinese Studies of Chinese Popular Religion." *Cahiers d'Extrême-Asie* 12 (2001): 103–126. A critical discussion of the nascent Chinese scholarship, clarifying many complex terminology and conceptual issues.

Poo, Mu-chou. *In Search of Personal Welfare: A View of Ancient Chinese Religion.* Albany, N.Y., 1998. A comprehensive discussion of early Chinese common religion.

Sangren, Steven P. "Traditional Chinese Corporations: Beyond Kinship." *Journal of Asian Studies* 43, no. 3 (1984): 391–415. An excellent argument for a comparative approach of the different forms of religious organizations in Chinese society.

Schipper, Kristofer. "Neighborhood Cult Associations in Traditional Tainan." In *The City in Late Imperial China,* edited by William G. Skinner, pp. 651–676. Stanford, Calif., 1977. A seminal study on territorial communities.

Schipper, Kristofer. "Structures Liturgiques et société civile à Pékin." *Sanjiao wenxian* 1 (1997): 9–23. The religious organization in early modern Beijing.

Sutton, Donald. "From Credulity to Scorn: Confucians Confront the Spirit Mediums in Late Imperial China." *Late Imperial China* 21, no. 2 (2000): 1–39. The growing Confucian fundamentalism turning against the most important specialists of popular religion.

Wolf, Arthur P. "Gods, Ghosts, and Ancestors." In *Religion and Ritual in Chinese Society,* edited by Arthur P. Wolf, pp. 131–182. Stanford, Calif., 1974. The classical study on popular theology.

Yang, C.K. (Yang, Qingkun). *Religion in Chinese Society.* Berkeley, Calif., 1961. The classical analysis of Chinese popular religion as diffuse religion.

Yü, Chün-fang. *Kuan-yin: The Chinese Transformation of Avalokitesvara.* New York, 2001. A superb history of how the Buddhist *bodhisattva* Guanyin became a popular Chinese goddess.

VINCENT GOOSSAERT (2005)

CHINESE RELIGION: MYTHIC THEMES

"Who was there to pass down the story of the beginning of things in the remote past? What means are there to examine what it was like before heaven above and earth below had taken shape?" (Hawkes, 1959, p. 46). These cryptic queries, the very first of the "Heavenly Questions" found in the *Chuci* anthology of the early third century BCE, simultaneously suggest the significant presence and problematic nature of ancient Chinese mythology. The fact that myths—stories of the beginning of things—were an important subject in the life and literature of ancient China is indicated by the tantalizing diversity of mythic episodes and personnel so familiarly alluded to in the *Chuci* and in other early Chinese literary and artistic works. At the same time, the interrogative format and enigmatic terseness of the "Heavenly Questions" aptly dramatize the overall riddle posed by ancient Chinese mythology.

The Problem of Chinese Myth. There are allusive mythological references in archaic Chinese literature but they are almost always fragmented and disguised in ways that make it very difficult to determine the character and import of specific myths. Moreover, while the rich zoomorphic iconography found on the Shang and Zhou dynasty bronze ritual vessels suggests a dualistic system of shamanistic symbolism, the highly stylized and formulaic nature of the evidence (e.g., the bipartite animal mask design known as the *taotie*) and the lack of any consistent correlation between artistic and literary evidence allow for only very tentative conclusions as to the prevailing mythological universe of meaning. Instead of coherent stories of the gods, animal ancestors, and semi-divine sage-kings of the sacred time of the beginnings, there are only bits and pieces of various myths that pointedly raise the difficult methodological question of knowing what means there are to examine such an apparently unmythical deposit of myth.

This situation is compounded by the fact that, while China is not wholly unusual in possessing only fragmented and composite mythological materials from the ancient period, early sinological scholarship tended to portray China as uniquely deficient in mythology. Indeed, assumptions concerning the special poverty of Chinese mythology, especially in relation to creation myths, were generally used to support scholarly judgments concerning the essentially philosophical, humanistic, or historical nature of the ancient tradition. Such opinions about the largely nonmythological and nonreligious character of early China have a long pedigree in the history of scholarship that was reinforced by both orthodox Chinese scholiasts and enlightened Western academicians who equated ancient Chinese culture with the great tradition of the Confucian classics and agreed on the irrational and degenerate role of religion and myth in human culture.

This discussion will be limited to mythic materials and themes specifically related to the ancient origins, early cultural development, and ultimate political coalescence of Chinese tradition—that is, the formative historical period that extends from the Xia (tentatively identified with the preliterate Erlitou culture) and Shang dynasties of the late third and second millennia, down through the feudal conditions and intellectual ferment in the Zhou period (tenth through third centuries), and to the rise of the early Qin and Han imperial traditions during the last few centuries before the common era. In contrast to notions of a monolithic classical tradition going back to the prehistoric beginnings of sinitic civilization and as indicated by the southern provenance of the *Chuci,* cultural development during the foundational period is best viewed as a dynamic amalgamative process that gradually incorporated various local and barbarian cultures.

Broken Stories and Thematic Function. It may be possible to find a culture or religion without myths, or with very weakly developed mythological traditions, and it is true that ancient China did have a special preoccupation with ritual behavior. Be this as it may, the pioneering work of Henri Maspero, Marcel Granet, Gu Jiegang, Carl Hentze, and Edouard Erkes in the 1920s and 1930s—along with the corroborating efforts of Bernhard Karlgren and Wolfram Eberhard in the 1940s—showed that the supposed absence or special poverty of Chinese mythic fabulation was a view that could not be sustained. As is seen in the clash between Karlgren's historicist perspective and the various comparative methods of some of the other scholars, there was no final agreement as to what could actually be known of the ancient myths, but it is demonstrably certain that mythological traditions played an important role in early Chinese culture.

The increased interdisciplinary study and appreciation of the early Chinese religion and mythology in contemporary scholarship (especially noteworthy is the work of Kwang-chih Chang, Sarah Allan, Rémi Mathieu, Jean Levi, Michael Loewe, and John Major) confirm the conclusions from the first part of this century. This work, together with the unavoidable judgment that recent archaeological discoveries (including epigraphical, textual, and extraliterary evidence) clearly document the centrality of cosmological and religious ideas in ancient China, collectively underscore the vital significance of mythic themes not only for nonorthodox materials like the *Chuci, Shanhai jing,* or *Zhuangzi,* but also for the classically standardized works espoused by Confucian and imperial tradition. In addition to this, and despite the caution that must be employed when analyzing ancient Chinese documents, there is a growing consensus that Karlgren's strictures against using the systematized Han dynasty materials for reconstructing ancient mythology, and his idea that much of Han mythology was an *ad hoc* product of that period, need to be amended. Thus, it is unreasonable to suppose that mythological materials found primarily in Han sources were a fabrication disconnected from earlier traditions. Furthermore, the very fact of a cosmological system of thought in the Han dynasty often indicates something important about the nature and function of earlier myths.

Ancient Chinese culture is not an example of an ancient religious or ritual tradition without mythology. The question one must ask is how and why the myths—or the particular recurrent and overlapping constellations of mythic themes, figures, and images from various local cultures—were preserved, combined, and transformed in certain patterned ways within different textual traditions. Given the compelling assumption that there were active oral traditions of myth-telling in both aristocratic and folk circles, it is probably the case that myths in a coherent storied form were present in ancient China. But the more addressable and interesting question is why the broken shards of mythic narratives were so often used in particular thematic ways in different written documents. The very fact that myths were written down in a fractured and composite way most likely indicates that individual mythic traditions were losing some of their original sacred, cultic, or religiously functional character. It still must be asked, however, whether or not the thematic glosses on myth, or the skeletal remains of mythic narratives, found in written sources may still function mythically—even when they appear in the profanized guise of history or philosophy.

In this sense, also, it may be questioned whether the oft-repeated claim that Chinese texts represent a curious instance of the reverse euhemerization of earlier mythic stories has any real significance. If reverse euhemerization refers to the false historicization of myth, making myths appear real, rather than the making of myths from actual historical events as the standard definition of euhemerization would have it, then it nevertheless seems that the intellectual and imaginative process involved was still primarily mythical in nature. In both cases history was fit to the demands of mythic form. Both types of euhemerization are made up yet are to some degree historically factual.

Ancient Chinese literature is basically nonnarrative in any extended sense and is not informed by myth in the overarching, dramatic, and epic way of some other ancient literatures. From a structural point of view, however, mythological thought may be seen primarily as an intellectual and imaginative strategy of bricolage that constantly juggles, rearranges, and transforms assorted mythological signs—bits and pieces—according to a deeper code of relational contrast and dynamic synthesis. The cultural function and communicative power of myth is to be found at the structural level that perdures beneath the shifting surface dimension of particular mythic images or narrative plot development. What is preserved, and what continues to function mythically in early Chinese literature, therefore, are the thematic structures of different myths that most generally stress formulas of order and disorder, qualities, relations, and states of being as opposed to an interconnected narrative flow of motivations, action, and consequences. It is this basic emphasis on mythic structure over mythic narrative in Chinese literature that may be related, as Andrew Plaks suggests, to the distinctive Chinese concern with ritual issues of correlative spatial relationship.

Thus understood, the bits and pieces of myth found in ancient Chinese texts betray a kind of slated thematic pattern, or repetitive static structure, that functions as an exemplary frame for determining the significance of the past for the present and future. In this way, the constantly changing reality of nature and social life only demonstrated to the ancient Chinese that history, like the Dao as the first principle of mythic transformation, always stays relatively and structurally the same. Aside from the different manipulations of selected mythical themes seen in particular textual traditions, the underlying abstract logic of mythical thought—stressing binary structural opposition, tertiary synthesis, and numerically coded relational permutation—dwells at the heart of the *yinyang wuxing* cosmological system that became universal in the Han dynasty.

These considerations concerning the thematic presence and structural function of myth in China are helpful in providing some means of answering the *Chuci*'s "Heavenly Questions," but they do not obviate the fact that formidable problems of content and method still complicate the study of ancient Chinese mythology. Suffice it to say that the basic thematic contours of archaic mythology may be known with reasonable confidence for periods as early as the Western and Eastern Zhou dynasties and that it is possible, and desirable, to work with this material inasmuch as it reflects on, and informs, the overall history of archaic Chinese religion; the differing visions of life seen among the various philosophical movements emerging during the Eastern Zhou period; the development of a shared tradition of correlative thought; and, most generally, the organismic Chinese worldview.

THEMATIC REPERTORY: BEGINNINGS AND RETURN. Working with the remnants of myths, or more accurately, with composite mythic units found variously in the earliest texts, makes it possible to reconstruct what may be called a typological sacred history of the beginning of things in the remote past. It must be stressed that this typology is only a partial digest of some of the more representative and recurrent mythic themes and that the sequential movement from cosmic to civilizational origins is an artificial construct of a generalized structural logic or mythic grammar inherent in much of early Chinese thought.

By the time of the Han dynasty all of the basic typological themes were shared as a common inheritance of mythic lore, but it is never the case that the different units were fully articulated in the manner presented here—although the eclectically Daoist compendium known as the *Huainanzi* (c. 100 BCE) comes close to being a comprehensive synthetic handbook of Chinese mythic history. It is also important to note that the use or exclusion of particular mythic units is a salient factor for distinguishing different textual and ideological traditions. Myth to some extent always refers to the issue of beginnings or world foundation. Where the archetypal beginnings are located in the remote past with respect to a particular conception of world and order will, therefore, have a significant relation to the different understandings of human nature and social life seen in various ideological movements emerging in the Eastern Zhou period.

The typology developed here also does not suggest any actual historical priority in the sequential arrangement of thematic units since, for example, it seems from the documentary evidence that full-fledged cosmogonic themes only coincided with the rise of philosophical speculation during the Eastern Zhou period, whereas various clan origin myths and cosmic disaster themes can be reliably traced to the much earlier Western Zhou dynasty, or perhaps even to the Shang period. In fact, in relation to the datable appearance of individual mythic units and images in extant literary and extra-literary sources, and as a counterpoint to the typological sequence, there was an apparent movement from the earliest myths of clan origin, animal ancestors, and the closeness of heaven and earth to the later myths of the Eastern Zhou period, where an antagonistic relationship among humans, animals, and the gods was often emphasized. It was in this later period (roughly after the eighth century BCE) that a diminished faith in an active sky or high god (Shangdi, Tian) and the appearance of nontheistic cosmogonic themes, hybrid human-animal mythological imagery, myths of the combat of cultural saviors with chaotic forces, and the accounts of sage-kings and model emperors as civilizational transformers came to the fore. There is an evident relation here with changes in the aristocratic religious tradition, social-political life, and kinship practices that may be linked with the emergence of philosophical and humanistic thought. It is, however, not so much a matter of philosophical or rational thought replacing mythic irrationality as a question of differing conceptualizations, still modeled on mythic structures and themes, as to what constitutes the fundamental principles of existential order.

With these various qualifications in mind, it is feasible to consider the overall typological repertory of mythic themes arranged under the four general headings of (1) cosmic and human beginnings, (2) cosmic disasters, beginning again, and cultural saviors, (3) civilizational beginnings, sage-kings, and model emperors, and (4) returning to the beginning as the cultivated renewal of individual and social life. This scheme of four phases of beginning has interrelated diachronic and synchronic implications. Diachronically, there is a progressive movement from the cosmic, natural, early cultural, and later civilizational orders or worlds, but structurally each stage represents a new beginning that recapitulates an earlier cosmic situation. The sacred history of the various human worlds as a series of new beginnings presupposes a constant return to some first condition of cosmic unity as the precondition for a new creation or renewal of life. In this way there is a kind of cosmogonic intentionality and cosmological methodology that, while not always stated, implicitly informs the ancient Chinese understanding of existence. While the literary use of myths may be broken from specific earlier cultic traditions, there is very much of a religiously salvational vision here that is designed to establish and maintain contact between humans and the cosmos. The idea of the sacred, as Mircea Eliade says, "does not necessarily imply belief in God or gods and spirits" (*Ordeal by Labyrinth,* Chicago, 1982, p. 154); rather, it is primarily the experience of existing in a world made meaningful and real by its connections with a greater cosmic order.

Cosmic and human beginnings. There are several clusters of mythic images and themes that are concerned with the question of existential origins and a kind of fall from the formative first order of things. From the standpoint of the mythic logic suggested by most of these materials, the primary structural category refers to the primordial, or very first, issue of world creation.

Cosmogonic origins. Contrary to claims that ancient China was devoid of any kind of authentic creation mythology, there was certainly a genre of explicit cosmogonic speculation during the Eastern Zhou period that was thematically rooted in the mythic image of a primal chaotic monad or raviolo known as *hundun* (variously imagined as a cosmic egg, gourd, rock, sac, dumpling, etc.; also personified as a strangely faceless and Humpty-Dumpty-like emperor of the center in the *Zhuangzi* or as a divine bird in the *Shanhai jing*). *Hundun* was that primordial condition or ancestral figure that gave rise to the multiplicity of the phenomenal world through a spontaneous process of separation (i.e., the splitting of the chaotic one into the dual cosmic structure of heaven and earth) or transformation (i.e., the metamorphosis of the one body of the primal animal ancestor into the multiple parts of the cosmos). The *hundun* theme also seems to have incorporated other mythic variants that told of the creative activites of world parents or some consanguineous male and female pair of deities (e.g., Fu Xi and Nügua) who generate the world through their incestuous sexual union. These themes, moreover, clearly represent the archaic prototype for the later (c. third to sixth century) depictions of Pangu as the primal man or chaos giant who was born from the embryonic *hundun.*

The theme of the primal unity and precivilizational innocence of the chaotic *hundun* is most prominent in the ancient Daoist texts as a metaphor for the chaotic order, untrammeled freedom, and wholeness of human nature and primitive society, which can be reattained by means of a kind of internalized mystical reversal of the cosmogony. In the guise of Pangu, the *hundun* theme is associated with the incarnate cosmic body of Laojun, the revealed savior in later sectarian Daoism. In the classics and other Confucian-inspired texts of the ancient period, on the other hand, the image of *hundun* is never presented in a cosmogonic context and is only rarely mentioned as a personified barbarian rebel (Hundun) who dangerously challenged the proper ritual order of civilizational life. The underlying structure and logic of the *hundun* creation scenario also may be related to the shared cosmological system of *yinyang* dualism and to the idea of a third term or mediating principle (i.e., the cosmological ether known as *qi* or the principle of man/shaman/emperor/priest) between the two things of heaven and earth. Most generally, the *hundun* theme of a self-generated creational process without a creator is most explicit in the early

Daoist texts, but may be said to inform the cosmological metaphysics associated with the ubiquitous ultimate principle of the Dao.

Lay of the land. Themes associated with the creative fashioning, cosmetic arranging, or cartographic determining of the cosmos are found more often than actual cosmogonic accounts; they most often imply that a world inhabited by humankind already existed. Despite this overt fixation on a preexisting human world, it seems that a prior world populated by gods and animal spirits is often intended. Whatever the case may be, the major thematic emphasis is placed on the sacred patterns of space and time that are common to gods or humankind and, in this sense, many different mythic units may be grouped together as cosmographical accounts of the first order of material existence.

Throughout most of the earliest texts, and as displayed by iconographical symbolism, there are a number of basic recurrent images that collectively describe the original divine form of things—for example, the image of the heavens as round and the earth as square and the tripartite division of a lower, middle, and upper realm together with the idea of an axis or pillar(s) that connects what is above and below. Various other themes link patterns of space and time so that the solar cycle is said to involve the sequential daily passage of one of ten suns from a sacred mulberry tree in the east to another tree in the extreme west. In general, themes of the sun and moon, as well as those of other celestial bodies, were important in classical sources as indications of the regular cycles of cosmic life as related to the ritual calendar and social order.

Although specific ancient myths of an earth deity are hard to identify (Yu and Huangdi betray some traces of this kind of figure), the cosmic structure of the natural landscape of the earth is suggested by the prominence given to sacred mountains such as Tai or Kunlun (and certain gourd-shaped islands in the eastern sea) that may be taken as the Chinese equivalent to the universal idea of an *axis mundi* connecting the heaven and earth. This emphasis on what is above and below the human landscape and on the sacred lay of the land, especially on those distant and hidden places on the earth that give access to the heavens or otherworld of the ancestors, is also thematically connected with the common motif of a shamanic and initiatory journey between the heaven and earth, or to the mountains, paradise islands, and chaos regions beyond the conventional order of the middle kingdom. Traveling in space in this way symbolically represents a journey back in time to the pristine conditions of the freshly created cosmos.

Human origins. Aside from a few minor references to Nügua, who was said to have created humankind by dragging a string in some mud, most of the accounts that deal with human origins recall clan origin myths that tell of the divine creation of the founding ancestor or first man of the ruling families of the early dynasties. Most of this material has been reworked and retrospectively systematized, but a general pattern that has some affinity with a kind of virgin birth motif related to the cosmogonic image of a primal egg, rock, or gourd can be detected (e.g., the fragmented origin accounts of the Si clan of the Xia dynasty and the Zi clan of the Shang dynasty). The most elaborate mythic remnants, as recounted in the *Shi jing,* tell of the descent of the Zhou dynasty from the "abandoned one" known as Hou Ji (Lord Millet) whose mother gave birth after she had stepped into the footprint left on earth by the heavenly supreme god (Tian, Shangdi?). Fragments of this nature thematically hint at very ancient totemic beliefs. As an assertion of the divine origins and chosen status of a particular ancestral grouping of humankind they were used to support the exclusivist political claims of aristocratic privilege. In this way they represent the contextual mythic prototype for the classical theory of the *tianming* ("mandate of Heaven") that from the Zhou period on was used by the *tianzi* ("son of Heaven") to sanction the legitimacy of dynastic authority.

Rupture and fall. In Chinese tradition there is no theme of the sinful fall of humankind or the intrinsic corruption of human nature comparable to what is seen in Western monotheistic traditions, but it is recognized that humans somehow do not enjoy the kind of regular harmony and spontaneous virtue that existed in some distantly past period. There is, therefore, a typical Chinese idea of a series of falls, some of which were not as inevitable, necessary, and permanent as others. Within a cosmic context there was the necessary separation of Heaven and earth that created the space that made both natural and human life possible. However, in the course of mythic time there was also a second separation, or rupture, of the ongoing communication between the divine world of the gods and ancestors and the earthly world of humankind. The best known example of this is seen in the two ancient accounts of Zhongli (or Zhong and Li as separate figures), who cut the cord binding Heaven and earth after Shangdi's displeasure over the disruption on earth caused by troublesome barbarian peoples. The issue here seems to be a clash between two rival ritual systems associated with different clan traditions, but the underlying implication is that a separation and distinction between two different orders, divine and human or civilized and barbarian, is inevitable and necessary. Aside from the passing reference to some divine unhappiness over the licentious practice of one rebellious group of humankind, the important point is that the incident was not interpreted as an act of wrathful divine retribution.

Another expression of the idea of a ruptured linkage between heaven and earth concerns the breaking of one of the cosmic pillars (Mount Buzhou to the northwest) by the chaos monster known as Gonggong (also associated with the deluge theme, and like Hundun often identified with rebels and barbarians that threaten the virtuous order of dynastic civilization). This rupture caused the tilt of the ecliptic (i.e., the orbital plane of the moving heavenly bodies—suggesting some affinity with pan-Eurasian astronomical origin myths) and required that rivers flow to the southeast. In one extant account Nügua is presented as a female fashioning deity who repairs the earth (after the disruption caused by Gonggong?) by smelting together multicolored stones and creating new heavenly props from a turtle's legs. Again, there is an acceptance of the necessarily flawed nature of things but no real suggestion that Gonggong's blundering actions were sinful in a way that utterly precludes any human access to the divine. It is always implied that in time there are ways to repair the breach, at least temporarily.

Philosophical expressions of this theme tend to describe humankind's alienation from the Dao as an almost inevitable process of losing an original innocence or faceless spontaneity (as in the face-giving operation on emperor Hundun in the *Zhuangzi* that is equated with death); as a matter of giving up primitive social life for the artificial ways of civilization (as in the *Laozi*); or, in contrast to the Daoist position, as a forgetting of the proper rituals and virtue of civilized human intercourse (as in Confucian literature). For both Daoists and Confucians there are different salvational methods (ways of mystical, ritual, and moral wisdom that emulate the cosmic knowledge of the mythic ancestors) for returning to the conditions that originally linked humans to the Dao.

Cosmic disasters, beginning again, and cultural saviors. Worldwide mythologies concerning some great natural disaster or combat between the forces of chaos and order often allude to a kind of permanent structural tension between the divinely created world of nature that cyclically requires regenerative periods of chaotic regression and the world of human culture that is threatened by the fickleness and chaotic ambiguity of nature and the gods. Combat mythology in this sense refers to the theme of the establishment of a human cultural order after the creation of some previous natural and divine world. The secondary creation, or recreation, of the cultural order, moreover, often implies a challenge to, or usurpation of, the cosmic powers of the chthonic gods and ancestors. The agent responsible for fixing the permanent cultural order is, however, frequently depicted as an ambiguous figure: someone who is partially related to the gods and has beastly characteristics, yet at the same time, a semihuman savior who insures the renewal and continuation of the human order.

In ancient China there are muted indications of this kind of combat mythology seen in the fragmented tales of Yu and Yi, but they are never accentuated in the epically dramatic, or heroic, fashion seen in Indo-European traditions. As with the Zhongli fragments and the clan origin myths, Yu and Yi were most commonly associated with the systematized sage-king and model emperor lore that recounted the establishment and progressive manifestation of the aristocratic order of dynastic civilization. Regardless of these transformations, the overall thematic pattern of the Yu and Yi fragments strongly suggest a more universal scenario of creation and cultural genesis that is not necessarily identified with a particular civilizational order.

The deluge and Yu the Great. The references to Yu, his taming of a great flood and the definitive organization of the human world, are attested in the earliest written sources (i.e., in the oldest sections of the classical *Shu jing* and *Shi jing,* as well as in the *Mengzi* and numerous other Eastern Zhou and Han dynasty documents). In extant sources the deluge is set in the predynastic time of Yao and tells of the diluvian labors of the semi-beastial figures known as Gun and Yu (both names etymologically reveal traces of their totemic status as aquatic, reptilian, or avian animal ancestors). The unexplained occasion of the flood causes the sage emperor Yao (or the sky deity Shangdi) to charge his minister Gun with the task of controlling the wanton waters that were "swelling up to heaven." After laboring unsuccessfully for nine years, Gun was summarily executed and Shun replaced him with Yu, miraculously born after three years from the split open body of Gun (in some accounts the body had been transformed into a rock). Yu wisely did not try to employ his father's method of damming up the waters, but sought out the hidden channels in the earth and allowed the waters to drain away naturally. Yu then erected mountains, adjusted the flow of the rivers, made the earth suitable for agriculture, conquered various barbarian rebels, and divided up the landscape according to a ninefold plan. In recognition of these accomplishments, Shun established Yu as the founder of the Xia dynasty, traditionally the first civilized state in ancient China.

There are other random details that can be culled from various sources, but in general terms the story of Yu stresses not the actual flood, or its causes, but the necessary methods of ordering the human world in a way that maintains a harmonious relationship with the secret structure of the cosmos. It is said that Yu assumed the form of an animal, limped from his titanic labors (the so-called step or dance of Yu), received the sacred *Luoshu* (Luo River Writing) and *Hetu* (Yellow River Chart) cosmic diagrams, and cast the nine *ding* cauldrons; these are all symbolic details that suggest Yu's shamanic function and his use of an esoteric methodology. In this way, the theme of Yu's mastery of the techniques of the creative reordering of the world may be associated with the sacred duties of the king and emperor who was responsible for insuring the continuation of the human order. In later liturgical Daoism this same mythic theme, with its emphasis on the hidden methods of recreating the world, was assimilated into the figure and ritual of the Daoist priest.

The method of Yu, his way or *dao,* was taken as a model for the fundamental moral principle that human nature *(xing)* can only be effectively cultivated by following the inborn channels of humans' natural, or original, dispositions. In fact, the theme of Yu's cosmological methods and cosmogonic power constitutes a paradigmatic reference point for political, religious, and moral techniques designed to renew corporate social life and the human body. From this perspective, then, it may be said that the theme of Yu the Great is not just the classical mythos of the origins of dynastic civilization; rather, it most basically tells of the semidivine technological prowess of human culture. By reading the blueprint of the world correctly as a kind of cosmic engineer, and by going with the flow of things, a meaningful cultural and personal order can be created out of the experience of chaos.

The ten suns and the archer Yi. The extremely meager plot of the sun theme tells of the unexplained simultaneous appearance of ten suns during the reign of Yao, and of the resulting conditions of a life-destroying drought. Nine of the suns were shot out of the sky with arrows by the ambivalent salvational figure known as Yi (or Hou Yi; there is some confusion between a good and evil Yi). Further details given in the *Huainanzi* relate that Yi, besides shooting the suns, killed and tamed various wild beasts that were disrupting the world. In a manner akin to the labors of Yu, Yi therefore established the conditions that allowed for the flourishing of human civilization.

The theme of the ten suns and the archer Yi has, like the deluge theme, many worldwide parallels. In the context of the standarized dynastic tradition, the deluge and sun themes can be linked respectively with the Xia and Shang cultural orders in a way that suggests a fundamental antagonistic pairing, or cyclic contrast, between the primal forces of water, flood, earth, west, aquatic ancestors (Xia associations) and the forces of fire, sun, drought, heaven, east, and avian ancestors (Shang associations). There is a hint of the standardized *wuxing* cosmological system here (the five phases that were aspects of the dual cycle of *yinyang*), but this kind of emblematic symbolism also points at more archaic traditions of totemic classification related to different clan origin mythologies. Thus, there is some possibility that the ten suns theme represents a dim remnant of early clan mythology connected with the founding ancestors and ritual calendar of the Shang tradition. This kind of analysis is most appealing, but the broader structural implications of the ten suns and deluge theme should not be overlooked: that dynasties, like nature and human nature, follow a dualistic cyclic pattern, and that moments of the overaccentuated presence of any one duality must be combated to ensure the continuation and harmony of the total cycle.

Civilizational beginnings, sage-kings, and model emperors. The sun and flood myths were incorporated into the sequence of civilizational development classically associated with the sage-kings and model emperors of antiquity. There is an important thematic difference, however, between the more demiurgic salvational struggles of Yi and Yu and the relatively placid unfolding of the civilizational order. Even though they are artificially presented as bureaucrats under Yao and Shun, Yu and Yi may be said to represent cultural creators. The sage-kings and model emperors, on the other hand (and despite their original mythological identities), are more prosaic examples of what might be called civilizational transformers whose accomplishments depend to some degree on the prior establishment of a foundational cosmic landscape and cultural methodology.

In the evolving classical interpretation of the beginnings there is a tendency to incorporate increasingly remote periods of mythical time into a single process of civilizational development. Thus Confucius especially honors the foundational figures of the early Zhou period (the kings Wen and Wu, and the sage-minister Zhou Gong), but by the Han period the semistandard grouping included three sage-kings (the San Huang) and five model emperors (the Wu Di) who were held to be the direct predynastic precursors of the founders of the Xia, Shang, and Zhou dynasties. Different figures, all revealing animal traits and other mythic characteristics, were included in these cosmologically coded groupings of three and five, but one fairly typical list would designate Fu Xi, Suiren/Zhurong, and Shen Nong (the inventor of agriculture) as the San Huang; and Huangdi (the Yellow Emperor), Zhuanxu, Ku, Yao, and Shun as the Wu Di.

These figures were used to trace out a pseudo-historical pattern of cultural development and genealogical inheritance that can be said to have run from the Mesolithic (especially Fu Xi, Nügua, and Suiren, who domesticated animals, established marriage ritual, invented fire, and contributed other basic cultural technologies), to the neolithic (Shen Nong, who as the Divine Farmer invented the plow and cleared the land), down to the late Neolithic threshold of city-state civilization (the Wu Di, who are responsible for creating the ritual principles of state governance). Thus the Yellow Emperor, among his other achievements, is said to have arranged the sixty-year cycle of the calendar and to have instituted the cult of state sacrifice. It should be noted that the Yellow Emperor, as the first of the Wu Di, often assumes a paradigmatic, though ambivalent, role similar to Yu's function as a primordial cultural creator and, like Yu, the Yellow Emperor became a model for salvational techniques found in both Daoist and Confucian tradition.

The scheme of the San Huang and Wu Di is largely the result of the confucianized attempt to charter a particular vision of the cosmic regularity of the dynastic cycle and the sacral implications of aristocratic rule (the Confucian implications are especially seen in the role given to founding ministers; both Shun and Yu were said to have started their careers as virtuous bureaucrats). One of the basic structural applications of the predynastic cycle (and its dynastic extension to the rise and fall of Xia, Shang, and Zhou) is to mediate the tension surrounding the problem of political succession. The crucial issue, therefore, often concerns the conflict between a hereditary principle of rule (associated with dynastic continuity) and rule by meritorious virtue (associated with dynastic change). This structural pattern and the use of model kings and emperors as a transformative set of myths is, however, not limited to Confucian tradition. The fundamental question of the meaning of virtue *(de)* as a principle of creativity could, for example, be evaluated in different ways based on which aspects of the mythic cycle were emphasized. In this way, references to the sage-kings and model emperors are found throughout both classical and nonclassical literature of the Eastern Zhou and Han dynasties and, depending on how certain figures were treated or ignored, can be used to characterize a particular ideological position.

Returning to the beginning. The sacred history of the beginnings traced above has already indicated that in ancient China (making some exception for the Fa jia, or Legalists) the ways of cultivating human life in the present depend on the different cosmic methods of remembering and emulating the mythic models from the remote past. This refers especially to the ways or methods of returning to the Dao that are modeled on cosmogonic and cosmological notions concerning the *creatio continua* of natural and human life, and the cyclic waxing and waning of dynasties. The inner structure of all forms of existence, it seems, is mythic in nature since change is fundamentally understood as a constant series of new beginnings or sets of structural permutations, that return to the recapitulate the first processes of creation. The problem of living after the mythic age is from this perspective primarily a problem of forgetting one's mythical ancestry and continuing linkages with cosmic life. The possibility of living a creatively virtuous life, one that is in tune with the rhythm of regeneration, depends therefore on humankind's interpretive ability to detect the cosmic signs left in the world by the mythic ancestors. Living a meaningful life, it may be said, hinges on the imaginative perception of the traces of cosmic structure hidden amidst the flux of experience.

Connected with the general principle of return are various golden age or paradise themes that serve as both individual and social ideals. In the Han dynasty utopian visions of the time of the Datong (great unity) and Taiping (great peace) were common phenomena that, upon the collapse of the dynasty, became associated with a messianic and apocalyptic future. In the ancient period, however, such utopian realms were firmly located in the past and early Confucian and Daoist longings can be differentiated in terms of where the golden age is located in mythic time and how it is characterized in relation to the prevailing social order. Thus, in contrast to the Confucian nostalgia for the perfect ritual propriety of the earliest dynastic states, the early Daoists tended to stress the sacredness of an egalitarian rural society.

Another expression of the theme of return is seen in the ancient ideas of the afterlife and the destiny of the dead. By the Han dynasty, one basic aristocratic view imagined death as a kind of journey back into mythic space and time. This is most impressively and graphically illustrated by the Mawangdui funerary banners dating to the second century BCE. The iconography of this silk painting generally shows that death was understood as a kind of voyage of the dead through a mediating cosmic realm shaped like a vase (or, perhaps calabash; a possible allusion to the paradise of Kunlun Mountain or Penglai Island), accompanied by a host of mythical animal spirits and servants. The dead person's final destination was reached by entering gates that led to the celestial regions associated with the mythical imagery of the ten suns and other mythical creatures and heavenly deities. Death was seen, in other words, as a navigation of a sacred landscape that led back to the heavenly bliss of mythic time when humans, animals, and gods lived in total harmony. Finally, it may simply be noted here that the salvational possibility of "no-death" or "long life," as related to the development of immortality cults in the Han period (such as those associated with the goddess Xi Wang Mu) most often implied the use of methods that would allow for this kind of mythic journey before one's natural death.

MYTH AS THE DIVINATION OF STRUCTURE. To return to the beginning of this essay, it would appear that the *Chuci's* "Heavenly Questions" can only be answered in the spirit that they were asked: as a puzzling out of an underlying code of meaning known only through the relative shape and fit of individual bits and pieces of myths. Although most of the pieces have been lost, it can still be said that much of the fascination and significance associated with the enigma of Chinese myth is exactly that, as more of the facts of the Chinese past are accumulated and comparatively analyzed, the more it seems that the cultural configuration of those very facts depends on the forms of life imagined mythically and enacted ritually.

At the very outset of Chinese civilization, the Shang dynasty oracle bones suggest that human life was fundamentally perceived as a riddle that could only be deciphered by a method that attended to the pattern of cracks, the divine signs of hidden structure in existence, made manifest on the skeletal remains of animals. In relation to the inscribed form of both the human question and heavenly answer, emphasis was placed on a structural methodology that allowed the technically proficient to divine the holy writ that was secretly traced in the bare bones of animals from the very beginning. In ancient China, it seems, knowing the past or future was not a matter of telling a story; rather, it involved a divination of the mythical structure of meaning. If China does not offer us a heady narrative broth to feast on, it certainly provides us with bones and marrow to gnaw.

SEE ALSO Afterlife, article on Chinese Concepts; Axis Mundi; Chaos; Confucianism; Dao and De; Historiography, overview article; Huangdi; Liu An; Myth, article on Myth and History; Shangdi; Structuralism; Taiping; Tian; Xi Wang Mu; Yao and Shun; Yinyang Wuxing; Yu.

BIBLIOGRAPHY

General Studies

Allan, Sarah. *The Heir and the Sage: Dynastic Legend in Early China.* San Francisco, 1981.

Bodde, Derk. "Myths of Ancient China." In *Essays on Chinese Civilization,* edited by Charles Le Blanc and Dorothy Borei, pp. 45–84. Princeton, 1981.

Chang, Kwang-chih. *Early Chinese Civilization: Anthropological Perspectives.* Cambridge, Mass., 1976.

Chang, Kwang-chih. *Art, Myth, and Ritual: The Path to Political Authority in Ancient China.* Cambridge, Mass., 1983.

Eberhard, Wolfram. *The Local Cultures of South and East China.* Translated by Alide Eberhard. Leiden, 1968.

Girardot, N. J. "The Problem of Creation Mythology in the Study of Chinese Religion." *History of Religions* 15 (May 1976): 289–318.

Girardot, N. J. "Behaving Cosmologically in Early Daoism." In *Cosmology and Ethical Order,* edited by R. W. Lovin and Frank E. Reynolds. Chicago, 1985.

Henderson, John B. *Development and Decline of Chinese Cosmology.* New York, 1984.

Jacobson, Esther. "The Structure of Narrative in Early Chinese Pictorial Vessels." *Representations* 8 (Fall 1984): 61–83.

Kaltenmark, Max. "La naissance du monde en Chine." In his *La Naissance du monde.* Paris, 1959.

Karlgren, Bernhard. "Legends and Cults in Ancient China." *Bulletin of the Museum of Far Eastern Antiquities* 18 (1946): 199–365.

Major, John S. "Myth, Cosmology, and the Origins of Chinese Science." *Journal of Chinese Philosophy* 5 (1978): 1–20.

Maspero, Henri. "Légendes mythologiques dans le *Chou King.*" *Journal asiatique* 204 (January–March 1924): 1–100.

Mathieu, Rémi. "Introduction à l'étude de la mythologie de la Chine ancienne; Considerations théoriques et historiques." In his *Étude sur la mythologie et l'ethnologie de la Chine ancienne.* Paris, 1983.

Soymié, Michel. "China: The Struggle for Power." Translated by Patricia Beardsworth. In *Larousse World Mythology,* edited by Pierre Grimal, pp. 271–292. New York, 1965.

Studies on Particular Thematic Topics

Allan, Sarah. "Sons of Suns: Myth and Totemism in Early China." *Bulletin of the School of Oriental and African Studies* 44 (1981): 290–326.

Bauer, Wolfgang. *China and the Search for Happiness: Recurring Themes in Four Thousand Years of Chinese Cultural History.* Translated by Michael Shaw. New York, 1976.

Boltz, William G. "Kung-kung and the Flood: Reverse Euhemerism in the *Yao tien.*" *T'oung pao* 67 (1981): 141–153.

Eliade, Mircea. *Ordeal by Labyrinth: Conversations with Claude-Henri Rocquet: with an Essay on Brancusi and Mythology.* Translated by Derek Coltman. Chicago, 1982.

Girardot, N. J. "Myth and Meaning in Early Taoism." Berkeley, 1983.

Graham, A. C. "The *Nung-chia* 'School of the Tillers' and the Origins of Peasant Utopianism in China." *Bulletin of the School of Oriental and African Studies* 42 (1979): 66–100.

Hawkes, David. *Ch'u Tz'u: The Songs of the South.* Oxford, 1959.

Levi, Jean. "Le mythe de l'âge d'or et les théories de l'évolution en Chine ancienne." *L'homme* 17 (January–March 1973): 73–103.

Loewe, Michael. *Ways to Paradise: The Chinese Quest for Immortality.* London, 1979.

Mathieu, Rémi. *Le Mu tianzi zhuan: Traduction annotée, étude critique.* Paris, 1978.

Plaks, Andrew H. *Archetype and Allegory in the Dream of the Red Chamber.* Princeton, 1976.

Schneider, Laurence A. *A Madman of Ch'u: The Chinese Myth of Loyalty and Dissent.* Berkeley, 1980.

New Sources

Allan, Sarah. *The Shape of the Turtle: Myth, Art, and Cosmos in Early China.* Albany, 1991.

Birrell, Anne. *Chinese Mythology: An Introduction.* Baltimore, 1993.

Birrell, Anne. "Studies on Chinese Myth since 1970: An Appraisal." *History of Religions* 33 (1994): 380–393 and 34 (1994): 70–94.

Birrell, Anne. "James Legge and the Chinese Mythological Tradition." *History of Religions* 38 (1999): 331–353.

Cahill, Suzanne. "The Goddess, the Emperor, and the Adept: The Queen Mother of the West as Bestower of Legitimacy and Immortality." In *Goddesses Who Rule,* edited by Elisabeth Benard and Beverly Moon, pp. 197–214. New York, 2000.

Hansen, Valerie. "The Law of the Spirits." In *Religions of China in Practice,* edited by Donald S. Lopez Jr., pp. 284–292. Princeton, 1996.

Henricks, Robert G. "On the Whereabouts and Identity of the Place Called 'K'ung-Sang' (Hollow Mulberry) in Early Chinese Mythology." *Bulletin of the School of Oriental & African Studies* 58, no. 1 (1995): 69–90.

Lai, Whalen. "Recent PRC Scholarship on Chinese Myths." *Asian Folklore Studies* 53, no. 1 (1994):151–161.

Lai, Whalen. "Unmasking the Filial Sage-King Shun: Oedipus at Anyang." *History of Religions* 35 (1995): 163–184.

Nyitray, Vivian Lee. "Becoming the Empress of Heaven: The Life and Bureaucratic Career of Mazu." In *Goddesses Who Rule,* edited by Elisabeth Benard and Beverly Moon, pp. 165–180. New York, 2000.

NORMAN J. GIRARDOT (1987)
Revised Bibliography

CHINESE RELIGION: HISTORY OF STUDY

The study of Chinese religion is connected intimately with the overall history of Western fascination with Chinese tradition. In the most obvious sense, the important historical role of Christian missionaries in China testifies to a pronounced and not always strictly apologetic interest in the subject of non-Christian forms of belief and practice. The question of the nature and significance of Chinese religion has also had a special (and at times contradictory) prominence in the rise of Western secular scholarship. Thus the early awareness of and debate over the meaning of Chinese and Asian traditions—especially concerning the comparative similitude of "other" cultural manifestations of religion—can be associated with both missionary sentiment and the intellectual revolution in Western thought during the Enlightenment.

In the case of China, these developments took a unique turn. The eighteenth-century skeptical spirit toward "superstitious" and "idolatrous" forms of religion found distinct comfort in the image (conveyed by the Jesuits) of a Confucian China politically ministered to by a special class of moral philosophers who condemned the "degeneracy" and "superstition" of Buddhism, Daoism, and popular religion. China was often seen by Voltaire and other Enlightenment thinkers as a special exception to the principle that religious irrationality and priestcraft ruled the history of all major civilizations. This imaginary vision of the classical purity of China is strongly reflected in the history of Sinology and is responsible for traditional difficulties in fully appreciating the rich history of Chinese religious experience.

Although the study of Chinese religion has been broadly intertwined with Western intellectual and cultural history since the seventeenth and eighteenth centuries, this discussion will focus only on the history of certain key figures and movements that have specifically contributed to the scholarly study of Chinese religions. In this regard Chinese religions will be taken to mean the three literate traditions known as Confucianism, Daoism, and Buddhism (and their interactions); the common body of beliefs and practices that characterize Chinese communities and are sometimes referred to as popular religion; the syncretic sectarian movements of late imperial China, the ancestral cult, and various associated thematic issues, such as archaic religion, ritual, myth, and cosmological symbolism, and related topics of comparative method and interpretation. But this straightforward listing of topics must be tempered with the understanding that the history of the study of Chinese religions has always involved the definitional ambiguities associated with the categories of religion, salvation, and the sacred (for example, the significance of such terms as Dao, Tian, and Shangdi). Further difficulties concern the porous interrelationships of different literate traditions (thus the problematic nature of the common "three religions" rubric) and the diffuse functional relation between Chinese religions and social and familial life. These considerations have often resulted in overly facile assertions about the syncretic and eclectic nature of Chinese religions or about the fundamental hierarchical dichotomy between "great" traditions (that is, aristocratic, civic, literate, orthodox, and those that are usually equated with state Confucianism) and "little" rituals (folk, popular, oral, nonorthodox, and those practices associated with regional sectarian religions).

The history of the study of Chinese religions has therefore contributed to Western and East Asian intellectual history, Christian missionary tradition, and the emergence of comparative religion and Sinology as distinct academic disciplines. Given this complex historical and intellectual legacy, it will be necessary to condense and organize the following discussion under three general phases of development: (1) seventeenth- and eighteenth-century contributions by Jesuit missionaries and the French Enlightenment roots of academic Sinology, (2) European Orientalism and Protestant missionary scholarship in the nineteenth century, and (3) the emergence of the interdisciplinary study of Chinese religions as an academic area in the twentieth century.

By way of setting the stage for the coming of the Jesuit mission at the end of the sixteenth century, it is sufficient to recognize that the medieval European image of China was mythically associated with legends telling of its fantastic, monstrous, or paradisiacal nature. Such a vision of the "marvels of the East" is most characteristically observed in the semifictitious fourteenth-century work known as the *Travels of Sir John Mandeville*. At about this same time more realistic firsthand accounts of religions in Mongolian-ruled Cathay appeared in the travel reports of early Franciscan missionaries and most notably in Marco Polo's *Description of the World.* But it was not until the great Portuguese trade efforts of the sixteenth century that detailed reports about China and Japan became available in Europe. This new wealth of knowledge is especially exemplified by the widely distributed *Historia . . . del gran Reyno de la China* (1585), written and compiled by the Spanish Augustinian Juan González de Mendoza. This work's grudging concern with the hidden similitude of Chinese religion in relation to the "holy, sacred, and Christian religion" typifies a kind of interpretive strategy that was to be reflected in different ways throughout the centuries of Western intercourse with China.

SEVENTEENTH AND EIGHTEENTH CENTURIES. In the same decade that Mendoza's work was published, Matteo Ricci (1552–1610), an Italian Jesuit priest, arrived in the China of the late Ming dynasty and, drawing upon the tradition of Jesuit missions to Asia (already established by Francis Xavier and Alessandro Valignano), inaugurated a new era in the Western understanding of Chinese civilization. Indeed Ricci may be considered not only the founding father of Sinology as the specialized, linguistically proficient study of China but also the first great interpreter of Chinese religions. The work fostered by Ricci was carried on and enriched by a long line of distinguished Jesuit scholars whose efforts span the early seventeenth century and extend to the second period of the French Jesuit mission at the end of the seventeenth century and into the eighteenth century. The pioneering translations of the Chinese classics and the detailed observations of Chinese life and religion produced by these indefatigable missionary-scholars gave rise to the European vogue of chinoiserie and, even more profoundly, influenced the intellectual and religious ferment of the Enlightenment, especially in France and Germany.

Ricci's studied openness to Chinese tradition was not as plainly objective as it seemed, however, because the Jesuits tended to adopt the intellectual biases as well as the dress and etiquette of China's lettered class, the Confucian scholars and bureaucrats. These men promulgated a canon of classical writings that expressly excluded Buddhist, Daoist, and other heterodox points of view. To study Chinese tradition therefore meant first and foremost to peruse the classics, modeled upon the neo-Confucian vision of the unity of Chinese civilization and on Zhu Xi's methods of commentarial exegesis. This mandarin perspective meshed with Ricci's own education in a Renaissance and Counter-Reformation tradition of Christian humanism that honored the philosophical and moral worth of classical Greek thought.

In the spirit of Mendoza's concern for similitude, Ricci examined the classics and found that ancient China shared a special sympathy with Christianity because of its apparent reverence for the one God, called Shangdi (ruler, lord on high, supreme ruler) or Tian (heaven). For Ricci, these appellations revealed the remnants of an archaic tradition of monotheistic belief and practice that had been lost, it seemed, under the baleful influence of Buddhist and Daoist idolatry. To be successful in China therefore, Christianity needed only to purify the false pantheistic accretions of latter-day Confucianism and to complete and fulfill the literati's philosophical appreciation of the natural law with the missionaries' gift of divine revelation.

Most of the Jesuit commentators tended to share Ricci's accommodationist methodology, but his sympathetic attitude toward Confucianism, the classics, and ancestral ritual was not universally accepted by all Jesuits (see, for example, Niccolo Longobardo's *Traité sur quelques points de la religion des Chinois,* 1701, which stressed the materialistic atheism of neo-Confucian thought) or by the other, ecclesiastically contentious orders of Catholic missionaries. In fact issues of missionary policy toward Chinese religions, including the "term question"—whether Shangdi (Tian) could be considered authentically theistic—gave rise to the embittered "rites controversy," which led eventually to the papal suppression of the Jesuit order in 1773. The rites controversy can also be associated in many ways with the growing European debate over the definitional or essential nature of religion as reflected, for example, in the theory of deism as a "natural religion" of reason. Thus the whole rites episode and its related intellectual environment can help explain why Sinologists have often found the Chinese to be less intrinsically religious than other traditions.

A second phase in the crystallization of a self-conscious Sinological tradition in the West is seen in the French Jesuit mission sent to China toward the end of the seventeenth century under the royal consent of Louis XIV. This effort continued into the "enlightened" climate of the eighteenth century and was favored by the newly tolerant rule of the Manchu emperor of the Kangxi period during the early Qing dynasty. Like the remarkable clerics of the first part of the seventeenth century, this new wave of missionaries included a roster of truly accomplished scholars who focused on Confucian classical tradition in the broad humanistic spirit of Ricci. These scholar-priests took special care to communicate the fruits of their Sinological labor back to Europe—for example, the impressive translations of the classics by Antoine Glaubil and the still useful compilations of miscellaneous translations and descriptive material about Chinese life and letters known as the *Lettres édifiantes et curieuses* (1703–1776) and the *Mémoires concernant l'histoire, les sciences, les arts, les mœurs, les usages, etc., des chinois* (1776–1814).

The interpretive perspective of the works found in the *Lettres* and *Mémoires* often reflected the old quest for hidden similitude so that, for example, J.-J. Amiot and J.-H. Prémare argued that chapter 14 of the *Laozi* revealed a phonetically encoded reference to Jehovah. More substantial than the occult presence of Jehovah in early Daoist texts, though very much related as an interpretive genre, was the so-called Figurist movement associated with Joachim Bouvet, J.-F. Foucquet, and Prémare. Inspired by the biblical tradition of allegorical interpretation, the Figurist movement took Ricci's approach to the Chinese classics to the extreme; it tried to show how the ancient Chinese texts disclosed not only hidden vestiges of monotheism and Trinitarian belief but also remnants of ancient Hebrew law and, prefiguring the New Testament, allusions to an incarnate future redeemer.

In Paris during this same period academics took the first steps in the direction of a secular tradition of professional Sinological scholarship. Various scholars of the Académie des Inscriptions et Belles-Lettres, such as Nicolas Fréret (1688–1749), the Arabist Étienne Fourmont (1683–1745), and the Syriac specialist Joseph de Guignes (1721–1800), turned their attention from the Near East to the Far East. Making use of the communications coming from the Jesuits—and aided by Arcade Hoang, a native Chinese who had been sent to Paris for training as a priest—these academicians sought to catalog, edit, publish, and sometimes plagiarize the rapidly accumulating materials coming from China. Other more original efforts concerning religion include in particular de Guignes's studies on the Indian origins of Buddhism based on his study of Chinese sources. Other works by de Guignes, such as his treatise entitled *Observations sur quelques points concernant la religion et la philosophie des égyptiens et des chinois* (1780), represented only a secularized version of the Jesuit fathers' Figurist view and to some degree anticipated the nineteenth-century pan-Babylonian diffusionists.

NINETEENTH CENTURY. In the face of the West's growing confidence in its imperial destiny, racial superiority, and dynamic progress, the old infatuation with Confucian China gave way to a more negative, and at times contemptuous, conviction that Chinese culture was inherently stagnant. This belief culminated philosophically in the mid- to late nineteenth century with the German philosopher G. W. F. Hegel's idea of the retarded spiritual development of Confucianism in particular and of Chinese civilization in general as well as with Leopold von Ranke's conclusion that China represented a realm of the "eternal standstill." This more negative evaluation of China, however, was only a special instance of a broader, antipodal Orientalist mode of nineteenth-century scholarship that tended to view all Near and Far Eastern cultures as manifestations of monolithic and backward entity: the Orient, the East, or Asia.

The subject of Oriental religions was particularly important in Western scholarship because it seemed to give access to the underlying and essentially desiccated "national spirit," or *Volksgeist,* of other cultures. The study of "other" religions, whether Asian or primitive, became central to many new nineteenth-century humanistic sciences, such as folklore studies, comparative philology, sociology, and anthropology, as well as in other comparative historical pursuits, such as *Religionswissenschaft.* But the specific study of Chinese religions was not as relevant to these endeavors as was the study—influenced by pervasive currents of German romanticism—of the Indo-European traditions that seemed to share a common linguistic heritage with the West. In this way the "mystery" and "perennial philosophy" of Indian and "Aryan" religion (and the resultant stereotype of Eastern mysticism, typically identified with Buddhism and Upaniṣadic Hinduism) were often found more stimulating than what the American philosopher Ralph Waldo Emerson called the arid moralism and "doleful monotony" of Confucian China.

French academic scholarship. The rapid establishment of academic Sinology in France came about as the direct inheritance of the Jesuit tradition and the embryonic eighteenth-century Parisian school of Sinological Orientalism. The fruition of these developments took place in 1814 with the installation of Abel Rémusat (1788–1832) in the first European chair of "langues et littératures chinoises et tartares-mandchoues" at the Collège de France and with the founding in 1822 of the Société Asiatique. An autodidact of the Chinese written language, Rémusat (like almost all of the French Sinologists until Chavannes) was wholly dependent on *livresque* scholarship. Within the sanctuary of his library, however, Rémusat displayed multifaceted interests and can take credit for being the first academic Sinologist to pay some serious though misguided attention to the nature and significance of *Laozi* and early Daoism. In addition Rémusat should be remembered for his translation and study of Chinese sources dealing with Buddhist history outside of China.

Rémusat and de Guignes's oblique concern for Chinese sources as they illuminated Buddhist origins became the general approach among French Sinologists and tended to prevent a full analysis of Chinese Buddhism on its own terms. Another factor that contributed to the neglect of East Asian Buddhism was the increasing emphasis later in the nineteenth century on the Pali canon. The Pali scriptures were held to be the original expression of authentic Buddhist tradition and were considered moral and philosophical, in contrast to the idolatrous degeneracy of the sūtra literature and religious practices of the Mahāyāna school. In like manner the philosophical mysticism and moral purity of the classical Daoist texts were generally preferred to what were viewed as the corrupt religious superstition and ritual excess of later Daoism. This kind of overemphasis on the earliest Daoist texts and the almost total neglect of the sectarian religious traditions of later Daoism typified the field of Daoist scholarship until the late twentieth century.

Several other prominent figures in Paris published on Chinese philosophy and religion during the first part of the nineteenth century (e.g., Léon de Rosny, the pioneer Japanologist who also wrote on Chinese religions), but Jean-Pierre Guillaume Pauthier (1801–1873) and Stanislas Julien (1797–1873) may be singled out as having been especially influential in the academic discourse of the period. Pauthier, the less-substantial scholar of the two, commands notice for his voluminous and popular works. His controversial partial "translation" of the *Laozi (Daodejing)* in 1838 led to Julien's more careful translation and commentary in 1841; his publication of *Les livres sacrés de l'orient* (1852) anticipates F. Max Müller's monumental series *Sacred Books of the East.*

Stanislas Julien, the inheritor of Rémusat's chair at the Collège de France, epitomized the best kind of philologically oriented scholarship of the day. He was moreover a tireless and combative promoter of academic Sinology throughout Europe and through the work of his students influenced several generations of European scholarship. Much of Julien's work concerned Chinese religion and philosophy. While maintaining the traditional exegetical interest in classical Confucianism, he also produced the first philogically competent translation of the *Laozi* and a detailed study of the Song dynasty *Taishang ganying pian* (The Most High's text of actions and response), a tract on popular morality. In keeping with the interests of the French tradition, Julien also published important studies on the celebrated seventh-century Buddhist pilgrim Xuanzang and on the philological principles used in the transcription of Sanskrit Buddhist terms from Chinese texts.

Anglo-American missionary scholarship. In comparison with French and continental scholarship (in addition to the French scholars, J. H. Plath, August Pfizmaier, Gustave Schlegel, and Charles-Joseph De Harlez should be noted), English tradition generally emphasized the gifted amateur over the professional pedant and tended to display a singular listlessness with respect to Sinological scholarship. By the mid–nineteenth century, however, the best and most extensive scholarly work was being done along the coast of China by a sedulous group of British and American Protestant missionaries. As a part of their evangelical faith and by taking full advantage of their direct exposure to the living Chinese tradition, the missionary scholars made the careful study of Chinese language and culture a significant and sometimes overriding aspect of their work. To bring the gospel to China—understood as the "land of Sinim" (*Is.* 49:12)—was to them most of all a divine calling that had been recorded prophetically in the Old Testament. The diligence of these missionaries cannot be questioned, but it should be noted that the Protestant evangelical theology was most often premised on a Calvinist view of the essentially depraved nature of pagan nations and religions. This view differed significantly from the accommodationist perspective and humanistic sympathy of the Jesuits.

The dominant passion of the Anglo-American missionaries, from Robert Morrison in 1807 until those at the end of the century, was to make the one and only true classic, the Bible, available in Chinese translation. To this end an incredible amount of missionary scholarship was devoted to producing a definitive interdenominational edition of the Scriptures. These labors had important repercussions because the need to find equivalent Chinese religious terms and concepts for an accurate and intelligible translation of the Scriptures led to broad investigations of Chinese religious tradition. In the most pointed sense such questions led to the heated debate known as the term question.

Like the earlier Jesuit controversy, the term question revolved around the problem of whether the classically sanctioned terms *Shangdi* and *Tian* were appropriate for expressing the true meaning of the creator God in the Bible. Despite the rancor, this controversy did have the virtue of forcing the combatants to argue etymology and semantics on the basis of Chinese sources and, in the case of the more liberal faction, to invoke fashionable nineteenth-century philological and comparative theories linking linguistic and cultural development. Thus a series of curious diffusionist works that argued for the Mesopotamian origins of Chinese civilization—a Babylonian variation on de Guignes's old Egyptian theories—appeared during the last part of the nineteenth century.

More important than these quaint examples of early Orientalist license were the general attitude and work of the liberal faction of missionary scholars, a group whose intellectual breadth was especially manifested in such popular China coast periodicals as the *Chinese Respository,* the *Chinese Recorder,* and the *China Review.* Many of the leading figures in this group (such as Walter Medhurst, S. Wells Williams, W. A. P. Martin, John Chalmers, Ernst Eitel, and Joseph Edkins) produced not only responsible scholarship about general aspects of Chinese tradition but also haphazardly objective appraisals of Chinese religions. Especially noteworthy in this regard are Eitel's studies on Buddhism and the popular geomantic art of *feng-shui* and Edkins's influential accounts of the general nature of Chinese religions, his studies on the *Yi jing,* and his various writings on Chinese Buddhism.

The greatest scholarly figure among the missionaries was the Scottish Congregationalist James Legge (1815–1897). Best known for the *Chinese Classics* (1893–1895), his massive (five volumes) and still-standard translations, with copious notes based on traditional neo-Confucian commentaries, Legge is the Protestant missionary equivalent of Ricci and the scholarly equal of Julien. Starting out as a conventionally pious missionary with a talent for languages and rigorous habits of study, Legge became embroiled in the term question in the 1850s, about the same time he decided to embark on his translation project. It was the combination of these two factors—the bitter recriminations engendered by the term debate and his growing Riccian respect for Confucius and the classics—that progressively alienated Legge from his more parochial colleagues in the mission field and caused him by the 1860s to redefine his vocation primarily in scholarly terms.

After assuming the first British chair of Chinese at Oxford University in 1876 and accepting Max Müller's commission to undertake the Chinese volumes for the *Sacred Books of the East* series (1879–1904), Legge produced translations of various Confucian classics, including a controversial rendition of the *Yi jing.* As a new and surprisingly congenial venture for him, he translated the *Laozi* and *Zhuangzi,* together with several short sectarian works. Like the extensive prolegomena to his Confucian translations, Legge's long introduction to the Daoist volumes is a valuable overview of classical Daoist studies up to his time (summarizing the work of Julien, John Chalmers, F. H. Balfour, and Herbert Giles). Legge also wrote a rather desultory popular overview of Chinese religions and, in emulation of French scholarship, produced a translation and study bearing on the travels of the Buddhist Faxian. But Buddhist studies were never even a minor vocation for Legge; in this area one must turn to the influential work of Edkins and Eitel as well as to the relatively more sympathetic studies of Samuel Beal and Timothy Richard.

Jesuit and other amateur scholarship. The nineteenth century is the great age of the Protestant apostolate to China, but after the reconstitution of the Jesuit order in 1814, a renewed Jesuit mission, starting in 1842, again made substantial contributions to the study of Chinese religions. Commendable in this regard are the copious studies found in the *Variétés sinologiques* (established in 1892), which revived the old encyclopedic spirit of the *Mémoires.* Individually important for their emphasis on Chinese philosophy and religion were three outstanding Jesuit scholars: Séraphin Couvreur (1835–1919), Léon Wieger (1856–1933), and Henri Doré (1859–1931). Couvreur and Wieger produced important scholarly translations and studies concerning the classics, Daoism, and Buddhism; Henri Doré is primarily remembered for his eighteen-volume *Recherches sur les superstitions en Chine* (1911–1938). This was a copious though not always representative descriptive handbook on multifarious popular "superstitions" current at the end of the Qing dynasty. The good father, it should be noted, seems to have partly cribbed his findings from the work of the Chinese Jesuit priest Pierre Hoang (Huang Bailu).

Doré's work reflects the fact that, toward the end of the nineteenth century, popular religious tradition was at last receiving some extensive if often bemused attention. Representing the earliest ethnographic and folkloric investigation of Qing regional religion, mythology, and ancestral ritual were several outstanding works by Anglo-American and European amateur scholars (Justus Doolittle, N. B. Dennys, J. Dyer Ball, and Arthur H. Smith) who lived in Chinese coastal cities. The most significant figure who can be loosely identified with this scholarly trend is the Dutchman J. J. M. de Groot (1854–1921). After a year in the field preparing for a career as a government interpreter, he published an observant analysis of the seasonal round of popular religious festivals in Amoy (*Les fêtes annuellement célébrées à Emoui: Étude concernant la religion populaire des Chinois,* 1886). De Groot is most famous, however, for his incomplete, six-volume magisterial synthesis titled *The Religious System of China* (1892–1910), which moved away from popular religion to a consideration of classical sources and the ancient substratum of all later forms of Chinese religion. This work was intemperate in tone and essentially sought to debunk what de

Groot had come to regard as the retarded pretensions of the elite tradition (see also his *Sectarianism and Religious Persecution in China,* 2 vols., 1903–1904). However, de Groot's idea of the *universismus* (or the underlying archaic unity of elite and popular manifestations of Chinese religion, especially popular Daoism) represented an important yet mostly ignored methodological counterpoint to the artificial "three religions" rubric of classically inspired Sinology.

TWENTIETH CENTURY. The beginning of the twentieth century saw the passing of the old apologetic missionary movement, which, as a reaction to internal disillusionment and external Chinese antagonism, had moved away from an interest in Chinese religion and pure scholarship. Within academic circles French scholarship continued as the premier Western Sinological tradition, although important work was also done by other European, Russian, and American scholars as well as by Japanese and Chinese scholars who, in the modernizing spirit of Western critical analysis, had transformed the conservative traditions of Confucian classical exegesis.

Early twentieth-century French Sinology. Édouard Chavannes (1865–1918) was the first to demonstrate the technical by combining amazingly encyclopedic interests with both philological rigor and humanistic sensitivity. More so than ever before Chavannes made use of native Chinese textual scholarship and emphasized the importance of linguistic and anthropological field experience in Asia (facilitated by the École Française d'Extrême-Orient, founded in Hanoi at the beginning of the century). Chavannes is particularly remembered for *Mémoires historiques de Se Ma Tsien* (1895–1905), his erudite partial translation of Sima Qian's *Shiji.* The elaborate annotations to this five-volume translation often constitute miniature dissertations on multifarious issues concerning ancient Chinese religion and testify to Chavannes's belief in the importance of religion to an understanding of early China. This belief is also seen in his work on the cultic foundations of archaic religion, *Le dieu du sol dans la Chine antique* (1910), and on the popular religious traditions associated with the sacred mountain Tai. Later works on religion included several studies of Buddhism, Buddhist folklore, and during his last years Daoist ritual.

The work of Chavannes's colleague and collaborator Sylvain Lévi (1863–1935) along with the even more impressive contributions of the Belgian scholar Louis de La Vallée Poussin (1869–1938) marked the emergence of a Franco-Belgian school of Buddhology. Concerned with the overall cultural context of Buddhist history, the school demanded philological training in all of the requisite canonical languages (Sanskrit, Pali, Tibetan, and Chinese). Along with its emphasis on the non-Pali Mahāyāna texts and commentaries associated with the East Asian tradition, the Franco-Belgian school distinguished itself from German and English scholarship by characteristically stressing the broad philosophical implications of Buddhist thought.

Cast in the mold of Chavannes but possessing even greater linguistic facility, bibliographical erudition, and breadth of interests was the peripatetic polymath Paul Pelliot (1878–1945). More intently than any of the other scholars of the period, Pelliot took as his mission the social, religious, and intellectual interrelationships of all of the Asian cultures—especially the rich historical interconnections between Central and East Asian traditions. Given this versatility, Pelliot produced a diverse stream of articles and reviews, many of which dealt with aspects of Chinese religious history that often broke with the old classical fixation. One of the most celebrated of Pelliot's accomplishments was his participation in the exploration and appropriation of the Dunhuang manuscripts during the years from 1907 to 1911. In terms of importance for understanding Chinese history and religion, the discovery of a cache of thousands of fragmented Buddhist texts (along with some rare Daoist and Confucian texts) dating from the fifth to the tenth centuries is comparable only to the archaeological recovery of the Shang dynasty in the 1920s and 1930s and the discovery of the Mawangdui burial deposit of early Han dynasty texts and artifacts in the 1970s.

Following in the grand tradition of Chavannes and Pelliot but making more significant methodological contributions to the study of Chinese religions were Marcel Granet (1884–1940) and Henri Maspero (1883–1945). Granet was the more methodologically innovative of the two in that his approach was couched within a broad sociological framework that often lent itself to venturesome speculation. From this perspective Granet, making use of the broadest assortment of textual materials from differing periods, attempted to reconstruct the social and religious life of ancient feudal China. Religious data of the most diverse sort, especially information relating to the archaic folk tradition, was crucial for Granet's understanding of Chinese civilization and resulted in a series of brilliant and sometimes overly intuitive interconnected studies on the cultic and folkloric implications of the *Shi jing* (Book of poetry), on the mythic and ritual structures at the heart of the feudal tradition of the Chou period, and on the overall religious and intellectual system (*La religion des Chinois,* 1922; and *La pensée chinoise,* 1934).

Maspero shared Granet's passion for a synthetic understanding of Chinese history and wrote with great technical mastery about a varied array of topics. Especially noteworthy for its methodological implications is Maspero's long monograph "Légendes mythologiques dans le 'Chou king'" in the *Journal asiatique* (1924). By making use of ethnographic data from Tai tribes to reconstruct ancient Chinese mythology and religion only partially preserved in early Chinese literature, Maspero showed that the classical "history" of the *Shu-jing* (Book of history) was fundamentally informed by myth and ritual themes. After 1926 Maspero began to explore the largely untapped history and meaning of religious Daoism. Anticipating and to some degree inspiring the broad interest in the overall Daoist tradition that would emerge in the

1960s, Maspero's work surveyed various aspects of sectarian Daoism and generally argued for a continuity between the mysticism of the early Daoist classics and the esoteric practices of the later religious tradition.

Continental and British scholarship before World War II. Besides the French contributions there were significant works by Scandinavian scholars (such as J. G. Andersson, M. W. de Visser, and Bernhard Karlgren) and by German scholars (such as Otto Franke, Adolph Forke, Bruno Schindler, August Conrady, Ernst Boerschmann, Eduard Erkes, and Carl Hentze). By far the greatest of these scholars was Karlgren, who is justly renowned for his work on the phonological development of the Chinese language as well as for his studies of archaic bronze iconography; also important was his long article "Legends and Cults in Ancient China" in the *Bulletin of the Museum of Far Eastern Antiquities* (1946). This article established strict historical criteria for the determination of authentic archaic mythology. In pointed contrast to Karlgren's approach was the work of Erkes and Hentze, which showed the impact of various comparativist schools of German anthropology. The most exaggerated and controversial example of the German influence is found in the work of Hentze. Based on his diffusionist comparisons with primitive cultures and early Mesoamerican civilizations, Hentze found an elaborate religious system of lunar symbolism in the zoomorphic and geometric glyphs on the bronze vessels of the Shang dynasty. Within German circles special mention must also be made of Max Weber and Richard Wilhelm. As a non-Sinologist, Weber admittedly based his work on China (see his *The Religion of China: Confucianism and Taoism,* translated by Hans H. Gerth, 1951) on secondhand information and was often ignored by specialists; nevertheless this work demonstrated the relevance of a comparative sociological method for understanding Chinese religions. The Sinologist Richard Wilhelm produced a number of influential studies and translations concerning classical philosophy and religion, but he is best known for his "scriptural" translation of the divinatory *Yi jing.* Through the enthusiastic patronage of Carl Jung, this work achieved a broad cultural following in Europe and North America during the 1960s and 1970s.

In England Legge's classically staid ruminations largely prevailed, although the works of William Soothill, L. C. Hopkins, Perceval Yetts, Herbert A. Giles, and Lionel Giles represent partial exceptions to the rule. It was really not until the maverick genius of Arthur Waley emerged that British scholarship rose above mere academic competence. Early American scholarship also tended to reflect the amateurish character and methodological narrowness of English Sinology. Outstanding, however, was the pioneering work on Daoist alchemy by the historian of science Tenney L. Davis and the anthropological studies of Chinese local culture and religion by Daniel Kulp and David Crockett Graham. Finally, Friedrich Hirth, Berthold Laufer, and Paul Carus should be mentioned as immigrant scholars whose work frequently dealt with religious topics. The most important of these figures was Laufer, whose erudition and synthetic abilities rivaled those of the French masters. His studies on ancient Chinese religion (e.g., *Jade: A Study in Chinese Archaeology and Religion,* 1912), which made brilliant use of comparative linguistics, archaeology, and ethnography are still valuable. In more of an ephemeral vein was the work of Paul Carus, who, besides bringing the famous Zen Buddhist scholar D. T. Suzuki to the United States, wrote a number of semipopular books on Daoism and Buddhism.

Prewar Japanese scholarship. In Japan the adoption of Western scholarly methods progressed more rapidly than in China. By the early Meiji period at the end of the nineteenth century the old Kangaku School of neo-Confucian scholarship had given way to various intellectual movements that emphasized a newly critical approach to classical Chinese civilization and its relation to Japanese tradition. A nationalistic cast often colored these fledgling adaptations of Western historiography, often combined with an element of Eastern Orientalism that typically relegated Chinese and Japanese religions to the margins of the historical process. At the same time Japanese philological and bibliographical mastery of Chinese sources and the newly engendered passion for a universal understanding of China independent of orthodox dynastic views established the foundations for a truly critical historiographical and social scientific appraisal of Chinese religions.

During the first few decades of the twentieth century Japanese works devoted to religious issues were generally few in number. Blandly bibliographical and descriptive in approach, they were usually confined to compartmentalized studies of textual filiation or to restricted sectarian aspects of Buddhist and Daoist history (particularly valuable were the descriptive surveys of Chinese and aboriginal religions on Taiwan conducted during the Japanese occupation). But by the 1920s and 1930s Japanese scholarship, while maintaining its superior talent for critical textual analysis, manifested more of a willingness to study the history of religions as an integral aspect of Chinese sociopolitical history. This new interpretive climate was signaled by the founding in 1936 of the Japanese Society for Historical Research on Chinese Buddhism, which brought together scholars interested in the history of Buddhism and Daoism as related to the larger institutional framework of Chinese tradition.

During this period Japanese scholars, especially in the area of Buddhology, started to engage in cooperative research, as is exemplified by the four-volume *Hôbôgirin* (1929–1931), the joint French-Japanese Buddhist encyclopedia project edited by Paul Demiéville under the supervision of Sylvain Lévi and Takakusu Junjiro. Another factor, which paralleled related developments in China, was the rise of the Japanese school of folklore studies under the tutelage of Yanagita Kunio. Concerned with anthropological and sociological methods of comparison that in this period often reflected German *Kulturkreiselehre* diffusionism, it is the Japanese folkloristic tradition of scholarship that constituted the foundation of the important Japanese participation, after World War II, in the history of religions as an international academic discipline of study.

Prewar Chinese scholarship. Given the greater degree of instability in Chinese political life, it is not surprising that a coherent, Western-style scholarship at first flourished more successfully in Japan than in China. The missionary experience had left many Chinese intellectuals acutely antagonistic toward the relevance of religion, whether Christian or traditional, in Chinese history; this attitude, coupled with the classical Confucian aloofness toward the "spirits" and the more modern secular implications of Western scholarly methods, resulted in a situation that was hardly conducive to the dispassionate study of Chinese religions. The eventual triumph of an officially atheistic, Marxist orthodoxy tended only to reinforce this prejudicial approach to the history of native religions.

In addition to such well-known figures as Liang Qichao and Hu Shi, who were imbued with Western notions of social Darwinism, a number of other prominent scholars were influenced by modern methodologies and made lasting, although sometimes rather indirect and polemical, contributions to the academic study of Chinese religions. Perhaps most important in terms of his iconoclastic impact on traditional Chinese historiography was Gu Jiegang. Gu was identified with the so-called Doubting Antiquity movement of the 1920s and 1930s, which produced the seven-volume *Gushi bian* (Critiques of ancient history, 1926–1941). This work signaled the end of the Confucian classical paradigm in historical and textual scholarship and remains in the early twenty-first century a storehouse of miscellaneous materials pertinent to the study of Chinese religion, mythology, and folk tradition. Along with articles and monographs published by the *Yenching Journal of Chinese Studies* and other periodicals influenced by Western social science, *Gushi bian* definitively established the relevance of ancient Chinese mythology and religion to an understanding of the foundations of the very classical tradition that denied them. In addition to his concern with ancient history, Gu also became involved in the analysis of modern popular tradition and religion through his relationship with the Folklore Studies movement, which appeared in South China in the late 1920s. Although its motivations were often more political than scholarly in nature, this loose group of scholars produced the first substantial scholarly collections of Chinese folk tales and songs and, drawing upon Arnold van Gennep's Durkheimian *Le Folklore* (1924), established the value of a folkloristic theory of culture for Chinese tradition.

Postwar to the present. The postwar years witnessed the growing dominance of social scientific methodologies and the establishment of specialized academic disciplines, departments, and area studies—especially in American universities. As a result of these developments scholars abandoned the old ideal of Sinology as a holistic pursuit concerned primarily with classical language and literature; instead, the field splintered into particular subdisciplines that were defined in terms of various discrete historical periods and methodological perspectives. These developments moreover tended to reinforce the old devaluation of the history of Chinese religions because, as a part of the growing emphasis on modern and revolutionary China, it seemed self-evident that religion had little importance for understanding Communist China. In the study of Chinese tradition then the rational and secular presuppositions of Western academic scholarship and social scientific methodology were especially strengthened by a whole set of apparent verifications coming from the conflation of the classical Confucian, early-twentieth-century Chinese modernist, and Chinese Communist self-images.

Consequently from the 1940s to the 1950s the focused Sinological study of religion was at a low ebb. Yet these relatively quiescent years laid the foundations for the upsurge of interest in Chinese religions in the decades that followed. During this transition a loose international group of scholars often dealt with selected religious topics while maintaining something of the old notion of Sinology as a comprehensive discipline. These academics included the Americans Derk Bodde, H. G. Creel, Schuyler Cammann, Arthur Wright, Alexander Soper, and Wing-tsit Chan; those continuing the French tradition, such as Paul Demiéville, Rolf Stein, and Étienne Balasz; and other European and Asian scholars such as Arthur Waley, J. J. L. Duyvendak, Werner Eichhorn, R. H. van Gulik, and Fung Yu-lan.

A second category of scholars during this same period more directly inspired the kind of specialized approach to religion in terms of subject area and methodology that characterized the 1970s and 1980s. Thus Buddhist and Daoist scholars included Max Kaltenmark, Michel Soymié, Erwin Rousselle, and Erik Zürcher in Europe; Yanagida Seizan, Kimura Eiichi, Yoshioka Yoshitoyo, Tang Yongtong, and Chen Guofu in Asia; and Kenneth Ch'en, Richard Robinson, Walter Liebenthal, Arthur Link, and Holmes Welch in the United States. Lastly, some researchers studied popular and local tradition from novel social scientific perspectives: Francis L. K. Hsu, who examined village culture and ancestral religion from a social-psychological frame of reference, and Wolfram Eberhard, who studied traditional Chinese religion, mythology, morality, and folklore in relation to the sociocultural history of local cultures.

In the 1960s the overall climate concerning the relevance of religion to modern life and the general academic significance of the study of world religions changed in dramatic ways. For the first time the specialized study of Chinese religions became recognizable as a specific professional focus for scholars working in different academic disciplines. This was a gradual, largely unconscious development throughout most of that decade and the next, but by 1974 public acknowledgment came in the form of the founding of the international Society for the Study of Chinese Religions by three American scholars: Holmes Welch, Daniel Overmyer, and Laurence Thompson.

Although the overt emergence of the study of Chinese religions as a field of concentration occurred in the 1970s, several earlier formative developments deserve note. One of these was the appearance of C. K. Yang's *Religion in Chinese Society* (1961), which applied a neo-Weberian sociological analysis to Chinese tradition and, arguing against prevailing attitudes, showed the intrinsic significance of religion within even the Confucian milieu of the "great tradition." Even more important for its grand compass, international impact, and interdisciplinary implications was the publication of the first few volumes of Joseph Needham's monumental and still appearing *Science and Civilisation in China* (1954–). Volume 2, which discusses Daoism as a part of the "history of Chinese science," was particularly important. First published in 1956, it did not really capture scholarly attention until the 1960s.

The interest in Daoism stimulated by Needham was also complemented by the work being done in the 1960s on the living liturgical traditions of sectarian Daoism in Taiwan by Kristofer Schipper, a Paris-trained scholar and the first Westerner to be initiated as a Daoist priest. Schipper's revolutionary fieldwork—along with the work of Needham, Nathan Sivin, and others who had been working on Daoist tradition—culminated in the first international conference on Daoist studies, held in Italy in 1968. This event was doubly significant. It not only signaled the rapid development of Daoist studies, which continues in the early twenty-first century, but also—as is shown by the presence of the Romanian-born American religious scholar Mircea Eliade at the conference and by the publication of the conference papers in the journal *History of Religions*—marked the emergence of a new spirit of cooperation between scholars of Chinese religions and those working in the comparative history of world religions, a discipline previously preoccupied with primitive and Indo-European traditions. This kind of collaborative approach was ratified by the establishment of the Society for the Study of Chinese Religions and tends to characterize the interdisciplinary range of articles on Chinese religion found currently in older, established journals in Sinology and in comparative religion, folklore, and philosophy as well as in several specialized journals started in the 1970s and 1980s (such as *Journal of Chinese Religions, Journal of Chinese Philosophy, Early China, Journal of the International Association of Buddhist Studies*).

In the late twentieth century and early twenty-first century a veritable flood of outstanding scholarship concerning Chinese religions has led to the rejection of many outdated assumptions about Chinese civilization. Fortunately this scholarly enterprise is also on the verge of becoming fully international in scope. Besides the continuing contributions of Japanese scholarship and the efforts of Chinese scholars in Taiwan, Singapore, and Hong Kong, the mainland Chinese Academy of Sciences and its affiliated Institute for Research on World Religions have been revitalized.

TRENDS IN SINOLOGY. Five areas may be singled out for their prominence in research in the early twenty-first century. The first concerns the archaic religion of ancient China. Continuing work on received texts, including oracle bone and bronze inscriptions, as well as the archaeological discovery of original and in many cases previously unknown texts has revolutionized this field of study. Japanese scholars like Akatsuka Kiyoshi, Ito Michiharu, and Shirakawa Shizuka combined traditional paleographic skills with anthropological and sociological insights to reenvision ancient China as a land where religious concerns were paramount. In an insightful series of studies David Keightley has applied a stricter methodology to reconstruct the mentality of the Shang, finding there the origin of Chinese bureaucracy and much of the later Chinese religious outlook. New bronze inscriptions have also transformed scholars' understanding of the Western Zhou. Jessica Rawson has drawn on inscriptions and material remains to delineate a ritual reform in the mid-Western Zhou, and Lothar von Falkenhausen has combined inscriptional and textual evidence to reassess the shamanic tradition in ancient China and its possible ties to later Daoism.

Turning to excavated manuscripts of the Warring States period, the discovery of Mawangdui in 1973 was followed rapidly by major troves of texts from Shuihudi, Baoshan, and Guodian. The philosophical works in these tombs attracted immediate attention from scholars like Ikeda Tomohisa, Robert Henricks, William Boltz, and Robin Yates. The more surprising element in these tombs was a genre of technical literature, including divinatory and medical texts, that, though common at the time, was not transmitted to later generations. Jao Tsung-I (Rao Zongyi), Li Ling, Mu-chou Poo, Mark Kalinowski, and Donald Harper have done groundbreaking work in this area. Grave goods and other material remains from this period, like jade suits and funereal banners, as well as Han funerary documents, like grave-quelling texts and land contracts, are also important reflections of Warring States religious belief and have been studied by Ikeda On, Anna Seidel, and Michael Loewe.

The second major area of research is China's indigenous organized religion, Daoism. Early scholarship in this field centered on Japan and Paris, with the studies of Yoshioka Yoshitoyo, Ōfuchi Ninji, Miyakawa Hisayuki, and Kubo Noritada leading the way for Rolf A. Stein, Kristofer Schipper, Anna Seidel, Isabelle Robinet, and Michel Strickmann. The primary focus of these scholars, with the exception of Kubo, was the early pre-Tang period of Daoist history. The next generation took these studies further, focusing on the early Celestial Master church (Angelika Cedzich, Stephen Bokenkamp, Terry Kleeman), the *Taipingjing* (Barbara Hendrischke, Jens O. Petersen), the system of precepts and monastic regulations (Benjamin Penny, Livia Kohn), fourth- and fifth-century reformation movements within Daoism (Yamada Toshiaki, Kobayashi Masayoshi, Kamitsuka Yoshiko), Daoism's relationship to popular cults (Peter Nickerson, Lai Chi Tim), and hagiography (Robert Campany). The Tang has still received little attention, with most of that focused on the small coterie of Daoists at court

(T. H. Barrett, Russell Kirkland), but studies of Song Daoism have flourished with important studies of Song scriptural sources (Piet van der Loon, Judith Boltz), the Quanzhen movement (Hachiya Kunio, Mori Yuria, Stephen Eskildsen, Vincent Goossaert), internal alchemy (Fabrizio Pregadio, Lowell Skar), and ecstatic religion (Edward L. Davis). Daoism in late imperial China remains largely unexplored, but the important work of Kenneth Dean seeks to link modern practice to Qing and earlier antecedents, and scholars like Li Fengmao, Maruyama Hiroshi, Shiga Ichiko, and Asano Haruji bring a command of canonical sources to their fieldwork on living practitioners. Important developments in the field include the first major exhibition of Daoist art, organized by Stephen Little; the publication of the *Daoist Handbook,* edited by Livia Kohn; the publication of the *Encyclopedia of Taoism,* edited by Fabrizio Pregadio; and the publication of Kristofer Schipper and Franciscus Verellen's annotated catalog of the Daoist canon.

A third major field of inquiry has been Buddhism. Early Western research focused on the transmission of Buddhism to China and the early schools (Erik Zürcher, Leon Hurvitz, Arthur Link, Lewis Lancaster), but a younger generation, raised on Alan Watts and often practicing Buddhists themselves, has given Chan studies pride of place in Western Buddhology. The influence of Yanagida Seizan is felt through students like Peter Gregory, John McRae, and Bernard Faure, but other scholars have questioned the influence of Japanese sectarian scholarship on the early history of Chan (Griffith Foulk) and on the idea of schools as an important element of Chinese Buddhism (Robert Sharf). Philologically based doctrinal scholarship continues, particularly with regard to Yogācāra (Daniel Lusthaus) and Huayan (Robert Gimello, Daniel B. Stevenson), but much interest has shifted to apocryphal scriptures (Robert Buswell, Kyoko Tokuno) and the influence of Tantric texts and practices in China (Michel Strickmann, Iyanaga Nobumi, Charles Orzech). One important trend of research has been to look at Buddhism within Chinese society. Chikusa Masaaki's studies of Song Buddhism and sectarian movements were followed by Stephen Teiser's studies of the Ghost Festival and mortuary ritual, Victor Mair's works on Dunhuang popular literature and the use of images in popular preaching, John Kieschnick's exploration of Buddhism's influence on Chinese material culture, and Timothy Brook's study of Buddhism in late imperial society. Buddhist art and architecture have provided another point of access to lived Buddhism for scholars like Marsha Weidner, Angela Howard, and Nancy Steinhardt. Chinese scholarship on Buddhism since Tang Yongtong has been constrained by political factors, but the late twentieth century saw the emergence of major scholars like Yang Cengwen, Wei Daoru, and Sun Changwu. Finally, Buddhism is also a vibrant living religion, and the work of Charles B. Jones and others has shed light on modern developments like the belief in a "human Pure Land" (*renjian jingtu*).

A fourth area of interest in the field of Chinese religions centers on the sectarian societies of later imperial and modern China. Pioneering work on these groups by Li Shiyu, Sawada Mizuho, and Marjorie Topley was followed by the substantial historical studies of Daniel Overmyer and Susan Naquin, but Barend ter Haar has shown the need for great care in using external accounts of such groups. Song Guangyu and David Jordan deserve special mention for their work on Yiguandao. Although these groups were initially identified as "folk Buddhism," many self-identify as Daoist; Philip Clart has dubbed these movements "maternist" because of their shared focus on the Unborn Venerable Mother (Wusheng laomu) as supreme deity, and he argues forcefully for spirit writing groups as self-cognizant modern Confucians. Whatever nomenclature is ultimately adopted, studies make clear that these are organized religious movements quite distinct from both the community-based common religion and the institutionalized religions of Buddhism and Daoism. Some are comparable in size and history to Protestant Christian denominations, have a distinct theology and canon, and deserve greater recognition and study.

The fifth major area of interest is the mass of traditional beliefs, practices, and observances that is sometimes dismissed as popular superstition; this compendium is now understood to be a distinct religion, the Chinese common religion, and to be an essential element of Chinese society from its earliest times to the present. The primary manifestation of this religion is the worship of deities in periodic and occasional observances involving communal ritual performance. Detailed synchronic and diachronic studies have appeared of specific deities, like Mazu (Li Xianzhang), Guanyin (Chünfang Yu), Guandi (Prasenjit Duara, Barend ter Haar), Wenchang (Terry Kleeman), Xuanwu Zhenwu (Pierre-Henry de-Bruyn), Lü Dongbin (Isabelle Ang, Paul Katz), Linji (Meir Shahar), Wutong (Angelika Cedzich, Richard von Glahn), and the Stove God (Robert Chard). Anthropology has always been an important source of information on Chinese religious life, and the fieldwork of scholars like Gary Seaman, Stephan Feuchtwang, William Watson, David Jordan, and Stevan Harrell have greatly expanded the understanding of the role of religious observances in daily life. The emergence of a corps of foreign-trained native anthropologists, like Yihyuan Li, Mei-rong Lin, and Hsun Chang, has led to more detailed studies focused specifically on religion and to indigenous analytical concepts like the "sacrificial circle" (*jisiquan*) and "belief circle" (*xinyang quan*).

Modernity has not been kind to Chinese religion, which has suffered persecutions beginning with the Taiping Revolution and carrying through the Republican New Life Movement and the Cultural Revolution. Nonetheless much of traditional practice has survived or been revived, and there is an active program of rescue ethnography trying to document the local Chinese religious world. The *Minsu quyi* (Folklore and performing arts) series edited by C. K. Wang has preserved a large body of local ritual drama. John Lagerway and Tam Wai-lun have mounted a massive project to document religious life in South China villages, concentrating on

Hakka areas of Guangdong and Fujian; Daniel Overmyer is organizing a similar project for North China. Opening up of the mainland has also permitted the first in-depth studies of local religion (Xiaofei Kang, Thomas DuBois). This local material, once accumulated in sufficient detail, will inevitably enrich and transform the understanding of Chinese religions.

Finally, something must be said about the phenomenal rise of the Falun Gong movement. Within the course of a single decade, this organization became the largest and fastest-growing of the world's new religions. The religious character of the Falun Gong is evident to any student of Chinese religions despite the disavowals of its members, but it is a unique organization, drawing institutionally on both the tradition of Chinese secret societies and the organizational principles of the Chinese Communist Party. For several years it has been the object of a sustained program of religious suppression unparalleled in scope since the Inquisition. Although a few Sinologists have published on this topic (notably David Ownby), this new and successful form of Chinese religious organization has to date largely escaped the notice of the field.

SEE ALSO Confucianism, article on History of Study; Daoism, article on History of Study; Granet, Marcel; Jesuits; Ricci, Matteo.

BIBLIOGRAPHY

Bibliographical Sources

The most important bibliographic resources for Chinese religions are the ongoing series of bibliographies compiled by Laurence G. Thompson and his colleagues, Lin Meirong's bibliography of primarily Chinese-language sources, and the on line bibliography on Chinese popular religion edited by Philip Clart.

Clart, Philip. "Bibliography of Western Language Publications on Chinese Popular Religion (1995 to Present)." Available from http://web.missouri.edu/~religpc/bibliography_CPR.html.

Cohen, Alvin P. "A Bibliography of Writings Contributory to the Study of Chinese Folk Religions." *Journal of the American Academy of Religion* 43 (1975): 238–265.

Cordier, Henri. *Bibliotheca Sinica.* 5 vols. Paris, 1904–1924.

Lin, Meirong. *Taiwan min jian xin yang yan jiu shu mu.* 2d ed., rev. Taipei, Taiwan, 1997.

Marceron, Désiré. *Bibliographie du taoïsme.* Paris, 1898.

Pas, Julian F. *A Select Bibliography on Taoism.* Stony Brook, N.Y., 1988.

Pfister, Louis. *Notices biographiques et bibliographiques sur les jésuites de l'ancienne mission de Chine, 1552–1773.* 2 vols. Shanghai, 1932–1934.

Seaman, Gary, ed. *Chinese Religion: Publications in Western Languages, 1981 through 1990.* Ann Arbor, Mich., 1993.

Seaman, Gary, and Zhifang Song. *Chinese Religions: Publications in Western Languages,* vol. 3: *1991–1995.* Edited by Gary Seaman. Ann Arbor, Mich., 1998.

Seaman, Gary, and Zhifang Song. *Chinese Religions: Publications in Western Languages,* vol. 4: *1996–2000.* Edited by Gary Seaman. Ann Arbor, Mich., 2002.

Thompson, Laurence G. *Chinese Religion in Western Languages: A Comprehensive and Classified Bibliography of Publications in English, French, and German through 1980.* Tucson, Ariz., 1984.

General Historical Studies and Early Period

The various specialized studies of Sinology or the study of Chinese religions include the following.

Brear, Douglas. "Early Assumptions in Western Buddhist Studies." *Religion* 5 (Autumn 1975): 136–157.

Dehergne, Joseph. "Les historiens jésuites du taoïsme." In *Actes du Colloque International de Sinologie: La mission française de Pékin aux dix-septième et dix-huitème siècles,* pp. 59–67. Paris, 1976.

Demiéville, Paul. "Aperçu historique des études sinologiques en France." *Acta Asiatica* 11 (1966): 56–110.

Girardot, N. J. "Chinese Religion and Western Scholarship." In *China and Christianity,* edited by James D. Whitehead et al., pp. 83–111. Notre Dame, Ind., 1979.

Honey, David B. *Incense at the Altar: Pioneering Sinologists and the Development of Classical Chinese Philology.* New Haven, Conn., 2001.

Lach, Donald F. *Asia in the Making of Europe.* 4 vols. Chicago, 1965–1977.

Lancashire, D. "Buddhist Reaction to Christianity in Late Ming China." *Journal of the Oriental Society of Australia* 6 (1968–1969): 82–103.

Maspero, Henri. "La sinologie." In *Société asiatique: Le livre du centenaire, 1822–1922,* pp. 261–283. Paris, 1922.

Pinot, Virgile. *La Chine et la formation de l'esprit philosophique en France, 1640–1740.* Paris, 1932.

Rule, Paul A. "Jesuit and Confucian? Chinese Religion in Journals of Matteo Ricci, S. J., 1583–1610." *Journal of Religious History* 5 (December 1968): 105–124.

Soymié, Michel. "Les études chinoises." *Journal asiatique* 261 (1973): 209–246.

Spence, Jonathan D. *The Memory Palace of Matteo Ricci.* New York, 1984.

Sprenkel, Otto Berkelback van der. "Western Sources." In *Essays on the Source for Chinese History,* edited by Donald D. Leslie, Colin Mackerras, and Wang Gungwu, pp. 154–175. Columbia, S.C., 1973.

Thompson, Laurence G. "American Sinology, 1830–1920: A Bibliographical Survey." *Tsing-hua Journal of Chinese Studies* 2, no. 2 (June 1961): 244–290.

Young, John D. *Confucianism and Christianity: The First Encounter.* Hong Kong, 1983.

Modern Period Studies

The following works include helpful discussions of particular aspects of historical and intellectual developments in China in the twentieth century.

Barrett, T. H. "Change and Progress in Understanding Chinese Religion." *Numen* 29 (December 1982): 239–249.

Barrett, T. H. *Singular Listlessness: A Short History of Chinese Books and British Scholars.* London, 1989.

Ch'en Yao-shen and Paul S. Y. Hsiao. *Sinology in the United Kingdom and Germany.* Translated by William W. G. Wan and T. W. Kwok. Honolulu, 1967.

Demiéville, Paul. "Henri Maspero et l'avenir des études chinoises." *T'oung pao* 38 (1947): 16–42.

Eberhard, Wolfram. "Studies in Chinese Religions: 1920–1932." In *Moral and Social Values of the Chinese: Collected Essays,* pp. 335–399. Taipei, 1971.

Eliasberg, Danielle. "Maspero: L'histoire de la religion populaire chinoise." In *Hommage à Henri Maspero, 1883–1945,* pp. 55–60. Paris, 1983.

Franke, Herbert. *Sinologie An Deutschen Universitäten.* Wiesbaden, Germany, 1968.

Freedman, Maurice. "On the Sociological Study of Chinese Religion." In *Religion and Ritual in Chinese Society,* edited by Arthur A. Wolf, pp. 19–41. Stanford, Calif., 1974.

Honey, David B. "The Foundation of Modern German Sinology." *Phi Theta Papers,* 1984, 82–101.

Jong, J. W. de. "A Brief History of Buddhist Studies in Europe and America." *Eastern Buddhist,* n.s. 7, no. 1 (May 1974): 55–106, no. 2 (October 1974): 49–82.

Kaltenmark, Max. "Henri Maspero et les études taoïstes." In *Hommage à Henri Maspero, 1883–1945,* pp. 45–48. Paris, 1983.

Lagerwey, John. "Questions of Vocabulary; or, How Shall We Talk about Chinese Religion?" In *Daojiao yu minjian zongjiao yanjiu lunji,* edited by Lai Chi Tim, pp. 166–181. Hong Kong, 1999.

Lalou, Marcelle. "Onze années de travaux européens sur le bouddhisme (mai 1936–mai 1947)." *Museon* 61 (1948): 245–276.

Maspero, Henri. "Édouard Chavannes." *T'oung pao* 21 (1922): 43–56.

Nakamura Hajime. "A Survey of Mahāyāna Buddhism with Bibliographical Notes." *Journal of Intercultural Studies* 3 (1976): 60–145, 4 (1977): 77–135, 5 (1978): 89–138.

Overmyer, Daniel L., ed. *Ethnography in China Today: A Critical Assessment of Methods and Results.* Taipei, 2002.

Peiris, William. *The Western Contribution to Buddhism.* Delhi, 1973.

Strickmann, Michel. "History, Anthropology, and Chinese Religion." *Harvard Journal of Asiatic Studies* 40 (June 1980): 201–248.

Wright, Arthur F. "The Study of Chinese Civilization." *Journal of the History of Ideas* 21 (1960): 232–255.

Yu, David C. "Present-Day Taoist Studies." *Religious Studies Review* 3 (October 1977): 220–239.

East Asian Scholarship
Useful studies of East Asian scholarship include the following:

Beasley, W. G., and E. G. Pulleyblank, eds. *Historians of China and Japan.* London, 1961.

Fogel, Joshua A. *Politics and Sinology: The Case of Naito Konan (1866–1934).* Cambridge, Mass., 1984.

Goto Kimpei. "Studies in Chinese Religion in Postwar Japan." *Monumenta Serica* 15 (1956): 463–511.

Jan Yün-hua. "The Religious Situation and the Studies of Buddhism and Taoism in China: An Incomplete and Imbalanced Picture." *Journal of Chinese Religions* 12 (Fall 1984): 37–64.

Overmyer, Daniel L. "From 'Feudal Superstition' to 'Popular Beliefs': New Directions in Mainland Chinese Studies of Chinese Popular Religion." *Cahiers d'Extrême-Asie* 12 (2001): 103–126.

Sakai Tadao, and Noguchi Tetsuro. "Taoist Studies in Japan." In *Facets of Taoism,* edited by Holmes Welch and Anna Seidel, pp. 269–287. New Haven, Conn. 1979.

Schneider, Laurence A. *Ku Chieh-kang and China's New History.* Berkeley, Calif., 1971.

NORMAN J. GIRARDOT (1987)
TERRY F. KLEEMAN (2005)

CHINESE RELIGIOUS YEAR.

CHINESE RELIGIOUS YEAR. The religious year of traditional China may be visualized as a circular base that is the calendar, upon which three overlays are superimposed. The first overlay shows the annual pan-Chinese observances; the second shows the celebrations of local, popular cults centered on the birthdays of particular deities; the third shows the schedule of official state sacrifices. I shall discuss each of these cycles of observances in turn.

THE RELIGIOUS YEAR AND THE CALENDAR. Traditionally, the dates of religious significance in the year were made known through a calendar issued by the Bureau of Astronomy in the Ministry of Rites. This calendar combined lunar and solar calculations, but for the religious year the former were more important. The waxing and waning of the moon was the most conspicuous indicator of change in the heavens, and the new and full moons thus formed focal points in the nexus of natural and human time. Solstices and equinoxes, as determined by the astronomers, were not so obvious, but were nevertheless important moments in the religious year because of their connection with the dominant or recessive phase of yin and yang.

The official calendar also indicated other kinds of time, of which two were most important in the religious year. The first was the marking of hours, days, months, and years by a cycle of two-character designations formed by sixty combinatory permutations of two series of symbols called the ten celestial stems (*tiangan*) and the twelve terrestrial branches (*dizhi*). The second was the division of the year into twenty-four climatic periods. The pairs serve not simply as a method of marking, but, from the correlations of the stems and branches with other factors in the cosmos, they also hint at the many occult forces affecting the fate of humankind. The division of the year into fortnightly climatic periods is intimately connected with the timing and meaning of major events in the ritual year. These fortnightly periods are called nodes (*jie*) or breaths (*qi*). They derive from observations, both celestial (division of the heavens into degrees) and terrestrial (meteorological phenomena), already made in ancient times. Widely applied throughout China, their descriptive names—clear and bright, a little warm, frost descends, a lot of snow—show their origination in the northern regions, where four distinct seasons obtain. The term *jie,* which came to designate the fortnightly periods, has retained its correlative meaning of the celebration of rites at fixed times. Hence, the festivals of the year, particularly those tied to the twenty-four climatic periods, are also called *jie.*

The calendar was not merely a schedule of times and seasons, but was more in the nature of an almanac, spelling out behaviors suitable, and indeed essential, for every season. Eventually it developed into a handbook containing medical lore, moral guidance, and techniques for prognostication and divination. The issuing of the imperial calendar was an act of religious import in itself, in that it was taken as evidence of the divine mandate possessed by the ruling dynasty. In effect, only such a divinely commissioned ruler could reveal the times and influences according to which all people must govern their lives. The concept of a religious year in the Chinese case must thus be understood as a yearlong effort on the part of ruler and people to grasp the complicated processes of the cosmos and make them work for humans. In this overall context the observances of the religious year underline the moments of greatest significance to family, community, occupational group, and state.

Pan-Chinese Observances. Rather than present a schematic overview, the following outline focuses on the island province of Taiwan, where the traditions have been fully preserved amidst the changes of modernization. A Chinese summary of the religious year, the section titled "Suishi yu Shendan" in Ruan Changrui's *Zhuangyandi shijie* (Taibei, 1982), has been relied upon here.

The twelfth and first months: the New Year. By far the most protracted, the busiest, and the most important of the annual festivals, the New Year begins in the middle of the twelfth month with the Weiya (tail end of the year) observance and continues through to the full moon of the first month. In former times all business came to a virtual standstill during most of this period; nowadays the length of the holiday has been considerably curtailed, but many traditional practices are continued. On "tail end of the year," the twelfth day of the twelfth month, sacrifices are made to Tudigong (the local earth god), the all-important tutelary deity of household and community. On this evening the proprietors of businesses hold feasts for their employees to thank them for their hard work and to wish for a successful new year.

On the twenty-fourth day of this month, Zaojun (lord of the cooking stove) leads the various deities assigned to terrestrial duties to the court of Yuhuang Shangdi (supreme emperor of jadelike augustness), ruler of the bureaucratic pantheon in Heaven; there he makes the required annual report. Zaojun is in effect the spirit overseer of the household. Presumably because his report will influence the life span recorded in the heavenly registers, he also is considered one of the *siming fujun* (arbiters of longevity). On this day, the deity's mouth is smeared with something sweet so that he will have only sweet things to report. The paper icon of Zaojun, found above each stove, is then burnt, the smoke conveying the report directly to Heaven. Once the deities have left for the court of Heaven, the house undergoes a thorough cleaning, which also gets rid of any *huiqi* (inauspicious breaths). The next day, celestial deities, deputed by the Supreme Emperor of Jadelike Augustness, arrive to make their inspection during the absence of the terrestrial deities. Everyone is on good behavior during this inspection period.

New Year's Eve is called Guonian (the passing of the old year) or Chuxi (the eve of the passing year). It is observed by seven traditional practices:

1. *Ci nian* (bidding farewell to the old year). Sacrifices are offered to gods and ancestors, to Zaojun, and to Chuangmu, the tutelary mother of the bed. Propitiary sacrifices are also placed at the gate for *haoxiong* (good elder brothers), that is, bereaved spirits, souls denied their rightful sacrifices, whose resentment constitutes a menace to the living. On the family altar in the main hall are set offerings of cooked rice, other foods, and strings of money. After the sacrifices have been made, firecrackers are set off to scare off demons.

2. *Tuanyuanfan yu weilu* (family reunion meal and surrounding the stove). The gathering of the family from far and near for the communal meal is also called *shousuijiu* (wine that safeguards the New Year). A brazier placed under the round table is festooned with coins and described as "warm as spring, the prospering breath of wealth." The family gathering is thus called "surrounding the stove"; should there be a family member who cannot attend the feast, some of his clothing is draped over an empty chair to indicate his symbolic presence and that the family is thinking of him. At this meal the last course is a fish, which must not be eaten, however, for fish is homophonous with having abundance (*yu*).

3. *Yasuiqian* (money of the year that is given away). After the communal feast the elders hand out money to the youngsters. This is also called *fen guonianqian* (dividing the money of the passing year). In the past, one hundred cash were strung together (the old coppers had a square hole in the center), and even though these have now been replaced by paper money, the meaning is still "may you live one hundred years."

4. *Shousui* (safeguarding the year). After the elders give money to the children, the family sits around the stove, chatting, joking, and playing games to see the old year out. Safeguarding the year is said to contribute to the longevity of the parents.

5. *Tiao huopen* (jumping over the fire pan). After the feast, all male members of the family take turns jumping over a pan filled with burning rice straw in front of the family gate. They call out certain auspicious phrases as they do so. The passing over fire signifies purification or making a new beginning.

6. *Tie chunlian* (pasting up spring scrolls). To welcome the new year, spring scrolls bearing auspicious words are pasted on the gateposts. Pieces of lucky red paper with the graph for spring written on them are pasted on such places as the leaves of the gate and the rice barrels. Other felicitous phrases are pasted elsewhere. The pasting up of spring scrolls derives from the ancient practice of hanging apotropaic peachwood amulets at the gate. There are colored paper

scrolls hung over the lintel on blue paper if a male infant has died during the year or on yellow paper if a female infant has died.

7. By ancient custom, on New Year's Eve people attended plays held in front of a temple. If a debtor stayed until dawn of New Year's Day, his creditor would not dare to disturb the gathering by trying to collect the debt. The debt, collectible before the new year, could then be postponed because the new year had arrived. These events were thus called *pizexi* (fleeing-from-debt plays).

The first five days of the new year are called Xinzheng (correct, or fixed, beginning) or Xinchun (beginning of the new spring). They are greeted with the spring scrolls, firecrackers, and music, while people crowd the streets in a happy bustle. On the first day people eat long noodles symbolic of their hope for longevity. Dressed in new clothes and bearing fruits and other offerings, they go to the temples to burn incense and worship the deities. Then they pay a New Year's call on friends and relatives. On this day everyone takes care to avoid saying or doing things of bad omen. No work is done, and everyone enjoys himself. On the second day newly married girls pay a visit to their natal homes. On the fourth day the deities who had been away at their annual audience at the court of Heaven return to this world and are received with offerings and prayers for good fortune during the new year. With day five life returns temporarily to normal, but the season is not yet over. On the evening of the eighth day everyone takes a bath and observes a fast called Shoushou (safeguarding longevity) until midnight. Then, led by the head of the family, all members of the household perform Dali, the great ritual, consisting of three kneelings and nine knockings (*ketou*, or kowtow as it is known in the West) and the presentation of incense. Thus is marked the beginning of the ninth day, the birthday of the Supreme Emperor of Jadelike Augustness, by whose indulgence all beings are born and nurtured.

The fifteenth day marks the close of the New Year festivities. It is called Shangyuan Jie (festival of the First Primordial). The triad Shangyuan, Zhongyuan, and Xiayuan, of whom the first is recognized here, are otherwise known in Daoism as the San Guan (three controllers), supervisors of the realms of Heaven, earth, and the waters. In popular religion they are also identified with the three sage-kings of legendary antiquity: Yao, who attained perfect goodness, is the Celestial Controller; Shun, who reclaimed the land, is the Terrestrial Controller; and Yu, who tamed the floods, is the Controller of the Waters. The birthday of each controller is widely celebrated. Sacrifices to the Celestial Controller are presented at dawn on the fifteenth.

The major event of the day, however, takes place in the evening and is called Yuanxiao Jie (festival of the First Primordial night) or Dengjie (lantern festival). The family again gathers at a communal feast, and special round dumplings of the First Primordial night (*yuanxiao yuanzi*) are eaten. The roundness of the dumplings is like this first full moon of the year and symbolizes the complete family circle as well as completeness or perfection in general. After dark everyone takes to the streets and temples to show and view ingeniously designed lanterns and to enjoy the boisterous dragon and lion dances accompanied by the din of gongs and drums, and the acrobatics of martial arts troupes. With this festival the season comes to an end.

Second month. On the second day of the second month a minor observance balances the tail end of the year, which, as we saw, falls on the twelfth day of the twelfth month. On the occasion of Touya (head of the year), as on the earlier occasion, the main events are sacrifices to Tudigong and the giving of a feast by the shopkeeper for his employees.

Third month. The second major festival of the year, Qingming Jie, takes place at the beginning of the climatic period called Qingming (clear and bright) and is dedicated to the ancestors. On the first of the month, families visit the ancestral tombs to tidy them up. A sacrificial meal including auspicious red-colored rice, called *yimu guo* (saluting-the-tomb rice), is offered. The family head divides up longevity noodles and red-colored rice among all the junior relatives. In general, the services at the tomb, called *peimu* (shoring up the tomb), are quite solemn and impressive. Sacrifices include twelve dishes of edibles in addition to the rice. A peeled egg is left atop the grave to express the idea that the old gives way to the new (*xin chen dai xie*). The children share some of the saluting-the-tomb rice and some money. This is called *yinmu guo* (rice with the seal of the tomb), and shows the abundant virtue of the ancestors, which in turn abides forever among their descendants. When the visit to the grave is ended, a strip of red paper is left on top in commemoration.

Fourth month. The eighth day is the festival of washing the Buddha, whose birthday it is said to be. The image of the Buddha in every temple is ceremonially washed, incense is burned, and scriptures are chanted.

Fifth month. The fifth of this month is called Duanwu (double *wu*) because both month and day contain the fifth celestial stem (*wu*) in their designations. The great event of the day in the South is the dragon boat races. These are popularly said to be a reenactment of the search for the body of Qu Yuan, a loyal statesman and poet of ancient times who drowned himself when his advice was no longer heeded by his lord. For this day people make a special kind of sweet dumpling wrapped in bamboo leaves that was originally supposed to have been thrown into the water for Qu Yuan's spirit to consume. Nowadays, people exchange such dumplings as presents on Duanwu.

Because the fifth month marks the junction of spring and summer and was associated with the onset of epidemic diseases, it has the reputation of being the *duyue* (poisonous month). Precautions are taken against the depredations of disease-causing spirits: strong yellow wine is drunk; a package of calamus, mugwort, and banian branches wrapped in lucky red paper is suspended above the gate; colored threads are tied around the wrists of children and bags of incense are hung by a red string around their necks. The proximity of the double fifth to the summer solstice, the moment when the ascendancy of yang will begin to give way to yin, no doubt has something to do with the prominence of the Duanwu festival.

Sixth month. The first and fifteenth of this month are occasions for celebrating the completion of the first half of the year. The deities and ancestors receive sacrifices and thanks for their help, with wishes for their continued support during the remainder of the year. On the sixth day, clothing, books, and paintings are aired to rid them of mildew from the spring rains. Old people also air their *shouyi* (longevity garments), the special coats, embroidered with the graph for longevity, that they will wear to the grave. On the nineteenth of the month many women go to the temples to offer sacrifices to Guanyin (the *bodhisattva* Avalokiteśvara), their most venerated protectress, who is said to have attained the Way (*de dao*) and to have ascended to Heaven on this day.

Seventh month. On the seventh day of this month the charming legend of the weaving maid and the cowherd (originally simply the names of two stars) comes alive again. This celestial couple can only meet on this one night each year when magpies form a bridge across the Celestial River (Milky Way). On this day, Qi Niangma (seventh imperial mother, the deity of the weaving-maid star) receives special sacrifices because she is considered an important protector of children. The fifteenth day is Zhongyuan Jie (festival of the Second Primordial). This day is considered the birthday of the Daoist Controller of Earth, or, in popular view, the ancient sage-king Shun. Sacrifices are offered to deities and ancestors at the family altars.

Despite these festivals, the central concern of the seventh month is the problem of bereaved spirits and damned souls. During this month the gates of the dark realm are open, and hungry ghosts (from the Indian concept of *preta*) are free to roam about in that invisible but very real dimension that impinges upon the world of the living. Three times during this month religious rituals are performed to counter this danger. On the first day every household sets out generous offerings of food at the entranceway. Incense sticks are placed in bowls, special burial clothes and silver paper spirit-money are burned to send into the invisible dimension. At the gateway is hung a lamp on which are written auspicious words. At the same time that this hospitable attitude is being exhibited, people take good care not to expose themselves to danger.

On the fifteenth, the second and by far the most important of the rituals to cope with the wandering ghosts takes place. The entire community invites these pitiable (and dangerous) visitors to a great feast at which not only will they be able for once to eat their fill, but also will receive the merits that accrue from the religious services held. *Pudu*, the ritual that assists all souls to cross over to the other shore of salvation, is performed on a large scale both by households and in temples. Altars are erected, sacrifices are offered to the poor souls, and priests, both Buddhist and Daoist, chant their sacred texts. Tall beacon posts are hung with lanterns and pennants to guide the spirits to the ritual places; paper and bamboo rafts take candles or small lamps out on the waters to attract the attention of the souls of the drowned. Finally, on the last day of the month, the spirits must return to their subterranean prisons and the gates are closed for another eleven months. The beacon lanterns are taken down, final sacrifices are presented, and the worlds of the living and the dead return to their normal condition of separation.

Eighth month. This month sees the minor birthday celebrations of two deities, humble in rank, but intimately involved in the daily life of the people. On the third day sacrifices are offered to Zaojun. On the fifteenth day sacrifices are made to Tudigong and also to the ancestors. The offerings include *yue bing* (moon cakes), for the fifteenth is also the night of the birthday of Yin Niangniang (the goddess of the moon). The full moon of this month is one of the most enjoyable festivals of the year, with fine weather contributing to the pleasure of moon-viewing parties. It no doubt originally had specific connections with the harvest, but that connection is no longer apparent.

Ninth month. Despite the promise that the Chongjiu or Chongyang (double-nine) day seems to hold, with its implication of the fullness of yang (nine is the number given to yang lines in the *Yi jing*), nothing seems to remain of any former religious significance of this day. The activities traditionally characterizing double-nine are going for a hike in the hills and flying kites.

Tenth month. Like the ninth month, the tenth is not a time of much religious celebration. On the fifteenth day occurs the Xiayuan Jie (festival of the Third Primordial), and hence the birthday of the Daoist Controller of the Waters or, in popular understanding, the ancient sage-king Yu.

Eleventh month. The important observance of the eleventh month is the Dongjie (winter festival), marking the solstice. Just prior to this day there is another gathering of the family to sacrifice to ancestors, called Qiuji (autumn sacrifice). Then, as winter begins, feasts mark the solstice with special foods such as *butong* (winter supplements). Soups with dumplings again play on the meaning of the word *yuan* (round, hence perfect or complete).

Popular Cults and the Birthdays of Their Deities. Practically every day of the year is designated as the birthday of one or more of the deities. These deities are of varied origins and may be classified in different ways. Aside from those actually deriving from popular, local religions, they include supernaturals originally connected with the traditions of Confucianism, Daoism, and Buddhism. These have largely lost their original significance and are integrated into popular religion where they acquire attributes that suit popular needs. An example of this phenomenon was the identification of the

Daoist San Guan (three officials) as the ancient sage-kings Yao, Shun, and Yu. The most famous case is the transformation of the *bodhisattva* Avalokiteśvara (Chin., Guanshiyin) into the most popular deity of all, the compassionate mother-figure, Guanyin, whose birthday is celebrated on the nineteenth day of the second month.

A few of the deities that originated in popular cults became so important that they were adopted by the state and became objects of official sacrifices as well. The most outstanding example on Taiwan is Mazu (granny), who was given the highest imperial rank of Tianhou (consort of Heaven). Her most important function is to protect all who must venture upon the waters. (Her birthday is celebrated on the twenty-third day of the third month.) Guan Sheng Da Di (holy great emperor Guan), originally a famous general of the Three Kingdoms period (third century CE), became the greatest of the military gods and protector of the empire; his birthday is celebrated on the thirteenth day of the fifth month. While many popular deities are pan-Chinese, their birthdays celebrated everywhere, there are also many others whose cults are only local, or of importance chiefly to certain groups or occupations.

Religious Year of the State. Since ancient times the state has considered the ritual offering of sacrifices to be one of its most basic duties and prerogatives. The calendar issued by the imperial Bureau of Astronomy gave the annual schedule of official sacrifices, which formed a separate system from the universal festivals and from the birthdays of deities celebrated in the popular cults.

In China, as elsewhere, some observances have become more or less drained of religious content and their original significance forgotten by all but scholars or obscured by later rationalizations. In the religious year as a whole a few themes are conspicuous: concern for unity of the family, including filiality to the ancestors and protection of the children; desire for longevity; hopes for blessings in general; and fear of resentful ghosts and attempts to propitiate them. Aside from these hopes and fears, the colorful practices marking the course of the year may be understood as one of the clearest expressions of traditional popular culture.

See Also Chinese Religion, article on Popular Religion; Confucianism, article on The Imperial Cult; Yuhuang.

Bibliography

A complete calendar of the religious year can be found in Henri Doré's *Recherches sur les superstitions en Chine,* 18 vols. (Shanghai, 1911–1938). Doré's opus has been translated by M. Kennelly as *Researches into Chinese Superstitions,* 13 vols. (1914–1938; reprint, Taipei, 1966); see volume 5, pages 563–656. An abbreviated calendar can be found in Doré's *Manuel des superstitions chinoises,* 2d ed. (Shanghai, 1936), pp. 132–137. The festival year observed in different localities is described in Justus Doolittle's *The Social Life of the Chinese,* vol. 2, edited by Paxton Hood (New York, 1868), chaps. 1–3; J. J. M. de Groot's *Les fêtes annuellement célébrées à Émoui (Amoy),* 2 vols. (1886; reprint, Taipei, 1977); *Annual Customs and Festivals in Peking,* (1936; reprint, Hong Kong, 1965), an annotated translation by Derk Bodde of a work by the Manchu author Tun Li-ch'en; Lewis Hodous's *Folkways in China* (London, 1929); C. S. Wong's *A Cycle of Chinese Festivities* (Singapore, 1967); and Henry Yi-min Wei and Suzanne Coutanceau's *Wine for the Gods; An Account of the Religious Traditions and Beliefs of Taiwan* (Taipei, 1976). Wolfram Eberhard's *Chinese Festivals* (1952; reprint, Taipei, 1972) discusses the origins and significance of some of the major observances. More specialized treatments include Marcel Granet's *Fêtes et chansons anciennes de la Chine* (Paris, 1919), translated into English by E. D. Edwards as *Festivals and Songs of Ancient China* (New York, 1932), in which see especially part 2; Derk Bodde's *Festivals in Classical China: New Year and Other Annual Observances during the Han Dynasty, 206 B.C.–A.D. 220* (Princeton, 1975); Göran Aijmer's *The Dragon Boat Festival on the Hupeh-Hunan Plains, Central China* (Stockholm, 1964); and Carole Morgan's *Le Tableau du Boeuf du Printemps: Étude d'une page de l'almanach chinois* (Paris, 1980).

New Sources

Chang, P. F. *Chinese Festivals Customs and Practices in Sarawak.* Sarawak, Malaysia, 1993.

Grayson, James H. "Is There an East Asian Millennium? East Asian Conceptions of Time." In *Calling Time,* edited by Martyn Percy, pp. 61–73. Sheffield, 2000.

Holzman, D. *Immortals, Festivals, and Poetry in Medieval China: Studies in Social and Intellectual History.* Brookfield, Vt., 1998.

Jian, T. *Strukturen, Funktionen und Symbole des chinesischen Festes Frühlingsanfang im historischen Wandel.* New York, 1999.

Kurihara, Keisuke. "The Hsia Hsiao-cheng, the Earliest Chinese Agricultural Calendar" tr. by Barry Steben. In *Contacts between Cultures,* edited by Bernard Hung-Kay Luk, pp. 276–278. Lewiston, N.Y., 1992.

Maheu, Betty Ann. "Welcome to the Year of the Dragon." *Tripod* 20, no. 115 (2000): 45–50.

Stepanchuk, C. *Red Eggs and Dragon Boats: Celebrating Chinese Festivals.* Berkeley, 1994.

Wong, C. S., and R. Pinsler. *An Illustrated Cycle of Chinese Festivities in Malaysia and Singapore.* Singapore, 1987.

Laurence G. Thompson (1987)
Revised Bibliography

CHINGGIS KHAN

CHINGGIS KHAN (1162–1227), great Mongol leader and founder of a vast empire in Asia. One of the extraordinary personages of world history, Chinggis Khan is a striking example of an emperor who became a god.

Born in Mongolia, northeast of present-day Ulan Bator, and called Temüjin in his youth, he was the eldest son of a chieftain of the Mongol Borjigit clan. Having succeeded in uniting the Mongol and Turkic tribes of the area, he adopted the title of Chinggis Khan and set out to conquer the world. He subdued the Chin empire in North China, the Hsi-hsia kingdom northeast of Tibet, the Turkic states in Turkistan, and the empire of Khorezm, comprising Transoxiana as well as Afghanistan and Eastern Iran. Mongol units even advanced as far as India and the Crimea. When Chinggis Khan died in 1227 near Ning-hsia, capital of Hsi-hsia, he left the broad foundations of an empire that would extend, under his sons and grandsons, from Korea to the Near East and southern Europe and from southern Siberia to Indochina.

The story of Chinggis Khan's life reads like that of an epic hero. Indeed, the thirteenth-century *Secret History of the Mongols,* the first work of Mongolian literature, patterns Chinggis Khan's biography after the model of the hero-king, and thus reflects the indispensable qualities of a ruler and the hopes set upon him. Chinggis Khan possesses the mandate of Heaven and Heaven's support to restore law, order, and peace on earth. He is of noble totemistic descent: his forefather, the ancestor of the Mongol royal family, is a blue-gray wolf whose son is born on the holy mountain Burkhan Qaldun. It is this "good place," the center of the world, where Chinggis Khan's career begins as well. From here he goes forth to conquer nations and peoples in all directions, and to this same place his dead body returns. He has a good wife, a good horse, and good companions, and he finds himself in a situation favorable for his activities.

After Chinggis Khan's death, his character develops in three ways: Chinggis Khan becomes a means of political identification, a figure of political theology, and a deity. Chinggis Khan is used as a means of political identification by the Mongols as well as by the Chinese. To the Mongols, as the founder of their unified state, he is a symbol of Mongol national independence, or at least autonomy. To the Chinese, he is the glorious first emperor of a Chinese dynasty of Mongol nationality, a symbol of the multinational character of Chinese history.

Chinggis Khan's association with political theology is twofold. It was probably during the time of Kublai, grandson of Chinggis, that the concept of a dual Buddhist world government was introduced: the ruler of the state is the king, as represented by Chinggis Khan and his successors, the Mongolian great khans; the head of the religion is the religious teacher, the lama, as represented by Buddha Śākyamuni and his successors, the Tibetan hierarchs. The two orders of state and religion, based on mutual harmony and distribution of functions, guarantee secular and spiritual well-being. This concept, however, has never been fully realized. Kublai became not the ruler of a Tibeto-Mongol Buddhist state, but rather the first Mongol emperor of China.

Another notion of Chinggis Khan that links political and religious images proved to be more successful. In this view, Chinggis Khan, protected by Heaven, becomes the son of Heaven (Tengri) or the son of Khormusta, the lord of the gods *(tengri),* the Indian Indra, whose attribute is the thunderbolt. In Mahāyāna Buddhism, Indra developed into the *bodhisattva* Vajrapāṇi, the "bearer of the thunderbolt," a figure symbolic of power. It is power that is the principal quality of Chinggis Khan and his people, the Mongols. At the same time, however, in ideological or even genealogical terms, Chinggis Khan becomes a successor to the first king of humankind, the Indian Mahasammata.

There are three aspects to the deification of Chinggis Khan. First, he became the ancestral deity of the ruling Borjigit clan, the state, and the whole Mongol people, guarding them against all evil. Sacrifices to Chinggis Khan, his family, and his war genies *(sülde)* seem to be offered even today in his main sanctuary, the Eight White Yurts, in the Ordos district of Inner Mongolia. He is also still officially venerated by Mongolian refugees in Taiwan. Second, Chinggis was incorporated into the Lamaist-Buddhist pantheon as a local guardian deity of comparatively low rank. In the practice of folk religion he became fused with the ancestral deity. Third, traits of an initiatory god were imputed to Chinggis Khan; as this deity, he introduced marriage customs, seasonal festivals connected with the nomadic economy, and certain ritual practices of daily life.

See Also Inner Asian Religions; Mongol Religions.

Bibliography

Basic observations on the religious role of Chinggis Khan have been made by Walther Heissig in his *Die Religionen der Mongolei* (Stuttgart, 1970), translated by Geoffrey Samuel as *The Religions of Mongolia* (Berkeley, 1980). The ideological development of Chinggis Khan's character is dealt with by Herbert Franke in his excellent study *From Tribal Chieftain to Universal Emperor and God: The Legitimation of the Yüan Dynasty* (Munich, 1978). Indispensable for everyone interested in Chinggis Khan's biography and thirteenth-century Mongol political and religious thought are the anonymous *Secret History of the Mongols* and two Persian chronicles written by al-Juwaynı and Rashīd al-Dīn. The following English translations are available: *The Secret History of the Mongols, for the First Time Done into English out of the Original Tongue and Provided with an Exegetical Commentary,* 2 vols., by Francis Woodman Cleaves (Cambridge, Mass., 1982–); *The History of the World-Conqueror, by ʿAla-ad-Din ʿAta-Malik Juvaini,* translated by John Andrew Boyle in two volumes (Cambridge, Mass., 1958); and *The Successors of Gengis Khan,* translated from the Persian of Rashīd al-Dīn Ṭabīb by John Andrew Boyle (New York, 1971). An excellent biography of Chinggis Khan written by a Western historian is René Grousset's *Le conquérant du monde* (Paris, 1944), translated into English by Denis Sinor and Marian MacKellar as *Conqueror of the World* (Edinburgh, 1967). The most recent study on Chinggis Khan's life and activities is Paul Ratchnevsky's *Činggis-Khan: Sein Leben und Wirken* (Wiesbaden, 1983).

New Sources

Onon, Urgunge. *The Secret History of the Mongols: The Life and Times of Chinggis Khan.* Richmond, 2001.

Ratchnevsky, Paul. *Genghis Khan: His Life and Legacy.* Translated and edited by Thomas Nivison Haining. Oxford, 1992.

Turnbull, Stephen. *Genghis Khan & the Mongol Conquests, 1190–1400.* New York, 2003.

Klaus Sagaster (1987)
Revised Bibliography

CHING-T'U SEE JINGTU

CHINUL

CHINUL (1158–1210), also known as National Master Puril Pojo; founder of the indigenous Chogye school of Korean Sŏn (Chin., Chan; Jpn., Zen). Chinul was born in 1158 to a gentry family in the Koryŏ capital of Kaesŏng. When seven years old, he was ordained into the Sagul-san lineage of the Nine Mountains school of early Sŏn and soon distinguished himself in both meditation and scriptural study. Chinul became dissatisfied with the quality of practice within the degenerate Sŏn schools of his time, however, and increasingly turned for guidance to the sources that he considered to contain authentic information on Buddhist meditative culture: scriptures and commentaries and the records of early Sŏn and Chan masters. Prompted by his vision of the basic unity of Sŏn and the scriptural teachings (*kyo*; Chin., *jiao*), Chinul developed an approach to Buddhism that combined the theoretical aids of Hwaŏm (Chin., Huayan) doctrine, especially as formulated in works by the Huayan commentator Li Tongxuan (635–730), with the practical concerns of Chan meditation, as typified in the instructions of Dahui Zonggao (1089–1163). This unique synthesis is rightly regarded as one of the most distinctively Korean contributions to Buddhist thought and illustrates the ecumenical penchant that is so characteristic of the Korean church. Chinul's insights provided a modus operandi for consolidating the divided Koryŏ Buddhist church, which remained bifurcated between the Sŏn and scholastic schools despite Ŭich'ŏn's attempts at unification a century before. More important for the future of the tradition, however, Chinul's thought also served as the inspiration for the development of a truly indigenous Korean school of Sŏn, the Chogye school, of which he is considered the founder.

Chinul outlined an approach to Buddhist practice that begins with the intuitive grasp of the significance of the scriptural teaching that an ordinary person (i.e., the practitioner himself) is already identical to the buddhas (enlightened beings). This sudden awakening of understanding (*haeo*; Chin., *jiewu*) brings about the provisional entrance into the Buddhist path of practice (Skt., *mārga*) at the first of the ten levels of faith. Awakening was then to be refined continuously in order to remove defilements and develop salutary qualities of mind. This gradual training finally culminates in the awakening of realization (*chŭngo*; Chin., *zhengwu*), the direct experience of the truths that are originally understood intellectually, which takes place at the first of the ten abidings (*daśavihāra*), the formal entrance into the *bodhisattva* path. This approach of sudden awakening/gradual cultivation (*tono chŏmsu*; Chin., *dunwu jianxiu*) was heavily indebted to the insights of the Chinese Chan/Huayan master Zongmi (780–841), another of the main influences on Chinul's thought.

Three principal meditative techniques were used by Chinul to bring about the consummation of this soteriological process: the dual cultivation of concentration and wisdom, as explained in the *Liuzu tanjing* (Platform scripture of the sixth patriarch); faith and understanding according to the complete and sudden school of Hwaŏm; and the distinctively Sŏn approach of investigating the critical phrase (*hwadu*; Chin., *huatou*). Chinul was the first Korean master to teach the formal *hwadu* technique developed by Dahui Zonggao, which is better known by the synonymous term *kongan* (Chin., *gong'an*; Jpn., *kōan*). In several of his writings Chinul provides an exhaustive outline of the correct approach to investigating the *hwadu*, while emphasizing its affinities with more traditional soteriological schemes. The initial investigation of the meaning of the *hwadu* (*ch'amŭi*; Chin., *canyi*) counteracts the discriminative tendencies of thought by focusing the mind on a single insoluble question. This concentration ultimately removes the obstacle of understanding and catalyzes the awakening of understanding. Continuing to investigate only the word itself devoid of any conceptual content (*ch'amgu*; Chin., *canju*) engenders the state of no-thought (*munyŏm*; Chin., *wunian*), which brings about the awakening of realization and the adept's initiation into the formal *mārga*.

SEE ALSO Buddhism, article on Buddhism in Korea; Chan; Huayan; Zongmi.

BIBLIOGRAPHY

Buswell, Robert E., Jr. *The Korean Approach to Zen: The Collected Works of Chinul.* Honolulu, 1983.

Buswell, Robert E., Jr. "Chinul's Systematization of Chinese Meditative Techniques in Korean Sŏn Buddhism," in *Chinese Buddhist Traditions of Meditation*, Studies in East Asian Buddhism, no. 4, edited by Peter N. Gregory, pp. 199–242. Honolulu, 1986.

Buswell, Robert E., Jr. "Ch'an Hermeneutics: A Korean View," in *Buddhist Hermeneutics*, edited by Donald S. Lopez, Jr., pp. 231–256. Honolulu, 1988.

Buswell, Robert E., Jr. "Chinul's Ambivalent Critique of Radical Subitism in Korean Sŏn." *Journal of the International Association of Buddhist Studies* 12, no. 2 (1989): 20–44.

Buswell, Robert E., Jr. "Chinul's Alternative Vision of Kanhwa Sŏn and Its Implications for Sudden Awakening/Gradual Cultivation." *Pojo sasang* 4 (1990): 423–447.

Buswell, Robert E., Jr. *Tracing Back the Radiance: Chinul's Korean Way of Zen.* Honolulu, 1991.

Gregory, Peter N. "The Integration of Ch'an/Sŏn and the Teachings (*Chiao/Kyo*) in Tsung-mi and Chinul." *Journal of the International Association of Buddhist Studies* 12, no. 2 (1989): 7–19.

Kang, Kun Ki. *Moguja Chinul yŏn'gu (A Study of Chinul).* Seoul, 2001.

Keel, Hee-Sung. *Chinul: The Founder of the Korean Sŏn Tradition.* Berkeley, 1984.

Shim, Jae-ryong. *Korean Buddhism: Tradition and Transformation.* Seoul, 1999.

Yi, Chongik. *Kangoku Bukkyō no kenkyū (A Study of Korean Buddhism).* Tokyo, 1980.

ROBERT EVANS BUSWELL, JR. (1987 AND 2005)

CHINVAT BRIDGE, the "crossing" or "bridge of the separator" or of the "decision"—the meaning is not certain—is, in the Zoroastrian tradition, a mythical bridge that souls must cross to go to Paradise. They succeed in crossing it only if they are souls of the *asha-van,* that is, faithful followers of *asha,* truth and order (Vedic, *ṛta*), the fundamental principle of Indo-Iranian religion. If they are souls of the *dregvant,* that is, followers of *druj* (falsehood), they will fall off the bridge, which for them will narrow itself to a razor's edge, and they will forever reside in Hell. Indeed, Chinvat Bridge stretches over the infernal abysses. One of its ends is on the peak of Mount Harā, also known as Alburz or Harā Berez ("high Harā")—a mythical mountain that figures importantly in Indo-Iranian cosmological conceptions; the other end reaches Paradise *(garōdman),* which the soul of the *ashavan* will enter after passing through the "Region of the Mixed" *(hamistagān)* and then through the halls of Good Thought, Good Word, and Good Deed.

Awaiting the soul on Chinvat Bridge is a divine tribunal composed of the deities Mithra, Sraosha ("discipline"), and Rashnu ("the judge"), assisted by Arshtāt ("justice"). It is then that the soul confronts its own inner self, its *daēnā,* the sum of its thoughts, words, and deeds. The *daēnā* can take the form of a magnificent maiden or of a horrible witch, according to the individual case. It serves as psychopomp for the rest of the voyage, accompanying the soul of the *ashavan* to paradise, where it is received by Vohu Manah ("good thought"), one of the Amesha Spentas, or beneficent immortals, and comforted for the difficult and painful test it experienced during its separation from the body.

This scenario is very ancient: Chinvat Bridge and the *daēnā* are both mentioned in the *Gāthās.* Many aspects of this belief—in particular, that of the bridge—are reminiscent of conceptions in other religious traditions, above all those of the shamanistic variety.

A passage to the beyond, Chinvat Bridge can also be considered the path of the soul to heaven during an ecstatic experience (Nyberg, 1938). It thus figures not only in conceptions of the afterlife but also in the religious transports that occur during initiations, which are analogous to death.

BIBLIOGRAPHY

Boyce, Mary. *A History of Zoroastrianism,* vol. 1. Leiden, 1975.

Corbin, Henry. *Terre céleste et corps de résurrection.* Paris, 1961.

Eliade, Mircea. *Shamanism: Archaic Techniques of Ecstasy.* Rev. & enl. ed. New York, 1964.

Gnoli, Gherardo. "Ašavan: Contributo allo studio del libro di Ardā Wirāz." In *Iranica,* edited by Gherardo Gnoli and Adriano V. Rossi, pp. 387–452. Naples, 1979.

Kellens, Jean. "Yima et la mort." In *Languages and Cultures. Studies in Honor of Edgar C. Polomé,* edited by M. A. Jazayery and W. Winter, pp. 329–334. Berlin–New York–Amsterdam, 1988.

Lommel, Herman. *Die Religion Zarathustras nach dem Awesta dargestellt.* Tübingen, 1930.

Molé, Marijan. "Daēnā, le pont Činvat et l'initiation dans le Mazdéisme." *Revue de l'histoire des religions* 158 (1960): 155–185.

Nyberg, H. S. *Die Religionen des alten Iran.* Leipzig, 1938.

Pavry, J. D. C. *The Zoroastrian Doctrine of a Future Life.* New York, 1926.

Widengren, Geo. *Stand und Aufgaben der iranischen Religionsgeschichte.* Leiden, 1955.

Widengren, Geo. *Les religions de l'Iran.* Paris, 1968.

GHERARDO GNOLI (1987)

Translated from Italian by Roger DeGaris

CHIPPEWA RELIGIOUS TRADITIONS SEE ANISHINAABE RELIGIOUS TRADITIONS

CHI-TSANG SEE JIZANG

CH'ŎNDOGYO (Religion of the Heavenly Way) is an indigenous Korean religion influenced by Confucianism and Daoism. It was founded in 1860 by Ch'oe Suun (Che-u; 1824–1864) in reaction to the traditional religions of Korea and in an attempt to offer a new religious dispensation to the masses. Originally known as Tonghak (Eastern Learning), the movement was also a reaction to Christianity, known as Sohak (Western Learning). The name was changed to Ch'ŏndogyo in 1905.

Suun was born in Kyŏngju, the ancient capital of the kingdom of Silla. According to Ch'ŏndogyo tradition, he received from God a revelation of *ch'ŏndo* (the Heavenly Way), a new universal truth. His teaching attracted a large following, but it was regarded as dangerous by the government, and he was martyred. Nevertheless, the movement continued to grow under the leadership of Suun's successor, Ch'oe Haewŏl (Si-hyŏng; 1827–1898), and under the third leader, Sohn Ŭiam (Pyŏng-hŭi; 1861–1922), Ch'ŏndogyo became one of the major religions of Korea. The writings of these first three leaders form the Ch'ŏndogyo scripture (*Ch'ŏndogyo kyŭngjŭn*). The most important part of this canon is Suun's writings, known as Tonghak Scripture or even Ch'ŏndogyo Scripture.

The antigovernmental Tonghak Revolution of 1894, a popular uprising under Tonghak leadership, helped to modernize Korean society. Ch'ŏndogyo also played a leading role among Korean religions in the Samil (March 1) Independence Movement of 1919 against Japanese colonialism. Since the demise of Sohn Uiam, Ch'ŏndogyo has remained a religion with a democratic system of ecclesiastical government. Currently, Ch'ŏndogyo membership is approximately one million and its headquarters are in Seoul. The church plays no active role in South Korean politics. In North Korea, Ch'ŏndogyo has been persecuted under communism since 1945.

Beliefs and Practices. The common term for God in Ch'ŏndogyo is Hanullim, or Heavenly Lord, although scripture also uses the epithet Ch'ŏnju, a Chinese form of Hanullim. (The latter is related to other Korean names for God, Hanŭnim and Hananim.) Ch'ŏndogyo conceives God as the totality of life or the universe, and his immanence is emphasized more than his transcendence.

The Ch'ŏndogyo view of human nature is expressed in two key phrases, "Si Ch'ŏnju" ("Man bears divinity") and "In nae Ch'on" ("Man is God"). Man is one with God in essence and in potentiality, and realizes this oneness in the practice of sincere faith and morality. These ideas reflect a mystical as well as a humanistic tendency. Since man is essentially divine, one must treat others with the utmost concern, respect, sincerity, dignity, equality, and justice. Thus the injunction "Sain yŏch'ŏn" ("Treat man as God") has been the central ethical teaching of Ch'ŏndogyo. This democratic principle was a revolutionary one in nineteenth-century feudalistic Korean society.

The Ch'ŏndogyo concept of human destiny is basically this-worldly, expressed in terms of a divine life or kingdom of heaven on earth. Ch'ŏndogyo emphasizes a cooperative community of humankind.

In Ch'ŏndogyo, the spiritual life is fostered by observance of the Five Practices (*ogwan*):

1. Incantation (*chumun*). Ch'ŏndogyo devotees seek oneness with God by chanting a formula that translates: "Ultimate Energy being here and now, I yearn for its great descent. Bearing God, I become firm and well. Never forgetting, I become aware of all." It is chanted at 9:00 PM every day and also at other times on special occasions. At the Sunday worship service, the second half of the incantation ("Bearing God . . .") is chanted.
2. Pure Water (*ch'ŏngsu*). In all ceremonies and at 9:00 PM daily, a bowl of pure water is placed on a table and the worshipers meditate on the significance of water as a symbol of spiritual purity.
3. Service Day *(siil).* The Sunday worship service includes prayer, hymns, scripture reading, and a sermon.
4. Sincerity Rice (*sŏngmi*). Believers put aside some rice each day and offer it to the church at the end of the month.
5. Prayer (*kido*). Prayer expresses the worshiper's wishes. A silent meditative prayer called *simgo* (heart address) is also practiced at mealtimes, before and after sleeping, and in all ceremonies.

Finally, Ch'ŏndogyo stresses moral discipline. It requires of its followers that they keep a steadfast mind, avoid materialistic desires, and cultivate sincerity, respect for others, and faith.

Bibliography

My book on Ch'ŏndogyo thought, *The Ch'ŏndogyo Concept of Man: An Essence of Korean Thought* (Seoul, 1978), contains a glossary and an extensive bibliography. Benjamin B. Weems's *Reform, Rebellion, and the Heavenly Way* (Tucson, 1964) deals mainly with the role that Ch'ŏndogyo played in Korean politics, but it also contains much of Ch'ŏndogyo history and cites some Ch'ŏndogyo ideas and practices. It includes a useful glossary, bibliography, and index. These two studies are the only books in English that deal exclusively with Ch'ŏndogyo.

The following books in Korean are good sources for understanding Ch'ŏndogyo: Che-u Ch'oe's *Ch'ŏndogyo Kyŏngjŏn* (*Tonghak Kyŏngjŏn*) (Seoul, 1961), Paek Se-myŏng's *Tonghak sasang kwa Ch'ŏndogyo* (Seoul, 1956), and Ch'oe Tong-hŭi and Kim Yong-ch'ŏn's *Ch'ŏndogyo* (Iri, 1976).

New Sources

An, Sang-jin. *Continuity and Transformation: Religious Syntheses in East Asia.* New York, 2001.

Belrene, Paul. "The Eclectic Mysticism of Ch'oe Cheu." *Review of Korean Studies* 2 (1999): 159–182.

Lee, Sang-Chan. "A Critical Study of the Popular View of the 'Righteous Army Movement' of 1896." *Seoul Journal of Korean Studies* 12 (1999): 124–151.

Yong-choon Kim (1987)
Revised Bibliography

CHŎNG YAGYONG (1762–1836), foremost representative of Korea's Sirhak (Practical Learning) movement and creator of a theistic Confucian philosophy. He is best known by his honorific name, Tasan. The Sirhak movement was characterized by a spirit of seeking evidence to establish fact, as opposed to more speculative modes of thought, and a spirit of practicality as seen in studies concerned with administrative and economic reform. Contemporary Koreans look to Sirhak as a kind of indigenous proto-modernity within their own tradition, although the movement seems to have largely dissolved by the second half of the nineteenth century. Tasan is especially revered as the preeminent intellectual figure of the movement, a polymath who mastered the principles of Western mechanics to build a town wall, wrote insightful treatises on government and social reform, and in his many works passed in critical review some two thousand years of Confucian learning. He was also one of East Asia's most prolific authors: his collected works, written in literary Chinese, come to more than eighteen thousand pages.

In his youth Tasan was a member of the small group of scholars that became interested in the Chinese writings of the Jesuit missionary Matteo Ricci (1552–1610). In 1784, while on a tribute mission to Beijing, one of the members of the group, Yi Sŭnghun, visited a European missionary and was baptized; he returned to Korea and baptized a number of other members in the group, including Tasan's two brothers. The movement spread rapidly, and when the first priest arrived in Korea in 1794 there were already some four thousand Korean Catholics.

It is not clear whether Tasan was ever baptized, but his connections to Catholicism were close enough to implicate him in the first large-scale purge of Catholics from government in 1801. The nineteen years of exile that followed these persecutions were a period of enforced seclusion in which Tasan devoted himself completely to study and writing, a style of life he maintained after the ban was lifted. During this long period he occupied himself not only with the practical studies typical of Sirhak but with the whole tradition of Confucian scholarship. In fact more than half of his voluminous collected works is devoted to commentary on the Confucian classics and related matters.

Tasan's reappraisal of the Confucian tradition is unusual, perhaps unique, for he took his viewpoint from the earliest classics, those that preserved an early Chinese theism that was already waning by the time of Confucius. On this basis, he reconstructed not just a primitive theistic Confucianism but a philosophically systematic Confucian theism that matched the sophisticated metaphysical and ascetic systems of the neo-Confucians. His work in this regard is notable especially for the completeness and maturity with which he grasped the ramifications of a theistic perspective.

Tasan's Confucianism had no intellectual heir. In part this is because he spent his last thirty-five years under a cloud of suspicion and in relative isolation, in part because his accomplishments occurred when Korea was on the threshold of a tumultuous change that dislocated the tradition he had accepted as authoritative.

See Also Confucianism in Korea; Ricci, Matteo.

Bibliography

For general introductions to Sirhak, see *The Traditional Culture and Society of Korea: Thought and Institutions*, edited by Hugh H. W. Kang (Honolulu, 1975), and my article "An Introduction to Silhak," *Korea Journal* 15 (1975): 29–46. A biographical account of Chŏng Yagyong's life can be found in Gregory Henderson's "Chŏng Ta-san: A Study in Korea's Intellectual History," *Journal of Asian Studies* 16 (1957): 377–386. A discussion and analysis of the meeting of theistic and nontheistic worldviews in Chŏng's work is my "Chŏng Tasan's Philosophy of Man: A Radical Critique of the Neo-Confucian World View," *Journal of Korean Studies* 3 (1981): 3–38.

New Sources

Kalton, Michael C. et al., trans. *The Forty-Seven Debate: An Annotated Translation of the Most Famous Controversy in Korean Neo-Confucian Thought.* Albany, 1994.

Kim, Sunghae. "Chŏng Yagyong (Tasan): Creative Bridge between the East and the West." In *Confucian Philosophy in Korea*, edited by Haechang Choung and Hyong-jo Han, pp. 213–291. Songnam, 1996.

Setton, Mark. *Chŏng Yagyong: Korea's Challenge to Orthodox Neo-Confucianism.* Albany, 1997.

Michael C. Kalton (1987)
Revised Bibliography

CHOSEN PEOPLE See ELECTION

CHOU TUN-I See ZHOU DUNYI

CHRIST See JESUS

CHRISTENSEN, ARTHUR

CHRISTENSEN, ARTHUR (1875–1945), Danish Orientalist and folklorist. Arthur Emanuel Christensen was born in Copenhagen, where, apart from short periods of study and travel, he spent his life. He studied in Berlin and Göttingen, passing his *Studentereksamen* in 1893 and obtaining his *candidatus magisterii* (master's degree) in French, history, and Latin in 1900. During his university years, Christensen was also a fervent student of Persian, Avestan, Arabic, Sanskrit, and Turkish. He studied under the famous Iranologist F. C. Andreas, and, in 1903, he obtained his Ph.D. He became a teacher and journalist, specializing in foreign politics. In 1919, he was appointed professor extraordinarius of Iranian philology at the University of Copenhagen, an office that he held for the rest of his life.

Christensen was a prolific writer who wrote on many aspects of Iranian cultural history, including language (dialect studies), folklore, general history, history of religions, philosophy, and music. His magnum opus, *L'empire des Sassanides: Le peuple, l'état, la cour* (1907), was written from a religio-historical point of view. Though Christensen elaborated various points in Sassanid history, he was chiefly concerned with chronological and purely historical and legendary elements. Examples of this interest are his *Le règne du roi Kawādh I et le communisme masdakite* (1925), which deals with the fifth-century communalist reformer Mazdak, and "La légende du sage Buzurjmihr" (*Acta Orientalia* 8, 1930), which examines one of the strangest figures of the Sassanid tradition.

Of religious life as such Christensen seems to have had no real sense; in his heart he doubted that it was possible to gain secure knowledge of what had once been a living religion in ancient Iran. His intention was to give a complete representation of the Iranian legendary history, the religious and national heritage that the Sassanids took over and attempted to legitimate as their own. He carried out his plan in a series of works of extraordinary importance for Indo-Iranian research in the areas of legend and religion, and for the understanding of legends and folktales in general. Through his endeavors to provide a theoretical and practical foundation for the study of tradition, legend, and myth, Christensen encountered the works of folklorists such as Axel Olrik and C. W. von Sydow, which led him into studies of general folklore, folk psychology, and philosophy. Christensen's foremost contribution to the study of folklore is his *Trebrødre- og Tobrødre Stamsagn* (1916), which gives a simple and natural psychological explanation of national ancestral legends.

To Avestan studies Christensen brought new understanding and inspiration. Problems concerning the time and environment of Zarathushtra (Zoroaster) and the chronology of the *Gatha* and the *Yashts* were his main concern. The systematic expression of his thought is given in several works: "Quelques notices sur les plus anciennes périodes du Zoroastrisme" (*Acta Orientalia* 4, 1926, pp. 81–115), *Études sur le Zoroastrisme de la Perse antique* (1928), and *Le premier chapitre du Vendidad et l'histoire primitive des tribus iraniennes* (1943). These works reveal Christensen as a bold interpreter whose theses would both inspire and irritate his contemporaries and future scholars.

BIBLIOGRAPHY

Christensen's *Recherches sur les Rubāʿiyāt de ʿOmar Ḫayyām* (Heidelberg, 1905) was written as his doctoral thesis; it was published in Danish in 1903. Later, he returned to this topic with *Critical Studies in the Rubáiyát of Umar-i-Khayyám* (Copenhagen, 1927). His great work, *L'empire des Sassanides: Le peuple, l'état, la cour* (Copenhagen, 1907) was twice revised and expanded under the title *L'Iran sous les Sassanides*, 2d ed. (1944; Osnabrück, 1971); it has also been translated into Persian. An examination of the shortcomings of Christensen's *magnum opus* can be found in Phillipe Gignoux's article "Die religiöse Administration in sasanidischer Zeit: Ein Überblick," *Archäologische Mitteilungen aus Iran* (suppl. 10, 1983): 253ff.

Among Christensen's works on the legendary history of Iran, the following deserve mention: "Reste von Manu-Legenden in der iranischen Sagenwelt," in *Festschrift Friedrich Carl Andreas* (Leipzig, 1916), pp. 63–69; *Les types du premier homme et le premier roi dans l'histoire légendaire des Iraniens*, 2 vols. (Stockholm, 1917–1934); *Les Kayanides* (Copenhagen, 1931); and *Les gestes des rois dans les traditions de l'Iran antique* (Paris, 1936). Notable among Christensen's studies of Iranian folklore are the following: *Contes persans en langue populaire* (Copenhagen, 1918); "Les sots dans la tradition populaire des Persans," *Acta Orientalia* 1 (1922): 43–75; and *Essai sur la démonologie iranienne* (Copenhagen, 1941) in which he shows how ancient Iranian elements of folk belief survive within the framework of present-day Islam. A significant example of Christensen's work of general folklore and folk psychology is his *Politik og masse-moral* (Copenhagen, 1911), which was translated by A. Cecil Curtis under the title *Politics and Crowd-Morality* (London, 1915).

A biographical appreciation of Christensen by Kaj Barr and H. Andersen appears in *Oversigt over Det Kongelige Danske Videnskabernes Selskab: Forhandlinger* (Copenhagen, 1945–1946), pp. 65–102; it includes a complete bibliography of 327 items. A biographical note by myself and Frank le Sage de Fontenay appears in *Dansk biografisk leksikon*, 3d ed., vol. 3 (Copenhagen, 1979), pp. 233–236.

JES P. ASMUSSEN (1987)

CHRISTIAN ETHICS.

The three primary manifestations of Christianity—Eastern Orthodoxy, Roman Catholicism, and Protestantism—have recognized that Christian faith involves a particular way of life. The good news of salvation in Jesus Christ calls for a life of discipleship. The scriptures point out that Christian believers are to live and act in certain ways. Conversion to Jesus Christ and membership in the Christian community involve moral exigencies.

CHRISTIAN ETHICS IN GENERAL. The Bible is the book of Christianity, but it does not contain Christian ethics as such. The Bible does include moral teachings and descriptions of the moral life of believers in Yahveh and in Jesus. The distinction between morality and ethics is significant. Morality refers to the actions, dispositions, attitudes, virtues, and ways of life that should characterize the moral person and society, in this case the Christian person and the Christian community. Christian ethics operates on the level of the theoretical and the scientific and tries to explain the Christian moral life in a thematic, systematic, coherent, and consistent manner. It is possible for one to attempt a biblical ethic that makes such an explanation of biblical morality, but that ethic would be based on the moral teaching found in Scripture. Biblical ethics and Christian ethics are not coextensive. The subject matter of Christian ethics is the Christian moral life and teaching, which is much broader than biblical moral life and teaching.

The relationship between Christian ethics and philosophical ethics is important. The significant differences between the two result from the different sources of ethical wisdom and knowledge employed. Philosophical ethics is based on human reason and human experience and does not accept the role of faith and revelation that is central to Christian ethics. However, Christian ethics poses the same basic questions and has the same formal structure as philosophical ethics. All ethics attempts to respond to the same questions: What is the good? What values and goals should be pursued? What attitudes and dispositions should characterize the person? What acts are right? What acts are wrong? How do the individual and society go about making ethical decisions? What are just societal structures?

Contemporary ethicists speak about three generally accepted formal approaches to ethics. The classical forms are teleology and deontology. The teleological approach determines what is the end or the good at which one should aim and then determines the morality of means in relationship to that end. The deontological model understands morality primarily in terms of duty, law, or obligation. Such an approach is primarily interested in what is right. In the twentieth century, some ethicists (e.g., H. Richard Niebuhr) have proposed a third model: the responsibility model, which is primarily interested in what is "fitting." Within Christian ethics all these different models have been employed. Teleology, for example, sees the end of the moral life as union with and participation in God, which becomes the good and the end of the moral life, thus specifying as good those means that attain that end. Deontological Christian ethics has often seen the moral life in terms of the Ten Commandments or the revealed word of God as the law Christians are to follow.

God's law determines what is right and wrong. The responsibility model understands the moral life on the basis of the Christian's response to the action and working of God in the world and in history.

The vast majority of Christian ethicists would agree that theological ethics is truly a form of ethics, that it asks the same questions and has the same formal structure as philosophical ethics. However, some Christians working out of a more fundamentalistic approach to the scriptures or out of a Barthian perspective might not agree that Christian ethics is a species of ethics as such.

SOURCES. What distinguishes Christian ethics from philosophical ethics and other religious ethics are the sources of wisdom and knowledge that contribute to Christian ethics. All Christian ethics recognizes the Christian scriptures, tradition, and church teaching as the revelatory sources of moral wisdom and knowledge. However, there is much discussion as to how these sources relate to one another and to the nonrevelatory sources of Christian ethics. The three major expressions of Christianity—Eastern Orthodoxy, Roman Catholicism, and Protestantism—and their corresponding ethical traditions emphasize different sources of Christian ethics. At least in theory, all these traditions give primary emphasis to sacred scripture, but there is no general agreement about how the scriptures should be used in Christian ethics.

The role accorded scripture in Christian ethics depends heavily on one's understanding of scripture's relationship to other sources of wisdom and knowledge. On such questions as those having to do with conversion or change of heart, the general attitudes a Christian should have, and the goals and dispositions of the Christian life, the scriptures can give much content to Christian ethics. On the question of precise norms and rules of moral action, however, many Christian ethicists are cautious in their attempts to find specific concrete norms that are absolutely binding in all circumstances. Protestantism's emphasis on the primacy of scripture and downplaying of tradition and church teaching distinguishes its ethics from that of the other two major forms of Christianity.

Since the church is a living communion proceeding through different historical and cultural circumstances under the guidance of the continuing presence of the Holy Spirit, God's self-revelation comes also through tradition as the preaching, teaching, celebration, and practice of the Christian faith. Within the general category of tradition, special emphasis is given, especially by the Eastern Orthodox churches, to the teachings of the patristic period and to the councils and legislation of that time. Authoritative or authentic church teaching is a special form of tradition that is found in the councils and synods of the churches, and in Roman Catholicism it is connected with the teaching office of the bishops, especially of the pope as the bishop of Rome and pastor of the universal church.

Christian ethics has always grappled with the question of whether human nature, human reason, and human experience can be sources of ethical wisdom and knowledge. The Roman Catholic tradition has emphasized natural law based on the ability of human reason to arrive at ethical wisdom and knowledge. This emphasis has often been more primary than the influence of revelatory sources. Eastern Orthodox and Protestant ethics have been more suspicious of human reason and experience, although today many ethicists in these traditions give reason and experience an important, though still subordinate, role.

EARLY HISTORY. In the first one thousand years of Christianity, there was no discipline of Christian ethics as such. Moral teaching was primarily pastoral, apologetical, homiletical, and catechetical, although at times there were systematic studies of particular issues. An early problem for the Christian church was the relationship of Christian mores to the culture and mores of the wider society. Pedagogical devices such as "the two ways" (elaborated on in the *Didache* and *Shepherd of Hermas*) and catalogs of virtues and vices were used by the early Christian writers. Often the patristic authors borrowed from Stoic and Neoplatonic philosophies of the times. The apologists of the second century attempted to show that Christian morality was in keeping with the best pagan understandings of morality.

In the third century, Tertullian stressed the differences between pagan and Christian moral teaching and proposed a rigorous and legalistic morality. The early church fathers relied heavily on scriptural teaching and often understood moral life in terms of the imitation of Christ. Exhortation to perseverance in the face of martyrdom, the avoidance of any type of idolatry, and the need for prayer, fasting, almsgiving, chastity, patience, and justice were stressed. Eastern moral thought, as reflected in that of Athanasius and the Alexandrians, stressed the divinization of human beings through the gift of the Holy Spirit. The Antiochian school understood justification in terms of sharing in the suffering, death, and resurrection of Jesus. Throughout the period of persecution great emphasis was put on martyrdom, but afterward substitutions for martyrdom (the word originally meant "witness") were proposed: the monastic life or strict obedience to God's will, sometimes called "the martyrdom of conscience."

In the West after the third century, the most significant figures were Ambrose, Augustine, and Pope Gregory I. Ambrose's *De officiis* is perhaps the most systematic, scientific approach to Christian morality, with its basis in the treatise of Cicero. Gregory, in his homilies and his *Moralia in Job,* often relies on the moral teaching of Augustine but emphasizes the practical and pastoral aspects of Christian morality. Augustine defends a Christian moral understanding against the dualism and pessimism of Manichaeans on the one hand and the optimism of Pelagians on the other. Augustine devoted a number of works to specific moral questions, such as lying, continence, marriage, and concupiscence. His major works, the *Confessions* and the *City of God,* also contain some methodological and substantive considerations in Christian ethics, even though there is no fully systematic treatise on moral theology. Augustine stresses the centrality of the grace of God, which delivers sinners from evil and makes the Christian life possible. The moral life is described in terms of love. The love of God aims at the enjoyment of God for God's own sake and uses everything else for the love of God, whereas desire involves attempts to enjoy self, neighbor, and earthly things without reference to God. These two different loves are the sources of the good life and the bad life, respectively. Augustine's eschatology emphasizes a great difference between the present world and the future reign of God at the end of time, a recognition that grounds his profound realism about life in this world.

In the East, the fathers showed a great interest in contemplation. Obedience to God's commandments, the practice of asceticism, and contemplation were proposed not only for monks but for all Christians. At the end of the patristic era in the East, John of Damascus (d. 749) summarized patristic teachings on the moral life by using Aristotelian concepts.

Before the end of the first millennium an important development occurred in the practice of the sacrament of penance. In the West, the new form of private penance spread from Ireland to the continent, and with the new repeatable private penance the *libri poenitentiales* (penitential books) came into existence. These books assigned a particular penance for a particular sin and were often used in a very mechanistic way. There were also penitentials in the East, such as the *Penitential of John the Faster* and others, which were borrowed from the West. However, the sacrament of penance in the East always emphasized the spiritual direction aspect of the relationship between penitent and monk-confessor, thereby avoiding, at least in theory, the dangers of legalism and ritualism. A scientific and systematic Christian ethic developed only in the second millennium.

THE EASTERN ORTHODOX TRADITION. Eastern Orthodox theology, in both its Greek and Russian approaches, is distinguished from other Christian ethics by its emphasis on tradition, especially the teachings of the church fathers, as important sources of moral wisdom and knowledge. The most distinctive characteristic of Orthodox ethics is its relationship to spirituality. Pastoral practice has emphasized the role of monks and confessors as spiritual directors who help guide the spiritual life of the faithful. The goal or end of the moral life is to become like God. The way to this full deification (*theosis* in the Greek) is through asceticism and prayer. Contemplation and contemplative prayer as parts of the struggle for deification are stressed. This perfectionist ethic calls for constant deepening of the believer's participation in divine life.

The anthropological basis for this movement toward deification is the creation of human beings in the image and likeness of God. "Image" consists in the human moral capacities of virtue, intellect, ethical judgment, and self-determination. The image of God is darkened and wounded by sin but still remains. "Likeness" refers to the human potential to become like God. In the Orthodox tradition, as in the Roman Catholic tradition, Christian morality is not heteronomous, for Christian morality brings the human to its fullest perfection. In the same way such an ethics stresses both the providence of God and the responsibility of Christians.

Within the Orthodox tradition there is doubt that natural law is a source of ethical wisdom and knowledge. Many affirm such knowledge on the basis of creation and the image of God embodied in human moral capacity, but others strongly deny this knowledge. At times the polemical nature of discussions between the Orthodox and Roman Catholic traditions seems to have influenced the Orthodox denial of natural law.

Law in general has a significant but not exclusive role to play in Orthodox ethics. Law is found in the Ten Commandments, the Beatitudes, the teachings of the New Testament, and the sayings of the church fathers. Although some Orthodox ethicists might have become legalistic or ritualistic, the tradition itself generally guards against legalism, especially by invocation of the principle of "economy." Economy allows exceptions to the law when the law stands in the way of the higher values of human persons and communities.

Orthodox ethics has been accused of lacking a world-transforming aspect and failing to develop an adequate social ethic, but many defenders of the Orthodox tradition deny this charge. In the past, social ethics was colored by recognition of a "symphony" between the church and the state in the single organism of the Christian empire. Today, the diverse settings in which the Orthodox church functions have forced it to try to work out a social ethic and the church's relationship to the state. Russian Orthodoxy in the twentieth century often found itself in relationship to communist governments, but the situation dramatically changed after 1989. In Europe and the United States, Russian and Greek Orthodox churches now also find themselves in a diaspora situation in which they, as a minority, must develop their own approach to social ethics. The Greek Orthodox church and the Russian Orthodox church have joined the World Council of Churches, so that Orthodoxy now participates, though not without tensions, in the current discussions and positions taken on contemporary social questions by the World Council.

HISTORICAL DEVELOPMENT OF EASTERN ORTHODOX ETHICS. Christian ethics as a separate discipline emerged comparatively late in the Orthodox tradition. After the Great Schism of the ninth century, the penitentials continued to be an important genre of moral teaching in the East. Despite some legalistic and ritualistic tendencies, Orthodoxy's emphasis on spirituality and striving for perfection served as a safeguard against a minimalistic legalism.

In Russian Orthodoxy the seventeenth-century Kiev school attempted to refute Roman Catholicism and its ethics by developing a theology strongly influenced by scholasticism. The *Orthodox Confession* of Petr Moghila (d. 1646), which was approved with slight modifications by the Greek patriarch at the Synod of Jerusalem (1672), explains Christian moral teaching on the basis of the nine precepts of the church, the seven sacraments, the Beatitudes, and the Ten Commandments. However, even the Kiev school stressed more distinctly Russian and patristic theology in its ascetical and spiritual works.

The eighteenth and nineteenth centuries in Russian Orthodox ethics again saw both dialogue and polemics with Roman Catholic and Protestant ethics in the West. Feofan Prokopovich (d. 1736) ignored the Orthodox tradition, rejected Catholic scholasticism, and turned to Protestant authors for his ethical principles. Some subsequent authors followed the same approach, but F. Fiveiskii (d. 1877) returned to more patristic sources and to a more Catholic methodology in his manual of moral theology, the official textbook in all seminaries until 1867.

The years from 1860 to 1863 saw the publication of P. F. Soliarskii's moral theology, which tried to combine patristic, Roman Catholic, and Protestant approaches to ethics. An abridged edition of this influential work was used in the schools for forty years. In the late nineteenth century the influence of modernism and its stress on the role of the natural moral sense influenced some approaches to moral theology. However, in addition to these manuals of moral theology, there was also a spiritual and mystical literature that drew heavily from patristic sources. In the twentieth century, Nikolai Berdiaev and Sergei Bulgakov appealed to the Russian Orthodox tradition in developing what can be called a communitarian personalism with emphasis on subjectivity, freedom, love, and the need to transform the objective world.

According to Stanley S. Harakas, Christian ethics as a separate theological discipline in Greek Orthodoxy developed in the modern period and emerged as a separate, distinct, scientific discipline only in the nineteenth century. Three different schools or approaches characterize Greek Orthodox moral theology from that time. The Athenian school, strongly influenced by philosophical idealism, sees no vital differences between Christian ethics and philosophical ethics. The Constantinopolitan school is Christocentric and depends heavily on Scripture and the church fathers. The Thessalonian school is apophatic in character, stresses a personalist perspective, and is heavily dependent on the monastic tradition. In his *Toward Transfigured Life,* Harakas tries to bring these three schools together.

THE ROMAN CATHOLIC TRADITION. The characteristics of Roman Catholic "moral theology," as Christian ethics has come to be called in the Catholic tradition, are insistence on mediation, acceptance of natural law, and the role of the church. Mediation is perhaps the most characteristic aspect of Roman Catholic theology in general. There is a distinctive Catholic emphasis on conjunctions—of Scripture and tradition, faith and reason, faith and works, grace and nature, the divine and human, Jesus and the church and Mary and the saints, love (as well as the virtues) and the commandments. This approach is an attempt to be universal and to embrace all elements, but it may fall into dichotomy. For example, rather than seeing tradition as a mediation of revelation whose privileged witness is in sacred Scripture, Scripture and tradition were seen as two separate fonts of revelation. Further, faith and works, properly understood, mean that the gift of salvation is mediated in and through the human response; a perennial danger is to absolutize works. Likewise, mediation insists on the importance of love, but love mediated through all the other virtues and commandments, which, however, must not be emphasized only in themselves.

In the Roman Catholic tradition, natural law can best be understood as human reason directing human beings to their end in accord with their nature. In the classic tradition based on Thomas Aquinas (d. 1274), human nature has a threefold structure: that which is shared with all substances, that which is common to humans and all the animals, and that which is proper to human beings as such. Human nature has its innate teleology on these three levels, and human reason discovers these ends and directs all human activity to them. In practice, Catholic moral theology often considered life in this world or in the temporal sphere as almost totally governed by natural law and not by the gospel, or by any explicitly Christian considerations. Before Vatican II, Catholic moral theology was dependent on reason and philosophical ethics and downplayed the role of the Scriptures and specific theological understandings.

The third characteristic of Roman Catholic moral theology is its insistence on relationship to the church. Catholic ecclesiology recognizes a special teaching office in matters of faith and morals that is given to the church, specifically the pope and the bishops. Since the seventeenth century there has been a growing intervention of authoritative papal teaching in moral matters. Catholic ecclesiology in accord with the teaching of Vatican I (1870) recognizes an infallible teaching function that is exercised through ecumenical councils and the ex cathedra teaching of the pope, as well as definitive teachings by the pope and the bishops. A noninfallible, authoritative teaching office is also exercised by the councils and especially by the pope through encyclicals, allocutions, and the various offices of the Curia Romana. The vast majority of Catholic moral theologians agree that there has never been an infallible papal teaching on a specific moral matter.

The authoritative church teaching offices have also served to keep the methodology of Catholic ethics somewhat monolithic. In the late nineteenth century, and subsequently, the popes have authoritatively directed that Roman Catholic theology and philosophy be taught according to the principles and the approach of Thomas Aquinas. Until comparatively recently, Catholic theology in general and moral theology in particular followed a Thomistic philosophical approach.

Church rites and practice have also influenced Catholic moral theology. Ever since the seventeenth century the primary purpose of moral theology textbooks has been to train confessors for the sacrament of penance, with emphasis on their role as judges of sinful actions. This narrow orientation resulted in an act-centered approach that was casuistic, based primarily on law, and aimed at determining the existence and gravity of sins.

HISTORICAL DEVELOPMENT OF ROMAN CATHOLIC ETHICS. Roman Catholic moral theology or Christian ethics developed into a scientific discipline earlier than in Eastern Orthodoxy. In the thirteenth century, systematic and scientific theology appeared with the work of the great Scholastic theologians, especially Thomas Aquinas. Moral theology in Thomas's thought is an integrated part of his systematic theology, not a separate discipline. The basic structure of Thomas's moral theology is teleological. The ultimate end of human beings is a happiness attained when the intellect knows perfect truth and the will loves the perfect good. For the Christian, the beatific vision fulfills and perfects human nature. The Franciscan school, represented by Alexander of Hales (d. 1245), Bonaventure (d. 1274), and John Duns Scotus (d. 1308), affirmed the primacy of the will and of charity and emphasized moral theology as wisdom.

The fourteenth century saw a criticism of Thomas from a nominalist perspective that grounded the good not in ontological reality but solely in the will of God and employed a more deontological approach to ethics. After the thirteenth century there appeared the *Summae confessorum,* very practical handbooks without any philosophical basis or analysis, which often arranged in alphabetical order the problems that the confessor would face in practice.

The *Institutiones theologiae moralis* appeared in the seventeenth century. These manuals, which became the standard textbooks of Catholic moral theology until Vatican II, began with a brief description of the ultimate end, which was followed by treatises on human acts, law as the objective norm of morality, and conscience as the subjective norm of morality. The virtues are mentioned, but sinful acts, often described on the basis of the Ten Commandments, remain the central concern. The sacraments are discussed, but almost exclusively from the viewpoint of moral and legal obligations. In the seventeenth and eighteenth centuries a controversy that arose between rigorists and laxists was finally resolved after papal intervention through the moderate approach of Alfonso Liguori (d. 1787), who was later named the patron of Catholic moral theology and of confessors.

Beginning with Leo XIII's encyclical *Rerum novarum* in 1891, a series of official teachings on the social question appeared. Leo and his immediate successors used a natural-law methodology, understood the state as a natural human society, proposed an anthropology that insisted on both the personal and communitarian aspects of human existence (thus avoiding the extremes of capitalism and socialism), recognized the right of workers to organize, and called for the state to intervene when necessary to protect the rights of workers or any particular class that was suffering. The tradition of hierarchical social teaching still exists, but now it stresses some of the newer methodological emphases in Catholic theology and deals with contemporary political and economic problems, especially in a global perspective.

There were attempts at renewal in moral theology, especially from the scriptural and Thomistic perspectives, but Bernhard Häring's *The Law of Christ* (1954) was the most significant single work in the renewal of Catholic moral theology in the pre–Vatican II period. Häring proposed a biblically inspired, Christocentric approach to moral theology based on the divine call to be perfect even as the gracious God is perfect.

The Second Vatican Council (1962–1965) greatly influenced the renewal of moral theology. Now there was greater dialogue with other Christians, non-Christians, and the modern world in general. Contemporary Catholic moral theology, while upholding the goodness of the natural and of the human, has tried to overcome the dichotomy or dualism between the supernatural and the natural. The gospel, grace, Jesus Christ, and the Holy Spirit are related to what happens in daily life in the world. Contemporary moral theology recognizes the need to consider more than acts and lays more emphasis on the person and on the virtues and attitudes of the person. No longer is there a monolithic Catholic moral theology based on a Thomistic natural law; instead, many different philosophical approaches are used. In general, there has been a shift from classicism to historical consciousness, from the objective to the subjective, from nature to person, from order to freedom. In addition to developments in methodology, there are also widespread debates in contemporary Catholic moral theology about the existence of intrinsically evil actions, absolute norms, and the possibility of dissent from noninfallible church teaching. As a result of these differences, some contemporary Catholic moral theologians are calling into question some official Catholic teachings in such areas as sexual and medical ethics, but the official teaching office has not changed on these issues.

THE PROTESTANT TRADITION. Protestant Christian ethics has as its distinctive characteristics an emphasis on freedom, an anticasuistic approach, the primacy of Scripture, and an emphasis on the theological nature of the discipline. Martin Luther (d. 1546) and the reformers in general stressed the freedom of the Christian, and freedom has characterized much of Protestant life and ethics. In Protestantism there is no central church teaching authority to propose authoritative teaching on specific issues or to insist upon a particular approach, as in Roman Catholicism. Consequently, in Protestant ethics there is a great pluralism and a diversity of approaches.

The emphasis on freedom colors the Protestant understanding of God and how God acts in human history. God is free to act and to intervene in history. Generally, Protestant ethics opposes any attempt to claim that God must always act in a particular way. The stress on God's freedom has also influenced a general Protestant unwillingness to base absolute norms on human reason and nature. The freedom of the believer as well as God is safeguarded in Protestant ethics.

The early reformers objected to the Roman Catholic emphasis on merit. They held that salvation comes from faith, not from human works. Protestantism ultimately rejected the Catholic sacrament of penance and thus never developed the casuistry involved in carrying out the role of the confessor as judge. Protestant ethics has been described as an ethics of inspiration, primarily because it does not usually get into a minute philosophical discussion of the morality of particular acts.

The Reformation insistence on the importance of Scripture characterizes much of Protestant ethics, but Scripture has been used in different ways. When God's immanence is stressed, there is a tendency to find in Scripture a moral message that can be lived by Christians in this world. When the transcendence of God is stressed, Scripture tends to be used more dialectically to include a judging and critical role with regard to every human enterprise. Perhaps the greatest change in Protestantism came to the fore in the nineteenth-century dispute over a critical approach to Scripture. Whereas liberal Protestantism—and soon most of mainstream Protestantism—employed literary and historical criticism to understand the Bible, fundamentalist Protestantism has continued to see the Bible primarily in terms of propositional truths or ethical norms and rules that God has revealed for all time and that Christians are called to obey. Such a deontological approach based on God's absolute laws given in Scripture cannot be accepted by Protestants who approach Scripture with the hermeneutical tools of biblical scholarship. Many contemporary Protestants see in Scripture the description of the mighty acts of God in history to which followers of Jesus must respond, and they consequently adopt a responsibility model of Christian ethics rather than a deontological approach.

Protestantism in general gives more significance to the theological aspects of Christian ethics than did traditional Roman Catholic ethics. Catholic ethics tended to see the moral life of all in this world in the light of natural law, whereas Protestantism has generally understood life in this world in relationship to the Bible and to theological concerns. Soteriology, Christology, and eschatology all have some influence on much of Protestant ethics. For example, Protestant ethics tends to see sin primarily in theological categories as a lack of faith, whereas Roman Catholicism understands sin primarily as actions that are morally wrong.

For some Protestants the primacy of grace and of Christ rules out any significant role for the human and the natural in Christian ethics. For others the effects of sin are so strong that human reason and human nature cannot be valid sources of ethical wisdom and knowledge. Even those Protestant ethicists who would be more open to the human on theological grounds shy away from the ontology and metaphysics that undergird Roman Catholic natural-law thinking. Protestants have also tended to give more significance to history than to nature, because history is more compatible with biblical categories and with the insistence on the freedom of God and of human beings.

Historical Development of Protestant Ethics. The first systematic, scientific, and independent treatment of Protestant ethics separated from dogmatic theology was produced by Georg Calixtus (d. 1656). Although the early reformers did not write scientific Christian ethics as such, they dealt with significant methodological and substantive issues affecting Christian ethics.

Justification by faith active in love stands at the heart of Lutheran theology and is opposed to merit, justification by works, and legalism. The emphasis on Scripture, even to the point of accepting the axiom "scripture alone," is another characteristic of the Reformation. Luther stressed freedom above all, but the dialectical aspect of his thought is seen in his famous saying "A Christian is a perfectly free lord of all, subject to none. A Christian is a perfectly dutiful servant of all, subject to all."

Lutheran social ethics is based on the two-realm theory, referring to the realm of creation and the realm of redemption. In the realm of creation, which involves the social life of human beings, there are true vocations for Christians, but the content of these vocations and what one does are not affected by Jesus, faith, or grace. Redemption affects only one's motivations. For this reason, Lutheran social ethics has often been accused of passivism and acceptance of the status quo.

John Calvin (d. 1564) shared much of Luther's theological presuppositions, but he gave greater emphasis to the will, both in God and in human beings. God is primarily sovereign will. Justification does not involve a pietistic response in trust; it means that the will of God becomes active in believers. Calvin came closer to a Roman Catholic understanding, and Calvinists (like Catholics) have tended to become legalists. Calvin was also more open than Luther to a natural-law approach, although not to the Catholic metaphysics of natural law. Like Luther, Calvin stressed the secular vocation of Christians, but he interpreted Christian work in the world in a more active and transforming way. Some later Calvinists have seen in worldly success a sign of God's predestining will for the individual. In the twentieth century, Max Weber proposed the controversial theory that the spirit of capitalism was compatible with and abetted by Calvinist ethics.

The Anabaptist-Mennonite tradition, or the left wing of the Reformation, from its sixteenth-century origins has stressed the radical call of discipleship, believer's baptism, and a committed, inflexible following of the radical ethical demands of the gospel. The believers form a sect that stands in opposition to the existing culture and society and bears witness to the gospel, especially the call to peace and nonviolence.

There has been no dominant figure in Anglican ethics, and thus no established pattern of doing Anglican ethics. However, in the Anglican community there have been important ethical thinkers who have served as a bridge between Roman Catholic ethics and Protestant ethics. Methodism developed a moral theory calling for spiritual growth and moral renewal.

The Enlightenment had a great influence on Protestant theology and ethics. Nineteenth-century Protestantism saw the emergence of liberal theology. Friedrich Schleiermacher (d. 1834), the most outstanding theologian in the nineteenth century, stressed experience and has been called the founder and most famous proponent of Protestant liberalism. Schleiermacher proposed an ethical theory dealing with goods, duties, and virtues, and he saw moral concerns as present and influencing all other areas of life, especially political, intellectual, aesthetic, and religious. Late-nineteenth- and early-twentieth-century liberal theology stressed the immanence of God working in human experience and history, the possibility of Christians living out the ethics of Jesus, and evolutionary human progress, while it downplayed divine transcendence and the power of sin. Within the context of liberal Protestant theology, the Social Gospel movement came to the fore in the first two decades of the twentieth century in the United States, especially under the leadership of Walter Rauschenbusch (d. 1918). In response to the problems created by the industrial revolution and in response to the privatism and individualism of past Christian ethics, the Social Gospel stressed that the kingdom of God should be made more present on earth and that the social order can and should be Christianized. In England and Germany many Christian thinkers embraced a moderate Christian socialism.

The harsh realities of World War I and the Great Depression occasioned the rise of the neo-orthodoxy of Karl Barth in Europe and the Christian realism of Reinhold Niebuhr in the United States. The reaction stressed the transcendence of God, the dialectical relationship between the existing world and the kingdom of God, the power of sin, and the fact that the fullness of God's kingdom lies outside history. In respect to the contemporary international scene, the World Council of Churches has addressed many contemporary social issues with strong support for liberation movements and has called for just, participative, and sustainable societies.

Even greater diversity characterized Protestant ethics in the latter part of the twentieth century. Methodologically, teleological, deontological, and responsibility models continued to thrive. Some newer methodological approaches have also appeared—an emphasis on praxis, narrative approaches, virtue theory, and on the particularity of Christian ethics as directly addressing only the Christian church and not the world. In terms of content or substance, conservative, liberal, and radical approaches have appeared in both personal and social issues.

Contemporary Scene. It is impossible to summarize the developments in Christian ethics since the mid-twentieth century. Paradoxically, greater diversity exists in Christian ethics in general and in each of its three traditions, but at the same time the boundaries separating the three traditions are disappearing and a more ecumenical approach has come to the fore. There are many reasons for this greater diversity. No longer does the European–North American world totally dominate the field of Christian ethics, especially in the Catholic and Protestant traditions. South America, Africa, and Asia have produced an increasing number of Christian ethicists. The emphasis on context and particularity intensifies the diversity as Christian ethicists deal with the realities of their own cultures and ethos. The industrialized world has also witnessed a growing number of women teaching and writing in Christian ethics. Until the latter half of the twentieth century, the seminary was the primary home of Christian ethicists, but now the discipline exists in colleges and universities. As a result, the number of people teaching and writing in the area of Christian ethics has grown considerably. The move to the academy means that Christian ethics now addresses both the church and the academy with different emphases according to different individuals. In this milieu, methodological diversity has flourished. The field of Christian ethics has become so vast and complex that different specializations, such as personal ethics, sexual ethics, bioethics, economic ethics, and political ethics, have come into existence. It is difficult now for any one person to claim to embrace the whole area of Christian ethics.

But the ecumenical aspect of Christian ethics has also increased dramatically, together with shared concerns and approaches even in different cultures and countries. In the United States, Europe, France, and England, ecumenical societies of Christian ethicists exist, hold annual meetings, and encourage greater professionalization in the discipline. These groups both exemplify and facilitate a more ecumenical way of doing Christian ethics. In the diaspora situation, Eastern Orthodox ethicists are a small minority, but they are actively involved in many of these societies.

The important moral issues facing the world in the political, economic, technological, biomedical, and personal areas are the same for all Christians. Addressing issues such as violence, poverty, justice, and bioethical experimentation brings Christian ethicists from diverse traditions closer together. Not only content but also methodological approaches have blurred the lines separating the different traditions and have emphasized common traits. Liberation theology well illustrates a methodological approach that is found today in different religious traditions. Liberation theology began primarily with Catholic theologians in South America in the late 1960s who emphasized the option for the poor, praxis, and the scriptural account of *Exodus* as paradigmatic for understanding salvation and the role of the church today. Various forms of liberation theology now exist in practically all countries of the world, especially in those with a large number of poor, oppressed, and marginalized people. In the United States, black liberation theology began around the same time, originally as a black Protestant approach, though one which has now influenced both black and white, and both Protestant and Catholic, churches in the United States. Feminist liberation theology originally developed primarily in the United States and quickly spread across the globe and across religious traditions and boundaries. Diverse groups of women have occasioned the development of more particular forms of feminist liberation theology, such as womanist (African American women) and *mujerista* theology (Latina and Hispanic women). Thus, on the contemporary scene, Christian ethics has become much more diverse, but, at the same time, communalities and more ecumenical approaches among the three traditions have come to the fore.

SEE ALSO Discipleship; Free Will and Predestination, article on Christian Concepts; Grace; Justification; Merit, article on Christian Concepts; Political Theology.

BIBLIOGRAPHY

There is no in-depth contemporary overview of the history of Christian ethics. The best available work remains Ernst Troeltsch's *The Social Teaching of the Christian Churches,* 2 vols., translated by Olive Wyon (New York, 1931; Louisville, Ky., 1992), which was originally published in German in 1911 but is still valuable today despite its datedness and somewhat biased perspectives. Troeltsch, like most Westerners writing on the subject, does not discuss Eastern Orthodox ethics. H. Richard Niebuhr's *Christ and Culture* (New York, 1951) is a frequently cited analysis of Western Christian ethics in the light of five possible models for understanding the relationship between Christ and culture. J. Philip Wogaman's *Christian Ethics: A Historical Introduction* (Louisville, Ky., 1993) is a concise and informative historical overview of Christian ethics from biblical times in the light of contemporary perspectives.

There are many studies of individual thinkers in the patristic era, but the best history of the period written by a Christian ethicist is George W. Forell's *History of Christian Ethics,* vol. 1, *From the New Testament to Augustine* (Minneapolis, 1979).

There is comparatively little literature on Eastern Orthodox ethics in modern Western languages. In addition to encyclopedia articles, George A. Maloney's *A History of Orthodox Theology Since 1453* (Belmont, Mass., 1976) and *Man: The Divine Icon* (Pecos, N. Mex., 1973) provide both historical details and anthropological considerations for Christian ethics. Georges Florovsky's *Collected Works,* 5 vols. (Belmont, Mass., 1972–), and John Meyendorff's *Byzantine Theology,* 2d ed. (New York, 1979), include helpful chapters dealing with Christian ethics. Stanley S. Harakas's *Toward Transfigured Life* (Minneapolis, 1983) and *Wholeness of Faith and Life: Orthodox Christian Ethics,* 3 vols. (Brookline, Mass., 1999), provide a systematic Christian ethics from the Greek Orthodox tradition that includes valuable historical data.

No one has written a definitive history of Catholic moral theology. Louis Vereecke, the recognized authority in the field, has published four volumes of printed notes for students at the Accademia Alfonsiana with the general title *Storia della teologia morale moderna* (Rome, 1979–1980). Vereecke has also published a collection of essays on the history of moral theology—*De Guillaume d'Ockham à Saint Alphonse de Liguori: Études d'histoire de la théologie morale moderne* (Rome, 1986). John Mahoney's *The Making of Moral Theology: A Study of the Roman Catholic Tradition* (Oxford, U.K., 1987) does not pretend to be a complete history but is the best historical volume available in English. Thirteen volumes of the series *Readings in Moral Theology* (New York, 1979–2003), originally edited by Charles E. Curran and Richard A. McCormick, indicate the contemporary developments and discussions within Catholic moral theology.

In the contemporary era, various authors have dealt with the historical development of Protestant ethics, in addition to earlier works by Troeltsch and H. Richard Niebuhr mentioned above. William H. Lazareth's *Christians in Society: Luther, the Bible, and Social Ethics* (Minneapolis, 2001) explains and defends Lutheran ethics from a contemporary perspective. Eric Fuchs's *La morale selon Calvin* (Paris, 1986) takes a similar perspective with regard to John Calvin. James M. Gustafson's *Christ and the Moral Life* (New York, 1968) explains and criticizes six different approaches taken in Christian ethics to the role of Jesus Christ. Edward LeRoy Long Jr.'s *A Survey of Christian Ethics* (New York, 1967) elucitates the history of Christian ethics in the light of three motifs for formulating the ethical norm and three motifs for implementing ethical decisions. Gary J. Dorrien's *Soul in Society: The Making and Renewal of Social Christianity* (Minneapolis, 1995) provides an overview of the development of Christian social ethics in the twentieth century.

CHARLES E. CURRAN (1987 AND 2005)

CHRISTIAN IDENTITY MOVEMENT is an offshoot of Protestantism found mostly in the United States and other English-speaking countries. The movement is characterized by an anti-Semitic and racist theology. Once the dominant religious orientation on the extreme right in the United States, Christian Identity now appears to be in decline.

HISTORY. Christian Identity developed out of British-Israelism (also known as Anglo-Israelism). British-Israelism emerged in Great Britain during the second half of the nineteenth century. It was neither a church nor a sect but rather an interpretive tendency among Protestants, largely members of the Church of England. Its distinctiveness rested upon its revisionist approach to sacred history. According to Anglo-Israelites, the British Isles had been populated by the Lost Tribes of Israel, who had wandered west from their original place of exile in the Middle East. In many versions of British-Israelism, the tribes were also said to have populated much of northwest Europe. British-Israelites, active at the summit of empire, saw British imperialism as both a divine mission and a demonstration of God's favor.

British-Israelism quickly spread to the United States, where it fitted well with conceptions of manifest destiny. Indeed, as the power of the United States increased, American

Anglo-Israelites began to suggest that the country might be the inheritor of Britain's divine role.

The heyday of British-Israelism came in the 1920s and 1930s, a time when many fringe religious movements gained a hearing. Its chief spokesperson was a Massachusetts lawyer, Howard Rand, whose Anglo-Saxon Federation of America organized chapters throughout the country. Rand's proselytizing was significantly aided by William Cameron, a Ford Motor Company executive. Cameron was the editor of Henry Ford's newspaper, the *Dearborn Independent*, notorious for its anti-Semitic articles in the early 1920s. Cameron's close association with Rand and the Anglo-Saxon Federation anticipated Christian Identity's fusion of British-Israelism and anti-Semitism.

Gradually, the links between British-Israelism in the United States and its English parent weakened. The separation was facilitated by the increasing links between the American extreme right and Anglo-Israelism. This was especially the case in southern California, among individuals associated with Gerald L. K. Smith, the most prominent anti-Semite in the country during the 1940s. Although Smith does not appear to have been a British-Israelite, he and his followers were clearly sympathetic to its rising antipathy toward Jews.

Three individuals in Smith's circle finally created a variation on British-Israelism that definitively marked it off from both its original version and Rand's Americanized form. These three—Wesley Swift, William Potter Gale, and Bertrand Comparet—represent the first leadership cadre of Christian Identity. Their ideas took shape between the end of World War II and the late 1960s, by which time a second generation of leadership was beginning to emerge.

WORLDVIEW AND DOCTRINES. British-Israelism had originally been philo-Semitic, seeing Jews as partners of the Anglo-Saxon peoples in God's plan. Indeed, British-Israelism strongly supported Jewish settlement in Palestine, and saw Britain's administration of Palestine under a League of Nations' mandate as a divine sign that Anglo-Jewish cooperation was predestined. However, the opposition of Zionists to British administration of Palestine after World War II engendered hostility in Anglo-Israelites, who could not understand why Jews did not see them as kin. This feeling of betrayal was notably strong in Rand and his followers.

The shift from philo-Semitism to anti-Semitism presaged the major doctrinal innovation of Christian Identity, the so-called two-seed theory. The two-seed theory, most closely associated with Swift, asserts that two lines of descent emanate from Eve: One consists of the offspring of Eve and Adam, Abel and Seth; the other comes from the child of Eve and Satan, Cain. For most Identity believers, Cain's father was Satan, not Adam, and the sin in the Garden of Eden was the sexual union of Eve with a humanoid "serpent."

The two corollaries drawn from this interpretation are, first, that the primal sin was miscegenation; and, second, that the Jews are Cain's descendants. By claiming Jewish ancestry to be satanic, Identity seeks to completely delegitimize any Jewish claims to God's promises. Instead, divine promises belong to the "true" Israelites, that is, whites of northwestern European heritage. Jews thus come to be seen as literally demonic, and history, both sacred and secular, is recast as a cosmic battle between the white race and its Jewish adversaries. Jews are also seen as counterfeit Israelites, seeking to wrest control of the divine promise from its rightful white bearers.

Nonwhites are said to be the result of separate acts of creation, not involving Adam or Eve. They are considered morally inferior to whites and easily manipulable, and are thought to inhabit some status intermediate between humans and nonhumans. To the extent that they perform any roles in the Identity worldview, they are allies to Jews and sources of racial impurity.

The vision of racial struggle (white "Israelites" versus Jews and nonwhites) supports Identity's version of millennialism. The struggle will reach its climax in an imminent battle between the forces of light and the forces of darkness—Armageddon defined in racial terms. However, Identity rejects the premillennial dispensationalism that dominates Protestant evangelicalism. The rejection is in part based on the prominence dispensationalists give to the fulfillment of prophecies concerning the Jewish people, and their support for the State of Israel. It is also a function of Identity's unwillingness to accept the concept of the Rapture (i.e., the moment at which the saved will be taken up to be with Christ during the chaos of the Tribulation).

Rejection of the Rapture means that Identity believers expect to have to survive the Tribulation, with its seven years of war and persecution. They will, in other words, need to remain on earth through the reign of antichrist until the second coming. Since they must endure the Tribulation, much attention goes to the details of living during a coming period of disorder. That accounts for the frequent overlap of Identity with survivalism, that is, a lifestyle characterized by separation and self-sufficiency, geared to a time when the normal routines of life can no longer be maintained.

PATTERNS OF CONDUCT. Racialism and survivalism have often been reflected in the Identity movement's preference for parts of the country characterized by low population density and very small numbers of Jews and nonwhites. Pockets of believers may thus be found in such areas as the Pacific Northwest east of the coastal cities, and the Missouri-Arkansas Ozarks. At its most extreme, Identity sometimes has been used as a rationale for total withdrawal from the larger society ("going off the grid"). A conspicuous example was the paramilitary Ozark commune, the Covenant, Sword, and Arm of the Lord (also called Zarephath-Horeb), founded in 1976. This group maintained its insularity until a law enforcement raid in 1985.

As self-proclaimed Israelites, Identity groups believe themselves to be governed by the precepts of the Hebrew Bible. They often celebrate such traditionally Jewish holidays as Passover and Sukkot and may observe some biblically-sanctioned dietary laws. They likewise frequently refer to God in biblical terms as Yahweh, YHWH, or YHVH. In other liturgical respects, however, they resemble nondenominational evangelicals.

Organization and Authority. British-Israelism never became a sect. It always advised adherents to remain members of their accustomed churches. This tendency was maintained in the United States by the Anglo-Saxon Federation. Indeed, Rand never presented himself as other than a layperson. However, the post–World War II development of Identity took a different course.

The key figures in the movement's early development—Swift, Gale, and Comparet—all had ministries of some sort, ranging from Swift's church in Antelope Valley, California, to Comparet's less conventional mail and tape ministry. None had formal seminary training, although Swift appears to have attended a Bible college. Nonetheless, they presented themselves as spiritual leaders and, especially in the cases of Swift and Gale, had congregations.

The pattern set at that time persisted: independent ministries linked only by personal ties and doctrinal similarities. These ministries have included small churches with regular services, Bible study groups, and various types of outreach using printed materials, audio and video recordings, and websites. As a result, power in the movement has always been highly diffused. Given the tendency of individual pastors to resist encroachments on their autonomy, attempts to impose even minimal coordinating mechanisms have failed. Relations among Identity notables have consequently been characterized by a high level of personal rivalry.

The demographic profile of rank-and-file adherents is difficult to determine with any exactness. Identity organizations tend to be secretive and suspicious, since many have attracted the attention of law enforcement agencies. In addition, the size of the body of believers (most estimates have ranged from about five thousand to thirty thousand) makes the movement too small to register in even the largest-sample religious identification surveys.

Anecdotal evidence suggests, however, that the membership (ethnicity and race aside) closely tracks that of the general populations in areas of Identity activity. There seems to be no convincing evidence that believers display unusual levels of social or personal pathology. Some Identity pastors have made significant efforts to recruit particular populations, including Midwestern farmers, unemployed urban youth, and white prison inmates. Only the latter appears to have been productive, as a function of racial polarization in many correctional facilities.

Christian Identity and the State. Although the great majority of Identity believers appear to be entirely law-abiding, a significant minority have been implicated in violent crimes and other law violations. These include many members of the insurgent group known as the Order, active in the West in the early 1980s; Eric Robert Rudolph, charged with the 1996 Centennial Olympic Park bombing in Atlanta; and Richard Wayne Snell, executed in 1995 for murder.

By the mid-1980s, both federal and state law enforcement agencies had become increasingly concerned about threats posed by Identity believers. This fear was exacerbated by dramatic confrontations between the FBI and Identity adherents; notably, the standoff in 1992 with Randy Weaver and his family at Ruby Ridge in Idaho, and the standoff in 1996 with the Montana Freemen, many of whose members were affiliated with Identity.

The rising tempo of surveillance and prosecution appears to have had an impact on Identity in several ways. First, activities have become less visible. Second, growth appears to have either stopped or continued at a much lower rate. Third, believers have sought to destigmatize themselves by rejecting the term *Identity* in favor of more acceptable terms, such as *Israel, Kingdom,* and *Covenant.* This has been the case with two of the most prominent clergy, Pastor Dan Gayman of the Church of Israel in Schell, Missouri, and Pastor Pete Peters of the LaPorte Church of Christ in LaPorte, Colorado.

Identity has also faced increasing competition within its own constituency of white racial separatists. It now confronts active recruiting efforts from racist faiths unrelated to either Identity specifically or Christianity in its other manifestations. These rivals include racial forms of Neopaganism, such as Odinism and Ásatrú, which seek to reconstitute pre-Christian northern European religion, and the World Church of the Creator, a nontheistic belief system built around the sacred nature of race.

In one respect, Identity has been able to secure some recognition, in federal and state prisons. Despite resistance by prison administrations, anxious to avoid the intensification of racial animosity, Identity inmates have pushed religious claims based on legislation that expands rights of free exercise, notably the Religious Freedom Restoration Act (1993) and the Religious Land Use and Institutionalized Persons Act (2000).

Bibliography

Aho, James A. *The Politics of Righteousness: Idaho Christian Patriots.* Seattle, 1990. Based on extensive interviews with both Identity and non-Identity members of the Idaho radical right.

Barkun, Michael. *Religion and the Racist Right: The Origins of the Christian Identity Movement.* Rev. ed., Chapel Hill, N.C., 1997. Describes the historical development of Identity concepts and organizations.

Flynn, Kevin, and Gary Gerhardt. *The Silent Brotherhood: Inside America's Racist Underground.* New York, 1989. Journalistic account of the Order.

Jeansonne, Glen. *Gerald L. K. Smith: Minister of Hate.* New Haven, Conn., 1988. Detailed biography of Smith.

Kaplan, Jeffrey. *Radical Religion in America: Millenarian Movements from the Far Right to the Children of Noah.* Syracuse,

N.Y., 1997. Discussion of Identity and other fringe theologies.

Levitas, Daniel. *The Terrorist Next Door: The Militia Movement and the Radical Right.* New York, 2002. Examination of William Potter Gale's career.

Noble, Kerry. *Tabernacle of Hate: Why They Bombed Oklahoma City.* Prescott, Ont., 1998. Unusual first-person account of the Covenant, Sword, and Arm of the Lord.

MICHAEL BARKUN (2005)

CHRISTIANITY

This entry consists of the following articles:

AN OVERVIEW
CHRISTIANITY IN THE MIDDLE EAST
CHRISTIANITY IN NORTH AFRICA
CHRISTIANITY IN EASTERN EUROPE
CHRISTIANITY IN WESTERN EUROPE
CHRISTIANITY IN LATIN AMERICA
CHRISTIANITY IN THE CARIBBEAN REGION
CHRISTIANITY IN NORTH AMERICA
CHRISTIANITY IN SUB-SAHARAN AFRICA [FIRST EDITION]
CHRISTIANITY IN SUB-SAHARAN AFRICA [FURTHER CONSIDERATIONS]
CHRISTIANITY IN ASIA
CHRISTIANITY IN AUSTRALIA AND NEW ZEALAND
CHRISTIANITY IN THE PACIFIC ISLANDS [FIRST EDITION]
CHRISTIANITY IN THE PACIFIC ISLANDS [FURTHER CONSIDERATIONS]

CHRISTIANITY: AN OVERVIEW

Christianity is defined by one of its leading modern interpreters, Friedrich Schleiermacher (1768–1834), as "a monotheistic faith . . . essentially distinguished from other such faiths by the fact that in it everything is related to the redemption accomplished by Jesus of Nazareth." While many interpreters of the meaning of Christianity would dispute the content that Schleiermacher gave to each of the crucial terms in that definition, the definition as such would probably stand. It is beyond the scope of this article, or even of this encyclopedia, to present an exhaustive summary of all that Christianity is and has ever been: entire encyclopedias several times the size of this one (some of them listed in the bibliography, below) have been devoted to such a summary, and even they have been far from exhaustive. What this article can do, supported by other articles throughout this work, is to sketch some of the main points in the history of Christianity and then to identify some of the features of Christianity that most students of the movement, whether professing personal allegiance to it or not, would probably recognize as belonging to its "essence." Although both the "history" and the "essence" are, unavoidably, controversial in that not everyone would agree with this (or with any) account of them, such an account as this can claim to represent a majority consensus.

THE HISTORY OF CHRISTIANITY. Christianity is a historical religion. It locates within the events of human history both the redemption it promises and the revelation to which it lays claim: Jesus was born under Caesar Augustus and "suffered under Pontius Pilate," at particular dates in the chronology of the history of Rome (even though the specific dates of those two events may be impossible to determine with absolute precision). In this respect Christianity shows its continuing affinities with the Judaism out of which it came, for there too the historical process becomes the peculiar arena of divine activity. The primal revelation for Judaism—and for Christianity—is the divine declaration to Moses (*Ex.* 3:6): "I am the God of Abraham, Isaac, and Jacob." To this primal revelation Christianity adds the assertion (*Heb.* 1:1–2) that the God who in past times had spoken through the prophets and acted through the exodus from Egypt has now spoken definitively and acted decisively in the life, death, and resurrection of Jesus, seen as the "Christ," the anointed and chosen one of God.

Early Christianity. It is, then, with Jesus of Nazareth that the history of Christianity takes its start. Almost everything that is known of him, however, comes from those who responded, in loyalty and obedience, to the events of his life and the content of his teaching. Therefore the history of the earliest Christian communities, to the extent that we are in a position to reconstruct it, is at the same time the history of Jesus as they remembered him. His own immediate followers were all Jews, and it is within that framework that they interpreted the significance of what they had received and perceived: he was the Christ, or Messiah, who had been promised to the patriarchs of Israel. As the record of those promises, the Hebrew scriptures were sacred for early Christians no less than for Jews, enabling them to claim a continuity with the history of the people of God since the creation of the world. The apostle Paul both summarized and reinterpreted the message of the first generation of believers. Together with the written deposit of their memories of Jesus in the Gospels, the writings of Paul and several other documents were circulated widely in Christian communities throughout the Mediterranean world, eventually becoming the Christian addendum (or "New Testament") to the Hebrew scriptures (or "Old Testament").

Paul was also responsible for the transformation of Christianity from a Jewish sect to a Gentile movement by the end of the first century of the common era. The importance of this change for Christian history is impossible to exaggerate. Jesus had been born in an obscure corner of the Roman Empire, but now his followers took upon themselves the assignment of challenging that empire and eventually of conquering it in his name. The opposition between empire and church during the second and third centuries sometimes took the form of persecution and martyrdom, but all that was replaced in the fourth century by the creation of a Christian Roman Empire, when the emperor Constantine (306–337) first made the new faith legal, then made it his own, then made it the official religion of the realm. As part of their political and philosophical defense against their adversaries, the apologists for Christianity in the second and third centuries had also sought to clarify its relation to Greek and Roman thought, but with its official adoption their successors in the fourth and fifth centuries undertook to interpret Christian theology as the perennial philosophy in which the aspirations of all religions were now corrected and fulfilled. Among these later apologists, Augustine of Hippo (354–430) in his *City of God* articulated the Christian case against those who charged that by undermining the traditional values of Roman religion the church had been responsible for the decline and fall of the Roman Empire. On the contrary, he said, Christianity was the support of just rulers and legitimate governments, and by its faith in the God of history, as well as by its moral teachings about work and the family, it promoted the welfare of society; the City of Earth would function best if it acknowledged the transcendent reality of the City of God, which was beyond history but which had made its presence known within this particular history.

The century that began with Constantine and ended with Augustine also saw the stabilization of the internal life and structure of the Christian movement. One by one, alternative ways of thought and belief that were adjudged to be aberrations were sloughed off or excluded as "heresies" or "schisms." Some of these (particularly the various species of apocalyptic or millenarian expectation) were efforts to perpetuate ways of being Christian that no longer suited the needs of the life of the church when the long-expected second coming of Jesus Christ failed to materialize, while others (notably the several Gnostic systems) involved the adaptation to the Christian message of schemes of revelation and salvation that were also manifesting themselves in other religions. In opposition to these alternative ways of thought and belief, Christianity, since before the days during which the books of the New Testament were being written, identified the content of orthodox belief and fixed its form in a succession of creedal statements. The earliest of these, including that eventually formulated as the Apostles' Creed, are put into the mouth of one or another or all twelve of the apostles of Jesus, and the most important creedal statement was adopted (under Constantine's patronage) at the Council of Nicaea in 325 (see "The Pattern of Christian Belief," below).

During those same early centuries, Christianity was also identifying the structures of authority that were thought to guarantee the preservation of "apostolic" faith and order: the Bible and the bishops. As already noted, the Bible of the Christians consisted of two parts (or "testaments"): the books they had inherited from Judaism, and the combination into a "New Testament" of four gospels about the life and teachings of Jesus, epistles attributed to Paul and other apostolic figures, the *Acts of the Apostles*, and (from among the many extant apocalyptic writings) the *Revelation to John*. The bishops through their uninterrupted succession were believed to certify the continuity of the church with its apostolic foundations. As the church that could claim to have been shepherded by all twelve apostles, Jerusalem held a unique place; but as the church that Peter had governed and to which Paul had written (and where both Peter and Paul had been martyred), and as the congregation at the capital of the civilized world, Rome early acquired a special position as "*the* apostolic see," which it would consolidate by the leadership in faith and life that it exercised during the crises of the fourth and fifth centuries. Actually, the criterion of "apostolicity" was a circular one: apostolic foundation of episcopal sees, apostolic authorship of biblical books, and apostolic orthodoxy of creedal belief supported one another, and no one of them was ever sufficient of itself—even in the case of the see of Rome—to serve as such a criterion in isolation from the others.

Official establishment of Christianity. Constantine's acceptance of Christianity and the eventual establishment of it as the official faith of the Roman Empire is rightly seen as the most portentous event—for good or ill or some combination of the two—in all of Christian history; conversely, "the end of the Constantinian era," which is how many thoughtful observers have characterized the twentieth century, has brought about the reshaping and rethinking of all the structures of faith and life that Christianity evolved in the aftermath of its new status from the fourth century on. Both in the Roman West, where Constantine prevailed in 312 "by the power of the cross," as he believed, and in the Byzantine East, where Constantine established the new capital of the Christian Roman Empire two decades later, Christianity undertook to create a new civilization that would be a continuation of ancient Greece and Rome and yet would be a transformation of those cultures through the infusion of the spiritual power of Christ as Lord.

The Christian culture of Byzantium. That pattern of continuation with transformation took a special form in the Christian culture of the Byzantine Empire, whose history persisted for more than a thousand years from the creation of Constantinople as "New Rome" in 330 CE to its fall to the armies of the Turkish sultan Mehmed II (and its change of name to Istanbul) in 1453. Constantine and his successors—and, above all, the emperor Justinian (r. 527–565)—saw themselves in their Roman capacity as the legitimate heirs of the ancient pagan caesars, but at the same time in their Christian capacity as "equal to the apostles" (*isapostolos*). In the exercise of this special authority, they frequently became involved in the administrative, liturgical, and doctrinal affairs of the church, and often without opposition and with great success. Contemporary historians tell us that it was the emperor Constantine who came up with the formula "one in being [*homoousios*] with the Father," which resolved, at the Council of Nicaea in 325, the dispute over the metaphysical relation between Christ and God. Later historians have coined for this special status of the Byzantine emperor the term *Caesaropapism*, implying that what the pope was in the West, the caesar was in the East. While the reign of Constantine, and even more that of Justinian, may have merited such a designation, the patriarch of Constantinople repeatedly asserted the authority of the church to determine its own destiny, above all in the areas of belief and worship. Most notably, in the iconoclastic controversies of the eighth and ninth centuries, which were brought on by the campaign of a series of emperors to remove images from the worship of the church, the defenders of the church's autonomy, who included especially monks and empresses, eventually carried the day, and the authority of the emperor to legislate unilaterally for the church was significantly curtailed.

One reason for this success in the iconoclastic disputes was the special place of icons in Byzantine (and later in Slavic) Orthodoxy, which one scholar has called its "distinctive identity." As interpreted by its defenders, the cult of the icons was anything but the relapse into idolatrous paganism of which it was accused by the iconoclasts; instead it represented the commitment of Orthodoxy to the reality of the full incarnation of the Son of God in the human figure of Jesus: worship of the image of Jesus Christ was in fact addressed to one who was in his single person completely God and completely man. Thus, to a degree unknown in the West even in the high Middle Ages, Greek Christianity defined itself by its liturgy and devotion, not only (perhaps not primarily) by its dogma and life. The very term *orthodoxia* in Greek, and its Slavic counterpart *pravoslavie*, meant in the first instance "correct worship," which also included "correct doctrine." Embodied as it was in the curriculum of Byzantine educational institutions at all levels, the continuing hold that a christianized Neoplatonism exercised over its expositors enabled them to make use of its metaphysics and epistemology in the service of the church's message. The Byzantine icons were only one part of a total Christian culture, in which architecture, poetry, and music also contributed their special part. One feature of this culture was a commitment to preserving the indigenous culture of each people to which the Christian message came: while the Western missionaries, in introducing the Mass, taught each nation Latin when they taught it the gospel (and thus, even without intending to do so, gave it at least some access to pre-Christian Roman culture), Eastern missionaries translated not only the Bible but also the liturgy into the language of the people. It was, above all, in the Byzantine missions to the Slavs (where the two philosophies about the proper language of the liturgy clashed) that this peculiarity of the Eastern church served to create an integrally Slavic Orthodoxy, through which the Ukraine, Bulgaria, Russia, and Serbia came of age as nations.

Christianity in the Middle Ages. In the Latin West, by contrast, the outcome of the Constantinian settlement took a radically divergent form, in which it was not principally the Christian emperor and the Christian empire, but the bishop of Rome and the papacy, that was to set the tone of the historical development of Christianity. With the transfer of the capital to Constantinople, the pope came to symbolize and to embody the continuity with ancient Rome. Within less than a century after that transfer, the bishop of Rome was calling himself "supreme pontiff" (*pontifex maximus*), a title that had belonged to the pagan caesars. When the various Germanic tribes arrived in western Europe, they found the papacy already present as a political and cultural force. Those tribes that chose to ignore that force by clinging too long to Germanic paganism or to forms of Christianity that had been outlawed as heretical also lost the opportunity to shape the future of European history, but the Franks, by allying themselves with the bishop of Rome, were to determine its subsequent course through much of the Middle Ages. The symbolic high point of the alliance came on Christmas Day in the year 800 with the crowning of the Frankish king Charles, known to history as Charlemagne (c. 742–814), as "emperor" at the hands of Pope Leo III in Rome, even though there was still an emperor in Constantinople. With its own emperor—and, above all, its own bishop and supreme pontiff—the West was free to pursue its own destiny. And although the schism between West and East, in a technical and canonical sense, did not take place until several centuries later, and in a spiritual sense may be said to have happened in 1204, the historical intuition that located it as having originated in the ninth century was in many ways sound.

Confrontation with Islam. Each in its own way, both Eastern and Western Christendom were compelled, from the seventh century onward, to come to terms with the reality of Islam. During the one hundred years after the death of the prophet Muḥammad in 632 CE, the geographical spread of Islam was both more rapid and more effective than that of Christianity had been during its first several centuries. Several of the major centers of the Eastern churches—Antioch, Alexandria, Jerusalem itself—became Muslim in government, although a large Christian population was able to practice its faith under varying degrees of pressure. Eventually, in 1453, Constantinople also became a Muslim city. The Muslim conquest of Palestine was likewise responsible for the most historic confrontation ever between Christianity and another faith, in the Crusades, as successive armies of Western Christians sought to reconquer the "holy places" associated with the life of Jesus—an enterprise that eventually failed.

The monks. Because its administrative structure and intellectual tradition were so different from those of the Byzantine East, the medieval Christianity of the West expressed its relation to society and culture in a distinctive fashion as well. In even greater measure than in the East, the bearers of its civilizing force were monks. The missionaries who brought the gospel to the barbarians—for example, Boniface (673–754), the "apostle of Germany" sent from Rome, and Cyril (c. 826–869) and Methodius (c. 815–c. 884), the "apostles to the Slavs" sent from Constantinople—were monks. So were the scribes who then brought Classical civilization to the same barbarians; thus the Benedictine monk the Venerable Bede (c. 673–735) laid many of the foundations of scholarship in England. Most of the reformers who throughout the Middle Ages recalled the church to its primitive faith and its ancient loyalties came from monasticism, as was evident above all in the work of Bernard of Clairvaux (1090–1153), "the unmitered pope" of the twelfth century, and then in the program of Francis of Assisi (1181/2–1226). The cloisters likewise supplied most of the theologians who systematized and defended the faith: Anselm of Canterbury (c. 1033–1109) was a Benedictine abbot, Thomas Aquinas (c. 1225–1274) was a Dominican friar, and Bonaventure (c. 1217–1274) and Duns Scotus (c. 1266–1308) were both Franciscans.

Repeatedly, of course, the monastic communities themselves needed to be reformed, and in virtually every century of the Middle Ages there arose movements of renewal dedicated to the purification of the monastic ideal and, through it, renewal of the life of the total church. When the leaders of such movements managed to establish themselves as leaders of the total church, the result was often a great conflict. Thus in the eleventh century the reformer Hildebrand became Pope Gregory VII (in 1073) and set about renewing the administration, the morals, and the faith and life of the church. He sought to enforce the law of clerical celibacy, to root out financial and political corruption, to free bishops and prelates from the dominance of secular princes, and to purge the church of heresy and schism. This brought him into collision both with his own ecclesiastical subordinates and with the empire, but it also gave him the opportunity to formulate for all time the special prerogatives of the church and the bishop of Rome (see "The Community of Christian Worship," below).

Reformation Christianity. Such reform movements, it seemed, could always be counted on to rescue the church in times of crisis—until, through Martin Luther (1483–1546) and the Reformation, a crisis arose in which the primary impetus for reform was to express itself not *through* monasticism or the papacy, but *against* both monasticism and the papacy (although it must be remembered that Luther, too, was originally a monk). Already in various late medieval reformations, such as those of the "Spiritual" Franciscans and the Hussites, there was the sense that (to cite the four standard "marks" of the church enumerated in the Nicene Creed) Christendom could be neither one nor holy nor catholic nor apostolic until it had replaced the secularized and corrupt authority of the bishop of Rome with the authenticity of the word of God, for which some looked to a church council while others put their confidence in the recovery of the message of the Bible. That sense finally found its voice in the program of the Protestant reformers. Beginning with the belief that they were merely the loyal children of Mother Church recalling her to her genuine self, they soon found themselves so alienated from the structures and teachings of the church of their time that they were obliged to look for, and if need be to invent, alternative structures and teachings of their own.

The structures and teachings of the several Protestant groups covered an extremely wide spectrum, such that those at one end of the spectrum (Lutherans and Anglicans) were in many ways closer to Roman Catholicism and even to Eastern Orthodoxy, despite the schisms both of the Middle Ages and of the Reformation, than they were to Socinianism or even to Anabaptism or even perhaps to Calvinism. In their ecclesiastical structures, the churches that came out of the Reformation ranged from a retention of the historic episcopate (e.g., in England and Sweden) to a presbyterian form of church government (e.g., in Scotland and in many, though by no means all, of the Calvinist churches on the European continent) to an insistence on the primacy and autonomy of the local congregation (e.g., in various of the dissenters from Anglicanism in the seventeenth and eighteenth centuries, including the Congregationalists and Baptists, especially in the New World). While the mainstream of Protestantism has in its doctrine maintained a loyalty to the doctrines of the Trinity, of the person of Christ, of original sin, and of salvation through the death of Christ, as these had been developed in the early and medieval church, it has diverged from earlier development (and thus from Roman Catholicism and Eastern Orthodoxy) above all in its understanding of the nature of the church and of the meaning (and hence the number) of the sacraments, with only baptism and the Lord's Supper being regarded as authentic sacraments by most Protestants. (See "The Pattern of Christian Belief," below.) The principal difference, at least as seen both by the Protestant reformers and by their Roman Catholic adversaries, lay in the area of religious authority: not the church or its tradition, not the papacy or a church council, but the Bible alone, was to be the norm that determined what Christians were to believe and how they were to live.

The Roman Catholic response to the Protestant Reformation is sometimes called the "Counter-Reformation," although that term has come to be regarded by many scholars as excessively negative in its connotations because it seems to ignore the positive reforms that were not merely a reaction to Protestantism. "The Roman Catholic Reformation" is in many ways a preferable designation. First through a series of responses to the theology and program of the reformers, then above all through the canons and decrees of the Council of Trent (1545–1563), the Catholic Reformation took up the issues addressed by Luther and by his most eminent successor, John Calvin (1509–1564), both in the area of church life and morals and in the area of church teaching and authority. Many of the corruptions that had acted as tinder for the Reformation received the careful attention of the council fathers, with the result that Roman Catholicism and the papacy emerged from the crisis of the Reformation diminished in size but chastened and strengthened in spirit. The creation of the Society of Jesus by Ignatius Loyola (c. 1491–1556) in 1534 provided the church with a powerful instrument for carrying out the program of reform and renewal, and many of the tools employed by the reformers (e.g., the printing press and the catechism) lent themselves to that program just as effectively. A deepening mystical devotion gave new life to medieval spirituality, particularly in sixteenth-century Spain, and the theology of Thomas Aquinas acquired new authority as the defenders of the faith closed ranks against

Protestant thought. The historical coincidence of the discovery of the New World and the Protestant Reformation, which both Protestants and Roman Catholics interpreted as providential, enabled Roman Catholic missionaries to recoup in North and South America the losses in prestige and membership caused by the Reformation. It was above all in Latin America that this recovery became a decisive religious and cultural force. Although divided (by the papal Line of Demarcation of 1493) between Spain and Portugal, Latin America was "united" in the sense that it was colonized and converted by Roman Catholic Christianity; the process of the Christianization of native populations was a gradual one, and many beliefs and practices of their pre-Christian history were carried over into their new faith. The effect of these and other missionary campaigns in the sixteenth and seventeenth centuries was to make the term *catholic* in *Roman Catholic* begin to mean in fact what it had always meant in principle: present throughout the known world.

The Christian East. Throughout the Middle Ages and the Reformation there were sporadic efforts in the West to establish (or reestablish) contact with the East; these ranged from the dispatch of various legations, to the translation of various classic works in one direction or the other, to marriages between Western monarchs and Byzantine or Russian princesses. The Crusades, which the East sometimes invited and sometimes dreaded, did at least reacquaint many members of the two traditions with one another, although the most unforgettable instance of such reacquaintance was the catastrophe of the sack of Christian Constantinople by the armies of the Fourth Crusade in 1204. Followed as it was two and a half centuries later by the Muslim capture of Constantinople and the end of the Byzantine Empire, the tragedy of 1204 is probably better entitled than any other event to the dubious distinction of being the point at which the Eastern and Western churches came into schism—a schism that, except for repeated but short-lived attempts at reunion (the most notable of which was probably the Union of Florence in 1439), has persisted ever since. Although the loss of Constantinople to the Turks drastically reduced its sphere of influence, the ecumenical patriarchate of Constantinople continued to enjoy a preeminence of honor within Eastern Orthodoxy, as it does to this day. Numerically as well as politically, however, it was Slavic Orthodoxy, above all in Russia, that became the "heir apparent," uniting itself with Russian culture as it had with medieval Greek culture. Plagued though it was by internal schisms, and caught in the political and cultural upheavals of the tsarist empire, the church in Russia went on producing saints and scholars, and through the icons and the liturgy it suffused the faith and life of the common people with the meaning of the Christian faith: the icon painter Andrei Rublev (c. 1360–c. 1430) and, in more modern times, the novelist and spiritual thinker Fyodor Dostoevsky (1821–1881) were among the products of this tradition best known in the West. The nineteenth and twentieth centuries witnessed an upsurge of interest in Eastern Orthodoxy throughout Western Christianity, as a consequence partly of the ecumenical movement and partly of the Russian Revolution, as both Protestants and Roman Catholics looked to Orthodoxy for the correction of what had come to be seen as Western deficiencies and overemphases in the aftermath of the Reformation.

Post-Reformation Christianity. The ecclesiastical map of the West after the Reformation shows a Europe divided between an almost solidly Roman Catholic south and a predominantly Protestant north, with the latter in turn divided between Anglican, Lutheran, and Reformed or Calvinist forms of Christianity. The same competition was exported into Christian missions in Africa and Asia and into the Americas. Among the most influential developments of the centuries following the Reformation was the effort, which took a distinct form in each denomination but nevertheless manifested a similarity of spirit, to encourage a deeper seriousness about the claims of the Christian gospel upon personal faith and life: Jansenism within French (and then North American) Roman Catholicism, Puritanism (and later on Methodism) within English Protestantism, and Pietism within the Lutheran and Reformed churches of the continent and of the New World. Especially during the eighteenth century, these movements had it as one of their primary goals to combat and counteract the influence, both in the church and in public life, of the rationalism, freethinking, and "infidelity" associated with the Enlightenment. Combining as it did the application to Christian history and biblical literature of the methods of historical criticism (particularly in German theological scholarship) with the reexamination or even the rejection of the special claims of Christianity to a privileged place in Western society (particularly in the legislation of the French Revolution), the Enlightenment came to represent the campaign for the secularization of culture. An important feature of that combination of emphases in Enlightenment thought was a fundamental reconsideration of the traditional Christian assertions of finality and uniqueness. As the philosophical and historical basis for such assertions was coming under increasing attack from within such traditionally Christian institutions as the theological faculties of universities, the discovery of other religions both in the historical past and in the distant parts of the present world was bringing such concepts as the uniqueness of the Christian message into serious question. The special privileges that Christianity had enjoyed since the Constantinian era were gradually withdrawn. Separation of church and state, as developed especially in the United States, and the growth of religious toleration and religious liberty were the social and political expressions of the new situation that was beginning to become evident at the end of the eighteenth century.

The nineteenth century. Despite the losses in both influence and numbers that it suffered in the period of the Enlightenment, Christianity entered the nineteenth century with a strong sense of its continuing relevance and special mission. The critical reexamination of the Christian toleration of slavery—long overdue, in the opinion of observers inside and outside the church—came to full realization in the nineteenth century, even though a civil war in the United States was necessary to bring this about. It was likewise in the nineteenth century, surnamed "the great century" in the leading history of Christian missions, that most of the major Christian denominations of the West, Protestant as well as Roman Catholic, set out to evangelize the globe. Although the Christian missionary and the colonialist conqueror often marched arm in arm across that globe, the results for native cultures were quite ambiguous: sometimes a loss of national identity and cultural deracination, but on the other hand no less often a deepening sense of historical particularity and the acquisition of scholarly instruments for understanding it and thus of overcoming both the colonialism and the missions. Significantly, it was from the mission schools founded in the nineteenth century that a disproportionately high number of the revolutionary leaders of the twentieth century in developing nations were to emerge. On the home front, the confrontation between traditional Christian beliefs and the discoveries of modern science engaged the attention of the churches. The most violent such confrontation was brought on by the work of Charles Darwin, whose books *The Origin of Species* (1859) and *The Descent of Man* (1871) called into question the traditional Christian belief in a special creation of the human species in the image of God as based on the biblical accounts of creation in the *Book of Genesis.* Yet as the nineteenth century ended, there was a widespread expectation that the next would truly be "the Christian century." *Christianizing the Social Order* by Walter Rauschenbusch (1861–1918), first published in 1912, was a representative statement of that expectation.

The twentieth century. As things turned out, the twentieth century proved to be the age of two world wars, of the coming to power of Marxist regimes throughout most of historic Eastern Christendom, and of moral and intellectual crises (including the Nazi Holocaust and the issues raised by modern technology) that would shake the traditional beliefs and historical confidence of Christians with unprecedented force. The reaction was, if not an overt loss of faith, then a growing indifference in many traditionally Christian groups. The most influential Christian theologian of the twentieth century, Karl Barth (1886–1968), protested the synthesis of the gospel with human culture and called for a reassertion of that gospel in its native power and uniqueness. At the same time, however, the most influential Christian event of the twentieth century, the Second Vatican Council of 1962–1965, undertook a reform of Christian faith and life that reached out to other Christians and to other religious traditions with a new openness. The council was the manifestation within Roman Catholicism of a new ecumenical consciousness that had its origins in Protestantism; the divisions that had followed in the wake of the Reformation now came under question in the light of the recognition that what separated Christians from one another was less significant than all the things that still held them together. That ecumenical consciousness throughout the Christian movement found expression in the recovery of historic Christian beliefs, in the creation of contemporary forms of worship, and in the reexamination of patterns of Christian life both individual and corporate. It remains to consider these three areas of belief, worship, and life, which, taken together, may be said to constitute the essence of Christianity.

THE ESSENCE OF CHRISTIANITY. Christianity has manifested an almost infinite variety of expressions as it has spread its presence and influence into all the major cultures of the Western world and into most of those of the East as well. With a billion or more adherents throughout the human race, it continues to be heterogeneous and pluralistic in its forms of organization and worship, belief, and life—so much so that it appears difficult or foolhardy or impossible to attempt to identify any characteristics as the distinctive genius or continuing essence of Christianity. A well-known criterion was the one proposed by Vincent of Lérins in the fifth century—what has been accepted "everywhere, always, by all" (*ubique, semper, ab omnibus*)—but the welter of detail about the history of Christianity scattered across the hundreds of articles dealing with the subject in the volumes of this encyclopedia should convince even the most casual reader that if there is an "essence of Christianity" it cannot possibly be everything that Christianity has ever been to everyone in every time and every place. Therefore, to quote again from Schleiermacher, "the only pertinent way of discovering the peculiar essence of any particular faith and reducing it as far as possible to a formula is by showing the element which remains constant throughout the most diverse religious affections within this same communion, while it is absent from analogous affections within other communions."

The search for an essence of Christianity is as old as the primary deposits of Christianity themselves. Already in the Hebrew scriptures, which Christianity took over as its Old Testament, the prophet Micah had declared: "God has told you what is good; and what is it that the Lord asks of you? Only to act justly, to love loyalty, to walk wisely before your God" (NEB *Mi.* 6:8). And an unknown first-century Christian writer, author of what came to be called the letter to the Hebrews in the New Testament, stated that "anyone who comes to God must believe that he exists and that he rewards those who search for him" (*Heb.* 11:6). The most successful formula for the essence of Christianity, however, was that of the apostle Paul: "In a word, there are three things that last for ever: faith, hope, and love; but the greatest of them all is love" (*1 Cor.* 13:13). Already in the second century, Irenaeus (c. 130–c. 200), bishop of Lyons, was invoking this formula as a summary of what "endures unchangeably," and in the fifth century it became the basis and the outline for Augustine's *Enchiridion,* to which Augustine himself usually referred as *On Faith, Hope, and Love.* From Augustine, in turn, the formula went on to provide the table of contents for the early catechisms in the age of Charlemagne and then for the rapid expansion in the number and use of catechisms by all parties in the age of the Reformation. Hence it may serve as a device for organizing this description of the essence of Christianity in its historical sweep, its geographical expansion, and its genius. Considered both in its history and in its contemporary expressions, Christianity has been, and is, a system of faith, of hope, and of love, a pattern of belief (and thought), a community of worship (and culture), and a way of life (and society). Paul's triad of faith, hope, and love may thus be used to correspond to the even more universal schema of the true, the beautiful, and the good.

The pattern of Christian belief. As a system of faith, Christianity manifests "faith" in all the various meanings that this term has acquired in the history of religion: as loyalty to the divine, based on the prior loyalty of the divine to the world and to humanity; as the confidence that God is trustworthy in truth and love; as dependence on the Father of Jesus Christ, who is the source of all good in this life and in the life to come; as the commitment to direct thought and action in accordance with the divine word and will; and as the affirmation that certain events and declarations, as given by divine revelation, are a reliable index to that will and word. It is the last of those meanings that provides a basis for describing in an epitome what it is that Christianity believes, teaches, and confesses.

"Whoever wishes to be saved must, above all, hold to the catholic faith." These opening words of the so-called Athanasian Creed (not in fact written by Athanasius, but a Latin and Western creed, compiled perhaps in the fifth century) would not, as they stand, automatically elicit the assent and support of all Christians; nor, for that matter, would all Christians who do accept such a statement be agreed on the precise content and extent of that "catholic faith." Differ though they do on these questions, however, Christians throughout history have affirmed the importance of the act of believing, as well as of the content of what is believed, as a mark of identification by which believers would be known.

The person of Jesus Christ. Christian belief began with the need to specify the significance of the person of Jesus, seen as the "Christ." The initial stages of that process are visible already in the pages of the New Testament. Its titles for him—in addition to Christ, such titles as Son of man, Son of God, Word of God (Logos), and Savior—were an effort to account for that significance, for within the events of Jesus' human life the God of Israel and the creator of the world had been disclosed. Before the theologians had invented ways of defining the content of these titles in any satisfying detail, the devotion and worship of the church were already identifying Jesus with God. This is evident, for example, from the earliest non-Christian account of the church that we possess, the letter of Pliny the Younger (62–113), governor of Bithynia, to the Roman emperor Trajan (r. c. 98–117), which describes Christians as gathering for worship and "addressing a song to Christ as to God" (*Christo ut deo*). But this devotional practice had yet to be squared both with the monotheism that the church inherited from and shared with Israel and with the concrete events of the life of Jesus as these were described in the Gospels. During the second and third centuries the reality of his human life needed to be defended; during the fourth century the divine dimension of his being demanded attention; during the fifth and sixth centuries the relation between the divine and the human in him required clarification. What emerged from the process of debate and definition—especially in the creeds formulated at the councils of Nicaea in 325, Constantinople in 381, and Chalcedon in 451—was a picture of Jesus Christ as having two "natures," divine and human: he was simultaneously "one in being" with God and "one in being" with humanity, and therefore able to mediate between them. The full content of the two natures and of the relation between them has continued to engage the speculative talents of Christian theologians ever since.

The Trinity. The final creedal statement of the relation between Christ and God was part of a more complete statement of belief, the Christian doctrine of the Trinity, which many theological exponents of Christianity would regard as the central teaching of the Christian faith. Its fundamental outline is already given in the "great commission"—which, according to the Gospels, Jesus entrusted to his disciples before withdrawing his visible presence from them (*Mt.* 28:19)—to baptize "in the name of the Father and of the Son and of the Holy Spirit." Threefold though that single "name" was, it was the relation of the Son to the Father that carried the principal weight in the clarification of the formula. Thus the original creed adopted at Nicaea, after enumerating the various "titles of majesty" belonging to Jesus Christ as the Son of God, simply added "And [we believe] in the Holy Spirit," with no similar elaboration of how and why the Third Person was entitled to stand alongside the Father and the Son. But before the fourth century was over, the status of the Holy Spirit, and thus the complete dogma of God as Trinity, had achieved the form it has held in Christian orthodoxy throughout the history of the church. The dogma presents itself as strictly monotheistic. The opening words of the Nicene Creed are "We believe in one God," and everything that follows about Father, Son, and Holy Spirit is set into that framework. The technical philosophical term for the oneness of God was *ousia* in Greek, *substantia* or *essentia* in Latin. But this single divine *ousia* had its being in three *hupostaseis,* or "persons."

The doctrine of the Trinity has from the beginning been one of the most productive—and one of the most problematic—points of contact between Christian theology and speculative philosophy. Both the Greek Neoplatonist Plotinus (c. 205–270) and the German idealist G. W. F. Hegel (1770–1831), with many others between them, taught a philosophical version of the Trinity with which many theologians felt obliged somehow to come to terms. The metaphysical ingenuity of philosophers and theologians—from the first of Latin theologians, Tertullian (160?–225?), and the boldest of Greek theologians, his contemporary Origen (c. 185–c. 254), to philosophical theologians of the twentieth century, such as the Protestant Paul Tillich (1886–1965) and the

Roman Catholic Karl Rahner (1904–1984)—has therefore continually experimented with new ways of accounting for (if not of "explaining") the relation between the One and the Three. Perhaps the most creative of such speculations was that of Augustine's *On the Trinity*, which constructed a series of trinitarian analogies in the universe and in the human mind as "images [or footprints] of the divine Trinity."

Sin and grace. All the councils that formulated these basic doctrines of the Trinity and of the person of Christ were held in the Greek-speaking eastern part of the Christian Roman Empire under the patronage of the Christian emperor, who was from the year 330 onward resident at Constantinople, and the creeds, which are in Greek, bear the marks of that origin. Still it is a mistake to ignore the role of the Latin West in the determination of normative Christian teaching: both at Nicaea and at Chalcedon there were decisive interventions from Western theologians and bishops. Nevertheless, the most distinctive and original Western contributions during the first five centuries came not in the doctrines of God and Christ but in the doctrines of sin and grace. With significant anticipations in various Western thinkers, it was once again Augustine who formulated these latter doctrines in the concepts and terms that were to dominate most of subsequent Christian teaching in the West, that of Roman Catholicism but no less the theology of Protestantism. Many early interpreters of Christian belief—for example, Gregory of Nyssa (c. 335–c. 395) in his treatise *On the Creation of Man*—had articulated the biblical teaching (*Gn.* 1:26–27) that, among all creatures on earth, humans alone possessed the special prerogative of having been created "in the image of God," with the promise of immortal life and of a "participation in the divine nature" (*2 Pt.* 1:4). But in so doing they had often spoken more explicitly about human free will than about human sinfulness. Yet this did not imply, Augustine insisted, that every human being faced the same choice between good and evil that Adam and Eve had faced. On the contrary, humanity had since Adam and Eve been under a curse of what Augustine called "the sin of origin" (*peccatum originis*), which infected every human being except Jesus Christ (and perhaps his mother, the Virgin Mary). Even without committing acts of sin, therefore, each member of the human race was corrupted from birth; the traditional practice of infant baptism (see "The Community of Christian Worship," below) was for Augustine evidence of the universality of this sinful condition.

Redemption. Neither the belief in God as Trinity nor the dogma of Christ as divine and human in nature nor the doctrine of humanity as created in the image of God but fallen into sin is, however, an end in itself for Christian faith. As a religion of redemption, Christianity presents itself as the message of how, through Christ, reconciliation has been achieved between the holiness of God and the sin of a fallen humanity. But while the Trinity, the person of Christ, and (though less universally or explicitly) the doctrine of original sin all have been subjects of a public and ecumenical confession of the church, the manner of this reconciliation has not received such attention. It has been left more to hymnody and preaching than to dogma and metaphysics to supply the metaphors for describing it. One of the most widely distributed such metaphors in early Christian writers, beginning with the sayings of Jesus himself (*Mt.* 20:28), is the description of redemption as "ransom" (which is, of course, what *redemption* means): the death of Christ was paid (to God or to the devil) as the price for setting humanity free. The difficulties that such a notion entailed for the Christian picture of God made a modification of the ransom theory seem imperative: the death of Christ took place in the course of a battle between God-in-Christ and the devil with his allies, a battle in which death triumphed initially by the nailing of Christ to the cross but in which Christ was victorious in the end through his resurrection. It remained once again for the medieval West to provide the most inventive of these theories. According to Anselm in his *Why God Became Man*, the reconciliation of the human race with God was fundamentally the reconciliation between the justice of God, which was committed to upholding "the moral order of the universe" (*rectitudo*) and therefore could not ignore human sin or forgive it by a simple fiat, and the mercy of God, which was bent on restoring humanity to the condition for which God had intended it by its creation. God became man in Christ, because as man he would be able, by his death, to produce the satisfaction demanded by divine justice, but as God he would render a satisfaction of infinite worth that could thus be applied to the entire human race. With some modifications and refinements, Anselm's theory has established itself both within Roman Catholicism and within most of classical Protestantism.

Justification. Classical Protestantism differs from Roman Catholicism in the interpretation of redemption not on the way redemption was achieved by God in Christ, but on the way it is appropriated by the Christian. Luther's doctrine of justification by faith—or, more fully and more precisely, justification by grace through faith—directed itself against what he perceived to be the widespread tendency of medieval Christianity to give human works part of the credit for restoring the right relation between God and man. This he attacked as a denial of the purely gratuitous character of salvation. The role of the human will in salvation was purely passive, accepting the forgiveness of sins as a sheer gift and contributing nothing of its own goodness to the transaction with God. Faith, accordingly, was not (or, at any rate, not primarily) an act of the intellect accepting as true what God has revealed but an act of the will entrusting itself unconditionally to the favor of God as conferred in Christ. Such unconditional trust led to the transformation of human life from the self-centered quest for gratification to the God-centered service of others (see "The Christian Way of Life," below). Partly in response to Luther's doctrine, the Council of Trent at its sixth session affirmed that "faith is the beginning of human salvation, the foundation and the root of all justification," but it condemned anyone who "says that the sinner is justified by faith alone, as though nothing else were required to cooperate."

The community of Christian worship. As a system of hope, Christianity holds forth the promise of eternal life through Jesus Christ. In the words of what has been called "the gospel in a nutshell" (*Jn.* 3:16), "God loved the world so much that he gave his only Son, that everyone who has faith in him may not die but have eternal life." But that promise and hope of life for those who have faith does not stand in isolation from the full range of Christian hope, the expectation of all the gifts of God for time and for eternity, and the acceptance of those gifts in thankfulness and praise. Hope, consequently, expresses itself chiefly in prayer and worship, both the personal prayer of the individual Christian believer and the corporate worship of the Christian community.

The holy catholic church. One integral component of Christianity both as " a pattern of belief" and as "a community of worship" is expressed in the words of the Apostles' Creed: "I believe in the holy catholic church, the communion of saints." According to the accounts of the New Testament, it was the intention of Jesus to found a church (*Mt.* 16:18): "I will build my church." Whether one accepts the literal historicity of those accounts or not, Jesus did, in fact, gather a community of disciples and establish a table fellowship. The earliest Christianity we are able to uncover is already a churchly Christianity, to which in fact we owe the Gospels and all the other books of the New Testament. For Christians of every persuasion and denomination, the church is at the same time the primary context of worship.

There is, however, far less unanimity about the nature of the church or about its organization and its authority. The tripartite complex of authority that emerged from the conflicts of early Christianity (see "The History of Christianity," above) vested in the office of the monarchical bishop the visible governance of the church and defined the church accordingly. Two formulas of Cyprian (d. 258), bishop of Carthage, summarize this definition: "Where the bishop is, there the church is" (*Ubi episcopus, ibi ecclesia*) and "There is no salvation apart from the church" (*Extra ecclesiam nulla salus*). For Cyprian himself, as became evident in his disputes with Stephen I (bishop of Rome from 254 to 257), each bishop carried the authority of the office on his own and was answerable to the authority of Christ and of his brother bishops, but not to any one bishop as monarch of the entire church. But there were already signs of a developing pyramidal structure of authority, with certain centers having clear jurisdiction over others. Among these, the see of Rome had, and has, preeminence. As noted earlier, this understanding of authority led in the Middle Ages to a definition of the church as a visible monarchy, analogous in some ways to other monarchies, of which the pope was the absolute ruler—"judging all, but being judged by none," as the *Dictatus papae* of Gregory VII said. Orthodoxy, by contrast, has resisted the pyramidal model of church authority, preferring to see the entire company of the church's bishops, particularly when they are in council assembled, as a corporate and collegial entity, with the bishop of Rome as "first among equals" (*primus inter pares*) but not as monarch. One of the major accents of the Second Vatican Council was a new emphasis on episcopal collegiality but not at the expense of the primacy of the bishop of Rome within the college. That accent was closely joined in the decrees of the council to a recovery of the definition of the church as principally the community of Christian worship.

Protestant views of the church. The Protestant rejection of the authority of the pope is closely joined to a redefinition of the nature of the church. There had always been the recognition in the medieval doctrine of the church, particularly as this had come down from Augustine, that the organizational, empirical church was not coextensive with the church as it exists in the eyes of God: some who participate in, or even preside over, the church as an institution today will ultimately perish, while others who now persecute the church are destined to become members of the body of Christ. That definition of the true church as "the company of the elect," and hence as invisible in its membership and in its essence, appears in one form or another in the thought of most of the Protestant reformers. It did not imply, except in the polemics of a radical few, that there was no visible church. With differing forms of ecclesiastical administration (see "Reformation Christianity," above), the reformers took over or adapted patterns of organization that would suit the church for its function as the community of Christian worship and the center of Christian instruction. A favorite Protestant term for the church, therefore, is the phrase in the Apostles' Creed, "the communion of saints."

The preaching of the word of God. Although they would agree that the church is the community of Christian worship, the several denominations disagree about the structure of that community—and about the content of that worship. It is characteristic of most Protestant groups that in their liturgies and forms of worship they assign centrality to communication of the Christian message through preaching: "Where the word of God is, there the church is" (*Ubi verbum Dei, ibi ecclesia*) is how they have recast Cyprian's formula. As the leader of the worshiping community, the minister is principally (though never exclusively) the proclaimer of the word of God, a word of God that is found in, or identified and even equated with, the Bible. The emphasis on biblical preaching has sometimes led to a didactic understanding of worship, but this has been counterbalanced in Protestantism by the literally tens of thousands of "psalms and hymns and spiritual songs" (*Col.* 3:16) that the Protestant churches have developed because of their equally great stress on the participation of the congregation and of each individual worshiper in the service. The traditional concern of Protestant Christianity with the authentic faith and experience of the individual—expressed in Luther's axiom "You must do your own believing as you must do your own dying"— is likewise audible in these hymns, many of which, typically, are cast in the language of the first person singular.

The sacraments. It would, however, be a grave distortion (albeit a distortion to which even sympathetic interpreters of Protestant Christianity have sometimes been subject) to interpret Protestantism as a thoroughgoing individualism in its understanding of worship, for the definition of the church as "the community of Christian worship," in Protestantism as well as in Orthodoxy and in Roman Catholicism, is embodied above all in the celebration of the sacraments. Except for certain details (e.g., whether it is the recitation of the words of institution or the invocation of the Holy Spirit in the epiclesis that effects the transformation of bread and wine into the body and blood of Christ in the Eucharist), Eastern Orthodoxy and Roman Catholicism stand in basic agreement on the nature of sacramental worship and the meaning of the seven sacraments. Among the many definitions of *sacrament* that have appeared in the Christian tradition, two (one from the East and one from the West) may suffice here: "the mystery of faith," since in Christian Greek *mustērion* means both "mystery" and "sacrament"; and, in a formula based on Augustine, "sacred sign," which by a visible means represents (or represents) an invisible divine grace.

The Eucharist. The primary sacrament and the center of Christian worship is, for both the Eastern and the Western tradition, the Eucharist or Lord's Supper, which is, in one form or another, celebrated by all Christian groups. Although the celebration is also a memorial and an expression of community, what sets the Roman Catholic and Orthodox understanding of the Eucharist apart from that of most other groups is their definition of this sacrament as real presence and as sacrifice. In fulfillment of the words and promise of Jesus, "This is my body" and "This is my blood," the bread and wine presented for the sacrament become the very body and blood of Christ, identical in their substance with the body born of Mary, even though the taste, color, and other attributes or "accidents" of bread and wine remain. The Fourth Lateran Council in 1215 defined this doctrine as "transubstantiation," and it was reaffirmed by the Council of Trent in 1551. As the real presence of the body and blood of the one whose death on the cross and resurrection effected the redemption of the world, the Eucharist is as well a sacrifice—not as though the first sacrifice were inadequate and Christ needed to be sacrificed over and over, but "in union with the sacrifice" of Calvary. The daily offering of that sacrifice for the living and the dead is at the center of Roman Catholic worship, devotion, and doctrine; and although Orthodoxy is, characteristically, less explicit in some of its detailed formulations about the metaphysics of the presence and more content to speak of it as a "mystery," its representatives, when pressed, will come up with language not far removed from that of the West—especially of the West as in the twentieth century it has, thanks to a repossession of the tradition of the Greek fathers, come to speak about the mystery of the Eucharist.

Whatever differences of emphasis there may be between Roman Catholicism and Eastern Orthodoxy about the Eucharist, they are much smaller than the differences among the several Protestant groups. Luther objected to transubstantiation as an excessively philosophical formula, and above all to the sacrificial understanding of the Eucharist as a diminution of the redemptive work of Christ, but he vigorously defended the real presence against his fellow Protestants. They in turn laid stress on the "true presence" of Christ in his spirit and power rather than on the "real presence" of the actual body and blood. Within Protestantism, consequently, the memorial aspects of the celebration of the Lord's Supper, which Christ according to the Gospels instituted to be eaten in his remembrance, have been prominent and sometimes even central. The other historic accent of Christian eucharistic worship that has found a new emphasis in Protestant practice and devotion is the understanding of the Lord's Supper as a corporate expression of the "communion" of Christian believers with one another. "Body of Christ" in the New Testament refers sometimes to the Eucharist, sometimes to the church, and sometimes (notably in *1 Corinthians*) to both at the same time. Compared with those two themes of memorial and communion, the specification of just how the body and blood of Christ can be present in the sacrament is of lesser significance.

Baptism. The other action of the community of Christian worship on whose "sacramental" character all Christians would agree is baptism. Throughout the *Acts of the Apostles*, baptism functions as the means of initiation into the Christian movement and into the reality of Christ himself, and in the epistles of Paul baptism is the way of appropriating the benefits of the death and resurrection of Christ. Although all the explicit references in the New Testament to the practice of baptism mention only adults as its recipients, and that generally only after a profession of their faith, the custom of administering it also to children began quite early; just how early is a matter of controversy, but by the end of the second century infant baptism was sufficiently widespread to have called forth objections from Tertullian. Except for that difference from subsequent tradition, Tertullian formulated in his treatise *On Baptism* what can be regarded as an all but universal consensus about the effects of baptism: remission of sins, deliverance from death, regeneration, and bestowal of the Holy Spirit. Eastern and Western Church Fathers, all the medieval scholastics, and many of the Protestant reformers would be able to subscribe to that formulation. Because of their misgivings about any view of any of the sacraments that might appear magical, Protestants have tended to avoid describing the conferral of these effects as something automatic. The Anabaptists of the sixteenth century on the continent, and the several bodies of Baptists in England and especially in the United States since the seventeenth century, have carried that position to the conclusion of repudiating the practice of infant baptism and insisting on "believers' baptism" as the only form of administering the sacrament that is consistent both with the original intention of Jesus and with the true nature of the Christian community.

Other sacraments. Although baptism and the Lord's Supper are for most Protestants the only two ordinances that qualify as sacraments, the medieval development in the West led to a system of seven sacraments, which Eastern Christianity, when obliged to become specific, has likewise affirmed. The sacrament of penance (together with the reception of absolution) developed as a way of coping with sins committed after the reception of forgiveness in baptism. As the contrition of the heart, the confession of the mouth, and the satisfaction of a work restoring what had been taken away by the sin, penance became, in the Latin Middle Ages, one of the principal means by which the imperatives and the promises of the Christian gospel were applied to individuals and communities. With the universal acceptance of infant baptism, the individual's assumption of the responsibilities of Christian discipleship, originally associated with adult baptism, came to be the central content of the sacrament of confirmation. As infant baptism attended the beginning of life with sacramental grace, so at death, or in a crisis or illness that might portend death, the anointing of the sick (or the sacrament of "extreme unction") brought that grace to the end of life as well. The only one of the seven "sacraments" to which the name was applied in the New Testament (*mustērion* in Greek, *sacramentum* in Latin) was marriage (*Eph.* 5:32); on that authority, it became part of the sacramental system. And as the ordinance by which all the other sacraments were usually made possible, the ordination of priests itself was defined to be a sacrament. Each of the seven, therefore, combines in a special way what is also the special emphasis of Christian hope and of Christian worship: the sacredness of each person, but in the context of the sacred community.

The Christian way of life. As a system of love—and love is, in the formula of Paul, the "greatest" of the three (*1 Cor.* 13:13)—Christianity presented itself to its hearers as a way of life; especially in *Acts*, "the way" became a standard designation for Christianity itself. In its symbiosis with the societies and cultures in which it has taken root, the Christian way of life has been characterized by even greater heterogeneity than Christian belief or Christian worship. That heterogeneity makes generalizations about it in such a summary as this even more hazardous, and the specifics of the forms of Christian ethics in society must be left for treatment elsewhere in this encyclopedia. It is nevertheless possible to single out briefly certain leitmotifs that run across the varieties of Christian morality, both individual and social.

The imitation of Christ. Ever since the New Testament, the human life of Jesus Christ has served as an example set forth for imitation; it has usually been more than an example, but never less. "Bend your necks to my yoke, and learn from me, for I am gentle and humble-hearted; and your souls will find relief" the New Testament (*Mt.* 11:29) represents him as commanding. Just what that imitation implies concretely for the Christian in the world has been, however, a continuing issue and problem, for the Christ whom the believer is invited to imitate was not married, did not hold public office, and was not supported chiefly from a trade or profession. The imitation of his example has come to mean, therefore, the application to one's own situation of the love and faithfulness that Christ brought to his. Repeatedly, when the demands of society or, for that matter, the requirements of the church have proved to be too complex or abstract, "the imitation of Christ" has become a way of reducing them to their essence. Thus, in what has probably been, except for the Bible itself, the most widely circulated book in Christian history, *Imitation of Christ* by Thomas à Kempis (1379/80–1471), the summons of the figure in the Gospels rises above the intervening voices with a clarity and directness that has spoken to followers in every century; and in the twentieth century, *The Cost of Discipleship*, by the young Lutheran theologian and martyr under the Nazis, Dietrich Bonhoeffer (1906–1945), has applied that New Testament summons of "Follow me" to a new generation of disciples.

Obedience. The imitation of Christ has also implied obedience to his will, as this was expressed both in his own teachings and in the Mosaic law. In its treatment of that law, the New Testament manifests an ambivalence: Christ is seen as "the end of the law" (*Rom.* 10:4), and yet he himself is represented as warning in the sermon on the mount (*Mt.* 5:17), "Do not suppose that I have come to abolish the law and the prophets." The ambivalence manifests itself likewise in the descriptions of the Christian way of life as obedience. The Christian catechisms that have proliferated especially since the sixteenth century (see "Reformation Christianity," above) have usually incorporated an exposition and application of the Mosaic Decalogue as their description of what it means in practical terms to be a Christian. That has been perhaps even more true of Protestant than of Roman Catholic catechisms, despite the polemic of Protestants against "moralism" and "legalism" in Roman Catholic theology and ethics. But both Roman Catholic and Protestant ethicists and teachers have also repeatedly defined Christian obedience as not the strict observance of a legal code, not even of the legal code in the Ten Commandments, but as the spontaneity of the Spirit. "Love God, and do what you will" was Augustine's characteristically epigrammatic way of describing that spontaneity; but that same Augustine is at the same time one of our earliest authorities for the use of the Ten Commandments in Christian pedagogy. Augustine is as well an early source for the adaptation to Christian purposes of the philosophical consideration of the nature and the number of the "virtues": to the classical (or, as they came to be called in Christian parlance, "cardinal") virtues of prudence, temperance, fortitude, and justice, Christian ethical thought added the three "theological" virtues of faith, hope, and love. Obedience to the will of God and the cultivation of these seven virtues were seen as the content of the Christian way of life.

The transformation of the social order. Each of the "cardinal" and "theological" virtues makes sense only in a social context, and obedience to the will of God has traditionally been seen as pertaining to society as well as to the individual. The petitions of the Lord's Prayer, "Thy kingdom come, thy will be done, on earth as it is in heaven," have been taken to mean that the reign of God and the will of God have as their object here on earth the creation of a social order that conforms as closely as possible to the reign of God in heaven. That is indeed how both the East (see "The Christian Culture of Byzantium," above) and the West (see "Christianity in the Middle Ages," above) have interpreted their mission through most of Christian history, and that was how they carried out their mission within those societies. Calvinism and Puritanism were especially committed to the creation of social and political institutions that lived up to the will of God, and the pacifism of Anabaptist and Quaker groups during the sixteenth and seventeenth centuries was inspired by a similar commitment. During the nineteenth and twentieth centuries, however, such an interpretation of the Christian mission took on new urgency—and occasioned new controversy—in a society where the institutions of Christianity no longer command attention or widespread obedience. The Social Gospel associated with the name of Rauschenbusch (see "The Nineteenth Century," above) was the most ambitious of modern efforts to rethink the fundamentals of the Christian way of life in relation to the situation of an industrial society and to define the very meaning of salvation (as well as of other themes of Christian teaching and devotion) in social terms. Although the Social Gospel has in greater or lesser measure affected the ethical thought of most Protestant groups, Roman Catholicism was, during most of the twentieth century, the major center for the development of new social and political theory. In a series of "social encyclicals" beginning with the *Rerum novarum* of Pope Leo XIII (1810–1903) of May 15, 1891, the papacy itself has often taken the lead in stimulating such development. But the application of the theory to modern society—the phenomenon of "worker priests" in France, and especially the creation of "liberation theology" by Roman Catholic theologians in Latin America—has often produced confusion and provoked controversy. Even those whose political or theological conservatism finds such trends dangerous, however, usually speak in the name of a particular definition of the social order that they regard as conforming, at least in some measure, to the same ideals.

Christian universalism. The Christian way of life as love is conventionally seen as finding its ultimate fulfillment in the church as the loving community of believers set apart from the world. But alongside that strain in the Christian tradition there has always stood a concern and a love for the entire world, a Christian universalism no less pronounced than is Christian particularism. It has sometimes expressed itself in a sense of urgency about Christian missions, to "bring the world to Christ." But a less prominent, yet no less persistent, expression of Christian universalism has sought to probe the implications of the unavoidable statements of the New Testament about the entire world as the object of the love of a God "whose will it is that all men should find salvation and come to know the truth" (*1 Tm.* 2:4). Origen in the third century, Gregory of Nyssa in the fourth century, Nicholas of Cusa in the fifteenth century—these and other theologians, committed though they were to the church and to its orthodoxy, have taken up the exposition of a universal vision in which the love of God revealed in Christ cannot be completely fulfilled until all God's creation has been reconciled.

Faith, hope, and love. The complex, sometimes labyrinthine, interactions of faith, hope, and love with one another throughout Christian history and throughout Christianity as a system suggest the absence of a set of universal principles that could, in the fashion of Euclid's geometry, yield *the* Christian worldview. Christianity is, rather, the product of a continuing and organic history. Its principal institutional expression has been the church in its various organizational forms, but Christianity is more than the church. Although its chief intellectual product has been a theological development that spans twenty centuries, the Christian message is not coextensive with its theology. Its most telling effect on history has been in the faith and life of its celebrated saints and seers, but Christianity has consistently declared that its power and spirit can be found as well among the silent in the land, the meek who shall inherit the earth.

SEE ALSO Apostles; Atonement, article on Christian Concepts; Baptism; Biblical Literature; Christian Ethics; Christian Liturgical Year; Church; Community; Confession of Sins; Constantinianism; Councils, article on Christian Councils; Creeds, article on Christian Creeds; Crusades; Deity; Denominationalism; Discipleship; Dogma; Drama, articles on European Religious Drama, Modern Western Theater; Eastern Christianity; Ecumenical Movement; Enlightenment, The; Eucharist; Evil; Faith; Fall, The; Free Will and Predestination, article on Christian Concepts; Gnosticism, articles on Gnosticism as a Christian Heresy, Gnosticism from Its Origins to the Middle Ages; God, articles on God in Postbiblical Christianity, God in the New Testament; Gospel; Grace; Heresy, article on Christian Concepts; Hope; Hypostasis; Iconoclasm; Iconography, article on Christian Iconography; Icons; Incarnation; Jesus; Justification; Literature, article on Religious Dimensions of Modern Western Literature; Marriage; Merit, article on Christian Concepts; Missions, article on Christian Missions; Monastery; Monasticism, article on Christian Monasticism; Music, article on Religious Music in the West; Ordination; Papacy; Persecution, article on Christian Experience; Poetry, article on Christian Poetry; Political Theology; Prayer; Priesthood, article on Christian Priesthood; Protestantism; Reformation; Religious Communities, article on Christian Religious Orders; Repentance; Roman Catholicism; Sacrament, article on Christian Sacraments; Schism, article on Christian Schism; Sin and Guilt; Soul, article on Christian Concepts; Ten Commandments; Theology, article on Christian Theology; Trent, Council of; Trinity; Vatican Councils, article on Vatican II; Worship and Devotional Life, article on Christian Worship.

BIBLIOGRAPHY

Christianity is fortunate in having had more works of general reference published about it than any other world religion. Probably the most convenient of these is *The Oxford Dictionary of the Christian Church*, 3d ed., rev. (Oxford, 1997). Also in English, and especially helpful for its bibliographies, is *The New Catholic Encyclopedia*, 15 vols. (Detroit, 2001). With more articles, a good many of which, however, are relatively brief, the *Lexikon für Theologie und Kirche*, 11 vols., 2d ed., edited by Michael Buchberger (Freiburg, 1957–1967), is a masterpiece of condensation. The succeeding editions of the *Realenzyklopädie für protestantische Theologie und Kirche*, 24 vols., 3d ed. (Leipzig, 1896–1913), whose fourth edition is now in preparation, have contained status reports on research into most of the themes treated in this article. And the *Dictionnaire de théologie catholique*, 15 double vols. (Paris, 1909–1950), presents comprehensive articles, some of them entire monographs, on many of the same themes.

The monographic literature on the history and the theology of Christianity is, quite literally, incomprehensible in its scope and cannot engage our attention here. But among more general works, perhaps the best overall treatment of its history is in *Histoire de l'église depuis les origines jusqu'à nos jours*, edited by Augustin Fliche, Victor Martin, and others (Paris, 1934–1964). *The Pelican History of the Church*, 6 vols., edited by Owen Chadwick (Harmondsworth, 1960–1970), is excellent, except for its omission of a volume on the Christian East, and always readable and often incisive. The more ambitious *Oxford History of the Christian Church* may well be a collaborative work destined to match Fliche-Martin in comprehensiveness. *Atlas zur Kirchengeschichte*, edited by Hubert Jedin, Kenneth Scott Latourette, and Jochen Martin (Freiburg, 1970), provides a sense of place for ideas and books that in the theological literature sometimes seem to be suspended in mid-air. The history of those ideas is the concern of my work *The Christian Tradition: A History of the Development of Doctrine*, 5 vols. (Chicago, 1971–), and the books are chronicled with a sureness of touch and with great fairness in Johannes Quasten's *Patrology*, 4 vols. (Utrecht, 1950–1960).

Of the many thousands of attempts at a systematic formulation of Christianity as a religion of faith, hope, and love (and therefore not only of Christian dogmatics, but of the entire Christian message), it may seem presumptuous to select only five: John of Damascus's *On the Orthodox Faith* in the eighth century, which has played a significant part in all three major segments of Christendom, Orthodox, Roman Catholic, and Protestant; Peter Lombard's *Sentences* in the twelfth century, which, with the more than one thousand commentaries that have been written on it, shaped Christian teaching for centuries; Thomas Aquinas's *Summa theologiae* in the thirteenth century, which many students of Christian thought would regard as the climax of its development; John Calvin's *The Institutes of the Christian Religion* in the sixteenth century, which summarized the principal tenets of the Protestant Reformation more masterfully than any other book of theology; and Friedrich Schleiermacher's *The Christian Faith* in the nineteenth century, which, both by its successes and by its failures, is an eloquent statement of the predicament and the promise of the Christian message.

New Sources

Barraclough, Geoffrey, ed. *The Christian World.* New York, 2003.

Campenhausen, Hans, Freiherr von. *The Fathers of the Church.* Combined edition of the Fathers of the Greek Church and the Fathers of the Latin Church. Peabody, Mass., 1998.

Chadwick, Henry, and Gillian Rosemary Evans, eds. *Atlas of the Christian Church.* New York, 1988.

Chadwick, Owen. *A History of Christianity.* London, 1995.

Crossan, John Dominic. *The Birth of Christianity.* San Francisco, 1998.

Ehrman, Bart D. *Lost Christianities: The Battles for Scripture and the Faiths We Never Knew.* Oxford, 2003.

Horsley, Richard A., ed. *Paul and Empire: Religion and Power in Imperial Society.* Harrisburg, Pa., 1997.

Koester, Helmut. *Ancient Christian Gospels: Their History and Development.* Philadelphia, 1990.

O'Mahoney, Kieran J., ed. *Christian Origins: Worship, Belief, and Society.* London and New York, 2003.

Sheehan, Thomas. *The First Coming: How the Kingdom of God Became Christianity.* New York, 1986.

JAROSLAV PELIKAN (1987)
Revised Bibliography

CHRISTIANITY: CHRISTIANITY IN THE MIDDLE EAST

The origins of the Christian communities in the Middle East are rooted in the birth and first development of Christianity in the old cities of Jerusalem, Antioch, and Damascus. Several million Christians continue to live in the Middle East at the beginning of the twenty-first century; most are scattered in Egypt (3.5 million), Jordan (150,000), Israel (105,000), the Palestinian territories (76,000), Syria (950,000), Lebanon (1.35 million), Iraq (615,000), Turkey (115,000), and Iran (150,000). Although their numbers have declined considerably in modern times, these communities represent an autochthonous Christian presence whose origins date further back than the birth and spread of Islam in the Middle East. Most Middle Eastern Christians are Arabs or, to a lesser extent, belong to such long-established groups as the Assyrians or the Armenians.

A PLURAL PRESENCE. Middle Eastern Christianity is characterized by a plurality of churches, bearing witness to the rich cultural and religious life and the historical evolution of the Christian communities of the early centuries. The division into independent churches was the result of doctrinal disputes linked to the Christological debates of the fourth and fifth centuries as well as to relations with the Latin Catholic Church. Beginning in the fifteenth century the latter tried to reunite with the Eastern churches by forming new Catholic churches that would maintain their own hierarchy and oriental liturgy but remain in dogmatic communion with the Church of Rome, recognizing the jurisdictional primacy of the pope (the so-called Uniat churches). In the nineteenth century, due in part to the increasing political and economic presence of the European states in the Middle East, many more Protestant and Latin missionaries arrived. The Latin Patriarchate of Jerusalem was restored in 1847, and at the same time Eastern Protestant communities were formed. After twenty centuries of historical evolution, the Eastern churches have been divided into four great families.

The Oriental Orthodox family. The Oriental Orthodox family is the most important in terms of the number of faithful living in the Middle East. It includes the Coptic Orthodox Church (at least 3,200,000 members), the Syrian Orthodox Church (177,000), and the Apostolic Armenian Church (540,000 in the Middle East). These churches separated from other churches of the Roman Empire in the fifth century (the beginning of the sixth century for the Armenian Church) when they refused to accept the diophysite Christological doctrine. This doctrine, as expressed by the Council of Chalcedon in 451, recognized in Christ two natures coexisting in one divine person. The three Oriental Orthodox churches instead remained faithful to the definition given by Cyril of Alexandria (c. 378–444), who spoke of "the one incarnate nature of the Word of God."

The Assyrian Church or Church of the East (120,000 members in the Middle East) also forms part of the Oriental Orthodox family. It separated from the other churches at the time of the Council of Ephesus (431 CE), rejecting the condemnation of the position of Nestorius, who held that in Christ there were two natures closely linked through a moral, not an ontological, bond.

The Oriental Orthodox churches are completely independent of each other and do not have juridical or disciplinary links with either the Roman Catholic Church or the Eastern Orthodox communion represented by the Patriarch of Constantinople.

The Orthodox (Chalcedonian) family. The Orthodox (Chalcedonian) family is represented in the Middle East by four autocephalous churches comprising approximately one million members. These four churches are all members of the Eastern Orthodox communion. They have been divided from the Catholic Church since 1054, the date of the mutual excommunication of the Church of Rome and the Patriarchate of Constantinople. The Orthodox Patriarchates of Antioch, Jerusalem, and Alexandria were set up in the fifth century by Christians and clergy who accepted the ruling of the Council of Chalcedon. The Middle Eastern Orthodox family also includes the Patriarchate of Constantinople in Turkey.

The Catholic family. The Catholic family comprises seven churches: Maronite (550,000 members), Chaldean (417,000), Melkite (450,000), Coptic Catholic (150,000), Armenian Catholic (60,000), Syrian Catholic (100,000), and the Latin Patriarchate of Jerusalem (86,500). These seven churches are fully united with the Church of Rome and recognize the jurisdictional primacy of the pope. In the late 1980s the Council of the Catholic Patriarchs of the Middle East was established to provide a forum for addressing the common problems of the Catholic communities in the region.

The Reformed family. The Reformed family, in existence since the nineteenth century, comprises thirteen different Protestant denominations, all of them modest in size. This family includes Lutheran, Evangelical, and Presbyterian communities as well as the Union of the Armenian Evangelical Churches of the Middle East for a total of about 81,000 members, mainly in Egypt, Lebanon, and Syria.

Council of the Churches of the Middle East. The various churches have their own institutions, including eparchies, community councils, various kinds of pastoral structures, ecclesiastical courts, and schools (in countries where confessional schools are allowed). One church's institutions often extend into the geographical regions of the other churches. The desires of individual churches to maintain their own identities and liturgical traditions has not prevented ecumenical activities, which led to the formation of the Council of the Churches of the Middle East (CCME) in 1974. All Middle Eastern Christian churches participate in the CCME, which helps to promote a more unified approach to the problems and issues facing Middle Eastern Christians. The prospect of ecumenism, even if it is sometimes difficult to achieve in concrete terms, is one of the few remaining sources of renewed energy for the Arab and Eastern churches in the long term.

THE HISTORICAL STATUS OF NON-MUSLIMS IN MUSLIM COUNTRIES. By the end of the seventh century Arab Muslims had conquered every part of the Middle East, and a new period began for the region's Christian communities. From the start Islam had to face the problem of its relations with members of other religions because there were Jews and Christians living in cities where Muslims first organized their own political and social structures. In addition Muslims had taken control of predominantly Christian areas that were previously under Byzantine control as well as Zoroastrian regions that had been part of the Sassanian Empire.

***Dhimma* system.** To accommodate non-Muslims, Islam adopted a system that was already in place in the Byzantine and Sassanian Empires, according to which different groups of people were accepted into society under a special status. Called *dhimma*, which means "protection" in Arabic, this system mandated that Muslims were obliged to protect groups on whom *dhimma* status had been conferred. In turn the *dhimmī* (protected) people had to submit absolutely to Muslim rule, recognizing Islam as the supreme power.

Islamic rulers conferred the status of *dhimmī* on members of the religions of the book, that is, those religions that had a sacred book as the basis of their doctrine, which included Judaism and Christianity as well as Sabaism and Mazdaism. In concrete terms the *dhimma* system aimed to enable Muslims and non-Muslims to live alongside one another within the Muslim state, yet it guaranteed the absolute supremacy of Islam and reduced non-Muslims to a lower legal and social status. Although the *dhimmī* were free to practice their own religion, they were forbidden any role in politics, government, or the military, which were reserved exclusively for Muslims. Furthermore the *dhimmī* were subjected to heavier taxes than those levied on Muslims, including the *jizya*, a special per capita tax, as well as taxes on land and business activities.

To guarantee the supremacy of Islam, non-Muslims were not allowed to engage in any kind of missionary activity, and Muslims were prohibited by law from converting to another religion. Under Islamic law both the missionary and the convert could be punished by death. The imposition of a death penalty for conversion (*ḥadd al-riddah*) guaranteed the integrity and growth of the Islamic community and prevented the expansion of other religious communities within Muslim regions. Islamic law on mixed marriages had a similar function, and the Muslim partner in such a marriage was clearly privileged. The law provided for the conversion to Islam of a non-Muslim man who wanted to marry a Muslim woman; the children were obliged to be Muslim. A non-Muslim woman married to a Muslim man was forbidden to teach her own religion to her children, who had no choice but to follow the creed of their Muslim father.

The provisions governing the *dhimmī* were made even stricter by conditions outlined in a document attributed to Caliph Omar (d. 644). These conditions were probably elaborated in subsequent decades and were eventually absorbed into traditional Islamic law. According to these rules Christians and Jews were forbidden to profess their faith in a manner that was considered excessively public. In addition they were prohibited from wearing crosses or other overtly religious symbols and from openly practicing certain rites, such as processions or the ringing of bells. Churches and synagogues were also expected to be simple in appearance and smaller than nearby Muslim buildings to correspond to the legally and socially inferior status of the religious communities to which they belonged and to express their submission to the dominance of Islam. Tight restrictions were imposed on the construction of new churches and the restoration of old ones.

Such legal provisions, through which Islam regulated the coexistence of Muslims and non-Muslims within the Muslim state, reveal Islam's tolerance toward other religious communities. It is clear, however, that although the *dhimma* system allowed peoples of different faiths to live side by side in the past, such a system could not but clash with modern sensibilities, for the *dhimma* sanctioned a model of legal inequality between Muslims and non-Muslims in which only the former enjoyed full rights, whereas the latter had to accept an inferior status that prohibited them from entering politics or gaining full legal rights.

***Millet* system.** The *millet* (nation) system remained in force throughout the Middle East until the end of the nineteenth century, although an important change in the status of Christians took place with the rise of the Ottoman Empire in the fourteenth century. No radical changes were made to laws governing Christians, but the status of Christians changed as religious communities became increasingly institutionalized within the *millet* system, in which the inhabitants of the Ottoman Empire were grouped on the basis of religion.

Along with the Muslim and Jewish *millet*, two Christian *millet* were recognized: the Greek Orthodox and the Gregorian Armenian. Within each *millet*, the representative authority was made up of members of the religious hierarchy, who had jurisdiction over their community for all matters regarding religion, cult, and family law. Thus the *millet* system identified the religious communities as intermediary bodies between the individual and the state. The *millet* system also allowed religious communities broader financial autonomy, as well as more control over the organization of community life and the management of the community's assets. The *millet* system thus gave greater organizational freedom to Christians and Jews while preserving the political and social dominance of Islam and the Muslim *millet*. Only with the Ottoman *tanzimats* (reforms) of 1839 and 1876 did the supreme political and religious Muslim power, the sultan caliph, decree for the first time in Muslim history the legal equality of all the subjects of the Empire.

SOCIAL AND POLITICAL DYNAMICS OF CHRISTIANS IN THE MODERN MIDDLE EAST. The situation of Christian communities in the modern Middle East is highly complex. Christians came to exercise an important political and cultural role in the Arab states that were established after the collapse of the Ottoman Empire in 1922. Christians were among the leading supporters of the *nahḍa*, a cultural and political renaissance that arose in the Arab world at the end of the nineteenth century. The *nahḍa* promoted the concept of "Arabianness," the common historical identity of both Arab Muslims and Christians. The cultural development that Middle Eastern Christians had enjoyed in the preceding decades, due to their relations with Western societies and their openness to democratic and liberal ideas, allowed them to exercise an indisputable influence within the various movements for national independence. It was a renaissance that involved many fields: economics, politics, philosophy, culture, and art. Modern ideas proliferated throughout Middle Eastern societies largely because Christian Arabs, who founded newspapers and magazines, initiated a new intellectual debate. In politics the majority of the opposition parties were established by or initiated with the help of the Christian Arabs.

The aim of this cultural and political movement was to create modern states in which one's right to full citizenship would depend on nationality, not on religion. Arab Christian elites emphasized their national Arab identity, which they felt united them culturally with all Arabs, regardless of their religious beliefs. This new political culture, which was supported by many Muslim intellectuals and politicians who were open to modernity, was especially favorable to Christians because it enabled them to overcome the traditional sociopolitical arrangement of the Muslim state, in which non-Muslims were treated as second-class citizens and denied a political role.

Starting in the 1930s and especially after World War II, a number of new Arab national states, which were potentially secular, were set up and obtained independence. But the young democratic systems in these states were not stable, and several nations evolved in the direction of nationalistic, authoritarian forms of government. This occurred in Syria and Iraq and to some extent in Egypt. Furthermore the dialectic of conflict grew between supporters of reform and modernization and those who advocated a return to traditional Islamic state institutions and Islamic law (*sharīʿah*), a movement represented by such groups as the Muslim Brotherhood founded in 1928 and the radical Islamic groups of the late twentieth century and early twenty-first century.

These complex political and cultural dynamics have led to a change in the relations between Middle Eastern Christian communities and the states to which they belong. A typology of four main sociopolitical situations reveals the status of Christian communities in the various states of the Middle East, showing how these communities evolved during the twentieth century and where they stand at the beginning of the twenty-first.

The first type is a well-established "national" church. Egypt, for example, is home to the largest Christian community in the Middle East, and the Egyptian Coptic Church, which has existed for much of the country's history, has the appearance of a national church. For this reason the Copts, despite being a minority, identify strongly with the Egyptian state, even though their actual participation in social and political life is restricted.

The second type is a state with a majority Christian population. In Lebanon, for example, which was established with French support as an independent country in 1943, Maronite Christians, along with other Christians, made up the majority. Thus their role in Lebanese politics was dominant for decades. During the 1990s, however, Lebanese Christians lost their demographic majority to Muslims, and the country's 1975 to 1990 civil war weakened the Maronite community. The political power of Lebanese Christians was further weakened by Syrian military intervention in Lebanon in 1989 and by the consequent Syrian political influence on the country.

The third type is characteristic of Syria, Jordan, and Iraq as well as, to some degree, the Palestinian and Israeli area, where there is no single dominant Christian church but rather a mosaic of Christian communities, all of which are in the minority. These churches are closely dependent on the government and the group that holds political power, and the attitudes assumed vary according to the context. In Jordan the Christian community is strongly attached to the monarchy. In Palestine, Christians have joined Muslims in the struggle for national liberation. Syrian Christians, together with other minorities, exercise a modest share of power. It is worth noting that in Syria, as in Iraq until April 2003, the government was ruled by the Baath Party, which holds a secular ideology in which people are involved in politics on the basis of nationalism, not religion. Many Christians are members of the Baath Party, which they consider a bulwark against Islamization.

A fourth type reflects the situation of Middle Eastern Christian communities that were subjected to political and military action by governments aimed at eliminating them. The most striking case is that of Armenian Christians in Turkey, up to one million of whom were massacred or deported on the order of the government of the Young Turks in 1915. When the war between Greece and Turkey ended in 1923, the Turkish government took part in a population exchange in which some 1.344 million Orthodox Christians in Turkey were sent to Greece, whereas 464,000 Muslims entered Turkey from Greece. The Christians who remained in Turkey were further oppressed by the Turkish state during the 1940s and the 1950s. The result was the emigration of almost all of Turkey's remaining Christians. Although in 1915 there were approximately 2.5 million Christians in Turkey, by 2000 there were only about 100,000.

A similar fate lay in store for Assyrian Christians in Iraq, who were massacred in 1933 by Iraqi troops and irregular bands supported by the government. These Assyrian Christians had been allied with the British, who had promised them their own independent state and then failed to support them.

The Crisis at the Beginning of the Twenty-First Century. Declining birthrates, widespread instability and conflict, and the threat of Muslim fundamentalism are the primary causes behind the crisis in the Christian communities of the modern Middle East. In 1915 Christians made up an estimated 20 percent of the population of the area that includes present-day Turkey, Syria, Iraq, Lebanon, Jordan, Israel, Palestine, and Egypt. By 2000 the most optimistic estimates calculated the number of Christians at 10 percent, whereas the more pessimistic estimates calculated that Christians made up no more than 6 or 7 percent of the population in these regions.

There are many reasons behind this decline. Some of them are sociodemographic, with Christians and Muslims displaying different birth and mortality patterns. The lower demographic growth among the region's Christians, along with the aging of the population, has been a major reason for the decrease in their numbers relative to the Muslim population.

However, the decrease in the number of Christians in the Middle East has been influenced by another important factor closely linked to the region's contemporary political and cultural context: emigration. The scale of Christian emigration from the countries of the Middle East is massive. It has been calculated that, since the middle of the twentieth century, approximately three million Middle Eastern Christians have emigrated to Europe, the Americas, and Australia. That figure accounts for one-quarter to one-third of the total Christian population of the area. The causal factors behind this tide of emigration have mainly been the difficult sociopolitical conditions within many Middle Eastern countries, the authoritarianism of their governments, and the general instability of the area, characterized since the 1950s by a continuous series of conflicts, including the long-standing Arab-Israeli conflict, the war in Lebanon from 1975 to 1990, and the Gulf War from 1990 to 1991, which led to an embargo and ultimately to the difficult postwar situation in Iraq in 2003.

To these factors must be added the long-standing influence of Muslim political and legal tradition and the emergence of new Islamist movements, which have made it difficult for Christians to enjoy full citizenship rights in most Middle Eastern countries. The reemergence of Islam as a political and social solution leading to the formation of Islamic states cannot but increase the fears of Christians, who in this kind of political structure would be reduced to the status of a protected minority, without political freedom and subject to discrimination. The formation of such a state was the reason for the massive emigration of Christians from Iran after the Islamic revolution of 1979.

The impact of the region's wars on Middle Eastern Christians is even more serious and long-lasting. The Israeli-Palestinian conflict has been responsible for a large-scale emigration of Palestinians, a high percentage of whom are Christian. The Arab-Israeli War of 1948 led to the exodus of approximately 726,000 Palestinians, of whom about 60,000 were Christians. Between 1967 and 2003 more than 20 percent of the total number of Christians living on the West Bank or in the Gaza Strip chose to emigrate.

Just as decisive in causing the emigration of large numbers of Christians was the Lebanese conflict, which began in 1975 and lasted for more than fifteen years. This conflict evolved into a real civil war in which fighting occurred not just between different religious groups but also between different factions within religious groups. Lebanon became the theater of a conflict that was influenced by the various political dynamics of the bordering countries, especially the conflict between Israel and the Palestinians, which caused the emigration to Lebanon of large numbers of Muslim Palestinians. The presence of these immigrants helped destabilize a society and a state that was based on a delicate balance between religious confessions and that was already feeling the pressure of changing social and demographic circumstances.

The long civil war in Lebanon also caused a major wave of emigration from the country. It has been estimated that between 1975 and 1990 approximately one million Lebanese emigrated, among whom were at least 300,000 Maronite Christians. Even the Armenians, who were a flourishing community in Lebanon, emigrated in large numbers. Although the emigration involved the broader Lebanese population and not just Christians, the percentage of Christians who left the country, especially during the first ten years of the war, was higher than that of Lebanese Muslims. Although the emigration of Lebanese Christians has decreased substantially since the beginning of the peace process, the demographic loss has been significant and will have an impact on future developments with repercussions for the political, social, and economic role of Christians in Lebanon.

The experience of Lebanese Christians is particularly serious because not only does it concern life in Lebanon itself, it also has negative symbolic value for all Christians in the Middle East. Lebanon has been the only Middle Eastern nation in which Christians played a determinant political role. This role is evidenced by the fact, unique in the Arab world, that the president of the Lebanese Republic is, according to the constitution, a Maronite Christian (with a Muslim holding the position of prime minister), whereas all other Arab countries require the head of state to be a Muslim. Lebanon was therefore a concrete symbol of freedom from a political system in which Muslims subordinated Christians. Moreover the Lebanese system, despite its limitations, has so far been the only Arab country to guarantee a democratic government.

The long war between Iran and Iraq and the international conflict involving Iraq since 1990 have played a significant role in speeding up the emigration of Iraqi Christians. Statistics confirm that, whereas in 2000 Christians made up only 3.2 percent of the total Iraqi population, over 30 percent of Iraqi emigrants that year were Christian.

The greater propensity of Middle Eastern Christians to emigrate—in comparison with Muslims—is also influenced by the higher educational level of the Christian population, which makes Christians less inclined to bear difficult economic situations and facilitates their integration into Western societies. Their emigration is also encouraged by the existence in many countries of well-organized diaspora communities of Eastern Christians. This emigration of Middle Eastern Christians, which generally involves younger generations, is also a factor in aging and the decrease in the fertility rate among the remaining Christians in the region. In addition emigration of young, well-educated Christians may lead to the impoverishment of the Middle Eastern Christian community's professional and intellectual resources. Such a "brain drain" may have a negative effect on the community's social and political influence.

The future of the Christian communities in the Middle East is linked to the various conflicts in the region and the consequent economic problems as well as the dynamics within Islam in its encounter with modernity. The success of the peace processes in the Middle East and the movement toward democratic and egalitarian forms of government are factors of fundamental importance to the future stability of a meaningful Christian presence in the Middle East.

BIBLIOGRAPHY

An-Na'im, Abdullahi A. "Religious Freedom in Egypt: Under the Shadow of the *Dhimma* System." In *Religious Liberty and Human Rights in Nations and in Religions*, edited by Leonard Swidler, pp. 43–59. Philadelphia, 1986.

Betts, Robert Brenton. *Christians in the Arab East: A Political Study*. Athens, Ga., 1975. Rev. ed., Atlanta, 1978.

Braude, Benjamin, and Bernard Lewis, eds. *Christians and Jews in the Ottoman Empire: The Functioning of a Plural Society*, vol. 2: *The Arabic-Speaking Lands*. New York, 1982.

Chabry, Laurent, and Annie Chabry. *Politique et minorités au Proche-Orient: Les raisons d'une explosion*. Paris, 1987.

Courbage, Youssef, and Philippe Fargues. *Christians and Jews under Islam*. Translated by Judy Mabro. New York, 1997.

Cragg, Kenneth. *The Arab Christian: A History in the Middle East*. Louisville, Ky., 1991.

Dadrian, Vahakn. *The History of the Armenian Genocide: Ethnic Conflict from the Balkans to Anatolia to the Caucasus*. Providence, R.I., 1995.

Fattal, Antoine. *Le statut légal des non-musulmans en pays d'Islam*. Beirut, Lebanon, 1958.

Haddad, Robert M. *Syrian Christians in Muslim Society: An Interpretation*. Princeton, N.J., 1970.

Haddad, Robert M. "Detribalizing and Retribalizing: The Double Role of Churches among Christian Arabs in Jordan, a Study in the Anthropology of Religion." *Muslim World* 82 (1992): 67–95.

Labaki, Boutros. "Confessional Communities, Social Stratification, and Wars in Lebanon." *Social Compass* 35 (1988): 533–561.

Pacini, Andrea, ed. *Christian Communities in the Arab Middle East: The Challenge of the Future*. Oxford, U.K., 1998.

Roberson, Ronald. *The Eastern Christian Churches: A Brief Survey*. 6th ed. Rome, 1999.

Valognes, Jean-Pierre. *Vie et mort des Chrétiens d'Orient: Des origines à nos jours*. Paris, 1994.

Wessels, Antonie. *Arab and Christian? Christians in the Middle East*. Kampen, Netherlands, 1995.

ANDREA PACINI (2005)

CHRISTIANITY: CHRISTIANITY IN NORTH AFRICA

Although we lack written sources, archaeological evidence suggests an early origin for the North African churches. However, we must distinguish between two obvious centers in the first century of the preaching of Christianity on the southern shores of the Mediterranean. One center was in Cyrenaica, within reach of the influence of Alexandria. The other was in Carthage, undoubtedly influenced from neighboring Rome across the sea.

Tradition associates the emergence of Christianity in Cyrenaica with the evangelization of Egypt by the apostle Mark. The existence of a considerable Jewish community in that area even before the birth of Christ surely established continuous communications with Jerusalem during the first century. Participation of Libyans and people from Cyrene in the religious controversies at Jerusalem is confirmed by the *Acts of the Apostles* (2:10, 6:8–9). Moreover, archaeological work has revealed the existence of catacombs in Cyrene that substantiate the development of an organized church with ties to Alexandrian Christianity prior to the third century.

The first mention of the church in Carthage came in the year 180, when Tertullian declared that his native Carthage was directly related to Roman apostolic authority. The church that, during the second century, produced so great a giant in the field of Christian theology as Tertullian must have had deep roots in the first century. Carthaginian Christianity was so strong and foundational that it had great influence on the theological controversies of the next several centuries within Western and Eastern Christendom.

CYRENE. Cyrenaica (the easternmost part of Libya) was known as the Pentapolis, or the five towns: Cyrene (modern-day Shaḥḥāt), Apollonia (Marsa Gona), Ptolemaïs (Tolmeta), Berenice (Benghazi), and Barce (Barka). Geographical location and the patterns of caravan trade tied these five towns more closely to Egypt than to Carthage and the rest of the western states of North Africa.

According to tradition, the evangelist Mark was a native Jew of Cyrene, who came to Alexandria by way of the Pentapolis and, after laying the foundations of the new church in Egypt, returned to Cyrene to evangelize. The First Council of Nicaea (325) decreed that Cyrenaica should be considered an obedientiary of the see of Alexandria. To this day the Coptic patriarch carries the five western towns in his title as a province of the see of Mark. We must assume that there was a continuous flow of ecclesiastical and missionary personnel between the two regions, much like the interaction between Carthage and Rome. The overwhelming Greek element in both Cyrene and Alexandria also facilitated communication between them.

Most clerics of Cyrenaica received their education in Alexandria, formerly in the Museion and later in the catechetical school. Alexandrian culture, both philosophically and theologically, had its representative in the Pentapolis in the person of Synesius of Cyrene (c. 370–413), bishop of Ptolemaïs, whose name has come down in history as one of the fathers of the Eastern church.

Synesius was born of wealthy pagan parents in Cyrene around the year 370. After obtaining all the education available in his country he went to Alexandria, where he attended the classes of Hypatia (c. 370–415), the best of the pagan Neoplatonist professors in the Museion. Synesius was captivated by the spell of her teaching and became one of her Neoplatonist disciples. From Alexandria, Synesius went to Athens but was disappointed by the lack of educational opportunities there. On return, his fellow citizens commissioned him to go to Constantinople to plead with the Byzantine emperor for relief from heavy taxation. The success of his mission increased his popularity and paved the way for his leadership of the Libyan people.

At this point Synesius went back to Alexandria, where he was married by Patriarch Theophilus (385–411). This is sufficient proof that he had become a Christian, though there is no evidence of baptism until 410. At that point, in appreciation for his success in Byzantium and for his organization of military defense against the Berbers, his people unanimously elected him to the episcopate. But Synesius was a married man and a staunch Neoplatonist, and he was unwilling to give up either his marriage or his philosophy for the proffered privilege of elevation to bishop. Finally, both the clergy and the people of Ptolemaïs made a strong appeal to the patriarch to consecrate him as their bishop, and their appeal was granted, an exception to Coptic Church tradition holding celibacy a requirement for the episcopate.

In the latter decades of his life, Synesius built fortified churches to which his people resorted for prayer and for defensive purposes when harassed by Berber marauders from the south. Remains of these buildings are still standing in the area of the Green Mountains in Cyrenaica. He also composed religious hymns and homilies that inspired his congregations. Yet he retained his sense of humor and found time to write a treatise in praise of baldness. In the realm of literature, however, he is better known for a set of 156 letters, addressed to many people, including Hypatia and the patriarch Theophilus, which he wrote between the years 399 and 413. These letters, which have been translated into English, are a rich source of information about the social life of the period, geography, and the economy of the world he knew. They show elements of syncretism in their considerations of Neoplatonist philosophy and Christian theology. Synesius may have been the greatest personality in the history of the Pentapolis.

On the whole, the Pentapolis followed Alexandria in all phases of its development during the Christian period. It was subjected to the same wave of persecutions under Roman rule. Even in heresy, there arose the same divisions in Cyrenaica as in Alexandria. During the Arian controversy, there were followers of Athanasius and supporters of Arius, including two bishops, Theonas of Marmarica and Secundus of Ptolemaïs. The third-century heresy of Sabellianism, or subordinationism, which made a distinction between the Son and the Father, the Logos and the Creator of the Logos, arose from a discussion by Sabellius, bishop of Ptolemaïs, and was opposed by two other bishops from the Pentapolis, Amon and Euphranor.

Cyrenaican Christianity appears to have been concentrated almost entirely among the Greek population, who fought the Berber natives along the southern frontier of the Sahara. The Berbers were considered a race of marauders whom the Greeks wanted to push into the desert. Thus the Berbers lived as foreigners beyond the border of their homeland. Outside the pale of the church, they retained their old practices. Arab conquest forced Greek emigration, and there was greater rapport between Berbers and Arabs than between Berbers and Greeks. This accounts in part for the sudden disappearance of Christianity from the Pentapolis and the spread of Islam after the advent of the Arabs.

CARTHAGE. Carthage was founded in the eighth century BCE by the Phoenicians, accompanied by Jewish traders. After the Roman conquest and the fall of the city in 140 BCE, other European settlers came to stay, but the Berber natives remained on the periphery of the agricultural territories. Archaeological work has revealed the extent of Roman culture in North Africa from Leptis Magna (near present-day Tripoli) in the east to Caesarea (northern Algeria) on the Mediterranean shore. The Romans established series of forts along the southern frontier, and these were strengthened by the Byzantines and in particular by the emperor Justinian for defensive purposes. North African agricultural land supplemented Egypt as the granary of the Roman Empire. The natives spoke what may be described as Libyan Punic, though the Romanized inhabitants and the Roman settlers conversed in Latin, which came to be the official language of the country and the church, in contrast to Greek in Cyrenaica.

Pagan religions of varied character from the Phoenician worship of Baal and Astarte to the animistic beliefs of the natives, later joined by the gods of the Roman pantheon, were in use at the coming of the Christian preachers of the gospel. It is difficult to fix precise dates for the introduction of Christianity into the western section of North Africa, though we may assume that the preaching of the gospel initially came from Rome. This is confirmed by the later demonstrations of close relationship with the see of Rome. The first concrete record of Roman registers revealing the existence of an organized and well-developed church surfaced suddenly just a couple of decades before the end of the second century. Christianity was largely concentrated in Carthage and its adjacent territories. From east to west, these included Tripolitania, Africa Proconsularis, Numidia, Mauretania Caesariensis, and Mauretania Tingitana, covering roughly modern-day Tripolitania, Tunisia, Algeria, and northern Morocco. The spread of Christianity must have taken place rapidly among the Carthaginian population, but it never took root among the Berbers, who remained outside the fold of Roman civilization and were systematically besieged by the church. The position of the church reached a high degree of efflorescence in the following few centuries, thanks to a number of people whose contributions to Christian thought and culture remained a standing monument for Carthaginian Christianity in spite of its sudden disappearance after about five centuries of existence.

In its early days, the church at Carthage was subjected, with the rest of the Roman Empire, to persecutions and contributed its full share in martyrdom. Namphamo of Numidia claimed to be the first martyr for his faith, and he could have been of Punic origin. However, the majority of the martyrs of Carthage were either Romanized natives or Roman settlers. Despite persecution, the church grew. At the death of Tertullian around 225, Carthage already had more than seventy bishoprics. In the year 250, during Cyprian's episcopate, the number increased to about 150. When the Edict of Milan was issued in 313, the number rose to 250 bishops. The country teemed with new churches. Cyprian mentions eighty-eight in his works, and twenty-nine more were added before the year 325.

In spite of its significant progress, the church began to suffer from internal division with the appearance of the Donatist movement. Though the source of the division was theological, Donatism began to assume the shape of nationalism, which was concentrated in Numidia against Carthage. The controversy dragged on until the coming of the Vandals in 429. The Vandals were of Arian confession and would have nothing to do with either catholics or Donatists, who were stifled under Vandal rule until the recovery of the country by the Byzantines in 533 on behalf of Emperor Justinian. In keeping with his imperialist policy, Justinian aimed at a unified church and state and discouraged all schismatic tendencies in his provinces, including North African Donatism. Donatism was weakened, but it flickered until the destruction of the church by the Arabs in the seventh and eighth centuries.

SHAPERS OF CHRISTIAN THOUGHT. The sudden extinction of Carthaginian Christianity could not minimize the glories of the North African church in the first centuries. Foremost among those who gave that church great stature in the annals of Christian civilization are Tertullian, Cyprian, and Augustine of Hippo.

Tertullian (160?–225?) lived in the age of Roman persecutions, and this is reflected in his writings. He was born a pagan in Carthage, but became a Christian in 193. The first Church Father to write in Latin, Tertullian fought idolatry and heresy in all its forms, whether Gnostic, Manichaean, or Marcionite. A prolific theologian, he used his gift of eloquence to defend Christian martyrs. To him we owe the first use of the word *trinity*, a creation of his lucid logic in the definition of the unity of God. He drew the main basic lines of Western theology, parallel to Origen's efforts in the East at the catechetical school of Alexandria. Subsequent generations of theologians continued to build on Tertullian's illuminating trinitarianism and Christology after his death.

Born a pagan and educated in rhetoric, Cyprian (c. 205–258) ultimately became a Christian some decades after the death of Tertullian, whose work he knew. Like Tertullian, Cyprian became an ascetic. He was elected bishop of Carthage shortly after his conversion (c. 248). Cyprian wrote numerous letters, which are among the best sources of the history of the church in the third century, as well as short treatises dealing with practical theological matters, such as the enforcement of rebaptism on heretics. His real strength lay in his pastoral genius as a man of action and a superb organizer. He led a stormy life within the church as well as without, and he was continuously beset with danger. In the year 258, a new wave of persecutions swept the empire by the order of Emperor Valerian, whose agents pursued the bishop. Cyprian did not flee, and he was martyred in 258.

Approximately a century after Cyprian's martyrdom, the genius of the North African church reached its peak in Augustine of Hippo (354–430), whose life and work became one of the greatest landmarks in the development of Christian theology. A native of North Africa and born of a pagan father and a Christian mother, Augustine was bishop of Hippo from 396 until his death in 430. He wrote against many heresies, including Manichaeism, Donatism, and Pelagianism. The two principal works that made Augustine the foremost writer of his age are his spiritual autobiography, the *Confessions*, and the *City of God*, a work seminal for medieval Christian thought. In the *City of God*, Augustine labors to vindicate Christianity against the attribution that the calamitous fall of Rome to the hordes of Alaric in 410 was due to the advent of the new religion. According to Augustine, the kingdom of God, the celestial Jerusalem, was the eternal kingdom that no earthly ravages or philosophical intellectualism could impair, and its only visible form on earth was the catholic church. In this way Augustine was able to substantiate all the elements of patristic thought in the service of catholic Christianity more effectively than any of his predecessors.

If the North African church had produced no creative writers beyond Tertullian, Cyprian, and Augustine, it would have more than justified its major importance in Christian antiquity. But North Africa contributed even more in a smaller way through the works of other minor authors. Of these may be cited Arnobius of Sicca (253–327), well-known rhetorician and teacher who was a Christian convert from paganism. Another was Lactantius, also a professor of rhetoric, who lived during the reign of Diocletian (284–304). After Christianity had been declared the state religion, the emperor Constantine in 317 appointed Lactantius to be tutor of his own son Crispus. Lactantius was already advanced in years and died about 320.

ADVENT OF ISLAM. After the conquest of Egypt in 640–642, a further thrust westward into the Pentapolis and the rest of North Africa by the Arabs became inevitable, initially to safeguard the fairest of their acquisitions, the Nile Valley. Cyrenaica surrendered to the Arab conquerors without difficulty and Carthage fell into their hands in 698. As the Arabs came in, the Greek and Roman populations went out, emigrating en masse to Byzantium, Sicily, Italy, and Spain. With their exit, the churches of North Africa vanished with surprising rapidity.

First among the factors that precipitated the disappearance of Christian foundations in North Africa, despite their remarkable development and past glories, was that the church had remained embedded in urban districts. Its congregations never really cared to undertake missionary work amid the Berber tribes. In contrast, the Arabs, who were nomads like the Berbers, offered the Berbers Islam with equality and full brotherhood. The Berbers accepted the offer and even participated with the Arab armies in further conquests. Second, waves of emigration from Arabia to North Africa came to fill the vacuum created by Christian departure from these regions. Instances of the advent of whole tribes settling in North Africa include the accounts of Banū Hilāl and Banū Sālim, whose adventures in these provinces are still the subject of Arabic folklore. A third factor was that most of the heterodox parties among the Arabs took off to the distant west, where they could pursue their doctrines undisturbed and even launch missionary work for their beliefs. The Khariji faction inaugurated the movement, and the Shīʿī followed suit; the latter were eventually able to establish their own caliphate and build an empire of their own. Fourth, the economy of the romanized provinces of North Africa was essentially founded on slavery and slave trade, while Islam offered full enfranchisement to all slaves willing to convert. Finally, there was the burden of Byzantine taxation, which was continually on the ascendance. Though it would be a mistake to contend that total relief accompanied the advent of the Arabs, the Berbers were assured of Arab leniency, and, at any rate, had nothing to lose by the change of masters.

It is therefore no wonder that the Berber population found it more to their advantage to accept the new situation readily and even participate with the conquerors in the extermination of all remaining pockets of Roman settlers, and with them the vestiges of a church that they regarded as the symbol of their past humiliation. These factors account for the precipitous downfall of Carthaginian Christianity and the almost total disappearance of churches from North Africa by the twentieth century.

Even though the door was left ajar for the reappearance of Christian elements from the West during the modern period of European colonization, these do not appear to have had any real impact on the prevalent status of Islam. Although stray Christians mainly of Coptic origin remain, in the present day, all the countries of North Africa, from Libya to Morocco, must be regarded as totally Muslim and without any surviving Christian element.

See Also Augustine of Hippo; Berber Religion; Cyprian; Donatism; Tertullian.

Bibliography

Altaner, Berthold. *Patrology.* Translated from the fifth German edition. New York, 1960.

Atiya, A. S. *A History of Eastern Christianity.* Rev. ed. Millwood, N.Y., 1980.

Bardenhewer, Otto. *Patrology: The Lives and Works of the Fathers of the Church.* Saint Louis, 1908.

Buonaiuti, Ernesto. *Il Christianesimo nell'Africa Romana.* Bari, 1928.

Groves, C. P. *The Planting of Christianity in Africa* (1948–1958). 4 vols. Reprint, London, 1964.

Julien, Charles-André. *Histoire de l'Afrique du nord.* 2 vols. Paris, 1956. Translated by John Petrie as *History of North Africa,* 2 vols. (London, 1970).

Leclercq, Henri. *L'Afrique chrétienne.* 2d ed. 2 vols. Paris, 1904.

Quasten, Johannes. *Patrology.* 3 vols. Utrecht and Westminster, Md., 1950–1960.

Synesius. *Letters and Hymns.* Edited by Dionysius Petavius. Paris, 1612. Available also in *Patrologia Graeca,* edited by J.-P. Migne, vol. 66 (Paris, 1859). See also by Synesius: *Hymni,* 2 vols., edited by Nicolas Terzaghi (Rome, 1939–1954), translated by Augustine Fitzgerald as *The Essays and Hymns of Synesius of Cyrene,* 2 vols. (Oxford, 1930); and his letters, in Rudolf Hercher's *Epistolographi Graeci* (Paris, 1873), translated by Augustine Fitzgerald as *The Letters of Synesius of Cyrene* (Oxford, 1926).

Azize Suryal Atiya (1987)

CHRISTIANITY: CHRISTIANITY IN EASTERN EUROPE

The story of Christianity in eastern Europe and northern Eurasia is complex—a tangled web of changing peoples, nations, and church allegiances; of political, military, and cultural conflicts; and of ideological, social, and spiritual forces in a seemingly perpetual flux. This article traces the course of twenty centuries of Christian history in this region, which is bounded on the south by the tip of the Greek Peninsula, ringed roughly by the Adriatic, Aegean, Black, and Caspian Seas; on the north by the Baltic Sea and the Finnish Peninsula; on the east by the Ural Mountains; and on the west by the eastern slopes of the Alps and the river Elbe.

The history of the Christian Church in eastern Europe and northern Eurasia can be understood through the interplay over the centuries of four major factors: Greek-Byzantine, Latin-Roman, and Frankish-German influences, and the migrations of peoples who eventually settled in eastern Europe and northern Eurasia, primarily the Slavs. These factors represent distinctive religious, cultural, and ethnic traditions that molded the development of the Christian Church over the centuries in this region. There are others, of course, including the Muslim Ottoman Empire in the fifteenth through nineteenth centuries and the Soviet Union in the twentieth century. Nevertheless, the story of how Christianity developed in this area can be told by describing the motives, mind-sets, interests, and policies together with the successes and failures of these four major forces.

Historically, the first actor at work in the molding of Christianity in eastern Europe and northern Eurasia was the Greek-Byzantine tradition. Highlighted by the apostle Paul's mission to the Gentiles and his crossing over into Europe, the Christian church abandoned the exclusivism of its Jewish roots to become a world religion. To be sure, he was not alone in this effort. Many anonymous evangelists and laypersons, including traveling businesspeople, contributed to the spread of the Christian faith from its origins in Palestine to as far as Rome and Spain. Although the Christian faith moved outward in all directions—toward Africa, Asia, and the Indian subcontinent—the church's major growth came as it entered the Greco-Roman world of the Mediterranean basin. As it sought to preach the message of salvation in Jesus Christ, it used not only the lingua franca of its day, the spoken and written Greek of the first century, but also Greek concepts, problematics, and philosophical traditions to communicate, understand, and interpret the faith. Beginning with the New Testament idea of Christ as the Logos (*Jn.* 1), there is an ongoing record of the incarnation of the Christian message into the Greco-Roman cultural milieu. What came out of this process, Orthodox Christianity, certainly could not be identified with any specific Greek philosophical system; it was uniquely Christian, but it formulated its faith and practice with the tools of the Greek heritage. Strongly concerned with clear doctrinal formulation of the teachings regarding the Holy Trinity and the person of Jesus Christ, the Greek tradition emphasized the transcendent dimension of faith, the reverence and awe of worship, the conciliar understanding of church life, and the ascetic spirituality of monasticism. This early tradition of Christianity, formulated in the writings of the Church Fathers primarily within the eastern part of the Roman Empire known as Byzantium, was embodied and essentially preserved in what much later came to be called the Eastern or Greek Orthodox Church, with all its various local expressions.

However, while accepting and defending as Christian orthodoxy the formulations of doctrine described above, Christianity in the western part of the Roman Empire quickly gave to the Christian message and life nuances and emphases that characterized its Latin heritage. Less theologically speculative, the sober Latin tradition focused on the practical and on the sense of order and pattern required in an increasingly unstable cultural, political, and social milieu produced by the inroads of numerous barbarian tribes beginning in the fourth century. While the Greek tradition concerned itself with the subtleties of church doctrine, frequently generating new heresies, Latin Christianity became a stronghold of fundamental Christian orthodoxy while concurrently remolding this orthodoxy according to its own genius. In practice, that meant an understanding of the Christian faith largely colored by legal concepts. For example, while the Greek East generally tended to understand sin in relational terms (sin as the breaking of the appropriate relationship between the Creator and the creature), the Latin West emphasized its legal dimensions (sin as guilt). This difference, and the exigencies of the breakdown of cultural unity and civil authority in the West between the fourth and eighth centuries, favored the development of a monarchical understanding of the church, leading to the rise of the Roman papacy as the single, supreme ecclesiastical (and frequently secular) authority in the West. The combination of an early reputation for careful orthodoxy in doctrine, with the centralization of authority in the Roman see, became the source of what eventually would come to be called the Roman Catholic Church.

The third group of actors in the drama of Christianity in eastern Europe and northern Eurasia were the Frankish and Germanic kingdoms, which while Roman Catholic in faith were primarily concerned with their military, economic, and political expansion in the area of eastern Europe. It is not that these concerns were unique to the Frankish and Germanic kingdoms, but that these interests affected the development of Christianity in significantly different ways from that of the see of Rome or of Byzantine Orthodoxy. The reason for this is that Roman Catholicism in the western European region sought actively to differentiate Western Christianity from Eastern Christianity, especially through espousal and promulgation of the *filioque* clause in the creed, which asserts that the Holy Spirit proceeds from the Father and the Son.

In 691 CE Clovis III (682–695 CE) became king of all Franks, beginning a process of consolidation of political power in the West. With Charles Martel's (c. 688–741 CE) victory over Arab forces at the Battle of Tours (732 CE), the integrity of western Europe was assured. A formal political split between the eastern and western parts of the Roman empire, exemplifying the cultural division of Eastern and Western Christianity, occurred with the crowning of Charlemagne (742–814 CE) by Pope Leo III (r. 795–816 CE) in the year 800 CE as the first emperor of the Holy Roman Empire. From that point on, Frankish and Germanic forces perceived the Byzantine Empire and its Greek church as rival powers opposed to their interests.

With the inclusion of *filioque* in the Nicene-Constantinopolitan Creed, at the insistence of the Franks (not originally by the Roman see) the stage was set for a long, drawn-out process of schism between the Western (eventually Roman Catholic) Church and the Eastern (eventually Eastern or Orthodox) Church. (*Filioque* literally means "and the Son," referring to the claim made mainly in the West that the Holy Spirit proceeded from the Son as well as from the Father; the doctrine was rejected by Eastern Churches.) Much of the conflict between East and West played itself out in eastern Europe and northern Eurasia. From the point of view of the history of the church from the ninth through the sixteenth centuries, Frankish and subsequently Germanic interests in the region translated into efforts to make Roman Catholicism dominant at the expense of Eastern Orthodoxy. In contradistinction, during this and subsequent periods, Eastern Orthodoxy became one of the major forces in the struggle of the peoples in the region to retain their cultural, spiritual, and political identity and autonomy. In the sixteenth century the Germanic influence in eastern Europe was expanded with the rise of the Reformation. From that time on, church history was strongly influenced by Protestant interests in the area.

The final actors in the story of Christianity in eastern Europe and northern Eurasia are the various peoples who historically had lived in the region or who came from elsewhere to settle there. Southeastern European peoples, primarily in Macedonia, Achaia, Crete, the Aegean Islands, and Byzantium, were able to trace the continuity of their ecclesiastical and cultural roots to early Christianity and beyond. In contrast, central and northern Europe was an area repeatedly overrun by peoples from the Asian steppes. As a result, the continuity of Christian history was repeatedly broken and reestablished, formed and reformed, in eastern Europe.

Primarily, though not exclusively, it was Slavic peoples who began the invasion of Europe by attacks on Asia Minor and the Balkans around the year 220 CE. Appeased in part by a Byzantine policy that combined military strength, payment of tribute, and settlement, the waves of invaders moved westward in the third to fifth centuries beyond the effective boundaries of the Byzantine Empire. In eastern Europe the newcomers were displaced by new conquerors, and the groups often mingled. Eventually, a measure of identity with particular geographic areas was achieved by the settlers.

The history of the Christian Church in eastern Europe and northern Eurasia can largely be told in terms of the competition of Greek-Byzantine, Latin-Roman, and Frankish-Germanic efforts to gain the loyalty of these largely Slavic peoples. Or, conversely, the history of the church in this area can be understood as the response of the Slavic and other peoples of the region to what the first three had to offer.

EARLY CHRISTIANITY. Christianity entered eastern Europe through the missionary work of the apostle Paul as well as the influence of countless Christians who shared the good news of the redemption of humankind by God in Christ through the Holy Spirit. They planted the Christian seed primarily in cities. Illustrative is Paul's dramatic entry into Europe as a result of a dream in which a Macedonian begged him to "Come over to Macedonia and help us," as described in *Acts* 16. The Christian Scriptures indicate the first-century establishment of Christianity in cities, such as Philippi in Macedonia; Thessalonica, Veroia, and Nicopolis on the western coast of the Greek Peninsula; Athens in Attica; Patras, Corinth, and Sparta in the Peloponnese; on the Aegean Islands of Chios and Samos; and on the island of Crete.

The northern boundary of the Roman Empire in the last decades of the second century extended to the Danube in Illyricum and beyond in the province of Dacia (present-day Romania). On either coast of the Adriatic Sea and the Black Sea there were small enclaves of Christians, but the vast numbers of Thracians, Moesians, Illyrians, and Dacians in the region had not been Christianized. Nevertheless, conditions existed favorable to their eventual conversion. For example, the northern branch of the Thracians, the Geto-Dacians (considered the ancestors of the Romanian people), although polytheists, believed in a supreme god whom they called Zalmoxis, the god of heaven and light. The Geto-Dacians were known to ancient Greek historians, such as Herodotos (c. 484–between 430 and 420 BCE), who described, in addition to this concept of a supreme god, their strong belief in the immortality of the soul. It is not at all unlikely that during this early period a scattering of Christians existed among the Geto-Dacians as a result of Christian influence in the armies of Trajan (53–117 CE; ruled 98–117 CE), who had subdued them.

A legend recorded by Eusebius of Caesarea (c. 260–c. 330 CE) and attributed to Origen (c. 185–c. 254 CE) holds that the apostle Andrew preached in the land of the Geto-Dacians, then referred to as Scythia. The *Passion of Saint Andrew,* included in the Constantinopolitan *Sunaxarion* (lives of saints for liturgical use), claims that Andrew preached in Pontus, Thrace, and Scythia. Although there is a ninth-century legend that Andrew ordained a certain Apion as bishop of Odessus (present-day Varna, Bulgaria), the first historical record of a bishop of the region was made by the historian Socrates (c. 380–450 CE) regarding Theodore the Thracian at the Synod of Sardica (343–344 CE). A bishop from the area named Terentius participated in the ecumenical council at Constantinople in 381 CE. A Bishop Timothy was recorded in attendance at the ecumenical council held in Ephesus (431 CE).

LEGITIMIZATION AND THE BARBARIAN INROADS. After Constantine (d. 337 CE), together with the coemperor Licinius (d. 325 CE), proclaimed Christianity to be a legal religion in 313 CE with the Edict of Milan, more and more of the population within the boundaries of the Empire began to be Christianized. But the appearance of the barbarians caused the boundaries of the Roman Empire to contract, and whatever earlier Christian presence existed in the area was severely weakened or destroyed. Among the earliest of the barbarian tribes to appear were the Goths.

During the period from 230 to 240 CE the Goths came out of southern Russia to attack the Roman provinces. A succession of Roman emperors fought against them, including Claudius (214–270 CE), Aurelian (c. 215–275 CE), Diocletian (245 or 248–313 or 316 CE), and Constantine. Christianity in its Arian form seems to have been introduced to the Goths through prisoner exchanges in Cappadocia around the year 264 CE, but it was at least a century before Christians were of any great number among them. By the mid-fourth century there seemed to be an adequate Christian population among the Goths to require a bishop. Thus in 341 CE Ulfilas (c. 311–c. 382 CE) was ordained first bishop of the Goths by the patriarch of Constantinople, Eusebius. Ulfilas's work was primarily in Plevna (in modern-day Bulgaria), and he translated the Scriptures and services into the Gothic tongue. It should be noted here that the orientation of these early efforts at Christianization was from the East. Yet over the next few centuries the constant incursions and displacement of tribes in a westward direction meant that little permanency of the Christian presence could be expected.

MISSIONS IN CONFLICT. It was not until the ninth century that Christianity began to gain a permanent foothold in the area. By this time not only had the foundations of Christian doctrinal understanding been formalized through seven ecumenical councils, but the four factors described above had also been clearly defined. As they met on the eastern European stage, they determined the organized forms that Christianity would take there and, in turn, much of its ethnic and political identity as well.

The barbarians, although intent on expansion and the acquisition of land, were also attracted by the quality of the Greco-Roman culture of the Empire, which they respected. The chief ingredient of this attraction was Christianity. In many cases these peoples were seized with a strong desire to embrace the faith because of what they had seen and heard in terms of the quality of life of Christians, the development of a Christian civilization base on Hellenic *Paideia*, and the power and influence of the Church in society as well as through the missionary efforts of the church. Among these in the ninth and tenth centuries were the peoples of Bulgaria to the south, Moravia to the north, and Russia to the east. The spirit of competitive choice among the recipients of the faith, as well as conflict among the transmitters of the faith, became evident during this period.

In the East the dominant power was the Byzantine Empire, whose fortunes had improved sufficiently in this period to permit consideration of missionary efforts; that is, the spreading of the Greek or Eastern form of Orthodox Christianity. In the West the Frankish Empire was divided in 843 CE at the Treaty of Verdun into three parts, the most eastern of which was to become Germany. Louis I (778–840 CE) the German became the founder of the German Carolingian dynasty, which lasted until 911 CE. This dynasty pursued vigorous missionary efforts in eastern Europe and northern Eurasia.

The first area in which the two missionary efforts came into conflict was Bulgaria. Both German and Byzantine missionaries saw the Bulgarian Slavs as ripe targets for missionizing. The Bulgars, however, in their choice between Western and Eastern forms of Christianity, were motivated by their own ethnic, cultural, and political perspectives, with independence as a prime concern. In the year 860 CE the drama began to unfold. Although at first attracted to the German missionaries, Khan Boris (d. 907 CE) accepted baptism from the Greeks. Later, feeling that his church was not independent enough, he turned from Constantinople to the West, admitting German missionaries whose policies even more strongly curtailed the independence of the Bulgarian church. These policies included the imposition of Latin in worship, subjugation of the hierarchy to the pope, celibacy of the clergy, and the *filioque* doctrine, even though it was not current in Rome at the time. By 870 CE Khan Boris had reacted to these restrictions by expelling the German missionaries and inviting back those from Constantinople. Since then Eastern Orthodoxy has been the dominant religion in the Bulgarian nation.

During this same period a somewhat similar drama played itself out to the north, but with opposite results. The major difference here was that Rome and Constantinople supported the same missionary policy in contrast to the rival efforts of the Germans.

Around 860 CE Prince Rostislav (846–c. 870 CE) of Moravia appealed to Patriarch Photios (Photius, c. 820–891 CE) of Constantinople for missionaries who could preach in the language of the people and conduct worship in Slavonic. Constantine, known later as Cyril, (c. 827–869 CE) and Methodius (c. 825–c. 884 CE), two Greek brothers from Thessalonica, were chosen for the task. Before going to the mission field, they created a Slavonic alphabet, into which they translated the Bible and the service books. Their mission policy thus included worship in the language of the people, the preaching of the Eastern form of Christianity (without the *filioque*), and the rapid indigenization of the clergy with its consequent spirit of local autonomy in church government. When they came into inevitable conflict with the German missionaries, Cyril and Methodius appealed to the pope and obtained his approval for their methods in Moravia. The Germans not only ignored this approval but even jailed Methodius for over a year. Following Methodius's death, the Germans expelled the Byzantine missionaries and imposed Western Christianity in the region.

During this same period Patriarch Photios also sent missionaries to Russia, and a short-lived mission survived there until 878 CE. As in the past, Christianity nevertheless continued to infiltrate the populace through ordinary contacts from Byzantium in the south, Bulgaria in the west, and Scandinavia in the north. Thus, when Prince Vladimir (c. 956–1015) was baptized in 988 CE, the Christianization of the land was readily accomplished, at least in the cities and especially in the region around the capital city of Kiev. As Vladimir had married the sister of the Byzantine emperor, Christianity was adopted in its Byzantine form. Originally centered in Kiev, Christianity gradually spread north and east, developing deep and strong roots among the people, and social concern, liturgical piety, and monasticism united with the culture and language of the Russian peoples. Nevertheless, Western influences were also present in Russian Christianity, influences that found resonance many centuries later.

SCHISM AND IMPERIAL CONTENTION. The eleventh century and early twelfth century were marked by the definitive Great Schism between the Eastern and Western Churches. Begun in the ninth century, it is traditionally marked by the mutual excommunications of Patriarch Michael Cerularios (c. 1000–1059) and Cardinal Humbert (c. 1000–1061) in 1054 and considered completed by the capture of Constantinople in 1204 by the Crusaders. The Venetians, at the head of the Fourth Crusade, established a Latin empire with a Latin patriarch in Constantinople. The Byzantines set up their capital in Nicaea and were unable to return to Constantinople until 1261. The result was that the pattern of conflict in the Christianization of the peoples of eastern Europe was intensified over the next few centuries.

On the southwestern shores of the region, the Croatians had long been subjected to efforts at Christianization by Latin missionaries in the sixth through eighth centuries, even though the Eastern empire held nominal control over the area. After 800 CE, however, the Franks brought the Croatians fully within the orbit of the West, completing the task by the tenth century. On their eastern border, however, another people—the Serbs—opened themselves up to the disciples of Cyril and Methodius. On the dividing line between Eastern and Western Christendom, the ninth-century Prince Mutimir (r. 865–891 CE), after some vacillation, looked toward Constantinople for the form of the faith to be practiced by the Serbs. Slavonic worship and Orthodox practices were accepted, and a strong Slavo-Byzantine culture was formed. In 1219 Sava (c. 1176–c. 1236) was consecrated as archbishop of Serbia in Nicaea, then the Byzantine capital. This consecration reflected the strength of the Serbian Empire at the time. In 1375 Constantinople recognized the Serbian patriarchate that had been proclaimed three decades earlier.

To the east of Serbia lay Romania, whose early Christian history has been noted. The Romanians are not Slavs but, as their name indicates, a Latin people. Clearly within the Greek-Byzantine ecclesial tradition, they have maintained much of their orderly Latin heritage. At the same time they have adopted a great deal from their Slavic neighbors, especially in the area of worship. The Romanian church is a fruitful amalgam of these various influences. By the fourteenth century, metropolitanates had been set up in various parts of the Romanian region.

At this same time, the Ottoman (Turkish) Muslim forces began to spread into the region from the southeast. They conquered the Bulgarian center of Taburnovo in 1393, took control of Serbia in 1441, captured Constantinople and destroyed the last vestige of the Byzantine Empire in 1453, subdued Bosnia in 1463, captured the Albanian fortress town of Kruje in 1478, put down the last resistance in Moldavia and Walachia (Romania) by 1490, and conquered Dyrrachium in 1501. The majority of the Christian peoples in this area were Eastern Orthodox in faith. The Muslims governed the conquered peoples in accordance with a system that identified each religion as a "nation." Known as the *millet* system, it required that all Orthodox Christians under Ottoman domination be governed through the patriarchate of Constantinople. This system, over the whole area south of the Danube, lasted for approximately four hundred years, to the mid-nineteenth century.

The major Orthodox nation not conquered by the Muslims was Russia. However, the history of the Russians was not without severe disturbances. The establishment of Kievan Orthodox Christianity in the tenth century was followed by a genuine flowering of church life for the next few centuries in Kiev (present-day Ukraine) and by active missionary work to the north. Notable were the establishments in Novgorod and Pskov. However, Kievan influence was broken in the thirteenth century with the coming of the Mongols. When Kiev fell to them in 1240, a century and a quarter of survival struggle aimed at maintaining Russian life was begun by the church. Gradually, power and strength returned to the Russians, but they then came to be centered in Moscow. The church figured strongly in the rebuilding of the Russian nation, and by the time of the death of Sergii of Radonezh (c. 1314–1392), Moscow was clearly the center of Russian Orthodoxy. In the north, Novgorod and Pskov, while free from the Mongols, were attacked in the mid-thirteenth century by westerners—the Swedes and the Germanic Teutonic Knights—intent upon imposing Western Christianity in the area. The Russians, under Prince Aleksandr Nevskii (c. 1220–1263), maintained the relative independence of the area. With the fall of Constantinople, the Russians began to think of Moscow as the "Third Rome," and the metropolitan of Moscow was honored with the rank of patriarch in 1589. The Russians emerged stronger and more united as an Orthodox nation as a result of their response to the Mongol threat.

To the northwest the power in the region in the fifteenth century was Hungary, which contained the Muslim advance northward. Christianity was introduced into Hungary in the ninth and tenth centuries by Western missionaries; King Stephen I (977–1038) set down a formal constitution for the church in 1001. In 1279 Esztergom (German, Gran) was named the see of the primate of the Hungarian church, and, until the Reformation, Christianity in the area was Western in form with no real influence from the East.

To the northeast of Hungary were the Poles. The history of the Polish people has been turbulent, and this turbulence has had a great impact on the form of Christianity in that land. Scholars once believed that Christianity began in Poland in the tenth century in conjunction with the German see of Magdeburg, but modern scholarship now holds that in all likelihood Christianity came to Poland from Moravia; that is, from the missionary impetus inaugurated by Cyril and Methodius. Situated between northwestern Russia and powerful Roman Catholic neighbors to the west, Poland was subject to influences from both sources. In the eleventh century the civil leaders were allied with the West, although many elements of Eastern Christianity were present in their church. Thus the Gregorian reforms of the Western Church were imposed by civil authorities in the face of stiff episcopal and lower-clergy opposition. The influence of Orthodox Russia was also felt, and there was a significant Eastern Orthodox population in Poland. Nevertheless, until the Reformation, the church of the Poles was generally under control of the West, while at the same time it was marked by significant Eastern influence. Its borders often shifting, Poland sometimes had larger, sometimes smaller populations of Orthodox Christians in its eastern regions.

In a similar fashion the area north of Poland along the eastern coast of the Baltic Sea—known historically as Lithuania, and subsequently as Lithuania, Latvia, and Estonia—was from the beginning of its history caught between the rivalry of Western and Eastern forces with all its ecclesiastical consequences. Lithuania came into being at the time of the Mongol conquest of Russia, and its first and only king, Trointen (r. 1259–1282), received Christianity from the

Germans. By 1341, Lithuania had become a large empire as a result of the king's expansionist policies. Russian Orthodoxy and Polish Catholicism vied for Lithuania's loyalty, but in 1385 a political union of Lithuania with Poland led to the baptism of the Lithuanians into Roman Catholicism by Polish clergy. This Polish-Lithuanian relationship continued into the sixteenth century. Nevertheless, a significant Orthodox population to the east remained ecclesiastically under the jurisdiction of the metropolitan of Kiev. These Orthodox became the occasion for the inception of a new phenomenon in church history—Uniatism, also known as Eastern Rite Catholicism.

Conceived as a means of unifying the religion of the populace, Uniatism subjected the Orthodox population to the primacy of the pope and Western doctrine while allowing the retention of the liturgical forms and customs of Eastern Orthodoxy. The Council of Brest (1596) split into Eastern and Western factions, with the Western faction opting for the Uniate approach and many Orthodox bishops accepting it. The Polish king approved the move and initiated a severe persecution of those Orthodox who refused to join. With Jesuit support, the Polish king, Sigismund III Vasa (1566–1632), took Moscow in 1607, forcing a short-lived union with Rome on the Russian Orthodox. This effort came to an end in 1613 with Czar Mikhail Romanov's (ruled 1613–1645) restoration of Russian sovereignty. Uniatism, or Eastern Rite Roman Catholicism, was henceforth a complicating force in the relations of Roman Catholicism and Eastern Orthodoxy.

Northernmost of the nations of the region under discussion here is modern-day Finland. Christianity came to this area in the late eleventh century and early twelfth century concurrently from both the East and the West. Roman Catholicism was introduced by the Crusaders and Eastern Orthodoxy by Orthodox monks from Novgorod, who established the famous Monastery of Valamo in 1100. The area was subject to the competition of its Roman Catholic Scandinavian neighbors to the west and its Orthodox Russian neighbors to the east.

In the sixteenth century the whole religious map of Europe was changed by the Protestant Reformation. Although the Reformation was primarily a western European phenomenon, it did have significant impact in eastern Europe, in some areas achieving dominance and in others remaining a minority factor. In the north, Finland became largely Lutheran, with only a minority of Orthodox. Lutheranism was introduced into Estonia and Latvia and soon became dominant, even under Russian control, in the eighteenth century. Protestantism in its Lutheran form entered Poland from Germany but was nearly erased by the Counter-Reformation. When Poland was partitioned in 1795, with Austria and Prussia assuming control of its western regions, Lutheranism returned to favor. It has remained a "remnant" church in this predominantly Roman Catholic nation.

Protestantism in the geographical area of the Czech Republic and Slovakia has deep roots going back to the fourteenth-century work of Jan Hus (1372 or 1373–1415) and the Brethren of the Common Life. In 1609 the Hapsburgs granted the Brethren freedom, but they were soon persecuted anew. Protestantism survived among the Brethren in Reformed and Lutheran forms, albeit among a few, until the establishment of the Czechoslovak state in 1918. Lutheran Protestantism came to Hungary in 1518 but shortly thereafter was supplanted by Reformed Protestantism. Both forms suffered under the Counter-Reformation until their adherents were granted civil rights in 1790 and 1791, and relations with the predominantly Roman Catholic nation were established in 1867.

Protestant churches in small numbers were established in Romania, particularly in Transylvania. Unitarianism began in this area. The Lutheran bodies there have strong German ethnic ties. Although early Reformed Protestantism in Transylvania had Hussite and Lutheran connections, in 1567 it adopted the Second Helvetic Confession of Faith. The small number of both Reformed and Lutheran Protestants in modern-day Yugoslavia were incorporated into the nation from border areas, primarily Hungary. The Reformation did not reach Greece, Bulgaria, or Russia until the nineteenth century, and then with only modest results, primarily in evangelical and Baptist forms.

Modern Nation-States. The eighteenth and nineteenth centuries saw the formation of the modern nation-states. The French Revolution set a pattern for self-government along national lines. In Orthodox Russia, czardom reigned, but the influence of the West, both Protestant and Roman Catholic, was strong. Peter the Great (1672–1725) removed the canonical head of the Russian church, the patriarch of Moscow, through his Ecclesiastical Regulation of 1721, substituting a state church patterned after German Protestant models. Scholastic theology, along with Italian Renaissance music, art, and architecture, was incorporated into Russian church life. This anomalous situation lasted until the Bolshevik Revolution of 1917, when the patriarchate was restored.

During the early nineteenth century, as the Ottoman Empire began to dissolve, the various Balkan peoples obtained their freedom through revolutions. Each Orthodox Balkan nation as it came into being sought an independent status for the Orthodox Church within its boundaries, and the nations that had patriarchates before the Ottoman conquest sought to reinstate them. In 1833 the patriarchate of Constantinople acknowledged the independence of the church of Greece. Following in quick succession, the Bulgarian church received its independence in 1870, the Serbian in 1879, and the Romanian in 1885. In these nations the Orthodox Church was recognized as the state church.

Of importance for religious life in Hungary was the creation in 1867 of an Austro-Hungarian "dual monarchy" that allowed a measure of religious freedom for Protestants—a pattern of church-state relations that lasted until World War

II. The partition of Poland by Russia, Austria, and Prussia during the second half of the eighteenth century meant the Orthodox in that country came under the jurisdiction of the Russian church, and the Uniates were compelled to return to Orthodoxy. Although the western part of Poland remained subject to Austria and Prussia, Polish Roman Catholics were severely restricted, and Rome was no longer able to exercise control over them. Similarly, Finland was to a large extent occupied by Russia (beginning in 1809), and a strong Russian influence on church life resulted. By the end of the century, however, the Orthodox Finns had asserted their national identity with the institution of services in Finnish.

Eastern Europe and northern Eurasia assumed a definitive national shape in the period just prior to and following World War I. Most notable for church history were the emergence of Finland, Poland, Czechoslovakia, Yugoslavia, and Albania as new nations, primarily as a result of the dissolution of the Austro-Hungarian Empire. Finland was over 90 percent Lutheran with a small Orthodox population that was also recognized as a state church. In 1923 the Finnish Orthodox achieved autonomy under the patriarchate of Constantinople. Similarly, in Poland the Roman Catholic Church became totally dominant, but there remained small Lutheran, old Catholic, Polish Catholic (which came into existence in 1897), and Orthodox Churches. The Polish Orthodox Church was recognized by the patriarchate of Constantinople as autonomous, that is, self-governing under supervision of the mother church, in 1924. In 1980, 92 percent of the population of Czechoslovakia was Roman Catholic. Small Hussite and Brethren Churches also existed, along with a small autonomous Orthodox Church recognized by the ecumenical patriarchate in 1922. Albania became an independent nation in 1912 but was always subject to threats of dismemberment by its neighbors. Its population prior to World War II was predominantly Muslim—the only such nation in eastern Europe—with a Roman Catholic minority in the north and an Orthodox minority in the south. The paradigm of the religious situation in eastern Europe at the time was that of Yugoslavia during and up to the end of the communist era. An amalgam of a number of peoples, Yugoslavia included Roman Catholics in its western provinces of Slovenia and Croatia and Orthodox in its eastern provinces of Serbia and Montenegro, thus reflecting the divided status of the church in eastern Europe and northern Eurasia as a whole.

After World War II. Although the redrawing of national boundaries as a result of World War II, primarily at the expense of the Soviet Union's western neighbors, had an impact on church order, the geographical demography of Orthodox, Roman Catholics, and Protestants did not change radically. Affecting all churches, however, were the forces of secularism, communism, and ecumenism. For more than two millennia the primary struggles of the various churches were among themselves. In the twentieth century the churches came to share common enemies that discounted the significance of religious faith. Secularism has taken many forms, but the most militant was Marxism. In the Soviet Union and the nations under its influence, Marxism was ideologically antireligious. However, the Communist bloc nations approached the Christian church with varying degrees of opposition. Albania during this period declared itself the first "atheist state," claiming that all vestiges of religion had been eliminated. The Soviet Union constitutionally granted freedom of worship but prohibited all other church activity. The rest of the nations in the bloc followed this policy but made less-restrictive accommodations with the church. For some nations, such as Poland, this took place out of political reality, and for other nations, such as Romania and Serbia, accommodations were worked out as a result of undeniable ethnic and cultural necessity. In these countries the dominant number of believers and the identification of the national culture with religious tradition made necessary a more lenient religious policy by the Marxist governments.

The dissolution of the Soviet empire had powerful influence in changing the political and religious face of Eastern Europe. In Russia the fall of Soviet Marxism was intimately supported by the Russian Orthodox Church, which sought, and in a significant measure obtained, its pre-Soviet role in public life. Though not proclaimed the official religion of the state, it is recognized as the dominant religious force in the nation, whereas a few other religions, among them Roman Catholicism, Lutheranism, and Islam, are also recognized. Perhaps the most striking change has taken place with the disintegration of Yugoslavia. The process began in 1989 with the efforts of Slobodan Milosević to remove the autonomy of the province of Kosovo, in the face of its Albanian Muslim majority, to prevent its secession. This eventually led to military action and efforts to expel its Muslim population. In 1991 the constituent provinces of the nation, Croatia, Slovenia, and Macedonia, declared independence, provoking a widening war among the ethnic groups. The former two developed Roman Catholic identities and the last an independent national Orthodox identity. When Bosnia-Herzogovina voted for independence the same year, an all-out war for control of the former province pitted Roman Catholic Croatians, Serbian Orthodox, and Muslims against each other under their ethnic identities. The conflict ended a year later with North Atlantic Treaty Organization action, forcing an uneasy peace.

In Poland the dominant Roman Catholic Church and the smaller Lutheran and Polish Orthodox Churches sought an ecumenical solution to their national political life in the postcommunist period. In tiny Estonia, rival church groupings of Estonian Orthodox and Russian Orthodox sought to work out relations. This resolution, however, provoked stressful relations between the ecumenical patriarchate of Constantinople (Istanbul) and the Moscow patriarchate.

Of great influence was the establishment of the European Union, to which several of the nations of eastern Europe have been admitted. The essentially "borderless" character of the European Union has challenged old presuppositions of nationhood and, especially for Christianity, the assumption of close church and national identities.

The story of Orthodox, papal, and Franco-German Roman Catholic and Protestant competition in the great expanse of eastern Europe and northern Eurasia may have largely come to an end. The twentieth-century ecumenical movement brought together in previously unimagined ways the disparate Christian churches. In the post–World War II era, Orthodox, Roman Catholics, and Protestants of all kinds struggled to replace confrontation and conflict with dialogue, understanding, and cooperation. It may be that the return to a pre-Constantinian status vis-à-vis the state may contain within it the seeds of a new unity for Christendom. What can be affirmed is that in the twenty-first century the various churches, after twenty centuries of conflict, relate to each other with difficulty but of necessity in an unaccustomed spirit of increased cooperation.

SEE ALSO Cyril and Methodius; Eastern Christianity; Ecumenical Movement; Greek Orthodox Church; Marxism; Russian Orthodox Church; Schism, article on Christian Schism; Uniate Churches.

BIBLIOGRAPHY

Byrnes, Timothy A. *Transnational Catholicism in Postcommunist Europe.* Lanham, Md., 2001. Studies Croatia, Poland, and Slovakia, showing deep involvement of the Roman Catholic Church in ethnic conflicts.

Chadwick, Owen. *The Christian Church in the Cold War.* Penguin History of the Church, vol. 7. New York, 1993. Covers the period from World War II to the collapse of the Soviet Union.

Dvornik, Francis. *The Slavs: Their Early History and Civilization.* Boston, 1956. A thorough introduction.

Dvornik, Francis. *Byzantine Missions among the Slavs: SS. Constantine-Cyril and Methodius.* New Brunswick, N.J., 1970. The major historical source in English on the topic.

Geanakoplos, Deno John. *Byzantine East and Latin West: Two Worlds of Christendom in Middle Ages and Renaissance.* New York, 1966. Important insights on the cultural sources of ecclesiastical conflicts. Excellent study.

Greinacher, Norbert, and Virgil Elizondo, eds. *Churches in Socialist Societies of Eastern Europe.* Concilium, no. 154. New York, 1982. Centers on Roman Catholic concerns. A collection of articles of varying quality.

Hösch, Edgar. *The Balkans: A Short History from Greek Times to the Present Day.* Translated by Tania Alexander. London, 1972. Readable, and a good introduction.

Hussey, Joan M., ed. *The Byzantine Empire.* Vol. 4 of *The Cambridge Medieval History,* 2d ed. Cambridge, U.K., 1966–. A standard reference volume. See parts 1 and 2, "Byzantium and Its Neighbours" and "Government, Church, and Civilisation."

Jelavich, Charles, and Barbara Jelavich. *The Balkans.* Englewood Cliffs, N.J., 1965. A clearly narrated introduction with a number of helpful maps.

Lanckorońska, Karolina. *Studies on the Roman-Slavonic Rite in Poland.* Orientalia Christiana Analecta, no. 161. Rome, 1961. Provides evidence of early Eastern influence in Poland.

Latourette, Kenneth Scott. *The Thousand Years of Uncertainty, a.d. 500–a.d. 1500.* Vol. 2 of *A History of the Expansion of Christianity.* New York, 1937–1945. Chapters 3 and 4 cover the early history of the spread of Christianity in eastern Europe from both the West and the East.

Mylonas, George E. *The Balkan States: An Introduction to Their History.* St. Louis, Mo., 1946. A good overview. Argues the Greek position on Macedonia.

Nowak, Frank. *Medieval Slavdom and the Rise of Russia* (1930). Westport, Conn., 1970. A readable short history of Russia to Catherine the Great.

Obolensky, Dimitri. *The Byzantine Commonwealth: Eastern Europe, 500–1453.* London, 1971. A history of Byzantium with a focus on the cultural, political, and ecclesiastical cohesion with the peoples of eastern Europe.

Purmonen, Veikko, ed. *Orthodoxy in Finland: Past and Present.* Kuopio, Finland, 1981. A collection of essays written by Orthodox Finns regarding their church.

Russell, James C. *The Germanization of Early Medieval Christianity: A Sociohistorical Approach to Religious Transformation.* Oxford, 1994. Argues that through history there has been a basic rewriting of the Christian message to conform with German culture.

Sutton, Jonathan, and William Peter Van Den Bercken, eds. *Orthodox Christianity and Contemporary Europe.* Dudley, Mass., 2003. Selected papers of an international conference held at the University of Leeds, England, in June 2001.

Tachiaos, Anthony-Emil N., ed. *The Legacy of Saints Cyril and Methodius to Kiev and Moscow.* Proceedings of the International Congress on the Millennium of the Conversion of Rus' to Christianity, November 1988. Thessalonike, Greece, 1992.

Ware, Timothy. *The Orthodox Church.* Rev. ed. London and New York, 1993. A clear, detailed introduction to the Orthodox Church.

Yannaras, Christos. *The Church in Post-Communist Europe.* Berkeley, Calif., 2003. A critique of consumerism, which the author claims has supplanted communion as a lynchpin of modern Orthodox Church life.

STANLEY SAMUEL HARAKAS (1987 AND 2005)

CHRISTIANITY: CHRISTIANITY IN WESTERN EUROPE

Although the history of Christianity in each of the regions to which it has spread manifests certain special characteristics that set it apart, the development of Christianity within the history of western Europe has in many decisive ways shaped its development in all other regions. The English man of letters Hilaire Belloc (1870–1953) formulated the significance of that development—as well as a highly idiosyncratic and debatable philosophy of history—in his epigram of 1912: "Europe will return to the [Christian] faith, or she will perish. The faith is Europe. And Europe is the faith." Belloc's pronouncement is partly historical and partly hortatory, and even those who would vigorously reject the first and hortatory half of his formulation would probably acknowledge the historical force of the second half. Through most of its history, what most people, insiders or outsiders, have identified as the Christian faith has been the particular form that the Christian faith has acquired in its European experience. Asia, Africa, and the Americas have imported most of their Christianity from western Europe or Britain, and while Christianity did indeed begin in Asia Minor, most Christians in Asia Minor now practice and believe versions of Christianity that have come there only after having first been filtered through Europe. The history of Christianity in western continental Europe and the British Isles is, therefore, indispensable to the understanding of Christianity wherever it exists today. It is no less indispensable to the understanding of the history of western Europe itself. And in that sense at least, Belloc was right.

In recounting the history of Christianity in western Europe and the British Isles from the time of the apostle Paul to the present, this article is designed to account for the identification of Christianity with Europe and to describe its later significance. Therefore, various incidents and individual details of persons and places are selected as they illustrate the several stages of the process, and much more must be omitted than can be included.

Beginnings of Christianity in Europe. The coming of Christianity to Europe may in some ways be read as the leitmotif of the *Acts of the Apostles* in the New Testament. The entire life and ministry of Jesus had taken place in Palestine. He did not speak a European language, and except for a few Romans, such as Pontius Pilate, he did not meet any Europeans. *Acts* also begins within Palestine, in Jerusalem, but the story of the second half of the book is set largely in Europe, one of its high points being the confrontation of the apostle Paul with an audience in Athens (*Acts* 17) and its climactic conclusion coming in the final chapter with his arrival at Rome. It was either to Europe or from Europe that Paul addressed the bulk of his letters, including the three longest ones (*Romans* and *1* and *2 Corinthians*), and he wrote all of them in Greek. From the Gospels it would have been difficult to predict that Christianity would become European, much less that Europe would become Christian, but with the career of Paul that direction had begun to become clear.

For the period of two and a half centuries between the career of Paul and the conversion of the emperor Constantine (r. 306–337) there exist many items of information about the appearance of Christianity in one or another part of Europe. One of the most instructive of these is the account, preserved by Eusebius of Caesarea (c. 260/270–c. 339) in book 5 of his *Church History*, of the persecution of a Christian community at Lyons, in Gaul, in 177–178. The church in Gaul is thought by many scholars to have been the source of the earliest Christian missions to the British Isles, which date from the second or third century, when some of the Celtic inhabitants of Britain were converted (hence the usual designation "Celtic church"). The apostle Paul wrote to the church in Rome, "I hope to see you in passing as I go to Spain" (*Rom.* 15:24). Although the evidence for his having ever actually made such a journey to Spain is tenuous, tradition was quick to attribute one to him.

As that reference indicates, however, the most powerful Christian center in Europe was, from the beginning, at the most powerful city in Europe: Rome. One tradition attributes the founding of that community to the apostle Peter around 42 CE, but critics of the credibility of that tradition have often pointed to the absence of any reference to Peter in the letter that Paul addressed to Rome fifteen years later (even though the final chapter of that letter is a catalog of proper names). But whoever it was that founded it, the Christian church at Rome was prominent enough both for Paul to send it his most important letter and for the emperor Nero to instigate a persecution of it, during which both Peter and Paul were said to have suffered martyrdom. That persecution did not diminish the power and prestige of the Roman church, which became a significant presence in the city and (especially after the capture of Jerusalem in 70 CE and its consequent decline as the mother city of Christianity) first among the Christian centers of Europe—indeed, of the Mediterranean world.

Although many of the most notable leaders of Christian thought during the second, third, and fourth centuries were not located in Europe but either in Alexandria (Clement, Origen, Alexander, Athanasius, Cyril) or in Roman North Africa (Tertullian, Cyprian, Augustine) or still in Asia Minor (Justin Martyr, Irenaeus, Cyril of Jerusalem, Jerome), most of them had some sort of European connection: Athanasius found asylum in Rome when he was driven out of Alexandria; before Jerome went to Palestine, he had undertaken the translation of the Vulgate at the behest of Pope Damasus, whom he served as secretary; Augustine was brought to Christianity in Europe through the teaching of Ambrose, bishop of Milan. Similarly, although the first seven ecumenical councils of the church were held at such Eastern cities as Nicaea, Constantinople, Ephesus, and Chalcedon, rather than in Rome or any other European city, it was in fact the power and prestige of Christian Europe that often determined their outcome. The Spanish bishop, Hosius of Cordova, was in many ways the most authoritative of the bishops at Nicaea in 325, and when, according to the contemporary account, the bishops at Chalcedon in 451 declared that "Peter has spoken through the mouth of [Pope] Leo," they were acknowledging once more the special status that European Christianity had achieved as early as the beginning of the fourth century.

The event with the most far-reaching consequences for the history of European Christianity, indeed for the history of Christianity everywhere, was the conversion of the emperor Constantine and the ensuing transformation of the Roman Empire into a Christian empire. That change took place on European soil when, in the Battle of the Milvian Bridge on October 28, 312, Constantine defeated the forces of his rival Maxentius, who was emperor for Italy and Africa, and thus became sole emperor. Attributing his victory to the

Christian God, Constantine identified the cross of Christ as the "sacred sign" by which the Senate and the Roman people had been restored to their ancient glory. Christianity rapidly moved from being persecuted to being tolerated to being preferred to being established. Constantine in 330 transferred the capital of his newly christianized empire from Rome to Byzantium, renamed Constantinople, or "New Rome." For the history of Christianity in Europe, this move away from Europe served, somewhat ironically, to endow Europe with a position of even greater consequence for the future, for much of the aura that had surrounded Rome and the Roman emperor continued to surround Rome, but now descended instead upon the Roman bishop, who from Europe would declare and enforce his position in the collegial company of bishops as "first among equals" (equals who would become less equal in the process).

Simultaneous with the developing establishment of a Christian empire and of a Christianized European society, and in part as a reaction against it, monasticism both Eastern and Western gave institutional form to the ascetic imperatives of primitive Christianity. Now that the sharp line of differentiation between the church and "the world" had been blurred, it was necessary to find a new and more striking way to draw the line by "forsaking the world" and going into a monastery. Above all, it was the work of Benedict of Nursia (c. 480–c. 547), through his *Rule*, that gave European monasticism a settled form. The monks were to become the principal missionaries to the new populations of Europe as well as the principal transmitters of the cultural heritage, classical as well as Christian, and thus the educators of medieval Europe. It was in recognition of this role that Benedict has been designated "patron saint of Europe."

MEDIEVAL EUROPE. In all of these ways European Christianity was developing in the direction of the forms and structures it was to have when it came to deal with the new populations that arrived in Europe. The beginning of the Middle Ages may be defined for our purposes here as the period during which those new populations were becoming Christian.

Some of these, most notably the Goths, had already become Christian before their arrival: Ulfilas, the fourth-century "apostle of the Goths," had worked among them as a missionary, translating the Bible into Gothic. Paradoxically, however, the christianization of the Goths was to work against them when they came to Europe, because the form of Christianity that Ulfilas had brought them was tainted with the Arian heresy and therefore stood in the way of an immediate political alliance between the Goths and the bishop of Rome. The future of Christian Europe belonged to such an alliance, in which all the Germanic, Celtic, and western Slavic tribes would eventually share. Among these tribes it was the Franks who came to assume a position of leadership when, in a reprise of Constantine's conversion, their king, Clovis, became an orthodox Catholic Christian in 496. With the support of the Catholic episcopate, Clovis set about the task of subduing the "heretical" Visigoths, militarily and then ecclesiastically, in the name of the orthodox faith. As a consequence, in the course of the two centuries after Clovis, the Frankish crown became the principal protector of the Roman see, which reciprocated by supporting Frankish political and territorial ambitions. The coronation as Holy Roman Emperor of the Frankish king Charles, known to history as Charlemagne, by the pope in the year 800 was as much the recognition of an already existing status quo as it was the creation of anything new, but it has served ever since as perhaps the primary symbol of the spiritual unity of "Christian Europe" as a cultural entity.

The Christianization of Europe and of the nations that came into Europe was at the same time the conquest of their indigenous religious traditions, sometimes by missionary activity and sometimes by military victory. Formally and externally, the conquest was taken to mean the total obliteration of the old faith. Thus, when in the early 720s Boniface, the Benedictine monk who bears the title "apostle of Germany," chopped down an oak sacred to the worship of the German god Thor at Geismar, this was interpreted to be the replacement of the "false gods" of paganism with the Christian deity. Yet the same Thor or Donar, god of thunder (*Donner*), was to give his name to the Germanic designations for the sixth day of the Christian week ("Thursday" or "Donnerstag"), the very week that began with a Sunday devoted to the weekly commemoration of the resurrection of Jesus Christ. Similarly, Friday's name came from Freyja, Germanic goddess of love and counterpart of Venus, who gave her name to that same day in French. The names of gods were sometimes transformed into the names of saints who often had the same provenance and some of the same functions as the gods. In sending Augustine to Kent, Pope Gregory I (r. 590–604) gave instructions that the new centers of Christian worship should be at the places already revered as holy by the native population; thus, sacred springs and streams became the sites of Christian baptisms. "Conquest," therefore, involved some measure of continuity as well as the more obvious forms of discontinuity.

Conversely, Christianity became European at the cost of increasing discontinuity between itself and Christian churches elsewhere. Such ruptures of continuity took place even within Western Christianity, as the centralized authority of Rome—administrative, liturgical, sometimes also doctrinal—clashed with older regional systems. Much of the *History of the English Church and People* by Bede "the Venerable" (c. 673–735) is devoted to the process by which older "Celtic" practices on such questions as monastic tonsure and the date of Easter had to surrender to customs developed on the continent and enforced by the papacy. Even more dramatic and far-reaching in their implications were the deepening differences between East and West. As "New Rome," Constantinople developed forms of organization and worship that gave to Byzantine Christianity a special character that it was to transmit to its daughter churches in eastern Europe. The dream of a single Christian empire reaching from one end of the Mediterranean to the other, all held together by a Greco-Roman Christian culture, never became a reality for any significant length of time, not even under the emperor Justinian (r. 527–565), who strove to achieve it by every means available, from armies to dogmas to jurisprudence. And as the Christianity of western Europe began to come of age, its family resemblance to Byzantium became less discernible. The rise and rapid expansion of Islam in the seventh and eighth centuries had, among many other consequences, the result of isolating Eastern Christendom and the Christianity of western Europe from each other. Fundamental differences of missionary methodology asserted themselves, most prominently in the Christianization of the Slavs during the ninth and tenth centuries. Byzantium sought to make a nation Christian by translating the Bible and the liturgy into that nation's language, Rome sought to do so by teaching it to pray in Latin and to accept Roman primacy. The collision between these two methodologies on the Slavic mission field coincided with increasing tensions over jurisdictional questions (such as the proper titles for the patriarchs of Old and New Rome) and doctrinal disputes (such as that over the procession of the Holy Spirit from the Father and the Son). All of these were symptomatic of the growing alienation—or, to put the matter more positively, of the growing self-awareness of western Europe as a Christian civilization in its own right rather than a Byzantine outpost.

One other difference between Byzantine Christianity and the Christianity of western Europe during the Middle Ages was political. Although the Eastern church was not the servile department of state that Western polemics have often described it to have been, its vision of the Christian empire did view the imperial power as having been transmitted directly from God through Christ to the emperor, without the mediation of church and hierarchy. By contrast, as the symbolism of the coronation of Charlemagne by the pope suggested, the mediation of the church was seen in the West as essential to the legitimacy of political power; it was seen that way by a succession of popes, but also by many emperors and kings, who invoked papal authority to validate their political sovereignty. Claiming the right to "bind" and "loose" (cf. *Mt.* 16:18–19) not only the forgiveness of sins but also political office, the papacy repeatedly came into conflict with the civil power, which often made use of the territorial church in its own land as an instrument of power politics. In the conflict between Pope Gregory VII and Emperor Henry IV, climaxing in their encounter at Canossa in 1077, one of the issues was the tension between the particularistic ambitions both of the German emperor and of the German church and the universal claims of the pope, who, as part of his campaign to purify and reform the church, strove to secure its independence from the economic and political entanglements of the feudal system. A century later, Thomas Becket, archbishop of Canterbury, defended those universal claims against the king of England, Henry II, and was murdered in 1170.

Combining as they did religious zeal, military ambition, national rivalry, and a yearning for the exotic, the Crusades, beginning at the Council of Clermont in 1095 and ending with the Turkish victory over the Christian forces at Nicopolis in 1396, were, on one level, an expression of the medieval ideal of a united Western Christian Europe: England, France, Germany, and Italy joined forces under the cross of Christ and with the inspiration and blessing of the church to rescue the "holy places" in Palestine. On another level, however, the Crusades are frequently interpreted as a disaster both for Christianity and for Europe, for they not only failed to achieve their goal in Palestine but also proved to be divisive within Christendom itself. The Crusades, as well as the confrontations between "spiritual" and "secular" authority, for which parallels can be found throughout the history of European and British Christianity both in the Middle Ages and since, illustrate the church's paradoxical role as simultaneously the patron of national cultures (whose kings were said to rule "by the grace of God") and the embodiment of a cultural ideal transcending all national boundaries.

That paradox was also at work in other aspects of medieval culture. In the millennium from Boethius (c. 480–c. 525) to Martin Luther (1483–1546), the intellectual history of Europe during the Middle Ages is, to a remarkable extent, the history of Christian thought in its interaction with philosophy, science, and political theory, as these came into medieval Europe both from classical antiquity and from contemporary Islam and Judaism; the Scholasticism of the twelfth and thirteenth centuries, whose most influential spokesman was Thomas Aquinas (c. 1225–1274), was an important chapter in the history of philosophy no less than in that of theology. Much of the architecture of the Middle Ages was made possible by the needs of the church for basilicas, abbeys, and cathedrals, and its art by the themes of Christian worship and devotion. Sacred music and secular music not only coexisted but interacted, both in the monastery and in the community. Early monuments of the literatures of Europe, such as *Beowulf* and the Norse sagas, document the blending of Christian and non-Christian elements in western Europe, and so, under more explicitly Christian inspiration, do late monuments such as *Piers Plowman* and Dante's *Commedia.* Here again, the relation between universal and particular—a Latin literature, which is European, versus the several vernacular literatures, which are national—manifests the ambivalence of the Christian role in what the medieval historian Robert S. Lopez has called "the birth of Europe."

EUROPE IN THE REFORMATION. Thus there were in medieval Europe, and in the Christianity of medieval Europe, centrifugal forces far more powerful than could be acknowledged by the political and ecclesiastical rhetoric of the oneness of the *corpus Christianum.* Such oneness as there was had probably reached its zenith in 1215 at the Fourth Lateran Council, when political and ecclesiastical representatives from all over western Europe had hailed the authority of Pope Innocent III. But both before and after that council, this authority and the unity it symbolized were in jeopardy. National churches pledged their allegiance to the pope—and went their own way in polity, liturgy, and religious practice. Kings and emperors craved anointing from the church, but often craved its property and power even more. And theologians opened their treatises with affirmations of their creedal orthodoxy, but manipulated the ambiguities of creedal language to ignore or revise or even undermine the dogmatic tradition.

But whatever cleavages of nations, parties, and schools of thought there may have been in medieval Europe, the principle—and the illusion—of unity-within-diversity remained. All of that was shattered by the Reformation of the sixteenth century. Conditions in the church throughout western Europe during the later Middle Ages had convinced nearly everyone that some sort of reform *in capite et membris* ("in head and members"), as the saying went, was needed; there were widespread complaints about episcopal and clerical negligence, abuses of authority at all levels were perceived to be rampant, ignorance and superstition among the people were being overlooked or even encouraged by the church, and even the most responsible voices in ecclesiastical positions acknowledged that almost every high official (sometimes up to and including the pope) could be suspected of having bought his office and thus of having committed the sin of simony. The spectacle of a schism between two popes, one at Rome and the other at Avignon, seemed to prove that the medieval tradition of reform, as enunciated in the eleventh century by Gregory VII, was inadequate to the crisis of the fifteenth century. During that century, a series of church councils (Pisa, 1409; Constance, 1414–1417; Basel-Ferrara-Florence, 1431–1445) sought to achieve reform by legislating changes in church life, reestablishing (unsuccessfully) ties to the Eastern churches, formulating orthodox doctrine on various issues, such as purgatory, that had not been set down before, and clarifying the relation between the authority of the pope and the authority of the council. This last issue led to new schisms, this time between pope and council. Some advocates of reform, notably Jan Hus in Bohemia, even set into motion forces that would produce separate churches.

In the intellectual and cultural life of Europe, this was at the same time a period of intense activity and of vigorous change. Although it is historically incorrect to interpret the humanism of the Renaissance, whether Italian or Northern, as a rejection of the essential content of Christianity, it did represent an attack on many of its received traditions. Thus the humanists attacked medieval Scholasticism both for its ignorance of classical culture and for its distortion of Christianity. They made the monks the object of ridicule for caricaturing the ethical imperatives of the New Testament, and they pointed to the contradictions between those imperatives and a great deal that was going on in the institutional life of European Christianity. In keeping with the humanistic motto "Back to the sources!" Italian humanists like Lorenzo Valla (1406–1457) and northern humanists like Erasmus (1469?–1536) devoted their scholarly attention to recovering the original text and the authentic message of the New Testament, and in this sense they also belong to the history of late medieval reform. Humanist and churchman at once, Francisco Jiménez de Cisneros (1436–1517) demonstrated the possibility of holding together Roman Catholic orthodoxy and a commitment to educational and ecclesiastical reform.

What kind of evolution of Christianity all these various reform movements would have brought about on their own is a subject only for speculation. For it was revolution, not evolution, that swept across Christian Europe during the sixteenth century, transforming both the map of Europe itself and the character of European Christianity in the process. The one church of the Middle Ages became the several churches of the Reformation. Each of these reformations was to shape the history of European Christianity in a distinct way.

The Lutheran Reformation carried out into cultural, political, and ecclesiastical structures the impulses set in motion by Martin Luther's struggle for faith. Although Luther began that struggle on the assumption that he could find salvation only within the institutional forms of the Western church, he ended by repudiating many of them, even denouncing the pope as antichrist. A right relation with God was the consequence not of human moral striving but of the divine gift of forgiving grace. That gift, moreover, was appropriated by faith alone, faith being understood as confidence and trust in the divine promise. And the authority for knowing this promise and being assured of this grace was not the voice of the church, but the word of God in the Bible. To be sure, these three Reformation principles—often cited in their Latin formulations as *sola gratia, sola fide, sola Scriptura*—became the common property of much of Protestantism, not only of Lutheranism, even though Lutheranism often claimed to be alone in carrying them out consistently. But in the Lutheran churches of Europe, above all in Germany and Scandinavia, these principles, enunciated officially in the Augsburg Confession of 1530, served as the foundation for new developments in many fields of culture. The Lutheran chorale, which began with the hymns of Luther himself, flourished from the sixteenth to the eighteenth century, producing not only hundreds of new liturgies and hymnals but also the sacred music of Johann Sebastian Bach (1685–1750). In formulating the implications of the Reformation principles, the theologians of the Lutheran church constructed systems of Christian doctrine that sometimes rivaled those of the medieval Scholastics for comprehensiveness, if not for philosophical sophistication.

The Calvinist tradition—or, as it has often preferred to identify itself, the Reformed tradition—shared many of the central emphases of the Lutheran Reformation, but sought to carry them out with greater consistency. As worked out in the career and thought of John Calvin (1509–1564), it took *sola Scriptura* to mean an elimination of those features in worship and Christian culture that could not claim explicit biblical warrant. The primacy and sovereignty of divine grace implied that not only salvation, but also damnation, was the consequence of the will of God. Perhaps most important of all was the Reformed belief that the social order, no less than the life of the individual believer, must be brought into conformity with the revealed word of God. In the Calvinist lands of Europe, therefore, far more than in the Lutheran ones, the Reformation brought about a concerted effort to reshape politics and economics in accordance with this standard. Whether or not this helped to create a spiritual climate in which modern European capitalism was able to take seed, as Max Weber and other scholars have contended, is still a matter of controversy, but Calvinism certainly did shape attitudes toward work, property, social justice, and public order not only in the Swiss and other non-Lutheran forms of Protestantism on the continent, but far beyond the borders of western Europe (including North America).

One of the regions in which the Calvinist Reformation became a major cultural force was the British Isles. Through the reformatory work of John Knox (c. 1514–1572), it was the Reformed version of Protestantism that prevailed in Scotland. Doctrinally this meant that the Scots Confession of 1560, which Knox composed together with several colleagues, was to be the first official statement of the teaching of the Reformed Church of Scotland, until it was replaced by the Westminster Confession of 1647. Liturgically, the Reformed character of the Church of Scotland was guaranteed by *The Book of Common Order* (1556–1564), in which Knox and his associates set down forms of worship that in their judgment conformed to the scriptures and affirmed the evangelical commitments of Reformation faith.

The relation of England to the Reformed tradition was considerably more equivocal. Although the earliest influences of the continental Reformation came to England through the writings and the disciples of Luther, the terms of the settlement that emerged from the break with Rome occasioned by the divorce of Henry VIII (1491–1547) avoided putting the Church of England unambiguously into any one confessional camp. *The Book of Common Prayer*, the retention of the apostolic succession of ordaining bishops, and the Thirty-nine Articles, taken together despite their deep differences of approach, defined the settlement. It was only with the rise of Puritanism and its protest against such ambiguity that Reformed patterns of churchmanship and theology began to press for control within Anglicanism. The established church of the sixteenth and seventeenth centuries left a permanent imprint on English culture through such literary monuments as the Authorized Version of the Bible and (despite profound divergences) the works of John Milton (1608–1674).

Unless the term *Reformation* is understood in a polemical and denominational sense as coextensive with the term *Protestantism*, however, it is necessary to include in it the history of the Roman Catholic reformation as well, and not simply to interpret this as a "counterreformation." The Protestant Reformation did not exhaust the imperative sense of reform within the church. In every country of Europe, therefore, Luther's activity evoked not only a defense of Roman Catholic doctrine and order but also a call for greater dedication to the cause of reform. The most abiding expression of that dedication came at the Council of Trent (1545–1563), which reaffirmed the church's teaching by identifying which positions among the many being espoused by churchmen and theologians lay within the bounds of orthodoxy and which did not. No less urgent an item on the council's agenda was the elimination of the abuses to which its fifteenth-century predecessors had already addressed their attention. Bishops were now obliged to be resident in their dioceses, instead of collecting the income and leaving the duties to surrogates. Preaching and teaching were prominent among those duties, and therefore the professional training of future clergy in seminaries was incumbent on the church everywhere. Implementation of the Catholic reformation was entrusted not only to a revitalized episcopate and clergy and a reformed papacy but also to the renewal of the religious orders and to the development of a new religious order, indeed, a new kind of order, in the Society of Jesus, founded by Ignatius Loyola (1491–1556). In part to compensate for the losses of European territory to Protestantism, the Jesuits and other religious orders undertook an intensification of missionary activity in the New World, as well as in Asia.

Also a part of the Reformation in Europe, despite their exclusion from conventional accounts, were the representatives of the several radical reformations. Anabaptism criticized Lutheranism and Calvinism for not having gone far enough in their rejection of traditional Roman Catholic forms, and it pressed for a "believers' church," in which only those who made a public commitment and confession would be members; since that excluded infants, the practice of infant baptism was repudiated. To be consistent, many of the Anabaptists, notably the Mennonites, likewise disavowed the Constantinian union between church and state, and some of them even repudiated the definition of "just war" and hence the theory that Christians could wield the sword. Although such groups as the Mennonites retained the orthodox doctrines of the Trinity and the divinity of Christ, the radical critique of traditional Christianity led others to question these as well. Despite their relatively small numbers, the churches and sects of the radical Reformation were expressing misgivings about the forms of institutional and orthodox Christianity, misgivings that appear to have been widespread, though unacknowledged, throughout Europe, both Roman Catholic and Protestant. Thus the end result of the Reformation was a Europe balkanized into confessions and denominations that continued to divide among themselves, a Europe in which the assumptions of a thousand years about a common Christian worldview were less and less valid.

European Christianity in the Modern Period. If it is correct to characterize the era of the Reformation as a time when revolution began to replace evolution as a means of dealing with the problems of church and state, it is even more appropriate to see the situation of European Christianity in the modern period as one of coping with an age of revolution—or, more accurately, of revolutions in every sphere of human activity. One of the most widely used histories of Christianity in the modern period bears the title *The Church in an Age of Revolution.*

Politically, the Europe that emerged from the conflicts of the Reformation would seem to be the negation of revolution. When history textbooks speak of this as "the age of absolutism," they are referring to the achievement, under such monarchs as Louis XIV of France (r. 1643–1715), of a level of royal authority seldom witnessed before or since, in which the church, though with some reluctance, acted as a buttress of the secular power. Yet before the century that began with Louis XIV on the throne of France had ended, the overthrow of monarchy in France and the proclamation of a new order (even of a new calendar) symbolized the end of secular absolutism, and increasingly the end of Christian hegemony. Many of the leaders of the French Revolution were openly hostile not only to the institutional church but also to the principal teachings of the Christian tradition as a whole; others sought a more positive relation between Christianity and revolution. Both overt opposition and the quest for rapprochement were to play a part in Christian reactions to the successive revolutions of modern Europe, for example in 1848. Christianity was identified, by friend and foe alike, as allied with the ancient regime; and by the time it had come to terms with the revolutionary regime, that was already being overthrown by a new revolution, with which Christianity must once more come to terms. A permanent outcome of those seemingly constant shifts was the creation, in many countries of Europe, of Christian democratic parties, sometimes at the conservative end of the political spectrum but often centrist in their policies, and even of various forms of Christian socialism. The condemnation of socialism and of other modern revolutionary movements in the *Syllabus of Errors* issued by Pope Pius IX in 1864 must be seen in counterpoint with the "social encyclicals," especially those of Pope Leo XIII (r. 1878–1903), which articulated a reconciliation of Christian teachings with the best in the democratic systems; a similar range of political opinion, and thus of response to the revolutions of the time, was present as well in the various branches of European Protestantism during the eighteenth and nineteenth centuries.

What Christians of all denominations found objectionable in much of revolutionary ideology was not only its attack on political regimes with which the institutional church had made its peace, but also its alliance with intellectual and social movements that seemed bent on undermining the Christian faith itself. Thus the theoretical foundations of both the French and the American revolutions contained many elements of the philosophy of the Enlightenment. Against the traditional Christian insistence on the need for revelation, Enlightenment thought defended the capacity of the natural mind to find the truth about the good life, and against the Christian distinction between the capacities of human nature and the superadded gift of divine grace, it ascribed to human nature the ability to live in accordance with that truth. Enlightenment science, and above all the philosophy that both underlay much of the science and was based upon it, seemed increasingly to make the Christian doctrine of creation irrelevant.

Enlightenment thought was the most vigorous expression of the more general attack on traditional European Christianity known as "secularism," which may be defined as the belief that, here in this world (Lat., *saeculum*), religious ideas about revelation and eternal life are not necessary to the development of a good life for the individual or society. Philosophically that belief has expressed itself in the construction of rational systems of thought and of conduct that attacked or simply ignored the claims of supernatural grace and revelation. Politically it took the form of gradually withdrawing from the church the privileged status it had held in the countries of Europe. Public education excluded Christian teaching from its curriculum and Christian ceremonies from its practice. The state would determine the criteria for what made a marriage valid, and the church ritual would at best serve only as a public attestation of a status defined by secular criteria. The clergy, who in medieval Europe had been tried in their own courts even for offenses against the political order (the issue on which Becket had clashed with the English crown) lost their special legal standing. Of the many instances in modern European history when secularism and Christianity clashed, the most renowned was probably the *Kulturkampf* in nineteenth-century Germany, in which the newly united German empire took drastic steps to curb the cultural and political status of the Roman Catholic Church. Although most of those steps were in fact eventually reversed, the *Kulturkampf* has come to symbolize a pattern widespread throughout Europe.

The case of the *Kulturkampf* suggests another closely related phenomenon that has also been a major force in redefining the place of Christianity in modern European culture, the dominance of nationalism. The nineteenth century, the "great century" of Christian missions, was as well the century of nationalist expansion into the European colonial empires. As the custodian of nationality and the patron of the national cultures of Christian Europe, Christianity had long maintained a dual role in fostering and yet restraining the devotion to the nation. Now that such devotion was assuming the proportions of a principal rival to the church for the deepest loyalties of European populations, this dual role meant that Christianity sometimes expressed itself in national terms so exclusive as to obscure its universal significance. One of the most frequent arenas for the clash between Christianity and national aspirations has been the effort of national governments to control the governance of the church within their own territories on such questions as episcopal appointments: Gallicanism was the effort by French ecclesiastics and statesmen to assert what were taken to be the historic rights of the church in France against the centralized ultramontane authority of the papacy. The most notorious expression of national religion came in the program of the German Christians in Nazi Germany, who identified the Christian gospel with Germanic ideology and Aryan purity.

As the supreme expression of nationalistic devotion, modern warfare has also been the ultimate test of Christianity's relation to European culture. From Augustine and Thomas Aquinas had come the definition of just war, which Christianity applied, with greater or lesser appropriateness, to modern European wars from the Thirty Years' War to World War II. Church leaders in European nations on both sides during those wars invoked the blessing of the same Christian God not only on the individuals who fought but also on the nationalist cause for which they fought. The same church leaders, however, often reminded their nations of the moral demands of a humanity beyond the nation, and in the efforts for peace and reconstruction after a war Christianity has often played a constructive role. The archbishop of Uppsala, Nathan Söderblom (1866–1931), received the Nobel Peace Prize in 1930 for his work after World War I. In the aftermath of the invention of nuclear weapons, Christianity in Europe—joined then by both Roman Catholicism and Protestantism elsewhere—took the lead in the task of rethinking the very notion of just war. It was also from Christianity in Europe that there came the reminder of what Pope John Paul II called "the common Christian roots of the nations of Europe" and the summons to find in those roots a vision of the continuing relation between Christianity and European culture. Thus, in a sense quite different from Belloc's own, the thesis that "Europe is the faith, and the faith is Europe" has continued to find support.

SEE ALSO Crusades; Enlightenment, The; Humanism; Modernism, article on Christian Modernism; Monasticism, article on Christian Monasticism; New Religious Movements, article on New Religious Movements in Europe; Papacy; Reformation; Scholasticism.

BIBLIOGRAPHY

Bainton, Roland H. *The Reformation of the Sixteenth Century.* New ed. Foreword by Jaroslav Pelikan. Boston, 1985. Deceptively clear yet complex and profound, a splendid introduction to the subject, with bibliographies that carry the reader to the next level.

Cambridge Medieval History. 8 vols. Cambridge, 1911–1936. There is no volume of this comprehensive work without direct relevance to the understanding of the history of Christianity in Europe.

Cambridge Modern History. 13 vols. Cambridge, 1902–1912. Antiquated though it is in both methodology and facts, this remains the most useful account of the entire story. Its very quaintness makes its discussions of Christianity especially helpful.

Chadwick, Owen. *The Reformation.* The Pelican History of the Church, vol. 3. Baltimore, 1964. Together with the other volumes of the series listed below (Cragg, Neill, Southern, and Vidler), the best place for the English reader to begin.

Cragg, Gerald R. *The Church and the Age of Reason, 1648–1789.* Baltimore, 1960. Remarkably free of animus, a thoughtful and provocative reading of the Enlightenment.

Fliche, Augustin, and Victor Martin, eds. *Histoire de l'Église, depuis les origines jusqu'à nos jours.* 21 vols. Paris, 1935–1964. Each volume of this learned set provides information and insight; Émile Amann's *L'époque carolingienne* (Paris, 1937), the sixth volume, stands alone as an account of the Carolingian period and its aftermath.

Latourette, K. S. *A History of the Expansion of Christianity.* 7 vols. New York, 1937–1945. As Stephen Neill (see below) has said, "It is baffling to his successors that, when we think we have made some specially bright discovery of our own, we nearly always find that he has been there before us."

Neill, Stephen C. *A History of Christian Missions.* Baltimore, 1964. European without being Eurocentric, it puts European Christianity into a world context.

Nichols, James. *History of Christianity, 1650–1950.* New York, 1956. As its title suggests, this volume makes "secularization" its central theme.

Pelikan, Jaroslav. *The Christian Tradition: A History of the Development of Doctrine.* 4 vols. Chicago, 1971–1984. Not exclusively, but primarily, European in its focus.

Southern, Richard W. *Western Society and the Church in the Middle Ages.* Harmondsworth, 1970. Unlike most histories of medieval Christianity, Southern's narrative concentrates on society and culture in the Middle Ages.

Vidler, Alec. *The Church in an Age of Revolution.* Baltimore, 1961. A judicious selection of persons and events to interpret the history of Christianity, especially in Europe, during the past two centuries.

Wand, J. W. C. *A History of the Modern Church from 1500 to the Present Day.* London, 1946. An interesting contrast to the viewpoint set forth by other volumes in this bibliography.

New Sources

Hastings, Adrian. *History of English Christianity.* London, 1991.

Phillips, Paul T. *A Kingdom on Earth: Anglo-American Social Christianity, 1880–1940.* University Park, Pa., 1996.

JAROSLAV PELIKAN (1987)
Revised Bibliography

CHRISTIANITY: CHRISTIANITY IN LATIN AMERICA

The discovery of Santo Domingo in 1492 marks the beginning of Latin American church history. There were no priests among the one hundred men aboard the *Pinta,* the *Niña,* and the *Santa Maria;* nevertheless, the seamen were Spanish Christians. To be Spanish or Portuguese around the beginning of the sixteenth century meant being impregnated with that particular concept of church and state that had spawned the Crusades, with tragic consequences for the indigenous American peoples. Only ten months before Columbus's landing, Spain had expelled the Moors from Granada and thus concluded its eight-centuries-old war of liberation. Fired by the conviction that the Spanish crown was the divinely chosen instrument for the salvation of the New World, Isabel and Ferdinand, and, later, Philip, promoted the Conquest wholeheartedly. They sent fifteen hundred men in a convoy of seventeen ships on the second expedition in 1493, including civil representatives, an ecclesiastical delegation (headed by the famous Benedictine Bernard Boyl), and a contingent of nobles to garner lands and servants for Christ. The decadent feudal society thus imposed artificially extended Spanish structures and indelibly stamped the organization and future of Latin American society, to the great detriment of both.

The "enemy" to be conquered in the New World bore no resemblance to the evicted Moors. Anthropologists and historians differ widely among themselves as to the nature of the cultural disparity between the Spanish and the higher Indian civilizations. Some estimate that the Indians had reached approximately the level of the first Egyptian dynasty; others reject such cultural comparisons as unilateral. The Aztec, the Maya, and the Inca lived in basically sedentary, agricultural communities, some of which were subject to the higher cultural influence; others were nomadic and tended to be more primitive in culture and religion. The syncretic Indian religions incarnated traditional dualisms: day and night, sun and moon, good and evil, subject to an overarching, implacable fate. The amazing rapidity with which these cultures were destroyed resulted, at least in part, from the superiority of Spanish weaponry, the use of horses (which had disappeared in indigenous prehistory), and the brutal annihilation of ancient beliefs and customs in order to impose a religion and form of life incomprehensible to the Indian peoples.

Agreements between the popes and Iberian Catholic kings go back to the thirteenth century, when Portugal was given ecclesiastical, political, and economic rights over countries discovered and to be discovered. Near the end of the successful reconquest of Granada, two papal bulls were issued, giving the Spanish kings extensive powers over ecclesiastical matters there. In 1493 the Roman pope conceded rights of jurisdiction to the Spanish and Portuguese crowns over discoveries on either side of an imaginary line drawn from north to south 100 leagues (556 km) west of the Azores, moved 370 leagues (2,054 km) farther west in 1494. Although there have been different interpretations as to whether the rights dispensed by the pope were territorial or solely ecclesiastical, the Catholic kings understood both to be included and acted accordingly. The right to the lands was coupled with the duty to evangelize the native peoples. The extension of the kingdom of God was the goal.

The royal rights conferred by the papal concordat included the establishment of bishoprics in the conquered territories, the nomination of bishops, the reception of tithes for the furtherance of evangelical work, the building of convents and churches, the appointment of all clergy, and the sending of missionaries. Thus both civil and ecclesiastical concerns were united under one head, the king, and the pope was effectively excluded from all decision making in the conversion of the Americas. The creation of the Supreme Council of the Indies (1524) facilitated the execution of the king's rights and will through civil authorities: viceroys and their various subordinates were appointed for New Spain (Mexico) in 1535, for Peru (the Andean region) in 1544, for Granada (greater Colombia) in 1717, and for the Plata (River Plate area) in 1776.

Colonial Church (1492–1808). The conquistadors were fired by a medieval devotion to the extension of Christendom. The Catholic monarchs, Ferdinand of Aragon and Isabel of Castile, supported by the staunch integralist Francisco Jiménez de Cisneros and succeeded by Charles I (as Holy Roman Emperor, Charles V) and Philip II, molded Spain into a unified nation that would be capable of what each believed to be a divine mission—the Christianization of the Americas. Together they directed the political-ecclesiastical enterprise for 124 years.

Foundations of the colonial church. The first twenty-five years following the discovery of Santo Domingo saw the implantation of Spanish colonies in the Caribbean basin. Few priests accompanied the first voyages. In the ten years following, 125 priests (including 89 Franciscans and 32 Dominicans) went to the West Indies to evangelize an estimated 250,000 natives. Their equipment included materials for the building of churches and monasteries, books, trinkets for opening communication with the Indians, and subsistence items. Of particular significance during this initial period were the prophetic denunciations of the abuse of the Indians made by two Dominicans, Antonio de Montesinos (in 1511) and Bartolomé de Las Casas (from 1514 until 1566). The greatest obstacles to the mission were the use of armed force in the subjection of the natives and the *encomienda* system by which the Indians were assigned to the care of those who received lands for the purposes of work and instruction in the Christian faith.

The conquest and Christianization of the mainland began with Hernando Cortés in Mexico (1519) and was extended to Peru by Francisco Pizarro (1531). These men were accompanied by priests, both regular and secular clergy. For the most part the regulars (monastic orders) concentrated on the mission, while the secular clergy served as parish priests of the Spanish, Creole, and, later, much of the mestizo, population.

Church organizations proliferated during the sixteenth century. By the close of the century, some fifteen bishoprics had been established in each of the two then-existing viceroyalties, Mexico and Peru. Soon after the conquest, diocesan and provincial meetings were held to determine polity and practice for institutional and mission work. Of the fifteen provincial councils held during the colonial period, the four of greatest importance were Lima I (1551) and III (1582–1583) and Mexico I (1555) and III (1585).

In Lima I the first forty resolutions established the organization of the Inca Indian Church on the basis of the original tribal and regional divisions of the empire. Also, catechetical instruction in the language of the people was required prior to baptism. The eighty resolutions that followed set forth the colonial ecclesiastical structure, marking clearly the division between Spanish and Indian sectors of society.

The first Mexican council treated with deep concern such matters as the indoctrination of the indigenous peoples, the use of their native languages in evangelization, their need for sacraments, the regulation of their traditional feasts and dances, the establishment of separate villages for them, and their freedom in choosing spouses. The councils of Lima III and Mexico III were influenced by the Council of Trent (1545–1563) and indicated a continuing concern about ecclesiastical and clerical reforms and the welfare of the Indians, whose numbers had dropped substantially during this period.

Civil authorities and churchmen agreed that the separation of the Indians into their own villages was the best policy. For the colonists it assured better control of the native tribes and family groups, and for the missionary priests it made their indoctrination and christianization more effective. As early as 1539 the Franciscan Fray Juan de Almeda established such a village in Huejotzingo, near Puebla in Mexico, for over forty thousand Indians. The Franciscans were soon followed by the Dominicans, Augustinians, and Mercedarians, but many areas in the wide expanses of territory were without spiritual care. Near the end of the sixteenth century, the priest Juan de Mendieta wrote that some priests traveled more than 100 miles to minister to groups of over one hundred thousand Indians.

Quarrels were frequent between the religious orders over jurisdiction in the villages, but were even more frequent between the orders and the secular priests of the church. Schools, trades, civil government, and hospitals were established in the villages. Early attempts were made to prepare indigenous clergy, but after disheartening experiences, most of the church authorities agreed that the natives were not sufficiently dependable. Several early councils and for a time several monastic orders specifically forbade the ordination of non-Spanish priests.

The church in Brazil developed more slowly than in the Spanish colonies. Although six Jesuits arrived as early as 1549, only seven bishoprics existed at the time of independence. As in Spanish America, the religious orders bravely supported royal edicts commanding decent treatment for the Indians, but the practice of royal governors and landholders, who wanted Indians as slaves, won out over theory. The Jesuits, often criticized for amassing economic power, were expelled from Brazil in 1759.

An explosive situation and a significant number of uprisings both in the black and Indian populations resulted from the large numbers of Africans brought as slaves to Brazil. By 1818 more than half the population (excluding the Indians in the interior) was black; 23 percent were white; 17 percent, mestizo; and 7 percent, Indian.

Missions. Real efforts were made by the kings to christianize the indigenous population, as stipulated in the concordat. After the initial discovery of the Americas, the conquistadors were always well accompanied by priests, chiefly Franciscans, Dominicans, and Augustinians. Within fifty years members of these orders numbered over eight hundred in Mexico alone. Thereafter, the Jesuits and other orders added strength to the missionary effort.

The method of the missionaries, in general, was to uproot old rites and most external manifestations of Indian religion (on the principle of *tabula rasa*) in order to teach the true, Catholic religion. After an initial and not too successful attempt to use translators, many of the priests determined to learn the native languages. Evangelization was carried out in two different ways in the sixteenth century: (1) in the *encomienda* a priest was assigned large numbers of natives for pastoral care, indoctrination, and administration of the sacraments; (2) itinerant priests went from village to village, often suffering great hardships, preaching, baptizing, and defending the Indians against abuse. Although force was still used when necessary, many Indians were converted by peaceful means through the direct approach of the priests. Unfortunately, the good done was often subverted by the subsequent incorporation of the new Christians into the forced labor system.

Historians differ as to the culpability of the Spaniards in their Christianization of New Spain (Mexico, which included what is now Texas and the southwest United States) and of Peru (which included parts of Colombia, Ecuador, Bolivia, and Chile). That there was unspeakable cruelty and that large sections of the Indian population were decimated are clear historical facts. It is equally clear that many priests, like Las Casas (e.g., Montolinia, Valdieso, Anchieta, Zumárraga, and Juan del Valle) fought for Indian rights against civil leaders, plantation and mine owners, and even other clerics. A body of ordinances called *New Laws for the Indies* was adopted in 1542, papal encyclicals were issued (e.g., that of Paul III in 1537), and royal edicts were emitted by both Spanish and Portuguese kings, all of which required just treatment of the Indians.

A key point at issue is the number of Indians present in the Americas at the time of the Conquest. Estimates vary from six million to nearly a hundred million. The Brazilian J. V. Cesár, a member of the National Indigenist Council, estimates thirty-five million both at the time of the Conquest and in the late twentieth century (*Atualização* 12, Belo Horizonte, 1981, p. 27). Sherburne F. Cook and Woodrow Borah carefully estimated that the nearly seventeen million Indians in central Mexico in 1532 were reduced to just over one million by 1608 (*The Indian Population of Central Mexico, 1531–1610*, Berkeley, 1960, p. 48). The exaggerated claims for baptisms must be viewed critically: Pedro de Gante claimed fourteen thousand in one day; Bishop Zumárraga of Mexico reported that Franciscans alone had baptized more than one million by 1531. Another chronicler claimed that more than ten million had been baptized solely by Franciscans and Dominicans by the mid-seventeenth century.

The Jesuits, admitted to Brazil in 1549, Peru in 1568, and Mexico in 1572, largely displaced the Mercedarians as a missionary agency. They joined the Franciscans, Augustinians, and Dominicans as the chief executives of mission in the seventeenth and eighteenth centuries. While all the orders served sacrificially and in diverse ways of evangelization, the secular priests tended to the Spanish and mestizo population, and the Jesuits dedicated much of their effort to education and to the establishment of reductions, Indian villages established by the Spanish. They, as well as the other orders, studied the native languages, wrote grammars and dictionaries, and published texts for study. They founded universities to prepare professionals in law and medicine, implant Tridentine theology, and teach arts and languages. The colleges and seminaries founded by the monastic orders paralleled the colonial universities established by royal license, such as the universities of Mexico, Santo Domingo, and Lima. The latter prepared candidates for the secular clergy, while the religious orders each prepared their own candidates. The Jesuits were never really integrated into the episcopal system.

The schools were often developed on land received by royal concession, donated by rich ranchers, given as payment for crimes or as testaments, or contributed by the clergy or members of the order. The efficient operation of these estates covered the cost of the schools and generated capital for further investments and for the respective orders. For example, the landed property of forty-five of the largest Jesuit estates, distributed in diverse regions of Mexico, included a total of 1,100,874 hectares (1 hectare = 2.471 acres) in 1767, less than two centuries after the arrival of the Society of Jesus in Mexico. The greatest concentrations of Indians and mestizo workers were in the smaller plots (500 to 1,000 hectares), while the larger ones (100,000 to 200,000 hectares) were in largely unpopulated areas.

Throughout Latin America the Indian villages organized in the sixteenth century frequently took on the more ordered form called reductions in the seventeenth and eighteenth centuries. In particular, the Franciscans, Dominicans, and the Jesuits established reductions in the areas of California and Mexico, Colombia and Venezuela, Ecuador and Peru, and Brazil and Paraguay. Most noted for their organization and extension were those among the Guaraní people of Brazil, Paraguay, and northern Argentina.

The social organization of the reductions reflected the theocratic character of the Jesuit order: a religious communism strictly ordered and based upon absolute obedience to the Jesuit fathers. The more than thirty reductions of Paraguay, with 3,500 or more Indians in each, occupied a total area of 53,904 square kilometers, with an additional zone of influence comprising over 315,000 square kilometers. The total population reached 150,000 in 1743.

The Indians who entered the reductions were like indentured servants: some entered by personal choice or as a penalty for crimes; as prisoners of war; as purchased property; and some were born in the village. They were bound for life to the mission; their life and work were strictly controlled, and their passive obedience tended to result in an attitude of stoical fatalism. Such was their dependence that after the expulsion of the Jesuit order in 1767 by the Portuguese and Spanish kings, the missions fell into decadence. Natives had not been schooled to provide leadership, to ward off the attacks of the encroaching Spanish or Portuguese seeking lands and slave labor, or to adapt to the new social and political context. Within thirty years half the Indians in Paraguay and Brazil had scattered, many to the nearly inaccessible interior. By the early nineteenth century, no missions remained. By the exclusion of the more than 2,200 Jesuits, the empire lost one of its most cohesive forces.

The success of the missions in colonial times remains a highly controversial issue. The positions taken by various scholars disagree with respect to the relative degree of adaptation or change accomplished by the evangelization. Some basic views are the following:

1. Only an external imposition of liturgy and ecclesiastical forms upon the pagan religion was accomplished. (George Kubler, Julio Jiménez Rueda, J. C. Mariátegui)
2. A kind of syncretism was attained, either by a mixture or a juxtaposition of the Christian and pagan religions. (Pedro Borges Morán)
3. An incomplete evangelization was effected, producing a genuine change through progressive catechesis. (Enrique Dussel)
4. The Indians essentially became Christians; the purity of their faith depended much on the methods of evangelism used. (Constantino Bayle, Fernando de Armas Medina)

The missionary strategy of Catholics and Protestants in the nineteenth and twentieth centuries was profoundly affected by their views on this question.

Later conflicts and crises. The church in the New World faced seemingly insuperable difficulties. The royal claims to the lands in the Americas and to its peoples were contested by many. The Indians and blacks often revolted; the Inquisition was needed to maintain internal order and loyalty; the Protestant nations, through pirates and colonists, contested Iberian exclusiveness; and, finally, local crises shattered the empire.

In the eighteenth century, a major Indian rebellion erupted under the leadership of Tupac Amarú (1742–1781), a lineal descendant of the great Inca chieftain of the same name. Educated by the Jesuits and accorded royal honors and wealth, he was recognized by his people as the heir of the Inca, but he defended them in vain before the Spanish authorities.

Finally, he organized an army of seventy to eighty thousand poorly equipped men. Bolivia, southern Peru, and the north of Argentina soon were under the control of his forces. He hoped that the Spanish could be conciliated and the two peoples could live side by side in peace, but the Spanish authorities called for reinforcements from Buenos Aires and Lima, and within six months Túpac Amaru was captured, horribly tortured, and torn apart by horses tied to his limbs, which were later displayed on poles in rebellious Indian villages. Thousands had joined the revolt, plundering and destroying everything Spanish they could find. Estimates of the total number of victims on both sides reached eighty thousand. The superior arms and power of the Spanish and the Portuguese proved, as always, to be decisive.

The title of apostolic inquisitor was officially given to Zumárraga, bishop of Mexico, in 1535, although Cisneros had conceded the power of inquisitor to all the bishops of the "Indies" in 1517. Other inquisitors were named and exercised their function later in the sixteenth century. The Holy Office of the Inquisition was established by royal decree in 1569 for Mexico and Lima and in 1610 for Cartagena. Its principle objectives were to combat (1) depraved customs (cursing, immorality, witchcraft, lack of respect for civil or ecclesiastical authorities, etc.); (2) heresy (religious or political); and (3) Jewish beliefs and customs. In the sixteenth century 902 cases were processed, 600 were found guilty, and 17 were executed. Estimates place the total number killed at about a hundred. The Inquisition served as a police court for the church in the reforming of wayward clergy, the censure of objectionable literature and plays, the securing of orthodox doctrine, and the punishment of captured sea pirates from Protestant nations. In all this it was largely successful. Some Indians were executed for idolatry before 1575, but thereafter they were judged to be too new in the faith, too weak, and too much like children to be subject to the judgment of the Inquisition.

Between 1529 and 1550 the Protestant Welser Colony settled in northern Venezuela, having received extensive political territory from Charles V. The plan included colonization and trade, especially of black slaves. Three hundred colonists arrived in 1530 and five hundred in 1535, but a lack of workers, anarchy, misery, and bankruptcy practically ended the project, with revocation of the royal concession occurring in 1550.

A French colony of three hundred, mostly Huguenots, with some Catholics, arrived in Brazil in 1555 and 1558, accompanied by pastors from Geneva. The French vice-admiral in charge of the colony broke the agreement of nonintervention in religious matters, and tried and executed three Calvinists. The remaining colonists were totally defeated by the Portuguese in 1567, and the colony came to an end.

Dutch colonists established plantations and factories in northeastern Brazil around 1630. Two "classes" (presbyteries) were founded, and two missionaries, with the help of seven fellow pastors, established mission posts, translated the Bible into Tupí, and took steps for the evangelization of the blacks. The Protestant governor was too tolerant of diverse religious views for some and was recalled. The project came to an official end in 1654. Two chiefs of Indian tribes converted by Dutch missionaries were severely persecuted by the Portuguese authorities.

The church in Latin America faced a growing crisis toward the end of the colonial period. The decadence of the Spanish Bourbon dynasty and its loss of control of the seas contributed to the weakening of the royalist position in the colonies, and Enlightenment thought challenged the existing social structures. Widespread libertinism and immorality, as well as jealous criticism of the church for its extensive possessions (nearly half of the land in Mexico by 1800), aggravated anticlericalism. Finally, the shift from an economy built on trading precious metals to an agriculturally oriented system created serious difficulties for many businessmen and laborers. The church was to struggle for its place in a new world of independent nations.

Church and National States (1808–1960). The liberation of Spanish and Portuguese America from European political control began a radically new period of Latin American church history. No longer did the kings function as the official heads of the church and its mission. The wealthier, educated Creoles (Spanish people born in the Americas) took over the reins of government (both in the church and state) from the Spanish-born elite. The Creoles formed about 20 percent of the population in 1800 and exercised control over the mestizos (mixed Indian and white, 26 percent), Indians (46 percent), and blacks (8 percent).

By the end of the nineteenth century the majority of the population in Guatemala and Bolivia was indigenous; the majority in Mexico, El Salvador, Honduras, Nicaragua, Colombia, Venezuela, Ecuador, Peru, and Paraguay was mestizo; that in Costa Rica, Cuba, Puerto Rico, Chile, Argentina, Uruguay, and Brazil was white; and that in Panama and the Dominican Republic was mulatto.

A different situation existed in the Protestant lands of British Guiana and Dutch Guiana (Surinam). Both had been governed by the Dutch until Britain took the part that was to bear its name during the Napoleonic wars. Blacks and mulattos formed over half of the population in British Guiana, and over 20 percent in Surinam. However, with the abolition of slavery, Hindus, Javanese, Portuguese, and Chinese were brought in as laborers. Indigenes were few. Most of the population became Christian, except for the Hindus. The majority were Protestants; some were Roman Catholics. In Surinam, the Moravians, who had begun work in 1738, were the largest group. In British Honduras and French Guiana the greater part of the population was Roman Catholic, with Protestant minorities.

Identity crisis. It is clear that the emancipation from Spanish rule in Spanish and Portuguese America was a rebellion of the elite. Scarcely 4 percent of the masculine population could vote. The great mass of the population reacted to the change of "lords" with indifference. At times some fought or served as cannon fodder in the cause of emancipation, but socioeconomic structures remained basically unaltered for the great majority. A liberal facade concealed the awful reality of the misery and slavery of the masses.

The rising spirit of nationalism, stimulated and exploited by foreign interference, destroyed hopes for a confederation of Latin American nations, and, consequently, for a united church. Simon Bolívar's plan to unite Colombia, Venezuela, and Ecuador failed, as did the attempted union of Bolivia and Peru in 1838 and the confederation of Central America in 1839.

The majority of the episcopacy, which had been named by the king, initially opposed the independence movement, while many (in some countries, most) of the regular and secular clergy actively participated in it. The patriots wanted to foster a national church but had no patience with those who had militated against the revolution. Many of the new states, such as Argentina (1824), Bolivia (1826), Nicaragua (1830), Colombia (1861), and Mexico (1917), confiscated ecclesiastical properties, especially in rural areas.

The leaders of the new nations believed they inherited the rights of the crown, including its authority over the churches. Religious hospitals passed to state control; the state was the administrator of the tithes (in some cases, they were discontinued); the religious and secular priests were declared responsible to their new "lords" and not to any foreigner; and the Inquisition was suspended. Many national constitutions affirmed that "the Catholic Roman Apostolic religion is the religion of the nation," as it was expressed in Argentina (1813). Nine years later Argentine president Bernardino Rivadavia canceled the right of priests to be tried in eccelesiastical courts, abolished tithes, and closed the smaller monasteries. Such actions eventually took place in most of the republics, but they were considered reforms and not a rejection of the church.

Many bishops, priests, and monks voluntarily left the revolutionary situation for reasons of conscience and loyalty to the previously constituted authorities; others were expelled. In many places this occasioned a severe shortage of priests and a lack of bishops. Pope Pius VII first ordered obedience to the restored Spanish king Ferdinand in 1816. This proved to be an impossibility, creating a crisis for the national churches. The process of official recognition of the new republics began with the naming of bishops by Gregory XVI in 1831.

Thus, during the first part of the nineteenth century, the political tendency of the republics was conservative; the church was recognized, but was subject to state control. The second half of the century and the first decades of the twentieth, however, marked a progressive rupture between church and state. The influx of European liberalism and positivism, the Masonic movement, and the increasing spirit of secularization were decisive factors in promoting the crisis. Such reforms as the official adoption of civil jurisdiction over education, the public use of cemeteries, and freedom of worship became realities in different countries at different times (in Colombia as late as 1930). The struggle of the church in this period was to conserve and restore the church of Christendom, what is often called the *corpus Christianum*, or the integralist vision, akin to the medieval model of the union of the (Catholic) church and state. This, however, proved to be a losing battle.

In the revolutionary period, the crisis between church and state demanded primary attention, and mission played a secondary role. The expulsion of priests and religious orders, repeated across the Americas, caused disruption. In the latter half of the nineteenth century, many religious orders returned to engage in traditional missionary activity. As in previous centuries, however, sickness, wars, and poverty caused the Indian population to decline, from 35 percent of the total inhabitants in 1800 to 8.8 percent in 1950.

The arrival of large contingents of immigrants, mostly Catholics, particularly from Italy, Spain, and Portugal, rapidly increased the relative size of the minority group—the whites. From 19 million in 1800 (fewer than 20 percent of the total population), the white population rose to 63 million in 1900 (over 35 percent) and 163 million in 1950 (44.5 percent). This surge of immigration also promoted the colonization of large untapped areas of Latin America.

The history of the Protestant churches in Latin America took a new turn as a result of the wars of independence. The opposition to the hegemony of Spain and Portugal (and control of the seas by the British and Dutch), which opened doors to commerce with and immigration from northern Europe; the surge of anticlericalism because of the negative attitudes of much of the episcopacy toward the revolution; and the new currents of thought favoring secularization, liberty, and tolerance all prepared the way. Progress, however, was slow; estimates place the number of Protestant missionaries in all Latin America by the end of the nineteenth century at less than nine hundred.

Most of the growth of the Protestant church in the twentieth century occurred because of immigration. Though by far the greatest number of immigrants were Latin and Catholic, the majority of the English and German immigrants were Protestant. The English tended to settle in the cities, while the Germans settled in rural areas. The River Plate region in Argentina and Uruguay early received large numbers of Protestants, and worship services were established, in their respective languages, for Anglicans in 1820, for Scottish Presbyterians in 1825, for German Lutherans in 1843, and for Italian Waldensians in 1859. They were followed by Russian-German contingents, Swiss and Dutch Reformed, Scandinavian Lutherans, Armenian Congregationalists, and Slavic Baptists. In general, these immigrant groups ministered pastorally to their own people without any real interest in the evangelization of others.

The first Protestant missionary to arrive in Spanish America was James Thomson of the British and Foreign

Bible Society. He came to Argentina in 1818 and, using the English community as a base, promoted the Lancaster system of education, with the Bible as a study text for reading. The new governments were open to this method, as were some Catholic clergy. Thomson and his associates sold thousands of Bibles in Spanish, made visits to at least nine of the Latin American republics, and established centers for Bible distribution in key cities. Throughout the century representatives and missionaries of the Bible societies frequented many cities across the continent. By 1900 they had distributed two million Bibles, testaments, and scripture portions.

In addition to the work of the Bible societies and the impulse given by immigration groups, missionaries from the various denominations overseas constituted a third factor in evangelization. Reports of the work of the Bible societies had aroused much interest in Protestant lands. The earliest mission boards to begin work were English, followed by missionaries from the United States, Canada, and Sweden.

The methods used included public preaching and personal witnessing directed toward a radical conversion from Catholicism. Methodists and Presbyterians in particular established both primary and secondary schools. With the rise in the level of education, religious publications became more important. Only nine medical institutions were established during the nineteenth century in Latin America, as compared to 94 in Africa and 415 in Asia. Little work was done among the indigenous peoples in this period, except by English Anglicans and, in Argentina, Bolivia, Paraguay, and Chile, by the South American Missionary Society. Especially noteworthy was the conversion of the Miskito Indians of Nicaragua through the work of the Moravians and the formation of a Moravian community of fifteen thousand in that country.

A characteristic inclination of the missions, in addition to their strong anti-Catholicism, was to become replicas of the sending agencies with the missionary as the director and teacher; there was only a partial adaptation to the receiving culture. This marked the Protestant church as foreign and exogenous to Latin society.

Conflict and growth. Several new factors profoundly affected the history of the church near the turn of the twentieth century. First, the center of gravity for commercial and political power shifted from Europe and England to the United States. In 1880 Great Britain had four times more investments in Latin America than the United States; in 1920 they were equal; but by 1950 the United States had four times more investments than Britain. The governments of the Latin American nations were controlled by oligarchies and dictators who frequently maintained close relations with their big northern neighbor.

Second, the twentieth century brought a serious confrontation between the Catholic and the Protestant churches. The Catholics accused the Protestants of introducing liberal individualism that disintegrated the family and community, and of serving as an instrument of North American imperialism. The Protestants denounced Catholicism as pagan and unfit to evangelize the Latin American peoples, as well as being responsible in large part for their poverty.

Third, the rapid population growth of Latin America increased the Catholic church membership to nearly half the worldwide total, while the Protestant churches likewise experienced rapid expansion through immigration and the missions.

Fourth, the character of society was changing rapidly from rural to urban. With the industrialization of the large cities, increasing numbers of people migrated toward metropolitan centers in hopes of improving their marginal social situation. This migration created shanty towns called *villas de miseria* or *favellas.* Church ties and loyalties were much weaker in the city than they were in rural areas (Azevedo, 1980, pp. 121, 122).

Catholicism. The nineteenth century had been marked by hostility to the church in most of the republics; frequently modified concordats were signed beginning in 1852. In the twentieth century new constitutions and/or concordats brought increasing liberty for most religious groups, but Catholicism continued to receive official recognition in countries such as Peru, Argentina, and Paraguay. Many of the national Catholic churches received state subsidies and were subject to varying degrees of state control. Other countries (Chile, Uruguay, Brazil) progressively introduced a separation of church and state that permitted freedom of worship as long as this did not oppose Christian morality and public order. Until Vatican II, however, such permission often remained an empty promise because of strong anti-Protestant popular sentiment and controls exercised by the Roman church. State funds supported missions to the Indians in order better to exercise national control and to use the mission as an instrument of civilization and culture, as in the Concordat of Colombia in 1902. Mexico is an exception to this general trend. The revolution of 1917 resulted in the confiscation of all church properties and the termination of the church's role in education and government. Many priests were deported and church buildings damaged. The relation between the churches and the state remains strained.

The conservatism of Latin American Catholicism at the turn of the century is clearly reflected in the first plenary Latin American Council held in Rome in 1899. The 998 articles produced examine the evils of contemporary society—liberalism, superstition, Masonry, paganism, Protestantism, socialism—and the methods of combating them. No new approaches to these problems were defined by the thirteen archbishops and forty-one bishops from Latin America. The agenda did indicate, however, the revival of Rome's interest in the long-neglected continent.

From this point on, the church began to deepen its intellectual and cultural foundations in the republics. Through new agreements made during the first decades of the century, educational rights were restored to the Catholic church. Many church schools were founded on primary and secondary levels, crowned by the establishment of many church universities, as in Bogotá (1937), Lima (1942), Medellín (1945), Río de Janeiro and São Paulo (1947), Quito (1956), Buenos Aires and Córdoba (1960), and Valparaíso and Guatemala (1961).

One result of this intellectual revival was the study of the neo-Thomism propounded by Jacques Maritain (1882–1973), which provided the foundation for a new social consciousness. A broad movement called Catholic Action, born in Europe and promoted by Pius XI (1922–1939), took root in the Latin American republics after 1929, with strong youth participation. Catholic Action was basically a lay movement under clerical control, directed at the raising of the Christian conscience, particularly that of the upper class with respect to the needs of the common people. It was also aimed at gaining political and civic control for the Catholic church, thus restoring by democratic means the power lost during the tumultuous nineteenth century. The way was prepared for this movement by the organization of Catholic labor unions, agricultural cooperatives, and other groups, stimulated by the papal encyclical *Rerum novarum* (1890). The Christian Democratic political parties that emerged in Latin America after 1930 owe their inspiration to this attempt to reinstate Catholic Christendom by the ballot box. The movement has been basically reformist in character and includes many of the conservative sections of the church. Between 1930 and 1950 the church and state sometimes cooperated for the victory of populist movements (for instance, those of Eduardo Frei in Chile and Juan Domingo Perón in Argentina).

Since 1960 new winds have blown across the continent. The century began with compromises and agreements between church and state; next, Catholicism tried to restore its *corpus Christianum* in conformity to the new situation: and then came the meeting of Vatican II, followed by the meeting of the Latin American Council of Bishops at Medellín (1968), where clear steps were taken toward an identification with the poor.

This last change did not occur all at once. Innovating currents had been present since the fifties, particularly in France and northern Europe, with repercussions in Latin America. The Catholic Action groups shifted from the Italian model to that of the French, from a concentration on doctrinal correctness to existential priorities. Additional contributing factors were the formation of community reflection groups, a new openness to biblical studies, liturgical renewal, and catechetical instruction directed toward responsible living. This marked a significant break from the traditional alignment with the elite and powerful.

Those who favored the new options were of two groups: the progressives, who leaned toward a development model of social reform, and the revolutionaries, who believed that radical structural change, with or without violence, was essential. A third group supported by such organizations as Opus Dei and the Cursillos de Cristiandad, was reactionary, striving to restore Tridentine theology and medieval structures. The majority of Catholics, however, may be considered conservative, being disinclined to identify with any of the other three groups. These four groups—the progressives, the revolutionaries, the traditionalists, and the conservatives—characterize the attitudes of the Catholic Church toward society up to the present.

Two types of organization characterize the Catholic churches: the regular dioceses, archdioceses, and congregations, on the one hand, and the mission territories on the other. The number of dioceses and mission territories increased in all of Latin America from about 100 in 1900 (organized during four centuries) to 547 by 1965. In Brazil in particular, the number of ecclesiastical districts increased from 12 in 1889 to 217 in 1975. According to CELAM (Council of Latin American Bishops), the total number of priests in 1967 was 42,589, of whom 15,381, or 36 percent, were foreign, mainly from Spain (54 percent) and the United States (20 percent). The heavy dependence on foreign assistance indicates the more basic problems of the lack of new priests and the abandonment of the office. In 1900 the ratio of priest to population was 1 to 3,829; in 1963 it had dropped to 1 to 4,891. One must remember that only 66.6 percent of the diocesan priests and 31.7 percent of the orders are in congregational service. Thus the number of members under the care of each priest should be doubled to give a true picture.

Since the priests tend to concentrate in the cities, the rural areas feel the shortage more. Prien (1978, p. 1067) gives statistics for Guatemala, from the largest city to the smaller ones: in Guatemala City there is one priest for 5,970 members; in Quetzaltenango, the ratio is 1 to 9,374; in Zacapá, 1 to 16,216; in Jalapa, 1 to 20,556; and in Maturín, 1 to 24,200. The percentages of the monks and nuns working in the capitals of their respective countries in the sixties were as follows: Santiago, 46 percent; Montevideo, 78 percent; San José (Costa Rica), 75 percent; Caracas, 53 percent; and Quito, 45 percent. Estimates vary in placing the number of active Catholics from 10 to 25 percent of the total membership. Papal statistics indicate that in 1970 about 90 percent of the Latin American population was Catholic. David B. Barrett (1982) estimated in mid-1980 over 329 million affiliated Catholics in all Latin America, or 88.6 percent of the population (p. 783).

Some countries, such as Brazil, Peru, Ecuador, and Colombia, have missionary territories. These function directly under the jurisdiction of the papal Sacred Congregation of the Doctrine of the Faith. Most of the missionaries have come from the monastic orders; some of them were prepared in the Pontifical Seminary for Foreign Missions established in 1920. The number of Christians in areas considered mission districts (largely Indians) has multiplied rapidly: in 1911, there were 472,000; in 1925, 1,675,000; and in 1938, nearly two million.

As of 1980 the vast majority of the total Latin American Indian population was found in five lands: Bolivia (70 percent of its population), Guatemala (60 percent), Peru (55 percent), Mexico (20 percent), and Ecuador. The largest homogeneous language group is the Aymares in Bolivia (one million) and Peru (a half million). Catholic missionary orders have made significant advances among these populations. During World War II the American Catholic Missionary Society shifted much of its efforts to Latin America, bringing in missionaries with previous experience in Asia and Africa. Many entered unchristianized areas in the Amazon and the Andes, regions of difficult access for white civilization. Others worked in Central America, Colombia, Venezuela, Chile, and Bolivia. On occasion they met with opposition from nationalistic governments, though this was more frequent in the case of Protestant missionaries.

Anthropologists and sociologists have criticized the mission effort severely, claiming the unnecessary destruction of Indian cultural and tribal values and accusing the church of collaborating, albeit inadvertently, with the state. Church authorities are sharply divided over the issue, some placing a higher priority on preserving Indian values and others on a vigorous program of evangelization and catechization.

Protestantism. Protestantism in Latin America may be divided into three groups: the historic churches, which arrived through immigration; the mission churches, which were begun by missionaries and foreign resources; and the popular churches or movements that grew spontaneously, without significant outside assistance. Most of the immigrant groups arrived in the nineteenth and early twentieth centuries; in 1914 they constituted about one half of the Protestant community. These groups are strongest in Brazil, Argentina, Chile, Uruguay, and Bolivia, where lands and opportunities for a new life had opened in a temperate zone.

The mission groups represented most of the other half of the total Protestant community in 1914, when their membership was estimated at approximately 470,000. They, more than the historic churches, dedicated their efforts to the Latin population, particularly to the Roman Catholics, but also to the Indians. The increase of Protestant missionaries sent to the southern countries was dramatic: there were 1,438 missionaries in 1903; 2,951 in 1938; 4,488 in 1949; and 11,363 in 1969. This meant an increase of 690 percent, compared with 283 percent for Africa and 39 percent for all of Asia in the same period. What was true for personnel was equally true for the efforts expended in money, religious education, Bible institutes, schools, and seminaries.

The third group of Protestants consists almost exclusively of the Pentecostal churches. Their rise coincides with the growth of popular religiosity in the Catholic Church. Those attracted to the Pentecostals tend to be from the lower economic class—the socially segregated, laborers, and the unemployed. There is an emphasis on spontaneous participation in worship, prayers with audible sharing by all, healing, speaking in tongues, opening ministry to everyone qualified by the Holy Spirit, and meetings in homes. The recognition of every member as a bearer of God's Spirit gives a sense of belonging and personal recognition. The growth has been phenomenal. Having begun in 1910, Pentecostalism in 1980 constituted about 70 percent of the estimated eighteen million in the Latin American Protestant community.

The relatively small contingent of evangelicals (the term equivalent to Protestants in Latin America) at the beginning of this century stimulated movements of cooperation among the denominations. The Panama Conference of 1916, with few Latin Americans participating, affirmed what the planners of the 1910 Edinburgh mission conference did not accept, namely, that Latin America was a mission field. The Panama delegates resolved that responsibility for mission in the Latin American countries should be divided among the various mission societies to avoid competition and duplication of efforts. Cooperation was sought in publication of literature, education, regional conferences, missionary meetings, university work, social reform, and preparation of new missionaries. Great efforts were made to approach and convert the elite through education. Three-fourths of the Latin American population could not read in 1900. An effort was made to teach the illiterates in order to give them personal access to the Bible. Other continental meetings were held in Montevideo (1925) and Havana (1929). Later, the Conferencia Evangélica Latinoamericana (CELA) met in Buenos Aires (1949), Lima (1961), and Buenos Aires (1969), with chiefly Latin American participation.

Beginning in 1920, Henry Strachan (later followed by his son, Kenneth) and Juan Varetto launched the mass campaigns that for several decades marked the new approach of the missions. Many of the evangelical churches presented their preaching and teaching in the public arena, some for the first time. This helped to overcome the sense of inferiority and lethargy that had characterized many of the historic churches as well as some of the mission groups.

Reasons given for the increased Protestant activity at this time include the following:

1. the rapid growth of the economic and cultural penetration of the United States into Latin America, which awakened the interest of the churches in mission possibilities there and opened the doors to the coming of the missionaries;
2. the changing social and intellectual situation in Latin America, which made the peoples more accessible to a different presentation of the Christian faith;
3. the active participation of Latin Americans in the promotion and direction of the work, which made Protestantism better adapted to the Latin American situation;
4. the Asian wars, causing large numbers of Asian missionaries from faith missions to come to Latin America and contribute new methods and policies for the work;
5. the growing economic power of the churches in the

United States, which made possible the large investments in personnel and funds over a sustained period (Azevedo, 1980, p. 133).

These last factors apply more to the first two Protestant groups than to the Pentecostals, for whom the second and third are most relevant.

Like the Catholics, the Protestant churches in general have been divided on social problems. In most countries during the last few decades positions have had to be taken with reference to military dictatorships and the doctrine of the national security state. Often Protestants and Catholics have suffered persecution, torture, and death for their convictions. Protestant attitudes may be divided into three groups: traditional (obedience to the state in all except false worship); progressive (the right to disobey the state on questions of social justice and the duty to struggle for the establishment of a just society); and radical (a recognition of the need to overthrow unjust social structures by violence, if necessary).

It is impossible to state with accuracy the number of Protestants in Latin America. Barrett (1982, p. 783) affirms that in 1980 they constituted 4.9 percent of the population, or approximately eighteen million in the total community. Dussel (1974, p. 192) gives the following percentages of total population for 1961:

>10%	Chile, British Guiana, Surinam, French Guiana
5–10%	Brazil
2–5%	Mexico, Guatemala, El Salvador, Nicaragua, Panama
1–2%	Argentina, Uruguay, Paraguay, Bolivia, Honduras
1%	Peru, Ecuador, Colombia, Venezuela, Costa Rica

Read, Monterroso, and Johnson estimate the number of Protestant adult communicant members at 4,915,477 in 1967.

Orthodox churches. A variety of Orthodox churches are represented in Latin America. Around 140,000 Arabic-speaking Syrians had come to Argentina and Brazil by 1915. Most were under the spiritual guidance of the patriarch of Antioch, though some priests came from Russia to provide pastoral care. Somewhat less than half a million Orthodox came as refugees in the years following the Russian Revolution and World War II. Many were lost to Orthodoxy, some identifying with spiritism, others with Protestantism. Greek, Russian, and Syrian congregations and dioceses have been organized in Mexico, Brazil, Argentina, Uruguay, Peru, Colombia, Ecuador, and Chile, while the Russian Orthodox also have churches in Venezuela and Paraguay. There is a Russian bishop in São Paulo and an archbishop for Latin America in Buenos Aires. A relatively few number of Uniates, Maronites, and Ruthenians (groups that maintain their national liturgy but acknowledge the supremacy of the pope in Rome) are also present, particularly in Brazil, Argentina, and Chile.

The Church and Signs of New Life. Since the mid-twentieth century, signs of new life have begun to appear both in Roman Catholic and Protestant churches. Efforts to identify with the realities of the Latin American situation do not exclude strong currents of traditional conservatism which, on the Catholic side, continue to support elitist power groups and, on the Protestant side, reject responsibility for societal improvement. But the new movements clearly point to significant changes in church attitudes and programs.

Catholicism. The organization of the Latin American Council of Bishops (CELAM) in 1955 gave to the Roman Catholic churches of the region a formal unity and coherence not found on other continents. This time the unity was not buttressed by civil force or restricted by the *patronato* that had given the national states certain rights over the churches. The chief characteristic of CELAM was its concern for the whole of human life and society.

Evidence of the new weight accorded to the Latin American churches was the large representation at Vatican II (1962–1965). The 601 Latin American bishops (22.33 percent of the total) were second in number only to the Europeans, with 31.6 percent. No Latin American priests had been present at Trent (1545–1563), and only 61 bishops had been at Vatican I (1870).

Catholic scholars judge the second general conference of CELAM at Medellín in 1968 to be a watershed in its history. Before Medellín the pastoral task had been conceived as the dispensation of sacramental grace within the contours of a Christian society. Medellín recognized that society was pluralistic, and that in this society a transformation of traditional values was possible and necessary. The popular manifestations of the faith needed to be impregnated by the word of the gospel. Devotional acts to the saints had to be changed from intercessory devices to models for life in imitation of Christ. The fatalism nurtured by the traditional sacramental view was rejected, and in its place an emphasis was placed on the pastoral task of educating people to become active collaborators with God in the fulfillment of their destiny. A call was made for organizing grass-roots community groups for Bible study and joint action in meeting social needs, especially in marginal economic areas.

In the eleven years between Medellín and CELAM III in Puebla (1979), more than two hundred thousand small ecclesiastical communities began to function effectively, particularly in Brazil, but also in other countries across the continent. Lay groups, sometimes with pastoral presence, were questioning the unchangeableness of their social plight in the light of biblical teaching and were becoming active participants for change. The Puebla Conference took up these concerns by first analyzing the Latin American situation, then making its recommendations. Recognition of the dignity of the human person, and particularly of the rights of the poor and oppressed, was declared to be at the heart of the gospel message.

The Puebla bishops were united in their harsh judgment of capitalism, Marxism, and the national security state: capitalism, for increasing the distance between rich and poor people and nations; Marxism, for sacrificing many Christian values and creating false utopias sustained by force; and the national security state, for supporting dictatorships that abuse police power to deprive human beings of their rights. Differences arise among Christians, however, when basic causes of poverty and oppression are defined and concrete programs for change proposed.

The theology of liberation was formulated after 1960 by theologians and social scientists through reflection on Latin American social and political reality and attempts to transform its oppressive structures. The best-known Catholic exponents include Gustavo Gutierrez (Peru), Juan Luis Segundo (Uruguay), Segundo Galilea (Chile), José Miranda (Mexico), Hugo Assman and Leonardo Boff (Brazil), Jon Sobrino (El Salvador), and Enrique Dussel (Argentina). They affirm the necessity of moving toward a social system characterized by priority for the poor, use of the social sciences in the analysis of reality, recognition of the ideological base from which every person develops religious understanding; and importance given to praxis—active and obedient discipleship, supported by theory, with the eventual goal of the transformation of society. This theology has been variously interpreted in Latin American church hierarchy. The fervor with which it is debated, the mutual concern about the large majority of marginalized peoples, and the evangelical zeal for ministry mark a significant renovation in Catholicism.

Protestantism. Protestantism has likewise developed differently from its mother institutions. The dramatic growth of the Pentecostal church bears a resemblance to other moments in church history when the chief advances were made among the poor. In their search for identity, fulfillment, and meaning there is a strong similarity between the small, spontaneous Pentecostal groups and the Catholic grass-roots communities. The Pentecostals lack the structural cohesiveness and the social commitment of the Catholics, but the inner spiritual vitality, the concern for healing in the church's ministry, and the forthright heralding of the word of the gospel that characterize the Pentecostals have awakened responses from sectors of society largely unresponsive to the historic and mission churches.

In addition to the three Protestant consultations for Latin America (CELA) mentioned earlier, other Protestant ecumenical groups that have arisen since 1960 in response to social and spiritual crises and a felt need for cooperation include a Latin American youth organization (ULAJE, founded in 1941), various university student organizations, an educational commission (CELADEC, 1961), and an association of Protestant churches (UNELAM, 1965). This later group was subsumed into the Latin American Church Council (CLAI), officially organized in 1982, with a broad representation from the three sectors of the Protestant churches. A group of churches with less emphasis on social responsibility formed a parallel organization called the Evangelical Confraternity of Latin America (CONELA) the same year.

Theological education slowly became a priority for Protestantism. The movement called Seminary by Extension was born in Guatemala in an effort to further train a large percentage of pastors and laity who already lead churches. This new educational model has spread rapidly throughout Latin America, Africa, and Asia. Economic problems have made more traditional Western methods of theological education difficult. Hundreds of Bible institutes and theological seminaries were established to prepare pastoral leadership. A Latin American Committee for Theological Education (CLAET), composed of three regional groupings of institutions, was established in 1979.

Protestant theology has developed slowly. Most of the publications in Latin America have been translations from European and especially United States sources with more local writing in recent decades. The movement Church and Society in Latin America (ISAL) attempted to provide a theological basis for a Christian attitude toward oppressive social structures. Some of its early efforts formed part of the Protestant contribution to the theology of liberation; among its leading exponents are José Miguez-Bonino (Argentina), Rubem Alves (Brazil), and Sergio Arce (Cuba). Publications featuring reflections on this theme have come chiefly from centers of theological education in Buenos Aires, San José, Mexico City, and Puerto Rico. The Latin American Theological Fraternity (FTL) has stimulated writing by theologians across a wide spectrum of positions. These manifestations of the life of the church confirm the increasing integration of Protestantism into Latin America, the identification of its concerns on many pastoral levels with those of the Catholic Church (as on human rights issues), and the continuing missionary zeal characteristic of its heritage.

See Also Afro-Brazilian Religions; Afro-Surinamese Religions; Kardecism; Las Casas, Bartolomé de; Mesoamerican Religions, article on Contemporary Cultures; Political Theology.

Bibliography

General

The best single volume on Roman Catholic church history is Enrique D. Dussel's *Historia de la iglesia en América Latina*, 3d ed. (Barcelona, 1974), translated into English as *History of the Church in Latin America* (Grand Rapids, Mich., 1982). The book has an excellent bibliography according to geographical area but hardly refers to churches other than the Roman Catholic. On both Catholic and Protestant history, the Brazilian Israel Belo de Azevedo gives an excellent recent summary in Portuguese, *As Cruzadas inacabadas* (Rio de Janeiro, 1980). In the preparation of this article I found these two books particularly helpful.

Covering the whole of Latin America will be the series of ten regional volumes published by CEHILA, Comisión de Estudios de Historia de la Iglesia en América Latina, under the general editorship of Enrique D. Dussel, who will write an introductory volume. The goal is to interpret church history from the perspective of the poor and oppressed. Volume 7, *Colombia y Venezuela* (Salamanca, 1981), has appeared in Spanish; volumes 2.1 and 2.2, *Brazil* (Petropolis, Brazil, 1977–1980), have appeared in Portuguese. *Latin American Church Growth* by William R. Read, Victor M. Monterroso, and Harmon A. Johnson (Grand Rapids, Mich., 1969) presents a detailed compilation of statistics from the evangelical Protestant perspective with heavy emphasis on numerical growth. This book also appears in Spanish, *Avance evangélico en la América Latina* (El Paso, Tex., 1970), and in Portuguese, *O crescimiento da igreja no América Latina* (São Paulo, 1969). Prudencio Damboriena does much the same from the Catholic viewpoint in his *El protestantismo en América Latina,* vol. 1, *Etapas y métodos del protestantismo Latinoamericano,* and vol. 2, *La situación del protestantismo en los países Latino-americanos* (Bogotá, 1962–1963). These form numbers 12 and 13 of the valuable series FERES (Federación Internacional de los Institutas Católicos de Investigaciónes Sociales y Socio-religiosas), which provides documentation and socioreligious studies about Latin America published in forty-two volumes during the decade of the sixties. See also number 21 of the same series, *La iglesia en América Latina* by Isidoro Alonso (Bogotá, 1964), for a description of recent ecclesiastical structures of the Catholic Church. Some of the best general descriptions remain those of the veteran historian K. S. Latourette in his *Christianity in a Revolutionary Age: A History of Christianity in the Nineteenth and Twentieth Centuries,* 5 vols. (1958–1962; reprint, Westport, Conn., 1973); see volume 3, pages 284–352, and volume 5, pages 158–240. See also volumes 5 and 7 of his *A History of the Expansion of Christianity,* 7 vols. (1937–1945; reprint, Grand Rapids, Mich., 1970), pages 68–129 and 164–185, respectively. Two extensive works from the perspective of the United States are Donald M. Dozer's *Latin America: An Interpretative History* (New York, 1962), which has been translated into Portuguese as *América Latina: Una perspectiva histórica* (Porto Alegre, 1966); and Hubert Herring's *A History of Latin America from the Beginnings to the Present* (New York, 1961), which has been translated into Spanish as *Evolución histórica de América Latina* (Buenos Aires, 1972). Herring offers a comprehensive bibliography (pp. 831–845) with emphasis on English titles up to 1960. His history is ably complemented by Germán Arciniegas's *Latin America: A Cultural History* (New York, 1967). After working several years in El Salvador and Brazil, Hans-Jürgen Prien wrote his monumental 1,302-page *Die Geschichte des Christentums in Lateinamerika* (Göttingen, 1978), which has been translated into Spanish as *La historia del cristianismo en América Latina* (Salamanca, 1981). The series "Biblioteca de Autores Cristianos" (Library of Christian Authors) elucidates the Catholic interpretation of the church's history from the Conquest to independence in the two-volume *Historia de la iglesia en la América Española desde el Descubrimiento hasta comienzos del siglo XIX:* no. 248, *México, América Central* by Léon Lopetegui and Félix Zubillaga (Madrid, 1965), and no. 256, *Hemisferio Sur* by Antonio de Egana (Madrid, 1966).

Special Themes

Two brief but excellent analyses of the receiving cultures at the time of the Conquest are Laurette Séjourné's *América Latina: Antiguas culturas precolombinas* (Mexico City, 1971), which has been translated into German as *Altamerikanische Kulturen* (Frankfurt, 1971), and Henri Lehmann's *Les civilisations précolombiennes,* 7th ed. (Paris, 1977), which has been translated into Spanish as *Las culturas precolombinas* (Buenos Aires, 1960). One of the best histories of the relation between the church and state remains J. Lloyd Mecham's *Church and State in Latin America: A History of Politico-Ecclesiastical Relations,* 2d rev. ed. (Chapel Hill, N.C., 1966). The rising phenomenon of Pentecostalism receives careful attention in the studies of Christian Lalive d'Epinay, *El refugio de las masas: Estudio sociológico del protestantismo chileno* (Santiago, 1968), and Emilio Willems, *Followers of the New Faith: Culture Change and the Rise of Protestantism in Brazil and Chile* (Nashville, 1967). For a description of the *encomendero* system and other relevant themes, see Lewis Hanke's *The Spanish Struggle for Justice in the Conquest of America* (Pittsburgh, 1949). Gustavo Gutierrez describes the history of Latin American theology and formulates a new theological perspective in *Teología de la liberación: Historia, política y salvación* (Lima, 1971), which has been translated as *A Theology of Liberation: History, Politics and Salvation* (Maryknoll, N.Y., 1973). For statistics, see the *World Christian Encyclopedia,* edited by David B. Barrett (Oxford, 1982). A complete indexed bibliography of all theological works in Spanish and Portuguese is published annually in the *Bibliografía teológica comentada* (Buenos Aires, 1973–) by the Instituto Superior Evangélico de Estudios Teológicos (ISEDET). Introductions to sections are in Spanish with English summaries. See also *Latin America: A Guide to the Historical Literature,* edited by Charles C. Griffin (Austin, 1971).

New Sources

Boff, Leonardo. *Eccleiosogenesis: The Base Communities Reinvented the Church.* Translated by Robert R. Barr. Maryknoll, N.Y., 1986.

Ingraham, John M. *Mary, Michael, and Lucifer: Folk Catholicism in Central America.* Austin, Tex., 1986.

Ireland, Rowen. *Kingdom Come: Religion and Politics in Brazil.* Pittsburgh, 1992.

Levine, Daniel. *Popular Voices in Latin American Catholicism.* Princeton, N.J., 1992.

Martin, David. *Tongues of Fire: The Explosion of Protestantism in Latin America.* Oxford and Cambridge, Mass., 1990.

Míguez Bonino, José. *Faces of Latin American Protestantism.* 1993 Carnahan Lectures. Grand Rapids, Mich., 1997.

Stephen, Lynn, and James Dow, eds. *Class, Politics, and Popular Religion in Mexico and Central America.* Washington, D.C., 1990.

Stoll, David, and Virginia Garrard-Burnett, eds. *Rethinking Protestantism in Latin America.* Philadelphia, 1993.

SIDNEY H. ROOY (1987)
Revised Bibliography

CHRISTIANITY: CHRISTIANITY IN THE CARIBBEAN REGION

One of the distinctive characteristics of Caribbean Christianity is the racial and ethnic diversity of its adherents. A high proportion of the people of the region is either black or African American (mixed African and non-African descent). Although a large proportion of the black population was exposed only superficially to Christian teachings during the period of slavery beginning in the sixteenth century and continuing into the nineteenth, and despite extensive disillusionment with the historical churches in the decades immediately after emancipation, Christianity has continued to spread widely in the region. The long and close relationship between religion and sociopolitical doctrine in the societies from which the dominant class in the colonial period came has persisted in many parts of the Caribbean to the present day.

The Early Years. The sixteenth and seventeenth centuries have been called the missionary centuries in the New World. Priests accompanied the explorers, and Catholic and Protestant missionaries were an important part of pioneer settlements. In 1685 the Code Noir prescribed that all slaves in the French islands were to be instructed and baptized in the Roman Catholic religion. The colonists paid little attention to the code, especially the sections dealing with religious obligations that were opposed to their economic interests. Priests varied greatly during the first half of the eighteenth century; some were zealous about their duties, others attended only to the external aspects of religion. In 1764 the Jesuits in Haiti were accused of stirring up the slaves and were expelled from the colony. With the revolt of the slaves in 1791, the Catholic religion in Haiti almost disappeared.

The first Lutheran congregation was established in Saint Thomas, Danish West Indies, in 1666 and for two and one-half centuries the Lutheran church was the state church. In the late 1750s, a Lutheran mission for the slaves was established in the island. In some parts of the West Indies, in Barbados, for example, the early slaves brought from Africa were not permitted to become Christians. In 1700 the Anglicans organized the Society for the Propagation of the Gospel in Foreign Parts to preach to the heathen, that is, slaves and free men in North America and the West Indies.

Moravian (United Brethren) missionaries arrived in Saint Thomas in December 1732. Count Nikolaus von Zinzendorf, founder of Moravian missions, opposed the emancipation of the slaves and did not favor teaching them to read and write. In addressing the converts at a mass meeting in 1739, he exhorted them to be obedient to their masters, adding that "your conversion will make you free, not from the control of your masters, but simply from your wicked habits and thoughts, and all that makes you dissatisfied with your lot."

The work of Methodist missionaries in the Caribbean began in 1770, but the Methodist Missionary Society was not founded until 1789. Because it was difficult for missionaries to gain permission from the planters to enter many of the estates in the West Indies, both the Methodists and the Baptists used a system of slave leaders to supervise their followers. The black assistants visited the sick, held prayer meetings, and oversaw the conduct of the members in their charge.

One of the first Baptist missionaries to reach the West Indies was a manumitted slave from Virginia, George Liele (Lisle). Liele organized a church in Jamaica in 1783, and by 1791 had enrolled 450 members, all blacks and most of them slaves. In 1813 the Baptist Missionary Society began to send out missionaries from London. Despite the hostility they encountered, regular services were conducted and schools opened at Kingston, Spanish Town, Falmouth, and other places. Three missionaries were sent to Jamaica in 1800 by the Scottish Missionary Society, a nondenominational body. The established Church of Scotland began its work in Kingston in 1819, a program that was carried on later by the United Presbyterian church.

Social Structure and Caribbean Christianity. Differences in world view that developed in the Caribbean as religions there changed have been related, by Raymond T. Smith, to social structural factors. In one such relation the main characteristics are hierarchial structure of offices and the solemn quality of religious proceedings. The model in this trend has been the Church of England, but the nonconformist churches also became establishment-oriented after the controversy over emancipation had passed. A second trend, ethical and sectarian individualism, is represented in European Protestantism but also in sects originating in the United States, including the Seventh-day Adventists and Jehovah's Witnesses. The third trend involves more demonstrative types of worship and includes such neo-African cults as Shango and such ancestral cults as Kumina; revivalist cults such as the Revival Zionists, the Spiritual Baptists, and the Shakers; and such groups as Pentecostalism, the Salvation Army, and the Nazarenes.

Roman Catholic Church. From the beginning of the Republic of Haiti in 1803 until 1858, a schism existed between the state and the Roman Catholic Church. Because the Constitution of 1805 provided for the complete separation of church and state, the Vatican refused to recognize Haiti as a state and forbade priests to enter the country. In 1860 an agreement between the pope and Haitian officials ended the long break. However, Catholicism had not developed deep roots in Haiti, and, during the schism, folk belief was combined with Christianity. Since that time, vodou has continued to maintain its hold on the Haitian mass. After President François Duvalier came to power in 1957, the state increasingly exercised control over the Catholic Church through intimidation and violence, including the expulsion of the archbishop of Port au Prince and dozens of French and Canadian missionaries, the closing of the major Catholic seminary, the banning of the Catholic daily paper, and the dissolution of the Christian trade union.

The Catholic Church has never been as influential in the national life of Cuba as in other Latin American countries. Its decline during the last years of Spanish rule continued after Cuba became independent in 1902. The shortage of priests, the fact that most of the priests and nuns were foreigners, the meager education of the priests, identification of the church with conservatism, its reputation for corruption and antipopular policies alienated it from a large part of the Cuban population.

The situation of the Catholic church in the former British West Indies has been somewhat different. The first Catholic priest to serve in Jamaica came to the island in 1792, but for many years the number of Catholics in the country remained small. Roman Catholics constitute fewer than 10 percent of the population, but the church is influential in Jamaican life. Catholics comprise 36 percent of the population of Trinidad and Tobago, including spiritist Catholics (Catholics who are involved in such cults as Shango).

Anglican Church. Unquestionably the Church of England in Jamaica in the eighteenth century was not a missionary church for the slaves; it was the religion of the white settlers and officials. The twenty Anglican churches in Jamaica in 1800 were small, and probably fewer than three hundred persons attended religious services each Sunday. The Church of England, disestablished in most of the colonies between 1868 and 1870, continues to be an important force in the life of the former British colonies.

Protestant Churches. The United Brethren (Moravian) church in Saint Thomas grew rapidly after 1740, and mission stations established in Saint Johns, Antigua, and in Basseterre, Saint Kitts, became quite successful. Those in Jamaica, Barbados, and Tobago were much less successful. In February 1755 King Frederick V of Denmark ordered that instruction in Christianity be given to the slaves in Saint Thomas, and by 1785 the Lutheran mission in the Virgin Islands was small only by comparison to the Moravian program. Separate services were conducted for the Danish and the black congregations.

In the forty years prior to emancipation, Methodist and Baptist missionaries in the West Indies were harassed for allegedly provoking insubordination among the blacks. Despite this persecution, by the time the Emancipation Act was passed in London in 1833 the Methodist membership in the West Indies had grown to 32,000, two-thirds of whom were slaves. Confusion and suspicion arose in the British West Indies by the time the apprenticeship system came to an end in 1838. Methodism entered a period of decline in membership and enthusiasm when many former slaves became disillusioned by the continuing gulf between whites and blacks. The Methodist church in the West Indies revived somewhat after the excesses of the Great Revival of 1861–1862 had passed. Never among the largest Protestant denominations in the Caribbean, the Methodist church is, nevertheless, an important religion in the region.

The Baptists quickly acquired a following among the slaves, and following emancipation their congregations grew even more rapidly. The Presbyterian church has remained one of the smaller religions in the Caribbean. In the past forty years, Pentecostalism, a part of the fundamentalist movement in American Protestantism, has been the fastest growing religion in the Caribbean. Offering hope of deliverance from unjust social orders, this faith is almost ideally adapted to the needs of the disadvantaged. The Pentecostal style of worship has spread to small supplementary prayer groups within both the Roman Catholic Church and a number of the historical Protestant churches.

DEMOGRAPHICS. The proportions of adherents to various forms of Christianity differ in each of the Caribbean countries. For example, in Cuba the population of professing Catholics dropped from almost nine-tenths at the beginning of the twentieth century to less than three-fourths by the time Fidel Castro came to power in 1959. Two decades later, only one-third of Cubans were professing Catholics; one-fourth of that number were also involved in Santería and other Afro-Cuban cults. Protestants constitute about 1 percent of the Cuban population, the nonreligious and atheists more than half, practicing Christians who keep their religion private approximately one-tenth, and those who are adherents only of Afro-Cuban syncretistic cults less than one-thirtieth.

In Haiti, more than four-fifths of the population is Roman Catholic (nine-tenths of whom are also involved in vodou). Approximately one-seventh are Protestants, and less than one-thirtieth belong to indigenous black sects and other religions.

In Jamaica, seven-tenths of the population is Protestant, while Roman Catholics, black indigenous church members, revivalists and other cultists each constitute approximately one-tenth. Finally, in Trinidad and Tobago, Roman Catholics constitute somewhat more than one-third of the population; Protestants three-tenths, and black indigenous sectarians, Shangoists, and other religionists about one-thirtieth.

SEE ALSO Caribbean Religions, article on Afro-Caribbean Religions; Santería; Vodou.

BIBLIOGRAPHY

Barrett, David B., ed. *World Christian Encyclopedia: A Comparative Study of Churches and Religions in the Modern World, A.D. 1900–2000.* Oxford, 1982. An excellent reference volume that provides data on religions throughout the world.

Calley, Malcolm J. C. *God's People: West Indian Pentecostal Sects in England.* New York, 1965. A study of West Indian immigrants to England with valuable commentary on Pentecostalism.

Curtin, Philip D. *Two Jamaicas: The Role of Ideas in a Tropical Colony, 1830–1865* (1955). Reprint, New York, 1968. A leading historian's analysis of the roles of Christianity and of Afro-Christian religions in Jamaica in the period before and after emancipation.

Gonzales, Justo L. *The Development of Christianity in the Latin Caribbean.* Grand Rapids, Mich., 1969. A critique of the programs of Christian churches in the French-speaking and Spanish-speaking countries of the Caribbean.

Hollenweger, Walter J. *The Pentecostals: The Charismatic Movement in the Churches.* London, 1972. A lucid account of the Pentecostal movement by a prominent theologian.

Simpson, George Eaton. *Black Religions in the New World.* New York, 1978. A study of religions that have been important to blacks in the New World.

Simpson, George Eaton. *Religious Cults of the Caribbean: Trinidad, Jamaica and Haiti.* 3d ed. Rio Piedras, Puerto Rico, 1980.

Smith, Raymond T. "Religion in the Formation of West Indian Society." In *The African Diaspora: Interpretive Essays,* edited by Martin L. Kilson and Robert I. Rotberg, pp. 312–341. Cambridge, Mass., 1976. This volume includes chapters on slavery and on the religions of blacks in the Caribbean.

GEORGE EATON SIMPSON (1987)

CHRISTIANITY: CHRISTIANITY IN NORTH AMERICA

Christianity came to North America with European explorers, colonizers, and settlers, expressing in a New World version enduring continuity but also substantial change. In what became Canada and the United States (the limits of North America for this article), national and political considerations proved important, but smaller, regional forms of Christianity also flourished. North American Christianity struggled with its plurality, perhaps, ironically, achieving its greatest unity in its large-scale dedication to mission.

CHRISTIANS MADE AND BORN. Intrinsic to the Christian vision was a commitment to mission—to the task of bringing all peoples to God through the saving power of his son Jesus Christ. So far did the ideology of mission extend in North America that, even in the case of those reared ostensibly as Christians, the mission to convert became in many instances a major concern.

Conversion of native North Americans. Aims for the conversion of indigenous North American peoples figured large in the rhetoric of the colonizing nations. But the religious impulse was also molded by the political ambitions of European nation-states. Hence, conversion went forward as an arm of the colonial ventures of the Spanish, French, and English governments.

In an often-cited debate between Juan Ginés de Sepúlveda and the Dominican Bartolomé de Las Casas (1550), the Spanish had pondered the question of whether native North Americans were slaves by nature or fit subjects for Christianization. The outcome, supporting Sepúlveda and Aristotle's theory of natural slavery, was not surprising, since the Spanish already considered Aztec religion, with its human sacrifice, worship of the devil. Similarly, both English and French called the Indians "savages," wild men without law or religion. Puritans in the Massachusetts Bay Colony saw them as "minions" of the devil, heathen who practiced nefariously in the forests. French Franciscans argued that until Indians were civilized they were not capable of Christianity. And French Jesuits, in the most positive estimate, saw a natural nobility in the "savage" peoples. These early opinions, if expressed more subtly, continued to inform the ideas and work of missionaries who, after Canada and the United States became political realities, carried on their work among the Indians.

Spanish missions. As early as the 1520s, Roman Catholic priests were in Florida and the Chesapeake, and by 1595 there was serious missionary work in Florida. Meanwhile, in New Mexico, Franciscan friars had accompanied the Spanish conquerors, and in 1598 they began an era of forced mission presence among reluctant Pueblo peoples. In California, efforts to convert the Indians proceeded less violently under the missionary leadership of the fabled Franciscan priest Junípero Serra (1713–1784). At its height, the system of missions established by Serra attracted over 21,000 Indians, who settled around the missions, Christianized and living according to Spanish order in farm communities.

French missions. If the Spanish arrived in the New World as *conquistadores,* the French came, especially, as fur traders. In this context, both Franciscan Recollets and Jesuits evangelized, the Jesuits particularly among the Hurons, living with them and speaking their language. Although for a time Iroquois hostility effectively ended the work of the Jesuits, by 1668 they were preaching among their former Iroquois persecutors. When the French opened the Mississippi to Europeans, Indians in southern New France heard the gospel, while those at the other end of the French empire also knew the mission presence. Still, by the close of the French era in Canada, the missionaries had been more successful in making the Indians loyal to France than in converting them.

English missions. Evangelization of Indian peoples appears clearly among English intentions in colonizing North America. Yet the English were demonstrably slower and feebler in implementing their aims than either the Spanish or the French. The Mayhew family worked successfully among native North Americans at Martha's Vineyard and Nantucket, and in seventeenth-century New England John Eliot (1604–1690) preached in the Massachuset tongue and translated the Bible and other works for his converts, settling fourteen villages of "praying Indians." Eliot was in at least one sense representative, for Protestant missions in British North America were tied to a deep sense of the importance of the word. Introducing Indians to Christianity meant, above all, introducing them to a sacred book.

Canadian and American (U.S.) missions. After Canadian confederation, Protestant missionary efforts went forward in the West, encouraged in part by the development of the Canadian Pacific Railway. Meanwhile, Roman Catholics had achieved a solid presence among certain groups in the West as well. In the United States, by 1787 the interdenominational Society for Propagating the Gospel among the Indians had been established, to be followed in 1810 by the American Board of Commissioners for Foreign Missions and later, in 1881, by the National Indian Association. As in Canada, Protestants and Roman Catholics alike evangelized, and in both countries the twentieth century saw Christian denominations still at work. Much of the effort continued to be traditional, but there was growing awareness of the problem of cultural imperialism. Christian missionaries learned that cultural contact was a two-way process and that Indians had much to contribute to a renewed Christianity.

Conversion of African North Americans. The Christianization of African North Americans largely occurred in the United States. In Canada, economic conditions did not favor slavery, and only a small free black population struggled along. In the United States, the majority of converted slaves embraced some form of Protestantism.

At first, many slaveholders were reluctant to allow proselytizing among their slaves, fearing that Christian baptism might render slaves materially equal or doubting that blacks had souls to save. For their part, blacks did not readily adopt the Anglican Christianity of the early eighteenth century. In time, however, slaveholders became more convinced of the practical value of converting slaves for social control, while by the end of the eighteenth century, Baptist and Methodist missionaries brought a revivalist Christianity that blacks found more attractive.

In the years that followed, two kinds of Christianity evolved. First, there was the official church Christianity that slaveholders fostered and controlled. Second, there was the so-called invisible institution, a form of unchurched Christianity created and controlled by blacks, blending elements of their African past and their lived experience on the plantations with Christian language. An "instant" (conversion-oriented) Christianity, unlike the gradualism of the Anglicans, it was shared in part by European North Americans in the revivals.

Meanwhile, black churches arose not merely at the initiative of white slaveholders. In the northern United States, free blacks had already begun to form their own churches in the late eighteenth century. In the South, prior to the 1830s, Baptist congregations had also enjoyed a measure of independence and control. However, only after the Civil War did black churches, both North and South, proliferate. By the late nineteenth century, the Holiness movement flourished among blacks, and by the early twentieth century, Pentecostalism had become popular. Beyond these, massive immigration to northern cities helped to spawn a series of small but intense religious movements based in Christianity but including new revelation. Yet for the most part, blacks who counted themselves church members in the twentieth century were Baptists or Methodists, usually belonging to separate black congregations of larger white denominations. As a rough estimate, almost two-thirds were Baptists and nearly one-quarter were Methodists.

In Canada, the situation for blacks had been in many ways different. When the imperial parliament abolished slavery in 1833, British North America had already long been free of the institution. But without the long and oppressive incubation period of slavery, Canadian blacks evolved a perhaps less distinctive religious life than American blacks had. Still, by 1840 racial prejudice meant that black congregations were separated from white ones, and blacks willingly fostered distinct institutions within the larger churches. They joined a range of denominations including the Baptist and Methodist as well as the Presbyterian and Anglican. Often, too, blacks in Canada, as in the United States, left the mainstream denominations to form their own sectarian groups. But overall, Baptist fellowships predominated among blacks in Canada as in the United States.

Conversion of European North Americans. Although the American Board of Commissioners for Foreign Missions worked to an extent among native North Americans, it had been founded for work abroad. Other denominational and nondenominational organizations followed, and by late in the nineteenth century the Student Volunteer Movement was aiming at "the evangelization of the world in this generation." Reflective of the tenor of its times, it joined other missionary societies in mingling evangelical zeal with expansionist political ambitions. Similarly, in British North America the Canada Foreign Missionary Society had been established as a nondenominational agency in 1854, and by the beginning of the twentieth century the major Christian groups in Canada were engaged in serious mission work abroad. From 1893, foreign mission boards from the United States and Canada came together in New York, meeting annually until, in 1911, they formed the Foreign Missions Conference of North America.

Despite the clear commitment these nineteenth- and twentieth-century efforts expressed, the more important missionary focus remained the unconverted at home. Typically raised in a Christian milieu and even holding Christian theological beliefs, the unconverted were those who had not experientially encountered the gospel. For a variety of historical and sociological reasons, this mission to the unconverted was most noticeable in the United States. Here the Puritan and revolutionary heritage intensified a religious situation already volatile in all of North America, separated from European culture and institutions and undergoing other forms of change.

Puritanism. The Puritan movement had arisen in England as various separatist and nonseparatist groups sought to purify the Anglican Church. Imbued with Calvinism and also with elements from the left wing of the continental Reformation, Puritans sought simplicity in worship and in life, and they preached a free, or gathered, church of the elect. In the English Atlantic colonies, Puritan presence was a major factor, with key colonial governments controlled by different Puritan groups. Moreover, Puritanism in the colonies fostered significant developments in the movement's religious teaching and practice. Increasingly, a doctrine of special chosenness and covenantal relationship with God prevailed. Puritans paid greater and greater attention to inner, emotional states, stressing the necessity for an experience of conversion before one could become a full member of the church. From this perspective, Puritans faced a generation of unbelievers not only among peers who were strangers but even among their children. Puritans could not expend resources converting Indians because, in part, they were already too busy converting their own.

Revivalism. Influenced by this understanding and by frontier conditions and economic forces, in the early middle decades of the eighteenth century the Great Awakening spread in the English Atlantic colonies. Under the preaching, especially, of the itinerant Methodist George Whitefield (1714–1770) and the latter-day Massachusetts Puritan Jonathan Edwards (1703–1758), emotional and physical manifestations became outward signs of God's inward work among thousands. Then, by the turn of the century, the Second Great Awakening brought visible signs of conversion to a new generation. In Kentucky and Ohio, lengthy camp meetings attracted massive crowds who fell under the power of the Spirit, experiencing strong physical and emotional manifestations.

Throughout the nineteenth century and into the twentieth, American revivals followed cyclically. Each regeneration brought converts to the churches, but over time enthusiasm waned and there was need for further missionary effort. With Charles G. Finney (1792–1875) and his deliberate use of "new measures," revivalism became a technique for mass evangelism. Later, as more and more people moved to the cities, urban revivalism found its chief organizer and innovator in the lay preacher Dwight L. Moody (1837–1899). The greatest of the twentieth century's preachers, William A. (Billy) Sunday (1862–1935) and Billy Graham (b. 1918), built on Moody's work and adapted it to new technologies and times. And throughout the century a flourishing Holiness-Pentecostal movement institutionalized physical and emotional religion so that even regular worship services became revivals.

In Canada, revivalism never achieved the spectacular presence that it had in the United States. It is significant that the first notable revival in British North America took place in Nova Scotia, the place to which New Englanders in large numbers immigrated before and during the Revolution. At the opening of the nineteenth century, a great revival spread through Upper Canada (Canada West), with many of the same physical and emotional expressions that characterized the American frontier revival. Itinerating Methodists who crossed the border built a rapidly growing denominational connection, especially among the large numbers of American immigrants to the area. Then, from roughly 1885 to 1900, the Holiness movement and the Salvation Army brought their brand of aggressive revivalism to the disinherited and competed effectively in urban settings. In the twentieth century, emotional religion grew with increasing Pentecostal membership. During the Great Depression a religious awakening spread in the West, and during the fifteen years after World War II a revival swept through Canada, paralleling one in the United States.

Evangelicalism and moral crusades. Revivalism provided a condensed version of what evangelicalism worked to achieve in North American culture more broadly. The religious imperative of mission meant commitment to transform both individual and society. Canadians and Americans alike responded energetically, and a common moralism pervaded their cultures. Already in New France, Roman Catholic moral rigorism had blended with harshness of land and climate to produce a quality of asceticism in public life. Later, in the British era, Canadian Protestants displayed even greater rigor. Mid-nineteenth-century ministers denounced alcohol and behavioral impropriety in general, particularly rebuking abuses of the Sabbath. After confederation, the war against alcohol became the great evangelical cause, and sabbatarianism also grew as a public cause. A more collective social concern was evidenced in the nineteenth-century condemnation of slavery—less of an issue in Canada than in the United States—but it was only in the twentieth century that moralism was effectively transmuted into social witness. The new Social Gospel was more subdued on issues like temperance and sabbatarianism and more emphatic on questions of economic organization and social service. By 1907, Canadian Protestants had established a Social Service Council, while Roman Catholics, in the wake of the social teachings of Pope Leo XIII, inaugurated a visibly successful epoch of Catholic trade unionism. In the United States, the Puritan legacy of moralism remained, and in the nineteenth-century atmosphere of nonestablishment, the need for public witness to propriety seemed the stronger. From other quarters, the Arminian teachings of religious liberals emphasized personal responsibility in Christian life, while Enlightenment deism, with its stress on the moral life, fostered the moralistic ethos. Two great public crusades for moral purity, the antislavery and temperance movements, flourished side by side, the former ended by the Civil War, the latter successfully culminating in the Prohibition amendment of 1919. By the second half of the twentieth century, new abolition crusades achieved public prominence, both in conservative struggles to end legal abortion and in liberal challenges to environmental pollution. The Social Gospel, with its calls for the coming of the kingdom of God on earth, was an American movement that spread to Canadian shores. After the Civil War and in the early twentieth century, its concerns were clearly articulated, and in the 1960s it again found a voice in the militant civil rights movement. Meanwhile, from the Roman Catholic side the social teachings of the church had their impact, although in the early century much less prominently than in Canada. Still, the Catholic Worker movement, arising during the depression, offered a telling witness to social concern within Catholicism. In the post–Vatican II era, that concern became a leading feature of the American church.

CHURCHES, DENOMINATIONS, AND INDEPENDENT RELIGIOUS GROUPS. The Christian genius for organization was nowhere more apparent than in North America. Here the old European church establishments became problematic. In the late eighteenth-century United States, the diversity of colonial establishments made a national church impractical. In New France, military defeat ended official church establishment. And in British Canada, the Anglican establishment found it impossible to become the religion of all or most of the people. Hence, denominationalism became the hallmark of North American Christianity: whatever the claims of an Old World church to universality, now the term *church* became simply a label of convenience. Still, the denominations understood themselves as participating in something larger—a universal church to which all Christian groups belonged. Beyond the denominations, other forms of Christianity flourished. There were sectarian movements, which maintained strong barriers against the outer world and held to a more intensive religious regimen than the mainstream. There were other religious groups that claimed sources of revelation in addition to Christian scripture or, at least, offered a major reinterpretation of it. The cultural climate of the United States, more than that of Canada, fostered these groups and, likewise, encouraged the multiplication of denominations.

Roman Catholicism. Roman Catholic spirituality stressed tradition as much as the written word of the Bible. Strongly authoritarian, the Roman Catholic Church had the most to lose in the evolving denominational situation. Yet in some ways it was more compatible with the North American setting than was Protestantism. With its strong sacramental cast, Roman Catholicism could see nature and the material world as the vehicle for spiritual reality. Hence, in its dealings with Indian peoples, Catholicism perhaps expressed less contempt for native ways and more willingness to incorporate aboriginal forms into a native North American Catholicism. Moreover, among the European immigrants, Catholicism provided the highly tangible institutional and ritual structures that could reassure those who were homesick for cultures and countries left behind.

New France. Catholicism in New Spain had been the religion, mostly, of Spanish conquerors and Indian converts. In New France, however, white settlement meant a transplanted European church that learned quickly to adapt to life on the frontier. Religious orders of men and women had come, the nuns making New France a pioneer in social concern and the French clergy forming a dedicated core. Their flock evidently responded. Although the settlers were remembered for their gaiety and enjoyment of life, European travelers were also impressed by their piety. There were, indeed, tensions between various religious orders and problems arising from the absenteeism of a series of bishops in Quebec, but Catholicism was in northern North America to stay.

British North Atlantic colonies. Roman Catholicism came to the British North Atlantic colonies in a far less privileged position. With a royal charter granted to George Calvert, the first Lord Baltimore (1580?–1632), the Maryland colony was founded as a refuge for Catholics persecuted in England. Laws passed in 1639 and a decade later guaranteed religious liberty, but Puritans quickly took control of the government and in 1654 repealed Maryland's Act of Toleration. Even in the first days of the colony, Catholics had been a minority, and by the early eighteenth century they were denied voting rights although they were paying taxes to support an Anglican establishment. Likewise, New England proved to be hostile ground for Catholic growth.

Growth and change in North American Catholicism. After Quebec fell to the British in 1760, the Church of England was the official established church, but in practice Roman Catholicism enjoyed the privileges of establishment. Closely bound to the culture and ethos of the French Canadians, it became a badge of ethnic identity, the sign of the French nation still flourishing in the heart of British North America. The Quebec Act of 1774 brought a vast territory of British North America into the French Canadian province, retained much of the old French legal and customary structure, conferred citizenship and ability to hold office on Roman Catholics, and permitted their church to maintain its tithing policy. After the Union Act of 1840 made Upper and Lower Canada (Canada West and East) one governmental unit, Catholics in 1845 obtained a return to denominational schools, a pattern that continued—not without challenge—in the Canadian system. By the end of the nineteenth century, French Canadians considered themselves a sacred, if beleaguered, people, with a special destiny to preserve their faith.

Outside French Canada, Roman Catholicism grew apace, brought in part by other immigrants. In the Maritimes, three distinct traditions—Acadian, Irish, and Scottish—flourished despite the tensions between them and despite the largely Protestant environment. To the west, French missions served the settlers, but English-speaking Catholics were not absent. Although their church continued to be dominated by the French, with time the role of the minorities increased. In the last quarter of the twentieth century, Catholicism was Canada's majority religion, and in 1975 some 52 percent of the population counted themselves Roman Catholic.

To the south, the American Revolution had inaugurated an era of religious toleration. To be sure, there was anti-Catholic feeling and, at times, violence against Catholics in the nineteenth and even the twentieth centuries. But the larger saga of Roman Catholicism was one of increasing integration into national life. Indeed, one of the biggest problems Catholics faced was that of becoming too well-integrated, too much like the Protestant majority. Thus, the trusteeship controversy of the early national period centered around the initiatives of Catholic laymen who attempted to follow the Protestant congregational model, calling and dismissing their pastors at will. And later efforts by liberal bishops led in part to Leo XIII's *Testem benevolentiae* (1899), warning against the heresy of "Americanism."

Not only did American Catholicism encounter the Protestant majority with its denominational plurality, but the church also found an abundant ethnic plurality within its own ranks. By the 1840s, a massive Irish immigration was changing the character of American Catholicism, and over time other groups joined the Irish: Germans, Italians, Poles, and Hispanics (the last through territorial acquisition as well as through immigration). There were marked tensions among these groups, but in the end the Irish form of Catholicism won, dominating the hierarchy and imprinting its character on American Catholic life.

Protestantism. Reformation spirituality had been born in protest against sacramentalism and traditionalism in the medieval church. It preached collective return to biblical sources of revelation and individual reliance on the grace of God in winning salvation. In fact, it was only a matter of time before the centrifugal tendencies implicit in the Reformation came to realization. Thus North America, settled largely by dissenting Protestants, proved fertile ground for a series of separate and at times competing denominations. At the same time, with its emphasis on the priestly vocation of all Christians in whatever worldly station, Reformation spirituality encouraged new sources of linkage between religion and culture. If church and state eventually became separated in North America, unofficially they sustained each other.

American denominationalism. The Virginia colony was settled by nondissenting members of the Church of England, but New England and Pennsylvania were colonized by sectarian groups—nonseparatist Puritans, separatist Pilgrims, and separatist Quakers. These "outsider" groups moved from quasi-sectarian status in England to the religious and political center in the New World. But when church nonestablishment was safeguarded by the new constitution, there were officially no religious "insiders" in the nation. Hence, from two directions there was movement toward homogenization.

For the Puritans of New England, however, something of the sectarian character remained. With their emphasis on congregational autonomy, Puritans quickly became Congregationalists. But their moralism and righteousness, their sense of destiny and chosenness, and their millennialism spread throughout religious and political culture. On the one hand, these attitudes engendered in the early republic a public Protestantism with a heavy ideological tinge. On the other hand, these attitudes encouraged, by their clarity, the self-definition of others and the multiplication of religious groups. Moreover, immigrants continued to bring Old World religions to the United States, further increasing the plurality.

After the Revolution, the American Church of England reconstituted itself as the Protestant Episcopal Church (1789). Meanwhile, Presbyterian and Baptist groups continued the Puritan vision, while Methodists, as new arrivals, achieved a separate American organization. The years of the early republic were times of spectacular Methodist development and growth, but Baptist fellowships, Methodism's closest competitors, also flourished, and restorationism (to the primitive New Testament church) grew with the Disciples of Christ, or "Christians" (1832). Thus, the evangelical character of these and other denominations was heavily imprinted on the culture. Nonetheless, a small but important liberal movement in religion had also arisen from Puritanism, assuming institutional form in 1825 as the American Unitarian Association. Liberalism likewise appeared in the popular religion of rural New England as Universalism, so called because of its teaching of universal salvation.

The Civil War brought serious denominational splits, and the post–Civil War epoch yielded new tensions between liberals and conservatives within denominations. With the new science of the era and the growing prestige of Charles Darwin's evolutionary theory, some preached world acceptance, welcoming "higher criticism" of the Bible and propounding a theology of immanence. Others, deeply troubled by these developments, welded millennial and rationalistic themes to shape a fundamentalism stressing biblical literalism and inerrancy. In this milieu, too, a "gospel of wealth," enjoining material prosperity, and a critique of poverty, preaching the Social Gospel, seemed to pull in opposite directions.

The results, for the twentieth century, included a denominationalism that often concealed within the ranks of the same religious organization individuals and groups of quite different theological and ethical bent. After 1925, fundamentalism for a time seemed less important, but the movement enjoyed a widespread resurgence by the last quarter of the century. At the same time, the twentieth century saw the development of a world ecumenical movement in which American denominations participated, especially through the World Council of Churches (1948) and the National Council of the Churches of Christ (1950).

Canadian denominationalism. In the territory that became the Dominion of Canada, Protestantism first came with Huguenot traders and settlers. Nearly two centuries later, in 1760, the Church of England officially became the established church. Establishment, however, was mostly a legal fiction. Anglican clergy were insufficient in numbers and enthusiasm, the Anglican relationship to government often proved a liability, and the formal character of worship and gradualist model of Christian life were poorly adapted to life on the frontier.

Protestant groups that reaped benefits from Anglican problems were largely Presbyterians, Methodists, and, to a lesser extent, Baptists. With this denominational spectrum, and with the far greater Roman Catholic population (four times as numerous as Anglicans in 1842), resentment flared periodically over government aid to the Church of England through lands set aside as clergy reserves. When, in 1854, legislation proclaimed the desirability of ending any appearance of connection between church and state and commuted parts of the reserves as a permanent endowment, dissatisfaction remained. But the Church of England, the Church of Scotland, and the Wesleyan Methodist Church—along with the Roman Catholic Church—all received a share of the commutation. The voluntary principle, in the end, had won.

Generally, if not officially, the Protestant and Roman Catholic churches supported the Confederation of 1867. By 1881, the four major Protestant denominations could count over half the Canadian population as members. Methodists had established themselves as the largest among these churches, while Presbyterians were a close second. Moreover, both denominations, through a series of unions and reorganizations, successfully brought together nearly all groups in their respective denominational families.

These late-century mergers to form national bodies paved the way for the union, in 1925, between the Methodist and Presbyterian churches and the much smaller Congregational Union to form the United Church of Canada. The new church became, in effect, the "national" Protestant church, the body that, of all Protestant bodies, provided a counterweight for Catholicism. A liberal evangelical communion, it supported the Social Gospel. Likewise, when union sentiment arose anew with the ecumenical organization of the Canadian Council of Churches in 1944, the United Church was part of the undertaking. Since close to four out of five Canadian Protestants were United Church members or Anglicans, the denominational center seemed even stronger.

Eastern Orthodoxy. Wherever it existed in North America, Eastern Orthodox spirituality grew in national churches that enjoined continuity with the past. Formality and ritual splendor in the Divine Liturgy mediated a familial closeness, as the mystical Christianity of traditional Orthodoxy blended with the often intense nationalism of its congregations. Although it never became mission-minded, Orthodoxy did adapt to its new setting, introducing English into the Divine Liturgy, erecting pews in churches (unlike the traditional arrangement), and bringing feasts and holy days into conformance with the Western calendar.

The third major branch of Christianity first came to North America in the eighteenth century: Russian Orthodoxy grew in Alaska until, in the beginning of the twentieth century, some one-sixth of its people were Orthodox. Meanwhile, after Alaska became a possession of the United States, Russian Orthodoxy moved to San Francisco (1872) and then, by the end of the century, to New York. In the twentieth century, Greek Orthodoxy—present even before the turn of the century with immigration—grew larger than its Russian cousin, so that by 1975 there were almost two million Greek Orthodox Christians in the United States. Together with one million Russian Orthodox and still another million or so in separate national Orthodox churches, American Orthodoxy had solid grounds for its claim to be the fourth major faith in the nation (after Protestantism, Roman Catholicism, and Judaism).

Early twentieth-century immigration brought Eastern Orthodoxy to Canada as well, when Russians, Greeks, Serbians, and especially Ukrainians came. In 1918, the Ukrainian Greek Orthodox Church of Canada was established, providing a religious center for its adherents in western Canada. Meanwhile, Russian Orthodoxy grew, particularly in Alberta, despite the differences, as in the United States, between various factions. By the late twentieth century, Eastern Orthodox adherents in Canada numbered over 362,000.

Independent religious groups. The spirituality of independent religious groups, in general, stressed intensity of commitment and the transforming power of religion in every aspect of life. Frequently millennial in orientation, these groups often expected the dawn of a new age. Moreover, the line between them and the Protestant denominations is difficult to draw. From one point of view, many of the sectarian movements may be considered Protestant, provided that they are not considered closely related to mainstream Reformation churches and, on the other hand, that any roots in Reformation churches are taken into account. Even more, when such sectarian movements lose their exclusiveness and move in a more denominational direction, their inclusion with other Protestant groups becomes virtually automatic. Beyond the sects, religions like Mormonism and Christian Science fall outside the scope of Protestantism, although for practical purposes these religions are also often lumped together with the Protestant churches.

Sectarian movements. Marking their boundaries with the outside world far more strongly than do denominations, sects form tightly knit groups of committed coreligionists. Yet they are often intensely conversionist, with a powerful missionary urge, a sense of impending end to the present era, and an accompanying doctrine and experience of new birth. In short, what the evangelical denominations in North America in many ways adumbrated, its sectarian movements carried to logical and psychological completion. Moreover, in the United States, where sects appeared in far greater number and variety than in Canada, the national ideology of newness helped to foster the experience of new birth.

Some sects in the two countries were simply European imports, attracted by promises of religious freedom and abundance of land. But because of the isolation of such groups (e.g., the Amish, the Mennonites, and the Hutterites) and their relatively smaller numbers, they did not have nearly so much impact on culture as sectarian movements closer in spirit to mainstream Protestantism. Thus, Adventist movements like the Millerites of the early 1840s attracted wide public notice in the United States and Canada—and a following difficult to number, much of it within the Baptist and other evangelical denominations.

In another example, the American Holiness-Pentecostal movement grew from Methodist perfectionism and other sources until, by the late nineteenth century, the expulsion of Holiness associations or their secession from the Methodist churches came about. In congregations like the Church of the Nazarene, Holiness people were, religiously, relatively conservative, but a more radical expression of perfectionism came early in the twentieth century in Pentecostalism. For Pentecostals, the signs of the Holy Spirit—speaking in tongues and added biblical gifts like prayer, prophecy, and healing—descended in an atmosphere of miracle and millennialism. Their movement, interracial at first but then separated along color lines, spread to Canada and throughout the world. In Canada, Holiness had developed indigenously, but it also migrated northward from the United States just at the time that the Canadian West was experiencing a rapid growth of cities. The Nazarenes quickly rose to prominence among the Holiness sects, even as Pentecostalism entered from both the United States and Great Britain, finding a favorable climate for increase.

New religious movements. Like the sects, new religious movements arose far more often and more prominently in the United States than in Canada. In fact, one such movement, the Mormons, by the late twentieth century had established itself as among the largest religious organizations in the United States. In Canada, the Mormons also achieved a presence, appearing in Ontario and Upper Canada and building a temple in Cardston, Alberta. Eventually they could be found throughout Canada. The major development, though, was in the United States, where Mormon founder Joseph Smith (1805–1844) preached a new revelation transmitted to him on golden plates, a salvation history that centered on early America. Smith's written transcription, the *Book of Mormon*, grounded the movement, which evolved a distinctive theology of materialism, supporting the American venture and pronouncing a final goal of deification.

Similarly, the founder of Christian Science, Mary Baker Eddy (1821–1910), in *Science and Health* gave her followers a book that they ranked beside the Bible. Built on a Congregational heritage of Puritanism and a resurgence of Platonism in the nineteenth century, Eddy's teaching stressed the illusory nature of the material realm and encouraged followers to look to divine Truth, experiencing physical healings and other material goods as signs of their apprehension of spiritual reality.

Eddy's Christian Science church was relatively small in size, but it was the best organized of a series of movements in the United States that preached and practiced mental healing. These metaphysical movements often expressed in more concentrated form a general idealism in American culture, and, in their growing emphasis on themes of prosperity, from their own perspective they too taught a theology of materialism. At the same time, Christian Science and New Thought (the general name for other metaphysical movements such as Unity) traveled across the border into Canada where, in missions and churches, they spread their message.

Numbers of other new religious groups, based at least partially in Christianity, prospered and grew in North America. The typical pattern was foundation in the United States and subsequent migration into Canada, where the movement had a much smaller following. Many of these groups seemed bizarre and exotic to more conventional Christians, but, typically, their members linked themselves to Christianity.

Such disparate groups as the nineteenth-century Oneida community that taught a regulated pluralism of sexual partners in complex marriage, the enduring Spiritualist churches from the second half of the nineteenth century that sought to establish contact with the spirits of the departed, and the apocalyptic Children of God organization from the late 1960s that embraced a totalitarian patriarchalism, all expressed currents in the religious culture of North America. They took religious freedom seemingly as far as it would go—even to a commitment that, paradoxically, sometimes became willing bondage. They announced an alienation from tradition and a yearning for identity and community in a North American society grown perhaps too plural and too large. In short, the spread of new religious movements, from Mormonism to the Unification Church of Sun Myung Moon, must be linked to the history and sociological base of North American Christianity.

NATIONAL AND REGIONAL CHRONICLES. By the late twentieth century, the United States and Canada had long since divided sovereignty over North America between them. Christianity was the predominant religion in both countries, and in both it exhibited characteristics suggesting the political and cultural ambience of North America. At the same time, each country showed marked differences from its neighbor in the forms its Christianity assumed.

Canadian Christianity. Because of their special history, Canadians generally thought of themselves as two nations—groups bound by ties of blood, tradition, and ethnic identity—in one political state. The political balance of power between French Canadians and English Canadians had a religious counterpart in the more or less equal division between Roman Catholic and Protestant Christians (although a large proportion of Catholics were English-speaking and not French at all). Protestant Christians comprised fewer denominations than in the United States, historically most belonging to the three or four biggest churches. Hence, it is fair to say that Canadian Christianity was both more and less plural than Christianity in the United States.

Canadian Christianity was more plural because the concentration of Christians into fewer religious groups fostered greater visibility and leverage for denominations with sufficient power and status in the community to count. But Canadian Christianity was also less plural than its American counterpart, for the obvious reason that there were fewer groups in absolute numbers, but also because of an ecumenism especially apparent in Protestant Christianity. It was less plural, too, because of the subtle Erastianism that en-

COSMIC VISIONS

Images offer viewers a special advantage: not only can they compact and transmit information with great economy, they offer a commanding perch from which to survey vast transits of time and expanses of space. Schematic images serve as maps of the cosmos, of history, of the night sky, and of the wanderings and pilgrimages of the soul. Visual imagery can also present to a single view, for purposes of meditation or memorization, extensive bodies of thought and teaching. Such images are often diagrams or charts that serve as mnemonic devices, teaching aids, or prompts for visualization in meditation. This manner of imagery is able to condense a complex array of information into a single visual field and to serve as a graphic shorthand for referring to or recalling teachings.

Itinerant Buddhist teachers in Tibet and other Himalayan regions make use of diagrams like the Wheel of Existence **(a)**, in which are encoded in symbolic imagery and scenes the fundamental teachings of Buddhism as practiced by Tibetan followers. Nearly one meter high, the image serves as a teaching aid for explaining the cycle of life, the structure of the Buddhist cosmos, the forces of evil and good, and such essential doctrines as karma, rebirth and its causes, and the levels of rebirth.

(a) A Tibetan cloth diagram of the Buddhist Wheel of Existence, from the eighteenth or early nineteenth century. *[©The Newark Museum/ Art Resource, N.Y.]*

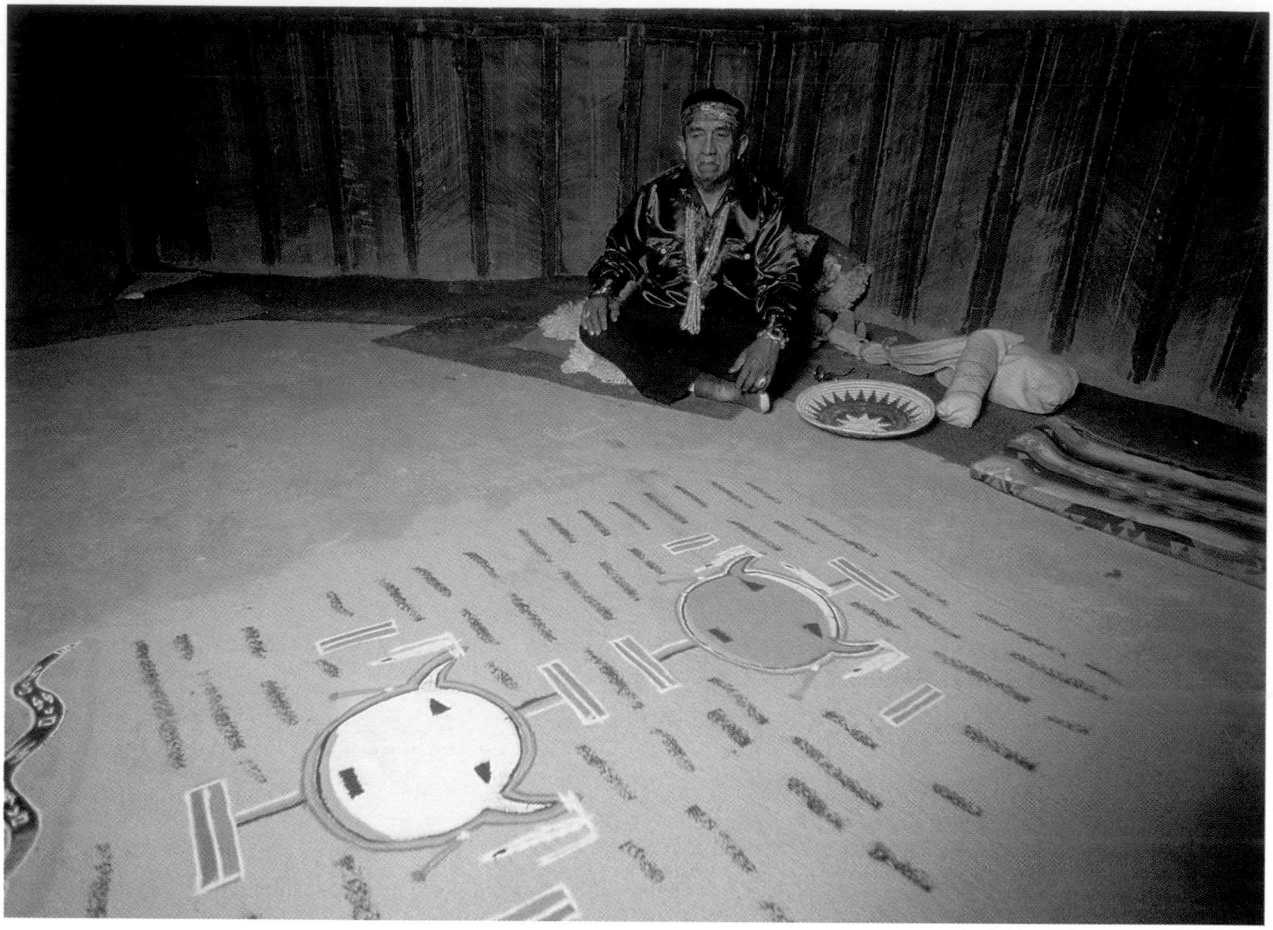

(b) Navajo medicine man Victor Begay with a sand painting he created for a healing ritual. *[©Arne Hodalic/Corbis]*

Other images reproduced here are cosmic maps created for various purposes. The Navajo sand painting **(b)** is a temporary device produced for the purpose of healing, fecundity, and the restoration of order. The diagram configures the ideal, balanced relations among natural forces and divine beings, which, when they slip into imbalance by human action, cause evil and ill health. The creation of the sand painting and its quick and ritual destruction bring about the resumption of cosmic balance and human well-being. A Daoist hanging scroll from China **(c)** also signifies the search for well-being conceived as balance and protection from evil. Zhenwu, the perfected warrior, is a savior figure who confronts evil on behalf of all souls by achieving the Dao's ideal balance of yin and yang, symbolized in the eight trigrams above the central figure. The rest of the image consists of seventy-two talismans, each of which is a star diagram with script that explains the particular protection against malevolence provided by each configuration.

Diagrams are an especially effective way of mapping a relationship between the scale of the human form and the corresponding macrocosm. The human body is transformed into a microcosm of larger forces. Robert Fludd's hermetic diagram **(d)** is an example of this graphic way of discerning occult relationships between the human form and the cosmic. The image conveys a prevailing sense of harmony among spiritual and material domains, described as a continuum that stretches from the divine (the Hebrew tetragramaton at the top) to the human body centered in the genitals. A different kind of diagram that represents in abstract linear form the embodied connection of different levels of the cosmos appears on many Olmec *celts* or stone axe heads that were illustrated and

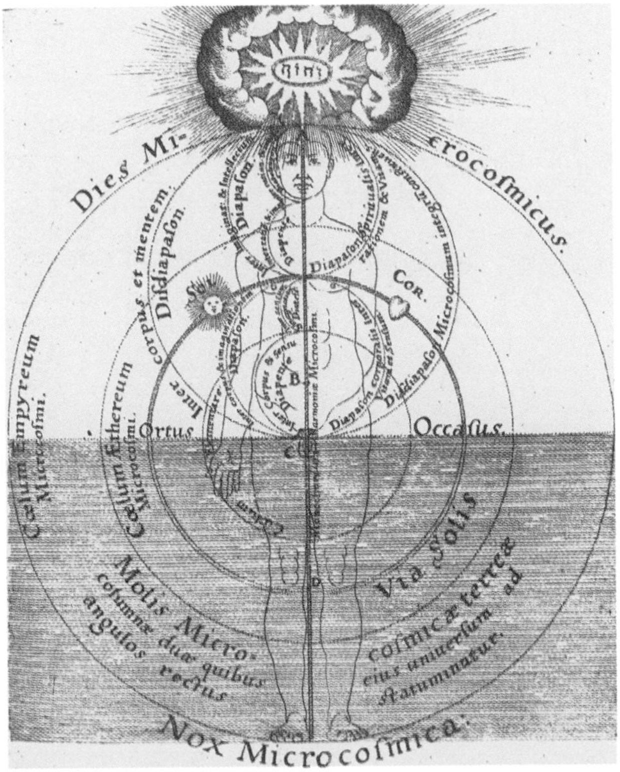

(c) Above. Chinese hanging scroll depicting Zhenwu with the Eight Trigrams, the northern dipper, and talismans, Qing dynasty, seventeenth or early eighteenth century. ***[Russell Tyson Endowment, 1999.566; reproduction, The Art Institute of Chicago]*** **(d) Left.** *The Diapason Closing Full in Man*, an illustration from Robert Fludd's *The Macrocosm*, volume 1: *Metaphysics and Cosmic Origins* (1617). ***[The Granger Collection, New York]***

vertically displayed as the *axis mundi*, or vertical alignment of earth, sky, and underworld. *Celts* mounted on wooden handles were used to prepare land for crops. The figure on some *celts* represents a shaman applying the tools of his trade to effect travel to the different levels of the cosmos for the benefit of the *celt's* owner.

Diagrams are often thought to possess power of their own. Several examples appear here. The investment of arcane diagrams with power and hermetic significance clearly informs the Jewish mystical or qabbalistic symbols assembled on a single folio and portrayed with Hebrew script **(e)**, presumably to avoid the Bible's injunction against graven images, but also to charge the images with greater spiritual potency. The hand-shaped form, for instance, called *hamsa*, provides protection against the evil eye. The elaborate printed page dedicated to the rosary **(f)** offers 230 years off from the soul's time in purgatory (note

(e) Above. A qabbalist print by Samuel Habib, used as a *mizrach*, an indicator of the direction toward Jerusalem, 1828. *[©The Jewish Museum, N.Y./Art Resource, N.Y.]* **(f) Right.** Erhard Schön, *The Great Rosary*, hand colored woodcut. The Metropolitan Museum of Art, Rogers Fund, 1920. (20.34.1) *[Photograph ©1997 The Metropolitan Museum of Art]*

the angels snatching souls from flames at the bottom) for those who pray the rosary, prescribed and guided by the print's compacted gathering of heavenly hierarchies who form the "brotherhood of the rosary," that is, those celestial worthies to whom one joins one's devotion. The circle of colored roses signifies the different kinds of prayer and the number of repetitions to ensure the rosary's promised efficacy. A Hindu practice of combining a diagram or *yantra* with supplication is shown here **(g)**, where a woman is creating the image of a lotus bloom from rice flour on the floor of a temple, while she invokes a goddess to assist her search for a good husband. The elaborate diagram is understood to attract divine energy and enable beneficial contact. A similar linear intricacy characterizes the Native American dream catcher **(h)**, a delicate mesh of fiber stretched on a willow frame and hung above sleeping children to attract the ephemeral stuff of good dreams and filter out bad dreams.

Diagrams are perhaps most widely used as maps. Eighteenth-century Muslims could envision the organiza-

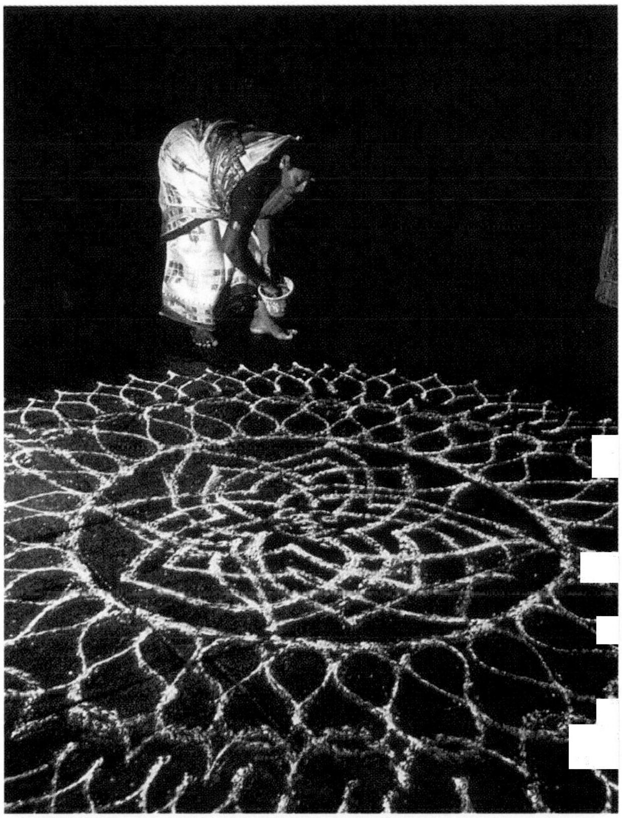

(g) RIGHT. An Indian woman creates a *yantra* of a lotus for aid in finding a good husband, Samayapuram, Tirchirappalli district, Tamil Nadu, India. *[©Photograph by Stephen P. Huyler]* **(h)** BELOW. A Yurok woman holds a dream catcher during the 1994 Salmon Festival in Klamath, California. *[©Catherine Karnow/Corbis]*

tion of the mosque in Mecca by the map **(i)** provided in manuscripts, showing the location of the Kaʿbah at the center and the entrances to the inner court of the mosque. Jains frequently used another kind of map found in stone relief in temples or painted portrayals. These structures present in highly symmetrical, concentric form the hall (*samavasaraṇa*) that is built by the gods for the delivery of a sermon by a Jina, one of twenty-four teachers who have achieved liberation from rebirth and gather monks and laity alike about them in order to teach the way to salvation. The image maps out the key ideas of Jainism, in particular tranquility (*santarasa*) and nonviolence (*ahiṃsā*), symbolized by the peaceful pairing of natural antagonists, such as the deer and tiger or the snake and mongoose.

Mapping the astral realm and the passage of time is perhaps one of the most universal uses for diagrammatic structures. Stonehenge **(j)** is a Neolithic structure whose functions included a precise coordination of astronomical events with human ritual. Tibetan lamas rely on astrological charts, such as the one reproduced here **(k)**, to consult

(i) **Left.** An eighteenth-century map of the Ḥaram Mosque in Mecca. *[©Giraudon/Art Resource, N.Y.]* **(j)** **Below.** Stonehenge, on Salisbury Plain in Wiltshire, England, constructed of sandstone and bluestone c. 2000 BCE. *[©Jason Hawkes/Corbis]*
(k) **Opposite.** Srid pa ho (Divination Chart), Tibet, late twentieth century, paint on cloth. Tibetan Collection, Asian Division (82). *[Library of Congress]*

(l) Late-fifteenth-century Aztec sun or calendar stone depicting the Five Eras, Tenochtitlan, Mexico. *[©Bettmann/Corbis]*

the horoscope of those undertaking a journey in order to determine an auspicious day for departure. The large Aztec stone diagram **(l)**, uncovered in Mexico City in 1790, is, according to recent study, a portrayal of an earth deity surrounded by depictions of the major periods of cosmic history. Outer circles represent cardinal directions and a calendrical system of notating recent Aztec history that affirmed the cosmic centrality of the Aztec empire and appears to have declared the importance of combat and human sacrifice as the destiny of the empire.

BIBLIOGRAPHY

Godwin, Joscelyn. *Robert Fludd: Hermetic Philosopher and Surveyor of Two Worlds*. Boulder, Colo., 1979.

Leidy, Denise Patry, and Robert A. F. Thurman. *Mandala: The Architecture of Enlightenment*. New York, 1997.

Little, Stephen, with Shawn Eichman. *Taoism and the Arts of China*. Chicago, 2000.

Menzies, Jack. *Buddha: Radiant Awakening*. Sydney, 2001.

Mills, Kenneth, and William B. Taylor, eds. *Colonial Spanish America: A Documentary History*. Wilmington, Del., 1998.

DAVID MORGAN (2005)

couraged all denominations to uphold a central cultural order. Christianity in Canada tended to be "social" Christianity, more conservative than in the United States and less rigid in its boundary between church and state.

Mission-minded and voluntaryistic like the American Christian churches, the Canadian denominations had worked on a huge geographical scale, and so—perhaps more than and ahead of their country's politicians—they thought in terms of the North American continent as a whole. Moreover, with the imposing strength of Roman Catholicism before them, Canadian Protestants were particularly urged in cooperative directions. Thus, in some sense they provided the public unity that the state could not give because of its divisions between English and French. Much more than Christianity in the United States, Canadian Christianity maintained its ties with the past, favoring continuity and tradition over religious change and novelty.

Finally, Canadians overwhelmingly counted themselves denominational Christians, exceeding even the high American church membership (nearly 70 percent of the people) in the late twentieth century. At the beginning of the twentieth century, 90 percent of Canadians belonged to six major Christian groups (including as the largest the Roman Catholic). By the 1960s, with some substitutions, the figure was higher still, and by the early 1970s over three-quarters of the population were Roman Catholic, United Church, or Anglican Church members.

American Christianity. The Puritan ethos left its mark on American religion, and numerical, political, and cultural balance made the United States distinctly Protestant. Although the nation was far more plural than Canada in the number of its Christian groups (a conservative estimate includes more than two hundred), public Protestantism meant that, with less overt cooperation between church and state, the country could become in some ways far more Christian, far less secular, than its northern neighbor.

Thus, while the Canadian system accommodated itself to the support of denominational schools, in the United States the nineteenth-century public schools openly taught Protestant Christianity. Similarly, even as Puritanism faded into other denominational forms, its spirit remained to transform public and political life. Manifest destiny and political imperialism became the harvest of the Puritan past.

Explicitly present in Puritanism, millennialism resurfaced time and again—in liberal expectations of a new era, in sectarian beliefs that the millennium had already come or was just about to break, in fundamentalist announcements of the signs of the swift return of Christ. Nationally, too, political millennialism suffused foreign and domestic policy, so that wars were generally read as epochal events that would determine the future of the nation and even the world.

Tied to this generalized cultural millennialism, ultraism flourished in American social history. The ultraism was evident in the moralistic crusades—which were more strident in the United States than in Canada—over antislavery, temperance, civil rights, and other social issues. Yet for all the mass emotion, the rhetoric of religious individualism became uppermost in the United States. This rhetoric went hand in hand with the ideology of newness and evangelical mission and hand in hand, too, with a pronounced ahistoricism and, in restorationist sentiment, a willingness to skip over long centuries of Christian history. Linked to a search for religious simplicity and sometimes to anti-intellectualism, restorationist movements expressed in institutional form a general spirit in American Christianity.

Certainly, as early as the mid-nineteenth century, Roman Catholicism was the single largest Christian denomination in the United States, and by 1983 it included some 29 percent of the population. But, with a different history and a lesser size, Catholicism never achieved the impact on American culture that had been its birthright in Canada. Simultaneously more and less established than in Canada, public Christianity continued to be Protestant Christianity.

Finally, this public Christianity assumed explicitly political form in what many scholars have called civil religion. While the Enlightenment ideology present at the time of the American Revolution encouraged a form of religious nationalism that was not specifically Christian, later a public alliance between gospel and flag became commonplace. By the 1970s and 1980s, a new Christian Right was working to shape political events. Conservative Christians were probably the fastest-growing Christian groups in Canada as in the United States, but again, because of the different histories of the two countries, they could not capture the public space in Canada in the same way as in the United States. Hence, in American religion, public Protestantism, civil religion, and cultural religion became aspects of the same center.

Regional Christianity. Living together in one area, Christian peoples may share a common history as well as a common religion. Likewise, they sometimes develop ties that, in effect, constitute them as a new "particular people." European sectarian groups that settled in North America offered striking cases of the growth of such religious regionalism. Rural places and urban centers alike often assumed the character of a religious and ethnic group. Meanwhile, more diffused throughout larger areas, identifiable forms of regional Christianity flourished. This was clearly true in the French Canadian Catholicism of the province of Quebec, but it was also true in, for example, the Eastern Cherokee Christianity of western North Carolina after the Indian Removal of 1838. The pattern could be noticed distinctly in the fundamentalist Protestantism of southern Appalachia, and it was strikingly present in black religion as, in sections of the American South, it joined to its Christianity inherited African thought forms and indigenous folk religion.

The larger North American landscape. In the end, however, North American Christianity should be seen from a continental perspective. With its voluntaryism, activism, and moralism, it has been generally evangelistic in tone. The call to mission clearly gave it a distinct identity: Roman Catholic and, more, Eastern Orthodox strains of mystical piety never made their mark on Christian culture as a whole. Denominational in organization, the essence of North American Christianity has been at once its plurality and its seeking for a genuine pluralism, a state of pleased acceptance of the plural situation. At the same time, North American Christianity modified the plurality to reflect political and national needs for unity.

With the second half of the twentieth century, religion in North America encountered the increasing secularization of culture. Although in both the United States and Canada Christian church membership included the large majority, it also seemed that, except for the fundamentalist political thrust of the New Right, Christianity had a diminished connection with everyday life. In a certain sense, the mission-minded evangelical ethos seemed more a style or habit than a substantive transformer of the world. On the other hand, North American Christianity has perhaps grown more modest, chastened by a new awareness of the danger of cultural imperialism. At the start of the twenty-first century, it has turned inward to find spiritual roots in its biblical heritage and outward to listen to the words and messages of non-Christian others at home and abroad.

SEE ALSO Christian Science; Denominationalism; Mormonism; New Religious Movements, article on New Religious Movements in the United States; North American Indian Religions, article on New Religious Movements.

BIBLIOGRAPHY

The one book that deals with all of North American Christianity as defined in this article is Robert T. Handy's *A History of the Churches in the United States and Canada* (New York, 1977). It is clear and straightforward, written from the perspective of church history and with meticulous attention to detail.

For American (U.S.) Christianity, the most exhaustive source, highlighting the theme of Puritanism, is the monumental work by Sydney E. Ahlstrom, *A Religious History of the American People* (New Haven, 1972). More concise but also informative is Winthrop S. Hudson's *Religion in America*, 3d ed. (New York, 1981). My book *America: Religions and Religion* (Belmont, Calif., 1981) offers a different approach from the previous works, employing the perspectives of history of religions and interdisciplinary history to study the counterpoint between the manyness and oneness of American religion(s).

As a collection of essays that masterfully explores denominationalism and other central themes in American religious history, the classic work by Sidney E. Mead, *The Lively Experiment: The Shaping of Christianity in America* (New York, 1963), is insightful and rewarding. The *Historical Atlas of Religion in America*, rev. ed. (New York, 1976), by Edwin S. Gaustad, is invaluable as a religious atlas. The book is especially useful for its careful charts and graphics. Another invaluable work of historical craftsmanship, edited by Edwin S. Gaustad, is his two-volume documentary collection, *A Documentary History of Religion in America*, vol. 1, *To the Civil War*, and vol. 2, *Since 1865* (Grand Rapids, Mich., 1982–1983). The documents, selected to show a pluralism present in American religious history from the first, contain a wealth of materials for the beginner or the more advanced student. With the possible exception of Mead's essays, all the works above consider American Christianity not exclusively, but as the largest theme in the religious mosaic of the United States, which they seek to describe comprehensively.

Among more specialized studies in American Christianity, *Righteous Empire: The Protestant Experience in America* (New York, 1970) by Martin E. Marty, republished in a second edition as *Protestantism in the United States: Righteous Empire* (New York, 1986), is still the best treatment of Protestantism, reading it in terms of its impact on culture and cultural imperialism. For Roman Catholicism, the account by John Tracy Ellis, *American Catholicism*, 2d ed., rev. (Chicago, 1969), is yet the classic short work. The book by Henry Warner Bowden, *American Indians and Christian Missions: Studies in Cultural Conflict* (Chicago, 1981), is sensitive to the contact situation but suggestive more than comprehensive as a treatment of the Christianization of Amerindian peoples in American territory. Still, its account of Huronia provides a highly readable introduction to the work of the Jesuits in New France. The pathbreaking work by Albert J. Raboteau, *Slave Religion: The "Invisible Institution" in the Antebellum South* (Oxford, 1978), considerably advances the study of black Christianity. More comprehensive in scope but written to argue a distinct theological agenda is Gayraud S. Wilmore's *Black Religion and Black Radicalism: An Interpretation of the Religious History of Afro-American People*, 2d ed., rev. and enl. (Maryknoll, N.Y., 1983). Even with the theological *tour de force*, it is the best survey presently available.

Lamentably, Canadian Christianity has not received nearly the scholarly attention that its American counterpart has. The most useful short history, though dated, is H. H. Walsh's *The Christian Church in Canada* (Toronto, 1956). More recent and more expansive is the three-volume work, *A History of the Christian Church in Canada*, produced under the general editorship of John Webster Grant. The first volume of this trilogy, *The Church in the French Era: From Colonization to the British Conquest* (Toronto, 1966), also by H. H. Walsh, intersperses nuanced biographical sketches in its chronicle of events and offers an absorbing, contextualistic account. The second volume, by John S. Moir, *The Church in the British Era: From the British Conquest to Confederation* (Toronto, 1972), continues the chronicle to 1867 within a crisp and comprehensive church historical framework. The third volume, *The Church in the Canadian Era: The First Century of Confederation* (Toronto, 1972), by John Webster Grant, completes the series in somewhat more discursive fashion. For a more popular and colloquial introduction, there is the handsome and illustrated *Religion in Canada: The Spiritual Development of a Nation*, by William Kilbourn, A. C. Forrest, and Patrick Watson (Toronto, 1968). Its impressionistic surveys sweep through Canadian religious history, virtually all of it Christian, to good effect; and its photo essays prove rewarding complements to the text. And for a useful documentary collection, see the volume edited by John S. Moir, *The Cross in Canada* (Toronto, 1966).

More specialized accounts of Canadian Christianity include the important work of John Webster Grant, *Moon of Wintertime* (Toronto, 1984), chronicling the ambiguous encounter between Christian missionaries and Canadian Indians since 1534. More regionally specific, the brief but impressive study by Cornelius J. Jaenen, *The Role of the Church in New France* (Toronto, 1976), supersedes the Walsh volume on New France and argues the role of Catholic Counter-Reformation piety in its cultural formation. Likewise studying Catholicism in Quebec is the work by Nive Voisine with the collaboration of André Beaulieu and Jean Hamelin, *Histoire de l'Église catholique au Québec, 1608–1970* (Montreal, 1971). It is regrettably without notes or index. *L'Église catholique au Canada, 1604–1886* (Trois-Rivieres, 1970) by the Abbé Hermann Plante is more widely ranging but unfortunately ends in the late nineteenth century and also contains neither notes nor index.

The short introduction by Douglas J. Wilson, *The Church Grows in Canada* (Toronto, 1966), although it purports to be a general study, almost entirely concerns Protestantism. Its thumbnail sketches of denominations and sectarian movements are useful, but there are inaccuracies. A classic study of evangelism and revivalism in Canada, dated in its interpretive framework but rich in its use of primary source materials and lively, if lengthy, in its account, is *Church and Sect in Canada* (Toronto, 1948) by S. D. Clark. Finally, *Church and State in Canada West: Three Studies in the Relation of Denominationalism and Nationalism, 1841–1867* (1959; reprint, Toronto, 1968) by John S. Moir surveys issues regarding the clergy reserves and education in Canada West (Upper Canada).

New Sources

Albanese, Catherine L. *America: Religion and Religions.* 2d ed., Belmont, Calif., 1992.

Brauer, Jerald C., ed. *The Lively Experiment Continued.* Macon, Ga., 1987.

Dorrien, George. *The Making of American Liberal Theology: Imagining Progressive Religion 1805–1900.* Louisville, Ky., 2001.

Dorrien, George. *The Making of American Liberal Theology: Idealism, Realism, and Modernity 1900–1950.* Louisville, Ky., 2003.

Eck, Diana. *A New Religious America.* New York, 2001.

Gausted, Edwin F., and Mark A. Knoll, eds. *A Documentary History of Religion in America.* 3d ed. Grand Rapids, Mich., 2003.

Hackett, David G., ed. *Religion and American Culture.* New York and London, 1995.

Hall, Donald A. *Lived Religion in America.* Princeton, N.J., 1997.

Lippy, Charles H. *Being Religious, American Style.* Westport, Conn., 1994.

Noll, Mark A. *A History of Christianity in the United States and Canada.* Grand Rapids, Mich., 1992.

Pinn, Anthony B. *The Varieties of African American Religious Experience.* Minneapolis, 1998.

West, Cornell, and Eddie S. Glaude Jr., eds. *African American Religious Thought.* Louisville, Ky., 2003.

CATHERINE L. ALBANESE (1987)
Revised Bibliography

CHRISTIANITY: CHRISTIANITY IN SUB-SAHARAN AFRICA [FIRST EDITION]

While it is impossible to obtain precise figures of religious allegiance, it is reasonable to state that the number of Christians in Africa in 1985 was not less than 150 million. Christianity is now either the majority religion, or about to become it, in almost all parts of the African continent south of the equator as well as in important parts north of the equator, notably along much of the west coast. Bantu-speaking Africa, in particular, is becoming overwhelmingly Christian. Some 150 years ago, there were only a handful of Christians, and those were mostly in a few European-controlled coastal settlements. A century ago, the missionary advance into the interior was still only just beginning, while Islam was far better established in both the west and east and set to spread further. The most likely religious future for the continent remained a slow but irresistible islamization like that which had been proceeding for centuries in the West African interior or as in eastern areas like Somalia. This did continue in some parts, such as the Tanzanian coast, among the Yao of Malawi and still more widely in much of West Africa.

Elsewhere, however, recent African history has witnessed the most extensive mass movement into Christianity anywhere in the world in modern times. Countries like Zaire, Ghana, Togo, Uganda, Kenya, Rwanda, Burundi, Zambia, Malawi, Zimbabwe, Namibia, Angola, and South Africa have a dominantly Christian sense of identity at the level of culture and popular religion, however mixed this may be with traditional religion—especially in remoter areas. This still inadequately recognized fact has not only profoundly affected the history and future of Africa but also altered the modern worldwide balance of Christianity. Increasingly the Christian churches must appear on the international scene as a racial alliance of white and black to a degree that could hardly have been envisaged in the early decades of the twentieth century.

BEGINNINGS OF CHRISTIANITY IN AFRICA. Before the last decades of the nineteenth century, there was nothing to suggest that Christianity would grow so explosively. Africa had time and again proved to be a continent in which Christianity failed to make a lasting breakthrough. The large and impressive early churches of Egypt and the North African coast were overtaken by Muslim conquest. In Egypt the Christian church survived, at times tenuously, as an underprivileged minority, but to the west it did not. Furthermore, it had failed to penetrate across the Sahara, unlike Islam in subsequent centuries. Certainly, it prospered in Ethiopia and also, for several centuries, in Nubia. Nevertheless, any spread southward was limited. Under Muslim pressure Nubian Christianity was extinguished by the fifteenth century while the Ethiopian church only just survived the sixteenth-century *jihād* of Ahmad Grañ.

From the sixteenth to the eighteenth century, under the patronage of the Portuguese empire, there was a considerable amount of evangelistic work undertaken in several parts of the continent—in some places, notably Warri, the Kongo, and the interior of Angola, with some apparent success. In the seventeenth century especially, the Kongo kingdom seemed deeply christianized in the period of the Capuchin missionaries. However, for a variety of reasons, such as the lack of a steady flow of missionaries, colonial politics and slave-trading, and the failure to establish truly indigenous institutions, almost nothing endured. Little by little, Christian practices were absorbed by the tolerant embrace of African traditional religion, until by the early nineteenth century they had simply faded away.

At this point Catholic missionary efforts were for a while taken over by Protestant efforts in the wake of the evangelical movement, the growth of British imperial power, and the campaign to abolish the slave trade. A small crowd of black people returning to Africa in 1787 under the aegis of a London emancipationist committee may be taken as inaugurating the new era. They were settled in Sierra Leone around what is now Freetown. Reinforced by further settlements, they made of Sierra Leone an Anglican and Methodist powerhouse. Fourah Bay College, founded at Freetown by the Church Missionary Society in 1827, developed into the first institution of higher education for black Africa. Sierra Leone became, for the nineteenth century, the source of a network of West African coastal Christian communities, English in speech and often in nomenclature, confident, and urban-based. Its most outstanding representative was the Yoruba-born Samuel Ajayi Crowther (1809?–1891), Anglican bishop on the Niger. This Krio (creole) Christianity proved highly vocal, the protagonist of a distinct African Christian identity, yet it did not mix easily with the rural multitude, and Sierra Leone as a whole remained one of the least christianized of African countries. A comparable black Christianity—though less elitist and vocal, and more rural—was growing up at much the same time in South Africa, especially among the Xhosa. With Crowther, one can here compare the Presbyterian minister Tiyo Soga (1829–1871), hymn writer and Bible translator.

Elsewhere, the institutional initiative would long remain with the white missionaries. The second half of the nineteenth century was their golden age, presided over by the brilliant, restless, and quite untypical spirit of David Livingstone (1813–1873). Henry Venn, secretary of the Church Missionary Society from 1841 to 1872 and the man responsible for Crowther's appointment, brought a new maturity to Protestant missionary thinking. So too did Cardinal Charles Lavigerie, founder of the White Fathers society for Africa missions (1868), and Bishop Melchior de Marion Brésillac, founder of the Society of Missions of Africa (SMA, 1856), for Roman Catholics.

From the 1870s on there was a marked increase in both the number and the educational level of missionaries. Yet for many years the effect of the new missionary wave may well have appeared to be not much greater than that of its predecessors. The new breed of missionaries on the west coast came into an ill-advised and destructive clash with Bishop Crowther and the Sierra Leoneans. The important legacy of this period was a significant start on translation of the Bible into scores of African languages, that would prove to be the true foundation for African Christianity. Missionaries like Robert Moffat (1795–1883) of Kuruman were often unimaginative, quarrelsome among themselves, and far from strikingly successful in terms of "conversions," but enough of them became remarkable linguists to ensure that the most widely available reading matter for the early generations of literate Africans would be the Christian scriptures. The formal preaching of missionaries seldom proved very convincing or even comprehensible (except to a more-or-less captive audience of house servants and ransomed slaves), but the Bible in its range of historic particularity, legal prescription, and deep mystery provided a compelling vision, and one seemingly more at home in traditional Africa than in nineteenth-century Europe.

By the start of the twentieth century there were several peoples, beyond Sierra Leonean Krios and the Xhosa, among whom a wide movement of Christian conversion was clearly under way: the Yoruba, Igbo, and other West Africa coastal peoples; the Kongo (renewing an old allegiance) and the Ngwato in the south; and the Ganda in the east (following the striking martyrdoms of 1886 under King Mwanga). The Ngwato and the Ganda were exceptional in that they lived in the interior. They remained the exceptions. But the circumstances of the continent as a whole were changing greatly.

The Colonial Period. In the 1890s Africa was parceled out among the European powers, and the fortunes of Christianity would, for a while, depend considerably upon its relationship with the colonial order. The latter undoubtedly helped missionary activity in various important ways, just as missionaries both pressed for, and facilitated, the colonial takeover, so that Christianity and colonial conquest could seem at times like two sides of a single coin. Modern anticolonialism has often branded Christianity in Africa, with some justification, as an accomplice of colonialism. But if the link between the two was often unhealthily close, it is also true that colonial conquest in no way required christianization— indeed, many colonialists would have preferred islamization. The British empire, in particular, had been too profoundly shaped by India to want to christianize its subjects, while the French government at the time was generally anticlerical. Missionaries could occasionally speak out against colonial proceedings on behalf of native rights; they did quite a lot to uncover the atrocities committed in the Congo Free State. They also began quite early in a few places (notably the Free Church of Scotland at Lovedale in South Africa and Livingstonia in Malawi) to provide a level of liberal education for Africans which colonists found both unnecessary and dangerous and which in fact served to cradle modern nationalism. Basically, however, missionaries were seldom a decisively influential part of early colonial society. By 1914, even though Africa was covered by a remarkable network of missions—often in intense rivalry with one another (especially Catholic versus Protestant)—there seemed to have been little decisive impact, except in a few places.

Nevertheless, an enormous religious change had begun to take place in thousands of different places. Three principal instruments were at work: the village school, the catechist, and the vernacular Bible. Colonial requirements, the pressures of modernity, and the deep vitality and adaptiveness of African societies combined to produce a sudden, quick-spreading urge for elementary Western education. No one but the missions tried to meet the demand, which they themselves saw as the hand of God. Everywhere, as a consequence, bush schools were opened and passages from the Bible were read. Baptism followed as a natural sequence. But in the face of the new demand, missionaries were few and none too mobile. The person who could cope with the new situation was the catechist—a poorly trained and more poorly paid village-level representative of both Christianity and modernity.

Besides the catechists, who were officially appointed by the churches, there were thousands of other self-appointed evangelists—miners, shopkeepers, migrant laborers—who spread elements of Christian life with enthusiasm: Bible reading, hymn singing, and even such concomitants as playing football. All this occurred in places well beyond the control of any missionary. The school and the catechist were, in secular terms, the agencies of a new economic and social order, but in religious terms they were the agency of a new biblically fed religious consciousness and sense of community.

The institutional structure and official statistics of the main churches were slow to reflect the deep underlying flow. Many churches imposed long periods of catechumenate before baptism, precisely to avoid the degenerating syncretism of an earlier age. This, together with stern rules of behavior (monogamy, abstinence from alcohol, appropriate dress), ensured that a high proportion of the people who were now coming to regard themselves as Christians were not accepted officially as church members. Training for ordination was far more severely circumscribed. The appointment of Bishop Joseph Kiwanuka as Roman Catholic vicar apostolic of Masaka, Uganda, in 1939 was absolutely exceptional. The number of the ordained before 1950 was in most countries and churches extremely small, where ordained clergy existed at all. Almost until the coming of political independence to the greater part of black Africa around 1960, official Christianity remained carefully controlled by white missionaries operating from a small number of complex missions—small denominational cities they had built up and ruled. Mission stations were of real importance because of the secondary schools and hospitals they contained, as well as because they provided the administrative and symbolic centers for the vast network of rural Christianity. Their boarding schools ensured that the new elite, as well as the masses, would be christianized in the very process of coming into existence. To a very large extent, Africa's new ruling class sprang from these schools. Even when most critical of missionaries and churches, African politicians seldom fail to express gratitude for their contribution toward secondary education.

But the effective (rather than symbolic) role of the central mission station and the missionaries (increasingly administrators) who staffed it remain secondary in importance for the understanding of the almost ubiquitous, rapid, yet largely uncharted evolution of modern African Christianity. The two levels could easily come into conflict. The character of popular Christianity inevitably left a great deal to be desired from the viewpoint of missionary orthodoxy. Should a zealous but polygamist catechist be retained? Could God be expected to address and instruct new converts through dreams and visions? Could the illnesses of Christians be explained and combated in terms of bewitchment? The missionary answer to such questions was most often a firm no. For their part, Africans frequently remained unconvinced on these matters, and from the end of the nineteenth century a multitude of independent churches began to arise, first in South Africa and Nigeria, then in many other parts of the continent where there was already a significant missionary presence.

Independent Churches. Independent church movements took roughly two chief forms. The first produced what in Nigeria have been called the "African" churches and in South Africa the "Ethiopian" churches. Early examples are the United Native African Church, founded in Lagos in 1891, and the Ethiopian Church, founded in Pretoria in 1892. These are essentially cases of schism, in which full members of an established church, often including some clergy, have divided from the missionary body over issues like the promotion of local leadership, nationalist sympathy and cultural ethos, and acceptance of polygamists in continuing membership. Such new churches sprang mostly from Methodist, Baptist, Presbyterian, or low church Anglican missions, and very seldom from Lutherans, high church Anglicans, or Roman Catholics. They have almost always retained substantial continuity in doctrine, liturgy, and church order with those from which they seceded. They fit closely enough within a pattern of bifurcation characteristic of nineteenth-century Protestantism in both Britain and the United States.

Churches of this sort, of African origin, are found in many parts of the African continent, and new ones have continued to come into existence in almost every decade of the twentieth century. From about the second decade of the century, however, there began the still more widespread development of prophet and healing churches, generally classed as "Zionist" in southern Africa, and in Nigeria called mostly "Aladura," or praying churches. These bodies generally grew out of the career of a prophet, yet they were also influenced by American or European Zionist and Pentecostal groups (e.g., the Christian Catholic Apostolic Church, with its headquarters at Zion City near Chicago, founded in 1896 by John Alexander Dowie). These links, such as they were, were easily left behind. Adoption of the name "Ethiopian" had no administrative or doctrinal significance. It was merely symbolic and persuasive, with its biblical foundation (Ps.

68:31, *Acts* 8:27) and reference to the one part of black Africa that had both been Christian for centuries and retained its political and ecclesiastical independence (Ethiopia's military victory over Italian invaders at Adwa in 1896 sent a thrill of excitement across the continent). So too the name "Zion" was appealing as a profound symbol of the immediate renewal of God's holy city as celebrated, for example, in Psalms 122–134.

African Zionist and praying churches were much more innovative than Ethiopian ones: their preoccupation was with healing instead of schooling (indeed, they were often opposed to Western education); they grew faster, their membership was poorer. In some places (though this was not true of Nigeria) they could be seen as a fairly typical expression of the religion of the deprived. At the start, they depended mostly upon the personal impact of prophetic founders and often continued to be ruled dynastically by the founders' families, although they were prone to more and more divisions into separate groups. If their prime secular concern was undoubtedly healing, the balance within them between healing, evangelism, and the appeal of a total religious community offering a complex liturgical life centered upon a "sacred city," a Zion of their own, has varied greatly between churches.

The first of the major African prophets of the twentieth century was the native Liberian William Wade Harris, a Grebo schoolteacher of Methodist and Episcopal background. During a period of imprisonment he experienced visions of the angel Gabriel commanding him to become an evangelist like John the Baptist. His subsequent months of peregrinatory preaching during 1914 in southern Ivory Coast and Ghana produced tens of thousands of baptisms and permanently altered the religious character of the area he traversed. The decisive effect was fully recognized both by missionaries and by colonial officials. Harris had abandoned his European ways, his shoes, and his trousers; he had also abandoned any particular church affiliation. He preached a very simple Christian monotheism, expelled devils, carried the Bible wherever he went, and baptized all who rejected and destroyed their pagan "fetishes." Harris insisted upon the observance of the Sabbath and the Ten Commandments, but not upon monogamy. He established no church of his own, and many thousands of his converts became Roman Catholic or Methodist, but he did leave "twelve apostles" in the villages he converted, and out of these communities the Harrist church subsequently grew.

At almost exactly the same time Garrick Braide, an Anglican catechist, carried on a similar mission in the Niger Delta. In the 1920s, the Aladura prophets (Moses Orimolade, Abiodun Akinsowon, Joseph Babalola, and others) were preaching, healing, and destroying "fetishes" up and down Yoruba country in western Nigeria. For a few months in 1921 Simon Kimbangu (1889?–1951), of Baptist background, set an immense prophetic movement afoot in the lower Kongo, west of Kinshasa. At much the same time, Isaiah Shembe was doing the same in Zululand, Ignatius Lekganyane in northern Transvaal, Samuel Mutendi in Rhodesia (present-day Zimbabwe). In the 1930s, John (Johane) Maranke and Johane Masowe were two striking John-the-Baptist figures in Rhodesia (each took the name of John after his vocation experience). In the 1950s it was the turn of Alice Lenshina (Mulenga) in Zambia. And there were many others.

The major prophets of this sort were frequently surrounded and followed by scores of lesser prophets. No single typology for the prophetic phenomenon in modern Africa can be established, but some general remarks can be made. One should distinguish between the prophet movement itself, especially in its initial outbreak, and the increasingly institutionalized church which usually, though not always, followed it. The latter has a consequential character, deriving from the need for a new community to cater to the prophet's clientele and the inability of existing churches to cope with either the prophet or his clientele, but it does not seem to be a primary intention of the prophet. At least initially, the prophets we have named probably did not see themselves as doing anything very different from many black evangelists working for the mission churches or, indeed, from the early white missionaries themselves. They may have simply taken the Bible more literally than the early white missionaries did, but the prophetic character of many an early missionary, with his long peregrinations, prayers for rain, healing skill, and apparently strange powers of many sorts, should not be overlooked. The prophetic vocation really came from the sheer impact of Bible and missionary upon the more imaginative. For new converts, lacking almost any other literature, the Bible could have an immediacy and an applicability which few of even the most fundamentalist of missionaries could really go along with. Visions, dreams, and miracles of healing seemed to be the staple of this strange book that had been translated into their tongue and presented as having an absolute authority; and these became the staple of early African prophetic Christianity, as they were not of missionary Christianity.

In many places there seemed to be a need for movements of this type regardless of whether any major figure was present or not. Just at the time Harris was making such an impact upon the Ivory Coast, a remarkably similar movement of conversion was developing without any central preacher at all, white or black, in the Usoko district of the Nigerian coast. Such movements, if handled one way, might produce massive new advances for a historic church; if handled another way, they led to an explosion of independency. Significant churches almost always developed from the major prophets: the Harrist church, the Church of Jesus Christ on Earth through the Prophet Simon Kimbangu, the Eternal Sacred Order of the Cherubim and Seraphim of Orimolade, the VaHosanna of Masowe, the Nazareth Baptist Church (Amanazaretha) of Shembe, the Lumpa of Lenshina. Many of these came to be centered upon a holy city—a Zion or

New Jerusalem—in which the founder had lived and was eventually buried, to which the sick came for healing, a center for pilgrimage and liturgy. Kimbangu's Nkamba, Shembe's Ekuphakameni, Lenshina's Kasomo are just a few of many examples. With the passing of time, however, in a second and third generation, many churches which were prophetic and Zionist in origin became increasingly administrative and "Ethiopian": spiritual healing was formalized or almost disappeared, schools became a preoccupation. The Kimbanguist church is one clear example. It is also true that some churches which began as "Ethiopian" and were rather Western in form subsequently developed in a more prophetic and healing direction.

African ecclesiastical independency is, then, an immensely varied response both to the scriptures and to the experience of missionary Christianity. It is also, to a greater or lesser extent, in continuity with traditional patterns of African religion and society. Modern African Christianity is heir to African traditional religions as well as to the nineteenth-century missionary movement, but here again the intricacies and varieties of the relationship must not be underestimated. There was a larger measure of harmony between the common pattern of African traditional religion and traditional Christianity (especially in its more Catholic forms) than missionaries recognized. The high god of African religions—Nzambi, Mulungu, Leza, Mwari, Katonda, or whatever name the god took—had attributes extremely similar to the God of the biblical tradition, even if the cult of ancestors often made him seem, especially to the outside observer, unduly remote. Christian theism came to support itself easily upon traditional theism. Nor was the moral law much of a problem area, although missionaries sometimes thought it was (the practice of polygamy provided a special case).

The main point of conflict was, and still largely is, the veneration of ancestral spirits and the many rites—domestic, agricultural, and communal—which involve the invocation of those spirits. Missionaries condemned participation in all such rites, and most churches continue to do so officially, but the majority of Christians probably return to traditionalism for at least some of these occasions. For the most part, independent churches are as opposed to such practices as the mission churches. Indeed, while the latter (especially the Roman Catholic Church) have tended to become accommodating with time, the former maintain the inflexibility of opposition of the nineteenth-century missionary.

In regard to some other aspects of traditional culture the case is different. On many points the Old Testament and African traditions appear to be somewhat allied against the New Testament and the missionary church: food taboos are a case in point. When these are recognized in an independent church, it is not clear whether it provides an example of the maintenance of traditional culture or a case of excessive Hebraism. Polygamy is another example. Many an independent church has rejected missionary insistence upon monogamy and appealed to the Old Testament for support, though it must be added that others (like the Kimbanguist and the Lumpa churches) have condemned polygamy without reserve.

Perhaps the most difficult area has been that of witchcraft beliefs. Throughout Africa—among some peoples a great deal more than others—sickness, death, and misfortune were and still are explained in terms of bewitchment. The traditional healer (*nganga* in most Bantu languages) then had to be someone who could both detect and counteract witchcraft. Most missionaries did not believe in the possibility of witchcraft (in this they conformed with colonial law) and countered traditional medicine with Western "scientific" practice. While for the missionaries the difference in kind between Western medicine and the *nganga*'s was clear, for Africans it often was not. Some independent churches have rejected both kinds of medicine in favor of faith healing alone, but others tend to interpret sickness in traditional bewitchment terms and the more concerned they are with healing the more they may be assimilable to a typical antiwitchcraft movement. The prophet can appear to be remarkably like the traditional *nganga*, however much the prophet may denounce the latter. The Holy Spirit to which the prophet appeals in the battle against witchcraft may seem no different from the spirit through which the *nganga* works.

If some independent churches do, then, represent some degree of merging of Christianity and African traditional religion, no generalization may be offered as to which eventually controls the symbiosis. In some of the better-known churches Christian orthodoxy prevails increasingly, but in many smaller groups it is African tradition which prevails. Each has proved naturally inclusive, not only in modern times but also down through the centuries, and it is as possible for elements of Christian thought, vocabulary, and ritual practice to be absorbed into an essentially non-Christian pattern of religion as it is for elements of traditional religion to be carried on, sometimes not incongruously, in the lives of believing and committed Christians. In much of this, the independent churches are no special category. We simply see in them, through the many studies conducted recently, processes which are almost equally at work in all the larger churches of Africa, for we must not forget that more than four-fifths of African Christians belong not to independent churches but to mission-founded churches. If the former may constitute as much as one-third of black Christians in South Africa, and are also very numerous in southern Nigeria, southern Ghana, and central Kenya, they are almost completely absent in some countries, such as Uganda and Tanzania, and in many others they are fewer than 10 percent of the Christian body.

Traditional Churches. As a whole, African Christianity is denominationally a highly complex reality, the field in which a thousand flowers are free to bloom. Beyond the independent churches, all the main European and American traditions are powerfully represented in one country or another. The Anglican communion is present wherever the

British empire used to be present and in Rwanda and Burundi as well, but it is particularly strong in Nigeria, Uganda, Kenya, and South Africa; Methodists are numerous in Nigeria, Ghana, South Africa, Zimbabwe, and Zaire; Presbyterians in Kenya and Malawi; Baptists in Zaire and Liberia; The Dutch Reformed Church in South Africa; Lutherans in Tanzania and Namibia; the Church of the Nazarene in Swaziland. And that is not a complete list. In Zambia the United Church of Zambia was inaugurated in 1965, the year of the country's political independence, with the blessing of President Kenneth Kaunda. It incorporated Presbyterians, Congregationalists, and Methodists, but such unions have not been favored. Ecumenical relations are mostly excellent but the desire to maintain an independent ecclesiastical identity—whether originally the church is mission-founded or independent—is extremely strong.

The nineteenth century was preeminently a period of Protestant mission, and the legacy of a multitude of African churches today reflects that fact. In the twentieth century Roman Catholicism has spread with great effectiveness. The systematic and disciplined efforts of the great Roman Catholic mission societies of priests, monks, and nuns cannot quite be paralleled upon the Protestant side. Today, not only is the Roman Catholic Church the church of the majority of all Christians in its older areas of predominance (French- and Portuguese-speaking especially), such as the Democratic Republic of the Congo, Togo, Rwanda, and Burundi, but it has also become the largest single church in almost every country of Africa (Namibia, with its Lutheran predominance, is perhaps—apart from Ethiopia—the most striking exception).

If almost all the main churches have an almost completely black leadership at the level of the episcopate or presiding ministers, it is equally true that almost all are extremely short of ordained men or women (and when they have them, they often find it difficult to pay them). But for the Roman Catholic Church, with its rigid pattern of celibate priesthood, this is above all the case. There are now some two hundred black Catholic bishops and half a dozen cardinals (the first being Rugambwa of Bukoba and later of Dar es Salaam, Tanzania). In a few areas, such as the Igbo dioceses of Nigeria, southern Uganda, and parts of Tanzania, there are also hundreds of African priests. Elsewhere the shortage is acute.

While the number of Roman Catholic missionaries in Africa is still remarkably large, it is declining steadily in most countries as a result of political pressures and a decline in the sense of missionary calling in the old sending countries of Europe. Meanwhile, the number of African Christians grows inexorably since political independence, still more than in colonial times. The typical Christian community in rural Africa is a priestless one, led today, as mostly in the past, by a catechist or committee of village elders. Baptism, not the Eucharist, is the sacrament of African Christianity.

African Theology. African theology, of a formal kind, remains a long way from this village reality. Written mostly by professors in university departments, like Kinshasa, Yaoundé, Ibadan, Legon, and Makerere, its principal concern has been with the relationship between traditional religion and Christianity. Harry Sawyerr (Sierra Leone), John Mbiti (Kenya), Bolaji Idowu (Nigeria), John S. Pobee (Ghana), and Ngindu Mushete (Democratic Republic of the Congo) are among its leading representatives. Their theological or academic contributions have not been of major world significance. In South Africa, African theology has developed less academically as black theology, with a more political and social orientation, a local version of liberation theology.

Elsewhere African theology has remained apolitical, despite the often anguished condition of contemporary Africa, a condition which has at times deeply affected the life of the church. The murder of Anglican Archbishop Janani Luwum in Idi Amin's Uganda and that of Cardinal Bayenda in Brazzaville, both in 1977, were symbolic of many other comparable events. In South Africa the long tradition of ecclesiastical criticism of racial discrimination, represented notably by Trevor Huddleston's *Naught for Your Comfort* (1956), is carried on by Bishop Desmond Tutu, formerly secretary of the South African Council of Churches and later the Anglican bishop of Johannesburg.

The strength of the African churches, however, does not lie at this formal and clerical level of written discourse and church organization, useful as it can be to have, for example, international links of the sort represented by the All Africa Conference of Churches (founded in 1963 in Kampala, with a general secretariat based in Nairobi and plenary conferences about every six years). In African Christianity, theologians and bishops are of limited importance. The growth of Christianity in Africa has been a popular and lay phenomenon, a shift in the underlying religious consciousness of half a continent in response to the modern missionary movement, the vernacular Bible, the pressures of colonialism, and the village school. The catechist remains its most characteristic figure, and the hymn, whether a European translation or an indigenous creation, is its most appropriate form of expression and vehicle of its theology. African Christianity is pietistic rather than political.

The future of African Christianity is uncertain, despite its vast vitality. Its northern flanks are being pressed increasingly hard by Islam. Elsewhere it is sure to continue to grow numerically for some time, but its intellectual expression, its ability to cope with secularization and Marxism, the competence of its clerical leadership, and the weight of its influence in future councils of world Christianity are all matters upon which it remains difficult to speak with confidence.

See Also African Religions, article on New Religious Movements; Ethiopian Church; Harris, William Wade; Kimbangu, Simon; Lenshina, Alice; Maranke, John; Political Theology; Shembe, Isaiah.

Bibliography

Charles P. Groves's *The Planting of Christianity in Africa*, 4 vols. (1948–1958; reprint, London, 1964), is in many ways outdated and concentrates too much upon the missionary role, but it is accurate, wide-ranging, and has not been replaced. For recent history, my *A History of African Christianity, 1950–1975* (Cambridge, 1979) is the standard work. The professional rewriting of nineteenth- and early twentieth-century missionary history is represented at its best by J. F. Ade Ajayi's *Christian Missions in Nigeria, 1841–1891* (London, 1965) and John McCracken's *Politics and Christianity in Malawi, 1875–1940* (Cambridge, 1977). Bengt Sundkler's *Bara Bukoba* (London, 1981) is a fine study of the development of a single church—the Lutheran church in Bukoba, Tanzania—by its scholar-bishop. The following four symposia all contain much valuable material: *Christianity in Tropical Africa*, edited by C. G. Baëta (Oxford, 1968); *Christianity in Independent Africa*, edited by E. Fasholé-Luke, R. Gray, A. Hastings, and G. Tasie (London, 1978); *Themes in the Christian History of Central Africa*, edited by T. O. Ranger and John C. Weller (Berkeley, 1975); and *The History of Christianity in West Africa*, edited by O. U. Kalu (London, 1980).

From the very extensive literature on African independent churches, the following may be selected. For South Africa, Bengt Sundkler's early *Bantu Prophets in South Africa* (1948; 2d ed., London, 1961) remains basic, though its approach is significantly modified in the author's much later *Zulu Zion and Some Swazi Zionists* (Oxford, 1976). M. L. Daneel's *Old and New in Southern Shona Independent Churches*, 2 vols. (The Hague, 1971–1974), is the most authoritative and detailed central African study; for West Africa, see Harold W. Turner's History of an *African Independent Church*, 2 vols. (Oxford, 1967), and J. D. Y. Peel's *Aladura* (London, 1968).

David B. Barrett's *Schism and Renewal in Africa* (Nairobi, 1968) attempts an overhasty but not-to-be-ignored continent-wide assessment. John S. Pobee's *Toward an African Theology* (Nashville, 1979) is the most up-to-date guide concerning religious thought, while my *Christian Marriage in Africa* (London, 1973) sums up the issues in one much-contested area. The *Journal of Religion in Africa* (Leiden, 1967–) is indispensable for the study of the whole subject.

ADRIAN HASTINGS (1987)

CHRISTIANITY: CHRISTIANITY IN SUB-SAHARAN AFRICA [FURTHER CONSIDERATIONS]

African Christianity is a complex topic, and the literature on the subject is voluminous. The historical metamorphosis and transmutation of African Christianity appears on a variety of interrelated levels: missions, conversions, struggles for autonomy, charismatic renewals, and the creative ways Africans have shaped Christianity for themselves and appropriated it within the context of their own worldview and culture. In terms of growth and ecclesiastical representation, African Christianity maintains a robust record. In fact, the ebb and flow of world Christianity in the twenty-first century will be largely determined by the trends and events within African Christianity. The creative genius of African Christianity is manifest in the exciting religious movements and models that have emerged in Africa.

Contemporary paradigms in African spirituality are challenging the traditional ways of studying theology and church history. This reality is a telling testimony to the fact that Africans have confidently claimed Christianity as their own. It is now intellectually moribund to contend that the Christian churches of Africa are alien institutions or that they are relics of colonial domination and control. It is imperative that scholars continue to ponder and probe the dynamic and unfolding experiences of African Christians in all their rich manifestations.

African Christianity evokes a protean image, always changing and persistently in the process of transformation and renewal. In the twenty-first century, African Christianity continues to experience remarkable growth and expansion. Indeed, the churches in Africa are bursting at the seams and exhibit an unprecedented diversity. Africa has become home to all the different denominations within the Christian faith. The Anglican Church in Nigeria has more members than in England, America, and Canada put together. By 1985, there were over 16,500 conversions a day in Africa, resulting in the addition of over 6 million new Christians annually. In 2000, the Christian population in Africa was 360 million. By the year 2025, the number of Christians in Africa will reach around 633 million.

CHRISTIANITY AROUND AFRICA. Christianity in contemporary Africa is a highly variable phenomenon. It continues to be a powerful force in politics, national integration, and the development of civil society. Since the 1980s the Roman Catholic Church has played a remarkable role in instituting constitutional reforms in Francophone Africa. In the case of Cameroon, Catholic theologians such as Jean-Marc Ela, Fabien Eboussi Boulaga, and the late Englebert Mveng have produced remarkable literature on African liberation theology.

In Anglophone African nations, the church has similarly been involved in politics and issues of social justice. For example, the Christian Association of Nigeria (CAN), which was established in 1986 as an ecumenical body of Protestants, Catholics, and African Initiated Churches (AIC, formerly called African Independent Churches), has been extremely critical of the sociopolitical anomalies in Nigeria. Even in the face of President Abacha's reign of terror (1993 to 1998), CAN remained outspoken and refused to be pummeled into submission. Likewise in Ghana, Mensa Otabil, the leader of Ghana's International Central Gospel Church, has been very critical of the International Monetary Fund and the World Bank's policies in Africa. His political theology underscores the importance of political consciousness, black pride, and self-empowerment.

Political leaders in Zambia have a new appreciation of the political clout of Zambian born-again Christians. The Evangelical Fellowship of Zambia accused Kenneth Kaunda of flirting with the demonic, and their persistent vitriolic criticisms eventually contributed to his political demise. Kaunda's successor, Frederick Chiluba, did not waste time in proclaiming his own evangelical credentials and had a flamboyant though short-lived romance with Zambia's evangelical and Pentecostal leaders.

In South Africa, the evangelical branch of the Dutch Reformed Church (DRC) presented a vocal and strident opposition to the odious nationalist agenda of this ecclesiastical body. The never-ending historical and theological justifications for apartheid by the Dutch Reformed Church were completely renounced by many outspoken evangelicals. The most forthright and distinguished representative of the evangelical tradition within the Dutch Reformed Church was David J. Bosch (1929–1992). Before his tragic death, he served as the dean of the theological faculty at the University of South Africa, Pretoria; general secretary of the Southern African Missiological Society (1968–1992); and editor of the renowned journal *Missionalia.* Bosch vigorously articulated the perversity of the obnoxious racial policies of the Dutch Reformed Church from a theological perspective.

African Christians are weary of the Western secular intellectual tradition and its mistrust of religion's crucial social influence. Although African Christians have embraced some of the ideals of democratic pluralism, Western liberal antipathy towards religious sensibilities does not find fertile soil in sub-Saharan Africa. The African experience boldly affirms that Christianity invigorates rather than undermines culture and society.

The Rise of Pentecostalism. The last decades of the twentieth century witnessed the veritable explosion of New Pentecostal churches all over Africa. Some of the new paradigms within these churches include American evangelical religious tenets, the gospel of prosperity, healing, deliverance from principalities and powers, and charismatic worship in a technologically stylish setting. These new dimensions underscore Paul Gifford's thesis on the pervasive presence of ecclesiastical externality in Africa Christianity. It is also a confirmation of what has been described as Africa's active engagement with external influences. The new gusto of Pentecostal zeal is especially appealing to urban youths.

The gospel of prosperity also provides a welcome message for the rich, since the accumulation of wealth is not considered anathema. Furthermore, it offers hope for the less financially successful, for whom it opens new vistas and infinite possibilities. This new wave of Pentecostalism arrogantly tends to reject some of the rituals and spiritual practices within the AIC because of their alleged pagan nature. Pentecostal diatribes are also directed at the mainline churches that they often portray as indulging in a form of Christianity that is bereft of power and Holy Ghost fervor.

Relations with Islam. One of the crucial challenges for African Christianity in the twenty-first century is its relationship with Islam. The interaction between these two Abrahamic religions has fluctuated dramatically over the centuries. It is truly a relationship saturated with both meaningful engagements and baffling ambiguities. It runs the gamut of thoughtful dialogue, lethargic encounters, open conflicts, and internecine violence. The intense politicization of religion in many African countries has continued to aggravate the deepening antagonism between Christians and Muslims.

Islam's persistent demand that religion and state should remain as mutually enforcing agents has likewise generated passionate responses from Christians in sub-Saharan Africa. In recent times, the imposition of full-blown *sharīʿah* (Islamic law) in many states in northern Nigeria has engendered violent religious riots in Nigeria. In fact, the *sharīʿah* issue has reawakened slumbering religious tensions in Nigeria and constitutes the greatest challenge to Nigeria's fledging democracy. One of the dilemmas facing Christians and Muslims in Africa is how to live amicably and in a way that accords respect to each group.

Conclusion. Pliny, the Roman historian, once said that there is always something new coming out of Africa. The aphorism is particularly relevant in the context of theology. As the center of Christianity inexorably shifts to the Southern Hemisphere, Africa provides an important venue for Christian development and experience. Among the challenges facing the churches in Africa is how they may become more self-critical and also be more responsive to the plethora of death-dealing problems plaguing Africans in the twenty-first century. These two agendas are quintessentially part of the good news of Jesus Christ.

Bibliography

Emmanuel A. Ayandele's *The Missionary Impact on Modern Nigeria, 1842–1914: A Political and Social Analysis* (London, 1966) provides important insights into the relationship between Christianity and the colonial powers. The book also examines the life and contributions of important figures like Bishop Ajayi Crowther, Edward Blyden, and James Johnson. Kwame Bediako's *Christianity in Africa: The Renewal of a Non-Western Religion* (Edinburgh, 1995) is an excellent analysis of the transformation of African Christianity into a non-Western religion. Richard Gray's *Black Christians and White Missionaries* (New Haven, Conn., 1990) offers a thorough study of how Africans have made Christianity uniquely African. Gray argues that many Christian themes are analogous to some of the salient themes in African religion. This is a very useful book for understanding the symbiotic role between religion and culture in Africa. Paul Gifford's *African Christianity: Its Public Role* (London, 1998) offers a valuable study of the sociopolitical engagement of Christianity in Ghana, Uganda, Zambia, and Cameroon. *The History of Christianity in Africa,* edited by Ogbu Kalu (Essex, U.K., 1980), is an impressive collection of essays on Christianity in West Africa. These essays cover such topics as the *modus operandi* of Christian missions in West Africa, the patterns of missionary expansion, Christianity and colonial society, and some examples of modern responses to Christianity in West Africa. Lamin Sanneh's *West African Christianity: The Religious Impact* (Maryknoll, N.Y., 1983) is indispensable for understanding the historical development of Christianity in West Africa. Sanneh's poignant reflection on Christian-Muslim encounters is also very useful and important. Harvey Sindima's *Drums of Redemption: An Introduction to African*

Christianity (Westport, Conn., 1994) offers an excellent introduction to the different stages in the Christian expansion in Africa. Sindima deals with issues such as the early African church, the Ethiopian church, African prophets and evangelists, and the rise of African theology. Bengt Sundkler's *History of the Church in Africa* (Cambridge, U.K., 2000) is a massive work on African Christianity. This 1,200-page book coherently covers all the different and complex historical developments, voices, models, and movements in African Christianity. Sundkler was a Swedish missionary in Tanzania and South Africa and later a professor at the University of Uppsala, Sweden. He died before this book was finished. Christopher Steed, also of the University of Uppsala, presided over the publication of this monumental work.

AKINTUNDE E. AKINADE (2005)

CHRISTIANITY: CHRISTIANITY IN ASIA

Christianity in Asia consists of a wide range of phenomena. It includes the mission churches, denominations, and related institutions established by Western missionaries, numerous independent and indigenous movements (churches or sects established by Asian Christians, which are organizationally independent of Western churches), as well as the personal beliefs and ritual practices adopted by individuals influenced by Christianity but unaffiliated with any of its organizational forms. In order to understand the significance of this religious tradition in Asia, the study of Christianity must include both the history of transplanted Christian traditions and foreign missionary efforts as well as the diverse "native" responses to and appropriations of Christianity that fall outside the framework of the Western churches. A review of the literature indicates that the history and impact of the Western mission churches has received the overwhelming attention and efforts of scholars, but that in recent decades there has been a broadening of research interests and more serious consideration of what Asians have contributed to the development of Christianity in their own countries and in the region as a whole.

This article will focus on three principal areas of Asia: (1) the Far East (the countries bordering the Pacific Ocean), which have been profoundly influenced by the Confucian worldview and by Buddhism; (2) Southeast Asia, where the dominant influence has been Buddhist, though not without Hindu and Islamic factors; (3) the Indian subcontinent, the home of Hindu culture, though with areas in which Hinduism has been almost completely submerged by Islam.

THE FAR EAST. The history of Christianity in the Far East is not one story. The introduction of Christianity and subsequent patterns of development have differed considerably in China, Taiwan, Japan, and Korea. In some instances there have been repeated introductions in response to the changing political climate of these lands.

China. By the seventh century CE, Nestorian Christians had made their way from Mesopotamia (Iraq) as far as western China. The discovery by the Jesuits in 1623 of the famous "Nestorian monument" in the precincts of the old Tang dynasty (618–907) capital, Chang-an, has made available reliable information as to the origins, arrival (635 CE), and fortunes of those engaged in this tremendous adventure. This church survived for about two centuries.

The second Christian incursion came with the Franciscan attempt to establish a mission in Khanbaliq (Beijing), with the hope of the conversion of Kublai Khan (1216–1294), hopes frustrated by the turning of the peoples of Central Asia to Islam and not to Christianity. John of Monte Corvino (d. around 1330) arrived in Beijing in 1294, gathered around him Christians of the Uighur people (who had been converted to the Nestorian form of Christianity), and secured consecration as archbishop. Other missionaries had joined him; however, distance from the home church made their work difficult, and after about half a century the mission ceased to exist.

The third attempt was made by Jesuits in the sixteenth century. Matteo Ricci (1552–1610) and his colleagues secured the favor of the Chinese by their achievements in astronomy and by introducing striking clocks, learning Chinese, and adopting many Chinese ways. In the opinion of their critics, Ricci and his colleagues were prepared to go too far in their adaptation of the Christian gospel to Chinese custom and tradition. In 1744 the pope forbade all such accommodation to non-Roman ways. The mission maintained itself, with varying fortunes, for a century and a half. It never completely died out, but at the end of the eighteenth century it was hardly more than a shadow of what it had been. The discovery of the diary of Andrew Li, a Chinese priest who had been trained in the seminary of Ayutthaya (Thailand), in which the students, from many lands, were allowed to talk with one another only in Latin, has shed a great deal of light on this period of decline.

The fourth missionary incursion, Roman Catholic and Protestant, followed the infamous Opium Wars of 1840 to 1842, and the unjust Nanjing treaty. Missionaries gradually managed to establish residence in all the provinces of China as far as the borders of Tibet, the Roman Catholics relying on the protection of the emperor Napoleon III and the Protestants for the most part following the advice of Hudson Taylor of the China Inland Mission in making their appeals only to the regularly constituted Chinese authorities. The church grew slowly but steadily through the adhesion of individuals and families. But the Christian mission was always under suspicion as being associated with the hated imperialism of the Western powers.

With the failure of the so-called Boxer Rebellion at the end of the nineteenth century, many Chinese felt driven to seek new moral resources for the restoration of China; they found an answer in the teaching of Jesus Christ, though with more emphasis on the moral and social teaching than on the specifically religious content. An astonishing number of young people accepted baptism; many of them were later to be distinguished in China's national life.

Then, in 1949, the communists overthrew the government of Chiang Kai-shek and took over rule of China. Their attitude was one of hostility to all religions, though some Christians succeeded in making a deal with this hostile government. Churches were closed; the Christians were driven underground. Many observers believed that for the fourth time China had rejected the Christian message and that the church was dead, except perhaps for small house groups. When the government loosened its restrictions on the practice of Christianity in 1979, it became clear that the churches were very much alive and in some areas had even increased their membership. The government's estimate of the Christian population in 1982, in fact, was three million, or three times the membership in 1949.

The Roman Catholics are in a particularly ambiguous position because many Chinese have refused the allegiance to Rome that Rome demands. The Protestants have formed a national council, which has brought them together without eliminating denominational differences and without allaying the anxieties of those who feel that the council has made too many concessions to the Marxist rulers.

Since the 1980s the fortunes of Christianity in China have changed dramatically. The demographic shift of masses from rural to urban areas has been accompanied by the rapid growth of Christian churches, underground house churches, and independent Christian movements. As in India, Christianity has also met with considerable success among minority tribal groups. A study in 1997 discovered that in Fugong County in southwest China, an area where the Lisu minority is concentrated, about seventy percent of the people were Christian. There is considerable disagreement on the actual number of Christians in contemporary China. As of 2003, the government estimated that there were at least sixteen million Christians; the China Christian Council suggests a number of at least twenty-five million, whereas experts from outside of China suggest figures ranging from forty million to one hundred million. Whatever the actual number, it is clear that Chinese Christianity is in a growth phase and its influence is spreading widely throughout society.

Taiwan. The Christian situation on the island is complicated. For a century the main Christian mission on Taiwan was Presbyterian (Canadian in the north, English in the south). When the Presbyterians came to the ninetieth anniversary of the founding of the mission, they asked themselves what they should do to celebrate the centenary and decided that, in the decade leading up to it, they would double their membership and double the number of their places of worship. Strong popular support achieved this goal.

During the period of Japanese colonial occupancy, and in the face of the strongest possible opposition from the Japanese, remarkable Christian movements began to take place among the peoples dwelling in the mountains. These people, who form a comparatively small percentage of the population of the island, speak their own languages and follow ancestral traditions entirely different from those of the lowland Taiwanese. In the twentieth century, entire communities have become Christian.

The whole situation on the island changed with the mass emigration from continental China that followed the collapse of the Kuomintang government. Chiang Kai-shek himself, with many of his leading followers, left their homes to begin a new existence in Taiwan, claiming that they, and not the Marxists, represented the true spirit and succession of China. This was by no means to the liking of the Taiwanese. Under the Japanese they had been compelled to learn the Japanese language; now they were compelled to learn the Mandarin form of Chinese, which is considerably different from the form of the Amoy dialect that the Taiwanese had traditionally spoken. With the continental Chinese came a proliferation of Christian churches and sects. Roughly one-third of the Catholics in Taiwan are Chinese who fled the mainland. In the last several decades of the twentieth century, the Pentecostal and charismatic renewal movements have been particularly influential. Roughly one-third of the 300,000 Taiwanese Protestants would identify themselves as Pentecostals or charismatic Christians.

Japan. Japan was almost wholly unknown to the West until Francis Xavier (1506–1552), with a small group of Jesuit colleagues, managed to land in the country in 1549 and remain for the greater part of three years. The Jesuit enterprise was crowned with astonishing success. Rulers were converted and were followed into the Christian church by their dependents. At the end of the sixteenth century it was reckoned that there were 300,000 Christians in Japan. Then the climate changed. During a period of terrible persecution, many missionaries died agonizing deaths, though a few recanted and denied their Christian faith. Almost all the faithful reverted to their previous religions; in 1638 it was concluded that "the Christian century in Japan" had come to an end with the elimination of the church. For more than two centuries Christianity was a proscribed religion. However, when at last in 1859 missionaries were able again to enter the closed land, they discovered with astonishment that a remnant of believers had maintained the faith in many of its essentials. Some of these so-called hidden Christians (*Kakure Kirishitan*) rejoined the Roman Catholic church once it was reestablished in Japan, whereas many others continued to practice their own version of the faith in small isolated communities on the island of Kyushu.

Never, since the sixteenth-century Jesuit success, has there again been anything like a mass movement of Japanese into the Christian church. Japanese Christians are often marked by three characteristics: intense intellectual activity, with faith depending on thoughtful conviction rather than on emotional decision; a strong spirit of independence, as in the non-church movement of Uchimura Kanzō (1861–1930), which refused to be tied to any kind of denominational organization; and a steady determination not to be subject to Western domination.

During World War II, the government decided that only three Christian bodies, the Roman Catholic, the Eastern Orthodox, and a Protestant amalgam called the United Church of Christ in Japan (Kyōdan), should be recognized. Some Anglicans, some Lutherans, and some Holiness churches refused to join the Kyōdan and lost all legal recognition, enduring varying degrees of official disapproval and even persecution. With the end of the war and establishment of religious freedom with the new constitution in 1947, some of the denominations that had been absorbed into the Kyōdan during the war withdrew and reestablished independent denominational identities. The Kyōdan remains the largest Protestant denomination, but smaller independent, evangelical, and Pentecostal groups tend to be more effective in attracting new members.

The Roman Catholic church in Japan has become an important source of support for many non-Japanese laborers and immigrants from countries such as the Philippines and Brazil, and their involvement in local parishes is creating new church dynamics and posing new challenges for pastoral care. Although church membership in modern Japan has never exceeded one percent of the population, the influence of Christianity remains significant in education, social work, and literature.

Korea. Korea has drawn much from Chinese culture and for a time was forced to endure Japanese rule, but the Korean language and many of the features of Korean life may have originated in Central Asia. After experiencing some rather ineffective attempts at Roman Catholic evangelization, the country remained entirely closed to foreign influences until the second half of the nineteenth century. Christian missionaries during that period were mostly Americans, notably Methodists and Presbyterians. The small Anglican mission distinguished itself by a special concern for the Korean traditions of language and culture.

After initial resistance, many Korean animists, whose adherence to Buddhism was largely formal, responded positively to the Christian message. From the start, the Korean Christians were encouraged to be independent and to serve as evangelists among their own people, the foreigners keeping in the background. In South Korea all churches are independent and self-governing, though many of them are linked to worldwide churches and denominations. The church has grown rapidly since the 1960s and is known for the development of mega-churches. The largest church in the world today, in fact, is the Yoido Full Gospel Church in Seoul, which claims over 700,000 members and a Sunday attendance of more than 200,000. The growth of the Korean church has also been accompanied by the development of numerous mission agencies and overseas missionary work. In the last decade of the twentieth century, the number of Korean missionaries serving overseas grew from 1,645 serving in 87 different countries in 1990 to 10,745 serving in some 162 different countries in 2002.

Little information is available regarding the fate of churches and Christians in North Korea. As far as is known, Christian churches have no visible existence under the Marxist regime. From occasional contacts that are possible between Christians in the south and relations and friends in the north, it seems that, as in China, Christians are maintaining their faith under conditions of extreme difficulty. Many Christians are active in the efforts for the political reunification of North and South Korea.

SOUTHEAST ASIA. The countries which stretch in a wide semicircle from the Philippines to Pakistan represent a great variety of races, languages, religions, and forms of culture. It is extremely difficult to reduce them all to any kind of common denominator. It is true that they all have come, at one time or another, under strong Buddhist influence, and that three of these countries have adopted Buddhism as their national religion. With the single exception of Thailand, all have come under colonial domination and have thus been bound to the West in about equal proportions of adaptation and resentment. Beyond that, generalization is difficult, and it will be best to address each country separately, especially as the degree of Christian influence varies greatly from one country to another.

The Philippine Republic. The Philippine Republic is the only Christian nation in Asia. The Spaniards arrived in 1538 and remained in power for three and a half centuries. In the course of those years, almost the entire population was brought within the Roman Catholic church, though a Muslim minority remained in the southern islands.

With the victory of the Americans in the war with Spain (1889–1902), sovereignty passed from the Spaniards to the Americans. To some Filipinos this change seemed like deliverance, for there had been increasing resentment among Filipinos at the domination of Spaniards in every part of the life of the people, not least in the life of the church.

Roman Catholics constituted the majority of the people, though at times restless and discontented. One sign of this was the uprising within the church, which led to the formation of the Philippine Independent Church, often called the Aglipayan Church after its first leader, Gregorio Aglipay (1860–1940). This church came under strong Unitarian influence, but in later times it restored more orthodox Christian tradition and recovered a regular Episcopal succession through the American Episcopal Church. In the early 1980s the church claimed three million members, though this may be an overestimate.

With the religious freedom brought by the Americans, Protestant missionaries poured in; they converted many discontented Catholics. Almost all the main American Protestant bodies are represented. The first Episcopal bishop, Charles Henry Brent, well known for his creative connection with the Faith and Order movement, told his missionaries to go to the mountain peoples, whom the Roman Catholic church had never succeeded in reaching.

It took time for the Roman Catholic church to adapt itself to the new situation. But gradually the lesson was learned, and an indigenous episcopate was brought into being. The church has produced some fine scholars. Ecumenical relations are far better than they were, and, though a number of tensions still exist, cooperation among Christians has been carried further than in many other countries. The charismatic movement has also had an impact on the Catholic and Protestant churches in the Philippines, with an estimated seven million or more involved in some way.

Vietnam and Cambodia. Roman Catholic missions had notable success in Vietnam in the seventeenth and eighteenth centuries. In the twentieth century, the Marxists took over, and many Christians fled from the north to the south. With the fall of the South Vietnamese government in 1975, Christians found themselves faced with the alternatives of accepting communist rule or again becoming refugees. Many died in their search for freedom. Because Cambodia was largely neglected by Christian missionaries, Cambodian Christians are few, and Buddhism has remained the major tradition.

Thailand, Burma, and Sri Lanka. Buddhism, wherever it exists, has proved resistant to Christian evangelism; Christians who are present in Buddhist countries in many cases have come from non-Buddhist peoples or communities. Thailand, squeezed in the nineteenth century between British and French dominions, has managed to preserve throughout history a somewhat precarious independence: its citizens would probably point to the Buddhist faith as the power that has preserved their country in its integrity. A Buddhist country ruled by a monarchy imbued with Buddhist tradition, Thailand is, however, a tolerant country, and the number of Christian missionaries increased greatly with the advance of the twentieth century. Conversions from Buddhism, however, have not been numerous. The majority of Christians in the country have come from the Chinese minority, not from among the Thais, and the total number of Christians represents less than one percent of the population.

Myanmar (known as Burma prior to the name change in 1989), after a century under British rule, obtained its independence in 1947 and declared Buddhism to be the national religion. Actually, large sections of the population are neither Burmese nor Buddhist; it is among these peoples that the Christian churches have made their greatest gains. Baptists are more numerous than any other Christian body in Burma. Their first great missionary, Adoniram Judson (1788–1850), who made himself a Burmese scholar and translated the Bible into that language, was imprisoned by the Burmese authorities and endured terrible sufferings from which he never entirely recovered. It was he who made contact with the Karens, a large non-Burmese group, and discovered among them a tradition concerning a sacred book which they had once possessed, and which one day would be brought back to them by white teachers.

This formed a point of entrance for Christianity, and Karens form a large part of the Christian population of Burma. Work has also been carried on successfully among the Chins, Kachins, and other peoples in the areas stretching up to the frontiers with China and India. Roman Catholic activity has also been vigorous. The best-known figure of the Roman Catholic church in Burma was Bishop Bigandet (vicar apostolic, 1856–1893), an eminent scholar whose works on Buddhism in its Burmese form are still authoritative.

Restrictions on the residence of foreigners in Myanmar have led to the withdrawal of all foreign Christian workers. The churches, forced to rely on their own resources, have suffered from a sense of isolation. But the Anglican Church, much smaller in number than the Baptists, has reported that its numerical progress is considerably more rapid than in the days when it was under the care and supervision of foreign missionaries. Christianity largely remains a religion of ethnic minorities (roughly five percent of the population), whereas the majority (eighty-nine percent) within Myanmar maintains their association with the Theravāda Buddhist tradition.

Sri Lanka is inhabited by adherents of four religions: Buddhism, Hinduism, Islam, and Christianity. But Buddhists prevail. The Buddhist priesthood has been extremely influential in political as well as in religious affairs. Serious attempts have been made to turn Sri Lanka into a Buddhist country and to make Sinhala the only official language. These attempts have led to grave dissensions between those who speak Sinhala and those who speak Tamil, among whom are many Christians.

During the Portuguese period, many inhabitants of the island became members of the Roman Catholic church. Under the Dutch a considerable number became Protestants; but, with the religious toleration introduced by the British at the end of the eighteenth century, a large majority of Protestants reverted to the Roman Catholic church, which embraces about four-fifths of all the Christians on the island. Since the 1980s a number of Pentecostal and charismatic churches and movements have been added to the traditional mix of Catholics and Protestants, and the older denominations have recorded gradual decline. Overall, the Christian population remains a small minority

Buddhism in Sri Lanka is marked by the excellence of its scholars and by the powerful influence of its teachings. A few Christians have become Buddhists, among them a former prime minister of the country. Christians in Sri Lanka have become aware of the vitality of their country's Buddhist tradition. A number of them have studied deeply and have qualified themselves as experts in Buddhism; such interreligious dialogue is perhaps more active in Sri Lanka than in any other part of the world.

Indonesia. Indonesia, a republic three thousand miles long and including about three thousand islands, stands somewhat apart from the rest of Southeast Asia, showing marks of Hindu, Buddhist, and Islamic religions. It has the largest Muslim population of any country in the world.

The Dutch, when they were dominant, carried on missionary work, with a good deal of success especially in Ambon and northern Sulawesi. Indonesia is the only country in the world in which there is a steady drift of Muslims into the Christian church. It seems that one cause has been the sharp reaction of many Muslims against the vengeance taken by Muslims against actual or suspected communists at the time of an attempted communist coup in 1965.

The most notable success has been obtained among the non-Muslim Batak people of northern Sumatra. Missionary Ingwer Nommensen (1834–1918), when he first saw beautiful Lake Toba in 1885, envisioned a time when the church bell in every village would call the faithful to worship. Since that time millions of Bataks have entered the Christian churches and evangelism continues. The skill and energy with which Indonesian Christians have freed themselves from Dutch and German influences is reflected in the sense of independence that marks Christians of that country, an independence which is being modified by an increasing willingness to enter into the life of the wider Christian world and to accept the help offered by other Christians.

The Indian Subcontinent. In 1757, at the battle of Plassey, the British established themselves as the strongest power in India. British unification of the subcontinent was complete in 1848. This unity lasted for almost a hundred years. In 1947 Muslims asserted their independence through the formation of Pakistan as an independent state (to be followed by the separation of East Pakistan), and the constitution, under the name Bangladesh, of a third independent state in the subcontinent.

The date at which the Christian faith first appeared in India has been the subject of many debates and still presents itself as a fascinating historical problem. It is certain that a Christian church has existed in Kerala (in southwestern India) for many centuries. The members of the various churches of the Thomas Christians are at one in their conviction that their church, in its original form, was founded by the apostle Thomas himself.

A number of scholars support the view that churches did exist in India not later than the second century; all but the most skeptical accept a date in the fourth century as almost certain. Through the centuries the church maintained its distinctiveness by retaining Syriac as the language of worship and receiving its bishops from Mesopotamia. Information for the medieval period is scanty; but when communication with the West was renewed, with the arrival of the Portuguese by the sea route in 1498, the church was found to be flourishing, Christians forming an accepted and respected element in Indian society. This ancient church remained, however, within the narrow compass of the region between the mountains and the sea, and, so far as is known, made no attempts to evangelize other parts of India. In fact, it made rather few attempts to convert local non-Christians.

When the Portuguese occupied Goa (1510) and made it the base for the establishment of their sea-borne empire, the situation was radically changed. The newcomers made no attempts to conquer extensive tracts of land as they had done in the Americas; but they did regard commerce and conversion to Christianity as intimately related to one another. By the end of the sixteenth century, as a result of special privileges for Christians and special hindrances for Hindus, the great majority of the population in the Portuguese possessions had entered the Roman Catholic church. In 1599, at the Synod of Udiyamperur (Diamper), the archbishop of Goa had persuaded the entire body of Thomas Christians to renounce the patriarch of Baghdad and accept the authority of the patriarch of Rome. Half a century later a third of the Thomas Christians, in rebellion against the autocracy of the Jesuits, reasserted their independence in the formation of the Malankara Syrian Orthodox Church, in which they still have their home.

A new complexion was given to missionary work by the great adventure of the Italian aristocrat Roberto de Nobili (1606–1656 in India), who set to work to turn himself into a brahman in order to win the brahmans. Nobili's considerable knowledge of Sanskrit and extensive literary activity in Tamil left a permanent mark on the Indian church.

With the support of the king of Denmark, the Protestants entered the field in 1706 in the small Danish territory of Tranquebar. Protestant missionary Christian Friedrich Schwartz served in India from 1750 until 1798 and left the indelible impression of a serene and gentle radiance upon Europeans and Indians alike.

In the first half of the nineteenth century, growth both for Roman Catholics and for Protestants was slow. The great period of expansion began in 1858, when the British government took over rule in India from the East India Company. Christians of many nations entered into the work, which in fifty years spread into almost every corner of India except in those areas where independent Indian rulers refused permission for any kind of Christian propaganda in their domains.

Three features of this period deserve special mention. First, the immense educational effort of the missionaries, aided by financial support from the government, produced a large Christian middle class, educated and professional, which prepared the way for the development of independent Indian churches. Second, the underprivileged "outcastes," seeing no hope of a better future under the Hindu system, began to press into the Christian churches. This movement was disapproved of by a great many missionaries and by the majority of educated Indian Christian leaders, but the pressure would not be stayed. These "untouchables" (*dalits*), in fact, represent well over half of all Protestant and Roman

Catholic church members. Third, many among the aboriginal peoples, having no wish to be incorporated into the Hindu caste system, saw in the Christian way a greater freedom than they could hope to enjoy elsewhere. Some whole peoples have become Christian and others greatly Christianized.

In the twentieth century, the great change was the transfer of power from foreign agents to indigenous leaders. The first Indian Anglican bishop, V. S. Azariah, was consecrated in 1912; the first Indian bishop of the Latin rite, Tiburtius Roche, was consecrated for Tuticorin in 1923. Rome showed its recognition of the maturity of the Indian church by the appointment of the first Indian cardinal, Valarian Gracias of Bombay, in 1953. The four fully united and independent churches of South India, North India, Pakistan, and Bangladesh have manifested an independent ecumenical spirit.

In the early 1980s, Christians numbered less than three percent of the population in India, much less in Pakistan and Bangladesh. But it may be argued that Christian teaching has had an impact upon contemporary Indian ethical thought. The government of independent India has abolished by law "untouchability." This righteous action owes much to the passionate advocacy by missionaries of the rights of the underprivileged. The Sarda Act, which raised the age of marriage for both boys and girls, was brought forward by Hindu reformers; these reformers were building on the work of Christians whose opposition to child marriage was well known.

British rule came to an end in 1947. When the change took place, both those who welcomed it with enthusiasm and those who viewed it with considerable alarm accepted it without question; not a single missionary left his or her post for reasons of political change. Nevertheless, political change was bound to affect the lives and prospects of Christians in a number of ways. While the Indian constitution contains a statement in favor of religious freedom, Christians often find life more difficult than it was in earlier days.

Pakistan has from the start been riven by dissensions. In any Muslim state Christians face a number of difficulties; Christians in Pakistan may have to face the possibility of increasing difficulties.

Conclusion. In 1948 the World Council of Churches and the International Missionary Council convened in Manila a meeting of leaders in the East Asian churches. The result of the meeting was the formation of the East Asia Secretariat, without any authority but with the expressed aim of promoting fellowship and mutual understanding. This was the beginning of a process which has proved highly productive. The Asian churches have come to feel that they ought to belong to one another. They have, for instance, held a meeting to discuss the problems of Christian faith and order in an Asian setting.

The missionary movement of the nineteenth and early twentieth century aimed at the development of an indigenous church in Asia defined by the "three selfs": self-control, self-support, and self-propagation, but usually understood as a duplication of the denominational expressions of churches in Europe or North America. There has been an overall decline in the number of missionaries related to the old established mainline churches and denominations of Europe and North America, although evangelical churches in the West maintain a strong missionary presence in Asia where legally permitted. Whereas there remain many examples of dependence on Western church theologies, creeds, and polities, most churches in Asia are under the direction of native rather than foreign leaders, and many new independent and post-denominational forms of Christianity have emerged in the last quarter of the twentieth century.

The transplantation of "normative" theologies from the West has largely been replaced by a serious concern to develop new forms of theological interpretation and Christian practice rooted in local cultures. Catholics refer to these theological developments as "inculturation," whereas Protestants usually use the term "contextualization." Just as Greek philosophy and categories shaped the early development of Western theologies, the Asian religious traditions—Hindu, Buddhist, and Confucian, for example—represent important resources for these new theological initiatives. Heroic and largely successful attempts to nurture a specifically Asian Christianity have been made. The full flowering of Asian theology may be yet to come, just as the full flowering of Christian thought and expression in the Syriac, Greek, and Latin languages did not begin until three centuries after the ministry of Jesus Christ. What has become abundantly clear is that Asians were not passive recipients of transplanted Christianity, but active agents who reinterpreted and reconstructed the Christian faith in terms that made sense to them.

In most of the multi-religious Asian societies considered here, Christians remain a minority group. In this situation, many church leaders have realized the importance of understanding the values and traditions that shape the larger majority with whom Christians must cooperate in order to build and sustain a civil society. Representatives of many churches and Christian institutions have invested considerable effort in dialogue with people of other faiths and established research and study centers that sponsor various activities and publications aimed at interreligious understanding. Inter-Religio, a network of sixteen Christian institutes and centers from eight countries in East Asia, is one example of this important development.

As has been the case in other non-Western contexts, the study of Christianity in Asia was initially burdened by a Eurocentric and North American orientation, and studies tended to focus on transplanted mission churches, missionary leaders, and institutions. A growing number of scholars are now seriously considering some additional ways in which Asians have engaged and reshaped Christianity throughout this region of the world.

SEE ALSO Chinese Religion, overview article; Japanese Religions, overview article; Jesuits; Korean Religion; Ricci, Matteo; Southeast Asian Religions, articles on Insular Cultures, New Religious Movements in Insular Cultures; Syriac Orthodox Church of Antioch; Uchimura Kanzō; Xavier, Francis.

BIBLIOGRAPHY

There are short summaries on all the countries dealt with in this survey in the *World Christian Encyclopedia*, edited by David B. Barrett (Oxford, 2001, second edition). Whereas this is a useful resource, readers should know that the membership data and figures for Christians tend to be on the high side. For statistical data on Catholics in Asia, see Bryan T. Froehle and Mary L. Gautier, *Global Catholicism: Portrait of a World Church* (Maryknoll, N.Y., 2003). An important reference work that serves as a useful guide to contemporary scholarship and bibliographical materials both on mission churches and indigenous Christian developments is Scott Sunquist, ed., *A Dictionary of Asian Christianity* (Grand Rapids, Mich., 2001). An indispensable resource on theology in Asia is John England, et al eds., *Asian Christian Theologies: A Research Guide to Authors, Movements, Sources*. Vols. 1 3 (Delhi, 2003). For recent events and developments in China, the best source is the periodical literature; see, for example, *The China Quarterly*, No. 174 (June 2003). Other useful resources include Daniel H. Bays, ed., *Christianity in China from the Eighteenth Century to the Present* (Stanford, Calif., 1996); Alan Hunter and Kim-Kwong Chan, *Protestantism in Contemporary China* (Cambridge, U.K., 1993); Samuel H. Moffett, *A History of Christianity in Asia, Vol. I, Beginnings to 1500* (Maryknoll, N.Y., 1998); and Nicolas Standaert, ed., *Handbook of Christianity in China, Vol. I* (Leiden, 2001). On Japan, see Mark R. Mullins, ed., *Handbook of Christianity in Japan* (Leiden, 2003), and on Korea and Japan, see Mark R. Mullins and Richard Young, eds., *Perspectives on Christianity in Korea and Japan* (Lewiston, N.Y., 1995). For a study of independent indigenous Christian movements, see Mark R. Mullins, *Christianity Made in Japan* (Honolulu, 1998). For India, see James Massey, *Roots of Dalit History, Christianity, Theology and Spirituality* (Delhi, India, 1996) and Stephen Neill, *History of Christianity in India*, 2 vols. (Cambridge, U.K., 1984–1985). On interreligious dialogue and relations in Asia, see Wesley Ariarajah, *Hindus and Christians: A Century of Protestant and Ecumenical Thought* (Grand Rapids, Mich., 1991); Judith M. Brown and Robert Eric Frykenberg, eds., *Christians, Cultural Interactions, and India's Religious Traditions* (Grand Rapids, Mich., 2002); Walen Lai and Michael von Bruck, *Christianity and Buddhism: A Multicultural History of Their Dialogue* (Maryknoll, N.Y., 2000); and Peter K.J. Lee, ed., *Confucian-Christian Encounters in Historical and Contemporary Perspective* (Lewiston, N.Y., 1991). An important book for locating recent trends in Asia within the larger context of world Christianity is Philip Jenkins, *The Next Christendom: The Coming of Global Christianity* (Oxford, 2002).

STEPHEN C. NEILL (1987)
MARK R. MULLINS (2005)

CHRISTIANITY: CHRISTIANITY IN AUSTRALIA AND NEW ZEALAND

Christianity has developed in Australia and New Zealand along broadly similar lines. Such similarities include the occurrence of colonization at about the same time, largely by emigration from the British Isles; the early presence of major Christian denominations, both locally and in extending missionary activity in the South Pacific; periodic sectarian strife; and, by the end of the twentieth century, the clearly evident effect of secularizing influences. Important differences include the much greater geographical extent of Australia, the situation of the respective indigenous inhabitants, and the partly different ethnic background and denominational affiliations of immigrants.

CONTACTS BETWEEN CHRISTIANITY AND INDIGENOUS CULTURES. British penal settlements were established in New South Wales on the east coast of Australia in 1788 and, on a smaller scale, in Van Diemen's Land (Tasmania) in 1803. During the nineteenth century, ex-convicts, free settlers, and government-assisted immigrants increased the population and spread it to Western and South Australia, Victoria, and Queensland.

The Aborigines—tribally and linguistically distinct groups scattered throughout Australia, with a population variously estimated between 300,000 and 750,000—were quickly displaced in the eastern colonies and reduced in numbers by disease, loss of hunting grounds, malnutrition, and brutality from settlers. Officials and missionaries found Aborigines to be enigmatic, and provision for religious observances in the settlements took slight account of them. Their seminomadism hindered missions and made it easy for settlers to assert that Aborigines had no substantive territorial claims. Missions, schools, and various measures, which sought simultaneously to isolate Aborigines from their own communities and segregate them from Europeans, had limited success during the nineteenth century.

From the late eighteenth century onward, whalers, sealers, and traders were attracted to New Zealand, inhabited by the Maori, who numbered between 70,000 and 100,000 in 1840. In that year New Zealand was annexed as a British colony, and Governor William Hobson signed the Treaty of Waitangi with northern Maori chiefs; subsequently, signatures were collected widely from other chiefs. The proceedings, the part played by missionaries, the meaning of the treaty's terms, and the treaty's contemporary relevance remain controversial. Disputes over land erupted into violence (at its most intense between 1860 and 1865), followed by extensive and unjust confiscation. Initial criticism of governmental action and settlers' attitudes by some church leaders, such as Octavius Hadfield, an Anglican missionary, became muted as the conflict proceeded. One legacy was widespread alienation of Maori from the British and their churches.

The Church Missionary Society had begun work among Maori in the far north of the North Island in 1814, partly at the behest of Samuel Marsden, a Church of England (Anglican) chaplain to the convict colony in New South Wales. In 1822, Wesleyan Methodists began work among the Maori, initially in the far north; both missions gradually extended southwards. Early Anglican and Methodist missionaries were firmly Protestant and evangelical, and the arrival in 1838 of Bishop Jean Baptiste Pompallier as the head of a Catholic mission generated anti-Catholicism and suspicion of French motives. Catholic missionaries, initially drawn from the Marist order, were, under Pompallier's guidance, more ready to accommodate native customs and often achieved closer identification with the Maori. Their impact was diminished by their relatively late arrival, the itinerant style of their ministry, Pompallier's administrative ineptitude, and, after 1850, the withdrawal of the Marist order from the diocese of Auckland, which comprised the upper half of the North Island and much of the Maori population.

By 1845 about half the Maori population was worshiping in Christian congregations. The general state of Maori society, the nature of the missionaries' impact, and the part played by other factors (e.g., war-weariness among the Maori, the attractions of literacy, improvements in the quality and methods of missionaries, and the role of Maori leadership) are debated by historians. Indigenous evangelists, catechists, and teachers significantly assisted conversions. The wives of missionaries played an important part in caring for their families, but also in having charge of mission stations when husbands were absent and in influencing Maori women and girls. The Maori often combined Christian ideas with their own traditional beliefs and practices, initially informally, but soon in reactive movements that combined secular and religious concerns. One of the earliest such movements, led by Papahurihia, later known as Te Atua Wera, emerged in the 1830s. Other movements followed, including that led by Pai Marire and Ringatu during the 1860s, and the movements associated with Rua Kenana and Tahupotiki Wiremu Ratana in the first and second decades of the twentieth century, respectively.

Church Development. By 1900 all the major denominations, and several minor ones, were represented in Australia. Anglican chaplains to the penal settlements arrived first; mostly evangelicals, they were precursors of the strong presence their version of Christianity has maintained in Australia. Their ministry to convicts, about a fifth of whom were women, was less successful than that offered to free settlers, where clergy initially found more support from laity than from military and civil authorities. An important stage was reached in 1836 when William Grant Broughton became the first and only Anglican bishop of Australia. His diocese was subsequently subdivided, and the dioceses (and later the general synod) were governed by synods of bishops, clergy, and laity.

Initially, no provision was made for Catholics, despite the presence of Irish convicts. In 1820, two Irish priests arrived in Sydney, but their activities were severely restricted. By 1828, Catholics in New South Wales constituted almost a third of the population. In 1833 William Ullathorne was appointed vicar-general; a year later John Bede Polding was designated bishop of Sydney. Dioceses for other Australian colonies were created in the 1840s. Governance remained the prerogative of bishops and clergy, among whom the Irish soon established a long-sustained predominance. Caroline Chisholm (1808–1877), a Catholic laywoman with a humanitarian concern for immigrants, provided a different style of leadership.

By 1803, Presbyterianism was established among Scottish immigrants in Sydney. John Dunmore Lang, who arrived in 1823, was a dominant, and sometimes dominating, figure in public and ecclesiastical life. By 1850, Presbyterianism was strongly represented, especially in Melbourne, but events in both Scotland and Australia made it prey to controversies and divisions, although these were mostly resolved over the next half-century. A national Presbyterian General Assembly first met in 1901 after wary negotiations over the respective functions of state and national assemblies. The initial Methodist class meeting was held in Sydney in 1812; the first minister arrived in 1815. An Australasian Conference first met in 1855; and in 1902 the Methodist Church of Australasia brought together the branches of Methodism, thirty years before Great Britain did so. By the 1830s several smaller denominations, notably Baptists, Congregationalists, and Quakers, were represented; Lutheranism brought by German migrants, was, like Methodism, especially strong in South Australia. By the close of the nineteenth century, Seventh-day Adventists, the Salvation Army, Brethren, and Unitarians added to denominational variety.

In nineteenth-century Australia the overwhelming majority of the population professed adherence to one of the major denominations. Anglicanism embraced many nominal adherents and infrequent worshipers, and it lost its quasi-establishment status to become one denomination among others. Methodism, on the other hand, shed vestiges of sectarianism to gain denominational status. Catholics and Methodists (especially the former), were initially overrepresented among the less affluent, while Anglicans and Presbyterians were slightly overrepresented among the more affluent.

Systematic colonization of New Zealand began in the 1840s. Two major settlements had ecclesiastical associations: Otago (1848) with Presbyterianism, and Canterbury (1850) with the Church of England; neither ended up religiously exclusive. George Augustus Selwyn, from 1841 to 1867 the first Anglican bishop of New Zealand, was a commanding, sometimes autocratic, figure. By 1869 the original diocese had been subdivided into six dioceses. A constitution of 1857, fostered by Selwyn and enacted without consulting the Maori, established the church in New Zealand as an autonomous province with close links to the Church of England and gave synodical representation to clergy and laity. In 1848 the Catholic Church in New Zealand was divided into two dioceses, based in Auckland and Wellington; dioceses in Dunedin and Christchurch followed later. Irish and Catholic identity were mutually reinforcing but were modified by the presence of English and French clergy and religious.

Presbyterianism, which began as a ministry to settlers, not a mission to the Maori, had its New Zealand beginnings in Wellington in 1840 and Auckland in 1842; during the 1850s and 1860s it spread more widely. Initially, Presbyterianism was organized in two separate bodies, one based in the southernmost provinces of Otago and Southland and the other covering the rest of New Zealand. Reunion moves faltered in the 1860s but succeeded in 1901. The early presence of Methodist missionaries, along with an emphasis on lay involvement, ensured that Methodism was active in the earliest years of settlement. The varieties of British Methodism were represented, but had united by 1913 when Methodism in New Zealand became an autonomous conference. The first Baptist church in New Zealand was formed in Nelson in 1851. The New Zealand Baptist Union was inaugurated in 1882. By 1900, other groups—Congregationalists, Churches of Christ, Quakers, Brethren, Seventh-day Adventists, Unitarians, and Lutherans—were represented in smaller numbers.

The social composition of the major churches in New Zealand was broadly similar to that of Australia, but the level of regular church attendance in New Zealand was lower than that in New South Wales, Victoria, and South Australia—as well as, for that matter, England and Scotland. The difference between Australia and New Zealand may be related to the slightly different denominational composition, since Methodists and Irish Catholics, more strongly represented in Australia, had higher church attendance figures than Anglicans.

Church, State, and Society. Debate on church-state relations in Great Britain extended to Australia and New Zealand. The most significant early measure in Australia was the New South Wales Church Act of 1836, which broke the Anglican monopoly of governmental financial aid and did not distinguish between the major denominations in providing funds to build churches and maintain clergy. Similar arrangements were made in other Australian colonies. South Australia began with a voluntary system and flirted briefly with state aid, but it set a precedent in 1851 by terminating such aid, which was phased out in other Australian colonies by 1895. Hobson, the first governor of New Zealand, was directed to guarantee "the most absolute toleration" to all denominations. Once representative government was in place in 1854, the House of Representatives affirmed "the privilege of a perfect political equality in all religious denominations" and declined responsibility for the Anglican bishop's stipend.

Controversy over the control and funding of education was also exported to the colonies. In Australia a pattern of state aid to denominational schools emerged. Erosion of such aid began in New South Wales in 1866 when separate boards for state and church schools were consolidated, existing denominational schools were regulated, and assistance was withheld from new church schools. In Victoria a secular public system was inaugurated in 1872, and in New South Wales state aid to denominational schools was withdrawn in 1880. Eventually all Australian colonies terminated state aid and established free, compulsory, and secular education at the primary level. In New Zealand aid was given to denominational schools during the Crown Colony period and was continued by some provincial governments until their abolition in 1876. The Education Act of 1877 stipulated that primary education should be free, compulsory, and secular; state aid was withdrawn.

While many Protestants in both countries supported state education in principle, Catholics and some Anglicans opposed it and developed schools at their own expense. Catholic schools, able to draw on religious orders for teaching staff, were more numerous and helped to reinforce Catholic community and identity. Especially in Australia, Protestant and Anglican secondary schools gained a long-lasting elite status. Behind the move to secularization in both countries was a dislike of sectarian squabbling, suspicion of Catholic and Anglican designs, fears of social divisiveness, inefficiencies and inequalities in existing systems, and the growing popularity in government circles of theories of secular education.

The secularizing of primary education, along with concerns about the effects of urbanization and falling church attendance, especially among workingmen, may have helped generate the sense of crisis among Christian leaders that arose in the 1870s. Moves to defend "Christian standards" were channeled into opposition to educational changes, evangelistic efforts, and moves to secure legislation on a range of issues including Sunday observance, temperance, gambling, prostitution, the age of consent, and indecent publications. Visions of what constituted a Christian society and how it was to be realized varied. Protestants and Catholics rarely cooperated. Few Catholics were prepared to support Protestant-led moves on gambling, sabbatarianism, and temperance. An economic depression during the 1890s helped generate concern about social justice, some of which was expressed in "Christian socialism." More generally, however, there was an emphasis on personal religion and morality and their outworking in public life. To this period belong the beginnings of church social-service agencies; Methodist "city missions" and the Salvation Army were conspicuous.

Although there were instances of denominational cooperation, which sometimes bridged the Catholic-Protestant divide, sectarian strife surfaced. Anti-Catholicism was evident in colonial New South Wales; in New Zealand suspicion first fastened on early French Catholic missionaries. Subsequent conflict was fed by various causes, including Protestant aversion to Catholicism, Catholic resentment of Protestant social and political ascendancy, the presence of a largely working-class Irish-Catholic subculture, strongly Protestant lodges and friendly societies, and disputes over education. On both sides were public figures with a propensity for inflammatory rhetoric: Daniel Mannix, archbishop of

Melbourne from 1917 to 1963 (and coadjutor from 1913 to 1917), personified militant Catholicism. During World War I, conscription and the 1916 Easter Rising in Ireland fueled sectarian strife, which continued into the postwar years, sustained by anti-Catholic organizations.

Leadership in church and society up to around 1900 and for some time thereafter was predominantly male. In a few smaller denominations—Primitive Methodists, Bible Christians (a branch of Methodism), Salvation Army, and Unitarians—women were allowed to preach; from the 1890s onward, some larger Protestant denominations appointed women as deaconesses. Women were active in many roles, including evangelism, pastoral care, charitable work, overseas missions, and teaching, particularly in Sunday schools, which gained added importance in the wake of the secularization of public education at the primary level. In Catholicism, and on a much smaller scale in Anglicanism, women's religious orders, some led by outstanding women—including Mary McKillop (1842–1909) in Australia and Suzanne Aubert (1835–1926) in New Zealand—worked effectively in education, nursing, and charitable enterprises. In the closing years of the nineteenth century, various women's organizations emerged, some church-based, others in which churchwomen worked alongside other women in matters of common concern, such as temperance and women's suffrage. Measures facilitating female participation in church government did not follow generally or quickly, even after female suffrage was granted, initially in New Zealand in 1893.

World Wars, Economic Depression, and the Churches. A sense of national identity (among Protestants particularly), combined with imperial loyalty, was evident from around 1900. It became apparent in moves leading to the federation of the Australian colonies in 1901, and in New Zealand in support for the South African War (1899–1902). With few dissentients, mostly from smaller Christian bodies such as Quakers and Brethren, church leaders and representative assemblies strongly supported participation in both world wars, although more soberly during World War II. The disastrous Gallipoli campaign in 1915 to 1916 was speedily memorialized in the annual Anzac (an acronym from Australian and New Zealand Army Corps) Day observance, which blends religious and secular elements and now commemorates the dead in other conflicts also. Australian Lutherans during World War I and conscientious objectors in both countries and conflicts were victims of prejudiced patriotism. For some—chaplains, combatants, and church leaders—World War I was an unsettling experience, strengthening support for pacifism and the League of Nations during the interwar years.

Between the two wars lay the economic depression of the late 1920s and early 1930s. Despite financially restrictive budgets the churches provided relief measures, although as the depression deepened some church members criticized government policies. In New Zealand the Labour Party capitalized on support from the churches, and this was a factor in the party's electoral victory in 1935. In Australia, Ernest Burgmann, the Anglican bishop of Goulburn from 1934, emerged as an outspoken social critic and supporter of working-class aspirations. Some Catholics, influenced by their church's social teachings, envisaged a more just social order, but they also sought to curb Communist influence in trade unions. These efforts, in which B. A. (Bob) Santamaria, a leading and controversial lay intellectual, played a key role, were one cause of a major split in the Australian Labour Party in the 1940s and early 1950s and its political defeat and ineffectiveness until the 1970s. These events strained a long-standing alliance between the Labour Party and Catholicism, which had weakened as Catholics moved up the socioeconomic ladder.

Missionary work among the Maori resumed towards 1900, in some areas competing with Mormons and the Ringatu and Ratana movements. Assimilative policies were only slowly abandoned; measures such as the Anglican appointment of Frederick Augustus Bennett as bishop of Aotearoa in 1928 typically gave the Maori an enhanced but still limited role. Church-related secondary schools contributed towards the emergence of Maori leadership. Aborigines were subjected to drastic assimilative measures, including the removal of Aboriginal children for adoption or institutional care. Protestant and Catholic missions among Aborigines in northern Australia were reestablished beginning around 1900, with varying success. Among Europeans, an understanding of Aboriginal culture remained rare, and protests against the conditions under which many Aborigines lived was rarer. More hopefully, significant indigenous ministry had real beginnings, notably with the evangelist Uraiakurai and with James Noble, the first Aboriginal Anglican deacon.

Women, often in significant educational, medical, and missionary roles, outnumbered men in overseas missions, but the roles that women could take locally changed only slowly. In 1927 Winifred Kiek, a South Australian Congregationalist, was the first woman ordained in either country, although deaconesses increasingly exercised ministry in major Protestant churches after about 1900. In the Catholic and, to some extent, the Anglican Church, laywomen's organizations were supervised by clergy and bishops and confined to devotional, missionary, and charitable activities. Anglican and Catholic leadership, including leading laywomen, remained strongly supportive of traditional patterns of marriage, family, and women's roles, and they were more resistant to changes in divorce law than other denominations.

A higher birth rate, along with immigration after World War II, especially from Italy and other predominantly Catholic countries in Europe, buttressed Catholic numbers in Australia. Migration brought numerical strength, ethnic and ecclesiastical variety, and concomitant tensions with the Orthodox churches. New Zealand was less affected by such immigration because numbers were smaller. There was some leveling off of active membership in Protestant churches in the interwar years, but the majority of children were baptized and attended Sunday school. In both countries about 90 percent of all marriages were performed by a religious celebrant. Liberalizing trends in theology, present from the late nineteenth century, gained added strength in Protestantism, but less so among Anglicans. Conservative evangelicals, edged from influential roles in some theological colleges and leadership positions, established a network of bible colleges, summer conferences, and transdenominational organizations. The diocese of Sydney and its theological college, Moore College, emerged as guardians of conservative, confessional, and firmly Protestant Anglicanism within and beyond Australia.

The years between approximately 1945 and 1960 were comparatively placid and prosperous. During the immediate postwar years there was a strong desire to return to normalcy; rising affluence benefited some, and suburbs mushroomed. Fund-raising schemes financed the construction of church buildings and Catholic schools. Church life was relatively stable: theology, structures, and piety were still largely intact from earlier times. Missions, notably those led in both countries by the Australian Methodist Alan Walker or by Billy Graham, expressed and enhanced Protestant confidence. Traditional Catholic devotionalism was similarly buoyed up by revivalist missions led by local clergy and religious, and by overseas visitors like Father Patrick Peyton, who preached a "rosary crusade" in both countries.

Controversy, Change, and Challenge. The 1960s were labeled the "hinge years"—their cultural turbulence generated by longstanding trends and catalytic events, and their legacy compounded during subsequent decades. Technological developments, notably in contraception, television, computing, and electronic media, helped engender far-reaching social consequences. Customary patterns of employment, recreation, censorship, women's roles, and family life underwent change. Christians were as polarized as their fellow citizens on questions of race, culture, gender, and national identity, and likewise on specific issues like the Vietnam War, abortion, homosexuality, and free-market policies. In addition, Catholics faced the upheaval precipitated by the Second Vatican Council (1962–1965), strains on schooling systems, reaction to the birth-control encyclical *Humanae Vitae* (1968), allegations of sexual abuse by clergy and other religious, the dilution of Catholic distinctiveness, and a decline in vocations to the priesthood and religious life—along with a high dropout rate from both. Some laity responded by adopting an autonomous attitude towards belief and practice, others by maintaining a traditionalist stance; one official response has been the appointment of such trusty conservatives as George Pell, archbishop, successively, of Melbourne and Sydney and a cardinal since 2001.

Moves towards organic union, first mooted about 1900 and never entirely shelved, slowed. In Australia the two Lutheran denominations united in 1966, and in 1977 the Uniting Church brought together Methodists, Congregationalists, and about two-thirds of Presbyterians. In New Zealand, moves to achieve organic union between Anglicans, Churches of Christ, Congregationalists, Methodists, and Presbyterians stalled by 1981. National councils of churches, founded in New Zealand in 1941 and Australia in 1946, continue functioning, but with diminished support and vigor. Since the Second Vatican Council, Catholics participated in some joint ventures, including theological education and local, less formalized ecumenical endeavors. At the same time that reunion moves abated, the internal unity of major Protestant denominations became strained over various theological and moral issues, including the ordination of persons in same-sex relationships. Moreover, Pacific Islanders, Indonesians, Chinese, Koreans, and Vietnamese have established church communities in the region that are strongly attached to traditional beliefs and morality.

Pentecostalism, represented from the 1920s by numerically small denominations, the largest being the Assemblies of God, burgeoned from the 1960s, but gains in this sector of Christianity do not outweigh losses elsewhere. Pentecostalism, along with the charismatic movement in major denominations, forms one aspect of a strong resurgence in conservative evangelicalism. The foundation of "Christian schools" and the increase in parental home schooling are important aspects of this revival. From the 1960s and 1970s, large increases in state aid to schools outside the public system have helped increase their number, sustain their viability, and widen educational options. Some denominational schools have rejected integration with the state system on the grounds that it propagates secular values. Despite sniping from teachers' unions and opposition from organizations such as the Australian Council for the Defence of Government Schools, the provision of governmental assistance to schools outside the public system has continued. Complete reversal of this policy seems unlikely, not least because it would be politically hazardous.

Maori and Aborigines, increasingly urbanized, have become more outspoken about discrimination and land issues. Some in the churches have taken up their cause, especially the Conference of Churches (formerly the National Council of Churches) in Aotearoa, New Zealand, the Uniting Church in Australia, and the National Council of Churches in Australia. Beginning in the 1960s, all major denominations in New Zealand made structural changes to give Maori more determinative roles. In Australia, as governmental and ecclesiastical policies shifted from assimilation to self-determination, some Aborigines have been ordained by major denominations, and more genuinely indigenous expressions of Christianity have emerged. In both countries these changes have helped open the way to the deployment of indigenous art in Christian contexts.

Women have increasingly undertaken theological study and wider roles in church governance and ordained ministry. In New Zealand, women were ordained in the Methodist (1959) and Presbyterian (1965) churches shortly before their Australian counterparts. Among Australian Anglicans, controversy over ordaining women to the priesthood was more divisive and protracted than in New Zealand, where the first such ordinations were held in 1977, compared with 1992 in Australia. Penelope Jamieson became the first woman diocesan bishop in Anglicanism on her appointment to Dunedin in 1990. The Catholic and Orthodox churches and, where priesthood is concerned, some sections of Anglicanism, notably the diocese of Sydney, have resisted this change while utilizing the ministry of women in other ways. Especially in some smaller denominations and independent congregations, traditional views of women's roles find support from the predominantly male leadership and associated women's groups. Conversely, feminism has led some women to various responses, including seeking reform of existing structures, developing feminist theologies and liturgies, or abandoning the churches.

In both countries most major denominations are experiencing a decline in numbers of adherents as a proportion of the total population. Major denominations are also seeing changing patterns of attendance, with fewer people attending services weekly. All such denominations, but some more than others, have an aging population, and as a result Sunday-school enrollments have plummeted. Churches and congregations of an evangelical or charismatic character have a lower age profile. Censuses from 1971 onward show substantial increases in those indicating "no religion" or opting for an increasing number of non-Christian options. Denominational loyalty is less of a concern for younger generations, including some church leaders. Except among relatively recent immigrants, the linkage between ethnic identity and ecclesiastical affiliation has weakened. Rites of passage are less often observed in Christian settings, and the number of people who attend church occasionally is probably falling. In explaining the downturn, some scholars invoke theories of secularization variously interpreted; others stress accelerating cultural and social changes dating back to the 1960s. Some scholars also note the decline in support for voluntary organizations and the alleged corrosiveness of liberal theologies, while others focus on evidence for the survival of religious beliefs—"believing without belonging"—and suggest strategies for church growth accordingly.

Concluding Perspectives. There was much in nineteenth-century church life in Australia and New Zealand that was derivative. Until about 1900, the churches in Australia and New Zealand were substantially dependent on clerical personnel from abroad. Overseas newspapers, periodicals, and books fuelled local theological debates. While some immigrants were eager to shake off the shackles of their past, real and imagined, others preferred to follow familiar ways in church life. The main sources of influence and personnel for Protestants and Anglicans were England, Scotland, and Wales; for Catholics, Ireland and Italy; and for Australian Lutherans, Germany. The United States, too, played its part with the arrival of Seventh-day Adventists, Mormons, and Jehovah's Witnesses; the visits of American Protestant and Catholic revivalists; and the precedent that the Episcopal Church provided for the constitutional arrangements of colonial Anglicanism. There were local initiatives before 1900, but they did not extend to the creation of new denominations or major sectarian movements, although significant Maori reactive movements emerged. While much local church architecture was imitative, timber was sometimes used effectively for construction, interior enhancement, and furnishings. Some local musicians, while influenced by overseas styles, contributed original compositions to hymnody and church music. Where ministry is concerned, lay preachers and, among Anglicans, lay readers were widely used, and in Australia the Australian Inland Mission (Presbyterian) and Anglo-Catholic Anglicans developed forms of ministry adapted for ministry to settlers in the outback.

Overseas influences remain important and pervasive. Air travel and speedier communication via electronic media, tape cassettes, the internet, and video ensure that this is the case. Liberal, radical, and conservative theologians, feminists and their critics, world leaders in Pentecostalism and the charismatic movement, spiritual guides, and church leaders visit Australia and New Zealand frequently. But the situation has changed in two respects. Australians and New Zealanders, now firmly ensconced in leadership positions, are part of an international interchange. Especially in Australia, which has more substantial financial, institutional, and personnel resources, there are now theologians of international standing, including Charles Birch in Sydney and Elaine Wainwright, an Australian and head of the school of theology at the University of Auckland. Church leaders, clerical and lay, participate in international commissions, conferences, and consultations. Along with much that remains derivative, significant local initiatives in architecture, liturgy, religious dance, church music, theology, and spirituality have emerged, some displaying the influence of indigenous cultures and sensitivity to local natural environments. The transition from colonial dependence has led to interdependence and interaction rather than complete independence.

Estimating the impact and significance of Christianity and the churches on cultural and public life is a complex task. In Australia the poet Francis Webb and the painter Arthur Boyd, and in New Zealand James K. Baxter and Colin McCahon (in the same roles, respectively), are examples of the artists, dramatists, novelists, and poets who have drawn on the Christian heritage in richly varied ways. Among historians, sociologists, and social commentators, some claim too much for the influence of Christianity and the churches, others too little. Some see the influence of Christianity and Christian churches as predominantly conservative, while others highlight the espousal of radical causes by groups and individuals, and yet others stress the historically ambiguous record of the treatment of indigenous peoples, children, and women by religious institutions and some professionals.

Where influence is concerned, there are differences in extent and character over time, between social groupings, and from one region to another, especially in Australia. Statistics of attendance and participation have their uses, especially where they disclose trends, but they hardly touch and test the inner essence of religious faith and practice. All this said, some things are clear. Legislative enactments governing Sunday observance, censorship, abortion, gambling, alcohol, and homosexual behavior, once strongly backed by many Christians, have been progressively eroded, despite the opposition of Christian conservatives. In this respect, and more generally, public life has become more secular. Church leaders no longer have the extent of informal contact with politicians they once had; with fewer members (and therefore fewer potential voters), church leaders have less clout with government. Anglican cathedrals in both countries are often still the setting for important national and civic occasions, but only remnants of quasi-establishment status linger.

Even apart from strictly religious considerations there is more to be said. Church-related institutions—hospitals, schools, university residence halls, city missions and other welfare agencies, and voluntary organizations— have made important contributions in areas where government assistance is sometimes parsimonious. It is difficult to point to any one major reform or protest movement sponsored solely by churches, but some leaders and members have participated in such moves, and, on the basis of local and overseas contacts, have contributed valuable perspectives. Christians involved in such activities have had their values shaped and efforts upheld by the worship and fellowship of church communities. Although the major churches still have substantial financial and personnel resources, as well as a degree of public goodwill, they face an uncertain future. Their current weaknesses mirror their diminished, although still significant, influence in the culture and public life of Australia and New Zealand.

SEE ALSO Australian Indigenous Religions, article on Aboriginal Christianity.

BIBLIOGRAPHY

Black, Alan W., ed. *Religion in Australia: Sociological Perspectives.* Sydney, 1991.

Breward, Ian. *A History of the Australian Churches.* Sydney, 1993. With extensive bibliography.

Breward, Ian. *A History of the Churches in Australasia.* Oxford, 2001. The best single treatment of the topic, with comprehensive bibliography.

Carey, Hilary M. *Believing in Australia: A Cultural History of Religions.* Sydney, 1996.

Crumlin, Rosemary. *Images of Religion in Australian Art.* Sydney, 1988.

Davidson, Allan. *Christianity in Aotearoa: A History of Church and Society in New Zealand.* 2d ed. Wellington, 1997. Comprehensive in coverage, with bibliography.

Davidson, Allan K., and Peter J. Lineham. *Transplanted Christianity: Documents Illustrating Aspects of New Zealand Church History.* 3d ed. Palmerston North, New Zealand, 1997.

Donovan, Peter, ed. *Religions of New Zealanders.* 2d ed. Palmerston North, New Zealand, 1996.

Emilsen, Susan, and William W. Emilsen, eds. *Mapping the Landscape: Essays in Australian and New Zealand Christianity, Festschrift in Honour of Professor Ian Breward.* New York, 2000.

Harris, John. *One Blood: 200 Years of Aboriginal Encounter with Christianity, A Story of Hope.* Sydney, 1990.

Hilliard, David. "Australasia and the Pacific." In *A World History of Christianity,* edited by Adrian Hastings, pp. 508–535. Grand Rapids, Mich., and Cambridge, UK, 1999. Succinct survey with useful bibliographical note.

Jackson, H. R. *Churches and People in Australia and New Zealand, 1860–1930.* Wellington, New Zealand, and Sydney, 1987.

Kaye, Bruce, Tom Frame, Colin Holden, and Geoff Treloar, eds. *Anglicanism in Australia: A History.* Melbourne, 2002.

McEldowney, Dennis, ed. *Presbyterians in Aotearoa, 1840–1990.* Wellington, New Zealand, 1990.

Moore, Albert C. *Arts in the Religions of the Pacific: Symbols of Life.* London and New York, 1995. Introductory survey of the arts of indigenous peoples, with bibliography.

O'Farrell, Patrick. *The Catholic Church and Community: An Australian History.* 2d ed. Sydney, 1985.

O'Farrell, Patrick, and Deirdre O'Farrell, eds. *Documents in Australian Catholic History, 1788–1968.* 2 vols. London, 1969.

Piggin, Stuart. *Evangelical Christianity in Australia: Spirit, Word, and World.* Melbourne, 1996.

Thompson, Roger C. *Religion in Australia: A History.* 2d ed. Melbourne, 2002. Lucid and compact, stresses the generally conservative role of the churches.

West, Janet. *Daughters of Freedom: A History of Women in the Australian Church.* Sydney, 1997.

COLIN BROWN (1987 AND 2005)

CHRISTIANITY: CHRISTIANITY IN THE PACIFIC ISLANDS [FIRST EDITION]

Christianity has become the religion of almost all the original peoples of the Pacific Islands. The Indo-Fijian population in Fiji and various immigrant groups in Hawaii are the only population groups that remain largely outside any Christian church. The following examples illustrate the fact that the indigenous island peoples hold to Christianity firmly and vigorously. Samoa has more ministers in proportion to its size than does any other country, and it is reported that 80 percent of the people of Vanuatu are in church on Sunday. In Tonga, until recently, the most common occupation after gardening and fishing was the Christian ministry. Both Papua New Guinea and Western Samoa refer to the Christian faith in their constitutions. Finally, in the country of Tuvalu, people not in church are presumed to be sick, and teams from the congregations visit them during the time of the church service.

INTRODUCTION AND DISTRIBUTION. The distribution of the various confessional groups in the Pacific reflects the processes by which Christianity was introduced to the region. Almost invariably the predominant church of any island or country is the church of the first missionaries to reach it. The move from the traditional religion to Christianity was normally made by the people as a whole—a whole island group in Polynesia or a whole village in Melanesia—thus preserving the religious unity that had existed previously and making for considerable religious uniformity within each land.

The first missionaries to work in the islands, the Spaniards who came with Sanvitores to the Mariana Islands in 1668, established Roman Catholicism as the religion of the Mariana peoples. That condition continues to the present time. The Catholicism of the Marianas is similar in many ways to that of the Philippine Islands, because the missionaries came from the Philippines and because in the following years there was much immigration from the Philippines. The Catholic missionaries also tried to penetrate the western Caroline Islands, but their work there was subject to many fluctuations, and as a consequence conformity to Roman Catholicism is not so general there.

The Spanish efforts died down, but a new missionary élan in Europe brought fresh Protestant and Catholic workers to the islands in the late eighteenth and early nineteenth centuries. The Protestant pioneer body was the London Missionary Society, and its first emissaries began work in Tahiti in 1797. After many disappointments the missionaries were surprised by a sudden shift to Christianity by the principal ruler, Pomare II, in 1815, and soon thereafter Pomare made himself the undisputed ruler of Tahiti and Christianity the undisputed religion of the island. The Protestant church begun then has continued as the majority religion of Tahiti and of the islands associated with it. The London Missionary Society missionaries then moved on to the Cook Islands and also to Samoa, where they established their largest and most flourishing church. From Samoa they reached out to Tuvalu and the Loyalty Islands, where again they became the church of the majority, and to Kiribati, where they eventually had to share the land equally with the Roman Catholics, who came from France at the end of the century.

Another Congregational body, patterned on the London Missionary Society, began missions in Hawaii. This was the American Board of Commissioners for Foreign Missions. When its first group of missionaries reached Hawaii in 1820, the traditional religion had already been repudiated, the great idols destroyed, and the sacred enclosures desecrated. This resulted from the influence of sailors and merchants from Europe and America who had broken the ancient taboos with impunity and had thus shaken the faith of the people. In the following years, Queen Kaahumanu took the lead in presenting Christianity to the people of Hawaii and gaining their adherence to it.

At about the same time, national movements into Christianity were taking place under the auspices of the English Methodists in Tonga and Fiji. The royal leader who made Methodism the church of Tonga was Taufa'ahau (later known as King George), who was converted in 1831 and thereafter brought the entire kingdom under his control by his military prowess. In Fiji there was a similar pattern. Thakombau, the most rapidly rising chief of the islands, made the decision for Christianity in 1854 and was able to defeat his non-Christian rivals. In both Tonga and Fiji the overwhelming majority of the indigenous people became and remain Methodists.

In the islands north and west of Fiji there are no large political units, so the spread of Christianity was slower—village by village. Vanuatu was the only country where the Presbyterians began the first churches and where they are now the major religious body. The Solomon Islands is the only country in the Pacific Islands where the Anglicans were the first to establish continuing work. Their Melanesian Mission began work not only in the Solomons but also in northern Vanuatu. The Anglican church continues as the largest church in the Solomons, though it divides the country with Methodists in the west, the Seventh-day Adventists in the Morovo Lagoon, the South Sea Evangelical Church on the island of Malaita, and the Roman Catholics on several islands. The South Sea Evangelical Church is unique among the churches thus far considered in that it was begun by a nonchurch mission, inspired and led by an Australian woman, Florence Young, who began her work in the islands in 1904.

After the Spanish decline Roman Catholic missionaries were usually from France. In most lands they came after the Protestants and so had only a minority status. This is true in Tahiti and most of French Polynesia (except the Marquesas), and in the Cook Islands, Samoa, Tonga, Fiji, Vanuatu, and the Solomons. In New Caledonia, however, the Catholics came first. Marist missionaries from France began continuing labors in that island in 1851 and, after many initial difficulties, began what is now the major religious community there. Large French and other Catholic immigrations have swelled this majority, and the church is now fairly evenly divided between the indigenes and the immigrants.

Papua New Guinea does not fit into the usual Pacific pattern of one original and predominant church. It contains as many people as all the other islands put together, and neither its history nor its geography has been conducive to a united Christian development. The London Missionary Society established the first continuing mission in 1871 and soon spread along nearly the whole of the south coast. Methodists, this time from Australia, came in 1875 to the Bismarck Archipelago and later to the islands east of Papua. French Catholics followed shortly in both Papua and the Bismarck Archipelago. After the British and German empires came to rule, the Anglican church established itself on the northeast coast of Papua and strong German-Lutheran and German-Catholic missions developed in German New Guinea. Out of these missions have come the five major church traditions of the country: Congregational, Methodist, Roman Catholic, Anglican, and Lutheran, with the Catholics by far the largest. The number of major religious bodies was reduced by one in 1968, when the Congregationalists and the Methodists combined to form the United Church, but that consolidation did not significantly counterbalance the proliferation of denominations that began in the 1950s, primarily in the New Guinea Highlands. The Highlands had been largely unknown and had been closed to Christian penetration before that time. But in the 1950s and 1960s there came a rush of many church and para-church missions into the area, making it the most variegated part of the Pacific Islands in terms of religion.

Indigenous Missionaries. The missionaries who came to New Guinea and to the other islands of the Pacific were not solely the Europeans who have received most of the attention; there were also Pacific-islanders in abundance. As soon as Tahiti and its neighbors were converted, missionaries radiated out from there to the Cook Islands and Samoa. Usually they were taken to their new posts by European missionaries, but once in place they did the major work of starting the new churches. Tonga sent early missionaries, with royal backing, to start Methodist churches in Samoa and Fiji. The Congregational church in Hawaii in the middle of the nineteenth century launched missions to the Marshall Islands and the eastern Caroline Islands, where they began what are still the principal churches of those islands.

The great challenge and opportunity for islander missionaries came in the late nineteenth and early twentieth centuries when New Guinea and the western Solomons were opening up. The Congregationalists of Samoa and the Cook Islands and the Methodists of Fiji and Tonga proved to be the great mission-senders for these new lands. Some 650 men, often accompanied by wives who were equally dedicated to missionary labors, went to the new areas. Much of the church life in the lands where they labored bears the imprint of their particular styles of Christianity. Within New Guinea itself the missionary tradition was continued by many hundreds of Christians who went from the coastlands and outer islands into the Highlands when they were opened. Notable are the hundreds of Lutheran pioneers, many of whom went even before the Highlands were officially opened. The Solomon Islands showed a similar activity in the work of the Melanesian Brotherhood, an Anglican order of young men begun in 1926 and numbering over one thousand through subsequent years, who were dedicated to bringing Christianity to the most isolated and resistant areas.

Folk Christianity. Most of the churches of the islands may be described as folk churches; that is, they are deeply intertwined with the societies around them and they are not inclined to distinguish themselves from or to stand out against those societies. Although they were originally the product of alien influences, they now believe themselves to be protectors of the island traditions and opponents of the newer alien influences that are pouring in.

Churches play a large role in village life and are often directly linked to village leadership. The church buildings are usually constructed by the village people and are maintained by them. Protestant pastors are selected, trained, and supported by the churches of which they are a part. Catholic priests are at present primarily expatriates, but the situation is changing steadily, so that the day of the indigenous priesthood is not far off in many countries. By the early 1980s it was already a reality in Samoa, Fiji, Tonga, Wallis-Futuna, and some parts of Papua New Guinea. The Roman Catholic church, of course, maintains its ties to Rome, but it also exercises much independence in national and regional structures. The major Protestant churches have all achieved full independence from the missions and handle their own affairs.

Interchurch Relations. During the nineteenth century the different Protestant missions worked, by design, in different territories and enjoyed fairly cordial relationships. Between Roman Catholics and Protestants, however, there was intense rivalry and much ill feeling. With the coming of the twentieth century the sense of hostility began to subside. After there were no more adherents of traditional religion who might be won by either camp, there was little point in further competition. People who were already Catholics or Protestants seldom changed sides.

New ecumenical attitudes in the wider world have begun to have their effect in the Pacific. Regional conferences of the Protestant churches began to be held in 1926, and eventually, in 1966, these led to the creation of the Pacific Conference of Churches, a body that includes nearly all the major Protestant denominations. The Catholic Bishops' Conference for the Pacific was formed in 1968, and a parallel organization for Papua New Guinea was also created. In 1973 this Conference took the unprecedented step of deciding to join the Pacific Conference of Churches. This was the first time Catholics anywhere determined to join Protestants in a regional church structure. Today all the major churches recognize each other and often engage in cooperative efforts.

New Religious Movements. The unity evidenced by the major churches does not extend to all the minor churches and sects, many of which have entered the islands in more recent years. The newer churches of the New Guinea Highlands have been brought together in a cooperative structure of their own, the Evangelical Alliance, but elsewhere in the Pacific the newer or smaller churches and sects are vigorously competitive and are growing at the expense of the older, established churches, especially in the urban areas. The largest of the smaller churches is that of the Mormons, which is by no means new and may not long be small. It has been growing rapidly and has become one of the larger minority bodies in most Polynesian countries.

In addition to the influx of new religious movements from outside the Pacific, many new movements have been created by the Pacific peoples themselves. These have usually been short-lived, emotionally intense movements that have combined features of traditional island religion and Christianity. The first of these appeared in Tahiti soon after the conversion of that country and was known as the Mamaia cult. Samoa, during the time of its conversion, saw a similar phenomenon in the cult of Sio Vili. Fiji produced a whole series of such movements that rose and fell in succession. In the years shortly before and after World War II, Papua New Guinea saw a plethora of new movements that drew worldwide attention. They were often called cargo cults, since many of them provided ritual ways of trying to secure the cargo that was seen coming to Europeans. These cults often emerged from the churches and were often led by former church officers. Many tried to enlist entire communities, since the effectiveness of the rituals was believed to require community-wide participation, and thus they damaged and even for a time destroyed church life in certain places. Typically, cult leaders tried to organize and control every aspect of their members' lives in an attempt to establish complete harmony and cooperation. When, however, their own communities developed divisions or the anticipated cargo failed to arrive, members gradually lost interest and the movements died down. In recent years they have largely disappeared, though a few continue in a quieter style and show signs of possible permanence—the Pa-liau movement in Manus, the Christian Fellowship Church in the western Solomons, the John Frum movement on the island of Tanna in Vanuata, and the Modekgnei movement in Belau.

See Also Cargo Cults.

Bibliography

The history and recent development of Christianity in the Pacific Islands is covered in two books: John Garrett's *To Live among the Stars: Christian Origins in Oceania* (Suva, Fiji, 1982), which concentrates on the nineteenth century, and my *The Island Churches of the South Pacific: Emergence in the Twentieth Century* (Maryknoll, N. Y., 1982), which concentrates on the twentieth. One of the few thorough analyses of Christianity in a Pacific country is Alan R. Tippett's *Solomon Islands Christianity: A Study in Growth and Obstruction* (London, 1967). A fine analysis of the work of an anthropologically sensitive missionary exploring what Christianity might mean to Pacific peoples is James Clifford's *Person and Myth: Maurice Leenhardt in the Melanesian World* (Berkeley, 1982). The basic study of the new religious movements has long been Peter Worsley's *The Trumpet Shall Sound: A Study of "Cargo" Cults in Melanesia* (London, 1957). Many fine studies of particular cults have followed. Of these the best known are Kenelm Burridge's *Mambu, a Melanesian Millenium* (London, 1960) and Peter Lawrence's *Road Belong Cargo: A Study of the Cargo Movement in the Southern Madang District, New Guinea* (Manchester, 1964).

Charles W. Forman (1987)

CHRISTIANITY: CHRISTIANITY IN THE PACIFIC ISLANDS [FURTHER CONSIDERATIONS]

During the 1960s mission organizations of the mainstream Christian churches backed away from "foreign control." This allowed for the formation of national Protestant churches. Among these, to illustrate, were l'Église évangélique in New Caledonia (1960), the Cook Islands Christian Church (1965), and the United Church in Papua New Guinea and the Solomon Islands (1968), all originating from a London Missionary Society base. The Evangelical Lutheran Church of Papua New Guinea is of interest for its stage-by-stage securing of complete autonomy between 1956 and 1976, as is the Pacific Christian Church (a Protestant concern independent in Papua New Guinea by 1966) in setting the goal for its Irian Jaya counterpart to pass beyond "mission status." In the Catholic sphere, Vatican II had the effect of generating a new council of bishops for the Pacific region (1966 for Polynesia and Melanesia; 1984 for Micronesia), localizing territorial control. With all these developments came the indigenization of church leadership. A strong stock of Melanesian bishops became manifest. Anglican George Ambo of Papua, for example, inspired austerity and personal discipline following the tightening of foreign purse strings that affected his church; New Guinea Lutheran Zuruwe Zurenuo and the United Church's Leslie Boseto of the Solomon Islands presented strong visions of postmission solidarity; while the controversial Bougainvillean Catholic Gregory Singkai ministered to different sides in the complex Bougainville crisis with extraordinary bravery (1990–1993). As a great man combining ecumenism and peacemaking across the Pacific (as well as astute pastoral care and engagement in the "democracy movement" in his own country), Tongan Catholic bishop Patelisio Finau (1934–1993) seems to tower above all such leaders in recent times.

Aside from mainline denominations, separatist or independent churches with indigenous leaders and homegrown concerns have also made a showing in the Pacific. In Melanesia, where over twenty such churches have emerged (some reminiscent of fixtures documented by Bengt Sundkler for southern Africa), the history of cargo cult movements provides an important background. Sizable examples of such movements like to appear as churches to enhance their legitimacy, as with the Pomio *kivung* on New Britain, for instance, with its indigenous messiah Koriam Urekit and the use of the Ten Commandments as its platform; and with Niu Apostolik in New Guinea's Sepik region, where local leaders have taken over the paraphernalia of a Canadian sectarian mission to flout the authority of the long-established Catholics. In Polynesia, a more socially conservative zone, a few special ecclesial independencies have manifested. The Cook Islands Christian Church is split down the middle over the place of the remarkable woman healer Apii Piho in the divine scheme of things. Her 1987 announcement that she was Jesus Christ himself created an impetus among her supporters to inject honorific references to her in worship, even while not making major departures from the liturgy.

The most important new trend across the whole Pacific, though, involves local initiatives to so intensify church commitment that they result in breakaway congregations or new worship groups. During the 1980s many small and previously unknown mission groups appeared in the region (or else consolidated after insignificant beginnings). In that decade, to illustrate, Papua New Guinea's Eastern Highlands, especially its capital, Goroka, constituted the most highly missionized place on earth, with over sixty organizations (at least half of them originating in the United States) contending for souls. Many such small missions were conservative Evangelical, if not self-defining Fundamentalist, organizations, with most being ready to join the Evangelical Alliance that had been founded in 1975. Such groups admittedly widened local ranges of religious choice, but they made only a small dent in preexisting structures. The smaller sectaries destined to have the most disturbing effects up until the present time, however, were Pentecostal (or Charismatic), and in Papua New Guinea, in the biggest and most populous part of Oceania, a Pentecostal Council was hastily put together in 1980.

Pentecostal missions—the Assemblies of God and the Four Square Gospel Church the best known and most sizable among them—combine old-style revivalism with a stress on spiritual gifts. The experience of altered states—such as glossolalia, group succumbing to a spirit wind, ecstatic prayer, and prophesying—chimes with islanders' expectations of real and dramatic contact with the spirit world, as in Africa and among African-originated communities of the Americas. Pentecostalism has consequently spread into the mainline churches and been the basis for large Christian gatherings that supplement or even break away from prevenient centers of worship. Manfred Ernst, researcher at Fiji's Pacific Theological College in Suva takes Pentecostalism as the most decisive of the *Winds of Change* in contemporary Pacific religion (as his 1994 book title has it). He takes both Fiji and Western Samoa as important centers of these shifts. One must appreciate, of course, that Pentecostal-type revivalism has had a prior history in the Pacific region, outbursts of fervor affecting the South Sea Evangelical Church on north Malaita (the Solomon Islands) in the 1970s and spreading to the Baptist mission area in the Enga area of the Papua New Guinea Highlands. A Maori and two Solomonese evangelists are prominent in this story, only going to show the attractions of Pentecostalism in drawing out colorful indigenous leadership styles.

A crucial feature of latter-day Pacific Christianity has been the emergence of indigenous theologies. Most of these have been contextual, in efforts either to provide identity for regional Christians (witness Tongan Sione Havea on "Coconut Theology," especially for Polynesians) or to divest introduced religion of its foreignness (the Papuan John Kadiba, for example, asking the islander faithful to consider using sweet potato and coconut juice for Communion rather than bread and wine). In some cases liberationist propensities are felt, with talk of revolution against land theft, paternalism, and demoralization on the lips of the Maori radical Anglican priest Hone Ka'a, or projections of the just society by Catholic (former Father) John Momis, the Bougainvillean activist and first minister for decentralization in an independent Papua New Guinea. A theology both to integrate the gospel and tradition while at the same time forestalling narrow conservatism and celebrating a multiethnic nation marks the achievement of Sevati Tuwere, with his work *Vanua* (2002), surely the most mature and systematic theological treatise by an islander scholar thus far.

SEE ALSO Cargo Cults; Oceanic Religions, article on New Religious Movements.

BIBLIOGRAPHY

Breward, Ian. *A History of the Churches in Australasia.* Oxford History of the Christian Church. Oxford, 2001.

Ernst, Manfred. *Winds of Change: Rapidly Growing Religious Groups in the Pacific Islands.* Suva, Fiji, 1994.

Salamonsen, Peter J. "Roman Catholic Participation in Pacific Islands Regional Ecumenism as Enhanced by the Leadership of Patelisio Finau, Bishop of Tonga." Ph.D. diss., University of Sydney, Sydney, 2002.

Trompf, Garry, ed. *The Gospel Is Not Western: Black Theologies from the Southwest Pacific.* Maryknoll, N.Y., 1987.

Wagner, Herwig, and Hermann Reiner, eds. *The Lutheran Church in Papua New Guinea: The First Hundred Years 1886–1986.* Adelaide. 1986.

GARRY W. TROMPF (2005)

CHRISTIAN LITURGICAL YEAR.

The Christian liturgical year consists of two cycles, differently defined in Eastern and Western traditions. The Eastern (Byzantine) rite distinguishes between movable and fixed festivals: the former are those whose dates vary each year with the date of Easter but always fall on the same days of the week; the dates of the latter are constant but may fall on any day of the week. Western tradition, on the other hand, includes with the movable festivals certain feasts whose date is fixed (most importantly, Christmas, December 25) and the seasons dependent on those. This whole cycle is known as the *temporale*, or (as in the present Roman Missal) the Proper of Seasons. The second cycle in Western tradition includes festivals of saints and other anniversaries on fixed dates and is called the *sanctorale*, the Proper of Saints.

EASTER, THE CHRISTIAN PASSOVER. The schematizations of the year refer to and are reflected in the organization of liturgical books. The roots of the distinction, however, reach back to the second century, when Easter (Pascha), which had been kept at Jerusalem on the fixed Jewish Passover date, was adjusted to the structure of the week so as to fall always on Sunday, the day of the resurrection. That adjustment renders Easter's date variable and is, therefore, the basis of the Christian cycle of movable feasts. The precise computation of the date of Easter was fixed at the Council of Nicaea (325 CE) as the Sunday following the full moon after the vernal equinox. Several factors, however, have disturbed that agreement, and the dates set for this major Christian festival differ between East and West in most years, yielding differing dates as well for those seasons and festivals dependent upon the Easter date.

The Paschal Fast. When the observance of Pascha was transferred from the Jewish date to Sunday, the original preceding one-day fast was extended to two days, the Friday on which Jesus was crucified and the Saturday on which he lay in the tomb. By the middle of the third century four more days were added in Syria and Egypt; this six-day total seems universal by the end of that century, yielding the Holy Week still observed by Christians. On Thursday of Holy Week the institution of the Eucharist at the last supper of Jesus with his disciples is celebrated, and the celebration often includes a reenactment of Jesus' washing of the feet of his disciples. In the West an anthem accompanying the ceremony had as its text the verse "A new commandment I give unto you, that you love one another as I have loved you" (*Jn.* 13:34). Its Latin incipit, "Mandatum novum," gave the name *Maundy* to the foot washing and to the Thursday on which it occurred.

A Western pilgrim named Egeria described the services at Jerusalem in 383. She noted that on Friday morning the wood of the cross (discovered in the course of excavating the tomb of Christ) was exposed for the veneration of the people who, one by one, passed by and kissed it. Such veneration attached as well to a major fragment of that wood at Rome in the sixth century, and this led to a similar veneration of a symbolic cross on Good Friday throughout the Western church, still encountered today. Egeria also described a service at Calvary during the hours from noon to three during which the passion narratives were read from the four Gospels. An extraliturgical service of preaching during these hours was instituted at Lima, Peru, in 1687, and has since achieved wide popularity in both Roman Catholic and Protestant churches, often consisting of seven sermons on Christ's words from the cross, interspersed with hymns.

The Paschal Vigil. Like Passover, the early Christian Pascha was a nocturnal observance, as testified to by the *Epistle of the Apostles*, a work from Asia Minor of the second half of the second century. The earliest detailed account of that vigil's content, the description coming from liturgical directories of the first half of the fifth century, relates activities in Jerusalem. After an initial lamp lighting, the vigil consisted of a series of twelve Old Testament lessons, each followed by prayer. These lessons recalled themes already traditionally associated with Passover: creation, the sacrifice of Isaac, the Exodus from Egypt, and so on. Similar series of twelve lessons are documented later in Spain and Gaul, retaining many of the Jerusalem readings. Such a series became standard in western Europe and was continued in the Roman Missal following the Council of Trent (1545–1563). That series of lessons is found today in the North American *Lutheran Book of Worship.* Similar but shorter series occur in recent revisions of the Roman Missal (1969) and *The Book of Common Prayer* (1979).

A climactic point in the paschal liturgy since the third century has been the conferral of baptism, that rite of initiation by which, as Paul said, we are buried with Christ and risen in him to new life (*Rom.* 6:4). Baptism was performed in a separate chamber during the Old Testament lessons in the fourth and following centuries, but today it is more likely to be performed after them in the presence of the congregation. Following the conferral of baptism, the first Eucharist of Easter is celebrated with exuberant rejoicing over the resurrection of Christ and for the sacramental realization of resurrection in the newly baptized.

In the West today the paschal vigil opens with the lighting of a new fire in the darkness. From this fire the paschal candle, a large candle representing the risen Christ, is lighted and carried into the church in a procession during which a minister proclaims at three points: "The Light of Christ." The same minister then sings over the paschal candle an ancient poem of praise called *Exultet.* The light ritual just described precedes the vigil readings today in Roman Catholic, Anglican, and Lutheran churches. A somewhat simpler light ritual precedes the readings in Orthodox churches now as it did in Jerusalem sixteen centuries earlier. At Jerusalem today, and since the tenth century, the light ceremony has been transferred to a point following the Old Testament readings. There, the Holy Light produced within the tomb of Christ is passed to the ministers and congregation outside the tomb and is carried by them to the other churches of the city in symbolic proclamation of the resurrection.

Pentecost. Already in the second century the paschal feast initiated a fifty-day period of rejoicing (Pentecost) during which fasting and kneeling were forbidden. But by the final two decades of the fourth century the unified celebration of Christ's resurrection and ascension and the outpouring of the Holy Spirit had given way to distinct festivals: the Pascha of the Resurrection on Easter Sunday, the Ascension on the fortieth day (a Thursday), and the sending of the Holy Spirit upon the church ten days later on Pentecost Sunday. In Gaul not only was fasting resumed after the ascension, but fasts were ordered on the three days preceding the ascension on which processions with rogations (litanies) were held to ask protection from natural disaster. Prior to twentieth-century liturgical reforms it was common to extinguish the paschal candle, symbol of the risen Christ's presence with the church, at the conclusion of the gospel reading on Ascension Day. Since Vatican Council II, however, in an effort to recover the integrity of the fifty-day period, the candle burns at all services through the day of Pentecost, and fasting is suspended throughout the period.

The conclusion of the paschal rejoicing at the end of Pentecost Sunday has been marked by a ceremonial return to fasting and kneeling for prayer. The resumption of fasting is noted by Egeria, and in the fifth century, notice is given of devotions performed (while kneeling) at the end of that Sunday on the Mount of Olives. Such a penitential service, called Gonuklisia ("the bending of the knee"), is still observed in the Eastern churches on the evening of Pentecost, marking the end of paschal festivity. The week following Pentecost Sunday is the occasion for one of four seasonal fasts at Rome called, in English, Ember Days, from the German term *Quatember* (Lat., *quatuor tempora*, "the four seasons"). Other Embertides, largely unobserved in Roman Catholic practice today but maintained in Anglican churches, fall in September, in late December, and in the first week of Lent.

Lent and Palm Sunday. Lent is the major fast season of the Christian year, a period of forty days commemorating the fast of Jesus in the wilderness. It is seen by Christians today as preparation for the celebration of Easter. Considerable variety has characterized this fast, stemming from two factors. First, in the West the last of the six weeks is Holy Week, while in the East Lent is the six weeks preceding Holy Week. Second, from the seventh century on there was a general concern that there be forty days of actual fasting. In the Eastern empire Saturday (Sabbath) was not a fast day, with the single exception of the day before Easter, and Sunday was never a fast day. Therefore, a week of fore-fast was added before the beginning of Lent to yield the desired total. In the West, where Lenten Sabbaths were fast days, the original six weeks yielded thirty-six days, and the beginning of the season was set on Wednesday of the preceding week.

Although the Byzantine Lent took on a penitential quality through monastic influence in the eighth century, that quality has never been so pronounced as in the Western church, where Lent was also the time of formal humiliation for those excluded from the community because of grave sins. Admitted to the order of penitents at the beginning of Lent, these separated sinners were solemnly restored to communion in the latter days of Holy Week. One of the ceremonial dimensions of admission to the order of penitents in Gaul was the sprinkling of ashes on their heads. By the eleventh century that penitential discipline had fallen into disuse, but the old ceremonies continued, now for all the faithful. By the end of the eleventh century the imposition of ashes was virtually universal in the West, giving the name *Ash Wednesday* to the first day of Lent. That ceremony continues to mark the beginning of the great fast. This general penitential tone is also manifested in the Western church by the suppression of the joyous acclamation "Alleluia" in all Lenten liturgical services, while "Alleluia" continues to be sung in the Byzantine liturgy during Lent.

The association of Lent with the forty-day fast of Jesus has been taken generally by scholars to be a secondary symbolic interpretation, unrelated to the origins of the great fast, since this time before Easter has no connection in Jesus' life to the temptation that followed immediately upon his baptism in the Jordan. Studies suggest, however, that the forty-day duration of the fast that we encounter after Nicaea may have originated in an earlier Alexandrian "Lent" that followed immediately after the celebration of the baptism of Jesus on January 6, the Feast of the Epiphany. That six-week period ended with the conferral of baptism in the sixth week and with a "feast of palms" celebrating Christ's triumphal entry into Jerusalem on the following Sunday, all separated from the paschal fast by several weeks. A similar six-week pattern is still visible in the Byzantine Lent, now prior to Holy Week rather than following Epiphany, hence making Palm Sunday the day before the Holy Week fast.

Egeria describes a procession down the Mount of Olives with palms on the afternoon of this Sunday at Jerusalem in 383, and such a procession was later adopted by other churches, which already called that day the Sunday of the Passion. Palm Sunday is now generally understood to be the beginning of Holy Week. Its focus is a procession with palms or other branches celebrating Christ's entrance into Jerusalem, followed by the Eucharist whose theme is the passion of Christ. In the Byzantine rite, the sixth week of Lent leading into Palm Sunday is called Palm Week, the individual days being similarly characterized, reinforcing the Coptic suggestion that Palm Sunday was originally the conclusion of Lent, rather than the beginning of Holy Week (as it is generally understood in the West today).

Christmas and Epiphany. The principal festivals of fixed date are those associated with the nativity of Jesus. In Rome by 336 such a festival on December 25 marked the beginning of the year. Earlier (perhaps from the beginning of the second century) in the Eastern churches the festival of the nativity known as Epiphania or Theophania, terms associated in classical Greek with the human manifestation of a deity, was set on January 6. In some churches the themes of Christ's baptism in the Jordan and his first miracle at Cana were celebrated on or near that same day.

The coincidence of the Roman date for the Feast of the Nativity, December 25, with the date of Natalis Solis Invicti, a winter solstice festival established by the emperor Aurelian in 274 CE, has encouraged the hypothesis that Christmas represents a Christian appropriation of the solstice festival, and similar pagan backgrounds have been proposed for the Epiphany festival on January 6. Contrary to this prevailing view, Louis Duchesne in his *Christian Worship* (London, 1903) suggests that those dates were computed as nativity dates from the inclusion of the Incarnation (i.e., the conception of Christ) in the themes celebrated at Pascha on known fixed dates, March 25 in Africa and Rome, April 6 in Asia Minor and elsewhere in the East. In modern times, March 25 is celebrated as the Feast of the Annunciation (the conception of Christ) nine months before Christmas, except among the Armenians, who continue to follow the tradition of Jerusalem by observing the Nativity on January 6 and the Annunciation nine months earlier. In the course of the later fourth and fifth centuries other Eastern churches adopted the Roman festival of December 25, thenceforward devoting January 6 only to the celebration of Christ's baptism. In that same period the January festival was adopted at Rome, and its nativity theme was narrowed to the visit of the Magi, from which it came to be considered the manifestation of Christ to the Gentiles.

In most Latin cultures, the Epiphany festival remains the occasion for the exchange of gifts, after the example of the Magi, while in northern Europe and English-speaking countries that custom, continued from pre-Christian year-end festivities, attaches rather to Christmas. In the Byzantine and other Eastern churches where Epiphany celebrates Christ's sanctification of water by his baptism, a major feature of the celebration is a blessing of water that is drawn by the faithful and carried to their homes, a custom for which pre-Christian roots are also claimed in modern scholarship.

ADVENT. Analogous to the period of preparation for Easter, a fast before the nativity developed in the West into a preparatory season. In addition to the Roman December Embertide, churches in Gaul observed fasts of six weeks or more; a common form was called Saint Martin's Lent, from its beginning on November 11, the Feast of Saint Martin of Tours. That season, known as Advent, developed themes associated both with the advent of Christ at his nativity and the second advent at the end of this world's history, the two advents having been expressed by the same term (*parousia*) since the Greek theologians of the second century. A forty-day fast is also kept before Christmas in the Eastern churches, but this never received the liturgical articulation of Advent in the West, where Advent today comprises the four weeks (or, in Milan, six weeks) before Christmas.

THE SANCTORAL CYCLE. From the death of Stephen (*Acts* 7), Christianity has honored those whose faith in Christ has brought them to martyrdom. The liturgical expression of this honor is documented as early as the second century, in the case of the martyrdom of Polycarp at Smyrna, and in the following centuries this veneration achieved a high level of local organization as the anniversaries of martyrs' deaths came to be observed by the celebration of the Eucharist at their tombs. A Roman martyrology of 354 includes a few North African martyrs, probably revealing the presence of an African community at Rome. That same document reveals memorial observances of bishops of Rome who were not martyrs. Both the bishops' list (first prepared in 336) and the list of martyrs present the dates of their memorial celebrations in calendrical order (beginning from December 25) and designate in each case the cemetery where the observance was held. A Syriac martyrology of the following century reveals an increasing unification of these local lists, conflating the martyrs' observances of a great many cities. This tendency to veneration over a wider area and the addition of revered Christians other than martyrs to liturgical calendars led in the Middle Ages to central control over the liturgical veneration of saints; this became in time a complex procedure for beatification and canonization. However, a uniform liturgical calendar of saints was never produced, for local interests continued to be selective. Revision of the Roman calendar in 1969 has given a much larger place to optional observances.

Many feasts represent anniversaries of the dedication of churches, and such a dedication festival at fourth-century Jerusalem is continued in modern calendars as the Feast of the Holy Cross. The dedications of churches also lie behind many other feasts (e.g., of various New Testament figures or angels) where there is no question of a known place of burial. Since the later Middle Ages, still other festivals have been instituted simply as an aid to the promulgation of particular theological or devotional concerns, but this approach to festival is less evident since the Second Vatican Council.

THE LITURGICAL YEAR SINCE THE REFORMATION. At the Reformation, churches of the reformed tradition placed a renewed emphasis on the weekly observance of Sunday as the primary liturgical articulation of time, while Lutheran and Anglican traditions continued to observe most of the traditional liturgical year but severely restricted the number of feasts of saints, limiting them to New Testament figures for the most part. Since the Second Vatican Council the reform of the Roman calendar has been widely adopted in the United States and Canada, with the general shape of its temporal cycle and accompanying lectionary followed by Roman Catholics, Episcopalians (Anglicans), Lutherans, Presbyterians, Methodists, and other participants in the Consultation on Church Union. Of these, the Episcopal and Lutheran churches have developed their own calendars of saints, following traditional principles.

LITURGICAL COLORS. In earlier times clergy were garbed in a frequently washed tunic of white linen and an overgarment (worn for warmth) that was usually of a dark colored wool. As these garments became more ceremonial in function, a wider range of colors and materials came to be used. All through the Middle Ages in the West color systems varied from place to place, while reflecting some general principles. The first attempt at standardization of liturgical colors is assigned to Pope Innocent III (d. 1216). He presented a system in which white was assigned to festivals of Christ, the Blessed Virgin, and saints who were not martyrs. Red was for feasts of apostles and martyrs, for feasts of the Cross, and for Pentecost. Black was to be used during Advent and Lent and at masses for the departed, with the option of violet as a substitute for black. For all other occasions, green was the assigned color. While other medieval color systems continue to be followed in some places, the Roman system outlined by Innocent is surely the predominant system in Western churches, except that violet now generally replaces black. The 1969 reform of the Roman Missal, however, assigns red for Palm Sunday and Good Friday, and urges the general principle of the Eastern traditions that on the most festive occasions one should use the richest materials available, without regard to color. While Eastern traditions have never sought to associate feasts and seasons with particular colors, there, too, the natural psychological tendency is to match colors to emotions, to associate, for example, dark with sorrow, bright with joy.

SEE ALSO Christmas; Easter; Epiphany.

BIBLIOGRAPHY

A useful but now somewhat dated general historical survey can be had in Allan MacArthur's *The Evolution of the Christian Year*

(London, 1953). A more recent presentation of historical development is Adolf Adam's *The Liturgical Year: Its History and Its Meaning after the Reform of the Liturgy* (New York, 1981). Another work arranged not historically but as a commentary through the Christian year is Adrian Nocent's *The Liturgical Year*, 4 vols. (Collegeville, Minn., 1977). For still more current scholarship, see the collection of papers of the 1981 Congress of Societas Liturgica published in *Liturgical Time*, edited by Wiebe Vos and Geoffrey Wainwright (Rotterdam, 1982). For more particular studies of individual festivals, see Patrick Cowley's *Advent: Its Liturgical Significance* (New York, 1960); John Gunstone's *Christmas and Epiphany* (London, 1967); Roger Greenacre's *The Sacrament of Easter* (New York, 1965); and John Gunstone's *The Feast of Pentecost* (London, 1967).

New Sources

Baggley, John. *Festival Icons of the Christian Year.* Crestwood, N.Y., 2000.

Beckwith, Roger T. *Calendar and Chronology, Jewish and Christian.* Leiden and New York, 1996.

Bellenir, Karen, ed. *Religious Holidays and Calendars: An Encyclopedic Handbook.* Detroit, 1998.

Bradshaw, Paul, and Lawrence A. Hoffman, eds. *Passover and Easter: Origin and History to Modern Times.* Notre Dame, Ind., 1999.

Bradshaw, Paul, and Lawrence A. Hoffman, eds. *Passover and Easter: The Symbolic Structuring of Sacred Seasons.* Notre Dame, Ind., 1999.

Roll, Susan K. *Toward the Origin of Christmas.* Kampen, Netherlands, 1995.

Talley, Thomas J. *The Origins of the Christian Liturgical Year.* 2d ed. Collegeville, Minn., 1991.

THOMAS J. TALLEY (1987)
Revised Bibliography

CHRISTIAN SCIENCE is a religious movement emphasizing Christian healing as proof of the supremacy of spiritual over physical power. Founded by Mary Baker Eddy, a New Englander of predominantly Calvinistic background, Christian Science emerged as a distinct phenomenon in American religious life during a period of both social and religious crisis. The dramatic conflict between science and faith, as witnessed in battles over Darwinism and critical biblical scholarship, was only the most obvious aspect of a developing breakdown in a Christian cosmology that pictured experience as split between a natural and a supernatural order. Christian Science, however, rejected traditional cosmology and was therefore free to address religious issues in a way that was limited neither by creedal formulas nor by assumptions based on nineteenth-century natural science.

Eddy from her earliest years showed a deep-seated longing for the divine that was broadly characteristic of the Christian tradition and especially prominent in Puritanism. She found it impossible, however, to reconcile her deepest religious feelings with the theology of a then decadent Calvinism. Yet while other revolts against Calvinism, such as those of Unitarianism and Transcendentalism, led to an attenuation or even an abandonment of Christian convictions, Eddy's Christianity was so deeply ingrained that she found it impossible to think of any ultimate answer to what she called the "problem of being" outside of a theistic, biblical context. In her own words, "From my very childhood, I was impelled, by a hunger and thirst after divine things—a desire for something higher and better than matter, and apart from it—to seek diligently for the knowledge of God as the one great and ever-present relief from human woe."

Running parallel to this search, and contributing heuristically to it, was Eddy's own long quest for health. She had exhausted the healing methods of the time, including homeopathy, and the techniques of the Maine healer Phineas Quimby, to whom she turned in 1862, and although she found useful hints concerning the mental causes of disease, she never found the permanent health for which she was looking. Her growing disenchantment with all curative methods returned her to her spiritual quest, which led to a radically different perception of God and creation from that held by Quimby, namely, that reality is, in truth, wholly spiritual.

Eddy identified the advent of this conviction with her "instantaneous" recovery in 1866 from the effects of a severe accident while reading an account of one of Jesus' healings. She described the event as follows: "That short experience included a glimpse of the great fact that I have since tried to make plain to others, namely, Life in and of Spirit; this Life being the sole reality of existence." This passage is reminiscent of much mystical writing, but Eddy saw the experience as the point at which she discovered a spiritual truth so concrete that it would be "scientifically" provable in the experience of others.

There can be no doubt that this moment of recovery marked an important turning point in Eddy's life, impelling the development of the theology and metaphysics to which she gave expression in her major book, *Science and Health with Key to the Scriptures*, first published in 1875. The primary purpose of the book was not to set forth a new systematic theology, but rather to serve as a textbook for religious practice. The focus throughout was on awakening the capacity of its readers to experience the presence of God directly; the "honest seekers for Truth," to whom the book was dedicated, were invited to explore the saving and physically healing effects of that experience.

A key point of Christian Science is that the understanding of God must include a changed view of reality itself. In effect, *Science and Health* challenged the traditional Christian view of God as the creator of a material world—not on philosophic grounds, even though Eddy's conclusions are partially articulated in philosophic terms—but on the grounds of a radical reinterpretation of the meaning of the gospel. Christian Science takes the works of Jesus, culminating in his resurrection and final ascension above all things material, as pointing to the essential spiritual nature of being. Accordingly, his life exemplifies the possibility of action outside of and contrary to the limits of a finite, material sense of existence. From the standpoint of traditional Christianity, Jesus' works constituted supernatural interruptions of natural process and law; from the standpoint of Christian Science, they resulted from the operation of divine power comprehended as spiritual law. In biblical terms this meant the breaking through of the kingdom of heaven—of the divine order of things—into ordinary sense-bound experience.

Nineteenth-century Protestant orthodoxy associated the kingdom of heaven with a realm in the beyond and the hereafter; Christian Science, however, views it as the spiritual potential of present experience to be actualized once sinning mortals cease to identify their own limited, erring perceptions as reality. Regeneration or spiritual awakening occurs as one sees through sense appearance to what Eddy called "the spiritual fact of whatever the material senses behold." The spiritual fact for her was not an otherworldly phenomenon, but a transforming power—a reality drastically obscured by the misconceived sense of life, substance, and intelligence, apart from God. So great is this error of misconceiving, or fundamental sin, that a revelatory breakthrough from outside material existence is required in order to manifest the true spiritual nature of creation. The advent of Jesus, according to Christian Science, constitutes the decisive spiritual event that makes possible the salvation of humanity from the flesh.

Christian Science does not deify Jesus, a point that its severest critics have sometimes said separates it conclusively from traditional Christianity. Yet Jesus' actual role in the achievement of humanity's salvation is as important to its theology as for traditional Christianity. His life of obedience and sacrifice is understood as the means through which the reality of being for humankind has broken through in the midst of ordinary human experience. This true spiritual selfhood is identified as the eternal Christ, as distinct from Jesus, although uniquely and fully incarnated in him. His mission is viewed as opening up the possibility for all men and women to make actual their own spiritual union with God. He did this by proving practically that neither sin nor suffering is part of authentic spiritual selfhood, or Christ.

While Christian Science holds that evil has no God-derived existence and therefore can be regarded ontologically as not real, it strongly emphasizes the need for healing rather than ignoring the manifold manifestations of the carnal mind, defined by the apostle Paul as "enmity against God," and as operating with hypnotic intensity in human experience. Such healing is to be accomplished not through personal will or effort but through yielding to the action of the divine Mind. Salvation, while seen as the effect of divine grace, requires prayer, self-renunciation, and radical, unremitting warfare against the evils of the mortal condition.

Salvation includes obedience to Jesus' command to heal the sick. Sickness is one expression of the fundamental error of the mortal mind that accepts existence as something separate from God. Healing, therefore, must be predicated on the action of the divine Mind or power outside of human thought. In Eddy's words, ". . . erring, finite, human mind has an absolute need of something beyond itself for its redemption and healing." Healing is regarded not merely as a bodily change, but as a phase of full salvation from the flesh as well. It is the normalization of bodily function and formation through the divine government of the human mentality and of the bodily system that that mentality governs.

The emphasis in Christian Science upon healing—primarily of sin, secondarily disease—is based on the concrete issues of everyday lived experience. The healing emphasis differentiates Christian Science from philosophies of idealism with which it is often carelessly identified, including the Emersonian transcendentalism that was part of its immediate cultural background. Indeed, departures from Eddy's teaching within the Christian Science movement itself have tended generally toward metaphysical abstraction, wherein her statements almost completely lose their bearings on daily experience.

In the context of Eddy's writings, however, such statements almost always point to the demand and possibility of demonstrating in actual experience what she understood as spiritual fact. Her abstract statement that "God is All," for instance, taken by itself could imply a pantheistic identification of humankind and the universe with God. Taken in the full context of her teachings, it indicates that God's infinitude and omnipotence rule out the legitimacy, permanence, and substantiality of anything contrary to God's nature as Principle, Mind, Spirit, Soul, Life, Truth, and Love, an assertion that is taken to be demonstrably practical in concrete situations, to some degree at least.

The radical claim as to the ultimate unreality of matter is to be assessed in these terms. Christian Science asserts that matter is not the objective substance it appears to be, but is rather a concept of substance shaped by the limitations of the human mind. This assertion no more denies the existence of humankind or natural objects than the challenge posed in physics to conventional views of perception and to the substantiality of matter denies the existence of the universe. But it does point to the necessity of bringing the true spiritual nature of humanity and the universe to light through progressive demonstration.

With this emphasis on practical regeneration and healing, one sees the clearest link between Christian Science and the American Puritan tradition. An undue emphasis on the practical aspect of Christian Science by some followers has sometimes led to a secularization of its teaching, with healing regarded as an end in itself rather than as one element of a full salvation. This tendency clearly characterizes the mind-cure and New Thought movements. These movements, in some respects akin to Christian Science, use similar terms, which, however, bear a notably different meaning.

As with any religious movement, the motives of those who call themselves Christian Scientists vary. Of the 350,000–450,000 who might so identify themselves, it is likely that a majority are not formal members of the Christian Science denomination. While many have made Christian Science a way of life and joined, others have sought it, sometimes intermittently, for comfort and support. There may be limited truth, too, to the hypothesis that activity in the Christian Science movement, in which women have been numerically predominant, has provided an outlet for women in a society that has otherwise restricted their role—particularly in the religious world. On the other hand, such an argument may reflect an unconscious male stereotyping that seeks reductionist explanations when women advance or espouse ideas.

Evidence of the religious experiences of long-term, committed adherents of Christian Science suggests that it may have survived for more than a century because it has met a more basic religious need. Disaffected Protestants, particularly, have seen in it a release not just from bodily suffering but also from spiritual malaise—an alternative to the attitude that accepts with Christian resignation the tragedies of present life in hope of compensation either in a life beyond or according to some transcendent scale of eternal values. Christian Science, however, regards the ultimate spiritual victory over evil prophesied in the Bible as requiring confrontation with all aspects of evil and imperfection in present experience.

Although Christian Science is explicitly committed to universal salvation, it focuses initially and primarily on the potential for transformation and healing within the individual. This focus, deviant as it has often seemed to conservative Christians, tends to associate it with the traditional Protestant concern over individual salvation, giving it a conservative cast in the eyes of more liberal Christians who wish to transform the social order. The identification of Christian Science with a conservative, well-to-do, middle-class ideology may be as misleading in a sociological sense as it is theologically. In fact, a greater segment of the movement comes from rural or lower-middle-class backgrounds than most outside accounts would suggest.

On the whole, the church does not share the social activism of many mainstream denominations, but its purpose in publishing the *Christian Science Monitor*—an international newspaper of recognized excellence—indicates a substantial commitment to an interest in the public good. Eddy founded the *Monitor* in 1908 as the most appropriate vehicle for the political and social expression of the practical idealism of her teaching. In addition, it was intended to educate Christian Scientists about the need for the healing of society at large, not just the individual.

The character of the *Monitor*, to a degree, reflects the educational purpose of the church that publishes it. Eddy, surprisingly sensitive to the dangers of institutionalized religion, conceived of the church in instrumental rather than ecclesiastical terms, shaping it to provide practical means for the study, communication, and teaching of Christian Science as a way of life. It was not part of her original purpose to found a separate denomination; rather, she and a group of her students founded the Church of Christ, Scientist, in 1879, when it became clear that other Christian churches were not disposed to accept her teaching. The overall structure of the church was laid out in a document of skeletal simplicity, the *Manual of the Mother Church*, which Eddy first published in 1895 and continued to develop until her death.

The central administrative functions of this "mother" church, the First Church of Christ, Scientist, in Boston, are presided over by a five-member, self-perpetuating board of directors. The Mother Church, with its branches, including some 3,000 congregations in fifty countries, constitute the Church of Christ, Scientist; the congregations are self-governing within the framework provided by the *Manual*.

Taken as a whole, the church's activities can best be understood as vehicles for disciplined spiritual education. These include the Bible "lesson-sermons" consisting of passages from the Bible and the Christian Science textbook studied by members during the week; the religious periodicals published by the church; and Christian Science lectures, Sunday schools, the intensive two-week course of class instruction, and follow-up refresher meetings attended by those seriously committed to the religion.

The absence of an ordained clergy, ritualistically observed sacraments, and all but the most spare symbols point to the almost Quaker-like simplicity of the Christian Science concept of worship, in which silent prayer has an important role and the sacraments are conceived of as a process of continuing purification and quiet communion with God. Spontaneous sharing of experiences of healing and spiritual guidance marks the Wednesday "testimony meetings."

Christian Science practitioners, listed monthly in the *Christian Science Journal*, are members who devote themselves full time to the ministry of spiritual healing, and a significant body of testimonies of healing—amounting to some 50,000 published accounts—has been amassed in Christian Science periodicals over the years. There is good evidence that this sustained commitment of an entire denomination over more than a century to the practice of spiritual healing has been a significant factor in the reawakening of interest in Christian healing among many denominations in the 1960s and 1970s.

By the 1979 centennial of the founding of the church, the Christian Science movement found itself experiencing greater challenges from the currents of secular materialism than it had encountered since the early days of its founding. The increasing secularization of Western society worked against the kind of radical Christian commitment it required, while at the same time its healing practices encountered new challenges in an increasingly medically oriented society.

The history of the church, however, confirms that it is no exception to the general tendency of religious movements to grow or decline according to inner vitality rather than external pressure. Nor are external signs of growth in themselves altogether valid indicators of spiritual strength; indeed, it was because of this that Eddy forbade the publication of church membership statistics at a time when the movement was growing rapidly. The great numerical growth of the movement in the decades after Eddy's death may well have been attributable more to sociocultural factors unrelated to and, in some respects, opposed to the specific religious and redemptive purposes of the church itself.

It is too soon to assess the long-term significance of some signs of decline of the Christian Science movement. Indeed, these signs must be qualified by other factors, among them the erosion of the insularity and complacency evident to some degree in the church's posture in earlier decades, the maturing of the movement, its willingness to position itself in relation to the rest of the Christian world, and the significant growth it has experienced in some developing nations.

SEE ALSO Eddy, Mary Baker.

BIBLIOGRAPHY

The basic document of the Christian Science movement is Mary Baker Eddy's *Science and Health with Key to the Scriptures* (1875; reprint, Boston, 1914), which contains the full statement of its teaching. Extensive historical background on Christian Science can be found in Robert Peel's trilogy, *Mary Baker Eddy: The Years of Discovery, The Years of Trial, The Years of Authority* (New York, 1966–1977). Peel's earlier *Christian Science: Its Encounter with American Culture* (New York, 1958) places Christian Science in its New England cultural context, relating it to both transcendentalism and pragmatism, while my own *The Emergence of Christian Science in American Religious Life* (Berkeley, 1973) gives a full account of Christian Science within the context of American religious development. An early, pathbreaking study of the theology of Christian Science is the essay by Karl Holl, "Szientismus," in *Gesammelte Aufsätze zur Kirchengeschichte*, vol. 3 (Tübingen, 1921–1928). A representative though reductionist treatment of Christian Science from a sociological perspective is the section on Christian Science in Bryan R. Wilson's *Sects and Societies: A Sociological Study of the Elim Tabernacle, Christian Science and Christadelphians* (1961; reprint, Westport, Conn., 1978). Charles S. Braden's *Christian Science Today: Power, Policy, Practice* (Dallas, 1958) attempts an overview of organizational developments, drawing largely on dissident sources. One reason for the paucity of adequate academic accounts of Christian Science is suggested in Thomas C. Johnsen's article "Historical Consensus and Christian Science: The Career of a Manuscript Controversy," *New England Quarterly* 53 (March 1980): 3–22. A popular but slapdash history of the early phases of the movement is Norman Beasley's *The Cross and the Crown* (New York, 1952). Basic documentation on Christian Science healing is given in the church-published *A Century of Christian Science Healing* (Boston, 1966).

New Sources

Christian Science Publishing House. *Christian Science: A Sourcebook of Contemporary Materials.* Boston, 2000.

Fraser, Caroline. *God's Perfect Child: Living and Dying in the Christian Science Church.* New York, 1999.

Harley, Gail M. *Emma Curtis Hopkins: Forgotten Founder of New Thought.* Syracuse, N.Y., 2002.

Schoepflin, Rennie B. *Christian Science on Trial: Religious Healing in America.* Baltimore, 2003.

STEPHEN GOTTSCHALK (1987)
Revised Bibliography

CHRISTIAN SOCIAL MOVEMENTS.

The richness of the Christian vision of God's transcendence and presence, the range of constituencies to which it appeals, and the variety of contexts into which it has moved have produced an enormous variety of social movements. Yet some main developments can be traced.

HISTORICAL BACKGROUND. In the ancient world, religions were linked to specific groups, primarily ethnic or political. Peoples and cities had their own deities, and religion secured stability and security. The defeat or victory of their warriors or rulers brought about the decline or ascendancy of their religion.

The ancient Hebrews shared many of these views. But specific aspects of that tradition pressed in a different direction. The "Lord" of the Hebrew Bible was understood to be the truly universal sovereign, not limited to any people, political order, or military destiny. Rather, the prophets inspired by this God demanded not only communal loyalty and rightly ordered worship for the well-being of the nation, but also witnesses to principles of justice that were universal in scope and required fair treatment of the stranger. Indeed they pointed to an expected "messianic age" that would bring a great transformation and a fulfilled righteousness for all peoples.

Christianity claimed that it was the true heir of these prophetic directions. In Jesus Christ the one universal and righteous God entered into the concreteness of human personhood and made transcendent reality into an accessible, immanent, and transforming presence. The life, teachings, death, and resurrection of this Son of God inaugurated the new age and manifest a new Spirit as the decisive animating factor in human affairs. The announcement and celebration of this divine immediacy became the good news that opened the door to liberation from sinful self-preoccupations, ritualistic compulsions, and obsessions with wealth and power. Moreover out of the precedents of the Jewish synagogue and the Greco-Roman "mystery cults," the early followers of Christ established a new social institution—a center of loyalty and fellowship outside the usual traditions of social participation, namely the church.

Particular population groups seem to have been most attracted to this new vision and new community of discipleship. The poor and the sick were given hope; widows and orphans found companionship; artisans and traders who were marginalized by aristocratic elites and priestly restrictions discovered new networks for creative interaction; intellectuals who found the old religions, cults, and speculations unsatisfying or sterile discerned a greater wisdom and vitality; and, later, on rulers of the Roman Empire and (still later) the princes of North Europe, who needed a moral and spiritual architecture to give shape to new civilizational developments, sought guidance in this faith's doctrines and legitimation from this church's leadership. This faith itself was a social movement from the start.

It is not that Jesus, Paul, or any other early Christian leader started a movement with specific social, political, or economic objectives in mind. The "kingdom" they sought was not, as Jesus said, "of this world." Nevertheless it was "in the world," and it altered perspectives on social life precisely because its sense of transcendence and its belief that the presence of that transcendent reality made a difference in life.

Wherever Christianity has gone it has brought with it an impulse, sometimes subverted, to form new centers of social existence distinct from ethnicity, any single cultural tradition, any particular political power, or any distinct economic caste or class. Whenever Christian communities have become too closely identified with one or another of these traditional orders of life, dissenting factions, alternative congregations, or paraecclesial movements, claiming to represent the true, prophetic faith, have challenged that accommodation. The relation of these alternative bodies to the majority developments of the tradition and their roles in society are decisive for understanding Christian social movements in the West.

Christianity seems always to have pressed in two directions. One is toward consolidation of the movement's growth by the establishment of a church that would take responsibility for guiding the moral and spiritual lives of the people and institutions in a territory where the movement gained influence. The other is sectarian in the sense that it draws people into an alternative lifestyle and communities of commitment that are self-consciously distinct from the established institutions of a society—including the church. The "sects" may seek to ignore the life of "the world," renouncing sex and the family, politics and power, and economics and wealth, or they may seek to transform "the world" and all of these spheres of life by "aggressive," even militant discipline.

In the medieval period of the West, alternative congregations were, for the most part, channeled into either monastic orders that claimed, with considerable success, to represent the ideal models of faithfulness or into various "confraternities"—guilds or lay orders for devotion and service without abandoning family, power, and wealth. Some orders, such as those founded by Saint Basil and Saint Benedict, were more withdrawing. Orders such as the Dominicans and Franciscans, by contrast, were gently aggressive in their efforts to touch and transform the everyday life of the laity. Some lay orders, meanwhile, such as the Templars and Hospitalers, were more aggressive in the conventional sense. In the late Middle Ages and increasingly during the Reformation, nonmonastic alternatives arose, some inspiring social movements with more intentionally overt sociopolitical overtones, such as those led by John Wyclif (c. 1330–1384), Jan Hus (1372 or 1373–1415), and Thomas Müntzer (1468 or 1489/90–1525), and a few people, such as Jon of Leiden, formed communities that held wives, husbands, and property in common. It is therefore impossible to understand the magisterial reformations of Martin Luther (1483–1546) and John Calvin (1509–1564) without seeing how much their sociopolitical thought continued that of their Roman predecessors.

What these Christian communions had in common was not only the confession of Christ but a social effect that was only partially intended. The formation of new organized bodies of believers, distinct from both political (royal or imperial) and familial (sib, clan, or tribal) authorities, gradually carved out a series of social spaces in which various interests claimed and eventually won the legal right to exist in independent institutions. It revolutionized social history.

That space was often not wide, but networks of scholars, leagues of peasants, and associations of artisans, mystics, traders, and bards found elbow room under the mantle of patrons and patron saints, in the shadow of monasteries or nunneries, or at the feet of the cathedrals in the free cities. These innovative organizations claimed the God-given right to address sociopolitical matters in terms of a Christian vision of righteousness and hope, often without the approval of established hierarchies. The very fact that they introduced new centers of organized conviction into late-feudal social settings brought about a reshaped and pluralistic constellation of moral and social authority into what were otherwise limited, often closed systems—a major change in itself. In this they followed what had already been anticipated in the early church when, as a tiny minority, it formed communities of commitment that differed from both the ethnic identities of Jews and Greeks, the political orders of both the old polis and the Roman imperium, and from the householders and servants in all the regional cultures. It is possible to discern the deepest roots of proto-democratic societies more clearly in these developments than in the polities of the ancient cities or the theories of the modern Enlightenment. Indeed, the latter is dependent on these antecedents.

MODERNIZING MOVEMENTS. Modern Christian social movements are distinguished from their earlier prototypes by their increasing ability to organize freely, by their more overt goals of addressing specific social problems or groups, and by the growth of a kind of historical consciousness that expects human agency, in the service of God's promises of redemption, to help the needy, empower the weak, establish justice, and resist injustice by concerted action. Movements sharing these characteristics have evolved in a variety of directions.

Some movements were organized in order to form institutions of charity, staffed by committed "sisters" or "brothers" who dedicated their lives to service. Christian hospitals, schools, orphanages, and homes for the mentally or physically handicapped were founded in nearly every sizable community in the Western world—as well as increasingly in developing countries, where mission movements have been active. Hospitals often still bear the names of their founding religious groups, even if their twenty-first-century support comes less from church-related sources and more directly from government, insurance companies, or foundations. The number of orphanages and homes for the handicapped has been reduced due to better medical care for mothers and for children with birth defects—and due to the increased options for safe abortion, sharply opposed by Catholics and many evangelicals, yet accepted in some circumstances by most Protestants. Adoption agencies, advocacy groups for and by handicapped persons, and pregnancy counseling services have increased, many under religious sponsorship or with their support Indeed, current advocates of governmental funding for "faith-based" groups as full partners in fighting certain social problems are seeking to extend this history into new channels of care and action.

Until the late nineteenth century most of the colleges and universities of the West were founded by churches, orders, or sects or by those political authorities who wanted to foster a specific religious perspective, improve the image of their city or region, and better prepare their citizens for a growing economy. Dedicated Christian educators extended the range of higher education by founding colleges and universities in nearly every country around the world. Believers also founded community organizations that sought to improve neighborhoods and cities and joined fraternal and service organizations, such as the Freemasons, Eastern Star, Rotary, or the Lions, that played similar roles in local communities.

Several movements on the Continent focused more on social action than on social service and echoed accents that came from the "Radical Reformation" of the sixteenth century (sometimes bloodily persecuted by the Catholic and early Protestant Churches). Later, in the Cromwellian revolution in England, certain parallels to the earlier examples also appeared. The Puritan "Chaplains" of the "New Model Army" and the lay "Diggers" and "Levelers" called for structural reform of authority, landownership, and status systems as well as the reform of the churches and the freedom of religion. More than a century later, after the American and French Revolutions, many Christians saw direct political involvement to support schools, good government, and the taming of the American frontier as duties of faith. Overtly Christian political parties were formed in many countries of Europe, and in the United States parties were formed not only to protect regional interests but to preserve the moral, spiritual, and democratic values of Protestantism as settlers moved west.

The Anglo-American dream of nations of yeoman farmers and village traders was shattered by the industrial revolution. It uprooted families, made traditional skills obsolete, and generated cities full of new classes, factories, immigrants, and misery. Specific churches became identified with particular minorities, and new sects developed special affinities for the new classes that replaced the older, hierarchically ordered status groups of aristocratic landlords, artisans, and peasants. Religious leaders ministered to these emerging class-conscious workers or bosses and became the advocates for their material interests. Comparable dynamics continue in developing nations, as worker or peasant movements protest, in the name of Christ, the identification of Christianity with bourgeois values and as new clusters of political, business, and professional leaders meet, also in the name of Christ, to increase their awareness of moral and spiritual values to guide them as they lead the world toward a new global order.

Many argue that post-Reformation Christianity was the key stimulus to democratic, technological, and economic societies, and also, indirectly, to the Enlightenment and modernity. Others argue that political, social, and technical changes brought about the religious developments. While each surely influenced the other, the weight of evidence seems to fall on the former contention. The religiously legitimated political revolutions of the seventeenth and eighteenth centuries and the technological revolutions of the nineteenth and twentieth ushered in new patterns of economic productivity and, ironically, new conceptions of the social order. Some of these conceptions became ideologically driven movements within established churches, new sects, and some denominations, each reflecting a somewhat distinctive understanding of the faith as well as the particular social interests of its constituency. The European history of militant Lutheranism among the Prussian Junkers, Catholic conservatism of the Iberian peoples, or nationalist Anglicanism of the British Tories could find parallels in the chauvinist movements among Protestants in the United States. Other parallels include the Pietistic *ecclesiolae* that developed in the Netherlands, the early Methodist "classes" among the coal miners of England, and later the Innere Mission in Germany, the Salvation Army among the urban poor in England and America, and the civil rights movements led by African American Christians and the (now mostly defunct) Christian labor organizations or "worker priest" movements in all industrializing countries.

In America, the pervasive early influences of the Reformed and the sectarian traditions stamped the structure of religious and civil life in distinctive ways, especially by the idea of "covenant." The notion of covenant, as it was distinguished in Protestant thinking from both voluntaristic "contract" and pre-given static "orders of society," suggested that people can construct or reform their social institutions but that the moral norms that must govern the agreements, reconstructions, and new institutions are established by God and must be discerned in community and implemented by concerted action. It was to fulfill the possibilities of covenantal forms of life that the early Pilgrims and Puritans came to the New World. The experience of leaving behind the old society and seeking to establish a new one in a new land reinforced biblical images of exodus and new covenant. It evoked expectations of historical change and made the quest for the new and better more important than satisfaction with the old and settled. But immigration and religious innovation brought a pluralization of religions that even such theocratic regimes as the one in Massachusetts could not contain. Further, the fact that American developments took place in a context without previous feudal or imperial traditions that had to be overcome produced widespread social experimentation with a priority of local freedom over centralized political order. Such factors interacted to produce a variety of alternative congregations, paraecclesial movements, and voluntary organizations unique in human history. In this context the famous fugitive from Puritan Massachusetts, Benjamin Franklin (1706–1790), started some two hundred associations for social betterment in Pennsylvania; the dissident Puritan, Roger Williams (1603?–1683), founded Providence, Rhode Island, on the principle of religious freedom and became the symbolic hero of the separation of church and state; and James Madison (1751–1836) argued in *The Federalist* that religious and party pluralism, supported by checks and balances in government, could preserve a new kind of freedom and prevent tyranny.

By the 1830s all the state constitutions in the United States were altered so that all churches were disestablished and legally viewed as voluntary associations. Even many who had fought the trend gradually became enthusiastic proponents of the idea that Christian social witness was to be carried out by voluntary, paraecclesial social organizations. That freedom of religion means not only tolerance but also the right and duty of committed people to organize movements for social service and social change outside the government and distinct from the worshiping congregation became the dominant view. It was believed that this was precisely what God had intended from the Exodus, through the prophets and the formation of the Jesus movement (with the calling of the disciples unrelated to the priesthood) to Pentecost in the New Testament, though only now were the fuller social implications of those events becoming actualized.

Missionary Movements. A veritable explosion of social movements took place on these foundations during the nineteenth and twentieth centuries. The United States became a nation of "joiners." "Home mission" societies ministered to the Native Americans who were being pushed ever westward, to the settlers on the semicivilized frontiers, and to the newly arrived immigrants in the growing American cities. Numerous "foreign mission" societies were formed as well to bring the faith and civilization to other lands. Many of the modern churches of Asia, Africa, and the Pacific Islands struggle to bring about open, democratic societies that respect human rights and foster economic development. They find their roots in the missionary efforts, although they often are also critical of those missionaries who cooperated with or were advocates of the imperialist policies of their home countries. Those who supported the missionary movements abroad were usually, however, among those who resisted imperialism and supported antislavery, labor, and child protection movements. They also often supported movements against liquor, gambling, pornography, and prostitution. In fact many "morally uplifting crusades" were soon to arise in the wake of revivalisms, themselves paraecclesial movements that offered the possibility of liberation from personal sin (by decision for Christ) and of the empowerment to transform the social habits and individual vices that sapped the spirits of ordinary people.

The most important social movement of the nineteenth century, however, was the struggle to free the slaves in the West. In the United States a number of slave uprisings, political struggles over the extension of slavery into new states, and humanitarian emancipation movements had raised the question to visibility from the early 1800s, but not until the northern churches began to mobilize at midcentury did the movement gain momentum. Although there were some slaves in the north as well, the rising tide of moral objection converged with sharp debates about how to interpret Scripture on social issues, how to understand apparent racial differences, how to chart the economic future of the nation, and how to understand the U.S. Constitution and the Bill of Rights. Several Protestant Churches split on these issues, setting the stage for persistent theological tensions. The resulting Civil War freed the slaves, defeated the confederated states, and accelerated the late entry of the United States into the industrial revolution. It also made the attempt by southern plantation owners to replicate a landed aristocracy with a feudal peasantry in a land without peasants obsolete economically as well as morally.

Many of the old practices, however, did not die the day Abraham Lincoln (1809–1865) issued the Emancipation Proclamation, for efforts were made to keep the old quasi-feudal system in revised form, not by chattel slavery but by instituting new patterns of servitude enforced by custom and discriminatory statute. Still, the end of the saddest era in American history was announced. In the wake of these events an enormous number of missionaries, teachers, and nurses went to the South from northern churches to evangelize the former slaves and to build schools, colleges, clinics, and hospitals for (and with) the newly freed black Americans. Newly formed black churches, especially Baptist and Methodist, provided opportunities for the cultivation of a new generation of leaders who not only led worship but also became central figures in community organization and social advocacy.

After the war, Christians organized advocacy and cooperative associations, such as the Farmers' Alliance and the Colored Farmers' National Alliance and Cooperative Union. Less overtly rooted in Christian thought was the Patrons of Husbandry (the "Grange"), which drew some patterns of ritual from the Freemasons. In the northern cities Christian paraecclesial movements attempted to address the new class conflicts arising with rapid industrialization by using evangelism techniques combined with social service and social action strategies. The immigrants to the cities from the farms and from Europe were met with city missionary societies and "settlement houses," the innovative Young Men's Christian Association (YMCA) and the younger but also growing Young Women's Christian Association (YWCA), plus nascent Christian labor unions. Such organizations were subsequently established around the world.

The methods of raising funds to sustain these organizations in the late nineteenth century and early twentieth century were innovative. The voluntary associational character of church organization produced a new interpretation of the biblical concept of stewardship, one that called upon church members to not only pledge regular contributions to sustain the church, but also to support mission, outreach, cultural activities, social action work, and benevolence agencies that were thought to serve the wider purposes of the Kingdom of God in society.

Funds to support these missionary and social movements were often raised by women's groups. Victorian women of means and charitable intent were sometimes satirized as "Lady Bountiful," but many struggling families kept body and soul together because of their gifts in an age before welfare. Moreover the wives of workers and farmers organized literary and musical events, bake sales, quilting bees, and knitting parties "for good Christian causes." Informal networks of cooperation to help the poor became more formalized and focused in such organizations as the Women's Rights Convention (1848), the Women's Christian Temperance Union (1873), the Women's Missionary Society, the Christian Women's Action Guild, the Women's Society for Christian Service, and a host of similar bodies. The full effect of these organizations is undocumented, but the existing literature suggests that, besides helping the needy, they provided an opportunity for the development of organizational skills and perspectives on family, political, and social issues. These were the training grounds for those who were to lead the struggles for suffrage and later causes identified as feminist. Some contemporary women's movements have been hostile to Christianity, but such women's organizations have been forceful advocates of social development and equal opportunity in both church and society.

Many concerns of the period began to congeal into a wider theological-social realignment at the end of the nineteenth century under the general rubric the "Social Gospel." This was less a single social movement than a congeries of movements signaled by a social understanding of faith that demanded institutional transformation toward economic democracy. While Washington Gladden (1836–1918), Richard T. Ely (1854–1943), and Walter Rauschenbusch (1861–1918) are among the more memorable apologists for the Social Gospel, the enormous variety of social concerns addressed under this mantle, from the perspective of the meaning of the term for social movements, are well cataloged in W. D. F. Bliss's *New Encyclopedia of Social Reform* (1910). All the mainline churches were deeply stamped by this movement.

World War I and the Great Depression shattered the tendency toward an overheated optimism in parts of the Social Gospel and brought other developments that modified the direction of Christian social movements. Several of the movements generated out of the Social Gospel began to lose their distinctive Christian bases and became little more than groups of liberal civic-minded activists, while others simply became interest groups struggling to get as many material gains for their constituents as possible. Simultaneously, and partly in reaction to these trends, evangelical movements and fundamentalism arose as fresh social and religious forces specifically critical of evolutionary biological, anthropological, social, and ethical theories, which they felt displaced the Gospel and overturned the authority of Scripture.

Catholic Developments. During this same period two European movements of considerable consequence were also underway. Socialist proletarians of the Marxist left engaged in increasingly sharp criticism of any connection between religion and socially progressive movements, sometimes targeting democratic politics and capitalist economics as the enemies of radical social change and the ideological masks of Protestant, bourgeois self-interest. Simultaneously, a series of aristocratic conservatives, from John Ruskin (1819–1900) in England to Bishop Wilhelm Ketteler (1811–1877) in Germany, Comte de Mun (1841–1914) in France, and Cardinal Gaspard Mermillod (1824–1892) in Switzerland, also undertook the study of emerging social problems and wrote a series of critiques of democracy, which they saw as the legacy of the antireligious French Revolution, taken over by a conspiracy of Jewish bankers and Protestant factory owners to reduce the workers and farmers to industrial servitude. Both democracy and capitalism, they said, were based on nothing more than individualistic and utilitarian "contracts" without any moral or spiritual bases. These Anglo-Catholic and Roman Catholic leaders developed positive proposals on the duties of the "Christian state," the "Christian family," and the "Christian Church" as organic, comprehensive communities based on natural law and revealed dogma by which the lives of all persons were to be sustained and guided and the restoration of a Christian society attained.

One of the great ironies of these two developments was that the actual programs of the antireligious, socialist left and of the "social Catholic" premodernist right converged to produce attitudes and political policies in many European countries that promoted workers' organizations and limited but did not prohibit the development of free markets. When these themes were officially propagated by Pope Leo XIII (reigned 1878–1903), a new course was set for Catholic engagement with modern social issues, one that had great consequence in the post–World War II period with the rise of "political theology" and later "liberation theology" in Latin America. These were adopted by religious leaders in decolonializing nations around the world and by many heirs of the Protestant Social Gospel, who took them as the unofficial standards of faith in the last quarter of the twentieth century.

These developments could not fully erase the memories of earlier hostilities between Catholics and Protestants. The flood of Catholic immigrants into the industrializing cities of the United States, especially from Ireland and, later, Italy, also sparked anti-Catholic movements. For most of the nineteenth century and much of the twentieth, Catholic populations were in a defensive and difficult position, and the energy expended and the sacrifices made to find jobs, to build churches, and to establish Catholic schools as an alternative to the largely Protestantized public schools are a monument to faith. Catholic lay leaders also formed paraecclesial lay fraternal orders, such as the Knights of Columbus, that echoed conservative views on social and religious questions even as their members swelled the ranks of left-leaning unions and political parties.

As these Catholics endeavored to form social movements, some adopted motifs from the essentially Protestant Social Gospel. However, when they became too enthusiastic about the virtues of religious pluralism, lay leadership in both church and society, secular democratic government, or the formation of religiously neutral unions, their efforts were condemned by Rome as "Americanism" and "modernism." Still, papal teachings had opened the door to modern economics, and new patterns of Catholic social thought and activity were stimulated. A new generation of American Catholic scholars and activists fomented social service and social advocacy within a decidedly democratic framework and toward a new form of welfare capitalism in the twentieth century. The Bishops' Program of Social Reconstruction (1919) is a landmark of this direction.

Figures such as Fr. John A. Ryan (1867–1945) and Fr. John Courtney Murray (1904–1967) provided intellectual and moral guidance for Catholic involvement in the democratization of economic opportunities and for Catholic participation in democratic political life. The line from these roots to contemporary Catholic social movements in the United States is not difficult to draw. Catholic movements against abortion, for peace and justice, and in support of human rights continued to grow, especially after Vatican II (1962–1965) spoke of the ministry of the laity and Popes John XXIII (reigned 1958–1963) and John Paul II endorsed these motifs. The U.S. Roman Catholic Bishops' Pastoral Letter on War and Peace (1982), issued at the height of the cold war, has been widely adopted as almost a manifesto for numerous Protestant and Catholic antinuclear movements. The U.S. Catholic bishops drafted a Letter on the Economy (1986), which both commends the achievements of capitalism and demands active engagement, in the name of Christ, to redress its negative effects. John Paul II, the Polish pope who was clearly involved in efforts to overthrow communism in Eastern Europe, cautiously but firmly accented the relative benefits of capitalism and democracy, strongly linked these to the defense of human rights, and approved sharp Vatican critiques of liberation theology.

Political Activism. Internationally the rise of National Socialism in Germany and Stalinism in the Soviet Union forced Christian social movements at mid-twentieth century to become increasingly and overtly political in defense of democracy. In the United States, extremist organizations such as the Ku Klux Klan and the White Citizens Councils attributed the ills of the world to blacks, Catholics, Jews, and communists, and they attempted to use Christian symbols to legitimate their hate. Nearly all church bodies preached against such organizations, and many threw their attention instead to a wide variety of religiously based efforts on the other end of the political spectrum, such as the Fellowship of Socialist Christians and the Fellowship of Reconciliation. More notable, however, is the fact that Christian Realism—a tough-minded theological orientation usually associated with Reinhold Niebuhr (1892–1971)—became the reigning mode of articulating the Christian vision for social justice during the Great Depression, World War II, and the cold war.

The building of vast armies to meet international threats and the increased involvement of the government in economic matters increased the size and scope of political, administrative, and regulative bureaucracies in the United States. These developments in government deeply affected Christian theology and church-related social movements. They supported national policies that institutionalized on nonreligious bases many of the programs begun in voluntary, faith-based movements, they modified church and religious organizations as the agencies providing services for the needy in local communities, and they evoked a general turn to political strategies of advocacy for specific public policies in the emerging welfare society.

After World War II these trends continued, but other trends also became prominent. A new generation of leaders arose from the black churches, the most famous of whom was Martin Luther King Jr. (1929–1968). King organized a new Christian social movement—the Southern Christian Leadership Conference—to confront the "betrayal of the American dream" and the racist customs and organizations that had established discriminatory laws after the end of slavery nearly a century before. He initiated a series of nonviolent marches and demonstrations that "called the country to its highest ideals" and "the faith to its first principles of justice." (Lincoln, 1970, p.13). Although the National Association for the Advancement of Colored People and the National Urban League had already worked for racial justice for decades and U.S. military forces had been integrated after it was recognized as absurd to fight the racist policies of Adolf Hitler (1889–1945) with segregated forces, King's movement touched the festering conscience of the world more deeply, and his strategies were soon adopted by other minority groups and activists with other agendas.

The U.S. involvement in Vietnam brought about another spate of church and paraecclesial efforts to alter common habits of mind and public policy. The organization Clergy and Laity Concerned about Vietnam was perhaps the most important national organization to protest the Vietnam War, but local organizations seemed to spring from the chaplains' offices on nearly every university campus. Many of the people engaged in the antiwar protests were those who had marched with King. After the war they organized boycotts against growers who employed migrant workers at below-standard pay rates, clothing manufacturers who resisted unionization, and infant-formula manufacturers who utilized questionable marketing techniques in poor countries. Others attempted to pressure stockholders of corporations doing business in, say, the Republic of South Africa in the days of apartheid to change policies or divest entirely, or to influence those operating in Central American or Southeast Asian countries to raise the minimal wages paid to workers there. Such authors as Rachel Carson (1907–1964) brought to public attention potential damage to the environment, and soon a variety of Christian "eco-justice" efforts were under way to protect God's creation. These issues were all taken up by the "mainline churches" as major causes, and concern about them survived, slightly modified, in the handbooks of church bureaucracies and slogans at antiglobalization demonstrations.

More often than not, in those church circles inclined to mount social movements, the source of the world's problems has been identified as "capitalism," usually understood in quasi-Marxist terms. However, the collapse of the Soviet Union, the privatization and deregulation of the economies in most countries, the resurgence of conservative religions as the guide to social development and public policy, and conflicting views of the nature of capitalism have brought frustration to "mainline" Christian social movements. Indeed it is almost a cliché to say that the "mainline" has been "sidelined" by its predictable and passé social analysis. Nowhere is this clearer than in the critiques of globalization as merely the result of Western forms of predatory capitalism. The fact that globalization involves the spread of human rights, the development of international law, the adoption of democracy, increased international cooperation to control disease and hunger, the striking formation of new middle classes, and the spread of technology along with access to education and means of communication is hardly mentioned. Globalization also involves a shift in perspective about sociological existence that is as dramatic as the shift Galileo Galilei (1564–1642) brought to cosmological existence. Ironically, many church leaders are as eager to condemn this shift as vigorously as their predecessors did Galileo. That is not to say that the churches are socially irrelevant, but it is to suggest that what they do on the ground is more effective and more dependent on more globalized perspectives than those that dominate the antiglobal theologies of many mainline national and ecumenical church bodies.

These brief references to political activism should not obscure the fact that liberation theology engendered several social movements, not only in Latin America but also in almost every part of Africa and Asia as the "new countries" sought independence from the colonial powers that previously governed them, and then from the internal hegemonies that emerged in one-party states after the colonialists were deposed. Scholars disagree on whether the views developed in these regions of the world can be considered "theology" in any enduring sense of the word, or whether they are instead a form of baptized ideology combined with local religiosity. But even critics acknowledge liberation theology's social importance in giving a voice to those who were previously only recipients of other people's perspectives.

Still, many wonder if this combination of piety and analysis, having made its witness against colonialism, imperialism, and hegemony, can also provide models for the reconstruction and development of liberated societies. In the Philippines after Ferdinand Marcos (president 1965–1986), in Indonesia after Suharto (president 1967–1998), in central Africa after successive coups, in southern Africa after apartheid, and in much of Latin America after right-wing dictators and guerrilla oppositions, ideas of liberation may engender effective models of democratic order with human rights, economic viability, racial justice, sexual equality, and freedom of religion, but the record has not proven promising.

Nevertheless the liberation movements did give people at the margins of the dominant institutions and traditions the courage to speak up. Two groups the liberationists did not expect to take that challenge have in fact exercised that option with vigor and effect. One is the feminists, and the other is the evangelicals.

Much of feminism traces its origins to the Enlightenment and can take one of two forms: liberal (accenting individual rights and moral autonomy) or radical (accenting social solidarity and the interdependence of sexism with classism, racism, and ecological domination). But not all modes of feminism are liberal or radical in these senses. A large literature has been developed by and about feminist Christians, heirs in a way of the nineteenth-century missionary movements. They join their liberal and radical sisters in that they too are critical of patriarchal religion and the ways in which clergy have subordinated or exploited women's gifts and leadership abilities both in church and society, but they see aspects and dynamics in the classical texts and traditions that are indispensable to both personal identity and community formation. All seek the recognition that women have been subordinated, oppressed, or simply viewed as sexual objects in much of human history, and all want the restructuring of authority and work in household and economy, access to political power and professional opportunity, and more control of reproduction.

The confluence of Enlightenment and Christian ethical norms has had a wide effect in the use of ordinary language, in the use of theological symbols, in expectations of shared duties in the home, and, more widely, in the way in which women are perceived and conduct themselves in the workplace—from the research lab to the battlefield, from the judge's bench to the pulpit. They have made what once were considered "private" issues matters of public awareness and policy, and they have forced those who thought they were doing "objective" analysis of medical, social, and political problems to acknowledge the presence of bias in the presuppositions and perceptions of problems. This movement has had worldwide repercussions, and women from every religious background have followed parallel paths to those already cut through the thickets of exegesis, tradition, debate, and role conflict by feminist Christians.

Parallel to the influence of feminism, evangelical Protestantism, with some wings essentially Pentecostal and others fundamentalist (and often in conversation and ethical agreement with conservative forms of Catholicism) have also had great effects. The interaction of these groups is evident in *Christianity Today* and *First Things*, two of the liveliest and most widely circulated Christian journals in the world. Whereas the views of these groups were obscured by mainline development in the past, they are obscure no more, to the chagrin of many ecumenical and liberal Christians. They have founded a series of academic and research institutions, they have bought a number of radio and television stations, they have become a major force in national politics in North and South America, and they have missionary and human services organizations that reach into most of the countries of the world and into the center of the most difficult urban subcultures.

Evangelical Protestantism's new public activism seems to have come in reaction to a series of public developments—the *Roe vs. Wade* ruling allowing abortion, the removal of public prayer from the public schools, the acceptance of gay relationships as equal in moral value to heterosexual marriage, and the neglect of religious, biblical, and theological influences in social and intellectual history due to a presumption that modernity means secularism. The fact that religious freedom, constitutional democracy, human rights, modern science, and modern technological and economic advances developed in cultures shaped by evangelical forms of Christianity, and only secondarily anywhere else, is not noted. Yet as mainline Christian interpretations of life and social history fall into relativism and missionary zeal erodes, perspectives appreciative of Christianity and new missionary movements are spreading throughout the world at the hands of Catholic, Evangelical, and Pentecostal theologies. They in fact have grown at exponential rates in Africa, Asia, and the many parts of the Americas. For these movements the crucial issues are openness to faith, a positive evaluation of religious freedom, and the theological cultivation of those patterns of life that can form a wholesome civil society, generate social capital, and empower marginalized peoples to participate in the cultural and economic dynamics of globalization.

While these two movements differ in a great number of respects, they share a recognition that the earlier sharp line between personal and public issues and between faith and secular social philosophy is fading, and that lifestyle issues and theology are central to public debates. In addition, many feminists realize that a majority of women are deeply religious, and many evangelical Christians recognize that the patriarchal treatment of women is contrary to the deeper strands of the faith. Both of these movements, like the growing consensus about the importance of human rights, ecological responsibility, and concern for the inequalities of economic opportunity around the world, also supported by feminist and Christian groups, show no sign of fading. It is doubtful that any social movement that does not recognize the vitality and validity of much that these two movements emphasize can flourish.

See Also Denominationalism; Evangelical and Fundamental Christianity; Freemasons; King, Martin Luther, Jr.; Leo XIII; Methodist Churches; Missions, article on Missionary Activity; Modernism, article on Christian Modernism; Niebuhr, Reinhold; Pietism; Political Theology; Rauschenbusch, Walter; Reformation; Religious Broadcasting; Religious Communities, article on Christian Religious Orders; Salvation Army; Troeltsch, Ernst; Williams, Roger.

Bibliography

Biblical and Early Church Traditions

Bammel, Ernst, and C. F. D. Moule. *Jesus and the Politics of His Day.* Cambridge, U.K., 1984. Major essays on the sociopolitical context and effects of the early Christian movement.

Hays, Richard B. *The Moral Vision of the New Testament.* San Francisco, 1996. A leading biblical scholar treats the social and ethical implications of biblical texts.

Malina, Bruce J., and Richard L. Rohrbaugh. *Social Science Commentary on the Synoptic Gospels.* Minneapolis, 2003.

Theissen, Gerd. *Sociology of Early Palestinian Christianity.* Philadelphia, 1978. One of the leading scholars of the social context of early Christian movements.

European Developments

Berman, Harold J. *Law and Revolution: The Formation of the Western Legal Tradition.* Cambridge, Mass., 1983. The legal history of social change in European developments.

Himmelfarb, Gertrude. *The Idea of Poverty: England in the Early Industrial Age.* New York, 1983. An interpretation of the development of the idea of "the poor" as an "oppressed" group.

Klinken, Jaap van. *Diakonia: Mutual Helping with Justice and Compassion.* Grand Rapids, Mich., 1989. A documented history of the growing Protestant sense of the moral duty to help those with less opportunity.

Stark, Rodney. *The Rise of Christianity.* Princeton, N.J., 1996. A sociological understanding of the reasons various groups turned to the Christian faith.

Thompson, E. P. *The Making of the English Working Class.* New York, 1966.

Troeltsch, Ernst. *The Social Teaching of the Christian Churches* (1911). 2 vols. Chicago, 1981. First published in English in 1931. The now classic Protestant interpretation of the interaction of doctrinal development and social influences.

Weber, Max. "The City." In *Economy and Society*, vol. 3, chap. 16. New York, 1968. A suggestive hypothesis about the pre-Protestant development of modernizing forces in medieval cities.

Williams, George Hunston. *The Radical Reformation.* 3d ed. Kirksville, Mo., 1992. A collection of the primary documents of the non-Lutheran, non-Calvinist Protestant movements that established the "free church" traditions of "disestablished religion."

Woodhouse, A. S. P., ed. *Puritanism and Liberty.* London, 1938.

American Developments

Ahlstrom, Sydney E. *A Religious History of the American People.* New Haven, Conn., 1972. The most exhaustive single volume of American church history in existence.

Carter, Paul Allen. *The Decline and Revival of the Social Gospel.* Ithaca, N.Y., 1956. The historical treatment of the transition from the early Social Gospel to the "Christian realism" of midcentury Christian activism versus the Nazi threat.

Donaldson, Dave, and Stanley Carlson-Their. *A Revolution of Compassion.* Grand Rapids, Mich., 2004. A challenging defense of the idea of "faith-based" subsidies.

Evans, Christopher H. *The Social Gospel Today.* Louisville, Ky., 2001. Collected essays on the importance of continuing influence of the "social gospel" in liberal Protestanism.

Hopkin, Charles Howard. *The Rise of the Social Gospel in American Protestantism, 1865–1915.* New Haven, Conn., 1940. The best overview of the rise of "social Christianity" in the industrial age.

Lincoln, C. E., and Lawrence Mamiya. *The Black Churches in America.* Boston, 1970. To date, the most comprehensive interpretation of the role of African American religion in American life.

McKelvey, Blake. *The Urbanization of America, 1860–1915.* New Brunswick, N.J., 1963. A key representative documentation of the social and religious effects of urbanization in the United States.

Niebuhr, H. Richard. *The Social Sources of Denominationalism.* New York, 1929. A widely used introduction to the interaction of social thought and theological understanding in modern America.

Smith, Timothy L. *Revivalism and Social Reform in Mid-Nineteenth-Century America.* New York, 1957. The primary text for the resurgence of the evangelical tradition as a major force in social science in the United States.

Modern and Contemporary Movements

Aikman, David. *Jesus in Beijing: How Christianity Is Transforming China and Changing the Global Balance of Power.* Washington, D.C., 2003. A journalistic account of the growth of Christianity in China as an example of the explosion of conservative faith in the developing world.

Jenkins, Philip. *The Next Christendom: The Coming of Global Christianity.* Oxford, U.K., 2002. An interpretation of the ways in which Christianity is changing the face of Africa.

May, Melanie A. *Bonds of Unity: Women, Theology, and the Worldwide Church.* Atlanta, 1989. Addresses the importance of feminist theology on the global scene.

Smidt, Corwin. *Religion as Social Capital: Producing the Common Good.* Waco, Tex., 2003. The rejection of religion as a product of social influences and an affirmation of religion as a personal, decisive social force.

Stackhouse, Max L., with Peter Paris, eds. *God and Globalization.* 4 vols. Harrisburg, Pa., 2000–2004. An attempt to identify the universalistic dynamics of religion, particularly Christianity, in shaping the new global civilization that is emerging in the early twenty-first century.

Wijaya, Yahya. *Business, Family, and Religion: Public Theology in the Context of the Chinese-Indonesian Business Community.* Oxford and New York, 2002. An example of the ways in which global forces are altering thought and action in non-Western societies.

MAX L. STACKHOUSE (1987 AND 2005)

CHRISTMAS is the Christian celebration of the birth of Jesus Christ. The name, English in origin, means "Christ's Mass," that is, the mass celebrating the feast of Christ's nativity. Names for Christmas in Romance languages are derived from the Latin *nativitas.* The French *Noël* comes from either *nativitas* or *nowell,* meaning "news." German employs the term *Weihnachten,* meaning "holy (or blessed) night." Another name for the whole season is *Yule.* Originally this name did not have Christian connotations but derived either from the Germanic *jol* ("turning wheel"), with reference to the gain of sunlight after the winter solstice, or from the Anglo-Saxon *geol* ("feast"). The name of this pre-Christian winter feast of the solstice was eventually applied to the whole of the Christmas season.

There is no certain knowledge of the origin of the Christmas feast. It may have been celebrated as early as the beginning of the fourth century in North Africa, but certainly it was observed at Rome by the middle of the same century. Two theories have been advanced for the occurrence of the feast on December 25. One theory argues that Christmas originated in opposition to or competition with the Roman Feast of the Invincible Sun (Sol Invictus) that had been celebrated on the old date of the winter solstice. The computation theory, on the other hand, argues that the birth of Christ was calculated on the basis of the idea that the conception of Christ coincided with his death, which supposedly occurred on March 25.

By the end of the fourth century the observance on December 25 of the feast of Christ's nativity had spread throughout most of the Christian world. At Antioch, Chrysostom regarded it as the actual date of Christ's birth. In the mid-fifth century the Jerusalem church, too, accepted the December 25 date, which then replaced the older celebration of the nativity there on January 6. The Armenians, however, have never accepted December 25 as the Feast of the Nativity.

The Western Christian observance of Christmas was strongly influenced by the celebration of this feast in the city of Rome. Three masses came to be celebrated by the pope on Christmas Day. The original mass was held at Saint

Peter's on Christmas morning. But in the course of the fifth century a second mass was added "in the middle of the night" (first at cockcrow and later at midnight) at the shrine of Christ's crib, which had been erected at the Church of Santa Maria Maggiore as a replica of the crib at Bethlehem. Finally, during the Byzantine period of the sixth century a third mass was added in Rome, this one at dawn at the Church of Sant' Anastasia, a martyr whose feast was celebrated in Constantinople on December 25. Probably for the sake of convenience, in the course of the eleventh century the original mass celebrated at Saint Peter's was transferred to Santa Maria Maggiore, already the site of the second mass. Since the eighth century the Western Christian celebration of Christmas has been provided with an octave, or eight days of liturgical observance, in imitation of the feasts of Easter and Epiphany.

In the early sixth century the emperor Justinian made Christmas a public holiday. The feast was extremely popular in all European countries during the Middle Ages, inspiring the composition of music and liturgical drama. The observance of Christmas received added impetus in the early thirteenth century when Francis of Assisi originated the devotion of the Christmas crib.

After the sixteenth century most of the Reformation churches retained the Christmas feast. Martin Luther, for example, showed great devotion to Christmas in his preaching. However, the English Puritans tried to do away with the celebration of Christmas altogether in the course of the seventeenth century. The feast was revived with the restoration of the English monarchy in 1660, but on a somewhat more secular basis. Under the Puritan influence in early America, especially in New England, Christmas was a regular workday until the middle of the nineteenth century.

The customs of Christmas in the Northern Hemisphere include, in addition to Christian religious practices and midwinter feasting, various celebrations of the returning light of the sun. In northern European folklore, the twelve days between Christmas and Epiphany are a time when the evil spirits are considered to be especially active, combating the coming of spring and the gradual victory of sunlight over darkness that follows the winter solstice; thus Christmas Eve is called there "the devil's funeral." To celebrate the victory of life over winter's death and to combat evil spirits, homes are decorated in this darkest period of the year with lights and evergreens of all kinds. Similarly, the Yule log was kindled on Christmas Eve in northern countries and kept burning until Epiphany, and remains of the log were kept to kindle the next year's Yule fire. The Christmas tree itself seems to be of rather recent origin: it may be as late as the sixteenth century that Germans first decorated a fir tree with lights, fruits, and tinsel. From Germany the custom spread quickly and became universally popular, even in the Southern Hemisphere.

The custom of sending special greeting cards at Christmas originated in nineteenth-century England. Giving gifts at Christmas probably originated with the pagan Roman custom of exchanging gifts (*strenae*) at the New Year. The popular gift bringer, Santa Claus, is an American invention; he combines features of the traditional children's saint, Nicholas of Myra, with some elements of the Germanic fire god, Thor, who fought the giants of ice and snow from his home in the polar regions.

Other customs of the Christmas season include the baking of special foods, the cooking of poultry dinners on Christmas Day, and the singing of special songs, notably carols, a species of simple song that originally had wider application than as Christmas music. The celebration of Christmas thus includes both Christian observances and wider folkloric customs, the latter relating to general festivity at the time of the winter solstice.

See Also Gift Giving; Sol Invictus; Winter Solstice Songs.

Bibliography

For a complete bibliography, see Sue Samuelson's *Christmas: An Annotated Bibliography of Analytical Scholarship* (New York, 1982). The most comprehensive treatment of the history of the Christmas celebration is still Hermann Usener's *Das Weihnachtsfest* (Bonn, 1889). For a survey of the liturgical development of the feast, see Ildephonso Schuster's *The Sacramentary* (New York, 1924). A good treatment of the customs associated with Christmas may be found in Francis X. Weiser's *Handbook of Christian Feasts and Customs* (New York, 1958), as well as in the same author's *The Christmas Book* (New York, 1952). For a treatment of the feast from the perspective of the history of religions, see E. O. James's *Seasonal Feasts and Festivals* (New York, 1961).

John F. Baldovin (1987)

CHRISTOLOGY See JESUS

CHRONOLOGY. The tendency to describe time in human terms inevitably leaves its mark on the various systems used for signifying time in all its widely varying forms and dimensions: from the identification of the period of light and the period of darkness within a day, to the artificial groupings of several days (seven-day week, ten-day week), the month (lunar or solar), the seasons, the year, cycles of many years, and the era. This tendency is found within the most diverse cultures and in everyday life as well as in the world of mythical traditions.

Scholars have long been gathering and analyzing a superabundant documentation relating to the concrete systems (mathematico-astronomical, economic, sacral) that in specific historical situations have been used to signify time. Unfortunately, scholars have not always asked themselves why such an activity should have been necessary. Rather than continuing to collect data of a phenomenological kind on the various methods of describing time, it seems more important to examine closely the ideology underlying them. Very useful for this purpose are historico-religious studies of the calendar, which have now made clear the decisions made in every type of culture to distinguish, within the otherwise vague, indistinct, and insubstantial temporal dimension of reality, that which is elevated to the rank of sacred from that which is deliberately left as profane.

Sacred time is saved from the anonymity of assimilation either to the perpetual self-renewal of nature or to the motionless stability of the mythical world, and is thereby rendered eternal in its periodic ritual scansions. Unlike profane time, sacred time tends to abstract not only from nature's inexorable rhythms (which it seeks in some way to control) but also from the rarefied and static character of the period of origins (which has now been left behind) and from the atmosphere of the festival (which, being out of the ordinary, is not congenial to it). As a result, sacred time always shows a face that is entirely its own, though in forms that vary according to the cultural environment and the historical situation. The phenomenology of sacred time ranges from the relatively simple impositions of taboos at specified times (which are thereby automatically removed from the everyday), to the prudent development of festive parentheses (inserted into profane existence as a means of linking this to the period of origins), and on to the infinitely more complex restructurings of calendrical rhythms. (The motives behind these rhythms—astronomical, economic, political, and/or social—are redeemed at the religious level, while the beginning and end of these rhythms are linked in the celebration of the New Year.)

History, for its part, presents us with well-defined instances of sacral descriptions of the temporal dimension. These include the dedication, in the true and strict sense, of limited periods of time to supreme beings (the "days of the gods" in ancient Egypt and the "week" of the *bolon ti ku* or "lords of the underworld" among the Maya); the indication of such days and months by name (as in the Zoroastrian religion and in the Roman, in which January was named after the god Janus, and March after the god Mars); and finally, the constant tendency to identify the beginning of linear time (time that is supremely profane by reason of the uniqueness of each instant) with events of exceptional religious importance. Such events included, for the Hebrews, creation and, for a more restricted period of time, the destruction of the Jerusalem Temple; for the Romans, the inauguration of the sanctuary of the supreme god, Jupiter Optimus Maximus; for the Western world, the birth of Christ; for Buddhist India and Indochina, the death of the Buddha and his attainment of *nirvāṇa;* and for the Islamic faithful, the emigration of Muḥammad from Mecca to Medina.

On the other hand, the consecration, and therefore surrender, of a period of time (which is thus removed from the crises of everyday life) brings the redemption, for man and for his existential needs and cultural requirements, of the remaining part of the temporal dimension, which is usually the larger part and which he seems anxious to regain possession of as soon as possible. In this context we may think of the care with which, by means of suitable indications on their epigraphical calendars, the Romans set apart the days that were *fasti* (i. e., on which it was permitted to administer justice), to the point of distinguishing within the twenty-four-hour period the time during which such activity was licit between the two phases of sacrifice. The Japanese set apart the *kannazuki* ("months without gods"), during which they, convinced that during these periods the Shintō *kami* neglect their faithful, consider it a duty not to waste time in cultic practices. Similarly, the civil authorities of various countries have brought mounting pressure to bear on the religious authorities to reduce the number of feast days and thus increase the number of workdays. The time that human beings reserve to themselves can—and by reason of existential difficulties must—be henceforth structured in a well-defined functional relation to productive activity.

It seems almost superfluous in our day to call attention to the important influence of various economic motivations on the progressive establishment and stratification of calendrical systems in the most diverse civilizations. Certain widespread phenomena in this area are obvious: the coincidence of the beginning and end of the year with the period when consumer goods are most available; the strategic location of festive periods in relation to essential work periods; and the close relation established between annual and seasonal rhythms and the needs created by human fatigue. I shall therefore only remind the reader of three considerations. First, the specific character of a calendrical structure is often determined by an agrarian economy (e.g., in ancient Egypt, where the New Year coincided with the flooding of the Nile, which was essential to the grain cycle and with which the three seasons of inundation, emersion, and repair of the irrigation system were likewise closely connected). Second, within one and the same civilization there are often several calendrical systems, each of which, with its different set of characteristics, looks to a different economic component of the society in question (e.g., at Rome, where the spelt harvest became fully available only in February, thus determining an agrarian-type New Year in March, whereas April 21 signaled the beginning of the work year for those engaged in pastoral activities). Finally, the names of the months often echo particular rural occupations (e.g., "The Garlic Harvest" in the Iran of the Achaemenids; "The Heaping of the Harvest" in pre-Columbian Peru; "The Sowing of the Rice" in China).

Our consciousness of the influence exercised by the economic factor on the cultural description of time is, moreover, such that we can see it already reflected in the sacral traditions of primitive cultures. In these cultures, myths abound showing that primitive man's anxiety focused not so much on the need of having time as on a concern that the time available be suited ("long enough" or "with daylight enough") for hunting (the Paiute of Nevada; the Caddo of eastern Texas) or for salmon-fishing (the Tlingit of the Northwest Coast).

But whether sacred or profane, time is essentially a reality that is conceived, planned, and activated in service of human beings and therefore must be adapted to their needs. Humans view as habitual and secure the limits represented by the day (among some peoples, only the period of daylight), the month (in some cultures, only the period of the waxing moon), the year (in some societies, only the seasons, which are defined in economic terms), and, sometimes, the century. Beyond these limits, human beings seem to feel displaced, lost, threatened, and crushed by the unnaturally vast dimensions that time appears to take on whenever it is geared no longer to them but to suprahuman beings who live in a "different" time or, more precisely, are thought of as "outside of time." Thus human beings can make nothing of a "day of Brahma," which in Hinduism is equivalent to an incommensurable *kalpa*, just as they cannot render useful to themselves, except in an ultimately apotropaic way, the vast eras in which, according to certain higher civilizations (Vedic India, the classical world, pre-Columbian America), phases of dissolution usually, and in significant ways, preclude a renewal of cosmic reality or even a termination of human reality. In the final analysis, human beings would even have a struggle appreciating properly the decidedly more restrained yet barely sufficient three millennia that, according to the Zoroastrian religion, the creator Ahura Mazdā needs in order to establish and then annihilate creation, after having imprisoned and destroyed evil within it.

The fact that time should be geared principally to man, tailored to his measure and defined in function of his needs, both existential and cultural, is constantly made clear precisely in those mythical traditions that, from time to time and in one civilization after another, emphasize this point at levels that are diverse but that, in every case, deal with the common necessity of turning absolute time into a human category. To begin with, great importance is attached in myth to the active role played by the human race in the acquisition of time during the period of origins, as compared with the more passive role played by the suprahuman powers. Those who request, take, conquer, or otherwise obtain time may be, according to circumstances, the First Man (natives of Vanuatu; the Sulka of New Britain); the earthly wife of the moon (the Aleut of Alaska); a child (the Micmac of Cape Breton); the carpenter and his sons (the Bambara of the Sudan); the shaman (the Caddo); or mythical kings (Rome and China). Or the social group in its entirety may play this active role by determining to couple peacefully in the dark (the Selk'nam of Tierra del Fuego); by turning in need to Wild Duck against the negative action of Coyote and the ineptitude of Wolf (the Paiute); by paying Bazzagro to keep the sun in the sky, while Coyote appears to play a secondary role in the entire event (the Pomo of California); by crying out their desire for "long days" so that Maikaffo, the master of atmospheric phenomena, cannot but hear and heed (the Hausa of the Sudan); or by claiming and obtaining a certain course of the sun through the sky, while the creator limits himself to granting their desire (the Tsimshian of the Northwest).

In short, individuals or social groups adapt time to their own use, whereas otherwise it would have other proportions, dimensions, and characteristics. There would, for instance, have been as many months of winter as there are hairs in the trickster's fur coat, instead of winters of only seven months (the Assiniboin of Canada); ten cold moons and, for sole nourishment, soup made of refuse, instead of two such moons, with sunflower seeds, roots, and berries to eat (the Atsugewi of California); lunar months of forty days, as Porcupine wanted, instead of months according to rule (the Tsimshian); excessively short days instead of "long days" (the Hausa); periods of either light alone or darkness alone, with either sleeping or fishing excluded, instead of the indispensable alternation of day and night (natives of Mota in Melanesia and the Tlingit).

It is also significant that time is made available in periods that are keyed to specifically human existence. In fact, time alone makes possible the existence of beds and sleep (natives of Mota); fire and the eating of cooked foods (the Sulka of New Britain); the present manner of making love (the Pomo and the Selk'nam); and death (the Luiseño of California and the Bambara). Prior to the acquisition of time, human beings had not yet carved out a special—that is to say, human and cultural—place for themselves that would differentiate them from the suprahuman and subhuman worlds. As long as time did not exist, either absolutely or in its definitive forms and with its definitive characteristics, mythical beings exercised governance (Rome); the gods were not yet born (Egypt); it was possible to marry the moon (the Aleut); men were still like the animals (the Tsimshian); and, finally, it was possible to use the channels of communication between earth and heaven (the Bambara, the Sulka, and natives of Vanuatu).

As for the acquisition or conquest of time as a function of elementary human needs, here, too, there is a widespread and much accentuated mythical motif. Claim was laid to a winter that was not too long and that was mitigated by the summer so that humans might endure the cold (the Assiniboin and the Micmac). There was a desire for daylight in order to obtain food and cook it (the Paiute, Caddo, Tlingit, and Atsugewi), and for the darkness of night in order to safeguard personal privacy (the Selk'nam) and to rest (the Caddo, natives of Mota, and the Sulka). And all manner of efforts were made to divide the year into months in order to have rest from fatigue (the Bambara) and to be able to commemorate the dead (the Luiseño).

Finally, one also finds a marked awareness that the acquisition of this human category of time had immediate and lasting repercussions in relation to the world of nature, which now received its definitive shape. With time, light first appeared (the Tlingit, natives of Vanuatu, Israel), and darkness as well (the Tlingit). With time, the moon rises and begins its successive phases (the Luiseño, Pomo, Aleut, Tlingit, and

Bambara), and plants and animals come into existence (the Tlingit and Sulka, natives of Vanuatu, Iran, Israel) and take on their definitive traits (the Paiute, Tsimshian, Tlingit). The gods can now be born and, in turn, generate the world (Egypt), and death comes upon the earth (the Bambara and Luiseño).

Paradoxically, time marks the real beginning of history and opens the way for nature to exist. Nature would otherwise have been different or would not even have existed at all. This enables us to understand how, among the rich and complex systems used for describing time in both primitive cultures and the higher civilizations, those systems that give material embodiment to time by specifically human and cultural means acquire special prominence. One such means in widespread use is the voice. In its most diverse forms, time can be announced in a loud voice to the collectivity by the qualified sacral personnel, or at least by individuals of exalted religious standing. We may think here of the solemn public proclamation of the new moon (on the basis of which the month now beginning acquired its special structure) by a *pontifex minor* (minor pontiff or subpontiff) in Rome; or of Muḥammad's reestablishment in Mecca in 631 of a lunar year uncontaminated by intercalations of any kind. Actions of this type, usually ritualized in various ways according to the particular cultural environment, seem to be found in a significant degree in those cultural traditions in which time has not yet become an integral part of the order of things. Time may make its first appearance as something announced and proclaimed (the Luiseño, Atsugewi, Paiute), but remember also *Genesis* 1:1–5, where God says: "Let there be light!" Or time may be repeated (the Assiniboin and Atsugewi), discussed (the Assiniboin, Paiute, Atsugewi, Nandi of northeastern Africa, and Tsimshian), or even obtained by shouting (the Maidu, Tlingit, and natives of Mota) on the part of suprahuman beings or primitive humankind.

Another system of circumscribing time is that represented by work and, in particular, the manual labor of craftsmen. In archaic societies such work soon acquired a properly creative value in relation to realities that are in themselves abstract and difficult, if not impossible, to regulate, as witnessed by the well-known Roman saying that the individual is the *faber* (creator) of his own destiny. The labor of a handworker and, more specifically, of a weaver, a carpenter, or an engraver—that is, the labor of individuals who are accustomed to using fibers, nails and hammer, or chisel and burin in order to produce something that is new, different, and, above all, irreversible (cloths; various objects; and marble and/or metals that are shaped and moved from one place to another) in relation to the raw material that human labor has now immobilized in a given form and thus rendered usable—is the kind of labor that seems to show through, even if sublimated to a henceforth symbolic level, in conceptions of time as something knotted, nailed, chiseled, or engraved. One can cite the knotted cords used for measuring time among various primitive peoples, as well as the "binding of the sun" into the arc of the seasons or into cycles of many years in pre-Columbian America; or the ritual hammering in of the *clavus annalis* ("nail of the year") at Rome, and the comparable way of marking the passage of the years in Etruria; or various epigraphic calendars.

Given the well-known fact that the specialization of trades appears with the rise of the higher civilizations, conceptions of the kind cited can be found only sporadically in primitive cultures, whereas other cultures give them a privileged place. In the myths of primitive peoples, the kind of toil by which time in its various forms is acquired is far from being the labor of a craftsman; rather, it is related to the habitual activities of the various sectors of these societies. In these stories time is hunted down and captured with bow and arrow (the Caddo); hoisted up by brute strength and ropes (the Aleut and Sudanese); ferried in a canoe (natives of Mota); given new form by means of an obsidian knife (natives of Mota); or even looked upon as something to be traded—for example, "bought" with a basket of pearls or a little necklace or even a pig (the Pomo, Paiute, and natives of Mota, respectively).

A further method of circumscribing or actuating time is even more human and cultural by comparison with the other systems. This is the system that actualizes time, in forms that vary constantly from civilization to civilization, through the more or less massive display of ludic activity. Scholars have long known and studied rituals in both primitive and higher cultures that focus on spectacle. Less well known, on the other hand, is the fact that such rituals (usually celebrated to highlight the salient moments of human, social, and cosmic existence and to create or recreate them from time to time at the sacral level) often specifically signal the passage of time by materially describing, characterizing, influencing, and even "realizing" its several and diverse forms and modalities. Among the Witóto, for example, the ritual game of soccer, in which the ball is identified with the moon, is played in precise relation to the various phases of this heavenly body. In the same context the Shasta of Oregon, try to "strike the moon" by hitting the ball with twelve vertebrae of a salmon, and thus to help the moon increase so that, month by month, it may travel the entire arc of the year; this action, in their view, even accelerates the moon's course in winter. The Pygmies of Africa annually dance around a fire to bring about the succession of the seasons; at the spring feast of Ysiah, the Yakuts of Siberia stage a combat between winter and the salutary season; and the Delaware of Oklahoma assign a clearly solstitial character, value, and purpose to the game of soccer.

Examples of this kind help us to grasp the ultimate function of the countless elements of spectacle (dances and songs, games and contests of every kind, dramatic representations, etc.) that, as is well known, are a constant component of New Year festivals both in the most widely varying primitive cultures and in the archaic higher civilizations. Even in these last, in fact, ludic activity, though tending to become what in the modern world is now simply sport and theatricals, still to a degree seeks to shape the varied and manifold formulations of time by describing its rhythms in the form of spectacles. To multiply examples here would carry us beyond the limits set for this article; we need only think of the Assyrian determination of the years by means of a game of chance, or the Greek custom of dating time in relation to the Olympiads celebrated every fifth year. Reflect, too, on the wealth and complexity of the elements offered by the inevitable projection of motifs of this kind in the mythic traditions of these civilizations. One can cite the Egyptian story told by Plutarch, according to which the five days added annually to the other 360 were made up by the god Thoth out of the fractions of time he had acquired by playing chess with the moon. Thoth's purpose in thus composing these days was to create a specific chronological space that would at last allow the divinities to enter the world, since the sun god Re would not allow them to be conceived and born during the regular year.

Given the limitations of space, I shall restrict myself to a brief consideration of how all this was verified in Roman society, where there were many rituals of a spectacular kind. If we keep in mind that the rotation and revolution of the heavenly bodies, which regulate the course of time, were assimilated in Roman culture to the special movement proper to *ludus* ("play"), we will readily understand the imposition of a complex astronomical symbolism on the space occupied by the circus, where every chariot race was intended to mime the course of the sun through the heavens. We will also see a more specific meaning in the fact that the periodic *ludi* served to mark in a solemn manner the expiration of fixed periods of time. Thus, the *lustrum*, or purificatory sacrifice, defined a regularly recurring cycle of four years; the *ludi saeculares*, or centennial games celebrated the end of a *saeculum;* and the various New Year festivals—the Saturnalia, Feriae Annae Perennae (festival of the goddess of the year), and Palilia (festival of Pales, the tutelary deity of shepherds and cattle)—abounded in spectacle.

When thus reduced to a mere product of a game, time seems to be rendered completely subordinate to a given culture. This does not mean, however, that time is undervalued in the slightest; on the contrary, there is always the greatest esteem for it, independent of cultural contexts and historical situations. The value assigned to time is extremely high in comparison with other categories, as seen in the widespread conviction that time is something "precious" that "must not be lost." This evaluation is independent of oscillations in value when moving from a merely economic level (in myth, time can be "bought," while in the modern world it becomes "money" pure and simple) to a highly ideological level. Thus time is equated with the uniqueness of existence in some myths (the Assiniboin, Luiseño, Bambara) in which the conquest of time has been made possible only by someone's sacrifice, suffering, and death.

See Also Calendars; History; Sacred Time.

Bibliography

Duval, Paul-Marie. "Observations sur le Calendrier de Coligny." *Études celtiques* 11 (1966–1967): 269–313.

Goudoever, J. M. van. *Fêtes et calendriers bibliques.* Théologie historique, vol. 7. 3d ed. Paris, 1967.

Hallo, William W. "The First Purim." *Biblical Archaeologist* 46 (Winter 1983): 19–26.

Hartner, Willy. "The Young Avestan and Babylonian Calendars and the Antecedents of Precession." *Journal for the History of Astronomy* 10 (1979): 1–22.

Herz, Peter. "Untersuchungen zum Festkalender der römischen Kaiserzeit nach datierten Weih- und Ehreninschriften." Ph.D. diss., University of Mainz, 1975.

Melena, José L. "Reflexiones sobre los Meses del Calendario Micénico de Cnoso y sobra la Fecha de la Caída del Palacio." *Emerita* 42 (1974): 77–102.

Michels, Agnes K. *The Calendar of the Roman Republic.* Princeton, 1967.

Mikalson, Jon D. *The Sacred and Civil Calendar of the Athenian Year.* Princeton, 1975.

Strobel, August. *Ursprung und Geschichte der frühchristlichen Osterkalendars.* Berlin, 1977.

Giulia Piccaluga (1987)
Translated from Italian by Matthew J. O'Connell

CHRYSOSTOM

CHRYSOSTOM (c. 354–407), bishop of Constantinople (397–404), father of the Eastern church, biblical commentator, and orator. Born John, he was given the name *Chrysostom* ("golden mouth") in the sixth century. Though probably the most popular of the Eastern church fathers, John Chrysostom is not the most accurately documented, and much remains to be elucidated concerning both his life and the number and authenticity of his works.

John was born at Antioch at an unknown date; 354 is the most likely. The only period of his life for which we have reliable information is that of his tenure as bishop of Constantinople and his trial and exile. The currently accepted version of his story is based on a seventh- or eighth-century biography ascribed to the patriarch George of Alexandria (c. 620–c. 630), which largely draws upon two sources: an apologetic dialogue (c. 408) by Palladius, bishop of Helenopolis in Bithynia and a friend of John, and the church history of Socrates Scholasticus of Constantinople (c. 380–c. 440). According to these sources, John was the son of Secundus, an officer in the Syrian army, and a Greek woman, Theousa, left a widow when John still was a child. The boy was sent to the best schools and was a pupil of the Greek rhetorician and sophist Libanius (314–393). At the age of eighteen he abandoned the pursuit of "vain verbosity" and became a Christian. At this time he was continually in the company of the bishop of Antioch, Meletius (360–381). He was baptized and three years later was advanced to the office of reader. After some time he withdrew from the city to lead an ascetic life, first, for four years, in the company of an old hermit, then, for two years, in solitude. Having ruined his health by immoderate austerities, he returned to Antioch, became a deacon in 381, and in 386 was ordained a priest by Meletius's successor, Flavian I (381–404).

John was a zealous priest and soon achieved a reputation as a pulpit orator. In 397, at the death of Nectarius, bishop of Constantinople, he was forcibly abducted to Constantinople at the emperor's order and elected a bishop. His early popularity as bishop and orator was soon adversely affected by the simplicity of his life, his endeavors to repress abuses in the clergy, his defense of the poor, and his criticisms of injustices and the display of wealth. He finally drew upon himself the hatred of the empress by accusing her openly of avarice and injustice. In 403, John's enemies joined in a mock synod (the Synod of the Oak), presided over by his worst enemy, Theophilus, patriarch of Alexandria, who then initiated a trial against John and declared him deposed. Ordered into exile, he was, however, recalled to Constantinople the following day because of a crisis at the palace, probably a miscarriage by the empress Eudoxia. He is said to have reentered the city immediately and been reconciled with the court. These restored relations were, however, soon impaired once more, after bitter complaints by John that the church offices were being disrupted by public festivities that followed the dedication of a statue of the empress. According to Socrates, the opening words of John's sermon, "Again Herodias raves," were interpreted as an insult to the empress and exploited by his enemies. He was subsequently suspended from his functions and finally banished by order of the emperor. For three years he remained in Cucusus, in Lesser Armenia; then, owing to his continued popularity, chiefly in Constantinople, he was sent to a more remote place near the Black Sea. On the road, he died of exhaustion and maltreatment at Comana on September 14, 407.

Beginning in 404 a bitter conflict arose in Constantinople between John's two successors, Arsacius and Atticus, and his followers, who refused to recognize those who had taken an important part in their bishop's eviction. After the death of Atticus (425) a reconciliation occurred. In 437 Chrysostom's relics were brought back to the capital, and he was venerated as a saint and a martyr.

In recent years, the study of a long unexplored source, the so-called *Life of Chrysostom* (attributed to Martyrius of Antioch), composed by an eyewitness and issued in Constantinople a few weeks after John's death, calls into question the previously unchallenged authority of Palladius and Socrates. Thus the commonly accepted accounts of the Synod of the Oak prove to be unreliable. Many other details of the events of John's life are similarly under reexamination.

John was known chiefly as an orator and composer of homilies, many of which are preserved only in the notes of scribes. Many of his sermons are commentaries on books of the Old and New Testaments: *Genesis,* the *Psalms,* the gospels according to Matthew and John, and the letters of Paul. Other sermons are dogmatical (e.g., baptismal catecheses) or practical and moral (*Against the Circus Games, On Almsgiving*). His eight homilies that bear the common title *Against the Jews* were primarily aimed at Christians who frequented the synagogues or indulged in the superstitious practices in which some Jews seem to have dealt at that time. He wrote occasional orations on liturgical feasts, in praise of saints, and on important political events (*On the Disgrace of Eutropius*). Some speeches relating to his difficulties and banishment, such as the famous sermon against the empress, may have been forged in later years by his enemies or his followers. John also left several treatises, for example, *On the Cohabitation of Clerics and Virgins, On Priesthood, On Vainglory and the* Education of Children. Dating from the time of his exile are his 236 extant letters, the most important of which are the seventeen addressed to Olympias, a widow, deaconess, and great benefactress of the poor. John's writings have been widely translated.

Though venerated as one of the four fathers of the Eastern church, John was not primarily a theologian. He was a pastor, concerned with the preservation of faith and morals in his flock. His teaching reflects the orthodox doctrine of the church in the period between the crises of Arianism and Nestorianism. He was successful in restoring unity among the divided Christians of Antioch and avoided in his orations and writings any statement that might endanger their mutual understanding. His popularity as a preacher and as a martyr, however, was such that in later times hundreds of works, even those of his opponents and of heretics, were circulated and preserved under his name.

BIBLIOGRAPHY

The most extensive biography of John Chrysostom is Chrysostomus Baur's *Der heilige Johannes Chrysostomus und seine Zeit,* 2 vols. (Munich, 1929–1930), translated as *John Chrysostom and His Time,* 2 vols. (Westminster, Md., 1959–1960). For John Chrysostom as a church father, see volume 3 of Johannes Quasten's *Patrology* (Westminster, Md., 1960), pp. 424–482. An edition of the most ancient source, the text attributed to Martyrius of Antioch, is to be issued in the near future in the series "Subsidia hagiographica" (Brussels). The first detailed studies have been published; see, for example, my "Que vaut le témoignage de Pallade sur le procès de saint Jean Chrysostome?," *Analecta Bollandiana* 95 (1977): 389–414.

An exhaustive list of the works of John Chrysostom and their editions can be found in Maurice Geerard's *Clavis Patrum graecorum,* vol. 2 (Turnhout, Belgium, 1974). The first edition of Chrysostom's complete works was made by Henry Savile in 8 volumes (Eton, 1612). The most complete edition was published by Bernard de Montfaucon in 13 volumes (Paris, 1713–1738); it was several times reprinted and finally reproduced in *Patrologia Graeca,* edited by J.-P. Migne, vols. 47–64 (Paris, 1858–1860). In recent times several of his works have been re-edited in various collections of patristic literature. For example, *Sources chrétiennes* includes thirteen separate volumes on Chrysostom (Paris, 1947–1983). *Corpus christianorum, series Graeca,* vol. 4 (Turnhout, 1978), reprints a spurious work; four volumes of Chrysostom's works are forthcoming. On spurious works, see J. A. de Aldama's *Repertorium pseudochrysostomicum* (Paris, 1965).

F. VAN OMMESLAEGHE (1987)

CHUANG-TZU SEE ZHUANGZI

CHU HIS SEE ZHU XI

CHU-HUNG SEE ZHUHONG

CHURCH

This entry consists of the following articles:

CHURCH POLITY
ECCLESIOLOGY
CHURCH MEMBERSHIP

CHURCH: CHURCH POLITY

The governance of the Christian churches has assumed a variety of forms based on historical factors as well as on theological positions regarding the origin or root of ministerial functions. In a descending degree of local autonomy, these forms are broadly classified as congregational, presbyterial, or episcopal, but within each category significant modifications exist. After a historical survey of church governance from its beginnings through the Middle Ages, the organization of the major denominations will be considered individually.

One cannot speak with precision or certitude about ministry in the early church because it is difficult to date and evaluate the documentary evidence, including the New Testament writings, and because of differences of organization in the primitive local communities. At the conclusion of an eighty-year evolutionary process there emerged, apparently first at Antioch around 110 CE, a threefold hierarchical leadership that gradually became normative throughout the Christian world. The hierarchy (sacred rule) consisted of three grades: a single bishop charged with the "supervision or oversight" (*episcopē*) of the community; a group of consultors called presbyters (elders); and a subordinate group of deacons, who assisted in the administration of property. Certain functions, such as presiding at the Eucharist, were ordinarily reserved to the bishop. The distinction was thus made between the people and their leaders, soon called "clergy," who were ordained; that is, set apart for the ministry by the imposition of the bishop's hands. The local church presided over by the bishop was in time known as a "diocese" or "eparchy."

Church organization gradually accommodated itself to the political divisions of the Roman Empire. The local churches in a Roman province constituted an ecclesiastical province under the presidency of an archbishop, or metropolitan, who was the bishop of the capital city of the province. By the fourth century the beginnings of a patriarchal system could be detected in the large regional groupings of provinces. Eventually, all the dioceses and provinces of the Empire were subject to one of five patriarchs (father-ruler), namely, the bishops of Rome, Antioch, Alexandria, Jerusalem, and Constantinople. The prominence of these bishoprics may be accounted for on grounds partly theological and partly political.

Among the five patriarchs, the bishop of Rome was accorded a certain primacy that was not clearly defined. The support of the Roman bishop, or pope (father), was particularly crucial in the fifth-century doctrinal disputes over the relation of the divine and human nature of Christ. These controversies were settled at ecumenical (worldwide) councils or synods of bishops held in Asia Minor. The conciliar condemnation of the monophysites and Nestorians greatly weakened the patriarchates of Antioch and Alexandria, in which they were largely concentrated. Constantinople emerged from these crises as the bastion of orthodoxy. After the Muslim conquests of the seventh century, only Rome and Constantinople survived as major churches. The growing estrangement of Eastern and Western Christianity became complete with the sack of Constantinople by the Crusaders in 1204.

In the West the position of the bishop of Rome, the only see (bishopric) to claim apostolic foundation, remained unchallenged for over thirteen hundred years. From the period of the Gregorian Reform (c. 1050), it embarked on a program of centralization, making effective use of councils, papal legates, and revivified canon law. In the wake of the Great Western Schism (1378–1417), during which there were three simultaneous claimants to the papacy, attempts were made to declare the ecumenical council the supreme authority in the church to which even the pope owed obedience. In the sixteenth century the failure to deal with abuses led to the Reformation and the establishment of a number of separate churches with divergent patterns of government.

EPISCOPAL FORM OF GOVERNMENT. The Roman Catholic, Orthodox, and Anglican churches, which considered the historical continuity of ministry from the beginning of Christianity to have the highest priority, retained the episcopacy as the key office in the church. The bishops were viewed as the successors of the twelve apostles. Each of these communions, however, has structured its episcopal commitment in a different way.

Roman Catholic. Echoing the Second Vatican Council, the *Code of Canon Law* promulgated by John Paul II (r. 1978–) in 1983 affirms: "Just as, in accordance with the Lord's decree, Saint Peter and the other apostles constitute one college, in like fashion the Roman Pontiff, Peter's successor, and the bishops, the successors of the apostles, are united with each other" (canon 330). The special responsibility of Peter continues in the bishop of Rome, the pope, who is head of the college of bishops, the vicar of Christ, and the shepherd of the universal church here on earth. He obtains full and supreme power in the church once he has accepted legitimate election by the cardinals. The college of bishops, whose head is the pope and whose members are sacramentally ordained bishops and officially recognized (i.e., in hierarchical communion), also possesses full and supreme power. The college exercises its power over the universal church in a solemn manner through an ecumenical council that can be convoked only by the pope.

The Second Vatican Council introduced a new structure known as the Synod of Bishops. Since 1965 this representative body of about two hundred bishops chosen from different regions of the world has met, usually every three years, to aid the pope in promoting faith and morals, in strengthening ecclesiastical discipline, and in directing the church's worldwide activity.

The cardinals of the Roman Catholic Church, who are appointed for life by a reigning pope, constitute a special college whose chief function is to elect the bishop of Rome. From 1586 until 1958 the number was limited to seventy; beginning, however, with the move of Pope John XXIII (r. 1958–1963) to promote representation from all areas in the world, the college of cardinals has expanded to about two hundred. Only those not yet eighty years of age, however, may participate in a papal election. The cardinals also act as a body of advisers when summoned to deal with questions of major importance, and they head the most important departments of the Curia Romana.

The pope usually conducts the business of the church through the Curia, which acts in his name and by his authority. The Curia consists of the Secretariat of State (which also performs a coordinating function), nine congregations (including the Doctrine of the Faith, Divine Worship and the Sacraments, the Causes of Saints, and the Evangelization of Peoples), three tribunals, twelve pontifical councils (e.g., for Promoting Christian Unity, for the Laity, for the Family, for Justice and Peace, and for the Interpretation of Legislative Texts), and a number of offices (especially, Economic Affairs) and institutes (e.g., the Vatican Library).

Furthermore, the papacy maintains a corps of representatives throughout the world. When these legates are only to the local churches, they are known as apostolic delegates. If they are accredited to states and governments, they are ranked nuncio, pronuncio, or internuncio. (Reciprocally, more than 170 governments, including the United States, maintain diplomatic relations with the Vatican.) In addition to serving a liaison function, the papal legates, in cooperation with the bishops, clergy, and laity of the country, transmit to Rome lists of potential candidates for the episcopacy.

The Roman Catholic Church, over which the pope presides, is made up of particular churches—certain portions of the people of God "in which and from which the one and unique Catholic church exists" (*Code of Canon Law*, canon 368). In current canonical terminology, a particular church is a diocese that is entrusted to a bishop assisted by a presbyterate. As a general rule, a diocese is circumscribed by territorial bounds so as to embrace all the faithful within that area.

It is the prerogative of the pope to appoint bishops to take charge of particular churches or to confirm those who have been legitimately elected. (In a few European dioceses and in the Eastern Catholic or Uniate churches, the right to elect a bishop is recognized.) At least every three years, the bishops of an ecclesiastical province are to draw up a list of priests suitable for the episcopacy that is then sent to Rome. A diocesan bishop governs the particular church committed to his care with legislative, executive, and judicial power according to the norms of the law. He exercises legislative power personally, executive power either personally or through vicars, and judicial power either personally or through a judicial vicar. He is aided in his government by the presbyterial council (a body of priests) and by his staff, including vicars, a chancellor, a finance council, a promoter of justice, and a defender of the bond (for suits alleging the nullity of marriage or of holy orders). Every five years the bishop is to send to Rome a report on the state of the diocese. Upon reaching the age of seventy-five, he is asked to submit his resignation to the pope.

Every diocese is divided into parishes, which are established by the bishop after consulting the presbyterial council. Parishes are usually territorial, but they may also be determined on a personal basis, incorporating, for example, all those of Korean nationality or all those belonging to a university community. The parish is to be entrusted to a pastor appointed by the bishop, who is considered an extension of the bishop bringing spiritual care to his people. Every parish must have a financial council in which the laity participates. In many dioceses a pastoral council (with only consultative voice) is organized. If the number of parishioners requires it, the bishop may appoint additional priests as parish assistants or curates. Parishes may also be entrusted to religious communities such as the Dominicans or Franciscans.

While the diocese is the basic administrative unit in the Roman Catholic Church, there is some provision for supradiocesan structures. These include provinces, a grouping of neighboring dioceses presided over by the metropolitan or archbishop, and the episcopal conference, which includes all the bishops of a given nation or territory. While an archbishop has only a general supervisory role in the province, a conference may make deliberative and binding decisions in particular matters, while on other issues the diocesan bishop has freedom regarding implementation.

Of the approximately 1.07 billion Catholics in the world, about 17 million belong to the Eastern churches. Except for the Maronites, these churches represent various groups that have reunited with Rome since the sixteenth century. Almost all of them have larger counterparts that are Eastern Orthodox or non-Chalcedonian Orthodox. The Eastern churches, Catholic as well as non-Catholic, follow different rites, which entail a special liturgy, law, and spiritual tradition. Thus, in addition to the Latin church, to which the vast majority of Catholics belong, there are also twenty-one Catholic Eastern churches. These churches, with considerable autonomy, especially in the choice of bishops, are in six instances headed by patriarchs who acknowledge the primacy of the pope.

Orthodox and other Eastern churches. The Eastern Orthodox and other Eastern churches are firmly committed to apostolic succession and the episcopacy. The Eastern Orthodox churches accept the first seven ecumenical councils (through the Second Council of Nicaea in 787), as do Roman Catholics. The smaller Eastern churches, refusing to recognize the third (Ephesus [432]) and fourth (Chalcedon [451]) ecumenical councils, are divided into two Nestorian churches and four others known collectively as non-Chalcedonian Orthodox.

The Eastern Orthodox Church is not centrally organized but is a federation composed of fifteen autocephalous, or self-governing, churches and four others, which are known as autonomous. "Autocephaly" connotes the right possessed by a group of eparchies (dioceses) to settle all internal matters on their own authority and to elect their own bishops, including the head of the church. The boundaries of autocephalies are usually coterminous with those of a state or nation. Four of these autocephalies (Constantinople, Alexandria, Antioch, and Jerusalem) are based upon ancient Christian tradition, as has already been noted. The remaining eleven have resulted from modern political developments: Russia, Romania, Serbia, Greece, Bulgaria, Georgia, Cyprus, Poland, the Czech lands and Slovakia, Albania, and North America. The autonomous churches—Finland, Japan, and Ukraine—while to a large degree self-governing, have not yet achieved full independence. The head of the monastery of Saint Catherine in the Sinai Peninsula has the rank of archbishop of Sinai; his jurisdiction over the immediate neighborhood constitutes an autonomous church.

From antiquity the heads of the churches of Constantinople, Alexandria, and Antioch have been known as patriarchs. That title is also accorded the heads of the Russian, Romanian, Serbian, and Bulgarian churches. The head of the Georgian church is known as catholicos-patriarch; the heads of the others are metropolitans or archbishops. Ecclesiastical provinces in western Europe, North and South America, and Australia depend upon one of the autocephalous churches or one of the emigrant Russian jurisdictions. There is no bishop among the Orthodox churches who holds a position analogous to that of the pope in the Roman Church, but the patriarch of Constantinople is recognized as the ecumenical or universal patriarch. He holds a place of honor and precedence, and his authority over the Orthodox world is a moral one, the first among equals. Supreme authority belongs only to a pan-Orthodox council.

The Greek Orthodox Church in North and South America, the largest body of Orthodox in the Western Hemisphere with two million communicants, was originally incorporated in 1921 as the Greek Orthodox Diocese in North and South America. It eventually embraced the Archdiocese of New York, nine dioceses in the United States, and one each in Canada and South America. On July 30, 1996, the Holy Synod of the Ecumenical Patriarchate provided separate metropolitanates for Canada, South and Central America, so that the Archdiocese of America subsequently exercised jurisdiction only over the United States. The archdiocese, with its seat in New York City, includes the Direct Archdiocesan District (New York) and eight metropolises (Atlanta, Boston, Chicago, Denver, Detroit, New Jersey, Pittsburgh, and San Francisco). It numbers one and a half million members.

According to a new charter approved by the patriarch on January 18, 2003, the archbishop and the metropolitans make up the eparchial synod that governs the archdiocese, subject to the superior authority of the ecumenical patriarchate. The synod ordinarily meets twice a year and has exclusive jurisdiction over all legal issues that affect the archdiocese as a whole and its metropolises.

In each archdiocesan district and in each metropolis, there is a spiritual court of first instances to, as the 2003 charter stipulates, to deal with family problems, as well as with moral and disciplinary charges against clergy and lay persons. The eparchial synod comprises a second instance or appeals court. The ecumenical patriarchate is the final court of appeals. Archdiocesan clergy-laity congresses are convened at least triennially. "Except for dogmatic or canonical matters," says the charter, "they are concerned with all other matters which affect the life, mission, growth and unity of the archdiocese" (Article 10 a). There is also a clergy-laity assembly for the archdiocesan district and each metropolis to treat local matters, "including the uniform governance of the parishes, educational programs, financial programs and philanthropic concerns, as well as with the better organization and effectiveness of the parishes" (Article 11 b). Councils at both the archdiocesan and local levels, comprising representatives of clergy and laity, meet at least twice a year to function in an advisory and consultative capacity. The election of the archbishop is the "exclusive privilege and the canonical right of the Holy Synod" (Article 13 a), though the eparchial synod and the archdiocesan council have an advisory role. For the election of other bishops, three names are submitted to the Holy Synod, which chooses one of them.

The second largest Orthodox body in the New World is the Orthodox Church in America, with approximately one million members. It received independent status from the Patriarchate of Moscow in 1970, against the will of the ecumenical patriarch, who refused to recognize its autocephaly. It adopted a new statute in 1971. The supreme canonical authority is the Holy Synod, which includes as voting members all the diocesan bishops under the presidency of the metropolitan. It meets twice annually and is competent to treat "all matters involving doctrine, canonical order, morals and liturgical practice" (*The Statute of the Orthodox Church in America,* Article 2, Official Text 1974). The synod regulates the election of bishops and the establishment of new dioceses.

The All-American Council is "the highest legislative and administrative authority within the Church" (Statute, Article 3). It is composed of the metropolitan and all bishops (who must approve all resolutions by a majority), the priests of each parish (and an equal number of lay delegates); priests not having parishes; two delegates from each seminary; and one representative from each organization officially accredited by the Holy Synod. It convenes every three years. The metropolitan is elected by the All-American Council with the approval of the Holy Synod. He is assisted by the Metropolitan Council, the permanent executive body of the church. He is the bishop of one of the dioceses.

The diocese, the basic church body, comprising all the parishes of a determined geographical area, is governed by a diocesan bishop with the advice of an assembly and council. The Diocesan Assembly nominates a candidate for an episcopal vacancy. If the candidate is unacceptable to the Holy Synod, it elects its own candidate. The Diocesan Assembly is made up of all the clergy and an equal number of elected lay delegates. For validity, all resolutions of the assembly must be approved by the diocesan bishop. The Diocesan Council, the permanent body of diocesan administration, meets at least twice a year. Its decisions become effective upon approval by the diocesan bishop. The bishop, as head of all parishes within the diocese, appoints the parish clergy. The rector, the head of a parish, is assisted by a parish council elected by a meeting of all the parishioners.

Besides the two main bodies of the Orthodox Church, there are a number of smaller national and language jurisdictions, such as an archdiocese dependent upon the Arab-speaking patriarchate of Antioch and dioceses under the patriarchates of Serbia, Romania, Bulgaria, and Albania. There is also a Standing Conference of Canonical Orthodox Bishops, which seeks to coordinate the activities of the various jurisdictions throughout the Americas.

Anglican and Episcopalian churches. The episcopal constitution of the church and apostolic succession are also fundamental to the Anglican Communion, which is made up of thirty-eight provinces found mainly in English-speaking countries and former colonies of England. The communion has been described as a federation without a federal government. Usually every ten years, an assemblage of archbishops and bishops of the entire communion, called the Lambeth Conference, convenes in the Lambeth Palace, London, under the presidency of the archbishop of Canterbury. The conference, which does not publish details of its debates, issues resolutions with only morally binding force. At the 1968 conference, a body representing the laity and the clergy as well as the bishops was formed. The Anglican Consultative Council, headquartered in London, meets biennially with about fifty delegates.

The parent body, the Church of England, is an established church with the sovereign of the country as its supreme governor. Acting upon the advice of the prime minister, the sovereign appoints the archbishops and bishops. Since the 1970s, however, procedures that give more weight in the selective process to ecclesiastical authorities have been followed. The church is divided into the province of Canterbury, whose archbishop is styled Primate of All England and Metropolitan, and the province of York, whose archbishop is called Primate of England and Metropolitan. The archbishop oversees all the dioceses within the province, confirms the election of every bishop and is his chief consecrator, and hears appeals in his provincial court. The archbishop of Canterbury, with the approval of the crown, may grant licenses and dispensations that are valid throughout the province of York as well. The jurisdiction of the bishop in his diocese is similar to that of a Roman Catholic bishop. He can promulgate binding rules of discipline, but in the matter of parochial appointments he is limited by extensive rights of patronage held by laity and certain corporate bodies. At the parish level, church councils elected by the lay members cooperate with the incumbent in developing church activities.

Each province, not more than three times a year, holds a convocation that, subject to the supreme authority of Parliament, determines policy with regard to doctrine and practice. The convocation, under the presidency of the archbishop of Canterbury, has an upper house of bishops and a lower house made up of senior archdeacons, representatives from each cathedral chapter, and elected representatives from the clergy. Both provinces together form the General Synod or Church Assembly, composed of a third house of laity in addition to the house of bishops and the house of clergy. The Assembly deals with legal and administrative matters but not with doctrine.

In the United States the church affiliated with the Anglican communion is the Protestant Episcopal Church. It is governed by a bicameral General Convention meeting triennially or at special call. The House of Bishops consists of all bishops; with the approval of the other house, it elects one of its members as presiding bishop, an office held until retirement. The presiding bishop is entrusted with general executive power over the whole Episcopal Church. The House of Deputies comprises not more than four priests and four laypeople elected from each diocese. All legislation must be passed by both houses. Between sessions of the General Convention, the church is governed by the presiding bishop in consultation with the Executive Council, whose members are elected by the General Convention and the Provincial Synods. The council is organized into a number of departments, with staff to coordinate activities at home and abroad.

To establish a diocese there must be at least six parishes and six voting presbyters. The diocese meets in convention annually with all diocesan clergy and representatives from each parish as members. The convention elects clerical and lay delegates to the provincial synod and to the General Convention. Each diocesan convention also elects a standing committee to advise the bishop between sessions. The convention lays down rules and procedures for filling an episcopal vacancy. The person chosen must be confirmed by a majority of the standing committees of all the dioceses as well as of the diocesan bishops in the United States. A bishop must retire at the age of seventy-two.

The diocesan convention is responsible for defining the boundaries of parishes and for establishing new ones. Each parish is governed by a vestry and wardens selected according to diocesan law. The number and qualifications vary from one diocese to another. Similarly, there is no canon specifying their specific duties, term of office, or voting rights. The vestry elects the pastor or rector and notifies the bishop of its choice. The bishop may try to dissuade the vestry but has little option in the matter. The appointment is considered to be for life; the rector cannot be removed unwillingly except with the consent of the bishop.

Methodist churches. The vast majority of the Methodists in the United States recognize the centrality of the episcopacy in their governing structure, although they do not accept it as an order different from the presbyterate. (Churches deriving from British Methodism do not have bishops.) Apostolic succession in the sense of historic continuity in the ministry is not viewed as necessary. The ordained ministry consists of elders (presbyters) and deacons who are "set apart by the Church for the specialized ministry of Word, Sacrament, and Order," as stated in the *Book of Discipline of the United Methodist Church* (par. 302, 1972) It also states that "to be ordained to the ministry of Order is to be authorized to equip the laity for ministry, to exercise pastoral oversight, and to administer the Discipline of the Church" (par. 309.1).

The Annual Conference corresponds to a diocese in the Episcopal and Roman Catholic churches. It consists of all the presbyters in a given geographical area plus an equal number of elected lay representatives. A bishop presides over the conference. He is responsible for appointing ministers to parishes after consultation with the district superintendents as well as with representatives of the local congregations. The appointments do not convey tenure but must be renewed annually. Each parish or local congregation has a Charge Conference, which serves as a liaison with the general church; the Charge Conference elects lay members of the Annual Conference and all local officers.

The Annual Conferences are grouped into Jurisdictional Conferences made up of an equal number of lay and clerical delegates. In the United States there are five regional jurisdictions, which normally meet once every four years. Their chief responsibility is to fill vacancies in the ranks of the bishops, to determine the boundaries of the Annual Conferences, and to provide for the work of the church within the jurisdiction.

The highest legislative authority in the United Methodist Church is the General Conference, composed of from six hundred to one thousand delegates, ministers and lay, chosen by the Annual Conferences based on size of membership. The General Conference also meets quadrennially before the Jurisdictional Conferences. It defines and fixes the powers and duties of all ministers, bishops, and subordinate conferences. It regulates the boundaries of jurisdictional conferences with the concurrence of the Annual Conferences involved. The General Conference initiates and directs all connectional enterprises of the church and provides boards for their implementation.

Presbyterial Form of Government. Presbyterians do not admit as normative a historically validated episcopal succession. They hold that there is no New Testament warrant for a distinct office of bishop; presbyters (elders) and bishops designate the same leadership body in the church (*Acts* 20:17–28, *1 Tm.* 3:1–13). The polity of Presbyterian churches rests on three constitutive principles: (1) "the parity of presbyters" (both clergy and lay); (2) "the right of the people through their representatives or lay elders to take part in the government of the church"; and (3) "the unity of the Church, not simply in faith and order, but in a graduated series of Church Courts [session, presbytery, synod, General Assembly] which express and exercise the common authority of the Church as a divine society" (Moffatt, 1928, p. 2).

The basic governing body is the session, which is made up of the minister or ministers of the local church and a group of ordained laity (ruling elders) elected by the congregation. Administrative authority rests with the representative body, not with the whole congregation. The session is charged with the "spiritual oversight of the congregation." While the minister presides, all elders have equal rights of discussion and vote. All congregations in a given geographical area belong to a presbytery, which is composed of all the ordained ministers in the area and elders from each congregation. The presbytery has several key responsibilities similar to those of a diocesan bishop in Roman Catholicism. The presbytery supervises ministerial candidates, ordains ministers, concurs in a "call" to specific pastorates, and in general oversees the discipline of the local congregations. The presbytery elects a moderator and a stated clerk, who may be either clerical or lay. The stated clerk functions as a chief administrator.

The presbyteries of a region are grouped into a synod. A synod must have at least three presbyteries. Elected representatives, both clerical and lay, from each of the presbyteries constitute a synod, which meets once a year. It serves as a court of appeal from actions taken by the presbyteries and stands in an intermediary position between the presbyteries and the General Assembly. The General Assembly, the highest representative body, meets annually for about one week. Its members are elected directly by the presbyteries, on the basis of one ministerial commissioner and one ruling elder commissioner for a determined number of church members in the presbytery. It is the supreme court of appeal in matters of doctrine and discipline. The General Assembly elects a moderator, a largely honorary official, who acts as titular head of the church for the next year. In fact, however, the stated clerk holds the most powerful leadership position.

In 1983, the two largest Presbyterian bodies in the United States merged to form the Presbyterian Church (USA). Presbyterians are joined with other churches of the Calvinist tradition in an international confessional group, the World Alliance of Reformed Churches, with headquarters in Geneva.

Congregational Form of Government. Opposed in principle to any form of control above or outside the local church, a third group of Christian denominations is organized along congregational lines so that each community is independent. The defenders of this ecclesial pattern of government maintain that the New Testament does not recognize any higher structure. Paul, for example, sent a general letter to the several churches in Galatia (*Gal.* 1:1–2). The author of *Revelation* was told to write to the seven churches in Asia Minor (*Rv.* 1:4). The *Acts of the Apostles* indicates that each congregation has the right to choose its own leaders (6:3, 13:2). The congregation can also regulate discipline without reference to any bishop, presbytery, or council (*1 Cor.* 5:12, *Mt.* 18:17).

In the United States, the Baptists have been the most conspicuous advocates of a democratic polity. Although Baptists do not have an official creed, they generally subscribe to two important confessions of faith, the Philadelphia Confession (1742) and the New Hampshire Confession (1833). Each congregation is self-constituting: the members bind themselves together by covenant, accepting as the sole rule of faith the Bible, which the members interpret according to their own lights. The members choose their own leaders—variously called elders, bishops, or pastors—who are set apart for the ministry. The laity retains full control so that all business is determined by majority vote.

Congregational autonomy, however, has had to be accommodated to the needs of fellowship and cooperation with other churches. Historically, the chief impetus leading to the formation of "conventions" was the concern for foreign missions that swept the United States at the beginning of the nineteenth century. Baptist churches are grouped into associations at local, state, and national levels. The five largest of the thirty-one bodies in the United States, embracing about 90 percent of the denomination, are the Southern Baptist Convention; the National Baptist Convention, USA; the National Baptist Convention of America; the American Baptist Churches, USA; and the Progressive National Baptist Convention, Inc. In addition there is the Baptist World Alliance, founded in 1905 to discuss matters of common concern; it meets every five years. The delegates, or messengers, who participate in the meetings of the associations have no power to bind the groups they represent. Even with this understanding there have been protests that the Baptists are drifting toward denominational centralism or Presbyterianism. One important function of the associations is to give counsel in the selection of ministers. Ministerial standards are set and recommendations are made to the congregations, who proceed to elect and ordain the ministers.

Congregationalism is also espoused by the United Church of Christ, which was formed by the merger of four denominations in 1957: the Congregational Church, the Christian Church, the Evangelical Synods, and the Reformed Church. Each of the uniting churches has maintained its own theological position and form of worship. The constitution of the United Church of Christ states explicitly that "the autonomy of the local church is inherent and modifiable only by its own action" (Horton, 1962, p. 135) The local congregations, however, are joined together for mutual support.

The organization resembles that of the Presbyterian Church. The churches of an area are grouped into an association that meets annually and that is made up of all the clergy and elected lay delegates. It accepts new churches into membership and is responsible for licensing, ordaining, and installing ministers. Associations within a region are joined in a conference composed of the ministers and elected lay delegates; meeting annually, it serves as a coordinating body. The "minister" of the conference, also called the superintendent or president, acts as the executive officer.

The highest body in the United Church of Christ is the General Synod, which assembles biennially. The conferences elect delegates to the General Synod, which has an equal number of clergy and lay people. The synod chooses a president for a four-year term and a moderator to preside over the synodal sessions. An executive council is elected to transact business between synods.

Contingent Polities. Not all churches fit neatly into one system or another. The Lutheran Church, the third largest body of Christians in the world after the Roman Catholics and the Eastern Orthodox, does not hold that any polity is divinely sanctioned. The sixteenth-century reformers were prepared to continue such existing institutions as the episcopacy, provided that the gospel was preached and the sacraments were administered. Thus, at the start of the twenty-first century there are bishops in the Scandinavian countries where, except for Sweden, Lutheranism is the established church. In general, however, apostolic succession and episcopal ordination are not considered essential to the church.

An early treatise of Martin Luther (1483-1546) suggests that he advocated a congregational type of government (*On the Right and Power of a Christian Congregation or Community to Judge All Doctrine and to Call, Install, and Depose Ministers,* 1523). Although every Christian is a priest (*Rv.* 5:10) and has the same right with respect to Word and sacraments, no one may use this right publicly except by the consent of the community. Otherwise there would be a "shameful confusion," a kind of "Babylon in the Church, as the Apostle teaches" (Luther, *Concerning the Ministry,* 1523, Works 40, pp. 34–35). The congregation retained the right to remove any minister who should preach falsely.

In the United States the three largest denominations, about 95 percent of the nine million Lutherans in the country, acknowledge varying degrees of local autonomy. Parishes are generally grouped into districts, which in turn are organized into territorial synods. The powers exercised by the synod are specified in a constitution. At all levels, pastors and lay representatives participate in the government. Synodal authority is concerned chiefly with the ordination and discipline of the clergy and ownership of property.

ECUMENISM. Despite the diversity of views about the ministry and government in the church, the ecumenical movement in the twentieth century uncovered a certain compatibility and explored the possibility of reconciliation. In the early 1960s nine church bodies in the United States—including Methodist, Disciples of Christ, Presbyterian, Episcopal, and United Church of Christ—formed an association known as the Consultation on Church Union (COCU). On a number of occasions over the next thirty years, representative committees attempted to formulate a detailed plan for union. Though the member churches could subscribe to the theological consensus presented, they were unwilling to ratify the structures or the nature of the ordained ministries, especially the episcopacy, proposed for the new uniting church. Finally, at Memphis, Tennessee, on January 19, 2002, the consultation, COCU, was formally superceded by a simpler relationship, Churches Uniting in Christ (CUIC). As reported by Thomas F. Best, each church retained its own identity and decision-making structures, but with the anticipation that the participating churches will achieve "mutual recognition and reconciliation of ordained ministry by the members of Churches Uniting in Christ by the year 2007" (2002, p. 403).

The status of ministry is central in any discussion of church polity. The most thorough investigation of ministry was undertaken by the Faith and Order Commission of the World Council of Churches. In 1982 it submitted to all Christian churches for an official response the document, long in preparation, entitled *Baptism, Eucharist, and Ministry.* After receiving and analyzing almost two hundred responses, the commission published a summary report of its consultation *Baptism, Eucharist, and Ministry 1982–1990* (Faith and Order Paper no. 149, 1990). According to that report, the vast majority of the responses affirmed that the church, from its earliest existence, has needed ministers, "persons ordained through the invocation of the Spirit and the laying on of hands and holding specific authority and responsibility" (p. 75). While there was "considerable appreciation for the description of the development of the threefold pattern of bishop, presbyter and deacon," many of the Reformation and Free churches "question its normative character" (pp. 80–81) and hold deep differences over episcopal succession.

Despite disparate polities, a number of churches have sought common ground for unity. At a service on October 4, 1998, the Evangelical Lutheran Church of America, the Presbyterian Church (USA), the United Church of Christ, and the Reformed Church of America formally entered into full communion. In *A Formula of Agreement,* the four bodies acknowledged, as reported by their committee of theologians, that though the sixteenth-century differences "regarding Eucharist, Christology, and predestination continue to shape and reflect our identities, they cannot claim to be church-dividing today and should not stand in the way of achieving 'full communion' among us. In addition, we affirm that the differences among these churches of the Reformation on questions of confessional commitment, ministry, and ecclesial polity fall within the bounds of allowable evangelical diversity and are therefore not church-dividing" (Nickle and Lull, eds., 1993, p. 65).

On January 6, 2001, after twenty-five years of dialogue, the Evangelical Lutheran Church in America and the Episcopal Church entered into full communion. The ecumenical accord, "Called to Common Mission," provided for the recognition of the present clergy of both denominations as equal, but stipulated that in the future all ordinations were to include the laying on of hands of a bishop ordained in a historic line of succession. However, because Lutheran tradition had sanctioned ordination by pastors, some Lutheran synods almost immediately sought an exemption so that "for pastoral reasons in unusual circumstances" a synod president could authorize a pastor to preside at an ordination. The Lutheran position has always been that polity is essentially adiaphoral (something indifferent, neither prescribed nor forbidden by scripture). At the same assembly at which they approved full communion with the Episcopalians, the Lutherans also sanctioned the agreement with the Moravian Church in America. The historian Martin Marty has noted that "it is the first time in U.S. religious history that a church has bridged the gap between churches so diversely governed—congregational, Presbyterian, synodical, conferencial and episcopal" (1999, p. 797). Undoubtedly the major polity issue yet to be resolved among Christians is that of a primatial authority.

SEE ALSO Apostles; Armenian Church; Coptic Church; Denominationalism; Eastern Christianity; Ethiopian Church; Greek Orthodox Church; Nestorian Church; Papacy; Reformation; Russian Orthodox Church; Schism, article on Christian Schism; Syriac Orthodox Church of Antioch; Uniate Churches.

BIBLIOGRAPHY

Baima, Thomas A. *The Concordat of Agreement between the Episcopal Church and the Evangelical Church in America: Lessons on the Way toward Full Communion.* Lewiston, N.Y., 2003. Analyzes method and content of negotiations.

Brand, Chad O., and R. Stanton Norman, eds. *Perspectives on Church Government: Five Views on Church Polity.* Nashville, 2004. Representatives support their own and respond to other traditions.

Campenhausen, Hans von. *Ecclesiastical Authority and Spiritual Power in the Church of the First Three Centuries.* Translated by J. A. Baker. Stanford, Calif., 1969. Treats the relationship between ministerial office and charismatic gifts.

Dulles, Avery. *Models of the Church.* New York, 1974. Discusses five major approaches, types, or models through which the character of the church may be grasped.

Gray, Joan, and Joyce Tucker. *Presbyterian Polity for Church Officers.* Louisville, Ky., 1999. Treats the impact of Reformed theology on church government.

Kirby, James E. *The Episcopacy in American Methodism.* Nashville, 2000. Traces the evolution of Itinerating General Superintendents into residential diocesan officials.

Kirk, Kenneth E., ed. *The Apostolic Ministry: Essays on the History and the Doctrine of Episcopacy.* London, 1946. A team of writers explores the Christian doctrine of ministry.

Kretschmar, Georg, et al. *The Councils of the Church: History and Analysis.* Edited by Hans J. Margull. Philadelphia, 1966. After a historical treatment of councils, authors from various churches present their respective theologies on the subject.

Longenecker, Richard N., ed. *Community Formation in the Early Church and in the Church Today.* Peabody, Mass., 2002. Following nine scriptural and historical essays, the final three "assess modern episcopal, Presbyterian, and congregational polities in light of their biblical and theological roots."

Maring, Norman H., and Winthrop S. Hudson. *A Baptist Manual of Polity and Practice.* Rev. ed. Valley Forge, Pa., 1991.

Mead, Frank S., and Samuel S. Hill, eds. *Handbook of Denominations in the United States.* 11th rev. ed. Revised by Craig D. Atwood. Nashville, 2001. Describes the historical background, main teachings, and governmental organization of more than 250 religious bodies.

Meyendorff, John. *The Orthodox Church: Its Past and Its Role in the World Today.* 3d ed. Crestwood, N.Y., 1981. Chapter 8 discusses the autocephalous churches in the post–World War II era.

Niebuhr, H. Richard, and Daniel D. Williams. *The Ministry in Historical Perspectives.* New York, 1956. Nine authors treat the ministry from the primitive church to the twentieth century, with emphasis on Protestantism.

Pelikan, Jaroslav. *Spirit versus Structure: Luther and the Institutions of the Church.* New York, 1968. After sketching Luther's rejection of sacramental ordination, monasticism, and canon law, Pelikan considers the struggles of the reformers to deal with the need for concrete structures.

Puglisi, James F., ed. *Petrine Ministry and the Unity of the Church: Toward a Patient and Fraternal Dialogue.* Collegeville, Minn., 1999. Twelve Protestant and Catholic scholars comment on recent papal overtures.

Sykes, Stephen, et al. *The Study of Anglicanism.* Rev. ed. London and Minneapolis, 1998. A collection of essays that introduce "the history and ethos of the Churches which constitute the Anglican Communion."

JOHN E. LYNCH (1987 AND 2005)

CHURCH: ECCLESIOLOGY

The word *church* refers to the visible community in which Christians come together for worship, prayer, communal sharing, instruction, reflection, and mission. Most Christian bodies, but not all, see this visible community as imperfectly representing on earth an invisible communion of saints called together by God in Jesus Christ. The church can thus be viewed as one social institution among many, but also as a shared form of life shaped by profound theological self-understandings. Seen institutionally, the church has subsisted in a variety of communal forms and structures of governance throughout a long and very complex history. Understood theologically, the church has been the object of many varying images, descriptions, terminologies, and conceptualities interwoven with the circumstances of that history. The systematic study of the church in all these interacting dimensions constitutes the field of ecclesiology. This realm of inquiry relates constructively to most of the other principal themes of Christian thought, among them the doctrine of God, Christology, soteriology, theological anthropology, and theological ethics.

CHURCH IN THE NEW TESTAMENT. The English word *church* translates the New Testament (NT) Greek *ekklesia* (assembly), the commonest equivalent for the Hebrew *qahal* (assembly, gathering, or congregation) in the Septuagint or Greek translation of the Jewish Scriptures, the Bible of the NT writers. It is possible that *ekklesia* was used of early church gatherings to distinguish them from the Jewish synagogues (Greek *synagoge*, translating the Hebrew term *edah* [assembly, or gathering] as virtually synonymous with *qahal)* to which many early Christians still belonged. The term *ekklesia* in this sense is found among the earliest Christian writings: see for example the phrase *ekklesia tou theou* (assembly of God) in *1 Thessalonians* 2:14.

The NT provides myriad images of this *ekklesia.* Several stand out: "people of God," "body of Christ," "communion of faith, hope, and love," "creation of the spirit," and "new Israel." Another image, the "kingdom (or rule) of God," central to the preaching of Jesus, becomes understood as the eschatological fulfillment of the church's life.

Whether Jesus of Nazareth intended (or could indeed have envisioned) anything like the "church" that in fact followed on his words and work has been a topic of continuing debate. The definitive factor in inaugurating this new community of faith seems not to have been Jesus' intention as such but rather the experience of the living presence of the risen Messiah, an experience variously described by the Gospel writers and by Paul. Jesus' life, death, and resurrection, as interpreted by his followers, gave rise to the movement that rather quickly became the NT *ekklesia.* But how, and by what stages, this band of believers evolved so as to become the church, with all the latter's institutional and doctrinal complexity and eventual multiplicity, is a matter of much controversy.

What can be said with certainty is fairly meager. By the middle of the first century Paul was freely using the term *body of Christ* and other theologically significant expressions to refer to the community of believers. The traditional account of "birthday of the Church" on the Day of Pentecost, as described in *Acts* 2, may certainly contain historical elements. But it came, in its present form, from a much later tradition. The same later tradition also gave us what is sometimes described as the first universal council (*Acts* 15), an event during which Paul's mission to Gentiles was affirmed, along with minimum conditions for their admission to the new community. It is this event that launched the community's transition from being one of many Jewish sects to being a self-standing body, yet one still without obvious signs of becoming what it did in fact become, a "church" for the Roman Empire as a whole.

Geographical Dispersion, Episcopacy, and the Formation of the Canon. Evidence exists within the NT for the early emergence of a variety of geographically dispersed centers of Christian activity—Damascus, Antioch, Alexandria, and others—whose ecclesiological self-understandings evidently varied. Many of these places are linked by being recipients of Paul's letters, in which they are urged to see themselves as members of "one body in Christ." But a connected ecclesial community across the Empire did not begin to be a reality until diocesan bishops—for example, Irenaeus (c. 130–203) and Cyprian (c. 205–258)—considered as successors to the apostles, took up their tasks of indicting heretical communities (Gnostics, Montanists, Novatians, Marcionites), regulating a common doctrinal patrimony, and taking steps toward defining a single canon of Scripture. By the late second century, nearly the whole of what became the NT was authoritative in the church for practical purposes. Yet the first known list of canonical writings corresponding to the present NT was made by Athanasius, Bishop of Alexandria (296–373), in 367. Wholly uniform agreement on the content of the canon was achieved still later.

It has become increasingly clear to modern scholars that this canon-forming process may have excluded more writings than it allowed in. Expressions of the faith existed that were deemed inconsistent with the apostolic tradition handed down in the major dioceses. Some scholars argue that writings approved for inclusion in the canon of Scripture tended to be those that affirmed Jesus Christ, one way or another, as God, leaving aside communities more inclined to see Jesus as only a Gnostic or prophetic teacher.

In sum, by the fourth century the church was beginning to take on a determinate form as to structures of leadership, canonical sources, and the outlines of doctrine. Even so, different ecclesiological tendencies were evident. In Tertullian (c. 160–225) one finds what would today be termed a thoroughly sectarian ecclesiology. In the work of Eusebius of Caesarea (c. 264–340) one finds an ecclesiology suitable for the then new relationship between church and Empire.

It is plain that the Christian community's emerging structure rested substantially upon the theory and practice of episcopacy, from the time when the bishop was, in effect, pastor of the local congregation (the so-called Ignatian pattern) to the period of multicongregational dioceses. The ecclesiological significance of episcopacy had already been clearly expressed in the letters of Cyprian (200–258), third-century bishop of Carthage, who held that the bishop was necessary to the very being (*esse*) of the church, not merely to its well-being (*bene esse*): "The church is in the bishop, and the bishop in the church." Bishops were successors to the apostles. But Cyprian also proclaimed the essential equality of bishops, resisting the already growing power of the bishop of Rome. A century later Eusebius, in support of this emphasis on continuity, made lists of the bishops who had served in several key dioceses.

Constantine and Creeds. By the early fourth century the church was well positioned to take advantage of the emperor Constantine's (c. 274–337) unexpected move in 312 or 313 CE granting toleration and many other legal favors to the church within the Empire. Constantine's personal "conversion," as described by Lactantius (c. 260–340) and Eusebius, was not itself ecclesiologically important. But the new and growing relation of the church to the Roman state was, leading as it did to complex and portentous developments. In 380, for example, the emperor Theodosius (346–395) did what Constantine had not: he made Christianity the only licit religion of the Empire. Roman emperors had previously claimed the title *pontifex maximus;* that is, chief priest of the state-sanctioned pagan cults. It was natural that once they had become Christian, they should claim similar power in the church, not as priests, but as protectors, enforcers, and legitimators. Constantine's calling of the Council of Nicaea and his enforcement of its decrees was a case in point. Above all, the emperors wished to maintain a voice in appointments to high church office.

Still, there had not as yet emerged any authoritative ecclesiology, any doctrinal definition of the church's nature as such. "The church" was not yet what was later called a theological *locus*, a topic of doctrinal reflection. Cyprian's creed (c. 250) named the church not as an object of belief in itself but only as the community "through" which members believe in the forgiveness of sins and eternal life. The earliest versions of the Nicene and Apostles' Creeds made no mention of the "holy catholic church" as such. That reference was added in the Constantinopolitan supplement of 381 to the Creed of the Council of Nicaea of 325, and the church was now to be not only "believed" as a reliable witness to the truth but also "believed in"—a significant further step: "We believe in one holy, catholic and apostolic church. . . ." With these words there emerged for the first time what came to be called the four "marks" of the church, later prominent in Catholic attempts to counter Orthodox and Protestant claims.

Augustine of Hippo. A full theological reflection on the church's nature was to come only in the work of Augustine of Hippo (354–430). This bishop and saint believed deeply in the Catholic Church as a visible, worldwide institution continuous with the church of the apostles. The word *catholic* was henceforth no longer just an adjectival "mark" of the church in the Creed. Now it was part of a proper name: the Catholic Church. Augustine could now say that he believed in the gospel only on the authority of this church, whose character and historical role the saint adumbrated at several points in his writings, notably those arguing (against the Donatists) that ordination, baptism, absolution, and other acts of the church are not dependent on the moral character of the one who administers them but rather on the church's objective being and authority as expressed in these acts. Here was an anticipation of the Council of Trent's declaration that, in the sacraments, grace is conferred *ex opere operato* (by the act performed).

Augustine contributed further to Catholic ecclesiology by locating the church significantly in his world-historical drama *The City of God.* The true membership of that city, he taught, consists of God's chosen and predestined ones and is in principle invisible. The Church on earth visibly represents the heavenly City, although not all church members are actually citizens of the holy commonwealth, for not all belong to the company of the elect. The earthly church, notwithstanding its representative function, is therefore a *corpus permixtum,* a mixed body of the elect and the nonelect, and likewise of sinners and saints. Elect persons may belong in either of the latter categories. The earthly church's sacraments are nevertheless necessary for salvation. In principle, Augustine agreed with Origen (c. 185–c. 254), Cyprian, and the very similar language of the Athanasian Creed, *extra ecclesiam nulla salus* (no salvation [occurs] outside the church).

THE PAPACY. The character of the Catholic Church, early and late, is inseparable from the history of the papacy. According to tradition Peter was the first pope, but the whole early history of the papal institution, and with it the roots of the power and preferment of the See of Rome in relation to other dioceses, is shrouded in obscurity and controversy. By the close of the second century, however, if not earlier, the bishop of Rome had achieved a significant degree of primacy over other bishops. Irenaeus, Bishop of Lyons, writing near the year 200, approvingly relates the story of this primacy, holding the See of Rome to have been founded by Peter and Paul, followed by other bishops in an unbroken line to his own day. Even so, at this time and for some centuries afterward, sees such as Jerusalem, Alexandria, and Antioch remain important centers of power and influence.

Political events from the fourth century onward offered opportunities for strengthening the papal institution. This, in turn, accentuated the relative administrative autonomy of the church, as well as its hierarchical character. Constantine's removal of his imperial administration from Rome to Constantinople gave the bishop of Rome added scope for independent action, as did the shift, in 404 CE, of the official imperial residence remaining in the West from Rome to Ravenna. Leo I "the Great" (440–461) took notable advantage of these circumstances to strengthen the Petrine office.

Other developments of ecclesiological importance occurred not long afterward. Among other things, the establishment of monastic and other orders, beginning with the Benedictine order about 528 or 529, protected by papal favor and rapidly proliferating across Europe, added a new and vital dimension to Catholic ecclesiology. Meanwhile, the popes continued their efforts to define and maintain ecclesiastical independence in the civil realm. The reigns of two popes in particular illustrate this point. With Gregory I "the Great" (590–604) the papacy began to take over many of the functions previously lodged in the state. Four hundred years later, Gregory VII (1073–1085), codified his conception of papal power in twenty-seven affirmations—not all of them new, but none before made explicit in this manner. This pope is especially remembered for his encounter with the Holy Roman Emperor, Henry IV, over the authority of secular princes to create bishops, the so-called investiture controversy. Henry made a symbolic submission to the pope but won a tactical political victory. Tensions over this and related church–state issues continued for centuries to shape the Western Church's character and self-understanding.

THE EASTERN CHURCHES. No such centralized and politicized ecclesiology emerged in the East. Circumstances did not demand them. Constantinople's patriarch ruled in the shadow of the emperor and the power of the civil authorities. Furthermore, it appeared that the genius of the Eastern Church was not for wrestling with the contingencies of human events but for reflecting on humanity's relationships with divinity. The ecclesiology of the East was far more tied to the liturgy and to a conception by which the church became a doorway to *theosis,* humanity's spiritual pilgrimage toward unity with God. While the church of the West up to the time of the Reformation maintained its administrative, liturgical, and theological unity, the Eastern Church expanded the variety of its expressions and relationships, each "autocephalous" body representing a different political history and set of cultural traits. "Oriental" Orthodox churches were already well established in Egypt, Syria, Armenia, India, and elsewhere. As early as the fourth or fifth century an Eastern Christianity, with a Latin culture, existed in what is now Romania. By the seventh century Eastern Christianity was spreading into the Slavic territories of Eastern Europe, giving rise to the Bulgarian and other Orthodox churches. By the tenth century orthodoxy was spreading into Russia, where it eventually became the largest of the Orthodox bodies.

As this expansion proceeded, tensions between the Eastern and Western branches of the Church were growing more marked. Specific differences—liturgical, canonical, theological—played their part. Among these, but hardly alone, was the theological question raised by the addition in the West of the word *filioque* (and the Son) to the clause in the Nicene-Constantinopolitan Creed having to do with the "procession" of the Holy Spirit. Such tensions were exacerbated by ecclesio-political pressures, including the presence of unruly crusaders from the West in the eastern territories and competition for ecclesiastical control over southern Italy and Sicily.

Matters came to a head over the claim of Pope Leo IX to supremacy by the See of Peter over the entire Catholic Church, a supremacy the pope deemed incompatible with the autonomy of territorial churches in the East. Despite the desire of the emperor to maintain the religious unity of his realm, successive attempts to negotiate these disputes went nowhere.

In 1054 a papal sentence of excommunication of the patriarch and his followers was followed by an act of excommunication in return. Events were to prove that this was not a final breach. Negotiations went on for nearly four hundred years, to be ended finally by the conquest of Constantinople by the Ottoman Turks in 1453.

Thus was established a separation that has continued to the present day, perpetuating two broad ecclesiological cultures in East and West, with much in common but marked differences owing to historical and cultural experience. The overriding characteristic of the Eastern churches has consistently been their maintenance of continuity with the ecclesiastical forms and teachings of the Church Fathers and of the first seven ecumenical councils, from Nicaea (325) to Second Nicaea (787). These churches, apart from their diaspora communities in the West, including the Americas, have over the years been relatively little influenced by Western cultural phenomena such as the Renaissance, the Reformation, and the Enlightenment. This isolation has begun to be overcome by these churches' participation in the modern ecumenical movement.

The Rise of Protestantism. It would be simplistic to claim that significant ecclesiological development in the West halted from the time of the great popes to the coming of the Reformation. Medieval theologians refer from time to time to this subject. But it is only with the Protestant reformers that ecclesiology again became a foreground issue in the church, with markedly varied outcomes in different parts of Europe.

Martin Luther (1483–1546). Early in his career, Luther sought to reform, but not divide, the church of the West. He regarded the division his activities in fact brought about as temporary, pending correction of certain abusive practices in the parent body. Therefore, he did not set out to formulate an alternative ecclesiological position. But Luther soon found himself at the heart of a movement of German princes, merchants, bishops, and priests, all with reasons for wishing to be free of Roman authority. Theological discovery coincided with practical political and economic interests. In 1520 Luther attacked the papal institution in a series of tracts denouncing the alleged superiority and privileges of the clergy over the laity, the pope's claim to have exclusive authority to interpret Scripture, and the claim that only the pope could call a council of the church. Papal doctrine, he said, held the church in a kind of Babylonian captivity, especially where the sacraments were concerned. Luther maintained that in pressing these views he and his followers were simply reasserting historic Christianity as it had been before its corruption by Rome.

Excommunication by the pope followed in 1520, and an imperial ban came in 1521. Faced with the challenge of reconstituting a church for Germany independent of papal authority, Luther turned first to Augustine's distinction between the church as a visible gathering, on the one hand, and an invisible company of those predestined for salvation from before the world's beginning on the other. For Luther, as for Augustine, the visible church contained a mixture of the elect and the nonelect. Yet, being the nominalist that he was, Luther rejected the seeming metaphysical realism of Augustine's notion of the church of the elect. He preferred to see this notion rather as a critical principle for judging the fidelity of all historical expressions of the church. Specific types of ecclesiastical structure and governance were to him *adiaphora*, matters of indifference, so long as the Word was rightly preached and the Eucharist and baptism rightly administered, implying communion with the true Body of Christ. Luther later added to these primary signs several secondary ones: the power of the keys, ministry, public prayer, and Christian life shaped by the cross.

One infers that this reformer would in principle have preferred a church consisting of congregations of committed believers. Yet, for the sake of consistency and order, he held to the principle of the territorial church to which all inhabitants were admitted by baptism. Moreover, with the old ecclesiastical structure dissolving, Luther gave the lay princes of these territories reason to disregard the episcopal and papal courts. The princes, in turn, were not slow to exercise administrative authority over the parish clergy. Hence the system of German *Landeskirchen*, or territorial churches that has persisted to the present day. In the outcome, some *Landes*, especially in the south, remained Catholic, while others in various ways embraced the Reformation, following in each case the religious allegiance of the prince in question.

John Calvin (1509–1564). A generation later, John Calvin found himself in an analogous but yet significantly different situation. He was summoned to the independent city-state of Geneva as a theological mentor in that community's effort to become a self-standing Christian community on Reformation principles. Calvin was therefore preoccupied with the organization of a community that gathered at one moment as church and at another as civic commonwealth. Calvin's ecclesiology and his statecraft therefore interpenetrate. The state was to uphold pure doctrine and the Church's temporal interests. Yet church and state were not to be confused or to interfere with one another.

While he extended, even radicalized, Augustine's notion of predestination, Calvin did not see the visible and invisible churches as two different realms, but rather as two ways of speaking about the one church. For Calvin the church existed where the gospel was properly preached and the sacraments administered according to God's Word. But Calvin was unwilling to lay upon others the specific ecclesiological and political provisions that Geneva had found suitable for regulating its own Christian life. The Calvinist or "Reformed" ecclesiology is therefore open to being expressed in many different outward forms. This is what happened as versions of Calvinism spread across Europe, to North America, and to other parts of the globe.

The "left wing" of the Reformation. Within Europe, the church structures built on the work of Luther and Calvin remained territorial—intended, that is, to embrace the *corpus permixtum* represented by whole populations. But the European continent also saw a proliferation of separatist, "free church," or "believers' church" ecclesiologies. The "radical reformers" behind these movements—Anabaptists, Mennonites, Hutterites, and many others—in effect collapsed the classical distinction between the visible, imperfect church on earth and the invisible church of the true saints, making the demand for visible conformity with Christ's teachings a central tenet of the earthly Christian community. This meant a separation from the territorially conceived Lutheran and Reformed bodies, a rejection of infant baptism, and a policy of withdrawal from the affairs of the state and the practices of warfare and judicial violence. The radical reformers saw precedents for their vision in the life of groups in the early church. Bodies with comparable ecclesiological convictions have continued to exist through the centuries to the present day.

Ecclesiological developments in Britain. The ecclesial expressions that emerged in Britain under the influence of Lutheran, Calvinist, and "free church" conceptions were shaped by the particular histories of those islands in the sixteenth and seventeenth centuries.

In England, King Henry VIII proclaimed himself "supreme head on earth of the English church," replacing the pope in this role and thereby launching the history of Anglicanism. This body retained the episcopal form of church governance and the claim to apostolic succession, yet it entertained a variety of theological self-understandings from "protestant" or "evangelical" to "catholic" in tendency. Simultaneously, Roman Catholicism continued through changing fortunes in Britain. The rise of "Anglo-Catholicism" in nineteenth-century Anglicanism brought a part of that communion close to Catholicism in virtually every respect but formal allegiance to the pope. Indeed, the rise of this position in Anglicanism may have been responsible for the rise in English of the term *Roman Catholic Church,* as opposed to merely *Catholic Church,* in order to distinguish the latter from its Anglican counterpart.

Meanwhile, a Congregational ecclesiology grew, by a lengthy process, out of sixteenth-century "Puritan" attempts to purify the Church of England. Many leaders of this effort had been in contact with Protestants in centers such as Basel, Strasbourg, and other cities of the Rhine Valley. Some of the former hoped to replace the episcopal governance of the English church with an essentially Presbyterian system. Failing this, some of this opinion joined separatist, or independent, groups of various kinds. Congregationalism as a distinct body was the product of a coalition of these impulses joined in support of the Cromwellian revolution of the seventeenth century and developed institutionally in the wake of that revolution's collapse.

Congregationalists practiced the autonomy of the local congregation within a loosely overarching church structure. The emphasis on decision making by the local gathering was generally shared by the various sorts of English nonconformists; Congregationalism thus came to represent the more conservative wing of nonconformity, while on the left arose such groups as the Society of Friends, the Levellers, the Diggers, and the apocalyptically oriented Fifth Monarchy Men.

A fully Presbyterian ecclesiology, though favored by many sixteenth-century English Puritans, was to become dominant only in Scotland, as articulated in John Knox's *First Book of Discipline* (1561), and achieving its classical shape under an act of 1690 establishing the Church of Scotland as it was to remain for generations in that nation. This polity was characterized by the rule of "presbyteries" (regional governing bodies composed of ministers and elders), held to the principle of "parity" of clergy—recognizing no higher order of ministry in the church than that of presbyter or elder—and to governance by a hierarchy of church "courts" from the "session" of a local congregation to the General Assembly.

The character of Scottish Presbyterian anti-episcopal sentiment was shaped by centuries of highly intricate political conflict between Scotland and England in the course of which episcopacy became associated with rule by the English sovereign. Scottish Presbyterians made common cause with the English Parliamentary Party against King Charles I and with the Puritans of the Cromwellian period, helping to embody their theological and ecclesiological principles in the Westminster Confession of Faith (1646).

Transitions beyond Europe: the "denomination." Virtually all of the European churches—Roman Catholic, classical Protestant, and free church alike—leapt across the Atlantic to North America, and then, at a later date, to mission fields across the globe. Colonial America saw several instances of territorial domination and formal establishment of religious bodies, such as Anglicanism in Virginia and Congregational Puritanism in Massachusetts. But Christian bodies that had previously been territorially established in conception and practice eventually found themselves living alongside many others in the same districts, cities, and towns. This, combined with various understandings of the "separation of church and state," the disappearance of ecclesiastical establishments, and nineteenth-century immigration from the European continent gave birth to a new notion, that of the "denomination." It was now impossible to consider all the inhabitants of a territory to be church members by baptism. Denominations were now competing with one another in open markets as alternative ecclesial possibilities.

Sometimes, of course, certain denominations became numerically dominant in their regions—Baptists or Methodists in the American South, Lutherans in the upper Midwest—leading them to function like European territorial churches. In other cases, they were forced to function as if they were independent or separatist bodies whether or not their original ecclesiologies would have supported such a notion. Even Roman Catholicism came to be looked upon as one "denomination" among others in many parts of America and the rest of the world.

From the notion of "denomination" as an American adaptation of ecclesiastical bodies born elsewhere, it was an easy step to forms of the church, having little or no continuity with European origins, arising to meet local or freshly identified needs. A significant example, among others, would be the emergence of the "black church" in America, going back as far as the seventeenth century to what has been called the "invisible institution" among the transplanted African slaves—a "clearing of freedom" in a world of oppression. After emancipation, the black churches became "denominations" in their own right, with the vitally important social role of being "a nation within a nation," forming a new paradigm of what it meant to be a church.

Likewise, missionary efforts transplanting churches from Europe and the New World to other parts of the globe, beginning with Spanish colonization enterprises in the sixteenth and seventeenth centuries and being undertaken in earnest, if differently, by American and European Protestants in the later nineteenth century, generated ecclesiastical polities resembling the former ones but with histories of their own. The rise of nineteenth- and twentieth-century American evangelicalism, which gave much impetus to these missionary efforts, produced a new, effectively postdenominational consciousness that paid little attention to ecclesiological matters but in fact represented an ecclesiology in which most of the older categories and barriers simply disappeared. In their place arose a broad evangelical culture in which one could, as it were, reach a direct, institutionally unmediated relationship to God in Jesus Christ. Revivalist enthusiasm for spreading the gospel cut across all ecclesiastical lines and exported this spirit to other parts of the world.

TWENTIETH-CENTURY DEVELOPMENTS. The twentieth century was marked by a new self-consciousness about the importance of ecclesiological issues and the means of pursuing them. It began to be seen that these issues have to do with the visible form of the presentation of the Christian message to the world. The impact of ecclesiastical divisions on this presentation began to be felt particularly by nineteenth-century Protestants in the mission fields, where historical reasons for such divisions meant little and the divisions themselves came to be seen as scandalous.

The rise of the ecumenical movement. Such realizations began to resonate in the sending churches of Europe and North America, coming to expression particularly in World Missionary Conference at Edinburgh in 1910 and in the founding of the Life and Work movement (Stockholm, 1925) and the Faith and Order movement (Lausanne, 1927). Further decades of consultation led to the founding of the World Council of Churches (WCC) in Amsterdam in 1948. All this brought about profound changes in ecclesiological attitudes, despite the fact that the WCC never professed to be a churchly body in itself and always made clear that membership in it did not involve any compromise of a church's ecclesiological convictions. A wide range of ecclesiastical bodies joined, including most mainstream Protestant churches in Europe, North America, and the former mission fields, as well as most of the Orthodox communions of the East. Many evangelical groups and the Roman Catholic Church remained formally outside. But Rome has for years been officially represented on the WCC's Commission on Faith and Order, devoted to church unity matters.

The Second Vatican Council. Meanwhile, the Second Vatican Council of the Roman Catholic Church, meeting from 1963 to 1965, not only dealt profoundly and innovatively with ecclesiological issues but also became an event of great ecclesiological importance by demonstrating the significance of the conciliar strand in the structure and governance of that body.

The council's "Dogmatic Constitution on the Church," *Lumen Gentium*, opens with the affirmation that "the church, in Christ, is in the nature of sacrament—a sign and instrument that is—of communion with God and of unity among all men." This church is both the mystical body of Christ and also a visible community. These are not two realities but one, in which a divine and a human element come together, much as do the divine and human natures of Jesus Christ. This church "constituted and organized as a society in the present world, subsists in the Catholic Church, which is governed by the successor of Peter and by the bishops in communion with him. Nevertheless, many elements of sanctification and of truth are found outside its visible confines."

At the same time this church is heir to the whole biblical tradition concerning the "people of God," from God's covenant with Israel to the new people of God inaugurated by Christ. This messianic people, although it does not include all human beings, is the "most sure seed of unity, hope and salvation for the whole human race."

Liberation theology and the "base communities." The rise of "liberation theology," largely a product of Latin American Catholicism but also represented by Protestant writers, has been in many ways a product of the Second Vatican Council's "people of God" ecclesiology. The most important ecclesiological product of this movement has been a "reinvention" of the church in the form of ecclesial "base communities."

Most such communities began as neighborhood gatherings designed to respond to the absence of enough priests to offer the sacraments in the parish churches. In these settings, lay leadership sought to connect the gospel with the practical needs and aspirations of the people. There emerged a view of the church as sacramental and communal as opposed to juridical and hierarchical, an ecclesiology with political implications of a new kind, as recognized by the 1968 Medellín, Colombia, conference of Latin American Catholic bishops, and restated by the 1979 Puebla, Mexico, bishops' gathering as a "preferential option for the poor."

Meanwhile, the ecclesio-genetic notion of the base communities has been borrowed by other groups in other parts of the world. Among the most prominent are gatherings of women determined to "reinvent the church" in their own way. These groups vary widely in style and thought, but are united in the perception that the entire patriarchally dominated development of the church's self-understanding has been fundamentally distorted by a systematic exclusion of women's voices and contributions.

End-of-century ecumenism: ecclesiology and ethics. The impact of liberation themes on ecumenism had the effect, from roughly the 1970s onward, of affirming the intimate connection of ecclesiology with social ethics. Explorers of the meaning of this connection added human-science perspectives to ecumenical insights to portray a church that expressed its being, its *esse,* as an alternative moral community in the world. Here was a vision of the church as disciplined moral community, as opposed to churches largely assimilated to the values of the cultures around them. This vision in turn raised the question whether churches separated by differences with regard to ministry and sacraments might find a kind of moral communion with one another, or at least discover a moral dimension in their search for sacramental communion.

AT THE DAWN OF THE TWENTY-FIRST CENTURY. The twenty-first century has begun with considerable convergence in the formal, classical arenas of ecclesiological thinking. The work of the WCC's Commission on Faith and Order, called by some "the most comprehensive theological forum in Christendom," has continued, together with a wide range of bilateral dialogues among the different communions. The WCC document *The Nature and Purpose of the Church: A Stage on the Way to a Common Statement* (1998) comes closest to articulating the "state of the question" in twenty-first-century ecumenical discussions of ecclesiology. There exists a broad convergence in biblical and theological terms about the church's nature and purpose. But seemingly intractable differences remain as to how these insights should shape visible institutional structures and strategies. The discussion of these issues continues, as does work on ecclesiology-and-ethics matters, where common agendas are hard to reach.

Meanwhile, the primary institutional context for ecumenical thinking, the WCC, is coming under increasing ideological and financial pressures. The Orthodox churches are pressing the council for greater recognition of their traditional claims. Other member churches are distracted by internal issues, notably conflict over conservative versus liberal visions and the roles of openly homosexual persons in the leadership of the church.

It is not clear that the twentieth-century achievements of ecumenism and conciliarism can be preserved. At the very least, the whole configuration of organized interchurch relationships is in a process of change. At this writing, it cannot be known how these questions will be resolved. Profound changes are taking place in the world that are bound to have an impact on the global shape of the *ekklesia.* The diminishing influence of traditional churches in Europe and North America contrasts with the rising profile of evangelical movements there and across the globe. The shift of major centers of Christian population toward the southern hemisphere brings traditional ecclesiologies under the pressure of new cultural assumptions.

Churches are questioning the justice, and the consequences, of their traditional alliances with Western power centers. Overcoming violence worldwide has become a priority issue. And finally, the possibility of new, more positive relationships with other world faiths over issues concerning humanity in general opens directions for inquiry and action whose consequences cannot be foreseen.

SEE ALSO Christian Social Movements; Ministry; Missions, article on Christian Missions; Monasticism, article on Christian Monasticism; Nuns, article on Christian Nuns and Sisters; Priesthood, article on Christian Priesthood.

BIBLIOGRAPHY

Congar, Yves M. J. *The Mystery of the Church.* Translated by A. V. Littledale. Baltimore, 1960.

Congar, Yves M. J. *A History of Theology.* Edited and translated by Hunter Guthrie. Garden City, N.Y., 1968.

Dulles, Avery R. *Models of the Church.* Garden City, N.Y., 1978.

Dulles, Avery R. *The Church: A Bibliography.* Wilmington, Del., 1985.

Florovsky, Georges. *Bible, Church, Tradition: An Eastern Orthodox View.* Belmont, Mass., 1987.

Kinnamon, Michael, and Brian F. Cope, eds. *The Ecumenical Movement: An Anthology of Key Texts and Voices.* Geneva and Grand Rapids, Mich., 1997.

Meyendorff, John. *Catholicity and the Church.* Crestwood, N.Y., 1993.

Minear, Paul. *Images of the Church in the New Testament.* Philadelphia, 1960.

Moltmann, Jürgen. *The Church in the Power of the Spirit,* Minneapolis, 1993.

Mudge, Lewis S. *The Church as Moral Community: Ecclesiology and Ethics in Ecumenical Debate.* New York, 1998.

Niebuhr, H. Richard. *The Social Sources of Denominationalism.* New York, 1929.

Rahner, Karl. *The Church after the Council.* New York, 1966.

Schillebeeckx, Edward. *The Church and Mankind.* Glen Rock, N.J., 1965.

Schmemman, Alexander. *The Historical Road of Eastern Orthodoxy.* New York, 1963.

Troeltsch, Ernst. *The Social Teachings of the Christian Churches and Groups.* Translated by Olive Wyon. New York, 1960.

Welch, Claude. *The Reality of the Church.* New York, 1958.

WCC Commission on Faith and Order. *The Nature and Purpose of the Church: A Stage on the Way to a Common Statement.* Geneva, 1998.

LEWIS S. MUDGE (2005)

CHURCH: CHURCH MEMBERSHIP

The question of church membership may be approached from various points of view: the theological, the juridical, and the sociological. The theological approach, which will be emphasized here, grows out of the biblical foundations of the Christian faith.

OLD TESTAMENT. The "people of God" are identified with Israel as an ethnic group and a nation in various books of the Old Testament (*Dt.* 7:7–8, *Is.* 41:8, 51:2, etc.). By birth the individual received the call to live up to the religious heritage of the people. Especially in the Judaism of the Diaspora, non-Israelites who believed in the God of Israel were admitted to the ranks of the proselytes and could, through circumcision and immersion, become Israelites in the full sense. A person who was once an Israelite could be put under the ban, or could apostatize, but could not cease to be a member of the people of God.

NEW TESTAMENT. There is no discussion of church membership as such in the New Testament, but certain conditions for membership seem to be implied in metaphors such as the net, the flock, the vine and branches, the olive tree, and the New Israel. In *Romans* 12:4–8 and *1 Corinthians* 12:12–31, Paul compares the members of the church to which he is writing to organs or limbs of a body. His letter to the Ephesians speaks of Christians as members of the body of Christ and of one another (*Eph.* 5:30, 4:25). In the New Testament, baptism is seen as the basic sacrament of incorporation, and it is regularly linked with the profession of Christian faith (*Acts* 2:38, 8:37, etc.). According to Paul, baptism makes one a son of God "through faith" (*Gal.* 3:26–27). The Eucharist further unifies the community insofar as all partake of the one bread (*1 Cor.* 10:17). All members of the community are seen as having an active role in keeping with their personal spiritual gifts (*Rom.* 12:6–18, *1 Cor.* 12:7, *1 Pt.* 4:10).

In various ways the New Testament authors indicate that membership or some of its effects may cease. For certain grave offenses, believers are ostracized (*2 Thes.* 3:14), shunned (*Ti.* 3:10), avoided (*1 Cor.* 5:11), treated as heathen (*Mt.* 18:17), and excluded from the homes of the faithful (*2 Jn.* 10). It is even taught that those who quit the Christian fellowship can never have been true Christians (*1 Jn.* 2:19).

CHRISTIAN ANTIQUITY. As the ancient church wrestled with problems of orthodoxy and discipline, it made provision for the exclusion of heretics, schismatics, and other serious offenders. Once the Roman Empire became officially Christian, membership in the church increasingly became a condition for rights of citizenship.

The fathers of the Greek church connected membership with baptism and the Eucharist—sacraments that they viewed as effecting union with Christ and participation in his divine life through faith and charity. These themes continue to be vital, especially in Eastern Christian churches, which emphasize chrismation as a necessary complement to baptism.

Augustine (d. 430) and the later Western fathers, notably Gregory I (d. 604), distinguished two aspects of the church. On the one hand, it is a communion of grace and spiritual gifts; on the other, a visibly organized society with doctrinal, sacramental, and ministerial structures. For the followers of Augustine the visible structures were a sign of, and a means of entry into, the invisible community, which had primary importance. Against the Donatists, Augustine insisted that sinners were still members of the church, though they belonged to it only in an external way. The church in its visible aspect, Augustine recognized, does not perfectly coincide with the communion of the just or of the predestined, who constitute the church in its deeper dimensions.

MIDDLE AGES. Early medieval theologians such as Bede the Venerable (d. 735), following Augustine, spoke of the universal church as having existed from the time of Abel and as including the angels and the souls of the blessed. But they regarded the visible structures of the church as essential to its present historical phase. Before the reforms of Gregory VII (d. 1085), the church was closely identified with the Christian people, who were held to be under two sets of rulers, temporal and spiritual. After Gregory VII a clearer line was drawn between membership in the church and membership in the state.

In the high Middle Ages the great scholastic theologians, including Thomas Aquinas, saw the church primarily as a communion of grace, and consequently they looked on membership principally as a grace-relationship to Christ. Thomas held that all human beings except those already damned are in one way or another united to Christ as head (*Summa theologiae* 3.8.3c). Those gifted with faith and charity are most perfectly members of the church on earth; those who have faith but not charity are imperfectly members; and infidels are members only in potency. Some scholastic theologians, such as Albertus Magnus, held that although sinners are members of the church, they are not members of Christ's mystical body.

In the late Middle Ages some saw membership as a purely individual relationship to God and as being hidden from human eyes. John Wyclif (d. 1348) and Jan Hus (d. 1415) spoke of the church as the "multitude of the predestined" (*numerus praedestinatorum*) known to God alone. For them, reprobates (i.e., those not predestined to glory) were only putative members.

Reformation and Counter-Reformation. The sixteenth-century Protestant reformers Martin Luther, Philipp Melanchthon, and John Calvin held that although the church is visible by reason of its functions of proclaiming the word of God and administering the sacraments, membership in the church is hidden. For practical purposes, they held, we must treat as members those who profess to believe in God and Christ, who partake of the sacraments, and who live as Christians. But God alone knows who belongs to him by sincere faith and election. Reformation theologians often stated that no one could be saved without belonging to the church, but by *church* in this context they meant "communion of saints" rather than a given socially organized institution. Repeating a well-known medieval axiom, they denied that God is bound to the means of grace he has instituted.

In reply to the reformers, Roman Catholics accented the visibility of the church and the guarantees of apostolic succession. For Roberto Bellarmino (d. 1621), church membership required three conditions: external profession of the true faith, sacramental communion, and subjection to the legitimate pastors, especially the pope as vicar of Christ. Whoever is unbaptized or excommunicated or guilty of manifest heresy or schism is not a member of the church of Christ (*De controversiis* 4, *De ecclesia,* bk. 3, chap. 2). Bellarmino, however, recognized that non-Catholics and non-Christians, if they were living in the grace of God, could belong to what he called the "soul" of the church.

For Francisco Suárez (d. 1617), the church had existed in some form since Adam. From the time of Christ, however, it was the "political or moral body of those who profess true faith in Christ" (*De fide,* disp. 4, sec. 1, n. 3). Whereas Bellarmino held that occult infidels were members of the church, Suárez denied this—yet the difference was not sharp, because even for Bellarmino such secret unbelievers were not "true" members (*De controv.* 4.3.10).

Modern Period. Until recently Roman Catholic theologians continued to adhere in substance to the positions of Bellarmino and Suárez. Bellarmino's doctrine was a major influence on Pius XII, who in his encyclical *Mystici corporis Christi* (1943) equated "real" (*reapse*) membership in the mystical body of Christ with being a Roman Catholic. Vatican Council II (1962–1965) modified this stance by avoiding the category of membership and by speaking instead of degrees of relatedness and incorporation. According to the Constitution on the Church (*Lumen gentium*), non-Christians who live by the grace of God are positively related (*ordinantur*) to the people of God (no. 16). All baptized Christians are joined (*conjunguntur*) with Christ and with Catholics (no. 15), as are also catechumens who explicitly intend to become incorporated into the church (no. 14). To be fully incorporated in the church, however, one must accept the visible structures of Roman Catholicism, be in sacramental communion with the pope, and be gifted with the grace of the Holy Spirit (no. 14). In effect, therefore, Vatican II reserved full membership to Roman Catholics who are living up to their professed faith. The council accepted the Augustinian theme that sinners are in the church in a bodily way but not in their hearts (no. 14). Vatican II's Decree on Ecumenism stressed baptism as the fundamental sacrament of incorporation (nos. 3, 22). The 1983 Code of Canon Law returns to Bellarmino's three conditions for full communion in the Catholic Church: the bonds of professed faith, sacraments, and ecclesiastical governance (can. 205).

The concept of church membership in Protestantism has undergone notable changes since the Reformation. The "free churches" that arose in the succeeding centuries were often nonaggressive sects or "denominations"—that is to say, voluntary, nonobligatory associations reflecting certain preferences with regard to doctrine, worship, or organization. Membership in a denomination is seen as implying a willingness to abide by the rules of the organization, even though one might wish to change some of those rules. Denominational membership is not equated with belonging to the community of salvation. In some denominations infant baptism is rejected in favor of a "believers' baptism" administered to adolescents. In such denominations small children are not considered church members.

The World Council of Churches in 1961 referred to the mutual recognition of members as an essential of Christian unity. Various ecumenical organizations have taken up this theme. In the United States, the Consultation on Church Union has been pressing since 1974 for a recognition that baptism in any one of the participating churches effects membership in the universal church. A few Christians have practiced or advocated dual or plural church membership as a means of manifesting that the church is one in spite of the multiplicity of the denominations.

Juridical Aspects. The juridical consequences of membership may be inferred by scrutiny of the constitutions of particular ecclesiastical bodies. Some recognize more than one kind of membership, distinguishing, for instance, between communicant and noncommunicant members. To be a communicant (i.e., to be entitled to receive the sacraments), one must have attained a certain minimum age (e.g., thirteen years) and live up to certain requirements, such as church attendance and financial support. Most churches have procedures for excommunication or exclusion from the rights and privileges of membership.

Spelled out to some degree in canon law, the juridical consequences of membership are theologically rooted in the status of being reborn in Christ. Among the duties of members the following are commonly mentioned: professing the true faith, participating in the worship of the church, rendering obedience to pastors, maintaining communion with the church, defending the freedom of the church, supporting its ministers, fostering Christian unity, and promoting peace and justice in the world. Among the rights of church members the following are frequently asserted: to hear the word of God, to receive the sacraments, to exercise the apostolate, to inquire freely into theological questions, to have freedom of expression, association, and assembly, to enjoy personal privacy and a good reputation, and to be protected against arbitrary deprivation of office. Some of these "Christian rights" coincide with human rights recognized in secular society.

Sociological Aspects. Sociologists commonly recognize various kinds and degrees of membership depending on the extent to which the individual is identified with, committed to, and active in the church. Joseph H. Fichter, for example, distinguishes four categories: the nuclear member, who is exceptionally active and committed; the modal, who is ordinary; the marginal, who is somewhat alienated or disaffected; and the dormant, who does not believe or practice but has not positively defected. Dormancy, as explained by Fichter, is more a matter of religious ignorance or apathy than of active rejection.

These sociological observations could be applied to non-Christian or nonreligious organizations, such as political parties, and they do not focus on what is specific to the church as a mystery or sacrament of the divine. But sociological analysis raises certain questions of a theological character—for example, whether dormant members should be considered members from a theological point of view.

Present Perspectives. Looking over the history of the theology of membership, one is struck by the correspondence between changes of theory and shifts in the actual situation of the churches. Organic models of membership, developed from such vitalistic metaphors as *body of Christ,* had their strongest appeal when society in general was highly organic and when the individual had little autonomy against the group. Juridical models, which came into vogue in the early modern period, corresponded to the fragmentation of Europe into highly organized competitive groups, such as nation-states and confessional churches, in which the sovereign rulers exercised strong coercive power. Voluntarist theories of membership came to prevail when freedom and individuality were cultivated, especially in the nineteenth century. In a period such as our own, when the social determinants of human existence are keenly felt, such religious individualism may seem inadequate.

Current thinking about membership will presumably be influenced by the contemporary situation of religious pluralism and rapid social change, as well as by the fact that membership in a church and membership in civil society no longer imply each other in most countries. Many Christians, subjected to a variety of influences, seem to be only partially identified with their religious community, yet they are unwilling to leave that community, which they cherish for its positive values. Some suspect that as secularization continues, the church will increasingly consist of a minority who have made an explicit choice, often against the tenor of society.

By forcing new reflection on the idea of membership, the present complex situation makes it evident that the term *membership* does not correspond to any single objective reality. Membership, subjected to analysis, includes various components—for instance, communion with God through grace, faith, hope, and charity; relationship to one's fellow believers; sharing the ideals and doctrines officially professed by the community; eligibility for sacramental life; and active participation. Members who are marginal by some of these criteria may be modal or nuclear by other criteria.

See Also Community; Denominationalism; Excommunication.

Bibliography

Carrier, Hervé. *The Sociology of Religious Belonging.* Translated by Arthur J. Arrieri. New York, 1965. A valuable, highly objective study of attitudes toward religious groups, conversion, integration, and disaffiliation, from the standpoint of social psychology. Requires some updating.

Congar, Yves. *L'église: De Saint Augustin à l'époque moderne.* Paris, 1970. A history of ecclesiology from a Roman Catholic perspective, with informative comments on changing concepts of church membership.

Les droits fondamentaux du Chrétien dans l'église et dans la société. Acts of the Fourth International Congress on Canon Law. Edited by Eugenio Corecco, Nikolaus Herzog, and Angelo Schola. Fribourg, 1981. A massive collection (1,328 pages) of papers on the rights of Christians, chiefly in connection with the canon law of the Roman Catholic Church.

Dulles, Avery. *Church Membership as a Catholic and Ecumenical Problem.* Milwaukee, 1974. A short study that attempts to correlate theological and sociological aspects, taking account of Vatican Council II and the ecumenical movement.

Gassman, Benno. *Ecclesia Reformata: Die Kirche in den Reformierten Bekenntnisschriften.* Freiburg, Basel, and Vienna, 1968. A Tübingen dissertation on the ecclesiology of the Reformed confessional writings, with comparisons between them and Vatican II. The question of church membership is adequately handled.

Internationale katholische Zeitschrift "Communio" 5 (May/June 1976). A theme issue on church membership with articles by Karl Lehmann, Matthäus Kaiser, Yves Congar, Joseph Ratzinger, and Hans Urs von Balthasar.

Kilcourse, George. *Double Belonging: Interchurch Families and Christian Unity.* New York, 1992.

Moberg, David O. *The Church as a Social Institution.* Englewood Cliffs, N.J., 1962. A standard textbook on the sociology of religion in the American context with several chapters touching on church membership.

Die Zugehörigkeit zur Kirche. Report of the Seventh International Conference on the Sociology of Religion, Königstein im Taunus, June 30 to July 2, 1962. Edited by Walter Menges and Norbert Greinacher. Mainz, 1964. Papers by European scholars on various aspects of membership—historical, sociological, theological, and pastoral.

Avery Dulles (1987 and 2005)

CHURCHES OF CHRIST emerged from the Stone-Campbell movement (also called the Disciples, or Restoration, movement) during the half-century following the American Civil War. Opposition to instrumental music in worship, missionary societies, and a professional ministry characterized the views of conservatives who had essentially coalesced by the time of the first U.S. Religious Census in 1906.

The majority of Churches of Christ were then located in the states of the former Confederacy, with a membership of approximately 160,000. By 1926 this number had grown to over 435,000, with estimates of 600,000 in 1941. This growth was largely the result of evangelism by traveling preachers and ordinary members who were convinced Churches of Christ had restored New Testament Christianity. In 2000 the *Atlas of American Religion* listed Churches of Christ as one of seven national denominations, partially based on the group's presence in every part of the nation, a reflection of this early persistent evangelism.

The fiercely congregational Churches of Christ have no official denominational structures or binding creeds. In the twentieth century their identity and uniformity was largely formed around three unofficial loci: religious schools, journals, and influential traveling evangelists.

Five colleges became important centers of learning and identity for Churches of Christ. Lipscomb University, originally Nashville Bible School, was founded by David Lipscomb and James A. Harding in Nashville, Tennessee, in 1891. The school embodied the educational model of Alexander Campbell, who opposed the creation of a clergy class through narrowly focused theological training. Instead, all students studied the Bible in the context of a liberal arts education. This model has prevailed in schools affiliated with Churches of Christ. The other major institutions established in the early twentieth century are Abilene Christian University in Abilene, Texas (1906); Freed-Hardeman University in Henderson, Tennessee (1908); Harding University in Searcy, Arkansas (1924); and Pepperdine University in Malibu, California (1937).

With the absence of official statements of belief, journals functioned as a major locus for creating and maintaining doctrinal consensus. The most influential journals in Churches of Christ in the twentieth century were the *Gospel Advocate,* established in 1855 by Tolbert Fanning in Nashville, Tennessee, and the *Firm Foundation,* established in 1884 by Austin McGary in Austin, Texas. Both continued to shape and reflect mainstream positions for the body until the 1970s.

The most important early thought-shaper was David Lipscomb (1831–1917), editor of the *Gospel Advocate* for nearly half a century. His opposition to the "innovations" introduced by those in what would become the Disciples of Christ and his strict ideas of congregational polity became identifying characteristics of Churches of Christ, though his beliefs on Christian nonparticipation in government were not universally accepted. Other important leaders included N. B. Hardeman (1874–1965), G. C. Brewer (1884–1956), and Foy E. Wallace Jr. (1896–1979). All were widely known evangelists who through their preaching, writing, and teaching exercised a powerful conservative influence on the churches.

A series of controversies and small schisms occurred in the first half of the twentieth century, reflecting the literalistic biblical hermeneutic then characteristic of Churches of Christ. All legitimate beliefs and practices, members believed, were discerned from the New Testament through a three-fold hermeneutic of direct command, apostolic example, and necessary inference. Debates arose over the scripturalness of full-time preachers, Sunday schools, multiple cups in the Lord's Supper, and dispensational premillennialism. The mainstream accepted the first three as expedient, but rejected premillennial eschatology as inimical to its conviction that the restored church is the kingdom of God on earth.

The attitude that Churches of Christ were the only true Christians, coupled with the socioeconomic reality that the membership was largely rural and working class, contributed to its cultural and religious isolation in the first half of the twentieth century, with the exception of a few southern cities like Nashville and Louisville. In the 1940s, however, Churches of Christ began to take on national stature and an international presence.

Members of Churches of Christ who served in World War II returned home promoting evangelism and benevolent assistance to Europe and Asia. In 1946 the Broadway Church of Christ in Lubbock, Texas, called a national meeting to discuss cooperation for these purposes, and some larger congregations took the role of "sponsoring church" for specific nations. The group's colleges grew with the postwar influx of students under the GI Bill, and an increased desire for trained ministers prompted the establishment of new schools. In 1943, Olan Hicks established the *Christian Chronicle* as a communion-wide newspaper, and it eventually became the largest circulated paper in Churches of Christ. A national radio program, the *Herald of Truth,* began in 1952 under the sponsorship of the 5th and Highland Church of Christ in Abilene, Texas.

Some viewed these moves with alarm, seeing them as evidence of growing institutionalism and modernization. A noninstitutional movement, led by individuals like Fanning Yater Tant (1908–1997), editor of the *Gospel Guardian,* attacked church support of colleges, cooperative mission efforts, and orphans homes as unscriptural and indicative of a desire for worldly prestige. By the end of the 1950s, approximately two thousand noninstitutional congregations had formed a separate communion.

Separate black congregations were formed when African Americans who opposed instrumental music and missionary societies withdrew from the Disciples in the early twentieth century. Two leaders symbolized different approaches to segregation in Churches of Christ. Marshall Keeble (1878–

1968), an evangelist who baptized over thirty thousand people, represented an accommodationist stance, acting deferentially to whites and thereby securing their support. G. P. Bowser (1874–1950) consistently attacked white racism as contrary to the gospel. He was known especially for his work as an educator and editor, operating several schools and founding the *Christian Echo* in 1902. In 1945, African American Churches of Christ established an annual National Lectureship, and in 1950 founded Southwestern Christian College in Terrell, Texas. At the beginning of the twenty-first century, these churches numbered over 169,000 members in more than 1,200 congregations.

In the 1960s a growing rift could be detected between conservatives and progressives in mainstream Churches of Christ. In 1966, conservative Ira Y. Rice Jr. (1917–2001) published the first of three volumes titled *Axe on the Root,* in which he attacked leaders he believed were abandoning traditional positions. The next year progressives began *Mission* magazine to challenge the body's biblical hermeneutic and the assumption that Churches of Christ were the only true Christians. *Wineskins* magazine, begun in 1992 and renamed *New Wineskins* in 2001, has become the most important progressive journal. The rift continued to develop so that at the beginning of the twenty-first century a de facto division existed, though nowhere officially recognized.

In 1993, congregations of the International Church of Christ (ICOC), formerly known as the Boston Church of Christ, asked not to be included in church directories. These churches had become a source of controversy for their aggressive evangelism, cultic control of members, and rigid hierarchal structure. In late 2002 a shakeup of the ICOC's leadership resulted in more prerogative for local congregations, most of which are located in major world cities.

Churches of Christ in the United States grew from 915,000 members in 1965 to over 1.24 million in 1980. Growth has been slow in the United States since then, with a count of slightly over 1.26 million in 2000. Growth outside the United States, however, has been dramatic in the same period. By 2003, studies indicated almost one million members of Churches of Christ in Africa alone, with several hundred thousand in India. Missionaries and indigenous evangelists supported directly by individual American congregations was the rule, though many national churches are now self-supporting.

Three major bodies share the Stone-Campbell heritage: Churches of Christ, the Christian Church (Disciples of Christ), and the "independent" Christian Churches/ Churches of Christ, the last two dividing over issues surrounding the twentieth-century fundamentalist-modernist controversy. In 1984, talks labeled the "Restoration Forum" began between Churches of Christ and independent Christian Churches, and in 1999, leaders from all three groups inaugurated the Stone-Campbell Dialogue to explore ways they might minister together.

See Also Campbell, Alexander; Disciples of Christ.

Bibliography

The first major effort at a history of Churches of Christ was undertaken by Earl Irvin West in two volumes titled *The Search for the Ancient Order: A History of the Restoration Movement,* first published by the Gospel Advocate Company in 1949 and 1950. West's treatment, eventually expanded to four volumes, reflected the triumphalistic attitude characteristic of Churches of Christ in the early twentieth century. In the 1990s a new, more self-critical, historiography arose that reflected an identity shift in the mainstream that had begun at least by the 1960s. Among the chief representatives of this new approach are:

Childers, Jeff W., Douglas A. Foster, and Jack R. Reese. *The Crux of the Matter: Crisis, Tradition, and the Future of Churches of Christ.* Abilene, Tex., 2002.

Foster, Douglas A. *Will the Cycle Be Unbroken? Churches of Christ Face the 21st Century.* Abilene, Tex., 1994.

Harrell, David Edwin, Jr. *The Churches of Christ in the Twentieth Century: Homer Hailey's Personal Journey of Faith.* Tuscaloosa, Ala., 2000.

Holloway, Gary, and Douglas A. Foster. *Renewing God's People: A Concise History of Churches of Christ.* Abilene, Tex., 2001.

Hooper, Robert E. *A Distinct People: A History of the Churches of Christ in the Twentieth Century.* West Monroe, La., 1993.

Hughes, Richard T. *Reviving the Ancient Faith: The Story of Churches of Christ in America.* Grand Rapids, Mich., 1996.

Because of the congregational polity of Churches of Christ, accurate statistics have been difficult to obtain. Mac Lynn, working with the Glenmary Institute's efforts to gather extensive national religious data, has produced reliable statistics on the body in his directories *Churches of Christ around the World: Exclusive of the United States and Her Territories.* Nashville, Tenn., 2003; and *Churches of Christ in the United States: Inclusive of Her Commonwealth and Territories.* Nashville, Tenn., 2003.

Douglas A. Foster (2005)

CHURCH OF ENGLAND See ANGLICANISM

CHURCH UNIVERSAL AND TRIUMPHANT is a modern movement that has its roots in various New Age predecessor groups, such as Theosophy, New Thought, and the Saint Germain Foundation. The movement started its existence in 1958 as Summit Lighthouse, a Washington, D.C.-based group founded by Mark L. Prophet (1918–1973). Prophet was a follower of the teachings of Guy Ballard (1878–1939) and Edna Ballard (1886–1971), founders of the Saint Germain Foundation, and of two spin-off groups, Bridge to Freedom and Lighthouse of Freedom. The mission of these three groups was to publish hidden spiritual teachings from higher planes of existence to guide the world at a critical moment in human history. The Ballards alone published over three thousand discourses given to them by the "ascended masters," who were seen as disembodied adepts responsible for the spiritual progress of humankind. For the Ballards, the key ascended master was Saint Germain, who was believed to have contacted Guy Ballard on Mount Shasta in northern California in a 1930 vision. Saint Germain designated Ballard the messenger of the ascended masters for the coming Seventh Golden Age of spiritual realization. Following Guy Ballard's death in 1939 and a prolonged prosecution of the Saint Germain Foundation for mail fraud, the Bridge to Freedom was founded by a disgruntled New York member, Geraldine Innocente (d. 1961). Innocente claimed contact with the ascended masters and published her "dictations" under the pseudonym of Thomas Printz. Prophet, a one-time follower of Innocente, became another claimant to messenger status and decided to publish his own "dictations" through Summit Lighthouse. Prophet announced that he had received the mantle of "messenger" from the ascended masters for the dawning Age of Aquarius.

During this early period, Prophet published *Pearls of Wisdom*, small booklets containing his messages from the ascended masters. He also organized the Keepers of the Flame Fraternity for a committed inner core of disciples. The Keepers made a monthly tithe and were sent a graded series of spiritual instructions that laid out Summit Lighthouse's central teachings.

The first of these teachings concerned a practice known as *decreeing*. This practice has its roots in the New Thought movement of the late nineteenth and early twentieth centuries. Emma Curtis Hopkins (1849–1925), a prominent purveyor of New Thought doctrines, taught that verbal affirmations using the biblical name of God, "I Am," connected students with their inner divine nature and assured that what was affirmed would manifest in the material universe. Both the Saint German Foundation and Summit Lighthouse adopted this practice and made it central to their respective ritual repertoire. The attraction of decreeing was the belief it gave students that they could overcome negative conditions in their lives and bring about both physical and psychological healing. A derivation of this teaching would be adopted by modern-day "prosperity gospel" proponents such as Robert Tilton, Kenneth Copeland, and Robert Schuller. In Summit Lighthouse's version of decreeing, the affirmations were vocalized at a rapid pace that sounded like a buzzing with indistinct phrases. To take one example:

> I AM Light, glowing Light, Radiating Light, intensified Light. God consumes my darkness, Transmuting it into Light. This day I AM a focus of the Central Sun. Flowing through me is a crystal river, A living fountain of Light That can never be qualified By human thought and feeling. I AM an outpost of the Divine. Such darkness as has used me is swallowed up By the mighty river of Light which I AM!

A second central teaching detailed the path of ascension. This teaching traces its roots to Christianity and to the writings of New Thought teacher Annie Rix Militz (1856–1924). Militz taught that the goal of human existence was the union of the human soul with the divine being in heaven, an experience she termed *ascension*. This exalted state was the birthright of every human soul and the crowning stage of evolution. Summit Lighthouse adopted this concept and articulated it in a spiritual anthropology that posited a tripartite human nature consisting of the I AM presence (the divine spark or God self), the Christ consciousness (an interior mediator between the human and divine planes of existence), and the human soul (a mortal component that could become immortal if ascension was achieved). Summit Lighthouse (and later Church Universal and Triumphant) taught that the carefully graded path of initiation freed disciples from negative karma, wed them to the Christ consciousness, and led them to final ascension.

A third central teaching of Summit Lighthouse concerned the collective mission of the ascended masters, Summit Lighthouse, and the United States in spearheading a Golden Age of spiritual freedom and illumination for humankind. This mission had its roots in Prophet's Gnostic-inspired version of creation, in which a creator deity had emanated perfect replicas of itself into the universe at the beginning of time. These divine sparks, in turn, had become enmeshed in the material world and had forgotten their true identity and ancestry. It was the mission of the ascended masters and of Summit Lighthouse to reveal the truth of the human condition and to furnish a path whereby humanity could be restored to its spiritual heritage.

The United States played a central role in this mission. According to Summit teachings, America has been sponsored since its beginnings by the ascended master Saint Germain, the Lord of the Seventh Ray of Freedom. Prophet claimed that Saint Germain was the inspiration behind the U.S. Constitution and that he had anointed George Washington as the country's first president. The country's unique role as a "New Atlantis" and forerunner of planetary spiritual illumination, however, was threatened by "fallen ones," who were seeking to weaken the United States through socialism, rock and jazz music, tobacco, alcohol, gambling, and abortion. Summit Lighthouse (and later Church Universal and Triumphant) adopted a nationalistic political outlook that cast the movement as a spiritual army commissioned by the ascended masters to do battle with the "dark forces" threatening the nation's entry into the prophesied Golden Age. The church's elitism, utopianism, and millennialism would result in an increasingly paranoid outlook and a cycle of apocalyptic extremism that threatened its very existence in the late 1980s and early 1990s.

During the early 1960s, Prophet had a small coterie of followers who attended his classes in Washington, D.C., or who belonged to Summit study groups around the country. In 1963, Prophet divorced his first wife and married a young student, Elizabeth Clare Wulf (b. 1939). While Mark Prophet was clearly the public spokesperson and "messenger" for the movement, behind the scenes he began training his new wife as "comessenger." The couple left Washington and moved to Colorado Springs, Colorado, in 1966. As the counterculture emerged during this period, many young people were drawn to Summit's teachings. A select group of these students moved into the Prophets' handsome mansion, La Tourelle, where they lived in spartan simplicity and assisted the Prophets' increasingly ambitious national outreach.

Part of this outreach included four seasonal conclaves, at New Year's, Easter, the Fourth of July, and Columbus Day, which brought together disciples from around the world. In 1970, the Prophets established Montessori International, an alternative educational system based on the teachings of Maria Montessori (1870–1952) and a potpourri of progressive educational theories. They also founded Ascended Master University (later called Summit University) in 1972 to provide new members with an intensive and extended exposure to the group's spiritual teachings. Students lived and ate in common, participated in decreeing and dictation sessions, and enjoyed one-to-one sessions of spiritual counseling with the Prophets. Summit University would undergo myriad refinements in both curriculum and mission over the next thirty years, perhaps reaching its apex in 1977 with Camelot, the movement's New Age mystery school constructed on the 218-acre campus of the former Thomas Aquinas College near Malibu, California.

Following Mark Prophet's sudden death in 1973, Elizabeth Clare Prophet took firm control of the movement, which she renamed Church Universal and Triumphant in 1974. Summit Lighthouse became the movement's increasingly successful publishing subsidiary. The key movement publications of this period were *Climb the Highest Mountain* (1972) by Mark and Elizabeth Clare Prophet, and *The Great White Brotherhood in the Culture, History, and Religion of America* (1976) by Elizabeth Clare Prophet. While acknowledging the movement's roots in Theosophy and the I AM Activity, these books were asserted as crucial new revelations from the Ascended Master El Morya for the Aquarian Age. They also proclaimed Church Universal and Triumphant as the true church of the "ascended masters" Gautama Buddha and Jesus Christ. Elizabeth Clare Prophet moved the church to southern California in 1976 and was successful in establishing study groups and teaching centers across the United States.

During the late 1970s and early 1980s, Elizabeth Clare Prophet was a nationally known purveyor of New Age spirituality who made regular appearances on television and radio. Her national tours, billed as "Stumping for Higher Consciousness," used state-of-the-art audiovisual technology and included dramatic dictations, decreeing, and initiatory blessings. Prophet advocated her conservative positions on such controversial social issues as pornography, abortion, terrorism, and America's need for a strong civil defense. Although nationalistic and nativistic in the tone of its public pronouncements, the church was inclusive in its membership, which reflected a wide spectrum of socioeconomic, ethnic, and national backgrounds.

Following a bitter lawsuit brought by a disgruntled exmember and a spate of negative publicity, the church moved its international headquarters to southern Montana in 1986. The move was also occasioned by fears of earthquakes in California and of nuclear attack by the Soviet Union, and by zoning battles with the church's Malibu neighbors. Prophet extolled the new Royal Teton Ranch property as a site where members could work together under the ascended masters' protection to neutralize impending negative karma for the earth and thus ensure the safe entry of the planet into the Golden Age of Aquarian illumination.

The church entered a period of increased apocalyptic anxiety during the late 1980s after warnings from the ascended masters about a possible nuclear war with the Soviet Union between 1989 and 1991. Members frantically constructed a network of fallout shelters on ranch property high in the foothills of the Teton mountains and called on its farflung membership to move to the adjacent Paradise Valley. When a series of prophesied events failed to materialize in early 1990, the group found itself dubbed as a "doomsday cult" by the international media. Prophet tried to calm fears that the group was a "dangerous cult" about to implode by appearing on national television programs such as *The Oprah Winfrey Show*, *Nightline*, and *Larry King Live*, and defending her church as a patriotic group that wished to live in harmony with its neighbors. She also publicly disavowed any specific doomsday prophecies, while maintaining that the Soviet Union still posed dangers to the United States.

This period of intense apocalyptic expectation and subsequent collective exhaustion resulted in a mass exodus of church members and a severe downsizing of the organization's Montana staff. By the mid-1990s, the church was beginning to sell off parcels of its property simply to meet ongoing operational expenses. In 1996, Church Universal and Triumphant's board of directors appointed Gilbert Clairbault, a Belgian management consultant, as its president and began a wholesale reconstitution of the church and its mission. The group has moved away from its prior ideology of apocalyticism and hyper-patriotism and now represents itself as a mainstream church whose mission is to make the Prophets' considerable body of New Age teachings available to an international audience in the form of both print and electronic media. Another aspect of its new mission is to engender the creation of spiritual communities around the world whose members embrace the church's esoteric teachings and alternative healing, educational, and spiritual practices.

A further crisis enveloped the church in 1999 when Prophet disclosed that she was suffering from Alzheimer's disease. This was a severe blow to a movement that had seen its leader as the one true spokesperson for the ascended masters and as a spiritual master who had balanced her karma and was ready for ascension. In July 1999, Prophet turned over both her temporal and spiritual authority to a leadership group consisting of a president, a board of directors, and a 24-member council of elders. The church has embraced entrepreneurial currents found in other New Age religious groups and is actively marketing its myriad products around the world. To keep its worldwide membership in regular communication, the church broadcasts its decreeing rituals and public meetings to subscribers via the internet.

Elizabeth Clare Prophet is now fully retired from church work and resides in Bozeman, Montana. As the movement strives to routinize her considerable charisma in various ministerial and organizational offices, she remains a revered figure in the movement. Groups of disgruntled members maintain contact through various newsletters, chat rooms, and conferences, and there has been an ongoing battle between those who advocate a more corporate culture for the group and those who seek to retain the charismatic atmosphere and governance of the church's founding period.

SEE ALSO Hopkins, Emma Curtis; New Thought Movement; Prophet, Mark and Elizabeth Clare; Theosophical Society.

BIBLIOGRAPHY

Lewis, James R., and J. Gordon Melton, eds. *Church Universal and Triumphant in Scholarly Perspective.* Stanford, Calif., 1994.

Prophet, Elizabeth Clare. *The Great White Brotherhood in the Culture, History, and Religion of America.* Colorado Springs, Colo., 1976.

Prophet, Elizabeth Clare. *The Lost Years of Jesus: Documentary Evidence of Jesus' 17-Year Journey to the East.* Livingston, Mont., 1984.

Prophet, Elizabeth Clare. *The Lost Teachings of Jesus.* 2 vols. Livingston, Mont., 1986.

Prophet, Mark L., and Elizabeth Clare Prophet. *Climb the Highest Mountain: The Everlasting Gospel.* Colorado Springs, Colo., 1972.

Prophet, Mark L., and Elizabeth Clare Prophet. *Science of the Spoken Word.* Colorado Springs, Colo., 1974.

Whitsel, Bradley C. *The Church Universal and Triumphant: Elizabeth Clare Prophet's Apocalyptic Movement.* Syracuse, N.Y., 2003.

PHILLIP CHARLES LUCAS (2005)

CHURINGA SEE TJURUNGAS

CHUVASH RELIGION.

The nearly two million Chuvash-speaking peoples inhabit the Chuvash Republic, Tatarstan, and Bashkortostan, all autonomous republics within the Russian Federation. The Chuvash have had a long history of contact with Islam and Christianity that has in varying degrees affected the traditional indigenous religion.

In the first few centuries BCE the Turkic language family separated into two groups: the first now includes the Turkish spoken in Turkey and the Turkic languages spoken in the Russian Federation, Poland, Iran, Afghanistan, and China. The second group, which included Khazar and Bulgar until they became extinct in the Middle Ages, is now made up solely of Chuvash. Thus the Chuvash language and people play a key role in reconstructing most of what is known today of ancient Turkic religion.

In the eighth century the Chuvash moved from the south to the middle Volga region, where they formed the major part of the Volga Bulgar empire, a state that came under Khazar jurisdiction. A gradual Islamization from the region of Khorezm, however, led to the Volga Bulgar emperor's acceptance in 922 of the religious authority of the caliph in Baghdad. The empire flourished until the Mongol invasion of 1236, when the Chuvash found shelter and a fair degree of autonomy in the forested regions on the right bank of the middle Volga. The Kipchaks of the Kazan region, however, posed a constant threat and tried to spread Islam. By the middle of the sixteenth century Russian colonization reached the Chuvash territory; after their occupation of Kazan, the Russians began attempts to Christianize the Chuvash, who tried to evade conversion by fleeing to the lands between the Volga and the Ural.

The Chuvash joined forces with Muslim Tatars and Bashkirs in several unsuccessful uprisings against the Russians in the eighteenth century. By the 1860s large numbers of Chuvash tried to convert to Islam as a last resort, but these efforts were also thwarted by the Russians, who, in addition to their existing policy of translating the Bible and Russian Orthodox religious books into Chuvash, began to set up schools that featured Chuvash as the medium of instruction and a curriculum that was almost entirely religious. By the end of the nineteenth century more than fifty such schools had been established among the Chuvash. Although many Chuvash finally converted as a result, the indigenous traditions, amalgamated with some Christian and Islamic elements, continued to flourish into the twentieth century.

Chuvash popular religion comprises traditional elements to which have been added significant layers of Islamic influence and a certain, though superficial, stratum of Russian Orthodox Christianity. The core of the traditional religion has preserved elements of the ancient Turkic religion.

The central figure of the Chuvash pantheon is Tura, whose name is a Chuvash derivative of the Old Turkic deity name *Tängri (Tengri).* The name *Tură* is also used for the Muslim and Christian God and was adopted in the Chuvash translations of the Bible. The Old Turkic name *Tängri* denoted both "God" and "sky." The latter meaning is now absent from Chuvash, but its earlier presence can be inferred, and its disappearance can be attributed to a transformation of beliefs through the influence of Islam and Christianity. The concept is still retained to a certain extent; "to thunder," for example, is expressed in Chuvash by *Tură aśatat,* where *aśa-* carries the original meaning of "father, grandfather, God the father, thunder." Tură, like Tängri prior to contact with

Christianity and Islam, is qualified also as the creator, Śuratakan.

The Chuvash medicine man is called *yumśă* and can be either male or female. The *yumśă* s cure various types of disease, perform particular rituals, trace stolen or lost animals, take part in weddings, and assist at childbirth. Some scholars have identified the *yumśă*s with shamans, but this hypothesis is unacceptable, for the *yumśă*s feature none of the salient characteristics of the shaman, for example, trance, journey to the otherworld, and use of a special garment and a sacred drum. Additionally, it has been recognized that if the *yumśă* were indeed a shaman, the term itself would be etymologically identical to the Turkic *qam*, "shaman." Szalontai-Dimitrieva (1982, pp. 171–178) has pointed out the difficulties of this identification and suggests that the term may be a recent loan from a Tatar term that can be traced to the Old Turkic form, *yumči*, which has a corresponding Mongolian form, *domči* ("sorcerer, medicine man"). Another important Chuvash figure is a different type of sorcerer, the *tuxatmăš*. In this case there is no doubt that the concept and role of the *tuxatmăš* is borrowed. The term can ultimately be traced to the Arabic *duʿāʾ* ("prayer"). In Chuvash *tuka tu-* or *tuxat* denotes "to cast a spell or charm," and thus the *tuxatmăš* is the person who casts the spell; the prayer of the Muslim muezzin came to be identified with the sorcerer's incantation. In its present linguistic form, the term appears to have been a recent loan, perhaps from the southern Bashkirs.

Some traits of the Old Chuvash religion can be reconstructed only with the help of other sources. A certain type of sorcerer (Old Turkic, *bögüči*) is no longer extant among the Chuvash but most likely was a part of old Chuvash culture. The evidence for this comes from the Hungarians, who borrowed and preserved the concept and role of the *bögüči* from the Chuvash during their close contact from the sixth to ninth centuries.

Other influences can be found among the Finno-Ugric Mari (Cheremis) people, whose term for sin (*sulak*) is derived from the Chuvash *śilăx*. The Christian Tatars have borrowed their word for prayer, *keläü*, from the Middle Chuvash. Chuvash also borrowed from contacts with other peoples; their word for human being (*śin*) is a loan from the Middle Persian *jān* ("soul"). Later, the same Iranian term came as a New Persian loan into Chuvash a second time through the Tatar in the form of *cun* and retained the meaning of "soul."

Not only comparative linguistics but also contemporary Chuvash folk practices serve as a source for reconstructing traditional Chuvash religion. One of the incantations spelled by a *yumśă* on a sick person refers to a pillar that stands in the middle of the world and supports the sky with the sun and moon on either side. The sky is said to be like the roof of a nomadic tent whose roof cover is closed with a ring. This fits the description of a yurt, although the Chuvash have not lived in yurts for more than seven hundred years. In contrast, the world beneath is not said to be the steppes of the early Chuvash, who were nomads. Rather, this world is said to consist of four types of forest: the "black forest" of leafy trees, the spruce forest, the poplar forest, and the juniper forest. Thus there is a conjunction of the Inner Asian concept of the four cardinal points with the typical "forested" world image of the Finno-Ugric peoples.

The dominant elements of contemporary Chuvash popular religion, however, do not originate from traditional Chuvash religion but from Islam. In some places Chuvash peasants worshiped a god called Xărpan, to whom they sacrificed a white ram. It is thought that the role of this deity, or at least his name, was influenced by Islamic sacrifice, called *qurbān* in Arabic. The lord of the wolves that protect the sheep is venerated as Pixampar, a name derived from the New Persian *payghamber* ("prophet"). The Chuvash recognize an evil spirit, who is called Šuytan, from the Arabic *shayṭān*.

The most respected of all spirits is the *kiremet*. The *kiremet* is the soul of a deceased person. Some Chuvash groups specify that it is the soul of someone who was wicked or evil or who died a violent death. *Kiremet*s dwell beneath the earth, and all localities have their own *kiremet*s. In many regions, forest clearings, meadows, cemeteries, hills, or brooks may be worshiped as *kiremet*s; in this sense the word bears the closest resemblance to its Arabic cognate, *karāmah* ("miracle"). Usually the area is encircled with a fence and cannot be plowed or used for secular purposes. Periodically, sacrifices are offered within this area. In some regions of northern Chuvashia *kiremet*s inhabit trees and have a special guard, the *kiremet ketüśi* ("herdsman of the *kiremet*"). This designation indicates the influence of the nomadic herdsmen on the nonnomadic forest peoples of northern Chuvashia.

The Chuvash also derived their notion of the angel of death from Islam. He is known both as Esrel (cf. Arab. ʿIzrāʾīl) and Masar Puśĕ ("ruler of the cemetery," cf. Arab. *mazār*). The central orientation in prayer, however, is not toward Mecca, but toward the east, following the Türk tradition. Thus during prayers or sacrifice the Chuvash faces east, and in the grave one's head is positioned on the western side because one must look eastward. The eyes of the dead, and sometimes also the nose, mouth, and ears, are covered with small linen patches. Excavations in the Volga region and in Hungary indicate similar burial customs dating to the ninth century. Until recent times the Chuvash also placed money and food in the grave, and sometimes the saddle, harness, and parts of the horse as well. These practices can be traced to burial customs in southern Russia and Hungary between the eighth and tenth centuries. In some parts of southern Chuvashia the funeral feast is not held until the Friday of the seventh week after death.

In northern Chuvashia the funeral ceremonies include placing a plank between a chair and a table that serves as a "bridge." The soul of the deceased must travel from the chair across the bridge to the table and from there to God. The ceremony is called the Feast of the Grave-post and is derived and transformed from Islam and early Iranian religion. The various elements contributing to Chuvash popular religion are evident in different Chuvash practices; many aspects of this religion, however, remain to be studied systematically by scholars.

SEE ALSO Islam, article on Islam in Central Asia; Tengri; Turkic Religions.

BIBLIOGRAPHY

Denisov, Petr Vladimirovich. *Religioznye verovaniia chuvash.* Cheboksary, 1959. A historical overview of Chuvash religion with attention to the political history of these peoples.

Magnitskii, Vasilii Konstantinovich. *Materialy k ob'iasneniiu staroi chuvashskoi very.* Kazan, 1881. One of the first descriptions of the "black faith" of the Chuvash, with original texts and Russian translations.

Mészáros, Gyula. *Csuvas népköltési gyüjtemény,* vol. 1, *A csuvas ősvallás emlékei.* Budapest, 1909. Materials collected in 1906 in Chuvashia on religion, customs, and folklore; contains original texts with Hungarian translations.

Nikol'skii, Nikolai Vasil'evich. *Khristianstvo sredi chuvash srednego Povolzh'ia v XVI–XVIII vekakh.* Kazan, 1912. Working with original documents, the author describes not only the Christianization of the Chuvash but also their popular beliefs.

Szalontai-Dimitrieva, Judith. "The Etymology of the Chuvash Word *Yumśă* 'Sorcerer.'" In *Chuvash Studies,* edited by András Róna-Tas, pp. 171–178. Budapest and Wiesbaden, 1982. Includes an analysis of the functions of the *yumśă.*

New Sources

Braslavskii, Leonid. *Religioznye i okkul tnye techeniia v Chuvashii.* Cheboksary, 2000.

Salmin, Anton Kirillovich. *Religiozno-obriadovaia sistema chuvashei.* Cheboksary, 1993.

Trofimov, Aleksei Aleksandrovich. *Chuvashskaia narodnaia kultovaia skulptura.* Cheboksary, 1993.

Vovina, Olesia Petrovna. *In Search of the National Idea: Cultural Revival and Traditional Religiosity in the Chuvash Republic.* Washington, D.C., 2000.

Werth, Paul William. "Subjects for Empire: Orthodox Mission and Imperial Governance in the Volga-Kama Region, 1825–1881." Ph.D. diss., University of Michigan, Ann Arbor, 1996.

ANDRÁS RÓNA-TAS (1987)
Revised Bibliography

CICERO (106 BCE–43 BCE) was a lawyer and public figure who undertook the senatorial *cursus honorum,* reaching the consulship in 63 BCE. He was subsequently involved in the civil war between Pompey and Caesar before falling victim to the purge of the Second Triumvirate (Octavian, Lepidus, Mark Antony). In discussions of Cicero and religion one should avoid the temptation to anachronistically confuse what may be defined as the religion of the ancient Romans with the common idea of religion in modern times, and one should be careful to distinguish what might be termed ancient "personal religion" from public and private devotion and cult (*sacra publica, sacra privata*). Personal religion for a man of learning such as Cicero meant philosophical speculation. For him, investigation into the nature of the gods and personal opinion on divinity belonged to the sphere of philosophy, while "religion" indicated an official institution with the purpose of paying homage to the essential values of the *res publica.*

If the diverse interests of Cicero converge upon everything involving public life and the public figure, religion, from his point of view, was an inalienable part of this. The laws on religion that form the opening of his ideal constitution in the work *De legibus* show how far from his mode of thought was the notion of the independence of the clergy from the state. But religion, consisting of *sacra publica,* did not require speculative thought. In *De natura deorum* the pontifex Cotta compares the immutable contents of the mores handed down by their parents with the transient nature of philosophical speculation regarding divinity. Religion signifies an entire collection of customs, festivals, rites, sacrifices, prayers, processions, and feasts, all serving to express the essence of productive, civic human society. For Cicero, religion was an institution, not a creed; it was an institution of protection that permitted and ensured social stability, a safeguard of law and constitutional order. Ethical values, emphasized by Cicero, are independent of religion: gods and human beings have the same rational ability. On the other hand, the problem of transcendence was discussed philosophically and without any particularly personal contribution or involvement. Cicero provides a more or less contemporary bibliography, so to speak, on the subject, and the discussion on divinity is unfolded in minute, scholarly detail.

In *De natura deorum,* the existence of the gods is seen as a social, political, and philosophical problem, but it does not have any bearing upon religious feeling: the problem of the existence of the gods is resolved via a patriotic list of political occurrences. A member of the pontifical college, Cotta, is entrusted with the refutation of the Stoic theory of the *Pronoia.* Religion is the servant of ethics and the patriotic sentiments and institutions created by the empire. But the inherently fragmentary and compartmentalized nature of ancient religion makes it inaccessible to the modern mind, which sees religion as a kind of system complete in itself.

Ancient religion is open and dynamic. The *res divinae* are not a complete self-contained corpus. Four centuries later, Augustine makes fun of the pedantic and muddled account of Varro. The emperor Julian counted 300,000 gods. For the ancients, religion was an uninterrupted and endless discovery of divine powers, which could be in turn individually identified and worshiped. Religion neither concerns itself with nor explains the afterlife. In Seneca, the investigation of the nature of god and the creation of the world is completely devoid of any religious content whatsoever. Again, the gods of Cicero, as simply gods of his own age, are ephemeral in character and they fall short of modern expectations, which have been formed by two millennia of subtle and detailed speculation on divinity. Christian apologists had great sport contrasting the sublime and profound nature of speculation on God with the weak and disorganized nature of the gods. The discussion of the Stoic Balbo in *De natura deorum* ends up as a naturalistic treatise and a doctrinal summary in which the gods are in effect everything that humanity sees and considers admirable. Besides, the ancient names of the gods are closely derived from the power they represent. Jupiter, Neptune, and Minerva are names behind which are hidden powers, made legitimate and institutionalized by *pietas*, via ancestral ceremonies and rites. Thus, syncretism is a defining characteristic of ancient religion. These gods do not possess ideological or philosophical depth; they are not, in effect, the subject of speculation.

The reader is surprised by the Ciceronian passages discussing the numerous and confused nature of the gods and their realms of competence (a catalog of the various spheres of influence of the Catholic saints would be similarly disorganized). Cicero's approach is quantitative because research on divinity is either focused upon the religious principle of "manifestation" (*epiphania*) or else on the popular discussion of the main findings of Greek philosophical knowledge. The theme of destiny and predestination assigns to the gods an instrumental and secondary role. As with every polytheist, so with Cicero: the divine may be broken down into an infinite number of powers and aspects, which are often ascribed by ancient traditions to legendary figures with various names, depending upon time and place.

The mystical note that Cicero introduces in *Somnium Scipionis* is in defense of the civic virtues of a man who goes to heaven because he has behaved on earth not as a saint but as a man of state. Even the philosophical consideration of transcendence is proposed in terms of the well-trodden path of Greek philosophy. It is a handbook on research into the divine. Prayer and interior contemplation to seek the divine within oneself are not properties of Ciceronian thought. Religious discourse is constantly and firmly linked to civic values and the merit of an active public life. Fate, of which the gods are instruments, is the subject of speculation in the light of its reflection and influences on public life. In short, there exists a preordained order or an inaccessible fate that is interested in the political events of the state and of no great relevance per se. Cicero is well aware that the gods must be invoked, not so as to become better, but for the sake of good health and prosperity. As Seneca notes (*Epistulae ad Lucilium* 10, 5), acknowledgment of one's own weakness to a god was not unknown to the religious sensibility of the ancient world. This form of religion was unacceptable to the nobles, however, and they criticized this attitude amongst any in their ranks who endorsed this approach. For example, the frequent attendance of Scipio Africanus to the temple of Zeus Capitolinus was regarded by Valerius Maximus (I, 2, 2) as a case of "fake religion."

See Also Ambrose; Apocatastasis; Apotheosis; Atheism; Augustine of Hippo; Casuistry; Conscience; Roman Religion; Skeptics and Skepticism; Superstition; Theology.

Bibliography

There is little recent work concerning religion in Cicero (in the sense of analyzing all his works), although the numerous commentaries on the works of Cicero on this subject may be of use. See, for example, *The Nature of the Gods*, translated with an introduction by P. G. Walsh (Oxford, 1997). The commentary of Arthur Stanley Pease remains essential: *M. T. Ciceronis: De natura deorum, I–II* (Cambridge, Mass., 1955–1958; reprint, 1979). See also Pease's commentary on *De divinatione* (Urbana, Ill., 1923; reprint, Darmstadt, Germany, 1963) and *De fato* (reprint, Darmstadt, 1963). For various aspects of Cicero's concern with religious matters, see:

Auvray-Assayas, Clara. *Modèles anthropologiques romains dans le De natura deorum.* Paris, 1994. See pages 207–219.

Fontanella, Francesca. "L'interpretazione ciceroniana del culto degli eroi e delle virtù." *Rivista storica Italiana* 102 (1995): 5–19.

Guillaumont, François. *Philosophe et augure: Recherches sur la théorie cicéronienne de la divination.* Brussels, 1984.

Mandel, Joshua. "State Religion and Superstition as Reflected in Cicero's Philosophical Works." *Euphrosyne* 12 (1983–1984): 79–110.

Troiani, Lucio. "La religione e Cicerone." *Rivista storica Italiana* 96 (1984): 920–952.

Turpin, Jean. "Cicéron: De legibus I-II et la religion romaine." In *Aufstieg und Niedergang der römischen Welt II* 16, no. 3. Berlin, 1986. See pages 1877–1908.

Lucio Troiani (2005)
Translated from Italian by Paul Ellis

CIJI, or Tzu Chi (from the Wade-Giles transliteration; in English, Compassion Relief), is a lay Buddhist movement founded in Taiwan under monastic leadership that has a mission of relieving suffering through secular action. Since the 1990s the movement has become one of the largest formal associations in Taiwan; it is also growing internationally, mainly within the Chinese diaspora. The founder and the leader is the Venerable Zhengyan (Cheng Yen) (1937–), a Buddhist nun hailed as "the Mother Teresa of Asia" who has received international awards for "reawakening Taiwan's modern people to the ancient Buddhist teachings of compassion and charity." Her work and influence through Tzu Chi provides disaster relief for victims throughout the world. The movement is commonly known in Chinese as *[Fojiao] Ciji gongde hui* ([Buddhist] Compassion Relief Merits Society, or, as translated by the organization, the Buddhist Compassion Relief Tzu Chi Association), although its official title is *Fojiao ciji jijinhui* (The Buddhist Compassion Relief Tzu Chi Foundation).

Founding. Compassion Relief's origins emerged from the experiences of Zhengyan. Born in 1937 in the town of Chingshui (Qingshui), Taizhong county in west central Taiwan, Zhengyan grew up in a middle-class mercantile family. Compassion Relief literature says that at age sixteen, Zhengyan vowed to Bodhisattva Guanyin (Avalokiteśvara) that she would give up twelve years of her life in exchange for her mother's recovery from a stomach ulcer. Her mother was, ostensibly, cured miraculously without surgery—surgery that was life-threatening at that time—and Zhengyan became a vegetarian, as she had also vowed to do. However, the idea of pursuing the Buddhist priesthood did not occur to her until her father suddenly died of a stroke in 1960, and after she had encountered a local Buddhist nun, the Venerable Xioudao. This nun inspired her to restore the priesthood's economic autonomy and, most importantly, to see Buddhism as the path toward a universal vocation—a vocation that can never be achieved by a woman within the limit of a family.

Zhengyan left home to become a Buddhist nun. After two years of wandering around various temples, she arrived in 1962 at a small temple of Bodhisattva Dizang (Kṣitigarbha) in Hualian, a town located in a backwater section of eastern Taiwan. Following the local practice, she took a learned layperson as her teacher, though she shaved her own head and studied scripture by herself.

At an accidental encounter in 1963 in Taipei, the well-known secularizing and reformist scholar-monk Yinshun (1906–) granted Zhengyan's request that he be her tonsure master. Yinshun gave her a new Dharma-name, "Zhengyan" and the advice that would later guide her immense vocation, telling her, "Be committed to Buddhism and to all living beings!"

Zhengyan completed the precepts, returned to Hualian, and meditated daily on the *Lotus Sūtra* for half a year in solitude and austerity in a humble straw hut behind the Bodhisattva Dizan temple. In 1964 Zhengyan began to lead her few disciples and to lecture on the Four Books, the *Lotus Sūtra,* and the Emperor Liang's Penance. In contrast to the traditional Chinese Buddhist priests who rely on alms, Zhengyan and her disciples supported themselves by subcontracting handicraft work from factories, thus abiding by the Baizhang Huaihai's dictum of "no toil, no meal."

Two events in Hualian in 1966 induced Zhengyan to found Compassion Relief. One day at a hospital, Zhengyan saw a pool of blood in the hallway and inquired about it. She was told that an aboriginal woman had experienced a miscarriage. Although her family spent eight hours carrying her to the hospital, she received no treatment because she could not afford the NT(New Taiwan)$8,000 (about U.S.$200) deposit. The unfortunate woman had died, leaving the blood on the floor. Zhengyan nearly fainted upon learning about such a tragedy and asked herself: "How could humans be so cruel to each other?" (Chen Huijian, 1998, p. 28).

The second trigger occurred when three missionizing Catholic nuns came to convert Zhengyan and "save the betrayal of the God" (Chen Huijian, 1998, p. 29). Instead, Zhengyan convinced them that Buddha's compassion was as great as the universal love of the lord God. But the Catholic nuns then asked why Buddhists, with their concept of universal love, tended to concentrate only on improving themselves rather than build schools or hospitals as the Christians did?

On April 14, 1966, Compassion Relief was founded in Hualian. At that time, it consisted of Zhengyan, her five monastic disciples, and thirty housewives. Their goal was to establish a charity fund to provide relief and defray medical costs for the poor. The housewives each donated NT$0.50 (about U.S.$0.013) every day from their grocery money and proselytized among their families and friends. The nuns made handicrafts whose sale supported the monastic order and added to the relief fund.

DEVELOPMENT. Compassion Relief developed slowly in its first decade. By 1979, the Venerable Zhengyan had resolved that building a general hospital should be the long-term mission of Compassion Relief. The nine-hundred-bed hospital was open in Hualian in 1986, one year before Taiwan lifted martial law. This was followed by Compassion Relief's rapid growth across the island at the start of the 1990s, when Taiwan was emerging as a developed economy and democratic polity. By 2000, Compassion Relief claimed over four million members worldwide (of these, about two million were in Taiwan). Although these numbers may have been exaggerated, Compassion Relief is clearly one of the largest Buddhist organizations in Taiwan, where the total Buddhist population was about 4.9 million as of 2000. In Taiwan at the start of the twenty-first century, Compassion Relief was running two state-of-the-art Western hospitals (the second one in Dalin, in Jiayi county in western Taiwan), a secular educational system ranging from elementary school to a university with a medical school, a television channel and publishing houses, and the largest databank of bone-marrow donations in Asia. The foundation was also giving away NT$5.4 billion (over US$157 million in 1999 dollars) in charity each year, much of it internationally.

Since 1990, Compassion Relief has become increasingly transnational. It has overseas branches among Chinese communities in about thirty countries and has delivered relief to disaster victims in over thirty countries around the world. Compassion Relief runs free clinics in California and Hawai'i and a dialysis center in Penang, Malaysia. Large branches in Western countries such as the United States run weekend schools that teach Mandarin and traditional characters to youngsters of Chinese heritage. Since 1991, Compassion Relief has delivered help to disaster victims in over fifty countries around the world. Such accomplishments have won Zhengyan several international awards, among them the Philippine Magsaysay Award, a nomination for the Nobel Peace Prize, the Noel Foundation Life Award, and an honorary doctorate in the social sciences from the University of Hong Kong.

Zhengyan's mission has expanded to include the Four Great Compassion Relief Missions and the four "footprints." The Four Great Missions (*si da zhiye*) are charity (on-site investigation, evaluation, and long-term care); medical care (e.g., building hospitals); education (e.g., building a university and organizing a Compassion Relief teachers' association and youth corps); and culture (e.g., Compassion Relief publications and television). The additional four footprints (*jiaoyin*) are international disaster relief, bone-marrow drives (collecting bone-marrow samples for an international database and transplantation), environmentalism (e.g., sorting garbage for recycling), and community volunteerism (e.g., cooperating with government social workers to provide local elders with long-term care). In contrast with the often ad hoc nature of Buddhist charity and its emphasis on spiritual rather than material relief in Chinese societies, Compassion Relief has established a reputation for searching out causes and mobilizing for effective implementation of concrete assistance.

The Compassion Relief headquarters remains in Zhengyan's residential monastery in Hualian, called the Still Thoughts Abode (*jinsi jinshe*). A triad configuration depicting Buddha Śākyamuni and the *bodhisattvas* Avalokiteśvara and Kṣitigarbha is enshrined in the main hall, and the monastery consisted of fewer than two hundred nuns in 2003. Under Zhengyan's charismatic leadership, the Compassion Relief umbrella organization has basically two divisions: the foundation and its staff on the one hand; and the volunteers, including the nuns, on the other hand. The foundation consists of six hundred staff members and has the largest endowment of any foundation in Taiwan, controlling about NT$12 billion (U.S.$350 million) in funds, solely from fund-raising. The volunteer organization has about seventeen thousand commissioners (*weiyuan*) worldwide who proselytize for Compassion Relief, seeking to follow its principles of sincerity, integrity, trust, and honesty. About 70 percent of the commissioners are women. Male participation has rapidly increased, however, since around 1990, resulting in the formation of a male auxiliary team, the Faith Corps, in 1992. At the beginning of the twenty-first century, the team had about eighteen hundred members. All Compassion Relief core members, including commissioners and members of the Faith Corps and Youth Corps, abide by the Ten Compassion Relief Precepts that consist of the five basic Buddhist precepts and another five precepts, which include such modern disciplines as not smoking, not drinking, not gambling, following traffic regulations, respecting parents, and speaking gently. The disciplines also bar participation in politics or demonstrations.

Compassion Relief followers concentrate on building a "pure land" in this world through secular actions. Their objectives are incorporated in the expression, "May all minds be purified, may society be peaceful, and may there be no disaster in this world." The Buddhist teaching is to be carried out; in Compassion Relief, only action counts, and its followers often say, "Just do it!" They view Zhengyan's mission as providing skillful methods that enable thousands of people to walk on the path of *bodhisattva,* to embody the *bodhisattva's* ideal of relieving the suffering, that is, to humanize Buddhist teachings and bring the *bodhisattvas* into this world. Compassion Relief collectivity embodies the *bodhisattva's* thousand eyes and thousand hands that carry out relief projects across political and ethnic borders; as exemplified in the Buddha's words: "Great compassion for those who are known and unknown, boundless mercy for all beings."

Zhengyan teaches classic Buddhist texts, but the most important book in Compassion Relief is her book, *Still Thoughts.* First published in 1989, it had gone through one hundred printings by 1992, with over one million copies having been sold by 2001. *Still Thoughts* is a collection of quotes from Zhengyan's teaching and sermons given at various times throughout her career. The quotes are brief paragraphs and concise sentences of Buddhist teaching, in plain words and set in the context of modern life. It is considered the "bible" upon which Compassion Relief followers model their speeches and conduct. *Still Thoughts* has been translated into English and German.

The significance of Compassion Relief for contemporary Buddhism is many-faceted. It is not only an example of Buddhist women's leadership and secularized Buddhism but also demonstrates a model of contemporary Buddhism's response to globalization: the global vision of its mission was an adaptation to, and a manifestation of, the role of religion in a context of intensified global communications. The result of Compassion Relief's global mission has been to put Buddhism on the world map, crossing borders through international outreach programs. This global mission is made possible by organizing the resources of the Chinese, and especially the Taiwanese, diaspora and channeling it into an active religious diaspora for universal causes.

SEE ALSO Buddhist Ethics; Missions, article on Buddhist Missions; Nuns, article on Buddhist Nuns.

BIBLIOGRAPHY

Primary Sources

Buddhist Compassion Relief Tzu Chi Foundation. *Let Ten Thousand Lotuses of Heart Blossom in This World: Dharma Master Cheng Yen [Zhengyan] and the Buddhist Compassion Relief Tzu Chi [Ciji] Foundation.* Taipei, 1994.

Buddhist Compassion Relief Tzu Chi Foundation. *Buddhist Compassion Relief Tzu Chi [Ciji] Foundation.* Taipei, 1999.

Buddhist Compassion Relief Tzu Chi Foundation. *Ciji Yuhui.* Taipei, 1999.

Cai Cixi et al., eds. *Tzu Chi [Ciji] USA 10th Anniversary: Annual Report.* Monrovia, Calif., 1999.

Chen Huijian. *Zhengyan Fashi de Ciji Shijie* (The Venerable Zhengyan's world of Ciji). Taipei, 1998.

Faun, Peter. *The Miracle World of Compassion.* Taipei, 1991.

Pen, Shu-chun. "Reflecting Mountains When Facing Mountains, Reflecting Water When Facing Water: The Story of Dharma

Master Cheng Yen [Zhengyan]." In *Still Thoughts by Dharma Master Cheng Yen [Zhengyan]*, pp. 242–263. Taipei, 1992.

Shaw, Douglas, ed. *Lotus Flower of the Heart: Thirty Years of Tzu Chi Photographs.* Taipei, 1997.

Shaw, Douglas, ed. *Ten Thousand Lotus Blossoms of the Heart: Dharma Master Cheng Yen and the Tzu Chi World*, Taipei, 1997.

Tzu Chi Foundation. "About Tzu Chi." Available from http://www.tzuchi.org.

Secondary Sources

Chen, Meikuei. "Buddhism in Taiwan: The Interactive Relationship between Buddhism and Social Change." Master's thesis, University of Oregon, 1994.

Chen, S. J. "Understanding the Buddhist Tzu-Chi Association: A Cultural Approach." Ph.D. diss., University of Southern California, 1990.

Ching Yu-ing. *Master of Love and Mercy: Cheng Yen [Zhengyan].* Nevada City, Calif., 1995.

DeVido, Elise. "Project Hope: Ciji's Post 921 Earthquake School Reconstruction Plan." *RICCI Bulletin* no. 6 (2003): 23–36.

Hu, William. "Glorious Honor for Humble Nun Chen Yen." *Sakyadhita: International Association of Buddhist Women* 5, no. 2 (1994): 12–13.

Huang, Chien-yu, and Robert P. Weller. "Merit and Mothering: Women and Social Welfare in Taiwanese Buddhism." *Journal of Asian Studies* 57, no. 2 (1998): 379–396.

Huang, C. Julia. "The Buddhist Tzu-Chi Foundation of Taiwan." In *Action Dharma: New Studies in Engaged Buddhism*, edited by Christopher Queen, Charles Prebish, and Damien Keown, pp. 136–153. London, 2003.

Huang, C. Julia. "Weeping in a Taiwanese Buddhist Charismatic Movement." *Ethnology* 42, no. 1 (Winter 2003): 73–86.

Huang, C. Julia. "'Sacred or Profane?' The Compassion Relief Movement's Transnationalism in Taiwan, the United States, Japan, and Malaysia." *European Journal of East Asian Studies* 2, no. 2 (Autumn 2003): 13–38.

Huang, C. Julia. "The Compassion Relief Diaspora." In *Buddhist Missionaries in the Era of Globalization*, edited by Linda Learman. Honolulu, 2005.

Huang, Chien-yu Julia. "Recapturing Charisma: Emotion and Rationalization in a Globalizing Buddhist Movement from Taiwan." Ph.D. diss., Boston University, 2001.

Jones, Charles B. *Buddhism in Taiwan: Religion and the State, 1660–1990.* Honolulu, 1999.

Laliberté, André. "Tzu Chi and Buddhist Revival in Taiwan: Rise of a New Conservatism?" *China Perspectives* no. 19 (September/October 1998): 44–50.

Laliberté, André. "The Politics of Buddhist Organizations in Taiwan, 1989–1997." Ph.D. diss., University of British Columbia, 1999.

Laliberté, André. 2001. "Buddhist Organizations and Democracy in Taiwan." *American Asian Review* 19, no. 4 (Winter 2001): 97–129.

Laliberté, André. "'Love Transcends Border' or 'Blood Is Thicker Than Water'? The Charity Work of the Compassion Relief in the People's Republic of China." *European Journal of East Asian Studies* 2, no. 2 (December 2003): 39–58.

Lu, Hwei-syin. "Self-Growth, Women's Power, and the Contested Family Order in Taiwan: An Ethnographic Study of Three Contemporary Women's Groups." Ph.D. diss., University of Illinois, Urbana-Champaign, 1991.

Lu, Hwei-syin. "Gender and Buddhism in Contemporary Taiwan—A Case Study of the Tzu Chi Foundation." *Proceedings of the National Science Council, Part C: Humanities and Social Sciences* 8, no. 4 (1998): 539–550.

Ting Jen-chieh. "Helping Behavior in Social Context: A Case Study of the Tzu-Chi Association in Taiwan." Ph.D. diss., University of Wisconsin, Madison, 1997.

Yang, C. H. "Tzu-Chi Buddhism Management Application to Small and Medium Size Real Estate Forms." Master's thesis, College of Management, Metropolitan State University, 1997.

Zhiru. "The Emergence of the Saha Triad in Contemporary Taiwan: Iconic Representation and Humanistic Buddhism." *Asia Major* (Taiwan), third series, 13, part 2 (2000): 83–105.

C. Julia Huang (2005)

CINEMA See FILM AND RELIGION

ČINGGIS KHAN See CHINGGIS KHAN

CINNABAR See ALCHEMY, *ARTICLE ON* CHINESE ALCHEMY

ČINVATŌ PERETU See CHINVAT BRIDGE

CIRCLE. The circle is used as a polyvalent symbol (commonly representing the cosmos and cosmic movement) as well as a pattern of ritual action (in which macrocosmic realities are transformed into microcosmic space with various meanings). As a symbol and as a ritual pattern, the circle is a cross-cultural form occurring in the round shapes of houses, public buildings, tombs, cult objects (such as altars), and ritual spaces. The circle is used ritually by inscribing circles on the ground, on amulets, or other objects and as a pattern for processions around altars, temples, spaces, and towns for various reasons. Circular shapes are often understood as patterned after the solar and lunar disks, and circular movements are frequently thought to replicate the circular motion of heavenly bodies; both circular shapes and motions are frequently assigned a sacred or religious function. In the past, scholars frequently indulged in the vain pursuit of the origins of the ritual use of circular shapes and motions, falsely assuming that such traditions have a unified origin providing a key to understanding their meaning. However, the meaning of such ritual patterns is probably polyvalent and must be based on contextual analysis, combining the emic explanations found in ancient interpretations and the etic explanations arrived at through cross-cultural comparison by modern theorists.

Neolithic and Bronze Age. The megalithic passage tombs in eastern Ireland, at Newgrange, Knowth, and Dowth (c. 3200 BCE), built by Neolithic farming communities, exhibit a ritualistic architecture. They are laid out in large circular shapes that have clear astronomical alignments, such as the winter solstice sunrise at Newgrange and the equinox sunrise at Loughcrew. According to ancient Roman sources, the Gauls associated the moon with death, and it may well be that the shape of the moon with this symbolic significance is replicated in circular megalithic tomb architecture. The same is true of the megalithic stone circle constructed somewhat later at Stonehenge in the vicinity of Salisbury, Wiltshire, England (constructed in three stages during the Late Neolithic and Early Bronze Age, c. 1800–1400 BCE). Stonehenge IIIa (c. 1600 BCE) consists of a circle of thirty upright monoliths capped by a continuous ring of carefully dressed stone lintels. The solstitial alignment of the various phases of the construction of Stonehenge suggest that it functioned as a place of worship involving the sun and moon, though little more is known. John North, in *Stonehenge: Neolithic Man and the Cosmos,* argues, "The aim [of the Neolithic builders] was not to discover the patterns of behaviour of the sun, Moon or stars but to *embody* those patterns, already known in broad outline, in a religious architecture" (North, 1996, p. xxxvi).

Unusual evidence for the cults of prehistoric Cyprus is in a clay sanctuary model of polished red earthenware found in a dromos tomb, part of an extensive necropolis dating to the Early Bronze, c. 2000 BCE. Described in detail in "The Excavations at Vounous-Bellapais in Cyprus, 1931–32" (Dikaios, 1938), the model consists of an open-air temenos or sacred precinct enclosed by a circular wall with a large arched entrance. On the floor is a semicircular curb that separates three statues of divinities from the rest of the temenos. Numerous seated and standing figures suggest that a ceremony of some type is depicted, which somehow involves the symbolic significance of the bulls, heads, and snakes that decorate the wall opposite the entrance. The circular temenos wall contrasts with other Early and Middle Bronze domestic architecture in which the rectangle predominates. Since the fundamental architectural principle in the Neolithic and Chalcolithic periods in Cyprus is the circle, the round temenos of this clay model represents a survival from an earlier period (the circular form also characterizes some Early Bronze age tombs at Vounous).

Ancient Greece and Rome. The Greeks had several words for "circle," including *gyros* (a trench around trees, used for the circle of the heaven or earth in LXX Iob 22.14 and Is 40.22), *kyklos* (the circle of the sky in Herodotos 1.131), and *trochos* (wheel, circular race); the terms *kirkos* and *krikos* both mean circle in the sense of a "ring" or "hoop." The preposition *peri* is prefixed to a number of verbs with variations on the meaning "to encircle," "surround" (e.g., *periechō, periistēmi, perikykloō, peritechizō, peritithēmi, peritrechō*). The primary Latin word for "circle" or "circular course" is *circus* and its diminutive form *circulus,* which describes "a circular figure or form." The preposition *circum* (around, about) is used as a prefix for a large number of verbs to describe various types of circular movement. According to the dominant pre-Hellenistic cosmology, the earth was shaped like a circular disk, encircled by Ocean (Herodotos 4.36), flowing in one direction (clockwise); the river Acheron, further out, flowed in the opposite direction, and Tartarus, the land of the dead, was located below the earth (Plato, *Phaedo* 112e). Concentric circles dominate this cosmology. According to Plato (*Philebus* 62a), Socrates speaks of the person who has knowledge of the divine circle and sphere (*kyklou men kai sphairas*)—based on the Platonic doctrine of ideas—but is ignorant of the human sphere and circle, even when building a circular house. Here Plato's theory of ideas provides a basis for distinguishing between microcosmic imitations of the macrocosmic circle or sphere.

In the lengthy description (*ekphrasis*) of the shield of Achilles in *Iliad* 18.483–608, one design depicts a city at peace where a dispute has arisen between two men. Heralds keep back the crowd from the area where elders sit upon polished stones "in a sacred circle" (*Iliad* 18.504). The scholiast explains that "the law courts are sacred." The reason they are sacred, thus rendering the circle of stone seats as sacred, is the belief that Zeus presides over judicial proceedings (*Iliad* 9.98–99). Eustathius, expanding on the scholiast, comments in *Eustathii Commentarii ad Homeri Iliadem Pertinentes,* "A sacred circle is the kind in the agora, where because of local law and custom, such a circle is understood to be sacred" (Eustathius, 1997–1987, p. 4.236). This reflects a link between the "sacred sircle" consisting of "smooth stones," sometimes with a sacred hearth or pit at the center (*Odyssey* 6.266), where the speaking and debating was done, and the "encircling agora" (Euripides, *Orestes* 919), where the assembly was gathered. Speakers within the "sacred circle" customarily held a scepter and enjoyed a limited immunity.

In Plutarch's narrative of the founding of Rome by Romulus (Romulus 9), he relates how a circular trench (*bothros kykloteres*) was dug around what later became the Comitium (a place of public assembly for the Comitia Curiata, which by the third century CE became a circular amphitheatre), into which each participant placed fruits and some earth from his native land. This trench was called *mundus,* reflecting a conscious cosmic symbolism. With this center, the city was marked out in a circle indicating the *pomerium,* leaving unplowed the places for the gates. The wall was thought to be sacred, for the city was the dwelling place of gods and people. The mythical character of this story is underlined by the fact that, although the city was traditionally called Roma Quadrata, the plowed trench is described as circular.

Round Altars and Temples. Vitruvius has a brief discussion of circular temples (*aedae rutundae*) in which he focuses exclusively on architectural matters (*On Architecture* 4.8). Servius claims that round temples were usually dedicated to Vesta, Diana, Hercules, and Mercury (*Commentarii in Aeneidem* 4.8.3). While there appears to be a close association between circular spatial and architectural forms and hero cults, there are no hard and fast rules or associations. In the Greek world of the classical period, round temples were commonly found in connection with the cult of Hestia, where the hearth of the polis was located. The hearth of individual homes as well as the hearths of cities clearly symbolized the sacred center of both.

The Greek term *tholos* generally referred to a round building with a conical roof in the archaic and classical periods, but in the Hellenistic period the same term is used for a variety of complex round architectural forms. In Athens, the term *tholos* was used of the rotunda or *prytaneion*, called the "Skias" in inscriptions, in which the magistrates dined (Plato *Apology* 32c; Andocides 1.45; Demosthenes 19.249; Aristotle *Athenian Constitution* 43.3; Pausanias 1.5.1). The *prytaneion* at Epidauros was also called the Thymela in inscriptions and *tholos* by Pausanias (2.27.2–5), constructed in the 380s BCE. Important *tholoi* of the Hellenistic period include the Rotunda of Arsinoe in Samothrake in the sanctuary of the Great Gods, built in the 280s BCE; the *tholos* near Kepoi on the Black Sea; and the round court with three annexed *tholoi* in Pella. The temple of Vesta (*aedes Vestae*) in Rome was a rotunda where the city hearth was located. It contained no image of the goddess and was part of a complex of buildings called the Atrium Vestae. It was circular and thought to have originated as a structure of wattles with a thatched roof, for example, preserving the tradition of a primitive Italic round hut (Ovid *Fasti* 6.261–266).

The most famous round temple in Rome is the Pantheon, actually the third in a succession of three buildings, the last built after 118 CE by Hadrian. Rather than a temple sensu stricto, the Pantheon in its three reincarnations was a dynastic monument (Hadrian reportedly held court there), a *templum mundi* (i.e., a "temple of the world") with Rome and its emperor at the center of the Roman world. The cosmic symbolism of the enormous dome as representing the celestial home of the gods struck Dio Cassius (59.27.2–4). The *oculus* ("eye") at the top of the dome provides all the illumination for the building, which would have spotlighted different parts of the floor and walls with the movement of the sun.

Two round temples of Hercules were erected in Republican Rome, a temple of Hercules Victor ad Forum Boarium (Livy 10.23.3) and a temple of Hercules Victor ad Portam Trigeminam (Macrobius Sat. 3.6.10). Though Augustus did not erect any significant cultic rotundas in Rome, the arch and exedra shapes were used extensively during his principate. In Augustan temples, apses framed cult statues delimiting a divine realm.

Round shapes were closely associated with the graves, shrines, and temples of heroes in Greco-Roman antiquity, though there is little evidence that either a consistent association with heroes or with cosmic symbolism determined the architectural use of circles, apses, and domes. The grave of Aeptytus was reportedly a mound surrounded by a circular base of stone (*Iliad* 2.592; Pausanias 8.16.3); the oracle of Trophonius was a circular construction of white marble (Pausanias 9.39.9), and Osiris reportedly had a circular tomb (Herodotos 2.170). The Maussolleion, the monumental tomb of Maussollos of Caria (d. 353 BCE) and his wife Artemisia was constructed in the vicinity of Halicarnassus (Strabo 14.656; Diodorus 16.45; Pliny hist. nat. 36, 30–31). The Mausoleum Augusti, the first Augustan building on the Campus Martius was begun in 28 BCE but not completed until several years later. The circular marble base measured more than eighty-five meters in diameter and surrounded a mound about forty-five meters high (Suetonius *Aug.* 100.4; Strabo 5.3.8 [236]). A bronze statue of Augustus was located at the summit. Alexander the Great also had a circular tomb. The Mausoleum Hadriani was constructed with a square base eighty-seven meters on each side and ten meters high. Mounted on this base is a drum sixty-four meters in diameter and perhaps twenty-one meters high. The Mausoleum Hadriani had only the circular shape in common with the Mausoleum Augusti.

The ritual of marching around a sacred place, often carrying ritual objects, whether an altar or shrine, as a preliminary means of setting such a sacred place apart for cultic purposes was widespread throughout the ancient world. One aspect of the protocol of classical Hellenic sacrifice involved the ritual encirclement of the sacred space containing the altar, the worshipers, and the victim before the killing of the victim. Two ritual objects which are frequently mentioned as being carried around the altar are a basin containing lustral water and a basket containing barley corns, a fillet, and a knife (Aristophanes *Peace* 948–962, 971, *Birds* 850, 958; *Lysistrata* 1129–1131). In a festival called Laphria in honor of Artemis, logs of green wood were arranged in a circle around the altar (Pausanias 7.18.11).

Ancient Mediterranean Magic. The ritual circle, when used by individuals for private and antisocial purposes, becomes a magic circle. The *ouroboros*—the figure of a snake "biting" (*bora*) its "tail" (*oura*), thus forming a circle—is a polyvalent ancient Egyptian symbol representing many things, including the sun, the moon, an earth-surrounding boundary, rejuvenation and rebirth, eternity, or a cartouche for the names of kings with claims to be world rulers. Two *ouroboroi* were incised on the walls of a shrine of Tutankhamen (1357–1349 BCE), one encircling his feet and the other his head. The serpent about the head is named Menen the Enveloper. In a papyrus of the twenty-first dynasty, the deceased woman (named Her-Uben) adores the solar disk surrounded by an *ouroboros* representing eternity. The "Book of Overthrowing Apep," from the Ptolemaic period in Egypt, describes one use of the *ouroboros* figure, which is pierced with a knife and thrown to the ground to destroy the evil beings associated with Apep.

While the *ouroboros* is rarely mentioned in classical and Hellenistic Greek texts, Plato relates a cosmology in which he describes certain rivers as coiling around the earth one or more times in a circle like serpents (*Phaedo* 112e7), which seems to reflect the *ouroboros* mythology. The *ouroboros* is commonly found on magical amulets, typically functioning as a border providing sanctity to that which is depicted within it, sometimes functioning as a symbol for the universe, eternity, or the year. Such an amulet is described in *The Greek Magical Papyri in Translation*: "And engraved on the stone is: Helios as a lion-faced figure, holding in the left hand a celestial globe and a whip, and around him in a circle is a serpent biting its tail [*ouroboros*]" (Betz, 1992, p. 7). Another magical text gives instructions for an amulet on a lamella or papyrus containing a sequence of magical words, magical characters, and an inscription: "Protect my body and the entire soul of me [insert name]," all written inside an *ouroboros* serpent (Betz, 1992, p. 134). This protective charm placed the bearer in the protective cosmic circle framed by the *ouroboros,* symbolizing protective encirclement. The *ouroboros* continued to be popular through the Middle Ages. A fourteenth-century CE Venetian alchemical manuscript is pictured in *Gnosis: The Nature and History of Gnosticism*, depicting the *ouroboros* encircling an inscription in Greek meaning "the All is One" (Rudolf, 1983, p. 70).

Acts of Thomas 32 (a third-century CE Christian document) refers to the *ouroboros* serpent, for the snake speaking to Thomas claims to be related to "the one who is outside the ocean, whose tail is set in his own mouth." A similar *ouroboros* conception is in the Coptic Gnostic *Pistis Sophia* (126): "The outer darkness is a great serpent whose tail is in its mouth, and it is outside the whole world, and it surrounds the whole world." In Christian Coptic magical texts, mention is made of the drawing of a magic circle around a person to prevent demons from entering. The comparative rarity of these references suggests that the ritual and magical use of the circle played only a minor role in early Christian ritual practices.

Rings were often used as magical objects because of the inherent power of the circular shape. *Greek Magical Papyri in Translation* (Betz, 1992) contains instructions for preparing a *defixio* in which the inside and outside of an iron ring (*kirkos*) are traced on papyrus with formulas and symbols to be inscribed within the outline of the ring as well as inside and outside the outline. In another text in the *Greek Magical Papyri* (Betz, 1992, XII, pp. 270–350), there are instructions for making a ring, also called a *kyklos* or "circle," on which an *ouroboros* serpent is engraved on heliotrope stone. This ring is said to be useful for opening doors, breaking chains, and performing exorcisms. Some magical procedures are written, like the script on magical bowls, in a tight spiral from inside to outside with a figure in the middle. Magical formulas can also be written in a circle on various materials, including an olivewood table (Betz, 1992, III, p. 292), the hide of an ass (Betz, 1992, IV, p. 2016), a papyrus sheet (Betz, 1992, IV, p. 2070), and a shell (Betz, 1992, VII, pp. 468–470). The one performing a magical procedure can also stand in the center of a protective circle drawn on the ground with chalk (Betz, 1992, VII, p. 858).

ANCIENT ISRAEL AND EARLY JUDAISM. The verb *chûgh* belongs to the semantic field of "circles and circular motion" and is distinguished from other lexemes in this field by its geometrical meaning "to draw a circular line [with a compass]." The term is used in cosmological contexts for describing two concentrical circular boundaries, the earth disk and the heavenly mountain island. The circle of the horizon is described in *Proverbs* 8:27: "When he established the heavens, I was there, when he drew a circle on the face of the deep." *Isaiah* 40:22 refers to God as "he who sits above the circle of the earth," while *Job* 26:10 says that God "has described a circle upon the face of the waters." The heavens also are circular in *Job* 22:14, which describes God as "walking on the circle of heaven." These important texts attest to the Israelite perception of the circle as a cosmological shape, which can serve as a pattern for ritual imitation. There is meager evidence for Israelite ritual circumambulation of the altar prior to sacrifice in *Psalms* 26:6: "I wash my hands in innocence and go about thy altar, O Lord," where the purpose is to enclose a sacred area so that evil influences cannot penetrate. *Joshua* 6:3–4, a fragment of a liturgical or ceremonial text, contains divine instructions to march around Jericho once each day for six days, culminating in seven encirclements on the seventh day. The Septuagint *Joshua* 6:3 is much shorter than the Masoretic text: "And you arrange the fighting men in a circle [*kyklōi*] around it [the city]." This circumambulation ritual, in which the number seven plays an important role, can be interpreted as a ritual means of laying claim to territory or as a ceremony of ritual cursing.

In *Mishnah Taanith* 3:8, the story is told of how Honi ha-Me'aggel ("the Circle-Drawer"), a first century BCE holy man, prayed for rain. When his prayer was not answered, he drew a circle (Hebrew, *me'aggel),* swearing an oath by God's great name that he would not step outside the circle until God sends rain. When a few drops fell, he complained that this was not enough. When it rained torrentially, he complained that it was too much. It then began to rain moderately. This story is summarized in Josephus (*Ant.* 14:22), who calls him Onias, but with the magical features suppressed. The fact that he is addressed in rabbinic sources as "the circle-drawer" suggests that this epithet reflected a fixed feature of his prayer ritual.

Circular and spherical shapes were combined in the magical bowls made and used by Jews, Mandaeans, Christians, and Manichaeans from the fifth to the seventh centuries CE in Mesopotamia for apotropaic and exorcistic purposes. The *ouroboros* is occasionally found in the center of Aramaic incantation bowls, however, in these cases the circle does not circumscribe a place of protection but is rather a place for trapping a demon, specifically depicted within the *ouroboros,* at the bottom center of the bowl. The adjurations are written in a long, tight spiral beginning from the bottom of the bowl and ending up near the rim. These inscriptions are often framed by two circles, one at the bottom of the bowl (sometimes replaced with the *ouroboros*) and near the rim of the bowl.

NATIVE AMERICAN CULTURES. The Adena culture, an Early Woodland culture of eastern North America, consisting of numerous small communities of ancient North American Indians who occupied the middle Ohio River Valley (c. 800 BCE to c. 200 CE), used circular architecture in the construction of houses of poles and bark and ceremonial circles constructed of earth. There are approximately five hundred extant Adena cites, three hundred in the central Ohio Valley and the rest scattered in Pennsylvania, West Virginia, Kentucky, and Indiana. Some of the larger Adena sites consist of large earthworks in the shapes of circles and other geometric figures. The Grave Creek Mound (Moundsville, West Virginia), the largest Adena burial mound, is 240 feet in diameter and 62 feet high, with an encircling ditch (40–45 feet wide; 4–5 feet deep). The Dominion site (located in present-day Columbus, Ohio) is the oldest Adena circle (dated some time after 500 BCE). Other Adena circles include the Mount Horeb site in Kentucky and the Anderson site in Indiana. These circular structures have no obvious or certain interpretation, though astronomical and cosmological symbolism is highly likely.

The term *medicine wheel* was first applied to the stone circle, cairn, and spoke configuration called the Big Horn Medicine Wheel ten thousand feet above sea level on Medicine Mountain in Wyoming. Medicine wheels were originally small decorative hoops—3 inches to 4 inches in diameter—made by the Cheyenne or Ojibwa with a web in the middle or two or more spokes bridging the circle and with several bird feathers attached to the lower perimeter. The term *medicine* indicates the ritual significance of both the miniature hoops and by extension the stone circle configurations. The Big Horn Medicine Wheel, which is about eighty-five feet in diameter with a central circular cairn thirteen feet in diameter, has twenty-seven stone spokes corresponding to the twenty-seven days of the lunar month. Following the identification of the Big Horn Medicine Wheel, about seventy-five similar artificially constructed stone surface forms were identified (in the northern Plains from Wyoming to South Dakota and north into Canada), characterized by a variety of stone circle, central cairn, and spoke configurations. These medicine wheels have several common features: they are made of unmodified chunks of stone, and they include a central cairn, two or more stone spokes, and one or more concentric stone rings arranged in a symmetrical form. The medicine wheels were frequently added to, making dating difficult. The earliest medicine wheels were constructed by the Oxbow complex in southeastern Saskatchewan (and extending somewhat into Alberta, Manitoba, Montana, and North Dakota), dating from 2750 to 1050 BCE. These were later embellished by subsequent cultures. Some of the medicine wheels clearly had solar and calendrical functions, and all of them were the sites of special ceremonies.

The Lakota and several other Plains tribes depict the sacred cosmic order represented by Wakan-Tanka ("Great Spirit") with the circle, and they understand the circle as a key symbol representing the whole of the universe and their part in it. The centrally important significance of the circle is emphasized in the following statement by Black Elk, in *Black Elk Speaks:*

> You have noticed that everything an Indian does is in a circle, and that is because the Power of the World always works in circles, and everything tried to be round. In the old days when we were a strong and happy people, all our power came to us from the sacred hoop of the nation, and so long as the hoop was unbroken, the people flourished. The flowering tree was the living center of the hoop, and the circles of the four quarters nourished it. (Neihardt, 1979, p. 194)

The largest representation of the circle among a number of Plains tribes (including the Arapaho, Kiowa, Cheyenne, and Sioux) were their encampments, called "the sacred hoop," just as they speak of the "hoop of the world." Everything within the camp circle was Lakota, while outside were enemies, evil spirits, and eventually the white people. Tribal divisions among the Cheyenne were located at the same place in the circular encampment, and the lodge of medicine arrows and the lodge of the buffalo cap were placed within the circle at predetermined locations. According to Black Elk, Buffalo Calf Woman gave the peace pipe (with its round bowl) and prescribed the camp circle, both of which share comparable degrees of sanctity. The pipe bowl was decorated with seven circles, representing the seven major rituals of the Lakota. The centers of the sweat lodges and of the bowls of the sacred pipes, where fires were made, represented the sun at the center of a circular cosmos. When the world is perceived as disordered, it can only be restored to its proper balance by sacred ritual, which the Lakota refer to as "making roundness."

The Teotihuacan civilization of Mesoamerica (c. 400–800 CE) oriented major urban sites using astronomical observations. Evidence for this survives in the form of "pecked" crosses (so-called because cross petroglyphs are "pecked" using a percussive device producing cuplike depressions in stone or plaster floors of important buildings and in rock outcroppings outside of buildings), indicating astronomical orientations. The form of pecked crosses typically consists of a double circle (sometimes single or triple) centered on a pair of orthogonal axes (Aveni, 1980, p. 227). In Teotihuacan (which was the location for such important buildings as the Pyramid of the Sun and the Pyramid of the Moon), the axes of the crosses align with the grid of that ceremonial city (the peculiar clockwise deviation from true north in the axial plan of Teotihuacan is shared by sites all over Mesoamerica), some apparently functioning as architectural benchmarks. The combination of pecked crosses and circles (reminiscent of calendar wheels) seems to unite spatial and calendrical with religious functions, though no single hypothesis can account for their origin.

SEE ALSO Circumambulation.

BIBLIOGRAPHY

Allcroft, A. H. *The Circle and the Cross.* London, 1927. A rich and lavishly illustrated collection of circular architectural, somewhat marred by a fixation on the problem of origins.

Altmann, Walter. *Die italischen Rundbauten.* Berlin, 1906. A classical discussion of round architectural forms in ancient Italy, particularly Rome.

Aveni, Anthony F. *Skywatchers of Ancient Mexico.* Austin, Tex., and London, 1980.

Betz, Hans Dieter, ed. *The Greek Magical Papyri in Translation.* 2d ed. Chicago, 1992.

Bonner, Campbell. *Studies in Magical Amulets, Chiefly Graeco-Egyptian.* Ann Arbor, Mich., 1950. A large collection of magical amulets including pictures and descriptions of many contained the *ouroboros* ("snake biting its tail").

Brown, Joseph Epes. *The Gift of the Sacred Pipe.* Norman, Okla., 1982. A transcription of some of the revelations of Black Elk, the Lakota medicine man.

Brumley, John H. *Medicine Wheels on the Northern Plains: A Summary and Appraisal.* Manuscript Series no. 12. Edmonton, Canada, 1988. An authoritative anthropological analysis of the native American stone circles in the northern Plains states and Canada.

Burl, Aubrey. *Great Stone Circles: Fables, Fictions, Facts.* New Haven, Conn., and London, 1999. A comprehensive treatment of stone circles in Britain, Ireland, and Brittany.

Castleden, Rodney. *The Making of Stonehenge.* London and New York, 1993.

Dikaios, P. "The Excavations at Vounous-Bellapais in Cyprus, 1931–32." *Archaeologia* 88 (1938): 1–174.

Eustathius. *Eustathii Commentarii ad Homeri Iliadem Pertinentes.* Edited by M. van der Valk. Leiden, 1971–1987.

Gaster, T. H. *Myth, Legend, and Custom in the Old Testament.* New York, 1969. An important work focusing on many of the magical traditions of the Hebrew Bible, including the use of circular shapes and circular processions.

Grinnell, George Bird. *The Cheyenne Indians: Their History and Ways of Life.* 2 vols. New Haven, Conn., 1924.

Montgomery, James A. *Aramaic Incantation Texts from Nippur.* Philadelphia, 1913. An early and comprehensive publication of the corpus of magical bowls.

Naveh, Joseph, and Shaul Shaked. *Amulets and Magic Bowls.* Jerusalem, 1985. The publication of some incantation bowls discovered after Montgomery's 1913 publication.

Neihardt, John Gnelsenau. *Black Elk Speaks.* Lincoln, Neb., and London, 1979.

North, John. *Stonehenge: Neolithic Man and the Cosmos.* London, 1996. Important work on the cosmological symbolism of Stonehenge.

Paper, Jordan. *Offering Smoke: The Sacred Pipe and Native American Religion.* Moscow, Idaho, 1988.

Rakob, Friedrich, and Wolf-Dieter Heilmeyer. *Der Rundtempel am Tiber in Rom.* Mainz am Rhein, Germany, 1973. Architectural and archaeological analysis of one of the ancient round temples in Rome.

Richardson, L. *A New Topographical Dictionary of Ancient Rome.* Princeton, N.J., 1992.

Robert, Fernand. *Thymélè: Recherches sur la signification et la destination des Monuments circulaires dans l'Architecture religieuse de la Grèce.* Paris, 1939. A comprehensive discussion of circular architecture and its symbolism in the world of ancient Greece.

Rudolf, Kurt. *Gnosis: The Nature and History of Gnosticism.* San Francisco, 1983.

Seidenberg, Abraham. "The Ritual Origin of the Circle and Square." *Archive for History of Exact Sciences* 25, no. 4 (1981): 270–321. An important article on the ritual uses of the circle, flawed by an emphasis on unknowable origins.

DAVID E. AUNE (2005)

CIRCUMAMBULATION is a ritual term meaning literally "to walk a circle around" a holy place, person, or object. Such rituals are related to the widespread significance of the sacred circle, which is the architectural ground plan and ideational scheme of such monuments as the stupa, such cities as Banaras and Jerusalem, and such ritual constructions as the medicine lodges and Sun Dance lodges of the North American Plains Indians. Thus, this topic is related to that of the sacred circle or the *maṇḍala* and is its ritual extension. One walks around what is set apart, circumscribed as charged or sacred; one might even say that circumambulation sets something apart by circumscribing it with one's own body. It is also to be noted that circumambulation, as a rite of both centering and bonding, is related in some ways to the many types of circle dancing such as the Ghost Dance of the Plains Indians, the maypole dances of the British Isles, and the circular dances and marches of the Shakers; such dance forms, however, will not be discussed here.

Circumambulation is a fundamental rite of orientation, and is often thought of as a human repetition of the apparent movement of the sun. The Lakota would walk "sunwise" around a fire or a ritual arena. The sense of this direction as the natural order also appears in Hindu ritual texts such as the *Śatapatha Brāhmaṇa* and the Gṛhyasūtras, which speak of the sunwise movement of ritual performance in rites meant to secure the blessings of the gods. This sunwise circling is known as *pradakṣiṇa*, "going to the right." *Pradakṣiṇa* around the sacred fire or the teacher, and later around the temple, became an act of centering and honoring in the Hindu tradition.

In Native American and Hindu traditions, as in many others, reversing the direction of circling was considered a reversal of the natural order and was associated with catastrophe or death. This circling to the left, contrary to the apparent course of the sun, was called *prasavya* in the Hindu tradition and was associated with the left hand and with rites for the dead, for the ancestors, and for the *nāgas*, or serpents. Anticipating or recovering from disasters, the Lakota circle counterclockwise after the fashion of the "thunder beings," whose movement, unlike that of the sun, is antinatural. In sixteenth-century England this turning in an unnatural direction came to be called *widdershins* and was associated with danger, magic, and witches.

In the Hindu tradition today, *pradakṣiṇa* is simultaneously an act of taking a place, deity, or person as one's center and of honoring that center, keeping it ever on the side of the auspicious right hand. The most concise *pradakṣiṇa* honoring the sacred place on which one stands, is simply to turn all the way around in place, as pilgrims do at the very southern tip of India at Kanyā Kumārī. The most extensive is the *pradakṣiṇa* of the entire subcontinent of India, from the north at Badrināth, to the east at Purī, to the south at Rāmeśvaram, to the west at Dvārakā (Dwarka), and back to the north again. One of India's great rivers, the Narmadā of central India, has a traditional circumambulation in which pilgrims, beginning wherever they wish, walk its entire length of 801 miles from Amarakaṇṭaka to the Bay of Cambay and back again. Mountains too are circumambulated, as in the well-known routes around Kailāsa in the Himalayan north, Arunācala in the Tamil country of the south, and Kamadgiri and Govardhan in the northern sanctums of Rāma and Kṛṣṇa, respectively. Many of India's sacred cities also have *pradakṣiṇa* routes, the best known being the Pañcakrośī *pradakṣiṇa* of the city of Banaras (modern-day Varanasi). This sacred circuit of the city takes pilgrims five days to perform, passing 108 shrines along the way and circumscribing with their footsteps the perimeter of the sacred zone of the city where simply to die is to attain *mokṣa* ("liberation").

More common, however, is simply the *pradakṣiṇa* of the sanctum sanctorum, the *garbhagṛha*, in a Hindu temple. Depending upon the size of the temple, the pilgrim will circumambulate either the entire complex or merely the inner courts before approaching the deity for *darśana*. There may be several circumambulatories, which usually will include their own circuit of ancillary shrines. In some popular temples, especially in the North, this is a very "close" circumambulation, with the devout running their hands along the temple walls, frequently stopping to touch the place at the back of the temple nearest the image of the divine inside. In the South, however, especially in Kerala and Karnātaka, there are often circumambulatory markers, outside of which the honorific circuit must be made, at a respectful distance of several feet from the temple itself.

The circumambulation of a center also formed a strong part of the early Buddhist tradition of worship, especially the circling of the stupa with its hemispherical dome, originally said to house a relic of the Buddha. The dome of the stupa, called the *aṇḍa* ("egg"), was said to have cosmic significance as the dome of heaven: the smaller superstructure on top was Mount Meru, and the surmounting umbrellas signaled the Buddha's world-kingship. The entire stupa was surrounded by a fence, with gates in the four principal directions. Between the fence and the *aṇḍa* was a *pradakṣiṇapatha*, a circumambulatory path. Very often, as in the case of the stupa of Amaravati in the Andhra area of India, there was an upper circumambulatory of the *aṇḍa* itself, with its own enclosing rail. The famous stupa of Borobudur in Java was built in nine levels, with a circumambulatory around each of the lower six levels that took the pilgrim not only around the stupa but also past bas-reliefs depicting the earthly life, the previous lives, and the instructive deeds of the Buddha.

The circling of the stupa, called the *chedi* in modern Thailand, continues as a common part of festival rituals. In the evening during the Thai celebration of Viśākha Pūjā (the day of the Buddha's birth, enlightenment, and death) monks and laity circle the *chedi* three times, holding lighted candles. Other festival days are marked with a similar threefold circumambulation.

The divine also circumambulates, reaffirming the sacred claim upon the territory circumscribed by the route. In Sri Lanka, for example, the annual procession of the relic from the Temple of the Tooth takes a circumambulatory route through the city of Kandy. In South India, such annual circuits of the gods are common. During the Chittarai festival in Madurai, for example, when the goddess Mīnākṣī moves in her giant chariot through the concentric rectangular circumambulatory streets of the city, she reclaims the four directions as her own.

In the ancient Hebrew tradition, the story of Joshua's siege of Jericho displays the power of the Lord in encircling the city. For six days Joshua's army, led by the ark of the covenant and seven priests with seven trumpets of rams' horns, made one circuit a day around the city; on the seventh day they made seven circuits and the city wall fell (*Jos.* 6). In the later tradition, circumambulatory circuits (*haqqafot*) are performed both to mark holy ground and, it would seem, to remember the power of the Lord that was with the children of Israel in the siege of Jericho.

The most festive *haqqafot* take place during the Feast of Booths, Sukkot, when those present make seven ceremonial circuits carrying the festal bouquet of willow branches and lemons around the altar in the synagogue. In the time of Philo Judaeus the procession, like that of Joshua, took place once a day for six days and seven times on the seventh. At Simḥat Torah, *haqqafot* are performed with the scrolls of the Torah being carried around the synagogue.

Christian worship has tended to focus the attention of the worshiper directionally toward the east or vertically toward the vaulting heavens, rather than inward toward an encompassed center. Even so, Christian architecture displays a tension between the center, which can be circumambulated, and the "transcendent" or the "east," which cannot. In the Middle Ages, churches were built with ambulatories to facilitate the movement of pilgrims through the church and around the altar, beneath which or near which a relic was enshrined. Circumambulation is an important part of pilgrimages, such as that of Saint Patrick's Purgatory on an islet in Lough Derg in Ireland, where pilgrims walk around the basilica four times, saying seven decades of the rosary beads. In the Christian tradition, as in others as well, circumambulation is often part of rites of consecration. For instance, when the new basilica of Our Lady of Guadalupe in Mexico City was consecrated in 1976, the consecrating procession circled the building sprinking it with sanctified water, anointing it with holy oil, and fumigating it with incense.

The Muslim *ḥājj* has the circumambulation *(ṭawāf)* of the Kaʿbah as one of its central rites. The original meaning of *ḥājj* is "to describe a circle," and this circling of the Kaʿbah is a pre-Islamic rite, said to have been done naked, a practice that was prohibited by the Prophet. Here the circles are made with the left side, said to be the side of the heart facing toward the sacred Kaʿbah. The *ṭawāf* consists of seven circuits of the Kaʿbah. The full pilgrimage contains three *ṭawāfs:* the initial *ṭawāf* on arrival, which is part of the ordinary *ʾumrah,* or lesser pilgrimages; a *ṭawāf* on return from the journey to Arafat; and a farewell *ṭawāf* before leaving.

The *ṭawāf* is interpreted in a spiritual way by theologians such as al-Ghazālī, who describes *ṭawāf* as a form of prayer. *Ṭawāf* is not merely the circling of the body around the Kaʿbah but the circling of the heart around God. In doing *ṭawāf,* the faithful are like the angels circling the throne of God. Some Sūfīs were believed to have reached such a high peak that the Kaʿbah came to circumambulate them, and not they the Kaʿbah.

In many traditions, circumambulation is associated not only with places of holiness or of worship, but also with life-cycle rites. Marriage rites often involve circling, since a wedding is preeminently a rite of bonding and union. In some traditional Jewish communities, the bride makes either three or seven *haqqafot* around the groom at the wedding. The circling establishes a common world for the couple. Roman weddings, for instance, called for the circling of the bride and groom around the family altar. In the Agni Pradakṣiṇa rite of the Hindu marriage, the bride follows the groom three times around the sacred fire, her sari tied to his dhoti. The rite immediately precedes the "seven steps," the legal culmination of the marriage ceremony. Interestingly, this rite repeats the groom's three circuits around the sacred fire during his initiation rite, the Upanayana, just before he received the sacred Sāvitrī mantra from the *gurū* and thus established the primary bond of his years of education.

In addition to being a rite of honoring, centering, and bonding, circumambulation also can set apart what is circumscribed. This is especially the case for the "dangerous holy," that is, the dead. Both the dead and places associated with the dead are circumambulated, sometimes counterclockwise, as a protective or apotropaic rite to keep the spheres of the living and dead apart.

In the Sephardic and Hasidic traditions of Judaism, seven *haqqafot* are made around a cemetery prior to burial. It has also been the custom in Ireland, Holland, Germany, and elsewhere in northern Europe to carry the casket in procession three times, sunwise, around the cemetery before burial. According to the *Mahāparinirvāṇa Sūtra,* five hundred of the Buddha's disciples circled his body before his cremation pyre was lit. The Hindu cremation rite today begins as the chief mourner, usually the eldest son, circles the pyre four times counterclockwise, carrying the flaming bundle of sacred *kuśa* grass and touching the body symbolically with each round, finally lighting the pyre at the head. In Buddhist Thailand as well the body is circumambulated three times before the cremation. In the case of a king or member of the royal family, a special palace-mountain pavilion called the *phra meru* is built for the cremation. On arrival, the body is borne around the *phra meru* three times, *uttaravatta,* in a "left-hand direction," before being placed upon the elaborate pyre. While the threefold circumambulation in the Buddhist tradition ordinarily marks reverence for the Buddha, the Dharma, and the Samgha, here it is said to remind the living of the three wearisome worlds of *saṃsāra*—that of earth, of heaven, and of hell.

See Also Circle; Maṇḍalas; Pilgrimage, article on Muslim Pilgrimage.

Bibliography

Heiler, Friedrich. *Erscheinungsformen und Wesen der Religion.* Stuttgart, 1961.

Pandey, Raj Bali. *Hindu Saṁskāras.* 2d rev. ed. Delhi, 1969. A description of the major *saṃskāras,* or sacraments from birth to death of the Hindu Brahmanical tradition.

Turner, Victor, and Edith Turner. *Image and Pilgrimage in Christian Culture.* New York, 1978. An anthropological study of Christian pilgrimages, looking at both Mexican and Irish pilgrimages as well as Marian pilgrimages in other countries.

Von Grunebaum, G. E. *Muhammadan Festivals.* New York, 1951. A discussion of Muslim worship, including the rites of the pilgrimage to Mecca, the *ḥājj.*

Wells, Kenneth E. *Thai Buddhism: Its Rites and Activities* (1939). Reprint, Bangkok, 1960. A study of daily, weekly, and yearly Buddhist rites and festivals in Thailand, with discussions of major life crisis rites such as ordination to the monastic order and funerals.

New Sources

Deegan, Chris. "The Narmada: Circumambulation of a Sacred Landscape." In *Hinduism and Ecology: The Intersection of Earth, Sky, and Water,* edited by Christopher Key Chapple and Mary Evelyn Tucker, pp. 389–400. Cambridge, U.K., 2000.

Nakamura, Susumu. "Pradakshiṇā, A Buddhist Form of Obeisance." In *Semitic and Oriental Studies: A Volume Presented to William Popper on the Occasion of His Seventy-Fifth Birthday,* edited by Walter J. Fischel, pp. 345–354. Berkeley, 1951.

Peters, Francis. *The Hajj: The Muslim Pilgrimage to Mecca and the Holy Places.* Princeton, 1994.

Sudhi, Padma. "An Encyclopaedic Study on Circumambulation." *Annals of the Bhandarkar Oriental Research Institute* 65, nos. 1–4 (1984): 205–226.

DIANA L. ECK (1987)
Revised Bibliography

CIRCUMCISION is the surgical removal of the foreskin from the penis; sometimes it also refers to less common practices of uncovering the glands of the penis by removing some of the foreskin and leaving the remainder as a flap, as practiced by the Maasai and Ki-kuyu of East Africa, or cutting the foreskin away but retaining it as two flaps, as practiced by the Tikopia of Polynesia. Early social theorists speculated about circumcision's origins, suggesting that it may have (1) marked captives, thereby signifying subjection, (2) attracted the opposite sex, (3) been a tribal or ethnic mark, (4) been hygienic, (5) increased sexual pleasure, (6) removed men from maternal bonds, (7) tested bravery, (8) sacrificed part of the self to ensure future rebirth, (9) been a form of symbolic castration to support the domination of youths by their elders, or (10) even simulated menstruation. None of these theories is accepted today, though various combinations of them may be cited by those groups who circumcise.

GEOGRAPHIC DISTRIBUTION. Circumcision is commonly associated with Semitic religions (Islam, Judaism, and Coptic Christianity), but, in fact, it predates all of these. It was practiced among ancient Egyptians, although not universally. It is widespread among peoples in Africa, western Asia, and the Pacific, including Australia. Early travelers' records and encyclopedias report circumcision among some New World peoples, but these accounts seem dubious, and, at most, the practice there appears to have been rare. Circumcision was not common in Europe or North America (except among Jews) until the 1870s and became widespread only at the turn of the century. Today about 85 percent of newborn American males undergo the operation, but it is far less common elsewhere in the English-speaking world and in Europe. It is our only form of prophylactic surgery, and currently members of the medical profession are in disagreement as to whether it is scientifically justifiable. Some cite its prevalence in America as an indication of a misconceived preoccupation with medicine and hygiene.

SEMITIC CIRCUMCISION. Muslims, Jews, and Coptic Christians usually circumcise during infancy. Ideally Jews circumcise on the eighth day of life. Among Orthodox Jews circumcision is performed by a professional circumciser (*mohel*) rather than a physician, and blood must be drawn from the wound either by mouth or, today, through a suction pump. In America, Jews have figured significantly in developing surgical devices that facilitate the operation. Circumcision is not strictly necessary to make one a Jew: since 1892, for example, Reform Jews have not required it of converts. Before the Hellenistic period circumcision among Jews took a less radical form than it does today. Because some Jews would "blister" the portion of their foreskin that remained in order to appear uncircumcised to the Greeks and Romans, the rabbinate advocated a fuller circumcision. Some hellenized Jews sought to appear uncircumcised because the Greeks and Romans viewed the practice with revulsion and periodically enacted laws to make the custom difficult for Jews and Egyptians under their rule.

Muslim circumcision usually occurs on what is termed the seventh day (in fact it is the eighth day, since the day of birth is not counted). In practice, the time varies widely. Some Muslims perform circumcision within the first five or six years; others delay it until as late as adolescence. While circumcision is not discussed in the Qurʾān, Muslims agree that it must occur before marriage and is required of male converts. In many cases, it is accompanied by lavish feasts and celebrations. A few Arabs combine circumcision with radical flaying and scarification of the lower abdomen.

Coptic Christians (including Ethiopians) circumcise in imitation of Old Testament Jews, but the time at which circumcision is performed varies from the first week of life to the first few years.

CIRCUMCISION AND ETHNICITY. Besides signifying membership in a religion, circumcision may indicate ethnicity or merely a human condition properly marked by the creativity of culture. Thus the Yoruba and Igbo of Nigeria usually circumcise during infancy; for them the operation signifies no religious or moral commitments nor does it distinguish them from their neighbors, who also circumcise. Even in respect to a single society generalizations about circumcision may be formulated with difficulty, as examples from Africa will illustrate. The western Dinka of the Sudan circumcise while the eastern Dinka do not. Their neighbors, the Nuer, do not ordinarily circumcise, but on rare occasions they may, in order to purify someone who has committed incest. Among the Azande of the Sudan and Zaire circumcision was introduced by neighboring peoples, with the result that within even the same village or extended kin group some will be circumcised while others will not. Among the Amba of Uganda circumcision was unknown until an unexplained interest in the custom, learned from neighbors to the west, led to sporadic waves of circumcision among youths and even adults. Among the Sotho of southern Africa circumcision was once universal, but under government and mission influence many have abandoned the practice while others continue to observe it. Among some migratory pygmies in Zaire circumcision has been interpreted as a mark of cultural subjugation to their sedentary African overlords. Even where circumcision is a traditional practice and remains prevalent it now often takes place in hospitals, despite protests from elders, who advocate the old ways.

CIRCUMCISION AND RITES OF SEXUAL INITIATION. Where circumcision is associated with a world religion, it rarely marks sexual maturity. Such an association is common, however, among preliterates, although even among these many peoples circumcise infants or children rather than adolescents. Early circumcision may be a mark of ethnicity, or it may be considered hygienic or aesthetically attractive, but it does not provide a means by which trauma may be harnessed to the inculcation of moral and metaphysical values, as occurs in many rituals of initiation. Nor can infantile circumcision serve as a test of bravery. These aspects of circumcision, however, are of special interest to the anthropologist of religion.

Among the societies that practice circumcision as a rite of passage to adulthood, those of central Australia and East Africa provide the most complex and dramatic examples.

In central Australia circumcision is the primary operation in defining male adulthood, although it is often accompanied by tooth evulsion, bodily scarification, and, a year or two later, subincision. Much pressure is exerted on the initiate to show no fear or pain. Among those Australian Aborigines who practice circumcision (and not all do), the operation marks the beginning of a youth's indoctrination into the men's secret ceremonial life, the preservation of which is believed to be vital for maintaining social and natural harmony. At this time novices witness complex ceremonies in which the mythical origins of the world are enacted and, thereby, the order of the world is reasserted. The initial rites convey only basic features of this information; only after a man has witnessed many such ceremonies over the years, first as a spectator-novice, then as an actor-participant, and finally as an organizer, does he become truly knowledgeable. Circumcision, therefore, is not only the occasion when a youth passes into the circle of informed adults, but it also provides repeated opportunities for him to continue to acquire deeper knowledge of traditions.

Australian circumcision furthers male solidarity by forever separating youths from their mothers. The initiates receive ritual objects that are forbidden to the sight of women. Admitted to frequent and complex secret male ritual activities, they begin to spend longer periods away from camp at ceremonies that exclude women. It is only after these rituals that a youth is likely to have heterosexual relations and marry. Male solidarity sometimes involves a homosexual experience, since a circumciser may be obliged to have sexual relations with a newly recovered novice to whom he will later give a wife.

Aborigines associate circumcision with marriage not simply to prepare a man to take a wife but to reinforce the bonds the man enjoys with the men of his wife's family. Thus a man's potential father-in-law and brothers-in-law, his own father, and his uncles (his father's affinal ties and members of the group that helped to circumcise his father) often figure in his circumcision. Male solidarity and hierarchy are closely associated with the bestowal of and submission to pain, a prevalent theme in Aboriginal belief and ritual. This in turn relates to the fact that periodically in a society circumcision and subincision involve the shedding of male "genital blood," a blessing with deep mystical value for the reestablishment of social and moral order through altruistic, sacrificial suffering.

Circumcision is widespread in East Africa. Among sedentary speakers of Bantu language it is usually performed annually on groups of youths approaching adolescence. These groups are segregated in the bush (the sphere of disorder) apart from villages and women. Novices are stripped, shaved, bathed, and sometimes marked with ashes or white earth, all to denude them of their previous status and to place them in a liminal state, neither minor nor adult. The actual operation is often performed by an expert who is outside or peripheral to the group. Bravery under pain is usually required. The shedding of blood is viewed as polluting, a "hot" procedure that temporarily creates disorder so as to achieve a greater eventual order. Rituals and medicines are therefore applied to "cool" the wound and allow it to heal.

During their weeks of recovery, novices are hazed by older circumcised youths or by elders. They fast and observe numerous prohibitions, as may also their kin, in order to ensure recovery. In their isolated quarters, the novices—vulnerable and impressionable because of the wounds, fasting, and exposure that they have suffered—are subjected to intensive instructions about sexual behavior, moral attitudes, and proper conduct. Toward the end of their confinement, the novices may don strange garb and tour nearby villages representing their status of being nameless, nonsocial creatures. Upon recovery, they return to their homes and enjoy the company of women at dances and feasts that celebrate their new adulthood. Circumcision marks their ritual death as minors and their rebirth as responsible adults.

In other East African societies, especially Para-Nilotes such as the Maasai, rites of circumcision are not held every year. Instead, they are held for several successive years until a sufficient group is recruited; then the rites are not practiced for some time. Through circumcision men enter named tribal age groups whose members provide mutual aid and hospitality and, when young, form fighting units.

In East Africa and Australia circumcision is understood to remove the vestiges of polluting femininity (the foreskin) from a youth, converting him into an adult male. It provides a powerful measure of commitment to group values in the face of considerable suffering, and it represents a permanent moral and physical transformation. Women are afforded no comparable process, and (despite any physical operation) they remain minors subordinate to men, according to the norms that govern social organization. Where such initiation occurs we find the belief that society improves upon nature by transforming the male body into a more proper vehicle for a moral person to inhabit. The social person and the natural body are brought into closer conjunction. The endurance of pain and the observance of ritual restrictions express both a willingness and a capacity to subject personal appetites and feelings to collective ends. At the same time the powers that shape the cultural process assume a physical reality in the experience of bodily suffering.

SEE ALSO Castration; Clitoridectomy.

BIBLIOGRAPHY

Beidelman, T. O. *The Cool Knife.* Bloomington, 1997. Detailed description of male and female circumcision and initiation among Bantu people of East Africa, useful bibliography.

Bleich, David. *Judaism and Healing.* New York, 1984. An apology for Jewish circumcision.

Dunsman, W. D., and E. M. Gordon. "The History of Circumcision." *British Journal of Urology International* 83, *Supplement* 1: 1–12. Restriceted to Western cultures.

Eilberg-Schwarts, Howard. *The Savage in Judaism.* Bloomington, 1990. Jewish practices compared to those of preliterate societies.

Friedman, David M. *A Mind of Its Own.* New York, 2001. Cultural history of the penis, excellent bibliography.

Glass, J. M. "Religious Circumcision: A Jewish View." *British Journal of Urology International* 83, *Supplement* 1: 11–12. An apology for Jewish circumcision.

Gollaher, David L. "From Ritual to Science." *Journal of Social History* 28 (1994): 5–36. Circumcision argued as a justified medical treatment.

Gollaher, David L. *Circumcision.* New York, 2000. Valuable survey.

Hoffmann, Lawrence J. *Covenant of Blood.* Chicago, 1976. Semitic circumcision.

Meggitt, M. J. *Desert People: A Study of the Walbiri Aborigines of Central Australia.* Sydney, 1962. Most reliable account of circumsion among Australian Aborigines.

Morgenstern, Julian. *Rites of Birth, Marriage, Death, and Kindred Occasions among the Semites.* Cincinnati, 1966. Contains a useful survey of Jewish and Muslim circumcision.

Spencer, Paul. *The Samburu: A Study of Gerontocracy in a Nomadic Tribe.* Berkeley, 1965. Contains a useful description of circumcision among para-Nilotes of East Africa.

Strage, Mark. *The Durable Fig Leaf.* New York, 1980. Survey of the history of the penis.

Thorn, Mark. *Taboo No More.* New York, 1990. Short and witty survey of the history of the penis.

Turner, Victor. "Three Symbols of *Passage* in Ndembu Circumcision Ritual: An Interpretation." In *Essays on the Ritual of Social Relations,* edited by Max Gluckman, pp. 124–173. Manchester, England, 1962. Influential essay on symbolism of circumcision in Central Africa.

T. O. BEIDELMAN (1987 AND 2005)

CIRCUMPOLAR RELIGIONS SEE ARCTIC RELIGIONS

CISTERCIANS. The Cistercians are an order of monks and nuns that arose in the twelfth century to foster the integral observance of the rule of Benedict of Nursia (d. 525). The order takes its name from the first community to adopt the reform, the Abbey of Cîteaux in Burgundy, France. Benedict's *Rule for Monasteries,* written around the year 500, became virtually the exclusive rule for monasteries in western Europe after the time of Charlemagne (d. 814). With the foundation of Cluny in 909, a reform to bring about a more observant monastic practice was effectively forwarded by a succession of great, holy, and long-lived abbots; however, this was achieved at the cost of local autonomy and the balance of liturgy, sacred reading, personal prayer, and manual work that is so characteristic of Benedict's *Rule.* At Cluny and many of its dependent monasteries, the liturgy was celebrated with great splendor and duration, while manual labor became for the monks a nominal exercise.

In the time of the Gregorian reform, many monastic founders arose who drew their inspiration from the Gospels, monastic traditions, and in some cases Benedict's *Rule.* They laid great stress on poverty, solitude, and simplicity of lifestyle. Most notable among these monks was Robert of Molesme (d. 1110), who, after entering the order at Moutier-la-Celle, near Troyes, attempted reforms in various monasteries and finally succeeded in gathering the hermits of Collan into a notable Benedictine community at Molesmes. The community's fervor brought fame and fortune, and then a more relaxed observance of the rule. Again Robert, with the permission of the legate, Hugh of Die, set out to seek the fullness of the Benedictine way of life, establishing the New Monastery at Cîteaux in 1098. He was accompanied by the prior and subprior from Molesmes, and nineteen others.

Within two years Robert was required by papal authority to return to Molesmes, but the reform was carried forward by Alberic, his prior (d. 1109), and then by Stephen Harding (d. 1135), who had been his subprior. Under the latter, an expansion began that accelerated rapidly with the arrival of Bernard of Clairvaux (d. 1153).

To Stephen is largely attributed the *Charter of Charity,* which bound together Cîteaux and the many monasteries that would spring from it directly or indirectly, forming them into an order. The federated nature of this order respected the autonomy of the local community, while ensuring ongoing regularity of observance by an annual gathering of the college of abbots in a chapter and by a system of annual visitation of all the monasteries. As early as the 1130s these successful elements of the Cistercian reform began to find their way into other Benedictine federations; later, in various forms, chapters and visitation became part of the structure of almost every religious order.

While the concern of the Cistercian reformers to live to the full Benedict's rule too often descended to bickering over observances (see *A Dialogue between a Cluniac and a Cistercian*), its true aim as powerfully expressed by the leading Cistercian fathers—Bernard of Clairvaux, William of Saint-Thierry (d. 1148), Guerric of Igny (d. 1157), and Ælred of

Rievaulx (d. 1169)—was to attain to the experience of God through mystical love, the goal pointed to by Benedict in the prologue and epilogue to his *Rule* and in its central chapter, the seventh, "On Humility."

The Cistercian order experienced very rapid expansion with the founding or affiliation of over three hundred monasteries in all parts of western Europe prior to the death of Bernard of Clairvaux. This expansion continued through the following centuries until there were over seven hundred Cistercian abbeys of monks, as well as innumerable convents of nuns following their observance. The order was slow to incorporate communities of women; only in the wake of the Second Vatican Council have the abbesses emerged as fully equal members of the college of superiors.

In order that monks might have the opportunity to live the Benedictine rule to the full and strive after a truly contemplative life, the lay-brother vocation was promoted; this system provided larger workforces to build the monasteries and care for the order's ever-growing landholdings. The tensions that inevitably arose between the increasingly clericalized choir monks and the hardworking brothers could even erupt at times into violence.

Through the influence of the schools, scholastic scholarship began to replace a contemplative patristic theology. With the great geographical expansion of the order, the reform structure began to break down, and observance declined. The unlettered who had been attracted to the Cistercian lay brotherhood began, in the thirteenth century, to turn to the new fervent mendicant orders. The Cistercians began to fragment into national or regional congregations. The Protestant Reformation wiped out monastic life in many countries. An attempted reform within the order in the seventeenth century led to a "war of observances" and the emergence of the Strict Observance, prior to further losses through the French Revolution and other secularizing movements. The policies of Emperor Franz Josef forced the monks in the Austrian Empire to take up tasks left off by the Jesuits when they were temporarily suppressed.

The Cistercians experienced a renewal in France in the nineteenth century that spilled over to the rest of the world in the next century. In 1892 Leo XIII sought to reunite all the Cistercians, but the pope's efforts resulted instead in the formation of two Cistercian orders, one now known as the Cistercians of the Strict Observance (Trappist), which includes both monks and nuns, and another composed of twelve congregations of monks and over eighty convents of nuns. A number of these congregations suffered extensively at the hands of the Communists in Eastern Europe and Vietnam and found refuge in other countries.

The Strict Observance was brought to new prominence by the writings of one of its members, Thomas Merton (Father Louis of Gethsemani Abbey, Trappist, Kentucky). As the largest order of contemplative men in the church today, it has played an increasingly significant role in the contemporary spiritual renewal of the Roman Catholic Church.

See Also Benedict of Nursia.

Bibliography

The most complete work on the Cistercians is that of Louis J. Lekai, *The Cistercians: Ideals and Reality* (Kent, Ohio, 1977). For a complementary study from the point of view of the Strict Observance, see Jean de la Croix Bouton's *Histoire de l'Ordre de Cîteaux,* 3 vols. (Westmalle, Belgium, 1959–1968). However, the most extensive study of the origins of the Strict Observance is Lekai's *The Rise of the Cistercian Strict Observance in Seventeenth Century France* (Washington, D.C., 1968). Its later development is found in Anselme Le Bail's *L'Ordre de Cîteaux* (Paris, 1924). Thomas Merton in *Waters of Siloe* (New York, 1949) treats the American segment of Cistercian history most completely. For a deep and authoritative presentation of the spirituality that animates the Cistercian life, see Jean Leclercq's *Bernard of Clairvaux and the Cistercian Spirit* (Kalamazoo, Mich., 1976). Louis Bouyer's *The Cistercian Heritage* (London, 1958) is a more comprehensive and popular presentation of the spirituality of the order. *A Dialogue between a Cluniac and a Cistercian* can be found in *Cistercians and Cluniacs: Documents in the Feud between White Monks and Black Monks,* translated by Jeremiah F. O'Sullivan and Irene Edmonds (Kalamazoo, Mich., 1986).

New Sources

Berman, Constance H. *The Cistercian Evolution.* Philadelphia, 1999.

Elder, E. Rozanne, ed. *New Monastery: Texts and Studies on the Early Cistercians.* Kalamazoo, Mich., 1998.

McGuire, Brian Patrick. *Friendship and Faith: Cistercian Men, Women, and their Stories, 1100-1200.* Aldershot, U.K., 2002.

Newman, Martha G. *The Boundaries of Charity: Cistercian Culture and Ecclesiastical Reform, 1098-1180.* Stanford, Calif, 1996.

Pennington, M. Basil. *The Cistercians.* Collegeville, Minn., 1992.

Pennington, M. Basil. *The School of Love: The Cistercian Way to Holiness.* Harrisburg, Pa., 2001.

Scholl, Edith, ed. *In the School of Love: An Anthology of Early Cistercian Texts.* Kalamazoo, Mich., 2000.

Tobin, Stephen. *The Cistercians: Monks and Monasteries of Europe.* Woodstock, N.Y., 1996.

M. Basil Pennington (1987)
Revised Bibliography

CITIES. In order to obtain the deepest historical understanding of urban religiosity, one may begin with the Neolithic site of Çatal Hüyük, located on Turkey's Anatolian Plateau. The main mound represents the continuous habitation of a coherent cultural group between about 7000 and 5700 BCE, making this one of the oldest known cities in the world. The earliest excavations exposed residential abodes adjoining structures identified as shrines in a section of the city described by James Mellaart, the principal excavator (1967), as a sacred or priestly quarter. The remarkably preserved shrine rooms reveal a dominant female image, molded on the walls in plaster with arms upraised and legs extended, sometimes portrayed as pregnant and sometimes portrayed with an animal's head emerging from her womb. Other images of animal heads in plaster adorn the walls of the shrines, and short pillars with mounted bulls' horns adorn the edges of raised platforms. Multiple plaster representations of breasts molded around animal skulls, or with animal skulls protruding from them, hang on the walls of some shrines, while stone statuary of a female image associated with leopards coincides with painted plaster images of leopards in other rooms. Detailed paintings in a single shrine portray giant vultures swooping down on decapitated human figures. Burials under the raised platforms of shrines and residences indicate initial exposure of the dead and elimination of flesh through the action of birds, before the final interment of bones, sometimes with red ochre or grave goods.

A different vision of early urban religiosity comes from the ancient site of Jericho, well known from a number of biblical passages and excavated repeatedly since the nineteenth century. Excavations in the 1950s found what may be the oldest monumental architecture in the world: a circular watchtower 28 feet in diameter and surviving to a height of 24.5 feet behind fortification walls. A population of perhaps 3,000 people lived here in the early eighth millennium BCE. Settlers at this site in the following millennium were using small female figurines with hands supporting their breasts, often interpreted as fertility goddesses. They also were burying their dead beneath the floors of houses, but removing their skulls in order to plaster and paint them in a lifelike manner, insert shells in their eye sockets, and exhibit them (Kenyon, 1970, pp. 39–57, 331).

These first cases of population concentration, civic architecture, and occupational specialization introduce several recurring themes in the discussion of religion and its relationship to cities. The first theme concerns the style of religiosity connected with urbanization: death and the invocation of fertility seem to constitute fundamental problems at the origins of town life. The second theme concerns the disposition of sacred and public space, represented in the case of Çatal Hüyük by the presence of buildings apparently dedicated to the performance of rituals. One may ask whether the multiplicity of sites indicates many publics oriented around specific kinship groups or priestly lineages, or whether this multiplicity connotes a concept of the sacred and ritual practice uniting all members of the settlement within an overarching community of citizens. The two examples of burial practices mentioned above suggest ritual practice occurring within more restricted social environments based on kinship or participation within specific rituals.

City-Gods and Rulers: Mesopotamia. The first detailed portrait of urbanization on a regional scale becomes possible during the fourth millennium BCE in Mesopotamia—old Sumer and Akkad, the territories that would become Babylonia. Archaeological work has traced here the transition from village farming communities to cities, and the study of the earliest cuneiform writing from the end of the millennium has allowed a deeper look at belief systems and social organization. Thorkild Jacobsen (1976) describes Sumerian religiosity as being based on an understanding of the entire universe in terms of its "numinous" qualities. The different features of the natural world follow patterns of change and growth that corresponded to the many attributes of sacred power, resulting in thousands of names for spiritual entities linked to natural and artificial phenomena. The attempts to understand these entities through their signs and to manipulate the rules for their manifestation form the background for massive numbers of cuneiform records concerned with divination and correct behavior. The attempts include astronomical observation and various performances in which groups of people invoked or placated sacred forces, including the calendar-based agrarian festivals celebrating the death and rebirth of anthropomorphic images of fertility. Tendencies toward representation of the sacred in human form seem to have become more prominent when larger populations concentrated in central places. As the Mesopotamian plain became dotted with cities, along with places dedicated to subsidiary sacred forces conceived as divine persons, each settlement created the "house" of a god associated with the life of the entire community.

The center of the divine presence was the temple, a quadrilateral roofed structure with an image of a deity, which most sources describe as an anthropomorphic statue made of wood and ornamented with precious substances. When a statue was installed with the correct rituals, the god entered into it and became one with it. As a living presence, the statue/deity enjoyed a daily round of services, including baths, offerings of food and drink, music, incense, and the worship of devotees. The temple household included kitchens for food preparation and habitation quarters for functionaries who prepared offerings, performed worship, and maintained the temple infrastructure. In order to support offerings and the personnel of the gods, temples came to control economic resources in the form of land or investments in commercial undertakings. The earliest written sources from the late fourth and early third millennia mostly describe economic transactions involving temples. This characteristic of the source material has supported the theory that the administration of the earliest cities was theocratic, with temples performing the management and distribution functions that allowed expansion of agriculture and trade (Wiggermann, 1995, pp. 1861–1862).

The perennial scholarly problem is tracing the interactions between the theocratic model of early urbanization and a model based on kingship. The earliest rulers of Sumerian city-states were "lords" *(en)* selected from a restricted body of citizens after rites of divination. The installation of the ruler occurred through a sacred marriage with the deity, at times represented by a priest or priestess of the city god's temple. The preponderance of temple economic transactions, the absence of buildings clearly identifiable as "palaces," and the primarily honorific actions of the lords suggest that their ability to wield independent power initially remained limited. Armed conflict among Sumer's cities in the early third millennium, a time when "city-states" emerged, indicates that war leaders were becoming more important in determining the outcomes of economic or territorial struggles. In the city of Lagash, for example, administrative texts dating between 2500 and 2350 BCE suggest that the king controlled the city's economy through the domains of the city's main temples. The person regarded as the fulfiller of this tendency was Sargon of Akkad (Agade), who in the late twenty-fourth century BCE brought all Mesopotamian city-states under his authority, reputedly campaigning as far as the Mediterranean Sea. Sargon claimed to be an appointee of the supreme god Enlil, and arranged for his daughter's appointment as priestess of the moon-god Sin in the city of Ur, thus posing as a traditionalist who preserved the archaic hegemony of independent cities. His grandson, Naram-Sin, initiated major renovations at Enlil's temple in Nippur, but also appointed governors over cities and appeared as a divine being in his own right (Franke, 1995). Even after the eclipse of Naram-Sin's empire, kings of Sumerian city-states represented themselves with divine attributes, while still claiming that their power derived from the favor of their city's leading deity. The many deities of Mesopotamian sites came to constitute a pantheon governed by the king-like Enlil, who ruled from the temple city of Nippur in conjunction with an assembly of the gods and through Enki, the master of intelligence, whose hometown was Eridu.

By the eighteenth century BCE, when Sumeria came under the hegemony of emperors based in Babylon or Assyria, a radical transformation of urban sacrality had taken place. A ranked hierarchy of personified deities now stood behind the phenomena of nature, dictating the fate of the world within a complex array of laws that required obedience and observation of ritual injunctions (Bottéro, 1992, pp. 208–231). Adjacent to now-expanded temples at the centers of major cities stood massive stepped pyramids or ziggurats, which probably included shrines on their summits accessible by long flights of stairs. Religious institutions, especially in northern Mesopotamia, appeared less like the organic outgrowths of the urban fabric and more like massive interventions of wealth and power located on heights above the population, culminating in massive urban planning projects of the "neo-Babylonian" kings in the seventh and sixth centuries (Van De Mieroop, 1997, pp. 84–86). The Babyonians placed Marduk at the head of the pantheon and the Assyrians placed Assur on top, each representing his capital city as in the older dispensation, but now portrayed as lords of the universe supported by emperors as their divinely appointed representatives on earth, demanding conformity from those below them. Thus, urban religion came to legitimize empire, and the city became a cosmogram constructed by and for political leaderships. Paradoxically, as the imperial motif was coming to dominate the city's sacred center during a period of expanding social and economic complexity, we notice the creation of architecture of privatized worship (Crawford, 1991, pp. 71–73, 101), an increasing attention to the human individual, and a concern with a personal god.

CEREMONIAL CENTERS: CHINA AND THE AMERICAS. Perhaps the most influential body of scholarship concerned with religion and the city has engaged in a comparative study of the cosmographic qualities of the ceremonial center, as originally exemplified in Mesopotamia. Paul Wheatley's classic study of the Chinese Shang and Zhou cities (second–first millennia BCE) propounded the study of the ceremonial center as a program for understanding "traditional" urbanization in Asia and, by extension, throughout the world:

> Whenever, in any of the seven regions of primary urban generation . . . , we trace back the characteristic urban form to its beginnings we arrive not at a settlement that is dominated by commercial relations, a primordial market, or at one that is focused on a citadel, an archetypal fortress, but rather at a ceremonial complex. . . . Beginning as little more than tribal shrines, in what may be regarded as their classic phases these centers were elaborated into complexes of public ceremonial structures, usually massive and often extensive, and including assemblages of such architectural items as pyramids, platform mounds, temples, palaces, terraces, staircases, courts, and stelae. Operationally they were instruments for the creation of political, social, economic, and sacred space, at the same time as they were symbols of cosmic, social, and moral order. (1971, p. 225)

Wheatley's particular interest concerned the change of the Zhou city center from a ceremonial enclave—a walled enclosure for an altar of the god of the soil and a temple of ancestors—toward a multifaceted administrative, military, and economic hub for a "spatially integrated hinterland" (pp. 175–178, 186–187). For this project he built on the centuries-old doctrines of geomancy *(feng-shui),* scholarship linking Chinese city planning to "cosmo-magical" elements already visible in Shang or Zhou divination records, and the orientation of excavated cities toward the cardinal directions. The project, however, had the more ambitious goal of linking Chinese materials to comparative theories of "astrobiology" that aligned earthly prosperity to a cosmic order, manifest in the stars, through orientation of the built environment around a universal axis. Wheatley was interested in constructing an urban progression from village farming community through dispersed ceremonial center to compact city, considering the "ideal-type ceremonial center . . . as a functional and developmental stage in the evolution of city life" (p. 329). The goal of this effort, shared by many in the social sciences of the twentieth century, was an understanding of these "foci of orthogenesis" as characteristic of the premodern, distinct from the "uniqueness of the present-day city" (pp. 478–482).

The framework of the ceremonial center has proven particularly durable in the study of precontact Mesoamerica, where urbanization originated in the early first millennium

BCE in Mexico's Olmec culture and achieved its "classic" form between the second and tenth centuries CE in central Mexico and the Maya world. The heart of the early Mesoamerican city consisted of shrines on raised platforms dedicated to the worship of deities and often associated with burials accompanied by grave goods. The most spectacular city was Teotihuacan in central Mexico, which emerged as a significant site around 100 CE and reached its peak around 500 CE, when its population was between 125,000 and 200,000. A primary road (called by the later Aztecs the Street of the Dead) bisected Teotihuacan beginning in the north at the giant Temple of the Moon, passing by the giant Temple of the Sun, and ending after 1.5 miles at the Great Enclosure and the Citadel housing the Temple of Quetzalcoatl. There were more than one hundred religious structures along the Street of the Dead alone. In addition, the city included over two thousand "apartment compounds" associated with their own platforms, suggesting that every residential unit of sixty to a hundred persons had its own shrine or temple (Marcus, 2000, p. 67; Cowgill, 2003, pp. 41–44).

The hypercentralization of Teotihuacan stands in contrast to settlements in eastern Mexico, Belize, Guatemala, and Honduras, where dozens of states arose, each focused on its own ceremonial complex. One example is Tikal, one of the superpowers of the classic Maya world, where more than 4,000 structures dispersed over an area of 6.2 square miles housed a population of between 50,000 and 90,000 inhabitants in the sixth century CE. The central area known as the Great Plaza, about 100 meters square, included high pyramids with surmounting temples on the west and east sides, and an array of lower pyramids on the north side. The south side of the plaza included an extensive palace complex or "acropolis" and, between the palace and the eastern pyramid, a ball court. Four main causeways linked the plaza to seven more large complexes within a 1.2-mile radius (Escobédo and Valdés, 1998; Grube, 2000, pp. 219–221).

Intensive research on landscapes and the decipherment of Maya hieroglyphic script in the late twentieth century have provided understandings of sacred cosmological concepts and the organization of space in the Mesoamerican city (Arellano Hernández et al., 1999, pp. 34, 108–113, 129–133, 136–139). The universe is tripartite, consisting of a middle world on the surface of the earth, the starry sky of the gods above, and an underworld of death below. It is also quadrilateral, oriented to the four cardinal directions associated with the sun's equinoxes, special colors, and characteristics, and revolving around a central axis where the world tree grows. The gods are natural forces and also superhuman beings connected with specific geometric positions in the universe and controlling different natural phenomena. People pay close attention to their spatial position in order to align themselves most effectively with natural powers and also to enable through their alignments the auspicious aspects of creation. These alignments occur in daily life and in every household, but appear most forcefully in the architecture of the urban center. Major monuments demonstrate orientation to sacred caves or mountains in the surrounding environment, and to the positions on the horizon where celestial bodies rise or set (Šprajc, 2004). Pyramids are mythical mountains, centers of the universe, surmounting caves where deceased ancestors and beings from the underworld reside. The gods presiding over their "places of sleep" in palace temples and on the summits of pyramids, like honored ancestors, are distant beings contacted through rituals of petition and supplication. The ball games played on the ubiquitous courts of the Maya cities seem closely connected to stories of the descent of the hero-twins to the underworld and their triumph over death, known from surviving Maya artwork or literature and from ethnographic study (Grube, 2000, pp. 186–189, 200, 270, 291). The plazas of the ceremonial center are described as oceans, lakes, or standing water, and the city of Izapa in Chiapas demonstrates the cosmological significance: about 2,000 years ago, the citizens diverted water from the nearby river into channels that fed reservoirs surrounding an enormous pyramid, transforming the site into the primordial sea at the world's creation, from which the pyramid-mountain of sustenance rises to support the first maize (Kappelman, 2001, pp. 83–86).

Earlier scholarship on the classic Maya envisioned a theocratic society concerned with the cyclical rhythms of cosmic time and pursuing the peaceful goals of an agrarian economy. More recent research, based on the comparative study of material culture and epigraphy, has portrayed an economically complex world involving long-distance trade, dominated by nobilities and royal families of fifty warring states who supervised the assembly of the ceremonial centers. With the adoption of divine names at their enthronement, rulers took the position of *ajaw* (leader, priest, and king), and after 400 CE they often described themselves as the "divine kings" *(k'uhul ajaw)* of particular territories. Rulers saw themselves as the personification of the world axis, and iconography displays them in the costume of the world tree flanked by serpents' heads representing branches and a headdress of the bird of heaven. The kings enacted public dance dramas in costume, taking the roles of deities such as the god of maize in the stories of creation. Royal men and women, at times under the influence of hallucinatory substances, pierced their bodies in order to collect their blood, aiming simultaneously at visionary experiences. Their blood, dropping on paper, would be burned along with copal, the sweet-smelling "blood" of trees—an activity connected to the idea of the breath-soul, related to aromas and also to sound—that is, to music. There are numerous references to smearing the mouths of gods with blood—in effect, feeding the gods—which involved the public sacrifice of animals and captured enemies. Success in military campaigns correlates closely with construction projects at the end of calendar periods, occasions for the reenactment of the destruction and re-creation of the world order (Arellano Hernández et al., 1999, pp. 92–93; Grube, 2000, pp. 149–153, 292). In these ways the geography of the sacred center became entwined with the public rituals and militaristic ambitions of hereditary political elites.

Attempts to understand the ceremonial center through material culture have underlain the study of various preliterate societies of North America, ranging from the Southwestern pueblo cultures of the Anasazi, oriented around sacred subterranean halls (and peaking between the ninth and thirteenth centuries CE), to the Eastern cultures oriented around artificial mounds. Among the latter, the Mississippian complexes (peaking between the ninth and fourteenth centuries) typically include central plazas adjoining earthen mounds, surrounding clusters of family habitation structures, and protective wooden stockades sometimes with defensive ditches. Population estimates for these sites range from 500 at the smallest to perhaps 25,000 at the largest in Cahokia, Illinois. Within the matrix of political, commercial, and environmental factors that could have supported these complexes, making the surviving architecture a "sociogram" providing clues to stratification, these monuments were obviously sacred sites embodying concepts of centrality, symmetry, boundaries, and domains. The largest, flat-topped mounds seem to have supported shrines or the habitations of elites who performed sacerdotal functions. The alignment of wooden post circles at Cahokia suggests orientation with celestial bodies. Many objects of daily or special ritual use (e.g., pipes) provide a rich body of imagery, including animal figurines, cross-in-circle motifs, and a recurring birdman image. Several examples of more spectacular human statuary provide insights into agrarian ritual iconography. Early travelers' accounts and ethnographic studies, along with archaeological evidence from burials within and around mounds, suggest that rituals of death and renewal were important. Religious beliefs among the contemporary Creek Nation provide illuminating, if speculative, links to the monumental landscape through narratives of human origins in the earth beneath mounds, associations with mountains, and ritual alignments of human groups along axes of a central square (Brown, 1997; Wesson, 1998; Dalan et al., 2003, pp. 149, 184).

The concept of the ceremonial center remains an important tool for describing the relationship between cosmological systems and the organization of space, as well as the relationship between ritual performances and the geography of the city, especially for social elites. In general, the study of earlier time periods has relied necessarily on the interpretation of the built environment as an expression of such systems, and thus the landscape of the cosmogram appears more often as an overarching principle of social organization. With access to written records, scholars tend to highlight the interactions of stratified social groups under conditions of political struggle and economic development, within the parameters of varying ecosystems.

Temple Urbanism in South Asia. The study of urbanization in South Asia reveals the varying fate of the cosmogram within a variety of social and environmental variables. In the case of the earliest cities within the Harappan (Indus Valley or Saraswati) Civilization, which reached its mature stage between 2500 and 1900 BCE, there are no indications of temples or other religious monuments. Amid hundreds of sites scattered over the largest geographic expanse of any primary urbanization, only the Great Bath complex at Mohenjo-Daro provides a hint of ritual purpose (Possehl, 2002, pp. 148–152). With the resurgence of urban sites in northern India during the early first millennium BCE, despite strong indications of religiosity provided by the "mother goddess" figurines available from many excavations, sacred centers are not visible in the urban fabric within the concentrated habitation patterns of walled cities (Allchin, 1995, pp. 224–225, 268–272). Truly monumental religious architecture emerges only in the late first millennium BCE in the form of Buddhist monastic institutions, which do display, in the stupa complex associated with Buddhist relics, features of the world axis and orientation to the cardinal directions (Mitra, 1971). Early Buddhist monasteries are not urban centers, however; generally they stand in the suburbs of cities or along commercial routes.

We do not encounter the centrally located sacred center in South Asian cities until the late first millennium, with the transition from monastic to temple architecture. All the features of the cosmogram appear in the temple, beginning with the consecration of the *maṇḍala* at its base, with a sacred axis and deities at the cardinal and intermediate points. The foundation and square "womb room" built above, with the main image of the deity at the center and subsidiary images on the outer walls, combine with quadrilateral pillared halls and the surrounding walls of compounds to create a unified geometry of the gods manifested on earth. The towering spire over the central shrine represents the Himalayan mountain home of the gods; the shrine becomes the *vimāna* or chariot of the deity moving through space (Michell, 1977).

By the eleventh century, with an urban revival in full swing throughout the subcontinent, temples were attracting resources from kings, agrarian leaders, and merchants who were looking for markers of legitimacy. In places like Tanjavur or Bhubaneswar, temple gigantism emerged at the heart of the cities; in other areas, multiple temple nodes with surrounding habitation sites created a distributed urban pattern reminiscent of classic Maya urbanism. A distinctive style of urban planning in southern India produced "temple cities" through the accumulation of additional surrounding walls (resulting in compounds hundreds of yards in width), or through the accumulation of concentric streets, each inhabited by different occupational specialists or castes, surrounding the temple grounds (Kulke, 1995; Champakalakshmi, 1996). Within the temple cities, the experience of sacred space provides clues to history and structure. For example, at the temple of Suchindram near the tip of peninsular India, the east-west axis of the complex creates a haptic experience of moving towards the town, connecting the devotee with the collective memory of the town's foundation. The bathing tank beside the temple creates a polarity between the upper, "male" town located around the temple of Śiva and the lower, "female" town located near the bathing tank and the goddess shrine—part of a configuration including four other goddess shrines on the periphery of the city. Festivals at the temple also preserve these urban memories (Pieper, 1980, pp. 65–80).

Between the fourteenth and sixteenth centuries, Vijayanagara, the "city of victory," became capital of an empire uniting southern India within a single political formation for the first time. The archaeological remains of the city include dozens of temples and civic structures enclosed in part within massive defensive walls; combined with literary sources, they provide an unparalleled view of the relationship between sacred and administrative geography. The performance of kingship within the capital exemplified concepts of the ruler as upholder of law, agent of material prosperity, and mediator within cycles of good and evil. Annual alternations between a period of rest, when the court, army, and king resided at the capital, and a period of movement (which included war, pilgrimage, or peaceful missions in the empire and beyond), created specific configurations of action within space. The transition between the two periods witnessed the celebration of the Mahānavami festival that commemorated the propitiation of the goddess Durgā by the epic hero-king Rāma before he marched against the evil Rāvaṇa, involving the display of the king's military strength, the wealth of his household, and his marital alliances. Simultaneously, the festival represented the reorganization of an older sacrality and memories of place. During the early phases of their rule, when they operated as little kings, the Vijayanagara kings had obtained the support of Pampā, a local goddess associated with a small shrine. When the kings emerged as a regional power, they adopted a male deity, Virūpākṣa (a manifestation of the pan-Indian deity, Śiva), as their dynastic emblem. They constructed for this god a temple lying west of a newly laid-out administrative zone and south of their old seat of power, and celebrated his "marriage" to the local goddess, Pampā. When Vijayanagara became the capital of an empire, the kings and their city took on cosmic significance associated with Rāma, an incarnation of the pan-Indian god Viṣṇu. A newly constructed Rāma temple in the royal core divided the "zone of performance" to the east from the "zone of residence" to the west, splitting the king's two bodies, as it were. Displays of the king's office and festivals occurred in the former zone, whereas the latter contained the royal quarters and the old temple dedicated to Śiva, now the protector of the household rather than the kingdom. Road construction now oriented the royal core towards a mythic landscape of Rāma, rather than Śiva or the goddess Pampā. Shrines of various members of the court and of other communities allied themselves with this new orientation, many being located on the main road that led out of the Rāma shrine (Fritz et al., 1984, pp. 146–154).

Courts, Markets, and Performance in South Asia. Muslims had long been active within South Asia, mostly as traders, but Turkish military campaigns from the northwest beginning in 1000 resulted in two additional models of sacred space based on Islam, resembling urban developments typical of southwest Asia (Lapidus, 1969; Bianca, 2000). The first model revolves around the royal or administrative court, and places the mosque *(masjid)* at the center of urban life within the fortified center. This model is visible by the fourteenth century in the capital of the Sultanate at Delhi, including the mosque and spectacular Quṭb Minar in Tughluqabad, as well as the provincial capitals of Islamic successor states such as Bidar, Bijapur, and Golconda in peninsular India. Recent research on old Delhi or Shahjahanabad, founded in the mid-seventeenth century, highlights not only the major public monuments established by an imperial master plan but a variety of subsidiary mosques, gardens, and utilities laid out by political subordinates. A hierarchical matrix of neighborhoods *(mahalla)* including semi-public and private spaces revolves around local mosques, temples, Sikh shrines *(gurdwara),* and, later, Christian churches (Ehlers and Krafft, 2003). The second model is based on the Ṣūfī shrine *(dargāh),* where the memory of a saint's holiness leads to a concentration of buildings around his burial place. An early example is the shrine of Bābā Farīd al-Dīn Ganj-i Shakar in the Punjab town of Pakpattan, where the saint settled down at the site of a river ferry during the thirteenth century. After his death and the passing down of his spiritual power to family successors, his hermitage became the site for monumental architecture, pilgrimage, and a network of social interactions based on economic development or the legitimacy of political leadership within emerging caste formations (Eaton, 2000, pp. 203–246). A similar phenomenon happened in Delhi, where the thirteenth-century hermitage of the saint Niẓām al-Dīn Awliyā' became the focus for a *kasbah* that eventually became part of the expanding city.

The roles of urban commercial interests in the construction of religious centers have become of greater interest to researchers focusing on recent centuries. A study of Chennai (Madras) between the seventeenth and eighteenth centuries identifies three types of dialogue between communities, the marketplace, and sacred sites. The first produced eclectic or generic all-community temples, "a celebration of the common mercantile nature" of the trading communities of the "native" settlement called Georgetown and of the personnel of the British East India Company. The second involved different castes constructing community-only temples, where social rivalry was manifested through processions, flags, or debates over the rights to use certain streets. The third produced temples that served as a "branch offices" of more impressive or older shrines. The three types of temple demonstrate how "foreigners" could find a place in South Asia, and how social difference and similarity could find voice through the vocabulary of religious architecture and community space (Waghorne, 1999a, pp. 654, 682).

Another study of Chennai during colonial and postcolonial times examines the relationship between the more prominent Beeri Chettiar merchants, who were largely

Tamil-speaking worshipers of Śiva, and their rivals, the Komati Chettiars and Balijas, who were Telugu-speaking worshipers of Viṣṇu. Their economic competition led to a number of community conflicts and riots during the eighteenth and nineteenth centuries, and also to the division of Georgetown into a western part occupied by the Komatis and an eastern part occupied by the Beeris. Temples associated with one of these communities, displaying their prestige, wealth, and status, shaped not only the boundaries of "community" but also the forms in which authority functioned. Even today, processions from the Kandasami temple in Park Town, earlier considered a "satellite" area of the Beeri Chettiar community, travel to the older "center" where the community no longer has houses, businesses, or control over the main community temple. Through controversies over the processional route, extensions of it into new areas, and the patronage of the festival, new leaders seek to direct the caste—now a citywide community—from the power base of a new temple that was once spatially peripheral and ritually subordinate (Mines, 1994).

The relayering of spatial and social histories within sacred centers and performances accompanies the growth of cities into manufacturing, technology, and service hubs. For example, the city of Bangalore began as a fort-settlement in the sixteenth century consequent to the decline of Vijayanagara, became a "garden city" in the colonial period, and popularly appears now as "India's Silicon Valley." In the high-tech city, public religious performances remain modes of civic life that attract devotion while preserving urban memories. The Karaga festival, Bangalore's largest religious extravaganza, occurs for nine days in the month of March or April every year. The key moment is the incarnation of the goddess Draupadī, wife of the Pāṇḍava brothers from the epic *Mahābhārata,* who is simultaneously cosmic power *(śakti).* She manifests herself in the form of a sacred icon and within the body of a male priest from the Tigala community who, by carrying the icon, becomes conjoined with her. The annual "birth" of the goddess occurs in Bangalore's Cubbon Park at a small covered well, the remainder of a large lake eliminated by office buildings and sports complexes. Her birth is a reminder of the city's earlier environment—a network of lakes, wells, and ponds—and the processions of the goddess over a nine-day period include visits to the former locations of water bodies, many of which were destroyed through construction activities, pollution, or neglect after 1950. The daily festival processions also visit various Hindu temples and the tomb of the Ṣūfī saint, Hazrat Tawakkal Mastan, signaling the participation of diverse publics in this "theater of the civic." The festival, which conjures for participants an alternative urban landscape, attracts over 100,000 participants on its final day, and is spreading in smaller versions throughout the suburbs of the metropolis (Srinivas, 2001).

Urban Violence and Religion. The focus of this article so far has been on the pacific embedding of the sacred, but religion in the city also seems to cause deadly conflict, providing justification for riots, bombings, and civil war in places such as Beirut, Belfast, or Sarajevo. No single theory can explain all instances of "religious terrorism," but Mark Juergensmeyer (2000) suggests that they are performative and function as "theater." Most of the groups and individuals behind these events work from a "script" of cosmic war, and social struggle is perceived in terms of a spiritual confrontation. They perceive themselves as martyrs and heroes, rather than terrorists, and satanize or depersonify the "enemy." They engineer events for their graphic and emotional impact on witnesses and various audiences through transnational media. The "stage" of theatrical terror is often urban because the events target symbols or hubs of modern societies: embassies, markets, subways, airports. During the 1995 gas attack on the Tokyo subway system by Aum Shinrikyō, for example, bags of poisonous sarin were meant to do the most damage when the train lines converged at Kasumigaseki subway station located close to the main buildings of the government, humiliating national security organizations. The repeated attacks on the World Trade Center in New York City aimed simultaneously at a symbol of global capitalism and at the U. S. government, viewed as an imperialist power.

Perhaps the deepest scholarship on urban religious violence concerns Europe during the Reformation of the sixteenth and seventeenth centuries, when the Wars of Religion pitted Catholic and Protestant against each other. Cities are crucial to all discussions of the Reformation, for it is mostly in urban centers that the leading reforming figures found ministerial positions, publishers, or followings, even if (as in the case of the Peasants' War of 1524–1525) there were important interactions with the countryside. Some of the most egregious cases of religious violence occurred within urban environments: the Anabaptist kingdom of Münster (1534–1535), which evolved into a totalitarian communism before its extermination, or the Saint Bartholomew Day's Massacre (1572), which began in Paris and spread throughout the major cities of France. Theological tracts and city archives have allowed scholars to investigate the players in religious violence—persons from artisanal or manufacturing trades and the urban proletariat, who interacted with clergy, the urban patriciate, and the nobility. During the late twentieth century, numerous local histories have shed light on these struggles to redefine the City of God and the New Jerusalem.

The scholarship ranges between two approaches, one concentrating on intellectual or theological ideas and the other concentrating on social, political, or economic variables. Some authors who try to blend these approaches use the latter as an envelope for discussing the writings of theologians (whose biographies are important parts of analysis) and the deliberations of ministerial councils (e.g. Williams, 1962, pp. 241–298; Strayer, 1976, pp. 206–207). Analyses informed by political economy remain sensitive to theology but focus on class struggle or the attempts by urban communes to preserve their political freedom and order within an incipient world system (Ozment, 1975; Heller, 1991). Influenced by the French *Annales* school, the "linguistic" and "cultural" turns in historiography, and a new social history crossing disciplinary boundaries, Natalie Davis embeds her work within the concrete conditions of production and class but situates the Reformation in Lyon within a symbolic analysis of "the moment of social interaction." Approaching Protestantism and Catholicism as two languages attempting to grasp the challenges of the city, she presents their alternative visions of sacred space, time, and the body as a prerequisite for understanding the "rites" of violence and a concern with pollution (Davis, 1975, pp. 152–188; Davis, 1981; Benedict, 1981, pp. 63–64). Another classic study of the city of Romans demonstrates that the class struggle in the late sixteenth century achieved public expression and was comprehensible for townspeople only through religious idioms that are amenable to analysis through comparative anthropological discourse (Ladurie, 1979). Finally, as part of a movement back to religion through sociology and poststructuralism, a major study of Reformation violence begins with an examination of cases where children committed atrocities. Violence becomes a ritual performance expressing a code, "prophetic because implicated in a prophetic collective consciousness, in a mental eschatological conjuncture, for which it is necessary to research the constitutive schemas" (Crouzet, 1990, vol. 1, p. 93). A continuing stream of studies on the urban Reformation attempt to blend culture and society, theology, and the built environment, within the context of institutions or communities (e.g., Roberts, 1996; Tittler, 1998).

In more recent times, South Asia has been the scene of the world's most intractable "communal" rioting, peaking in 1947, when approximately one million people died in massive demographic shifts, but continuing at the rate of several hundred recorded incidents annually within India. The roots clearly go deep into doctrinal, theological, and social phenomena of the nineteenth century, the intellectual categories developed under colonialism, and the problematic of "secularism" in the postcolonial nation-state. The major religious confrontations since independence (the civil war between Sinhalese and Tamils in Sri Lanka, the 1984 anti-Sikh riots after Indira Gandhi's assassination, the 1992 Hindu-Muslim riots in India after the demolition of the Babri Masjid) clearly occured as responses to political events. The main scholarly issue concerns the many clashes that occur regularly in cities, constituting a persistent source of religious animosity that may erupt into civil war. A veritable industry of research and analysis has grown around this problem, ranging from the official reports of governments, journalists, and citizens' bodies after each occurrence to scholarship from social scientists aimed at understanding the etiology of individual events, common patterns, and the potential for preventative public policy. Detailed studies by Asghar Ali Engineer and associates (e.g., 1984) have demonstrated a complex interaction of sociocultural and economic variables, and a process by which neighborhood incidents lead to violent action, typically with the instigation of male activists and local politicians. Some scholars have attempted to categorize these variables in order to determine the "riot-proneness" of specific communities (Varshney and Wilkinson, 1996), although Paul R. Brass (1997, 2003) also implicates security forces as major players in the production of the "institutionalized" communal riot. Stanley Tambiah (1996) compares incidents with religious overtones in Sri Lanka and India to riots in Pakistan that feature coreligionists, in an attempt to create a comparative understanding of "ethnic" conflict within sociological categories.

Pilgrimages and Religious Movements in the City. If the daily social practices within cities divide, differentiate, or hierarchize the specialized zones frequented by their citizens, then religious pilgrimages, which break down the division between citizens, can work to eliminate class categories and transgress urban boundaries. One could argue, in fact, that the movement through space to participate in collective celebrations is one of the primary manifestations of religiosity and urbanism alike. Many pilgrimage destinations originated as cities or became cities when people clustered around sacred attractions. Mass public transportation has made pilgrimage, this gravitation toward sacred spaces, one of the most significant manifestations of religious localization.

Scholars have been especially interested in the modes through which pilgrimage has altered the understanding of urban space. As Maurice Halbwachs (1992, pp. 193–235) has pointed out in his essay "The Legendary Topography of the Gospels," early Christian embedding of Jerusalem's meaning in the narratives of the Gospels occurred through pilgrims' exercises of spatial localization. A new way of moving through space affirmed the Christian reading of Jerusalem, where places were already commemorated and associated with ancient memories of Jewish history. Christian pilgrimages through Jerusalem, making use of sites already part of collective memorabilia, endowed them with different meanings by situating them within new narratives or actions. In a similar process, the Qurʾān reinscribed an originally pantheistic pilgrimage site, the Kaʿaba, as the activity space of Abraham, linking Islam with Judaism and Christianity, while pilgrimage to Mecca established a series of conceptual categories and somatic experiences that remapped the city and its environs. This process is happening constantly in the contemporary world, as new pilgrimage sites regularly appear alongside the manifestation of charisma by saints and other spiritual figures.

In a phenomenon similar to that which occurred in thirteenth-century India, Sufism is still proving a rich ground for the generation of sacred cities and pilgrimage networks. For instance, Shaykh Aḥmad (Amadou) Bamba (1853–1927) of Senegal rests in a mausoleum in the city of Touba, the early development of which he oversaw. This city and its Great Mosque (inaugurated 1963) is a place of pilgrimage for his disciples, or Mourides. Supported by contributions to its infrastructure from Mourides, in less then a century Touba has become Senegal's second largest city. Devotees have produced a thriving visual culture that includes devotional icons, murals, cosmological architecture, writing, and other forms that grace homes, businesses, vehicles, junkyards, walls, and clothes in the city. This visual culture has also been a crucial part of the social and expressive explosion in the capital, Dakar, since Senegalese independence in 1960, and it features in public debates about identity, memory, and an alternative modernity. Although the saint belongs to the colonial period, he reveals new messages even today for his followers and is a conduit for healing and miracles. The potency of his image works through the transnational chains that link Senegal to other cities through migration, import-export economies, and employment networks (Roberts and Roberts, 2003).

The example of Aḥmad Bamba demonstrates the relevance of pilgrimage phenomena to the study of "religious movements," a branch of scholarship that forms part of a larger "social movements" literature examining intersections between religion and political and cultural processes such as postcolonialism and transnationalism. This scholarship looks at the contemporary proliferation of what are sometimes described as "New Age movements," "new religions," "revitalization movements," and "fundamentalist movements," many of which flourish on urban soil. Some of these movements, such as the Bahāʾīs, propound an avowedly universal message and attempt to create novel, transurban forms of expression. Others, such as the Swaminarayan movement originating in Gujarat (and globalized through Gujarati merchant communities), or evangelical Christian missionary efforts in Asia and Africa, preserve a universal message within an envelope of older "Hindu" or "Christian" traditions.

Japan has been the scene for intensive studies of many "new religions" emerging in the twentieth century under conditions of hyperurbanization. Sōka Gakkai, perhaps the best known, has been most successful at crossing national boundaries and becoming a global organization. It began in the 1930s as a religious organization meant to propagate doctrines of one of the smaller Nichiren Buddhist sects. It grew rapidly as a lay evangelist organization promising meaning and comfort in postwar Japan, becoming a national and global movement with about eight to ten million middle- and upper-class followers (over a million outside Japan) in the 1990s. It sponsors an educational system, art museums, newspapers, and various cultural organizations and is involved in social activism including the fostering of world peace and antiwar activities. It is heavily urban-based (tightly organized into prefectural, city, district, and block groups). Members are encouraged to improve their material conditions and also spend time in daily prayer, meetings of the groups, and proselytizing. The Sōka Gakkai belief is that religion must be the basis of a moral and just society; social institutions need to be purified; and modern, rationalized Buddhist beliefs must fuse with all features of society. Despite the continued embedding of ritual within a Japanese Buddhist format, the envelope of rational peacefulness and acceptance of material success have allowed Sōka Gakkai to attract members from a variety of cultural and national backgrounds (Metraux, 1996).

Some religious movements support distinct "ethnic" identities even when they try to avoid them, contributing to or perpetuating a layer of cultural segmentation within urban environments. The movement dedicated to the Indian guru Sathya Sai Baba (b. 1926) has expanded to include perhaps ten million people worldwide, most of them in urban areas. In a study of this movement in Trinidad, Morton Klass (1991) focused on its roles among urban and suburban Indian (and Hindu) Trinidadians who form the overwhelming majority of devotees. He points out that there are political differences between Indian Trinidadians and Afro-Trinidadians attributable to different notions of their cultural resources and pancultural affiliations; Afro-Trinidadians, therefore, remain a minority in the Sai Baba movement. A separate study of the Malaysian Sai Baba movement in the city of Kuala Lumpur in the mid- to late 1990s explored the way the Indian-dominated leadership attempts to include Chinese devotees. A nonsectarian and multiethnic profile including Chinese devotees "enhances the hope which this neo-Hindu movement offers to members of the marginalized Indian minority to win an audience among the Malay majority and thus achieve recognition as the rightful proprietors of an eternal, all-subsuming and unifying spiritual vision." Nonetheless, ethnic boundaries in Kuala Lumpur tend to be reproduced (Kent, 2000, p. 5).

MODERN IMAGINARIES AND URBAN RELIGIOSITY. Are there religious imaginations and practices distinctive to contemporary cities? In *Gods of the City* (1999) Robert Orsi argues that the dynamic interaction between religious traditions, contemporary cityscapes, and their social conditions results in specific maps, styles, and idioms of "urban religion." In *The Madonna of 115th Street* (1985), Orsi examines street behavior, processions, and festivals, like the *festa* of the Madonna of 115th Street in New York's Italian Harlem, as modes of boundary-making by immigrants, the creation and negotiation of ethnic identities, the production of community, and the theater or social drama of urban lives. Others, looking at recent diasporas in American cities, have examined strategies through which immigrant groups make sense religiously of an urban landscape that differs considerably from the spaces they left. Thus, Mama Lola, a Brooklyn Vodou priestess discussed by Karen McCarthy Brown (1999), travels back and forth between Haiti and Brooklyn and maintains social and spiritual loyalties in two places. She, like others, transposes Haitian places onto New York: Brooklyn's Prospect Park sometimes functions as the sacred forest of Vodou rituals. Such religious identities may retreat into basements, or are practiced behind closed doors, while signs of more acceptable Catholic identity appear publicly. The more affluent South Asian diaspora in the United States, normally with greater social and cultural capital than the Haitians, construct temples as a largely suburban phenomenon located close to freeways rather than within an "ethnic" part of the city (Waghorne, 1999b). Unlike the temple in India where one god or goddess or a sectarian tradition usually predominates, in the United States several deities live in harmony under one roof, in a manner that parallels the multiple religious affiliations of their suburban devotees.

Globalization and economic restructuring, combined with massive shifts of population, have reconfigured "place-based religious identities" in cities throughout the world. For example, in the small town of Dacula in Gwinnett County, Georgia—the fastest-growing county in the United States in the 1980s—one study has explored the relationship of urban deconcentration to the institutional dynamics of Christian congregations. Until the early 1980s, eleven out of twenty-four churches (such as Pleasant Hill Methodist and the black Mt. Zion Methodist) still traced their origins to the time before the town's founding, and five were founded subsequently. Within a period of thirteen years, however, eight new congregations were established, almost "as if locals had placed a sign on Highway 316 designating the area 'Church Growth Parkway'" (Eiesland, 2000, p. 48). As industrial and corporate jobs mushroomed around transportation infrastructure, the new congregations evolved strategies for attracting members, ranging from an exuberant mega-church to specialized ministries. Meanwhile, in Africa, Kano in northern Nigeria changed during the 1970s from a mercantile center into a large industrial metropolis with new suburbs growing around the old walled city. The crash of oil prices in the early 1980s resulted in a recession that produced challenges for local Muslim identity and practice in the face of state-based corruption and capitalist commodification. Michael Watts (1996) describes the rise of a fundamentalist (though not antimodern) Muslim leader in Kano among subaltern classes, such as migrant workers, for whom the state and its elites symbolized moral bankruptcy. The two paths of urban economic development elicit, on the one hand, the marketing of religion, and on the other, the use of religion as a source of revitalization.

Religion plays an important role in the heritage politics of various cities as they wrestle with the rise of the nation-state, socialism, democracy, globalization, and explosive demographic growth. Istanbul, for instance, has been a world city since the fourth century, serving as an imperial capital for the Roman, Byzantine, and Ottoman empires and a major commercial node for Afro-Eurasia. Just before World War I, it had about a million people—a majority non-Muslim—including many Italian, Turkish, Greek, or Tartar inhabitants. Muslims, Christians, and Jews coexisted without intermarriage under Ottoman administrators, their religious and cultural lives compartmentalized within corporate entities. When the state adopted the project of modernization, binary constructs (East versus West, Islam versus Christianity, Turk versus non-Turk, local versus global) began to dominate public discourse. During the early twentieth century, anticolonial and nationalist policies took on ethnic content, and religion rationalized ethnic purification of Jews, Armenians, and Greeks. Thus, the vast majority of Istanbul's citizens were Muslims in the 1980s, when the state adopted a strategy aimed at transforming it into a world city. The capture of the city government by an Islamicist party that pushed for changes in public culture (such as dress codes for women) became an embarrassment for an avowedly secularist nation-state, aligned with financial interests in a concern that Islamicist culture could jeopardize Turkey's membership in the European Union. In a city with multiple pasts, the question of historic preservation during urban renewal projects became a deeply contested issue involving the interplay of nationalist and religious tropes. The nationalist discourse pushing for urban renewal viewed the neighborhood of Pera, for example, as a symbol of a non-Turkish "Europe in Istanbul," while Islamicists advocated the destruction of older buildings (some of considerable architectural merit) for the building of a mosque (Keyder, 1999). How the inhabitants of the city appeared and behaved in public and the nature of their buildings remained issues intimately connected with religious conceptions.

Urban planning thus struggles with the reinsertion of sacred spaces by several publics. In her study of Aboriginal claims to space in Perth, Australia, Jane Jacobs (1996, p. 127) provides another viewpoint on political agitations that "reactivated a (pre-) modern knowing of space within the specific conditions of modernity." The contests she describes concerned an area near the Swan River in Perth that had been used previously by the colonial government to establish a depot in 1833 excluding the Aborigines. In the 1980s this area was developed by corporate interests into a brewery and a hotel chain with theaters, office spaces, and a theme park—the quintessential signs of the service economy. Laws concerning Aboriginal land in Australia had tended to designate territory as sacred only when it was far away from urban centers, but Aboriginal claims in this case located the spiritual firmly within the area of the Swan Brewery. Aborigines occupied the area for a while in 1989. While their action ultimately failed and the area was given over to development, Jacobs argues that the Aboriginal occupation not only brought the sacred back to the city but set off an "anxious" politics of occupation by the government and developers. The controversy between "beer, work, tourism and sport" and "urban dreamings," as Jacobs categorizes it, puts into relief the binary imaginings of planners and the unpredictable potential for sacred upsurges within the city.

Rather than a steady decline of religion under conditions of urban anomie, we are witnessing the rise of spiritual leaders and religious movements who claim an authority that rivals the authority of nations, transnational corporations, and secular ideologies. For many believers among a world population that will be mostly urban after 2007 (United Nations, 2002, p. 5), religion provides alternative sources of value, critiques of capitalism, and avenues of cultural modernity.

SEE ALSO Marduk; Maya Religion; Mesopotamian Religions, overview articles; Mosque, article on Architectural Aspects; Olmec Religion; Pilgrimage, overview article; Violence.

BIBLIOGRAPHY

Allchin, F. Raymond. *The Archaeology of Early Historic South Asia: The Emergence of Cities and States.* Cambridge, U.K., and New York, 1995.

Arellano Hernández, A., M. Ayala Falcón, B. de la Fuente, M. de la Garza, L. Staines Cicero, and B. Olmedo Vera. *The Mayas of the Classical Period.* Translated by Kim López Mills and Sergio Negrete. Milan, 1999.

Benedict, Philip. *Rouen during the Wars of Religion.* Cambridge, U.K., 1981.

Bianca, Stefano. *Urban Form in the Arab World: Past and Present.* London and New York, 2000.

Bottéro, Jean. *Mesopotamia: Writing, Reasoning, and the Gods.* Translated by Zainab Bahrani and Marc Van De Mieroop. Chicago and London, 1992.

Brass, Paul R. *Theft of an Idol: Text and Context in the Representation of Collective Violence.* Princeton, N.J., 1997.

Brass, Paul R. *The Production of Hindu-Muslim Violence in Contemporary India.* New Delhi, 2003.

Brown, James A. "The Archaeology of Ancient Religion in the Eastern Woodlands." *Annual Review of Anthropology* 26 (1997): 465–485.

Brown, Karen McCarthy. "Staying Grounded in a High-Rise Building: Ecological Dissonance and Ritual Accommodation in Haitian Vodou." In *Gods of the City: Religion and the American Urban Landscape,* edited by Robert A. Orsi, pp. 79–102. Bloomington and Indianapolis, Ind., 1999.

Champakalakshmi, Radha. *Trade, Ideology, and Urbanization: South India 300 B.C. to A.D. 1300.* New Delhi, 1996.

Cowgill, George L. "Teotihuacán: Cosmic Glories and Mundane Needs." In *The Social Construction of Ancient Cities,* edited by Monica L. Smith, pp. 37–55. Washington, D.C., and London, 2003.

Crawford, Harriet. *Sumer and the Sumerians.* Cambridge, U.K., 1991.

Crouzet, Denis. *Les guerriers de Dieu: La violence au temps des troubles de religion, vers 1525–vers 1610.* 2 vols. Seyssel, France, 1990.

Dalan, Rinita A., George R. Holley, William I. Woods, Harold W. Watters Jr., and John A. Koepke. *Envisioning Cahokia: A Landscape Perspective.* Dekalb, Ill., 2003.

Davis, Natalie Zemon. *Society and Culture in Early Modern France.* Stanford, Calif., 1975.

Davis, Natalie Zemon. "The Sacred and the Body Social in Sixteenth-Century Lyon." *Past and Present* 90 (1981): 40–70.

Eaton, Richard M. *Essays on Islam and Indian History.* New Delhi, 2000.

Ehlers, Eckart, and Thomas Krafft, eds. *Shâjahânâbâd/Old Delhi: Tradition and Colonial Change.* 2d ed. New Delhi, 2003.

Eiesland, Nancy L. *A Particular Place: Urban Restructuring and Religious Ecology in a Southern Exurb.* New Brunswick, N.J., and London, 2000.

Engineer, Asghar Ali, ed. *Communal Riots in Post-Independence India.* Hyderabad, India, 1984.

Escobédo, Hector, and Juan Antonio Valdés. "Archaeology of the Central Lowlands: Tikal." In *Maya Civilization,* edited by Peter Schmidt, Mercedes de la Garza, and Enrique Nalda, pp. 356–371. London, 1998.

Franke, Sabina. "Kings of Akkad: Sargon and Naram-Sin." In *Civilizations of the Ancient Near East,* vol. 2, edited by Jack M. Sasson, pp. 831–841. New York, 1995.

Fritz, John M., George Michell, and M. S. Nagaraja Rao. *Where Kings and Gods Meet: The Royal Centre at Vijayanagara, India.* Tucson, Ariz., 1984.

Grube, Nikolai, ed. *Maya: Divine Kings of the Rain Forest.* Cologne, 2000.

Halbwachs, Maurice. *On Collective Memory.* Edited and translated by Lewis A. Coser. Chicago and London, 1992.

Heller, Henry. *Iron and Blood: Civil Wars in Sixteenth-Century France.* Montreal and Kingston, Ontario, 1991.

Jacobs, Jane. *Edge of Empire: Postcolonialism and the City.* London and New York, 1996.

Jacobsen, Thorkild. *The Treasures of Darkness: A History of Mesopotamian Religion.* New Haven, Conn., and London, 1976.

Juergensmeyer, Mark. *Terror in the Mind of God: The Global Rise of Religious Violence.* Berkeley, Calif., 2000.

Kappelman, Julia Guernsey. "Sacred Geography at Izapa and the Performance of Rulership." In *Landscape and Power in Ancient Mesoamerica,* edited by Rex Koontz, Kathryn Reese-Taylor, and Annabeth Headrick, pp. 81–111. Boulder, Colo., 2001.

Kent, Alexandra. "Creating Divine Unity: Chinese Recruitment in the Sathya Sai Baba Movement of Malaysia." *Journal of Contemporary Religion* 15, no. 1 (January 2000): 5–27.

Kenyon, Kathleen M. *Archaeology in the Holy Land.* 3d ed. New York and Washington, D.C., 1970.

Keyder, Çaglar, ed. *Istanbul: Between the Global and the Local.* Oxford, 1999.

Klass, Morton. *Singing with Sai Baba: The Politics of Revitalization in Trinidad.* Boulder, Colo., 1991.

Kulke, Hermann. "The Early and the Imperial Kingdom: A Processural Model of Integrative State Formation in Early Medieval India." In *The State in India, 1000–1700,* edited by Hermann Kulke, pp. 233–262. Delhi, 1995.

Ladurie, Emmanuel Le Roy. *Carnival in Romans.* Translated by Mary Feeney. New York, 1979.

Lapidus, Ira M., ed. *Middle Eastern Cities: A Symposium on Ancient, Islamic, and Contemporary Middle Eastern Urbanism.* Berkeley, Calif., and Los Angeles, 1969.

Marcus, Joyce. "On the Nature of the Mesoamerican City." In *The Ancient Civilizations of Mesoamerica,* edited by Michael E. Smith and Marilyn A. Masson, pp. 49–82. Malden, Mass., 2000.

Mellaart, James. *Çatal Hüyük: A Neolithic Town in Anatolia.* London, 1967.

Metraux, Daniel A. "The Sōka Gakkai: Buddhism and the Creation of a Harmonious and Peaceful Society." In *Engaged Buddhism: Buddhist Liberation Movements in Asia,* edited by Christopher S. Queen and Sallie B. King, pp. 365–400. Albany, N.Y., 1996.

Michell, George. *The Hindu Temple: An Introduction to Its Meaning and Forms.* Bombay, 1977.

Mines, Mattison. *Public Faces, Private Voices: Community and Individuality in South India.* Berkeley, Calif., and Los Angeles, 1994.

Mitra, Debala. *Buddhist Monuments.* Calcutta, 1971.

Orsi, Robert A. *The Madonna of 115th Street: Faith and Community in Italian Harlem, 1880–1950.* New Haven, Conn., and London, 1985.

Orsi, Robert A., ed. *Gods of the City: Religion and the American Urban Landscape.* Bloomington, Ind., 1999.

Ozment, Steven E. *The Reformation in the Cities: The Appeal of Protestantism to Sixteenth-Century Germany and Switzerland.* New Haven, Conn., and London, 1975.

Pieper, Jan. "The Spatial Structure of Suchindram." In *Ritual Space in India: Studies in Architectural Anthropology,* edited by Jan Pieper, pp. 65–80. London, 1980.

Possehl, Gregory L. *The Indus Civilization: A Contemporary Perspective.* Walnut Creek, Calif., 2002.

Roberts, Penny. *A City in Conflict: Troyes during the French Wars of Religion.* Manchester, U.K., and New York, 1996.

Roberts, Allen F., and Mary Nooter Roberts. *A Saint in the City: Sufi Arts of Urban Senegal.* Los Angeles, 2003.

Šprajc, Ivan. "Perpetuating Celestial Order in an Earthly Environment: Astronomy in Mesoamerica around 1000." In *The World in the Year 1000,* edited by James Heitzman and Wolfgang Schenkluhn, pp. 87–102. Lanham, Md., 2004.

Srinivas, Smriti. *Landscapes of Urban Memory: The Sacred and the Civic in India's High-Tech City.* Minneapolis, Minn., 2001.

Strayer, James M. *Anabaptists and the Sword.* 2d ed. Lawrence, Kans., 1976.

Tambiah, Stanley J. *Leveling Crowds: Ethnonationalist Conflicts and Collective Violence in South Asia.* Berkeley, Calif., 1996.

Tittler, Robert. *The Reformation and the Towns in England: Politics and Political Culture, c. 1540–1640.* Oxford, 1998.

United Nations Department of Economic and Social Affairs, Population Division. *World Urbanization Prospects: The 2001 Revision.* New York, 2002.

Van De Mieroop, Marc. *The Ancient Mesopotamian City.* Oxford, 1997.

Varshney, Ashutosh, and Steven I. Wilkinson. *Hindu-Muslim Riots, 1960–1993: New Findings, Possible Remedies.* New Delhi, 1996.

Waghorne, Joanne Punzo. "The Diaspora of the Gods: Hindu Temples in the New World System, 1640–1800." *Journal of Asian Studies* 58, no. 3 (August 1999a): 648–686.

Waghorne, Joanne Punzo. "The Hindu Gods in a Split-Level World: The Sri Siva-Vishnu Temple in Suburban Washington, D.C." In *Gods of the City: Religion and the American Urban Landscape,* edited by Robert A. Orsi, pp. 103–130. Bloomington, Ind., 1999b.

Watts, Michael. "Mapping Identities: Place, Space, and Community in an African City." In *The Geography of Identity,* edited by Patricia Yaeger, pp. 59–97. Ann Arbor, Mich., 1996.

Wesson, Cameron B. "Mississippian Sacred Landscapes: The View from Alabama." In *Mississippian Towns and Sacred Spaces: Searching for an Architectural Grammar,* edited by R. Barry Lewis and Charles Stout, pp. 93–122. Tuscaloosa, Ala., and London, 1998.

Wheatley, Paul. *The Pivot of the Four Quarters: A Preliminary Enquiry into the Origins and Character of the Ancient Chinese City.* Chicago, 1971.

Wiggermann, F. A. M. "Theologies, Priests, and Worship in Ancient Mesopotamia." In *Civilizations of the Ancient Near East,* vol. 3, edited by Jack M. Sasson, pp. 1857–1870. New York, 1995.

Williams, George Huntston. *The Radical Reformation.* Philadelphia, 1962.

JAMES HEITZMAN (2005)
SMRITI SRINIVAS (2005)

CIVIL RELIGION. The word *religion* is derived from two Latin terms, *religio* and *religare.* The first term designates a quality of prudence, regard, and seriousness as an attitude toward ancestral founders. The second term means to bind, to tie—as a mode that gives a specificity, concreteness, and cohesion—an identity to a human community. The binding is always related to a myth that reveals the nature and meaning of ancestors who were involved in the founding of the city.

This meaning of religion can be seen in ancient foundings of cities and towns. In his book *The Ancient City* (1873) Fustel de Coulanges described religions associated with founding Greek and Roman city-states. This sense of founding took into account the ancestors and gods that existed prior to the organization of the city. Joseph Rykwert's *The Idea of a Town* (1976) provides a similar discussion of sacred symbols, rituals, and meanings that were essential to the foundation of Greek and Roman communities.

The term *civil religion* was first introduced by Jean-Jacques Rousseau in his book *The Social Contract* (1762). Rousseau used the term in the context of the European Enlightenment and the revolutionary movement toward democratic statehood. The concept applied to the ordering and organization of modern democracies preceeding the French Revolution and the overthrowing of religious and political hierarchies as the ordering principles of the state. Rousseau, as did many founders of modern democracy, nevertheless thought that a shared sense of essential moral and religious beliefs must still serve to provide cohesion for the general citizenry of the French nation. Such beliefs were girded in Enlightenment Christianity and consisted of "essential" prescriptive values:

1. the idea of a benevolent deity,
2. the existence of an afterlife,
3. the faith in justice and divine retribution,
4. sacred correspondence of the social contract with the state's laws.

Rousseau was writing before the French Revolution and was attempting to locate a basis for the integrative principle of society that would replace the monarchy and the church. But even after their revolutions democratic European states still possessed the residue of ancient traditions embedded in their histories and institutions. In other words, they were already "a people" prior to the foundation of democratic institutions. The difference between European and American identities was noted by Alexis de Tocqueville when he toured the United States in the 1830s. "Up to the present," he noted, "I don't see a trace of what we generally consider faiths, such as customs, ancient traditions, and the power of memories" (Pierson, 1938, p. 153).

None of these cultural forms of customs, ancient traditions, or the power of memories was present in the American nation; thus the basis for a civil society was always rather tenuous. What was present was a historical style of Protestantism, which was embraced by the majority population. Although the U.S. Constitution denies the meaning of any positive religion as the "religion of the Republic" and all specific religions are entitled to have the right of full expression and freedom, it was assumed by the "majority" of Americans that the proper lens of interpretation for important national issues was through a Protestant point of view.

Introduction of "Civil Religion" in the American Academy. Will Herberg's 1960 work *Protestant, Catholic, Jew* was an attempt to break through this Protestant sense of America by offering an alternative and plural understanding of the nature of American religiosity. The title of his book is taken from one of the popular identifiers on identification tags of American soldiers in World War II. Along with the soldier's serial number and blood type was one of these religious identifiers. An apocryphal story is told that if a soldier declared himself or herself an atheist, then his or her tag was stamped "p" for Protestant. This story goes to the heart of the matter, for the designation was only a sign of religion and carried with it no serious meaning or commitment. The designation expressed a sentimentality associated with religious rhetoric rather than any efficacious religious meaning.

Robert Bellah's article "Civil Religion in America," published in *Daedalus* in 1967, brought to the surface the problematical nature of the foundational principles of American society. Bellah made clear that his article grew out of a concern occasioned by the public debate that had grown out of the candidacy of Senator John F. Kennedy for president of the United States. Kennedy was a Roman Catholic, and therefore the issue of both his adherence to a hierarchical religious church whose administrative center lay outside of the United States as well as the fact that he was not a member of the Protestant majority raised questions about the de facto meaning of what constitutes an American.

As a sociologist, Bellah focused his meaning of American civil religion in the symbols and rituals that provided a sense of cohesion and continuity for Americans. He drew attention to the founding documents and the rhetoric of the American Republic in the Declaration of Independence and the Constitution, which he argued made possible the existence of a civil society in the United States. He pointed to Abraham Lincoln's Second Inaugural Address and Gettysburg Address as examples of civil religion. In particular the first few presidents had set the tenor in their words and deeds. Bellah argued that American civil religion, although derived from Christianity, is not to be equated with a positive religion. The "God of the Republic" can be characterized as having more of a concern for "order, law, and right, than to salvation and love" (Demerath and Hammond, p. 172). This God is active in history and shows a "special concern for America." (Demerath and Hammond, p. 172). A higher law and a transcendent force exist by which to judge the political processes of the American people (Demerath and Hammond, p. 172).

In a subsequent discussion, "American Civil Religion in the 1970's," published in the *Anglican Theological Review*, Bellah asserted that he had invented the notion of "civil religion" as a social science category of interpretation, stating, "In a sense, and not in a trivial sense, civil religion in America existed from the moment the winter 1967 issue of *Daedalus* was printed" (Bellah, 1973, p. 8). He admitted that there had been other interpretations on the topic prior to the publication of his article, but he took credit for the specific contextualization of this notion. Prominent in these prior interpretations of an American religion was the American church historian Sidney E. Mead, who referred to the United States as a "nation with the soul of a church," a phrase he took from G. K. Chesterton (Mead, 1975). Mead showed that while there was nothing like a "church" in the Constitution of the first pluralistic and "secular" democracy, there was a strong tradition of voluntary association imbibed through the Puritan Dissenters in the seventeenth century and early eighteenth century that was not to be seen as entirely at odds with the beliefs in popular sovereignty later propounded by the likes of Thomas Jefferson and Benjamin Franklin.

In *The Nation with the Soul of a Church* (1975) Mead argues that a principle of religious freedom began with the Lutheran Reformation and continued through a variety of Calvinist sects. The American sects emphasized covenant theology, which resembled social contracts and reflected the idea that voluntary consent of the governed was the basis of all good government. The Puritans were able to wed this democratic formulation to a sense of chosenness, with their Calvinist notions of "election" or sainthood as the condition of the governing bodies or theocracy. Thus voluntary consent to the laws of the Puritan state coalesced with consent to divine laws and "destiny" for a "peculiar people." Mead's formulation is based upon the history of American religion from the Puritans through American denominationalism into the mid–twentieth century. He discerns that through this history Americans have been able at various times to appeal to a meaning of their destiny as it is revealed beyond the empirical historical situations. They have been within these spaces at various moments able to discern unique and qualitative meanings of freedom as they relate to the very constitution of an American self.

Historical Background and Manifestations of American Civil Religion. Catherine Albanese (1999), following closely upon Mead, has delineated several modes civil religion has taken during American history. She has shown that the Enlightenment and Puritan traditions combined to shape the rhetoric, symbols, and structure of American civil religion. The Puritans laid the groundwork for a national symbology that could be drawn upon by subsequent revolutionaries and later generations of Americans in times of war and crises.

John Winthrop imagined the 1630 Puritan crossing of the Atlantic in terms of a biblical typology—the crossing was a reenactment of the Exodus story of Israelites from Egyptian captivity and the crossing of the Red Sea. He compared the colony to the "chosen" people and a "city set upon a hill"; their duty was to be a light unto Europe so all could follow their example. The American people may inherit what Albanese calls a "melodramatic" edge from the Puritans along with a strong sense of suffering and guilt (Albanese, 1999, p. 439). Perhaps the guilt was occasioned by their departure from Britain; perhaps their sense of failure stemmed from the imminent British Reformation, which as Perry Miller claimed in his famous book *Errand into the Wilderness*, may have left uncertainty as to whether their "errand" was not more similar to that of an errand boy (Miller, 1956, p. 3). In any case, the Puritans developed their chosenness with gravity, guilt, and a sense of the imminence of their own failure and depravity, the latter of which was also grounded in the Calvinist focus on predestination and original sin.

Although the Puritan focus on innate depravity would seem to be at odds with the language of the Declaration of Independence, during the eighteenth century the situation of Puritans had changed. As can be witnessed in the sermons of the Northampton clergyman Jonathan Edwards, the experience of conversion or chosenness gained closer proximity to a language of the senses and nature. According to many critics, the First Great Awakening (1730–1740) that Edwards initiated can be seen as a forerunner to the American Revolution. To be sure, for many itinerant preachers and the general populace involved in mass revivalist democracy, the focus on a sensuous experience of conversion often converged with Puritan millennialism and a sense of imminent natural redemption of the American land as the "Promised Land" and the place in which the new millennium would begin. While Jonathan Edwards maintained a balance between millennialist rhetoric and the ordering of the township space of Northampton into a space for cultural expressions of religious concern, in the hands of those less concerned with local communities the typologies could be adapted to the Enlightenment belief in individual and national rationality, prosperity, and progress.

Benjamin Franklin may be one such figure who recognized the utility of revivalism for the creation of moral and "civil" citizens. Natural law seemed to coincide with God's law. And God, for the Enlightenment founders, was understood within the register of deism as a benevolent and "great governor." Freemasonry, a semisecret society, flourished as a method for the spread of deism and "fifty-two of the fifty-six signers of the Declaration of Independence were Masons" (Albanese, 1999, p. 440). During the Revolutionary War, the Puritan rhetoric of chosenness converged with natural law, and drawing on Puritan symbols, many revolutionaries depicted themselves as involved in a millennial battle with Great Britain. This adaptation of Puritan rhetoric and typologies to "America," or what Ralph Waldo Emerson called "Nature's Nation," increased during the nineteenth century after the Louisiana Purchase and the expansion of the continent. As Giles Gunn pointed out, Sidney Mead claimed that with the Second Great Awakening came a "reactionary evangelical enthusiasm" that "sever[ed] religious life in America from intellectual life" (Gunn, 1992, p. 225). Indeed the varieties of denominations and sects that developed during this period seemed to turn inward and focus on individual purity. Nonetheless in the nineteenth century expansion gave impetus to the continuation of Enlightenment notions of progress adapted to millennialism.

American civil religion finds its most intense expression during periods of crises and wars. The "War of 1812, like the Revolution, was a holy war" (Albanese, 1999, p. 450). Moreover in 1845 John L. O'Sullivan coined the term "manifest destiny" to justify American expansion and the annexation of Texas. The Civil War furthered the attachment of millennial rhetoric associated with New England Puritans to the Civil War between the North and the South. Julia Ward Howe's "The Battle Hymn of the Republic" was sung with its martial rhythms and its casting of the South as the anti-Christ over which the righteous North would prevail (Albanese, 1999, p. 451). During this time there was also a construction of the sacredness of the "founding fathers." Lincoln's Gettysburg Address was, however, one attempt to interrogate the meaning of the American Revolution in terms of the promises for civil religion that attended to the ordering of the nation. In the twentieth century many critics argued that there was a decline in the efficacy of American civil religion. Through ceremonies like Memorial Day, an attempt was made to connect Americans to their foundations, but "as veterans began to die, a bond with the past was broken" (Albanese, 1999, p. 455). Although civil religion may have emerged in times of "trial" through successive generations, and especially during the Vietnam War, Albanese claims that the "many" of the United States were losing faith in the "oneness" that civil religion symbolized.

E Pluribus Unum: Founding a "Novus Ordo Seclorum." At this juncture where the story of American civil religion seems to end, the notion of the many and the one needs to be revisited. In addition to her delineation of the various historical forms of civil religion in the United States, Albanese paid attention to the "religion" and rituals of the founding. She noted the conscious imitation of Rome and Roman rituals in the festivals and early celebrations of the founding of the nation. A mingling of Puritan and Roman elements served in the symbolism and rituals surrounding George Washington. He was both a Moses figure and a Roman hero, who like "Cincinnatus, the Roman general, . . . left his plough to fight for the country and then, when the task was done, had dropped the sword to return to his farm" (Albanese, 1999, p. 443). In Albanese's opinion the Roman allusions, such as the motto *e pluribus unum,* were an attempt to capture the spirit of a republic that would attend to the plurality of creeds and nations united by the oneness of a state.

In another vein Hannah Arendt also analyzed the meaning of the founding of the American Republic. She noted that the language of the founding works almost in a formulaic manner as it determines a structure of meaning and constitution. Arendt undertook a philosophical analysis of the language of the founding as a basis for the civil religion in the United States. Arendt's analysis shows that though the American Republic was the first of the modern democracies, its founding could not totally shed the problem of founding, as Rykwert and de Coulanges set forth in ancient cultures. For in the founding of a modern state the revolutionaries underwent a unique experience of novelty and the issue of beginning anew. "Novus Ordo Seclorum" (a new secular order) is the title of a chapter in Arendt's *On Revolution* (1963); it is the Latin motto on the Great Seal of the United States and on the American dollar bill. Arendt clarified that if the founders' attitude was "religious," that sense of religion was closer to *religare,* which consists of binding "back to a beginning." For the Romans that beginning entailed a binding "to the beginning of Roman history, and the foundation of the eternal city" (Arendt, 1963, p. 198). The modern revolutionaries faced the problem of a free act, which, in their case, did not consist of binding oneself to a "distant past" (as in Rome). Rather, they faced the problem of manifesting the specific novelty of the "American" situation. Their beginning needed to account for the plurality and the aboriginal ordering of the land that immediately surrounded them. This means that if they were to legitimate a foundation premised on revolution, they would have to provide spaces for the voluntary association and public debate to continue.

While the founders did provide a "constitution," they were not as successful in providing spaces for the spirit of revolution and freedom to continue. According to Arendt, even the founders immediately worried that their foundation would encourage apathy. While the ritual of "voting" might serve to activate some of the population in the spirit of political freedom, it was too infrequent an occurrence to maintain the revolutionary spirit of the Republic. Many critics have pointed out that this failure to provide spaces for novelty to continue to appear coincides with the retention of slavery in the founding of the Republic. While slavery was one of the main topics of discussion during the Constitutional Convention, it was not mentioned in the Declaration of Independence, and the mention of it in the Constitution was the basis for the famous three-fifths compromise. This compromise at the founding of the Republic on the meaning of freedom was repeated throughout American history. Thus one might return to the critical debate on the decline in the commitment to American civil religion in the twentieth century, most aptly characterized by Bellah's title of his 1975 book *The Broken Covenant.* From this perspective, that sense of betrayal of not only the authenticity of the words but also the acts of founding a revolutionary democracy has been present for much longer.

CRITICAL UNDERSTANDINGS OF AMERICAN CIVIL RELIGION. In his essay in the *Anglican Theological Review,* Bellah in response to his critics made it clear that it had not been his intent to define civil religion as a good thing. He said, "Like all things human, civil religion is sometimes good and sometimes bad, but in any case, it seems likely to be with us for a very long time" (Bellah, 1973, p. 10). Almost every notion of civil religion or one of its predecessors or derivatives has been established with a positive quality while allowing for ambiguities that move toward a negativity. Arendt has pointed to the fact that this quality of civil religion was present in the founding itself. Mead noted that this negative quality might be found in the emphasis Americans have given to space over time. Given such an emphasis, Americans seem to have had little patience with memories—with the meaning of the actual events that took place in the land. While Herberg's formulation of Protestant-Catholic-Jew attempted to show that an Americanness could be expressed in any of these forms, the formula was always in danger of turning into an innocuous triviality because any of these designations or all of them together might be understood as a kind of religion in general (see Demerath and Hammond, 1969, p. 172).

Ambiguity around the notion of American civil religion persists, and the attempt to connect it to normative or positive religious expressions has been unsatisfactory. The reason for this might be located in the problematic of founding a revolutionary democracy. Arendt argued in subsequent reflections on the American Revolution in her book *Willing* (1978) that the revolution itself created a "hiatus" or a radical break with the past; the hiatus is the revolutionary time of possibility and freedom, a space in between the "no more" of the old order and the "not yet" of the new (Arendt, 1978, p. 204). The problem of the constitution of a civil religion based on a revolutionary spirit that had detached itself from the meaning of ancestors or sacred space may be viewed next to the problems of constituting a religion of the Republic that would also take into account the presence of aboriginal people, Native Americans, and African Americans. In terms of revolutionary beginnings and civil religion, a long and hopeful, while often prophetic and judgmental, tradition has existed with African Americans.

And yet these traditions have for the most part been left out of most formal discussion of American civil religion. Charles H. Long noted this exclusion in his essay "Civil Rights—Civil Religion: Visible People and Invisible Religion" (1974). This essay is included in the collection *American Civil Religion* edited by Russell E. Richey and Donald G. Jones in 1974 with the approaching bicentennial of the signing of the Declaration of Independence. Bellah, Mead, and Herberg contributed as well. Here Long noted that the issue of "American" civil religion brought to the fore questions of what it means to be American and in particular what it means to be invisible in the telling of the national story, which has gained a well-nigh "cosmogonic language, a language of beginnings; it structures the American myth of beginnings, and has continued to express the synchronic dimensions of American cultural life since that time" (Long, 1974, p. 214). From this perspective, the issue of American civil religion is one of contestation, "concealment," and exclusion in the telling of a myth of origins.

Myth, as Long notes, is a "true story," and African American versions of American civil religion often used the language of religio-political symbols while defining another space for freedom of expression through music, art, and the cultural redefining of a transnational "America" to emerge. This tradition begins at least as early as the black music of the spirituals and the oral traditions of speaking and preaching, later finding written expression as *Walker's Appeal in Four Articles* (1829), in which David Walker challenged the Jeffersonian natural hierarchies and "Nature's God."

A sense of importance is also brought to Africa in the creation of the United States, while European Christians were challenged on their hypocritical understandings of an "equality" before God. Slave revolts, such as those led by Gabriel Prosser and Denmark Vesey and especially the 1831 revolt led by Nat Turner, often relied on biblical typologies of the Israelites in Egypt, and the leaders became Moses figures for their people. While an eschatological and often violent protest tradition emerged to challenge the white Protestant civil religious tradition in the United States, Frederick Douglass and other black abolitionists seemed to share more closely the Enlightenment values of natural equality and the Protestant work ethic. One might also cite W. E. B. Du Bois's *The Souls of Black Folk* (1903) and his later *Black Reconstruction* (1935) as major documents of American civil religion. In the former Du Bois addressed both the issue of ordering American society and the telling of its myth of beginnings. "Your country?" he asked and then inserted a black presence into the sacred story by reminding Americans that "before the Pilgrims landed [Africans] were here" (Du Bois, 1903, p. 275). The stories, music, spirit, and folk traditions of both Africans and aboriginal tribes were present, Du Bois claimed, and were "gifts," added and intermingled in blood, sweat, and wars in the formation of the "Promised Land." Finally, one must mention the last great documents of this tradition as the speeches, events, and works of Martin Luther King Jr.

The African American tradition is a reminder that whatever form civil religion takes, its more hopeful organization includes that enunciated by Edwards in his "awakening" of active and free persons who are provided with a place for public debate over the issues of the day. While it may seem clear that "American civil religion" in its more positive Christian orientations and its faith in national heroes has declined in the twentieth century, the problematic of the nation's religio-political identity and the meaning of its revolutionary founding remains central as the nation further reflects on its powerful status in international affairs and the increasing diversity within its borders.

See Also Politics and Religion.

Bibliography

The ideological and intellectual foundations of the new Western democratic states stem from the Reformation and Enlightenment critiques of hierarchical and sacredotal authority as the ordering principle for society and in the drive for a form of freedom defined for and located in the individual person. New democratic governments were brought into being to establish and maintain the rights of the individual. Democratic states, for the most part, did institute new human rights for the individual but this left open the meaning of a binding that would hold together a group of individuals into an abiding bond of unity. The United States of America is a case in point.

In addressing this issue, many revolutionaries had recourse to models from ancient societies, such as those in Fustel de Coulanges, *The Ancient City* (Garden City, N.Y., 1956; originally published 1873); and Joseph Rykwert, *The Idea of a Town* (Princeton, N.J., 1976), which show how religious rituals and beliefs created the "common bond" that held societies together. Jean-Jacques Rousseau, *The Social Contract* (Baltimore, 1968; originally published 1762), notes that revolutionary democratic societies, like ancient societies, needed some form of religion to guarantee the integration and cohesion of modern democratic societies. Émile Durkheim, *The Elementary Forms of the Religious Life*, translated by Karen Fields (New York, 1995), in his description of Australian Aboriginal religion, alludes to a similar notion about the social integrative meaning of religion. Catherine L. Albanese, *Sons of the Fathers* (Philadelphia, 1976), discusses the imitation of Roman rituals in the ceremonies connected with the inauguration of George Washington as the first president.

The Puritan dimensions of American cultural and religious institutions have been ably set forth in Perry Miller's essays, *Errand into the Wilderness* (Cambridge, Mass., 1956), a good introduction to the range of his scholarship on the Puritans. Discussions of the rhetoric of chosenness and New England Covenant theology commonly begin with analyses of John Winthrop's lay sermon preached aboard the *Arabella* in 1630, "A Modell of Christian Charity." *Winthrop Papers: Volume II, 1623–1630.* New York, 1968, 282–295. Stephen A. Marini, *Radical Sects of Revolutionary New England* (Cambridge, Mass., 1982), indicates the radical and intense fragmentation within the religious and secular parts of society prior to the Revolutionary War. Sidney E. Mead, *The Lively Experiment* (New York, 1963), discusses the "shape of Protestantism" in relation to the expansion in geographical space of the American Republic. Jonathan Edwards is often cited as setting the precedent for an enduring form of Puritanism as the basis for a "secular" religious polity, as seen in his writings on revivalism, especially *The Works of Jonathan Edwards,* vol. 4: *The Great Awakening,* edited by Perry Miller (New Haven, Conn., 1972), in which C. C. Goen provides an introduction that addresses Edwards's often disputed "post-millennialism," pp. 1–94. An analysis of this transition is in Alan Heimert, *Religion and the American Mind, from the Great Awakening to the Revolution* (Cambridge, Mass., 1966). Along with Miller, Joseph Haroutunian, *Piety versus Moralism: The Passing of the New England Theology* (New York, 1932), offers an examination of the more "progressive" use of Edwards's theology by his New Divinity followers. Alexis De Tocqueville commented on the importance of the Puritan townships and municipalities to the formation of a democratic spirit in the United States in his two volume work, *Democracy in America* (New York, 1990; Volume I originally published 1835; Volume II originally published 1840). George W. Pierson alludes to De Tocqueville's comments on the disregard of ancient traditions and cultures in the United States in *Tocqueville and Beaumont in America* (New York, 1938).

Broader interpretive works that deal with the history of religion in America include Martin E. Marty, *Righteous Empire* (New York, 1970); and Sydney E. Ahlstrom, *A Religious History of the American People* (New Haven, Conn., 1972). Albanese's textbook, *America: Religion and Religions* (Belmont, Calif., 1999), gives prominence to the various expressions of civil religion in American cultural history. The sociologists N. J. Demerath III and Phillip E. Hammond survey the religious situation in America in *Religion in Social Context* (New York, 1969).

H. Richard Niebuhr puts forth theologically critical positions regarding the plurality of religious institutions in the United States in *The Social Sources of Denominationalism* (New York, 1957). Given the constitutional principle of the separation of church and state and the fact that American culture was a Protestant culture in terms of style and history, the many immigrants from other parts of the world, the progeny of the Africans enslaved within the country, and the aboriginal populations, one looked for a meaning of America that could provide the serious binding that is necessary for a functional society. Sidney E. Mead, *The Nation with the Soul of a Church* (New York, 1975), explains the meaning that could provide the serious binding necessary for a functional society within the structures of a form of secular Protestantism. Will Herberg attempts to extend a meaning of America in terms of a pluralistic religious meaning in *Protestant, Catholic, Jew* (Garden City, N.J., 1960).

Within this context one must understand Robert N. Bellah's programmatic "Civil Religion in America," *Daedalus* 96 (Winter 1967): 1–21. Bellah responds to some of his critics in "American Civil Religion in the 1970's," *Anglican Theological Review,* supp. ser., 1 (July 1973): 8–20, and continues his exposition of civil religion in *The Broken Covenant* (New York, 1975) and with Richard Madsen, William M. Sullivan, Ann Swidler, and Steven M. Tipton in *Habits of the Heart* (New York, 1986). Trenchant critiques of American civil religion are in John Murray Cuddihy, *The Ordeal of Civility* (New York, 1974) and *No Offense: Civil Religion and Protestant Taste* (New York, 1978). Another critical examination of Bellah's position is in John F. Wilson, *Public Religion in American Culture* (Philadelphia, 1979). Giles B. Gunn, *Thinking across the American Grain,* chap. 9, pp. 212–236 (Chicago, 1992), is an interrogation of the concept from a literary perspective informed by the tradition of American pragmatism. Hannah Arendt examines the philosophical meaning of the founding documents and rituals of the United States in *On Revolution* (New York, 1963) and in *Willing* (New York, 1978), the latter published posthumously.

Hardly any discussion of civil religion in the United States has emphasized the issue of slavery as an institution or the existence of enslaved Africans in the country at the time of its founding. Though this is a perennial issue of the country, having been one of the major causes of one the greatest wars in human history, it is seldom mentioned in relationship to either a religious or civil ordering of the country. Slavery was discussed almost every day in the constitutional convention and provisions were made to count the number of slaves for representation, but the founding made no change in their status. For the institution of slavery and the enslaved in the Constitutional Convention, see Paul Finkelman, *An Imperfect Union* (Chapel Hill, N.C., 1981). Charles H. Long, "Civil Rights—Civil Religion: Visible People, Invisible Religion," pp. 211–221, in *American Civil Religion,* edited by Russell E. Richey and Donald G. Jones (New York, 1974), contributes to this discussion. There is, however, a long tradition of African American thought concerning the civil ordering of the country, including David Walker, *Walker's Appeal in Four Articles* (1829), which has been reprinted as *David Walker's Appeal to the Coloured Citizens of the World,* edited by Peter P. Hinks (University Park, Pa., 2000); W. E. B. Du Bois, *The Souls of Black Folk* (Chicago, 1903) and *Black Reconstruction* (New York, 1935); and Martin Luther King Jr., *Strength to Love* (New York, 1963), *Where Do We Go From Here?* (New York, 1967), and *Why We Can't Wait* (New York, 1964). In addition a great deal of the contemporary Black Theology movement can be seen as contributing to the meaning of a civil religion. See especially James H. Cone, *Black Theology and Black Power* (New York, 1969) and *A Black Theology of Liberation* (Philadelphia, 1970). Gayraud S. Wilmore's interpretive discussion of African American Christianity, *Black Religion and Black Radicalism* (Maryknoll, N.Y., 1998) also makes a major contribution to this discussion.

Carole Lynn Stewart (2005)

CLASSIFICATION OF RELIGIONS is necessitated by the diversity, complexity, and greatly increased knowledge of religions and by the development of the scientific study of religion during the past hundred years. The student of religion seeks to find or bring some system of intelligibility to the manifold expressions of religious experience, not only to make the data manageable but to discern common characteristics by which religions and religious phenomena can be grouped together and compared with or distinguished from others. Basically, there are two kinds of classification. One orders historical religions in terms of their similarities and differences; the other orders religious phenomena into categories (e.g., sacrifice, purification, rites of passage).

Early Modern Classification Schemes. The work of F. Max Müller (1823–1900), the father of the comparative study of religions, gave impetus to the classification of religion. Primarily a linguist, Müller used his philological method as a model for the comparative study of religions and the classification of religions along racial-genetic lines. In his view, racial, linguistic, and religious "families" (Aryan, Semitic, and Turanian) coincided. Language provided the primary evidence for this coincidence.

The Dutch scholar C. P. Tiele (1830–1902), one of the founders of the scientific study of religion and a contemporary of Müller, also gave particular attention to the classification of religions. Tiele was impressed by the moral and ethical qualities he found in religions. He saw these qualities as expressions of a "religious idea" that had evolved in the course of history. He distinguished between "nature religions" and "ethical religions." The former were those in which ethical elements were either absent or, at most, minimally present. These religions included polyzoic naturalism (a belief that all nature is endowed with life), polydemonistic-magical religions (animism), therianthropic polytheism (gods in the form of animals), and anthropomorphic polytheism (gods in the form of men). The ethical religions ("spiritualistic ethical religions of revelation") were divided into two categories: natural nomistic (legalistic) religious communions (including Daoism, Confucianism, Brahmanism, and Judaism) and universalistic religious communions (Buddhism, Christianity, and Islam). Of the former category Judaism was considered transitional in the direction of universalistic religions. To the latter category only Buddhism and Christianity fully belong, for Islam is thought to retain some particularistic and nomistic elements.

Tiele's emphasis on the ethical as a new and decisive religious element came to be used frequently in distinguishing the "higher" from the "lower" religions. While it is true that the monotheistic religions emphasize ethics and morality, it is not the case that a concern for morality is absent in so-called primitive religions. The judgment of Tiele and others of his time, and the classifications based on it, reflected prejudices concerning "primitive" peoples.

Types of Classification. Some classifications of religions are extraordinarily broad, the broadest being binary or bipartite. Familiar bipartite classifications give such contrasting pairs as true-false, natural-revealed, literate-preliterate, Eastern-Western, and Christian–non-Christian. The most obvious difficulty with such broad classifications is that they do not distinguish sufficiently to do justice to the diversity and complexity of the religious world.

Normative classification. The most common type of classification, historically, has been normative. Religions have been classified according to the norms or standards of the classifiers. Typically, these norms were religiously, culturally, and historically conditioned, if not derived, and tended to be subjective and arbitrary.

A persistent binary normative classification has been the division of religions in relation to "truth," yielding the two categories: "true religion" and "false religion." This division has appeared frequently among the great monotheistic religions (Judaism, Christianity, and Islam) but has not been limited to them. Normative classifications do not increase understanding.

The use of normative classification by Christians goes back at least to the church fathers. It arose in the context of the religious competition of the early centuries, a time of great religious ferment and rivalry, to meet the needs of Christian apologetics. Thus, for example, other religions were said to exist as the result of divine condescension to the needs and weaknesses of humans and no longer had any validity after the appearance of Christianity. Judaism with its Torah, it was said, had been a "schoolmaster" preparing its adherents for the coming of the Gospel, and the other religions were merely imperfect copies of the true religion, plagiarisms at best.

Other Christian classifications of religions originated in the Middle Ages, and received a status that they retained in large measure through the magisterial authority of Thomas Aquinas (1225–1274). Thomas taught a basic distinction between natural religion and revealed religion, the former based on religious truth that can be known through the use of reason itself and the latter on divinely revealed truth. This distinction coincides in part with the distinction between religions based on "general revelation" and those based on "special revelation."

Protestantism has also provided various binary classifications of religions. Examples from the Reformation include Martin Luther's norm of justification by faith and John Calvin's *sola gratia;* a later instance is the distinction between "heathen religions" and the Christian religion, commonly made at the beginnings of the Protestant missionary movement.

Less obviously normative are classifications of religions that are ostensibly scientific, particularly those classifications based on theories about the origin and development of religion that appeared during the late nineteenth and early twentieth centuries. The theory that enjoyed the greatest vogue, E. B. Tylor's "animism," argued that the earliest form of religion was based on belief in anima or souls, spiritual entities capable of separation from the body. Tylor theorized that this primitive belief was based on certain real but misinterpreted universal human experiences (sleep, dreams, trances, hallucinations, and death). He admitted, however, that religion as it is found in the world is more than this, for everywhere it has undergone development. It evolves through various stages, which Tylor tried to sketch out, thereby accounting for the various kinds of theism, including polytheism and monotheism.

The theories of Tylor and others who developed evolutionary schemes typically postulated not neutral stages but scales having normative significance. Evolution was seen as a movement from simple, rudimentary, indeed crude, beginnings, through successive stages, each exhibiting increasing complexity, toward completion and perfection. "Earlier" meant lower and inferior; "later" meant higher and superior. Chronology was given valuative meaning. Not surprisingly, monotheism was seen as the highest religious stage yet attained. Each religion could be distinguished and classified in terms of its place on the scale, the several great monotheisms coming at the top. At the same time, one could reveal the "primitive" foundations and beginnings of all religions, including the highest. The evolutionists, like the later Freudians, believed they could disclose the secret that lay at the beginning. Moreover, they assumed that the nature, the essence of religion, is identical with its origin.

Geographical classification. Geography has been a ready means of classification of religions, especially since many religions and types of religion can be observed to belong exclusively or mainly to certain geographical areas. Again, simply binary classifications have appeared, the most common being "Eastern religions" and "Western religions." Often "Western" means Judaism and Christianity (religions of "Near Eastern" origin, actually), with Islam conveniently forgotten by many classifiers. "Eastern" or "Asian" may mean India and China and the lands under their cultural and religious influence. This simple bipartite division not only groups together religions (especially those of the "East") which differ greatly from one another, but omits important areas of the world and their religions.

The actual geographical distribution of some of the major religions renders problematic classification by geographical distribution. Some, for example Christianity, may be found in most regions of the world, although the proportion of adherents to the general population will vary widely. In this regard Islam is a particularly difficult case. Originating in the Near East, it quickly became a religion of wide geographical distribution, generating the "Islamic world," a great band stretching at least from Morocco in the West to Indonesia in the East, with important communities in the North (the Soviet Union and China) and South (sub-Saharan Africa). The fact that some religions have become virtually extinct in the lands of their origins (e.g., Indian Buddhism) also complicates geographical classification.

Further, it is difficult to stay simply with geographical criteria. Many textbooks on "comparative religion" (under such titles as *Religions of the World* and *Religions of Mankind)* combine the geographical and the historical in their outlines, utilizing such headings as "Religions of Middle Eastern Origin," "Religions of Ancient Rome," and "Religion in the Islamic World" as well as headings of purely geographical designation (e.g., "Religions of the Indian Subcontinent"). Such textbooks tend to leave out some important geographical regions. They may present religions of India, the Near East, the Far East, and perhaps religions of Greece and Rome. They are much less likely to include African religions and the religions of the Amerindians and the Pacific islands peoples.

Geography appears at first to afford the possibility of a convenient, intelligible, neutral classification of religions but turns out not to do so. In any case, its value is doubtful, for the significance of geographical considerations, especially on a large scale, is minimal for the understanding of particular religions and groups of religions, recent studies in the ecology of religion notwithstanding.

PHILOSOPHICAL CLASSIFICATION. The philosophical consideration of religions led in the modern period to some attempts in the West to classify religions on a philosophical rather than a theological or geographical basis. Perhaps the most wide-ranging and best-known effort is that of the German philosopher G. W. F. Hegel (1770–1831), especially in his *Lectures on the Philosophy of Religion* (1832). Briefly, Hegel saw religions in relation to the dialectical movement of the whole of human history toward the ultimate realization of freedom. He envisioned a vast scheme of evolution in which Spirit progressively realizes itself through the ongoing dialectical process of thesis, antithesis, and synthesis.

Hegel classified religions in terms of the stages they represent in the progressive self-realization of Spirit. Contrasting self and nature, he considered as the lowest level of religion the religions of nature. In these religions humans are completely immersed in nature and have only such consciousness as derives from sense experience. A higher stage of religion is represented, according to Hegel, by those religions in which humans have begun to emerge from nature and become conscious in their individuality. Specifically, this stage is represented by Greek and Roman religions and Judaism. The highest stage of religion is that in which the opposites of nature and individuality are transcended in the realization of what Hegel called Absolute Spirit. This is the level of Absolute Religion, which he did not hesitate to identify with Christianity.

Hegel's general scheme, as well as his classification of religions, has been criticized for its assumption that human history exhibits continuous progress. Further, Hegel's classification of religions is value-laden, most obviously in its claim that the Christian religion is the absolute religion. One sees again that normativeness is not the sole preserve of theologians.

A somewhat different philosophical approach to classification is found in the work of another nineteenth-century German thinker, Otto Pfleiderer (1839–1908), especially in his *Die Religion, ihr Wesen und ihre Geschichte*, 2 vols. (1869). Pfleiderer's approach focused upon the essence (*Wesen*) of religion. In his view, the essence is found in two elements, freedom and dependence, which are variously interrelated in the religious consciousness generally and in specific historical religions. Some religions (e.g., Egyptian and ancient Semitic religions) emphasize the religious sense of dependence, whereas other religions (e.g., the religions of the Aryans, Greeks, and Romans) stress the opposite pole, freedom. Still other religions clearly contain both elements but in unequal proportion (Brahmanism, Buddhism, Zoroastrianism). In Pfleiderer's view the highest manifestation of religion is one in which the two elements, freedom and dependence, are in equilibrium, reconciled in an ultimate harmony. This possibility he believed is found only in the monotheistic religions, Judaism, Christianity, and Islam. The possibility is fully realized, however, only in Christianity, for Islam is still inclined toward dependence and Judaism toward freedom. Here again a Western Christian thinker's classification of religions is used as a means of affirming the religious superiority of Christianity.

Phenomenology of religion. The term *phenomenology* can mean several things. It can refer to the twentieth-century philosophical school initially associated with the German philosopher Edmund Husserl, and later with Martin Heidegger, Maurice Merleau-Ponty, Paul Ricoeur, and others. In this sense it is phenomenological philosophy devoted to the study of religion. However, the term *phenomenology of religion* refers to the application of phenomenological methods to the study of the history of religions, as, for example, by W. Brede Kristensen, Gerardus van der Leeuw, C. Jouco Bleeker, and Mircea Eliade. In the hands of these scholars phenomenology is less a philosophy than a method for the study of religions.

The interest of phenomenologists of religion is in the classification of religious phenomena that are not limited or specific to a particular historical religion but cross the religious lines. For example, the phenomenologist of religion is interested in such categories as rites of sacrifice, myths of origin, and fertility deities. Further, phenomenologists seek to discern the "meaning" of religious phenomena in a nonreductionistic and nonnormative manner, believing that the phenomena will disclose their meanings to those who approach them "phenomenologically," that is, in a disciplined but open and nonprejudicial way.

W. Brede Kristensen (1867–1953), a Dutch scholar of Norwegian origin and a pioneer of phenomenology of religion, understood phenomenology as a new method of organizing data in the study of religion. One could, of course, organize the data historically or geographically as had been done in the past. But one could also organize data phenomenologically, in which case one would attempt to discern common themes and to describe the meanings of these themes among religions, regardless of their historical tradition or geographical location. Ultimately, one seeks the *essence* of the religious phenomena. In *The Meaning of Religion* (1960), Kristensen described the task of phenomenology of religion as that of classifying and grouping the divergent data of religion in such a way that one may obtain an overall view of their religious content and the religious values therein. The phenomena should be grouped according to characteristics that correspond to the essential and typical elements of religion. Kristensen classified the subjects of the phenomenology of religion into three broad groups: religious cosmology (the world), religious anthropology (humans), and cultus (acts of worship). Within their scope he was able to treat such specific phenomena as the worship of earth gods, conceptions of the soul, and ritual purifications.

Another Dutch phenomenologist of religion was Gerardus van der Leeuw (1890–1950), whose *Religion in Essence and Manifestation* (*Phänomenologie der Religion*, 1933) is considered a classic. His broadest phenomenological categories were the object of religion (which he analyzed in terms of power and the forms of power), the subject of religion (sacred man and community), and object and subject in reciprocal operation. Using these categories, he was able to classify and interpret an impressive number and variety of specific religious phenomena: sacred stones and trees, demons, priests, saints, sects, souls, sacrifices, taboo, sacred times and spaces, festivals, myth, mysticism, faith, and many others.

Unlike Kristensen, van der Leeuw gave some attention to "religions" (i.e., historical religious wholes), quoting Heinrich Frick's assertion that "religion actually exists only in religions." His classification was twelvefold. It was, however, curious and mixed, for it included not only historical religions but types of religion without specific historical form, and forms of religious dynamic. Specifically, van der Leeuw distinguished eight historical forms of religion: (1) religion of remoteness and flight (Confucianism and eighteenth-century Deism); (2) religion of struggle (Zoroastrian dualism); (3) religion of strain and form (Greek religion); (4) religion of infinity and asceticism (Indian religion, especially Hinduism); (5) religion of nothingness and compassion (Buddhism); (6) religion of will and obedience (Jewish religion); (7) religion of majesty and humility (Islam); and (8) religion of love (Christianity). To these forms he added religion of repose and religion of unrest. The former he associated with mysticism and the latter with theism. Both are elements in historical religions but have no proper historical form of their own. Finally, van der Leeuw distinguished two forms of the "dynamic of religions." One manifests itself by syncretism and mission, the other by revivals and reformations.

The usual criticism of phenomenology of religion, including its classifications, whether of phenomena or historical religions, is that it is not sufficiently historical. While phenomenologists of religion often begin with the historical data and seek to understand the data "historically," at least initially, the tendency is often toward abstraction, and then toward reification of these "forms" of religious dynamic, with the result that the phenomenologist's attention is drawn away from the religions in their historical particularity.

RECENT ATTEMPTS AT CLASSIFICATION. The enterprise of classifying religions is no longer in vogue. It is not often that one finds students of religion devoting their energies to this task. While the need to order data continues, other reasons that encouraged classification have diminished. As intimated above, one reason for classification has been to provide a framework for the assertion of the superiority of Christianity. That motive, whether consciously or unconsciously held, has faded. Another reason was directly connected with the vogue of evolutionism, for it encouraged and facilitated classification in terms of religious stages. That, too, has declined.

Nevertheless, there have been some recent attempts to classify religions. Illustratively, attention may be called to three. The sociologist of religion, Robert N. Bellah, has sought to construct an evolutionary interpretation of religion. In an essay titled *Religious Evolution* (1964) he proposed a sequence of five ideal typical stages of development: primitive, archaic, historic, early modern, and modern. These stages are examined in terms of their religious symbol systems, religious actions, religious organizations, and social implications. He maintains that the symbol systems have evolved from the simple to the complex. Also, religious collectivities have become progressively differentiated from other social structures. Finally, beginning with the historic stage, the consciousness of the self as a religious subject has increasingly developed. Religious evolution is thus seen as a process of differentiation and development that can best be understood historically and sociologically.

The influential and prolific historian of religions Mircea Eliade has delineated two fundamentally different religious orientations: cosmic and historical. The former is the principal topic of *The Myth of the Eternal Return* (1949). It is the type of orientation characteristic of so-called primitive and archaic religions and, in fact, of all "traditional" religion. Cosmic orientation is distinguished by its experience and conception of time (as cyclical and reversible). Sacred time is mythical, not historical. History is deprecated in favor of transcendental models provided by myth. By means of return to the powerfully creative, mythical time of origins, humans are enabled to overcome the deleterious effects of ordinary, profane time. Moreover, the objects and structures of the world ("nature") are means by which the sacred manifests itself ("hierophanies"). In striking contrast to the cosmic religious orientation, with its distinctive ontology, is the historical religious orientation. It, too, involves a conception of time. Time is linear, chronological, historical. It is irreversible, and historical events are unique (not typical, as in cosmic time). History is affirmed, for it is primarily in and through historical events that the sacred manifests itself. Myth is understood as sacred history. In Eliade's view, this second type of religious orientation is characteristic of the monotheisms—Judaism, Christianity, and Islam—and is largely confined to them. However, even within these religions the contrasting religious orientation makes itself felt, as, for example, in the "cosmic Christianity" of Eastern Europe.

A third recent attempt to classify religions is found in an essay ("Primitive, Classical, and Modern Religions," 1967) by Joseph M. Kitagawa. It relates to both Eliade's and Bellah's classifications. According to Kitagawa, religions can be distinguished by the kinds of religious experience and apprehension characteristic of them. Primitive religion is characterized by an orientation in which the ultimate purpose of life is participation in the creation of "cosmos" out of "chaos" by imitating mythical models. The classical religions, which include the religions of the ancient Near East, Iran, India, the Far East, and the Greco-Roman world, evidence a significant emancipation of *logos* from *muthos*. These religions are further marked by a change in man's view of himself— no longer is he only a part of nature—and by a sophistication and systematization of the theoretical, practical, and sociological expressions of his religious experience.

A completely satisfactory classification of religions continues to elude scholars. Some general requirements for more adequate classification of religions, however, are the following. First, the classification should be comprehensive, that is, inclusive ideally of all religions. Second, the classification should be objective and descriptive, not subjective and normative. Third, the effort should be made to do justice to particular religions and to avoid misrepresenting or caricaturing them because of prejudice or the desire to make them fit a particular scheme of classification. Fourth, judgments should be made in order to distinguish what is essential or fundamental in religions from what is accidental or incidental. Fifth, one should be alert equally to similarities and differences among religions. Finally, it is imperative to recognize that "living religions" are indeed alive and always changing and that "dead religions" have had a history: both, in short, are categories of dynamic entities. This dynamism is one factor that makes the classification of religion an unending task.

Bibliography

Two studies of the problem of classification appeared in the twentieth century. They are Duren J. H. Ward's *The Classification of Religions: Different Methods. Their Advantages and Disadvantages* (Chicago, 1909) and Fred Louis Parrish's *The Classification of Religions: Its Relation to the History of Religions* (Scottdale, Pa., 1941). The latter is especially complete and contains a useful bibliography for the study of classification. Additional relevant, though less focused, works include Morris Jastrow's *The Study of Religion* (1901; reprint, Chino, Calif., 1981), containing chapters on classification; C. P. Tiele's *Elements of the Science of Religion*, 2 vols. (Edinburgh, 1897–1899), especially the first volume; P. D. Chantepie de la Saussaye's *Manual of the Science of Religion* (London, 1891), which is Beatrice S. Colyer Ferguson's translation of volume 1 of his *Lehrbuch der Religionsgeschichte* (1887); Henri Pinard de la Boullaye's *L'étude comparée des religions*, 2 vols. (Paris, 1922–1925), especially volume 2, *Ses méthodes;* F. Max Müller's *Introduction to the Science of Religion* (London, 1873), a clear presentation of his influential views on the comparative method; and, finally, Gustav Mensching's *Die Religion: Erscheinungsformen, Strukturtypen und Lebensgesetze* (Stuttgart, 1959), containing a more recent discussion of the classification of religions.

New Sources

Broughton, Vanda. "A New Classification for the Literature of Religion." Paper presented at the 66th IFLA Conference, 2000. Available at http//www.ifla.org/IV/ifla66/papers/034–130e.htm.

Mills, Jack, and Vanda Broughton, eds. *Bibliographic Classification: Class P: Religion, The Occult, Morals and Ethics.* 2d ed. London, 1997.

HARRY B. PARTIN (1987)
Revised Bibliography

CLEANLINESS SEE PURIFICATION

CLEMEN, CARL

CLEMEN, CARL (1865–1940), Protestant theologian and historian of religions. Carl Christian Clemen was one of the founders of research in the science of religion and of its institutionalization in Germany. After qualifying for a lectureship in New Testament studies in Halle, he taught there from 1892 to 1903 and in Bonn from 1903 to 1908. After visiting the United States as a guest lecturer in 1908 and 1909, he became in 1910 associate professor and in 1920 professor of the history of religions in the philosophy department of the University of Bonn. The breadth of his scholarship is indicated by the fact that his publications number approximately six hundred titles, that he lectured on the Old Testament and on systematic and practical theology, and that he taught Avestan.

His publications first concerned the New Testament and its background in the history of religions. His inaugural lecture at Bonn, published as *Die religionsgeschichtliche Methode in der Theologie* (1904), outlined his program, first, of summarizing the different challenges confronting theology from the religio-historical method, especially that of the *Religionsgeschichtliche Schule,* and second, of tracing the derivation of religious views in the New Testament. For him the religio-historical method is a principle of research that Christian theology simply must apply if it is to be considered a field of knowledge. In this, however, Clemen believed that the comparison of Christianity with other religions (1) does not hinder the researcher, despite a temporary presumption of the equality of religions, from being convinced of the advantage of a certain religion and church; (2) does not promote the relativization of Christianity or, in its historical observation of Christianity, exclude the confirmation of its absoluteness; and (3) will lead, in fact, in its attempt to explain Christianity by means of other religions, to the verification of Christianity's originality and of its possession of content that was already present and only poured into borrowed forms.

Research is indebted to Clemen, in connection with these arguments, for a more precise definition of the idea of "influence" among religions through his application of three criteria. One can speak of "influence" if any one of the following criteria is met: (1) if a special religious view cannot be explained completely from the original ideas of the religions concerned; (2) if any hypothesized influence of one religion is actually demonstrable in another religion, and the precedence of the former is plausible; and (3) if the manner in which a religious view is transmitted is comprehensible (otherwise a correspondence must be shown to be so far-reaching that the former has to be regarded as the model, even if the way of influence is unknown). A broadly conceived exposition of these ideas appeared in his *Religionsgeschichtliche Erklärung des Neuen Testaments: Die Abhängigkeit des ältesten Christentums von nichtjüdischen Religionen und philosophischen Systemen* (1909; translated as *Primitive Christianity and Its Non-Jewish Sources,* 1912). A German revision of *Religionsgeschichtliche Erklärung* published in 1924 also incorporates his work *Der Einfluss der Mysterienreligionen auf das älteste Christentum* (The influence of mystical religions on primitive Christianity; 1913), while his book *Die Reste der primitiven Religion im ältesten Christentum* (Traces of primitive religion in primitive Christianity; 1916) adds a portrayal of concepts originating in nature religions. A summary view of the opposite relationships is provided by the late work *Der Einfluss des Christentums auf andere Religionen* (The influence of Christianity on other religions; 1933). Clemen's summary work, *Die Religionen der Erde: Ihr Wesen und ihre Geschichte* (1927), was translated into English as *Religions of the World: Their Nature and Their History* (1931). The broad scope of his approach to method is seen in writings such as *Die Anwendung der Psychoanalyse auf Mythologie und Religionsgeschichte* (The application of psychology to mythology and the history of religion; 1928) and *Grundriss der Religionsphilosophie* (Outline of the philosophy of religion; 1934). Yet his ideal was strongly source-oriented historical research, and his edition of *Fontes historiae religionum ex auctoribus Graecis et Latinis collecti,* beginning with his collection of sources and published as *Die griechischen und lateinischen Nachrichten über die persische Religion* (Greek and Latin accounts of Persian religion; 1920), has become an aid of lasting importance to religio-historical research.

BIBLIOGRAPHY

Mensching, Gustav. "Carl Clemen." *Die christliche Welt* 54 (August 3, 1940): 353–354.

Rühle, Oskar. "Clemen, Carl." In *Die Religion in Geschichte und Gegenwart.* 2d ed., vol. 1. Tübingen, 1927.

Schrey, Heinz Horst. "Clemen, Carl Christian." In *Neue deutsche Biographie,* edited by Erich Angermann et al., vol. 3. Berlin, 1957.

Waardenburg, Jacques. *Classical Approaches to the Study of Religion,* vol. 2, *Bibliography.* The Hague, 1974. See pages 39–40.

CHRISTOPH ELSAS (1987)
Translated from German by Roger Norton

CLEMENT OF ALEXANDRIA

CLEMENT OF ALEXANDRIA (150?–215?), Christian theologian. Little is known about the life of Titus Flavius Clemens. A few details can be gathered from Clement's allusion to his education (*Miscellanies* 1.1, 2.2) and from the report of the fourth-century Christian writer Eusebius of Caesarea (*Ecclesiastical History* 5.10–11, 6.6, 6.11.5–6). Born in the mid-second century to pagan parents, perhaps in Athens, Clement traveled extensively as a young man, seeking an intellectual mentor. This he found in Pantaenus, who, according to Eusebius, served as head of a Christian school in Alexandria. Clement is said to have succeeded Pantaenus as chief of the school in the late second century, probably remaining a layperson after his conversion to Christianity. In 202 or 203, at the time of the emperor Septimius Severus's persecution of Christians, Clement left Alexandria for Asia Minor. Presumably he died before 215.

The following treatises of Clement are extant: *Exhortation to the Greeks* (*Protrepticus*); *The Instructor* (*Paedagogus*); *Miscellanies* (*Stromateis*); *Who Is the Rich Man That Is Saved?* (*Quis dives salvetur?*); a collection of excerpts from Valentinian teachings, with Clement's comments (*Excerpta ex Theodoto*); and a work of exegetical notes on the Old Testament (*Eclogae propheticae*). Only fragments remain of other treatises. Although scholars disagree on the precise dating of Clement's works, the period 195–210 probably encompasses them all. He wrote the *Protrepticus* first, followed by the *Paedagogus*, the *Stromateis*, and the *Quis dives salvetur?* Clement's influence on later theology was largely channeled through the writings of his brilliant successor, Origen.

Clement's works testify to the diversity of Christians in Alexandria around the year 200. There were "simple believers," wary of speculation, who understood Scripture literally and thought ecclesiastical authority enough to direct their lives. Those able to embrace a more advanced theology sought to align the best of classical culture with their faith. (Perhaps this group included those Clement hoped to comfort with his assurance that riches did not automatically debar them from salvation if they practiced inward detachment from their wealth and heeded Christianity's call for charity.) In addition to Alexandrians within the Catholic Christian fold, there were many Gnostics, especially the followers of Valentinus and Basilides, who self-identified as Christians, but whom Clement considered heretics. Clement, following his predecessors, the second-century Apologists, also addressed pagan critics who mocked Christianity as a religion for the uneducated. The pagan writer Celsus's searing attack on Christianity, *The True Word,* had been composed only about fifteen years before Clement began his writing career.

Although Clement did not reject the "simple believers," he advocated higher theological education and an allegorical interpretation of Scripture, conceding that the Bible was stylistically inelegant and was replete with anthropomorphic depictions of God. Responding to more theologically educated Christians and to pagan critics, Clement argued that Christianity was a species of philosophy, far superior to Greek myth or to the mystery religions. (Recent scholars have emphasized Clement's indebtedness to various philosophical traditions, especially Middle Platonism.) Clement attempted to display his erudition by quoting several hundred passages from classical authors in his writings, although he probably derived many of his citations not from the original sources, but from the handbooks popular in his day. Like the Gnostics, Clement valued religious knowledge highly, but he argued, allegedly against them, that God's creation, the material world, was good. He accused Gnostics of holding either overly ascetic or, conversely, libertine positions regarding the use of the body and material things, thus he (somewhat lukewarmly) endorsed the virtues of Christian marriage. Moreover, since Clement understood Gnostic notions of "election" to mean "fatalistic determinism," he championed the freedom of the will and freely chosen good deeds as necessary components of Christian salvation.

Among the more prominent themes in Clement's works are the following: the progressive revelation of truth through the Logos (the Word) from ancient to early Christian times; Greek philosophers' plagiarism of ideas from the Old Testament; humans' creation in the "image of God" that constantly recalled them to more virtuous lives; the incorporeality of God, misrepresented by Scripture's anthropomorphisms (although Clement sometimes engaged feminine images for God); the necessity of allegorical interpretation of Scripture; detailed guidelines provided by the Logos as "Instructor" for daily activities such as eating and sleeping; the benefits that preparatory instruction in philosophy and other secular disciplines provided for Christians; the possibility of advancement in the Christian life from belief to knowledge and from self-control to impassability (although good deeds and love were incumbent upon Christians at all stages); and the claim that the appellation "Gnostic" was more appropriately applied to those advanced in Catholic orthodoxy than to those he deemed heretics.

Bibliography

Bardy, Gustave. *Clément d'Alexandrie.* Paris, 1926. A standard older biography of Clement, with discussion of his writings.

Buell, Denise Kimber. *Making Christians: Clement of Alexandria and the Rhetoric of Legitimacy.* Princeton, 1999. Explores Clement's metaphors of procreation and kinship which authorize power relations.

Chadwick, Henry. *Early Christian Thought and the Classical Tradition: Studies in Justin, Clement, and Origen.* New York, 1966. An insightful study of Clement's relation to the classical tradition.

Countryman, L. William. *The Rich Christian in the Church of the Early Empire: Contradictions and Accommodations.* New York, 1980. An examination of Clement's treatise *Who Is the Rich Man That Is Saved?* in relation to early Christian attitudes toward wealth. See especially Chapter 1.

Dawson, David. *Allegorical Readers and Cultural Revision in Ancient Alexandria.* Berkeley, 1992. Analyzes Clement's hermeneutic and the social purposes of his allegorical reaings. See especially Chapter 4.

Hoek, Annewies van den. "The 'Catechetical' School of Early Christian Alexandria and Its Philonic Heritage." *Harvard Theological Review* 90 (1997): 59–87. Discusses the debate over whether there was a "school" at Alexandria and its possible origins.

Hunter, David G. "The Language of Desire: Clement of Alexandria's Transformation of Ascetic Discourse." *Semeia* 57 (1992): 95–111. Shows how differentiating the terms Clement uses for "desire" creates a more nuanced view of his discussion of marriage.

Kovacs, Judith L. "Divine Pedagogy and the Gnostic Teacher according to Clement of Alexandria." *Journal of Early Christian Studies* 9 (2001): 3–25. Analyzes how Clement's notion of teaching relates to his view of the Logos as an "instructor."

Lilla, Salvatore R. C. *Clement of Alexandria: A Study in Christian Platonism and Gnosticism.* Oxford, 1971. A detailed investigation of Clement's philosophical interests and his relation to gnosticism.

Méhat, André. *Étude sur les Stromates de Clément d'Alexandrie.* Paris, 1966. A comprehensive study of the *Miscellanies,* Clement's major work.

ELIZABETH A. CLARK (1987 AND 2005)

CLEMENT OF ROME, supposed author of a letter sent from the church of Rome to the church of Corinth in the last years of the first century CE. The date most commonly given for the letter is 96–97. In the course of the second century the author of this letter came to be identified as Clement and was thought to have been the third bishop of Rome, after Peter and Paul. Although there is no particular reason to doubt that the person who actually penned the letter was so named, there is some doubt as to whether at this time Rome had a bishop in the later sense of the word, that is, a single head of the church.

The letter, known as *1 Clement,* tells us nothing about the person who wrote it. Indeed, the letter is intended to be understood as the expression of a church rather than an individual. In response to disagreements at Corinth, it focuses on the need for harmony and the evils of discord. The author draws upon materials from the Bible (the Hebrew Bible in the Septuagint Greek translation) and from Greco-Roman tradition. He knows several of Paul's letters, perhaps including *Hebrews.* He also uses material similar to what we find in the synoptic Gospels, but it is doubtful whether he knew the Gospels in their present form.

First Clement gives early expression to ideas that would subsequently be very important in the Roman tradition and elsewhere. The leadership of the church is seen as standing in a chain of authority extending from God, through Christ, on through the apostles, and finally to the bishops or presbyters (the terms seem to be used interchangeably), who now stand as a group at the head of the individual churches. To overthrow the established ministers (as apparently had been done at Corinth) when they have been blameless in the performance of their duties is to rebel against God.

Some have interpreted *1 Clement* as the earliest expression of Roman primacy, and Clement of Rome therefore as the first pope on record as having acted papally. This, however, is to exaggerate the authoritarian character of the letter and the individual importance of its author. It is a letter of exhortation from one church to another, both of which shared the tradition of having been evangelized by Peter and Paul.

Clement of Rome was subsequently but erroneously credited with a second "letter" (*2 Clement*), really a sermon, probably written around the middle of the second century, and two third-century letters on virginity. In addition, the fourth-century pseudo-Clementine *Homilies* and *Recognitions* feature Clement as the protagonist of their dramatic narratives. There seems to be no reason to suppose that any historically reliable information about the first-century Clement can be derived from these materials. Subsequent to the time of the pseudo-Clementines, Clement of Rome seems not to have played a large role in Christian tradition. He was remembered as the first pope of whom more than the name alone was known, and as the author of the earliest extant piece of Christian literature outside the New Testament.

BIBLIOGRAPHY

For the English-speaking reader, *1 Clement* is most accessible through the translation and commentary in Robert M. Grant and H. H. Graham's *The Apostolic Fathers,* vol. 2, *First and Second Clement* (New York, 1965). The Greek text is available in Franz X. Funk's *Die apostolischen Väter,* revised by Karl Bihlmeyer (1924), new ed., edited by Wilhelm Schneemelcher (Tübingen, 1970). The scholarly discussion of *1 Clement* is largely a German affair. The most useful monographs are Otto Knoch's *Eigenart und Bedeutung der Eschatologie im theologischen Aufriss des ersten Clemensbriefes* (Bonn, 1964); Karlmann Beyschlag's *Clemens Romanus und der Frühkatholizismus* (Tübingen, 1966); and Gerbert Brunner's *Die theologische Mitte des ersten Klemensbriefs* (Frankfurt, 1972). These books also illustrate the impact of Catholic-Protestant polemics on the study of early Christianity.

JAMES F. MCCUE (1987)

CLITORIDECTOMY. The term *clitoridectomy* covers a range of ritual surgical operations: (1) drawing blood from the clitoral prepuce or removal of the prepuce, (2) excism of the clitoris, (3) excism of the clitoris and labia minora, and (4) infibulation, requiring removal of the clitoris, the labia minora, and the anterior two-thirds of the labia majora, the two sides of which are then joined so that a small posterior opening is left for the passage of urine and menstrual blood. The first type occurs in Islamic countries of the Middle East, Africa, and Asia. The second type occurs in East, West, and central Africa, on the Arabian Peninsula, and in Brazil, eastern Mexico, and Peru. The third type occurs throughout Africa, in Arab countries, and in parts of Aboriginal Australia. Infibulation occurs in Sudan, Ethiopia, Djibouti, Eritrea, southern Egypt, northern Nigeria, Mali, and the Central African Republic.

In countries where clitoridectomy is practiced, the rite may be performed virtually universally or it may have a sparse and patchy distribution. For example, in northern Ghana almost all women in the Kusase ethnic group will have had clitoridectomy, while none in the neighboring Tallensi group will have undergone this ritual. Nor is there a clear relationship between clitoridectomy and religion: in an area of southern Nigeria five contiguous ethnic groups perform the rite, but the Etsako are Muslim, the Esan and Ijan are predominantly Christian, and the Bini and Ukwuani primarily observe their traditional religion.

In Sudan, few women in the south are infibulated, but from 90 to 95 percent of the women in the Arabic north are (Dareer, 1983, p. 41). In neighboring Egypt an estimated 95 percent of women have had some kind of clitoridectomy, but most is of the third type and only relatively few, near the Sudan border, have been infibulated (Aziza, 1983, p. 13). In both countries urban, better-educated women tend to have minimal surgery or no clitoridectomy. Egyptian mummies dated 200 BCE show evidence of clitroidectomy (Dareer, 1983, p. 41), and present-day Coptic Christian as well as Muslim women in Egypt have clitoridectomy, suggesting that it is a pre-Islamic custom. This speculation is further supported by the fact that the Islamic countries of Saudi Arabia, Iraq, Iran, and Afghanistan do not practice clitoridectomy.

There is no mention of clitoridectomy in the Qurʾān, but more or less authentic *ḥadīth*s mention its practice in pre-Islamic Arabia. Although texts and dictionaries are not very explicit, evidence suggests minimal excision of the prepuce of the clitoris (Bosworth, 1978, p. 913). In an Islamic tradition preserved by Ahmad ibn Hanbal (d. 855), circumcision is called *sunnah* for males and honorable for females (Wensinck, 1979, p. 20). *Sunnah* means to follow the traditions of the prophet Muḥammad, who according to tradition was circumcised. The commentaries of al-Nawawī, edited in Cairo in 1283, say, however, that circumcision is equally obligatory for males and females, specifying removal of a small part of the skin in the highest part of the genitals (ibid.). Some contemporary Muslim teachers cite the general Islamic rule that forbids cutting parts of the body unless the benefits exceed the pain and injury, and the Sudanese religious and political leader El Sayed Abdel Rahman El Mahadi explicitly forbade infibulation (Dareer, 1983, p. 44). Thus one can understand the confusion revealed in a Sudanese survey where 60 percent of the women said religion and custom demanded infibulation, but of those who disagreed, 50 percent did so on religious grounds (ibid., p. 43).

Clitoridectomy was not practiced in the ancient Jewish religion, and it is not mentioned in either testament of the Bible.

Clitoridectomy is a rite and in its minimal form is performed on girls individually, accompanied by gifts. Or girls may be initiated in a large class with accompanying rites that involve all the women of a village or indeed a whole chiefdom (MacCormack, 1979). The age at which girls experience clitoridectomy varies, but in all cases it should be done by the time of puberty and marriage. Although some Islamic texts prohibit clitoridectomy before the tenth year (Wensinck, 1979, p. 20), in Sudan it is done between two and eleven years, and in Egypt between three and eleven years of age, although there are cases of it being done before the age of one.

Clitoridectomy is usually performed by a traditional midwife. In Egypt the decision is primarily taken by the girl's mother, then in descending order of importance, by both parents together, an aunt, a sister or grandmother, and the father alone (Aziza, 1983, p. 14). However, fathers usually pay for the ceremony, and in the case of infibulation, husbands pay for re-fibulation following each childbirth.

There is no single meaning of clitoridectomy. In all societies that circumcise females, males are also circumcised. The reasons given for both sexes is that it is a ritual of membership into a religious tradition, an ethnic group with the status of adult, or a prerequisite for legitimate and moral marriage, sexuality, and procreation.

In Mediterranean and Islamic countries clitoridectomy is often explained as an aspect of family honor. The phrase "son of an uncircumcised woman" is considered injurious in the sense that it is synonymous with "son of a whore"—that is, a woman of excessive sexual appetite caused by her not being circumcised. In Egypt, for example, clitoridectomy is thought to protect a girl's chastity by reducing her libido, thus maintaining the family's honor and the girl's suitability for a good marriage. In Muslim Java a mild pricking of the prepuce is associated with ritual filing down of teeth, suggesting a symbolic statement about curbing all appetites.

In countries concerned with female modesty as a sign of family honor, public evidence of defloration is often an important rite following marriage. A woman who cannot demonstrate virginity by blood on the marriage bed may be divorced or even put to death at the hands of her own family to preserve their honor. Infibulation may be associated with an extreme expression of that honor.

Nawal El Saadawi (1980) has suggested a Marxist interpretation, following Engels, whereby in societies with patrilineal inheritance an emphasis on female chastity protects inheritance of private property by ensuring that a man's heirs are his own children. Just as ruling classes impose the moral values of renunciation of pleasure on laborers, while they value extravagance themselves, so men constitute a "ruling class" over women and impose the renunciation of sexual pleasure on them while they enjoy sexual freedom and seduction with impunity. This Marxist interpretation cannot be a universal explanation for clitoridectomy because there are societies with patrilineal inheritance of property where women may be punished or even put to death for an infringement of sexual rules, but which lack rites of clitoridectomy.

In a wider comparative framework, the explanation that genital surgery is universally a by-product of male suppression of women is called into question. For example, in coastal West Africa there are groups that practice clitoridectomy but also allow a considerable amount of premarital freedom to women. In the patrilineal Mende area of Sierra Leone, for example, women may even hold overt political office, and the pain of clitoridectomy, experienced in a group, may serve to bond women together into potentially cohesive chapters of a women's secret society, thus enhancing their political power and control of wealth (MacCormack, 1979). Among some Aboriginal Australian and some Melanesian ethnic groups, men undergo much more extreme and painful ritual genital surgery than women, and this usually occurs in societies with patrilineal descent where men are described as being dominant.

Virtually everywhere, clitoridectomy is described as an act of purification, making women clean. On the Sherbro coast of Sierra Leone, women say that without this puberty rite a girl can achieve womanhood biologically but will remain a girl socially. Using a functional model of analysis, we might say that the ritual scar and body modification are the sign of being brought within an adult moral sphere. The man with whom an initiated woman shares an intimate relationship will know that she has been taught the responsible role of potential procreator.

Using a structuralist model of analysis, "making women clean" removes the clitoris, the small male penis, making women fit unambiguously—purely and "cleanly"—within the female category. Furthermore, the pain of clitoridectomy might be seen as a metaphor for childbirth. In Sierra Leone, the position assumed for clitoridectomy is the same as the position assumed in childbirth. The place is the same, since ideally a woman returns to her natal initiation place to give birth, under the hand of the midwife who initiated her. The social group is similarly constituted of local female kin and other townswomen, all being members of the women's secret society. The pain of clitoridectomy, controlled by time, place, and the technical skill of the midwife, is a metaphor for the pain of childbirth. As the midwife controls bleeding and protects against infection in clitoridectomy, so she does in childbirth. Womanhood is symbolically achieved in clitoridectomy and is confirmed, under the midwife's hand, in childbirth. In Sierra Leone the two events are logically related as part of the same message, although they are separated in time (MacCormack, 1979, 1982; see also Griaule, 1965, p. 158).

SEE ALSO Androgynes; Bodily Marks; Circumcision; Initiation, article on Women's Initiation.

BIBLIOGRAPHY

Aziza, Hussein. *Facts about Female Circumcision.* Cairo, 1983. Issued by the Cairo Family Planning Association.

Bosworth, C. E., et al. "Khafd." In *The Encyclopaedia of Islam,* new ed., vol. 4, pp. 913–914. Leiden, 1978.

Dareer, Asma El. "Epidemiology of Female Circumcision in the Sudan." *Tropical Doctor* 13 (1983): 41–45.

Griaule, Marcel. *Conversations with Ogotemmêli: An Introduction to Dogon Religious Ideas.* London, 1965.

MacCormack, Carol P. "Sande: The Public Face of a Secret Society." In *The New Religions of Africa,* edited by Bennetta Jules-Rosette, pp. 27–37. Norwood, N.J., 1979

MacCormack, Carol P. "Health, Fertility and Birth in Moyamba District, Sierra Leone." In *Ethnography of Fertility and Birth,* edited by Carol P. MacCormack, pp. 115–139. London, 1982.

Myers, R. A., et al. "Circumcision: Its Nature and Practice among Some Ethnic Groups in Southern Nigeria." *Social Science and Medicine* 21 (1985): 581–588.

Saadawi, Nawal El. *The Hidden Face of Eve: Women in the Arab World.* Translated and edited by Sherif Hetata. London, 1980.

Wensinck, A. J. "Khitān." In *The Encyclopaedia of Islam,* new ed., vol. 5, pp. 20–22. Leiden, 1979.

New Sources

Genital Cutting and Transnational Sisterhood: Disputing U.S. Polemics. Edited by Stanlie M. James and Claire C. Robertson. Urbana, 2002.

Hosken, Fran P. *The Hosken Report: Genital and Sexual Mutilation of Females.* Lexington, Mass, 1994.

Lightfoot-Klein, Hanny. *Prisoners of Ritual: An Odyssey into Female Genital Circumcision in Africa.* New York, 1989.

Manresa, Kim. *The Day Kadi Lost Part of Her Life.* North Melbourne, Victoria, 1998.

Walker, Alice, and Pratibha Parmar. *Warrior Marks: Female Genital Mutilation and the Sexual Blinding of Women.* New York, 1993.

CAROL P. MACCORMACK (1987)
Revised Bibliography

CLOTHING

This entry consists of the following articles:

CLOTHING AND RELIGION IN THE EAST
CLOTHING AND RELIGION IN THE WEST
DRESS AND RELIGION IN AMERICA'S SECTARIAN COMMUNITIES

CLOTHING: CLOTHING AND RELIGION IN THE EAST

Clothing in the East communicates a wide range of personal and collective information about religious practice. A Buddhist monk's tonsure and saffron robes or a Hindu *guru's* choice not to wear any clothing are religiously sanctioned costumes that reinforce the distinctiveness of an observant community as separate from the larger, secular society. Other kinds of clothing also speak to religious affiliation.

IDENTITY. A Jewish male's yarmulke and tallith, a Muslim woman's *hajib,* or a Parsi's white cotton shirt and white lamb's wool cord may be sanctioned for worship, but in daily life they signify a personal covenant with the divine, empowering the individual and at times serving political and cultural ends. By the same token, the traditional use of colored turbans by Islamic societies—white for believers, yellow for Jews, and blue for Christians—have in effect discriminated against ethnic and religious minorities.

The unbleached hemp garments worn by the eldest Chinese son signify his withdrawal from society in order to attend to the duties prescribed for mourning. As chief mourner he leads the ceremonies honoring the memory of the departed and conducts the rites associated with the ancestor cult. As the mourning period passes, the gradual reentry into the world is marked by changing the sack cloth to undyed or white garments of varying degrees of refinement, then to blue-trimmed white garments and eventually blue clothing.

Coiffure and headgear are particularly important symbols. In East Asia, from at least the second millennium BCE, hair dressed in knots on the top or at the back of the head distinguished populations of the urbanized south from the shaved heads or plaited tresses of northern nomads. Letting one's hair hang free or go undressed was a sign of disengagement from Chinese civilized society. For this reason the tonsure and queue that Manchu rulers enforced upon all populations of the Chinese Empire during the seventeenth century through the early twentieth century was an overwhelming symbol of political and cultural domination. Tonsure could also demonstrate commitment to Buddhist monastic practices. In other instances hair styles reflect folk beliefs. Binding hair at the "four corners" of the head into tufts was thought to ward off the danger of Chinese children falling into the hands of demons, as the tufts provided a convenient grip for Buddhist deities or good spirits to retrieve the child.

In western Asia, shaving the head or letting certain parts of the hair grow helped distinguish Muslim and Jewish populations.

Gender. In many Eastern religions, clothing addresses issues of gender. For Buddhist and Muslim societies, clothing de-emphasizes or obscures feminine identity by altering or completely negating notions of beauty or sexuality. In most Muslim cultures some form of head covering or veil is prescribed for women. In Pakistan, for example, a large scarf or shawl called a *dupatta* is worn over the head to cover the hair and affords proper modesty. In contrast, the Afghan veil, called a *burka,* is an all-enveloping garment that a woman is required to wear in public, reducing all women to an anonymous, generic, nonmale presence.

Cross-gender. Within Buddhist practice, nuns and members of female lay groups undergo tonsure and wear plain garments based on those worn by male members of monastic orders. In appearance they become male, yet the transformation also underscores their secondary place as women within the karmic cycle of rebirth through which sentient beings evolve from lower to higher forms on the path to *nirvāṇa*. The message of such cross-gender attire is conspicuously ambiguous, reflecting some of the larger cosmological principles at the core of Indian esoteric beliefs, in which the avatars of deities appear in many forms: some bestial, some feminine, some masculine, some theologically neuter. The artistic transformation of Bodhisattva Avalokiteśvara in East Asia during the late eighth century and the ninth century from a neuter but essential masculine form into a female deity initially had less to do with costume than with the emphasis on female physical attributes—sweet face, elaborate hairdo, and female body type—but over time the deity's attire also changed. Such developments affected the appeal of this deity among female Buddhist devotees.

Cross-gender dressing among the *hijras,* a community of male-to-female transgenders in India and among related groups throughout South and Southeast Asia, sets them apart and contributes to their own identity as a third gender, neither female nor male. Traditionally, they conduct ceremonies within the larger community associated with birth.

Shamanism. Cross-gender dressing is also conspicuous among some Tunguz-speaking tribal culture groups of eastern Siberia, where male shamans wear feminine garments. In North Asian cultures shamanic practitioners may be either male or female. Yet for both genders clothing is intended to transform the wearer into an intermediary capable of bridging the gap between the physical world and the world of the spirits. Masks and garments tend to be highly personal, crafted by the shaman after a vision or intervention of the spirit world. In eastern Siberia they often take the form of a bird, bear, or stag. The cut of these garments, whether of animal skin or cloth, is significantly different from normal clothing, in part demonstrating the otherworldliness of shamanic practice. For example, coats may incorporate construction features, such as fringes or gussets, to simulate the animal they represent. Symbols for the sun, moon, and earth may be painted, appliquéd, or made of iron and attached to the upper body garment. Other decorative devices may evoke the sky gate, the goal of the spirit journey of the shaman. In addition, snakes, birds, horses, and other auspicious beasts are often part of the decorative program. A second common shaman garment type is decorated with bonelike forms that create an X-ray impression of the wearer's body.

Dance and performance. Among the dance costumes worn at Chinese folk festivals one can also find garments marked with bone diagrams and garments that imitate the animal protectors of shamanist power. The Cham dances of Tibet arose in pre-Buddhist times and were later incorporated into Tibetan Buddhist ritual. They employ forms of ecstatic dancing that evoke shamanistic practice. Cham costumes include masks, headgear, and garments that evoke birds, stags, horses, and other beasts familiar to the Siberian pantheon. The bone diagram garments were also used in Tibetan Buddhist ceremonial dancing. Although the surviving examples of these costumes are made of imported Chinese and Indian silks, the fluttering scarves and pendant sleeves as well as other construction features differentiate these coats from lay or clerical attire. Similar garments were in use among Mongol populations that converted to Tibetan Buddhism in the fourteenth century.

In contrast, in the secular Hindu world throughout South Asia, dance dramas are the focus of public ceremonies and celebrations associated with religious events, although the dramas themselves are not forms of worship. The colorful costumes, headdresses, and masks used in these performances constitute highly specialized costumes that suggest links between religion and political culture. Many are consciously archaic, evoking the mythic times, which are often the settings for these dramas. Similarly the garments and accessories worn by court dancers in Thailand and Indonesia evoke the bejeweled costumes seen on representations of Buddhist deities.

RITUAL CLOTHING. In those communities where a clergy acts as intermediary between the human and the divine there are often prescribed public rituals or displays. Here special clothes are used to transform the priest into a ritual celebrant.

Throughout Asia, clothing used within religious contexts is often among the most primitive garment types preserved by a culture. At one extreme are the palm-fiber garments worn by medicine men on the island of Buru in eastern Indonesia. The material is used as it comes from the source without further processing. The capes and mantles of green leaves, or their embroidered imitations worn by images of some of the Daoist immortals, reflect similar primitivism. Although made of luxury silk and greatly embellished, the highest-ranking Daoist priests' robes described below are among the most basic East Asian garment constructions. From the point of view of structure, these garments that are simply made of two lengths of fabric folded over the shoulder, seamed up the back and at the sides leaving space for the wearer's hands, contrast sharply with the more complex constructions having sleeves that are worn by second-ranking priests.

At another level this conservativism is reflected in the preservation of ancient textile forms within religious contexts. The tendency is particularly marked in Southeast Asia. Among the Batak tribes in Sumatra the most prestigious fabrics are those called *ragidup.* These large rectangular cloths are composed of three loom lengths joined along their selvages. Often the center panel is wider and is made of lighter-colored fiber. The cloth is produced on a simple loom, despite the presence of more sophisticated weaving equipment within the culture. These cloths are used in ritual gift giving and within religious ceremonies. A similar three-panel cloth with a light-colored central panel called a *khamar* is preserved in Bhutan. It is used by Tibetan Buddhists as a mark of esteem. It parallels the use of the *chaksay pankhep* reserved for royalty that is placed over the lap when the owner sits in audience and that is used as a napkin for wiping the hands.

VESTMENTS. When a priesthood interacts with the larger society, its authority is often tied to issues of status and rank. As is often the case, when clerical authority is set up in opposition to political culture, the attributes of patriarchal power and control are similar. The value system ascribed to secular power—luxury, magnificence, and conspicous consumption—are co-opted to serve the divine.

Shintō. Vestments worn by Shintō clergy—white kimono and white or red trousers (*hakama*) as well as the outer coats (*kariginu*) and black lacquered silk hats—are based on tenth-century Japanese court attire. While color signifies purity, the style of these garments and their political identification coincide with the period of centralization of priestly power in the hands of clan heads and the more structured form of worship that evolved in reaction to Buddhism and Confucianism from China. Shintō worship began to incorporate public ceremonies in which priests and priestesses conducted ritual observances. Other public gatherings were marked by events such as *kagura* dances that utilized specialized costumes and masks.

Daoism. Although it was also transformed into a much more sophisticated state religion as a result of the influence of Buddhism, Daoism as practiced in late imperial China used vestments linked to Siberian shamanism. When officiating at public celebrations, the highest-ranking Daoist priests wear a mantle called *jiang-i* (robe of descent), bearing cosmological symbols similar to those found in Siberian contexts.

This Daoist vestment is a full-length garment formed of two lengths of cloth seamed up the back and the sides and left open at the front. The back of the garment is decorated with astral symbols, ranked by registers from top to bottom and from center to edge. Symbols for the principle luminaries are arranged across the top of the garment. At the right shoulder the sun is represented by a red disk with a three-legged cock symbol; the moon at the left shoulder is depicted as a white disk in which a rabbit pounds the elixir of immortality; and a constellation, conventionally depicted as three balls joined by lines, is placed between. Explanation for these astral symbols can be documented to the first century BCE. Through these symbols, daily, monthly, and annual time could be calculated, and a calendar—one of the prime requirements for agrarian societies—could be fixed.

The decoration of the rest of the garment conveys notions of an unseen heaven. Prominent in this celestial diagram is a central image of paradise, often depicted as a multistoried tower within an ovoid frame of circular disks representing stars. This refers to the Three Isles of the Immortals located in the Eastern Sea. Five abstract forms arranged in a semicircle beneath the tower represent the five mythical peaks of the world. They guard the five principal directions: East, South, West, North, and Center. Below these, four mountain or pavilion structures symbolize the physical directions of the earth gates. Such association with paradise is often enhanced by figural imagery depicting various deities within complex pantheons. The hem may display the universal ocean with dragons, horses, tortoises, serpents, and other mythical beasts. The front of the coat is generally plain except for a dragon symbolizing the East and a tiger symbolizing the West. These figures flank the front opening and act as protective devices. Unlike shamanic garments, which assist the spirit journey of the individual, Daoist vestments function symbolically, transforming the wearer into an animator of political and religious systems that promoted control and stability.

Buddhism. Buddhism appropriated existing secular costume. Like Hinduism, from which it developed, it was initially a religion isolated from the population at large. Buddhist devotees lived within monastic communities and adopted clothing that stressed the rejection of worldly society. Over time the three-part costume based on the common attire of the Indian subcontinent became ritual attire. The lower body was covered with a sarong (*antaravasaka*). A shawl (*uttarasanga*), utilizing a length of loom-woven fabric, was draped in various manners around the upper body. A third garment called *sanghati*, literally "a twelve-fold cloth," was worn over the left shoulder.

The shawl became the most significant garment for Buddhism. It evolved into a rectangle constructed of smaller pieces, thus symbolizing the tattered and patched garments of the mendicant Buddha. The patchwork mantle, also called *kasaya*, was formalized to differentiate and identify its wearer as a member of a religious community and became the subject of monastic regulation.

Originally the name *kasaya* referred to a color distinction, which set the "impure" colored mantles of monks apart from the normal bleached white clothing of Indian laity. In time the "impure" colored clothing of monks of the Hīnayāna sect was enhanced by yellow dye, which still distinguishes the clothing of the Buddhist monks of Sri Lanka and Southeast Asia.

The specialized patchwork form of the garment spread north and east across Asia, accompanying proselytizing Buddhist missionaries. As the faith moved north and east, public worship evolved. In the less temperate regions of Central Asia, China, Korea, and eventually Japan, the simple three-part Buddhist costume was abandoned. The mantle was retained as symbolic apparel and worn over the normal dress typical of each region. The monastic clothing used in Tibet among Buddhist communities is a notable exception. There the sarong and mantle made of red-dyed wool was used. In all the Mahāyāna sects in East Asia a hood offered the tonsured heads of monks protection and conveyed public status. In Tibet the color of the hood distinguished the sect within the larger Buddhist community.

In East Asia, monastic costume continued to be regulated by prescription according to function and rank of the wearer. Most regulations focused on the mantle. In Japan, for example, the meanings of the original names of Buddhist garments were appropriated to describe variations of the pieced mantle. The *antaravasaka* became a five-paneled working outer mantle; the *uttarasanga* (the original shawl) defined a seven-paneled mantle worn at assembly. The *sanghati* was a large mantle used for travel composed of nine panels; two more panels were added for each advance in grade, reserving the twenty-five-panel *kasaya* for the highest-ranking clergy.

In Central Asia, China, and Japan the patchwork mantle acquired a significant secondary feature. Additional patches at the corners and along the longer side worn closest to the head added symbolic protection. The corner patches, usually in contrasting fabric, were associated with the *deva* kings who serve as guardians of the Buddhist law at each of the cardinal points of the compass. The large patches on the long side, a characteristic of the *uttarasanga* type, in China and Japan are named after the *bodhisattvas* Samantabhadra and Mañjuśrī, the principal attendants of Śākyamuni, the historical Buddha. These garments, often made of sumptuous secular silks donated to temples by pious devotees, created colorful focus for public ceremonies and demonstrated the power and authority of the Buddhist church. The magnificence of the fabrics used for making these vestments are seemingly in conflict with the principles of renunciation and poverty. However, through the destruction of secular goods by cutting them into pieces and reconstructing them as vestments, the goods metaphorically shed their worldly associations.

PRIVATE WORSHIP. Eastern religious traditions include sects that place a major emphasis on communal ritual and those for which religious practice is of a more private, individual nature. This division affects the manner in which clothing promotes notions of religious belief. Where religious practice is largely self-determined and reclusive, a clergy, if it exists, is less involved with public demonstration; hence clothing plays a less conspicuous role, and the notion of vestment is largely absent.

Islam. Islam has produced no vestments. The central religious leaders, whether mullahs, *mujtahids*, or ayatollahs, are in effect jurists who interpret Islamic law and serve as teachers. Clothing types used by these groups, regardless of ethnic origin, reflect the basic attire of the Arab founders of the faith: a cotton or wool caftan, a wool mantle (*ʿabaʿ*), and a cotton turban. Worship is an obligation of the faith, and when possible worship is practiced communally, but the prayer leader or *imām* does not function as intermediary between God and man. His clothing remains undifferentiated from that of the congregation. Individuals are expected to practice their religion while remaining active participants of society. Those who have made the pilgrimage to Mecca are entitled to wear special clothing, although it plays no liturgical role.

Hinduism. Within the Hindu tradition of India, public worship, although extremely complex, also occurs without the intervention of priests. Hinduism is without founder or prophets. It has no ecclesiastical or institutional structures. As a result there are virtually no specialized Hindu religious garments. Traditionally, the Brahman class was the source of the priesthood, but individual adherents practiced priestly vocation outside society based largely on the study of scriptural sources. For them, ritual was largely private, such as the placing of a sacred cord across the shoulder, both binding the devotee to religion and cutting the individual off from society. The central religious figure for Hinduism is the *guru,* or teacher, who follows a self-determined, often reclusive way of life that aims at purification and extinction from the cycle of rebirth. Clothing worn by *brahmans,* minimal and plain, reflects this distancing.

SECULAR ATTIRE. Until the late nineteenth and early twentieth centuries the attire of political elites often retained vestiges of ritual obligations that had been associated with rulers of antiquity.

South Asia. Court attire within the Hindu-Muslim courts of Java utilized a set of restricted batiked patterns on the sarongs and shawls to distinguish royalty and the higher ranks of the aristocracy. Many of these designs symbolized cosmic principles and underscored the significance of court ceremony and its relationship to religious belief.

China. The link between religion and politics is particularly evident in the court attire of imperial China and in the Chinese-influenced court attire in Korea, Japan, Vietnam, and various Central Asian kingdoms. Motifs symbolizing water, land, and sky were placed on these garments to represent the physical world over which the ruler held sway. In addition, fabulous mythical beasts, of which the dragon was the most common, represented the supernatural power and moral authority of imperial rule. The arrangement of these motifs conveyed a sense of universal order by reflecting notions of geopolitical control with reference to the points of the compass. Wearing the garment also demonstrated cosmic control and underscored the balance of forces in the universe. The wearer's body symbolized the world axis, while the neck of the garment symbolized the gate of heaven, separating the physical world represented by the coat from the spiritual represented by the wearer's head. In effect, the garment was only animate when worn, making each courtier an active participant in imperial rule.

The emperor's sacrificial obligations on behalf of the state were confirmed through clothes decorated with a special set of twelve symbols. These included the sun, moon, stars, earth, elements of the natural world, and symbols of political authority. Their use was reserved exclusively for the emperor.

These official garments had impacts throughout society. Chinese wedding attire in particular imitated court costume and prerogatives. Other types of quasi-official attire were used in conjunction with Buddhist and Daoist festivals and for the special garments made for religious images.

SEE ALSO Calendars; Hair; Masks; Textiles.

BIBLIOGRAPHY

Data about clothing used as vestment or as religious dress within Eastern traditions are scattered and diverse, varying considerably from culture to culture. In those religions with extensive scriptures, such as Islam, Buddhism, Hinduism, or Judaism, descriptions as well as specific proscriptions affect clothing choices. Issues of ritual and clothing are discussed in Catherine M. Bell, *Ritual: Perspectives and Dimensions* (New York, 1997); and Linda B. Arthur, ed., *Undressing Religion: Commitment and Conversion from a Cross-Cultural Perspective* (Oxford and New York, 2000). Ruth Barnes and Joanne B. Eicher, eds., *Dress and Gender: Making and Meaning in Cultural Contexts* (New York, 1992), discusses the ramifications of gender when considering clothing and religion.

One of the best discussions of dress in Islam is Fadwa El Guindi, *Veil: Modesty, Privacy, and Resistance* (New York, 1999). A good source on shamanic practice is Mircea Eliade's *Shamanism: Archaic Techniques of Ecstasy,* rev. and enl. ed. (New York, 1964), which has exhaustive bibliographic references. Particular references and illustrations of Mongolian shamanic and Lamaist dress are in Henny Harald Hansen's *Mongol Costumes* (Copenhagen, 1950). Additional information on Tibetan Buddhist practice is in Newark Museum, *Catalogue of the Tibetan Collection and Other Lamaist Articles in the Newark Museum,* 5 vols. (Newark, N.J., 1950–1971).

A comprehensive reference to East Asian religious practices in English is J. J. M. de Groot's *The Religious System of China: Its Ancient Forms, Evolution, History, and Present Aspect, Manners, Customs, and Social Institutions Connected Therewith,* 6 vols. (Leiden, 1892–1910). This massive study remains one of the best standard references to traditional religious practices in China. Data on Daoist practices are summarized in Stephen Little with Shawn Eichman, *Taoism and the Arts of China* (Chicago, 2000). An interesting account of some Buddhist practices is P. Steven Sangren, "Female Gender in Chinese Religious Symbols: Kuan Yin, Ma Tsu, and the 'Eternal Mother'," *Signs: Journal of Women in Culture and Society,* vol. 9, no.1, pp. 4–25 (Chicago, 1983).

Political and religious functions of Chinese court attire are discussed in Schuyler V. R. Cammann's *China's Dragon Robes* (New York, 1952), and in John E. Vollmer's *Ruling from the Dragon Throne: Costume of the Qing Dynasty, 1644–1911* (Berkeley, Calif., 2002). A discussion of Japanese Shintō practices and vestments is in International Congress for the History of Religions Shintō Committee, *Basic Terms of Shinto,* rev. ed. (Tokyo, 1985).

For discussions of South Asian garments and religions see Emma Tarlo, *Clothing Matters: Dress and Identity in India* (Chicago, 1996); and Serena Nanda, *Neither Man nor Woman: The Hijras of India* (Belmont, Calif., 1998). Henk Schulte Nordholt, *Outward Appearances: Dressing, State, and Society in Indonesia* (Leiden, 1997), and Penny Van Esterik, *Materializing Thailand* (Oxford and New York, 2000) include discussions of religious clothing in Southeast Asia. Articles by international scholars documenting clothing and textiles throughout the Indonesian Archipelago, including descriptions of religious usages, are in Mattibelle Gittinger, ed., *Indonesian Textiles: Irene Emery Roundtable on Museum Textiles, 1979 Proceedings* (Washington, D.C., 1980). This volume contains a bibliography and extensive citations to a considerable literature in Dutch, German, French, and English.

JOHN E. VOLLMER (2005)

CLOTHING: CLOTHING AND RELIGION IN THE WEST

Christianity, Judaism, and Islam all have individual forms of dress that visibly identify members of the religion and that help maintain the traditions, customs, and hierarchies of the religion. *Dress* is defined, and will be discussed here in relation to religious clothing, as an assemblage of modifications or supplements to the body (Eicher and Roach-Higgins, 1992). This definition includes a long list of modifications to the body, including hair, body art (piercing and tattooing), scents, and plastic surgery. Jewelry, accessories, and other categories of items added to the body as supplements are also included as dress. When examining religious dress, the cultural, economic, historical, and political context must be understood and analyzed to gain an appreciation of the meaning of dress within each religion. Christianity, Judaism, and Islam have dominant ideologies that guide decisions about dress. For example, beliefs about dress within Christianity are influenced by the biblical account of Adam and Eve in the Garden of Eden; therefore modesty is a goal, particularly for women. This double standard may reflect the patriarchal nature of the European cultures in which Christianity evolved (Renbourn, 1972). A woman's head or hair was thought to be provocative, and by the third century CE the church required women to cover their heads when attending church (Storm, 1987).

Judaism is based on the philosophy that individuals exist to glorify God; to be appropriately well dressed is therefore a religious duty, not one of personal preference. Ancient Jews divided the "pure" upper body from the "impure" lower body by wearing a girdle (Storm, 1987). Islamic philosophy emphasizes the group over the individual and promotes the separation of the sexes. Women's bodies should be covered and their movements within society restricted in the public sphere. The Islamic fundamentalist movement reflects a concern over the westernization of dress and promotes a return to traditional dress and behavior.

In *Dress, Drinks, and Drums* (1931), Ernest Crawley provides a historical perspective by segregating clothing into two categories: sacred and profane. Profane dress is that which is not related to religion or religious matters, while sacred dress involves religion. Crawley identified four kinds of sacred dress: sanctified, priestly, godly, and sacrificial. In terms of Western religions, sacrificial and godly dress is nonexistent. Priestly dress includes that of Roman Catholic priests or monks whose dress indicates the diminished importance of "maleness" and shows their rejection of worldly desires and goods. For example, most priests wear no facial hair, which symbolizes their voluntary departure from sexual relationships (Storm, 1987). The shaven head of a Roman Catholic nun prior to the dress reforms of Vatican II in 1962 (and of some nuns who are members of cloistered orders) demonstrates her turning away from worldly pleasures for a life of celibacy and spiritual pursuit. Dress can also reflect a priest's or a nun's life of poverty. Ironically, some vestments in high-church status can be highly elaborate rather than humble and can symbolize the priest's divine character.

Dress of sanctity differentiates the wearer from the profane. This is usually accomplished by using different colors or forms that are different from the secular. One of the most familiar dresses of sanctity is that of the worshiper or "churchgoer." In the United States, church dress is frequently a person's newest, and perhaps most elegant, but it otherwise is like secular dress. Until the mid-1960s, women wore hats and gloves to church, but this tradition has vanished. In the West, symbols of dress are consistently worn in the Jewish synagogue. The yarmulke worn by most Jewish men indicates their reverence to God. Muslim worshipers remove shoes before entering a mosque so as to not soil the holy place. Consequently, slipper-type shoes are frequently worn (Storm, 1987). The fez allows the men to cover their heads and touch their heads to the floor in prayer.

SACRED DRESS. There are many examples of articles of dress that are considered sacred by their wearers. For Orthodox Jews, the *halakhah* (traditional Jewish law) governs daily and ritual acts. It separates the sacred from the profane. In terms of *halakhic* law, the Bible contains a prohibition on cross-sex dressing and forbids the mixing of flax and wool (*sha'atnez*) in the construction of fabrics for clothing (Baizerman, 1992). There are specifications about tying tzitzit (corner tassels) on the prayer shawl, or tallith. Women cover their hair and heads based on custom. To some this is an expression of modesty, while to others, "exposed hair equals nudity, and seeing it would therefore be sexually provocative to men" (Schneider, 1984, p. 236).

Within the Roman Catholic Church, vestments of both priests and nuns are considered sacred. For example, the chasuble is the chief garment of a priest celebrating Mass. It is worn outside the other vestments. In the West all who celebrate Mass wear the same chasuble. In France, Ireland, the United States, and frequently England, a cross is marked on the back. Protestant clergy dress more to emphasize their role as pastor (meaning shepherd) or minister (one who serves), so their clothing tends to be similar to that of the congregation. However, among some denominations, such as Lutherans or Presbyterians, the dress of the clergy may be more formal, including a surplice and cassock.

DRESS, HIERARCHY, AND GROUP MEMBERSHIP. Dress is an important way of marking the hierarchy and group membership within religious organizations. The history of the Catholic priesthood shows that religious garb was in opposition to the lay dress. With the vestment the priest establishes a persona of divinity. "The changing of vestments has a powerful psychical appeal. The dress is a material link between his person and the supernatural; it absorbs, as it were, the rays of Deity, and thus at the same time inspires the human wearer" (Crawley, 1931, p. 164).

Clothing of contemporary Hasidic Jews is considered identical to the traditional Jewish garments that were once the apparel of all Jews. The type of Hasidic clothing and the way of looking Hasidic varies from class to class—that is, the extent of affiliation within Hasidism determines the particular type of garments worn, and these garments serve as an identifier of social rank (Poll, 1962). Garments vary from *zehr Hasidish* (extremely Hasidic) to *modernish* (modern). When a person wears clothing symbolizing a higher status, the frequency and intensity of his or her religious behavior should be consistent with the type of garment he or she wears. Wearing a garment symbolizing a higher status creates a chain reaction of more and more intensified religious observance. Items of dress include *shich* and *zocken* (slipper-like shoes and white kneesocks), *shtreimel* and *bekecher* (fur hat and long silk coat), *kapote* (overcoat), *biber* hat (large brimmed hat), and *bord* and *payes* (beard and side locks) (Carrel, 1999, p. 164).

Jewish women who strictly observe *halakhah* (Jewish law) frequently wear wigs to cover their hair, which, according to the Talmud, exudes sensual energy. However, there is nothing to say that these wigs cannot be stylish. In New York the most fashionable hairdressers create wigs for Orthodox women. They work to make them modest, not matronly, and definitely not "wiggy," the word Orthodox women use to describe the heavy appearance of wigs (Hayt, 1997). Covering real hair with a wig (whether the wig is made of the woman's own hair or not) is perfectly modest to these Jewish women who follow the laws of the Torah. As frequently happens in cultures throughout the world, what might seem an illogical contradiction to outsiders is completely sensible to an insider of the religious group.

Dress and Religious Traditions. Religious dress can be separated from secular dress by using different colors or forms. Dress is frequently associated with the Christian sacraments of baptism, communion, marriage, and ordination, which symbolize the individual's religious development. For a first communion, for example, girls frequently wear an ornate white dress with a white veil or hair covering, and boys wear a blue or white suit. Dress for marriage is designed to symbolize the virtue of the two individuals being "eternally" united (Storm, 1987).

Dress acts as a visible symbol for the precepts of Protestant fundamentalism, including the facts that religious principles govern all aspects of their lives (including dress) and that women's roles are frequently more "traditional," with individual needs and beliefs relinquished to the greater good of the family and religious group. In 1986, Concerned Women of America, a group of female religious advocates drawn from both the fundamentalist and the evangelical movements, wrote of the "supernaturalism" inherent in a woman's beauty and its potential for good or evil in the workplace (Edwards, 1993). However, since the 1980s fundamentalist Protestant women have had to adapt to the new economic realities of entering corporate America. For example, at Bob Jones University, a conservative Protestant college in South Carolina, classes begin with prayer, but young women are also taught to be Christian, competitive, and fashionable. Since the 1980s these women have successfully entered the more competitive business world and have learned how to dress fashionably to both fit in and move ahead. This trend encompasses a broad swath of society and is having an increasingly influential impact on consumer America, including the market for more modest fashions in retail settings.

Religious Dress, Social Control, and Morality. Religious dress can provide social control and is an important method to structure behavior, particularly as it relates to morality. Christianity has historically handed down a code of morals, including strict rules about clothing. Early Christian teachings stress the link between the outward appearance of the body and the state of the person's soul (Ribeiro, 1986). An important example of this is the process of becoming a nun, in which dress symbolizes the transition from secular life to spiritual. This involves relinquishing the individuality of dress choice by deferring to the uniform appearance of the habit. At each stage before taking final vows, women are encouraged to give up their prior self-images, accompanied by a commitment to learn to conform to the demands of the new religious life. Postulancy is the first stage, where they receive black uniforms and give up personal possessions. The postulant's uniform varies slightly from order to order but mainly consists of a short white veil, blouse, and black skirt.

Upon successful completion of this initial period, the postulant proceeds to become a novitiate, a year spent isolated from everyone except other novices. In a ceremonial rite of passage, a novice receives the habit, a religious name, and a new identity as a "bride of Christ." As stated in the Ceremonial for the Reception of Novices of the Sisters of Providence, each component of the habit is symbolically linked to the vows. The habit symbolizes an enduring state of humility; the cincture is a sign of chastity and temperance; the tunic is a sign of gravity and modesty; and the white veil is a sign of innocence. During the final period the woman takes vows of poverty, chastity, and obedience and retains limited access to the outside world. Heads are shaved prior to making final vows as a symbolic gesture related to the vow of chastity. In the 1960s and 1970s many nuns in noncloistered orders relinquished habits for secular dress as part of larger reforms dictated by Vatican II in 1962. Women religious in non-cloistered orders and their transition to secular clothing provide a model for understanding how religious dress can identify social role as well as personal identity (Michelman, 1998).

Traditional practices for Muslim men making the pilgrimage to Mecca call for the wearing of no other garment other than the *iḥrām*, which consists of two seamless wrappers, one passed around the legs, the other over the shoulder, with the head left uncovered. The ceremony of putting them on at a pilgrims' station is *al-iḥrām*, "the making unlawful" (of ordinary clothing, behavior, and occupations). The ceremony of taking them off is *al-ihlal*, "the making lawful." The pilgrim shaves his head when the pilgrimage is over. The *iḥrām* is the shroud prepared in the event of the pilgrim's death. More likely it is preserved and used as a shroud when he dies (Crawley, 1931).

Some fundamental religious groups believe that female sexuality is dangerous if left uncontrolled. This belief leads to the religious practice of prescribing modest and proper dress for female members. Modesty is generally understood to be the covering of certain parts of the body that, according to the belief system of individuals, have a sexual connotation if exposed in public. J. C. Flugel, in *The Psychology of Clothes* (1930), suggests that dress serves three main purposes—decoration, modesty, and protection. James Laver (1969) contends that until the late twentieth century it was almost universally agreed that the fundamental reason for wearing clothing was modesty. The *Book of Genesis* in the Bible recounts that Adam and Eve, having eaten of the fruit of the Tree of Knowledge, "knew that they were naked" and made themselves "aprons" of fig leaves.

Modesty is culturally relative. Research on dress of the Kalabari people of Nigeria in West Africa shows that dress for women became much more modest after Christian missionaries from Europe introduced the concept of sin and shame associated with the nude body (Michelman and Erekosima, 1992). Previously, young girls had exposed and drawn attention to their developing breasts and buttocks as part of the cultural norms of dress. Although now done only for ceremonial reenactment, this was a stage of dress that exhibited a girl's ability to move to a higher social status through the process of physical maturation and her potential for bearing children. This example demonstrates that, at least from an anthropological perspective, exposure of body parts is not inherently shameful.

Modesty is also frequently related to the religious beliefs of a group of people and is associated with holiness. For example, many Muslim women cover their heads, necks, arms, legs, and even faces in public, believing that it is proper for a woman to show these "sexual" parts of her body only within the confines of her home. Worldwide attention was focused on the proscribed attire for men and women under the rule of the Taliban in Afghanistan. Since the downfall of the Taliban, these restrictions have lessened. Much of the publicity, particularly regarding Afghani women, who were required to wear a complete covering of the body in public, have raised concerns among non-Muslims of oppression of women, particularly as it regards the political control of their bodies.

Mennonites have many religious proscriptions about women's dress that relate to their belief that clothing is "a mirror of the soul," reflecting their inner attitudes and values. In contrast, there is much immodesty in American movies, television, and music. In the United States there is an increasing "backlash" to immodesty, particularly among the more fundamental religious groups that are developing a wider influence on the broader American culture.

DRESS, SOCIAL CHANGE, AND CLASS DIFFERENCE. Although changes in religious dress occur with much less frequency than changes in the dress of the general population, forces of social, economic, and political change do influence sacred dress. For example, in Iran some Islamic women wear Chanel-style suits (secular dress) under a chador (sacred dress) (Sciolino, 1997). These women are described as the cultural elite, women who have both a Western education and growing political influence in their country. Education and wealth provide social agency to individuals, so limits on movement and role-taking in society may seem more problematic to women in the cultural elite than to poorer women who lack access to political and social power.

Religions have used sumptuary laws to regulate the conduct of members as well as to designate social class. Sumptuary laws include regulations restricting extravagance in food, drink, and dress, usually on religious or moral grounds. Muslim sumptuary rules followed those of Jewish tradition and proscribed against tattooing, nudity, and the potential idolatry of representing the human form in pictures. Dress dictated by religion means the individual does not make complicated decisions over current fashion and can devote time to his or her social identity, in particular his or her religious life.

Christianity, Islam, and Judaism use dress to perpetuate their beliefs and organizations by maintaining their traditions and customs. Dress can be considered sacred by the religion's members and is separated from the profane or secular. Hierarchy and group membership can be expressed within religious organizations through dress. Religious traditions, morality, and modesty are frequently prescribed through dress. "While dress is commonplace, it is not ephemeral, vacuous or meaningless. We wear our identities on our bodies and our bodies are used by religions to visually communicate world views" (Arthur, 1999, p. 6).

SEE ALSO Textiles.

BIBLIOGRAPHY

Arthur, Linda B. "Dress and Social Control of the Body." In *Religion, Dress, and the Body.* New York, 1999, pp. 1–7.

Baizerman, Suzanne. "The Jewish Kippa Sruga and the Social Construction of Gender in Israel." In *Dress and Gender: Making and Meaning in Cultural Contexts,* pp. 92–105, edited by Ruth Barnes and Joanne B. Eicher. New York, 1992.

Crawley, Ernest. *Dress, Drinks, and Drums: Further Studies of Savages and Sex.* London, 1931.

Edwards, Lynda. "Worldly Lessons." *New York Times,* May 30, 1993, pp. C1, C9.

Eicher, Joanne B., and Mary Ellen Roach-Higgins. "Definition and Classification of Dress." In *Dress and Gender: Making and Meaning in Cultural Contexts,* edited by Ruth Barnes and Joanne B. Eicher, pp. 8–28. New York, 1992.

Flugel, John Carl. *The Psychology of Clothes.* London, 1930.

Hayt, Elizabeth. "For Stylish Orthodox Women, Wigs That Aren't Wiggy." *New York Times,* April 27, 1997, pp. 43, 48.

Laver, James. *Modesty in Dress: An Inquiry into the Fundamentals of Fashion.* Boston, 1969.

Michelman, Susan O. "Breaking Habits: Fashion and Identity of Women Religious." *Fashion Theory* 2, no. 2 (1998): 165–192.

Michelman, Susan O., and Tonye Victor Erekosima. "Kalabari Dress in Nigeria: Visual Analysis and Gender Implications." In *Dress and Gender: Making and Meaning in Cultural Contexts,* edited by Ruth Barnes and Joanne B. Eicher, pp. 164–182. New York, 1992.

Poll, Solomon. *The Hasidic Community of Williamsburg.* New York, 1962.

Renbourn, E. T. *Materials and Clothing in Health and Disease.* London, 1972.

Ribeiro, Aileen. *Dress and Morality.* London, 1986.

Schneider, Susan Weidman. *Jewish and Female: Choices and Changes in Our Lives Today.* New York, 1984.

Sciolino, Elaine. "The Chanel under the Chador." *New York Times Magazine,* May 4, 1997, pp. 46–51.

Storm, Penny. *Functions of Dress: Tool of Culture and the Individual.* Englewood Cliffs, N.J., 1987.

SUSAN O. MICHELMAN (2005)

CLOTHING: DRESS AND RELIGION IN AMERICA'S SECTARIAN COMMUNITIES

America is home to numerous sectarian religious groups, most of whom immigrated to the United States from their original homes in Europe, the Middle East, and Asia. They are sects, rather than organized religions, as their beliefs focus on separation from the dominant religions, power systems, and culture at large. In spite of their relocation to the United States, many of these groups intentionally avoid assimilation into the larger American culture. Whereas they may be physically located in the United States, they symbolically indicate their uniqueness. Sectarian religious groups use cultural boundary markers such as dress, language, and other customs that focus on maintaining their ethnic and religious heritage; hence they are often referred to as "ethno-religious" groups.

Dress is one of the most interesting cultural boundary markers because it is a visual manifestation of cultural identity. As a window into the social world, dress is bound by a tacit set of rules, customs, conventions, and rituals that guide face-to-face interaction. To many of America's sectarian religious groups, clothing is an important symbol of religious identification. However, for most of these groups the regulation of personal appearance goes beyond clothing. The term *dress,* as it is used here, includes clothing, grooming, and all forms of body adornment. Dress also includes behaviors related to the control of the body, such as dieting, plastic surgery, and cosmetics. Holistically, then, dress functions as an effective means of nonverbal communication. Ideas, concepts, and categories fundamental to a group, such as age, gender, ethnicity, and religion, help define a person's identity that is then expressed outwardly through a person's appearance. Both individual and group identity are projected through dress because self-presentation and self-promotion are used by people to visually present identity that is congruent with their belief systems. Members of religious groups actively construct their own lives and use dress symbolically to express religious beliefs, adaptation to social change, and the conformity to social norms and religious authority.

Many of America's sectarian religious groups fit into the sociological notion of high-context cultures; in such communities, social cues are clearly embedded in expectations having to do with members' daily lives. In high-context cultures, visible symbols provide for a rich coding system that is readily understood by the culture's members. Dress is the most visible symbol for America's sectarian societies—they have developed cultural norms with regard to defining what forms of dress are considered acceptable to their specific groups. Dress codes, both formal and informal, exist as a means of showing identity. In the case of the most stringently enforced dress codes found in America's ethno-religious groups, an individual's own personal identity is subsumed by group identity.

RELIGIOUS IDEOLOGIES. Fundamentally, dress codes are less about clothing than about the control of the body by the more powerful members of a group who enforce ideologies pertinent to that religious culture. America's ethno-religious groups are based on patriarchy that is divinely ordered. They subscribe to the notion that God ordained male power. Where religious dress codes exist, they express group identity and simultaneously function as a means of reinforcing male patriarchal control within the group. Dress codes are related to gendered power; in essence, dress codes within most of America's ethno-religious groups are a reflection of male control over women's bodies.

To examine how dress can be expressive of religious ideologies, it is helpful to understand how each of America's major religions perceives the role of dress as a means of identity expression. These values are based on long-standing beliefs found in each group's history. Judaism is based on the concept that people exist to glorify God, and to be appropriately dressed, then, is a religious duty. Similarly for Christianity, modesty with regard to body exposure is an important value that is a key indicator of religious conservatism. For fundamentalist Christians, such as the Anabaptist groups (Amish, Mennonites, and Hutterites) whose religious precepts include the requirement that they be uniquely separate from the larger society, dress is used to show that separation. In these ethno-religious sectarian groups, dress is often hyper-conservative or may even be a form of fossilized fashion, where the garments look much like those worn by their ancestors hundreds of years ago.

Islamic ideology focuses on male power and requires separation of the sexes in public and private spheres. Among American sectarian religious groups, codes of modesty go beyond the covering of women's bodies to include restriction of women's behavior. America is home to a disparate group of people who fled their original countries seeking more freedom and issues of dress codes in the home country have often been cited as unduly restrictive. For example, when in public, Saudi Arabian women cover everything but the eyes with cloaks (*abbaya*) and veils, referred to as "life's uniform." Throughout the larger cities in Iran, posters announce the specifics of the dress code requiring Iranian women to dress similarly to Saudi women. Iranian women are required to wear chadors that cover all but their faces. In Afghanistan under Taliban control, women were killed if they did not wear the all-enveloping *burka* or *chadaree.* Muslim women who have immigrated to the United States continue to wear clothing that meets standards of modesty acceptable to the woman, her family, and her religious community. It is much more rare to see Muslim women in America who are completely veiled; whereas loose, modest clothing and head veils are common in the United States, face veils are not.

Modesty and Female Sexuality in Dress. Among all of the major ethno-religious groups in America, modesty in women's dress is associated with gender norms; this is a major issue to sectarian societies. Gender issues are paramount in the dress codes of conservative religious groups, because the control of female sexuality is often of great importance in patriarchal societies. The dress codes generally relate to modesty and require clothing to cover the contours of the female body.

As used by religious groups, the issue of modesty goes beyond the covering of women's bodies in order to disguise female curves and secondary sexual characteristics; in the conservative strains of all of the major religions, dress codes also deal with the care and covering of women's hair, as it is associated with women's sexuality. Further complicating matters, dress codes are conflated with gender and power issues in America's ethno-religious groups. At the root of this issue is the control of female sexuality that is perceived to be necessary by some religious groups as a means to maintain social order.

An understanding of how dress works within religious groups calls attention to the complexity of meanings surrounding visible symbols such as dress and sheds light on the ways bodies can communicate social and religious values. The dress of America's sectarian religious groups can be used to facilitate social and ideological agendas. In these societies clothing and personal adornment are used for establishing and maintaining personal and social identities, social hierarchies, definitions of deviance, and patriarchal systems of power, which is evidenced in social control measures, and these are subtly expressed in dress codes. As a consequence, dress within conservative religious groups is a symbol of the individual's commitment to his or her ethno-religious society, while it also symbolizes the group's control over its individual member's lives. For America's fundamentalist Christian groups, and the Anabaptist groups in particular, dress is important with regard to its role as a cultural boundary marker that has an active role in maintaining the social control system and in greatly retarding social change and acculturation.

Dress and Social Control. With many of America's sectarian societies, dress is an immediate and visible indicator of how a person fits into his or her religious sect. As a marker of identity, dress may be used to gauge the person's commitment to the group and to the religious value system. In many of the most conservative groups, suppression of individuality is expected in order to show obedience to the rules of the religious organization. Ethno-religious groups frequently use clothing to simultaneously express ethnicity, gender norms, and level of religious involvement (religiosity). Through conformance to a strict religious value system, the most conservative of the American sectarian groups exert control over their members' spirituality and simultaneously control their bodies. Since strict conformity is often equated with religiosity, compliance to strict codes of behavior is demanded. The internal body is subject to control by the religious culture, especially with regard to food and sex. The external body, however, is much more visibly restrained. Strict dress codes are enforced because dress is considered symbolic of religiosity. Clothing becomes a symbol of social control as it controls the external body. Whereas a person's level of religiosity cannot be objectively perceived, symbols such as clothing are used as evidence that the member of the religious group is on the "right and true path."

Normative social control begins with personal social control through self-regulation, followed by informal social control. The member wants to fit into the group and expresses role commitment by following the social norms, visibly expressed in the group's dress code. When the individual begins to offend, for example, by wearing a garment that is too revealing of body contours, peers may disapprove and use subtle methods of informal control to pressure the individual to conform to the group norms. Finally, the threat an offender introduces to the social order is managed through formal social control measures, such as disciplinary actions and expulsion administered by specialized agents, including ministers, rabbis, and other moral arbiters. Thus, norms are managed through social control to inhibit deviation and insure conformity to social norms at even the most minute level.

Through symbolic devices, the physical body exhibits the normative values of the social body. Symbols such as dress help delineate the social unit and visually define its boundaries because they give nonverbal information about the individual. Unique dress attached to specific religious and cultural groups, then, can function to insulate group members from outsiders while bonding the members to each other. Normative behavior within the culture reaffirms loyalty to the group and can be evidenced by the wearing of a uniform type of attire.

Within American culture there are specific ethno-religious groups that intentionally separate themselves from the rest of society and attempt to reestablish the small, face-to-face community. Many originated in Europe and moved to America when religious freedom was promised to immigrants. Shakers, Mennonites, Hutterites, and Amish are such groups. These groups are often perceived by the outside world as quite unusual, but that derives more from their unique customs and behaviors than from their religious differences from mainstream Christianity. An essential factor in ethno-religious groups, social control is significant in terms of the survival prospects of the group. Among Orthodox Jews in Williamsburg, New York, social control was achieved in ways remarkably similar to those used by the Amish and conservative Mennonites. The most important features included isolation from the external society; emphasis on conformity with status related to religiosity (symbolized by clothing status markers); a powerful clergy; and rigorous sanctions to insure conformity to norms.

Some of America's sectarian ethno-religious groups use fossilized fashion to separate themselves from the outside world. Notable among these are the Shakers, Amish, Hasidic Jews, Hutterites, and several conservative Mennonite groups. Fossilized fashion has been explained as a sudden "freezing" of fashion, whereby a group continues to wear a style long after it has gone out of style for the general population. This phenomenon has been explained as expressing dignity and high social status or the group's religious, old-fashioned, sectarian identity. Within certain ethno-religious groups, fossilized fashion is used in contemporary settings as a visual symbol of traditional gender roles for women; this generally occurs in societies that find change to be a threat.

SECTARIAN DRESS. Some of America's sectarian groups are referred to as "plain people" because they believe that simplicity is a prerequisite for Christian living. Their religious mandate that they live separate from the world is visibly manifest in their use of "plain dress" that identifies them as uniquely different from other Americans. In 1986 there were just under 800,000 people living in these sectarian societies. In spite of assimilation pressures, however, at that time over half of these groups still dressed plain or semiplain.

Among the best known of America's plain people are the Amish, Hutterites, and Mennonites who are descended from the Anabaptists, a radical group that originated during the Protestant Reformation in the 1500s. As the Anabaptists migrated from Europe to America in the eighteenth and nineteenth centuries, schisms occurred, and frequently the concept of how the group was to maintain its separation from the larger American culture was at issue. Cultural boundary markers that are visual, such as dress, figured into many of these schisms. Today there are a wide range of dress standards in the approximately 3,000 communities of Amish, Hutterites, and Mennonites in the United States; 65 percent of these groups use plain dress.

Amish. Among America's sectarian societies is the Old Order Amish, whose dress is used to visually separate them from outsiders. Amish women and girls are known for wearing long, loose dresses made from solid-colored fabric that are pinned rather than buttoned. These dresses are covered with a cape over the bust and apron; in winter a shawl is worn for warmth. Following the perceived biblical mandate of *1 Corinthians* 11:2–6, their hair is not cut but is parted and put in a bun; over that a white prayer covering is worn. Differences between Amish communities are seen in the pleating of the prayer covering. Pants, cosmetics, and jewelry are not allowed.

Amish men and boys are allowed to have buttons on their solid-colored shirts, but they often have hooks and eyes on outerwear such as jackets and vests. They wear dark-colored suits, "plain coats" (straight-cut coats without lapels) and broad-fall trousers with suspenders, like those worn centuries ago. Hats are broad-brimmed. In winter, black felt hats are worn, in summer the hats are of straw. Their hair is worn in a bowl cut, and they are not allowed to wear mustaches. Once married, men grow beards.

Mennonites. Only one-fourth of the Mennonite groups dress plain in the twenty-first century. Like the Quakers and many Brethren groups, many Mennonite groups began to eliminate clothing restrictions in the late nineteenth century as they began to assimilate into the larger American culture. Mennonite ministers had concerns with regard to assimilation and the perception that it might draw Mennonites away from their spiritual roots; as a result these concerns led to a revival of plain dress between the 1920s and 1940s. Nonetheless, by the 1980s most Mennonite groups had nearly abandoned plain dress. Those wishing to maintain plain dress standards frequently joined more conservative Mennonite groups. Plain dress is still used in the most conservative Mennonite communities, such as among the Holdeman Mennonites (Church of God in Christ, Mennonite) and among the Old Order Mennonites.

Modesty and gender segregation are the prevailing features for women's dress in the plain Mennonite groups. Dress styles are regulated by tradition; they are quite similar to those worn by their forebears in the previous centuries. Dresses are loose, high-necked, often long-sleeved, with skirts worn at calf length or longer. The most conservative Mennonite women also wear an apron and cape to disguise the bust and abdomen. A head covering (black for Holdeman women, white for other Mennonites) is required to be worn over uncut hair, which is pinned up in a bun. Fabric for dresses may be of subtle prints or patterns. Slacks and shorts are not allowed. Similarly, jewelry, fancy buttons, and cosmetics are prohibited as worldly.

In the plain Mennonite groups, dress is more restrictive for women than for men; it is the women's responsibility to maintain the tradition of plain dress. Mennonite men in the plain groups are not as distinctly dressed. In some groups a plain suit is worn to church, and men are prohibited from wearing ties and shaving beards, though some may trim their beards. Outside of church, plain Mennonite men often dress much like non-Mennonite neighbor men, in denim pants and plaid shirts. In contrast, Hasidic Jewish men wear more distinctive clothing than their wives.

Hasidic Jews. Among the most visibly orthodox of the Jewish groups, Hasidic Jews are easily distinguishable by their dress: men with beards and long side curls typically wear broad-brimmed black hats, black suits, and even black topcoats. Their dress is sometimes confused with that of Amish men, as both groups wear fossilized fashion that originated from the 1600s. Hasidic Jews wear the same clothes as centuries ago in order to protect themselves against assimilation and to reinforce their respect for the teachings of the Torah.

A Hasidic man's everyday wardrobe consists of a wool suit in a dark color with a long tailored jacket (*bekeshe*), under which he wears a white shirt. He wears a felt hat most days. On the Jewish Sabbath, dress is more formal. The *bekeshe* is black satin or silk, and the hat *(streimel)* is a round hat made of fur. Under the jacket he wears a rectangular prayer shawl.

Hasidic Jewish women take care to dress modestly but have no prescribed garments. Skirts and sleeves are long, and they wear stockings. If they are married, their natural hair must be covered, even in the home. Hair is perceived as a sexual element appropriate only for the husband's view. Prior to immigration to the United States, Hasidic women covered their hair with kerchiefs or wigs that were obviously artificial. However, the use of fine human hair has made the wigs often look as good as or better than women's own hair, and the rabbis have started questioning whether these wigs now meet the religious requirements of modesty.

Dress and Social Change. With changing social, political, and economic environments, even the most sectarian religious group has to contend with the impact of social change. Changes in dress often signal underlying changes in social roles as well as gender roles. Traditional gender roles can be marked by a particular form of dress where the roles are stable for long periods of time; when dress changes suddenly in these groups, one can expect to find a change in gender roles. A good example is that of the change in the dress of Roman Catholic priests and nuns following the changes instituted by Vatican II in the 1960s. The changes were more pronounced for nuns, and as their roles within the church dramatically changed, so too did their dress. Additionally, when roles are restrictive, one can expect to see a restriction in women's dress in the form of either dress codes or physically restrictive clothing.

In conclusion, dress in America's sectarian societies can be used visually to provide distinction between the sacred and the profane, especially in the symbolic separation of the ethno-religious subculture from a dominant culture. As ethno-religious groups encounter social change, dress often symbolically becomes important as certain items of a religious group's clothing may be classified as sacred in contrast to what is considered profane. Due to their symbolic manifestation of religious values, dress codes can be seen as sacred rules. Dress in these groups is used intentionally to visually separate these religious groups from the larger culture.

See Also Anabaptism; Christianity; Islam; Judaism; Protestantism; Sexuality.

Bibliography

Arthur, Linda B. "Clothing Is a Window to the Soul: The Social Control of Women in a Holdeman Mennonite Community." *Journal of Mennonite Studies* 15 (1997): 11–29.

Arthur, Linda B., ed. *Religion, Dress, and the Body.* Dress, Body, Culture Series. Oxford, 1999.

Arthur, Linda B., ed. *Undressing Religion: Commitment and Conversion from a Cross-Cultural Perspective.* Dress, Body, Culture Series. Oxford, 2000.

Damhorst, Mary Lynn, Kimberly A. Miller, and Susan O. Michelman. *The Meanings of Dress.* New York, 1999.

Gingerich, Melvin. *Mennonite Attire through Four Centuries.* Breinigsville, Pa., 1970.

Goffman, Erving. *The Presentation of Self in Everyday Life.* Garden City, N.J., 1959.

Hostetler, John A. *Amish Society.* Baltimore, 1980.

Poll, Solomon. *The Hasidic Community of Williamsburg.* New York, 1962.

Scott, Stephen. *Why Do They Dress That Way?* Intercourse, Pa., 1986.

Linda B. Arthur (2005)

CLOTILDA (c. 470–545), queen consort of Clovis, king of the Franks. Her Christian faith of the Nicene, or catholic, tradition greatly influenced her husband and all of northern Gaul. Clotilda was born a Bergundian, in the Rhone valley in eastern France; her grandfather was Gundioc, king of the Bergundians. Her father, Chilperic, a Christian, was one of four heirs to the king. A violent dispute among the heirs led to Chilperic's death and to Clotilda's having to live with an uncle in Geneva. Commerce between the Bergundians in Geneva and the Salians, a group of Franks living in Paris under King Clovis, led to Clotilda's meeting Clovis and to their eventual marriage.

Clotilda was a Christian devoted to the orthodox faith, as opposed to Arianism. Clovis disdained her faith until the Alemanni, a formidable Germanic people, invaded northern Gaul. He vowed that if he defeated the Alemanni he would accept Clotilda's Christ. His victory in 495 led to his baptism, along with that of three thousand of his warriors, on Christmas Day of 496. The Franks were the first Germanic tribes to convert to the orthodox faith; most of the tribes to the south of them were Arians. With Clotilda's help, Clovis expanded the area of his rule, defended the Catholic faith against Arianism, and became an important link in the spread of Christianity in northwestern Europe.

After the death of her husband in 511, Clotilda's four sons engaged in a bitter feud that led to several deaths. Deeply saddened, Clotilda retired to a convent in Tours, a town where the famous Martin had been bishop in the fourth century. She maintained her keen interest in civic matters and became fabled for her piety and her practical deeds of generosity.

BIBLIOGRAPHY

The best biography, and one that is quite readable, is Godefroi Kurth's *Saint Clotilda,* translated by V. M. Crawford (London and New York, 1913).

H. MCKENNIE GOODPASTURE (1987)

CLOWNS. The term *clown* is used here as a gloss for a cluster of figures that appear in the religious events of various peoples and that have certain attributes in common. It is, therefore, a term of analysis employed in thinking about the place of such figures in religious performance. This usage is not intended to be homologous with the perceptions of any given people, whose culture is likely to connote more particularistic significance to such characters and their cognates. Instead, it is suggested in this article that what ritual-clown figures have in common with one another is a certain logic of composition. Characters of such composition then have crucial functions for the rituals and dramas within which they perform.

The etymology of the word *clown* in the English language suggests the logic of composition for such figures. According to the *Oxford English Dictionary,* the term appeared in English usage in the second half of the sixteenth century: it originally meant "clod," "clot," or "lump." *Clod* and *clot* were long synonymous. *Clod* connotes the coagulation of liquids and a lumpish adhesion of materials. *Clot* connotes a semisolid lump formed by congelation and coagulation. Put together, *clown, clod,* and *clot* connote an entity that is unfinished or incomplete in its internal organization: one that hangs together in a loose and clumsy way. The clown is lumpish in its imperfect—but congealing and adhering—fusion of attributes. It also has a sense of frozen motion, of congealed liquidity, that connotes processuality and dynamism rather than structure and stasis. In the European tradition, the clown had affinities to festival fools, folk fools, and holy fools, all of whom had the tendency to melt the solidity of the world. The word *fool,* according to the *Oxford English Dictionary,* derives from the Latin *follis,* which literally means "bellows" but is also used in the sense of "windbag." The term *buffoon,* with connotations similar to those of *fool,* is cognate with the Italian *buffare,* "to puff." In the derivation of *fool* there is a sense of lightness and motion, and so of processuality. Given the likely affinity between the clown and the fool, there is in the clown a figure that is integrated in a clumsy fashion and that adheres to itself with an incipient sense of internal movement.

Clowns are ambiguous and ambivalent figures. Within their variegated composition they subsume attributes that contradict and invert one another. The clown in ritual is at once a character of solemnity and fun, of gravity and hilarity, of danger and absurdity, of wisdom and idiocy, and of the sacred and the profane. The interior logic of composition of such a figure is not homogeneous. It is neither wholly one attribute of a set nor another. Given this sense of neither/nor, such figures subsume holistically, albeit lumpishly, all of their contradictory sets of attributes.

These contradictions within the ritual clown rarely are resolved. Instead, whichever attribute a clown presents in performance, the projection of its contrary always is imminent. Thus the opposing attributes within the figure continuously oscillate among themselves. Given this attribute of internal oscillation, such clown figures can be said to subsume within themselves a notion of border or boundary that they straddle and across which they move, back and forth, for as long as they remain true to type. The ritual clown is an eminently paradoxical figure: It is neither wise nor foolish, yet it is both without being wholly one or the other. As a paradoxical being, the figure evokes inconsistencies of meaning and referential ambiguities in ritual contexts that otherwise have an appearance of solidity and stability. The clown is a construct with a sense of incompleteness, yet whole (a lump), that is in a condition of transformation (congelation) but that is somehow out of place in context (a clod).

Externally, the ritual clown appears as an ill-formed unity. Pueblo Indian clowns of the American Southwest are lumpish in form or painted in stripes of contrasting colors. Other clowns often are particolored or piecemeal beings that hang together loosely. Internally, the ritual clown manifests qualities of multiplicity and fluidity: it is fluctuating and unstable. This interior organization can be summated as a condition of self-transformation: the figure is continually in motion within itself, and so it remains permanently unfinished. It is a powerful figurative rendition of processuality. This makes it a powerful solvent of contexts and structures within which it is located. These attributes are crucial to the roles it performs within ritual and ceremonial occasions.

Clowns seem to have especial affinities to the boundaries of ritualistic occasions. In European folk rites and dramas that were associated with seasonal transitions, especially those from winter to spring, and so with notions of the regeneration of natural and social orders, folk fools at times played the role of master of ceremony. These characters tended to be killed and revived in these events, and so they bridged and mediated cosmic transitions. Among the Tewa, Hopi, and Zuni Pueblo Indians of the American Southwest, ritual clowns were indisputable masters of the boundary. More generally, where such clown figures are common in ceremonials, they either control the overall organization of sequencing of events or they appear during the interludes between phases of rites. In either instance, they are located in transitional zones that connote the sequential movement or transformation of ritual from one context to another. Given that these figures encompass a notion of boundary within the composition of their being—one through which they endlessly oscillate—their affinity to the external boundaries of ritual events, and to those within ritual, should be clear. They are ambulatory manifestations of boundariness, for their composition resonates with, and so is keyed to, borders of ritual in terms of its spatial and sequential ordering.

This delineation of ritual clowns is quite distinct from those modern clowns of the European tradition of the circus and from stock figures of comedy. Circus clown performances usually consist of at least a pair of clowns who are distinguished categorically from one another. The white-faced clown is an epitome of "culture": he is formal, elegant, authoritative, rigid, and overcivilized. By contrast, the "auguste" clown is thoroughly sloppy, ill kempt, amoral, and chaotic: he inverts the attributes of the white-faced clown and is identified with those of "nature." In performance these two clowns are viable in tandem, so that their respective sets of characteristics complement each other.

These clowns also have an intimate relation to boundaries; but theirs is an exterior one, for a sense of boundary is established by their interplay in performance rather than by their being part of the logic of composition of either or both of them. Thus the boundary between, say, categories of "nature" and "culture" becomes located somewhere between these two figures instead of within one or both of them. Each figure itself has a homogeneous and stable composition, and so the contrast of opposites is evident only when they are together: they manipulate boundaries only as a duo. By way of contrast, the ritual clown dissolves boundaries by itself. Stock comic figures that appear in ritual dramas, and whose ethnographic provenance seems much more extensive than that of ritual clowns, also tend to have homogeneous and internally stable compositions. In general they lack, in and of themselves, the transformative capacities that are integral to clowns in ritual.

Nonetheless, figures that approximate the attributes of ritual clowns, as these are delineated here, do have a fairly widespread distribution among peoples of the world, some of whom are mentioned here, although lack of space prevents adducing these. Clowns in ceremonial and ritual are reported for the Mayo and Yaqui peoples of northern Mexico, for the Pueblo Indian peoples of the American Southwest, and for other native peoples of California, the Great Plains, and the Northwest Coast of North America. In European traditions, festival fools were prominent in various English dramas of springtime and in the Swiss-German *Fastnachtsspiele;* they had affinities to the Italian tradition of *buffo* and perhaps to picaresque literary works. Clownlike figures are reported in the Turkish puppet theater, in some Iranian improvisatory folk theater, and in the traditional Szechwan theater of China. Such figures also are found in modern Javanese *ludruk* performances and in the Javanese puppet theater. They appear quite elaborated in various South Indian traditions: in Carnatic puppet performances, in Kannada *yaksagana* dance dramas, in the *kutiyattam* dramatic tradition of Kerala, and in Tamil *karakam* dances and *terukkuttu* street dramas as well as in the stories of the sixteenth-century Tamil and Telugu court jester Tenali Rama. The provenance of such figures extends south to Sri Lanka and north to the tradition of dance dramas in Tibetan monasteries.

There is a multiplicity and duplicity in clowns, a radical emphasis on the disharmonic that at first sight appears out of place in many of the ceremonies and dramas in which they appear. And a sense of unease pervades many of the explanations of why they are there. The commonest, and the least satisfactory, is that clowns provide comic relief, either from the seriousness and tedium of the ritual medium itself or from the everyday suppression of forbidden themes that clowns raise to overt and conscious scrutiny. There are various versions of this thesis. Thus, such figures are said to enable members of audiences to think or to behave in otherwise repressed ways, or it is said that these clowns exist in order to violate taboo, given the need to evoke themes that must be suppressed in the everyday contexts of life. These approaches readily lend themselves to varieties of psychologistic reductionism, such that clowns are said to concretize and to release unconscious psychic tensions by bringing them to conscious thought. An added explanation is that these figures reduce the tension and anxiety that are generated by awesome and mysterious sacrality, since, through harmless burlesque, the frightening is made familiar and known.

Clowns in ritual and drama do indeed invert, mock, and satirize both taken-for-granted conventions of life and those that are sacralized and venerated, whether through gentle irony, through dramatic allegory, or through scatological burlesque. Yet, within the same occasions, they often are the righteous upholders of morality and propriety. Such groups as the Hopi Indians of the American Southwest explicitly recognize that clowns underline moral precepts by their amoral antics. The Hopi state that clowns show life as it should not be. Others, such as the Tewa, Zuni, and Mayo Indians, accord explicit sacred and moral stature to their clowns. Among the Mayo, these are more figures of fright than of amusement. Still other peoples seem to refrain from exegesis and simply summate clowns in ritual as figures of fun.

There are two signal difficulties with discussions of ritual clowning that rely on one or another version of catharsis or of satirical inversion to explain the existence of these contrary characters. In the first instance, either or both of these functions can be and are performed by figures of much simpler composition. Stock comic characters, who appear in ceremonial and dramatic activities, and whose composition is homogeneous and not transformative, often meet such requirements. These are the quintessential butts, bunglers, and schemers, whose rollicking antics and exaggerated amorality serve onlookers with a license to frolic with the unspeakable, and perhaps with the unthinkable, in the security of knowing or feeling that these are unnatural and temporary versions of order that will revert to their moral counterparts and so will reaffirm righteous values and conduct. Why then should clown figures of such complex and inconstant composition be equated in role and function with these facile and straightforward stock comic characters? The likely answer is that they should not be, and that ritual clowns carry out other tasks more in keeping with their own interior organization.

The second difficulty in discussions of ritual clowning is that these clowns are treated as if they reflect, in unmediated ways, themes of more general cultural and psychological significance. In other words, clowns are torn from the contexts of their appearance and performance without any explanation of their presence there. Yet, first and foremost, and prior to a consideration of their significance for more abstract motifs of psychic balance and cultural values, it is in terms of the occasions of their appearance that the presence of clowns should be explicated.

That clowns in ritual are living studies in vivid contrast and in shades of comparison is indicative of their status in performance. As interlocutors and as commentators, their affinities are to boundaries that separate ceremonial or narrative action from the mundane or that distinguish between different phases or contexts within ritual performance itself. In a sense, they keep one foot within an ongoing context of participation and experience, while the other foot is already leading into another. As such, they are agents of change, mediators who dissolve and transform the fixity of categories of performance and narrative that boundaries organize and integrate.

Ritual and ceremonial occasions have programs or texts, prescribed or inscribed, that are their elementary organization. Occasions in which clowns appear are always composed of more than a single adumbrated context of meaning and experience. That is, these occasions are constituted of a number of phases that contrast with one another in their programmatic purpose and that must be shifted, one into another, in sequence. Written or oral texts and programs often suggest that such transitions are accomplished simply because they are inscribed or prescribed. Yet, in the practice of performance, each phase or context of an occasion has the tendency to adumbrate and to reify itself in stable and seamless ways that wholly engross participants in its experience. This lack of discordance works against the necessary decomposition or deconstruction of context, in order to make way for the next, and so to enable the overall occasion to be shifted in sequence through its constituent phases, as specified by program or text.

The design of the clown is precisely that of a whirligig—one that swirls in counterpoint to the adumbration and concordance of any ritual context in which it is located. As it revolves within itself, the clown gathers up the interwoven strands of the coherence of context, mixes them up, and so contradicts their integration and unravels them. Just as the clown upends any configuration of meaning into which it enters, so it takes apart context and opens the way to the cohering of alternative patterns of meaning.

Such occasions often have a sense of climax that arouses within the participants the recognition of some transcendent reality and seamless truth. Then the inherently reflexive properties of the clown must be stilled. Otherwise, true to its own rhythm and logic, it would continue to raise questions and doubts about such contexts, and so it would signify that even the experience of transcendence is artificial and transitory. This likely would destroy the significance of the truths of transcendence for the participants. Therefore, a common fate of clowns in ritual is their demise as contrary, oscillating, reflexive characters. Either they are tamed and brought to heel, or their internal composition is made homogeneous. Then they no longer arouse reflectiveness among participants, for their presence no longer causes the participants to doubt the validity of transcendent experiences. At this point, clowns simply reinforce the values of such truths or revelations in straightforward ways.

This depiction of the clown in ritual recognizes that the especial properties of this figure are a function of its unusual design, and so, too, of its place during religious and dramatic occasions. If the figure of the clown is apprehended as a complex device that unlocks perception to an awareness of the artifice of textual coherence, then it is comprehended also as a dynamic device that enables certain religious occasions to be enacted and accomplished. It is then incumbent upon further thought to search other ceremonial media, in which clowns have no place, for analogous mechanisms that accomplish transformation of context and transitions between contexts and so enable these occasions to progress in sequence through their programs.

See Also Drama; Masks; Tricksters.

Bibliography

Useful overviews of fools and of clownlike figures in European traditions are found in Enid Welsford's *The Fool: His Social and Literary History* (London, 1935) and in Barbara Swain's *Fools and Folly during the Middle Ages and the Renaissance* (New York, 1932). The complex and contrastive characters of clown figures are discussed evocatively in William Willeford's *The Fool and His Sceptre* (London, 1969). The clown as a solvent of perception and of structure is implied strongly in Wolfgang M. Zucker's "The Clown as the Lord of Disorder," in *Holy Laughter,* edited by M. Conrad Hyers (New York, 1969). The logic of composition of ritual clowns discussed in this article is expanded and elaborated in my article "The Ritual-Clown: Attributes and Affinities," *Anthropos* 76 (1981): 321–370. Paul Bouissac makes a semiotic analysis of the nature-culture distinction in modern European circus clown performances in "Clown Performances as Metacultural Texts," a chapter in his *Circus and Culture* (Bloomington, Ind., 1976), pp. 151–175. A clear, if simple, example of a cathartic explanation of ritual clowning is John J. Honigmann's "An Interpretation of the Social-Psychological Functions of the Ritual Clown," *Character and Personality* 10 (1941–1942): 220–226. The view that the activity of ritual clowns should be explicated first and foremost with reference to wider themes of culture, outside the contexts of performance, is put ably by Laura Makarius in her article "Ritual Clowns and Symbolical Behavior," *Diogenes* 69 (1970): 44–73. In an ethnographic vein, there are few accessible and complete accounts of ritual clowning in context. One decent description is of a Tewa Pueblo Indian rite, in Vera Laski's *Seeking Life* (Philadelphia, 1958). Louis A. Hieb's "The Ritual Clown: Humor and Ethics," in *Forms of Play of Native North Americans,* edited by Edward Norbeck and Claire R. Farrer (Saint Paul, Minn., 1979), pp. 171–188, argues against cross-cultural delineations of ritual clowns, since the meanings of such figures are highly specific to particular cultures. *Clowning as Critical Practice: Performance Humor in the South Pacific* (Pittsburgh, 1992), edited by William R. Mitchell, is a rich and insightful collection on the prominent roles of clowning practices in Pacific societies. Chapter Five, on "Clowning and Chiasm," in Claire R. Farrer's, *Living Life's Circle: Mescalero Apache Cosmovision* (Albuquerque, 1991) contains a fertile discussion of clowns in ritual. Abdellah Hammoudi's, *The Victim and Its Masks: An Essay on Sacrifice and Masquerade in the Mahgreb* (Chicago, 1993) has a rich analysis of a ritual in which clowning is prominent.

DON HANDELMAN (1987 AND 2005)

COATLICUE ("serpent skirt") was one of an array of Aztec earth-mother goddesses, the Teteoinnan, who represented the notion of maternal fertility associated with the earth. Coatlicue's monumental stone image, excavated in 1790 in the heart of Mexico City, is one of the finest and most monstrous achievements of Mesoamerican religious art. It is an eight-foot-tall stone figure consisting of a female form draped with a blouse of severed human hands and hearts, a skirt of intertwined serpents with skull belt buckles in front and back, ferocious rattlesnakes for hands, and a head composed of two giant rattlesnake heads facing one another. According to art historians, these two giant serpent heads emerge from spurts of blood resulting from Coatlicue's decapitation. Her feet are giant jaguar claws. A serpent of blood flows from beneath her skirt of serpents. This masterpiece of Mesoamerican sculpture, located today in the Museo Nacional de Antropología in Mexico City, reflects the combined qualities of terror and destruction associated with some aspects of the goddess cult of the Aztec capital, Tenochtitlán (1325–1521).

Coatlicue's primary creative act, told in book 3 of Fray Bernardino de Sahagún's *Historia general de las cosas de la Nueva España* (compiled 1569–1582; also known as the Florentine Codex), consisted of the dramatic birth of the war god Huitzilopochtli. This *teotuicatl* ("divine song") tells how Coatlicue was sweeping out a temple on Coatepec ("serpent mountain") when a ball of feathers made her pregnant with Huitzilopochtli. Her children, the *centzon huitznahua* ("four hundred southerners"), became outraged at this and prepared for war against their mother. Led by Coatlicue's aggressive daughter, Coyolxauhqui ("she of the golden bells"), the four hundred warriors began their march toward Coatepec. When Coatlicue became frightened, a voice from her womb comforted her, saying, "Do not worry, I know what must be done." When the warriors arrived at Coatepec, Coatlicue gave birth to Huitzilopochtli, fully grown and dressed as a warrior. Using his *xiuhcoatl* ("serpent of lightning"), he dismembered his sister Coyolxauhqui and slaughtered most of the rest of his siblings as well.

Along with the goddess Cihuacoatl ("serpent woman"), Coatlicue represents the aggressive mortuary aspect of Aztec goddesses.

BIBLIOGRAPHY

Brundage, Burr C. *The Fifth Sun: Aztec Gods, Aztec World.* Austin, 1979. See especially Brundage's helpful chapters on "The Quality of the Numinous" (pp. 50–79) and "The Goddesses" (pp. 153–175). Brundage's work takes seriously the religious factor in Aztec society and develops in this book a framework to relate specific aspects of the sacred to a general understanding of the religious system.

Fernandez, Justino. *Coatlicue: Estética del arte indígena antiguo.* 2d ed. Mexico City, 1959. Fernandez's work, with a stimulating prologue by Samuel Ramos, discusses Coatlicue's aesthetic character in relation to a general model of Aztec art.

New Sources

Matos Moctezuma, Eduardo. *Piedras negadas: de la Coatlicue al Templo Mayor.* (*Neglected Stones: From Coatlicue to the Great Temple*). Mexico City, 1998.

DAVÍD CARRASCO (1987)
Revised Bibliography

COCKS. The cock is preeminently a sun symbol. In western Asia the crowing cock is closely associated with solar rituals; in the ancient Near East it became an integral part of the solar iconography during the second millennium BCE, and the mythology of the "fire cock" has spread widely and survived in the folklore of western Asia. The solar cock is also attested among some of the most primitive peoples of Asia; the Nagas of Assam, for example, believe that the sun is lured out of darkness by the cock's crowing. According to the Miao of southern China, the sun, which hides itself behind the mountain and darkens the whole world, shows itself again with the crowing of a cock. Similarly, Japanese myths tell how Amaterasu, the sun goddess, hides in the heavenly cave but comes out again on hearing the crowing of cocks.

The symbolic importance of the cock is well attested in the Greco-Roman world. There, the motif of the crowing cock, the bird of dawning, was enriched by the motif of the cock as fighter. The fighting cock, although associated with warrior divinities (such as Ares and Athena), was especially connected with Dionysos, in whose theater the official fights occurred. Significantly, the pugnacity of the cock was taken as an aspect of its sexual life; representations of the cock with a human phallus as head and neck are quite numerous. Especially interesting are three associations of the cock with Greco-Roman funerary symbolism: (1) it was one of the animals offered to the deities of the underworld in connection with the cult of the dead; (2) as is suggested by its representation together with Persephone and Hades, the cock was viewed as the herald of the dawn of the new world, the future life; as such, it symbolized hope of life after death; and (3) as the victor of a fight, the cock symbolized the soul of the departed; it was commonly associated, especially on tombstones, with Hermes, the psychopomp who escorted the soul to a blessed life after death. In Mithraism, the cock was frequently used in cult meals, where presumably its connection with the rising sun and immortality or future life was significant.

In Judaism the cock has been used in the Kapparah, a practice designed as a means of ritual atonement for sins. The cock has also been regarded as a charm that could exorcise demons; at the dedication of a new house, Jews used to kill a cock on the spot to purge the house of a demonic presence. Moreover, the crowing cock at dawn was a symbol of the redemption of the messianic age.

Christianity has continued this idea, making the cock a symbol of the risen Lord, Jesus Christ, the new light. In announcing the approach of day, the cock reminds Christians not only of Peter's denial but also of their own resurrection in a future life. Even cockfighting has found its Christian representations, which inspire believers to win the struggle with their own lower nature so that they can inherit eternal life.

In Islam, too, the cock is a benevolent bird. Muslims have believed that a cock would crow when it became aware of the presence of jinn, evil spirits. And, as the bird of dawning, the cock still serves to awaken the sleeping faithful for morning prayer.

BIBLIOGRAPHY

The best treatment of the cock in Greek tradition remains Sir D'arcy W. Thompson's *A Glossary of Greek Birds* (1895; reprint, London, 1936), pp. 33–44. See also Erwin R. Goodenough's admirable account of cock symbolism in *Pagan Symbols in Judaism,* volume 8 of his *Jewish Symbols in the Greco-Roman World* (New York, 1958), pp. 59–70.

New Sources

Baird, Merrily. *Symbols of Japan: Thematic Motifs in Art and Design.* New York, 2001.

MANABU WAIDA (1987)
Revised Bibliography

CODES AND CODIFICATION.

While codes and codification are only rarely discussed in broad studies of religion, there are nevertheless preliminary studies that allow us to outline the subject with some accuracy. Henry Sumner Maine, in his *Ancient Law,* first published in 1861, tried to describe the evolution of human society by comparing all preserved collections of ancient laws. With the discovery and diffusion of the art of writing, laws engraved on tablets took the place of the customary law recollected by privileged aristocracies, and "democratic sentiment" added to their popularity. "Inscribed tablets," Main notes, "were seen to be a better depository of law and a better security for its acccurate preservation than the memory of the aristocracies" (1905, p. 12).

In 1901–1902, when French archaeologists discovered in former Susa the stela with the text of the code of Hummurabi from the eighteenth century BCE, it became clear that Maine's connection of codification with the struggles of plebeians against aristocrats was much too simple. On the other hand, the finding did confirm the existence of the literary genre of the law code. The law code was in widespread use as a means to make legal regulations accessible to the public. We can thus broadly define law codes as collections of laws (in casuistic style) written on stones, papyrus, or parchment and made accessible to the public.

There also existed, however, cultures that did not attach much value to recording their traditions in writing. Among the Celts, for example, the powerful priesthood of the druids considered it fitting that their holy traditions be transmitted only in oral and not in written form, as reported by Caesar in the *Gallic Wars* (4.14). The Zoroastrians handed down their holy texts by word of mouth for centuries until, forced by external circumstances, they wrote them down in the third century CE. In rabbinic Judaism some rabbis advocated that written and oral tradition should be separated. "You are not permitted to recite from writing things that are transmitted orally; those that are written you are not permitted to say orally" (B. T., *Temurah* 14b). And some Islamic *ʿulamāʾ* advanced the view that the *ḥadīth* should not be written down. In these cases oral traditions could become public without being written down.

MEANS OF CODIFICATION: STELA, SCROLL, AND CODEX. The oldest texts of law codes of the ancient Near East were written down on stelae, large stones that were inscribed and publicly displayed. In some cases the texts of these stelae were copied on clay tablets by pupil-scribes. By means of these clay tablets Mesopotamian codes were preserved, even though the original stelae had disappeared. In the Hebrew scriptures (Old Testament) two tables (*luḥot*) are mentioned, on both sides of which the text of the Decalogue has been engraved (*Ex.* 32:15–16). The prophet Isaiah received the order to write the word of the Lord on a tablet (made of wood or ivory with a layer of plaster or wax on it), that it might "become an eternal witness for a day to come" (*Is.* 30:8; cf. *Hab.* 2:2). The *Book of Isaiah* (eighth century BCE) also testifies to the transition to writing on papyrus, the pith of an Egyptian water plant. For in *Isaiah* 8:1 the Lord asked the prophet to take a papyrus leaf (*gillayon*) and write on it. The oldest Hebrew papyrus is a palimpsest found in the Wadi Murabbaʿat that goes back to the eighth century BCE. The sheets of papyrus (*chartes*) were stuck together to form a scroll with the text on the inside. In the second century BCE parchment came into use. It was prepared from the skin of various animals and turned out to be stronger than papyrus. Pergamon exported parchment of particularly fine quality. Sheets of parchment that could be inscribed on both sides were since the first century BCE put in layers and folded as a codex. Christians promoted the use of the codex, while Jews stuck to the scroll.

Scroll and codex, then, were used in addition to the stela to record collections of laws. The Hebrew Book of the Covenant (*sefer ha-berit; Ex.* 24:7) should be imagined as a scroll; the same holds true for the "book of the *torah*" (*sefer ha-torah; 2 Kgs.* 22:8, 23:2) discovered at the time of the Judahite king Josiah (639–609 BCE), which is partly identical with *Deuteronomy.* The Codex Justinianus, on the contrary, was a manuscript in the form of a codex.

There are some differences between these means of codification. Laws written down as edicts could be sent to bureaus throughout the empire. But there was always the problem of authenticity. "A law that has been sent must be accepted and must undoubtedly be valid, and the power to emend and to revoke shall be reserved to our clemency [i.e., that of the Emperor]" (Codex Theodosianus 1.1.5). The scrolls indeed enabled scribes to make emendations. The scribe could add glosses to the text or introduce new authorized regulations at the end of the transmitted ones. Stelae could scarcely be falsified, but they were not easily used for the dissemination of edicts. It is therefore not surprising that laws sometimes were edited in both fashions. The Jewish law of purification, prohibiting foreigners to enter the Temple, was made public by means of slabs, one of them reading: "No alien *[allogenēs]* shall enter the holy place; if he is caught, he shall die" (Gerhard Pfohl, *Griechische Inschriften*, Munich, 2d ed., 1980, no. 135). In the beginning of the second century BCE, a local official ordered stelae to be set up in his villages recording letters of King Antiochos III that protected these villages from molestation. Stelae inscribed and publicly displayed could make such orders respected.

CUSTOM AND LAW, RESTITUTION AND PUNISHMENT. When laws were codified and written down their institutional context was changed. There is a process of assimilation and elimination that is typical of oral transmission in a nonliterate society: what continues to be of social relevance is stored in the memory while the rest is usually forgotten. Literacy puts an end to this process. The tradition becomes a fixed object, and inconsistencies within it become obvious. If systems of writing are complex, as in the ancient civilizations, then a deep gulf may develop between the esoteric literate culture and the popular culture. In the ancient Near East, scribes formed a class of their own, separate from the priesthood and in the service of the king. They became the experts in law and dislodged the elders previously responsible for the transmission of oral tradition (Goody and Watt, 1968).

It is common to discriminate custom from law. We call "custom" any habitual or usual course of action, any established practice. We call "law" a rule of conduct administered by a ruler or his subordinates. Laws are enforced by explicit sanctions while customs are enforced by social control. These are merely logical distinctions. But it is evident that the historical factor of writing worked in favor of laws sanctioned from above. Even if customs remained unchanged, their incorporation in an official code reinforced the power sustaining them. Often the institution of a law code became an opportunity to select from among customary practices. When in 303 BCE Antigonus I granted the citizens of Teos and Lebedos the right to write down their laws, he asked them to draw up only those laws they deemed the best. Sometimes there are clear cases of breaching custom. Solon prohibited in 594–593 BCE loans on the person of the debtor. The regulations concerning debt-slavery in Mesopotamian and Jewish codes show similar attempts to temper severe customs concerning debtors. They reflect efforts to subordinate private power to public control.

We must further discern between two sanctions: restitution and punishment. The law codes are full of examples of this distinction. The codes have the form of a collection of casuistic laws: conditional sentences in the third person. The dependent clause contains the facts supposed and the main clause the sanction. The arrangement of topics conforms to no general logic but seems random and includes homicide, battery, theft, slavery, sexual offenses, property rights, brideprice, inheritance, and so on. The difference between restitution and punishment concerns the sanction. A thief could be forced to restitute what he had stolen. In this case his action was regarded as a civil breach. In other cases theft was regarded as a serious offense, and the thief was made to restitute a multiple value of the thing stolen (as in *Exodus* 21:37–22:3). And finally theft could be judged as a crime to be punished by death or mutilation (as in code of Hammurabi 6f). Stanley Diamond maintains, as previous scholars have, that the customary law followed only the principle of restitution. Only with the rise of the state and legislation did homicide and theft become punishable crimes. The institution of the state was responsible for the severity of sanctions (*In Search of the Primitive*, 1974, chap. 6). Émile Durkheim argued precisely the opposite. He drew a distinction between two types of sanctions: restitutive sanctions and repressive ones. These two types are supposed to correspond to two types of social solidarity: the mechanical and the organic. In societies based on mechanical solidarity there is a predominance of repressive law, whereas restitutive (cooperative) laws prevail in societies based on organic solidarity. Though it holds true that Durkheim vastly overstated the role of repressive law and understated the degree of reciprocity in primitive societies, there remains much testimony that primitive societies are disposed toward penal sanctions. It is therefore improbable that with the creation of the state came repressive sanctions.

On this issue the reflections of Henry Sumner Maine are still valid. He discerned two types of offenses: offenses against one's neighbor and offenses against God (Maine, 1905, pp. 307–309). Offenses against one's neighbor (torts) gave rise to an obligation that was fulfilled by payment. In the Hittite laws, for example, the general sanction for homicide is the handing over of a number of persons. Offenses against God (sins), on the contrary, are punished with severity. Take for example the Jewish laws regarding homicide: "Ye shall take no ransom for the life of a manslayer liable to death, for he shall surely die. . . . So ye shall not pollute the land wherein ye are, for blood polluteth the land and no expiation can be made for the land for the blood which is shed therein but by the blood of him that shed it" (*Nm.* 35:31–33). Durkheim advanced a similar idea: "In primitive societies, criminal law is religious law" (*The Division of Labor in Society*, New York, 1947, p. 92). E. Adamson Hoebel (1954) also subscribed to the view that in primitive society criminal law coincides with certain notions of sin (p. 259).

A. S. Diamond (1935) used this distinction to classify preserved law codes. He arranged them in three groups. In the first group (early codes) the sanctions imposed are only pecuniary, including those for homicide and battery (e.g., the early laws of the peoples of western Europe). The second group ("central" codes) comprises codes in which some civil wrongs are regarded as criminal offenses and others not (e.g., the Hittite laws of the sixteenth century BCE). The last group (late codes) is formed of codes that regard the more serious wrongs—homicide, adultery, rape, and theft—as crimes (e.g., the code of Hammurabi, eighteenth century BCE). Diamond postulated an evolution according to which the field of the law of criminal offenses gradually expanded. Considering the historical dates of the law codes mentioned it seems far more appropriate to speak of logical types of codes.

COMPARISON OF LAW CODES. A review of extant law codes should attempt to address two main scientific problems: Did the codes contribute to public control of private power, as exercised, for example, in the enslavement of others? What are the reasons that law codes differ, principally with regard to sanctions for the same offense?

Mesopotamian codes. The most important Mesopotamian law codes are the following: the laws of the Sumerian king Urnammu (hereafter called LU, 2111–2094 BCE); the laws of King Lipit-Ishtar (LL, 1934–1924 BCE); the code of the city Eshnunna (CE, eighteenth century BCE); the code of the Akkadian king Hammurabi (CH, 1793–1750 BCE); the Hittite laws (HL, c. 1600 BCE); the Assyrian laws (AL, eleventh century BCE). (These texts are collected in Borger, 1982.)

The most famous code is of course the code of Hammurabi. It was written on a diorite stela, topped by a bas-relief showing Hammurabi receiving from Shamash, the sun god and god of justice, the commission to write the law book. The stela was carried off as a trophy of war to the Elamite capital Susa. The code of Hammurabi is particularly valuable because it reveals something of how such a code was intended to function. The epilogue speaks about the motives of the king and the function of the stela. The king set up the stela with the aim of protecting the weak against the strong, procuring justice for the orphan and the widow, and establishing equity in the land (CH 47). The motivations given in the LU (104–116, 162–168) and in the LL (1f., 19.6ff.) are similar. A citizen who has been injured shall read the stela, recognize his legal claims, and thank Hammurabi. If a subsequent king disregards the words of the stela, kingship shall be taken away from him (CH 48f.). The epilogue of LL blesses him who does not damage the stela (19.36–45). It has to be mentioned that among the hundreds of thousands of extant cuneiform tablets the number of copies of these codes is surprisingly small. The codes did not leave clear traces in Mesopotamian jurisdiction. J. J. Finkelstein (1961) concludes that the purpose of these codes was not legislation. Of course a litigant could appeal to the provisions of a code, but such an appeal would have carried moral rather than legal force. The codes must be regarded as political justifications of kingship.

The three codes proclaiming in prologue and epilogue protection of the weak against the strong belong together even in terms of their contents. In the Hittite laws the sanction of killing a free man or woman is the handing over of four persons (HL 1). For theft of cattle the sanction is payment of a stated multiple of the value (HL 45.57ff.). If a man steals from a house, "in former times he restituted for the theft one mine of silver. But now he gives twelve shekels [one-third of a mine] silver" (HL 94). A similar alleviation of punishment is decreed in HL 166–167: here a capital sanction has been replaced by a restitutive one. Only adultery, rape, and sexual offenses are punished with death (HL 187f., 197f.). Herein the code of Hammurabi is in accordance with the Hittite laws (CH 129f; cf. CE 26.28; LU 6f.). But in the other cases the code of Hammurabi inflicts heavy penalties. The following offenses are regarded as crimes punishable by death: an unproved accusation of murder (CH 1), murder (LU 1), false testimony (CH 3), theft of property (CH 6f.; only by night, CE 12f.), kidnapping (CH 14), hiding of a slave (CH 16), burglary (CH 21), robbery (CH 22; LU 2), sorcery (CH 2, AL 47). These severe penalites are imposed only in cases of offenses against citizens. The rape of a female slave, for example, can be requited by a pecuniary payment (LU 8; CE 31, to be compared with 26). The Assyrian laws very often prescribe mutilations—the removal of ears, fingers, eyes, or lips, for example, sanctions quite rare in the code of Hammurabi, which prescribes amputation of a hand only if an overseer steals the seed or fodder of an owner (CH 253).

Did criminal law arise from religion, as Maine, Durkheim, and Hoebel maintain? The codes themselves refer to a more specific concept: The king established justice (*misharum*) on behalf of the gods (LU, prologue; LL, epilogue; CH 5.14ff., 47.84ff.). It is not so much religion in general but the specific idea of a divine, just order that lies behind these codes. We must therefore explain the differences between sanctions (pecuniary versus capital) in terms of different concepts concerning this order. The case of debt slavery can elucidate the essence of these differences. The Hittite laws do not deal at all with enslavement of citizens, though such enslavement did exist. The Assyrian laws, the code of Eshnunna, and the code of Hammurabi, on the other hand, presuppose as a fact that a creditor who has a claim to corn or silver seizes persons of the debtor's family (CH 115; AL 39, 44, 48). This is only illegal if the claim is not substantiated, in which case a fine must be paid (CH 114). The code of Eshnunna gives more details: if the seized person is a female slave, the pledger shall pay silver in full compensation for her; if he doesn't return her and she dies, he shall give two female slaves as replacement; if he distrains the wife or children of a citizen and causes their death, he shall die (CE 22–24). The code of Hammurabi goes beyond these regulations and introduces laws protecting the person legally seized. "If the distress dies in the house of him who has taken him as a distress through blows or ill-treatment, the owner of the distress shall convict his merchant, and if [the distress is] a [free] man's son, his son shall be put to death or, if [he is] a [free] man's slave, he shall pay one-third mine of silver and forfeits anything whatsoever that he has lent" (CH 116). "If a man has become liable to arrest under a bond and has sold his wife, his son or his daughter or gives [them] into servitude, for three years they shall do work in the house of him who has brought them or taken them in servitude; in the fourth year their release shall be granted" (CH 117). These regulations were an effort to establish a public control over the harsh and merciless practice of debt slavery. The customary law of enslaving the debtor's family yields to statute law decreed by the emperor. Some of these emperors ordered at the beginning of their rule a remission of debts. "Whoever has given barley or silver to an Akkadian or an Amorite as an interest-bearing loan . . . because the king has invoked the *misharum* for the land, his document is voided" (Edict of Ammisaduqa 4). "Because the king has instituted *misharum* in the land, he [the enslaved citizen or his wife or his children] is released" (20). The release (*anduraru*) of the debt-slaves is due to justice. As J. J. Finkelstein cogently argued, the *misharum* and the law codes drew from the same concept, a concept of divine, just order that secured the citizen's property (human and otherwise) and reputation from infringement. The code of Hammurabi added to these rights the protection against permanent enslavement.

Jewish codes. The most important Jewish codes were the Book of the Covenant (*sefer ha-berit; Ex.* 24:7) incorporated into *Exodus* (20:22–23:19) and the legal part of *Deuteronomy* (12–26), perhaps identical with the "book of the *torah*" (*sefer ha-torah*), discovered at the time of Josiah (639–609 BCE) in the Temple (*2 Kgs.* 22:8, 23:2). As compared with the Book of the Covenant, the genre of the law code in *Deuteronomy* has lost its genuine form.

The Book of the Covenant contains casuistic law and apodictic law. Albrecht Alt has argued that the Israelites took over from the Canaanites the secular casuistic law, while the sacral apodictic law belonged to their own heritage. But Alt understated the religious background of the casuistic law in the code of the ancient Near East (see Alt, *Kleine Schriften zur Geschichte des Volkes Israel*, Munich, 1959, pp. 278–332). The Book of the Covenant starts with a prologue. Yahveh commissions Moses to erect an altar and to give the Israelites laws (*mishpatim; Ex.* 21:1) with regard to slaves (21:2–11); the capital offenses, including intentional homicide, abduction, beating and cursing of one's parents (21:12–17); inflicting bodily injuries (21:18–36); and theft, property delicts, and seduction (21:37–22:16). Thereupon follow apodictic laws on different subjects (22:17–23:19).

The Book of the Covenant belongs to the group of codes that regard private wrongs as capital offenses. A comparison with the code of Hammurabi, however, shows similarities and differences. Murder and abduction are in both codes capital crimes. But not all the capital offenses enumerated in the code of Hammurabi are regarded as such in Israel. In Judaism, the thief caught stealing livestock and selling them shall return fivefold (for oxen) or fourfold (for sheep) the number he stole. If the cattle are found in his possession alive he shall pay double. If he has not the means to do so he himself shall be sold. If the owner kills the thief there is no blood revenge, except if it happened in broad daylight (*Ex.* 21:37–22:3). On the other hand, the code of Hammurabi did not regard offenses against parents as crimes deserving death. In Israel offenses against persons and their status seem to weigh more heavily than offenses against property.

The Book of the Covenant acknowledged loans on the person and enslavement of debtors. But it made an attempt to temper the severe customs regarding the Hebrew debtors. The Hebrew slave shall be released after six years. A female slave that doesn't please her master may not be sold to a foreign people (21:7–8). Assault of a debt slave shall be avenged if he dies immediately. Bodily injuries shall lead to his release (21:20–21, 21:26–27). We recognize efforts similar to those in the Mesopotamian codes to alleviate the harsh fate of debt slaves and to institute a public control over it.

Deuteronomy departs from the genuine form of law codes. But Moshe Weinfeld (1972) has cogently argued that it still reflects this genre, maintaining that the book marks the transition from a narrow casuistic law corpus to a humanistic law code. Laws concerning property are nearly completely lacking. The Deuteronomic legislator aimed at setting forth a code of laws assuring protection for individuals and particularly persons in need. The debt slave is regarded as a citizen, a brother (*aḥ*), who only sells his service—but not his person—to his master. He conducts an independent family life. His master is obliged to manumit him after six years (*Dt.* 15:12–18). A slave who seeks refuge shall not be turned over to his master (23:15f.)—an offense punished by death in the code of Hammurabi (CH 16). The code in *Deuteronomy* still follows the casuistic form, but it introduces a new element unparalleled in the codes of ancient Near East: the motive clause. The release of the debt slaves is not only a command of God. The Deuteronomic legislator adds a further reason to follow the law: "Remember that you were a slave in Egypt and your Lord has released you" (15:15). He does not base the political recognizance of his code on the power of kingship but on the personal conviction of citizens.

Greek and Roman codes. The most important codifications are the laws of Solon, the laws of Gortyn, and the Roman Twelve Tables. The legislation of Solon was preceded by that of Draco (seventh century BCE). The *thesmoi* of Draco addresses the prosecution of homicide. Intentional homicide was avenged by the kin of the victim, manslaughter was compensated by payment of a wergild. The laws of Draco had officially been published on wooden tablets, set up on revolving pillars (*axones*). The laws of Solon were published in the same way.

The legislation of Solon (594/3 BCE) is only transmitted fragmentarily by Greek historians. The archonship of Solon (594 BCE) was preceded by civil strife in which the enslavement of poor Athenians by wealthy ones seems to have been an important issue. Solon at first ordered a cancellation of debts (*seisachtheia*); afterwards he enacted laws. His laws prohibited loans on the person of the debtor, arranged the population according to property qualifications into four classes, and established rules for electing the magistrates. Solon also made the curious law that whoever in a time of political strife did not take an active part on either side of a conflict should be deprived of his civic rights. He prohibited dowries and changed the rule of inheritance. Citizens without children could convey by testament their property to anyone they wished. Previously the heritage had to remain in the *genos* (kin group) of the deceased. He enacted a law saying that a son who had not been given the chance to learn a craft by his father was not obliged to sustain him later. Another law inhibited the export of agricultural products except olive oil.

Aristotle may have committed a historiographical error when he assigned to Solon the setting up of a constitution (*politeia*); only since the fourth century has Solon been regarded as founder of a constitution. But Aristotle referred rightly to the democratic feature of the laws of Solon (*Athenaiōn Politeia*, 9.1). The law that nobody could contract a loan secured on a person was a breach of the custom of debt slavery. This breach didn't occur all over the Greek world, but the view that law that could breach custom seems fairly common. Law was identified with statute law, and this identification remained characteristic of the whole Greek world. "Unwritten law" (*agraphos nomos*) should not be used by the court. The conflicts that could arise between custom and statute law are illustrated by the *Antigone* of Sophocles. This preference for statute law was a natural corollary of democracy. Justice, to which Solon also had appealed, became subject to the political discourse of citizens.

The most important source of pre-Hellenistic legislation is that found in the city of Gortyn (Crete). An inscription from the fifth century BCE begins with an injunction against taking the law into one's own hands: "Gods! He who will institute legal proceedings regarding a freeman or a slave shall not take him away before the judgement." But a condemned man or a debtor (*katakeimenon*) can be taken away without punishment. The inscription gives laws concerning rape and adultery (punished with a fine); conveyance of property in case of divorce, adoption, and death; ransom of compatriots; marriage, especially of an heiress; security and liability; and adoption.

There are some texts elucidating the process of codification of Greek law. After the liberation of Chios from the Persians in 333–332 BCE, Alexander ordered that the expelled democrats should return, that Chios should be a democracy, and that scribes should draw up and systematize the laws. I have already suggested that the *sunoikismos* of Teos and Lebedos in Asia Minor should be recognized as an act of common legislation. After his victory over the Egyptian forces in 200 BCE the Seleucid ruler Antiochos III recognized the Jewish customs and laws as *patrioi nomoi*. It was a privilege of political communities to dispose a written law code. The law code—in the ancient Near East a justification of kingship—had in the Hellenic and Hellenistic culture the function of a constitution.

According to Livy, the Roman law of the Twelve Tables was compiled in 450–449 BCE in an attempt to control the struggle between plebeians and patricians and to secure equal liberty for the two groups (Livy, 3.31.7). His account can hardly be considered satisfactory in view of its inconsistencies and improbabilities. The Twelve Tables are known only from later sources. The law code begins with a number of short rules indicating how to start and pursue legal proceedings (cf. the law of Gortyn). They proceed to debt slavery: "Unless they make a settlement, debtors shall be held in bonds for 60 days. On the third market day they shall suffer capital punishment or be delivered up for sale abroad, across the Tiber" (table three). Tables four to six contain fundamental principles of conveyance and of property law. Table eight deals with criminal law. Intentional homicide is a capital offense. For theft the sanctions vary, from paying double the amount of the stolen object's value to a capital sentence.

SOME FINAL REMARKS. The later codices of the Roman Empire deviated fundamentally from the preceding ones. The Theodosian Code was a compilation of laws issued by the emperors from 313 until 438 CE. In 429 Theodosius ordered such a compilation be made, and nine years later the code was solemnly promulgated. The code contained the legislative enactments issued by the emperors on given dates. These imperial laws (called constitutions) had been *edicta* (official proclamations), *decreta* (decrees in the settlement of lawsuits), *rescripta* (decisions in answer to officials and private persons) and *epistulae* (letters to officials). The emperor was conceived as the sole source of law, and his enactments were considered divine. His orders were called *constitutiones*, since they formed the fundamental law. The contravention of a given statute would be considered a crime, punishable usually be death. The fundamental Greek identification of justice and law was thus fused with monarchy. Again, as in the Mesopotamian codes, there is an emphasis on punishment. And again, not religion in a general sense, but specific notions of justice, had given rise to the code.

Other famous codes are the Syrian lawbooks and the Zoroastrian Madigani Hazar Dadastan. In the Islamic community a law code as such did not develop. The Qurʾān was regarded as the supreme source of Islamic law. Besides this source, the *sunnah*, the *ḥadīth*, the consensus of the Islamic community, and the analogical method were used to develop rules.

SEE ALSO Law and Religion; Revenge and Retribution.

BIBLIOGRAPHY

Borger, Rylke, Heiner Lutzmann, Wilhelm H. P. Römer, and Einar von Schuler. "Rechtsbücher." In *Texte aus der Umwelt des Alten Testaments,* vol. 1, pp. 15–125. Gütersloh, 1982. A fresh translation of Mesopotamian law codes provided with explanations and a list of recent studies.

Diamond, A. S. *Primitive Law, Past and Present* (1935). London, 1971. An attempt to describe the general development of law by studying the offenses regarded as crimes and by arranging the codes in different classes.

Fikentscher, Wolfgang R., Herbert Franke, and Oskar Köhler, eds. *Entstehung und Wandel rechtlicher Traditionen.* Freiburg, 1980. A collection of profound essays dealing with the great cultures and attempting a historical anthropology of law.

Finkelstein, J. J. "Ammiṣaduqa's Edict and the Babylonian 'Law Codes.'" *Journal of Cuneiform Studies* 15 (1961): 91–104. Tries to establish the relationship between reform acts and law codes of Mesopotamian kings.

Fried, Morton. *The Evolution of Political Society: An Essay in Political Anthropology.* New York, 1967. A meritorious study that defines the essential notion of social control and sanction, power and authority, custom and law.

Goody, Jack, and Ian Watt. "The Consequences of Literacy." In *Literacy in Traditional Societies,* edited by Jack Goody, pp. 27–68. Cambridge, U.K., 1968. A prolific article that sets forth the differences between memorizing in oral cultures and in literate cultures and that evaluates the systems of writing with regard to their spread.

Hoebel, E. Adamson. *The Law of Primitive Man: A Study in Comparative Legal Dynamics.* Cambridge, Mass., 1954. A fundamental study in the anthropology of law.

Kohler, Josef, and Erich Ziebarth. *Das Stadtrecht von Gortyn und seine Beziehungen zum gemeingriechischen Rechte* (1912). Hildesheim, 1972. A valuable study that gives text, translation, and commentary of the inscription of Gortyn and adduces other relevant Greek legal texts.

Maine, Henry Sumner. *Ancient Law: Its Connection with the Early History of Society and Its Relation to Modern Ideas* (1861). London, 1905. Maine's early study, still in print in various editions, recognized the ancient law codes as systems of their own.

Rendtorff, Rolf. *Das Alte Testament: Eine Einführung.* Neukirchen-Vluyn, 1983. A useful overview of the Old Testament, including the legal codes incorporated into it.

Weinfeld, Moshe. *Deuteronomy and the Deuteronomic School.* Oxford, 1972. A comprehensive study comparing the "Book of the Covenant" with *Deuteronomy* and tracing the relation of *Deuteronomy* to Mesopotamian law codes.

H. G. KIPPENBERG (1987)

CODRINGTON, R. H. (1830–1922), Christian missionary to Melanesia and scholar of Melanesian languages and cultures. The second son of an Anglican rector, Robert Henry Codrington was educated at Charterhouse and at Wadham College, Oxford, where, as his later high church views suggest, he may have been touched by the Oxford Movement. In 1857, two years after he was ordained, he gave up excellent prospects in England to go to New Zealand with his vicar, Edmund Hobhouse, who had been elevated to the bishopric of Christchurch. In 1863 he accompanied Bishop John Coleridge Patteson on the island voyage of the mission ship *Southern Cross,* and in 1867 he joined the peripatetic Melanesian Mission, which advocated a policy of racial equality and minimal interference in traditional native culture. When Patteson was killed in 1871 by Melanesians previously victimized by Australian "blackbirders" (kidnappers), Codrington declined the bishopric, but he served for some years as acting head of the mission. Despite a propensity to severe sea-sickness, he did on several occasions make the island voyage; he preferred, however, to direct the mission school on Norfolk Island, to which young Melanesians were brought for training as native teachers. There he also took over the linguistic studies Patteson had begun (in part under the stimulus of the German-born Oxford philologist and comparative religionist F. Max Müller). Through the intermediacy of Lorimer Fison, a Wesleyan missionary-anthropologist with whom he had become acquainted during the public furor surrounding Patteson's death, Codrington established contact with the British social evolutionary anthropologist E. B. Tylor. By 1880 he had begun to send ethnographic material to the *Journal of the Anthropological Institute.*

Returning on leave to England in 1883 to complete the translation of the Bible into Mota (the Melanesian lingua franca), Codrington resided for two years in college at Oxford, where he attended lectures by Tylor. While there he published one of his two major works, *The Melanesian Languages* (1885), which long remained a standard reference; the companion study of their culture, *The Melanesians* (1891), was published after a second truncated tour of duty with the mission. After a brief period as rector of a country parish, Codrington served the remainder of his long life as prebendary of the cathedral in Chichester.

As a religious scholar, Codrington is best known for the idea of *mana,* which he saw as the basis of all Melanesian religious belief. Despite his contact with Tylor, Codrington remained closer to the philologically oriented pre-Darwinian "ethnological" tradition to which Müller, too, was tied. Unlike his friend Fison, he was little concerned with evolutionary problems. He remained dubious of the evolutionary socioreligious concept of totemism, and though he did not explicitly reject Tylor's rationalistic doctrine of animism, by implication he called it into question. Suspicious of received anthropological categories, Codrington saw ethnography as a matter of "setting forth what natives say about themselves." It was in this context (as well as in an effort to find a universal substructure for Christian missionizing) that he focused on *mana:* "the persuasion that there is a supernatural power belonging to the region of the unseen"—a power emotionally experienced rather than rationally surmised, which natives could turn to their benefit. Offered originally in a letter to Max Müller, Codrington's definition of *mana* was used by Müller to attack Tylorian intellectualist views in a series of lectures published as *The Origin of Religion* (1878). Subsequently adopted by R. R. Marett as the basis for the concept of "preanimistic" religion, the concept of *mana* played an important role in the critique of social evolution that developed in British anthropology after 1900. It was also manifest in such major critiques of evolutionary rationalism as Durkheim's *Elementary Forms of the Religious Life* (1912) and Freud's *Totem and Taboo* (1912).

BIBLIOGRAPHY

Codrington has not yet found a biographer, and biographical material must be sought in obituaries and standard biographical sources, notably the article by Ernest Beaglehole in the *International Encyclopedia of the Social Sciences* (New York, 1968). A considerable body of his correspondence and relevant printed materials are preserved in Rhodes House, Oxford. A bibliography of his writings is contained in the obituary by Sidney Ray, in *Man* 97 (1922): 169–171. Codrington is also the subject of my article "Robert Henry Codrington: Melanesian Man and Evolutionary Categories," in *After Tylor: British Social Anthropology, 1888–1951* (Madison, Wis., 1995).

GEORGE W. STOCKING, JR. (1987 AND 2005)

COHEN, ARTHUR A. Arthur A. Cohen (1928–1986) was an American Jewish theologian, novelist, essayist, editor, and publisher. Born in New York City, Cohen grew up in an affluent, assimilated Jewish home and was educated at the University of Chicago where he studied philosophy and religion. His first year at Chicago, on realizing "that Western culture is a Christian culture" (Stern and Mendes-Flohr, 1998, p. 34) he underwent a spiritual crisis and seriously considered converting to Christianity. To save their son from taking this path, his horrified parents enlisted the help of their rabbi, Milton Steinberg (1903–1950; arguably the most original Jewish American religious thinker of his day), and under Steinberg's tutelage, Cohen began to study Hebrew and Jewish texts. In 1949, after receiving a master of arts degree from the University of Chicago, Cohen spent six months in Jerusalem where he met Martin Buber (1878–1965) whose theology subsequently became the subject of Cohen's first book, published in 1958). He later studied briefly at the Jewish Theological Seminary of America in New York. In 1951, he left academia for good to cofound the Noonday Press, the first of several publishing ventures in which Cohen was involved—the others were Meridian Books (where Cohen pioneered the publication of high-quality paperbacks), World Publishing House, and Holt, Rhinehart, Winston, where he eventually became editor-in-chief and vice-president. At Holt, Cohen commissioned a number of extremely important Jewish books including the English translation of Franz Rosenzweig's (1886–1929) *The Star of Redemption.*

In 1969 he retired from publishing to write theology and fiction full time (although in the 1980s he re-entered business with his wife, the celebrated designer and artist Elaine Lustig Cohen, and became a very successful dealer in rare early twentieth-century art documents and books). Although he occasionally taught a course at universities and participated intensely in New York literary and intellectual circles, Cohen eschewed most institutional, educational, and organizational ties in the Jewish world. In 1986, at the age of fifty-eight, he died of leukemia.

EARLY THEOLOGY. Cohen first won major attention with his second book, *The Natural and Supernatural Jew* (1962), which sets out the basic structure of his religious thinking. The foundation of that structure, intimated in the book's title, is the distinction between the natural and the supernatural Jew. The natural Jew, Cohen wrote, is "a creature situated in nature and activated by history" (Stern and Mendes-Flohr, 1998, p. 44)—that is, one whose fate is essentially defined by his or her cultural and social circumstances and who cannot alone transcend the determinations of nature and history. In contrast, the supernatural Jew is a messianic being, the Jew aware of being called by God to the transhistorical vocation of bringing redemption, who must testify that "there is *no* redemption until *all* history is redeemed" (Stern and Mendes-Flohr, 1998, p. 45). These two types, Cohen emphasized, are not to be understood as opposites or as mutually exclusive: they "are joined in every Jew" (Stern and Mendes-Flohr 1998, p. 48). Although "the supernatural Jew may occasionally forget that he is also flesh and blood"—that is, fated to live in history—such a Jew, Cohen wrote, "is as much in error as is the natural Jew who forgets what links him to eternity" (Stern and Mendes-Flohr, 1998, p. 48). The renewal of the Jewish vocation lies in the reuniting in the Jew of both selves, natural and supernatural, and in turning Judaism toward history and culture in such a way that they will be made into "bearers of ultimate and consummate meaning" (Stern and Mendes-Flohr, 1998, p. 49).

In distinguishing between the natural and the supernatural, the historical and the meta-historical, Cohen's work both drew on the new existentialist philosophy coming out of Europe at the time and represented a rejection of the ideological rationalism that had characterized the Jewish theologians of the previous generation, preeminently Mordecai M. Kaplan (1881–1983), the naturalist Jewish theologian and founder of Reconstructionism. Cohen and his contemporaries—such other Jewish thinkers as Will Herberg (1901–1977), Eugene Borowitz (b. 1924), and Emil Fackenheim (1916–2003)—argued for a renewal of Jewish theology as a prerequisite for the renewing of Judaism itself and reasserted the centrality of supernaturalist categories like faith, revelation, chosenness, and messianism.

More than his contemporaries, however, Cohen emphasized the messianic, eschatological side of Judaism, which for him meant the quintessentially unredeemed condition of the present world. Like Rosenzweig (whose adolescent near-conversion to Christianity clearly anticipated, if not served as the model for Cohen's own early experience), Cohen predicated his understanding of the Jewish vocation on a repudiation of Christianity, indeed on an essential theological enmity between Judaism and Christianity. The latter was always for Cohen a promise and a reality to be denied by the Jew. This theme was the primary subject of his second major early work, a collection of related essays entitled *The Myth of the Judeo-Christian Tradition* (1970).

POST-HOLOCAUST THEOLOGY. Beginning in 1974, Cohen's theology became increasingly concerned with the Holocaust. In a lecture delivered that year to the Leo Baeck Institute in New York, Cohen argued that the Holocaust represented an unprecedented manifestation of absolute evil that fundamentally changed the terms of God's relationship to the Jewish people. Because it defied all the traditional categories of Jewish theodicy (e.g., sin and punishment, divine retribution, and so on) the Holocaust was, in Cohen's terminology, the *Tremendum,* a term Cohen borrowed from the nineteenth-century German theologian Rudolph Otto (1869–1937), who had used it to define God's presence as a *mysterium tremendum,* a terrifying and unfathomable mystery. Cohen analogously identified the Holocaust as a manifestation of sheer terror—although one unaccompanied by the presence of God.

In Cohen's view, for the Jew living after the Holocaust, the *Tremendum* was the defining event of his or her relationship to God, hence of Jewishness itself. Drawing on the Passover Haggadah (as Julian Levinson has pointed out), Cohen wrote that a Jew must feel as though he or she "was really, even if not literally, present in Egypt, and really, if not literally, present at Sinai" (Stern and Mendes-Flohr, 1998, p. 248). As such, the Holocaust represented a challenge to traditional conceptions of the Jewish God. Even so, Cohen was adamant in his belief that Jewish theology could meet that challenge. "The time is now to build again upon the wreckage of previous understandings" of Jewish theology, and particularly its conception of the divinity. Even if "the God who will endure may . . . prove to be less imperious and authoritarian, . . . [He] may gain in credibility and truth what He has lost in unconditional absoluteness" (Stern and Mendes-Flohr 1998, p. 101).

FICTION AND LITERARY ESSAYS. The most remarkable feature of Cohen's theological work was his career as a novelist. In the course of this career, Cohen published five novels and one book of three novellas. Although only one of these books is on an explicitly Jewish and theological theme—*In the Days of Simon Stern* (1973)—Cohen's turn to fiction as a medium for Jewish theology was not entirely surprising. Even his explicitly theological writing possessed the rare eloquence and passion of poetry, what he called "the language of existence—the means by which the paradoxes of theology can be rendered into life" (Cohen, 1962, p. 146), as he wrote about the dedication to language shared by his own literary-theologian models, the German-Jewish theologian Rosenzweig and the medieval Jewish poet and philosopher Judah Halevi (1086–1145). Rosenzweig once remarked that Judaism must be smuggled into life; Cohen used fiction to smuggle Judaism into art.

Although he is often described as a novelist of ideas, it would be more accurate to say that Cohen's fictions are all about characters—poets, artists, intellectuals, messiahs—obsessed with ideas. Thus, *Simon Stern* recounts the history of its protagonist, the Simon Stern of the book's title, a millionaire real estate dealer on the Lower East Side who, in the aftermath of the Holocaust, attempts to save the remnants of European Jewry (a select number of survivors chosen for their capacity to "endure" history) by rescuing them from Europe, bringing them to New York and building for them a temple-like sanctuary in New York City. By the novel's end, however, this project of redemption has failed, and the temple itself has been destroyed in a fire (once again!). Cohen's protagonist, Simon Stern, although certainly a failure, is a genuine, messiah. However, his particular messianic mission in the novel is ultimately not to save humanity but to prove the impossibility of redemption so long as history lasts. In this way, through the novel, Cohen succeeded in recreating a classic Jewish myth that was also a perfect expression of Cohen's own personal theological obsessions.

As a novel, *Simon Stern* is often creaky, heavy-handed, and shapeless, but its enormous intellectual and spiritual energy, epitomized in the book's sprawling, massive shape, encompasses the boundless Jewish yearning for redemption and the equally boundless messianic disappointment. Even if the book fails on purely literary grounds as a novel, it is an extraordinary epic of the theological imagination.

The impossibility of neatly categorizing *Simon Stern* is almost a perfect correlative for Cohen's own exceptionality as an American Jewish thinker. In his numerous essays, Cohen wrote about nearly every conceivable subject—from Franz Kafka (1883–1924) and George Frederick Handel's (1685–1759) *Jephthah* to architecture, art, and the history of modern typographical design (about which he happened to be a world-recognized authority). As a single corpus, all of his writings, although hardly adhering to any conventional generic classification, were inhabited and enlivened by a single literary and intellectual persona.

Perhaps the most unusual example of the deep coherence of Cohen's literary-theological oeuvre is an essay he wrote titled "The Typographic Revolution: Antecedents and Legacy of Dada Graphic Design" (1979). On its surface, this dense and complex study traces the prehistory and influence of Dada typography—those chaotic and inventive arrangements of letters and print familiar to all students of early twentieth-century art. As Cohen argues, however, the Dadaist letters are actually ideograms come alive, and the Dadaist ambition to enliven letter types so that they can be "reapprehended as living voice, speaking volumes, shouting and making love" (Stern and Mendes-Flohr, 1998, p. 475) should be understood in conjunction with the inquiries of such contemporary philosophers and theologians as Ferdinand Ebner, Nicolai Berdyaev, Buber, and Rosenzweig, all of whom, Cohen asserts, sought to reconceive the direct speech between humans and God and thus to reclaim those "realms of intimacy" in which the living voice of the divine once spoke. The brilliance of this essay, with its unexpected connections between avant-garde typography and modern theology, exemplifies the uniqueness of Cohen's own voice as a religious thinker. The writing produced by that voice was like nothing else in American Jewish culture.

SEE ALSO Jewish Thought and Philosophy, article on Modern Thought.

BIBLIOGRAPHY

Cohen, Arthur A. *The Natural and the Supernatural Jew: An Historical and Theological Introduction.* New York, 1962.

Katz, Steven T. *Historicism, the Holocaust, and Zionism: Critical Studies in Modern Jewish Though and History.* New York, 1992. See pp. 251–273.

Levinson, Julian. "Arthur A. Cohen's Resplendent Vision." *Prooftexts* 23 (2003): 259–267.

Morgan, Michael L. *Beyond Auschwitz: Post-Holocaust Jewish Thought in America.* Oxford, 2001. See pp. 14–54.

Stern, David, and Paul Mendes-Flohr, eds. *An Arthur A. Cohen Reader: Selected Fiction and Writings on Judaism, Theology, Literature, and Culture.* Detroit, Mich., 1998.

DAVID STERN (2005)

COHEN, HERMANN (1842–1918) was a Jewish philosopher of religion and founder and exponent of Marburg Neo-Kantian philosophy. Born into a cantor's family in the small-town Jewish community of Coswig/Anhalt, Germany, Cohen received intense religious training from his father in addition to the general education typical of his time and place. The transition from these beginnings to the modern rabbinical seminary of Breslau was natural. Part of the seminary's curriculum was the requirement of university studies, and while at the University of Breslau, Cohen decided that philosophy, rather than the rabbinate, was his vocation.

SCHOLAR. Transferring to the University of Berlin, Cohen first fell under the influence of the folk-psychological epistemologists Heymann Steinthal (1823–1899) and Moritz Lazarus (1824–1903), but he quickly progressed toward the ideas of Immanuel Kant (1724–1804) and a more logistic outlook. His habilitation thesis on Kant's theory of experience was published in 1871, and in the context of the "back to Kant" movement of the day, his ideas had a revolutionary impact. He particularly impressed the radical social reformer and professor of philosophy at Marburg, Friedrich Lange (1828–1875; author of the famous idealistic *History of Materialism*). Through Lange, a committed Protestant, Cohen, a committed Jew, received his first appointment at the University of Marburg in 1873. He stayed there until his voluntary, albeit disgruntled, retirement in 1912. Thereafter he taught at the Liberal rabbinical seminary in Berlin, the Hochschule für die Wissenschaft des Judentums, where he wrote his last works. Shortly after his arrival in Marburg he married Martha Lewandowski, daughter of the chief cantor of the Berlin Jewish community and liturgical composer, Louis Lewandowski (1821–1894). (She later died in the concentration camp of Theresienstadt.)

During his long incumbency in Marburg, Cohen not only produced the bulk of his own philosophic oeuvre but also gathered around him a group that came to constitute the Marburg School of Neo-Kantianism. Among the many scholars associated with him in this undertaking were his student and subsequent colleague Paul Natorp (1854–1924) and, later, Ernst Cassirer (1874–1945). Cohen attracted many devoted students and disciples, particularly Jews from German-speaking countries, from Eastern Europe, and even America. However, his personal, philosophical, and social relations at the university became increasingly strained down through the years, not least because of growing political reaction during that period against the overtly ethical (i.e., Kantian), anti-Marxist, and antimaterialist socialism of the Marburg school. In the politics of the time the names of Cohen's students Kurt Eisner (1876–1919) and Eduard Bernstein (1850–1932) became quite well known.

Throughout his life Cohen never ceased to be active in Jewish matters. For example, he published his *The Love of Neighbor in the Talmud: Affidavit before the Royal Court of Marburg* in 1888 (in German) in response to the notorious Rohling/Delagarde anti-Semitic episode in which the old "blood libel" and Jewish xenophobism combined with the then nascent German racism. He wrote voluminously on Jewish subjects; in 1924 his writings were collected in three volumes, edited and introduced by Franz Rosenzweig, author of *The Star of Redemption.* Just before the outbreak of World War I Cohen made a triumphal tour of the largest Jewish communities in Russia, a trip that the German government supported for political reasons. Cohen hoped also by means of this tour to advance in the East the enlightened Jewish social and educational values of the Jews of the West.

COHEN'S WRITINGS. Cohen's work can be divided into three parts: his exegetical readings of Kant, his system of philosophy, and his specifically Jewish work.

Exegetical readings of Kant. Several of Cohen's books crystallized and solidified the aprioristic, transcendental, critical foundations of the Kantian system: *Kants Theorie der Erfahrung* (1871), *Kants Begründung der Ethik* (1877, 1910), and *Kants Begründung der Ästhetik* (1889). In 1883 he published *Das Prinzip der Infinitesimalmethode und seine Geschichte: Ein Kapitel in der Begründung der Erkenntniskritik* (The Principle of the Infinitesimal Method and Its History: A

Chapter in the Foundation of the Critique of Cognition), in which he argues that the (sensuous) given, which Kant treated as the separate, empiricist source of knowledge, is also a rational construction, and thus that reality is a totally aprioristic, regulative product.

The system of philosophy. Cohen's radicalized, Neo-Kantian understanding of reality and of ethics that developed directly from his critiques of Kant found expression in his *Logik der reinen Erkenntnis* (Logic of Pure Cognition; 1902, 1914), *Ethik des reinen Willens* (Ethics of the Pure Will; 1904–1907), and *Ästhetik des reinen Gefühls* (Aesthetic of Pure Feeling; 1912). Here the universe is determined by the three "interests" of reason (i.e., cognition, will, and feeling), which strive for the traditional ideals of truth, goodness, and beauty. All three operate under what Kant had called "the primacy of practical (i.e., ethical) reason." The infinite task of the attainment of practical reason produces the unending history of regulative progressive science, progress toward the good society (as in ethical socialism), and the synthesis of the two in a world perfectly true and perfectly good, that is, messianically beautiful.

Cohen's Jewish philosophy. Cohen's work in the area of Jewish studies—intimated in his philosophizing and, increasingly, explicitly identified with it—was systematically elaborated in the final decade of his life and was consummated in the posthumously published *Religion der Vernunft aus den Quellen des Judentums* (Religion of Reason out of the Sources of Judaism; 1919, 1929). Cohen's Jewish philosophical theology (although he did not use this terminology) consists of a translation back into classical Jewish terms of the philosophical position Cohen held he had extracted from Judaism with the help of the progressive line of thought running from Plato (c. 428–348 or 347 BCE) through Moses Maimonides, (1135/8–1204) to Kant. Thus God is the idea (in the Neo-Kantian, regulative sense) of the normative, infinite realization of the good in the world. This realization is known in religion as the establishment by means of the imitation of God of the messianic kingdom on earth. The Law (*halakhah*) is the historical Jewish specifications of the categorical imperative and the foundation of the universal human moral brotherhood of the "Noachide covenant," which is also the religious, prophetic goal of socialism. The last third of *Religion of Reason* leading up to the religious virtues of truthfulness and peacefulness is, together with the cited and appended texts, a Jewish restatement of the last third of *Ethics of the Pure Will.* The role of the Jewish people in history is then to represent "ethical monotheism" physically and to disseminate it morally throughout the world. Therefore, Cohen rejected the Zionism that was nascent at the time: The conflict between the two views is well expressed in the classic debate between Cohen and Martin Buber (1878–1965) in "Answer to the Open Letter of Dr. M. Buber" (1917) and in the writings of Cohen's former student Jakob Klatzkin, who became the leading theoretician of the radical Zionist "negation of the Diaspora."

Influence of Cohen's Work. Cohen's influence in matters of religion was not limited to Jewry, although here it was magisterial. At the University of Marburg he interacted closely with the Protestant theology faculty, first with Julius Wellhausen (1844–1918), whose Bible criticism he esteemed highly as a good scholarly undergirding to prophetic Judaism, and then especially with the liberal, proto-Social Gospel philosophical theologian Wilhelm Herrmann (1846–1922). Natorp himself became increasingly active in liberal Protestantism. A second generation of Christian thinkers resulted from what might be called this Marburg school of Kantian liberal theology, albeit largely by way of dialectical antitheses: Karl Barth (1886–1968) and Rudolf Bultmann (1884–1976) deliberately place primary emphasis on the subjectivity of faith in place of Cohen's argument for the objectivity of ethical and social values.

Cohen's philosophical and Jewish influence is scattered in diverse and embattled manifestations. Around the turn of the century a rebellion emerged against what was perceived as the extreme scientific, rationalistic theoreticism of Marburg Neo-Kantianism. In reaction, there appeared positions that asserted the ultimate power of "reality" over reason in "life-philosophy," re-Hegelianizing historicism, positivism, and nascent existentialist phenomenologism. In German circles the value of historical and even metaphysical Germanism (*Deutschtum*) was apostrophized, and in Jewish circles a parallel affirmation of the peoplehood of Israel and the historical or even metaphysical genius of the Jewish people was pitted against bloodless and lifeless assimilationist universalism. The fact that Franz Rosenzweig (1886–1929), a disciple of Friedrich Meinecke (1862–1954) and author of important studies on G. W. F. Hegel (1770–1831), became Cohen's last important, brilliant disciple added another complicating element, for Rosenzweig interpreted the "late Cohen" as the precursor of a total break with systematic rationalism in favor of a form of metahistoricism inspired by Friedrich Schelling (1775–1854).

Politically, religiously, and philosophically very different extrapolations continue to be made from Cohen's fundamental analyses. Leading Jewish Orthodox authorities like Joseph Ber Soloveitchik (1903–1993) and Yitzchok Hutner (1906–1980) never ceased drawing on their Cohenian studies in the 1920s, whereas rationalistic reformers like Benzion Kellermann (1869–1923) and fully acculturated Westerners like Cassirer struck out in their own directions from Cohen. These varied approaches demonstrate how decisive the intellectual experience of Cohen has remained for subsequent Jewish thought. Cohen's Jewish writings have been translated into Hebrew, English, and other languages, but the technical philosopher Cohen has remained within the confines of German-language culture. Even there he has suffered many depredations. The Weimar backlash against rationalism as too cold and intellectual forced a number of Marburg-influenced figures such as Natorp, Nicolai Hartmann (1882–1950), and José Ortega y Gasset (1883–1955) toward the positions of Edmund Husserl (1859–1938), Martin Heidegger (1889–1976), and others. The Nazi period saw the final destruction of the Neo-Kantianism of Marburg. Since World War II, however, a new, qualified appreciation of transcendental philosophy has arisen, through the work of men such as Hans Wagner, Helmut Holzhey, Werner Flach, Wolfgang Marx, and others. But the contributions that Cohen's work can still make toward a fully developed and effective constructionalism in the areas of philosophy of science, ethics, and even of religion have not yet been fully realized.

In the last decades of the twentieth century, interest in Cohen's thought surged. Rosenzweig's misleading yet entrenched interpretation of Cohen's late philosophy of religion as a break with systematic idealism resulted in the bifurcation of Cohen interpretation into a systematic Neo-Kantian and a Jewish religious line. In more recent interpretations, however, scholars such as Michael Zank, Robert Gibbs, Hartwig Wiedebach, and Andrea Poma have built on the post-World War II generation above, overcoming the separation of Cohen's Neo-Kantian system and his specifically Jewish thought. The result is a recognition of the continuities in Cohen: The messianic age, for example, as the ideal future of the peace of humankind, was prefigured in the concept of time postulated in the ethics of the early Cohen.

In the midst of the age of nationalism and of the politics of identity, Cohen's ideal of the state is also receiving renewed attention as an ethical union of citizens that ought to supersede aspirations for the sovereignty of the primordial nation. Nonetheless, despite the resurgence in the study and appreciation of Cohen, it remains an open question whether his thought will serve as a foundation for constructive work in the future outside the sphere of Jewish philosophy.

SEE ALSO Cassirer, Ernst; Jewish Studies, article on Jewish Studies from 1818 to 1919; Jewish Thought and Philosophy, article on Modern Thought; Kant, Immanuel; Maimonides, Moses; Rosenzweig, Franz; Schelling, Friedrich.

BIBLIOGRAPHY

Under the general editorship of Helmut Holzhey, director of the Hermann-Cohen-Archiv at the University of Zurich, publication of Cohen's *Werke* (Hildesheim, Germany, 1978–) is nearing completion. Cohen's writings on religion available in English are limited: His major work of philosophy of religion, *Die Religion der Vernunft aus den Quellen des Judentums* was published posthumously in 1919 as *Religion of Reason out of the Sources of Judaism,* translated by Simon Kaplan (New York, 1972). Selections from Cohen's writings on Jewish themes, *Jüdische Schriften,* 3 vols. (Berlin, 1924), have been published as *Religion and Hope: Selections from the Jewish Writings of Hermann Cohen,* translated by Eva Jospe (New York, 1971; reprint, Cincinnati, 1993) and Alan Mittleman, "'The Jew in Christian Culture' by Hermann Cohen," *Modern Judaism* 23 (2003): 51–73; Mittleman has also translated "'The Significance of Judaism for the Religious Progress of Humanity,' by Hermann Cohen," *Modern Judaism* 24 (2004): 36–58.

For Cohen's place in modern Jewish thought, see Julius Guttmann's *Philosophies of Judaism,* translated by David W. Silverman (New York, 1964) and Kenneth Seeskin, "Jewish Neo-Kantianism: Hermann Cohen," in *History of Jewish Philosophy,* edited by D. H. Frank and O. Leaman (London, 1997). The writings of Steven Schwarzschild (1924–1989) sustained Jewish thought in a Cohenian key; see Menahem Kellner, ed., *The Pursuit of the Ideal: Jewish Writings of Steven Schwarzschild* (Albany, N.Y., 1990). The revival of interest in Cohen's thought at the close of the twentieth century is evidenced by new studies in German, Italian, French and English, including Andrea Poma, *The Critical Philosophy of Hermann Cohen,* translated by John Denton (Albany, N.Y., 1996) and Michael Zank, *The Idea of Atonement in the Philosophy of Hermann Cohen* (Providence, R.I., 2000).

STEVEN S. SCHWARZSCHILD (1987)
ROBERT S. SCHINE (2005)

COKE, THOMAS (1747–1814), chief associate of John Wesley in the organization of worldwide Methodism. Born in Brecon, Wales, Coke attended Jesus College, Oxford, and earned in 1775 the degree of doctor of civil law. Having been ordained a deacon of the Church of England in 1770 and a priest in 1771, he served as curate of South Petherton, Somerset, from 1771 to 1777. In 1776 he fell under the spell of John Wesley and in 1777, largely because of his Methodism, was dismissed from his curacy. Becoming Wesley's colleague, he took over most of the supervision of the Irish societies, served as Wesley's secretary and agent, and employed his legal acumen in 1784 to draw up the deed poll incorporating the British Methodist Conference. In the same year he helped Wesley prepare and publish his revision of *The Book of Common Prayer.*

Wesley conveyed his own ecclesiastical authority to Coke in a form of ordination as "superintendent" for America, and thus transmitted ministerial orders to the Methodists there. Coke ordained Francis Asbury as his episcopal colleague—an act confirmed, at Asbury's insistence, through election by the American preachers—but Coke was the leader in formulating the American preachers' original *Discipline* on the basis of Wesley's "large" *Minutes.* Altogether, Coke spent less than three years in America, so that eventually Asbury took precedence over him, especially after it was discovered that in 1791 Coke had clandestinely sought a union of American Methodism with the Protestant Episcopal Church.

However, Coke had other irons in the fire. Among his many published works were a commentary on the Bible (1801–1807) and a *History of the West Indies* (1808–1811). He formed a tract society in 1782, advocated a missionary society in 1784, began to evangelize the West Indies in 1786, and was traveling to a mission in India at the time of his death. It was he more than any other who kindled Methodism's missionary zeal.

SEE ALSO Methodist Churches.

BIBLIOGRAPHY

Easily the best biography is *Thomas Coke, Apostle of Methodism* (Nashville, 1969) by John Ashley Vickers. Additional insights and information can be found in chapter 9 of my book *From Wesley to Asbury: Studies in Early American Methodism* (Durham, N.C., 1976) and in *The Encyclopedia of World Methodism*, 2 vols., edited by Nolan B. Harmon (Nashville, 1974).

FRANK BAKER (1987)

COLERIDGE, SAMUEL TAYLOR (1772–1834),

English Romantic poet, literary critic, journalist, philosopher, and religious thinker. With William Wordsworth, Coleridge helped inaugurate the Romantic era with the publication of *Lyrical Ballads* (1798). A devoted writer, he later worked sporadically as a journalist and lecturer. His life was shadowed by an unhappy marriage, ill health, and a lifelong drug addiction.

Raised in the Church of England by his minister father, Coleridge became a Unitarian during his student years at Cambridge, but he returned definitively to a trinitarian theology in 1805. Although essentially orthodox in his adherence to Church of England doctrine, Coleridge was often daringly innovative in his theological speculations on such concepts as the Logos, the Trinity, original sin, and the church. *Aids to Reflection* (1825) contains profound insights into the nature of faith and the relationship between faith and reason; *On the Constitution of the Church and State* (1830) offers a conservative view of the nature of the church and its "clerisy"; and *Confessions of an Inquiring Spirit* (published 1840) introduces into England the approaches to scripture of the German "higher criticism." His *Notebooks* (published 1957–) and *Marginalia* (published 1980–) also contain perceptive reflections on doctrine, church history, and theological controversy.

Coleridge was one of the most widely read men of his century. Hence, the influences on him were many, including David Hartley, Joseph Priestley, and William Godwin (whose necessitarianism he later rejected); Plato and the seventeenth-century Cambridge Platonists; the medieval Schoolmen; mystics like Jakob Boehme and (to a lesser extent) Emanuel Swedenborg; philosophers in the so-called pantheist tradition like Giordano Bruno and Barukh Spinoza; and the German transcendental philosophers, especially Immanuel Kant and Friedrich Schelling. Each was interpreted, however, according to the needs of Coleridge's own organic philosophy and used to further his own theological speculations.

Coleridge's influence on subsequent religious thought was widespread, both in England and in the United States. He is commonly seen as a forerunner of the Broad Church movement through such disparate thinkers as Thomas Arnold, Julius Hare, and, especially, F. D. Maurice. There are also strong affinities between Coleridge and John Henry Newman, particularly in the two writers' approaches to religious epistemology. Through the writing of George MacDonald, Coleridge had—especially in his views on symbol, which are deeply grounded in his theology—an indirect influence on the imaginative literature of such writers as G. K. Chesterton, Charles Williams, J. R. R. Tolkien, and C. S. Lewis. Among Coleridge's poems, *The Rime of the Ancient Mariner*, with its anguished spiritual odyssey, became a paradigm for imaginative and spiritual journeying. In the United States, *Aids to Reflection* was particularly influential, made known especially by James Marsh, by W. G. T. Shedd (who published a seven-volume edition of Coleridge in 1853), and by Ralph Waldo Emerson. Through Emerson, Coleridge's influence on American Transcendentalist thought was considerable.

Coleridge struggled against rationalism—both within the Protestant tradition and in the secular world—and against materialism, and he wrote vigorously of the need for a renewal of the spiritual dimensions of society and culture. His most important contribution to the religious thought of his own time may well be his introduction into England of German idealist thought and of higher criticism of scripture, while his most lasting contribution may be his reflections on the nature of religious language, especially on the role of symbol in religious experience.

BIBLIOGRAPHY

The central resource for the study of Coleridge is *The Collected Works of Samuel Taylor Coleridge*, 16 vols., edited by Kathleen Coburn (Princeton, 1970–); the lengthy introductions to these volumes are especially helpful. The most complete studies of Coleridge's religious thought are James D. Boulger's *Coleridge as Religious Thinker* (New Haven, 1961) and my work *Coleridge and Christian Doctrine* (Cambridge, Mass., 1969; 2d ed., 1987). Basil Willey's *Samuel Taylor Coleridge* (New York, 1972) is, in the author's own words, an "intellectual and spiritual biography"; it brings both learning and good sense to Coleridge's complex life. Stephen Prickett's *Romanticism and Religion: The Tradition of Coleridge and Wordsworth in the Victorian Church* (Cambridge, U.K., 1976) traces skillfully and perceptively the influence of Coleridge, especially his analysis of religious language, in religious writing of the later nineteenth century. James Cutsinger's *The Form of Transformed Vision: Coleridge and the Knowledge of God* (Macon, Ga., 1987) is a helpful analysis of Coleridge's theological foundations, and my book *Romanticism and Transcendence: Wordsworth, Coleridge, and the Religious Imagination* (Columbia, Mo., 2003) explores the role of the religious imagination in Coleridge's work.

J. ROBERT BARTH (1987 AND 2005)

COLONIALISM AND POSTCOLONIALISM.

Religion, as well as the study of religion, can be located in colonial contexts. Colonialism is the use of military and political power to create and maintain a situation in which colonizers gain economic benefits from the raw materials and cheap labor of the colonized. More than merely a matter of military coercion and political economy, however, colonialism represents a complex intercultural encounter between alien intruders and indigenous people in what Mary Louise Pratt calls "contact zones." In analyzing colonial encounters, scholars need to consider both their material and cultural terms and conditions. In the political economy of colonialism, cultural forms of knowledge and power, discourse and practice, techniques and strategies, played an integral role in the formation of colonial situations.

European explorers, traders, conquerors, and colonial administrators operated with an ideology of territorial expansion and intercultural negation that became thoroughly integrated into European modes of thinking about and engaging the larger world. According to the early nineteenth-century German philosopher G. W. F. Hegel, for example, all great nations "press onward to the sea" because "the sea affords the means for the colonizing activity—sporadic or systematic—to which the mature civil society is driven" (Hegel, 1974, pp. 282–283). By taking to the sea, Hegel argued, colonizers solved certain internal problems, such as poverty, overpopulation, and limited markets, that blocked the development of a mature civil society. But they also encountered "barbarians" in strange lands who were allegedly incapable of developing the maturity of civilization. In relation to such permanent children, Hegel insisted, "the civilized nation is conscious that the rights of the barbarians are unequal to its own and treats their autonomy as only a formality" (Hegel, 1967/1821, p. 219). In this formulation, with its thematics of distance and difference, denial and domination, the philosopher only recapitulated the basic ingredients of a European culture of colonialism.

On colonized peripheries, however, indigenous people deployed a range of strategies for engaging these European territorial claims and cultural representations. On the one hand, reversing the alien terms of European religious signification was an option. During the era of sixteenth-century Spanish conquests in the Americas, for example, the conquistadors were armed with a theological formula, the *Requirement,* that was designed to be read before a gathering of natives to enact a ceremony of possession that certified Spanish claims on new land. In a carefully constructed chain of references, the *Requirement* announced to Native Americans that the Spanish conqueror who stood before them represented the authority of the king of Spain in Castile, who represented the authority of the pope in Rome, who represented the authority of the apostle Peter in Jerusalem, who represented the ultimate authority of the supreme God who had created heaven and earth. Although the *Requirement* invited the natives to freely convert to Christianity, the text concluded that those who refused would experience the force of total warfare and that the deaths and damages that resulted would be their fault (Seed, 1995, p. 69).

In response to this colonial ultimatum, indigenous people could submit or resist. But people also found ways to reappropriate and reverse the chain of references that spanned the Atlantic Ocean to link the New World with the Old. For example, the Andean nobleman Guaman Poma, who had lived through the Spanish conquest of the Inca empire, the subjugation of the Andean people, and the dispossession of native lands, published a book in 1621 that reversed the terms of the *Requirement.* Drawing upon the new Christian resources, Guaman Poma argued that under colonial conditions the world was "upside-down." To restore the proper order of the world, he proposed, the chain of references established by Spanish colonization had to be reversed. According to Guaman Poma, the restoration of Inca political sovereignty would reveal the order of a world in which the mineral wealth of Peru supported the Spanish king in Castile, who supported the Catholic pope in Rome, who supported the religion of the God of heaven and earth. In reversing these alien religious terms, therefore, Guaman Poma tried to intervene in a world that had been turned upside down by Spanish colonization (Adorno, 2000).

On the other hand, reworking the familiar terms of indigenous religious signification was also an option. In Africa, for example, indigenous myths of sea and land were recast to make sense out of the strange encounters and violent oppositions of colonial contact. During the seventeenth century, many Africans concluded that white people who came from the sea actually lived under the ocean. Drawing on earlier mythic themes, this identification of Europeans with the sea became a symbolic template for interpreting the colonial encounter. Using this symbolic framework, Africans could reconfigure the encounter in terms of the mythic opposition between sea and land.

Under the impact of British colonization in nineteenth-century southern Africa, myths of the sea were reworked to make sense of the military incursions, dispossession of land, and new relations of power. As the Xhosa chief Ngqika observed, since the Europeans were people of the sea—the "natives of the water"—they had no business on the land and should have stayed in the sea. The Xhosa religious visionary and war-leader Nxele developed this political observation about sea and land into an indigenous theology that identified two gods, Thixo, the god of the white people, who had punished white people for killing his son by casting them into the sea, and Mdalidiphu, the god of the deeps, who dwelled under the ground but had ultimate dominion over the sea. Similarly, during the first half of the nineteenth century, a Zulu emergence myth was reworked in terms of this colonial opposition between land and sea. In the beginning, uNkulunkulu created human beings, male and female, but also black and white. Whereas black human beings were created to be naked, carry spears, and live on the land, white human beings were created to wear clothing, carry guns, and live in the sea.

For these African religious thinkers, therefore, the mythic origin—the primordium—was clearly located in the new era that opened with the colonial opposition between people of the sea and people of the land. By appropriating foreign religious resources and recasting local religious resources, indigenous people all over the world struggled to make sense out of colonial situations.

An important facet of the European colonial project, however, was the assertion of control over not only material but also symbolic, cultural, and religious resources. In nineteenth-century southern India, for example, British colonial interventions in religion on the Malabar coast succeeded in reifying religious differences and separating religious communities of Hindus and Christians that had lived in harmony for centuries. Tracing their traditional origin to the first-century apostle of Jesus and their spiritual power to ongoing connections with Christian holy men of West Asia, the Saint Thomas Christians of the Malabar coast had maintained close relations with the Hindu rulers of the region. Sharing the same military disciplines and upper-class status with the Hindu rajas, the Saint Thomas Christians received patronage, financial support, and royal protection for their churches, shrines, and festivals. In exchange, the Christians supported the shrines and participated in the festivals of the Hindu ruling class.

This interreligious cooperation changed dramatically, however, after the British East India Company established its domination of the region in 1795. Between 1810 and 1819, under the authority of the British resident Colonel John Monro, the network of economic, social, and religious exchange between Christians and Hindus was broken. Directing state funds for the construction and repair of their churches, Monro exempted Saint Thomas Christians from paying taxes and tributes to Hindu officials. Since these funds were also used to support Hindu temples, shrines, and festivals, Saint Thomas Christians were thereby removed from the system of mutual exchange by which high-caste Hindus and Christians had cooperated in supporting religion. Increasingly, Saint Thomas Christians became targets for the animosity of high-caste Hindus. By the 1880s, riots frequently broke out between them, and annual religious festivals, which had been events of interreligious celebration, became occasions for interreligious provocation. During these festivals, Hindus and Saint Thomas Christians marched past each other's shrines, as one observer reported, "howling, screaming, and crying out obscene words" (Bayly, 1989, p. 294).

British colonial interventions, therefore, had succeeded in reifying the boundaries between two religions—Hindu and Christian—that had been part of the same network of social class, martial culture, and religious worship in southern India. As many analysts have observed, the British colonial reification of religious boundaries not only reinforced a certain kind of European Christianity in India but also produced the modern religious classification "Hinduism." Under colonial conditions, the primary categories of the study of religion—"religion" and "religions"—emerged as potent signs of identity and difference.

Colonial Comparative Religion. As a sustained reflection on religious difference, the study of religion has its historical roots not only in the European Enlightenment but also in this long history of colonialism. On the frontiers of colonial encounter, European explorers, travelers, missionaries, settlers, and colonial administrators recorded their findings on indigenous religions all over the world. With remarkable consistency over a period of five hundred years, these European observers reported that they had found people in the Americas, Africa, and the Pacific Islands who lacked any trace of religion. At the beginning of the sixteenth century, the explorer Amerigo Vespucci observed that the indigenous people of the Caribbean had no religion. In the seventeenth century, the traveler Jacques le Maire insisted that among the inhabitants of the Pacific Islands there was "not the least spark of religion." In the context of expanding trading relations in eighteenth-century West Africa, the trader William Smith reported that Africans "trouble themselves about no religion at all." Well into the nineteenth century, European observers persisted in claiming that the aboriginal people of Australia had "nothing whatever of the character of religion, or of religious observance, to distinguish them from the beasts that perish" (Chidester, 1996, pp. 12–13).

As this global litany of denial accumulated, it developed multiple layers of strategic significance in European colonial encounters with indigenous people. Because they supposedly lacked such a defining human characteristic as religion, indigenous people had no human rights to life, land, livestock, or control over their own labor that had to be respected by European colonizers. In this regard, the denial of the existence of any indigenous religion—this discovery of an absence—reinforced colonial projects of conquest, domination, and dispossession.

Obviously, the discovery of an absence of religion implied that European commentators in colonial situations were operating with an implicit definition of religion, a definition that was certainly informed by Christian assumptions about what counted as religion. More significantly, however, these denials indicated that the term *religion* was used as an oppositional term on colonial frontiers. In its ancient genealogy, of course, *religio* was always a term that derived its meaning in relation to its opposite, *superstitio.* On contested colonial frontiers, however, the conceptual opposition between religion and superstition was often deployed as a strategic denial of indigenous rights to land, livestock, or labor. In the eastern Cape of southern Africa, for example, the beliefs and practices of indigenous Xhosa people were explicitly denied the designation "religion" during the first half of the nineteenth century by European travelers, missionaries, settlers, and colonial magistrates who were trying to establish British military control over the region. Supposedly lacking any trace of religion, the Xhosa allegedly were immersed in superstition. Invoking the defining opposite of religion in this particular colonial situation, the traveler Henry Lichtenstein, for example, reported that the Xhosa's "superstition, their belief in magic or enchantment, and in omens and prognostics, is in proportion to their want of religious feelings" (Lichtenstein, 1928, pp. 301, 311–313). As a recurring motif in European reflections on religious difference in open frontier zones, this opposition between religion and superstition served the colonial project by representing indigenous people as living in a different world.

How did European observers move from the denial to the discovery of indigenous religions in colonial situations? Although that question has to be investigated through detailed attention to historical conditions in specific regions, a general answer can be suggested by the experience of the Xhosa in the eastern Cape of southern Africa. According to the reports of every European commentator, the Xhosa lacked any trace of religion until 1858, when they were placed under a colonial administrative system—the magisterial system—that had been designed by the Cape governor, Sir George Grey, for the military containment, surveillance, and taxation of indigenous people in the eastern Cape. Following his researches on indigenous traditions in Australia and New Zealand, Grey was both a professional colonial administrator and an amateur scholar of religion. It was the new context of colonial containment, however, that inspired the magistrate J. C. Warner to be the first to use the term *religion* for Xhosa beliefs and practices. Insisting that the Xhosa had a religious system, Warner worked out a kind of proto-functionalist analysis by determining that Xhosa religion was a religion because it fulfilled the functional "purposes" of providing psychological security and social stability. Although Warner hoped that the Xhosa religion would ultimately be destroyed by military conquest and Christian conversion, he concluded that in the meantime their indigenous religious system could function to keep them in their place just like the colonial magisterial system.

Throughout southern Africa, the European "discovery" of indigenous religions can be correlated with the colonial containment of indigenous people. While the discovery of a Zulu religious system followed the imposition of the colonial location system in Natal in the 1840s, the recognition of a Sotho-Tswana religious system was delayed until the colonial reserve system was imposed after the destruction of their last independent African polity in the 1890s. By that point, however, when colonial administrators assumed that every African in the region was contained with the urban location system or the rural reserve system, European commentators found that every African in southern Africa had been born into the same "Bantu" religion.

The southern African evidence suggests, therefore, that the "discovery" of indigenous religions under colonial conditions was not necessarily a breakthrough in human recognition. As a corollary of the imposition of a colonial administrative system, the discovery of an indigenous religious system was entangled in the colonial containment of indigenous populations.

Ironically, the colonial project of containment that sought to keep people in place at the same time generated theoretical terms for the displacement of indigenous people. Throughout the colonized world, European observers developed theories of history, genealogy, and descent that traced indigenous people back to cultural centers in the ancient Near East. In the Americas, for example, European travelers, missionaries, and colonizers during the seventeenth century argued that Native Americans were descended from ancient Israel, a claim that was stated succinctly in 1650 in the title of Thomas Thorowgood's book, *Jews in America, or Probabilities That the Americans Are of That Race.* By implication, if they were actually Jews from ancient Israel, then Native Americans did not actually belong in America.

In southern Africa, European commentators also traced the genealogy of indigenous people back to the ancient Near East. Anticipated by the early eighteenth-century findings of the German visitor Peter Kolb, who traced the Khoikhoi or "Hottentot" religious system of the subjugated indigenous people of the Cape back to the Judaism of ancient Israel, nineteenth-century European commentators argued that all Africans in southern Africa came from the north. The Xhosa had been ancient Arabs, the Zulu had been ancient Jews, and the Sotho-Tswana had been ancient Egyptians. Besides transposing the religious differences of the ancient Near East onto the southern African landscape, thereby reifying the ethnic, cultural, and religious differences that had been shaped by colonialism, this fanciful genealogy also implied that indigenous Africans were not actually indigenous to southern Africa because they originally belonged in the Near East. Similarly, a British colonial comparative religion that traced Hinduism back to ancient Indo-European migrations that originated in Siberia or Persia could work not merely as a historical reconstruction but also as a strategy of displacement. Pursuing this contradictory dual mandate of structural containment and historical displacement, colonial comparative religion operated throughout the world to deny, discover, locate, and displace the beliefs and practices of the colonized.

IMPERIAL COMPARATIVE RELIGION. In his inaugural lectures on the science of religion in 1870, F. Max Müller, who has often been regarded as the "founder" of the modern study of religion, demonstrated that the culture of British colonialism and imperialism permeated his understanding of the academic study of religion. First, the study of religion was a science of distance and difference. The distance between the metropolitan center and the colonized periphery was conflated with the difference between the civilized and the barbarian, the savage, or the primitive. In developing a comparative method for the study of religion, Müller and other metropolitan theorists played on this theme of distance and difference in order to infer characteristics of the "primitive" ancestors of humanity from reports about contemporary "savages" living on the colonized periphery of empire. "Though the belief of African and Melanesian savages is more recent in point of time," as Müller observed in his 1870 lectures, "it represents an earlier and far more primitive phase in point of growth" (Müller, 1873, p. 25). In similar terms, E. B. Tylor, the "father of anthropology," asserted that the "hypothetical primitive condition corresponds in a considerable degree to modern savage tribes, who, in spite of their difference and distance. . .seem remains of an early state of the human race at large" (Tylor, 1871, vol. 1, p. 16). Whatever their differences, nineteenth-century metropolitan theorists of religion, such as Müller, Tylor, John Lubbock, Herbert Spencer, Andrew Lang, W. Robertson Smith, and James Frazer, employed a comparative method, which came to be known as *the* comparative method, that used reports about the different, the exotic, and the savage from distant colonized peripheries to draw conclusions about the evolutionary origins of religion.

Second, the study of religion was a science of denial and domination. "Let us take the old saying, *Divide et impera*," Müller proposed, "and translate it somewhat freely by 'Classify and conquer'" (Müller, 1873, pp. 122–123). More than merely a rhetorical flourish, this "old saying" provided legitimation for an imperial comparative religion that aspired to global knowledge over the empire of religion. Classification according to language gave Müller a measure of conceptual control over the library of the sacred texts of the world. But imperial conquest enabled him to develop theories of religion that were anchored in British India and British South Africa. In his last work to be published before his death, the pamphlet *The Question of Right between England and the Transvaal* (1900), which was printed and widely distributed by the Imperial South African Association, Müller asserted that the British Empire "can retire from South Africa as little as from India" (p. 11). These two imperial possessions, he suggested, were essential for maintaining the global power and authority of the British Empire.

But they were also essential for Müller's imperial comparative religion that mediated between "civilized" Great Britain and the "exotic" and "savage" peripheries of empire. While his edition of the *Rig Veda* and his expertise on the religious heritage of India were made possible by the financial support of the East India Company, Müller's imperial comparative religion rested on comparative observations that depended heavily on the British possession of South Africa. Although he observed that in the empire of religion there was "no lack of materials for the student of the Science of Religion" (Müller, 1873, p. 101), Müller knew that those raw materials had to be extracted from the colonies, transported to the metropolitan centers of theory production, and transformed into the manufactured goods of theory that could be used by an imperial comparative religion.

In his relations with South Africa, for example, Müller was engaged in a complex process of intercultural mediation in order to transform raw religious materials into theory. First, Africans on the colonized periphery were drawn into this process as informants—often as collaborators, sometimes as authors—as they reported on religious innovations, arguments, and contradictions in colonial contexts. The Zulu informant Mpengula Mbande, for example, reported arguments about uNkulunkulu, tracking African disagreements about whether he was the first ancestor of a particular political grouping, the first ancestor of all people, or the supreme god who created all human beings.

Second, local European "experts" on the colonized periphery synthesized these religious conflicts and contradictions into a "religious system." Relying heavily on Mbande's local fieldwork, the Anglican missionary Henry Callaway became the leading authority in the world on Zulu religion, and, by extension, on "savage" religion in general, by publishing his classic text, *The Religious System of the Amazulu* (1868–1870). Like other "men on the spot" in colonized peripheries, Callaway corresponded with the metropolitan theorists in London.

However, his exposition of the Zulu "religious system" was dissected by those metropolitan theorists in the service of a third mediation, the mediation between the "primitive" ancestors of humanity, who could supposedly be viewed in the mirror of the Zulu and other "savages" on the colonized peripheries of empire, and the "civilized" European. What was construed as a religious system in the colony, therefore, was taken apart and reassembled in London as religious data that could be used in support of an evolutionary progression from the primitive to the civilized.

The colonial situation, as Jean Paul Sartre observed, "manufactures colonizers as it manufactures colonies" (Sartre, 1965, pp. xxv–xxvi). On colonial peripheries and at imperial centers, nineteenth-century comparative religion played a role in manufacturing European colonial discourse, especially through its representations of "others" in colonized regions such as "exotic" India and "savage" South Africa. As Nicholas Dirks has proposed, these efforts contributed to manufacturing colonizers as "agents of Western reason" (Dirks, 1992, p. 6). In the twenty-first century, we must still wonder about the colonial and imperial legacies that have been inherited by the academic study of religion. In our attention to structure and history, morphology and genealogy, psychological and social functions, and other analytical concerns, do we reproduce the containments and displacements of "others" that were so important to European colonial and imperial projects? However this question might be answered, it is clear that a critical academic study of religion must be self-reflexive and self-critical of the political implications of its theory and practice.

Postcolonial Prospects. As we find in postcolonial studies generally, postcolonial prospects for the academic study of religion are largely a matter of location. In *Orientalism* (1978), Edward Said used the analytical term *strategic location* to capture the subject position of European authors in relation to the broad discursive formations of European colonialism and imperialism. In more recent developments within postcolonial theory, however, attention has shifted away from the critique of European colonial representations of "others" to a recovery of the subjectivity and agency of the colonized. At the risk of oversimplifying the complex theoretical controversies that have raged in this emergent field, we can identify two extreme positions in postcolonial studies—*indigeneity* and *hybridity*—that are relevant to the future of the academic study of religion.

First, indigeneity represents a range of analytical strategies based on the recovery of place, the authenticity of tradition, and the assertion of self-determination in a project to forge postcolonial meaning and power on indigenous terms. Privileging the self-representation of indigenous people who have passed through the experience of colonization, indigeneity generates analytical terms for recovering the purity of local traditions from the defiling effects of global imperialism. Drawing inspiration from political struggles against colonialism, indigeneity engages the precolonial not merely through a romantic politics of nostalgia but also through the liberation movements of the colonized world.

In this respect, the work of the radical psychiatrist Frantz Fanon, who actively identified with the liberation struggles of colonial Africa, has informed an understanding of indigenous tradition that is both postcolonial and postromantic. "Colonization is not satisfied merely with holding a people in its grip and emptying the native's brain of all form and content," Fanon observed. "By a kind of perverted logic, it turns to the past of oppressed people, and distorts, disfigures and destroys it" (Fanon, 1963, p. 170). While the recovery of a "pure" tradition from colonial distortions and disfigurements was therefore part of his postcolonial project, Fanon linked that recovery of the past with a present of struggle—armed, violent struggle—against colonialism. Although Fanon's position has been characterized as a type of "nativism," it was an indigeneity that sought to forge a new humanity in the modern world by means of a militant anticolonialism.

Certainly, many examples could be cited of postcolonial religious indigeneity in which religious "traditionalists" have deployed "modern" means to assert their power, place, purity, and authenticity. Insisting that the only indigenous religion of India is Hinduism, the Rashtriya Swayamsevak Sangh has actively engaged in electoral politics on the platform of "Hinduness" (*Hindutva*) in ways that have not just recovered but have actually redefined what it means to be a Hindu in contemporary Indian society. Rejecting colonial constructions of African mentality, a variety of African movements have nevertheless promoted visions of African humanity and personality, communalism and socialism, in the interests of a postcolonial African renaissance. Arguing that indigenous land should be regarded as sacred and communal rather than alienable property, Native Americans continue to press cases for the recovery of traditional sacred land in the modern courts of law in the United States. The failure of almost all of these land claims has suggested to many scholars of Native American religion that the long history of colonial occupation, with its denial, containment, and displacement of indigenous religion, has not ended in America.

While some scholars of religion have embraced indigeneity as their own strategic location, they have had to contend with trends in postmodern, post-structural, and other postcolonial analysis that have generally undermined any confidence in the continuity or uniformity of tradition. With respect to historical continuity, influential research on the "invention of tradition" has shown how supposedly timeless traditions—even the primitive, the archaic, or the exotic traditions that fascinated colonial and imperial comparative religion—can turn out to have been recent productions. For example, the Indian caste system, which has supposedly been a perennial feature of Hinduism from time immemorial, has been investigated in recent research as a complex product of indigenous interests and colonial order. In defense of indigeneity, however, as Rosalind O'Hanlon has argued, it is possible to reject the British colonial "notion of an ageless caste-bound social order" while not attributing the entire historical process to a "colonial conjuring" that produces a picture of Indians "who are helpless to do anything but reproduce the structures of their own subordination" (O'Hanlon, 1989, pp. 98, 104, 100). In this respect, indigeneity has made an important contribution by stressing the agency of the colonized as historical actors in the formation of religious, social, and political structures.

The "invention of structures," however, has also been called into question, most effectively in the work of Benedict Anderson on "imagined communities," which analyzed colonial instruments—the census, the archive, the administrative system, and so on—for the production of an imaginary sense of social uniformity, but also in the general distrust of any "essentialism" that has been the result of postmodern theory. However, even anti-essentialist critics can propose that in some situations a "strategic essentialism" might be necessary to intervene on behalf of the marginal, oppressed, or "subaltern" in struggles over representation in colonial relations. For advocates of indigeneity in the academic study of religion, some form of "strategic essentialism" seems to be necessary in order to pursue an authentic recovery of traditions that however much they might be "invented" or "imagined" nevertheless produce real effects in the real world.

Second, hybridity captures a range of analytical strategies that follow a logic not of place but of displacement. As a strategic location, hybridity is dislocated in migration and diaspora, contact and contingency, margins and mixtures. As a theoretical intervention in both colonial situations and the postcolonial horizon, attention to hybridity rejects the binary distinction between the colonist and the colonized. According to the most vigorous proponent of colonial hybridity, the cultural theorist Homi Bhabha, the analysis of colonial situations should focus on neither "the hegemonic command of colonial authority" nor "the silent repression of native traditions." Rather, analysis should be directed toward the cultural space in between, the intercultural space of contacts, relations, and exchanges. According to Bhabha, intercultural relations in colonial situations are based, "not on the exoticism of multiculturalism or the *diversity* of cultures, but on the inscription and articulation of culture's *hybridity*." In the colonial contact zone of intercultural relations, Bhabha insists, "it is the 'inter'—the cutting edge of translation and negotiation, the *in-between* space—that carries the burden of the meaning of culture" (Bhabha, 1994, pp. 38–39).

As Bhabha and other postcolonial theorists have developed this analysis of cultural hybridity, emphasis has shifted from the self-representation of indigenous people in their traditional places to the translations, negotiations, and improvisations of the displaced. Migrants, exiles, and diaspora communities have received special attention. For example, cultural theorist Stuart Hall has adapted the notion of hybridity as a strategic location for analyzing a dispersed Afro-Caribbean identity that was formed out of the New World that was "the beginning of diaspora, of diversity, of hybridity and difference" (Hall, 1990, p. 235). In clarifying the New World origin of this diaspora identity, Hall has insisted that it does not entail a politics of nostalgia that evokes myths of "scattered tribes whose identity can only be secured in relation to some sacred homeland to which they must at all costs return, even if it means pushing other people into the sea. This is the old, the imperializing, the hegemonizing, form of 'ethnicity'" (Hall, 1990, p. 235). By contrast to such an ethnic, dominating, imperializing, or even indigenous sense of place, purity, and essence, which Hall identifies with the hegemonic constructions of colonialism and imperialism, the diaspora identity that he is interested in exploring "is defined, not by essence or purity, but by the recognition of a necessary heterogeneity and diversity; by a conception of 'identity' which lives with and through, not despite, difference; by hybridity" (Hall, 1990, p. 235).

In the study of religion, this postcolonial notion of hybridity has been anticipated by the term *syncretism*. Although the term has borne the burden of suggesting impure or illicit mixtures of religion, it has more recently been recovered as a medium of religious innovation. For religious studies, as Ella Shohat has noted in postcolonial studies, "'Hybridity' and 'syncretism' allow negotiation of the multiplicity of identities and subject positionings which result from displacements, immigrations and exiles without policing the borders of identity along essentialist and originary lines" (Shohat, 1992, p. 108). Liberated from the "policing of borders" inherent in colonial constructions of genealogical origins and systemic essences, a postcolonial study of religion can engage the complex and contested negotiations over person, place, and power that inevitably arise in intercultural relations.

See Also Orientalism; Politics and Religion; Primitivism; Transculturation and Religion, overview article.

Bibliography

Adorno, Rolena. *Guaman Poma: Writing and Resistance in Colonial Peru.* 2d ed. Austin, Tex., 2000.

Anderson, Benedict. *Imagined Communities: Reflections on the Origin and Spread of Nationalism.* 2d ed. London, 1991.

Bayly, Susan. *Saints, Goddesses, and Kings: Muslims and Christians in South Indian Society, 1700–1900.* Cambridge, UK, 1989.

Bhabha, Homi. *The Location of Culture.* London, 1994.

Callaway, Henry. *The Religious System of the Amazulu.* Springvale, South Africa, 1868–1870; reprint, Cape Town, 1970.

Chidester, David. *Savage Systems: Colonialism and Comparative Religion in Southern Africa.* Charlottesville, Va., 1996.

Dirks, Nicholas, ed. *Colonialism and Culture.* Ann Arbor, Mich., 1991.

Fanon, Frantz. *The Wretched of the Earth.* Translated by Constance Farrington. New York, 1963.

Hall, Stuart. "Cultural Identity and Diaspora." In *Identity, Community, Culture, Difference*, edited by Jonathan Rutherford, pp. 222–237. London, 1990.

Hegel, G. W. F. *Philosophy of Right* (1821). Translated by T. M. Knox. Oxford, 1967.

Hegel, G. W. F. *The Essential Writings.* Edited by F. Weiss. New York, 1974.

Hobsbawm, Eric, and Terrence Ranger, eds. *The Invention of Tradition.* Cambridge, UK, 1983.

King, Richard. *Orientalism and Religion: Postcolonial Theory, India, and "the Mystic East."* London, 1999.

Lichtenstein, Martin Karl Heinrich. *Travels in Southern Africa in the Years 1803, 1804, 1805* (1811–1812). 2 vols. Translated by Anne Plumptre. Cape Town, 1928.

Lopez, Donald S., Jr., ed. *Curators of the Buddha: The Study of Buddhism under Colonialism.* Chicago, 1995.

MacGaffey, Wyatt. "Dialogues of the Deaf: Europeans on the Atlantic Coast of Africa." In *Implicit Understandings: Observing, Reporting, and Reflecting on the Encounters between Europeans and Other Peoples in the Early Modern Period*, edited by Stuart B. Schwartz, pp. 249–267. Cambridge, UK, 1994.

Martin, Joel W. "Indians, Contact, and Colonialism in the Deep South: Themes for a Postcolonial History of American Religion." In *Retelling U.S. Religious History*, edited by Thomas A. Tweed, pp. 149–180. Berkeley, Calif., 1997.

Müller, F. Max. *Introduction to the Science of Religion: Four Lectures Delivered at the Royal Institution; with Two Essays, On False Analogies and the Philosophy of Mythology.* London, 1873.

Müller, F. Max. *The Question of Right between England and the Transvaal: Letters by the Right Hon. F. Max Müller with Rejoinders by Professor Theodore Mommsen.* London, 1900.

O'Hanlon, Rosalind. "Cultures of Rule, Communities of Resistance: Gender, Discourse, and Tradition in Recent South Asian Historiography." *Social Analysis* 25 (1989): 94–114.

Parry, Benita. "Resistance Theory/Theorising Resistance or Two Cheers for Nativism." In *Colonial Discourse/Postcolonial Theory*, edited by Francis Barker, Peter Hulme, and Margaret Iverson, pp. 172–193. Manchester, UK, 1994.

Pratt, Mary Louise. *Imperial Eyes: Travel Writing and Transculturation.* London, 1992.

Said, Edward. *Orientalism.* New York, 1978.

Sartre, Jean-Paul. "Introduction." In *The Colonizer and the Colonized*, by Albert Memmi. New York, 1965.

Seed, Patricia. *Ceremonies of Possession in Europe's Conquest of the New World 1492–1640.* Cambridge, UK, 1995.

Shohat, Ella. "Notes on the Post-Colonial." *Social Text* 31/32 (1992): 99–113.

Tylor, E. B. *Primitive Culture.* 2 vols. London, 1871.

Van der Veer, Peter. *Imperial Encounters: Religion and Modernity in India and Britain.* Princeton, N.J., 2001.

Warner, J. C. "Mr. Warner's Notes." In *A Compendium of Kafir Laws and Customs,* edited by John MacLean, pp. 57–109. Mount Coke, South Africa, 1858.

DAVID CHIDESTER (2005)

COLORS. Like other forms of religious symbolism, the symbolism of color emerges from the immediate material experience of human beings. Common elements of life are the basis for reflections on the meaning of color. Various plants (flowers, trees, medicinal herbs, etc.), animals, insects, the human body, celestial and climatological phenomena are just a few things that orient the meanings of color symbolism. This implies that there are universal themes in color symbolism that are involved with local knowledge of particular geographies. The naive and immediate experience of color gives rise to complex speculations about the nature of the cosmos. Beginning with a basic distinction of primary from secondary colors, one is soon led on to such notions as warm and cold colors, for example. There are no set universal characteristics of color symbolism just as there are no completely cultural-specific meanings of color. Nevertheless, exploring color symbolism of religions other than one's own is valuable because it informs commonly held meanings. Indeed, various artists and cultures play with the organic connections between colors and their referents.

For example, in Paul Klee's (1879–1940) work primary colors are associated with different sounds, geometrical forms, and even subjective experiences. According to Klee, blue is associated with the circle and with the experience of stability; yellow, with the triangle and the sensation of speed; and red, with the square and the experience of power. Similarly, Wassily Kandinsky (1866–1944), one of the greatest abstract painters, observed that a yellow circle seemed to develop outward in an expansive movement so that it appears to approach the observer, whereas a blue circle seemed to contract and move away from the viewer. In the world of fashion, it is well known that the colors of black and white have opposing effects on human perceptions: White is experienced as expansive whereas black is contractive. Both Klee and Kandinsky played with associations that were well-grounded in specific phenomena to induce a perceptual experience in the viewer. In other words, they played with human associations between color and its various conceptual meanings. This strategy has been utilized in various cultural contexts as well.

Red, white, and black are the three most used colors in Ndembu ritual. At first glance these colors are representative of blood, milk (or semen), and feces. In different contexts, however, (e.g., in ritual or artistic contexts) these representations expand to other associations. For example, in the context of the circumcision rite, red is a prominent color and could certainly be associated with blood. From its specific and universal association with blood, however, are formed other meanings having to do with lineage, male potency, hunting, and warfare. Likewise, during the Ndembu female initiation rite, red has equally powerful but opposite meanings such as menstruation, childbirth, and matrilineage. From the specific associations of red and blood other meanings of the color have developed that are specific to particular cultural contexts. Over the course of several weeks of seclusion, young boys and girls are formed into adult members of Ndembu society through color symbolism.

MESOAMERICAN COLOR USE. As is true for many ancient monuments around the world, in Mesoamerican archaeological sites the gray and lifeless stone monuments seen today were originally plastered in white and awash in vibrant colors. The architectural remnants of today are but dim reminders of the vitality of these ceremonial centers. Colors of black, blue, red, and yellow decorated ancient Mesoamerican temples and palaces. Murals of deities, animals, kingly exploits, as well as numerous other topics, were painted with an assortment of colors. Ancient cities such as Tikal, Bonampak, Tula, Teotihuacan, Cholula, Chichén Itzá, and Tenochtitlan were all brightly painted.

Pre-Columbian picture books and texts were composed of a series of images. Often these images depicted the activities of gods, heroes, divinatory calendars, and conquests and tribute. Invariably, artisans who crafted these books used brilliant colors to better communicate their messages. Ceramics, stone carvings, and other art objects were also adorned with an assortment of colors. Pre-Columbian texts often feature body painting, and specific colors and arrangements of colors represented the activities of gods and humans. For example, a red-striped body represented human sacrifice. Black stripes on the face and yellow hair were associated with the fire god Xiuhtecuhtli or Ixcozauhqui (Yellow Face). White was often associated with the bleached bones of the god Mictlanteuchtli, the lord of the dead who resided in the underworld. Painted images in these books indicate that body painting was an important feature of Mesoamerican ritual life. Just as colors adorned the temples that served as the central focus of ceremonial activity, likewise practitioners of the ceremonies used colors to adorn their bodies.

Color was therefore an important feature of Mesoamerican symbolism. At the level of practice, colors could symbolize specific material phenomenon, including yellow for the sun, red for blood, and blue for water. Often certain colors were associated with specific cardinal directions. However, no one-to-one correlation existed between color and a particular aspect of material life. Colors would often be associated with several things at once, thus the meaning of specific colors was multivalent. At the level of ideology colors could be intimately associated, for example, with a deity, a geographical location, or a specific ritual activity.

Blue and red were often directly associated with water and blood. For example, on temples in which human sacrifices took place and on picture books that represented the activities of the gods, blue and red consistently refer to water and blood. Ceremonies dedicated to fertility deities, such as Chac for the Maya and Tlaloc for the Aztec, underscored the relationship between water and blood. Thus, stylized depictions of these deities and adornments on their temples, in particular, prominently utilized blue and red.

The use of colors was part of the total sensual experience of being in the city. One's participation in ceremonial events, as well as everyday activities, meant being surrounded by rich sensory stimuli including music and sound, light and dark, smells and tastes, and colors. The affective use of color, therefore, gave people the sense of being intimately integrated into Mesoamerican social and cosmological realities.

CHRISTIAN SYMBOLISM. In contrast—and yet related—to Hellenistic and Roman traditions, Christian color symbolism was generally based on white, which was associated with purity and innocence. In the Catholic Church color most often symbolized the virtues of purity and spiritual hierarchy. As such, more attention is paid to the universal aspects of color associations. White was the color of the martyrs, the *candidatus exercitus* (white-clad army). Opposed to white was black, considered to be the color of sadness and later introduced into funeral liturgies. Cobalt blue was the color of darkness and the devil, whereas red was the color of the empyrean sky and of the angels. Purple, the imperial color of ancient Rome, became the color of the cardinal's robe. The comparative difficulty in attaining purple led to its associations with social prestige and power, which became connected with the spiritual hierarchy of the Catholic church. In addition to these associations, color is also associated with the yearly passage of time. Use of color in the vestments of officiant, on the altar, and in the attire of the attendants also leads to symbolism that is part of the Christian liturgical year.

From the ninth century on, colors were a constant element of Christian ritual. Despite early attempts to standardize church usage, variations persisted. In Greece, for example, red was the color of mourning (perhaps associated with blood), but in Milan, where the local Ambrosian ritual was celebrated, red was connected with the Holy Sacrament. In France, red was the liturgical color on All Saints Day (November 1; a clear reference to the blood of martyrs) whereas in Rome white, the symbol of triumph, was used for the same feast.

The first codification of the liturgical colors began under Innocent III (1198–1216) and reached its definitive form under Pius V (1566–1572) after the Council of Trent (1545–1563). In the final codification, white is a primary color and is used in the great festivities of the liturgical year to symbolize triumph, innocence, and purity; red is reserved for the feast of the martyrs, symbolizing the blood of sacrifice and eternal life; green is a symbol of hope and is to be regarded between white and red; violet is used during periods of penance (i.e., Lent) and in funeral services; and black has fallen into disuse (except on Good Friday, when it is used to symbolize Christ's descent into death prior to his resurrection) because of its associations with the devil by Church Fathers, particularly during the late Middle Ages. On occasion silver may replace white, and gold may be used instead of white, green, or red. In other words, the symbolism of white, silver, and gold have a preeminent place in the color symbolism of the Catholic Church. Codification of the ceremonial uses of color attempted to reduce the local associations for the sake of maintaining global unanimity.

THE COLOR GOLD. The polyvalence of gold is worth noting. Throughout Christendom, mysticism is often expressed by use of gold. Byzantine mosaics and icons, as well as medieval paintings utilize gold to articulate the high spiritual value of specific individuals In his *Speculation in Colors* (1915), the Russian Orthodox philosopher Evgenii Trubetskoi (1863–1920) noticed the influence of a solar Christological mysticism in the golden backgrounds of the icons, because only the color of gold can reflect the supreme sunlight of the heavenly world. Artists devised the *assist*—the insertion of shining golden lines radiating the dress of divine figures—for this reason. The *assist* is especially common in depictions of Christ and, above all, in depictions of the transfiguration, the resurrection, and the ascension, and the other post-resurrection events. It is clearly intended as a symbol of Christ's superhuman glory. Behind it lies the speculative metaphysics of light exemplified in the golden backgrounds of the Byzantine mosaics in churches in Ravenna and Byzantium (modern Istanbul) aimed at turning the inner space of the Roman basilicas into space-light and lightening the heaviness of the architectural material. The golden background produces an atmosphere pervaded with immaterial light (*phos to aulon*) and draws the believers out of material concerns toward the contemplation of the divine mysteries. Gold symbolism in the development of Christianity associated solar symbolism with the universality of Christ's liberating presence in the world. The promise of Christian salvation was directly associated with the heavens—above and outside earthly confines. Many of the world's great and global religions have utilized solar symbolism to promote the universality of their message. For example, in the Buddhist text, the *Supreme Sūtra of the Golden Brilliance*, the Buddha's immaterial body is presented as shining gold and is identical with the *dharmakāya* (the body of the Law). The essence of the universe is thus compared to a golden light that shines forth like sunlight. In several Gandharan traditions (defined as an area of Afghanistan and Pakistan from the first to fifth centuries CE), they speak of the Buddha's shadow as golden and shining.

The golden backgrounds of mosaics, icons, and paintings on wood were created by applying very thin sheets of gold to a prepared surface. Because this method cannot be used on the larger scale of frescos, some painters, notably Giotto (1267–1337), filled the backgrounds of murals with a blue pigment made by powdering the gemstone lapis lazuli to create the most precious color of that time. In Giotto's frescoes the blue of lapis lazuli can be compared to the golden backgrounds of the Byzantine Siensese tradition, with the resulting orientation toward a heavenly mysticism and away from the fundamental realism of the paintings. Nevertheless, in the ancient Christian tradition, azure and blue had a negative value. The high values of gold, silver, and lapis lazuli over and against other materials are connected with their associations to salvation, resurrection, and heaven. Not only were the materials that were used for making these colors comparatively rare in the West, but their associations with the spiritual values of the church make them seem intrinsically valuable.

Compared with blue, gold is free of the ambiguity associated with other colors, but the blue of lapis lazuli was widely used in the area of Central Asia. Many Buddhist paintings found in the area of Kuqa have this blue appearing alongside green. On one hand, it was used in Tibetan Buddhist art to depict terrifying gods with enormous powers. In the sole surviving wall painting of Tumshuq, and in several others around Kuqa, inauspicious figures either are completely blue or have blue beards. On the other hand, ascetics and monks are also depicted with blue beards.

ALCHEMY AND NATIVE AMERICAN TRADITIONS. Color plays an important role in the Western alchemic tradition. According to this tradition, the alchemic process passes though four stages, each associated with a color: the *nigredo* (black) or initiatory death, the *albedo* (white) or beginning of rebirth, the *rubedo* (red) or sublimation, and the *auredo* (gold), the almost unreachable final stage that represents spiritual perfection. The series seems to coincide with the elementary set of colors that the Greek philosophers Pythagoras (571–497 BCE) and Empedocles (492–432 BCE) regarded as the only ones allowable on a palette, namely, black, white, red, and yellow.

As with the Mesoamericans and alchemy, the Lakota-speaking people of the Great Plains of North American associate colors with different aspects of life. In the Pipe Ceremony, the colors red, yellow, black, and white are associated with the cardinal directions. A variety of ceremonies performed for the fertility of the earth, for healing, human life stages, and so on utilize this color symbolism. The Oglala healer Black Elk's vision emphasized the colors associated with the six grandfathers, which were the deities associated with foundational elements of the universe. During these difficult times of the early reservation, Black Elk's community performed his Great Vision in a ceremony. A tipi was erected in the middle, elaborately painted to reflect his boyhood vision. Horses of specific colors—yellow, red, black, and white—were used in the ceremony. Black Elk's vision was performed by his community and thereby brought out of the realm of the human mind into activity. His Oglala people invested significant resources in reproducing the colors of the vision accurately so as to reestablish proper relationships with deities that controlled their world.

Similarly, for the Haudenosaunee (People of the Longhouse; better known as the Iroquois), of upstate New York and Canada, the colors purple and white have deep significance. These are the colors of wampum, which is a bead carved from the quahog shell found along the New England Atlantic coast. As with ancient people of the Mediterranean basin, purple is regarded as a precious color. The colors of wampum symbolize cosmological attributes—black of night and light of day. The purple and white signify the opposing forces of the universe that come together in the working of creation. Wampum belts and strings, therefore, are items of human manufacture that establish proper relationships with the Creator. Wampum has been used continuously by the Haudenosaunee in Longhouse ceremonies. Because of the religious significance of wampum, it has been used in forming international and intercultural alliances between the Haudenosaunee and the Dutch, English, French and American governments, as well as a number of indigenous nations. Today the purple and white Confederacy Belt, which symbolizes the unity of the original five nations (Seneca, Cayuga, Onondaga, Oneida, and Mohawk), can be seen everywhere throughout Haudenosaunee territory and serves as the flag of the Haudenosaunee.

The meaning and use of color is a universal human phenomenon. Yet the orientations that individual human communities have to color symbolism is specific to their local contexts and environments. Color has a powerful effect on human emotions and can unify and divide groups of people. It is an integral part of ceremonial life triggering a range of emotional responses that is often referenced to a sacred reality. There is no color code of religious meanings but rather specific colors can mean a range of things depending on the context of their use. Certainly, without color religion would be a much less urgent and powerful phenomenon in human life.

SEE ALSO Alchemy, overview article; Art and Religion; Christian Liturgical Year.

BIBLIOGRAPHY

Barreiro, José, ed. *Indian Roots of American Democracy.* Ithaca, N.Y., 1992.

Neihardt, John G. *Black Elk Speaks.* Lincoln, Neb., 1932; reprint, 1979.

Turner, Victor. *The Forest of Symbols: Aspects of Ndembu Ritual.* Ithaca, N.Y., 1967.

PHILIP P. ARNOLD (2005)

COMENIUS, JOHANNES AMOS (1592–1670),

the "grandfather of modern education." Born Jan Amos Komenský in Nivnitz, Moravia, he was orphaned early and did not begin school until the age of sixteen. He died in Amsterdam, a lifelong refugee from religious wars, the last bishop of the Moravian and Bohemian Brethren, formerly known as the Old Church.

Said to be unoriginal in philosophy, Comenius's genius lay in teaching. His philosophy and his teaching were forged from personal experience with both religious intolerance and bad schooling. He was convinced that international tensions were grounded in religious differences, which in turn were grounded in lack of knowledge of the order of nature as well as of others' religions.

His grand strategy was "Pansophia," a philosophy of universal knowledge based on a universal language built on a universal education that included women. Invited to England to develop a system of education, he was prevented from carrying out his program by the Civil War. He visited Sweden and planned the reformation of schools there only to flee the outbreak of war in 1648. He returned to Leszno, Poland, whence he had fled from Nivnitz as a young man, and where he had done most of his writing, but was forced by the war between West Prussia and Poland to escape to Amsterdam in 1655, losing in this final move all his manuscripts.

For Comenius, schools as he found them were "the slaughterhouse of the mind," devoted as they were to the dreary and sometimes desperately enforced study of Latin in a world where that language was no longer used. In his schools there was to be no "stuffing and flogging," but, rather, a reasonable following of "the lead of nature." "A rational creature should be led," he wrote, "not by shouts, imprisonment and blows, but by reason." Nothing was to be learned "for its own sake," but "for its usefulness in life." Everything was to be learned by practice: "Let the students learn to write by writing, to talk by talking, to sing by singing, to reason by reasoning." Comenius likened education to nature, where the existence of objects was prior to the development of language. "The principle of succession," he wrote, in which "nature prepares the material before giving it form, develops everything from within, always ending in particulars, makes no leaps [and] advances only from strength." Knowledge, therefore, comes most naturally through the senses: "The sense of hearing should be conjoined with that of sight, and the tongue should be trained in coordination with the hand." Objects were to be brought into the classroom for use in teaching.

His plans for state schools, radical in his century, are now generally accepted. Schools were to open at a uniform date each year and holidays were to be frequent but short. According to his plans, a definite learning task would be assigned to each hour of the day; after each class there was a recess. The length of the day was longer the higher the grade. Comenius proposed that each teacher have a separate room and all learning be done under the teacher's supervision; there was to be no homework. Comenius hoped for the establishment of a central college which was to be provided with facilities for both advanced learning and teacher preparation. From a generation so trained, he believed, a Christian republic might grow. "There is no more certain way under the sun," he wrote, "to raise a sunken humanity."

Comenius's *Dictionary of Tongues and All Sciences* was translated into Arabic and Russian, as well as into other European languages, and the students of three continents thumbed its pages. *Orbis pictus* (The visible world), published in 1658, was his most famous text; it was illustrated, featured parallel passages in Latin and in the student's vernacular, and was intended to be employed by students at a rate commensurate with their individual abilities. These texts were based on earlier works: *Gate of Tongues Unlocked* (1631) and *Labyrinth of the World* (c. 1623). His best-known work is *Didactica magna*, written between 1628 and 1632. It has influenced teaching methods in the Western world more, perhaps, than any other book of educational theory.

Bibliography

A good biography of Comenius is Matthew Spinka's *John Amos Comenius: That Incomparable Moravian* (Chicago, 1943). A good analysis of his contribution to education is John E. Sadler's *J. A. Comenius and the Concept of Universal Education* (London, 1966).

WAYNE R. ROOD (1987)

COMMUNION SEE EUCHARIST

COMMUNITY.

Although groupings or community formations are a regular feature of the phenomenon of religion, it is important to recognize that they are neither necessary nor equally prominent in all religions. There are situations otherwise completely typical of the category "religion" wherein the communal element is lacking, and others wherein it is loosely structured, evanescent, or deemed unimportant. For example, even though monasteries constitute a rigorous and elaborate kind of community, the name for them in Western languages derives from the Greek *monos*, meaning "single, alone." Hermit monks and wandering *saṃnyāsins* take as a major element in their piety and ascetic practice the renunciation of community. Also, many people in modern, industrialized societies consider themselves religious because of certain attitudes, practices, and beliefs but do not take part in a communal structure in which these religious factors are shared or are decisive.

Therefore, in the following paragraphs, as various types of religious communal organization are reviewed and their dynamics analyzed, one must remember that these groups vary in intensity and importance in their respective cultures and traditions, and that they do not exhaust the possibilities for religious life. Nevertheless, it is not too much to say that nearly all religious situations do have a communal dimension and that in many the community is the decisive factor.

It is a prejudice of modern society to speak of "organized religion" as if organization added an extraneous element to what legitimately exists without it. It is possible, of course, to define or to believe in a religion that is a matter of one's aloneness. It should also be recognized, however, that for many other people the social factor—belonging to and having a place in a religious community—may be the dominant aspect of their religious life and that, further, it may be a hidden factor even in the life of the one who rejects its significance.

The following description and typology of religious communities is highly abstract and theoretical. It describes poles, although most groups actually lie somewhere on a continuum between such poles; it speaks of pure types, even though most of life is compromised and blended; it isolates factors and structures that are in actuality mixed with other social patterns as well as influenced and changed by belief, rite, and experience. All this notwithstanding, focusing on these social structures, abstracted from their living contexts, may be helpful in sorting out the communal element from among the many contributing factors in a religious phenomenon and so may lead to a better understanding of the whole.

CHARACTERISTICS OF RELIGIOUS COMMUNITY. Some form of initiation usually marks entrance into a religious community. Entrance rituals may also be duplicated, reinforced, or elaborated on subsequent occasions. Later transition ceremonies often mark the beginning of new status within a group (e.g., ordination or monastic profession). There are also rituals and procedures for leaving a group, by incorporation into a higher status beyond the perimeters of the former group, or by censure and repudiation. Even death, which would seem to end an individual's membership in a community, can be understood as an initiation into a yet higher degree of existence in the group. In such cases, certain ceremonies during the ritual year may celebrate the return of the dead to participate in the life of the community.

Communal ritual activities for other purposes or on other occasions than initiation or ordination are also characteristic marks of religious communities. These rituals may be focused on seasonal change, agricultural processes, famous events of history, and doctrines, usually with all these elements blended together. Gathering as a group for such rites is perhaps the most persistent aspect of religious community, and is arguably its reason for being.

Differentiation of function and of merit or value is often recognized in communal structure. In some cases special functions within the group, especially leadership in ritual activities, are assumed by individuals specially selected and consecrated; in other cases leaders emerge from the group charismatically. That is, some religious traditions are highly sensitive to structural arrangements and carefully delineate lines of command and authority, carefully categorizing all functions and degrees. In other traditions the patterns of authority are quite casual, very much dependent on individual initiative and lacking ritual recognition.

Religious communities often validate, or give religious meaning to, natural or social distinctions. Gender, for example, is often a significant determinant of an individual's role in a religious community. One's role in the family (as mother, son, etc.) or one's lineage (e.g., in a caste system) may also determine religious status, and one's political office or status as a leader in the society at large tends to take on religious significance.

Religious communities are different from other social groups in their concept of the community as a sacred phenomenon. Instead of conceiving of the community in practical or casual terms, the distinctly religious group sees itself as part of a larger structure, plan, or purpose, one that transcends the immediate or basic needs of humanity. Conscious correlation of the community with patterns of symbols that are not social in their primary reference is a signal of the presence of religious rather than secular community.

Where nature and its processes are the focal point of religious attention, the community is conceived and structured with reference to the natural world. The subgroups within a tribe, for example, are linked in the mind with animals, stars, and the like. This totemism does not indicate an obliteration of the distinction between nature and culture in such peoples but rather shows an attempt to correlate one with the other or to use the elements of the natural world as a means of labeling and systematizing society.

Among religious groups for whom nature is not the primary concern, the concept of the community as a sacred entity takes a variety of forms. A special relationship with one or more gods or goddesses may be expressed by seeing the group as the servants, the messengers, or perhaps the coworkers of the divine beings. There is a fine line between metaphors and ontological assertions in theological language, so one often does not know how precisely to take images, such as the church as the "body" of Christ, that seem to give a group a kind of organic participation in the sacred.

A concept of the group as sacred can be linked with the merit or attainments of adepts with various degrees of skill. Those who are most advanced in ascetic practice, meditation, or yoga may constitute a sacred core around or below which those of lesser attainments are ranked. This arrangement leads to a pattern illustrated by Buddhism, according to which the term for the community, *saṃgha*, may refer to the inner circle of monks (*bhikkhus*) or to the larger group, the laity, who subscribe to the doctrine but practice it less exclusively.

It is possible, of course, for a religious community to be structured along lines that are not particularly religious from the point of view of believer or observer, as is so, for example, in the military model of the Salvation Army and the constitutional administrative arrangement of some American Protestant denominations. In such cases, concepts of the group as a sacred entity might become almost entirely separate from its actual structural appearance. Tensions can develop in religious groups when the social structure and the theology become too divergent. It is odd, for example, to have a monastic pattern that is almost inevitably based on merit and attainment existing within a tradition that doctrinally asserts equality before God or some alternate kind of sacred hierarchy.

To summarize, we can assume that we are observing a religious community, whether it is so labeled or not, when most or all of the following characteristics are evident in reference to the sacred: rituals of initiation and incorporation (as well as those of rejection); other communal rituals; and status levels and functional distinctions.

"NATURAL" RELIGIOUS GROUPS. One of the clearest distinctions to be made among religious communities is that between groups specifically and self-consciously organized around religious beliefs and activities and those societies or "natural" groups wherein whatever is religious is part of the whole social structure. This distinction may also be made by noting that the specific religious groups are typically or theoretically voluntary, while one is born into the latter type of community, and there is no choice about joining it. A further way of making the distinction is by observing the relationship between the religious dimension and the political or governmental dimension: specific religious groups are not involved per se in governing, whereas the natural religious group is identical with the social group as a whole, including its political functions.

These broad categories have been labeled in many ways; for example, the terms *differentiated* and *undifferentiated* have been used, based on the degree to which the religious group is differentiated from the society as a whole. Sometimes it seems better to designate the natural, or undifferentiated, type of religious community as "folk" religion and, by contrast, to see the specific religious community as "universal" in character. Folk religion is part of the culture of a particular group of people and is not easily distinguished from all the other patterns and practices that define the culture. A universal religious group, however, tries to cross cultural and ethnic boundaries by assuming that all people everywhere can become members of its community.

The terms *specific* and *natural* are used in this article to name these groups, even though the latter term presents a problem of multiple meanings. Many presuppositions lie behind any use of *nature*, and most of these are irrelevant to their present use. One should not assume, for example, that natural religious groups are sociobiologically based in a way that specific groups are not. In fact, nothing that follows need be understood as affecting theories concerning the biological determination of human social behavior. All that is meant by the use of *natural* in this context is the identity of the religious community with those forms of social organization that are mostly inevitable in human life: family, clan, ethnic group, and nation.

Even though one is born into such social structures, initiation into "real" participation in the community is one of the signs that the social unit is also a religious community. At birth or puberty, or at both of these life passages, a ceremony such as circumcision or some act of consecration marks the official (or ontological) entrance into society. In many places such initiation is more marked for boys than for girls, although there may be rituals connected with the onset of menstruation. It is to be expected that gender, lineage, and comparable identifications will be more significant in natural religious groups than in others.

In natural religious groups the religious leaders or functionaries are generally the leaders of the society as a whole. It is rare, however, to find a community that does not also have its religious specialists, perhaps a shaman or medicine man, whose appearance and role depend on a special recognition that is not determined by "nature" in the sense used here.

It should also be noted that specific religious organizations may exist within natural religious groups. The primitive secret society is an example of such a group: it has its own dynamics as a voluntary group with special religious functions and rites apart from the society as a whole. Similarly, groups based on family, gender, ethnic background, and related natural factors may be found within or alongside specific religious communities or may even seem to merge with them. Men's fraternities are a common example of a gender-based grouping, and the practical identity (at least in former years) of Spanish background and Roman Catholicism is an example of the apparent merging of the natural with the specific religious community.

Humans face a special situation in the phenomenon of the nation as a religious community—special in that the basis of community is not necessarily "natural" in the way that it is for gender, family, or lineage. In a nation, unrelated peoples can be joined together, slaves or slave populations may be incorporated into the political unit, and foreigners may have a place in the society as merchants or mercenaries. When the nation is also a religious community, however, it typically develops a set of stories (a mythology) to make the diverse groups appear to be a family. It is not at all certain, for example, that the ancient Israelites were all descended from Jacob; but new tribes could be included by having their patriarchs included among Jacob's sons. Emphasis on the "natural" in this type of religious nation may also be seen in the Israelites' insistence on the number twelve (the names of the sons of Jacob vary, but they are always twelve in number); this probably reflects a desire to repeat in human society the pattern of the heavens: twelve lunar cycles within a single solar cycle.

To the Israelites and other ancient peoples, political and religious functions were indistinguishable. While in modern times people differentiate between religious and civil law, ancient lawgivers recorded both in the same codes and in the same manner. The king was political, military, and religious functionary in one. Society, nature, and the gods were all seen as part of one interrelated organism. This outlook led to such phenomena as blaming crop failure on the weakness or immorality of the king. The king was characteristically seen as a god, the son of a god, or a representative and link from the heavens to earth and society.

This set of concepts is not entirely limited to the past. Some modern nations take on many of these characteristics (for some of their people) and thus become religious communities of a sort. Nations, both ancient and recent, have been known to cultivate epics of their origin, promote their peculiar concepts of the world, claim special connection with a god or gods, and link their success (or failure) to divine purpose. Not all of these nation-religions are generally recognized as such, but the Shintō tradition of Japan clearly exemplifies this phenomenon.

The religious and political dimensions of human life may be connected in another way as well, one that goes beyond the nation as a political unit. Islam, the most recent of the major religions, exhibits some of the characteristics of the very ancient natural religious community. It is based on the premise that the religious regulation and the civil regulation of life are to be derived from one source and litigated in one way. The international community of Islam thus presumes that a family of nations or peoples can be Muslim in law and belief. Some Muslim nations have begun to reject the notion of a secular government (i.e., one that is determined not by religious belief but by human deliberation) in favor of a religious government based on the Qurʾān. Although Islamic government of this sort does not necessarily have a kinglike figure or a theology of agriculture, in most other ways it is like the ancient nations, a natural religious community.

Specific Religious Communities. Specific religious communities are sometimes called "founded" religions because they have appeared within the scope of recorded history as the result of efforts of a particular person or small group. As noted above, this category could also be termed "universal," "differentiated," or "voluntary." Contemporary pluralistic societies include religious communities of this type, even though some characteristics of natural religious communities can be observed on occasion.

Sociologists of religion, mainly Westerners interested in Christian groups, have put most of their energies into analyzing specific religious groups. As the examination of the social dimensions of religion became a recognized scholarly discipline, the categories "church" and "sect" were developed to distinguish between religious communities. This terminology applied well to sixteenth-century Europe but was insufficient elsewhere. For America it was necessary to add at least the category "denomination." One widely used typology of religious groups that developed out of the earlier distinctions lists six major types of religious community: cult, sect, established sect (or institutionalized sect), denomination, ecclesia, and universal church. These categories were developed particularly with reference to the ways in which the religious community is integrated into the society as a whole and to a lesser degree with reference to the internal dynamics of each group or its theology. Nevertheless, these six types can provide a framework for understanding Christian communities and can be applied with some adjustments to other religions as well.

The kind of group that is least involved in the rest of society is called a "cult." A cult may comprise barely more than the audience for a charismatic leader or healer. It is loosely organized; often it is small and short-lived. Its religious style is personal and emotional.

A "sect" is a religious community that is more clearly organized than a cult, that provides a great amount of religious value to its members (in terms of social relationships, ritual activities, ethical and doctrinal direction, and so forth), but that plays little role in the society at large. Taken to its extreme, a sect can form a completely separate miniature state either mixed into the society geographically or located in its own separate territory.

It is also possible, however, for a sect to move in a different direction and become more stable within the larger society. A sect so changed would be an "established sect," or an "institutionalized sect." In this situation the wider society's acceptance of the sect can be great even though the sect remains exclusive and self-centered. An established sect has lost its appearance of opposition to the rest of the society and other religious groups, but it remains doctrinally or theoretically exclusive.

At this point the "denomination" assumes its place in the six-type scheme as another type of Western religious community. It is the kind of group that maintains separate and distinct organization despite its acceptance of the legitimacy of other denominations or communities. It may conceive of itself as the best, but hardly the only, community in which adequate religious practice can be found. It is also relatively more involved with and accepted by the larger society.

Students of American religious communities have been struck by the tendency of each Christian sect and denomination to be made up of people from a single socioeconomic class. Furthermore, they note that a sect tends to become an established sect or a denomination and that as it does, the class composition of its members tends to change. Some of the characteristics of the transition from sect to its more established form or to a denomination are an increase in the members' and the institution's wealth; movement toward the center of the surrounding culture and away from criticism of it; less ridicule of other religious communities and more cooperation with them; less exclusion of potential members for being thought potentially unworthy; fewer casually prepared part-time leaders and more professionally trained full-time ministers; more concern for children and education; less emphasis on death and the next world and more attention to life in this world; and less spontaneity and emotion in worship and more use of hymns and texts from the liturgical traditions. The established sect and the denomination might be similar in most of these departures from the patterns of a sect, but the denomination has a different theology, while the established sect, no matter how institutionalized or accepted, retains its exclusive and condemnatory thought and speech.

The next two categories, beyond denomination, represent the most established and, culturally and socially, the most prominent kinds of religious community. One has been called the "ecclesia" and consists of the established national churches, for example, the churches of England and of Sweden. The other is termed "universal church." It is as well established as the ecclesia but exists in many nations and cultures; the classic example is the Roman Catholic church of the thirteenth century.

One of the characteristics of the specific religious community as compared with the natural religious community is its voluntary character. Yet this characteristic is almost completely absent in the ecclesia and universal church and is of little importance in the denomination and the established sect. The sect is noted for its emphasis on conversion, a voluntary, adult decision to join the group. The more established churches, however, incorporate the children of members almost automatically into the community, thus operating somewhat like a natural religious group. Furthermore, kings and other political functionaries tend to become semireligious officials in the ecclesia and the universal church categories.

As noted above, most of the terminology used here has been derived from studies of Western Christian religious communities, but it can be applied to Eastern Christianity and other religions with some limited success. Sunnī Islam can be seen as a universal church; Shīʿī Islam in Iran can be seen as an ecclesia; other Shīʿī groups can be seen as sects or established sects, and so on. Eastern Christian groups are usually of the ecclesia type in their home countries and have had to shift character in order to be denominations in America. In Thailand and Sri Lanka, Buddhism has had ecclesia status; its role in China can be analyzed in various periods as taking the forms of sect, denomination, and so on—all this despite its essentially monastic structure.

It is more important in examining non-Western religious communities to note their patterns of internal relationships and their role in the larger religious tradition than to concentrate on their relationship to the state or society. In non-Western societies, the different mix of natural and specific groups must be considered, as well as the recent and incomplete phenomenon of secularity (the separation of civil from religious jurisdiction). For example, Hinduism is, for the most part, a natural religious community, but some associations within it are of the specific type. These groups (*sampradāyas*) select a certain god or family of gods, a certain style of worship, and certain temples from the whole range of Hinduism, and these elements become the basis for the group's religious life. Thus a community with its own leaders and priests emerges. This phenomenon has many of the characteristics of the denomination in its recognition of other (almost as good) practices and gods in Hinduism, but it is sectarian in its lack of involvement with the society as a whole and in its governmental structures.

The different circumstances of non-Western religious communities can be understood better in terms and categories other than the six reviewed above. The following categories have been developed especially by anthropologists and ethnologists, and they help people to understand the subgroups within larger religious communities or traditions.

Communities within Communities. One large distinction that can be made within both natural and specific religious groups is that of "great" and "little" traditions. The professional leadership of a society or a specific religious community promotes a literate, fairly sophisticated, and often transcultural understanding and practice of its religion. The ordinary members of the group, however, may be imperfectly incorporated into this tradition. They may maintain some notions and practices from older religions or participate in the tradition in a way that is based on different media. These two strata do not form clearly separate communities but constitute a pattern in many countries.

On a much smaller scale there are other communal formations that can be found in both natural and specific religious communities. Prominent among these is the master, guru, or teacher with his following. This is the basic format of the cult as defined above, but it is also both a regular phenomenon in almost all religions as well as the point of origin for many new religious communities. The master with his disciples is an evanescent phenomenon. Beyond the first generation it must become something like a sect, pursuing a separate identity; it must institutionalize the master-pupil pattern in a more or less monastic structure; or it may do both (as does, for example, Buddhism). The model of the Hindu ashram or of the Muslim Ṣūfī shaykh with his disciples indicates a recognition of this kind of religious community in their respective traditions but without much regularization or institutionalization.

The monastic community is often to be found within larger religious communities. It may be defined as a group of people drawn from a larger religious community who live together for shorter or longer periods of time in order to cultivate religious techniques and disciplines. This inclusive definition can apply to secret societies or to men's groups within tribal societies as well as to the institutions prominent in Buddhism, Hinduism, and Christianity. Islam displays a variation of this kind of community in the Ṣūfī orders.

Monastic communities may be at the center of their larger traditions, as in Buddhism. Here the monks may be the only leaders of the religious community and thus take on functions characteristic of priests and ministers in other traditions. Within Christianity, however, monasticism has been a supplementary pattern of religious leadership that exists alongside the priestly hierarchy. Often monastic communities as well as other subgroups have originated in a protest against prevailing practices or doctrines in the larger group.

When such a protest becomes estranged, a new religion is formed, but often the protest is institutionalized and becomes another option within the larger community.

Certainly the most common subgroup in any large religious community is the worshiping unit. This can be quite an independent group with little involvement in the larger tradition (such as the Christian "congregationalist" polity), or it can be a casual association of people whose primary communal identity is with the larger group (e.g., those Hindus who happen to be at the same temple at any given time). Pilgrimage to a certain shrine can give a very large community the sense of being essentially one worshiping group even when most religious practice actually takes place in various localities. Islam's concept of the *ummah,* with its *ḥājj* and orientation of prayer toward Mecca, is the most prominent example.

See Also Church; Cults and Sects; Excommunication; Expulsion; Jewish People; Monasticism; Religious Communities; Saṃgha; Schism; Secret Societies; Society and Religion; Ummah.

Bibliography

The most comprehensive typology of religious communities that attempts to cover all religions and cultures is Joachim Wach's *Sociology of Religion* (1944; reprint, Chicago, 1962). There is a shorter typology in Gerardus van der Leeuw's *Religion in Essence and Manifestation,* 2 vols., translated by J. E. Turner from the 2d German ed. (1938; reprint, Gloucester, Mass., 1967). Werner Stark's *The Sociology of Religion: A Study of Christendom,* 5 vols. (New York, 1966–1972) discusses the forms of community extensively, but it ignores non-Christian examples and structures. The distinction between church and sect was formulated by Ernst Troeltsch in *The Social Teaching of the Christian Churches,* 2 vols., translated by Olive Wyon (1911; reprint, New York, 1931). The form of the denomination was added to Troeltsch's pattern by H. Richard Niebuhr in *The Social Sources of Denominationalism* (New York, 1929). The sixfold typology of religious communities was developed by J. Milton Yinger in *Religion, Society, and the Individual* (New York, 1965) and elaborated by him in *The Scientific Study of Religion* (New York, 1970). A survey of the attempts to develop a typology of religious groups is to be found in Roland Robertson's *The Sociological Interpretation of Religion* (New York, 1970) and in Michael Hill's *A Sociology of Religion* (London, 1973). The dichotomy of the great and little traditions was created by Robert Redfield in *The Primitive World and Its Transformations* (Ithaca, N.Y., 1953) and *The Little Community: Viewpoints for the Study of a Human Whole* (Chicago, 1955). Examples of sects, mostly Christian but from many places around the world, are given in Bryan R. Wilson's *Religious Sects: A Sociological Study* (London, 1970).

New Sources

Cross, Mike. *Communities of Individuals: Liberalism, Communitarianism, and Sartre's Anarchism.* Burlington, Vt., 2001.

Etzioni, Amitai. *The New Golden Rule: Community and Morality in a Democratic Society.* New York, 1996.

Fergusson, David. *Community, Liberalism, and Christian Ethics.* New York, 1998.

Gross, Rita. "Some Reflections about Community and Survival." *Buddhist-Christian Studies* 23 (2003): 3–20.

Kramer, Matthew. *John Locke and the Origins of Private Property: Philosophical Explorations of Individualism, Community, and Equality.* New York, 1997.

Tan, Sor-hoon. "From Cannibalism to Empowerment: An *Analects*-Inspired Attempt to Balance Community and Liberty." *Philosophy East and West* 54 (January 2004): 52–71.

Warner, R. Stephen, and Judith Wittner, eds. *Gatherings in Diaspora: Religious Communities and the New Immigration.* Philadelphia, 1998.

Wurthnow, Robert. *The Restructuring of American Religion.* 1988; reprint, Princeton, 1990.

George Weckman (1987)
Revised Bibliography

COMPARATIVE-HISTORICAL METHOD [FIRST EDITION].

A means of studying religion as a whole, as well as the particularities of each tradition or subtradition, the comparative-historical method draws on historical data in comparing religions. As Wilhelm Schmidt (1868–1954) argued, the method aims to show not only the interplay of the general and the particular elements of religion, but also the interplay of influences between religious phenomena and the secular factors in human culture.

General Considerations. The comparative-historical method differs from purely historical approaches because it is cross-cultural. "Pure history" can deal, for example, with the unfolding of European pietism or South Indian *bhakti* without getting involved in comparisons and contrasts between the two phenomena. Obviously the comparative-historical method presupposes "pure history" which, together with ancillary disciplines such as philosophy and archaeology, supplies the facts upon which comparisons depend. It differs from psychology and phenomenology of religion, however, insofar as these disciplines content themselves with exploring timeless patterns or types of religious phenomena. Thus these disciplines may be concerned with patterns of mystical experience, for example, but not with how these patterns arise historically or to what extent they are affected by social and cultural conditions. In the discipline of psychology of religion, religious data are selected in a way that is distinct from the comparative-historical method, but the distinction between phenomenology of religion and the comparative-historical method cannot be put always so clearly. Insofar as phenomenology also deals with various types of changes in religious phenomena over the course of history, the distinctions begin to vanish.

The difference between the comparative-historical method and theology stems less from the selection of data than from the special way that theology approaches data. Theology (a term that usually is shorthand for Christian theology, but that in principle can include other varieties) is essentially the systematic exploration of the truth of a particular religious tradition or subtradition. The comparative-historical method does not begin from the assumption of the truth or falsity of any one religious position. Thus, although the ancillary disciplines of theology (such as church history, the history of ideas, philology, and so on) may overlap with those of the comparative study of religion, their essential aim and ethos are different. The comparative-historical method aims to be as objective as possible about the nature and power of religion; it is not concerned with whether a particular faith is true. Its objective is to relate religion's actual influences and effects within the world of human history.

The comparative study of religion, in the sense indicated, has a forceful rationale: there is an aspect of human culture, namely religion, that calls for interpretation, explanation, and delineation in ways similar to other aspects of human culture, such as politics and economics. This examination is called for whether or not a religion is transcendentally derived—whether, in short, its claims about its origin are true or not. The comparative-historical method considers it important to explore recurrent patterns of religious thought, symbolism, ritual, and experience that can be found cross-culturally. This approach suggests that religions have a relatively independent occurrence—whatever the theory at which we might ultimately arrive regarding their ultimate origin—and so may be used to explain various historical developments. Thus, for example, the occurrence of devotional religion might help to explain certain patterns of social organization.

Problems in Comparative Studies. There are at least two major problems, however, with the comparative study of religion. One has to do with objectivity, and the other with the definition of religion. The first problem has a particular as well as a general form. In particular, there was a reaction in the early twentieth century against the use of the term *comparative*, since Western and colonialist assumptions often entered into the making of comparisons. This criticism contributed to the fashionability of the phrase "phenomenology of religion" as an alternative way of labeling the enterprise. In general, some scholars have doubted whether it is possible to be genuinely objective about religion since religion has necessarily to do with subjectivity, and the study of religion is full of value judgments. In response to this criticism, two considerations are important. On the one hand, objectivity may be better defined as "descriptive success," and so the question is, Can we be descriptively successful in describing different forms of subjectivity? On the other hand, though complete neutrality may not be possible, it is possible to be relatively neutral in regard to value judgments. In a qualified manner, therefore, descriptive success and a kind of detachment are feasible. Here the charge of bias can be turned into an advantage: it stimulates us to examine our assumptions, and thus to generate a new level of self-awareness that is necessary for the practice of *epochē*, or phenomenological detachment.

The other main problem with the comparative-historical method concerns definition. This is a complex problem, for if it is not possible to gain a common definition of religion, can we be sure that we are talking about a "religious factor" in human affairs? Perhaps this factor is merely a chimera based on the conventions of European languages. Further, can we be sure that, given that the religious factor exists, we are not excluding phenomena that are of the same kind, though they may not be conventionally labeled "religious"? The two sides of this problem are interrelated. We might, for instance, define religion as relating to a transcendent being or state (e.g., God or *nirvāṇa*). This definition may adequately group some of the "great" traditions, but it leaves doubt about other religions (Stoicism, some religions of small-scale societies in Africa and elsewhere, etc.), and excludes the symbolic and "religiously functioning" aspects of secular ideologies and ways of life. Pragmatically, it seems best to begin with a religious core and draw into our analysis worldviews and elements of symbolism that exhibit analogies with the religious properties of this core. In this way, we use the comparative method to arrive at a field of inquiry. The field in its widest form is worldview analysis, or the delineation and interpretation of worldviews that are both religious (in the traditional, transcendentally oriented sense) and secular. This approach, however, begins with the kinds of analysis that are specially relevant to the exploration of traditional religious worldviews.

Some scholars, because of the invidious implications of the term *comparative*, prefer *cross-cultural*. This term has some drawbacks, but it also has two considerable merits. First, obviously, it avoids the term *comparative*; and, second, it suggests that analogies are drawn from different cultural traditions, and so may make use of terminology and attitudes that are not Western. As greater numbers of scholars from religious traditions other than those of the West make their contributions to worldview analysis, and as we become in general more globally conscious, a new cross-cultural vocabulary will in all probability emerge. Already there are signs of the appearance of this vocabulary: terms such as *taboo*, *totem*, *yoga*, *bhakti*, *Dao*, *nirvāṇa*, and *karma* are in general use in English.

Aims of Comparative-Historical Study. Generally speaking, the comparative-historical method has two preliminary aims: to demonstrate historical connections, and to point out independent occurrences of similar phenomena. The tracing of historical connections indicates the scope of the diffusion of key concepts, rites, institutions, and so on. Often such diffusion is the first hypothesis of many investigators. For example, early investigators who saw the similarities between ideas in the *Bhagavadgītā* and in the New Testament supposed that a single influence, one way or another, informed both. The use of the swastika symbol both in India and among American Indian groups is also suggestive of very ancient diffusion. But the most interesting cases from the theoretical angle are those where a strong degree of independence of cultural origins can be shown and yet the phenomena are similar. It is, for example, striking when the utterances of mystics in apparently independent traditions are similar.

Such similarity is suggestive of at least a perennial phenomenology—that is, the existence of certain recurring, characteristic patterns of human experience—if not of a perennial philosophy. It is partly on this basis that scholars build up their phenomenologies of religion.

But the comparative method is also historical. This introduces two complications into any typology of religious factors or themes. The first complication is particularity. Though it may be that a certain recurrent theme occurs in two traditions, it nevertheless has a different contextual meaning in each. For instance, there may appear to be a similar mystical experience described in Sufism and Mahāyāna Buddhism. But the meaning of the two experiences will diverge: the one involves a close unity with God, the other the attainment of ultimate emptiness. The meaning of each experience affects the way each is perceived, both because the Sufi and the Mahāyāna Buddhist have different expectations leading into their experiences and also because, *ex post facto*, the experiences suggest differing accounts of the ultimate. More generally, it may be said that each tradition or subtradition is organic, in that the meaning of each of the particular elements woven together into a whole is affected by the meanings of all the other elements associated with it within the whole. Thus, because the comparative method is historical, it recognizes the importance not only of general similarities but also of the particularity of each historical context. Comparisons are therefore never quite exact but are analogical in character. Although the method upholds the value of comparisons, it nevertheless recognizes the need for contextual modification.

The other complication is that the traditions or elements of traditions under consideration are examined in time; they are the consequences of change, and they themselves give rise to changes. A religious ideology may indeed retain some "original message" or primordial revelation in an unchanged manner. Nevertheless, any such relatively unchanged revelation is still transmitted by a process that can only be described historically. Indeed, it seems as though an element that has been transmitted from an ancient culture down to modern times, in order to have retained its identity through changing contexts, must have had to change its overt message if it has managed to retain the same meaning. Likewise, an overtly unchanged element that has been transmitted "without change" through differing contexts might well have undergone a change in meaning because of the altered context. In either case the historical method involves the exploration of changes.

It follows then that in addition to relatively time-free typological comparisons there are comparisons of kinds of changes. Such a typology, which can be called a "dynamic phenomenology," blurs the distinction between the comparative-historical and phenomenological methods. It also takes us back to some of the early preoccupations of the comparative study of religion, namely, the delineation of the evolution of religion from animism through monotheism. Although the evolutionary model is less fashionable now than in the latter part of the nineteenth century, which saw the emergence of comparative religion as a discipline, there is still an interest in the dynamic patterns of development in society that are generated by religion—an interest stimulated by the work of Max Weber (1864–1920). An example of a recent evolutionary scheme is found in Robert N. Bellah's paper "Religious Evolution" (*American Sociological Review* 29, 1964, pp. 358–374).

INTRA- AND EXTRARELIGIOUS EXPLANATIONS. Of greater importance, however, are more detailed studies of the modes under which different religious themes interact both within and outside the bounds of religion, strictly defined. It is, for instance, important to see the ways in which doctrines reflect aspects of experience and myth, or ritual reflects aspects of doctrine and ethics, and so on. These interactions within the boundaries of religion can be called *intrareligious*, and explanations that refer to them might be termed *intrareligious explanations*. It is also important to consider how doctrines, myths, and the rest impinge upon or are affected by social and economic factors in society. Such relations are *extrareligious*, and explanations referring to them are *extrareligious explanations*. The most extreme cases of extrareligious explanations are "projection" theories of religion (an example would be Freud's theory of religion), in which religion is understood to be "caused" by deep structures in nonreligious human nature or human society. Cases of intrareligious explanations include the understanding of "negative" theology as a consequence of mystical experience, worship as a consequence of the numinous experience, priesthood as a consequence of sacramental ritual, and humility as an ethical consequence of worship. Extrareligious interactions can be seen in such phenomena as the erosion of the liturgical year by the new, indifferent rhythms of industrial society; the increase of pilgrimage in South Asia due to the development of buses and railways; and the pressure for gender-related changes in ecclesiastical organization due to women's movements. Cases of the reinforcement of religious symbolism by symbolic factors associated with nonreligious worldviews and ideologies (such as nationalism) can be seen in modern Iranian nationalism, the Buddhist revival in Sri Lanka, and so on.

The period from World War II onward, and especially from the mid-1960s until the mid-1980s, saw an immense expansion in both historical and comparative studies in the field of religion, notably in the English-speaking world, and particularly in North America. The consequence of this expansion has been a fine array of monographs and studies on varied aspects of religion. But although there has been intensive work in cross-cultural dialogue between religions, there have been few large-scale comparative studies. The times are clearly ripe for such endeavors, which would build upon excellent foundational studies in particular religious traditions. The most flourishing aspect of recent comparative studies has been in the field of mysticism, which has attracted the interest of scholars involved in hermeneutical and philosophical studies as well as historians and others. The interfaces of comparative study in religion with anthropology and sociology as they relate to ritual process has also proved fruitful, as in the influence and work of Victor Turner (1920–1983). The most influential phenomenological synthesis remains Gerardus van der Leeuw's *Religion in Essence and Manifestation* (1938), an indication that the field awaits a new synthetic overview after a period of intense, but on the whole less broad, activity. Already, however, the comparative-historical method is beginning to be seen as a vital tool not only for the framing of new hypotheses about the patterns of religious developments both in the past and today, but also for the testing of older ways of thinking about the nature and provenance of religion.

See Also Comparative Religion; Evolution, article on Evolutionism; Hermeneutics; History of Religions; Phenomenology of Religion; Psychology, article on Psychology of Religion; Religionsgeschichtliche Schule; Sociology; Study of Religion; Women's Studies in Religion.

Bibliography

The series "Religion and Reason," edited by Jacques Waardenburg (The Hague, 1971–), is an invaluable collection of monographs on the theory of religion; it includes an excellent anthology of classical readings, *Classical Approaches to the Study of Religion*, vol. 1, *Introduction and Anthology* (The Hague, 1973), compiled by Waardenburg. The most up-to-date survey of recent work is Ursula King's monograph-long essay, "Historical and Phenomenological Approaches," in *Theory and Method in Religious Studies: Contemporary Approaches to the Study of Religion*, edited by Frank Whaling (Mouton de Gruyter, Berlin/NY, 1995), pp. 41–176. A complement to the Waardenburg volume is a reader in sociology and anthropology titled *Sociology of Religion*, edited by Roland Robertson (Baltimore, 1969). The most useful history of the field is Eric J. Sharpe's *Comparative Religion: A History* (London, 1975). A discussion of some of the central themes of this article can be found in my book *The Science of Religion and the Sociology of Knowledge* (Princeton, 1973).

Ninian Smart (1987)

COMPARATIVE-HISTORICAL METHOD [FURTHER CONSIDERATIONS].

The central focus of the comparative-historical method is to develop comparisons between religious formations (comparative) while accounting for their development within particular contexts through time (historical). As such, the method can be distinguished from the following: the phenomenology of religion, which tends toward ahistorical typologies; theology, which operates within single traditions; social scientific (psychological, sociological) approaches, which are usually not as rigorously historical; and from formalist, philosophical approaches to religion. The comparative-historical method converges unavoidably on other articles from the *Encyclopedia of Religion* besides Ninian Smart's, most notably "History of Religions" (Ugo Bianchi), and to a lesser extent "Comparative Method" and "Comparative Religion" (Eric Sharpe). It is reasonable to say that Bianci viewed the comparative-historical method as the dynamic fulcrum of the history of religions.

The comparative-historical method is very much at the heart of the academic discipline of religion. The process of comparative religion proper, taking its place beside traditional biblical theology around 1870, marks the inauguration of the academic study of religion. Theology itself has increasingly become historicized and comparative since that time. As a recent series of articles in the journal *Numen* have argued from a variety of perspectives, comparison is a primary rather than secondary process within analytical inquiry; it is inevitable, marking one of a number of theoretical options. Definitions of particular phenomena are not plausible without reference to, or comparison with, more general categories through which they can be comprehended. Comparison and generalization thus need not be confused with the quest for theoretical infallibility and belief in universal principles. Used properly, comparison simply starts scholars thinking—it need not prevent them from it.

In the years that have passed since Smart's original article was written, the emphasis of religious scholarship has gradually shifted from a preoccupation with religion as a potential object of analytical inquiry to the many subjective processes by which something designated as "religion" has been conceived. As applied to the comparative-historical method, this has resulted in an increased emphasis on the historical half of the equation, while the drawing of comparisons has become theoretically conservative. Increased historicism has resulted in some degree of decline in the production of compelling theoretical work. Generalization within and about particular religious traditions has become difficult; generalization about the nature of religion has become almost impossible.

Solutions to this problem have not been altogether satisfying and have spawned a literature, often languid and unproductive, that questions whether the study of religion is adequately substantive as an academic genre. The highly technical linguistic considerations that permeate scholarship on non-Western religions, the increasingly myopic historical approach, and the recourse to semantics and semiotics in all genres of religious study arose in response to legitimate concerns about the excessive breadth of scholarship in the field. It may be time for the pendulum to swing, however, and for questions to be asked about the limitations of these new trends. As Jonathan Z. Smith has noted, philological expertise has become the standard for achieving professional status in the field, but this direction has come with hidden costs: "Philology is the vocation; generalization the avocation. This has led to the wholesale adoption of a sort of common-sense descriptive discourse as a major rhetoric for work in the field" (Smith, 2001, p. 140). Debate within each unique academic locus can easily become internalized and accessible (or of interest) only to scholars working within fields of close enough proximity.

Little attention has been paid to why this may particularly be a problem within the field of religion. The study of religion has been, especially in terms of the way it originated, one of—if not the—most truly global of all the academic disciplines. It addresses all of the major civilizations of the world, and though its focus on small-scale societies has lamentably decreased, this genre has formed a significant part of the disciplinary history as well. The very breadth of the discipline makes comparative statements of any depth tenuous, and this would appear to be a legacy with which the field is destined to grapple. As a softer discipline whose net is cast wide and which is poised between any number of epistemologies, a willingness to persist in asking the question of what religion is across daunting theoretical chasms may define the heart of its enterprise.

The emergent emphasis on historical context forces the recognition that the concept "religion" at which the comparative-historical method is aimed is not a monolith, and the results of applying the method are diverse because of this. As a new form of intellectual inquiry, religion went through various transformations within the varying European national traditions from its earlier usages. Definitions of religion revolved primarily around its relationship to its cultural settings. While other countries certainly claimed variations on the theme, the reconceiving of religion in Britain and Germany, in particular, makes for an informative case study.

In Germany, *Kultur* indicated a more organic understanding of social organization that located its roots within a particular geographical space. A people's *Kultur* gained its depth, meaning, and potency through historical development in that place. Cultural legitimacy was inherent and internal—a property right, so to speak. Comparison with other peoples was not the principal means of conferring authenticity. So it was with the early German approach to religion as a new cognitive category—at least for those who did not seek to dismiss religion altogether. In the tradition of Kant and Hegel, and eventually Otto, religion and the religious impulse were both primordial and obvious. From the German context, there emerged the notion of *Religionsgeschichte*, roughly "history of religions," and also the more prevalent *Religionswissenschaft*, or "science of religions." The combining of history and science in Germany, following the historiographical vision of von Ranke, involved the art of establishing, through an intuitive synthesis, the pivotal and compelling aspects of a given historical datum. With this background, it is more understandable that the notion of a science of religion, specifically, never was encumbered by the scientific literalism that has predominated in a place like the United States. The concept of religion in Germany was comparative only in a secondary sense. Primarily, it grew out of the collective embrace of *Kultur*, which was grounded in a deep sense of geographical identification that had gained force through time. Where religions were compared, it was more to reinforce or embellish an existing notion of religion that was not primarily comparative.

In Britain the term *civilization*, borrowed from the French, grew in usage as F. Max Mueller began to shape a field of religion through his philological endeavors and implied something very different than *Kultur*. Civilization indicated a broader and more comparative conception of social organization where a society becomes what it is by demonstrating cognizance of how it differs from other societies. The rise of Britain to a position of global eminence corresponded with the colonial phenomenon, and modern British society was built significantly around its perceived position as global organizer. Normative notions of what it meant to be "civilized" were made possible by establishing what was not civilized. Thus comparison, to a much greater extent than geographical identification and history, became the hallmark for cultural orientation. Comparative religious categories mirrored the emerging intercultural hierarchies, a point made clear by the time of the first world's fair, which took place in London in 1851. Evolutionary theory was spawned during this period, and all of the world's cultures became located within a schematic that was at once a spatial *typology* of cultures, descending from civilized to primitive according to the culture's perceived industrial sophistication, and also a temporal *chronology* ascending from primitive to civilized based on perceived degrees of natural evolution. This ubiquitous heuristic device for organizing the world's cultures was known as social evolution. Along with F. Max Muller's forays into comparative philology that focused more precisely on compartive religious understanding emerging out of the larger civilizational context of India, social evolution increasingly became a pivotal theoretical principle around which early comparative religion in Britain was built in a more global sense. It also helped to shape British society as a globally minded "civilization" rather than a more organic *Kultur*.

The early use of the comparative-historical method in Germany and Britain shows that its application can vary widely depending from where and toward what it is being applied. In a context like the history of religions within the Chicago School, a bridge was established to some degree between the British and German approaches to studying religion. Comparing religions in the Americas has proved a virtual necessity in maintaining a constructive social dialogue. Ideally, a pragmatic historical approach to understanding religion in context would combine with a keen conceptual awareness of the problems of comparative-historical categories to produce scholarship that is adequately balanced between the two aspects of the method. Specific studies would then emphasize either the historical or the conceptual, depending on their datum.

Any method results in the need for interpretation, and the comparative-historical method needs to be applied to interpretive strategies as well. Interpretation must itself be located within an intellectual context and confined to some degree so that scholars dealing with obscure historical materials do not argue from some latent form of common sense, as Smith has cautioned. To remain relevant, comparative-historical epistemologies should bear some connection to identifiable hermeneutical systems that comprise the ancestry of the study of religion.

Finally, the comparative-historical method must be able to address the object of religion as well as account for the more subjective processes that have generated the concept in modernity. William Paden and Ferren MacIntyre have made theoretical suggestions in this direction. In a more historical sense, the epistemological basis of the study of religion needs to demonstrate flexibility to accommodate the wide range of historical studies that mark the field. Without some willingness to "imagine religion," potentially informative aspects of the field of religion where historical reconstruction is challenging, such as the exploration of nonliterate cultures or a crucial datum like African American slave religion, run a strong risk of being inadequately represented or tacitly dismissed. In France, for instance, where historical method can perhaps be considered as having reached its apogee with the *Annales* School, there exist in church archives superior historical records extending back to the medieval period. In this circumstance, the notion of moving backward in time with a precision that borders on the scientific appears tenable and attractive. Yet if this kind of standard is made the benchmark for authentic historical work in religion globally, much data will be inassimilable and fruitful opportunities for comparative religious understanding will be lost. Cross-cultural gender studies face similar challenges, where the process of tapping more comprehensive meanings within what is rapidly developing into a global gender revolution is vital. Given the breadth of the field of religion as it has developed, more imaginative approaches to historical work and its interpretation appear crucial if the comparative-historical method is to be put to its full use in moving the study of religion into the future.

SEE ALSO Comparative Mythology; Comparative Religion; History of Religions.

BIBLIOGRAPHY

For current perspectives on the problem of comparison, see the useful articles in *Numen* 48 (July 2001), especially Robert Segal's "In Defense of the Comparative Method," and William Paden's "Human Behaviors and Cultural Variations," as well as Jonathan Z. Smith's "A Twice-Told Tale: The History of the History of Religions' History," in *Numen* 48 (April 2001), and Ferren MacIntyre's speculative yet provocative "Was Religion a Kinship Surrogate?" in *Journal of the American Academy of Religion*, 72, no. 3 (September 2004). See also John P. Burris's article "Text and Context in the Study of Religion," in *Method and Theory in the Study of Religion* 15, no. 1 (2003), the responses to it by David Chidester and Russell McCutcheon in *Method and Theory in the Study of Religion* 15, no. 3 (2003), and Burris's rejoinder in *Method and Theory in the Study of Religion* 16, no. 2 (2004).

There has been a proliferation of edited volumes on comparison in the field of religion in recent years, but these volumes, though containing useful articles, are inevitably inconsistent and potentially take readers away from the idea that the comparative-historical method can be identified and used in anything approaching a methodical manner. Recent book-length studies employing or examining the comparative-historical method tend to approach it indirectly and demonstrate it rather than announce it. A look at the new radical historicism can be found in Ivan Strenski's *Four Theories of Myth in the Twentieth-Century History* (Iowa City, Iowa, 1987). Regarding historiography in Germany and America and how much national traditions vary in conducting historical study, see Peter Novick's *That Noble Dream: The "Objectivity Question" and the American Historical Profession* (Cambridge, U.K., 1988). In regard to Asia, see Richard King's *Orientalism and Religion: Post-Colonial Theory, India, and "The Mystic East"* (London and New York, 1999). An interesting study of the comparative-historical method in a colonial context can be found in David Chidester's *Savage Systems: Colonialism and Comparative Religion in Southern Africa* (Charlottesville, Va., 1996). An example of the method applied to the metropole can be found in John P. Burris's *Exhibiting Religion: Colonialism and Spectacle at International Expositions, 1851–1893* (Charlottesville, Va., 2001).

JOHN P. BURRIS (2005)

COMPARATIVE MYTHOLOGY.

An early form of comparative mythology is the so-called *interpretatio Graeca*, that is, the use of Greek names for gods of other peoples. Thus, for instance, Near Eastern storm gods were interpreted by Greek authors as Zeus, who shared essential features with them. Similarly, Roman authors identified Celtic or Germanic gods as Jupiter, Mars, or Mercury. Such identifications, employing *interpretatio Romana*, are readily apparent in the English and French names of the days of the week; the English names are derived from the Germanic gods, the French from the Roman: thus *Tuesday*, Týr's (or Tiu's) day, corresponds to *mardi*, day of Mars; *Wednesday*, Woden's day, corresponds to *mercredi*, day of Mercury; and *Thursday*, Thor's day, corresponds to *jeudi*, day of Jupiter.

As a technical term, *comparative mythology* was introduced in 1856 by the German-born British philologist F. Max Müller. He based his argument on the observation that the Indo-European languages were related to each other and obviously should be derived from one common language. Since, according to Müller, myths originated through literal interpretations of metaphoric expressions leading to a personification of such natural phenomena as the sun and the dawn, it would be useful to compare not only the languages but also the myths of Indo-European peoples. Strangely enough, he made little use of his observation for a comparison of divine names in the various religions; he was more interested in combating evolutionistic interpretations of mythology based on material from "primitive" peoples.

When two or more myths are similar in some respects, there are, roughly speaking, three possible theories. One is that they form part of a common heritage; another is that a myth or mythological motif has spread from one religion to another ("diffusion"); a third is that parallel, independent development has produced similar results in two or more different places. Following the third line of reasoning, we might assume one of two possible explanations: either that similar ecological conditions produce similar myths or that the human mind contains archetypes that are expressed in similar symbols everywhere. However, a combination of these two explanations should not be entirely ruled out.

INDO-EUROPEAN RELIGIONS. A common heritage can be assumed in the various Indo-European religions. Linguistic comparison of divine names reveals several interesting facts. For instance, the Vedic *Dyaus* corresponds to the Greek *Zeus*, the Roman *Jupiter* (*Iovpater*, "father Jove"), the Nordic *Týr*, and perhaps also the Latvian *Dievs*. Parjanya is an Indian rain god; the Baltic peoples have a god of the thunderstorm called Perkūnas or Pērkons, while Fjǫrgynn is a somewhat obscure Nordic god. In India, Yama is the first man, in Iran Yima, while Ymir in Nordic mythology is the giant from whose body the world was created. The relationship is especially close between Indian and Iranian religions. The Indian god Mitra corresponds to the Iranian Mithra, with very similar functions: Vedic mythology uses *Vṛtrahan* in the epithet of Indra as the killer of the dragon Vrtra; in Iran, Verethraghna is a god of war and kingship. The fact that Sanskrit *deva* means "god" but Iranian *daiva* is "demon," while Sanskrit *asura* means "demon" and Iranian *ahura* is the name of the highest god, indicates an early conflict between the two religions. It is worthy of notice that the functions of gods with related names are not always identical.

A different and more promising approach to the comparative mythology of the Indo-European peoples was suggested by the French scholar Georges Dumézil (1898–1986). He started from the observation that most Indo-European religions have a myth about the preparation of a drink of immortality, which was stolen and recovered and then became the object of ritual drinking. Continued researches, however, resulted in the observation that behind the mythology of most of these peoples a tripartite structure could be detected.

As a matter of fact, the gods of the pantheon are organized in such a manner that they reflect the tripartite social structure of Indo-European society. There are the functions of rulership, of warfare, and of fertility and wealth. The first function has two aspects: the mysterious and magical on one side and the orderly and lawful on the other. It is represented by Varuṇa and Mitra in India, by Jupiter and Dius Fidius in Rome, and by Odin and Týr in Scandinavia. The warlike function is represented by Indian Indra, Roman Mars, and Scandinavian Thor. The gods of the third function are admitted to the circle of gods only after a battle, followed by a settlement, which makes the pantheon complete; they are, for instance, the Vedic twin gods Aśvins or Nāsatyas and the Nordic Vanir (Freyr, Freyja, etc.), while in Rome the lesser-known god Quirinus may belong here. Celtic evidence is scanty but can probably be fit into the same pattern. The same structure is reflected in the functions of the Zoroastrian "archangels," the Amesha Spentas, which replace the old gods in Zoroastrian monotheism, and in the characters of the legendary kings of early Rome. Thus Romulus represents the orderly ruler; Numa Pompilius, the priest, is the mysterious one; Tullus Hostilius is the warrior; and Ancus Marcius represents material welfare. It should also be noticed that the Sabinians were admitted into Roman society after a war, just as were the gods of the third function, and only then was the Roman community complete. In other words, mythology has been transformed into legendary history.

An interesting detail is the fact that of two Roman heroes in the wars against the Etruscans, one, Horatius Cocles, is one-eyed, and the other, Gaius Mucius Scaevola, loses his one hand. The Irish war god Nuadha has a silver hand instead of the one he lost in battle, and among the Nordic gods, Odin is one-eyed and Týr has only one arm.

That Greek mythology has only a few traces of this pattern is probably due to influence from pre-Greek Aegean religion. Dumézil's method is not primarily based on philological evidence and is thus not open to criticism based on difficulties in establishing the exact relationship between the Indo-European languages. On the other hand, there is a difficulty in the fact that the names of the gods of one particular function are not always linguistically related, and that related names may appear in different functions.

NEAR EASTERN MYTHOLOGIES. Comparison of Semitic mythologies can also be based in part on linguistic evidence. *Il* or *el* is in all Semitic languages (except Ethiopic) either the common word for "god" or the name of the highest god. But there are also problems. For instance, in South Arabia, Athtar is a god, perhaps connected with the morning star, but Babylonian and Assyrian Ishtar is a goddess, also connected with the morning star, while the early Canaanite texts from Ugarit know both a god Athtar and a goddess Athtart, the latter identical with the Astarte of the Old Testament. It may be assumed that an originally androgynous deity, perhaps a sky god (like Ethiopian Astar), has been differentiated in two directions as male and female. A similar shift of gender is known also in the case of the sun, sometimes worshiped as a male god (Babylonian Shamash), sometimes as a goddess (South Arabia, Ugarit). The male form in Babylonia may be due to Sumerian influence.

Three themes of ancient Near Eastern mythology are of particular interest here: (1) the dying and reviving god, (2) the killing of the dragon, and (3) death and immortality.

The dying and reviving god. The Sumerian god Dumuzi (Akkadian, Tammuz), the god of flocks and grain, is killed and carried to the netherworld, but it is finally decided that he shall spend part of the year on earth to promote fertility. Baal, the Canaanite god of thunder and fertility, is killed by his enemy Mot, and while he is dead, vegetation withers, but his sister Anat defeats Mot, and Baal is finally restored to life. The story of Aqhat seems to reflect the same pattern:

Aqhat is offered immortality by the goddess Anat in exchange for his fine bow but refuses and is killed, which results in the withering of vegetation. His sister seeks him, but here the tablet is broken, and we do not know the outcome. If the point of the story is man's mortality, we should expect him to remain dead; if the vegetation motif is predominant, as in the Baal myth, it is likely that he was revived.

The Egyptian Osiris is somewhat different: he is king and connected with the grain; he is killed by his brother Seth, but his wife Isis finds his dismembered body and restores it to life, and Osiris becomes the ruler of the dead. We know that the god's death and resurrection were celebrated in seasonal festivals. Different again is the Hittite myth of Telepinu: he disappears and vegetation withers and procreation fails; he is found sleeping and brought back, and life returns to normal.

There is a common pattern in these myths, probably reflecting the vicissitudes of vegetation in the seasonal cycle, but the actual form of the myth differs from country to country insofar as the common features have been combined with local elements to form a new unity. The problem is further complicated by the fact that some of the characteristic elements of the pattern reappear in connection with the Nordic god Baldr, who is supposed to be invulnerable but is killed with the only weapon that can hurt him, namely, a twig of mistletoe. Baldr, however, remains dead, though nearly everything weeps for him. Dumézil has found a parallel to this myth among the Ossets, a tribe in the Caucasus, probably descended from the ancient Scythians. Here the willful Syrdon finds out the only way to kill the supposedly invulnerable Soslan (or Sosryko). In both myths Dumézil finds traits that point to some connection with the rites of the summer solstice. It is not clear whether we have here a case of the migration of myths or an example of common Indo-European heritage.

Furthermore, in the Finnish national epic, the *Kalevala*, we are told that the hero Lemminkäinen was killed by means of an inconspicuous plant. His mother found him, reassembled the parts of his body, and brought him back to life. Here is an element that is strongly reminiscent of the Osiris myth. It is also interesting that a bee plays a significant role at the resuscitation of Lemminkäinen, just as a bee wakes up the Hittite Telepinu. It is hard to prove any historical connection among the three myths involved, but it seems that elements from different sources have been combined into a new story.

The killing of the dragon. In the Babylonian epic of creation the god Marduk kills a monster, Tiamat, representing the primeval ocean, and creates the world out of her body. In Canaanite myth where Baal kills Prince Sea, the result is not creation but the establishment of his rulership and the building of a temple. There are also fragments in Canaanite mythology that tell of the killing of a being called Lotan or *tannin* ("dragon"). Reminiscences of the battle motif are also found in the Old Testament in connection with creation. The defeated party is here called either Leviathan (Lotan) and *tannin* or *tehom* ("the deep"; i.e., Tiamat). The elements of the myth recur, but they are combined differently. Since the motif is absent in the Sumerian myths of creation, it may be of West Semitic origin. The enemy slain is the sea, but the results differ.

Death and immortality. The hero of the Gilgamesh epic, seeking eternal life, finds the "plant of life," but it is snatched away by a serpent, and he remains mortal. In another Babylonian myth, Adapa is offered the "food of life" but he refuses to eat it and remains mortal. In the Old Testament, Adam and Eve have access to the "tree of life" but are deprived of it through a serpent and are henceforth mortal. The problem is the same: why is man mortal? The symbols of eternal life differ—plant, food, tree—but the result is the same. In other words, the intention of the myth is the same in all three cases, but the concrete expressions differ.

To sum up: myths intend to answer existential questions; the symbols used are sometimes identical, sometimes differing in details; and mythical motifs can be combined in different ways in different contexts.

MYTHOLOGIES OF OTHER CULTURES. Similar observations can be made in comparative study of mythologies in many other parts of the world. Three mythic themes provide interesting examples: (1) the origin of death, (2) the earth diver, and (3) the flood.

The origin of death. In most parts of Africa there is a myth of the origin of death. Common to most of them is the idea that man was originally intended to live forever. God sent a message to that effect, but the messenger was delayed and overtaken by another messenger, who brought the message of death. Other myths report that the message was distorted so as to imply death instead of life. Other tribes say that man was offered two bundles, one containing life, the other death; by mistake, man chose death. There are also myths that ascribe death to the disobedience of man. In the last case, one might suspect Christian influence, but the other myths, which occur in several versions in several tribes, are certainly indigenous and provide a good example of how the outward form of a myth may vary, though the intention is the same.

The earth diver. Creation myths among many North American Indian tribes tell of a primeval sea: a bird or animal dives into the water and brings up some soil from which the earth is created. This myth of the earth diver is known also from several peoples in Northeast Asia. It has the idea of the primeval sea in common with Babylonian, Israelite, and, to some extent, Egyptian cosmogony; but is any historical relationship possible? Such relationship does exist, however, between North America and Northeast Asia. In some North Asian versions of the earth-diver myth, the motif is combined, rather illogically, with the myth of the great flood. According to one Samoyed myth, seven men who have been saved from the flood send a bird to the bottom of the sea to fetch a turf to form the earth. This is obviously a combination of two elements of different origin.

The flood. The myth of the flood, on the other hand, is a problem in its own right. It is well known from the Bible and from ancient Mesopotamia. A study of the biblical and the three Mesopotamian versions reveals that they have several conspicuous details in common (the god reveals the secret of the coming flood to one righteous man, he builds a ship, he sends out birds to see if the water has receded, and he offers sacrifices after being saved); but it can be shown that the story has been modified in each case to suit the context of a larger narrative complex into which it has been inserted (Gilgamesh epic, Atrahasis epic, the primeval history of *Genesis*). But flood stories are known from many other parts of the world, both in Asia and in North and South America. Have they originated independently in areas where large rivers cause inundations from time to time, or is there any kind of connection? The latter alternative can be proved in the ancient Near East, but the other stories show differences too great to make direct borrowing likely.

CONCLUSION. Thus, comparative study of mythology raises questions that are difficult to answer. Similar myths appearing in different parts of the world seem to have no communication with one another. Neither common heritage nor diffusion seems probable. Myths that are strikingly similar to the Greek myth of Orpheus, who tried to bring his wife, Eurydice, back from the netherworld but failed to do so, appear in several North American Indian tribes, but no historical connection can be shown. Is it possible that such a characteristic myth can develop independently in two distant places? The New Zealand Maori are reported to have a creation myth, according to which there was first darkness and water, but the god Io pronounced a word and there was light, he pronounced a second word and the sky came into being, and a third word and the earth was there. In this case, it seems likely that Christian ideas have influenced either the myth or the one who recorded it. But in other cases we may ask if there is not some truth in Jung's theory of archetypes in the human mind whereby similar existential questions are answered by similar symbols. Or, as Mircea Eliade puts it in a somewhat different terminology, essential aspects of reality appear in the human mind as images and symbols forming certain patterns that meet a need and fulfill a function, that of revealing the hidden modalities of our existence.

A new approach to the study of myth has been suggested by the French structuralist Claude Lévi-Strauss. He breaks down the myth into small units and analyzes their mutual relationships. The units are meaningful only in terms of the positions they occupy in the total structure of the myth and in the context of the culture concerned. Thus there emerges a pattern consisting of thesis, antithesis, and synthesis. In the myth of Oedipus, for instance, there is an overvaluation of kinship (e.g., Oedipus marries his mother), an undervaluation of kinship (e.g., Oedipus kills his father), and a synthesis implying that contradictory kinship relations are contradictory in a similar way. In analyzing a specific myth, Lévi-Strauss often explains the significance of a unit by adducing comparative material from the same culture, but only in the third volume of his *Mythologiques* does he bring in a global perspective.

SEE ALSO Comparative Religion; Cosmogony; Death; Dragons; Dying and Rising Gods; Grimm Brothers; Indo-European Religions, article on History of Study; Müller, F. Max; Myth; Myth and Ritual School.

BIBLIOGRAPHY

Max Müller's essay "Comparative Mythology" is found in the second volume of *Chips from a German Workshop* (London, 1868). Together with Åke Ström, I have reviewed the comparative work done in Indo-Iranian and Indo-European studies in *Religions of Mankind Yesterday and Today* (Philadelphia, 1967). In *Arische Religion* (Leipzig, 1914), Leopold von Schroeder deals with the same material.

Georges Dumézil sets forth his theories in many places. Several general introductions are available: *L'idéologie tripartie des Indo-Européens* (Brussels, 1958), *L'héritage indo-européen à Rome* (Paris, 1949), and *Les dieux des Indo-Européens* (Paris, 1952).

My own observations on the comparative mythology of the ancient Near East are published in numerous places: "Remarks on the Method of Comparative Mythology," in *Near Eastern Studies in Honor of William Foxwell Albright*, edited by Hans Goedicke (Baltimore, 1971); "Israel's Place among the Religions of the Ancient Near East," in *Supplements to Vetus Testamentum* 23 (1972): 1–8; and "The Impact of the Ancient Near East on Israelite Tradition," in *Tradition and Theology in the Old Testament*, edited by D. A. Knight (Philadelphia, 1977). For a treatment of Athtar and related deities, consult my *Word and Wisdom* (Lund, 1947), and for a discussion of dying and reviving gods, it is valuable to look at the classic work by James G. Frazer that has been edited by Theodor H. Gaster and published as *The New Golden Bough*, abr. ed. (1959; London, 1980).

African myths about the origins of death are the subject of Hans Abrahamsson's *The Origin of Death* (Uppsala, 1951). Anna Birgitta Rooth has published the article "Creation Myths of North American Indians," *Anthropos* 52 (1957): 497–508, and Åke Hultkrantz sets forth his views on Orpheus traditions among Native Americans in *The North American Indian Orpheus Tradition* (Stockholm, 1957). Flood stories are dealt with by Richard Andree in *Die Flutsagen* (Braunschweig, 1891) and also by Ruth E. Simoons-Vermeer in "The Mesopotamian Flood Stories: A Comparison and Interpretation," *Numen* 21 (1974): 17–34. For an introduction to the theories of Lévi-Strauss and structuralism, see two works by Edmund Leach: *The Structural Study of Myth and Totemism* (London, 1967) and *Lévi-Strauss* (London, 1970).

New Sources

Doniger, Wendy. *Other Peoples' Myths: The Cave of Echoes.* 1988; reprint, Chicago, 1995.

Doniger, Wendy. "Myths and Methods in the Dark." *Journal of Religion* 76 (October 1996): 531–537.

Doniger, Wendy. *Splitting the Difference: Gender and Myth in Ancient Greece and India.* Chicago, 1999.

Doty, William. *Mythography: The Study of Myths and Rituals.* 1986; reprint, Tuscaloosa, Ala., 2000.

Golden, Kenneth, ed. *Uses of Comparative Mythology: Essays on the Work of Joseph Campbell.* New York, 1992.

Napier, David. *Foreign Bodies: Performance, Art, and Symbolic Anthropology.* Berkeley, 1992.

Worthen, Thomas. *The Myth of Replacement: Stars, Gods, and Order in the Universe.* Tucson, Ariz., 1991.

HELMER RINGGREN (1987)
Revised Bibliography

COMPARATIVE RELIGION. The term *comparative religion* broadly signifies the study of all traditions and forms of religious life, as distinguished from the study or exposition of just one. Ideally, and more specifically, it is the disciplined, historically informed consideration of commonalities and differences among religions. Indeed, such cross-cultural or global perspective is entailed in the notion of an academic study of religion.

Comparison is a fundamental mental activity: grouping some things together under a common class or pattern, but also noticing how the examples vary in relation to each other. Such connections and relationships are the basis of thought and science. Without them, there are only isolated, contextless facts. It is on the basis of comparison that generalizations, interpretations, and theories are formed. Hence, comparative frames can create new ways of perceiving and organizing the world.

One cannot generalize about religion on the basis of a single case, just as geologists do not construct geological science on the basis of the rocks that simply happen to be in one's backyard. The local rocks, like the local religions, are themselves instances of certain universal chemistries and patterned formations. Accordingly, without identifying these recurring factors it is not possible to know what any particular religious tradition or phenomenon has in common with others and, consequently, how it differs from them.

At the same time, the comparative enterprise has been used for many different purposes. Thus, while cross-cultural perspective has been considered one of the great achievements of religious studies, it has also come under criticism as a source of distortion and cultural bias. Indeed, a whole range of religious and scientific motivations have driven comparative religion, and that has made it an area of controversy. For example, it has been used to demonstrate the superiority of one's own religion; to show that all religions are "the same"; to demonstrate that one can understand each religion from its own point of view; or to simply map a variegated landscape of different traditions. Likewise, it has been used to demonstrate any number of competing theories about the origin and nature of religion. Insofar as it has taken an even-handed approach to all religions, religious conservatives have perceived it as a relativizing of belief, and hence a threat to religious convictions.

While travelers and theologians have always formed views about other peoples' religions, the notion of an academic field of comparative religion emerged in the late nineteenth century in European and American universities, reflecting scholarly goals. It addressed the need to synthesize the enormous amount of information that was accumulating about the religions of the world, past and present, including new knowledge about non-Western traditions. This involved not only analyzing commonalities, differences, and types of religious life, but also postulating stages of historical or evolutionary development. This entry gives an overview of some salient points in the history of comparative religion (see Sharpe's *Comparative Religion: A History*, 1986, for a comprehensive account) and then addresses issues that had surfaced by the beginning of the twenty-first century.

SOME RELIGIOUS VERSIONS OF "COMPARATIVE RELIGION." The nineteenth-century founders of academic comparative religion faced provincial, heavily biased Euro-Christian maps about "other" religions. For example, until the early nineteenth century, Western culture still divided all religion into four kinds: Christianity, Judaism, Islam, and paganism. In that schema, everything outside the biblical traditions was "idolatry"—the supposed worship of false gods, or idols—and Christianity was given a place of automatic superiority to Judaism and Islam. Likewise, other religious cultures have also conducted the study of religions through the standard of their own faith.

Historically, and to take a Western example, Christian theologians developed specific strategies for explaining the existence of other religions. These ranged from outright negative accounts (other religions were the work of demons) to relatively positive ones (other religions resulted from an innate human capacity to know God, even though the special revelation of Christ was the fulfillment of that capacity). In between were a host of "historical" explanations: polytheistic religions were originally monotheistic, traceable to the sons of Noah, but deteriorated due to human depravity; religions that appeared "like" Christianity must have borrowed or received the ideas through historical contact; other gods were simply deified kings and heroes and hence not really gods at all. Allegorical interpretation was another form of comparison. Here the gods and myths of other religions could be construed as containing "signs" of Christian truths; for example, Athena could be said to stand for God's wisdom.

In the latter third of the twentieth century, the notion of interfaith dialogue gained some currency, featuring a "listening" stance toward other religions, and not merely a prejudging position that stereotypes others. Wilfred Cantwell Smith (1916–2000), an influential Christian comparativist and specialist in Islam, emphasized that the comparative study of religion needed to responsibly describe the living qualities and values of other peoples' faiths in a way that those persons themselves would be able to recognize.

Alongside such views of other religions, another religious approach existed, one that could broadly be called *uni-*

versalism. In that version of comparison, all religions refer to the same underlying spiritual reality, manifest through varying cultural forms—just as water remains water regardless of what it is called in different languages. Even in the world of ancient Greece, there was a well-known doctrine of "the equivalence of the gods." Thus, the fifth-century BCE historian Herodotus could report that the gods of Egypt were basically Egyptian names for Greek divinities. In the Far East, Buddhists commonly interpreted native Chinese and Japanese gods as "manifestations" of cosmic buddhas. Universalism remains a popular form of comparative religion for those interested in sameness and unity rather than difference.

THE RISE OF ACADEMIC COMPARATIVE RELIGION. From the mid-nineteenth century, in contrast to explicitly normative approaches, an academic version of comparative religion emerged. This was made possible by expanding knowledge of non-Western religions and preliterate cultures, and also by evolutionary rather than scriptural views of human history. An influential advocate was F. Max Müller (1823–1900), a German-born and Oxford-based scholar of the Sanskrit language, sometimes regarded as the "father of comparative religion." Müller, who edited a fifty-volume translation series titled *The Sacred Books of the East* (1879–1910), made a particularly strong case that the study of religion should outgrow in-house Western mappings and take into account the great civilizational religions of Asia. He also advocated that comparative religion is to any one religion as comparative philology is to the study of any particular language, and as comparative anatomy is to the anatomy of any one species. He applied to religion what the poet Goethe said of language, that "he who knows one, knows none" (Müller, 1872, p.11). Thus the study of one religion could shed light on the study of another. Müller outlined a broad program that included learning about a religion through its own writings, grouping religions according to regional and linguistic patterns, exercising critical historical methods, understanding the nature of religious and metaphoric language, and avoiding the common tendency to compare positive aspects of one religion with negative aspects of another.

Another of the best known of these premodern comparativists was the Scottish classicist and anthropologist James G. Frazer (1854–1941), particularly through his work *The Golden Bough*, first published in 1890 and later to grow to twelve volumes. The work is a vast compendium of worldwide patterns of ritual and myth—motifs that Frazer interpreted as marking stages of human thinking prior to the age of science. A primary theme of the book is the renewal of the world through ritual or symbolic deaths, deaths that in turn lead to the rebirth of nature or society. Frazer examined the topic through cyclical rites of succession to sacred kingship, but also through the symbolisms of seasonal festivals, mythologies of "dying and rising gods," rites of scapegoating and expulsion, and related themes such as sympathetic magic and taboo. He also held that once some of these patterns are understood as ways that the "archaic" human mind worked, then particular historical practices and beliefs, otherwise obscure, might become intelligible. The field of anthropology, in sharp contrast, went on to focus on field studies of particular cultures and tended to reject the grand, armchair approach to comparison represented by Frazer's encyclopedic lists of parallels.

As students of religion aspired to develop an academic field, they began to map their subject matter not only historically but structurally. From the end of the nineteenth century to the mid-twentieth century, so-called phenomenologies of religion tried to catalog and describe every kind of religious phenomenon, including types of objects of veneration (e.g., sky, sun, fire, ancestors) and kinds of ritual practice. What a Linnaeus had done for the botanical world was now to be done for religion: its many species or "classes of phenomena" needed to be named and organized. By the latter part of the twentieth century, after the age of these encyclopedic collections, creative comparative work tended to focus on particular topics, such as origins myths, evil, mysticism, sacrifice, pilgrimage, rites of passage, theology, violence, women's rites, and the body.

Theories of religion, whether of a sociological or psychological kind, all engaged in identifying recurrent patterns and typologies in religion, though not necessarily under the banner of "comparative religion." Examples can be seen in the psychological archetypes of the school of C. G. Jung (e.g., the Great Mother, the Hero, the Trickster); or Max Weber's typologies of ways that religions reflected social values in various cultures; or Claude Lévi-Strauss's "structuralism," which identified patterned binary oppositions in the language of mythology. In the field of religious studies per se, arguably the most influential comparativist of the last generation was the Romanian-born scholar Mircea Eliade.

MIRCEA ELIADE (1907–1986). Eliade's "history of religions" approach at the University of Chicago (he joined the faculty in 1956) produced a notable generation of scholars oriented to cross-cultural, thematic studies and provided an expansive, creative vision about the cultural importance of a global, comparative perspective. Eliade's "new humanism" represented the culmination of the classic tradition, but also an approach that many of the newer generation in the last two decades of the century either contested or tried to modify.

Eliade's work had exceptional range. He was equally interested in the elite and popular forms of religious culture, projecting a fascination with the sheer variety of "modalities of the sacred." He sometimes likened this diversity to the many creative universes constructed by the arts. His view was that religions are not just philosophical beliefs, but inhabited, engaged worlds defined by ways that the sacred is perceived and ritually enacted. Nonreligious worlds lack this dimension of sacrality. Eliade was well known for his descriptions of thematic ways that religious cultures symbolize their worlds through representations of sacred space, sacred time, and natural symbols, and his ideas here may be summarized briefly.

Many religious cultures endow certain spaces or objects with the function of being "the center of the world," an "axis of the world" (*axis mundi*), or an "opening" to the world of the gods. These become sites of orientation and ritual, linking "heaven and earth." The comparison of religions shows innumerable such centers of the world, side by side, each absolute for their respective believers. A grand-scale example would be the great Muslim shrine, the Kaʿbah, in Mecca, the place toward which Muslims face in their daily prayers and toward which they are faced at burial.

As with space, religious cultures ground themselves in their own sacred histories. In the "great" times of origin, the gods or ancestors created all the significant religious institutions and teachings that adherents still live by and that they still rehearse. This is not just chronological time, but a world that can be accessed periodically and continually re-presented through ritual and festival times. In this way, one's present world is reconnected to its origins. To this extent, religious people live out of the archetypes, laws, and narratives of their past, whether in oral or scriptural form.

Eliade also held that sacrality is expressed through and incorporated in various symbolisms of the natural world. These include the transcendence of the sky, the fecundity and periodic renewal of the earth and its vegetation, the power of the sun, the waxing and waning cycle of the moon, the durability of stone, and the solubility and regenerative qualities of water—all described at length in his comprehensive *Patterns in Comparative Religion* (first published in French, 1949). In turn, however, these universal or archetypal values were to become a point of criticism, namely, that they were too ahistorical and "Platonic."

OBJECTIONS TO COMPARATIVISM. Eliade's work, and that of all who drew generalizations from cross-cultural materials, elicited a set of issues about the nature of the comparative enterprise. In a benchmark critical essay published in 1971 in *History of Religions*, Jonathan Z. Smith challenged the lack of methodological foundation and control for what usually passed as comparison. Indeed, in the last two decades of the twentieth century, where an age of specialization was replacing an age of generalization and a postmodern ideological climate challenged Western metalanguages, comparativism came under full suspicion—even though global, multicultural "understanding" was emerging on another, popular front. A number of critical issues surfaced and may be summarized under five points.

The first criticism is that comparison suppresses cultural difference. It can do this in two ways. The first is by imposing a false, superficial homogeneity on all its examples. Universal patterns, with their preestablished meanings, are then allowed to override specific contexts of meaning. In this sense, the distinctiveness of religious cultures would seem to remain elusively off the comparative grid, for the representation of others is reduced to only those points that illustrate and replicate the scholar's own categories, themes, or molds.

An example of the issue of cultural difference is pointed out in Jonathan Z. Smith's critique (*To Take Place*, 1987, pp. 1–23) of Eliade's attribution of the "center of the world" motif to the totemic pole of the Australian Arunta. Eliade had interpreted the pole as a kind of portable "world axis" that could be carried from place to place, allowing the tribe to remain "at the Center." Smith argued that a more careful examination indicated a different contextual orientation. He tried to show that aboriginal Australian notions of space were based on memorialized ancestral "traces" and "tracks" rather than constructed, hierarchic edifices, and thus differed from the kinds of Near Eastern imagery Eliade had based his category on. The latter featured notions of a "Center" based on strong political centralization and significant ritual templates about constructed vertical relations between upper and lower worlds, such as city-state temples. Smith concluded that "the 'Center' is not a secure pattern to which data may be brought as illustrative; it is a dubious notion that will have to be established anew on the basis of detailed comparative endeavors" (p. 17).

Another form of suppressing differences is the kind that has a "colonialist," politically hegemonizing function. Critics here are concerned about a conceptual imperialism exercised by one culture, religion, gender, or class on others. It is charged that the comparativists' maps can subordinate, obliterate, or render invisible the subjectivity and voices of others. Generalizations about initiation rites, for example, might in fact be based entirely on male examples, and descriptions of "origins" mythologies may only draw illustrations from the traditions and interests of the socially elite classes.

A second criticism of comparativism is the argument of incomparability. Religious phenomena, it is claimed, are indelibly embedded in unique sociocultural settings. If removed from those wholes—plucked out, so to speak, and set alongside similar pieces from other cultures—they will lose their original meanings, meanings that are always linked to local and contextual behaviors. An alternative approach would be to build a specialist's knowledge of a particular religious tradition, through its own self-representations and categories. In this sense, area specialists have always been wary of comparativists encroaching on and decontextualizing their subject matter.

A third objection to comparative work stems from the postmodern challenge to the very notions of objectivity and neutrality. Many would deny that there are such things as objective cultural "facts." It would follow that comparativists cannot draw valid generalizations simply by lining up supposed data, because all cultural descriptions and patterns are ultimately invented, or at best imagined, by the scholar.

A fourth kind of criticism is that comparativism has typically been too theological in the way it organizes its material. While it is not surprising that many scholars interested in religion have religious interests themselves, Eliade's work and that of the phenomenology of religion tradition have often assumed that religion is ultimately based on a general divine reality that is then manifest in various forms. Consequently, religious life is represented as a kind of encounter with divine revelation. Critics with a naturalistic view of religion take this to be an unwarranted reference to a metaphysical foundation of all religion. Instead of taking an outsider's analytical viewpoint, the comparativist is thus accused of simply assuming or replicating the language of religious insiders.

Finally, and in contrast, there is the argument that comparative religion is not objective enough: it is merely descriptive and not explanatory, and thus lacks scientific value. In order to contribute to cumulative knowledge, as opposed to just positing individualistic interpretations, comparativism would need to show in a testable way how specific religious ideas and practices recur and vary in relation to specific social and historical conditions. The challenge here is not just to assert commonality or difference, not just to list parallels, but rather to explain them, and the charge is that comparative religion scholarship has yet to incorporate and apply the canons of empirical and analytical methods.

RECONSTRUCTING COMPARATIVISM. Important critiques of comparison meant that the method and rationale of cross-cultural descriptions have had to be defined and controlled more carefully and plausibly. Hence, the post-Eliadean period has seen several emergent articulations that attempted to address, if not remediate, some of the problems just listed.

Aspectual, limited comparative focus. One element of a reconstituted comparativism has been to secure greater definition of the act of comparison itself. Thus, focusing on and controlling the exact, stipulated point of analogy, the comparativist should acknowledge that the objects—the things compared—may be quite incomparable in other respects and for other purposes. As Fitz John Porter Poole put it in the seminal article "Metaphors and Maps" (1986), restrained comparison "does not deal with phenomena *in toto* or in the round, but only with an aspectual characteristic of them. . . . Neither phenomenologically whole entities nor their local meanings are preserved in comparison" (pp. 414–415). Comparisons, like all explanations, maps, and generalizations, are necessarily abstractions, and no comparative pattern covers the complexity of the objects to which it applies. For example, to describe or explain someone as a Canadian does not pretend to assume that the person's individual complexity, special voice, or "difference" is accounted for under that generic trait. Nor is the individual's particularity obliterated by such a trait designation: it is simply not addressed. Apples and oranges may not be "the same," but they *do* share some common aspects—for example, they both are round, edible, and belong to the class "fruit." Canadians, or sacred space, or "the paradigmatic function of myth," are also such classes.

One outcome of this approach is that large-block, essentialized comparisons, such as Asian versus Western religion, can give way to specific, controlled analogies between particular kinds and aspects of religious behavior. For example, research such as that of Barbara Holdrege in *Veda and Torah* (1996) breaks down the otherwise stereotyped difference between Hinduism and Judaism by identifying common aspects of these two traditions. Hence, both are "textual communities" that have codified the norms of orthodoxy in the form of scriptural canons; both are cultural systems concerned with blood lineages and intergenerational transmission of tradition; and both involve regimens with strict regulations concerning purity, impurity, and dietary laws. Again, these traditions are not "the same," but they do have significant patterns and points of resemblance.

Affirmation of differences. Comparison involves not only connecting two or more examples to illustrate a common factor, but also showing how the examples differ in relation to that factor. The differences then reveal the variability of the pattern in cultural contexts. In turn, the many variations enrich understanding of the pattern and can lead to differentiating the pattern into its subtypes. Thus many *kinds* of sacred space or origins myths can be identified.

Using culturally defined topics as a basis of comparison, such as "God," or "Saviors," privileges those religious ideas by making them the standard. But what if the unit of comparison lies at the panhuman rather than cultural level? Are there not common forms of human behavior shared by all societies? New lines of comparativism have therefore looked for species-level continuities of human behavior and cognition. For example, in *The Implied Spider* (1998) Wendy Doniger advocates a "bottom-up" rather than a "top-down" approach, meaning that instead of assuming commonalities regarding broad culturally infused topics such as sacrifice or "high gods," comparativists could find certain shared panhuman factors such as gendered sexuality, body, desire, and procreation and their concomitant story motifs or shared human problems, and then identify individual diversity in relation to them. This variety is endless, even among individuals in given cultures.

Human universals, here, do not refer to preexisting, ahistorical meanings but to shared predispositions and kinds of social behaviors found in all cultures. For example, humans not only sleep, procreate, and eat, they also form societies that fashion laws and moral orders, create "histories," perform periodic rites, and endow objects and persons with special charisma or authority. Cultures will improvise on these common social dispositions in their own manner and with their own contents. Thus religious groups articulate "pasts" and "origins," but each of these histories is different and comprises its own worldview; and every religion has a kind of sacred moral order, but what it is that constitutes order and its violation will differ. Likewise, members of every religion remember their past in periodic rites and festivals, but the content of what is recalled is different in every case, revealing what is of value to that particular group. For example, the content of major annual rites may variously have to do with the sacred authority of a social hierarchy (e.g., kings, emperors, ancestors), or the display of ideal military values, or the prestige of the religious founder. In this sense, cultural difference is not suppressed but showcased.

Debates about the relation of particularity and commonality will continue. Also evolving are more clearly defined protocols of comparison and fresh theoretic frameworks for synthesizing cross-cultural material. The emerging global orientation of the study of religion in higher education will provide a setting for those developments. Just as comparative perspective contains the risks of distortion, it also has the potential to add new contexts of intelligibility to the history of religions, and to foster intercultural understanding.

See Also Comparative-Historical Method [Further Considerations]; Phenomenology of Religion; World Religions.

Bibliography

Carman, Jon B., and Steven P. Hopkins, eds. *Tracing Common Themes: Comparative Courses in the Study of Religion.* Atlanta, 1991. Shows various ways that comparative topics and perspectives can be addressed in college religion courses.

Doniger, Wendy. *The Implied Spider: Politics and Theology in Myth.* New York, 1998. Example of how the "webs" of universal human dispositions can contextualize individual variations.

Eliade, Mircea. *Patterns in Comparative Religion.* Translated by Rosemary Sheed. Cleveland, Ohio, 1958. A classic, encyclopedic account of recurrent types of religious symbolism.

Eliade, Mircea. *The Sacred and the Profane.* Translated by Willard R. Trask. New York, 1959. Widely read summary statement by the best-known comparative religion scholar.

Frazer, James G. *The Golden Bough,* abridged ed. New York, 1963. First published in 1922. Frazer's own abridgment of his twelve-volume work on ritual and mythic motifs.

Holdrege, Barbara. *Veda and Torah: Transcending the Textuality of Scripture.* Albany, N.Y., 1996. A major comparative study of Judaism and Hinduism, showing some profound commonalities.

Jay, Nancy. *Throughout Your Generations Forever: Sacrifice, Religion, and Paternity.* Chicago, 1992. Exemplary comparative study of the role that gender plays in the institution of sacrifice.

Jones, Lindsay. *The Hermeneutics of Sacred Architecture: Experience, Interpretation, Comparison.* 2 vols. Cambridge, Mass., 2000. Chapters 10 to 12 of volume 1 address two distinct, complementary, often sequential modes of comparison: synchronic morphological comparison and diachronic historical comparison.

Jordan, Louis Henry. *Comparative Religion: Its Genesis and Growth.* Edinburgh, 1905. Comprehensive survey of comparative religion scholarship at the turn of the twentieth century.

Martin, Luther H., ed. "The New Comparativism in the Study of Religion: A Symposium." *Method and Theory in the Study of Religion* 8, no. 1 (1996): 1–49. Debate on the function of comparison by scholars representing different approaches.

Martin, Luther H. "Comparison." In *Guide to the Study of Religion,* edited by Willi Braun and Russell T. McCutcheon, pp. 45–56. London, 2000. Reviews the critical role that theory plays in the uses of comparative religion.

Müller, F. Max. *Lectures on the Science of Religion.* New York, 1872. Seminal charter statement advocating the comparative study of religion as a new field of study.

Neville, Robert Cummings, ed. *Ultimate Realities: A Volume in the Comparative Religious Ideas Project.* Albany, N.Y., 2001. A major collaborative consideration of the processive nature of comparison and the vulnerability of comparative categories to correction and specification.

Numen: International Review for the History of Religions 48, no. 3 (2001). The entire issue is devoted to essays on new approaches to comparativism.

Paden, William E. *Religious Worlds: The Comparative Study of Religion.* 2d ed. Boston, 1994. Overview of common patterns of religious "worldmaking" and the ways those patterns are exemplified through different cultural values.

Patton, Kimberley C., and Benjamin C. Ray, eds. *A Magic Still Dwells: Comparative Religion in the Postmodern Age.* Berkeley, 2000. Essays by fourteen scholars on the importance of comparative perspective in relation to the challenges of postmodernism.

Poole, Fitz John Porter. "Metaphors and Maps: Towards Comparison in the Anthropology of Religion." *Journal of the American Academy of Religion* 54 (1986): 411–457. Cogent analysis of the epistemological basis of comparative method by an anthropologist of religion.

Saler, Benson. *Conceptualizing Religion: Immanent Anthropologists, Transcendent Natives, and Unbounded Categories.* Leiden, 1993. Extensive review of resources for conceptualizing comparative categories.

Sharpe, Eric C. *Comparative Religion: A History.* 2d ed. La Salle, Ill., 1986. A richly informative account of the general development of comparative religion as an academic field.

Smart, Ninian. *Dimensions of the Sacred: An Anatomy of the World's Beliefs.* Berkeley, 1996. Outline of comparative themes by a well-known figure in the field.

Smith, Jonathan Z. "*Adde Parvum Parvo Magnus Acervus Erit.*" *History of Religions* 11 (1971): 67–90. Now classic essay calling for more serious attention to the methodology of comparison.

Smith, Jonathan Z. *Imagining Religion: From Babylon to Jonestown.* Chicago, 1982. Chapters 1 and 2 review and pose critical issues about comparative method.

Smith, Jonathan Z. *To Take Place: Toward Theory in Ritual.* Chicago, 1987.

Smith, Jonathan Z. *Drudgery Divine: On the Comparison of Early Christianities and the Religions of Late Antiquity.* Chicago, 1990. Addresses issues of method in comparison, by way of a critique of Christian interpretations of Hellenistic period religions.

Wach, Joachim. *The Comparative Study of Religions.* Edited by Joseph M. Kitagawa. New York, 1958. Midcentury classic.

Waldman, Marilyn Robinson. *Prophecy and Power: A Comparative Study of Islamic Evidence.* Cambridge, Mass., 2004. Though focused on Islam, addresses broad questions about the comparison of religions as a strategic sociopolitical act as well as an academic method.

William E. Paden (2005)

COMPASSION See KARUNĀ

COMTE, AUGUSTE

COMTE, AUGUSTE (1798–1857), French philosopher, founder of positivism. Born into a Roman Catholic, royalist family in Montpellier, France, Comte completed his early education by preparing for the École Polytechnique under the direction of Daniel Encontre, from whom Comte learned that philosophy is a complete view of reality. Comte ranked high in the Polytechnique entry competitions, but he studied there only a few years. Republican political opinions, later expressed in his memoirs, moved him to participate in the student rebellions that were instrumental in causing the royalist government to close the school for reorganization.

In 1817 Comte became secretary to Claude-Henri de Rouvroy Saint-Simon, the social philosopher. Comte's writing appeared in numerous publications edited by Saint-Simon. Indeed, Comte's *Sommaire appréciation de l'ensemble du passé moderne* (Summary Evaluation of the Impact of the Recent Past; 1820) came out under Saint-Simon's signature. In this work Comte describes the *ancien régime* as having two poles, or capacities, the theological and the military; these are being superseded by two new poles: the scientific and the industrial.

In *Prospectus des travaux scientifiques nécessaires pour reorganiser la société* (Prospectus of the Scientific Tasks Necessary for the Reorganization of Society; 1822), Comte presented a law of three states through which human history and each of the sciences must pass in their development; he gave one hundred examples. Revised as *Système de politique positive* (System of Positive Polity; 1824), this theory appeared with one thousand examples, unsigned, in a publication of Saint-Simon's. After he left Saint-Simon, Comte gave lessons in mathematics. In 1825 he married Caroline Massin.

Considérations philosophiques sur les sciences et les savants (Philosophical Considerations concerning Sciences and Scientists; 1825) and *Considérations sur le pouvoir spirituel* (Considerations concerning Spiritual Power; 1826) were published while Comte prepared his *Cours de philosophie positive* (Course on Positive Philosophy). He gave the first lesson in this course on April 2, 1826. Among those present were the zoologist Henri-Marie de Blainville, the scientist Louis Poinsot, the economist Charles Barthelemy, and the naturalist Alexander von Humboldt. The course ended with its third meeting because of Comte's mental problems. Melancholic, he attempted to drown himself in the Seine, but was rescued. He took up his work again in the spring of 1828.

The course resumed, and the first volume based on these lectures was published in 1830. In this same year, Comte inaugurated a free public course on astronomy that continued for seventeen years. Beginning in 1832, he served as assistant master at the École Polytechnique, but the minister of instruction offered no reply to Comte's queries about a chair at the Collège de France. In 1842, the sixth and concluding volume of the *Cours* appeared, followed by *Discours sur l'esprit positif,* which appeared as part of his treatise on popular astronomy. Although his request for a chair in the history of positive sciences met with no success, publication of his *Discours sur l'ensemble du positivisme* (Discourse on the Unity of Positivism; 1848), and the creation of a subsidy by Émile Littré through Comte's Société Positiviste (founded 1848), provided financial support for the philosopher.

Comte's four-volume *Système de politique positive* (System of Positive Polity) appeared during 1851–1854. In the preface to his *Catéchisme positiviste* (Positivist Catechism; 1852), Comte presented himself as founder of the religion of humanity. Littré, unable to follow in this new development, broke with him. Also in 1852, the second volume of the *Système* was issued, which contained an important chapter on religion: "General Theory of Religion, or Positive Theory of Human Unity."

The two aims of religion, according to Comte, are regulation of the individual and unification of individuals. For him, the etymology of the Latin *religio* is *religare:* to connect and unite. This unity depends upon both an intellectual and a moral condition; the first determines dogma, the second cult. Beyond individual and social unity lies an external world, here considered as the foundation of faith, as the aim of activity, and as an object of affection. "Faith is but an auxiliary of love" (*Système*, vol. 2, p. 48). Moral unity rests entirely in sociability prevailing over personality (*Catéchisme positiviste*, in the dialogue between the priest and the woman). Positivism is a religion of relation and does not propose a merely individual synthesis. It is rather the great being, or humanity as a whole, that is loved for its perfectibility. Humanity, the positivist God, is behind and before us as the progressive realization of the ideal that reveals itself in realization.

See Also Positivism.

Bibliography

The writings of Comte can be found in his *Œuvres*, 12 vols. (Paris, 1968–1970). The works available in English translation include *The Positive Philosophy of Auguste Comte*, 2 vols., a condensation of the *Cours* by Harriet Martineau (London, 1853); *The System of Positive Polity*, 4 vols., translated by J. H. Bridges et al. (London, 1875–1877); and *The Catechism of Positive Religion*, translated by Richard Congreve (London, 1858). Henri Gouhier's *La vie d'Auguste Comte*, 2d rev. ed. (Paris, 1965), and Joseph Lonchampt's *Précis de la vie et des écrits d'Auguste Comte* (Paris, 1889) are informative biographies.

New Sources

Comte, Auguste, Oscar A. Haac, and John Stuart Mill. *The Correspondence of John Stuart Mill and Auguste Comte.* New Brunswick, 1995.

Harp, Gillis J. *Positivist Republic: Auguste Comte and the Reconstruction of American.* Liberalism, 1865–1920. University Park, 1995.

Kennedy, Emmet. "The French Revolution and the Genesis of a Religion of Man, 1760–1885." In *Modernity and Religion.* Notre Dame, Indiana, 1994.

Pickering, Mary. *Auguste Comte: An Intellectual Biography.* Cambridge, U.K., 1993.

Scharff, Robert C. *Comte after Positivism.* Cambridge, U.K., 1995.

Wernick, Andrew. *Auguste Comte and the Religion of Humanity: The Post-Theistic Program of French Social Theory.* Cambridge, U.K., 2001.

Wright, T. R. *The Religion of Humanity: The Impact of Comtean Positivism on Victorian Britian.* Cambridge, U.K., 1986.

ANGÉLE KREMER-MARIETTI (1987)
Revised Bibliography

CONALL CERNACH. The father of Conall Cernach was Amhairghin, the famous poet and hero of the Ulstermen, and he himself is represented as the most important of the Ulster heroes save Cú Chulainn. He is also sometimes named as a foster brother of Cú Chulainn, though evidently more mature in years: at the time of Cú Chulainn's birth he was already one of the Ulster warriors, and it was he who guarded the southern border of Ulster when the youthful Cú Chulainn came there to perform his first initiatory exploit in the epic *Táin Bó Cuailnge* (The cattle raid of Cuailnge). But whereas Cú Chulainn died without progeny, Conall Cernach appears in the genealogies as the ancestor of the Cruthin or Pictish tribes of Ireland. In *Fledh Bhricrenn* (The feast of Bricriu) he contests the prize of the "champion's portion" with Cú Chulainn but has to give best to the younger hero. It was Conall Cernach who avenged Cú Chulainn's death, beheading his slayer Lughaidh mac Con Roí. When he himself was slain and beheaded by his lifelong foes the Connachtmen, it is said that his head was so large that it could have held four men playing "chess" *(fidhchell)* or a couple lying together.

He is sometimes described as *cloen* ("crooked") because his inveterate enemy, the Connachtman Cet mac Mághach, to whom he was a nephew, had stamped his heel upon his neck after his birth, for it was prophesied that he would kill half the men of Connacht. The name *Conall* derives from a Celtic form, **cuno-valos* ("strong as a wolf"), and, appropriately, his epithet *cernach* may mean "triumphant" and is so understood in early texts. But there was also an alternative interpretation. According to the *Cóir Anmann* (Fitness of names), the word *cern* means "bump, protuberance" as well as "victory," and Conall's epithet is said to refer to the fact that he had "a lump on one side of his head as big as the boss of a shield." Because of this and an episode in the tale of *The Cattle Raid of Fróech*, Anne Ross has suggested that there is an affinity between Conall Cernach and the Gaulish horned god Cernunnos (*Pagan Celtic Britain*, London, 1967, pp. 149ff.). Though she does not advert to it, her argument is supported by the fact that Irish *cern* is etymologically related to Irish *corn*, Latin *cornū*, Old High German *horn*, and so on.

BIBLIOGRAPHY

Further information on Conall Cernach can be found in Rudolf Thurneysen's *Die irische Helden- und Königsage bis zum siebzehnten Jahrhundert*, 2 vols. (Halle, 1921), the classic study of *Táin Bó Cuailnge.*

PROINSIAS MAC CANA (1987 AND 2005)

CONCENTRATION SEE ATTENTION; MEDITATION

CONFESSION OF FAITH SEE CREEDS

CONFESSION OF SINS. The word *confession* has a twofold meaning that can be partially explained by etymology. The Latin *confiteor*, from which *confession* derives, means specifically "to confess a sin or fault," but also, in a more general sense, "to acknowledge or avow." Thus one may speak both of the sinner who confesses his sins and of the martyr who confesses his faith. Since the confession or witness of a martyr normally took place before a tribunal, it did in fact bear a formal resemblance to the confession of sins. The resemblance should prevent us from separating the two basic meanings of the word *confession* too sharply. Nevertheless, this entry will be concerned solely with an examination of the confession of sins in the strict sense, in other words as utterances concerning sins or offenses that are made in order to escape from these sins and their consequences. Confession in this strict sense normally occurs in a ritualized context that transcends the individuality of the sinner or offender. It must be done before a "recipient" who hears the confession. In many cases, it is performed in the interest not only of the one confessing but also of the community (familial, social, ecclesiastical) to which both the confessing person and the recipient belong.

Two principal approaches to the study of confession can be distinguished. On the one hand, one may view the confession of sins as one of many elements, such as prayer, sacrifice, the priesthood, and so forth, in the phenomenology of religion. These common elements can be recognized within various religions throughout the ages in different cultural areas, though they may have been motivated and shaped quite differently. On the other hand, one may view the partial phenomenological similarities of the different rituals that are conventionally labeled confessions of sins as the products of historical convergences.

In the first approach, the comparative-historical study of confession may transcend the purely phenomenological classification of the different forms and functional interpretations of confession to suggest hypotheses concerning the process of its formation. It may study the relative antiquity of the various subtypes of confession and the particular cultural-historical contexts in which confession originates as a more or less structured institution. This was the approach of Raffaele Pettazzoni (1883–1959), who developed the theory that the confession of sins originated from forms of magic, specifically from the magic of the spoken word. Confession, in this theory, was originally a ritual intended to expel or eliminate a sin by means of its verbal expression. The sin itself could be unconscious and involuntary; it was conceived of as a kind of substance that was charged with destructive or obstructive power. Pettazzoni believed that such rites were well adapted to cultural contexts such as those found in agricultural, matriarchal societies. This theory elicited scholarly objections, particularly from scholars belonging to the Viennese cultural-historical school. They pointed out that Pettazzoni's unilinear reconstruction of the history of confession—leading from the magical to the theistic and assigning an ethical character only to the latter, with its stress on the voluntary character of sin and the value of contrition—could in fact mean a return to a farfetched evolutionism.

Moreover, if one explains the similarities observed among the different forms of confession as being the result not of a unilinear evolution but rather of occasional convergences in the history of religions, as in the second approach, one can avoid appealing to such a general theory. In fact, magical and theistic forms of confession, far from being products of a single unilinear evolution, are sometimes found together within a single cultural-historical milieu. Their relative antiquity cannot be determined merely by citing the frequency with which they are mentioned in extant religious documents. To be sure, it is necessary to distinguish between a sin conceived as the infringement of a moral code, emanating from (or at least guaranteed by) a deity, and a sin resulting from the neglect of a taboo, a law not necessarily motivated by the will of a suprahuman, personal agency. A distinction must also be made between voluntary and involuntary transgression, both of moral codes and of mere taboos. But the coexistence of these alternatives in some religions does not necessarily imply that one is chronologically later than the other. Furthermore, the motivation for apparently identical eliminatory or deprecatory ritual gestures may differ according to the context: magical techniques can be used to reinforce theistic motivations, while theistic beliefs sometimes motivate magical practices.

Confession of Sins in Nonliterate Cultures. An interpretation of the confession of sins among nonliterate peoples must consider that there is indeed a tension between theistic conceptions of confession, where the goal is divine forgiveness, and nontheistic conceptions, where the efficacy of confession is intrinsic to the act itself. The Sanpoli and Nespelen (Salish Indians), whom Wilhelm Schmidt (1868–1954) ranked among the *Urvölker*, in other words among the people of the greatest possible antiquity, practice a theistic form of confession, accompanied by prayer to the supreme being. The purpose of the confession is the sinner's attainment of heaven and presupposes the positive disposition of the person confessing. By contrast, among the Kikuyu, an agricultural people of East Africa, one finds a nontheistic form of confession. Here the transgression of a taboo or other ceremonial regulation can be eliminated by "vomiting" it, that is, confessing it to the sorcerer.

This distinction between theistic and nontheistic forms of confession should not be overemphasized, however, important though it is in the history of religions. As already noted, fundamentally identical gestures and expressions may be found in both forms, but they receive particular meaning only from the context of their use.

The study of the content of confession is no less important than the study of its general forms. One of the most typical, perhaps the most typical subject of confession, is a woman's confession of adultery, particularly when the confession is occasioned by the act of childbirth. The recipient of the confession may be a priest, a sorcerer, the husband, or perhaps another woman. The woman making the confession must either enumerate her partners or identify them by name. This requirement may be intended to allow the offending partner to redress his wrong by offering a sacrifice or paying a fine (as among the Luo of Dyur and the Nuer of East Sudan respectively). This requirement reflects the belief that the concrete effects of a wrong action can be eliminated only through an equally concrete confession of each act. Unconfessed adultery possesses an inherently obstructive power that must be removed by means of ritual confession. The Luo, the Nuer, and also the Atcholi of Uganda believe that the destructive power of unconfessed adultery may become manifest through the death of the delivered child. These regulations and beliefs presuppose the ethical value of marriage, a standard that influences the understanding of confession. To explain the negative effects of adultery in the case of the child's death as due to sickness deriving from the material effects of libertinage would be clearly reductive. In New Caledonia, young male initiands are questioned by elders concerning any previous sexual behavior. They must confess cases of illicit sexual relations with women; not doing so would cause danger to the society as a whole.

Another typical occasion for making a confession in nonliterate societies is the activity of hunting or fishing. The magical practices associated with these activities are well known. For example, women must observe particular taboos while their husbands are away hunting in order not to compromise the success of the expedition. The husbands themselves, during the days preceding departure, must abstain from various activities, in particular from cohabitation with their wives. Confession is another preparatory practice. Individual members of the hunting or fishing party must confess their sins prior to departure, since the unacknowledged breaking of a taboo or a persistent condition of impurity and culpability would endanger the success of the entire expedition. One who resisted making the required confession would be excluded from participating.

Another peculiarity of confession of sins in nonliterate societies is the fact that the transgression to be confessed need not be voluntary or conscious, particularly a transgression of taboos or of ritual regulations. The same is true of other purificatory rituals. As shall be discussed below in greater detail, the need for confession of sin to be circumstantial and at the same time thorough (i.e., not achieved through generic formulations) led to the construction of long lists of possible sins or offenses. Such lists were to be recited by the one confessing in order to avoid the omission of any committed sin. This clear example of the elaboration of sacral techniques demonstrates how the original need for confession may be eventually overshadowed by the need for completeness. Yet this need to be complete does not essentially contradict the nature of confession, whether theistic or magical. Confession is characterized not by generic utterances of culpability but by the necessity to be concrete and specific, to evoke and destroy the very existence and malignant efficacy of a particular sin.

Characteristic of confession among preliterate peoples is also that it may be associated with the rhythms of the astronomical year as well as with the production cycle. Among the Lotuko of East Sudan, there is a public confession by warriors at the beginning of the great hunting season. Their confessions are made individually with lowered voice and then repeated by the priest serving the rain god. The reason for this procedure cannot be to avoid exposing the warriors to shame; more probably, the custom is meant symbolically to preserve, to the extent that it is possible, the originally individual character of confession. Other instances of confession on the occasion of annual ceremonies of renewal are found among the Bechuana, the Algonquin, and the Ojibwa.

New Year rituals of confession are clearly eliminatory. Faults and their evil efficacy must not be allowed to extend beyond the close of the expiring year; they must be abolished. Other eliminatory rituals or customs may take place on such occasions, such as throwing away or destroying old and damaged implements. In confession, however, elimination concerns things not exterior to humans but interior to them. This remains true whether the interiority of sin is conceived of magically (as a substance, fluid, or influx) or theistically, as a condition of being and a reality reflected in the conscience of the person confessing. Such annual confessions, though remaining fundamentally an act of the individual, also have collective, even cosmic, implications. These are all the more evident when a confession is made by the king as an authorized representative of the collectivity, bound to it by the bonds of "sympathy." This common idea is found in other well-known rites where the very person and life of the king are involved in rituals ensuring the perpetuity of the world and the smooth transition from one season to the next. The king as an individual sinner, as the proper subject of confession, paradoxically becomes the representative of the multitude and acts in the people's interest. Thus, even here, the individual nature of the act of confession is preserved.

Finally, we must note the connection of confession of sins with the ordeal that may be used to test the sincerity of the confessing person. Here two different ritual procedures are intermingled. Evil is not the consequence of a sin that goes unconfessed; it is rather the consequence of a confession that was not sincere. The ethical side of confession becomes paramount; a reference to the elimination of occult sin would be out of place here. This instance makes clear the inadequacy of reducing confession strictly to a material utterance having magic, autonomous effects.

Confession is also found in association with other rituals. Among the Nandi, a solemn form of confession is associated with circumcision. Among the Sulka (New Britain) and the Maya (Yucatan), confession is associated with initiation, and in Chiapas (Mexico) with marriage. In other words, confession may be an element in rites of passage, both individual and seasonal.

Confession is sometimes associated with such ritual and ascetic procedures as fasting, abstinence, and chastity, evidently because of their importance in achieving ritual or ethical purity. Confession has also been associated with the scapegoat ritual, but it is preferable, in this instance, to speak not of confession but of the magical or juridical transfer of sin onto an animal destined to be eliminated from the community. Confession as an explicit acknowledgment of sin is quite different; moreover, it requires a recipient, a more or less qualified "hearer" or counterpart. In confession among primal cultures, there is an efficacy not only in the word that is spoken, but also in the word that is heard. The dialogical context is thus crucial. Both speaker and hearer embody a circle that functions, whether theistically, magically, or both, to consume the sin confessed.

Confession of Sins in Traditional High Cultures and World Religions. We pass now to the significance of confession of sins in traditional high cultures (both past and present), which are mostly polytheistic, and to the world religions. It is worth recalling that the term *confession* is here used not as a univocal, but as an analogical term in accordance with classical logic. This means that the term *confession* overshadows sets of concepts and realities having in common some typical characteristics or aspects, not always the same, sets separated by differences that reach to the same depth as the similarities. Thus there is a kind of "family resemblance" that is different from a strictly definable "universal."

Mexico and Peru. Confession was practiced in old Mexico in connection with Tlacolteótl, the goddess of impurities. She symbolized the sexual offenses (particularly adultery) that were the main object of confession. The priests of the goddess acted as the recipients of confession, and the confession itself was understood as taking place before the great, omniscient god Tezcatlipoca. The confession was secret and was followed by the imposition of a complicated penance, to be performed on the festival day of the goddess. The penance involved drawing blood from the tongue or ear, and it was accompanied by symbolic eliminatory acts, such as casting away wooden sticks that had been in contact with the wound. Extraction of blood was frequent in the religious life of the Mexicans, having an eliminatory and perhaps sacrificial meaning. Another object of confession was intoxication on the sacred drink, *pulque.*

In modern Mexico, confession is practiced by the Huichol at the time of the annual expedition to collect the *hikuli,* a sacred plant. This expedition requires a condition of purity in the participants, which is achieved through confession of sexual offenses. For mnemonic purposes, knots corresponding to sins are tied in a rope that is then burned at the end, a typical symbolic form of elimination.

Confession was also practiced in Peru, where it was associated with the bath (*upacuna*) and with other eliminatory or symbolic acts, such as blowing away powders. The recipient of confession was the *ichuri,* who was not a priest but belonged, rather, to a low class of diviners. The typical occasion for confession was sickness, whether of oneself or one's relatives, and the integrity of the confession could be tested by ordeal. Other occasions included bad weather and times of preparation for festivals. The emperor (the *inca*) and the high priest ordinarily confessed their sins directly to the sun and to the great god Viracocha, respectively. This fact reduces the value of these examples for the study of the typology of confession, since confession normally has a human recipient. Nevertheless, if this irregularity is attributed to the special status of the emperor, the confession of the *inca* may continue to be looked upon as genuine.

The sickness of the *inca* was an occasion for his subjects to practice confession, not only in homage to the emperor's dignity, but to show the sympathetic connection between the emperor and his people. In China the reverse happened. There, the emperor confessed to the people.

The site of confession in Peru was the peninsula that provided access to the shrine of the sun, located on a sacred island in Lake Titicaca. A long and detailed list of sins was employed, and some had to be confessed before the high priest. Generally speaking, the practice of confession in Peru did not involve secrecy.

Japan and China. The biannual Shintō ceremony of Oho-harahi resembles a rite of confession, but it is only a recitation of a complete list of possible sins or impurities by the *nakatomi,* a high dignitary, or by other priests. The ceremony is accompanied by such symbolic eliminatory acts as throwing impure objects into running water. Cases of individual confession are attested.

In China, eliminatory rituals were related to the grand conception of the Dao, the universal, heavenly order. A disturbance of this order, whether caused by the emperor or by his people, had serious consequences. It was the emperor's duty to redress the wrong, often through the vicarious performance of penance and a written confession of sins. Individual confession was also practiced in China, particularly in the context of the Daoist tradition, especially in the case of sickness. Sins were written down, perhaps in imitation of the emperor's confession or as a means of reinforcing their expression, and were then thrown into water.

India. In contrast to the political character it acquires in the Inca, Japanese, and Chinese empires, the confession of sins or dismeritorious deeds in India belongs to the mainstream of religious speculation and practice. In the Vedas there is an insistence on the purifying properties of fire and water together with faith in Varuṇa, a heavenly and omniscient god. Varuṇa punishes sinners by entangling and binding them in his net. He can also liberate the sinner from these bonds. He is connected with ethical laws, especially with the eternal order of *ṛta,* yet his *modus operandi* is clearly magical, and his jurisdiction extends to involuntary offenses. Nevertheless, the Vedas know nothing of confession proper; they know only of generic declarations of fault. It is in the Brāhmaṇas, which exalt the magical omnipotence of sacrifice, that confession is found, with particular reference to adultery; here confession is accompanied by eliminatory rituals. Brahmanic confession occurs at the summer feast of Varuṇapraghāsa; the name of the god may indicate a partial continuity with the ethical sphere of the Vedic Varuṇa. Starting this ceremony without having first confessed adultery is believed to create an insupportable burden for one's conscience, even in the context of an objective or material conception of sin. The confession of adultery must be complete, including the names or the number of lovers, since otherwise it could cause evil to the confessing woman's relatives. Confession is followed by an eliminatory sacrifice. An important feature of this ritual is its mythic motivation: it was created by the god Prajāpati. Similar motivation exists in the case of the Shintō ritual described above, which is connected with the figure of Susano-o.

In the sūtra literature, as in classical antiquity, what is alleged to be a confession of sins is actually an individual's public proclamation that he is a sinner, a proclamation that does not involve a specific recipient. It is more a notification, as Pettazzoni rightly noted when he criticized the theory of Franz Boas (1858–1942) that such a procedure constituted the most ancient form of confession.

Jainism. Confession in Jainism (*alocana* and, more generally, *pratikramana*) is mainly a monastic institution, performed twice daily. The laity make confession before their respective *gurūs.* Jainism combines the elimination of impurities (sin) with the doctrine of the annihilation of *karma,* conceived of as something substantial. Confession before death is considered important, and an insincere confession can perpetuate the cycle of rebirths.

Buddhism. The *prātimokṣa* is a gradated list of possible transgressions (sins) of the monastic rules governing the life of individual Buddhist monks or nuns; it is recited bimonthly at night services called *uposatha.* The participant monks must be in a state of purity; transgressions must be confessed in an individual and reciprocal form. Similar occasion for confession was the *pavāraṇa* ("invitation"), which occurred during the rainy season, when the monks led a sedentary life. Monks would invite their fellows to make statements concerning their (i.e., the inviter's) individual conduct. Both celebrations were originally public confessions, made in response to the reading of the list of transgressions at the *prātimokṣa* and to the threefold interrogation by the presiding monk. In the classical form of the ritual, however, it was presupposed that the monks had achieved the required state of purity through confession prior to the *prātimokṣa* recitation, so that no one was expected actually to accuse himself of transgression during the ritual. The purpose of repeated interrogation was to confirm this state of purity formally. These formal, silent answers, based as they were on previous confessions, were also a kind of negative confession designed to reveal sincerity of conscience: a proclamation of purity.

With Buddhism, the objective conception of transgressions and purification, found in both Jain and Brahmanic conceptions of *karma*, was abolished. *Karma* was now understood to be produced through the subjective element of volition, and there was a corresponding modification of the meaning of confession. With time, however—it would seem—monastic casuistry tended to lower this new moral emphasis in the Buddhist conception of confession.

Western Asia and Greece. It is difficult to assimilate the practices described in some of the epigraphic and literary texts of the religions of antiquity to the category of confession of sins. These texts mention the mere acknowledgment and subsequent public declaration of a sin or other offense by an individual. It is scarcely possible to speak of the confession of sins when the regent of Byblos writes to Amenophis IV that he has confessed his fault to the gods, or when the Hittite king Mursilis confesses a sin before the god of heaven. The same applies to the repeated confessional utterances (*homologein, exomologeisthai*) of the "superstitious man" described by Plutarch, a man continually and scrupulously resorting to purificatory rituals in the sanctuary. Similarly, the Galli of the Magna Mater, when participating in the procession of the goddess, enthusiastically and repeatedly declared the particular misdeeds of their past life, as well as describing the punishment (usually some form of sickness) that the god had inflicted upon them. This repeated evocation of past faults is the exact opposite of a ritual of confession, which is meant to eliminate the dangerous presence of sin once and for all. Nor can the term *confession* be applied to certain texts of Roman poets concerning personal experiences in the context of the cult of Egyptian deities or describing the vicissitudes of mythic or legendary characters: Ovid, *Metamorphoses* 11.129–143 (esp. v. 134, "*peccasse fatentem*," [confessed his fault] referring to the sinful King Midas) and *Fasti* 4.305–327 (esp. v. 321, "*si tu damnas, meruisse fatebor*," [if you do condemn me, I will confess my guilt] referring to the falsely accused Roman matron Claudia Quinta, who introduced the sacred stone of the Magna Mater to Rome in 204 BCE).

None of these records mentions the recipient of an oral confession, a necessary element of any penitential structure or institution. The texts present no more than a free initiative by the concerned sinner. The same is true of writings related to the confession of sins in Greek and Roman Orphism. Vergil (*Aeneid* 6.566–569) speaks of a "confession" in the otherworld, imposed by the judge of souls, Rhadamanthys, on those who persisted in enjoying their bad deeds until the end of their lives without having been purified. This does not necessarily imply an allusion to the neglected confession of sins during life. The same situation is found in Dante's *Commedia (Inferno* 5.7–10), where the souls come before Minos, the judge of the dead in the netherworld, and "confess," that is, declare their sins in order to be sent to the appropriate eternal penance. The same holds for Thespesius's episode in Plutarch, where the *homologein* ("acknowledgment of sinfulness") of a sinner in the netherworld is mentioned: a man who had always refused to reveal his sin on earth is condemned to confess it continuously.

The sole testimony of a confession of sins in Greece seems to consist of two anecdotes concerning the mysteries of Samothrace, which are told about two Spartan admirals, Antalkidas and Lysandros, who were requested by the priest in charge of the ritual of initiation (or perhaps purification) to mention the worst deed they committed in their lives. Possibly the so-called confession inscriptions of Phrygia (also of Lydia and Knidos) are evidence of a genuine confession of sins. Here persons of lower estate confess their transgression of some ritual regulation or their violation of some sacral person or property and dedicate a confessional inscription at the sanctuary as a record of the misdeed. According to Pettazzoni, these inscriptions testify to a particular connection of the Anatolian form of confession with the local great goddess. In another instance, an inscription recording a perjury is placed in the Anatolian sanctuary of Zeus Asbamaios. But these inscriptions are, in fact, testimonies to a popular pattern of behavior rather than to a ritual structure. All in all, it is with good reason that Pettazzoni criticized the belief of Richard Reitzenstein (1861–1931) that confession of sins was a phenomenon diffused throughout the Greek world.

Southern Arabia, Babylon, and Egypt. Some confessional inscriptions have been discovered in southern Arabia, although their chronology is uncertain. They seem similar to the confessional inscriptions of Phrygia, but with a peculiar emphasis on sexual sins.

Babylonian religion recognized several theistic and magical means for eliminating ethical and ritual offenses. For instance, lists of sins were written on tablets and were then destroyed. Nevertheless, a ritual of confession properly so called is far from clearly attested. The same holds for the Babylonian penitential psalms, despite their ritual background. Herodotus attributed to the people of Babylon the custom of placing the sick in the public square so that they might confess their sins publicly; this is nearer to the repetitious declarations of the enthusiastic Galli, mentioned above, than to ritually structured confession. Among other things, there is here no appointed recipient of confession.

More akin to present typology is the negative confession of the king at the beginning of the New Year festival in Babylon, the Akitu festival. True, a negative confession in which the king declares his innocence of a series of offenses against the city and the people is in a sense the opposite of a confession of sins. Yet both establish an immediate connection between the evocation of sin and the annihilation of it and its consequences. The most famous example of a negative confession is found in the Egyptian *Book of Going Forth by Day* (no. 125) where two complete lists of possible sins are used for the examination and weighing of the soul in the afterlife. This kind of totalitarian confession encompasses all kinds of possible sin, whether conscious or unconscious, in order to omit none of them. Although this is not confession in the strict sense, it nevertheless achieves its purpose.

Israelite religion and Judaism. The Old Testament texts, including the penitential psalms, are sometimes mistakenly conceived of as evidence of an institutionalized ritual of the confession of sins within the vast array of purification rituals. This also applies to the so-called collective confessions, in which the general wording "we have sinned" (corresponding to the "I have sinned" of the former texts) does not properly fit into our typology. As far as the scapegoat ritual is concerned, it has already been remarked that this is not a proper form of confession, but rather the religiously valorized transfer of sin for the purpose of expelling it. Although the procedure has an oral, declaratory element, it cannot be assigned to the typology of confession.

Israelite religion and Judaism consider sin to be a secondary issue. It is linked to the monotheistic belief in one God and the mythical fall of the first man, Adam, which is described concretely and is pictorially devoid of any theological or theoretical speculation. The most commonly used root for sin-related words in the Old Testament is *ḥaṭṭ*, meaning to miss the mark, to fall short of the goal, especially in maintaining unity between persons. Sin, then, is something very ordinary that is committed in everyday life. The relation to God is envisaged as analogical to relations between humans. Consequently, sin is a personal failing in one's relation to God and his commandments.

Sin, depicted as an inherited consequence of the fall in Judaism (*Gn.* 3), refers (1) to the conduct of being disobedient to God and his commandments, (2) to the turning away from the right path and right way of life, and (3) to failing to fulfill the purpose that God intended when he created the world. In rabbinical literature it refers both to disobedience in the sense of "not doing" what one is supposed to do and to transgression or the "actual doing" of what is forbidden. Sin is conceived of as an attitude of defiance or hatred of, even revolt against, God.

Sin leaves its mark not only on the sinner, but also on nature itself, and on all humankind universally. The sinner encounters a sense of guilt. The deluge, the plagues of Egypt, and the curses on unfaithful Israel are conceived of as marks on nature. As a result of the fall, all human beings were considered sinners. This universality of sin was the cause of the flood and of the inclination in the hearts of men and women towards evil from their youth. The prophets see the whole nation of Israel as sinful. The psalmists and sages also proclaim this universality: "But all are unfaithful, altogether corrupt; no one does good, no, not even one" (*Ps.* 14.3).

Judaic law determines the notion of sin. Every transgression of the law is a rebellion against the will of God and is therefore a sin. A distinction is made between sinning defiantly and sinning through ignorance. There is also a tendency to put the burden of guilt on both the individual and the community. As sin is regarded as having the world in its grip, observing the law is considered to be the only way to overcome the inclination to sin. The consequence of sin is punishment, which may manifest itself as sickness, death, and eternal damnation. But repentence and the return to God is possible at any stage in life, thanks to God's mercy.

Christianity. The mission of the Old Testament prophets was to awaken in the people a sense of sinfulness and a recognition of their personal and collective guilt. Sin, then, was regarded as a deliberate violation of the will of God attributed to human pride, self-centeredness, and disobedience. The New Testament discusses confession in many places, but there is no mention of its having to be specific or detailed, or that it has to be made to a priest. The activity of John the Baptist, who baptized ordinary people and also prepared Jesus for his public ministry by baptizing him, is often referred to as the origin of confession in Christianity: at that time baptism was accompanied by a public confession (*Mt.* 3:6).

Generally sin is portrayed in the context of forgiveness, as in the parable of the prodigal son (*Lk.* 15:11–32), where sin is manifested in the son's leaving his father to enjoy a debauched lifestyle. The forgiveness that the father shows at his son's return is seen as analogical to the heavenly Father's forgiveness. The son's sin was an offence not only against his father, but also against heaven. The miserable servitude the son suffered was the natural consequence of his sin. However, by returning he passed from death to life.

In its first centuries of existence, the Christian church practiced a canonical penance for sins considered *mortal* or *capital*. The penitential act started with the sinner entering the order of penitents through a confession rendered before the bishop, or at least with the acceptance of the assigned penance. With the gradual introduction of the private form of confession, from the seventh century onward, a new form of the celebration of reconciliation came into practice. The private form of confession necessarily emphasized the "accusation" made by the penitent.

Later on, theologians distinguished between *actual* and *original* sin. *Actual* refers to sin in the ordinary sense of the word. It is a category covering evil acts, whether of thought, word, or deed. The somewhat misleading expression *original sin* refers to the morally vitiated condition in which humans find themselves at birth as an inherited consequence of the first human sin.

Actual sin is subdivided into *mortal* and *venial* sin, the gravity of the sin being used as a criterion. A mortal sin, then, is a deliberate turning away from God, an act committed in full knowledge and with full consent of the sinner's will. Until the turning away is repented it cuts the sinner off from God's grace. In contrast, a venial sin is often committed with less awareness of wrongdoing. Although it weakens the sinner's union with God, it is not a deliberate turning away and therefore does not entirely block the inflow of God's grace. Originally anyone who had been baptized was expected to refrain from committing serious sins, but if they did so, expulsion from the Christian community was irrevocable. The practice of readmitting sinners to the community after penance was instituted during the third century CE despite strong protest from the Novatians and others. The excommunicated were received on Maundy Thursday by the bishop after having done penance during Lent.

A new form of penance, which became part of the ascetic life, was adopted in Irish monasteries: monks regularly confessed to a priest and received absolution, and penance appropriate to the sin was prescribed. This monastic practice spread to the continent of Europe in the seventh century and also became popular among the laity. The origin of the practice of the confession of sins that still prevails in the Orthodox and Roman Catholic churches lies in this monastic habit. Penance was made one of the seven sacraments in the fourth Lateran Council of 1215.

The Roman Catholic Church initially considered penance obligatory only for mortal or capital sins, that is, sins committed in full awareness of their being violations of the will of God. It was enough to repent of venial sins and to adopt a penitent attitude. However, over time the church began to encourage the confession of minor sins at least once a year as part of Christian spiritual life.

In principle, valid confession requires complete repentance (*contritio*) out of love of God, although incomplete repentance (*attritio*) may become complete through the sacrament of confession. Before absolution is given, the confessor is ordered to do penance, which was originally quite severe. The practice of easing penance through indulgence arose during the Middle Ages.

The practice of repentance is connected to the sacrament of confession, which has many names: the confession of sins, the remission of sins, and penance. Repentance aptly describes the content and character of the sacrament. It is founded on Christ's promise to his apostles: "If you forgive anyone's sins, they are forgiven. . . ." (*Jn.* 20:22); "If your brother does wrong, reprove him; and if he repents, forgive him" (*Lk.* 17:3–4).

The process of repentance is illustratively described in the parable of the prodigal son: his leaving and turning away from his father and his subsequent return to his father's house, the goal of which was to find God and his kingdom. The sacrament of confession does not imply forgiveness of sins that allows the sinner to go on as before. In true repentance there is an aspiration for a lasting resolve: "Now that you are well, give up your sinful ways, or something worse may happen to you" (*Jn.* 5:14). The sacrament may be regarded as the "medical examination of the soul": it concerns our relation to God, to our neighbors, and to our union with God.

Confession is virtually nonexistent in the Protestant tradition, although there has been a slight revival of the habit in recent years in connection with spiritual retreats and pilgrimages. Nowadays, penance is a Roman Catholic sacrament that is considered to be instituted by Christ. The confession of all serious sins committed after baptism is imperative. In the tradition of Eastern Christianity, private confession is usually made regularly to a personal spiritual father, who thus is able to follow and guide the individual's spiritual struggle and development.

Zoroastrianism, Mandaean religion, and Manichaeism. From Sassanid times on, Zoroastrianism recognizes a form of the confession of sins, the *patet* ("expiation"), made before a priest or, in his absence, before the sun, the moon, and the divine fire. An annual confession is encouraged in the month of Mihr (after Mihr, the god Mithra). According to Pettazzoni, Zoroastrian confession was actually derived from Christian confession, but alternative explanations are possible. It resembles the form of confession found in the Manichaean *Xastvanift*, a book preserved in the Uighur language of Central Asia. The meaning of confession in Manichaeism depended upon the Manichaean concept of sin, which was based on belief in a radical dualism of soul and body. The soul was believed not to be responsible for the actions of the body. Salvation was accordingly attained by means of the soul's complete separation from the body, a separation effected through a knowledge, or gnosis, of the soul's heavenly origin and a series of radical abstentions from bodily activities.

There are three main Manichaean texts used in confession. (1) The *Xastvanift*, mentioned above, consists of a list of sins and is intended for the laity (the "hearers"); it contains the recurrent formula "*Man astar hirza*" ("Forgive my fault"), which was used in the liturgy, read aloud, perhaps, by the priest to the faithful. Also employed were (2) a prayer composed in Chinese and used for communal confession, and (3) a form of confession composed in Sogdian and intended for the elite, bearing the title *Manichaean Book of Prayer and Confession*. Possibly this latter text was read during Bema, the annual festival of the Manichaeans.

The Mandaeans, adherents of a gnostic, ethnic religion that survives still in Iraq, recognize a confession for sins that can be repeated no more than two times before the sinner is excommunicated. The Mandaean confession covers both conscious and unconscious faults. It is similar to the Parsi and Manichaean forms of confession.

See Also Purification; Repentance.

BIBLIOGRAPHY

For a discussion of the topic by one of its major interpreters, see Raffaele Pettazzoni's *La confessione dei peccati,* 3 vols. (Bologna, Italy, 1929–1936; reprint, 1968). Pettazzoni's *La confession des péchés,* 2 vols. (Paris, 1931–1932), is the enlarged translation by René Monnot of volume 1 of the work mentioned above. For the Viennese school's criticism, see Leopold Walk's "Pettazzoni, Raffaele's 'La Confessione dei peccati,'" *Anthropos* 31 (1936): 969–972, and a series of articles by Michele Schulien listed in *Etnologia religiosa* (Turin, Italy, 1958), p. 286, note 7, by Renato Boccassino. Further studies by Pettazzoni on the theme are found in his *Essays on the History of Religions* (Leiden, 1954): "Confession of Sins and the Classics," pp. 55–67, and "Confession of Sins: An Attempted General Interpretation," pp. 43–54, with a further bibliography found on page 54, note 12. P. Wilhelm Schmidt's *Der Ursprung der Gottesidee,* vols. 5, 7, and 8 (Münster, Germany, 1934, 1940, 1949), discusses the concept among most primitive, as well as pastoral, cultures (consult the indexes). See Franz Steinleitner's *Die Beicht im Zusammenhange mit der sakralen Rechtspflege in der Antike* (Leipzig, Germany, 1913) for the Anatolian confessional inscriptions and related topics.

On the confession of sins in other traditions and cultures, see Arthur Darby Nock's *Essays on Religion and the Ancient World,* 2 vols., edited by Zeph Stewart (Cambridge, Mass., 1972; reprint, Oxford, 1986), pp. 66 and 427, note 77; Jacques Duchesne-Guillemin's *La religion de l'Iran ancien* (Paris, 1962), pp. 113ff.; and Kurt Rudolph's *Die Mandäer,* vol. 2: *Der Kult* (Göttingen, Germany, 1961), pp. 247–254. The last work cited includes an extensive bibliography concerning confession in Zoroastrianism, Manichaeism, and Mandaeism. On doctrine and practice in contemporary Catholicism, see John J. O'Brien's *The Remission of Venial Sin* (Washington, D.C., 1959); Charles J. Keating's *The Effects of Original Sin in the Scholastic Tradition from St. Thomas Aquinas to William Ockham* (Washington, D.C., 1959); G. Vandervelde's *Original Sin: Two Major Trends in Contemporary Roman Catholic Reinterpretation* (Amsterdam, 1975); and Pope John Paul II's *Reconciliatio et Paenitentia: Post-synodal Apostolic Exhortation of John Paul II to the Bishops, Clergy, and Faithful on Reconciliation and Penance in the Religion of the Church Today* (London, 1984). For the discussion of sin by the spiritual masters of the Orthodox Christian tradition, see *The Philokalia,* 4 vols. (London, 1979–1995). On the discussions of sin from a modern perspective, see Richard J. Bautch's *Developments in Genre Between Post-Exilic Penitential Prayers and the Psalms of Communal Lament* (Atlanta, Ga., 2003); Kay Carmichael's *Sin and Forgiveness: New Responses in a Changing World* (Aldershot, U.K., 2003); Anselm Schubert's *Das Ende der Sünde: Anthropologie und Erbsünde zwischen Reformation und Aufklärung* (Göttingen, Germany, 2002); and Patricia A. Williams's *Doing without Adam and Eve: Sociobiology and Original Sin* (Minneapolis, 2001). For a historical outline, see "Confession des péchés" in *Dictionnaire de théologie catholique* (Paris, 1923–1950), and "Beichte" in *Theologische Realenzyklopädie* (Berlin and New York, 1980). See also Roberto Rusconi, *L'ordine dei peccati: La confessione tra Medioevo ed età moderna* (Bologna, Italy, 2002), which includes a useful bibliography from the perspective of ecclesiastical history.

UGO BIANCHI (1987)
RENÉ GOTHÓNI (2005)

CONFUCIANISM

This entry consists of the following articles:

AN OVERVIEW
THE CLASSICAL CANON
THE IMPERIAL CULT
HISTORY OF STUDY

CONFUCIANISM: AN OVERVIEW

Over the two and a half millennia since the death of Kongzi (trad. 551–479 BCE), the figure whose name was latinized into "Confucius" by Jesuit missionaries in the sixteenth century, diverse groups have identified him as the source of their texts and practices. As a result, a wide variety of phenomena are called "Confucianism," many of which appear to have only a distant connection to one another. The term "Confucian" is applied to religious traditions grounded in the transmission and interpretation of sacred texts and practices, as well as to educational, ethical, and social systems. While some have argued that Kongzi's primary message was philosophical and secular, historians are increasingly questioning the justification for considering the ethical dimension of Confucianism as either more original than, or as separate from, its other aspects. Wing-tsit Chan's entries—"Foundation of the Tradition" and "Neo-Confucianism"—in the first edition of the *Encyclopedia of Religion* are among the most cogent yet nuanced treatments of Confucianism viewed as the legacy of a genealogy of philosophers. Instead of trying to rewrite his classic treatment, this article shifts perspectives to portray Confucianism as a set of plural and diverse strands that different interests have woven together (and occasionally unraveled) over the course of several millennia of East Asian history.

The following description begins with three topics central to the formative period of most strands of Chinese Confucianism: the legacies of the former sages; Kongzi and the disciple traditions; and the attempts to define the link between ethical self-transformation and rulership in the centuries immediately after Kongzi's death. In this period, expertise in a set of practices based in the rites, music, and classics of antiquity became the basis of vocations in advising rulers and teaching potential officials. Through the filter of dialogs transmitted in multiple disciple traditions, Kongzi came to be considered the paragon of these specializations. The second phase saw a redefinition of the relationship between the state and the legacies that Kongzi represented, as the study of the classics bifurcated into official academic positions sponsored by the state and private institutions, where transmissions of the classics gradually were cast as alternatives to very different kinds of Daoist and Buddhist lineages. In the early imperial and medieval period, the authority of Kongzi's representation of antiquity was grafted onto a variety of novel social institutions. In the third phase, as the dynasties of late imperial China alternated between rule by indigenous and foreign powers, and as the spread of monastic institutions transformed society, Kongzi's project was seen as a model for a quest to recover the indigenous traces of the early sages. Under the influence of the redefinition of the tradition sparked by Zhu Xi (also romanized as Chu Hsi, 1130–1200 CE), competing scholastic lineages theorized the connection between practice and politics, and between knowledge and the study of the classics. Confucianism today both receives support and is subject to restrictions in the People's Republic of China, even while its adaptation to modernity has continued in the communities of the East Asian diaspora.

LEGACIES OF THE EARLY SAGES. Even prior to the birth of Kongzi in 551 BCE, many of the elements that are today associated with Confucianism had long been present in Chinese society. Both the textual record of antiquity and the writings associated with Kongzi and his disciples credit the development of principal political and religious ideals and institutions to the great sage kings of antiquity, such as the third millennium BCE rulers Yao, Shun and Yu, and the more recent founders of the Zhou dynasty (trad. 1027–221 BCE). The central political narrative of pre-imperial China was the receipt of the sanction of Heaven (*tian*) by the eleventh century BCE Zhou founders, Kings Wen and Wu, on account of their virtue (*de*). References to this mandate (*ming*) are ubiquitous in both the *Classic of Documents* (*Shujing*) and *Classic of Poetry* (*Shijing*), works that predate Kongzi and were considered authoritative by him. This implicit connection between personal virtue and political legitimacy informs Confucian traditions to the present day, even while the connotations of the term *Heaven* and the nature of the connection have changed over time. Kongzi also credited the Zhou founders with the codification of an archaic ritual system built on a set of normative hierarchical social networks. While early records testify to a developed system of ancestor worship that reinforced the value of intergenerational family loyalty, there is less evidence that many elements of the ritual code preserved in works like the *Zhou Rituals (Zhouli),* the *Ceremonies and Rituals (Yili),* and the *Records of Ritual (Liji)* actually date to the early Zhou period. Regardless of their actual age, the antiquity of the political and ritual order associated with the ancient sages and, in particular, with the reforms of the Zhou, was a central religious assumption of the age into which Kongzi was born.

The identity of religion and politics dates back to the earliest records in China, the "oracle bone" inscriptions (*jiaguwen*). The Shang court (trad. c. 1750–1027 BCE) used inscribed cattle scapulae and tortoise plastrons to record inquiries addressed to the ancestors of the ruling clan. The application of heat produced a crack in the bone or shell that was interpreted as a divine communication, and the political authority of the ruler derived in part from an ability to contact the ancestral spirits. In the oracle bones, the ruler's "shining" virtue correlated with an ability to secure the support of the ancestors, and for this reason the term for virtue has also been translated as "power" and understood as a form of "moral charisma." The practice of carrying out divinations and sacrifice to assure good fortune continued after the Shang, and broadened to address anthropomorphic deities and celestial officials as part of Chinese popular religions.

In the Zhou, Shang reliance on the approval of the "Highest Ancestors" (*Shangdi*) was redirected to a concern with the conditional guidance of Heaven. Bronze inscriptions (*jinwen*) from Western Zhou vessels commemorate honors bestowed in such a way as to reveal an elaborate scheme of sumptuary rituals, records whose location in tombs suggest that they were directed to the ancestors. Records in the *Classic of Documents* in the voice of the Zhou rulers explain how the Shang lost the support of Heaven through immoral and irreverent actions. The Zhou's own usurpation of the Shang is cast as a matter of complying with the mandate, and the Zhou rulers' resulting claim to the title of "Son of Heaven" (*tianzi*) became both the prototype for divinely sanctioned political authority in imperial times and a paradigm for the ideal relationship between the human and nonhuman worlds. Through ritual, the Zhou continued to draw a parallel between state hierarchy and family hierarchy, and to affirm the continuity of loyalty on the part of the inferior and kindness on the part of the superior, even after the death of the superior.

The ritual system of the Zhou encompassed myriad seasonal and occasional rites and defined role-specific behavior both at home and at court. The rites defined a pattern of complementary obligations, while they reinforced social and familial hierarchies. The regularity of ancestral sacrifice and the elaborate and expensive nature of court funeral ceremonies illustrate the importance placed on situating the mourner in a proper relationship with the ancestral spirits, a practice that likely served both a therapeutic and a protective function. The Zhou religious system, at least as it existed in the imagination of early imperial China, was based on an elaborate regimen of sacrificial observances. According to the "Methods of Sacrifice" (*Jifa*) chapter of the *Records of Ritual,* the Zhou state had altars for sacrifice to Heaven and Earth (*tan* and *zhe*), temples for sacrifice to the imperial ancestors (*zongmiao*), and platforms for sacrifice to the spirits of the soil and grain (*she* and *ji).* There were also altars to the seasons, cold and heat, sun and moon, stars, floods and drought, and the four directions. The same chapter records sacrifices to the "hundred spirits," those animating the "mountains and forests, rivers and valleys, rises and hills. They can generate clouds, make the wind and rain, and appear as monstrous beings." In keeping with the need to secure blessings for specific or generalized actions that animated Shang religious practice, the emphasis in Zhou observance emphasized appropriate action toward the spirit world, rather than gathering specific information from it. Texts like the *Zuo Commentary [to the Spring and Autumn]* (*Zuozhuan*) contain what are generally accepted to be retellings of ancient records of how rulers conducted divination and sacrifice to eliminate baleful omens such as droughts or illnesses connected with nature deities such as particular mountain and river spirits. Sometimes, in the *Zuo Commentary*, such sacrifices are condemned by an interlocutor who favors action directed at Heaven because the latter's reach is universal rather than local, as in the case of nature deities. Hierarchies in the pluralistic Zhou pantheon influence later religious developments, such as the Confucian veneration of Heaven and an emphasis on ritual purity. The particular henotheism of Zhou sacrificial practices formed the background for attempts at communicating with ancestral or celestial spirits to neutralize dangers from rogue or terrestrial spirits. In addition, elements of the language and form of the ritual purification (*zhaijie*) ceremony, entailing abstinence from certain foods and actions, turn up in later discussions of self-transformation.

Beyond their specific discussions of the sages' reception of the mandate and the necessity of ritual performance, the Zhou worldview also drew a connection between the two. The attitude of reverence (*jing*) in the presence of the ancestral spirits was the same one the *Classic of Documents* says the current ruler should have when listening to the words of the rulers of the past. More generally, proper ritual performance demonstrates reverence in the eyes of the ancestral spirits and of Heaven, in effect a domestication of the way that proper court behavior was evidence that the sages of antiquity were qualified to rule as kings. Historically, the qualities of familial piety (*xiao* and *di*) displayed by the sage king Shun's subjecting himself to harsh abuse at the hands of his father and elder brother was testimony to his virtue and qualities as ruler. The connection between political authority and ancestor worship that derived from the Zhou identity of clan and political authority is also demonstrated by Liu Zehua's observation that in the Zhou period, familial piety was a matter of revering both one's ancestors and parents and one's lineage founder. These elements of early Zhou religion were adapted and preserved by the classical tradition that grew out of the teachings of Kongzi, and they therefore represent a selective prehistory of Confucianism rather than a comprehensive portrayal of the Zhou religious landscape.

The degree to which Kongzi looked to Zhou institutions as a model in his teachings is apparent in the *Analects.* In the eighth century BCE, infighting and incursions on the western border forced the removal of the Zhou capital east from Hao to Luoyang, setting the stage for the two major divisions of the Eastern Zhou period (770–256 BCE): the Spring and Autumn period (722 – 481 BCE) and the Warring States period (403 – 221 BCE). By the sixth century BCE, the old Zhou polity was weakened and shared power with a set of increasingly autonomous states competing for authority, and both ritual forms and moral justifications for authority were often sacrificed in the face of military expediency. In the *Analects* (*Lunyu*), the text that today is identified most closely with the historical Kongzi, he nostalgically argues that the virtue of the rulers of Zhou was the highest of all (*Analects* 8.21), writing: "I follow Zhou" (*Analects* 3.13). In particular, he identified himself with the Duke of Zhou, whom he saw as the epitome of the gifted sage (*Analects* 8.11), and who appeared to him in his dreams (*Analects* 7.5). There is no question that such claims served to confer the authority of a usable past on Kongzi's teachings; at the same time, his re-conceptualization of systems and attitudes inherited from the Zhou was the heart of his project of developing a model for rulership and public service.

EARLY TRADITIONS SURROUNDING KONGZI AND HIS DISCIPLES. While the traditions of Confucianism contain many elements that predate Kongzi, the centrality of his role is illustrated by the fact that many of these components later became identified with his name. Observers outside of China have exaggerated this point by translating as "Confucian" a number of terms that do not reference Kongzi in the original Chinese, such as *Ru* (more accurately, classicists), the derivative terms *Rujia* and *Rujiao* (bibliographical and ceremonial sub-traditions based on classical texts and practices), *jingxue* (the exegesis of the classics), and even *daoxue* (the study of the indigenous Way, which overlaps with the English term neo-Confucianism). Narratives about Kongzi were among the focal points that these traditions used to clarify their own projects, although they were not the only ones used in this way. Defining Kongzi's life and thought was at the heart of the contest over the appropriation of his authority by these burgeoning multifocal traditions.

After Kongzi's death around 479 BCE, works purporting to record dialogs, teachings, and biographical narratives of the sage began to appear. Collections based on material from the early Zhou period, such as the songs of the *Classic of Odes* and the terse chronicles of the state of Lu in the *Spring and Autumn* (*Chunqiu*), were identified as having been edited by him. Recent archaeological discoveries confirm that narratives and chapters concerning Kongzi circulated independently in the fourth and third centuries BCE. The third century BCE collection *Han Feizi* records the existence of eight distinct disciple traditions and notes that what each group "adopted and discarded (from Kongzi) was different and contradictory, but each claimed to represent the authentic Kongzi." The project of taking these diverse sources and assembling a complete picture of Kongzi and his teachings was undertaken in earnest after the early imperial dynasties of Qin (221–206 BCE) and Han (206 BCE–220 CE) unified the Warring States–period patchwork of independent kingdoms that had grown up as Zhou central authority waned. Influential collections of dialogs and narratives organized in the second and first centuries BCE, such as the *Analects* and the *Records of Ritual,* were based on selections from disciple-specific traditions or independently circulating stories, as was the first biographical treatment of Kongzi in the *Records of the Historian* (*Shiji*), compiled around 100 BCE. Portraits of Kongzi transmitted through later history were generally based on principles of selection from this distant vantage point, several centuries after his death and after the transition to an imperial government. This is one reason why, while few call into question the historicity of Kongzi, there is growing scholarly awareness of the ways in which his teachings and biography have been mediated. This also explains an important facet of the emphasis in later Confucian scholarship on textual dating and authenticity. Debates over the provenance and age of individual works of antiquity are secondarily debates about the nature of the biography of Kongzi, and indeed about the very nature of his project and his teachings. The following section introduces how three influential early imperial collections selected and transmitted early materials associated with Kongzi, and then triangulates the views of self-transformation practice, theories of ritual performance, and ethics of government service implicit in these sources.

The earliest biographical arrangement of Kongzi materials, some of which overlap the *Analects*, was made by Sima Qian (c.145–c.86 BCE). Two chapters of his *Records of the Historian* portray Kongzi as an advisor to rulers and as a teacher who trained his disciples to become moral officials, a division that likely reflects two dominant narratives about Kongzi. In the "Hereditary House of Kongzi," Kongzi is portrayed as an advisor who, due to his own integrity and the jealousies that his abilities inspired, was forced to move from state to state in search of patronage. While Sima Qian generally placed treatments of individuals in the "arranged traditions" (*liezhuan*) section of the *Records of the Historian*, he placed Kongzi among the treatments of "hereditary noble lineages" (*shijia*), something that the Tang dynasty commentator Zhang Shoujie explained was because scholars and all those who cultivate themselves through the "six arts" (*liuyi*) revered Kongzi and recognized him as the epitome of sagehood. According to the "Hereditary House of Kongzi," Kongzi was born in the state of Lu and as a small child displayed an unusual interest in and knowledge of the rites, causing at least one member of the Lu nobility to seek his guidance in ritual forms. Kongzi was given the sobriquette Zhong Ni, literally "second-born Hill," because of a rise on his forehead. In Sima Qian's time, these aspects of the biography would have been read as omens of his extraordinary ability. In adulthood, however, Kongzi only rose to occupy technical and clerical offices, directing ceremonies and managing provisions and animals.

Sima Qian arranges Kongzi's advice to rulers about adhering to ritual and self-control in a narrative framework that stresses the way Kongzi was slandered, overlooked, or treated in a ritually improper way. Kongzi journeyed from Lu to Zhou, returned to Lu, and subsequently went through the states of Qi, Wei, Song, Zheng, Chen, Cai, and She in a futile search of a patron who would recognize his extraordinary abilities and heed his advice. The picture of how the age never recognized Kongzi's talents reflects Sima Qian's own self-conception as a victim of mistreatment by Emperor Wu of the Han (r. 140–87 BCE).

A second set of Kongzi narratives is related in the "Arranged Traditions of Zhong Ni's Disciples" chapter of the *Records of the Historian*, mostly instructive conversations arranged under the names and short biographies of each disciple. The names are divided into three categories: "virtuous actions" (*dexing*), "government service" (*zhengshi*), and "learning in cultural forms" (*wenxue*). In these conversations, particular attention is paid to the way Kongzi addressed the particular strengths and concerns of each of his students. The bipartite structure of the *Records of the Historian* reflects the fact that at the end of the second century BCE, Sima Qian was reliant on two kinds of dialogs: pedagogical ones transmitted through the disciple traditions and political anecdotes preserved in diverse Warring States sources.

The *Records of Ritual* mixes these two types of text in a composite collection that reflects the different genres and viewpoints surrounding ritual at the time of its collation in the early empire. The *Records of Ritual* was likely compiled in the first century BCE. Kongzi is cast as a ritual expert in many of its chapters, but there are at least three distinct ways in which he treats the subject. Chapters like "Tan Gong," and "Disciple Zeng asked" (*Zengzi wen*) record questions from disciples about the authenticity of specific funerary and sacrificial practices and Kongzi's definitive answers. These dialogs pay particular attention to issues such as the actions, clothing, gait, and carriages suitable to particular ranks, and relationships to the deceased. By contrast, the "Transformations of the Rites" (*Liyun*) and "Vessels of the Rites" (*Liqi*) chapters tend to historicize ritual practices in the context of the governance of the sage kings, explaining the function and adaptation of ritual. These chapters contain narratives about the proper attitude to ritual as well anthropologies that explain the reason for sacrifice, such as the "Transformations of the Rites" explanation of sacrificial ceremonies as attracting the spirits in order to secure the blessings of Heaven. A third set of chapters locates the rites less historically and more cosmologically. "Duke Ai asked" (*Aigong wen*), "Black Robes" (*Ziyi*), "Records of Dykes" (*Biaoji*), "Great Learning" (*Daxue*) and "Doctrine of the Mean" (*Zhongyong*) contain wide-ranging dialogs and essays stressing the importance of ritual hierarchies for social order, often relating this to notions of cosmic order. Ritual is related to good government by the assumption that proper behavior and correct measures on the part of a ruler create complementary responses on the part of the ruler's subjects. Indeed, the ability of the sage ruler to transform his people is only one aspect of the sage's special relation to Heaven that is explored in some of these chapters. Because it was collated in imperial China, the *Records of Ritual* contains several distinct layers that likely represent either different schools of thought or distinct stages in the development of early views on the nature of Kongzi's teachings on ritual.

Made up of compact statements and dialogs that are often only loosely related from one to the next, the twenty chapters of the *Analects* derive from the records of the disciple traditions. The dating of the *Analects* is controversial. Han dynasty historian Ban Gu (32–92 CE) dates it to the fifth century BCE, writing: "At the time, each disciple kept his own records. After the master died, the second-generation disciples together collated them, then considered and selected from among them." However, references to the title of the *Analects* only appear in works from the second century BCE; the earliest excavated version, the first commentaries, and evidence that it had taken on a fixed form come from the first century BCE. While there is no single theme in the *Analects*, many of its chapters see Kongzi exhort his disciples to pursue the noble ideal (*junzi*, often translated as "gentleman") by cultivating a set of moral dispositions. The description of the noble ideal often turns on the presence of particular ethical dispositions of benevolence (*ren*, a sensitivity to the personhood of others) and ritual propriety (*li*, regulating speech and demeanor as befits one's status). These two dispositions are intimately linked: Kongzi tells his disciple Yan Yuan, "To control one's self and return to ritual propriety is to act with benevolence" (*Analects* 12.1), while elsewhere he asks rhetorically, "Being human but not benevolent, how could this accord with the rites?" (*Analects* 3.3). At other times, the noble ideal of the *Analects* is distrustful of others' words when actions can also be examined, and it possesses a capacity to judge people and circumstances that comes from wisdom (*zhi*, a knowledge of the past that allows one to assess the present). Personally, the noble ideal is loath to speak and scrupulous about trustworthiness (*xin*, being true to one's word). In public life, the *Analects* expects the noble ideal to be steadfast in resisting coercion and preserving righteousness (*yi*, conducting oneself impartially and fairly) even if it imperils the prospects for advancement. Finally, in private life, the noble ideal is reflective about study and practices familial piety, because the constancy of both the self-transformation process and the omniscience of Heaven means that ethical action cannot be compartmentalized. In this way, the noble ideal cultivates the Way (*dao*), a normative path to personal or political perfection. The *Analects* is perhaps most concerned with the application of ritual and ethics in public life, and Kongzi continually examines the motives and conduct of his disciples from their preparation for an official career through their service in that career.

These three early imperial repositories of lore about Kongzi share significant features and derive from a common fund of stories in wide circulation, and are reinforced by more fragmentary accounts in Warring States texts and archaeologically discovered materials. Warring States collections of essays—such as the *Mencius* (*Mengzi* or *Meng Tzu*), *Xunzi* (also romanized as *Hsün Tzu*), and *Zhuangzi* (also romanized as *Chuang Tzu*)—all contain passages that credit Kongzi as the originator of their own perspectives, although sometimes the content of their teachings differ significantly from those in early imperial collections. Materials excavated in the 1990s from tombs sealed at the end of fourth century BCE include material from the *Records of Ritual* (e.g., the "Black Robes" chapter), alternate versions of chapters in the *Analects* (e.g., a text named "Zhong Gong" that appears to have been abridged as *Analects* 13.3), and new works (e.g., "Kongzi discusses the *Odes*," a pedagogical exegesis of selected poems in the *Classic of Odes*). Taken together with the collections described above, these works provide a more robust picture of early approaches to moral self-transformation, ritual performance and public service.

The course of self-transformation that Kongzi advocated is predicated on a model wherein a mastery of the classical arts, rites, and music leads to the development of a set of cultivated moral dispositions. Proficiency in the "six arts" of the rites, music, archery, charioteering, writing and mathematics led one to behave consistently with the noble ideal. Scholars of religious ethics like Philip J. Ivanhoe have treated the cultivation of dispositions like benevolence as an example of classical "virtue ethics" (since *de* is usually translated as "virtue," the term "excellence" will be used where one might apply the category of a virtue like the Greek arête in a comparative context). Characteristically for such a system, evaluation of actions is not based on outcomes but on the presence of authentic moral motivation. That is, Kongzi would criticize seemingly good actions that are really the result of desires for personal gain or fear of punishment. This is the basis for the famous condemnation of punishment in the *Analects*: "Lead them by government and equalize them through punishment, and people will know to avoid it but not to be ashamed. Lead them by virtue and equalize them through ritual, and they will have shame and so regulate themselves" (*Analects* 2.3). A contrast with this virtue ethics model is the radically different ethical system of Kongzi's rough contemporary Mozi (trad. 480–390 BCE, also romanized as Mo Tzu), who counseled rulers in defensive warfare and the frugal use of resources. Mozi's ethic looked only at the consequences and not the motivations of action. Chapter 16 of the posthumous collection *Mozi* rejects traditional norms like familial piety as partial and therefore unjust, arguing for impartial distribution of resources instead: "one must treat one's friend's body as if it were one's own, and one must treat one's friend's parent as if he or she was one's own." Because Mozi's cosmology held that good acts are automatically rewarded by Heaven, he had no patience for programs for the cultivation of excellences, such as chanting the *Classic of Odes* and practicing ritual forms. Conversely, Kongzi's advocacy of gradual training to develop dispositions was precisely because he held that good behavior did not always benefit the actor. The disciple Zixia's statement that "life and death are a matter of the mandate, while wealth and noble rank are a matter of Heaven" (*Analects* 12.5) illustrates Kongzi's redeployment of the Zhou concept of Heaven's mandate to describe the fragility of the moral person's situation in the world, a microcosm of the Zhou view of the contingency of divine support for the ruler.

Beyond the efficacy of ritual in the context of a program of personal self-transformation, Kongzi also justified reinstituting the ritual system of the Zhou on the basis of its social utility. The value of reverence, inherited from the Zhou, is an important facet of Kongzi's treatment of ritual (*Analects* 2.7), and it is applied not only to sacrificial contexts but also to the context of official service (*Analects* 13.19). With its emphasis on self-transformation, the *Analects* draws a distinction between formally proper ritual, and authentic ritual performance with proper feelings: "When one says 'The rites this, the rites that . . .' is it really only a matter of jade and silk?" (*Analects* 17.10). A related facet of Kongzi's discussions of ritual is his criticism of excessive sacrifice, either directed at ritually improper contemporary rulers (*Analects* 3.1, 3.6) or at those who sacrifice to other than their own ancestors (*Analects* 2.21). By contrast, chapters of the *Records of Ritual* that justify the rites based on cosmology argue that the rites replicate an ideal balance between humans and the ancestors and support a natural hierarchy in society that leads to harmony. In the "Duke Ai asked" chapter, Confucius tells the duke: "In order to enact good government one must first attend to ritual, because ritual is the root of good government." While ritual performance is theorized in several different ways, rarely is it justified by simple appeal to tradition.

The political perspective of the early dialogs borrows the notion of rule by virtue from Zhou religion but adapts it to the particular sociological status of Kongzi and his early disciples. No longer genuinely in the service of regional kings, the minor official Kongzi's education of his disciples effected the adoption of an unconventional set of values that rendered them immune to the temptation to take advantage of their official status. In the *Analects*, Kongzi explains: "Wealth and noble rank are what all people desire, but if they are not attained in a way consistent with the Way, then one cannot accept them" (*Analects* 4.4). When one of his disciples in the service of a wealthy clan helps them collect excessive taxes to augment their already exceptional wealth, Kongzi disavows him, and says: "It is now suitable for the younger disciples to shriek at him and play the drums to chastise him" (*Analects* 11.17). Kongzi stressed to his disciples that they not be ashamed of poverty, and that he himself preferred to be paid not in luxury items, but in meat, rejecting standards of conventional economic exchange but accepting an item of value in a sacrificial context. In a similar way, Kongzi observes: "The noble ideal understands righteousness, while the petty person understands profit" (*Analects* 4.15). The cultivation of the excellences is in effect an alternative system of value that renders initiates incorruptible in official contexts. This version of the Zhou notion of Heaven mandating rule by the virtuous was in effect an argument for administration by the benevolent, modified in a context in which kingship was effectively the product of military success.

SELF-TRANSFORMATION AND RULERSHIP IN THE FOURTH AND THIRD CENTURIES BCE. The florescence of diverse perspectives on politics, religion, and philosophy known in Chinese history as the "many masters and hundred experts" (*zhuzi baijia*), and included by Karl Jaspers in his description of the "Axial Age," led to the development of both alternatives to and elaborations of Kongzi's views. In this period, the pivot of disagreements over methods of government and personal self-transformation was a lively debate over the content of human nature (*xing*, the course of development characteristic of all members of a species or kind). Kongzi's defense of Zhou institutions was explicitly challenged by the moral skepticism of the *Zhuangzi* and the political absolutism of the *Han Feizi*, even while the *Mengzi* and *Xunzi* grounded it in distinct theories of human nature. Their adaptations demonstrated a growing attention to human psychology and to the mechanisms by which the inner cultivation of the sage was related to the external authority of the ruler. Because the *Mengzi* and *Xunzi* rhetorically situate themselves in the tradition of Kongzi's advocacy of the cultivation of moral dispositions, they are often seen as the second major stage of Confucian traditions.

The phrase "inside a sage and outside a king" (*neisheng waiwang*) is often invoked to refer to one of the central concerns of later Warring States texts: the need to examine and account for the link between self-transformation and rulership. This phrase is common to both ritual texts and late Warring States works like the *Zhuangzi*. Central to this inquiry were accounts of the sage kings of antiquity and theories about the origin and nature of sagehood. Two works that address this concern by taking related but ultimately different approaches are the excavated "Five Kinds of Action" (*Wuxing*) and the *Mencius*. Both texts locate four of Kongzi's cardinal excellences (benevolence, righteousness, wisdom, and ritual propriety) in cultivated dispositions present at birth in the inner mind (*xin*, the locus of cognition and emotion located in organ of the heart). However, they differ in the way they relate this to the debate over the exceptional characteristics of the sage.

The *Mencius* is attributed to the disciples of the fourth and third century BCE writer Mengzi (Meng Ke or Mencius, c. 380–c. 290 BCE), and both its content and form depict Mengzi as a latter-day Kongzi, an advisor to the rulers of different states and a teacher of various disciples. It embeds the character traits advocated in the *Analects* into a model of the body in which a disposition to morality is part of one's make-up at birth. "Sprouts" (*duan*) of moral reactions are already present in the inner mind, as the *Mencius* notes: "people have these four sprouts just like they have four limbs" (*Mencius* 2A6). Proof of their existence lies in the natural, spontaneous reaction to the sight of another person in danger, such as an infant about to fall in a well (*Mencius* 2A6). Yet the *Mencius* admits that it is possible that a person who is continuously exposed to the depredations of a hostile environment might end up as bereft of their original moral dispositions, like a bare mountainside whose trees and topsoil have been lost to deforestation (*Mencius* 6A8). For this reason, despite its common currency, it is simply not the case that the *Mencius* holds that "human nature is good" (*xing shan*). Instead, the text argues that the inner mind has dispositions to goodness at birth, which need to be cultivated in order to flourish. What the *Mencius* does say that is not a part of Kongzi narratives is that the biological model in which all people are born, with the sprouts of morality in their inner mind, is what makes sagehood a possibility for all people (even members of the border nations) at birth (cf. *Mencius* 4B1). Numerous times the *Mencius* contains statements to the effect that the sage king "Shun was a person, and I, too, am a person," (*Mencius* 3A1, 4B28, 4B32, 6A7, 6B2). Yet the fact that people begin life with the same sprouts of moral reactions does not assure they all end up as sages.

Archaeologists have excavated two manuscript versions of the "Five Kinds of Action," one in Hunan province in 1973 and one in Hubei province in 1993. A complex, and at times obscure treatise on moral psychology, this text adds a fifth term associated with "the Way of the cosmos" (*tiandao*, with *tian* here translated as "cosmos" connoting a naturalistic version of the previously anthropomorphic "Heaven") to the four cardinal excellences listed in chapter two of the *Mencius.* In positioning "sagehood" as the culmination of the human excellences, the "Five Kinds of Action" addresses problems of plural and conflicting values common to virtue ethics systems by arguing that sagehood harmonizes moral actions in a way that eliminates potential quandaries. The Five Kinds of Action also develops a metaphorical vocabulary to describe the way that sagehood is transmitted across generations through "hearing," establishing a model in which cultural forms that express the intentions of the sages of the past can "activate" people in the present similar to the way one instrument can cause another to sound through the phenomenon of resonance. The resultant changes in an activated person's inner mind are observable as changes in the voice, according to section six of the "Five Kinds of Action": "if one is sharp-eared then one can hear the Way of the noble ideal. If one can hear the Way of the noble ideal then one will have a jade tone." This view of sagehood as the result of a special endowment from the cosmos, making a person physically different from others, takes a step away from the universality of the more biologically oriented *Mencius* in explicating its model of self-transformation.

The above descriptions of an intuitive, and at times mystical, approach to self-transformation illustrates the affinities between certain threads of Warring States Confucianism and texts such as the fourth through second century BCE *Zhuangzi,* classified as "Daoist" (*daojia*). The phrase "the Way of the cosmos" is part of the basis of the *Zhuangzi*'s challenge to methods of self-transformation associated with the Zhou founders and with Kongzi. Much of that composite text advocates a return to an innate human nature, one imagined to have existed prior to the forced imposition of the distinctions inculcated by ritual performance. Reading the term for Heaven as something closer to modern conceptions of the cosmos, the *Zhuangzi* advocates that people return to an original, spontaneous, and Heaven-given human nature. By elevating a cosmically endowed disposition to sagacity above the four innate dispositions of the *Mencius,* the "Five Kinds of Action" argues that for the sage, the cultivation of these dispositions may lead to a spontaneous level of action in harmony with the cosmos. While the author of "Five Kinds of Action" is unknown, there are other early texts that associate similar views with Kongzi. The phrase "the Way of the cosmos" only has one controversial appearance in the *Analects,* but it plays a significant part in the chapters of the *Records of Ritual* that explain ritual in cosmological terms. In the "Duke Ai asks" chapter, when the duke asks why the noble ideal is to value the Way of the cosmos, Kongzi's reply points out the ways in which the ideal acts like the sun and moon, including "not acting intentionally yet completing things, as with the Way of the cosmos." This self-negating language recalls a section of another chapter of that text, "Kongzi was at leisure" (*Kongzi xianju*), and a parallel passage in an early-third-century excavated text called "Father and Mother to the People" (*Min zhi fumu*), which record Kongzi's advice that the ruler put into practice "soundless music, disembodied ritual, and sacrifice without offerings." This apophatic mode implies an early stage of cross-fertilization between Confucianism and its erstwhile Daoist critics.

The intuitionist aspects of the *Mencius* may have been similar to the *Zhuangzi,* but they are also the key to the text's disagreements with the *Xunzi.* The contents of the *Xunzi* are diverse, but the chapters thought to be authentically the work of Xunzi (Xun Qing, c.310–c.220 BCE) are chiefly essays that argue that sagehood can only be accomplished by the process of externally oriented habituation through ritual and music. According to the *Records of the Historian,* Xun Qing was patronized by the King of Qi at Jixia from 285 – 275 BCE, where he held a ritual-related post. The "Encouraging Learning" (*Quan xue*) chapter of the *Xunzi* explains that: "In terms of its process, [learning] begins with reciting the classics and ends with reading the rites. In terms of its significance, [learning] begins with being a candidate for office, and it ends with being a sage." Where the *Mencius* locates morality in the inner mind, the *Xunzi* looks to cultural forms. Since human nature has none of the dispositions that *Mencius* thought it did, society is wont to fall into chaos as people compete for resources to sate their unlimited appetites. Only the Zhou solution to this predicament, the rites and music developed by the sage kings, hold the possibility of changing behavior. In addition to ritual and music, a person needs the influence of a teacher to habituate the proper set of reactions to external stimuli, in effect transforming the person's affective dispositions (*qing*). The *Xunzi*'s view of affective dispositions dovetails with that of an early third century excavated text called "A discussion of human nature and affective dispositions" (*Xingqing lun*) which holds that "study and acculturation shift one's intentions" and that the shift is not simply a matter of human nature. By properly training a person in ritual, music, and the classics, one may systematically alter affective responses to external stimuli and in so doing change that person's behavior. Similar to the excavated text's denial that self-transformation is only a matter of human nature, the *Xunzi* directly criticizes the quasi-mystical notion of "hearing" the Way of the noble ideal: "Just because their eyes are clear-sighted and their ears sharp of hearing, does not mean they understand what they are taught." Instead, the text celebrates the effect of ritual and music in both limiting one's appetites and transforming them into an intention to pursue sagehood.

Epistemologically, the two alternatives provided in the *Mencius* and *Xunzi* differ in where they locate morality: in the inner mind versus in the cultural creations of the sage kings. While the *Mencius* enjoyed a renaissance in the Song dynasty (960–1279 CE), the views of the *Xunzi* exerted more influence in the early imperial period. In part, this influence was through the secondary influence of Xunzi's student Prince Fei of the state of Han (c.280–c.233 BCE), associated with the third century "Legalist" (*fajia*) work *Han Feizi.* Like the *Xunzi,* the *Han Feizi* argues that people struggle and compete for their livelihoods because of population growth combined with a scarcity of goods, and that one must adopt the most efficacious system to avoid a state of social chaos. In a way more similar to some sections of the *Zhuangzi,* however, the *Han Feizi* concluded that, "benevolence and righteousness were useful in ancient times, but not in the present." Instead, a ruler should apply a strict code of penal law and a precise set of assignments for officials indexed to a clear set of models of behavior (*fa,* a term also used to refer to law). While this conclusion, giving up as it did on the possibility of self-cultivation for the majority, was diametrically opposed to that of his mentor, Prince Fei shared many of Xunzi's assumptions about the malleability of human behavior and the importance of training. This was a point on which most early imperial writers also agreed.

The *Han Feizi*'s influence on the Qin dynasty (221–206 BCE) may be seen in its detailed legal codes, a large part of which was adopted in the following Han dynasty, to the consternation of some who worried about its effect on people's ability to develop a sense of shame (cf. *Analects* 2.3 above). This is just one of the many ways in which social and economic changes in the early imperial period exerted pressure on the reception of the texts and practices of the Zhou as revitalized by Kongzi, and as grounded in human nature by the *Mencius* and *Xunzi.*

HAN CONFUCIAN TRADITIONS AND THE INFLUENCE OF THE IMPERIAL STATE. The 221 BCE unification under the Qin led to major changes in the system of patronage and in the nature of official service, two major aspects of the social background of the pre-imperial works associated with Kongzi, Mengzi, and Xunzi. Not only would Kongzi's movement from state to state as he fled unprincipled patrons have been impossible in the unified empire, but the rejection of conventional economic exchange within the master-disciple community was undermined by the bureaucratization of the fields in which advisors, teachers, and experts in the classics had once specialized. In addition, the link between self-transformation and sagehood became a sensitive topic, since the imperial clan's reliance on hereditary succession did not fit well with transmitted narratives that celebrated nonhereditary transfers of power based on virtue. In the following treatment of the Qin, Western Han (206 BCE – 9 CE), and Eastern Han (25 CE–220 CE) dynasties, the emphasis will be on the ways that the legacy of Kongzi was appropriated by the imperial state, and on early attempts to transmit the classics through independent channels.

As the state took control of access to the vocations of advising rulers, and to the teaching of potential officials based on expertise in the rites, music, and classics, service as an imperial official was increasingly associated with mastery of the texts and practices that Kongzi had refashioned out of the cultural memory of the Zhou. The Qin and early Han emperors appointed Erudites *(boshi)* as experts in important classical texts, even though Sima Qian's *Records of the Historian* relates the story that the Han founder, Emperor Gao, was not very fond of the scholar-officials of his age. Gao remarked that since he had unified the empire on horseback he had little need for the classics of *Odes* and *Documents.* The major institutionalization of the study of those classics did not happen until two imperial edicts were issued by Emperor Wu (r. 140–87 BCE). A 136 BCE edict added Erudites in the *Classic of Documents, Classic of Ritual* (probably a reference to the *Rituals of Zhou*), and *Classic of Changes* (*Yijing*) to the existing ones in Master Gongyang's commentary to the *Spring and Autumn* (*Chunqiu Gongyangzhuan*) and the *Classic of Odes.* In 124 BCE, he established an Imperial Academy (*taixue*) under the supervision of the Master of Rites (*taichang*), modeled on the institutions of the early Zhou. The Imperial Academy functioned to evaluate a candidate's knowledge of these Five Classics (*wujing*) to determine their suitability for service in office. In less than a generation, however, critics like Sima Qian offered veiled criticisms of the way in which the institutionalization of the study of the classics had co-opted the tradition that he traced back to Kongzi. Many of the Western Han writers that are today identified as Confucian were celebrated in their day primarily for their expertise in the classics and their assembly of collections of explanatory material about the classics. Examples are Fu Sheng (fl. 200 BCE), an expert in the *Classic of Documents,* and Han Ying (c. 200–120 BCE), an expert in the *Classic of Odes,* who both served as Erudites.

Two particularly influential Western Han exegetes were Jia Yi (200–168 BCE) and Dong Zhongshu (c.179–c.104 BCE), both of whom adapted thinking about cultivating excellences to the new imperial cosmology of the Han. In the early empire, the epistemological project of synthesizing "many masters and hundred experts" texts and different regional practices, was conceptualized as a search for an overarching "Way" behind the validity and efficacy of what were at one time competing schemes. In his essay titled "Protecting and Tutoring," Jia Yi, the outspoken Erudite and Palace Grandee for Emperor Wen (180–157 BCE), explains the failure of short-lived Qin dynasty as being a matter of failing to value yielding and righteousness, and of abrogating ritual in favor of punishment. At the same time, in his ethical theory Jia Yi accepted the idea that self-transformation is a matter of an externally oriented habituation: "The fate of the people of the world depends upon the crown prince and, in turn, the competence of the crown prince is determined by early instruction and the selection of the prince's attendants." In accepting the *Xunzi*'s understanding of the origins of morality, Jia Yi well represents the Han view that human nature is malleable and self-transformation a matter of practice. In the Han, Dong Zhongshu was most famous for his interpretation and transmission of the Gongyang commentary to the *Spring and Autumn*, but today he is recognized as the person who adapted Kongzi's ethics to the Han belief that "the cosmos and human beings resonate with one another" (*tianren ganying*). In his discussion of the human nature debate in "An in-depth investigation into names" (*Shencha minghao*), Dong Zhongshu used the dualistic model of a balance between the feminine and masculine principles of *yin* and *yang* to effect a compromise in which affective dispositions (which need to be regulated) and human nature (which may be good, but needs to be awoken) together are responsible for moral behavior. The Warring States controversy between the *Mencius* and *Xunzi* was thus bypassed by a cosmologically justified compromise view of self-transformation. Like Jia Yi, Dong Zhongshu was less interested in identifying the content of human nature than describing the correct environment and method for self-transformation.

Following the brief interregnum of the Xin dynasty (9–23 CE), the Eastern Han saw the maturation of trends begun in the first centuries of the early empire, magnifying the stature of Kongzi both in educational and religious contexts. Besides establishing fourteen new Erudites and continuing the practice of basing the official examinations on texts associated with Kongzi, students at regional schools and scholars at the Imperial Academy sacrificed to Kongzi as the founder of the scholarly traditions. Emperor Ming (r. 57–75 CE) combined the sacrifice to Kongzi with sacrifices to the Sage's disciples in 59 CE. Observances at the Master's birthplace were first augmented by official sacrifices at the capital in 241 CE. In the first century BCE, the imperial court began to favor a compilation that included shorter pieces long associated with Kongzi, the *Analects*, in contexts such as the education of the crown prince. The Eastern Han exegete Zheng Xuan (127–200 CE), who is credited with commenting on eighty texts and established an authoritative school of *Analects* interpretation, claimed to have been visited by Kongzi in a dream. Other Han works, such as Yang Xiong's (53 BCE–18 CE) imitation of the *Analects* called the *Model Sayings* (*Fayan*), the partially extant *Records of Kongzi in the Three Courts* (*Kongzi sanchao ji*), a lost eight-chapter work called *Zheng's Treatises* (*Zhengzhi*) devoted to Zheng Xuan's answers to questions about the *Analects*, and the *Sayings of Kongzi's School* (*Kongzi jiayu*) attributed to Wang Su (195–256 CE) show that a connection with Kongzi was of increasing interest to writers and readers, even as Kongzi was increasingly invoked by the imperial state.

At the same time, Kongzi was also a potent symbol for those who questioned the prerogatives of the imperial state. In the Western Han, a number of non-official schools provided alternatives to the official network, beginning with the second-century example of the unjustly punished imperial advisor, Master Shen. Shen was an expert in the *Classic of Odes* who established a school after retiring to his home in Kongzi's old state of Lu and became recognized as a teacher of the major Han exegetes of that classic. By the Eastern Han, the *History of the Latter Han* (*Hou Hanshu*) records that the *Odes* specialist Wei Ying had several thousand registered students. Besides the popularity of private academies for the teaching of the Five Classics, a related phenomenon was the development of a set of prophetic texts ancillary to each of those classics. The reign of the Eastern Han founder, Emperor Guangwu (r. 25–57 CE), began in an atmosphere strongly influenced by a view of Kongzi as the "pure king" (*suwang*) who had encoded his method of rulership between the lines of the classic *Spring and Autumn* chronicle. Not only Guangwu, but other pretenders to the imperial crown sought to ground their claims to authority in prophecies associated with Kongzi from texts with titles like *Kong Qiu's Secret Classic* (*Kong Qiu mijing*). The intellectual historian Feng Youlan observed of the Han view of Kongzi that "if these views had prevailed, Kongzi would have held in China a position similar to that of Jesus Christ." These prophecies became the models for a new genre of writing called "apocrypha" *(chenwei),* actually a combination of two types of work: "charts and proofs" (*tuchen*) or prophecy texts and "weft books" (*weishu*) or texts ancillary to the classics. The many texts in the latter category constitute a shadowy complement to each of the Five Classics, often using numerology and correlations to obliquely comment on the relations of the classic to kingship.

MEDIEVAL CONFUCIAN TRADITIONS AND THE ENCOUNTER WITH BUDDHISM. The secret methods of a prophetic Kongzi must have been especially attractive in an Eastern Han dynasty weakened by a combination of natural disasters, infighting between eunuchs, aristocratic clans and the ruling house, and religious rebellions. Following the gradual demise of central authority in the second century CE, the strands of official and unofficial Confucianism responded in different ways to the initial stages of major changes in the Chinese religious landscape. While sacrifices connected with Kongzi continued in the Imperial Academy in Luoyang, the city was also home to the first translators of Buddhist sūtras from the West, and to refugees fleeing the rebellions in the Southwest and Northeast that eventuated in the community of healers that became the basis for the Celestial Masters (*Tianshi*) tradition of organized Daoism (*daojiao*). As the Han gave way to the Six Dynasties period (222–589 CE), few would have predicted that it would be four centuries until a similarly unified dynasty would emerge. Spurred on by the way in which Buddhism's independent institutional existence allowed it to maintain its integrity without relying on a precarious social organization, the other previously diffuse traditions emerged from this period of disunity having copied those characteristics to become part of the "Three Teachings" (*sanjiao*): Confucianism, Buddhism, and Daoism.

Records of the early reception of Buddhism in China are limited to brief mentions in official histories, providing only occasional glimpses of the way that it affected culture outside the imperial court. Some of these indicate that Buddhist practice was first received as a method of controlling desires along the lines of early Daoist practices like "preserving the one" (*shouyi*). The response of classical scholars to Buddhism changed during the Six Dynasties, with initial strategies of accommodation to other traditions giving way to criticism. While exegetes like He Yan (190–249 CE) and Wang Bi (226–249 CE) of the Wei (220–265 CE) dynasty developed a hybrid "Study of the Mystery" (*Xuanxue*, also translated as "Abstruse Learning" or "Mysterious Learning") that integrated elements from works like the *Zhuangzi*, scholar officials in the Eastern Jin (317–420 CE) and Southern Dynasties periods (420–529 CE) developed a broad attack on Buddhist cosmology. Study of the Mystery applied classical exegetical principles to the mysteries of the *Classic of Changes*, the *Laozi*, and the *Zhuangzi*. It also applied terms deriving from the latter texts, such as "naturalness" (*ziran*) and "nothingness" (*wu*), to the understanding of classical texts like the *Analects*. Finally, in what some scholars argue is an accommodation to Buddhism, but which also owes much to the interpretations of the *Classic of Changes*, Study of the Mystery drew new ontological distinction such as those between "substance" (*ti*) and "function" (*yong*), with which one may distinguish between the essential featureless substance of a thing, containing all of its potential permutations, and its function in a given situation at a specific time and place. The sage was able to realize the identity of substance and function, and thereby adapt a knowledge of the past to any situation in the future. While Study of the Mystery had a major influence in Six Dynasties period commentaries, it also rather quickly attracted criticism from Confucian scholars in their official capacities. The conservative reaction is seen in writings attributed to Sun Sheng (302–373 CE), a chronicler of the early Six Dynasties period who attacked the Study of the Mystery claim that the Daoist patriarch Laozi was a sage comparable with Kongzi, and who argued against the notion that any aspect of consciousness could survive death (as Buddhist cosmology held). Fan Ning (339–401 CE) specifically criticized Wang Bi for allowing "benevolence and righteousness to sink into darkness," holding that Kongzi's "subtle" or "esoteric" (*wei*) doctrines could be learned from the study of the early commentaries to the *Spring and Autumn*.

Following the division of the former Han state into separate lines of successive kingdoms in the north and south from the fifth and sixth centuries, the continuity of interpretive traditions became even more closely associated with the careers of individual scholars. On the popular level, this period is identified with the growth and consolidation of Buddhism, the accelerated translation of Sanskrit texts, and the increased, accuracy of translations by Kumārajīva (344–409 CE) and his disciple Seng Zhao (374–414 CE) led to a sense of its deeper differences from Daoism. The transmission and exegesis of the legacy of the Zhou as synthesized by Kongzi continued in official schools and private academies, but as imperial patronage became increasingly unreliable, more modest goals of consolidation and preservation took precedence. The retrospective concern with preserving the order of the Zhou and Han also contributed to a turn toward bibliography, taxonomy, and the assembly of comprehensive commentaries on the classics. Nevertheless, the Liang Erudite Huang Kan (488–545 CE) surpassed the precedent set by He Yan by not only assembling the glosses of prior commentators on the *Analects*, but also incorporating them into his own synthetic interpretation of the text based in part of the *Xunzi*'s view of human nature and affective dispositions. Individual courts such as the Liang (502–557 CE) continued to establish Erudites and authorize textual lineages in the classics, while others like the Cheng Han (302–347 CE) in the southwest derived their authority from association with Daoist lineages. Famous anti-Buddhist polemics were written by Fan Zhen (450–510 CE) and Xing Shao (496–c. 563 CE), and the competition between the Three Teachings for patronage was institutionalized in a set of debates in the Northern Qi (550–557 CE) about the relative merits of different traditions.

Even while nominal affiliation with one of the three teachings became increasingly important for individuals intent on securing patronage, the pluralistic atmosphere led to cross-fertilization of doctrines and practices between the traditions. Critics of elements of Buddhism like Liu Jun (462–521 CE) enlisted aspects of Daoist cosmology when he refuted the Buddhist notion of karma. Liu Jun argued that natural endowments of pneumas and unpredictable environmental influences determined the outcome of people's lives, reading the Zhou notion of the "mandate of Heaven" in terms of the Study of the Mystery notion of "naturalness." Other scholars consciously sought to bring Buddhist ideas into Confucianism. Examples include Yan Zhitui's (b. 531 CE) integration of the "five precepts" (*wujie*) of Buddhism into discussions of ethical behavior and Wang Tong's (584 – 617 CE) advocacy of a unification of the Three Teachings. In addition, the very terms of debates with Buddhism shifted the Confucian discourse toward issues like cosmology and the social consequences of religious institutions, and away from late Warring States concerns with moral psychology and the nature of self-transformation. It was only after the reunification of China in the sixth century CE and the development of a nativist impulse to revive the pre-Buddhist transmission of Confucianism that the first attempts were made to recover those notions and use them to create "indigenous" alternatives to increasingly popular Buddhist and Daoist practices.

TANG AND SONG CONFUCIAN TRADITIONS AND THE STUDY OF THE INDIGENOUS WAY. While the idea of interpretive lineages had been a part of Confucianism since the institutionalization of the study of the classics in the early empire, the reunification under the Sui (581–618 CE) and Tang dynasties (618–907 CE) saw the rise of more general conceptions of the "transmission of the Way" (*daotong*) and the "transmission of good governance" (*zhengtong*) that had been abandoned during the preceding period of disunity. When Tang writers attempted to rejuvenate classical ideals in an effort to recover a transmission from the sage-kings that had not been corrupted by foreign doctrines, they began to look outside the canon of the Five Classics for records of the early period. Han Yu (768–824) traced the transmission of the Way from the ancient sage kings to the rulers of the Zhou dynasty to Kongzi and then to Mengzi. Later writers such as Pi Rixiu (833–883 CE) and Liu Kai (947–1000 CE) amended the transmission so as to identify the first figure in the revival of the transmission as Wang Tong, but they also identified Han Yu as Wang's successor. In addition to attacking the validity of Buddhist ideas of karma and rebirth, Han Yu's rhetoric also centered on the proper origins of knowledge, holding that Buddhist traditions were invalid because they did not derive from the Way of the ancient sage kings. As a result, Buddhism lacked the proper connection between knowledge and action, and so contradicted Confucian values of ritual propriety and social engagement. Tang writers like Han Yu and Li Ao (d. c. 844 CE) began to reweave disparate strands of the traditions associated with Kongzi in such a way as to emphasize earlier concerns with idealism and human nature.

Complementing this classical revival, the emperors of the Tang established an official network of temples dedicated to Kongzi in all prefectural and county schools, while simultaneously supporting and exercising control over Daoism and Buddhism. Yan Shigu (581–645 CE) was commissioned by Emperor Taizong (626–649 CE) to direct the compilation of an authoritative edition and commentary on the Five Classics, resulting in the "Corrected Meanings of the Five Classics" (*wujing zhengyi*), which took sixteen years to complete. During the Tang, however, the classics began to take second seat to the revival of interest in Warring States "many masters and hundred experts" texts. In an atmosphere that acknowledged a plural approach to the traces of the sage kings, influential figures like Liu Zongyuan (773–819 CE) applied a similar approach to Buddhism when he criticized Han Yu's sole focus on the social effect of monastic institutions. Liu Zongyuan wrote that Chan (in Japan, *Zen*) Buddhism as expressed through Huineng's (638–713) *Platform Sūtra of the Sixth Patriarch* (*Liuzu tanjing*), with its condemnation of popular practices in favor of reflection in order to remove the desires that obscure self-nature, was in agreement with Confucianism on some key points, such as what he characterized as the *Mencius*'s view that "human nature is good." At the same time, the Tang expanded the corpus of the imperial service examination system to include texts like the *Zhuangzi*, as pre-imperial texts of all kinds were increasingly seen as a means to recover the ancient past.

In the Northern Song dynasty (960–1127 CE) this culminated in an official redefinition of the canon, in part through the efforts of the pivotal figure Zhu Xi (1130–1200 CE). The Five Classics gave way to the "Four Books" (*sishu*), which elevated the *Analects* to canonical status along with the *Mencius* and two chapters of the *Records of Ritual*: the "Great Learning" and the "Doctrine of the Mean." The latter two works had already attracted interest both inside and outside Confucian traditions, in part because the interplay between psychology and cosmology implicit in their use of concepts such as the quality of sincerity (*cheng*) linking the sage to the cosmos, and the strategy of "attending to oneself in solitude" (*shendu*), read by Zhu as a type of enhanced self-scrutiny. Read in this way, these works lent themselves to the concerns and practices of the time. Zhu Xi held that each of the four was written in a different generation, and so each represented a successive stage in the transmission of the Way. The four began with Kongzi's version in the *Analects*, followed by the disciple Zengzi's "Great Learning," the second generation disciple Zisi's "Doctrine of the Mean," and finally Zisi's student Mengzi's *Mencius*. Even though the canon no longer centered on the Zhou classics associated with Kongzi, this reading of the Four Books illustrated the way that the interpretation of the Way changed from one generation to the next, and so shed light on the process of teaching and learning in an inductive fashion. As Song interpretations of the Four Books became the basis of the imperial examination system, the reception of the classics was dramatically changed through the imposition of Zhu Xi's new interpretive orthodoxy.

While Song writers developed a new interpretive paradigm for recovering the meaning of pre-Buddhist texts, the method was only partially developed from the vocabulary of early texts themselves. In particular, the dual concepts of "principle" (*li*, a different character than the *li* for ritual) and "matter" (*qi*, a neutral description of the animating pneumas of the cosmos that came to be especially associated with human desires) were central to Zhu Xi's reading of the Four Books, even though their currency in Confucian traditions largely dates from early imperial times. Zhu Xi was the son of a local official who was exposed to Chan Buddhism, but at twenty he turned his attention to the classical scholarship of the Cheng brothers (Hao, 1032–1085 CE and Yi, 1033–1107 CE) and their new explanation of human nature. Scholars sometimes trace their explanation to Zhou Dunyi (Zhou Lianxi, 1017–1073 CE) and Zhang Zai's (Zhang Zihou, 1020–1077 CE) conception of a "supreme ultimate" (*taiji*). Zhou Dunyi's supreme ultimate imbues all things, both animate and inanimate, but expressed in its purest state it is simply the nature of human beings, as outlined in his "Explanation of the Diagram of the Supreme Ultimate" (*Taijitu shuo*). The Chengs developed and elevated the notion of human nature to subsume related notions of fate, mind, affective dispositions, the Way, and the cosmos. Cheng Yi held that morality inheres in the part of one's nature that is an expression of the natural pattern of principle, but is obscured by material. "Settling one's nature" (*ding xing*) and cultivating an attitude of reverence refines the matter of the inner mind, making it possible to discover the purity of cosmic principle contained therein. Because human nature, once settled, reflects the same cosmic principle that underlies ritual and the

Way, social hierarchies implicit in the rites are then also implicit in the cosmos.

Zhu Xi adopted the Cheng brothers' view of a human nature that contains cosmic principle, and integrated this with a concrete approach to self-transformation. For this reason, Zhu's rereading of Confucian traditions is sometimes called the "Study of Principle" (*lixue*), or the Cheng-Zhu school. Some scholars have applied terms like *rationalist* or *metaphysical* to what has also been called Zhu Xi's "neo-Confucian" position. While these terms fail to capture certain aspects of the cosmological basis for Zhu Xi's readings, it is true that human nature was an expression of a cosmic principle that transcended the category of human beings. Zhu Xi's noble ideal attains benevolence through discovery of the cosmic principle that had been understood by past sages, and so self-transformation was a matter of rediscovering their system of ritual and the study of the classics. To accomplish this, he promoted a program that combined quiet sitting (*qingzuo*) to settle the inner mind and a method of studying the classics that stressed the need to "penetrate things" (*gewu*). "Penetrating things" is a phrase adapted from a description of the way the ancient sages moved from self-transformation to ordering the state in the "Great Learning," and for Zhu Xi it was the method that allows one to "fully comprehend principle" *(qiongli).* In engaging the affairs and things of the past, "penetrating things" depends on fostering a resonance between the principle in the subject's mind and the principle of the object being interpreted. According to Chen Lai, one need not experience actual situations or develop concrete rules, but instead one must develop the capacity to infer such rules from study and ethical practice. A cross between meditation and hermeneutics, this view of learning through mutual activation meant that exegesis was a crucial part of the process of becoming a moral person. Zhu Xi established an academy called "White Deer Hollow" (*Bailu dong*), where moral instruction, commentary, and sacrifice were all part of the curriculum. While Zhu Xi was critical of study undertaken in order to attain office, graduates of his academy went on to take the civil service examination, and in the middle of the thirteenth century his commentaries came to be regarded as the best guarantee of success on the examination.

While a variety of factors, including nativism, led to this emphasis on recovery of an indigenous Way, no scholarly consensus exists on the degree to which Zhu's reconceptualization itself was influenced by Buddhism. In part this is because underlying issues of cultural identity are still being contested. The lack of consensus is also because the possibility of isolating purely "Confucian" and "Buddhist" figures in the whirling dance of translated Sanskrit sūtras, hybrid Chinese Buddhist works, Buddhist commentaries on pre-Buddhist classics, and Daoist-influenced anti-Buddhist polemics, is so remote. It is true that some of the central differences between late imperial Confucianism and what came before it—such as the notion of the recovery of "cosmic principle" or an "original inner mind" prior to its becoming obscured by matter—appear to show a movement in the direction of Chan Buddhism. However, even critics of Zhu Xi, such as the twentieth century "New Confucian" (*xin Ru*) Mou Zongsan (1909–1995), rejected the notion that the Song revival was "equal parts Confucian and Buddhist" (*yang Ru yin Shi*). Mou argued that while the two traditions shared certain generic conceptual schemes and attitudes to practice, these were external to the distinctly Confucian inner essence of Zhu Xi's thought. On one level, Mou is echoing Cheng Hao's Song dynasty critique of Buddhism—that it includes comportment by which to control oneself internally, but not the excellences by which to order oneself externally. On another level, his testimony is itself evidence of how a tradition predicated on the intergenerational transfer of sagely knowledge resists the imposition of models that call into question the integrity of this transfer. What is certain is that in scholastic conflicts throughout the early imperial period, the accusation of Buddhist influence was a partisan charge leveled against most Confucian writers. Zhu Xi himself hesitates in accepting Xie Liangzuo's (1050–c.1121 CE) use of the term "awakening" (*jue*) to explain benevolence because it has too much of a Chan Buddhist flavor. The compilation of his writings compiled by his disciples called *Classified Utterances of Master Zhu* (Zhuzi yulei) contains condemnations of the writings of Zhu Xi's contemporary Lu Jiuyuan (Lu Xiangshan, 1139–1193 CE) along the same lines. Lu Jiuyuan's call for a return to the "inner mind" is ridiculed as revealing a lack of understanding of the *Analects* phrase "control one's self and return to ritual propriety," as well as a neglect of the importance of the records of past sages and worthies. As such, "inner mind" was considered nothing more than Chan Buddhism.

Zhu Xi's "Study of Principle" became the orthodoxy for the study of the classics through the institution of the civil examination system, yet even after the abolition of that system, his commentaries continued to be regarded as authoritative. Imperial edicts in 1415 and 1715 led to the sponsorship of the issue and reissue of versions of *The Great Collection on Human Nature and Principle* (*Xingli daquan*) based on Zhu's writings. In part this was a testament to his own exegetical flair and the clarity of his presentation. Yet despite a major challenge in the Ming dynasty (1368–1644 CE), the dominance of the "Study of Principle" continued well into the Qing dynasty (1644–1911 CE), in part because it provided a model that fused scholarship with practice, and in part because it revived the early goals of moral self-transformation without challenging dynastic authority.

MING AND YUAN CONFUCIAN TRADITIONS AND THE RELATION BETWEEN PRACTICE AND POLITICS. In the Yuan (1206–1368 CE) and Ming dynasties, the gap between official service and the study of the classics was reflected in the critique of a lack of social engagement on the part of "School of Principle" adherents made by Wang Yangming (born Wang Shouren, or Wang Bo'an, 1472–1529 CE), the major figure in the alternative "Study of the Inner Mind" (*Xinxue*) tradition. Although the Yuan Dynasty was ruled by the Mongols, a dual-track civil service examination system was reinstituted in 1314, and the curriculum for both Chinese and non-Chinese tracks included "School of Principle" commentaries on the Four Books, causing it to gain wide currency. Yuan scholar officials, like Jin Lüxiang (Jin Jifu, 1232–1303 CE), a representative of the southern Jinhua school who accentuated the importance of commentary in the study of the classics, with few exceptions saw themselves as continuing in the "School of Principle" tradition.

When Zhu Yuanzhang (1328–1398 CE), the founding emperor of the Ming, replaced the Mongol Yuan with a highly centralized and autocratic state, his xenophobia and anti-intellectualism boded at best a continuation of the conservative Yuan scholarship. Yet even the first generation of Ming scholars showed a greater willingness to innovate within the "Study of Principle" framework than might have been expected. Xue Xuan (Xue Dewen, 1392–1464 CE), associated with the Hedong School of the "Study of Principle," served in office until retiring to teach for the last eight years of his life. He revived the idea of "returning to human nature" (*fuxing*), promoted by Li Ao in the Tang dynasty, in such a way as to deny the notion that principle preceded matter and argue that principle and matter arise simultaneously. This had the effect of moving the "School of Principle" even further from a focus on the discovery of principle in an untouched inner mind as advocated by Lu Jiuyuan, toward Xue Xuan's explicit emphasis on the training of the senses and the body through ritual and daily activities. Chen Xianzheng (Chen Gongfu, 1428–1500 CE) emphasized bodily training though quiet sitting, but connected it to a revival of Lu Jiuyuan's equation of the inner mind and cosmic principle. Chen Xianzheng's success in the civil service examination late in life and his positive message of returning to a natural state to access the cosmic principle in the inner mind made him the first Ming voice in what developed into a genuine alternative to the "School of Principle."

Echoing the criticisms of Lu Jiuyuan and Chen Xianzheng that Zhu Xi artificially divided the inner mind and cosmic principle, the "Study of Inner Mind" (also called the Lu-Wang School) posited a necessary relationship between knowledge *(zhi)* and action *(xing)*, and a superiority of experiential knowledge gained through action over ordinary knowledge gained through study. This emphasis on accessing an intuitive level of understanding has led some to label it (somewhat misleadingly) as "idealism." The founder of the school was Wang Yangming (1472–1529), who passed the civil examination at the age of twenty and went on to serve in a variety of official positions. Wang appropriated the phrase "true knowing" *(liangzhi)* from *Mencius* 7A15: "What a person is able to do without having to learn is what he can truly do; what a person knows without having to reflect is what he truly knows." In its original context, true knowing is identified with caring for parents and respect for elders, and Wang Yangming used this to explain the way that knowledge of principle is incipient in the original substance of the inner mind.

This imperative to social engagement coincided with a different approach to classical traditions. In his critique of Zhu Xi's program, Wang Yangming returns to the "Great Learning" in arguing that the "investigation of things" must be in service of "arriving at knowing" *(zhizhi)* of morality and so refers to investigating the principles that were already present in the inner mind. Wang eschewed complex textual exegesis, arguing that classics are but commentaries on the mind. Instead, he focused on character formation through realizing "original substance" *(benti)* by the cultivation practice (*gongfu*) of applying morality by being sincere in daily life. Philip J. Ivanhoe has likened Wang Yangming's view of moral self-transformation to a model of acting on affections, and Wang himself quotes the "Great Learning" when he likens moral action to "loving pretty colors or hating bad stench." Just as with Zhu Xi, modern scholars have compared Wang Yangming's view that moral knowledge depends on clearing away the dust of the desires to reveal the mind's inherent moral principles to Chan Buddhist notions of the "original mind" (*benxin*). Despite his vociferous criticism of Buddhists as living a life of emptiness and silence, lacking any engagement with society, the revisionist "Study of Inner Mind" scholar Liu Zongzhou (Liu Qidong, 1578–1645 CE), acknowledged the mutual influence when he wrote that Wang Yangming "resembled Chan but then condemned Chan." Indeed, criticisms of "Study of Inner Mind" by later Confucians sometimes read like criticisms of Chan by later Buddhists.

Even viewed in the context of the orthodoxy of Zhu Xi's intellectualism, Wang Yangming's reification of intuition was a radical epistemological position, and the later history of the "Study of Inner Mind" school is one of different degrees of accommodation with prior views concerning the legacies of the past sages. While Wang Yangming's early disciples—such as Wang Ji (Wang Longxi, 1498–1583 CE), whose theory of the inner mind led to a version of reincarnation, and Wang Gen (Wang Xinzhai, 1483–1540 CE)—were dedicated to making their teacher's intuitionism more robust, others tried to temper it. Chen Xianzhang's student Zhan Ruoshui (Zhan Yuanming, 1463–1557) argued that there was no correction possible once one has arrived at one's inner mind's true knowing, and so integrated that goal into the more general project of "in every place realizing cosmic principle" *(suichu tiren tianli)*. While Zhan Ruoshui agreed that the inner mind was central to the discovery of principle, his understanding of the inner mind was of a nexus between the external world full of the resources that the "Study of Principle" drew on, and the intuitions favored in "Study of Inner Mind." Liu Zongzhou reread the phrase "attend to oneself in solitude" from the "Doctrine of the Mean" to refer to a solitary disposition to goodness in the original mind that must first be made sincere through self-cultivation practice before embarking on external study. That Wang Yangming's viewpoint was developed in numerous directions is shown by Liu Zongzhou's student, Huang Zongxi (Huang Taichong, or Huang Lizhou, 1610–1695 CE), who delineates eight regional "Study of Inner Mind" schools in his chronicle of Ming scholasticism, *Examples of the Studies of Ming Classicists* (*Mingru xue'an*). Huang Zongxi's own rejection of pure intuitionism is illustrated by his description of Wang Ji and Wang Gen as promoters of Chan Buddhism. As Zhu Xi's writings had, Wang Yangming's works also had a major impact on Confucianism, as well as literature and politics in Yi Korea as well as Tokugawa (1600–1868) Japan.

QING CONFUCIAN TRADITIONS AND THE STUDY OF THE CLASSICS. In late imperial China, issues of national identity and academic and political authority were all bound up in the identification of Kongzi as a ritualist and a scholar. When, in 1644, the Manchu Qing dynasty replaced the Ming, the new rulers recognized the legitimacy that might be conferred by continuing patronage of classical scholarship. While discourse on the Chinese past was increasingly limited to a discussion of ritual and exegesis, new trends in interpretation and a valuation of evidence-based scholarship (*kaozheng*) over Song and Ming scholasticism led to a new orientation to classical traditions. While scholars associated with "School of Principle" and "Study of Inner Mind" traditions of self-transformation still taught students and held office, a dissatisfaction with those traditions gave rise to a new kind of exegete who did not aspire to sagehood, but instead to accurately understand the past. Later and more iconoclastic Qing scholars developed new perspectives on the classics that elevated proper engagement with texts to the highest level of experience.

The "Han Studies" (*Hanxue*) movement associated with Gu Yanwu (Gu Yinglin, 1613–1682 CE) was begun in the atmosphere of the anti-Manchu sentiment of the early Qing. Han Studies may be linked to resistance to foreign rule, in that it sought to return to an authentic Chinese worldview, before it was polluted by what many Qing scholars called the Buddhist-inspired "Song Studies" (*Songxue*). Because careful research into the early meanings of the classics had the effect of undermining the anachronistic cosmologies that earlier imperial scholars had used to interpret them, Han Studies was a pragmatic reaction against the academic tendency to focus on abstract concepts like cosmic principle, and a turning away from what was seen as a sterile and failed approach to the past. The earliest Han Studies scholars were iconoclasts who generally rejected affiliation with established lineages and pursued different approaches like historical study, philology, or natural philosophy as pragmatic alternatives to earlier and narrower models of classical scholarship. The Ming loyalist Wang Fuzhi (Wang Chuanshan, 1619–1692 CE) sought to use Zhang Zai's "supreme ultimate" to provide School of Principle cosmology a more materialistic basis, rejecting Zhu Xi's view of the primacy of principle over matter, and arguing, for instance, that desires also contained an expression of principle. An autodidact, Wang Fuzhi criticized the more abstract elements of Daoism and Buddhism, but read the classics alongside historical and literary works and wrote a commentary on the *Zhuangzi*. Gu Yanwu, like Wang Fuzhi, a Ming official who refused to serve under the Qing, developed a number of new approaches to classical studies, making contributions in phonology, textual criticism, and historical geography. While he grounded this approach in Kongzi's imperative to "study widely in literature" (*boxue*, see *Analects* 6.27, 9.1, 12.15, and 19.5), Gu Yanwu's valuation of the work of early imperial commentators like Zheng Xuan signaled a major shift in Confucian hermeneutics toward a more historical approach. Other Ming loyalists broadened the subjects of classical research, with Fu Shan (Fu Qingzhu, 1607–1684 CE) focusing on medical and "many masters and hundred experts" texts, and Lü Liuliang (Lü Zhuangsheng, 1629–1683 CE) making pointed observations about foreign relations in historical texts. The explicit justification for such broad study was its potential application in contemporary society, in spite of the fact that these authors eschewed official service under the Manchus.

The middle period of the Qing was characterized by the further development of independent scholarly fields that each identified itself with the tradition of Kongzi, and it continued the focus on the issue of the social relevance of classical learning. Yan Yuan (Yan Yizhi, 1635–1704 CE) was an early critic of the exegetical emphasis of Han Studies for their neglect of practical knowledge in other fields. Yan Yuan's view of the classics was that they should be seen as an expression of intentions that under different historical circumstances might have been expressed through concrete actions. By contrast, Dai Zhen (Dai Dongyuan, 1723–1777 CE) took the developing Han Studies emphasis on philological method and, in his "Tracing the Origins of Goodness" (*Yuanshan*), argued that it was a necessary antidote to the subjectivity inherent in later imperial readings of the classics. He attacked the differentiation of principle and matter, the hierarchy between which was the cosmological justification for longstanding social hierarchics that he maintained had to end. What the approaches of Yan Yuan and Dai Zhen had in common was a genuine disregard for the dualism that informed the writings of both Zhu Xi and Wang Yangming, and by the eighteenth century the bitter disagreements between their followers had been replaced by a view that they shared common shortcomings. Nonsectarian approaches like that of Peng Dingqiu (Peng Qinzhi, 1645–1719 CE) promoted not only the essential unity of the "Study of Principle" and "Study of Inner Mind," but also a synthesis of the Three Teachings that emphasized conduct and a vegetarian diet. The Qing's dissemination of "morality books" (*shanshu*) that promoted a syncretic moral system that stressed values like loyalty to the state reinforced the idea that the Three Teachings were based on a common moral foundation.

It was in the Qing Dynasty that several tendencies cemented Kongzi's status as the founder of the diverse strands of scholarship, service, and practice with which he had previously been associated. Kongzi was increasingly viewed as the founder of the projects in which both private and official scholars were engaged. In the words of the Qing scholar Pi Xirui (Pi Lumen, 1850–1908 CE), the author of *History of the Study of the Classics* (Jingxue lishi), "The first age of the study of the classics began with Kongzi's editing of the Six Classics." Here the "Six Classics" refer to the Five Classics plus the lost classic of Music (*Yuejing*). When classical scholars like Pi Xirui constructed genealogies from which they claimed authority, Kongzi was always placed at the beginning. What both proponents of evidence-based scholarship and those who tried to reconcile the approaches of Zhu Xi and Wang Yangming had in common was the search for a pure past whose interpretation had been politicized by the disagreements of late imperial scholars. The assumed unity of Kongzi's intentions became the basis for postulating the existence of a common source from which the many strands of Qing Confucianism once derived. The period also saw a renewal of interest in Kongzi as a prophetic figure and religious founder, a renewal tied to late Qing encounters with the west.

The culmination of the emphasis on social relevance of the classics was Kang Youwei's (1858–1927 CE), portrait of Kongzi as a prophetic social reformer. Kang Youwei was classically trained at a time when European, American, and Japanese imperial aspirations convinced most Chinese of the need to promote scientific and military development. In his 1897 *Kongzi as a Reformer* (*Kongzi gaizhi kao*), Kang Youwei turned back to early commentaries on the *Spring and Autumn* and the Confucian apocrypha to construct a view of Kongzi as a religious founder along the lines of Jesus Christ, and to reject the orthodox Study of Principle reading of Kongzi as a teacher and advisor. His direct influence on the young Qing emperor Guangxu (r. 1875–1908) led to a series of explicit measures intended to transform China into a constitutional monarchy, which were ended by what was effectively a coup d'état by the Empress Dowager Cixi in September of 1898. While Kang Youwei fled to Japan, his student Liang Qichao (1873–1929 CE) revived a reformist constitutional movement in the period from 1905 through 1911. Qing intransigence frustrated these reforms up until the success of the Republicanism espoused by Sun Zhongshan (i.e., Sun Yat-sen, 1866–1925 CE) in ending the Qing and most aspects of the imperial system in 1911.

The 1919 May Fourth movement was critical of many aspects of traditional culture, but it was far outdone by the 1949 revolution that established the Communist People's Republic of China. As the locus of Confucian thinking and scholarship moved to Taiwan, Hong Kong, and the Chinese diaspora, the fraying of ties between the state and both the performance of ritual and the mastery of the classics significantly changed the nature of the tradition. Institutionally, the home of some of the most versatile forms of modern Confucianism is the international university, and its voice is identified with that of academics such as Tu Weiming (or Tu Wei-ming, b. 1940). In this context, inter-religious dialog and attempts to accommodate traditional views to the concerns of modernity have come to the fore. At the same time, there is interest in a revival of Confucian ethics as a resource for combating official corruption in the People's Republic of China, while particular Confucian traditions, such as evidence-based scholarship and sacrifice at temples to Kongzi, continue in many traditional venues.

Throughout history, the traditions drawn upon by people who today identify themselves with Confucianism were woven and unwoven in response to outside influences. These traditions have adapted in response to criticisms by Warring States thinkers like Mozi and Zhuangzi, to the popularity of early Buddhist institutions, or to the perception that religion played a role in the technological progress of nineteenth-century imperial powers. While recent scholarship on the historical development of Confucianism has called into question the notion that Kongzi founded the multiple threads of the tradition, there is no question that, for the past several centuries, contests over his biography and teachings have been the dominant common feature of these threads. Going back in time, however, other common features may be found: a theory of history based on a particular model of familial and social relations; an ethic of stewardship; a view of archaic ritual practice; and a set of texts and interpretations that form the curriculum of the civil service examinations. Whether one considers Confucianism a religion or not is ultimately a question of whether one is looking at the "humanistic" thread isolated out by Jesuits looking for natural theology and reformers looking for natural philosophy, or at other threads at other times.

SEE ALSO Chinese Religion, overview article.

BIBLIOGRAPHY

Brokaw, Cynthia. *The Ledgers of Merit and Demerit: Social Change and Moral Order in Late Imperial China.* Princeton, N.J., 1991.

Chafee, John. *The Thorny Gates of Learning in Song China: A Social History of Examinations.* New York, 1985.

Chen Lai. *Song Ming lixue.* Shenyang, China, 1991.

Csikszentmihalyi, Mark. *Material Virtue: Ethics and the Body in Early China.* Leiden, 2004.

Elman, Benjamin A. *From Philosophy to Philology: Intellectual and Social Aspects of Change in Late Imperial China.* Cambridge, Mass., 1990.

Feng Youlan (Fung Yu-lan). *A Short History of Chinese Philosophy.* Translated By Derk Bodde. New York, 1953.

Graham, A. C. *Two Chinese Philosophers: The Metaphysics of the Brothers Ch'eng.* La Salle, Ill., 1992.

Goldin, Paul. *Rituals of the Way: The Philosophy of Xunzi.* Chicago, 1999.

Guo Yi. *Guodian zhujian yu xianQin xueshu sixiang.* Shanghai, 2001.

Hall, David L., and Roger T. Ames. *Thinking Through Confucius.* Albany, N.Y., 1987.

Hummel, Arthur, et al. *Eminent Chinese of the Ch'ing Period, 1644–1912.* 2 vols. Taiwan, 1970.

Ivanhoe, Philip J. *Confucian Moral Self-Cultivation.* 2d ed. Indianapolis, 2000.

Ivanhoe, Philip J. *Ethics in the Confucian Ttradition: The Thought of Mengzi and Wang Yangming.* 2d ed. Indianapolis, 2002.

Jaspers, Karl. *Origin and Goal of History.* New Haven, Conn., 1953.

Jensen, Lionel. *Manufacturing Confucianism: Chinese Traditions and Universal Civilization.* Durham, N.C., 1997.

Kanaya, Osamu. *ShinKan shisoshi kenkyu.* Tokyo, 1960.

Lau, D. C., trans. *Analects.* Harmondsworth, U.K., 1979.

Liu Zehua. *Zhongguo zhengzhi sixiang shi,* 2 v. Hangzhou, China, 1996.

Machle, Edward. *Nature and Heaven in the Xunzi: A Study of the Tian Lun.* Albany, N.Y., 1993.

Mou Zongsan. *SongMing Ruxue de wenti yu fazhan.* Taibei, China, 2003.

Nylan, Michael. *The Five "Confucian" Classics.* New Haven, Conn., 2001.

Ren Jiyu. *Zhongguo zhexue fazhan shi,* vol. 1. Beijing, 1983.

Shun, Kwong-Loi. *Mencius and Early Chinese Thought.* Stanford, Calif., 1997.

Tu Weiming. *Confucianism in an Historical Perspective.* Singapore, 1989.

Van Norden, Bryan. *Confucius and the Analects: New Essays.* New York, 2002.

Wilson, Thomas A. *Genealogy of the Way: The Construction and Uses of the Confucian Tradition in Late Imperial China.* Stanford, Calif., 1995.

Yang Bojun. *Mengzi yizhu.* Beijing, 1984.

Zhang Xuezhi. *Mingdai zhexue shi.* Beijing, 2000.

Zhu Xi. *Sishu zhangzhu.* Beijing, 1982.

MARK CSIKSZENTMIHALYI (2005)

CONFUCIANISM: THE CLASSICAL CANON

A focus on the ritual, music, and texts of a bygone era of social harmony has been a central feature of many of the traditions now identified as Confucian, from classical studies to moral education for government service. In teaching disciples and rulers Kongzi (Confucius, 551–479 BCE) relied on songs preserved in the *Classic of Odes* (Shijing) and myriad forms of ceremony and etiquette believed to date back to the earliest years of the Zhou dynasty (c. 1150 to 256 BCE). Since Kongzi's time the task of preserving the culture of the ancient sages has been understood to require the transmission and interpretation of a normative set of texts and practices. While different eras used different taxonomies for the canon, from the Five Classics (*wujing*) to the Thirteen Classics (*shisanjing*) to the Four Books (*sishu*), a certain attitude and approach to these works was basic to the training that aspiring scholars and officials received. In the *Analects,* Kongzi tells his son, "If you do not study the odes, you will have nothing to use when you speak. . . . If you do not study the rites, you will have nothing to use to establish yourself." On hearing this a disciple remarks that he has learned about three important things: the odes, the rites, and how Kongzi kept the proper distance from his son. Since a "proper distance" exemplified the normative relationship between teacher and student, Kongzi's insistence on it even in the case of teaching his son illustrates the way Kongzi was seen not only as valuing the past, but how he was the paradigm for the right means of teaching the classics and applying the practices of the past.

At the core of debates about canon and orthodoxy in China is the word *jing,* which, although its connotations shift over time, will here be consistently translated as "classic." John B. Henderson borrows Wang Chong's (27–c. 100 CE) distinction between the classics (*jing*) of the "sages" (*shengren*) and the commentaries (*zhuan*) of the "worthies" (*xianren*) and argues that the hierarchical distinction between classic and commentary is made less on the basis of content than "according to their respective sources" (1991, p. 71). Henderson says the resulting one is similar to the Hindu distinction between "revealed scripture" (*sruti)* and "explanations" (*smirti)* of saints and prophets (p. 71). Because the role of the classical canon both within Confucian traditions and Chinese society as a whole changed over time, this treatment of the classical canon is divided into three chronological sections: the Five Classics of the preimperial and early imperial periods (through 220 CE), redefinitions of the canon culminating in the Tang (618–907) and Northern Song (960–1127 CE) dynasty establishment of the Thirteen Classics, and the recognition of the Four Books by Zhu Xi (1130–1200). The reformulations of the canon reflect different assumptions about the relationship of text and tradition, which were translated into new commentarial practices, culminating in a modern situation in which the approach to the Confucian classics is intertwined with that of other traditions to their canons.

THE FIVE CLASSICS. The Five Classics (*wujing*), established as the basis of the imperial curriculum in the second century BCE, were seen as vehicles for the preservation of the norms and practices of the Zhou dynasty, a goal that was seen as a continuation of a project begun by Kongzi. As such, training oneself using these texts was an undertaking that was itself traditional, and the word for a person who had received such training was *classicist (ru).* While the term *ru* is usually translated as "Confucian" based on the traditional view of Kongzi as the first classicist, this article will attempt to distinguish between the several Chinese terms translated as "Confucian" to preserve distinctions made by practitioners themselves. The earliest records of classicists connect them specifically to the teaching and performance of the *Classic of Odes* and the *Classic of Documents* (Shujing), which, with the *Classic of Changes* (Yijing), *Spring and Autumn* (Chunqiu), and the *Records of Rites* (Liji), comprise the Five Classics.

Classic of Odes. The *Classic of Odes* is a collection of 305 songs (excluding six titles transmitted without text), dating from the beginning through the middle of the Zhou dynasty, with the final compilation thought to have taken place in, or slightly before, Kongzi's time. Both the form and content of these songs varies and the classical division of the collection into sections reflect a generic distinction, and perhaps signal that these divisions were once independent texts. Modern scholarship has used particular songs as evidence for Zhou ancestral sacrifice and popular religious festivals. In pedagogical contexts their narration of affective dispositions (*qing*) in particular situations in the past has been seen as a guide for training one's reactions so as to conform with the dispositions of the sage kings.

The earliest references to the *Classic of Odes* mention the sections "Airs" (*feng*), "Elegantiae" (*ya*), and "Hymns" (*song*), with the Elegantiae section further divided into "Lesser" (*xiao*) and "Greater" (*da*) subsections. In the "Prefaces to the *Odes*" (*Shi xu*), associated with early imperial members of the disciple traditions of Zixia (507–400 BCE), this four-part structure is called the "four beginnings" *(sishi)*. The folksong-like Airs are divided into subsections associated with different states, and the "Great Preface" (*Da xu*) explains that its songs "take a given country's affairs and tie them to their sources in particular individuals." The Elegantiae sections contain court pieces about the culture heroes of the Zhou dynasty, as well as pieces for special occasions and, occasionally, criticisms and plaints. The "Great Preface" explains that "elegantiae means 'correct'" and explains their function as describing "the origins of the rise and fall of kingly government." The Hymns, many of which likely were performance pieces for sacrificial occasions, are described in the "Great Preface" as "praising the form and appearance of flourishing virtue in order to report completed accomplishments to the luminous spirits." Similarly, discovered in the 1990s, the early third-century BCE "Kongzi's discussion of the *Odes*" (*Kongzi Shilun*) says, "The Hymns are (about) sagely virtue." An example of these last forty songs is the "Great Brightness" song, addressed to the people or soldiers of Zhou, justifying their rule with the phrase "There is a mandate (ming) that comes from Heaven, that mandates [the rule of] our own King Wen."

Classic of Documents. The concept of "Heaven's mandate" (*tianming*) is also at the core of many of the proclamations that make up the fifty-eight-fascicle *Classic of Documents* (Shujing), also known as the Books of the Predecessors (*Shangshu*). Among the core chapters widely accepted as genuine are the "Great Announcement" (*Da gao*), "Announcement of Kang" (*Kang gao*), "Announcement of Shao" (*Shao gao*), "Many Officials" (*Duo shi*), and "Lord Shi" (*Jun shi*), traditionally dated to the reign of King Cheng of Zhou (d. 1006 BCE). While Heaven's mandate was historically the command issued to the Zhou founders to overthrow the last corrupt ruler of the Shang dynasty (c. 1500–1050 BCE), the term is also used more generally for a divine justification for authority claimed by both rulers and rebels alike. The "Great Announcement" records how divination using tortoise shells conveyed Heaven's mandate to the imperial regent, the duke of Zhou (Zhougong). Because the basis of Heaven's endorsement of the dynasty was the personal virtue (*de*) of its founders and rulers, politics was intimately linked to a discussion of character and to the possession of particular traits such as reverence (*jing*). The "Announcement of Kang" argues that since Heaven's mandate may change, the ruler must always keep the possibility of its withdrawal in mind, which causes him to be reverent.

For much of modern Chinese history the authenticity of a large portion of the *Classic of Documents* has been contested. Following the literary purges of the Qin dynasty (221–206 BCE), there were several discoveries of lost portions of the text, beginning with Fu Sheng's (c. 245–c. 180 BCE) claim to have preserved twenty-nine fascicles of the text in the wall of his house. The discovery of other materials transmitted by Kongzi's descendents resulted in an "ancient text" (*guwen*) version of the Fu Sheng materials with twenty-four fascicles of other material. In the first century CE Liu Xiang (79–8 BCE) championed this version of the classic, and in the fourth century CE the Fu Sheng chapters were redivided into thirty-four fascicles, resulting in the fifty-eight-fascicle text transmitted today. Beginning in the late Tang and Northern Song dynasties textual scholars noted discrepancies that caused them to question the authenticity of the "ancient text" chapters. Nevertheless, the archaeological discovery of attributed quotations of "ancient text" chapters dating to the late Warring States period (403–221 BCE) indicates that even sections of the *Classic of Documents* that are not authentic records of the early sage kings may well be forgeries of great antiquity.

Classic of Changes. The use of divination to provide justification for rule is one instance of the use of the divination or omen text the *Classic of Changes* (Yijing). The *Classic of Changes* is a layered text consisting of an early Zhou dynasty omen manual transmitted alongside a set of increasingly abstract commentaries dating to the Warring States and early imperial periods. Its title (and its alternate title *Changes of the Zhou,* or *Zhouyi)* refers to the "change" inherent in the moment of performance of casting and counting out milfoil stalks or, probably in its earliest form, reading cracks produced by heat in cattle scapulae or tortoise plastrons. These media were seen as particularly sensitive membranes between the natural or spirit worlds and that of human beings, and skilled diviners could use them to read incipient patterns. In the context of producing and reading these patterns the *Classic of Changes* is used to interpret the resulting symbols: a hexagram or hexagrams (*gua*) diagnostic for particular questions or concerns. In its history as one of the Five Classics, however, the original practical aspect of the *Classic of Changes* was less important than its status as a description of a natural system that subsumed considerations of change and contingency and so could be applied to analyze history, alchemy, and a host of other areas.

The base text of the *Classic of Changes* consists of sixty-four named hexagrams, each constructed of six solid or broken lines, a brief "hexagram statement" *(guaci),* and a series of "line statements" *(yaoci)* indexed to numbers generated as part of the process of determining each line of the hexagram. The first two hexagrams, *qian* and *kun,* are made up of six solid and six broken lines, respectively, and each is followed by a terse and somewhat opaque hexagram statement, and then six-line statements that apply only if the lines of the hexagram are solid or broken lines of a certain kind. The attached commentaries to the base text are also collectively known as the "Ten Wings" *(Shiyi).* The earliest layers of commentary are devoted to the further elucidation of the symbolic features of the hexagram, such as the *Judgements (Duan)* and *Greater and Lesser Images (Da/Xiao Xiang).* Later layers are essays on the hexagrams and the cosmos, such as the bipartite *Commentary on the Appended Phrases (Xici),* the *Explanations of the Trigrams (Shuogua),* and the *Order of the Hexagrams (Xugua).* The *Words about the Patterns (Wenyan)* commentary contains detailed commentary on the first two hexagrams only, and the *Miscellaneous Hexagrams (Zagua)* provides pithy explanations of the meanings of pairs of hexagrams. While these commentaries have become part of the *Classic of Changes* itself, commentary on the *Yijing* has been a feature of Chinese literature of all types and affiliations. Han dynasty (206 BCE–220 CE) commentaries are classed as "image and number" (*xiangshu*) because they correlated each element of the hexagram to an image and a set of numbers. Wang Bi (226–249 CE) initiated a strategy of reading the text in isolation from the universe of correlations previously employed. This type of commentary, known as "meaning and pattern" *(yili),* became dominant by the Northern Song dynasty.

Spring and Autumn. The *Spring and Autumn (Chunqiu)* is a concise chronicle of diplomatic, political, and other noteworthy happenings in Kongzi's home state of Lu from the period 722 to 481 BCE. The term *annals* is often added as a suffix to the translation to express the sense in which the terms *spring* and *autumn* signify the passage of the year, and the nature of the text as a year-by-year description of events. Although its content appears to have been based on official Lu records, later traditions recount that Kongzi composed it shortly before his death, as a means to preserve his normative vision once he had given up on transforming the society in which he lived. This view, which emphasizes the political import of the *Spring and Autumn* among the Five Classics, is seen in the *Mengzi* (*Mencius,* c. 380–c. 290 BCE), which quotes Kongzi as saying, "Those who understand me will do so on account of the *Spring and Autumn,* and those who berate me will also do so on account of the *Spring and Autumn.*" Indeed, for the commentarial schools that developed in the early imperial period, the style of the work was seen to contain subtle clues to moral evaluations of historical figures, and small deviations were read as indications of Kongzi's praise or censure. Zhao Qi (c. 107–201), in commenting on Kongzi's speech in the *Mengzi,* uses the term *unsullied king (suwang)* to express a view that became associated with the "new text" (*jinwen*) school of Confucianism, that Kongzi was the ideal ruler and the *Spring and Autumn* was the key to his method of government.

In the early imperial period three commentaries to the *Spring and Autumn* defined three separate schools of interpretation of the events and of Kongzi's historiography: the Gongyang, Guliang, and Zuo traditions. Each of these schools developed around a particular commentary to the *Spring and Autumn.* The two commentaries most representative of the "praise and censure" approach are the Gongyang and Guliang commentaries, which formally resemble a catechism: simple questions and answers about the judgments behind choices of words made by Kongzi. The Gongyang commentary, supposedly written by the late Warring States period figure Gongyang Gao from the state of Qi, but actually dating to the second century BCE, is allegedly based on centuries of esoteric transmission through the lineages of disciples of Kongzi. The Guliang commentary is associated with Guliang Chi, supposedly an early Warring States period figure from the state of Lu, who Yang Shixun, the Tang dynasty subcommentator, claims received training in the *Spring and Autumn* from Kongzi's disciple Zixia. The most influential commentary, however, is the one associated with the fifth-century BCE state of Lu historian Zuo Qiuming, although it probably is an amalgam of a number of sources, both historical and fictive. The Zuo commentary differs from the other two because of its incorporation of detailed narratives and by the fact that its coverage of the *Spring and Autumn* events extends to 469 BCE, while the Gongyang and the Guliang commentaries both extend to 482 BCE. That the Zuo version covers events that postdate the traditional death of Confucius was explained by Du Yu (222–284), the Jin dynasty (265–420) commentator, as being the result of the master's disciples having completed his work based on the archives of Lu. Modern scholars tend to see these differences as reflecting a more basic difference in the nature of the source material on which the commentaries were based.

Records of Ritual. The "Three Ritual Compendia" *(sanli)* are ostensibly collections of record of the archaic ritual system of the Zhou period, called *Zhou Rituals (Zhouli),* the *Ceremonies and Rituals (Yili),* and the *Records of Ritual (Liji).* The six sections of the *Zhou Rituals* formulaically reconstitute the governmental structure of the Zhou, with each section containing short descriptions of sixty offices under the jurisdiction of a different state bureau. While modern scholars generally do not think the *Zhou Rituals* predates the Han period (206 BCE–220 CE), for much of Chinese history it has been treated as a source, albeit somewhat idealized, for information on predynastic China. The seventeen sections of the *Ceremonies and Rituals* provide a more practical description of ritual protocol in different situations, from capping rites for the children of members of the official class to guidelines for receiving and hosting the impersonator of the deceased during a funeral. While traditionally associated with the eleventh-century BCE figure the duke of Zhou (Zhougong), the actual record of transmission of the *Ceremonies and Rituals* may only be verified as of the Han period. The forty-nine sections of the *Records of Ritual*, by contrast, are acknowledged to have been edited after the beginning of the dynastic period in 221 BCE, although the discovery in the last two decades of exemplars of chapters of the work in preimperial tombs shows that it is constituted of older materials. Dai De (first century BCE) and his nephew Dai Sheng (73–49 BCE) are credited with paring a collection of ritual writings into the current diverse collection of dialogues about ceremony and etiquette between Kongzi and his disciples or the rulers he advised, abstract discussions of the minutiae and origins of particular ritual forms, and cosmological or psychological essays that integrate ritual into the discussion of other themes.

Early discussions of the Five Classics are vague about which of the "Three Ritual Compendia" were included, but the *Records of Ritual* soon gained prominence. While it is a composite text that contains many different views of the function and significance of ritual, its account of the importance of ritual both reflected and informed the central role that ritual plays in many forms of Confucianism. In one dialog between Kongzi and Duke Ai of Lu in chapter 48 of the *Records of Ritual*, Kongzi explains, "Inside, it is the way to govern the rites of the ancestral temple, sufficient to allow one to match the spirit luminances of Heaven and Earth. Outside, it is the way to govern the rites of correcting and instructing, sufficient to establish reverence between superior and inferior." Sun Yirang (1848–1908) explains that "matching the spirit luminances" in this passage refers to copying the movement of the sun and moon in the ancestral temple rites. This quotation reflects how ritual oriented the performer in both a cosmologically and socially optimal way and implies that there is a relationship between correct ritual behavior on the part of the ruler and maintenance of social order in the state.

***The Five Classics* in Chinese history.** While the Five Classics came from diverse origins both generically and chronologically, in the early empire their reception became inextricably bound with the reputation of Kongzi. The establishment of a "Confucian orthodoxy" by the Martial Emperor (Wu, r. 140–87 BCE) beginning in 136 BCE led to the institutionalization of an examination system that made a knowledge of the Five Classics the requirement for an official career. Because of Kongzi's reputation as teacher and advisor, the ethical foundation in the Five Classics with which he came to be associated was seen to be necessary training for officials. As the preparatory system for the examinations became increasingly institutionalized, the commentary on and transmission of the classics became a path to salary and office.

Drawing on the authority of the orthodox classics, a new genre of text often called the "Confucian apocrypha" developed in the first century CE. While the classics were seen as the exoteric transmission of Confucius for use by everyone, and the *Spring and Autumn* was the exoteric transmission encoded for use by future sages, the apocrypha were seen in the Han as part of a genuinely esoteric transmission. The corpus generally referred to as the "apocrypha" *(chenwei)* is actually a combination of two types of work: "charts and proofs" or prophecy texts (*tuchen*) and "weft books" (*weishu*) or texts ancillary to the classics. The distinction between "charts and proof" texts and "weft books" is now made on the basis of whether or not the title includes the title of a companion "classic," but it is unclear whether this formal distinction actually reflects differences between the genesis of the two genres. In the latter part of the Han period many of the prophetic texts that had been used by different factions at the beginning of the dynasty to furnish political omens had the name of one of the Five Classics added as prefixes to their titles. As a result, while these texts came to be associated with particular classics, their origins and content generally have little to do with the classic with which they are associated.

After the decline of the Han the long period of political disunity known as the Six Dynasties period (220–589) saw a variety of administrative structures come and go as short-lived kingdoms established themselves in a land divided for most of the period between north and south. This was also the period in which Buddhism took root in China, and during which organized Daoism became established. It saw the rise of the *Classic of Filial Piety* (Xiaojing) and the *Analects* (Lunyu) to the level of classic, leading to the occasional use of the term *Seven Classics* (Qijing) to refer to the *Classic of Filial Piety* and *Analects* added to the Five Classics. The terse, eighteen-section *Classic of Filial Piety* is likely a Han-period composition, although it is traditionally associated with Kongzi's disciple Zengzi (505–435 BCE) and is largely composed of dialogues between the two. It centers on the importance of the virtue of "familial piety" (*xiao*, also translated as filial piety), both for individual development and for social order. The twenty sections of the *Analects*, while perhaps compiled as late as the early Han, are largely composed of dialogs featuring Kongzi, his disciples, and their patrons that probably date from the time of Kongzi through the Han. The *Analects*'s discussion of the noble ideal (*junzi*, often translated "gentleman") centers on the cultivation of a set of virtues that constitutes the Way (Dao), a means to achieving personal and political ideals. The expansion of the Five Classics attests to the beginning of the redefinition of the canon, one that had much to do with the expansion of the category of sacred texts to include works that were sacred for reasons other than their pedigree as a continuation of the golden age of the Zhou.

The *Analects* became increasingly important as the primary source of Kongzi's ethics and his view of service, and is now perhaps the best known of the Confucian classics. Collected from a body of diverse sayings and anecdotes written on bamboo slips and circulated in the late *Spring and Autumn* and Warring States periods, its aphoristic passages were likely originally intended as a guide to proper ritual behavior for princes and officials charged with maintaining court etiquette. The extant *Analects* was collated by Zheng Xuan (127–200), although one excavated version of the text unearthed in 1973 indicates it circulated in something close to its current form in 55 BCE. The *Analects* discusses development of the character traits such as benevolence (*ren*), which it explains in particular contexts. In chapter twelve Kongzi tells different disciples different things: for example, "If something goes against ritual propriety, do not look at it" (12.1); "When abroad, behave as though you were at home receiving an important guest" (12.2); and "The mark of benevolence is that one is hesitant to speak" (12.3). Traditional commentaries explain this as an example of Kongzi's use of expediencies directed at the strengths and weaknesses of particular disciples. Alternatively, this might represent the compilation of the *Analects* from diverse sources, perhaps transmitted in different disciple traditions.

REDEFINING THE CANON: THE THIRTEEN CLASSICS AND THE FOUR BOOKS. The reunification under the Sui (581–618) and Tang dynasties saw redefinitions but not reconceptualizations of the canon based on the model of the Five Classics. Emperor Wen (r. 179–157 BCE) of the Tang dynasty sponsored the inscription of the Twelve Classics (*shi'erjing*) on stelae at the Imperial Academy in what is today called Xi'an. The only major addition, however, was the *Approaching Elegance* (Erya), a nineteen-section systematic compilation of commentarial glosses that is effectively a dictionary. While the *Approaching Elegance* is thought to date from the third or second centuries BCE, its inclusion among the classics was relatively late. Besides the *Approaching Elegance*, the *Analects*, *Classic of Filial Piety*, and Twelve Classics were either members of the Five Classics or commentaries thereon. Instead of only the *Records of Ritual*, the Twelve Classics also includes the *Zhou Rituals* and the *Ceremonies and Rituals*. Instead of the *Spring and Autumn*, the Twelve Classics includes the Gongyang, Guliang, and Zuo commentaries. These moves may best be seen as an expansion of the Five Classics rather than as a basic change in the canon.

At the same time the Tang imperial house had changed the civil examination system in significant ways. The Tang rulers traced their descent to the mythical sixth- or fifth-century Daoist sage Laozi and elevated several Daoist texts to the status of classics. This happened to both the *Master Zhuang (Zhuangzi)*, which was renamed *True Classic of Southern Splendor (Nanhua zhenjing)* and the *Master Lie (Liezi)*, renamed the *True Classic of the Ultimate Virtue of the Void (Chongxu zhide zhenjing)*. At the same time, views of canon were influenced by the translation of the Buddhist Tripitika (*sanzangjing*). The imperial house sponsored the publication of Buddhist and Daoist works, even as Emperor Taizong (599–649) commissioned Yan Shigu (581–645) to create a definitive annotated edition of the Five Classics. These developments signaled that the traditional rationale for the status of the Five Classics, their connection to the Zhou dynasty, could no longer be considered the sole operant ground for entry into the canon.

The culmination, and perhaps the most influential reformulation of the classics in later imperial China, was the Thirteen Classics (*shisanjing*), which was established during the Northern Song dynasty. The chief change was the addition of the *Mengzi*, a late fourth- or early third-century BCE work in the style of the *Analects* that located the latter work's self-cultivation program in a model of human nature. According to the *Records of the Historian* (*Shiji*, c. 100 BCE) Mengzi (Mencius, 391–308 BCE) "withdrew and together with the followers of [his disciple] Wan Zhang, put in order the [classics of] *Odes* and *Documents* and interpreted the intentions of Kongzi. They wrote the [*Mengzi*] in seven chapters" (73.2343). This description of the composition of the *Mengzi* accurately identifies Mengzi as continuing the "intentions of Kongzi."

At the same time, the elevation of the *Mengzi* reflects the Confucian need for resources to address psychological claims made by Buddhists that the *Analects* did not contain. For example, *Mengzi* 2A2 argues that within each person's mind are incipient bases of the virtues of benevolence, righteousness *(yi)*, ritual propriety *(li)*, and wisdom *(zhi)*. *Mengzi* 2A6 argues that people have these incipient dispositions to goodness "just like they have four limbs." By grounding morality in the human nature and the body the *Mengzi* was perhaps more consonant with the Buddhist goal of returning to an original "nature" unclouded by desires. The *Mengzi*'s place in the canon may be traced back at least to Han Yu's (768–824) contention that Mengzi was the last classical representative of the Transmission of the Way (Daotong).

A more radically alternative formulation of the canon was created by the Song scholar Zhu Xi. Zhu Xi singled out two chapters of the *Records of Ritual*—*Great Learning (Daxue)* and *Doctrine of the Mean (Zhongyong)*—along with the *Analects* and the *Mengzi* as members of the Four Books (*Sishu*). The *Great Learning* and *Doctrine of the Mean* had some of the same appeal that the *Mengzi* had in the later imperial post-Buddhist period. Both texts, products of the Han synthetic combination of morality and cosmology, link psychology and ethics using concepts such as the magnetic power of "sincerity" (*cheng*) and a quasi-divine conception of the "sage" (*sheng*). Associating these three texts so closely with the *Analects* allowed Zhu Xi to read the latter text in a new way, one that proved immensely influential even through the present day.

In 1190 Zhu Xi published his commentary on the Four Books, called the *Collected Commentaries on the Sentences and Sections of the Four Books (Sishu zhangju jizhu)*. Because of his intellectual stature, Zhu Xi's formulation had immediate influence on his contemporaries, and his *Collected Commentaries on the Sentences and Sections of the Four Books* became orthodox parts of the civil service examination system at the start of the fourteenth century. This happened despite Zhu Xi's criticism of the examination system as leading people to pursue training in the classics out of self-advancement.

Models of Canon Formation in China. The legacy of the Song dynasty today is two alternate Confucian canons. From the viewpoint of the history of Chinese literature the category of the Thirteen Classics is still widely used today. While there was a broadening of the canon as a result of the movement to historicize the classics in the Qing dynasty (1644–1911), the benchmark of "evidentiary scholarship" *(kaozheng)* is the *Commentaries and Subcommentaries to the Thirteen Classics (Shisanjing zhushu),* edited by Ruan Yuan (1764–1849) in 1815. From the viewpoint of the history of Chinese thought Zhu Xi's reformulation of the Four Books is still widely influential, and the Four Books are still the basis of elementary education in many parts of the Chinese diaspora.

At the same time, in contexts where classical scholarship is taught, the category of the Five Classics is often still used. This perhaps best reflects the fact that these three canons were selected and have authority for different reasons: the Five Classics based on the authority of the Zhou-period institutions and later on Kongzi's status as the transmitter of those institutions; the Thirteen Classics based on the authority of the late imperial sponsorship of authoritative and distinctively Confucian texts and commentaries that grew out of the Five Classics; and the Four Books based on the authority of Zhu Xi and his engagement of issues relevant to the post-Buddhist religious climate.

These three models of canon formation indicate the variety of functions that religious and philosophical literature fulfilled in traditional China. The inclusion of the Five Classics as translated by James Legge (1815–1897) in Max Müller's *Sacred Books of the East* (1879–1910) drew attention to their points of similarity to the canons of other religious traditions. In part as a result of such comparisons, the twentieth century saw changes in the reception of Confucianism both inside and outside of China. Imputing aspects of the role of the canon in other traditions led to the de-emphasis of ritual and the ritual classics in Confucianism, as well as an emphasis on Kongzi's role as a religious founder and on the *Analects* as an expression of his founding vision. At the same time, an appreciation of the way that the Confucian canon changed and developed within the tradition has led to a new emphasis on understanding the role of commentary and hermeneutics in the formation of meaning in Confucian traditions.

Bibliography

Chen Mengjia. *Shangshu tonglun.* Beijing, 1985.

Cheng, Anne. *Étude sur le confucianisme Han: L'élaboration d'une tradition exégétique sur les classiques.* Paris, 1985.

Henderson, John B. *Scripture, Canon, and Commentary: A Comparison of Confucian and Western Exegesis.* Princeton, N.J., 1991.

Hong Zhanhou. *Shijing xueshi.* 2 vols. Beijing, 2002.

Loewe, Michael. *Early Chinese Texts: A Bibliographical Guide.* Berkeley, Calif., 1993.

Lynn, Richard John, trans. *The Classic of Changes: A New Translation of the I Ching as Interpreted by Wang Bi.* New York, 1994.

Makeham, John. *Transmitters and Creators: Chinese Commentators and Commentaries on the Analects.* Cambridge, Mass., 2003.

Nylan, Michael. *The Five "Confucian" Classics.* New Haven, Conn., 2001.

Pi Xirui. *Jingxue lishi.* Rev. ed. Taibei, 1987.

Pi Xirui. *Jingxue tonglun.* Beijing, 1998.

Mark Csikszentmihalyi (2005)

CONFUCIANISM: THE IMPERIAL CULT

From early imperial times to the twentieth century, the emperor and officers of the court and civil bureaucracy offered cult sacrifice to the gods that governed the cosmos. The rituals that serviced these gods were based on and authorized by the ritual canons of the Confucian classics, and, as such, were the privileged domain of classically educated men called *Ru,* or "Confucians," who mastered that canon. Sacrifices were performed according to a regular calendar in temples inside the imperial capital, at open altars outside of the capital walls, and at ritual spaces throughout the empire down to the county level. The geographic expanse of these ritual complexes constituted the most visible signs of the extent of the Chinese imperium and provides concrete evidence of interaction between elite and popular religious practices. Successive dynasties drew from the precedents of the ancient canon to define and regulate imperial cults by specifying the amount and type of foods offered to each god, the rank or status of the sacrificer, the music played, hymns sung, and prayers chanted during the ceremony. The aim of sacrifice—or what might be more appropriately understood as ritual feasting—was to satiate the gods to enlist their cooperation in the proper maintenance of the cosmic order in ways favorable to the well-being of the living. In addition to realizing these aims, the effect of proper performance of these rites was the demonstration of the sovereign's virtue and affirmation of the dynasty's legitimacy in ruling the empire.

Formation of the Imperial Cult. Prior to the imperial era, which began with the unification of China under a single emperor in 221 BCE, there were numerous royal cult traditions associated with the courts that ruled various parts of China. These traditions were distinguishable by the language of their practitioners and their liturgical arrangements, as well as by their basic conceptions of the gods and their relationships with the living. Shamanism and trance-induced, intimate commingling between gods and mortals characterized some of these early courtly traditions, whereas studied separation and reverent distance between humans and gods predominated in other traditions, particularly those that eventually formed the basis of Confucian ritual.

Inscriptions on bones and, later, on bronze vessels provide material evidence of an ancient royal cult during the

Shang dynasty (c. 1500–1050 BCE) based on divination, oracular communication with the royal ancestors, and sacrifice to gods and ancestors. While the use of oracles had declined by the Zhou dynasty (c. 1150–256 BCE), inscribed bronze vessels for sacrifices to gods and ancestors were used in a thriving royal cult. Ritual specialists of the late Zhou and early Han (206 BCE–220 CE) dynasties variously selected, coopted, omitted, and redefined elements of these heterogeneous cults to form the imperial cult that thrived until the end of the nineteenth century and then dissolved in the early twentieth century. Detailed elaborations of and critical reflections upon Zhou ritual traditions appear throughout the ritual canons—principally in the *Li ji* (Record of rites) and the *Zhouli* (Rites of Zhou)—of the Five Classics. The most salient characteristic of the royal cult as codified in the classics was the primary role of Heaven as the highest deity ruling the cosmos and the most exalted in the ritual hierarchy to receive sacrifice from the king. Another conspicuous feature of imperial cults was the central role of royal ancestors as crucial mediators between the reigning emperor and the highest gods. The Han conquest of the empire brought about the unification of these royal and regional cults under the authority of a single court, although many inconsistencies, contradictions, and redundancies persisted. The Han dynasty nonetheless probably marks the first period about which one can speak of a single pantheon, understood as a conception of the gods coexisting collectively within a relatively cohesive whole.

During the period of disunity that followed the fall of the Han, ritual specialists debated cult liturgies at the royal courts of regional kingdoms. By the eighth century the Tang court (618–907) systematized these liturgies into a coherent official ritual system that would remain the foundation of the imperial cult until the end of the imperial era, although virtually every aspect of cult practice continued to be subject to frequent debate and reform, especially during the Song (960–1279) and Ming (1368–1644) dynasties.

The most far-reaching changes to the system of imperial cults took place in the sixteenth century, largely precipitated by repercussions of a succession crisis—or complication—that led to Ming Shizong's (r. 1521–1567) coronation as emperor. Although historians are suspicious of his personal motives in provoking a series of important reforms known by his reign name, Jiajing, it is clear that he tapped into controversies over the imperial cult's canonical precedents that had erupted intermittently and with fierce intensity among ritual scholars both in and out of the court for at least five hundred years.The description of the pantheon that follows is largely based on the Jiajing reforms, which were retained with few major changes until the early twentieth century.

The gods of the imperial pantheon governed specific realms of the cosmos. The correlation between gods and mortals was painstakingly regulated through exact prescriptions of the locations and type of ritual space where each god was to receive sacrifice and the person by whom it would be offered. The hierarchical system of cults, ranked into three tiers of great, middle, and miscellaneous, makes clear that the power of the gods and the realms over which they governed at times overlapped, usually because a more ancient god's power was superseded by that of another, more recent, one. By reading the pantheon of the Ming dynasty as a guide, it is possible to gain insight into the cosmic order that enveloped the gods, the stars, the natural forces, and the world of the living.

Cult of Heaven/Shangdi. Heaven occupied the pinnacle of the imperial pantheon. Heaven received Great Sacrifice *(dasi)* on the winter solstice at a round open-air altar (*yuanqiu,* "round mound") south of the city only from the Son of Heaven, the emperor. The spirit seat upon which the god was invited to sit bore the name "Lofty Heaven Lord on High" (Hao Tian Shangdi). The altar was open so that all celestial spirits, such as Heaven, could gain access to the ritual feast at the altar only after it was rendered into smoke and dispersed into the ether. The altar was round because Heaven was itself construed as round. Only the emperor could offer a Great Sacrifice because he was the highest living being and because he had exclusive access to Lofty Heaven Shangdi through the intermediary presence of his own ancestor, the founding emperor of the dynasty, whose spirit tablet faced west next to that of Heaven on the highest platform of the altar. The presence of lesser deities invited to share in this ritual feast as correlates suggests that the cosmic realm over which Heaven reigned was further subdivided into other subordinate realms. The sun received secondary sacrifice as Great Light, and the moon as Evening Light. Gods of the stars occupying the twenty-eight heavenly spheres, the five planets (Venus, Jupiter, Mercury, Mars, and Saturn), Lord Wind, and commanders Cloud, Thunder, and Rain received secondary sacrifice at the Great Sacrifice. The power of these gods affected the human world from above as it circulated throughout the heavens, above the world of the living. All of these correlate deities also received Middle Sacrifice from officers of the court as the chief deities at their own altars.

Cult of Earth. Heaven was not omnipotent in the cosmos, it was simply the highest of all gods. As a yang force, it initiated all things and thus required a receptive yin force—the Earth—to bring all things to fruition. Earth received sacrifice as August Earth God (Huangdi chi) on the summer solstice at an open square mound/altar (because Earth was seen as square) north of the city. As in the cult of Lofty Heaven Shangdi, the emperor observed a three-day purification fast, then offered Great Sacrifice to Earth, again with the intermediary presence of his ancestor, the dynastic founder. The presence of lesser gods who received correlate sacrifice at the square altar reveals the properly terrestrial quality of the cosmos governed by Earth. The Five Sacred Peaks and other lesser mountains, the Four Seas and the Four Rivers (Yangzi, Yellow, Huai, and Ji) constituted subservient, more particularized forces subsumed under the power of Earth. Some of these, such as Mount Tai among the Five Sacred Peaks, were historically more ancient objects of cult veneration than Earth, an overtly less particularized cosmic force associated with things terrestrial. These cosmic forces exerted powerful, yet more circumscribed, influence in relation to celestial gods, along Earth's "square" surface.

These separate sacrifices to Heaven and Earth at altars dedicated to each during the Ming and Qing (1644–1911 CE) were based on the precedents established in the *Record of Rites* and the *Rites of Zhou*. During most of the imperial era, however, Earth received joint sacrifice with Heaven at the round altar in the southern suburb. The rationale for joint sacrifices was initially not based on canonical precedent but on the intuitive conviction that as coeval forces in the cosmos they should be combined. The joint rites were vigorously debated in the Song, when opponents appealed to the canonical authority of the *Rites of Zhou*, and proponents to the less lofty, but apparently more compelling, argument of precedents set by long-standing dynastic practice. Joint sacrifices were continued in the Yuan and early Ming dynasties, although vigorous debate began anew in the first year of the Ming and culminated in the ritual reforms of the Jiajing era, when separate liturgies were formulated. Even after these changes, and in spite of the zealousness of the debates, sacrifice to Earth was not, in practice, scrupulously observed, while that to Heaven most certainly was.

Cult of imperial ancestors. The cults of Heaven and Earth shared the status of the highest-ranking Great Sacrifice in the Ming ritual statutes with the imperial ancestors. The ancestors of Ming emperors and their principal consorts received sacrifice five times a year in a walled complex in the southeastern quarters inside the imperial city. The main gate of the Imperial Temple opened from the south into the compound where three enclosed halls were arrayed along a north-south axis that paralleled the layout of the imperial city. The first hall called the Great Shrine (*taimiao*) was the location of combined rites for former emperors (*dixia*). The second building, the Inner Apartments (*qindian*), housed the spirit tablets of no more than seven imperial ancestors, kept in niches housed in seven halls according to the ritual precedents found in the *Record of Rites*. Behind the Inner Apartments was the Hall of Removed Tablets (*tiaomiao*) for the dynastic founder's ancestors, extending back five generations; other former emperors who were removed from among the seven emperors housed in the Inner Apartments as the most recently deceased rulers were also installed there.

The arrangement of the tablets in the Ming Imperial Temple clearly illustrates the intersection of cult practice and court politics. The founding emperor, Ming Taizu (r. 1368–1398), occupied the middle, superior position in the Inner Apartments, followed by his successor, seated to his left, then the five most recent ancestors of the reigning emperor, who led the ceremony. The tablet to Taizu's left was that of Ming Taizong—the Yongle emperor (r. 1402–1424), later canonized as Ming Chengzu—who killed his nephew, the second emperor, burned the palace in Nanjing, and relocated the capital in Beijing. The reign of the second emperor was expunged from the court annals and his name tabooed in the hallowed ancestral halls. The conventions of imperial succession are again interrupted in the sequence of tablets with the presence of an ancestor who never reigned at all. He was posthumously granted the status of emperor, amid tumultuous court controversy, after Ming Shizong succeeded his cousin, who had left no heir, as emperor. Rather than allow himself to be adopted into his cousin's line, Shizong insisted upon retroactively inserting his parents into the line of emperors. Historians have debated his motives for centuries, but at the very least, filial piety, ancestral cult devotion, and political legitimation are inextricably tangled together in this affair.

The official ancestral cult of the imperial court descends from ancient rites that date to as early as the Shang dynasty. Extant oracle-bone inscriptions record sacrifices to the royal ancestors and entreaties by kings for their ancestors to intercede in their requests to the gods to bring rain, bountiful harvests, or military victories. By the Zhou dynasty, the cult of ancestors was widely practiced among the lower hereditary lords, when ritual scholars began to codify these rites. By the Song dynasty, ancestral cult practices were nearly universal among virtually all people throughout China. Even before the Ming—when the court began to regulate cult practices of commoners for the first time—the canonical rites of serving the spirits of the ancestors found in the Confucian classics profoundly influenced the religious consciousness of peasants. Commoners, Confucian literati, and the Son of Heaven all believed that the spirits of departed ancestors required sustenance, which only male descendants could proffer. The ritual feasting of ancestral spirits by the living constituted the primary means of communication with the spirit world. Cult feasting served to sustain the ancestors in the netherworld, which they requited by exercising influence over the fate of their living descendants. In addition to material benefits and emolument, high status among the living brought expanded privileges to offer sacrifices to ever-greater numbers of ancestors.

Notwithstanding Confucian criticisms of popular customs as licentious, it is often difficult to distinguish elite from popular religious practice, particularly on the crucial level of the relationship between the living and the spirits of their ancestors. Licentiousness largely referred to the mixing of sexes across lineage and affinal lines or to noncanonical, usually sexual, relations between gods and shaman priestesses. The religious sensibilities of commoners tended to be more overtly intertwined with local and noncanonical religious ideas—in the specific sense of ideas not found in the Confucian canon—from Daoism and Buddhism than those of the classically educated elite. But the Confucian literati were hardly free from such influences. Were one to distinguish elite from popular religion at all, one would need to do so as a difference of degree of "strict canonical purity" at one end of a spectrum and increasingly dense saturation of regional, local custom or Daoism and Buddhism at the other, rather than as a difference of kind. Although Confucian classical learning and philosophy no doubt influenced commoners, particularly through the examination system, it was largely through the spread of ancestor worship into virtually every household in China that Confucianism had its most profound and permanent impact.

Cult of soils and grains. A fourth cult ranked as Great Sacrifice is that of the gods of soils (*she*) and grains (*ji*), which are among the most ancient of the imperial cults. They are also among the most complex in that they are simultaneously local—grounded in the very soils of the community—and overtly tied to the ruler's sovereignty. In ancient times, the *she* altar was synonymous with the king, the land of his kingdom, and the welfare of his subjects. To destroy the altar once used to honor the soils gods was unthinkable, and to use it was either usurpation or confusion of different polities. The *she* cult of many ancient ritual traditions substituted for, or overlapped with, the cult of Earth as Heaven's counterpart, as seen in the "Single Victim Suburban Sacrifice" (*jiao tesheng*) chapter of the *Record of Rites*, which states, "*She* sacrifice takes the way of Earth as the deity." In the second month of the spring and autumn during Ming times, Great Sacrifice was offered by the emperor to gods of soils and grains on separate altars at a two-tiered open, square altar (thus replicating Earth's square mound in the northern suburbs) within a walled complex inside the imperial city. Rites at the *she* altar, built on an earthen mound with different colored soils from the five cardinal directions (North, South, East, West, and Center), included correlate sacrifices to Lord Soil (Houtu goulong). Rites at the *ji* altar for grains, built on an earthen mound with yellow soil and (at least during the Yuan dynasty) no spirit tablet, included correlate sacrifices to Lord Millet (Houji), ancestor of the Zhou royal family.

The cults of Heaven, Earth, the imperial ancestors, and soils and grains occupied the highest level of the imperial pantheon. As recipients of Great Sacrifice, they are distinguishable from all other cults in at least four interrelated ways: (1) they were the most exalted and powerful gods ruling the cosmos, and thus the emperor alone could offer sacrifice, except under extraordinary circumstances when either the heir apparent or a high-ranking official acted as surrogate; (2) they were most closely tied to the virtue and legitimacy of the ruler who led the rites, and any ruler who was not virtuous was not legitimate; (3) they were all located in the imperial city or outside its walls—their exact location was geographically and cosmically fixed not only by the surrounding terrain as ascertained by geomancy, but also by their proximity to the emperor's throne; and (4) they were all sanctioned by the Confucian canon. Although the canonical sources contain more than one version of some of these cults—which partly explains why controversies about them never ceased—there was no doubt in anyone's mind that they originated in the golden era of the Zhou dynasty.

Middle-level and miscellaneous cults. The second level of the imperial pantheon was occupied by lesser gods that received middle-level sacrifices (*zhongsi*) from officers of the court, and, on some occasions, by the emperor or the heir apparent. Some middle-level cults were regional variations of the higher cults, such as soils and grains, stars, wind and rain, mountains and rivers. Other middle-level cults developed later, with little, or at best a tenuous, canonical foundation. Two agricultural cults began in the Eastern Han (25–220 CE). The First Farmer received sacrifice at a shrine, followed by the principal consecration officer's ceremonious turning of the first three furrows of the planting season. Although court debates questioned if this was not a conflation with the soils god, it continued, with occasional participation by the emperor, until the Qing dynasty, when Manchu rulers performed this rite assiduously. Parallel sericulture rites performed by the empress also date to the Eastern Han period.

Confucius was venerated as the principal deity in a middle-level cult of civil culture. Initially a local cult observed by Confucius's descendants and disciples in Qufu, Shandong, where he lived, the cult of Confucius was patronized by imperial entourages since the early Han. By the Tang dynasty it was integrated into the imperial pantheon, with a temple cult in the capital. From the Tang until the early Ming, Taigong Wang, a general who served the founders of the Zhou dynasty, was the primary deity of a military cult. He was enshrined as a correlate in the cult of past rulers in 1388 and replaced by Guandi, a heroic minister at the end of the Han dynasty to whom miraculous powers were attributed and who had acquired an enormous popular following throughout the empire. The kings and emperors of past dynasties also received cult sacrifice in the Temple of Former Dynasts beginning in the Ming. This consolidated various local rites performed since the Sui (581–618) at tomb sites of past rulers scattered throughout north China, beginning with the legendary sage-kings of high antiquity. The liturgy and temple layout followed that of the Imperial Temple, except that court officials were usually dispatched to perform these rites. The gods of walls and motes (usually referred to as "city gods" in English), and those of the flags and banners of the southern wall and instruction halls of provincial capitals, also received middle-level sacrifice.

Most of these middle cults had counterparts as miscellaneous cults (*qunsi*) and received minor sacrifices (*xiaosi*) from local officials at the district and county levels. Local officials also offered sacrifices to the ghosts of abandoned ancestors and those who died violent deaths at special altars outside the walls of towns and cities. In addition to these official cults, the Ming court also passed sumptuary prescriptions regulating private cults, such as those for the gods of soils and grains of individual plots of land, for ancestors extending back two generations at altars in the homes of commoners or shrines operated by larger clan organizations, and for the spirits that inhabited kitchen stoves. The Ming court was more inclined than its predecessors to prescribe ritual duties to commoners, thereby formally linking the loftiest of imperial cults, which were tended by the emperor at the center, with cult activities of merchants and artisans in towns, as well as cultivators in villages, within a cohesive, overarching pantheon.

Ritual Purity. In the Confucian world of cults, the orderly operation of the cosmos required proper performance of the rites of sacrifice to the gods. Proper performance of the rites entailed observing distinctions among the gods, who were divided into a three-tiered hierarchy based on criteria of antiquity, canonicity, and cosmic power. Ritual distinction was marked by a number of indicators: the kind and location of the ritual space where a cult was practiced; the kind and amount of offerings; the music, dance, and prayers of the liturgy; and the position or rank of the person who offered the sacrifice. And what of the living persons who came before the gods offering gifts of supplication at the altar? What qualifications must the sacrificer possess to earn such a privilege? A key to understanding the religious import of the rites of the imperial cult is that the sacrificer did not act for his own benefit but for that of the entire community for which he was responsible. An imperial cult conducted by a formal, governing body, by definition, is public; it is "civil," not private. The sacrificer acts for the well-being of a people and does not seek nor expect personal gain, such as salvation, enlightenment, or inner, spiritual transformation. It is clear from the relationship between the living and the gods that such things were not in the offing, even if the sacrificer sought them.

How are we to understand the inner state of the sacrificer? Surely there was a range of interpretations of cult rites among those who practiced them, but the canonical description of the inner state of the sacrificer found in the *Record of Rites* was repeatedly endorsed in later ritual texts and discussions of the rites, which emphasize ritual efficacy. These sources stress the necessity of undergoing purification rites before the sacrifice in order to realize a state of reverence and single-minded concentration on the spirit that is to receive sacrifice. This state of ritual purity makes it possible to communicate the sacrifices to the gods. Ritual purity is realized in the days before the actual sacrifice through observing regulations and a fast. A ritual specialist explained the process to the first emperor of the Ming by saying:

> The regulations delimit the external and the fast orders the internal. The regulations prescribe a bath and change of clothes. In your comings and goings, do not drink wine, eat meat, inquire about the illness of others, observe mourning, listen to music, or pass judgment on criminals. The fast concentrates the mind on the sacrifice; it is to be strict, cautious, and fearful. Think only of the spirit that is to receive the sacrifice, as if it is there above you or to your left or right. The fast means to be perfectly pure and completely sincere without a moment's lapse. (*Mingshi* 47.1239–1240)

Thus the ritual purity of the sacrifice is not achieved through extirpating defilement or purging sin—a concept that is noticeably absent in writings on imperial cults—but by so concentrating one's consciousness on the spirits that one can "almost certainly see them at the altar." The virtue of one's reverence toward the spirits is a precondition of the rite. Upon completing the rite, what one has accomplished or gained is the success of communicating the feast to the gods.

Political Legitimation and the Imperial Cults. Some twentieth-century social scientists have argued in a functionalist mode that imperial cult rituals were simply a means employed by the ruling elite to control the populace. As with other religions with direct connections to regimes of political power, successful performance of the rites of the imperial cult brought prestige and enhanced political legitimacy to those who performed them. Not to perform the rites was a clear indication of illegitimacy, and they were apparently rarely if ever abandoned by ruling dynasts, except in times of grave trouble when it was not possible to perform them. As such, these cult rituals were a sine qua non of legitimate rule during imperial times because the gods were believed to possess great power and their assistance was deemed necessary.

Suburban Sacrifice to Heaven/Shangdi at the Round Altar. The following description of the sacrifice to Heaven is based on the imperial liturgy of the Ming dynasty after the Jiajing reforms. Understanding a complex ritual such as this depends not only upon grasping its numerous details, but also obtaining a clear sense of the sequence of its parts and of the duration of ritual time involved in performing the liturgy. Although all elements of the rite were necessary, some carried more weight, as demonstrated by, for example, the emperor's repeated visits to the Imperial Shrine to notify his ancestors of his intention to perform this rite and to request the founding emperor's presence at the altar. The materials offered to the god, such as jade and the animals used for the feast, were carefully selected and inspected. Incense was used to attract the gods, who were invited to partake in the feast no less than three times. The fastidious attention to the person of the sacrificer, his clean and proper clothes, pure mental state, and appropriate corporeal demeanor all attest to the singular importance of each.

Preparation for the ceremony began ten days beforehand when the Office of Imperial Sacrifice sent officers to inspect the animals to be used in the sacrifices: nine calves, three sheep, and three pigs. Five days before the ceremony, imperial guards escorted the emperor to the cleansing pen to inspect the victims. Imperial sacrifice focused on presenting food to the gods—not on killing—and thus these animals were not slaughtered at the altar, but were carefully prepared in the temple kitchen in advance as part of a feast for the gods. The night before this the emperor, wearing ordinary dress, went to the Imperial Shrine inside the Forbidden City, where he offered incense to each of the imperial ancestors, beginning with the dynastic founder. He then announced his intention to offer sacrifice to August Heaven Shangdi. Four days before the ceremony, erudite members of the Office of Imperial Sacrifice drafted the prayer that was to be read at the ceremony.

Three days before the ceremony, the emperor, wearing ritual garb, resided in the bedchambers of the Imperial Shrine. Holding a jade scepter tablet that identified him, the emperor formally greeted the ancestral spirits at the main incense table by prostrating himself and offering incense. Before the niche of the founding emperor's spirit tablet he offered libation and read a prayer stating his intention to offer sacrifice to Shangdi, and his request for the founding emperor's presence at the ceremony. On this same day, the emperor and other celebrants began to follow regulations to bathe, wear clean clothes, and refrain from engaging in any activity that might distract them from concentrating on the impending ceremony, such as consoling the bereaved, drinking wine, listening to music, and interacting with their wives. They also observed a purification fast that aimed to bring unified order to their hands, feet, and mind.

On the day before the sacrifice, the emperor went to the Hall for Receiving Heaven in the inner court of the Forbidden City to personally write out the prayer on a new green mulberry-wood board. At this time he also placed green jade and green silk in boxes (shades of blue-green were associated with the color of the heavens). He then offered incense three times and performed one set of three kowtows. Wearing ritual dress, the emperor informed the spirits of his ancestors that he was heading to the Altar of Heaven, then he rode the carriage to the Round Altar. After inspecting the victims, he went to the fasting quarters attached to the altar complex, where he observed a strict fast during which he devoted himself entirely to the pending sacrifice.

Before dawn on the morning of the sacrifice, the minister of rites led the collected officers to the incense altar before the spirits. All knelt to perform three kowtows, then took the spirit tablets out of their niche cupboards, beginning with the lowest-ranking spirit. The officers lined up along the spirit path leading to the Round Altar, and the drums were sounded three times; the emperor left the fasting quarters, entered the altar complex, and assumed his position at the foot of the stairs of the three-tiered Round Altar. A fire was set to stacked wood and the entire victim was cooked so that it was rendered into smoke. The emperor bowed while the minister for ceremonial said, "Having observed a fast and the regulations, sacrifice is offered this morning. With this cleansing, we come before the gods and spirits." The emperor put his jade tablet in his belt, washed and dried his hands, held his tablet and ascended the Round Altar. The minister then said, "The spirits are above us, observe the ceremony carefully!"

The emperor then approached the spirit tablet of Lofty Heaven Shangdi, which faced south on the north side of the highest of the three tiers. Arrayed in front of the tablet was a feast consisting of the single cooked calf, a dark green jade disc, twelve bolts of dark green silk, a bowl of broth, glutinous millets and millet grains, nuts and cakes, sauces and edible grasses, and three tripods for the libation offering (these same foods were offered in lesser amounts to other gods of the pantheon, so it is difficult to read particular symbolic significance into these items). The emperor knelt at the altar, and offered up incense three times; he then bowed, proceeded to the altar of the dynastic founder, and performed the same offerings, then returned to his position on the south side of the third tier. He repeated the same sequence of actions, then presented the first offering (*chuxian*): He washed and dried a tripod, filled it with wine, knelt before the spirit tablet, offered incense, raised the tripod as offering (*dianjue*), poured some of the wine at the base of the altar to guide the spirit to the precise location of the feast, and placed the tripod on the altar in front of the tablet. He performed the same sequence when presenting the first offering to the dynastic founder. The prayer was then read while the emperor prostrated himself, rose, bowed, then returned to his position.

At this point, the secondary consecration officers went to the altars for the other gods on the middle tier and offered incense, silk, and libation. The emperor then presented the second (*yaxian*) and final offerings (*zhongxian*) to Shangdi and the dynastic founder, which was followed each time by the secondary consecration officers' presentation of offerings to the other gods. The emperor drank some of the blessed wine and received a portion of the sacrificial meat; the viands were then cleared away and the spirits escorted away from the Round Altar. The text of the prayer and the silk were finally burned as a means of commuting them to the world of the spirits. Once these had been at least half consumed by fire, the ceremony ended.

SEE ALSO Chinese Religion, overview article, article on Mythic Themes.

BIBLIOGRAPHY

Bilsky, Lester James. *The State Religion of Ancient China.* Taipei, 1975.

Chang, K. C. *Art, Myth, and Ritual: The Path to Political Authority in Ancient China.* Cambridge, Mass., 1983.

Fisher, Carney. *The Chosen One: Succession and Adoption in the Court of Ming Shizong.* London, 1990.

Ho Yun-yi. *The Ministry of Rites and Suburban Sacrifices in Early Ming.* Taipei, 1980.

Keightley, David. *The Ancestral Landscape: Time, Space, and Community in Late Shang China, ca. 1200–1045 B.C.* Berkeley, 2000.

Lewis, Mark Edward. *Sanctioned Violence in Early China.* Albany, N.Y., 1990.

McDermott, Joseph P., ed. *State and Court Ritual in China.* New York and Cambridge, UK, 1999.

McMullen, David. *State and Scholars in T'ang China.* Cambridge, UK, 1988.

Meyer, Jeffrey. *The Dragons of Tiananmen: Beijing as a Sacred City.* Columbia, S.C., 1991.

Naquin, Susan. *Peking: Temples and City Life, 1400–1900.* Berkeley, 2000.

Neskar, Ellen. "The Cult of Worthies: A Study of Shrines Honoring Local Confucian Worthies in the Sung Dynasty, 960–1279." Ph.D. diss., Columbia University, 1993.

Puett, Michael. *To Become a God: Cosmology, Sacrifice, and Self-Divinization in Early China.* Cambridge, Mass., 2002. A provocative explanation of the formation of gods in early China.

Rawski, Evelyn S. *The Last Emperors: A Social History of Qing Imperial Institutions.* Berkeley, 1998. Chapter six describes imperial cult practices of the Manchu emperors.

Stuart, Jan, and Evelyn Rawski. *Worshiping the Ancestors: Chinese Commemorative Portraits.* Stanford, Calif., 2001.

Taylor, Romeyn. "Official and Popular Religion and the Political Organization of Chinese Society in the Ming." In *Orthodoxy in Late Imperial China,* edited by Kwang-ching Liu, pp. 126–157. Berkeley, 1990.

Wechsler, Howard. *Offerings of Jade and Silk: Ritual and Symbol in the Legitimation of the T'ang Dynasty.* New Haven, 1985. A thorough examination of the formation of rituals in the Tang with particular concern for the issue of political legitimacy.

Wilson, Thomas, ed. *On Sacred Grounds: Culture, Society, Politics and the Formation of the Cult of Confucius.* Cambridge, Mass., 2003. A collection of essays on the formation of the cult of Confucius in imperial times to the post-Mao era.

Yang, C. K. *Religion in Chinese Society: A Study of Contemporary Social Functions of Religion and Some of Their Historical Factors.* Berkeley, 1961. A functionalist account of Chinese religion.

Zito, Angela. *Of Body and Brush: Grand Sacrifice as Text/Performance in Eighteenth-Century China.* Chicago, 1997. A semiotic reading of imperial sacrifice that shows the ritual construction of the Manchu emperor's filial body.

The description of imperial cult rituals is based on the ritual treatises (*lizhi*) in dynastic histories of the Han (*Hanshu*), Latter Han (*Hou Hanshu*), Tang (*Jiu Tangshu*), Song (*Songshi*), Ming (*Mingshi*), and Qing (*Qingshi gao*), and the following sources:

Li Dongyang and Shen Shixing, comps. *Da Ming huidian.* 5 vols. (1587 ed.). Taipei, 1976.

Long Wenbin. *Ming hui yao.* 2 vols. Taipei, 1956.

Mukedeng'e, Wang Tingzhen, et al., eds. *Da Qing tongli.* Rev. ed. 1824.

Wang Bo et al., eds. *Tang huiyao.* 2 vols. Shanghai, 1992.

Zheng Xuan and Kong Yingda, eds. *Liji zhengyi.* In *Shisan jing zhushu,* 3 vols. (1816), edited by Ruan Yuan. Beijing, 1980. vol. 1: 1221- vol. 2: 1696.

Thomas A. Wilson (2005)

CONFUCIANISM: HISTORY OF STUDY

Any effort to describe Confucianism (*ru,* literally "weakling" but conventionally glossed as "scholar") as an object of study requires one to acknowledge that it is a historically related symbolic complex made from the fateful conjunction of early modern European and Chinese curiosity. The greater weight of the scholarly output of this conjunction has been borne by Western interpreters. The reason for this is obvious: *ru* was never actually a subject of conscious investigation by the Chinese until around 1900, and *Confucianism* is, as Lewis Hodous declared in the 1911 edition of the *Encyclopedia Britannica,* "a misleading general term for the teachings of the Chinese classics upon cosmology, the social order, government, morals and ethics." A celebrated case of metaphor as mistake yielded four centuries of analysis, commentary, and most importantly, translations through which Confucianism and the essential China it metonymically contained were exactingly documented for purposes of admiration or attack. Over this interval the figure of "Confucius" acquired global fame, while the native figure, Kongzi, was revered for millennia as Chinese culture's greatest sage and teacher. In the context of this great encounter, the meaning of which was slowly distilled through Confucianism, the place of China and Confucianism has shifted within Western cultural self-consciousness. China's value for the West has changed, and along with it the significance of Confucianism; however, the one salient constant has been the global character of this complex.

The term *Confucianism* familiar to most early twenty-first century readers is the nominal equivalent of the expressions *ru, rujia, ruxue,* the meanings of which are scholar, classical tradition, and classical teaching, rather than the teaching of Confucius (Kongzi, 551–479 BCE). Confucianism has meant, most notably: (1) a system of thought; (2) a mechanism of social control or state ideology; and (3) China's civil religion or ethos, in this sense being indistinguishable from China itself and thus a very worthy subject of study. Confucianism stands for a great number of things both enabling and disabling of any effort to compile a history of it as an object of study.

Prior to the eighteenth century and the intellectual debates between scholars of the new and old script traditions of Chinese classical scholarship, there was really no effective study of Confucianism. Instead, there were the manifold traditions of textual communities underwritten by exegesis and commentary on any of the *jiujing,* or nine classic works (Book of Documents, Book of Odes, Classic of Change, Spring and Autumn Annals, Record of Rites, Guliang Commentary, Gongyang Commentary, Zuo Commentary, and the Rites of Zhou) all believed to have been edited, inspired, or written by Kongzi. The work on these texts, the form of study about which one might write a history, is best understood as an inspired scholarly practice analogous to biblical hermeneutics in the West. The history of this engagement with texts in the interest of getting at the timeless truths of antiquity has been eloquently retold by John Henderson in *Scripture, Canon and Commentary* (1991) and Benjamin Elman in *From Philosophy to Philology* (1984), but it is not really about Confucianism per se.

***Ru:* A Chinese Context of Confucianism Study.** The life Confucianism has lived as a form of study in the West was distinct, and until very recently largely different, from the scholarly history of *ru* in China. The epistemic status of the *ru* as an object of study was registered in the first "history" of China, Sima Tan (d. 110 BCE) and Sima Qian's *Shiji* (Grand Scribe's Records, c. 90 BCE). Here the category *rujia* was explicitly identified as one of the primary traditions of Chinese antiquity. *Ru* was a native tradition self-consciously attested to in the writings of the Warring States (479–256 BCE) and achieved a degree of national prominence in the first two imperial dynasties Qin (221–206 BCE) and Han (206 BCE–221 CE), when scholars (*boshi*) of specific classical works (*Shijing* [Book of Poetry], *Shangshu* or *Shujing* [Book of Documents], and *Yijing* [Book of Changes]) were appointed to government posts, a practice that continued, somewhat fitfully with well-noted interruptions, until the abolition of the official examination system in 1905. With the advent in the Han of an elaborate scholastic enterprise involving the cataloguing of all extant written works and the writing of an official history of civilization, *ru*—the de facto classicists of this time—assumed an official presence disproportional to their numbers among the plural intellectual traditions of the early imperial period.

The Chinese Empire was built upon texts—astronomical, divinatory, legal, medical, philosophical, ritual, and strategic—and was as much a semiotic system as a political entity. With classicists such as *ru* serving as prominent producers and interpreters of texts, they were, as Christopher Connery has argued, drawn into the care of the empire. In the Han capital of Chang'an an imperial academy, the Guozi jian, was founded with a syllabus organized around favored *ru* texts. An imperial sacrifice to Kongzi was initiated at his natal home of Qufu more than 750 miles to the east of the capital (in the second century BCE) along with a panoply of other official celebratory rites, by means of which the emperor sought legitimacy with both man and nature. This particular cultural concatenation of the appointment of *ru* and the formation of the imperial Kongzi cult may be taken as the Chinese foundation of "Confucianism"; it was also a phenomenon that, at a much later period, drew the attention of the Jesuit missionaries and became the focus of scholarly inquiry, as some sought in this confluence evidence of so-called Oriental Despotism or of a distinctive modern conjunction of royal authority and religious tolerance.

The official rise to prominence of the previously undistinguished *ru* fellowship is dated at 136 BCE, a moment that is considered epochal, because it is here that the monolithic myth of a two-thousand-year marriage of "Confucianism" and the Chinese imperium began. Beyond the nascent national prominence of metropolitan *ru* celebrated in the imperial cult to Kongzi, there were a number of other *ru* textual communities—eight according to Han Feizi (c. 280–233 BCE)—all inspired by the memory of the culture hero. On evidence provided by the *Shiji*, it is also known that by the time of the Han dynasty's founding there were myriad autochthonous temple cults to Kongzi. By the dawn of imperial times, the tradition of *ru* meant classical study (*jingxue*).

The earliest uses of *ru* are found just before the formation of the first Chinese imperial state, when it meant "pliable" or "weak" in the sense of disinclined to physical work; yet the term was clearly associated with the story traditions of an honored teacher, Kongzi. An eponymous discourse or a school of thought, *Kongjiao*—"Kong teaching," with perhaps "Confucianity" being better—did not exist until the first years of the twentieth century, when it was an antidote self-consciously administered by the state to combat the effects of foreign religious and social doctrines. This later invention, more literally Confucianism, was conceived as a national ethos distinct from *ru*, which referred to scholars of the *Wujing* (Five Classics—Book of Documents, Book of Changes, Book of Odes, Record of the Rites, Spring and Autumn Annals) and, later in the Yuan and Ming eras, the *Sishu* (Four Books—Selected Sayings [of Kongzi], Book of Mengzi, Doctrine of the Mean, Great Learning).

THE AGONISTIC RELATION OF *RU* AND THE IMPERIUM. This political tradition of administrative dependence on *ru* texts and ethos was noted with admiration by Western observers, but there was even more evidence conducive to their judgment that Confucianism was the *clavis Sinica,* or key to China. In 1313 the Mongols, ruling as the Yuan dynasty, reestablished the metropolitan examination, which promoted the annotations and commentaries on the *Wujing* and the *Sishu* of the southern Song classicist Zhu Xi (1130–1200), founder of a fundamentalist *ru* sect called *daoxue* (learning of the path), as the required texts for preparation for official service. The vernacular quality of Zhu's commentaries made them especially suitable for use by conquest elites, and their particular recensions endured until the twentieth century. This six-century continuity of use, and especially the exclusive reliance on the *Sishu,* ensured the regnancy of *daoxue*—and by association *ru*—as an intellectual orthodoxy indefeasibly linked to the operations of the imperial bureaucracy. Moreover, the formal enshrinement of Zhu Xi and the elevation of *daoxue* and its prominent followers in the hierarchy of the Kongzi temple by the Yuan (1279–1368), Ming (1368–1644), and Qing (1644–1911) dynasties effected the canonization of *ru* as an orthodoxy whose transmission was a concern of the state.

For the most part, self-identified followers of the *ru* tradition filled the ranks of classical scholars, both independent and official; however, there was no systematic study of *ru* until perhaps the *Mingru xue'an* (Cases of Ming Scholars) of Huang Zongxi (1610–1695). Published in 1676, within the same interval as Jesuit translations in Latin of Chinese scriptural texts were first being published in Europe, the *Mingru xue'an* inaugurated a new genre of historical scholarship. The popularity of Huang's critical review of the lives and teachings of an apostolic succession of *ru* exemplars inspired similar compilations on the Song (960–1279) and Yuan periods (*Song-Yuan xue'an*), all construed as records of intellectual descent, providing a historical sketch of the diversity and proliferation of *ru* over imperial time. In Huang's hands *ru* was a prominent object in an historical field, a tradition whose elaboration could be documented through subsequent generations of practitioners. His genealogical reconstruction used the methods of standard philology, not merely to parse obscure classical phrasing but to historicize the present *ru* as active appropriators of the traditions they received. This subtle shift in interpretive agency relocated authority to the reader and away from the government-sanctioned canon, and anticipated the remarkable intellectual developments of eighteenth-century classicism, developments advanced by *ru* but in a manner inconsistent with the honored synarchy of state and scholarship.

Yet just as late Ming *ru*, like Huang, moved to dissolve the heteronomy of research and regime and scholar-official and state, Jesuit missionaries—standing outside the reach of this emergent critical culture—reasserted the identity of *ru* and the empire while insisting that in an era of scholarly disenchantment with inherited tradition, they, too, could engage the texts of antiquity as legitimate readers. And from this point the story of the study of the Confucianism with which we are familiar develops.

CONFUCIANISM: INVENTION AND INTERCULTURAL COMMUNICATION. Since the mid-seventeenth century, when transmission of native Chinese texts to Europe became possible, Confucius and Confucianism have been interpreted as the core of the *sapientia sinica*, or the wisdom of the Chinese, a unique object of aesthetic and religious apprehension avidly sought by linguists, missionaries, philosophers, and scientists. Thus, to study Confucianism was to pursue even greater understanding of China itself, and with proper attention, to disclose the implicit theological unity of East and West. This meant that such scholarly attention was equally animated by the prospects of compatibility and dissimilarity on the grounds of reason and faith, entities of great value in a period of cultural crisis and religious conflict.

The study of Confucianism as we know it begins with the work of a handful of missionaries of the Society of Jesus, who between 1582 and 1610 insinuated themselves into southern Chinese life at the invitation of regional Chinese officials. The missionaries sought converts through a process of thorough enculturation (described by modern scholars as "accommodationism") by which they sought to prove the theological compatibility of Christianity and native Chinese faith. Indeed, it can be argued that the apologetic catechisms, letters, and translations generated by these Jesuits represented the origin of Confucianism. The first work demonstrating an awareness of the figure from whom the term *Confucianism* was derived was a Latin draft of the first Jesuit catechism for prospective Chinese converts, *Vera et brevis divinarum rerum expositio* (True and brief explanation of the divine things). The seventh chapter of this primitive xylographic pamphlet—produced between 1579 and 1583 by Michele Ruggieri (1543–1607) and Matteo Ricci (1552–1610)—was organized as a dialogue between a native philosopher and a Christian priest and included a single mention of "Confutius." Over a little more than a decade, missionary awareness of this cultural icon grew in proportion with the Jesuits' deepening interest in the original teaching of Kongzi and his disciples, who they described as the *legge d'letterati* (order of the literati), *i veri letterati* (true literati) and *xianru* (the primordial *ru*). Throughout the second, and authoritative, catechism written and published in Chinese by Ricci in 1596, *Tianzhu shiyi* (The real significance of the Heavenly Master), Kongzi's tradition was assimilated by the missionaries who increasingly identified themselves as defenders of *zhenru* or the "real *ru*."

Their identification was occasioned by a belief that the texts attributed to Confucius—the *Lunyu* (Selected Sayings, or Analects), the *Zhongyong* (Doctrine of the Mean), and the *Daxue* (Great Learning)—bore witness to an ancient belief in the one God, *shangdi* (lord on high), but more commonly referred to by the Jesuits' Chinese neologism, *tianzhu* (Master of Heaven). Between 1596 and 1608, when Ricci was asked to prepare a history of the Jesuit mission in China, *ru*, *legge d'letterati*, and the Jesuits were indistinguishable, so much so that interpretation of Chinese cultural phenomena was inflected with the Jesuit favor for this tradition, which in their eyes was so much like their own. The understanding of Confucianism as a body of texts and a discipline of study founded by Confucius slowly emerged from the Jesuits' Chinese enculturation and was documented in the history of the mission's entrance into China compiled by Matteo Ricci between 1608 and 1610, *Della entrata della Compagnia di Giesù e Christianità nella Cina* (On the Entrance of the Jesuit Company and Christianity into China), but not published until 1615, after Nicolá Trigault (1577–1628) had completed a tendentious Latin translation (*De Christiana expeditione apud Sinas* [On the Christian Expedition among the Chinese]). Here, in an exposition on the *tre leggi diverse* (three different orders) of Chinese religion, readers learned that:

> the greatest philosopher among them is Confutio [Confucius], who was born 551 years before the coming of the Lord to the world and for more than seventy years lived a very good life teaching this people through words, works, and writings. . . . Not only the literati but the kings themselves venerate him through so many centuries measuring backwards in time . . . and they avow that they themselves display a soul grateful for the doctrine received from him.

What the early missionaries welcomed in Kongzi's teaching were those things they esteemed in their own sodality: the importance of undying fraternal affection; the role of rites in molding meaningful life; elected service to the wise in achieving social harmony; and study as a mechanism of moral self-fashioning. Such appreciation of what would later be called Confucianism as the religious *doppelgänger* of Christianity inspired subsequent efforts to illuminate Chinese religious understanding through translation of scriptural texts from Chinese into Latin and French. Indeed, from the first bilingual (Latin and Chinese) translation of the *Sishu* through the publication of the Reverend David Collie's *The Four Books* (1828) and beyond, the bulk of missiological and scholarly work on Confucianism consisted of efforts to translate and interpret these texts, often without the aid of Chinese commentary. This was the principal legacy of the Sino-Jesuit mission, something borne out well in the reliance of James Legge (1815–1897) on Catholic missionary translations in his encyclopedic translation of the *Sishu* and the *Wujing* between 1865 and 1895.

Less than a decade following Ricci's death in 1610, however, the interest in indigenous sources of Chinese Christianity was aggressively contested by a new generation of missionaries who, along with their Vatican patrons, believed that Confucianism had been willfully misrepresented by the first Sino-Jesuit translators and commentators. Consequently, in the early decades of the seventeenth century and continuing through the eighteenth, a theological debate raged over the possibility of regarding Chinese religion as compatible with Christianity, specifically the popular ancestral rites of Chinese families and the established native terms for God: *shangdi*, *tian*, and *tianzhu*. Strictly literal interpreters like Niccolò Longobardo (1565–1655), whose *De Confucio ejusque doctrina tractatus* (1623; A treatise on Confucius and his doctrine) denounced the apologetic tendency of Ricci's followers to accommodate Chinese and Christian conceptions of God in the term *tianzhu*. Longobardo's was the first of a number of texts devoted to the demolition of interpretative sympathy and the reaffirmation of Catholic orthodoxy, but accommodationist views continued to exist.

The favored texts of Confucianism, specifically the *Lunyu*, *Zhongyong*, *Daxue*, *Mengzi*, and *Yijing*, continued to draw the interest of theological and linguistic speculation. Accommodationism underwrote the production of substantial works of annotated translation such as *Sapientia Sinica* (1662; Wisdom from China), *Sinarum scientia politico-moralis* (1687; The politico-moral learning of the Chinese), *Confucius Sinarum philosophus* (1687; Confucius, philosopher of the Chinese), and *Sinensis imperii libri classici sex* (1711; The authoritative six classics of the Chinese).

As the first translations of selected texts from the Chinese canon appeared in seventeenth-century Europe, Confucius—the cherished Jesuit symbol of archaic monotheism—became a favorite figure among the educated. Very technical translations and interpretive works produced by the missionaries in China were hastily republished and even popularized. Many of these texts, translated from Latin to native vernaculars and republished, circulated widely. For example, the *Sinarum scientia politico-moralis* was translated into French as *"La Science des Chinois"* and republished in 1672 by Melchisedec Thévenot in a popular four-volume work of travel literature titled *Relations de divers voyages curieux* (Accounts of various strange journeys).

The increasing popularity of travel literature in the late seventeenth century was a consequence of the rise of something akin to ethnographic authority that was, in turn, part of a larger epistemological shift away from faith and insight to experiment and observation as the basis of reliable knowledge. In this intellectual context the Jesuits and their Chinese texts were construed as scientific authorities providing testimony on behalf of the universality of divinely authored creation. The local, self-constituting character of the Jesuit mission in China ensured that the Jesuits' texts were widely read, because their authority lay in their having been there "among the Chinese," as the message they were believed to convey about intimations of the divine in China transcended the particular.

Upon its publication in 1687 the *Confucius Sinarum philosophus* was met with intellectual excitement from its lay audience, despite its conceptual sophistication and awkward Latin equivalents of Chinese terms. The work was immediately abridged and translated into French, appearing the following year in Amsterdam as *La Morale de Confucius, Philosophe de la Chine*. An English translation of the French abridgement, *The Morals of Confucius, A Chinese Philosopher*, was published in 1691 in London. Both books were reprinted and, like the first editions, were published as leather-bound parchment pocket books. Each was less than 125 pages and offered an abbreviated sampling of the Jesuit translations of the *Daxue*, *Zhongyong*, and *Lunyu*, a shortened biography of Confucius, a preface by the editors, and an introductory essay titled, "On the Antiquity and Philosophy of the Chinese." This abbreviation and publication of significant portions of the *Confucius Sinarum philosophus* occurred alongside the abridgment and republication of the *Philosophical Transactions* of the Royal Society, which were translated into national vernaculars. So, in the same way that the multilingual European scientific community was sustained by the rapid circulation of the summary volumes of the Royal Society, an educated lay community was joined through the movements of an information network.

Confucius could offer more than a political vision of reasoned stability and civil order; in fact, Confucius and the written language of which he was the most learned representative were conceived of by some natural philosophers and scientists in Europe as features of a semiotic system analogous to mathematics, a universal system of real characters. As an unmediated reflection of nature or the universe, the cogency of this system was dependent on textual evidence of the very sort provided by Philippe Couplet (1623–1693) and others in the *Confucius Sinarum philosophus*.

CONFUCIANISM, COMPARATIVE THEOLOGY AND THE *CONFUCIUS SINARUM PHILOSOPHUS*. The *Confucius Sinarum philosophus*, or *Scientia Sinensis* (Chinese learning), like Isaac Newton's *Principia Mathematica* that was published in the same year, sought to establish the one-to-one correspondences between God's providential order and other signifying systems. It represented the accumulation of one hundred years of translation and exegesis in its demonstration of China's archaic monotheism and offered the first documented use of the descriptive term *Confucian*. Earlier missionary scholarship had similarly focused on history and geography, cartography, or language and grammar, but this work was different: it was a massive annotated translation in service to a more ambitious ecumenical program of comparative theology. It contained detailed chronological tables of Christian and Chinese history, an incomplete translation of a recension of the *Sishu,* an exhaustive critical introduction including a disquisition on popular religion, and a biography of Confucius.

The Jesuit compilers assembled this heterogeneous fund of plural schools, practices, texts, and interpretations into a system identified as the legacy of the mythic philosopher-hero. It was just this metonymic reduction of the many to the one that was responsible for the political significance of the *Confucius Sinarum philosophus* for new states seeking to articulate, justify, and enforce absolute claims to nationhood. Confucius was, in fact, China, and so too could Louis XIV (r. 1661–1715) be France or William III (r. 1689–1702) be England. The Jesuits could not have foreseen such an interpretation of their work, but they did believe that China could be reduced to Confucius, offering at least two reasons that would justify this equivalence.

First, they argued that because he was the author of the *libri classici* (the classics), which are the literary summation of China's ancient culture, Confucius had been immemorially honored. While he was described by Ricci and Trigault as the Chinese equal of "ethnic philosophers" like Plato or Aristotle, a living icon of a system of thought, the authors of the *Confucius Sinarum philosophus* compared Confucius to the Oracle at Delphi, though in higher regard than the latter because he enjoyed more authority among the Chinese than that attributed to the Oracle by ancient Greeks. In this way they presumed Confucius's teachings were a good propaedeutic to Christianity, suggesting the necessary evolution of one into the other.

Second, like the early accommodationists, they saw Confucius's teaching, *ju kiao* (*rujiao*), as a distillation of the ancient belief in *Xan ti* (*Shangdi*), or what the authors now called *Religionem Sinensium* (The Chinese religion.) Here they exceeded the ground-level ethnographic notations on religious practice made by Ricci, demonstrating a compelling cognate philological link between *Xan ti,* Deus, Elohim, and Jehovah. The authors claimed that these four terms were etymologically derived from the same source. It was just such curious philology in support of ecumenism that especially appealed to Leibniz, whose efforts to create a *characteristica universalis* (universal system of characters) were justified by the testimony of these translations.

Revealing something of the indistinguishability of theology and contemporary politics, the authors remind us that the Chinese monarchy had been in place for more than four thousand years, seventeen hundred of which were continuously under the *Magistratum Confucium* (Magistracy of Confucius). The essential equation of China and Confucianism and Christianity as the inevitable singular belief system of China was reinforced in the European imagination by the testimony of "*Siu* Paulus," or Paul Xu (Guangqi, 1562–1633), that "[Christianity] fulfills what is lacking in our Master Confucius and in the philosophy of the literati; it truly removes and radically extirpates nefarious superstitions and the cult of the demons [Daoism, Buddhism, and neo-Confucianism]." In the instability of Europe after the religious wars of the sixteenth century, a reasoned defense of national faith in a single religion or ideology, such as the Jesuits described for China, was read politically as a justification for the peaceful coexistence of national singularity and religious uniformity.

This same interpretive mechanism of unequal complementarity—Christianity as the "high religion" supplemented by the "lower religions" of ethnic others like the Chinese—would soon be found in a host of works on pagan religion and world chronology written by figures like Isaac Newton and David Hume as the quarrel between the Ancients and the Moderns raged among European *philosophes.* The semiotic taxonomies of the imperial genealogy and the *Tabula Chronologica* (a comparative chronology of Chinese and biblical time) included as appendices of the *Confucius Sinarum philosophus* were readily admitted into the rhetoric of authentic representation of the physical world that occupied the energies of seventeenth-century lay intellectuals. The perplexing chasm they faced between the fallen languages of man and the work of God provoked a search by way of linguistics, experimental science, mathematics, and natural philosophy to invent new semiotic forms capable of representing God's creation while avoiding the sin of hubris.

And, once Chinese scriptural texts of Confucianism were understood as semiotic forms representative of nature, then the Jesuits' translations and interpretive commentaries could serve the same pious function as the strategies of Leibniz and Newton. Moreover, Jesuit translations of the "real characters" of Chinese offered evidence of the reasonableness of the contention of European scientists that real characters, the calculus, or a universal language could be deduced from the "natures of things" as unmediated expressions of God's intention. In so doing, the Jesuits named the Chinese system that some Europeans believed was isomorphic with nature and about which, as Umberto Eco has shown, the Europeans increasingly expounded in a search for "the perfect language." These missionaries called this religious system "Confucian."

In inventing this eponymous term the accommodationist compilers of the *Confucius Sinarum philosophus* achieved the fateful reduction of China to Confucius. The "Dedicatory Letter" addressed to Louis XIV that opens the work asserts that "by the blood of Chinese rulers, he who is called Confucius . . . is the wisest moral philosopher, politician, and orator." Elsewhere, Couplet and his coauthors chronologically document the transmission of the genuine *ru* teachings from the heralded moral philosopher to themselves when they write, "the lineage of this one [Confucius] has been propagated with a not-uninterrupted series in this year 1687." At the close of the *Confucii Vita,* the compilers summarize Chinese dynastic descent from the Han dynasty to the present, taking care to note the millennial tribute to Confucius paid by a succession of imperial families. Further, in obvious deference to the self-conception of *le Roi Soleil* (the Sun King), they report that, although Confucius was symbolic of Chinese religion, the rites performed to him were thoroughly secular—"*civiles sunt honores ac ritus illi Confuciani*" (civil are the honors and those Confucian rites)—and here the authors deliver the inevitable neologism, "Confucian."

A paragraph below this phrase, a similar formulation appears. It reads "*vero magis confirmat ritus illos Confucianos merè esse politicos*" (he confirms those Confucian rites are truly political), which again affirms the secular character of the rites in honor of Confucius. These were assurances that the worship of Confucius was not idolatrous and therefore worthy of comparison with the cultlike adulation rendered to Louis XIV by his people. Consequently, the invocation of Louis XIV, "*MAGNI LUDOVICI* [LOUIS THE GREAT]," in the summary paragraph of *Confucii vita*, was intended as a way for Couplet and colleagues to pay homage to their monarch and benefactor by deliberately drawing a comparison between the undying symbol of the Chinese people and the living icon of the French and their enlightened culture. In this way the Chinese dependency complex of *ru* and imperial government was reproduced by Jesuit missionaries. Confucianism was the key to China and it was the language of God among the Chinese. For this reason, above all, whether one wished to extol or repudiate Chinese civilization, Confucianism and Confucius influenced Europe's intellectual agenda.

CONFUCIANISM: THE WILLFUL DIVERGENCE OF CHINA AND THE WEST. In seventeenth- and eighteenth-century works, Confucianism and China were either lionized as exemplifying the light of reason, as in *Novissima Sinica, Nouveaux mémoires sur l'état présent de la Chine* (1696), *Portrait historique de l'empereur de la Chine* (1698), *China Illustrata*, and *Recherches philosophiques sur les Egyptiens et les Chinois* (1773), or denounced for superstitions as in *Lettres Persanes* (1721) and *De L'Esprit des lois* (1748), or extolled for enlightened despotism in "Despotisme de la Chine." Nevertheless, Confucianism remained a touchstone from which Chinese civilization was judged to be enlightened or retrogressive. By the time Leibniz penned his "Remarks on Chinese Rites and Religion" (1707) in which he defended the secular, performative quality of Chinese rituals, the century-long war that had broken out within the church itself over the heretical qualities of Chinese rites and terms (the Rites and Terms Controversy) was resolved with the Nanjing Decree against Chinese practice by papal legate Charles-Thomas Maillard de Tournon (1668–1710), coinciding with a decline in European interest in Confucianism as antidote to the poisons of religious war and inchoate linguistic nationalism.

The two views of Confucianism persisted through the eighteenth and nineteenth centuries, with the sympathetic one grandly proclaimed in 1758 with the publication of a French edition of Diogenes Laertius's (fl. third century CE) *Lives of the Philosophers,* which included a ninety-page exposition of the life and doctrines of Confucius. Yet, this Enlightenment encomium of Confucius did not easily endure as the changing politics of global contact and of the Vatican caused the less sympathetic view to supersede accommodationism. A rising tide of authoritarianism and the active repression of popular cults and Western religions under the Qing moved in sequence with the insistence of Catholic authorities on the fundamental incompatibility of Christianity and Chinese religion, culminating in Pope Clement XIV's (1705–1774) ruling *Dominus ac Redemptor* (Master and Redeemer) of 1773 that dissolved the Society of Jesus.

When Protestant missionaries made inroads into China's hinterland in the early decades of the nineteenth century, arguments for a global theologico-cultural compatibility were silenced by the gunships of China's colonial trading partners; Confucianism, with its deference to patriarchal authority, was identified as a fundamental cultural weakness. By the first years of the twentieth century, China was no longer the site of exotic imaginings, wanderlust, and curiosity it had been for Jesuit missionaries and European accommodationists. It was "opened" by the Western nations that had established a commanding economic, political, and religious presence along China's coast. The meaning of Confucianism and the nature of its study changed. Confucianism became a symbol of local obstruction of a vast cultural space made continuous through the operation of the market. The Jesuit melding of native Chinese practice and Christianity, which undergirded the seventeenth-century search for the perfect language and drew China and the West closer, was replaced by nineteenth-century ideas of greater currency and scientific weight—nationalism, imperialism, and evolution—making the imaginative space between China and the West as great as their geographic distance.

The history and politics here are quite complex, but they tell us little about Confucianism, that is until Max Weber (1864–1920) turned his attention to the sociology of Chinese religion. The publication in 1915 and 1920 of his two-volume *Konfuzianismus und Taoismus*—more commonly known by the problematic title of its English translation, *The Religion of China* (1951)—drew benefit from the equation of China and Confucianism and from the interpretive predilection to hold Confucianism accountable for China's cultural stagnation. *The Religion of China* marks a turning point in the study of Confucianism. It returned China to meaningful engagement with the West as it cast the specific history of Confucianism's mediation of capitalism against the backdrop of world secularization. Weber's comparative sociology was motivated by an historical interest in determining the specific conditions for the rise of rational capitalism in Europe. His study of China was premised on a negative question—why rationalization did not give rise to capitalism—the answer to which cast light on both Europe's Protestant and China's Confucian spiritualities.

Weber's conclusion that the development of rational entrepreneurial capitalism in China was undermined by Confucianism's distinctive ethos of rational, world accommodation, in contrast with Protestantism, whose impulses toward transcendence displayed a productive, world-renouncing tension, has been contested for a century. And yet by calling attention to Confucianism as a mediating spirituality by means of which the Chinese, especially the literati (*ru* scholar-officials), processed the dramatic changes in consciousness and material life brought by modernization, he provided the analytical tools used in all subsequent study of Confucianism, especially the scholarly work on neo-Confucianism of the 1950s through the 1970s and even the contemporary intellectual movements of *xinrujia,* or New Confucianism.

Twentieth-Century Repudiation and Recovery. Even though the twentieth century may be considered the most productive period of scholarly work on Confucianism, its scholarship has displayed a certain defensiveness due in part to the collapse of the Chinese dynastic state and its reactionary *ru*-infected ideology, Kongjiao. Nativist, nationalist radicals and student revolutionaries between 1880 and 1919 saw in *ru* the entire sordid history of their civilization's cultural effeteness and political sterility. For these pro-Western, "New Culture" intellectuals, insofar as *ru* and Kongzi were symbolically wedded to the ritual theater of Chinese autocracy, they could not be recuperated. China's humiliating position vis-à-vis the world was attributed by these figures to the inherent weakness of Kongjiao, which they saw as lying at the center of the Chinese imperium, a bulwark against the advance of modernity. Nothing symbolized this national helplessness more than the ceding of Chinese territories to Germany and Japan in the Treaty of Versailles ending the Paris Peace Conference.

On May 4, 1919 the May Fourth Movement was launched with the cries of more than 3000 of Beijing University's students and professors who took to the streets to protest this imperialist compromise of Chinese national sovereignty. Seized by a populist urge to forge a new culture governed by science and democracy, they inveighed against the regressive traditionalism of Confucianism, calling on the nation to "smash the shop of the Kong clan" *(pohuai Kongjia dian).* Still, in the first years after World War II, cultural defenses of Confucianism and *ru* were advanced by Chinese and by Western scholars of Chinese intellectual history. The effort to restore dignity and respect to a once-vital intellectual tradition was aimed at reversing the rueful, dismissive trajectory of May Fourth and to counter the conclusions of Max Weber on Chinese religion.

For the radicals, *ru* symbolized a culture so corrupt it required eradication. Against these impulses of rejection, scholars like Hu Shi (or Shih; 1891–1962) contended that the demonization of *ru,* not *ru* itself, was a pathology. In "Shuoru" (An explication of *Ru*), an essay notable for its courage and insight, Hu advanced a theory that *ru* was a religious force, a fount of world civilization on a par with Christianity in the West. This striking reformulation, based on a creative reading of the Book of Changes, selective interpretation of key Warring States' texts, and a critical exegesis of the Bible, was provocative among a circle of Chinese scholars writing from the late 1930s to the 1950s. However, this inspired reconception of *ru* would not secure wider scholarly favor until the 1980s, when Western scholars of Confucianism appropriated the vestiges of Hu's argument and redefined *ru* as a religion definitive of Chinese and East Asian modernity.

Since the 1950s the study of Confucianism has prospered in the United States in particular. Works in the early 1950s on intellectual history focused on Chinese thought, though sometimes without sufficient context, but always to the greater credit of Confucianism. In 1953 alone, several significant publications appeared. *Studies in Chinese Thought,* edited by Arthur Wright (1913–1976) under the auspices of Robert Redfield (1897–1958) aimed to bring about "intercultural communication" through a thoroughly historical account of the dispositions of the Chinese mind in a broadly comparative context. A complete translation by Derk Bodde (1909–2003) of Feng Youlan's (1895–1990) magisterial history of Chinese philosophy, *Zhongguo zhexue shi* (1934; *A History of Chinese Philosophy*), provided Western readers an organized interpretation of certain key figures and texts in Chinese thought. Also in 1953, *Études sociologiques sur la Chine* (Sociological studies of China), by Marcel Granet (1884–1940), was similarly comparative yet more analytical.

These several volumes succeeded in establishing the fundaments of the Chinese worldview within a larger history of ideas, avoiding the narrow equivalence of Confucianism and Chineseness, thereby advancing scholarship beyond the earnest exploration of religio-cultural common ground by Jesuit missionaries and proto-sinologists. Later conference volumes, beginning with John K. Fairbank's (1907–1991) *Chinese Thought and Institutions* of 1957, were to unfold the elaborate, diverse and interlocking connections of time, space, and community in China. Instead, works such as *Confucianism in Action* (1959), *The Confucian Persuasion* (1960), and *Confucian Personalities* (1962) displayed a striking preponderance of the unitary cultural ideal metonymically encapsulated in Confucianism and its nominal derivative, Confucian. A chrestomathy of the essays from these Confucianism collections was produced under Arthur Wright in 1964, bearing the title *Confucianism and Chinese Civilization,* thus revealing the limits of scholarly imagination to compass a grand territory of Chinese experiences. The reduction of Chinese diversity to ideological unity represented by these anthologies provoked a countermovement to explore the full range of China's unrepresented popular cultures that would not come of age until the new social history of the early 1980s.

Confucianism Restored: Indigenous Values and Religion. William Theodore de Bary (1919–) and Wing-tsit Chan (1901–1994) together inveighed prolifically against the notion that Confucianism accounted for China's weakness. They reasserted Confucianism, or more specifically, neo-Confucianism, as definitive of Chinese modernity, a resource of humanitarianism and liberalism denied by the iconoclastic excesses of early twentieth-century radicalism. Their work was challenged by the common twentieth-century revolutionary conclusion that the great tradition of China's ancient civilization was irrelevant and that Confucianism had failed—a failure doubly reinforced by the iconoclastic ideology and politics of the nation's two national parties, the Communists and the Nationalists. Also, the rediscovery of a materialist, scientific Marx and the intellectually creative rage of protesting students in the 1960s and 1970s in Europe and the United States problematized the notion of a broad civic culture of Confucian *shidafu* (scholar-officials) that, through the universality of civilization, overcame the particularity of class.

Furthermore, the trend of postwar area studies scholarship encouraged by the U.S. government was toward social science and contemporary politics, with a focus on the causes and consequences of the Chinese revolution. Chan and de Bary's work bucked all these trends in claiming that the cultural context of twentieth-century China was generated in the Song era with the advent of Zhu Xi's *daoxue*, otherwise known as "neo-Confucianism." The study of Confucianism via neo-Confucianism accelerated in the 1970s and 1980s, with additional conference volumes as the principal vehicle for its development. Politics and cultural struggles drove U.S. scholars to advance a defense of Confucianism and the Chinese civilization through a reappraisal of neo-Confucianism and the compensatory redescription of Chinese philosophy through common western philosophical terms.

Picking up on Hu Shi's early-twentieth-century view, while developing Chan and de Bary's interests in neo-Confucianism, Tu Weiming (1940–) has become one of the principal representatives for the creative reinvention of Confucianism as religion. Tu and other Confucian-values advocates place themselves self-consciously in what he has termed a "Third Wave" of rejuvenation of the *ru* tradition. This contemporary incarnation of the tradition must be recognized, he insists, as a new ethical world religion on par with Islam, Judaism, and Christianity and capable of generating a similar fundamentalism: "Confucianism so conceived is a way of life which demands an existential commitment on the part of Confucians no less intensive and comprehensive than that demanded of the followers of other spiritual traditions such as Judaism, Christianity, Islam, Buddhism, or Hinduism."

In this particular context Tu's argument for equal theological status with world religions resembles the formalistic equating of Chinese and Western philosophy found in Wing-tsit Chan's *Sourcebook of Chinese Philosophy,* where one learns that "in order to understand the mind of China, it is absolutely necessary to understand Chinese thought, especially Neo-Confucianism." The Tu Wei-ming fundamentalist reading of a "New Confucianism" (*xinruxue*) has been embraced by social scientists as definitive of late-twentieth-century Asian modernity and is fully in evidence in recent essay collections such as Joseph B. Tamney and Linda Hsueh-Ling Chiang's *Modernization, Globalization, and Confucianism in Chinese Societies* (2002) and Daniel A. Bell and Hahm Chaibong's *Confucianism for the Modern World* (2003). Such works regard China's impressive economic transformation as caused by its system of values, that is, "Confucianism," thus using Weber's own conception of mediating spirituality to turn on its head his argument about the lack of capitalism in China.

Consequently, the term *Confucianism,* meaning here traditional values of social hierarchy and familial tranquility, exerts considerable influence over academic commentary on the political and economic reforms that have brought China unforeseen prosperity, as seen in recent works by André Gunder-Frank, Samuel Huntington, and David Landes. This common reading has achieved conceptual assent in the West and elaboration in China, Singapore, Taiwan, and Hong Kong as an ideology of sensible capitalist development under the watchful eye of Kongzi/Confucius and managed by authoritarian governments. An editorial in *Renmin ribao* (*People's Daily*) in 1996 declaimed the harmony of Confucianism and China's market Leninism, asserting that "Confucianism's rule of virtues and code of ethics and authority" were "the soul of the modern enterprise culture and the key to gaining market share and attracting customers." Such is the complex and sometimes contradictory rhetorical context of today's New Confucianism.

NATIVISM AND NEW CONFUCIANISM. The term *xinrujia* (or *xinruxue*), loosely translated as "New Confucianism," refers to an intellectual and cultural phenomenon of the last decades of the twentieth century, coinciding with the Chinese economic reforms begun in the early 1980s. Cited by foreign pundits and Communist Party officials as a significant determining factor in China's rapid and largely successful economic transformation, this postmodern Confucianism has growing numbers of followers and advocates, principally in academic institutions in Beijing, Hong Kong, Taipei, and the United States. The increasingly self-proclaimed existence of these *dangdai xinrujia* (contemporary New Confucians) is evidence of a revolution in cultural politics and emergent global intellectual affinities generated by the search of a deracinated intelligentsia for moral justification and the accidental advent of the Chinese economic miracle. By turns considered a matter of cultural identity, religion, philosophy, and social ethos, "New Confucianism"—in its vast range of contemporary cultural reference— is, not unlike its predecessor, "Confucianism," everything and yet no-thing.

Arguably, any Confucianism put forward with good faith at any time after China's twentieth-century revolution must be "new"; there have certainly been currents of *ru* advocacy running in the broader tumultuous stream of Chinese culture in the twentieth century and indeed in previous centuries. Nevertheless, New Confucianism in China at the turn of the twenty-first century is a distinct product of China's economic reforms, particularly the capitalist triumphalism of the Deng Xiaoping era (1979–1997). It unites the diverse contemporary constituencies of the meta-national entity that is *wenhua Zhongguo* (cultural China), while explaining in a mild chauvinist temper the rapid economic expansion of China and the four "mini-dragons" of Hong Kong, Singapore, South Korea, and Taiwan.

In the creative convulsion of the 1980s, *Ruxue* or "Confucianism" returned to respectability as China opened *(kaifang)* to the outside world while looking inward in search of cultural resources that might offer moral solace and regenerate indigenous models for community in the wake of a broader spiritual crisis (*jingshen weiji*). *Ru* revivalism first took its place as a discrete movement to reassess cultural identity, quickly thereafter metamorphosing into a state-supported research institute in Beijing, the China Confucius Research Institute (Zhonghua Kongzi yanjiusuo). And, of the manifold cultural exuberances of this anxious era, New Confucianism, perhaps because of its alignment with the party-state, was one of the few that survived the massacre at Tiananmen in 1989 and the subsequent campaign against bourgeois liberalism. It endured and became a discourse with multiple constituencies as scholars in China who had long worked on the subject in isolation or self-censorship learned of a larger academic dialogue in East Asia and the United States over the restitution of Confucian studies.

This late-twentieth-century frenzy of reinvention followed a longer interval of multiple forms of conceptual invention by Chinese scholars. The very term *New Confucianism* may be traced to He Lin (1902–1992), the Chinese idealist who, writing in the early 1940s about *xinrujia*, saw in the unfolding of a "new" Confucianism (that is, the *xin xinxue* [new learning of the mind] of Wang Yangming, 1472–1529), a cultural path for China's reconciliation of subjective and objective spirit in a manner parallel to that sketched out by Hegel's phenomenology for Europe. His vision was blocked by decades of oscillating violence against "revisionism," bourgeois sentiment, and tradition, most spectacularly the prolonged national campaign of the 1970s to criticize Lin Biao (1908–1971) and Kongzi (*piLin piKong*), wherein everything that was wrong with China was placed at the feet of Confucianism.

Owing to the simultaneous emergence of the revival of Confucianism (*fuxing ruxue*) and of Asian regional hypergrowth, many Communist Party officials have concluded that this coincidence indicates causation. This view directly and fiercely confronts Max Weber's argument that late Qing Confucianism exhibited an ethic of accommodation with the world that inhibited the growth of capitalism and its modern rationality. The capitalist Confucians contend that Confucianism, properly understood—that is, New Confucianism—is as world transforming as Puritanism, but without its otherworldly, transcendent yearnings. Capitalist Confucians, then, represent but one of a growing number of *xinruxue* manifestations in the post–Cultural Revolution era, in which the urge for a secure native identity by Chinese both at home and abroad is paramount.

The faith of this form of New Confucianism is likely to remain prominent in explaining the eminence of Asia in the twenty-first century, given the widespread acceptance of the facticity of Confucianism and of its principal explanatory role in the sophisticated accumulation of Asian capital and Chinese modernization. However, China's capitalist Confucian achievement, that some characterize as "harmony above all," or of the "pervasiveness of the Confucian mentality in contemporary East Asia," occludes a broader vision of the nation's definitive religious pluralism. In this way the scholars of New Confucianism, whether in Boston, Hong Kong, Beijing, or Taipei, commit the grievous error of Han-era orthodoxy—namely, aligning themselves and their readers with the official country, as Kristofer Schipper has pointed out, against "the real country, the local structures being expressed in regional and unofficial forms of religion."

This, of course, was the legacy of Matteo Ricci's elevation of *la legge d'letterati* above the sects of Buddhism and Daoism, as it was the logical interpretive consequence of Max Weber's valorization of the Confucian life orientation over that of Daoism. So it is that all turn-of-the-twenty-first-century talk about a "spiritual Confucianism" or of "Confucian humanism" and any of the other manifestations of essentialist cultural self-definition in fact continues the four-century-old tale of intercultural (transnational) communication. The invention of Confucianism is one of the significant moments in the cultural politics of modernity. Our instinctive familiarity with the figure of Confucius and the ethics and social order for which it stands is testament to the conjoined cultural consciousness of the modern era. Confucianism's invention and reinvention at the hands of its many makers, West and East, has occurred in circumstances of crisis or tumultuous change—late-sixteenth-century Europe, seventeenth-century Europe, late-nineteenth-century China, mid-twentieth-century United States, and late-twentieth-century China. Its development as a field of study thus bears the marks of these times and conveys past and present interpretation forward, with the religious lives of authentic China just beyond our representative reach.

SEE ALSO Chinese Religion, article on History of Study; Daoism, article on History of Study.

BIBLIOGRAPHY

Bell, Daniel A., and Hahm Chaibong, eds. *Confucianism for the Modern World.* Cambridge, U.K., 2003.

Bresciani, Umbero. *Reinventing Confucianism: The New Confucian Movement.* Taipei, Republic of China, 2001.

Cai Shangsi. "Kongzi sixiang de xitong" (The system of Kongzi's thought). In *Chu Hsi and Neo-Confucianism,* edited by Wing-tsit Chan. Honolulu, 1986.

Chan, Wing-Tsit. *A Source Book in Chinese Philosophy.* Princeton, 1969.

Ching, Julia, and Fang Chaoying, eds. *Records of Ming Scholars,* by Huang Tsung-hsi. Honolulu, 1987.

Ching, Julia, and Willard J. Oxtoby. *Moral Enlightenment: Leibniz and Wolff on China.* Leiden, 1992.

Cohen, Paul A. *Discovering History in China: American Historical Writing on the Recent Chinese Past.* New York, 1984.

Connery, Christopher Leigh. *The Empire of the Text: Writing and Authority in Early Imperial China.* Lanham, Md., 1999.

Cook, Daniel J., and Henry Rosemont Jr. *Gottfried Wilhelm Leibniz: Writings on China.* LaSalle, Ill., 1994.

Couplet, Philippe, et al. *Confucius Sinarum philosophus, sive Scientia Sinensis.* Paris, 1687.

Dangdai Ruxue zhi ziwo zhuanhua (The subjective turn in New Confucianism). Taipei, Republic of China, 1994.

de Bary, William Theodore. "A Reappraisal of Neo-Confucianism." In *Studies in Chinese Thought,* edited by Arthur F. Wright, pp. 81-111. Stanford, Calif., 1959.

de Bary, William Theodore, ed., *The Unfolding of Neo-Confucianism.* New York, 1975.

de Bary, William Theodore, and Tu Wei-ming, eds. *Confucianism and Human Rights.* New York, 1998.

Dirlik, Arif. "Confucius in the Borderlands: Global Capitalism and the Reinvention of Confucianism." *boundary 2,* 22 no. 3 (1995): 229–273.

Eber, Irene, ed. *Confucianism: The Dynamics of Tradition.* New York, 1986.

Eco, Umberto. *The Search for the Perfect Language,* trans. by James Fentress. London, 1995.

Elman, Benjamin A. *From Philosophy to Philology: Intellectual and Social Aspects of Change in Late Imperial China.* Cambridge, Mass., 1984.

Elman, Benjamin A., John B. Duncan, and Herman Ooms, eds. *Rethinking Confucianism: Past and Present in China, Japan, Korea, and Vietnam.* Los Angeles, 2002.

Esherick, Joseph. "Harvard on China: The Apologetics of Imperialism." *Bulletin of Concerned Asian Scholars* 4, no. 4 (December 1972): 9–16.

Fairbank, John K., ed. *Chinese Thought and Institutions.* Chicago, 1957.

Fairbank, John K., and James Peck. "An Exchange." *Bulletin of Concerned Asian Scholars* 2, no. 3 (April–July 1970): 51–66.

Fang, Keli, and Li Jinquan, eds. *Xiandai xin Ruxue yanjiu lunji* [Collected Essays on New Confucianism Studies]. Beijing, 1989.

Farquhar, Judith B., and James L. Hevia. "Culture and Postwar American Historiography of China." *positions: east asia cultures critique,* vol. 1, no. 2 (Fall 1993): 486–525.

Feng, Zusheng, ed. *Dangdai xin Rujia* [Contemporary New Confucianism]. Beijing, 1989.

Fung Yu-lan (Feng Youlan). *A History of Chinese Philosophy* I and II, trans. by Derk Bodde. Princeton, N.J., 1952–1953.

Furth, Charlotte, ed. *The Limits of Change: Essays on Conservative Alternatives in Republican China.* Cambridge, Mass., 1976.

Granet, Marcel. *Études sociologiques sur la Chine.* Paris, 1953.

Gunder-Frank, André. *Re-ORIENT: Global Economy in the Asian Age.* Berkeley, Calif., 1998.

Guoji Ruxue yanjiu [International Confucianism Studies]. Beijing, 1999.

Hanshu buzhu [Former Han History with Supplementary Commentaries], comp. by Wang Xianqian. Reprint, Taibei, 1974.

He, Lin. *Rujia sixiang de xinkaizhan: He Lin xinruxue lunzhu jiyao* [The New Unfolding of New Confucian Thought: He Lin's Key Works on New Confucianism]. Beijing, 1995.

Henderson, John B. *Scripture, Canon, and Commentary: A Comparison of Confucian and Western Exegesis.* Princeton, N.J., 1991.

Hsia, Adrian, ed. *The Vision of China in the English Literature of the Seventeenth and Eighteenth Centuries.* Hong Kong, 1998.

Huang Zongxi. *Mingru xue'an* [Cases of Ming Scholars]. Reprint. Taibei, 1969.

Huang Zongxi and Quan Zuwang. *Zengbu Song-Yuan xue'an* [Cases of Song and Yuan Scholars with Supplements]. Sibu beiyao edition. Shanghai, 1920–1937.

Huntington, Samuel P. *The Clash of Civilizations and the Remaking of the World Order.* New York, 1998.

Hu Shi. "The Establishment of Confucianism as a State Religion during the Han Dynasty." *Journal of the North China Branch of the Royal Asiatic Society* 60 (1929): 20–41.

Hu Shi. "Shuo ru" [An Elaboration on *Ru*] (1934). In *Hu Shi wencun* [The Literary Preserve of Hu Shi], Vol. 4. Taibei, 1953.

Jensen, Lionel M. *Manufacturing Confucianism: Chinese Traditions and Universal Civilization.* Durham, N.C., 1997.

Jensen, Lionel M. "Among Fallen Idols and Noble Dreams: Notes from the Field of Chinese Intellectual History." *Studies in Chinese History* 7 (December 1997): 33–67.

Jensen, Lionel M. "Human Rights, Chinese Rites, and the Limits of History." *The Historian* (Winter 2000): 378–385.

Kang, Youwei. *Kongzi gaizhi kao* [Researches on Kongzi, the Reformer]. Reprint, Beijing, 1958.

Lancashire, Douglas, and Peter Hu Guo-chen, trans. *The True Meaning of the Lord of Heaven.* St. Louis, Mo., 1985.

Landes, David S. *The Wealth and Poverty of Nations: Why Are Some So Rich and Others So Poor?* New York, 1998.

Legge, James, trans. *The Chinese Classics.* 5 vols. Reprint. Hong Kong, 1971.

Levenson, Joseph R. *Confucian China and Its Modern Fate: A Trilogy.* Berkeley, Calif., 1969.

Li Madou (Matteo Ricci). *Tianzhu shiyi* [Real Significance of the Heavenly Master]. In *Tianxue chuhan* vol. 1, 351–635.

Li Zhizao, ed. *Tianxue chuhan* [The Essentials of the Heavenly Learning]. 6 vols. Reprint, Taibei, 1965.

Makeham, John, ed. *New Confucianism: A Critical Examination.* London, 2003.

Mendoza, Juan González. *Historia de las cosas, ritos y costumbres, del gran Reyno de la China* [A History of the Most Notable Things, Rites and Customs of the Grand Kingdom of China]. Valencia, 1596.

Metzger, Thomas. *Escape from Predicament: Neo-Confucianism and China's Evolving Political Culture.* New York, 1977.

Montesquieu. *De L'esprit des lois.* Geneva, 1748.

Montesquieu. *Lettres Persanes.* Amsterdam, 1721.

The Morals of Confucius: A Chinese Philosopher. London, 1691.

Moyers, Bill. "A Confucian Life in America." Public Broadcasting System, 1991.

Mungello, D. E. *Curious Land: Jesuit Accommodationism and the Origins of Sinology.* Honolulu, 1985.

Myers, Ramon H., and Thomas A. Metzger. "Sinological Shadows: The State of Modern China Studies in the United States." *Australian Journal of Chinese Affairs,* vol. 4 (Spring 1980): 1–34.

Neville, Robert. *Boston Confucianism: Portable Tradition in the Late-Modern World.* Albany, N.Y., 2000.

Nivison, David S., and Arthur F. Wright, eds. *Confucianism in Action.* Stanford, Calif., 1959.

Pauw, Cornelius de. *Recherches philosophiques sur les Egyptiens et les Chinois.* Berlin, 1773.

Quesnay, François. "Despotisme de la Chine." Paris, 1767.

Ricci, Matteo. *Fonti Ricciane (Storia dell'Introduzione del Christianesimo in Cina).* 3 vols. Edited by Pasquale M. d'Elia, S.J. Rome, 1942–1949.

Saussy, Haun. *Great Walls of Discourse and Other Adventures in Cultural China.* Cambridge, Mass., 2002.

Schipper, Kristofer. *The Taoist Body.* Translated by Karen C. Duval. Berkeley, Calif., 1993.

Shryock, John K. *The Origin and Development of the State Cult of Confucius.* New York, 1932.

Sima Qian. *Shiji.* 10 vols. Reprint, Beijing, 1975.

Smith, Wilfred Cantwell. *The Meaning and End of Religion.* New York, 1978.

Tamney, Joseph B., and Linda Hsueh-Ling Chiang, eds. *Modernization, Globalization, and Confucianism in Chinese Societies.* Westport, Conn., 2002.

Taylor, Rodney L. *The Religious Dimension of Confucianism.* Albany, N.Y., 1990.

Taylor, Rodney L., and Gary Arbuckle. "Confucianism." *Journal of Asian Studies* 54, no. 2 (May 1995): 347–354.

Thévenot, Melchisédec. *Relations de divers voyages curieux* [Accounts of Varied Strange Journeys]. 4 vols. Paris, 1696.

Trigault, Nicolá, and Matteo Ricci. *De Christiana expeditione apud Sinas ab Societate Iesu Suscepta, es Matthaei Ricci commentarus libri* [On the Expedition of Christianity among the Chinese undertaken by the Society of Jesus, a book by Matteo Ricci]. Augsburg, 1615.

Tu, Wei-ming. *Humanity and Self-Cultivation: Essays in Confucian Thought.* Berkeley, Calif., 1979.

Tu, Wei-ming. "The Search for Roots in Industrial East Asia: The Case of the Confucian Revival." In *Fundamentalisms Observed,* edited by Martin E. Marty and R. Scott Appleby, pp. 740–781. Chicago, 1991.

Tu, Wei-ming, ed. *The Triadic Concord: Confucian Ethics, Industrial Asia, and Max Weber.* Singapore, 1991.

Tu, Wei-ming. *Way, Learning, and Politics: Essays on the Confucian Intellectual.* Albany, N.Y., 1993.

Tu, Wei-ming, ed. *The Living Tree: The Changing Meaning of Being Chinese Today.* Stanford, Calif., 1994.

Tu, Wei-ming, and Mary Evelyn Tucker, eds. *Confucian Spirituality.* New York, 2002.

Webb, John. *Historical essay endeavoring a probability that the language of the Empire of China is like Primitive Language.* London, 1669.

Weber, Max. *The Religion of China.* Edited and trans. by Hans Gerth. New York, 1964.

Wilson, Thomas A., ed. *On Sacred Grounds: Culture, Society, Politics, and the Formation of the Cult of Confucius.* Cambridge, Mass., 2002.

Wolff, Christian. *De Sinarum Philosophia Practica,* Frankfurt, 1726.

Wright, Arthur F., ed. *The Confucian Persuasion.* Stanford, Calif., 1960.

Wright, Arthur F., ed. *Studies in Chinese Thought.* Chicago, 1953.

Wright, Arthur F., and Denis Twitchett, eds. *Confucian Personalities.* Stanford, Calif., 1962.

Wright, Arthur F., ed. *Confucianism and Chinese Civilization.* New York, 1964.

Xinzhong, Yao. *An Introduction to Confucianism.* Cambridge, U.K., 2000.

Xinzhong, Yao, ed. *Encyclopedia of Confucianism.* 2 vols. New York, 2003.

Xu, Yuanhe. *Ruxue yu dongfang wenhua* [Confucianism and Eastern Culture]. Beijing, 1994.

Yu, Yingshi. "Zhongguo jinshi zongjiao lunli yu shangren jingshen" [Modern China's Religion and Ethics and the Spirit of Merchants]. *Zhishi fenzi* [Intellectuals] 2, no. 2 (1986): 3–45.

Yu, Yingshi. *Xiandai Ruxue lun* [On Contemporary Confucian Studies]. Shanghai, 1998.

Zhongguo Ruxue baike quanshu [Encyclopedia of Confucianism in China]. Beijing, 1997.

LIONEL M. JENSEN (2005)

CONFUCIANISM IN JAPAN.

The earliest Japanese chronicles tell us that Confucianism was introduced to Japan near the end of the third century CE, when Wani of Paekche (Korea) sent the Confucian *Analects* (Chin., *Lun-yü;* Jpn., *Rongo*) to the court of Emperor Ōjin. Although the actual date of this event may have been a century or more later, it is also likely that continental emigrants familiar with Confucian teachings arrived in Japan prior to the formal introduction of Confucianism.

JAPANESE CONFUCIANISM TO 1600. The Confucianism to which the Japanese were first exposed represented more than the humble ethical dicta of Confucius himself. By this time, those doctrines had been overlaid and to some extent obscured by the doctrines of Daoism and Yin-yang dualist speculation, which combined to form a sophisticated cosmology. Prior to the seventh century it is likely that these Confucian teachings remained a virtual monopoly of scribes and literati attached to the Yamato court where they probably assisted with quasi-diplomatic correspondence and record keeping.

Both supporting and being supported by the political forces of centralization in the nascent Japanese state, Confucian teachings first achieved prominence in Japan during the time of Shōtoku Taishi (573–621), who served as regent to his aunt, the empress Suiko (592–628). In 604, Shōtoku Taishi issued the Seventeen-Article Constitution, which was intended to centralize further the administration of Japan by emphasizing administrative efficiency and harmony among contending factions. The constitution reflected the Confucian cosmology that regarded the universe as a triad composed of heaven, earth, and man, with each element having specific and mutual responsibilities. Again under Confucian influence, the cause of centralization and unification was furthered by the Taika Reforms of 646, which asserted the Confucian imperial principle of unified rule, and by the introduction of a complex legal and administrative system patterned after the codes of the Chinese Tang dynasty during the eighth century.

The influence of Confucian principles in government administration declined during the ninth and tenth centuries along with the political power of the imperial court. Confucian advice on how to regulate the state and the affairs of man was secondary to the more superstitious uses to which the Confucian cosmology could be applied. The Korean monk Kwalluk (Jpn., Kanroku) had brought books on geomancy and divination as early as the year 602, and "Confucian" advice on where to build a home or when one might auspiciously marry was more familiar at the popular level than were other Confucian principles. Perhaps disillusioned by this trend, Japanese Confucians of the eleventh and twelfth centuries engaged more in textual analysis and criticism than in original thought or interpretation.

The Neo-Confucian doctrines of Zhu Xi (Jpn., Shuki, more commonly, Shushi; 1130–1200) were introduced to Japan, if the sources are to be believed, soon after Zhu Xi's death. Institutionally, the doctrines were taught in Zen monasteries where such Neo-Confucian practices as "maintaining reverence and sitting quietly" (*jikei seiza*) were regarded as intellectually stimulating variations of what Zen practitioners already knew as "sitting in meditation" (*zazen*). Though Neo-Confucian doctrines were from time to time favorably received at the imperial and shogunal courts, particularly during the reigns of the emperors Hanazono (r. 1308–1318) and Go-Daigo (r. 1318–1339), and despite the attempts of the Ashikaga Academy to propagate Neo-Confucian teachings, Neo-Confucianism would remain largely in the shadow of its Zen patrons through the sixteenth century. Nonetheless, since Neo-Confucianism originally arose in China as a secular and rational alternative to the teachings of Buddhism, it may have been inevitable that a rupture would eventually occur between the two, and it was out of that rupture that Neo-Confucianism achieved independent status in Japan.

Tokugawa Confucianism (1600–1868). Perhaps the only positive result of the abortive Japanese invasions of Korea in the 1590s was the consequent introduction of new texts from the Confucian tradition into Japan. Fujiwara Seika (1561–1619) was made aware of this new tradition during his study in a Zen monastery. He had his first interview with Tokugawa Ieyasu (1542–1616), the future empire builder, in 1593, a decade before Ieyasu would be granted the title of *shōgun*. Regarding Neo-Confucianism as a possible basis for stable international relations, Ieyasu invited the philosophically eclectic Fujiwara Seika to join his government, but Seika declined and recommended in his stead a young student of his, Hayashi Razan (1583–1657).

Like his teacher, Hayashi Razan had studied Zen but was soon drawn to the orthodox teachings of Zhu Xi. With his appointment to Ieyasu's government, a degree of official attention was conferred on these teachings, and his descendants would serve as official Confucian advisers to the Tokugawa government throughout the period. Known for the quality of their scholarship and their initial fidelity to the teachings of Zhu Xi, Hayashi Razan's descendants succeeded in securing further official recognition for their doctrines. Tokugawa Yoshinao (1600–1650) erected the Seidō (Sages' Hall) near the Hayashi residence in Edo (Tokyo), and the fifth Tokugawa shōgun, Tsunayoshi (r. 1690–1709) endowed the Hayashi school, the Shōheikō (School of Prosperous Peace) alongside the Seidō. Nonetheless, after Hayashi Razan the most important Tokugawa Confucians all came from outside the Hayashi family.

The final important champion of fidelity to the teachings of Zhu Xi in Japan was Yamazaki Ansai (1618–1682). His school, the Kimon, had as its goal the popularization of the ethics of Zhu Xi. Like other Neo-Confucians, this school generally took a dim view of human emotions and feelings, regarding them as potentially disruptive to the delicate balance that must lie at the heart of both man and the cosmos.

Another center for seventeenth-century Confucianism was the domain of Mito, where the daimyo, Tokugawa Mitsukuni (1628–1701), began a major historiographical enterprise seeking to reinterpret the Japanese polity in terms of Confucian imperial principles. He was assisted in this venture, titled the *Dainihonshi* (History of Great Japan), by the Chinese Ming loyalist and refugee Zhu Shun-shui (Jpn., Shushunsui; 1600–1682).

During the second half of the seventeenth century, Neo-Confucian assumptions and vocabulary penetrated the new popular culture of Japan, but what has been called the "emotionalism" of the Japanese at this time made the puritanical Neo-Confucian stance on emotions and feelings incompatible with the mainstream of Japanese culture. These teachings had dominated long enough, however, to leave a lasting legacy of humanism and rationalism that enriched later Tokugawa thought.

In China, the most compelling Confucian alternative to the orthodox teachings of Zhu Xi were the teachings of the fifteenth-century figure Wang Yang-ming (Jap., Ōyōmei).

His teachings, known in Japan as Yōmeigaku, were first propagated by Nakae Tōju (1608–1648), who emphasized the Wang school's teachings on intuition and action. Kumazawa Banzan (1619–1691), a pupil of Tōju, interpreted these activist teachings in terms of their relevance to the samurai class. These teachings would have their greatest impact in Japan during the nineteenth century when such leaders as Sakuma Shōzan (1811–1864) and his disciple Yoshida Shōin (1830–1859) became ideological leaders of the Meiji restoration. Both tried to stow away on one of Commodore Perry's vessels in 1854 but were caught and imprisoned. Sakuma's advocacy of "Eastern ethics and Western science" inspired generations of later reformers. Yoshida went so far as to plan to assassinate a shogunal emissary to the imperial court who was seeking the emperor's approval of a treaty with the United States. His plot was exposed, and he was beheaded in 1859, but he continued to serve as a model for loyalist activism.

In Japan, however, the most intellectually compelling alternative to Neo-Confucian teachings was presented by a succession of schools known collectively as Ancient Learning (Kogaku). Yamaga Sokō (1622–1685), the first proponent of Ancient Learning, argued that if the goal of Confucian exegesis was to find the true message of the sages, then that end might better be served by reading the works of Confucius and Mencius (Meng-tzu) directly rather than by reading the commentary on those works by Zhu Xi or others. Yamaga was drawn to the relevance of Confucian teachings in a military age, and he is regarded as the modern founder of the teachings of Bushidō, the Way of the Warrior. His publication in 1665 of a frontal attack on the orthodox teachings of Zhu Xi resulted in his banishment from Edo during the years 1666–1675. He insisted that Japan, and not China, was the true "central kingdom" and repository of Asian culture.

Itō Jinsai (1627–1705) and his son Itō Togai (1670–1736) further developed the fundamentalist assumptions of Ancient Learning. In their school, the Kogidō (School of Ancient Meanings), located in Kyoto, Confucius was revered as the supreme sage of the universe, and the school openly showed disdain for the metaphysical explanations of the Sung and Ming Confucians in China.

The most important Ancient Learning figure, however, was Ogyū Sorai (1666–1728), whose methodology was known as Kobunjigaku (School of ancient words and phrases). An ardent Sinophile, Sorai regarded ancient Chinese writings as the repository of intellectual resources for establishing the organization of social institutions, the performance of ancient rituals, and principles of governmental administration. He revolutionized Confucian teachings in East Asia by insisting that the principles of the Confucian way were not a priori principles but were, rather, the products of the sages' own inventive wisdom. Sorai thus insisted that aspiration to sagehood was at the least irrelevant to, and at worst destructive of, the polity.

With the decline of the school of Ogyū Sorai during the mid-eighteenth century, Confucianism as a whole began to decline. After Hayashi Razan, the most influential Confucian adviser to the government was Arai Hakuseki (1657–1725), who served as mentor to the sixth shōgun, Ienobu, and as adviser to the seventh, Ietsugu, during the years 1709–1715. He was instrumental in revising the Laws Governing Military Households and was known as an able administrator who sought to tighten fiscal policy and management. Known for the high degree of rationalism in his thought, he was also a gifted historian.

Aware of and concerned over the decline of fidelity to the Neo-Confucian teachings in the official *bakufu* (military government) college of the Hayashi family, Matsudaira Sadanobu (1758–1829), head of the Council of Elders (*rōjū*), promulgated in 1790 the Prohibition of Heterodox Studies (*Kansei igaku no kin*). This attempt at ideological reform enjoyed some measure of success in the *bakufu* college, the edict had limited effect on the more important regional schools scattered throughout Japan.

CONFUCIANISM IN MODERN JAPAN. During the mid-nineteenth century, the historical, emperor-centered nationalism of the Mito school came to find points of agreement with the xenophobic, Shintō-influenced patriotism of the nativist (Kokugaku) schools. Spurred into action by the philosophy of Yōmeigaku, Confucian activists took the lead in restructuring the Japanese polity in the Meiji restoration of 1868, in which direct rule was returned to the imperial court. Nonetheless, Confucianism as an independent doctrine declined during the decades immediately following the restoration, in part because Confucian teachings had been identified so strongly with the previous Tokugawa government. Further, most prominent Tokugawa Confucians died during the first twenty-five years of the Meiji period, and only a scant handful had satisfactory successors to carry on the teachings. Still, the Confucian ideals of loyalty, duty, filial piety, and harmony persisted well into this period.

Motoda Eifu (1818–1891), Confucian tutor and adviser to the Meiji emperor, was the last important Japanese Confucian. He regarded Confucianism as a remedy for excessive infatuation with Western methods and served as Confucian lecturer in the Imperial Household Ministry from 1871 to 1891. Concerned over the lack of ethical teachings in the new public school curriculum, he was responsible for issuing in 1890 the Imperial Rescript on Education that introduced Confucian teachings on loyalty and filial piety into the standard curriculum.

Confucianism played a relatively passive role through the end of World War I. By this time the originally Confucian notions of loyalty and filial piety had come to be regarded as native Japanese virtues, and in 1937 these virtues were propounded in a work entitled *Kokutai no hongi* (Essentials of the national polity) as the cardinal principles of Japanese national morality. Confucianism served Japanese imperialist aims in Korea after its annexation in 1910, in Manchuria after 1932, and in the Japanese-controlled portions of North China after 1937. Japanese militarist rulers in these territories regarded Confucian teachings as one way to emphasize a common cultural heritage in East Asia. They felt that the survival of such teachings in Japan indicated not only that Confucian civilization was superior to Western civilization but that Japanese civilization was the primary form of civilization in East Asia.

After World War II, Confucian teachings were removed from the Japanese curriculum by the occupation authorities, and Confucianism has not yet recovered from this blow. Nonetheless, to the extent that an abiding emphasis on education and such ideals as harmony and loyalty can be said to belong to Confucianism, these qualities may be fundamental to Japanese culture and society and are likely to survive.

BIBLIOGRAPHY

A most valuable source book of materials on Japanese Confucianism is *Sources of Japanese Tradition,* 2 vols., compiled by Ryusaku Tsunoda, Wm. Theodore de Bary, and Donald Keene (New York, 1958). Joseph J. Spae's *Itō Jinsai* (New York, 1967) is helpful for information on the Ancient Learning school, as is John Tucker's *Ito Jinsai's Gomo Jigi and the Philosophical Definition of Early Modern Japan* (Amsterdam, 1998). Other helpful studies of individual Tokugawa Confucians include Mary Evelyn Tucker's *Moral and Spiritual Cultivation in Japanese Neo-Confucianism: The Life and Thought of Kaibara Ekken* (Albany, N.Y., 1989), and Kate Wildman Nakai's *Shogunal Politics: Arai Hakuseki and the Premises of Tokugawa Rule* (Cambridge, Mass., 1988). From a methodological point of view, an important work is Maruyama Masao's *Studies in the Intellectual History of Tokugawa Japan,* translated by Mikiso Hane (Princeton, 1975). See also the volume that I have edited, *Confucianism and Tokugawa Culture* (Hawai'i, 1997). Herman Ooms's *Charismatic Bureaucrat: A Political Biography of Matsudaira Sadanobu, 1758-1829* (Chicago, 1975) is a superb account of this important late Tokugawa figure. Finally, two helpful studies of the modern fate of Confucian thought in Japan, are *Confucianism in Modern Japan,* 2d ed. (Tokyo, 1973), by Warren W. Smith Jr., and Wei-Ming Tu's (ed.) *Confucian Traditions in East Asian Modernity: Moral Education and Economic Culture in Japan and the Four Mini-Dragons* (Cambridge, Mass., 1996).

PETER NOSCO (1987 AND 2005)

CONFUCIANISM IN KOREA. While Confucianism did not achieve status as a dominant thought system in Korea until the founding of the Yi dynasty (1392–1910), the introduction of the Confucian classics to the peninsula predates the common era. In the seventh century, the Silla government, at first a tribal federation, turned to Confucianism as a tool of centralization. In 651, the Royal Academy was established, in which officials, drawn from the aristocracy, were exposed to the Confucian classics. Furthermore, Confucian precepts found their way into aristocratic codes of behavior, even becoming incorporated into the rules of conduct for the *hwarang*, a knightly class instrumental in the Silla unification of the Korean Peninsula in 668.

Under the Unified Silla (668–935), Confucianism found a more fertile environment. Government examinations were instituted at the Royal Academy in 788 and close relations with Tang China led late in the dynasty to the rise of a group of scholars who were steeped in Confucian learning there, and who returned to Korea with a Confucian vision of government and a resolve to restore the deteriorating social order. An example is Ch'oe Ch'iwŏn (b. 857), who passed the Tang government examinations but returned hoping to end anarchic conditions in the provinces. Disillusioned, he died a recluse.

From the inception of the Koryŏ dynasty (918–1392) an expanded role for Confucian doctrine was envisioned. In the celebrated "Ten Injunctions" addressed to his descendants by the dynastic founder, Wang Kŏn (r. 918–943), Buddhism was chosen to govern spiritual matters, geomancy was to be used for prophecy and prognostication, and Confucianism was chosen as the guiding principle in the sociopolitical sphere. Two of the injunctions are direct restatements of traditional Confucian precepts. One declares that the people's livelihood and welfare should be the foremost concern of government while another admonishes the occupant of the throne to heed ministerial advice in fulfilling this task.

In the late tenth century the government was reorganized into a centralized bureaucratic structure. Local officials were appointed by the central government. Among the long-term results were the emergence of the civil and military bureaucracy as a social force and the transformation of the Koryŏ polity into an aristocratic-bureaucratic state in which the power of the ruling elite derived from government position rather than an ancestral seat. This change reflected the Confucian rhetoric of government; it conformed to the hierarchical order at whose summit reigned the sovereign as paterfamilias of the state with corresponding responsibilities to and respect from his subject-children.

Under this Confucian system, civil officials served in the capital, where the mode of life included the pursuit of scholarly and literary activities. Educational institutions such as the National Academy, established in 992, and twelve private academies, the first founded by Ch'oe Ch'ung (984–1068) in the eleventh century, arose to serve this group. This early Koryŏ civil elite is often characterized as having been more interested in the literary rather than the philosophical aspect of Confucian studies. This group seems to have accepted the Confucian precepts of civilization with its moral and political implications. The *Samguk sagi* (Historical record of the Three Kingdoms), the first extant dynastic history in Korea, written by the twelfth-century Confucian scholar Kim Pusik, expresses this outlook. The work is an attempt to place Korean history in the context of Confucian civilization.

Moral appraisal is the foremost criterion for evaluating the legitimacy of historical states or depicting events or persons.

The military coup of 1170 disrupted this Confucian social order. The Mongols, who invaded Korea in 1231, were instrumental in bringing about the end of military rule in 1259. Koryŏ kings, married to Mongol princesses and devoid of power, spent a great deal of time prior to their accession and after their retirement in the cosmopolitan Yuan capital. Establishments such as that of the scholar-king Ch'ungsŏn (r. 1289, 1308–1313) served as meeting places for Chinese and Korean scholars, and Korean scholars for the first time had firsthand exposure to Song dynasty (960–1279) neo-Confucian scholarship, particularly that of the Zheng-Zhu school, so-called for its putative founders, Zheng Yi (1033–1108) and Zhu Xi (1130–1200). The result was an impressive array of scholars beginning with An Hyang (1243–1306) and Paek Ijŏng (fl. 1300), commonly regarded as having introduced neo-Confucianism to Korea, and including, by the mid-fourteenth century, such scholars as Yi Saek (1328–1396), Chŏng Mongju (1337–1392), and Yi Sungin (1347–1392). They succeeded in including the neo-Confucian texts—the Four Books and Five Classics—in the civil service examination and in the curriculum at the Royal College and in reinstituting the royal lecture, complete with neo-Confucian texts and teacher-officials who lectured to the king-student.

FOUNDING OF THE YI NEO-CONFUCIAN POLITY. Neo-Confucianism was posited on a holistic vision of the moral universe in which a unifying moral principle operated in the phenomenal as well as the nonphenomenal world, particularly in the human world. Society should be organized to conform to this moral order and an individual should try to live in accordance with its principles. Commitment to neo-Confucianism rendered it impossible for its practitioners to concede the religious realm to Buddhism. The founding of the Yi dynasty was, in this sense, not merely a change in political power. Its founders were all confirmed neo-Confucians and they sought to create a new sociopolitical order based on their moral vision. Chŏng Tojŏn (1342–1398), the leader of this group, campaigned to discredit Buddhism. Motivated by the neo-Confucian belief in the centrality of man, Chŏng challenged the Buddhist view that this world, the phenomenal world, was illusion, terming such a view invalid and harmful. His theoretical attack was accompanied by institutional sanctions against the Buddhist establishment, which undermined its special position. Chŏng articulated the new political ideology in the coronation edict he composed for Yi T'aejo (r. 1392–1398). The *raison d'être* of the government was the attainment and maintenance of a Confucian moral order. Thus, it should be staffed with people who understood Confucian moral principles. The legitimacy of the Yi monarchy was based on the claim that it had received from Heaven a mandate to carry out this task.

Beginning with changes in the political structure, the Yi government launched a massive transformation of Korean society that was not fully realized for several centuries. The most conspicuous changes were the adoption of a new system of education, a restructuring of social organization along patrilineal groups, the adoption of Confucian ritual, and the propagation of Confucian ethics through local associations. In order to disseminate Confucian values more widely to the educated class, the Yi government sought to establish a nationwide public school system. Four schools in the capital and one school in each county supposedly would make primary education widely available, while the Royal College in the capital would provide advanced education for qualified students. This departed from Koryŏ practice, in which education was limited to a small elite. Private schools and academies began to appear in the mid-fifteenth century; although government-supported, they became alternatives to government service for renowned scholars. Thus, the relationship between the private academies and the state became ambivalent—mutually supportive but competitive for influence and the opportunity to define orthodoxy.

The civil service examination became the accepted channel of entry to an official career. Almost all high officials passed the *munkwa*, the final stage of the civil service examinations; of the two preliminary examinations, the one in the exposition of classics became more important than the one in literary composition. Nonetheless, the rigid class structure of Korean society precluded the development of the strict meritocracy envisioned by the Yi founders and power still remained confined to a relatively small elite. But the examinations did have the effect of confucianizing the governing elite; by the mid-sixteenth century, Confucian ideology was no longer just a means by which the governing class ruled but rather the system of values by which they were measured. From the king down to the lowest officials, all had to justify their actions and intentions in the context of Confucian rhetoric and ideals. This Confucianization of the official class was paralleled by an attempt to disseminate Confucian normative values among the peasantry.

THE DEVELOPMENT OF CONFUCIAN SCHOLARSHIP. By the sixteenth century, Korean scholars turned to the more purely intellectual and speculative aspects of Confucian learning, looking directly to the Zheng-Zhu school. Despite close ties with Ming dynasty (1368–1644) scholarship, Korean Neo-Confucianism developed independently of contemporary scholarship there. While Korean scholars accepted the authority of the Zheng-Zhu school, they defined issues in their own way, adding insights and interpretations. The scholars Pak Yŏng (1471–1540), Sŏ Kyŏngdŏk (1489–1546), and Yi Ŏnjŏk (1491–1553) reflect the diversity and independence of the Korean school. Pak devoted himself to the question of *ihak* (Chin., *lixue*, "learning of principle"), one of the main themes of Neo-Confucian philosophy. Based on his study of the *Daxue* (Great Learning), he asserted that principle and knowledge should be sought entirely within one's self. Later scholars found in this assertion a resemblance to the works of the Ming-dynasty thinker Wang Yangming (1472–1529) and for this reason found his thinking heterodox. Sŏ Kyŏngdŏk, on the other hand, turned to Zhang Zai's (1020–1077) *t'aehŏ* (Chin., *taixu*, "great void"). Speculating on the cosmology of creation, it was natural that he should grant primacy to the role of *ki* (Chin., *chi*, "material force"). Primarily interested in observing natural phenomena and unconcerned with the moral implications of the role of principle, he parted from Zhu Xi. Unlike So, who lived as a recluse and shunned bookish learning, Yi Ŏnjŏk had a long official career and left copious writings. His erudition, his interests in a broad range of topics, and his laborious textual studies set new standards for scholars of future generations.

It was Yi Hwang (1501–1570), better known by his pen name, T'oegye, who brought Korean neo-Confucianism to maturity. Working at a time when Wang Yangming's thought seemed to be gaining influence in the Korean scholarly community, he devoted himself to defining orthodoxy, to distinguishing "right learning" from deviant thought. The definition of a Korean orthodoxy within the tradition of the Zheng-Zhu school, one that excluded the ideas of the Wang Yangming school, is often attributed to his efforts. T'oegye accepted Zhu Xi's dual theory of principle and material force and the relationship between them. While Zhu Xi acknowledged that principle and material force cannot exist in isolation, he held that principle is prior and material force posterior. The superiority of principle was a defining feature of his philosophy: principle was identified with the Way (*dao*) and the nature (*xing*), which are permanent and unchanging, while material force was identified with physical entities, which constantly change. But Zhu Xi's position proved somewhat ambiguous. One could ask whether the priority of principle was existential or evaluative, that is, did it exist first or did it just have a superior moral value? Further, in what sense did principle exist prior to material force if it could not manifest itself without material force? Much of T'oegye's work was devoted to this question. He concluded that the priority of principle applied in the realm of ethical values, and that principle exerted a positive ethical influence. He wrote, for instance, that "Good occurs if principle manifests itself and material force follows, while evil occurs if material force veils principle and principle recedes."

Like the Song neo-Confucians, Korean scholars including T'oegye were deeply concerned with the problem of human evil. If man's original nature was good, then how can one explain evil? T'oegye again accepted Zhu Xi's concept of human nature based on his dual theory of principle and material force. Principle is immanent in everything in the universe. What individuates one thing from another is material force. Since principle is good, what determines the moral quality of an entity is its material force. Man has an original nature and a physical nature and only when he returns to original nature does he act in accordance with moral principle. What determines the morality of human action is mind. The mind possesses innate knowledge of moral principle and has the cognitive capacity to discern it. Yet, this capacity of mind can be prevented from functioning when it becomes clouded by selfish desire. T'oegye used the terms *tosim* (Chin., *daoxin*, "moral mind") and *insim* (Chin., *renxin*, "human mind") to describe the two aspects of mind. The term *moral mind* described a mind rectified and discerning of moral principle while human mind referred to a mind containing seeds of selfish desire and prone to error. Moral cultivation was necessary to develop mind into a moral state.

Korean scholars seized upon this question of mind and the result was one of the characteristic themes of Korean neo-Confucian thought. The debate centered around the *sadan* (Chin., *siduan*, "four beginnings") and the *ch'ilchŏng* (Chin., *qiqing*, "seven emotions"). The Four Beginnings, which appear in *Mengzi* (*Mencius*), are the moral qualities of man that give rise to the original goodness of human nature. The Seven Emotions, mentioned in the *Zhongyong* (Doctrine of the mean), are human feelings. The questions debated were whether both the Four and the Seven were feelings, how they were related to the moral mind and the human mind, and their relationship to principle and material force. T'oegye took Chŏng Chiun's (1509–1561) position that the Four issued from principle and therefore must be good while the Seven issued from material force and therefore could be either good or evil. The Four were the basis of the moral mind and the Seven the basis of the human mind. Challenged by Ki Taesŭng (1527–1572) in their famous "Four-Seven" debate, T'oegye acknowledged that both involved principle and material force and that both were feelings, but he insisted that their origins were different. The Four are initiated by principle and material force follows them while the Seven are initiated by material force and principle rides on them. In order to posit that the four are initiated by principle, T'oegye had to endow principle with a generative power. Principle does not merely constitute human nature; it guides the mind toward the realization of goodness.

T'oegye later used the same theory to take issue with Wang Yangming's theory of the unity of knowledge and action. In his emphasis on innate knowledge, Wang dismissed the need for acquiring knowledge through examination and inquiry. T'oegye argued that this was applicable to the emotional activity of the mind but not to rational thought.

While Yi T'oegye chose to limit himself to what was explicit in Zhu Xi, Yi I (1536–1584), known by his pen name, Yulgok, preferred a more independent and creative approach to scholarship. Taking the formula "obtain truth through one's own effort" as his credo, he regarded adhering too rigidly to previous masters' positions as contrary to the spirit of neo-Confucian learning. He accepted Zhu Xi's authority, but he was willing to differ with him on specific issues. Yulgok is regarded as having established the school of Material Force in Korea. Yulgok conceded that, at least logically, principle and material force were distinct. What is referred to as the primacy of material force in Yulgok is his theory of the inseparability of principle and material force in both function and manifestation. As principle cannot be expressed without material force and material force has no root without principle, they are interrelated. Thus, to him it was illogical to conceive of them as prior and posterior and he denied that principle has its own generative power. Principle is passive and material force is active and they always manifest themselves together. His belief in their inseparability led him to object to the notion that principle is unchanging and always in a pure state. Departing from Zhu Xi, he held that principle was not a unified entity but that the principle in each thing was distinct, conditioned, and determined by its material force. Hence an individuating principle in a thing is always changing and in varying states of purity.

Yulgok's ideas of the Four Beginnings and the Seven Emotions were also developed along these lines. In a celebrated debate with Sŏng Hon (1535–1598) on the subject, he denied that the Four are associated with principle and the Seven with material force. They both are manifestations of material force that contains principle. The difference is that the Four are "good" manifestations of material force or, more specifically, the Seven themselves manifested as good. Likewise, the "moral mind" and the "human mind" do not rise from different origins but are rather purely descriptive terms referring to different states. In positing that an entity—the Four Beginnings—could be a good manifestation of material force, Yulgok was challenging the dichotomy that made material force the source of evil and principle the source of good.

Yi T'oegye and Yi Yulgok are regarded as the founders respectively of the school of Principle and the school of Material Force. T'oegye's philosophy was developed by the Yŏngnam school while Yulgok's was developed by the Kiho school, which emerged as political as well as scholarly rivals. Continuing refinements in the study of principle and material force and new interpretations of the Four Beginnings and the Seven Emotions constituted the mainstream of Korean neo-Confucian scholarship. The scholars of the school of Principle emphasized the generative power of principle that T'oegye proposed. Yi Hyŏnil (1627–1704), Yi Sangjong (1710–1781), and Yi Chinsang (1811–1878) assigned ever greater roles to principle, endowing it with priority in existential sequence and in function as well. This tendency culminated in Yi Hangno (1792–1868) who identified principle with creative force, divinity, and mind.

The scholars of the school of Material Force correspondingly attributed even greater function to material force. Song Siyŏl (1607–1689), for example, posited that mind, which acts, is material force and the nature, which does not move, is principle. Han Wŏnjin (1682–1750) refined this theory, but Im Sŏngju (1711–1788) went one step further. He declared that since mind and the nature are one then the latter should also be material force. He denied that principle could exist at all without material force. Hence man could not be good because of principle but must be good because his material force is good. This flies in the face of the Zheng-Zhu school dictum that the (original) nature, being perfectly good, is principle.

As T'oegye emphasized the universality of principle and Yulgok spoke of individuating principle, their successors pushed to extremes in developing these opposing views. Ultimately, this led to the eighteenth-century debate concerning man's relationship to the cosmos. If principle is universal and omnipresent then man is connected to other things through principle sharing the nature. If, however, principle is completely determined by material force then man, who possesses different material force than other things, would not share the same nature. The debate, known as the Nak-Ho debate, began between Yi Kan (1677–1727) and Han Wŏnjin. Yi took the position that men share their natures with other things in the universe while Han maintained that man was separated from other things with respect to original nature. This debate generated an intense discussion, which eventually came to involve much of the Korean scholarly community of the time.

Both the school of Principle and that of Material Force, despite their differing interpretations, were viewed both by themselves and by others as firmly within Zheng-Zhu orthodoxy, this, even though both schools had views that sometimes departed from the original Zheng-Zhu teachings. Reinterpreting specific issues within the tradition was one thing, but a direct challenge to orthodoxy was another. Pak Sedang (1629–1703) was termed a heterodox thinker for his work *Sabyŏnnok*, in which he directly opposed Zhu Xi's scholarship and offered his own views. As a result of the fall of the Chinese Ming dynasty to the "barbarian" Qing dynasty (1644–1911), seventeenth century Korean intellectuals became concerned with orthodoxy in an attempt to redefine Korea's role in the Confucian world. Perhaps the conflict between Song Siyŏl and Yun Hyu (1617–1680) indicates this process. Song Siyŏl's position can be characterized by his desire to maintain Zhu Xi orthodoxy intact in Korea. As a follower of Yulgok, his philosophy differed somewhat from that of Zhu Xi, but he maintained an unswerving loyalty and commitment to the supremacy of the Zheng-Zhu school. Yun Hyu, on the other hand, preferred a wider definition of orthodoxy. He regarded Zhu Xi as a great scholar, but felt that measuring one's scholarship by him or, for that matter, even by Confucius, was too confining and harmful. He wrote his own commentaries on several of the Four Books, for which he was ostracized by Song and his followers as heterodox.

The intellectual scene in the eighteenth century was somewhat freer and more diverse. Chŏng Chedu (1649–1736), who received high honors from King Yŏngjo (r. 1724–1776), openly espoused ideas of Wang Yangming which had long been suppressed in Korea. This period also witnessed the flowering of the Sirhak ("practical learning") school. Centuries of factional struggle and growing competition for office had left many scholars outside the mainstream of political power. Practical Learning scholars were disaffected intellectuals who wrote treatises on social and economic reform. They fall largely into two groups. Yu Hyŏng-wŏn

(1622–1673) and Yi Ik (1681–1763) accepted the Confucian vision of an agrarian society presided over by the rule of virtue and urged social improvement through land reform and moral rule. Pak Chi-wŏn (1737–1805), Hong Taeyong (1731–1783), and Pak Chega (b. 1750), on the other hand, searched for alternatives. They addressed themselves to such issues as commerce, trade, and technology. Pak Chi-wŏn's biting satire of the class system, Hong Taeyong's interest in science as it was expressed in his notion of the moving earth, and Pak Chega's belief in technology founded on a startling theory of a consumer economy clearly departed from the conventional mode of thinking. Chŏng Yagyong (1762–1836), often considered the greatest Practical Learning scholar, encompassed both trends in his reform ideas. His attention to the improvement of local government is well known. While these scholars worked within the Confucian political and value system, they are regarded as precursors of modernization for their critique of contemporary society and their innovative proposals for reform.

In the late nineteenth century as Korea came under increasing pressure from the major powers and the Confucian value system itself came under attack, Confucian thinking turned defensive. Confucian scholars committed to preserving the orthodox tradition became conservatives who opposed treaties and modernizing measures. Seeing themselves as the defenders of the only true civilization, they put up real resistance. Ch'oe Ikhyŏn (1833–1906) was a representative scholar of this generation. His fearless memorials objecting to the government's domestic and diplomatic policies resulted in frequent banishment. When Korea became a protectorate of Japan in 1905, he organized what is known as the Righteous Army and fought against Japanese and Korean royal troops. Arrested by the Japanese and imprisoned in Tsushima Island, he died of starvation, considering it unprincipled to accept food from the enemy. The role of Confucianism in Korea's modernization process, however, remains to be examined.

See Also Buddhism, article on Buddhism in Korea; Cheng Hao; Cheng Yi; Chinese Religion; Chŏng Yagyong; Korean Religion; Sŏ Kyŏngdŏk; Wang Yangming; Yi T'oegye; Yi Yulgok; Zhang Zai; Zhu Xi.

Bibliography

Works in Korean

For an overview of the history of Korean Confucianism, see Youn Sa-soon's *Han'guk yuhak yŏn'gu* (Seoul, 1980). Works by the major thinkers include: Ch'oe Ikhyŏn's *Myŏnamjip* (Seoul, 1906); Chŏng Tojŏn's *Sambongjip* (reprint, Seoul, 1961); Chŏng Yagyong's *Chŏng Tasan chŏnsŏ*, 3 vols. (reprint, Seoul, 1960–1961); Hong Taeyong's *Tamhŏnsŏ*, 2 vols. (reprint, Seoul, 1969); Ki Taesŭng's *Kobong munjip* (reprint, Seoul, 1976); Pak Chega's *Pukhagŭi* (Seoul, 1971); Pak Chiwŏn's *Yŏnamchip* (1932; reprint, Seoul, 1966); Pak Sedang's *Sabyŏnnok* (Seoul, 1703); Song Siyŏl's *Songja taejŏn*, 7 vols. (1929; reprint, Seoul, 1971); Yi T'oegye's *T'oegye chŏnsŏ*, 2 vols. (reprint, Seoul, 1958); Yi Yulgok's *Yulgok chŏnsŏ*, 2 vols. (reprint, Seoul, 1961); Yi Ik's *Sŏngho saesŏl*, 2 vols. (reprint, Seoul, 1967); Yi Ŏnjŏk's *Hoejae chŏnsŏ* (reprint, Seoul, 1973); Yu Hyŏngwŏn's *Pan'gye surok* (reprint, Seoul, 1958); and Yun Hyu's *Paekho chŏnsŏ*, 3 vols. (Taegu, 1974).

Works in English

Articles in English include Martina Deuchler's "The Tradition: Women during the Yi Dynasty," in *Virtues in Conflict*, edited by Sandra Matielli (Seoul, 1977), pp. 1–47; Park Chong-hong's "Historical Review of Korean Confucianism," *Korea Journal* 3 (September 1963): 5–11; and Key P. Yang and Gregory Henderson's "An Outline History of Korean Confucianism," *Journal of Asian Studies* 18 (November 1958 and February 1959): 81–101 and 259–276. *The Rise of Neo-Confucianism in Korea*, edited by Wm. Theodore de Bary and me (New York, 1985), contains a number of important essays. See Julia Ching's "Yi Yulgok on the 'Four Beginnings and the Seven Emotions'" (pp. 303–322); Chai-sik Chung's "Chŏng Tojŏn: 'Architect' of Yi Dynasty Government and Ideology" (pp. 59–88); Martina Deuchler's "Reject the False and Uphold the Straight: Attitudes toward Heterodox Thought in Early Yi Korea" (pp. 375–410); Tomoeda Ryūtarō's "Yi T'oegye and Zhu Xi: Differences in Their Theories of Principle and Material Force" (pp. 243–260); and Tu Wei-ming's "Yi T'oegye's Perception of Human Nature: A Preliminary Inquiry into the Four-Seven Debate in Korean Neo-Confucianism" (pp. 261–282).

New Sources

Chong, C.-s. *A Korean Confucian Encounter with the Modern World: Yi Hang-no and the West.* Berkeley, 1995.

Chung, E.Y.J. *The Korean Neo-Confucianism of Yi T'oegye and Yi Yulgok: A Reappraisal of the "Four-Seven Thesis" and Its Practical Implications for Self-Cultivation.* Albany, N.Y., 1995.

Haboush, J. K. *The Confucian Kingship in Korea: Yongjo and the Politics of Sagacity.* New York, 2001.

Haboush, J. K., and M. Deuchler. *Culture and the State in Late Choson Korea.* Cambridge, Mass., 1999.

Kim, Y.-G. *Karl Barth's Reception in Korea: Focusing on Ecclesiology in Relation to Korean Christian Thought.* New York, 2003.

Ko, D., J. K. Haboush, and J. R. Piggott. *Women and Confucian Cultures in Premodern China, Korea, and Japan.* Berkeley, 2003.

Kum, C.-t.a. *Confucianism and Korean Thoughts.* Seoul, 2000.

Palais, J. B. *Confucian Statecraft and Korean Institutions: Yu Hyongwon and the Late Choson Dynasty.* Seattle, 1996.

JaHyun Kim Haboush (1987)
Revised Bibliography

CONFUCIUS (552?–479 BCE), known in Chinese as Kong Qiu (also styled Zhongni); preeminent Chinese philosopher and teacher. The name *Confucius* is the Latin rendering of *Kong Fuzi* ("Master Kong"). Confucius was born in the small feudal state of Lu, near modern Qufu (Shandong Province). Little can be established about his life, forebears, or family, although legends, some of very early origin, are abundant and colorful. The biography in Sima Qian's *Shi ji* (Historical Annals, second century BCE) is unreliable. The *Lunyu* (*Analects*), a record of Confucius's conversations with his disciples, likely compiled in the third century BCE, is probably the best source, although here, too, apocryphal materials have crept in. The *Analects* may be supplemented by the *Zuo zhuan*, a commentary to the *Chun qiu* (Spring and Autumn Annals; also third century BCE), and by the *Mengzi* (Mencius; second century BCE).

In all these accounts, fact and legend are difficult to separate. The *Zuo zhuan* makes Confucius a direct descendant of the royal house of the Shang dynasty (c. 1766–1123 BCE), whose heirs were given the ducal fief of the state of Song by the succeeding Zhou dynasty (1111–256 BCE). According to this account, three to five generations prior to the sage's birth, his forebears moved to the neighboring state of Lu. His father is said to have been a soldier and a man of great strength; his mother, to have been a woman much younger and not the first wife. Some accounts make Confucius the issue of an illegitimate union. Tradition has it that at his birth dragons appeared in his house, and a unicorn (*lin*) in the village. These may command as much belief as the description of Confucius that endows him with a forehead like that of the sage-king Yao, shoulders like those of the famous statesman Zichan, the eyes of Shun, the neck of Yu, the mouth of Gaoyao, the visage of the Yellow Emperor, and the height of Tang, founder of the Shang dynasty.

Of Confucius's childhood and youth, we hear little even from legends, except for references to the early loss of his father, followed later in his youth by the death of his mother. His favorite childhood game was reportedly the setting up of sacrificial vessels and the imitation of ritual gestures. He married young; some accounts allege that he later divorced his wife, although that cannot be proved and is unlikely to be true. He is also supposed to have visited the capital of the Zhou dynasty (present-day Luoyang) and to have met Laozi, from whom he sought instruction. But this report as well appears to be unfounded.

In the *Analects*, Confucius says that he was of humble status. Perhaps he came from the minor aristocracy, as he received an education—although not from a famous teacher—and also trained in archery and music. He probably belonged to an obscure and impoverished clan. He would say of himself that by age fifteen he had fixed his mind on studying (*Analects* 2.4). As a young man, he held minor offices, first overseeing stores with the task of keeping accounts, and later taking charge of sheep and cattle (*Mengzi* 5B.5). Confucius probably served in a junior post at the Lu court, if the *Zuo zhuan* is correct about his encounter in 525 with the viscount of Tan, a visitor in Lu, of whom he asked instructions regarding the ancient practice of naming offices after birds. At this point Confucius would have been twenty-seven years old.

Confucius lived in an age of great political disorder. The Zhou royal house had lost its authority and the many feudal lords were competing for hegemony. He himself was concerned with the problems of restoring order and harmony to society and of keeping alive the ancient virtues of personal integrity and social justice. For him, a good ruler is one who governs by moral persuasion and who loves the people as a father loves his children. Confucius was especially learned in rites and music, finding in them both the inspiration and the means for the achievement of moral rectitude in society. He reflected deeply on the human situation about him in the light of the wisdom of the ancients. By about the age of thirty he felt himself "standing firm" (*Analects* 2.4) on his insights and convictions.

Like others of his time, Confucius viewed service in the government—the opportunity to exert moral suasion on the king—as the proper goal of a gentleman *(junzi)*. At about thirty-five, he visited the large neighboring state of Qi. He stayed there for about one year and was so enthralled by the *shao* music (attributed to the sage-king Shun) that for three months, he claimed, he did not notice the taste of the meat he ate (*Analects* 7.14). Clearly, he hoped to be of use at the ducal court. The *Analects* (12.11) reports his conversations with Duke Jing of Qi about government, and his emphatic belief that a ruler should be a good ruler, the minister a good minister, the father a good father, and the son a good son. The duke decided not to use him (*Analects* 18.3).

In Lu again, Confucius hesitated some time before accepting public office, perhaps because of the complexity of Lu politics. The Ji family, which had usurped power, was itself dominated by its household minister, Yang Hu (or Yang Huo), and Confucius was reluctant to ingratiate himself with this man (*Analects* 17.1; *Mengzi* 3B.7). Perhaps it was at this point that he determined to develop his ideas and to teach disciples. He said of himself that "at forty, I had no more doubts" (*Analects* 2.4). But some time after 502 (*Mengzi* 5B.4), at about age fifty, he accepted the office of sikou (police commissioner): "At fifty I knew Heaven's decree" (*Analects* 2.4). In 498 he attempted in vain to break the power of the three leading families of Lu and restore power to the duke. Perhaps this failure caused him to leave Lu the following year. The *Analects* (18.4) claims that Confucius left because the head of the Ji family of Lu had been distracted from his duties by dancing girls, while the *Mengzi* (6B.6) gives as the reason the fact that the head of Lu had failed to heed his advice. (The *Shi ji* reports that Confucius became prime minister of Lu, but there is reason to question the authenticity of the account.)

After leaving Lu, Confucius traveled for some thirteen years with a small group of disciples. He first visited the state of Wei (*Analects* 13.9). Although Duke Ding of Wei did not have a good reputation, Confucius took office under him, but left his service when the duke asked his advice on military rather than ritual matters (*Analects* 15.1). To avoid assassins sent by an enemy, he had to disguise himself while passing through the state of Song (*Analects* 7.23; *Mengzi* 5A.8). In Chen he accepted office under the marquis; but his stay in Chen was marred by many difficulties and he was once near starvation (*Analects* 15.2; *Mengzi* 7B.18). In 489 he went on to the state of Cai, where he met the governor of She, a visitor from Chu. When the governor asked Confucius's disciple Zilu about his master, Confucius offered this description of himself: "[Tell him I am] the kind of man who forgets to eat when trying to solve a problem, who is so full of joy as to forget all worries, and who does not notice the onset of old age" (*Analects* 7.19). He was then about sixty-three years old. He also said of himself: "At sixty, my ears were attuned [to truth]" (*Analects* 2.4).

From Cai, Confucius traveled to Wei via Chen and found it in disorder as the deceased duke's son sought to oust the new ruler, his own son, from the ducal throne. Such disputes help us to understand Confucius's insistence on the "rectification of names" (*zheng ming*)—that fathers should be paternal and sons filial. After extensive travel through states that lay within present-day Shandong and Henan, Confucius returned to Lu around 484. He was given an office, perhaps as a low-ranking counselor (*Analects* 14.21). He also occupied himself with music and poetry, especially the *ya* and the *song*, which now make up two of the sections of the *Shi jing* (Book of Poetry). During this period he conversed with Duke Ai of Lu and with the head of the Ji family on questions of government and ritual.

It is known that Confucius had at least one son, Kong Li (Boyu), and one daughter, whom he married to his disciple Gongye Chang. He also married the daughter of his deceased elder brother to another disciple, Nan Rong (*Analects* 5.1, 11.5). Of his son little is known, except that the father urged him to study poetry and rites (*Analects* 16.13). Although he is popularly portrayed as a severe moralist, the *Analects* show Confucius as fond of classical music and rituals, informal and cheerful at home, affable yet firm, commanding but not forbidding, dignified and yet pleasant, with an ability to laugh at himself. In his old age, he devoted more and more time to his disciples. He also knew that he had reached spiritual maturity: "At seventy I could follow my heart's desires without overstepping the line" (*Analects* 2.4). But his last years were saddened by the successive deaths of his son, his favorite disciple, Yan Hui, and the loyal though flamboyant Zilu.

According to the *Zuo zhuan*, Confucius died in 479 at the age of seventy-three. While no description exists concerning his last hours, the account of a previous illness shows how Confucius probably faced death. At that time Zilu wanted the disciples to attire themselves like stewards in attendance upon a high dignitary. Confucius rebuked him, saying, "By making this pretence of having stewards when I have none, whom do you think I shall deceive? Shall I deceive Heaven? Besides, is it not better for me to die in the hands of you, my friends, than in the hands of stewards?" (*Analects* 9.12). When Zilu requested permission to pray for him, Confucius replied, "I have already been praying for a long time" (*Analects* 7.35). The word *praying* here has been understood to mean living the life of a just man.

Confucius's political ambitions remained largely unrealized; he is remembered by posterity above all as a teacher, indeed as the greatest moral teacher of East Asia. He is said to have accepted students without regard to their social status or ability to pay. While the *Shi ji* credits him with three thousand disciples, the more conservative number of seventy (or fewer) is more likely. With two known exceptions, most of the disciples were of humble station and modest means. The majority came from Confucius's own state of Lu, although a few were from the neighboring states of Wei, Chen, and Qi.

The modern scholar Qian Mu divides the disciples into two groups—those who had followed Confucius even before he left Lu for ten years of travel and those who came to him after his return to Lu. The earlier disciples include Zilu, Yan Hui, and Zigong. Zilu was the oldest in age, only some nine years younger than Confucius himself; his valor and rashness stand out in the *Analects*. Yan Hui, the favorite of Confucius, was about thirty years his junior. His early death at about forty caused much sorrow to Confucius. Zigong, about Yan's age, was an enterprising and eloquent diplomat. Zilu perished—in a manner that had been predicted by Confucius—during a rash effort to rescue his master in the state of Wei (480). Zigong served at the Lu court and was leader of the disciples at the time of Confucius's death. He is reported to have stayed on at his master's grave in Qufu for three years longer than the mourning period of twenty-seven months prescribed for the death of one's parents, vivid testimony to the depth of his commitment to his teacher.

The later disciples were mostly much younger, sometimes forty years Confucius's junior. Those mentioned in the *Analects* include Ziyou, Zixia, Zizhang, Youzi, and Zengzi, who was only about twenty-seven at the time of his master's death. All five men played important roles in spreading Confucius's teachings, but Zengzi, exemplary for his filial piety, is remembered as the principal spiritual heir through whom Confucius's essential message reached later generations.

Traditionally, Confucius has been credited with the editing of the Five (or Six) Classics: the *Shi jing* (Book of Poetry); the *Yi jing* (Book of Changes), a divination manual with metaphysical accretions; the *Shu jing* (Book of History), a collection of speeches and documents; the *Li ji* (Book of Rites); the *Chun qiu* (Spring and Autumn Annals), historical records of the state of Lu during the years 722 to 481, said to have been compiled by Confucius; and the now lost *Yue jing* (Book of Music). Modern scholarship does not support these traditional attributions. Although the *Analects* mentions Confucius's knowledge of the *Poetry*, *History*, and *Changes*, there is no evidence that he had a part in editing these texts; nor was it his immediate disciples who, in their study of these texts, started the traditions of transmission for them. Of his relation to antiquity, one can say that Confucius loved the ancients—above all the duke of Zhou, to whom the dynasty allegedly owed its rituals and other institutions—and that he read widely in the ancient texts and passed his understanding on to his disciples.

Confucius's place in history derives from his activities as a teacher and from the teachings that he crystallized and transmitted. In an age when only aristocrats had access to formal education he was the first to accept disciples without regard to status. He instructed them—according to each disciple's ability—not only in the rituals, knowledge of which was expected of all gentlemen, but also in the more difficult art of becoming one who is perfectly humane (*ren*). Although none of his disciples attained high political office, Confucius the teacher wrought a real social change. Because of his teaching, the word *gentlemen* (*junzi*, literally, "ruler's son") came to refer not to social status but to moral character. A new class gradually emerged, that of the *shi* (originally, "officers" or "government counselors"), a class of educated gentry. Those among the *shi* especially distinguished for scholarship and character were known as the *ru* (originally meaning "weaklings"). Hence the Confucian school is known in Chinese as "the Ru school."

Confucius had a clear sense of his mission: he considered himself a transmitter of the wisdom of the ancients (*Analects* 7.1), to which he nonetheless gave new meaning. His focus was on the human, not just the human as given, but as endowed with the potential to become "perfect." His central doctrine concerns the virtue *ren*, translated variously as goodness, benevolence, humanity, and human-heartedness. Originally, *ren* denoted a particular virtue, the kindness that distinguished the gentleman in his behavior toward his inferiors. Confucius transformed it into a universal virtue, that which makes the perfect human being, the sage. He defined it as loving others, as personal integrity, and as altruism.

Confucius's teachings give primary emphasis to the ethical meaning of human relationships, finding and grounding what is moral in human nature and revealing its openness to the divine. Although he was largely silent on God and the afterlife, his silence did not bespeak disbelief (*Analects* 11.11). His philosophy was clearly grounded in religion, the inherited religions of Shangdi ("lord on high") or Tian ("heaven"), the supreme and personal deities of the Shang and Zhou periods, respectively. He made it clear that it was Heaven that protected and inspired him: "Heaven is the author of the virtue that is in me" (*Analects* 7.23). Confucius believed that human beings are accountable to a supreme being, "He who sins against Heaven has no place left where he may pray" (*Analects* 3.13); nevertheless, he showed a certain scepticism regarding ghosts and spirits (*Analects* 6.20). This marked a rationalistic attitude that became characteristic of the Confucian school, which usually sought to resolve problems by active human involvement rather than by hoping or praying for divine intervention.

Confucius himself was devoted to the civilization of the Zhou dynasty, although he might have been a descendant from the more ancient Shang royal house. The reason for this may have derived from the fact that Chinese civilization assumed a definitive shape during the Zhou dynasty, or from the special relationship Confucius's native state of Lu enjoyed as a custodian of Zhou culture. Its rulers were descended from the duke of Zhou, the man who established the institutions of the dynasty and who acted as regent after the death of his brother, the dynasty's founder.

Confucius's emphasis on rituals is significant, as it is ritual that governs human relationships. Rituals have a moral and social function as well as a formal and ceremonial one. The Chinese word *li* refers also to propriety, that is, to proper behavior. Confucius teaches also the importance of having the right inner disposition, without which propriety becomes hypocrisy (*Analects* 15.17).

Confucius's philosophy might appear unstructured to those who cast only a cursory glance at the *Analects*, perhaps because the book was compiled several generations after Confucius's death. But the teachings found in the *Analects*, with all their inner dynamism, assume full coherency only when put into practice. Confucius did not attempt to leave behind a purely rationalistic system of thought. He wanted to help others to live, and by so doing, to improve the quality of their society. In defining as his main concern human society, and in offering moral perfection as the human ideal, Confucius has left behind a legacy that is perennial and universal. On the other hand, his teachings also show certain limitations that derive from his culture, the authoritarian character of government, and the superior social status enjoyed by men, for instance. These limitations do not, however, change the validity of his central insights into human nature and its perfectibility.

SEE ALSO Chinese Religion, article on History of Study; Laozi; Li; Ren and Yi; Shangdi; Tian.

BIBLIOGRAPHY

For information on Confucius in English, a useful reference work is the *Encyclopaedia Britannica (Macropaedia)* (Chicago, 1982). His life is well summarized in Richard Wilhelm's *Confucius and Confucianism*, translated by George H. Danton and Annina Periam Danton (New York, 1931); in H. G. Creel's *Confucius: The Man and the Myth* (New York, 1949), reprinted under the title *Confucius and the Chinese Way* (New York, 1960); in the introduction to James Legge's translation of the *Analects* (1893; 3d ed., Tokyo, 1913), which is not critical enough of the sources; in the introduction to Arthur Waley's translation, *The Analects of Confucius* (London, 1938), which is definitely better; and in the introduction and appendixes to D. C. Lau's much more recent translation, *Confucius: The Analects* (London, 1979), which is a further improvement. A summary of Confucius's teachings is also given in Liu Wu-chi's *A Short History of Confucian Philosophy* (Harmondsworth, 1955), and in the relevant chapters in Fung Yu-lan's *A History of Chinese Philosophy*, translated by Derk Bodde, vol. 7 (Princeton, 1952). (Volume 2 has excellent chapters on Neo-Confucianism.) My *Confucianism and Christianity* (Tokyo, 1977) is a comparative study from a theological perspective.

Certain Chinese works are indispensable for a study of Confucius's life. Cui Shu's (1740–1816), *Zhusi kaoxin lu*, a small work in three *juan* (with a three *juan* supplement), offers an excellent critical study. Qian Mu's *Xian Qin zhuzi xinian,* vol. 1 (Hong Kong, 1956), is immensely useful. Gu Jiegang's *Gushibian,* vol. 2 (Shanghai, 1930–1931), should also be consulted.

There are interesting Japanese studies of Confucius's life. Kaizuka Shigeki's *Koshi* (Tokyo, 1951) has been translated into Chinese (Taibei, 1976); Geoffrey Bownas's English translation, *Confucius* (London, 1956), is also recommended. Morohashi Tetsuji's *Nyoze gamon Koshi den* (Tokyo, 1969) reports both facts and legends while distinguishing between them wherever possible.

New Sources

Gier, Nicholas. "Whitehead, Confucius, and the Aesthetics of Virtue." *Asian Philosophy* 14 (July 2004): 171–191.

Henderson, John B. *Scripture, Canon, and Commentary: A Comparison of Confucius and Western Exegesis.* Princeton, N.J., 1991.

Jensen, Lionel. *Manufacturing Confucianism: Chinese Traditions and Universal Civilization.* Durham, N.C., 1997.

Mou, Bo. "A Re-Examination of the Structure and Content of Confucius's Version of the Golden Rule." *Philosophy East and West* 54 (April 2004): 218–249.

Olberding, Amy. "The Consummation of Sorrow: An Analysis of Confucius's Grief for Yan Hui." *Philosophy East and West* 54 (July 2004): 279–302.

Sim, May. "The Moral Self in Confucius and Aristotle." *International Philosophy Quarterly* 43 (December 2003): 439–463.

Van Norden, Bryan W. *Confucius and the Analects: New Essays.* New York, 2002.

JULIA CHING (1987)
Revised Bibliography

CONGREGATIONALISM.

Congregational churches arose in England in the late sixteenth and seventeenth centuries. In their early days, Congregationalists were also known as Independents. They are most numerous in the United States, England, and Wales, but recently most of them have joined with others to form united churches in several parts of the world.

Among churches, they have stood somewhere between the Presbyterians and the more radical Protestant groups, with a distinctive emphasis on the rights and responsibilities of each properly organized congregation to make its own decisions about its own affairs without recourse to any higher human authority. This, along with an emphasis on freedom of conscience, arose from convictions concerning the sovereignty of God and the priesthood of all believers.

HISTORICAL SURVEY. The "Congregational way" emerged as a major factor in English life during the English Civil War, but its roots lay in Elizabethan Separatism, which produced Congregationalism's first three martyrs, Henry Barrow, John Greenwood, and John Penry. Some of the Separatists settled in Holland, and it was from among these that the *Mayflower* group set out for New England in 1620. During the English Civil War, Congregationalists, then usually called Independents, were particularly prominent in the army, reaching the peak of their influence during the Commonwealth through Oliver Cromwell and such outstanding ministers as John Owen and Hugh Peter. The Restoration of Charles II was a disaster for their cause, and the Act of Uniformity of 1662 was the first of many efforts to suppress them. Most of the two thousand ministers ejected from livings in the Church of England at that time were Presbyterians, but many Independent ministers who did not hold livings also suffered. Persecution was not so severe as to prevent creative work being done, and the major theological works of John Owen, the greatest poems of John Milton, an Independent, and John Bunyan's *Pilgrim's Progress* (although Bunyan's closest affinities were with the Baptists) all appeared after the Restoration. The works of the latter two, along with some of the hymns of Isaac Watts, have become part of the furniture of the English imagination.

The accession of William and Mary in 1688 made life more tolerable for Congregationalists, and, after a threatened setback in the reign of Queen Anne, they played a significant minor part in eighteenth-century England. They were particularly active in education, where the Dissenting Academies were educational pioneers at a time when Oxford and Cambridge languished. The spiritual influence of such leading ministers as Philip Doddridge and Isaac Watts helped prevent Congregationalists from becoming Unitarians, as most Presbyterians did at that time. Congregationalists received a considerable spiritual quickening toward the end of the century through the influence of the Methodist revival. One result was the founding in 1795 of the London Missionary Society, through whose agency churches were established in Africa, India, Madagascar, China, Papua, and the South Sea Islands.

English Congregationalism shared fully in nineteenth-century ecclesiastical prosperity. As members of the emerging lower middle classes crowded into the churches, they became more politically minded. Voluntarism, opposing state support of denominational education, and the Liberation Society, advocating the disestablishment of the Church of England, were influential. The Congregational Union, linking the churches in a national organization, was formed in 1832, and the Colonial (later Commonwealth) Missionary Society for promoting Congregationalism in English-speaking colonies in 1836. Many large new churches were erected, and some ministers, like R. W. Dale of Birmingham, were well-known public figures. Civic disabilities were steadily removed. Mansfield College was founded at Oxford in 1886. Thriving churches in city centers and residential neighborhoods were hives of social, philanthropic, and educational activities, which anticipated many of the services taken over by the state in the twentieth century. The victory of the Liberal Party in the 1906 election represented the peak of the political and social influence of Congregationalism. After that, numerical and institutional decline began, hastened by the upheaval of World War I and the increased mobility of population. Although churches were losing much of their popular appeal, the emergence of several distinguished theologians and ecumenical leaders in the interwar period provided evidence of continuing vitality. In 1972 the majority of Congregationalists joined with the Presbyterian Church in England to form the United Reformed Church.

In the rest of Britain, Congregationalists have been strongest in Wales, where the Welsh-speaking churches, known as the Union of Welsh Independents, retain their identity. These churches were transplanted successfully from the countryside to industrial Wales during the industrial revolution and became strong centers of distinctively Welsh life, cherishing their traditions of preaching, hymns, and poetry. The numerically smaller Scottish churches acted as a liberalizing influence in Scottish life and gave much to the wider church through such outstanding figures as Robert Moffat, David Livingstone, George McDonald, and P. T. Forsyth.

It is in the United States that Congregationalism achieved its greatest public influence and numerical strength. The New England experiment has been a major factor in determining the character of the nation. The Separatists of the Plymouth Colony were more radical than the Puritans of Massachusetts Bay, but they had enough in common to form a unified community and to repudiate the more radical views of Roger Williams and Anne Hutchinson. Their statement of faith, the Cambridge Platform of 1648, accepted the theology of the English Presbyterian Westminster Confession of 1646 but laid down a Congregational rather than a Presbyterian polity. In this, it was followed by the English Savoy Declaration of 1658.

The original New Englanders were not sectarian; they worked out an intellectually powerful and consistent system of theology and church and civil government that they strove, with considerable success, to exemplify. John Cotton's *Keyes of the Kingdom of Heaven and the Powers Thereof* (1644) is a classic statement of their view of the church. The very success of the New England settlement made it difficult for succeeding generations to retain the original commitment, and the Half-Way Covenant was devised to find a place for those who were baptized but could not make a strong enough confession of faith—permitting them a form of church membership that did not confer a place at the Lord's Table or in church government. Education was seen as vital from the outset. Harvard College was founded in 1637 to maintain the succession of learned ministers. Yale and others followed later, the precursors of a long succession of distinguished colleges founded under Congregational auspices across the country.

New life came with the Great Awakening, the revival movement begun in 1734, in which Jonathan Edwards, a minister at Northampton, Massachusetts, and one of the greatest American theologians, was prominent. Differences began to emerge at the turn of the century between the two wings of Congregationalism, those who continued to accept the modified Calvinism represented by Edwards and those who were moving toward Unitarianism. Unitarianism became dominant in the Boston area but not in Connecticut, where Congregationalism remained the established church until the early nineteenth century.

Despite the loss to the Unitarians, who took with them many of the most handsome colonial churches, Congregationalism flourished in the nineteenth century and was active in the westward expansion of the nation. It adopted in 1801 a Plan of Union with the Presbyterians, who were concentrated chiefly in the Middle Atlantic states, for joint home missionary activity. One factor in the ultimate breakdown of this agreement was the growing theological liberalism of Congregationalism. Horace Bushnell was a representative theologian who challenged the traditional substitutionary view of the atonement and whose influential book *Christian Nurture* (1847) questioned the need for the classic conversion experience. The so-called Kansas City Creed of 1913 summed up this liberalism, which represented a break with the Calvinist past. This liberalism continues to prevail, although substantially modified after World War II by the influence of neoorthodoxy.

The mainly Congregational American Board of Commissioners for Foreign Missions (1810) promoted missions in China and the Near East. A national Congregational organization was founded in 1871, and its boards of Home Missions and Education have done much to start schools and colleges among the black community in the South. Modern Congregationalism has been exceptionally active in the ecumenical movement. Union with the Christian Churches in the United States was achieved between the wars and with the substantial Evangelical and Reformed Church in 1961, to form the United Church of Christ.

Beliefs and Practices. The beliefs and practices of most Congregationalists have been broadly similar to those of other mainline evangelical Protestant churches of the more liberal kind. The English historian Bernard Manning described them as "decentralized Calvinists," but this fails to allow for their emphasis on the free movement of the Holy Spirit, which gives them some affinity with the Quakers as well as with Presbyterians. In its origin, their notion of the "gathered church" was not a form of secular voluntarism but an attempt, as against Anglican territorialism, to recognize "the crown rights of the Redeemer" and the primacy of the free Spirit's action in gathering together the covenant people of God. Their strong emphasis on this freedom has not only led them to be reluctant to give binding authority to creeds but also served indirectly to promote the rights of minorities of many kinds, especially in England. The long-faced, repressive Puritan of legend is largely a caricature.

Preaching is important in Congregationalism because the word in scripture is thought of as constitutive of the church. The ministry derives its authority from the word, not vice versa. Baptism and the Lord's Supper are the only recognized sacraments, and infant baptism is customary.

Traditionally, public prayer has been *ex tempore*, but more recently set forms have been widely used. Hymns are important. The English *Congregational Praise* (1952), with many hymns by Isaac Watts, the greatest Congregational writer of hymns, is an outstanding compilation.

Congregational polity is sometimes charged with promoting spiritual individualism, but this is based on a misunderstanding. It is an attempt to give the most concrete expression to the church as a local visible community. It must be properly organized, with Bible, sacraments, a duly called and trained ministry, and deacons and members in good standing. With these, no body can be more fully the church, because all necessary means of grace are available. Congregationalism has never concluded that this has meant spiritual isolation or indifference to "the communion of the churches with each other." This is shown by the fact that no group of churches has shown a greater readiness to enter schemes of reunion.

One of the most distinctive Congregational institutions is that of the church meeting, a regular gathering at which all church members have the right and responsibility to participate in all decisions. This has not always had the vigor that its place in the polity demands, but strong efforts have been made to revive it in recent times. Women have always been active in Congregational churches, which were among the first of the American and British denominations to admit women to the full-time ministry of the word and sacraments.

Until they merged with other bodies, Congregational churches were linked in associations or unions, at local and national levels, and in an International Congregational Council, to which such related bodies as the Swedish Mission Covenant Church and the Dutch Remonstrant Brotherhood also belonged. In the course of the twentieth century, churches in the United States appointed officials called state superintendents, and those in England officials called moderators, to exercise a general ministry to churches over a wide area. When a covenant with the Church of England and the Methodist Church was proposed by the United Reformed Church in England in 1980–1982, it was implied that the moderators should be made into bishops. This was hotly challenged by a substantial minority as a denial of the Reformed understanding of the ministry. The failure of the Church of England to ratify the covenant meant that this particular proposal was abandoned.

Congregational churches have existed chiefly in English-speaking countries and in communities related to them, and they have not been among the larger Christian groups. Their ideas and practices, however, have had a greater influence than their size might suggest. The Congregational tradition continues to exercise influence as one element in the life of larger reunited churches in many lands.

BIBLIOGRAPHY

Williston Walker's *Creeds and Platforms of Congregationalism* (New York, 1893) is a classic sourcebook. Douglas Horton's *Congregationalism: A Study in Church Polity* (London, 1952) and *The United Church of Christ* (New York, 1962) are two works by the most representative American Congregationalist of the twentieth century. Geoffrey F. Nuttall's *Visible Saints: The Congregational Way, 1640–1660* (Oxford, 1957) emphasizes the "spiritualizing" element in Congregationalism, and R. Tudur Jones's *Congregationalism in England, 1662–1962* (London, 1962) is a comprehensive tercentenary history. A fresh view of Congregationalism in the light of the ecumenical movement is presented in my book *Congregationalism: A Restatement* (New York and London, 1954), and essays on modern Congregationalism can be found in *Kongregationalismus* (Frankfurt, 1973), edited by Norman Goodall as volume 11 of "Die Kirchen der Welt."

New Sources

Long, Edward Le Roy. *Patterns of Polity: Varieties of Church Governance.* Cleveland, 2001.

Sell, Alan P. F. *Visible, Orderly and Catholic: The Congregational Ideal of the Church.* Alison Park, Pa., 1986.

DANIEL JENKINS (1987)
Revised Bibliography

CONSCIENCE, as commonly understood, is the faculty within us that decides on the moral quality of our thoughts, words, and acts. It makes us conscious of the worth of our deeds and gives rise to a pleasurable feeling if they are good and to a painful one if they are evil.

ORIGIN OF THE NOTION. Three articulations of human experience appear to be at the basis of the Western notion of conscience: the Hebrew scriptures, the writings of Cicero, and the writings of Paul.

Hebrew scriptures. In the Hebrew scriptures God is presented as someone who knows and evaluates our entire being. Psalm 139 develops the theme:

> O Lord, thou has searched me and known me! Thou knowest when I sit down and when I rise up; thou discernest my thoughts from afar. . . . If I take the wings of the morning and dwell in the uttermost parts of the sea, even there thy hand shall lead me, and thy right hand shall hold me. . . . Search me, O God, and know my heart! Try me and know my thoughts! And see if there be any wicked way in me, and lead me in the way everlasting! (*Ps.* 139:1–2, 9–10, 23–24)

The pious psalmist is confident that the divine scrutiny will vindicate him. Others, the enemies of Israel, are the wicked ones who will be found wanting. (See also *Job* 34:21–23.)

The idea of divine omniscient scrutiny leads, however, to vigorous self-scrutiny: "the spirit of man is the lamp of the Lord, searching all his innermost parts" (*Prv.* 20:27). The prophet Jeremiah is appalled by what he sees when he looks inside himself:

> The heart is deceitful above all things, and desperately corrupt; who can understand it? "I the Lord search the mind and try the heart, to give to every man according to his ways, according to the fruit of his doings." (*Jer.* 17:9–10)

But, here again, the prophet is confident that God is his refuge (see vv. 17–18). That God, not the self, judges the self is good news: the Strong One who sees me all (in my interiority as well as my outward acts) is a good protector, and I am safe in his hands.

Writings of Cicero. Cicero uses *conscientia* in another sense, to refer to an internal moral authority on important issues. Most of the time conscience is consciousness of something, agreeable consciousness of one or many good deeds (*Orationes Philippicae* 1.9; *Res publica* 6.8) or disagreeable consciousness of a trespass (*Tusculanae disputationes* 4.45, where he speaks metaphorically of the bite of conscience). He speaks with zeal of the force of this inner testimony: "Great is the power of conscience, great for bliss or for bane" (*Pro Milone* 61; see also *De natura deorum* 3.85, where it is specified that the workings of conscience unfold without our having to assume divine design). Some passages speak of bad conscience as if it were the internalization of a disapproval voiced by others or by public opinion in general (*In Catilinam* 3.25; *Tusculanae* 4.45). Good conscience, however, is presented as independent of public opinion. (Here, he speaks mainly of his own.) Cicero, for instance, has a good conscience about withdrawing from public life and devoting himself to writing (*Epistulae ad Atticum* 12.28.2) and is determined never to stray from the straight path of conscience. In such cases conscience is referred to without stating what it is consciousness of. While one text stresses to the juror that he should follow his conscience alone but that he should also take comfort from the fact that he is not alone in his judging (*Pro Cluentio* 159), most texts make the good conscience a rather isolated self-approval. A stunning metaphor states that no theater, no audience offers an applause that has more authority than that of conscience (*Tusculanae* 2.64). Finally, we should note that Cicero speaks of conscience in a rhetorical context and with moralizing intent; he inveighs against evil men, commends good ones, and voices his assurance of his own worth.

Writings of Paul. In the New Testament, Paul uses the notion of conscience (Gr., *suneidēsis*) as he finds it in everyday speech and common moral reflections. He puts forward his own unshakable good conscience (*Rom.* 9:1, 2 *Cor.* 1:2; see also *Acts* 23:1); he urges respect for the conscience of others, especially when that conscience is weak and judges matters erroneously (*1 Cor.* 8:7, 8:10); he appeals to conscience (*2 Cor.* 4:2); he allows that in evil people conscience is corrupted (*Ti.* 1:15). *Romans* 2:15 launched a momentous new understanding of it: conscience is a witness within all men, including pagans; it states what the law of God requires (it is "the law written in their hearts"), and it accuses all men. So far, Paul speaks of *suneidēsis* very much like Philo (who speaks mainly of *elenchos*, "reproof"). The Jewish philosopher found in all men a "true man" who should be ruler and king, who is a judge and umpire, a silent witness or accuser. Human beings live thus with a court of law inside them, and they should behave in such a way as to keep their internal judge pleased. Philo, like Paul, sees this internal authority as a gift of God, but he also accepts immanent views of it (Wallis, 1975).

But there is in Paul something else that is peculiar to him and was to prove very influential on all subsequent developments. Though he seems to have had a morally rather robust conscience, not haunted by feelings of guilt (Stendahl, 1976), Paul frequently wrote in a manner that revealed a troubled self-consciousness. He feels pain at not being acknowledged for what he is (*Gal.* 1:10); a physical handicap humbles him (*2 Cor.* 12:7). We thus find in his writing a new sort of literary voice: a self-consciousness bruised by despairing self-humiliation. His will is divided; his body does not obey him; his urgent convictions are challenged by adversaries, his life's work nearly overthrown. Under his pen, all this is not trivial autobiographical detail but is made to reflect a cosmic crisis. Paul feels that he and others are caught in the transition between a passing age and a new dispensation. His inner troubles interiorize the death of Christ. Still caught up in the age that is passing, he feels impotent, worthless; but this conviction of despair is considered by him to be a form of suffering through which he—and, he believes, all men—must pass before they can share in new life with the risen Christ (Altizer, 1983). Inner pains are thus inevitable birth pangs. A subtle shift has occurred: the notion that God welcomes a contrite heart (*Ps.* 34:18) is in the process of becoming indistinguishable from the notion that God likes—or requires—a broken heart. In *Romans*, conscience, the accuser, caught up in an eschatological drama, always convicts (3:9, 7:15–20). Good conscience before God means surrender of what men call good conscience. This eschatological turmoil gives to Paul's writings on conscience a ring very different from Philo's serene utterances.

Historical Developments. The church fathers adopt the notion of conscience as an inner voice of divine origin. The assumption is that all human beings have it, and only Christians obey it and thus please God. The firmness of the Christians' conscience enables them to obey God rather than men, live as people who do not belong to this world, and accept martyrdom with joy. Augustine compares conscience to a tribunal in the mind and speaks of it with a tone of restive introspection. He thus confirms the blending, initiated by Paul, of the three notions of divine judgment, moral self-evaluation, and the troubled forays into the hidden recesses of one's heart. A classic passage links the three realities with the Latin *conscientia:*

> "What O Lord could be hidden from you, even if I wanted not to confess it, since the abyss of human conscience is naked before your eyes? I should only be hiding you to me, not me from you. Now that my tears testify how disgusted I am with myself, you only are my light and please me; you are the object of my love and desire. I am ashamed of myself so that I cast myself aside to choose you and want to please myself or you only through you." (*Confessions* 10.2.2)

That God knows the self is a source of comfort that overcomes the intense discomfort the introspective self feels. The misery of self-rejection seems to be the necessary price to be paid before one reaches divine acceptance.

The Middle Ages use the notion of conscience primarily to elaborate a theory of moral judgment. In their systematic construction, the Scholastics use two terms to designate two functions. *Synderesis* (the word probably appears first as an erroneous reading; medieval ignorance of Greek let it become established) is the faculty that knows the moral law; it remained unaffected by the fall. The Franciscan school makes of it a *potentia affectiva*, namely a disposition of the heart. The Dominicans make of it a sort of cognition; it exists in the reason. *Conscientia* applies the moral law to concrete cases. It is a *habitus* of the practical intellect, say the Franciscans; an act, according to the Dominicans, which applies knowledge to action. To Thomas Aquinas (c. 1225–1274) *synderesis* decides; it always orients us to the good. *Conscientia* controls; we can set it aside. When it functions, *conscientia* is a witness; it says what we have done or not done. It binds or motivates; it says what we should or should not do. Finally, it excuses or accuses; it tells us whether what we have done was well or not well done. While *synderesis* cannot err, *conscientia*, a sort of decree of the mind, is fallible (*Summa theologiae* 1.79.12–13). Conscience now is no longer an occasional voice at important moments, but a concomitant of all morally relevant action.

Medieval theologians also examine whether one is obligated to follow an erroneous conscience. It is allowed that some consciences are invincibly erroneous, that is, their error cannot be overcome by the use of moral diligence or thorough study. Even in these circumstances the self must obey conscience. *Romans* 14:23 is the norm: whatever is not from faith is deemed sinful. One must, however, at all times seek to correct one's conscience by instruction. Thomas Aquinas teaches that to hold in contempt the dictates of an erroneous conscience is a mortal sin and that conscience binds, even when it contradicts the precepts of a superior, if it endures.

This intellectual clarification is accompanied by a system of practical guidance. In 1215, the Fourth Lateran Council made it an obligation for all Christians to confess their sins and receive the sacrament once a year. This came to be known as the tribunal of conscience. A practice was required and an occasion offered: the self had to embark upon intellectual deliberation on its behavior and could obtain expert advice or counsel. Benjamin Nelson (1981) described this system of spiritual direction under a threefold heading: conscience, casuistry, and the cure of souls. The individual, like all men, is obligated by the universal moral law. Like some other men, he has peculiar dilemmas related to his age, his class, his role in life; casuistry studies these cases of conscience and enlightens the individual by drawing upon the experience of those whose lot is comparable. Finally, the individual is unlike everyone else; he has his own sorrows and fears; his soul needs to be ministered to in a therapeutic way and comforted. The system reaped behavioral fruit: the lives of Western Christians were progressively ordered in conformity with Christian moral principles. Consciences were slowly educated. Fear of divine judgment loomed large among the motivational forces. While the theologians' *synderesis* and *conscientia* were purely moral principles, the pastoral tribunal of conscience often functioned in an atmosphere of religious anguish: God would be angry if sins were not confessed and corrected. His searching of the hearts was felt to be a perilous affair; sinners were threatened with outright condemnation.

While canon lawyers instituted the tribunal of conscience and while pastors appealed to or pounded on individual consciences, the national monarchies and the royal law of France and England developed in such a way as to give an increasing social relevance to the notion of moral conscience. Frenchmen in the twelfth and thirteenth centuries began to be aware of themselves as one people, living together civilly in a good land under the rule of a just and Christian king. This emergence of national consciousness came simultaneously with urbanization, with an increased practice of prudence and courtesy in social relations (the arts of peace), and with the rise of an ethics of intention, such as that discussed by Abelard (1079–1142). Now new collective representations give expression to a shared will to live together for the sake of peace and to the happy sense of forming together a good society. The sense of the sacred has begun to shift from a largely supernatural realm to the national Christian society that provides a good, secure life. A sacred bond now unites the righteous king and the loyal people. And a man can now encounter people he has never seen before (and with whom no one in his village has ever had dealings) and still have civil relations: strangers are conscious at the outset of belonging to the same people. In England, the old Aristotelian notion of equity is introduced into the royal law: law is said always to aim at justice and to be corrigible whenever principles of equity are violated, for instance, whenever the helpless are dealt with unfairly, or whenever widows and orphans are oppressed. Correction is said to be introduced "for the sake of conscience." In France and in England, society can henceforth be said to have a collective and civil conscience, to be sensitive to the moral demands of common peace and universal justice, to visualize royal power as not simply heroic but merciful as well. (This Western confidence that human beings can collectively govern themselves well is reflected in Calvin's *Institutes* 2.2.13.)

The stage is now set for the great crises and transformations of the sixteenth century. For the first time conscience has become a culturally central, crucial notion among Christians. The three notions of it we originally identified now merge to define the problem: the man of conscience is "spiritual," he lives "before God"; he is also moral and has obligations to his fellow men; he has a rapport with himself and feels condemned or saved. The Protestant Reformation saw itself as a defender of conscience. The word became one of its most militant terms.

The reformers spoke of conscience as being oppressed by the medieval system. While considering itself obliged to obey "the pope's commandments," conscience saw itself weighed down by the burden of bad and illegitimate laws of human origin, which it was impossible to obey. There was anguish in trying to obey and anguish in disobedience because of the nagging sense of fearsome consequences. Luther articulated his own scrupulous monastic experience of anguish over every action and involuntary impulse by indentifying with Paul. He vibrated in unison, he thought, with Paul's and Augustine's autobiographical statements. Conscience and the law jointly accused him and brought him death. (Unlike Paul, Luther was under the yoke of bad law; identifying with Paul, he overlooked the difference in the objective content of the laws.) The monk Luther, however, was not alone. Henry VIII, a Catholic king, was afraid his marriage to Catherine of Aragon was sterile because it had been cursed by God. (Catherine had been engaged to Henry's brother; even though the brother was dead, the marriage was incestuous by canonical if not dynastic rules.) Was his conscience genuinely troubled or was his second marriage expedient or self-indulgent? (It is significant that the issue is still debated.)

In any case, the medieval burden of being trapped by a guilty conscience was thrown off by many who broke their vows or changed their lifestyles. The religious authorities' guiding conscience had ceased to be credible in the eyes of many of the people of God. Most theological reformers also rejected the very principle of trying to please God with deeds (works); no action was conceivable that could give man a joyful conscience before God. Thus the Protestant Reformation also rejected the whole system of the tribunal of conscience. Freed by grace, living in faith, the Christian immediately receives a good conscience from his God. He thus recaptures the sense of the covenant found in the Hebrew scriptures: that God can fathom our hearts and that he alone judges us once again becomes good news. We are not accountable to ecclesiastical authorities, and they should not haunt our consciences and enrich themselves at our expense. Thus with good consciences, redeemed Christians walk straight in the paths of righteousness. Activities of public reform persuade these Christians that they are indeed setting up a more moral order. For its part, the Roman Catholic Church maintains the system of casuistry and cure of souls. But in time, with a more saintly clergy, the authority of the spiritual directors is restored. Consciences are again more guided than tyrannized.

It must be seen that the Protestant Reformation fostered a new Western assurance of conscience. Conscience became safe, certain. The system of casuistry was dealing in probabilities, constantly weighing pros and cons, and every authority was liable to be overthrown by other authorities. The civil conscience was also always open to correction. Reading his Bible, the Protestant Christian gained subjective certainty once and for all: he was God's child and his path was straight. (The sixteenth century began many moves toward certainty: the Protestant Reformation gave subjective assurance and the scientific revolution began to give objective certainty; Galileo did not weigh the relative merits of authorities; he knew for sure. See Nelson, 1981.) Luther's conscience is lyrical: he is ultimately safe in God's arms and above pleasing men or worrying about their opinions. All the reformers agree: he who has faith has good conscience. No human forum can accuse him. Conscience has nothing to do with a man's dealing among his fellow men but only with his reception of divine forgiveness. Paul Tillich (1948) coined the term *transmoral conscience* to refer to this notion of man's innerness as it meets God. Calvin is clear: conscience must not be confused with "police." Its business is not with men but with God (*Institutes* 3.19.15–16; 4.10.3). It must be unhappy at first. "It is necessary that conscience drive our misery home to us before we can have some sense of God" (*Institutes* 1.1.1 and 4.19.15–16). While Calvin as an elect does not let others challenge his own conscience, he openly distrusts the conscience of others: "Nothing is more common, just as nothing is easier than to boast of faith and a good conscience" (Neal, 1972). The notion of conscience as a subjective absolute is reinforced by the practice of religious privatism: sins are remitted by private confession to God, without confession to a fellow human being or reparation to the victim. With Calvin, the assurance of conscience among the elect is coupled with a particularly vigorous moral action in the world. The concept that had been used to detach the individual from the world now presides over the conscientious effort to shape the world according to the Christian's moral aspirations. The stage is set for the polemics in which Protestants blame Catholics for the erroneous precepts they impose on conscience, and Catholics blame Protestants for their unbridled "conscientious" energies.

The sixteenth century witnessed also the rise of a fresh, vigorous articulation of conscience in the civil tradition. Surrounded by wars waged for the sake of conscience, the French moralist Montaigne (1533–1592) inaugurated the art of writing for oneself the story of an observant, rigorously honest conscience (Brunschwicg, 1953). Both moral and introspective, this conscience ponders the actions of the self and of others and looks at the relations and roles the self is involved in. Self-critical, open to instruction and correction from those who have experience of the world, this conscience treasures selected friendships and enjoys a measure of self-acceptance. It holds on to the few truths and rare marks of humanity it believes itself to be capable of. The dramas of acceptance and rejection at the hands of the biblical God recede in the background. Front stage belongs to the dramas of human likes and dislikes. Descartes (1596–1650) puts an analysis of conscience at the center of his philosophy. In his case, conscience is troubled or disturbed by the experience of its fallibility and by the idea of the infinite; the goodness of God provides decisive reassurance on both points. In the ambit of French civilization, conscience will henceforth keep these crucial characteristics: it is autonomous, moral, and social, somewhat skeptical, worldly wise, and it has a modest but firm pride.

The authority of conscience receives its fullest religious legitimacy in the theory of inner light common to many seventeenth-century English sects. Instead of being an act of interpretation of a law, this conscience is an absolute and final insight. It is also British philosophy that gave to moral conscience its most ample philosophical underpinnings. The theory of moral sense identifies the consciousness of right and wrong with the voice of an inner moral law (the unwritten, inborn law of which Cicero spoke in *Pro Milone* 10). Inner voices or feelings are described as edicts of one's conscience. L. Butler (1692–1752; *Sermons*) affirms that it has a natural authority; it is the voice of God within us. Conscience has become a faculty of the mind that judges immediately and finally on moral matters. In the Middle Ages conscience was a function: people had more or less of it, and tried more or less to exercise it. With the reformers it was a fact of spiritual life: people had a troubled or a joyful one; it became an individual organ—you have your conscience and I have mine, just as each of us has his own stomach. This conscience was said to be infallible and generally philanthropic. It was also inviolate. No serious conflicts of conscience were foreseen. The stage was set for the good conscience of the West to be applied in colonial expansion. All human beings have conscience, it was thought. Western Christians liberated what they deemed to be inferior races from the fears to which their idolatrous and superstitious consciences were prone; they established liberty of conscience (freedom of religion) wherever they ruled, and they did all this without violating consciences. Being most developed, the Western consciences helped others develop too. Western expansion was optimistically expected to moralize the world.

Modern Conflict between Conscience and Consciousness. Theoreticians declare what conscience always says to the inner man. Conscience may in fact behave according to theory; but also it might not. Or, more commonly, the individual realizes that what conscience pronounces clashes with some other inner state he is aware of at a given moment. Distinctions need to be made among the voices in one's inner debate. Luther translated the medieval *conscientia* with *das Gewissen.* Two centuries later, Christian Wolff (1679–1754), the founder of German philosophy, translated the *conscientia* of the Cartesians with *das Bewusstsein.* In sixteenth-century English, *conscience* can denote authoritative, secure moral conscience or simple, trivial consciousness. (The French language still uses *la conscience* to speak both of the moral rationales the self fully accepts and of fleeting mental events.) With the eighteenth century, the sense of a separation between conscience and consciousness became widespread. While moral beings naively went on believing in their stable, good, unerring conscience, literature (the novel especially) increasingly explored the chasm between conscience and the vagaries of consciousness. The semiblind yet massive good conscience of the modern theoreticians of conscience and their followers could now become manifest. Moralists became aware of time, of the necessary distinction between what is abiding and what is transitory in a man's sense of himself. Conscience then came to be seen as a firm statement that the self utters before others or privately, a plea entered in a public or inner forum. Like consciousness, conscience is an event; but unlike it, it is also a moral discourse, a public claim. Hence, the critical question: is this discourse fully aware of the actualities of the case? Is conscience conscious? (Engelberg, 1972).

Nineteenth-century probings ordinarily shared the conviction that human beings should always be as fully conscious as possible, with actions completely lucid and deliberate. Rousseau (1712–1778) believed he could derive norms for political life from the assumption that politics consists of free, conscious, virtuous interaction among autonomous, independent individuals. (He even believed the whole of social life could consist of such interaction.) Kant (1724–1804) pursued the point with theoretical thoroughness. All moral action proceeds from good will and is conscientious. *Das Gewissen* never errs. It is "the moral faculty of judgment, passing judgment upon itself . . . a state of consciousness which is itself a duty" (*Religion within the Limits of Reason Alone* 4.2.4). With each action, the individual should reflect and proceed only if he is sure that this action obeys the dictates of conscience. The consequence does not escape Hegel (1770–1833): consciences will be in conflict, each vibrating with its assurance, each alone in its certainty of obeying the moral law (Despland, 1975). Far from being a reliable guide, conscience now appears to be potentially immoral arrogance.

The nineteenth century is full of denigrations of conscience. The poet William Blake (1757–1827) is sarcastic: "Conscience in those that have it is unequivocal" ("Annotations to Watson"). Goethe (1749–1832) commends an alternative: Faust heals himself, grows by purging himself of conscience (he does not let himself be crippled by the episode with Marguerite) and ever widening his consciousness. Nietzsche (1844–1900) attempts to show that conscience only imitates ready-made values; the hard human task is to embody knowledge in ourselves, to create conscious values; and consciousness is not given gratis.

But the claims of conscience remain tenacious even in the post-Romantic age. Conscience, however, becomes more tragic, more solitary. Rare are those who see in it the workings of an other-regarding instinct. To Kierkegaard (1813–1855), the inwardness of conscience is demonic: more conscience means more consciousness and deeper despair. Such is also the case in Dostoevskii's *Notes from the Underground* (1864): conscience has become an obsessive inner court; the self is the accuser, the accused, the judge, and the executioner. In a bizarre extension of Paul's and Luther's autobiographical pages, self-consciousness merges into compulsive self-humiliation, with no redemption in sight. Conscience is no longer active knowledge immersed in the social flow of life but purely retrospective, solitary self-condemnation, or entirely fearful anticipation.

More balanced statements of this construction are found in the writings of Coleridge (1772–1834) and Conrad (1857–1924). The poet-critic Coleridge stresses that conscience no longer acts "with the ease and uniformity of instinct"; rather, consciousness is the problem. In *Lord Jim*, Conrad shows us his protagonist haunted by a conscience that prevents his awareness of the good new life he has built for himself, while in *Heart of Darkness* we see Kurtz surrendering conscience and letting his consciousness be flooded by instinctual experience. Without conscience, Kurtz is all awareness and lacks an interpreter; he stands thus naked before horror.

APPLICATION OF THE NOTION TO THE STUDY OF RELIGIOUS AND ETHICAL SYSTEMS. Hindu and Buddhist philosophies have very articulate and complex theories of consciousness. All religious traditions have notions of moral law and moral judgment. All encourage reflectivity and offer conceptual tools and practical techniques for self-evaluation. But the notion of conscience as internal organ is not found outside of Christianity. As commonly understood, it is peculiar to the West. The generalization of the tribunal of conscience, the universal legal requirement for annual confession and penance, is a uniquely Western phenomenon. Westerners seem to have taken on a special burden of responsibility. (This was probably not particularly helpful morally.) I must have a vision of myself—of my vocation, for instance—for which I alone will be accountable. Consider, for instance, the notion of conscience found in the writings of the German existentialist philosopher Heidegger (1889–1976): that there is an objectless call of conscience that summons us, not to be in a particular manner, but to choose in what manner we shall be. The wars against guilty thoughts and the self-condemnatory forays into self-consciousness seem also linked to the unique history of Western man (the Gnostic and the celibate monastic episodes being probably particularly influential). Recall that most of the decisive articulations of conscience were autobiographical statements focusing on inner turmoils.

Nineteenth-century founders of the science of religion used the idea of evolution of conscience to bridge the gap between themselves, the Western scholars able and desirous to know all mankind, and the people they studied, whose outlook was perceived as regional, if not primitive. So they wrote about the dawn of conscience in the ancient Near East and about the various stages of conscience reached in non-Christian religions. The moral and religious dignity of man was commonly tied to the functioning of this individual organ. The evolutionary view was self-serving and is now discarded, but it had the merit of affirming a commonality among all humankind.

Articles on conscience in James Hastings's *Encyclopaedia of Religion and Ethics* (vol. 4, 1911) illustrate this stage of scholarship. There is a polemic against the nascent sociological reductionist view that sees in conscience an interiorization of social rules. A lengthy article seeks to establish the Jewish view of conscience. The article is not in the least embarrassed by the fact that rabbinic Judaism has no such notion. (For a respected account of Jewish morality, see Neusner, 1981: the will has some power to affect the world, and its intention should be good.) Attempts to find everywhere notions of conscience comparable to the Western one have now largely been abandoned. Current influential works in the discipline of comparative religious ethics have no recourse to it (Little and Twiss, 1978; Bird, 1981). In contrast, the concept is important in current philosophical ethics (Childress, 1979).

ANTHROPOLOGICAL AND THEOLOGICAL CONSIDERATIONS. Etymology may once again be suggestive. Conscience is "knowledge-with," that is, a shared knowledge of something. The foundational experience is the awareness that somebody else is aware of what I have done; I have been seen, and I know that he knows, and I know that he knows that I know that he knows. There is, for a fleeting moment, a shared awareness between us. There is intelligence in the birth of conscience: the other can be a clever accomplice or an articulate critic. But there is also co-feeling: my action is endorsed or disapproved of. The mutual awareness is not just mental. There is also compassion: he knows how it feels to do what I have done, and I know how it feels to observe this being done. Conscience, then, is not just a matter of sight and scrutiny; there is also sensitivity and heart in it. And if conscience makes us potentially morally liable, it makes us also aware of potential moral support.

After this initial point, conscience becomes an interpretive activity. Thus, I own my act and articulate its meaning, serenely, aggressively, or defensively. But while I interpret, others (the initial fellow-feeler or some third party) also interpret. My interpretation will be happy and secure if it agrees in detail or broadly with a wider community of interpretation. It was the merit of the medieval "domestication" of conscience (Lehmann, 1963) that an authoritative, plausible community was always near. Conscience was the court of first instance to adjudicate the worth of my action, and it was the court of last instance. But there was guidance from intermediate courts, which could function in a human manner, with intellectual stability and a measure of understanding. It was the weakness of the Kantian theory that conscience became the only (first and last) tribunal. (Paul had had the good sense to admit that God, not his conscience, judges him. See *1 Corinthians* 4:4.) Kant prepared the "decline and fall" of conscience: solitary conscience is either hostile to self and cruel, or self-righteous and insensitive to others. Freud (1856–1939) could only spell out the irrelevance and uselessness of this conscience (Lehmann, 1963).

The interpretive activity of conscience must therefore always be an account to the other, to others. De Jaucourt (*Encyclopédie*, 1765) emphasized quite soundly that what is important about conscience is the quality of the reasons it can put forward. Hegel saw quite correctly that, to be moral, an action must be owned and expressed: it must be said that it is from conscience. Accountability before somebody else (the one or those affected, or an ideal observer) is intrinsic to morality; the effort of persuasion directed toward others in their otherness is bound with the aspiration to worth. The self needs to be at least symbolically endorsed by others, to be supported at least in words. It is the utmost hypocrisy to claim that conscience can judge itself with skill and authority. Conscience does not produce a private hell or heaven but a public person. When conscience is alive it evaluates the action of the self as part of a continuing moral action (and interaction and further interaction). It is a diseased conscience that carries out nothing but introspective, retrospective self-appraisal. The healthy conscience lives in the present. (In the moment of conscience, consciousness becomes conscious of its past social unconsciousness, and moves on.) And conscience lives in the presence of another human being or beings. It forges an intention, takes an initiative, faces others with a proposal, issues forth in a public act (Jankélévitch, 1933, 1950). Wise and foolish consciences, happy and unhappy ones, are not immobile, self-enclosed realities. They are stages in conscious histories. Healthy consciences share their stories. Each narrates old stories and listens to old stories: in the process, a new story is shared and action shaped. It takes a story to account for one's conscience, and it takes a shared, ongoing story for conscience to form—and enjoy forming—action.

On the interreligious scene today, it is to be wished that dialogue and encounter shall proceed from conscience. And the notion of conscience may well be—or become—part of the account that each will give to the other of his or her own humanity. Such meeting of consciences cannot occur without the labor of consciousness: each trying to communicate over a period of time what he is aware of.

Any attempt in the West to develop a theologically relevant notion of conscience must overcome two traditional tendencies. First of all, religious conscience should be purged of its tendency to reject the fellowship of men and become absorbed in the private dialogue of the soul with God. Conscience, wrote Luther, is the place where we must live with God as man and wife (*Lectures on Psalms* 3.593.28–29). It must also heal itself of the tendency to assume that God will love us if we hate ourselves. From Augustine on, the notion has persisted that to lay bare before God our innermost hearts, admit we find there utter corruption, and profess to feel pain will miraculously turn a bad conscience into a good one. Such self-serving self-humiliation is either an insincere act or an abject one. Self-torture does not make man morally better. A bad conscience may prevent worse sins, but it never brings joy.

A reconstruction might proceed from the biblical sense that conscience and heart are interchangeable. Conscience is then constituted by the hearing of—or sensitivity to—a call, a commandment. The idea of conscience can be built on what happens in an encounter between persons, rather than on the notion of a moral experience. Such a notion mistakenly assumes that a moral subject is already established, before hearing the claims of the other; one might recall here that Paul told the Corinthians not to advance their own (strong) consciences but to heed the (weaker) consciences of others. What is heard in the depths of the encounter with the widows, the orphans, and the poor of the land is the infinite call of vast human need. Within the compass of being, there are persons who are not beings; that is, they are not beings one should simply adapt oneself to or exercise power on. In each person there is also an infinite with which one can and should talk, in lucid awareness of one's own strength. The primal condition of conscious human freedom is to be unfree because claimed by the presence of a weaker other. He who is conscious of the nature of ordinary human relations has just put food in his mouth and a roof over his head: he has time to think. The mere fact of his respite makes him infinitely liable to those who are still hungry. And the infinite that meets us in other concrete human beings is an infinity of demands that cannot be answered by a mere rule of what is right and sufficient; it is also an infinity of stories that cannot be reduced to one plot. Thus there is in every other being an excess of possibilities over the possibilities that are inherent in me; something new should result from our encounter. Scripture affirms that God meets us in the lowest among our brethren. Only in these meetings are found the birthplace of morality and the voice of God. (See the analyses of Lévinas, presented in Smith, 1983.) Kierkegaard praised the faith that clung to the divine promise and readied itself to disobey the law. In contrast, Emmanuel Lévinas urges us to give up the hope of a warm rapport with God and love the law instead, austerely. This is what God requires; what we (both we the strong and we the weak) most need in order to fulfill God's requirement are some firm exterior rules of justice (Lévinas, 1976, pp. 189–193).

See Also Christian Ethics; Conversion; Morality and Religion; Religious Experience; Sin and Guilt; Theology, article on Christian Theology.

Bibliography

Altizer, Thomas J. J. "Paul and the Birth of Self-Consciousness." *Journal of the American Academy of Religion* 51 (September 1983): 359–370.

Bird, Frederick. "Paradigms and Parameters for the Comparative Study of Religious and Ideological Ethics." *Journal of Religious Ethics* 9 (Fall 1981): 157–185.

Brunschwicg, Léon. *Le progrès de la conscience dans la philosophie occidentale* (1927). 2d ed. 2 vols. Paris, 1953.

Childress, James F. "Appeals to Conscience." *Ethics* 89 (July 1979): 315–335.

Despland, Michel. "Can Conscience Be Hypocritical? The Contrasting Analyses of Kant and Hegel." *Harvard Theological Review* 68 (July–October 1975): 357–370.

Engelberg, Edward. *The Unknown Distance: From Consciousness to Conscience, Goethe to Camus.* Cambridge, Mass., 1972.

Jankélévitch, Vladimir. *La mauvaise conscience* (1933). Paris, 1982.

Jankélévitch, Vladimir. *L'ironie ou la bonne conscience.* 2d ed. Paris, 1950.

Lehmann, Paul L. *Ethics in a Christian Context.* New York, 1963.

Lévinas, Emmanuel. *Difficile liberté.* 2d ed. Paris, 1976.

Little, David L., and Sumner Twiss, Jr. *Comparative Religious Ethics.* New York, 1978.

Neal, J. R. "Conscience in the Reformation Period." Ph.D. diss., Harvard University, 1972.

Nelson, Benjamin. *On the Roads to Modernity.* Totowa, N.J., 1981.

Neusner, Jacob. *Judaism: The Evidence of the Mishnah.* Chicago, 1981.

Smith, Steven G. *The Argument to the Other: Reason beyond Reason in the Thought of Karl Barth and Emmanuel Lévinas.* Chico, Calif., 1983.

Stendahl, Krister. "Paul and the Introspective Conscience of the West." In *Paul among Jews and Gentiles, and Other Essays.* Philadelphia, 1976.

Tillich, Paul. "The Transmoral Conscience." In *The Protestant Era.* Chicago, 1948.

Wallis, R. T. *The Idea of Conscience in Philo of Alexandria.* Berkeley, 1975.

New Sources

Adler, Jacob. *The Urgings of Conscience: A Theory of Punishment.* Philadelphia, 1992.

Hall, Amy Laura. "Self-Deception, Confusion, and Salvation in Fear and Trembling with Works of Love." *Journal of Religious Ethics* 28, no. 1 (2000): 37–61.

Hammond, Guy. "Conscience in Public and Private." In *Religion in a Pluralistic Age: Proceedings of the Third International Conference on Philosophical Theology,* edited by Donald A. Crosby and Charley D. Hardwick, pp. 173–187. New York, 2001.

Hoose, Jayne, ed. *Conscience in World Religions.* Notre Dame, Ind., 1999.

McLaren, John, and Harold Coward, eds. *Religious Conscience, the State, and the Law: Historical Contexts and Contemporary Significance.* Albany, 1999.

Redmond, Walter. "Conscience as Moral Judgment: The Probabilist Blending of the Logics of Knowledge and Responsibility." *Journal of Religious Ethics* 26 (1998): 389–405.

Rittgers, Ronald K. *The Reformation of the Keys: Confession, Conscience, and Authority in Sixteenth-Century Germany.* Cambridge, U.K., 2004.

Zachman, Randall C. *The Assurance of Faith: Conscience in the Theology of Martin Luther and John Calvin.* Minneapolis, 1993.

MICHEL DESPLAND (1987)
Revised Bibliography

CONSCIOUSNESS, STATES OF. Consciousness is the great enigma. We experience it in the present moment. Yet when one tries objectively to understand it within oneself, it becomes amorphous and changing. Sometimes changes from one state of consciousness to another are not recognized until the change has occurred, as if these states were separated by a zone of forgetfulness. When one observes changes in consciousness in someone else, the description always seems colored with one's own biases and preconceptions, in spite of attempts to be objective. A physiologist sees only a range from stupor through sleep and from the normal everyday waking state to hyperexcitability. A psychiatrist who subscribes to depth psychology sees waking consciousness as the mere tip of the iceberg, the rest being composed of a vast domain of the unconscious lying below the surface of awareness, all of which is considered more primitive than rational consciousness. The religious adept wants to acknowledge the reality of hellish as well as transcendent states, the former considered lower and darker and more painful, and the latter higher and deeper or more subtle and more highly refined, than that of the normal waking condition. Hence one's model of consciousness depends largely on the scope of one's personal experience and the context of one's worldview.

Most scientists remain firmly committed to a positivist and reductionist epistemology in their approach to the study of consciousness. Traditionally, this view demands adherence to the idea that there is no other state than the normal everyday waking one. All phenomena are merely variations of this one single state. When one is asleep, according to this view, there is no consciousness. Consciousness and awareness are identical. There is nothing else. There is no such thing as an unconscious, nor is there any reality to the idea of states of consciousness, let alone higher or lower ones, as these are all thought to be mere projections of the waking state.

Psychologists and psychiatrists who subscribe to the psychodynamic view at least acknowledge the reality of the unconscious. Thoughts, words, and deeds may be influenced by images held below the surface of consciousness, many of which are representations of past traumatic experiences or other forms of intrapsychic conflict. The prevailing view in the social sciences, however, is that the unconscious is more primitive and undeveloped than the waking rational state. The model only ranges from the normality of the waking state through the maladjustment of the neurotic to the complete disintegration of consciousness in psychopathology. The very acknowledgment of different states of consciousness, perforce, implies a disintegration of the essential continuity of waking consciousness.

Most of the major religions and philosophies of the world, on the other hand, speak, most often in symbolic terms, about higher and lower states of consciousness other than those of ordinary experience. These are the realms of the heavens and hells—the highest ecstatic states of expanded consciousness possible for humans to experience or the lowest states of suffering even beyond imagination. According to these teachings, people have the potential to experience qualitatively different and superior levels of perception, awareness, and orientation toward themselves, others, and the universe. Indeed in such states the ultimate nature of reality may be revealed.

But the problem is always the same with each of these teachings, namely that religious traditions tend to advocate that transformation from a lower state to a higher state of consciousness may result from adherence to the ideas, methods, and prescribed meditations of only one's own authentic spiritual discipline, whereby consciousness is refined, converted, and realigned from "the coarse to the fine." The question still remains, however, about the extent to which such experiences can only be mediated through a specific religious tradition, or whether or not this is a generic transformation toward spiritual consciousness possible in each individual regardless of the tradition or cultural context. Individuals, not institutions, after all, experience states of consciousness. Institutions meanwhile can foster the experience of interior states or either actively or inadvertently repress them.

Most contemporary histories, however, do not delve into the religious literature but look more toward the objective, scientific approach to the study of states of consciousness in the West, which they maintain begins only with Franz Anton Mesmer in the late eighteenth century.

FRANZ ANTON MESMER. A remarkable healer of what are called psychosomatic and hysterical illnesses, Mesmer (1734–1815) was knowledgeable in medicine, psychology, hermeticism, and alchemy. He postulated that people possess two distinct realms of consciousness, the ordinary waking state and an underlying unseen realm. In this invisible realm two related powers seem to be activated. The first is an exchange of rarefied energies or "fluids" between individuals that allows certain sensitive persons to influence others by their presence; that is, to influence them in more subtle ways than are generally believed operative in human exchanges. The second is a faculty of superior intelligence and will. The recognition of these submerged potentials as put forth by Mesmer and the psychologists who succeeded him led to investigation into the powers, scope, and subtleties of the unconscious as opposed to the functioning of normal everyday waking consciousness.

In his healing endeavors, Mesmer found himself capable of affecting other people by his presence. He was able to transmit a mysterious energy that he named "animal magnetism" to his patients. He believed he had the ability to transfer surplus energy from himself to others. While treating a woman who vacillated between episodes of illness and periods of relative calm, he was reminded of the endless oscillations of the tides and the seasons. This gave Mesmer the idea that these bouts, like the ebbs of the tides, might be essential components of a more complete process. That insight generated his strategy of inducing an "artificial tide" in his patient (with the aid of magnets) to evoke a cathartic ebb or "crisis," a therapeutic convulsion to enhance the body's "fluid" circulation and bring about a cure. The cures he effected in this way persuaded him that the cure of illness caused by mental factors was facilitated by circulating this subtle fluid and rebalancing the underlying realm within the patient. Such a realignment seemed to be induced by Mesmer's own magnetism and internal balance, for it was inexplicable by the prevailing theories of the day. The inferences are that one's state of consciousness, balance, or sensitivity may profoundly affect another person, and that this balance corresponds to the fundamental order of the universe itself. He wrote:

> Man's sleep is not a negative state, nor is it simply the absence of wakefulness; modifications of this state have taught me that the faculties of a sleeping man not only are not suspended, but that often they continue to function with more perfection than when he is awake. One can observe that certain persons walk, and conduct their affairs with more planning and with the same reflection, attention, and skill as when they are awake. It is still more surprising to see faculties which are called "intellectual" being used to such an extent that they infinitely surpass those cultivated in the ordinary state. (Mesmer, 1980, p. 112)

GUSTAV THEODOR FECHNER. A German mathematician, physicist, and philosopher, Fechner (1801–1887) is often credited as the founder of modern psychophysics for his expression of the Weber-Fechner Law, in which the just noticeable difference between two weights can be detected. Intensely interested in the mind-body problem, Fechner's true intent, however, was to measure the threshold between any two different states of consciousness, but this idea was lost on later reductionists in experimental psychology who claimed him as their patron saint. Fechner experienced a nervous breakdown in 1839 as an aftereffect from experiments gazing into the sun, and he spent a year in a condition of blindness, during which time he had various Asian scriptures read to him. In 1851 he produced his own text outlining a theory of universal consciousness. Borrowing his main title from the great Zoroastrian scripture by the same name, he called it *Zend Avesta: Oder über die Dinge des Himmels und des Jenseits.*

William James later became enamored with Fechner's writings on the subject. In his Hibbert Lectures at Oxford in 1907, James summarized Fechner's doctrine of the earth soul and of beings intermediary between God and man. James also wrote a preface to the fourth edition of the English translation of Fechner's *Little Book of Life after Death* (1907), in which Fechner outlined the three great spheres of evolutionary consciousness—a womb consciousness characterized by the fetus immersed in amniotic fluid, waking rational consciousness in the physical body, and a higher spiritual consciousness after death. Fechner believed that each stage presaged and was therefore preparation for the next, but that all stages were available simultaneously in human beings while still alive in the body.

WILLIAM JAMES. James (1842–1910) is the most noted modern psychologist to have seriously investigated altered states of consciousness and the influence of states of consciousness on the perception of reality. An avid physiologist, psychologist, philosopher, and psychical researcher, James studied trance states in mediums from an early age. He also experimented throughout his professional life with mind-altering drugs, including ether, chloral hydrate, nitrous oxide, and peyote. He was an expert hypnotist and often encouraged people to try automatic writing. In his monumental *Principles of Psychology* (1890) he defined consciousness as a stream and investigated subconscious conditions at the periphery of awareness, such as fugue states in somnambulism. He also studied the hypnogogic zone—the twilight period between waking and sleeping—in his 1896 Lowell Lectures on exceptional mental states. In *The Varieties of Religious Experience* (1902) James discussed ultimately transforming mystical states that, although inaccessible to purely rational consciousness, impart exceptional meaning and understanding to experience. The enhanced powers of cognition exhibited in such states suggest that human beings possess faculties beyond those of the ordinary mind for attaining certainty and wisdom:

> One conclusion was forced upon my mind at that time, and my impression of its truth has ever since remained unshaken. It is that our normal waking consciousness, rational consciousness as we call it, is but one special type of consciousness, whilst all about it, parted from it by the filmiest of screens, there lie potential forms of consciousness entirely different. . . . No account of the universe in its totality can be final which leaves these other forms of consciousness quite disregarded. How to regard them is the question—for they are so discontinuous with ordinary consciousness. . . . At any rate, they forbid a premature closing of our accounts with reality. (James, 2002, p. 318)

James defined mystical states by demarcating four of their salient qualities. The first is the "noetic" or cognitive aspect of the mystical state. This is not the rational, discursive, comparative function of thinking, however. It is, rather, visionary understanding or wisdom—a power of heightened intellectual discernment and relational understanding in which positioning, valuation, and function are apprehended and seemingly disparate facts are properly ranked and organized into meaningful entities. The second quality he characterized as "ineffability." Because they are ineffable, these transformations in consciousness cannot be verbalized in a manner that ever does justice to the nuances of the experience. The third quality is "transience." Mystical states usually are short-lived. Having their own distinctive flavor, they appear to be connected and continuous with each other, and those who experience them generally report a new and vivid awareness of being in the present moment. Fourth, mystical states are characterized by a feeling of "passivity," as if one's personal will were suspended and one had opened oneself to a higher or superior force. The experience is of not quite being oneself; there is another force, power, or "person" operating through one.

At the end of this groundbreaking work James postulated the need for a cross-cultural dynamic psychology of mystical states in order to grasp psychology's true contribution to the religious sphere and to understand the experience of higher states of consciousness as central to the evolution of human spirituality in different cultures.

But what is the relationship between altered states of consciousness, the superior intellectual faculties described by James, and the evolution of this power of sustained directed attention toward ultimate reality? On the whole, these questions—so central to the esoteric traditions—were only slightly addressed at the interface between depth psychology and religious studies, and largely ignored by mainstream scientific psychologists, until interest in the neurosciences forced the issue of different states of consciousness on reductionistic theorists. Other scientific and medical men, both around James and since James's time, have also been interested in the reality of different states of consciousness, however.

PIERRE JANET. Phenomena such as dissociation and somnambulism—the waking fugue state—and the study of hysteria and other "neuroses," including multiple personality, brought the French neurologist Pierre Janet (1859–1947) into the international spotlight in the late 1880s through the so-called French experimental psychology of the subconscious. This school of thought flourished between 1880 and 1910 as a driving force behind a larger French, Swiss, English, and American psychotherapeutic axis that dominated developments in scientific psychotherapy in the West long before psychoanalysis came into international prominence. In such works as *L'automatisme psychologique* (1889), *L'état mental des hysteriques* (1894), and *The Major Symptoms of Hysteria* (1907), Janet postulated that human beings are either in control of themselves if they are psychologically strong or operate under the control of the subconscious if they are psychologically weak.

The separation of subconscious from conscious awareness through psychological weakness creates a debilitated person, exemplified by the dissociated personalities and amnesiacs Janet treated. Such a person is compelled to live in a distorted corner of reality. This nonintegrated person becomes enslaved by the impulses and fears buried in the subconscious and succumbs to its cunning power to constrict and obfuscate reality into piecemeal fragments. The subconscious absorbs the very fragments it has manufactured, and these fragments are in turn present for the next event, creating still further splintered replacements for reality. This process condemns its victims to a life of intellectual distortion and neurotic symptoms.

Optimal human functioning, according to Janet, is the rule of the conscious mind over the subconscious. It is the sublimation and integration of the subconscious into ordinary consciousness. He calls the apex of his "hierarchy of the mind" a "grand synthesis," which he counterposes against the automatic actions or motor discharges of "psychological automatism," that which is relegated to the lowest rung of his system. Later in his career, under the influence of James Mark Baldwin, Janet reworked his theories into a developmental model of the normal personality and, turning away from an exclusive focus on pathology, also applied his model to an understanding of religious phenomena.

Théodore Flournoy. Another figure in the late nineteenth century associated with the so-called French, Swiss, English, and American psychotherapeutic axis, Flournoy (1854–1920) was a professor of experimental psychology at the University of Geneva. He was a close friend of James and an important influence on C. G. Jung and Jean Piaget. His major contribution to the psychology of the subconscious was an investigation of Helene Smith, a case of multiple personality with speaking in tongues (Flournoy, 1899). His final conclusion was that, whereas an experimental psychology of the subconscious had failed to prove the spiritualists' claim for the reality of life after death, there was concrete evidence for the development of exceptional human abilities beyond what seemed normally possible (Flournoy, 1911).

Richard Maurice Bucke, F. W. H. Myers, and Roberto Assagioli. The Canadian psychiatrist Richard Maurice Bucke (1837–1902) took the issue much further by postulating an evolutionary model of consciousness similar to that of Fechner (Bucke, 1901). Humans are emerging from the domain of the primitive and instinctual into the rational and are evolving toward a more cosmic and expanded spiritual state. Possibly the most important theorist of the time in this regard was F. W. H. Myers (1843–1901), the British psychical researcher. Myers postulated a spectrum of states of consciousness ranging from the psychopathic to the transcendent, with waking consciousness appearing merely as one state among many, its primary function being the preservation of the biological vehicle that experiences those other states. Dissolutive states tended toward personality disintegration, while evolutive states showed the higher spiritual possibilities of the race in the future. Myers's work had a major influence on James, Flournoy, Jung, and others, such as the young Italian psychiatrist Roberto Assagioli (1888–1974), who associated himself with this axis and the idea of a growth-oriented dimension of personality as early as 1909.

Sigmund Freud. Freud (1856–1939), however, is generally recognized in mainstream Western history as the purveyor of a theory of different states of consciousness in psychology and psychiatry. Fallaciously, he is said to have discovered the unconscious, when in actuality he was the first to succeed in injecting a dynamic language of the unconscious into Western reductionistic science. His task was to establish the conscious, rational functions of the ego as the controlling factor in the growth of civilization. The ego is moderated by two opposing forces, the ethical boundaries of right and wrong set by the superego, and a dynamic tension created by immediate sexual gratification of primitive, instinctual needs of the id, the basic force of the unconscious.

Consciousness, for Freud, was the ego's awareness and mediation of the unconscious in relation to forces in the external world. What was preconscious was what the ego could consciously represent from the unconscious. What was unconscious had never and could never come directly to consciousness. One approached the unconscious, rather, indirectly, through the method of symbolism. Thus, whereas the goal of psychoanalysis was a return to the ability to love and to work, the heart of Freud's method was an exploration of the unconscious through free association, the interpretation of dreams, and analysis of other unconscious behavior, such as humor, slips of the tongue, and recurring symptoms where the unconscious suddenly interposes itself into the field of waking consciousness.

In *Civilization and Its Discontents* (1930) Freud was inclined to identify the mystical experience as merely one more self-deception to which humans, in their desperation and naïveté, fall prey. There Freud wrote of a friend who was opposed to his idea that religion is a crutch allowing psychologically weak people, enfeebled because of their ignorance of scientific truths, to project a father figure in the form of God onto the universe. The solace provided by this wishful thinking assuages their fears in the face of a terrifying and unintelligible world. Freud considered himself a scientist first, and therefore declared himself to one correspondent as "a God-forsaken incredulous Jew." But other interpreters, such as David Bakan (1991), have analyzed Freud's theories in light of an unconscious legacy from the Jewish mystical tradition.

C. G. Jung. As a younger colleague of Freud from 1906 to 1912, a close correspondent with Freud, and at one point heir apparent to the psychoanalytic throne, Jung (1875–1961) can be considered the twentieth-century exponent of the symbolic hypothesis. He took the method of symbolism much further than Freud, but epistemologically he is more accurately placed within the context of the late-nineteenth-century psychologies of transcendence. This places him more centrally within the psychologies of James, Flournoy, and Myers than as a mere acolyte of Freud. Jung's entire psychology is a commentary on different states of consciousness. He spoke about a dialogue between consciousness and the unconscious, individuation, wholeness, and the development of the "self" rather than the "ego" as the mature center of personality. In "The Spiritual Problem of Modern Man," chapter ten of *Modern Man in Search of a Soul* (1933), he described the modern person as the rare, exceptional human being who, completely conscious and having fully integrated the solutions of the past and faced the problems of the future, is free to break with all constraints and live wholly in the present.

For Jung, consciousness consisted of three realms. The first is the everyday, waking rational state, which includes the functions of the ego, contact with the proverbial objects of one's material identity, and the many masks a person wears in society at large that are the ways he or she wishes to be seen, as opposed to the way he or she really is. The second most accessible layer is the personal unconscious, which contains one's motivations for personal survival and the largely repressed material that violates the self-image he or she can tolerate for himself or herself. It also contains the cultural habits and heritage that condition him or her unawares. The third and fundamental layer is the collective unconscious. This is a transcendent, primordial realm that contains a person's impersonal aspirations, cunning adversaries, and ultimate possibilities. Access to it is mediated by the archetypes, inborn biologically conditioned modes of perceiving and thinking that have to be penetrated and transcended if one is to prevail in confrontation with the unconscious and achieve psychic growth and health, a process Jung called individuation.

The collective unconscious helped Jung account for the plethora of parapsychological phenomena—such as psychokinesis, clairvoyance, and synchronicity—that captivated him. If a person's psychic life is somehow linked to that of all humanity, then reports of apparently inexplicable events such as extrasensory perception are not quite so unintelligible.

EXISTENTIAL-HUMANISTIC AND TRANSPERSONAL PSYCHOLOGIES. In the 1960s, transpersonal psychology emerged from its existential-humanistic and phenomenological roots as a movement devoted in part to the study of meditation and alternative states of consciousness. Though by no means representative of the mainstream of psychological research in the West, transpersonal psychologists are intrigued by the possibility that human beings possess transcendent powers of consciousness. Some speculate about the brain's untapped potential and hold a view of the universe as continuous with oneself, being both conscious and purposive. They are convinced that one can be motivated by broader and less-selfish impulses than physiological needs and egoistic emotions. For these psychologists, the most important motivations spring from a selflessness that revolves around the pondering of ultimate questions—questions about the meaning, purpose, and value of human life. Often influenced by the influx of Eastern psychologies and philosophies into the West, transpersonal psychology seeks to reverse what it considers the disproportionate attention given to psychological afflictions at the expense of great potentialities as human beings. This movement may be understood as an attempt to reconnect the science of psychology with the perennial metaphysical teachings of the spiritual traditions.

ABRAHAM MASLOW. Maslow (1908–1970) was particularly interested in fully developed or "self-actualized" people who frequently undergo "changes in consciousness" that he called "peak experiences." Believing people have an inherent inner core that strives for growth (cf. Carl Rogers, Rollo May), Maslow developed a hierarchy of human motivations that seeks to encompass the entire spectrum of personality. Thus there are not only self-actualizing personalities but a self-actualizing dimension to all personalities.

Maslow designated the lowest and most basic needs as physiological and safety needs; these are fundamentally personal, selfish, and self-serving. The next stages include aesthetic and cognitive impulses. At the top of Maslow's hierarchy are "beta" or "being" needs. These operate in the self-actualized person who surpasses all personal motivations and strives for the good of humanity by acting from feelings of "wholeness," "justice," "self-sufficiency," and "aliveness," strivings capable of affecting all aspects of life. These fortunate people have thoroughly developed the inner self with which all people are born but which is generally squelched, obfuscated, or distorted by societal and parental conditioning. Such conditioning can be overcome, however.

Peak experiences are most often the prerogative of Maslow's self-actualized persons. These experiences are held to be transformations of consciousness and perception wherein life is imbued with a sense of transcendent meaning. In *Toward a Psychology of Being* (1968), Maslow reported that they are states where vision is whole rather than partial, where perception is based upon reality rather than subjective projection, and where life's meaning and goodness are experienced directly and with certainty. Time appears to be suspended, and the experiencer escapes the stress of "becoming." He or she seeks a tension-free life in the calm of "effortless being." Through such self-actualizing development and peak experiences, one is then able to live a completely engaged life.

Fueled by the writings of such thinkers as Aldous Huxley, who was involved with the Vedanta Society in Southern California from the 1940s; Alan Watts, an Episcopal priest and disciple of D. T. Suzuki who became a leading interpreter of Zen; and even the existential Christian theology of Paul Tillich (a major influence on both Rollo May and Carl Rogers); Asian concepts of consciousness, particularly the epistemological idea of states higher than the normal everyday waking condition, entered the scientific lexicon through humanistic and transpersonal psychology. Maslow talked about a Daoistic attitude of noninterference and comfortability with paradox in the self-actualizing personality. Gardener Murphy and Lois B. Murphy published *Asian Psychology* (1968). Elmer Green and Alyce Green at the Menninger Foundation began studying yogic adepts, such as Swami Rama. Indeed, a new dialogue seemed to be emerging at the interface between psychology and comparative religions.

The Hindu Vedantic tradition, for example, speaks of four states of consciousness. The first (*jāgrat*) is the habitual waking consciousness, analogous to that experienced by Plato's shackled prisoner. The second (*svapna*) occurs when one experiences reality as the product of one's subjective projections rather than as random, inexplicable, and either indifferent or cruel in its circumstances. *Svapna* conforms to the experience of the unchained prisoner seeking escape. The third state (*susupti*) is one of "divine wisdom"—clearly the purview of the liberated person. The fourth (*turīya*) is, fittingly, ineffable.

According to the philosophy of Sāṃkhya Yoga, the mind can be found in any one of five habitual states of consciousness: *Ksipta*, or restless; *Mudha*, meaning stupefied; *viksipta*, or distracted; *ekagra*, meaning one-pointed; and *niruddha*, referring to the concentration of *samādhi*. Yoga, relative to attaining the concentration of *samādhi*, pertains only to the last two. One-pointed concentration weakens the afflictions, loosens the bonds of *karma,* and paves the way toward *samādhi* or complete absorption. In the various stages of *samādhi* the mind produces a continuously flowing stream of insights into all objects (*samprajnatasamadhi*), whereas the highest state of consciousness is described as a complete separation of lifeless inert matter (*prakṛti*) from pure consciousness (*puruṣa*); that is, a separation of the illuminating quality (*sattva*) of consciousness from the stream of all objects themselves, a condition called *asamprajnatasamadhi.* This last is *chittavrittiniruddha* or a complete cessation of the fluctuations of all mental activity.

According to the philosophy of Buddhism, which originally borrowed heavily from the Yoga tradition, the perfection of meditative concentration is described. According to the Tibetan teachings of the *Jewel Ornament of Liberation* (Sgam-Po-Pa, 1959), the first stage is overcoming restlessness. The second stage is the promotion of insight coupled with tranquility. The third leads to compassion for all sentient beings. The fourth is to abide in the oneness of thought without swerving between the opposites of being and nonbeing. The fifth is transcendence, which means the arising of discriminative awareness born from wisdom and transmutation. The sixth is that same state but now purified through emptiness and compassion. The seventh is the attainment of unsurpassable enlightenment.

The idea of levels of consciousness is also evident in the work of the Ṣūfī teacher Javad Nurbakhsh Shaykh of the Niʿmatullahīyah order, who delineates four stages of development:

1. self becoming emptied,
2. self becoming illuminated,
3. self becoming adorned,
4. self having passed away (*fanā*).

Through a spiritual training revolving around an exceptional master-pupil relationship, an initiate on the path (*ṭarīqah*) may penetrate the sufferings, confusions, and convolutions inherent in egoism—represented by life in the Platonic cave—and pass beyond them to bliss, truth, and communion with God.

Such interest soon directed attention back to the Western mystical tradition. Jakob Boehme, Meister Eckhart, Hildegard of Bingen, Saint Ignatius, Saint Teresa, Maimonides, and numerous others have all come in for study of their deep contemplative spirituality and its meaning for understanding of profound and transforming states of consciousness. Fueled by the possibility of a dynamic, transcendent psychology of interior experience, humanistic and transpersonal psychologists then delved more deeply into not only their own cultures but the mystical traditions of all world cultures.

The new emphasis on alternate states of consciousness was also influenced through dramatic developments in physiological monitoring. The field of biofeedback, for instance, became one of the primary technologies through which the scientific study of techniques such as Yoga and meditation was conducted. From the 1970s onward, an exponential progression of scientific studies on meditation then appeared in the scientific literature.

The earliest work was conducted at Harvard Medical School by the cardiologist Herbert Benson, who first identified the relaxation response, and at Maharishi International School of Management in Iowa by scientific researchers who were studying the effects of transcendental meditation (TM). Based primarily on data from the study of the electroencephalogram and other physiological differences noted between sleep and meditation, these investigators postulated the existence of a fourth state of consciousness beyond waking, sleeping, and sleep with dreams.

The meditative state, they maintained, was a wakeful hypometabolic state of parasympathetic dominance; that is, a relaxed, wakeful state of sustained attention. Benson maintained that periodic entry into this state could have measurable effects on improving health, especially from stress-related illnesses. Based on almost thirty years of studying advanced meditation practitioners, the TM researchers have gone a step further and claimed that additional experimental evidence they have collected on this fourth state suggests that it is a higher state of consciousness, such as those described in the inner sciences of Asian cultures.

Psychedelic drugs also contributed significantly to the modern revolution in the scientific study of consciousness. Psychedelics were first introduced into the general population in the United States in the late 1950s. This occurred first through physicians and scientists in the military working with various U.S. government intelligence agencies, who disseminated psychoactive substances, such as lysergic acid diethylamide (LSD), among prisoners, soldiers, and test groups of civilians before dispersing such substances throughout the medical establishment. Within a short time, in an unprecedented occurrence within the research community, scientists began to experiment personally with these agents. Psychiatrists, psychologists and nonprofessionals in others countries then followed suit as word spread about the drug and its effects on consciousness throughout popular culture.

Soon a scientific literature developed that was radically split in the interpretation of the empirical evidence defining the physiochemistry and effects of various substances such as the cannabinols, LSD, mescaline, and fungi such as psilocybin. Scientists and physicians associated jointly with the military and medical establishments universally declared that psychedelics were psychotomimetics, suitable only for mind control and the artificial induction of insanity in warfare. An entirely different group of scientists, however, began experimenting with these drugs on themselves and their patients in controlled clinical settings and came to the conclusion that particularly psychedelic compounds were invaluable aids in the treatment of other chemical addictions, such as alcoholism and morphinism, that psychedelics immeasurably deepened the experience of psychotherapy and contributed significantly to accelerating the process of self-knowledge, and moreover that such substances held the promise of opening science up to an entirely new understanding of altered states of consciousness.

Two of the foremost models of consciousness in this vein have been proposed by Charles Tart, now a professor of psychology, emeritus, at the University of California at Davis, and Stanislav Grof, former psychiatrist at the Maryland Psychiatric Institute. Tart, a parapsychologist, psychedelic researcher, and personality theorist, in a series of pioneering works in the 1960s and 1970s proposed that the framework of traditional science was sufficient only for an understanding of the rational waking state. Newer forms of science were required that were internally consistent with and exclusive to the state of consciousness in which they were applied. Tart's call for the development of state-specific sciences was accompanied by the assertion that scientists needed to have experienced the particular conditions they were studying as a necessary prerequisite for objectivity. Grof undertook a variety of different investigations of altered states of consciousness, including the recovery of birth memories, the study of transformative religious visions, and shamanic states of healing, especially in non-Western cultures.

CONTEMPORARY NEUROSCIENCE, NEUROPHILOSOPHY, AND NEUROTHEOLOGY. *Neurotheology* refers specifically to modern attempts to study religious experience using the techniques and theories of the neurosciences, which include neuroimaging of meditative and contemplative states of consciousness. Neurotheology in this sense is an extension of the more recent term *neurophilosophy*, in which cognitive scientists, such as Daniel Dennett, Patricia Churchland, Paul Churchland, and Robert Searl, have dominated the discussion about the philosophical implications of the biology of consciousness. Here again, however, is the paradox that the neuroscience revolution is generating humanistic implications that demand a return to the kind of philosophical discussions long banned from the discourse of reductionistic science. The problem is that the new breed of scientific philosophers are all trained in cognitive behaviorism and Aristotelian and Kantian thought, the very epistemologies that the scientific revolution in consciousness is fast transcending, and if these so-called neurophilosophers know any philosophy at all, it is the analytic philosophers from Alfred North Whitehead and Bertrand Russell through Ludwig Wittgenstein to Rudolf Carnap, Herbert Figel, and Willard van Orman Quine, whose overemphasis on the logical ordering of sense data alone may become the approach in science most vulnerable to extinction.

Meanwhile a surge of interest in neurotheology has come from the work of Andrew Newberg and the late Eugene D'Aquili. Studying Buddhist meditators and Franciscan nuns, D'Aquili and Newberg employed SPECT scans (single photon emission computed tomography, as opposed to positron emission tomography [PET] scans or functional magnetic resonance imaging [fMRI]) to get a picture of the brain's activity during peak meditative states of oneness or union. From a neurophysiological perspective, they have proposed a heightening of the attentional areas in the frontal cortex, which they associate with activities of the will, and a diffuse, quiescent blurring of the boundaries between self and not-self mediated by the posterior superior parietal lobe. Moreover they have proposed that the parietal lobe is a major controlling factor in the experience of a continuum ranging from pleasure of an aesthetic moment, including everyday insights, to the heightened, transforming experience of religious ecstasy. They have also proposed an evolutionary role for such experiences relating the peak experience to ritual and mythmaking that have become wired-in to the nervous system.

THE CORRELATION BETWEEN BRAIN STATES AND MENTAL STATES. As noted, the idea that human beings have access to higher realms of consciousness is prevalent in all esoteric contemplative traditions. To speak in purely Western terms, in Plato's remarkable allegory the ordinary human condition is portrayed as existence in a cave, where shackled prisoners with limited vision—able to look only at the wall in front of them—mistake shadows and echoes for reality. Liberation, the ascent into the real world, is arduous and requires loosening the chains, turning around, overcoming the initial confusion, and persisting in a quest that brings knowledge and freedom. The prisoner must become realigned so that he or she can control his or her dark fears and shadowy thoughts and so escape from the cave. Once he or she is out of the cave, complete vision is possible through the liberation of the higher mind (nous). Higher consciousness evolves in its encounter with reality, thereby apprehending the laws of the universal order—the True, the Beautiful, and the Good.

Modern science has progressively attempted to penetrate into this domain, but to what end? The trend has been to reduce all phenomena to scientific terms, still elevating the objectivist stance and denigrating the experiential. But now engaged in the scientific study of consciousness and the organ that created science in the first place, scientists are confronted with the phenomenology of their own enterprise. One result is that science itself may in the end become transformed.

The quintessential example is the physiological monitoring of advanced meditators. Tibetan monks skilled in the techniques of *G tumo* Yoga are able to raise their body temperature in frigid conditions and sleep on the snow. They also engage in a meditation practice where they compete to see how many wet sheets they can dry on their backs outside in the cold. Advanced physiological monitoring confirms this phenomenon and further shows that their meditations are quite specific in that the internal core body temperatures remain the same but they raise their skin temperatures sometimes as much as 18 degrees centigrade, which accounts for the warming effect. When queried individually, each monk recounts entering a meditative state according to his own idiosyncratic practices, but all achieve the state of *G tumo* by employing the same advanced visualizations. These are described in detail in a classic Tibetan text, Tsong kha pa's *Six Yogas of Naropa* (Zhang, 1963).

How is it then that the monks, without a knowledge of Western science, achieve such drastic alterations of normally unconscious physiological processes? The answer is that the physiological measures demonstrate a correlation of brain states that can be quantified with states of mind described metaphorically. In other words which state is accessed through a particular spiritual practice in a religious tradition is likely dependent on the particular advanced teachings of that specific tradition as far as the voluntary control of internal states is concerned (Taylor, 2003).

The implications for the neurosciences seem clear. Scientists have always presumed in biochemistry that there cannot be a thought without some chemical reaction somewhere. This example offers similar confirmation that thoughts not only are driven by body chemistry, but that they can alter it as well, in ways not normally deemed possible by normative science. The monks obviously did not enter into a lifetime of training just to be able to dry wet sheets on their backs. Their goal was the teachings and their effects on transforming consciousness. One's epistemology therefore, the core of one's belief system, must be tied into the outcome where the problem of consciousness is concerned, a thought altogether new for the way science is normally conducted.

CONCLUSION. Virtually unheard of in the middle of the twentieth century, the expression "states of consciousness" has entered the common vocabulary. How this idea will present itself in the years to come, how a subject so intimately wedded to metaphysical and religious concerns will fare in modern culture, and how religion, philosophy, and psychology may meet in their concern over this subject may prove decisively important to all who seek answers to the larger questions of human life, who one is and why one is here. At the least the struggle to understand what happens to consciousness when it becomes more conscious of itself will contribute to the ongoing dialogue between science and religion.

SEE ALSO Dreams; Ecstasy; Enthusiasm; Frenzy; Inspiration; Sleep; Visions.

BIBLIOGRAPHY

Aranya, Hariharananda. *Yoga Philosophy of Patañjali.* Albany, N.Y., 1983.

Bakan, David. *Maimonides on Prophecy: A Commentary on Selected Chapters of the Guide of the Perplexed.* Northvale, N.J., 1991.

Balzer, Marjorie Mandelstam, ed. *Shamanic Worlds: Rituals and Lore of Siberia and Central Asia.* Armonk, N.Y., 1997.

Bucke, Richard Maurice, ed. *Cosmic Consciousness: A Study in the Evolution of the Human Mind.* Philadelphia, 1901.

Budge, E. A. Wallis. *Osiris and the Egyptian Resurrection.* Illustrated after drawings from Egyptian papyri and monuments. 2 vols. London and New York, 1911.

Budge, E. A. Wallis, ed. *The Book of the Dead.* New introduction by David Lorimer. London, 1989.

Bynum, Edward Bruce. *The African Unconscious: Roots of Ancient Mysticism and Modern Psychology.* New York, 1999.

Combs, A., and S. Krippner. "Process, Structure, and Form: An Evolutionary Transpersonal Psychology of Consciousness." *International Journal of Transpersonal Studies* 22 (2003): 47–60.

Darnton, Robert. *Mesmerism and the End of the Enlightenment in France.* Cambridge, Mass., 1968.

Desoille, R. "The Directed Daydream." *Bulletin du la Societe de Researches Psychotherapeutique de Langue Francoise* 3, no. 2 (May 1965): 27–42.

Dobkin de Rios, Marlene. "From Tribal Shaman to Urban Spiritualist in the Peurvian Amazon." Paper presented at the 1983 Annual Meeting of the American Psychological Association (August 15, 1983, Los Angeles, California) cosponsored by Division 36 and the Transpersonal Psychology Interest Group as part of the symposium "The Dialogue between Psychology and World Religions."

Du Bois, W. E. B. *The Philadelphia Negro: A Social Study* (1899). With a new introduction by Elijah Anderson together with a special report on domestic service by Isabel Eaton. Philadelphia, 1996.

Du Bois, W. E. B. *The Souls of Black Folk* (1904). With an introduction by Donald B. Gibson and with notes by Monica M. Elbert. New York, 1996.

Eliade, Mircea. *Shamanism: Archaic Techniques of Ecstasy.* Translated from the French by Willard R. Trask. London, 1964.

Ellenberger, Henri F. *The Discovery of the Unconscious: The History and Evolution of Dynamic Psychiatry.* New York, 1970.

Epstein, Ronald, trans. "The Transformation of Consciousness into Wisdom: The Path of the Bodhisattva according to the *Chen Wei-Shr Lun.*" *Vajra Bodhi Sea* 15, no. 176 (1985): 22–23; no. 177 (1985): 15–17; no. 178 (1985): 14–15.

Flournoy, Théodore. *Spiritism and Psychology.* Translated, abridged, and with an introduction by Hereward Carrington. New York and London, 1911.

Flournoy, Théodore. *From India to the Planet Mars: A Case of Multiple Personality with Imaginary Languages.* Edited and introduced by Sonu Shamdasani; foreword by C. G. Jung; commentary by Mireille Cifali. Princeton, N.J., 1994.

Freud, Sigmund. "The Unconscious." In *Collected Papers of Sigmund Freud,* edited by E. Jones, vol. 4, pp. 98–136. New York, 1915.

Freud, Sigmund. *Civilization and Its Discontents.* Authorized translation by Joan Riviere. New York, 1930.

Govinda, Anagarika. "The Functions of Consciousness and the Process of Perception." In *The Psychological Attitude of Early Buddhist Philosophy and Its Systematic Representation according to the Abhidhamma Tradition,* pp. 129–412. London, 1969.

Gray, John, comp. *Àshe, Traditional Religion and Healing in Sub-Saharan Africa and the Diaspora: A Classified International Bibliography.* Foreword by Robert Farris Thompson. New York, 1989.

Harding, M. Esther. *Woman's Mysteries, Ancient and Modern: A Psychological Interpretation of the Feminine Principle as Portrayed in Myth, Story, and Dreams.* 1935; reprint, New York, 1972.

Heinze, Ruth-Inge. *Shamans of the Twentieth Century.* New York, 1991.

Heinze, Ruth-Inge. *Trance and Healing in Southeast Asia Today.* 2d rev. and expanded ed. Bangkok and Berkeley, Calif., 1997.

James, William. *The Principles of Psychology.* 2 vols. New York, 1890.

James, William. *The Varieties of Religious Experience: A Study in Human Nature.* 1902; centenary ed. with new introductions by Eugene Taylor and Jeremy Carrette. New York and London, 2002.

Johansson, Rune E. A. "Nibanna and Consciousness." In *The Psychology of Nirvana.* London, 1969.

Jung, C. G. *Modern Man in Search of a Soul.* New York, 1933.

Jung, C. G. "The Concept of the Collective Unconscious" (1936). In *Collected Works of C. G. Jung: Archetypes and the Collective Unconscious,* vol. 9, pt. 1, pp. 42–53. London, 1959.

Katz, Richard. *Boiling Energy: Community Healing among the Kalahari Kung.* Cambridge, Mass., 1982.

Katz, Richard. *The Straight Path: A Story of Healing and Transformation in Fiji.* Reading, Mass., 1993.

Katz, Richard, Megan Biesele, and Verna St. Denis. *Healing Makes Our Hearts Happy: Spirituality and Cultural Transformation among the Kalahari Ju/'hoansi.* Rochester, Vt., 1997.

Krippner, S. "Psi Research and the Brain's 'Reserve Capacities.'" In *Mind in Time: The Dynamics of Thought, Reality, and Consciousness,* edited by Allan Combs, Mark Germine, and Ben Goertzel, pp. 313–329. Cresskill, N.J., 2004.

Legge, James. *The Chinese Classics.* Translated with exegesis, prolegomena, and copious notes. Hong Kong, 1960.

Magon, Jane. "The Shaman as Tree." Paper presented at the 1998 Annual Meeting of the American Academy of Religion, Orlando, Fla., sponsored by the Mysticism Study Group.

Maslow, Abraham H. *Toward a Psychology of Being.* 2d ed. New York, 1968.

May, Rollo. "Tillich, Paul, 1886–1965." *Pastoral Psychology* 19 (1968): 7–10.

Mesmer, Franz Anton. *Mesmerism: A Translation of the Original Scientific and Medical Writings of F. A. Mesmer.* Translated and compiled by George Bloch. Los Altos, Calif., 1980.

Needleman, Jacob. *Consciousness and Tradition.* New York, 1982.

Nurbakhsh, Javad. *Sufism.* Tehran, 1977.

Schimmel, Annemarie. *Mystical Dimensions of Islam.* Chapel Hill, N.C., 1975.

Sgam-Po-Pa. *The Jewel Ornament of Liberation.* Translated by Herbert V. Guenther. London, 1959.

Silberer, H. "Report on a Method of Eliciting and Observing Certain Symbolic Hallucination-Phenomena." In *Organization and Pathology of Thought,* edited by David Rapaport, pp. 195–207. New York, 1951.

Sri Krishna Prem. *The Yoga of the Bhagavat Gita.* New York, 1949.

Tart, Charles T. "States of Consciousness and State-Specific Sciences." *Science* 176 (1972): 1203–1210.

Taylor, Eugene. "Asian Interpretations: Transcending the Stream of Consciousness." In *The Stream of Consciousness: Psychological Investigations into the Flow of Human Experience,* edited by Kenneth S. Pope and Jerome L. Singer, pp. 31–54. New York, 1978.

Taylor, Eugene. *William James on Exceptional Mental States.* New York, 1983.

Taylor, Eugene. "A Perfect Correlation between Mind and Brain: The Influence of James's *Varieties* in the History of Mind/Body Medicine." *Journal of Speculative Philosophy* 17, no. 1 (2003): 40–52, Special James centennial issue.

Van Dusen, W. "Wu wei, No Mind, and the Fertile Void in Psychotherapy." *Psychologia* 1 (1958): 253–256.

Velmans, M. "A Reflexive Science of Consciousness." In *Experimental and Theoretical Studies of Consciousness,* pp. 81–99. Ciba Foundation Symposium 174. Chichester, U.K., 1993.

Walters, Orville. "Psychodynamics in Tillich's Theology." *Journal of Religion and Health* 12 (1973): 342–353.

Zhang, Zhenji. *Teachings of Tibetan Yoga.* Translated by Garma C. C. Chang. New York, 1963.

EUGENE TAYLOR (2005)

CONSECRATION. As a cross-cultural concept, consecration refers to the practice of investing particular objects with extraordinary religious significance. The significance of any single instance of consecration depends in good part on the type of object consecrated. Places and buildings are made into habitations for spiritual beings; higher powers enliven icons and food; kings and hierarchs are recognized as maintainers of a higher order on earth. Yet despite the diversity of both consecrated objects and the traditions from which their religious meaning derives, most instances of consecration reveal some basic structural resemblances. First, an act of consecration is at root a creative act. It is a deliberate attempt to alter the environment, to establish in the visible world some definite, concrete means for fruitful interaction with the divine. Second, a consecrated object, now represented as a link to higher reality, is often itself understood to be transformed—purified or empowered, transmuted into divine substance or given over to the divine. And third, as something extraordinary in its environment, a consecrated object is often ritually marked off, delimited from the mundane, everyday

MAKING PLACES HOLY. The power of limits themselves to consecrate holy places is evident in the practical significance of the Theravāda Buddhist concept of *sīmā* ("boundary"). In Theravāda Buddhism monks and laity are represented as two orders in society, each with its own role in the economy of salvation. The monks, through observing their ascetic code, help maintain the cosmic order; the laity should serve the monks. These two roles are played out in different physical spaces, with a boundary between them. Thus, in the villages of modern Thailand, the monastic compound is set clearly apart. Monks may leave the compound for specific monastic duties but not to gossip in the village; villagers should enter the compound to serve the monks. In addition to the definite but sometimes unmarked boundary around the extended monastic compound, the observance hall, where monks are ordained and make group confession, has a marked boundary of its own. This boundary is denoted by stones—called *sīmā* stones—that are installed according to prescribed rites; it is normally respected by laypersons, who must remove their shoes to enter the observance hall. Here, then, ritual consecration expresses a crucial socioreligious division visible in this world.

When interaction with sacred reality is seen to demand traffic between worlds, the consecration of a physical structure on earth may instill in it the presence of an otherworldly being. Sometimes this link between worlds is forged with the help of material traces left by a holy person who has passed beyond the earthly realm. Relics of the Buddha are ideally embedded in the great stupas of ancient India and the pagodas still found in Southeast Asia. In reverencing these structures, built as memorials to the Buddha, devotees revere the Buddha's person. In the consecration of Roman Catholic churches, usually named after saints, installation of the relics of the patron saint plays a part in a larger ceremony through which the building is literally marked out for, and consigned to, the crucified Lord.

Each of the three major parts of the ceremony presents a phase in the building's transformation. The bishop begins by marking off and purifying the church externally, circumambulating it three times and sprinkling its walls with water. He then has the door unlocked and makes the sign of the cross with his staff on the threshold; inside, a cross of ashes is drawn joining the four corners of the church. Through the cross on the door and on the floor during this first phase of the ceremony, Christ the crucified is understood to take possession of the church. The second phase of the ceremony makes the church a suitable dwelling place for the Lord through both negative and positive means: first evil is banished through the sprinkling of specially prepared holy water, and then a solemn prayer for grace and sanctification is offered. The third phase, in which relics are enclosed in the altar, materially links the spiritual focus of the church to the power of a divine intercessor.

PUTTING LIFE INTO THE IMAGE OF A DEITY. In Hindu temples, the central physical repositories of spiritual power are not relics but images. Devotees often see the image as a manifestation of the deity itself. In their ritual worship, devotees interact with the deity as a person with whom they attempt to come into intimate terms. In large temples, long-hallowed images are enthroned and revered as sovereigns. At the temple to Śrīnāthjī in Nāthdwāra, Rajasthan, for example, people are allowed to see the image only at the times of day an important personage would be pleased to grant audience. Śrīnāthjī wears clothes suited to the time of day and season and is treated to lavish banquets. Deities in household shrines, on the other hand, are treated more like guests who may only be visiting for a particular festive occasion. In order to perceive the divinity in these household images, the performance of a consecratory rite may be particularly crucial. Grand images at major temples are sometimes understood to have arisen spontaneously: Śrīnāthjī, they say, emerged from Mount Govardhan, sacred to Kṛṣṇa. But a clay image from the bazaar brought into the house for a temporary period must be visibly transformed in order to be seen to embody the deity's person.

The household consecration ceremony performed for Gaṇeśa, the elephant-headed deity, by Hindus of Maharashtra reveals how human beings can put life into divine images. When the image is brought home it is put on an altar, around which designs of powdered chalk have been drawn and ceremonial implements laid out. Special space has thus been demarcated for the deity to be embodied, but the image itself remains lifeless clay. In the ritual's central act (*prāṇapratiṣṭhā*) the worshiper installs vital breath into the image. But to do this the worshiper himself must first take on the aspects of the divine through preliminary consecrations. To align his microcosmic world with the macrocosm, the worshiper makes brief utterances while touching parts of his body and his ritual implements, identifying himself as the primal cosmic being and the implements as cosmic elements. The breath is installed in the deity when, to the accompaniment of a priest's recitation of particular utterances, the worshiper touches the image with a kind of grass understood to be a potent conduit. At the climax of this rite, the worshiper understands both himself and the deity to have a common identity in the cosmic life force. This identity is then invoked in further ritual worship that includes feeding the deity and sprinkling it with water, both important aspects of consecratory ritual in many Indian traditions.

The installation of the image of Gaṇeśa in Maharashtrian homes takes place on the day of his annual festival, which falls in August or September. The consecration of the day itself is thus marked by the visit of Gaṇeśa, which may be extended for some time longer. As long as the image of the deity continues to remain in the house it is offered daily ceremonial hospitality, with flowers, songs, and incense. Both the image and the time remain sanctified. But when Gaṇeśa's visit is over, usually within ten days, the worshiper symbolically closes the image's eyes by brushing them with the same kind of grass he used to enliven it. The breath is then said to leave the clay image, which is immersed in a nearby source of water and dissolves. In separating from each other, both breath and clay return to a state that is both formless and timeless; but through their interpenetration in the enlivened image, the ritual transformation of a material form has helped consecrate a particular time.

One of the most important media through which Hindus interact with a deity like Gaṇeśa is consecrated food. Devotees offer food to the god in hospitality and later eat what are then seen as the deity's leavings. Through eating the deity's leavings, the devotee partakes of his substance and his power. The idea that something of the deity's person inheres in these leavings derives from pervasive Hindu cultural presuppositions. For traditional Hindus see the world as a hierarchy of interpenetrating substances, and food, ingested in the body, is a potent medium for transmitting psychic substance between individuals. Thus, food prepared by people of low spiritual status is degrading to those above, food offered by brahmans and gurus can offer spiritual benefits, and food left over from the plate of the deity is likely to be the most powerful of all. Through contact with a higher being, food is consecrated naturally in Hindu eyes, sometimes without any special ritual at all. In Hindu tradition, communion with the deity through consecrated food takes place without mystery.

Giving Persons Divine Authority. Communion via the sharing of consecrated food in Roman Catholic tradition is deliberately identified as a mystery and requires a consecrator legitimately ordained in the church to be effective. Although the precise meaning of transubstantiation remains an issue of theological speculation, the rite effecting this transformation of bread and wine into the physical substance of Christ—a daily, worldwide occurrence—is fairly simple. The priest, reenacting the role of Jesus at the last supper, utters over the offerings a formula taken from the Gospels: "Take, eat; for this is my body." During the act of consecration, the priest is understood to represent Jesus, and for his act to be valid, he must be unambiguously acknowledged by hierarchs recognized as true successors to the apostles. Thus the consecrator himself needs to be consecrated.

While the rite conferring priesthood for a long time highlighted the priest's sacramental authority, it has always expressed his spiritual inheritance through apostolic succession. As an essential element of the ordination rite, the tradition of instruments—which distinctly expresses sacramental power—is known only from the twelfth century. In this tradition ordinands touch a chalice filled with wine and a paten containing bread (the "instruments") while the bishop utters a formula that bestows on the applicants the power to celebrate Mass. But the tradition of instruments was always accompanied by that of the laying on of hands, which dates from early Christian times, and is accompanied with prayer by a spiritual elder for the personal religious welfare of the ordinand. Now understood to be the only essential rite of ordination for bishops and deacons as well as for priests, the laying on of hands expresses the continuity of saving grace, from senior to junior, through the generations. From the consecration of a bishop as successor to the apostles of Jesus to the transformation of ordinary foodstuffs into the body of Christ, the rituals of consecration in Roman Catholic tradition make the power of a divine personage of the past present in today's world.

In premodern societies, the religious authority of the priest often exists in tension with that of a monarch, who may claim a divine status of his own. The Christian West has known a series of contests and accommodations between papal and royal power, which led in the early Middle Ages to the celebration of royal consecration as a sacrament of the church. God was understood to empower the king through the bishop, and the king, transformed, was given status in the clergy. In ancient India, on the other hand, though clergy performed the consecration of the king, his religious status was of a different order from theirs. From the beginning, rituals of royal consecration in India have closely resembled rituals performed for divinities. In fact the essential part of the ritual, the anointing—*abhiṣeka* in Sanskrit, literally "sprinkling"—seems to have been preeminently a royal ceremony that was later applied to the consecration of divine images. But more than the consecration of images, royal consecrations were also likely to have a visible social and political import. However deified he might sometimes appear, the king was also very much a man subject to the flux of worldly affairs, and his consecration was usually marked by prayers for his popularity, the prosperity of himself and his people, and the extent and stability of his dominion. To maintain all these potentially fleeting goods, the consecration of early Indian kings was ideally repeated annually, a custom that finds parallels in the royal New Year festivals of ancient Mesopotamia and the Chinese imperial sacrifice performed on the winter solstice. The brilliance of the ancient king's reign was usually in practical fact as well as religious belief closely linked to the welfare of his people, and both could use regular, visible signs of renewal.

Personal Consecrations and Renewal. The renewal and repetition of consecration becomes increasingly important in tradition to the extent that consecration is understood to be a human act and a personal one. In Indo-Tibetan Tantra, the consecration of a deity—referred to as *abhiṣeka,* like the royal anointing—expressly ties outer ritual to inward contemplation and is performed as a regular spiritual exercise. In some instances, moreover, the outer ritual may be dispensed with and only the inward consecration remain. As in Roman Catholic practice, the power to perform consecrations in most Buddhist traditions requires a legitimate source: initiations into both the powers of deities and the sanctity of monkhood need to come through a recognized lineage. But the established channels of sacramental authority in Catholicism and Buddhism are oriented in different directions. In the Roman rite, the power to consecrate is bestowed largely for the good of others, not for the personal benefit of the recipient, who as consecrator becomes a public instrument for the distribution of grace in the world. Once given, the power is supposed to be permanent; a force of its own working through the individual consecrator, it is not closely dependent on his spiritual state. In Buddhism, on the other hand, sacraments are more inwardly oriented: in Buddhist Tantra people perform regular consecrations largely for their own spiritual benefit; in Theravāda, the value of the monk for the community lies in his inner purity, and if this cannot be maintained it is thought best for all that he leave the order.

For people in ritual and devotional traditions everywhere, consecration in its most general sense can become a way of life. In the orthodoxies of Hinduism and Judaism all vital acts are ideally carried out according to divinely ordained precepts and are usually attended by ritual or prayers. In this way, rising, eating, sex, and even elimination become consecrated, that is, made part of the sacred world. For ardent devotees, consecration can mean surrender, a giving up of one's person and one's goods to the Lord. Through dedication, the Christian religious attempt to consecrate themselves fully to the service of God; Hindus following the path of the *Bhagavadgītā* give up the fruits of their works to Kṛṣṇa. Entailing an infinite succession of individual acts, consecration as a way of life demands perpetual vigilance, an acting out of the tension between divine absolutes and temporary realities that lies at the heart of consecration's religious meaning.

CONCLUSION. Deriving from Latin roots that connote an act of bringing particular things "together with" (*com*) the "sacred" (*sacrum*), the very word *consecration* implies a dichotomy between what is sacred and what is profane. Marking this dichotomy, moreover, is an important aspect of consecratory acts in many religious traditions. But in cross-cultural perspective the concept of consecration also suggests other continuities in the religious thought and practice of diverse peoples. When accompanying the enshrinement of relics of the dead or the initiation of living persons into hallowed spiritual lineages, an act of consecration in the present maintains the efficacy of specific divine sources revealed in the past. The efficacy of the act may also demand a consecration of the consecrators themselves, whose ritual performance presents some of their most exalted religious potentials: while celebrating Mass, the priest already ordained in the church is seen to be most fully representative of Jesus; to enliven an image, the Hindu worshiper is identified with the primordial cosmic person. Finally, the difference between temporary and permanent consecration that emerges from a global perspective highlights the continuing religious problem people face in attempting to establish the divine in the material world: consecrations taken as permanent express the absoluteness of divine presence; those seen as temporary reveal the limits of human effort and the impermanence of material embodiments.

SEE ALSO Blessing; Images; Ordination; Relics.

BIBLIOGRAPHY

Most ready material on consecration is to be found in works on specific traditions. Monastic ordinations and the concept of boundary in Theravāda Buddhism are approached through their classical sources by John Holt in *Discipline: The Canonical Buddhism of the Vinayapiṭaka* (New Delhi, 1983) and examined in contemporary Thai tradition by S. J. Tambiah: *Buddhism and the Spirit Cults in North-east Thailand* (Cambridge, U.K., 1970). The meanings of enlivened images in different Hindu traditions are presented in *Gods of Flesh, Gods of Stone* (Chambersburg, Pa., 1985) edited by Joanne Waghorne and Norman Cutler in association with Vasudha Narayan. The work of Paul Courtright on the worship of Gaṇeśa, a description of whose consecration is condensed into an article for the last-mentioned volume, is found in fuller form in his *Gaṇeśa: Lord of Obstacles, Lord of Beginnings* (New York, 1984). In *Ancient Indian Kingship from the Religious Point of View* (Leiden, 1966), J. Gonda summarizes accounts of Indian royal consecrations found in diverse Sanskrit sources. A detailed account of the rite described in the priestly srauta sutras with a valuable socio-religious interpretation is presented by J. C. Heesterman in *The Ancient Indian Royal Consecration* (The Hague, 1957). On the complex rituals of Buddhist Tantra see Yael Bentor, *Consecration of Images and Stupas in Indo-Tibetan Tantric Buddhism* (Leiden, 1996).

A full treatment of ritual consecrations and their historic development in Catholicism is given in *The Liturgy of the Roman Rite* by Ludwig Eisenhofer and Joseph Lechner, translated by A. J. and E. F. Peeler, ed. H. E. Winstone (Freiburg, Edinburgh-London, 1961). The development and meaning of the Catholic priest's sacramental authority is concisely described by Joseph Lécuyer, C.S.SP. in *What Is a Priest?*, translated by P. J. Hepburne-Scott (New York, 1959). On the relationship between the divine authority of kings and hierarchs in Western Europe, the classical account remains Gerd Tellenbach's *Church, State and Christian Society at the Time of the Investiture Contest*, translated by R. F. Bennett (New York, 1959).

DANIEL GOLD (1987 AND 2005)

CONSERVATIVE JUDAISM evolved out of the desire of Eastern European Jewish immigrants to find their way in the United States; it was one of a myriad of syntheses of Jewish identity and modernity invented by acculturating Jews. While its intellectual and institutional origins lie in the nineteenth century, the Conservative Jewish denomination rests on the confluence of modernizing rabbis trained at the Jewish Theological Seminary in New York City, Americanizing Eastern European Jewish immigrant masses, and the national organizational infrastructure that emerged to inculcate Conservative Judaism to Jewish men, women, and children.

IDEOLOGICAL AND INSTITUTIONAL ORIGINS. Conservative Judaism considers European rabbi and scholar Zacharias Frankel (1801–1875) to be its ideological founder. In 1845, in Frankfurt am Main, at a conference of rabbis engaged in reforming Judaism, the men agreed to amend the traditional worship service to dispense with the Hebrew language in all but a handful of prayers. Although Frankel was open to adapting Judaism in response to the challenges posed by the encounter of Jews with modernity, such a drastic break with the Jewish past was an anathema. He seceded from the conference, advocating an alternative response to modernity: positive-historical Judaism. The response prioritized reason based on scholarship and a deep appreciation for conserving the traditions of the past, as opposed to the will of the laity, to guide the process of accommodating Judaism to the new realities of the nineteenth century. In 1854 Frankel became the founding president of Breslau's Jüdisch-Theologisches Seminar, a new rabbinical school whose graduates espoused positive-historical Judaism. When, in 1886, the Jewish Theological Seminary of America was established in New York City, its founders not only evoked the Breslau school in choosing a name, they also saw it as a model.

At the same time, nineteenth-century American Jews and their rabbis were engaged in reforming Judaism. Responding to their increasing distance from tradition and their desire to transmit Judaism to the next generation, virtually every synagogue by 1870 had adopted some reforms. But twentieth-century labels do not neatly fit nineteenth-century American Jewish realities. In some synagogues, led by immigrant rabbis whom historian Moshe Davis dubbed "men of the Historical School," English-language prayers and sermons, and Sunday schools that educated girls as well as boys, emerged. Other synagogues went further, ending the practice of separating men and women in worship and abolishing the head covering and ritual garb traditionally worn by Jewish men.

Events in the 1880s suggested that those advocating the most extensive reforms would soon triumph. In July 1883, as the first rabbis ever trained on American soil prepared to be ordained, prominent Jews journeyed for the historic occasion to Cincinnati's Hebrew Union College. Invited to a celebratory banquet, the traditionalists among them were appalled to find clams, shrimp, and frog's legs, all decidedly unkosher or *treyf* foods in violation of Jewish law, on the menu. The traditionalists stormed out of the *treyfah* banquet and were soon calling for a new rabbinical seminary. In January 1886, after Reform rabbis had rejected Jewish law and tradition in the Pittsburgh Platform of 1885, a coalition of traditionalist leaders and moderate reformers founded the Jewish Theological Seminary of America for those Jews who would both uphold Mosaic law and adhere to a historical Judaism resting upon the great interpretations of rabbinic literature codified in works like the Talmud.

The Early Seminary. The "early Seminary," as the school in the years between its founding in 1886 and its reorganization in 1902 has since become known, was not intended to be a denominational institution promulgating Conservative Judaism. Although at its opening exercises, Professor Alexander Kohut (1842–1894), a graduate of the Jüdisch-Theologisches Seminar, spoke of Conservative Judaism, and although its founders pledged their allegiance to historical Judaism, this rhetoric cannot camouflage the fact that Conservative Judaism, as such, did not yet exist. In fact, many of the early Seminary's first leaders, including its president Sabato Morais (1823–1897), would, if labels must be assigned, more properly be termed *Orthodox.* And well into the 1920s, when a merger of the Jewish Theological Seminary and Orthodoxy's Yeshiva College was contemplated, the boundaries between Conservative Judaism and a modernizing Orthodox Judaism remained poorly defined.

This early Seminary, which distinguished itself by its embrace of the English language and secular education, graduated seventeen rabbis and cantors between 1894 and 1902. Its first graduates included Mordecai M. Kaplan (1881–1983), who became professor of homiletics at the Seminary and who led an influential wing within the Conservative movement that eventually became a separate denomination called Reconstructionist Judaism. In 1901 these Seminary graduates founded an alumni association, which grew into the Rabbinical Assembly, the union of Conservative rabbis. But, even as they did, their alma mater, the early Seminary, which had long suffered a lack of financial support, was on the verge of collapse.

What saved the Jewish Theological Seminary from extinction was its reorganization in 1902. A group of wealthy New York Jews, most of them personally committed to Reform Judaism and all engaged with other institutions advancing the Americanization of Eastern European Jewish immigrants, were persuaded to endow the Seminary and to bring to the United States the renowned Cambridge University scholar Solomon Schechter (1847–1915) as its president.

The Schechter Years. Although Schechter led the Seminary for only thirteen years, until his death in 1915, he left so clear an imprint on the school that it became known, both in his lifetime and afterwards, as Schechter's Seminary. Envisioning the Seminary as a great Jewish academy, Schechter hired a distinguished faculty, including Louis Ginzberg (1873–1953) as professor of Talmud. He also revamped the rabbinical curriculum to make it a postgraduate school; launched a teachers course, which evolved into the Teachers Institute, to train educators to work alongside Seminary rabbis; transformed the library into one of the largest and most valuable collections of Judaica ever owned by Jews, an indispensable resource for advancing Jewish scholarship in America; and moved the Seminary to its new home in Manhattan's Morningside Heights in the heart of the academic setting bounded by Union Theological Seminary and Columbia University. Schechter's presidency thus charted the Seminary's future by setting the training of rabbis, teachers, and scholars at the heart of its mission.

Schechter had hoped that the Seminary he revisioned would unify the diverse elements of American Jewry. But as Orthodox rabbis prohibited Orthodox synagogues from hiring Seminary graduates—who, they asserted, were tainted by the critical scholarly methodologies of Ginzberg—and as Reform leaders openly expressed criticism, Schechter realized the impossibility of this dream. Moreover, his espousal of Zionism, which he considered a bulwark against assimilation, had alienated many among his own board of directors, who were either neutral towards Zionism or who even opposed it. Needing to extend his base of support, Schechter ultimately did what he had hoped to avoid. Joined by Seminary rabbis who felt isolated in their pulpits out in the field, he launched a new federation of synagogues—the third in the United States, since both Reform and Orthodoxy already had their own synagogal unions—to support the Seminary and advance its vision of Judaism.

In 1913, twenty-two congregations formed the United Synagogue of America (renamed in 1991 the United Synagogue of Conservative Judaism), which embraced Schechter's vision and welcomed any congregations that were not avowedly Reform (that is, those using Reform's *Union Prayer Book* and where men worshiped without covering their heads with skullcaps or hats). The new union would advance Jewish life in the United States, especially the observance of the Sabbath and the dietary laws of *kashrut.* It would foster Jewish education and promote Jewish religious life in the home as well as in the synagogue. Its members would pray in Hebrew, but their synagogues would maintain decorous behavior in worship (in contrast to an unmodernized, immigrant-style prayer). Their rabbis would preach in English, and they would welcome women to assist in their work.

The Emergence of the Conservative Synagogue. By 1929, less than two decades later, the United Synagogue had expanded to 229 member congregations. It had become the central address for American Jewish men and women who, as they left behind immigrant ghettos for the comfort of middle-class apartments in new urban neighborhoods, sought a new expression of Judaism for themselves and especially for their American-born children. United Synagogue leaders deliberately sought out these upwardly-mobile Jewish men and women who were equally distanced from the Yiddish-speaking Orthodoxy of their youth and the dramatic ritual and ideological transformations of Reform Judaism. Conservative rabbis promised moderate reforms—for example, a late Friday evening service with its greater reliance on English for prayer; Sunday schools, Hebrew schools, and adult education classes; and the seating of men and women side-by-side in prayer in contravention of the customary Jewish practice of separating the sexes in worship. But these reforms were balanced by retaining the traditional Hebrew Saturday morning service, albeit with an English-language sermon; mandating intensive preparation for the ceremony of bar mitzvah; and maintaining allegiance to Jewish law and expecting Conservative Jews to continue to usher in the Sabbath in their homes by lighting candles and blessing wine, to walk to synagogue on Sabbath mornings and on holidays, and to adhere to *kashrut.*

In general, concedes Jack Wertheimer, Seminary provost and historian of Conservative Judaism, services in these new synagogues were poorly attended since, in the years between World War I and World War II, most men worked on Saturday mornings. That meant that women filled the pews and assumed from the inception of the Conservative synagogue an active role in its congregational life.

Many of these new synagogues were lavish synagogue-centers—"*shuls* [synagogues] with pools," a unique Jewish-American invention. Synagogue-centers offered sanctuaries and chapels for worship, social halls for fellowship, classrooms for study and meetings, and gymnasiums and swimming pools for recreation. Although the idea of the synagogue-center had its roots in earlier nineteenth-century American Jewish settings, including Reform synagogues and the Young Men's Hebrew Associations (YMHAs), the prototype of the interwar synagogue-center was the Jewish Center, founded in 1917, by Seminary professor Kaplan. As Jewish immigrants and their children flocked to these new institutions, they became ethnic enclaves where American Jews could pray and play together.

Organizational Growth. Even as the United Synagogue reached out to pioneer new congregations, it simultaneously created the umbrella organizations of Conservatism's various lay groups, essentially developing different structures, often, but not always, modeled on those Reform Judaism's Union of American Hebrew Congregations had already organized, for connecting the various segments of the American Jewish community to the synagogue and Conservative Judaism. In 1918 the National Women's League of the United Synagogue of America (now the Women's League for Conservative Judaism) became the umbrella for the sisterhoods that flourished as gendered spaces in these new synagogues. The organization's founding president and guiding spirit was Solomon Schechter's widow and intellectual companion, Mathilde Schechter (1859–1924). In 1929 another deliberately gendered entity emerged, the National Federation of Jewish Men's Clubs. The first of a variety of Conservative Jewish youth organizations dates to 1921, but this early association was abandoned in favor of new models after World War II when a different kind of teen culture emerged in a rapidly suburbanizing United States.

These different entities offered programs geared to their specific constituencies and presented a path to national leadership for Conservative laity. They sponsored conventions and retreats, developed new educational programs, and published an array of movement literature, including institutional magazines, all meant to foster a greater awareness of how it was indeed possible, even in the midst of secular American culture, to live a full Jewish life at home and in the synagogue. All remained dedicated to Conservative Judaism's principles of upholding historic Jewish observances and advancing knowledge of Hebrew and Torah. In so doing they helped shape a specific Conservative Jewish denominational identity.

The Great Depression and World War II. The promising expansion of Conservative Judaism through the United Synagogue came to a grinding halt with the onset of the Great Depression. The economic crisis affected both Conservative synagogues and the national organizations and institutions. With the world moving towards war, the energies of American Jews focused on an endangered Jewry across the Atlantic and embattled Zionists in British-mandate Palestine. As a result, the era of the depression and the early years of World War II were years of stasis, at best, for much of the Conservative movement.

That began to change, however, with America's entry into the war in December 1941. Helping the war effort occupied Conservative men, women, and youth at home and in their synagogues. But as the war sent tens of thousands of American Jews into the military, many met there, for the first time, Conservative rabbis serving as chaplains in the U.S. armed forces. When these soldiers returned home after the war, they formed the nucleus of a new generation of Conservative Jews, paving the way for a second era of remarkable movement growth.

IDEOLOGICAL AND THEOLOGICAL DIVIDES. A careful look at those Conservative rabbis—on the eve of World War II they numbered just over three hundred, most, but not all, ordained at the Seminary (by 1944, a third were military chaplains)—would have then revealed significant ideological and theological divisions within the Conservative movement. Conservative rabbis were united by their belief in the historic body of Jewish law which, they asserted, must govern a Jew's life from birth to death. But they knew that modernity, secularization, and Americanization had deeply affected Jews' attachment to *halakhah*. (*Halakhah*, literally "the way," refers to the entire corpus of Jewish law and includes laws found in the Bible, the many classics of rabbinic literature, and modern interpretations too.) American Jews, including Conservative Jews, had fashioned their own Jewish tradition, picking and choosing from *halakhah*, observing certain holidays and forgetting others, upholding certain rites and rituals, even inventing new ones, and ignoring others. This *halakhic* anarchy undermined the tradition Conservative rabbis upheld. The solution, they believed, was for them to take charge of shaping *halakhah*. They would be the ones to guide American Jewry to strike the proper balance between the forces of *Tradition and Change* (the title of a significant collection of movement essays, edited by Mordecai Waxman and published in 1958). If they succeeded, then Conservative Jews could and would volunteer to adhere to Jewish law and praxis.

Conservative rabbis all agreed that *halakhah* must be adjusted, adapted to meet modern realities and changing circumstances. They also shared an opposition to Reform Judaism's deliberate abrogation of Jewish law, even as they claimed that the Orthodox had erred in maintaining a rigid, unadjusted *halakhah*. But if these stances united Conservative rabbis they were nevertheless deeply divided over the extent to which Jewish law could and should be properly accommodated to contemporary realities, over the best way to forge a synthesis of modernity with *halakhah*.

Almost from its inception, Conservative Judaism was wracked by different visions of the acceptable methods of adjusting tradition to the modern world. For many rabbis *halakhah* could be adapted only through time-honored processes of reinterpretation of classic texts to prove that innovations remained within the basic spirit of Jewish law, and that they would, therefore, be acceptable to all of Jewry, which Schechter had considered the will of "Catholic Israel." But others asserted that Conservative rabbis had the right to enact new legislation and must abrogate old laws that had become irrelevant and were, moreover, ignored by most Conservative Jews.

Behind Conservatism's disputes over interpreting *halakhah* were diametrically opposed theological understandings of God and revelation. They are perhaps best understood as emanating from the two polestars of the Seminary faculty at midcentury, Kaplan and Abraham Joshua Heschel.

In his magnum opus *Judaism as a Civilization* (1934), Kaplan proposed a total revolution in Jewish theology, demanding that it be "reconstructed" to naturalism. He rejected the notion of a supernatural God, redefining God as the Power in the universe that makes for salvation, the sum of the forces that enable men and women to make the most of their lives. For Judaism to survive the challenges of modernity, there could be no miracles, no supernatural revelation. Since no authoritarian God could have revealed the commandments to the nation at Sinai, Kaplan revisioned the commandments as folkways, understanding Judaism's sacred seasons, rites, and rituals as existing to answer human needs. Consequently, they must be adapted to meet the changed circumstances of contemporary life. Concomitantly, he also rejected the historic concept that the Jews were God's chosen people.

To many Conservative leaders, in the decades when those embracing Kaplan's Reconstructionism remained within the movement, this theology was utterly anathema. They understood belief in a supernatural God and his revelation as fundamental theological concepts, though they also understood the difficulties these beliefs posed for moderns. Many of these rabbis were deeply influenced by the spiritual pietism and personal traditionalism of the charismatic Seminary professor of Jewish ethics and mysticism Heschel.

Heschel's philosophical and theological writings related directly to the moral dilemmas of the moment. His Depth Theology went below the surface phenomena of modern doubt and rootlessness to illumine the Living God, not as a philosophical abstraction or psychological projection but as the Most Moved Mover, the God of pathos who stands in a dynamic and reciprocal relationship to creation, who is overwhelmingly real and shatteringly present. Depth Theology explored the ongoing encounter between man and God, showing it to be an arduously difficult dialogue in which God remained a constant partner in man's work in the world.

ADJUSTING JEWISH LAW. These differences over theology and ideology were reflected in the three wings of the Conservative movement. By 1927, when the Rabbinical Assembly formed its first Committee on Jewish Law to answer for the movement the myriad of *halakhic* questions congregants and rabbis raised, the divisions had crystallized among the movement's elites—its rabbis and Seminary professors—into a religious and ideological right, center, and left. Those on the right, which included most of the Seminary faculty, favored the maintenance of tradition over any but the most essential changes. Those on the left, represented by the Reconstructionists who followed Kaplan's philosophy, considered major adaptations essential to meet the radically changed world inhabited by a modernizing Jewry. In the middle stood a large center trying valiantly to balance the sometimes shaky coalition.

As Conservative leaders established a series of committees on Jewish law to answer the enormous number of questions raised—in some years they exceeded 170—the rabbis were careful to balance committee members from among the conservative and liberal wings of the Rabbinical Assembly. The committees answered a host of questions about dietary laws, synagogue customs, architecture, Shabbat and holiday observance, funeral practices, conversion, circumcision, and intermarriage. Could unfermented wine be used for ritual purposes in order to comply with Prohibition? Was it permissible to withhold a *get,* the Jewish bill of divorcement, until a civil court had dissolved the marriage? Could intermarried Jews join a synagogue? Was eating broiled fish in restaurants and hotels permissible? What could the rabbis do about the plight of a wife chained to a husband who no longer lived with her but who refused or was unable to grant her a divorce, which, under Jewish law, only he could do? Was it permissible to drive to synagogue services on the Sabbath? What could be done, within the confines of Jewish law, to adjust the unequal status of women?

If the committee on Jewish law ruled unanimously on a question, then all Conservative rabbis, and presumably all Conservative Jews, must abide by the ruling (note the rabbis had little coercive power over the laity). But if the law committee published a majority and minority report, then the rabbis were free, according to Jewish custom and tradition, to follow either opinion. Thus all Conservative rabbis were prohibited from officiating at intermarriages. But Conservative synagogues have the option of abrogating the second day of observance of certain holidays and of completing the reading of the Torah, the Five Books of Moses chanted on Sabbath morning, over either one or three years.

As World War II was ending, the Conservative movement's coalition of the right, center, and left continued to hold, and it would hold throughout the first postwar decades when a new era of remarkable expansion required the energies of all in the movement.

Postwar Expansion. By the late 1930s, Seminary leaders, notably Louis Finkelstein (1895–1992), who became its president in 1940 and retired as its chancellor in 1972, recognized that the hegemony of world Jewry was shifting from Europe to the United States. Determined that Conservatism must become *a,* if not *the,* leading force guiding American and even world Jewry, Finkelstein set a course to raise funds and develop new initiatives to extend Conservative Judaism's reach.

As the war broke out, the Seminary began admitting larger classes to train the increasing number of rabbis needed to serve at home and at the front. As the war ended, the need for Conservative rabbis became so acute that the Rabbinical Assembly began admitting more and more rabbis trained in Reform and Orthodox settings who preferred to be Conservative rabbis.

As Jewish servicemen returning home joined the urban exodus, they organized new synagogues for their growing families in the burgeoning suburbs. Many decided that middle-of-the-road Conservative Judaism, whose chaplains they had first encountered during the war, would attract the widest swathe of suburbanizing Jews. While the number of Reform synagogues grew in these years, the growth in the Conservative movement was greater. By 1949 the United Synagogue had 365 congregations, nearly a 100 percent increase in just four years. By 1971, with the era of remarkable growth over, the United Synagogue counted 832 congregations, comprising some 350,000 families with an estimated 1.5 million members.

A National Identity. The explosion of synagogues was accompanied by a simultaneous expansion of movement activities and new initiatives designed to solidify Conservatism's presence as a national movement among American Jewry. The United Synagogue advised emerging congregations on synagogue management, budget, personnel, youth work, and successful synagogue programs. By the end of the 1940s, Conservative cantors, synagogue administrators, and Jewish educators had formed new professional associations. In 1947 the Seminary established a West Coast branch, the University of Judaism, in Los Angeles. Moreover, after many years of false starts, a prayer book for the movement, *The Sabbath and Festival Prayer Book,* was at last published in 1946. As it became almost universally accepted in Conservative synagogues, it contributed to a clearer sense of national movement identity among the laity.

Conservative leaders already had ambitions beyond the United States, and in 1957 they established a World Council of Synagogues (now the World Council of Conservative Synagogues) to extend their unique vision of Judaism around the globe. In 1962 they launched a rabbinical seminary in Argentina to train modern Spanish-speaking rabbis. As increasing numbers of Conservative rabbis made their homes in Israel, the movement grew there too. In 2003 the Masorti movement, as Conservative Judaism is known in Israel (*masorti* means "traditional"), numbered fifty congregations and included a kibbutz and educational institutions. This is a significant achievement, given that early in the history of the new state full jurisdiction over marriage, divorce, and burial for all Israeli Jews was handed over to the Orthodox, and its rabbinate has yet to recognize the authority of rabbis ordained outside Orthodox settings.

Education and Conservative Youth. Perhaps the greatest of Conservative Judaism's successes in these first postwar decades lay in the field of Jewish education. Abiding by the dictum, "And you shall teach them diligently unto your children" (*Dt.* 6:7), the movement invested extraordinary resources in an array of formal and informal programs of Jewish education at a time when American women were giving birth to the demographic bulge known as the baby boom. The Conservative synagogue became a central site for educating young Jews as nursery schools and Sunday schools were held on its premises. At the same time, Conservative leaders and laity created their first Jewish parochial schools, known as day schools; by 1958, there were fourteen Conservative day schools. In these settings children and teens spend approximately 40 percent of every day immersed in Jewish studies, including Hebrew language and classical Jewish texts. In 2003 over seventy schools in twenty states and Canada were affiliated with the movement's Solomon Schechter Day School Association.

New youth programs in these first postwar decades provided informal Jewish education. They included not only United Synagogue Youth, founded in 1951 for high school students, but also programs for teens seeking advanced Jewish education and other programs for the increasing numbers of Jewish youth attending college. The first of what would become a network of movement camps, Camp Ramah, opened in Wisconsin in 1947. Designed as Hebrew-speaking camps where campers would pray daily and live Judaism during the long, hot summers, they were expected to propel the next generation of Conservative Jews to lives filled with Judaism, observance, and study. United Synagogue Youth and especially Camp Ramah (both included Israel travel experiences) became training grounds for those who would go on to become lay leaders and for the next generations of Conservative rabbis.

Yet, in terms of its reach to the greatest number of Conservative youth, surely the pinnacle of Conservatism's educational achievements was the three-day-a-week afternoon congregational school, the Hebrew school. Prior to its emergence, most boys learned what they needed to know for bar mitzvah (the rite of passage to adult status in the synagogue, which occurs at age thirteen) in community Hebrew schools. The shift from the community school to the congregational Hebrew school began in the 1920s during the Conservative synagogue's first period of expansion, but the three-day-a-week congregational Hebrew school, which eventually absorbed the Sunday school for all but the youngest children, became the pillar of the new Conservative suburban synagogue. It became the medium by which Conservative children, and in the educationally egalitarian suburbs they included girls as well as boys, acquired the knowledge and skills necessary to fit into congregational life. Here children learned Hebrew prayers, studied the Bible, and were introduced to Jewish history, literature, and culture. They came to understand the centrality of Israel to the Jewish people and to comprehend Jewish values and ethics. By moving the Hebrew school to the synagogue and requiring attendance three times a week for five years before bar mitzvah, the Hebrew school became the nucleus of the family-centered suburban congregation, drawing parents and children together to the synagogue.

Bat Mitzvah. It also had unintended and unanticipated consequences, for not only was Hebrew school the path to bar mitzvah, it also became the path to bat mitzvah. Bat mitzvah was a new Jewish rite marking the transition from childhood to adolescence among American girls. In 1922, Kaplan created the first bat mitzvah in the United States for his daughter Judith. In the decades that followed, bat mitzvah won limited acceptance on an individual basis in Conservative synagogues. Its form—whether it took place at the Friday evening or Saturday morning Sabbath service, and which portions of the service the bat mitzvah girl read—differed from synagogue to synagogue. By 1948 a third of Conservative synagogues had adopted bat mitzvah, and by 1960 almost all celebrated both bar and bat mitzvah, even though it would take another decade or two for bat mitzvah to parallel exactly the bar mitzvah rite in most Conservative congregations.

Yet, even as bat mitzvah was becoming the norm for Conservative synagogues, it nevertheless signaled the end of a girl's public participation and leadership of the service. Boys could continue, if they wished, to use what they had learned in Hebrew school. They could, as teens and adults, bless the Torah scroll and read from it. They could even continue their Jewish learning and become rabbis. In these years no one expected that the bat mitzvah girl would ever again ascend to the pulpit, and surely she would never think of becoming a rabbi. Thus, Conservatism's educational triumphs, the creation of strong institutions for youth education, unwittingly helped set the stage for its most significant public crisis.

Years of Unease. By 1968, with the war in Vietnam raging, the youth rebellion in full swing, and the end of the demographic baby boom that had caused the suburban synagogue explosion, the era of enormous movement growth was at an end. As the 1960s have come to stand for years of turmoil in American society, when Americans launched a war on poverty, struggled to bring civil rights to all, and began a remarkable revisioning of gender roles, the Conservative movement too experienced its own years of unease.

In 1968 the Reconstructionists, long the most ardent champions of Conservatism's liberal wing, defected. As long as Kaplan remained a professor at the Seminary—and he taught rabbinical students there for more than five decades (from 1909 to 1963)—he refrained from creating the structures that would proclaim Reconstructionism's independence. Gradually, over the course of the 1960s, they had emerged. The final step was the establishment of the Reconstructionist Rabbinical College in Philadelphia in 1968. Its founding meant that those who would have become the standard bearers of Conservatism's liberal wing in the next generation could now become Reconstructionist, rather than Conservative, rabbis.

At the same time Conservative leaders experienced another defection, that of their best and brightest youth. In 1968 in Boston, Jews in their twenties, mostly graduate students and many, perhaps most, raised in elite Conservative institutions, founded the first *havurah* (plural, *havurot*), a small intimate group for prayer, celebration, and study. Creating a Jewish expression of the wider American counterculture, by the mid-1970s *havurot* flourished in all major Jewish communities. The young men and women of the *havurot*, and they included at least one former national president of United Synagogue Youth, rejected the grand suburban synagogues in which they had come of age, depicting them as spiritually arid temples to the hollowness of affluence.

Many Conservative leaders perceived the rebellion of their youth as indicative of the movement's weaknesses. They charged that their congregational schools had, despite their best efforts, failed. With the exception of the climactic experience of bar and bat mitzvah, they had not won over the youth who must become the next generation of Conservative Jews. Yet, Rabbi Wolfe Kelman (1923–1990), known as "the rabbi of the rabbis" for his long tenure as executive director of the Rabbinical Assembly, argued that the Conservative youth who were the chief architects of the Jewish counterculture were actually a sign of the movement's success. They had learned enough in Conservative settings to criticize the institutions in which they were raised and were so committed to Judaism that they demanded more from it.

Nevertheless, as the size of the movement stabilized, as the Reconstructionists seceded, and as the youth who should have become the next generation of Conservative synagogue members seemed to defect, the late 1960s and early 1970s became years of unease within Conservatism. This unease was compounded in the 1970s as many of the grand old synagogue-centers built in the 1920s, which had survived the early migrations to the suburbs, declined, and as the first suburban congregations built in the 1950s and early 1960s faced hard choices about refurbishing aging buildings in the hopes of attracting new members. But these concerns would pale before the conflict that was about to emerge—the demand to ordain women as Conservative rabbis.

THE CRISIS OVER WOMEN'S ORDINATION. Conservative Judaism had already responded to several questions about the status of women. Mixed seating, the sitting of men and women together in worship, which had become characteristic of the Conservative synagogue as it emerged, also became the denominational boundary distinguishing Conservative from modern Orthodox congregations. Conservative rabbis, long uncomfortable with praying each morning "Blessed be He who did not make me a woman," emended this prayer in the 1946 *Sabbath and Festival Prayer Book.* Bat mitzvah and a 1955 ruling permitting females to have an *aliyah*, the honor of blessing the Torah scroll, gave Conservative girls and women new, albeit limited, roles in the synagogue service. Finally, Conservative elites had wrestled for decades over the *agunah*, which chained the wife to an untenable marriage that only her husband could end. Even when American courts had issued a civil divorce, if a husband refused to grant a Jewish divorce the wife remained unable, as Conservative rabbis understood Jewish law, to remarry. In the late 1960s the Rabbinical Assembly took steps to resolve this *halakhic* impasse.

Marshall Sklare (1921–1992), who wrote the definitive sociological study of the Conservative movement, understood well that the inferior position of women in Jewish law transgressed Western norms. But, as he wrote at midcentury, he observed that Conservative women were not agitating for full equality. They seemed then, to Sklare, quite satisfied with the changes in women's status already made in Conservative Judaism.

By the early 1970s, however, that was no longer true. In March 1972, three months before the first American woman was ordained by Reform Judaism's Hebrew Union College, a group of women in New York, riding the crest of the new wave of American feminism and deeply committed to Conservative Judaism, appeared at the annual meeting of the Rabbinical Assembly. As girls, they had received the same educations as their brothers in Conservative schools and camps. As women, they were denied the opportunity to use that knowledge. As feminists, they deemed this a gross affront to their intelligence and sensibilities. They called for an end to the second-class status of women in Jewish life, demanded that women be allowed to participate fully in all religious observances, and launched an agonizing public debate over whether or not the Conservative movement would ordain women rabbis.

From 1972 to 1983, Conservative leaders found themselves inextricably engaged in an intricate political dance of shifting alliances, studies undertaken, commissions formed, hearings held, motions tabled, and votes counted. Each twist and turn of the question of women's ordination in these years, as the ball was thrown from one arena of Conservative Judaism to another, reflected just how divisive and painful the prospect of women rabbis was for those enmeshed in the debate.

For example, the movement convened the Commission for the Study of the Ordination of Women as Rabbis, and it held public hearings in five cities to gather the opinions of Conservative Jews. In December 1978 its members divided. Eleven believed that Jewish law did not prohibit women's ordination, and they recommended their admission to the rabbinical school the following September. Three commission members dissented, arguing ominously that women's ordination would disrupt the unity of the movement. A year later, the Seminary faculty, fearing schism within their ranks, tabled the question of admitting women to the rabbinical school for the foreseeable future.

But by the fall of 1983, when it was evident that the Rabbinical Assembly would soon admit a woman ordained at Hebrew Union College (she would have been a Conservative rabbi if she could have been), the Seminary faculty convened again. This time they voted to admit women to the rabbinical school. The vote propelled some from the right wing of the movement to break off. Decrying Conservatism's selective loyalty to *halakhah*, they established the Union for Traditional Judaism. In May 1985, Amy Eilberg, who had accumulated advanced standing through prior coursework as she waited patiently for Conservative leaders to allow women's ordination, was ordained a rabbi.

Judaism in the Center. The bitter debate over women's ordination was "a struggle for the soul of the movement" (Wertheimer, 1993, p. 348). Indeed, in the wake of women's ordination, the Conservative movement was transformed. By the 1990s it had at last moved firmly to the center. The secessions, first of the Reconstructionists on the left and then of the opponents of women's ordination on the right, explain the shift, but only partially. The successful suburbanization of Orthodox Judaism, which occurred later than that of Conservative Judaism and which Conservative leaders had not anticipated during the heyday of suburban synagogue expansion in the 1950s and 1960s, also contributed significantly to moving Conservatism to the center. New suburban Orthodox synagogues allowed traditional Jews to create strong Sabbath-observant communities of like-minded families who once would have become the more traditional elements in Conservative congregations. The result was a shift to the center in the movement, which in the past had to balance its coalition so carefully that the presidents of the Rabbinical Assembly rotated among the right, center, and left.

Now egalitarianism won the day in Conservative worship. By 1981, less than a decade after the 1973 decision to count women in the quorum necessary for prayer—an early concession to the demand for women's ritual equality, only 47 percent of Conservative congregations had done so. By 1995 to 1996, 83 percent counted women in the prayer quorum, and in more than three-quarters of congregations women led services and read from the Torah. Rather than egalitarianism muting Conservatism's loyalty to *halakhah*, it likely increased overall levels of observance and knowledge in every synagogue community.

Even as Conservatism's new commitment to women's full and equal participation paralleled that of Reform and Reconstructionist Judaism, its adherence to tradition and loyalty to *halakhah* continued to parallel Orthodoxy. Nevertheless, Conservative Judaism has long been characterized by a striking gap in observance. In public movement settings, in its synagogues, schools, and camps, loyalty to Jewish tradition, to Sabbath observance, and to *kashrut* was and is the norm. But Conservative Jews, with the exception of the elites (the Seminary professors and rabbis), by and large violate these norms personally and in their homes. For example, of all those who identified as Conservative in the 1990 National Jewish Population Survey, only 23 percent report lighting Sabbath candles regularly and less than 15 percent keep kosher.

To close the gap in observance, Conservative leaders have repeatedly tried to convey to the laity the movement's position on loyalty to Jewish tradition. In 1979 Isaac Klein (1905–1979), one of Conservatism's most important legal experts and long a leader of its right wing, published *A Guide to Jewish Religious Practice*, a modern code for Jewish living that incorporated many of the movement's decisions on Jewish law. In 1988 the movement published *Emet Ve-Emunah: Statement of Principles of Conservative Judaism.* Earlier attempts to reach consensus on such a statement had always failed. This one succeeded largely because *Emet ve-Emunah* (truth and faith) conveyed its centrist stance by presenting the divergent theological views on God, revelation, Jewish law, and the election of Israel that had evolved among Conservative thinkers. For example, it reported that "Conservative Judaism affirms the critical importance of belief in God, but does not specify all the particulars of that belief" (p. 18).

As the twentieth century gave way to the twenty-first, thorny *halakhic* issues emerging from the new sociological and behavioral patterns of American Jews continued to challenge Conservative leaders. As the intermarriage rate soared in the late twentieth century, it forced Conservative rabbis to think ever more carefully about the position of the intermarried family in the synagogue. Could the non-Jewish spouse become a member and vote and eventually hold synagogue office? What roles would the non-Jewish parent play in the children's bar mitzvah? in their weddings? Could the non-Jewish spouse be buried in the synagogue cemetery? Even as Conservative leaders grappled with these specific questions, they continued to uphold the historic Jewish principle of matrilineal descent, recognizing any child of a Jewish mother as a Jew, and refusing to embrace patrilineality, according to which the child of a Jewish father and a non-Jewish mother is recognized as a Jew.

The shift to the center and the stances on intermarriage may help explain changes in the position of Conservatism within the spectrum of American Jewry and the decline in the size of the movement. At one time Conservative Judaism was the largest denomination in American Jewry. In 1971, 42 percent of Jews choosing a denominational label identified themselves as Conservative. By the time of the 1990 National Jewish Population Survey, 35 percent identified themselves as Conservative, whereas 38 percent described themselves as Reform. Only slightly more than half of Conservative Jews actually belong to a Conservative synagogue. (American Jews affiliate voluntarily with a synagogue and must pay annual dues and synagogue fees, which, in 2003, typically exceeded $2,000 a year for a family with children). In 2003 the United Synagogue of Conservative Judaism numbered 760 synagogues, a decline from the nearly 850 congregations at its peak.

These synagogues differed in another significant way from those of the 1950s and 1960s. The Conservative synagogue of the 1990s had come to reflect the Jewish sensibilities of its generation of congregants, many of whom came to their synagogues with more intensive Jewish educations than their parents had. Not only had they studied in Jewish schools as children, celebrated bar and bat mitzvah as teens, and attended Jewish youth groups and summer camps, but many had also taken Jewish studies courses in college and had visited Israel at some point in their lives. This new generation of Conservative synagogue members was the generation of the postwar baby boom, and they had, at last, turned to the synagogue as they became parents and needed its structures and settings for their own children. Yet, like the children of their peers who had founded the Jewish counterculture in their youth, they expected greater spontaneity and informality in the synagogues they would join, as they did elsewhere in their lives.

Consequently, many late-twentieth-century Conservative synagogues tried to respond to their different constituencies and their needs. One answer was to institute a variety of worship services designed to bring greater intimacy to the synagogue. Depending on the congregation, these might include a traditional service for those who remained uncomfortable with egalitarianism, a main egalitarian service where bar and bat mitzvah were celebrated, various *havurot* meeting within the congregation, different children's services, and a learners' service to give those who wished to do so a chance to discuss the liturgy and weekly biblical readings.

Moreover, the late Friday evening service, which had characterized the Conservative synagogue in its founding era, was starting to fade. By 1995 fewer than two-thirds of Conservative congregations still regularly held this service. The circumstances which had brought about its creation in American Jewish life had changed, and Conservative Judaism was, once again, adapting to new sociological realities, this time that of the two-career family and a desire by many, especially Conservative rabbis, to turn back to the customary early service on the eve of the Sabbath followed by the traditional meal with family at home. This process of adaptation had long been and will likely remain a hallmark of this centrist religious movement of American Judaism.

SEE ALSO Jewish Thought and Philosophy, article on Modern Thought; Orthodox Judaism; Reconstructionist Judaism; Reform Judaism; Zionism.

BIBLIOGRAPHY

Among the most important writings on the history of Conservative Judaism are those by Abraham Karp, especially "A Century of Conservative Judaism in the United States" in *American Jewish Year Book* 86 (Philadelphia, 1986): 3–61, and "The Conservative Rabbi," *American Jewish Archives* 25 (1983): 188–262. The definitive sociological study of the movement is Marshall Sklare's *Conservative Judaism: An American Religious Movement* (1955; rev. ed., 1972; reprint, Lanham, Md., 1985). Conservative institutions have a strong sense of historical consciousness and have published their own histories. See, for example, Jack Wertheimer, ed., *Tradition Renewed: A History of the Jewish Theological Seminary,* 2 vols. (New York, 1997), and Robert E. Fierstien, ed., *A Century of Commitment: One Hundred Years of the Rabbinical Assembly* (New York, 2000). Since the study of Conservative Judaism belongs to the fields of American religion and American Judaism broadly, it is often presented in larger studies. See especially Jonathan D. Sarna, *American Judaism: A History* (New Haven, 2004). See also Nathan Glazer, *American Judaism* (1957; rev. ed., Chicago, 1972); Jack Wertheimer, *A People Divided: Judaism in Contemporary America* (New York, 1993); and Marc Lee Raphael, *Judaism in America* (New York, 2003).

Specific aspects of this article are based on the following. The standard work on the nineteenth-century origins of Conservative Judaism is Moshe Davis, *The Emergence of Conservative Judaism: The Historical School in 19th Century America* (New York, 1963). On American synagogues instituting reforms in the nineteenth century, see Leon A. Jick, *The Americanization of the Synagogue, 1820–1870,* (1976; reprint, Hanover, N.H., 1992). On the early Seminary, see Robert E. Fierstien, *A Different Spirit: The Jewish Theological Seminary of America, 1886–1902* (New York, 1990). On the emergence of the Conservative synagogue, see several of the essays in Jack Wertheimer, ed., *The American Synagogue: A Sanctuary Transformed* (New York and Cambridge, UK, 1987), especially those by Karp and Wertheimer. On the synagogue-centers, see Deborah Dash Moore, *At Home in America: Second Generation New York Jews* (New York, 1981), and David Kaufman, *Shul with a Pool: The "Synagogue-Center" in American Jewish History* (Hanover, N.H., 1999). On the ideological divisions within the movement, see especially the essays on *halakhah* and the Rabbinical Assembly in Pamela S. Nadell, *Conservative Judaism in America: A Biographical Dictionary and Sourcebook* (New York, 1988). On the emergence of bat mitzvah, see Paula E. Hyman, "The Introduction of Bat Mitzvah in Conservative Judaism in Postwar America," *YIVO Annual* 19 (1990): 133–146, and Regina Stein, "The Road to Bat Mitzvah in America" in *Women and American Judaism: Historical Perspectives,* edited by Pamela S. Nadell and Jonathan D. Sarna (Hanover, N.H., 2001). On the *havurot,* see Riv-Ellen Prell, *Prayer and Community: The Havurah in American Judaism* (Detroit, 1989). On women's ordination, see Pamela S. Nadell, *Women Who Would Be Rabbis: A History of Women's Ordination, 1889–1985* (Boston, 1998), and Beth S. Wenger, "The Politics of Women's Ordination: Jewish Law, Institutional Power, and the Debate over Women in the Rabbinate" in *Tradition Renewed: A History of the Jewish Theological Seminary,* edited by Jack Wertheimer (New York, 1997), pp. 485–523. For studies utilizing the data of the North American Study of Conservative Synagogues and their members, 1995–1996, see Jack Wertheimer, ed., *Jews in the Center: Conservative Synagogues and Their Members* (New Brunswick, N.J., 2000).

The literature produced by the Conservative movement is voluminous. It includes conference proceedings, journals, and magazines published by the various institutions of the movement. Among the most useful of these are the annual *Proceedings of the Rabbinical Assembly* and the journal *Conservative Judaism.* Other movement publications of importance are the essays by the key figures in the movement's first half century collected in Mordecai Waxman, ed., *Tradition and Change: The Development of Conservative Judaism* (New York, 1958); Isaac Klein, *A Guide to Jewish Religious Practice*

(New York, 1979); Jewish Theological Seminary of America, Rabbinical Assembly, United Synagogue of America, Women's League for Conservative Judaism, and Federation of Jewish Men's Clubs, *Emet Ve-Emunah: Statement of Principles of Conservative Judaism* (New York, 1988); Simon Greenberg, ed., *The Ordination of Women as Rabbis: Studies and Responsa* (New York, 1988); and Nina Beth Cardin and David Wolf Silverman, eds., *The Seminary at 100: Reflections on the Jewish Theological Seminary and the Conservative Movement* (New York, 1987).

PAMELA S. NADELL (2005)

CONSTANTINE (272/273–337), known as Constantine the Great, Roman emperor and agent of the Christianization of the Roman Empire. Born at Naissus, the only son of Helena and Flavius Constantius, Constantine was assured a prominent role in Roman politics when Diocletian, the senior emperor in the Tetrarchy, appointed his father Caesar in 293. Educated in the imperial court at Nicomedia, and permitted to accompany the eastern emperors on provincial tours and military campaigns, he doubtless expected to succeed to his father's position when Diocletian and Maximian abdicated in 305. But Galerius, who may have contrived the abdication and as the new eastern emperor controlled the succession, ignored Constantine—and Maxentius, the son of Maximian—and instead nominated as Caesars his own nephew and the praetorian prefect Severus. Constantine could not challenge this decision immediately, but when his father died at York in July 306, he reasserted the claim, this time backed by the British and Gallic armies, and requested confirmation from the eastern emperor. Galerius resisted, preferring Severus as Constantius's successor, but to avoid a confrontation offered Constantine the lesser rank of Caesar. When Maxentius rebelled at Rome in October 306, however, he refused to grant a similar concession, and for the next seven years civil war disrupted the western half of the empire.

In the end it was Constantine who dislodged the resilient Maxentius from Rome, defeating his army at the Milvian Bridge on October 28, 312. For Lactantius and Eusebius of Caesarea, Christian observers who produced accounts of the event a few years later, this was more than a political triumph. On the eve of the battle, they insisted, Constantine had experienced the vision (or visions) that inspired his conversion to Christianity. Constantine's motives are beyond reconstruction, but it is clear that he believed the victory had been won with divine assistance. Even the inscription on the triumphal arch in Rome erected by the Senate in 315 to mark the event attributed his success to the "prompting of a deity." If the language is ambiguous, perhaps in deference to the sentiments of the pagan majority, Constantine's legislation and activities after 312 attest the evolution of his Christian sympathies.

Whether the "conversion" represented a dramatic break with the pagan past is more problematic. Constantine had never been a persecutor; indeed, in 306 he had ordered the restoration of property in Britain and Gaul that had been confiscated from Christians during the Great Persecution (303–305). Unlike Galerius, who had vigorously persecuted Christians in the East, Constantine was a tolerant pagan, content with the accumulation of heavenly patrons (Sol Invictus, Apollo). In 312 he may well have considered the God of the Christians simply another heavenly patron, demonstrably more powerful than others but not necessarily incompatible. Though he refused to participate after 312 in distinctly pagan ceremonies, Constantine retained the title *pontifex maximus* and evidently did not find the demands of government and religion irreconcilable. Exclusive commitment and a sense of mission, however, would develop over time. Early on he expressed his gratitude and allegiance through special exemptions and benefactions; after 324 he did not hesitate to use his office to condemn pagan beliefs and practices and to promote the christianization of the empire.

Politics accounts in large measure for Constantine's transformation from benefactor to advocate. The conversion did not alienate pagans, for religion had not been an issue in the civil war, and nothing indicates that Licinius, whom Galerius had chosen as co-emperor in 308, objected to Constantine's evident Christian sympathies in 312. At Milan the following year, in fact, the two survivors joined in the publication of Galerius's edict of toleration, drafted just before his death in 311, and ordered the restoration of Christian property in the East. As political rivalry developed over the next few years, however, the religious policies of the emperors diverged, especially after the inconclusive civil war of 316/7. Politics and religion became so entangled that Constantine, using attacks on Christians in the East as pretext, could declare his campaign against Licinius in 324 a crusade against paganism. His victory at Chrysopolis (September 18) simultaneously removed the last challenge to his authority and legitimized his emerging sense of mission.

Denunciations of pagan practices followed immediately, coupled with lavish grants for the construction of churches and preferential treatment of Christian candidates for administrative posts. Constantine also took the lead in efforts to restore order in an increasingly divided church. The Council of Nicaea (325), which three hundred bishops attended, was not his first attempt at ecclesiastical arbitration. A decade earlier he had summoned fractious North African bishops to a council at Arles (314) to decide a disputed election in Carthage and to rule on the orthodoxy of the Numidian bishop Donatus. The latter was condemned, but his partisans (Donatists) continued for the remainder of Constantine's reign to resist the council's decision. The prospects for settlement in 325 were bleaker still. The nature of Christ, not simply a disputed election or the propriety of rebaptism, was the question at issue. Arius, a presbyter of Alexandria in Egypt, had repeatedly argued that Christ was a created being, a view that seemed to deny his divinity. The bishops assembled in Nicaea (Bithynia), responding to the counterarguments of Alexander (bishop of Alexandria) and others, condemned Arianism and adopted a creed (the Nicene Creed) that declared the Father and Son to be of the same essence. This language satisfied the majority in attendance, but it did not silence Arians. By midcentury, in fact, the Arian position, not the Nicene, had been accepted by most of the eastern churches represented at Nicaea and by the successors of Constantine.

Pagans, of course, would not have found much to applaud in all this; their prosperity was determined by Constantine's handling of everyday affairs, not by his performance in church councils. Victories over the northern barbarians, reform of the coinage, rationalization of the bureaucracy—these were the issues that shaped their sense of well-being. That the emperor, especially during the last decade of his reign, was attentive to these concerns is clear, so much so that he can be credited with the refinement and implementation of the reforms introduced by his pagan predecessors. And yet, it is his Christianity that sets him apart. His reputation rests on his skillful manipulation of Christian symbols—the Milvian Bridge, the Council of Nicaea, the foundation of Constantinople (the "second Rome" that served as the principal capital after its dedication in 330). He was both the new Augustus and the thirteenth apostle, the pagan emperor who, after his encounter with the God of the Christians, adopted as his personal mission the Christianization of the empire. In pursuit of this objective, he had created by his death in 337 a Christian Roman empire that would endure for a thousand years.

Bibliography

Barnes, Timothy D. *Constantine and Eusebius.* Cambridge, Mass., 1981.

Barnes, Timothy D. *The New Empire of Diocletian and Constantine.* Cambridge, Mass., 1982.

Dörries, Hermann. *Constantine the Great.* Translated by Roland H. Bainton. New York, 1972.

Jones, A. H. M. *Constantine and the Conversion of Europe.* Rev. ed. New York, 1962.

Momigliano, Arnaldo, ed. *The Conflict between Paganism and Christianity in the Fourth Century.* Oxford, 1963.

John W. Eadie (1987)

CONSTANTINIANISM is a policy establishing a particular Christian church as the religion of the state, also known as Caesaropapism. Formulated originally by the Roman emperor Constantine I, the Great (d. 337), it was continued in the Byzantine Empire (until 1453), the Frankish kingdom, the Holy Roman Empire (962–1806), and numerous states of Europe, being modified in most states since the Protestant Reformation but persisting in some even today. According to this policy, state and church should form a close alliance so as to achieve mutual objectives.

Constantinianism Conceived. Following his "conversion" in 312, Constantine proceeded by stages to establish Christianity as the sole religion of the empire. From 312 to 320 he tolerated paganism but he elevated the standing of Christianity with increasing vigor. From 320 to 330 he thrust the organization of the church into the foreground and directed a frontal attack on polytheism. From 330 to 337, after moving the capital from Rome to Byzantium, he waged an open war on the old religion.

Constantine, whatever the exact nature of his conversion, believed that the supreme God whom Christians worshiped had given him the victory at the Milvian Bridge and dominion over the empire. He hoped that by doing God's will he would obtain further prosperity for himself and his subjects and feared that if he offended God he would be cast down from power and pull the empire down with him. In a letter to an official charged with responsibility for healing the Donatist schism, the emperor confessed he would feel secure "only when I see all venerating the most holy God in the proper cult of the catholic religion with harmonious brotherhood of worship." This concern for right worship prompted him to seek not merely the establishment of Christianity but the conservation of a united and orthodox Christianity. Bitterly offended by division among Christians, he felt duty-bound to impose unity, first in the Donatist controversy and then in the Arian. To resolve the latter, he summoned a universal council representing the whole church to meet at Nicaea, and presided over it himself. In an opening address he deplored the internecine strife in the church as a disaster greater than war or invasion. During the crucial part of the debate, he himself chaired and took an active part in guiding the proceedings. He used his imperial presence to secure an inclusive formula with which all except ardent Arians could agree, proposing the phrase "of one essence" *(homoousios)* to express the Son's relation to the Father.

Though Constantine's peacemaking efforts within the church turned out rather badly both for his and later generations, he put in motion a program that would eventually secure the triumph of Christianity over its competitors. When his co-emperor Licinius turned sour toward Christianity and backed away from the tolerance guaranteed by the Edict of Milan (313), Constantine initiated against him a virtual crusade culminating in his defeat and death in 324. Thenceforth, as Constantine once remarked in a speech to bishops he was entertaining, he considered himself "a bishop established by God of those outside [the church]." He thought of himself, too, as a "thirteenth apostle." If he did not undertake to promote missionary work outside the empire, he did so within its boundaries. He grew increasingly impatient with the unwillingness of his subjects to accept the Christian faith until finally, in 330, exasperated with the tenacious grip of paganism on old Rome, he established a new Christian capital at Byzantium. Thereafter he held back nothing, razing and looting temples and lavishing public monies on the churches, forcing pagans to return property confiscated from

Christians under Licinius, building churches of great splendor in important cities, and enticing soldiers and public officials with lavish favors. His successors, Julian (361–363) excepted, followed suit, and by the time of Justinian (527–565), intolerance toward non-Christians had become a public virtue.

Constantinianism Controverted. Constantinianism was never seriously contested in the Byzantine Empire, but it has been in other nations, especially in the West. The so-called Donation of Constantine, a spurious document composed between 752 and 778 in the Carolingian (Frankish) kingdom, inaugurated a long history of debate over relations between church and state with strong advocacy of the superiority of popes to princes by grant of Constantine himself. Charlemagne, king of the Franks from 778 to 814, and his successors operated on the Constantinian model, aiding the church in its evangelism but using it to achieve royal aims and freely interfering in ecclesiastical affairs. Their practice of lay investiture, secular rulers handing symbols of office to the clergy at their installation, however, touched off a fierce battle with the papacy on which compromise was not achieved until 1122. Subsequently, Innocent III during his years as pope (1198–1216) stood Constantinianism on its head by liberal interference in matters of state in the Holy Roman Empire and virtually every nation in Europe.

The strongest objections to Constantinianism, however, have been voiced by sects that have suffered from its emphasis on uniformity. The ancient Donatists, ruing their request for imperial involvement in ecclesiastical disputes, soon advocated separation of church and state. So too did some medieval sects. The most persistent and consistent voice against Constantinianism, however, has come from the so-called free churches that emerged at the time of the Protestant Reformation in the sixteenth century and after. Many of these, especially Anabaptists and Baptists, have denounced the alliance of church and state that Constantine effected as a "fall" of the church, resulting not only in religious intolerance and persecution but also in an adulteration of Christianity. According to a Hutterite chronicle, this well-intended alliance is how "the disease of craftiness, which creeps about in darkness, and the corruption which perverted at high noon, [was] introduced by violence" and "the Cross was conquered and forged to the sword." In opposition to Constantinianism, the free churches espoused voluntary association in congregations and separation of church and state. "Gathered churches" composed of "regenerate members," and not the state or its magistrates, would, by this plan, exercise discipline in doctrine and behavior over their constituents. Although government has a legitimate role to play, the free churches further stated, it should restrict its activities to the civil realm and leave religion to the churches. God alone is Lord over the human conscience in religious matters.

See Also Anabaptism; Arianism; Constantine; Donatism; Heresy, article on Christian Concepts; Innocent III; Reformation.

Bibliography

Constantine's Christian intentions have been the subject of many recent books. Most helpful in interpreting his policy are Andrew Alföldi's *The Conversion of Constantine and Pagan Rome,* translated by Harold Mattingly (Oxford, 1948), and A. H. M. Jones's *Constantine and the Conversion of Europe* (London, 1948). A critical assessment of Constantinianism can be found in Hermann Dörries's *Constantine and Religious Liberty,* translated by Roland H. Bainton (New Haven, 1960).

E. Glenn Hinson (1987)

CONTARINI, GASPARO

CONTARINI, GASPARO (1483–1542), Venetian statesman, author of philosophical and theological works, proponent of Roman Catholic church reform, and cardinal. Born in Venice on October 16, 1483, he died in Bologna on August 24, 1542. Belonging to an ancient patrician clan, Contarini received a solid education first in Venice and then, from 1501 to 1509, at the University of Padua, where he studied philosophy, mathematics, and theology. In 1511, during a period of inner turmoil and search for personal vocation, he arrived at the conviction that humankind is justified before God by faith, not works. This belief, similar to Martin Luther's, later enabled him to deal sympathetically with Protestantism.

His career in the service of Venice began in 1518. Among its highlights were embassies to Emperor Charles V from 1521 to 1525, and to Pope Clement VII from 1528 to 1530. Dispatches from both missions show the development of Contarini's considerable diplomatic skill. Between 1530 and 1535 he was a member of the Venetian government's inner circle, holding high office almost continuously, including that of the head of the Council of Ten. This period also saw the completion of his best-known work, *De magistratibus et respublica Venetorum,* which contributed to the widespread diffusion of the idea of Venice as a perfectly ordered state.

On May 21, 1535, Pope Paul III appointed Contarini cardinal. He became the center of a group of reformers at the papal court, heading a commission to propose reforms in the church before the calling of a general council. As a member of subsequent commissions for the reform of various curial offices, he was an insistent spokesman for the necessity of removing abuses and clashed with his conservative colleagues. In January 1541, he was chosen as papal legate to the religious colloquy between Catholics and Protestants in Regensburg. In an unsuccessful effort to break down the differences between the two confessions, Contarini proposed a theory of double justification. It was eventually rejected by both sides. He spent the last months of his life as papal legate in Bologna, suspected by intransigents in Rome of having been too accommodating to Protestants and of leaning toward their ideas. Contarini remains perhaps the most attractive personality among Catholic reform thinkers before the Council of Trent.

BIBLIOGRAPHY

Franz Dittrich's *Gasparo Contarini* (Braunsberg, 1885) is still the fullest biography. Contarini's works have been issued under the titles *Gasparis Contarini cardinalis opera* (1571; microfilm reprint, Rome, 1964) and *Regesten und Briefe des Cardinals Gasparo Contarini, 1483–1542,* edited by Franz Dittrich (Braunsberg, 1881). Useful studies include Hubert Jedin's "Gasparo Contarini," in *Dictionnaire d'histoire et de géographie ecclésiastiques,* vol. 13 (Paris, 1956), pp. 772–784; James B. Ross's "The Emergence of Gasparo Contarini: A Bibliographical Essay," *Church History* 41 (1972): 22–46; and Gigliola Fragnito's "Gasparo Contarini," in *Dizionario biografico degli Italiani,* vol. 28 (Rome, 1983), pp. 172–192.

ELISABETH G. GLEASON (1987)

CONTEMPLATION SEE ATTENTION; MEDITATION; PRAYER

CONTRITION SEE CONFESSION OF SINS; REPENTANCE

CONVERSION. The nature and definition of conversion elicits enormous controversy. Given the complexity, and to some, the transcendent mystery of conversion, it is no surprise that scholarly consensus has yet to be achieved. For some, conversion is a form of pathology. For others, it is an example of human manipulation and coercive power. It is important at the outset of this article to note that Buddhism, Christianity, and Islam have been traditionally identified as conversionist (or missionary) movements. However, conversion studies necessarily deals with a much broader array of religions and topics than those confined to any of these three religions. The subject of conversion, once the exclusive franchise of evangelical Protestants and psychologists of religion, is now investigated by scholars in anthropology, history, missiology, religious studies, theology, and sociology.

Fundamentally, conversion is religious change. Since the 1980s, however, the very definition of conversion erupted as a zone of contention. What changes? Who changes? How does one change? How much change is necessary for the change to be considered conversion? What is authentic conversion? These debates permeate the extensive and growing literature on the nature of conversion. The word *conversion* itself is a source of debate. Especially in areas where missionaries from a variety of religious traditions have been active, the specter of forced, or at the very least, manipulated conversions, elicit a desire to reject the word *conversion* as a symbol of the colonial missionary enterprise.

Two common English definitions of conversion originated from the Greek terms *epistrophe,* which can mean "conversion" or "turning around," and *metanoia,* which can mean "repentance" or "to turn around," with an emphasis on the inner transformation of the convert. The term *conversion* was employed initially within Judeo-Christian circles to describe a believer's self-identification with a religious tradition either through faith in God and/or through commitment to new beliefs, rituals, and a religious community. Comparatively, converts to Buddhism, especially in its earliest Indian environs hundreds of years before the emergence of Christianity, described their own experience not as "converting" but as "enlightenment." To the faithful within monotheistic religious traditions, conversion was seen positively as testimony to the truth of the religion as well as guarantor of salvation. Pejoratively, conversion often meant sacrificing personal or social identity, a rejection of local lifeways and customs, through the "turning to" another religious tradition that may have been associated with a dominant political, social, or religious power.

Constructing theories and interpretations of conversion can be an arduous enterprise. "Insiders" assume that people convert to the insider's religion because the religion is, of course, true. "Outsiders" to a particular religion will not assert that a person converts to another religion because it is true. Moreover, the secular person may use explanations that are related to psychological needs, sociological factors, cultural forces, economic incentives or deprivations, and/or political constraints or inducements to make sense of the phenomena, thereby reducing the concept of conversion to a monocausal force rather than recognizing its pluriform nature. Facile definitions of such robust and dynamic phenomena fail to account for the multifaceted process that affects social, psychological, religious, and political life. Definitions of conversion abound, yet the use of theory helps human beings to begin to intellectually grasp its meaning. Given the inherent complexity of conversion, there exists no single comprehensive theory that successfully disentangles the numerous threads that together give rise to religious change. For instance, not all conversions entail inner transformation—some require adherence to divine laws revealed to human beings. Furthermore, some scholars suggest that conversion entails an abrupt and radical religious reorientation or intensification, while others assert that conversion processes are gradual, with the convert progressively entering a new religious tradition or deepening their commitment to their present tradition.

The study of conversion has dramatically expanded. In addition to numerous articles and monographs, the most common format is the edited book with articles addressing various dimensions of the phenomenon. In some cases the books are organized according to disciplines, in other cases they are focused on a particular religion or a region of the world. Recent contributors to this genre include Robert W. Hefner, Andrew Buckser, and Stephen D. Glazier in anthropology; Christopher Lamb, M. Darrol Bryant, and Peter van der Veer in religious studies; and Rowena Robinson and Sathianathan Clarke in the study of conversion in India. Others have added to the extensive literature in historical studies, including Steve Kaplan, Kenneth Mills, Anthony Graftson, and James Muldoon, while Kenneth J. Collins and John Tyson have written about Wesleyan studies. These studies are valuable in providing rich detail and texture to descriptions of conversion processes. There is a need for students of conversion to work more systematically in interdisciplinary studies in order to build a more coherent, cumulative approach to theory and research.

This article on conversion focuses on a number of theoretical orientations currently deployed in the study of conversion. Various theories elucidate different dimensions and processes involved in the phenomenon of conversion, and each theory grows out of different sets of assumptions and methods of research. No single theory currently dominates the field of conversion studies. By exploring a wide array of conversion theories, the diversity and complexity of conversion will be illumined. The theories are organized according to broad categories that focus on the person, social and cultural approaches, religious and theological approaches, and convergent models; the latter are theoretical approaches that seek to be interdisciplinary and inclusive.

Personalistic Theories. Personalistic theories include:

Psychoanalytic theory. According to the psychoanalytically oriented scholar, the phenomena of conversion is driven and shaped by the primal forces within the personality. Sigmund Freud suggested that the id, ego, and superego engage in constant conflict, giving rise to the human urgency to seek gratification of powerful desires, where culture, religion, and conscience (superego) serve to constrain. In Freud's view, conversion processes are fragile compromises in the ongoing conflict of the life and death instinct, where the drama of infant, mother, and father are mirrored in the dynamics of conversion. Religious rituals, beliefs, and relationships are motivated by such powerful emotions as guilt, grief, terror, emotional deprivations, and all kinds of suffering that propels the person into religion. Adherents of psychoanalytic theory interpret conversion as inherently pathological, interpreting it as a means to overcome childhood fears and conflicts rooted deep within the personality.

Archetypical theory. Carl G. Jung developed the archetypical theory that asserts that there are fundamental, universal patterns within the human psyche that give form to human experience. Based upon his work, scholars of archetypical theory postulate that conversion takes place when a person is captivated by a powerful religious symbol or experience that meets profound needs within that person's psyche. Scholars following archetypical theories take seriously the symbol systems of religion in order to understand the attraction and impact upon a convert.

Attachment theory. Some scholars of conversion assert that human beings form emotional ties reflecting the connection of an individual with their original primary caregiver. Building on some of the foundational notions of Freud and evolutionary theory, John Bowlby's work asserts that conversion in part compensates for severely deprived and distorted parenting patterns or it can be congruent with parental modes of relating to the dependent child. Attachment theory emphasizes the primacy of affective and emotional relationships as formative.

Attribution theory. Attribution theory is based on the universal human need to create and/or find meaning in life, including meaning for inexplicable daily events as well as more profound issues of the human predicament, such as undeserved suffering and death. Adopting a new system of attributions about the nature of self, others, and God is a significant aspect of what happens for many converts. Attribution theory asserts that religion or a religious perspective provides meaning and a sense of purpose to those issues that haunt human consciousness. This theory stresses the cognitive and intellectual spheres of conversion processes.

Social/Cultural Theories. Social and cultural theories include:

Multicultural theory. Increasingly, scholars of conversion recognize the importance of the cultural dimensions of the conversion process. Previously the bulk of theoretical work on conversion was derived from people of European racial and cultural heritage. Unquestioned assumptions about patterns of family life, modes of selfhood, and norms of mental health were either ignored or were assumed to be superior to people of other racial, ethnic, and national origins. While most Euro-American scholars previously tended to universalize their perceptions of self, personality, and motivation, more recently there has been growing interest in researching non-Western settings or people with Asian, Latin American, African, or Pacific Island backgrounds.

Alan Roland's self theory postulates variable dimensions of self that are virtually universal but have different valence or importance in various cultures. Roland suggests that the five dimensions constituting the whole self are the individual self, the family self, the spiritual self, the developing self, and the private self. For instance, in India and Japan, the family self is more developed and most people in those countries tend to be focused on the family aspect of selfhood. Multicultural theories of conversion take into account, for instance, the norms of individual self and family self in their assessment of conversion dynamics. Whereas in the West, where the norm is the isolated, autonomous convert, people from some non-Western cultures may convert "en masse," as a group mirrors their contours of selfhood. A viable theory of conversion requires recognition of different forms of selfhood in the person and group and the contours of selfhood subsequent to conversion. Likewise, other social scientific theories of conversion, namely those from anthropological and sociological perspectives, require sensitivity to the perspective of the Western or non-Western assumptions regarding the role of culture and society in the motivations to convert. Conversion theories will be enhanced significantly when people from various parts of the world develop theories reflective of and relevant to indigenous cultures and religions.

Postcolonial theory. This approach seeks to investigate the experience of Africans, Asians, and Latin Americans with imperialism and colonialization. Scholars working in postcolonial theory examine the processes by which the presence of military, economic, and cultural power have shaped the infrastructures and superstructures of societies, cultures, economies, and subjectivities of people in post-colonial nation states. Conversion to a world religion, such as Islam or Christianity, is interpreted as a part of the "colonization of the mind and spirits" of the dominated peoples. Submission and resistance of the colonized in the conversion process are important themes for postcolonial theorists. Furthermore, the blending of the local religious tradition with the world religion, sometimes understood as syncretism, often creates a robust and creative religious experience. That is to say, understanding conversion in a postcolonial context involves recognizing human actors as actively engaged in negotiating strategies and tactics of submission as well as resistance and innovation.

Identity theory. With increased urbanization and modernization, along with ethnic and religious pluralism, old notions of self, communities, relationships, and convictions are changing. In social psychology and sociology, identity theory suggests that conversion is a process of gaining convictions and values that consolidate understandings of the self to structure the relationships with others and to provide a sense of continuity in a fragmented world. In this sense, conversion consolidates identity and helps to maintain it through time, providing a sense of meaning in a world characterized by social mobility and anomie.

Intellectualist theory. According to Robin Horton, human actors seek to understand, predict, and control space-time events. Horton proffered a theory of microcosm and macrocosm based on his work in Africa. In the African context, the microcosm consisted of the quotidian world occupying most of a community's daily activities. Their religious life concerned the explanation, prediction, and control of their concrete world. However, virtually all groups, according to Horton, had a macrocosm—the wider world—that was only minimally developed because their daily energy was focused on the microcosm. With increasing social mobility small-scale African communities interacted with people from a wider social world, which expanded the myths, rituals, and symbols of the small-scale societies to include the macrocosm—a broader world of a high god, rationalized religion, and often a formal scripture. Horton's theory reflects evolutionary motifs, since the theory assumes that conversion entails a movement from microcosm to macrocosm based on active cognitive decision-making.

Narrative theory. Some scholars assert that conversion involves, among other things, learning a new narrative that reconstructs a person's biography in light of a new allegiance, a new theology, and a new set of rituals. Biographical reconstruction and the resulting narrative provides new meaning to a person's self, God (or other transcendent reality of a particular tradition), relationships, community, and world. Conversion in this sense means adopting a new story that resonates with the convert, finding connections between "my" story and "the" story, and incorporating the story into one's own life narrative. Conversion stories among evangelical Christian traditions frequently present themselves as personal testimonies, often weaving biblical stories and themes into the convert's own narrative, and thus making past biblical truths contemporaneous with the current believer's own experience. Likewise, a convert to Buddhism can speak of a personal experience of awakening along the lines as prescribed in the Buddhist scriptures.

Globalization theory. The increasing interconnectedness and ease of global communication systems, such as television, radio, and the Internet, and ease of mobility through airlines, automobiles, and trains have invigorated and, in some cases, made possible the growth of new religious movements, the spread and intensification of world religions, and the global revitalization of such movements. Globalization has enabled unprecedented mass communication, through which the yearnings for spiritual renewal and transformation are contacted and cultivated. For example, through globalized media even hinterland villages may have access to religious programming and watch images of the Muslim pilgrimage *(ḥājj)*, Christian televangelists healing the sick, or Hindu devotees chanting sacred text, all beamed in from distant locations. Scholars of the globalization theory of conversion stress not only the content of the message but the form of the communication.

Religious/Spiritual Theories. Religious and spiritual theories include:

Theological theories. Whenever scholars employ theory to illuminate their data, it is important to keep in mind that all attempts at understanding complex phenomena are inherently reductionist. Theoretical biases and perspectives come into play in all theory construction. As such, some scholars of conversion note the normative issues within each religion. Historically, earlier discussions of the theologies of conversion were dominated by evangelical Christians, whereas liberal Christians emphasized social concerns. The Roman Catholic Church, following the reforms of the Second Vatican Council (1962–1965), also began to reexamine the phenomena of conversion. Historically, Buddhism, Christianity, and Islam have been the "missionary religions" aimed explicitly at converting others. Newer religious movements, such as the Church of Jesus Christ of Latter-day Saints and the Unification Church, each have their own set of normative guidelines for what constitutes authentic conversions. For one, conversion may entail accepting a God as revealed by a prophet (e.g., Joseph Smith and Mormonism), but for others, conversion may consist in accepting the prophetic insight of a founder that may be focused less on a transcendent being than on an immediate experience of belonging and community.

Whether scholars write from within a particular religious tradition or from a variety of theoretical perspectives, many recognize the crucial role of religious experience, divine intervention, and transcendence. They apply descriptions and definitions of the process of conversion according to their theological anthropology, their doctrine of human nature. These normative theologies disclose their assumptions regarding the deep structures of the human being and focus on the way in which human beings were created, their desires and aspirations, the human predicament, and, in some traditions, the urgent need for a relationship with a transcendent being or law that gives meaning, orientation, and, indeed, even their salvation.

Translation. Another feature of the phenomenon of conversion is the relationship between sacred texts and the convert. Some religions affirm the sacred quality of a particular language as it is used for prayer, worship, and reading, while others emphasize the inherent translatability of scriptures, with the assumption that the Divine endorses mother-tongue communication. Islam, which affirms the distinctively sacred role of Arabic, exemplifies the former and Christianity and Buddhism, which has since their beginnings emphasized translation into vernacular languages, the latter. The translatability and untranslatability of sacred texts plays a significant role in understanding the conversion process as lives of converts are shaped and guided in part by sacred texts and the cultural and revelatory traditions that in part gave rise to them.

Convergence Models. Convergence models include:

Process theory. Lewis R. Rambo developed a stage model of conversion as a heuristic device that attempts to illuminate the phenomena by highlighting crucial dynamics and elements of religious change. It is important to note that while Rambo's theory is neither unilinear nor universal, the usefulness of his model lies in its ability to systematically organize the complex phenomena of religious change as well as some of the technical issues emerging in conversion scholarship. It should be noted that this stage model does not assume a discrete, unidirectional movement through the stages, but rather a dynamic process of interplay between the stages.

Rambo lays out seven stages of the converting process. Stage one identifies the context in which converting takes place, which functions as the matrix of conversion. Stage two is crisis, where disordering and disrupting experiences call into question a person's or group's taken-for-granted world. This crisis is often triggered by the interaction of external or internal forces, exemplified by colonial contact in the former case and the words of a charismatic religious leader in the latter. Stage three is quest, which encompasses different ways people actively respond to crises. Stage four is encounter, which describes the contact between the potential convert and the advocate of a new religious option. Stage five is interaction, in which the converting person or group learns more about the teachings, lifestyle, and expectations of the group, and is required to begin making alterations in beliefs, rituals, and relationships that are consistent with the prescriptions and proscriptions of a new religious community. Stage six is commitment, where a decision is required and, in many cases, a public demonstration of the status change is expected. Stage seven is consequences. Given the fact that converts are in the process of changing many different aspects of their life, discernment of the nature of these changes is important. Indeed, some religious traditions seek to assess the authenticity of a conversion based on these changes. The criteria are based on the expectations of specific religious communities, including such dimensions of affective, intellectual, ethical, religious, and social/political domains. Scholars of conversion assess the consequences based on criteria derived from their own disciplines, whether from history, social sciences, religious studies, or otherwise. Many scholars of conversion believe that authentic conversion is a continuous process of transformation.

Feminist theory. Feminist theory elucidates the influence of gender inequality in all aspects of life. In Western society, patriarchy has generally dominated society, culture, and religion, giving priority to male perspectives in religious, social, cultural, and economic domains. As a result, feminist studies of conversion have only recently emerged. Feminist theory points to issues that need to be addressed in the study of religious change. For instance, do women experience conversion differently from men, and, if so, in what ways? Do religious models of conversion constrict and distort women's motivations, needs, and desires? Is religious conversion healing and helpful to women, or just another mode of domination? Preliminary studies indicate that, indeed, women do experience conversion differently than men, have significantly different motivations for conversion, and often approach the process of religious change in different ways. Future conversion studies must incorporate feminists' concerns in research and writing.

Christianization and Islamization theory. In the conversion studies literature there is a growing body of work that falls under the broad headings of Christianization and Islamization theories. These studies explore the religious, historical, cultural, social, political, economic, and ideological factors and forces that create and sustain comprehensive processes by which religions, in these cases Christianity and Islam, are disseminated, cultivated, consolidated, and sustained by a wide range of forces that create an environment in which individual religious change takes place. These processes have parallels in discussions of other inclusive processes called Sankritization, Buddhization, Confucianization, Hellenization, modernization, and secularization. Some scholars of conversion would reject this all-embracing process as being called conversion. It is, however, accurate to say that in many studies of conversion and in the ordinary use of the term, it is common to speak of the conversion of Armenia, the Roman Empire, the Philippines, Syria, and so forth. Conversion must be seen as more than merely individual religious change because it usually entails the transformation of political, social, and cultural environments that create what might be described as an ecology of conversion that makes individual conversion possible.

All-inclusive studies often focus on geographical areas in which Christianity or Islam gain ascendancy. In the case of Christianity, these include explorations of the Christianization of the Roman Empire, British Isles, Europe, Russia, Latin America, the Philippines, and Korea. Studies of conversion to Islam include such geographical areas as Arabia, Iran, Egypt, Africa, Southeast Asia, India, the Malay Archipelago, Britain, Europe, and so forth. Few of these studies emphasize individual experience but rather the roles persons might play as missionaries, emissaries, leaders (charismatic or otherwise), or traders. Most focus on Christianization or Islamization, in other words, the creation of social, cultural, religious, and political environments in which individuals, families, communities, and societies flourish as Christian or Muslim zones of influence and power. Many such studies are, of course, historical, but there are also examinations of the processes of Christian or Islamic conversion using various interpretative models such as the diffusion of innovation theory by Richard W. Bulliet.

In the study of Islamization, other theoretical explanations for Islamic conversion include the use of force, attractiveness of Islam as a movement for the liberation of slaves and soldiers, compliance with new political regimes, desire for the privileges of Islamic political power (e.g. tax relief), influence of traders (through intermarriage and patronage relationships), attractiveness of monotheism (especially for those from "pagan" and "primal" religions), and the provision of mystical and transcendent experiences through such things as Ṣūfī modes of spirituality. In the case of Christianization, explanations for conversion, in addition to some of the same interpretations as those used for Islam, include experiences of healing, the attraction of communities of grace and fellowship, the appeal to women of new understandings of the role of women, and the deployment of various forms of persuasion, coercion, and force.

BRIEF ILLUSTRATIONS. Conversion to Christianity in the archipelagic nation of Indonesia, the largest Muslim country in the world, during the mid-1960s illustrates the complexity of the phenomena, combining elements of globalization, postcolonial, and identity theories. Since its independence on August 17, 1945, Indonesia, with more than 13,000 islands, has experienced a series of social, political, and economic crises that threaten to pull the country apart. September 30, 1965, marks the failed coup attempt on President Sukarno by left-wing officers. The Indonesian Communist Party (PKI) was held responsible for the coup attempt, and military and Muslim organizations responded by purging the communist threat in the nation. Most reports estimate that about 500,000 people were killed. Some converted to Hinduism. More striking is the fact that roughly two million Javanists and Chinese converted to Christianity to quickly unite themselves with a government-recognized religion and thereby distance themselves from any association with the PKI. Social and political realities, along with personal concerns, play an important role in understanding conversion. Conversion patterns in Indonesia during the unstable period of 1965–1966 suggest that sometimes conversion may be appealing because it distances the convert from the larger population. For instance, in the Indonesian case, Javanist and Chinese converts became Christians rather than Muslims, who were part of the punishing forces.

Throughout the history of conversion worldwide there have been moments where conversions were imposed by force or, at least, strongly encouraged in order for people to prosper in a newly established social order. The use of military force, social pressure, and economic incentives has been employed by followers of world religions at least at some point in their histories to bring people into the fold. These external forces of conversion can be potent motivators for religious change, and sometimes the fundamentalist interpretation of a religion can in part provide legitimation for such aggression. The history of colonialism is replete with instances of forcible conversions, where external forces played a significant role in conversion patterns.

While it is true that all conversions are both contextual and personal, scholars can also discern whether a conversion is caused and experienced primarily within in the personal sphere and which are influenced primarily by contextual dynamics. Another way to state this issue is to what degree is a conversion primarily internal and which is fundamentally contextual? Moreover, many theistic traditions would simply suggest that conversion is the result of a god who calls people to join the community of faithful followers of truth, thus recognizing a force (i.e., God) that is beyond both personal and contextual domains. It must be expressed, however, that all personal conversions are influenced by the context and all contextual conversions are experienced personally.

The contemporary social and political world is shaped in part by the pervasive influence of conversion. Buddhism pervades Thailand, Burma, Cambodia, Vietnam, and continues to have an important impact on China, Korea, Japan, and much of Asia. Islam is the dominant religion of the Middle East, Indonesia, parts of south Asia, and in many areas of Africa. Christianity is predominant in Europe, the Americas, Australia, and the Philippines, and has experienced significant resurgence in the non-Western world. The presence of world religions on all six continents represents members from diaspora communities but also converts to those religions. Latin America exemplifies a region where conversion within a religion, that is, from Roman Catholicism to Pentecostalism, has given way to significant social change, with about half of Latin America's Pentecostals living in Brazil. The religious world is a dynamic force field of dissemination, conflict, establishment, decline, renewal, and reversals of various religious movements, institutions, and ideologies. Conversion is integral to these transformations. The cultural geography of the world continues to be shaped by the dynamics of religious change.

Bibliography

Buckser, Andrew, and Stephen D. Glazier, eds. *The Anthropology of Religious Conversion.* Lanham, Md., 2003.

Bulliet, Richard W. *Conversion to Islam in the Medieval Period: An Essay in Quantitative History.* Cambridge, Mass., 1979.

Collins, Kenneth J., and John Tyson, eds. *Conversion in the Wesleyan Tradition.* Nashville, 2001.

Davidman, Lynn. *Tradition in a Rootless World: Women Turn to Orthodox Judaism.* Berkeley, Calif., 1991.

Farhadian, Charles E. "Comparing Conversions among the Dani of Irian Jaya." In *The Anthropology of Religious Conversion,* edited by Andrew Buckser and Stephen D. Glazier, pp. 55–68. Lanham, Md., 2003.

Gelpi, Donald L. *The Conversion Experience.* New York, 1998.

Hefner, Robert W., ed. *Conversion to Christianity: Historical and Anthropological Perspectives on a Great Transformation.* Berkeley, Calif., 1993.

Horton, Robin. "African Conversion." *Africa* 41, no. 2 (1971): 85–108.

James, William. *The Varieties of Religious Experience* (1902). Cambridge, Mass., 1986.

Juster, Susan. "'In a Different Voice': Male and Female Narratives of Religious Conversion in Post-Revolutionary America." *American Quarterly* 41, no. 1 (March 1989): 34–62.

Kahn, Peter J., and A. L. Green. "Seeing Conversion Whole: Testing a Model of Religious Conversion." *Pastoral Psychology* 52, no. 3 (January 2004): 233–257.

Kaplan, Steve, ed. *Indigenous Responses to Western Christianity.* New York, 1996.

Kapstein, Matthew T. *The Tibetan Assimilation of Buddhism: Conversion, Contestation, and Memory.* New York, 2000.

Kirkpatrick, Lee A., and Philip R. Shaver. "Attachment Theory and Religion: Childhood Attachments, Religious Beliefs, and Conversion." *Journal for the Scientific Study of Religion* 29, no. 3 (1990): 316–334.

Kose, Ali. *Conversion to Islam: A Study of Native British Converts.* London, 1996.

Levtzion, Nehemia, ed. *Conversion to Islam.* New York, 1979.

MacMullen, Ramsay. *Christianizing the Roman Empire (AD 100–400).* New Haven, Conn., 1984.

Montgomery, Robert L. *The Diffusion of Religions.* Lanham, Md., 1996.

Montgomery, Robert L. *The Lopsided Spread of Christianity: Toward an Understanding of the Diffusion of Religions.* Westport, Conn., 2001.

Mills, Kenneth, and Anthony Grafton, eds. *Conversion in Late Antiquity and the Early Middle Ages: Seeing and Believing.* Rochester, N.Y., 2003.

Mills, Kenneth, and Anthony Grafton, eds. *Conversion: Old Worlds and New.* Rochester, N.Y., 2003.

Muldoon, James, ed. *Varieties of Religious Conversion in the Middle Ages.* Gainesville, Fla., 1997.

Nock, Arthur Darby. *Conversion: The Old and New in Religion from Alexander the Great to Augustine of Hippo.* Oxford, 1933.

Popp-Baier, Ulrike. "Conversion as a Social Construction." In *Empirical Studies in Theology,* edited by Chris A. M. Hermans, Jan van der Lans, Aad de Jong, and Gerrit Immink, pp. 41–61. Leiden and Boston, 2002.

Porton, Gary G. *The Stranger within Your Gates: Converts and Conversion in Rabbinic Literature.* Chicago, 1994.

Poston, Larry. *Islamic Daʿwah in the West: Muslim Missionary Activity and the Dynamics of Conversion to Islam.* New York, 1992.

Rambo, Lewis R. *Understanding Religious Conversion.* New Haven, Conn., 1993.

Rambo, Lewis R. "Theories of Conversion." *Social Compass* 46, no. 3 (September 1999): 259–271.

Rambo, Lewis R. "Anthropology and the Study of Conversion." In *The Anthropology of Religious Conversion,* edited by Andrew Buckser and Stephen D. Glazier, pp. 211–222. Lanham, Md., 2003.

Rambo, Lewis R., and Charles E. Farhadian. "Converting: Stages of Religious Change." In *Religious Conversion: Contemporary Practices and Controversies,* edited by Christopher Lamb and M. Darrol Bryant, pp. 23–34. London, 1999.

Robinson, Rowena, and Sathianathan Clarke, eds. *Religious Conversion in India: Modes, Motivations, and Meanings.* New Delhi, 2003.

Roland, Alan. *In Search of Self in India and Japan: Toward a Cross-Cultural Psychology.* Princeton, N.J., 1988.

Sandos, James A. *Converting California: Indians and Franciscans in the Missions.* New Haven, Conn., 2004.

Sanneh, Lamin. *Translating the Message.* Maryknoll, N.Y., 1998.

Smith, Curtis D. "Religion and Crisis in Jungian Analysis." *Counseling and Values* 34 (April 1990): 177–185.

Smith, Gordon T. *Beginning Well: Christian Conversion and Authentic Transformation.* Downers Grove, Ill., 2001.

Spilka, Bernard, and Daniel N. McIntosh. "Attribution Theory and Religious Experience." In *Handbook of Religious Experience,* edited by Ralph W. Hood, Jr., pp. 421–445. Birmingham, Ala., 1995.

Stewart, Charles, and Rosalind Shaw, eds. *Syncretism/Anti-Syncretism: The Politics of Religious Synthesis.* New York, 1994.

Stromberg, Peter G. *Language and Self-Transformation: A Study of the Christian Conversion Narrative.* New York, 1993.

Ullman, Chana. *The Transformed Self: The Psychology of Religious Conversion.* New York, 1989.

van der Veer, Peter, ed. *Conversion to Modernities: The Globalization of Christianity.* New York, 1996.

Viswanathan, Gauri. *Outside the Fold: Conversion, Modernity, and Belief.* Princeton, N.J., 1998.

Lewis R. Rambo (1987 and 2005)
Charles E. Farhadian (2005)

COOMARASWAMY, ANANDA (1877–1947),

Sinhala art historian and religious thinker who spent the last three decades of his life in the United States.

Coomaraswamy's work falls into three periods, distinguished less by topic than by purpose and sensibility. From 1903 to 1916, as a young scholar and idealistic author, Coomaraswamy was a well-known proponent of traditional Indian and Sinhala culture and a stirring essayist on behalf of cultural and political independence in both countries, then under British rule. He was also an extraordinarily perspicacious art historian who discovered and restored in historical perspective one of the great schools of Indian painting. In his middle years, from 1917 to 1931, when he was curator of Indian and Muslim art at the Museum of Fine Arts in Boston, he applied his erudition to the production of a series of scholarly books and articles on Asian art; many of these works are still consulted for both fact and interpretation. Unlike the publications of his youth, which show more than a trace of late romantic idealism and a concern for literary finesse, the works of his middle period are scientific in the best sense: directed toward factual knowledge and coolly analytical in approach. In 1932 Coomaraswamy began to combine his early, value-oriented scholarship with the factuality of his middle period; this synthesis led to the masterful works of his old age. In book after book, essay after essay—he was once described as "New England's most prolific author"—Coomaraswamy undertook a scholarly and yet visionary exploration of traditional religious art and culture, primarily of India and medieval Europe. These works, his final contribution, have an eloquence, a force of conviction, and a stunning erudition that make them still, and perhaps classically, a literature to which both scholars and seekers may turn for guidance and inspiration.

Born in Ceylon (present-day Sri Lanka) to a distinguished Hindu legislator and his English wife, Ananda Kentish Coomaraswamy was educated in England. He earned the degree of doctor of science in geology from London University and in 1902 returned to Ceylon as a geologist. There he combined professional work with a growing interest in the indigenous, precolonial culture of the island, which had been weakened by nearly a century of British rule. Deeply influenced by William Morris (1834–1896), the British craftsman, author, and humanitarian socialist, Coomaraswamy toured the island, making observations and taking photographs that became the substance of his first major nongeological publication, *Mediaeval Sinhalese Art* (1908). The book was a pioneering effort to inventory and interpret a traditional and inherently religious art.

Coomaraswamy's geological career gave way to his authentic vocation. Shifting his interest and residence to the larger world of India, where he became an intimate of the family of the poet Rabindranath Tagore (1861–1941) and an active polemicist on behalf of *swadeshi* ("home rule"), Coomaraswamy also engaged in studies of art history that gradually drew near a major discovery. His *Indian Drawings* (1910) and its companion *Indian Drawings, Second Series, Chiefly Rajput* (1912) are primarily portfolios of illustrations and are of limited textual interest, but they mark the beginning of a reversal in British (and Western) opinion of Indian art that was largely due to the efforts of Coomaraswamy and his colleagues, such as the British critic Roger Fry, in the newly founded India Society.

Coomaraswamy's next major publication in the field of art history, *Rajput Painting* (1916; reprint, 1975), formally disclosed to the world the Hindu painting of Rajasthan and the Punjab, now universally admired and widely studied but essentially unknown until Coomaraswamy's research. Confused with contemporaneous Muslim painting, the masterworks of this art lay unrecognized in obscure collections throughout India and had hardly been valued until Coomaraswamy traveled far and wide, built a splendid collection, and for the first time interpreted them in historical and aesthetic terms.

During these predominantly Indian years, broken by sojourns in England, where he maintained a home, Coomaraswamy also published *Myths of the Hindus and Buddhists* (1913) and *Buddha and the Gospel of Buddhism* (1916). The latter is an early and graceful summary of Buddhism for general readers, published in an era that had seen few if any studies of its quality. Essays from this period were collected a few years later for his first American publication, *The Dance of Shiva* (1918; reprint, 1957). Coomaraswamy had recently moved to the United States, and this widely read book established his popular reputation there as an authority on Indian culture.

Accepting a curatorial post at the Boston Museum, which acquired his unique collection of Indian painting, Coomaraswamy now entered his period of rigorous scholarly effort. His work in the 1920s is epitomized by two publications, the multivolume *Catalogue of the Indian Collections in the Museum of Fine Arts, Boston* (1923ff) and his *History of Indian and Indonesian Art* (1927; reprint, 1972). Both works of exact scholarship in art history were written as a much-needed service to the field he had helped to found.

As noted above, Coomaraswamy's work—and undoubtedly his person—underwent a major transformation in about 1932. While he continued to write art history at nearly his customary pace, he also began to publish studies of the religions, myths, aesthetics, and traditional cultures of India and medieval Europe—indeed, of tradition wherever he encountered it. The art historian ceded some ground to the religious thinker and philosopher; the scientist ceded to the man of conviction, who contrasted the secular, industrialized way of life in the modern world with the traditional order of life in which knowledge is primarily religious and art is visible religion. Although the books and essays of this period were born of a powerful conviction that modern man must remember and allow himself to be moved by the depth and light of tradition, Coomaraswamy's writings were not predominantly polemic in character; for the most part they are encyclopedic works that explore the metaphysics and theology, the iconography and symbols, and the artistic and social forms of the East and West, often on a comparative basis.

Coomaraswamy was one of the first erudite practitioners of cross-cultural study and interpretation to be biased—if he was at all—toward the East. His later works initiate the reader unforgettably into both the general structure and the countless details that constitute traditional religious culture in the premodern world. Occasional polemic essays drive home, with wit and passion, the importance that this lesson in ancient things holds for modern man. No brief summary can do justice to his works in this period. It must suffice to say that they blend remarkable scholarship with the dispassionate quality of religious passion known in Indian tradition as jñana. As he once asked in an essay, "Can we imagine a perfected ardor apart from understanding, or a perfected understanding without ardor?"

BIBLIOGRAPHY

The major works from Coomaraswamy's late period include *The Transformation of Nature in Art* (1934; New York, 1956), *Elements of Buddhist Iconography* (1935; New Delhi, 1972), *Why Exhibit Works of Art?* (1943; reprinted as *Christian and Oriental Philosophy of Art*, New York, 1956), *Hinduism and Buddhism* (1943; Westport, Conn., 1971), *Figures of Speech or Figures of Thought* (London, 1946), *Am I My Brother's Keeper?* (New York, 1947), and *Time and Eternity* (Ascona, 1947). A three-volume collection entitled *Coomaraswamy* (vol. 1, *Selected Papers: Traditional Art and Symbolism*; vol. 2, *Selected Papers: Metaphysics*; vol. 3, *His Life and Work*), respectively edited and written by me (Princeton, 1977), gathers additional writings from the late period and explores Coomaraswamy's life and mind, with emphasis on the later years.

New Sources

Coomaraswamy, Ananda K. "The Interior Image." *Parabola* 11, no. 2 (May 1986): 14–19.

Coomaraswamy, Ananda K. *Early Indian Architecture: Huts, and Related Temple Types.* Cambridge, Mass., 1988.

ROGER LIPSEY (1987)
Revised Bibliography

COPERNICUS, NICOLAUS

COPERNICUS, NICOLAUS (1473–1543), Polish cleric and astronomer, was born Mikołaj Kopernik in Torún, Poland, on February 19, 1473. He was raised in the comfortable circumstances of a wealthy burgher family and was educated at the cathedral school. Upon the death of his father in 1583, Copernicus and his younger brother Andreas were taken under the guardianship of their maternal uncle, Canon Lucas Watzenrode, who had been trained in the cosmopolitan humanist atmosphere of Bologna and later was made prince bishop of the Diocese of Warmia. Copernicus matriculated in the Collegium Maius of the renowned Jagiellonian University of Kraków, which at that time was strong in mathematics and had an endowed chair of astronomy dating from 1410. Copernicus's study of the theories of such luminaries as Ptolemy, Euclid, Sacrobosco, and Regiomontanus was complemented by his own observation in Kraków of the comets of 1491 and 1492 and of four lunar and solar eclipses during the next two years.

In 1496 Copernicus and his brother were sent to Bologna by their uncle to further their educations. During his decade in Italy, Copernicus studied medicine at Padua, continued his observations of the heavens, and became well enough versed in philosophy and classical literature to translate the letters of a Byzantine poet into Latin. In 1503 Copernicus took his degree in canon law from the University of Ferrara. Watzenrode had arranged for Copernicus's election to a benefice in the Diocese of Warmia to ensure his nephew's financial independence, and Copernicus returned to Poland to embark upon his duties as a canon of Frombork Cathedral. For the next four decades he was engaged in ecclesiastical administration and other service to the diocese. He wrote an important treatise on coinage, painted a self-portrait, and conscientiously practiced medicine. Astronomy remained his passion, however, and in 1510 he built a modest observatory in a tower near the cathedral.

COPERNICUS AND ASTRONOMY. In order to evaluate Copernicus's significance in relation to religion, one must first understand how he transformed astronomy. His enduring legacy was the rehabilitation of the long-neglected heliocentric hypothesis. The concept of a moving earth was not new of course, having been proposed in the third century BCE by Aristarchus of Samos and discussed by Archimedes, although Philolaus and Ecphantus the Pythagoreans are the ancients whom Copernicus mentions in connection with the idea. But the ancient arguments against heliocentrism, both from common sense and from lack of observed stellar parallax, had been so overwhelming that the alternative geocentric cosmology prevailed from antiquity through the late Middle Ages.

Aristotle (384–322 BCE) envisioned a set of nested concentric spheres bearing the planets, the sun, the moon, and the stars around a spherical, stationary earth. This system was enlarged and codified by the second-century Egyptian astronomer Ptolemy in the *Almagest*, which became the basic astronomical text of the scholastic canon. In order to preserve uniform circular motion while accounting for the periodic retrograde motion of the planets against the backdrop of the fixed stars, the system invoked a scheme of epicycles and eccentrics that revolved on the deferent circle about the equant point. Ptolemaic astronomy was integrated with Aristotelian physics in scholastic science, in which circular motion was proper to the heavens and rectilinear motion to the earth and in which the four terrestrial elements (earth, water, fire, and air) were disposed appropriately according to their degrees of levity or gravity. The pre-Copernican cosmology was in turn integrated with theology to form an orderly scholastic synthesis of physics, astronomy, and theology. Each science in this hierarchy of disciplines operated from its own set of principles, and together they governed everything from the nature of matter and planetary motion to the geographic location of heaven and hell.

By the sixteenth century Ptolemaic astronomy had begun to encounter difficulties in accurately predicting celestial phenomena. The system of eccentrics and epicycles revolving about the equant point "saved the appearances" in accounting for retrograde planetary movements without sacrificing uniform circular motion. But the minute inaccuracies of this system when compounded annually over more than a millennium had pushed astronomical reckoning off by ten days. This cumulative error posed serious calendrical problems, including the difficulty of correctly calculating the date of Easter, the central Christian feast on which much of the church year was based.

As Copernicus continued his quest for improving predictive accuracy in astronomy, he gradually turned his attention to the possibility of a moving earth, sketching his system in the *Commentariolus.* This unpublished outline circulated widely in draft form among his students before 1514 and challenged established tradition by proposing three kinds of terrestrial motion: (1) real diurnal rotation of the earth to account for the apparent diurnal rotation of the heavens; (2) annual revolution about the stationary sun to account for the solar year; and (3) motion in declination to account for the precession of the equinoxes.

Copernicus continued to elaborate his planetary theory during the next quarter century. In 1539 a Lutheran scholar from Wittenberg named Georg Joachim Rheticus (1514–1574) learned of Copernicus's theory and traveled to Frombork to study it in detail with the Catholic astronomer. He became Copernicus's first disciple, published his own sketch of the system, *Narratio Prima,* in 1540, and finally persuaded Copernicus to offer his theory to the world. The latter in 1541 authorized Rheticus to carry a copy of the manuscript to Nuremberg, where it was published by Johannes Petreius under the title *De revolutionibus orbium coelestium libri sex* (1543). As circumstances did not permit Rheticus to remain in Nuremberg to oversee publication, that duty was entrusted to the Lutheran theologian Andreas Osiander (1498–1552), who added an unauthorized preface stating, "These hypotheses need not be true nor even probable; if they provide a calculus consistent with the observations, that alone is sufficient." Osiander emphasized the hypothetical nature of astronomy used as a calculating device, apparently for the purpose of protecting the work from overzealous censors. But whether or not Copernicus was aware of this preface when *De revolutionibus* was presented to him in 1543 as he lay dying, he almost certainly would not have agreed with Osiander's disclaimer that heliocentrism should be treated as a mathematical convenience rather than as a genuine claim about the true physical nature of the cosmos.

De revolutionibus sits in the paradoxical position of being on the one hand essentially a conservative work in the classical tradition of astronomy and on the other hand a book that sparked a major revolution in scientific thought. With the exception of an engaging broad exposition of the system in the first of its six books, *De revolutionibus* is a highly mathematical treatise that made few initial converts. Although it was widely read in astronomical circles, fewer than a dozen committed Copernicans before 1600 can be identified.

As a conservative reformer, Copernicus preserved the assumption of uniform circular motion and continued to employ Ptolemy's epicycles and eccentrics. Indeed he has been referred to as the last great Ptolemaic astronomer. Where he departed from the tradition of Ptolemy was in pursuing the insight that shifting the reference frame from the earth to the sun not only increased observational accuracy but for the first time made logical sense out of the order of the planets. Rather than viewing the sun, moon, and planets with their varying dimensions as arbitrarily assigned to widely divergent periods and orbital angles, a heliocentric system generated an intrinsic order. The planets farthest from the sun had the longest orbital periods and the widest orbital angles, while those closest to the center revolved most tightly and rapidly around the sun. Likewise the Copernican model also made coherent sense of retrograde motion. Instead of interpreting the looping paths of the planets against the sidereal backdrop as actual celestial occurrences, Copernicus understood these motions to be mere optical illusions resulting from the annual revolution of the terrestrial observatory inside or outside the orbits of its fellow planets. Copernicus offered a remarkably prescient rebuttal to Ptolemy's objection that a moving earth would leave any loose objects drifting westward. He suggested two possible explanations, one based on an Aristotelian mingling of qualities and another on the idea of momentum: "The reason may be either that the nearby air, mingling with earthy or watery matter, conforms to the same nature as the earth, or that [this] air's motion, acquired from the earth by proximity, shares without resistance in its unceasing rotation" (*DR* I.8).

Astronomers appreciated the increased predictive accuracy of Copernicus's system, although initial reaction to his revolutionary postulate was guarded. More significantly the fruitfulness of his effort may better be measured by the range and diversity of theories he stimulated. *De revolutionibus* gave free rein to an incremental rethinking of astronomy and physics that challenged the existing hierarchy of disciplines and that within a century blossomed into a full-scale scientific revolution. Ptolemaic astronomy no longer offered a satisfactory architectonic vision of the cosmos, and Copernicus was not the only thinker prepared to suggest an alternative model. The Danish astronomer Tycho Brahe (1546–1601) proposed a "geo-heliocentric" model in which the five planets revolve around the sun, which in turn revolves with the moon around the earth. Brahe appreciated Copernicus's success in circumventing the most discordant aspects of the Ptolemaic system, but he personally could not overcome a revulsion of ascribing to the sluggish earth the quick motion shared by the "ethereal torches." But Brahe did initiate a break with the Aristotelian assumption of celestial immutability when he claimed that the nova of 1572 was in fact a new star and when he concluded that, because the comet of 1577 looped around the sun in an orbit closer than that of Venus, there could be no crystalline spheres.

Copernicus and Brahe inhabited a pre-Newtonian, predynamical age, and their respective modifications of geocentrism remained committed to uniform circular motion as a perfection proper to the heavens. A more remarkable departure from classical astronomy was initiated by Brahe's student Johannes Kepler (1571–1630), whose close observation of Mars led him to postulate elliptical planetary orbits with the sun occupying one focus of the ellipse. The psychological impact of this "breaking of the circle" was arguably a challenge greater even than the shift to heliocentrism, and the introduction of a dynamic element was a significant step on the path to the eventual Newtonian synthesis.

Further challenges unfolded with the telescopic observations of Galileo Galilei (1564–1642). Galileo's publication of *Sidereus nuncius* (1610) provided physical evidence that seemed to confirm the mathematical theory of heliocentrism, although genuine empirical proof of the earth's annual orbital motion only arrived with Friedrich Wilhelm Bessel's (1784–1846) establishment of stellar parallax in the 1830s and the confirmation of diurnal axial rotation awaited Jean-Bernard-Léon Foucault's (1819–1868) pendulum in 1851. Nevertheless Galileo's charting of the revolutions of the moons of Jupiter and the phases of Venus suggested, by analogy, the plausibility of the heliocentric cosmological model. Likewise his observation of lunar craters implied the similarity of the moon to the earth, and his discovery of sunspots furthered the argument that mutability is not confined only to the terrestrial realm.

REACTIONS TO COPERNICUS'S THEORY. The fortunes of the Copernican hypothesis were shaped not only by its incremental scientific acceptance but also by factors such as the flexibility of intellectual culture and the circumstances of ecclesiastical politics. Since the Condemnations of 1277 the church had wisely refrained from committing itself to a single cosmological model, and Nicole d'Oresme (c. 1325–1382), bishop of Lisieux, had felt free to consider a number of arguments for diurnal rotation in his 1377 commentary on Aristotle's *De caelo.* Copernicus himself dedicated *De revolutionibus* to Pope Paul III, and the immediate response on the part of the post-Tridentine church was such that no particular restrictions were imposed on Catholic astronomers. However, whereas the Counter-Reformation was not in itself antiscientific, it was certainly not about to embrace innovations that would undermine its dogmas. One consequence of this was the papal mandate to carry out policies of the Council of Trent (1545–1563), including reinforcing exegesis that emphasized wherever possible the literal interpretation of the Bible.

Moreover astronomical speculation could also carry heterodox implications, as in the case of Giordano Bruno (1548–1600), who postulated a plurality of worlds and the infinity of the universe. Although Bruno was executed for theological heresy rather than for his scientific views, he was a vehemently anti-Aristotelian admirer of Copernicus, and from the 1590s astronomical innovation became associated with heterodoxy. In the decades after the Council of Trent the Catholic Church entered what William Shea has referred to as a period of restrictive orthodoxies in which Aristotelianism became applied as a mechanical criterion of the truth. In such an atmosphere it is not surprising that the initially favorable reception of Galileo's telescopic discoveries should have been accompanied by suspicion of his Copernicanism and ultimately by the suspension of *De revolutionibus,* "until corrected," by the Congregation of the Index in 1616. This suspension was honored mostly in the breach, and Owen Gingerich has shown that only about 8 percent of the five hundred extant copies of the first edition were censored by their owners in full compliance with the index.

Copernicus's deceptively simple insight in *De revolutionibus* carried with it enormous implications for a wide range of disciplines and questions. In physics and astronomy it played an important role in initiating the process of scientific discovery that has led from Kepler and Galileo through Sir Isaac Newton (1642–1727) and Pierre-Simon de Laplace (1749–1827) to the twenty-first century. In epistemology the Copernican revolution upset the established order of the scholastic curriculum by daring to use mathematics, a lower science, to correct astronomy, a science of higher dignity. An extension of this epistemological challenge was Galileo's elevation of sense experience—in the form of experiment and observation—into a more important role than it had enjoyed under Scholastic Aristotelianism.

Copernicus and his successors also contributed to the secularization of modernity through the disenchantment of cosmology, the removal of the earth from its central location, and the relativization of human concerns by contrast with the infinity of time and space. Copernicus contended that the size of the universe was "similar to the infinite." Theologically an intriguing swing occurred from the church's relative neutrality on cosmology before Copernicus to its rigid adherence to the Aristotelian-Ptolemaic worldview during the Galileo affair and back again to a relative independence from cosmological commitment. Although theology cannot remain wholly apophatic about the world in which it is embedded, too close an adherence to a particular worldview will leave the believer high and dry when the paradigm changes, as inevitably it will. From a modest and relatively self-contained pre-Copernican cosmos focused on the human drama of salvation, scholars have moved to a vast and much less obviously anthropocentric universe. In Copernicus's prophetic words, "So vast, without any question, is the divine handiwork of the most excellent almighty" (*DR* I.10).

SEE ALSO Galileo Galilei; Kepler, Johannes; Newton, Isaac; Ptolemy.

BIBLIOGRAPHY

Copernican studies were enriched with numerous publications surrounding the quincentenary of the astronomer's birth in 1973. The English translation of Copernicus's writings is Nicolaus Copernicus, *Complete Works*, 3. vols. (London, 1972–1992). Edward Rosen, translator, *Three Copernican Treatises,* 3d ed. (New York, 1971), includes an accessible *Commen-*

tariolus and supporting materials. Concise biographical sketches include Wanda M. Stachiewicz's *Copernicus and His World* (Montreal, 1972); and Jan Adamczewski's nicely illustrated *Nicolaus Copernicus and His Epoch* (Philadelphia, 1972). Many of Rosen's meticulous examinations of specific details are in his *Copernicus and His Successors* (London, 1995).

A classic account of Copernicus's astronomical science in a traditional "revolution" context is Thomas S. Kuhn's *The Copernican Revolution* (Cambridge, Mass., 1957). See also Rosen, *Copernicus and the Scientific Revolution* (Malabar, Fla., 1984). Noel M. Swerdlow and Otto Neugebauer provide a detailed analysis in *Mathematical Astronomy in Copernicus's "De revolutionibus"* (New York, 1984), which includes a definitive biographical study by Swerdlow. Various features of Copernicus's science are treated in Owen Gingerich's *The Eye of Heaven: Ptolemy, Copernicus, Kepler* (New York, 1993).

Kenneth J. Howell examines the reception of Copernicanism in light of scriptural exegesis in *God's Two Books: Copernican Cosmology and Biblical Interpretation in Early Modern Science* (Notre Dame, Ind., 2002). For an important study of Protestant and Catholic attitudes to Copernicanism before Galileo, see Robert S. Westman, "The Copernicans and the Churches," in *God and Nature: Historical Essays on the Encounter between Christianity and Science,* edited by David C. Lindberg and Ronald L. Numbers (Berkeley, Calif., 1986). James M. Lattis shows the importance of the Jesuit influence in *Between Copernicus and Galileo: Christoph Clavius and the Collapse of Ptolemaic Cosmology* (Chicago, 1994).

Indispensable to the study of the early fortunes of the heliocentric hypothesis is Gingerich's *An Annotated Census of Copernicus' "De revolutionibus" (Nuremberg, 1543, and Basel, 1566)* (Leiden and Boston, 2002), an examination of over six hundred extant copies of Copernicus's book. Gingerich recounts this quest as an engaging intellectual adventure in *The Book Nobody Read: Chasing the Revolutions of Nicolaus Copernicus* (New York, 2004).

PETER M. J. HESS (2005)

COPTIC CHURCH.

The Coptic church is the ancient church of Egypt; the name *Copt* derives from the Greek *Aiguptioi* ("Egyptians"). According to tradition within the church, its founder and first patriarch was Mark the Evangelist, who first preached Christianity in Alexandria in the forties of the first century CE. For several centuries the new faith interacted in various ways with Judaism, traditional Egyptian religion, Hellenistic philosophy, and Gnosticism, amid sporadic waves of Roman persecution. The consummation of the persecutions came under Diocletian, from the beginning of whose reign in 284 CE the Copts began their own calendar "of the martyrs" (1 *Anno Martyrum*). This church calendar remains in use to the present day.

Biblical and other Christian texts preserved in second- and third-century papyrus manuscripts are testimonies to the penetration of the new faith into Egypt long before the end of the age of persecutions. With the Edict of Milan (313), whereby the emperor Constantine guaranteed freedom of worship to Christians, Alexandria gained in prestige as a major Christian ecclesial and theological center.

THE CATECHETICAL SCHOOL OF ALEXANDRIA. The catechetical school of Alexandria, which appears to have taken shape late in the second century, became a center of Christian scholarship under the leadership of some of the greatest church fathers. Pantaenus, credited with being its first head, is reported to have traveled as an evangelist as far east as India. Clement of Alexandria, who succeeded him, advocated the reconciliation of Christian doctrine and the Bible with Greek philosophy.

The school of Alexandria came of age under Origen, one of the most prolific authors of all time, whose exegetical, philosophical, and theological writings had broad influence on the early church, including such pillars of orthodoxy as his pupils Heraclas (patriarch 230–246, and the first in the annals of the Coptic church to bear the title "pope") and Gregory Thaumatourgos, as well as Antony, Athanasius, the Cappadocian Fathers, and Jerome. The school of Alexandria proved to be an arena of free scholastic endeavor, defending the "catholic" faith in a "pagan" environment, offering the first attempts at a Christian systematic theology, and paving the way for ecumenical developments in the early church.

ECUMENICAL COUNCILS. An ecumenical movement intended to unify the church and combat heresy was inaugurated by Constantine with the Council of Nicaea (325). At this and subsequent councils, "orthodox" teaching was defined for theological questions concerning the (triune) identity of God and the (divine and human) person of Christ. Alexandria played a major role in the early councils, in which the teachings that the Son is *homoousios* ("of one being") with the Father (championed by Athanasius, patriarch 326–373), that the incarnate Word is one Lord and one Son, and that Mary is therefore the *theotokos* or "God bearer" (championed by Cyril, patriarch 412–444) were upheld.

Alexandrian authority appeared to have been cemented at the Second Council of Ephesus (449)—dismissed as a "Robber Council" by Rome—which was dominated by Cyril's nephew, Dioscorus (patriarch 444–454). However, a change of emperors and an alliance of the sees of Rome and Constantinople challenged the Alexandrian ecclesiastical hegemony. The new, pro-Western emperor Marcion called a council in Chalcedon in 451, which promptly condemned Dioscorus (although not on doctrinal grounds), who was consequently deposed and exiled.

Henceforth, the place of the Coptic church in the Christian world was curtailed. Two parallel lines of succession to Mark the Evangelist gradually came into existence. One, allied to the Byzantines (and eventually labeled *melkite*), accepted the "two nature" formula of the Council of Chalcedon for describing the divine and human Christ; the other, which gained strong local support, held to Cyril's "one nature of the incarnate Word" formula, a position called *monophysite* by its opponents.

MONASTICISM. Though several social and economic factors must have played a role in accelerating the withdrawal of Egyptian Christians to the desert, it remains true that early monasticism was principally a movement of piety that, in its earliest stages, was practiced close to home by "village anchorites." Early Christian imagination was captured, however, by the figure of Antony (c. 250–356), who fled to the solitude of the eastern desert from his native village on the Nile after hearing *Matthew* 19:21 ("Jesus said to him, 'If you would be perfect, go, sell what you possess and give to the poor, and you will have treasure in heaven; and come, follow me.'"). Others followed Antony's example and a monastic colony arose around his cave in the Red Sea mountains. There they practiced a life of austerity, prayer, and meditation on scripture. Although committed to solitude, they found it spiritually profitable to be within sight of their great mentor for guidance, and advantageous in a variety of ways to be within reach of other brothers. These circumstances led to the development of a form of monastic life that may be called communal eremiticism. This form of monastic life is familiar from many of the sayings of the Desert Fathers (including such giants as Macarius the Great), many of whom inhabited the monastic centers of Nitria, Cellia, and Scetis (present-day Wādī al-Naṭrūn), to the west of the Nile Delta.

Another form of monastic life, the cenobitic, is associated with the name of Pachomius (d. 346). Originally a pagan legionary, he was inspired by the goodness of Christian villagers who ministered to the needs of the soldiers and was baptized a Christian. After spiritual training by a desert ascetic, Pachomius developed a community and subsequently an original rule. The rule prescribed a carefully regulated communal life and stressed productive labor in addition to the study of scripture, prayer, meditation, and discussion. Pachomian monasteries multiplied rapidly during their founder's life, including foundations for women as well as men, and attracting persons from afar.

The holy men and women of Egypt came to be a source of inspiration throughout the Christian world. Athanasius wrote the *Life of Antony*, which provided a new model of holiness for the world. Visitors to the monks in the late fourth century included Rufinus of Aquileia, who made a Latin translation of the *History of the Monks in Egypt*; Melania the Elder, a great monastic leader and "female man of God;" Palladius, who compiled the lives of the Desert Fathers in *The Lausiac History*; Cassian, who wrote the *Institutes* and the *Conferences* in order to bring Egyptian monasticism to Gaul; and Jerome, who translated the rule of Pachomius into Latin.

MISSIONARY ENDEAVOR. Those who brought the way of life of the Egyptian monks to their homelands may be regarded as unchartered ambassadors of early Egyptian Christianity, but, further, Egyptian Christians themselves were active in an extensive missionary enterprise. The sphere of influence of the patriarch of Alexandria came to include the easternmost part of Libya (the Pentapolis), Nubia, and Ethiopia. The influence of Egyptian Christianity on Nubia, in the upper reaches of the Nile, is confirmed by archaeological excavations. While the Byzantine emperor Justinian (r. 527–565) aimed at winning the northern Nubian kingdom of Nobatia to the Chalcedonian cause, Egyptian anti-Chalcedonians, with the support of the empress Theodora, were able to arrive in the Nobatian capital before the Chalcedonian delegation, and won the Nobatian king for the "one nature" Christian confession.

The conversion of the kingdom of Ethiopia took place in the fourth century. Two Syrian Christian brothers, shipwrecked on their way to India, were taken into the household of the Ethiopian monarch. One of them, Frumentius, was eventually ordained bishop by Athanasius himself, beginning a long association of the Ethiopian church with the See of Saint Mark.

Isolated cases provide instances of Egyptian missionary work in Asia. As mentioned earlier, Pantaenus is said to have preached the gospel in India. Eugenius of Clysma, according to legend, had been a Pachomian monk before he became the founder of monasticism in Mesopotamia.

In Europe, the ideals of the Egyptian desert ruled in the monasteries of southern Gaul and elsewhere, and spread widely: sea, forest, and swampland often played the role of "desert." A popular story concerning Egyptian Christians in present-day Switzerland is that of the Theban Legion, a group of Christian legionaries from Egypt led by Mauritius. They were martyred by Maximian (286–305) for refusing to sacrifice to Roman deities and for refusing to kill Christian converts. Verena, a saintly woman who had accompanied the legion, is commemorated for healing the sick and baptizing new converts in the region of Zurzach. Three martyred saints who were baptized in defiance of imperial command are the subject of the coat of arms of the city of Zurich.

In late antiquity Egypt boasted one of the great Christian pilgrimage centers of the Mediterranean world, the shrine of the Egyptian martyr Menas (southeast of Alexandria). Terra-cotta ampullae bearing the image of the saint have been discovered throughout Europe, bearing witness to the great number of European visitors who flocked to his shrine, especially in the fifth and sixth centuries.

FROM CHALCEDON TO THE ARAB CONQUEST. The Council of Chalcedon in 451, with its condemnation of the Alexandrian patriarch Dioscorus and with its dyophysite ("two nature") interpretation of Cyril's Christological legacy contrary to the miaphysite ("one nature") interpretation of many of Cyril's most ardent supporters, led to the cleavage of Christendom into two divergent camps. To this day, Chalcedon is bitterly remembered by the Copts of Egypt, as well as by others (the Syrian, Ethiopian, and Armenian Orthodox). The outcome of Chalcedon was immediately felt in Egypt: the Byzantine emperors who aimed at unity within the church as the primary bearer of cohesion in the empire attempted to impose that unity through imperial sanction and military support of pro-Chalcedonian patriarchs. In opposition to this, the majority of Egyptian bishops remained faithful to the anti-Chalcedonian position of Dioscorus and elected patriarchs accordingly, although these patriarchs seldom led an untroubled existence: Timothy Aelurus ("the Cat") spent much of his tenure (457–477) in exile, while his successor Peter Mongus (477–490) spent years in hiding until an imperially promulgated doctrinal compromise (the *Henoticon* of Zeno, 482) allowed him to surface. In the next century, under the pro-Chalcedonian emperor Justinian, the anti-Chalcedonian patriarch Theodosius spent long years (537–566) in exile in Constantinople. On the other hand, Coptic tradition recalls that his contemporary, the pro-Chalcedonian patriarch Apollinaris (551–570), began his patriarchate by revealing the priestly robes under his military uniform.

The early seventh century was a period of great disruption in the life of the Egyptian church: a period of Persian occupation (616–629) was followed by Byzantine recovery and the reassertion of coercive pro-Chalcedonian policies in Egypt by the emperor Heraclius, who appointed Cyrus, a bishop from the Caucasus, as Chalcedonian patriarch (631–642). For ten years his anti-Chalcedonian rival Benjamin (patriarch 622–662) was a fugitive within Egypt, moving from monastery to monastery. With the Arab conquest of Egypt in the early 640s, however, a new era began for Egyptian Christians (who were called *al-Qibṭ* by the Arabs). The Arab Muslims promised significant religious freedoms to the "People of the Book," that is, to Christians and Jews, in exchange for acceptance of Arab Muslim rule and the payment of the poll tax or *jizyah*. In fact, after the fall of Alexandria, the conquerors offered the fugitive Coptic patriarch Benjamin honorable safe-conduct and possession of churches hitherto held by the Chalcedonians: the frequently retold story of the friendly meeting between Benjamin and the Muslim general and governor ʿAmr ibn al-ʿĀṣ is foundational to the modern Egyptian discourse of *al-waḥdah al-waṭaniyyah*, "national unity" or good relations between Muslims and Copts.

Life in a "New World Order." Muslim rule created a new barrier between the Christians of the "East" and those of the "West": for Byzantine Christians, or those of the Latin West, the Coptic church (and its Christological teachings) now fell on the other side of the border and largely out of mind. Within the Islamic empire or *Dār al-Islām*, Christians had to adjust to what turned out to be not a temporary incursion like that of the Persians, but a new Islamic world order. Coptic civil servants carried on in their work for new superiors, while church leaders learned new forms of interaction with Muslim governors (and their demands for revenue). The monasteries became more important than ever as centers of Coptic identity and spiritual power, even as Christianity in Alexandria and in the Delta, in particular, began a long period of decline. Periodic Coptic revolts in the Delta (between 725 and 831) failed, and with their failure the Islamization of the region accelerated. In the mid-ninth century, pilgrimage to the shrine of Saint Menas effectively came to an end (as did the revenues it brought the bishop in Alexandria). In the tenth century, the patriarchal residence was displaced from the city of Alexandria to the Delta.

The Shīʿī Fāṭimid dynasty (969–1171 CE) appears to have ushered in a period of stabilization and recovery for the Copts. Coptic civil servants enjoyed high positions in the Fāṭimid administration and Coptic craftsmen flourished. The patriarchal residence was eventually established in churches near the Fāṭimids' new city of *al-Qāhirah* (Cairo). At the end of the tenth century, bishop (and former civil servant) Sāwīrus ibn al-Muqaffaʿ became the first Coptic theologian to write extensively in the Arabic language, while in the late eleventh century both clergy (including patriarchs Christodoulos and Cyril II) and leading laymen (such as Mawhūb ibn Manṣūr ibn Mufarrij) contributed to a project of translation of fundamental documents, including the accounts that became the *History of the Patriarchs* (a primary source for Egyptian church history), from Coptic into Arabic.

The process of Arabization of the Copts (and their literature) continued through the eleventh and twelfth centuries, a period marked with difficulties from the chaos at the end of Fāṭimid rule, periodic drought and famine, and Crusader incursions. At the beginning of the thirteenth century there was a nearly twenty-year vacancy in the patriarchate (1216–1235). These factors make all the more remarkable the cultural flowering that took place within the Coptic community at that time, in which the patronage of wealthy Copts, a revival of patristic tradition, cross-fertilization by outside Christian traditions available in Arabic, and the extraordinary theological, artistic, and scientific talents of clergy (such as Bishop Paul of al-Būsh) and laity (such as the renowned Ibn al-ʿAssāl brothers) came together to usher in a golden age of Copto-Arabic theology, history, and philology, as well as a period of great accomplishment in art (gloriously on display in the recently restored wall paintings in the Monastery of Saint Antony, in the eastern desert near the Red Sea).

The Mamlūk era (1250–1517 CE) was difficult for the Copts. Coptic administrators were indispensable but resented, and Copts were frequently the victims of excessive taxation, discriminatory legislation, or even mob violence (especially in 1321 and 1354) in which churches and monasteries were destroyed. Many Copts converted to Islam. In terms of literature, the brilliant creativity of the early thirteenth century gave way to compilations and encyclopedias, and then to only the very occasional original work. We have but short notices about the patriarchs of this era, with the exception of the saintly Matthew the Poor (1378–1409), a burst of holiness in the midst of a precarious and sometimes chaotic existence.

The Mamlūk era came to an end with the Ottoman conquest of Egypt in 1517. Egypt became something of a political and cultural backwater under Ottoman administration. However, the Coptic nobility (*arākhinah*) gained influential administrative and financial positions close to the local decision-makers, and by the eighteenth century were able to provide patronage to numerous activities within the community including the building and restoration of churches, the copying of manuscripts, and the painting of icons, with results that can be seen throughout the churches and monasteries of Egypt today.

THE MODERN PERIOD. The French expedition of 1798 to 1802 marks the beginning of intensive Egyptian contacts with the West. Under the modernizing policies of Muḥammad ʿAlī (r. 1805–1848) and his successors, Copts came to be treated as full Egyptian citizens: in 1855 the *jizyah* was abolished (and soon Copts were for the first time conscripted into the Egyptian army), and in 1879 the full equality of all Egyptians was declared. Pope Cyril IV (1854–1861), known as "the father of reform," provided impetus to a Coptic "awakening"—one in which the Coptic laity played a major role—that led to the establishment of schools and a theological college, benevolent societies, and book production. Competition from Protestants and Catholics (who established Coptic Evangelical and Coptic Catholic communities, with schools, hospitals, development agencies, and theological institutions) also challenged the Coptic Orthodox community to effective organization, teaching, and literary endeavor.

In the early twentieth century, Copts could aspire to full participation in Egyptian social and political life. Buṭrus Ghālī Pasha served as prime minister from 1908 to 1910, and the Copts openly aired their grievances at a Coptic Congress in 1911. Copts participated with Muslims in the nationalist movement, and (after World War I) the struggle for independence and the development of democratic politics: two Copts were in the cabinet that nationalist hero and Wafd Party leader Saʿd Zaghlūl formed in 1924.

The liberal experiment, with its hope of "the nation for all," did not live up to its early promise. Following the revolution of 1952 the position of the Copts was affected by reforms that cut into the Coptic elite's landholdings, wealth, and dominance in certain professions. The Copts' sometimes precarious sense of national belonging was challenged by a revival of the politics of specifically Islamic identity in Egypt, beginning with the remarkable growth of the Muslim Brotherhood (founded in 1928) and continuing throughout the century with demands for the implementation of the Islamic *sharīʿah* and the development of specifically Islamic institutions and forms of life. Incidents of intercommunal violence increased in frequency in the 1970s and still flare up from time to time, while in the 1990s a militant Islamist insurrection in Middle Egypt sometimes claimed Coptic lives and property.

If the political road beyond the heady accomplishments of the nationalist movement was strewn with disappointments for the Copts, the community was energized by other developments. A Coptic "Sunday School Movement" begun in the mid-1930s led to the rise of a cadre of remarkable leaders, many of whom (including Pope Shenouda III, who become pope in 1971) became monks and contributed to a monastic revival. Pope Cyril VI (1959–1971) was a charismatic monk who has come to be revered as a saint and miracle worker. Since the 1960s the number of monastic professions has soared, monasteries have been greatly expanded, deserted ones have been repopulated, and new ones—including convents for nuns—have been established. Throughout the country, Coptic sacramental life, catechesis, artistic production, and charitable work have been enlivened. New bishoprics have been established, and totaled around eighty in Egypt and the Coptic diaspora in 2004 (up from thirty-two in 1977). Bible studies (such as those regularly led by the pope) and other educational opportunities draw great crowds, while centers of scholarship and publication (such as the Orthodox Centre for Patristic Studies and the Saint Mark Foundation) are admired for their work both at home and abroad.

The role of the Egyptian church in the ecumenical movement has been resumed, with active Coptic Orthodox membership in the World Council of Churches and the Middle East Council of Churches. Beginning in 1973, joint Christological statements have been arranged with Chalcedonian Christians of Orthodox, Catholic, and Reformation backgrounds. A very significant development of the late twentieth century is the internationalization of the Coptic church: while Coptic emigration has posed the challenges of brain drain to the community in Egypt, the church has moved vigorously to establish bishoprics and scores of congregations in Europe, the Americas, and Australia, while continuing missionary activity in sub-Saharan Africa. In many cities around the globe, the Coptic Orthodox have become part of the local Christian mosaic.

The re-invigoration of Coptic identity in the twentieth century in many ways reflects phenomena in the Muslim community. As Christians and Muslims in Egypt increasingly find their identity in their specific religious traditions rather than in a sense of shared Egyptianness, the possibility of conflict remains; a challenge for the twenty-first century will be the discovery of renewed content for the old slogan of *al-waḥdah al-waṭaniyyah*. Egyptian Christians look to the future, however, with a remarkable record of survival, aided by several factors. They have developed a profound spirituality, rooted in scripture and tradition, nourished by the stories of saints and martyrs, and given concreteness by sacred geography—the network of ancient churches and monasteries blessed by the saints and, indeed, by the holy family itself. As the largest Christian community in the Middle East (with an estimated seven million adherents), Copts are bearers of a torch that they are determined to hand on to posterity.

SEE ALSO Monasticism, article on Christian Monasticism; Pachomius.

BIBLIOGRAPHY

The fundamental resource for Coptic studies is Aziz Suryal Atiya, ed., *The Coptic Encyclopedia* (New York, 1991). Nearly as encyclopedic in scope is the work of Otto F. A. Meinardus in such volumes as *Monks and Monasteries of the Egyptian Desert* (Cairo, 1961; rev. ed., 1992); *Christian Egypt, Ancient and Modern* (Cairo, 1965); *Christian Egypt, Faith and Life* (Cairo, 1970); *Two Thousand Years of Coptic Christianity* (Cairo, 1999); and *Coptic Saints and Pilgrimages* (Cairo and New York, 2002).

There is a vast literature on particular topics in Coptic studies: one may consult the congress reports of the International Association of Coptic Studies or the volumes in the series Études Coptes for recent developments and bibliographies. Some older monographs remain indispensable, including Hugh G. Evelyn-White, *The Monasteries of the Wadi'n Natrûn* (New York, 1926); and O. H. E. Khs-Burmester, *The Egyptian or Coptic Church: A Detailed Description of Her Liturgical Services* (Cairo, 1967).

General surveys of the history of the Coptic Orthodox Church include Aziz Suryal Atiya, *A History of Eastern Christianity* (London, 1968); and Theodore Hall Partrick, *Traditional Egyptian Christianity: A History of the Coptic Orthodox Church* (Greensboro, N.C., 1996). Studies of early Egyptian Christian history include Colin H. Roberts, *Manuscript, Society, and Belief in Early Christian Egypt* (London, 1979); Birger A. Pearson and James E. Goehring, eds., *The Roots of Egyptian Christianity* (Philadelphia, 1986); C. Wilfred Griggs, *Early Egyptian Christianity: From Its Origins to 451 C.E.* (Leiden, and New York, 1990); and James E. Goehring, *Ascetics, Society, and the Desert: Studies in Early Egyptian Monasticism* (Harrisburg, Pa., 1999).

For the Coptic "sacred geography" see David Frankfurter, ed., *Pilgrimage and Holy Space in Late Antique Egypt* (Leiden, 1998); Gawdat Gabra, ed., *Be Thou There: The Holy Family's Journey in Egypt* (Cairo and New York, 2001); Elizabeth S. Bolman, ed., *Monastic Visions: Wall Paintings in the Monastery of St. Antony at the Red Sea* (Cairo and New Haven, Conn., 2002); Massimo Capuani, *Christian Egypt: Coptic Art and Monuments through Two Millennia* (Collegeville, Minn., 2002); and Gawdat Gabra, *Coptic Monasteries: Egypt's Monastic Art and Architecture* (Cairo and New York, 2002).

For the Coptic community today see Nelly van Doorn-Harder and Kari Vogt, eds., *Between Desert and City: The Coptic Orthodox Church Today* (Oslo, 1997); John H. Watson, *Among the Copts* (Brighton, U.K., 2000); and Mark Gruber, *Journey Back to Eden: My Life and Times among the Desert Fathers* (Maryknoll, N.Y., 2002).

AZIZ SURYAL ATIYA (1987)
MARK N. SWANSON (2005)

CORBIN, HENRY (1903–1978), French writer, philosopher, and Iranologist. After early training in music and philosophy, Corbin eventually attained the *diplôme des études supérieures de philosophie* of the University of Paris in 1927. From 1925 he began the study of Near Eastern languages and received the diploma in Arabic, Persian, and Turkish in 1929 when he was already employed as a librarian working with oriental manuscripts in the Bibliothèque Nationale. In 1930 he made the first of several journeys to Germany and established contacts there with leading thinkers. For almost a year (1935–1936) he was attached to the French Institute in Berlin. Much of Corbin's early publication consisted of translations from German or reviews of German works. In 1931 he met Martin Heidegger and became the first to translate Heidegger into French. The translation appeared in 1939 as *Qu'est-ce que la métaphysique?* The early writings also evidenced other interests, ranging from the spiritual tradition of the Reformation to contemporary Protestant theology and the hermeneutics of Martin Luther.

The determinative event for Corbin's career was his meeting Louis Massignon in the Bibliothèque Nationale in the autumn of 1929, for it was Massignon's presentation of a lithographed edition of *Ḥikmat-al Ishrāq* of Shihāb al-Dīn Yaḥyā Suhrawardī that first made Corbin acquainted with the work of this great Iranian philosopher. Corbin saw the presentation as a symbolic act, the transmission of wisdom from master to disciple. He followed Massignon's courses in the university and in 1954 was appointed as his replacement in the chair of Islam and the religions of Arabia at the École Pratique des Hautes Études. Corbin published the first of his numerous works on Suhrawardī in 1933 and in the same year married Stella Leenhardt, who was his helper as well as companion through the succeeding years.

In 1939 Corbin was seconded from the Bibliothèque Nationale to the French Institute in Istanbul where he intended to spend six months. Because of World War II, however, six years were to elapse before he returned to France. During this long period Corbin explored the numerous and rich libraries of Turkey and laid the foundation for his later studies in Iranian philosophy. The most basic development of these years was his discovery of the corpus of Suhrawardī's works. The first volume of the first of his editions of Suhrawardī, *Opera metaphysica et mystica* (1945), containing three treatises of the master, was prepared in Istanbul and published there.

Corbin paid his first visit to Iran in the autumn of 1945, even before returning to France. The visit brought him into contact with Iranian scholars who became his collaborators in later years, but, more important, it planted the seeds from which sprang the department of Iranology of the new Institut Franco-Iranien in Tehran. In 1946 he was appointed head of the department of Iranology, a post that he held until retirement in 1973. The enduring fruit of Corbin's work in Tehran is the monumental "Bibliothèque iranienne," founded in 1949, a series of text editions, translations, and studies offering unparalleled resources for the analysis of Iranian and Islamic philosophy. From his appointment as professor in Paris in 1954 onward, it was Corbin's custom to pass each autumn in Iran and to return to Paris for his teaching in the winter and spring. From 1949 also began his association with the annual Eranos conferences, which he attended faithfully; many of Corbin's more important writings were contributions to the Eranos meetings and first appeared in the pages of the *Eranos Jahrbuch.*

Corbin's scholarly work may be classified into five principal categories: first is his contribution to knowledge of the philosophy of Suhrawardī. Not only did he publish and study the long-neglected works of the Iranian thinker, but he adopted the latter's philosophy of light as his own. Suhrawardī had professed his purpose to be the resurrection of the ancient Iranian philosophy of light, and Corbin shared that purpose. He was most interested in Suhrawardī's angelology, which presented the gradations of reality in the cosmos in terms of hierarchies of angels. The angelology provided a link between the thought of ancient Iran and Twelver Shiʿi gnosis, enabling Corbin to hold there to be a distinct Irano-Islamic philosophy. The scholarly attention that Suhrawardī receives today is largely due to Corbin's influence.

The second focus of Corbin's work was Shiism. He did important studies on the Ismāʿīlīyah, but greater attention went to the Twelvers, whose mystical and philosophical aspects in particular he explored. Here also he was a pioneer in his work on imamology, studying the *ahadith* of the Twelver imams, and in his work on such groups as the Shaykhīyah. He was the first to describe the so-called School of Isfahan, a group of thinkers responsible for the revival of Iranian philosophy in Safavid times and whose principal thinker was Mulla Ṣadra (Ṣadr al-Dīn al-Shīrāī). Corbin believed Twelver Shiism to be the complete or integral Islam since it was concerned with the esoteric as well as the esoteric aspect of the prophetic revelations, as other branches of Islam were not.

Corbin is also responsible for redirecting the study of Islamic philosophy as a whole. In his *Histoire de la philosophie islamique* (1964), he disputed the common view that philosophy among the Muslims came to an end after Ibn Rushd, demonstrating rather that a lively philosophical activity persisted in Iran and, indeed, continues to our own day.

Sufism also attracted Corbin's interest, his principal contribution being the study of *L'imagination créatrice dans la soufisme d'ibn ʿArabī* (1958). Again rejecting the common opinion, Corbin did not believe Sufism to be the unique vehicle of spirituality in Islam. He found an even more significant spirituality among the Twelver Shiʿah, one that refused the approach of the Ṣūfī orders but was, nonetheless, deeply and genuinely mystical. In genetic terms he thought Shiism to be the origin of all other mysticism in Islam. In this light Sufism appears as a kind of truncated Shiism, possessed of Shiism's spirituality but lacking its essential basis, the doctrine of the imams.

Finally, Corbin was concerned with a broad spiritual philosophy of contemporary relevance. He was primarily a philosopher, and his Iranian and Ṣūfī studies, though they have a historical aspect, were attempts to answer questions that he thought to have been raised for all men at all times. His purpose was not merely to describe a spiritual philosophy but to advocate it. The central concept of this philosophy was the *mundus imaginalis* or imaginal world, where the soul has its life, and which is known through visions and dreams. He discerned a strong bond and parallelism between the spirituality of the West exemplified in such as Jakob Boehme, the stories of the Grail, or Emanuel Swedenborg, and that of Iran, and he called for a universal spiritual chivalry *(javānmardī)* that would preserve mankind's ancient spiritual heritage, its inner life, against the corrosion of modernity, secularism, and historicism.

See Also Images.

Bibliography

A number of Corbin's books are available in English translation. These include *Avicenna and the Visionary Recital* (New York, 1960), *Creative Imagination in the Sufism of Ibn ʿArabi* (Princeton, 1969), *Cyclical Time and Ismīʿīli Gnosis* (London, 1983), *The Man of Light in Iranian Sufism* (Boulder, Colo., 1978), and *Spiritual Body and Celestial Earth: From Mazdaen Iran to Shiite Iran* (Princeton, 1977).

Biographical notes and bibliographies of Corbin's works are to be found in *Les Cahiers de l'Herne,* in the number entitled *Henry Corbin,* edited by Christian Jambet (Paris, 1981), and in *Mélanges offerts à Henry Corbin,* edited by Seyyed Hossein Nasr (Tehran, 1977). Both volumes also contain appreciations of his work by scholars and associates.

New Sources

Corbin, Henry. "A Subtile Organ." *Parabola* 26, no. 4 (2001): 75.

Corbin, Henry, Vladimir Ivanow, and Sabine Schmidtke. *Correspondance Corbin-Ivanow: Lettres échangées entre Henry Corbin et Vladimir Ivanow de 1947 à 1966.* Paris, 1999.

Nasr, Seyyed Hossein. "Henry Corbin (1903–1978): souvenirs et reflexions sur son influence intellectuelle vingt ans apres." *Esoterisme, Gnoses and Imaginaire Symbolique,* edited by Richard Caron, et al., pp 783–796. Leuven, 2001.

Shayegan, D. *Henry Corbin: la topographie spirituelle de l'Islam iranien.* Paris, 1990.

Wasserstrom, S. M. *Religion after Religion: Gershom Scholem, Mircea Eliade, and Henry Corbin at Eranos.* Princeton, 1999.

Charles J. Adams (1987)
Revised Bibliography

CORDOVERO, MOSHEH

CORDOVERO, MOSHEH (1522–1570), Jewish mystic of Safad. Mosheh Cordovero is among the most prominent individuals in the history of Qabbalah, or Jewish mysticism. The likelihood is that Cordovero was born in Safad, a small Galilean city north of Tiberias in Israel where an important renaissance of Jewish mysticism occurred in the sixteenth century. From his name it appears that his family was Spanish in origin.

Cordovero studied rabbinic law with the outstanding legal authority Yosef Karo (1488–1575), but it is in the sphere of Qabbalah that he attained widespread fame as a teacher and author. His master in qabbalistic studies was his brother-in-law Solomon Alkabetz. It appears, however, that a reversal of roles took place and pupil became teacher. Cordovero quickly succeeded in becoming the principal master of esoteric studies in Safad. His disciples included most of the great mystics of that city: Eliyyahu de Vidas, Avraham Galante, Hayyim Vital, Avraham ben Eliʿezer ha-Levi Berukhim, Elʿazar Azikri, Shemuʾel Gallico, and, for a short while, Isaac Luria.

Cordovero was a highly prolific writer; his most important works include *Pardes rimmonim, Ellimah rabbati,* and *Or yaqar,* a massive commentary on the classic text of thirteenth-century Qabbalah, the *Zohar.* Cordovero's major literary contribution was his construction of a highly systematic synthesis of qabbalistic ideas: he may be considered the foremost systematizer of qabbalistic thinking.

At the same time, however, Cordovero addressed creatively the theoretical problems raised by qabbalistic theology and speculation. For example, one central theoretical issue in the qabbalistic system concerns the nature of the relationship between the aspect of the godhead that is utterly concealed and beyond human comprehension. Ein Sof ("the infinite"), and the ten qualities of divine being that emanate from within the depths of Ein Sof, known as the *sefirot* ("divine radiances"). Are the *sefirot* of the same "substance" as Ein Sof, which is, after all, the source of their existence, or are they separate and differentiated from Ein Sof? Cordovero offered a compromise: the *sefirot* should be conceived as both separate from Ein Sof as well as possessing substantive identification with it. Whereas from the divine point of view Ein Sof embraces all reality, from the human perspective the *sefirot* are perceived as lower stages, constituting a secondary reality that has an existence separate from Ein Sof.

Besides being a subtle and master theoretician of Qabbalah, Cordovero was a spiritual mentor, as evidenced by the rules of piety that he established for his disciples. Testimony is also preserved concerning his experiences of automatic speech, which he had when he and Alkabets would wander among the gravesites of departed teachers. It was on these occasions that he and Alkabetz would, in the manner of sudden motor automatism, utter qabbalistic mysteries and words of esoteric knowledge.

Bibliography

A valuable full-length study of Mosheh Cordovero's speculative system is Yosef Ben Shlomo's *Torat ha-Elohut shel R. Mosheh Cordovero* (Jerusalem, 1965). Useful information on Cordovero can be found in Gershom Scholem's *Kabbalah* (New York, 1974), especially pages 401–404. An essay on Cordovero's doctrine of evil is Kalman Bland's "Neoplatonic and Gnostic Themes in R. Moses Cordovero's Doctrine of Evil," *Bulletin of the Institute of Jewish Studies* 3 (1975): 103–130. An excellent translation of a short but influential ethical treatise written by Cordovero is *The Palm Tree of Deborah,* translated and edited by Louis Jacobs (1960; New York, 1974). Cordovero's rules of mystical piety and ethics are found in my own *Safed Spirituality: Rules of Mystical Piety, The Beginning of Wisdom* (New York, 1984).

New Sources

Sack, Bracha. *Kabbalah of Rabbi Moshe Cordevero* (in Hebrew). Be'er-Shevaʿ, Israel, 1995.

Lawrence Fine (1987)
Revised Bibliography

COSMOGONY. The word *cosmogony* is derived from the combination of two Greek terms, *kosmos* and *genesis. Kosmos* refers to the order of the universe and/or the universe as an order. *Genesis* means the coming into being or the process or substantial change in the process, a birth. Cosmogony thus has to do with myths, stories, or theories regarding the birth or creation of the universe as an order or the description of the original order of the universe. One type of narrative portraying meanings and description of the creation of the universe is the cosmogonic myth. These myths, which are present in almost all traditional cultures, usually depict an imaginative religious space and time that exist prior to the universe as a normal habitation for human beings. The beings who are the actors in this primordial time are divine, superhuman, and supernatural, for they exist prior to the order of the universe as known by the present generation of human beings.

Cosmogonic myths in their narrative form give a rhetorical, stylistic, and imaginative portrayal of the meaning of the creation of the world. These myths set forth a tonality and stylistics for the modes of perception, the organizing principles, and provide the basis for all creative activities in the cultural life. While these myths are always specific to the cultures in which they are found, it is possible to classify them in various ways. One may classify them according to the cultural-historical strata in which they appear; thus, one might place together myths from hunter-gatherer cultures, or from early Neolithic cultures, agricultural societies, and so on. Myths may also be classified in terms of specific religions or cultural-geographical areas (e.g., ancient Near Eastern myths, Hindu myths, etc.), or in terms of linguistic groups (e.g., Indo-European myths).

Myths may be classified further according to the symbolic structures and relationships portrayed and narrated in the myths. In the cosmogonic myth the symbols give expression to the religious imagination of the creation of the world. As the prototypical story of founding and creation, the cosmogonic myth provides a model that is recapitulated in the creation and founding of all other human modes of existence. In this sense, it expresses, to use Bronislaw Malinowski's phrase, a charter for conduct for other aspects of the culture. As such some creation myths find extended expression in ritual actions that dramatize certain symbolic meanings expressed in the myth. Myths should not, however, be thought of simply as the theoretical or theological dimension of a ritual. Even when analogous meanings are portrayed in myth and ritual, these meanings may arise from different modes of human consciousness. There are mythic meanings that may arise from ritual activity. R. R. Marett, the English anthropologist, surmised that myths might have arisen as attempts to give order to the dynamic rhythms and experiences of life that first found expression as ritual activities. Pierre Bourdieu, the French ethnologist, has refined interpretations of this kind by making a distinction between two types of theories. There is a theory that is the result of speculative human thought and there is another kind of theory that arises out of practical activity. Myth as theory may be of either type, but in each case the myth is a distinctive expression of a narrative that states a paradigmatic truth; this is especially true in the cosmogonic myth.

Creation myths are etiological insofar as they tell how the world came into existence, but what is important in the etiology of the creation myth is the basis for the explanation, that is, the basis of the explanation is in the founding or creation of the world itself. In other etiological stories the ultimate cause is not of primary importance.

TYPES OF COSMOGONIC MYTHS. Cosmogonic myths may be classified into the following types according to their symbolic structures: (1) creation from nothing; (2) from chaos; (3) from a cosmic egg; (4) from world parents; (5) through a process of emergence; and (6) through the agency of an earth diver. Cosmogonic myths are seldom limited to any one of these classifications; several symbolic typological forms may be present in one myth. For example, in the *Viṣṇu Purāṇa,* the creation myth shows how Viṣṇu evolves from the primordial reality of *prakṛti;* how Viṣṇu as a boar dives into the waters to bring up earth for the creation (earth diver); how the creation is produced from austerities and meditation; how creation results from the churning of the primordial ocean. There is in addition the symbolism of the cosmic egg as a meaning of the creation. The classification of myths into these types is thus meant not to be a stricture of limitations but rather to emphasize a dominant motif in the myth.

Creation from nothing. Though the type of cosmogonic myth recounting creation from nothing is usually identified with the monotheistic religions of the Semitic traditions, it is a more pervasive structure. However, its identification with these religions opens up a fruitful line of study. It is clear that the monotheistic religions—Judaism, Christianity, and Islam—presuppose a religious history prior to their coming into being: for Judaism, the western Semitic tradition as expressed in Mesopotamia; for Christianity, the Hebrew tradition; and, finally, for Islam, the traditions of Hebrews and Christians.

Given this history, it is legitimate to raise the issue of the relationship of prior empirical cultural history as a background to the religious imagination of creation *de novo,* or creation from nothing, in these traditions. The facticity of the Near Eastern religions enables us to more easily recognize the issue of the prehistory of those cultures in which this kind of myth appears. As a matter of fact, the very powerful symbolism of a deity who creates from nothing is a symbolic *tour de force* against the impacted empirical cultural histories as the basis for a new founding and ordering of the world and the human community. The power of the deity in myths of this type establishes the cosmos as unrelated to, and discontinuous from, all other structures prior to the statement of the creation of the cosmos and the human condition as enunciated in the myth. To the extent that older structures are present they are reintegrated within the new mode of creation.

Thus in the Egyptian myth of Khepri, it is stated, "I spat out what was Shu, and I sputtered out what was Tefnut." In the Hebrew myth the action is just as direct: "And God said, 'Let there be light'; and there was light" (*Gn.* 1:3). In the Polynesian myth, one of the names of the creator god is Io-matua-te-kora, which means "Io, the parentless"; this deity has no parents, brothers, or sisters. The deity exists in the void in himself and by himself; the autonomous and self-created nature of the deity appears out of the void or out of nothingness, which are understood to be potent realities. Thus in a Tuomotuan myth it is stated that "Kiho mused all potential things whatever, and caused his thought to be evoked." The notion of nothingness as a creative potency is related to the mode of creation as a conscious, deliberate act; it is either stated explicitly or defined by the style of the narrative. The deliberate process of the creation signifies willful volition and the fact that the creation is brought forth as a form of perfection from a supreme being.

The creator deity in myths of this kind is often symbolized by the sky or sky deities. In such cases the sky symbolism shows that the deity who creates from nothing is not contingent to the world although the created order is contingent to the deity. Ultimately, the creation from nothing emphasizes that the creation is not a mere ordering or even founding but has come forth as a powerful religio-magical evocation from a powerful supreme being.

Creation from chaos. Some creation myths describe how the creation arises out of a prior matter or stuff that is either negative or confused. The chaotic condition may be variously depicted as water, a monster, or as the qualities of coldness, sterility, quiescence, repression, and restraint. In any case, the situation of chaos inhibits creation.

In a number of Near Eastern and Indian myths, chaos is in the form of a serpentlike monster. Mary Wakeman has classified such myths into two types, a space model and a time model. In the space model the monster is a withholder of water, sun, and fertility. The monster is repressive and acts as a tyrant in relation to its subjects. The monster prevents vital forces and energies from finding expression in a created order. The restraint and repressive nature of the monster does not allow the place and space for a created order to come forth. Chaos is thus defined as a holding back of the orders and energies of creation; this is a situation of primordial confusion and indeterminacy. It is clear, however, that there is power and potency in this confused situation. The repressive and restraining nature of chaos is equally the expression of an inertia in the face of a definitive order; chaos in this sense defines a stasis.

In the time model all the potencies are similarly contained within a primordial chaos. There is no change, no movement, and no differentiation. Conversely, some myths portray the chaos as a constant state of flux in which everything changes so fast that no distinguishable ordered form is possible. In the time model of myths of chaos, the drama shows how the forces and potencies of creation are energized to move and also how the constant flux is reduced to a measured movement in which the tendency to dissipation is balanced by a force of cohesion and integration, and this tendency is complemented by the deployment and expansion of the order. Human existence is seen as a mean between these extremes; thus the meaning of ordered human time appears from the regulation of this original chaos.

In some myths of this type the chaos is never completely overcome. While order may emerge from the chaos in the forms of space and time, vestiges of the chaos remain and the created order is always in danger of slipping back into chaos or chaos appears as the destiny of the cosmos when it has exhausted the meaning of its time and space.

Creation from a cosmic egg. In many myths involving creation from chaos there is also the symbolism of a cosmic egg or an ovoid shape out of which creation or the first created being emerges. Myths of this kind are found in Polynesia, Africa, India, Japan, and Greece. The egg is obviously a symbol of fertility. In egg myths the potency for creation is contained within the form of the egg. The incubation of the egg implies a time-ordered creation and a specific determination regarding the created order.

Hermann Baumann has suggested that one motif of the egg symbolism has to do with the statement and resolution of the problem of sexual antagonism, and has its origin in megalithic cultural circles. For Baumann there is, first of all, an early stage in megalithic cultures in which the meaning of creation is expressed in the form of a sky father and earth mother as sexually differentiated deities; there is another stage in which the parents are separated and may reside within the egg as twins. A third stage portrays the meaning of sexuality as abstract principles such as *yin* and *yang* in China. In this stage the gods possess these abstract principles as attributes. In the final stage there is the attempt to recover the antagonism of sexual differentiation and to resolve it. This is the myth of androgyny.

The symbolism of the egg also connotes a state of primordial perfection out of which the created order proceeds. In a Dogon myth from West Africa, the god Amma created a world egg as the first order of creation. Within the egg twins were incubating. In time these twins were supposed to come forth as androgynous beings, indicating perfection on the level of sexuality. Other aspects of the created order were correlated with this mode of perfection. For example, instead of the dualism of day/night, the world was to be in perpetual twilight, and instead of either wet or dry, the world was supposed to be damp, and the twins were supposed to be amphibious. Due to a mishap this perfection was not attained and thus the created order as we know it is a compromise alternating between the dualism of day and night, wet and dry, land beings and water beings, male and female sexes. A philosophical statement of this myth of dualism stated in terms of androgyny is found in Plato's *Symposium* (190–192).

World-parent myths. In some myths creation is the result of the reproductive powers of primordial world parents. The birth of offspring from the world parents is often portrayed as an indifferent or unconscious activity. Even the sexual embrace of the world parents is without passion or intent. The sexual embrace does not appear as the result of a desire or an intention; it is simply the way things are. In this way the sexual embrace of the world parents is like the twins contained within the world egg, and the embrace itself recapitulates an original androgyny. As a matter of fact, the Dogon myth states that the male and female in sexual embrace is an imitation of the original androgynous archetype. In myths of this kind there is a reluctance on the part of the primordial couple to separate from this embrace. The embrace has no beginning or climax; it is perpetual and the world parents are indifferent or unaware of the offspring produced from this embrace.

In world-parent myths the world parents are, in most cases, the second phase of the primordial ordering. Prior to the appearance of the world parents there is a chaotic or indeterminate phase. For example, in *Enuma elish*, the Babylonian creation myth, it is stated that waters commingled as a single body in a state of indeterminacy; the Polynesian myth of Rangi and Papa speaks of a darkness resting over everything. In a similar fashion, in the Egyptian myth of Seb and Nut primeval chaotic waters precede the coming into being of the world parents. From this point of view, the world parents are part of the ordering of the cosmos, a specific stage of its coming into being as a habitat for the human community.

The offspring of the world parents tend to be aliens to their parents. The close embrace of the parents allows no space and thus no reality for their mode of being. The world parents are for the most part indifferent to the needs and desires of their offspring. A tension comes about because of this alienation and the offspring become the agents of the separation of the world parents. In some cases the agent of separation is another deity or one of the offspring, but in most cases the separation marks the beginning of a community and a discourse among the offspring. In *Enuma elish* this community and discourse have to do with a battle between the offspring and the world parents. The same sequence takes place in the Polynesian myth of "the children of heaven and earth." In cases of this sort the community of offspring are the archetypal models for the human community.

The separation of the world parents is a rupture in the order of creation. In *Enuma elish* the mother's body is made into the earth that human beings now inhabit. This is similar to a theme in the Dogon world-egg myth, where one of the twins leaves the egg before maturity, tearing the yolk of the egg off with him; this yolk becomes the earth. Amma must then sacrifice the other twin to make the earth habitable for human beings. In other versions of this type of myth the separation comes about when a woman who is pounding grain needs more room for her pestle and pushes the world parents apart so that she can have more room for her work.

The agents of separation in the world-parent myths are the cultural heroes who make space for the specific tasks of the human community. They bring light where there was darkness, and they set forth a certain meaning and destiny for the human community. The symbolism of light in the form of the sun is prominent in these myths, for it refers to human knowledge and the destiny of the human community. The separation of the world parents presages the human community as a distinct mode of being, but the price of this separation is the remembrance of the tragic rupture between the parents and the offspring as a necessary condition for the human mode of being.

Emergence myths. The emergence myths describe the creation of the cosmos in the symbolism of gestation and birth. The most prominent symbol in myths of this kind is that of the earth as a mother. The earth is depicted as the source of all powers and potencies. Within this womb of the earth are all the seeds and eggs of the world; they exist in embryonic form within the earth. The emergence of the forms of the world from the womb describes a process whereby the maturation of the forms within the earth take place before appearing on the face of the earth. The movement through the layers and strata of the earth is a gradual and cumulative one; at each stage some new forms are added to the growing embryos. The process is also one of integration and harmony, which has an ethical and logical meaning, for the meaning of the ethical is understood in terms of the harmonious relationship among all the forms of the created order. The capacity for the ethical is acquired during the process of the emergence upward through the strata of the earth.

In emergence myths hardly any prominence is given to the meaning of the male principle as father. The myths of this kind emphasize the earth as womb and mother, the container of all powers and potential realities. When the maturation is complete and humans emerge from the earth they are exposed to the light for the first time. The light at the last emergence is the symbol of the sun, which is the male ordering principle, but the basic formation of humans has taken place within the bowels of the earth.

Earth-diver myths. In earth-diver myths water constitutes the primordial stuff of the beginning. Water, in its undifferentiated indeterminacy, covers everything in the manner of a chaos. A culture hero, usually an animal, dives into the primordial waters in an attempt to bring up a particle of sand, mud, or earth, any substantial form of matter out of which a more stable mode of order might be established. Several animals make the attempt and fail; finally, one of the animals succeeds in bringing up a piece of earth, mud, or sand. Upon coming to the surface of the water the bit of matter, which is usually so minuscule that it is lodged under the animal's fingernails, expands to great proportions, thus constituting the landmass of the world on which all beings reside.

Some myths of this kind tell the story of the antagonism between two creative primordial beings. In some of the myths, which bear certain Christian elements, God and Satan have created the primordial waters. God sends Satan to dive into the waters to bring back a piece of earth. After several attempts Satan brings back a small portion of earth, which expands into the world. But after this landmass is created, God does not know how to make further determinations of directions, valleys, mountains, and so on. Satan seems to have this knowledge and muses to himself how stupid God is, for he does not know how to order the landmass. God sends a bee over to eavesdrop on Satan's musings. The bee overhears Satan giving the proper knowledge as he muses to himself; he flies back and gives this knowledge to God, who then orders the world in its proper proportions. In another version, it is a human being who dives into the waters to bring up earth. He brings up earth and gives it to God, but he secretly hides a piece of earth in his mouth, thinking that he will make a world on his own. When God orders the earth to expand, the hidden earth in the mouth of the human also begins to expand and the human must expose his secret. God then orders him to give him that piece of earth, and out of it God makes the swamps and boggy places of the earth.

Earth-diver myths are widespread, but there is a preponderance of them in the aboriginal cultures of North America. In these cultures the myths are part of the trickster-transformer-culture hero cycle of myths. This type of cultural figure is somewhat unique to myths of this kind. In these myths the antagonism and tensions between the creator deity and a culture hero in the form of an animal or a human being is made clear. The antagonism is not a direct one of confrontation as in the separation motif in the world-parent myths; it is subtle, indirect, and subdued, but nevertheless intense. There is obviously a desire on the part of the culture hero to create a different world in a different mode from that of the creator deity.

The American folklorist Alan Dundes interprets this meaning in a psychoanalytical manner. He interprets the diving into the waters to bring up a piece of substantial matter according to Freud's suggestion that what is ejected from the body as waste is at the same time experienced as a source of value and the basis for a new creative order. Insofar as the trickster-transformer-hero exhibits male characteristics, Dundes speculates that this is an expression of birth envy on the part of the male. The waters, which can be seen as a symbol of the primordial womb, are potent but cannot give birth; it is only through the earth diver that the necessary form of matter is brought to the surface as a basis for the creation. But once brought to the surface there is still an antagonism or a distrust between the creator deity and the earth diver.

Mac Linscott Ricketts, a historian of religions, interprets these motifs as a new and paradoxical meaning of sacrality. The trickster-transformer-hero is for him the religious symbol of the human being who is independent of the gods and their power. It expresses the desire to know on the part of the human, and this desire for knowledge does not follow the pattern of archetypal participation in the sacredness of that which has been created in primordial times by the gods. The trickster-transformer-hero figure represents for Ricketts the rejection of the ways of the gods as a mode of life and knowledge; his way is a kind of "primitive humanism," wherein knowledge is sought through experiments that reveal the foolishness and the humorous, even comical nature of the human being who attempts to know apart from the sacred power and forms of the creator deities.

IDEOGRAMS, THEMES, AND STRUCTURES. Rudolf Otto, in his classic work *The Idea of the Holy*, speaks of ideograms as modes of expression that lie somewhere between experience and concept. It is possible to discern from the cosmogonic myths such orderings of meaning that will color more systematic thought concerning the meaning of the creation of the world.

Primordiality. The primordial has to do with the problem of the basic stuff out of which the creation has emerged. In one sense what is before the creation may always be understood as chaos, for the only modes of order are those that are forthcoming in the created order itself. However, the meaning of this primordial order expresses in symbolic terms the intention of the creation. The primordial order may be spoken of in neutral terms or as alien and inimical or it may, as in the emergence myths, connote a nurturing womb.

Mircea Eliade has spoken of two meanings of primordiality; one is the original primordiality, which may be seen in the symbols of water, earth, darkness, or nothingness. The other mode of primordiality is the first mode of ordering in the creation; this may be through a world egg, world parents, a creator deity, and so forth. It is at this stage that a specific meaning and direction is given to the creation of a world for human habitation, for this is the stage at which cultural heroes appear.

Ruptures. Ruptures and discontinuities are present at several points in cosmogonic myths. There is first of all the rupture between the primordial stuff and the first mode of ordering. In some cases this discontinuity is stated as the word of power of a powerful deity whose very power breaks through the inertia of the first primordiality. In other cases a new form simply appears, as in a world egg that appears upon the waters. The other stage of rupture is occasioned by the desire of the embryonic and prehuman forms, which are the result of this first stage of ordering, to exist. These are the offspring of the world parents, or the twins who are maturing in the egg, or the earth diver who does not wish to be subject to the imitation of deities and divine models for existence.

In the world-parent and egg myths the impatience of the offspring and the twins leads to tragic results, for in both cases there is a tearing, killing, and violation of the primordial order for the sake of existence. This tragic element explains the finitude of the human community and introduces death as a cosmogonic structure of human existence. It furthermore qualifies the perfection of the primordial order, for with the coming of human existence the meaning of the primordial order itself is changed.

This is turn raises the issue of the mutual contingency of the human order and the primordial order. While a case for mutual contingency and dependence could be made for a myth such as *Enuma elish*, the Egyptian myth of Khepri with its powerful evocation of creation from the power of the deity does not lend itself to any mode of dependence of the creator upon the creation. The aseity of the deity and the relationship of the deity to the created order thus becomes a meaning that receives theoretical and practical forms in most communities.

Dualisms. What is the meaning of the distinction between the two modes of primordiality, and which possesses the greater qualitative power? Is the first ordered form of the primordial time an absolute victory and advance over the primordial chaos? This is an initial issue of dualism in cosmogonic myths. There is also the dualism of the structure of the first order and the offspring of that order. There is the dualism of partners in the creation. In the Dogon myth there is ostensibly a good twin and a malevolent one, and the human condition is constituted by a mixture of both of them.

The human condition is thus riddled with ordinary and qualitative dualisms—that of night and day, wet and dry, male and female, and so on. Are these the marks of finitude of lesser beings or does the human condition represent the original intention of creation? These dualism are also between the nonhuman creators, as in the case of God and Satan in the earth-diver myths. How can these dualisms be handled on the human level? Are they to be harmonized and alternated, or do they represent fundamental differences and orientations in the cosmos?

ETHICS. The ethical has to do with the proper, appropriate, and right conduct of a community. It is obvious that such behavior must be based upon some principles, and those principles in one way or another presuppose an explicit or implicit understanding of the nature of the world in which one lives. Cosmogonic myths are narrative statements of the origin of the various worlds of humankind. The origin of the world is often the basis for the principles that define the resources, possibilities, limitations, and validities of the meaning of human existence for the human community. There is not, however, a one-to-one relationship between the structures and themes of cosmogonic myths and the ethics of a community.

The cosmogonic myths, more often than not, serve as background and context for thinking about the issue of ethics. It is not only those elements of the cosmogonic myth that may lead to explicit philosophical and ethical principles that are important. Equally important are the style and rhythms of these stories of the ordering of the world that are a basis for reflection and creative thinking in a community. There may be similar structures in the cosmogonic myths of different communities, but these similar structures may very well lead to quite different ethical reflections and modes of behavior. The philosopher of religion Paul Ricoeur has put forth the notion that the "symbol gives itself to thought." By this he means to set forth a basis for religious and ethical thought within a religious community. Thought can arise as a reflection upon a tradition of thought within a community, but thought may also arise out of that which is not understood as simply a part of the traditional thought of the community. The symbol and the myth define a more archaic mode of presentation, expression, and style that engenders thought within a community. There may be some cosmogonic myths that are inimical to ethical reflection or that set forth ethical options that are to be rejected by the community, as well as cosmogonic symbols that appear to be neutral or indifferent as far as ethical reflection is concerned. This does not mean that such myths and symbols cannot constitute part of the ethical reflection of the community, for the myths do not simply present principles that are to be carried out in behavior. The relationship between symbol and myth on the one hand, and modes of thought, behavior, and conduct, on the other, is a much more problematic one.

Cosmogonic myths form the horizons of meaning in cultures where they still have their original power and efficacy. In this way the meaning of thought and behavior is shaped by them. It is instructive to understand the term *shaped* in an aesthetic sense, as something being created within the context of certain resources of materials that are suggested by the cosmogonic myth, for it is necessary for ethical thought and moral conduct not only to be right but to be appropriate, to fulfill aesthetic concerns, and to fulfill some of the possibilities adumbrated as possible orders for the world.

SEE ALSO Androgynes; Chaos; Culture Heroes; Dragons; Egg.

BIBLIOGRAPHY

For a general discussion of cosmogony within the framework of cosmogonic myths, see Charles H. Long's *Alpha: The Myths of Creation* (New York, 1963) and Barbara C. Sproul's *Primal Myths: Creating the World* (San Francisco, 1979). For ancient Near Eastern myths of creation, see *Ancient Near Eastern Texts Relating to the Old Testament*, edited by J. B. Pritchard (Princeton, 1950); Theodor H. Gaster's *Thespis: Ritual, Myth, and Drama in the Ancient Near East*, 2d rev. ed. (Garden City, N.Y., 1961); Hermann Gunkel's *The Legends of Genesis* (Chicago, 1901); Mary K. Wakeman's *God's Battle with the Monster* (Leiden, 1973); *Before Philosophy: The Intellectual Adventure of Ancient Man*, by Henri Frankfort, Henriette A. Frankfort, John A. Wilson, and Thorkild Jacobsen (Harmondsworth, 1963); and Henri Frankfort's *Kingship and the Gods* (Chicago, 1948).

For a general philosophical and comparative study of ancient Near Eastern and Greek cosmogonies, see Paul Ricoeur's *The Symbolism of Evil* (New York, 1967). Langdon Gilkey's *Religion and the Scientific Future* (New York, 1970) deals with ancient cosmogonic themes in light of contemporary philosophy and Christian theology.

W. K. C. Guthrie's *In the Beginning: Some Greek Views on the Origins of Life and the Early State of Man* (London, 1957) is one of the best introductions to Greek cosmogonic thought. Louis Gernet's essays in his *The Anthropology of Ancient Greece*, translated by John Hamilton and Blaise Nagy (Baltimore, 1981), relates certain cosmogonic notions to law, social institutions, and the beginnings of Greek philosophy. The origins of the Greek style of thinking within ancient Greece and its basis for Western thought are explored in Richard B. Onians's *The Origins of European Thought* (Cambridge, 1954) and in Bruno Snell's *The Discovery of Mind* (New York, 1960).

For the trickster figure in cosmogonic myths, see the following works: Daniel G. Brinton's *The Myths of the New World: A Treatise on the Symbolism and Mythology of the Red Races of America* (New York, 1868); Mac Linscott Ricketts's "The North American Indian Trickster," *History of Religions* 5 (Winter 1966): 327–350; Robert D. Pelton's *The Trickster in West Africa* (Berkeley, 1980); and Stanley Walens's *Feasting with Cannibals: An Essay on Kwakiutl Cosmology* (Princeton, 1981). See also *The Trickster: A Study in American Indian Mythology*, edited by Paul Radin (New York, 1956).

The most thorough discussion of the distribution and meaning of the egg as a symbol in cosmogony is Anna-Britta Hellbom's article "The Creation Egg," *Ethnos* 28 (1963): 63–105. For earth-diver myths, see Alan Dundes's "Earth-Diver: Creation of the Mythopoeic Male," in his *Sacred Narrative* (Berkeley, 1984). This anthology of interpretive essays on cosmogonic myths also contains Mircea Eliade's "Cosmogonic Myth and Sacred History," Franz Kiichi Numazawa's "The Cultural Background of Myths of the Separation of Sky and Earth," and Anna Birgitta Rooth's "The Creation Myth of North American Indians."

For a general survey of Indo-European creation myths, see Bruce Lincoln's "The Indo-European Myth of Creation," *History of Religions* 15 (1975): 121–145. In this article Lincoln describes and compares the structures of the Puruṣa myth of *Ṛgveda* 10.90, the *Bundahishn* of the Zoroastrian Avesta, the *Prose Edda* of Germanic mythology, and the creation myth of the *Śatapatha Brahmana*. Hans H. Penner's article analyzes in detail the creation myth in the *Viṣṇu Purāṇa* in "Cosmogony as Myth in the Vishnu Purana," *History of Religions* 5 (Winter 1966): 283–299. Since the creation myth sets forth the origin of all modes and forms of life, the origin of death and evil are often narrated in the cosmogony. Wendy Doniger O'Flaherty's *The Origins of Evil in Hindu Mythology* (Berkeley, 1976) discusses this meaning in Hindu myths; Hans Abrahamsson's *The Origin of Death* (Uppsala, 1951) classifies a wide variety of myths of death in Africa.

Most speculative, philosophical, and theological works of religious cultural traditions proceed from a theme or structure in the culture's cosmogonic or cosmological tradition. Charles Hartshorne and William L. Reese's *Philosophers Speak of God* (Chicago, 1953) is an example of this type of discussion in the Western tradition. A group of essays discussing the relationship of cosmogony to ethics can be found in *Cosmogony and Ethical Order*, edited by Robin Lovin and Frank E. Reynolds (Chicago, 1985). C. F. von Weizsäcker's *The Relevance of Science: Creation and Cosmogony* (Chicago) is still the best introduction to the relationship of religious mythical cosmogonies and those of modern physics.

New Sources

Anderson, Gary. "The Interpretation of Genesis 1:1 in the Targums." *Catholic Biblical Quarterly* 52 (1990): 21–9.

Bowler, Peter J. *Evolution: The History of an Idea.* 3d ed. Los Angeles, 2003.

Clifford, Richard. *Creation Accounts in the Ancient Near East and in the Bible.* Washington, D.C., 1994.

Currid, John D. "An Examination of the Egyptian Background of the Genesis Cosmogony." *Biblische Zeitschrift* 34 (1990): 18–40.

Drees, Willem B. *Beyond the Big Bang: Quantum Cosmologies and God.* La Salle, Ill., 1990.

Keller, Catherine. *Face of the Deep: A Theology of Becoming.* London and New York, 2003.

North, John David. *Measure of the Universe: A History of Modern Cosmology.* New York, 1990.

Reeves, John C. *Jewish Lore in Manichaean Cosmogony: Studies in the Book of Giants Traditions.* Cincinnati, 1992.

CHARLES H. LONG (1987)
Revised Bibliography

COSMOLOGY

This entry consists of the following articles:

AN OVERVIEW
AFRICAN COSMOLOGIES
AUSTRALIAN INDIGENOUS COSMOLOGY
OCEANIC COSMOLOGIES
INDIGENOUS NORTH AND MESOAMERICAN COSMOLOGIES
SOUTH AMERICAN COSMOLOGIES
HINDU COSMOLOGY
JAIN COSMOLOGY
BUDDHIST COSMOLOGY
SCIENTIFIC COSMOLOGIES

COSMOLOGY: AN OVERVIEW

Cosmology is the term for the study of cosmic views in general and also for the specific view or collection of images concerning the universe held in a religion or cultural tradition. The twofold meaning of the term is reminiscent of the double meaning of mythology, which is at the same time the study of myths and the dominant or representative assemblage of myths in a given tradition. However, the double usage of the term *cosmology* is still wider in one respect: Quite explicitly, it also relates to inquiries in the natural sciences. The natural sciences customarily associate the term with the study of cosmic views; more specifically, these sciences reserve cosmology for the scientific study of the universe considered as a whole. Thus, it is the most encompassing task of astronomy and is distinct from, even if presupposed by, sciences with a comparatively more limited object, such as physics or geology.

IMAGES OF THE WORLD AS SUBJECTS FOR HISTORIANS. For historians, including historians of religions, the study of cosmology surveys and tries to classify and understand the significance of mythical images and religious conceptions concerning the cosmos and the origin and structure of the universe. The variety of images held, historically and globally, leads to one central question: What is the relation between human views of the world and the validity and authority of the tradition in which these views are held? Invariably, the two are related—despite the contemporary uncritically held views concerning a separation between the sciences and the humanities. Hence the two meanings of cosmology noted previously do not present an ambiguity: The study of the structure of the universe and the history of cosmological imagery are interrelated and inseparable. In their study of cosmology, natural scientists do not usually need to concern themselves with images of the world held in past civilizations and in regions distant from the centers of modern scientific learning. For the historian of religions, however, the opposite is true: The cosmic views held by modern scientists cannot be ignored for they are but the latest in a long series of views and are thus as worthy of consideration as those, for instance, of the tribes of central Australia or the Hindus of India. Nicholas of Cusa (1401–1464) was an early student of the world's structure, but also a theologian and cardinal. It remains important to keep in mind that the separation between the sciences and the humanities is a recent (nineteenth century) academic idea, which epistemologically is still under debate.

The history of religions is the only discipline seeking to relate two branches of learning that have been kept apart for a considerable time, that is, the humanities (including history) and the natural sciences. With respect to images and theories of the universe, the borderline between science and myth has fluctuated throughout history. The significance of religious and historical studies in cosmology is largely due to this fluctuation, because the investigations of the historian of religion must overstep the boundaries that normally divide basic disciplines of study (i.e., specialized disciplines precisely delineated and separated from each other in objective and method) and can thereby illuminate features and themes or provide insights that in any given specialization can hardly be surmised.

In most instances, every aspect of a culture or religion presupposes a view of the cosmos. Nevertheless, even this generalization should be made with some caution. In the case of the modern natural sciences, there is no doubt about the pervasiveness of an implicit worldview, even though many of the details of this view may be open to debate. However, in the study of religious images of the world, the presupposition of a cosmic view does not necessarily apply. The sacred and the phenomenal world are related, but they are by no means identical. Certainly, notions of what is sacred vary widely from one tradition to another, yet in every tradition one notion or configuration of the sacred is prominent and forms the *sine qua non* of that particular religion and constitutes the vantage point for understanding it. The same is not true for images of the cosmos, for in certain traditions cosmic imageries are of mere secondary importance (as in Christianity and Buddhism). In the case of the biblical texts alone, images of the cosmos change several times without affecting the religious tradition. A hierophany (a manifestation of the sacred) can lead to an image of the cosmos, but images of the cosmos do not necessarily take on a sacred significance.

COSMOLOGY AND WORLDVIEW. According to this explanation of cosmology, the terms *cosmology* and *worldview*, although related, cannot often be used interchangeably. Worldview is the term for a more general, less precisely delineated but commonly accepted set of ideas (i.e., an ideology) concerning life and world. Cosmology refers to more consciously entertained images, doctrines, and scientific views concerning the universe. In religious traditions, the natural place to look for cosmology is the myths of creation or birth of the world (cosmogony), whereas questionnaires might be the best means to arrive at a dominant worldview. The philosopher Immanuel Kant (1724–1804) introduced the term *Weltanschauung* (worldview), but he used it as a synonym for cosmology or image of the world. The more nebulous term (especially as used by English-speakers) *Weltanschauung* is to a large extent the result of philosophical discussions and disagreements that have taken place for the most part outside of theological circles. The meaning of the term *worldview* in common use at the beginning of twenty-first century is a generally sensed answer to a question concerning the meaning of life that is felt rather than expressed. Its lack of articulation distinguishes it from cosmology. No wonder that so much discord has continued to exist among philosophers on the meaning and definition of worldview, although it has been accepted as a philosophical concept (e.g., by Karl Jaspers, 1883–1969). It is easy to see that a worldview, precisely to the extent that it is held uncritically, can be a remnant of an earlier cosmology.

The relation between scientific views of the universe and worldview—and the influence of the former on the latter—are strikingly exemplified in developments of the twentieth century and, if anything, increasingly so in the twenty-first century. Discoveries in astronomy, the popularization of unimaginable distances in space, and the beginning of space travel have contributed to a new anxiety.

Human beings have become conspicuously lonesome creatures in the universe. Typically, in science fiction literature, space travelers risk the danger of literally getting lost in space. This anxiety is part of a widespread worldview, which is tied to a new cosmology produced by scientific discoveries. A relation to traditional religious systems might seem completely absent, if it were not for the accompanying fully conscious realization that the central place of humans in the cosmos has faded. Thus, the anxiety concerns precisely the cardinal point in all traditional religious imageries: In more than one manner the world seems to have become less human, if not inhuman. It is, however, not correct to assume that all the cosmologies held on to by people in ancient and distant cultures were stories of perfect peace. It should be remembered that the biblical creation account ends with the entrance of evil and the expulsion of the first people from paradise, and, according to many African myths, an accidental forgetfulness in the conveyance of a message causes the mortality of people.

CLASSIFICATION OF COSMOLOGIES. Cosmic worldviews may be examined from two distinct perspectives: geographical location and culturally evolved themes.

Geography. The most obvious grouping of cosmic views is given according to the continents of the earth, the various regions within them, and their ethnic and linguistic divisions. Although a necessary first step that appeals to the quest for empirical knowledge, this method is most valuable in showing the extreme difficulty of making generalizations and is useful in demonstrating the impossibility of finding helpful answers to a number of elementary questions. The greatest problem for the longest period of time has been the self-overestimation of Westerners who regarded themselves as very well-educated indeed—never having had a primitive thought in their minds and the natural inheritors of the classical Greeks. It took Europeans and Americans a long time to pay proper attention, intellectually, to Africa, which was so often maltreated and exploited, especially during colonization—worse than any other continent.

At the same time, however, one cannot help but observe in Africa a variety of traditions and a great dissimilarity in historical influences and levels of culture. Although there may seem to be in African traditions few pure cosmologies in the sense of myths explicitly dealing with the origin and structure of the universe when compared with, for instance, traditions in the Pacific or the sheer beauty of Indonesian myths, this deficiency is more than made up for by a pronounced significance given to human acts in the world from its inception. In particular, the discovery and presentation of Dogon myths have opened Western eyes to the philosophical profundity of African thought. The choices made by people as reflected in their acts obviously concern the world, even when the cosmos itself is not described in its origin and structure with the poetic beauty characteristic of, for example, many Indonesian myths. Marcel Griaule's *Conversations with Ogotemmêli, an Introduction to Dogon Religious Ideas* (1965) opened Western eyes for the profundity and philosophical depth of the Dogon myths in the West.

A geographic compilation of cosmic views leads to a very natural and necessary first conclusion: Humanity is an important theme in traditional cosmologies. Whether poetic visions of primordial mountains and oceans or a preoccupation with the risks or failures in human acts prevail, the world of human beings is the theme of all traditional mythology, including the narratives and the symbolism that refer expressly to nature, the universe, the cosmos, and the earth. This basic conclusion must indeed be drawn; it eliminates much unnecessary confusion on cosmological and cosmogonic myths as supposed steps toward satisfying innate human scientific curiosity or cravings for establishing causes.

Cultural themes. Any worldwide survey of cosmological views must consider as a crucial factor the variety of cultural levels on which views of the cosmos have developed. At first glance, this variety may seem only to increase the almost overwhelming abundance and complexity of the material to be studied; however, in the end it provides the only sturdy vantage point for a thematic classification on which some scholarly agreement might exist. This is not to say that the various livelihoods (hunting–gathering, tilling the soil, livestock raising) are presented as ironclad systems in myths. Yet to quite an extent, views of the cosmos are in harmony with the social order in a tribe or tradition and, as a rule, reflect the prevailing mode of production (and may shed light on the legal customs of the society as well).

The generating earth. Even though no unambiguous examples of matriarchy have been found, many examples of female cosmic principles and deities do exist. In certain very early agricultural societies, as in prehistoric Eastern Europe, it is likely that supreme goddesses to some extent mirrored the importance of women in society. However, much more is at stake than a mere projection of society. There are indications that a mother deity functioned at one time as the sole generative principle, giving birth without the participation of a male counterpart. It is not necessary to think of the peoples holding such ideas as ignorant concerning impregnation; obviously, such ignorance, wherever it existed, could not be the point of the cosmogony.

Evidence of the imageries of a sole maternal figure comes from well-developed early and classical cultures, including those of the Greeks, Egyptians, Hittites, and Japanese. The earth—constituting "the whole place" in which humans found themselves—evidently was conceived as the center or foundation of the cosmos. A Sanskrit word for earth, *prthivi,* is feminine and literally means "the one who is wide." Taking all evidence together, caution is advised in speaking without further qualification of motherhood as the cause of all these imageries. Less socio-psychologically but not less concretely, the preoccupation with the fact and act of generating seems central in all examples of the generatrix (she who brings forth). In the settled, archaic society of the Zuni, but also among many other Indians of the New World, myths speak of people emerging from the earth in very early, mythical times. Here the subject of originating is much more emphatically presented in the tradition than is the principle of motherhood.

The predominant significance of the earth in a number of traditions is commonly referred to with the adjective *chthonic.* Derived from the Greek word *chthon* (earth), it was first used by classicists to describe the quality of many deities in Greece, whether female (such as Gaia and Semele) or male (such as Ploutos, identified with Hades). Gaia (from *earth*) is the equivalent of Tellus in Roman mythology, and Ploutos, called Pluto by the Romans, is the provider of wealth that comes from the earth. Gaia is regarded as the oldest of the deities in Greek tradition, arising by her own power out of chaos. In many cosmogonic myths in the ancient Mediterranean world, the theme of the spontaneity of life and life arising from death is repeated and elaborated. Its variations are not limited to the classical civilizations in the Mediterranean but occur wherever agricultural life exists.

Divine male fashioner. Many nonliterate traditions know of a primordial celestial god who created the world and then withdrew after having accomplished that act (*deus otiosus,* lit., god without work). The great monotheistic systems (those of ancient Israel, Judaism, Christianity, Islam, as well as Zoroastrianism) that also speak of a supreme creator are very different because they brought into existence an understanding of monotheism proper that extends beyond the idea of a god who merely creates. Their monotheism is the result of their fight against polytheism of one type or another and is a matter of a revolution in the development of religion. Not by chance are they historically rooted in pastoral traditions and in civilizations far more extensive than those of early hunters and gatherers. Here, the father is the undisputed head of the family. The world is governed strictly by the creator, Yahweh, the biblical god who sets the course for the celestial bodies. However, societies of a pronounced patriarchal type with a monotheistic religion are relative latecomers in history, and their diversity is striking. One would hesitate to emphasize similarities between them beyond a few general lines linking cosmic structure, social structure, and their type of deity.

The *pater familias* (father as head of the household) in Roman religion may focus the attention on a striking feature yet brings to mind the complexity of an ideologically pastoral, agriculturally based, and advanced urban society. Also, it is a reminder that the most typical examples of monotheism (as in Israel and Islam) are not an inevitable product of one homogeneous socio-cultural development. After all, Rome did not itself yield to monotheism until Christianity's gradual conquest in the third, fourth, and fifth centuries CE.

World parents. Enlarging on the themes of the earth's generative power and a supreme fashioner is the theme of the world parents. The primordial union out of which all there is was born is often that of sky and earth, that is, the primal pair of parents. Iconographically, the pair is often depicted as if in shorthand form through a square or rectangle (the earth) and a circle (the sky). Here also, an inadequate scientific knowledge and fanciful illusions concerning the structure of the universe is not under question but rather the fundamental issues in a lasting religious quest. In addition to the immediate world of humans, there exists the sky, at the same time undeniably there and yet unreachable. The sky is the first image of what in philosophy will come to be called *transcendence.* Out of the opposites of earth and sky, the world (perhaps more precisely called "the human world") is born.

Pointing to the theme of the world parents as an expression of the mystery of all creation is far from exhausting the subject. This theme occurs with infinite variations. In ancient Egypt, for example, the earth and the sky are male and female, respectively, unlike the vast majority of traditions. In the ancient Near East, in their relationship the primordial pair, Tiamat and Apsu, exist distinct from and prior to the establishment of sky and earth; they are portrayed as a series of opposites, one of which is the opposition of the primeval salt water and fresh water oceans that were crucial to Babylonian existence. The two form the beginning of the god's life and the beginning of organization necessary for the world that is yet to come. Hence, the pair of deities is both theogonic (related to the study of the origins of gods) and cosmogonic.

OTHER MOTIFS. Traditionally, especially since the nineteenth century, anthropologists and historians of religions have been interested in social structures and cultural structures and generally were neither trained for nor interested in typically exact science questions. In recent decades however, more scientists have begun to look at ancient cultures and at societies that not long ago were generally understood to be primitive. In so doing, they have found evidence of much greater interest in the skies in early ages than anthropologists and historians of religions had previously realized. Moreover, in the science of astronomy more and more voices are speaking of mysteries.

Several other themes that deal with the origin of the world and its structure may be related with certainty to the specific cultural environments in which they are narrated. Nevertheless, they cross-cultural boundaries or occur with modifications that can be expected by cultural anthropologists and historians. However, with chthonic creativity and the world parents, it is not necessary here to think in terms of diffusion from one point of the globe to another. On the basis of observation and experience, one may conclude that independent origins are not uncommon and in fact are often more likely. Among the notable exceptions are the variations within the cosmos of conflicting dualisms that are observable in many areas of the world and that are attributable directly or indirectly to Iranian or Manichaean influences.

A number of archaic hunters' traditions know of an earth diver, a creature that descends to the bottom of the primordial ocean to pick up the earth from which the dry land is to be fashioned on the surface of the water (for example, the theme occurs in North America among the Huron). In some regions, the motif appears with the addition of a character, often divine, who orders the earth diver to descend and fetch the required particles of earth. Finally—and herein lies the striking example of a historically traceable influence—the theme recurs with an earth diver who attempts to keep the earth to himself or who sets himself up in opposition to the divine creator. There is little doubt that a dualism of Iranian (Zoroastrian) or Manichaean origin is making itself felt here. In the new versions, the earth, in the end, is the product of both the good maker and the helper, who turns out to be a satanic figure. Thus the existence of evil is acknowledged, but the (good) god is not held responsible for it. Such a dualistic cosmogonic procedure is described in various ways in Eastern European and Siberian traditions.

Again, caution is in order in making generalizations, for the opposition of good and evil is not alien to any human society, even though in some cases specific historical influences can be inferred. Of general importance is the realization, first, that all myths are subject to historical changes, even if these changes have not been traced in detail and, second, that a cosmogonic myth of any thematic type is not necessarily wiped out or replaced but can be merely modified when a great religious system is superimposed on a civilization. For example, in the myth of the earth diver, first a dualistic change came about (no doubt from outside) and yet the new, dualistic version continued its life after Christianity had gained ascendancy in Eastern Europe.

Themes that in all probability were created independently in various traditions include the world egg, the cosmic tree, creation ex nihilo (out of nothing), creation from chaos, and creation from sacrifice. Each of these usually occurs in conjunction with other themes. The tree of the world and of life occurs in one form or another from the ancient Germanic and Celtic peoples to ancient Babylonia and to classical and modern Java. Perhaps even more than the others, this symbolism allows for interpretations of the cosmos at large (the macrocosm) and the "world" of a person's body and existence (the microcosm). Many traditions elaborate on such double application. Chapter 15 of the ancient text the *Bhagavadgītā* (c. 200 BCE) is an excellent example.

The imagery of the world egg occurs also in many places (e.g., Africa, Polynesia, Japan, and India) that are far apart and cannot be expected to have been in contact in such a way as to explain the similarity. The power of the imagery must be sought in the imagery itself. Just as water is always and everywhere given as a basic ingredient expressive of perfect potentiality because it takes on any form given to it, having no form of its own (hence symbolically interchangeable with chaos) and plays an essential role at birth, the egg is given as a cosmogonic image precisely because it represents a form that contains all there is "in principle" and produces life. The creation out of nothing, well known from the traditional Christian interpretation of *Genesis* 1, occurs unambiguously and articulately in a Tuamotuan tradition (Polynesia). Sacrifice as an act resulting in the creation of the world is especially well developed in early India (Vedism and Brahmanism).

COMMON CHARACTERISTICS OF RELIGIOUS COSMOLOGIES. When symbolism and mythology depict cosmogony and cosmology, the view is confirmed that the cosmos is always the world of humanity and is not an external object of inquiry. Additionally, an ethical concern, which by itself has no evident part in the study of nature or of astronomy, is very much in evidence in religious views of the world. The behavior required of human beings is often described and always implied in the account of the world's structure.

Even if certain features do not make an obvious ethical impression on many modern and Western readers, they nevertheless may illuminate something concerning the rules that govern human behavior. Sacrificial or headhunting techniques are given within the structure of the cosmos. The renewal of the world celebrated in the Babylonian New Year festival is a cosmological event that has little, if anything, in common with modern scientific researches, most obviously so because it implies a renewal that must be observed in human existence. Another example is the teachings concerning many births and rebirths in Hinduism, Jainism, and Buddhism; they fit in traditions that speak of world cycles, successions of worlds, and multiple worlds. Finally, the intimate relationship of the macrocosm and the microcosm, which is widely attested, is a striking formal link between various views of the cosmos.

DO SCIENCE AND RELIGION VIEW THE COSMOS DIFFERENTLY? Contrary to popular opinion, pondering the conflicts between science and religion is not often necessary. It is more to the point to think of differences in questions asked and in subject matter. Pre-Islamic Indian literary sources are almost unanimous with respect to the conception of the continents of the earth. They depict the continents geometrically rather than empirically, and India itself occurs in the center of the world's map. The idea of many long ages and periods with truly astronomical numbers and the concept of many worlds existing both in succession and simultaneously are pan-Indian. As indicated, the center is and remains the human world and the human quest for liberation. This does not mean that the large figures of years given in the Purāṇas are figments of the imagination or betray a disregard for science. Quite the reverse is true, despite earlier fashions in scholarship that disparaged India's talent for science (a tradition fostered by some eminent Sanskritists). On this score scholarship has been set right by recent investigations in the history of science, with David Pingree in the forefront of this work.

On a wider scale, a comparable correction has been made with respect to the generally held opinion that prehistoric people and, in their wake, members of every nonliterate tradition were wanting in intellectual power capable of raising scientific questions. This correction has been made through the work of Alexander Marshack, who persuasively interpreted prehistoric data as records of precise astronomic observations. None of this suggests oppositions between religion and science; such oppositions are in fact a very recent phenomenon in history and are restricted to very few sciences and only to specific religious traditions. Only in recent times have antiscientific, fundamentalist religious movements occurred. It is certainly impossible on the basis of the cumulative evidence to regard religious and mythical views of the cosmos merely as precursors to science or as preliminary or inadequate endeavors that are discarded with the development of science. Moreover, not only from the point of view of the historian of religions but also from that of the historian of science, no single moment in history can ever be established to pinpoint the supposed fundamental change from myth to science. In fact, no such moment exists. The relation between clearly recognizable religious views and scientific views is complex, but much clarity can be gained by looking critically at the sort of questions that are asked, the nature of the assumptions questioners make under the influence of their own culture, or the intellectual habits of their age.

One tradition, fundamentalism, although largely limited to the history of American Protestantism, illuminates the study of the problem of science and religion with regard to cosmology. Fundamentalism is rooted in America's frontier experience and in rural life, yet ideologically it has had an emotional impact on urban communities and educational institutions. The public evil of religious illiteracy is the root cause of most questionable ideas concerning religion and science. Taking biblical statements about the cosmos literally, fundamentalists build up a supernaturalism that does not replace naturalism so much as it is superimposed on it, while the religious character of religious accounts is obscured in the process. In a legal procedure in 1981 and 1982, a group of fundamentalists known as creationists tried to provide educational institutions with the right to spend equal time on creation science (i.e., based on biblical statements about the physical universe) alongside the teaching of generally accepted modern scientific inquiries. The assumption was that religious accounts can be viewed for their factual, that is, verifiable and inferential accuracy. The question of the religious intention is not raised, because the creation scientist postulates a factuality that is positivistic in nature—in the sense of the French philosopher, Auguste Comte (1798–1857) and after the manner of the English social philosopher, Herbert Spencer (1820–1903) for whom religion covered everything not yet figured out by science.

Rather than holding up ideas of this sort for ridicule, scholars have used them to show more clearly the weakness of ideas shared in the widest intellectual circles. The modern intellectual problem of creating a dichotomy in which documents show a unity or seem to indicate no more than aspects of the same thing cannot be ignored. The contrast between modern science and traditional religious ideas concerning the world and cosmogony has occupied the minds of many Westerners, especially since the eighteenth century. This contrast has blurred the intention of world images given in religious traditions.

It would not be appropriate to allow a conflict generated by the French Enlightenment and repeated and modified since then in Western intellectual history to distort perception of all religious symbolism concerning the world, its nature, and origin. Instead, religion and science should be viewed together in their development, with the understanding that every attempt to view religious cosmologies side by side with modern scientific cosmologies fails if the cardinal point mentioned before is missed: The former are human-centered, whereas the latter is only human-observed and human-calculated. However, this distinction, with which modernity should be familiar, is not a division, and few ages and communities have found it necessary to make the distinction into a special subject for discourse or emphasis.

The ancient Babylonians thought of the earth as the center of the universe and conceived of it as a mountain, hollow underneath and supported by the ocean, whereas the vault of heaven kept the waters above from those below; the waters above explained the phenomenon of rain. Roughly the same cosmic scheme occurs throughout the entire ancient Near East and returns in the creation account in the *Book of Genesis*. Another example is Thales of Miletus (c. 600 BCE), the Ionian natural philosopher, who is famous for positing water as the primal substance of the universe. Although this schematization may appear scientifically primitive, such a scheme was, in fact, never presented in any tradition and is only the summary that the modern mind draws from far more complex mythologies.

Although the study the development of the natural sciences can (mistakenly) take place in isolation, the documents of the exact sciences, available from the ancient Babylonians (the period of the Hammurabi dynasty, 1800–1600 BCE) and the ancient Egyptians on are recorded not only in mathematical signs, as one might expect, but are also surrounded by mythological images. Mythological images simultaneously absorb and appropriate scientific discoveries, calendrical calculations, and established views of the world, stars, and planets as their symbols. Although a distinction must be drawn between the two sciences, the documents make no such separation and establish no contrast. Various scholars (e.g., Mircea Eliade and Werner Müller) have stressed the cosmic character of all archaic religious traditions. It is of great importance, however, to add that the history of science points to the interwovenness of science (notably astronomy and physics) and religion.

Epistemological considerations are not separable from socio-religious traditions and cannot be kept for long from the work of a modern scientist. Basic definitions functioning in scientific research are not central in scientific education, yet typically normal, consensus-bound research ultimately results in revolution. The process of change in religion is quite analogous. As a rule, renowned mystics, prophets, and great reformers have followed their tradition so persistently as to arrive willy-nilly at a change that in some cases amounted to a rebirth or total overhaul of a tradition (e.g., the great reformers in Christianity; Nāgārjuna, second century CE, in Buddhism; the great *bhakti* philosophers, especially Rāmānuja, traditionally dated to 1017–1137 CE, in Hinduism; and Abū Ḥāmid al-Ghazālī, twelfth century, in Islam). Any such great change is reflected in the image of the world.

The breakdown of the classical, Aristotelian world image, shaken by Nicolaus Copernicus (1473–1543), Tycho Brahe (1546–1601), Galileo Galilei (1564–1642), Johannes Kepler (1571–1630), and Isaac Newton (1642–1727), is principally due to René Descartes (1596–1650), the initiator of philosophy in modern Western history. Instead of being a human environment and accessible through the senses, the world now becomes a definite object of rational inquiry of a new, truly objective character of which humans are no longer the unquestionable center. The conflict between Galileo and the church is well known and has been given so much attention as to obscure the structures of both science and religion. This conflict is limited to only one science (astronomy) and only one religion (Christianity) in a particular phase of each. Other sciences, such as the science of music or the science of crystals, have never found themselves in a comparable predicament with Christianity. It stands to reason that a religion such as Buddhism, in which the subject of the world's creation and the earth's central position in it has no significant part at all, could not be expected to provoke comparable polemics between astronomers and defenders of the religious tradition.

Two final points must be made to complete the subject of the distinctive place of religion with respect to cosmology. First, an absolute break between religion and the sciences after Copernicus and Descartes is not a meaningful division. From Gottfried Leibniz (1646–1716) to Pierre Teilhard De Chardin (1881–1955), Carl F. von Weizsäcker (b. 1912), Stephen Hawking (b. 1942; widely known through his *A Brief History of Time*), and Karl Jaspers, writers, scientists, and theologians have dealt with the unity and meaning of the world, a world designed to be religiously and scientifically comprehensible. Second, significantly (and complementary to the first one point), in considering the cosmos under two aspects in the religious documents that exist, the religious view—wherever it does come to the fore—tends to show a certain priority. This is not only true in the temporal sense that the historical development shows religious assumptions concerning the world before the first recognizable scientific strides are taken, but also in terms of relative importance. Karl Barth (1886–1968) rightly emphasized (in part in opposition to theories by the New Testament theologian Rudolf Bultmann, 1884–1976) that the histories of Israel and of the church have unfolded under the impact of various dominant views of the cosmos without being disturbed by them. Characteristically, in the entire history of the church, no creed ever made the structure of the universe an item worthy of concern. The same holds true for other religious traditions as well. Even though in archaic traditions the sacred can be expressed primarily through cosmic forms, the sacred supersedes the cosmic in all religions.

SEE ALSO Ages of the World; Cosmogony; Deus Otiosus; Dualism; Earth; Egg; Eschatology, overview article; Evangelical and Fundamental Christianity; Goddess Worship, overview article and article on Theoretical Perspectives; Hieros Gamos; Metaphysics; Monotheism; Science and Religion.

BIBLIOGRAPHY

In many, if not most creation myths, one finds notions of human or political power. For this reason alone, it is useful to look at Said Amir Arjomand, ed., *The Political Dimensions of Religion* (Albany, 1993). For African creation accounts, the most helpful work is Herman Baumann's *Schöpfung und Urzeit des Menschen im Mythus der afrikanischen Völker* (Berlin, 1936). Jean Bayet's *Histoire politique et psychologique de la religion Romaine,* 2d ed. (Paris, 1969) has a special eye for the interwovenness of human orientations and conceptions of the world throughout Roman history. Hendrik Bergema's *De boom des levens in schrift en historie* (Hilversum, Netherlands, 1938) is the most extensive collection of tree symbolisms in religious traditions. Jean Bottéro, *The Birth of God. The Bible and the Historian,* translated by Kees W. Bolle (University Park, Pa., 2000) is mandatory reading for all who have a religious or theological interest in this subject. Kenneth Brecher and Michael Feirtag, eds., *Astronomy of the Ancients* (Cambridge, Mass., 1980) is a collection of essays by experts in astronomy and history of science. The collection is not only interesting in itself but also is useful reading for all students of the mythology in ancient and tribal cosmogonies. Following the lead of the earlier work by Hertha von Dechend and Giorgio de Santillana, *Hamlet's Mill; an Essay on Myth and the Frame of Time* (Boston, 1969), the contributors point to evidence of exact observation of the sky, found in the earliest cultures, that is clearly present in the materials.

A sociological attempt to show that human beings by nature orient themselves toward a more encompassing world than that of their observable social and psychological reality is made by Peter L. Berger and Thomas Luckmann in *The Social Construction of Reality* (Garden City, N.Y., 1966). Eduard J. Dijksterhuis's *The Mechanization of the World Picture* (Oxford, 1961) is the classic study of philosophies and discussions leading from antiquity to the birth of science in modern history. Mircea Eliade's *Cosmos and History: The Myth of the Eternal Return* (New York, 1954), *Myth and Reality* (New York, 1963), and *Patterns in Comparative Religion* (New York, 1958) offer the most comprehensive religio-historical studies of cosmic symbolism, especially in archaic societies, with special emphasis on cosmogony as the fundamental myth in any tradition and on the significance of world renewal. Eliade's *Australian Religions: An Introduction* (Ithaca, N.Y., 1973) elaborates on these and other themes in the particular compass of some culturally most archaic tribal traditions. Adolf E. Jensen's *Myth and Cult among Primitive Peoples* (Chicago, 1963) is especially concerned with the relation between cosmic views and human behavior. Marcel Griaule's *Conversations with Ogotemmêli, an Introduction to Dogon Religious Ideas* (London, 1965) is the work that more than any other made it difficult to speak seriously anymore about "primitive thought." The Dogon people of western Sudan, the preface sums up, "live by a cosmogony, a metaphysic, and a religion which put them on a par with the peoples of antiquity, and which Christian theology might indeed study with profit" (p. 2). Noel Q. King, *Religions of Africa, A Pilgrimage into Traditional Religions* (New York, 1970) remains one of the most sympathetic introductory works on the religions of Africa. Willibald Kirfel's *Die Kosmographie der Inder* (Bonn, 1920) treats views of the world among Hindus, Buddhists, and Jains.

The most influential works in the history of science in the illumination of the wider philosophical and religious context of the origins of modern science are by Alexandre Koyré: *Entretiens sur Descartes* (New York, 1944) and *From the Closed World to the Infinite Universe* (Baltimore, 1957). Samuel Noah Kramer, ed., *Mythologies of the Ancient World* (Garden City, N.Y., 1961) discusses different mythologies, including cosmic views, ranging from the ancient Near East to ancient Mexico and to India, China, and Japan. The best observations made within the context of Vedic and Brahmanic ritual concerning the cosmos are available in Herta Krick's *Das Ritual der Feuergründung* (Vienna, 1982). W. Brede Kristensen's *Het leven uit de dood* (Haarlem, Netherlands, 1926) is the unsurpassed study on the relation of cosmogonies to the spontaneity of life as a central issue in ancient Egyptian and Greek religion. Reprinted and revised several times since its first publication in 1934, Harvey Brace Lemon's *From Galileo to the Nuclear Age* (Chicago, 1965) is quite educational for anthropologists and historians of religions concerned with the development of physics and scientific cosmologies. Including all periods and many civilizations yet with most relevance to cosmogonies in nonliterate traditions, one of the most attractive collections is Charles H. Long's *Alpha: The Myths of Creation* (New York, 1963).

Henry Margenau and Roy Abraham Varghese, eds., *Cosmos, Bios, Theos: Scientists Reflect on Science, God, and the Origins of the Universe, Life, and Homo Sapiens* (LaSalle, Ill., 1992) contains essays and answers concerning life and the universe by eminent astronomers, mathematicians, physicists, biologists, and chemists and does not at all abstain from pronouncements dealing with religion.

Alexander Marshack's *The Roots of Civilization* (New York, 1972) was the first work to break down artificial barriers between religion and scientific views of the universe on the basis of prehistoric data. Jacques Merleau-Ponty and Bruno Morando's *The Rebirth of Cosmology* (New York, 1976) is a detailed reflection on the limits of modern astronomy. A collection of studies on cosmos and myth in seventeen different nonliterate traditions, plus one playful attempt at a structural analysis of the *Book of Genesis* as myth by Edmund Leach, are collected in John Middleton, ed., *Myth and Cosmos* (Garden City, N.Y., 1967). Marijan Molé's *Culte, mythe et cosmologie dans l'Iran ancien* (Paris, 1963) presents a full discussion of ancient Iranian cosmology, with elaborate textual documentation. Werner Müller's *Die heilige Stadt: Roma quadrata, himlisches Jerusalem und die Mythe vom Weltnabel* (Stuttgart, Germany, 1961) discusses the tenacity of cosmic views forming the model of city planning and includes a lengthy bibliography. Teachings concerning the cosmos and its hierarchy, with special attention to microcosmic views, are given in Seyyed Hossein Nasr's *An Introduction to Islamic Cosmological Doctrines* (Cambridge, UK, 1964). Volume 2 of Joseph Needham's *Science and Civilisation in China,* 7 vols. (Princeton, N.J., 1956) is the best study available on any civilization that illuminates the rise of science, cosmology, views of nature within the course of religious traditions and change. Otto Neugebauer's *The Exact Sciences in Antiquity,* 2d ed.

(New York, 1969) is a classic work on the topic. Martin P. Nilsson's *Geschichte der griechischen Religion,* 3d ed., 2 vols. (Munich, 1967–1971) is indispensable for the study of religious complexities within which cosmic views in Greece arose and changed. F. S. C. Northrop's *Man, Nature and God* (New York, 1962) deals with the problem of cosmology, science, and nature within a world that is religiously, culturally, and philosophically diverse yet has no option but to come to terms with its unity. Jacob K. Olupona, ed., *African Traditional Religions in Contemporary Society* (St. Paul, Minn., 1991) is a collection of essays mainly by scholars of African universities.

The best available text on astronomy from classical India is David Pingree, ed., trans., and comm., *The Yavanajataka of Sphujidhvaja,* 2 vols. (Cambridge, UK, 1978). For the problem of monotheism and the origin of the cosmos, see Raffaele Pettazzoni's *Essays on the History of Religions* (Leiden, 1954) and *The All-Knowing God* (London, 1956). In view of the great importance of myths of creation and cosmologies and their significance for the notion of power in the world, see the world-encompassing Raffaele Pettazzoni, *Miti e leggende* (New York, 1978). Don K. Price's "Endless Frontier or Bureaucratic Morass?" *Daedalus* 107 (Spring 1978): 75–92, and Robert L. Sinsheimer's "The Presumptions of Science," *Daedalus* 107 (Spring 1978): 23–36, both present indirect but eloquent arguments for the necessity of a more significant framework for science than science itself can provide. James B. Pritchard, ed., *Ancient Near Eastern Texts relating to the Old Testament,* 3d ed. with supp. (Princeton, N.J., 1969) is a large collection of myths, laws, and epic texts in which cosmological ideas are embedded. Dualistic views characteristic of Manichaeism are described in Henri-Charles Puech's "Le manichéisme," in *Histoire des religions,* vol. 2, edited by d'Henri-Charles Puech (Paris, 1972). Joseph Silk, *The Big Bang: The Creation and Evolution of the Universe* (San Francisco, 1980) provides a readable account of the famous theory—very useful for humanists and social scientists who wish to be informed. Carl F. von Weizsäcker's *The History of Nature* (Chicago, 1949) is a balanced and thoughtful account of the modern natural sciences between philosophy and religion and is of abiding interest. A. J. Wensinck, *Studies of A. J. Wensinck* (New York, 1978), interprets a number of cosmological symbols in Mesopotamian, ancient West Semitic, and Arabic traditions.

KEES W. BOLLE (1987 AND 2005)

COSMOLOGY: AFRICAN COSMOLOGIES

An account of African cosmologies must first come to terms with a set of issues likely to generate controversy. Foremost has been the scholastic predisposition to regard them as of less interest because of their supposed comparative simplicity and lack of theoretical sophistication in articulating visions of a cosmos generally, even in mythical terms. This is linked to a view of indigenous religions in the African context as anachronisms that are the vestigial remains of cultures whose precolonial authenticity has been in a state of decline for several centuries. Christianity and Islam, on the other hand, are often portrayed as dynamic missionary enterprises, almost inevitably destined to prevail and thereby bring Africa and Africans into the domain of respectably articulated "world" religions—and cosmologies.

To counter these questionable yet still all too common stereotypes it is helpful to begin by pointing out that there are in the early twenty-first century at least eight hundred distinct language cultures in sub-Saharan Africa alone. The time is long past when scholars of these cultures could feel comfortable with cosmological and religious generalizations, supposedly common to all, on the basis of detailed studies of a few. Texts that were for too long taken as definitive accounts of African "traditional" religion are therefore challenged by new generations of scholars who reject the negative value judgments implicitly justified by cosmological paradigms derived from predominantly non-African sources. There is a growing consensus that Africa and Africans must finally speak for themselves, from the standpoints of indigenous believers, rather than defer to the potentially methodologically distorted interpretations of purely academic fieldworkers.

This means that a substantial body of established scholarly texts is now directly challenged. Cosmological paradigms patched together from such disparate sources as the accounts of explorers, missionaries, colonial administrators, traders, folklorists, anthropologists, historians, and art historians increasingly are deconstructed by scholars of religion with a social scientific predisposition and by philosophers in the African context. This can mean that there are more than ideological motives involved when Africa reclaims Egyptian civilization (cosmology included) as part of its intellectual heritage. This can also mean that pioneering portrayals of African cosmologies, such as Placide Tempels's *Bantu Philosophy* (a hierarchical, pantheistic, vital force ontology extending from a Supreme Being downward to the lowliest forms of matter) or Marcel Griaule's *Conversations with Ogotemmêli: An Introduction to Dogon Religious Ideas* (an elaborate symbolist rendering of a Dogon cosmology and cosmogony that includes and interrelates everything from stellar constellations to the patterns of plowed fields), are coming to be treated as the systematized, empathic renderings of Western devotees and the elaborated images of idiosyncratic sources whose ideas were thereafter presented as if representative of an entire culture.

Consequently noncontroversial accounts of authentically African cosmologies—past or present—are not easy to identify. Nevertheless in what follows attempts will be made to represent contemporary, even if not entirely methodologically compatible, viewpoints on the cosmologies of three African ethnic groups: the Yoruba of West Africa (principally Nigeria), the Maasai of East Africa (principally of Kenya), and the Kongo of Central Africa (principally as located in the Democratic Republic of Congo, formerly known as Zaire).

YORUBA COSMOLOGY. It has become a truism that more has been written about the Yoruba and their culture than any other in sub-Saharan Africa. Nevertheless this should not be taken to imply that a consensus has been reached about how best to represent Yoruba cosmological beliefs, even if the many accounts of a Yoruba cosmology that have been published might lead one to believe otherwise.

Most of these standardized accounts represent the cosmology as a pantheon. At its head or top is the "sky" god, Olodumare. He "reigns" over the spiritual (*orun*) and material (*aye*) worlds he ultimately is responsible for creating through many lesser (a step down the pantheon) divinities (*orisha*). Olodumare is portrayed as distant from both these lesser divinities and the created world with which they principally interact. The Yoruba have any number of splendid, elaborate myths detailing the story of creation and various encounters between these lesser divinities and between the divinities and the material world, human beings included of course (Courlander, 1973). A step further down the pantheon is reserved for the ancestors (*ara orun*), an exceptional few of whom may have been elevated to *orisha* status, whereas most are in between lifetimes in the physical world. The Yoruba traditionally believe that the individual human "life" consists of an indefinite series of reincarnations within the same family line.

Taking yet another step down the pantheon, one enters the physical world, where human beings as well may be rated or ranked on one of seven different levels, depending on their talents and abilities (Hallen, 2000). Events within that world are frequently attributed to the activities of the lesser divinities, and therefore it is of critical importance that there be an avenue or pathway of communication between the spiritual and physical worlds, which is provided by the agency of the diviner (*babalawo*). The underlying system of divination is known as *Ifa* and consists of an intricate and extensive body of oral literature to which diviners refer when providing information to their clients (Abimbola, 1976). In this Yoruba pantheon there is no personified force of evil, especially one comparable to the Christian or Muslim Satan or devil. Therefore on the level of humanity, individuals usually bear the ultimate responsibility for their immoral (not "evil") behavior, especially when such behavior manifests a publicly identifiable pattern (Hallen, 2000; Olupona, 2000, p. xix).

Beginning in the latter part of the twentieth century, this model of a Yoruba cosmology was challenged by a number of scholars who saw it as a distorted overview—though it may contain many accurate elements—of a still vital cultural tradition. The distortion is due primarily to the imposition of something like a Greek or Roman spiritual and physical pantheon on a cultural context, where it is out of place because it misrepresents the ways in which people in that context relate to and act out their views of the cosmos. These scholars pointed out that religion and its component cosmological beliefs in Yoruba culture are not the product of a "received" body of doctrine, as is the case with Christianity and the Bible or Islam and the Qurʾān (Olupona, 1991). There is also no prophetic figure corresponding to Christ or Muḥammad. In addition the qualitative distancing between the spiritual and the physical introduced by such a hierarchical model does not do justice to Yoruba sensitivities about such relationships. In fact the spiritual is not somehow "up there." It too is "here," constantly intermixed with the so-called physical realm, even if from a different dimension that involves having recourse to specialized techniques (ritual ceremonies, divination, dreams, and offerings—a more interculturally neutral term than the implicitly pejorative "sacrifices") to communicate and interact with it (Soyinka, 1976).

Doctrine or Ritual? Jacob K. Olupona's 1991 *Kingship, Religion, and Rituals in a Nigerian Community*, a study of religion in the Yoruba cultural context, stands out as designed specifically to accommodate a religion and view of the cosmos that does not arise from a body of received doctrine. This shift in the religious substratum is more revolutionary than it might at first seem. In received religions a body of religious doctrine forms the bedrock, whereas rituals and ceremonies are treated as comparatively peripheral and therefore of secondary importance. Now the converse becomes the case, and what was peripheral becomes the bedrock. This also serves to redeem the intellectual character of Yoruba indigenous religion by suggesting that it has never been done justice in conventional fieldwork studies, because again the basis on which it was approached was skewed so as to favor doctrinal-based religions as paradigmatic. Therefore a religion that expressed itself principally via ritual ceremonies did not receive the methodologically specialized treatment it deserved. This could also help to explain the persistent concerns of academic field-workers to construct a systematized pantheon of Yoruba spiritual and physical elements, because the cosmology then could be reconstituted (even if misleadingly) in a discursive format that imitated the architectonics of doctrinal-based religions.

Yet another negative consequence of the pantheon approach is that it gives the impression that the same religious and cosmological views are shared by all Yoruba. But as Olupona points out, it is the Yoruba themselves who acknowledge that they are divided into different cultural groups, and each of these groups can in turn be subdivided into its constituent elements (e.g., individual cities and towns). Therefore one sensible way to reestablish a basis for a systematic approach to assessing the possible universality as well as the potentially culturally relative meanings of myths, ritual ceremonies and their cosmological portents would be to begin on a microcosmic level—what myths are told and how rituals are enacted in a particular city or town—before proceeding to hazard generalizations about some sort of Pan-Yoruba religion or cosmos.

Another stereotype of Africa's indigenous societies that must be challenged is the idea that they are static, oriented exclusively toward "traditions" inherited from the past and therefore resistant to change. For what Olupona finds in present-day Ondo is indeed a "traditional" culture but one that is changing to adapt to and come to terms with present-day realities. In religious and cosmological terms, the introduction of Christianity and Islam has had the most profound consequences. But the institutions of indigenous Ondo religion, most importantly as personified by the town's traditional ruler or king (*Oshemawe*), have recast the annual cycle of public ritual ceremonies involving the king so that they serve a civic as well as a religious function. In other words, indigenous religion in the Ondo Yoruba context is now sustained and perpetuated by the wider social and cultural contexts with which its rituals, ceremonies, and myths have become intimately associated. Indeed Olupona goes so far as to speak of a civic dimension to these public ritual ceremonies that complement the viewpoints of those (Christians, Muslims, and so on) who have no reason to view them in more conventionally religious terms.

What this means is that the annual cycle of religious ceremonies can now also be regarded as occasions in which the entire town—indigenous practitioners, Christians, and Muslims—can all actively participate in some form or other because they serve to renew and to energize the Ondo cosmos in the most general terms (Olupona, 1991, p. 21). Effectively the king has supplanted the Supreme Being as the principal agent of that cosmos. Yet his status as an *orisha* or divinity as well as a temporal ruler instills these proceedings with a spiritual force that attracts the participation of other, purely spiritual *orishas*: the ancestors, the chiefs who rule under him, and the body of the townspeople. Rather than the townspeople factionalizing along religious lines, this localized, revisionist role of the king and the ritual ceremonies with which he is involved have enabled the town to retain a robust sense of unity. Olupona suggests that this might not have happened were it not for the fact that Yoruba religion can be so eclectic and that this eclecticism can in large part again be attributed to the fact that the religion is not based on a fixed body of doctrine or dogma, cosmology included.

Maasai Cosmology. The solitary Maasai warrior (*moran*) fashionably festooned with ochre and a red tunic, standing on one or two legs with spear or staff upright while guarding a grazing herd of cattle, has become one of the Western icons of sub-Saharan Africa. The once mighty Maasai military confederation, thanks to colonialism and the rise of independent African nation-states, has been compelled to recast itself as a nomadic, pastoralist society devoted primarily to raising the cattle their myths tell them were originally a gift from God (Nkai).

There is considerable controversy as to what their religious and cosmological beliefs may have been in the past. But Paul Spencer's 2003 study, *Time, Space, and the Unknown: Maasai Configurations of Power and Providence*, written essentially from a structuralist viewpoint, sets out to document them in the present. This contemporary Maasai cosmology effectively reflects their current lifeworld, a term that is understood in phenomenological-hermeneutical circles to refer to a socially constituted, everyday, cultural universe. This means that the views attributed to them about space and time and the cosmology of which they are constituent elements are said to arise from the world the Maasai inhabit as empirically firsthand.

Although the Maasai are nomadic, they are said to have a refined sense of spatial order—within certain empirical limits. This extends from the precisely detailed layouts of their huts and homesteads to the uninhabited grazing lands for their herds—still sometimes referred to by those who write about Africa's cultures as the "bush." By day the bush may constitute an environment that offers obvious benefits and usually identifiable dangers, but by night it becomes a place where many natural and supernatural hazards (sorcery among them) may victimize the unwary, so that it is primarily groups of *moran* who may on occasion undertake ritual ceremonies there in relative safety.

By the early twenty-first century the pastoral Maasai consisted of sixteen separate but federated territorial groups. Although there must obviously be a sense of spatial identity arising from the territory of the federation as a whole, the individual Maasai is said to more or less view the space that is within his or her ethnic domain as the one that is truly privileged to him or her. What lies beyond is the relatively unfamiliar, though there is acknowledgment of an other, hidden dimension to a space of indefinite, also supernatural, extension that cannot be known in straightforward empirical terms.

Time in the Maasai cosmos is said to be most importantly determined by the cycle of ritual ceremonies that take place every fourteen to fifteen years and govern groups of males' progression through childhood to *moran* status and finally to that of elders who are entitled to marry and settle down (nomadically) in an individual homestead, raising families and building up herds of cattle. The model of time is said to be lived by the individual Maasai, so it is not so much cyclical in nature as it is spiral. This is because the individual lifetime progresses through the cycle of ritual ceremonies only once as it advances from childhood to elder status, even if the ceremonies continue to be performed for other individuals and groups. Consequently the Maasai are said to be a "very age-conscious people" (Spencer, 2003, p. 15). Although the *moran* may be more vigorous physically, the elders govern and determine the ritual cycle. Therefore their status in the community is, in the end, supreme—as a source of both political stability and morality.

The elders, as those who control the timing and organization of the ritual ceremonies, are also looked to as those best qualified to deal with the wider, spiritual dimensions to the Maasai cosmos (Spencer, 2003, p. 65). They determine when the offerings are to be made to Nkai to ensure his continued providence, because he is said to be ultimately responsible for everything that happens in the Maasai world. But although Nkai may have once been in close contact with the Maasai, for example, when he first provided them with cattle, he has since withdrawn in a manner that makes it difficult to determine whether and why fortune or misfortune will affect a particular individual's lifetime. And that lifetime constitutes everything that the individual has to look forward to, because the Maasai are said not to believe in an afterlife and therefore in any forms of ancestral spirits.

When the Maasai feel the need to turn to a higher authority than the elders for guidance or counsel, they turn to diviners (*il-oibonok*). The oracles used by qualified diviners are said never to lie, but it can also prove difficult to get them to give a clear and unambiguous diagnosis of the underlying problem. The most prominent lineage among families who claim to have special powers in this regard are the Loonkidongi, who trace their origin back to Kidongoi, a boy with extraordinary powers who is said to have come down from the sky. Within the ranks of diviners, the most powerful—communally announced and acknowledged—are said to be analogous to prophets in that their powers to "see" the truth about any situation are held in awe and are believed by many to be infallible. These are the specialized professionals to whom even the elders turn when faced with a delicate or difficult situation.

Spencer's (2003) account of Maasai cosmology contains several recurrent themes that suggest it may have more in common with that of the Yoruba than originally thought. He remarks repeatedly on the Maasai inability or unwillingness to elaborate many of their most important cosmological beliefs. With reference to any subject beyond the immediately empirical, words or phrases such as "reticence," "beyond human comprehension," "dimly perceived," "unknowable," "avoid the topic," "enigmatic," and "reluctant to elaborate" pepper his text. Yet when it comes to descriptions of the ritual ceremonies in Maasai culture, they are said to be elaborate and even "flamboyant." Therefore one cannot help wondering whether this is another example of a religion and cosmology that is based on and expressed by its ritual ceremonies rather than a body of received doctrine. If this is the case, it would explain the Maasai inability to elaborate on their religion and cosmology in discursive fashion and therefore make efforts to get them to do so of indeterminate value.

KONGO COSMOLOGY. The traditional cultures of Zaire were subjected to one of the most disruptive forms of colonialism when that nation was part of the Belgian Congo. Therefore what is truly remarkable about modern-day Kongo cosmology is how many of its precolonial elements have survived, even if the institutions and agents through which they are expressed have been dramatically transformed. Even though colonialism did not directly suppress Kongo cosmology at the local, village level, what this perhaps testifies to is the passion, the depth of feeling and commitment on the part of the Kongo to their indigenous religion and cosmology.

As Wyatt MacGaffey (1983, 1986) states, it is the abstracted academic study of select behavior and beliefs that transforms things that are lived realities, that are literally worth living and dying for, into "subjects" like "African cosmology" or "African traditional religion." Therefore to reinvent them it is necessary to put them back into the wider social and cultural contexts of which they are intrinsically and dynamically constituent. Kongo cosmology and religion are also said to be expressed primarily via myths and ritual ceremonies, and the two combined create a distinctive cosmology. In Kongo cosmology the universe consists of the land of the living (*nza yayi*, "this earth") and the land of the dead (*nsi a bafwa*), which are separated by a body of water. Interaction between these two realms is vigorous and constant. Unlike the Yoruba, the Kongo do not believe in reincarnation or, like the Maasai, that there is no afterlife. The individual dead (*bafwa*) remain in the world of spirits, of whom the most powerful is Nzambi Mpungu, not a prominent figure or causal agent in the indigenous Kongo cosmology but later conscripted by missionaries to serve as the Christian "God." Yet it is the land of the dead that is regarded as the primary source of power (*kindoki*), so ritual interaction with it is assigned a high priority for maintaining order in both their land and that of living human beings. Other inhabitants of the land of the dead that are important as sources of power are the "nature spirits" (*bisimbi*), who are attended to by priests (*banganga*) on behalf of local communities.

Although this basic model has been somewhat degraded by the hostile onslaughts of colonialism, missionary Christianity, and even the bureaucratic institutions of an independent Zaire—which all recast it as pagan superstition—it has managed to survive in revitalized form in that country's African Christian churches. In Kongo cosmology myth and ritual correspond to the words and actions used to maintain order and to control and to exercise power in and between the lands of the living and the dead. Because the land of the dead is regarded as the major source of such power, it is the human agents who interact with it via rituals that play the most prominent role in the cosmology. Before colonialism these were said to have been the chiefs (*mfumu*), priests (*banganga*), witches (*ndoki*), and magicians (*nganga*). The former two were associated with those who exercise their powers in a socially benevolent manner, whereas the latter two were thought susceptible to a degree of individualized self-interest that might result in the victimization of their fellow human beings.

The onset of colonialism, missionary Christianity, and then the nation-state led to the abolition of chieftaincies as independent political agencies and of diviners as independent spiritual agents, for reasons that should be obvious in an arena where power itself was being contested. Although missionary Christianity sought to fill the resultant spiritual vacuum, it was the rise of independent African Christian churches, most notably that of the self-announced prophet Simon Kimbangu in 1921, that provided a politically correct institutional home and outlet for the framework of a Kongo cosmology that had endured in the hearts and minds of the people. In this contemporary adaptation the church-based prophet (*ngunza*) assumes the role of the priest-diviner, and the various rituals as modified (principally by the removal of traditional ritual objects) now provide the same high-priority services—mediation with the dead, protection against witchcraft and sorcery, explanations of past misfortune or fortune, and projections of the same with regard to the future—as before. For example, it is noteworthy that interactions between the Kongo and Europeans, such as the slave trade and colonialism, are now regarded as periods during which the Congolese people generally were victimized by European witchcraft. Therefore one point of MacGaffey's (1983, 1986) texts is that the phenomenon of Kimbanguism is indisputable evidence that an indigenous cosmology, expressed principally by myth and ritual ceremony rather than by doctrine, can survive sustained, deliberate attempts to extinguish it and can reemerge and refashion itself, so as to structure and inform a new social institution that will provide it with the public forum it fully deserves, in fact demands.

CONCLUSION. Africa's indigenous religions and cosmologies are neither dying, nor are they operating as anachronisms. They have proved themselves capable of adapting to changing circumstances over which they may have little or no control. Furthermore African cosmologies are diverse, and therefore it is best to avoid unwarranted generalizations about their common characteristics or attributes. This also means that cosmologies expressed via myth and ritual ceremonies have their own integrity and should not be regarded as the products of cultures that are somehow less sophisticated. The religions with which they are associated, Africa's indigenous religions, should therefore be accorded the same respect and integrity as the so-called, self-designated world religions. Last but far from least, there is the as yet unresolved issue of whether African-inspired Christian churches are best regarded as a further manifestation of Africa's indigenous religions.

BIBLIOGRAPHY

Abimbola, 'Wande. *Ifá: An Exposition of Ifá Literary Corpus.* Ibadan, Nigeria, 1976.

Courlander, Harold. *Tales of Yoruba Gods and Heroes.* New York, 1973.

Deng, Francis Mading. *Dinka Cosmology.* London, 1980.

Fu-Kiau, Kimbwandènde Kia Bunseki. *African Cosmology of the Bântu-Kôngo.* 2d ed. Brooklyn, N.Y., 2001.

Griaule, Marcel. *Conversations with Ogotemmêli: An Introduction to Dogon Religious Ideas.* Oxford, 1965.

Hallen, Barry. *The Good, the Bad, and the Beautiful: Discourse about Values in Yoruba Culture.* Bloomington, Ind., 2000.

MacGaffey, Wyatt. *Modern Kongo Prophets: Religion in a Plural Society.* Bloomington, Ind., 1983.

MacGaffey, Wyatt. *Religion and Society in Central Africa: The BaKongo of Lower Zaire.* Chicago, 1986.

Mudimbe, V. Y. *Tales of Faith: Religion as a Political Performance in Central Africa.* London, 1997.

Olupona, Jacob K. *Kingship, Religion, and Rituals in a Nigerian Community.* Stockholm, 1991.

Olupona, Jacob K., ed. *African Traditional Religions in Contemporary Society.* New York, 1990.

Olupona, Jacob K., ed. *African Spirituality: Forms, Meanings, and Expressions.* New York, 2000.

Soyinka, Wole. *Myth, Literature, and the African World.* Cambridge, U.K., 1976.

Spencer, Paul. *Time, Space, and the Unknown: Maasai Configurations of Power and Providence.* London, 2003.

Tempels, Placide. *Bantu Philosophy.* Paris, 1959.

BARRY HALLEN (2005)

COSMOLOGY: AUSTRALIAN INDIGENOUS COSMOLOGY

In 1788, when Captain Arthur Phillip raised the Union Jack on the eastern coast of Australia, he did not know that he had just entered a land that had at least 250 distinct languages. Potentially this meant that there were 250 unique ways to view the land and sea that indigenous Australians called home. Sadly many of these languages are now extinct, and many are in perilous condition with only a few speakers. Each language reflects its own cosmology, its own way of understanding the land to which it belongs. It is, therefore, dangerous to generalize about anything in indigenous Australia. Thus, in this description of indigenous Australian cosmology I will draw on two regional examples, one from the Yolngu-speaking people of northeast Arnhem Land and the other from the Yanyuwa people of the southwest Gulf of Carpentaria.

Indigenous people in many parts of Australia all use the term *dreaming* to refer to the relationship between people and their environment and the laws that set out the realm of Aboriginal experience; the same term can also be used to describe cosmological processes. It is the law that embodies their beliefs, and the law is said to be derived from "the dreamtime" or "the dreaming." The term is misleading because it carries connotations of an imaginary or unreal time. Despite its popular currency among both indigenous and nonindigenous people, the terms *dreaming* and *dreamtime* carry a series of ideological and political connotations stemming from colonial discourses of conquest and dispossession. These issues are discussed and highlighted by Wolfe (1991).

While indigenous people still continue to use the word *dreaming*, it is important, while we need to keep the word, to move beyond the word and explore what is really meant by it. In a more detailed rendering the dreaming and its law refer to a body of moral, jural, and social rules and correct practices that are believed to derive from the cosmogonic actions by which ancestral beings—with the ability to change from animal and phenomenal forms into humans—shaped and named the land, sea, and waterways, transforming parts of their bodies into landscape features, natural phenomena, and plants. Along their journeys they also gave life to people at particular places, bestowed these places upon them, and taught each group the correct manner of doing things: from hunting and foraging, processing of food, and the making of tools to the performance of paintings, songs, and dances. These actions thus constitute the knowledge associated with a place, a knowledge that is respected and observed by being followed in everyday practices as well as reenacted in ritual.

The life worlds of indigenous people in Australia are replete with images of relatedness that are used in many idiomatic expressions; the sea, for example is used as a powerful symbol for establishing identity and notions of strength and in some instances of separateness from the mainland. For example, the Yanyuwa people of the southwest Gulf of Carpentaria call themselves li-Anthawirriyarra, "a people whose spiritual origins are derived from the sea" (Bradley, 1997), while for the Yolngu people of the Galiwin'ku area the Arafua Sea itself is seen to provide ways for the Dhuwa and Yirritja moieties to relate to each other. The Yolngu of this area speak of two distinct bodies of salt water: *gapu dhulway,* a body of shallow inshore water that belongs to the Yirritja moiety and associated clans, and *gapu marmaba,* a body of open sea water belonging to the Dhuwa moiety and associated clans. These two distinct bodies of salt water are known by the terms *Mambuynga* and *Rulyapa;* they "play" with one another as they join together, become separate, and then come together again (Sharp, 2002; see also Bagshaw, 1998).

The actions of creator beings demand a different way of doing things; in some communities they demand a different way of speaking, cooking, or eating (Memmot, 1982; Bradley, 1997). The law of the sea, for example, while similar to that of the mainland, is not the same as that of the mainland. However, despite cultural differences and languages and differing nuances about the law of the land and sea for indigenous people, they all provide an overpowering sense of connectedness and images of the "journey" and "transformation." Ancestral beings first traveled the land and sea, some in the image of species such as kangaroos, eagles, snakes, sharks, marine turtles, dugong, and sea birds, for example. Others are humanlike in form, such as the *Djang'kawu* sisters of northeast Arnhem Land, the *Kilyiring-kilyiring* women in the Numbulawar and Roper Rivers areas, and the *li-Maramaranja,* dugong hunters of the southwest Gulf of Carpentaria. These are among the numerous beings that made journeys, all of which founded groups of people who are their direct descendants today. As these beings traveled, they transformed their bodies, or moved their bodies in certain ways, creating hills, trees, sand ridges, rivers, reefs, sandbars, the tides, and tidal currents. It is images such as these that dominate the cosmogonies and cosmologies of indigenous people throughout Australia. These images are in fact central in illustrating how relatedness is at the basis of the law. A critical aspect of this law is that it provides an understanding of how names and naming are crucial to its activation, transference, and negotiation. People carry names from their country, they know the names of the different parts of their land and sea, they know the names of the hills, ridges, creeks, rivers, sand dunes, reefs and sandbars, the channels and beaches, and they have names for the winds, rain, the waves, and the calm sea. It is an environment full of a particular vocabulary and other ways of thinking and knowing.

Each cosmogonic action of the ancestral beings establishes a relationship among an ancestral being, a place, and a group of people who identify with the land and own it. The image of the journey is held to be the mechanism that orders, distributes, and differentiates groups' rights to and ownership of particular tracts of land or countries. These are important issues; the images of journey cross many hundreds of kilometers. For example, the Groper Ancestor, who began her travels in northwest Queensland at a place called Ngurdurri in Ganggalida country, close to the old Dommadgee mission, traveled looking for country and found it on South West Island in Yanyuwa country. She then traveled northwest and came to a place near Numbulwar before going south and traveling up the Roper River and finishing her travels among the Marra and Wandarrang people at a place called Nyamarranguru. Thus, while there may be no known links of blood kinship among these people, the people who share the Groper as an ancestral being are seen to share a substance derived from the common ancestor. They are kin; there is a regional network established by such actions that daily transform themselves into duties of regional obligation and sharing of ritual.

Similarly, in northeast Arnhem Land the Shark Ancestor is said to have come from Umbukamba on Groote Island and then traveled to Dhurrputjpi and Wandawuy of the Djapu clans; from there to Rorruwuy of the Datiwuy clan; then to Garratha of the Djambarrpuyngu clan; and then to Ngangalala of the Djinang Murrungun clan (Tamisari, 1995, 1998). Thus, all of these clans share in the common essence of the shark, and because of this they are kin; they share in the wealth of the shark, and they come together to celebrate and demonstrate this during times of ritual. What is important in both of the above examples is the ways in which ancestral actions of transformations and of the journey are pervasive images that convey different levels of relatedness among ancestral events, a group owning a given place, and the places that constitute the trajectory of any ancestral journey.

The law that Shark or Groper, for example, put down establishes a series of overlapping local and spatio-temporal connections: first of all between places that they shaped and named along their journeys—a stretch of sea, an area of the coast shaped by hitting the ground with their heads, and further on, a depression they imprinted with their tails. Second, these bodily transformations at each place also connect the plants, animals, and phenomena with which they have interacted. The plants that grow there, like the place itself, are imbued with their power. Third, by bestowing these places upon different groups of people, they related the groups that are positioned at different stages of the journey. These groups identify with Shark and Groper; they are Shark and Groper people, yet they are associated with and are responsible for different aspects of the practical teaching and esoteric knowledge given to them.

These journeys do more than establish kinship links between humans; they also provide a basis by which kinship is established to place for land living and "nonliving" things.

In this way a place or an animal is one's mother because it belongs to one's mother's group. Similarly, a dugong is kin to the particular sea grass species, and sea birds are kin to fish. In other words, animals and plants are considered to be kin and to be related to their environment and other animals rather than having a particular behavior and inhabiting a biological habitat. It is indicative that, as coastal indigenous people would say, the law of an animal refers not only to its biological and behavioral characteristics such as diet, size, coloring, and habitat but also to what is perceived to be its temperament, moral orientation, and intentionality or "cleverness." The nature of relatedness established between place, ancestral events, and people goes beyond what is usually characterized as observable biological phenomena. Because of contemporary issues associated with maritime and coastal management, it needs to be stressed that "putting down the law" encompasses the classification of animals according to both their biological characteristics and their potential to be cultural, moral, and social beings who indeed created humanity. We are dealing here with a non-human-centered moral ecology premised on attributions of intentionality, obligation, responsibility, and reciprocity (cf. Rose, 1992; Bradley, 2001; Yanyuwa families et al., 2003). It is only by understanding this that it is possible to even come close to understanding how indigenous people may frame their concerns. These are issues, as stated above, of cross-cultural communication that cannot be taken for granted. Thus, land and sea are ancestors in themselves; they are sentient, they watch, and if provoked by wrongful action by indigenous kin or nonindigenous people they will release their wrath, hold back desired food, and create tempestuous seas that no boat can cross. Entities living on the land will cause people to become blind so that they will not find the place they are looking for.

All indigenous people see the land and sea they call home as being distinctive, as having a specialness rooted in the actions of ancestral beings and in the actions of their human ancestors. Different groups of indigenous people see themselves as distinctive; their own perception and other people's perceptions of them are as a people apart. Sea people are people who hunt dugong, sea turtle, and fish and who are ecologically, economically, technologically, and ancestrally distinct, while for land-based people it will be the particular species that inhabit their country. There are still great contrasts between the life of people who call the sea home and those that do not.

Amid all of the important discussion that people have had, and continue to have, about their land, there are also the less intimate but no less important relationships of people, creatures, and environment. As senior Yanyuwa woman Annie Karrakayn has commented concerning sea birds, in particular the white-bellied sea eagle, "They make me think about my country, my island, my sea, my mother, poor things." What is being demonstrated in such a statement is the deep and enduring emotional links between people and their country, highlighting an evocative and emotional attachment of "things" to people. The indigenous people of Australia stand within an ecological system dominated by thoughts of their country, their land, and the sea, which has as a part of its integral components human and nonhuman kin, ancestral beings, special knowledge, and power.

BIBLIOGRAPHY

Bagshaw, G. "Gapu Dhulway, Gapu Maramba: Conceptualisation and the Ownership of Saltwater among the Burrarra and Yan-nhangu Peoples of Northeast Arnhem Land." In *Customary Marine Tenure in Australia,* edited by N. Peterson and B. Rigsby, pp. 154–177. *Oceania Monograph 48* (1998).

Bradley, John. "Li-Anthawirriyarra, People of the Sea. Yanyuwa Relations with Their Maritime Environment." Ph.D. diss., Northern Territory University, Darwin, 1997.

Bradley, John. "Landscapes of the Mind, Landscapes of the Spirit: Negotiating a Sentient Landscape." In *Working on Country: Contemporary Indigenous Management of Australia's Lands and Coastal Regions,* edited by R. Baker, J. Davies, and E.Young, pp. 295–307. Oxford, 2001.

Memmot, P. "Rainbows, Story Places and Malkri Sickness in the North Wellesley Islands." *Oceania* 53, no. 2 (1982): 163–182.

Rose, D. *Dingo Makes Us Human: Life and Land in an Australian Aboriginal Culture.* Cambridge, U.K., 1992.

Tamisari, F. "Body, Names and Movement: Images of Identity Among the Yolngu of North-East Arnhem Land." Ph.D. diss., London School of Economics and Political Science, University of London, 1995.

Tamisari, F. "Body, Vision and Movement: In the Footprints of the Ancestors." *Oceania* 68, no. 4 (1998): 249–270.

Wolfe, P. "On Being Woken Up: The Dreamtime in Anthropology and in Australian Settler Culture." *Comparative Studies in Society and History* 33, no. 2 (1991): 197–224.

Yanyuwa Families, J. Bradley, and N. Cameron. *"Forget about Flinders": A Yanyuwa Atlas of the South West Gulf of Carpentaria.* Brisbane, Australia, 2003.

JOHN J. BRADLEY (2005)

COSMOLOGY: OCEANIC COSMOLOGIES

Since over a quarter of the world's discrete religions are found in Oceania or on the islands of the Pacific Ocean, generalizations about their worldviews do not come easily. Because the languages of Polynesia, and virtually all Micronesia, belong to the Austronesian (formerly Malayo-Polynesian) phylum, it is easier to detect a certain culturo-religious homogeneity across these regions, astoundingly scattered though their isolated protrusions of land may be. In the southwest Pacific, on the other hand, Melanesia harbors the most complex mix of languages on earth, concentrated in larger islands, and reflecting a great variety of small-scale traditional pictures of the cosmos. One may safely concede a common social structure pertains in Polynesia and Micronesia; their peoples are governed by chiefs, with chiefly seniority usually being established through tracing one's ancestry to the leader of the first canoe arriving on a given island. Distinctly hierarchical societies have arisen from this arrangement, with Hawai'i, Tahiti, New Zealand, and especially Tonga, being known for their monarchs ruling over nobles (including priests) and commoners. In Melanesia, by comparison, chieftain societies are in the minority (albeit a significant one), and more common is a competition between skillful "managers" of exchanges and war, one among the other contenders rising to the top as a clan leader or "bigman." In this more characteristically Melanesian situation no one ever secures supreme power over a whole culturolinguistic complex, which therefore remains acephalous and unstable. Only rarely in Melanesian chiefly societies, moreover, as in Viti Levu, Fiji, and in the Trobriand Islands, did one chief achieve virtual paramountcy over various others.

As a rule of thumb (while also being wary of sociological reductionism), Oceanic cosmologies tend to reflect this relative contrast in social structure. The Austronesian world pictures of the wider Pacific tend to be more "vertical," tending more to differentiate the upper from the lower world and often distinguishing the land inhabited by humans from an underworld. In southwest Pacific Melanesia the outlook is more "horizontal," with most of the nonhuman powers that matter seen to surround settlements in the visible and proximate environment. Starting from two extreme points will help our orientation. In Tonga one finds two kinds of grave, one for commoners known as *fonua,* with burials under plain mounds of coral sand, and the other *langi,* for royals and nobles, more impressive for being hedged about by blocks of rock. Significantly, *fonua* denotes land and the earth, which commoners have served and to which they return, becoming vermin under the ground. *Langi,* in contrast, means heaven (and its great beings), to which sovereigns and those of noble blood are destined, a vertical cosmic picturing and a hierarchical power structure thus reinforcing each other. Taking a well-known Papua New Guinea Highlands case, in stark contrast, the Wahgi recognize no major deities like the Tongans—though the powers behind prehistorically polished round stones were taken as war gods—and their cosmology is defined exclusively by the ancestors. The dead were deposited high in the mountains, and it is the departed who were thought to push the clouds backwards and forwards across the sides of the great Wahgi Valley, allowing for the sun and moon to be seen, or not. The spirit powers, in any case, including harmful place spirits (Tok Pisin: *masalai)* were basically environal, or largely horizontal in relation to humans, being "out there" rather than above or below.

In the Austronesian *Weltanschauungen* of Polynesia and Micronesia, therefore, one may expect cosmogonic narratives in which levels of the universe are given their places. In Maori myth (of Aotearoa/New Zealand), to illustrate, Rangi (heaven) and Papa (earth) were in an inextricable embrace until Tanemahuta, god of forests, birds, and insects, and one of the primal pair's six children, raised up his father to the skies with his strong back and limbs, his feet firmly grounded in his mother the earth. Here we find a cosmic *Trennung,* a common motif of cosmogenesis around the globe, one underscored by recognition of an underworld, supervised by the formidable Hine-nui-te-po, Goddess of the Dead. On Rarotonga (Cook Islands), the cosmos was conceived as arising out of an enormous coconut shell. It grew up from "Ancient Dirt" (that betokened the netherworld and the ancestral base of humanity, as well as earth) and reached its completion in the heavens. In the Micronesian Gilbertese (now Kiribati) genesis, the young hero Naareau Riiki snares the cosmic eel so as to uproot the sky, propping it up as separate from the sinking land and sea below.

Common in the wider (non-Melanesian) Pacific is the sense of the surface of both earth and sea lying between two major spirit realms of sky and the undersea depths. This imaging pertains rather naturally to an island context, in which upthrusts of land sit under a vast sky that reaches down to distant watery horizons like a huge upturned bowl. The most vital sources of positive power typically lay above; the middle arena usually contained spirit powers along with humans, and strategies were taught as to the best means of interaction because forces were a mixture of the well disposed and the difficult; while the netherworld was most often a domain of uncertainty, if not anxiety. The sky realm could be conceived as having compartments (of the four directions), as well as layers, with the lowest "brow of heaven" (as the Micronesian Chuukese of the Caroline Islands put it) peopled by deities connected to everyday activities—fishing, weaving, lovemaking, and the like. Debate surrounds the authenticity of Maori traditions of a deity called Io, who sits above all the layers of heavens like the removed ultimate mystery of the ancient Gnostics; but the picturing remains consistent with Austronesian vertical orientations and is commensurate with the insistence that chiefs become stars after death and still influence earthly affairs from afar.

In Melanesia such socio-cosmological correlations are more uneven. The mixture of Austronesian and many non-Austronesian groups, and the greater number of inland-based cultures, make it hard to spot patterns. Most typical is the preconceptual "feel" of an environment that decreases in security the further one is away from a home base. What Peter Lawrence (1984) has described as the "security circle" usually consists of a cluster of hamlets, or lineages dwelling close enough to constitute a clan. Each clan worked inherited land available for gardening, in proximity to blood-related clans that made up an acephalous tribal complex. The jural group and the political executive were at the clan level, and religious ceremonies were put on by clans, albeit sometimes simultaneously, even together with others. Security diminished as one passed into bushland that separated tribes, into tribal areas that were neighboring and often hostile to one's own, and then on into swamps, deep forests, and across rivers and mountains where powerful spirits dwelt or where one became a truly vulnerable stranger. The spirit world generally manifested at "ground level," and encounters with problematic *masalai* and ghosts were expected if wild areas were traversed. Fears of such encounters often relate to assumptions about defensible territory. Ghosts connected to other tribal areas would be presumed to be highly inimical to outsiders. In the case of the Papuan Highland Fuyughe, notions of any roundabout raids on enemy hamlets were forestalled by beliefs that each tribe was protected by *sila* (place spirits in the form of huge serpents), beings who dwelt in the mountain overshadowing each tribal territory and who were ready to destroy any trespassers.

It is not that the sense of transcendence was completely absent from Melanesian traditional religions. Among the Enga, for instance, to the west of the New Guinea Highland Wahgi and in a society comparably preoccupied with the aid of the ancestors, one finds talk of an apparent "high god" Aitawe. While Aitawe sustains all things, however, he receives barely any ritual attention and does not figure in the religious foreground—in the *Tee* festival (for the ceremonial prestation of pigs), initiations, even rites to avert crises. This relative inattention to "overarching" deities is typical of Melanesia. If there are creator gods, they often put the basic environment in place and let other beings—often "culture heroes"—show creativity thereon (as with Anut of the Sor, Sengam, and related coastal Madang peoples), or, like the bisexual sky deity Ugatame of the Irian Jayan Kapauka, they set a "predetermining scheme of things" (*ebijata*) but do nothing to police it. On the other hand, creative deities' original acts can be forgotten so that instead what comes to the fore is their role of bringing succor in war or their close-to-hand sanctions against delicts—as with Yabowahine for Goodenough and Bonarua Islanders respectively (in the East Papuan Massim cultural complex).

Powers that are high above are likely to be "brought down" in Melanesia to have special connections to a people's very ground, and any conceived high planes of existence were made quite comparable to the human one. Thus, among the Southern (Papua New Guinea) Highland Huli, the sun is Ni, one of two cosmic brothers, but it is more important that he looks over Huli territory (from the Huli point of view not staying long to watch anywhere else) and that he laid his "eggs," shiny smooth black stones revealed in ritual and signifying the protection of tribes. At the same time the most powerful spirits for the Huli dwelt in caves, and certain sacred cave sites (*gebeanda*) became the focus of more than one tribe. Whereas in the wider Pacific places of worship suggest "open spaces," with stone platforms and fenced arenas more than impressive temples being the key architectural feature, Melanesia is famous for preoccupation with eerie "natural" shrines (such as caves and crevices), to which offerings will be brought with the utmost caution, or with temples that bear darkened interiors and contain hidden, awesome paraphernalia of a cult deity or else the trophies (oftentimes skulls) of the ancestors' previous victories.

What of planes of existence? In a strange, broken line from mountainous Enga country down to the swamplands of the Fly River Delta, there are notions of the sky people and sky villages. Among the Enga a special class of beings (the *yalyakali)* are thought to occupy the sky realm, yet their appearance in the lives of humans is almost always connected to a change in material existence—a special opportunity in hunting, for instance. In the Roku (western Trans-Fly) area, the dead are supposed to live in the sky, yet again their capacity to act as conduits of material blessing on earth is the paramount point. Rocks, for example, are not found in Roku terrain, yet the Roku dead are imagined to create them and then send them to the beginning of those trade routes in the West, whence they arrive to fulfil a material need.

In Melanesia, indeed, one even finds such concrete interactions with spirit beings that some of them can only be brought into being by human actions and others are discarded when their purpose has been served. The war god called Kakar among the Murik Lakes tribes (at the mouth of the Sepik), for example, is only brought to life when the carved war clubs that "constitute" him are put in a line. The accoutrements signifying the ancestral being known as the Sir Ghost among the Manus (New Guinea Islands) are taken from rafters and thrown into the sea once the head of a household dies and takes on the role of a new Sir. Whereas in the wider Pacific, spiritual presences tend to be more confined to worship areas or open-faced meeting houses (such as the elaborately carved *whare whakairo* among the Maori), in Melanesia such presences extend to the poles and rafters of houses' interiors (whether communal or familial). The spiritual energy in these poles is in various cultures conceived as a protective shield against sorcery, the fear of which is more prevalent in Melanesia than elsewhere in Oceania. Moreover, whereas in Austronesian languages terms for spirits are more indicative than symbolic, many non-Austronesian languages nuance the natural environment in highly subtle ways. The Southern Highland Foi, for example, "feel" damp places and valleys as feminine, while dry spots and high, airy terrain intimate masculinity (a dichotomy familiar in Chinese sensibilities).

Cosmological differences can be expected to bear implications for pictures of afterlife states. In the main, admittedly, the other world is expected to be an extension of the living community and to hold all of those who are deceased, whether good or bad, so long as their "soul" or "spirit" is released in funerary rites or their journey to the place of the dead made without mishap. Thus, for the coastal Papuan Roro those whose spirits reach the eastern horizon have been individuals escaping some traumatic, sudden death. A surprise attack from behind by an enemy, or being taken to one's death by a crocodile, prevented this blessing, condemning the deceased to the state of an angry wandering ghost near the place of the sad incident. In the belief of the Raiateans of Tahiti, for a Polynesian case, whether the dead went to the realm of Light (*Ao*) or Darkness (*Po*) simply depended on whether the soul perched itself on the right rock of final departure or not. Culturally between, on the (Austronesian) Papuan Muju Island, admission to "the Isle of the Blest" (Tum) came only through precariously balancing on the great serpent Motetutau who took one there and by showing two special lines of tattooing to get around the hag guarding this (horizontally placed) "heaven."

Only occasionally do ethical dimensions show up in visions of post-mortem conditions. The Micronesian Wuvulu hold that each hamlet is guarded by *puala*-spirits whose reactions to human behavior are interpreted by priests. The *puala* send bad people down to Mani Pino Pino directly below each settlement, where waste drips down and evildoers live in agony eating snakes and lizards, until the *puala* grant mercy and bring them up to the wonderful villages of the dead. If cases like this in Melanesia have horizontally placed purgatories—the Papua coastal Motu naming two islands where malefactors have to work off the punishments they deserve—a few of them project more vertical images. The Southern Highland Erave, for instance, speak of a red place in the sky—a kind of Valhalla—receiving those who die on the field of battle (and those women supporting them), while a brown place of estrangement on earth level awaits the rest.

The general cosmological polarity suggested in the above survey can be accepted only as a useful heuristic devise, certainly not as a watertight generalization. The honoring of the (sculptured) ancestor chiefs of Polynesia's Easter Island, or Rapanui, for example, and the Orongo bird cult that developed more recently in the island's history, did not intimate transcendental or vertical conceptions; while some groups of Melanesia's north Papuan Orokaiva conceived of Asisi as a God high above humans, with the ancestors mediating in between. On the balance of the evidence, moreover, the smaller the scale of the culture in the Pacific, the less likely social hierarchy and a tiering of the cosmos will appear reinforcing each other, and the more special features of the landscape will call for sacralization or beckon ritual attention. One litmus test here would be caves, which are not uniformly doors to the underworld in Polynesia and Austronesian cultures. In Melanesia, however, whether on land or under water, they are most likely to be entrances to mysterious treasure or material blessing. Famous stories in this latter connection concern Manamakeri, of the Biak-Numfor cultural complex (Irian Jaya), a hero who reveals that the access to eternal life and permanent material blessing *(koreri)* is under the ground; and also Edai Siabo, who found the secrets to generate the Hiri trade expeditions (of coastal Papua) when diving into the depths of the sea.

Islander movements in response to outside intrusions and colonialism have reflected the tendencies here being plotted. Among the most famous new religious movements in the colonized world are the Melanesian cargo cults. In these, the followers of "prophet-visionaries" are convinced that European-style commodities—from tinned meat to automobiles—will arrive in abundance at the hands of returning ancestors, even Jesus in his Second Coming (as inferred from mission teaching). The stress in such cults is on material prosperity and tangible riches, reflecting Melanesian horizontal cosmologies. Prophets (*konoors*) among the Biakese, to illustrate, proclaimed access to Koreri, and in the context of the Second World War members of a makeshift army protesting against the Japanese believed that the magical touch of eternity made them invulnerable to foreigners' bullets. Other, comparable protest actions in Melanesian occurred in the hope that guns would be included in the cargo to drive colonial intruders from their land.

In new religious movements of the wider Pacific, by comparison, we find prophets presenting themselves as mediators between heaven and earth, even if the same Protestant and cargoist themes can also be found. In the context of the second Maori War (1864–1865), for example, with so-called Hauhau "extremists" also taking themselves to be impervious to British firepower, the prophet Marire reassured his followers of Gabriel's message that fallen fighters would be "glorified" and "stand on the roof of clouds." The message of the freelance missionary Siovili of Eva on Samoa (1840s) was that he had direct access to the "Great Spirit" above and that a cargo ship would arrive, not over an ordinary horizon, but from "the King of the Skies." In the following century, when a new sect sprang up on Onotoa in the southern Gilberts (Kiribati), the leader Ten Naewa promised that God himself would descend directly to the island, and later announced himself to be "father of God" and his close protectors, "Swords of Gabriel." The contrasting cosmological tendencies detectable in such movements now continue behind different ecclesiastical and theological styles as Christianity consolidates in the region.

SEE ALSO Caves.

BIBLIOGRAPHY

Bennardo, Giovanni, ed. *Representing Space in Oceania: Culture in Language and Mind*. Canberra, 2002.

Goldman, Irving. *Ancient Polynesian Society*. London, 1970.

Goodenough, Ward. *Under Heaven's Brow: Pre-Christian Religious Tradition in Chuuk*. Memoirs of the American Philosophical Society 246. Philadelphia, 2000.

Handy, Craighill. *Polynesian Religion*. Bernice P. Bishop Museum Bulletin 34. Honolulu, 1927.

Lawrence, Peter. *The Garia: An Ethnography of a Traditional Cosmic System in Papua New Guinea*. Melbourne, 1984.

Moore, Albert. *Arts in the Religions of the Pacific*. London, 1997.

Swain, Tony, and Garry Trompf. *Religions of Oceania*. Library of Religious Beliefs and Practices. London, 1995.

Trompf, Garry. *Melanesian Religion*. Cambridge, U.K., 1991.

GARRY W. TROMPF (2005)

COSMOLOGY: INDIGENOUS NORTH AND MESOAMERICAN COSMOLOGIES

There are relatively few generalizations that can legitimately be made about Native American cosmology as a whole. Perhaps the most important, if apparently contradictory generalization, is that all cosmologies are local. In other words, each people, each nation, each pueblo, each city maintains its own cosmos. On some level, then, to understand Native American cosmology as a whole one must comprehend a multiplicity of individual Native American cosmologies. There are scholarly works that provide an overview of Native American cosmology through broad surveys of the various traditions. Some of these books are mentioned at the end of this essay, but no such endeavor is attempted here. Instead, the intent here is to blend conventional scholarly methods with indigenous methods of communicating cosmological knowledge in order to give the reader a substantive yet concise sense of the character of Native American cosmology.

Rather than selecting traditional narratives that are intended to symbolize all Native American cosmologies, we turn to two specific indigenous histories. In both cases, we will see how calendric and astronomical practices reflect cosmological views. The first story comes from a late-nineteenth-century Zuni pueblo; the second from the Late Classic Maya city of Copán. Although separated by over a thousand miles and a thousand years, these two events provide insight into the means by which Native American cosmologies might be conceptualized as representing a single Native American cosmology.

For Native Americans, the universe is generally considered to consist of three realms. The region below the surface of the earth comprised the lower world. The region above the reach of the highest trees constitutes the upper world. The region in between is, approximately, the middle world. There is a further "division" of the cosmos based on the movements of the upper realm's inhabitants, the most important of which is the sun. Frequently this division is correlated to the concept of the four cardinal directions. Native American conceptualizations, however, explicitly tie these directions to the reference frame of the sun's motion: east is associated with the sun's entry into the sky; west with the sun's entry into the Underworld; north is the right hand of the sun; and south the left hand of the sun.

All three levels of the cosmos are inhabited by different entities. Most entities make a single realm their permanent home, but some entities have the ability to move between realms, or at least communicate across "boundaries." Within this cosmography, time is controlled by the members of the upper realm. Generalizations about the role of the Underworld in Native American cosmologies are more difficult to make, although it is most frequently considered to be the abode of deceased human beings. The deceased, or ancestors, often play active roles in the lives of the "living," but the precise roles vary according to the tradition and the era. In each tradition, however, there is some ritually maintained center that allows a people to communicate with the different realms. Because each form of communication is specific to a people, many different cosmic centers—and accordingly, cosmologies—must coexist.

It is in this general cosmographic context that we may consider two indigenous histories. For the Zuni case, we turn to the year 1896 and the newly initiated state of New Mexico. At this time, the Zuni pueblo in question consisted of a few thousand people occupying multi-room adobe houses and dependent on rainfall irrigation of agricultural crops. Social life was organized by clans, each of which had specific roles in Zuni ritual life. From among these clans, a council of A'shiwanni, or rain priests, would select a *pe'kwin,* or sun priest, charged with maintaining the ritual calendar for all Zunis. Although a religious leader of his people, the *pe'kwin* was elected and so was subject to removal from office should he not fulfill his duties.

Such a case transpired shortly before the appointment of a new *pe'kwin* in 1896. A severe drought had brought suffering to the Zuni pueblo, and the Shi'wano'kia ("Priestess of fecundity") placed the blame for the failed crops on the incumbent *pe'kwin* (Stevenson, 1970, p. 108). A trial of sorts was held, accusations of sorcery were leveled, and the *pe'kwin* was removed from office. Matilda Coxe Stevenson described the succeeding events as follows:

> He was impeached and removed and, after much discussion, a young man of the Raven division of the Dogwood clan was selected to fill the place. The Kia'kwemosi dispatched the elder and younger brother Bow priests to make the announcement to the chosen party. The mother, who was present, wept bitterly and begged her son not to accept the position, saying to the elder brother Bow priest: "He is so young, and he might make some mistake, and then perhaps he would be condemned as a sorcerer." The mother's grief touched the heart of the son, and he declined the honor which he most earnestly desired to attain. Another meeting of the A'shiwanni was held, when a man of the Macaw division of the Dogwood clan was chosen, and in due time he was installed in his high office. (Stevenson, 1970, p. 166)

This new *pe'kwin* did find himself in a predicament shortly after being installed. The Shi'wano'kia questioned whether he had correctly set the ritual calendar, which required an accurate identification of the summer solstice. Fortunately for the young *pe'kwin,* the council of rain priests discussed the case and came down in favor of his calculations.

The above story provides an entry into Zuni cosmology, for it tells us that "natural" phenomena were ultimately subject to "social" determination. From the "modern," "scientific" point of view the date of the summer solstice is in the realm of observable fact; there is really no discussion required: either the sun was at astronomical solstice, or it was not.

But there is obviously more to it in the Zuni case. For one thing, Zuni astronomy itself is of necessity partly based on interpretation given the inaccuracy of naked-eye observation, and their mathematical model of the sun's course. Determining when the summer solstice has arrived by observing the sunrise is difficult, given that the sun appears to rise over the same geographical feature along the horizon for a period of approximately four days (Zeilik, 1985, p. S17). It is up to the priest to determine on which of these four days the sun "changed its course," a determination based in turn on computation and other solar observations. An element of arbitrariness is thus inherent in the setting of the calendar.

Moreover, the process of setting the date of summer solstice had direct impact on the ceremonial life of the pueblo. Namely, harvests and ceremonies were set by the solar calendar, and that calendar was initiated with the observation of the summer solstice by the *pe'kwin.* Zuni ceremonial life, then, was intimately tied to the agricultural cycle and to agricultural productivity, and thus, in turn, to the survival of the pueblo. A poor agricultural yield was thought to result from problems in the relationship between the gods and the populace. The *pe'kwin* was the mediator, so in the end, he was held accountable.

The Zuni gods were neither entirely benevolent nor entirely malicious. Some, in fact, seemed to randomly switch back and forth between reasonableness and juvenile mischief. The *pe'kwin* had the difficult job of navigating these mood swings to obtain the best possible results for his people. It was his job to read the clues wherever he might find them, and to lay a course accordingly. The setting of the ritual calendar comprised an assessment on the *pe'kwin's* part of both the capriciousness of the gods and the needs of his community. The ambiguity inherent in the setting of the date of the summer solstice allowed for flexibility and adjustments to compensate for whatever set of circumstances the *pe'kwin* perceived.

Furthermore, when the Shi'wano'kia in the story above suggested that sorcery might have been the source of the *pe'kwin's* poor guidance, numerous allegations from the populace supported this claim. This tells us that there was a concurrent social negotiation underlying the *pe'kwin's* responsibilities. When the Shi'wano'kia relieves the old *pe'kwin* of his duties and suggests a replacement, she is setting up a social dynamic that affects her people. Namely, if the drought that had begun in the time of the former *pe'kwin* were to continue, the people could still blame it on his ill practices. If, on the other hand, agricultural yield increased, then the new *pe'kwin* could be hailed as the reason for the renewed agricultural production. Either way, the psychological health of the community is maintained, either through a release of grievances—with the old *pe'kwin* as the scapegoat—or through the creation of a new focus for community optimism—the new *pe'kwin* who is seen as righting the course.

We must be careful, however, to note that this does not imply that the job of the *pe'kwin* was strictly political. If his calculations of the sun's movements were significantly in error, for example, the rain priests, who were also observing the sun's course, would not have supported his case. The point is that the *pe'kwin* was forced to intimately know his environment—physical, ecological, religious, and social—in order to maintain the livelihood of the pueblo.

A similar set of negotiations can be observed in the history of another indigenous polity—although this consisted of some 30,000 people and thrived some one thousand years earlier. At the Classic Maya city of Copán, during the seventh century CE, the twelfth ruler of the dynasty, or *ajaw,* found himself and his city at a moment of opportunity. Through alliances with its nearest neighbors, and likely profiting greatly from trade goods that passed from the south into the Mayan region, this city experienced a boom in prosperity. Undoubtedly this caused tensions among the local nobility, and the archaeological record provides us with a demonstration of Ruler 12's efforts to ameliorate the conflicts and generate a cohesion that would maintain the health of the polity in the face of rapid change. A quick review of these efforts demonstrates an overlap in cosmological conceptions between the Copánec and Zuni cases that will aid us in characterizing indigenous views of the universe.

During the middle of the Classic period, the twelfth *ajaw* had begun building up the monumental architecture of Copán systematically. He did not restrict his focus to the civic-ceremonial center, however, but also built monuments among the foothills framing the Copán Valley. These outlying monuments (known as stelae) were critical to maintaining order among the local nobility and populace.

The stelae themselves are unremarkable artistically relative to the far more elaborate monuments raised in the city center. They were carved with long hieroglyphic texts, but did not bear mythological iconography, or a royal portrait as did their counterparts. In fact, their placement was far more important than the textual message they carried. That is, the stelae had been raised in locations that would allow for a marking of the sun's transit along the horizon. In Copán the reasons for observing the sun's movements were different than they were in the Zuni pueblo mentioned above. The stelae did not mark the summer solstice; instead, stelae alignments pointed toward a more detailed integration of sky, earth, and Underworld mediated by Mayan calendrics (Aldana, 2002, pp. S29–S39).

To understand this point, we must first recall that each of the Mayan calendric components—the Long Count, the 365-day count, and the 260-day count—shared a basis in the number twenty. The Long Count tallied days according to accumulations of twenty-day periods; the 365-day year was comprised of 18 months of 20 days each (with one final period of 5 days); and the 260-day count was based on the relationship of 13 numbers to 20 day signs. Not surprisingly, then, the stelae at Copán were set up to observationally and mathematically partition the year into 20-day periods (Aldana, 2002, pp. S29–S39; Aveni, 1980, p. 243).

What made this more than a simple astronomical curiosity was that these monuments were set up in the foothills framing the Copán Valley, among the lands occupied by the commoners in Copánec society. Furthermore, the specific hillocks on which the stelae were placed appear to have held sacred associations for the various lineages that comprised Copán nobility (Proskouirakoff, 1973; Aldana and Fash, 2001). Given the explicit records of Ruler 12's forged alliances with nearby polities, and his need to manage a rapidly growing city, we may see a parallel between his position and that of the Zuni *pe'kwin*: both sought to meet the social and economic needs of their people through observing the activities of celestial deities and by mediating between these deities and the human world. Namely, the twelfth *ajaw* drew together the various noble clans of Copán by ritually connecting socially affiliated geographic regions through the movements of the sun. Because the sun was itself rhetorically tied to the legitimacy of Classic Mayan rulership, Ruler 12 was creating a cosmic metaphor: just as the sun set the order of the celestial realm, so would Ruler 12 set the order in the social realm.

Furthermore, the stelae were public and outside of the city center, making the observation of this celestial order available to all members of the polity. Here, then, the Copán *ajaw* was using astronomy to present a model of order to his polity in order to ameliorate the tensions that arose from economic change. The recurrent rise of the sun behind the stelae on prescribed days exemplified the order that ideally should govern the city of Copán.

In the case of the ancient Mayan city, we see the elaboration possible in a large polity, whereas the Zuni case shows us the intimacy of life in a smaller pueblo. Each case, however, reflects a specific example of a number of concurrent negotiations taking place in indigenous cosmological spaces. An orientalizing view of these native cultures might divide the Native American cosmos into realms whose separation had some physical meaning. We have seen here, however, that an indigenous view of the universe requires a different type of categorization. Rather than think of the sky, the earth, and the Underworld as three physical realms, we may now see them as three social realms, or three polities that require the same types of negotiations within and across them as do human polities. In the above cases, the sun played a particularly important role in the negotiation of what modern society would characterize as political and economic issues. In indigenous terms, we might better conceptualize the negotiation as one between the sky clan and the human clan, with the ruler/*pe'kwin* as the mediator. Cosmology thus becomes the description of personalities and of the relationships among them. In this context, the "laws of nature" can be seen as contracts among clans or lineages—contracts the leaders of communities are charged with maintaining under varying conditions.

Bibliography

Aldana, Gerardo. "Solar Stelae and a Venus Window: Science and Royal Personality in Late Classic Copán." *Archaeoastronomy Supplement* 33, no. 27 (2002): 29–50.

Aldana, Gerardo, and William L. Fash. "Art, Astronomy, and Statecraft of Late Classic Copán." Forthcoming in a collection of papers presented at "Science, Art, and Religion in the Maya World," a conference at Copán, Honduras, July 14, 2001.

Aveni, Anthony F. *Skywatchers.* Austin, Tex., 2001. Revised and updated edition of *Skywatchers of Ancient Mexico* (Austin, Tex., 1980).

Irwin, Lee. *The Dream Seekers: Native American Visionary Traditions of the Great Plains.* Norman, Okla., 1994.

Proskouirakoff, Tatiana. "The Hand-Grasping-Fish and Associated Glyphs on Classic Maya Monuments." In *Mesoamerican Writing Systems: A Conference at Dumbarton Oaks, October 30th and 31st, 1971,* edited by Elizabeth P. Benson, pp. 165–178. Washington, D.C., 1973.

Stevenson, Matilda Coxe. *The Zuñi Indians.* New York, 1970. Originally published in the *Twenty-Third Annual Report of the Bureau of American Ethnology* (Washington, D.C., 1905).

Sullivan, Lawrence E., ed. *Native American Religions: North America.* New York and London, 1989.

Sullivan, Lawrence E., ed. *Native Religions and Cultures of Central and South America.* New York, 2002.

Zeilik, Michael. "The Ethnoastronomy of the Historic Pueblos (1): Calendrical Sun-Watching." *Archaeoastronomy* 16, no. 8 (1985): 1–24.

Gerardo Aldana (2005)

COSMOLOGY: SOUTH AMERICAN COSMOLOGIES

The complex spatial and temporal constructions of South American cosmologies, and the values associated with them, allow only the broadest of generalizations. Vertical structures of the universe vary widely in composition from three-layer arrangements to massive twenty-five layer compositions inhabited by a great variety of beings. In general, the upper worlds are associated with the creative and life-renewing forces of light, lightness, and liquids (river, lakes); the underworlds, associated with places of darkness, the netherworlds of the dead, and animal spirits; and this world, the center of the universe, associated with human life. Different kinds of space and places of being in the universe are systematically associated with one another so as to constitute a whole. Horizontal space highlights the center (or centers), associated with a wide variety of images (cosmic trees, mountains, waterfalls, ladders, vines) symbolizing communication between spatial planes; the periphery, or outer margin, which often expresses in inverted form key values of the center; and a variety of mediating elements, openings, and penetrations connecting inner and outer realms. The places where sacred beings first appear often become models for innumerable spatial constructs.

Such spatial constructions are intrinsically dynamic. For example, the Kogi (contemporary descendants of the ancient Chibchan-speaking Tairona of the Sierra Nevada area of Colombia) universe consists of nine different levels, from zenith to nadir, and is shaped like a spindle, centered on the all-important vertical axis. Like an immense whirling spindle, the universe weaves life from its male (central shaft) and female (whorl) elements, spinning the thread from which the universe's fabric is woven. The beam of sunlight which, during the year, is cast onto the floor of the Kogi temples is considered to be the pattern of life woven by the sun in the universe. A highly respected class of priests, the *mama*, during some eighteen years of training, learn the lore and practice necessary to maintaining *yuluka* (harmony or balance) in the universe as the "law of the mother." The essence of their task is to turn back the sun when it threatens to burn the world, or to avert rain when it threatens to flood it. The cardinal directions of the universe are associated with colors, emotions, animals, mythical beings, the ideal village-plan, the structure of the temple with its four ceremonial hearths, the four principal clans, and so on. The center of space is where the *mama* communicate with divinity.

South American cultures recognize multiple types and units of time independently of chronological history. Cosmic, meteorological, and sonic cycles, the seasonal ripening of fruits, the appearance of animal species, and so on, all represent different modes of time. Festival rounds, ordered in calendric cycles, maintain the order of the universe, reenacting the mythic events that created temporal order in the first place. In these rounds, distinct cycles of time are interwoven—solar and lunar, seasonal, flowering cycles, cycles of song and sounds, the human life cycle, and periodic manifestations of emotions and colors. Ritual music, above all, is the symbol of cosmic time, transforming spaces (dwellings, bodies, etc.) into dynamic containers of changing life. Ritual drunkenness, combat and noise, all prominent aspects in religious festivities, refer to temporal constructs rooted in the primordium and its demise.

One of the central motifs of cosmology among the indigenous peoples of the Upper Xingu of central Brazil is the difference between the original models of beings, present in the myths, and their later renewals. For example, it is customarily said that the original pequi tree produced much larger fruits, with abundant pulp and small seeds; and that the first flutes were aquatic spirits, but the one who discovered them hid them, making wooden imitations, which never could reproduce the potent voice of the original. The first human beings were carved out of wood by the demiurge, who also tried to bring them back to life; because he failed, irreversible death was then commemorated in the ceremony of the Kwarup, in which trunks of the same wood serve as symbols for the dead. The twins Sun and Moon, beyond being the modelers of the Indians of the upper Xingu, are also models for them, since the majority of their mythic adventures consists of the inaugural realization of practices that were later adopted by humans: wrestling, scarification, and shamanism.

Thus, myth is not only a collection of founding events that were lost in the dawn of time; myth constantly guides and justifies the present. The geography of the region is dotted with sites where mythic actions unfolded; the ceremonies are explained by the initiative of mythic beings; the world is peopled by immortal beings that go back to the origin of the world; and the creators of humanity still live in a specific place in the region. In short, myth exists as a temporal—but, above all, a conceptual—reference.

The primordial making of humans, according to upper Xingu mythology, was the work of a demiurge who gave life to wooden logs placed in a seclusion compartment by blowing tobacco smoke over them. Thus were created the first women, among whom was the mother of the twins, Sun and Moon, archetypes and authors of present-day humanity. In homage to this woman, the first festival of the dead was celebrated, which is the most important festival of the Upper Xingu and which thus consists of a reenactment of the primordial creation, at the same time it is the privileged moment for public presentation of the young women who have recently come out of puberty seclusion. Thus, it is a ritual that ties together death and life—the girls who come out of seclusion are like the first humans, mothers of men.

The first humans were thus made in a seclusion chamber. The wooden girls were transformed into people after being closed up in straw compartments similar to those that shelter adolescents in their parents' house. Echoing this myth of origin, the making of the person in the upper Xingu involves various periods of seclusion, all of which are conceived of as moments for making the body: the *couvade* (restrictions imposed on married couples with newborn children), puberty, sickness, shamanic initiation, and mourning. This making of the person is also a process of modeling the ideal personality, above all in the case of puberty seclusion, the most important of all seclusions.

A Transformational Universe. Two key notions for understanding South American cosmologies are transformation and perspective. Various ethnologists of Lowland South America, and also historians of religion, have noted the central importance of the notion of transformation for indigenous traditions. Peter Rivière, for example, in his article "AAE na Amazônia" (1995), discusses the notions of transformation as found in mythic narratives, cosmologies, and social practices. Human nature is seen as varied and complex, which is symbolically expressed through clothing, masks, and body ornaments, which are understood, in turn, as ways of domesticating an "animal" component, which is essential to human nature. Clothing and body decoration mediate between the interior self, society, and the cosmos. "The native peoples of Amazônia live in a highly transformational world, where appearances deceive" (p. 192).

In many creation myths—for example, those of the Mbyá-Guarani, Desána, Xavante—creation blooms from the thought, dream, or intention of the original divinity, but the very notion of "blooming" implies a transformation of something that already exists. Thus, creation is more of a self-transformation than a creation, as in the Christian tradition.

For example, in the Xavante traditions, the primordial beings, through their powers, transform themselves into the sun, moon, animals, and plants. They are able to do this because they possess the principles of manifestation of certain cosmological possibilities, which are contained in their ontological nature. The primordial beings conjugate in their own nature the duality of being and becoming, for they manifest phenomenal beings (the sun, moon, animals, etc.) from their own beings, but without losing their original nature.

Transformations were also critical for the introduction of periodicity, cyclicity, and differentiation in the universe. Many creation myths begin with the description of a prior condition of stasis, which, due to the actions of the primordial beings, comes to an abrupt end, a watershed moment that initiates change in the cosmos. In traditions of the Northwest Amazon, for example, night did not exist in the beginning; it was always day, and the routine of the creator was always the same until, one day, his wife advised him that her father was the owner of night and that night was a good thing. The creator sought night and ended up introducing night into the world. From that moment of rupture, two cycles were initiated, diurnal and nocturnal, each with its own order.

Native views of the world are also defined by what Viveiros de Castro (1996) has called *perspectivism.* According to this theory, the way in which humans see animals and other subjective entities that populate the universe—gods, spirits, the dead, inhabitants of other levels of the cosmos, meteorological phenomena, and at times even objects and artifacts—is profoundly different from the way in which these beings see them and see themselves. "Typically, humans see humans as humans, animals as animals and spirits as spirits; the animals (predators), however, and spirits see humans as animals (game), while game animals see humans as spirits or as predatory animals. Further, the animals and spirits see themselves as humans" (p. 117). This perspectivism has profound implications for the way in which indigenous peoples understand relatedness among the beings of the universe and its dynamics.

TRANSFORMATION AND METAMORPHOSIS IN THE LIFE CYCLE: THE KULINA. The Kulina are an Arawá-speaking people of the Amazon region in Brazil. Their cosmography defines spaces for the spirit beings, plants, human beings, and animals. This cosmography presupposes the existence of layers and, in each layer, places. The layers are basically: *meme* (sky), *nami* (earth), and *nami budi* (below the earth). There is also *dsamarini* (the place of the water) and two other differentiations of the sky that are infrequently mentioned.

Human beings, animals, and plants live on *nami*, the earth, while the spirits occupy the underworld, *nami budi.* The animals and game animals also live in *nami budi*, coming up to the earth to be hunted by the men. The shaman, when he drinks *rami* (ayahuasca) or through his dreams, makes contact with the world of *nami budi*, visiting the great subterranean villages where the spirits live or bringing the animals up to the surface, near the village. To do this, he transforms himself into an animal, given that the animals of *nami budi* are metamorphosed spirits.

For the Kulina, transformation refers to the process of modification of an animal into a person, while metamorphosis is the process of modification of a spirit into an animal. This cycle of transformations is based on a system of oppositions that can be synthesized in the following manner: spirit/metamorphosis; shaman/death; body/transformation; and newborn/game animal. According to the cycle, an undomesticated being, the newborn *nono*, represented by the forest (nature, male), is domesticated through the ingestion of foods produced in the gardens through female substances (maternal milk and saliva), and through learning and understanding the myths and music, until it becomes a social being. After passing through adult life, this social being—*maqquideje* or *jadahi*—has two ways in which he may return to nature, his origin: after death, when his spirit will go to *nami budi*, to the villages of his ancestors, being transformed into a game animal, or through the metamorphosis of the shaman into a wild animal (normally a peccary).

The shaman, assisted by his *tokorimé* (spirit, double, image, normally the peccary), goes to *nami budi*, the place of the dead, and, by identifying his animal *tokorimé* with that of the other spirits of the dead metamorphosed into peccaries, succeeds in bringing them to the surface, near the village, where they then will be, by indication of the shaman, hunted and later devoured. In the final cycle of transformations, the spirits are hunted and eaten by the living, which suggests a kind of endocannibalism, but this is necessary in order for the spirit of the dead to be incorporated once again into the system of reciprocity, which it abandoned abruptly upon dying. During this cycle, the physical undomesticated body goes in the direction of the village, the world of sociability. The other part, the spiritual domesticated part, goes in the direction of the forest, the savage undomesticated world. There is a relation between the physical body and the social world, as well as between the spiritual body and the world of nature, where the world of sociability is that of the living, while the wild world of the forest is related to the spirits, the dead. In this way, the spiritual domesticated body, in its highest degree, goes in the direction of the world of nature and returns as a physical wild body, through shamanic practices or death—the transformations of each occurring in the extremities of each place.

RITUAL RELATEDNESS AND TRANSFORMATION: THE ENAWENÊ NAWÊ. For the Enawenê Nawê, Arawak-speaking peoples of southwestern Brazil, rituals are associated with two categories of spirits: the Enore, spirits of the sky, and the Yakairiti, spirits that live underground, in the hills, and in generally inhospitable places. When an Enawenê Nawê gets sick, he attributes his misfortune to the Yakairiti spirits, whom he believes are upset with something and are threatening to take him to the other world. In the Yãkwa ritual, there is a generalized exchange between humans and the Yakairiti spirits, enacted by ritual groups involving all the village inhabitants. Everything is done with the intent of satisfying the desires of the Yakairiti, so that, on the one hand, they will have no reason to threaten life in the village and, on the other, to maintain the harmony of the world.

The Enawenê Nawê perform several rituals during the year: from January to July, the Yãkwa, and from July to September, the Lerohi (both dedicated to the Yakairiti); in October, the Salumã; and in November and December, every other year, the Kateokõ (dedicated to the Enore). The Yãkwa is the longest and most important of the Enawenê Nawê rituals. It begins with the harvest of the new corn and ends with the planting of the collective manioc (cassava) garden. Each of the nine Enawenê Nawê ritual groups—collectively known as Yãkwa (and which, in reality, are the Enawenê Nawê clans)—is associated with a specific group of Yakairiti spirits. The Enawenê Nawê believe that the Yakairiti spirits are likewise organized in groups and inhabit a specific part of their traditional territory.

To perform the Yãkwa, the groups divide into the Harikare (hosts) and the Yãkwa (clans). The Harikare (or hosts) are responsible for the organization of the ritual and have to fetch firewood, light the fires, and offer the food, while the others (the Yãkwa) sing and dance on the plaza together with the Yakairiti. For a two-year period, one of the ritual groups is the main host and is in charge of the garden, making vegetal salt (an offering to the Yakairiti), and organizing the ritual. At the beginning of the ritual, following mythical traditions, a group of men and boys leave the village for a two-month fishing expedition, during which they construct a dam and set fish traps. The Enawenê Nawê believe that large quantities of fish are provided by the Yakairiti in exchange for the vegetal salt they receive in the course of the ritual. On returning to the village, the men and boys dress and adorn themselves to represent (that is, transform into) the Yakairiti and, carrying the large quantities of fish, they enter the village, at which time there occurs a mock battle between the Harikare and the Yakairiti. After that, the Yãkwa and Yakairiti dance and play the flutes together. Each of the nine ritual groups plays instruments specific to the group. During the course of the ritual, it is as though the Yakairiti become humanized, thus dramatizing the relation of ambivalence and symbiosis that characterizes their coexistence with humans in the cosmos.

A Violent Universe. In many native South American cosmologies, there exists a dialectical tension between dark and light consciousness, manifest as two historically opposed forces: witches, or predatory spirits that kill; and shaman prophets, or priests, with direct access to the sources of creation. Both are represented symbolically in mythical consciousness and both are necessary, the traditions seem to say, to the dynamics of cosmological and historical existence, illustrating the point that dark and light, predatory killing and curing, are complementary opposites rather than antagonistic possibilities of the cosmos. Thus, among the Carib-speaking peoples of the region of the Guianas and Orinoco, we find myth cycles that recount the story of creation as the struggle between two brothers whose deeds set the framework and conditions for human society and individual destiny. One is associated with darkness, evil, and the creation of plants and animals; the other with light, shamanism, and patronage to humanity. These mythic struggles set the stage for the unceasing warfare between *kanaimà* sorcerers ("dark shamans" who specialize in violent killings) and *piai* (light) shamans. Similar sorts of dialectical tensions between the benevolent and malevolent forces of the cosmos may be seen among the Warao of the Orinoco delta, the Baniwa of the Northwest Amazon, and among many Tupian groups.

For the Tupian Cinta Larga of the Juruena River region in Brazil, for example, the universe is seen through the prism of unity. The creation myth is a detailed account of how Gorá created human beings, members of different tribes who populate the region, and conferred on them specific identities and characteristics. Animals, birds, and other living beings were created through the transformation of human beings—some became jaguars, others tapirs, and so on, all through the work of Gorá. Gorá and other minor heroes of Cinta Larga mythology are responsible for all that is positive in the social and cultural universe. The counterpart of these beneficial acts of creation is a spirit called Pavu that inhabits the forest and incarnates the dark side of existence. Pavu wanders through the forest in search of victims and, as soon as it comes upon a solitary hunter or anyone passing through, it launches its mortal attack. No one can resist its power, and, from this encounter, victims get fever that is inevitably followed by death.

Bibliography

Instituto socioambiental (Socio-Environmental Institute). *Povos indígenas no Brasil.* Available in Portuguese and English at http://www.socioambiental.org/website/povind. A basic, though incomplete, reference on indigenous peoples in Brazil.

Rivière, Peter. "AAE na Amazônia." *Revista de antropologia* (São Paulo, USP) 38, no. 1 (1995): 191–203. A brief but important article highlighting the importance of the notion of transformation to South American cosmologies.

Sullivan, Lawrence. *Icanchu's Drum: An Orientation to Meaning in South American Religions.* New York, 1988. Outstanding source on native South American religions by a historian of religions. Examines the cosmogonies, cosmologies, anthropologies, and eschatologies of native peoples across the continent. Masterful work of interpretation of myths, rituals, and beliefs.

Viveiros de Castro, Eduardo. "Os pronomes cosmológicos e o perspectivismo Ameríndio." *Mana* 2, no. 2 (1996): 115–144. Classic article on Lowland South American Indian cosmology, defining key notions of perspectivism, multinaturalism, and animism.

Viveiros de Castro, Eduardo. *A inconstância da alma selvagem e outros ensaios de antropologia.* São Paulo, 2002. Collection of the author's most influential articles in ethnology, including revised versions of articles on the Xingu rituals.

Whitehead, Neil. *Dark Shamans: Kanaimà and the Poetics of Violent Death.* Durham, N.C., 2002. Superb historical and cosmological analysis of the Kanaimà complex (dark shamanism) among Carib-speaking peoples of the Guyanas region and Roraima in Brazil.

Wright, Robin. *Cosmos, Self, and History in Baniwa Religion: For Those Unborn.* Austin, Tex., 1998. Monograph on the Baniwa peoples of the Northwest Amazon, focusing on cosmogony, cosmology, eschatology, and conversion to Protestant evangelicalism.

ROBIN M. WRIGHT (2005)

COSMOLOGY: HINDU COSMOLOGY

Hindu tradition possesses one of the richest and most continually evolving cosmologies in the global culture. From the most ancient Indian religious compositions, the Vedas, to contemporary twenty-first-century Indian theories combining science and religion, time and space have been lavishly narrated and meticulously calculated. Moreover moral, social, and philosophical meanings underlie these cosmologies in compelling ways.

This article will focus on six major frames for Hindu cosmology: the Vedic, Upaniṣadic, epic, Purāṇic, non-Sanskritic, and contemporary scientific-philosophical. Although through the millennia Hindu thinkers have dramatically redrawn notions of time, space, and person, they also share a wealth of common imagery: the reciprocal effects between natural and human affairs, the central idea of a cycle, and the divisions of space into particular realms and spheres. Each new cosmology does not completely replace the old but stands alongside of it as yet another cosmological option.

VEDIC COSMOLOGY. The Vedas and Brāhmaṇas are texts that existed before the idea of "Hinduism" per se emerged as a world religion. Present scholarly consensus puts the earliest date of the Vedas at 1500 BCE, but there remains debate on the topic that might place the Vedas earlier. The Brāhmaṇas are placed around 900 BCE. These texts were almost entirely oral, guarded by the priestly Brahmanic tradition as the basic supporting texts of the sacrifice. The cosmology of the Vedas speaks of the cosmos as Father Sky (Dyaus Pitṛ) and Earth (Pṛthivī). In other texts the cosmos is divided into three realms: *bhūr* (earth), *bhuvaḥ* (air), and *svaḥ* (heaven). The sacrifice and not the gods is considered the source of time, space, and all things that make up the universe. The Agnicayana, or the building of the fire altar, as well as many other forms of sacrifice are viewed in the Brāhmaṇa texts as symbolic reconstructions of the cosmos. Moreover the right placement of sacrificial implements and correct chanting of *mantras* allows the unimpeded turning of the year, the months, and the seasons as well as the correct placement of the three realms. At times cosmological thinking is so present and deeply assumed in Vedic texts that the "earthly realm" (as opposed to the other realms) is simply referred to as *iha,* "here."

VEDIC SPACE. Following from above, the basic form of cosmological space is the sacrificial arena. However, many of the Vedic gods, such as Agni, the fire god, have three different forms corresponding to the three Vedic realms. These "realms" are not only spatial but can also be described as mental states of mind: *loka,* or world, in its earliest meanings, can mean the "freedom to exist unimpeded" or "expansiveness" as much as it can mean a physical location. Yet these three realms are not the only form of imagined space: at death, the Vedic funeral hymns assert, the various elements within a person are scattered to various parts of the natural world. Alternatively the person can go to the realm of Yama, the overlord of the dead.

VEDIC TIME. The sacrificial world understood time as a kind of simple cycle in which the year, the months, and the day are products of the work of the sacrifice. The passing of time is also homologized with death, and in later periods both death and the year were created by Prajāpati, the "Lord of Creatures," who also gave instructions about the correct procedures of the sacrifice. If one sacrificed well and long enough, one attained status oneself as an ancestor deity to be propitiated by other living sacrificers on earth. Therefore once one attained this status, the Vedic texts express a wish to avoid a "re-death." In addition Vedic texts show a high awareness of the motion and rhythm of the sun, moon, and stars and imagine them in a variety of colorful ways: the sun as a horse crossing the sky in a chariot, night and the dawn as rivalrous sisters, and so on. There is evidence that astronomical knowledge, such as the marking of the lunar asterisms, might well have been fairly advanced, even at this early stage of known religious history.

VEDIC PERSON AND MORALITY. In one famous Vedic hymn (*Ṛgveda* 10:90), which proved to be influential in a number of later Hindu schools of thought, the universe itself is understood as a cosmic person (Puruṣa). This Puruṣa is sacrificed in a primordial ritual procedure, and from parts of his body emerge the various creatures of the earth, elements of time and space, elements of the sacrifice, and most importantly categories of the social world, called *varṇa.* These four *varṇas* (brahmin priest; *kṣatriya* warrior; *vaiśya* agriculturalist or trader; and *śūdra* servant) become the basis of social organization expressed in later legal and religious texts. The model earthly Vedic person is one who studies the Vedas, sacrifices, and tends to the sacrificial fires and therefore becomes ritually and morally responsible for the cosmos.

And yet such a person is also a seeker. *Ṛgveda* 10:90 ends with a philosophical paradox: "with the sacrifice the gods sacrificed to the sacrifice." This enigma also sets the tone for much of Vedic cosmology: acceptance of multiple versions of creation; Vedic cosmology is questioning and searching, not doctrinal or creedal in nature. One of the most famous cosmological hymns, the Nasadīya hymn (*Ṛgveda* 10:129), speaks of the world beginning from nothingness, where "the One breathed, windless," and then coming into existence through the power of heat. Desire is the primal seed, and the sages create by stretching a cord across the void. Yet even this spare, poetic cosmology ends with a query:

> Who really knows? Who will here proclaim it? Whence was it produced? Whence is this creation? The gods came afterwards, with the creation of the universe. Who then knows whence it has arisen? . . . perhaps it formed itself, or perhaps it did not—the one who looks down on it, in the highest heaven, only he knows perhaps he does not know. (O'Flaherty, 1981, pp. 25–26)

UPANIṢADIC COSMOLOGY. While the activity of sacrifice is still presumed in the period of composition of the Upaniṣadic texts, the object of sacrificial knowledge is no longer the actual procedures of the sacrifice or the gods per se but a new force called *brahman. Brahman* is thought of as the power behind the sacrifice, and as the Upaniṣadic thought developed, it was described as the power behind every living thing and every element in the universe. *Brahman* is "the Whole" (*Bṛhadāraṇyaka Upaniṣad* 2:5) and transcends even the gods. It also exists beyond all known things in this world, and yet is also present within them as well. It is set apart from beings and yet dwelling within beings at the same time. This basic identification between the selves of beings and *brahman* leads to the famous Upaniṣadic equation that the self *(ātman)* is the same as the power behind the universe *(brahman).* As the sage Yājñavalkya puts it, "The self within all is this self of yours." The larger *brahman* is also spoken of as the *ātman* or "self" of the universe, thus giving rise to the poetic nineteenth-century translation "the World-Soul."

The earliest Upaniṣads probably originated around 600 to 500 BCE and were composed in prose. They shared a common focus on many topics, such as the nature of *brahman,* the nature of sacrificial speech and the verses, the various forms of breath, and the homologization of parts of the body to the powers in the universe. The teaching of the five fires as the essence of the major parts of the cosmos (e.g., fire as man, woman, and the three worlds) is especially distinctive in these early prose compositions. The later Upaniṣads are composed in verse and develop the theme of *brahman* into a theistic rather than monistic conception. They also focus on the idea of liberation through meditation. Both are themes common in later Purāṇic cosmologies.

UPANIṢADIC SPACE. Many of the Upaniṣads continue the idea of the three worlds in the Vedas but add to this cosmology an inner, more existential meaning. When the student Aśvala asks how many oblations there will be, the sage Yājñavalkya responds that each oblation has its own modality and is therefore connected to the specific world that shares that modality. The oblations that flare will win the world of the gods, for the world shines that way. The oblations that overflow *(atinedante)* will go to the world of the ancestors, for that world is "over above" *(ati).* The oblations that lie down *(adhiśerate)* will go to this human world, for that world is here below *(adha).*

This imagery continues a basic cosmology that one sees in earlier Vedic texts of the worlds of the gods, the fathers, and the ancestors. However, it attributes, through etymologies, different modes of being to each of the offerings and each of worlds. In other passages the three-fold world is described in a progression of size from one to sixty-four, a numerology that is recurrent in many later cosmological texts. Finally, in other passages the three levels *(bhūr, bhuvaḥ, svaḥ)* of the Vedic world are expanded into seven realms, many of the additional realms again connoting "modes of being": *mahas, janas, tapas* (meditative heat), and *satyam* (truth).

The second kind of Upaniṣadic space is the body itself. Each of the basic sacrificial procedures, present from the earliest Vedic ritual texts, becomes homologized with the individual breathing body as well as the world itself. In the *Bṛhadāraṇyaka* and other Upaniṣads the sacrificial fires are seen as part of the inner workings of the body; the role of the Adhvaryu priest is identified with their eyes and the process of sight itself, and this sight can see the nature of the whole world (*Bṛhadāraṇyaka Upaniṣad* 3:1:5). In other passages it is not only the cosmology of the sacrifice that is given to the body but also the cosmology of the entire world and its topography. For instance, rivers of the world are identified as the rivers contained within the body (*Bṛhadāraṇyaka Upaniṣad* 1:1:1; *Śvetāśvatara Upaniṣad* 1:4:5), the eye of the world is also the sight of the body (*Chāndogya Upaniṣad* 1:7:4), and so on.

The third kind of Upaniṣadic space is that of *brahman* itself. *Brahman* is also spoken of as a formulation of truth—a truth that is to be attained by wise men and women who have practiced meditation and focused on the forest teachings for a long time. *Brahman* is the highest object of the teachings on hidden connections—an object rooted in austerity and the knowledge of the self (*Śvetāśvatara Upaniṣad* 1:9). The imagery here is not simply that of a truth to be attained but of an abode in its own right, where the sun never sets nor rises (*Chāndogya Upaniṣad* 3:11). Similarly other Upaniṣads also describe *brahman* as a stainless realm (*Praśna Upaniṣad* 1.16) in its own right—a world of unending peace, an ancient formulation that is heard in the heavenly abodes.

UPANIṢADIC TIME: THE CYCLE OF BIRTH AND DEATH. One sees emerging in the Upaniṣads a theory of death and birth that is strikingly different than the Vedic sacrificial fear of "re-death" *(punarmṛtyu).* The Upaniṣads contain the earliest records of what has been called *saṃsāra,* or the endless cycle of birth and death, as well as *mokṣa,* or the path that leads away from *saṃsāra.* The story of Jabālā is instructive on this point (*Chāndogya Upaniṣad* 3:4:1–4). Jabālā is ashamed that his native learning, gleaned at his father's knee, is not sufficient in the court to which he travels. He must learn an entirely new set of metaphors, in which each aspect of life (man, woman, semen, food) is said to be identical with the sacrificial fire. While such matters are not unusual for many sections of the Upaniṣads, the subsequent section is startlingly new. Those whose conduct is good but who choose to offer sacrifices in the village will go on the path of the moon and be reborn accordingly. Those who choose the path of the forest and the knowledge of *brahman* will go on the path of the sun and leave this life altogether. And those whose conduct is reprehensible will be reborn into a lesser, probably repugnant womb. In other accounts the two paths are described as the path of the gods *(devayāna)* and the path of the father *(pitṛyāna).*

UPANIṢADIC PERSON AND MORALITY. Despite their variations, the Upaniṣads all share the concept of a cycle of infinitely recurring births and deaths in which the nature of a rebirth depends upon a person's actions in life. The only way to escape this cycle of time is through knowledge of *brahman,* the infinite, which can be gained through slow and painstaking mastery of meditation under the guidance of a teacher. Each Upaniṣad had a different method for teaching this knowledge, but all used the basic imageries of the sacrifice to show the ways in which bodily processes and processes of awareness allowed the student to conceive of the sacrifice as going on inside his body. In the *Bṛhadāraṇyaka Upaniṣad* 3:1:8–10, Aśvala the *hotṛ* (a priest trained in sacrifice and sacrificial recitation), asks Yājñavalkya the teacher about how many deities will be used by the Brāhmaṇ priest to protect the sacrifice that day. He answers, "One, the mind." Yajñavalkya argues that this is possible because the mind is without limit, the all-gods are without limit, and the world one gains by it is also limitless. Thus the deities become identified with mind itself—and by implication the Brāhmaṇ priest, the controller of the sacrifice, can earn his authority through the machinations of his own mind. Finally, in discussing the hymns that are used in the sacrifice, Aśvala asks what these hymns are with respect to the "self-body" *(ātman).* Yājñavalkya replies that the hymn recited before the sacrifice is the out-breath, the hymn that accompanies the sacrifice the in-breath, and the hymn of praise the inter-breath.

The *Bṛhadāraṇyaka Upaniṣad* puts the relationship between self, body, and cosmos eloquently: "This self is the honey of all beings, and all beings are the honey of this self. The radiant and immortal person in the self and the radiant and immortal person connected with the body [here, also referred to as *ātman*]—they are both one's self. It is the immortal; it is Brahman, it is the Whole" (2:5:9).

EPIC COSMOLOGY. The two great Indian epics, the *Rāmāyaṇa* and the *Mahābhārata,* were probably composed between 200 BCE and 200 CE. Both of these narratives act as a kind of bridge between the worlds of the Vedas and the Upaniṣads and that of classical, Purāṇic Hinduism. This same period saw the development of the early Śāstras or legal texts, which also contain cosmological information. The cosmology of the epics and the early Śāstras incorporates an increasing systematization of the idea of samsaric time for the individual and expands the idea of the universe into one that dissolves and regenerates. Epic cosmology also incorporates the ideas of Sāṃkhya and Yoga philosophy, such as the "qualities," or *guṇas*, that are inherent in all beings and elements in the universe. Such a cosmology involves an entirely new pantheon of gods, the triad of Viṣṇu, Śiva, and Brahmā, and the Devī, or goddess. These gods were probably part of the popular religious worlds of North India, even during the period of Vedic sacrificial practice. However, as sacrificial practice waned and the patronage of temples increased, these gods emerged as the larger, cosmological deities in their own right. Devotion *(bhakti)* toward these deities is also an emerging theme in the epics, in which the deity is seen as the creator and sustainer of the universe. The body of the deity is the frame of the cosmos, and time (also an agent of the deity) moves beings toward their final state.

At the basis of these ideas is an early Hindu philosophy called Sāṃkhya, which means "counting." In the sense that its aim is to enumerate everything in the universe, it could also be called a cosmology. According to Sāṃkhya, the universe evolves from a feminine "natural matter" and becomes entangled with the masculine *puruṣa,* which is an individual soul (and not to be confused with the earlier "cosmic person"). Thus in these entanglements twenty-four "evolutes" emerge, including the senses and the elements. Sāṃkhya is the basis of the practice of Yoga, whereby the yogin gradually extricates the soul from the evolutes of *prakṛti.* After eight stages, the soul realizes its eternal nature and is no longer subject to the laws of action *(karma)* or transmigration *(saṃsāra).* Time, however, is not an agent in itself. Sāṃkhya's ordering of the universe of *prakṛti* is generally not hierarchical, although one text—the *Yoga Bhāṣya*—sees the lower evolutes of *prakṛti* as the hells and the higher ones as the heavens. The extrication of the soul from *prakṛti* in the practice of Yoga is seen as the soul's movement toward the higher realms, and when it leaves the world altogether, it also dissolves it. On a smaller cosmological scale, Sāṃkhya Yoga philosophy contributes the basic idea that there are universal qualities or *"guṇas"* inherent in every element on earth. These *guṇas* are *sattva* (truth, light); *rajas* (passion, force) and *tamas* (weight, darkness) are inherent in every particle of the universe.

EPIC SPACE. The epics and Dharmaśāstras and related texts of this period give an idea of how those heavens and netherworlds might be inhabited. In the *Mahābhārata,* Arjuna visits Śiva and obtains a weapon from him in one of his heavenly abodes; so too the gods dwelling in heaven remind Rāma of his duty toward his wife at the end of the *Rāmāyaṇa.* The great *Mahābhārata* heroes, the Paṇḍava brothers, also make ascents and descents to heaven and hell at the end of the great battle. Most importantly it is during this transitional period that one sees the intimation that the land of Bhārata is to be identified with Indian civilization and the entirety of the earth.

EPIC TIME. The *Bhiṣmaparvan* of the *Mahābhārata* (4–12) contains an entire depiction of the cosmos, which involves the beginnings of the devotional, or *bhakti,* tradition. So too the *Śantiparvan* introduces the idea of the division of time into *kalpas* and *yugas,* as does the *Manu Smṛti,* one of the more well-known legal Dharmaśāstric texts developed during this time. The epic texts also introduce explicit teachings on the doctrine of the *avatāras,* or "descents" of god. These *avatāras* appear at various points when time has lost its power to fight the demons and to restore the *dharma,* or moral order, of the universe. As early as the great *Bhagavadgītā,* or "Song of the Lord," contained in the *Mahābhārata,* Kṛṣṇa apparently refers to the notion of time and to the integration of the idea of the *avatāra* with that of the descending ages, or *yugas.* As Kṛṣṇa puts it:

> Son of Bhārata, whenever there is a decline in *dharma,* and the absence of *dharma* increases, I create Myself. I come into being from age to age with the purpose of fixing *dharma*—as a refuge for those who do good and as a doom for those who do wrong. (4:7–8; in Patton, 2005)

Epic Person and Morality. Kṛṣṇa's words lead directly to a new understanding of the relationship between cosmology and the morality of the human world. That relationship is conceived of in terms of *dharma* (sacred role or duty). Kṛṣṇa is beyond time and space and yet at the same time incarnates himself in order to make sure that *dharma* is in the correct order and format. The cosmos is perceived as directly responsive to any change in the correct pattern of *dharma.* So too the reverse is the case: as one of the Dharmaśāstras argues, if one follows the *dharma* of hospitality toward a brahmin guest, one can gain various heavens depending upon the number of days the guest stays in one's home. Entertaining a brahmin guest forever allows one to attain *svargaloka.*

Purāṇic Cosmology. The medieval Hindu texts called Purāṇas ("of the ancient times") contain Hindu cosmology at its most exuberant and efflorescent. Emerging during the early first millennium CE as a genre in their own right, Purāṇas were sponsored by each temple or kingdom and usually focused on a particular deity, which gave its own account of the world and its destruction. In the Purāṇas, the basic themes introduced in the epics and the Śāstras are elaborated upon imagistically, poetically, and mathematically. Moreover the theme of *bhakti,* or devotion, which was dramatically introduced in the epics and Yoga texts, becomes paramount.

Purāṇic Space. Many Purāṇas, including the relatively early *Viṣṇu Purāṇa,* describe a flat disk of earth, which is itself composed of a series of circles. These are in fact seven concentric islands that keep doubling in size as one moves outward. (The first is an actual circle, and the concentric islands are ring-shaped.) The islands are separated from each other by a series of oceans, each of which has the width of the island it encircles. The center-most island is the most well known and is called Jambudvīpa (Rose Apple Island). And at the center of the world, the golden mountain called Meru anchors the entire arrangement. Meru is unusual in that it is an inversion of the usual mountains and points downward. Jambudvīpa is further divided into nine *varṣas,* or regions, that consist of mountain ranges. The lines are latitudinal, running from east to west.

The region of Jambudvīpa that is the farthest north is called Uttarakuru and may well be Kurukṣetra, where the central battle of the *Mahābhārata* took place. Moving southward, one encounters the other *varṣas:* Hiranmaya, Ramyaka, Ketumāla, Ilavṛta, Bhadrāśya, Harivarṣa, Kiṃpuruṣa, and Bhārata. The final region, Bhārata, is assumed by many scholars to be India, as this is the same name for India in the twenty-first century. In the Purāṇic cosmograph, however, it is a *karmabhūmi,* or realm where the laws of *karma* apply. As such one can only attain *mokṣa,* or liberation from these laws, in this region. Bhārata is also the only place on earth where rain falls. Bhārata itself is divided into nine sections. Moreover the celestial river Ganges also divides into seven branches—the traditional seven rivers found in ancient Vedic texts.

The full series of seven islands then begins with Jambudvīpa, whose diameter is 100,000 *yojanas.* Jambudvīpa forms an actual circle with a radius of fifty thousand *yojanas.* (A *yojana* is a word that occurs as early as the *Ṛgveda;* it has been variously measured as two, four, five, or nine English miles, although it also has an etymological link to Yoga and *yuga* that makes its connotations metaphysical.) The rest of the ring-shaped islands are named as follows: Plakṣadvīpa, Sālmaladvīpa, Kuśadvīpa, Krauṇcadvīpa, Śākadvīpa, and Puṣkaradvīpa. All the islands are named after some species of the trees and plants that grow on them. Each concentric ring island is double the width of the previous one, so that the outermost, Puṣkaradvīpa, ends up with a width of 6.4 million *yojanas.* Finally, just as Jambudvīpa is divided into nine *varṣas,* or regions, of mountain ranges, so too each of the five inner ring-shaped islands also is divided into seven mountain-range *varṣas.* The outer most island, Puṣkaradvīpa, is delineated by a ring of mountains called Mānassottara.

The oceans that separate the ring islands from one another have the same width as the diameter they surround, with the same expansion of measurement up to 6.4 million for the last ocean. Their names are drawn from the substance of the oceans themselves: Lavaṇoda (Salt Ocean), Ikṣura (Molasses Ocean), Suroda (Wine Ocean), Ghṛtoda (Ghee Ocean), Dadhyoda (Curd Ocean), Kṣīroda (Milk Ocean), and Svādūdaka (Freshwater Ocean). The Freshwater Ocean flows beyond the last ring island, Puṣkaradvīpa, and separates it from the end of the universe *(lokasaṃsthiti).* The realm at the end of the universe is a golden realm that divides the world from the nonworld, similarly to the way in which being and nonbeing are distinguished even in the earliest Vedic cosmologies. The golden realm also has a mountain, Lokakāloka (World and non-World). After this mountain is a region of perpetual darkness, where, the texts seem to suggest, only the elements of earth, wind, air, and fire exist. After that realm is the shell of the egg of Brahmā, which envelopes the universe in its entirety. The entire diameter of this universe is said to be 500 million *yojanas.*

What of the stars and other heavenly bodies? The stars move around Mount Meru in a circular direction, with the

North Star *(dhruva)* as their pivot. Below them lies the flat disk of the earth. The sun, moon, and planets move about in chariots drawn by horses, as was the case even in the earliest Vedic texts. They are attached to the North Star by bands of air that allow them to travel in their proper orbits.

The Hindu cosmograph, with its conical center, Mount Meru, and the chariot of the sun and disk of stars circulating above the disk of concentric islands and oceans may be based on a projection of the celestial sphere onto a flat surface. In such an analysis the circle of the sun is the mythographic expression of the circle of the ecliptic. Mount Meru represents the projection of the celestial Tropic of Cancer, while the Mānassottara Mountain represents the projection of the Tropic of Capricorn. The prominence of the North Star, the conspicuous absence of the south polar star, and the stories about the exile of Agastya (Canopus) to the Southern Hemisphere to preserve the cosmograph all support the idea that the Hindu cosmograph is a northern, planispheric projection of the sort used to construct such instruments as the astrolabe.

As for a vertical cosmology, there are seven worlds with the same names as those of the Upaniṣads, although the Purāṇas make considerable elaboration on these. The *bhūrloka* contains the cosmograph of the seven islands outlined above, with Bhārata as the only land where the law of *karma* applies and liberation is possible. Most significantly, there are seven Pātalas, or netherworlds: Atala, Vitala, Nitala, Gabhastimat, Mahātala, Sutala, and Pātala. Below these are twenty-eight hell realms.

The *bhuvaṣḥ,* or intermediate realm, is the realm of the sun, which moves through its annual course in its chariot. Above this is the *svarloka,* which contains, in ascending order, the moon; its twenty-seven or twenty-eight Nakṣatras, or houses of the moon; Mercury (Buddha); Venus (Śukra); Mars (Angārika); Jupiter (Bṛhaspati); Saturn (Śani); and the Seven Ṛṣis (the Great Bear) and Dhruva (the North star, mentioned above).

The three basic realms of *bhur, bhuvaḥ,* and *svaḥ* are described as *kṛtika*—meaning they are "created" worlds and therefore transitory. They are the regions where consequences are experienced and renewed with every *kalpa.* In these three realms the fruits of *karma* that are acquired in Bhārata manifest themselves, and souls are reborn to enjoy these fruits. These are the enjoyment realms *(bhogabhūmi)* as opposed to the *karmabhūmi* of Bhārata. Above the *svarloka* is the realm of *mahas,* which is considered a mixed realm because it is a deserted by beings at the end of *kalpa* but is not destroyed. Finally, the three highest realms—*janas, tapas,* and *satyam*—are described as *akṛittika:* that which is uncreated. They perish only at the end of the life of Brahmā.

PURĀṆIC TIME. The Purāṇas divide time into such components as *yugas,* as four age cycles, and *kalpa*s, which are a day and a night of Brahmā. The Purāṇas provide a very thorough analysis of these components. Together with doctrines concerning the various destructions *(pralayas),* they are the glue that holds this cosmology together and provides it with a coherent drama of salvation. Indeed *Viṣṇu Purāṇa* asserts it is not space but time that constitutes the body of the deity.

Hindu divisions of time are as follows. Fifteen "twinklings of the eye" make a *kāṣṭhās,* or one *kalā;* and thirty *kalās* equal one *muhūrtta.* Thirty *muhūrttas* constitute a day and a night of mortals; thirty such days make a month, which is divided into two halves (waxing and waning). Six months form an *ayana,* and two *ayanas* compose a year.

The southern *ayana* is a night and the northern a day of the gods. Twelve thousand divine years, each comprising 360 such days, constitute the period of the *yugas (caturyuga).* The *kṛtayuga* consists of four thousand divine years, the *tretāyuga* of three thousand, the *dvāparayuga* of two thousand, and the *kaliyuga* of one thousand. The period that precedes a *yuga* is called a *sandhyā;* it lasts for as many hundred years as there are thousands in the *yuga.* The *sandhyānsa,* at the end of the *yuga,* is of similar duration. Together the four *yugas* constitute a *kalpa.* A thousand *kalpas* is a day of Brahmā, and fourteen Manus, or descendants of man, reign during that time period, which is known as Manvantara. At the end of a day of Brahmā, the universe is consumed by fire, and its dissolution occurs. Brahmā then sleeps for a night of equal duration. Three hundred and sixty such days and nights constitute a year of Brahmā, and one hundred such years equal his entire life *(mahākalpa).* One *parārddha,* or half his life, has expired.

The various *pralayas* epitomize the agency of time by moving the soul—and the universe—from its current state to its eventual salvation. The Purāṇas distinguish four types of dissolution, or *pralaya,* each reversing the process of creation at different levels. These include:

1. *Nitya pralaya,* or physical death of the individual caught in the cycle of transmigration;
2. *Ātyantika pralaya,* or spiritual liberation *(mokṣa)*;
3. *Prākṛta pralaya,* or dissolution of the elements at the end of the life of Brahmā;
4. *Naimittika pralaya,* or occasional dissolution associated with the cycles of *yugas* and descents of *avatāras.*

Yet calculations of time also had a meditative quality: the contemplation of infinity, or the largest number next to infinity, was meant to be close to a vision of God. The *Brahmavaivarta Purāṇa* tells the well-known story of the dialogue between Viṣṇu and Indra. In the form of a young boy, Viṣṇu tells Indra that a parade of ants crawling on the earth have all had lives as Indras—each ruling over their own solar systems in different ages.

PURĀṆIC PERSON AND MORALITY. In the Purāṇic texts, the four *yugas* progress as a kind of inevitable decay in the moral quality of the universe. The *Kūrma Purāṇa* (1:27, 16–57; 28:1–7) states it elaborately. The text describes the meditational bliss, lack of self interest, and natural habitat of human beings in the first *yuga, kṛtayuga;* the arising of pleasure and greed in the *tretāyuga;* the lack of firm resolve and the introduction of war, death, and suffering in the *dvāparayuga;* and the rampant hunger, fear, and inversion of social order in the final present age of the *kaliyuga.* Happiness, beauty, homes in the forest, and food dropping from trees gradually give way to the moral decay of the world and then to the development of practices aimed at liberation from such decay.

The *kaliyuga* is considered the worst of the four *yugas*—the moment right before the final destruction and renewal of the universe. The Purāṇas and many contemporary Hindu thinkers understand the present to be the *kaliyuga.* The decadence, greed, and confusion of social categories is both inevitable and part of the turning of the cycles of time, and yet the Purāṇas and other Hindu texts exhort each individual to be the moral exception in this period of decay.

NON-SANSKRITIC COSMOLOGIES. It is important to note, however, that the extended discussion of cosmology above is based mainly on the Sanskrit textual tradition and that there are many important cosmologies within Hinduism that may depart from these basic ideas in significant ways. In South India, for example, Tamil, Telugu, and Karnatak traditions have developed complex and sophisticated classical cosmologies of their own. Such texts focus on the meaning of the temple and the city surrounding it as a center and origin of the world and on a regional deity as its creator. The temple spires and surrounding tanks frequently function in ways similar to, and are sometimes even compared with, Mount Meru and its surrounding islands in the Sanskrit texts. So too South Indian texts describe deities like Murukaṉ (Murugan) residing in these temples as if they were a kind of paradise created at the beginning of the world. At a village level, guardian deities of ponds, wells, and the intersections of roads are also credited with cosmological powers and roles in creation.

Finally, the *ādivasis,* or "tribal" communities of India, such as the Muṇḍa, Santal, and others, also possess unique cosmologies, some of which incorporate Hindu deities such as Rāma, others of which involve completely separate deities who have created and preside over the natural world and look after the welfare of human beings. Many tribal cosmologies incorporate narratives of the victory of good over evil. The Muṇḍa, for example, tell the story of Singbonga, who tried to stop the iron smelters from working as it was causing pollution in the universe. When they refused, he had to destroy them in order to keep the world safe. So too the Kokna, Bhil, and Varli peoples understand that before humans the world was filled with *rakṣasas,* or demons; Rāma and Sītā then passed through the area, killed the demons, and gave birth to humans.

SCIENCE AND COSMOLOGY. Any discussion of Hindu cosmology would be empty without a discussion of astronomy and related sciences. As mentioned previously, the astronomical sciences appear as early as the Vedic period in the form of Jyotiḥśāstra, or "the science of light." Though there is considerable debate as to the range and nature of astronomical knowledge, it is known that the lunar mansions are mentioned in the Brāhmaṇas and that the Hindu science of calculation began with the cosmological Vedic altars and developed into the elaborate calculations of the *yugas, kalpas,* and *mahākalpas* in the Purāṇas. Jyotiṣḥśāstra encouraged thinkers to assign dates to the grand conjunctions of the middle planets at Aries, and the date February 18 (or 19) of 3101 (or 3102) BCE is frequently cited as marking the beginning of the *kaliyuga.* One astronomical text, in the *Viṣṇudharmottara Purāṇa* (2:166–174), is the earliest of this genre and is the basis of the *Brahmāpakṣa.* Together with the *Aryapakṣa* and the *Ardharatrikapakṣa,* these three texts form the canonical schools of Hindu astronomy.

The great astronomer-sage Āryabhaṭa (fifth–sixth centuries CE) calculated the rotations of the earth and the sun in terms of the *yugas.* His treatises *(siddhantas)* sketch his mathematical, planetary, and cosmic theories and include a sine table, astronomical computations, divisions of time, and rules for computation for eclipses as well as the longitude of planets. Among the other theorists, Varāhamihira (sixth century CE), Brahmagupta (seventh century CE), Bhāskara (twelfth century CE), and Mādhava (fourteenth century CE) all gave calculational and astronomical theories that contributed to overall ideas about the universe, such as the rotational powers of the planets and the centrality of the sun.

Indeed by the time of Bhāskara (c. twelfth century CE) the old Purāṇic cosmology was being questioned with the construction of a different model of the solar system. In the debates one can detect a conflict between the Purāṇic cosmology and the cosmology of the Jyotiṣas. There are some discussions that remind one of the contemporary cosmological debate between creationism and the Big Bang. For instance, the astronomical writers asked: If, as some of the Purāṇas state, a tortoise is holding up the earth, then what being or substance might be supporting that tortoise? Or if one is assuming the gigantic height of Mount Meru and a flat, disk-like earth, then would not one be able to see Mount Meru from every point on the disk of the earth?

Around 1200 CE al-Bīrūnī, an Arab astronomer and translator, noted the debates and problems of Purāṇic cosmology that were present in the discussions of Indian astronomers. Relatedly it is clear that there was a great deal of scientific collaboration between Hindus and Muslims in Mughal India, especially in seventeenth- and eighteenth-century Jaipur, where the appropriate description of the cosmos was argued out at great length.

Finally, in the contemporary period various more and less controversial attempts have been made to correlate scientific advances with Hindu cosmology. In the more controversial cases textual exegetes argue about whether it is appropriate to view certain descriptions of "vehicles" in the epics as referring to space travelers or whether the ancient word *yojana,* mentioned above, refers to the speed of light. In a more speculative and less controversial vein Yoga theorists draw parallels between the theory of the three *guṇas* and James C. Maxwell's theories of electromagnetism; between the relation of space and time in Sāṃkhya theory and the theory of relativity; between the idea of the cosmic egg and the theory of curved space in the general theory of relativity; and so on.

Many contemporary philosophers and historians, such as S. Radhakrishnan, B. K. Motilal, A. N. Balslev, and W. R. Kloetzli, have written of the parallels (not equivalencies) between scientific and Hindu philosophical thinking. The Hindu philosophical school of Nyāya Vaiśeṣika and its views on the atom's role in the universe is one particularly salient example. Finally, the cosmological writings of astrophysicist Jayant Viṣṇu Narlikar land more squarely in the world of physical science and cosmology. Considered a leading expert and defender of the steady state cosmology against the more popular Big Bang cosmology, Narlikar has also drawn some intriguing parallels with Hindu mythology—not in order to "prove" the existence of scientific knowledge in ancient texts but rather to show the power of the cosmological imagination in both science and mythology. Many of the cosmological myths referred to above, involving expansion and contraction, the in-breathing and out-breathing of Brahmā, and so on, seem to involve metaphors of a "steady state" similar to Narlikar's physical and mathematical arguments in scientific cosmology.

BIBLIOGRAPHY

General Works on Hindu Cosmologies

For a general overview of cosmology, the best resources are of course the original texts themselves. In translation, Wendy Doniger O'Flaherty's *Rig Veda* (Harmondsworth, U.K., 1981) and Walter Maurer's *Pinnacles of India's Past: Selections from the Rgveda* (Amsterdam and Philadelphia, 1986) both have good discussions of cosmogonic themes; Patrick Olivelle's introduction to his *Upanisads* (Oxford and New York, 1995) also has a good discussion. The classic treatment of Purāṇic cosmology remains Cornelia Dimmitt and J. A. B. Van Buitenen's *Classical Hindu Mythology: A Reader in the Sanskrit Purānas,* rev. ed. (Philadelphia, 1995), which devotes entire sections to space and to time. The *Bhagavadgītā* is also an excellent resource for Hindu cosmological thinking, especially chapters 10 and 11. See Laurie Patton's translation of *The Bhagavad Gita* (Harmondsworth, U.K., 2005).

For treatment of the themes of the cycle of time, the end of the world, and the renewal of the world, one might consult three works: Horst Bürkle's "Geschichtliche Einmaligkeit und zyklische Wiederkehr," *Internationale katholische Zeitschrift "Communio"* 17, no. 4 (1988): 327–336; Michel Hulin's "Décadence et renouvellement: La doctrine des âge du monde dans l'hindouisme," in *Der geheime Strom des Geschehens,* edited by Rudolf Ritsema (Frankfurt am Main, Germany, 1987), pp. 177–208; and Vasudha Narayanan's "Y51k and Still Counting: Some Hindu Views of Time," *Hindu-Christian Studies Bulletin* 12 (1999): 15–21. Mariasusai Dhavamony's "Hindu Eschatology," *Studia Missionalia* 32 (1983): 143–180, has a rather more Christian view. A little more updated in is theoretical perspective on "end of time" scenarios is Tom Forsthoefel's "Uses and Abuses of Apocalypticism in South Asia: A Creative Human Device," *Journal of Dharma* 26, no. 3 (2001): 417–430. For an integration of basic ritual themes and cosmological ideas, see Samarendra Saraf's "Hindu Ritual Idiom: Cosmic Perspective and Basic Orientations," in *The Realm of the Extra-Human: Ideas and Actions,* edited by Agehananda Bharati (The Hague, 1976), pp. 151–163. The locus classicus for the relationship between theodicy, or justice, and Hindu cosmology remains Wendy Doniger O'Flaherty's *The Origins of Evil in Hindu Mythology* (Berkeley, Calif., 1976). There is also a series of more comparative treatments of Hindu cosmology that take on the themes of "worldview" and "nature." Neither term is indigenous to the Hindu texts, but nonetheless they are excellent starting points for the comparativist. One could begin with Heinrich von Stietencron's "Welt und Gottheit: Konzeptionen der Hindus," in *Christentum und Weltreligionen,* edited by Hans Küng, Josef Van Ess, and Heinrich von Stietencron (Munich, 1984), pp. 271–310. A. Syrkin's two-part series in *Numen* gives a nice discussion of the avatar in Hindu cosmology; see "The Salutary Descent," *Numen* 35, no. 1 (1988): 1–23 and no. 2 (1988): 213–237. Non-Western scholars have also contributed to efforts to think about cosmology comparatively and to engage Hindu themes—see, for example, G. P. Pokhariyal's "The Hindu View of God, Humanity, and Mother Nature," in *God, Humanity, and Mother Nature,* edited by Gilbert E. M. Ogutu (Nairobi, Kenya, 1992), pp. 165–171; and Tadakazu Yamada, James Dator, and Russell Schweickart's *Cosmos, Life, Religion: Beyond Humanism* (Tenri, Japan, 1988.)

Relatedly contemporary writing on the environment and Hindu cosmology blossomed in the last decade of the twentieth century. One of the most central authors, O. P. Dwivedi, began with his "Environmental Stewardship: Our Spiritual Heritage for Sustainable Development," *Journal of Developing Societies* 12, no. 2 (1996): 217–231. David R. Kinsley's "Reflections on Ecological Themes in Hinduism," *Journal of Dharma* 16, no. 3 (1991): 229–245, is also important. Following Dwivedi's initiative are Augustine Thottakara, ed., *Eco-Dynamics of Religion: Thoughts for the Third Millennium* (Bangalore, India, 2000); Christopher Key Chapple and Mary Evelyn Tucker, eds., *Hinduism and Ecology: The Intersection of Earth, Sky, and Water* (Cambridge, Mass., 2000); and Lance E. Nelson, ed., *Purifying the Earthly Body of God: Religion and Ecology in Hindu India* (Albany, N.Y., 1999).

There is also a long tradition of scholarship that, while not specifically environmentalist, addresses the idea of the Hindu cosmos as the body of God. Many such works are comparative in nature, beginning with Ninian Smart's "God's Body," *Union Seminary Quarterly Review* 37 (1981): 51–59; Alex Wayman's "The Human Body as Microcosm in India, Greek Cosmology, and Sixteenth-Century Europe," *History of Religions* 22, N (1982): 172–190; Julius J. Lipner's "The World as God's 'Body': In Pursuit of Dialogue with Rāmānuja," *Religious Studies* 20 (1984): 145–161; and George A. Chalmers's "Rāmānuja and Alexander: The Concept of the Universe as the Body of God," *Scottish Journal of Religious Studies* 6, no. 1 (1985): 26–33. More recent work has connected the bodies of gods and goddesses with politics; see, for example, Konrad Meisig's "'Mutter Indien' (Bhāratamātā): Zur Personifizierung kosmologischer Vorstellungen im politischen Hinduismus," in *Religion im Wandel der Kosmologien,* edited by Dieter Zeller, pp. 281–285 (Frankfurt am Main, Germany, and New York, 1999). Kapila Vatsyayan's book series, "Prakriti" (Indira Gandhi National Center for the Arts) contains a number of excellent collections of essays on cosmology by Indian and Western authors alike.

Finally, George Michell, *The Hindu Temple: An Introduction to Its Meanings and Forms* (London, 1977) and *Hindu Art and Architecture* (New York, 2000), and Stella Kramrisch, *The Hindu Temple* (Delhi, 1976), remain the loci classici among examinations of the relationship between architecture and cosmology. However, more specific, local treatments with important theoretical implications include Anthony Good's "The Burning Question: Sacred and Profane Space in a South Indian Temple Town," *Anthropos* 94, nos. 1–3 (1999): 69–84; Adam Hardy's "The Hindu Temple: A Dynamic Microcosm," in *Sacred Architecture in the Traditions of India, China, Judaism, and Islam,* edited by Emily Lyle (Edinburgh, 1992), pp. 41–57; and K. R. Van Kooij's "The Concept of Cosmic Totality in the Ancient Art of India," in *Approaches to Iconology,* edited by Hans G. Kippenberg, L. P. van den Bosch, and L. Leertouwer (Leiden, 1986), pp. 37–49. Most compelling is Michael W. Meister's "Symbology and Architectural Practice in India," in *Sacred Architecture in the Traditions of India, China, Judaism, and Islam,* edited by Emily Lyle (Edinburgh, 1992).

Vedic and Upaniṣadic Cosmologies

Two early works by Sadashiv Ambadas Dange and Richard F. Gombrich, respectively, remain excellent resources for Vedic ritual cosmology. See Dange's "Cosmo-Sexualism in the Vedic Ritual," in *Charudeva Shastri Felicitation Volume,* edited by Suniti Kumar Chatterji, Triloki Nath, Satya Vrat, and Dharmendra Kumar Gupta (Delhi, 1974), pp. 23–44; and Gombrich's "Ancient Indian Cosmology," in *Ancient Cosmologies,* edited by Carmen Blacker and Michael Loewe (London, 1975), pp. 110–142. M. A. Mehendale's short "Sapta Devalokāh," in *Charudeva Shastri Felicitation Volume,* edited by Suniti Kumar Chatterji, Triloki Nath, Satya Vrat, and Dharmendra Kumar Gupta (Delhi, 1974), also gives a good basic introduction to the idea of the seven worlds. For more detailed, thematic studies of Vedic cosmology, see Marius Schneider's "Das Schöpfungswort in der vedischen Kosmologie," in *Musicae Scientiae Collectanea: Festschrift Karl Gustav Fellerer zum 70. Geburtstag,* edited by Heinrich Hüschen (Cologne, Germany, 1973), pp. 523–526, and his "Die Grundlagen der Kultsprache in der vedischen Kosmologie," in *Sprache und Sprachverständnis in religiöser Rede: Zum Verhältnis von Theologie und Linguistik,* edited by Thomas Michels and Ansgar Paus (Salzburg, Austria, 1973), pp. 13–60. Albrecht Wezler's "Thin, Thinner, Thinnest: Some Remarks on Jaiminīya Brāhmana 1:144," in *India and Beyond: Aspects of Literature, Meaning, Ritual, and Thought: Essays in Honour of Frits Staal,* edited by Dick Van Der Meij (Leiden, 1997), pp. 636–650, engages the important question of worldview in the Brāhmaṇa literature. Henk W. Bodewitz gives a good sense of how early Vedic themes might give rise to later Purāṇic ones in "Pits, Pitfalls, and the Underworld in the Veda," *Indo-Iranian Journal* 42, no. 3 (July 1999): 211–226. Moving forward to the Upaniṣads, Joel P. Brereton's excellent "Cosmographic Images in the Brhadāranyaka Upaniṣad," *Indo-Iranian Journal* 34 (1991): 1–17, gives a good specific case study of a single Upaniṣad that can be used as a launching point for the study of other Upaniṣads. For another integrative view of earlier and later texts, see Petteri Koskikallio's "When Time Turns: Yugas, Ideologies, Sacrifices," in *Studia Orientalia* 73, edited by Palva Heikki, Tapani Harviainen, Asko Parpola, and Harry Halén (Helsinki, Finland, 1994), pp. 253–271.

Epic and Purāṇic Cosmologies

John E. Michiner's *Traditions of the Seven Ṛṣis* (Delhi, 1981) gives an excellent overview of the various cycles of time in the Vedas, the epics, and the Purāṇas, especially the Ages of Manu and the role of the Vedic sages in creating and maintaining the cosmos. Also addressing both epic and Purāṇic understandings of time is R. K. Dwivedi's "A Critical Study of the Changing Social Order at Yuganta; or, the End of the Kali Age," in *D. D. Kosambi Commemoration Volume,* edited by Lallanji Gopal, Jai Prakash Singh, and Nisar Ahmad (Varanasi, India, 1977), pp. 276–297. Wendell C. Beane's "Cosmological Structure of Mythical Time: Kālī-Sakti," *History of Religions* 13 (1973): 54–83, connects these time cycles with the goddess concept of *shakti.* Tracy Pintchman builds on these insights in "Gender Complementarity and Gender Hierarchy in Purānic Accounts of Creation," *Journal of the American Academy of Religion* 66 (1998): 257–282. For conceptions of place, Ian W. Mabbett's "The Symbolism of Mount Meru," *History of Religions* 23 (1983): 64–83, is a good introduction to the issues at stake, as is Adalbert J. Gail's "Die neun Abschnitte Bhāratavarsas: Eine textgeschichtliche Untersuchung," *Wiener Zeitschrift für die Kunde südasiens und Archiv für indische Philosophie* 17 (1973): 5–20. To see all of these cosmological traditions tied together into a philosophical point of view, one might read Alfred Collins's "From Brahma to a Blade of Grass: Towards an Indian Self Psychology," *Journal of Indian Philosophy* 19 (1991): 143–189. For more local Purāṇas and their cosmologies, see Don Handelman's "Myths of Murugan: Asymmetry and Hierarchy in a South Indian Puranic Cosmology," *History of Religions* 27 (1987): 133–170; William L. Smith's "The Celestial Village: The Divine Order in Bengali Myth," *Temenos* 18 (1982): 69–81; and David C. Scott's "Radha in the Erotic Play of the Universe," *Asia Journal of Theology* 12, no. 2 (1998): 338–357.

No discussion of Purāṇic cosmology would be complete without a discussion of the related medieval tradition of Tantric cosmology. Most scholarly works concentrate on Śaivite (Shaivite) traditions, as do S. Arulsamy's "Spiritual Journey in Shaiva Siddhanta," *Journal of Dharma* 11, no. 1 (1986): 37–61; Gavin D. Flood's "Shared Realities and Symbolic Forms in Kashmir Shaivism," *Numen* 36 (1989): 225–247; and Paul E. Muller-Ortega's "Aspects of Jīvanmukti in the Tantric Shaivism of Kashmir," in *Living Liberation in Hindu Thought,* edited by Andrew O. Fort and Patricia Y. Mumme (Albany, N.Y., 1996), pp. 187–217. Glen Alexander Hayes turns to cosmological Tantra in Bengal in his "Cosmic Substance in the Vaisnava Sahajiyā Traditions of Medieval Bengal," *Journal of Vaisnava Studies* 5 (1996): 183–196.

Non-Classical Cosmologies

The field of "folk" cosmology in Hindu traditions is just beginning to emerge. Earlier works include Stuart H. Blackburn's

"Domesticating the Cosmos: History and Structure in a Folktale from India," *Journal of Asian Studies* 45, no. 3 (1986): 527–543; and Dieter B. Kapp's "The Concept of Yama in the Religion of a South Indian Tribe," *Journal of the American Oriental Society* 102, no. 3 (1982): 517–521. The familiar theme of body and cosmos comes up in Lise F. Vail's "Founders, Swamis, and Devotees: Becoming Divine in North Karnataka," in *Gods of Flesh, Gods of Stone: The Embodiment of Divinity in India,* edited by Norman Cutler, Vasudha Narayanan, and Joanne Punzo Waghorne (Chambersburg, Pa., 1985), pp. 123–140; this is also one of the concerns in Hilde Link's "Das Unbegreifbare begreifbar machen: Südindische Baumeister gestalten einen sakralen Platz," *Anthropos* 88, nos. 1–3 (1993): 194–201.

Science and Cosmology

For more general treatments of science and cosmology, see Anindita Niyogi Balsley's "Cosmology and Hindu Thought," *Zygon* 25, no. 1 (1990): 47–58. For specific connections between Purāṇic and medieval scientific discourse there are two excellent resources: W. Randolph Kloetzli's "Maps of Time—Mythologies of Descent: Scientific Instruments and the Puranic Cosmograph," *History of Religions* 25 (1985): 116–147; and David Pingree's "The Purāṇas and Jyotihshāstra: Astronomy," *Journal of the American Oriental Society* 110 (1990): 274–280. Rory Fonseca's "Constructive Geometry and the Shrī-Cakra Diagram," *Religion* 16, no. 1 (1986): 33–49, is helpful with mathematical treatments of the cosmos. Also see Chris Minkowski's recent "Astronomers and their Reasons: Working Paper on Jyotishastra," *Journal of Indian Philosophy* 30, no. 5 (2002): 495–514; and his "The Pandit as Public Intellectual: The Controversy of Virodha or Inconsistency in the Astronomical Sciences," in Axel Michaels, ed., *The Pandit: Proceedings of the Conference in Honour of Dr. K. P. Aithal.* Heidelberg, 2001, pp. 79-96.

For more contemporary philosophical treatments, see Anindita Niyogi Balsley's "Cosmos and Consciousness: Indian Perspectives," in *Science and Religion in Search of Cosmic Purpose,* edited by John F. Haught (Washington, D.C., 2000), pp. 58–68; and Karl E. Peters's "Cosmology and the Meaning of Human Existence: Options from Contemporary Physics and Eastern Religions," *Zygon* 25, no. 1 (1990): 7–122. Jayant Viṣṇu Narlikar's basic scientific writings include *The Primeval Universe* (Oxford, 1988) and *Seven Wonders of the Cosmos* (Cambridge, U.K., 1999).

W. RANDOLPH KLOETZLI (1987)
LAURIE LOUISE PATTON (2005)

COSMOLOGY: JAIN COSMOLOGY

Jainism, a renunciatory tradition that emerged in the Ganges basin of India around the seventh and sixth centuries BCE, produced a model of the universe virtually unrivalled in complexity among ancient cosmologies. Without beginning or end, this vast system is not controlled by any overseeing deity and is one in which human beings are restricted to an extremely delimited location. As such, it serves to remind Jains of the rarity of human birth, which alone can bring about liberation.

The rich textual sources for Jain cosmology span almost two millennia. It is possible to trace the early development of Jain cosmological ideas in scriptural texts like the *Vyākhyāprajñapti* and *Sthānāṅga Sūtra* (c. first century BCE–third century CE) and detailed descriptions are found in the various subsidiary (*upāṅga*) scriptures of the canon such as the *Jambūdvīpaprajñapti Sūtra* which date from around the fourth century CE. Umāsvāti"s *Tattvārtha Sūtra* (c. fourth century CE) provides an authoritative systematization of ancient trends. Since medieval times knowledge of traditional cosmology has been mediated to ascetic and lay Śvetāmbara Jains through a genre of texts called Saṃgrahaṇī. The earliest recension is the *Bṛhatsaṃgrahanī* of Jinabhadra Ganin (sixth century CE), while the *Laghusaṃgrahaṇī,* compiled by Candra Sūri in 1136, proved the most influential throughout the late medieval period and after. Manuscripts of these texts are usually lavishly illustrated.

BEGINNINGS. The Jain term for the universe, *loka,* is a Sanskrit word found in the *Ṛgveda* (c. twelfth to tenth centuries BCE), where it has the sense of "open space" (cf. Latin *lucus,* "sacred space"). However, descriptions of the *loka* in the form of a detailed cosmology developed only gradually in the course of the Jain canonical period (between c. 400 BCE and 400 CE) and it is uncertain to what extent Mahāvīra, the twenty-fourth *tīrthaṅkara* (or teacher), was responsible for communicating anything beyond the bare rudiments of the system. Early Jain texts simply contrast the *loka* with the non-*loka* without any explanation, and unquestionably there are aspects of developed Jain cosmology, such as the structure of the continents of the Middle World, which derive from Hindu models that emerged near the beginning of the common era.

The Vyākhyāprajñapti Sūtra contains a passage (5:9) in which Mahāvīra concedes that the basic structure of the *loka* had been taught by the twenty-third *tīrthaṅkara,* Pārśva, who supposedly flourished around the seventh century BCE. Since the *Vyākhyāprajñapti* most likely does not antedate the first century BCE, this may be an anachronistic attempt to confirm the existence of a linkage between Pārśva and Mahāvīra. Nonetheless, the description given of the *loka* as broad at the top and bottom like a bed and an upturned drum respectively and narrow in the middle like the god Indra's thunderbolt weapon is one that was not substantially altered thereafter. Only after the beginning of the second millennium CE did Jain artists start to represent the loka in the form of a (male or female) cosmic giant.

The *Sūtrakṛtāṅga Sūtra* (1:5) and the *Uttarādhyayana Sūtra* (chapter 19), ancient texts of the Śvetāmbara canon, describe a variety of hells that were probably essential to early Jain teachings about the perils of violence and the consequent fall from human state, although there is no attempt to provide either the elaborate systematization found at a later date or any linkage of them to a larger cosmic structure. These hells are presented as places of torment of various kinds, encompassed simultaneously by darkness, blazing fire, and cold, where demonic torturers and tortured alike experience the consequences of their previous violent actions.

Mention is made of a hellish river called Vaitaraṇī, whose waves are like razor blades, and also of a huge mountain that looms over the suffering.

The Structure of the Loka. What follows represents the standardized picture of the Jain universe, although there are many differences concerning detail between the Śvetāmbara and Digambara sects. To pious Jains the vast complexity and detail recorded by monastic cosmologists reflect the omniscient and all-encompassing perception of the *tīrthaṅkaras,* the saving teachers.

The *loka* is envisaged as being a finite tripartite structure set in the non-*loka,* like a boat in water, consisting of an upper tier of heavens, at the summit of which lies the realm of the liberated souls, a lower tier of hells, and, in between, a narrow band wherein is located a system of island-continents and oceans. Immediately outside the *loka* are atmospheric layers of various types of air. Beyond these is nothing, empty space in which no entity exists.

The basic unit of cosmological measurement given in the scriptural texts is the yojana, loosely speaking, "a league." Later Jain cosmologists employ the *rajju,* or "rope," to measure the dimensions of the *loka.* This represents the distance traversed by a god flying in a straight line for six months at a speed of 2,057,152 *yojanas* an instant. Overall, the loka is estimated as being fourteen *rajjus* in height from top to bottom, seven *rajjus* wide at top and bottom, in its middle section a mere one *rajju* wide, and seven *rajjus* thick throughout.

Connecting the three realms of the *loka* is a vertical channel called the trasanāḍī, in which all moving creatures are located.

In recent years, noteworthy large-scale models of the *loka* and the central island-continent of Jambūdvīpa (see below) have been erected at Pālitānā and Hāstinapur respectively.

The Middle World. The configuration of the Middle World (madhyaloka) takes the form of a horizontal disk containing a system of circular oceans, each of which abuts onto a circular island-continent *(dvīpa).* The water of all the oceans is not uniformly salty; some taste of wine, milk, or sugarcane. Although the constituents of this system are technically regarded as being beyond normal calculation *(asaṅkhyātaṅā),* in actuality Jain cosmology is concerned only with the central sixteen oceans and sixteen island-continents.

At the center of the Middle World are the "Two-and-a-Half Island-continents" (Aḍhāīdvīpa) that constitute the world of human beings, namely the island-continent of Jambūdvīpa, spatially a disc of 100,000 *yojanas* in width (as opposed to the ring shape of the other continents), the island-continent of Dhātakīkhaṇḍa, which is 400,000 *yojanas* in width, and half of the island-continent of Puṣkara, which is 800,000 *yojanas* in width. Jambūdvīpa, which is located at the very center of the Middle World, is separated from Dhātakīkhaṇḍa by the Salt Ocean (Lavaṇasamudra), while Dhātakīkhaṇḍa is separated from Puṣkara by the Black Water (Kālodadhi) Ocean. At the center of Puṣkara is a range of mountains beyond which, that is to say as far as the outermost island-continent of the Middle World called Svayambhūramaṇa, no human beings live, only animals which are reborn in the heavenly realms after death. Furthermore, the normal operations of time cease at Puṣkara's central mountain range.

Jambūdvīpa, "The Island of the Rose-apple Tree," is the most precisely described area of the *loka.* It is named after the rose-apple *(jambū)* tree that stands beside Mount Meru, which is 100,000 *yojanas* in height and constitutes the central axis of the island-continent. On the perimeter of Jambūdvīpa is an encircling adamantine wall of eight *yojanas* height in which four huge doors are set at the cardinal direction points and through which the rivers of the island-continent flow into the Salt Ocean.

Jambūdvīpa is divided into seven regions *(varṣa),* separated from each other by six mountain ranges that extend outwards from Mount Meru from east to west. These regions are called Bhārata, Haimavata, Ramyaka, Videha (sometimes Mahāvideha), Hari, Hairaṇyaka, and Airāvata. Of these regions, Bhārata, Airāvata, and half of Videha are *karmabhūmis,* where religious actions are fully efficacious in terms of possible rebirth and ultimate salvation, whereas the remaining regions are *bhogabhūmis,* where human beings can flourish in worldly comfort but cannot advance seriously on the path to liberation. Five *karmabhūmis* are also found on both the island-continents of Dhātakīkhaṇḍa and Puṣkara.

The region of Bhārata is located at the south of Jambūdvīpa and is effectively the equivalent of the contemporary geographical entity called South Asia, as can be seen by its two rivers, the Sindhu (Indus) and the Gaṅgā (Ganges), both of which flow in the west and east into the Salt Ocean, and the presence to the north of the Himavat range, or the Himalayas. The influence of terrestrial geography can also be seen from the fact that the capital city of Bhārata called Ayodhyā, the name of the hero-god Rāma's capital and from the third century CE the capital of the Gupta Empire that dominated north India.

To the south of the Himavat range is a further range of mountains called Vaitāḍhya, which contains cities inhabited by *vidyādharas,* semi-divine beings with the power of flight who can traverse the whole continent, but lack the ability to gain deliverance. The Vaitāḍhya mountains, in conjunction with the Sindhu and Gaṅgā, divide Bhārata into six parts. Five of these are barbarian *(mleccha)* regions where inclination to follow Jain teachings is weak and the possibility of deliverance absent, while only one is "aryan," inhabited by people who are naturally susceptible to Jainism and the birthplace of all twenty-four *tīrthaṅkaras* of this age. The region of Airāvata in the north of Jambūdvīpa evinces exactly the same structure and constituents as Bhārata, with its two rivers being called the Raktodā and the Raktā. More broadly, the continents of Dhātakīkhaṇḍa and Puṣkara mirror the geographical structure of Jambūdvīpa.

The largest region of Jambūdvīpa is the central strip called Videha (sometimes Mahāvideha, "Great Videha," because of its importance), which divides the island-continent and at whose center is Mount Meru, while two rivers, the Sitā and Sitodā, flow through it to the east and west. Videha, which is divided into thirty-two parts mirroring Bhārata and Airāvata, is immune from any sort of disaster and its inhabitants, Jain laypeople and ascetics, live morally responsible lives. Cycles of time do not hold sway there as elsewhere and *tīrthaṅkaras* appear continually, from four to thirty-two simultaneously. Of the four currently preaching in Videha at present, Sīmandhara is a significant object of devotion to Jains in India. Videha and its *tīrthaṅkaras* are not directly accessible to human beings in other regions of Jambūdvīpa. One must either be reborn there or, exceptionally, be transported there by supernatural means, as in the case of the Digambara teacher Kundakunda (early common era), whose hagiographies claim that he was able to visit Sīmandhara and hear the doctrine being preached by him.

Highly significant in Jain cosmology is the eighth island-continent from Jambūdvīpa, which is known as Nandīśvara. Inaccessible to human beings, this island-continent contains fifty-two mountains, each of which has on its peak a Jina temple of great magnificence. The gods visit Nandīśvara on regular festival days to worship the images in these temples. It is common for Jain temples today to contain representations of the shrines at Nandīśvara.

Around nine hundred *yojanas* above Jambūdvīpa are the celestial bodies: the planets and stars and their stations, conceived of as the chariots of the gods of light *(jyotiṣa)*. In keeping with the mirroring structure of the north and south parts of Jambūdvīpa, the Jain cosmologists assert that two moons and two suns hold sway over the periods of darkness and light.

THE LOWER WORLD. Around one thousand *yojanas* beneath the Middle World is the Lower World *(adholoka)*, seven *rajjus* high, which consists of seven tiers *(bhūmi)* constructed of an earth-like material substance. Each tier has within it a number of hells, with the highest containing three million and the lowest only five. These seven realms are called Ratnaprabhā ("Jewel-colored"), Śarkaraprabhā ("Gravel-colored"), Vālukāprabhā ("Sand-colored"), Paṅkaprabhā ("Mud-colored"), Dhūmaprabhā ("Smoke-colored"), Tamaḥprabhā ("Darkness-colored"), and Tamastamaḥprabhā ("Most Intense Darkness-colored"). The bottom of each tier of the Lower World fits into the top of the one below, with the whole structure being supported upon space.

Ratnaprabhā, the highest tier of the Lower World, is relatively bright, but darkness increases at each successively lower level, as does the amount of suffering endured by those who are spontaneously born and live there. Such beings are commensurately greater physically and more long-lived the further they descend. Animals can be reborn in most of the hells. Female human beings cannot be reborn below the sixth hell, while only male human beings and species of water-dwelling creatures can be reborn in the seventh hell.

The hells of the Lower World represent a terrifying extension of the basic Jain principle that negative *karma*, the result of evildoing in previous existences, has to be eliminated by the practice of austerities. In Jainism the Lower World has no central ruler equivalent to the Hindu god Yama. Rather, a superficial chaos seems to prevail, though in actuality the suffering inflicted by hell-beings on themselves and each other is in precise accord with evil previously committed, so that when the karmic penalty has run its course, the hell being dies and is then reborn in the Middle World as animal or human. While Jainism does posit the possibility of eternal rebirth for some unfortunate predestined beings, unceasing residence in any one of the hells is not a possibility.

In the space between the Middle World and Ratnaprabhā, the first hellish realm of the Lower World, live varieties of (sometimes) antinomian deities. The "Palace-dwelling" (Bhavanavāsin) gods experience lives of princely luxury similar to their terrestrial counterparts. The "Interstitial" (Vyantara) gods are often found in rock clefts or within trees. Both categories of god frequently visit the world of humans and they might best be classified as demiurges, similar to the tutelary deities who form part of the Jain pantheon.

THE UPPER WORLD. Above the Middle World and the gods of light is located the Upper World *(ūrdhvaloka)*, which is seven *rajjus* high (including the negligible height of the Middle World). This consists of a series of tiered heavens *(kalpa)* inhabited by the Vaimānika gods, so called because of the celestial chariots *(vimāna)*, effectively palaces, in which they ride. According to the Śvetāmbara sect, the first, second, seventh, and eighth heavens are divided into northern and southern halves, thus constituting separate heavenly regions, while for the Digambaras the first eight heavens are divided in this way. Further divisions are also found within the higher heavenly tiers. Thus for the Śvetāmbaras there are twenty-six heavens in total, for the Digambaras thirty-nine.

The Vaimānika gods, whose period of existence and mental attainments are governed by *karma*, are divided into two main categories. The lower category does not invariably possess correct faith *(samyagdṛṣṭi)* in Jain principles and inhabit the twelve lower heavens. The higher category lives above the lower heavens and possesses the necessary faith that will eventually lead to the attainment of deliverance. The higher the level a god inhabits, the greater his psychic and spiritual attainments. The lower heavens are variously colored (black, blue, red, yellow, and white), but the higher heavenly realms are increasingly white in token of their purity and distance from the passions. This reflects a doctrine of Jain *karma* theory that holds that the life-monad *(jīva)* assumes colors *(leśyā)* according to the influence of the types of *karma* it has accrued.

The Vaimānika gods live in conformity to a hierarchical structure replicating that of the cities, courts, and kingdoms of the human world. Many of their heavens are ruled by a category of gods called Indra, whose name derives from that of the Vedic warrior-god. Another category of god called *kilbiṣaka* functions in a serving capacity, effectively the equivalent of human untouchables. Jain narratives frequently refer to Vaimānika gods who are able to travel to the Middle and Lower Worlds to visit and counsel former relatives and acquaintances living there.

The goddesses of the Upper World cannot inhabit a heaven beyond the second level, although they are capable of reaching as high as the eighth level on a temporary basis. The gods and goddesses conduct sexual relations in the two lowest heavenly levels in the same manner as human beings. However, sexual activity becomes progressively more refined amongst the higher Vaimānika deities and passion plays no part in the upper heavenly levels where the deities are very close to that final human birth which will bring about deliverance.

A noteworthy feature of the Upper World is the Black Fields (Kṛṣṇarājī). Located within the fifth heaven, they constitute a dark heavenly region consisting of eight masses of water and coagulated vegetable matter, portrayed in Jain cosmological art as triangular, oblong, hexagonal and circular in shape, which flow up from the Aruṇavara ocean of the Middle World. Rain and thunder are produced in the Black Fields and they serve as an inevitable and repeated staging post for all living beings in the beginningless rebirth process.

The Realm of the Liberated. Twelve leagues above Pañcānuttara, the highest heavenly level of the Upper World, is Īṣatprāgbhāra, the "Slightly Curving Place," so called because it has the shape of a parasol. This is the permanent abode of those who have achieved liberation *(siddha)* and freedom from rebirth.

Jain cosmology depicts Īṣatprāgbhāra in concrete terms, although its inhabitants are without physicality. The whole of this realm is made of white gold. It is eight *yojanas* high at its middle point and (according to Śvetāmbara cosmology) 4,500,000 *yojanas* wide. In the middle of Īṣatprāgbhāra there is a circular rock, eight *yojanas* in height and width. One *yojana* above this rock is the very edge and end of the *loka* and it is in this area that the liberated dwell, in number beyond calculation.

Time. For Jainism, the universe has no beginning or end. As a consequence, the tradition evinces a major preoccupation with time. Although Jainism subscribes to the basic system of time-units found in Brahmanic tradition and on occasion utilizes the model of time as divided into epochs *(yuga)* elaborated in Purāṇic Hinduism, it evolved its own system of cosmic reckoning in which huge periods of duration were enumerated.

The central unit of time for Jainism is envisaged as being equivalent to the turning of a wheel continually repeated throughout eternity and providing a totalizing explanation of human progress and decline. This is divided into two half-motions, a "down-moving" *(avasarpiṇī)* succeeded by an "up-moving" *(utsarpiṇī)* to be followed by a "down-moving" and an "up-moving," and so on *ad perpetuum.* These movements of time, sometimes also defined as six "spokes of a wheel" *(ara)* hold sway in the various *karmabhūmi,* but not in the five Videha regions of the innermost two-and-a half continents of the Middle World.

Each downward motion commences with an "extremely happy" *(suṣamā-suṣamā)* period that lasts 4×10^{14} *sāgaropama* years (one *sāgaropama,* literally "ocean-like" period of time, is equal to $8{,}400{,}000 \times 10^{19}$ years). This is succeeded by the "happy" *(suṣamā)* period that lasts for 3×10^{14} *sāgaropama* years. During this period human beings, who are of massive physical dimensions and live for vast periods of time, exist in a sexually undifferentiated state and have all their physical needs satisfied by wishing trees.

The third stage of a downward movement, the "more happy than unhappy" *(suṣamā-duḥṣamā),* lasts for 2×10^{14} *sāgaropama* years. The fourth stage, "more unhappy than happy" *(duḥṣamā-suṣamā),* lasts 1×10^{14} *sāgaropama* years, less 42,000 calendrical years. During these stages, decline sets in and human beings progressively diminish in size, lifespan, and intellectual attainment, becoming sexually differentiated and without any practical abilities. The first of twenty-four *tīrthaṅkaras* appears, who preaches the eternal Jain doctrine and teaches human beings cultural skills. It is only during the third and fourth stages, in which there is neither an extremity of knowledge nor of ignorance, that human beings can obtain liberation. During these periods there also appear the various universal emperors *(cakravartin),* nonviolent heroes *(baladeva),* warlike heroes *(vāsudeva),* and their enemies *(prativāsudeva)* whose careers mesh with those of the first twenty-two *tīrthaṅkaras* and provide the substance of an extensive Jain legendary history.

The fifth stage, called "unhappy" *(duḥṣamā),* is the one in which those inhabitants of the Middle World subject to the influence of time are located at present. It lasts for 21,000 calendrical years. During this time human beings assume "normal" physical dimension and longevity, no *tīrthaṅkaras* are born, the Jain community goes into decline, and receptivity to Jain teachings diminishes, until at the end, with the almost complete disappearance of knowledge of the scriptures, there remain only a single monk, nun, layman, and laywoman.

The sixth stage, the "very unhappy" *(duḥṣamā-duḥṣamā),* lasts for 21,000 calendrical years. During this stage, human beings degenerate completely and are reduced to the status of short-lived dwarves without any social skills who exist as troglodytes. Eventually, the sixth stage ends in a conflagration and the succeeding upward movement of time starts, with its six stages in reverse order to those of the downward motion.

BIBLIOGRAPHY

Caillat, Colette, and Ravi Kumar. *The Jain Cosmology.* Basel, Paris, and New Delhi, 1981. Contains outstanding illustrations of Jain cosmological art.

Jnanmati, Aryika. *Jaina Geography.* Hāstinapur, India, 1985. A detailed account of the configuration of the Middle World by a prominent Digambara nun.

Kirfel, Willibald. *Die Kosmographie der Inder.* Hildesheim, Germany, 1967. See pp. 208–331. The definitive treatment of Jain descriptions of the universe, containing full details of cosmological enumeration and measurement.

Ohira, Suzuko. *A Study of the Bhagavatīsūtra: A Chronological Analysis.* Ahmedabad, India, 1994. Important for the early development of Jain cosmology.

PAUL DUNDAS (2005)

COSMOLOGY: BUDDHIST COSMOLOGY

There is no single system of Buddhist cosmology. Virtually every theological tendency within the Buddhist tradition addressed the cosmological sciences from its special perspective—seeing the universe as the stage for a drama of salvation cast in terms of its own particular philosophical and theological predilections. Buddhist systems are related not only to other Indian systems, for example, Hindu, Jain, Ājīvika, and so forth, but to Hellenistic speculations as well.

The single-world system that is particularly prominent in the oldest Buddhist texts pictures the cosmos as a flat disk with heavens and meditation realms above and hells below. Although the oldest tradition apparently limited its interest to a single-world system, a grandiose cosmic structure developed on the perimeter of this single universe. Traces of themes associated with multiple-world systems appear in texts of the Pali canon. A ten-thousand-world system is mentioned in the Jātakas, though with little elaboration, and in a more systematic way in Buddhaghosa's *Visuddhimagga* (sec. 414ff.). These and other similar cosmologies are variants of the *sāhasra* cosmology, or "cosmology of thousands." They focus on themes of cosmic time and belong to the Hīnayāna schools of Buddhism.

The cosmology of the Mahāyāna, characterized by innumerable world systems distributed throughout the ten regions of space, can be characterized as an *asaṃkhyeya* cosmology, or "cosmology of innumerables." Although certain of these world systems lack the presence of a Buddha, most are buddha fields (*buddhakṣetras*) where a fully and perfectly enlightened Tathāgata resides and teaches the law for the benefit of countless beings. Generally speaking, there are three types of *buddhakṣetras*: "pure" (*viśuddha*), "impure" (*aviśuddha*), and "mixed" (*miśraka*). Sukhāvatī is the best known among the Pure Lands, although in some texts it is clearly subordinated to others. Sahā is the most important of the Impure Lands—although from another perspective, Sahā may be considered a "mixed" land, alternately ornamented (pure) and unornamented (impure). Located in the region of the south, Sahā is our universe and is the field of the Buddha Śākyamuni.

At the core of each of these cosmologies is a drama of salvation. It is this drama of salvation, implicit in all the Buddhist cosmologies, that allows for the integration of the scientific and theological bases of these cosmologies, represented in images of motion and light. More specifically, these cosmologies transform the astronomical themes of motion and light into the mytho-philosophic themes of journey and soul. The seemingly fantastic numbers characteristic of these cosmologies are grounded in the power of mathematics that allows the astronomers to measure the motions of the heavens and enables the faithful to comprehend the theological and mystical implications of these measurements.

SINGLE-WORLD SYSTEM. The basic outlines of the single-world system are generally agreed upon throughout a broad spectrum of Buddhism and are a prominent feature of the Pali texts as well as the Buddhist Sanskrit literature. Buddhist text designate it as the *cakravāla,* after the mountain of iron that surrounds it. Single, circular world systems are prominent in the Puranic and Jain cosmologies as well and have a wide dispersion throughout the classical world in general. This article ignores variations of detail in the Buddhist texts and is restricted to the extensive and systematic testimony of Vasubandhu's *Abhidharmakośa* (hereafter *Kośa*), a Sautrāntika work composed in the fourth or fifth century of the common era.

The *cakravāla*. The *cakravāla* is represented as a disk ringed with a series of seven circular, golden mountain ranges, arranged concentrically with Mount Meru at the center and the *cakravāla* wall of iron at the perimeter. Proceeding outward from the center, the mountains are known as Meru, Yugandhara, Īṣadhāra, Khadirika, Sudarśana, Aśvakarṇa, Vinataka, Nimindhara, and Cakravāla. Mount Meru has a height of eighty thousand *yojanas* and penetrates the waters in equal measure; each of the mountain ranges is half the height and depth of the preceding range. The waters of various seas (*sītā*) fill the regions between the mountain ranges.

The landmasses are situated in the great ocean (*mahāsamudra*) that flows within the area bounded by Nimindhara and Cakravāla. The four landmasses, located at the points of the compass, are spoken of as "islands" (*dvīpa*) and are named Pūrvavideha (in the east), Jambudvīpa (in the south—named after the Jambu tree that is found there), Aparagodānīya (in the west), and Uttarakuru (in the north). The names of these islands are suggestive of theological directions as well: for example, Videha is the name of disembodied deities and suggests the goal of yoga, which is to liberate the soul from its bondage to the body; the Jambu tree is suggestive of the fruits of the path of Buddhism, Godānīya of Kṛṣṇa's heaven, the Goloka, and Uttarakuru of the Kurukṣetra, the "field of the Kurus," on which was fought the great battle of the *Mahābhārata.*

All of these entities rest on a layer of golden earth (*kāñcanamayībhūmi*), and all of the mountains except the *cakravāla* are composed of excrescences of this golden earth. While the islands are not similarly composed, the *vajrāsana* ("diamond throne") situated in the middle of Jambudvīpa is said to rest on the golden earth. The golden earth of the *cakravāla* rests on a circle of water (*ābmaṇḍala*); a layer of wind (*vāyumaṇḍala*) supports the water and in turn rests on empty space (*ākāśa*).

The four islands of the *cakravāla* are distinguished from each other in a number of ways, particularly with regard to their size and shape and the life span of their inhabitants. Uttarakuru is square, measuring 2,000 *yojanas* on a side, and life there has a duration of 1,000 years. (A *yojana* has been defined variously as the equivalent of 2.5, 4, 5, or 9 English miles, although its etymological link to *yoga* and *yuga* suggests a metaphysical significance as well.) Godānīya is shaped like a full moon measuring 7,500 *yojanas* around with a diameter of 2,500 *yojanas*, and life there lasts 500 years. Pūrvavideha has the shape of a half moon with three sides said to be 2,000 *yojanas* in length and a fourth that is 350 *yojanas* in length. Duration of life there is equal to 250 years. Jambudvīpa, too, measures 2,000 *yojanas* on three sides, but its fourth side is only 3.5 *yojanas* long. It is said to be shaped like a chariot. (In addition to the four main islands, the *Kośa* recognizes eight intermediate islands, two of which are similar in shape to each of the four main islands, although they are only one-tenth the size. The shape of the faces of the inhabitants of each of the islands is said to resemble the shape of the island.)

Jambudvīpa provides an important exception to the superhuman and unchanging durations of life found in the other islands. The length of human life in Jambudvīpa varies; at the beginning of the *kalpa* it is incalculable, but eventually it diminishes to only ten years and continues to fluctuate throughout the *kalpa*. Because of these irregular life expectancies, the inhabitants of Jambudvīpa are particularly aware of the workings of *karman*. Moreover, it is only in Jambudvīpa during a time of declining life spans that a Buddha will appear. Another distinguishing feature of Jambudvīpa is that all the hells are situated beneath this island. The *Kośa* distinguishes eight hot hells and eight cold hells, although other systems are attested.

A series of heavens is arrayed above the *cakravāla* in three great divisions: (1) those heavens in the "realm of desire" (*kāmadhātu*) corresponding to the six classes of the "gods of desire" (*kāmadeva*); (2) the seventeen heavens belonging to the "realm of form" (*rūpadhātu*), grouped into four classes of "meditation realms" (*dhyāna*); and (3) the four "infinities" of the "realm of nonform" (*ārūpyadhātu*). The significance of these divisions is uncertain except for the fact that they form a schematic representation of Buddhist philosophy and doctrine related to meditation. Nevertheless, several of the heavens have characteristics worth noting. The ruler of the Trāyastriṃśa is Indra, or Śakra, whose abode rests atop Mount Meru. The Tuṣita is distinguished by the fact that it is here that the *bodhisattva* is born immediately prior to being born as a Buddha in Jambudvīpa. The duration of life in the Tuṣita corresponds to the ages in which a Buddha appears. The uppermost heaven is the Akaniṣṭha; the fourth infinity is designated *bhavāgra* ("pinnacle of being").

Associated drama. In its simplest form, the drama of the single-world system depends on the fact that the universe is limited and continuous. The monk travels through all the realms of the universe in the course of his meditations, eventually getting beyond it—detaching himself from it—to take possession of an individual *nirvāṇa* and achieve the state of *arhat*. For the most part, neither the presence of a buddha nor the divisions of cosmic time are central to this drama.

Cosmology of Thousands. There exist countless variations within this general heading, but the combination of thousands of worlds and the superimposition of one cosmic level upon another is a fundamental characteristic of the *sāhasra* cosmology. A second characteristic is the ultimate unity of these various combinations of worlds in the realm of a single buddha, a single *buddhakṣetra* (buddha field), or another similarly unifying entity.

The *Majjhima Nikāya* (3.101) describes a division of the *brahmaloka* into multiples of thousands of worlds, making a distinction between a *sahasso-brahmā* governing a *sahassīi lokadhatu*, and equivalent realms governed by a *dvisahasso-brahmā*, a *trisahasso-brahmā*, a *catussahasso-brahmā*, a *pancassahasso-brahmā*, and a *satasahassobrahmā*, gods that rule over worlds numbering between 1,000 and $1{,}000^{100}$.

Another example from the Pali texts is found at *Aṅguttara Nikāya* 1.227, which describes (1) a system of one thousand universes, *sahassīi chūḷanikā lokadhātu* ("small chiliocosm"); (2) a system of one million universes, *dvisahassī majjhimikā lokadhātu* ("middle chiliocosm"), embracing one thousand "small chiliocosms"; and (3) a system of one billion universes, *tisahassī mahāsahassi lokadhātu* ("great chiliocosm"), embracing one thousand "middle chiliocosms." The *Kośa* (vol. 3, pp. 138–141) describes the *trisāhasramahāsāhasralokadhātu* in virtually identical terms.

From this description it appears that a *trisāhasramahāsāhasralokadhātu* (*tisahassī mahāsahassī lokadhātu*) consists of one billion universes like the one in which we live, each consisting of four islands, a *cakravāla* wall, seven concentric ring mountains, a sun, a moon, and a Mount Meru. This arrangement of thousands of worlds is the most representative expression of the *sāhasra* cosmology and emerges as the formulaic expression of a *buddhakṣetra*. Even Mahāyāna texts that recognize the existence of innumerable *buddhakṣetras* acknowledge the fact that each is a *trisāhasramahāsāhasralokadhātu*.

Interpretation of the meaning of the *trisāhasramahāsāhasralokadhātu* remains problematic. However, it is closely associated with speculations on the great division of cosmic time. Because of this association, it is reasonable to assume a connection between the thousands of the *sāhasra* cosmology and the manner in which astronomers measured the movements of the planets, multiplying the fractional measurements of their observations by thousands of years to determine the beginning and end of the world, that is, that time when all planets were (will be) in a straight line. Based on these associations, we may regard the universe as "ever-measuring," constantly productive of the divisions of time grounded in the powers of discrimination.

This association with measurements of time is strengthened by the parallels between the *sāhasra* cosmology and the cosmologies of the Hindu Purāṇas, since the "thousands of worlds" (i.e., one billion) of the *sāhasra* cosmology exactly equal the divisions of time of the Puranic cosmos—if one leaves out references to days and nights and counts only years. The Puranic *yugas* consist of ten divine years, each equal to one thousand human years, for a total of ten thousand years in a *māhayuga.* One thousand *māhayugas* are the equivalent of a *kalpa*, which is also a "day of Brahmā," and one hundred years of such days equal the life of Brahmā or a *mahākalpa.* (The full reckoning is: 10 x 1000 x 1000 x 100 = 1,000,000,000.) The *trisāhasramahāsāhasralokadhātu* apparently spatializes the temporal divisions of Hindu cosmology.

Associated drama. In contrast to the drama of the single-world system, the manner whereby salvation occurs within the structures of the *sāhasra* cosmology is inextricably related to the divisions of cosmic time and the appearance of a buddha.

The largest division of time, corresponding to the duration of the universe, is a *mahākalpa.* A *mahākalpa* in turn consists of four "moments" (*kalpas*), each of which contains twenty *antarakalpas*. Thus, the *mahākalpa* consists of (1) a *kalpa* of creation (*vivartakalpa*), which extends from the birth of the primordial wind to the production of the first being that inhabits the hells; (2) a *kalpa* that consists of the duration of the creation (*vivartasthāyikalpa*), which begins with the appearance of the first being in the hells; (3) a *kalpa* of dissolution (*saṃvartakalpa*), commencing with the moment when beings cease to be reborn in the hells and ending with the moment when the "receptacle world" (i.e., the world inhabited by sentient beings) is destroyed; and (4) a *kalpa* during which the world remains dissolved (*saṃvartasthāyikalpa*) and during which nothing remains but space (*ākāśa*) where the world was. Each of the four *kalpas* are sometimes designated *asaṃkhyeya* ("incalculable") *kalpas*.

The twenty small or "intermediate" *kalpas* (*antarakalpas*) are characterized as follows: In a period of creation, the receptacle world (*bhājanaloka*) is created during the first *antarakalpa*; beings appear during the remaining nineteen. A reverse process occurs during a period of destruction. At the end of a period of creation, humankind has a life that is infinite in duration. During the first *antarakalpa* of the creation, it diminishes (*apakarṣa*) to ten years. Each of the next eighteen *antarakalpas* consists of an augmentation (*utkarṣa*) of life span from ten years up to eighty thousand years and a subsequent diminution back down to ten years again. The twentieth *antarakalpa* consists solely of augmentation up to eighty thousand years.

While not specifically mentioned in the *Kośa*, it should be noted that messianic traditions within Buddhism focus on the figure of Maitreya, the future and last Buddha of our age, who will provide a new *dharma* ("teaching") to replace the degenerated teaching of Śākyamuni. This will occur when the duration of life has reached eighty thousand years.

When all beings have disappeared from the inferior realms and are reunited in a meditation realm, presumably through the power of meditation and possibly the attainment of *nirvāṇa*, the "destructions" (*saṃvartānis*) take place. The agents of the destructions are the "great elements" and are of three kinds: those by fire, those by water, and those by wind. The second meditation realm (*dhyāna*) is the limit (*sīmā*) of the destruction by fire; everything lower is burned and scorched. The third *dhyāna* is the limit of the destruction by water; everything lower is decomposed or dissolved. The fourth *dhyāna* is the limit of the destruction by wind; everything below it is scattered. There is no destruction by earth because the receptacle world consists of earth. The destructions succeed one another in the following sequence: Seven destructions by fire are followed by a destruction by water; this cycle of eight destructions is repeated a total of seven times. Then follow seven more destructions by fire and a final destruction by wind. Thus there are seven times eight, or fifty-six destructions by fire, seven by water, and a final (sixty-fourth) destruction by wind.

While the soteriological drama associated with this cosmology is framed by the speculations on cosmic time, the drama proper divides itself into four discrete "moments." The first is that of the progress of the *śrāvaka*, or one who has undertaken the religious vocation toward becoming an *arhat.* Second is the exercise of miraculous powers. Third is the career of the *bodhisattva*, who makes a vow in the presence of a buddha to pursue buddhahood rather than pass into the extinction of *nirvāṇa.* The fourth moment in the drama is the appearance of a Buddha.

The progress of the *śrāvaka* toward the state of *arhat* consists of a series of practices, teachings, and meditations designated in a general way as "the path." Briefly stated, the *śrāvaka* on the way to arhatship masters a path that consists of sixteen "moments" of the four Holy Truths (*abhisamaya*) and 182 moments of the stages of meditation (*bhāvanāmārga*) including taking possession of the "four fruits" of the path: *srotāpanna* ("stream winner"), *sakṛdāgāmin* ("once-returner"), *anāgāmin* ("nonreturner"), and *arhat.*

Following the exercise of certain miraculous powers obtained as a result of meditation, and having made a vow to become a buddha, the *bodhisattva* then perfects the various virtues (*pāramitās*) during three *asaṃkhyeya* s of *mahākalpas.* After countless rebirths among the excellent destinies, the *bodhisattva* is born in the Tuṣita Heaven, during which time he develops the acts that are productive of the thirty-two marks of a great and almost certainly cosmic person (*mahāpuruṣa*). During the course of one hundred supplementary cosmic ages (*kalpaśate śese*), he exhibits in Jambudvīpa the marks of a *mahāpuruṣa.* This he does only in the presence of a buddha.

The final stage in the drama involves the appearance of a buddha. While there is considerable doctrinal disagreement on many points relating to this subject, it is generally agreed that a buddha only appears during a period when the length of human life is declining and when it is between eighty thousand and one hundred (sometimes, eighty) years. Lifespans greater than this are too long to afford beings awareness of the impermanent nature of things; less than this and life is too brief and the five corruptions (*kaṣāyas*) too powerful for the teaching to be mastered. Since the buddha is clearly of a different order from the *arhat,* and since both are necessarily in possession of *nirvāṇa,* we must conclude that the *nirvāṇa* of the buddha is of a different order from that of the *arhat.*

Since it is more important to provide a general means of interpreting these systems than to provide ever greater detail, I suggest the following. The single-world system in isolation serves as an aid to monastic meditation in much the same way as Sāṃkhya philosophy serves as a cosmological framework for the practice of yoga. Time (motion) and the cosmos are essentially contained within the body of the individual in its unliberated mode. Time and space are the products of the movements of the primordial matter (*prakṛi*) agitated by the presence of a soul.

As a corollary, there is little need for the great divisions of time—*kalpas, yugas, mahākalpas,* and so forth. Where these appear, time (and the cosmos) have been incorporated into the body of the deity. While arhatship or the attainment of the individual *nirvāṇa* is the essential drama of the single-world system in the Pali texts, the Sarvāstivādin texts establish a drama involving the relationship between the individual *nirvāṇa* (*arhat*) and the *nirvāṇa* of the Buddha as a cosmic figure whose body contains the elements of time. This suggestion is supported in part by the fact that the Pali Abhidhamma recognizes a single unconditioned *dharma* and a single *nirvāṇa,* whereas the Sarvāstivādin literature recognizes three unconditioned *dharmas,* including space and two types of *nirvāṇa.*

Alternative dramas. Along with three classes of saints—*arhat, bodhisattva,* and buddha—the *Kośa* recognizes a fourth class of saint known as the *pratyekabuddha,* or person who achieves enlightenment in isolation. The grouping of four is noteworthy for its transformation in the *Saddharmapuṇḍarīka Sūtra (Lotus Sūtra).*

The *Lotus Sūtra* describes a "path" to salvation known as the *ekayāna,* or "single path." By means of "devices" (*upāya*), the cosmic Buddha projects three paths—those pursued by the *arhat,* the *pratyekabuddha* and the *bodhisattva*—to suit the differing spiritual capacities of creatures. While these three goals are pursued independently by beings according to their sensibilities, it is after having achieved these various provisional *nirvāṇas* that the true *nirvāṇa* is bestowed upon them by the Buddha.

There are additional continuities between this drama and that found in the Pure Land traditions. There the faithful are admonished to think at the moment of death of the Buddha Amitābha ("infinite light"), whose field, Sukhāvatī (the Land of Bliss), lies in the west. In so doing, they will be reborn there in what will be their last birth; to live lives without interruption and to hear the *dharma* preached perfectly and thence to obtain final *nirvāṇa.* I shall simply note that Sukhāvatī is the realm of *sukha* ("bliss"), set over against this world of *duḥkha* ("suffering"). The fundamental tenet of the Hīnayāna, of course, is that all existence is suffering (*duḥkha*). The *sukha* world is therefore the visionary representation of all duality and of all striving. It is thus an accommodation to the sensibilities of all creatures and in some ways a provisional *nirvāṇa.* From Sukhāvatī the second stage of the drama unfolds, which is the *ekayāna,* or the *nirvāṇa* granted as a result of the *nirvāṇa* of the Buddha.

With the same thought in mind, but using the stick rather than the carrot, the Japanese monk Genshin (942–1017) compiled extensive and horrible descriptions of the hells associated with the single-world system in order to turn people's minds toward rebirth in Sukhāvatī lest they remain in the realm of *duḥkha* and become subject to its worst torments.

The Tiantai school of Chinese Buddhism utilizes the *trisāhasramahāsāhasralokadhātu* in another way, basing its interpretation on the second chapter of the *Lotus Sūtra.* Here we are told that it represents the three thousand worlds used as a model for the interpenetrating nature of all reality. These three thousand worlds are also known as *dharmas* and are organized in the following manner. There are ten realms of existence—those of the buddhas, *bodhisattvas, pratyekabuddhas,* direct disciples of the Buddha (*śrāvakas*), heavenly beings, spirits, human beings, departed beings, beasts, and depraved men. Each of these shares the characteristics of the others, thus making one hundred realms. Each of these in turn is characterized by ten "thusnesses" or "such-likenesses" through which the true state is manifested in phenomena. This makes one thousand realms of existence. Each realm is further constituted by the three divisions of living beings, space, and the (five) aggregates (*skandhas*) that constitute *dharmas,* thus making a total of three thousand realms of existence or aspects of reality. Because the interpenetration of these three thousand realms (*trisāhasramahāsāhasralokadhātu*) is immanent in a single instant of thought, all beings have the buddha-nature in them and can thus be saved.

While comparison of these variations in drama with that of the *sāhasra* cosmology is useful, they are better understood in the context of another set of general cosmological structures known as the *asaṃkhyeya* cosmology.

COSMOLOGY OF INNUMERABLES. The *asaṃkhyeya* cosmology belongs to the Mahāyāna and is characterized by the "innumerable" (*asaṃkhyeya*) buddhas and *buddhaksetras* filling the ten regions of space in place of the single *buddhakṣetra* of the Hīnayāna.

Images of space. While the *sāhasra* cosmology was dominated by the temporal categories of the *kalpa*, the *asaṃkhyeya* cosmology is dominated by spatial categories and images. The emphasis on spatial imagery is carried to the point where the Mahāyāna can argue that time does not exist. Just as the appearance of the Buddhas in the *sāhasra* cosmology was linked to the passage of time, the Buddhas are now associated with the directions or points of space and are referred to as the "Buddhas of the ten regions" (*daśadigbuddha*). As a result, the appearance of a buddha in this cosmology is not a rare event. Instead, it is repeatedly stated that the Buddhas are "as numerous as the sands of the Ganges."

Associated drama. A new drama is expressed in a mytheme that finds wide currency in Mahāyāna texts. It revolves around the "great concentrations" of the buddha Śākyamuni in his cosmic form and the manner in which the concentrations result in the exercise of miraculous powers, most notably the issuance of rays of light from the body of the Buddha. While the mytheme varies from text to text, it is analyzed with scholastic thoroughness in the *Mahāprajñāpāramitā Śāstra* (chaps. 14–15), a text traditionally attributed to Nāgārjuna. The essential tenets of this drama may be summarized as follows.

The Buddha enters into a concentration in which are contained all the concentrations. Departing therefrom he practices a variety of magical powers, the most notable of which is the issuance of rays of light from his body. Touched by these rays of light, all beings become intent upon enlightenment and are prepared to hear the great sermon of the cosmic Buddha; the world is transformed into a Pure Land, and beings are either able to see and hear the *dharma* being preached in other buddha fields or are transported to one of those fields where they can hear the *dharma* without obstacle, distraction, or interruption. The Buddha utilizes the magical powers gained through concentration for the welfare of all beings. The power of the rays of light is so great that it is likened to the destruction of the universe by fire at the end of a *kalpa*. As a result of his extinction in concentration, the Buddha exercises miraculous powers that benefit all beings in accordance with their sensibilities. Just as the Hindu cosmologies explore the multivalence of the term *pralaya* (death/destruction of the universe/liberation) the Buddhist cosmologies explore the multiple meanings of *nirvāṇa*.

In the last analysis, it is the *nirvāṇa* of the cosmic Buddha that alone results in salvation, not the *nirvāṇas* of individuals. According to the *Lotus Sūtra*, "he does not teach a particular Nirvāṇa for each being; he causes all beings to reach complete Nirvāṇa by means of the complete Nirvāṇa of the Tathāgata" (Kern, 1965, p. 81).

The drama of the *sāhasra* cosmology and that of the *asaṃkhyeya* cosmology can be contrasted on many points. The journey of the *sāhasra* cosmology is one that moves arduously and laboriously through each of the abodes of the cosmography and extends indefinitely in time. The journey of the *asaṃkhyeya* cosmology on the other hand occurs in an instant, transporting the individual to one of the many worlds separated from each other by the void of infinite space. In the former, Buddhas are rare and quiescent, in the latter, numerous and active. Just as the Hindu cosmologies play with a juxtaposition of the term *puruṣa* in its two meanings of multiple individual souls on the one hand and a single, all-encompassing soul on the other, the Buddhist cosmologies are concerned with individual and cosmic *nirvāṇas*.

It may be argued that all of Buddhist cosmological speculation falls into one of these two traditions. Those that accept time as the fundamental cosmological reality belong to the Hīnayāna. Those that embrace metaphors of space belong to the Mahāyāna. It is also likely that the *cakravāla* cosmology and the Pure Land cosmologies actually constitute shorthands or simplifications of these two great traditions, the one for the benefit of the monastic vocation, and the other for the benefit of the devotional traditions of the Mahāyāna.

SEE ALSO Buddhas and Bodhisattvas, article on Celestial Buddhas and Bodhisattvas; Pure and Impure Lands; Soteriology.

BIBLIOGRAPHY

Texts and Translations

Abhidharmakośa, translated by Louis de La Vallée Poussin as *L'Abhidharmakośa de Vasubandhu*, 6 vols. (1923–1931; reprint, Brussels, 1971).

Mahāprajñāpāramitā Śāstra, translated by Étienne Lamotte as *Le traité de la grande vertu de sagesse de Nāgārjuna*, 5 vols. (Louvain, 1949–1980).

Ōjōyōshū, translated by August Karl Reischauer as "Genshin's Ojo Yoshu: Collected Essays on Birth into Paradise," *Transactions of the Asiatic Society of Japan*, 2d ser., 7 (1930): 16–97.

Saddharmapuṇḍarīka Sūtra, translated by Hendrik Kern as *Saddharma-Puṇḍarīka; or the Lotus of the True Law* (1884; reprint, Delhi, 1965). The Chinese version of this text was translated by Leon Hurvitz as *Scripture of the Lotus Blossom of the Fine Dharma (Lotus Sutra)* (New York, 1976).

Sukhāvatīvyūha Sūtra, translated by F. Max Müller and edited by E. B. Cowell in *Buddhist Mahāyāna Texts*, Sacred Books of the East, vol. 49 (1894; reprint, New York, 1969).

Traibhūmikathā, translated by Frank E. Reynolds and Mani Reynolds as *Three Worlds according to King Ruang* (Berkeley, 1982).

Visuddhimagga, by Buddhaghosa, translated by Bhikkhu Ñyāṇamoli as *The Path of Purification*, 2d ed. (Colombo, 1964).

Other Works of Interest

Andrews, Allan A. *The Teachings Essential for Rebirth: A Study of Genshin's Ōjōyōshū.* Tokyo, 1973.

Basham, A. L. *History and Doctrine of the Ājīvikas: A Vanished Indian Religion.* London, 1951.

"Butsudō." In *Hôbôgirin: Dictionnarie encyclopédique du bouddhisme d'après les sources chinoises et japonaise,* 4 vols., edited by Paul Demiéville. Tokyo, 1929–1931.

Hurvitz, Leon. *Chih-I.* Brussels, 1962.

Kirfel, Willibald. *Die Kosmographie der Inder* (1920). Reprint, Bonn, 1967.

Kloetzli, W. Randolph. *Buddhist Cosmology: From Single World System to Pure Land; Science and Theology in the Images of Motion and Light.* Delhi, 1983.

Lamotte, Étienne. *The Teaching of Vimalakīrti (Vimalakīrtinirdeśa).* Translated from French by Sara Boin. London, 1976. See especially "Note 1: The *buddhakṣetra.*"

La Vallée Poussin, Louis de. "Cosmogony and Cosmology (Buddhist)." In *Encyclopaedia of Religion and Ethics,* edited by James Hastings, vol. 4. Edinburgh, 1911. A lucid and highly detailed discussion of Hīnayāna cosmology.

New Sources

French, Rebecca R. "The Cosmology of Law in Buddhist Tibet." *Journal of the International Association of Buddhist Studies* 18, no. 1 (1995): 97–116.

Gethin, Rupert. "Cosmology and Meditation: From the *Agganna-Sutta* to the Mahayana." *History of Religions* 36 (1997): 183–217.

Hamilton, Sue. "The 'External World': Its Status and Relevance in the Pali Nikayas." *Religion* 29 (1999): 73–90.

Kong sprul, B. g. m. ī, and R. Bokar. *The Treasury of Knowledge. Book One: Myriad Worlds.* Ithaca, N.Y., 2003.

Mitchell, Donald W. "The Trinity and Buddhist Cosmology." *Buddhist Christian Studies* 18 (1998): 169–180.

Sadakata, Akira. *Buddhist Cosmology: Philosophy and Origins.* Tokyo, 1997.

Walker, J. L. "This Quiet Place That Buddhas Love." *Parabola* 24 no. 1 (1999): 35–39.

W. Randolph Kloetzli (1987)
Revised Bibliography

COSMOLOGY: SCIENTIFIC COSMOLOGIES

General speculations about the nature of the world are as old as the Greek pre-Socratic philosophers, but a truly scientific cosmology could not be formulated until there was some knowledge of the basic laws of nature. Isaac Newton's discovery of universal inverse-square-law gravity afforded the first serious opportunity for such an endeavor. Because gravity is attractive, an immediate problem was to explain why the universe did not collapse in upon itself. Planetary motions stopped this happening in the solar system, but what about the "fixed stars"? The answer first suggested was that in a universe of infinite extent, populated uniformly by stars, the attractive forces in different directions would cancel each other out, giving equilibrium.

However, there was a problem with the idea of a limitless cosmos. Every line of sight would have to terminate somewhere on the surface of a star. In 1823 Wilhelm Olbers pointed out that this would imply that the night sky was everywhere uniformly bright. The modern resolution of this paradox relies on the fact that the finite speed of light and the finite age of the universe together mean that only a finite number of stars are actually visible to us.

An important discovery was made at the end of the eighteenth century by Sir William Herschel. He discovered that the band of light known as the Milky Way is actually composed of a multitude of stars, constituting a vast galaxy of which the solar system is only a tiny component. Early speculators, including Immanuel Kant (1724–1804), had proposed that this might be the case. They also suggested that the luminous patches called nebulae might be other "island universes," similar to the Milky Way but at great distances from it. The issue was not finally settled until the twentieth century, but the idea was already in the air that created reality might be much vaster than had earlier been supposed.

Distances to nearby stars can be measured by parallax, the slight shift in apparent celestial position as the Earth moves around its orbit. Beyond that range, estimating distance depends upon establishing a *standard candle,* a source of light of known intensity whose observed dimming then affords a measure of its distance. Stars of regularly fluctuating brightness, called Cepheid variables, provide this measure, for it is known that their intrinsic brightness is strictly correlated with the period of their variation. In 1924 Edwin Hubble used this method to establish that the Andromeda nebula is a distant galaxy, now known to be about two million light-years away from the Milky Way.

Hubble then went on to make his biggest discovery. Light from distant galaxies is found to be reddened in comparison with the same light from a terrestrial source. This is interpreted as due to the effect of recessional motion, and the degree of reddening induced is correlated to the speed of recession. The effect (Doppler shift) is similar to the change in frequency of an ambulance siren due to the motion of the vehicle. Hubble discovered that the rate at which a galaxy is receding is proportional to its distance. This was then interpreted as an effect due to the expansion of space itself. Just as spots on the surface of a balloon move away from each other as the balloon is inflated, so as space expands it carries the galaxies with it. Hubble's discovery of the expanding universe had a profound effect upon the development of cosmological theory.

Relativistic Cosmology. Newton regarded space as a container within which the motion of material atoms took place in the course of the flow of absolute time. Albert Einstein's discovery of the theory of general relativity completely changed this picture.

In 1908 Einstein had what he regarded as his happiest thought. He realized that if he were to be falling freely, he would be completely unaware of gravity. This seemingly rather insignificant observation led him to recognize the principle of equivalence, which lies at the root of general relativity. There are two conceptually distinct meanings of mass: inertial mass (measuring a body's resistance to having its state of motion changed) and gravitational mass (measuring the strength of the body's interaction with a gravitational field). Despite their conceptual distinctness, these two measures are always numerically identical. Quantitatively, inertial and gravitational mass are equivalent. This implies that all bodies move in the same way in a gravitational field. Doubling the mass will double the inertial resistance to a change of motion, but it also doubles the gravitational force effecting the change. In consequence the resulting motion is the same. This universal behavior means that the effects of gravity on individual bodies can be reinterpreted as a general consequence of the properties of space itself, or more accurately, taking into account Einstein's earlier discovery of special relativity's close mutual association of space and time, the properties of four-dimensional spacetime. The concepts of space, time, and matter, held quite distinct by Newton, were united by Einstein in a single package deal. He turned gravitational physics into geometry. Matter curves spacetime and the curvature of spacetime in turn affects the paths of matter. There is no time without space and matter, a point Augustine had realized fifteen centuries earlier.

Einstein set to work to discover the equations that would give quantitative expression to his idea. The search was long, but in November 1915 he hit upon them. Immediately he was able to show that they predicted a small deviation in the behavior of the planet Mercury, which had already been observed but which had defied Newtonian explanation. Later, in 1919, observations of a total solar eclipse confirmed another prediction, relating to the bending of starlight by the Sun. Overnight Einstein became in the public's imagination the iconic scientific hero.

This integration of space, time, and matter in a single theory afforded the opportunity to construct a truly scientific account of the whole universe. However, there seemed to be a problem. At the time, physicists still believed that cosmological theory should yield a static picture. Physics was to be the last of the sciences to recognize the true significance of temporality and unfolding process. The geologists had got there at the end of the eighteenth century, and by mid-nineteenth century the biologists, with the publication of Charles Darwin's *Origin of Species* in 1859, had followed suit. In the early twentieth century, the physicists still held the Aristotelian notion of an eternally changeless cosmos. Einstein could not find a static solution of his equations. Consequently, when he published his cosmological proposals in 1918 he tinkered with the equations, adding an extra term (the cosmological constant). It represented a kind of anti-gravity, a repulsive force designed to counterbalance over great distances the attractive force of conventional gravity.

Einstein later called this addition the greatest blunder of his life. He had missed the chance to predict an expanding universe, for his unmodified equations had solutions (discovered by the Russian meteorologist Alexander Friedmann and the Belgian priest Georges Lemaître) that corresponded to the behavior later observed by Hubble. Moreover, his proposed static solution did not really work, for it was unstable and would have collapsed under disturbance.

BIG BANG COSMOLOGY. If the galaxies are presently moving apart, then in the past they must have been closer together. This leads to the conclusion that the universe we observe today appears to have emerged from the Big Bang, a primeval state of immensely condensed and energetic matter. Current estimates date this emergence at 13.7 billion years ago.

Taken literally, the Big Bang itself is an instant of infinite density and energy, a singularity that is beyond the power of conventional science to analyze. (Some highly speculative ideas about the very early universe, close to the Big Bang, will be discussed below.) Although some religious people (including Pope Pius XII) succumbed to the temptation to speak of the Big Bang as "the moment of creation," this was clearly a theological mistake. The Judeo-Christian-Islamic doctrine of creation is concerned with ontological origin (why is there something rather than nothing?), rather than temporal origin (how did it all begin?). God is as much the Creator today as God was 13.7 billion years ago. Big Bang cosmology is very interesting scientifically, but not critically significant theologically.

Nevertheless, three cosmologists, Hermann Bondi, Fred Hoyle, and Thomas Gold, feared that Big Bang cosmology might favor religion, and so in the 1960s they proposed an alternative *steady state* theory, the picture of an everlasting universe always broadly the same. This return to Aristotelian ideas was reconciled with the recession of the galaxies by the supposition of the continuous creation of matter, taking place at a rate too small to be observed but sufficient over time to fill in the gaps left by the motion of the already existing galaxies. Further observational results have disposed of this idea.

As the universe expands, it cools. By the time it was a microsecond old, its temperature was already at the level where the cosmic processes taking place had energies sufficiently low for scientists to possess a reliable understanding of their nature. Discussion is further simplified by the fact that the early universe was almost uniform and structureless, making it a very simple physical system to consider.

By the time it was about three minutes old, the universe had cooled to the extent that nuclear interactions ceased on a cosmic scale. As a result the gross nuclear structure of the world got fixed at what it still is today, three-quarters hydrogen and one-quarter helium. By the time the cosmos was about half a million years old, further cooling had taken it to the point where radiation was no longer energetic enough to break up any atoms that tried to form. Matter and radiation then decoupled and the latter was left simply to cool further as cosmic expansion continued. Today this radiation is very cold, three degrees above absolute zero. It was first observed in 1964 by Arno Penzias and Robert Wilson. Known as cosmic background radiation, it forms a fossilized deposit left over from the big bang era, telling us what the universe was like when it was half a million years old. One of the things we learn is that the cosmos was then very uniform, with fluctuations about the mean density amounting to no more than one part in ten thousand. This background radiation put paid to the steady state theory, which could not explain its properties in the natural way that was possible for Big Bang cosmology.

Gravity has the long-term effect of enhancing small fluctuations. A little more matter here than there produced a little more attraction here than there, thereby triggering a snowballing effect by which the universe eventually became lumpy with galaxies and stars. By a cosmic age of one billion years this process was in full swing. As stars condensed, they heated up and nuclear reactions began again on a local scale. Initially, stars burn by converting hydrogen into helium. At a later stage of stellar development, heavier elements, such as carbon and oxygen, are formed by further nuclear processes. Inside a star this sequence cannot get beyond iron, the most stable of the nuclear species. At the end of their lives, however, some stars explode as supernovae, not only scattering the elements they have made out into the environment, but also, in the explosive process itself, generating the missing elements beyond iron. In this way the ninety-two chemical elements eventually became available. One of the great triumphs of twentieth-century astrophysics was unraveling the details of the delicate processes of nucleosynthesis. When a second generation of stars and planets formed, there was available a chemical environment sufficiently rich to permit the development of life. Thus began one of the most remarkable developments in cosmic history known to us. With the eventual dawning of self-consciousness the universe became aware of itself.

The Anthropic Principle. As scientists came to understand the evolutionary processes of cosmic history, they began to realize that the possibility for the development of carbon-based life depended critically on the details of the laws of nature actually operating in the universe. The collection of insights pointing to this conclusion has been given the name of the anthropic principle, though carbon principle would have been a better choice as it is the generality of life, rather than the specificity of *Homo sapiens*, that is involved. Many examples have been given of these anthropic "fine-tunings."

One is provided by the stellar processes by which the elements necessary for life have been formed. Every atom of carbon in every living body was once inside a star, and the process by which that carbon was made depends critically on the quantitative details of nuclear physics. Three helium nuclei have to combine to make carbon. One would expect a two-step process, two heliums first fusing to form beryllium, and then a third helium being added on to make carbon. However, there is a problem because beryllium is very unstable and this makes the second step problematic. In fact it is only possible because there turns out to be a substantial enhancement effect (a resonance) occurring at exactly the right energy. If the nuclear forces were different from what they actually are, this resonance would be in the wrong place and there would be no carbon at all. When Hoyle discovered this remarkable coincidence, he felt it could not just be a happy accident but there must be some Intelligence lying behind it.

Examples can be multiplied. Developing life on a planet depends upon its star providing a long-lived and reliable source of energy. Stars burn in this way in our universe because the force of gravity is such as to permit it. The most exacting anthropic fine-tuning relates to Einstein's cosmological constant. Modern thinking has revived this notion, but its strength has to be extremely weak to prevent the universe either collapsing or blowing apart. Many cosmologists believe the force (usually called *dark energy*) is actually present, but at a level that is only 10^{-120} of what one would regard as its natural value. Anything larger than this tiny number would have made the evolution of life, or any complex cosmic structure, quite impossible.

These scientific insights are uncontroversial, but what their deeper, metascientific significance might be held to be has been highly contended. Few are prepared to treat these anthropic coincidences as merely happy accidents, and so two contrasting explanatory proposals have been widely canvassed. One views the universe as a divine creation, explaining its finely tuned specificity as an expression of the Creator's will that it should be capable of having a fruitful history. The other is the multiverse approach, supposing that this particular universe is just one member of a vast portfolio of different existing worlds, each separate from each other and each possessing its own natural laws and circumstances. Our universe is simply the one in this immense cosmic array where, by chance, the development of carbon-based life is a possibility. Although there are highly speculative scientific ideas that might to a degree encourage multiversal thinking (see below), the unobservable prodigality of the multiverse approach makes it seem a metaphysical proposal of considerable extravagance, which appears to do only one piece of explanatory work in defusing the threat of theism.

The Very Early Universe. The closer scientists try to press to the Big Bang, the more extreme are the regimes involved and therefore the more speculative their thinking.

Many believe that when the universe was about 10^{-36} seconds old, a kind of boiling of space occurred, called inflation, which expanded the universe very greatly and with immense rapidity. The idea is not only supported by some theoretical arguments, but also gains credibility through its ability to explain some significant facts about the universe. One is cosmic isotropy: the background radiation appears virtually the same in all directions despite the fact that the sky contains many regions which, on a simple extrapolation back to the Big Bang, would never have been in causal contact with each other. On an inflationary picture, however, these different regions derive from an initially much smaller domain where there would have been the causal contact necessary to produce uniformity of temperature and density. Inflation would also have had a smoothing effect, thereby explaining the large-scale homogeneity of the universe and the close balance between expansive and gravitational effects that is actually observed (and which, in fact, is another anthropic necessity).

Much more speculative is the attempt to understand the Planck era, before 10^{-43} seconds, when the universe was so small that it has to be understood quantum mechanically. The proper unification of quantum theory and general relativity has not been achieved. In consequence there are many different hypothetical accounts of quantum cosmology. A frequent theme is that universes may continually arise from the inflation of fluctuations in the ur-vacuum of quantum gravity, and our universe is just one member of this proliferating multiverse. The assertion that this process would represent science's ability to explain creation out of nothing, is merely an abuse of language. A quantum vacuum is a highly structured and active medium, very different from *nihil.*

COSMIC DESTINY. On the largest scale, the history of the cosmos involves a tug of war between the expansive tendencies of the Big Bang and the contractive force of gravity. If in the end gravity wins, what began with the Big Bang will end in the big crunch, as the universe collapses in upon itself. If expansion wins (the currently favored option), the universe will continue to expand forever, becoming progressively colder and more dilute, eventually decaying in a long drawn out dying whimper.

In its eschatological thinking, theology must take account of these reliable scientific prognostications of the eventual futility of current process. Ultimately, a simple evolutionary optimism is not a viable possibility.

SEE ALSO Physics and Religion.

BIBLIOGRAPHY

Barrow, John, and Frank Tipler. *The Anthropic Cosmological Principle.* Oxford, 1986. An encyclopedic survey of anthropic insights and arguments.

Drees, Willem. *Beyond the Big Bang: Quantum Cosmologies and God.* La Salle, Ill., 1990. A careful and quite technical survey of possible connections between quantum cosmologies and theology.

Hawking, Stephen. *A Brief History of Time: From the Big Bang to Black Holes.* London, 1988. Famous exposition of the author's particular version of quantum cosmology.

Leslie, John. *Universes.* London, 1989. A concise and careful account of scientific and philosophical issues relating to the anthropic principle.

Leslie, John, ed. *Physical Cosmology and Philosophy.* New York, 1990. A useful collection of reprinted papers.

Miller, James, ed. *Cosmic Questions.* New York, 2001. A wide-ranging collection of papers given at a conference sponsored by the American Association for the Advancement of Science.

Polkinghorne, John. *Science and Creation: The Search for Understanding.* London, 1988. A scientist-theologian looks at the universe considered as a creation.

Polkinghorne, John, and Michael Welker, eds. *The End of the World and the Ends of God: Science and Theology on Eschatology.* Harrisburg, Pa., 2000. A collection of papers considering eschatological issues in the light of modern science.

Rees, Martin. *Before the Beginning: Our Universe and Others.* London, 1998. Readable account of modern cosmological ideas; supportive of the idea of a multiverse.

Weinberg, Steven. *The First Three Minutes: A Modern View of the Origin of the Universe.* 2d ed. New York, 1988. Classic and moderately technical account of early universe cosmology.

Worthing, Mark. *God, Creation, and Contemporary Physics.* Minneapolis, 1996. Creation considered in the light of modern physics.

JOHN POLKINGHORNE (2005)

COUNCILS

This entry consists of the following articles:

BUDDHIST COUNCILS
CHRISTIAN COUNCILS

COUNCILS: BUDDHIST COUNCILS

Accounts considering the final events in the life of Siddhārtha Gautama, the historical Buddha, are often quick to point out that his last injunctions to his community include exhortations to remember that all compounded things are impermanent and to work diligently for the attainment of salvation. What these accounts sometimes fail to emphasize is that the Buddha also enjoined the community to appoint no successor in his stead. The Buddha was explicit in arguing that his teaching (Dharma) and disciplinary training (Vinaya) would provide sufficient guidance for the attainment of *nirvāṇa.* He further granted the community authority to abolish all lesser and minor precepts of conduct, although he failed to identify precisely which precepts he deemed minor and lesser. In the absence of an appointed or hereditary successor to leadership of the Buddhist community, and with an obvious uncertainty as to which disciplinary rules were to be retained, much confusion could be expected in the days and years following the leader's demise. To combat the anticipated disorientation, it was suggested that a council be convened whose purpose would be to solidify basic Buddhist doctrine and discipline. In this way, the transition from the ministry of the Buddha's charismatic leadership to one of a newly established social identity was softened and advanced. Further, convocation of this first Buddhist council helped to establish a precedent upon which future Buddhist communities could draw for sanction in resolving disputes.

COUNCIL LITERATURE. Literature on these various Buddhist councils derives from both primary and secondary sources.

Initially, one looks to the canonical sources, and this avenue of inquiry yields fruitful results. Appended to the Vinaya Piṭaka, or disciplinary portion, of each Buddhist school's canon is a section devoted to a consideration of the Buddha's death and the first two Buddhist councils. Noncanonical sources also unearth a mine of useful material. In this regard, we can consult such texts as the Pali *Dīpavaṃsa,* as well as the *Samayabhedoparacanacakra* of Vasumitra, the *Nikāyabhedavibhaṅgavyākhyāna* of Bhavya, the *Mahāprajñāpāramita Śāstra,* (often wrongly attributed to Nāgārjuna), Ji-zang's *San-lun hsüan-i* (based on an earlier work of Paramārtha), the *Mahāvibhāṣā Śāstra,* the *Śāriputraparipṛcchā Sūtra,* and others. There is also a wealth of secondary material in Western languages, for which the reader is referred to the appended bibliography.

MAJOR INDIAN COUNCILS. Current buddhological research enables the documentation of no fewer than five Indian Buddhist councils, each of which must be described in order to unearth its import for the history of the tradition.

The first council: Rājagṛha. The first Indian Buddhist council was allegedly held during the rainy season immediately following the Buddha's death in, according to the most popular reckoning, 483 BCE. It was held in the capital city of King Bimbisāra, ruler of Magadha and a chief royal patron of the Buddha and the Buddhist community. With food and shelter provided, Rājagṛha proved to be an ideal site for the Buddhists' deliberations. Most accounts tell that a leading Buddhist monk of the time, Kāśyapa, was selected to convene the council and charged with the task of inviting an appropriate assemblage of monks. There are, however, some indications that the Buddha's first enlightened disciple, Ājñāta Kauṇḍinya, was chosen to preside, thus raising a later scholarly debate as to whether personal merit or seniority was the basis for leadership selection. In any case, as the records recount the story, five hundred monks, all having attained the status of *arhats* (Pali, *arahants*; "enlightened ones"), were selected to participate in the council proceedings. The plan for the enactment of the council was to have the president of the event question first Upāli, a disciple known for his mastery of the disciplinary materials, on Vinaya, and then Ānanda, allegedly the Buddha's most beloved disciple, on the various sermons of the Buddha. Sources recount, however, that at the time of his selection Ānanda was not yet enlightened. (This fact in and of itself casts some doubt on the accuracy of the account.) In due course, however, Ānanda is reported to have attained *nirvāṇa,* thus enabling him to participate in the expected fashion.

During Kāśyapa's questioning of Ānanda, reference was made to the Buddha's suggestion that the lesser and minor precepts be abolished. With the community in a quandry as to the best course of action, Kāśyapa decided to leave all disciplinary rules intact, lest the community fall into disrepute in such matters. After the recitation of the doctrinal and disciplinary materials, other issues of business were entertained and various penalties imposed on individuals who had acted incorrectly. As the convocation prepared to adjourn, a traveling monk, Purāṇa, arrived in Rājagṛha and was invited to join the proceedings. He declined, noting that he chose to remember the Dharma and Vinaya precisely as spoken by the Buddha. In so noting, further suspicion is thrown on the authority and impact of the council. Finally, the council concluded, referring to itself as the *vinayasaṃgīti,* or "chanting of the Vinaya."

At least three major functions for this first council at Rājagṛha can be distinguished. In the first place, there is the practical concern. The council established authority for the fledgling religious community in the absence of its founder, and solidarity was enhanced as well. There was also a secondary concern to begin the post-Buddha period with communal purity confirmed. The meting out of formal penalties assured such a condition. Third, there is the obvious mythic function. A formal religious event effected a renewal of the cosmic and social order, thus providing an auspicious beginning for the religious organization's new mission. Furthermore, in the recitation of the Dharma and the Vinaya (in nothing like their later forms, however), an infant Buddhist canon was established.

The general consensus of scholarship devoted to the first council almost uniformly concludes that the canonical accounts are at best greatly exaggerated and at worst pure fiction. On a small scale, it may be safe to assume that several of the Buddha's intimates gathered after his death to consider their future plight in the Indian religious climate, but the authenticity of the dramatic event presented in the canon is highly questionable.

The Second Council: Vaiśālī. One hundred years pass before there is any further information on the historical development of the Buddhist community. The occasion for this new look into the ongoing progress of the still-infant Buddhist religion was a council held in the town of Vaiśālī. The various Vinaya accounts record that a Buddhist monk named Yaṣas wandered into Vaiśālī and observed the resident monks, or *bhikṣus* (formally identified as the Vṛjiputraka *bhikṣus*), engaged in ten practices that seemed to conflict with Yaṣas's understanding of injunctions made explicit in the Vinaya. Yaṣas, the tale has it, formally protested indulgence in these ten apparently illicit practices, but was rejected by the community of monks and sentenced to a penalty known as the *pratisaṃharaṇīya-karma.* This punishment required that he beg the pardon of the monks he had offended by his accusation and obtain their forgiveness. Although initially intending to comply with the penalty, Yaṣas eventually changed his mind, resolving to convince the local laity that the Vṛjiputraka monks were at fault. Upon learning of Yaṣas's renewed attack on their conduct, the resident monks further punished this young agitator with the *utkṣepaṇīya-karma,* literally banishing him from the community.

Undaunted by the formal act of banishment, Yaṣas journeyed to Kauśāmbī, seeking the support of a learned monk known as Saṃbhūta Śāṇavāsin. Another well-respected monk, Revata, also decided to come to Yaṣas's support on the issue of the ten practices. All the while, the Vṛjiputraka *bhikṣus* were gathering supporters to their side as well. The conflict was brought to a conclusion in the convocation of a formal council in Vaiśālī. Revata was selected to preside over the proceedings. Sarvagāmin, an elder monk who had had the Buddha's direct disciple Ānanda as his *upādhyāya*, or teacher, was questioned on each of the ten points. One by one, Sarvagāmin rejected each point on the basis of various scriptures. With the ten practices condemned and concord renewed, the council concluded, again referring to itself as the "recital of the Vinaya" (*vinayasaṃgīti*) or as the "recital of the seven hundred," the number of monks who attended the gathering.

Of course it is necessary to consider just what these ten illicit practices were and why this particular event seems to have had so great an impact on the early Buddhist community. The ten points include: (1) preserving salt in a horn; (2) taking food when the shadow is beyond two fingers wide; (3) after finishing one meal, going to another town for another meal; (4) holding several confession ceremonies within the same monastic boundary; (5) confirming a monastic act in an incomplete assembly; (6) carrying out an act improperly and justifying it by its habitual performance in this way; (7) after eating, drinking unchurned milk that is somewhere between the states of milk and curd; (8) drinking unfermented wine; (9) using a mat without a border; and (10) accepting gold and silver. Although there is considerable scholarly disagreement concerning the meaning and implications of these practices, it is abundantly clear that each of the ten points was fully rejected by the Vinaya of each Buddhist *nikāya*, or school. Based on such scriptural certainty, then, is it possible to make any sense out of these points and their implications for Buddhist history?

Although a reconciliation was effected by the council of Vaiśālī, the very occasion of the council suggests forcefully that there were significant tensions and disagreements already operative in the Buddhist community. That it was divided by various factions must be assumed. To make general statements, it may be summarized that the various differences that were emerging as reflecting (1) rigorist versus laxist tendencies; (2) monastic versus lay emphases; and (3) sacred versus secular concern in the community.

Virtually all scholars conclude that the council of Vaiśālī was a historical event. Almost all sources place the event one hundred years after the Buddha's *nirvāṇa* (although two sources cite 110 years) at the Vālukārāma Monastery in Vaiśālī. Wilhelm Geiger and others have suggested that the council of Vaiśālī is the beginning point of Buddhist sectarianism, the point at which the *saṃgha* split into the Sthavira and Mahāsāṃghika schools. This premise, however, has been persuasively rejected by Marcel Hofinger, André Bareau, myself, and others. Thus, at the conclusion of the council of Vaiśālī, the Buddhist community remained bound together, albeit in a rather tenuous and uncertain union.

Pāṭaliputra I: the noncanonical council. By the time of the consecration of King Aśoka (c. 270 BCE), the Buddhist sectarian movement was already well advanced. Attempts to locate the beginnings of Buddhist sectarianism in the scriptures have continually failed. Nonetheless, through the painstaking efforts of Bareau, it has been possible to reconstruct the evidence of a council from which the Buddhist sectarian movement had its birth. By using primarily noncanonical sources, Bareau has been able to conclude that another council followed that of Vaiśālī by less than half a century, and it is this event that must be considered here.

In the study of this new council, only one issue can be found about which all the texts concur: that it was held in Pāṭaliputra. Both the date of the council and the occasion for its convocation are troublesome. Four possible dates appear in the various texts: 100 AN (i.e., after the *nirvāṇa* of the Buddha), 116 AN, 137 AN, and 160 AN. Bareau dismisses the extreme dates as "manifestly aberrant," and initially concludes that the event must have occurred either in 137 AN or 116 AN. According to Bareau, the former date would locate the council under the reign of King Mahāpadma the Nandin, while the latter would place the proceedings in the reign of Kālāśoka. Bareau prefers the former figure, assuming that it would take thirty-seven years or so for the cause of the council to develop fully: namely, disciplinary laxity and five disparaging theses about *arhats* promulgated by an apparently renegade monk named Mahādeva. In other words, Bareau feels quite certain as to the cause of the convocation, and infers the date from the cause.

As to the specifics of the council, Bareau tells us that by the reign of Mahāpadma the Nandin, the Buddhist community had divided itself into two camps, one lax in discipline and supporting the tenets of Mahādeva, the other rigorous and strongly opposed to him. Unable to resolve their dispute internally, the Buddhists approached King Mahāpadma and asked him to mediate the dispute. The king assembled the two groups in his capital of Pāṭaliputra, but being incompetent in religious matters, decided to put the matter to a simple vote. The "laxist" party was apparently in the majority and withdrew, calling itself the Mahāsāṃghikas, or "Great Assembly." The minority party referred to itself as the Sthaviras, or "Elders." Each group then began to develop its own canon and religious community.

Virtually all the early sources in Buddhist literature conclude that the council described above was a historical event. Further, they consider this initial council of Pāṭaliputra to be the true starting point of the sectarian movement in Buddhism. Recently, however, Bareau's conclusions as to the date and cause of the council have been questioned. Janice J. Nattier and Charles S. Prebish have suggested that the council took place in 116 AN, under the reign of Kālāśoka, and that disciplinary laxity and Mahādeva's theses had nothing at all to do with the schism (1977). Based on a reevaluation of Bareau's sources and a consideration of the *Śāriputraparipṛcchā Sūtra*, Nattier and Prebish argue that the chief issue of the council, and the resulting sectarian split, was unwarranted Vinaya expansion on the part of the future Sthaviras. They are unable, at this time, to ascertain which hypothesis, if either, is correct. Nevertheless, it is clear that the sectarian movement in Buddhism emerged sometime in the century following the Vaiśālī council; by 200 BCE more than a dozen sects were evident in the Buddhist community.

Pāṭaliputra II: the third canonical council. No king has been more important for the early history of Buddhism in its native land than Aśoka. Although the traditional Buddhist legends tend to conflict somewhat with the picture of Aśoka revealed by his numerous rock edicts and inscriptions, it has generally been concluded that Aśoka was a pious ruler, sympathetic to the many Buddhists in his domain. By utilizing materials in the Pali *Dīpavaṃsa*, *Mahāvaṃsa*, *Mahābodhivaṃsa*, and *Samantapāsādikā*, one can construct a fairly accurate account of the events leading up to the third Buddhist council, and of the council itself.

The *Mahāvaṃsa* (v. 280) indicates that the close of the council was in the seventeenth year of Aśoka's reign. The *Dīpavaṃsa* notes the date as 236 AN, or 247 BCE. Apparently, "heretics" had been entering the Buddhist community for some time, undermining the Dharma, and therefore weakening the entire social and religious structure of the *saṃgha*. In order to remedy the situation, Aśoka chose a famous monk, Moggaliputtatissa, to preside over a huge assembly of a thousand monks, who were to determine and restore orthodoxy. Under Tissa's guidance the offending viewpoints were rejected; eventually it was concluded that the Buddha was a *vibhajyavādin*, or "distinctionist." The viewpoints under discussion were recorded in a now well-known Abhidharma text, the *Kathāvatthu*.

There is no question that this council was a historical event. It is curious, however, that it is mentioned only in the Pali accounts, lending weight to the supposition that the council may have been only a "party meeting" of the Vibhajyavāda sect. It is now well known that this sect was the parent of the Theravāda *nikāya*. Other possibilities for the function of the council include the separation of the Sarvāstivādin group (the heretical faction under this interpretation) from the Sthavira proper.

The council of Kaniṣka. Near the end of the first century CE, Kaniṣka became the ruling monarch of the great Kushan dynasty. He tried hard to emulate Aśoka's example of ruling in accord with the Buddhist Dharma, and championed the Sarvāstivādin school of Buddhism. From his capitals of Purusapura and Mathura, he wielded much power in the Buddhist world. Near the end of his reign, about 100 CE, Kaniṣka sponsored a council, probably in Gandhara (but possibly in Kashmir), to consider the doctrines of the Sarvāstivādin school.

Following the suggestion of the Sarvāstivādin scholar Pārśva, invitations were sent to all the learned Buddhists of the time, from whom 499 were finally chosen to attend the conference. Great debates were held on various aspects of Buddhist doctrine, and especially on the Abhidharma. The venerable scholar Vasumitra was president of the council, assisted by Aśvaghoṣa. A new Vinaya was committed to writing at the conference, and a great commentary, known as the *Mahāvibhāṣā*, on the Abhidharma text of the *Jñānaprasthāna* was compiled. There is no question but that the position this council occupies in the history of the Sarvāstivāda *nikāya* is analogous to that of the council convened by Aśoka nearly four centuries earlier for the history of the Theravāda *nikāya*.

No collective meeting in Indian Buddhism ever attained the importance of the five heretofore considered. All of the other major convocations were to take place outside of the Buddhist homeland.

OTHER ANCIENT COUNCILS. Recognizing the impact the Indian Buddhist councils have had on the continued growth of the religion in its native land, councils have periodically met in other Buddhist countries as well. Of course Aśoka was renowned for exporting Buddhism through a series of missionary endeavors, with Sri Lanka at the forefront of his enterprise. Equally, within several centuries of the close of King Kaniṣka's reign in India, Buddhism had spread into Central Asia, China, and Tibet. It is no surprise then, that Sri Lanka and Tibet were the sites of other ancient Buddhist councils.

The fourth Theravādin council. Records indicate that Aśoka's son Mahinda, a Buddhist monk, was sent to Sri Lanka to propagate the religion. Upon receiving Mahinda's teaching, King Devānampiyatissa became a lay disciple and established a Buddhist monastery, called the Mahāvihāra, in his capital city of Anurādhapura. A branch of the bodhi tree was exported to Sri Lanka, and an ordination lineage was started for monks and nuns.

During the first century the Buddhist order was threatened by invading Tamils from South India and King Vaṭṭagāmaṇī was forced into exile for fourteen years (43–29 BCE). After reassuming the throne, the king found his land threatened by famine and the religious tradition split by schismatic rumblings. To combat rising religious unrest, it was decided to convene a conference in the capital city (in 25 BCE), in the by then old and famous Mahāvihāra. The prime function of the proceedings was to write down the scriptural texts of the Theravādin school of Buddhism in the Pali language. Thus the formal Tipiṭaka ("three baskets," i.e., the Buddhist canon) was established, providing an institutionalized basis for the continued growth and development of the Theravāda tradition. In addition, the Mahāvihāra community had an apparently orthodox, authoritative textual ground from which to refute their rivals in the Mahāyāna-leaning community of the Abhayagiri Monastery. Eventually, the Pali scriptures compiled at this council found their way into all the Theravādin countries of South and Southeast Asia.

The Lhasa council in Tibet. By the middle of the seventh century of the common era Tibet had an unusual political and religious relationship to India and China. King Srong bstan sgam po of Tibet seems to have been married to both Nepalese and Chinese wives, and there was a clear influx of Buddhist ideas from each of these countries. After the great monastery at Bsam yas was completed in 787, a Sarvāstivādin ordination lineage was established, and the institution became a lively place for the discussion of a wide variety of religious viewpoints.

Although King Khri srong lde btsan (r. 759–797?) was able to undermine the claims to state religion of the indigenous Bon religion, his reign was further aggravated by internal disputes among the Buddhists in his kingdom. Not only did the Tantric tradition advanced by Padmasambhava conflict with older Indian ideas maintained by Śāntirakṣita, but a Chinese monk (generally called Hva-shang, or simply Mahāyāna) argued against Śāntirakṣita as well.

As a resolution to the problem, it was suggested that a council be held at court (in 792–794 CE), with the king in attendance. To present the traditional Buddhist viewpoint, Śāntirakṣita's pupil Kamalaśīla was invited to Tibet. Mahāyāna argued the Chinese position. Two chief issues were considered. First, the Chinese monk argued that buddhahood was attained suddenly, intuitively, while the Indian monk maintained that the path to enlightenment was gradual. Second, the Indian representative argued, as a corollary to the prior point, for the positive value of meritorious action, while Mahāyāna offered a radical opposition. In a lively debate, the Chinese position was clearly defeated (so say the prevailing accounts of the Indian faction), establishing the efficacy of the Indian standpoint for Tibetan Buddhism. The Chinese were forced in no uncertain terms to leave the country, as is reported through both a Chinese source in the Dunhuang manuscripts and the works of Kamalaśīla (preserved in Sanskrit and Tibetan), but the memory of this monumental debate persisted in the minds of many Tibetan Buddhists for generations.

MODERN COUNCILS. In the millennium between 800 and 1800 CE little mention was made of Buddhist councils. To be sure, there were numerous proceedings of local import in the various Buddhist countries, but it was not until the latter half of the nineteenth century that another council took place of major impact for the entire Buddhist world.

The fifth Theravādin council. In the Buddhist culture of Southeast Asia it is not at all unusual for royal monarchs to be religious scholars, with prior training from within the Buddhist monastic order. Rama IV of Thailand, for instance, developed extensive scholarship in the Pali texts during his twenty-seven years as a monk. It was in this tradition that King Mindon Min of Burma (r. 1852–1877) convened the fifth Theravādin council in Mandalay in 1871. The purpose of the council was explicit: to revise the Pali texts. To insure the survival of the new scriptures the king had all the texts entombed in stupas, thus preserving the 729 marble tablets upon which the texts were inscribed.

The sixth Theravādin council. In 1954, nearly one hundred years after the Mandalay council, the sixth Theravādin council was convened in Rangoon, Burma, by the prime minister, U Nu. The fact that the twenty-five hundredth anniversary of the Buddha's death was approaching made the notion of a council even more auspicious. The basic function of this sixth council was to recite and confirm the entire Pali canon. Nearly two years of preparations were made prior to its inauguration on May 17, 1954.

U Nu delivered the initial address, charging the twenty-five hundred monks in attendance to work diligently at reciting and editing these important scriptural resources. For two years recitation proceeded, culminating with closure on the twenty-five hundredth anniversary of the Buddha's death (according to Burmese reckoning). The council, in addition to having tremendous religious significance, was a national festival in Burma, and established solidarity among all Theravāda Buddhists there and throughout Asia.

The World Fellowship of Buddhists. In an attempt to carry on the spirit demonstrated by the various Buddhist councils, the World Fellowship of Buddhists was established in 1950 as an expression of true religious ecumenism. The Fellowship has exercised its lofty intention through a series of conferences in various Buddhist countries. These conferences have sometimes expressed political as well as religious concerns, but they nonetheless reflect a spirit of cooperation that is thoroughly consistent with the very first Buddhist conclave, held in the rainy season following the Buddha's death in 483 BCE.

SEE ALSO Aśoka; Buddha; Devānaṃpiyatissa; Kamalaśīla; Moggaliputtatissa; Śāntarakṣita; Theravāda.

BIBLIOGRAPHY

The best general, comprehensive work on the issue of Indian Buddhist councils is André Bareau's *Les premiers conciles bouddhiques* (Paris, 1955). Much of this material, and the work of other researchers, is summarized in Charles S. Prebish's "A Review of Scholarship on the Buddhist Councils," *Journal of Asian Studies* 33 (February 1974): 239–254. A useful study of the Rājagṛha council is presented in Jean Przyluski's *Le concile de Rājagṛha* (Paris, 1926–1928). An equally valuable resource for the Vaiśālī council is Marcel Hofinger's *Étude sur la concile de Vaiśālī* (Louvain, 1946). The Vaiśālī council is also discussed in Paul Demiéville's "À propos du concile de Vaiśālī, " *T'soung pao* 40 (1951): 239–296, and Nalinaksha Dutt's "The Second Buddhist Council," *Indian Historical Quarterly* 35 (March 1959): 45–56. For a somewhat dated but still important viewpoint, consult Louis de La Vallée Poussin's "The Buddhist Councils," *Indian Antiquary* 37 (1908): 1–18, 81–106. The most recent and controversial material on Indian Buddhist councils is presented in Janice J. Nattier and Charles S. Prebish's "Mahāsāṃghika Origins: The Beginnings of Buddhist Sectarianism," *History of Religions* 16 (February 1977): 237–272. For non-Indian councils, Demiéville's *Le concile de Lhasa* (Paris, 1952) effectively covers the Tibetan materials. Donald Smith's *Religion and Politics in Burma* (Princeton, 1965) is helpful for Theravādin proceedings, and *Buddhism in the Modern World,* edited by Heinrich Dumoulin and John Maraldo (New York, 1976), offers a constructive overview.

New Sources

Bechert, Heinz. "The Importance of Asoka's So-Called Schism Edict." In *Indological and Buddhist Studies: Volume in Honour of Professor J. W. de Jong on His Sixtieth Birthday,* edited by L. A. Hercus et al., pp. 61–68. Canberra, 1982.

Bechert, Heinz, ed. *Zur Schulzugehörigkeit von Werken der Hīnayāna-Literatur.* Göttingen, 1985–1987.

Cousins, Lance. "The 'Five Points' and the Origins of the Buddhist Schools." In *The Buddhist Forum: Seminar Papers 1987–88,* edited by T. Skorupski, pp. 27–60. London, 1991.

Lamotte, Étienne. *History of Indian Buddhism: From the Origins to the Śaka Era.* Translated by Sara Webb-Boin. Louvain-la-Neuve, 1988. See pages 124–139.

Prebish, Charles S. "Buddhist Councils and Divisions in the Order." In *Buddhism: A Modern Perspective,* edited by Charles S. Prebish, pp. 21–26. Delhi, 1995.

Prebish, Charles S. "Saiksa-Dharmas Revisited: Further Considerations of Mahasamghika Origins." *History of Religions* 35 (1996): 258–270.

Ruegg, D. Seyfort. *Buddha-nature, Mind and the Problem of Gradualism in a Comparative Perspective: On the Transmission and Reception of Buddhism in India and Tibet,* London, 1992.

Wang, B. "Buddhist Nikayas through Ancient Chinese Eyes." In *Buddhist Studies Present and Future (IABS 10th International Conference 1991),* edited by Ananda W. P. Guruge, pp. 65–72. Sri Lanka, 1992.

Charles S. Prebish (1987)
Revised Bibliography

COUNCILS: CHRISTIAN COUNCILS

Since the beginning of Christian history, designated leaders of Christian communities have from time to time gathered to make authoritative decisions on common teaching and practice. Such gatherings are usually called councils or synods (from the Greek *sunodos,* "a coming together"). Although these two terms are sometimes used synonymously, especially in Greek-Christian literature, *synod* normally designates the gathering of representatives from a local church or a single denomination, as distinct from *council,* which usually means a meeting at which representation is intended to be universal. Although only seven such meetings, all held in Greek cities in Asia Minor between the fourth and eighth centuries, are recognized by most Christian churches today as worldwide, or "ecumenical," councils (from the Greek *oikoumenē,* "the inhabited world") and as classically authoritative in their articulation of Christian faith and church order, the conciliar pattern of decision making has remained a constant feature in the life of most churches. The Roman Catholic Church, in fact, has traditionally regarded fourteen later councils, most of them Western gatherings held under papal auspices, as also ecumenical and normative. Christian councils have varied greatly in size, procedure, composition, and the way in which they have been convoked and ratified. The only criterion for determining their authority and importance is the practical norm of "reception": that a council's decisions are subsequently accepted by a church or a group of churches as valid and binding.

Councils in the Early Church. Precedents for early Christian conciliar practice lay in the Jewish Sanhedrin, or national council of priests and elders, which regulated the religious affairs, as well as some secular matters, of postexilic Israel until the destruction of Jerusalem in 70 CE, and in the collegial bodies of priests and leading citizens that ruled most local cults in the Hellenistic and Roman world. The first recorded gathering of Christian leaders to rule in a doctrinal and disciplinary dispute was the "council" of apostles and elders held in 48 or 49 CE and described in *Acts of the Apostles* 15:6–29. That council decided not to require full observance of the Mosaic law from Gentile converts. As the Christian church established itself in other regions of the Greco-Roman world, special meetings of the bishops in a particular province or region were occasionally called to deal with disputed issues, such as the prophetic Montanist movement (Asia Minor, c. 170), the date of the celebration of Easter (Asia Minor, Palestine, Gaul, and Rome, c. 190), the readmission to Christian communion of those who had "lapsed" in persecution (Rome, c. 230–250; Carthage, c. 240–250), or the scandalous behavior of Paul of Samosata, bishop of Antioch (Antioch, 264–268).

During the late second and third centuries, episcopal synods probably met regularly in most regions, although the evidence is fragmentary. As the end of the illegal status of the Christian churches drew near, however, their leaders became bolder in organizing such meetings. A synod of Spanish bishops held in Elvira, near Granada, some time in the first decade of the fourth century enacted eighty-one canons on church discipline that remained widely influential, particularly on the indissolubility of marriage and clerical celibacy. Another local synod, at Arles in southern Gaul (August 314), called to consider the response of Catholics to the schismatic Donatist church in Africa, ruled against rebaptizing Donatists who wished to enter the Catholic Church.

Early Ecumenical Councils. The first attempt to gather a body of bishops representing the whole Christian world was the council called by the emperor Constantine I at Nicaea, in northwest Asia Minor, in the summer of 325 (June 18–August 25). The Council of Nicaea is still recognized as the first ecumenical Christian council and as the model for later authoritative gatherings. With the style and procedure of the Roman senate likely in mind, Constantine commissioned the 318 bishops who had assembled near his residence in Nicaea, including several representatives from the Latin church of the West, to settle the controversy raised by Arius's denial of the eternity and full divinity of Jesus. In asserting that Jesus, as Son of God, is "begotten, not made" and "of the same substance as the Father," the council's creedal formula laid the groundwork for the classical development of Christian trinitarian theology in the half century that followed. The Nicene council also excommunicated Arius and his followers, determined a unified way of reckoning the date of Easter, and issued twenty disciplinary decrees or canons, mainly regulating the appointment and jurisdiction of bishops. Although the emperor's influence was strongly felt at Nicaea, it was the bishops themselves—under the leadership of Constantine's adviser, Bishop Hosius of Cordova, and of the young Alexandrian priest Athanasius—who formulated common theological and practical decisions. The bishops of the whole Christian world were now publicly recognized as the senate of the church.

After more than fifty years of sharp controversy over the reception and interpretation of the Nicene formula, a period that saw the proliferation of local synods and the production of many new creeds, the emperor Theodosius I convoked a meeting of some 150 Greek-speaking bishops at Constantinople in 381 (May–July) for what later was recognized as the second ecumenical council (Constantinople I). In addition to confirming Nicaea's insistence on the full divinity of Jesus as Son, this council condemned those who denied that the Holy Spirit is a distinct individual within the trinitarian mystery of God. An expanded version of the Nicene Creed, probably professed by the patriarch-elect Nectarius during the council before his installation in the see of Constantinople, was taken by the Council of Chalcedon (451) to be the official creed of the whole gathering and is still used as the standard profession of faith in many Christian liturgies (the "Niceno-Constantinopolitan Creed"). This council also enacted four disciplinary canons, including one that accorded second place in ecclesiastical honor, after that of "old Rome," to the new imperial capital, Constantinople. That provision was to become a cause of contention between the Eastern and Western churches.

As a result of a bitter dispute between Nestorius, bishop of Constantinople, and Cyril, bishop of Alexandria, over the proper way of conceiving the relationship of the divine and human aspects of Jesus, the emperor Theodosius II summoned a meeting of bishops at Ephesus on the coast of Asia Minor, in the summer of 431, to resolve the issue, and more particularly to judge the propriety of calling Mary "Mother of God" (*theotokos*), as Cyril insisted on doing. Representatives of the opposing groups could not agree to meet, and the would-be council ended abortively in mutual excommunication. Later (April 433) Cyril came to an agreement with the more moderate of Nestorius's supporters to excommunicate Nestorius and to accept the title *theotokos* as valid, but also to recognize that in Jesus two distinct natures—the human and the divine—are united without confusion in a single individual. On the basis of this agreement, the meeting of Cyril's party at Ephesus in 431 later came to be regarded as the third ecumenical council, and the dossier assembled there by Cyril's supporters was used as a classical anthology of christological documents.

The fullest articulation of the early church's understanding of the person of Christ was made at a council held at Chalcedon, across the Bosporus from Constantinople, in the fall of 451 (October–November). In response to continuing controversy over whether the humanity of Jesus constituted a distinct and operative reality or "nature" after the incarnation of the Word, the emperor Marcian convoked this meeting of over 350 bishops (including three legates from Pope Leo I and two North African bishops) and forced it to formulate a doctrinal statement on Christ that accommodated a variety of theological traditions. The chief inspiration of the document, however, was the balanced "two-nature" Christology articulated by Leo in his letter to Bishop Flavian of Constantinople in 449. The council also enacted twenty-eight disciplinary canons, the last of which confirmed the second rank of the see of Constantinople and awarded it jurisdictional primacy in Asia Minor and northeastern Greece. This meeting, regarded as the fourth ecumenical council, is the first for which we possess detailed minutes as well as final documents.

Chalcedon's formulation of the Christian understanding of Christ proved to be only a new beginning for controversy. After more than a century of recriminations, especially in the East, the emperor Justinian I convoked another meeting at Constantinople (Constantinople II) in the year 553 (May 5–June 2) and persuaded the 168 bishops present to reformulate the Christology of Chalcedon in terms that more clearly emphasized the centrality of Jesus' divine identity. They also condemned the speculative theology of Origen (third century) and his followers, as well as that of the chief opponents of Cyril of Alexandria from the previous century. The Roman bishop, Vigilius I, was present in Constantinople during the council but refused to attend, suspecting—along with most Western bishops—that it was being forced to weaken the stated faith of Chalcedon in the interests of political unity. In February 554, however, he agreed to accept the decisions of Constantinople II, a step that resulted in decades of controversy in Italy and Africa. This synod has generally been accepted since then as the fifth ecumenical council.

In the century that followed, Greek theologians continued to look for ways of reconciling the monophysites, Christians who had broken from the official church after Chalcedon by emphasizing the dynamic unity of the two-natured Christ as a divine person. One such attempt, favored by several seventh-century Byzantine patriarchs and emperors, was the ascription to Christ of a single divine will and "activity," or range of behavior. Led by the exiled Greek monk Maximos the Confessor, a local Roman synod of October 649 rejected this new Christology as a subtle weakening of the integral affirmation of Jesus' humanity. This condemnation was confirmed by a small gathering of mainly Eastern bishops in the rotunda of the imperial palace in Constantinople between November 7, 680, and September 16, 681, a synod subsequently recognized as the sixth ecumenical council (Constantinople III).

Ten years later, the emperor Justinian II summoned another gathering of bishops in the same rotunda to discuss disciplinary issues and formulate practical canons that would supplement the authoritative theological decisions of Constantinople II and III. Hence its customary titles, the "Quinisext" (fifth-and-sixth) synod or the synod "in the rotunda" (Gr., *en trullō),* also known as the Trullan Synod. The membership of this meeting was also entirely Greek, and a number of its canons explicitly rejected Western practices. Although this gathering is not regarded as ecumenical, its legislation became one of the main sources of Orthodox canon law and was also frequently cited by Western medieval canonists.

The main theological controversy in the eighth- and ninth-century Eastern church was no longer directly over the person of Christ, but over the related issue of the legitimacy of using and venerating images in the context of worshiping a transcendent God. In 726, Emperor Leo III began the policy of removing and destroying the images in churches (iconoclasm), and his successor, Constantine V, convoked a synod of 338 bishops in Constantinople in 754 to ratify this practice, excommunicating those who defended the use of images, including the theologian and monk John of Damascus. In 787 (September 24–October 7), however, the empress Irene convoked another synod at Nicaea (Nicaea II), attended by some 350 Greek bishops and two papal representatives. This synod reversed the decision of the year 754 and affirmed the legitimacy of venerating images and of asking for the intercession of the saints, while insisting also that worship, in the strict sense, is due to God alone. A resurgence of iconoclastic influence in the early ninth century delayed full acceptance of this council's decrees in the East, while the rivalry of the emperor Charlemagne and the poor Latin translation of the acts of Nicaea II that reached his court led to resistance in the West and even to condemnation of the council's decisions at a synod of 350 bishops at Frankfurt in June 794. However, Nicaea II was recognized as the seventh ecumenical council at the Council of Constantinople (869–870), a recognition that was endorsed for the West by Pope John VIII in 880. It is the last of the ancient councils recognized as authoritative by virtually all Christian churches.

Medieval Councils. After the death of Theophilus, the last iconoclastic emperor, in 842, controversy in mid-ninth-century Constantinople over the manner of reinstating the veneration of images led to the forced abdication of the patriarch Ignatius in 858 and to the appointment of the learned civil servant Photios, a layman, as his successor. A local synod of 861, attended by two representatives of Pope Nicholas I, confirmed Photios's elevation and declared that the election of Ignatius had been uncanonical; the pope, however, was persuaded by Ignatius's followers to break communion with Photios two years later. Tension between Rome and Constantinople grew, both over the role of the pope as a source of legitimation and a court of appeal for Eastern bishops and over competing missionary activities of the two churches in Bulgaria. A synod summoned by the Greek emperor Michael in 867 condemned Roman incursions in the East, as well as the Roman church's introduction of the word *filioque* into the creed; it asked the Frankish emperor Louis II to depose Pope Nicholas. Another council in Constantinople, summoned by the new Greek emperor, Basil I, in 869–870, deposed Photios in an effort to win the pope's support, but Photios became patriarch again after Ignatius's death in 877 and was recognized by the pope in a council of reunion held in Constantinople in 879–880. This last meeting annulled the decisions of the council of 869–870, but Western canonists in the twelfth century included the earlier gathering among the ecumenical councils, as Constantinople IV, because its twenty-second canon, forbidding the appointment of bishops by laypeople, provided a precedent for their own case against lay investiture. None of the Photian councils is recognized as ecumenical by other churches.

After the synod of 879–880, Eastern and Western bishops ceased to meet over common concerns for almost four centuries. Local and regional synods, however, continued to play an important role in civil and ecclesiastical life. In Constantinople, the "residentiary synod" (Gr., *sunodos endēmousa*) of the patriarch functioned as the administrative cabinet of the Byzantine communion. Synods in North Africa in the early fifth century (especially at Carthage in 418) and in southern Gaul in the early sixth century (especially at Orange in 529) made important formulations of the Western church's doctrine of grace. And provincial synods, attended by both bishops and secular lords, became an increasingly important instrument of government in the Frankish kingdoms of the sixth and seventh centuries. In Visigothic Spain, eighteen synods were held at Toledo between 589 and 702, dealing with both church and civil discipline and with the doctrinal issue of later Arianism. The Celtic and Roman traditions of church order in Britain were unified by the Synod of Whitby in Northumbria in 664. For the Carolingian empire, national synods were an important instrument for fostering political and doctrinal unity.

It was only in the time of the "Gregorian reform," however, in the eleventh and twelfth centuries, that the popes, as part of their program of strengthening the power and independence of the ordained clergy in ruling the church, thought again of convoking councils with a more than regional representation. Gregory VII, in his canonical summary known as *Dictates of the Pope*, insisted that only the bishop of Rome has the right to convoke an ecumenical council—a principle preserved ever since by Western canon law. Corresponding to his vision of the papacy as the active center of a universal and politically independent church, Gregory and his successors began to invite bishops and abbots from other parts of Europe to participate in Roman synods and also took the lead in mobilizing European forces to regain the Christian holy places in Palestine from Muslim occupation.

Three twelfth-century Roman synods—the Lateran councils of 1123, 1139, and 1179—demonstrated the concern of the popes of this period to assert the independence of the hierarchy from lay control by enacting a variety of measures that insured the moral and social integrity of the clergy. The council of 1179 also condemned the emerging Catharist or Albigensian heresy (a Western form of Gnosticism), regulated the activities of monastic and military orders, and established the lasting rule that a pope must be elected by a two-thirds majority of the senior Roman clergy, who were known as "cardinals." These three Lateran synods, increasingly international in membership and deliberately modeled on the councils of the early church, were and are regarded as ecumenical councils by the Roman Catholic Church. Far more important, however, was the Fourth Lateran Council, convoked in 1215 (November 11–30) by Innocent III. Innocent invited not only all bishops and heads of religious orders from the Western church, but also bishops of the Armenian, Maronite, and Greek churches. Only Latin bishops attended, however, and the council's seventy canons included a strong assertion of papal primacy and a complaint against the Greek church for rebaptizing Latin converts. The meeting—recognized in the West as the twelfth ecumenical council—not only continued the disciplinary reforms of its three predecessors but also issued doctrinal statements on the Trinity and the sacraments (introducing the word *transubstantiation* into official church vocabulary), forbade secret marriages, and instituted the requirement of annual confession for adult Catholics.

Continued conflict between the popes and the Hohenstaufen emperors led Innocent IV to convoke a council of some 150 bishops at Lyons in June and July 1245. Besides calling for renewed efforts to reconquer the holy places, this synod excommunicated the German emperor Frederick II, absolving his subjects from the moral duty of obeying him. Western canonists regard this synod as the thirteenth ecumenical council. Gregory X summoned a second council at Lyons in the summer of 1274 (May 5–July 17), in the hope of restoring communion between the Eastern and Western churches, a bond broken by mutual anathemas in 1054. The Greek emperor, Michael VIII Palaeologus, who had recaptured Constantinople from Latin occupiers in 1261, accepted the invitation to attend, hoping to prevent further Western attacks on his capital. Delegates of the Mongol khan also attended, as did some two hundred bishops and the nonvoting representatives of most Western rulers. Thomas Aquinas, invited to participate as a theological expert, died en route to Lyons. The Greek delegation participated in the papal Eucharist on June 29, the Feast of Saints Peter and Paul, and agreed to a formal reunion of the churches on July 6, raising no objection to the traditionally disputed Western doctrines of the procession of the Holy Spirit, purgatory, and papal primacy, or to the new Western understanding of seven sacraments. The council is regarded in the West as the fourteenth ecumenical council. In 1283, however, a synod in Constantinople repudiated the union and deposed the patriarch, John Beccus, who had agreed to it at Lyons. Michael Palaeologus who had never succeeded in winning Greek support for the council, was excommunicated by Pope Martin IV in 1281, and his own church even denied him a Christian burial on his death in 1282.

In the face of the increasing attempts of Philip IV ("the Fair") of France to control the church. Clement V—the first pope to reside at Avignon—summoned a council to meet in the independent French town of Vienne in 1311–1312 (October 16–May 6). Eager to acquire the wealth of the Knights Templars, Philip had exerted strong pressure on the pope, even before the council, to suppress the military order on allegations of venality, heresy, and immoral practices. The council found no grounds to support these charges, but Clement suppressed the Templars by a bull of March 1312. The council also discussed plans for a new crusade, issued regulations for the growing number of new religious orders, and condemned the strict interpretation of the poverty of Jesus being advanced by the Spiritual Franciscans. Attended by 132 bishops and 38 abbots, all from western Europe, the Council of Vienne was the first to prepare documents in subcommissions and to delegate a standing committee to finish drafting documents still incomplete at the council's dissolution. Western canonists consider it the fifteenth ecumenical council.

In the Greek church a series of local synods in Constantinople (c. 1340) took up the controversy between Gregory Palamas, a monk of Mount Athos, and the Calabrian monk Barlaam about the value of hesychastic prayer (contemplative prayer prepared for by repetition of a mantra) and the possibility of experiencing the presence of God in this life. A synod in July 1351 recognized as orthodox Palamas's doctrine that God's "energies" or activities, if not God's essence, can be experienced in a quasi-visual way by a soul purified through constant prayer, a teaching that has been of central importance for Orthodox monasticism ever since.

In the West, the years of the Avignon papacy (1308–1378) saw continued centralization of papal authority, as well as increasing opposition to papal rule by the German emperors, independent cities, and certain charismatic and millenarian groups within the church. With the beginning of the Great Western Schism in 1378, in which two rival popes claimed the church's obedience, support began to grow among canonists and theologians for a more corporate system of church government, by which the pope would be understood as an executive appointed by and held accountable to the whole church, represented in a carefully appointed general council. This "conciliarist" theory, first proposed in practical terms by William Durandus of Mende at the time of the Council of Vienne, was seen by a number of prominent theologians in the last decades of the fourteenth century as the only way to end the schism. In 1409, a council at Pisa attempted to put conciliarism into practice by deposing both rival popes and electing a new one (John XXIII). The result, however, was simply that three claimants now vied for the Roman see. In 1414, the emperor Sigismund allied with John XXIII to convoke another council at Constance to resolve the issue (November 5, 1414–April 22,

1418). Following the representative system of the medieval universities, the voting members of the council—who included over 325 bishops, 29 cardinals, more than 100 abbots, several princes, and several hundred doctors of theology—decided to divide into four blocks, or "nations," each of which would have one corporate vote in the council's final decisions. These "nations" were the Germans (including eastern Europeans), the French, the English (including the Irish and Scots), and the Italians; from July 1415 the cardinals at the council were allowed to vote as a fifth unit, and a Spanish "nation" was added in October 1416. Debate was conducted within the "nations," and the whole council was managed by a joint steering committee, in which each "nation," as well as the cardinals, was represented. The council's decree, *Sacrosancta,* enacted on April 6, 1415, declared that the gathering was a general council of the church and that it therefore had supreme authority of itself, despite the absence of John XXIII, who had fled two weeks earlier. The council then condemned the reformist teachings of English theologian John Wyclif (1330?–1384) and his Bohemian disciple Jan Hus, the latter of whom was publicly burned in Constance on July 6, 1415. The decree *Frequens* (October 5, 1417) stipulated that another council was to meet five years after the dissolution of the gathering at Constance, followed by a third council seven years later and by subsequent councils at ten-year intervals. Having devised these limitations on papal power, the council appointed a joint conclave of cardinals and delegates from the "nations," who elected Martin V on November 11, 1417. After further measures for structural reform, the council adjourned in April 1418. Although Martin had previously rejected some aspects of conciliar theory (including the idea of appeal to a further council) and never formally endorsed *Sacrosancta* or *Frequens,* he did declare, at the closing session, that he would observe what the whole council had declared on matters of faith.

After an abortive attempt to summon a council at Pavia in 1423, in accordance with the decrees of Constance, Martin convoked another meeting at Basel in 1430. Eugenius IV, who succeeded Martin in March 1431, hoped once again to effect a reunion with the Greek church and believed that an Italian setting would be more appropriate for that purpose. As relations with the delegates at Basel grew more strained, Eugenius ordered the council transferred to Ferrara in September 1437, although most of the members refused to go and remained in Basel as a rival assembly until 1448. The Greek delegation arrived in Ferrara in March 1438, and after preliminary discussions the council was moved to Florence in January 1439, where the city had offered to underwrite its costs. Led by Bessarion, metropolitan of Nicaea, the Greek delegation recognized the legitimacy of the Latin doctrines of the procession of the Spirit, purgatory, and papal primacy without prejudice to the validity of the Greek tradition, which differed on these points. A decree of union between the churches was signed on July 6, 1439. Subsequent decrees of union were signed with the Armenian church (November 22, 1439) and with the Copts and Ethiopians (February 4, 1442). The date of closure of the council is uncertain. It is regarded by the Western church as the seventeenth ecumenical council. In Byzantium, however, strong opposition led by Mark Eugenikos, metropolitan of Ephesus, who had also been a delegate to the council, was voiced against the union. A synod in Constantinople in 1484 officially repudiated the Florentine decree in the name of the Greek church.

AGE OF REFORMATION. Conciliarism had died as a practical force in the Roman church with the end of the Council of Basel. The Renaissance papacy continued to grow in power and wealth, although throughout Europe the demand for "reform in head and members" continued to grow as well. Faced with the attempt of Louis XII of France to convoke the antipapal reform synod at Pisa in 1511, Julius II summoned a Roman council (the Fifth Lateran Council) on May 15, 512, which continued under his successor, Leo X, until March 16, 1517. Aside from a few decrees aimed at correcting financial abuse and encouraging popular preaching, this council—recognized as ecumenical by the Western church—achieved little.

The wave of institutional and theological reform set in motion by Martin Luther in the 1520s brought new pressure to bear on the popes to convoke a council to deal seriously with "Protestant" issues. Paul III called a council at Mantua in 1537, for which Luther prepared the theses that were later accepted by German Protestants as a kind of manifesto and known as the Smalcaldic Articles. This meeting was transferred to Vicenza in the same year and then suspended in 1539. After several delays, it was reconvened at the Alpine town of Trent, in imperial territory, on December 13, 1545. Rejecting the conciliar structure agreed on at Constance and Basel, the Council of Trent allowed only cardinals, bishops, and heads of religious orders voice and vote in its full sessions. During its first period (December 1545–March 1547), the council discussed the relation of scripture and tradition, the canon of scriptural books, the doctrines of original sin and justification, and various proposed reforms in church administration. Transferred to Bologna (papal territory) in 1547, to escape the plague, the council continued to discuss the Eucharist and the other sacraments, but Paul III agreed not to let it formulate final decisions until it could return to Trent, where Protestants could participate more freely. A second set of sessions was held in Trent from May 1, 1551, until April 28, 1552, in which documents on these topics were finished. After a ten-year hiatus due largely to continued warfare among the German principalities, Pius IV reconvoked the council on January 18, 1562, for a third and final period, during which documents were issued on the sacrificial character of the Mass, on Holy Orders and the education of the clergy, on the sacramental nature of marriage, and on purgatory, as well as numerous disciplinary decrees. The Council of Trent, recognized by Roman Catholics as a nineteenth ecumenical council, was closed on December 4, 1563. Its decrees laid the foundation for the doctrines and practice of the Roman church for the next four centuries.

The sixteenth and seventeenth centuries, an age of rapid, often violent change in religious and civil institutions throughout western Europe as well as a time of bitter theological controversy, also witnessed a number of gatherings within and between the new Protestant communities. At the Synod of Dort in the Netherlands (November 13, 1618–May 9, 1619), representatives of the Reformed churches affirmed, against the theories of the Leiden professor Jacobus Arminius, a strict Calvinist doctrine of the predestination of both the saved and the damned, the total depravity of unredeemed humanity, and the limited scope of Jesus' atoning death. In 1643, the English Parliament commissioned a group of Calvinist divines to revise the Thirty-nine Articles of the Church of England along Puritan lines and to draw up a Puritan confession of faith for the British Isles. On December 4, 1646, this Westminster Assembly completed its document, known as the Westminster Confession. It comprised thirty-three articles, largely based on the teaching of Dort and the covenant theology of English Puritanism. Accepted by the Church of Scotland in 1647, it became the chief confessional document of Scottish Presbyterianism. Protestant theology also made its influence felt in the Eastern churches at this time. Synods at Constantinople in 1638 and 1641 condemned the writings of the Western-educated Byzantine patriarch Cyril I (d. 1638) for their Calvinist teaching, and this condemnation was repeated at Orthodox synods in Jassy (Iaşi, Romania) in 1642 and Bethlehem in 1672.

THE MODERN ERA. The Roman Catholic Church showed little interest in large-scale conciliar gatherings during the seventeenth and eighteenth centuries. A regional synod held in Pistoia in Tuscany in September 1786, under the leadership of Bishop Scipione Ricci, demanded a variety of administrative and pastoral reforms in the church but was rejected by Roman authorities as antipapal and Jansenist in inspiration. Eighty-five propositions taken from its documents were condemned by Pius VII on August 28, 1794. As the spirit of political revolution and scientific positivism swept through European culture in the mid-nineteenth century, however, Catholic interest in a general council that would confront these attacks on religious tradition and give confident expression to the church's teaching again grew. Pius IX appointed a commission to prepare for such a council in 1865 and opened it solemnly—as the First Vatican Council—on December 8, 1869. The 774 bishops who attended from around the world discussed prepared drafts on faith and revelation, authority in the church, reform of the Curia Romana, and other subjects. On April 24, 1870, the constitution *Dei filius* was approved. It affirmed the compatibility of faith and reason and the necessity of supernatural revelation (contained both in scripture and in the church's oral tradition) for a full knowledge of God. After prolonged debate on the opportuneness of a conciliar statement on papal primacy and infallibility, a constitution on the church, *Pastor aeternus*, was approved on July 18, declaring the "immediate, universal jurisdiction" of the pope over all Christians and affirming that when he acts solemnly as spokesman for the universal church in doctrinal matters, the pope "possesses that infallibility with which the divine Redeemer wanted his Church to be endowed in articulating its teaching of faith and morality." Because of the outbreak of the Franco-Prussian War, the French troops that had been protecting the Papal State were withdrawn that same summer, and on September 20 Piedmontese troops occupied Rome. With most of the delegates gone, Pius IX suspended the council on October 20, 1870, despite the unfinished state of its agenda. Although a number of subsequent interpretations of *Pastor aeternus*, recognized approvingly by Pius IX himself, stressed that papal infallibility, as the council had envisaged it, was simply a special, highly restricted exercise of the assurance of faith in which the whole church believed itself to share, the effect of the council's decrees was to widen the gulf between the Roman church and the other churches, as well as to emphasize Catholicism's critical attitude toward secular values. Vatican I is recognized in the Roman Catholic Church as the twentieth ecumenical council.

By contrast with much of previous Christian history, the conciliar principle has come to be used increasingly as a means for fostering unity between Christian groups and mutual understanding between Christians and nonbelievers. The modern ecumenical movement began, on the institutional level, with the World Missionary Conference, a meeting of Protestant missionary groups, at Edinburgh in 1910. Two other cooperative bodies within Protestantism—Life and Work, founded in 1925 to foster common social and political action, and Faith and Order, established in 1927 to discuss doctrinal and liturgical issues—agreed in 1938 to form a World Council of Churches. Delayed by World War II, the constitutive assembly of the council was held in Amsterdam in 1948; the International Missionary Council joined it in 1961. Not a jurisdictional or legislative body, the World Council seeks to facilitate common action and dialogue in faith among all Christian churches with ten thousand members or more and to be an intermediate step toward a more formal Christian unity.

Although it is not yet a full member of the World Council of Churches, the Roman Catholic Church took its own decisive step toward Christian unity in the documents and reforms of the Second Vatican Council (October 11, 1962–December 8, 1965), which it recognizes as the twenty-first ecumenical council. Conceived by John XXIII in January of 1959 as a way of leading the Catholic Church toward spiritual renewal, toward greater cooperation with other Christian churches and other religions, and toward a more open attitude to contemporary culture, the council was attended by between 2,100 and 2,400 bishops and heads of religious orders from within the Roman communion, as well as by invited observers from other Christian churches and religious bodies. Vatican II produced sixteen documents on a wide range of pastoral, institutional, and theological issues. Affirming the ancient principle of the collegial responsibility of bishops for the governance of the whole church, in union with the pope, the Constitution on the Church (*Lumen gentium*) opened new possibilities for conciliar government in the Catholic tradition, a step that has led to the regular convening of a worldwide synod of bishops in the years since the council. Vatican II's call for liturgical reform, its stress on the centrality of the scriptures to Christian doctrine and practice, and its recognition of the validity of modern methods of biblical criticism have lessened some of the centuries-old differences between Protestants and Catholics and have given a model for practical reform to other churches. The council's declaration on religious freedom (*Dignitatis humanae*), as well as its decrees on ecumenism, on the Eastern churches, and on relations with Jews and other non-Christians, have greatly altered official Catholic attitudes toward people of other faiths. Its Constitution on the Church in the Modern World (*Gaudium et spes*) expressed, in addition, a positive, welcoming attitude toward the potentialities and aspirations of modern society that invites Roman Catholics to move beyond the defensiveness of the nineteenth century. Although much clearly remains to be accomplished, the revolution in Roman Catholic thought and practice since Vatican II and the continued growth of both the World Council and of individual dialogues between churches, suggest that Christian councils may in the future both become genuinely ecumenical once again and lead to the unity in plurality that is essential to the Christian ideal of community.

See Also Creeds, article on Christian Creeds; Ecumenical Movement; Iconoclasm; Sanhedrin; Trent, Council of; Vatican Councils, articles on Vatican I, Vatican II.

Bibliography

A convenient one-volume edition of the decrees of the twenty-one councils recognized as ecumenical by the Roman Catholic Church, in their Latin or Greek original, is *Conciliorum oecumenicorum decreta*, 3d ed., edited by Giuseppe Alberigo and others (Bologna, 1972). The most complete collection of Christian synodal and conciliar documents is the *Sacrorum conciliorum nova, et amplissima collectio,* begun in 1759 by the Italian canonist Giovanni Domenico Mansi and continued through Vatican I by Louis Petit and Jean-Baptiste Martin, 57 vols. (1759–1798; reprint in 53 vols., Paris, 1901–1927); the text is often defective, however, and modern critical editions exist of the documents of most major councils.

The most complete history of the Christian councils is still Karl-Joseph von Hefele and Josef Hergenröther's *Conciliengeschichte,* 10 vols. (Freiburg, 1855–1890), especially in its expanded French translation, *Histoire des conciles d'après les documents originaux,* 11 vols., by Henri Leclerq and others (Paris, 1907–1952); the first part of the German original, dealing with the seven ecumenical councils of the early church, has also been translated into English by William R. Clark as *A History of the Christian Councils,* 5 vols. (Edinburgh, 1871–1896). An excellent recent series of monographs on all the councils up to Vatican I, edited by Gervais Dumeige, is "Histoire des conciles oecumeniques" (Paris, 1962–1973). Outstanding studies of individual councils include: on Constantinople I, Adolf Martin Ritter's *Das Konzil von Konstantinopel und sein Symbol* (Göttingen, 1965); on Chalcedon, Robert V. Sellers's *The Council of Chalcedon: A Historical and Doctrinal Survey* (London, 1953); on Constance, Louise R. Loomis, John H. Mundy, and Kennerly M. Woody's *The Council of Constance: The Unification of the Church* (New York, 1961), a translation of the main diaries and documents of the council, with thorough introduction; on Florence, Joseph Gill's *The Council of Florence* (Cambridge, 1959); on Trent, Hubert Jedin's *Geschichte des Konzils von Trient,* 4 vols. (Freiburg, 1949–1975), a monumental work of scholarship, of which the first two volumes have been translated into English by Ernest Graf as *A History of the Council of Trent* (London, 1957–1961), and Remigius Bäumer's *Concilium Tridentinum* (Darmstadt, 1979), a useful collection of historical essays; on Vatican I, Theodor Granderath and Konrad Kirch's *Geschichte des Vatikanischen Konzils,* 3 vols. (Freiburg, 1903–1906); on Vatican II, Giovanni Caprile's *Il Concilio Vaticano II,* 5 vols. (Rome, 1966–1969), the best general history of the council to date, Henri Fesquet's *The Drama of Vatican II* (New York, 1967), a lively diary of the council, *Vatican II: An Interfaith Appraisal,* edited by John H. Miller (Notre Dame, 1966), a useful symposium by representatives of different faiths, and *Commentary on the Documents of Vatican II,* edited by Herbert Vorgrimler, 5 vols. (New York, 1968–1969).

Good brief histories of Christian councils include Edward I. Watkin's *The Church in Council* (London and New York, 1960), Francis Dvornik's *The Ecumenical Councils* (New York, 1961), and Philip Hughes's *The Church in Crisis: A History of the General Councils* (New York, 1961). A useful collection of essays on the history and theology of councils, by Protestant scholars, is Hans-Jochen Margull's *The Councils of the Church* (Philadelphia, 1966). No comprehensive history of local synods exists, but there is a full bibliographical survey of publications on individual meetings: Jakub T. Sawicki's *Bibliographia synodorum particularium* (Vatican City, 1967).

On the history of the theory of councils, the most thorough surveys are those of Hermann-Josef Sieben, *Die Konzilsidee der alten Kirche* (Paderborn, 1979), *Die Konzilsidee des lateinischen Mittelalters* (Paderborn, 1983), and *Traktate und Theorien zum Konzil: Vom Beginn des grossen Schismas bis zum Vorabend der Reformation, 1378–1521* (Frankfurt, 1983). The classic study of the origins of conciliarism is Brian Tierney's *Foundations of Conciliar Theory* (Cambridge, 1955); an excellent recent work on conciliarism in the period before Constance is Giuseppe Alberigo's *Chiesa conciliare: Identità e significato del conciliarismo* (Brescia, 1981).

New Sources

Albergio, Giuseppe, ed. *History of Vatican II.* 5 vols. English version edited by Joseph A. Komonchak. Maryknoll, N.Y., 1995.

Coppa, Frank J., ed. *Encyclopedia of the Vatican and Papacy.* Westport, Conn., 1999.

Frend, W. H. C. *The Donatist Church: A Movement of Protest in Northern Africa..* Oxford and New York, 1952; reprint, 2000.

Latourelle, René, ed. *Vatican II: Assessment and Perspectives: Twenty-Five Years Later.* 3 vols. New York, 1988–89.

L'Huillier, Peter. *The Church of the Ancient Councils: The Disciplinary Work of the First Four Ecumenical Councils.* Crestwood, N.Y., 1996.

Pottmeyer, Hermann Josef. *Towards a Papacy in Common: Perspectives from Vatican Councils I and II.* Translated by Matthew J. O'Connell. New York, 1998.

Stevenson, James, and W. H. C. Frend, eds. *Creeds, Councils and Controversies: Documents Illustrating the History of the Church, A.D. 337–461.* Rev. ed. London, 1989.

Stump, Phillip M. *The Reforms of the Council of Constance, 1414–1418.* Leiden and New York, 1994.

Torrance, Iain R. *Christology after Chalcedon: Severus of Antioch and Sergious the Monophysite.* Norwich, U.K., 1988.

BRIAN E. DALEY (1987)
Revised Bibliography

COUVADE is the name given to various ritual acts performed by a husband during his wife's pregnancy, delivery, and postpartum period. In their most extreme form, couvade customs are said to involve the male's mimicking of or experience of pregnancy symptoms and labor pains, followed by his postpartum recovery. Meanwhile, the woman's actual physical experience is given minimal attention, and she continues her regular activities with little interruption. This extreme form of couvade seems to be more hypothetical than actual. The term *couvade* is more generally used to refer to symbolic behaviors engaged in by men during and immediately after their wives' pregnancies and deliveries.

Since in most, if not all, societies men's activities are affected to some extent by their wives' pregnancies and deliveries, it might seem reasonable to conclude that some form of couvade is universal. However, that usage would make the term so broad that some other term would then be needed to refer to the more specific and more demanding practices engaged in by men in certain tribal societies. One of the most recent discussions of couvade suggests that the term not be used to refer to activities such as giving a birth feast or helping the wife with daily chores during pregnancy. It is suggested that a mild form of couvade is involved when the husband keeps food taboos during the pregnancy or postpartum period. A more intensive form of couvade would involve behavior changes in the postpartum period, such as work taboos and restrictions, or staying close to home for varying lengths of time. The most intensive form of couvade involves ritual seclusion of the husband during pregnancy or the postpartum period, sometimes with his wife and sometimes in his own household or the men's house.

These kinds of behaviors are fairly widespread among small-scale societies, with a concentration of such practices in South American and Caribbean societies. However, theoretical discussions of couvade also rely on reports of the practice among the Ainu (the aboriginal tribal inhabitants of Japan) and among some Pacific Island groups.

A condensed summary of couvade among the Kurtachi, a people of the Pacific Islands, provides a specific example of couvade. During delivery, husband and wife are secluded in separate huts. This seclusion continues for six days, during which the man keeps food taboos, ignores his normal subsistence chores, and does not handle sharp tools. After three days he is allowed to see the child, and gives it medicine to make it strong. On the sixth day he ends his couvade by again entering the wife's seclusion hut, this time carrying a large knife with which he pretends to slash the infant.

Couvade among the Black Carib has also been studied and analyzed somewhat extensively. Their couvade observances vary in length from two days to a full year, with three months being the most typical duration. Various work taboos are considered an important part of couvade, as is a taboo on sexual intercourse, both marital and extramarital. However, food taboos play almost no part in Black Carib couvade.

A superficial approach to couvade would involve rather commonsense interpretations. Many men practicing couvade customs might be likely to see these practices as helping to protect the infant from harm, and ethnographers studying couvade could well see these practices as promoting the bonding of the father with his infant. Within a psychoanalytic framework the institution of couvade might be considered an expression of womb envy, of men's attempt to participate more directly in, or even to usurp, the essential birth-giving task of females. However, the need to protect young infants, to promote the bonding of fathers with their infants, and to defuse cross-gender envy of males, who unconsciously long for more direct participation in the birth process, exists in all societies. Yet only some societies practice couvade as defined and described by most anthropologists. Thus most recent students of couvade seek the rationale of couvade in other, less universal, factors.

By and large, these analysts find the rationale of couvade in specific features of a lifestyle's social structure. One hypothesis regarding couvade has made more refined use of psychoanalytic analysis. Proponents of this hypothesis have suggested that couvade can result from "low male salience," a combination of factors especially involving arrangements in which the mother sleeps with her children while the father sleeps elsewhere, or is absent altogether. It is hypothesized that the absence of significant contact with the father and the absence of other male role models, combined with such intense contact with the mother, promotes a cross-gender identity that encourages the male to engage in vicarious childbirth observances. Advocates of this explanation of couvade also stress that although other societies may also exhibit "low male salience," they do not have strongly institutionalized couvade. These societies, it is claimed, cope with "low male salience" by means of rigorous and demanding male puberty initiation ceremonies. Through these rigorous initiations, young males are supposedly swayed from any cross-gender identification and take on a kind of masculine identity that relieves them of tendencies toward couvade. It has been pointed out that few if any societies practice both intensive couvade and intensive male puberty rituals.

Alternative theories of couvade stress other causal factors that explain the presence of couvade in some but not all societies. It is claimed that in societies with weak fraternal interest groups a man has no reliable legal or economic means to claim paternity rights to a woman's children. He cannot rely on a loyal kin group to back up his claims to the child, nor can he refer to large economic exchanges or binding legal agreements made prior to the marriage and childbirth. Therefore, he engages in a ritual behavior to establish his claims over the child, and this ritual show gains for him a communal consensus regarding his paternity claims. According to this hypothesis, couvade is a form of ritual bargaining rather than a magico-religious attempt to influence biological processes or a ritual expression of unconscious psychodynamics. However, it would also seem that such political expressions cannot occur without some religious or psychological predisposition toward them.

Couvade seems best explained by looking to varying hypotheses rather than by focusing on only one factor as the sole rationale for these practices. It may be worthwhile to recognize the impulse toward couvade as universal, even though that impulse does not always result in the specific practices associated with "the couvade." Males are universally interested in the genesis, birth, and survival of infants whom they perceive as important. Thus, in varying degrees, males in all societies could be expected to experience some pregnancy symptoms or observe some pregnancy taboos, become involved in the childbirth process, and engage in special behaviors in the immediate postpartum period. Although the term *couvade* refers to specific male childbirth practices in some societies, the institution itself is the expression of a universal impulse rather than a strange practice limited to some small-scale societies.

SEE ALSO Birth.

BIBLIOGRAPHY

Theoretical discussions of couvade stressing psychodynamics are found in Robert L. Munroe, Ruth H. Munroe, and John W. M. Whiting's "The Couvade: A Psychological Analysis," *Ethos* 1 (Spring 1973): 30–74, and Ruth H. Munroe and Robert L. Monroe's *Cross-Cultural Human Development* (Monterey, Calif., 1975). Couvade as a political ritual to establish paternity rights is discussed in Karen Ericksen Paige and Jeffery M. Paige's *The Politics of Reproductive Ritual* (Berkeley, 1981). All these theoretical papers cite more descriptive literature concerning couvade. A typical ethnographic account of couvade is found in Allan R. Holmberg's *Nomads of the Long Bow: The Siriono of Eastern Bolivia* (Garden City, N.Y., 1969).

RITA M. GROSS (1987)

COVENANT.

COVENANT. The translation of the Hebrew notion of *bᶜrît* by *covenant* originates from its Latin rendering as *foedus/pactum* in Hieronymus's *Vulgata.* Although there is a controversy about the etymology of *bᶜrît,* the linguistic link with the Accadian *birītu(m)* (string, tie) seems to be the most acceptable solution. The literary contexts of *bᶜrît* confirm that the rendering in the *Vulgata* and thus the translation as *covenant* fits well. It depends on the particular context what is meant by this notion: Either two partners with equal rights mutually bind themselves (*1 Kings* 5:26; 15:19) or a stronger partner imposes unilateral claims upon a weaker one or the stronger partner voluntarily binds himself without any claims towards someone else (*1 Kings* 20:34; *Hos.* 12:2; *Ezek.* 17:13).

CONTRACT, TREATY AND LOYALITY OATH IN THE ANCIENT NEAR EAST. The legal order of the Middle East is based on laws of contract. As transfers of ownership (such as the sale of estates) and changes of marital status (marriage, adoption) are laid down in a written contract (Accadian *riksātu[m]),* mutual obligations are suable at a law court. Furthermore, in late Assyrian contracts breach of contract is identified with oath-breaking, for which divine sanction is effected by means of curse and penalty for the benefit of the temple. Laws of contract are also applied to settle international relations between states with equal rights as well as between a supreme power and vassal states (e.g. Hittite vassal treaties; Korošec). Opposite to private contracts, international contracts are loyalty obligations mutually or unilaterally affirmed upon by an oath. There are two distinctive types of these contracts: first, a western type of Hethite and Syrian contracts (Sfire; Lemaire, 1984) that include a section of blessings in addition to the curse; second, an eastern type of late Assyrian contracts (Parpola and Watanabe, 1988) in which only the curse can be found. This second type is different from late Assyrian loyalty oaths, such as that of King Esarhaddon (Watanabe, 1987). In these oaths, the officials of the Assyrian state and its tributary vassals—among them the king of Judea—swear unconditional loyalty to the Assyrian king and to the crown prince by the gods.

In the seventh century BCE a new and special form of late Assyrian laws of contract emerges for the first time. Now the contracts are not only subject to divine protection, but the deity himself is a party to the contract. In a collection of prophetic oracles spoken on the occasion of Esarhaddon's accession to the throne (Parpola, 1992), the god Ashur enters in a covenant (Accadian, *adê)* with the king; the other gods of the pantheon join as well. Later, the citizens and vassals of Assyria ought to be reminded of this covenant by the oath ceremony of cultic water drinking. In return for the divine support against enemies the king has to engage in ritual duties.

CONTRACT, LOYALTY OATH, AND COVENANT IN THE HEBREW BIBLE. According to the practice in the Ancient Middle East, the Hebrew Bible also mentions contracts of sale (e.g. *Jer.* 32:10–11), rent (e.g. *Gen.* 29:15–20, *Exod.* 2:9) and marriage (*Mal.* 2:14, *Prov.* 2:17). In ancient Palestine the different lifestyles and interests of Nomads, shepherds, farmers, urban people, craftsmen, and Levites coexisted in a cramped space where economical and political relations had to be constituted across family borders (e.g. *Gen.* 21:22–34; 26:23–33; 31:44–53). Therefore laws of contract were of special significance in ancient Israel surpassing the rules for changes in ownership and marital status. With reference to William Robertson Smith, Max Weber marked the ancient idea of making a covenant between JHWH, the God of Israel, and his people as a starting point of Israelite history of religion; however, this idea was not introduced because of an "elective affinity" *(Wahlverwandtschaft)* of the federal structure prevalent in prenational Israel as confederacy of oath *(Eidgenossenschaft)* in the thirteenth through the tenth centuries BCE.

Expanding Weber's theory, Martin Noth put forward the statement of an alliance of tribes organized on the model of the ancient Greek amphictyony as *Sitz im Leben* of the covenant theology. He and George Mendenhall were aiming to corroborate this statement by an analogy between the structure of an early Israelite covenant schedule and Hethite vassal treaties from the second millennium BCE. There was much argument against this early dating of the covenant between God and His people at the beginning of Israelite history of religion. On the one hand it is opposed to the covenant silence *(Bundesschweigen)* of the prophets in the eighth century BCE. Thus in *Hosea* 2:4–15 and 3:1–4, where the relationship of the people and Israel towards JHWH is interpreted as a marriage, the covenant theology is merely prepared. On the other hand the covenant theology of the Sinai pericope (*Exod.* 19–24) is known to be a late creation of Israelite literary history. Therefore Lothar Perlitt, who refers to Julius Wellhausen, came to the conclusion that the covenant theology ensued from preexile prophesy, taking its rise in the time of crisis of the late Assyrian Empire, and thus dated in the seventh century BCE.

Motifs of the late Assyrian royal ideology were partially accepted, but also partially rejected in Judah. In modern times this process—especially concerning the covenant theology—can be described in a more exact way (Otto) than in the previous centuries. In Judah they adopted the motif of a covenant with a divine partner from Ashur in the seventh century BCE in order to legitimate the reign of kings (*Ps.* 89:4–5). The authors of preexile *Deuteronomy* accept the loyalty oath of the Assyrian king in a subversive way by transforming the demand for unconditional loyalty to this king into the demand of the same kind to JHWH (*Deut.* 13:2–10; 28:20–44). The claim of the state for absolute power was thereby set in bounds and the ground prepared for a reinterpretation of the idea of covenant. As a result, within the Deuteronomistic framework of *Deuteronomy* the entire people of Israel became a partner of the covenant with JHWH at Horeb, God's mount (*Deut.* 26:16–19), and in the land of Moab (*Deut.* 29:9–14).

In the time of exile the covenant with JHWH at Horeb replaced the king. As in *Deuteronomy* the law is linked to blessing and curse; it is not modeled upon the Assyrian tradition, but rather upon a Hethite type of contract that was transmitted to Israel via Syria. Thus JHWH gets the character of a Grand King and His vassal Israel owes Him loyalty of legal obedience. If the nation, by making the covenant, is to be held liable for the law of *Deuteronomy,* the authors of the Deuteronomistic *Deuteronomy* yet are aware of the possibility that the people may fail to keep the law due to disobedience (*Deut.* 9:9–10:5).

In the tale of *Deuteronomy* the authors let the people of Israel enter into the covenant after their failure, so they express their hope that God is willing to adhere to his covenant in spite of the people's failure to obey the law—that is, JHWH does not revoke His covenant even though Israel failed the law. In this way the Israelites overcome their experience of defeat against the Babylonians and their trauma of exile.

A second version of the origin of Israel. The Priestly Code dating from the time of Exile represents a second major version of the tale of Israel's origin and is the counterpart to the covenant theology in *Deuteronomy.* It deals with universal history and designs the final goal of creation and the world history of all peoples (*Gen.* 1–11). The underlying concept of the Priestly Code is the immanent presence of Israel's God in the tabernacle of the congregation, the establishment of the expiatory cult of offerings at the altar, and, along with the cult, the priest's office ministered by the Aaronites at Mount Sinai—God's mount (*Exod.* 29:42–46). Additionally, the Priestly Code aims to prove that since the Flood, mankind has overcome the former possibility to fail God's law once for all. After the Flood, God imposed the Noachian Laws on mankind, making a covenant with them in which he commits himself to guarantee the preservation of the earth and all humans (*Gen.* 9:1–17). Israel and mankind as a whole cannot fail the covenant by which JHWH made Israel stand out from the world of the other peoples.

The Priestly Code does not locate the covenant at Mount Sinai; further, it dates the Code back to the time of the patriarchs; here it is Abraham with whom God makes a covenant (*Gen.* 17). Thus the covenant is not linked any longer to binding laws, but instead represents a mere act of divine grace. This covenant comprises God's promise of numerous descendants and of the possession of the land of Canaan. Henceforth the nation of Israel is unable to fail the covenant. An individual Israelite may, however, fail if he refuses circumcision—the token of this covenant—and will consequently be excluded from the ethnic community. Scribes of postexilic times combine both programmatic texts, *Deuteronomy,* and the Priestly Code, thus forming a Hexateuch (*Gen.* 1–*Josh.* 24); its final goal is the making of a covenant between JHWH and Joshua, who acts on behalf of the people of Israel (*Josh.* 24:25–27).

Referring to *Deuteronomy,* Joshua delivers a speech of admonition that precedes this covenant and points out the consequences of its breach if the ban on worship of foreign gods is violated. Thus he pursues the course that adds the liability for the law and the possibility of Israel's failure to the covenant theology of the Priestly Code based upon mere grace. Its sequel is realized by the extension of the Sinai pericope (*Exod.* 19–*Num.* 10) in the final form of the Pentateuch (*Gen.* 1–*Deut.* 34) that is structured by the sequence of making, breaking, and re-making the covenant (*Exod.* 19–34). God's will to adhere to His covenant with Israel, despite their failure to the law (*Exod.* 32), remains the main statement in the Pentateuch.

In contradiction to the author-scribes of the Pentateuch, prophetic circles in Jeremiah's tradition regard the Sinai covenant of old as being broken beyond repair. They instead hope for a new covenant between JHWH and His people. In their view it is this new covenant that Israel will finally not be able to break; JHWH will write the law straight into the human heart. Circles in Ezekiel's tradition expect, in a similar way, that JHWH will give Israel a new heart—as well as His spirit—so that they may comply with the law. The law itself should not be altered.

COVENANT IN EARLY JUDAISM AND IN THE NEW TESTAMENT. The covenant theology has preserved its importance in post-canonical Judaism that picks up the thread of the Pentateuch theology. According to the *Book of Sirach*, the story of JHWH with Israel consists of a series of eternal covenants reaching from Noah to David (*Sir.* 44–45); the Mosaic Law—in its role as the "Book of the Covenant"—is the expression of the preexistent wisdom in this world. In the *Book of Jubilees* those who keep the covenant made with Abraham and who undergo circumcision will not come to grief (*Jub.* 15:25–28). The feast of Shavuot becomes the date of the covenant at Mount Sinai (*Jub.* 1:1) and of the covenants made with Noah and Abraham. Moreover, theologians of the Essenes refer to the prophetic expectation of a new covenant that they consider to be realized in their community. This is also the case when membership with the Essene community—that is, participation in the New Covenant—stands for compliance with the written Torah according to Essene exegesis, including the Manual of Discipline (Sektenregel). The new covenant also needs a regular renewal at Shavuot, and on this occasion the members of the Essene community receive the blessing, whereas those who do not participate in the New Covenant are cursed.

In the Septuagint—the Greek translation of the Hebrew Bible—the notion *bʿrît* is rendered not by *synthēkē* or *spondē* (treaty/covenant), but by a term from the law of descent: *diathēkē* (testament/last will). It says that God's promise is staunch and unchangeable. Yet the Septuagint has overtones of the possibility that during his lifetime the testator can dispose of the estate bequest by will, despite the appointment of the heir. Thus JHWH is depicted as the giving father and Israel as the receiving son without God's sovereignty ever being restricted.

The New Testament continues the linguistic usage of the Septuagint. The saying on the cup (Becherwort) at the last supper (*Mark* 14:24, *Mattt.* 26:28) typologically resumes the verses in *Exodus* 24:8, *1 Corinthians* 11:25, *Luke* 22:20, and *Jeremiah* 31: 31–34. God establishes the eschatological community of the New Covenant (Latin: *novum testamentum*) on the basis of Jesus' expiatory death. It is the dedication of the last supper. In *Galatians* 3:15–18 Paul argues with the term *diathēkē* from the law of descent in order to institute his gospel, which is not tied to the condition of the law. Like a testament, the covenant with Abraham cannot subsequently be altered by the law, which was given later at Mount Sinai. In *2 Corinthians,* 3:14, Paul calls the Torah read at the synagogue service "old covenant" and contrasts it with the New Covenant, which is not based on the letter of the law but on God's spirit. In *Romans,* chapters 9–11, Paul expresses his hope that Israel will likewise become part of the eschatological New Covenant and that in this way God's covenant with Israel will not be cancelled (*Rom.* 11:29). The Epistle of the Hebrews sets the obsolete "old covenant" of the Levitical Torah at Mount Sinai (*Heb.* 8:7–13; 10:15–18), understood as the "first covenant," against the New Covenant and thus continues the tradition of Jeremiah 31:31–34. The New Covenant is supposed to be the "better covenant" and the "eternal covenant" that belongs to the divine order of God's roaming people. By Christ's death on the cross this order was established as an antithesis to Exodus 24:8 (*Heb.* 9:11–22), but its final completion has yet to come (*Heb.* 8:6; 11:1–12:3).

COVENANT IN POSTBIBLICAL CHRISTIANITY. In the second century CE the antagonism between the old and the new covenant gains even more severity. In postcanonical texts like the letter of Barnabas (9:1–5) and in the dialogue of Justin with Tryphon the Jew, the old covenant—intended for the Jews—was replaced by the new covenant of the Christian church. Yet in the third century the church had to contend against Gnostic and Marcionitic heresies that, with reference to the Old Testament, considered the Creator in a theologically negative way. The covenants of the Old Testament again gained in importance; they were part of the permanent salvation acts (Heilsökonomie) of God. Ireneus of Lyon substantiated the unity of both Testaments as belonging to the one Christian canon. Only in the combination of both, God's plan of salvation, consisting of the laws from Mount Sinai as well as the redemption through Christ, could be carried out.

Theologians of the Reformation, proceeding from Ireneus's thought, developed a federal covenant theology (Föderaltheologie). Heinrich Bullinger (1504–1575), a reformer from Zurich, Switzerland, was the first to project a Protestant federal covenant theology. To him the history of salvation from Abraham to Christ represented one single covenant with two aspects: the first concerning law and ritual in the Old Testament, the second concerning a covenant of divine grace in the New Testament.

In the seventeenth century CE the covenant theology of orthodox Calvinism reached its climax in the Netherlands, especially due to Johannes Coccejus (1603–1669). He developed his dogmatics by going beyond Aristotelian notions, preferring to elaborate a system of the history of salvation according to which, step by step, the covenant of works (*foedus operum*) with Adam will be replaced by the covenant of grace (*foedus gratiae*). This process is said to prepare mankind for the coming of God's kingdom.

From the eighteenth to the twentieth centuries, theologians in different countries were influenced by reformist covenant theology: Thomas Boston (1676–1732) in Scotland, Charles Hodge (1797–1878) in America, as well as the Swiss theologians Karl Barth (1886–1968) and Walther Eichrodt (1890–1978). Eichrodt was a reformist scholar of Old Testament studies and developed Old Testament theology based on the patterns of covenant terminology.

COVENANT IN RABBINIC JUDAISM AND IN ISLAM. Rabbinic Judaism interprets the Biblical *bʿrît* in particular with "law/commandment" in the contents of which the sign of covenant—that is, the circumcision—is meant (compare *Gen.* 17:10) first of all. In accordance with that meaning the Israelites may be called *bʿnê bʿrît* (sons of circumcision). Referring to Exodus 34:27, the commitment to the law including oral traditions can be qualified as *bʿrît*, as well. In the Middle Ages the explicit idea of *bʿrît* only plays a minor role in Jewish theological thought. In Maimonides (c. 1135–1204), the covenant describes the union of Moses and the biblical patriarchs with God, a union directed at acquiring cognition, the goal of which is to have the insights transmitted to all women and men.

The biblical covenants are a main subject for apology in order to either reject Christian theory about the replacement of God's old covenant with Israel by Christ's salvation work, or to reject the Islamic claim that the revelation of the Prophet Muhammad exceeds the biblical covenants. Modern Jewish philosophy and theology again attaches more importance to the notion of covenant; it serves as an expression of ethic autonomy based on mutual obligations between God and mankind, or on a dialogic behavior between both of them as explained in Martin Buber (1878–1965).

According to the Qurʾān (*sūrah* 7:134–135), which adopted the biblical conception of *bʿrît*, Moses' covenant (Arabic: *ʿahd mūsā*) with God enables Moses to intercede with God and to receive the tables of testimony (*sūrah* 7:144–145). Moreover, God made a covenant with the prophets (*sūrah* 3:81; 33:7), and in particular with the Israelites at Mount Sinai, as he had previously done with Moses. The Israelites, however, broke this covenant (e.g. *sūrah* 2:63–66). After all, God had entered into a covenant with all women and men, calling upon all people to adhere to the revealed laws and to accept the reign of the one God (*sūrah* 7:171–172). Islamic traditional exegesis of these Qurʾanic verses links God's granting humans the ability to speak to the following demand of the covenant on Adamite mankind: They have to accept God as the single One and at the time of resurrection nobody can claim ignorance of the conditions of the covenant in order to exculpate himself.

SEE ALSO Biblical Literature, article on Hebrew Scriptures; God, article on God in Postbiblical Christianity.

BIBLIOGRAPHY

Eichrodt, Walther. *Theology of the Old Testament* (1933–1939). 2 vols. London, 1961–1967. Organizes Old Testament thought around the idea of a covenant.

Jobert, Anni. *La notion d'Alliance dans le Judaisme aux abords de l'ère chretienne.* Paris, 1963. Basic study of early Jewish covenant theology.

Kalluveettil, Paul. *Declaration and Covenant: A Comprehensive Review of Covenant Formulae from the Old Testament and the Ancient Near East.* Rome, 1982. A form-critical study of language and form of contracts in the ancient Near East and the Bible.

Korošec, Viktor. *Hethitische Staatsverträge: Ein Beitrag zu ihrer juristischen Wertung.* Leipzig, 1931. Legal interpretation of Hittite international treaties.

Lemaire, André Durand. *Les inscriptions araméennes de Sfiré et l'Assyrie de Shamshi-Ilu.* Geneva, 1984. Text, translation, and commentary of the Syrian Sfire-treaty.

McCarthy, Dennis. *Treaty and Covenant: A Study in Form in the Ancient Oriental Documents and in the Old Testament.* 2d ed. Rome, 1978. Reliable interpretation of key-texts of ancient Near East treaties and biblical covenants.

Mendenhall, George. *Law and Covenant in Israel and the Ancient Near East.* Pittsburgh, 1955. A pioneer study that initiated much discussion of the relations between the Hittite vassal treaties and the Hebrew Bible.

Noth, Martin. *Das System der zwölf Stämme Israels.* Stuttgart, Germany, 1930. Important study of the "setting in life" of early Israelite covenant theology.

Otto, Eckart. *Das Deuteronomium: Politische Theologie und Rechtsreform in Juda und Assyrien.* Berlin, 1999. Study of the reception of neo-Assyrian loyality oaths and covenant motifs in Judah.

Otto, Eckart. *Das Deuteronomium im Pentateuch und Hexateuch.* Tübingen, Germany, 2000. Study of the postexilic pentateuch and covenant theology.

Parpola, Simon. *Assyrian Prophecies.* Helsinki, 1997. Transliteration and translation of neo-Assyrian prophecies that include motifs of a covenant between the god Ashur and the Assyrian king.

Parpola, Simon, and Watanabe, Kazuko. *Neo-Assyrian Treaties and Loyalty Oaths.* Helsinki, 1988. Transliteration and translation of neo-Assyrian treaties and loyality oaths.

Perlitt, Lothar. *Bundestheologie im Alten Testament.* Neukirchen-Vluyn, Germany, 1969. Basic study of the origin of biblical covenant theology.

Robertson Smith, William. *Lectures on the Religion of the Semites: The Fundamental Institutions.* 2d ed. London, 1894. Study of covenant motifs in early biblical and Arabic thought.

Tucker, Gene M. *Contracts in the Old Testament.* Ph.D. diss. Yale University, 1963. Study of profane contracts in Israel.

Watanabe, Kazuko. *Die adê-Vereidigung anläßlich der Thronfolgeregelung Asarhaddons.* Berlin, 1987. Text and translation of Esarhaddon's loyality oath.

Weber, Max. *Die Wirtschaftsethik der Weltreligionen: Das antike Judentum* (1920). Edited by Eckart Otto. Tübingen, Germany, 2004. Translated by Hans H. Gerth and Don Martindale as *Ancient Judaism.* Glencoe, Ill., 1952. Study of the economic contexts of biblical covenant theology.

ECKART OTTO (2005)

COWS See CATTLE

CRANMER, THOMAS

CRANMER, THOMAS (1489–1556), archbishop of Canterbury (1533–1556), a principal figure in the reformation of the Church of England. Born of a gentry family in Nottinghamshire, Cranmer entered Jesus College, Cambridge, at the age of fourteen. After taking his B.A. (1511) and M.A. (1515), he became a fellow of the college. His marriage to a gentlewoman named Joan cost him the fellowship, but it was restored when Joan, with her baby, died in childbirth.

After his ordination (before 1520), he was appointed one of twelve university preachers and, on obtaining his B.D. (1521) and D.D. (1526), a university examiner in divinity. Cranmer kept aloof from other Cambridge scholars who met frequently to discuss Luther's writings. Instead, he privately tested these writings by his own independent study of the Bible and early church fathers.

Cranmer left Cambridge in 1529 to serve the cause of King Henry VIII's annulment of his marriage to Queen Catherine. During an embassy to Emperor Charles V in 1532 he became acquainted with several Lutheran leaders, among them Andreas Osiander at Nuremberg, whose niece Margaret he secretly married. She bore him a daughter and a son. Few were privy to this marriage until the next reign.

When Archbishop William Warham died in 1532, Henry decided that Cranmer would succeed him at Canterbury. The king was convinced that Cranmer would be dutiful not for any personal convenience, much less ambition, but from his sincere (and somewhat extreme) belief that scripture taught obedience to the divine right of kings and princes. This conviction explains many compromises and vacillations in Cranmer's life. Privately he would advise and admonish Henry and plead for mercy for the king's victims, but he would never openly disobey him.

In January 1533, Henry's secret marriage to Anne Boleyn, already pregnant, made the annulment issue urgent. Although Pope Clement VII suspected Henry's intentions, he consented to Cranmer's consecration, which took place on March 30. Both before and twice during the rite Cranmer read a protestation that his oath of obedience to the pope did not bind him if it was against the law of God, the laws and prerogatives of the Crown, or the reformation of the church.

Within a few weeks, Cranmer pronounced the marriage to Catherine null and that to Anne valid. In July the pope issued but did not publish excommunications of Henry, Anne, and Cranmer. Any hope of reconciliation ended when the Act of Supremacy (1534) declared the king and his successors "the only supreme head in earth of the Church of England."

Cranmer supported but did not initiate the major reforms of Henry's reign: the dissolution of all monastic and religious houses between 1536 and 1539 (carried out more because of the Crown's greed for their vast properties than for the sake of any principle) and the official authorization in 1539 of the English "Great Bible," for which Cranmer wrote a notable preface in 1540.

The stringent Act of Six Articles (1539) closed the door to any reforms in doctrine or practice. Cranmer spoke against it in the House of Lords, but he voted for it because the king willed it. By now Cranmer was commonly believed to be a Lutheran. In 1543 the privy council voted to arrest him as a heretic, but Henry intervened and saved him. Until Henry's death Cranmer worked quietly on projects of liturgical reform, but of these only the *English Litany* of 1544 was authorized.

Reformers dominated the privy council of King Edward VI (1547–1553), Henry's precocious young son, who was educated by Protestant tutors. Among the councillors committed to religious reform were the young king's uncle the duke of Somerset and Lord Protector, and Cranmer, his godfather. Cranmer soon published a *Book of Homilies,* one part to be read every Sunday, and translated a Lutheran catechism by Justus Jonas. Clerical celibacy was abolished. Communion including both bread and wine was ordered, for which Cranmer prepared *The Order of the Communion* (1548), a vernacular devotion for the people's Communion at Mass.

At Pentecost 1549 *The Book of Common Prayer* came into use under an act of uniformity. The book's reforming principles were derived from Lutheran sources; but its Catholic heritage was preserved by Cranmer's skillful adaptation and translation of liturgical forms and prayers from Latin service books. The daily offices were reduced to two, matins and evensong, with one chapter from both the Old and New Testaments read at each. The Holy Communion eliminated all sacrificial references except "praise and thanksgiving" and forbade any elevation of the consecrated elements. The prayer book was not popular, however, with either conservatives or radical reformers.

After Somerset's fall from power, the duke of Northumberland became Lord Protector. He was more interested in the church properties he acquired than in the radical reforms he promoted. In 1550 Cranmer published *The Form and Manner* for ordaining bishops, priests, and deacons, based on the Latin *Pontifical* and a work of Martin Bucer, and also his principal theological work, *A Defence of the True and Catholike Doctrine of the Sacrament of the Body and Bloud of Our Saviour Christ.*

A revised prayer book was issued in 1552 under an act of uniformity. Most of the old vestments and ceremonies were abolished, and the Communion service was rearranged and conformed to the Swiss reformers' doctrine. All images, crosses, rood screens, and other ornaments were smashed, removed, or sold; and a wooden "holy Table" replaced all altars.

While Edward lay dying, Northumberland plotted to place his cousin Lady Jane Grey (granddaughter of King Henry VII) on the throne. Cranmer strongly opposed this until Edward commanded him to submit. But the coup was short-lived. Mary I, the elder daughter of Henry VIII, was acclaimed queen. Many reformers fled to the continent, and Cranmer sent his family back to Germany.

An ardent Roman Catholic, Mary persuaded Parliament to revoke all reforms of Edward's reign. Cranmer was arrested, tried, and condemned as a traitor; but Mary had other plans. When Cardinal Reginald Pole, papal legate and archbishop-designate of Canterbury, arrived in 1554, he absolved the kingdom and restored papal authority. The burning of heretics then began.

Under pressure, Cranmer wrote several recantations, but to no avail. On the day of his degradation and burning, March 21, 1556, he publicly recanted all his recantations, hastened to the stake, thrust his fist into the fire crying "This hand has offended," and soon collapsed. His monument lives in *The Book of Common Prayer*, often amended and enriched, which is used in the worship of all churches of the Anglican communion.

Bibliography

The principal collections of Cranmer's writings can be found in *The Remains of Thomas Cranmer, D. D., Archbishop of Canterbury*, 4 vols., edited by Henry Jenkyns (Oxford, 1833), and the two volumes edited by John Edmund Cox for the Parker Society, *Writings and Disputations of Thomas Cranmer, Archbishop of Canterbury, Martyr, 1556, Relative to the Sacrament of the Lord's Supper* (Cambridge, U.K., 1844) and *Miscellaneous Writings and Letters of Thomas Cranmer, Archbishop of Canterbury, Martyr, 1556* (Cambridge, U.K., 1846).

Many other sources and later assessments of Cranmer are evaluated in the biography by Jasper Ridley, *Thomas Cranmer* (Oxford, 1962), with full bibliography and index of names. On the controversies over Cranmer's doctrine of the Eucharist, with much bibliographical detail, see Peter Brooks's *Thomas Cranmer's Doctrine of the Eucharist: An Essay in Historical Development* (London, 1965). A learned, fair, and readable account of the background of Cranmer's work can be found in W. K. Jordan's *Edward VI: The Young King* (Cambridge, Mass., 1968) and *Edward VI: The Threshold of Power* (Cambridge, Mass., 1970).

Massey H. Shepherd, Jr. (1987)

CREATION MYTHS See COSMOGONY

CREEDS

This entry consists of the following articles:

AN OVERVIEW
CHRISTIAN CREEDS
ISLAMIC CREEDS

CREEDS: AN OVERVIEW

A creed is a confession of faith; put into concise form, endowed with authority, and intended for general use in religious rites, a creed summarizes the essential beliefs of a particular religion. The notion of creed comes from the Christian thought world, and it is not possible to identify in other religions the exact parallel, in form and function, of what Christians call a creed. However, approximate parallels may be noted.

According to the definition given above, there are three Christian creeds: the Apostles', the Nicene, and the Athanasian. Here is the text of the shortest and, as far as its sources are concerned, the oldest of the three, the Apostles' Creed, as found in the Anglican *Book of Common Prayer* (1945):

> I believe in God the Father Almighty, Maker of heaven and earth: And in Jesus Christ his only Son our Lord: Who was conceived by the Holy Ghost, Born of the Virgin Mary: Suffered under Pontius Pilate, Was crucified, dead, and buried: He descended into hell; The third day he rose again from the dead: He ascended into heaven, And sitteth on the right hand of God the Father Almighty: From thence he shall come to judge the quick and the dead. I believe in the Holy Ghost: The Holy Catholic Church: The Communion of Saints: The Forgiveness of sins: The Resurrection of the body: And the Life everlasting. Amen.

The three Christian creeds are authoritative in large segments of the church, although Eastern Orthodoxy considers only the Nicene Creed as completely authoritative. Certain branches of Protestantism (those that emphasize freedom from traditional rites, a rational approach to religion, or the autonomy of individual religious experience) ignore creeds altogether.

In Judaism, a formula taken from *Deuteronomy* 6:4 and called the Shemaʿ (from the first word, meaning "Hear!") is the expression of monotheistic faith:

> Hear, O Israel: The Lord our God is one God.

Recited liturgically, the Shemaʿ includes, in addition, *Deuteronomy* 6:5–9, 11:13–21, and *Numbers* 15:37–41.

In the *Yasna,* the chief liturgical work of the Avesta (the sacred writings of the Zoroastrian religion), are found several short confessions of faith, summarizing in various wordings the principal beliefs of that religion. One of these (*Yasna* 12:1) is:

> I drive the *daēvas* hence; I confess as a Mazdā-worshiper of the order of Zarathushtra, estranged from the *daēvas*, devoted to the love of the Lord, a praiser of the Bountiful Immortals; and to Ahura Mazdā, the good and endowed with good possessions, I attribute all things good, to the holy One, the resplendent, to the glorious, whose are all things whatsoever which are good.

In Hinduism, the widely used Gāyatrī Mantra, based on *Ṛgveda* 3.62.10, corresponds in some ways to the definition of creed:

> Oṃ [the supreme power]! O earth! O air! O heavens! Let us meditate on the resplendent glory of Savitṛ [the sun god] that it may awaken our thoughts.

This formula is more precisely an invocation of the gods, but implicit in it is a confession of faith. The recitation of a creed functions as prayer in other religions as well.

Buddhism's Triple Refuge is a profession of faith in the wisdom of the Buddha, in the truth of his teaching, and in the significance of the community:

> I take refuge in the Buddha; I take refuge in the Dharma [doctrine]; I take refuge in the Saṃgha [community of believers].

In Islam, the creed is recited as a twofold witness:

> I witness that there is no god but God and that Muḥammad is the Messenger of God.

In Sikhism, the opening words of Japji, the guru Nānak's prayer, are expressive of basic Sikh doctrine and are universally recited by that religious community:

> There is but one God whose name is true, the Creator, devoid of fear and enmity, immortal, unborn, self-existent; by the favor of the Guru. The True One was in the beginning; The True One was in the primal age. The True One is now also, O Nānak; The True One also shall be.

FUNCTIONS OF CREEDS. Creeds function in different ways: (1) as the basis for membership in a religious community, whether accompanying a rite of initiation (Christian baptism) or constituting one of the elements of religious distinctiveness (Buddhism, Islam, Judaism, Sikhism); (2) as a test of orthodoxy, in formal opposition to heresy (Christianity); (3) as a type of prayer used in private or public worship (Hinduism, Zoroastrianism, Christianity; in Alsace, Lutherans are invited in their liturgy to "pray the creed"); (4) as a basis for religious instruction; (5) as a corporate or individual response in faith to divine revelation leading to conduct of commitment (Jews call their creed "the acceptance of the yoke of the kingdom of heaven"); (6) as an expression of self-understanding by the religious community; (7) as an assertion and confirmation of the unity of the community (Islam, Christianity, Judaism); or (8) as a witness to the world, expressing the core of belief (Judaism, Islam, Christianity).

SOURCES OF AUTHORITY. Only in Christianity has the authority of creeds been legislated formally by conciliar action. The creed of Islam draws its authority from the fact that its elements are found in the Qurʾān, and from its express wording in the *ḥadīth,* or from reports of the prophet Muḥammad where he affirms that the creed is one of the five pillars upon which Islam is built. The Shemaʿ of Judaism is an exact quotation from the Bible. In other religions, the formulas functioning as creeds base their authority on communal unanimity.

TERMS DESIGNATING CREEDS. Besides the word *creed*—not strictly a name in its origin, since it is derived from the Latin verb *credo* ("I believe"), with which the Apostles' Creed and the Nicene Creed open—Christians use the phrase "symbol of the faith" to designate a creed.

In Islam, the creed is called the Shahādah, meaning "witness." Sikhs refer to their creed as the Mul Mantra or "root formula." In the Avesta, the term *fravarāne* is used for "confession of faith."

EXTENSION OF THE DEFINITION. Sometimes the definition of creed is broadened to include longer, more detailed statements of doctrine. These are more precisely called "articles of faith" or "confessions of faith" in Christianity and *ʿaqīdah*s in Islam. Examples of such doctrinal treatises are likewise seen in Judaism, attributed to such great scholars as Philo Judaeus, Josephus Flavius, and Moses Maimonides. Contrary to the strict definition of creed given above, articles of faith are not recited orally in liturgical settings, and their authority has been limited to certain segments of a religious community.

The advent of Protestantism in sixteenth-century Christendom prompted the preparation and use of several important confessions of faith that distinguish one denomination from another. Examples are the Augsburg Confession of Lutheranism (1530) and the Westminster Confession of the Reformed tradition (1646).

Islamic *ʿaqīdah*s have often served to emphasize controverted points of doctrine and practice or to attack heretical tendencies, so they do not necessarily deal with the full range of doctrine. Such statements of faith emerged from the five schools of Sunnī jurisprudence that predominate in the Muslim world today, as well as from schools of thought that have disappeared, and from theologians, legal scholars, mystics, and philosophers, both ancient and modern.

BIBLIOGRAPHY

The article "Creeds and Articles" in the *Encyclopaedia of Religion and Ethics,* vol. 4, edited by James Hastings (Edinburgh, 1911), is not so much an overview of the subject as a series of unconnected descriptions of beliefs in the various religions, with quotations from original sources. The overall nature of creeds is much more clearly set forth in the article "Bekenntnis" by Gustav Mensching et al., in *Die Religion in Geschichte und Gegenwart,* 3d ed., vol. 1, edited by Kurt Galling (Tübingen, 1957). Most of the article is devoted to Christian creeds, and this rightfully, since the notion of creed is most specifically a Christian phenomenon.

The exhaustive and still irreplaceable source of information about Christian creeds is Philip Schaff's *The Creeds of Christendom, with a History and Critical Notes,* 3 vols., 6th ed. (1919; reprint, Grand Rapids, Mich., 1983). A more accessible work, containing a good introduction on the nature and function of creeds, is *Creeds of the Church: A Reader in Christian Doctrine from the Bible to the Present,* 3d ed., edited by John H. Leith (Atlanta, 1982). J. N. D. Kelly, in *Early Christian Creeds,* 3d ed. (New York, 1972), gives a fine study of the origins and development of creed making in Christendom. The entry by Louis Jacobs, "Shema, Reading of," in *Encyclopaedia Judaica,* vol. 14 (Jerusalem, 1972), describes the historical background, liturgical function, and theological meaning of the Jewish creedal formula.

A. J. Wensinck's *The Muslim Creed: Its Genesis and Historical Development* (New York, 1965) deals with the subject in a broad way, analyzing the content of several ancient *'aqīdahs.* Some attention is given to the significance and function of the Shahadah.

Perceptive remarks on the general nature of creeds, strictly defined as a special type of holy word, can be found in Gerardus van der Leeuw's *Religion in Essence and Manifestation,* vol. 2 (1938; reprint, Gloucester, Mass., 1967), pp. 441–443.

R. MARSTON SPEIGHT (1987)

CREEDS: CHRISTIAN CREEDS

Christian usage tends to apply the word *creed* preeminently to the Apostles', Nicene, and Athanasian creeds (the so-called ecumenical symbols), to use *dogma* for specific ecclesiastical pronouncements, and to use *confession of faith* for the comprehensive manifestos of the Protestant Reformation. But the terminology remains fluid, and *creed* may be taken in a broad, generic sense to include any official codification of a belief, or the beliefs, of a religious community. Distinctions must then be made among the Christian creeds with respect to their functions, their degree of comprehensiveness, their authority, and their several authorizing bodies.

The various churches differ markedly on the status claimed for their respective pronouncements. Creeds may be invested with the authority of divine revelation. But at the opposite end of the scale, the entire notion of a normative, as distinct from a purely descriptive, statement of belief has often been rejected outright as a threat to the unique authority of scripture, the freedom of faith, or new communications from the Holy Spirit. Since the late nineteenth century, there has also been a tendency to disparage creeds on the ground that they occasion discord in the church and misrepresent the nature of Christian belief.

The greatest number of Christian creeds date from the Reformation era: they were by-products of the division of the Western church, serving to legitimate the several groups that claimed to be, or to belong to, the true or catholic church. For precisely this reason, the sixteenth-century confessions asserted their continuity with the past; many of them expressly reaffirmed the three ecumenical symbols, and some endorsed as well the pronouncements of the ecumenical councils. But there was, and is, no unanimity on which creeds and which councils may legitimately be classed as ecumenical.

The themes to be considered are, accordingly, the nature and authority of Christian creeds in general, the ecumenical creeds and councils, the Lutheran and Reformed confessions, other creeds of the Reformation era, and Christian creeds in the modern world.

NATURE AND AUTHORITY OF CHRISTIAN CREEDS. It is often assumed that a creed is a catalog of authorized beliefs designed as a test of orthodoxy. But the history of the origin and use of Christian creeds proves that such an interpretation is too narrow. A useful clue to this complex history may perhaps be taken from one possible meaning of the word "symbol," by which the Apostles' Creed was known from the earliest times. Tyrannius Rufinus (c. 345–410) thought the creed was so termed because it was intended as a kind of password or means of identification (Lat., *symbolum*). The basic creedal function that underlies all the others is to establish the identity of a community or to identify oneself with it.

Types of creed. The several types of Christian creeds are generated by the diverse situations that demand the affirmation, or the reaffirmation, of identity. The roots of Christian creeds, so understood, must be sought in biblical faith—in the self-understanding of the people of God. A clear prototype of the earliest Christian creeds is to be found in such Old Testament declarations as *Deuteronomy* 26:1–11, which may be described as a historical credo or confession of faith for liturgical use. In content, it is a grateful recital of the redemptive deeds of God—the deliverance from bondage and the gift of the Promised Land—by which the people of Israel were, and still are, constituted. And it is expressly designed as a liturgical formula for the sanctuary—to accompany the presentation of an offering to the Lord. Similarly, the core of the early Christian creeds was recital of the so-called Christ-*kerygma,* the deeds of God in Jesus Christ understood as continuous with the Old Testament story. (Compare the second article of the Apostles' Creed with, e.g., *1 Corinthians* 15:3–7 and *Acts* 13:16–41.) And the Christian creeds too had their original place in a liturgical rather than a legal setting: they celebrated the identity of the church as the community called into being by the crucified and risen Lord. From the earliest times there was a close connection between creed and baptism, and in most of the historic liturgies of the churches, in both East and West, a creed has been recited or sung as part of the eucharistic service.

It would be a mistake, however, to link Christian creeds exclusively with liturgy (the forms prescribed for corporate worship) or with any particular element in it, such as baptism or the Eucharist. Creeds also served the church's educational needs. Here, too, the Old Testament appears to offer a prototype: in *Deuteronomy* 6:20–25 there is a historical credo without a liturgical context, and the recital of God's marvelous deeds is simply for the instruction of the young, lest future generations forget the events that brought the people into existence. Early Christian creeds likewise found their place not only in the worship but also in the instruction of the church, including catechetical instruction before baptism.

Besides the constant requirements of worship and education, periodic divisions within a church and threats from outside have provided special occasions for the development and use of creedal formulas. Indeed, it is sometimes said that creeds and confessions are most properly born in times of crisis. Although this too is an oversimplification (like the notion that creeds are tests of orthodoxy), it is certainly true that defense against the peril of false belief—in the form of heresy, persecution by another church, or paganism—has been one stimulus to creed-making throughout Christian history. And it must be added that not only the desire to exclude competing beliefs but also the desire to overcome divisions has produced creeds, in which previous recriminations are laid aside in a new sense of unity.

The diverse uses of Christian creeds are reflected in the traditional nomenclature. An affirmation of communal identity having symbolic authority might be called "creed," "confession," "articles of faith," "canons," "decree," "catechism," "declaration," "covenant," "consensus," "platform," "apology," and so on. But in practice, function and title do not invariably coincide, and many creeds have been put to more than one use.

Authority of creeds. The status of creeds in the Roman church is closely bound up with the Roman Catholic understanding of the church, its magisterium and its infallibility. Though degrees of authoritative statement are differentiated, the highest ecclesiastical pronouncements have a juridical character and are binding on the church's members: to deviate openly and obstinately from any truth of the catholic faith is heresy. The tendency of Rome to accumulate dogmas is not approved by the Eastern Orthodox churches, but they invest the Nicene Creed and the pronouncements of their seven ecumenical councils with much the same authority that Rome accords its more abundant dogmatic norms. By contrast, the status of creeds in Protestantism is not uniform, and in view of the Protestant appeal to the sole authority of scripture, it is often seen as a problem.

The followers of Martin Luther (1483–1546) wanted a common form of doctrine to which all the evangelical churches could be expected to subscribe. Their Formula of Concord (1577) drew an explicit parallel between the authoritative ancient symbols and their own Augsburg Confession (1530), "the symbol of our time." This raised questions about the relationship of the Augsburg Confession and other Lutheran symbols to the authority of scripture. The Formula drew a line between the word of God and postapostolic witness to it, but allegiance to the symbols presupposed that they were no more than summaries of scriptural truth required by the threat of false teaching. An identity of content was claimed between scripture as the *norma normans* and the Lutheran confessions as the *norma normata*, so that an actual critique of the Lutheran church's doctrine would appear to be, in principle, as hard to undertake from within as Luther found it to launch a critique of the Roman church's doctrine. Irreformability of the Lutheran church's dogmatic standpoint was implied in the assertion "We do not intend, either in this [the Formula of Concord] or in subsequent doctrinal statements, to depart from the aforementioned [Augsburg] Confession or to set up a different and new confession." Some of the Lutheran churches regard their *Book of Concord* (1580) as a now-closed collection of symbolic books: no subsequent statement, after 1580, could attain symbolic status. Others, however, never endorsed the Formula of Concord or, with it, the *Book of Concord*.

It is sometimes asserted that the authority of confessions is weaker in the Reformed church than in the Lutheran. But the historical evidence is ambivalent. On the one hand, the absence of a single preeminent confession and a closed symbolic collection among the Reformed does appear to invite continuous revision of their confessional stand. To this extent, an admission of reformability is tacitly built into Reformed confessionalism; and the authors of Reformed confessions have sometimes expressly disowned any exclusive claim for their particular terminology, or have invited correction if in any respect they should be found to have departed from the word of God. On the other hand, subscription to the prevailing local creed or creeds has commonly been demanded of pastors and sometimes of schoolteachers—or even of entire populations (as happened in Geneva in 1537). The history of the Westminster Confession (1647), the principal creed of the English-speaking Reformed (the "Presbyterians"), is particularly instructive. The Westminster Divines seem not to have wanted it to become the rule of faith and practice rather than a "help," but that is exactly how the Scots used it north of the border, and Scottish influence became paramount. The Presbyterian appetite for heresy trials presupposed that the Westminster Confession had a legal status not unlike that accorded by the Roman church to Roman Catholic dogmas.

An unmistakable shift can be observed within Protestantism when one moves from the Lutheran and Reformed churches to what may be broadly, if loosely, called the "free church" tradition. For instance, in their Savoy Declaration (1658) the Congregationalists adapted the Westminster Confession to their own use but they expressly disavowed any intention to bind consciences, since that would belie the very name and nature of confessions of faith and turn them into exactions and impositions of faith. Since 1970, Congregationalists have belonged to the World Alliance of Reformed Churches. But Congregationalism has generally, if not always, affirmed a descriptive rather than a normative view of creeds. They "declare, for general information, what is commonly believed among" Congregationalists (English Declaration, 1833). In this manner the agony of heresy hunts is avoided, but the more strictly confessional churches are likely to argue that the basic creedal function of preserving the community's identity is here in peril of being surrendered.

Churches that renounce the use of creeds altogether may differ from the confessional churches in little more than the refusal to commit their beliefs to formal, written definitions; they may in practice be just as intolerant of any deviations from the approved language of the community. If unwritten creeds are set aside, however, it may perhaps be concluded that there are three types of Protestant attitude to formulas of belief: a closed confessionalism that requires allegiance to a past symbol or a completed collection of symbols, an open confessionalism that calls for the drafting of present symbols of belief, and a purely descriptive confessionalism that denies to "human formularies" any binding or symbolic authority at all. While these three types appeared among the Lutherans, the Reformed, and the Congregationalists, respectively, they cannot be simply identified as denominational positions. All three communions have had a complex history of subscription controversies. And the three types do not exhaust the options. The Anglican communion, for example, understands itself largely as a worshiping community, and its leaders often point to *The Book of Common Prayer* (1662) and the historic episcopate rather than the Thirty-nine Articles (1563–1571) as the pledge of corporate identity.

ECUMENICAL CREEDS AND ECUMENICAL COUNCILS. In the New Testament, faith, confession, and salvation are inseparable (*Mt.* 10:32, *Rom.* 10:10). The simplest formula of Christian confession is the assertion that Jesus is Christ (*Mk.* 8:29) or Lord (*Rom.* 10:9, *1 Cor.* 12:3), and the Western text of *Acts* 8:37 evidently reflects early use of a similar formula ("Jesus Christ is the Son of God"; cf. *Mt.* 16:16) in connection with baptism. But it was the conviction of the early Christians that Jesus himself enjoined baptism in the triadic name of Father, Son, and Holy Spirit (*Mt.* 28:19), and summaries of Christian belief emerged, known as "rules of faith" but fluid in their wording, as the Christ-*kerygma* came to be incorporated into a triadic framework. Similar to them in basic structure, only more fixed in wording, two major families of creed developed, culminating in the Apostles' Creed in the West and the Nicene Creed in the East.

The Apostles' Creed. The legend that the twelve apostles themselves jointly composed the creed named after them, each in turn contributing one clause, was not seriously doubted before the critical labors of Lorenzo Valla (c. 1405–1457) and Reginald Pecock (c. 1393–c. 1461). In its present wording, the Apostles' Creed makes its first verifiable appearance in the West no earlier than the eighth century, in a treatise by the monk Pirminius (or Priminius, d. 753), and it has remained strictly a Western creed. But a long history certainly brought it to its final form. It is generally agreed that the historical roots of the Apostles' Creed are in the ancient baptismal confession of the Roman church, the "Old Roman Creed" (R), which Archbishop James Ussher (1581–1656) first attempted to reconstruct from Marcellus (d. around 374) and Rufinus.

More recent scholarship suggests that the earliest version of R was a Greek creed in interrogative form ("Do you believe . . .?") and that it dates back to about CE 200, when Greek was still in use in the Roman church. Behind it there probably lies a still earlier trinitarian confession, also of the interrogative type but without the Christ-*kerygma.* It may simply have asked the candidate for baptism: "Do you believe in God, the Father, Almighty? And in Christ Jesus, his only Son, our Lord? And in the Holy Ghost, the holy church, the resurrection of the body?" (Another explanation of the term *symbol* is that the triple interrogation was understood to be symbolic of the Trinity.) The insertion of the Christ-*kerygma* into this presumed early-Roman baptismal confession may have been encouraged by the need to refute docetism, the denial of Jesus' humanity. The received text of the Apostles' Creed makes the point cumulatively: Jesus was conceived, was born, suffered, "was crucified, dead, and buried." Finally, the shift to the declarative form ("I believe . . ."), which required recital from memory, perhaps was made initially in catechetical preparation for baptism, then carried over into the baptismal rite itself.

The Nicene Creed. Until modern times, it was traditionally assumed that the so-called Nicene Creed was the creed promulgated by the Council of Nicaea (325), as revised and endorsed by the Council of Constantinople (381). Especially since the researches of Eduard Schwartz (1858–1940), the tradition has been generally abandoned, but much scholarly disagreement remains. Perhaps tradition was right in linking the Nicene Creed with the Council of Constantinople; hence modern scholarship designates it "the Niceno-Constantinopolitan Creed" (C). But it does not seem to have been a mere revision of the creed promulgated at Nicaea (N); rather, the two creeds must be said to belong to a common Eastern type, as does the creed of Caesarea, which was once supposed to have been adopted at Nicaea as the first draft of N.

The Eastern creeds are distinguished from R by their greater interest in the preexistence of Christ before the incarnation: they place the Christ-*kerygma* in a cosmic setting. Hans Lietzmann (1875–1942) thought it was possible to reconstruct an Eastern or "Oriental" prototype (O) analogous to R, but it remains uncertain whether O, or something like it, actually existed as the model for other Eastern creeds. In any case, N advances beyond O in the attempt to exclude Arianism: it affirms that the Son of God was "God from God . . . of the same substance *[homoousion]* as the Father" and concludes with anathemas against the Arian watchwords (that there was a time when the Son was not, etc.). C, in turn, advances beyond N in affirming, against the Macedonian heresy, the equality of the Holy Spirit with the Father and the Son, although the technical term *homoousios* is not used of the Spirit as well. Some time in the sixth or seventh century, the word *filioque* was inserted into the Latin text of C, so that the Holy Spirit was said to proceed from the Father *and the Son.* The insertion became a bone of contention between Rome and the Eastern churches, which firmly rejected it.

The Nicene Creed (C) came to be used liturgically in the Eastern church in both baptism and the Eucharist; in the West it was adopted as the eucharistic confession. The creed of Nicaea (N), by contrast, was designed not for instruction or worship but as a test of orthodoxy, which could be invoked even against a bishop of the church. In this respect, the Council of Nicaea marked a new stage in creedal history: its creed was the first to be promulgated by an ecumenical council with a claim to universal authority throughout the entire church.

The Athanasian Creed. The so-called Creed of Saint Athanasius (also known as the Quicunque Vult, from its opening words in Latin) was probably composed in southern France during or after the post-Nicene debates on the incarnation. After the Council of Nicaea, theological interest shifted from the eternal relations of Father, Son, and Spirit within the divine Trinity to the relationship between the divine and human natures of the incarnate Son. Arianism, now officially condemned, was succeeded by the Apollinarian, Nestorian, and Eutychian heresies. While the provenance of the Athanasian Creed can be inferred from the evidence of its earliest use and influence, the date assigned to it depends chiefly on the answer to the question which of the three christological heresies it was intended to oppose. It was indeed argued by Daniel Waterland (1683–1740) that even its statements on the doctrine of the Trinity require a date no earlier than 420, because they reflect the language of Augustine's (354–430) trinitarian speculations. In any case, the Christological statements almost certainly allude not only to Apollinarianism but also to Nestorianism, possibly to Eutychianism; and the three heresies were condemned respectively at the councils of Constantinople (381), Ephesus (431), and Chalcedon (451). The attribution of the creed to Athanasius, who died in 373, is clearly impossible and was already discredited in the seventeenth century by Gerrit Jansz Voss (1577–1649). Alternative suggestions have been made; perhaps the most persuasive case points to Lérins, the island abbey opposite Cannes, as "the cradle of the creed" (J. N. D. Kelly), and someone close to Vincent of Lérins (d. around 450) and Caesarius of Arles (d. 542) as its author.

The first part of the Athanasian Creed presents the doctrine of the Trinity, and the second part places the Christ-*kerygma* in the protective setting of propositions against the christological heresies. Although the creed came to be sung regularly in the West, it most likely originated not as a hymn but as a form of instruction for clergy; and its technical, metaphysical, and threatening style has gradually reduced its liturgical use. In the East it was unknown until the twelfth century and never won very high regard. The Chalcedonian definition, though never added to the number of the ecumenical symbols, actually enjoys wider authority as a defense against christological heresy because of its association with an ecumenical council.

Recognition of the creeds and councils. Most of the major churches recognize the ecumenical creeds and councils insofar as they present fundamental Christian beliefs about God and Christ. But only the Nicene Creed can fully claim the rank of ecumenical symbol, and it is unfortunate that its significance is tarnished by debate over the *filioque* insertion. Ecumenical status is assigned by the Eastern Orthodox church to seven councils: two of Nicaea (325, 787), three of Constantinople (381, 553, 680), Ephesus, and Chalcedon. The Roman church claims ecumenical rank also for its own synods, the last of which, Vatican II (1962–1965), was counted the twenty-first ecumenical council; and Rome considers the decrees of an ecumenical council to be "an infallible witness to the Catholic rule of faith." Protestants tend to single out the first four "general councils" as especially worthy of reverence, but deny that their decrees are in principle infallible; rather, they are to be tested by the word of God.

LUTHERAN AND REFORMED CONFESSIONS. The Protestant confessions of the Reformation era were intended to restore to the church its true image and identity, which, it was widely agreed, had been obscured by the errors and abuses of the later Middle Ages. The heart of the Reformation creeds is the rediscovery of the gospel as, in Luther's memorable phrase, "the real treasure of the church." The church, Luther held, is the creation of the gospel; it is the word of God in Jesus Christ that makes the church the church. And he believed that the church's confession of the divinity of Christ was fatally impaired wherever this gospel was displaced or misconstrued.

Lutheran confessions. Of the ten symbols included in the Lutheran *Book of Concord*, the first three are the ecumenical creeds; the rest, in chronological order of publication, are Luther's Large and Small Catechisms (1529), the Augsburg Confession, Philipp Melanchthon's (1497–1560) *Apology for the Augsburg Confession* (1531), Luther's Smalcald Articles (1537), Melanchthon's *Treatise on the Power and Primacy of the Pope* (1537), and the Formula of Concord. Among the distinctively Lutheran symbols, all German in origin, the Augsburg Confession holds a special place. Lutheranism was granted legal recognition by the Peace of Augsburg (1555) as "the religion of the Augsburg Confession." The spread of Lutheranism beyond Germany always meant adoption of this confession, and the Formula of Concord itself claimed to be simply the correct and final explanation of it in response to certain inner-Lutheran controversies.

The confession was presented to Emperor Charles V on June 25, 1530, at the Diet of Augsburg (whence the name by which it is familiarly known). Although earlier documents by other hands lay behind it, in its final form its principal author was Melanchthon, whose ecclesiastical strategy it reflects. According to the Formula of Concord, the Augsburg Confession "distinguishes our reformed churches from the papacy and from other condemned sects and heresies." But that by no means conveys the author's intention. He was certainly eager to disown the Zwinglians and the Anabaptists, but precisely in order to confirm the essential Lutheran agreement with Rome. The confession (or "apology," as it was initially called) set out to accomplish two goals: to defend the catholicity of Lutheran doctrine and to justify the innovations in Lutheran practice. Part one (arts. 1–21), the confession of faith proper, contains a summary of the doctrines taught in the Lutheran churches. It claims to present the faith of the catholic church, not of a particular Lutheran church, and it insists that there can be no disagreement with Rome if Rome's teaching, too, conforms to antiquity. The contention is not over articles of faith but over a few usages, and these are taken up in part two (arts. 22–28), which lies outside the confession of faith in the strict sense.

Melanchthon's design required the suppression of several controversial issues, including the authority of scripture, papal primacy, and the priesthood of all believers. How well he succeeded is open to question, but it is significant that in 1980, when the 450th anniversary of his confession was celebrated, there were widespread discussions between Roman Catholic and Lutheran theologians on the possibility that Rome might recognize the Augsburg Confession as a catholic confession. Still, it is undeniable that the confession bears a distinctively Lutheran stamp precisely in the regulative place it assigns to the gospel, understood as the message of justification through faith without any merits of our own. It is this "chief article" that provides one implicit definition of an "abuse" for part two of the confession: any usage implying that grace can be earned is an abuse (art. 15). The same chief article constitutes the actual core of part one, shaping the doctrines of church, ministry, and sacraments as well as the Lutheran understanding of the Christian life, neighborly love, and the earthly callings.

It is not surprising that the Roman Catholic critics of the confession, while they welcomed the affirmation of the real presence in the Eucharist (art. 10), found uncatholic the pivotal notion that the sacraments in general are testimonies of God's good will for the purpose of arousing faith, that is, the faith through which we are justified (art. 13). Sacraments are thereby interpreted (or reinterpreted) as functions of the word of God, forms of the gospel proclamation; and the entire medieval conception of the church and its ministry is transformed accordingly. This was one strictly doctrinal issue that lay behind the Lutheran charge, in part two of the confession (art. 24), that it is an abuse to celebrate the Mass as a sacrifice for sin. It would be unfair to conclude (as has sometimes been done) that Melanchthon was devious or naive. The point, rather, is that his concern was to reaffirm the gospel of grace without letting the Lutheran reform rend the unity of the catholic church.

The Reformed confessions. Unlike the Lutherans, the Reformed churches of the sixteenth and seventeenth centuries were not held together by a single confession of faith. Though they often acknowledged one another's confessions—sometimes even the Lutheran Augsburg Confession—in general each national or regional church drew up its own standard or standards of belief. The most comprehensive collection of Reformed creeds (E. F. K. Müller, 1903) contains fifty-eight items, and the editor remarks that the number could be doubled without achieving completeness. Other individual collections have appeared from time to time, but none has ever acquired, or could have acquired, ecclesiastical endorsement as the Reformed "Book of Concord." It was a new departure—and the act of only one branch of the Reformed family—when the United Presbyterian Church in the United States of America in 1967 authorized its *Book of Confessions*, a selection of Reformed creeds of international origin. In the 1983 edition, the *Book of Confessions* of what had become the Presbyterian Church (USA) included six documents from the Reformation era (along with the Nicene and Apostles' creeds and two twentieth-century confessions): the Scots Confession (1560), the Heidelberg Catechism (1563), the Second Helvetic Confession (1566), the Westminster Confession (rev. ed., 1958), and the two Westminster Catechisms (1647). None of these six creeds stands very close to John Calvin (1509–1564), an omission that could be remedied with the French (Gallican) Confession of 1559, perhaps the outstanding Reformed creed of the declarative type. Originally conceived as an apology of the persecuted French Protestants to the king of France, the confession was not a creed for theologians only but a confession of the church, and it came to be printed inside the Bibles and Psalters of the French Reformed congregations.

Dogmatic uniformity is hardly to be expected throughout the total Reformed *corpus confessionum*, and no one confession can be taken as regulative for them all. But they were first and foremost, like other Protestant confessions, "evangelical"—that is, reaffirmations of the gospel of Christ, or (what for them was the same thing) of the lordship of Christ, as alone constitutive of the church's identity. This is particularly clear in the documents from the early years. The very first Reformed confession, the Sixty-seven Articles (1523) of Huldrych Zwingli (1484–1531), sounds the characteristic note in its opening assertions (cf. Ten Theses of Bern, 1528; Lausanne Articles, 1536). In subsequent confessions the primacy of the gospel comes to be set in a more systematic framework, but it is still affirmed, either within the confessions (e.g., First Helvetic Confession, 1536, art. 12; cf. art. 5) or in preambles to them (e.g., the French and Scots confessions), and serves as the constant norm for sifting out truth from error in the prevailing beliefs and practices of the church.

The dogma of double predestination, sometimes imagined to be the center of Reformed or Calvinistic theology, is not emphasized in the sixteenth-century confessions; in some (e.g., the First Helvetic Confession and the Heidelberg Catechism) it is not even mentioned. If one looks for a distinctively Reformed emphasis, it might more plausibly be located in the concern for the order, discipline, and worship of the church. The "parity of presbyters" (i.e., the equality of all ordained clergy in rank) and the need for elders to assist the pastors in maintaining discipline are expressly included in some of the confessions—apparently as matters of faith. But here too the fundamental principle is the sole lordship of Christ, the only universal bishop of the church, the ever-present and life-giving head of the body, who needs no "vicar" (French Confession, arts. 29–30; Scots Confession, chap. 16; Belgic Confession [1561], art. 31; Second Helvetic Confession, chap. 17; etc.). And the same line of thinking prevents Zwingli's memorialist conception of the Lord's Supper, which occasioned the breach with Lutheranism, from intruding into the major Reformed confessions. In the Lord's Supper the living and present Lord feeds and strengthens his people "with the substance of his body and of his blood" (French Confession, art. 36; cf. Scots Confession, chap. 21, Second Helvetic Confession, chap. 21, and so on).

OTHER CREEDS OF THE REFORMATION ERA. Besides the Lutherans and the Reformed, other non-Roman churches in the West produced statements of belief during the Reformation era. The Church of England had its Thirty-nine Articles, the Unitarians their Racovian Catechism (1605), the Mennonites their Dordrecht Confession (1632); the Congregationalists, the Baptists, and even the Quakers continued to add to the confessional literature of the earlier Reformation. But none of these groups has invested its statements with the doctrinal authority the Lutherans and the Reformed accord to theirs; most of them would say that their confessions are for instruction, not for subscription. Sometimes the new statements borrowed freely from the old. Already in the sixteenth century the Thirty-nine Articles were largely derived from continental Protestantism, and in the following century the Congregationalists and the Baptists (both "Particular" and "General" Baptists) made their own recensions of the Presbyterian Westminster Confession, as John Wesley (1703–1791) was later to make a Methodist recension of the Anglican articles (the Twenty-five Articles of 1784).

Eastern Orthodox churches. The Eastern churches remained aloof, as far as possible, from the Reformation crisis, judging it to be an internal problem of the Western church. Some exchange did take place, however, and it generated more or less official Orthodox responses to Protestantism. Most important among them was the Confession of Dosítheos, issued by the Synod of Jerusalem (1672) to combat the Calvinizing opinions advanced by, or attributed to, Cyril I (Kyrillos Loukaris, 1572–1638), former patriarch of Constantinople. It is generally assumed that the patriarch of Jerusalem, Dosítheos (1641–1707), was the principal author of the confession, which constitutes chapter 6 of the synod's decrees. He avoided Roman Catholic doctrines and practices that Orthodoxy does not accept (papal supremacy, the celibacy of all clergy, withholding the cup from the laity) and took essentially the same stand as Rome against the Protestant views of authority and justification. The Calvinist doctrine of the Eucharist is opposed (decree 17) not only by affirming a propitiatory sacrifice but also by borrowing the Latin idea of transubstantiation.

In addition to promulgating its own confession, the Synod of Jerusalem endorsed the earlier replies of Jeremias II (c. 1530–1595), patriarch of Constantinople, to overtures from the Lutheran theologians of Tübingen. The replies (published in 1584) rejected the distinctive doctrines of the Augsburg Confession on everything except the marriage of priests. The synod also gave its sanction to a catechism drafted (c. 1640) partly in opposition to the Calvinizers by Petr Moghila (1596–1647), metropolitan of Kiev, which was probably the most influential witness to the Orthodox faith of the Greek and Russian churches until superseded in 1839 by the Catechism of Filaret (1782–1867), metropolitan of Moscow. But neither Filaret's catechism nor the documents promulgated or endorsed by the Synod of Jerusalem have the same authority in Eastern Orthodoxy as the Nicene Creed, which commended itself all the more because it was safe from the conflict in the Western church. Insofar as the Eastern church faced the Reformation at all, it has usually considered its responses to be strictly contextual; use of the Latin dogma of transubstantiation, for example, in the Confession of Dosítheos did not make it an Orthodox dogma.

The Roman Catholic Church. The Roman church, by contrast, produced its most comprehensive standard of belief (until that time) precisely in response to the Protestant Reformation. In 1545, fifteen years after the Diet of Augsburg, the long-hoped-for council that was to settle the religious questions was finally convened at Trent. Its last session took place in 1563, eighteen years later. The Orthodox and the Protestants were not represented, but Trent is considered by the church of Rome to be the nineteenth ecumenical council. (The Lutherans were invited, and delegates from Saxony and Württemberg did appear briefly in the spring of 1552, but they could be received only as errant children of the church, which had condemned Luther three decades before.) The canons and decrees of the Council of Trent were published in their entirety in 1564. Not all twenty-five sessions produced decrees on doctrine. Those that did were mainly interested in three matters of faith: authority, justification, and the sacraments.

After adopting the Nicene Creed as its confession of faith and shield against heresies (sess. 3), the council proceeded to specify the two witnesses to which it would appeal in confirming dogmas and restoring morals in the church: scripture and unwritten traditions (sess. 4). The express concern of Trent, like that of the Protestants, was for "the purity of the gospel." But there could be no question of appealing to the gospel against the traditions or teaching of the church. For the truths of the gospel, according to Trent, are contained both in scripture and in the unwritten traditions handed down from the apostles; both are to be received with the same devout reverence. And the scriptures themselves are not to be interpreted by anyone's private judgment contrary to the sense that holy mother church has held and holds.

It did not follow that the Roman church wished to stand behind the practices and beliefs that the Protestant confessions had judged to be violations of the gospel. Trent did reject the Lutheran protest in principle, and it could not accept the Lutheran inventory of abuses without discrimination. But in its decrees on reform the council inaugurated a Catholic reformation, which dealt extensively with many of the alleged abuses, eradicating some and purging others. And in its decrees on doctrine it defined positions that cannot be simply identified with positions the Lutherans and the Reformed had attacked. In particular, the decree on justification (sess. 6), which took seven months to complete, seems to deny forthrightly the very opinion against which the Lutherans had most vehemently protested: that the grace of justification can be merited (chap. 8). Trent's denial of merit before justification has been the subject of divided interpretation among twentieth-century historians, and in any case other confessional differences concerning justification, or possible differences, certainly remain, but the dividing lines are not as sharp as sixteenth-century polemics made them out to be. The same holds true for sacramental theology.

Among the controverted sacramental issues, none ranks higher in importance than the debate over the sacrificial character of the Mass. Both the Lutheran confessions (e.g., Augsburg Confession, art. 24) and the Reformed confessions (e.g., Scots Confession, art. 22) presumed that in the Roman Mass the priest was credited with sacrificing Christ to appease God. The Mass, they alleged, therefore detracted from Christ's self-sacrifice on the cross and violated the heart of the gospel—that grace is not obtained through human works. The language of the Tridentine response (sess. 22) is neither uniform nor wholly transparent. But no competition between cross and altar is implied. The once-for-all offering on the cross is said to be "represented" in the Mass and its benefits applied to daily sins, "so far is the latter from derogating in any way from the former" (chaps. 1–2). And though the sacrifice of the Mass is carried out "by the church through the priests," the decree adds: ". . . the same now offering by the ministry of priests who then offered himself on the cross" (chaps. 1–2).

Confessional legacy of the Reformation. The Tridentine decrees must be seen in relation to subsequent dogmatic pronouncements of the Roman Catholic Church, especially the constitutions of the First and Second Vatican Councils (1869–1870; 1962–1965). But the confessional legacy of the Reformation era appears less totally and irrevocably divisive than might be supposed. Just as the Reformed confessions did not perpetuate the Zwinglian sacramental views that the Lutherans found so offensive, so also the Tridentine decrees did not simply immortalize the errors and abuses with which the Protestants charged the late medieval church. And a more irenic age would have to ask, in turn, how just were the Tridentine anathemas hurled against the Protestants.

CHRISTIAN CREEDS IN THE MODERN WORLD. Although the Reformation era may be singled out as the most productive period of Christian creed-making, dogmas have continued to be defined and confessions drafted down to the present time. The Roman church's dogmas of the Immaculate Conception (1854), papal infallibility (1870), and the Assumption of the Virgin Mary (1950) were important developments of traditional Roman Catholic beliefs about Mary and the papacy. Other creedal statements have been self-conscious attempts to rethink confessional positions in the modern world. But it is also during the last three centuries that the very idea of a creed has become most precarious.

Modern anticreedalism. The problem of what may be termed "anticreedalism" has naturally made itself felt more especially in Protestantism. From the first, even the most staunchly confessional of the Protestant churches, the Lutheran, was not entirely of one mind about its symbolic books. Distinctions were made between one confession and another, and not all the Lutheran bodies adopted the Formula of Concord. Moreover, in the non-Lutheran churches there was a tendency to contrast all human formularies much more sharply with the divinely inspired scriptures. Modern anticreedalism, however, has other roots besides biblicism. Most important is the drift toward a less dogmatic variety of Christian religion. With roots in sixteenth-century humanism and antitrinitarianism and in seventeenth-century Arminianism, aversion to distinctively Christian dogmas flourished in English Deism and was nurtured by the theologians of the German Enlightenment. In the course of the eighteenth century, Protestant orthodoxy, already weakened by Pietism, retreated before enlightened disdain for inherited superstitions and dogmatic particularism. Friedrich Schleiermacher (1768–1834) tried to deal more sympathetically with the old creeds as authentic, though reformable, deliverances of the Christian consciousness. But the resurgence of Lutheran confessionalism in the early nineteenth century was directed against Schleiermacher as well as against the rationalists, and it was carried by German immigrants to the New World.

By the end of the nineteenth century, the beleaguered antidogmatic line in Protestant theology found new resources in the work of Ritschlian church historian Adolf von Harnack (1851–1930), who argued with massive erudition that Christian orthodoxy arose as a corruption of the gospel by Hellenic metaphysics and intellectualism. Dogmas, as he put it, are "a work of the Greek spirit on the soil of the gospel"; by them, confidence in the Father God of Jesus is transformed into intellectual assent to metaphysical propositions about the inner life of the godhead and the two natures of the incarnate Son. From this standpoint, Harnack considered himself free to subject even the Apostles' Creed to detailed criticism and to oppose its continued use as a legal ordinance.

Strictly speaking, Harnack and the liberal Protestants who rallied around him did not want to abolish the Apostles' Creed, or creeds in general. Harnack in fact made a classic case for what we have termed "open confessionalism." While he deplored what he saw as the "catholicizing" of Lutheranism, he judged the opposite demand for a totally undogmatic Christianity to be a mistake. The church's task, he believed, was not to dispense with creeds but to add a new creed to the old. "Upon the path of the old Creeds we must remain," he wrote. "Satisfied with them we cannot be. The entanglements of history divide us from them."

The objection is sometimes made that such a program, despite the disavowals, abrogates the entire notion of a creed: a temporary dogma is no dogma at all, and adoption of a new confession is tacit denial of the old. But in the centuries that separate the Reformation from the present, another danger, more surely fatal to the life of a confessing church, has become increasingly clear: an old creed may be retained only as a sacred relic, a token of outward conformity, to be invoked on rare occasions for some shibboleth that it conveniently enshrines—and not as the living confession of a church. And there is a growing readiness among Christians of every communion, even among those who do not object either to creeds in principle or to the specific dogmas of the traditional creeds, to admit that every confession of faith is conditioned by the circumstances of its historical origin, and none is therefore likely to serve as the sufficient confession of another day. This admission has made it easier in practice for the churches to reappraise the historic creeds of other traditions, while accepting the responsibility to add to their own.

Modern creeds. Four twentieth-century documents represent the continued activity of Christian creed-making in the modern world. Two of them address specific political and social crises by reaffirming, sharpening, and applying elements already present in the confessional tradition: the lordship of Christ (the original Christian confession), and reconciliation through Christ, respectively. The Barmen Declaration (1934) was adopted by a synod of representatives from the Lutheran, Reformed, and United churches in Germany to address the crisis of National Socialism. Largely inspired by Karl Barth (1886–1968), it was the response of the Confessing church to the so-called German Christians. Its six terse affirmations and corresponding condemnations asserted the sole lordship of Jesus Christ, the one word of God, over every area of life against the encroachments of the Nazi state and its *Führer*. Broader in scope, but still a declaration rather than a comprehensive confession of faith, the Confession of 1967 was adopted by the United Presbyterian Church in the USA to reaffirm the message of reconciliation and bring it to bear on four urgent social issues: racial discrimination, international conflict, enslaving poverty, and alienation between the sexes.

The opening message (1962) of the Second Vatican Council also singled out two issues as especially urgent: peace between peoples and social justice. But the council's sixteen dogmatic constitutions, decrees, and declarations are not a response to a particular crisis or to critical issues; they are a broad and detailed attempt at an "updating" (*aggiornamento*) of the Roman church's entire stand in the twentieth century—her self-understanding and her relationships with other Christian groups, the non-Christian religions, and the whole human community. They call for all Christians and men of goodwill to join the Catholic Church in "building up a more just and brotherly city in the world." In issuing this call, the council made up for an omission in the work of Trent and for what many Roman Catholics perceive as one-sidedness in the work of the First Vatican Council.

The Council of Trent did not undertake to define the nature of the church at all; differences among the fathers themselves made any such venture impolitic. The First Vatican Council, on the other hand, which Rome counts as the twentieth ecumenical council, did produce a Constitution on the Church of Christ (1870), but it was concerned exclusively with the primacy of the pope and with his infallibility when he defines a doctrine concerning faith or morals. Vatican II, especially in its Dogmatic Constitution on the Church (*Lumen gentium*, 1964), presents a much fuller doctrine of the church, in biblical rather than juridical language. The hierarchical structure of the church and the primacy of the pope are reaffirmed. But Vatican II places a stronger emphasis than Vatican I on the regular and collective, or "collegial," office of all the bishops in communion with the pope, and it takes "the church" to mean the whole body of the Lord, the people of God, laity as well as clergy. All the faithful in their several ways share in the priestly, prophetic, and kingly functions of Christ. By her relationship with Christ, the church is a kind of sacrament—that is, a sign and instrument—of union with God and the unity of all humankind. Not only the Catholic faithful but all who believe in Christ are in some way united with this people of God in the Holy Spirit, who is operative among them too with his sanctifying power.

Finally, the Lima Document on Baptism, Eucharist, and Ministry (1982), which approaches the creedal type of a union statement, may serve as a useful indication of the consensus and dissensus between the inherited confessional positions at the present time. Ecumenical dialogue has repeatedly shown the possibility of agreement on traditionally divisive issues, including the doctrines of justification and the sacraments. The Lima Document, produced for the Commission on Faith and Order of the World Council of Churches by representatives of all the major confessional traditions (including Roman Catholics, who have no official participation in the World Council itself), faces some of the most divisive issues of all. Its main text establishes a large measure of agreement, mainly by appeal to the common biblical heritage, and the additional commentaries indicate the differences that either have been overcome or are still in need of further discussion. Even on two of the most intractable differences—between infant and believer baptism, and between episcopal and nonepiscopal ministry—the way is pointed out toward mutual recognition as a step in the direction of greater unity of doctrine, order, and practice. It has thus become a dominant concern of modern Christian creed-making, not only to meet the political, social, and intellectual problems of the day but also to reverse the tendency of the sixteenth- and seventeenth-century creeds toward inflexibility and separation.

See Also Councils, article on Christian Councils; Theology, article on Christian Theology.

BIBLIOGRAPHY

Despite its age (it was first published in 1877), the best resource for the study of Christian creeds and confessions is still Philip Schaff's monumental *Bibliotheca Symbolica Ecclesiae Universalis: The Creeds of Christendom, with a History and Critical Notes,* 6th ed., 3 vols. (New York, 1931), which has been reissued (Grand Rapids, Mich., 1983). *The Faith of Christendom: A Source Book of Creeds and Confessions,* edited by myself (Cleveland, 1963), is a modest introduction to symbolics (the study of creeds) through analysis of the ecumenical creeds and six documents from the Reformation period. *Creeds of the Churches: A Reader in Christian Doctrine, from the Bible to the Present,* edited by John H. Leith, first published the same year (1963), includes many more documents with shorter historical introductions, and the third, revised edition (Atlanta, 1982) contains important additions from the intervening two decades. All three of these general works provide further bibliographical guidance.

The standard English work on the ecumenical symbols is J. N. D. Kelly's *Early Christian Creeds,* 3d ed. (New York, 1972). Kelly is also the editor and translator of Rufinus's *A Commentary on the Apostles' Creed,* "Ancient Christian Writers," vol. 20 (Westminster, Md., 1955), and he has published a separate study of the third of the ecumenical symbols (barely mentioned in *Early Christian Creeds*), *The Athanasian Creed* (New York, 1964).

The best English edition of the Lutheran confessions is *The Book of Concord: The Confessions of the Evangelical Lutheran Church,* translated and edited by Theodore G. Tappert and others (Philadelphia, 1959). A useful collection of Reformed creeds in English is *Reformed Confessions of the Sixteenth Century,* edited by Arthur C. Cochrane (Philadelphia, 1966). The seventeenth-century Westminster standards are included in *The Constitution of the Presbyterian Church (USA.),* part 1, *Book of Confessions* (New York, 1983). For free-church creeds, see Williston Walker's *The Creeds and Platforms of Congregationalism* (1893; reprint, Boston, 1960); W. J. McGlothlin's *Baptist Confessions of Faith* (Philadelphia, 1911); and William L. Lumpkin's *Baptist Confessions of Faith* (Chicago, 1959). An able commentary on the *Book of Concord* is Edmund Schlink's *Theology of the Lutheran Confessions* (Philadelphia, 1961). Nothing comparable is available in English on Reformed creeds, but a useful symposium, occasioned by the proposal for the new Presbyterian Confession of 1967 and published as an issue of *McCormick Quarterly* (vol. 19, no. 2, January 1966), provides extensive guidance on the corpus, theological character, and function of the Reformed confessions.

For the reasons indicated, one cannot point to any collection of Eastern Orthodox symbols. A translation of the Confession of Dosítheos was given in *The Acts and Decrees of the Synod of Jerusalem,* translated and edited by J. N. W. B. Robertson (London, 1899), and is reproduced in both Leith's and my work. An English version of the Catechism of Filaret will be found in Schaff. The Roman Catholic Church, by contrast, has a semiofficial collection of authorized symbols, including the doctrinal decrees of Trent, in Heinrich Denzinger's *Enchiridion symbolorum,* translated from the thirtieth edition by Roy J. Deferrari as *The Sources of Catholic Dogma* (Saint Louis, 1957). The most important guide to Trent is Hubert Jedin's history, *Geschichte des Konzils von Trient,* 4 vols. in 5 (Freiburg, 1959–1975). The translation by Ernest Graf, *A History of the Council of Trent* (Saint Louis, 1957–), is unfortunately still incomplete.

Harnack's position on the modern use of creeds is succinctly outlined in his somewhat neglected writing, *Thoughts on the Present Position of Protestantism* (London, 1899). Reappraisal of creeds across the confessional divide may be illustrated from the discussions of the Augsburg Confession as a catholic document in *The Role of the Augsburg Confession: Catholic and Lutheran Views,* edited by Joseph A. Burgess (Philadelphia, 1980), and *Augsburgisches Bekenntnis im ökumenischen Kontext,* edited by Harding Meyer (Stuttgart, 1980). The Barmen Declaration will be found in Cochrane, Leith, and the Presbyterian *Book of Confessions.* For the complete text of the Confession of 1967, see the *Book of Confessions* or *Reformed Witness Today: A Collection of Confessions and Statements of Faith Issued by Reformed Churches,* edited by Lukas Vischer (Bern, 1982). Denzinger-Deferrari includes the Marian dogmas of 1854 and 1950 and the dogmatic constitutions of Vatican I, but does not reach Vatican II, for which see *The Documents of Vatican II,* edited by Walter M. Abbott (New York, 1966). Leith reproduces the Lima Document in his third edition.

New Sources

Pelikan, Jaroslav, and Valerie Hotchkiss. *Creeds and Confessions of Faith in the Christian Tradition.* 4 vols. New Haven, Conn., 2003.

Stevenson, James, and W. H. C. Frend, eds. *Creeds, Councils and Controversies: Documents Illustrating the History of the Church, A.D. 337–461.* Rev. ed. London, 1989.

Westra, Liuwe H. *The Apostle's Creed: Origin, History, and Some Early Commentaries.* Turnhout, Belgium, 2002.

Young, Frances M. *The Making of the Creeds.* London and Philadelphia, 1991.

B. A. GERRISH (1987)
Revised Bibliography

CREEDS: ISLAMIC CREEDS

An *ʿaqīdah* is an Islamic creed or creedal statement; the plural, *ʿaqāʾid* ("articles of belief"), is used in a similar sense. Since there is no Islamic body corresponding to the Christian ecumenical councils, Islamic creeds do not have the official status of the Christian creeds and thus are not used liturgically. What might be regarded as an exception to these assertions is the Shahādah, or confession of faith ("There is no deity except God; Muḥammad is the messenger of God"), which is universally accepted by Muslims and is repeated in the formal worship or prayers (*ṣalāt*). The Shahādah is not generally regarded as an *ʿaqīdah,* however, though it might be considered the basis of all later creeds. The terms *ʿaqīdah* and *ʿaqāʾid* are applied to works of greatly varying length, ranging from those with fewer than a dozen lines to voluminous theological treatises.

THE DEVELOPMENT OF THE ISLAMIC CREEDS. Although they hold no ecumenical councils, the Sunnīs, who are the great majority of all Muslims, have come to a large measure of agreement about the articles of belief through informal consensus. Each legal/theological school, and notably the Ḥanafī and Ḥanbalī schools, has developed creeds which the school has accepted and often attributed to its founder, even when the composition might date from several centuries later. The various subdivisions of Shīʿī Islam have also produced their creedal statements, as have some of the minor sects.

The process by which the Sunnī creed was elaborated is similar to that in Christianity, namely through argument against the views of some believers which were felt to be heretical by the main body of believers. Among the views excluded by the Sunnīs were the Shīʿī belief that the prophet Muḥammad had designated ʿAlī to succeed him and that each of the following (Shīʿī) imams had been similarly designated by his predecessor, the Khārijī belief that a person who commits a grave sin is thereby excluded from the community, and the Muʿtazilī belief that human acts are independent of God's control.

The Main Doctrines of the Sunnī Islamic Creed. The following are the main articles of belief accepted by Sunnīs, though the wording does not follow any specific creed. The order is roughly that of the Ḥanafī creed (found in Wensinck, 1932); comments have been added.

1. *God is one and unique in the sense that there is no deity other than God; he has neither partner nor associate, and neither begets nor is begotten.* This is the first clause in the Shahādah and also appears in the Qurʾān, though not in the earliest portions. *Allāh* is the Arabic word for God, used also by Arabic-speaking Christians, but some of Muḥammad's contemporaries recognized Allāh as a "high god" alongside other deities. It is against such people, and polytheists in general, that this article emphasizes the uniqueness of God, which became one of the distinctive features of Islam.

2. *He has been from all eternity and will be to all eternity with all his names and attributes.* These attributes may be essential or active (attributes pertaining to activity): among the former are life, power (or omnipotence), knowledge (or omniscience), speech, hearing, sight, and will; and among the latter, creating, sustaining (with food), giving life, and raising (from the dead). All these attributes are eternal; they are not God and yet not other than God. The Qurʾān frequently applies names to God, such as the Merciful, the Forgiving, the Creator, the Knowing. Ninety-nine such "beautiful names" are commonly recognized and used in devotions. The theologians held that God possesses the qualities or attributes (*ṣifāt*) corresponding to these names, as the quality of mercy corresponds to "the Merciful." The seven essential attributes listed above were much discussed by theologians in the third and fourth centuries AH (ninth and tenth centuries CE). Some, especially the Muʿtazilah, held that the attributes are not distinct from God's essence, so that, for example, he might be said to know by his essence; others held that the attributes have a hypostatic character (not unlike the three hypostases of the Christian Trinity), so that it is by his knowledge rather than his essence that God knows. The latter view, which made allowance for the special position of the Qurʾān as God's attribute of speech, came to be the standard Sunnī position and was accepted by the Ashʿarīyah, the Māturīdīyah, and others. With regard to the active attributes, the Ashʿarīyah held that these are not eternal, since, for example, God cannot be creator until he has created. The Māturīdīyah, on the other hand, held that these names and attributes apply to God eternally. There was also some discussion, especially in later times, when there was greater familiarity with philosophical ideas, as to whether existence, eternity, and the like were to be regarded as attributes.

3. *God created the world and all that is in it; he did not create things from any preexisting thing.* God's creation of the world *ex nihilo* is always implied in the creeds, although it is not always stated explicitly.

4. *God is unlike all created things: he is neither body nor substance nor accident (of a substance); he has no spatial limit or position.* Nevertheless, as the Qurʾān indicates, he has two hands, two eyes, and a face, and he is seated on the throne. The otherness and, in this sense, transcendence of God are clearly expressed in the Qurʾān ("No thing is like him" [42:11]), and this point received much emphasis in later times. It was a serious problem for the theologians to reconcile this otherness of God with the anthropomorphisms in the Qurʾān, which include not merely such terms as *hands* and *face*, but also most of the names and attributes. Some of those who insisted on the otherness and incorporeality of God, like the Muʿtazilah, held that the anthropomorphic terms were to be understood metaphorically, and they called those who understood them literally *mushabbihah* ("those who make [God] resemble [humanity]"). Most Sunnī theologians, following Aḥmad ibn Ḥanbal, said they were to be accepted *bi-lā kayf*, or "amodally" (literally "without [asking] how [they were to be understood]"), that is, neither literally nor metaphorically. Some later Ashʿarī theologians allowed metaphorical interpretation, within limits however.

5. *The Qurʾān, as it is written down, remembered, and recited, is the speech of God and uncreated.* Our writing and reciting of it, however, are created. This matter was the subject of violent discussions in the ninth century. In the so-called inquisition (*miḥnah*) begun by Caliph al-Maʾmūn around 833, prominent jurists and other officials were obliged to state publicly that they believed the Qurʾān to be the created speech of God. Among those who refused to make the profession was Aḥmad ibn Ḥanbal, and for a time he was the main defender of the uncreatedness of the Qurʾān. The point at issue seems to have been that, if the Qurʾān is created, God could have created it otherwise, and so it is not unthinkable that the caliph, if regarded as inspired by God, could alter its rules. On the other hand, if it is uncreated, it expresses something of God's being and cannot be humanly altered; this implies that the final decision about the application of Qurʾanic rules to practical matters is in the hands, not of the caliph, but of the accredited interpreters of the

Qur'ān, namely the *ʿulamā'*, or religious scholars. The Shīʿah, who believe their imams are inspired, still hold the Qur'ān to be created, but since the end of the inquisition around 850, the Sunnīs have adhered firmly to the doctrine of the uncreatedness of the Qur'ān.

6. *God's will is supreme, and he controls all mundane events. No good or evil comes about on earth except as God wills, but although he wills all events, good and evil, he does not command or approve what is evil. Actions are good or bad, not in themselves, but because God commands or forbids them; he could, if he so willed, change what is good and bad. Human acts are created by God and "acquired" by the individual.* Belief in the absolute sovereignty of God (for which there are precedents in the Bible and in pre-Islamic Arabia) enabled Muslims to face life with assurance, knowing that no disaster could happen to them unless God willed it. The Muʿtazilī assertion of human free will was seen to threaten God's sovereignty, and so many Sunnī theologians tried to find a way of reconciling God's omnipotence with human freedom. The Muʿtazilah and their opponents agreed that when a people acted, it was through a "power" or "ability" which God created in them, but while the Muʿtazilah held that this was a "power" to do either the act or its opposite and was created before the act, the others insisted that it was the "power" to do only the act in question and was created in the moment of acting. Many Sunnī theologians, especially the Ashʿarīyah, further held that while God created the act, the human agents only "acquired" (*kasaba*) it, meaning that they somehow "made it theirs" or had it "credited" to them as their act. The Muʿtazilah had shown that if the act was not the individuals' act and was sinful, God could not justly punish them for it. Most Sunnīs held that whether people were believers or unbelievers depended on their own acts and not on God. At the same time they thought that God could, in his goodness, help people to belief, yet also in his justice lead them astray or abandon them, in the sense of withdrawing guidance from them, but ultimately such treatment followed on sins by the people in question.

7. *God will judge all human beings on the Last Day after they have been raised from the dead. Among the realities of the Last Day are the balance (*mīzān*), the bridge (*ṣirāṭ*), and the pool or basin (*ḥawḍ*). Before the Last Day sinners will be exposed to the punishment of the tomb.* God's judgment on the Last Day is prominent in the Qur'ān and is implied in all creeds even when not explicitly stated. A balance to weigh a person's good deeds against bad deeds is spoken of in the Qur'ān, but there are no clear references there to the pool from which Muḥammad quenches the thirst of the believers or to the knife-edge bridge over Hell from which evildoers fall down: these are popular eschatological conceptions which have found their way into some creeds, as is also the belief in a punishment in the tomb (*ʿadhāb al-qabr*).

8. *Muḥammad and other prophets are permitted to intercede with God on the Last Day for sinful members of their communities.* Although the Muʿtazilah held that the Qur'anic references to intercession did not justify this belief, it came to be generally accepted.

9. *Paradise and Hell are already created, and will never cease to exist.* This was a denial of some sectarian views attributed to the Jahmīyah and others.

10. *God will be seen by the believers in Paradise.* This is asserted in the Qur'ān, but it is difficult to understand literally since God is incorporeal. It was eventually held to be true "amodally" *(bi-lā kayf)*.

11. *God has sent messengers (*rusul*) and prophets (*anbiyā'*) to human communities with his revelations. Prophets are preserved (*maʿṣūm*) from sin by God; Muḥammad is the seal of the prophets.* Prophets are sometimes said to be very numerous, reaching as many as 120,000, although only a small number, sometimes 313, are messengers. According to the Māturīdīyah, prophets are preserved from all sins; according to the Ashʿarīyah, only from grave sins. The phrase "seal of the prophets" is now always taken to mean "last of the prophets," but originally it may have meant the one who, like a seal, confirmed previous prophets.

12. *The most excellent of the community after Muḥammad is Abū Bakr, then ʿUmar, then ʿUthmān, then ʿAlī.* This apparently nontheological assertion is a denial of the Shīʿī view that ʿAlī was most excellent after Muḥammad, and thus it is an essential element of Sunnīsm. It was agreed upon only after much discussion, especially regarding the place of ʿUthmān because of criticisms of his conduct.

13. *Faith (*īmān*) consists in assenting with the heart, confessing with the tongue, and performing works; it may increase or decrease.* This is the Ashʿarī and Ḥanbalī understanding of faith, or what makes a person a believer. The Māturīdīyah and other Ḥanafīyah, on the other hand, exclude performing works from the definition and then insist that faith can neither increase nor decrease.

14. *A believer who commits a grave sin does not thereby cease to be a believer.* This is directed against the Khārijīs, who held that the grave sinner is excluded from the community of believers. Sunnīs generally came to hold that a grave sinner of the community might be punished in Hell for a time, but would eventually go to Paradise through the intercession of Muḥammad.

SHĪʿĪ BELIEFS. Whereas for Sunnī Muslims true doctrine is what is asserted in the Qur'ān and *ḥadīth* as interpreted by accredited *ʿulamā'*, for Shīʿī Muslims authority in matters of doctrine rests with the divinely inspired imam. There are three main subdivisions of the Shīʿah, namely the Imāmīyah (Twelvers), the Ismāʿīlīyah (Seveners), and the Zaydīyah. All believe that ʿAlī was the rightful imam, or leader of the Muslims in succession to Muḥammad, and was followed by his sons, Ḥasan and Ḥusayn, and that thereafter each imam designated his successor, usually a son. The Twelvers, with their center in Iran, hold that in 874 the twelfth imam went into occultation (*ghaybah*), but is still alive and will return as the Mahdi at an appropriate moment to set things right in the world. The Ismāʿīlīyah accept the first six Twelver imams, but hold that the seventh was a son of the sixth named Ismāʿīl, and that the series of imams continues until today. The present Aga Khan is the imam of the best-known subsection of the Ismāʿīlīyah. The original Zaydī view was that the rightful imam was a descendant of Ḥasan or Ḥusayn who claimed the imamate and made good his claim by the sword. The Shīʿah in general reject the twelfth of the articles presented above and also hold that the Qurʾān is created, but they accept most of the rest of the creed, although the Zaydīyah, and to a lesser extent the Twelver Shīʿah, tend to the position of the Muʿtazilah. The strength of the Twelver *ʿulamāʾ* in Iran today is in part due to the fact that they represent the Hidden Imam.

SEE ALSO Attributes of God, article on Islamic Concepts; Polemics, articles on Christian-Muslim Polemics, Muslim-Jewish Polemics.

BIBLIOGRAPHY

The only book devoted to the topic is the pioneer work of A. J. Wensinck, *The Muslim Creed: Its Genesis and Historical Development* (1932; reprint, New York, 1965). This is built around translations of three Ḥanafī creeds and includes long scholarly commentaries on them. Much more is now known about later developments of the creeds, and it should be noted that Wensinck was not clearly aware of the differences between the Ḥanafīyah (including the Māturīdīyah) and the Ashʿarīyah, as seen in article 13 above. Creeds by al-Ashʿarī, al-Ghazālī, Abū Ḥafṣ al-Nasafī, and al-Faḥālī are translated by D. B. Macdonald in his *Development of Muslim Theology, Jurisprudence and Constitutional Theory* (1903; reprint, New York, 1965), but otherwise the book is somewhat out of date. Two versions of al-Ashʿarī's creed are translated and edited by Richard J. McCarthy in *The Theory of al-Ashʿarī* (Beirut, 1953).

For the development of dogma, there is a brief account in Wensinck's book; I have given a much fuller account of the early period in *The Formative Period of Islamic Thought* (Edinburgh, 1973), and I present a survey up to the present in my *Islamic Philosophy and Theology*, 2d rev. ed. (Edinburgh, 1984).

For the beliefs of the Twelver Shīʿah, the creed by Ibn Bābawayhi (d. 991) is contained in *A Shi'ite Creed*, translated by A. A. Fyzee (London, 1942); that of ʿAllāmah al-Ḥillī (d. 1326) appears in *Al-Bābu'l-Ḥādī ʿAshar, a Treatise on the Principles of Shīʿite Theology*, translated by William Miller (London, 1928). A modern work is *A Shi'ite Anthology*, edited by William C. Chittick (Albany, N.Y., 1981). For the Ismāʿīlīyah there is a summary of a long creed from about 1200 in *A Creed of the Fatimids* by Vladimir A. Ivanov (Bombay, 1936). The most important work on the Zaydīyah is Wilferd Madelung's *Der Imam al-Qāsim ibn Ibrāhīm und die Glaubenslehre der Zaiditen* (Berlin, 1965).

New Sources

Rahman, Fazlur. *Major Themes of the Qur'an*. Minneapolis, 1989.

W. MONTGOMERY WATT (1987)
Revised Bibliography

CREMATION SEE FUNERAL RITES

CREOLIZATION.

The term *creolization* describes the process of acculturation in which Amerindian, European, and African traditions and customs have blended with each other over a prolonged period to create new cultures in the New World. Creole cultures are found in the southern United States, parts of Latin America, and in the Caribbean. These regions share a similar history that includes long periods of European colonial rule, a history of slavery and resistance to slavery, and the cultivation of sugar cane by forced labor. The creolizing process that accompanied these events has created rich forms of cultural expression that have been woven together like the diverse strands in a tapestry to create new cultures. These traditions may bear a resemblance to the older forms from which they derive, but they are distinct in the varying ways they blend with one another.

The term *Creole* was used initially in the sixteenth-century Caribbean to designate people of mixed race (also called mulattos) who were born of African and European parents. By the seventeenth century, it came to be applied to anyone of European and African descent born in the New World. Since the colonial period, the term has been applied to many aspects of culture. In the culinary arts it designates a highly seasoned type of food cooked with ingredients like okra and tomatoes. It refers to styles of dress that is reminiscent of the colonial era, and in the arts certain musical rhythms and dance steps are identified as Creole.

LANGUAGE. Creolization's most distinctive contributions to the cultures of the New World are in the areas of linguistics and religion. The Creole languages derive from earlier pidginized tongues that developed during the colonial period to allow African slaves and their masters to communicate. Pidgins evolved into more sophisticated languages with more complex grammatical and syntactical structures. Modern Creole languages make extensive use of words from the European languages and may also include some African and Amerindian words.

Most Creole grammatical structures are based on the languages native to West Africa, and their forms vary depending on which ethnic groups were brought from Africa or Europe to which regions of the New World. Based upon the extent of their borrowings, the Creole languages may be referred to as English-derived (as is Gullah in the United States), or French-derived (such as Haitian or Martiniquane Creoles), or Dutch-derived (Papiamento in Curaçao). Their linguistic and literary forms, oral or written, express distinctive cultural and social realities that are unique to each region.

RELIGION. Creolization has influenced many indigenous religions in the New World. Like the Creole languages, the creolization process combines religious traditions from the peoples of Africa, Europe, and the New World. Creole religions are found in the Brazilian state of Bahia, the countries on the northern coast of South America, and in the Caribbean, Central America, and the southern parts of the United States. These regions share common historical and socioeconomic circumstances related to colonialism, the plantation system, and slavery. The religions that developed in these regions are divided by scholars into several categories.

Roman Catholicism. In various parts of Central America, Amerindian and African religious traditions have been intermixed with Roman Catholic beliefs and practices, including many of the local rituals associated with various saints and the Virgin. These practices are found in various parts of Brazil and in the Spanish-speaking countries on the western shore of the Gulf of Mexico.

Neo-African. The Neo-African religions developed within the context of slavery and preserve a considerable number of African religious traditions and some Amerindian traditions, combined with Roman Catholicism. They include Vodou in Haiti and some parts of Louisiana, Santería in Cuba, the Dominican Republic, and Puerto Rico, Candomblé in Brazil, and the Orísha sects in Trinidad and Grenada.

Ancestral religions. The ancestral religions have preserved fewer African traditions and derive from various forms of Protestantism imported from the United States to the Caribbean by Christian missionaries in the nineteenth and twentieth centuries. They include Orísha in Trinidad, Kumina and Convince in Jamaica, Big Drum in Grenada, and Carriacou and Kele in Saint Lucia.

Revivalist religions. The Revivalist religions are nineteenth and twentieth century phenomena, and are related to charismatic Protestant movements imported from the United States. They encompass Pentecostals, Baptists, Seventh Day Adventists, and Revival movements throughout the Caribbean and in parts of South America. This class includes Shouters and Spiritual Baptists (a Creole sect distinct from Baptists) in Trinidad and Tobago, Saint Vincent, Grenada, Guyana, and Venezuela; the Shakers and Streams of Power in Saint Vincent, the Tie Heads (members of the Jerusalem Apostolic Spiritual Baptist Church) in Barbados and Saint Lucia; the Jordanites of Guyana; the Spirit Baptists of Jamaica; and the Cohortes and the Holiness Church and other Pentecostal movements in Haiti.

Divination Another group of Creole religions emphasizes divination (the intuitive reading of one's future in an object) and folk healing through mediums. It includes Myalism and various Revival movements in Jamaica, Espiritismo and the various spiritist sects in Puerto Rico, Umbanda in Brazil, Maria Lionza in Venezuela, and various healing sects in Central America.

Asian religions. Another set of Creole religions were brought to the New World beginning around 1850 by indentured laborers from Asia. They include Hindu sects in Trinidad, Tobago, and Guyana.

The divisions that exist between these categories are merely theoretical, for in reality these religions are not mutually exclusive but take diverse local forms, and the theology of one region may influence that of another. These religions are shaped by their devotees, who may give their allegiance to more than one tradition simultaneously. Their practitioners' religious lives reflect the religious diversity and syncretic nature of the Creole cultures.

CREOLIZATION AS RELIGIOUS ACCULTURATION. The process of creolization that resulted in the blending of various religious traditions began shortly after the establishment of the first European settlements in the late fifteenth century. The new settlers encountered native Amerindian peoples who possessed their own religious traditions. The colonists, obsessed with the need to acquire land and the prospect of finding gold, enslaved the indigenous peoples and forced them into hard labor. The work was so onerous that by the seventeenth century the number of Amerindians was reduced by more than half.

The rapid decrease in the indigenous population necessitated a new source of labor, and Amerindians were replaced with African laborers. Africans were first brought to the Caribbean around 1512, and the total number transported to the New World since then has been estimated at more than twelve million. Most of the Africans came from West Africa and belonged to diverse ethnic groups whose religious traditions they wove into the fabric of the New World's colonial life. In their contacts with each other, they shared their religious traditions and succeeded in fashioning religious amalgams that have left indelible marks on the cultures of the New World, and eventually engendered a process of creolization that combined diverse African, Amerindian, and European religious traditions.

Creolization varied from region to region and depended upon a number of variables. The ethnic mix and historical circumstances in different regions of the New World are important considerations in the process of creolization. The uneven demographic distribution of various ethnic groups in the colonies resulted in the prominence of some cultures and the preeminence of their religious traditions. The unique mixture of ethnic religious traditions in each colony contributed to the marked diversity in beliefs and practices in different regions. The large number of Nigerians brought to Cuba and Brazil resulted in the preeminence of Yoruba beliefs and practices in Cuban Santería and Brazilian Candomblé. Africans brought from Benin and the Congo had a significant impact on the theology of vodou in Haiti and Louisiana.

The African names of these ethnic groups were preserved in many of the Creole religious traditions of the New World. Words for geographical locations or ethnic groups in West Africa, like *Arada* (or *Rada*), *Guinea, Kongo, Nago,* and *Ibo,* are used in Vodou, Candomblé, and Santería today. But they now characterize different pantheons of African spirits who function as sustainers of the cosmos, providers, or healers. Santería, Espiritismo, and Umbanda all incorporate their own pantheons of spirits who are wholly New World inventions. They developed to fill the needs of colonial societies and include Amerindian spirits from Taino, Arawak, and Carib religions.

The length of the period of colonialism and the extent to which Europeans exercised a strong cultural presence in various regions had a significant impact on the process of creolization. A prolonged European cultural influence in a country, such as Jamaica, tended to curtail its people's ability to maintain strong Amerindian or African religious traditions. In Haiti, however, where European colonial domination and cultural contact ended following the slave revolt in 1804, the people managed to maintain many more African traditions than most other nations in the New World, which remained colonies well into the twentieth century. Other nations refused to recognize Haiti for a period of fifty-six years after independence, and the country's relative isolation from foreign cultural influences allowed African traditions to entrench themselves profoundly in the culture.

Catholic traditions. The way Creole religions incorporated Christian traditions into their theology is a further consideration. The prominence of Christianity in these religions varies from region to region and especially from Catholic to Protestant colonial territories. In the French, Spanish, and Portuguese colonies, Catholic religious beliefs and practices were incorporated into Candomblé, vodou, Espiritismo, and Santería. Catholicism in these religions is visible in both theology and in ritual. Theologically, the slaves in these areas created a system of reinterpretation in which symbols associated with saints in Christian hagiology were made to correspond with similar symbols associated with the gods in African mythology. Saint James the Great, for example, the patron saint of the Spanish campaigns against the Moors, becomes Ogún, Nigeria's Yoruba god of war, in vodou and Santería. Saint Peter, believed to hold the keys to the kingdom of heaven, becomes Eleggua (or Legba), who in Yoruba and Beninese traditions is the guardian of human destiny. Catholic symbols also found a home in the religions of the New World, which make extensive use of crucifixes, missals, incense, holy water, and lithographs of various saints (and by extension of African or Amerindian spirits) in their religious rituals.

Protestant traditions. The mainly British Protestant colonies present a different picture. By and large, the British possessions tended to be less syncretic than the Catholic, mainly because the Protestants undertook the evangelization of the slaves at a much later period. The British thought that Christianity was too sophisticated for Africans to understand, and therefore considered their slaves unfit for it. The Anglican Church of England did not make any systematic efforts to evangelize the slaves in the Caribbean until the 1820s, shortly after the arrival in Jamaica of Moravian and Methodist missionaries from the United States. In contrast, the French began to convert their slaves to Christianity as early as the sixteenth century, and redoubled their efforts in the seventeenth and eighteenth centuries.

Evangelical influences. Protestantism was relatively rare in the Catholic colonies until the late eighteenth and early nineteenth centuries. Some Protestant denominations flourished in Latin America and the Caribbean in the twentieth century thanks to their evangelical nature. They included Pentecostals, Baptists, Seventh Day Adventists, Jehovah's Witnesses, and more recently the Church of the Latter Day Saints (Mormons). The number of Pentecostals and Baptists in Latin America and the Caribbean today probably exceeds those of the other established Protestant denominations, not only because of their religious zeal but also because of their ardent recruitment methods. The Pentecostals and Holiness groups believe in engaging directly with the spirit world through spiritual trances and glossolalia (speaking in tongues), akin to the African ritual styles entrenched in the southern United States, the Caribbean, and the state of Bahia in eastern Brazil. This similarity may have contributed to the conversion of so many thousands of devotees.

Pentecostalism and the Holiness sects are based on the New Testament story in which the Holy Spirit descended on Christ's disciples after his death, empowering them to prophesy and to preach the gospel in different tongues (Acts 2:1–4). Charismatics believe that the miracle at Pentecost can be replicated today and that their bodies can be filled with the Holy Spirit. Speaking in tongues is a profound spiritual achievement that makes it possible to receive divine revelations and to prophesy to the community, heal the sick, and interpret dreams.

Pentecostal theology has inspired the formation of religious Creole movements throughout the Caribbean and Latin America, many combining traditional African rituals with evangelical Protestant theology. Because these groups are independent of each other it is difficult to estimate their number, but there are probably about a hundred charismatic movements in the Caribbean, each slightly different. The best-known are the Tie Heads of the Jerusalem Apostolic Spiritual Baptist churches in Barbados, the Shouters and Spiritual Baptists in Trinidad, the various Cohortes and Holiness churches (mainly Pentecostal) in Brazil, Haiti, and the Dominican Republic, the Shakers and Streams of Power in Saint Vincent, and the Native Baptists and Kumina sects in Jamaica.

These sects are unusual in combining aspects of African and Protestant traditions. They share a reverence for ancestors, a style of worship that includes antiphonal calls and answers between leader and congregants, hymns sung in rhythmic patterns accompanied by drums, and cadenced swaying of the congregants' bodies, all reminiscent of African traditional religions and part of the Creole ritual practices. Like African rituals, Pentecostal and Baptist styles of worship use every possible visible and auditory vehicle to engage the congregants. The rituals are "danced out" rather than conceived intellectually; they do not separate the mind from the body by leading a participant to high-flown intellectual exercises, but claim the entire person. But despite their Africanness, these religions are not merely replicas of their African counterparts. The Creole religions in the New World are no longer Amerindian, Christian, or African, but uniquely new creations.

Hinduism. Hinduism too has played an important role in the creolization of religions in the New World, and especially in the Caribbean. Although there are small communities of Hindus throughout the Caribbean, the largest concentrations are in Trinidad, Guyana, and Suriname. The religious presence of Hinduism in the Caribbean came about because of the abolition of slavery. After the British Emancipation Act of 1834, English colonizers imported East Indian indentured laborers. Their importation to the New World spanned a period of seventy-two years (1838–1910) in which some 143,000 people came to Trinidad alone. More were brought to Suriname, Guyana, Martinique, and Guadeloupe. These immigrants originated in the northwestern part of India and belonged to several social castes. About 15 percent of them were priests *(brahmins)* who founded support organizations in an effort to maintain Hindu traditions. Today these organizations have sought to standardize Hindu worship and supervise the teaching of its traditions in some sixty Hindu schools in Trinidad alone. Like other Creole religions, Hinduism in the Caribbean is no longer an Asian religion transplanted to the New World. It has created new myths, rituals, and festivals, such as the annual *Holi Pagwa,* that bear little resemblance to those of India. Hinduism has evolved into a Creole religion original to the New World.

CREOLE RELIGIONS IN THE DIASPORA. Since the 1950s hundreds of thousands of Caribbean and Latin American people have migrated to other parts of the Caribbean and to the United States, Canada, and the United Kingdom. Among some several million emigrants are priests and priestesses of the various Creole religions. They have established temples wherever they are and continue to wield considerable authority over the people they serve.

Religion plays an important part in peoples' lives in the diaspora, and their spiritual leaders assist them in celebrations and in times of hardship. Devotees recreate their rituals by adapting them to their new cultural milieu. The day devoted to the Virgin Mary in the Catholic liturgical calendar, for example, July 16, is reserved for Ezili in Vodou and Oshún in Santería. On that day, many Haitians in New York will make pilgrimages to Our Lady of Mount Carmel Church in New York, where they will honor the Virgin in her many aspects.

The Creole religions in the diaspora are noteworthy for their multiethnic character. Ritual participation is open to members of all cultural and ethnic groups, whites as well as blacks. African Americans who seek to integrate aspects of black nationalism with an authentic African worldview are particularly attracted to the Creole religious communities. The energy, creativity, and resourcefulness of these communities will undoubtedly further alter the Creole religions as they adapt their cultural and religious traditions to suit their new communities. The Creole traditions in the diaspora will very likely continue to diversify. How they do so will depend upon their demographic composition and the theological inclinations of their members.

SEE ALSO Syncretism; Transculturation and Religion.

BIBLIOGRAPHY

Bastide, Roger. *African Civilisations in the New World.* Translated by Peter Green. New York, 1971.

Bastide, Roger. *The African Religions of Brazil: Toward a Sociology of the Interpenetration of Civilizations.* Translated by Helen Sebba. Baltimore, 1978.

Bourguignon, Erika. *Possession.* San Francisco, 1976.

Brandon, George. *Santeria from Africa to the New World: The Dead Sell Memories.* Bloomington, Ind., 1993.

Brown, Diana deG. *Umbanda: Religion and Politics in Urban Brazil.* New York, 1994.

Brown, Karen McCarthy. *Mama Lola: A Vodou Priestess in Brooklyn.* Berkeley, 1991.

Desmangles, Leslie Gérald. *The Faces of the Gods: Vodou and Roman Catholicism in Haiti.* Chapel Hill, N.C., 1992.

Fernández Olmos, Margarite, and Lizabeth Paravisini-Gebert. *Creole Religions of the Caribbean: An Introduction from Vodou to Santeria to Obeah and Espritismo.* New York, 2003.

Glazier, Stephen D. *Marchin' the Pilgrims Home: Leadership and Decision-Making in an Afro-Caribbean Faith.* Westport, Conn., 1983.

Lewin, Olive. *Rock It Come Over: The Folk Music of Jamaica.* Kingstown, Jamaica, 2000.

Look Lia, Walton. *Indentured Labor, Caribbean Sugar: Chinese and Indian Migrants to the British West Indies, 1838–1918.* Baltimore, 1993.

Lum, Kenneth Anthony. *Praising His Name in the Dance: Spirit Possession in the Spiritual Baptist Faith and Orisha Work in Trinidad, West Indies.* Amsterdam, 2000.

McDaniel, Lorna. *The Big Drum Ritual of Carriacou: Praisesongs in Rememory of Flight.* Gainesville, Fla., 1998.

Moreau de Saint-Méry, Médéric Louis-Elie. *Description topographique, physique, civile, politique, et historique de la partie française de l'isle de Saint-Domingue* (1797). 3 vols. Paris, 1958.

Murphy, Joseph M. *Working the Spirit: Ceremonies of the African Diaspora.* Boston, Mass., 1994.

Rey, Terry. *Our Lady of Class Struggle: The Cult of the Virgin Mary in Haiti.* Trenton, N.J., 1999.

Schuler, Monica. "Myalism and the African Religious Tradition in Jamaica." In *Africa and the Caribbean: The Legacies of a Link,* edited by Margaret E. Crahan and Franklin W. Knight. Baltimore, 1979.

Simpson, George Eaton. *Black Religions in the New World.* New York, 1978.

Thomas, Eudora. *A History of the Shouter Baptists in Trinidad and Tobago.* Tacarigua, Trinidad, 1987.

Zane, Wallace W. *Journeys to the Spiritual Lands: The Natural History of a West Indian Religion.* New York, 1999.

LESLIE G. DESMANGLES (2005)

CRESCAS, ḤASDAI (c. 1340–1410/11), Spanish rabbi, philosopher, natural scientist; author of the anti-Aristotelian Hebrew classic, *Or Adonai* (The Light of the Lord). Son of a distinguished family of scholars and merchants, Crescas was raised in Barcelona, studying there under the renowned Talmudist and homilist Nissim ben Re'uven. He served as rabbi in Barcelona and from 1387 was an adviser to the king and queen of Aragon, Joan I and Violant. In 1389, Crescas assumed the post of rabbi of Saragossa, and the next year he was recognized by the throne as judge of all the Jews of Aragon. Following the anti-Jewish mob riots of 1391, in which thousands of Spanish Jews—including his only son—were murdered and more than a hundred thousand were converted to Christianity, he devoted himself to the physical and spiritual reconstruction of the Jewish communities of Aragon and of Spain as a whole. His *Epistle to the Jewish Community of Avignon* (translated from the Hebrew in Kobler, 1952), dated 20 Heshvan 5152 (October 19, 1391), is a terse chronicle of the massacres that may have been written as background for entreaties to the papal court. The *Epistle* bears somber biblical allusions: the great Jewish communities of Spain are desolated Jerusalems (allusions are made to *Lamentations* 2:2, 2:4, 2:7, 5:4); Crescas's son is an Isaac sacrificed upon the altar (allusions are made to *Genesis* 22:2, 22:7–8). His *Refutation of the Dogmas of the Christians* (1397–1398), written in Catalan but surviving only in the Hebrew translation of Yosef ibn Shem Ṭov (*Biṭṭul ʿiqqarei ha-Notsrim,* 1451; Frankfurt, 1860; Kearny, N.J., 1904; translated in Lasker, 1992), was intended to combat christianizing literature aimed at Jews and *conversos.* It is a nonrhetorical logical critique of ten basic elements of Christianity: original sin, salvation, the Trinity, the incarnation, the virgin birth, transubstantiation, baptism, the messiahship of Jesus, the New Testament, and demons. Even his profound philosophical treatise, *The Light of the Lord* (1410; Ferrara, 1555; Vienna, 1859–1860; Johannesburg, 1861; and Jerusalem, 1990, ed. S. Fisher), written in Hebrew, was to some extent a response to the troubles of his times. Its assault on Aristotelianism was in part motivated by the belief that Aristotelian philosophy was weakening the commitment of Jewish intellectuals to Judaism and thus facilitating their apostasy. Crescas is also the author of a philosophic homily on the Passover, which inquires into the epistemological status of faith based on miracles, such as the splitting of the Red Sea (Jerusalem, 1988).

The Light of the Lord, a counterblast to Maimonides' *Guide of the Perplexed,* was planned as the philosophical first part of a two-part work. The unwritten second part was to have been an analytic codification of rabbinic law and was intended to supersede Maimonides' rabbinic masterwork, the *Mishneh Torah* (Code of Law). The *Light* is divided into four books. Book 1 discusses three roots (*shorashim*) of the Torah: God's existence, his unity, and his incorporeality. (In grouping these three principles together, Crescas followed Maimonides; cf., e.g., *Guide of the Perplexed,* intro. to part 2.) Book 2 discusses six fundaments (*pinnot*) of the Torah: God's knowledge, providence, and power; prophecy; human choice; and the purposefulness of the Torah. The fundaments are concepts that follow necessarily (i.e., analytically) from Crescas's definition of the Torah as "the product of a voluntary action from the Commander, Who is the initiator of the action, to the commanded, who is the receiver of the action" (*Light* 2, intro.). Book 3 discusses eleven nonfundamental obligatory beliefs of the Torah: God's creation of the world, the immortality of the soul, reward and punishment, resurrection of the dead, the eternality of the Torah, the uniqueness of Moses' prophecy, the efficacy of the Urim and Tummim, the coming of the messiah, the efficacy of prayer, the spiritual value of repentance, and the special providential nature of the High Holy Days and the festivals. Book 4 examines thirteen nonobligatory beliefs held by sundry groups of Jews; for example, the Jewish Aristotelian proposition that God is the Intellect and the qabbalistic doctrine of metempsychosis *(gilgul).*

The *Light* is best known for its revolutionary logico-conceptual critique of Aristotelian physics (e.g., theories of space, time, motion, the vacuum, infinity), important parts of which were translated into Latin in Gianfrancesco Pico della Mirandola's *Examen vanitatis doctrinae gentium* (1520). In place of Aristotle's closed world, Crescas suggested that both space and time are infinite extensions *in actu* in which many worlds—an infinite number?—are continuously being created by the infinitely good, infinitely loving God. Crescas rejected Maimonides' Aristotelian proofs of God, but did offer a short metaphysical proof of his own: whether causes and effects are finite or infinite, there must be a cause of the whole of them; for if all are effects, they would have merely possible (i.e., contingent) existence, and thus they must have something that determines their existence over their nonexistence, and this is the first cause or God (*Light* 1.3.2, quoted in Spinoza, *Epistle* 12). Such rationalistic reflection, Crescas held, can incline one toward belief in the true God of religion, but only revelation can establish that belief firmly. In a celebrated discussion of human choice (*Light* 2.5), Crescas upheld the determinist view that the notion of human choice coheres with both divine omniscience and strict physical causality. In his theologically significant discussion of teleology (*Light* 2.6), he argued that love is the purpose of man, the Torah, the created universe, and God. Against the Aristotelians, he maintained that love is not intellectual, that the immortal essence of the human soul is not intellect, and that God is to be understood not as passionless Intellect but as joyfully loving.

Crescas's own highly original philosophy emerges out of his radical critique of Aristotle and of Aristotelians such as Maimonides, Ibn Rushd (Averroës), and Levi ben Gershom (Gersonides) and is argued in their vocabulary. In some areas, it is significantly influenced by Ibn Sīnā. Its spirit, however, recalls Abū Ḥāmid al-Ghazālī, Yehudah ha-Levi, and Nissim ben Re'uven. It is also colored by Qabbalah. Its precise relationship to Latin and Catalan writers is a subject for speculation.

Among Crescas's students was the well-known philosophical popularizer Yosef Albo, who in his Hebrew *Sefer ha-'iqqarim* (Book of Roots; 1425) adapted and simplified some of his master's teachings. Crescas's *Light of the Lord* had an appreciable influence on later Jewish philosophers, notably Judah Abravanel (c. 1460–1521) and Barukh Spinoza (1632–1677).

SEE ALSO Jewish Thought and Philosophy, article on Premodern Philosophy.

BIBLIOGRAPHY

For Crescas's life, see Yitzhak Baer's *A History of the Jews in Christian Spain,* 2 vols. (Philadelphia, 1961–1966). Crescas's critique of Aristotelian physics is the subject of Harry A. Wolfson's monumental *Crescas' Critique of Aristotle* (Cambridge, Mass., 1929); the volume includes Hebrew texts from the *Light* with facing English translation. Shlomo Pines explored the connection between Crescas's science and that of Nicole d'Oresme and other Latin authors in "Scholasticism after Thomas Aquinas and the Teachings of Hasdai Crescas and His Predecessors," *Proceedings of the Israel Academy of Sciences and Humanities* 1 (1967), n. p. See also Warren Zev Harvey's *Physics and Metaphysiscs in Ḥasdai Crescas* (Amsterdam, 1998). Crescas' philosophic homily is edited and analyzed in Aviezer Ravitzky, *Dershat Ha-Pesaḥ le-Rabbi Ḥasdai Crescas* (Jerusalem, 1988). On Crescas's critique of Christianity, see Daniel J. Lasker's *The Refutation of the Christian Principles by Ḥasdai Crescas* (Albany, N.Y., 1992) and his *Jewish Philosophical Polemics against Christianity in the Middle Ages* (New York, 1977). On his influence on Spinoza, see Wolfson's *The Philosophy of Spinoza,* 2 vols. (Cambridge, Mass., 1934). Crescas's *Epistle to the Jewish Community of Avignon* is found in English translation in Franz Kobler's *Letters of Jews through the Ages* (London, 1952), pp. 272–275.

WARREN ZEV HARVEY (1987 AND 2005)

CREUZER, G. F.

CREUZER, G. F. (1771–1858), German Romantic mythologist. Educated at Marburg and then Jena, Georg Friedrich Creuzer was appointed professor of philology at Marburg in 1802, and in 1804 professor of philology and ancient history at Heidelberg, where he taught for almost forty-five years. Creuzer's major work was *Symbolik und Mythologie der alten Völker, besonders der Griechen* (1810–1812).

Creuzer argued that ancient Greek religion derived from a spiritually pure and noble monotheism carried from India by wandering priests. But this high monotheism needed to be adapted to the crude, native polytheism. There thus arose an exoteric and popular teaching for the vulgar many, one that spoke of many gods, and an esoteric teaching for the initiated and refined worshiper. Creuzer claimed that this esoteric tradition informed Eleusinian and Samothracian mysteries, Orphism and Pythagoreanism, and Neoplatonism. His book quickly became famous and was both admired and criticized. There was much speculation on the part of German Romantics—often extravagant or fantastic—about India as the homeland of all true religion and wisdom. Creuzer seemed to give solid historical support to this enthusiasm for the East and its synthesis with Greece. But because Creuzer's work claimed to be accurate history, it also became the chief target of scholarly attacks on the excesses and defects of the Romantic mythologists. This quarrel between "romanticists" and "rationalists" is a major episode in early nineteenth-century history of religion. Creuzer's data and methods were rebutted, from various positions, by such famous scholars as Gottfried Hermann (1819), Karl Otfried Müller (1825), Christian Lobeck (1829), and Ludwig Preller (1854). One result of this controversy was that "rationalistic" and philological study of myth often disdained "romantic" enthusiasm and speculation about myth as a living religious force.

Creuzer's views on myth also met opposition in the Romantic camp. He firmly distinguished between myth and symbol. Divine meaning shone forth first of all in the symbol. The first interpretations here (as by Indic sages) took the form of images or pictographs, so as to preserve the symbol's union of spirit and matter. Only later, and on a lower level, came the narrated stories found in myth. Creuzer suggests these are concessions to popular taste. For Creuzer, the symbol embodies monotheism; myths are the vehicles of polytheism. One general criticism is summed up in the judgment of the German idealist philosopher and mythologist Friedrich Schelling, who suggests Creuzer simply reduced myth to allegory, and did so because he reproduced in Romantic terms the old Christian charge that polytheistic myth only plagiarized (and confused) the original monotheistic revelation.

BIBLIOGRAPHY

No English translation of Creuzer's *Symbolik* exists. There is a French translation by Joseph D. Guigniaut under the title *Religions de l'antiquité considérées principalement dans leurs formes symboliques et mythologiques,* 4 vols. (Paris, 1825–1841). For the controversy over Creuzer's *Symbolik,* see Ernst Howald's *Der Kampf um Creuzers Symbolik* (Tübingen, 1926), which contains excellent selections and commentary. Henri Pinard de la Boullaye's *L'étude comparée des religions,* 4th ed., vol. 1 (Paris, 1929), pp. 261–268, discusses Creuzer as a religious historian. In *The Rise of Modern Mythology, 1680–1860* (Bloomington, Ind., 1972), Robert Richardson and I discuss Creuzer as mythologist, with translated selections.

New Sources

Donougho, Martin. "Hegel and Creuzer; or, Did Hegel Believe in Myth?" In *New Perspectives on Hegel's Philosophy of Religion,* pp. 59–80. Albany, NY, 1992.

BURTON FELDMAN (1987)
Revised Bibliography

CROSSROADS

CROSSROADS in religion belong to the general phenomenon of sacred places and are a specific instance of the sacrality of roads. Wherever two or more roads intersect—forming a T or a fork or, most significantly, a junction of two roads at right angles to form a cross—there religious people often feel that the divine has intersected with the mundane. The nature of this divine presence may be positive but is very often negative. Most often, however, the divinity associated with a crossroads is paradoxically both good and evil: It seems that the meeting of different roads attracts and then expresses very well the meeting of opposites within the god.

Buddhist pilgrims travel with pleasure to a crossroads, for it is there that they are likely to find a reliquary structure containing precious remains of the cremated body of the Buddha. The Lord himself stated in the *Mahāparinibbana Sutta* that the remains of all great beings should be treated alike: "At the four crossroads a stupa should be erected to the Tathāgata" (5.26–28). Expectations were different for a pious Greek or Roman who came to a meeting of three roads, for that was the domain of the goddess Hekate, whose name, Vergil says, "is howled by night at the city crossroads" (*Aeneid* 4.609). Associated with death as well as with darkness, Hekate could be propitiated by the burial of the body of a criminal at her favorite place. This helps to explain the English custom, prevalent until modern times, of burying suicides and criminals at a meeting of roads. The execution of criminals there probably gave rise to the phrase "dirty work at the crossroads."

The folk deity Dōsojin of Japan and the Olympian Hermes of ancient Greece are gods of boundaries and of roads, but also of crossroads. They are both commonly represented by phallic images that express uneasily, even for their worshipers, the unexpected union of spirit and nature. Dōsojin may be found at the crossroads in the shape of an upright stone phallus or—capturing the god's ambivalence—a pair of phalli or a male and female holding hands. Hermes' quadrangular stone pillars are topped by the god's head and fronted by his erect penis. Located at the juncture of roads, these herms were supposed to guide and protect travelers, but might just as easily bring them grief. As the Homeric *Hymn to Hermes* puts it, "And even though he helps a few people, he cheats an endless number." Something similar must be said of the Vedic god Rudra, whose "favorite haunt," according to the *Śatapatha Brāhmaṇa* (2.6.2.8), is the crossroads. Rudra is fierce but must be addressed as "Śiva" (Auspicious One) if he is to heal the wounds that he himself inflicts. Rudra is not himself phallic, but he provides a name and an ambivalent character for the later Hindu deity Śiva, whose chief image is the phallus. Thus, one can understand the ancient advice to an Indian bridegroom traveling with his bride: "On the way, he should address crossroads. . . . 'May no waylayers meet us'" (*Gṛhyasūtra of Gobhila* 2.4.2). In so doing, he is calling to Rudra for help, yet asking him to stay away.

Crossroads also appear, with a different level of meaning, in the boyhood vision of Black Elk, the Oglala Lakota holy man, described in his life story, *Black Elk Speaks* (Lincoln, Nebr., 1932). Looking down from a high place, he saw the earth and two roads crossing, a red one and a black. These roads symbolized the good times and the troubled times that his people must necessarily experience; yet the crossing of them provided a center where there bloomed a "holy stick" by which his people would flourish. It was this image that provided Black Elk himself with a center and an orientation for the rest of his life.

BIBLIOGRAPHY

After consulting the sources given and the standard scholarship for each religion mentioned, one might read the two essays on "Cross-roads" by J. A. MacCulloch and Richard Wünsch in the *Encyclopaedia of Religion and Ethics,* edited by James Hastings, vol. 4 (Edinburgh, 1911). For accounts of crossroads rites, see James G. Frazer's *The Golden Bough,* 3d ed., rev. & enl., 12 vols. (London, 1911–1915).

GEORGE R. ELDER (1987)

CROWLEY, ALEISTER (1875–1947), was a British poet, novelist and occultist, infamous throughout England and the United States as "the wickedest man in the world." Reviled as a drug fiend and debauchee and proclaiming himself the "Great Beast, 666," Aleister Crowley was also one of the most important figures in the revival of modern Western occultism in the twentieth century. Although seldom taken seriously by most scholars today, Crowley was not only an accomplished poet and mountain climber, but one of the first Western students of yoga and a major influence on the rise of Neopagan witchcraft in Europe and the United States.

In many ways, Crowley might be said to embody some of the deepest tensions in late Victorian English society as a whole. The son of a preacher in the highly puritanical Plymouth Brethren sect, Crowley would later turn to the most extreme forms of sensual excess, apparently not resting until he had shattered every imaginable social and religious taboo. Born Edward Alexander Crowley, he studied at Trinity College in Cambridge, where he would change his name to Aleister, taken from Percy Bysshe Shelley's poem, "Alastor, or, The Spirit of Solitude" (1816). Having inherited a large sum of money as a young man, Crowley was able to spend much of his time pursuing his two passions, poetry and mountain climbing. During his travels in India and Sri Lanka, Crowley also studied Hinduism and Buddhism, and would publish some of the first English works on Raja Yoga.

Crowley's first initiation into the world of occultism occurred in 1898 when he was introduced to the esoteric group known as the Hermetic Order of the Golden Dawn. An eclectic blending of Rosicrucianism, Freemasonry, and Qabbalah, the Golden Dawn attracted a number of prominent artists and intellectuals, including W. B. Yeats. In 1904, however, Crowley received his own first great revelation and the knowledge that he was to be the herald of a new age in world history. According to his account, Crowley's guardian angel, Aiwass, spoke through Crowley's wife and dictated to him *The Book of the Law* (*Liber AL vel Legis*). *The Book of the Law* announces the dawn of a third eon of human civilization: the first was the age of Isis, dominated by matriarchy and worship of the mother-goddess; the second was the age of Osiris, when the patriarchal traditions of Judaism and Christianity were dominant; and the third is the age of the son, Horus, when the individual human will is supreme. The only law in this age is the law of Thelema (derived from the Greek, meaning "will"): "do what thou wilt shall be the whole of the law."

Crowley's ritual practices centered first and foremost around the art of *magick*, which he spelled deliberately with a *k* in order to distinguish it from popular ideas of magic. In Crowley's definition, magick is the science and art of causing change to occur in conformity with one's will. Influenced in part by Friedrich Nietzsche's "will to power," Crowley saw the will as the most powerful force in creation, which, when properly directed, can accomplish anything the individual desires.

One of the primary reasons for the scandal and titillation that surrounds Crowley is his practice of sexual magick. Rejecting the prudish Victorian morality in which he was raised, Crowley identified sex as the most powerful expression of the will and the most potent source of magickal energy. Taking an apparent delight in violating social taboos, Crowley also employed explicitly transgressive acts, such as masturbation, homosexuality, and bestiality, in his magickal practice. After 1910, Crowley also became involved with the esoteric group known as the Ordo Templi Orientis (OTO). The higher degrees of the OTO employed a variety of sexual rites, influenced in part by a somewhat distorted form of Hindu Tantra, a tradition that also involves sexual and transgressive rituals as a means to spiritual power. Crowley and the OTO, however, would employ sexual rites in ways that no Indian *tāntrika* would probably have dared to imagine.

The peak of Crowley's magickal career was the period after 1920, when he founded his own spiritual community called the Abbey of Thelema in Sicily. The original inspiration derived from François Rabelais's *Gargantua and Pantagruel* (1534), which describes an ideal community that would transcend the hypocrisy of Christian monasteries. Crowley took Rabelais's ideal a good deal further, however, by creating a utopian community in which every desire could be expressed through free experimentation in drugs, sex, and physical excess. During this period, he would also publish his infamous *Diary of a Drug Fiend,* a semiautobiographical novel written at top-speed in order to fuel his own growing drug habit.

By the end of his life, Crowley had exhausted most of his wealth and his own seemingly infinite will to power. Though he continued to believe that his *Book of the Law* might have a decisive role to play in the unfolding of global events during World War II, he would spent his last years in a small guest house in London, increasingly addicted to heroin, until his death in 1947.

Despite the general neglect of Crowley by most historians of religions today, he has clearly had a formative impact on almost all forms of occultism, magic, and Neopaganism in the West since the mid-twentieth century. Gerald Gardner, the founder of the Neopagan Witchcraft revival in England in the 1950s, was a great admirer of Crowley and borrowed freely from him in his rituals. At the same time, Crowley's version of sexual magic and his rather skewed interpretation of Indian Tantra has had a profound influence on the many contemporary forms of sex magic and "Western Tantra" so popular in the United States and Europe today.

Finally, on a broader historical level, Crowley could be said to embody many of the central trends in modern Europe itself in the first half of the twentieth century. With his emphasis on the power of the individual human will, his ideal of a liberated sexuality, and his hope for a utopian new age beyond all the old gods, Crowley epitomizes what Marshall Berman calls the modern Faustian self. And with Crowley's own decline into drug addiction and poverty in the 1940s, he perhaps reflects the exhaustion of those Faustian ideals and the chaos of modern Europe amidst the disaster of World War II.

See Also Wicca.

BIBLIOGRAPHY

Among the few academic studies of Crowley are Bradford Verter, "Dark Star Rising: The Emergence of Modern Occultism, 1800-", PH.D. Dissertation, Princeton University, 1997; and Hugh B. Urban, "The Beast with Two Backs: Aleister Crowley, Sex Magic and the Exhaustion of Modernity," *Nova Religio*, 7, no.3 (2004): 7-25. Despite the lack of academic scholarship on Crowley, his vast body of works exist in numerous editions; the most important include *The Law is for All: The Authorized Popular Commentary on Liber AL sub figura CCXX, The Book of the Law* (Tempe, Ariz, 1996), and *Magick in Theory and Practice* (Paris, 1929). In addition to his autobiography, *The Confessions of Aleister Crowley: An Autohagiography*, edited by John Symonds (New York, 1969), there are numerous biographies, the most recent of which is Lawrence Sutin, *Do What Thou Wilt: A Life of Aleister Crowley* (New York, 2000). Other nonacademic works include Kenneth Grant, *The Magickal Revival* (New York, 1973), and John Symonds, *The Magic of Aleister Crowley* (London, 1958). On Crowley's literary works, see Martin Booth, *Aleister Crowley: Selected Poems* (London, 1986).

Hugh Urban (2005)

CROWN. The significance of the crown lies chiefly in its place on top of the head, where it marks the bearer's relationship to what is above, to what is transcendent. At the same time the crown represents the joining of what is above to what is below, the divine and the human, the celestial and the terrestrial. The crown symbolizes access to rank and to superior force, and therefore to dignity, royalty, and power.

From a very early time crowns were associated with the sun, especially with its rays. On a third-century bas relief from the Roman city of Virunum the sun is shown receiving his radiant crown from Mithra, who has beat him in a wrestling match. In alchemy the spirits of the planets receive their light in the form of crowns from their king, the sun. In the ancient religions of Mexico and Egypt, the king in his divine aspect is the sun.

The crown's meaning can also be discovered in its circular shape, which signifies perfection and eternity. The material of the crown may represent the divinity with which its wearer is associated or even assimilated. Thus, the laurel wreath often related its wearer to Apollo, while oak leaves were emblems of Zeus. At the end of the harvest in Europe celebrants have traditionally worn wreaths of ears of grain.

During a Tibetan ceremony that seeks to eliminate the spirits of the dead, the priest wears a crown that guarantees the cosmic worth of the sacrifice by bringing together symbolically the five Buddhas and the material universe, as well as the four cardinal points with their center. In the West the Crown of Charlemagne, made for Otto I, founder of the Holy Roman Empire, is octagonal in shape, recalling the walls of Rome and the ramparts of heaven.

Crowns, often in the form of wreaths, have been awarded to victors in war or contests where the honored hero is identified with a divine patron of the contest or with a warrior god. Another religious dimension is added when—as in Mithraism and Christianity—the souls of the elect are crowned like athletes or soldiers as victors over death.

In some religious sacrifices the sacrificer wears a crown; in others the victims, even animal victims, do the same. The dead may also be crowned: in Egypt both the mummy and the statue that represented the deceased were crowned for the triumphant entry into the next life. In Christianity the crowning of martyrs is often pictured: the wearer of the crown is always related through it to a greater transcendent power.

Objects, as well as persons, can be crowned. Holy scriptures, icons, pictures, and statues are frequently honored and dedicated with crowns. Crowns sometimes assume significance independent of the crowned. Among the Yoruba of West Africa sheep were occasionally sacrificed to the crown, which had magical powers. In ancient Egypt a crown or diadem representing the highest sovereignty could execute the king's secret purpose or inflict vengeance. In one version of the legend of Ariadne and Theseus, a crown of light guides Theseus through the labyrinth after he has killed the Minotaur.

Bibliography

The image of the crown appears extensively in most religious literature, but no single source begins to explore the whole range of material with both examples and interpretation. G. F. Hill's long essay, "Crowns," in the *Encyclopaedia of Religion and Ethics,* edited by James Hastings, vol. 4 (Edinburgh, 1911), describes mostly Western history and tradition and says relatively little about the religious symbolism of the crown. Nonetheless, the article is good background material. J. E. Cirlot, in *A Dictionary of Symbols,* 2d ed. (New York, 1971), and Jean Chevalier and Alain Gheerbrant, in their *Dictionnaire des symboles* (Paris, 1982), have written interesting discussions without pretending to cover the subject.

New Sources

Joseph Lowin. "Crown: A Hebrew Lesson." *Jewish Heritage Online Magazine* 6 (November 2003). Available from http://www.jhom/hebrew/crown_h.html.

Elaine Magalis (1987)
Revised Bibliography

CRUMMELL, ALEXANDER (March 3, 1819–September 12, 1898), Episcopal priest and missionary, was a significant figure in both African American and West African Christianity. In *The Souls of Black Folks,* W. E. B. Du Bois devoted a chapter to analyzing Crummell's intellectual and moral strength. Crummell believed that Christianity had a providential role to play in the development of Africa.

Crummell was born in New York City. His father was an African prince from the Temne people who had been kidnapped and sold into slavery at the age of thirteen. Alexander Crummell attended the African Free School and Canal Street High School. In 1835 he traveled, with Henry Highland Garnet, to Canaan, New Hampshire, to attend a new experimental interracial college. However, the town's people burned the college to the ground after he and Garnet gave some inflammatory speeches during the town's observance of Independence Day. Therefore Crummell attended Oneida Institute in Whitesboro, New York, from 1836 to 1839. Because he was denied admission to Union Theological Seminary in New York City, he had to be privately tutored to pursue his goal of Episcopalian ordination. He was ordained a deacon in 1842 and a priest in 1844.

Crummell's first call was as an organizing pastor to poor blacks in New York City. From 1848 to 1853 he traveled throughout England, preaching and lecturing to raise funds for his ministry. While he was in England he was encouraged to acquire additional education at Queen's College, Cambridge, which he did. Although he raised monies for the congregation in New York, he did not return there himself but went to Liberia as an Episcopal missionary. He became a citizen of that country and married there shortly after his arrival. After establishing a number of churches in Liberia he accepted the job of principal of the Mount Vaughn High School at Cape Palmas in 1858. Crummell became a member of the faculty of Liberia College in Monrovia in 1861 and was also active in promoting the interests of the American Colonization Society, making several visits to the United States to generate interest in emigration among blacks. He published *The Relations and Duties of Free Colored Men in America to Africa* (1861) and *The Future of Africa* (1862).

Dismissed from Liberia College in 1866 due to disagreements with the administration over curriculum and other matters, Crummell formed his own school. But a period of political turmoil in the country prompted him to return to the United States in 1872. Settling in Washington, D.C., he founded Saint Luke's Episcopal Church, and in 1882 he published a collection of his sermons, *The Greatness of Christ and Other Sermons.* He founded the Conference of Church Workers among Colored People in 1883 to promote the advancement of blacks in the Episcopal ecclesial structure. After he retired from the church, in 1894, he accepted a teaching position at Howard University, which he held from 1895 to 1897. In 1897 he founded the American Negro Academy, whose purpose was to provide mutual support among black scholars and intelligentsia. His autobiography, *The Shades and the Lights of a Fifty Years' Ministry,* was published in 1894.

BIBLIOGRAPHY

Crummell, Alexander. *The Relations and Duties of Free Colored Men in America to Africa.* Hartford, Conn., 1861.

Crummell, Alexander. *The Future of Africa.* New York, 1862.

Crummell, Alexander. *The Greatness of Christ and Other Sermons.* New York, 1882.

Crummell, Alexander. *The Shades and the Lights of a Fifty Years' Ministry.* New York, 1894.

Du Bois, W. E. B. *The Souls of Black Folk.* Edited by Henry Louis Gates Jr. and Terri Hume Oliver. New York, 1999.

Moses, Wilson Jeremiah. *Alexander Crummell: A Study of Civilization and Discontent.* New York, 1989.

Murphy, Larry G., J. Gordon Melton, and Gary L. Ward, eds. *Encyclopedia of African American Religions.* New York, 1993.

Oldfield, John R. *Alexander Crummell (1819–1898) and the Creation of an African American Church in Liberia.* Lewiston, N.Y., 1990.

Rigsby, Gregory U. *Alexander Crummell: Pioneer in Nineteenth-Century Pan-African Thought.* New York, 1987.

JAMES ANTHONY NOEL (2005)

CRUSADES

This entry consists of the following articles:

CHRISTIAN PERSPECTIVE
MUSLIM PERSPECTIVE

CRUSADES: CHRISTIAN PERSPECTIVE

Crusades were military expeditions against various enemies of the church; the term refers particularly to the medieval campaigns aimed at liberating the Holy Land from the Muslims. The word *crusade* (Span., *cruzada;* Fr., *croisade*) derives from the Latin *crux* (cross); the Latin term *cruciata* does not occur before the thirteenth century. It recalls the ceremony of "taking the cross" (*Mt.* 10:38), the public act of committing oneself to participate in a crusade. Crusaders wore a red cloth cross sewn to their cloaks as a sign of their status. In modern times the word *crusade* is used metaphorically to designate evangelistic efforts at promoting all kinds of religious or moral causes.

ROOTS AND CAUSES. While the roots of the movement were complex, a major religious impulse came with the fusion of pilgrimage and holy war. The Crusades continued the old tradition of pilgrimage to the Holy Land that was often undertaken in fulfillment of a vow or as a penance; its earlier designations were *via, iter,* or *peregrinatio.* Attractive for pilgrims were not only the holy places themselves but their relics, above all the Holy Sepulcher, to which the emperor Heraclius had restored the True Cross in 627 CE. The finding of the Holy Lance at Antioch (June 1098) revitalized the First Crusade. In the Christian *terra sancta* mythology the name of Jerusalem ("vision of peace") evoked the image of the heavenly city, the goal of the Christian life (cf. *Gal.* 4:26, *Heb.* 12:22, *Rv.* 21:10–27). As "navel of the world" Jerusalem also figured in apocalyptic expectation; according to the Tiburtine Sibyl, the last battles would be fought and the last emperor hand over his rule to Christ in Jerusalem.

During the twelfth century armed pilgrimages began to be regarded as just wars fought in defense of the Holy Land against its illegitimate occupation by the Muslim infidel. The notion of a just war as revenge for an injury done to Christ had been invoked in the fight against Muslims in Spain and Sicily and, even earlier, in the Carolingian expeditions against pagans and Saracens. In 878, Pope John VIII offered spiritual incentives to those who would arm themselves against his foes in Italy. Gregory VII (1073–1085) envisaged a *militia Christi* for the fight against all enemies of God and thought already of sending an army to the East. An additional factor was the expectation of religious benefits. In the popular perception, the Crusade indulgence offered nothing less than full remission of sins and a sure promise of heaven. In a feudal society of warriors, crusading for God's sake under the banner of Saint Michael ranked as the ultimate fulfillment of the ideal of Christian knighthood.

Among the political causes of the Crusades, the appeals for help from the Byzantine emperors were prominent. The year 1071 saw the defeat of the Byzantine army at Manzikert in Asia Minor. Jerusalem fell to the Seljuk Turks in 1077. There is no clear evidence that these events led to increased harassment of Christian pilgrims. Nevertheless, they caused great alarm and spurred papal offers of assistance. Moreover, in dealing with the fighting spirit of the aristocracy, reform movements such as the Cluniac and the Gregorian were promoting the "Peace of God" (protection of unarmed persons) and the "Truce of God" (*treuga Dei,* suspension of all fighting during specified times). In this situation, participation in holy warfare provided an outlet for the martial vigor of Christian knights.

CAMPAIGNS. Any attempt at systematizing the Crusades remains arbitrary. Nevertheless, for clarity's sake, we shall follow the customary numbering of the main expeditions.

First Crusade (1096–1099). Urban II's call for participation in an expedition to the East at the Council of Clermont on November 27, 1095, met with an enthusiastic response. He himself declared the acclamation "God wills it!" to be the divinely inspired battle cry for the Crusaders. Thousands took the cross, especially French, Norman, and Flemish knights. Several bands of badly armed pilgrims from France and Germany, most of them poor and inexperienced, set out for Constantinople even before the army gathered. Some started by massacring Jews on their way through Germany. Many died in Hungary, and the remnants perished in Anatolia. The main force, under the papal legate Bishop Adhémar of Le Puy and an illustrious baronial leadership (including Godfrey of Bouillon, Baldwin II of Flanders, Raymond IV of Toulouse, Robert II of Normandy, and Bohemond I of Taranto), assembled at Constantinople (December 1096 to May 1097) and set out on a long, arduous march through Asia Minor. After costly victories at Nicaea and Dorylaeum (June–July 1097) and enormous hardships, the Crusaders captured Antioch (June 3, 1098) and finally Jerusalem (July 15, 1099), consolidating their victory by the defeat of a Fatimid army at Ascalon (August 12, 1099). A side expedition under Baldwin had already taken Edessa to the north (February 6, 1098). Only Nicaea was returned to the Byzantine emperor, and four Crusader states were organized along the Syro-Palestinian coast: the counties of Edessa and Tripoli, the principality of Antioch, and the kingdom of Jerusalem. Measured against the original goal, the First Crusade was the only successful one. Its territorial gains, protected by inland ridges and a system of fortresses along the coast, formed the basis that future Crusades sought to defend against mounting Muslim pressure. Constant quarrels among the leaders and rival interests of the major European powers, however, prevented any effective cooperation and success.

Second Crusade (1147–1149). The preaching of the Second Crusade had its immediate cause in the loss of Edessa to the Muslims of Syria (1144). Moved by the preaching of Bernard of Clairvaux, Louis VII of France and Conrad III of Germany led separate armies through Asia Minor. The losses suffered by the troops were disheartening. Furthermore, rather than aiming at Edessa, the remnant joined the Palestinian knights in an unsuccessful siege of Damascus (July 1148), which had been at peace with the kingdom of Jerusalem. This diversion worsened the plight of Edessa, Antioch, and Tripoli. Even at home the crusade was soon recognized as a disaster.

Third Crusade (1189–1192). At the initiative of the archbishop of Tyre, the Third Crusade responded to the defeat of the Palestinian knights at Ḥiṭṭīn in Galilee (July 4, 1187) and the resulting loss of Jerusalem to the sultan, Saladin. The leadership included Frederick I Barbarossa, Philip II Augustus of France, and Richard I ("the Lionhearted") of England. But Frederick accidentally drowned during the march, and the crusading effort disintegrated through attrition, quarreling, and lack of cooperation. Only Acre was recaptured (July 1191) and some ports secured, mainly through the initiative of Richard, who also took Cyprus from the Byzantines and finally negotiated a three-year truce with Saladin (September 1192).

Fourth Crusade (1202–1204). Pope Innocent III (1198–1216) made the reorganization of the crusade under papal auspices one of the priorities of his pontificate. A first appeal went out on August 15, 1198. The response was slow, and the fervor aroused by the preaching of Fulk of Neuilly did not reach beyond France and Italy. The leaders contracted for transportation with the doge of Venice, Dandolo, but lack of funds forced a diversion from the original plan to attack the Muslims in Egypt. At the request of the Venetians, the Crusaders first attacked the Christian city of Zara in Dalmatia (November 1202) and then sailed on to Constantinople, where they hoped to enthrone Alexios, an exiled Byzantine pretender to the crown, and to receive the material assistance they needed. When these plans failed, the Crusaders laid siege to the city and finally stormed it (April 12, 1204). Byzantium was looted for its treasure of relics, art, and gold, and was made the residence of a Latin emperor, with Baldwin IX of Flanders as the first incumbent. A Byzantine army recaptured the city almost casually in 1261.

The Fourth Crusade was followed by the legendary Children's Crusade of 1212. A group consisting mostly of young people under the leadership of a boy named Nicholas tried to cross the Alps and find passage to the Holy Land. All trace of them was lost even before they reached the Mediterranean ports. Crusade preaching, religious fervor, and respect for children as instruments of God's power contributed to the phenomenon. Later sources confuse this crusade with a French movement led by a shepherd boy, Stephen of Cloyes, who wanted to deliver a heavenly letter to the king.

Fifth Crusade (1217–1221). In connection with his call for the Fourth Lateran Council in 1215, Innocent III tried to stir up new interest in the crusade. In the Levant, Acre had become the center of Christian activity. From there an expedition under baronial and clerical leadership (Cardinal Pelagius) attempted to strike at the heart of Ayyubid power in Egypt (May 1218). The harbor city of Damietta was forced to surrender (November 5, 1219), but further hopes were dashed by the defeat at al-Mansūra on the way to Cairo (July 24, 1221). A stunning novelty was the expedition of Emperor Frederick II of Hohenstaufen (the so-called Sixth Crusade, 1228–1229). Frederick sailed to Cyprus and Acre (June 1228), secretly negotiated a ten-year truce that included the return of Jerusalem, Bethlehem, and Lydda to the Christians, and crowned himself king of Jerusalem (March 18, 1229), although he had been excommunicated by Gregory IX for his failure to act on a Crusade vow earlier. The Holy City was retaken by Muslim allies in 1244 after an expedition of Count Thibaut IV of Champagne had failed to secure the diplomatic gain (1239–1240).

Seventh and Eighth Crusades. Two crusades of the thirteenth century are connected with the name of Louis IX (Saint Louis) of France. In fulfillment of a vow, Louis sailed to Cyprus with a splendid host of fifteen thousand men and attacked Egypt (Seventh Crusade, 1248–1254). Damietta was occupied again (June 1249) but had to be returned together with a huge ransom when the king and his army were routed and taken captive on their slow march south (April 6, 1250). Louis took up residence in Acre for four years, attempting to strengthen the Crusader states by, for example, working toward an alliance with the Mongol khan. Another expedition against the sultan of Tunis (Eighth Crusade, 1270–1272) also ended in failure. The king died in North Africa (August 25, 1270), and the Muslims succeeded in buying off the Crusaders. In the meantime, all of Palestine as well as Antioch was lost to the Mamluk sultan, Baybars. The last Christian bastion on the Syrian coast, Acre, was stormed by the sultan in 1291.

The fourteenth and fifteenth centuries saw several papal attempts to revive the crusade or support expeditions to the East. In 1365, King Peter I of Cyprus captured Alexandria; this victory was widely hailed but inconsequential. Soon the fight against the Ottoman Turks turned into a defense of Christian lands, especially after Muslim victories over the Serbs, the Hungarians (Nicopolis, 1396), and a last Crusader army under John Hunyadi and Julian Cardinal Cesarini (Varna, 1444). The fall of Constantinople in May 1453 led to a serious initiative on the part of Pius II, who wished to go on the crusade in person. He died on the way to joining the fleet at Ancona (July 1464).

OTHER CRUSADES. During the medieval period crusades were also used against internal foes in the West. The granting of Crusade indulgences for the fight against the Moors in Spain beginning with Alexander II (1072) and a crusade to convert the Slavic Wends in northern Germany (1147) set the precedent. These actions were followed by savage crusades against Albigensian heretics in southern France (1209–1229), northern German peasants (1232–1234), and the Hussites (1421–1435), by wars of conversion against the pagan Prussians in the Baltic region (after 1236), and similar expeditions. A different development came with the "political" crusades to protect the papal lands in Italy against the Hohenstaufens. Gregory IX proclaimed the crusade against Frederick II in 1240; Innocent IV followed in 1245; and the French Angevins took Sicily (1261–1264) with full Crusaders' privileges granted by Urban IV.

CHARACTERISTICS. From the beginning, the movement depended on the initiative of the papacy; as a result, the latter's claims to universal leadership were strengthened. Urban II preached the crusade himself, as did other popes. Generally, however, this task was delegated to bishops, papal legates, and specially commissioned Crusade preachers. Few examples of this preaching are known. We have, however, a manual for Crusade preachers written around 1250 by the Dominican master general, Humbert of Romans. A crusade was announced through papal bulls, the first of these having been issued by Eugenius III (December 1, 1145). They normally included exhortation, narration (of the situation in the East), and the enumeration of privileges. The last point was of particular importance. Canon law specified the Crusader's rewards: plenary indulgence, legal advantages such as protection of family and property and the right to be judged in ecclesiastical courts, and financial incentives like exemption from certain taxes and interest payments or the right to sell and mortgage property. Violations were subject to severe punishment, including excommunication, which also applied to those who failed to act on a crusading vow.

Originally, participants expected to pay their own way and to provision their vassals. As enthusiasm faded, the financing of a crusade became more complicated. Apart from using current income, popes from the mid-twelfth century on authorized special Crusade taxes of 1 to 10 percent on ecclesiastical income for up to five years; taxing rights or a share of the ecclesiastical tithe could be granted also to secular leaders. In 1187, Pope Gregory VIII began granting Crusade indulgences for persons assisting the effort at home, who soon came to include the wives of Crusaders.

A consequence of the growing financial involvement of the popes was the wish to have more direct control of the goals and operations. While Urban II still discouraged participation of the clergy, in practice the situation soon changed. Many clerics joined the expeditions, and papal legates regularly accompanied the armies. Conflicts over authority and leadership were inevitable. Yet the popes had to be flexible. No crusade could be conducted without popular support. The early enthusiasm probably was the expression of a genuine religious sentiment, often in response to charismatic preachers such as Peter of Amiens, Bernard of Clairvaux, Fulk of Neuilly, and Jacques of Vitry. But after the initial success and the later shock over the failure of the Second Crusade, a revival of the original zeal became more difficult despite increased incentives and propaganda efforts. From the middle of the twelfth century on, critical voices were heard, including imperial publicists, Rutebeuf, Roger Bacon, and William of Tripoli. Papal opinion polls (Gregory X, 1272; Nicholas IV, 1292) elicited many answers. As in the isolated event of Francis of Assisi's visit to Sultan al-Kamīl during the Fifth Crusade (spring and summer 1219), the need for a fundamental shift from military intervention to peaceful mission efforts was often stressed, leading to missionary initiatives in the late Middle Ages, especially from the mendicant orders.

OUTCOME. The results of the Crusades are difficult to assess. In terms of religion, the failures nourished doubts about God's will, church authority, and the role of the papacy. Religious fervor yielded to apathy, cynicism, and legalism. On the other hand, the Crusades stimulated religious enthusiasm on a large scale and gave Christendom a unifying cause that lasted for centuries. They inspired a great literature of tracts, chronicles, letters, heroic tales, and poetry, not only in Latin but in the vernaculars. Ignorance of Islam was replaced by a measure of knowledge, respect, and occasionally tolerance. An emphasis on informed apologetics (for instance those of Thomas Aquinas and Ramón Lull) and on Eastern languages (canon 11 of the Council of Vienne, 1311) as a prerequisite for mission was characteristic of the later Middle Ages.

Politically, the Crusades brought few lasting changes. The Crusader states and the Latin empire remained episodes. Their precarious status forced new diplomatic contacts with Eastern powers but also strengthened the Muslim conviction that holy war *(jihād)* could be carried farther west. In this sense the Crusades led directly to the Turkish wars of later centuries, during which Ottoman expansion threatened even central Europe.

The effect of the Crusades on relations with Byzantium was primarily negative. The Crusades needed Byzantine support as much as Byzantium needed Western armies. But what started as an effort to help Eastern Christians ended in mutual mistrust and enmity (for example, the Crusades against the Byzantines in 1237, 1261, and 1282). The shrewd moves of Byzantine diplomacy created the image of the "treacherous Greeks" among Crusaders, while the sack of Constantinople left the indelible impression of Western barbarity on the Greek mind. Thus, the "unions" of Eastern churches with the West (at the councils of Lyons, 1274, and Florence, 1439) had no support at home.

One novelty with an impact on European politics was the military orders founded in the East. The Templars' financial deals with the French crown led to their ruthless suppression (1307–1312); the Hospitalers' odyssey took them to the island of Rhodes (1309–1322) and to Malta (after 1530). The Teutonic Knights found a new task in the Baltic states, and several chivalrous orders in Spain and Portugal were to influence Iberian politics for centuries.

The Crusades imposed huge burdens on clergy and laity; at times the papacy was unable to support any other cause. Yet they also furthered the growth of a money economy, banking, and new methods of taxation. The widening of the geographic horizon prepared Europe for the age of discovery. Urban culture, especially in Italian city-states such as Genoa, Pisa, and Venice, received strong impulses through trade with the East. In the West, Islamic science, philosophy, and medicine deeply influenced intellectual life.

BIBLIOGRAPHY

Many general bibliographies on the Middle Ages feature sections on the Crusades. Two specialized bibliographies provide a thorough introduction to sources and literature: A. S. Atiya's *The Crusade: Historiography and Bibliography* (1962; reprint, Westport, Conn., 1976) and Hans Eberhard Mayer's *Bibliographie zur Geschichte der Kreuzzüge* (Hannover, 1960) with its supplement, *Literaturberichte über Neuerscheinungen zur ausserdeutschen Geschichte und zu den Kreuzzügen,* "Historische Zeitschrift, Sonderheft," vol. 3 (Munich, 1969).

The most comprehensive treatment of the Crusades in English is found in the excellent volumes of *A History of the Crusades,* under the general editorship of Kenneth M. Setton, with Marshall W. Baldwin, Robert Wolff, and especially Harry W. Hazard as editors (vols. 1–2, Philadelphia, 1955–1962; new edition and continuation, vols. 1–5, Madison, Wis., 1969–1984). Steven Runciman's *A History of the Crusades,* 3 vols. (Cambridge, 1951–1954), presents another comprehensive, though somewhat idiosyncratic, approach. The best short introduction is Hans Eberhard Mayer's *The Crusades* (Oxford, 1972).

Carl Erdmann's classic book on the roots of the movement is now available in English: *The Origin of the Idea of Crusade* (Princeton, 1977). Still the most thorough investigation of the religious aspects is Paul Alphandéry's *La Chrétienté et l'idée de croisade,* 2 vols. (Paris, 1954–1959). Benjamin Z. Kedar's *Crusade and Mission: European Approaches toward the Muslims* (Princeton, 1984) stresses the interaction of the two main strategies toward Islam.

Much recent attention has focused on canonical and legal aspects. Major studies are James A. Brundage's *Medieval Canon Law and the Crusader* (Madison, Wis., 1969); Maureen Purcell's *Papal Crusading Policy,* Studies in the History of Christian Thought, no. 11 (Leiden, 1975); and Joshua Prawer's *Crusader Institutions* (Oxford, 1980). A standard work on critical voices is Palmer A. Throop's *Criticism of the Crusade: A Study of Public Opinion and Crusade Propaganda* (1940; reprint, Philadelphia, 1975).

New Sources

Andrea, Alfred J. *The Encyclopedia of the Crusades.* Westport, Conn., 2003.

Brundage, James A. *The Crusades, Holy War, and Canon Law.* Aldershot, U.K., 1991.

Kedar, Benjamin Z. *Crusade and Mission: European Approaches toward the Muslims.* Princeton, N.J., 1984.

Madden, Thomas F., ed. *The Crusades: The Essential Readings.* Oxford, and Malden, Mass., 2002.

Mastnak, Tomaz. *Crusading Peace: Christendom, the Muslim World, and Western Political Order.* Berkeley, Calif., 2002.

Riley-Smith, Jonathan, ed. *The Oxford History of the Crusades.* Oxford, 2002.

Slack, Corliss Konwiser, compiler. English translations by Hugh Bernard Feiss. *The Crusade. Charters, 1138–1270.* Tempe, Ariz., 2001.

KARLFRIED FROEHLICH (1987)
Revised Bibliography

CRUSADES: MUSLIM PERSPECTIVE

The Muslims of Syria, who were the first to receive the assault of the Crusaders, thought the invaders were Rum, the Byzantines. Accordingly, they regarded the invasion as still another Byzantine incursion into Islamic territory, and, in fact, one inspired by previous Muslim victories in Byzantine domains. It was only when the Muslims realized that the invaders did not originate in Byzantium that they began referring to them as Franks, although never as Crusaders, a term for which there was no Arabic equivalent until modern times. Even a century later, the Arab historian Ibn al-Athīr (1160–1233) characterized that first invasion as a part of the general expansion of the Frankish empire that had begun with their conquests in Muslim Spain, Sicily, and North Africa a decade before the campaign in Syria. Nevertheless, the establishment of Frankish kingdoms in Islamic territory, the periodic reinforcement of troops from Europe, and the recurrence of invasion all contributed to a growing Muslim consciousness of the nature of the Frankish threat in Syria and Palestine.

This consciousness was reflected in the development of propaganda in Arabic designed to support the mobilization of Muslim forces against the infidel troops. The second half of the twelfth century saw the emergence of both a major Muslim leader and a literature to abet his efforts. The leader was Nūr al-Dīn (1118–1174), who succeeded in forging the political unity of the Muslims of northern Syria and upper Mesopotamia, thereby providing the basis of a military force strong enough to confront the Franks. Fatimid Egypt was brought under the control of Nūr al-Dīn's lieutenant, Ṣalāḥ al-Dīn, known to the West as Saladin (1138–1193). The literature consisted of poetry, *jihād* ("holy war") tracts, and books extolling the merits of Jerusalem and Palestine. Cumulatively, these works celebrated a Muslim warrior for the faith *(mujāhid)* who would unite the believers in a *jihād* to drive the soldiers of the Cross from the holy places. After the death of Nūr al-Dīn, Ṣalāḥ al-Dīn was able to build on the former's political and military accomplishments and exploit the fervor engendered for a Muslim hero as a means of achieving spectacular success against the Crusaders. Although no single Muslim leader of equal stature emerged under the Ayyubid or Mamluk dynasties that followed, literary support for prosecution of war against the Franks flourished until the very end, when the fall of Acre and the remaining Crusader fortifications on the coast was celebrated as a great victory for Islam, the culmination of a century-old struggle.

It should be emphasized, however, that with few exceptions active support for a concerted Muslim campaign against the Franks was limited to the areas threatened with occupation, namely Syria, Palestine, and Egypt. Various attempts to enlist the help of the Abbasid caliph of Baghdad were futile, partly, no doubt, because the institution of the caliphate was by this time virtually defunct. Even Ṣalāḥ al-Dīn, who was assiduous in seeking caliphal sanction for his activities, never received more than symbolic recognition from a reluctant caliph.

It should also be pointed out that war against the Franks was never total, that Muslim rulers often felt no compunctions about allying themselves with Crusader princes in order to gain their own ends, and that the call for *jihād* was muted when it was expedient, as in 1229 when the Ayyubid ruler al-Malik al-Kāmil (d. 1238) ceded Jerusalem to Holy Roman Emperor Frederick II. Ṣalāḥ al-Dīn himself did not hesitate to strengthen Egyptian ties with the Italian commercial cities in order to obtain the materials he needed from Europe for his campaigns.

With the exception of their fortresses and churches, the Franks left few traces in Muslim territory or consciousness. Although the Muslims looted columns and at least one portal from Crusader structures and incorporated them into their mosques as trophies of victory, Islamic architecture developed independently. Nor is there any evidence of significant influence of Crusader minor arts on Islamic counterparts or, for that matter, of substantial Crusader influence on any aspect of Islamic cultural and intellectual life. There are indications, certainly, in the memoirs of the Syrian knight Usāmah ibn Munqidh (1095–1188) and the Spanish traveler Ibn Jubayr (1145–1217) that Muslims observed their Frankish neighbors with interest, interacted with them on occasion, and even approved of some aspects of their behavior—their treatment of peasants, for example. But the Muslims apparently made no effort to imitate the Franks. While it is sometimes claimed that the Crusaders contributed to the persecution of Christians in Muslim territory, the evidence for this is by no means consistent. There are clear signs that the Muslims in Egypt could and did distinguish between the Copts and the Franks and treated each accordingly. Probably the main Crusader legacy to the Arab Muslims should be sought in the field of commerce. There is little doubt that the activities of European merchants in eastern Mediterranean ports continued to be tolerated, even encouraged, by the Muslim conquerors and thus kept commercial contacts between East and West alive. However, recent Arabic historiography depicts the Crusaders as precursors of modern European infiltrations of the Arab world.

BIBLIOGRAPHY

A detailed study of the Muslim response to the Crusades is Emmanuel Sivan's *L'Islam et la croisade: Idéologie et propagande dans les réactions musulmanes aux croisades* (Paris, 1968), which, though it focuses on the ideological reaction, relates it to political and military events as well. For a different perspective on some of the material discussed by Sivan, see Hadia Dajani-Shakeel's "Jihād in Twelfth-Century Arabic Poetry: A Moral and Religious Force to Counter the Crusades," *Muslim World* 66 (April 1976): 96–113. See also Amin Maalouf's *The Crusades through Arab Eyes* (London, 1984).

Attitudes of contemporary Arab Muslims toward the Crusades can be studied firsthand in *Arab Historians of the Crusades*, edited by Francesco Gabrieli and translated from the Italian by E. J. Costello (Berkeley, 1969), and in Usamah ibn Munqidh's *Memoirs of an Arab-Syrian Gentleman or an Arab Knight in the Crusades*, translated by Philip K. Hitti (1927; reprint, Beirut, 1964). For a comparative study of Muslim and Christian concepts of holy war see Albrecht Noth's *Heiliger Krieg und Heiliger Kampf im Islam und Christentum* (Bonn, 1966).

DONALD P. LITTLE (1987)

CÚ CHULAINN SEE TÁIN BÓ CUAILNGE

CULIANU, IOAN PETRU (January 5, 1950–May 21, 1991), a scholar of Romanian origin, was born in Iaşi, Romania. He descended from ancestors who played an important role in the cultural milieu of this city, the ancient capital of the province of Moldavia. His grandfather, Neculai Culianu, was the dean of the University of Iaşi in the late nineteenth century and the early twentieth century as well as a member of the influential cultural group *Junimea* (the Youthhood), founded in 1867 and directed by the literary critic Titu Maiorescu. Culianu's interest in the history of religions was precocious despite the political and ideological circumstances of his early scholarly career. In 1967 he left Iaşi for Bucharest, where he enrolled in the Faculty of Foreign Letters at the University of Bucharest. He studied Italian Renaissance thought under the guidance of Nina Façon and in 1971 delivered a thesis on the philosopher Giordano Bruno and the magical aspects of his works. Obtaining a short-term scholarship for Italy (University of Perugia) after graduating from Bucharest, Culianu decided to pursue his academic interests as an émigré rather than return to Romania. He spent the rest of his life outside his native country, living in Italy (1971–1978), the Netherlands (1978–1986), and finally the United States (1986–1991), where he died when he was shot in a bathroom at the Divinity School of the University of Chicago. According to Tereza Culianu-Petrescu, "of all the hypotheses regarding the murder, the only one privileged by evidence . . . is that of a political assassination" (in S. Antohi, Zool, p. 57). His biography also includes long stages of research in France and after 1986 frequent return trips to Europe.

Despite the interdictions of the communist-totalitarian regime of his Romanian youth, he discovered and pursued early the writings of Mircea Eliade (1907–1986) and placed himself for many years as a disciple of the great Romanian-born historian of religion. Culianu's first book (1978) was a monograph on Eliade as a historian of religions and as a writer. It was the first in western Europe to systematically discuss many of Eliade's important books and articles written in the Romanian period (1924–1940/1945). Culianu inherited from Eliade the interest for the comparative study of religion and groundbreaking themes, for different axial fields of the discipline, for literature—after 1967 Culianu published novels in Romanian as well as in Italian and English—and for modern Romanian culture. For a span of five years Culianu was also the administrator responsible for Eliade's legacy, his writings and archives preserved in Chicago, and was adopted in the 1980s as his most faithful disciple. Eliade and Culianu published together *The Eliade Guide to World Religions* (1991), which was translated into various languages, but despite its title, the project and the writing of this manual was entirely due to Culianu. The fourth and last volume of Eliade's *A History of Religious Ideas* was edited and published in German in 1990, and a long and significant scientific correspondence between the two scholars has been preserved in the Culianu family archive.

Culianu's Italian period was productive. In this epoch he was a steadfast contributor to journals like *Aevum* and *Studi e materiali di storia delle religioni*, writing many articles and book reviews pertaining to various fields of the history of religions, always with a sharp interest in methodology. The following orientation of his research can be discerned through his articles published in prestigious journals like *Numen* after 1975 and *Revue de l'histoire des religions* after 1976. In 1975 Culianu was appointed the assistant of Professor Ugo Bianchi (1922–1995), his mentor, at the Catholic University of Milan, and began his doctoral thesis. The results of many years of Italian research was collected and refined in a masterly synthesis on eros and magic in the Renaissance, which was finally published in Paris in 1984 as *Éros et magie à la Renaissance*. By analyzing the phantasmagorical background of different religious techniques of humanists like Marsilio Ficino and Giordano Bruno, Culianu demonstrated how the sixteenth- and seventeenth-century censure of Renaissance imagination played a huge role in evacuating from the European religious scene the baffling techniques of manipulation through magic. In Italy, Culianu published a book on Gnosticism, including an interview with Hans Jonas, that shows the great interest he developed for ancient Gnostic thought and its fictitious posterity in modern revivals (*Gnosticismo e pensiero moderno: Hans Jonas*, 1985). In the Netherlands, Culianu taught religious studies at Groningen University and taught Romanian language and literature while making several small contributions in neo-Latin and Romanian topics following the mentorship of Professor Willem Noomen, for whom Culianu edited a Festschrift in 1983.

Culianu then embarked upon a new doctoral thesis (*doctorat d'État*) at the Sorbonne on Gnostic mythical dualism under the supervision of Michel Meslin. This followed the writing of two very useful syntheses, one dealing with "the ascension of the soul" in historical and comparative perspectives (*Psychanodia I: A Survey of the Evidence concerning the Ascension of the Soul and Its Relevance*, 1983) and the other on the topic of ecstasy, ascension, and visionary description of the otherworld (*Expériences de l'extase: Extase, ascension, et récit visionnaire, de l'héllenisme au Moyen Age*, 1984), books that continue to be important for the clear exposition of all their sources, the lucid inquiry into most difficult and fascinating topics of religious studies, and the critiques they directed against the inadequacy, unfounded presuppositions, and factual errors of the German school of the history of religions. Starting in the early 1980s Culianu became more and more interested in different aspects of Gnosticism, yet he equally improved his skill in divergent disciplines like anthropology, cognitive science, literary criticism, and contemporary culture.

Arguably the most important turning point in Culianu's academic career was his departure for the United States in

1986. There he first worked as a fellow and then as an associate professor at the University of Chicago's Divinity School. He adopted a fresh approach to the study of different variants of Gnosticism, aiming to trace in his books on Western dualisms (the two editions of which are different from one another) the different types of Gnostic exegesis applied to the first paragraphs of the *Book of Genesis*, from the early Gnostics to some contemporary Gnostic-fashioned thinkers and artists. By classifying all the types of exegesis and all the possible combinations between the models adopted through the ages by the Gnostics, Culianu revealed the neglected parallel history of Christian dogmatic interpretation and their religious and mythological patterns. The discovery of invariants along two millennia in religious and secular paradigms concerning the exegesis of *Genesis* showed Culianu determined to engage a new type of approach to cognitive studies. In 1990 he founded, with the aim of combining historical and philological scholarship with the epistemology of cognitive studies, an international journal, *Incognita*, which did not survive after his premature death (only the first four volumes appeared in 1990 and 1991). Culianu's last writings include discussion on the hypothesis of determining the nature of religion as a mind game. In *Out of This World: Other-Worldly Journeys from Gilgamesh to Albert Einstein*, his last book (published posthumously), he convincingly combined fresh enquiries on the major transcendent journeys in the mythologies from the ancient Middle Eastern civilization to China with the epistemological speculation about the fourth dimension. In this research, sustained by a brilliant capacity of attracting the attention of different types of readers, Culianu met some of the current hermeneutical paradigms in Italy, France, and the United States, aiming like his mentor Eliade to conceive the history of religions as a total discipline, capable of interacting with a huge constellation of other disciplines and methods of enquiry.

The wide range of topics and academic skills Culianu expressed from his very youth to his death were the subject of internationally acclaimed exegesis. All his major books are accessible in English translation, and many of them have been translated into German, Italian, and other languages. Meanwhile some work of his last period pertaining to the introduction of cognitive sciences' methods into the frame of religious studies was sometimes criticized. *The Tree of Gnosis: Gnostic Mythology from Early Christianity to Modern Nihilism* (1992) is probably his masterpiece, but one can only guess the developments Culianu aimed to pursue. Because of his untimely death he was not able to accomplish several planned works, such as *A History of Magic* and an essay on Raimundus Llullus's *ars combinatoria*. His scholarly posterity remains vivid, as can be appreciated through the two-volume *Gedenkschrift* edited ten years after his death by Sorin Antohi, a Romanian historian of ideas, including more than forty scholarly and biographical contributions from Italy, Romania, and the United States (*Religion, Fiction, and History: Essays in Memory of Ioan Petru Culianu*, 2001). A subsequent Romanian edition was published in 2003. After 2000 a collection of Culianu's books began publication in Romanian by Bucharest's Nemira Publishing House and in Iaşi by Polirom; the latter editorial project aimed to present about forty volumes containing Culianu's collected papers translated into Romanian, of which fifteen have been published, including Culianu's minor writings edited and introduced by Antohi, Culianu's contributions to the *Encyclopedia of Religion* and other encyclopedias, edited by Eduard Irinischi, and the Eliade-Culianu corpus of correspondence, edited by Tereza Culianu-Petrescu and Dan Petrescu. These new volumes better expressed Culianu's solidarity with and, later, important divergences from, his Romanian master, as well as the difficulty in assuming the scholarly heritage of Eliade. The Ioan Petru Culianu Lectures on Religion, delivered by major scholars in the field, were established at the Central European University of Budapest, also through the effort of Sorin Antohi.

See Also Eliade, Mircea.

Bibliography

Culianu, Ioan Petru. *Mircea Eliade.* Assisi, Italy, 1978.

Culianu, Ioan Petru. *Iter in silvis: Saggi scelti sulla gnosi e altri studi.* Messina, Italy, 1981.

Culianu, Ioan Petru. "Religione e accrescimento del potere." In *Religione e potere*, edited by Gianpaolo Romanato, Mario Lombardo, and Ioan Petru Culianu, pp. 173–252. Turin, 1981.

Culianu, Ioan Petru. *Psychanodia.* Leiden, 1983.

Culianu, Ioan Petru. *Éros et magie à la Renaissance, 1484.* Paris, 1984. American ed., *Eros and Magic in the Renaissance.* Translated by Margaret Cook. Chicago, 1987.

Culianu, Ioan Petru. *Expériences de l'extase: Extase, ascension et récit visionnaire, de l'héllenisme au Moyen Age.* Paris, 1984.

Culianu, Ioan Petru. *Gnosticismo e pensiero moderno: Hans Jonas.* Rome, 1985.

Culianu, Ioan Petru. *I miti dei dualismi occidentali.* Milan, 1989. French ed., *Les gnoses dualistes de l'Occident: Histoire et myths.* Paris, 1990.

Culianu, Ioan Petru. *Dictionnaire des religions.* With Mircea Eliade, in association with H. S. Wiesner, Paris, 1990. English ed., *The Eliade Guide to World Religions.* San Francisco, 1991.

Culianu, Ioan Petru. *Out of This World: Other-Worldly Journeys from Gilgamesh to Albert Einstein.* Boston, 1991.

Culianu, Ioan Petru. *The Tree of Gnosis: Gnostic Mythology from Early Christianity to Modern Nihilism.* San Francisco, 1992.

Culianu, Ioan Petru. *Păcatul împotriva spiritului: Scrieri politice* (The sin against the Holy Spirit: Political writings). Bucharest, 1999. Contains political articles from 1989 to 1991, first published in New York.

Culianu, Ioan Petru. *Studii româneşti I: Fantasmele nihilismului; Secretul doctorului Eliade.* Bucharest, 2000. Translated by Corina Popescu and Dan Petrescu as *Romanian Studies I: The Phantasm of Nihilism; The Secret of Dr. Eliade.*

Culianu, Ioan Petru. *Jocurile minţii. Istoria ideilor, teoria culturii, epistemologie* (Mind games: History of ideas, theory of culture, epistemology). Edited by Mona Antohi and Sorin Antohi. Iaşi, Romania, 2002.

Culianu, Ioan Petru. *Iocari serio.* (Science and art in Renaissance thought). Translated by Maria-Magdalena Anghelescu and Dan Petrescu. Iaşi, Romania, 2003.

Culianu, Ioan Petru. *Cult, magie, erezii. Articole din enciclopedii ale religiilor.* Translated by M. M. Anghelescu and D. Petrescu. Iaşi, Romania, 2003. Includes a postscript by Edouard Irinischi about the Eliade-Culianu relationship in the making of the *Encyclopedia of Religion,* including useful previously unpublished material from Eliade's archives.

Culianu, Ioan Petru. *Dialoguri Întrerupte.* Corespondţă Mircea Eliade–Ioan Petru Culianu. Edited by Tereza Culianu-Petrescu and Dan Petrescu. Iaşi, Romania, 2003. Contains revelations concerning their relationship, 1972–1986, and for the historiography of the history of religions.

Eliade, Mircea. *Geschichte der religiösen Ideen.* Vol. 3, pt. 2. Edited by Ioan Petru Culianu. Freiburg, Germany, 1990.

Fiction

Culianu, Ioan Petru. *La collezione di smeraldi.* Milan, 1989.

Culianu, Ioan Petru. *Hesperus.* Bucharest, 1992.

Culianu, Ioan Petru. *Pergamentul diafan.* Bucharest, 1992.

Culianu, Ioan Petru. *Arta fugii: Povestiri* (The art of fugue: Short stories). Iaşi, Romania, 2002.

Works on Ioan Petru Culianu

Antohi, Sorin, ed. *Religion, Fiction, and History: Essays in Memory of Ioan Petru Culianu.* 2 vols. Bucharest, 2001.

Antohi, Sorin, ed. *Ioan Petru Culianu: Omul şi opera* (The man and the works). Iasi, Romania, 2003.

Anton, Ted. "The Killing of Professor Culianu." *Lingua Franca,* September–October, 1992.

Anton, Ted. *Eros, Magic, and the Murder of Professor Culianu.* Evanston, Ill., 1996.

Casadio, Giovanni. "Ricordo di Ioan Petru Culianu (1950–1991)." *Religioni e società* 8 (1993): 85–92. Republished with minor changes in *Manichean Studies Newsletter,* 1993, pp. 4–15.

Casadio, Giovanni. "Ioan Petru Culianu ou la contradiction." *Archævs* 5 (2001): 15–24.

Casadio, Giovanni. "Ioan Petru Culianu, ovvero la storia delle religioni come vita e come arte." *Archævs* 6 (2002): 313–324.

Eco, Umberto. "Murder in Chicago." *New York Times Review of Books* (April 10, 1997).

Idel, Moshe. "Ioan Petru Culianu." *Archævs* 5 (2001): 11–14.

Marchianò, Grazia. "Un uomo per altre latitudini: Ioan Petru Culianu." In *Estetica 1993: Oriente e Occidente,* edited by Stefano Zecchi. Bologna, 1993.

Marchianò, Grazia. "I primi dieci anni postumi di Culianu: Congetture su un pensiero fermato." *Archævs* 5 (2001): 7–10.

Zolla, Elémire. *Ioan Petru Culianu.* Turin, 1994. Reprinted in E. Zolla, *La filosofia perenne,* Milan, 1999, pp. 179–205.

EUGEN CIURTIN (2005)

CULT OF SAINTS.

The cult of saints in the early Christian church began with the commemoration and veneration of the victims of persecution. The earliest forms of this veneration were part of the traditional funerary *memoria* of the dead. The inclusion of the names of martyrs in the liturgies of early Christian communities and the earliest celebrations of the anniversaries of martyrs, often observed at their tombs, rapidly gave rise to specific cults that went far beyond mere commemoration of the dead. The practice of petitions addressed to martyrs on behalf of the living arose out of the belief in the communion of saints, the resurrection of the body, and the high status accorded those who had died for the faith, and who, through their remains, remained physically present among the living. The acceptance of the intercessory role of the martyrs can be seen as early as the *Passion of Saint Perpetua* (early third century).

Although the martyr epitomized the ideal type of saint for centuries, the end of the period of persecution (early fourth century) brought with it a new concept of sanctity: namely, that those persons who lived lives of constant self-martyrdom and extraordinary virtue—had there been persecutions they too would have been martyrs—were also worthy of veneration. Increasingly, first in Syria but then throughout Christendom, persons living lives of extraordinary asceticism were venerated as *sancti* (holy persons). *Sancti* were thought capable of exerting hidden supernatural powers through miracles and, as an extension of this, powers within human society. Thus, *sancti* functioned as mediators among local groups and between local communities and regional and central powers. The sort of human and supernatural patronage that these individuals provided was thought to continue at the site of their tombs after they had died. The bodies were preserved and honored as pledges (Lat., *pignora*) of their continued interest in the living. The sorts of veneration accorded to them—vows, petitions for cures and other miracles, incubation at their tombs, and offerings of goods and specie to the clerics who had charge of their tombs—closely resembled the practices associated with pre-Christian pagan cults, such as that of Asklepios.

The initial cult of saints was focused on their tombs, but the increasing demand for cult objects in the fourth century led, in the eastern part of the empire, to the practice of moving bodies of saints to new locations, although such translations and the practice of dismembering bodies and distributing the various parts as relics were against Roman law. Along with the veneration of saints through their corporeal remains, a cult of saints focusing on their images, or icons, developed in the East. This cult, apparently encouraged by emperors as an extension and reinforcement of the secular cult of the emperor's image, survived the violent iconoclastic attacks of the seventh and eighth centuries and became a major aspect of Eastern Christianity.

In the West, the cult of saints was more conservative and, throughout the eighth century, continued to focus on the tombs of martyrs and early confessors. Nevertheless, objects that had been in physical proximity to saints' tombs were distributed as relics, particularly by the bishops of

Rome, who gained much of their prestige from controlling large quantities of remains of Roman martyrs. Relics of the saints played a major role in the Christianization of the West because the relics were offered to new converts to replace their pagan gods. The locations where bodies or relics were found became primary sites for contact between the human and divine worlds and formed the basis for the reorganization of sacred geography. While the classical world had emphasized the sacrality of urban space and considered extraurban cemeteries unclean, the Christian cult of martyrs and saints gave priority to the suburban cemeteries at the expense of the city.

Churchmen such as Pope Gregory the Great (d. 604) and the bishop Gregory of Tours (d. 594), both of whom sought to establish indigenous Christian traditions, attempted to anchor the cult of saints within the control of the hierarchy by deemphasizing living saints, who were, after all, difficult to regulate, in favor of the dead and by writing lives of Western martyrs and confessors. In these lives and in early medieval hagiography (literature dealing with saints)—which included not only *passiones* ("accounts of martyrdom") but *vitae* ("lives"), *libri miraculorum* ("books of miracles"), and *translations* ("accounts of translations")—saints were largely presented as members of social elites elected before birth as instruments of divine power. The social roles of such saints were severely limited: aside from the early martyrs, the men were normally bishops or monks and the women were almost without exception members of religious orders who had spent their lives in the cloister. The saints' lives and the promotion of their cults, particularly those of Merovingian saints written in the seventh century, were often closely related to the efforts of aristocratic relatives to establish a sacred heritage on which to base their claims of lordship. Thus saints were presented less as models of the Christian life than as evidence of supernatural power.

Threats to Rome by the Lombards in the mid-eighth century led popes to translate the remains of many martyrs into the city from the undefended catacombs. The Franco-papal political and cultural alliances of the following century resulted in an unprecedented number of translations—both sanctioned and illicit—of saints from Rome, Spain, and Gaul to the northern and eastern territories of the Frankish empire.

The demand for the remains of the saints for the purpose of promoting Christianity was enormously important in the subsequent development of medieval religion. In the ninth through eleventh centuries Roman martyrs and local saints, who were often deemed responsible for the evangelization of specific regions, were the focus of much of religious life. Veneration centered on the tombs of the saints, usually buried under the sanctuary of a church. Access to these tombs was controlled by the clergy of the church, frequently monks or canons, who were responsible for the celebration of the liturgy of the saints and direction of the cult. The importance of saints as miracle workers, patrons, and protectors of the region in which their remains were found resulted in the advent of pilgrimages made on principal feast days as well as at other times in the fulfillment of individual vows. The need to accommodate numbers of pilgrims without disrupting the regular liturgical life of the church led to the development of the characteristic pilgrimage church, with its raised crypt and wide ambulatories allowing the faithful to reach the saint's tomb or shrine without disturbing the liturgical life of the community.

During the tenth century the popularity of three-dimensional images of saints began to increase, particularly in the south of France. These statues, which were not unknown earlier and probably developed from statue reliquaries, became increasingly important during the twelfth century, when expanded contact with the Near East and improved internal communication and centralization contributed to the growth of the cults of more international saints, particularly the Virgin and the apostles of Christ. Although relics of the saints maintained their importance, miraculous statues and paintings, particularly in Italy during the later Middle Ages, became the focus of devotions.

Some saints' cults, such as those of the martyrs in Rome, the cult of Saint James in Compostela, and the cult of Saint Foy (Faith) in Conques, became international in their appeal. Most cults, however, were primarily local and regional. Consequently, competition between cults of different saints and between different cult locations for the same saint could be fierce. Beginning in the twelfth century devotion to exclusively local saints gave way to more individual or group choices of patrons as both laity and religious chose specific patrons for their activities and organizations. Devotion to particular patrons became an integral aspect of solidarity and identity in religious orders and communities, lay fraternities, craft and trade guilds, communes, and nascent states. In addition, specific saints became identified with specific types of miracles and thus were sought for specialized assistance.

The competition among cults, as well as the concern of secular and religious authorities over the proper identification and recognition of saints, led in the course of the later Middle Ages to an increasingly formal means of authentication of saints. Prior to the ninth century the process had been extremely informal: the existence of a popular cult among the faithful was usually seen as proof of sanctity. Starting in the ninth century, however, church synods insisted that no new or previously unknown saints could be venerated unless their sanctity was proved by the authenticity of their lives and miracles. The determination of authenticity was the responsibility of the local bishop; recognition meant the inclusion of the saint's name and feast day (usually the traditional anniversary of his or her death) in the liturgical calendar of the diocese. As of the tenth century local groups increasingly sought the inclusion of the saint's feast in the Roman calendar as well, and in time this led to the customary request that the pope recognize the saint's cult with a solemn canonization. With the growth of papal centralization, this practice became more formalized, and from the time of the pontificate of Innocent III (1198–1216), the right of canonization has been reserved to the pope. This did not, however, change the primary role of the faithful in the development of the actual cult. On the contrary, the role of the faithful was of the utmost importance: without an existing cult and evidence of post mortem miracles, no individual, no matter how exemplary his or her life, could be canonized. Because of the enormous expense, political negotiations, and investment of time necessary to effect a papal canonization, very few of the hundreds of persons who were the objects of cults were ever actually canonized, and those who were tended to be members of princely or aristocratic families or important religious orders who could organize, finance, and sustain the canonization process.

The intervention of the papacy in the recognition of saints as well as the social and economic transformations of the later Middle Ages prompted a change in the popular image of saints. From the thirteenth century on, more emphasis was placed on the quality of life of the individual as an imitation of the life of Christ than on miracles. The spectrum of social backgrounds from which the venerated men and women came was also greatly broadened. Under the influence of mendicant spirituality there were more saints from the bourgeoisie, more women who had active roles outside the cloister, and more laity who were seen to have achieved sanctity.

Throughout the late Middle Ages there existed a broad consensus on both the existence of a sort of sensorial code by which one could recognize special servants of God and on a belief in the saint's ability to intervene in all areas of human need. However, from the twelfth century on, a widening gulf separated the mental structures of the laity and the majority of the clergy from the university-trained elite. In the later Middle Ages three groups of persons developed who were accorded sanctity based both on geography and social position. According to André Vauchez (1981), the popular saints were the first group. Venerated primarily in rural areas—generally in northern Europe—they were the closest to the archaic type of saint: persons who, regardless of life and piety, met violent and undeserved deaths. The second group, local saints, varied according to region. In northern Europe they were, as in the early Middle Ages, persons of high rank whose bodies produced miracles. In the Mediterranean world, the local saints were most often persons who had renounced a normal existence for voluntary asceticism, poverty, and chastity. The third group of saints most closely resembled the type of saints whose cults were promoted by the official church.

The official teaching concerning the communion of the saints, the efficacy of the saints as intercessors and, thus, the validity of the cult of saints, has always insisted that whereas saints may be the object of veneration (Gr., *dulia*), they must never be the object of adoration (Gr., *latria*). Since the virtues of the saints are the virtues of Christ, praise of the saints, prayers to them, and veneration of their relics are all ultimately directed to Christ. The reality of several of the specific cults of saints, however, was often at great variance with this official position, and throughout the Middle Ages orthodox reformers occasionally objected to excesses or deviations from the official stance. From the late twelfth century on, radical reformers, such as Pierre Valdès, founder of the Waldensians, went still further by rejecting the intercessory role of saints, thereby denying the validity of the cult. Sixteenth-century reformers, especially John Calvin, were even more forceful in rejecting the mediatory role of saints and condemning the cult of relics and images as idolatry. Despite these oppositions, the cult of saints, especially that of the Virgin, has continued to play an important role within the Catholic tradition, particularly in southern Europe and in Latin America, where the cult of Christian saints has merged with indigenous and African cults in a process similar to that which took place in Europe in late antiquity.

SEE ALSO Asklepios; Iconoclasm; Icons; Persecution, article on Christian Experience; Pilgrimage, articles on Eastern Christian Pilgrimage, Roman Catholic Pilgrimage in Europe, and Roman Catholic Pilgrimage in the New World.

BIBLIOGRAPHY

Peter Brown's *The Cult of the Saints: Its Rise and Function in Latin Christianity* (Chicago, 1981) is a brief, interpretative introduction to the cult of saints in late antiquity. More specialized are his articles on saints and holy men in his *Society and the Holy in Late Antiquity* (Berkeley, 1982). Ernst Kitzinger's "The Cult of Images in the Age before Iconoclasm," *Dumbarton Oaks Papers* 8 (1954): 83–150, reprinted in his *The Art of Byzantium and the Medieval West* (Bloomington, Ind., 1976), pp. 90–156, remains a fundamental introduction to the development of the cult of icons by a leading art historian. In Frantisek Graus's *Volk, Herrscher und Heiliger im Reich der Merowinger: Studien zur Hagiographie der Merowingerzeit* (Prague, 1965), the important Czech historian provides a classic study of the place of saints and hagiography in early medieval society. For the later, Carolingian, period, Joseph-Claude Poulin's *L'idéal de sainteté dans l'Aquitaine carolingienne d'après les sources hagiographiques, 750–950* (Quebec, 1975) examines the changing values of society as reflected in the cult of saints.

Three recent studies have examined the cult of saints in the later Middle Ages in relation to changing social forms and spiritual values. Michael Goodich's *Vita Perfecta: The Ideal of Sainthood in the Thirteenth Century* (Stuttgart, 1982) presents a computer-assisted prosopographical analysis of thirteenth-century saints as an ideal cultural type. Donald Weinstein and Rudolph M. Bell, in their *Saints and Society: The Two Worlds of Western Christendom, 1000–1700* (Chicago, 1982), examine saints between 1000 and 1700 in order to understand the transformation of late medieval and early modern piety. The most important of the three is that of André Vauchez, *La sainteté en Occident au derniers siècles du Moyen-Âge d'après les proces de canonisation et les documents hagiographiques* (Rome, 1981). This magisterial examination of the cult of saints in the later Middle Ages is essential for understanding the interplay of social, religious, political, and cultural factors in the cult of saints.

A number of recent anthologies have collected important articles on saints from specialized journals. The most significant of these are *Agiografia altomedievale*, edited by Sofia Boesch Gajano (Bologna, 1976), and *Saints and Their Cults: Studies in Religious Sociology, Folklore and History*, edited by Stephen Wilson (Cambridge, U.K., 1983). The latter is particularly valuable for its rich annotated bibliography on all aspects of saints and hagiography both Christian and non-Christian.

New Sources

Blumenfeld-Kosinski, Renate, and Timea Szell, eds. *Images of Sainthood in Medieval Europe.* Ithaca, N.Y., 1991.

Crook, John. *The Architectural Setting of the Cult of Saints in the Early Christian West.* Oxford and New York, 2000.

Howard-Johnston, James, and Paul Antony Hayward, eds. *The Cult of Saints in Late Antiquity and the Middle Ages: Essays on the Contributions of Peter Brown.* Oxford and New York, 1999.

Rollason, David W. *Saints and Relics in Anglo-Saxon England.* Oxford and Cambridge, Mass., 1989.

Thacker, Alan, and Richard Sharpe, eds. *Local Saints and Local Churches in the Early Medieval West.* Oxford and New York, 2002.

PATRICK J. GEARY (1987)
Revised Bibliography

CULTS AND SECTS. The terms *cult* and *sect* are regarded as stereotype-loaded terms that are associated with new or unpopular religious movements, and these terms are thus mostly avoided by scholars. They are, however, widely used by the media and by groups (especially so-called anticult groups) that perceive certain new religious movements as objectionable and dangerous. In contemporary English, *cult* functions as the derogatory word, with *sect* reserved for less controversial groups. In French, German, Spanish, and Italian, the derogatory word is the local equivalent of *sect*, and the word *cult* is rarely used. Some dictionaries now translate the French *secte* and similar non-English words with *cult* rather than with *sect.* Originally, however, the English *cult* and *sect* were nonpejorative, scholarly terms. Some earlier uses of *sect* and *cult* in sociology will be reviewed before discussing the current derogatory uses of these terms.

FROM TROELTSCH TO STARK AND BAINBRIDGE. Ernst Troeltsch (1865–1923), a German theologian and sociologist, elaborated in the early twentieth century an influential distinction between churches, sects, and mysticism. Churches, according to Troeltsch, are religious groups well integrated into the larger society. A typical mark of this integration is the fact that most members are born into churches, rather than converted to them. Coming to conclusions similar to those of Max Weber (1864–1920), Troeltsch saw the sect as a religious movement where most members are first-generation converts. Troeltsch's "sect" refers to a group that is typically hostile or indifferent to the larger society and that may criticize churches as being "this-worldly." Sects prefer to remain poor and comparatively small rather than compromise their integrity. Sects, however, may eventually evolve into churches and move toward the mainstream, being replaced at the margins of the religious field by new sects. This happens less often, according to Troeltsch, with mysticism, which is less structured and organized, and survives as a sum of individual experiences.

Troeltsch's typology remained influential in the sociology of religion until World War II. It was revised and refined in the 1940s and 1950s by J. Milton Yinger, who made further distinctions within the descriptions of both sects and churches. Yinger distinguished between "established sects," "sects," and "cults." The latter are small groups of believers sharing a religious experience but not yet organized into a structure. While some cults eventually disappear, others, according to Yinger, become sects, which he defined as religious organizations mostly made up of first-generation converts and existing in a significant degree of tension with the larger society. When second- and third-generation members appear, the sect moves to the stage of "established sect," a transitional position between the Troeltschian types of sect and church. What really differentiates sects from churches is, according to Yinger, "universalism." A sect, even an established sect, does not (yet) regard itself as universal. It only tries to organize a limited group of members. A "denomination" represents the first stage of the transformation of a sect into a church, because it at least proclaims a universal goal, although in fact it is not able to pursue it. "Ecclesiae" (churches) are more universal than denominations, but only "universal churches" are churches in the fullest sense of the word, having achieved their universal goal in practice and not only in theory. Although within Christianity only the Roman Catholic Church is, according to Yinger, a universal church, theoretically every cult can eventually pass through the various stages and become a church.

Troeltsch and Yinger clearly had in mind Christianity, and Christianity only. After World War II, the media often described as sects and cults movements that were not Christian but derived from Hinduism, Buddhism, or the occult tradition. Some sociologists, such as Bryan R. Wilson, tried to redefine *sect* as a word not necessarily connected to Christianity. In Wilson's view, the sect may be defined by its goal, which is both more and less ambitious than the typical goal of a mainstream church. A sect, unlike a church, does not aspire to be recognized by the state as an institution, nor as part of the organizational fabric of society. On the other hand, it wants to deeply change the life of its members, and will occasionally claim that this change will result eventually in a revolutionary change of society itself. These goals may be pursued inside or outside Christianity.

The latest influential sociological statement of the differences between church, sect, and cult was included in *The Future of Religion: Secularization, Revival, and Cult Forma-*

tion (1985) by American sociologists Rodney Stark and William Sims Bainbridge. A *church* is defined (following Troeltsch) as a religious group that accepts, and cooperates with, the dominant social milieu, while a *sect* is a religious group in a situation of tension or hostility with respect to the social mainstream. However, the same group may be regarded at the same time as a sect in one country and a church in another. A sect is by definition a group that exhibits some degree of deviance while remaining within a tradition perceived as nondeviant in a given society. According to this definition, Jehovah's Witnesses are a sect because they are perceived as deviant by mainstream Christianity, yet remain within a (heterodox) Christian tradition that is not perceived as deviant per se in the West. While sects, though deviant, remain within a nondeviant tradition, cults are perceived as both deviant and as belonging to a deviant tradition. For example, Western members of the International Society for Krishna Consciousness, popularly known as the Hare Krishnas, are regarded as belonging to a cult rather than a sect because not only are they perceived as deviant, but the Hindu tradition itself is perceived as deviant and nonmainstream by the general public in the West.

Stark and Bainbridge also proposed a vertical model distinguishing between "audience cults," "client cults," and "cult movements." Audience cults are non-organized (much as Troeltsch's mysticism was) and include the following of a popular author or lecturer. Their "members" may pray or meditate in a common way, but they do not feel the need to organize. Client cults are more organized, since they include the "clients" of a religious leader or group of leaders, who sell services (courses or rituals) on a regular basis, and who would like to keep their client constituency through some sort of organization. Only cult movements are full-blown religious movements, where the permanent organization is more important than the transitional leader-client relationship.

Eventually, Stark, Bainbridge, and Wilson all recognized that *cult* and *sect* were becoming ambiguous labels and should preferably be avoided. Sociologists may use them in a purely neutral, Troeltschian way, without implying that cults or sects are morally or socially "evil," or less acceptable than "genuine" religions. However, since the media, beginning in the 1970s, were using the words *cult* and *sect* to mean dangerous or even criminal religious organizations, most sociologists and historians of religion eventually accepted the proposal by Eileen Barker to use *new religious movement* as a value-free, nonderogatory substitute for *sect* or *cult.* The term *new religions* had already been introduced by various authors, but had gained more acceptance in literature written in French rather than in English. Although there are problems with the concept of "new religious movement," a large majority of scholars follow Barker's suggestion, and the small minority of academics still using *sect* or *cult* is in fact making an implicit statement of sympathy with the goals of the anticult movement.

THE ANTICULT MOVEMENT. For the anticult movement, the distinction is simple. Religions and churches are joined out of free will. Cults and sects (the distinction between the two being somewhat blurred) use mind control, or "brainwashing," in order to attract members and keep them within the fold. Although only a tiny minority of academic scholars throughout the world would take this distinction seriously, it has been used in parliamentary reports and laws (particularly in Europe) and is still widely quoted by the news media.

Prominent in the campaign to promote brainwashing theories in reference to new religious movements was Margaret Thaler Singer (1921–2003), a clinical psychologist who was an adjunct professor at the University of California, Berkeley. She often appeared in court cases and, in a sense, invented a new profession as a psychologist in the service of anticult lawsuits and initiatives. Based on the brainwashing arguments, private vigilantes started kidnapping adult members of new religious movements on behalf of their families, then subjected them to a sort of "counterbrainwashing" technique, which they called *deprogramming.* The largest organization of the American anticult movement, the Cult Awareness Network, was often accused of referring families to deprogrammers, although courts were initially tolerant of the practice.

Criticism of the brainwashing model was offered by the American Sociological Association and the American Psychological Association, as well as by several prominent scholars of new religious movements. Scholarly criticism eventually reversed the trend toward belief in brainwashing in U.S. courts, starting in the U.S. District Court for the Northern District of California in *United States v. Fishman* (1990). Some later decisions deviated in varying degrees from *Fishman,* so this ruling did not spell out once and for all the death of the brainwashing theory. Nevertheless, an important precedent had been set in the United States that later triggered a chain of events which led to the end of deprogramming and even of the largest American anticult organization, the Cult Awareness Network. Caught in the act of referring a family to deprogrammers, the Cult Awareness Network was sentenced to such a heavy fine that it was forced to file for bankruptcy. In 1996 the court-appointed trustee-in-bankruptcy sold by auction the organization's files, name, and logo to a coalition of religious liberty activists led by Church of Scientology members.

Although the brainwashing theory lost its momentum in U.S. courts in the 1990s, the suicides and homicides associated with the Temple Solaire in Switzerland and France in 1994 and 1995 gave the theory new impetus in Europe, where it influenced parliamentary reports (largely unaware of the complicated history of the U.S. controversy) and even resulted in a controversial amendment to the French criminal code in 2001. Paradoxically, although the concept of brainwashing was used during the Cold War in American anticommunist propaganda targeting Chinese Communists, the ideology of brainwashing was used in the People's Republic of China beginning in 1999 to distinguish between "evil cults" and legitimate "religions" in a campaign that initially targeted Falun Gong, but was extended to several underground Christian organizations. The same rationale was applied by the French government's several attempts to prevent "cults" such as the Church of Scientology from operating in France, starting from a parliamentary report published in 1996. In the United States, notwithstanding the prevailing attitude of the courts against the theory of brainwashing, brainwashing metaphors were widely used by the media to provide a quick explanation for why such groups as the Branch Davidians and even al-Qāʿidah should be seen as cults rather than religions.

Although only a handful of academics accept them, distinctions between legitimate "religions" and dangerous "cults" and "sects" remain popular in some European political milieus and in the media, while acquiring a new currency to explain suicide terrorism in the wake of the events of September 11, 2001.

See Also Anticult Movements; Brainwashing (Debate); Deprogramming; New Religious Movements, articles on History of Study, New Religious Movements in Europe, New Religious Movements in Japan; New Religious Movements in Latin America, New Religious Movements in the United States, and Scriptures of New Religious Movements; Temple Solaire.

Bibliography

Anthony, Dick Lee. "Brainwashing and Totalitarian Influence: An Exploration of Admissibility Criteria for Testimony in Brainwashing Trials." Ph.D. diss., University of California, Berkeley, 1996. The key criticism of the distinction between religions and cults based on brainwashing.

Barker, Eileen. *The Making of a Moonie: Choice or Brainwashing?* Oxford, 1984. A case study showing that, in the case of the Reverend Sun Myung Moon's Unification Church, distinctions between cults and religions are not easy to apply.

Introvigne, Massimo. *Il lavaggio del cervello: Realtà o mito?* Turin, Italy, 2003. A summary of controversies about the idea of cults.

Stark, Rodney, and William Sims Bainbridge. *The Future of Religion: Secularization, Revival, and Cult Formation.* Berkeley, Calif., 1985. An early sociological attempt to define the notion of cult.

Troeltsch, Ernst. *The Social Teaching of the Christian Churches.* 2 vols. Translated by Olive Wyon. New York, 1931. An early seminal work about the notion of sect.

Wilson, Bryan R. *Religious Sects: A Sociological Study.* Englewood Cliffs, N.J., 1970. Proposes a definition, and a typology, of sects.

Yinger, J. Milton. *Religion in the Struggle for Power: A Study in the Sociology of Religion.* Durham, N.C., 1946. A further work in the course of the definitional history of the term *sect.*

Yinger, J. Milton. *Religion, Society, and the Individual: An Introduction to the Sociology of Religion.* New York, 1957. Further comments by Yinger on the differences between sects and religions.

Yinger, J. Milton. *The Scientific Study of Religion.* London, 1970. A final word by Yinger on the notion of sect, taking into account later controversies.

Massimo Introvigne (2005)

CULTS OF AFFLICTION See AFFLICTION, *ARTICLE ON* AFRICAN CULTS OF AFFLICTION

CULTURE.

In its most basic sense, culture is that portion or aspect of thought and behavior that is learned and capable of being taught to others. Culture includes customs and worldviews that provide a mental model of reality and a guide for appropriate and moral action. Languages are cultural in that they are learned symbolic information sets and are one of the most important means of encoding ideas and knowledge for memory and communication. All religions are cultural and all forms of spirituality exist within broader traditions or *cultures.*

Culture becomes widely communicated and shared in social groups, and it serves as a foundation for general agreement and common acceptance of certain principles and perceptions as valid, normal, and natural. In this way, the influences on culture are often masked and it is not automatically apparent that one's own views and beliefs are not simply accurate apprehensions of reality, but are, in fact, artificial and, to a degree, arbitrary. Because of this characteristic, culture can be difficult to study, either in oneself or in others. Habitual use makes the cultural lenses that one continually wears disappear from awareness, so that what is seen falsely seems to be objective truth.

In observing foreign peoples and ways of life through one's own cultural lenses, people tend to automatically judge others—insofar as their ways are different from one's own—as erroneous and inferior. At the same time, adherents to other traditions or cultures tend to look upon their customs and beliefs using their own cultural assumptions, and they can misinterpret and judge both thought and action according to foreign standards. This natural human tendency is known as ethnocentrism, which is a major barrier to understanding other ways of life and value systems. Ethnocentrism is overcome through cultural relativism, an approach in which judgment is withheld in a measured fashion in an attempt to understand another people's way of life according to their own perspectives. Once an empathetic understanding is reached, one can begin to compare cultures more accurately according to some external scientific or humanistic standard, in order to discern patterns or make generalizations.

Culture is normally contrasted with instinctual modes of thought and behavior that are not learned, but rather are genetically inherited. While the distinction between biological and cultural inputs is heuristically useful and, indeed, necessary for an understanding of human emotion, cognition, motor behavior, social interaction, and institutions, culture does not exist independently of biologically inherited characteristics, including instinctual drives and behaviors. While some behaviors appear to be almost entirely instinctual (such as an infant's innate ability to suck) as a rule, both biology and culture are implicated in most mental and motor behavior. This can be seen, for example, in food preferences. The biological need for nourishment is culturally elaborated in the great variation in which particular foods are preferred, such that any two peoples may find each other's delicacies unpalatable. These differences, while partly attributable to genetic and constitutional factors, are largely explicable only in terms of cultural difference.

Culture could also be contrasted with individual learning that is incapable of being communicated to others, or with idiosyncratic ideas and preferences not widely shared by the social group. *Culture* is often used in this sense in the social sciences and humanities. When scholars stress a populational rather than an individual perspective, *culture* typically implies a shared perspective ostensibly held by an entire population, such as a religious group or an ethic group, referred to as a culture. However, this usage can mask the fact that learned information is not always shared.

While many animal species include learning and even social transmission of knowledge in their behavioral repertoires, humankind differs from other species primarily in our much greater neurological capacity for culture and the degree to which humans rely on socially learned information as a basis for both individual and group life. Human reliance on culture allows people to adapt to a great variety of environments and psychological stresses, to respond to innumerable challenges, and to transmit to others the lessons learned through experience. One consequence of this ability to both purposely and unconsciously transmit information is that ideas originating in one person's experience can become widely shared among members of social groups. Once cultural ideas are widely shared, they appear to acquire an added aura of truthfulness, supported by apparent mutual confirmation and elaboration. A second consequence of cultural transmissibility is that individuals' ideas can survive, albeit in somewhat altered form, beyond their lifetimes. The capacity for and reliance on culture thus allows traditions to come into existence by providing a means for their codification and transmission.

Particularly in anthropology, where the concept was refined, but also in the other social sciences and humanities, culture is central because of its pervasive relevance to everything that human beings think, feel, and do. Much is captured by the term *culture,* and the phenomena scholars seek to describe, interpret, and explain under its rubric are among the most complex in nature. Therefore, the term has meant different things to different scholars, and it has undergone repeated critiques, abandonments, and redefinitions. Nevertheless, it has proven an extremely useful term with which to discuss and model the great variety of ways of thinking and living that different groups and societies around the world display. This is nowhere more clear than in the study of religion, which has revealed both great diversity and remarkable similarities in the many religious traditions of the world. Contemporary social scientists would agree that differences between religions are differences of culture, though some would use different terms. For this reason, the study of culture must be central to understanding religion as a human phenomenon.

History of the Concept. In its earliest known English usages, *culture* refers to the cultivation of food plants. Philip Smith (2001, p. 1) writes that by the sixteenth century this meaning was metaphorically applied to people to signify proper education and human achievement. In this sense, the term *culture* in English carries a positive bias and refers only to those parts of learned ideals and behaviors that the observer considers good, proper, and refined, as when one speaks of a person being highly cultured, or of culture in the sense of fine arts. In other words, *culture* was originally meant to refer to one's own culture, carried to its most benevolent and ideal state of development.

Edward Burnett Tylor (1832–1917), the world's first professor of anthropology, was the most influential in adapting and changing this English term for the social sciences, humanities, and popular usage. Alfred L. Kroeber and Clyde Kluckhohn (1952/1963, p. 14) verified that Tylor derived these new meanings from the German term *Kultur* as used in the mid-nineteenth-century writings of Gustav E. Klemm. Tylor's definition, first proposed in the 1870s and still widely quoted, broadened the term by removing its ethnocentric bias and narrow reference to artistic achievement to include all socially learned knowledge and the behaviors, institutions, and artifacts that are produced as a result of that knowledge. For Tylor, "Culture . . . , taken in its wide ethnographic sense, is that complex whole which includes knowledge, belief, art, morals, law, custom, and any other capabilities and habits acquired by man as a member of society" (1877 [1871], p. 3).

Tylor's definition accomplished four things. First, with this usage, *culture* could be extended to people whose ideals and practices the scholar personally disapproves of or considers inferior, so that all peoples could be recognized as having culture. This element became central to the development of cultural relativism. Second, one could speak of multiple independent cultural traditions that develop in isolation from one another. This allowed scholars to speak of societies sharing ideas and beliefs as *cultures.* Third, the definition allowed one to treat all socially learned knowledge as part of a single, great body of wisdom produced by humankind as a whole. This allowed scholars to see all peoples as participating in a common project of advancing knowledge. Fourth, one could speak of culture writ large as something that develops and evolves at a level beyond that of the individuals who bear culture. This allowed scholars to analyze those learnable institutions, including religions, that do not reside in full in any individual's mind, but rather are distributed among people and artifacts and seem to transcend the individual.

From around the time that Tylor's new definition of culture was introduced, anthropologists began increasingly to believe that racial and biological explanations could not account for the differences between customs and religions throughout the world. Adopted babies grew up learning the language, religion, and skills of the people among whom they were raised, rather than inheriting those of their biological ancestors. In light of these observations, they made culture the central concept of their discipline—because through it one could explain differences in beliefs and morals in terms of learning, not innate characteristics. Fortuitously, this explanation carried with it the implication that all peoples have an equal potential to learn and develop.

Kroeber and Kluckhohn's detailed history of the term *culture* shows that Tylor's definition remained unelaborated for decades, following which a flurry of new definitions were offered (1952/1963, pp. 291–292). They cite 164 of these offered by 1950. Scholars developed new definitions of *culture* as a way of emphasizing certain elements of what was coming to be seen as an excessively broad concept, including such elements as ideas; learned behavior; symbols; problem-solving devices; normative rules or values; and patterns, systems, and organizations that are abstracted from observed behaviors. Kroeber and Kluckhohn correctly anticipated future revisions of these formulations in terms of "the interrelations of cultural forms[,] variability and the individual," and observed that some British and American anthropologists had avoided the concept altogether because of its vagueness (1952/1963, p. 357). These critiques were harbingers of developments in the second half of the twentieth century, in which the culture concept was further contested, particularly in relation to the problems of the locus, variability, and dynamics of culture.

CURRENT USE AND CONTESTATION IN THE SOCIAL SCIENCES AND HUMANITIES. Because of all its ambiguities and its uneven acceptance, the culture concept has come to be regarded with some suspicion, but nevertheless remains firmly fixed in scholarship. From the 1970s to the 1990s, scholars released a flurry of critiques of the concept. To summarize from Robert Brightman's 1995 review of this literature, several areas of semantic difficulty have been identified. Since the term can be used as a reified abstraction, or to refer to ideas and meanings, *culture* can deflect attention from actual, observable human behavior and interaction. *Culture* is often used to refer to a legalistic guide for behavior, which downplays the importance of individual agency or volitional choice, strategy, and improvisation. In the same vein, *culture* can imply that objective, grammatical systems of behavior control individuals like automatons. *Culture* is also often regarded as a holistic, homogeneous, coherent, functionally integrated pattern, when in fact there is a great deal of internal variation, fragmentation, disorder, contradiction, and contestation. The term *cultures* implies discrete, localized groupings, when in fact people and ideas often overlap and are not strictly bounded. Speaking of cultures can imply that these are ahistorical grouping systems, when in reality they are always changing. *Culture* can be used to mean a primordial, authentic, native way of life when in fact there is constant borrowing and mixing of ideas and practices. This usage can also falsely imply that cultures are discrete objects. Finally, viewing human variation as cultural difference can encourage scholars to exaggerate the differences between peoples, and to imply that these differences must be seen in hierarchical relationship with one another.

Brightman's citation of earlier literature makes it clear that, while many of these critiques have been presented as new, scholars have in fact wrestled with all of these complexities of the culture concept throughout the twentieth century. What is perhaps different in some of the newer critiques is that alternative terms have been suggested, either to replace or to supplement *culture* and to shift attention to processes considered more useful for the study of humanity. For example, Pierre Bourdieu uses *habitus* rather than *culture* to emphasize the disposition and practice of individuals as the proper locus of human social life (1977, pp. 72–95). Lila Abu-Lughod (1991) takes this a step further, suggesting that *culture* be abandoned altogether in favor of Bourdieu's *practice* and Michel Foucault's *discourse,* both of which emphasize the agency of individuals and observable behavior and speech rather than the supposedly timeless control of an abstract culture. Brightman (1995, p. 518) observes that another alternative term, Antonio Gramsci's *hegemony,* has come into common use among those who wish to emphasize the greater influence on ideals and behaviors exerted by people possessing disproportionate power in a society, while *counterhegemony* refers to areas of resistance within these spheres of domination.

Other threads of thinking on the culture concept can be seen in cognitive anthropology. Scholars like Claudia Strauss and Naomi Quinn (1998) have addressed the critique that *culture* is an abstract, timeless, and agentless concept by locating it in human perception, cognition, and shared experience. In this view, culture operates in the mind as generic images of reality, or schemas, that direct perception and alter in response to experiences, allowing culture to be relatively stable, but also capable of change.

Some scholars focus on cultural transmission and reception as a way to remove static or abstract implications from the culture concept. Some use analogies of genetic transmission and evolution, while others, like Dan Sperber (1996, p. 82), explain cultural processes, including the spread of religious beliefs, by using the metaphor of epidemiology. For certain thinkers, such metaphors imply that culture exists in units, sometimes called *memes* after Richard Dawkins's coinage, variously conceived of as songs, stories, or religious beliefs. Such theorized units of culture are controversial, however, and not widely accepted by scholars, who see them as arbitrary, unbounded, and changeable (see Aunger, 2001).

The interdependencies and relationships between the cultural and genetic information that contributes to each individual's capabilities and makeup, together with human agency as a force in its own right, are also pressing concerns for some scholars of culture, as Lee Cronk (1999) discusses. Despite the various critiques, *culture* continues to be a useful term in the social sciences and humanities, not only in spite of, but also because of, its multiple meanings and ambiguity.

THE RELATIONSHIP BETWEEN CULTURE AND RELIGION. Virtually all of the questions that scholars in the humanities and social sciences seek to answer involve cultural factors, and questions about religion are no exception. There are certainly biological components to religious behavior, including cognitive tendencies to anthropomorphize, or perceive humanlike attributes in nonhuman phenomena, which Stewart Guthrie (1993) sees as the source of religion. Cognitive constraints limit what kinds of perception and beliefs are conceivable, and, as Pascal Boyer (1994) argues, the combination of ideas that are memorably bizarre or "unnatural" with those that are believably ordinary or "natural" appears to be a characteristic of all religious beliefs. However, no religious belief or behavior can be understood by reference to biological factors alone, for culture overlays, stylizes, elaborates, and embellishes these foundations with meanings that are both deeply motivating and arbitrary. The capacity for religious thought and experience has its foundation in our biological makeup, but it can only come to full expression with cultural inputs and processes. Thus, cognitive constraints interact with culture to produce the range of specific supernatural beings and forces that are characteristic of the world's religions.

No specific religious system can be understood without recourse to culture, for particular religions are forms of culture and exist within broader cultures. Regardless of whether one takes a theological or an agnostic perspective on a particular religion, one must recognize that the stuff of religions is cultural—it is socially learned and widely shared, and it is made up of mental and public representations of reality that guide behavior and are changed by experience. Successful religions can be seen as more widely appealing than others, and therefore more likely to be culturally learned. The fact that religions operate within broader cultural contexts is profoundly relevant to the study of religion because the "same" religious ideas change when they are transmitted from one culture to another—as shown, for example, in Kenelm Burridge's 1960 study of how beliefs of European missionaries were interpreted very differently by their Melanesian recipients, creating a "cargo cult." Syncretism, or the mixing of elements from different religious in situations of culture contact, are an important area of cross-cultural religious studies—as explored, for example, in Charles Stewart and Rosalind Shaw's (1994) volume on this phenomenon. In other cases, religions appear to be transmitted wholesale across cultural boundaries, as exemplified in Joel Robbins's (2004) account of a Papua New Guinea people's adoption of Baptist Christianity and concepts of sin, modernity, and globalization.

To study religions—whether one's own or others'—with cultural sophistication necessitates awareness of multiple points of view. Awareness of the cultural perspective of both scholars of religion and the people they describe is vital to assessing any study of religion. Missiologists begin with a cultural assumption of the primacy of a particular religious tradition in relation to other religious cultures that they consider erroneous and in need of change. Some social scientists work from materialist assumptions that deny the existence of supernatural beings and forces for lack of evidence, while others either embrace the existence of spirits or consider such questions unanswerable. Theories about religion, like religions themselves, are cultural.

IMPLICATIONS OF THE COMPARATIVE STUDY OF CULTURES FOR THE STUDY OF RELIGION. Cross-cultural research indicates that religious thinking and behavior is found among all peoples and in all cultures. The basis of this commonality is sometimes attributed to a panhuman tendency to supernaturalism, which is elaborated differently from one culture to the next. However, others argue that the concept of supernaturalism is itself too culturally biased to describe all religions. Scholars engaging this debate have not reached consensus (see Lohmann, 2003). The degree to which culture determines human religiosity itself remains contested. However, there is no doubt that the particular beings, forces, and morals that people sense or believe in are culturally learned, since they differ from one religion to the next. Variation in specific religious ideas shows the degree of cultural malleability that humans possess with regard to religion. Perhaps the most important implication of the comparative study of cultures for the study of religion is that all religions appear to be true from the perspective of the cultural systems in which they are found; however, the arbitrariness and variability of cultures indicates that no religion is a flawless representation of absolute truth.

SEE ALSO Religion.

BIBLIOGRAPHY

Abu-Lughod, Lila. "Writing against Culture." In *Recapturing Anthropology: Working in the Present,* edited by Richard Fox, pp. 137–162. Santa Fe, N.Mex., 1991. An influential essay arguing that the term *culture* should be replaced with *practice* and *discourse.*

Aunger, Robert, ed. *Darwinizing Culture: The Status of Memetics as a Science.* Oxford, 2001. A volume in which a variety of scholars debate the utility of memes as models of culture's units and their implications for cultural transmission and evolution.

Bourdieu, Pierre. *Outline of a Theory of Practice.* Translated by Richard Nice. Cambridge, U.K., 1977. Broadly influential in social science, this book avoids the culture concept but describes cultural phenomena, emphasizing individual dispositions and decision-based behavior.

Boyer, Pascal. *The Naturalness of Religious Ideas: A Cognitive Theory of Religion.* Berkeley, Calif., 1994. This book cross-culturally explores common themes in all religious ideas, arguing that these point to constraints in human cognition.

Brightman, Robert. "Forget Culture: Replacement, Transcendence, Relexification." *Cultural Anthropology* 10, no. 4 (1995): 509–546. Usefully summarizes critiques of the term *culture,* its changing meanings, and its replacement with new terms.

Burridge, Kenelm. *Mambu: A Melanesian Millennium.* London, 1960; reprint, Princeton, N.J., 1995. A classic and readable account of a cargo cult—an example of how Christian beliefs altered when they entered a new cultural context.

Cronk, Lee. *That Complex Whole: Culture and the Evolution of Human Behavior.* Boulder, Colo., 1999. A book describing approaches to cultural transmission and change drawing on biological evolutionary theory, sociobiology, and memetics.

Guthrie, Stewart Elliott. *Faces in the Clouds: A New Theory of Religion.* Oxford, 1993. A book exploring the causes and prevalence of anthropomorphism, arguing that religion derives from this tendency to misperceive.

Kroeber, A. L., and Clyde Kluckhohn. *Culture: A Critical Review of Concepts and Definitions.* Cambridge, Mass., 1952; reprint, New York, 1963. A detailed tracing of the culture idea in the social sciences and humanities, including numerous quoted definitions.

Lohmann, Roger Ivar, ed. "Perspectives on the Category 'Supernatural.'" Special issue, *Anthropological Forum* 13, no. 2 (2003). A collection of essays debating the value of *supernaturalism* as a culture-neutral concept for describing religions cross-culturally.

Robbins, Joel. *Becoming Sinners: Christianity and Moral Torment in a Papua New Guinea Society.* Berkeley, Calif., 2004. An ethnographic description of the cultural changes brought about by the rapid adoption of Christianity by a remote people.

Smith, Philip. *Cultural Theory: An Introduction.* Malden, Mass., 2001. An excellent and readable overview of cultural theory, wide-ranging but emphasizing sociology.

Sperber, Dan. *Explaining Culture: A Naturalistic Approach.* Oxford, 1996. A lucid book that defines culture as mental and public representations of reality, arguing that to explain culture, one must show why certain ideas, including religious beliefs, become more common than others.

Stewart, Charles, and Rosalind Shaw, eds. *Syncretism/Anti-Syncretism: The Politics of Religious Synthesis.* London, 1994. A collection of essays on cross-cultural religious mixing, known as syncretism—at times a controversial term insofar as it is used to imply that mixed religions are less authentic than others.

Strauss, Claudia, and Naomi Quinn. *A Cognitive Theory of Cultural Meaning.* Cambridge, U.K., 1998. A sophisticated treatment of culture that responds to critics of the concept by drawing on cognitive theory to remove *culture's* abstraction.

Tylor, Edward B. *Primitive Culture: Researches into the Development of Mythology, Philosophy, Religion, Language, Art, and Custom.* 2d ed. 2 vols. New York, 1877. The Victorian source of the extremely influential first anthropological definition of culture, this book proposes a now dated evolutionary model of cultural and religious advancement, but nevertheless contains much of lasting value.

ROGER IVAR LOHMANN (2005)

CULTURE CIRCLES SEE KULTURKREISELEHRE

CULTURE HEROES. The culture hero is a mythical being found in the religious traditions of many archaic societies. Although the culture hero sometimes assists the supreme being in the creation of the world, the most important activity for the culture hero occurs after creation: making the world habitable and safe for humankind. The culture hero establishes institutions for humans, brings them cultural goods, and instructs them in the arts of civilization. Thus, the hero introduces culture to human beings.

The culture hero, unlike the supreme being, is neither omniscient nor omnipotent. In some cases, the hero's behavior resembles that of a clown or buffoon; in the myths of many North American Indian tribes the culture hero appears as the trickster. Various scholars have referred to the culture hero as transformer, demiurge, culture bringer, *héros civilisateur,* and, most frequently, *Heilbringer.*

HISTORY OF SCHOLARSHIP. The German historian Kurt Breysig first introduced the term *Heilbringer* in 1905. Since then, the idea of the culture hero has been interpreted in various ways. Early interpretations emphasized the place of the culture hero in the evolution of the idea of a supreme being. Breysig, for example, saw the culture hero as belonging to a stage of religious development that was not only earlier than, but also inferior to, humankind's awareness of a personal supreme being. The German ethnologist Paul Ehrenreich, in developing his theory of "nature mythology," interpreted the myths about culture heroes as attempts by primitive humans to understand their natural surroundings. Ehrenreich saw in the culture hero the embodiment of the structure and rhythms of natural phenomena, for example, the rising and setting of the sun, the waxing and waning of the moon, and the movement of the stars and constellations. On the other hand, Wilhelm Schmidt, an ethnologist and historian of religions, was the chief proponent of the doctrine of primitive monotheism (*Urmonotheismus*). Theorizing that even early humans believed in a supreme being, he contended that the *Heilbringer* was never a genuine creator and that the form appeared in archaic societies after, not before, the idea of the supreme being.

The interpretations of Breysig, Ehrenreich, and Schmidt have been rejected by later students of culture and historians of religions, who, having access to more and different ethnological data, have recognized the autonomy and complexity of the culture hero. Scholars such as Hermann Baumann, Adolf E. Jensen, Mircea Eliade, Otto Zerries, Raffaele Pettazzoni, and Harry Tegnaeus have made significant contributions to a new appreciation and understanding of the culture hero. Rather than pursue an evolutionary approach, these scholars have examined the relation between the details of the myths and the historical and cultural realities of the archaic societies—their economic activity, their political and social institutions, and their attitude toward space, time, and mortality.

CHARACTERISTIC ACTIVITIES. In many of the myths that tell of the culture hero's exploits, the culture hero is portrayed as setting the stage for human survival. The myth of the Jicarilla Apaches of the southwestern United States tells how the culture hero Jonayaiuin saved humanity by destroying huge monsters that were killing people. By removing this threat of annihilation, the culture hero made the world fit for human habitation. The Malecite Indians of northern Maine tell that long ago a monster, Aglabem, withheld all the water in the world, causing people to die of thirst. Their culture hero, referred to as "a great man," killed Aglabem and released the waters by felling a huge tree. This tree became the Saint John River; its branches, the tributaries of the river; its leaves, the ponds and lakes at the heads of the streams. To the tellers of this myth, the shape of the landscape is evidence that the culture hero made the world fit for human life.

In various ways, the culture hero creates distinctions between humans and animals. The Tupian peoples of the Amazon basin in eastern Brazil believe that Korupira, a deity who is referred to as "lord of the beasts," protects wild game against human hunters. Korupira has the power to close the forest to hunters and punish those who kill his animals needlessly. The Mbuti, hunters and gatherers who inhabit the rain forest of central Africa, are one of many groups who credit their culture hero with bringing them fire. The Mbuti hero, Tore, stole fire, much to the chagrin of the neighboring chimpanzees, and gave it to humankind. From that time on, humans have enjoyed the use of fire while chimpanzees have lived in the forest without it. In the stories of numerous societies, the culture hero introduced humans to speech and manners, established the social differences between males and females, and instituted the laws of society.

The culture hero is also perceived as making economic life possible for humans. According to the myths of the San (Bushmen), a hunting and gathering people living in South Africa and Namibia, the culture hero Kaang created all wild game and gave the animals their colors, names, and characteristics. He taught the San how to make bows, poisoned arrows, traps, and snares, and he instructed them in hunting techniques. Tudava, the culture hero of the Trobriand Islanders, not only taught the Trobrianders how to build canoes and to fish but introduced them to the cultivation of yams and taros, the first root crops. Nyikang, the culture hero and first king of the Shilluk, pastoral nomads of East Africa, is said to have been the son of a cow. He released the waters and provided grazing land for the Shilluk's cattle. Among the Dogon people of Mali, West Africa, the twin culture heroes known as Nommo are credited with bringing the first millet seeds from heaven to earth and with teaching the arts of blacksmithing and pottery.

In numerous myths, the culture hero is connected with the origin of death. In a story told by the Khoi (Hottentots) of South Africa, the moon sends an insect to tell humans that after they die they will come back to life, as the moon does. The culture hero, Hare, overtakes the insect and volunteers to carry the message. However, Hare delivers the opposite message to humans, saying that they will perish forever.

Through the adventures in which they ensure human survival, institute the difference between humans and animals, introduce humankind to social and economic activity, and originate human mortality, the culture heros save the human race from chaos. They order and arrange the world, introducing humankind to the possibilities of human creativity.

BIRTH OF THE CULTURE HERO. The culture hero is able to perform these feats because he is imbued with power; he comes from another world. His divine origin is revealed in his parentage and in the supernatural nature of his birth. Tudava, the culture hero of the Trobriand Islanders, was said to have been born of a mother who became pregnant while sleeping in a cave, when her vagina was pierced by water dripping from a stalactite. The mother of Manabozho, the culture hero of the Menomini tribe of North America, was made pregnant by the wind. The mother of the culture hero of the Dinka of East Africa came to earth already pregnant. Among several African peoples, the culture hero was born from the knee or thigh of a man or woman. Regardless of the way the culture hero is born, his origin is not of this world.

DISAPPEARANCE AND TRANSMUTATION. After setting the world in order for humankind, the culture hero usually disappears. Sometimes the culture hero is killed while conquering monsters; frequently returning to a point of origin—into the sky or earth. In the myths of several peoples, the culture hero is transformed into the moon or stars or constellations. In other instances, particularly among the Australian tribes, the culture hero disappears into the earth at a specific spot, which is marked by a stone, a plant, or a body of water. Such a place, imbued as it is with power, becomes the site of the tribe's initiation and increase ceremonies.

One of the dramatic myths of the disappearance and transformation of a culture hero is that of the people on the island of Ceram in Indonesia, reported by the German ethnologist Adolf E. Jensen. The principal culture hero, Hainuwele, who in this case was a maiden, was murdered by other beings in mythical times. Their punishment, imposed by Hainuwele's sister, was that they were forced to consume the body of their victim. Then the body of Hainuwele was transformed into useful root crops, which before that time had not existed. Her sister became mistress of the underworld. This primeval murder signaled the end of mythical time and the beginning of the historical world.

The events leading up to the murder and transformation of Hainuwele established the institution of cannibalism among the people of Ceram. It also established the initiation ceremony: The young men must kill, imitating the primordial murder of Hainuwele as part of their rite of passage to manhood. Further consequences of this murder were the cultivation of root crops, the delineation of the people into separate clans, the establishment of cult houses, the separation of humans from ghosts and spirits, and the establishment of rules governing entrance to the mythical land of the afterlife. Jensen's research demonstrated the significance of the murdered culture hero among those peoples who practice root crop cultivation.

In the mythology of the Cheyenne of North America, maize originated from the murdered body of their culture hero. The transmutation of the culture hero into food, however, is not limited to the myths of agricultural societies. The Central Inuit (Eskimo) tell of Sedna, a female culture hero, who was murdered by her father. Different sea animals emerged from parts of her mutilated body—whales from her fingers, whale bones from her fingernails, and seals from the second joints of her fingers. As in the case of Hainuwele's sister, Sedna became the mistress of the underworld.

VARIOUS MANIFESTATIONS. The culture hero often appears as twins, who usually symbolize opposites. They may be of different sexes. Frequently the elder is the hero while the younger is depicted as foolish and inept. The twin heroes of the Iroquois of North America are brothers who have different fathers: One, who represents good, is the son of the sun, while his brother, who represents evil, is the son of the waters.

While Hainuwele, Sedna, and many other culture heroes are anthropomorphic, the culture heroes of many societies are theriomorphic. In Oceania, the culture hero is frequently a snake; in South America he is often a jaguar. In many tribes of North America and Africa, the culture hero appears as an animal or insect and has the characteristics of a trickster. Ananse the spider, the culture hero of many of the peoples of West Africa, is popularly known as "the foolish one"; the southern African San's culture hero, Praying Mantis, is seen as a mischievous trickster. Among North American tribes, the coyote, the hare, the mink, the chipmunk, and the crow are common forms of the trickster.

In many instances, the activities of the trickster parallel those of other culture heroes: The trickster destroys monsters, creates animals, and introduces humans to various forms of technology and social institutions. However, the trickster's adventures are also marked by failures and stumblings, deceptions and lies, awkwardness and crudity. Tricksters are often portrayed as oversexed, gluttonous, and amoral. They continually violate the institutions and prohibitions they had established. They can be alternately gracious and cruel, truthful and mendacious.

The American anthropologist Paul Radin (1956) interprets the figure of the trickster and the trickster's adventures as symbolic of humankind's development from an undifferentiated psyche to a differentiated and individual one. The adventures of the trickster, Radin contends, are symbolic of the movement from a state of asociality or nonsociality to one of sociality, from isolation to being a part of the community. The trickster not only creates or modifies the physical and social environment of humankind; by violation of the social rules and the contempt the trickster exhibits toward sacred objects, the trickster creates a kind of internal space for humankind. The trickster legitimates rebellion and disobedience by constantly challenging the status quo of the cosmos.

The phenomenon of the culture hero is very complex. Although the hero usually appears as male, some cultures have a culture heroine. In some societies, the hero is the object of a cult; in others he or she is not. Sometimes the culture hero appears as the offspring of the supreme being and assists in creation; in other instances, the culture hero is the supreme being's adversary. Visible forms of the culture hero range from human to animal, from insect to heavenly body.

Having completed his or her task on earth, the culture hero disappears, sometimes ascending to the sky or descending to the underworld. Occasionally the culture hero is transformed into a natural phenomenon such as the stars or the moon, while in some religious traditions the hero's parting accounts for shapes in the landscape.

In spite of the multifarious forms and adventures of the culture hero as they appears in different cultures, the culture hero clearly discloses one characteristic: The culture hero's mode of being reveals the sacrality of cultural and social institutions and activities that constitute the context of ordinary life for humankind. Participation in these activities by the people of archaic societies provides meaning and value to their lives and enables them to live in a sacred cosmos.

SEE ALSO Animals; Cosmogony; Death; Lord of the Animals; Tricksters; Twins.

BIBLIOGRAPHY

A general discussion of the culture hero can be found in the chapter entitled "Mythische Urzeitwesen und Heilbringer" in Ferdinand Hermann's *Symbolik in den Religionen der Naturvölker* (Stuttgart, 1961), pp. 98–109. This book also contains an excellent bibliography. Two good books on the culture hero in Africa are Hermann Baumann's *Schöpfung und Urzeit des Menschen im Mythus der afrikanischen Völker* (Berlin, 1936) and Harry Tegnaeus's *Le héros civilisateur* (Stockholm, 1950). Otto Zerries's *Wild- und Buschgeister in Sudamerika* (Weisbaden, 1954) is an exhaustive study of the culture hero in the myths of hunting and gathering cultures in South America. The role of the culture hero among archaic cultivators is discussed in Adolf E. Jensen's *Myth and Cult among Primitive Peoples* (Chicago, 1963). This book also treats the relation of the culture hero to the supreme being. The pioneering work on the trickster figure among North American Indians in Paul Radin's *The Trickster: A Study in American Indian Mythology* (New York, 1956). A readable and enlightening critique of Radin's position can be found in Mac Linscott Ricketts's "The North American Indian Trickster," *History of Religions* 5 (Winter 1966): 327–350. Robert D. Pelton, in *The Trickster in West Africa: A Study of Mythic*

Irony and Sacred Delight (Berkeley Calif., 1980) extends the study of the trickster to the peoples of Africa and applies methods of literary criticism in his analysis.

JEROME H. LONG (1987)

CUMONT, FRANZ. Franz Valèry Marie Cumont (1868–1947) was a Belgian historian of religions, as well as a philologist, archaeologist, and epigraphist. He studied at Ghent (1886–1888) and in Germany and Austria (Bonn, Berlin, Vienna [1888–1890], with Usener, Diels, Mommsen, Benndorf, and Bormann), after which he made the classical "grand tour" in Greece and Rome (1891), followed by a year in Paris (École Pratique des Hautes-Études, IVe section, 1892, with Duchesne, Haussoullier, etc.). He became professor of classical philology and ancient history at the University of Ghent in 1892, a position he left in 1911 when the minister of education, supported by the Catholic lobby, denied him the chair of Roman history. Cumont's *Religions orientales dans le paganisme romain* (1906) had presented a new vision of the historical links between the diffusion of Oriental religions and the development of Christianity. Cumont had friendly relationships with several modernists, including Alfred Loisy, Louis Duchesne, and Ernesto Buonaiuti; he also published works in modernist journals in France and Italy, and was thus considered a "subversive" scholar by conservative Catholics. He retired in 1911, and in 1913 he decided to live in Rome and Paris as a private scholar, rejecting offers of several academic positions.

Cumont passed through the two world wars without fighting, but he tried to maintain intellectual activity as a sign of cultural resistance. He never married and died in 1947 near Brussels, without direct heirs. Cumont bequeathed his archive and rich library, in which the history of religions and the sciences were especially well represented, to the Belgian Academy in Rome. The more interesting part of the archive is the scholarly correspondence, which includes about twelve thousand letters received by Cumont from 1885 to 1947 from more than a thousand scholars around the world. These documents offer a rich and complex picture of the scientific, cultural, and political background of Cumont's period and activity, and of the scholarly "cartography" of his time.

Cumont's first major study is the Mithraic corpus *Textes et monuments figurés relatifs aux mystères de Mithra* (1894–1899), which was the foundation for the scientific study of Mithraism. Cumont published an abridged version, *Les mystères de Mithra*, in 1900, which was translated into German and English (*The Mysteries of Mithra*, 1910). In 1900 Cumont and his brother Eugène traveled to Asia Minor (Pontus and Armenia) in search of the Asiatic roots of Mithra, but, though he found and published a number of new inscriptions, he did not find answers to his questions about Mithra's origin. His *Textes et monuments figurés relatifs aux mystères de Mithra* remained the standard work on Mithraism for more than half a century.

In the 1970s Cumont's reconstruction of the Mithra's mysteries came under criticism by Richard Gordon and others. Three main problems were outlined: (1) The Anatolian, or more precisely Persian, origin of the Mithra cult, which seems to develop only in the Roman context; (2) the role attributed to the magi; that is, the Persian and Chaldean astrologers, in the cult's transmission and diffusion; and (3) the dating of Mithraism, which, according to Cumont, appeared in the Hellenistic period, though it was only documented in Roman times. However, after the discovery of the Mithraeum (Sanctuary of Mithra) in Dura-Europos in 1934 and then in Doliche (Commagene; c. 100 BCE), it seems that Cumont's ideas were not in error, and research tends to back up both the Anatolian origin and the Hellenistic dating.

In 1905 Cumont lectured at the Collège de France about Asiatic cults in Roman paganism, which led in 1906 to his famous book ("a little book about a great topic," as he said himself) *Les religions orientales dans le paganisme romain*. The book focuses first on the historical background and channels of the Oriental cults' diffusion in the Roman Empire; it also contains four chapters about major cults from Asia Minor (Cybele and Attis), Egypt (Isis and Serapis), Syria (Atargatis, Baal, Adonis), and Iran (Mithra). The book ends with a conclusion on the role of astrology and magic. In the fourth edition (1929), Cumont added a chapter on the Dionysiac mysteries. He was the first to point out the importance of the so-called Oriental cults for the evolution of Roman paganism, and he attempted to study them not only from the legal and public point of view, but also from the social and private one. Cumont emphasizes the multiethnic character of the Roman Empire, where the acculturative power of the religious practices was very strong. Cumont also tries to explain how the Oriental cults paved the way for the adoption of Christianity.

Though Cumont's work had a deep influence on the next generations, his vision must be revisited. First, the concept of "Oriental religions" is too imprecise and too general. The "Oriental cults" were in fact more "Greco-Oriental"—they passed first from Asia to Greece, where they were deeply Hellenized, and then from Greece to Rome. Thus, Cumont's vision is too linear and "diffusionist," and the diffusion from Asia to Rome seems to be an artificial reconstruction. The reception of the "Oriental cults" in different parts of the Roman Empire (for example, on the Danubian limes) provoked assimilations and syncretisms between the Roman, Greek, and Oriental cults and did not erase the Romans' ancient religious beliefs, but it encouraged cultural interactions, as demonstrated in Nicole Belayche's work (e.g., 2001) on this topic. Nonetheless, Cumont's *Les religions orientales dans le paganisme romain* remains a fundamental step in the history of ancient religions.

In 1911 Cumont lectured in Sweden and in the United States about *Astrology and Religion among the Greeks and the Romans* (1912). In this work Cumont underlines the importance of astrological determinism and its consequences on the religious conceptions of the soul's destiny and of its afterlife journey. This work is related to a great philological enterprise that Cumont began in 1898: the *Corpus codicum astrologorum graecorum.* The aim was to collect information about astrological manuscripts conserved in major European libraries. Cumont, with several collaborators (in particular Franz Boll), published several volumes on the Italian, German, British, and French libraries. He used the occasion to study ancient astrological conceptions and the relationship between philosophical and religious theories, especially Neoplatonism.

Cumont thereafter published numerous essays on Greek and Roman eschatology. In 1922 he published *Afterlife in Roman Paganism;* in 1942 *Recherches sur le symbolisme funéraire des Romains*; and in 1949 (posthumously) *Lux Perpetua,* a scientific testament that has not been supplanted as a standard work. Cumont traces the development of conceptions of the soul, especially in the Roman world. According to ancient popular belief, a dead person survived in the tomb or as a shadow in the netherworld and could return to earth as a ghost to haunt the living. Belief in a celestial immortality appeared to Cumont to have been borrowed from Irano-Chaldean magi by Greek philosophers. This belief, owing to Pythagorean, Platonic, and Stoic influences, gradually spread from the cultivated elite to the common people, although at this point the soul was still not conceived as nonmaterial; rather, it was believed to be a subtle fluid or vapor. It was not until the rise of Neoplatonism that the opinion arose, which prevailed in Christianity, that the soul was distinct from the conditions of space and time and reached, after death, beyond the limits of the world into eternity. As for funerary art, most was allegorical, though a small proportion was supposed to represent literally the afterlife in the netherworld. Cumont examines how Greek myths—such as the stories of Phaeton, Marsyas, or the Muses—came to be used, through philosophical interpretation, as themes for the decoration of the sarcophagi of the upper classes.

Different aspects of Cumont's reconstruction were challenged by Arthur Darby Nock and Paul Veyne, who doubt that such a symbolic value is actually perceptible. Veyne prefers to speak of an "aesthetic" atmosphere, while Nock stresses the fact that Cumont gives too much importance to philosophical and literary evidence, and consequently presents as a general phenomenon what was actually a conception among elites.

Cumont's works on Julian include *Recherches sur la tradition manuscrite des lettres de l'empereur Julien* (1898); with Joseph Bidez, *Imp. Caesaris Flavii Claudii Iuliani Epistulae, leges, poematia, fragmenta varia* (1922); *L'Égypte des astrologues* (1937); and, with Bidez, *Les Mages hellénisés* (1938). This last work is a critical edition of and an abundant commentary on texts (mostly in Greek) that were issued in antiquity under the authority of Zoroaster/Zarathushtra, or other so-called magi. The very existence of such Hellenized magi remains doubtful however: many if not all of those works were written by Greeks, Romans, and others, who were not magi.

Cumont also played a major role in the excavations of Dura-Europos (*Fouilles de Doura-Europos, 1923–1924,* 1926), begun in 1923 and later led by Cumont with Michael Rostovtzeff. Cumont also encouraged the Belgian excavations in Apamea.

From a methodological point of view, Cumont was a complete scholar able to make use of all the sources (literary and material) available to him to present a vivid and richly documented historical fresco. He was an excellent philologist (Hermann Diels's favorite pupil), epigraphist, and historian of religions, sciences, and art, and he was also deeply involved in geographical and institutional history. He believed that the study of Asia, through excavations and the discovery of archives, was a real revolution in historical science and that it was impossible to study the Greek and Roman world without taking Asian influences into account. His point of view was obviously that of a classicist who did not always have firsthand knowledge of the different aspects of the "Orient." Cumont learned Syriac, but he was not an Orientalist in the strict sense of the word; he asked Charles Clermont-Ganneau or Giorgio Levi della Vida to help him when he had to study Semitic inscriptions. Nevertheless, Cumont was a great scholar and a generous open-minded person who had a major influence on historians and philologists of the 1950s and 1960s, especially in France and Belgium, and including Pierre Boyancé, Jean Gagé, Henri-Irénée Marrou, André-Jean Festugière, and Jerome Carcopino.

BIBLIOGRAPHY

Biographical sketches are available in L. Canet, "Préface," in Cumont's *Lux Perpetua* (Paris, 1949), pp. vii–xxx; and Corinne Bonnet, "Franz Cumont," in *Religion und Geschichte in Gegenwart,* 4th ed. (Stuttgart, Germany, 1999), col. 504–505. On Cumont's life, works, and correspondence, see Bonnet, *La correspondance scientifique de Franz Cumont conservée à l'Academia Belgica de Rome* (Brussels and Rome, 1997); as well as Bonnet's "La formation de Franz Cumont d'après sa correspondance (1885–1892)," *Kernos* 11 (1998): 245–264. See also Aline Rousselle, ed., *Actes de la Table Ronde: "Franz Cumont et la science de son temps," Paris, 5–6/12/1997* (Paris, 1999; *MEFRIM* 111 [1999]); Bonnet, "Franz Cumont recenseur," in *Képoi: Mélanges en l'honneur d'André Motte,* edited by Vinciane Pirenne-Delforge and Edouard Delruelle (Liège, Belgium, 2001), pp. 309–335; Bonnet, *"Le grand atelier de la science": Franz Cumont et l'Altertumswissenschaft, Héritages et émancipations,* vol. 1: *Des études universitaires à la première guerre mondiale* (Brussels and Rome, 2004).

On Mithraism, see Richard Gordon, "Franz Cumont and the Doctrines of Mithraism," in *Mithraic Studies,* edited by John R. Hinnells (Manchester, UK, 1975), pp. 215–248; Roger Beck, "Mithraism since Franz Cumont," *Aufstieg und Niedergang der römischen Welt* (*ANRW*) II, 17, no. 4 (1984): 2002–2115; Robert Turcan, "Franz Cumont, un fondateur," *Kernos* 11 (1998): 235–244; and Roger Beck, "The Mysteries of Mithra: A New Account on Their Genesis," *Journal of Roman Studies* 88 (1998): 115–128.

On iconographical analysis, see Arthur Darby Nock, "Sarcophagi and Symbolism," *American Journal of Archaeology* 50 (1946): 14–170, and Paul Veyne, "L'empire Romain," in Philippe Aries and Georges Duby, eds., *Histoire de la vie privee*, vol. I, *De l'Empire Romaine à l'an mil* (Paris, 1985), pp. 221–222.

On Oriental religions, see Ramsey MacMullen, *Paganism in the Roman Empire* (New Haven and London, 1981); Nicole Belayche, "'Deae Syriae Sacrum': La romanité des cultes 'orientaux,'" *Revue Historique* 302 (2001): 565–592; and "L'Oronte et le Tibre: L''Orient' des cultes 'orientaux' de l'empire romain," in *L'Orient dans l'histoire religieuse de l'Europe*, edited by Mohammad Ali Amir-Moezzi and John Scheid (Louvain, Belgium, 2001), pp. 1–35.

JACQUES DUCHESNE-GUILLEMIN (1987)
CORINNE BONNET (2005)

CUNA RELIGION.

CUNA RELIGION. There are perhaps forty thousand Cuna Indians today, living mostly in the San Blas Reserve on Panama's Atlantic coast, with small groups along the interior Bayano and Chucanaque rivers and in three villages in Colombia. The Cuna survived the traumatic but ephemeral Spanish conquest of the Darien Isthmus (modern-day Isthmus of Panama) after 1510. They are thus one of the few remnants of the flourishing pre-Columbian chieftaincies of the circum-Caribbean. The Cuna maintained their autonomy partly by allying themselves with the buccaneers who harassed the Spaniards.

CULT ORGANIZATION. Institutionally, Cuna religion is organized in both communal and shamanic cults. The communal cult is maintained by the village chiefs (*sailakana*), who chant from oral mythological texts known as Pap Ikar ("god's way") some three nights a week to the assembled village. Official interpreters (*arkarana*) explain the arcane language of the chants, using homilies on contemporary morality. Female puberty feasts are collective rites sponsored by each village once a year.

The shamanic cult is not conducted communally, save for the rite of village exorcism that occurs during epidemics or other collective dangers. Shamans (*neles*) are credited with clairvoyance, through trance or dreams, into the four layers of the underworld. *Neles*, who may be male or female, are born to their role and are discovered by midwives through signs in their afterbirth. A born *nele* must nurture the gift and be apprenticed to an adult *nele*.

Other experts are not clairvoyants. All know a sacred text, *ikar* ("path" or "way"). These texts invoke spiritual helpers, such as stick dolls (*suar nuchu*) or magical stones (*akwanusu*), as allies in combating evil, meddlesome spirits, who usually have captured the patient's soul and who hold it in their stronghold at the fourth level of the underworld. In addition, there are herbalists (*inatuleti*) who know native plant medicines and brief incantations. Usually these specialists go to work only after a *nele* has clairvoyantly diagnosed the patient.

The various curing, exorcism, female puberty, and funerary texts are all recited verbatim as learned from an authoritative master. Not so with the texts of the chiefly God's Way. Chiefs are free to render myths as they see fit, or even to recount events from recent history. Some of their chants are not narratives, but complicated poetic metaphors.

COSMOGONY AND MYTHIC THEMES. Cuna cosmogony, as disclosed in God's Way, posits an original creation by God, who sends the first man, Wako, to earth. In a primordial paradise, Wako finds the earth to be his mother, and the rivers, the sun, the moon, and the stars to be his brothers. The trees are young women. Wako lives here blissfully until God calls him back. (This image of a primordial paradise resembles the childhood of a male Cuna in a matrilocal household belonging to his mother and composed of his brothers and sisters, the type of household that exists before marriage disperses the brothers to other households and brings in outsiders to marry the sisters. Thus Wako does not have to grow up.)

Wako is merely the first of many human sons or emissaries whom God sends to earth. Most of their descendants become corrupt, necessitating more emissaries to correct them. When this fails, God repeatedly visits catastrophic punishments upon mankind and the cycle begins again. This is not quite a creation cycle since mankind is never destroyed and created anew. Rather, emissary prophets attempt to correct wayward peoples. They succeed with some, for a time; others degenerate into evil spirits and—later—"animal people."

After Wako, God sends Piler, together with his wife, to found the human race. Piler's grandchildren become vainglorious and quarrelsome. After two successive groups of emissary teachers fail to correct them, God upturns the world, banishing Piler's descendants to the fourth layer of the underworld, where they remain as *ponikan* ("evil ones") ready to wreak illness upon mankind.

The next great emissary prophet is Mako, sent to correct the obstreperous *ponikan* who are making their way through tunnels up from the underworld. Like Piler, Mako is given a wife by God. Both he and his wife are called back to God unblemished. Their three morally ambiguous children, who are neither exemplarily good nor particularly evil, start the major cycle of Cuna mythology: that of Tat Ipelele ("grandfather lord shaman"; also, the personified sun).

Ipelele and his six siblings are born of an incestuous union between two of Mako's children. Forced by their crime to flee, Ipelele's father becomes the Moon, while Ipelele's mother takes refuge with Frogwoman. Frogwoman's animal sons devour Ipelele's mother, and Frogwoman raises the children as her own. Ipelele discovers the secret of his birth and journeys to the underworld to find the herbal medicines that will revive his mother. Able to restore her only temporarily, Ipelele then devotes his life to heroic struggles against the descendants of Piler, as well as against other enemies.

Ipelele marries the daughters of evil chiefs to learn their secrets. He gives his sister to Wind in order to make an ally of him. He discovers the powers inherent in tobacco, hot pepper smoke, and cacao incense to make the *ponikan* drunk and helpless during feasts he offers them. He turns many of them into "animal people," animal spirits with their own strongholds at the fourth layer of the underworld. He finds allies in magical stones and stick spirits (from the balsa tree), which are the magical allies of shamans today. At one point, he even defeats the *ponikan* in battle, leaving the battlefield strewn with their corpses. Finally, Ipelele is called back to heaven to become the Sun, riding each day in a giant canoe steered by his helmsman servant and accompanied by his sister.

After Ipelele's ascent, the cycle of emissary preachers, human corruption, and catastrophic punishment (by fire, wind, darkness, and flood) is repeated four more times. After the final flood comes the beginning of the present epoch. Here the great tribal culture hero, Ipeorkun ("lord gold kuna") arrives among the Cuna, who are at this time corrupt, ignorant, and little different from the "animal people" who surround them.

MYTHIC ORIGIN OF CUNA CULTURE. Now there is a reversal of the usual theme. Instead of the descendants of a prophet lord becoming corrupt, the Cuna (like Ipelele before them) discover their true identity as *olotule* ("golden people") and shed the filthy ways of the animal people. Ipeorkun, like Mako, is not a warrior but is rather a teacher who reveals the particulars of Cuna culture: female puberty ceremonies; bodily cleanliness and, closely associated with it, purity; "correct" (Cuna) kin terms; terms for parts of the body; how to use the magical spirit allies of the shamans and the texts that control them; how to mourn properly; how to build proper houses; how to sleep in hammocks; and, finally, the texts of God's Way. His sister teaches women the arts of cleanliness and sewing. Ipeorkun—like Wako, Mako, and Ipelele—is called to God.

After Ipeorkun come the eight Ipelerkan ("lord shamans") to continue his teachings. They grow vainglorious and corrupt, now in specifically Cuna ways. For instance, one of them who knows the female puberty text keeps the young initiates for himself. The eight Ipelerkan are corrected by a young son of one of them, Nele Kwani, who foresees a drought (another punishment from God) and bests them all in a contest of magical powers.

Although the Cuna are a horticultural people whose staple is the banana in various forms, and whose cash crop is the coconut, neither crop is sacralized or commemorated in any myths yet collected. Cacao, tobacco, balsa wood, and magical stones, all supernatural allies in the struggle against evil, are, however, richly attested in the Ipelele cycle of narratives.

COSMOLOGY. Cuna cosmology, with its four levels above and four below the earth, is continuously revealed by the *neles*, who mystically journey through the cosmos, often forging alliances with evil spirits to learn their secrets. In the underworld are the strongholds of the kings of the spiritual allies. Heaven itself, revealed by the *neles* through a chant that recounts the adventures of a soul brought back from the dead, is a stronghold at the fourth layer above. Its golden buildings not only evoke the ancient chiefly strongholds of nearby Colombia, but today heaven also includes skyscrapers, automobiles, and telescopes, which permit souls to gaze upon the living, the underworld, and the United States (located, by implication, somewhere near the underworld). Souls who arrive at God's golden house do so only after having been physically punished for their earthly sins as they journey through the underworld.

GOD AND MORALITY. The image of God, called Pap ("father") or Diosaila (from the Spanish *Dios* and the Cuna *saila*, "chief"), is that of a stern and distant paternal figure. He is never directly personified, unlike his sons and emissaries. His morality is consistent with the good and harmonious management of a matrilocal extended household and of a community made up of a number of such households. That morality, preached weekly in the local assemblies, enjoins a man to be hard-working, productive, and cooperative, and a woman to be fertile, clean, industrious, and nurturant. Women must avoid gossip, and men, quarrels. Minor conflicts must be dealt with promptly by wise, paternal chiefs, and punishment meted out swiftly—often in the form of verbal admonishments—after which all is forgiven and forgotten. To do otherwise raises the specter of backsliding into the evil ways of the "animal people."

MYTHOLOGY AND CULTURAL SURVIVAL. Armed with this religion, the Cuna were an insuperable foe to the Spaniards, whom the Cuna associated with the *ponikan*, and whom they correctly identified as the source of illnesses. Just as the *ponikan* steal men's souls, so did the Spaniards capture their bodies and enslave them. The Cuna borrowed their mythological strategy for dealing with the *ponikan* and applied it to the Spaniards. Just as *neles* ally themselves mystically with friendly spirits, get the *ponikan* drunk magically, and confine them to their proper strongholds, so too did the Cuna form alliances with the Atlantic enemies of Spain, feast the Spaniards, and keep them at arm's length. In 1925, the strategy was played out exactly. The great tribal chief Nele Kantule, who was also a shaman, formed an alliance with an American adventurer and organized an uprising against the Panamanian administration, which took place during Carnival. The plotters fell upon unsuspecting, drunken guardsmen and killed them. The United States imposed on Panama a treaty favorable to the Indians.

Cuna mythology is kept open-ended and vital through the *neles* and through the chiefs who incorporate recent history into their chants. The dominant ritual is the recitation of texts. Prayer and sacrifice are not practiced.

Cuna religion continues to be practiced vigorously despite the incursions of Christian missionaries and public health clinics. One community, however, has already appointed "singing chiefs" for a traditional congress house separate from the "administrative chiefs" who conduct secular affairs. It is possible that this development contains the seeds of a Cuna church or ecclesiastical cult separate from the civil government. Such a church could very well be the outcome of continuing acculturation and urbanization.

Bibliography

The single most important source for Cuna mythology is Norman MacPherson Chapin's *Pab Igala: Historias de la tradición Cuna* (Panama City, 1970). This comprehensive set of texts is arranged in a sequence that Chapin's chiefly informants agree is correct. The current edition is mimeographed, but a print edition is planned. There has been no such compilation of curing, puberty, or funerary texts. The text for childbirth appears in Nils M. Homer and S. Henry Wassen's *The Complete Mu-Igala in Picture Writing* (Göteberg, 1953). This is the subject of a celebrated essay by Claude Lévi-Strauss, "The Effectiveness of Symbols," in *Structural Anthropology* (New York, 1963). Chapin has corrected Lévi-Strauss's ethnographic errors in "Muu Ikala: Cuna Birth Ceremony," in *Ritual and Symbol in Native Central America,* edited by Phillip Young and James Howe (Eugene, Ore., 1976). This volume also contains Howe's cogent "Smoking Out the Spirits: A Cuna Exorcism," pp. 69–76. The best study of curing is Chapin's "Curing among the San Blas Cuna" (Ph.D. diss., University of Arizona, 1983).

Unfortunately, recent work has shown the texts of Erland Nordenskiöld's 1920s expedition to the Cuna to be garbled. His *An Historical and Ethnological Survey of the Cuna Indians,* written in collaboration with Ruben Pérez and edited by S. Henry Wassen (Göteberg, 1938), should be read only in connection with other works cited here.

James Howe, Joel Sherzer, and Norman MacPherson Chapin have published *Cantos y oraciones del Congreso Cuna* (Panama City, 1979) in a beautiful edition that presents a number of texts and excellent sociolinguistic and ethnological analyses. Sherzer expounds the different styles used in reciting Cuna sacred texts in "*Namakke, sunmakke, kormakke:* Three Types of Cuna Speech Event," in *Explorations in the Ethnography of Speaking,* edited by Richard Bauman and Joel Sherzer (New York, 1974).

The female puberty ceremony is described, without symbolic analysis and without the major sacred texts, in Arnulfo Prestán Simón's *El uso de la chicha y la sociedad Kuna* (Mexico City, 1975). The continuing open-endedness or *productivité* of Cuna sacred texts is explained in Dina Sherzer and Joel Sherzer's "Literature in San Blas: Discovering the Cuna *Ikala,*" *Semiotica* 6 (1972): 182–199. I have explicated the application of this mystical strategy to practical diplomacy in "Lore and Life: Cuna Indian Pageants, Exorcism, and Diplomacy in the Twentieth Century," *Ethnohistory* 30 (1983): 93–106. My "Basilicas and King Posts: A Proxemic and Symbolic Event Analysis of Competing Public Architecture among the San Blas Cuna," *American Ethnologist* 8 (1981): 259–277, explicates the peculiarly rectangular Cuna house construction both in mythological and symbolic terms. Finally, the single best ethnographic study of the Cuna is James Howe's "Village Political Organization among the San Blas Cuna" (Ph.D. diss., University of Pennsylvania, 1974).

Alexander Moore (1987)

CURSING, the antithesis of blessing, is a pan-global, pan-historical phenomenon in which language, spoken or written and with or without special accompanying actions, is directed at bringing down evil or misfortune upon an intended object, person, or community. Although in colloquial parlance *cursing* commonly refers to imprecations spoken as spontaneous outbursts of rage or to cold-blooded private wishes of malice, as well as to "profane" language generally, this article emphasizes not only expressiveness but also the presumed efficacy of such language. A curse can be considered efficacious in a given cultural context either because of an explicit or implicit appeal to a deity or spiritual power to endorse and realize the curse or because the spoken or written word in and of itself is recognized as efficacious by the sender and the object of the curse and/or by the cultural community. In the latter case, the curse may be considered operative upon being pronounced, and the object of the curse may henceforth consider him or herself, and be regarded by the community, as "accursed."

A middle ground between cursing as spontaneous oral outburst and culturally recognized or institutionalized ritual is the broad category of inscribed personal curses that serve exclusively private ends. Linguists and folklorists in many cultural contexts have collected private and personal curses, including modern Palestinian curses that follow biblical curse formulas. For example, a *da'weh* may call upon God (or sometimes Satan) to bring down affliction on an enemy's health, family, honor, or property: "may God make a disease, whose cure nobody knows, befall you," "may God destroy your tent and your pasture. . . . may God deprive you of all that throws a shadow" (Canaan, 1935, pp. 247, 259).

Among the richest sources of such private curses are the *tabellae defixiones* of the classical Greco-Roman world. Thousands of such tiny lead tablets, etched with inscriptions and sometimes diagrams and rolled and pierced by a nail, have been discovered at the bottoms of wells or buried at stadia, crossroads, marketplaces, and the thresholds of homes and shops. These *tabellae* use succinct and sometimes cryptic but often explicit subjunctive or optative language to call down mishap, misfortune, financial disaster, sexual dysfunction, bodily harm or death upon the object of the curse, whether a despised neighbor, a rival shop-owner, a courtroom adversary, a chariot-racing competitor (Gager items 66, 45, and 6, respectively), or the object of frustrated sexual desire: "I bind you, Theodotis, daughter of Eus, by the tail of the snake . . . and the penis of the god so that you may never be able to sleep with any other man, nor be screwed, nor be taken anally, nor fellate, nor find pleasure with any other man but me" (Gager item 54).

Sometimes the tablet includes a tiny lead doll, bound and pierced, and the written "binding" inscription implies an accompanying manipulative action that makes this more like a spell or charm than a purely linguistic curse. The most thorough and inclusive of all these *defixiones* curses is a Latin example c. 75–50 BCE against a woman in retribution for a curse she had put upon the scribe: it scrupulously enumerates her body parts, including "intestines, belly, navel, shoulder blades, sides" and concludes, "Terribly destroy her, terribly kill her, terribly ruin her" (Falco, 140–41). The roots of such punitive counter-curse formulae can be traced to the much earlier, first-century Mesopotamian *Maqlu* tablets, which contain extensive counter-witchcraft directives and incantations: "May their witchcraft, poisons, and charms that are not good, but rather evil. / Turn upon them and attack their heads and their faces. . . . May they dissolve, melt, drip ever away, / May their life force come to an end like water from a water skin" (Tablet AfO 18, 1957–1958, ll. 56–7, 76–7, in Abusch, 2002, pp. 73–74; cf. Cryer and Thomsen, 2001, p. 47).

EARLY SCHOLARSHIP. In the matter of cultural interpretation, scholarship on cursing in the mid-twentieth century was heavily influenced by the turn-of-the-century research of Sir James Frazer's *Golden Bough, A Study in Magic and Religion,* 12 vols. (London, 1911–1915) and the Cambridge school of ethnography. Their work globalized cultural studies, but from a very hegemonic perspective. Thus, the early classic studies of cursing by Edward Westermarck, Ernest Crawley, and others often display cultural and ethnic stereotyping that derives both from their theoretical perspective of cultural evolution and from their uncritical use of travel accounts, colonial memoirs, and ethnographies as sources of descriptive and anecdotal evidence. Canaan, for example, in his article on Palestinian cursing quotes with approval an earlier writer, Rihbany, who cautioned that in the matter of extravagant verbal outbursts one must "keep in mind the juvenile temperament of the Oriental" (Canaan, 1935, p. 260).

Early scholarship assumed a fundamental dichotomy between the mentalities of "primitive" cultures, which used magic, and the mentalities of "higher" civilizations, which developed religion. Scholars believed that cultures begin in magic and "progress" toward religion and that religion itself naturally "progresses" from animism through polytheism to monotheism (see, for example, Malinowski, 1948 and the critical responses to Malinowski reviewed by Tambiah, 1968; cf. Keim, 1992, chap. 1; Fox, 1914, p. 122; and Cryer and Thomsen, 2001, pp. 113–117). "Although the theoretical basis of this interpretive model has been largely discredited and abandoned by anthropologists today," as Keim concludes, "its legacy remains strong within the field of biblical studies. . . . [as] the idealistic framework remained intact, whereby the mythological and magical develops (in Israel) toward the historical and ethical" (p. 9).

Thus, until recently, biblical scholarship operated from similar presumed contrasts between the "higher" theocratic and ethical religious ideology assumed to be reflected in the Hebrew scriptures and the polytheistic, "idolatrous," and allegedly non-ethical religious ceremonialism of the neighboring cultures of Mesopotamia, Egypt, and Canaan (see, for example, Pedersen, 1926/1964; Mowinckel, 1962; Hempel, 1961; Alt, 1934; and Blank, 1950–1951; cf. the criticism and the review of scholarship in Keim, 1992, pp. 7–10; Gervitz, 1961, pp. 137–140; Brichto, 1963, chap. 7; and Crawford, 1992, chap. 2). According to this traditional reading, cursing was a God-dependent supplication for the biblical Hebrews, whereas it was a mechanical, magical contrivance for the other Ancient Near Eastern cultures When a biblical text described curses similar to those of neighbor cultures, the scholar might lament how "the common people of Israel even in the more mature stages of their religious development frequently relapsed into the gross practices of idolatry and witchcraft [including]. . . . practices closely akin to the extant Greek and Roman *tabellae defixionum,* or curse tablets" (Fox, 1914, pp. 111–112). Thus, Alt in his classic 1934 monograph on the origins of Israelite law, which influential scholar William Foxwell Albright endorsed in his review in the *Journal of Biblical Literature* (1936, pp. 164–169), promotes the chauvinistic idea that "Hebrew apodictic law was original and unique in Israel," whereas "less advanced" casuistic law was followed in Mesopotamian and Canaanite cultures.

The following comment by Westermarck is typical of the cultural evolutionist viewpoint on the distinction between mechanical and intentional curses: "It is not to be expected, then, that distinctions of so subtle a nature should be properly made by the uncultured mind. . . . But with the deepening of the religious sentiment this idea [of mechanically effective curses] had to be given up. A righteous and mighty god cannot agree to be a mere tool in the hand of a wicked curser" (1908, vol. I, pp. 235, 564; but cf. Thisleton, 1974; Lauterbach, 1939; and Blank, 1950–1951, p. 78). But as Graf has demonstrated in a study of Greek magical papyri, the Frazerian dichotomy is untenable (1991, p. 194). Contemporary scholarship tends to show, in fact, that there is no definable, consistent contrast between the curse-formulas and usages of ancient Israel and those of her neighbors (see, for example, Gervitz, 1961 and 1962; Hillers, 1964 and 1984; Keim, 1992, chap. 1; Crawford, 1992, pp. 231–235; and Cryer and Thomsen, 2001, pp. 120–34, 144–146).

CONTEMPORARY PERSPECTIVE. Current anthropological and cultural studies and scholarship in comparative religion are no longer tied to the Frazerian evolutionist paradigm or unaware of its colonialist biases, as Mary Douglas shows in *Purity and Danger: An Analysis of the Concepts of Pollution and Taboo* (London, 1966). Instead, Western scholarship has come to be as concerned with emic or indigenous self-representation and self-understanding, as with etic analysis and interpretation from the outside (see, for instance, the theoretical introduction by Frank Salomon and Stuart Schwartz to the *South America* volume of the *Cambridge His-*

tory of the Native Peoples of the Americas, 1999). Anthropologists no longer confidently plot a diachronic cultural progression from magic through religion to science (whose defining differences no longer seem self-evident, in any case) but are more inclined to see these as overlapping and synchronic mentalities, not only within cultures but within individual psyches. Moreover, in his seminal monograph *How to Do Things with Words,* John Austin offered a significant philosophical and linguistic contribution to the discussion of such speech acts as cursing and blessing, which seem to combine both utterance and performance. Although Austin's taxonomy of "performative language" continues to be critiqued by philosophers of language (see, for example, Tambiah, 1968; Searle, 1965, 1975, and 1979), it has nonetheless proved useful to analyses of ritual language, as in recent studies of West African ceremonialism (Finnegan, 1968; Ray, 1973–1974). The concept of performative language offers at least the beginning of a more productive way to think and talk about cursing or blessing as understood within given cultural contexts.

One way to create order out of the welter of ethnographic and literary sources on cursing is to survey the material thematically, the approach taken in Falco's dissertation on "The Malediction in Indo-European Tradition." Drawing upon Indic, Hittite, Mesopotamian, Greco-Roman, Germanic, and Celtic literary sources, Falco offers examples of curses that reference such universal themes as the body and its parts (particularly the eye), food and hunger, sex, childlessness, homelessness, and pursuit and also more culturally specific themes such as allusions to swine and the sea and metaphors of atavistic dissolution into water, earth, and ashes. Particularly elaborate is the so-called Hittite Soldiers Oath, actually more of a threat of sanction than an oath, which charges that any soldiers breaking the military code will be changed "into women, and may they dress them in a womanly fashion . . . and let them place in their hands a distaff and a spindle. . . . And let them be so cursed that their land not bear fruit, that their wives not bear children like unto their begetters, but monsters, that their cattle not increase according to nature, that they suffer defeat in battle and in lawsuits and in marketplace, and that they perish utterly" (Falco, 1992, pp. 89, 121).

In ethnographic study and popular culture, perhaps the most familiar category of curses as speech acts that happen are the reported instances of "vodou death." Haitian vodou, Brazilian Xango, and Cuban Santería derive from West African religious traditions syncretically combined with aspects of folk Catholicism, and all are popularly supposed to include traditions of casting charms and spells, including fatal curses that take effect instantaneously and across any distance (for Haitian vodou, see Metraux, 1959/1972; Rigaud, 1953/1985; Pluchon, 1987; Abrahams, 1983). Casting of powerful and deadly spells has been reported for Malaysia (Skeat, 1965, chap. VI) and for Melanesia (Codrington, 1891, pp. 51, 147) and is illustrated in the documentary film *Ongka's Big Moka,* which shows an oath-making ceremony intended to refute an accusation of death by sorcery in a village of Papua, New Guinea (dir. Charlie Nairn, Granada Television International, 1974).

Comparable traditions have been widely reported for other indigenous cultures of Native America, Africa, Oceania and, especially, Aboriginal Australia. Death brought about by Aborigine "bone pointing" became a fixture of early ethnographic reporting (Warner, 1941; Basedow, 1925) and of popular culture as well, as in the Australian mystery novel *The Bone Is Pointed* by Arthur Upfield (1947/1984). Similarly, it is reported that among the Maoris, "the anathema of a priest is regarded as a thunderbolt that an enemy cannot escape" (Polack, 1840, I.248; cf. Crawley, 1934, pp. 11–19 for other Maori citations). A healthy but inconclusive ongoing scholarly exchange on the subject of vodou death, with an emphasis on Australian Aborigine culture, has appeared over the years in the pages of *American Anthropologist* (Cannon, 1942; Lester, 1972; Lex, 1974; Eastwell, 1982; Reid & Williams, 1984), often looking for empirical explanations of such reported deaths or, in the case of Reid and Williams, charging that vodou death is a European/American construct and not an Aborigine reality.

Personal Curses and Institutionally Sanctioned Curses. Nonetheless, belief in the power of the word itself, independent of any separate invocation of a deity, can be attested in many cultural contexts, including the Indo-European. In fact, it is particularly distinctive of the Sanskrit tradition, in which numerous Vedic, Brahmanic, and Upaniṣads texts convey the idea that a primordial word, such as *Brahma* itself, embodies the fundamental creative and sustaining power of the universe that can accomplish all things (Zimmer, 1956, pp. 74–83; Westermarck, 1908, I.563; II.658, 716), and the idea of chanted *mantra* having all-pervasive efficacious power is common to Hindu, Buddhist and Tantric traditions alike. Not surprisingly, therefore, efficacious curses abound in Indic, Persian, and other Indo-European epic literature, as Falco demonstrates. A number of biblical passages imply an automatic potency to curses (e.g., *Num.* 21–22), although this remains a subject of scholarly controversy (see Fox, 1914, p. 122; Hillers, 1984, p. 185; Lauterbach, 1939; Thiselton, 1974; and Blank, 1950–1951, pp. 78, 86).

Similar beliefs in mechanically effective cursing speech acts have been documented from numerous cultures throughout the world (see especially Grimm, 1883–1886/1966; Frazer, 1911–1915; Westermarck, 1908 and 1933, Crawley, 1934; Hobley, 1967; Skeat, 1965; Kluckhohn, 1944/1967). The curse can be reified and treated as a baneful substance, as in reports of Irish folk opinion "that a curse once uttered must alight on something" (Crawley, 1934, p. 368) or of old Teutonic images of curses alighting, settling, and returning home to their sender like birds (Grimm, 1883–1886/1966 III.1227) or in the somewhat more symbolic notions that Arabs considered curses so polluting and contagious that they would lie flat on the ground so that a curse could fly over them, or that when forced to take an oath a Berber might undress entirely so that the oath could not cling to the clothing (Westermarck, 1908, I.57–59). The idea that curses can be contagious is the basis for two of Frazer's most prominent themes in *The Golden Bough*, sympathetic magic and the transference of evil. Actual personification of curses is familiar from the Greek myth of the pursuing Erinyes, who may be born of the blood of a murdered man, as in Aeschylus's *Eumenides* (cf. *Choephori* 283 seq.; Plato, *Laws* ix.866).

In contrast with private and personal cursing, culturally recognized and institutionally sanctioned cursing involves speech acts that depend not only on the power of the words or formulas themselves, or on the deity or spiritual power which may be invoked, but on the proper setting and circumstances and, above all, on the recognized empowerment of the (special) person delivering or pronouncing the curse—the "technician of the sacred." Depending on the religio-cultural context, such a person may be designated as priest, prophet, sage, shaman, wizard, or witch.

The "specialist" in cursing goes under many different cultural designations, along a spectrum of degrees of perceived positivity and negativity, ranging from the priest who heroically curses enemies on behalf of a community to the witch or sorcerer whose curses are wholly malicious. The major Mesopotamian text on witchcraft, *Maqlû*, consists of rubrics and incantations of an *asipu* or exorcist directed at subverting the negative powers of a *kassaptu*, a sorcerer or witch, one who performs destructive magic: "May the curse of my mouth extinguish the curse of your mouth" (Abusch, 2002, p. 132). In his writing about West African culture, Dominque Zahan emphasizes the polarity between magicians who are healers and sorcerers, whom he labels *nyctosophers*, or practitioners of night-wisdom (1970/1979, chap. 7). Both have fearful power that mediates between the community and that which is wild or extraordinary, but among such groups as the Azande or the Lugbara, the sorcerer represents the inversion of the idealized human image (Ray, 1976, p. 151; Evans-Pritchard, 1936/1976). A similar fundamental distinction between healer and witch as spiritual "technicians" holds for the Navajo, but in addition Clyde Kluckhohn states that four distinct kinds of witchery are designated by four distinct Navajo terms, with the sorcerer (*'inzi'd*) being the one to specialize in spells and curses (1944/1967, pp. 31–33; cf. Simmons, 1974/1980, chap. 9).

Alternatively, the person's power to curse may derive instead from some more existential circumstance: from his or her role as parent, a superannuated person, a stricken or dying person, or from the social role of stranger, guest, beggar, or victim of injustice. The curse of a parent is particularly dreaded in many cultures. According to a Moorish proverb, "If the saints curse you the parents will cure you, but if the parents curse you the saints will not cure you," and it is reported that among the Nandi of Uganda a father's curse, unless forgiven, is believed to be fatal (Westermarck,1908, I.622). Examples from Cameroon are given in Ngankam Fogue, *La malediction chez les Bamileke du Cameroun* (Baroussam, 1985; p. 14). Oedipus in exile delivers a terrible paternal curse against his disloyal sons (Sophocles, *Oedipus at Colonnus* 1299, 1434). In fact, the curses of parents were embodied as avenging spirits, as the Erinyes among the Greeks or as the *divi parentum* of the Romans (*Iliad* 9. 453–457;and 21.412 seq.). The final scene of the third act of Verdi's *Rigoletto* contains a highly dramatic malediction pronounced by a wronged father: Count Monterone curses his tormentor, the jester Rigoletto, a curse fulfilled at last against both Rigoletto and the count's own innocent daughter. By extension, many cultures privilege the curses (and blessings) of the elderly and especially the dying; Grimm reports that in old Teutonic ideology, the curse of a dying person was the strongest of all curses (1883–1886/1966, IV.1690; cf. Westermarck, 1908, II.637 for examples from Africa and classical Rome).

WOMEN AND CURSES. In cultures where women carry an aura of taboo or where witchcraft is widely credited, a woman's curse can be particularly feared. Alice Ahenakew tells the Cree story of "The Old Woman's Curse," about a mother who inflicts a terrible fate on the young man who robbed her of her daughter (Wolfart and Ahenakew, 2000, pp. 20–24 and chap. 11). Zahan emphasizes the role of women in *nyctosophy* among the Bambara of West Africa because of "woman's enigmatic and impenetrable character. . . . All the more amazing because of the psychological character of her soul" (1970/1979, pp. 94–5), without acknowledging the gender bias inherent in such a comment. Similarly, Westermarck reports that among the Berbers of Morocco, "a person who takes refuge with a woman by touching her is safe from his pursuer," explaining that the "reason why women are regarded as able to offer an asylum is obviously the belief in their magic power and the great efficacy of their curses" (1907, p. 367). There is a great deal of evidence of malevolent cursing in medieval and Early Modern Europe (see Kittredge, 1929; Thomas, 1997; Douglas, 1970), but scholars now discount the idea that there were active covens of female witches who consciously preserved elements of pre-Christian European religion (see the review of critical literature on European witchcraft in Thomas, 1997, chap. 16, esp. pp. 514–515).

SOCIAL JUSTICE AND CURSES. At the opposite pole from figures of authority and technicians of the sacred, is another group believed to have a special power to curse: the stranger, the guest, the poor and the needy, and the victim of injustice. Thus in many parts of the world—and numerous examples ranging from North Africa to the Tonga Islands and the Native American Southwest are presented in the surveys by Westermarck and Crawley—strangers who step over the threshold are not only welcomed, but given a position of privilege at bed and board, at least for a limited period of time, lest any dissatisfaction from a guest bring harm to the household. The Greeks believed that guests and suppliants and beggars had their Erinyes, or avenging spirits, which personified the curses they cast upon any who despised them or turned them away (Homer, *Odyssey* xvii.475; Aeschylus, *Suppliants* 349, 489). Ecclesiasticus warns, "Do not avert your eye from the needy, and give no one reason to curse you, for if in bitterness of soul some should curse you, their Creator will hear their prayer. . . . The prayer of the poor goes from their lips to the ears of God, and his judgment comes speedily" (*Sir.* 4:5–6; 21:5; cf. *Prov.* 28:27). A pair of Palestinian proverbs sums up the philosophy of social justice underlying this category of cursing: "Do not be an oppressor and you do not need fear curses," and "There is no veil separating heaven from the prayers and imprecations of the oppressed" (Canaan, 1935, p. 263).

A special case of the conditional curse as an appeal for social justice, protection, or sanctuary is the North African Arab concept of *l-'âr*, which signifies a compulsory relationship in which a claimant invokes support and protection at the implied risk of a curse in the event of being denied. As Westermarck explains, the "constraining character of *l-'âr* is due to the fact that it implies the transference of a conditional curse," mediated by what he calls "external conductors," such as sharing food, or grasping or touching a person, the person's child or horse, or grasping the person's tent-pole (1907, pp. 361–362). A similar claim and conditional curse can be represented by a heap of stones:

> A common practice among scribes is to make a cursing cairn for a wealthy man whom they have in vain asked for a present. They make a cairn either outside his house or in some open place, read over it some passages of the Koran, and, with the palms of their hands turned downwards, pronounce a curse upon the niggard. (p. 364)

A coercive claim can be made upon a saint by building a cairn or by tying a rag to a house or a tomb and declaring, "O saint, behold! I promised thee an offering and I will not release [literally *open*] thee until thou attendest to my business" (p. 369)—a threat/prayer analogous to that of Jacob wrestling with the angel (*Gen.* 32.26). Another method would be to sacrifice an animal at the threshold of the person whose benefits are sought, for "of all conductors of curses none is considered more efficient than blood" (p. 365). Westermarck reports that in the Great Atlas Mountains a Jew who settles in a Berber village "always places himself under the protection of some powerful man by putting *ār* upon him." Because a supplicant's declaration that "I am in the *ār* of God and your *ār*," implies a claim of sanctuary, Westermarck concludes that *lār* "is thus a great boon to weak and helpless people, criminals, and strangers" (p. 366).

Protective curses. On the other hand, the protective conditional curse is at the heart of prohibitive inscriptions and edicts of rulers and the elite, and of the traditions of oaths, treaties, and covenants in Egypt and the Ancient Near East. In each case, the conditional curse invokes stated or agreed sanctions in the event that a tomb or boundary marker is violated, or an oath, treaty, or covenant is broken. Curses as protective threat-formulae are a familiar feature of ancient Egyptian inscriptions. Represented in Western popular culture as "the mummy's curse," the textual threat-formulae (involving a variety of Egyptian word roots, including and others) encompass a vast lexicon of stipulations and injunctions and a vast array of threatened punishments for such criminal or sacrilegious acts as theft, defilement, effacements, and other violations of tombs, stelae and monuments (Morschauser, 1991; Nordh, 1996; Parrot, 1939). In the words of one Sixth Dynasty tomb inscription: "As for any noble, any official, or any man who shall rip out any stone or any brick from this tomb, I will be judged with him by the great God, I (will) seize his neck like a bird, and I will cause all the living who are upon the earth to be afraid. . . ." (Pritchard 1969, p. 327c; for other examples, see pp. 326–328). Similar protective curses are common in Mesopotamian and Iron Age Syro-Palestinian Semitic inscriptions (For Mesopotamian examples see Pomponio, 1990; Grätz, 1998, chap. 2; and Speyer, 1969, pp. 1170–1174. For Syro-Palestinian examples see Crawford, 1992, chaps. 4 and 5). An eighth-century Karatepe inscription carved in Phoenician upon a statue and pedestal of Baal, threatens any defacers of the name of King Azitiwada:

> Now if a king among kings, or a prince among princes, or any man who is a man of renown, effaces the name of Azitiwada from this gate and puts up his own name, or more than that, covets this city and pulls down this gate which Azitiwada made, and makes another gate for it and puts his own name on it, whether it is out of covetousness or whether it is out of hatred and malice that hew pulls down this gate—then let Baalshamem and El-Creator-of-Earth and the eternal Sun and the whole generation of the sons of the gods efface that kingdom and that king. . . . (Crawford, 1992, p. 162; cf. p. 165, and Beyerlin, 1975, pp. 242–243; also see the inscriptions of Hadad and Nerab, in Crawford pp. 200–207)

A sixth-century tomb found in Sidon tries to warn off potential tomb-robbers:

> I, Tabnit, priest of Astarte, king of the Sidonians, son of Eshmunazor, priest of Astarte, king of the Sidonians, lie in this sarcophagus. Whoever you may be who comes across this sarcophagus, do not open it and do not disturb me. For they have collected no silver for me, nor have they collected any gold nor any other kind of valuable. Only I am lying in this sarcophagus. You must not open it and you must not disturb me, for that would be taboo to Astarte. And if nevertheless you do open it and do destroy me, may (you) not have any seed among the living under the sun nor a resting place among the spirits of the dead. (Beyerlin, 1975, p. 245)

To maximize their efficaciousness, Egyptian curse-threats often were directed against the violator's own mortuary cult and ritual burial, his remembrance, his family, and his offspring: "As for anyone who shall violate my corpse in the Necropolis, or who shall damage my image in my chamber: he shall be a hated one of Re. He shall not receive water or ointment for an Osirian, nor shall he ever bequeath his goods to his children" (Morschauser, 1991, pp. 117–129, 179). Some inscriptions known as the execration texts, imply that magical actions accompanied the formulae (p. 142), and spells in medical papyri and curses in royal decrees are particularly prominent in the Rammesid period (Morschauser, 1991, p. 182; cf. Nordh, 1996, p. 103). A stock image in late New Kingdom texts is the threat against a perpetrator, his wives, or children of sexual violation by an ass or of their sexual violation of each other: "He shall violate an ass, an ass shall violate his wife, and his wife shall violate his children" (Morschauser, 1991, pp. 198–200, 227–229).

Harsh and even crude as such curses sound, both Morschauser and Nordh emphasize the functionality of the Egyptian curse-formulae as supplements to and guarantors of stipulations that, although having legal and moral standing, were nevertheless unenforceable, as in the case of the protection of the tombs, monuments, and inscriptions of the deceased. Nordh proposes further that curses were a way of propagating the orthodox ideology of living in accordance with the all-embracing Egyptian cosmovision subsumed under the name of *Maat* (Nordh, 1996, p. 104; cf. Morschauser, 1991, p. 266). As Keim insists,

> One of the things that must be asserted at the outset, and reasserted in the course of study, is that ancient Near Eastern maledictions are religious. . . . There can be no question of such practices arising out of magical practices and then developing into religious systems. If there was such a development, it was long before the dawn of history and is no longer recoverable. Everything we actually know about maledictions in the ancient Near East attests to the deeply religious nature of their forms and operations. (1992, p. 33)

Indeed, the most renowned legal inscription of the Ancient Near East, the Code of Hammurabi (c. 1675 BCE), concludes with an extended curse invoking the gods Adad, Sin, Innana, and others to inflict terrible punishments on any who disregard, distort, or efface the king's words (Pritchard, 1969, pp. 178–180). In addition, Tzvi Abusch argues that the counter-witchcraft ritual, the Mesopotamian *Maqlu*, was based on the fundamental social contract embodied in an oath, *mamitu*, whose violation by the witch brings down the punitive counter-curse (2002, pp. 236–245, 253; and see Mercer, 1912, pp. 26–28).

As many scholars have pointed out, any oath intrinsically implies a conditional self-curse calling down on oneself a sanction or punishment in the event that the oath-taker proves untrue to what has been sworn. Often the medium or vehicle of the oath embodies its assurance: the eye, the heart, the right hand, one's children, orone's parents are put at risk; or a weapon or a ritually slain animal are taken to represent either the means or the consequences of a violated oath, as with the custom of the Nagas of Assam in which each party to an oath lays hand on a dog chopped in two (Mercer, 1912, p. 40 n.3; Crawley, 1934, p. 47; cf. *Gen.* 15 and the discussion in McCarthy, 1981, pp. 93–95). Crawley (1934, pp. 39–48) and Westermarck (1908, chap. 50) present within a Frazerian evolutionist model numerous examples of such oaths, and the related convention of trial by ordeal, from worldwide cultural contexts.

***Kudurru* and Covenants.** The oath/curse formula characterizes two important, distinct yet related genres of Ancient Near Eastern literature: *kudurru*, or boundary-stone inscriptions, and vassal-treaties, or covenants (for examples and sources see Fensham, 1963; Grätz, 1998, chap. 2, esp. pp. 46–65; and Hillers, 1964, chap. 2). Scholars have differed over the commonalities and differences among these Ancient Near Eastern *kudurru* and treaty forms, but Dennis McCarthy has demonstrated "the essential elements of the form: stipulations, the god lists or invocations, and the curse formulae which are invariably found in the treaties from Eannatum of Lagash to Ashurbanipal of Assyria" (McCarthy, 1981, p. 122; cf. Fensham, 1962, p. 1–6; Hillers, 1964, chap. 1). McCarthy reviews and analyzes important examples of Hittite, Assyrian, and Syrian treaty texts, including the seventh-century Assyrian treaty of Esarhaddon and the eighth-century Aramaic-Syrian treaties of Sefiré (McCarthy, 1981, Part I; for original publication of texts see Wiseman, 1958; Dupont-Sommer, 1958, and Korosec, 1931; for translations and bibliography see Pritchard, 1969, pp. 534–541, 653–662). McCarthy's comparative study shows that although a verbal blessing and cursing formula typically concludes the Hittite texts (chap. 4), the Sefire treaties actually incorporate the rubrics of acted out or performed curse-actions (1981, chap. 5; cf. Hillers, 1964, pp. 21–24), and the Esarhaddan treaty includes an exceptionally long and graphic curse (a "baroque elaboration," as McCarthy calls it (p. 121), accompanied by demonstrative actions: "just as male and female kids . . . are slit open and their entrails roll down over their feet, so may the entrails of your sons and daughters roll down over your feet" (p. 117 and chap. 6). "The reason for this emphasis on the curses," McCarthy concludes, "is evident enough. They sought to secure the observance of the treaty by multiplying as it were the religious sanctions and by the use of rites which were thought infallibly to bring about the ruin of the transgressor" (p. 151).

The Ancient Near Eastern vassal-treaty and its attendant curse formulae provide an apt transition to analysis of the curse traditions of the Hebrew scriptures, specifically in relation to the central biblical idea of covenant (see Hempel, 1961; Alt, 1934; Fensham; Hillers; Keim, 1992; and McCarthy, 1981). The locus classicus is the blessing and cursing ritual at Shechem in *Deuteronomy* 27, and the expansion or midrash on the blessings and curses in *Deuteronomy* 28, with its overwhelming preponderance of curse sanctions threatened for disobedience to God's law (*Dt.* 28:15–68; cf. the parallel text in *Lev.* 26; see Lewy, 1962; Buis, 1967; Hillers, 1964 chap. 3; McCarthy, 1981, chap. 9 and sources). The curses of *Deuteronomy* 28 are compulsively thorough, promising every manner of illness, misfortune, destruction, abandonment, and disaster: "Cursed shall be the fruit of your womb, the fruit of your ground, the increase of your cattle and the issue of your flock. Cursed shall you be when you come in, and cursed shall you be when you go out" (*Dt.* 27: 18–19). Although scholars continue to debate the origins of cultic proclamation of covenant law, the cultic character of the Deuteronomic formulae is clear (see Alt, 1934; Mowinckel, 1962; Grätz, 1998, chap. 3; Schottroff, 1969, esp. pp. 217–230; and the review of scholarship in McCarthy, 1981, pp. 197–199). But, it is reported, so dread were the Deuteronomic maledictions in medieval synagogues that there were difficulties in obtaining readers at the appointed times; in one case, "on a Sabbath on which the 'chapter of maledictions' was to be read, the Scroll of the *Torah* was shamefully permitted to lie open for several hours, because no member of the congregation was willing to come up to the pulpit" (Trachtenberg, 1970, p. 59, sources on p. 284, notes on pp. 32–35).

Other Old Testament texts that focus on the covenantal relationship, notably the Sinai texts of *Exodus* and various prophetic texts that espouse a covenant theology, have recourse to the curse sanctions of the Near Eastern treaty model: "If the prophets of all periods knew the terms of the covenant with Yahweh," Hillers concludes, "they knew the curses associated with the covenant as well, for these, an essential part of the covenant between men . . . were also commonly attached to the covenant with God" (1964, pp. 84–85). Hillers adduces numerous parallels between Assyrian and Aramaic treaty-curses and such biblical passages as *Isaiah* 34:11–17 and *Jeremiah* 13:26–27 and 50, which call down curses of flood and desolation, devouring animals, broken weapons, incurable wounds, dry breasts, rape, and harlotry (1964, chap. 4). Fensham had earlier concluded that there "obviously exists a close connection between certain curses of the ancient Near East and various prophetic maledictions," focusing on examples of punitive maledictions from *Amos* 4 and *Isaiah* 13. "We have followed the line through from *kudurru*-inscriptions to treaties and hence to the Old Testament prophecies," Fensham continues, although the latter, he insists, substitute a moral/theological grounding for the "mechanical, magical execution of the treaty-curse" (1963, pp. 172–173). It is precisely this last point, however, that more recent scholarship calls into question. For example, Gervitz's survey of West-Semitic commemorative, funerary and votive inscriptional curses shows the contain the same mix of apodictic and casuistic forms as do the Hebrew scriptures.

Study of the topic of cursing in Old Testament contexts is complicated by the fact that several quite distinct Hebrew words are commonly translated as *curse* into English (or as malediction in French or Fluch in German.). The major Hebrew terms are *ʿalah, ʿarr, qillel,* and *qbb* (for major discussions see Brichto, 1963; Keim, 1992, pp. 15–20; Scharbert, 1977; Gordon, 1997). The preponderance of occurrences of the verb *qbb* in the OT occurs in the Balak/Balaam episode in *Numbers* 22–24 in which Balak futilely urges Balaam to curse, rather than bless, Israel; Balak's expectation is that such a curse (or blessing) would be automatically efficacious upon pronouncement, whereas Balaam assumes that it would be dependent upon God. *Qbb* as *revile* also occurs in *Proverbs* 11:26 and 24:24 as an unambiguous malediction upon bad behavior, and also in the familiar passage in which Job curses the night of his birth (3:8). In fact, the extended passage of Job's curse upon his birth (3:1–9) includes parallel uses of three of the Hebrew words for curse: *qbb, ʿarr,* and *qillel.* As a noun *qelala* is used to signify either that which is accursed or curse as the opposite of blessing (*baraka*—and sometimes *berek,* bless, is used euphemistically to mean *qillel,* curse, as in *I Kings* 21:13 and *Job* 1:5 and 9–11). As a verb *qillel* is generally used in the Old Testament in a rather defuse and imprecise way to convey personal contempt, disrespect, or abuse directed at a variety of objects, including parents, kings, and, in *Leviticus* 24:10–16 and *Exodus* 22:27, the Deity. In *Genesis* 8:21 God promises never again to *qallel* the earth, which as Brichto argues (1963, pp. 119–120), means abuse or treat injuriously, rather than curse (for full discussion on this root see Brichto, 1963, chaps. 4 and 5).

Thus, the two primary terms for curse in the Old Testament remain *ʿalah* and *ʿarr.* The *ʿalah* term usually has the force of conditionality and is associated with oaths and swearing, and it is deeply implicated in the curse-sanctions of treaties and covenant. As elsewhere in the Ancient Near East the *ʿalah* curse is associated with the protection of property (*Judg.* 17:2; *Lev.* 5:1; *Prov.* 29:24), with juridical oaths (*I Kings* 8:31) or trial by ordeal (*Num.* 5:21–28, where guilt of adultery is tested by the curse of bitter waters), and with royal commands (*1 Sam.* 14:24, where Saul precipitously puts a battlefield curse on anyone who eats before evening). But the most important association of *ʿalah* is as punishment upon Israel for betrayal of the covenant (*berith*), as set forth in *Deuteronomy* and a number of prophetic texts (*Deut.* 29:20; *Isa.* 24:6; *Jer.* 23:10; *Ezek.* 16:59; *Dan.* 9:11; and see Zechariah's vision of the flying scroll of curses, *Ezek.* 5:1–4).

The *ʿarr* term, cognate to the Arabic *lār* discussed earlier, forms the basic operative cursing rubric in the Old Testament in its *qal* passive participle: "cursed be. . . ." Its fearful efficacy is associated with utterance by a figure of authority (*Num.* 5:18–27); a professional curser (*Gen.* 27:29; *Num.* 24:7); a king (e.g., Jehu, who curses Jezebel in *2 Kings* 9:34); or the Deity, as in the paradigmatic curses in *Genesis* on the serpent, the ground itself, and Cain (*Gen.* 3:14, 17; 4:11); or the angel of the Lord who curses those who do not participate in a holy war (*Judg.* 5:23). Such a curse has the force of a spell, as in the Balak/Balaam sequence in *Numbers* 22–23, and it is the basis of the catalog of curses associated with violation of the covenant in *Deuteronomy* 27 and 28, discussed above. In one enigmatic passage God threatens to curse Israel's blessings (*Mal.* 2:2), in a passage that Gordon takes as a satire on the priestly blessing (1997, I.525). In other passages, a curse can be nullified by a blessing (*Judg.*

17:1–2), or it can be taken on by another person, as Rebekah does to protect Jacob (*Gen.* 27:13). Other uses of *ʿarr* include cursing the day one was born (*Jer.* 20:14–15; *Job* 3:1–9), or, as a noun, it is used to signify that which is cursed (*Gen.* 4:12 and 9:25; *Josh.* 9:23) or banned (*Jer.* 17:5). Compare it with the related term *herem* "identical with the curse in its most potent form" (Pedersen, 1926/1964, vol. 2, p. 272), meaning that which is placed under a ban, even to threat of extinction (*Exod.* 22:19; *Deut.* 7:6 and 13:13; *Judg.* 5:23 and 21:11).

CURSING IN THE OLD AND NEW TESTAMENTS. A special case of the use of cursing in the Old Testament, one that has been particularly problematical for pastoral theology, is the "cursing psalms," which Brueggemann has subsumed under the more general heading of "Psalms of Disorientation" (1984, chap. 3; cf. Pedersen, 1926/1964, vol. 1, pp. 446–452; Mowinckel, 1962, pp. 48–52). Here cursing is turned into a weapon against personal enemies (*Ps.* 35) or, more characteristically, into a weapon of Israel against its national enemies (*Pss.* 79, 109 and 137). Thus, the familiar Psalm 137, "By the rivers of Babylon. . . ." concludes with the violent wishful prayer that the hated Edomites be crushed for "what you have done to us!/Happy shall they be who take your little ones and dash them against the rock!" (8–9). Most extravagant of all is Psalm 109, an uninhibited prayer for Yahweh to visit every manner of cruel revenge upon the unnamed evildoers.

"Curses of the covenant" delivered by priests and Levites appear in the initiation ceremony of the Qumran community (1QS 2:16 and 5:12; and CD 1:17; 15:2–3), and whoever attacks the covenantal relationship is accursed (11QTemple 64:9–12). The Talmud permits cursing the wicked (*Men.* 64b), and acknowledges the efficacy of curses (*Ber.* 7a; *Meg.* 15a; *Sanh.* 105b), especially when uttered by a sage, and even if undeserved (*Ber.* 56a; *Mak.* 11a). Hence, there also are prohibitions against cursing, for example, by a wife (*Ket.* 72a), and against self-cursing (*Shebu.* 35a). A Jewish curse adapted from Psalm 109 that has retained currency is *Yimmah shemo (vezikhro)*: "May his name (and memory) be blotted out!," but the general rabbinic provision was to "Let yourself be cursed, rather than curse someone else" (*Sanh.* 49a). One well-known perpetuation of synagogue exclusion was the excommunication of Spinoza from the Portuguese synagogue of Amsterdam in 1656 (Little, 1993, pp. 277–278).

There is some continuity but not as much emphasis on cursing in the Old Testament Apocrypha and Intertestamental literature (see Van Den Doel, 1968, chap. 2). In the wisdom tradition, a well-known passage in *Sirach* parallels a mother's curse and God's curse (3:9, 16) and another warns against the curse of the neglected poor (4:5–6). The *Wisdom of Solomon* reiterates the *Genesis* curse on the Canaanites (12:11) and promises that the ungodly and idolatrous will be accursed (*Genesis* 3:12; 14:8), and *Tobit* 13:12 calls accursed all those who would dominate or harm Jerusalem. One distinctive cursing form found in the Intertestamental literature is the roll-call of woes: *2 Esdras* contains woes against Assyria (2:8); the Sibylline Oracles call down woes upon Babylon, Ethiopia, Libya (3:295–334), Phoenicia, Crete, Thrace (3:492–511), Lycia (5:1–26), and Greece (11:183–185). The *Apocalypse of Baruch* declares that in the last days the dead will be blessed (10:6, 11:7) and the living will be cursed (10:7, 14:14). Most impressively, the final judgment section of *1 Enoch* (94–105) contains a rolling denunciation of the foolish and the unrighteous, especially of the wealthy who oppress the poor, for they will be given over "to a great curse" (94:6–8; 97:8–10).

These Intertestamental apocalyptic themes and the rhetoric of the woes offer a direct connection to some of the most distinctive curse motifs in the New Testament. (Note that the NT, like the Septuagint (LXX), adopts the Greek words *anathematizo* and *kataraomoi* as equivalents to the various Hebrew words for cursing.) The apocalyptic woes spread over the earth in *Revelations* 9–12 directly carry over from the Intertestamental woes, as does Jesus' pronouncement of woes upon the towns of Galilee (*Matt.* 11:21–23; *Luke* 10: 13–15). On the other hand, Jesus' reiterated "Woe unto's" reflect a more intense focus on personal authenticity and spirituality, as when *Luke* parallels the beatitudes with woes unto the opposite behaviors (6:20–26). Jesus pronounces woes unto the betrayer of the Son of Man (*Mark* 14:21; *Luke* 22:22). But the major instance occurs when Jesus pronounces woes against the scribes and Pharisees as blind fools, hypocrites, and vipers (*Matt.* 23:13–36; *Luke* 11:42–52), a rolling denunciation that is the New Testament equivalent of the Deuteronomic curses in the Old Testament. Apart from these texts, the only direct curses Jesus utters are the apocalyptic words of judgment, "Depart from me" (*Matt.* 25:41), and the enigmatic cursing of the fig tree (*Mark* 11:12–22; *Matt.* 21:18–20), usually taken as an "acted out" parable denouncing the barrenness of Israel (see Van Den Doel, 1968, pp. 247–251; Hatch, 1923; Robin, 1962). Other than this, Jesus' main teaching on the matter of curses is to refrain from all oaths (*Matt.* 23:16–22; cf. *James* 3:9), and the *Book of Revelation* declares that in the Heavenly Jerusalem "Nothing accursed will be found there any more" (22:3). Paul, nevertheless, concludes his First Epistle to the Corinthians with the words, "Let anyone be accursed who has no love for the Lord" (*1 Cor.* 22; a similar Islamic execration is found in Qurʾān 2:161).

The New Testament does present a number of instances of individuals pronouncing oaths and curses, especially in the *Acts of the Apostles.* Examples include the oath of conspirators against Paul (*Acts* 23:12), Peter's implicit curses against Ananias and Simon Magus (*Acts* 5:1–11, 8:9–24), and similar punitive curses of a folkloric character that occur in a number of the New Testament Apocrypha (see Van Den Doel, 1968, p. 247). In *2 Peter* 2:14 the apostle denounces false teachers as "accursed children," and earlier Peter had sworn an oath against himself upon denying Christ (*Mark* 14:71; *Matt.* 26:74).

But the curse of greatest theological richness occurs in *Galatians* 3:10–14, in the teaching that "all who rely on the works of the law are under a curse" because justification is only by faith, but that "Christ redeemed us from the curse of the law by becoming a curse for us—for it is written, 'Cursed is everyone who hangs on a tree'" (citing *Deut.* 21:23). This radical doctrine of substitution (cf. *2 Cor.* 5:21) may have led certain Gnostics to honor only a spiritual Christ and to repudiate the earthly Jesus, leading to Paul's otherwise enigmatic admonition, "Therefore I want you to understand that no one speaking by the Spirit of God ever says, 'Let Jesus be cursed!'" (*1 Cor.* 12:3).

Early Christian writers wrestled with the question of the appropriateness of cursing, generally labeling it a pagan practice but allowing for it as an occasional moral corrective (Augustine, *De sermone Domine in monte* 1:63–4; *PL* 34 1261–62) or as a judgment of justice rather than revenge (Gregory the Great, *Moralia in Job* 6; *PL* 75:638–9). In the eighth century, Rhabanus Maurus Christianized the Deuteronomic presentation of blessings and cursings (*Deut.* 27) by associating the curses with the Law and the blessings with the Gospel (*Enarratio super Deuteronomium* 3:24–5; *PL* 108:947–61). Thomas Aquinas' scholastic solution was to conclude that justified curses were curses only in accident and not in substance when judged according to intentionality (*Summa theologiaa* IIa–IIae, q. 76).

Cursing and the Church. Moreover, the post-Constantinian Church, building upon Paul's comments in *1 Corinthians* 16:22 and *Galatians* 1:8, incorporated formal procedures for anathema and excommunication, ratified at the councils from Elvira (fourth century), Tours (sixth century), and Toledo (seventh century) to Toulouges (eleventh century). In his study of medieval cursing rituals, *Benedictine Maledictions*, Lester Little sets out the documentary history of liturgical maledictory formulas in the monasteries of northern France from the tenth through the thirteenth centuries. Little shows that in the context of deeply unsettled social structures, amid the threat of recurrent violence and disorder, and in the absence of effective instruments of law and justice, the Benedictine monasteries developed a pair of elaborate ritual responses: the Clamor and the Humiliation of the Saints. These rituals were influenced both by biblical precedent and by the Irish Christian folk culture that had earlier been carried by monks to the Continent. The rich tradition of Irish saints, beginning with Patrick, whose weapons in the wilderness were fasting and cursing combined with the strong language of the maledictory Psalms, produced a powerful ritual of prostration and cries unto the Lord for protection against enemies who ranged (in the eyes of the monks) from marauding Vikings to recalcitrant or peremptory local barons. (See Little, 1993, Appendix C for "A Miscellany of Curse Formulas"; Little also reminds us that a modern literary adaptation of the Clamor appears in Sterne's *Tristram Shandy*.)

The Clamor was made even more dramatic when combined with the Humiliation of the Saints, a tradition with far less ecclesiastical sanction (Geary, 1983), when the chief relics held by a monastic church were taken from their usual places of veneration and placed on the floor of the chancel and covered with thorns. This ritual, combined with the cessation of virtually all work and ritual at the monastery, apparently created enough distress on the part of the local community and the offending baron that a settlement of the relevant issue could be negotiated. The religious phenomenology of the ritual is complex and conflicted: although the prayers are directed to God, the successful outcome is attributed to the saint, who has, however, not been prayed to but in effect coerced and even punished for dereliction of duty. Verification of this interpretation comes from unauthorized versions of the Humiliation ritual in which peasants would angrily strike the relic (an interesting contemporary representation occurs in the Francine Prose novel *Household Saints* and its film adaptation). Behind all this, as Little argues, was the very real need for justice and protection against very real adversaries in a situation of extreme vulnerability. Nevertheless, by the time of the Second Council of Lyons in 1274, the church forbade the ritual of Humiliation, although the tradition of the Clamor continued in the form of special votive masses and prayers in time of trouble and in the Ash Wednesday *Commination* in the Book of Common Prayer.

Although the Protestant Reformers were understandably hostile to the Catholic Church's claim of authority to anathematize and excommunicate, many of the Reformed churches (basing themselves upon *Matt.* 18:15–18 and *1 Cor.* 5:11) arrogated to themselves comparable powers of "evangelical separation," usually referred to among the radical Anabaptist sects as banning or shunning. Characteristic expressions of this reformed version of exclusion can be found in several texts collected in George Hunston Williams's *Spiritual and Anabaptist Writers* (1957/1970), including Conrad Grebel's "Letters to Thomas Müntzer" (1524), Balthasar Hubmaier's "On Free Will" (1527), Caspar Schwenckfeld's "An Answer to Martin Luther's Malediction" (c. 1544), Dietrich Philips's "The Church of God" (c. 1560), and Ulrich Stadler's "Cherished Instructions on Sin, Excommunication, and the Community of Goods" (1537); and a systematic presentation is set out in Menno Simons's "On the Ban: Questions and Answers" (1550).

Cursing in the Early Modern Period to the Present. One of the most familiar carry-overs of the curse tradition in popular culture since the Early Modern period has remained the protective curse, famously called to the attention of tourists at Stratford-on-Avon, England, when viewing Shakespeare's tomb engraving:

> GOOD FRIENDS FOR JESVS SAKE FORBEARE,
> TO DIGG THE DVST ENCLOASED HEARE:
> BLESE BE ye MAN yt SPARES THES STONES,
> AND CVRST BE HE yt MOVES MY BONES.

In *Anathema!* Marc Drogin has collected hundreds of fly-leaf book curses from medieval to Early Modern times aimed at protecting books from theft, defacement, misuse, or even misreading, concluding with a contemporary British postal mailing carefully inscribed, "*PLEASE DO NOT BEND*/ if anyone shall bend this, let him lie under perpetual malediction. Fiat fiat fiat. Amen." To this someone in Her Majesty's Postal System succinctly appended, "FART" (1983, p. 111).

Finally, note that the corpus of world literature is full of curses that drive plots and provide dramatic and melodramatic dénouements, including: Enkidu's curse on the prostitute in *Gilgamesh* (vii.3); Oedipus's unwitting self-curse (Sophocles, *Oedipus Rex* 269–72); Dido's curse on Aeneas, who abandoned her (*Aeneid* IV.863–919); Medea's curse on Jason, who betrayed her (Euripides, *Medea* 160 seq.); Caliban's curse on his new island overlords (Shakespeare, *The Tempest* I.ii.353–67); Byron's denunciation of Lord Elgin in "The Curse of Minerva"; the bitter curses rained down upon Brother Lawrence in Browning's "Soliloquy of the Spanish Cloister"; and Dylan Thomas's plea to a dying father: "And you, my father, there on the sad height, / Curse, bless me now with your fierce tears, I pray / Do not go gentle into that good night. / Rage, rage against the dying of the light."

BIBLIOGRAPHY

A comprehensive survey of primary and secondary references to cursing in the ancient Mediterranean world (Mesopotamian, biblical, and Greco-Roman) is provided by Wolfgang Speyer's article "Fluch" in *Reallexikon für Antike und Christentum*, Bd. VII (1969): 1160–1288. Such an assemblage will not have to be done again. Cursing, however, is a thematic topic embedded in a vast range of other ethnographic literature of which there is no comparably complete or analytic survey. The widest ranges of reference are to be found in the work of two early surveyors of ethnographic sources: Edward Westermarck and Ernest Crawley. For Westermarck see *The Origin and Development of the Moral Ideas*, 2 vols. (London, 1908), especially chapters xxiii, xxiv, xxv, and l; *Pagan Survivals in Mohammedan Civilization* (London, 1933; Amsterdam, 1973) and his important article, "*L'Âr*, or the Transference of Conditional Curses in Morocco," *Anthropological Essays Presented to Edward Burnett Tylor* (London, 1907), pp. 361–374. For Crawley see *Oath, Curse, and Blessing*, edited by Theodore Besterman (London, 1934), extracted from Crawley's *The Mystic Rose* (London, 1902); the material is also abstracted in Crawley's article "Cursing and Blessing" for the *Encyclopaedia of Religion and Ethics*, edited James Hastings, vol. 4 (Edinburgh, 1908–1926; reprint, New York, 1970), pp. 367–374. Another comprehensive presentation occurs in the article "Maldición" in volume xxxii of the *Enciclopedia Vniversal Ilvstrada Evropeo-Americana* (Madrid, 1958): 486–492. Also see the early overview article by W. Sherwood Fox, "Cursing as a Fine Art," *Sewanee Review Quarterly* 27 (1919): 460–477. The classic expression of cultural evolutionism is James Frazer, *The Golden Bough: A Study in Magic and Religion,* 12 vols. (London, 1911–1915). A key example of early-twentieth-century anthropological perspective on magic and religion is Branislaw Malinowski, *Magic, Science and Religion and Other Essays* (New York, 1948).

There has been a good deal of scholarship on the motif of cursing in Ancient Near Eastern and Mediterranean literature. Egyptian material is covered in Katarina Nordh, *Aspects of Ancient Egyptian Curses and Blessings* (Uppsala, Sweden, 1996); Scott Morschauser, *Threat-Formulae in Ancient Egypt* (Baltimore, 1991); and André Parrot, *Malédictions et violations de tombes* (Paris, 1939). The Mesopotamian *Maqlû* ritual for countering a witch's curse is thoroughly analyzed by Tzvi Abusch in *Mesopotamian Witchcraft* (Leiden, 2002). Greek magical papyri are studied by Fritz Graf in "Prayer in Magic and Religious Ritual," in *Magika Hiera: Ancient Greek Magic and Religion,* edited by Christopher Faraone and Dirk Obbink, pp. 188–213 (Oxford, 1991). The major study of curse tablets or *tabellae defixionum* in the Greco-Roman world is John Gager's *Curse Tablets and Binding Spells from the Ancient World* (New York, 1992). Curses as a motif in the Indo-European literatures are the subject of Jeffrey Louis Falco's "The Malediction in Indo-European Tradition," Ph.D. diss. (UCLA, 1992). Cursing motifs in Germanic and Scandinavian folklore are dispersed throughout Jacob Grimm's classic early work, *Teutonic Mythology*, translated by James Steven Stallybrass, 4 vols. (1883–1888; reprint, New York, 1966). For examples from India, see Heinrich Zimmer, *Philosophies of India,* edited by Joseph Campbell (New York, 1956), pp. 66–83; and Paul Hockings, *Counsel from the Ancients: A Study of Badaga Proverbs, Prayers, Omens, and Curses* (Amsterdam, 1988), Index, p. 777.

Magical formulas, including curses, from Ancient Mesopotamia and Syria-Palestine, and from the Old Testament are illustrated and discussed in Frederick Cryer and Marie-Louise Thomsen, *Witchcraft and Magic in Europe: Biblical and Pagan Societies* (Philadelphia, 2001). Many relevant selections from Egyptian and Mesopotamian texts, legal, political, and literary, are conveniently available in James B. Pritchard, ed., *Ancient Near Eastern Texts Relating to the Old Testament,* 3d ed. with supplement (Princeton, N.J., 1969); Walter Beyerlin, ed., *Near Eastern Religious Texts Relating to the Old Testamentv* (Philadelphia, 1975); and Francesco Pomponio, ed., *Formule di maledizione della Mesopotamia preclassica* (Brescia, Italy, 1990). A major comparative study is Sebastian Grätz, *Der strafende Wettergott: Erwägungen zur Traditionsgeschichte des Adads-Fluchs im der Alten Orient und im Alten Testament* (Bodenheim, Germany, 1998). Thomas Crawford's *Blessing and Curse in Syro-Palestinian Inscriptions of the Iron Age* (New York, 1992) analyzes Semitic cursing inscriptions in Akkadian, Ugaritic, Aramaic, Phoenician, Hebrew, and Edomite. Contemporary Palestinian curses are the subject of T. Canaan's "The Curse in Palestinian Folklore," *Journal of the Palestine Oriental Society* 15 (1935): 235–279.

Of particular importance among the Ancient Near Eastern texts for Old Testament study are treaties and covenants. Important original texts were published in D. J. Wiseman, *The Vassal-Treaties of Essar-haddon* (London, 1958); A. Dupont-Sommer, *Les inscriptions araméennes de Sifré* (Paris, 1958); and V. Korosec, *Hethitische Staatsverträge* (Leipzig, Germany, 1931). Important studies include Dennis McCarthy, S. J., *Treaty and Covenant: A Study in Form in the Ancient Oriental Documents and in the Old Testament* (Rome, 1981); Paul Arden Keim, "When Sanctions Fail: The Social Function of Curses in Ancient Israel," Ph.D. diss. (Harvard, 1992); and Delbert Hillers, *Treaty-Curses and the Old Testament Prophets* (Rome, 1964). Also see Delbert Hillers, "The

Effective Simile in Biblical Literature," *American Oriental Series* 65 (1984); Samuel Mercer, *The Oath in Babylonian and Assyrian Literature* (Paris, 1912); F. Charles Fensham, "Malediction and Benediction in Ancient Near Eastern Vassal-Treaties and the Old Testament," *Zeitschrift für die Alttestamentliche Wissenschaft* 74.1 (1962): 1–9, and F. Charles Fensham, "Common Trends in Curses of the Near Eastern Treaties and *Kudurru*-Inscriptions Compared with Maledictions of Amos and Isaiah," *ZAW* 74.2 (1963): 155–175.

In addition to Speyer, already mentioned, major work on the subject of cursing in the Old Testament has been contributed by Josef Scharbert, including the articles "'Fluchen' und 'Segnen' im Alten Testament," *Biblica* 39 (1958): 1–26; "Curse," in the *Encyclopedia of Biblical Theology*, edited by Johannes Bauer (New York, 1981): 174–79; and articles in *Theological Dictionary of the Old Testament*, edited by G. Johannes Botterweck and Helmer Ringgren, translated by John Willis (Grand Rapids, Mich., 1977): I.261–266, 405–418; and his book *Solidarität in Segen und Fluch im Alten Testament und in seiner Umwelt* (Bonn, Germany, 1958). Other book-length studies focusing on cursing in the Old Testament include Willy Schottroff, *Der altisraelitische Fluchspruch* (Neukirchen-Vluyn, Germany, 1969); and Herbert Chanan Brichto, *The Problem of "Curse" in the Hebrew Bible* (Philadelphia, 1963). Robert Gordon is author of a series of articles on the various Hebrew words for *curse* in the *New International Dictionary of Old Testament Theology and Exegesis*, edited by Willem A. VanGemeren (Grand Rapids, Mich., 1997): vol. 1, items 457 and 826; vol. 3, items 7686 and 7837; and vol. 4, pp. 491–493.

An important article that offers a comparative analysis of cursing in the Hebrew scriptures and neighboring cultures is Stanley Gervitz, "West-Semitic Curses and the Problem of the Origins of Hebrew Law," *Vetus Testamentum* XI.2 (1961): 137–158 (and see his article "Curse" in the *Interpreter's Dictionary of the Bible*, 4 vols. [New York, 1962]: I, pp. 749–750). Earlier treatments of the same issue include: Albrecht Alt, *Die ursprünge des israelitischen Rechts* (1934); Johannes Hempel, "Die Israelitische Anschauungen von Segen und Fluch im Lichte altorientalisher Parallelen," *Beiheft zur Zeitschrift für die Alttestamentliche Wissenschaft* 81 (1961): 30–113; and, with respect to *Deuteronomy*, Immanuel Lewy, "The Puzzle of *Dt.* xxvii: Blessings Announced, but Curses Noted," *Vetus Testamentum* XII.2 (1962): 207–211; and Pierre Buis, "Deuteronome xxii 15–26: Malédictions ou Exigences de l'Alliance?," *Vetus Testamentum* XVII.4 (1967): 478–479. On the cursing element in the *Psalms*, see Johannes Pedersen, *Israel: Its Life and Culture*, 4 vols. in 2 (Copenhagen, Denmark, 1926; reprint, London, 1964); Sigmund Mowinckel, *The Psalms in Israel's Worship*, 2 vols., translated by D. R. Ap-Thomas (New York, 1962); Walter Brueggemann, *The Message of the Psalms* (Minneapolis, 1984); and Sheldon Blank, "The Curse, Blasphemy, the Spell, and the Oath," *Hebrew Union College Annual* XXIII.1 (1950–1951): 73–95. The question of whether Old Testament texts manifest a belief in the automatic efficacy of curses is addressed by W. Sherwood Fox, "Old Testament Parallels to *Tabellae Defixionum*," *American Journal of Semitic Languages and Literatures* 30.2 (1914): 111–124; by J. Z. Lauterbach, "The Belief in the Power of the Word," *Hebrew Union College Annual* XIV (1939); and by Anthony Thistleton, "The Supposed Power of Words in the Biblical Writings," *Journal of Theological Studies* 25 (1974): 283–299. For the biblical and later Jewish tradition, see Joshua Trachtenberg, *Jewish Magic and Superstition: A Study in Folk Religion* (New York, 1970), chaps. 4, 5, and 8; and the article "Cursing" in *The Jewish Encyclopedia*, edited by Isidore Singer et al. (New York, 1916): IV, pp. 389–390.

For the New Testament, the major studies, in addition to Speyer, are Anthonie Van Den Doel, "Blessing and Cursing in the New Testament and Related Literature," Ph.D. diss. (Northwestern Univ., 1968); and L. Brun, *Segen und Fluch in Urchristentum* (Oslo, Norway, 1932). Regarding the cursing of the fig tree; see A. De Q. Robin, "The Cursing of the Fig Tree in *Mark* XI: A Hypothesis," *New Testament Studies* 8.3 (1962): 276–281; and W. H. P. Hatch, "The Cursing of the Fig Tree," *Journal of the Palestine Oriental Society* III (1923): 6–12. Discussion of the various words for *curse* in the New Testament occur in articles by Behm and by Büchsel in *Theological Dictionary of the New Testament*, edited by Gerhard Kittel, translated by Geoffrey Bromiley (Grand Rapids, Mich., 1964): I, 355–356 and 448–451.

Aspects of ritual cursing in medieval Christendom, especially in monastic milieux, are the subject of studies by Patrick Geary, "Humiliation of Saints," in *Saints and Their Cults*, edited Stephen Wilson, chap. 3 (Cambridge, U.K., 1983); and by Lester Little, *Benedictine Maledictions: Liturgical Cursing in Romanesque France* (Ithaca, N.Y., 1993). Little is author of the article "Cursing" in the original edition of the *Encyclopedia of Religion*, edited by Mircea Eliade, vol. 4, pp. 182–185 (New York, 1987), which includes a focus on Catholic, and especially Irish, saint lore. Medieval book-curses are garnered in Marc Drogin, *Anathema!: Medieval Scribes and the History of Book Curses* (1983). Reformation traditions of banning as a Protestant form of excommunication occur in various texts collected in George Hunston Williams, ed., *Spiritual and Anabaptist Writers* (Philadelphia, 1957; reprint, 1970).

The role of cursing in European witchcraft appears intermittently in the discussion by George Lyman Kittredge, *Witchcraft in Old and New England* (Cambridge, Mass., 1929); and in the more recent essays by Norman Cohn, Peter Brown, Keith Thomas, and Alan MacFarlane collected in Part I ("The Context of Witchcraft in Europe") of *Witchcraft: Confessions & Accusations*, edited by Mary Douglas (London, 1970); and in Keith Thomas, *Religion and the Decline of Magic: Studies in Popular Beliefs in Sixteenth and Seventeenth Century England* (New York, 1997).

Cursing as an aspect of magic is a subject of ethnographic study in worldwide contexts. Classic studies of magic in Africa include: E. E. Evans-Pritchard, *Witchcraft, Oracles, and Magic among the Azande*, edited and abridged by Eva Gillies (1936; reprint, Oxford, 1976), esp. chaps. 3, 5, and 11; C. W. Hobley, *Bantu Beliefs and Magic*, 2d ed. (London, 1967), esp. chap. 7, "The Curse and Its Manifestation"; the essays collected in *Witchcraft and Sorcery in East Africa*, edited by John Middleton and E. H. Winter (London, 1963; reprint, 1969); Dominique Zahan, *The Religion, Spirituality, and Thought of Traditional Africa*, translated by Kate Ezra and Lawrence Martin (1970; reprint, Chicago, 1979), chap. 7, "Nictosophers and 'Healers'"; and Benjamin Ray, *African Religions* (Englewood Cliffs, N.J., 1976), chaps. 4 and 5. Relevant articles include: Ruth Finnegan, "How to Do Things with Words: Performative Utterances among the Limba of Sierra Leone," *Man* 4.4 (1969): 537–552; Benjamin Ray, "'Performative Utterances' in African Rituals," *History of Religions* 13 (1973–1974): 16–25; the essays by Alison Redmayne and R. G. Willis in *Witchcraft: Confessions and Accusations*: Part II, "Cleansing and Confession of Witches," and, on the subject of "cursing deaths" in East Africa, Godfrey Lienhardt, "The Situation of Death: An Aspect of Anuak Philosophy," in the same collection, chap. 13.

Curses, including death by cursing, is treated in studies of African-derived vodou traditions. For Haiti see Alfred Metraux, *Voodoo in Haiti*, translated by Hugo Charteris (1959; reprint, New York, 1972), Section V; Milo Rigaud, *Secrets of Voodoo*, translated by Robert Cross (1953; reprint, San Francisco, 1985), chap. 6; and Pierre Pluchon, *Vaudou: Sorciers Empoisonneurs* (Paris, 1987). Non-academic and exploitive literature on vodou abounds, as in the case of Robert Pelton, *Voodoo Charms and Talismans* (New York, 1973), which contains instructions, for instance, on how "To Place a Curse" (chap. 1). On performative language in the West Indies, see Roger Abrahams, *The Man-of-Words in the West Indies: Performance and the Emergence of Creole Culture* (Baltimore, 1983).

Related material on cursing traditions is found in studies of Southeast Asian and Oceanic cultures, including Walter William Skeat, *Malay Magic* (London, 1965), chap. vi, "Divination and the Black Art"; Francisco Demetrio, S.J., *Encyclopedia of Philippine Folk Beliefs and Customs* (Cagayan de Oro City, Philippines, 1991), pp. 52–54, 296; R. H. Codrington, *The Melanesians: Studies in Their Anthropology and Folklore* (Oxford, 1891), chaps. xi, "Prayers," and xii, "Magic"; and the book-length evangelizing work by Pieter Middelkoop, *Curse—Retribution—Enmity: As Data in Natural Religion, Especially in Timor, Confronted with the Scripture* (Amsterdam, 1960). For the Maori see J. S. Polack, *Manners and Customs of the New Zealanders* (London, 1840) and other nineteenth-century ethnographies cited in Crawley *Oath* 10–19.

For the extensive and controverted reporting on vodou death or bone-pointing among the Australian Aborigines, see, among the older works, H. Basedow, *The Australian Aboriginal* (Adelaide, Australia, 1925), pp. 178–179; and W. L. Warner, *A Black Civilization: A Social Study of an Australian Tribe* (London, 1941), p. 242; and, for the more recent scholarly debate in the pages of *American Anthropologist*: Walter Cannon, " 'Voodoo' Death," *AA* 44.2 (1942): 169–181; David Lester, "Voodoo Death: Some New Thoughts on an Old Phenomenon," *AA* 74.3 (1972): 386–390; Barbara Lex, "Voodoo Death: New Thoughts on an Old Explanation," *AA* 76.4 (1974): 818–823; Harry Eastwell, "Voodoo Death and the Mechanism for Dispatch of the Dying in East Arnhem, Australia," *AA* 84.1 (1982): 5–18; and Janice Reid and Nancy Williams, "'Voodoo Death' in Arnhem Land: Whose Reality?," *AA* 86.1 (1984): 121–133.

For classic studies of witchcraft and cursing traditions among Native Americans of the Southwest, see Clyde Kluckhohn, *Navajo Witchcraft* (Cambridge, Mass., 1944; Boston, 1967), sections 4, 5, and 10, Appendix II, "Sorcery," and Appendix III, "Wizardry"; Clyde Kluckhohn and Dorothea Leighton, *The Navajo* (Cambridge, Mass., 1946, 1974), chaps. 5 and 6; and Marc Simmons, *Witchcraft in the Southwest: Spanish and Indian Supernaturalism on the Rio Grande* (Lincoln, Neb., 1974, 1980). For other Native American examples, see *They Knew Both Sides of Medicine: Cree Tales of Curing and Cursing Told by Alice Ahenakew*, edited and translated by H. C. Wolfart and Freda Ahenakew (Winnipeg, 2000); and, for South America, Peter Riviere, "Factions and Exclusions in Two South American Village Systems," in *Witchcraft: Confessions and Accusations*, chap. 11.

The ur-text on performative language is John L. Austin, *How to Do Things with Words: The William James Lectures Delivered at Harvard University in 1955* (Cambridge, Mass., 1962). The on-going debate is reflected in S. J. Tambiah, "The Magical Power of Words," *Man* 3.2 (1968): 175–208; and in the essays gathered in *The Philosophy of Language*, 3d ed., edited by A. P. Martinich (New York, 1996), part II, "Speech Acts": J. L. Austin, "Performative Utterances" (1961); and John R. Searle, "What Is a Speech Act?" (1965), "A Taxonomy of Illocutionary Acts" (1979), and "Indirect Speech Acts" (1975) Although there is little direct discussion of the subject of cursing in this literature, the concept has been invoked in the studies of African ritual by Finnegan and Ray.

GEORGE SCHEPER (2005)

CUSANUS SEE NICHOLAS OF CUSA

CUSHITE RELIGION SEE KUSHITE RELIGION

CYBELE (Latin) or Kybele (Greek) is the Greek and Roman name given to a female deity of Anatolian origin whose worship was widely disseminated throughout the ancient Mediterranean world. The deity's name in her homeland was Matar, or Mother; in some cases this was modified by the Phrygian epithet Kybeliya, meaning "mountain," the source of the term *Cybele*. The Greeks and Romans also addressed the goddess as Mother (Meter in Greek, Mater in Latin), and the epithet Megale (Greek) or Magna (Latin), meaning "great," was frequently used, causing her to become known as the "Great Mother." Both the name and the visual image of the goddess first appear in Phrygia, in central Anatolia (modern Turkey), during the early first millennium BCE and spread from there, first to the Greek cities on the west coast of Anatolia, and then to mainland Greece and to Greek cities in the western Mediterranean. The goddess's cult was imported into Rome at the end of the third century BCE, and she became an important figure in Roman religion also. The deity remained a prominent figure in Greek and Roman religious practice until the dominance of Christianity in the fourth century CE.

THE ANATOLIAN BACKGROUND. The earliest clear evidence for the deity is found in ancient Phrygia. In this region there are numerous shrines to the goddess; frequently these contain an image of the deity, often placed within a sculptural relief that depicts the gabled end of a building in which the goddess appears as if standing in a doorway. Such shrines are particularly common in the region of Gordion, Ankara, and Boğazköy, and also further west in the Phrygian highlands, a region bounded by the modern cities of Afyon, Eskişehir, and Kütahya. The goddess is regularly shown wearing an elaborate gown and a high headdress, and often holds a predatory bird, perhaps a hawk; in a few cases the standing goddess is flanked by a composite human-animal figure, young male figures, or lions. In some shrines, only the architectural frame and doorway exist, suggesting that a portable image of the goddess (now lost) was placed there. Some of the doorway shrines are found on separate blocks, but others were carved directly into the natural rock of the landscape, where they form impressive monuments. Such monumental rock façades are particularly common in the Afyon-Eskişehir region; the façade at Midas City is the best known example. In several cases these façades bear inscriptions giving the name of the goddess, Matar, occasionally with a qualifying epithet, such as Kubeliya. Others bear the names of Phrygian kings, such as Midas and Ates, suggesting a close connection between the Mother goddess and Phrygian royalty. In urban centers the goddess's shrines are frequently located near the city gates. Shrines are also found along strategic transportation routes and passes, often in rural mountainous areas. Others are situated near springs and other water sources, or near burial tumuli.

The origins of the goddess are much disputed. While some have claimed that her roots lie in older Anatolian religious practice, there is no secure evidence for a mother goddess in this region during the Neolithic or Bronze ages. Female figurines from Neolithic sites such as Çatal Hüyük and Hacilar probably have no connection with Cybele, nor is there any direct antecedent for the goddess in Hittite or other second millennium BCE Anatolian cultures. The Phrygians immigrated into Anatolia from the Balkan region during the Early Iron Age, and the origins of the goddess may lie in their ancestral homeland in southeastern Europe. On the other hand, it is clear that the cult of the goddess as practiced in Phrygia was extensively influenced by the religious imagery of earlier and contemporary Anatolian cultures; the visual image of the Phrygian Mother goddess bears a close resemblance to sculptural images of a contemporary Anatolian deity, Kubaba, worshiped in neo-Hittite cities in southeastern Anatolia. In addition, the attributes of the Phrygian Mother goddess, especially the hawk and the association with mountains, have affinities with both earlier Hittite cultures and with early first millennium BCE Anatolian peoples, such as the neo-Hittites and Urartians. Yet the distinctive combination of name, physical appearance, and architectural shrines that characterize the cult of the Mother goddess is specific to Phrygia. The roots of the Greek and Roman Cybele lie in Phrygia.

CYBELE IN THE GREEK WORLD. From Phrygia, the cult of the Mother goddess passed to Lydia, in western Anatolia, where a fine marble image of the seventh or sixth century BCE depicting the goddess standing in a temple has been found in Sardis. During the same period, the earliest votive images of the goddess appeared in the Greek world, first in the Greek cities in Anatolia along the Aegean and Black Sea coasts, and then in numerous centers on mainland Greece and in Greek colonies in the western Mediterranean. In the Greek world the deity was addressed as Meter (Mother); *Homeric Hymn 14*, which probably dates from the sixth century BCE, calls her "the Mother of all gods and all human beings." She was regularly called the Mother of the Gods and was often conflated with the Greek goddesses Rhea and Demeter. In Greek votive images the goddess appears as a seated figure, usually holding a tympanum (drum) and phiale (ritual cup); often she has a lion cub in her lap, or two lions standing on either side of her throne.

Shrines to Meter are found in virtually every community in the Greek world. One prominent example was in the Agora of Athens, which contained a cult statue made by Agoracritus, pupil of Phidias. Here the shrine of Meter served as the repository of Athenian laws, a practice followed in some Ionian Greek cities as well. The goddess was also worshiped with nocturnal mystery rites limited to initiates. Briefly mentioned by Pindar (*Pythian Odes* 3), Herodotus (4.76), and Euripides (*Bacchae* 78–79), these rites seem to have been characterized by music, dance, and expressions of emotional intensity, features that were viewed with suspicion by some Greeks, including Demosthenes (*On the Crown* 260).

During the Hellenistic period the cult of Meter became even more widespread and appears in a number of new Hellenistic city foundations. It is particularly well attested in Asia Minor, especially in Pergamum, where the goddess had an urban shrine with a magnificent marble cult statue. She was also worshiped in rural mountain sanctuaries near Pergamum, a link with her Phrygian identity as a mountain goddess. Another prominent Asia Minor sanctuary is Pessinus, in Phrygia, where the sanctuary of the Mother goddess was the center of a temple state controlled by priests who bore the title Attis.

During the Hellenistic period the cult of the Greek Cybele was increasingly associated with that of a young male figure, Attis. According to a complex mythological tradition preserved in variant sources (especially Ovid, *Fasti* 4.223ff.; Pausanias 7.17, 9–11; and Arnobius, *Against the Pagans* 5.5–7), Attis was a beautiful Phrygian shepherd boy whom the goddess loved. When he proved to be unfaithful to her, the goddess drove him mad, whereupon he castrated himself. In this action he supposedly served as a model to the priests of the goddess, the Galli, who emasculated themselves in honor of Cybele. The origins of this mythological tradition and of the practice of ritual castration have been much discussed, and the source and meaning of both myth and ritual practice remain unclear. A god named Attis does not appear in Phrygian cult practice, and the name may refer to a member of the Phrygian royal family who had important priestly functions, functions that survived the collapse of the Phrygian kingdom and are reflected in the survival of the title Attis in the Mother's priesthood, such as that at Pessinus. A fourth-century BCE votive offering to Attis from the Piraeus forms the earliest indication of the cult of a god Attis in the Greek world, and his cult is attested there in the Hellenistic period as well. Votive images of Attis become common during the Hellenistic period; these depict him as a young man wearing a characteristic costume with a short tunic, leggings, boots, and a soft hat with a pointed tip. The costume, originally worn by Achaemenian Persians, became so closely associated with Attis that the dress, and especially the cap, are often called Phrygian.

CYBELE IN THE ROMAN WORLD. The cult of Roman Cybele, the Magna Mater, was imported to Rome, probably from Pergamum, in 204 BCE, toward the end of the Second Punic War. This step was taken by the Roman government after consultation with the Sibylline Books and was approved by Apollo's oracle at Delphi. From the first, the goddess was connected with the Trojan origins of Rome. Members of several prominent senatorial families, including the Cornelians and Claudians, assisted in the transfer of the goddess's image, said to be an unformed black stone. The goddess was given a temple on the Palatine, dedicated in 191 BCE, and an annual festival called the Megalesia was instituted. The cult of Attis was apparently introduced into Rome at the same time, as is suggested by the discovery of a great many images of Attis, dating from the second and first centuries BCE, in the precincts of the Palatine temple. The Galli, the emasculated priests of the goddess, also appeared in Rome. Their flamboyant costumes, feminine manners, and practice of ritual castration attracted much negative attention, and they became the archetype of the effeminate male, as described in Catullus 63. According to a passage of Dionysius of Halicarnassus, *Roman Antiquities* 2.19.5, from the first century BCE, the Roman senate at first prohibited the participation of Roman citizens in certain ceremonies of the cult of the goddess.

The Megalesia festival of the Magna Mater, celebrated April 4 through April 10, was characterized by a procession of the Galli through the streets, in which an image of the goddess seated in a chariot drawn by lions was carried aloft. Theatrical performances and banquets shared among members of the aristocracy also formed part of the festivities. Her cult was administered in Rome by the castrated Galli, under the control of the chief priest, the Archigallus; during the second century CE these offices were opened to Roman citizens. Religious fraternities, such as the Dendrophori ("tree bearers") and the Cannophori ("reed bearers"), assisted in the ceremonies. The liturgical language of the cult seems to have been Greek, and the surviving images of the goddess are similar to the Greek model. The cult of the Magna Mater spread widely throughout the Western Roman Empire, and important shrines are known in Italy, Gaul, Germany, Spain, and North Africa. The cult continued to be prominent in the Eastern empire as well.

Under the empire, the role of Attis in the cult became greater. His part in the cult may have been officially recognized for the first time by the emperor Claudius, according to information contained in Johannes Laurentius Lydus's *De mensibus* 4.59, written in the sixth century CE. The codex calendar of 354 CE mentions five days of festivities in March in honor of Attis, followed by the ceremonial washing of the black stone in the Almo, a little river outside Rome. The increased participation of Attis in the cult seems to have been celebrated with mystery rites. In the fourth century CE, the resurrection of Attis is explicitly affirmed by Firmicus Maternus (*De errore profanarum religionum* 3), although it is doubtful whether the potential for resurrection was extended to the cult's practitioners.

The ritual of the taurobolium came to be associated with the Magna Mater cult during the second century CE. Originally a bull sacrifice to the goddess, the rite was frequently performed as homage to the emperor. During the late third and fourth centuries CE, the taurobolium entailed a form of baptism by the blood of a sacrificed bull, as described by Prudentius (*Peri stephanon* 10.1001–1050). In the fourth century CE, the cult of Cybele and Attis formed a conspicuous rallying point for that part of the Roman aristocracy that had not been converted to Christianity; in the mid-fourth century it attracted the emperor Julian, who wrote an oration in honor of the Magna Mater. Public sacrifices to the goddess disappeared at the end of the fourth century, although in the fifth century the philosopher Proclus wrote a book, now lost, on Cybele.

SEE ALSO Castration; Dying and Rising Gods; Goddess Worship, article on Goddess Worship in the Hellenistic World; Virgin Goddess.

BIBLIOGRAPHY

Borgeaud, Philippe. *La Mère des dieux: De Cybèle à la vierge Marie.* Paris, 1996.

Cerri, Giovanni. "La madre degli dei *nell'Elena* di Euripide: Tragedia e rituale." *Quaderni di storia* 18 (1983): 155–195.

Graillot, Henri. *Le culte de Cybèle, Mère des dieux, à Rome et dans l'empire romain.* Paris, 1912. Old, but still has important data on Cybele in Rome.

Gruen, Erich S. "The Advent of the Magna Mater." In *Studies in Greek Culture and Roman Policy*, pp. 5–33. New York and Leiden, 1990.

Haspels, C. H. E. *The Highlands of Phrygia: Sites and Monuments.* Princeton, 1971.

Hepding, Hugo. *Attis, seine Mythen und sein Kult.* Giessen, Germany, 1903. Reprint, 1967.

Lancellotti, Maria Grazia. *Attis, between Myth and History: King, Priest, and God.* Leiden, 2002.

Lane, Eugene N., ed. *Cybele, Attis, and Related Cults: Essays in Memory of M. J. Vermaseren.* Leiden, New York, and Cologne, 1996.

Mellink, Matcheld J. "Comments on a Cult Relief of Kybele from Gordion." In *Beiträge zur Altertumskunde Kleinasiens: Festschrift für Kurt Bittel*, edited by R. M. Boehmer and H. Hauptmann, pp. 349–360. Mainz am Rhein, 1983.

Nauman, Friederike. *Die Ikonographie der Kybele in der phrygischen und der griechischen Kunst.* Tübingen, 1983.

Pensabene, Patrizio. "Nuovi indagini nell'area del tempio di Cibele sul Palatino." In *La soteriologia dei culti orientali nell'Impero Romano*, edited by Ugo Bianchi and Maarten J. Vermaseren, pp. 68–98. Leiden, 1982.

Roller, Lynn E. *In Search of God the Mother: The Cult of Anatolian Cybele.* Berkeley, Los Angeles, and London, 1999. A comprehensive treatment of the cult of Cybele in Anatolia, Greece, and the Roman Republic and early empire.

Rutter, Jeremy B. "The Three Phases of the Taurobolium." *Phoenix* 22 (1968): 226–249.

Sfameni Gasparro, Giulia. *Soteriology and Mystic Aspects in the Cult of Cybele and Attis.* Leiden, 1985.

Vermaseren, Maarten J. *Cybele and Attis: The Myth and the Cult.* Translated by A. M. H. Lemmers. London, 1977.

Vermaseren, Maarten J. *Corpus cultus Cybelae Attisdisque.* 7 vols. Leiden, 1977–1989. The most comprehensive collection of epigraphical and artistic sources for the Cybele cult; interpretations should be used with caution.

Wiseman, T. P. "Cybele: Virgil and Augustus." In *Poetry and Politics in the Age of Augustus*, edited by Tony Woodman and David West, pp. 117–128. Cambridge, UK, 1984.

LYNN E. ROLLER (2005)

CYBERNETICS. Cybernetics is the study of control and communication. Although it is often thought of as primarily the control systems in machines, cybernetic theory can also be applied to biological agents, to systems comprised of either mechanical or biological agents, or both. Of particular interest to cybernetics are systems that are complex, adaptive, and self-regulating through the use of feedback. Norbert Wiener coined the term in 1947 as a transliteration of the Greek *kybernetes*, which means "steersman," though it was originally used in a broader sense than merely locomotive. Plato used the term to denote the act of governing a populace as well as that of steering a boat. and the term *governor* derives from the same root. Both terms refer to the control and direction of complex systems.

Cybernetics describes the world in terms of systems and information. A mechanical or biological agent can be considered a hierarchy of interacting networks through which information is moved, created, or transformed. Similarly, a system of agents can also be described and studied through the same concepts of control and feedback. Cybernetics uses mathematical and logical models to describe the flow of information in a system. Since many systems are influenced by random factors, statistical methods are also used to forecast or describe information flow.

The goals of cybernetics are twofold. First, for any given system, cybernetics hopes to advance knowledge of that system by describing the processes that regulate its functioning. Second, the field of cybernetics also seeks to develop laws that describe control processes in general and that are applicable to all types of systems. Cybernetics focuses on the structure and functioning of any given system rather than on the physical makeup of its elements.

APPLICATIONS. The earliest applications of cybernetics were predominantly in engineering and computer science (robotics, circuit design, aiming artillery). Early work by Wiener, Claude Shannon, and John von Neumann was closely allied with the fledgling field of artificial intelligence and machine learning. Since any system that evidences both complexity and self-adaptation can be studied using cybernetics, the basic concepts were soon applied in a variety of fields, including economics (Kenneth Boulding), political science, management and industrial theory (Jay Forrester, Stafford Beer), biology (Warren McCulloch, Humberto Maturana, William Ross Ashby), sociology and anthropology (Gregory Bateson, Stein Braten), and ethics (Valentin Turchin). As cybernetics moved into the social sciences in the 1960s and1970s, descriptions in the field changed from those of an observer external to the system (e.g., a human observer of a mechanical system) to those of an internal participant (e.g., a human within a political or social community).

Whereas early cyberneticists thought of information as a commodity that flowed through systems, subsequent writers, such as Maturana, have viewed information as the product of a system. In a further step one can think of the system itself as consisting of information. The computer scientist Ray Kurzweil has applied this approach to his understanding of the human being, whereas the physicists Frank Tipler and Stephen Wolfram view information as the building block of the whole universe. For these writers the concept of information informs not only the system's outcomes or activities but is considered the very basis of the system itself.

PHILOSOPHICAL AND THEOLOGICAL IMPLICATIONS. This final understanding of both mechanical and biological agents as consisting essentially of information leads to the most important philosophical and theological implications of cybernetic theory. A cybernetic view of the human person sees that person as a system composed of information. The concept of cybernetic immortality is based on the assumption that thoughts, memories, feelings, and action define the human person. These are products of consciousness, which is considered an emergent property of the complex system of the brain. In other words, to the cyberneticist, human beings are basically biological machines whose unique identity is found in the patterns that arise and are stored in the neuronal structures of the brain. If these patterns could be replicated—in sophisticated computer technology, for example—the defining characteristics of the person would be preserved. In such an anthropology the soul is considered that part of consciousness that exerts the highest level of control on the system that makes up the human being.

The ability to isolate the cognitive part of the system and preserve its viability past the death of the body is held by some researchers as an alternative to the metaphysical immortality proposed by many religions. Kurzweil suggests the future possibility of a computer-based immortality, in which the contents of the human mind are downloaded to a silicon-based platform. Tipler envisions an eschatology in which the universe will contract to an "omega point" that will contain all the information that has ever existed, including that which makes up each human being. God is essentially the highest level of control in the cybernetic system of the universe, thus becoming identical with the omega point at the final contraction. Tipler notes that this omega point could allow for something not unlike the Christian concept of resurrection of the body, in that the information that makes up any given human being would be available, thus allowing for a reinstantiation of that individual. A cybernetic view of both God and the human person provides a way to maintain belief in a reductionistic materialism without giving up the hope of immortality.

Cybernetic theories have also been used to describe the origin of religion in societies and the development of ethical systems. In general, a cybernetic view of religion sees it as an adaptive mechanism for the survival of groups as they evolve and change in an atmosphere of physical and social competition. Religion becomes one of many feedback mechanisms for regulating the functioning of individuals within the social group.

SEE ALSO Artificial Intelligence.

BIBLIOGRAPHY

Norbert Wiener's *Cybernetics* (New York, 1948) introduced the term and the field. A more popular treatment of the field is in Wiener's *The Human Use of Human Beings* (New York, 1988). William Ross Ashby's *An Introduction to Cybernetics* (New York, 1956) remains the basic textbook in cybernetic theory. The Principia Cybernetica website, constructed by Frans Heylighen and available at http://pcp.lanl.gov, provides an excellent primer in both the theory and the philosophy of cybernetic thought. Humberto R. Maturana and Francisco J. Varela, *The Tree of Knowledge: The Biological Roots of Human Understanding* (Boston, 1992), apply cybernetic concepts to human cognition and to human social systems. Ray Kurzweil's *The Age of Spiritual Machines* (New York, 1999) explores the possibility of cybernetic immortality on a computer platform, whereas Frank J. Tipler's *The Physics of Immortality* (New York, 1994) combines cybernetics with modern physics to present an eschatological vision. Stephen Wolfram, in *A New Kind of Science* (Champaign, Ill., 2002), presents another view of the universe as cybernetic system.

NOREEN L. HERZFELD (2005)

CYCLADIC RELIGION SEE AEGEAN RELIGIONS

CYPRIAN

CYPRIAN (c. 205–258), also known as Thascius Caecilius Cyprianus; bishop of Carthage. According to his own testimony, Cyprian was raised in Carthage, where he was born probably in the first decade of the third century. Scion of a noble pagan family, he had the opportunity to become well trained in literature and rhetoric. Because he was a successful rhetorician, he acquired fame and friends in the ranks of high society.

Cyprian was already mature when in 246, attracted by the purity of Christian ethics, he was initiated into the Christian faith by the presbyter Caecilius, whose name he adopted. He found theological guidance in the works of Tertullian, whom he called "the teacher," even though he did not follow him in his extreme views.

Within a short period of time Cyprian had acquired such authority that in 248, after the death of Donatus, bishop of Carthage, he was elected his successor "by the voice of the people and the verdict of God." A year later the persecutions under Emperor Decius began. While the pagan mob cried, "Give Cyprian to the lion," he found refuge outside the city, whence he administered the church with the assistance of a committee of vicars.

The persecution badly disrupted the unity of the North African church. The edict of Decius invited all Christians either to sacrifice to the idols, whereupon they would receive a *libellus* ("certificate"), or to suffer martyrdom. Large groups of Christians everywhere became martyrs to the faith, but others (the *sacrificati*) offered some kind of sacrifice, while yet others (the *libellatici*) managed to obtain false documents stating that they had offered sacrifice. When these *lapsi*, or "backsliders," expressed the desire to return to the church, Cyprian instructed his clergy to grant full communion to the sick, but to give only pastoral care to the others until peace came, when a decision could be reached on how to receive the *lapsi*.

Cyprian found opposition to his policy, however, from a group of tolerant Christians under the layman, later deacon, Felicissimus, who advocated the immediate acceptance of all backsliders without restriction. They were backed by those presbyters who were displeased by Cyprian's election to the episcopate, as well as by numerous confessors, who promptly gave letters of recommendation to backsliders.

When he returned to his see fourteen months after he left, Cyprian convoked a synod that established in concert with Rome the fundamental principles for receiving the backsliders. The *sacrificati* should undergo penance of varying length, while the *libellatici* would be received immediately. However, there was a reaction on the part of the rigorists as well. Cyprian did not succeed in preventing a double schism, which resulted from the election of two new bishops as his rivals, Fortunatus and Maximus.

A new crisis, threatened during the reign of Gallus (252) by an outbreak of the plague, was averted by the self-sacrificing attitude of the Christians toward the victims of the misfortune, both Christian and pagan. In the period that followed, Cyprian carried out fruitful pastoral, social, and interchurch activities.

The validity of the baptism of heretics, an old problem exacerbated by the extension of the influence of Novatian, a leading presbyter in Rome, was to vex the church anew. How should the returning heretics be received? Cyprian, in accordance with the custom of the African church, and on the basis of his own ecclesiological persuasions, thought that no sacrament had any validity if performed outside the canonical church. Consequently, all heretics who returned would have to be rebaptized. His opinion was confirmed by three successive synods in 255 and 256. Pope Stephen, maintaining that acceptance should be made only by the laying on of hands, broke relations with Cyprian.

Under Valerian a new edict was issued against the Christians. Cyprian, not wishing to hide this time, was arrested, exiled to a place north of Carthage, and finally condemned to death. On hearing the decision, he said only "Deo gratias." He was beheaded on September 14, 258.

Though the Christian stage of Cyprian's life was short and troubled, he became one of the great writers of the church. He certainly did not possess the force and depth of Tertullian, whose terms and topics he borrowed extensively, but he showed greater understanding and moderation than the latter. His works are the product and proof of his practical interests and they reflect all the major issues and personalities of the day. Three ancient lists cite the titles of his writings, mostly short treatises and letters.

A friend of Cyprian's, Donatus, had difficulty in breaking away from old pagan customs. In *To Donatus*, Cyprian says that he himself also feared that he would find difficulty after his turn toward Christianity but that the water of regeneration had made him a new man. *To Quirinius*, later called *Testimonia*, is a collection of biblical passages with short comments for the training of new Christians. *On the Ornaments of Virgins* was written at the beginning of Cyprian's episcopate to praise the virtue of virginity and stress the need for modesty in dress. Cyprian issued *On the Lapsed* when he returned to his see in 251. In it he expresses his sorrow for the victims of the persecution and draws principles on the basis of which the problem of the backsliders should be solved.

On the Unity of the Catholic Church was written in 251, in face of the apparent danger of a split in the church, to stress that the church of Christ is one and that those who split it bring about an evil worse than the persecution. *On the Lord's Prayer*, written in 252, presents an edifying allegorical interpretation of the Lord's Prayer. The two treatises *To Demetrianus* and *On Morality* answer questions about suffering. The first is an answer to the accusations that arose during the plague, namely that Christian refusal to worship Roman deities was responsible for the present evils. Responsibility for these evils, states Cyprian, is to be found in the moral disorder of pagan society. *On Morality* was written during the same period to answer the question of why Christians endure the same evils as the pagans—dying prematurely from the plague and from hunger. Cyprian reasons that natural laws, established by the divine will, have universal bearing. Moreover, death is not a punishment for Christians: what travelers do not long to return to their homeland? Heaven is the home of Christians.

Other treatises cover almsgiving, baptism, jealousy, and envy, or are meant to enhearten Christians facing persecution. A number of other short treatises, mostly from the third century, have been falsely attributed to Cyprian.

The letters of Cyprian, some of them small treatises in themselves, are also important. Most refer to the problems of his episcopate: the consequences of persecution under Decius, the problem of the backsliders, the Novatian schism, and the question of the baptism of heretics. Popes Cornelius, Lucius, and Stephen, and the bishop of Caesarea in Cappadocia, are his most eminent correspondents.

A man of action, Cyprian was concerned exclusively with practical questions as aspects of the great problem of the church. "We struggle for the honor and the unity of the Church," he declares (*Letters* 73.11). His insistence that there is only one leader of the faith and his fear of the separatist movements within the church led him to stress the element of unity. He insisted that on a high level the church is one, because its founder is one, but simultaneously it is also universal. The one church is diffused into the universal through the multiplicity of bishops. The Petrine chair, the *cathedra*, is the one church; the sees of the local bishops constitute the universal church.

The fourth chapter of Cyprian's *On the Unity* examines unity on a second level, the unity of the body of bishops. The interpretation of this text, preserved in two recensions, has presented problems for theological research. The longer recension, because it is favorable to papal primacy, was once considered by many to be an interpolation. After the research of Othmar Perler, Maurice Bévenot, and others, however, both recensions are regarded as genuine. The long text stresses that "primacy was given to Peter" by Christ and that "those who abandon the chair of Peter cannot belong to the church." The mistake of earlier historians was that they identified the chair of Peter with the see of Rome. It appears that Cyprian was already aware of such a misunderstanding, and for this reason he removed those expressions and gave the text the short form. What Cyprian wished to say was that in the famous verse of *Matthew* 16:18, "Upon this rock [*petra*] I will build my Church," the rock and chair of Peter is the faith, and since the faith is one, the see is also one. In this one see all the apostles take part, as well as their successors. "Episcopatus unus est" ("The episcopate is one"), and the particular bishops are coparticipants in it. Further, the bishops are closely joined by the law of personal love and concord, and also through their common origin (*Letters* 43.5; 69.3). Therefore the important problems of the church can be solved only by a common decision of the bishops in synod.

On the local level, every church constitutes a unity achieved through the bond of the bishop, the clergy, and the laity. The faithful must be united with the bishop in the sense understood by Ignatius of Antioch; and he who is not one with the bishop is not even with the church. But the unity must operate reciprocally. Cyprian never acted without consultation with his clergy and people.

There are definite consequences of this kind of unity for the process of salvation. The church is the bride of Christ, pure and incorrupt; therefore, "no one can have God as Father, if he does not have the Church as mother" (*On the Unity* 6). In opposition to Tertullian, Cyprian insisted that the Holy Spirit is active only within the church: "Salus extra ecclesiam non est" ("There is no salvation outside the church," *Letters* 73.21). The church is the ark of Noah, whose passengers were the only ones saved from the great flood. The sacraments of the church, especially baptism, Eucharist, penance, and ordination, are valid only within the framework of the canonical ecclesiastical life.

Cyprian's feast is celebrated in the Western church on September 16, while in the Eastern church it is celebrated on October 2, and in the Anglican on September 26; the confusion occurs because of an Antiochian magician of the same name who converted to Christianity. At the time of Augustine, there were already three churches dedicated to Cyprian's name. His relics were transferred to Lyons under Charlemagne and were later deposited at Moissac in southern France.

The dissemination of Cyprian's writings in the Middle Ages shows that he was more honored than any other Latin church writer, except for the four great doctors of the Western church. He is one of the principal founders of Latin theology. Augustine was profoundly influenced by his views; the Council of Ephesus (431) used demonstrative passages from his works; the *Gelasian Decree* put him at the head of its list of orthodox bishops; and the *Decretum* of Gratian gave official weight to his treatise *On Unity*, which was widely used during the investiture controversy.

SEE ALSO Donatism.

BIBLIOGRAPHY

Works by Cyprian

The works of Cyprian were edited for the first time by Johannes Andreae in *Cypriannus opera* (Rome, 1471). This edition is unsatisfactory, as is that of Étienne Baluze and S. Mauri, *Sancti Caecilii Cypriani* (Paris, 1726), reprinted in *Patrologia Latina*, vol. 4, edited by J.-P. Migne (Paris, 1865). A critical edition, *S. Thasci Caecilii Cypriani Opera omnia*, 3 vols., "Corpus Scriptorum Ecclesiasticorum Latinorum," 3.1–3 (1868–1871), has been edited by Wilhelm Hertel. Robert Weber, Maurice Bévenot, Manib Simonetti, and Claudio Moreschini have edited the excellent *Sancti Cypriani episcopi opera*, 2 vols., "Corpus Christianorum, seria Latina," 3, 3A (Turnhout, Belgium, 1972–1976). The works of Cyprian have been translated by Robert E. Wallis in *Saint Cyprian: Writings*, 2 vols., "Ante-Nicene Christian Library," vols. 8, 13 (Edinburgh, 1868–1869).

Works about Cyprian

The comprehensive studies of Edward White Benson, *Cyprian: His Life, His Times, His Work* (London and New York, 1897), and Paul Monceaux, *Histoire littéraire de l'Afrique chrétienne*, vol. 2, *Saint Cyprien et son temps* (Paris, 1902), are still valuable, as is also the discussion of Cyprian's doctrine by Adehémar d'Alès, *La théologie de S. Cyprien*, 2d ed. (Paris, 1922). The recent study of Michael M. Sage gives a complete and good picture of his personality, times, and activity. The studies of Ulrich Wickert, *Sacramentum unitatis, Ein Beitrag zum Verständnis der Kirche bei Cyprian* (Berlin, 1971), Peter Hinchliff's *Cyprian of Carthage and the Unity of the Christian Church* (London, 1974), Charles Saumagne's *Saint Cyprien, évêque de Carthage, "pape" d'Afrique, 248–258: Contribution à l'étude des "persécutions" de Dèce et de Valérien* (Paris, 1975), and Michael A. Fahey's *Cyprian and the Bible: A Study in Third-Century Exegesis* (Tübingen, 1971) present particular aspects of Cyprian's activity. Hugo Koch has presented his research, which sheds new light on the evaluation of Cyprian's ecclesiology, in two writings, *Cyprianische Untersuchungen* (Bonn, 1926) and *Cathedra Petri: Neue Untersuchungen über die Anfänge der Primatslehre* (Giessen, 1930). Maurice Bévenot published, besides a number of small articles, a large work, *The Tradition of Manuscripts: A Study in the Transmission of Saint Cyprian Treatises* (Oxford, 1961).

PANAGIOTIS C. CHRISTOU (1987)
Translated from Greek by Philip M. McGhee

CYRIL I (1570/2–1638), surnamed Loukaris, known also as Cyril Lucar; Greek Orthodox patriarch of Constantinople. Next to Gennadios Scholarios, the first patriarch after the fall of Constantinople, Cyril was the most brilliant and influential head of the Greek church during the period of Turkish rule. Living at a time of intense conflict, when both Rome and the Protestants were seeking to bring Greek Orthodoxy under their control, Cyril strongly favored the Protestant side.

He was born at Candia (modern-day Heraklion) in Crete, then under Venetian sovereignty, and was given the baptismal name of Constantine. He studied at Venice under the celebrated Greek scholar Maximos Margounios, and then at the University of Padua. At his ordination (c. 1593) to the diaconate in Constantinople by Meletios Pegas, patriarch of Alexandria, who was probably his relative, Loukaris took the new name of Cyril. In 1594 he was sent to Poland to strengthen the Orthodox resistance against Roman Catholic propaganda and to help with education. In 1596, when the Synod of Brest-Litovsk ratified the union of the Orthodox church in Poland with the Roman Catholic church, Cyril took part in the countersynod held in Brest by those Orthodox who opposed the union. He stayed in Poland until 1598 and went for a second visit in 1600–1601. Returning in 1601 to Constantinople, Cyril was ordained priest, and in Egypt that autumn he was elected patriarch of Alexandria succeeding Pegas, an office he held until 1620, residing much of the time in Constantinople.

While in Poland, although siding with the antiunionist party, Cyril maintained friendly relations with leading Roman Catholics; in his early sermons (1599–1600) he draws on Catholic apologists such as Roberto Bellarmino and makes use of Latin scholastic categories, accepting among other things the doctrine of the Immaculate Conception. As late as 1608 he wrote to Paul V in terms implying a recognition of papal primacy. During his time as patriarch of Alexandria, however, Cyril came to feel increasing sympathy with Protestantism, particularly in its Calvinist form. His Protestant contacts were chiefly Dutch: he formed a close friendship with Cornelius van Haag (or Haga), Dutch ambassador at Constantinople; corresponded with the theologian Jan Uytenbogaert; and met David Le Leu de Wilhem. He also exchanged letters with George Abbot, archbishop of Canterbury, and in 1617 he sent a young Greek monk, Metrophanes Kritopoulos (1589–1639), to study at Oxford. Kritopoulos remained in England until 1624, later becoming patriarch of Alexandria (1636–1639).

In 1620 Cyril was elected patriarch of Constantinople (he had been patriarch briefly in 1612). He remained on the ecumenical throne until his death in 1638, though with some interruptions: he was deposed, reinstated in 1630, deposed a third time and restored in 1633, deposed and again reinstated in 1634, deposed in 1635 and not restored until 1637, thus serving altogether no fewer than seven different periods in office. The frequency with which he was ejected is an indication of the extreme instability of the ecumenical patriarchate at this time, subject as it was to constant interference from the Turkish authorities, and with its bishops deeply divided by internal strife. Throughout his years as patriarch, Cyril was the center of a bitter conflict between the anti-Roman and pro-Roman factions in the holy synod; behind this conflict lay the wider struggle between different states of western Europe for influence within the Ottoman empire. Cyril's opponents in the synod, the chief among them being Cyril (Kontaris) of Beroea, himself on several occasions patriarch, were supported by the Propaganda Fide in Rome and by the Jesuits in Constantinople, as well as by the French and Austrian ambassadors; on his side, Cyril relied upon the assistance of the Dutch and English embassies. He enjoyed the friendship of Thomas Roe, English ambassador during 1621–1628, through whom he donated the Codex Alexandrinus in 1628 to King Charles I of England. He also became close friends with Antoine Léger, chaplain at the Dutch embassy from 1628.

As patriarch, Cyril struggled to raise standards of education. In particular he opened a printing press at Constantinople in 1627, but this functioned for only a few months before it was closed by the Turks in 1628. He commissioned a translation of the New Testament into modern Greek, which was eventually published at Geneva in 1638. But he is chiefly remembered for his *Confession of Faith,* first published at Geneva in 1629. This work is openly Calvinist in its teaching, and many have denied its authenticity; yet, even if it was drafted by one of Cyril's Protestant friends, such as Léger, Cyril himself appended his signature to it and accepted it as his own.

Cyril's life came to a tragic end on June 27, 1638. He was arrested on an accusation of inciting the Don Cossacks to attack the Ottoman domains. After a few days in prison he was taken out to sea in a small boat and strangled. A man of vision and energy, and endowed with an able intellect, in calmer times Cyril might have succeeded in effecting a theological rapprochement between East and West, as well as in raising cultural and educational standards within the ecumenical patriarchate. As it was, his great gifts of leadership were largely wasted in an unremitting and futile struggle for power.

Cyril's *Confession of Faith* expresses to a considerable degree a reformed rather than an Orthodox viewpoint. He states that "the authority of scripture is higher than that of the church," since scripture alone, being divinely inspired, cannot err (sec. 2); and he denies the infallibility of the church (sec. 12). He adopts the standard Calvinist teaching on predestination and election (sec. 3) and insists on justification by faith alone, without works (sec. 13). He holds that there are only two "sacraments of the gospel," baptism and the Eucharist (sec. 15), and he dismisses "the vainly invented doctrine of transubstantiation," arguing that the faithful receive the body of Christ "not by crushing it with their physical teeth, but by perceiving it through the sense and feeling of the soul" (sec. 17). He rejects the doctrine of purgatory, denying that there can be change or progress after death (sec. 18), and he repudiates the veneration of icons (answer 4).

Cyril's *Confession* is the most far-reaching attempt ever made by an Eastern church leader to bring Orthodox teaching into line with Protestantism. It is hard to determine whether he was seeking merely to please his Calvinist supporters, or whether he was expressing his own deepest convictions in the hope of inspiring some sort of reformation within the Orthodox church. In fact the *Confession* found little favor and was condemned by no fewer than six Orthodox councils in the half century following Cyril's death (Constantinople, 1638, 1642; Jassy, 1642; Constantinople, 1672; Jerusalem, 1672; and Constantinople, 1691). The most significant of these condemnations was at the Jerusalem Council of 1672; this council ratified the *Confession* composed by Patriarch Dositheos of Jerusalem, which rebutted Cyril's *Confession* point by point. Even though Dositheos was influenced by Latin theology, his deviation from mainstream Orthodoxy was far less radical than Cyril's. The influence of Cyril's *Confession* was in this way largely negative, serving to push the Greek church in an anti-Protestant direction; but, if only by way of reaction, it also served to clarify seventeenth-century Orthodox thinking about the church, the sacraments, and the state of the departed.

BIBLIOGRAPHY

The Greek text of *The Eastern Confession of the Christian Faith* may be found in part 1 of Ernest Julius Kimmel's *Monumenta fidei ecclesiae orientalis* (Jena, 1850), pp. 24–44. It has been translated into English and edited by James N. W. B. Robertson in *The Acts and Decrees of the Synod of Jerusalem* (London, 1899), pp. 185–215; another translation is George A. Hadjiantoniou's *Protestant Patriarch: The Life of Cyril Lucaris, 1572–1638, Patriarch of Constantinople* (Richmond, Va., 1961), pp. 141–145. Some of Cyril's earlier sermons have been edited by Keetje Rozemond in *Sermons*, 1598–1602 (Leiden, 1974). Cyril's correspondence may be found in *Monumens authentiques de la religion des Grecs, et de la fausseté de plusieurs confessions de foi des chrétiens orientaux*, edited by Jean Aymon (The Hague, 1708), pp. 1–200; also, in Émile Legrand's *Bibliographie hellénique, ou Description raisonnée des ouvrages publiés par des Grecs au dix-septieme siècle*, vol. 4, Notices bibliographiques (Paris, 1896), pp. 175–521.

Source material on Cyril's career is to be found in Thomas Smith's *Collectanea de Cyrillo Lucario, patriarcha Constantinopolitano* (London, 1707) and in *The Negotiations of Sir Thomas Roe* (London, 1740). Among modern studies, the most scholarly are in Greek: see especially Chrysostom Papadopoulos's *Kurillos Loukaris*, rev. ed. (Athens, 1939) and Ioannis N. Karmiris's *Orthodoxia kai Protestantismos* (Athens, 1937), pp. 177–275. The work of Hadjiantoniou, cited above, is a readable but partisan account by a Greek evangelical. There is a briefer but more balanced treatment in Steven Runciman's *The Great Church in Captivity: A Study of the Patriarchate of Constantinople from the Eve of the Turkish Conquest to the Greek War of Independence* (Cambridge, U.K. 1968), pp. 259–288. On the political background, see Gunnar Hering's *Ökumenisches Patriarchat und europäische Politik, 1620–1638* (Wiesbaden, 1968).

KALLISTOS WARE (1987)

CYRIL AND METHODIUS. Cyril, also known as Constantine (c. 826–869), and Methodius (c. 815–844) were called the "apostles to the Slavs" because of their religious and cultural contributions to the people of the Danube basin and later to all Slavic-speaking people. Constantine (who took the name Cyril only in the last months of his life) and Methodius were born into a prominent Christian family in Thessalonica, Greece. The brothers learned Greek and probably also Slavic, since many Slavic people had migrated south into their area of Macedonia. After their father's death, Constantine moved to Constantinople. Then only fourteen, he was cared for by the family of a high government official. He later attended the imperial university and benefited from studying with the leading teachers in the region, including Photius, the future patriarch of Constantinople (858–867, 877–888). He became librarian of Hagia Sophia, the leading church in the East, and later professor of philosophy at the imperial university. He also participated in religious debates with church leaders and Muslim scholars.

Methodius, meanwhile, had been awarded the governorship of a Slavic-speaking district. After some years as governor, however, he withdrew into a Greek monastery in Bithynia (in Asia Minor), where Constantine joined him in 855. In 860, the patriarch sent Constantine and Methodius on a mission to the Khazars, a people occuping the territory northeast of the Black Sea, who had asked that the Christian message be explained to them. The result of their visit was that two hundred Khazars requested baptism. This success led to another, more important mission shortly thereafter.

In 862, Rastislav, duke of Greater Moravia, sent a request for help to the emperor in Constantinople, Michael III. Rastislav's Slavic-speaking subjects had already been widely evangelized by missionaries from western Europe, that is, from the East Frankish kingdom (modern-day West Germany and Austria). The Slavic peoples, however, had no written language and no strong cultural or church leadership, and Rastislav perceived a danger in the political and ecclesiastical influence of the neighboring Germanic tribes. He hoped that aid from Constantinople would enable Moravia to remain politically and religiously autonomous.

Recognizing the importance of the request, the Byzantine emperor and the patriarch, Photius, agreed to send Methodius and Constantine. In the months before their journey, Constantine prepared for the mission by developing a written language for the Slavs. He formed the alphabet from Hebrew and Greek letters (in its final form, this alphabet, the Cyrillic, is still used in modern Russian and in a number of other modern Slavic languages). Using this alphabet, Constantine translated the Gospels and later the epistles of Paul and the *Book of Psalms* into Slavic.

In late 863, the brothers began the mission. They sailed around Greece and up the Adriatic to Venice, then traveled overland to Moravia, where they were warmly welcomed. Their work included training a native clergy, instructing them in the newly written Slavic language, and translating liturgical textbooks. The latinized clergy in the area vigorously opposed the Slavic liturgy; they held to a "trilingualist" theory that only Latin, Greek, and Hebrew were acceptable for worship. To win papal support for their innovations, the brothers journeyed to Rome in 867. The also took along some trainees for ordination. On the way, they spent several months south of the Danube in Pannonia (modern-day western Hungary), where another Slavic chieftain, Kocel (r. 861–874), welcomed the brothers and entrusted to them a group of young men for training.

When the brothers reached Rome, Pope Adrian II welcomed them and granted full approval to their Slavic liturgy. After some months, and while still in Rome, Constantine became seriously ill. The brothers had been staying in a Greek monastery, and during his illness Constantine took a vow to remain a monk and at that point assumed the name Cyril. In less than two months, at the age of about forty-two, he died.

With papal encouragement, Methodius returned to work with the Slavic princes of Pannonia, Moravia, and the area around Nitra. Wishing to gain jurisdiction over the areas, Adrian II sent letters with Methodius approving the Slavic liturgy. The princes welcomed Methodius back, and in 869 the pope ordained him archbishop of Pannonia and Moravia, with his cathedral at Sirmium (near present-day Belgrade, Yugoslavia). Opposition to this appointment came from the neighboring Frankish (Bavarian) bishops, Hermanrich of Passau, Adalwin of Salzburg, and Anno of Fresing, all of whom had long worked for Frankish ecclesiastical and political influence in the area. In 870, with the help of Svatopluk, the ruler of Nitra, Bishop Hermanrich contrived to arrest Methodius and imprison him in a monastery in Swabia (southwestern Germany). In 873, Pope John VIII ordered his release, reinstalled him in his former diocese, and reaffirmed, with slight reservations, papal support for the Slavic liturgy.

The work of Methodius among the Slavs seems to have prospered, but opposition continued from the Frankish clergy and from Svatopluk, the new ruler in Moravia. Accused of heresy, Methodius successfully defended himself and won from John VIII a bull that praised his orthodoxy, reaffirmed the independence of his diocese, and expressly authorized the Mass in Slavic. During the last years of his life, Methodius continued to meet opposition. Nevertheless, with the help of two disciples, he completed the translation of the Bible into Slavic and codified both the civil and the ecclesiastical law. After Methodius's death in 884, his disciples were expelled by their Frankish opponents but found refuge in southern Poland, Bulgaria, and Bohemia. Through them the work of Constantine-Cyril and Methodius continued, contributing substantially to the growth of the Greek church and Slavic Christian culture in eastern Europe.

BIBLIOGRAPHY

A detailed study with notes, maps, and bibliography is Francis Dvornik's *Byzantine Missions among the Slavs: SS Constantine-Cyril and Methodius* (New Brunswick, N.J., 1970).

H. MCKENNIE GOODPASTURE (1987)

CYRIL OF ALEXANDRIA (c. 375–444), church father, theologian, and saint. Cyril succeeded his uncle Theophilus as bishop of Alexandria in 412. His aggressive nature involved him in a series of polemics against heretics. His rhetorical skills were sometimes stronger than his theological judgment, and he was often forgetful of evangelical moderation. In the early days of his studies in the humanities and in religion, he had not been trained to distinguish between the authentic treatises of Athanasius, his most admired predecessor, and those by Apollinarius, listed under Athanasius's name in the episcopal library of Alexandria. Thus he mistakenly urged a form of Christology best expressed by Apollinarius's phrase, which he believed to be Athanasian: "the unique incarnate nature of God the Logos."

Cyril's most famous controversy was with Nestorius, his colleague in the imperial metropolis of Constantinople. A monk from Antioch, made bishop of Constantinople by Emperor Theodosius II in 428, Nestorius preached against Arian and Apollinaristic factions in the monasteries surrounding the capital. Both groups called Mary *theotokos* (Mother of God) in claiming that the Logos incarnate was born, grew up, and suffered. Nestorius became suspicious of this epithet and preferred Mother of Christ. Denounced to Cyril, who ignored the local circumstances and was eager to interfere in the debates at Constantinople, Nestorius was accused by his powerful Alexandrian rival of dividing Christ into two beings, a mere man and the Logos. An exchange of several letters between January and June 430 did not help. Nestorius, with an obvious lack of needed theological acumen, was unaware of the coming storm. Cyril gained strength speedily, and now without diplomatic maneuvers, he garnered the full support of the Roman bishop Celestine and the ear of the emperor. The latter called for a general council in Ephesus, at Pentecost, on June 7, 431. Before numerous Eastern bishops, led by John of Antioch, could arrive—they were moderate supporters of Nestorius and opposed to the passionate initiatives of Cyril—Nestorius was condemned as a heretic and deposed, on June 22. It took Cyril two years to become reconciled with his Eastern colleagues. Nestorius was sent into a bitter exile in Petra, and later to the Great Oasis in southern Libya. His supporters were all sent to work camps as prisoners.

The literary and theological legacy of Cyril focuses on his christological system and on biblical exegesis. In the wake of anti-Nestorian polemics, he demonstrated a strong opposition to the Antiochene school of scriptural hermeneutics. The main teachers and actual founders of this school were Diodorus, bishop of Tarsus from 378 to around 394, and Theodore, bishop of Mopsuestia from 392 to 428. They were accused by Cyril of having paved the way for Nestorianism, and were condemned by the imperial court. Most of their invaluable biblical commentaries were destroyed.

Cyril's commentaries include an interpretation of christological evidences taken by him from the Pentateuch. These are known as *Glaphura,* which includes extensive interpretations of *Isaiah* and the Minor Prophets, as well as commentaries on *John, Luke, Matthew,* and the Pauline letters. In his exegesis he uses the traditional Alexandrian method, laying out the literal, typological, and moral teaching of scripture. His knowledge of different Greek versions and of the Hebrew text of the Old Testament was complemented by his familiarity with allegorical and etymological techniques of interpretation. His dogmatic works on trinitarian theology popularized the notion of one divine substance in three persons. The main contribution of Cyril in the christological debate was to prepare a clearer notion of the interrelated properties of God and man in the unity of Christ, the so-called *communicatio idiomatum.*

Through the centuries (in both the East and the West), Cyril has been regarded as one of the main defenders of imperial orthodoxy as it was transmitted into the Middle Ages.

See Also Nestorianism; Nestorius.

Bibliography

Grillmeier, Aloys. *Christ in the Christian Tradition.* 2d ed., rev. Atlanta, 1975.

Kerrigan, Alexander. *Saint Cyril of Alexandria, Interpreter of the Old Testament.* Rome, 1952.

Scipioni, Luigi I. *Nestorio e il concilio di Efeso: Storia, Dogma, Critica.* Studia Patristica Mediolanensia, vol. 1. Milan, 1974.

Charles Kannengiesser (1987)

CYRIL OF JERUSALEM (313–386), ecumenical doctor and father of the church. Born in or around Jerusalem, Cyril was ordained presbyter in 343 by Bishop Maximus II, whom he succeeded at the beginning of 348. Although seemingly indifferent to dogmatic subtleties, Cyril could not remain outside the climate of his time. He was acknowledged by the Arians because he avoided the term *homoousios* ("of the same substance"), but he disappointed them at the beginning of his episcopate by placing himself among the adherents of the Nicene dogma. This fact was one reason for his break with Acacius, the Arian metropolitan of Caesarea who had ordained him. A second reason for this rupture was the ambiguity of the seventh canon of the Council of Nicaea (325), which ordered that the bishop of Jerusalem be honored according to ancient custom but be subject to the metropolitan of Caesarea.

Acacius, a favorite of the Arian emperor Constantius, succeeded in banishing Cyril from his see (357), and, although he was recalled by the Council of Seleucia in 359, Cyril had to endure further banishments lasting many years. Having returned under the reign of Julian, he was not personally affected by the emperor's plans to degrade Christianity and promote paganism by all means possible. However, banishment under Valens kept Cyril far from his flock for eleven years. After returning to his see in 378, he remained undisturbed in his work until his death (386).

Cyril's chief work was his *Catecheses,* a collection of twenty-four instructions, delivered in the Church of the Resurrection before and after Easter 348. Their aim was to initiate the catechumens in the fundamental doctrines of Christian faith and life and to explain the main sacraments of the church to the newly baptized.

The collection contains three types of instruction. One preliminary teaching (the *Procatechesis*), which emphasizes the importance of the last stage of instruction, draws the new tasks of the catechumens and points out the need for their preparation for baptism. Next, eighteen catecheses to the *phōtizomenoi* (those who had reached the stage of awaiting baptism at the coming of Easter) deal with the subjects of repentance and baptism, describe the basic doctrines of Christianity and the rules of life, and offer a theologically edifying interpretation of the creed. Finally, five mystagogical catecheses to the newly baptized give a detailed interpretation of the sacraments of baptism, confirmation, and the Eucharist. Some manuscripts ascribe this third section to Cyril's successor, John of Jerusalem.

These instructions seem to have been delivered impromptu, as is noted in some manuscripts. However, their style is clear, vivacious, and cordial. Their mode of instruction is based on sound pedagogical principles; the author repeats a number of times the essential elements so that they may be consolidated in the minds of the hearers. The work has been translated into many languages, both ancient and modern.

Of the homilies of Cyril only one has been preserved; it deals with the cure of the paralytic (*Jn.* 5:5). A letter addressed to Emperor Constantius reports the miraculous apparition of a cross of light above Calvary on May 7, 351. Some other unimportant texts, including an anaphora, have been falsely attributed to him.

As an adherent of the Council of Nicaea, Cyril declared that he neither separated the persons of the Trinity nor confused them. He does not, however, use the critical term *homoousios.* This omission certainly is not owing to his insistence on the necessity of biblical language in doctrine, since the term *homoeos* ("like"), which he does use to define the relation of the Son to the Father, is also nonscriptural. Neither can it be attributed to a semi-Arian tendency, since his struggle against Arianism would therefore go unexplained. It may be ascribed to his fear of a deviation toward Sabellianism, a fear that possessed many adherents of the Nicene Creed. Indeed, Cyril said, "We should not either say there was a time when the Son was not, or put our faith in the doctrine of *huiopatoria* (that is, the Father and the Son are the same person); let us not deviate either to the left or to the right" (*Catecheses* 11.16). He might have been compelled to use the term later on as an indispensable weapon in the struggle against Arianism, but we have no such evidence.

Cyril characterizes the sacrament of baptism in two ways: first, according to the Pauline presentation, as a tomb from which the baptized are resurrected, dying and rising together with Christ; and second, according to the Johannine presentation, as mother of the new spiritual birth. In the eucharistic doctrine he emphasizes clearly the real presence of Christ in the elements: "in the *tupos* of bread" the body of Christ exists, and "in the *tupos* of wine" the blood of Christ exists. Therefore, the faithful, receiving both of these, become "co-bodily and co-bloodily" of Christ. Christ, who at Cana changed water into wine, would have no difficulty in changing wine into blood. Yet Cyril does not mention the words of institution in the Eucharist, probably because they are too sacred for such mention.

After his death Cyril was not often cited, but gradually, as knowledge of his theology spread, his major writings were widely used by theologians, who came to consider them one of the more valid sources for Orthodox theologizing. In 1893

Cyril was proclaimed a doctor of the church by Pope Leo XIII. His feast is celebrated in both the Eastern and the Western church on March 18.

BIBLIOGRAPHY

Dionysius Kleopas has edited the *Procatechesis* and the *Catecheses* in two volumes (Jerusalem, 1867–1868). A popular edition is F. L. Cross's *St. Cyril of Jerusalem's Lectures on the Christian Sacraments: The Procatechesis and the Five Mystagogical Catecheses* (London, 1951). William Telfer has translated the texts with introduction in *Cyril of Jerusalem and Nemesius of Emesu* (London, 1955).

Several studies treat particular aspects of Cyril's activity and teaching. W. J. Swaans attributes the five mystagogical pieces to John of Jerusalem in "À propos de 'Catéchèses mystagogique,' attribuées à S. Cyrille de Jerusalem," *Muséon* 55 (1942): 1–42. Jacob H. Greenlee treats the biblical sources in his *The Gospel Text of Cyril of Jerusalem* (Copenhagen, 1955). The educational methods of Cyril are treated in Demetrios Moraitis's *Cyril of Jerusalem as a Catechete and Pedagogue* (in Greek; Thessaloniki, 1949); in Elias Voulgazakis's *The Catechesis of Cyril of Jerusalem* (Thessaloniki, 1977), a very important work in modern Greek; and in Antoine Paulin's *Saint Cyrille de Jerusalem Catéchète* (Paris, 1959). Some aspects of Cyril's theological teaching are examined by Basilius Niederberger in *Die Logosidee des hl. Cyrillus von Jerusalem* (Paderborn, 1923); by Hugh M. Riley in *Christian Initiation: A Comparative Study of the Interpretation of the Baptismal Liturgy in the Mystagogical Writings of Cyril of Jerusalem, John Chrysostom, Theodore of Mopsuestia and Ambrose of Milan,* "Studies in Christian Antiquity," no. 17 (Washington, D. C., 1974); and by Edward Yarnold in *The Awe-Inspiring Rites of Initiation: Baptismal Homilies of the Fourth Century* (Slough, U.K., 1972).

PANAGIOTIS C. CHRISTOU (1987)

CYRUS II (c. 585–c. 529 BCE), called Cyrus the Great; builder and ruler of the Persian empire from 559 BCE until his death. A king of the Achaemenid dynasty, Cyrus (OPers., Kurush) combined great ambition, shrewd calculation, and military expertise to establish the largest empire in world history. From his base in Anshan he conquered neighboring Media in alliance with the Babylonian king Nabonidus in 550, overtook Lydia in Asia Minor in 547, defeated resisting areas in the Greek mainland, then returned to Persia and drove his armies eastward as far as India. With his power thus increased, he conquered Babylonia and proclaimed himself king of all Mesopotamia—indeed, of the world—in 539.

Nabonidus had alienated the Babylonian priesthood through his extraordinary devotion to the moon cult. Capitalizing on Nabonidus's heresy, Cyrus achieved popularity in Babylon by restoring the cult of its chief god, Marduk, and by reestablishing the shrines and proper worship of other gods in their former locations. In a proclamation composed in Babylonian, Cyrus asserts that Marduk delivered his lands to the conqueror and that Bel (Enlil) and Nabu, the local Babylonian gods, love his rule. The Hebrew scriptures preserve two versions of an edict by Cyrus in which the conqueror attributes his victories to the Israelite god, "YHVH God of Heaven" who "commanded me to build him a temple in Jerusalem" (*Ezr.* 1:1–3, 6:3–5). The Judeans living in exile in Babylonia saw Cyrus as their liberator because he permitted them in 538 to return to their homeland in Judaea and to rebuild the Temple, which had been destroyed by Babylonia in 587/6. A prophet of the Judean exile, the so-called Second Isaiah, portrayed Cyrus as the "shepherd" chosen by the Lord to subjugate nations and reestablish the Jerusalem Temple (*Is.* 44:28, 45:1ff.; cf. *Is.* 41:1ff.).

Subsequent Jewish traditions tend to play down Cyrus's personal rectitude while seeing him as an instrument of God (B.T., *Meg.* 12a). Christian exegetes have often regarded Cyrus as a prefiguration of the Messiah.

BIBLIOGRAPHY

Pierre Briant, *From Cyrus to Alexander: A History of the Persian Empire*, translated by Peter T. Daniels (Winona Lake, Ind., 2002), pp. 1–49, takes a somewhat more skeptical view of Cyrus's achievements than the more conventional account in Albert Ten Eyck Olmstead's *History of the Persian Empire: Achaemenid Period* (Chicago, 1948), pp. 34–58. The relationship between Cyrus's policies and his support of local cults is delineated by Joseph Blenkinsopp in "Temple and Society in Achaemenid Judah," in *Second Temple Studies, 1: The Persian Period*, edited by Philip R. Davies (Sheffield, 1991), pp. 22–53. Cyrus's Babylonian proclamation is translated by A. Leo Oppenheim in *Ancient Near Eastern Texts Relating to the Old Testament,* 3d ed. with suppl., edited by J. B. Pritchard (Princeton, 1969), pp. 315–316, and a good analysis of this text, with bibliography in the notes, is Amélie Kuhrt's "The Cyrus Cylinder and Achaemenid Imperial Policy," *Journal for the Study of the Old Testament* 25 (February 1983): 83–97. The Hebrew and Aramaic edicts of Cyrus are analyzed by Elias J. Bickerman in "The Edict of Cyrus in Ezra 1," *Journal of Biblical Literature* 65 (1946): 249–275.

EDWARD L. GREENSTEIN (1987 AND 2005)

ISBN 0-02-865736-5